STATS™
Pro Basketball Handbook
2000-01

STATS, Inc.

Published by STATS Publishing
A division of Sports Team Analysis & Tracking Systems, Inc.

Cover design by Ryan Balock, Marc Elman and Chuck Miller

Cover photo by Jed Jacobsohn/Allsport

First Edition: July, 2000

Printed in the United States of America

ISBN 1-884064-84-1

Acknowledgments

Publishing the sixth edition of the *Pro Basketball Handbook* is a collective effort that requires a heavy dose of teamwork. The STATS team is successfully anchored by CEO John Dewan and President Alan Leib, and lending invaluable assistance to the guys at the top is Jennifer Manicki. Sue Dewan and Bob Meyerhoff oversee our Research & Development/Special Projects efforts. Sue works on special projects and Bob directs a group composed of Athan Arvanitis, Jim Osborne, Joe Sclafani and Andy Tumpowsky. Arthur Ashley provides programming and project support for the development group.

Shaping the book into final form is the work of the Publications Department, led by newly appointed department director Marc Elman. Getting the numbers programmed appropriately fell into the hands of Jim Henzler, while Chuck Miller painstakingly manipulated the many columns and graphs that are key to the book's design. Tony Nistler and yours truly oversaw editorial responsibilities, with help from Taylor Bechtold, Marc Carl and Norm DeNosaquo. Getting the word out about the *Pro Basketball Handbook* and other STATS publications requires the hard work of Ryan Balock, Mike Janosi, Antoinette Kelly and Mike Sarkis. Ryan designed this book's cover. Tim Coletta lends assistance to Jim with day-to-day programming assignments.

We couldn't get the book out without our Operations Department. Managing the collection of these numbers is Allan Spear. His troup of ball-hawking defenders includes Jeremy Alpert, Scott Berg, Michelle Blanco, Les Briesemeister, Jon Caplin, Jeff Chernow, Mike Hammer, Derek Kenar, Tony Largo, Roger Liss, Jon Passman, Jeff Schinski, Matt Senter, Bill Stephens, Joe Stillwell, Stu Wiley and Chris Witt. Thanks especially to Jeremy, who oversees the accuracy of our NBA data, and to Allan, who coordinated the effort to expand our college statistics.

Standing beyond the arc waiting to knock down a three are our Commercial, Fantasy, Interactive and Sales departments. Vince Smith heads our Commercial staff, made up of Jim Blazek, Ethan D. Cooperson, Seth Johnson, Stefan Kretschmann, Dave Pinto and Nick Stamm. Steve Byrd oversees the Fantasy Department, which consists of Bill Burke, Sean Bush, Jim Corelis, Consilia DiBartolo, Mike Dreckmann, Dan Ford, Brian Hogan, Walter Lis, Marc Moeller, Mike Mooney, Oscar Palacios, Jim Pollard, Eric Robin, Jeff Smith, Jake Stein, Yingmin Wang and Rick Wilton. Robert Schur directs an Interactive group that includes Jake Costello, Chuck Durvis, Jay Fleck, Gregg Kosieniak, Scott Kraatz, Joe Lindholm, Patrick Markey, Will McCleskey, Dean Peterson, Pat Quinn, John Sasman, Mindy Singer, Morris Srinivasan and David Thiel. Jim Capuano heads Sales with the help of Greg Kirkorsky.

Keeping us in the game is the Financial/Administrative/Human Resources/Legal Department. Howard Lanin facilitates the financial and administrative concerns of the company with key assists from Kim Bartlett, Mary Ellen Gomez and Betty Moy. Susan Zamecheck contributes in finance and keeps our headquarters running smoothly. Tracy Lickton is in charge of human resources while Carol Savier aids with legal matters. Brian Spisak keeps our computers running.

And introducing our new Research Department for Fox Sports in Los Angeles headed by vice president Don Zminda and his team of sports researchers: Matt Brown, Eric Corwin, Khalid El-Bayoumy, Eddie Garcia, Tracey Graham, Ryan Gunn, Don Hartack, Fred King, Meghan Sheehan, Stephanie Sluke, Aneel Trivedi and Randy Williams. This team eagerly awaits the addition of newcomers Mike Berger and Sam Lubeck. We wish the new crew well.

—Thom Henninger

This book is dedicated to my parents, Philip and Cynthia,
and to my brother Greg, who have all given me a life full of endless love
and support in anything and everything I set my mind to.
I could not be happier with any other family in the world,
even though my mother may know more about sports than I do.
And to my incredible girlfriend Whitney,
who has been the most inspiring woman a man could ever know.
She has and will continue to hold my heart and soul
for as long as I shall live.

—Jeremy Alpert

Table of Contents

Introduction

While this is the sixth edition of the *STATS Pro Basketball Handbook*, it has been a work in progress since 1993-94. Following the 1992-93 NBA season, STATS published the first *STATS Basketball Scoreboard* which was similar to our current baseball and football editions. The following year the *Basketball Scoreboard* included a player register, which led to the first *Pro Basketball Handbook* in 1995-96. We've been adding content to it every year since.

This year, we've added college statistics for every player who played in the NBA during the 1999-2000 season. Did you know that Terry Cummings' .821 free-throw percentage last season was his best since he shot .832 during his first season with DePaul in 1979-80? We've also included four year's worth of college data for players taken in the 2000 NBA Draft. We think these improvements will give you a better flavor of a player's abilities.

As always, we give you player statistical splits that illuminate such things as Kobe Bryant's ability to shine in the second of back to back games. His shooting percentage and scoring average in such contests were better than his overall averages in those categories.

You'll get the standings, postseason results and team statistics for both the regular season and postseason and a special page devoted to team records based on certain criteria. On this page, you'll find such things as: the Dallas Mavericks had a winning record in games where they out-rebounded their opponent. However, they played in just 13 (7-6) such contests, by far the lowest figure in the league.

There's a section for team statistical splits, team game-by-game logs, team statistics by individual players and single-season and career leader boards to round out the book.

With the addition of the college information to what we've always offered in this publication, we hope you enjoy our biggest *Pro Basketball Handbook* ever!

—Chuck Miller

Career Register

This section lists all players who were active for at least one game in the NBA last season. In addition, you'll find four players who didn't play in an NBA game during the 1999-2000 campaign, but whom we anticipate could suit up in 2000-01: Bison Dele, Zydrunas Ilgauskas, Rony Seikaly and Hot Rod Williams. Also, we included the career register for Jayson Williams, who announced his retirement in June.

Age: We list seasonal age through January 31, 2001, the approximate midpoint of the 2000-01 season.

All-Stars: If a player was selected for an All-Star Game, a star appears following the team(s) for which he played that season. There was no All-Star Game during the 1998-99 season.

Multiple-Team Seasons: If a player saw action with more than one NBA team in a season, his stats for each team in that season appear just above the career-totals line at the bottom of each entry. The teams are listed in the order in which the player appeared.

League Leaders: Throughout the career statistics, any stat that led the NBA in a given season will be in boldface. In the Leader Boards section of the book, you'll find the minimum numbers required to qualify for leadership in any percentage category.

Profiles: For all players with more than 1,200 minutes last season, you will see a note just above the age, "(statistical profile on page 203)," for example. This directs you to the Player Profiles sections, where you'll find detailed situational statistics.

Draft Information: The Career Register section includes draft data on each player. You'll find the year he was taken in the NBA draft, the round taken, his overall position in the draft (in parentheses) and the team that *originally* drafted him.

Missed Seasons: Throughout the Register you'll occasionally find players with "Played in Italy" or "Did not play: injury—Ankle" listed in a season line. For every "missed" NBA season by a player in the Register, we've listed the *specific* reason he did not play in that particular year whenever possible. We also list leagues other than the NBA as a reason a player didn't play. The leagues used in this section are: Continental Basketball Association (CBA), Global Basketball Association (GBA), International Basketball League (IBL), United States Basketball League (USBL) and the World Basketball League (WBL). We think it gives a much more complete picture of a player's career, especially for the Dean Garretts of the world.

College Statistics: For a complete listing of the school abbreviations used in this section, please see page 437. The three-point shot was not officially recognized by the NCAA until the 1986-87 season.

Tariq Abdul-Wahad

(statistical profile on page 184)

Pos: G **College:** San Jose State **Drafted:** '97 1(11)—Sac
Ht: 6'6" **Wt:** 223 **Born:** 11/3/74 **Age:** 26

College Year Tm	G	GS	Min	Field Goals Md	Att	Pct	3-Pt FGs Md	Att	Pct	Free Throws Md	Att	Pct	Misc TO	Stl	Blk	Fouls PF	DQ	Assists Ast	Avg	Rebounds Off	Tot	Avg	Points Pts	Avg
93-94 Mich	32	1	418	49	96	.510	4	14	.286	13	23	.565	30	18	6	69	2	17	0.5	27	72	2.3	115	3.6
94-95 Mich	4	0	53	8	16	.500	1	2	.500	2	2	1.000	6	1	1	11	0	0	0.0	7	13	3.3	19	4.8
95-96 SJSU	25	—	698	148	332	.446	18	65	.277	117	158	.741	87	25	22	88	—	64	2.6	—	157	6.3	431	17.2
96-97 SJSU	26	26	868	225	457	.492	26	71	.366	143	196	.730	68	39	19	63	0	28	1.1	79	229	8.8	619	23.8
4 Years	87	—	2037	430	901	.477	49	152	.322	275	379	.726	191	83	48	231	—	109	1.3	—	471	5.4	1184	13.6

NBA Year Tm	G	GS	Min	Field Goals Md	Att	Pct	3-Pt FGs Md	Att	Pct	Free Throws Md	Att	Pct	Misc TO	Stl	Blk	Fouls PF	DQ	Assists Ast	Avg	Rebounds Off	Tot	Avg	Points Pts	Avg
97-98 Sac	59	16	959	144	357	.403	4	19	.211	84	125	.672	65	35	13	81	0	51	0.9	44	116	2.0	376	6.4
98-99 Sac	49	49	1205	177	407	.435	6	21	.286	94	136	.691	70	50	16	121	0	50	1.0	72	186	3.8	454	9.3
99-00 2Tm	61	56	1578	274	646	.424	3	23	.130	146	193	.756	106	59	28	147	1	98	1.6	101	291	4.8	697	11.4
Orl	46	46	1205	223	515	.433	2	15	.095	115	151	.762	87	53	16	116	1	72	1.6	77	239	5.2	563	12.2
Den	15	10	373	51	131	.389	1	2	.500	31	42	.738	19	6	12	31	0	26	1.7	24	52	3.5	134	8.9
3 Years	169	121	3742	595	1410	.422	13	63	.206	324	454	.714	241	144	57	349	1	199	1.2	217	593	3.5	1527	9.0

NBA Postseason

Year Tm	G	GS	Min	Md	Att	Pct	Md	Att	Pct	Md	Att	Pct	TO	Stl	Blk	PF	DQ	Ast	Avg	Off	Tot	Avg	Pts	Avg
98-99 Sac	5	5	99	15	33	.455	0	1	.000	13	16	.813	3	4	4	8	0	4	0.8	6	19	3.8	43	8.6

Shareef Abdur-Rahim

(statistical profile on page 184)

Pos: F **College:** California **Drafted:** '96 1(3)—Van
Ht: 6'9" **Wt:** 230 **Born:** 12/11/76 **Age:** 24

College Year Tm	G	GS	Min	Field Goals Md	Att	Pct	3-Pt FGs Md	Att	Pct	Free Throws Md	Att	Pct	Misc TO	Stl	Blk	Fouls PF	DQ	Assists Ast	Avg	Rebounds Off	Tot	Avg	Points Pts	Avg
95-96 Cal	28	28	972	206	398	.518	8	21	.381	170	249	.683	87	52	35	58	2	29	1.0	81	236	8.4	590	21.1

NBA Year Tm	G	GS	Min	Field Goals Md	Att	Pct	3-Pt FGs Md	Att	Pct	Free Throws Md	Att	Pct	Misc TO	Stl	Blk	Fouls PF	DQ	Assists Ast	Avg	Rebounds Off	Tot	Avg	Points Pts	Avg
96-97 Van	80	71	2802	550	1214	.453	7	27	.259	387	519	.746	225	79	79	199	0	175	2.2	216	555	6.9	1494	18.7
97-98 Van	82	82	2950	653	1347	.485	21	51	.412	502	640	.784	257	89	76	201	0	213	2.6	227	581	7.1	1829	22.3
98-99 Van	50	50	2021	386	893	.432	11	36	.306	369	439	.841	186	69	55	137	1	172	3.4	114	374	7.5	1152	23.0
99-00 Van	82	82	3223	594	1277	.465	29	96	.302	446	551	.809	249	89	87	244	3	271	3.3	218	825	10.1	1663	20.3
4 Years	294	285	10996	2183	4731	.461	68	210	.324	1704	2149	.793	917	326	297	781	4	831	2.8	775	2335	7.9	6138	20.9

Cory Alexander

Pos: G **College:** Virginia **Drafted:** '95 1(29)—SA
Ht: 6'1" **Wt:** 190 **Born:** 6/22/73 **Age:** 27

College Year Tm	G	GS	Min	Field Goals Md	Att	Pct	3-Pt FGs Md	Att	Pct	Free Throws Md	Att	Pct	Misc TO	Stl	Blk	Fouls PF	DQ	Assists Ast	Avg	Rebounds Off	Tot	Avg	Points Pts	Avg
91-92 UVa	33	33	1037	127	338	.376	44	149	.295	72	105	.686	94	41	3	74	—	145	4.4	13	106	3.2	370	11.2
92-93 UVa	31	31	1118	213	470	.453	64	174	.368	93	132	.705	106	26	7	75	—	144	4.6	30	107	3.5	583	18.8
93-94 UVa	1	1	11	0	4	.000	0	2	.000	0	2	.000	1	0	1	0	—	2	2.0	0	1	1.0	0	0.0
94-95 UVa	20	20	692	119	263	.452	34	97	.351	61	87	.701	78	32	3	40	—	110	5.5	9	84	4.2	333	16.7
4 Years	85	85	2858	459	1075	.427	142	422	.336	226	326	.693	279	99	14	189	—	401	4.7	52	298	3.5	1286	15.1

NBA Year Tm	G	GS	Min	Field Goals Md	Att	Pct	3-Pt FGs Md	Att	Pct	Free Throws Md	Att	Pct	Misc TO	Stl	Blk	Fouls PF	DQ	Assists Ast	Avg	Rebounds Off	Tot	Avg	Points Pts	Avg
95-96 SA	60	0	560	63	155	.406	26	66	.394	16	25	.640	68	27	2	94	0	121	2.0	9	42	0.7	168	2.8
96-97 SA	80	6	1454	194	490	.396	94	252	.373	95	129	.736	146	82	16	148	0	254	3.2	29	123	1.5	577	7.2
97-98 2Tm	60	22	1298	171	400	.428	66	176	.375	80	102	.784	112	70	11	98	2	209	3.5	17	146	2.4	488	8.1
98-99 Den	36	4	778	97	260	.373	30	105	.286	37	44	.841	69	35	5	77	0	119	3.3	7	74	2.1	261	7.3
99-00 Den	29	2	329	28	98	.286	9	35	.257	17	22	.773	28	24	2	39	0	58	2.0	8	42	1.4	82	2.8
97-98 SA	37	3	501	60	145	.414	20	64	.313	25	37	.676	47	25	5	53	2	71	1.9	7	47	1.3	165	4.5
Den	23	19	797	111	255	.435	46	112	.411	55	65	.846	65	45	6	45	0	138	6.0	10	99	4.3	323	14.0
5 Years	265	34	4419	553	1403	.394	225	634	.355	245	322	.761	423	238	36	456	2	761	2.9	70	427	1.6	1576	5.9

NBA Postseason

Year Tm	G	GS	Min	Md	Att	Pct	Md	Att	Pct	Md	Att	Pct	TO	Stl	Blk	PF	DQ	Ast	Avg	Off	Tot	Avg	Pts	Avg
95-96 SA	9	0	70	10	24	.417	1	5	.200	5	7	.714	6	2	0	8	0	9	1.0	4	9	1.0	26	2.9

Ray Allen
(statistical profile on page 185)

Pos: G **College:** Connecticut **Drafted:** '96 1(5)—Min   **Ht:** 6'5" **Wt:** 205 **Born:** 7/20/75 **Age:** 25

College				Field Goals			3-Pt FGs			Free Throws			Misc			Fouls		Assists		Rebounds			Points	
Year Tm	G	GS	Min	Md	Att	Pct	Md	Att	Pct	Md	Att	Pct	TO	Stl	Blk	PF	DQ	Ast	Avg	Off	Tot	Avg	Pts	Avg
93-94 Conn	34	0	735	158	310	.510	33	82	.402	80	101	.792	47	38	7	46	2	53	1.6	76	155	4.6	429	12.6
94-95 Conn	32	31	1051	255	521	.489	85	191	.445	80	110	.727	64	61	16	53	—	75	2.3	—	218	6.8	675	21.1
95-96 Conn	35	35	1215	292	618	.472	115	247	.466	119	147	.810	82	60	18	46	0	117	3.3	81	228	6.5	818	23.4
3 Years	101	66	3001	705	1449	.487	233	520	.448	279	358	.779	193	159	41	145		245	2.4	—	601	6.0	1922	19.0

NBA				Field Goals			3-Pt FGs			Free Throws			Misc			Fouls		Assists		Rebounds			Points	
Year Tm	G	GS	Min	Md	Att	Pct	Md	Att	Pct	Md	Att	Pct	TO	Stl	Blk	PF	DQ	Ast	Avg	Off	Tot	Avg	Pts	Avg
96-97 Mil	82	81	2532	390	908	.430	117	298	.393	205	249	.823	149	75	10	218	0	210	2.6	97	326	4.0	1102	13.4
97-98 Mil	82	82	3287	563	1315	.428	134	368	.364	342	391	.875	263	111	12	244	2	356	4.3	127	405	4.9	1602	19.5
98-99 Mil	50	50	1719	303	673	.450	74	208	.356	176	195	.903	122	53	7	117	0	178	3.6	57	212	4.2	856	17.1
99-00 Mil*	82	82	3070	642	1411	.455	172	407	.423	353	398	.887	183	110	19	187	1	308	3.8	83	359	4.4	1809	22.1
4 Years	296	295	10608	1898	4307	.441	497	1281	.388	1076	1233	.873	717	349	48	766	3	1052	3.6	364	1302	4.4	5369	18.1

NBA Postseason																								
Year Tm	G	GS	Min	Md	Att	Pct	Md	Att	Pct	Md	Att	Pct	TO	Stl	Blk	PF	DQ	Ast	Avg	Off	Tot	Avg	Pts	Avg
98-99 Mil	3	3	120	25	47	.532	9	19	.474	8	13	.615	11	3	1	9	0	13	4.3	8	22	7.3	67	22.3
99-00 Mil	5	5	186	40	90	.444	10	26	.385	20	22	.909	9	8	0	10	0	13	2.6	10	33	6.6	110	22.0
2 Years	8	8	306	65	137	.474	19	45	.422	28	35	.800	20	11	1	19	0	26	3.3	18	55	6.9	177	22.1

Rafer Alston

Pos: G **College:** Fresno State **Drafted:** '98 2(39)—Mil   **Ht:** 6'2" **Wt:** 173 **Born:** 7/24/76 **Age:** 24

College				Field Goals			3-Pt FGs			Free Throws			Misc			Fouls		Assists		Rebounds			Points	
Year Tm	G	GS	Min	Md	Att	Pct	Md	Att	Pct	Md	Att	Pct	TO	Stl	Blk	PF	DQ	Ast	Avg	Off	Tot	Avg	Pts	Avg
97-98 Fres	33	29	1030	124	309	.401	66	196	.337	50	66	.758	111	70	12	96	3	240	7.3	15	71	2.2	364	11.0

NBA				Field Goals			3-Pt FGs			Free Throws			Misc			Fouls		Assists		Rebounds			Points	
Year Tm	G	GS	Min	Md	Att	Pct	Md	Att	Pct	Md	Att	Pct	TO	Stl	Blk	PF	DQ	Ast	Avg	Off	Tot	Avg	Pts	Avg
98-99										Played in CBA														
99-00 Mil	27	0	361	27	95	.284	3	14	.214	3	4	.750	29	12	0	29	0	70	2.6	5	23	0.9	60	2.2

NBA Postseason																								
Year Tm	G	GS	Min	Md	Att	Pct	Md	Att	Pct	Md	Att	Pct	TO	Stl	Blk	PF	DQ	Ast	Avg	Off	Tot	Avg	Pts	Avg
99-00 Mil	4	0	16	0	3	.000	0	1	.000	0	2	.000	1	0	0	0	0	1	0.3	0	0	0.0	0	0.0

John Amaechi
(statistical profile on page 185)

Pos: C **College:** Penn State **Drafted:** '95 FA—Cle   **Ht:** 6'10" **Wt:** 270 **Born:** 11/26/70 **Age:** 30

College				Field Goals			3-Pt FGs			Free Throws			Misc			Fouls		Assists		Rebounds			Points	
Year Tm	G	GS	Min	Md	Att	Pct	Md	Att	Pct	Md	Att	Pct	TO	Stl	Blk	PF	DQ	Ast	Avg	Off	Tot	Avg	Pts	Avg
90-91 Van	24	0	311	26	57	.456	0	0	—	14	25	.560	26	10	11	36	0	6	0.3	15	65	2.7	66	2.8
92-93 PSU	27	27	897	114	241	.473	15	48	.313	130	182	.714	56	20	65	64	2	20	0.7	68	206	7.6	373	13.8
93-94 PSU	25	25	837	124	243	.510	4	15	.267	171	245	.698	64	23	58	59	2	37	1.5	71	223	8.9	423	16.9
94-95 PSU	32	32	1108	168	300	.560	2	6	.333	176	260	.677	100	21	68	67	0	55	1.7	87	316	9.9	514	16.1
4 Years	108	84	3153	432	841	.514	21	69	.304	491	712	.690	246	74	202	226	4	118	1.1	241	810	7.5	1376	12.7

NBA				Field Goals			3-Pt FGs			Free Throws			Misc			Fouls		Assists		Rebounds			Points	
Year Tm	G	GS	Min	Md	Att	Pct	Md	Att	Pct	Md	Att	Pct	TO	Stl	Blk	PF	DQ	Ast	Avg	Off	Tot	Avg	Pts	Avg
95-96 Cle	28	3	357	29	70	.414	0	0	—	19	33	.576	34	6	11	49	1	9	0.3	13	52	1.9	77	2.8
96-97										Played in Greece														
97-98										Played in Italy														
98-99										Played in France														
99-00 Orl	80	53	1684	306	700	.437	1	6	.167	223	291	.766	139	35	37	161	1	95	1.2	62	266	3.3	836	10.5
2 Years	108	56	2041	335	770	.435	1	6	.167	242	324	.747	173	41	48	210	2	104	1.0	75	318	2.9	913	8.5

NBA Postseason																								
Year Tm	G	GS	Min	Md	Att	Pct	Md	Att	Pct	Md	Att	Pct	TO	Stl	Blk	PF	DQ	Ast	Avg	Off	Tot	Avg	Pts	Avg
95-96 Cle	1	0	2	0	1	.000	0	0	—	0	0	—	0	0	0	0	0	0	0.0	0	0	0.0	0	0.0

Derek Anderson
(statistical profile on page 186)

Pos: G **College:** Kentucky **Drafted:** '97 1(13)—Cle   **Ht:** 6'5" **Wt:** 195 **Born:** 7/18/74 **Age:** 26

College				Field Goals			3-Pt FGs			Free Throws			Misc			Fouls		Assists		Rebounds			Points	
Year Tm	G	GS	Min	Md	Att	Pct	Md	Att	Pct	Md	Att	Pct	TO	Stl	Blk	PF	DQ	Ast	Avg	Off	Tot	Avg	Pts	Avg
92-93 OhSt	22	8	587	72	158	.456	9	35	.257	72	89	.809	50	43	5	65	4	59	2.7	27	72	3.3	225	10.2

Year Tm	G	GS	Min	Field Goals Md	Att	Pct	3-Pt FGs Md	Att	Pct	Free Throws Md	Att	Pct	Misc TO	Stl	Blk	Fouls PF	DQ	Assists Ast	Avg	Rebounds Off	Tot	Avg	Points Pts	Avg
93-94 OhSt	22	22	695	108	232	.466	21	62	.339	92	113	.814	64	45	2	57	1	107	4.9	54	108	4.9	329	15.0
95-96 Kty	36	24	701	117	230	.509	23	59	.390	80	102	.784	51	61	7	82	2	88	2.4	59	122	3.4	337	9.4
96-97 Kty	19	17	481	111	226	.491	38	94	.404	77	95	.811	32	37	2	39	0	67	3.5	36	77	4.1	337	17.7
4 Years	99	71	2464	408	846	.482	91	250	.364	321	399	.805	197	186	16	243	7	321	3.2	176	379	3.8	1228	12.4

NBA Year Tm	G	GS	Min	Field Goals Md	Att	Pct	3-Pt FGs Md	Att	Pct	Free Throws Md	Att	Pct	Misc TO	Stl	Blk	Fouls PF	DQ	Assists Ast	Avg	Rebounds Off	Tot	Avg	Points Pts	Avg
97-98 Cle	66	13	1839	239	586	.408	17	84	.202	275	315	.873	128	86	13	136	0	227	3.4	55	187	2.8	770	11.7
98-99 Cle	38	13	978	125	314	.398	21	69	.304	138	165	.836	82	48	4	73	0	145	3.8	20	109	2.9	409	10.8
99-00 LAC	64	58	2201	377	860	.438	55	178	.309	271	309	.877	167	90	11	149	2	220	3.4	80	258	4.0	1080	16.9
3 Years	168	84	5018	741	1760	.421	93	331	.281	684	789	.867	377	224	28	358	2	592	3.5	155	554	3.3	2259	13.4

NBA Postseason

Year Tm	G	GS	Min	Md	Att	Pct	Md	Att	Pct	Md	Att	Pct	TO	Stl	Blk	PF	DQ	Ast	Avg	Off	Tot	Avg	Pts	Avg
97-98 Cle	4	0	103	10	22	.455	0	0	—	23	26	.885	12	5	1	10	0	11	2.8	0	9	2.3	43	10.8

Kenny Anderson

(statistical profile on page 186)

Pos: G **College:** Georgia Tech **Drafted:** '91 1(2)—NJ   **Ht:** 6'1" **Wt:** 168 **Born:** 10/9/70 **Age:** 30

College Year Tm	G	GS	Min	Field Goals Md	Att	Pct	3-Pt FGs Md	Att	Pct	Free Throws Md	Att	Pct	Misc TO	Stl	Blk	Fouls PF	DQ	Assists Ast	Avg	Rebounds Off	Tot	Avg	Points Pts	Avg
89-90 GTch	35	35	1321	283	549	.515	48	117	.410	107	146	.733	143	79	3	66	—	285	8.1	51	193	5.5	721	20.6
90-91 GTch	30	30	1167	278	636	.437	65	185	.351	155	187	.829	113	89	2	69	—	169	5.6	56	171	5.7	776	25.9
2 Years	65	65	2488	561	1185	.473	113	302	.374	262	333	.787	256	168	5	135	—	454	7.0	107	364	5.6	1497	23.0

NBA Year Tm	G	GS	Min	Field Goals Md	Att	Pct	3-Pt FGs Md	Att	Pct	Free Throws Md	Att	Pct	Misc TO	Stl	Blk	Fouls PF	DQ	Assists Ast	Avg	Rebounds Off	Tot	Avg	Points Pts	Avg
91-92 NJ	64	13	1086	187	480	.390	3	13	.231	73	98	.745	97	67	9	68	0	203	3.2	38	127	2.0	450	7.0
92-93 NJ	55	55	2010	370	850	.435	7	25	.280	180	232	.776	153	96	11	140	1	449	8.2	51	226	4.1	927	16.9
93-94 NJ*	82	82	3135	576	1381	.417	40	132	.303	346	423	.818	266	158	15	201	0	784	9.6	89	322	3.9	1538	18.8
94-95 NJ	72	70	2689	411	1031	.399	97	294	.330	348	414	.841	225	103	14	184	1	680	9.4	73	250	3.5	1267	17.6
95-96 2Tm	69	64	2344	349	834	.418	92	256	.359	260	338	.769	146	111	14	178	1	575	8.3	63	203	2.9	1050	15.2
96-97 Por	82	81	3081	485	1137	.427	132	366	.361	334	435	.768	193	162	15	222	2	584	7.1	91	363	4.4	1436	17.5
97-98 2Tm	61	56	1858	268	674	.398	57	160	.356	153	194	.789	143	87	1	135	1	345	5.7	39	173	2.8	746	12.2
98-99 Bos	34	33	1010	161	357	.451	6	24	.250	84	101	.832	71	33	2	78	1	193	5.7	24	103	3.0	412	12.1
99-00 Bos	82	82	2593	434	986	.440	85	220	.386	196	253	.775	130	109	8	230	4	420	5.1	55	225	2.7	1149	14.0
95-96 NJ	31	28	1042	143	380	.376	36	99	.364	151	188	.803	58	52	8	73	0	247	8.0	37	101	3.3	473	15.3
Cha	38	36	1302	206	454	.454	56	157	.357	109	150	.727	88	59	6	105	1	328	8.6	26	102	2.7	577	15.2
97-98 Por	45	40	1472	204	527	.387	47	133	.353	112	145	.772	114	61	1	99	1	245	5.4	36	134	3.0	567	12.6
Bos	16	16	386	64	147	.435	10	27	.370	41	49	.837	29	26	0	36	0	100	6.3	3	39	2.4	179	11.2
9 Years	601	536	19806	3241	7730	.419	519	1490	.348	1974	2488	.793	1424	956	89	1436	11	4233	7.0	523	1992	3.3	8975	14.9

NBA Postseason

Year Tm	G	GS	Min	Md	Att	Pct	Md	Att	Pct	Md	Att	Pct	TO	Stl	Blk	PF	DQ	Ast	Avg	Off	Tot	Avg	Pts	Avg
91-92 NJ	3	0	24	3	9	.333	0	0	—	2	2	1.000	1	1	0	1	0	3	1.0	1	3	1.0	8	2.7
93-94 NJ	4	4	181	19	54	.352	3	10	.300	22	33	.667	9	9	0	11	0	27	6.8	2	12	3.0	63	15.8
96-97 Por	4	4	169	22	46	.478	5	19	.263	19	20	.950	11	7	1	10	0	19	4.8	2	17	4.3	68	17.0
3 Years	11	8	374	44	109	.404	8	29	.276	43	55	.782	21	17	1	22	0	49	4.5	5	32	2.9	139	12.6

Nick Anderson

(statistical profile on page 187)

Pos: G-F **College:** Illinois **Drafted:** '89 1(11)—Orl   **Ht:** 6'6" **Wt:** 228 **Born:** 1/20/68 **Age:** 33

College Year Tm	G	GS	Min	Field Goals Md	Att	Pct	3-Pt FGs Md	Att	Pct	Free Throws Md	Att	Pct	Misc TO	Stl	Blk	Fouls PF	DQ	Assists Ast	Avg	Rebounds Off	Tot	Avg	Points Pts	Avg
87-88 Ill	33	25	909	223	390	.572	2	6	.333	77	120	.642	57	37	28	70	0	53	1.6	—	217	6.6	525	15.9
88-89 Ill	36	32	1125	262	487	.538	24	66	.364	99	148	.669	59	57	32	69	0	72	2.0	—	285	7.9	647	18.0
2 Years	69	57	2034	485	877	.553	26	72	.361	176	268	.657	116	94	60	139	0	125	1.8	—	502	7.3	1172	17.0

NBA Year Tm	G	GS	Min	Field Goals Md	Att	Pct	3-Pt FGs Md	Att	Pct	Free Throws Md	Att	Pct	Misc TO	Stl	Blk	Fouls PF	DQ	Assists Ast	Avg	Rebounds Off	Tot	Avg	Points Pts	Avg
89-90 Orl	81	9	1785	372	753	.494	1	17	.059	186	264	.705	124	69	34	140	0	124	1.5	107	316	3.9	931	11.5
90-91 Orl	70	42	1971	400	857	.467	17	58	.293	173	259	.668	113	74	44	145	0	106	1.5	92	386	5.5	990	14.1
91-92 Orl	60	59	2203	482	1042	.463	30	85	.353	202	303	.667	126	97	33	132	0	163	2.7	98	384	6.4	1196	19.9
92-93 Orl	79	76	2920	594	1324	.449	88	249	.353	298	402	.741	164	128	56	200	1	265	3.4	122	477	6.0	1574	19.9
93-94 Orl	81	81	2811	504	1054	.478	101	314	.322	168	250	.672	165	134	33	148	1	294	3.6	113	476	5.9	1277	15.8
94-95 Orl	76	76	2588	439	923	.476	179	431	.415	143	203	.704	141	125	22	124	0	314	4.1	85	335	4.4	1200	15.8
95-96 Orl	77	77	2717	400	904	.442	168	430	.391	166	240	.692	141	121	46	135	0	279	3.6	92	415	5.4	1134	14.7
96-97 Orl	63	61	2163	288	725	.397	143	405	.353	38	94	.404	86	120	32	160	1	182	2.9	66	304	4.8	757	12.0

NBA				Field Goals			3-Pt FGs			Free Throws			Misc			Fouls		Assists		Rebounds			Points	
Year Tm	G	GS	Min	Md	Att	Pct	Md	Att	Pct	Md	Att	Pct	TO	Stl	Blk	PF	DQ	Ast	Avg	Off	Tot	Avg	Pts	Avg
97-98 Orl	58	44	1701	343	754	.455	77	214	.360	127	199	.638	85	72	23	98	1	119	2.1	98	297	5.1	890	15.3
98-99 Orl	47	39	1581	253	640	.395	96	277	.347	99	162	.611	83	64	15	72	0	91	1.9	51	277	5.9	701	14.9
99-00 Sac	72	72	2094	306	782	.391	132	397	.332	37	76	.487	95	94	16	118	0	123	1.7	83	339	4.7	781	10.8
11 Years	764	636	24534	4381	9758	.449	1032	2877	.359	1637	2452	.668	1337	1098	354	1472	4	2060	2.7	1007	4006	5.2	11431	15.0

NBA Postseason

Year Tm	G	GS	Min	Md	Att	Pct	Md	Att	Pct	Md	Att	Pct	TO	Stl	Blk	PF	DQ	Ast	Avg	Off	Tot	Avg	Pts	Avg
93-94 Orl	3	3	120	13	34	.382	8	20	.400	9	12	.750	5	5	2	8	0	10	3.3	2	10	3.3	43	14.3
94-95 Orl	21	21	814	107	239	.448	41	107	.383	43	63	.683	30	33	10	49	0	65	3.1	21	100	4.8	298	14.2
95-96 Orl	11	11	418	55	127	.433	18	63	.286	28	45	.622	21	21	5	22	0	21	1.9	16	55	5.0	156	14.2
96-97 Orl	5	5	130	12	36	.333	4	15	.267	0	2	.000	6	3	9	8	0	3	0.6	3	29	5.8	28	5.6
98-99 Orl	4	4	152	29	79	.367	11	42	.262	14	19	.737	10	9	0	12	1	9	2.3	7	27	6.8	83	20.8
99-00 Sac	5	5	132	11	34	.324	7	20	.350	7	8	.875	4	1	3	9	0	2	0.4	4	17	3.4	36	7.2
6 Years	49	49	1766	227	549	.413	89	267	.333	101	149	.678	76	72	29	108	1	110	2.2	53	238	4.9	644	13.1

Shandon Anderson

(statistical profile on page 187)

Pos: F **College:** Georgia **Drafted:** '96 2(54)—Uta **Ht:** 6'6" **Wt:** 210 **Born:** 12/13/73 **Age:** 27

College				Field Goals			3-Pt FGs			Free Throws			Misc			Fouls		Assists		Rebounds			Points	
Year Tm	G	GS	Min	Md	Att	Pct	Md	Att	Pct	Md	Att	Pct	TO	Stl	Blk	PF	DQ	Ast	Avg	Off	Tot	Avg	Pts	Avg
92-93 UGa	29	0	554	99	201	.493	9	26	.346	64	105	.610	65	52	7	59	1	44	1.5	—	103	3.6	271	9.3
93-94 UGa	30	30	859	157	324	.485	6	34	.176	93	141	.660	109	59	10	87	3	114	3.8	—	168	5.6	413	13.8
94-95 UGa	28	28	827	149	315	.473	17	53	.321	56	95	.589	86	45	7	72	3	83	3.0	—	145	5.2	371	13.3
95-96 UGa	31	31	891	176	327	.538	16	52	.308	94	143	.657	78	56	15	73	1	83	2.7	—	103	3.3	462	14.9
4 Years	118	89	3131	581	1167	.498	48	165	.291	307	484	.634	338	212	39	291	8	324	2.7	—	519	4.4	1517	12.9

NBA				Field Goals			3-Pt FGs			Free Throws			Misc			Fouls		Assists		Rebounds			Points	
Year Tm	G	GS	Min	Md	Att	Pct	Md	Att	Pct	Md	Att	Pct	TO	Stl	Blk	PF	DQ	Ast	Avg	Off	Tot	Avg	Pts	Avg
96-97 Uta	65	0	1066	147	318	.462	24	47	.511	68	99	.687	73	27	8	113	0	49	0.8	52	179	2.8	386	5.9
97-98 Uta	82	2	1602	269	500	.538	7	32	.219	136	185	.735	92	66	18	145	0	89	1.1	86	227	2.8	681	8.3
98-99 Uta	50	2	1072	162	363	.446	14	41	.341	89	125	.712	66	39	10	89	0	56	1.1	49	132	2.6	427	8.5
99-00 Hou	82	82	2700	368	778	.473	79	225	.351	194	263	.767	194	96	32	182	0	239	2.9	91	384	4.7	2503	9.0
4 Years	279	86	6440	946	1959	.483	124	345	.359	487	662	.736	425	228	68	529	0	433	1.6	278	922	3.3	2503	9.0

NBA Postseason

Year Tm	G	GS	Min	Md	Att	Pct	Md	Att	Pct	Md	Att	Pct	TO	Stl	Blk	PF	DQ	Ast	Avg	Off	Tot	Avg	Pts	Avg
96-97 Uta	18	0	296	29	66	.439	5	12	.417	20	28	.714	13	11	1	28	0	13	0.7	20	48	2.7	83	4.6
97-98 Uta	20	0	378	53	103	.515	3	11	.273	25	37	.676	30	5	1	30	0	19	1.0	26	63	3.2	134	6.7
98-99 Uta	11	0	297	37	77	.481	6	14	.429	24	34	.706	14	6	3	34	2	13	1.2	8	41	3.7	104	9.5
3 Years	49	0	971	119	246	.484	14	37	.378	69	99	.697	57	22	5	92	2	45	0.9	54	152	3.1	321	6.6

Chris Anstey

Pos: C **College:** None **Drafted:** '97 1(18)—Por **Ht:** 7'0" **Wt:** 249 **Born:** 1/1/75 **Age:** 26

NBA				Field Goals			3-Pt FGs			Free Throws			Misc			Fouls		Assists		Rebounds			Points	
Year Tm	G	GS	Min	Md	Att	Pct	Md	Att	Pct	Md	Att	Pct	TO	Stl	Blk	PF	DQ	Ast	Avg	Off	Tot	Avg	Pts	Avg
97-98 Dal	41	8	680	92	231	.398	3	16	.188	53	74	.716	41	31	27	95	1	35	0.9	53	157	3.8	240	5.9
98-99 Dal	41	4	470	50	139	.360	0	7	.000	34	48	.708	26	18	13	98	1	27	0.7	35	97	2.4	134	3.3
99-00 Chi	73	11	1007	161	364	.442	1	6	.167	116	147	.789	80	29	25	180	4	65	0.9	90	280	3.8	813	5.2
3 Years	155	23	2157	303	734	.413	4	29	.138	203	269	.755	147	78	65	373	6	127	0.8	178	534	3.4	813	5.2

Greg Anthony

(statistical profile on page 188)

Pos: G **College:** UNLV **Drafted:** '91 1(12)—NY **Ht:** 6'1" **Wt:** 180 **Born:** 11/15/67 **Age:** 33

College				Field Goals			3-Pt FGs			Free Throws			Misc			Fouls		Assists		Rebounds			Points	
Year Tm	G	GS	Min	Md	Att	Pct	Md	Att	Pct	Md	Att	Pct	TO	Stl	Blk	PF	DQ	Ast	Avg	Off	Tot	Avg	Pts	Avg
86-87 Por	28	—	923	147	369	.398	35	95	.368	100	144	.694	71	54	8	67	—	112	4.0	—	121	4.3	429	15.3
88-89 UNLV	36	—	1025	155	350	.443	47	125	.376	107	153	.699	107	85	8	111	—	239	6.6	—	102	2.8	464	12.9
89-90 UNLV	39	39	1160	145	317	.457	45	120	.375	101	148	.682	121	106	16	100	—	289	7.4	—	116	3.0	436	11.2
90-91 UNLV	35	35	1100	141	309	.456	45	114	.395	79	102	.775	68	84	14	68	—	310	8.9	—	89	2.5	1735	12.6
4 Years	138	—	4208	588	1345	.437	172	454	.379	387	547	.707	367	329	46	346	—	950	6.9	—	428	3.1	1735	12.6

NBA				Field Goals			3-Pt FGs			Free Throws			Misc			Fouls		Assists		Rebounds			Points	
Year Tm	G	GS	Min	Md	Att	Pct	Md	Att	Pct	Md	Att	Pct	TO	Stl	Blk	PF	DQ	Ast	Avg	Off	Tot	Avg	Pts	Avg
91-92 NY	82	1	1510	161	435	.370	8	55	.145	117	158	.741	98	59	9	170	0	314	3.8	33	136	1.7	447	5.5
92-93 NY	70	35	1699	174	419	.415	4	30	.133	107	159	.673	104	113	12	141	0	398	5.7	42	170	2.4	459	6.6
93-94 NY	80	36	1994	225	571	.394	48	160	.300	130	168	.774	127	114	13	163	1	365	4.6	43	189	2.4	628	7.9

NBA				Field Goals			3-Pt FGs			Free Throws			Misc			Fouls		Assists		Rebounds			Points	
Year Tm	G	GS	Min	Md	Att	Pct	Md	Att	Pct	Md	Att	Pct	TO	Stl	Blk	PF	DQ	Ast	Avg	Off	Tot	Avg	Pts	Avg
94-95 NY	61	2	943	128	293	.437	56	155	.361	60	76	.789	57	50	7	99	1	160	2.6	7	64	1.0	372	6.1
95-96 Van	69	68	2096	324	781	.415	90	271	.332	229	297	.771	160	116	11	137	1	476	6.9	29	174	2.5	967	14.0
96-97 Van	65	44	1863	199	507	.393	88	238	.370	130	178	.730	129	129	4	122	0	407	6.3	25	184	2.8	616	9.5
97-98 Sea	80	0	1021	150	349	.430	66	159	.415	53	80	.663	91	64	3	97	0	205	2.6	18	111	1.4	419	5.2
98-99 Por	50	0	806	104	251	.414	49	125	.392	62	89	.697	55	66	3	75	0	100	2.0	14	63	1.3	319	6.4
99-00 Por	82	3	1548	169	416	.406	88	233	.378	88	114	.772	85	59	9	143	0	208	2.5	17	133	1.6	514	6.3
9 Years	639	189	13480	1634	4022	.406	497	1426	.349	976	1319	.740	906	770	71	1147	3	2633	4.1	228	1224	1.9	4741	7.4

NBA Postseason																								
Year Tm	G	GS	Min	Md	Att	Pct	Md	Att	Pct	Md	Att	Pct	TO	Stl	Blk	PF	DQ	Ast	Avg	Off	Tot	Avg	Pts	Avg
91-92 NY	12	0	213	19	46	.413	5	12	.417	20	33	.606	13	16	1	28	0	41	3.4	4	17	1.4	63	5.3
92-93 NY	15	0	240	24	60	.400	3	14	.214	8	14	.571	11	13	1	26	0	52	3.5	4	30	2.0	59	3.9
93-94 NY	25	3	436	45	128	.352	18	61	.295	14	24	.583	31	19	8	52	0	59	2.4	4	27	1.1	122	4.9
94-95 NY	11	0	135	15	38	.395	7	23	.304	10	11	.909	6	2	2	27	0	15	1.4	2	10	0.9	47	4.3
97-98 Sea	9	0	118	12	40	.300	5	19	.263	3	8	.375	11	5	1	17	1	10	1.1	3	10	1.1	32	3.6
98-99 Por	13	0	225	18	55	.327	8	31	.258	23	34	.676	11	13	1	25	0	32	2.5	4	14	1.1	67	5.2
99-00 Por	15	0	213	19	52	.365	10	31	.323	12	16	.750	12	13	4	27	0	25	1.7	2	16	1.1	60	4.0
7 Years	100	3	1580	152	419	.363	56	191	.293	90	140	.643	93	81	18	205	1	234	2.3	28	124	1.2	450	4.5

B.J. Armstrong

Pos: G **College:** Iowa **Drafted:** '89 1(18)—Chi
Ht: 6'2" **Wt:** 185 **Born:** 9/9/67 **Age:** 33

College				Field Goals			3-Pt FGs			Free Throws			Misc			Fouls		Assists		Rebounds			Points	
Year Tm	G	GS	Min	Md	Att	Pct	Md	Att	Pct	Md	Att	Pct	TO	Stl	Blk	PF	DQ	Ast	Avg	Off	Tot	Avg	Pts	Avg
85-86 Iowa	29	3	232	32	66	.485	—	—	—	19	21	.905	19	8	0	17	0	41	1.4	—	16	0.6	83	2.9
86-87 Iowa	35	35	995	153	295	.519	28	54	.519	100	126	.794	82	50	1	55	1	148	4.2	—	89	2.5	434	12.4
87-88 Iowa	34	—	1023	203	421	.482	62	137	.453	124	146	.849	77	66	1	35	—	155	4.6	—	74	2.2	592	17.4
88-89 Iowa	32	31	1015	195	403	.484	46	116	.397	160	192	.833	77	59	7	50	0	173	5.4	—	79	2.5	596	18.6
4 Years	130		3265	583	1185	.492	136	307	.443	403	485	.831	255	183	9	157	—	517	4.0	—	258	2.0	1705	13.1

NBA				Field Goals			3-Pt FGs			Free Throws			Misc			Fouls		Assists		Rebounds			Points	
Year Tm	G	GS	Min	Md	Att	Pct	Md	Att	Pct	Md	Att	Pct	TO	Stl	Blk	PF	DQ	Ast	Avg	Off	Tot	Avg	Pts	Avg
89-90 Chi	81	0	1291	190	392	.485	3	6	.500	69	78	.885	83	46	0	105	0	199	2.5	19	102	1.3	452	5.6
90-91 Chi	82	0	1731	304	632	.481	15	30	.500	97	111	.874	107	70	4	118	0	301	3.7	25	149	1.8	720	8.8
91-92 Chi	82	3	1875	335	697	.481	35	87	.402	104	129	.806	94	46	5	88	0	266	3.2	19	145	1.8	809	9.9
92-93 Chi	82	74	2492	408	818	.499	63	139	.453	130	161	.807	83	66	6	169	0	330	4.0	27	149	1.8	1009	12.3
93-94 Chi*	82	82	2770	479	1007	.476	60	135	.444	194	227	.855	131	80	6	147	1	323	3.9	28	170	2.1	1212	14.8
94-95 Chi	82	82	2577	418	894	.468	108	253	.427	206	233	.884	103	84	8	159	0	244	3.0	25	186	2.3	1150	14.0
95-96 GS	82	64	2262	340	727	.468	98	207	.473	234	279	.839	128	68	6	147	0	401	4.9	25	184	2.2	1012	12.3
96-97 GS	49	17	1020	148	327	.453	25	90	.278	68	79	.861	53	25	2	56	0	126	2.6	7	74	1.5	389	7.9
97-98 2Tm	66	0	831	105	213	.493	9	35	.257	42	50	.840	42	29	0	74	0	150	2.3	16	76	1.2	261	4.0
98-99 2Tm	32	1	358	40	88	.455	7	15	.467	18	21	.857	25	12	0	31	0	61	1.9	2	39	1.2	105	3.3
99-00 Chi	27	18	583	83	186	.446	13	29	.448	22	25	.880	40	7	1	34	0	78	2.9	2	47	1.7	201	7.4
97-98 GS	4	0	59	6	19	.316	0	1	.000	5	7	.714	7	4	0	6	0	6	1.5	4	7	1.8	17	4.3
Cha	62	0	772	99	194	.510	9	34	.265	37	43	.860	35	25	0	68	0	144	2.3	12	69	1.1	244	3.9
98-99 Cha	10	1	178	21	43	.488	6	8	.750	9	10	.900	10	3	0	16	0	27	2.7	1	16	1.6	57	5.7
Orl	22	0	180	19	45	.422	1	7	.143	9	11	.818	15	9	0	15	0	34	1.5	1	23	1.0	48	2.2
11 Years	747	341	17790	2850	5981	.477	436	1026	.425	1184	1383	.856	889	533	47	1128	1	2479	3.3	192	1321	1.8	7320	9.8

NBA Postseason																								
Year Tm	G	GS	Min	Md	Att	Pct	Md	Att	Pct	Md	Att	Pct	TO	Stl	Blk	PF	DQ	Ast	Avg	Off	Tot	Avg	Pts	Avg
89-90 Chi	16	0	217	21	62	.339	0	4	.000	22	24	.917	12	10	0	22	0	29	1.8	3	20	1.3	64	4.0
90-91 Chi	17	0	273	35	70	.500	3	5	.600	20	25	.800	13	19	1	13	0	43	2.5	5	27	1.6	93	5.5
91-92 Chi	22	0	434	63	139	.453	5	17	.294	30	38	.789	18	14	0	33	0	47	2.1	2	24	1.1	161	7.3
92-93 Chi	19	19	643	88	168	.524	21	41	.512	20	22	.909	14	19	2	49	0	62	3.3	2	28	1.5	217	11.4
93-94 Chi	10	10	360	55	106	.519	7	12	.583	36	44	.818	9	8	0	21	0	25	2.5	2	24	2.4	153	15.3
94-95 Chi	10	10	288	36	79	.456	13	29	.448	18	22	.818	6	6	0	21	0	27	2.7	4	18	1.8	103	10.3
97-98 Cha	9	0	146	16	42	.381	2	5	.400	3	4	.750	6	6	0	11	0	18	2.0	2	10	1.1	37	4.1
98-99 Orl	2	0	3	0	1	.000	0	0	—	0	0	—	1	0	0	1	0	1	0.5	0	0	0.0	0	0.0
8 Years	105	39	2364	314	667	.471	51	113	.451	149	179	.832	79	82	3	171	0	252	2.4	24	151	1.4	828	7.9

Darrell Armstrong

Pos: G **College:** Fayetteville State **Drafted:** '94 FA—Orl
Ht: 6'1" **Wt:** 180 **Born:** 6/22/68 **Age:** 32
(statistical profile on page 188)

College				Field Goals			3-Pt FGs			Free Throws			Misc			Fouls		Assists		Rebounds			Points	
Year Tm	G	GS	Min	Md	Att	Pct	Md	Att	Pct	Md	Att	Pct	TO	Stl	Blk	PF	DQ	Ast	Avg	Off	Tot	Avg	Pts	Avg
88-89 Fay	27	—	662	131	255	.514	14	40	.350	93	116	.802	—	—	—	—	—	58	2.1	—	80	3.0	369	13.7

College

Year Tm	G	GS	Min	FG Md	FG Att	FG Pct	3P Md	3P Att	3P Pct	FT Md	FT Att	FT Pct	TO	Stl	Blk	PF	DQ	Ast	Avg	Off	Tot	Avg	Pts	Avg
89-90 Fay	27	—	800	125	235	.532	17	40	.425	83	106	.783	—	—	—	—	—	125	4.6	—	140	5.2	350	13.0
90-91 Fay	24	—	643	117	233	.502	44	107	.411	115	152	.757	—	—	—	—	—	113	4.7	—	86	3.6	393	16.4
3 Years	78	—	2105	373	723	.516	75	187	.401	291	374	.778	—	—	—	—	—	296	3.8	—	306	3.9	1112	14.3

NBA

Year Tm	G	GS	Min	FG Md	FG Att	FG Pct	3P Md	3P Att	3P Pct	FT Md	FT Att	FT Pct	TO	Stl	Blk	PF	DQ	Ast	Avg	Off	Tot	Avg	Pts	Avg
91-92	Played in GBA, Played in USBL																							
92-93	Played in GBA, Played in CBA, Played in USBL																							
93-94	Played in Cyprus, Played in USBL																							
94-95 Orl	3	0	8	3	8	.375	2	6	.333	2	2	1.000	1	1	0	3	0	3	1.0	1	1	0.3	10	3.3
95-96 Orl	13	0	41	16	32	.500	6	12	.500	4	4	1.000	6	6	0	4	0	5	0.4	0	2	0.2	42	3.2
96-97 Orl	67	0	1010	132	345	.383	55	181	.304	92	106	.868	99	61	9	114	1	175	2.6	35	76	1.1	411	6.1
97-98 Orl	48	17	1236	156	380	.411	25	68	.368	105	123	.854	112	58	5	96	1	236	4.9	65	159	3.3	442	9.2
98-99 Orl	50	15	1502	230	522	.441	69	189	.365	161	178	.904	158	108	4	90	0	335	6.7	65	180	3.6	690	13.8
99-00 Orl	82	82	2590	484	1119	.433	137	403	.340	225	247	.911	248	169	9	137	0	501	6.1	65	270	3.3	2925	11.1
6 Years	263	114	6387	1021	2406	.424	294	859	.342	589	660	.892	624	403	27	444	2	1255	4.8	219	688	2.6	2925	11.1

NBA Postseason

Year Tm	G	GS	Min	FG Md	FG Att	FG Pct	3P Md	3P Att	3P Pct	FT Md	FT Att	FT Pct	TO	Stl	Blk	PF	DQ	Ast	Avg	Off	Tot	Avg	Pts	Avg
96-97 Orl	5	0	143	20	42	.476	6	18	.333	11	13	.846	7	8	1	6	0	17	3.4	3	21	4.2	57	11.4
98-99 Orl	4	4	163	17	46	.370	9	24	.375	16	16	1.000	25	9	0	16	1	25	6.3	6	20	5.0	59	14.8
2 Years	9	4	306	37	88	.420	15	42	.357	27	29	.931	32	17	1	22	1	42	4.7	9	41	4.6	116	12.9

Ron Artest

(statistical profile on page 189)

Pos: G-F **College:** St. John's (NY) **Drafted:** '99 1(16)—Chi **Ht:** 6'7" **Wt:** 246 **Born:** 11/13/79 **Age:** 21

College

Year Tm	G	GS	Min	FG Md	FG Att	FG Pct	3P Md	3P Att	3P Pct	FT Md	FT Att	FT Pct	TO	Stl	Blk	PF	DQ	Ast	Avg	Off	Tot	Avg	Pts	Avg
97-98 StJn	32	12	870	139	335	.415	34	104	.327	60	114	.526	92	52	36	79	2	62	1.9	79	201	6.3	372	11.6
98-99 StJn	37	37	1265	196	418	.469	58	155	.374	85	132	.644	105	76	44	85	4	156	4.2	61	232	6.3	535	14.5
2 Years	69	49	2135	335	753	.445	92	259	.355	145	246	.589	197	128	80	164	6	218	3.2	140	433	6.3	907	13.1

NBA

Year Tm	G	GS	Min	FG Md	FG Att	FG Pct	3P Md	3P Att	3P Pct	FT Md	FT Att	FT Pct	TO	Stl	Blk	PF	DQ	Ast	Avg	Off	Tot	Avg	Pts	Avg
99-00 Chi	72	63	2238	309	759	.407	60	191	.314	188	279	.674	166	119	39	159	0	202	2.8	62	308	4.3	866	12.0

Chucky Atkins

(statistical profile on page 189)

Pos: G **College:** South Florida **Drafted:** '99 FA—Orl **Ht:** 5'11" **Wt:** 160 **Born:** 8/14/74 **Age:** 26

College

Year Tm	G	GS	Min	FG Md	FG Att	FG Pct	3P Md	3P Att	3P Pct	FT Md	FT Att	FT Pct	TO	Stl	Blk	PF	DQ	Ast	Avg	Off	Tot	Avg	Pts	Avg
92-93 SoFl	27	27	867	94	221	.425	41	101	.406	46	72	.639	83	26	2	51	1	108	4.0	16	93	3.4	275	10.2
93-94 SoFl	26	25	787	96	269	.357	37	134	.276	70	94	.745	65	19	1	48	2	104	4.0	13	62	2.4	299	11.5
94-95 SoFl	30	30	1067	161	389	.414	84	219	.384	98	131	.748	100	35	1	55	1	196	6.5	15	96	3.2	504	16.8
95-96 SoFl	28	28	1064	175	405	.432	82	220	.373	109	141	.773	92	35	7	54	0	111	4.0	17	85	3.0	541	19.3
4 Years	111	110	3785	526	1284	.410	244	674	.362	323	438	.737	340	115	11	208	4	519	4.7	61	336	3.0	1619	14.6

NBA

Year Tm	G	GS	Min	FG Md	FG Att	FG Pct	3P Md	3P Att	3P Pct	FT Md	FT Att	FT Pct	TO	Stl	Blk	PF	DQ	Ast	Avg	Off	Tot	Avg	Pts	Avg
96-97	Played in CBA																							
97-98	Played in Croatia																							
98-99	Played in Croatia																							
99-00 Orl	82	0	1626	314	741	.424	57	163	.350	97	133	.729	142	52	3	137	1	306	3.7	20	126	1.5	782	9.5

Stacey Augmon

Pos: F **College:** UNLV **Drafted:** '91 1(9)—Atl **Ht:** 6'8" **Wt:** 205 **Born:** 8/1/68 **Age:** 32

College

Year Tm	G	GS	Min	FG Md	FG Att	FG Pct	3P Md	3P Att	3P Pct	FT Md	FT Att	FT Pct	TO	Stl	Blk	PF	DQ	Ast	Avg	Off	Tot	Avg	Pts	Avg
87-88 UNLV	34	—	884	117	204	.574	2	2	1.000	75	116	.647	70	69	24	104	—	64	1.9	—	206	6.1	311	9.1
88-89 UNLV	37	—	1091	210	405	.519	41	98	.418	106	160	.663	89	59	27	104	—	101	2.7	—	274	7.4	567	15.3
89-90 UNLV	39	39	1246	210	380	.553	16	50	.320	118	176	.670	91	69	49	96	—	143	3.7	—	270	6.9	554	14.2
90-91 UNLV	35	35	1062	220	375	.587	38	81	.469	101	139	.727	62	78	28	76	—	125	3.6	—	255	7.3	579	16.5
4 Years	145	—	4283	757	1364	.555	97	231	.420	400	591	.677	312	275	128	380	—	433	3.0	—	1005	6.9	2011	13.9

Year Tm	G	GS	Min	FG Md	FG Att	FG Pct	3P Md	3P Att	3P Pct	FT Md	FT Att	FT Pct	TO	Stl	Blk	PF	DQ	Ast	Ast Avg	Off	Tot	Reb Avg	Pts	Pts Avg
NBA																								
91-92 Atl	82	82	2505	440	899	.489	1	6	.167	213	320	.666	181	124	27	161	0	201	2.5	191	420	5.1	1094	13.3
92-93 Atl	73	66	2112	397	792	.501	0	4	.000	227	307	.739	157	91	18	141	1	170	2.3	141	287	3.9	1021	14.0
93-94 Atl	82	82	2605	439	861	.510	1	7	.143	333	436	.764	147	149	45	179	0	187	2.3	141	394	4.8	1212	14.8
94-95 Atl	76	76	2362	397	876	.453	7	26	.269	252	346	.728	152	100	47	163	0	178	2.3	178	368	4.8	1053	13.9
95-96 Atl	77	49	2294	362	738	.491	1	4	.250	251	317	.792	138	106	31	188	1	156	2.0	157	304	3.9	976	12.7
96-97 2Tm	60	10	942	105	220	.477	0	0	—	69	97	.711	64	42	17	87	0	56	0.9	47	138	2.3	279	4.7
97-98 Por	71	23	1445	154	372	.414	1	7	.143	94	156	.603	81	57	32	144	0	88	1.2	104	235	3.3	403	5.7
98-99 Por	48	21	874	78	174	.448	0	2	.000	52	76	.684	30	57	18	81	0	58	1.2	47	125	2.6	208	4.3
99-00 Por	59	0	692	83	175	.474	0	2	.000	37	55	.673	38	27	11	69	0	53	0.9	47	116	2.0	203	3.4
96-97 Det	20	3	292	31	77	.403	0	0	—	28	41	.683	27	10	10	29	0	15	0.8	14	49	2.5	90	4.5
Por	40	7	650	74	143	.517	0	0	—	41	56	.732	37	32	7	58	0	41	1.0	33	89	2.2	189	4.7
9 Years	628	409	15831	2455	5107	.481	11	58	.190	1528	2110	.724	988	753	246	1213	2	1147	1.8	1044	2387	3.8	6449	10.3

Year Tm	G	GS	Min	FG Md	FG Att	FG Pct	3P Md	3P Att	3P Pct	FT Md	FT Att	FT Pct	TO	Stl	Blk	PF	DQ	Ast	Ast Avg	Off	Tot	Reb Avg	Pts	Pts Avg
NBA Postseason																								
92-93 Atl	3	3	93	14	31	.452	0	0	—	8	12	.667	4	4	0	7	0	5	1.7	3	8	2.7	36	12.0
93-94 Atl	11	11	324	46	89	.517	0	0	—	27	38	.711	15	7	2	26	0	28	2.5	13	29	2.6	119	10.8
94-95 Atl	3	1	52	6	14	.429	0	0	—	9	12	.750	2	3	0	8	0	5	1.7	3	7	2.3	21	7.0
95-96 Atl	10	10	314	35	72	.486	0	1	.000	33	40	.825	17	11	6	26	0	27	2.7	9	36	3.6	103	10.3
96-97 Por	4	0	35	2	6	.333	0	0	—	3	4	.750	1	1	0	6	0	3	0.8	1	1	0.3	7	1.8
97-98 Por	4	0	28	2	4	.500	0	0	—	1	2	.500	2	2	1	2	0	1	0.3	1	3	0.8	5	1.3
98-99 Por	13	0	176	10	28	.357	0	1	.000	15	18	.833	3	8	3	15	0	5	0.4	10	33	2.5	35	2.7
99-00 Por	7	0	34	4	12	.333	0	0	—	1	2	.500	0	0	0	6	0	0	0.0	0	2	0.3	9	1.3
8 Years	55	25	1056	119	256	.465	0	2	.000	97	128	.758	44	36	12	96	0	74	1.3	40	119	2.2	335	6.1

Isaac Austin

Pos: F-C **College:** Arizona State **Drafted:** '91 FA—Uta **Ht:** 6'10" **Wt:** 270 **Born:** 8/18/69 **Age:** 31

Year Tm	G	GS	Min	FG Md	FG Att	FG Pct	3P Md	3P Att	3P Pct	FT Md	FT Att	FT Pct	TO	Stl	Blk	PF	DQ	Ast	Ast Avg	Off	Tot	Reb Avg	Pts	Pts Avg
College																								
89-90 AriSt	31	27	848	164	300	.547	0	1	.000	97	150	.647	77	20	24	92	3	27	0.9	—	192	6.2	425	13.7
90-91 AriSt	30	30	906	189	331	.571	0	1	.000	112	178	.629	75	29	17	83	2	57	1.9	—	262	8.7	490	16.3
2 Years	61	57	1754	353	631	.559	0	2	.000	209	328	.637	152	49	41	175	5	84	1.4	—	454	7.4	915	15.0
NBA																								
91-92 Uta	31	0	112	21	46	.457	0	0	—	19	30	.633	8	2	2	20	0	5	0.2	11	35	1.1	61	2.0
92-93 Uta	46	3	306	50	112	.446	0	1	.000	29	44	.659	23	8	14	60	1	6	0.1	38	79	1.7	129	2.8
93-94 Phi	14	0	201	29	66	.439	0	1	.000	14	23	.609	17	5	10	29	0	17	1.2	25	69	4.9	72	5.1
94-95										Played in France														
95-96										Played in Turkey														
96-97 Mia	82	17	1881	321	639	.502	0	3	.000	150	226	.664	161	45	43	244	4	101	1.2	136	478	5.8	792	9.7
97-98 2Tm	78	50	2266	406	871	.466	0	8	.000	243	363	.669	206	61	56	231	5	175	2.2	199	557	7.1	1055	13.5
98-99 Orl	49	49	1259	185	453	.408	2	7	.286	105	157	.669	114	47	35	125	1	89	1.8	83	237	4.8	477	9.7
99-00 Was	59	23	1173	151	352	.429	1	4	.250	94	137	.686	107	17	38	128	0	74	1.3	64	282	4.8	397	6.7
97-98 Mia	52	25	1371	252	532	.474	0	3	.000	155	228	.680	117	43	34	162	5	87	1.7	119	330	6.3	659	12.7
LAC	26	25	895	154	339	.454	0	5	.000	88	135	.652	89	18	22	69	0	88	3.4	80	227	8.7	396	15.2
7 Years	359	142	7198	1163	2539	.458	3	24	.125	654	980	.667	636	185	198	837	11	467	1.3	556	1737	4.8	2983	8.3
NBA Postseason																								
92-93 Uta	1	0	3	1	2	.500	0	0	—	0	0	—	0	0	1	1	0	0	0.0	0	1	1.0	2	2.0
96-97 Mia	15	0	287	36	81	.444	1	4	.250	25	31	.806	22	6	7	35	0	6	0.4	16	66	4.4	98	6.5
98-99 Orl	4	4	112	9	23	.391	0	2	.000	8	12	.667	8	4	3	14	0	8	2.0	7	16	4.0	26	6.5
3 Years	20	4	402	46	106	.434	1	6	.167	33	43	.767	30	10	11	50	0	14	0.7	23	83	4.2	126	6.3

Anthony Avent

Pos: F **College:** Seton Hall **Drafted:** '91 1(15)—Atl **Ht:** 6'9" **Wt:** 240 **Born:** 10/18/69 **Age:** 31

Year Tm	G	GS	Min	FG Md	FG Att	FG Pct	3P Md	3P Att	3P Pct	FT Md	FT Att	FT Pct	TO	Stl	Blk	PF	DQ	Ast	Ast Avg	Off	Tot	Reb Avg	Pts	Pts Avg
College																								
88-89 SetHl	38	1	395	68	149	.456	0	0	—	32	49	.653	38	6	27	63	1	12	0.3	42	114	3.0	168	4.4
89-90 SetHl	28	28	842	119	244	.488	0	0	—	55	89	.618	84	15	53	117	1	47	1.7	78	262	9.4	293	10.5
90-91 SetHl	34	34	1114	228	395	.577	0	0	—	150	200	.750	91	32	41	102	1	53	1.6	125	335	9.9	606	17.8
3 Years	100	63	2351	415	788	.527	0	0	—	237	338	.701	213	53	121	282	9	112	1.1	245	711	7.1	1067	10.7

NBA				Field Goals			3-Pt FGs			Free Throws			Misc			Fouls		Assists		Rebounds			Points	
Year Tm	G	GS	Min	Md	Att	Pct	Md	Att	Pct	Md	Att	Pct	TO	Stl	Blk	PF	DQ	Ast	Avg	Off	Tot	Avg	Pts	Avg
91-92										Played in Italy														
92-93 Mil	82	78	2285	347	802	.433	0	2	.000	112	172	.651	140	57	73	237	0	91	1.1	180	512	6.2	806	9.8
93-94 2Tm	74	40	1371	150	398	.377	0	0	—	89	123	.724	85	33	31	147	0	65	0.9	144	338	4.6	389	5.3
94-95 Orl	71	3	1066	105	244	.430	0	0	—	48	75	.640	53	28	50	170	1	41	0.6	97	293	4.1	258	3.6
95-96 Van	71	32	1586	179	466	.384	0	0	—	57	77	.740	107	30	42	202	3	69	1.0	108	355	5.0	415	5.8
96-97										Played in Greece														
97-98										Played in CBA — Elbow Injury														
98-99 Uta	5	0	44	4	13	.308	0	0	—	1	2	.500	7	2	0	6	0	1	0.2	8	12	2.4	9	1.8
99-00 LAC	49	3	377	29	96	.302	0	0	—	23	32	.719	24	16	15	62	1	11	0.2	23	74	1.5	81	1.7
93-94 Mil	33	20	695	92	228	.404	0	0	—	61	79	.772	43	16	20	60	0	33	1.0	60	154	4.7	245	7.4
Orl	41	20	676	58	170	.341	0	0	—	28	44	.636	42	17	11	87	0	32	0.8	84	184	4.5	144	3.5
6 Years	352	156	6729	814	2019	.403	0	2	.000	330	481	.686	416	166	211	824	5	278	0.8	560	1584	4.5	1958	5.6

NBA Postseason

Year Tm	G	GS	Min	Md	Att	Pct	Md	Att	Pct	Md	Att	Pct	TO	Stl	Blk	PF	DQ	Ast	Avg	Off	Tot	Avg	Pts	Avg
93-94 Orl	2	0	40	6	13	.462	0	0	—	7	8	.875	1	0	0	2	0	1	0.5	8	11	5.5	19	9.5
94-95 Orl	7	0	40	3	7	.429	0	1	.000	3	4	.750	2	0	1	11	0	0	0.0	4	8	1.1	9	1.3
2 Years	9	0	80	9	20	.450	0	1	.000	10	12	.833	3	0	1	13	0	1	0.1	12	19	2.1	28	3.1

William Avery

Pos: G **College:** Duke **Drafted:** '99 1(14)—Min   **Ht:** 6'2" **Wt:** 180 **Born:** 8/8/79 **Age:** 21

College				Field Goals			3-Pt FGs			Free Throws			Misc			Fouls		Assists		Rebounds			Points	
Year Tm	G	GS	Min	Md	Att	Pct	Md	Att	Pct	Md	Att	Pct	TO	Stl	Blk	PF	DQ	Ast	Avg	Off	Tot	Avg	Pts	Avg
97-98 Duke	35	0	674	102	239	.427	32	108	.296	61	82	.744	60	34	1	54	0	87	2.5	22	69	2.0	297	8.5
98-99 Duke	39	39	1210	201	416	.483	76	185	.411	102	126	.810	102	57	1	86	1	196	5.0	27	137	3.5	580	14.9
2 Years	74	39	1884	303	655	.463	108	293	.369	163	208	.784	162	91	2	140	1	283	3.8	49	206	2.8	877	11.9

NBA				Field Goals			3-Pt FGs			Free Throws			Misc			Fouls		Assists		Rebounds			Points	
Year Tm	G	GS	Min	Md	Att	Pct	Md	Att	Pct	Md	Att	Pct	TO	Stl	Blk	PF	DQ	Ast	Avg	Off	Tot	Avg	Pts	Avg
99-00 Min	59	1	484	56	181	.309	18	63	.286	24	36	.667	42	14	2	60	0	88	1.5	8	40	0.7	154	2.6

Toby Bailey

Pos: G **College:** UCLA **Drafted:** '98 2(45)—LAL   **Ht:** 6'6" **Wt:** 213 **Born:** 11/19/75 **Age:** 25

College				Field Goals			3-Pt FGs			Free Throws			Misc			Fouls		Assists		Rebounds			Points	
Year Tm	G	GS	Min	Md	Att	Pct	Md	Att	Pct	Md	Att	Pct	TO	Stl	Blk	PF	DQ	Ast	Avg	Off	Tot	Avg	Pts	Avg
94-95 UCLA	33	13	827	137	283	.484	20	73	.274	53	94	.564	67	35	9	73	1	63	1.9	—	158	4.8	347	10.5
95-96 UCLA	31	31	1063	170	371	.458	62	157	.395	56	87	.644	113	27	12	67	0	105	3.4	35	134	4.3	458	14.8
96-97 UCLA	32	32	1148	166	360	.461	42	126	.333	76	115	.661	116	39	7	72	0	155	4.8	50	183	5.7	450	14.1
97-98 UCLA	33	32	1177	206	465	.443	47	145	.324	132	179	.737	106	38	23	94	4	135	4.1	78	195	5.9	591	17.9
4 Years	129	108	4215	679	1479	.459	171	501	.341	317	475	.667	402	139	51	306	5	458	3.6	—	670	5.2	1846	14.3

NBA				Field Goals			3-Pt FGs			Free Throws			Misc			Fouls		Assists		Rebounds			Points	
Year Tm	G	GS	Min	Md	Att	Pct	Md	Att	Pct	Md	Att	Pct	TO	Stl	Blk	PF	DQ	Ast	Avg	Off	Tot	Avg	Pts	Avg
98-99 Pho	27	10	249	34	86	.395	1	5	.200	9	13	.692	11	9	2	24	0	13	0.5	24	54	2.0	78	2.9
99-00 Pho	46	2	449	58	140	.414	2	10	.200	45	65	.692	24	13	4	55	0	30	0.7	26	72	1.6	163	3.5
2 Years	73	12	698	92	226	.407	3	15	.200	54	78	.692	35	22	6	79	0	43	0.6	50	126	1.7	241	3.3

NBA Postseason

Year Tm	G	GS	Min	Md	Att	Pct	Md	Att	Pct	Md	Att	Pct	TO	Stl	Blk	PF	DQ	Ast	Avg	Off	Tot	Avg	Pts	Avg
99-00 Pho	5	0	15	1	4	.250	0	0	—	2	4	.500	0	0	0	1	0	2	0.4	1	2	0.4	4	0.8

Vin Baker

(statistical profile on page 190)

Pos: F **College:** Hartford **Drafted:** '93 1(8)—Mil   **Ht:** 6'11" **Wt:** 250 **Born:** 11/23/71 **Age:** 29

College				Field Goals			3-Pt FGs			Free Throws			Misc			Fouls		Assists		Rebounds			Points	
Year Tm	G	GS	Min	Md	Att	Pct	Md	Att	Pct	Md	Att	Pct	TO	Stl	Blk	PF	DQ	Ast	Avg	Off	Tot	Avg	Pts	Avg
89-90 Hart	28	2	374	58	94	.617	0	0	—	16	41	.390	27	7	47	88	3	7	0.3	29	82	2.9	132	4.7
90-91 Hart	29	29	899	216	440	.491	0	0	—	137	202	.678	81	31	58	97	7	18	0.6	104	302	10.4	569	19.6
91-92 Hart	27	27	997	281	638	.440	14	214	.192	142	216	.657	88	35	100	63	4	36	1.3	103	267	9.9	745	27.6
92-93 Hart	28	28	1019	305	639	.477	32	119	.269	150	240	.625	81	39	74	79	2	54	1.9	97	300	10.7	792	28.3
4 Years	112	86	3289	860	1811	.475	73	333	.219	445	699	.637	277	112	279	333	15	115	1.0	333	951	8.5	2238	20.0

NBA				Field Goals			3-Pt FGs			Free Throws			Misc			Fouls		Assists		Rebounds			Points	
Year Tm	G	GS	Min	Md	Att	Pct	Md	Att	Pct	Md	Att	Pct	TO	Stl	Blk	PF	DQ	Ast	Avg	Off	Tot	Avg	Pts	Avg
93-94 Mil	82	63	2560	435	869	.501	1	5	.200	234	411	.569	162	60	114	231	3	163	2.0	277	621	7.6	1105	13.5
94-95 Mil*	82	82	3361	594	1229	.483	7	24	.292	256	432	.593	221	86	116	277	5	296	3.6	289	846	10.3	1451	17.7

NBA			Field Goals			3-Pt FGs			Free Throws			Misc			Fouls		Assists		Rebounds			Points	
Year Tm	G	GS Min	Md	Att	Pct	Md	Att	Pct	Md	Att	Pct	TO	Stl	Blk	PF	DQ	Ast	Avg	Off	Tot	Avg	Pts	Avg
95-96 Mil*	82	82 3319	699	1429	.489	10	48	.208	321	479	.670	216	68	91	272	3	212	2.6	263	808	9.9	1729	21.1
96-97 Mil*	78	78 3159	632	1251	.505	15	54	.278	358	521	.687	245	81	112	275	8	211	2.7	267	804	10.3	1637	21.0
97-98 Sea*	82	82 2944	631	1164	.542	1	7	.143	311	526	.591	174	91	86	278	7	152	1.9	286	656	8.0	1574	19.2
98-99 Sea	34	31 1162	198	437	.453	0	3	.000	72	160	.450	76	32	34	121	2	56	1.6	86	211	6.2	468	13.8
99-00 Sea	79	75 2849	514	1129	.455	2	8	.250	281	412	.682	213	47	66	288	6	148	1.9	227	605	7.7	1311	16.6
7 Years	519	493 19354	3703	7508	.493	36	149	.242	1833	2941	.623	1307	465	619	1742	34	1238	2.4	1695	4551	8.8	9275	17.9

NBA Postseason																							
Year Tm	G	GS Min	Md	Att	Pct	Md	Att	Pct	Md	Att	Pct	TO	Stl	Blk	PF	DQ	Ast	Avg	Off	Tot	Avg	Pts	Avg
97-98 Sea	10	10 371	71	134	.530	0	0	—	16	38	.421	22	18	15	38	1	18	1.8	41	94	9.4	158	15.8
99-00 Sea	5	4 177	30	75	.400	0	1	.000	10	17	.588	16	5	2	19	0	10	2.0	16	38	7.6	70	14.0
2 Years	15	14 548	101	209	.483	0	1	.000	26	55	.473	38	23	17	57	1	28	1.9	57	132	8.8	228	15.2

Charles Barkley

Pos: F **College:** Auburn **Drafted:** '84 1(5)—Phi **Ht:** 6'6" **Wt:** 252 **Born:** 2/20/63 **Age:** 37

College			Field Goals			3-Pt FGs			Free Throws			Misc			Fouls		Assists		Rebounds			Points	
Year Tm	G	GS Min	Md	Att	Pct	Md	Att	Pct	Md	Att	Pct	TO	Stl	Blk	PF	DQ	Ast	Avg	Off	Tot	Avg	Pts	Avg
81-82 Aub	28	— 746	144	242	.595	—	—	—	68	107	.636	—	—	51	99	4	30	1.1	—	275	9.8	356	12.7
82-83 Aub	28	— 782	161	250	.644	—	—	—	82	130	.631	—	—	45	102	9	49	1.8	—	266	9.5	404	14.4
83-84 Aub	28	— 794	162	254	.638	—	—	—	99	145	.683	—	—	49	89	4	58	2.1	—	265	9.5	423	15.1
3 Years	84	— 2322	467	746	.626	—	—	—	249	382	.652	—	—	145	290	17	137	1.6	—	806	9.6	1183	14.1

NBA			Field Goals			3-Pt FGs			Free Throws			Misc			Fouls		Assists		Rebounds			Points	
Year Tm	G	GS Min	Md	Att	Pct	Md	Att	Pct	Md	Att	Pct	TO	Stl	Blk	PF	DQ	Ast	Avg	Off	Tot	Avg	Pts	Avg
84-85 Phi	82	60 2347	427	783	.545	1	6	.167	293	400	.733	209	95	80	301	5	155	1.9	266	703	8.6	1148	14.0
85-86 Phi	80	80 2952	595	1041	.572	17	75	.227	396	578	.685	350	173	125	333	8	312	3.9	354	1026	12.8	1603	20.0
86-87 Phi*	68	62 2740	557	937	.594	21	104	.202	429	564	.761	322	119	104	252	5	331	4.9	390	994	14.6	1564	23.0
87-88 Phi	80	80 3170	753	1283	.587	44	157	.280	714	951	.751	304	100	103	278	6	254	3.2	385	951	11.9	2264	28.3
88-89 Phi*	79	79 3088	700	1208	.579	35	162	.216	602	799	.753	254	126	67	262	3	325	4.1	403	986	12.5	2037	25.8
89-90 Phi*	79	79 3085	706	1177	.600	20	92	.217	557	744	.749	243	148	50	250	2	307	3.9	361	909	11.5	1989	25.2
90-91 Phi*	67	67 2498	665	1167	.570	44	155	.284	475	658	.722	210	110	33	173	2	284	4.2	258	680	10.1	1849	27.6
91-92 Phi*	75	75 2881	622	1126	.552	32	137	.234	454	653	.695	235	136	44	196	2	308	4.1	271	830	11.1	1730	23.1
92-93 Pho*	76	76 2859	716	1376	.520	67	220	.305	445	582	.765	233	119	74	196	0	385	5.1	237	928	12.2	1944	25.6
93-94 Pho*	65	65 2298	518	1046	.495	48	178	.270	318	452	.704	206	101	37	160	1	296	4.6	198	727	11.2	1402	21.6
94-95 Pho*	68	66 2382	554	1141	.486	74	219	.338	379	507	.748	150	110	45	201	3	276	4.1	203	756	11.1	1561	23.0
95-96 Pho*	71	71 2632	580	1160	.500	49	175	.280	440	566	.777	218	114	56	208	3	262	3.7	243	821	11.6	1649	23.2
96-97 Hou*	53	53 2009	335	692	.484	58	205	.283	288	415	.694	151	69	25	153	2	248	4.7	212	716	13.5	1016	19.2
97-98 Hou	68	41 2243	361	744	.485	18	84	.214	296	397	.746	147	71	28	187	2	217	3.2	241	794	11.7	1036	15.2
98-99 Hou	42	40 1526	240	502	.478	4	25	.160	192	267	.719	100	43	13	89	0	192	4.6	167	516	12.3	676	16.1
99-00 Hou	20	18 620	106	222	.477	6	26	.231	71	110	.645	44	14	4	48	0	63	3.2	71	209	10.5	289	14.5
16 Years	1073	1012 39330	8435	15605	.541	538	2020	.266	6349	8643	.735	3376	1648	888	3287	44	4215	3.9	4260	12546	11.7	23757	22.1

NBA Postseason																							
Year Tm	G	GS Min	Md	Att	Pct	Md	Att	Pct	Md	Att	Pct	TO	Stl	Blk	PF	DQ	Ast	Avg	Off	Tot	Avg	Pts	Avg
84-85 Phi	13	2 408	75	139	.540	4	6	.667	40	63	.635	35	23	15	49	0	26	2.0	52	144	11.1	194	14.9
85-86 Phi	12	12 497	104	180	.578	1	15	.067	91	131	.695	65	27	15	52	2	67	5.6	60	189	15.8	300	25.0
86-87 Phi	5	5 210	43	75	.573	1	8	.125	36	45	.800	22	4	8	21	0	12	2.4	27	63	12.6	123	24.6
88-89 Phi	3	3 135	29	45	.644	1	5	.200	22	31	.710	11	5	2	9	0	16	5.3	8	35	11.7	81	27.0
89-90 Phi	10	10 419	88	162	.543	6	18	.333	65	108	.602	30	8	7	36	0	43	4.3	66	155	15.5	247	24.7
90-91 Phi	8	8 326	74	125	.592	2	20	.100	49	75	.653	25	15	3	23	0	48	6.0	31	84	10.5	199	24.9
92-93 Pho	24	24 1026	230	482	.477	10	45	.222	168	218	.771	50	39	25	73	0	102	4.3	93	326	13.6	638	26.6
93-94 Pho	10	10 425	110	216	.509	14	40	.350	42	55	.764	27	25	9	26	0	48	4.8	34	130	13.0	276	27.6
94-95 Pho	10	10 390	91	182	.500	9	35	.257	66	90	.733	25	13	11	28	0	32	3.2	39	134	13.4	257	25.7
95-96 Pho	4	4 164	31	70	.443	3	12	.250	37	47	.787	6	4	4	15	0	15	3.8	18	54	13.5	102	25.5
96-97 Hou	16	16 605	86	198	.434	11	38	.289	103	134	.769	43	19	7	52	1	54	3.4	64	192	12.0	286	17.9
97-98 Hou	4	0 87	12	23	.522	0	2	.000	12	21	.571	6	5	0	12	1	4	1.0	5	21	5.3	36	9.0
98-99 Hou	4	4 157	36	68	.529	2	7	.286	20	30	.667	8	6	2	12	0	15	3.8	13	55	13.8	94	23.5
13 Years	123	108 4849	1009	1965	.513	64	251	.255	751	1048	.717	353	193	108	408	4	482	3.9	510	1582	12.9	2833	23.0

Dana Barros

Pos: G **College:** Boston College **Drafted:** '89 1(16)—Sea **Ht:** 5'11" **Wt:** 163 **Born:** 4/13/67 **Age:** 33

College			Field Goals			3-Pt FGs			Free Throws			Misc			Fouls		Assists		Rebounds			Points	
Year Tm	G	GS Min	Md	Att	Pct	Md	Att	Pct	Md	Att	Pct	TO	Stl	Blk	PF	DQ	Ast	Avg	Off	Tot	Avg	Pts	Avg
85-86 BC	28	28 971	158	330	.479	—	—	—	68	86	.791	51	57	0	68	1	97	3.5	—	78	2.8	384	13.7
86-87 BC	29	29 1145	194	424	.458	70	173	.405	85	100	.850	77	36	3	56	1	110	3.8	—	85	2.9	543	18.7

College

Year Tm	G	GS	Min	Md	Att	Pct	Md	Att	Pct	Md	Att	Pct	TO	Stl	Blk	PF	DQ	Ast	Avg	Off	Tot	Avg	Pts	Avg
				Field Goals			3-Pt FGs			Free Throws			Misc			Fouls		Assists		Rebounds			Points	
87-88 BC	33	33	1223	242	504	.480	109	240	.454	130	153	.850	76	43	2	45	0	135	4.1	—	113	3.4	723	21.9
88-89 BC	29	29	1096	230	484	.475	112	261	.429	120	140	.857	66	45	3	51	0	96	3.3	13	103	3.6	692	23.9
4 Years	119	119	4435	824	1742	.473	291	674	.432	403	479	.841	270	181	8	220	2	438	3.7	—	379	3.2	2342	19.7

NBA

Year Tm	G	GS	Min	Md	Att	Pct	Md	Att	Pct	Md	Att	Pct	TO	Stl	Blk	PF	DQ	Ast	Avg	Off	Tot	Avg	Pts	Avg
				Field Goals			3-Pt FGs			Free Throws			Misc			Fouls		Assists		Rebounds			Points	
89-90 Sea	81	25	1630	299	738	.405	95	238	.399	89	110	.809	123	53	1	97	0	205	2.5	35	132	1.6	782	9.7
90-91 Sea	66	0	750	154	311	.495	32	81	.395	78	85	.918	54	23	1	40	0	111	1.7	17	71	1.1	418	6.3
91-92 Sea	75	1	1331	238	493	.483	83	186	.446	60	79	.759	56	51	1	84	0	125	1.7	17	81	1.1	619	8.3
92-93 Sea	69	2	1243	214	474	.451	64	169	.379	49	59	.831	58	63	3	78	0	151	2.2	18	107	1.6	541	7.8
93-94 Phi	81	70	2519	412	878	.469	135	354	.381	116	145	.800	167	107	5	96	0	424	5.2	28	196	2.4	1075	13.3
94-95 Phi*	82	82	3318	571	1165	.490	197	425	.464	347	386	.899	242	149	4	159	1	619	7.5	27	274	3.3	1686	20.6
95-96 Bos	80	25	2328	379	806	.470	150	368	.408	130	147	.884	120	58	3	116	1	306	3.8	21	192	2.4	1038	13.0
96-97 Bos	24	8	708	110	253	.435	43	105	.410	37	43	.860	39	26	6	34	0	81	3.4	5	48	2.0	300	12.5
97-98 Bos	80	15	1686	281	609	.461	100	246	.407	122	144	.847	107	83	6	124	0	286	3.6	28	153	1.9	784	9.8
98-99 Bos	50	16	1156	168	371	.453	64	160	.400	64	73	.877	88	52	5	64	1	208	4.2	16	105	2.1	464	9.3
99-00 Bos	72	0	1139	196	435	.451	59	144	.410	66	76	.868	66	31	4	80	0	133	1.8	13	99	1.4	517	7.2
11 Years	760	244	17808	3022	6533	.463	1022	2476	.413	1158	1347	.860	1120	696	42	972	3	2649	3.5	225	1458	1.9	8224	10.8

NBA Postseason

Year Tm	G	GS	Min	Md	Att	Pct	Md	Att	Pct	Md	Att	Pct	TO	Stl	Blk	PF	DQ	Ast	Avg	Off	Tot	Avg	Pts	Avg
90-91 Sea	3	0	25	9	13	.692	2	5	.400	3	4	.750	3	3	0	1	0	5	1.7	1	4	1.3	23	7.7
91-92 Sea	7	0	96	21	40	.525	10	17	.588	0	0	—	6	4	0	11	0	8	1.1	1	7	1.0	52	7.4
92-93 Sea	16	0	136	22	47	.468	5	16	.313	6	8	.750	8	5	0	6	0	12	0.8	0	12	0.8	55	3.4
3 Years	26	0	257	52	100	.520	17	38	.447	9	12	.750	17	12	0	18	0	25	1.0	2	23	0.9	130	5.0

Brent Barry

(statistical profile on page 190)

Pos: G **College:** Oregon State **Drafted:** '95 1(15)—Den **Ht:** 6'6" **Wt:** 215 **Born:** 12/31/71 **Age:** 29

College

Year Tm	G	GS	Min	Md	Att	Pct	Md	Att	Pct	Md	Att	Pct	TO	Stl	Blk	PF	DQ	Ast	Avg	Off	Tot	Avg	Pts	Avg
				Field Goals			3-Pt FGs			Free Throws			Misc			Fouls		Assists		Rebounds			Points	
91-92 OreSt	31	13	545	57	136	.419	25	77	.325	22	33	.667	54	30	11	49	0	70	2.3	—	47	1.5	161	5.2
92-93 OreSt	23	17	607	55	134	.410	15	64	.234	40	47	.851	76	33	21	63	2	83	3.6	—	49	2.1	165	7.2
93-94 OreSt	27	27	959	144	289	.498	38	104	.365	85	112	.759	93	64	23	84	4	94	3.5	—	141	5.2	411	15.2
94-95 OreSt	27	27	1012	181	352	.514	52	132	.394	153	186	.823	86	72	12	71	3	104	3.9	—	159	5.9	567	21.0
4 Years	108	84	3123	437	911	.480	130	377	.345	300	378	.794	309	199	67	267	9	351	3.3	—	396	3.7	1304	12.1

NBA

Year Tm	G	GS	Min	Md	Att	Pct	Md	Att	Pct	Md	Att	Pct	TO	Stl	Blk	PF	DQ	Ast	Avg	Off	Tot	Avg	Pts	Avg
				Field Goals			3-Pt FGs			Free Throws			Misc			Fouls		Assists		Rebounds			Points	
95-96 LAC	79	44	1898	283	597	.474	123	296	.416	111	137	.810	120	95	22	196	2	230	2.9	38	168	2.1	800	10.1
96-97 LAC	59	0	1094	155	379	.409	56	173	.324	76	93	.817	76	51	15	88	1	154	2.6	30	110	1.9	442	7.5
97-98 2Tm	58	36	1600	213	506	.421	90	229	.393	115	134	.858	104	64	27	118	0	153	2.6	29	171	2.9	631	10.9
98-99 Chi	37	30	1181	141	356	.396	52	172	.302	78	101	.772	72	42	11	98	2	116	3.1	39	144	3.9	412	11.1
99-00 Sea	80	74	2726	327	707	.463	164	399	.411	127	157	.809	142	103	31	228	4	291	3.6	50	372	4.7	945	11.8
97-98 LAC	41	36	1341	190	444	.428	78	195	.400	103	122	.844	95	50	23	88	0	132	3.2	27	143	3.5	561	13.7
Mia	17	0	259	23	62	.371	12	34	.353	12	12	1.000	9	14	4	30	0	21	1.2	2	28	1.6	70	4.1
5 Years	313	184	8499	1119	2545	.440	485	1269	.382	507	622	.815	514	355	106	728	9	944	3.0	186	965	3.1	3230	10.3

NBA Postseason

Year Tm	G	GS	Min	Md	Att	Pct	Md	Att	Pct	Md	Att	Pct	TO	Stl	Blk	PF	DQ	Ast	Avg	Off	Tot	Avg	Pts	Avg
96-97 LAC	3	0	84	11	27	.407	5	11	.455	8	9	.889	4	4	0	10	0	10	3.3	1	7	2.3	35	11.7
99-00 Sea	5	3	155	12	33	.364	8	20	.400	10	14	.714	7	3	3	20	2	15	3.0	3	13	2.6	42	8.4
2 Years	8	3	239	23	60	.383	13	31	.419	18	23	.783	11	7	3	30	2	25	3.1	4	20	2.5	77	9.6

Drew Barry

Pos: G **College:** Georgia Tech **Drafted:** '96 2(57)—Sea **Ht:** 6'5" **Wt:** 191 **Born:** 2/17/73 **Age:** 27

College

Year Tm	G	GS	Min	Md	Att	Pct	Md	Att	Pct	Md	Att	Pct	TO	Stl	Blk	PF	DQ	Ast	Avg	Off	Tot	Avg	Pts	Avg
				Field Goals			3-Pt FGs			Free Throws			Misc			Fouls		Assists		Rebounds			Points	
92-93 GTch	30	13	806	80	171	.468	25	78	.321	33	41	.805	91	42	9	41	—	164	5.5	12	102	3.4	218	7.3
93-94 GTch	24	22	787	61	145	.421	27	81	.333	45	58	.776	64	40	6	48	—	141	5.9	15	82	3.4	194	8.1
94-95 GTch	27	27	966	119	232	.513	50	117	.427	73	97	.753	81	46	13	53	—	181	6.7	25	131	4.9	361	13.4
95-96 GTch	36	36	1315	149	367	.406	77	209	.368	105	133	.789	130	65	13	68	0	238	6.6	24	167	4.6	480	13.3
4 Years	117	98	3874	409	915	.447	179	485	.369	256	329	.778	366	193	41	210	—	724	6.2	76	482	4.1	1253	10.7

NBA

Year Tm	G	GS	Min	Md	Att	Pct	Md	Att	Pct	Md	Att	Pct	TO	Stl	Blk	PF	DQ	Ast	Avg	Off	Tot	Avg	Pts	Avg
				Field Goals			3-Pt FGs			Free Throws			Misc			Fouls		Assists		Rebounds			Points	
96-97										Played in CBA														
97-98 Atl	27	0	256	18	38	.474	9	21	.429	11	13	.846	30	10	1	28	0	49	1.8	5	35	1.3	56	2.1

NBA				Field Goals			3-Pt FGs			Free Throws			Misc			Fouls		Assists		Rebounds			Points	
Year Tm	G	GS	Min	Md	Att	Pct	Md	Att	Pct	Md	Att	Pct	TO	Stl	Blk	PF	DQ	Ast	Avg	Off	Tot	Avg	Pts	Avg
98-99 Sea	17	0	183	10	32	.313	8	24	.333	9	13	.692	12	7	1	24	0	29	1.7	3	20	1.2	37	2.2
99-00 2Tm	16	0	159	15	33	.455	7	18	.389	4	5	.800	13	2	0	23	0	33	2.1	0	12	0.8	41	2.6
99-00 GS	8	0	85	9	18	.500	3	9	.333	1	2	.500	6	2	0	14	0	17	2.1	0	8	1.0	22	2.8
Atl	8	0	74	6	15	.400	4	9	.444	3	3	1.000	7	0	0	9	0	16	2.0	0	4	0.5	19	2.4
3 Years	60	0	598	43	103	.417	24	63	.381	24	31	.774	55	19	2	75	0	111	1.9	8	67	1.1	134	2.2

NBA Postseason

Year Tm	G	GS	Min	Md	Att	Pct	Md	Att	Pct	Md	Att	Pct	TO	Stl	Blk	PF	DQ	Ast	Avg	Off	Tot	Avg	Pts	Avg
97-98 Atl	2	0	5	0	1	.000	0	1	.000	0	0	—	0	0	0	0	0	0	0.0	0	1	0.5	0	0.0

Jon Barry

(statistical profile on page 191)

Pos: G **College:** Georgia Tech **Drafted:** '92 1(21)—Bos **Ht:** 6'5" **Wt:** 210 **Born:** 7/25/69 **Age:** 31

College				Field Goals			3-Pt FGs			Free Throws			Misc			Fouls		Assists		Rebounds			Points	
Year Tm	G	GS	Min	Md	Att	Pct	Md	Att	Pct	Md	Att	Pct	TO	Stl	Blk	PF	DQ	Ast	Avg	Off	Tot	Avg	Pts	Avg
87-88 Pac	29	—	809	100	269	.372	22	59	.373	53	71	.746	89	39	3	45	—	108	3.7	—	74	2.6	275	9.5
90-91 GTch	30	30	1088	180	405	.444	77	209	.368	41	56	.732	68	53	16	66	—	110	3.7	31	110	3.7	478	15.9
91-92 GTch	35	35	1231	201	468	.429	99	265	.374	101	145	.697	120	71	8	81	—	207	5.9	32	152	4.3	602	17.2
3 Years	94	—	3128	481	1142	.421	198	533	.371	195	272	.717	277	163	27	192	—	425	4.5	—	336	3.6	1355	14.4

NBA				Field Goals			3-Pt FGs			Free Throws			Misc			Fouls		Assists		Rebounds			Points	
Year Tm	G	GS	Min	Md	Att	Pct	Md	Att	Pct	Md	Att	Pct	TO	Stl	Blk	PF	DQ	Ast	Avg	Off	Tot	Avg	Pts	Avg
92-93 Mil	47	0	552	76	206	.369	21	63	.333	33	49	.673	42	35	3	57	0	68	1.4	10	43	0.9	206	4.4
93-94 Mil	72	7	1242	158	382	.414	32	115	.278	97	122	.795	83	102	17	110	0	168	2.3	36	146	2.0	445	6.2
94-95 Mil	52	0	602	57	134	.425	16	48	.333	61	80	.763	41	30	4	54	0	85	1.6	15	49	0.9	191	3.7
95-96 GS	68	0	712	91	185	.492	44	93	.473	31	37	.838	42	33	11	51	1	85	1.3	17	63	0.9	257	3.8
96-97 Atl	58	8	965	100	246	.407	48	124	.387	37	46	.804	59	55	3	56	0	115	2.0	26	99	1.7	285	4.9
97-98 LAL	49	1	374	38	104	.365	18	61	.295	27	29	.931	22	24	3	33	0	51	1.0	8	37	0.8	121	2.5
98-99 Sac	43	0	736	59	138	.428	24	79	.304	71	84	.845	47	53	5	61	1	112	2.6	25	96	2.2	213	5.0
99-00 Sac	62	1	1281	161	346	.465	66	154	.429	107	116	.922	85	75	7	104	1	150	2.4	38	159	2.6	495	8.0
8 Years	451	17	6464	740	1741	.425	269	737	.365	464	563	.824	421	407	53	526	3	834	1.8	175	692	1.5	2213	4.9

NBA Postseason

Year Tm	G	GS	Min	Md	Att	Pct	Md	Att	Pct	Md	Att	Pct	TO	Stl	Blk	PF	DQ	Ast	Avg	Off	Tot	Avg	Pts	Avg
96-97 Atl	2	0	9	0	3	.000	0	3	.000	0	0	—	0	0	0	0	0	0	0.0	0	0	0.0	0	0.0
97-98 LAL	7	0	18	0	8	.000	0	5	.000	0	0	—	0	1	0	1	0	0	0.0	2	0.3	0	0.0
98-99 Sac	5	0	112	12	34	.353	5	19	.263	11	12	.917	9	6	1	9	0	9	1.8	3	10	2.0	40	8.0
99-00 Sac	5	0	102	9	21	.429	7	12	.583	14	16	.875	4	3	0	7	0	12	2.4	2	12	2.4	39	7.8
4 Years	19	0	241	21	66	.318	12	39	.308	25	28	.893	13	10	1	17	0	21	1.1	5	24	1.3	79	4.2

Maceo Baston

Pos: F **College:** Michigan **Drafted:** '98 2(58)—Chi **Ht:** 6'9" **Wt:** 215 **Born:** 5/29/75 **Age:** 25

College				Field Goals			3-Pt FGs			Free Throws			Misc			Fouls		Assists		Rebounds			Points	
Year Tm	G	GS	Min	Md	Att	Pct	Md	Att	Pct	Md	Att	Pct	TO	Stl	Blk	PF	DQ	Ast	Avg	Off	Tot	Avg	Pts	Avg
94-95 Mich	30	2	549	89	132	.674	0	0	—	52	95	.547	55	22	30	98	6	6	0.2	72	165	5.5	230	7.7
95-96 Mich	32	28	785	137	201	.682	0	1	.000	101	149	.678	70	17	41	99	5	19	0.6	83	211	6.6	375	11.7
96-97 Mich	34	11	816	116	202	.574	0	1	.000	122	182	.670	67	29	35	97	4	15	0.4	106	231	6.8	354	10.4
97-98 Mich	30	24	811	129	219	.589	0	0	—	123	188	.654	88	25	33	99	7	35	1.2	75	223	7.4	381	12.7
4 Years	126	65	2961	471	754	.625	0	2	.000	398	614	.648	280	93	139	393	22	75	0.6	336	830	6.6	1340	10.6

NBA				Field Goals			3-Pt FGs			Free Throws			Misc			Fouls		Assists		Rebounds			Points	
Year Tm	G	GS	Min	Md	Att	Pct	Md	Att	Pct	Md	Att	Pct	TO	Stl	Blk	PF	DQ	Ast	Avg	Off	Tot	Avg	Pts	Avg
98-99									Played in CBA																
99-00 Mil									Active but did not play																

Tony Battie

(statistical profile on page 191)

Pos: F-C **College:** Texas Tech **Drafted:** '97 1(5)—Den **Ht:** 6'11" **Wt:** 240 **Born:** 2/11/76 **Age:** 24

College				Field Goals			3-Pt FGs			Free Throws			Misc			Fouls		Assists		Rebounds			Points	
Year Tm	G	GS	Min	Md	Att	Pct	Md	Att	Pct	Md	Att	Pct	TO	Stl	Blk	PF	DQ	Ast	Avg	Off	Tot	Avg	Pts	Avg
94-95 TxTch	29	3	368	47	96	.490	0	6	.000	18	27	.667	27	8	23	50	1	17	0.6	34	129	4.4	112	3.9
95-96 TxTch	30	29	806	114	221	.516	4	14	.286	60	95	.632	36	22	68	88	3	32	1.1	—	266	8.9	292	9.7
96-97 TxTch	28	28	978	206	356	.579	6	16	.375	107	163	.656	77	26	71	85	5	23	0.8	82	329	11.8	525	18.8
3 Years	87	60	2152	367	673	.545	10	36	.278	185	285	.649	140	56	162	223	9	72	0.8	—	724	8.3	929	10.7

14

NBA			Field Goals			3-Pt FGs			Free Throws			Misc			Fouls		Assists		Rebounds			Points	
Year Tm	G	GS	Min	Md	Att	Pct	Md	Att	Pct	Md	Att	Pct	TO	Stl	Blk	PF	DQ	Ast	Avg	Off	Tot	Avg	Pts	Avg
97-98 Den	65	49	1506	234	525	.446	3	14	.214	73	104	.702	98	54	69	199	6	60	0.9	138	351	5.4	544	8.4
98-99 Bos	50	15	1121	147	283	.519	0	3	.000	41	61	.672	45	29	71	159	1	53	1.1	96	300	6.0	335	6.7
99-00 Bos	82	4	1505	219	459	.477	1	8	.125	102	151	.675	67	47	70	249	4	63	0.8	152	410	5.0	541	6.6
3 Years	197	68	4132	600	1267	.474	4	25	.160	216	316	.684	210	130	210	607	11	176	0.9	386	1061	5.4	1420	7.2

Jonathan Bender

Pos: F College: None Drafted: '99 1(5)—Tor Ht: 6'11" Wt: 202 Born: 1/30/81 Age: 20

NBA			Field Goals			3-Pt FGs			Free Throws			Misc			Fouls		Assists		Rebounds			Points	
Year Tm	G	GS	Min	Md	Att	Pct	Md	Att	Pct	Md	Att	Pct	TO	Stl	Blk	PF	DQ	Ast	Avg	Off	Tot	Avg	Pts	Avg
99-00 Ind	24	1	130	23	70	.329	2	12	.167	16	24	.667	7	1	5	18	0	3	0.1	4	21	0.9	64	2.7

NBA Postseason																							
Year Tm	G	GS	Min	Md	Att	Pct	Md	Att	Pct	Md	Att	Pct	TO	Stl	Blk	PF	DQ	Ast	Avg	Off	Tot	Avg	Pts	Avg
99-00 Ind	9	0	21	4	6	.667	1	1	1.000	3	6	.500	0	1	0	2	0	0	0.0	0	3	0.3	12	1.3

Benoit Benjamin

Pos: C College: Creighton Drafted: '85 1(3)—LAC Ht: 7'0" Wt: 265 Born: 11/22/64 Age: 36

College			Field Goals			3-Pt FGs			Free Throws			Misc			Fouls		Assists		Rebounds			Points	
Year Tm	G	GS	Min	Md	Att	Pct	Md	Att	Pct	Md	Att	Pct	TO	Stl	Blk	PF	DQ	Ast	Avg	Off	Tot	Avg	Pts	Avg
82-83 Cre	27	25	871	126	292	.555	—	—	—	76	116	.655	79	12	92	71	2	28	1.0	—	259	9.6	400	14.8
83-84 Cre	30	30	1112	190	350	.543	—	—	—	107	144	.743	72	21	157	93	2	55	1.8	—	295	9.8	487	16.2
84-85 Cre	32	32	1193	258	443	.582	—	—	—	172	233	.738	88	27	162	100	2	68	2.1	—	451	14.1	688	21.5
3 Years	89	87	3176	610	1085	.562	—	—	—	355	493	.720	239	60	411	264	6	151	1.7	—	1005	11.3	1575	17.7

NBA			Field Goals			3-Pt FGs			Free Throws			Misc			Fouls		Assists		Rebounds			Points	
Year Tm	G	GS	Min	Md	Att	Pct	Md	Att	Pct	Md	Att	Pct	TO	Stl	Blk	PF	DQ	Ast	Avg	Off	Tot	Avg	Pts	Avg
85-86 LAC	79	37	2088	324	661	.490	1	3	.333	229	307	.746	145	64	206	286	5	79	1.0	161	600	7.6	878	11.1
86-87 LAC	72	61	2230	320	713	.449	0	2	.000	188	263	.715	184	60	187	251	7	135	1.9	134	586	8.1	828	11.5
87-88 LAC	66	59	2171	340	693	.491	0	8	.000	180	255	.706	223	50	225	203	2	172	2.6	112	530	8.0	860	13.0
88-89 LAC	79	62	2585	491	907	.541	0	2	.000	317	426	.744	237	57	221	221	4	157	2.0	164	696	8.8	1299	16.4
89-90 LAC	71	58	2313	362	688	.526	0	1	.000	235	321	.732	187	59	187	217	3	159	2.2	157	723	10.3	982	14.0
90-91 2Tm	70	65	2236	386	778	.496	0	0	—	210	295	.712	235	54	145	184	1	119	1.7	130	513	8.1	879	14.0
91-92 Sea	63	61	1941	354	740	.478	0	2	.000	171	249	.687	175	39	118	185	1	76	1.2	51	209	3.5	335	5.7
92-93 2Tm	59	6	754	133	271	.491	0	0	—	69	104	.663	78	31	48	134	0	22	0.4	135	499	6.5	718	9.3
93-94 NJ	77	74	1817	283	589	.480	0	0	—	152	214	.710	97	35	90	198	0	44	0.6	94	440	7.2	675	11.1
94-95 NJ	61	57	1598	271	531	.510	0	0	—	133	175	.760	125	23	64	151	2	38	0.6	141	539	6.5	728	8.8
95-96 NJ	83	71	1896	294	590	.498	0	3	.000	140	194	.722	144	45	85	224	1	64	0.8	95	469	12.0	13	3.3
96-97 Tor	4	3	44	5	12	.417	0	0	—	3	4	.750	2	1	0	5	0	1	0.3	3	9	2.3	13	3.3
97-98 Phi	14	0	197	22	41	.537	0	0	—	19	30	.633	12	4	4	26	0	3	0.2	18	53	3.8	63	4.5
98-99 Phi	6	0	33	2	7	.286	0	0	—	0	0	—	3	0	0	6	0	1	0.0	3	8	1.3	4	0.7
99-00 Cle	3	0	8	1	3	.333	0	0	—	0	0	—	0	0	1	1	0	0	0.0	0	1	0.3	2	0.7
90-91 LAC	39	38	1337	229	465	.492	0	0	—	123	169	.728	138	26	91	110	1	74	1.9	95	469	12.0	581	14.9
Sea	31	27	899	157	313	.502	0	0	—	87	126	.690	97	28	54	74	0	45	1.5	62	254	8.2	401	12.9
92-93 Sea	31	6	448	81	163	.497	0	0	—	47	67	.701	42	17	35	73	0	12	0.4	27	113	3.6	209	6.7
LAL	28	0	306	52	108	.481	0	0	—	22	37	.595	36	14	13	61	0	10	0.4	24	96	3.4	126	4.5
95-96 Van	13	13	404	71	161	.441	0	0	—	39	56	.696	34	10	15	40	1	16	1.2	31	103	7.9	181	13.9
Mil	70	58	1492	223	429	.520	0	3	.000	101	138	.732	110	35	70	184	0	48	0.7	110	436	6.2	547	7.8
15 Years	807	614	21911	3588	7224	.497	1	21	.048	2046	2837	.721	1847	522	1581	2292	27	1070	1.3	1459	6063	7.5	9223	11.4

NBA Postseason																								
Year Tm	G	GS	Min	Md	Att	Pct	Md	Att	Pct	Md	Att	Pct	TO	Stl	Blk	PF	DQ	Ast	Avg	Off	Tot	Avg	Pts	Avg
90-91 Sea	5	5	163	20	41	.488	0	0	—	29	32	.906	11	3	13	17	1	1	0.2	7	33	6.6	69	13.8
91-92 Sea	9	4	161	23	41	.561	0	1	.000	9	18	.500	8	5	13	20	0	5	0.6	10	46	5.1	55	6.1
93-94 NJ	4	4	108	7	17	.412	0	0	—	7	8	.875	5	2	8	16	0	1	0.3	5	21	5.3	21	5.3
3 Years	18	13	432	50	99	.505	0	1	.000	45	58	.776	24	10	34	53	1	7	0.4	22	100	5.6	145	8.1

Corey Benjamin

Pos: G College: Oregon State Drafted: '98 1(28)—Chi Ht: 6'6" Wt: 205 Born: 2/24/78 Age: 22

College			Field Goals			3-Pt FGs			Free Throws			Misc			Fouls		Assists		Rebounds			Points	
Year Tm	G	GS	Min	Md	Att	Pct	Md	Att	Pct	Md	Att	Pct	TO	Stl	Blk	PF	DQ	Ast	Avg	Off	Tot	Avg	Pts	Avg
96-97 OreSt	23	17	601	121	280	.432	35	111	.315	66	101	.653	78	25	12	80	4	31	1.3	26	92	4.0	343	14.9
97-98 OreSt	25	22	673	185	343	.539	29	99	.293	97	136	.713	69	46	17	78	1	56	2.2	46	125	5.0	496	19.8
2 Years	48	39	1274	306	623	.491	64	210	.305	163	237	.688	147	71	29	158	5	87	1.8	72	217	4.5	839	17.5

NBA			Field Goals			3-Pt FGs			Free Throws			Misc			Fouls		Assists		Rebounds			Points	
Year Tm	G	GS	Min	Md	Att	Pct	Md	Att	Pct	Md	Att	Pct	TO	Stl	Blk	PF	DQ	Ast	Avg	Off	Tot	Avg	Pts	Avg
98-99 Chi	31	1	320	44	117	.376	3	14	.214	27	40	.675	21	11	8	46	0	10	0.3	15	40	1.3	118	3.8
99-00 Chi	48	10	862	145	350	.414	31	89	.348	49	82	.598	74	31	22	122	2	54	1.1	21	88	1.8	370	7.7
2 Years	79	11	1182	189	467	.405	34	103	.330	76	122	.623	95	42	30	168	2	64	0.8	36	128	1.6	488	6.2

Mario Bennett

Pos: F **College:** Arizona State **Drafted:** '95 1(27)—Pho   **Ht:** 6'9" **Wt:** 220 **Born:** 8/1/73 **Age:** 27

College			Field Goals			3-Pt FGs			Free Throws			Misc			Fouls		Assists		Rebounds			Points	
Year Tm	G	GS	Min	Md	Att	Pct	Md	Att	Pct	Md	Att	Pct	TO	Stl	Blk	PF	DQ	Ast	Avg	Off	Tot	Avg	Pts	Avg
91-92 AriSt	33	25	889	159	277	.574	7	22	.318	86	140	.614	78	40	55	91	2	28	0.8	—	224	6.8	411	12.5
93-94 AriSt	21	20	706	134	226	.593	5	16	.313	67	132	.508	62	21	21	71	2	32	1.5	—	180	8.6	340	16.2
94-95 AriSt	33	33	1132	247	417	.592	8	30	.267	115	234	.491	101	34	115	96	2	79	2.4	—	271	8.2	617	18.7
3 Years	87	78	2727	540	920	.587	20	68	.294	268	506	.530	241	95	191	258	6	139	1.6	—	675	7.8	1368	15.7

NBA			Field Goals			3-Pt FGs			Free Throws			Misc			Fouls		Assists		Rebounds			Points	
Year Tm	G	GS	Min	Md	Att	Pct	Md	Att	Pct	Md	Att	Pct	TO	Stl	Blk	PF	DQ	Ast	Avg	Off	Tot	Avg	Pts	Avg
95-96 Pho	19	14	230	29	64	.453	0	1	.000	27	42	.643	11	11	11	46	0	6	0.3	21	49	2.6	85	4.5
96-97										Played in CBA														
97-98 LAL	45	4	354	80	135	.593	1	2	.500	16	44	.364	21	19	11	61	0	18	0.4	60	126	2.8	177	3.9
98-99 LAL	3	0	19	2	6	.333	0	0	—	3	4	.750	1	1	0	4	0	0	0.0	2	5	1.7	7	2.3
99-00 LAC	1	0	3	0	3	.000	0	0	—	0	0	—	0	0	0	1	0	0	0.0	1	2	2.0	0	0.0
4 Years	68	18	606	111	208	.534	1	3	.333	46	90	.511	33	31	22	112	0	24	0.4	84	182	2.7	269	4.0

			Field Goals			3-Pt FGs			Free Throws			Misc			Fouls		Assists		Rebounds			Points	
									NBA Postseason															
Year Tm	G	GS	Min	Md	Att	Pct	Md	Att	Pct	Md	Att	Pct	TO	Stl	Blk	PF	DQ	Ast	Avg	Off	Tot	Avg	Pts	Avg
95-96 Pho	2	0	8	2	4	.500	0	0	—	0	0	—	2	0	0	0	0	0	0.0	2	3	1.5	4	2.0
97-98 LAL	4	0	10	1	2	.500	0	0	—	2	2	1.000	0	0	1	2	0	0	0.0	2	6	1.5	4	1.0
2 Years	6	0	18	3	6	.500	0	0	—	2	2	1.000	2	0	1	2	0	0	0.0	4	9	1.5	8	1.3

Travis Best

Pos: G **College:** Georgia Tech **Drafted:** '95 1(23)—Ind   **Ht:** 5'11" **Wt:** 184 **Born:** 7/12/72 **Age:** 28

(statistical profile on page 192)

College			Field Goals			3-Pt FGs			Free Throws			Misc			Fouls		Assists		Rebounds			Points	
Year Tm	G	GS	Min	Md	Att	Pct	Md	Att	Pct	Md	Att	Pct	TO	Stl	Blk	PF	DQ	Ast	Avg	Off	Tot	Avg	Pts	Avg
91-92 GTch	35	33	1227	151	336	.449	56	145	.386	72	98	.735	143	48	0	83	—	198	5.7	12	89	2.5	430	12.3
92-93 GTch	30	30	1075	163	345	.472	80	175	.457	82	109	.752	85	51	6	73	—	176	5.9	15	94	3.1	488	16.3
93-94 GTch	29	29	1087	180	390	.462	49	144	.340	123	142	.866	69	58	3	84	—	167	5.8	22	104	3.6	532	18.3
94-95 GTch	30	30	1115	209	469	.446	73	192	.380	116	137	.847	69	60	6	71	—	151	5.0	17	95	3.2	607	20.2
4 Years	124	122	4504	703	1540	.456	258	656	.393	393	486	.809	366	217	15	311	—	692	5.6	66	382	3.1	2057	16.6

NBA			Field Goals			3-Pt FGs			Free Throws			Misc			Fouls		Assists		Rebounds			Points	
Year Tm	G	GS	Min	Md	Att	Pct	Md	Att	Pct	Md	Att	Pct	TO	Stl	Blk	PF	DQ	Ast	Avg	Off	Tot	Avg	Pts	Avg
95-96 Ind	59	1	571	69	163	.423	8	25	.320	75	90	.833	63	20	3	80	0	97	1.6	11	44	0.7	221	3.7
96-97 Ind	76	46	2064	274	620	.442	57	155	.368	149	197	.756	153	98	5	221	3	318	4.2	36	166	2.2	754	9.9
97-98 Ind	82	0	1547	201	480	.419	21	70	.300	112	131	.855	111	85	5	193	3	281	3.4	28	122	1.5	535	6.5
98-99 Ind	49	0	1043	127	305	.416	22	59	.373	70	83	.843	62	42	4	111	2	169	3.4	19	80	1.6	346	7.1
99-00 Ind	82	0	1691	271	561	.483	35	93	.376	156	190	.821	107	76	5	204	1	272	3.3	16	142	1.7	733	8.9
5 Years	348	47	6916	942	2129	.442	143	402	.356	562	691	.813	496	321	22	809	9	1137	3.3	110	554	1.6	2589	7.4

			Field Goals			3-Pt FGs			Free Throws			Misc			Fouls		Assists		Rebounds			Points	
									NBA Postseason															
Year Tm	G	GS	Min	Md	Att	Pct	Md	Att	Pct	Md	Att	Pct	TO	Stl	Blk	PF	DQ	Ast	Avg	Off	Tot	Avg	Pts	Avg
95-96 Ind	5	0	84	11	22	.500	1	6	.167	6	7	.857	10	6	0	10	0	9	1.8	3	11	2.2	29	5.8
97-98 Ind	16	0	280	27	72	.375	5	18	.278	38	43	.884	19	11	3	36	0	31	1.9	1	16	1.0	97	6.1
98-99 Ind	11	0	150	16	46	.348	2	10	.200	12	13	.923	14	4	1	34	1	21	1.9	7	17	1.5	46	4.2
99-00 Ind	23	0	463	77	179	.430	13	30	.433	37	44	.841	25	19	4	61	1	66	2.9	15	57	2.5	204	8.9
4 Years	55	0	977	131	319	.411	21	64	.328	93	107	.869	68	40	8	141	2	127	2.3	26	101	1.8	376	6.8

Mike Bibby

Pos: G **College:** Arizona **Drafted:** '98 1(2)—Van   **Ht:** 6'2" **Wt:** 190 **Born:** 5/13/78 **Age:** 22

(statistical profile on page 192)

College			Field Goals			3-Pt FGs			Free Throws			Misc			Fouls		Assists		Rebounds			Points	
Year Tm	G	GS	Min	Md	Att	Pct	Md	Att	Pct	Md	Att	Pct	TO	Stl	Blk	PF	DQ	Ast	Avg	Off	Tot	Avg	Pts	Avg
96-97 Ari	34	34	1110	151	339	.445	67	170	.394	89	127	.701	100	76	7	77	3	176	5.2	22	109	3.2	458	13.5
97-98 Ari	35	35	1124	209	450	.464	77	199	.387	108	143	.755	78	84	7	57	1	199	5.7	27	106	3.0	603	17.2
2 Years	69	69	2234	360	789	.456	144	369	.390	197	270	.730	178	160	14	134	4	375	5.4	49	215	3.1	1061	15.4

Year Tm	G	GS	Min	Md	Att	Pct	Md	Att	Pct	Md	Att	Pct	TO	Stl	Blk	PF	DQ	Ast	Avg	Off	Tot	Avg	Pts	Avg
				Field Goals			**3-Pt FGs**			**Free Throws**			**Misc**			**Fouls**		**Assists**		**Rebounds**			**Points**	
98-99 Van	50	50	1758	260	605	.430	15	74	.203	127	169	.751	146	78	5	122	0	325	6.5	30	136	2.7	662	13.2
99-00 Van	82	82	3155	459	1031	.445	77	212	.363	195	250	.780	247	132	15	171	1	665	8.1	73	306	3.7	1190	14.5
2 Years	132	132	4913	719	1636	.439	92	286	.322	322	419	.768	393	210	20	293	1	990	7.5	103	442	3.3	1852	14.0

Chauncey Billups

Pos: G **College:** Colorado **Drafted:** '97 1(3)—Bos **Ht:** 6'3" **Wt:** 202 **Born:** 9/25/76 **Age:** 24

College Year Tm	G	GS	Min	Md	Att	Pct	Md	Att	Pct	Md	Att	Pct	TO	Stl	Blk	PF	DQ	Ast	Avg	Off	Tot	Avg	Pts	Avg
95-96 Colo	26	25	919	145	351	.413	45	127	.354	130	151	.861	118	42	4	75	3	143	5.5	54	165	6.3	465	17.9
96-97 Colo	29	29	947	152	368	.413	75	187	.401	176	206	.854	84	62	4	53	0	139	4.8	33	141	4.9	555	19.1
2 Years	55	54	1866	297	719	.413	120	314	.382	306	357	.857	202	104	8	128	3	282	5.1	87	306	5.6	1020	18.5
NBA 97-98 2Tm	80	70	2216	280	749	.374	107	325	.329	226	266	.850	174	107	4	172	2	314	3.9	62	190	2.4	893	11.2
98-99 Den	45	41	1488	191	495	.386	85	235	.362	157	172	.913	98	58	14	115	2	173	3.8	24	96	2.1	624	13.9
99-00 Den	13	5	305	34	101	.337	7	41	.171	37	44	.841	24	10	2	27	0	39	3.0	8	34	2.6	112	8.6
97-98 Bos	51	44	1296	177	454	.390	64	189	.339	147	180	.817	118	77	2	118	1	217	4.3	40	113	2.2	565	11.1
Tor	29	26	920	103	295	.349	43	136	.316	79	86	.919	56	30	2	54	1	97	3.3	22	77	2.7	328	11.3
3 Years	138	116	4009	505	1345	.375	199	601	.331	420	482	.871	296	175	20	314	2	526	3.8	94	320	2.3	1629	11.8

Mookie Blaylock
(statistical profile on page 193)

Pos: G **College:** Oklahoma **Drafted:** '89 1(12)—NJ **Ht:** 6'1" **Wt:** 185 **Born:** 3/20/67 **Age:** 33

College Year Tm	G	GS	Min	Md	Att	Pct	Md	Att	Pct	Md	Att	Pct	TO	Stl	Blk	PF	DQ	Ast	Avg	Off	Tot	Avg	Pts	Avg
87-88 Okla	39	38	1347	241	524	.460	78	201	.388	78	114	.684	100	150	3	91	1	232	5.9	93	162	4.2	638	16.4
88-89 Okla	35	35	1359	272	598	.455	91	245	.371	65	100	.650	101	131	20	79	0	233	6.7	73	164	4.7	700	20.0
2 Years	74	73	2706	513	1122	.457	169	446	.379	143	214	.668	201	281	23	170		465	6.3	166	326	4.4	1338	18.1
NBA 89-90 NJ	50	17	1267	212	571	.371	18	80	.225	63	81	.778	111	82	14	110	0	210	4.2	42	140	2.8	505	10.1
90-91 NJ	72	70	2585	432	1039	.416	14	91	.154	139	176	.790	207	169	40	180	0	441	6.1	67	249	3.5	1017	14.1
91-92 NJ	72	67	2548	429	993	.432	12	54	.222	126	177	.712	152	170	40	182	1	492	6.8	101	269	3.7	996	13.8
92-93 Atl	80	78	2820	414	964	.429	118	315	.375	123	169	.728	187	203	23	156	0	671	8.4	89	280	3.5	1069	13.4
93-94 Atl*	81	81	2915	444	1079	.411	114	341	.334	116	159	.730	196	212	44	144	0	789	9.7	117	424	5.2	1118	13.8
94-95 Atl	80	80	3069	509	1198	.425	199	555	.359	156	214	.729	242	200	26	164	3	616	7.7	117	393	4.9	1373	17.2
95-96 Atl	81	81	2893	455	1123	.405	231	623	.371	127	170	.747	188	212	17	151	1	478	5.9	110	332	4.1	1268	15.7
96-97 Atl	78	78	3056	501	1159	.432	221	**604**	.366	131	174	.753	185	**212**	20	141	0	463	5.9	114	413	5.3	1354	17.4
97-98 Atl	70	69	2700	368	938	.392	90	334	.269	95	134	.709	176	183	21	122	0	469	6.7	81	341	4.9	921	13.2
98-99 Atl	48	48	1763	247	651	.379	77	251	.307	69	91	.758	115	99	9	61	0	278	5.8	45	224	4.7	640	13.3
99-00 GS	73	72	2459	327	837	.391	101	301	.336	67	95	.705	143	146	22	122	0	489	6.7	55	270	3.7	822	11.3
11 Years	785	741	28075	4338	10552	.411	1195	3549	.337	1212	1640	.739	1902	1888	276	1533	5	5396	6.9	938	3335	4.2	11083	14.1

NBA Postseason

Year Tm	G	GS	Min	Md	Att	Pct	Md	Att	Pct	Md	Att	Pct	TO	Stl	Blk	PF	DQ	Ast	Avg	Off	Tot	Avg	Pts	Avg
91-92 NJ	4	4	148	17	55	.309	1	6	.167	3	4	.750	7	15	2	16	0	31	7.8	5	16	4.0	38	9.5
92-93 Atl	3	3	99	9	25	.360	4	12	.333	5	6	.833	11	3	4	9	0	13	4.3	2	13	4.3	27	9.0
93-94 Atl	11	11	415	48	141	.340	22	64	.344	25	30	.833	32	24	5	22	0	98	8.9	16	55	5.0	143	13.0
94-95 Atl	3	3	121	18	49	.367	11	28	.393	7	11	.636	9	4	0	6	0	17	5.7	7	13	4.3	54	18.0
95-96 Atl	10	10	426	61	145	.421	33	84	.393	16	24	.667	29	22	8	15	0	64	6.4	13	43	4.3	171	17.1
96-97 Atl	10	10	441	61	154	.396	28	85	.329	14	21	.667	35	21	2	15	0	65	6.5	12	70	7.0	164	16.4
97-98 Atl	4	4	153	22	53	.415	8	27	.296	7	12	.583	9	7	1	8	0	33	8.3	6	20	5.0	59	14.8
98-99 Atl	9	9	358	44	135	.326	18	51	.353	7	15	.467	30	18	2	11	0	36	4.0	6	36	4.0	113	12.6
8 Years	54	54	2161	280	757	.370	125	357	.350	84	123	.683	162	116	24	102	0	357	6.6	67	266	4.9	769	14.2

Corie Blount

Pos: F **College:** Cincinnati **Drafted:** '93 1(25)—Chi **Ht:** 6'10" **Wt:** 242 **Born:** 1/4/69 **Age:** 32

College Year Tm	G	GS	Min	Md	Att	Pct	Md	Att	Pct	Md	Att	Pct	TO	Stl	Blk	PF	DQ	Ast	Avg	Off	Tot	Avg	Pts	Avg
91-92 Cin	34	21	864	114	238	.479	0	2	.000	50	90	.556	57	39	51	107	—	69	2.0	—	213	6.3	278	8.2
92-93 Cin	21	—	588	104	189	.550	0	0	—	30	53	.566	54	37	33	69	—	47	2.2	—	170	8.1	238	11.3
2 Years	55	—	1452	218	427	.511	0	2	.000	80	143	.559	111	76	84	176	—	116	2.1	—	383	7.0	516	9.4

NBA			Field Goals			3-Pt FGs			Free Throws			Misc			Fouls		Assists		Rebounds			Points	
Year Tm	G	GS	Min	Md	Att	Pct	Md	Att	Pct	Md	Att	Pct	TO	Stl	Blk	PF	DQ	Ast	Avg	Off	Tot	Avg	Pts	Avg
93-94 Chi	67	8	690	76	174	.437	0	0	—	46	75	.613	52	19	33	93	0	56	0.8	76	194	2.9	198	3.0
94-95 Chi	68	9	889	100	210	.476	0	2	.000	38	67	.567	59	26	33	146	0	60	0.9	107	240	3.5	238	3.5
95-96 LAL	57	2	715	79	167	.473	0	2	.000	25	44	.568	47	25	35	109	2	42	0.7	69	170	3.0	183	3.2
96-97 LAL	58	18	1009	92	179	.514	1	3	.333	56	83	.675	50	22	26	121	2	35	0.6	113	276	4.8	241	4.2
97-98 LAL	70	3	1029	107	187	.572	0	4	.000	39	78	.500	51	29	25	157	2	37	0.5	114	298	4.3	253	3.6
98-99 2Tm	34	3	530	36	100	.360	0	1	.000	28	54	.519	21	19	16	74	0	12	0.4	58	151	4.4	100	2.9
99-00 Pho	38	1	446	44	89	.494	0	2	.000	19	33	.576	28	15	7	78	0	10	0.3	52	113	3.0	107	2.8
98-99 LAL	14	3	162	13	33	.394	0	1	.000	6	12	.500	6	1	4	27	0	2	0.1	24	46	3.3	32	2.3
Cle	20	0	368	23	67	.343	0	0	—	22	42	.524	15	18	12	47	0	10	0.5	34	105	5.3	68	3.4
7 Years	392	44	5308	534	1106	.483	1	14	.071	251	434	.578	308	155	175	778	6	252	0.6	589	1442	3.7	1320	3.4

NBA Postseason

Year Tm	G	GS	Min	Md	Att	Pct	Md	Att	Pct	Md	Att	Pct	TO	Stl	Blk	PF	DQ	Ast	Avg	Off	Tot	Avg	Pts	Avg
94-95 Chi	8	0	20	0	3	.000	0	1	.000	0	0	—	1	0	0	5	0	0	0.0	1	5	0.6	0	0.0
96-97 LAL	3	0	8	1	1	1.000	0	0	—	1	2	.500	0	0	0	2	0	1	0.3	2	2	0.7	3	1.0
97-98 LAL	12	0	209	12	24	.500	0	0	—	7	11	.636	3	6	4	27	1	7	0.6	24	64	5.3	31	2.6
99-00 Pho	9	0	162	17	31	.548	0	0	—	10	18	.556	13	6	6	36	0	3	0.3	25	56	6.2	44	4.9
4 Years	32	0	399	30	59	.508	0	1	.000	18	31	.581	17	12	10	70	1	11	0.3	50	127	4.0	78	2.4

Muggsy Bogues

(statistical profile on page 193)

Pos: G **College:** Wake Forest **Drafted:** '87 1(12)—Was **Ht:** 5'3" **Wt:** 141 **Born:** 1/9/65 **Age:** 36

College			Field Goals			3-Pt FGs			Free Throws			Misc			Fouls		Assists		Rebounds			Points	
Year Tm	G	GS	Min	Md	Att	Pct	Md	Att	Pct	Md	Att	Pct	TO	Stl	Blk	PF	DQ	Ast	Avg	Off	Tot	Avg	Pts	Avg
83-84 Wake	32	0	312	14	46	.304	—	—	—	9	13	.692	33	31		50	—	53	1.7	—	21	0.7	37	1.2
84-85 Wake	29	28	1025	81	162	.500	—	—	—	30	44	.682	62	85	0	81	—	207	7.1	—	69	2.4	192	6.6
85-86 Wake	29	29	1101	132	290	.455	—	—	—	65	89	.730	96	89	3	84	—	245	8.4	—	90	3.1	329	11.3
86-87 Wake	29	29	1130	159	318	.500	35	79	.443	75	93	.806	106	70	1	62	—	276	9.5	—	110	3.8	428	14.8
4 Years	119	86	3568	386	816	.473	35	79	.443	179	239	.749	297	275	4	277	—	781	6.6	—	290	2.4	986	8.3

NBA			Field Goals			3-Pt FGs			Free Throws			Misc			Fouls		Assists		Rebounds			Points	
Year Tm	G	GS	Min	Md	Att	Pct	Md	Att	Pct	Md	Att	Pct	TO	Stl	Blk	PF	DQ	Ast	Avg	Off	Tot	Avg	Pts	Avg
87-88 Was	79	14	1628	166	426	.390	3	16	.188	58	74	.784	101	127	3	138	1	404	5.1	35	136	1.7	393	5.0
88-89 Cha	79	21	1755	178	418	.426	1	13	.077	66	88	.750	124	111	7	141	1	620	7.8	53	165	2.1	423	5.4
89-90 Cha	81	65	2743	326	664	.491	5	26	.192	106	134	.791	146	166	3	168	1	867	10.7	48	207	2.6	763	9.4
90-91 Cha	81	46	2299	241	524	.460	0	12	.000	86	108	.796	120	137	3	160	2	669	8.3	58	216	2.7	568	7.0
91-92 Cha	82	69	2790	317	671	.472	2	27	.074	94	120	.783	156	170	6	156	0	743	9.1	58	235	2.9	730	8.9
92-93 Cha	81	80	2833	331	730	.453	6	26	.231	140	168	.833	154	161	5	179	0	711	8.8	51	298	3.7	808	10.0
93-94 Cha	77	77	2746	354	751	.471	2	12	.167	125	155	.806	171	133	2	147	1	780	10.1	78	313	4.1	835	10.8
94-95 Cha	78	78	2629	348	730	.477	6	30	.200	160	180	.889	132	103	0	151	0	675	8.7	51	257	3.3	862	11.1
95-96 Cha	6	0	77	6	16	.375	0	1	.000	2	2	1.000	6	2	0	4	0	19	3.2	6	7	1.2	14	2.3
96-97 Cha	65	65	1880	204	443	.460	60	144	.417	54	64	.844	108	82	2	114	0	469	7.2	25	141	2.2	522	8.0
97-98 2Tm	61	31	1570	141	323	.437	4	16	.250	61	68	.897	105	67	3	58	0	331	5.4	30	132	2.2	347	5.7
98-99 GS	36	5	714	76	154	.494	0	6	.000	31	36	.861	47	43	1	44	0	134	3.7	16	73	2.0	183	5.1
99-00 Tor	80	5	1731	157	358	.439	17	51	.333	79	87	.908	59	65	0	119	0	299	3.7	25	135	1.7	410	5.1
97-98 Cha	2	0	16	2	5	.400	0	0	—	2	2	1.000	1	2	0	2	0	4	2.0	0	1	0.5	6	3.0
GS	59	31	1554	139	318	.437	4	16	.250	59	66	.894	104	65	3	56	0	327	5.5	30	131	2.2	341	5.8
13 Years	886	556	25395	2845	6208	.458	106	380	.279	1062	1284	.827	1429	1367	39	1579	6	6721	7.6	534	2315	2.6	6858	7.7

NBA Postseason

Year Tm	G	GS	Min	Md	Att	Pct	Md	Att	Pct	Md	Att	Pct	TO	Stl	Blk	PF	DQ	Ast	Avg	Off	Tot	Avg	Pts	Avg
87-88 Was	1	0	2	0	0	—	0	0	—	0	0	—	1	0	0	0	0	2	2.0	0	0	0.0	0	0.0
92-93 Cha	9	9	346	39	82	.476	0	2	.000	10	14	.714	17	24	0	21	0	70	7.8	6	36	4.0	88	9.8
94-95 Cha	4	4	145	14	45	.311	1	3	.333	5	5	1.000	9	4	0	8	0	25	6.3	3	6	1.5	34	8.5
96-97 Cha	2	2	58	11	19	.579	6	7	.857	4	4	1.000	6	1	0	5	0	5	2.5	1	3	1.5	32	16.0
99-00 Tor	3	2	87	6	21	.286	3	9	.333	1	3	.333	4	4	0	4	0	5	1.7	3	6	2.0	16	5.3
5 Years	19	17	638	70	167	.419	10	21	.476	20	26	.769	37	33	0	36	0	107	5.6	13	51	2.7	170	8.9

Etdrick Bohannon

Pos: F **College:** Auburn-Montgomery **Drafted:** '97 FA—Ind **Ht:** 6'9" **Wt:** 225 **Born:** 5/29/73 **Age:** 27

College			Field Goals			3-Pt FGs			Free Throws			Misc			Fouls		Assists		Rebounds			Points	
Year Tm	G	GS	Min	Md	Att	Pct	Md	Att	Pct	Md	Att	Pct	TO	Stl	Blk	PF	DQ	Ast	Avg	Off	Tot	Avg	Pts	Avg
92-93 Ari	24	0	203	23	52	.442	0	0	—	17	31	.548	15	8	14	23	0	12	0.5	28	52	2.2	63	2.6
94-95 Tenn	14	—	182	18	54	.333	0	0	—	19	36	.528	27	2	12	29	—	9	0.6	—	59	4.2	55	3.9
95-96 Ab-Mn	12	—	327	79	135	.585	0	0	—	56	97	.577	31	10	42	33	—	17	1.4	—	122	10.2	214	17.8
96-97 Ab-Mn	24	—	750	140	234	.598	0	0	—	92	166	.554	80	20	57	78	—	20	0.8	—	225	9.4	372	15.5
4 Years	74	—	1462	260	475	.547	0	0	—	184	330	.558	153	40	125	163	—	58	0.8	—	458	6.2	704	9.5

Year Tm	G	GS	Min	Md	Att	Pct	Md	Att	Pct	Md	Att	Pct	TO	Stl	Blk	PF	DQ	Ast	Avg	Off	Tot	Avg	Pts	Avg
	NBA			**Field Goals**			**3-Pt FGs**			**Free Throws**			**Misc**			**Fouls**		**Assists**		**Rebounds**			**Points**	
97-98 Ind	5	0	11	0	4	.000	0	0	—	0	0	—	3	0	2	3	0	1	0.2	2	6	1.2	0	0.0
98-99 Was	2	0	4	0	0	—	0	0	—	0	0	—	0	0	0	0	0	0	0.0	0	0	0.0	0	0.0
99-00 2Tm	13	0	118	7	13	.538	0	0	—	15	24	.625	10	2	6	25	0	5	0.4	13	31	2.4	29	2.2
99-00 NY	2	0	5	0	0	—	0	0	—	3	4	.750	2	0	0	1	0	0	0.0	1	1	0.5	3	1.5
LAC	11	0	113	7	13	.538	0	0	—	12	20	.600	8	2	6	24	0	5	0.5	12	30	2.7	26	2.4
3 Years	20	0	133	7	17	.412	0	0	—	15	24	.625	13	2	8	28	0	6	0.3	15	37	1.9	29	1.5

Calvin Booth

Pos: C **College:** Penn State **Drafted:** '99 2(35)—Was **Ht:** 6'11" **Wt:** 241 **Born:** 5/7/76 **Age:** 24

Year Tm	G	GS	Min	Md	Att	Pct	Md	Att	Pct	Md	Att	Pct	TO	Stl	Blk	PF	DQ	Ast	Avg	Off	Tot	Avg	Pts	Avg
	College			**Field Goals**			**3-Pt FGs**			**Free Throws**			**Misc**			**Fouls**		**Assists**		**Rebounds**			**Points**	
95-96 PSU	28	28	670	100	182	.549	0	0	—	61	96	.635	42	19	101	64	0	35	1.3	40	150	5.4	261	9.3
96-97 PSU	27	25	706	87	204	.426	1	3	.333	61	84	.726	65	15	90	66	0	15	0.6	40	134	5.0	236	8.7
97-98 PSU	32	32	990	156	294	.531	0	1	.000	65	97	.670	61	22	140	74	1	34	1.1	45	208	6.5	377	11.8
98-99 PSU	27	26	942	157	306	.513	0	6	.000	100	129	.775	62	17	95	53	1	24	0.9	46	236	8.7	414	15.3
4 Years	114	111	3308	500	986	.507	1	10	.100	287	406	.707	230	73	426	257	2	108	0.9	171	728	6.4	1288	11.3
	NBA			**Field Goals**			**3-Pt FGs**			**Free Throws**			**Misc**			**Fouls**		**Assists**		**Rebounds**			**Points**	
99-00 Was	11	0	143	16	46	.348	0	0	—	10	14	.714	6	3	14	23	0	7	0.6	15	32	2.9	42	3.8

Lazaro Borrell

Pos: F **College:** None **Drafted:** '99 FA—Sea **Ht:** 6'8" **Wt:** 220 **Born:** 9/20/72 **Age:** 28

Year Tm	G	GS	Min	Md	Att	Pct	Md	Att	Pct	Md	Att	Pct	TO	Stl	Blk	PF	DQ	Ast	Avg	Off	Tot	Avg	Pts	Avg
	NBA			**Field Goals**			**3-Pt FGs**			**Free Throws**			**Misc**			**Fouls**		**Assists**		**Rebounds**			**Points**	
99-00 Sea	17	6	167	28	63	.444	0	3	.000	6	11	.545	6	6	3	9	0	10	0.6	14	40	2.4	62	3.6
	NBA Postseason																							
99-00 Sea	2	1	26	4	7	.571	0	0	—	2	4	.500	1	0	0	2	0	1	0.5	3	11	5.5	10	5.0

Cal Bowdler

Pos: F **College:** Old Dominion **Drafted:** '99 1(17)—Atl **Ht:** 6'10" **Wt:** 245 **Born:** 3/31/77 **Age:** 23

Year Tm	G	GS	Min	Md	Att	Pct	Md	Att	Pct	Md	Att	Pct	TO	Stl	Blk	PF	DQ	Ast	Avg	Off	Tot	Avg	Pts	Avg
	College			**Field Goals**			**3-Pt FGs**			**Free Throws**			**Misc**			**Fouls**		**Assists**		**Rebounds**			**Points**	
95-96 ODU	23	0	204	16	47	.340	8	26	.308	9	13	.692	17	3	12	28	—	14	0.6	15	38	1.7	49	2.1
96-97 ODU	33	10	626	65	150	.433	14	44	.318	39	80	.488	44	9	42	64	4	11	0.3	54	161	4.9	183	5.5
97-98 ODU	28	28	830	102	242	.421	7	39	.179	74	133	.556	54	14	68	70	2	15	0.5	71	245	8.8	285	10.2
98-99 ODU	34	34	1021	179	364	.492	9	35	.257	133	182	.731	74	17	96	82	3	43	1.3	97	339	10.0	500	14.7
4 Years	118	72	2681	362	803	.451	38	144	.264	255	408	.625	189	43	218	244	—	83	0.7	237	783	6.6	1017	8.6
	NBA			**Field Goals**			**3-Pt FGs**			**Free Throws**			**Misc**			**Fouls**		**Assists**		**Rebounds**			**Points**	
99-00 Atl	46	0	423	49	115	.426	0	1	.000	24	38	.632	21	14	9	46	1	14	0.3	22	85	1.8	122	2.7

Bruce Bowen

Pos: G-F **College:** Cal State Fullerton **Drafted:** '96 FA—Mia **Ht:** 6'7" **Wt:** 200 **Born:** 6/14/71 **Age:** 29

Year Tm	G	GS	Min	Md	Att	Pct	Md	Att	Pct	Md	Att	Pct	TO	Stl	Blk	PF	DQ	Ast	Avg	Off	Tot	Avg	Pts	Avg
	College			**Field Goals**			**3-Pt FGs**			**Free Throws**			**Misc**			**Fouls**		**Assists**		**Rebounds**			**Points**	
89-90 CSF	18	0	98	9	22	.409	3	5	.600	10	13	.769	7	3	3	17	0	4	0.2	8	18	1.0	31	1.7
90-91 CSF	28	23	849	89	236	.377	14	60	.233	83	120	.692	61	26	24	80	4	60	2.1	76	169	6.0	275	9.8
91-92 CSF	28	27	969	138	311	.444	12	44	.273	120	161	.745	68	51	23	75	1	70	2.5	86	196	7.0	408	14.6
92-93 CSF	27	27	987	148	318	.465	14	43	.326	131	201	.652	73	53	21	75	3	62	2.3	72	176	6.5	441	16.3
4 Years	101	77	2903	384	887	.433	43	152	.283	344	495	.695	209	133	71	247	8	196	1.9	242	559	5.5	1155	11.4
	NBA			**Field Goals**			**3-Pt FGs**			**Free Throws**			**Misc**			**Fouls**		**Assists**		**Rebounds**			**Points**	
93-94										Did not play in NBA														
94-95										Played in France														
95-96										Played in CBA														
96-97 Mia	1	0	1	0	0	—	0	0	—	0	0	—	0	0	1	0	0	0	0.0	0	0	0.0	0	0.0
97-98 Bos	61	9	1305	122	298	.409	20	59	.339	76	122	.623	52	87	29	174	0	81	1.3	79	174	2.9	340	5.6

NBA			Field Goals			3-Pt FGs			Free Throws			Misc			Fouls		Assists		Rebounds			Points	
Year Tm	G	GS	Min	Md	Att	Pct	Md	Att	Pct	Md	Att	Pct	TO	Stl	Blk	PF	DQ	Ast	Avg	Off	Tot	Avg	Pts	Avg
98-99 Bos	30	1	494	26	93	.280	7	26	.269	11	24	.458	13	21	9	51	2	28	0.9	15	52	1.7	70	2.3
99-00 2Tm	69	2	878	72	194	.371	27	58	.466	25	43	.581	19	23	15	118	0	34	0.5	27	96	1.4	196	2.8
99-00 Phi	42	0	311	26	73	.356	1	2	.500	6	12	.500	5	9	5	37	0	16	0.4	14	36	0.9	59	1.4
Mia	27	2	567	46	121	.380	26	56	.464	19	31	.613	14	14	10	81	0	18	0.7	13	60	2.2	137	5.1
4 Years	161	12	2678	220	585	.376	54	143	.378	112	189	.593	84	131	54	343	2	143	0.9	121	322	2.0	606	3.8

NBA Postseason																							
Year Tm	G	GS	Min	Md	Att	Pct	Md	Att	Pct	Md	Att	Pct	TO	Stl	Blk	PF	DQ	Ast	Avg	Off	Tot	Avg	Pts	Avg
99-00 Mia	10	0	157	10	27	.370	5	22	.227	10	16	.625	6	7	4	27	1	8	0.8	1	10	1.0	35	3.5

Ryan Bowen

Pos: F **College:** Iowa **Drafted:** '98 2(55)—Den **Ht:** 6'7" **Wt:** 215 **Born:** 11/20/75 **Age:** 25

College			Field Goals			3-Pt FGs			Free Throws			Misc			Fouls		Assists		Rebounds			Points	
Year Tm	G	GS	Min	Md	Att	Pct	Md	Att	Pct	Md	Att	Pct	TO	Stl	Blk	PF	DQ	Ast	Avg	Off	Tot	Avg	Pts	Avg
94-95 Iowa	33	19	647	58	110	.527	0	1	.000	35	59	.593	32	38	34	65		16	0.5	—	148	4.5	151	4.6
95-96 Iowa	27	8	554	55	91	.604	0	0	—	39	58	.672	36	36	20	51	1	16	0.6	—	121	4.5	149	5.5
96-97 Iowa	29	26	827	120	217	.553	10	32	.313	93	135	.689	53	55	30	66	1	35	1.2	109	264	9.1	343	11.8
97-98 Iowa	31	30	852	164	272	.603	8	15	.533	111	161	.689	45	77	41	72	2	48	1.5	102	271	8.7	447	14.4
4 Years	120	83	2880	397	690	.575	18	48	.375	278	413	.673	166	206	125	254		115	1.0	—	804	6.7	1090	9.1

NBA			Field Goals			3-Pt FGs			Free Throws			Misc			Fouls		Assists		Rebounds			Points	
Year Tm	G	GS	Min	Md	Att	Pct	Md	Att	Pct	Md	Att	Pct	TO	Stl	Blk	PF	DQ	Ast	Avg	Off	Tot	Avg	Pts	Avg
98-99										Played in Turkey														
99-00 Den	52	0	589	46	117	.393	1	9	.111	38	53	.717	14	39	13	95	0	20	0.4	75	114	2.2	131	2.5

Ira Bowman

Pos: G **College:** Pennsylvania **Drafted:** '99 FA—Phi **Ht:** 6'5" **Wt:** 195 **Born:** 6/11/73 **Age:** 27

College			Field Goals			3-Pt FGs			Free Throws			Misc			Fouls		Assists		Rebounds			Points	
Year Tm	G	GS	Min	Md	Att	Pct	Md	Att	Pct	Md	Att	Pct	TO	Stl	Blk	PF	DQ	Ast	Avg	Off	Tot	Avg	Pts	Avg
91-92 Prov	28	9	354	40	82	.488	1	5	.200	46	72	.639	44	22	1	70	4	35	1.3	12	22	0.8	127	4.5
92-93 Prov	15	1	136	17	29	.586	0	0	—	12	18	.667	12	4	0	31	2	5	0.3	13	23	1.5	46	3.1
94-95 Penn	28	0	558	120	210	.571	11	34	.324	50	76	.658	37	56	3	66	1	46	1.6	28	85	3.0	301	10.8
95-96 Penn	27	27	950	149	328	.454	28	76	.368	118	166	.711	88	57	7	82	4	142	5.3	25	135	5.0	444	16.4
4 Years	98	37	1998	326	649	.502	40	115	.348	226	332	.681	181	139	11	249	11	228	2.3	78	265	2.7	918	9.4

NBA			Field Goals			3-Pt FGs			Free Throws			Misc			Fouls		Assists		Rebounds			Points	
Year Tm	G	GS	Min	Md	Att	Pct	Md	Att	Pct	Md	Att	Pct	TO	Stl	Blk	PF	DQ	Ast	Avg	Off	Tot	Avg	Pts	Avg
96-97										Played in CBA														
97-98										Played in CBA														
98-99										Played in CBA														
99-00 Phi	11	0	20	2	2	1.000	0	0	—	1	2	.500	1	1	0	0	0	1	0.1	0	2	0.2	5	0.5

NBA Postseason																								
Year Tm	G	GS	Min	Md	Att	Pct	Md	Att	Pct	Md	Att	Pct	TO	Stl	Blk	PF	DQ	Ast	Avg	Off	Tot	Avg	Pts	Avg
99-00 Phi	7	0	11	0	2	.000	0	1	.000	0	2	.000	0	0	0	0	0	2	0.3	0	0	0.0	0	0.0

Earl Boykins

Pos: G **College:** Eastern Michigan **Drafted:** '98 FA—NJ **Ht:** 5'5" **Wt:** 133 **Born:** 6/2/76 **Age:** 24

College			Field Goals			3-Pt FGs			Free Throws			Misc			Fouls		Assists		Rebounds			Points	
Year Tm	G	GS	Min	Md	Att	Pct	Md	Att	Pct	Md	Att	Pct	TO	Stl	Blk	PF	DQ	Ast	Avg	Off	Tot	Avg	Pts	Avg
94-95 EstMi	30	30	976	129	312	.413	34	99	.343	83	118	.703	70	50	4	39	0	136	4.5	26	73	2.4	375	12.5
95-96 EstMi	31	31	1029	156	361	.432	23	75	.307	144	179	.804	77	58	2	47	0	181	5.8	26	71	2.3	479	15.5
96-97 EstMi	32	31	1163	208	492	.423	39	130	.300	156	183	.852	115	60	1	58	0	147	4.6	21	67	2.1	611	19.1
97-98 EstMi	29	29	1070	266	563	.472	85	209	.407	129	158	.816	93	54	3	39	0	160	5.5	21	66	2.3	746	25.7
4 Years	122	121	4238	759	1728	.439	181	513	.353	512	638	.803	355	222	10	183	0	624	5.1	94	277	2.3	2211	18.1

NBA			Field Goals			3-Pt FGs			Free Throws			Misc			Fouls		Assists		Rebounds			Points	
Year Tm	G	GS	Min	Md	Att	Pct	Md	Att	Pct	Md	Att	Pct	TO	Stl	Blk	PF	DQ	Ast	Avg	Off	Tot	Avg	Pts	Avg
98-99 2Tm	22	0	221	30	79	.380	3	18	.167	2	3	.667	20	6	0	20	0	33	1.5	7	17	0.8	65	3.0
99-00 2Tm	26	0	261	56	116	.483	8	20	.400	18	23	.783	17	12	1	23	0	48	1.8	12	26	1.0	138	5.3
98-99 NJ	5	0	51	10	21	.476	1	5	.200	0	0	—	7	1	0	3	0	6	1.2	1	4	0.8	21	4.2
Cle	17	0	170	20	58	.345	2	13	.154	2	3	.667	13	5	0	17	0	27	1.6	6	13	0.8	44	2.6
99-00 Orl	1	0	8	3	4	.750	0	0	—	0	0	—	0	0	0	0	0	3	3.0	1	1	1.0	6	6.0
Cle	25	0	253	53	112	.473	8	20	.400	18	23	.783	17	12	1	23	0	45	1.8	11	25	1.0	132	5.3
2 Years	48	0	482	86	195	.441	11	38	.289	20	26	.769	37	18	1	43	0	81	1.7	19	43	0.9	203	4.2

Shawn Bradley

(statistical profile on page 194)

Pos: C **College:** Brigham Young **Drafted:** '93 1(2)—Phi   **Ht:** 7'6" **Wt:** 263 **Born:** 3/22/72 **Age:** 28

College Year Tm	G	GS	Min	Field Goals Md	Att	Pct	3-Pt FGs Md	Att	Pct	Free Throws Md	Att	Pct	Misc TO	Stl	Blk	Fouls PF	DQ	Assists Ast	Avg	Rebounds Off	Tot	Avg	Points Pts	Avg
90-91 BYU	34	—	984	187	361	.518	1	1	1.000	128	185	.692	77	23	177	109	—	41	1.2	—	262	7.7	503	14.8

NBA Year Tm	G	GS	Min	Field Goals Md	Att	Pct	3-Pt FGs Md	Att	Pct	Free Throws Md	Att	Pct	Misc TO	Stl	Blk	Fouls PF	DQ	Assists Ast	Avg	Rebounds Off	Tot	Avg	Points Pts	Avg
93-94 Phi	49	45	1385	201	491	.409	0	3	.000	102	168	.607	148	45	147	170	3	98	2.0	98	306	6.2	504	10.3
94-95 Phi	82	59	2365	315	693	.455	0	3	.000	148	232	.638	142	54	274	338	18	53	0.6	243	659	8.0	778	9.5
95-96 2Tm	79	68	2329	387	873	.443	1	4	.250	169	246	.687	179	49	288	286	5	63	0.8	221	638	8.1	944	11.9
96-97 2Tm	73	70	2288	406	905	.449	0	8	.000	149	228	.654	134	40	248	237	7	52	0.7	221	611	8.4	961	13.2
97-98 Dal	64	46	1822	300	711	.422	1	3	.333	130	180	.722	96	51	214	214	9	60	0.9	164	518	8.1	731	11.4
98-99 Dal	49	33	1244	167	348	.480	0	4	.000	86	115	.748	56	35	159	153	2	40	0.8	130	392	8.0	420	8.6
99-00 Dal	77	54	1901	266	555	.479	1	5	.200	114	149	.765	74	71	190	260	7	60	0.8	160	497	6.5	647	8.4
95-96 Phi	12	11	334	43	97	.443	0	0	—	19	25	.760	31	8	38	42	0	8	0.7	34	106	8.8	105	8.8
NJ	67	57	1995	344	776	.443	1	4	.250	150	221	.679	148	41	250	244	5	55	0.8	187	532	7.9	839	12.5
96-97 NJ	40	38	1228	199	456	.436	0	5	.000	81	122	.664	64	23	160	122	4	20	0.5	118	325	8.1	479	12.0
Dal	33	32	1060	207	449	.461	0	3	.000	68	106	.642	70	17	88	115	3	32	1.0	103	286	8.7	482	14.6
7 Years	473	375	13384	2042	4576	.446	3	30	.100	898	1318	.681	829	345	1520	1658	51	426	0.9	1237	3621	7.7	4985	10.5

A.J. Bramlett

Pos: F **College:** Arizona **Drafted:** '99 2(39)—Cle   **Ht:** 6'10" **Wt:** 227 **Born:** 1/10/77 **Age:** 24

College Year Tm	G	GS	Min	Field Goals Md	Att	Pct	3-Pt FGs Md	Att	Pct	Free Throws Md	Att	Pct	Misc TO	Stl	Blk	Fouls PF	DQ	Assists Ast	Avg	Rebounds Off	Tot	Avg	Points Pts	Avg
95-96 Ari	30	0	251	24	47	.511	0	0	—	10	28	.357	6	8	9	37	0	8	0.3	21	56	1.9	58	1.9
96-97 Ari	33	28	788	109	204	.534	0	1	.000	50	95	.526	50	25	22	105	4	19	0.6	90	229	6.9	268	8.1
97-98 Ari	35	35	936	143	278	.514	0	0	—	77	135	.570	47	30	36	107	6	39	1.1	100	259	7.4	363	10.4
98-99 Ari	29	29	909	160	299	.535	0	0	—	91	158	.576	57	24	37	94	2	32	1.1	95	273	9.4	411	14.2
4 Years	127	92	2884	436	828	.527	0	1	.000	228	416	.548	160	87	104	343	12	98	0.8	306	817	6.4	1100	8.7

NBA Year Tm	G	GS	Min	Field Goals Md	Att	Pct	3-Pt FGs Md	Att	Pct	Free Throws Md	Att	Pct	Misc TO	Stl	Blk	Fouls PF	DQ	Assists Ast	Avg	Rebounds Off	Tot	Avg	Points Pts	Avg
99-00 Cle	8	0	61	4	21	.190	0	0	—	0	0	—	3	1	0	13	0	0	0.0	12	22	2.8	8	1.0

Elton Brand

(statistical profile on page 194)

Pos: F **College:** Duke **Drafted:** '99 1(1)—Chi   **Ht:** 6'8" **Wt:** 260 **Born:** 3/11/79 **Age:** 21

College Year Tm	G	GS	Min	Field Goals Md	Att	Pct	3-Pt FGs Md	Att	Pct	Free Throws Md	Att	Pct	Misc TO	Stl	Blk	Fouls PF	DQ	Assists Ast	Avg	Rebounds Off	Tot	Avg	Points Pts	Avg
97-98 Duke	21	18	493	100	169	.592	0	0	—	81	134	.604	34	32	27	53	1	10	0.5	76	154	7.3	281	13.4
98-99 Duke	39	37	1141	255	411	.620	0	0	—	181	256	.707	67	49	86	97	1	41	1.1	139	382	9.8	691	17.7
2 Years	60	55	1634	355	580	.612	0	0	—	262	390	.672	101	81	113	150	2	51	0.9	215	536	8.9	972	16.2

NBA Year Tm	G	GS	Min	Field Goals Md	Att	Pct	3-Pt FGs Md	Att	Pct	Free Throws Md	Att	Pct	Misc TO	Stl	Blk	Fouls PF	DQ	Assists Ast	Avg	Rebounds Off	Tot	Avg	Points Pts	Avg
99-00 Chi	81	80	2999	630	1306	.482	0	2	.000	367	536	.685	228	66	132	259	3	155	1.9	348	810	10.0	1627	20.1

Terrell Brandon

(statistical profile on page 195)

Pos: G **College:** Oregon **Drafted:** '91 1(11)—Cle   **Ht:** 5'11" **Wt:** 180 **Born:** 5/20/70 **Age:** 30

College Year Tm	G	GS	Min	Field Goals Md	Att	Pct	3-Pt FGs Md	Att	Pct	Free Throws Md	Att	Pct	Misc TO	Stl	Blk	Fouls PF	DQ	Assists Ast	Avg	Rebounds Off	Tot	Avg	Points Pts	Avg
89-90 Ore	29	29	1067	190	401	.474	41	94	.436	97	129	.752	101	51	4	63	1	174	6.0	—	106	3.7	518	17.9
90-91 Ore	28	28	1108	273	556	.491	40	119	.336	159	187	.850	102	63	4	57	0	141	5.0	—	101	3.6	745	26.6
2 Years	57	57	2175	463	957	.484	81	213	.380	256	316	.810	203	114	8	120	1	315	5.5	—	207	3.6	1263	22.2

NBA Year Tm	G	GS	Min	Field Goals Md	Att	Pct	3-Pt FGs Md	Att	Pct	Free Throws Md	Att	Pct	Misc TO	Stl	Blk	Fouls PF	DQ	Assists Ast	Avg	Rebounds Off	Tot	Avg	Points Pts	Avg
91-92 Cle	82	9	1605	252	601	.419	1	23	.043	100	124	.806	136	81	22	107	0	316	3.9	49	162	2.0	605	7.4
92-93 Cle	82	8	1622	297	621	.478	13	42	.310	118	143	.825	107	79	27	122	1	302	3.7	37	179	2.2	725	8.8
93-94 Cle	73	10	1548	230	548	.420	7	32	.219	139	162	.858	111	84	16	108	0	277	3.8	38	159	2.2	606	8.3
94-95 Cle	67	41	1961	341	762	.448	48	121	.397	159	186	.855	144	107	14	118	0	363	5.4	35	186	2.8	889	13.3
95-96 Cle	75	75	2570	510	1096	.465	91	235	.387	338	381	.887	142	132	33	146	1	487	6.5	47	248	3.3	1449	19.3
96-97 Cle*	78	78	2868	575	1313	.438	101	271	.373	268	297	.902	178	138	30	177	1	490	6.3	48	301	3.9	1519	19.5
97-98 Mil	50	48	1784	339	731	.464	31	93	.333	132	156	.846	145	111	17	120	1	387	7.7	23	176	3.5	841	16.8
98-99 2Tm	36	34	1217	212	507	.418	12	47	.255	65	78	.833	74	63	10	82	0	309	8.6	27	134	3.7	501	13.9

NBA			Field Goals			3-Pt FGs			Free Throws			Misc			Fouls		Assists		Rebounds			Points	
Year Tm	G	GS	Min	Md	Att	Pct	Md	Att	Pct	Md	Att	Pct	TO	Stl	Blk	PF	DQ	Ast	Avg	Off	Tot	Avg	Pts	Avg
99-00 Min	71	71	2587	486	1042	.466	53	132	.402	187	208	.899	184	134	30	158	1	629	8.9	44	238	3.4	1212	17.1
98-99 Mil	15	14	505	85	208	.409	7	28	.250	26	31	.839	36	24	3	25	0	104	6.9	11	53	3.5	203	13.5
Min	21	20	712	127	299	.425	5	19	.263	39	47	.830	38	39	7	57	0	205	9.8	16	81	3.9	298	14.2
9 Years	614	374	17762	3242	7221	.449	357	996	.358	1506	1735	.868	1221	929	199	1138	5	3560	5.8	348	1783	2.9	8347	13.6

NBA Postseason

Year Tm	G	GS	Min	Md	Att	Pct	Md	Att	Pct	Md	Att	Pct	TO	Stl	Blk	PF	DQ	Ast	Avg	Off	Tot	Avg	Pts	Avg
91-92 Cle	12	0	157	22	55	.400	0	3	.000	3	4	.750	11	3	1	17	0	30	2.5	4	22	1.8	47	3.9
92-93 Cle	8	0	132	20	46	.435	2	5	.400	9	9	1.000	14	7	3	6	0	17	2.1	4	17	2.1	51	6.4
93-94 Cle	3	0	56	12	19	.632	0	0	—	2	3	.667	1	1	0	1	0	5	1.7	1	4	1.3	26	8.7
95-96 Cle	3	3	125	21	47	.447	3	9	.333	13	15	.867	11	4	1	10	0	24	8.0	1	9	3.0	58	19.3
98-99 Min	4	4	161	31	69	.449	3	5	.600	12	13	.923	14	9	2	11	0	28	7.0	2	30	7.5	77	19.3
99-00 Min	4	4	162	32	63	.508	4	11	.364	10	11	.909	8	3	0	11	0	34	8.5	4	23	5.8	78	19.5
6 Years	34	11	793	138	299	.462	12	33	.364	49	55	.891	59	27	7	56	0	138	4.1	16	105	3.1	337	9.9

Chucky Brown

Pos: F **College:** North Carolina State **Drafted:** '89 2(43)—Cle   **Ht:** 6'8" **Wt:** 225 **Born:** 2/29/68 **Age:** 32

College			Field Goals			3-Pt FGs			Free Throws			Misc			Fouls		Assists		Rebounds			Points	
Year Tm	G	GS	Min	Md	Att	Pct	Md	Att	Pct	Md	Att	Pct	TO	Stl	Blk	PF	DQ	Ast	Avg	Off	Tot	Avg	Pts	Avg
85-86 NCSt	31	5	310	38	80	.475	—	—	—	21	34	.618	13	8	6	30	—	13	0.4	—	67	2.2	97	3.1
86-87 NCSt	34	5	629	81	138	.587	0	1	.000	61	80	.763	32	9	6	49	—	12	0.4	—	145	4.3	223	6.6
87-88 NCSt	32	32	1024	226	395	.572	1	6	.167	77	121	.636	47	18	22	68	—	27	0.8	—	193	6.0	530	16.6
88-89 NCSt	31	31	1051	210	383	.548	6	21	.286	81	125	.648	54	27	29	62	—	42	1.4	—	274	8.8	507	16.4
4 Years	128	73	3014	555	996	.557	7	28	.250	240	360	.667	146	62	63	209	—	94	0.7	—	679	5.3	1357	10.6

NBA			Field Goals			3-Pt FGs			Free Throws			Misc			Fouls		Assists		Rebounds			Points	
Year Tm	G	GS	Min	Md	Att	Pct	Md	Att	Pct	Md	Att	Pct	TO	Stl	Blk	PF	DQ	Ast	Avg	Off	Tot	Avg	Pts	Avg
89-90 Cle	75	35	1339	210	447	.470	0	7	.000	125	164	.762	69	33	26	148	0	50	0.7	83	231	3.1	545	7.3
90-91 Cle	74	51	1485	263	502	.524	0	4	.000	101	144	.701	94	26	24	130	0	80	1.1	78	213	2.9	627	8.5
91-92 2Tm	42	2	431	60	128	.469	0	3	.000	30	49	.612	29	12	7	48	0	26	0.6	31	82	2.0	150	3.6
92-93 NJ	77	20	1186	160	331	.483	0	5	.000	71	98	.724	56	20	24	112	0	51	0.7	88	232	3.0	391	5.1
93-94 Dal	1	0	10	1	1	1.000	0	0	—	1	1	1.000	0	0	0	2	0	0	0.0	0	1	1.0	3	3.0
94-95 Hou	41	14	814	105	174	.603	1	3	.333	38	62	.613	29	11	14	105	0	30	0.7	64	189	4.6	249	6.1
95-96 Hou	82	82	2019	300	555	.541	1	8	.125	104	150	.693	94	47	38	163	0	89	1.1	134	441	5.4	705	8.6
96-97 2Tm	70	1	757	78	154	.506	1	6	.167	47	70	.671	19	9	22	100	1	28	0.4	41	148	2.1	204	2.9
97-98 Atl	77	8	1202	161	372	.433	2	8	.250	63	87	.724	51	23	13	100	0	55	0.7	57	183	2.4	387	5.0
98-99 Cha	48	21	1192	176	373	.472	15	40	.375	40	59	.678	38	16	19	106	0	57	1.2	36	174	3.6	407	8.5
99-00 2Tm	63	29	1096	148	328	.451	2	10	.200	36	52	.692	45	20	18	114	1	66	1.0	35	167	2.7	334	5.3
91-92 Cle	6	0	50	5	10	.500	0	0	—	5	8	.625	2	3	0	7	0	3	0.5	2	6	1.0	15	2.5
LAL	36	2	381	55	118	.466	0	3	.000	25	41	.610	27	9	7	41	0	23	0.6	29	76	2.1	135	3.8
96-97 Pho	10	0	83	13	26	.500	0	0	—	8	11	.727	4	0	2	14	0	4	0.4	3	16	1.6	34	3.4
Mil	60	1	674	65	128	.508	1	6	.167	39	59	.661	15	9	20	86	1	24	0.4	38	132	2.2	170	2.8
99-00 SA	30	27	602	82	176	.466	1	3	.333	25	31	.806	28	8	10	53	0	41	1.4	11	77	2.6	190	6.3
Cha	33	2	494	66	152	.434	1	7	.143	11	21	.524	17	12	8	61	1	25	0.8	24	90	2.7	144	4.4
11 Years	650	263	11531	1662	3365	.494	22	94	.234	656	936	.701	524	217	205	1128	2	532	0.8	647	2061	3.2	4002	6.2

NBA Postseason

Year Tm	G	GS	Min	Md	Att	Pct	Md	Att	Pct	Md	Att	Pct	TO	Stl	Blk	PF	DQ	Ast	Avg	Off	Tot	Avg	Pts	Avg
91-92 Cle	3	0	44	8	19	.421	0	1	.000	3	6	.500	1	0	2	3	0	2	0.7	3	11	3.7	19	6.3
92-93 NJ	4	0	62	9	22	.409	0	0	—	6	7	.857	2	3	3	2	0	1	0.3	3	9	2.3	24	6.0
94-95 Hou	21	1	326	34	76	.447	1	2	.500	25	37	.676	12	9	2	46	2	7	0.3	20	65	3.1	94	4.5
95-96 Hou	8	8	168	25	45	.556	0	0	—	15	18	.833	4	3	0	17	0	5	0.6	6	24	3.0	65	8.1
97-98 Atl	4	0	50	7	15	.467	1	2	.500	1	2	.500	2	0	0	5	0	4	1.0	1	6	1.5	16	4.0
5 Years	40	9	650	83	177	.469	2	5	.400	50	70	.714	21	15	7	73	2	19	0.5	33	115	2.9	218	5.5

Dee Brown

Pos: G **College:** Jacksonville **Drafted:** '90 1(19)—Bos   **Ht:** 6'2" **Wt:** 205 **Born:** 11/29/68 **Age:** 32

College			Field Goals			3-Pt FGs			Free Throws			Misc			Fouls		Assists		Rebounds			Points	
Year Tm	G	GS	Min	Md	Att	Pct	Md	Att	Pct	Md	Att	Pct	TO	Stl	Blk	PF	DQ	Ast	Avg	Off	Tot	Avg	Pts	Avg
86-87 Jac	21	—	186	28	65	.431	2	12	.167	13	22	.591	10	11	0	11	—	17	0.8	—	28	1.3	71	3.4
87-88 Jac	28	—	764	108	239	.452	12	45	.267	54	66	.818	67	46	5	74	—	56	2.0	—	125	4.5	282	10.1
88-89 Jac	30	—	1133	219	447	.490	43	101	.426	108	131	.824	88	56	12	71	—	112	3.7	—	228	7.6	589	19.6
89-90 Jac	29	—	1052	231	466	.496	30	80	.375	69	101	.683	82	88	16	77	—	151	5.2	—	192	6.6	561	19.3
4 Years	108	—	3135	586	1217	.482	87	238	.366	244	320	.763	247	201	33	233	—	336	3.1	—	573	5.3	1503	13.9

(continued)

NBA			Field Goals			3-Pt FGs			Free Throws			Misc			Fouls		Assists		Rebounds			Points	
Year Tm	G	GS	Min	Md	Att	Pct	Md	Att	Pct	Md	Att	Pct	TO	Stl	Blk	PF	DQ	Ast	Avg	Off	Tot	Avg	Pts	Avg
90-91 Bos	82	5	1945	284	612	.464	7	34	.206	137	157	.873	137	83	14	161	0	344	4.2	41	182	2.2	712	8.7
91-92 Bos	31	20	883	149	350	.426	5	22	.227	60	78	.769	59	33	7	74	0	164	5.3	15	79	2.5	363	11.7
92-93 Bos	80	48	2254	328	701	.468	26	82	.317	192	242	.793	136	138	32	203	2	461	5.8	45	246	3.1	874	10.9
93-94 Bos	77	76	2867	490	1021	.480	30	96	.313	182	219	.831	126	156	47	207	3	347	4.5	63	300	3.9	1192	15.5
94-95 Bos	79	69	2792	437	977	.447	126	327	.385	236	277	.852	146	110	49	181	0	301	3.8	63	249	3.2	1236	15.6
95-96 Bos	65	23	1591	246	616	.399	68	220	.309	135	158	.854	110	82	10	119	0	146	2.2	36	136	2.1	695	10.7
96-97 Bos	21	2	522	61	166	.367	20	65	.308	18	22	.818	24	31	7	45	0	67	3.2	8	48	2.3	160	7.6
97-98 2Tm	72	12	1719	246	562	.438	108	271	.399	58	71	.817	73	82	23	123	1	154	2.1	24	152	2.1	658	9.1
98-99 Tor	49	0	1377	187	495	.378	135	349	.387	40	55	.727	80	56	8	75	0	86	2.3	9	54	1.4	264	6.9
99-00 Tor	38	12	673	93	258	.360	67	187	.358	11	16	.688	39	24	5	62	1	53	1.3	10	62	1.5	280	6.8
97-98 Bos	41	10	811	109	255	.427	43	113	.381	19	28	.679	32	44	6	76	1	53	1.3	10	62	1.5	280	6.8
Tor	31	2	908	137	307	.446	65	158	.411	39	43	.907	41	38	17	47	0	101	3.3	14	90	2.9	378	12.2
10 Years	594	267	16623	2521	5758	.438	592	1653	.358	1069	1295	.825	894	793	204	1250	7	2213	3.7	319	1549	2.6	6703	11.3

NBA Postseason

Year Tm	G	GS	Min	Md	Att	Pct	Md	Att	Pct	Md	Att	Pct	TO	Stl	Blk	PF	DQ	Ast	Avg	Off	Tot	Avg	Pts	Avg
90-91 Bos	11	0	284	53	108	.491	0	5	.000	28	34	.824	22	11	6	32	0	41	3.7	9	45	4.1	134	12.2
91-92 Bos	6	0	120	22	44	.500	0	3	.000	4	6	.667	7	1	4	16	2	31	5.2	3	12	2.0	48	8.0
92-93 Bos	4	3	133	15	41	.366	1	7	.143	14	14	1.000	6	2	4	11	0	15	3.8	2	6	1.5	45	11.3
94-95 Bos	4	4	172	26	62	.419	9	26	.346	14	16	.875	7	5	1	13	1	19	4.8	6	20	5.0	75	18.8
99-00 Tor	3	0	19	0	4	.000	0	3	.000	0	0	—	1	2	0	4	0	2	0.7	0	2	0.7	0	0.0
5 Years	28	7	728	116	259	.448	10	44	.227	60	70	.857	43	21	15	76	3	108	3.9	20	85	3.0	302	10.8

Marcus Brown

Pos: G **College:** Murray State **Drafted:** '96 2(46)—Por   **Ht:** 6'3" **Wt:** 185 **Born:** 4/3/74 **Age:** 26

College			Field Goals			3-Pt FGs			Free Throws			Misc			Fouls		Assists		Rebounds			Points	
Year Tm	G	GS	Min	Md	Att	Pct	Md	Att	Pct	Md	Att	Pct	TO	Stl	Blk	PF	DQ	Ast	Avg	Off	Tot	Avg	Pts	Avg
92-93 Mur	30	—	591	81	166	.488	18	50	.360	86	109	.789	57	34	7	85	—	33	1.1	—	84	2.8	266	8.9
93-94 Mur	29	—	747	182	362	.503	37	121	.306	125	149	.839	40	57	10	86	—	79	2.7	—	111	3.8	526	18.1
94-95 Mur	30	—	973	219	429	.510	44	119	.370	189	211	.896	58	76	9	69	—	63	2.1	—	147	4.9	671	22.4
95-96 Mur	29	29	1080	254	536	.474	74	175	.423	185	220	.841	102	65	8	82	2	119	4.1	59	139	4.8	767	26.4
4 Years	118	—	3391	736	1493	.493	173	465	.372	585	689	.849	257	232	34	322	—	294	2.5	—	481	4.1	2230	18.9

NBA			Field Goals			3-Pt FGs			Free Throws			Misc			Fouls		Assists		Rebounds			Points	
Year Tm	G	GS	Min	Md	Att	Pct	Md	Att	Pct	Md	Att	Pct	TO	Stl	Blk	PF	DQ	Ast	Avg	Off	Tot	Avg	Pts	Avg
96-97 Por	21	0	184	28	70	.400	13	32	.406	13	19	.684	13	8	2	26	0	20	1.0	4	15	0.7	82	3.9
97-98 Van								Did not play: injury — Right Shoulder																
98-99								Played in France																
99-00 Det	6	0	45	4	14	.286	0	7	.000	2	2	1.000	3	0	0	8	0	3	0.5	3	7	1.2	10	1.7
2 Years	27	0	229	32	84	.381	13	39	.333	15	21	.714	16	8	2	34	0	23	0.9	7	22	0.8	92	3.4

P.J. Brown

(statistical profile on page 195)

Pos: F **College:** Louisiana Tech **Drafted:** '92 2(29)—NJ   **Ht:** 6'11" **Wt:** 240 **Born:** 10/14/69 **Age:** 31

College			Field Goals			3-Pt FGs			Free Throws			Misc			Fouls		Assists		Rebounds			Points	
Year Tm	G	GS	Min	Md	Att	Pct	Md	Att	Pct	Md	Att	Pct	TO	Stl	Blk	PF	DQ	Ast	Avg	Off	Tot	Avg	Pts	Avg
88-89 LaTch	32	—	569	61	147	.415	2	3	.667	25	44	.568	42	14	50	87	—	36	1.1	—	178	5.6	149	4.7
89-90 LaTch	27	—	672	94	204	.461	3	5	.600	48	81	.593	50	21	39	80	—	29	1.1	—	230	8.5	239	8.7
90-91 LaTch	31	—	936	170	315	.540	7	20	.350	98	150	.653	55	37	77	90	—	58	1.9	—	301	9.7	445	14.4
91-92 LaTch	31	—	931	151	309	.489	9	25	.360	84	115	.730	74	29	75	97	—	53	1.7	—	308	9.9	395	12.7
4 Years	121	—	3108	476	975	.488	21	53	.396	255	390	.654	221	101	241	354	—	176	1.5	—	1017	8.4	1228	10.1

NBA			Field Goals			3-Pt FGs			Free Throws			Misc			Fouls		Assists		Rebounds			Points	
Year Tm	G	GS	Min	Md	Att	Pct	Md	Att	Pct	Md	Att	Pct	TO	Stl	Blk	PF	DQ	Ast	Avg	Off	Tot	Avg	Pts	Avg
92-93								Played in Greece																
93-94 NJ	79	54	1950	167	402	.415	1	6	.167	115	152	.757	72	71	93	177	1	93	1.2	188	493	6.2	450	5.7
94-95 NJ	80	63	2466	254	570	.446	4	24	.167	139	207	.671	80	69	135	262	8	135	1.7	178	487	6.1	651	8.1
95-96 NJ	81	81	2942	354	798	.444	3	15	.200	204	265	.770	133	79	100	249	5	165	2.0	215	560	6.9	915	11.3
96-97 Mia	80	80	2592	300	656	.457	0	2	.000	161	220	.732	113	65	98	283	7	92	1.2	239	670	8.4	761	9.5
97-98 Mia	74	74	2362	278	590	.471	0	0	—	151	197	.766	97	66	98	264	9	103	1.4	235	635	8.6	707	9.6
98-99 Mia	50	50	1611	229	477	.480	0	0	—	113	146	.774	69	46	48	166	2	66	1.3	115	346	6.9	571	11.4
99-00 Mia	80	80	2302	322	671	.480	0	1	.000	120	159	.755	100	65	61	264	4	145	1.8	216	600	7.5	764	9.6
7 Years	524	473	16225	1904	4164	.457	8	48	.167	1003	1346	.745	664	481	633	1665	36	799	1.5	1386	3791	7.2	4819	9.2

NBA Postseason

Year Tm	G	GS	Min	Md	Att	Pct	Md	Att	Pct	Md	Att	Pct	TO	Stl	Blk	PF	DQ	Ast	Avg	Off	Tot	Avg	Pts	Avg
93-94 NJ	4	1	56	2	9	.222	0	0	—	8	8	1.000	3	0	2	13	0	3	0.8	4	8	2.0	12	3.0

23

Year Tm	G	GS	Min	Md	Att	Pct	Md	Att	Pct	Md	Att	Pct	TO	Stl	Blk	PF	DQ	Ast	Avg	Off	Tot	Avg	Pts	Avg
96-97 Mia	15	15	451	42	103	.408	0	0	—	38	53	.717	16	9	20	40	0	10	0.7	48	129	8.6	122	8.1
97-98 Mia	5	5	190	19	37	.514	0	0	—	8	22	.364	6	7	3	22	1	4	0.8	15	44	8.8	46	9.2
98-99 Mia	5	5	144	21	45	.467	0	1	.000	9	10	.900	3	2	2	17	0	5	1.0	14	31	6.2	51	10.2
99-00 Mia	10	10	308	35	82	.427	0	0	—	5	6	.833	11	8	4	42	3	11	1.1	26	82	8.2	75	7.5
5 Years	39	36	1149	119	276	.431	0	1	.000	68	99	.687	39	26	31	134	4	33	0.8	107	294	7.5	306	7.8

Randy Brown

(statistical profile on page 196)

Pos: G **College:** New Mexico State **Drafted:** '91 2(31)—Sac **Ht:** 6'2" **Wt:** 190 **Born:** 5/22/68 **Age:** 32

College				Field Goals			3-Pt FGs			Free Throws			Misc			Fouls		Assists		Rebounds			Points	
Year Tm	G	GS	Min	Md	Att	Pct	Md	Att	Pct	Md	Att	Pct	TO	Stl	Blk	PF	DQ	Ast	Avg	Off	Tot	Avg	Pts	Avg
86-87 Hou	28	—	578	42	83	.506	0	2	.000	21	36	.583	61	32	2	58	—	81	2.9	—	75	2.7	105	3.8
87-88 Hou	29	—	998	64	142	.451	0	4	.000	75	100	.750	100	77	8	91	—	162	5.6	—	83	2.9	203	7.0
89-90 NMSt	31	—	907	131	294	.446	16	42	.381	124	184	.712	100	91	14	97	—	109	3.5	—	106	3.4	409	13.2
90-91 NMSt	29	—	917	110	276	.399	10	36	.278	121	175	.691	103	71	6	85	—	187	6.4	—	116	4.0	351	12.1
4 Years	117	—	3400	347	795	.436	26	84	.310	348	495	.703	364	271	30	331	—	539	4.6	—	380	3.2	1068	9.1

NBA				Field Goals			3-Pt FGs			Free Throws			Misc			Fouls		Assists		Rebounds			Points	
Year Tm	G	GS	Min	Md	Att	Pct	Md	Att	Pct	Md	Att	Pct	TO	Stl	Blk	PF	DQ	Ast	Avg	Off	Tot	Avg	Pts	Avg
91-92 Sac	56	0	535	77	169	.456	0	6	.000	38	58	.655	42	35	12	68	0	59	1.1	26	69	1.2	192	3.4
92-93 Sac	75	34	1726	225	486	.463	2	6	.333	115	157	.732	120	108	34	206	4	196	2.6	75	212	2.8	567	7.6
93-94 Sac	61	2	1041	110	251	.438	0	4	.000	53	87	.609	75	63	14	132	2	133	2.2	40	112	1.8	273	4.5
94-95 Sac	67	4	1086	124	287	.432	14	47	.298	55	82	.671	78	99	19	153	0	133	2.0	24	108	1.6	317	4.7
95-96 Chi	68	0	671	78	192	.406	1	11	.091	28	46	.609	31	57	12	88	0	73	1.1	17	66	1.0	185	2.7
96-97 Chi	72	3	1057	140	333	.420	4	22	.182	57	84	.679	58	81	17	116	0	133	1.8	34	111	1.5	341	4.7
97-98 Chi	71	6	1147	116	302	.384	0	5	.000	56	78	.718	63	71	12	118	0	151	2.1	34	94	1.3	288	4.1
98-99 Chi	39	32	1139	132	319	.414	0	10	.000	78	103	.757	80	68	8	93	1	149	3.8	27	132	3.4	342	8.8
99-00 Chi	59	55	1625	157	435	.361	3	6	.500	62	84	.738	105	61	15	120	1	202	3.4	23	144	2.4	379	6.4
9 Years	568	134	10027	1159	2774	.418	24	117	.205	542	779	.696	652	643	143	1094	8	1229	2.2	300	1048	1.8	2884	5.1

Year Tm	G	GS	Min	Md	Att	Pct	Md	Att	Pct	Md	Att	Pct	TO	Stl	Blk	PF	DQ	Ast	Avg	Off	Tot	Avg	Pts	Avg
95-96 Chi	16	0	112	16	28	.571	3	6	.500	9	12	.750	7	5	1	18	0	7	0.4	3	10	0.6	44	2.8
96-97 Chi	17	0	98	9	30	.300	0	0	—	3	5	.600	4	8	2	22	0	6	0.4	3	10	0.6	21	1.2
97-98 Chi	14	0	71	2	12	.167	0	0	—	5	6	.833	7	2	0	6	0	9	0.6	3	9	0.6	9	0.6
3 Years	47	0	281	27	70	.386	3	6	.500	17	23	.739	18	15	3	46	0	22	0.5	9	29	0.6	74	1.6

Rick Brunson

Pos: G **College:** Temple **Drafted:** '97 FA—Por **Ht:** 6'4" **Wt:** 190 **Born:** 6/14/72 **Age:** 28

College				Field Goals			3-Pt FGs			Free Throws			Misc			Fouls		Assists		Rebounds			Points	
Year Tm	G	GS	Min	Md	Att	Pct	Md	Att	Pct	Md	Att	Pct	TO	Stl	Blk	PF	DQ	Ast	Avg	Off	Tot	Avg	Pts	Avg
91-92 Tem	30	—	537	41	128	.320	12	53	.226	53	87	.609	39	29	0	41	—	56	1.9	—	79	2.6	147	4.9
92-93 Tem	33	—	1205	147	371	.396	57	177	.322	112	171	.655	79	67	3	73	—	149	4.5	—	98	3.0	463	14.0
93-94 Tem	31	—	1221	128	346	.370	50	167	.299	77	119	.647	65	83	3	58	—	142	4.6	—	127	4.1	383	12.4
94-95 Tem	30	—	1149	164	448	.366	72	252	.286	100	143	.699	73	74	4	69	—	123	4.1	—	177	5.9	500	16.7
4 Years	124	—	4112	480	1293	.371	191	649	.294	342	520	.658	256	253	10	241	—	470	3.8	—	481	3.9	1493	12.0

NBA				Field Goals			3-Pt FGs			Free Throws			Misc			Fouls		Assists		Rebounds			Points	
Year Tm	G	GS	Min	Md	Att	Pct	Md	Att	Pct	Md	Att	Pct	TO	Stl	Blk	PF	DQ	Ast	Avg	Off	Tot	Avg	Pts	Avg
95-96							Played in Australia																		
96-97							Played in CBA																		
97-98 Por	38	10	622	49	141	.348	22	61	.361	42	62	.677	52	25	3	55	0	100	2.6	14	56	1.5	162	4.3
98-99 NY	17	0	95	6	21	.286	0	5	.000	5	18	.278	12	9	0	8	0	19	1.1	3	10	0.6	17	1.0
99-00 NY	37	0	289	29	70	.414	2	13	.154	11	18	.611	31	9	1	35	0	49	1.3	3	27	0.7	71	1.9
3 Years	92	10	1006	84	232	.362	24	79	.304	58	98	.592	95	43	4	98	0	168	1.8	20	93	1.0	250	2.7

Year Tm	G	GS	Min	Md	Att	Pct	Md	Att	Pct	Md	Att	Pct	TO	Stl	Blk	PF	DQ	Ast	Avg	Off	Tot	Avg	Pts	Avg
98-99 NY	9	0	18	2	5	.400	0	0	—	2	2	1.000	4	0	0	3	0	2	0.2	1	1	0.1	6	0.7
99-00 NY	3	0	4	0	1	.000	0	0	—	0	0	—	0	1	0	2	0	1	0.3	0	0	0.0	0	0.0
2 Years	12	0	22	2	6	.333	0	0	—	2	2	1.000	4	1	0	5	0	3	0.3	1	1	0.1	6	0.5

Kobe Bryant

(statistical profile on page 196)

Pos: G **College:** None **Drafted:** '96 1(13)—Cha **Ht:** 6'7" **Wt:** 215 **Born:** 8/23/78 **Age:** 22

	NBA			Field Goals			3-Pt FGs			Free Throws			Misc			Fouls		Assists		Rebounds			Points	
Year Tm	G	GS	Min	Md	Att	Pct	Md	Att	Pct	Md	Att	Pct	TO	Stl	Blk	PF	DQ	Ast	Avg	Off	Tot	Avg	Pts	Avg
96-97 LAL	71	6	1103	176	422	.417	51	136	.375	136	166	.819	112	49	23	102	0	91	1.3	47	132	1.9	539	7.6
97-98 LAL*	79	1	2056	391	913	.428	75	220	.341	363	457	.794	157	74	40	180	1	199	2.5	79	242	3.1	1220	15.4
98-99 LAL	50	50	1896	362	779	.465	27	101	.267	245	292	.839	157	72	50	153	3	190	3.8	53	264	5.3	996	19.9
99-00 LAL*	66	62	2524	554	1183	.468	46	144	.319	331	403	.821	182	106	62	220	4	323	4.9	108	416	6.3	1485	22.5
4 Years	266	119	7579	1483	3297	.450	199	601	.331	1075	1318	.816	608	301	175	655	8	803	3.0	287	1054	4.0	4240	15.9

NBA Postseason

Year Tm	G	GS	Min	Md	Att	Pct	Md	Att	Pct	Md	Att	Pct	TO	Stl	Blk	PF	DQ	Ast	Avg	Off	Tot	Avg	Pts	Avg
96-97 LAL	9	0	133	21	55	.382	6	23	.261	26	30	.867	14	3	2	23	0	11	1.2	1	11	1.2	74	8.2
97-98 LAL	11	0	220	31	76	.408	3	14	.214	31	45	.689	11	3	8	28	0	16	1.5	7	21	1.9	96	8.7
98-99 LAL	8	8	315	61	142	.430	8	23	.348	28	35	.800	31	15	10	24	1	37	4.6	13	55	6.9	158	19.8
99-00 LAL	22	22	857	174	394	.442	22	64	.344	95	126	.754	55	32	32	89	1	97	4.4	26	98	4.5	465	21.1
4 Years	50	30	1525	287	667	.430	39	124	.315	180	236	.763	111	53	52	164	2	161	3.2	47	185	3.7	793	15.9

Mark Bryant

(statistical profile on page 197)

Pos: F **College:** Seton Hall **Drafted:** '88 1(21)—Por **Ht:** 6'9" **Wt:** 250 **Born:** 4/25/65 **Age:** 35

	College			Field Goals			3-Pt FGs			Free Throws			Misc			Fouls		Assists		Rebounds			Points	
Year Tm	G	GS	Min	Md	Att	Pct	Md	Att	Pct	Md	Att	Pct	TO	Stl	Blk	PF	DQ	Ast	Avg	Off	Tot	Avg	Pts	Avg
84-85 SetHl	26	23	774	122	257	.475	—	—	—	74	114	.649	62	9	22	81	4	16	0.6	—	177	6.8	318	12.2
85-86 SetHl	30	28	901	169	323	.523	—	—	—	82	121	.678	53	18	29	99	4	16	0.5	—	226	7.5	420	14.0
86-87 SetHl	28	28	891	171	345	.496	1	1	1.000	127	180	.706	65	12	28	94	9	23	0.8	67	198	7.1	470	16.8
87-88 SetHl	34	30	1105	267	473	.564	1	2	.500	163	218	.748	81	36	32	107	2	32	0.9	107	311	9.1	698	20.5
4 Years	118	109	3671	729	1398	.521	2	3	.667	446	633	.705	261	75	111	381	19	87	0.7	174	912	7.7	1906	16.2

	NBA			Field Goals			3-Pt FGs			Free Throws			Misc			Fouls		Assists		Rebounds			Points	
Year Tm	G	GS	Min	Md	Att	Pct	Md	Att	Pct	Md	Att	Pct	TO	Stl	Blk	PF	DQ	Ast	Avg	Off	Tot	Avg	Pts	Avg
88-89 Por	56	32	803	120	247	.486	0	0	—	40	69	.580	41	20	7	144	3	33	0.6	65	179	3.2	280	5.0
89-90 Por	58	0	562	70	153	.458	0	0	—	28	50	.560	25	18	9	93	0	13	0.2	54	146	2.5	168	2.9
90-91 Por	53	0	781	99	203	.488	0	1	.000	74	101	.733	33	15	12	120	0	27	0.5	65	190	3.6	272	5.1
91-92 Por	56	0	800	95	198	.480	0	3	.000	40	60	.667	30	26	8	105	0	41	0.7	87	201	3.6	230	4.1
92-93 Por	80	24	1396	186	370	.503	0	1	.000	104	148	.703	65	37	23	226	1	41	0.5	132	324	4.1	476	6.0
93-94 Por	79	10	1441	185	384	.482	0	1	.000	72	104	.692	66	32	29	187	0	37	0.5	117	315	4.0	442	5.6
94-95 Por	49	0	658	101	192	.526	1	2	.500	41	63	.651	39	19	16	109	1	28	0.6	55	161	3.3	244	5.0
95-96 Hou	71	9	1587	242	446	.543	0	2	.000	127	177	.718	85	31	19	234	4	52	0.7	131	351	4.9	611	8.6
96-97 Pho	41	18	1018	152	275	.553	0	0	—	76	108	.704	46	22	5	136	4	47	1.1	67	212	5.2	380	9.3
97-98 Pho	70	22	1110	109	225	.484	0	1	.000	73	95	.768	58	36	15	180	3	46	0.7	92	244	3.5	291	4.2
98-99 Chi	45	29	1204	168	348	.483	0	1	.000	71	110	.645	68	34	16	149	2	48	1.1	92	232	5.2	407	9.0
99-00 Cle	75	50	1712	174	346	.503	0	0	—	76	94	.809	87	31	31	250	5	61	0.8	126	352	4.7	424	5.7
12 Years	733	194	13072	1701	3387	.502	1	12	.083	822	1179	.697	643	321	190	1933	23	474	0.6	1083	2907	4.0	4225	5.8

NBA Postseason

Year Tm	G	GS	Min	Md	Att	Pct	Md	Att	Pct	Md	Att	Pct	TO	Stl	Blk	PF	DQ	Ast	Avg	Off	Tot	Avg	Pts	Avg
89-90 Por	13	0	160	18	33	.545	0	0	—	6	8	.750	12	3	2	27	1	3	0.2	9	29	2.2	42	3.2
90-91 Por	14	0	137	10	22	.455	0	0	—	14	16	.875	4	2	1	25	0	2	0.1	14	32	2.3	34	2.4
91-92 Por	12	0	116	10	29	.345	0	0	—	3	4	.750	9	3	0	22	0	1	0.1	11	29	2.4	23	1.9
92-93 Por	4	4	83	17	37	.459	0	0	—	5	5	1.000	6	0	3	14	0	0	0.0	10	18	4.5	39	9.8
93-94 Por	4	1	64	5	17	.294	0	2	.000	0	0	—	3	2	2	7	0	2	0.5	6	12	3.0	10	2.5
94-95 Por	2	0	6	1	2	.500	0	0	—	0	2	.000	0	0	0	1	0	0	0.0	1	2	1.0	2	1.0
95-96 Hou	8	0	145	21	35	.600	0	0	—	12	15	.800	3	1	2	21	0	4	0.5	7	27	3.4	54	6.8
96-97 Pho	4	0	36	4	10	.400	0	0	—	3	3	1.000	2	0	0	4	0	0	0.0	1	4	1.0	11	2.8
97-98 Pho	4	1	93	17	34	.500	0	0	—	6	12	.500	3	4	2	16	1	1	0.3	9	23	5.8	40	10.0
9 Years	65	6	840	103	219	.470	0	2	.000	49	65	.754	42	15	12	137	2	13	0.2	68	176	2.7	255	3.9

Greg Buckner

Pos: G **College:** Clemson **Drafted:** '98 2(53)—Dal **Ht:** 6'4" **Wt:** 210 **Born:** 9/16/76 **Age:** 24

	College			Field Goals			3-Pt FGs			Free Throws			Misc			Fouls		Assists		Rebounds			Points	
Year Tm	G	GS	Min	Md	Att	Pct	Md	Att	Pct	Md	Att	Pct	TO	Stl	Blk	PF	DQ	Ast	Avg	Off	Tot	Avg	Pts	Avg
94-95 Clem	28	28	911	141	268	.526	13	44	.295	41	80	.513	38	63	12	69	—	58	2.1	46	165	5.9	336	12.0
95-96 Clem	29	29	950	144	305	.472	1	25	.040	92	137	.672	38	38	8	64	1	48	1.7	59	147	5.1	381	13.1
96-97 Clem	33	33	1071	190	393	.483	17	54	.315	119	168	.708	63	35	10	86	2	63	1.9	51	150	4.5	516	15.6
97-98 Clem	32	32	1022	204	380	.537	19	58	.328	94	135	.696	47	51	10	93	2	83	2.6	26	130	4.1	521	16.3
4 Years	122	122	3954	679	1346	.504	50	181	.276	346	520	.665	186	187	40	312	—	252	2.1	182	592	4.9	1754	14.4

NBA Year Tm	G	GS	Min	Field Goals Md	Att	Pct	3-Pt FGs Md	Att	Pct	Free Throws Md	Att	Pct	Misc TO	Stl	Blk	Fouls PF	DQ	Assists Ast	Avg	Rebounds Off	Tot	Avg	Points Pts	Avg
98-99										Played in CBA														
99-00 Dal	48	1	923	111	233	.476	10	26	.385	43	63	.683	36	38	20	148	1	55	1.1	56	174	3.6	275	5.7

Jud Buechler

Pos: G-F **College:** Arizona **Drafted:** '90 2(38)—Sea   **Ht:** 6'6" **Wt:** 228 **Born:** 6/19/68 **Age:** 32

College Year Tm	G	GS	Min	Field Goals Md	Att	Pct	3-Pt FGs Md	Att	Pct	Free Throws Md	Att	Pct	Misc TO	Stl	Blk	Fouls PF	DQ	Assists Ast	Avg	Rebounds Off	Tot	Avg	Points Pts	Avg
86-87 Ari	30	9	474	54	111	.486	10	25	.400	16	28	.571	27	10	3	34	0	35	1.2	27	68	2.3	134	4.5
87-88 Ari	36	0	422	64	124	.516	4	9	.444	38	58	.655	35	15	8	41	1	41	1.1	28	87	2.4	170	4.7
88-89 Ari	33	33	962	139	229	.607	1	5	.200	84	103	.816	47	51	12	85	0	51	1.5	87	219	6.6	363	11.0
89-90 Ari	32	32	1072	182	338	.538	25	66	.379	88	115	.765	87	40	12	67	2	129	4.0	79	264	8.3	477	14.9
4 Years	131	74	2930	439	802	.547	40	105	.381	226	304	.743	196	116	35	227	3	256	2.0	221	638	4.9	1144	8.7

NBA Year Tm	G	GS	Min	Field Goals Md	Att	Pct	3-Pt FGs Md	Att	Pct	Free Throws Md	Att	Pct	Misc TO	Stl	Blk	Fouls PF	DQ	Assists Ast	Avg	Rebounds Off	Tot	Avg	Points Pts	Avg
90-91 NJ	74	10	859	94	226	.416	1	4	.250	43	66	.652	26	33	15	79	0	51	0.7	61	141	1.9	232	3.1
91-92 3Tm	28	0	290	29	71	.408	0	1	.000	12	21	.571	13	19	7	31	0	23	0.8	18	52	1.9	70	2.5
92-93 GS	70	9	1287	176	403	.437	20	59	.339	65	87	.747	55	47	19	98	0	94	1.3	81	195	2.8	437	6.2
93-94 GS	36	0	218	42	84	.500	12	29	.414	10	20	.500	12	8	1	24	0	16	0.4	13	32	0.9	106	2.9
94-95 Chi	57	0	605	90	183	.492	15	48	.313	22	39	.564	30	24	12	64	0	50	0.9	36	98	1.7	217	3.8
95-96 Chi	74	0	740	112	242	.463	40	90	.444	14	22	.636	39	34	7	70	0	56	0.8	45	111	1.5	278	3.8
96-97 Chi	76	0	703	58	158	.367	18	54	.333	5	14	.357	27	23	21	50	0	60	0.8	45	126	1.7	139	1.8
97-98 Chi	74	0	608	85	176	.483	25	65	.385	3	6	.500	21	22	15	47	0	49	0.7	24	77	1.0	198	2.7
98-99 Det	50	0	1056	100	240	.417	61	148	.412	13	18	.722	21	37	13	83	0	57	1.1	29	133	2.7	274	5.5
99-00 Det	58	5	657	55	156	.353	18	83	.217	2	7	.286	13	25	16	50	1	33	0.6	30	91	1.6	130	2.2
91-92 NJ	2	0	29	4	8	.500	0	0	—	0	0	—	0	1	2	2	0	2	1.0	2	2	1.0	8	4.0
SA	11	0	140	15	30	.500	0	0	—	3	9	.333	5	8	3	18	0	11	1.0	6	22	2.0	33	3.0
GS	15	0	121	10	33	.303	0	1	.000	9	12	.750	7	9	3	11	0	10	0.7	10	28	1.9	29	1.9
10 Years	597	24	7023	841	1939	.434	210	581	.361	189	300	.630	257	272	126	596	1	489	0.8	382	1056	1.8	2081	3.5

NBA Postseason Year Tm	G	GS	Min	Md	Att	Pct	Md	Att	Pct	Md	Att	Pct	TO	Stl	Blk	PF	DQ	Ast	Avg	Off	Tot	Avg	Pts	Avg
94-95 Chi	10	0	104	9	21	.429	0	2	.000	2	4	.500	3	4	3	15	0	5	0.5	11	20	2.0	20	2.0
95-96 Chi	17	0	127	18	38	.474	8	21	.381	2	4	.500	8	7	0	13	0	6	0.4	2	10	0.6	46	2.7
96-97 Chi	18	0	138	13	31	.419	4	12	.333	3	5	.600	1	3	1	15	0	5	0.3	9	23	1.3	33	1.8
97-98 Chi	16	0	64	4	11	.364	3	5	.600	0	0	—	1	3	1	7	0	3	0.2	4	11	0.7	11	0.7
98-99 Det	5	0	84	3	15	.200	2	8	.250	0	0	—	3	3	1	6	0	3	0.6	4	13	2.6	8	1.6
99-00 Det	3	0	34	2	7	.286	2	5	.400	0	0	—	0	0	1	4	0	1	0.3	0	4	1.3	6	2.0
6 Years	69	0	551	49	123	.398	19	53	.358	7	13	.538	16	20	7	60	0	23	0.3	30	81	1.2	124	1.8

Rodney Buford

Pos: G **College:** Creighton **Drafted:** '99 2(53)—Mia   **Ht:** 6'5" **Wt:** 195 **Born:** 11/2/77 **Age:** 23

College Year Tm	G	GS	Min	Field Goals Md	Att	Pct	3-Pt FGs Md	Att	Pct	Free Throws Md	Att	Pct	Misc TO	Stl	Blk	Fouls PF	DQ	Assists Ast	Avg	Rebounds Off	Tot	Avg	Points Pts	Avg
95-96 Cre	29	11	752	158	342	.462	46	118	.390	59	81	.728	49	49	24	48	0	41	1.4	47	122	4.2	421	14.5
96-97 Cre	30	30	947	225	512	.439	58	153	.379	81	110	.736	63	44	18	60	0	48	1.6	50	168	5.6	589	19.6
97-98 Cre	28	28	864	189	446	.424	53	162	.327	99	138	.717	77	43	9	55	0	58	2.1	50	204	7.3	530	18.9
98-99 Cre	31	30	1011	206	439	.469	55	125	.440	109	133	.820	72	59	8	56	1	68	2.2	67	222	7.2	576	18.6
4 Years	118	99	3574	778	1739	.447	212	558	.380	348	462	.753	261	195	59	219	1	215	1.8	214	716	6.1	2116	17.9

NBA Year Tm	G	GS	Min	Md	Att	Pct	Md	Att	Pct	Md	Att	Pct	TO	Stl	Blk	PF	DQ	Ast	Avg	Off	Tot	Avg	Pts	Avg
99-00 Mia	34	0	386	62	151	.411	7	29	.241	16	22	.727	9	10	8	44	0	21	0.6	10	48	1.4	147	4.3

NBA Postseason Year Tm	G	GS	Min	Md	Att	Pct	Md	Att	Pct	Md	Att	Pct	TO	Stl	Blk	PF	DQ	Ast	Avg	Off	Tot	Avg	Pts	Avg
99-00 Mia	1	0	16	4	8	.500	1	2	.500	2	2	1.000	0	0	0	3	0	1	1.0	0	1	1.0	11	11.0

Matt Bullard

Pos: F **College:** Iowa **Drafted:** '90 FA—Hou   **Ht:** 6'10" **Wt:** 235 **Born:** 6/5/67 **Age:** 33

College Year Tm	G	GS	Min	Field Goals Md	Att	Pct	3-Pt FGs Md	Att	Pct	Free Throws Md	Att	Pct	Misc TO	Stl	Blk	Fouls PF	DQ	Assists Ast	Avg	Rebounds Off	Tot	Avg	Points Pts	Avg
85-86 Colo	28	—	869	142	235	.604	—	—	—	72	88	.818	64	22	32	94	—	86	3.1	—	179	6.4	356	12.7
86-87 Colo	28	—	938	182	349	.521	5	26	.192	95	128	.742	62	20	35	62	—	61	2.2	—	280	10.0	464	16.6

College

Year Tm	G	GS	Min	Field Goals			3-Pt FGs			Free Throws			Misc			Fouls		Assists		Rebounds			Points	
				Md	Att	Pct	Md	Att	Pct	Md	Att	Pct	TO	Stl	Blk	PF	DQ	Ast	Avg	Off	Tot	Avg	Pts	Avg
88-89 Iowa	20	13	498	66	117	.564	17	43	.395	32	40	.800	38	14	15	42	0	37	1.9	—	123	6.2	181	9.1
89-90 Iowa	18	8	366	72	166	.434	25	71	.352	36	50	.720	36	12	7	38	3	24	1.3	—	53	2.9	205	11.4
4 Years	94	—	2671	462	867	.533	47	140	.336	235	306	.768	200	68	89	236	—	208	2.2	—	635	6.8	1206	12.8

NBA

Year Tm	G	GS	Min	Field Goals			3-Pt FGs			Free Throws			Misc			Fouls		Assists		Rebounds			Points	
				Md	Att	Pct	Md	Att	Pct	Md	Att	Pct	TO	Stl	Blk	PF	DQ	Ast	Avg	Off	Tot	Avg	Pts	Avg
90-91 Hou	18	0	63	14	31	.452	0	3	.000	11	17	.647	3	3	0	10	0	2	0.1	6	14	0.8	39	2.2
91-92 Hou	80	7	1278	205	447	.459	64	166	.386	38	50	.760	56	26	21	129	1	75	0.9	73	223	2.8	512	6.4
92-93 Hou	79	4	1356	213	494	.431	91	243	.374	58	74	.784	57	30	11	129	0	110	1.4	66	222	2.8	575	7.3
93-94 Hou	65	0	725	78	226	.345	50	154	.325	20	26	.769	28	14	6	67	0	64	1.0	23	84	1.3	226	3.5
94-95								Played in Greece																
95-96 Atl	46	0	460	66	162	.407	26	72	.361	16	20	.800	24	17	11	50	0	18	0.4	18	60	1.3	174	3.8
96-97 Hou	71	12	1025	114	284	.401	67	183	.366	25	34	.735	38	21	18	68	0	67	0.9	13	117	1.6	320	4.5
97-98 Hou	67	24	1190	175	389	.450	96	231	.416	20	27	.741	39	31	24	104	0	60	0.9	25	146	2.2	466	7.0
98-99 Hou	41	0	413	43	114	.377	24	62	.387	7	10	.700	14	13	4	28	0	18	0.4	9	42	1.0	117	2.9
99-00 Hou	56	27	1024	139	340	.409	79	177	.446	25	30	.833	36	19	13	85	0	63	1.1	13	138	2.5	382	6.8
9 Years	523	74	7534	1047	2487	.421	497	1291	.385	220	288	.764	295	174	108	670	1	477	0.9	246	1046	2.0	2811	5.4

NBA Postseason

Year Tm	G	GS	Min	Md	Att	Pct	Md	Att	Pct	Md	Att	Pct	TO	Stl	Blk	PF	DQ	Ast	Avg	Off	Tot	Avg	Pts	Avg
92-93 Hou	12	0	169	20	42	.476	15	28	.536	6	6	1.000	9	4	5	11	0	13	1.1	4	23	1.9	61	5.1
93-94 Hou	10	0	55	4	19	.211	2	10	.200	6	8	.750	0	1	2	6	0	0	0.0	2	10	1.0	16	1.6
95-96 Atl	4	0	51	4	12	.333	4	8	.500	2	4	.500	2	0	2	6	0	0	0.0	0	6	1.5	14	3.5
96-97 Hou	2	0	7	2	2	1.000	2	2	1.000	0	0	—	0	0	0	1	0	0	0.0	1	2	1.0	6	3.0
97-98 Hou	5	4	70	6	18	.333	3	10	.300	2	2	1.000	0	1	0	5	0	5	1.0	3	8	1.6	17	3.4
98-99 Hou	2	0	8	2	2	1.000	1	1	1.000	2	2	1.000	0	0	0	0	0	1	0.5	0	0	0.0	7	3.5
6 Years	35	4	360	38	95	.400	27	59	.458	18	22	.818	11	6	9	29	0	19	0.5	10	49	1.4	121	3.5

Scott Burrell

(statistical profile on page 197)

Pos: F **College:** Connecticut **Drafted:** '93 1(20)—Cha **Ht:** 6'7" **Wt:** 218 **Born:** 1/12/71 **Age:** 30

College

Year Tm	G	GS	Min	Field Goals			3-Pt FGs			Free Throws			Misc			Fouls		Assists		Rebounds			Points	
				Md	Att	Pct	Md	Att	Pct	Md	Att	Pct	TO	Stl	Blk	PF	DQ	Ast	Avg	Off	Tot	Avg	Pts	Avg
89-90 Conn	32	20	826	88	228	.386	20	64	.313	66	106	.623	43	60	30	103	—	57	1.8	—	177	5.5	262	8.2
90-91 Conn	31	31	1075	136	309	.440	37	108	.343	84	142	.592	80	112	40	106	—	95	3.1	—	234	7.5	393	12.7
91-92 Conn	30	30	1059	175	386	.453	61	154	.396	77	126	.611	95	75	31	96	—	87	2.9	—	183	6.1	488	16.3
92-93 Conn	26	25	861	145	353	.411	50	145	.345	79	104	.760	63	63	28	76	—	54	2.1	—	156	6.0	419	16.1
4 Years	119	106	3821	544	1276	.426	168	471	.357	306	478	.640	281	310	129	381	—	293	2.5	—	750	6.3	1562	13.1

NBA

Year Tm	G	GS	Min	Field Goals			3-Pt FGs			Free Throws			Misc			Fouls		Assists		Rebounds			Points	
				Md	Att	Pct	Md	Att	Pct	Md	Att	Pct	TO	Stl	Blk	PF	DQ	Ast	Avg	Off	Tot	Avg	Pts	Avg
93-94 Cha	51	16	767	98	234	.419	2	6	.333	46	70	.657	45	37	16	88	0	62	1.2	46	132	2.6	244	4.8
94-95 Cha	65	62	2014	277	593	.467	96	235	.409	100	144	.694	85	75	40	187	1	161	2.5	96	368	5.7	750	11.5
95-96 Cha	20	20	693	92	206	.447	37	98	.378	42	56	.750	43	27	13	76	2	47	2.4	26	98	4.9	263	13.2
96-97 2Tm	57	2	939	98	271	.362	41	116	.353	57	76	.750	53	28	19	120	0	74	1.3	49	158	2.8	294	5.2
97-98 Chi	80	3	1096	159	375	.424	51	144	.354	47	64	.734	50	64	37	131	1	65	0.8	80	198	2.5	416	5.2
98-99 NJ	32	10	706	75	208	.361	28	72	.389	34	42	.810	23	40	11	82	2	45	1.4	32	119	3.7	212	6.6
99-00 NJ	74	9	1336	165	419	.394	82	232	.353	39	50	.780	38	67	44	173	1	72	1.0	65	256	3.5	451	6.1
96-97 Cha	28	2	482	45	131	.344	19	55	.345	42	53	.792	25	14	11	60	0	39	1.4	24	79	2.8	151	5.4
GS	29	0	457	53	140	.379	22	61	.361	15	23	.652	28	14	8	60	0	35	1.2	25	79	2.7	143	4.9
7 Years	379	122	7551	964	2306	.418	337	903	.373	365	502	.727	337	338	180	857	7	526	1.4	394	1329	3.5	2630	6.9

NBA Postseason

Year Tm	G	GS	Min	Md	Att	Pct	Md	Att	Pct	Md	Att	Pct	TO	Stl	Blk	PF	DQ	Ast	Avg	Off	Tot	Avg	Pts	Avg
97-98 Chi	21	0	261	32	73	.438	6	20	.300	10	11	.909	11	19	2	33	0	10	0.5	11	43	2.0	80	3.8

Jason Caffey

(statistical profile on page 198)

Pos: F **College:** Alabama **Drafted:** '95 1(20)—Chi **Ht:** 6'8" **Wt:** 256 **Born:** 6/12/73 **Age:** 27

College

Year Tm	G	GS	Min	Field Goals			3-Pt FGs			Free Throws			Misc			Fouls		Assists		Rebounds			Points	
				Md	Att	Pct	Md	Att	Pct	Md	Att	Pct	TO	Stl	Blk	PF	DQ	Ast	Avg	Off	Tot	Avg	Pts	Avg
91-92 Ala	30	0	331	31	73	.425	0	1	.000	10	30	.333	33	4	13	52	—	10	0.3	—	67	2.2	72	2.4
92-93 Ala	29	29	847	169	326	.518	3	11	.273	80	130	.615	92	27	20	85	—	39	1.3	—	252	8.7	421	14.5
93-94 Ala	29	24	784	140	269	.520	1	2	.500	90	143	.629	73	18	18	85	—	20	0.7	—	183	6.3	371	12.8
94-95 Ala	31	26	933	148	291	.509	0	4	.000	79	145	.545	85	18	16	78	—	51	1.6	—	249	8.0	375	12.1
4 Years	119	79	2895	488	959	.509	4	18	.222	259	448	.578	283	67	67	300	—	120	1.0	—	751	6.3	1239	10.4

NBA				Field Goals			3-Pt FGs			Free Throws			Misc			Fouls		Assists		Rebounds			Points	
Year Tm	G	GS	Min	Md	Att	Pct	Md	Att	Pct	Md	Att	Pct	TO	Stl	Blk	PF	DQ	Ast	Avg	Off	Tot	Avg	Pts	Avg
95-96 Chi	57	0	545	71	162	.438	0	1	.000	40	68	.588	48	12	7	91	3	24	0.4	51	111	1.9	182	3.2
96-97 Chi	75	19	1405	205	385	.532	0	1	.000	139	211	.659	97	25	9	149	0	89	1.2	135	301	4.0	549	7.3
97-98 2Tm	80	14	1423	226	466	.485	0	2	.000	131	200	.655	105	25	20	181	4	67	0.8	160	344	4.3	583	7.3
98-99 GS	35	32	876	123	277	.444	0	1	.000	62	98	.633	75	24	9	113	1	18	0.5	79	205	5.9	308	8.8
99-00 GS	71	56	2159	323	675	.479	0	2	.000	206	345	.597	170	62	20	269	11	119	1.7	189	482	6.8	852	12.0
97-98 Chi	51	8	710	100	199	.503	0	1	.000	68	103	.660	48	13	17	92	1	36	0.7	76	173	3.4	268	5.3
GS	29	6	713	126	267	.472	0	1	.000	63	97	.649	57	12	3	89	3	31	1.1	84	171	5.9	315	10.9
5 Years	318	121	6408	948	1965	.482	0	7	.000	578	922	.627	495	148	65	803	19	317	1.0	614	1443	4.5	2474	7.8

NBA Postseason

Year Tm	G	GS	Min	Md	Att	Pct	Md	Att	Pct	Md	Att	Pct	TO	Stl	Blk	PF	DQ	Ast	Avg	Off	Tot	Avg	Pts	Avg
96-97 Chi	17	5	167	15	33	.455	0	0	—	11	14	.786	12	3	3	27	0	15	0.9	25	42	2.5	41	2.4

Michael Cage

Pos: F-C **College:** San Diego State **Drafted:** '84 1(14)—LAC **Ht:** 6'9" **Wt:** 248 **Born:** 1/28/62 **Age:** 39

College				Field Goals			3-Pt FGs			Free Throws			Misc			Fouls		Assists		Rebounds			Points	
Year Tm	G	GS	Min	Md	Att	Pct	Md	Att	Pct	Md	Att	Pct	TO	Stl	Blk	PF	DQ	Ast	Avg	Off	Tot	Avg	Pts	Avg
80-81 SDSU	27	—	1031	115	206	.558	—			65	86	.756	—		20	—		11	0.4	—	355	13.1	295	10.9
81-82 SDSU	29	—	1076	123	252	.488	—			72	109	.661	—		—	—		44	1.5	—	256	8.8	318	11.0
82-83 SDSU	28	—	1070	191	335	.570	—			165	221	.747	—		—	—		31	1.1	—	354	12.6	547	19.5
83-84 SDSU	28	—	1085	250	445	.562	—			186	251	.741	—		47	—		12	0.4	—	352	12.6	686	24.5
4 Years	112	—	4262	679	1238	.548	—			488	667	.732	—		—	—		98	0.9	—	1317	11.8	1846	16.5

NBA				Field Goals			3-Pt FGs			Free Throws			Misc			Fouls		Assists		Rebounds			Points	
Year Tm	G	GS	Min	Md	Att	Pct	Md	Att	Pct	Md	Att	Pct	TO	Stl	Blk	PF	DQ	Ast	Avg	Off	Tot	Avg	Pts	Avg
84-85 LAC	75	41	1610	216	398	.543	0	0		101	137	.737	81	41	32	164	1	51	0.7	126	392	5.2	533	7.1
85-86 LAC	78	12	1566	204	426	.479	0	3	.000	113	174	.649	106	62	34	176	1	81	1.0	168	417	5.3	521	6.7
86-87 LAC	80	76	2922	457	878	.521	0	3	.000	341	467	.730	171	99	67	221	1	131	1.6	354	922	11.5	1255	15.7
87-88 LAC	72	70	2660	360	766	.470	0	1	.000	326	474	.688	160	91	58	194	1	110	1.5	371	938	13.0	1046	14.5
88-89 Sea	80	71	2536	314	630	.498	0	4	.000	197	265	.743	124	92	52	184	1	126	1.6	276	765	9.6	825	10.3
89-90 Sea	82	82	2595	325	645	.504	0	0	—	148	212	.698	94	79	45	232	1	70	0.9	306	821	10.0	798	9.7
90-91 Sea	82	55	2141	226	445	.508	0	3	.000	70	112	.625	83	85	58	194	0	89	1.1	177	558	6.8	522	6.4
91-92 Sea	82	69	2461	307	542	.566	0	5	.000	106	171	.620	78	99	55	237	0	92	1.1	266	728	8.9	720	8.8
92-93 Sea	82	66	2156	219	416	.526	0	1	.000	61	130	.469	59	76	46	183	0	69	0.8	268	659	8.0	499	6.1
93-94 Sea	82	42	1708	171	314	.545	0	1	.000	36	74	.486	51	77	38	179	0	45	0.5	164	444	5.4	378	4.6
94-95 Cle	82	21	2040	177	340	.521	0	2	.000	53	88	.602	56	61	67	149	1	56	0.7	203	564	6.9	407	5.0
95-96 Cle	82	80	2631	220	396	.556	0	1	.000	50	92	.543	54	87	79	215	0	53	0.6	288	729	8.9	490	6.0
96-97 Phi	82	24	1247	66	141	.468	0	0	—	19	41	.463	17	48	42	118	0	43	0.5	112	320	3.9	151	1.8
97-98 NJ	79	17	1201	43	84	.512	0	1	.000	20	36	.556	23	45	44	105	1	32	0.4	115	308	3.9	106	1.3
98-99										Did not play in NBA														
99-00 NJ	20	7	242	12	24	.500	0	0	—	3	3	1.000	4	8	8	30	0	9	0.5	33	81	4.1	27	1.4
15 Years	1140	733	29716	3317	6445	.515	0	25	.000	1644	2476	.664	1161	1050	725	2581	8	1057	0.9	3227	8646	7.6	8278	7.3

NBA Postseason

Year Tm	G	GS	Min	Md	Att	Pct	Md	Att	Pct	Md	Att	Pct	TO	Stl	Blk	PF	DQ	Ast	Avg	Off	Tot	Avg	Pts	Avg
88-89 Sea	8	0	175	24	40	.600	0	1	.000	9	22	.409	8	7	3	14	0	5	0.6	22	46	5.8	57	7.1
90-91 Sea	5	0	80	6	14	.429	0	0	—	13	17	.765	3	3	2	12	0	2	0.4	9	21	4.2	25	5.0
91-92 Sea	9	4	197	19	34	.559	0	0	—	1	1	1.000	8	6	8	22	0	4	0.4	18	51	5.7	39	4.3
92-93 Sea	19	2	378	42	80	.525	0	0	—	7	18	.389	16	13	7	43	1	10	0.5	47	111	5.8	91	4.8
93-94 Sea	5	5	93	6	16	.375	0	0	—	2	6	.333	3	4	5	15	0	4	0.8	10	27	5.4	14	2.8
94-95 Cle	4	0	81	8	18	.444	0	1	.000	0	2	.000	1	2	4	9	0	3	0.8	8	18	4.5	16	4.0
95-96 Cle	3	3	101	8	14	.571	0	0	—	3	5	.600	0	2	5	5	0	2	0.7	13	28	9.3	19	6.3
7 Years	53	14	1105	113	216	.523	0	2	.000	35	71	.493	39	37	34	120	1	30	0.6	127	302	5.7	261	4.9

Marcus Camby

(statistical profile on page 198)

Pos: F-C **College:** Massachusetts **Drafted:** '96 1(2)—Tor **Ht:** 6'11" **Wt:** 225 **Born:** 3/22/74 **Age:** 26

College				Field Goals			3-Pt FGs			Free Throws			Misc			Fouls		Assists		Rebounds			Points	
Year Tm	G	GS	Min	Md	Att	Pct	Md	Att	Pct	Md	Att	Pct	TO	Stl	Blk	PF	DQ	Ast	Avg	Off	Tot	Avg	Pts	Avg
93-94 Mass	29	12	634	117	237	.494	0	4	.000	62	104	.596	50	18	105	101	—	36	1.2	—	185	6.4	296	10.2
94-95 Mass	30	21	679	166	302	.550	1	1	1.000	83	129	.643	54	24	103	74	—	37	1.2	—	186	6.2	416	13.9
95-96 Mass	33	30	1011	256	537	.477	0	8	.000	163	233	.700	83	32	128	87	0	58	1.8	81	271	8.2	675	20.5
3 Years	92	63	2324	539	1076	.501	1	13	.077	308	466	.661	187	74	336	262	—	131	1.4	—	642	7.0	1387	15.1

NBA				Field Goals			3-Pt FGs			Free Throws			Misc			Fouls		Assists		Rebounds			Points	
Year Tm	G	GS	Min	Md	Att	Pct	Md	Att	Pct	Md	Att	Pct	TO	Stl	Blk	PF	DQ	Ast	Avg	Off	Tot	Avg	Pts	Avg
96-97 Tor	63	38	1897	375	778	.482	2	14	.143	183	264	.693	134	66	130	214	7	97	1.5	131	394	6.3	935	14.8

NBA

Year Tm	G	GS	Min	Md	Att	Pct	Md	Att	Pct	Md	Att	Pct	TO	Stl	Blk	PF	DQ	Ast	Avg	Off	Tot	Avg	Pts	Avg
97-98 Tor	63	58	2002	308	747	.412	0	2	.000	149	244	.611	134	68	230	200	1	111	1.8	203	466	7.4	765	12.1
98-99 NY	46	0	945	136	261	.521	0	0	—	57	103	.553	39	29	74	131	2	12	0.3	102	253	5.5	329	7.2
99-00 NY	59	11	1548	226	471	.480	1	2	.500	148	221	.670	72	43	116	204	5	49	0.8	174	461	7.8	601	10.2
4 Years	231	107	6392	1045	2257	.463	3	18	.167	537	832	.645	379	206	550	749	15	269	1.2	610	1574	6.8	2630	11.4

NBA Postseason

Year Tm	G	GS	Min	Md	Att	Pct	Md	Att	Pct	Md	Att	Pct	TO	Stl	Blk	PF	DQ	Ast	Avg	Off	Tot	Avg	Pts	Avg
98-99 NY	20	3	509	81	143	.566	0	1	.000	45	73	.616	15	24	38	76	2	6	0.3	51	153	7.7	207	10.4
99-00 NY	16	0	386	29	86	.337	0	1	.000	19	31	.613	12	8	23	51	1	6	0.4	34	111	6.9	77	4.8
2 Years	36	3	895	110	229	.480	0	2	.000	64	104	.615	27	32	61	127	3	12	0.3	85	264	7.3	284	7.9

Elden Campbell

(statistical profile on page 199)

Pos: F-C **College:** Clemson **Drafted:** '90 1(27)—LAL   **Ht:** 7'0" **Wt:** 255 **Born:** 7/23/68 **Age:** 32

College

Year Tm	G	GS	Min	Md	Att	Pct	Md	Att	Pct	Md	Att	Pct	TO	Stl	Blk	PF	DQ	Ast	Avg	Off	Tot	Avg	Pts	Avg
86-87 Clem	31	3	534	107	193	.554	0	0	—	59	84	.702	55	12	62	79	—	20	0.6	50	126	4.1	273	8.8
87-88 Clem	28	27	808	217	345	.629	0	4	.000	91	147	.619	53	32	88	85	—	15	0.5	65	207	7.4	525	18.8
88-89 Clem	29	25	814	205	373	.550	2	5	.400	95	138	.688	68	38	87	90	—	34	1.2	70	222	7.7	507	17.5
89-90 Clem	35	30	1038	225	431	.522	1	1	1.000	124	207	.599	93	54	97	98	—	44	1.3	85	281	8.0	575	16.4
4 Years	123	85	3194	754	1342	.562	3	10	.300	369	576	.641	269	136	334	352	—	113	0.9	270	836	6.8	1880	15.3

NBA

Year Tm	G	GS	Min	Md	Att	Pct	Md	Att	Pct	Md	Att	Pct	TO	Stl	Blk	PF	DQ	Ast	Avg	Off	Tot	Avg	Pts	Avg
90-91 LAL	52	0	380	56	123	.455	0	0	—	32	49	.653	16	11	38	71	1	10	0.2	40	96	1.8	144	2.8
91-92 LAL	81	47	1876	220	491	.448	0	2	.000	138	223	.619	73	53	159	203	1	59	0.7	155	423	5.2	578	7.1
92-93 LAL	79	13	1551	238	520	.458	0	3	.000	130	204	.637	69	59	100	165	0	48	0.6	127	332	4.2	606	7.7
93-94 LAL	76	74	2253	373	808	.462	0	2	.000	188	273	.689	98	64	146	241	2	86	1.1	167	519	6.8	934	12.3
94-95 LAL	73	59	2076	360	785	.459	0	1	.000	193	290	.666	98	69	132	246	4	92	1.3	168	445	6.1	913	12.5
95-96 LAL	82	82	2699	447	888	.503	0	5	.000	249	349	.713	137	88	212	300	4	181	2.2	162	623	7.6	1143	13.9
96-97 LAL	77	77	2516	442	942	.469	1	4	.250	263	370	.711	130	46	117	276	6	126	1.6	207	615	8.0	1148	14.9
97-98 LAL	81	28	1784	289	624	.463	1	2	.500	237	342	.693	115	35	102	209	1	78	1.0	143	455	5.6	816	10.1
98-99 2Tm	49	33	1459	222	465	.477	0	1	.000	172	269	.639	80	39	73	159	3	69	1.4	126	397	8.1	616	12.6
99-00 Cha	78	77	2538	370	829	.446	0	6	.000	247	358	.690	127	56	150	269	6	129	1.7	168	590	7.6	987	12.7
98-99 LAL	17	1	325	44	101	.436	0	0	—	38	62	.613	22	1	16	51	2	8	0.5	38	96	5.6	126	7.4
Cha	32	32	1134	178	364	.489	0	1	.000	134	207	.647	58	38	57	108	1	61	1.9	88	301	9.4	490	15.3
10 Years	728	490	19132	3017	6475	.466	2	26	.077	1849	2727	.678	943	520	1229	2139	28	878	1.2	1463	4495	6.2	7885	10.8

NBA Postseason

Year Tm	G	GS	Min	Md	Att	Pct	Md	Att	Pct	Md	Att	Pct	TO	Stl	Blk	PF	DQ	Ast	Avg	Off	Tot	Avg	Pts	Avg
90-91 LAL	14	0	138	25	38	.658	0	0	—	7	15	.467	6	6	8	23	1	3	0.2	8	29	2.1	57	4.1
91-92 LAL	4	2	117	14	37	.378	0	0	—	12	18	.667	4	3	6	14	0	6	1.5	9	25	6.3	40	10.0
92-93 LAL	5	5	178	29	69	.420	0	0	—	12	24	.500	12	6	12	15	0	7	1.4	17	42	8.4	70	14.0
94-95 LAL	10	10	376	64	132	.485	0	0	—	29	44	.659	15	4	30	44	2	16	1.6	26	73	7.3	157	15.7
95-96 LAL	4	4	129	20	39	.513	0	1	.000	8	16	.500	10	1	9	17	1	8	2.0	3	32	8.0	48	12.0
96-97 LAL	9	9	278	37	93	.398	1	1	1.000	31	38	.816	14	7	13	30	0	9	1.0	14	39	4.3	106	11.8
97-98 LAL	13	0	180	23	51	.451	0	0	—	22	34	.647	13	3	12	27	0	8	0.6	17	45	3.5	68	5.2
99-00 Cha	4	4	150	22	47	.468	0	1	.000	13	14	.929	8	2	4	16	0	4	1.0	9	33	8.3	57	14.3
8 Years	63	34	1546	234	506	.462	1	3	.333	134	203	.660	82	32	94	186	4	61	1.0	103	318	5.0	603	9.6

Antoine Carr

Pos: F-C **College:** Wichita State **Drafted:** '83 1(8)—Det   **Ht:** 6'9" **Wt:** 270 **Born:** 7/23/61 **Age:** 39

College

Year Tm	G	GS	Min	Md	Att	Pct	Md	Att	Pct	Md	Att	Pct	TO	Stl	Blk	PF	DQ	Ast	Avg	Off	Tot	Avg	Pts	Avg
79-80 Wich	29	—	818	178	355	.501	—	—	—	86	129	.667	—	—	40	—	—	64	2.2	—	171	5.9	442	15.2
80-81 Wich	33	—	1030	211	360	.586	—	—	—	101	132	.765	—	—	65	—	—	94	2.8	—	241	7.3	523	15.8
81-82 Wich	28	—	785	179	316	.566	—	—	—	91	115	.791	—	—	54	—	—	46	1.6	—	196	7.0	449	16.0
82-83 Wich	22	—	727	195	339	.575	3	5	.600	104	136	.765	—	—	50	—	—	39	1.8	—	168	7.6	497	22.6
4 Years	112	—	3360	763	1370	.557	3	5	.600	382	512	.746	—	—	209	—	—	243	2.2	—	776	6.9	1911	17.1

NBA

Year Tm	G	GS	Min	Md	Att	Pct	Md	Att	Pct	Md	Att	Pct	TO	Stl	Blk	PF	DQ	Ast	Avg	Off	Tot	Avg	Pts	Avg
83-84									Played in Italy															
84-85 Atl	62	15	1195	198	375	.528	2	6	.333	101	128	.789	108	29	78	219	4	80	1.3	79	232	3.7	499	8.0
85-86 Atl	17	0	258	49	93	.527	0	0	—	18	27	.667	14	7	15	51	1	14	0.8	16	52	3.1	116	6.8
86-87 Atl	65	2	695	134	265	.506	1	3	.333	73	103	.709	40	14	48	146	1	34	0.5	60	156	2.4	342	5.3
87-88 Atl	80	2	1483	281	517	.544	1	4	.250	142	182	.780	116	38	83	272	7	103	1.3	94	289	3.6	705	8.8

29

NBA				Field Goals			3-Pt FGs			Free Throws			Misc			Fouls		Assists		Rebounds			Points	
Year Tm	G	GS	Min	Md	Att	Pct	Md	Att	Pct	Md	Att	Pct	TO	Stl	Blk	PF	DQ	Ast	Avg	Off	Tot	Avg	Pts	Avg
88-89 Atl	78	12	1488	226	471	.480	0	1	.000	130	152	.855	82	31	62	221	0	91	1.2	106	274	3.5	582	7.5
89-90 2Tm	77	4	1727	356	721	.494	0	7	.000	237	298	.795	125	30	68	247	6	119	1.5	115	322	4.2	949	12.3
90-91 Sac	77	48	2527	628	1228	.511	0	3	.000	295	389	.758	171	45	101	315	14	191	2.5	163	420	5.5	1551	20.1
91-92 SA	81	27	1867	359	732	.490	1	5	.200	162	212	.764	114	32	96	264	5	63	0.8	128	346	4.3	881	10.9
92-93 SA	71	46	1947	379	705	.538	0	5	.000	174	224	.777	96	35	87	264	5	97	1.4	107	388	5.5	932	13.1
93-94 SA	34	0	465	78	160	.488	0	1	.000	42	58	.724	15	9	22	75	0	15	0.4	12	51	1.5	198	5.8
94-95 Uta	78	4	1677	290	546	.531	1	4	.250	165	201	.821	87	24	68	253	4	67	0.9	81	265	3.4	746	9.6
95-96 Uta	80	0	1532	233	510	.457	0	3	.000	114	144	.792	78	28	65	254	4	74	0.9	71	200	2.5	580	7.3
96-97 Uta	82	0	1460	252	522	.483	0	3	.000	99	127	.780	75	24	63	214	2	74	0.9	60	195	2.4	603	7.4
97-98 Uta	66	8	1086	151	325	.465	0	0	—	76	98	.776	48	11	53	195	3	48	0.7	42	131	2.0	378	5.7
98-99 Hou	18	0	152	21	52	.404	0	1	.000	5	7	.714	9	1	10	31	0	9	0.5	9	31	1.7	47	2.6
99-00 Van	21	0	221	28	64	.438	0	0	—	11	14	.786	9	3	6	42	0	7	0.3	8	32	1.5	67	3.2
89-90 Atl	44	0	803	128	248	.516	0	4	.000	79	102	.775	54	15	34	128	4	53	1.2	50	149	3.4	335	7.6
Sac	33	4	924	228	473	.482	0	3	.000	158	196	.806	71	15	34	119	2	66	2.0	65	173	5.2	614	18.6
16 Years	987	168	19780	3663	7286	.503	6	46	.130	1844	2364	.780	1187	361	925	3063	56	1086	1.1	1151	3384	3.4	9176	9.3

NBA Postseason																								
Year Tm	G	GS	Min	Md	Att	Pct	Md	Att	Pct	Md	Att	Pct	TO	Stl	Blk	PF	DQ	Ast	Avg	Off	Tot	Avg	Pts	Avg
86-87 Atl	9	0	162	39	56	.696	0	0	—	26	32	.813	10	3	8	36	1	13	1.4	11	27	3.0	104	11.6
87-88 Atl	12	0	210	36	68	.529	0	1	.000	9	14	.643	10	4	17	47	2	15	1.3	12	41	3.4	81	6.8
88-89 Atl	5	0	81	13	21	.619	0	0	—	8	11	.727	4	0	4	13	0	7	1.4	5	8	1.6	34	6.8
91-92 SA	3	3	109	24	44	.545	1	2	.500	10	16	.625	4	2	11	14	1	3	1.0	8	23	7.7	59	19.7
92-93 SA	8	8	171	39	74	.527	0	0	—	6	10	.600	7	3	9	28	1	9	1.1	13	38	4.8	84	10.5
93-94 SA	3	0	37	5	11	.455	0	0	—	8	9	.889	0	1	2	7	0	3	1.0	1	1	0.3	18	6.0
94-95 Uta	5	0	114	14	31	.452	0	0	—	20	24	.833	4	3	5	26	2	7	1.4	3	15	3.0	48	9.6
95-96 Uta	18	0	339	46	97	.474	0	0	—	17	25	.680	16	4	14	66	2	21	1.2	11	34	1.9	109	6.1
96-97 Uta	20	0	280	40	83	.482	0	0	—	18	24	.750	18	6	9	64	1	10	0.5	11	40	2.0	98	4.9
97-98 Uta	20	0	292	41	90	.456	0	0	—	6	8	.750	9	1	12	63	1	11	0.6	16	41	2.1	88	4.4
98-99 Hou	4	0	37	4	11	.364	0	0	—	0	0	—	4	0	1	19	1	4	1.0	3	7	1.8	8	2.0
11 Years	107	11	1832	301	586	.514	1	3	.333	128	173	.740	86	27	92	383	12	103	1.0	94	275	2.6	731	6.8

Chris Carr

Pos: G **College:** Southern Illinois **Drafted:** '95 2(56)—Pho **Ht:** 6'6" **Wt:** 220 **Born:** 3/12/74 **Age:** 26

College				Field Goals			3-Pt FGs			Free Throws			Misc			Fouls		Assists		Rebounds			Points	
Year Tm	G	GS	Min	Md	Att	Pct	Md	Att	Pct	Md	Att	Pct	TO	Stl	Blk	PF	DQ	Ast	Avg	Off	Tot	Avg	Pts	Avg
92-93 SIU	31	0	353	52	88	.591	0	4	.000	18	33	.545	23	9	20	53	0	15	0.5	47	110	3.5	122	3.9
93-94 SIU	30	30	946	156	301	.518	24	74	.324	88	109	.807	60	32	31	87	4	55	1.8	71	197	6.6	424	14.1
94-95 SIU	32	32	1069	250	521	.480	40	101	.396	165	214	.771	102	50	15	95	4	68	2.1	94	232	7.3	705	22.0
3 Years	93	62	2368	458	910	.503	64	179	.358	271	356	.761	185	91	66	235	8	138	1.5	212	539	5.8	1251	13.5

NBA				Field Goals			3-Pt FGs			Free Throws			Misc			Fouls		Assists		Rebounds			Points	
Year Tm	G	GS	Min	Md	Att	Pct	Md	Att	Pct	Md	Att	Pct	TO	Stl	Blk	PF	DQ	Ast	Avg	Off	Tot	Avg	Pts	Avg
95-96 Pho	60	10	590	90	217	.415	11	42	.262	49	60	.817	40	10	5	77	1	43	0.7	27	102	1.7	240	4.0
96-97 Min	55	10	830	125	271	.461	31	88	.352	56	73	.767	37	24	10	93	0	48	0.9	31	113	2.1	337	6.1
97-98 Min	51	40	1165	190	452	.420	40	127	.315	84	99	.848	69	17	11	129	1	85	1.7	43	155	3.0	504	9.9
98-99 2Tm	39	4	445	76	205	.371	28	75	.373	27	40	.675	28	8	2	45	0	23	0.6	23	71	1.8	207	5.3
99-00 2Tm	57	2	1166	196	496	.395	32	101	.317	107	125	.856	117	30	15	113	0	84	1.5	41	173	3.0	531	9.3
98-99 Min	11	2	81	9	26	.346	3	9	.333	2	4	.500	4	1	1	9	0	7	0.6	0	12	1.1	23	2.1
NJ	28	2	364	67	179	.374	25	66	.379	25	36	.694	24	7	1	36	0	16	0.6	23	59	2.1	184	6.6
99-00 GS	7	0	74	11	33	.333	1	8	.125	16	19	.842	5	0	1	12	0	3	0.4	5	13	1.9	39	5.6
Chi	50	2	1092	185	463	.400	31	93	.333	91	106	.858	112	30	14	101	0	81	1.6	36	160	3.2	492	9.8
5 Years	262	66	4196	677	1641	.413	142	433	.328	323	397	.814	291	89	43	457	2	283	1.1	165	614	2.3	1819	6.9

NBA Postseason																								
Year Tm	G	GS	Min	Md	Att	Pct	Md	Att	Pct	Md	Att	Pct	TO	Stl	Blk	PF	DQ	Ast	Avg	Off	Tot	Avg	Pts	Avg
95-96 Pho	3	0	36	9	14	.643	2	3	.667	4	5	.800	4	2	1	6	0	4	1.3	3	7	2.3	24	8.0
96-97 Min	1	0	8	0	2	.000	0	2	.000	0	0	—	1	0	0	0	0	1	1.0	0	2	2.0	0	0.0
2 Years	4	0	44	9	16	.563	2	5	.400	4	5	.800	5	2	1	6	0	5	1.3	3	9	2.3	24	6.0

Anthony Carter

(statistical profile on page 199)

Pos: G **College:** Hawaii **Drafted:** '99 FA—Mia **Ht:** 6'2" **Wt:** 185 **Born:** 6/16/75 **Age:** 25

College				Field Goals			3-Pt FGs			Free Throws			Misc			Fouls		Assists		Rebounds			Points	
Year Tm	G	GS	Min	Md	Att	Pct	Md	Att	Pct	Md	Att	Pct	TO	Stl	Blk	PF	DQ	Ast	Avg	Off	Tot	Avg	Pts	Avg
96-97 Haw	29	29	1005	211	426	.495	32	90	.356	89	138	.645	136	78	16	86	2	191	6.6	30	107	3.7	543	18.7
97-98 Haw	29	29	1042	191	422	.453	34	110	.309	111	142	.782	138	64	9	73	1	212	7.3	48	152	5.2	527	18.2
2 Years	58	58	2047	402	848	.474	66	200	.330	200	280	.714	274	142	25	159	3	403	6.9	78	259	4.5	1070	18.4

	NBA			Field Goals			3-Pt FGs			Free Throws			Misc			Fouls		Assists		Rebounds			Points	
Year Tm	G	GS	Min	Md	Att	Pct	Md	Att	Pct	Md	Att	Pct	TO	Stl	Blk	PF	DQ	Ast	Avg	Off	Tot	Avg	Pts	Avg
98-99										Played in CBA														
99-00 Mia	79	30	1859	201	509	.395	3	23	.130	93	124	.750	173	93	5	167	0	378	4.8	48	199	2.5	498	6.3

NBA Postseason

Year Tm	G	GS	Min	Md	Att	Pct	Md	Att	Pct	Md	Att	Pct	TO	Stl	Blk	PF	DQ	Ast	Avg	Off	Tot	Avg	Pts	Avg
99-00 Mia	10	3	275	32	77	.416	1	6	.167	12	16	.750	24	12	2	23	0	56	5.6	8	40	4.0	77	7.7

Vince Carter

(statistical profile on page 200)

Pos: G-F **College:** North Carolina **Drafted:** '98 1(5)—GS **Ht:** 6'6" **Wt:** 225 **Born:** 1/26/77 **Age:** 24

	College			Field Goals			3-Pt FGs			Free Throws			Misc			Fouls		Assists		Rebounds			Points	
Year Tm	G	GS	Min	Md	Att	Pct	Md	Att	Pct	Md	Att	Pct	TO	Stl	Blk	PF	DQ	Ast	Avg	Off	Tot	Avg	Pts	Avg
95-96 UNC	31	19	555	91	185	.492	19	55	.345	31	45	.689	36	20	18	57	0	40	1.3	51	119	3.8	232	7.5
96-97 UNC	34	31	937	166	316	.525	36	107	.336	75	100	.750	47	49	26	72	3	83	2.4	58	152	4.5	443	13.0
97-98 UNC	38	32	1185	224	379	.591	44	107	.411	100	147	.680	40	45	36	61	1	74	1.9	74	195	5.1	592	15.6
3 Years	103	82	2677	481	880	.547	99	269	.368	206	292	.705	123	114	80	190	4	197	1.9	183	466	4.5	1267	12.3

	NBA			Field Goals			3-Pt FGs			Free Throws			Misc			Fouls		Assists		Rebounds			Points	
Year Tm	G	GS	Min	Md	Att	Pct	Md	Att	Pct	Md	Att	Pct	TO	Stl	Blk	PF	DQ	Ast	Avg	Off	Tot	Avg	Pts	Avg
98-99 Tor	50	49	1760	345	766	.450	19	66	.288	204	268	.761	110	55	77	140	2	149	3.0	94	283	5.7	913	18.3
99-00 Tor*	82	82	3126	788	1696	.465	95	236	.403	436	551	.791	178	110	92	263	2	322	3.9	150	476	5.8	2107	25.7
2 Years	132	131	4886	1133	2462	.460	114	302	.377	640	819	.781	288	165	169	403	4	471	3.6	244	759	5.8	3020	22.9

NBA Postseason

Year Tm	G	GS	Min	Md	Att	Pct	Md	Att	Pct	Md	Att	Pct	TO	Stl	Blk	PF	DQ	Ast	Avg	Off	Tot	Avg	Pts	Avg
99-00 Tor	3	3	119	15	50	.300	1	10	.100	27	31	.871	8	3	4	12	0	19	6.3	9	18	6.0	58	19.3

Sam Cassell

(statistical profile on page 200)

Pos: G **College:** Florida State **Drafted:** '93 1(24)—Hou **Ht:** 6'3" **Wt:** 185 **Born:** 11/18/69 **Age:** 31

	College			Field Goals			3-Pt FGs			Free Throws			Misc			Fouls		Assists		Rebounds			Points	
Year Tm	G	GS	Min	Md	Att	Pct	Md	Att	Pct	Md	Att	Pct	TO	Stl	Blk	PF	DQ	Ast	Avg	Off	Tot	Avg	Pts	Avg
91-92 FlaSt	31	31	1046	206	454	.454	58	164	.354	100	142	.704	92	56	8	108	5	119	3.8	40	141	4.5	570	18.4
92-93 FlaSt	35	35	1298	234	466	.502	50	131	.382	123	162	.759	98	97	10	110	7	170	4.9	47	152	4.3	641	18.3
2 Years	66	66	2344	440	920	.478	108	295	.366	223	304	.734	190	153	18	218	12	289	4.4	87	293	4.4	1211	18.3

	NBA			Field Goals			3-Pt FGs			Free Throws			Misc			Fouls		Assists		Rebounds			Points	
Year Tm	G	GS	Min	Md	Att	Pct	Md	Att	Pct	Md	Att	Pct	TO	Stl	Blk	PF	DQ	Ast	Avg	Off	Tot	Avg	Pts	Avg
93-94 Hou	66	6	1122	162	388	.418	26	88	.295	90	107	.841	94	59	7	136	1	192	2.9	25	134	2.0	440	6.7
94-95 Hou	82	1	1882	253	593	.427	63	191	.330	214	254	.843	167	94	14	209	3	405	4.9	38	211	2.6	783	9.5
95-96 Hou	61	0	1682	289	658	.439	73	210	.348	235	285	.825	157	53	4	166	2	278	4.6	51	188	3.1	886	14.5
96-97 3Tm	61	44	1714	337	783	.430	81	231	.351	212	251	.845	168	77	19	200	9	305	5.0	47	182	3.0	967	15.9
97-98 NJ	75	72	2606	510	1156	.441	15	80	.188	436	507	.860	269	121	20	262	6	603	8.0	73	228	3.0	1471	19.6
98-99 2Tm	8	3	199	39	93	.419	2	10	.200	47	50	.940	20	9	0	22	1	36	4.5	5	15	1.9	127	15.9
99-00 Mil	81	81	2899	545	1170	.466	26	90	.289	390	445	.876	267	102	8	255	5	729	9.0	69	301	3.7	1506	18.6
96-97 Pho	22	9	539	100	241	.415	19	62	.306	106	124	.855	60	23	6	66	4	99	4.5	12	50	2.3	325	14.8
Dal	16	13	398	70	165	.424	15	49	.306	42	50	.840	41	17	6	48	2	57	3.6	14	50	3.1	197	12.3
NJ	23	22	777	167	377	.443	47	120	.392	64	77	.831	67	37	7	86	3	149	6.5	21	82	3.6	445	19.3
98-99 NJ	4	3	100	21	49	.429	1	7	.143	29	31	.935	12	3	0	13	1	19	4.8	1	6	1.5	72	18.0
Mil	4	0	99	18	44	.409	1	3	.333	18	19	.947	8	6	0	9	0	17	4.3	4	9	2.3	55	13.8
7 Years	434	207	12104	2135	4841	.441	286	900	.318	1624	1899	.855	1142	515	72	1250	26	2548	5.9	308	1259	2.9	6180	14.2

NBA Postseason

Year Tm	G	GS	Min	Md	Att	Pct	Md	Att	Pct	Md	Att	Pct	TO	Stl	Blk	PF	DQ	Ast	Avg	Off	Tot	Avg	Pts	Avg
93-94 Hou	22	0	478	63	160	.394	17	45	.378	64	74	.865	47	21	5	62	1	93	4.2	19	59	2.7	207	9.4
94-95 Hou	22	0	485	74	169	.438	24	60	.400	71	85	.835	33	21	2	66	1	89	4.0	8	42	1.9	243	11.0
95-96 Hou	8	0	206	26	81	.321	8	29	.276	23	29	.793	18	6	1	20	0	34	4.3	1	17	2.1	83	10.4
97-98 NJ	3	1	26	3	9	.333	0	0	—	0	0	—	2	0	1	7	0	5	1.7	1	3	1.0	6	2.0
98-99 Mil	3	3	102	16	32	.500	0	1	.000	14	16	.875	7	3	0	14	1	26	8.7	0	6	2.0	46	15.3
99-00 Mil	5	5	178	30	72	.417	1	5	.200	18	21	.857	9	4	0	19	1	45	9.0	0	17	3.4	79	15.8
6 Years	63	9	1475	212	523	.405	50	140	.357	190	225	.844	116	55	9	188	4	292	4.6	29	144	2.3	664	10.5

Kelvin Cato

(statistical profile on page 201)

Pos: C **College:** Iowa State **Drafted:** '97 1(15)—Dal   **Ht:** 6'11" **Wt:** 255 **Born:** 8/26/74 **Age:** 26

College				Field Goals			3-Pt FGs			Free Throws			Misc			Fouls		Assists		Rebounds			Points	
Year Tm	G	GS	Min	Md	Att	Pct	Md	Att	Pct	Md	Att	Pct	TO	Stl	Blk	PF	DQ	Ast	Avg	Off	Tot	Avg	Pts	Avg
93-94 SoAl	24	—	433	49	123	.398	0	0	—	45	79	.570	32	16	85	60	—	17	0.7	—	138	5.8	143	6.0
95-96 IaSt	27	26	697	94	187	.503	0	0	—	71	111	.640	48	25	71	87	4	17	0.6	74	209	7.7	259	9.6
96-97 IaSt	28	24	801	128	234	.547	0	1	.000	61	113	.540	48	26	118	81	4	15	0.5	83	235	8.4	317	11.3
3 Years	79	—	1931	271	544	.498	0	1	.000	177	303	.584	128	67	274	228	—	49	0.6	—	582	7.4	719	9.1

NBA				Field Goals			3-Pt FGs			Free Throws			Misc			Fouls		Assists		Rebounds			Points	
Year Tm	G	GS	Min	Md	Att	Pct	Md	Att	Pct	Md	Att	Pct	TO	Stl	Blk	PF	DQ	Ast	Avg	Off	Tot	Avg	Pts	Avg
97-98 Por	74	8	1007	98	229	.428	0	3	.000	86	125	.688	44	29	94	164	3	23	0.3	91	252	3.4	282	3.8
98-99 Por	43	0	546	58	129	.450	1	1	1.000	34	67	.507	27	23	56	100	3	19	0.4	49	150	3.5	151	3.5
99-00 Hou	65	32	1581	216	402	.537	0	4	.000	135	208	.649	71	33	124	175	1	26	0.4	102	389	6.0	567	8.7
3 Years	182	40	3134	372	760	.489	1	8	.125	255	400	.638	142	85	274	439	7	68	0.4	242	791	4.3	1000	5.5

NBA Postseason																								
Year Tm	G	GS	Min	Md	Att	Pct	Md	Att	Pct	Md	Att	Pct	TO	Stl	Blk	PF	DQ	Ast	Avg	Off	Tot	Avg	Pts	Avg
97-98 Por	4	0	58	9	17	.529	0	1	.000	8	11	.727	4	1	7	12	0	1	0.3	3	12	3.0	26	6.5
98-99 Por	8	0	43	1	9	.111	0	0	—	4	10	.400	2	1	1	13	0	2	0.3	6	7	0.9	6	0.8
2 Years	12	0	101	10	26	.385	0	1	.000	12	21	.571	6	2	8	25	0	3	0.3	9	19	1.6	32	2.7

Duane Causwell

Pos: C **College:** Temple **Drafted:** '90 1(18)—Sac   **Ht:** 7'0" **Wt:** 255 **Born:** 5/31/68 **Age:** 32

College				Field Goals			3-Pt FGs			Free Throws			Misc			Fouls		Assists		Rebounds			Points	
Year Tm	G	GS	Min	Md	Att	Pct	Md	Att	Pct	Md	Att	Pct	TO	Stl	Blk	PF	DQ	Ast	Avg	Off	Tot	Avg	Pts	Avg
87-88 Tem	33	—	399	27	55	.491	0	0	—	13	30	.433	17	10	31	78	—	3	0.1	—	85	2.6	67	2.0
88-89 Tem	30	—	1081	128	249	.514	0	1	.000	84	123	.683	41	30	124	92	—	19	0.6	—	267	8.9	340	11.3
89-90 Tem	12	—	416	52	107	.486	0	0	—	31	52	.596	12	5	48	32	—	9	0.8	—	99	8.3	135	11.3
3 Years	75	—	1896	207	411	.504	0	1	.000	128	205	.624	70	45	203	202	—	31	0.4	—	451	6.0	542	7.2

NBA				Field Goals			3-Pt FGs			Free Throws			Misc			Fouls		Assists		Rebounds			Points	
Year Tm	G	GS	Min	Md	Att	Pct	Md	Att	Pct	Md	Att	Pct	TO	Stl	Blk	PF	DQ	Ast	Avg	Off	Tot	Avg	Pts	Avg
90-91 Sac	76	55	1719	210	413	.508	0	0	—	105	165	.636	96	49	148	225	4	69	0.9	141	391	5.1	525	6.9
91-92 Sac	80	77	2291	250	455	.549	0	1	.000	136	222	.613	124	47	215	281	4	59	0.7	196	580	7.3	636	8.0
92-93 Sac	55	45	1211	175	321	.545	0	1	.000	103	165	.624	58	32	87	192	7	35	0.6	112	303	5.5	453	8.2
93-94 Sac	41	8	674	71	137	.518	0	0	—	40	68	.588	33	19	49	109	2	11	0.3	68	186	4.5	182	4.4
94-95 Sac	58	24	820	76	147	.517	0	1	.000	57	98	.582	33	14	80	146	4	15	0.3	57	174	3.0	209	3.6
95-96 Sac	73	26	1044	90	216	.417	0	1	.000	70	96	.729	53	27	78	173	2	20	0.3	86	248	3.4	250	3.4
96-97 Sac	46	8	581	48	94	.511	2	3	.667	20	37	.541	34	15	38	131	5	20	0.4	57	127	2.8	118	2.6
97-98 Mia	37	2	363	37	89	.416	0	0	—	15	26	.577	18	7	27	73	0	5	0.1	29	99	2.7	89	2.4
98-99 Mia	19	1	137	20	35	.571	0	0	—	4	12	.333	18	0	11	32	1	2	0.1	14	35	1.8	44	2.3
99-00 Mia	25	2	185	20	37	.541	0	0	—	26	38	.684	10	2	16	42	0	2	0.1	11	47	1.9	66	2.6
10 Years	510	248	9025	997	1944	.513	2	7	.286	576	927	.621	477	212	749	1404	29	238	0.5	771	2190	4.3	2572	5.0

NBA Postseason																								
Year Tm	G	GS	Min	Md	Att	Pct	Md	Att	Pct	Md	Att	Pct	TO	Stl	Blk	PF	DQ	Ast	Avg	Off	Tot	Avg	Pts	Avg
95-96 Sac	2	0	25	1	3	.333	0	1	.000	3	4	.750	2	0	0	3	0	1	0.5	1	5	2.5	5	2.5
97-98 Mia	1	1	5	0	0	—	0	0	—	0	0	—	1	0	0	0	0	0	0.0	0	2	2.0	0	0.0
98-99 Mia	4	0	20	1	2	.500	0	0	—	4	6	.667	0	1	0	2	0	1	0.3	0	2	0.5	6	1.5
3 Years	7	1	50	2	5	.400	0	1	.000	7	10	.700	3	1	0	5	0	2	0.3	1	9	1.3	11	1.6

Cedric Ceballos

(statistical profile on page 201)

Pos: F **College:** Cal State Fullerton **Drafted:** '90 2(48)—Pho   **Ht:** 6'7" **Wt:** 220 **Born:** 8/2/69 **Age:** 31

College				Field Goals			3-Pt FGs			Free Throws			Misc			Fouls		Assists		Rebounds			Points	
Year Tm	G	GS	Min	Md	Att	Pct	Md	Att	Pct	Md	Att	Pct	TO	Stl	Blk	PF	DQ	Ast	Avg	Off	Tot	Avg	Pts	Avg
88-89 CSF	29	29	986	241	545	.442	16	58	.276	117	174	.672	97	46	8	77	1	43	1.5	130	256	8.8	615	21.2
89-90 CSF	29	28	1071	247	509	.485	31	96	.323	144	215	.670	92	47	15	69	0	50	1.7	156	362	12.5	669	23.1
2 Years	58	57	2057	488	1054	.463	47	154	.305	261	389	.671	189	93	23	146	1	93	1.6	286	618	10.7	1284	22.1

NBA				Field Goals			3-Pt FGs			Free Throws			Misc			Fouls		Assists		Rebounds			Points	
Year Tm	G	GS	Min	Md	Att	Pct	Md	Att	Pct	Md	Att	Pct	TO	Stl	Blk	PF	DQ	Ast	Avg	Off	Tot	Avg	Pts	Avg
90-91 Pho	63	0	730	204	419	.487	1	6	.167	110	166	.663	69	22	5	70	0	35	0.6	77	150	2.4	519	8.2
91-92 Pho	64	4	725	176	365	.482	1	6	.167	109	148	.736	71	16	11	52	0	50	0.8	60	152	2.4	462	7.2
92-93 Pho	74	46	1607	381	662	.576	0	2	.000	187	258	.725	106	54	28	103	1	77	1.0	172	408	5.5	949	12.8
93-94 Pho	53	43	1602	425	795	.535	0	9	.000	160	221	.724	93	59	23	124	0	91	1.7	153	344	6.5	1010	19.1
94-95 LAL*	58	54	2029	497	977	.509	58	146	.397	209	292	.716	143	60	19	131	1	105	1.8	169	464	8.0	1261	21.7
95-96 LAL	78	71	2628	638	1203	.530	51	184	.277	329	409	.804	167	94	22	144	0	119	1.5	215	536	6.9	1656	21.2

32

NBA

Year	Tm	G	GS	Min	Field Goals Md	Att	Pct	3-Pt FGs Md	Att	Pct	Free Throws Md	Att	Pct	Misc TO	Stl	Blk	Fouls PF	DQ	Assists Ast	Avg	Rebounds Off	Tot	Avg	Points Pts	Avg
96-97	2Tm	50	40	1426	282	617	.457	26	102	.255	139	186	.747	85	33	23	113	0	64	1.3	102	330	6.6	729	14.6
97-98	2Tm	47	25	990	204	415	.492	21	70	.300	107	145	.738	72	33	16	88	0	60	1.3	75	221	4.7	536	11.4
98-99	Dal	13	5	352	59	140	.421	11	28	.393	34	49	.694	28	7	5	23	1	12	0.9	23	85	6.5	163	12.5
99-00	Dal	69	25	2064	447	1002	.446	44	134	.328	209	248	.843	125	56	24	165	3	90	1.3	172	462	6.7	1147	16.6
96-97	LAL	8	8	279	34	83	.410	5	21	.238	13	15	.867	17	5	6	19	0	15	1.9	11	53	6.6	86	10.8
	Pho	42	32	1147	248	534	.464	21	81	.259	126	171	.737	68	28	17	94	0	49	1.2	91	277	6.6	643	15.3
97-98	Pho	35	16	626	129	258	.500	15	50	.300	60	84	.714	39	22	8	59	0	35	1.0	51	149	4.3	333	9.5
	Dal	12	9	364	75	157	.478	6	20	.300	47	61	.770	33	11	8	29	0	25	2.1	24	72	6.0	203	16.9
10 Years		569	313	14153	3313	6595	.502	213	687	.310	1593	2122	.751	959	434	176	1013	6	703	1.2	1218	3152	5.5	8432	14.8

NBA Postseason

Year	Tm	G	GS	Min	Md	Att	Pct	Md	Att	Pct	Md	Att	Pct	TO	Stl	Blk	PF	DQ	Ast	Avg	Off	Tot	Avg	Pts	Avg
90-91	Pho	3	0	24	7	12	.583	0	0	—	2	6	.333	1	2	0	0	0	2	0.7	3	5	1.7	16	5.3
91-92	Pho	8	8	188	44	80	.550	0	0	—	20	30	.667	11	6	6	14	0	12	1.5	20	51	6.4	108	13.5
92-93	Pho	16	3	185	40	70	.571	0	0	—	16	22	.727	5	5	7	12	0	13	0.8	13	37	2.3	96	6.0
93-94	Pho	10	8	212	43	93	.462	0	2	.000	15	18	.833	11	8	2	9	0	16	0.8	16	44	4.4	101	10.1
94-95	LAL	10	10	340	48	126	.381	18	50	.360	28	38	.737	21	12	7	21	0	18	1.8	11	61	6.1	142	14.2
95-96	LAL	4	4	142	30	62	.484	5	16	.313	11	12	.917	8	4	1	9	0	5	1.3	11	33	8.3	76	19.0
96-97	Pho	5	0	107	11	33	.333	3	12	.250	8	8	1.000	8	4	3	12	0	3	0.6	9	26	5.2	33	6.6
7 Years		56	33	1198	223	476	.468	26	80	.325	100	134	.746	65	41	26	77	0	61	1.1	83	257	4.6	572	10.2

John Celestand

Pos: G **College:** Villanova **Drafted:** '99 2(30)—LAL **Ht:** 6'3" **Wt:** 175 **Born:** 3/6/77 **Age:** 23

College

Year	Tm	G	GS	Min	Md	Att	Pct	Md	Att	Pct	Md	Att	Pct	TO	Stl	Blk	PF	DQ	Ast	Avg	Off	Tot	Avg	Pts	Avg
95-96	Vill	30	0	340	35	93	.376	10	39	.256	18	26	.692	26	14	5	46	1	44	1.5	8	36	1.2	98	3.3
96-97	Vill	34	24	956	97	255	.380	29	102	.284	60	91	.659	106	52	6	77	2	121	3.6	24	90	2.6	283	8.3
97-98	Vill	29	21	1006	136	329	.413	47	144	.326	65	90	.722	109	48	10	62	0	148	5.1	31	120	4.1	384	13.2
98-99	Vill	31	29	1006	151	347	.435	58	153	.379	99	124	.798	92	41	8	70	2	137	4.4	20	96	3.1	459	14.8
4 Years		124	74	3308	419	1024	.409	144	438	.329	242	331	.731	333	155	29	255	5	450	3.6	83	342	2.8	1224	9.9

NBA

Year	Tm	G	GS	Min	Md	Att	Pct	Md	Att	Pct	Md	Att	Pct	TO	Stl	Blk	PF	DQ	Ast	Avg	Off	Tot	Avg	Pts	Avg
99-00	LAL	16	0	185	15	45	.333	2	9	.222	5	6	.833	16	7	0	22	0	20	1.3	1	11	0.7	37	2.3

Rex Chapman

Pos: G **College:** Kentucky **Drafted:** '88 1(8)—Cha **Ht:** 6'4" **Wt:** 195 **Born:** 10/5/67 **Age:** 33

College

Year	Tm	G	GS	Min	Md	Att	Pct	Md	Att	Pct	Md	Att	Pct	TO	Stl	Blk	PF	DQ	Ast	Avg	Off	Tot	Avg	Pts	Avg
86-87	Kty	29	—	962	173	390	.444	68	176	.386	50	68	.735	70	36	15	55	—	103	3.6	—	66	2.3	464	16.0
87-88	Kty	32	—	1108	231	461	.501	66	159	.415	81	102	.794	85	53	16	61	—	117	3.7	—	93	2.9	609	19.0
2 Years		61	—	2070	404	851	.475	134	335	.400	131	170	.771	155	89	31	116	—	220	3.6	—	159	2.6	1073	17.6

NBA

Year	Tm	G	GS	Min	Md	Att	Pct	Md	Att	Pct	Md	Att	Pct	TO	Stl	Blk	PF	DQ	Ast	Avg	Off	Tot	Avg	Pts	Avg
88-89	Cha	75	44	2219	526	1271	.414	60	191	.314	155	195	.795	113	70	25	167	1	176	2.3	74	187	2.5	1267	16.9
89-90	Cha	54	52	1762	377	924	.408	47	142	.331	144	192	.750	100	46	6	113	0	132	2.4	52	179	3.3	945	17.5
90-91	Cha	70	68	2100	410	922	.445	48	148	.324	234	282	.830	131	73	16	167	1	250	3.6	45	191	2.7	1102	15.7
91-92	2Tm	22	11	567	113	252	.448	8	29	.276	36	53	.679	45	15	8	51	0	89	4.0	10	58	2.6	270	12.3
92-93	Was	60	23	1300	287	602	.477	43	116	.371	132	163	.810	79	38	10	119	1	116	1.9	19	88	1.5	749	12.5
93-94	Was	60	59	2025	431	865	.498	64	165	.388	168	206	.816	117	59	8	83	0	185	3.1	57	146	2.4	1094	18.2
94-95	Was	45	29	1468	254	639	.397	86	274	.314	137	159	.862	62	67	15	85	0	128	2.8	23	113	2.5	731	16.2
95-96	Was	56	50	1865	289	679	.426	125	337	.371	83	113	.735	79	45	10	117	0	166	3.0	22	145	2.6	786	14.0
96-97	Pho	65	33	1833	332	749	.443	110	314	.350	124	149	.832	96	52	7	108	1	182	2.8	25	181	2.8	898	13.8
97-98	Pho	68	67	2263	408	956	.427	120	311	.386	146	187	.781	116	71	14	102	0	203	3.0	30	173	2.5	1082	15.9
98-99	Pho	38	35	1183	165	459	.359	53	151	.351	76	91	.835	54	34	9	46	0	109	2.9	12	104	2.7	459	12.1
99-00	Pho	53	19	957	124	320	.388	41	123	.333	59	78	.756	38	22	1	70	0	62	1.2	10	80	1.5	348	6.6
91-92	Cha	21	11	545	108	240	.450	8	27	.296	36	53	.679	42	14	8	47	0	86	4.1	9	54	2.6	260	12.4
	Was	1	0	22	5	12	.417	0	2	.000	0	0	—	3	1	0	4	0	3	3.0	1	4	4.0	10	10.0
12 Years		666	490	19542	3716	8638	.430	805	2301	.350	1494	1868	.800	1030	592	129	1228	4	1798	2.7	379	1645	2.5	9731	14.6

NBA Postseason

Year	Tm	G	GS	Min	Md	Att	Pct	Md	Att	Pct	Md	Att	Pct	TO	Stl	Blk	PF	DQ	Ast	Avg	Off	Tot	Avg	Pts	Avg
95-96	Mia	3	3	88	12	28	.429	3	13	.231	0	0	—	1	3	0	6	0	5	1.7	0	6	2.0	27	9.0
96-97	Pho	5	5	191	41	83	.494	22	48	.458	17	25	.680	15	2	0	14	0	13	2.6	2	16	3.2	121	24.2
97-98	Pho	2	2	58	6	23	.261	0	5	.000	6	7	.857	2	2	0	1	0	4	2.0	0	0	0.0	18	9.0

Year Tm	G	GS	Min	Md	Att	Pct	Md	Att	Pct	Md	Att	Pct	TO	Stl	Blk	PF	DQ	Ast	Avg	Off	Tot	Avg	Pts	Avg
98-99 Pho	3	3	57	6	21	.286	2	6	.333	3	4	.750	4	1	0	9	1	6	2.0	2	6	2.0	17	5.7
4 Years	13	13	394	65	155	.419	27	72	.375	26	36	.722	22	8	0	30	1	28	2.2	4	28	2.2	183	14.1

Calbert Cheaney

(statistical profile on page 202)

Pos: F **College:** Indiana **Drafted:** '93 1(6)—Was   **Ht:** 6'7" **Wt:** 217 **Born:** 7/17/71 **Age:** 29

College				Field Goals			3-Pt FGs			Free Throws			Misc			Fouls		Assists		Rebounds			Points	
Year Tm	G	GS	Min	Md	Att	Pct	Md	Att	Pct	Md	Att	Pct	TO	Stl	Blk	PF	DQ	Ast	Avg	Off	Tot	Avg	Pts	Avg
89-90 Ind	29	29	928	199	348	.572	25	51	.490	72	96	.750	51	24	16	78	1	48	1.7	57	133	4.6	495	17.1
90-91 Ind	34	34	1029	289	485	.596	43	91	.473	113	141	.801	77	24	13	97	2	47	1.4	45	188	5.5	734	21.6
91-92 Ind	34	32	991	227	435	.522	33	86	.384	112	140	.800	64	36	6	84	2	48	1.4	42	166	4.9	599	17.6
92-93 Ind	35	35	1181	303	552	.549	47	110	.427	132	166	.795	85	33	10	76	1	84	2.4	75	223	6.4	785	22.4
4 Years	132	130	4129	1018	1820	.559	148	338	.438	429	543	.790	277	117	45	335	6	227	1.7	219	710	5.4	2613	19.8

NBA				Field Goals			3-Pt FGs			Free Throws			Misc			Fouls		Assists		Rebounds			Points	
Year Tm	G	GS	Min	Md	Att	Pct	Md	Att	Pct	Md	Att	Pct	TO	Stl	Blk	PF	DQ	Ast	Avg	Off	Tot	Avg	Pts	Avg
93-94 Was	65	21	1604	327	696	.470	1	23	.043	124	161	.770	108	63	10	148	0	126	1.9	88	190	2.9	779	12.0
94-95 Was	78	71	2651	512	1129	.453	96	283	.339	173	213	.812	151	80	21	215	0	177	2.3	105	321	4.1	1293	16.6
95-96 Was	70	70	2324	426	905	.471	52	154	.338	151	214	.706	129	67	18	205	1	154	2.2	67	239	3.4	1055	15.1
96-97 Was	79	79	2411	369	730	.505	4	30	.133	95	137	.693	94	77	18	226	3	114	1.4	70	268	3.4	837	10.6
97-98 Was	82	82	2841	448	981	.457	15	53	.283	139	215	.647	104	96	36	264	4	173	2.1	82	324	4.0	1050	12.8
98-99 Was	50	18	1266	172	415	.414	8	37	.216	33	67	.493	42	39	16	146	0	73	1.5	33	141	2.8	385	7.7
99-00 Bos	67	19	1309	120	273	.440	18	54	.333	9	21	.429	46	44	14	158	3	80	1.2	23	138	2.1	267	4.0
7 Years	491	360	14406	2374	5129	.463	194	634	.306	724	1028	.704	674	466	133	1362	11	897	1.8	468	1621	3.3	5666	11.5

Year Tm	G	GS	Min	Md	Att	Pct	Md	Att	Pct	Md	Att	Pct	TO	Stl	Blk	PF	DQ	Ast	Avg	Off	Tot	Avg	Pts	Avg
96-97 Was	3	3	120	18	40	.450	0	2	.000	9	12	.750	5	3	2	10	0	4	1.3	6	11	3.7	45	15.0

Pete Chilcutt

Pos: F **College:** North Carolina **Drafted:** '91 1(27)—Sac   **Ht:** 6'10" **Wt:** 245 **Born:** 9/14/68 **Age:** 32

College				Field Goals			3-Pt FGs			Free Throws			Misc			Fouls		Assists		Rebounds			Points	
Year Tm	G	GS	Min	Md	Att	Pct	Md	Att	Pct	Md	Att	Pct	TO	Stl	Blk	PF	DQ	Ast	Avg	Off	Tot	Avg	Pts	Avg
87-88 UNC	34	3	573	66	117	.564	0	1	.000	36	51	.706	41	10	10	32	—	43	1.3	—	110	3.2	168	4.9
88-89 UNC	37	13	750	110	205	.537	3	8	.375	33	53	.623	56	23	8	31	—	51	1.4	—	200	5.4	256	6.9
89-90 UNC	34	28	917	132	257	.514	12	30	.400	30	42	.714	69	41	30	54	—	47	1.4	—	225	6.6	306	9.0
90-91 UNC	35	33	937	175	325	.538	5	19	.263	65	85	.765	60	41	35	38	—	47	1.3	—	231	6.6	420	12.0
4 Years	140	77	3177	483	904	.534	20	58	.345	164	231	.710	226	115	83	155	—	188	1.3	—	766	5.5	1150	8.2

NBA				Field Goals			3-Pt FGs			Free Throws			Misc			Fouls		Assists		Rebounds			Points	
Year Tm	G	GS	Min	Md	Att	Pct	Md	Att	Pct	Md	Att	Pct	TO	Stl	Blk	PF	DQ	Ast	Avg	Off	Tot	Avg	Pts	Avg
91-92 Sac	69	2	817	113	250	.452	2	2	1.000	23	28	.821	41	32	17	70	0	38	0.6	78	187	2.7	251	3.6
92-93 Sac	59	9	834	165	340	.485	0	0	—	32	46	.696	54	22	21	102	2	64	1.1	80	194	3.3	362	6.1
93-94 2Tm	76	24	1365	203	448	.453	3	15	.200	41	65	.631	74	53	39	164	2	86	1.1	129	371	4.9	450	5.9
94-95 Hou	68	17	1347	146	328	.445	35	86	.407	31	42	.738	61	25	43	117	0	66	1.0	106	317	4.7	358	5.3
95-96 Hou	74	0	651	73	179	.408	37	98	.378	17	26	.654	22	19	14	65	0	26	0.4	51	156	2.1	200	2.7
96-97 Van	54	1	662	72	165	.436	25	69	.362	13	22	.591	28	26	17	52	0	47	0.9	67	156	2.9	182	3.4
97-98 Van	82	0	1420	156	359	.435	54	130	.415	39	59	.661	62	53	37	158	0	104	1.3	77	306	3.7	405	4.9
98-99 Van	46	0	697	63	172	.366	26	68	.382	14	17	.824	28	22	12	52	0	30	0.7	29	117	2.5	166	3.6
99-00 3Tm	56	2	601	53	127	.417	6	26	.231	8	8	1.000	20	15	10	73	2	27	0.5	46	131	2.3	120	2.1
93-94 Sac	46	24	974	152	328	.463	0	1	.000	31	52	.596	56	43	28	116	2	71	1.5	100	271	5.9	335	7.3
Det	30	0	391	51	120	.425	3	14	.214	10	13	.769	18	10	11	48	0	15	0.5	29	100	3.3	115	3.8
99-00 Uta	26	0	224	22	62	.355	1	10	.100	2	2	1.000	9	5	4	31	0	10	0.4	15	43	1.7	47	1.8
LAC	24	2	347	31	63	.492	5	16	.313	6	6	1.000	11	10	6	39	2	16	0.7	27	79	3.3	73	3.0
Cle	6	0	30	0	2	.000	0	0	—	0	0	—	0	0	0	3	0	1	0.2	4	9	1.5	0	0.0
9 Years	584	55	8394	1044	2368	.441	188	494	.381	218	313	.696	390	267	210	853	6	488	0.8	663	1935	3.3	2494	4.3

Year Tm	G	GS	Min	Md	Att	Pct	Md	Att	Pct	Md	Att	Pct	TO	Stl	Blk	PF	DQ	Ast	Avg	Off	Tot	Avg	Pts	Avg
94-95 Hou	20	15	323	31	64	.484	14	36	.389	14	17	.824	11	7	4	39	0	18	0.9	15	58	2.9	90	4.5
95-96 Hou	1	0	10	1	4	.250	0	1	.000	0	2	.000	1	0	0	0	0	0	0.0	2	3	3.0	2	2.0
2 Years	21	15	333	32	68	.471	14	37	.378	14	19	.737	12	7	4	39	0	18	0.9	17	61	2.9	92	4.4

Chris Childs

(statistical profile on page 202)

Pos: G **College:** Boise State **Drafted:** '94 FA—NJ   **Ht:** 6'3" **Wt:** 195 **Born:** 11/20/67 **Age:** 33

College

Year Tm	G	GS	Min	Field Goals Md	Att	Pct	3-Pt FGs Md	Att	Pct	Free Throws Md	Att	Pct	Misc TO	Stl	Blk	Fouls PF	DQ	Assists Ast	Avg	Rebounds Off	Tot	Avg	Points Pts	Avg
85-86 Boi	28	28	792	109	264	.413	10	31	.323	72	91	.791	103	56	1	91	4	84	3.0	—	87	3.1	300	10.7
86-87 Boi	30	30	945	153	344	.445	47	116	.405	109	132	.826	74	68	12	—		87	2.9	—	77	2.6	462	15.4
87-88 Boi	30	30	944	147	316	.465	54	120	.450	81	95	.853	90	58	2	84	5	99	3.3	—	79	2.6	429	14.3
88-89 Boi	30	30	929	131	295	.444	52	119	.437	97	121	.802	92	33	1	92	1	122	4.1	—	101	3.4	411	13.7
4 Years	118	118	3610	540	1219	.443	163	386	.422	359	439	.818	359	215	16	—		392	3.3	—	344	2.9	1602	13.6

NBA

Year Tm	G	GS	Min	Field Goals Md	Att	Pct	3-Pt FGs Md	Att	Pct	Free Throws Md	Att	Pct	Misc TO	Stl	Blk	Fouls PF	DQ	Assists Ast	Avg	Rebounds Off	Tot	Avg	Points Pts	Avg
89-90						Played in CBA																		
90-91						Played in CBA																		
91-92						Played in CBA																		
92-93						Played in CBA, Played in USBL																		
93-94						Played in CBA, Played in USBL													14	69	1.3	308	5.8
94-95 NJ	53	11	1021	106	279	.380	41	125	.328	55	73	.753	76	42	3	116	1	219	4.1	14	69	1.3	308	5.8
95-96 NJ	78	54	2408	324	778	.416	95	259	.367	259	304	.852	230	111	8	246	3	548	7.0	51	245	3.1	1002	12.8
96-97 NY	65	61	2076	211	510	.414	70	181	.387	113	149	.758	180	78	11	213	6	398	6.1	22	191	2.9	605	9.3
97-98 NY	68	0	1599	149	354	.421	27	87	.310	104	126	.825	103	56	6	179	2	268	3.9	29	162	2.4	429	6.3
98-99 NY	48	0	1297	114	267	.427	36	94	.383	64	78	.821	85	44	1	156	0	193	4.0	18	133	2.8	328	6.8
99-00 NY	71	2	1675	146	357	.409	37	104	.356	47	59	.797	105	36	4	240	4	285	4.0	17	147	2.1	376	5.3
6 Years	383	128	10076	1050	2545	.413	306	850	.360	642	789	.814	779	367	33	1150	16	1911	5.0	151	947	2.5	3048	8.0

NBA Postseason

Year Tm	G	GS	Min	Field Goals Md	Att	Pct	3-Pt FGs Md	Att	Pct	Free Throws Md	Att	Pct	Misc TO	Stl	Blk	Fouls PF	DQ	Assists Ast	Avg	Rebounds Off	Tot	Avg	Points Pts	Avg
96-97 NY	10	10	328	38	87	.437	9	26	.346	19	23	.826	28	20	0	39	1	59	5.9	9	49	4.9	104	10.4
97-98 NY	10	0	254	24	58	.414	4	13	.308	11	15	.733	23	6	0	29	0	33	3.3	5	25	2.5	63	6.3
98-99 NY	20	0	494	33	93	.355	9	28	.321	19	26	.731	30	13	1	64	2	73	3.7	8	47	2.4	94	4.7
99-00 NY	16	0	334	27	70	.386	9	28	.321	24	28	.857	14	7	0	53	1	39	2.4	1	37	2.3	87	5.4
4 Years	56	10	1410	122	308	.396	31	95	.326	73	92	.793	95	46	1	185	4	204	3.6	23	158	2.8	348	6.2

Doug Christie

(statistical profile on page 203)

Pos: G **College:** Pepperdine **Drafted:** '92 1(17)—Sea   **Ht:** 6'6" **Wt:** 205 **Born:** 5/9/70 **Age:** 30

College

Year Tm	G	GS	Min	Field Goals Md	Att	Pct	3-Pt FGs Md	Att	Pct	Free Throws Md	Att	Pct	Misc TO	Stl	Blk	Fouls PF	DQ	Assists Ast	Avg	Rebounds Off	Tot	Avg	Points Pts	Avg
89-90 Pep	28	—	687	84	167	.503	12	47	.255	70	98	.714	100	44	34	64	—	112	4.1	—	115	4.1	250	8.9
90-91 Pep	28	—	913	188	401	.469	17	65	.262	143	187	.765	113	62	31	65	—	134	4.8	—	145	5.2	536	19.1
91-92 Pep	31	—	1058	211	453	.466	40	120	.333	144	193	.746	119	62	21	78	—	149	4.8	—	183	5.9	606	19.5
3 Years	87	—	2658	483	1021	.473	69	232	.297	357	478	.747	332	168	86	207	—	395	4.5	—	443	5.1	1392	16.0

NBA

Year Tm	G	GS	Min	Field Goals Md	Att	Pct	3-Pt FGs Md	Att	Pct	Free Throws Md	Att	Pct	Misc TO	Stl	Blk	Fouls PF	DQ	Assists Ast	Avg	Rebounds Off	Tot	Avg	Points Pts	Avg
92-93 LAL	23	0	332	45	106	.425	2	12	.167	50	66	.758	50	22	5	53	0	53	2.3	24	51	2.2	142	6.2
93-94 LAL	65	34	1515	244	562	.434	39	119	.328	145	208	.697	140	89	28	186	2	136	2.1	93	235	3.6	672	10.3
94-95 NY	12	0	79	5	22	.227	1	7	.143	4	5	.800	13	2	1	18	1	8	0.7	3	13	1.1	15	1.3
95-96 2Tm	55	17	1036	150	337	.445	46	106	.434	69	93	.742	95	50	19	141	5	117	2.1	34	154	2.8	415	7.5
96-97 Tor	81	81	3127	396	949	.417	147	383	.384	237	306	.775	200	201	46	245	6	315	3.9	85	432	5.3	1176	14.5
97-98 Tor	78	78	2939	458	1071	.428	100	307	.326	271	327	.829	228	190	57	198	3	282	3.6	94	404	5.2	1287	16.5
98-99 Tor	50	50	1768	252	650	.388	49	161	.304	207	246	.841	119	113	26	111	1	187	3.7	59	207	4.1	760	15.2
99-00 Tor	73	73	2264	311	764	.407	99	275	.360	182	216	.843	144	102	43	167	1	321	4.4	63	285	3.9	903	12.4
95-96 NY	23	0	218	35	73	.479	10	19	.526	13	22	.591	19	12	3	41	1	25	1.1	8	34	1.5	93	4.0
Tor	32	17	818	115	264	.436	36	87	.414	56	71	.789	76	58	16	100	4	92	2.9	26	120	3.8	322	10.1
8 Years	437	333	13060	1861	4461	.417	483	1370	.353	1165	1467	.794	989	789	224	1119	19	1419	3.2	455	1781	4.1	5370	12.3

NBA Postseason

Year Tm	G	GS	Min	Field Goals Md	Att	Pct	3-Pt FGs Md	Att	Pct	Free Throws Md	Att	Pct	Misc TO	Stl	Blk	Fouls PF	DQ	Assists Ast	Avg	Rebounds Off	Tot	Avg	Points Pts	Avg
92-93 LAL	5	0	39	4	11	.364	1	3	.333	0	0	—	4	2	2	5	0	6	1.2	1	4	0.8	9	1.8
94-95 NY	2	0	6	0	4	.000	0	0	—	0	0	—	1	0	0	3	0	0	0.0	0	0	0.0	0	0.0
99-00 Tor	3	1	61	3	13	.231	3	8	.375	3	6	.500	4	4	1	10	0	6	2.0	1	5	1.7	12	4.0
3 Years	10	1	106	7	28	.250	4	11	.364	3	6	.500	9	6	3	18	0	12	1.2	2	9	0.9	21	2.1

35

Keon Clark

Pos: F-C **College:** UNLV **Drafted:** '98 1(13)—Orl **Ht:** 6'11" **Wt:** 220 **Born:** 4/16/75 **Age:** 25

(statistical profile on page 203)

College				Field Goals			3-Pt FGs			Free Throws			Misc			Fouls		Assists		Rebounds			Points	
Year	G	GS	Min	Md	Att	Pct	Md	Att	Pct	Md	Att	Pct	TO	Stl	Blk	PF	DQ	Ast	Avg	Off	Tot	Avg	Pts	Avg
96-97 UNLV	29	5	816	168	302	.556	6	19	.316	88	140	.629	74	23	112	93	3	32	1.1	101	289	10.0	430	14.8
97-98 UNLV	10	10	320	57	104	.548	4	8	.500	30	45	.667	28	2	26	38	1	19	1.9	22	86	8.6	148	14.8
2 Years	39	15	1136	225	406	.554	10	27	.370	118	185	.638	102	25	138	131	4	51	1.3	123	375	9.6	578	14.8

NBA				Field Goals			3-Pt FGs			Free Throws			Misc			Fouls		Assists		Rebounds			Points	
Year	G	GS	Min	Md	Att	Pct	Md	Att	Pct	Md	Att	Pct	TO	Stl	Blk	PF	DQ	Ast	Avg	Off	Tot	Avg	Pts	Avg
98-99 Den	28	0	409	36	80	.450	0	1	.000	21	37	.568	21	10	31	52	0	10	0.4	36	96	3.4	93	3.3
99-00 Den	81	20	1850	286	528	.542	1	8	.125	121	176	.688	125	45	114	231	1	71	0.9	162	505	6.2	694	8.6
2 Years	109	20	2259	322	608	.530	1	9	.111	142	213	.667	146	55	145	283	1	81	0.7	198	601	5.5	787	7.2

Keith Closs

Pos: C **College:** Central Connecticut State **Drafted:** '97 FA—LAC **Ht:** 7'3" **Wt:** 215 **Born:** 4/3/76 **Age:** 24

College				Field Goals			3-Pt FGs			Free Throws			Misc			Fouls		Assists		Rebounds			Points	
Year Tm	G	GS	Min	Md	Att	Pct	Md	Att	Pct	Md	Att	Pct	TO	Stl	Blk	PF	DQ	Ast	Avg	Off	Tot	Avg	Pts	Avg
94-95 CenCt	26	—	761	109	197	.553	2	13	.154	45	84	.536	63	12	138	82	—	27	1.0	—	193	7.4	265	10.2
95-96 CenCt	28	—	884	147	283	.519	5	17	.294	80	124	.645	95	15	179	83	—	34	1.2	—	259	9.3	379	13.5
2 Years	54	—	1645	256	480	.533	7	30	.233	125	208	.601	158	27	317	165	—	61	1.1	—	452	8.4	644	11.9

NBA				Field Goals			3-Pt FGs			Free Throws			Misc			Fouls		Assists		Rebounds			Points	
Year Tm	G	GS	Min	Md	Att	Pct	Md	Att	Pct	Md	Att	Pct	TO	Stl	Blk	PF	DQ	Ast	Avg	Off	Tot	Avg	Pts	Avg
96-97																								
97-98 LAC	58	1	740	93	207	.449	0	0	Played in Atlantic Basketball Assoc.	46	77	.597	38	12	81	73	0	19	0.3	63	168	2.9	232	4.0
98-99 LAC	15	0	87	12	23	.522	0	1	.000	8	10	.800	6	3	9	14	1	0	0.0	5	25	1.7	32	2.1
99-00 LAC	57	6	820	96	197	.487	0	3	.000	46	78	.590	34	13	73	80	0	25	0.4	65	179	3.1	238	4.2
3 Years	130	7	1647	201	427	.471	0	4	.000	100	165	.606	78	28	163	167	1	44	0.3	133	372	2.9	502	3.9

Derrick Coleman

Pos: F-C **College:** Syracuse **Drafted:** '90 1(1)—NJ **Ht:** 6'10" **Wt:** 260 **Born:** 6/21/67 **Age:** 33

(statistical profile on page 204)

College				Field Goals			3-Pt FGs			Free Throws			Misc			Fouls		Assists		Rebounds			Points	
Year Tm	G	GS	Min	Md	Att	Pct	Md	Att	Pct	Md	Att	Pct	TO	Stl	Blk	PF	DQ	Ast	Avg	Off	Tot	Avg	Pts	Avg
86-87 Syr	38	38	1163	173	309	.560	0	0	—	107	156	.686	67	45	68	120		45	1.2	119	333	8.8	453	11.9
87-88 Syr	35	34	1133	176	300	.587	1	6	.167	121	192	.630	76	45	57	84	2	76	2.2	138	384	11.0	474	13.5
88-89 Syr	37	36	1226	227	395	.575	0	8	.000	171	247	.692	89	46	127	120	5	106	2.9	136	422	11.4	625	16.9
89-90 Syr	33	31	1166	194	352	.551	15	41	.366	188	263	.715	90	51	67	102	0	95	2.9	146	398	12.1	591	17.9
4 Years	143	139	4688	770	1356	.568	16	55	.291	587	858	.684	322	187	319	426	15	322	2.9	539	1537	10.7	2143	15.0

NBA				Field Goals			3-Pt FGs			Free Throws			Misc			Fouls		Assists		Rebounds			Points	
Year Tm	G	GS	Min	Md	Att	Pct	Md	Att	Pct	Md	Att	Pct	TO	Stl	Blk	PF	DQ	Ast	Avg	Off	Tot	Avg	Pts	Avg
90-91 NJ	74	68	2602	514	1100	.467	13	38	.342	323	442	.731	217	71	99	217	3	163	2.2	269	759	10.3	1364	18.4
91-92 NJ	65	58	2207	483	958	.504	23	76	.303	300	393	.763	248	54	98	168	2	205	3.2	203	618	9.5	1289	19.8
92-93 NJ	76	73	2759	564	1226	.460	23	99	.232	421	521	.808	243	92	126	210	1	276	3.6	247	852	11.2	1572	20.7
93-94 NJ*	77	77	2778	541	1209	.447	38	121	.314	439	567	.774	208	68	142	209	2	262	3.4	262	870	11.3	1559	20.2
94-95 NJ	56	54	2103	371	875	.424	28	120	.233	376	490	.767	172	35	94	162	2	187	3.3	167	591	10.6	1146	20.5
95-96 Phi	11	11	294	48	118	.407	7	21	.333	20	32	.625	28	4	10	30	0	31	2.8	13	72	6.5	123	11.2
96-97 Phi	57	54	2102	364	836	.435	32	119	.269	272	365	.745	184	50	75	164	1	193	3.4	157	573	10.1	1032	18.1
97-98 Phi	59	58	2135	356	867	.411	26	98	.265	302	391	.772	157	46	68	144	1	145	2.5	149	587	9.9	1040	17.6
98-99 Cha	37	29	1178	168	406	.414	7	33	.212	143	190	.753	90	24	42	96	1	78	2.1	76	328	8.9	486	13.1
99-00 Cha	74	64	2347	446	979	.456	51	141	.362	296	377	.785	173	34	130	195	2	175	2.4	124	632	8.5	1239	16.7
10 Years	586	546	20505	3855	8574	.450	248	866	.286	2892	3768	.768	1720	478	884	1595	15	1715	2.9	1667	5882	10.0	10850	18.5

NBA Postseason				Field Goals			3-Pt FGs			Free Throws			Misc			Fouls		Assists		Rebounds			Points	
Year Tm	G	GS	Min	Md	Att	Pct	Md	Att	Pct	Md	Att	Pct	TO	Stl	Blk	PF	DQ	Ast	Avg	Off	Tot	Avg	Pts	Avg
91-92 NJ	4	4	162	36	74	.486	1	6	.167	16	21	.762	11	7	4	12	0	21	5.3	13	45	11.3	89	22.3
92-93 NJ	5	5	225	50	94	.532	5	12	.417	29	36	.806	13	6	13	18	0	23	4.6	13	67	13.4	134	26.8
93-94 NJ	4	4	173	27	68	.397	5	9	.556	39	50	.780	18	2	5	12	0	10	2.5	19	57	14.3	98	24.5
99-00 Cha	4	4	169	27	57	.474	5	16	.313	22	28	.786	13	3	12	11	1	14	3.5	10	50	12.5	81	20.3
4 Years	17	17	729	140	293	.478	16	43	.372	106	135	.785	55	18	34	53	1	68	4.0	55	219	12.9	402	23.6

Bimbo Coles

(statistical profile on page 204)

Pos: G **College:** Virginia Tech **Drafted:** '90 2(40)—Sac **Ht:** 6'2" **Wt:** 182 **Born:** 4/22/68 **Age:** 32

College				Field Goals			3-Pt FGs			Free Throws			Misc			Fouls		Assists		Rebounds			Points	
Year	G	GS	Min	Md	Att	Pct	Md	Att	Pct	Md	Att	Pct	TO	Stl	Blk	PF	DQ	Ast	Avg	Off	Tot	Avg	Pts	Avg
86-87 VTch	28	—	752	101	245	.412	0	14	.000	78	109	.716	72	34	5	87	—	112	4.0	—	85	3.0	280	10.0
87-88 VTch	29	—	990	241	544	.443	20	62	.323	200	270	.741	91	60	7	92	—	172	5.9	—	103	3.6	702	24.2
88-89 VTch	27	—	924	249	547	.455	62	166	.373	157	200	.785	81	52	3	73	—	141	5.2	—	111	4.1	717	26.6
89-90 VTch	31	—	1147	280	693	.404	67	218	.307	158	214	.738	101	70	13	84	—	122	3.9	—	147	4.7	785	25.3
4 Years	115	—	3813	871	2029	.429	149	460	.324	593	793	.748	345	216	28	336	—	547	4.8	—	446	3.9	2484	21.6

NBA				Field Goals			3-Pt FGs			Free Throws			Misc			Fouls		Assists		Rebounds			Points	
Year Tm	G	GS	Min	Md	Att	Pct	Md	Att	Pct	Md	Att	Pct	TO	Stl	Blk	PF	DQ	Ast	Avg	Off	Tot	Avg	Pts	Avg
90-91 Mia	82	9	1355	162	393	.412	6	34	.176	71	95	.747	98	65	12	149	0	232	2.8	56	153	1.9	401	4.9
91-92 Mia	81	28	1976	295	649	.455	10	52	.192	216	262	.824	167	73	13	151	3	366	4.5	69	189	2.3	816	10.1
92-93 Mia	81	37	2232	318	686	.464	42	137	.307	177	220	.805	108	80	11	199	4	373	4.6	58	166	2.0	855	10.6
93-94 Mia	76	4	1726	233	519	.449	20	99	.202	102	131	.779	107	75	12	132	0	263	3.5	50	159	2.1	588	7.7
94-95 Mia	68	65	2207	261	607	.430	16	76	.211	141	174	.810	156	99	13	185	1	416	6.1	46	191	2.8	679	10.0
95-96 2Tm	81	55	2615	318	777	.409	88	254	.346	168	211	.796	171	94	17	253	5	422	5.2	49	260	3.2	892	11.0
96-97 GS	51	13	1183	122	314	.389	30	102	.294	37	49	.755	59	35	7	96	0	149	2.9	39	118	2.3	311	6.1
97-98 GS	53	44	1471	166	438	.379	13	57	.228	78	88	.886	89	51	13	135	2	248	4.7	17	123	2.3	423	8.0
98-99 GS	48	32	1272	183	414	.442	6	25	.240	83	101	.822	82	45	11	113	2	222	4.6	21	117	2.4	455	9.5
99-00 Atl	80	54	1924	276	607	.455	8	39	.205	85	104	.817	103	58	11	178	1	290	3.6	30	172	2.2	645	8.1
95-96 Mia	52	52	1882	231	559	.413	63	172	.366	139	173	.803	123	63	12	175	3	296	5.7	38	201	3.9	664	12.8
GS	29	3	733	87	218	.399	25	82	.305	29	38	.763	48	31	5	78	2	126	4.3	11	59	2.0	228	7.9
10 Years	701	341	17961	2334	5404	.432	239	875	.273	1158	1435	.807	1140	675	120	1591	18	2981	4.3	435	1648	2.4	6065	8.7

NBA Postseason				Field Goals			3-Pt FGs			Free Throws			Misc			Fouls		Assists		Rebounds			Points	
Year Tm	G	GS	Min	Md	Att	Pct	Md	Att	Pct	Md	Att	Pct	TO	Stl	Blk	PF	DQ	Ast	Avg	Off	Tot	Avg	Pts	Avg
91-92 Mia	3	0	45	7	10	.700	1	1	1.000	8	10	.800	5	3	0	5	0	6	2.0	2	7	2.3	23	7.7
93-94 Mia	5	0	140	25	47	.532	1	4	.250	18	23	.783	11	7	1	15	0	17	3.4	2	14	2.8	69	13.8
2 Years	8	0	185	32	57	.561	2	5	.400	26	33	.788	16	10	1	20	0	23	2.9	4	21	2.6	92	11.5

Marty Conlon

Pos: C **College:** Providence **Drafted:** '91 FA—Sea **Ht:** 6'11" **Wt:** 235 **Born:** 1/19/68 **Age:** 33

College				Field Goals			3-Pt FGs			Free Throws			Misc			Fouls		Assists		Rebounds			Points	
Year Tm	G	GS	Min	Md	Att	Pct	Md	Att	Pct	Md	Att	Pct	TO	Stl	Blk	PF	DQ	Ast	Avg	Off	Tot	Avg	Pts	Avg
86-87 Prov	34	0	487	43	96	.448	0	0	—	64	77	.831	42	11	7	87	2	16	0.5	41	100	2.9	150	4.4
87-88 Prov	11	10	282	45	88	.511	0	3	.000	55	66	.833	5	43	5	39	2	19	1.7	23	62	5.6	145	13.2
88-89 Prov	29	29	885	154	294	.524	16	42	.381	91	125	.728	94	29	14	95	4	60	2.1	79	202	7.0	415	14.3
89-90 Prov	29	29	866	136	271	.502	15	48	.313	138	187	.738	73	17	15	85	0	72	2.5	78	220	7.6	425	14.7
4 Years	103	68	2520	378	749	.505	31	93	.333	348	455	.765	214	100	41	306	8	167	1.6	221	584	5.7	1135	11.0

NBA				Field Goals			3-Pt FGs			Free Throws			Misc			Fouls		Assists		Rebounds			Points	
Year Tm	G	GS	Min	Md	Att	Pct	Md	Att	Pct	Md	Att	Pct	TO	Stl	Blk	PF	DQ	Ast	Avg	Off	Tot	Avg	Pts	Avg
90-91									Played in CBA															
91-92 Sea	45	1	381	48	101	.475	0	0	—	24	32	.750	27	9	7	40	0	12	0.3	33	69	1.5	120	2.7
92-93 Sac	46	0	467	81	171	.474	0	4	.000	57	81	.704	28	13	5	43	0	37	0.8	48	123	2.7	219	4.8
93-94 2Tm	30	9	579	95	165	.576	0	2	.000	43	53	.811	33	9	8	69	1	34	1.1	53	139	4.6	233	7.8
94-95 Mil	82	3	2064	344	647	.532	8	29	.276	119	194	.613	123	42	18	218	3	110	1.3	160	426	5.2	815	9.9
95-96 Mil	74	1	958	153	327	.468	5	30	.167	84	110	.764	79	20	11	126	1	68	0.9	58	177	2.4	395	5.3
96-97 Bos	74	15	1614	214	454	.471	2	10	.200	144	171	.842	109	46	18	154	2	104	1.4	128	323	4.4	574	7.8
97-98 Mia	18	0	209	28	62	.452	0	0	—	32	44	.727	11	9	5	27	0	12	0.7	16	46	2.6	88	4.9
98-99 Mia	7	0	35	3	13	.231	0	0	—	2	2	1.000	3	0	1	6	0	1	0.1	1	5	0.7	8	1.1
99-00 LAC	3	0	9	1	2	.500	0	0	—	0	0	—	0	0	0	1	0	0	0.0	1	2	0.7	2	0.7
93-94 Cha	16	8	378	66	109	.606	0	1	.000	31	38	.816	23	5	7	36	1	28	1.8	34	89	5.6	163	10.2
Was	14	1	201	29	56	.518	0	1	.000	12	15	.800	10	4	1	33	0	6	0.4	19	50	3.6	70	5.0
9 Years	379	29	6316	967	1942	.498	15	75	.200	505	687	.735	413	148	73	684	7	378	1.0	498	1310	3.5	2454	6.5

NBA Postseason				Field Goals			3-Pt FGs			Free Throws			Misc			Fouls		Assists		Rebounds			Points	
Year Tm	G	GS	Min	Md	Att	Pct	Md	Att	Pct	Md	Att	Pct	TO	Stl	Blk	PF	DQ	Ast	Avg	Off	Tot	Avg	Pts	Avg
91-92 Sea	1	0	1	0	1	.000	0	0	—	2	2	1.000	0	0	0	0	0	0	0.0	0	1	1.0	2	2.0
97-98 Mia	3	0	46	3	7	.429	0	0	—	1	2	.500	6	1	1	7	0	3	1.0	1	4	1.3	7	2.3
2 Years	4	0	47	3	8	.375	0	0	—	3	4	.750	6	1	1	7	0	3	0.8	1	5	1.3	9	2.3

Tyrone Corbin

Pos: F **College:** DePaul **Drafted:** '85 2(35)—SA   **Ht:** 6'6" **Wt:** 225 **Born:** 12/31/62 **Age:** 38

College			Field Goals			3-Pt FGs			Free Throws			Misc			Fouls		Assists		Rebounds			Points	
Year Tm	G	GS	Min	Md	Att	Pct	Md	Att	Pct	Md	Att	Pct	TO	Stl	Blk	PF	DQ	Ast	Avg	Off	Tot	Avg	Pts	Avg
81-82 DeP	28	0	602	43	103	.417	—	—	—	56	78	.718	68	27	6	75	5	30	1.1	—	172	6.1	142	5.1
82-83 DeP	33	28	1060	124	263	.471	—	—	—	102	132	.773	—	21	31	99	3	39	1.2	—	262	7.9	350	10.6
83-84 DeP	30	30	1070	166	316	.525	—	—	—	93	125	.744	—	42	9	79	2	89	3.0	—	223	7.4	425	14.2
84-85 DeP	29	29	1004	189	354	.534	—	—	—	83	102	.814	—	45	11	82	3	69	2.4	—	236	8.1	461	15.9
4 Years	120	87	3736	522	1036	.504	—	—	—	334	437	.764	—	135	57	335	13	227	1.9	—	893	7.4	1378	11.5

NBA			Field Goals			3-Pt FGs			Free Throws			Misc			Fouls		Assists		Rebounds			Points	
Year Tm	G	GS	Min	Md	Att	Pct	Md	Att	Pct	Md	Att	Pct	TO	Stl	Blk	PF	DQ	Ast	Avg	Off	Tot	Avg	Pts	Avg
85-86 SA	16	0	174	27	64	.422	0	1	.000	10	14	.714	12	11	2	21	0	11	0.7	11	25	1.6	64	4.0
86-87 2Tm	63	15	1170	156	381	.409	1	4	.250	91	124	.734	66	55	5	129	0	97	1.5	88	215	3.4	404	6.4
87-88 2Tm	84	5	1739	257	525	.490	1	6	.167	110	138	.797	104	72	18	181	2	115	1.4	127	350	4.2	625	7.4
88-89 Pho	77	30	1655	245	454	.540	0	2	.000	141	179	.788	92	82	13	222	2	118	1.5	176	398	5.2	631	8.2
89-90 Min	82	80	3011	521	1083	.481	0	11	.000	161	209	.770	143	175	41	288	5	216	2.6	219	604	7.4	1203	14.7
90-91 Min	82	82	3196	587	1311	.448	2	10	.200	296	371	.798	209	162	53	257	3	347	4.2	185	589	7.2	1472	18.0
91-92 2Tm	80	9	2207	303	630	.481	0	4	.000	174	201	.866	97	82	20	193	1	140	1.8	163	472	5.9	780	9.8
92-93 Uta	82	58	2555	385	766	.503	0	5	.000	180	218	.826	108	108	32	252	3	173	2.1	194	519	6.3	950	11.6
93-94 Uta	82	17	2149	268	588	.456	6	29	.207	117	144	.813	92	99	24	212	0	122	1.5	150	389	4.7	659	8.0
94-95 Atl	81	4	1389	205	464	.442	14	56	.250	78	114	.684	74	55	16	161	1	67	0.8	98	262	3.2	502	6.2
95-96 2Tm	71	2	1284	155	351	.442	3	18	.167	100	120	.833	67	63	20	147	1	84	1.2	81	244	3.4	413	5.8
96-97 Atl	70	65	2305	253	600	.422	74	208	.356	86	108	.796	85	90	7	176	1	124	1.8	76	294	4.2	666	9.5
97-98 Atl	79	79	2699	328	747	.439	49	141	.348	101	128	.789	86	105	7	197	1	173	2.2	78	362	4.6	806	10.2
98-99 Atl	47	6	1066	131	335	.391	38	119	.319	52	80	.650	43	31	7	74	0	43	0.9	37	145	3.1	352	7.5
99-00 Sac	54	5	941	88	247	.356	10	44	.227	33	39	.846	29	36	5	99	2	60	1.1	40	165	3.1	219	4.1
86-87 SA	31	15	732	113	264	.428	0	0	—	49	67	.731	46	38	3	81	0	80	2.6	52	119	3.8	275	8.9
Cle	32	0	438	43	117	.368	1	4	.250	42	57	.737	20	17	2	48	0	17	0.5	36	96	3.0	129	4.0
87-88 Cle	54	4	1148	158	322	.491	0	3	.000	77	98	.786	66	42	15	128	2	56	1.0	79	220	4.1	393	7.3
Pho	30	1	591	99	203	.488	1	3	.333	33	40	.825	38	30	3	53	0	59	2.0	48	130	4.3	232	7.7
91-92 Min	11	8	344	57	142	.401	0	1	.000	44	53	.830	26	12	6	31	0	33	3.0	24	69	6.3	158	14.4
Uta	69	1	1863	246	488	.504	0	3	.000	130	148	.878	71	70	14	162	1	107	1.6	139	403	5.8	622	9.0
95-96 Sac	49	2	930	117	259	.452	1	12	.083	77	92	.837	50	47	17	96	1	61	1.2	55	179	3.7	312	6.4
Mia	22	0	354	38	92	.413	2	6	.333	23	28	.821	17	16	3	51	0	23	1.0	26	65	3.0	101	4.6
15 Years	1050	457	27540	3909	8546	.457	198	658	.301	1730	2187	.791	1307	1226	270	2609	22	1890	1.8	1723	5033	4.8	9746	9.3

NBA Postseason

Year Tm	G	GS	Min	Md	Att	Pct	Md	Att	Pct	Md	Att	Pct	TO	Stl	Blk	PF	DQ	Ast	Avg	Off	Tot	Avg	Pts	Avg
85-86 SA	1	0	14	0	4	.000	0	0	—	0	0	—	0	0	0	0	0	1	1.0	0	1	1.0	0	0.0
88-89 Pho	12	12	310	45	86	.523	0	0	—	19	25	.760	14	24	4	37	0	26	2.2	43	85	7.1	109	9.1
91-92 Uta	16	0	447	69	137	.504	0	2	.000	42	54	.778	17	12	3	45	0	17	1.1	39	88	5.5	180	11.3
92-93 Uta	5	0	161	24	50	.480	0	0	—	11	17	.647	7	3	1	15	0	9	1.8	16	38	7.6	59	11.8
93-94 Uta	16	11	413	41	106	.387	4	12	.333	14	15	.933	11	21	3	31	0	15	0.9	25	79	4.9	100	6.3
94-95 Atl	3	2	79	12	26	.462	2	6	.333	8	9	.889	2	2	1	10	0	2	0.7	6	10	3.3	34	11.3
95-96 Mia	2	0	34	1	5	.200	0	0	—	3	4	.750	1	2	0	3	0	1	0.5	4	7	3.5	5	2.5
96-97 Atl	10	10	364	42	92	.457	13	37	.351	9	9	1.000	14	4	2	29	0	20	2.0	12	43	4.3	106	10.6
97-98 Atl	4	4	113	7	25	.280	1	6	.167	0	0	—	3	6	1	10	0	4	1.0	3	15	3.8	15	3.8
98-99 Atl	9	4	268	30	72	.417	6	23	.261	3	4	.750	8	6	0	20	0	16	1.8	7	33	3.7	69	7.7
99-00 Sac	3	0	23	2	5	.400	0	2	.000	0	1	.000	0	0	0	2	0	3	1.0	1	5	1.7	4	1.3
11 Years	81	43	2226	273	608	.449	26	88	.295	109	138	.790	77	80	15	202	0	114	1.4	156	404	5.0	681	8.4

Chris Crawford

Pos: F **College:** Marquette **Drafted:** '97 2(51)—Atl   **Ht:** 6'9" **Wt:** 235 **Born:** 5/13/75 **Age:** 25

College			Field Goals			3-Pt FGs			Free Throws			Misc			Fouls		Assists		Rebounds			Points	
Year Tm	G	GS	Min	Md	Att	Pct	Md	Att	Pct	Md	Att	Pct	TO	Stl	Blk	PF	DQ	Ast	Avg	Off	Tot	Avg	Pts	Avg
93-94 Marq	18	0	116	9	25	.360	6	13	.462	9	13	.692	7	1	5	26	0	3	0.2	6	11	0.6	33	1.8
94-95 Marq	33	18	611	72	163	.442	17	45	.378	43	67	.642	47	15	6	108	8	16	0.5	41	89	2.7	204	6.2
95-96 Marq	31	27	798	118	280	.421	29	84	.345	83	116	.716	52	20	10	86	4	29	0.9	58	126	4.1	348	11.2
96-97 Marq	31	31	961	165	352	.469	33	86	.384	100	130	.769	69	33	22	90	4	45	1.5	55	165	5.3	463	14.9
4 Years	113	76	2486	364	820	.444	85	228	.373	235	326	.721	175	69	43	310	16	93	0.8	160	391	3.5	1048	9.3

NBA			Field Goals			3-Pt FGs			Free Throws			Misc			Fouls		Assists		Rebounds			Points	
Year Tm	G	GS	Min	Md	Att	Pct	Md	Att	Pct	Md	Att	Pct	TO	Stl	Blk	PF	DQ	Ast	Avg	Off	Tot	Avg	Pts	Avg
97-98 Atl	40	0	256	46	110	.418	1	3	.333	57	68	.838	18	12	7	27	0	9	0.2	20	41	1.0	150	3.8
98-99 Atl	42	30	784	110	255	.431	11	33	.333	57	70	.814	48	10	13	106	1	24	0.6	37	90	2.1	288	6.9
99-00 Atl	55	11	668	91	229	.397	7	27	.259	63	81	.778	37	17	16	83	1	33	0.6	51	99	1.8	252	4.6
3 Years	137	41	1708	247	594	.416	19	63	.302	177	219	.808	103	39	36	216	2	66	0.5	108	230	1.7	690	5.0

Year Tm	G	GS	Min	Md	Att	Pct	Md	Att	Pct	Md	Att	Pct	TO	Stl	Blk	PF	DQ	Ast	Avg	Off	Tot	Avg	Pts	Avg
97-98 Atl	1	0	4	0	0	—	0	0	—	2	2	1.000	2	0	1	2	0	0	0.0	1	2	2.0	2	2.0
98-99 Atl	6	5	125	16	48	.333	4	14	.286	23	26	.885	6	1	1	19	2	5	0.8	6	19	3.2	59	9.8
2 Years	7	5	129	16	48	.333	4	14	.286	25	28	.893	8	1	2	21	2	5	0.7	7	21	3.0	61	8.7

Austin Croshere

(statistical profile on page 205)

Pos: F **College:** Providence **Drafted:** '97 1(12)—Ind   **Ht:** 6'9" **Wt:** 242 **Born:** 5/1/75 **Age:** 25

College				Field Goals			3-Pt FGs			Free Throws			Misc			Fouls		Assists		Rebounds			Points	
Year Tm	G	GS	Min	Md	Att	Pct	Md	Att	Pct	Md	Att	Pct	TO	Stl	Blk	PF	DQ	Ast	Avg	Off	Tot	Avg	Pts	Avg
93-94 Prov	25	1	233	38	95	.400	10	31	.323	29	40	.725	21	5	8	26	0	3	0.1	20	55	2.2	115	4.6
94-95 Prov	30	4	570	106	231	.459	29	85	.341	66	85	.776	50	17	16	50	0	33	1.1	67	147	4.9	307	10.2
95-96 Prov	30	30	858	151	359	.421	47	141	.333	109	128	.852	64	45	27	79	4	33	1.1	102	173	5.8	458	15.3
96-97 Prov	36	36	1192	200	440	.455	61	175	.349	182	205	.888	95	38	25	92	3	54	1.5	72	270	7.5	643	17.9
4 Years	121	71	2853	495	1125	.440	147	432	.340	386	458	.843	230	105	76	247	7	123	1.0	261	645	5.3	1523	12.6

NBA				Field Goals			3-Pt FGs			Free Throws			Misc			Fouls		Assists		Rebounds			Points	
Year Tm	G	GS	Min	Md	Att	Pct	Md	Att	Pct	Md	Att	Pct	TO	Stl	Blk	PF	DQ	Ast	Avg	Off	Tot	Avg	Pts	Avg
97-98 Ind	26	0	243	32	86	.372	4	13	.308	8	14	.571	13	9	5	32	1	8	0.3	10	45	1.7	76	2.9
98-99 Ind	27	0	249	32	75	.427	8	29	.276	20	23	.870	23	7	8	32	0	10	0.4	16	45	1.7	92	3.4
99-00 Ind	81	14	1885	288	653	.441	63	174	.362	196	231	.848	121	44	60	203	2	89	1.1	135	516	6.4	835	10.3
3 Years	134	14	2377	352	814	.432	75	216	.347	224	268	.836	157	60	73	267	3	107	0.8	161	606	4.5	1003	7.5

Year Tm	G	GS	Min	Md	Att	Pct	Md	Att	Pct	Md	Att	Pct	TO	Stl	Blk	PF	DQ	Ast	Avg	Off	Tot	Avg	Pts	Avg
98-99 Ind	1	0	1	0	1	.000	0	0	—	2	2	1.000	0	0	0	0	0	0	0.0	1	1	1.0	2	2.0
99-00 Ind	23	2	490	64	153	.418	15	37	.405	73	87	.839	25	9	16	51	0	19	0.8	31	109	4.7	216	9.4
2 Years	24	2	491	64	154	.416	15	37	.405	75	89	.843	25	9	16	51	0	19	0.8	32	110	4.6	218	9.1

John Crotty

Pos: G **College:** Virginia **Drafted:** '92 FA—Uta   **Ht:** 6'2" **Wt:** 194 **Born:** 7/15/69 **Age:** 31

College				Field Goals			3-Pt FGs			Free Throws			Misc			Fouls		Assists		Rebounds			Points	
Year Tm	G	GS	Min	Md	Att	Pct	Md	Att	Pct	Md	Att	Pct	TO	Stl	Blk	PF	DQ	Ast	Avg	Off	Tot	Avg	Pts	Avg
87-88 UVa	31	12	717	59	163	.362	26	75	.347	51	87	.586	55	18	1	73	—	92	3.0	24	70	2.3	195	6.3
88-89 UVa	33	33	1143	136	309	.440	41	112	.366	113	169	.669	92	42	6	79	—	208	6.3	16	85	2.6	426	12.9
89-90 UVa	32	32	1176	156	401	.389	66	194	.340	134	191	.702	116	32	4	65	—	214	6.7	19	94	2.9	512	16.0
90-91 UVa	33	33	1138	176	397	.443	46	136	.338	115	148	.777	84	35	6	70	—	169	5.1	23	78	2.4	513	15.5
4 Years	129	110	4174	527	1270	.415	179	517	.346	413	595	.694	347	127	17	287	—	683	5.3	82	327	2.5	1646	12.8

NBA				Field Goals			3-Pt FGs			Free Throws			Misc			Fouls		Assists		Rebounds			Points	
Year Tm	G	GS	Min	Md	Att	Pct	Md	Att	Pct	Md	Att	Pct	TO	Stl	Blk	PF	DQ	Ast	Avg	Off	Tot	Avg	Pts	Avg
91-92								Played in GBA																	
92-93 Uta	40	0	243	37	72	.514	2	14	.143	26	38	.684	30	11	0	29	0	55	1.4	4	17	0.4	102	2.6
93-94 Uta	45	0	313	45	99	.455	11	24	.458	31	36	.861	27	15	1	36	0	77	1.7	11	31	0.7	132	2.9
94-95 Uta	80	0	1019	93	231	.403	11	36	.306	98	121	.810	70	39	6	105	0	205	2.6	27	97	1.2	295	3.7
95-96 Cle	58	4	617	51	114	.447	8	27	.296	62	72	.861	51	22	6	60	0	102	1.8	20	54	0.9	172	3.0
96-97 Mia	48	0	659	79	154	.513	20	49	.408	54	64	.844	42	18	0	79	0	102	2.1	15	47	1.0	232	4.8
97-98 Por	26	2	379	29	90	.322	6	20	.300	32	34	.941	42	10	1	28	0	63	2.4	4	32	1.2	96	3.7
98-99 2Tm	27	0	382	51	124	.411	14	36	.389	43	50	.860	33	11	0	31	0	63	2.3	8	31	1.1	159	5.9
99-00 Det	69	0	937	106	251	.422	33	80	.413	80	93	.860	54	27	5	104	0	128	1.9	17	75	1.1	325	4.7
98-99 Por	3	0	19	4	8	.500	1	1	1.000	3	3	1.000	0	2	0	1	0	5	1.7	0	1	0.3	12	4.0
Sea	24	0	363	47	116	.405	13	35	.371	40	47	.851	33	9	0	30	0	58	2.4	8	30	1.3	147	6.1
8 Years	393	6	4549	491	1135	.433	105	286	.367	426	508	.839	349	153	19	472	0	795	2.0	106	384	1.0	1513	3.8

Year Tm	G	GS	Min	Md	Att	Pct	Md	Att	Pct	Md	Att	Pct	TO	Stl	Blk	PF	DQ	Ast	Avg	Off	Tot	Avg	Pts	Avg
92-93 Uta	1	0	3	2	2	1.000	0	0	—	0	0	—	0	0	0	0	0	1	1.0	1	1	1.0	4	4.0
93-94 Uta	8	0	38	4	11	.364	2	2	1.000	2	2	1.000	1	1	0	6	0	9	1.1	0	3	0.4	12	1.5
94-95 Uta	3	0	24	2	3	.667	0	0	—	3	5	.600	0	1	0	2	0	6	2.0	0	0	0.0	7	2.3
95-96 Cle	2	0	9	0	0	—	0	0	—	2	2	1.000	1	1	0	1	0	1	0.5	1	1	0.5	2	1.0
96-97 Mia	15	0	125	13	33	.394	5	12	.417	6	7	.857	14	4	0	15	0	11	0.7	5	11	0.7	37	2.5
99-00 Det	3	0	51	2	10	.200	0	3	.000	2	2	1.000	4	1	1	4	0	4	1.3	0	4	1.3	6	2.0
6 Years	32	0	250	23	59	.390	7	17	.412	15	18	.833	20	8	2	27	0	32	1.0	7	20	0.6	68	2.1

Terry Cummings

Pos: F **College:** DePaul **Drafted:** '82 1(2)—SDC   **Ht:** 6'9" **Wt:** 250 **Born:** 3/15/61 **Age:** 39

College			Field Goals			3-Pt FGs			Free Throws			Misc			Fouls		Assists		Rebounds			Points	
Year Tm	G	GS	Min	Md	Att	Pct	Md	Att	Pct	Md	Att	Pct	TO	Stl	Blk	PF	DQ	Ast	Avg	Off	Tot	Avg	Pts	Avg
79-80 DeP	28	—	861	154	303	.508	—	—	—	89	107	.832	—	—	—	—	—	40	1.4	—	263	9.4	397	14.2
80-81 DeP	29	—	994	151	303	.498	—	—	—	75	100	.750	—	—	—	—	—	47	1.6	—	260	9.0	377	13.0
81-82 DeP	28	28	1031	244	430	.567	—	—	—	136	180	.756	89	48	36	91	4	57	2.0	—	334	11.9	624	22.3
3 Years	85	—	2886	549	1036	.530	—	—	—	300	387	.775	—	—	—	—	—	144	1.7	—	857	10.1	1398	16.4

NBA			Field Goals			3-Pt FGs			Free Throws			Misc			Fouls		Assists		Rebounds			Points	
Year Tm	G	GS	Min	Md	Att	Pct	Md	Att	Pct	Md	Att	Pct	TO	Stl	Blk	PF	DQ	Ast	Avg	Off	Tot	Avg	Pts	Avg
82-83 SDC	70	69	2531	684	1309	.523	0	1	.000	292	412	.709	204	129	62	294	10	177	2.5	303	744	10.6	1660	23.7
83-84 SDC	81	80	2907	737	1491	.494	0	3	.000	380	528	.720	218	92	57	298	6	139	1.7	323	777	9.6	1854	22.9
84-85 Mil*	79	78	2722	759	1532	.495	0	1	.000	343	463	.741	190	117	67	264	4	228	2.9	244	716	9.1	1861	23.6
85-86 Mil	82	82	2669	681	1438	.474	0	2	.000	265	404	.656	191	121	51	283	4	193	2.4	222	694	8.5	1627	19.8
86-87 Mil	82	77	2770	729	1426	.511	0	3	.000	249	376	.662	172	129	81	296	3	229	2.8	214	700	8.5	1707	20.8
87-88 Mil	76	76	2629	675	1392	.485	1	3	.333	270	406	.665	170	78	46	274	6	181	2.4	184	553	7.3	1621	21.3
88-89 Mil*	80	77	2824	730	1563	.467	7	15	.467	362	460	.787	201	106	72	265	5	198	2.5	281	650	8.1	1829	22.9
89-90 SA	81	78	2821	728	1532	.475	19	59	.322	343	440	.780	202	110	52	286	1	219	2.7	226	677	8.4	1818	22.4
90-91 SA	67	62	2195	503	1039	.484	7	33	.212	164	240	.683	131	61	30	225	5	157	2.3	194	521	7.8	1177	17.6
91-92 SA	70	67	2149	514	1053	.488	5	13	.385	177	249	.711	115	58	34	210	4	102	1.5	247	631	9.0	1210	17.3
92-93 SA	8	0	76	11	29	.379	0	0	—	5	10	.500	2	1	1	17	0	4	0.5	6	19	2.4	27	3.4
93-94 SA	59	29	1133	183	428	.428	0	2	.000	63	107	.589	59	31	13	137	0	50	0.8	132	297	5.0	429	7.3
94-95 SA	76	20	1273	224	464	.483	0	0	—	72	123	.585	95	36	19	188	1	59	0.8	138	378	5.0	520	6.8
95-96 Mil	81	13	1777	270	584	.462	1	7	.143	104	160	.650	69	56	30	263	2	89	1.1	162	445	5.5	645	8.0
96-97 Sea	45	3	828	155	319	.486	3	5	.600	57	82	.695	45	33	7	113	0	39	0.9	70	183	4.1	370	8.2
97-98 2Tm	74	3	1185	200	428	.467	0	1	.000	67	98	.684	51	38	10	181	1	47	0.6	97	283	3.8	467	6.3
98-99 GS	50	0	1011	186	424	.439	1	1	1.000	81	114	.711	58	46	10	168	4	58	1.2	95	255	5.1	454	9.1
99-00 GS	22	0	398	76	177	.429	0	0	—	32	39	.821	27	13	8	74	0	21	1.0	45	107	4.9	184	8.4
97-98 Phi	44	2	656	97	212	.458	0	1	.000	39	58	.672	17	22	5	102	1	21	0.5	55	148	3.4	233	5.3
NY	30	1	529	103	216	.477	0	0	—	28	40	.700	34	16	5	79	0	26	0.9	42	135	4.5	234	7.8
18 Years	1183	815	33898	8045	16628	.484	44	149	.295	3326	4711	.706	2200	1255	650	3836	56	2190	1.9	3183	8630	7.3	19460	16.4

NBA Postseason

			Field Goals			3-Pt FGs			Free Throws			Misc			Fouls		Assists		Rebounds			Points	
Year Tm	G	GS	Min	Md	Att	Pct	Md	Att	Pct	Md	Att	Pct	TO	Stl	Blk	PF	DQ	Ast	Avg	Off	Tot	Avg	Pts	Avg
84-85 Mil	8	8	311	86	149	.577	0	1	.000	48	58	.828	26	12	7	33	1	20	2.5	21	70	8.8	220	27.5
85-86 Mil	14	14	510	130	253	.514	0	0	—	43	62	.694	39	20	16	52	0	42	3.0	33	138	9.9	303	21.6
86-87 Mil	12	10	443	105	215	.488	0	0	—	57	83	.687	15	12	13	51	1	28	2.3	29	95	7.9	267	22.3
87-88 Mil	5	5	193	50	89	.562	0	0	—	29	44	.659	12	9	3	16	0	13	2.6	12	39	7.8	129	25.8
88-89 Mil	5	4	124	25	69	.362	0	1	.000	14	16	.875	4	3	0	16	0	7	1.4	19	33	6.6	64	12.8
89-90 SA	10	10	375	103	195	.528	1	5	.200	42	52	.808	19	7	4	39	0	22	2.2	31	94	9.4	249	24.9
90-91 SA	4	4	124	25	49	.510	0	1	.000	9	18	.500	9	3	2	13	0	4	1.0	14	37	9.3	59	14.8
91-92 SA	3	3	122	34	66	.515	0	1	.000	10	20	.500	7	4	4	9	0	7	2.3	15	34	11.3	78	26.0
92-93 SA	10	0	138	31	70	.443	0	1	.000	5	8	.625	8	3	1	27	0	5	0.5	17	39	3.9	67	6.7
93-94 SA	4	1	72	11	22	.500	0	0	—	10	12	.833	4	5	3	10	0	2	0.5	10	25	6.3	32	8.0
94-95 SA	15	2	135	18	48	.375	0	1	.000	22	30	.733	7	5	0	25	0	4	0.3	12	31	2.1	58	3.9
96-97 Sea	12	6	292	45	92	.489	0	0	—	16	24	.667	14	11	6	39	1	14	1.2	28	72	6.0	106	8.8
97-98 NY	8	1	120	15	34	.441	0	0	—	2	8	.250	7	4	2	23	0	5	0.6	11	35	4.4	32	4.0
13 Years	110	68	2959	678	1351	.502	1	11	.091	307	435	.706	171	98	61	353	3	173	1.6	252	742	6.7	1664	15.1

Vonteego Cummings   (statistical profile on page 205)

Pos: G **College:** Pittsburgh **Drafted:** '99 1(26)—Ind   **Ht:** 6'3" **Wt:** 190 **Born:** 2/29/76 **Age:** 24

College			Field Goals			3-Pt FGs			Free Throws			Misc			Fouls		Assists		Rebounds			Points	
Year Tm	G	GS	Min	Md	Att	Pct	Md	Att	Pct	Md	Att	Pct	TO	Stl	Blk	PF	DQ	Ast	Avg	Off	Tot	Avg	Pts	Avg
95-96 Pitt	18	12	438	39	117	.333	10	42	.238	28	42	.667	36	15	6	35	0	52	2.9	15	62	3.4	116	6.4
96-97 Pitt	33	33	1129	189	414	.457	42	105	.400	119	167	.713	129	85	6	100	5	140	4.2	60	137	4.2	539	16.3
97-98 Pitt	26	26	1042	173	406	.426	41	130	.315	120	173	.694	115	66	12	74	3	154	5.9	32	107	4.1	507	19.5
98-99 Pitt	26	26	923	153	372	.411	41	124	.331	72	103	.699	84	69	11	76	5	112	4.3	27	106	4.1	419	16.1
4 Years	103	97	3532	554	1309	.423	134	401	.334	339	485	.699	364	235	35	285	13	458	4.4	134	412	4.0	1581	15.3

NBA			Field Goals			3-Pt FGs			Free Throws			Misc			Fouls		Assists		Rebounds			Points	
Year Tm	G	GS	Min	Md	Att	Pct	Md	Att	Pct	Md	Att	Pct	TO	Stl	Blk	PF	DQ	Ast	Avg	Off	Tot	Avg	Pts	Avg
99-00 GS	75	11	1793	265	655	.405	49	151	.325	127	169	.751	132	91	13	174	4	247	3.3	57	184	2.5	706	9.4

Bill Curley

Pos: F **College:** Boston College **Drafted:** '94 1(22)—SA **Ht:** 6'9" **Wt:** 245 **Born:** 5/29/72 **Age:** 28

College			Field Goals			3-Pt FGs			Free Throws			Misc			Fouls		Assists		Rebounds			Points	
Year Tm	G	GS	Min	Md	Att	Pct	Md	Att	Pct	Md	Att	Pct	TO	Stl	Blk	PF	DQ	Ast	Avg	Off	Tot	Avg	Pts	Avg
90-91 BC	30	27	873	141	260	.542	0	3	.000	96	139	.691	77	36	6	103	7	38	1.3	93	206	6.9	378	12.6
91-92 BC	31	31	1051	187	324	.577	0	1	.000	178	230	.774	88	26	25	115	3	29	0.9	68	250	8.1	552	17.8
92-93 BC	31	31	1052	181	312	.580	0	0	—	129	152	.849	69	32	29	93	5	37	1.2	78	235	7.6	491	15.8
93-94 BC	34	34	1140	233	418	.557	0	1	.000	215	271	.793	74	27	28	96	4	54	1.6	110	305	9.0	681	20.0
4 Years	126	123	4116	742	1314	.565	0	5	.000	618	792	.780	308	121	88	407	19	158	1.3	349	996	7.9	2102	16.7

NBA			Field Goals			3-Pt FGs			Free Throws			Misc			Fouls		Assists		Rebounds			Points	
Year Tm	G	GS	Min	Md	Att	Pct	Md	Att	Pct	Md	Att	Pct	TO	Stl	Blk	PF	DQ	Ast	Avg	Off	Tot	Avg	Pts	Avg
94-95 Det	53	1	595	58	134	.433	0	0	—	27	36	.750	25	21	21	128	3	25	0.5	54	124	2.3	143	2.7
95-96 Por							Did not play: injury — Left Ankle																	
96-97 Min							Did not play: injury — Right Knee																	
97-98 Min	11	1	146	16	33	.485	0	1	.000	2	3	.667	3	3	1	28	1	4	0.4	11	28	2.5	34	3.1
98-99 Min	35	7	372	29	72	.403	1	5	.200	19	22	.864	10	17	9	83	1	14	0.4	20	51	1.5	78	2.2
99-00 2Tm	28	0	309	29	68	.426	0	1	.000	18	25	.720	21	13	4	61	2	14	0.5	18	50	1.8	76	2.7
99-00 GS	24	0	259	23	57	.404	0	1	.000	18	25	.720	17	11	4	51	1	14	0.6	14	42	1.8	64	2.7
Hou	4	0	50	6	11	.545	0	0	—	0	0	—	4	2	0	10	1	0	0.0	4	8	2.0	12	3.0
4 Years	127	9	1422	132	307	.430	1	7	.143	66	86	.767	59	54	35	300	7	57	0.4	103	253	2.0	331	2.6

NBA Postseason			Field Goals			3-Pt FGs			Free Throws			Misc			Fouls		Assists		Rebounds			Points	
Year Tm	G	GS	Min	Md	Att	Pct	Md	Att	Pct	Md	Att	Pct	TO	Stl	Blk	PF	DQ	Ast	Avg	Off	Tot	Avg	Pts	Avg
97-98 Min	2	0	7	0	0	—	0	0	—	0	0	—	0	0	0	0	0	0	0.0	0	0	0.0	0	0.0

Dell Curry

Pos: G **College:** Virginia Tech **Drafted:** '86 1(15)—Uta **Ht:** 6'5" **Wt:** 205 **Born:** 6/25/64 **Age:** 36

College			Field Goals			3-Pt FGs			Free Throws			Misc			Fouls		Assists		Rebounds			Points	
Year Tm	G	GS	Min	Md	Att	Pct	Md	Att	Pct	Md	Att	Pct	TO	Stl	Blk	PF	DQ	Ast	Avg	Off	Tot	Avg	Pts	Avg
82-83 VTch	32	—	1024	198	417	.475	—	—	—	68	80	.850	101	58	20	78	—	107	3.3	—	95	3.0	464	14.5
83-84 VTch	35	—	1166	293	561	.522	—	—	—	88	116	.759	113	89	22	85	—	96	2.7	—	143	4.1	674	19.3
84-85 VTch	29	—	968	225	467	.482	4	7	.571	75	99	.758	85	69	19	90	—	91	3.1	—	169	5.8	529	18.2
85-86 VTch	30	—	1117	305	577	.529	—	—	—	112	142	.789	89	79	19	80	—	113	3.8	—	203	6.8	722	24.1
4 Years	126	—	4275	1021	2022	.505	4	7	.571	343	437	.785	388	295	80	333	—	407	3.2	—	610	4.8	2389	19.0

NBA			Field Goals			3-Pt FGs			Free Throws			Misc			Fouls		Assists		Rebounds			Points	
Year Tm	G	GS	Min	Md	Att	Pct	Md	Att	Pct	Md	Att	Pct	TO	Stl	Blk	PF	DQ	Ast	Avg	Off	Tot	Avg	Pts	Avg
86-87 Uta	67	0	636	139	326	.426	17	60	.283	30	38	.789	44	27	4	86	0	58	0.9	30	78	1.2	325	4.9
87-88 Cle	79	8	1499	340	742	.458	28	81	.346	79	101	.782	108	94	22	128	0	149	1.9	43	166	2.1	787	10.0
88-89 Cha	48	0	813	256	521	.491	19	55	.345	40	46	.870	44	42	4	68	0	50	1.0	26	104	2.2	571	11.9
89-90 Cha	67	13	1860	461	990	.466	52	147	.354	96	104	.923	100	98	26	148	0	159	2.4	31	168	2.5	1070	16.0
90-91 Cha	76	14	1515	337	715	.471	32	86	.372	96	114	.842	80	75	25	125	0	166	2.2	47	199	2.6	802	10.6
91-92 Cha	77	0	2020	504	1038	.486	74	183	.404	127	152	.836	134	93	20	156	1	177	2.3	57	259	3.4	1209	15.7
92-93 Cha	80	0	2094	498	1102	.452	95	237	.401	136	157	.866	129	87	23	150	1	180	2.3	51	286	3.6	1227	15.3
93-94 Cha	82	0	2173	533	1171	.455	152	378	.402	117	134	.873	120	98	27	161	0	221	2.7	71	262	3.2	1335	16.3
94-95 Cha	69	0	1718	343	778	.441	154	361	.427	95	111	.856	98	55	18	144	1	113	1.6	41	168	2.4	935	13.6
95-96 Cha	82	29	2371	441	974	.453	164	406	.404	146	171	.854	130	108	25	173	2	176	2.1	68	264	3.2	1192	14.5
96-97 Cha	68	20	2078	384	836	.459	126	296	.426	114	142	.803	93	60	14	147	0	118	1.7	40	211	3.1	1008	14.8
97-98 Cha	52	1	971	194	434	.447	61	145	.421	41	52	.788	54	31	4	85	2	69	1.3	26	101	1.9	490	9.4
98-99 Mil	42	0	864	163	336	.485	69	145	.476	28	34	.824	45	36	3	43	0	48	1.1	18	85	2.0	423	10.1
99-00 Tor	67	9	1095	194	454	.427	95	242	.393	24	32	.750	40	32	9	66	0	89	1.3	11	100	1.5	507	7.6
14 Years	956	94	21707	4787	10417	.460	1138	2822	.403	1169	1388	.842	1219	936	224	1680	7	1773	1.9	560	2451	2.6	11881	12.4

NBA Postseason			Field Goals			3-Pt FGs			Free Throws			Misc			Fouls		Assists		Rebounds			Points	
Year Tm	G	GS	Min	Md	Att	Pct	Md	Att	Pct	Md	Att	Pct	TO	Stl	Blk	PF	DQ	Ast	Avg	Off	Tot	Avg	Pts	Avg
86-87 Uta	2	0	4	0	3	.000	0	1	.000	0	0	—	0	0	0	1	0	0	0.0	0	0	0.0	0	0.0
87-88 Cle	2	0	17	1	4	.250	0	1	.000	0	0	—	0	0	1	1	0	2	1.0	1	1	0.5	2	1.0
92-93 Cha	9	0	222	42	97	.433	6	21	.286	9	11	.818	13	13	0	19	0	18	2.0	11	32	3.6	99	11.0
94-95 Cha	4	0	107	16	34	.471	9	21	.429	10	11	.909	6	0	0	11	0	6	1.5	5	9	2.3	51	12.8
96-97 Cha	3	1	50	5	17	.294	1	4	.250	3	3	1.000	1	4	0	5	0	5	1.7	1	1	0.3	14	4.7
97-98 Cha	9	0	171	21	52	.404	4	16	.250	6	7	.857	5	7	3	21	0	10	1.1	6	19	2.1	52	5.8
98-99 Mil	3	0	49	2	15	.133	1	8	.125	4	4	1.000	0	3	0	5	0	1	0.3	0	4	1.3	9	3.0
99-00 Tor	3	0	30	2	4	.500	2	3	.667	1	2	.500	2	2	0	4	0	1	0.3	1	2	0.7	7	2.3
8 Years	35	1	650	89	226	.394	23	75	.307	33	38	.868	27	29	4	67	0	43	1.2	25	68	1.9	234	6.7

Michael Curry

(statistical profile on page 206)

Pos: F **College:** Georgia Southern **Drafted:** '93 FA—Phi   **Ht:** 6'5" **Wt:** 210 **Born:** 8/22/68 **Age:** 32

	College				Field Goals			3-Pt FGs			Free Throws			Misc			Fouls		Assists		Rebounds			Points	
Year Tm	G	GS	Min	Md	Att	Pct	Md	Att	Pct	Md	Att	Pct	TO	Stl	Blk	PF	DQ	Ast	Avg	Off	Tot	Avg	Pts	Avg
86-87 GaSo	31	—	594	59	116	.509	—	—	—	31	45	.689	—	—	—	—	—	29	0.9	—	87	2.8	149	4.8
87-88 GaSo	31	—	836	82	151	.543	1	6	.167	33	51	.647	—	—	—	—	—	44	1.4	—	154	5.0	198	6.4
88-89 GaSo	29	—	1014	117	219	.534	0	3	.000	75	108	.694	—	—	—	—	—	89	3.1	—	211	7.3	309	10.7
89-90 GaSo	28	—	926	164	264	.621	0	3	.000	137	170	.806	—	—	—	—	—	58	2.1	—	196	7.0	465	16.6
4 Years	119	—	3370	422	750	.563	—	—	—	276	374	.738	—	—	—	—	—	220	1.8	—	648	5.4	1121	9.4

	NBA				Field Goals			3-Pt FGs			Free Throws			Misc			Fouls		Assists		Rebounds			Points	
Year Tm	G	GS	Min	Md	Att	Pct	Md	Att	Pct	Md	Att	Pct	TO	Stl	Blk	PF	DQ	Ast	Avg	Off	Tot	Avg	Pts	Avg
90-91										Played in Germany, Played in Belgium, Played in France														
91-92										Played in Germany, Played in Belgium, Played in France														
92-93										Played in CBA, Played in USBL														
93-94 Phi	10	0	43	3	14	.214	0	2	.000	3	4	.750	3	1	0	6	0	1	0.1	0	1	0.1	9	0.9
94-95										Played in CBA														
95-96 2Tm	46	1	783	73	161	.453	20	53	.377	45	62	.726	24	24	2	92	1	27	0.6	27	85	1.8	211	4.6
96-97 Det	81	2	1217	99	221	.448	23	77	.299	97	108	.898	28	31	12	128	0	43	0.5	23	119	1.5	318	3.9
97-98 Mil	82	27	1978	196	418	.469	4	9	.444	147	176	.835	77	56	14	218	1	137	1.7	26	98	1.2	543	6.6
98-99 Mil	50	4	1146	90	206	.437	1	15	.067	63	79	.797	37	42	7	134	0	78	1.6	19	108	2.2	244	4.9
99-00 Det	82	3	1611	182	379	.480	1	5	.200	141	168	.839	73	33	5	209	3	87	1.1	21	104	1.5	506	6.2
95-96 Was	5	0	34	3	10	.300	0	3	.000	4	4	1.000	1	1	0	3	0	1	0.2	2	5	1.0	10	2.0
Det	41	1	749	70	151	.464	20	50	.400	41	58	.707	23	23	2	89	1	26	0.6	25	80	2.0	201	4.9
6 Years	351	37	6778	643	1399	.460	49	161	.304	496	597	.831	242	187	40	787	5	373	1.1	116	515	1.5	1831	5.2

	NBA Postseason																							
Year Tm	G	GS	Min	Md	Att	Pct	Md	Att	Pct	Md	Att	Pct	TO	Stl	Blk	PF	DQ	Ast	Avg	Off	Tot	Avg	Pts	Avg
95-96 Det	3	0	43	3	7	.429	0	1	.000	0	0	—	0	1	1	5	0	1	0.3	1	3	1.0	6	2.0
96-97 Det	2	0	7	1	2	.500	0	0	—	0	1	.000	0	0	0	1	0	0	0.0	0	1	0.5	2	1.0
98-99 Mil	3	0	59	7	12	.583	0	1	.000	6	6	1.000	2	2	1	8	0	3	1.0	1	4	1.3	20	6.7
99-00 Det	3	1	79	12	23	.522	0	0	—	4	6	.667	2	1	1	5	0	3	1.0	0	3	1.0	28	9.3
4 Years	11	1	188	23	44	.523	0	2	.000	10	13	.769	4	4	3	19	0	7	0.6	2	11	1.0	56	5.1

Erick Dampier

Pos: C **College:** Mississippi State **Drafted:** '96 1(10)—Ind   **Ht:** 6'11" **Wt:** 265 **Born:** 7/14/74 **Age:** 26

	College				Field Goals			3-Pt FGs			Free Throws			Misc			Fouls		Assists		Rebounds			Points	
Year Tm	G	GS	Min	Md	Att	Pct	Md	Att	Pct	Md	Att	Pct	TO	Stl	Blk	PF	DQ	Ast	Avg	Off	Tot	Avg	Pts	Avg
93-94 MisSt	29	—	678	133	226	.588	0	0	—	78	159	.491	70	17	65	82	—	23	0.8	—	251	8.7	344	11.9
94-95 MisSt	30	—	853	153	239	.640	0	0	—	87	146	.596	80	25	78	99	—	28	0.9	—	291	9.7	393	13.1
95-96 MisSt	34	34	1112	195	354	.551	0	0	—	104	170	.612	93	16	106	86	1	77	2.3	125	317	9.3	494	14.5
3 Years	93	—	2643	481	819	.587	0	0	—	269	475	.566	243	58	249	267	—	128	1.4	—	859	9.2	1231	13.2

	NBA				Field Goals			3-Pt FGs			Free Throws			Misc			Fouls		Assists		Rebounds			Points	
Year Tm	G	GS	Min	Md	Att	Pct	Md	Att	Pct	Md	Att	Pct	TO	Stl	Blk	PF	DQ	Ast	Avg	Off	Tot	Avg	Pts	Avg
96-97 Ind	72	21	1052	131	336	.390	1	1	1.000	107	168	.637	84	19	73	153	1	43	0.6	96	294	4.1	370	5.1
97-98 GS	82	82	2656	352	791	.445	0	2	.000	267	399	.669	175	39	139	281	6	94	1.1	272	715	8.7	971	11.8
98-99 GS	50	50	1414	161	414	.389	0	0	—	120	204	.588	92	26	58	165	2	54	1.1	164	382	7.6	442	8.8
99-00 GS	21	12	495	70	173	.405	0	0	—	27	51	.529	29	8	15	75	1	19	0.9	48	134	6.4	167	8.0
4 Years	225	165	5617	714	1714	.417	1	3	.333	521	822	.634	380	92	285	674	10	210	0.9	580	1525	6.8	1950	8.7

Antonio Daniels

Pos: G **College:** Bowling Green **Drafted:** '97 1(4)—Van   **Ht:** 6'4" **Wt:** 205 **Born:** 3/19/75 **Age:** 25

	College				Field Goals			3-Pt FGs			Free Throws			Misc			Fouls		Assists		Rebounds			Points	
Year Tm	G	GS	Min	Md	Att	Pct	Md	Att	Pct	Md	Att	Pct	TO	Stl	Blk	PF	DQ	Ast	Avg	Off	Tot	Avg	Pts	Avg
93-94 BlGr	28	19	864	132	258	.512	6	19	.316	84	103	.816	67	28	5	38	—	110	3.9	—	81	2.9	354	12.6
94-95 BlGr	26	22	753	97	196	.495	16	38	.421	58	83	.699	74	18	4	32	—	100	3.8	—	73	2.8	268	10.3
95-96 BlGr	25	25	922	142	297	.478	17	51	.333	99	137	.723	70	47	11	46	0	147	5.9	—	77	3.1	400	16.0
96-97 BlGr	32	32	1161	279	510	.547	45	104	.433	164	211	.777	103	73	10	51	0	216	6.8	18	90	2.8	767	24.0
4 Years	111	98	3700	650	1261	.515	84	212	.396	405	534	.758	314	166	30	167	—	573	5.2	—	321	2.9	1789	16.1

	NBA				Field Goals			3-Pt FGs			Free Throws			Misc			Fouls		Assists		Rebounds			Points	
Year Tm	G	GS	Min	Md	Att	Pct	Md	Att	Pct	Md	Att	Pct	TO	Stl	Blk	PF	DQ	Ast	Avg	Off	Tot	Avg	Pts	Avg
97-98 Van	74	50	1956	228	548	.416	11	52	.212	112	170	.659	164	55	10	88	0	334	4.5	22	143	1.9	579	7.8
98-99 SA	47	0	614	83	183	.454	5	17	.294	49	65	.754	44	30	6	39	0	106	2.3	13	54	1.1	220	4.7
99-00 SA	68	1	1195	163	344	.474	22	66	.333	72	101	.713	58	55	5	73	0	177	2.6	16	86	1.3	420	6.2
3 Years	189	51	3765	474	1075	.441	38	135	.281	233	336	.693	266	140	21	200	0	617	3.3	51	283	1.5	1219	6.4

	NBA Postseason																							
Year Tm	G	GS	Min	Md	Att	Pct	Md	Att	Pct	Md	Att	Pct	TO	Stl	Blk	PF	DQ	Ast	Avg	Off	Tot	Avg	Pts	Avg
98-99 SA	15	0	106	9	21	.429	4	6	.667	5	6	.833	10	4	0	7	0	16	1.1	1	10	0.7	27	1.8
99-00 SA	4	0	82	9	23	.391	2	8	.250	9	13	.692	6	7	0	5	0	6	1.5	2	10	2.5	29	7.3
2 Years	19	0	188	18	44	.409	6	14	.429	14	19	.737	16	11	0	12	0	22	1.2	3	20	1.1	56	2.9

Kornel David

Pos: F **College:** None **Drafted:** '98 FA—Chi **Ht:** 6'9" **Wt:** 230 **Born:** 10/22/71 **Age:** 29

	NBA		Field Goals			3-Pt FGs			Free Throws			Misc			Fouls		Assists		Rebounds			Points	
Year Tm	G	GS	Min	Md	Att	Pct	Md	Att	Pct	Md	Att	Pct	TO	Stl	Blk	PF	DQ	Ast	Avg	Off	Tot	Avg	Pts	Avg
97-98							Played in CBA, Played in Hungary																	
98-99 Chi	50	6	902	109	243	.449	0	1	.000	90	111	.811	48	23	17	88	0	40	0.8	70	173	3.5	308	6.2
99-00 2Tm	32	5	474	67	157	.427	0	3	.000	45	56	.804	33	17	3	56	0	17	0.5	26	81	2.5	179	5.6
99-00 Chi	26	5	443	63	148	.426	0	3	.000	42	52	.808	31	13	2	49	0	16	0.6	22	73	2.8	168	6.5
Cle	6	0	31	4	9	.444	0	0	—	3	4	.750	2	4	1	7	0	1	0.2	4	8	1.3	11	1.8
2 Years	82	11	1376	176	400	.440	0	4	.000	135	167	.808	81	40	20	144	0	57	0.7	96	254	3.1	487	5.9

Antonio Davis

(statistical profile on page 206)

Pos: F-C **College:** UTEP **Drafted:** '90 2(45)—Ind **Ht:** 6'9" **Wt:** 230 **Born:** 10/31/68 **Age:** 32

	College		Field Goals			3-Pt FGs			Free Throws			Misc			Fouls		Assists		Rebounds			Points	
Year Tm	G	GS	Min	Md	Att	Pct	Md	Att	Pct	Md	Att	Pct	TO	Stl	Blk	PF	DQ	Ast	Avg	Off	Tot	Avg	Pts	Avg
86-87 UTEP	28	—	240	11	32	.344	0	0	—	13	30	.433	11	6	8	25	—	4	0.1	—	51	1.8	35	1.3
87-88 UTEP	30	—	907	108	183	.590	0	0	—	63	115	.548	56	19	36	82	—	20	0.7	—	195	6.5	279	9.3
88-89 UTEP	32	—	1014	162	298	.544	0	1	.000	135	218	.619	52	12	36	74	—	14	0.4	—	255	8.0	459	14.3
89-90 UTEP	32	—	991	119	228	.522	0	1	.000	106	165	.642	55	17	36	90	—	21	0.7	—	243	7.6	344	10.8
4 Years	122	—	3152	400	741	.540	0	2	.000	317	528	.600	174	54	116	271	—	59	0.5	—	744	6.1	1117	9.2

	NBA		Field Goals			3-Pt FGs			Free Throws			Misc			Fouls		Assists		Rebounds			Points	
Year Tm	G	GS	Min	Md	Att	Pct	Md	Att	Pct	Md	Att	Pct	TO	Stl	Blk	PF	DQ	Ast	Avg	Off	Tot	Avg	Pts	Avg
90-91							Played in Greece																	
91-92							Played in Greece																	
92-93							Played in Italy																	
93-94 Ind	81	4	1732	216	425	.508	0	1	.000	194	302	.642	107	45	84	189	1	55	0.7	190	505	6.2	626	7.7
94-95 Ind	44	1	1030	109	245	.445	0	0	—	117	174	.672	64	19	29	134	2	25	0.6	105	280	6.4	335	7.6
95-96 Ind	82	14	2092	236	482	.490	1	2	.500	246	345	.713	87	33	66	248	6	43	0.5	188	501	6.1	719	8.8
96-97 Ind	82	28	2335	308	641	.480	1	14	.071	241	362	.666	141	42	84	260	4	65	0.8	190	598	7.3	858	10.5
97-98 Ind	82	12	2191	254	528	.481	0	3	.000	277	398	.696	103	45	72	234	0	61	0.7	192	560	6.8	785	9.6
98-99 Ind	49	1	1271	164	348	.471	0	0	—	135	192	.703	50	22	42	136	3	33	0.7	116	344	7.0	463	9.4
99-00 Tor	79	78	2479	313	712	.440	0	0	—	284	371	.765	121	38	100	267	2	105	1.3	235	696	8.8	910	11.5
7 Years	499	138	13130	1600	3381	.473	2	20	.100	1494	2144	.697	673	244	477	1468	24	387	0.8	1216	3484	7.0	4696	9.4

	NBA Postseason																							
Year Tm	G	GS	Min	Md	Att	Pct	Md	Att	Pct	Md	Att	Pct	TO	Stl	Blk	PF	DQ	Ast	Avg	Off	Tot	Avg	Pts	Avg
93-94 Ind	16	0	401	48	89	.539	1	1	1.000	37	66	.561	22	11	18	47	0	7	0.4	37	106	6.6	134	8.4
94-95 Ind	17	0	367	32	71	.451	0	0	—	37	59	.627	23	9	11	61	0	7	0.4	38	97	5.7	101	5.9
95-96 Ind	5	0	127	13	25	.520	0	0	—	13	15	.867	10	3	6	12	0	3	0.6	12	31	6.2	39	7.8
97-98 Ind	16	0	459	42	91	.462	0	0	—	63	94	.670	25	12	18	65	5	14	0.9	37	108	6.8	147	9.2
98-99 Ind	13	0	326	31	75	.413	0	0	—	41	62	.661	20	5	14	39	0	8	0.6	23	92	7.1	103	7.9
99-00 Tor	3	3	105	14	24	.583	0	0	—	11	14	.786	4	1	4	9	0	3	1.0	7	25	8.3	39	13.0
6 Years	70	3	1785	180	375	.480	1	1	1.000	202	310	.652	104	41	71	233	5	42	0.6	154	459	6.6	563	8.0

Baron Davis

(statistical profile on page 207)

Pos: G **College:** UCLA **Drafted:** '99 1(3)—Cha **Ht:** 6'3" **Wt:** 210 **Born:** 4/13/79 **Age:** 21

	College		Field Goals			3-Pt FGs			Free Throws			Misc			Fouls		Assists		Rebounds			Points	
Year Tm	G	GS	Min	Md	Att	Pct	Md	Att	Pct	Md	Att	Pct	TO	Stl	Blk	PF	DQ	Ast	Avg	Off	Tot	Avg	Pts	Avg
97-98 UCLA	32	31	1003	137	259	.529	24	78	.308	75	111	.676	99	77	12	113	9	161	5.0	37	129	4.0	373	11.7
98-99 UCLA	27	26	828	150	312	.481	35	102	.343	94	157	.599	89	68	10	94	8	138	5.1	39	97	3.6	429	15.9
2 Years	59	57	1831	287	571	.503	59	180	.328	169	268	.631	188	145	22	207	17	299	5.1	76	226	3.8	802	13.6

	NBA		Field Goals			3-Pt FGs			Free Throws			Misc			Fouls		Assists		Rebounds			Points	
Year Tm	G	GS	Min	Md	Att	Pct	Md	Att	Pct	Md	Att	Pct	TO	Stl	Blk	PF	DQ	Ast	Avg	Off	Tot	Avg	Pts	Avg
99-00 Cha	82	0	1523	182	433	.420	25	111	.225	97	153	.634	140	97	19	201	1	309	3.8	48	165	2.0	486	5.9

	NBA Postseason																							
Year Tm	G	GS	Min	Md	Att	Pct	Md	Att	Pct	Md	Att	Pct	TO	Stl	Blk	PF	DQ	Ast	Avg	Off	Tot	Avg	Pts	Avg
99-00 Cha	4	0	57	10	23	.435	1	6	.167	2	4	.500	3	4	0	6	0	6	1.5	3	6	1.5	23	5.8

Ben Davis

Pos: F **College:** Arizona **Drafted:** '96 2(43)—Pho   **Ht:** 6'9" **Wt:** 240 **Born:** 12/26/72 **Age:** 28

Year Tm	G	GS	Min	Field Goals Md	Att	Pct	3-Pt FGs Md	Att	Pct	Free Throws Md	Att	Pct	Misc TO	Stl	Blk	Fouls PF	DQ	Assists Ast	Avg	Rebounds Off	Tot	Avg	Points Pts	Avg
College																								
91-92 Kan	32	7	564	82	173	.474	0	0	—	48	92	.522	41	18	7	89	3	15	0.5	—	145	4.5	212	6.6
94-95 Ari	21	7	440	85	158	.538	0	0	—	38	60	.633	34	11	5	53	0	8	0.4	44	124	5.9	208	9.9
95-96 Ari	33	33	1039	171	313	.546	0	0	—	127	184	.690	77	20	32	91	1	23	0.7	97	313	9.5	469	14.2
3 Years	86	47	2043	338	644	.525	0	0	—	213	336	.634	152	49	44	233	4	46	0.5	—	582	6.8	889	10.3
NBA																								
96-97 Pho	20	0	98	10	26	.385	0	0	—	9	20	.450	3	4	1	16	0	0	0.0	12	27	1.4	29	1.5
97-98 NY	7	0	13	2	10	.200	0	0	—	0	0	—	0	1	0	3	0	0	0.0	6	6	0.9	4	0.6
98-99 NY	8	0	21	7	17	.412	0	0	—	3	6	.500	1	0	0	4	0	3	0.4	9	11	1.4	17	2.1
99-00 Pho	5	0	22	2	6	.333	0	0	—	0	0	—	3	1	1	2	0	2	0.4	3	9	1.8	4	0.8
4 Years	40	0	154	21	59	.356	0	0	—	12	26	.462	7	6	2	25	0	5	0.1	30	53	1.3	54	1.4

Dale Davis

Pos: F **College:** Clemson **Drafted:** '91 1(13)—Ind   **Ht:** 6'11" **Wt:** 252 **Born:** 3/25/69 **Age:** 31   (statistical profile on page 207)

Year Tm	G	GS	Min	Field Goals Md	Att	Pct	3-Pt FGs Md	Att	Pct	Free Throws Md	Att	Pct	Misc TO	Stl	Blk	Fouls PF	DQ	Assists Ast	Avg	Rebounds Off	Tot	Avg	Points Pts	Avg
College																								
87-88 Clem	29	21	714	91	171	.532	0	0	—	45	89	.506	34	16	38	80	—	10	0.3	97	223	7.7	227	7.8
88-89 Clem	29	14	736	146	218	.670	0	0	—	93	144	.646	34	17	40	77	—	16	0.6	100	258	8.9	385	13.3
89-90 Clem	35	34	1077	205	328	.625	0	1	.000	127	213	.596	55	36	58	97	—	16	0.6	166	395	11.3	537	15.3
90-91 Clem	28	28	971	191	359	.532	0	2	.000	119	205	.580	66	37	74	94	—	21	0.6	122	340	12.1	501	17.9
4 Years	121	97	3498	633	1076	.588	0	3	.000	384	651	.590	189	106	210	348	—	84	0.7	485	1216	10.0	1650	13.6
NBA																								
91-92 Ind	64	23	1301	154	279	.552	0	1	.000	87	152	.572	49	27	74	191	2	30	0.5	158	410	6.4	395	6.2
92-93 Ind	82	82	2264	304	535	.568	0	0	—	119	225	.529	79	63	148	274	5	69	0.8	291	723	8.8	727	8.9
93-94 Ind	66	64	2292	308	582	.529	0	1	.000	155	294	.527	102	48	106	214	1	100	1.5	280	718	10.9	771	11.7
94-95 Ind	74	70	2346	324	576	.563	0	1	.000	138	259	.533	124	72	116	222	2	58	0.8	259	696	9.4	786	10.6
95-96 Ind	78	77	2617	334	599	.558	0	0	—	135	289	.467	119	56	112	238	0	76	1.0	252	709	9.1	803	10.3
96-97 Ind	80	76	2589	370	688	.538	0	0	—	92	215	.428	108	60	77	233	3	59	0.7	301	772	9.7	832	10.4
97-98 Ind	78	78	2174	273	498	.548	0	0	—	80	172	.465	73	51	87	209	1	70	0.9	233	611	7.8	626	8.0
98-99 Ind	50	50	1374	161	302	.533	0	0	—	76	123	.618	43	20	57	115	0	22	0.4	155	416	8.3	398	8.0
99-00 Ind*	74	72	2127	302	602	.502	0	0	—	139	203	.685	91	52	94	203	1	64	0.9	256	729	9.9	743	10.0
9 Years	646	592	19084	2530	4661	.543	0	3	.000	1021	1932	.528	788	449	871	1899	15	548	0.8	2185	5784	9.0	6081	9.4
NBA Postseason																								
91-92 Ind	3	0	69	4	10	.400	0	0	—	0	0	—	1	0	5	8	0	2	0.7	5	19	6.3	8	2.7
92-93 Ind	4	4	117	8	12	.667	0	0	—	1	4	.250	3	4	4	15	0	4	1.0	4	32	8.0	17	4.3
93-94 Ind	16	16	578	56	106	.528	0	1	.000	11	36	.306	30	18	17	52	0	11	0.7	63	159	9.9	123	7.7
94-95 Ind	17	17	490	56	105	.533	0	0	—	23	47	.489	22	7	14	56	0	6	0.4	53	136	8.0	135	7.9
95-96 Ind	5	5	184	16	31	.516	0	0	—	4	11	.364	10	3	6	16	0	4	0.8	20	56	11.2	36	7.2
97-98 Ind	16	16	466	56	86	.651	0	0	—	29	64	.453	21	5	18	42	0	12	0.8	44	120	7.5	141	8.8
98-99 Ind	13	13	394	45	77	.584	0	0	—	28	50	.560	21	10	18	42	0	11	0.8	45	132	10.2	118	9.1
99-00 Ind	23	23	714	79	151	.523	0	0	—	32	59	.542	18	11	31	83	4	17	0.7	83	263	11.4	190	8.3
8 Years	97	94	3012	320	578	.554	0	1	.000	128	271	.472	126	58	113	314	4	67	0.7	317	917	9.5	768	7.9

Emanual Davis

Pos: G **College:** Delaware State **Drafted:** '96 FA—Hou   **Ht:** 6'5" **Wt:** 195 **Born:** 8/27/68 **Age:** 32

Year Tm	G	GS	Min	Field Goals Md	Att	Pct	3-Pt FGs Md	Att	Pct	Free Throws Md	Att	Pct	Misc TO	Stl	Blk	Fouls PF	DQ	Assists Ast	Avg	Rebounds Off	Tot	Avg	Points Pts	Avg
College																								
88-89 DeSt	19	—	—	126	285	.442	58	172	.337	80	119	.672	77	42	13	50	—	83	4.4	—	128	6.7	390	20.5
89-90 DeSt	28	—	—	119	259	.459	54	138	.391	94	126	.746	—	57	19	—	—	156	5.6	—	135	4.8	386	13.8
90-91 DeSt	25	—	838	165	328	.503	41	106	.387	122	163	.748	94	84	13	78	—	139	5.6	—	118	4.7	493	19.7
3 Years	72	—	—	410	872	.470	153	416	.368	296	408	.725	—	183	45	—	—	378	5.3	—	381	5.3	1269	17.6
NBA																								
91-92										Played in USBL														
92-93										Played in American Basketball Assoc., Played in CBA														
93-94										Played in CBA														
94-95										Played in Italy														

NBA			Field Goals			3-Pt FGs			Free Throws			Misc			Fouls		Assists		Rebounds			Points	
Year Tm	G	GS	Min	Md	Att	Pct	Md	Att	Pct	Md	Att	Pct	TO	Stl	Blk	PF	DQ	Ast	Avg	Off	Tot	Avg	Pts	Avg
95-96									Played in CBA															
96-97 Hou	13	0	230	24	54	.444	12	27	.444	5	8	.625	17	9	2	20	0	26	2.0	2	22	1.7	65	5.0
97-98 Hou	45	0	599	63	142	.444	27	72	.375	31	37	.838	52	17	3	55	0	59	1.3	10	47	1.0	184	4.1
98-99									Played in France															
99-00 Sea	54	2	701	80	220	.364	31	103	.301	26	38	.684	44	38	5	72	0	70	1.3	15	100	1.9	217	4.0
3 Years	112	2	1530	167	416	.401	70	202	.347	62	83	.747	113	64	10	147	0	155	1.4	27	169	1.5	466	4.2

Hubert Davis

(statistical profile on page 208)

Pos: G **College:** North Carolina **Drafted:** '92 1(20)—NY   **Ht:** 6'5" **Wt:** 183 **Born:** 5/17/70 **Age:** 30

College			Field Goals			3-Pt FGs			Free Throws			Misc			Fouls		Assists		Rebounds			Points	
Year Tm	G	GS	Min	Md	Att	Pct	Md	Att	Pct	Md	Att	Pct	TO	Stl	Blk	PF	DQ	Ast	Avg	Off	Tot	Avg	Pts	Avg
88-89 UNC	35	0	248	44	86	.512	4	13	.308	24	31	.774	12	3	1	10	—	9	0.3	12	27	0.8	116	3.3
89-90 UNC	34	6	725	111	249	.446	44	111	.396	59	74	.797	31	33	6	42	—	52	1.5	27	60	1.8	325	9.6
90-91 UNC	35	20	851	161	309	.521	64	131	.489	81	97	.835	37	30	9	35	—	66	1.9	32	85	2.4	467	13.3
91-92 UNC	33	30	1095	241	474	.508	85	198	.429	140	169	.828	45	42	7	42	—	52	1.6	27	76	2.3	707	21.4
4 Years	137	56	2919	557	1118	.498	197	453	.435	304	371	.819	125	108	23	129	—	179	1.3	98	248	1.8	1615	11.8

NBA			Field Goals			3-Pt FGs			Free Throws			Misc			Fouls		Assists		Rebounds			Points	
Year Tm	G	GS	Min	Md	Att	Pct	Md	Att	Pct	Md	Att	Pct	TO	Stl	Blk	PF	DQ	Ast	Avg	Off	Tot	Avg	Pts	Avg
92-93 NY	50	2	815	110	251	.438	6	19	.316	43	54	.796	45	22	4	71	1	83	1.7	13	56	1.1	269	5.4
93-94 NY	56	27	1333	238	505	.471	53	132	.402	85	103	.825	76	40	4	118	0	165	2.9	23	67	1.2	614	11.0
94-95 NY	82	4	1697	296	617	.480	131	288	.455	97	120	.808	87	35	11	146	1	150	1.8	30	110	1.3	820	10.0
95-96 NY	74	14	1773	275	566	.486	127	267	.476	112	129	.868	63	31	8	120	1	103	1.4	35	123	1.7	789	10.7
96-97 Tor	36	0	623	74	184	.402	16	70	.229	17	23	.739	21	11	2	40	0	34	0.9	11	40	1.1	181	5.0
97-98 Dal	81	30	2378	350	767	.456	101	230	.439	97	116	.836	88	43	5	117	0	157	1.9	34	169	2.1	898	11.1
98-99 Dal	50	21	1378	174	397	.438	65	144	.451	44	50	.880	57	21	3	76	0	89	1.8	3	86	1.7	457	9.1
99-00 Dal	79	15	1817	217	464	.468	82	167	.491	67	77	.870	70	24	3	109	0	141	1.8	17	134	1.7	583	7.4
8 Years	508	113	11814	1734	3751	.462	581	1317	.441	562	672	.836	507	227	40	797	3	922	1.8	166	785	1.5	4611	9.1

NBA Postseason																							
Year Tm	G	GS	Min	Md	Att	Pct	Md	Att	Pct	Md	Att	Pct	TO	Stl	Blk	PF	DQ	Ast	Avg	Off	Tot	Avg	Pts	Avg
92-93 NY	7	0	96	14	25	.560	1	2	.500	2	3	.667	9	6	0	8	0	5	0.7	1	6	0.9	31	4.4
93-94 NY	23	7	396	44	121	.364	10	35	.286	23	32	.719	23	5	3	43	0	26	1.1	5	21	0.9	121	5.3
94-95 NY	11	0	184	17	48	.354	10	27	.370	2	2	1.000	9	1	5	20	0	10	0.9	0	7	0.6	46	4.2
95-96 NY	8	0	145	17	31	.548	10	19	.526	9	11	.818	7	0	0	12	0	4	0.5	4	12	1.5	53	6.6
4 Years	49	7	821	92	225	.409	31	83	.373	36	48	.750	48	12	8	83	0	45	0.9	10	46	0.9	251	5.1

Mark Davis

Pos: G-F **College:** Texas Tech **Drafted:** '95 2(48)—Min   **Ht:** 6'7" **Wt:** 205 **Born:** 4/26/73 **Age:** 27

College			Field Goals			3-Pt FGs			Free Throws			Misc			Fouls		Assists		Rebounds			Points	
Year Tm	G	GS	Min	Md	Att	Pct	Md	Att	Pct	Md	Att	Pct	TO	Stl	Blk	PF	DQ	Ast	Avg	Off	Tot	Avg	Pts	Avg
93-94 TxTch	28	28	995	186	375	.496	17	54	.315	130	197	.660	127	49	43	101	3	109	3.9	58	227	8.1	519	18.5
94-95 TxTch	30	29	971	199	399	.499	20	60	.333	102	166	.614	106	51	36	103	5	142	4.7	80	254	8.5	520	17.3
2 Years	58	57	1966	385	774	.497	37	114	.325	232	363	.639	233	100	79	204	8	251	4.3	138	481	8.3	1039	17.9

NBA			Field Goals			3-Pt FGs			Free Throws			Misc			Fouls		Assists		Rebounds			Points	
Year Tm	G	GS	Min	Md	Att	Pct	Md	Att	Pct	Md	Att	Pct	TO	Stl	Blk	PF	DQ	Ast	Avg	Off	Tot	Avg	Pts	Avg
95-96 Min	57	0	571	55	149	.369	4	13	.308	74	116	.638	68	40	22	92	1	47	0.8	56	125	2.2	188	3.3
96-97 Phi	75	17	1705	251	535	.469	24	93	.258	113	168	.673	118	85	31	230	7	135	1.8	138	323	4.3	639	8.5
97-98 Phi	71	12	906	109	244	.447	0	6	.000	64	101	.634	91	49	18	95	1	73	1.0	64	158	2.2	282	4.0
98-99 Mia	4	1	35	2	6	.333	0	0	—	5	6	.833	7	1	0	12	1	1	0.3	2	7	1.8	9	2.3
99-00 GS	23	7	464	56	137	.409	0	2	.000	31	47	.660	40	25	4	52	0	38	1.7	31	84	3.7	143	6.2
5 Years	230	37	3681	473	1071	.442	28	114	.246	287	438	.655	324	200	75	481	10	294	1.3	291	697	3.0	1261	5.5

Ricky Davis

Pos: G-F **College:** Iowa **Drafted:** '98 1(21)—Cha   **Ht:** 6'6" **Wt:** 195 **Born:** 9/23/79 **Age:** 21

College			Field Goals			3-Pt FGs			Free Throws			Misc			Fouls		Assists		Rebounds			Points	
Year Tm	G	GS	Min	Md	Att	Pct	Md	Att	Pct	Md	Att	Pct	TO	Stl	Blk	PF	DQ	Ast	Avg	Off	Tot	Avg	Pts	Avg
97-98 Iowa	31	26	825	173	371	.466	28	91	.308	90	129	.698	104	38	10	54	2	74	2.4	56	148	4.8	464	15.0

NBA			Field Goals			3-Pt FGs			Free Throws			Misc			Fouls		Assists		Rebounds			Points	
Year Tm	G	GS	Min	Md	Att	Pct	Md	Att	Pct	Md	Att	Pct	TO	Stl	Blk	PF	DQ	Ast	Avg	Off	Tot	Avg	Pts	Avg
98-99 Cha	46	1	557	81	200	.405	2	12	.167	45	59	.763	54	30	7	46	0	58	1.3	40	84	1.8	209	4.5
99-00 Cha	48	4	570	94	187	.503	0	4	.000	39	51	.765	46	30	8	39	0	62	1.3	29	83	1.7	227	4.7
2 Years	94	5	1127	175	387	.452	2	16	.125	84	110	.764	100	60	15	85	0	120	1.3	69	167	1.8	436	4.6

Todd Day

Pos: G **College:** Arkansas **Drafted:** '92 1(8)—Mil   **Ht:** 6'6" **Wt:** 195 **Born:** 1/7/70 **Age:** 31

College			Field Goals			3-Pt FGs			Free Throws			Misc			Fouls		Assists		Rebounds			Points	
Year Tm	G	GS	Min	Md	Att	Pct	Md	Att	Pct	Md	Att	Pct	TO	Stl	Blk	PF	DQ	Ast	Avg	Off	Tot	Avg	Pts	Avg
88-89 Ark	32	—	741	148	328	.451	31	90	.344	98	137	.715	73	48	27	86	—	49	1.5	—	129	4.0	425	13.3
89-90 Ark	35	34	1008	237	483	.491	71	176	.403	139	183	.760	83	82	33	93	—	89	2.5	—	188	5.4	684	19.5
90-91 Ark	38	—	1121	277	586	.473	67	189	.354	165	221	.747	99	85	25	93	—	111	2.9	—	201	5.3	786	20.7
91-92 Ark	22	—	711	173	347	.499	57	133	.429	97	127	.764	62	85	17	56	—	70	3.2	—	155	7.0	500	22.7
4 Years	127	—	3581	835	1744	.479	226	588	.384	499	668	.747	317	300	102	328	—	319	2.5	—	673	5.3	2395	18.9
NBA			**Field Goals**			**3-Pt FGs**			**Free Throws**			**Misc**			**Fouls**		**Assists**		**Rebounds**			**Points**	
Year Tm	G	GS	Min	Md	Att	Pct	Md	Att	Pct	Md	Att	Pct	TO	Stl	Blk	PF	DQ	Ast	Avg	Off	Tot	Avg	Pts	Avg
92-93 Mil	71	37	1931	358	828	.432	54	184	.293	213	297	.717	118	75	48	222	1	117	1.6	144	291	4.1	983	13.8
93-94 Mil	76	39	2127	351	845	.415	33	148	.223	231	331	.698	129	103	52	221	4	138	1.8	115	310	4.1	966	12.7
94-95 Mil	82	81	2717	445	1049	.424	163	418	.390	257	341	.754	157	104	63	283	6	134	1.6	95	322	3.9	1310	16.0
95-96 2Tm	79	12	1807	299	817	.366	100	302	.331	224	287	.780	109	81	51	225	2	107	1.4	70	224	2.8	922	11.7
96-97 Bos	81	27	2277	398	999	.398	126	348	.362	256	331	.773	127	108	48	208	0	117	1.4	109	330	4.1	1178	14.5
97-98 Mia	5	0	69	11	31	.355	2	12	.167	6	9	.667	3	7	0	10	0	7	1.4	4	6	1.2	30	6.0
98-99										Played in CBA														
99-00 Pho	58	1	941	130	330	.394	64	165	.388	72	108	.667	50	44	22	127	1	65	1.1	31	129	2.2	396	6.8
95-96 Mil	8	0	171	22	71	.310	5	25	.200	24	26	.923	11	4	3	27	1	5	0.6	8	22	2.8	73	9.1
Bos	71	12	1636	277	746	.371	95	277	.343	200	261	.766	98	77	48	198	1	102	1.4	62	202	2.8	849	12.0
7 Years	452	197	11869	1992	4899	.407	542	1577	.344	1259	1704	.739	693	522	284	1296	14	685	1.5	568	1612	3.6	5785	12.8
NBA Postseason																								
Year Tm	G	GS	Min	Md	Att	Pct	Md	Att	Pct	Md	Att	Pct	TO	Stl	Blk	PF	DQ	Ast	Avg	Off	Tot	Avg	Pts	Avg
99-00 Pho	9	0	100	16	35	.457	5	16	.313	5	10	.500	4	4	1	24	0	4	0.4	6	10	1.1	42	4.7

Andrew DeClercq

(statistical profile on page 208)

Pos: F-C **College:** Florida **Drafted:** '95 2(34)—GS   **Ht:** 6'10" **Wt:** 234 **Born:** 2/1/73 **Age:** 27

College			Field Goals			3-Pt FGs			Free Throws			Misc			Fouls		Assists		Rebounds			Points	
Year Tm	G	GS	Min	Md	Att	Pct	Md	Att	Pct	Md	Att	Pct	TO	Stl	Blk	PF	DQ	Ast	Avg	Off	Tot	Avg	Pts	Avg
91-92 Fla	33	—	825	117	231	.506	0	0	—	57	87	.655	67	19	47	106	—	26	0.8	—	203	6.2	291	8.8
92-93 Fla	28	—	715	118	208	.567	0	0	—	59	101	.584	59	47	44	93	—	15	0.5	—	198	7.1	295	10.5
93-94 Fla	37	—	998	129	237	.544	1	3	.333	68	104	.654	92	45	51	108	—	54	1.5	—	292	7.9	327	8.8
94-95 Fla	30	—	966	138	270	.511	5	15	.333	115	159	.723	85	36	34	101	—	42	1.4	—	265	8.8	396	13.2
4 Years	128	—	3504	502	946	.531	6	18	.333	299	451	.663	303	147	176	408	—	137	1.1	—	958	7.5	1309	10.2
NBA			**Field Goals**			**3-Pt FGs**			**Free Throws**			**Misc**			**Fouls**		**Assists**		**Rebounds**			**Points**	
Year Tm	G	GS	Min	Md	Att	Pct	Md	Att	Pct	Md	Att	Pct	TO	Stl	Blk	PF	DQ	Ast	Avg	Off	Tot	Avg	Pts	Avg
95-96 GS	22	1	203	24	50	.480	0	1	.000	11	19	.579	4	7	5	30	0	9	0.4	18	39	1.8	59	2.7
96-97 GS	71	1	1065	142	273	.520	0	0	—	91	151	.603	76	33	27	229	3	32	0.5	122	298	4.2	375	5.3
97-98 Bos	81	49	1523	169	340	.497	0	1	.000	101	168	.601	84	85	49	277	3	59	0.7	180	392	4.8	439	5.4
98-99 2Tm	47	32	1102	138	276	.500	0	0	—	95	141	.674	54	50	29	161	3	31	0.7	104	255	5.4	371	7.9
99-00 Cle	82	31	1831	225	443	.508	0	0	—	94	160	.588	108	63	66	275	6	58	0.7	156	439	5.4	544	6.6
98-99 Bos	14	1	258	28	57	.491	0	0	—	19	29	.655	22	13	9	51	1	10	0.7	33	63	4.5	75	5.4
Cle	33	31	844	110	219	.502	0	0	—	76	112	.679	32	37	20	110	2	21	0.6	71	192	5.8	296	9.0
5 Years	303	114	5724	698	1382	.505	0	2	.000	392	639	.613	326	238	176	972	15	189	0.6	580	1423	4.7	1788	5.9

Vinny Del Negro

(statistical profile on page 209)

Pos: G **College:** North Carolina State **Drafted:** '88 2(29)—Sac   **Ht:** 6'4" **Wt:** 200 **Born:** 8/9/66 **Age:** 34

College			Field Goals			3-Pt FGs			Free Throws			Misc			Fouls		Assists		Rebounds			Points	
Year Tm	G	GS	Min	Md	Att	Pct	Md	Att	Pct	Md	Att	Pct	TO	Stl	Blk	PF	DQ	Ast	Avg	Off	Tot	Avg	Pts	Avg
84-85 NCSt	19	0	125	12	21	.571	—	—	—	15	23	.652	14	4	0	14	—	22	1.2	—	14	0.7	39	2.1
85-86 NCSt	17	0	139	11	30	.367	—	—	—	7	11	.636	8	9	1	14	—	31	1.8	—	14	0.8	29	1.7
86-87 NCSt	35	21	918	133	269	.494	36	72	.500	63	71	.887	48	22	4	60	—	102	2.9	—	115	3.3	365	10.4
87-88 NCSt	32	32	1093	187	363	.515	31	78	.397	104	124	.839	48	56	6	64	—	115	3.6	—	158	4.9	509	15.9
4 Years	103	53	2275	343	683	.502	67	150	.447	189	229	.825	118	91	11	152	—	270	2.6	—	301	2.9	942	9.1
NBA			**Field Goals**			**3-Pt FGs**			**Free Throws**			**Misc**			**Fouls**		**Assists**		**Rebounds**			**Points**	
Year Tm	G	GS	Min	Md	Att	Pct	Md	Att	Pct	Md	Att	Pct	TO	Stl	Blk	PF	DQ	Ast	Avg	Off	Tot	Avg	Pts	Avg
88-89 Sac	80	2	1556	239	503	.475	6	20	.300	85	100	.850	77	65	14	160	2	206	2.6	48	171	2.1	569	7.1
89-90 Sac	76	29	1858	297	643	.462	10	32	.313	135	155	.871	111	64	10	182	2	250	3.3	39	198	2.6	739	9.7
90-91										Played in Italy														
91-92										Played in Italy														
92-93 SA	73	31	1526	218	430	.507	6	24	.250	101	117	.863	92	44	1	146	0	291	4.0	19	163	2.2	543	7.4
93-94 SA	77	56	1949	309	634	.487	15	43	.349	140	170	.824	102	64	1	168	0	320	4.2	27	161	2.1	773	10.0

(continued)

NBA			Field Goals			3-Pt FGs			Free Throws			Misc			Fouls		Assists		Rebounds			Points	
Year Tm	G	GS	Min	Md	Att	Pct	Md	Att	Pct	Md	Att	Pct	TO	Stl	Blk	PF	DQ	Ast	Avg	Off	Tot	Avg	Pts	Avg
94-95 SA	75	71	2360	372	766	.486	66	162	.407	128	162	.790	56	61	14	179	0	226	3.0	28	192	2.6	938	12.5
95-96 SA	82	82	2766	478	962	.497	57	150	.380	178	214	.832	100	85	6	166	0	315	3.8	36	272	3.3	1191	14.5
96-97 SA	72	53	2243	365	781	.467	44	140	.314	112	129	.868	92	59	7	131	0	231	3.2	39	210	2.9	886	12.3
97-98 SA	54	38	1721	211	479	.441	17	39	.436	74	93	.796	53	39	6	113	0	183	3.4	13	152	2.8	513	9.5
98-99 Mil	48	7	1093	114	270	.422	13	30	.433	40	50	.800	55	33	3	62	0	174	3.6	14	102	2.1	281	5.9
99-00 Mil	67	0	1211	153	325	.471	8	24	.333	35	39	.897	48	36	0	81	0	160	2.4	9	107	1.6	349	5.2
10 Years	704	369	18283	2756	5793	.476	242	664	.364	1028	1229	.836	786	550	62	1388	4	2356	3.3	272	1728	2.5	6782	9.6

NBA Postseason

Year Tm	G	GS	Min	Md	Att	Pct	Md	Att	Pct	Md	Att	Pct	TO	Stl	Blk	PF	DQ	Ast	Avg	Off	Tot	Avg	Pts	Avg
92-93 SA	8	0	112	17	38	.447	2	9	.222	4	4	1.000	3	1	1	13	0	24	3.0	6	19	2.4	40	5.0
93-94 SA	4	4	93	12	27	.444	2	4	.500	3	5	.600	3	1	0	6	0	18	4.5	1	7	1.8	29	7.3
94-95 SA	15	15	382	51	118	.432	9	20	.450	20	24	.833	16	8	2	23	0	37	2.5	4	32	2.1	131	8.7
95-96 SA	10	10	379	57	124	.460	16	27	.593	13	19	.684	6	13	3	19	0	29	2.9	4	26	2.6	143	14.3
97-98 SA	9	3	283	39	81	.481	2	10	.200	16	17	.941	13	8	0	30	0	29	3.2	2	24	2.7	96	10.7
99-00 Mil	5	0	93	13	30	.433	0	2	.000	0	0	—	3	3	0	4	0	9	1.8	0	8	1.6	26	5.2
6 Years	51	32	1342	189	418	.452	31	72	.431	56	69	.812	47	34	6	95	0	146	2.9	17	116	2.3	465	9.1

Bison Dele

Pos: C **College:** Arizona **Drafted:** '91 1(10)—Orl **Ht:** 6'11" **Wt:** 260 **Born:** 4/6/69 **Age:** 31

College			Field Goals			3-Pt FGs			Free Throws			Misc			Fouls		Assists		Rebounds			Points	
Year Tm	G	GS	Min	Md	Att	Pct	Md	Att	Pct	Md	Att	Pct	TO	Stl	Blk	PF	DQ	Ast	Avg	Off	Tot	Avg	Pts	Avg
87-88 Myld	29	—	813	156	260	.600	0	0	—	51	76	.671	68	17	36	90	—	22	0.8	—	173	6.0	363	12.5
89-90 Ari	32	27	693	130	235	.553	0	1	.000	80	110	.727	48	19	41	87	3	14	0.4	63	181	5.7	340	10.6
90-91 Ari	35	32	878	195	315	.619	0	0	—	99	147	.673	73	29	39	95	3	21	0.6	96	273	7.8	489	14.0
3 Years	96	—	2384	481	810	.594	0	1	.000	230	333	.691	189	65	116	272	—	57	0.6	—	627	6.5	1192	12.4

NBA			Field Goals			3-Pt FGs			Free Throws			Misc			Fouls		Assists		Rebounds			Points	
Year Tm	G	GS	Min	Md	Att	Pct	Md	Att	Pct	Md	Att	Pct	TO	Stl	Blk	PF	DQ	Ast	Avg	Off	Tot	Avg	Pts	Avg
91-92 Orl	48	2	905	171	324	.528	0	0	—	95	142	.669	86	41	53	139	2	33	0.7	115	272	5.7	437	9.1
92-93 Orl	21	0	240	40	78	.513	0	1	.000	16	20	.800	25	14	17	48	2	5	0.2	24	56	2.7	96	4.6
93-94 Den	80	1	1507	251	464	.541	0	3	.000	137	211	.649	104	18	87	221	3	50	0.6	138	446	5.6	639	8.0
94-95 Den	63	10	1261	196	333	.589	0	0	—	106	162	.654	114	38	43	210	7	53	0.8	98	298	4.7	498	7.9
95-96 LAC	65	65	2157	416	766	.543	1	6	.167	196	267	.734	190	70	55	226	4	122	1.9	149	492	7.6	1029	15.8
96-97 Chi	9	0	138	26	63	.413	0	0	—	11	15	.733	11	3	5	20	0	12	1.3	14	33	3.7	63	7.0
97-98 Det	78	78	2619	531	1040	.511	1	3	.333	198	280	.707	181	67	55	252	4	94	1.2	223	695	8.9	1261	16.2
98-99 Det	49	48	1177	216	431	.501	0	1	.000	81	118	.686	111	38	40	181	3	71	1.4	92	272	5.6	513	10.5
99-00									Did not play basketball															
8 Years	413	204	10004	1847	3499	.528	2	14	.143	840	1215	.691	822	320	355	1297	26	440	1.1	853	2564	6.2	4536	11.0

NBA Postseason

Year Tm	G	GS	Min	Md	Att	Pct	Md	Att	Pct	Md	Att	Pct	TO	Stl	Blk	PF	DQ	Ast	Avg	Off	Tot	Avg	Pts	Avg
93-94 Den	12	0	289	42	76	.553	0	0	—	27	41	.659	17	4	11	36	0	11	0.9	33	89	7.4	111	9.3
94-95 Den	3	0	44	10	18	.556	0	0	—	4	4	1.000	10	0	1	15	1	2	0.7	5	18	6.0	24	8.0
96-97 Chi	19	0	336	50	104	.481	0	0	—	16	31	.516	14	19	8	63	1	1	0.2	31	71	3.7	116	6.1
98-99 Det	5	5	122	24	40	.600	0	0	—	5	9	.556	7	3	2	25	1	11	0.6	12	32	6.4	53	10.6
4 Years	39	5	791	126	238	.529	0	0	—	52	85	.612	48	26	22	139	3	25	0.6	81	210	5.4	304	7.8

Tony Delk

Pos: G **College:** Kentucky **Drafted:** '96 1(16)—Cha **Ht:** 6'2" **Wt:** 189 **Born:** 1/28/74 **Age:** 27

College			Field Goals			3-Pt FGs			Free Throws			Misc			Fouls		Assists		Rebounds			Points	
Year Tm	G	GS	Min	Md	Att	Pct	Md	Att	Pct	Md	Att	Pct	TO	Stl	Blk	PF	DQ	Ast	Avg	Off	Tot	Avg	Pts	Avg
92-93 Kty	30	0	287	47	104	.452	18	51	.353	24	33	.727	19	17	3	24	—	22	0.7	—	57	1.9	136	4.5
93-94 Kty	34	34	957	200	440	.455	95	254	.374	69	108	.639	59	64	21	70	—	59	1.7	—	153	4.5	564	16.6
94-95 Kty	33	33	960	207	433	.478	77	197	.391	60	89	.674	51	53	9	67	—	65	2.0	—	110	3.3	551	16.7
95-96 Kty	36	36	947	229	464	.494	93	210	.443	88	110	.800	64	67	13	72	1	64	1.8	53	150	4.2	639	17.8
4 Years	133	103	3151	683	1441	.474	283	712	.397	241	340	.709	193	201	46	233	—	210	1.6	—	470	3.5	1890	14.2

NBA			Field Goals			3-Pt FGs			Free Throws			Misc			Fouls		Assists		Rebounds			Points	
Year Tm	G	GS	Min	Md	Att	Pct	Md	Att	Pct	Md	Att	Pct	TO	Stl	Blk	PF	DQ	Ast	Avg	Off	Tot	Avg	Pts	Avg
96-97 Cha	61	1	867	119	256	.465	52	112	.464	42	51	.824	68	36	3	71	1	99	1.6	31	99	1.6	332	5.4
97-98 2Tm	77	9	1681	314	798	.393	42	157	.268	111	151	.735	109	73	12	96	0	172	2.2	38	172	2.2	781	10.1
98-99 GS	36	13	630	92	253	.364	16	66	.242	46	71	.648	45	16	6	47	0	95	2.6	11	54	1.5	246	6.8
99-00 Sac	46	1	682	120	279	.430	9	40	.225	47	59	.797	32	35	5	58	0	55	1.2	36	88	1.9	296	6.4
97-98 Cha	3	0	34	3	4	.750	1	1	1.000	1	2	.500	4	0	0	8	0	3	1.0	0	2	0.7	8	2.7
GS	74	9	1647	311	794	.392	41	156	.263	110	149	.738	105	73	12	88	0	169	2.3	38	170	2.3	773	10.4
4 Years	220	24	3860	645	1586	.407	119	375	.317	246	332	.741	254	160	29	272	1	421	1.9	116	413	1.9	1655	7.5

NBA Postseason

Year Tm	G	GS	Min	Md	Att	Pct	Md	Att	Pct	Md	Att	Pct	TO	Stl	Blk	PF	DQ	Ast	Avg	Off	Tot	Avg	Pts	Avg
96-97 Cha	3	1	85	13	31	.419	5	13	.385	0	0	—	2	2	0	10	0	6	2.0	5	10	3.3	31	10.3
99-00 Sac	5	0	101	18	41	.439	3	5	.600	17	23	.739	8	3	0	11	0	7	1.4	11	18	3.6	56	11.2
2 Years	8	1	186	31	72	.431	8	18	.444	17	23	.739	10	5	0	21	0	13	1.6	16	28	3.5	87	10.9

Derrick Dial

Pos: G **College:** Eastern Michigan **Drafted:** '98 2(52)—SA   **Ht:** 6'5" **Wt:** 195 **Born:** 12/20/75 **Age:** 25

	College			Field Goals			3-Pt FGs			Free Throws			Misc			Fouls		Assists		Rebounds			Points	
Year Tm	G	GS	Min	Md	Att	Pct	Md	Att	Pct	Md	Att	Pct	TO	Stl	Blk	PF	DQ	Ast	Avg	Off	Tot	Avg	Pts	Avg
94-95 EstMi	30	16	767	104	258	.403	33	113	.292	53	69	.768	26	18	3	62	2	40	1.3	46	154	5.1	294	9.8
95-96 EstMi	31	30	915	161	332	.485	47	127	.370	56	80	.700	36	30	11	49	0	63	2.0	66	178	5.7	425	13.7
96-97 EstMi	32	32	1099	204	392	.520	55	130	.423	102	125	.816	58	39	19	69	2	73	2.3	50	165	5.2	565	17.7
97-98 EstMi	29	29	1030	222	459	.484	79	198	.399	84	107	.785	61	39	25	66	1	67	2.3	66	195	6.7	607	20.9
4 Years	122	107	3811	691	1441	.480	214	568	.377	295	381	.774	181	126	58	246	5	243	2.0	228	692	5.7	1891	15.5

	NBA			Field Goals			3-Pt FGs			Free Throws			Misc			Fouls		Assists		Rebounds			Points	
Year Tm	G	GS	Min	Md	Att	Pct	Md	Att	Pct	Md	Att	Pct	TO	Stl	Blk	PF	DQ	Ast	Avg	Off	Tot	Avg	Pts	Avg
98-99										Played in USBL														
99-00 SA	8	0	95	17	46	.370	3	12	.250	3	5	.600	6	1	1	10	0	5	0.6	14	26	3.3	40	5.0

NBA Postseason

Year Tm	G	GS	Min	Md	Att	Pct	Md	Att	Pct	Md	Att	Pct	TO	Stl	Blk	PF	DQ	Ast	Avg	Off	Tot	Avg	Pts	Avg
99-00 SA	2	0	8	2	4	.500	0	0	—	1	2	.500	0	0	0	1	0	0	0.0	2	2	1.0	5	2.5

Michael Dickerson

(statistical profile on page 209)

Pos: G **College:** Arizona **Drafted:** '98 1(14)—Hou   **Ht:** 6'5" **Wt:** 190 **Born:** 6/25/75 **Age:** 25

	College			Field Goals			3-Pt FGs			Free Throws			Misc			Fouls		Assists		Rebounds			Points	
Year Tm	G	GS	Min	Md	Att	Pct	Md	Att	Pct	Md	Att	Pct	TO	Stl	Blk	PF	DQ	Ast	Avg	Off	Tot	Avg	Pts	Avg
94-95 Ari	29	0	330	50	93	.538	10	19	.526	28	41	.683	24	9	2	21	0	18	0.6	24	58	2.0	138	4.8
95-96 Ari	32	11	736	144	329	.438	31	91	.341	62	84	.738	61	21	11	51	0	59	1.8	56	113	3.5	381	11.9
96-97 Ari	34	34	1079	233	565	.412	55	166	.331	121	170	.712	86	37	3	51	5	51	1.5	68	153	4.5	642	18.9
97-98 Ari	35	35	993	241	473	.510	57	141	.404	91	120	.758	76	38	8	79	0	62	1.8	67	156	4.5	630	18.0
4 Years	130	80	3138	668	1460	.458	153	417	.367	302	415	.728	247	105	24	242	5	190	1.5	215	480	3.7	1791	13.8

	NBA			Field Goals			3-Pt FGs			Free Throws			Misc			Fouls		Assists		Rebounds			Points	
Year Tm	G	GS	Min	Md	Att	Pct	Md	Att	Pct	Md	Att	Pct	TO	Stl	Blk	PF	DQ	Ast	Avg	Off	Tot	Avg	Pts	Avg
98-99 Hou	50	50	1558	215	462	.465	71	164	.433	46	72	.639	66	27	11	90	0	95	1.9	26	83	1.7	547	10.9
99-00 Van	82	82	3103	554	1270	.436	119	291	.409	269	324	.830	165	116	45	226	0	208	2.3	78	279	3.4	1496	18.2
2 Years	132	132	4661	769	1732	.444	190	455	.418	315	396	.795	231	143	56	316	0	303	2.3	104	362	2.7	2043	15.5

NBA Postseason

Year Tm	G	GS	Min	Md	Att	Pct	Md	Att	Pct	Md	Att	Pct	TO	Stl	Blk	PF	DQ	Ast	Avg	Off	Tot	Avg	Pts	Avg
98-99 Hou	4	4	82	6	22	.273	3	8	.375	2	4	.500	2	2	3	8	0	3	0.8	2	4	1.0	17	4.3

Vlade Divac

(statistical profile on page 210)

Pos: C **College:** None **Drafted:** '89 1(26)—LAL   **Ht:** 7'1" **Wt:** 260 **Born:** 2/3/68 **Age:** 32

	NBA			Field Goals			3-Pt FGs			Free Throws			Misc			Fouls		Assists		Rebounds			Points	
Year Tm	G	GS	Min	Md	Att	Pct	Md	Att	Pct	Md	Att	Pct	TO	Stl	Blk	PF	DQ	Ast	Avg	Off	Tot	Avg	Pts	Avg
89-90 LAL	82	5	1611	274	549	.499	0	5	.000	153	216	.708	110	79	114	240	2	75	0.9	167	512	6.2	701	8.5
90-91 LAL	82	81	2310	360	637	.565	5	14	.357	196	279	.703	146	106	127	247	3	92	1.1	205	666	8.1	921	11.2
91-92 LAL	36	18	979	157	317	.495	5	19	.263	86	112	.768	88	55	35	114	3	60	1.7	87	247	6.9	405	11.3
92-93 LAL	82	69	2525	397	819	.485	21	75	.280	235	341	.689	214	128	140	311	7	232	2.8	220	729	8.9	1050	12.8
93-94 LAL	79	73	2685	453	895	.506	9	47	.191	208	303	.686	191	92	112	288	5	307	3.9	282	851	10.8	1123	14.2
94-95 LAL	80	80	2807	485	957	.507	10	53	.189	297	382	.777	205	109	174	305	8	329	4.1	261	829	10.4	1277	16.0
95-96 LAL	79	79	2470	414	807	.513	3	18	.167	189	295	.641	199	76	131	274	5	261	3.3	198	679	8.6	1020	12.9
96-97 LAL	81	80	2840	418	847	.494	11	47	.234	177	259	.683	193	103	180	277	6	301	3.7	241	725	9.0	1024	12.6
97-98 Cha	64	41	1805	267	536	.498	3	14	.214	130	188	.691	114	83	94	179	1	172	2.7	183	518	8.1	667	10.4
98-99 Sac	50	50	1761	262	557	.470	11	43	.256	179	255	.702	131	44	51	166	2	215	4.3	140	501	10.0	714	14.3
99-00 Sac	82	81	2374	384	764	.503	7	26	.269	230	333	.691	190	103	103	251	2	244	3.0	174	656	8.0	1005	12.3
11 Years	797	657	24167	3871	7685	.504	85	361	.235	2080	2963	.702	1781	978	1261	2652	44	2288	2.9	2158	6913	8.7	9907	12.4

NBA Postseason

Year Tm	G	GS	Min	Md	Att	Pct	Md	Att	Pct	Md	Att	Pct	TO	Stl	Blk	PF	DQ	Ast	Avg	Off	Tot	Avg	Pts	Avg
89-90 LAL	9	1	175	32	44	.727	1	2	.500	17	19	.895	13	8	15	27	1	10	1.1	16	48	5.3	82	9.1
90-91 LAL	19	19	609	97	172	.564	1	6	.167	57	71	.803	41	27	41	65	2	21	1.1	49	127	6.7	252	13.3

NBA Postseason

Year Tm	G	GS	Min	Md	Att	Pct	Md	Att	Pct	Md	Att	Pct	TO	Stl	Blk	PF	DQ	Ast	Avg	Off	Tot	Avg	Pts	Avg
91-92 LAL	4	4	143	15	43	.349	0	2	.000	9	10	.900	18	5	3	17	1	15	3.8	6	22	5.5	39	9.8
92-93 LAL	5	5	167	37	74	.500	4	9	.444	12	22	.545	11	6	12	22	0	28	5.6	17	47	9.4	90	18.0
94-95 LAL	10	10	388	57	122	.467	2	9	.222	40	62	.645	28	8	13	44	2	31	3.1	34	85	8.5	156	15.6
95-96 LAL	4	4	115	15	35	.429	1	5	.200	5	8	.625	8	0	5	10	0	8	2.0	11	30	7.5	36	9.0
96-97 Cha	3	3	116	21	46	.457	0	3	.000	12	15	.800	6	3	6	11	0	10	3.3	13	26	8.7	54	18.0
97-98 Cha	9	9	345	42	87	.483	0	1	.000	20	33	.606	22	7	14	34	1	31	3.4	25	98	10.9	104	11.6
98-99 Sac	5	5	198	25	56	.446	1	5	.200	30	36	.833	19	8	4	17	0	23	4.6	9	50	10.0	81	16.2
99-00 Sac	5	5	160	20	56	.357	0	2	.000	16	23	.696	9	7	1	22	0	14	2.8	9	36	7.2	56	11.2
10 Years	73	65	2416	361	735	.491	10	44	.227	218	299	.729	175	79	117	269	7	191	2.6	189	569	7.8	950	13.0

Michael Doleac

(statistical profile on page 210)

Pos: C **College:** Utah **Drafted:** '98 1(12)—Orl   **Ht:** 6'11" **Wt:** 262 **Born:** 6/15/77 **Age:** 23

College				Field Goals			3-Pt FGs			Free Throws			Misc			Fouls		Assists		Rebounds			Points	
Year Tm	G	GS	Min	Md	Att	Pct	Md	Att	Pct	Md	Att	Pct	TO	Stl	Blk	PF	DQ	Ast	Avg	Off	Tot	Avg	Pts	Avg
94-95 Utah	32	1	547	81	179	.453	0	1	.000	72	97	.742	39	15	32	66	0	6	0.2	—	144	4.5	234	7.3
95-96 Utah	34	34	819	101	218	.463	0	0	—	92	116	.793	47	21	30	91	0	26	0.8	75	261	7.7	294	8.6
96-97 Utah	33	33	876	166	309	.537	8	18	.444	135	174	.776	61	22	29	87	3	25	0.8	95	253	7.7	475	14.4
97-98 Utah	32	32	876	165	338	.488	13	32	.406	173	215	.805	51	13	33	75	1	17	0.5	69	228	7.1	516	16.1
4 Years	131	100	3118	513	1044	.491	21	52	.404	472	602	.784	198	71	124	319	4	74	0.6	—	886	6.8	1519	11.6

NBA				Field Goals			3-Pt FGs			Free Throws			Misc			Fouls		Assists		Rebounds			Points	
Year Tm	G	GS	Min	Md	Att	Pct	Md	Att	Pct	Md	Att	Pct	TO	Stl	Blk	PF	DQ	Ast	Avg	Off	Tot	Avg	Pts	Avg
98-99 Orl	49	0	780	125	267	.468	0	0	—	54	80	.675	26	19	17	117	1	20	0.4	66	148	3.0	304	6.2
99-00 Orl	81	29	1335	242	535	.452	1	2	.500	80	95	.842	65	29	34	224	3	63	0.8	89	334	4.1	565	7.0
2 Years	130	29	2115	367	802	.458	1	2	.500	134	175	.766	91	48	51	341	4	83	0.6	155	482	3.7	869	6.7

NBA Postseason

Year Tm	G	GS	Min	Md	Att	Pct	Md	Att	Pct	Md	Att	Pct	TO	Stl	Blk	PF	DQ	Ast	Avg	Off	Tot	Avg	Pts	Avg
98-99 Orl	4	0	43	5	18	.278	0	1	.000	7	9	.778	3	0	1	6	0	0	0.0	5	12	3.0	17	4.3

Sherman Douglas

Pos: G **College:** Syracuse **Drafted:** '89 2(28)—Mia   **Ht:** 6'1" **Wt:** 198 **Born:** 9/15/66 **Age:** 34

College				Field Goals			3-Pt FGs			Free Throws			Misc			Fouls		Assists		Rebounds			Points	
Year Tm	G	GS	Min	Md	Att	Pct	Md	Att	Pct	Md	Att	Pct	TO	Stl	Blk	PF	DQ	Ast	Avg	Off	Tot	Avg	Pts	Avg
85-86 Syr	27	—	307	57	93	.613	—	—	—	32	44	.727	33	33	5	33	0	57	2.1	—	33	1.2	146	5.4
86-87 Syr	38	38	1240	246	463	.531	16	49	.327	151	203	.744	64	64	5	72	0	289	7.6	39	97	2.6	659	17.3
87-88 Syr	35	34	1195	222	428	.519	14	53	.264	104	150	.693	117	69	1	55	0	288	8.2	23	76	2.2	562	16.1
88-89 Syr	38	38	1348	272	498	.546	39	106	.368	110	174	.632	139	69	1	71	2	326	8.6	31	93	2.4	693	18.2
4 Years	138	—	4090	797	1482	.538	69	208	.332	397	571	.695	410	235	12	231	2	960	7.0	93	299	2.2	2060	14.9

NBA				Field Goals			3-Pt FGs			Free Throws			Misc			Fouls		Assists		Rebounds			Points	
Year Tm	G	GS	Min	Md	Att	Pct	Md	Att	Pct	Md	Att	Pct	TO	Stl	Blk	PF	DQ	Ast	Avg	Off	Tot	Avg	Pts	Avg
89-90 Mia	81	66	2470	463	938	.494	5	31	.161	224	326	.687	246	145	10	187	0	619	7.6	70	206	2.5	1155	14.3
90-91 Mia	73	73	2562	532	1055	.504	4	31	.129	284	414	.686	270	121	5	178	2	624	8.5	78	209	2.9	1352	18.5
91-92 2Tm	42	2	752	117	253	.462	1	10	.100	73	107	.682	68	25	9	78	0	172	4.1	13	63	1.5	308	7.3
92-93 Bos	79	36	1932	264	530	.498	6	29	.207	84	150	.560	161	49	10	166	1	508	6.4	65	162	2.1	618	7.8
93-94 Bos	78	78	2789	425	919	.462	13	56	.232	177	276	.641	233	89	11	171	2	683	8.8	48	170	2.6	954	14.7
94-95 Bos	65	43	2048	365	769	.475	20	82	.244	204	296	.689	162	80	2	152	0	446	6.9	55	180	2.3	890	11.3
95-96 2Tm	79	66	2335	345	685	.504	40	110	.364	160	219	.731	194	63	5	163	0	427	5.4	57	193	2.4	764	9.7
96-97 Mil	79	79	2316	306	610	.502	38	114	.333	115	172	.669	153	78	10	191	0	319	4.0	52	135	1.7	639	8.0
97-98 Mil	80	11	1699	255	515	.495	14	46	.304	115	172	.669	110	55	7	156	2	124	4.1	16	58	1.9	247	8.2
98-99 LAC	30	19	842	96	219	.438	0	11	.000	55	87	.632	61	27	3	54	0	34	1.7	13	29	1.5	120	6.0
99-00 NJ	20	2	309	45	90	.500	5	16	.313	25	28	.893	24	17	0	26	0	19	3.8	1	6	1.2	37	7.4
91-92 Mia	5	2	98	16	31	.516	0	1	.000	5	7	.714	8	4	0	10	0	19	3.8	12	57	1.5	271	7.3
Bos	37	0	654	101	222	.455	1	9	.111	68	100	.680	60	21	9	68	0	153	4.1	12	57	1.5	271	7.3
95-96 Bos	10	4	234	36	84	.429	1	7	.143	25	40	.625	29	2	0	16	0	39	3.9	6	23	2.3	98	9.8
Mil	69	62	2101	309	601	.514	39	103	.379	135	179	.754	165	61	5	147	0	397	5.8	49	157	2.3	792	11.5
11 Years	706	475	20054	3213	6583	.488	146	536	.272	1515	2246	.675	1682	749	72	1522	7	4392	6.2	537	1598	2.3	8087	11.5

NBA Postseason

Year Tm	G	GS	Min	Md	Att	Pct	Md	Att	Pct	Md	Att	Pct	TO	Stl	Blk	PF	DQ	Ast	Avg	Off	Tot	Avg	Pts	Avg
91-92 Bos	6	0	65	9	25	.360	0	2	.000	1	2	.500	4	0	0	8	0	10	1.7	1	4	0.7	19	3.2
92-93 Bos	4	4	166	17	45	.378	0	3	.000	10	15	.667	12	4	0	10	0	38	9.5	12	26	6.5	44	11.0
94-95 Bos	4	4	168	24	68	.353	4	12	.333	8	11	.727	17	4	1	12	0	33	8.3	4	20	5.0	60	15.0
97-98 NJ	3	2	125	23	44	.523	2	5	.400	7	10	.700	13	6	0	5	0	25	8.3	1	8	2.7	55	18.3
4 Years	17	10	524	73	182	.401	6	22	.273	26	38	.684	46	14	1	35	0	106	6.2	18	58	3.4	178	10.5

Bryce Drew

Pos: G **College:** Valparaiso **Drafted:** '98 1(16)—Hou **Ht:** 6'3" **Wt:** 185 **Born:** 9/21/74 **Age:** 26

(statistical profile on page 211)

College

Year Tm	G	GS	Min	Field Goals Md	Att	Pct	3-Pt FGs Md	Att	Pct	Free Throws Md	Att	Pct	Misc TO	Stl	Blk	Fouls PF	DQ	Assists Ast	Avg	Rebounds Off	Tot	Avg	Points Pts	Avg
94-95 Val	27	—	943	117	267	.438	78	170	.459	49	65	.754	71	37	3	59	1	162	6.0	—	64	2.4	361	13.4
95-96 Val	32	32	1136	178	401	.444	92	231	.398	103	119	.866	88	46	1	74	2	164	5.1	19	92	2.9	551	17.2
96-97 Val	31	31	1078	193	419	.461	100	219	.457	131	149	.879	77	50	4	71	2	145	4.7	16	94	3.0	617	19.9
97-98 Val	31	31	1114	208	462	.450	94	217	.433	103	130	.792	73	53	2	60	0	155	5.0	24	130	4.2	613	19.8
4 Years	121	—	4271	696	1549	.449	364	837	.435	386	463	.834	309	186	10	264	5	626	5.2	—	380	3.1	2142	17.7

NBA

Year Tm	G	GS	Min	Field Goals Md	Att	Pct	3-Pt FGs Md	Att	Pct	Free Throws Md	Att	Pct	Misc TO	Stl	Blk	Fouls PF	DQ	Assists Ast	Avg	Rebounds Off	Tot	Avg	Points Pts	Avg
98-99 Hou	34	0	441	47	129	.364	16	49	.327	8	8	1.000	31	12	4	61	2	52	1.5	3	32	0.9	118	3.5
99-00 Hou	72	5	1293	158	413	.383	59	163	.362	45	53	.849	66	41	1	79	2	162	2.3	23	103	1.4	420	5.8
2 Years	106	5	1734	205	542	.378	75	212	.354	53	61	.869	97	53	5	140	2	214	2.0	26	135	1.3	538	5.1

NBA Postseason

Year Tm	G	GS	Min	Field Goals Md	Att	Pct	3-Pt FGs Md	Att	Pct	Free Throws Md	Att	Pct	Misc TO	Stl	Blk	Fouls PF	DQ	Assists Ast	Avg	Rebounds Off	Tot	Avg	Points Pts	Avg
98-99 Hou	1	0	4	1	1	1.000	0	0	—	0	2	.000	0	0	0	1	0	2	2.0	1	3	3.0	2	2.0

Chris Dudley

Pos: C **College:** Yale **Drafted:** '87 4(75)—Cle **Ht:** 6'11" **Wt:** 260 **Born:** 2/22/65 **Age:** 35

College

Year Tm	G	GS	Min	Field Goals Md	Att	Pct	3-Pt FGs Md	Att	Pct	Free Throws Md	Att	Pct	Misc TO	Stl	Blk	Fouls PF	DQ	Assists Ast	Avg	Rebounds Off	Tot	Avg	Points Pts	Avg
83-84 Yale	26	—	498	45	97	.464	—	—	—	28	60	.467	30	8	17	81	—	10	0.4	—	132	5.1	118	4.5
84-85 Yale	26	—	795	131	294	.446	—	—	—	65	122	.533	78	19	51	102	—	22	0.8	—	266	10.2	327	12.6
85-86 Yale	26	—	756	171	317	.539	—	—	—	80	166	.482	75	7	37	70	—	27	1.0	—	256	9.8	422	16.2
86-87 Yale	24	—	749	165	290	.569	0	0	—	96	177	.542	57	15	67	85	—	14	0.6	—	320	13.3	426	17.8
4 Years	102	—	2798	512	998	.513	0	0	—	269	525	.512	240	49	172	338	—	73	0.7	—	974	9.5	1293	12.7

NBA

Year Tm	G	GS	Min	Field Goals Md	Att	Pct	3-Pt FGs Md	Att	Pct	Free Throws Md	Att	Pct	Misc TO	Stl	Blk	Fouls PF	DQ	Assists Ast	Avg	Rebounds Off	Tot	Avg	Points Pts	Avg
87-88 Cle	55	1	513	65	137	.474	0	0	—	40	71	.563	31	13	19	87	2	23	0.4	74	144	2.6	170	3.1
88-89 Cle	61	2	544	73	168	.435	0	1	.000	39	107	.364	44	9	23	82	0	21	0.3	72	157	2.6	185	3.0
89-90 2Tm	64	30	1356	146	355	.411	0	0	—	58	182	.319	84	41	72	164	2	39	0.6	174	423	6.6	350	5.5
90-91 NJ	61	25	1560	170	417	.408	0	0	—	94	176	.534	80	39	153	217	6	37	0.6	229	511	8.4	434	7.1
91-92 NJ	82	21	1902	190	472	.403	0	0	—	80	171	.468	79	38	179	275	5	58	0.7	343	739	9.0	460	5.6
92-93 Por	71	16	1398	94	266	.353	0	0	—	57	110	.518	54	17	103	195	5	16	0.2	215	513	7.2	245	3.5
93-94 Por	6	3	86	6	25	.240	0	0	—	2	4	.500	2	4	3	18	0	5	0.8	16	24	4.0	14	2.3
94-95 Por	82	82	2245	181	446	.406	0	1	.000	85	183	.464	81	43	126	286	6	34	0.4	325	764	9.3	447	5.5
95-96 Por	80	61	1924	162	358	.453	0	1	.000	80	157	.510	79	41	100	251	4	37	0.5	239	720	9.0	404	5.1
96-97 Por	81	14	1840	126	293	.430	0	0	—	65	137	.474	80	39	96	247	3	41	0.5	204	593	7.3	317	3.9
97-98 NY	51	22	858	58	143	.406	0	0	—	41	92	.446	44	13	51	139	4	21	0.4	108	275	5.4	157	3.1
98-99 NY	46	16	685	48	109	.440	0	0	—	19	40	.475	24	13	38	116	1	7	0.2	79	193	4.2	115	2.5
99-00 NY	47	3	459	23	67	.343	0	0	—	9	27	.333	18	7	21	95	2	5	0.1	63	136	2.9	55	1.2
89-90 Cle	37	22	684	79	203	.389				26	77	.338	47	19	41	83	1	20	0.5	88	203	5.5	184	5.0
89-90 NJ	27	8	672	67	152	.441				32	105	.305	37	22	31	81	1	19	0.7	86	220	8.1	166	6.1
13 Years	787	296	15370	1342	3256	.412	0	3	.000	669	1457	.459	700	317	984	2172	40	344	0.4	2141	5192	6.6	3353	4.3

NBA Postseason

Year Tm	G	GS	Min	Field Goals Md	Att	Pct	3-Pt FGs Md	Att	Pct	Free Throws Md	Att	Pct	Misc TO	Stl	Blk	Fouls PF	DQ	Assists Ast	Avg	Rebounds Off	Tot	Avg	Points Pts	Avg
87-88 Cle	1	0	24	2	4	.500	0	0	—	1	2	.500	1	0	0	3	0	2	0.5	4	6	1.5	5	1.3
88-89 Cle	1	0	4	0	1	.000	0	0	—	0	0	—	1	0	0	1	0	0	0.0	0	0	0.0	0	0.0
91-92 NJ	4	0	77	5	14	.357	0	0	—	4	8	.500	1	2	10	14	1	3	0.8	13	25	6.3	14	3.5
93-94 Por	4	2	81	4	10	.400	0	0	—	1	2	.500	1	6	16	16	0	0	0.0	5	15	3.8	9	2.3
94-95 Por	3	3	59	2	3	.667	0	0	—	3	8	.375	3	0	1	8	0	1	0.3	6	15	5.0	7	2.3
95-96 Por	5	0	92	5	13	.385	0	0	—	4	6	.667	4	2	2	18	0	1	0.2	9	27	5.4	14	2.8
96-97 Por	4	0	69	5	11	.455	0	0	—	2	6	.333	0	2	5	19	1	3	0.8	10	28	7.0	12	3.0
97-98 NY	6	3	53	3	9	.333	0	0	—	2	4	.500	2	2	1	16	0	0	0.0	6	18	3.0	8	1.3
98-99 NY	18	6	294	16	38	.421	0	0	—	11	28	.393	9	9	8	63	2	5	0.3	27	82	4.6	43	2.4
99-00 NY	5	2	43	1	2	.500	0	0	—	2	2	1.000	1	1	1	11	0	2	0.4	5	12	2.4	4	0.8
10 Years	54	16	796	43	105	.410	0	0	—	30	66	.455	23	24	28	169	4	17	0.3	85	228	4.2	116	2.1

Tim Duncan
(statistical profile on page 211)

Pos: F-C **College:** Wake Forest **Drafted:** '97 1(1)—SA **Ht:** 7'0" **Wt:** 260 **Born:** 4/25/76 **Age:** 24

College				Field Goals			3-Pt FGs			Free Throws			Misc			Fouls		Assists		Rebounds			Points	
Year Tm	G	GS	Min	Md	Att	Pct	Md	Att	Pct	Md	Att	Pct	TO	Stl	Blk	PF	DQ	Ast	Avg	Off	Tot	Avg	Pts	Avg
93-94 Wake	33	32	997	120	220	.545	1	1	1.000	82	110	.745	40	12	124	82	2	30	0.9	106	317	9.6	323	9.8
94-95 Wake	32	32	1168	208	352	.591	3	7	.429	118	159	.742	91	13	135	79	3	67	2.1	123	401	12.5	537	16.8
95-96 Wake	32	32	1190	228	411	.555	7	23	.304	149	217	.687	104	22	120	74	0	93	2.9	110	395	12.3	612	19.1
96-97 Wake	31	31	1137	234	385	.608	6	22	.273	171	269	.636	99	22	102	69	1	98	3.2	122	457	14.7	645	20.8
4 Years	128	127	4492	790	1368	.577	17	53	.321	520	755	.689	334	69	481	304	6	288	2.3	461	1570	12.3	2117	16.5

NBA				Field Goals			3-Pt FGs			Free Throws			Misc			Fouls		Assists		Rebounds			Points	
Year Tm	G	GS	Min	Md	Att	Pct	Md	Att	Pct	Md	Att	Pct	TO	Stl	Blk	PF	DQ	Ast	Avg	Off	Tot	Avg	Pts	Avg
97-98 SA*	82	82	3204	706	1287	.549	0	10	.000	319	482	.662	279	55	206	254	1	224	2.7	274	977	11.9	1731	21.1
98-99 SA	50	50	1963	418	845	.495	1	7	.143	247	358	.690	146	45	126	147	2	121	2.4	159	571	11.4	1084	21.7
99-00 SA*	74	74	2875	628	1281	.490	1	11	.091	459	603	.761	242	66	165	210	1	234	3.2	262	918	12.4	1716	23.2
3 Years	206	206	8042	1752	3413	.513	2	28	.071	1025	1443	.710	667	166	497	611	4	579	2.8	695	2466	12.0	4531	22.0

NBA Postseason																								
Year Tm	G	GS	Min	Md	Att	Pct	Md	Att	Pct	Md	Att	Pct	TO	Stl	Blk	PF	DQ	Ast	Avg	Off	Tot	Avg	Pts	Avg
97-98 SA	9	9	374	73	140	.521	0	1	.000	40	60	.667	25	5	23	24	1	17	1.9	20	81	9.0	186	20.7
98-99 SA	17	17	733	144	282	.511	0	3	.000	107	143	.748	52	13	45	50	1	48	2.8	55	195	11.5	395	23.2
2 Years	26	26	1107	217	422	.514	0	4	.000	147	203	.724	77	18	68	74	2	65	2.5	75	276	10.6	581	22.3

Howard Eisley
(statistical profile on page 212)

Pos: G **College:** Boston College **Drafted:** '94 2(30)—Min **Ht:** 6'2" **Wt:** 180 **Born:** 12/4/72 **Age:** 28

College				Field Goals			3-Pt FGs			Free Throws			Misc			Fouls		Assists		Rebounds			Points	
Year Tm	G	GS	Min	Md	Att	Pct	Md	Att	Pct	Md	Att	Pct	TO	Stl	Blk	PF	DQ	Ast	Avg	Off	Tot	Avg	Pts	Avg
90-91 BC	30	30	1011	95	264	.360	26	74	.351	81	108	.750	84	46	6	83	6	100	3.3	11	79	2.6	297	9.9
91-92 BC	31	31	1071	118	242	.488	37	75	.493	88	118	.746	102	61	3	99	5	135	4.4	18	111	3.6	361	11.6
92-93 BC	31	31	1162	131	296	.443	43	104	.413	121	145	.834	94	37	5	83	2	153	4.9	22	107	3.5	426	13.7
93-94 BC	34	34	1203	185	389	.476	91	188	.484	83	105	.790	86	51	2	93	2	156	4.6	16	116	3.4	544	16.0
4 Years	126	126	4447	529	1191	.444	197	441	.447	373	476	.784	366	195	16	358	15	544	4.3	67	413	3.3	1628	12.9

NBA				Field Goals			3-Pt FGs			Free Throws			Misc			Fouls		Assists		Rebounds			Points	
Year Tm	G	GS	Min	Md	Att	Pct	Md	Att	Pct	Md	Att	Pct	TO	Stl	Blk	PF	DQ	Ast	Avg	Off	Tot	Avg	Pts	Avg
94-95 2Tm	49	4	552	40	122	.328	9	37	.243	31	40	.775	50	18	6	81	0	95	1.9	12	48	1.0	120	2.4
95-96 Uta	65	0	961	104	242	.430	14	62	.226	65	77	.844	77	29	3	130	0	146	2.2	22	78	1.2	287	4.4
96-97 Uta	82	0	1083	139	308	.451	20	72	.278	70	89	.787	110	44	10	141	0	198	2.4	20	84	1.0	368	4.5
97-98 Uta	82	18	1726	229	519	.441	48	118	.407	127	149	.852	160	54	13	182	3	346	4.2	25	166	2.0	633	7.7
98-99 Uta	50	0	1038	140	314	.446	21	50	.420	67	80	.838	109	30	2	122	0	185	3.7	12	94	1.9	368	7.4
99-00 Uta	82	5	2096	282	675	.418	60	163	.368	84	102	.824	132	59	9	223	2	347	4.2	23	170	2.1	708	8.6
94-95 Min	34	4	496	37	105	.352	8	32	.250	31	40	.775	42	18	5	78	0	77	2.3	10	42	1.2	113	3.3
SA	15	0	56	3	17	.176	1	5	.200	0	0	—	8	0	1	3	0	18	1.2	2	6	0.4	7	0.5
6 Years	410	27	7456	934	2180	.428	172	502	.343	444	537	.827	638	234	43	879	5	1317	3.2	114	640	1.6	2484	6.1

NBA Postseason																								
Year Tm	G	GS	Min	Md	Att	Pct	Md	Att	Pct	Md	Att	Pct	TO	Stl	Blk	PF	DQ	Ast	Avg	Off	Tot	Avg	Pts	Avg
95-96 Uta	18	0	202	16	42	.381	3	9	.333	18	22	.818	11	3	2	29	0	44	2.4	4	22	1.2	53	2.9
96-97 Uta	20	0	217	38	76	.500	9	19	.474	27	28	.964	17	3	0	27	1	40	2.0	4	18	0.9	112	5.6
97-98 Uta	20	0	366	46	125	.368	8	27	.296	12	13	.923	31	12	5	42	0	81	4.1	4	40	2.0	112	5.6
98-99 Uta	11	0	241	26	71	.366	5	24	.208	24	29	.828	20	7	3	27	0	32	2.9	3	20	1.8	81	7.4
99-00 Uta	10	0	200	17	55	.309	9	19	.474	8	9	.889	13	6	1	24	0	19	1.9	1	18	1.8	51	5.1
5 Years	79	0	1226	143	369	.388	34	98	.347	89	101	.881	92	31	11	149	1	216	2.7	16	118	1.5	409	5.2

Obinna Ekezie

Pos: F **College:** Maryland **Drafted:** '99 2(37)—Van **Ht:** 6'10" **Wt:** 260 **Born:** 8/22/75 **Age:** 25

College				Field Goals			3-Pt FGs			Free Throws			Misc			Fouls		Assists		Rebounds			Points	
Year Tm	G	GS	Min	Md	Att	Pct	Md	Att	Pct	Md	Att	Pct	TO	Stl	Blk	PF	DQ	Ast	Avg	Off	Tot	Avg	Pts	Avg
95-96 Mryld	30	18	463	51	108	.472	0	0	—	33	60	.550	39	13	20	78	3	10	0.3	47	111	3.7	135	4.5
96-97 Mryld	32	32	858	115	209	.550	0	0	—	92	144	.639	80	23	33	106	4	22	0.7	75	212	6.6	322	10.1
97-98 Mryld	32	32	895	138	285	.484	0	0	—	134	200	.670	69	19	37	103	6	51	1.6	75	207	6.5	410	12.8
98-99 Mryld	24	23	614	104	213	.488	0	2	.000	97	140	.693	55	15	35	70	1	21	0.9	56	141	5.9	305	12.7
4 Years	118	105	2830	408	815	.501	0	2	.000	356	544	.654	243	70	125	357	14	104	0.9	253	671	5.7	1172	9.9

NBA				Field Goals			3-Pt FGs			Free Throws			Misc			Fouls		Assists		Rebounds			Points	
Year Tm	G	GS	Min	Md	Att	Pct	Md	Att	Pct	Md	Att	Pct	TO	Stl	Blk	PF	DQ	Ast	Avg	Off	Tot	Avg	Pts	Avg
99-00 Van	39	0	351	41	88	.466	0	0	—	43	64	.672	26	9	4	61	0	8	0.2	34	92	2.4	125	3.2

Mario Elie

(statistical profile on page 212)

Pos: G-F **College:** American Int. **Drafted:** '85 7(160)—Mil **Ht:** 6'5" **Wt:** 225 **Born:** 11/26/63 **Age:** 37

College

Year Tm	G	GS	Min	Md	Att	Pct	Md	Att	Pct	Md	Att	Pct	TO	Stl	Blk	PF	DQ	Ast	Avg	Off	Tot	Avg	Pts	Avg
				Field Goals			**3-Pt FGs**			**Free Throws**			**Misc**			**Fouls**		**Assists**		**Rebounds**			**Points**	
81-82 AmInt	25	—	754	157	268	.586	—	—	—	72	97	.742	—	—	—	—	—	—	—	—	207	8.3	386	15.4
82-83 AmInt	31	—	1060	188	357	.527	—	—	—	116	157	.739	—	—	—	—	—	50	2.0	—	239	7.7	492	15.9
83-84 AmInt	31	—	1174	225	398	.565	—	—	—	135	170	.794	—	—	—	—	—	99	3.2	—	256	8.3	585	18.9
84-85 AmInt	33	—	1208	252	459	.549	—	—	—	157	202	.777	—	—	—	—	—	59	1.9	—	299	9.1	661	20.0
4 Years	120	—	4196	822	1482	.555				480	626	.767	—	—	—	—	—	124	3.8	—	1001	8.3	2124	17.7

NBA

Year Tm	G	GS	Min	Md	Att	Pct	Md	Att	Pct	Md	Att	Pct	TO	Stl	Blk	PF	DQ	Ast	Avg	Off	Tot	Avg	Pts	Avg
				Field Goals			**3-Pt FGs**			**Free Throws**			**Misc**			**Fouls**		**Assists**		**Rebounds**			**Points**	
85-86										Played in Europe/Argentina														
86-87										Played in Europe/Argentina, Played in USBL														
87-88										Played in Europe/Argentina														
88-89										Played in Europe/Argentina														
89-90										Played in CBA, Played in WBL														
90-91 2Tm	33	0	644	79	159	.497	4	10	.400	75	89	.843	30	19	10	85	1	45	1.4	46	110	3.3	237	7.2
91-92 GS	79	32	1677	221	424	.521	23	70	.329	155	182	.852	83	68	15	159	3	174	2.2	69	227	2.9	620	7.8
92-93 Por	82	7	1757	240	524	.458	45	129	.349	183	214	.855	89	74	20	145	0	177	2.2	59	216	2.6	708	8.6
93-94 Hou	67	8	1606	208	466	.446	56	167	.335	154	179	.860	109	50	8	124	0	208	3.1	59	216	2.6	626	9.3
94-95 Hou	81	13	1896	243	487	.499	80	201	.398	144	171	.842	104	65	12	158	0	189	2.3	50	196	2.4	710	8.8
95-96 Hou	45	16	1385	180	357	.504	41	127	.323	98	115	.852	59	45	11	93	0	138	3.1	47	155	3.4	499	11.1
96-97 Hou	78	77	2687	291	585	.497	120	286	.420	207	231	.896	135	92	12	200	2	310	4.0	60	235	3.0	909	11.7
97-98 Hou	73	59	1988	206	456	.452	55	189	.291	145	174	.833	100	81	8	115	0	221	3.0	39	156	2.1	612	8.4
98-99 SA	47	37	1291	156	331	.471	40	107	.374	103	118	.866	61	46	12	91	0	89	1.9	36	137	2.9	455	9.7
99-00 SA	79	79	2217	195	457	.427	74	186	.398	126	149	.846	130	73	9	156	0	193	2.4	48	249	3.2	590	7.5
90-91 Phi	3	0	20	2	7	.286	1	2	.500	1	2	.500	3	0	0	2	0	1	0.3	0	1	0.3	6	2.0
GS	30	0	624	77	152	.507	3	8	.375	74	87	.851	27	19	10	83	1	44	1.5	46	109	3.6	231	7.7
10 Years	664	328	17148	2019	4246	.476	538	1472	.365	1390	1623	.856	900	613	117	1326	6	1744	2.6	482	1862	2.8	5966	9.0

NBA Postseason

Year Tm	G	GS	Min	Md	Att	Pct	Md	Att	Pct	Md	Att	Pct	TO	Stl	Blk	PF	DQ	Ast	Avg	Off	Tot	Avg	Pts	Avg
90-91 GS	9	7	197	28	56	.500	1	1	1.000	27	32	.844	10	5	1	32	0	13	1.4	17	32	3.6	84	9.3
91-92 GS	4	2	80	23	36	.639	2	2	1.000	2	3	.667	6	5	0	11	1	10	2.5	11	22	5.5	50	12.5
92-93 Por	4	0	52	5	10	.500	2	2	1.000	8	9	.889	5	2	1	1	0	4	1.0	2	6	1.5	20	5.0
93-94 Hou	23	0	382	42	106	.396	10	32	.313	40	47	.851	21	8	3	30	0	38	1.7	9	40	1.7	134	5.8
94-95 Hou	22	6	635	69	137	.504	28	65	.431	35	44	.795	21	21	1	55	0	54	2.5	19	62	2.8	201	9.1
95-96 Hou	8	0	233	29	66	.439	9	24	.375	11	12	.917	5	7	3	17	0	14	1.8	6	22	2.8	78	9.8
96-97 Hou	16	16	598	54	116	.466	24	60	.400	52	62	.839	30	14	4	52	3	61	3.8	19	56	3.5	184	11.5
97-98 Hou	5	1	133	12	27	.444	3	9	.333	6	9	.667	5	2	0	10	0	6	1.2	3	13	2.6	33	6.6
98-99 SA	17	17	526	43	112	.384	8	30	.267	41	49	.837	25	22	2	42	0	50	2.9	9	59	3.5	135	7.9
99-00 SA	4	4	115	6	22	.273	1	7	.143	17	18	.944	12	5	0	4	0	7	1.8	5	17	4.3	30	7.5
10 Years	112	53	2951	311	688	.452	88	232	.379	239	285	.839	140	91	15	254	4	257	2.3	100	329	2.9	949	8.5

Sean Elliott

Pos: F **College:** Arizona **Drafted:** '89 1(3)—SA **Ht:** 6'8" **Wt:** 220 **Born:** 2/2/68 **Age:** 32

College

Year Tm	G	GS	Min	Md	Att	Pct	Md	Att	Pct	Md	Att	Pct	TO	Stl	Blk	PF	DQ	Ast	Avg	Off	Tot	Avg	Pts	Avg
				Field Goals			**3-Pt FGs**			**Free Throws**			**Misc**			**Fouls**		**Assists**		**Rebounds**			**Points**	
85-86 Ari	32	32	1079	187	385	.486	—	—	—	125	167	.749	68	22	8	52	0	70	2.2	—	171	5.3	499	15.6
86-87 Ari	30	30	1046	209	410	.510	33	89	.371	127	165	.770	101	21	6	68	4	110	3.7	67	181	6.0	578	19.3
87-88 Ari	38	38	1249	263	461	.570	41	87	.471	176	222	.793	101	28	15	69	1	137	3.6	66	219	5.8	743	19.6
88-89 Ari	33	33	1125	237	494	.480	66	151	.437	195	232	.841	103	32	9	54	1	134	4.1	69	237	7.2	735	22.3
4 Years	133	133	4499	896	1750	.512	140	327	.428	623	786	.793	373	103	38	243	6	451	3.4	202	808	6.1	2555	19.2

NBA

Year Tm	G	GS	Min	Md	Att	Pct	Md	Att	Pct	Md	Att	Pct	TO	Stl	Blk	PF	DQ	Ast	Avg	Off	Tot	Avg	Pts	Avg
				Field Goals			**3-Pt FGs**			**Free Throws**			**Misc**			**Fouls**		**Assists**		**Rebounds**			**Points**	
89-90 SA	81	69	2032	311	647	.481	1	9	.111	187	216	.866	112	45	14	172	0	154	1.9	127	297	3.7	810	10.0
90-91 SA	82	82	3044	478	976	.490	20	64	.313	325	402	.808	147	69	33	190	2	238	2.9	142	456	5.6	1301	15.9
91-92 SA	82	82	3120	514	1040	.494	25	82	.305	285	331	.861	152	84	29	149	0	214	2.6	143	439	5.4	1338	16.3
92-93 SA*	70	70	2604	451	918	.491	37	104	.356	268	337	.795	152	68	28	132	1	265	3.8	85	322	4.6	1207	17.2
93-94 Det	73	73	2409	360	791	.455	26	87	.299	139	173	.803	129	54	27	174	3	197	2.7	68	263	3.6	885	12.1
94-95 SA	81	81	2858	502	1072	.468	136	333	.408	326	404	.807	151	78	38	216	2	206	2.5	63	287	3.5	1466	18.1
95-96 SA*	77	77	2901	525	1127	.466	161	392	.411	326	423	.771	198	69	33	178	1	211	2.7	69	396	5.1	1537	20.0
96-97 SA	39	39	1393	196	464	.422	42	126	.333	148	196	.755	89	24	24	105	1	124	3.2	48	190	4.9	582	14.9
97-98 SA	36	36	1012	122	303	.403	34	90	.378	56	78	.718	57	24	14	92	0	62	1.7	16	124	3.4	334	9.3
98-99 SA	50	50	1509	208	507	.410	39	119	.328	106	140	.757	71	26	17	101	0	117	2.3	35	213	4.3	561	11.2
99-00 SA	19	19	391	38	106	.358	13	37	.351	25	32	.781	19	12	2	34	0	28	1.5	6	47	2.5	114	6.0
11 Years	690	678	23273	3705	7951	.466	534	1443	.370	2191	2732	.802	1277	553	259	1546	12	1816	2.6	802	3034	4.4	10135	14.7

52

NBA Postseason

Year Tm	G	GS	Min	Md	Att	Pct	Md	Att	Pct	Md	Att	Pct	TO	Stl	Blk	PF	DQ	Ast	Avg	Off	Tot	Avg	Pts	Avg
89-90 SA	10	10	291	53	96	.552	0	1	.000	21	29	.724	15	9	6	37	0	18	1.8	11	41	4.1	127	12.7
90-91 SA	4	4	132	17	40	.425	0	3	.000	25	32	.781	9	4	1	9	0	16	4.0	8	22	5.5	59	14.8
91-92 SA	3	3	137	19	40	.475	5	8	.625	16	18	.889	6	3	4	6	0	8	2.7	4	13	4.3	59	19.7
92-93 SA	10	10	381	59	125	.472	3	14	.214	37	40	.925	22	8	3	22	0	36	3.6	8	48	4.8	158	15.8
94-95 SA	15	15	574	87	200	.435	20	55	.364	66	85	.776	27	10	6	38	0	40	2.7	23	72	4.8	260	17.3
95-96 SA	10	10	389	47	117	.402	10	34	.294	51	64	.797	30	11	4	24	0	25	2.5	11	39	3.9	155	15.5
98-99 SA	17	17	574	68	153	.444	22	55	.400	45	59	.763	21	9	4	50	0	45	2.6	11	58	3.4	203	11.9
99-00 SA	4	4	119	15	40	.375	5	13	.385	5	8	.625	4	0	2	13	0	5	1.3	1	22	5.5	40	10.0
8 Years	73	73	2597	365	811	.450	65	183	.355	266	335	.794	134	54	30	199	0	193	2.6	77	315	4.3	1061	14.5

Dale Ellis

Pos: G-F **College:** Tennessee **Drafted:** '83 1(9)—Dal **Ht:** 6'7" **Wt:** 215 **Born:** 8/6/60 **Age:** 40

College				Field Goals			3-Pt FGs			Free Throws			Misc			Fouls		Assists		Rebounds			Points	
Year Tm	G	GS	Min	Md	Att	Pct	Md	Att	Pct	Md	Att	Pct	TO	Stl	Blk	PF	DQ	Ast	Avg	Off	Tot	Avg	Pts	Avg
79-80 Tenn	27	—	573	81	182	.445	—	—	—	31	40	.775	—	—	—	—	—	34	1.3	—	96	3.6	193	7.1
80-81 Tenn	29	—	1057	215	360	.597	—	—	—	83	111	.748	—	—	—	—	—	21	0.7	—	185	6.4	513	17.7
81-82 Tenn	30	—	1134	257	393	.654	—	—	—	121	152	.796	—	—	—	—	—	22	0.7	—	189	6.3	635	21.2
82-83 Tenn	32	—	1179	279	464	.601	—	—	—	166	221	.751	—	52	—	—	—	32	1.0	—	209	6.5	724	22.6
4 Years	118	—	3943	832	1399	.595	—	—	—	401	524	.765	—	—	—	—	—	109	0.9	—	679	5.8	2065	17.5

NBA				Field Goals			3-Pt FGs			Free Throws			Misc			Fouls		Assists		Rebounds			Points	
Year Tm	G	GS	Min	Md	Att	Pct	Md	Att	Pct	Md	Att	Pct	TO	Stl	Blk	PF	DQ	Ast	Avg	Off	Tot	Avg	Pts	Avg
83-84 Dal	67	2	1059	225	493	.456	12	29	.414	87	121	.719	78	41	9	118	0	56	0.8	106	250	3.7	549	8.2
84-85 Dal	72	4	1314	274	603	.454	42	109	.385	77	104	.740	58	46	7	131	1	56	0.8	100	238	3.3	667	9.3
85-86 Dal	72	1	1086	193	470	.411	63	173	.364	59	82	.720	38	40	9	78	0	37	0.5	86	168	2.3	508	7.1
86-87 Sea	82	76	3073	785	1520	.516	86	240	.358	385	489	.787	238	104	32	267	2	238	2.9	187	447	5.5	2041	24.9
87-88 Sea	75	73	2790	764	1519	.503	107	259	.413	303	395	.767	172	74	11	221	1	197	2.6	167	340	4.5	1938	25.8
88-89 Sea*	82	82	3190	857	1710	.501	162	339	.478	377	462	.816	218	108	22	197	0	164	2.0	156	342	4.2	2253	27.5
89-90 Sea	55	49	2033	502	1011	.497	96	256	.375	193	236	.818	119	59	7	124	3	110	2.0	90	238	4.3	1293	23.5
90-91 2Tm	51	24	1424	340	718	.474	57	157	.363	120	166	.723	81	49	8	112	0	95	1.9	64	173	3.4	857	16.8
91-92 Mil	81	11	2191	485	1034	.469	138	329	.419	164	212	.774	119	57	18	151	0	104	1.3	92	253	3.1	1272	15.7
92-93 SA	82	76	2731	545	1092	.499	119	297	.401	157	197	.797	111	78	18	179	0	107	1.3	81	312	3.8	1366	16.7
93-94 SA	77	75	2590	478	967	.494	131	332	.395	83	107	.776	75	66	11	141	0	80	1.0	70	255	3.3	1170	15.2
94-95 Den	81	3	1996	351	774	.453	106	263	.403	110	127	.866	81	37	9	142	0	57	0.7	56	222	2.7	918	11.3
95-96 Den	81	52	2626	459	959	.479	150	364	.412	136	179	.760	98	57	7	191	1	139	1.7	88	315	3.9	1204	14.9
96-97 Den	82	51	2940	477	1151	.414	192	528	.364	215	263	.817	146	60	7	178	0	165	2.0	99	293	3.6	1361	16.6
97-98 Sea	79	0	1939	348	700	.497	127	274	.464	111	142	.782	74	60	5	128	0	89	1.1	51	184	2.3	934	11.8
98-99 Sea	48	9	1232	174	395	.441	94	217	.433	53	70	.757	45	25	3	77	1	38	0.8	25	115	2.4	495	10.3
99-00 2Tm	42	5	564	66	159	.415	37	100	.370	9	13	.692	20	13	0	45	0	14	0.3	13	56	1.3	178	4.2
90-91 Sea	30	24	800	181	391	.463	27	89	.303	62	84	.738	49	33	3	59	0	64	2.1	28	92	3.1	451	15.0
Mil	21	0	624	159	327	.486	30	68	.441	58	82	.707	32	16	5	53	1	31	1.5	38	81	3.9	406	19.3
99-00 Mil	18	0	324	47	101	.465	23	65	.354	6	9	.667	7	6	0	23	0	6	0.3	7	34	1.9	123	6.8
Cha	24	5	240	19	58	.328	14	35	.400	3	4	.750	13	7	0	22	0	8	0.3	6	22	0.9	55	2.3
17 Years	1209	589	34778	7323	15275	.479	1719	4266	.403	2639	3365	.784	1771	974	183	2480	10	1746	1.4	1533	4201	3.5	19004	15.7

NBA Postseason

Year Tm	G	GS	Min	Md	Att	Pct	Md	Att	Pct	Md	Att	Pct	TO	Stl	Blk	PF	DQ	Ast	Avg	Off	Tot	Avg	Pts	Avg
83-84 Dal	8	1	178	26	80	.325	1	12	.083	6	8	.750	5	10	2	17	0	4	0.5	19	42	5.3	59	7.4
84-85 Dal	4	1	68	10	23	.435	2	5	.400	1	2	.500	4	4	0	3	0	3	0.8	4	7	1.8	23	5.8
85-86 Dal	7	0	67	9	22	.409	7	12	.583	5	1	1.000	4	2	2	6	0	2	0.3	3	7	1.0	30	4.3
86-87 Sea	14	14	530	148	304	.487	13	36	.361	44	54	.815	33	10	6	54	1	37	2.6	37	90	6.4	353	25.2
87-88 Sea	5	5	172	40	83	.482	3	12	.250	21	29	.724	12	3	2	17	0	15	3.0	11	23	4.6	104	20.8
88-89 Sea	8	8	304	72	160	.450	15	37	.405	24	33	.727	21	11	1	19	1	10	1.3	14	32	4.0	183	22.9
92-93 SA	10	10	305	51	113	.451	10	32	.313	13	16	.813	10	4	0	25	0	11	1.1	9	35	3.5	125	12.5
93-94 SA	4	4	114	17	43	.395	5	17	.294	3	5	.600	4	3	0	6	0	1	0.3	3	10	2.5	42	10.5
94-95 Den	3	0	73	10	28	.357	4	13	.308	12	13	.923	2	2	1	6	0	3	1.0	6	14	4.7	36	12.0
97-98 Sea	10	0	170	20	53	.377	11	26	.423	5	6	.833	2	2	0	10	0	6	0.6	4	13	1.3	56	5.6
10 Years	73	43	1981	403	909	.443	71	202	.351	134	171	.784	97	51	14	163	2	92	1.3	110	273	3.7	1011	13.8

LaPhonso Ellis

(statistical profile on page 213)

Pos: F **College:** Notre Dame **Drafted:** '92 1(5)—Den **Ht:** 6'8" **Wt:** 240 **Born:** 5/5/70 **Age:** 30

College				Field Goals			3-Pt FGs			Free Throws			Misc			Fouls		Assists		Rebounds			Points	
Year Tm	G	GS	Min	Md	Att	Pct	Md	Att	Pct	Md	Att	Pct	TO	Stl	Blk	PF	DQ	Ast	Avg	Off	Tot	Avg	Pts	Avg
88-89 ND	27	—	819	156	277	.563	1	1	1.000	52	76	.684	—	22	53	78	—	31	1.1	—	254	9.4	365	13.5
89-90 ND	22	—	712	114	223	.511	2	6	.333	79	117	.675	—	21	37	75	—	33	1.5	—	278	12.6	309	14.0

College				Field Goals			3-Pt FGs			Free Throws			Misc			Fouls		Assists		Rebounds			Points	
Year Tm	G	GS	Min	Md	Att	Pct	Md	Att	Pct	Md	Att	Pct	TO	Stl	Blk	PF	DQ	Ast	Avg	Off	Tot	Avg	Pts	Avg
90-91 ND	15	—	495	90	157	.573	8	17	.471	58	81	.716	—	11	24	52	—	26	1.7	—	158	10.5	246	16.4
91-92 ND	33	—	1194	227	360	.631	4	9	.444	127	194	.655	92	37	86	112	—	51	1.5	—	385	11.7	585	17.7
4 Years	97	—	3220	587	1017	.577	15	33	.455	316	468	.675	—	91	200	317	—	141	1.5	—	1075	11.1	1505	15.5

NBA				Field Goals			3-Pt FGs			Free Throws			Misc			Fouls		Assists		Rebounds			Points	
Year Tm	G	GS	Min	Md	Att	Pct	Md	Att	Pct	Md	Att	Pct	TO	Stl	Blk	PF	DQ	Ast	Avg	Off	Tot	Avg	Pts	Avg
92-93 Den	82	82	2749	483	958	.504	2	13	.154	237	317	.748	153	72	111	293	8	151	1.8	274	744	9.1	1205	14.7
93-94 Den	79	79	2699	483	963	.502	7	23	.304	242	359	.674	172	63	80	304	6	167	2.1	220	682	8.6	1215	15.4
94-95 Den	6	0	58	9	25	.360	0	0	—	6	6	1.000	5	1	5	12	0	4	0.7	7	17	2.8	24	4.0
95-96 Den	45	28	1269	189	432	.438	4	22	.182	89	148	.601	83	36	33	163	3	74	1.6	93	322	7.2	471	10.5
96-97 Den	55	49	2002	445	1014	.439	95	259	.367	218	282	.773	117	44	41	181	7	131	2.4	107	386	7.0	1203	21.9
97-98 Den	76	71	2575	410	1007	.407	57	201	.284	206	256	.805	173	65	49	226	2	213	2.8	146	544	7.2	1083	14.3
98-99 Atl	20	20	539	80	190	.421	1	5	.200	43	61	.705	34	8	7	48	1	18	0.9	25	109	5.5	204	10.2
99-00 Atl	58	8	1309	209	464	.450	3	21	.143	66	95	.695	52	32	25	133	1	59	1.0	98	290	5.0	487	8.4
8 Years	421	337	13200	2308	5053	.457	169	544	.311	1107	1524	.726	789	321	351	1360	28	817	1.9	970	3094	7.3	5892	14.0

NBA Postseason																								
Year Tm	G	GS	Min	Md	Att	Pct	Md	Att	Pct	Md	Att	Pct	TO	Stl	Blk	PF	DQ	Ast	Avg	Off	Tot	Avg	Pts	Avg
93-94 Den	12	12	436	68	142	.479	3	6	.500	38	54	.704	19	9	11	46	2	26	2.2	27	97	8.1	177	14.8

Pervis Ellison

Pos: F-C **College:** Louisville **Drafted:** '89 1(1)—Sac   **Ht:** 6'10" **Wt:** 242 **Born:** 4/3/67 **Age:** 33

College				Field Goals			3-Pt FGs			Free Throws			Misc			Fouls		Assists		Rebounds			Points	
Year Tm	G	GS	Min	Md	Att	Pct	Md	Att	Pct	Md	Att	Pct	TO	Stl	Blk	PF	DQ	Ast	Avg	Off	Tot	Avg	Pts	Avg
85-86 Lou	39	39	1194	210	379	.554	—	—	—	90	132	.682	60	50	92	117	3	78	2.0	—	318	8.2	510	13.1
86-87 Lou	31	31	952	185	347	.533	0	0	—	100	139	.719	96	36	82	96	6	56	1.8	—	270	8.7	470	15.2
87-88 Lou	35	35	1175	235	391	.601	1	2	.500	146	211	.692	73	46	102	103	2	108	3.1	—	291	8.3	617	17.6
88-89 Lou	31	30	1014	227	369	.615	0	1	.000	92	141	.652	85	39	98	98	5	78	2.5	—	270	8.7	546	17.6
4 Years	136	135	4335	857	1486	.577	1	3	.333	428	623	.687	314	171	374	414	16	320	2.4	—	1149	8.4	2143	15.8

NBA				Field Goals			3-Pt FGs			Free Throws			Misc			Fouls		Assists		Rebounds			Points	
Year Tm	G	GS	Min	Md	Att	Pct	Md	Att	Pct	Md	Att	Pct	TO	Stl	Blk	PF	DQ	Ast	Avg	Off	Tot	Avg	Pts	Avg
89-90 Sac	34	22	866	111	251	.442	0	2	.000	49	78	.628	62	16	57	132	4	65	1.9	64	196	5.8	271	8.0
90-91 Was	76	30	1942	326	636	.513	0	6	.000	139	214	.650	146	49	157	268	6	102	1.3	224	585	7.7	791	10.4
91-92 Was	66	64	2511	547	1014	.539	1	3	.333	227	312	.728	196	62	177	222	2	190	2.9	217	740	11.2	1322	20.0
92-93 Was	49	48	1701	341	655	.521	0	4	.000	170	242	.702	110	45	108	154	3	117	2.4	138	433	8.8	852	17.4
93-94 Was	47	24	1178	137	292	.469	0	3	.000	70	97	.722	73	25	50	140	3	70	1.5	77	242	5.1	344	7.3
94-95 Bos	55	11	1083	152	300	.507	0	2	.000	71	99	.717	76	22	54	179	5	34	0.6	124	309	5.6	375	6.8
95-96 Bos	69	29	1431	145	295	.492	0	0	—	75	117	.641	84	39	99	207	2	62	0.9	151	451	6.5	365	5.3
96-97 Bos	6	4	125	6	16	.375	0	0	—	3	5	.600	7	5	9	21	1	4	0.7	9	26	4.3	15	2.5
97-98 Bos	33	8	447	40	70	.571	0	0	—	20	34	.588	28	20	31	90	3	31	0.9	52	109	3.3	100	3.0
98-99 Bos										Did not play: injury — Right Ankle														
99-00 Bos	30	5	269	19	43	.442	0	0	—	15	21	.714	13	10	8	67	1	13	0.4	29	67	2.2	53	1.8
10 Years	465	245	11553	1824	3572	.511	1	20	.050	839	1219	.688	795	293	750	1480	29	688	1.5	1085	3158	6.8	4488	9.7

NBA Postseason																								
Year Tm	G	GS	Min	Md	Att	Pct	Md	Att	Pct	Md	Att	Pct	TO	Stl	Blk	PF	DQ	Ast	Avg	Off	Tot	Avg	Pts	Avg
94-95 Bos	4	0	68	11	19	.579	0	0	—	2	2	1.000	4	2	5	17	1	2	0.5	11	17	4.3	24	6.0

Evan Eschmeyer

Pos: C **College:** Northwestern **Drafted:** '99 2(34)—NJ   **Ht:** 6'11" **Wt:** 255 **Born:** 5/30/75 **Age:** 25

College				Field Goals			3-Pt FGs			Free Throws			Misc			Fouls		Assists		Rebounds			Points	
Year Tm	G	GS	Min	Md	Att	Pct	Md	Att	Pct	Md	Att	Pct	TO	Stl	Blk	PF	DQ	Ast	Avg	Off	Tot	Avg	Pts	Avg
95-96 NW	27	25	691	94	168	.560	0	0	—	54	106	.509	44	21	26	105	10	16	0.6	85	178	6.6	242	9.0
96-97 NW	29	16	805	147	240	.613	0	0	—	116	178	.652	68	28	34	91	3	47	1.6	101	235	8.1	410	14.1
97-98 NW	27	27	1015	200	328	.610	0	0	—	185	302	.613	102	19	24	74	3	67	2.5	100	290	10.7	585	21.7
98-99 NW	29	29	938	180	308	.584	0	0	—	208	273	.762	94	24	48	100	4	76	2.6	96	292	10.1	568	19.6
4 Years	112	97	3449	621	1044	.595	0	0	—	563	859	.655	308	92	132	370	20	206	1.8	382	995	8.9	1805	16.1

NBA				Field Goals			3-Pt FGs			Free Throws			Misc			Fouls		Assists		Rebounds			Points	
Year Tm	G	GS	Min	Md	Att	Pct	Md	Att	Pct	Md	Att	Pct	TO	Stl	Blk	PF	DQ	Ast	Avg	Off	Tot	Avg	Pts	Avg
99-00 NJ	31	5	373	38	72	.528	0	0	—	15	30	.500	21	8	21	84	2	21	0.7	40	108	3.5	91	2.9

Patrick Ewing

(statistical profile on page 213)

Pos: C **College:** Georgetown **Drafted:** '85 1(1)—NY **Ht:** 7'0" **Wt:** 255 **Born:** 8/5/62 **Age:** 38

College

Year Tm	G	GS	Min	Md	Att	Pct	Md	Att	Pct	Md	Att	Pct	TO	Stl	Blk	PF	DQ	Ast	Avg	Off	Tot	Avg	Pts	Avg
81-82 GTwn	37	36	1064	183	290	.631	—	—	—	103	167	.617	75	40	119	117	5	23	0.6	—	279	7.5	469	12.7
82-83 GTwn	32	32	1024	212	372	.570	—	—	—	141	224	.629	81	49	106	102	7	26	0.8	—	325	10.2	565	17.7
83-84 GTwn	37	37	1179	242	368	.658	—	—	—	124	189	.656	89	36	133	108	2	31	0.8	—	371	10.0	608	16.4
84-85 GTwn	37	37	1132	220	352	.625	—	—	—	102	160	.638	81	42	135	109	2	48	1.3	—	341	9.2	542	14.6
4 Years	143	142	4399	857	1382	.620	—	—	—	470	740	.635	326	167	493	436	16	128	0.9	—	1316	9.2	2184	15.3

NBA

Year Tm	G	GS	Min	Md	Att	Pct	Md	Att	Pct	Md	Att	Pct	TO	Stl	Blk	PF	DQ	Ast	Avg	Off	Tot	Avg	Pts	Avg
85-86 NY*	50	50	1771	386	814	.474	0	5	.000	226	306	.739	172	54	103	191	7	102	2.0	124	451	9.0	998	20.0
86-87 NY	63	63	2206	530	1053	.503	0	7	.000	296	415	.713	229	89	147	248		104	1.7	157	555	8.8	1356	21.5
87-88 NY*	82	82	2546	656	1183	.555	0	3	.000	341	476	.716	287	104	245	332	5	125	1.5	245	676	8.2	1653	20.2
88-89 NY*	80	80	2896	727	1282	.567	0	6	.000	361	484	.746	266	117	281	311	5	188	2.4	213	740	9.3	1815	22.7
89-90 NY*	82	82	3165	922	1673	.551	1	4	.250	502	648	.775	278	78	327	325	7	182	2.2	235	893	10.9	2347	28.6
90-91 NY*	81	81	3104	845	1645	.514	0	6	.000	464	623	.745	291	80	258	287	3	244	3.0	194	905	11.2	2154	26.6
91-92 NY*	82	82	3150	796	1525	.522	1	6	.167	377	511	.738	209	88	245	277	2	156	1.9	228	921	11.2	1970	24.0
92-93 NY*	81	81	3003	779	1550	.503	1	7	.143	400	556	.719	265	74	161	286	2	151	1.9	191	980	12.1	1959	24.2
93-94 NY*	79	79	2972	745	1503	.496	4	14	.286	445	582	.765	260	90	217	275	3	179	2.3	219	885	11.2	1939	24.5
94-95 NY*	79	79	2920	730	1452	.503	6	21	.286	420	560	.750	256	68	159	272	3	212	2.7	157	867	11.0	1886	23.9
95-96 NY*	76	76	2783	678	1456	.466	4	28	.143	351	461	.761	221	68	184	247	2	160	2.1	157	806	10.6	1711	22.5
96-97 NY	78	78	2887	655	1342	.488	2	9	.222	439	582	.754	269	69	189	250	2	156	2.0	175	834	10.7	1751	22.4
97-98 NY	26	26	848	203	403	.504	0	2	.000	134	186	.720	77	16	58	74	0	28	1.1	59	265	10.2	540	20.8
98-99 NY	38	38	1300	247	568	.435	0	2	.000	163	231	.706	99	30	100	105	1	43	1.1	74	377	9.9	657	17.3
99-00 NY	62	62	2035	361	775	.466	0	2	.000	207	283	.731	142	36	84	196	1	58	0.9	140	604	9.7	929	15.0
15 Years	1039	1039	37586	9260	18224	.508	19	122	.156	5126	6904	.742	3321	1061	2758	3676	48	2088	2.0	2568	10759	10.4	23665	22.8

NBA Postseason

Year Tm	G	GS	Min	Md	Att	Pct	Md	Att	Pct	Md	Att	Pct	TO	Stl	Blk	PF	DQ	Ast	Avg	Off	Tot	Avg	Pts	Avg
87-88 NY	4	4	153	28	57	.491	0	1	.000	19	22	.864	11	6	13	17	0	10	2.5	16	51	12.8	75	18.8
88-89 NY	9	9	340	70	144	.486	0	0	—	39	52	.750	15	9	18	35	0	20	2.2	23	90	10.0	179	19.9
89-90 NY	10	10	395	114	219	.521	1	2	.500	65	79	.823	27	13	20	41	0	31	3.1	21	105	10.5	294	29.4
90-91 NY	3	3	110	18	45	.400	0	0	—	14	18	.778	11	1	5	12	0	6	2.0	2	30	10.0	50	16.7
91-92 NY	12	12	482	109	239	.456	0	1	.000	54	73	.740	23	7	31	49	1	27	2.3	33	133	11.1	272	22.7
92-93 NY	15	15	604	165	322	.512	1	1	1.000	51	80	.638	39	17	31	60	2	36	2.4	43	164	10.9	382	25.5
93-94 NY	25	25	1032	210	481	.437	4	11	.364	123	163	.755	83	32	76	94	1	65	2.6	88	293	11.7	547	21.9
94-95 NY	11	11	399	80	156	.513	1	3	.333	48	70	.686	30	6	25	51	1	27	2.5	17	106	9.6	209	19.0
95-96 NY	8	8	328	65	137	.474	1	2	.500	41	63	.651	30	1	25	22	0	15	1.9	11	85	10.6	172	21.5
96-97 NY	9	9	357	88	167	.527	0	1	.000	27	42	.643	27	3	22	30	0	17	1.9	26	95	10.6	203	22.6
97-98 NY	4	4	132	20	56	.357	0	0	—	16	27	.593	10	3	5	16	0	5	1.3	9	32	8.0	56	14.0
98-99 NY	11	11	347	58	135	.430	0	0	—	28	36	.778	10	7	8	35	0	6	0.5	14	96	8.7	144	13.1
99-00 NY	14	14	461	71	170	.418	0	0	—	62	89	.697	27	16	20	48	0	6	0.4	29	133	9.5	204	14.6
13 Years	135	135	5140	1096	2328	.471	8	22	.364	587	814	.721	343	121	299	510	5	271	2.0	332	1413	10.5	2787	20.6

Tony Farmer

Pos: F **College:** Nebraska **Drafted:** '97 FA—Cha **Ht:** 6'9" **Wt:** 244 **Born:** 1/3/70 **Age:** 31

College

Year Tm	G	GS	Min	Md	Att	Pct	Md	Att	Pct	Md	Att	Pct	TO	Stl	Blk	PF	DQ	Ast	Avg	Off	Tot	Avg	Pts	Avg
87-88 SJSU	14	—	108	13	38	.342	0	1	.000	6	11	.545	—	4	2	21		3	0.2	—	22	1.6	32	2.3
88-89 SJSU	16	—	339	52	111	.468	0	1	.000	35	55	.636	—	15	7	71		11	0.7	—	81	5.1	139	8.7
90-91 Neb	34	21	844	138	287	.481	7	30	.233	137	197	.695	61	36	19	94	2	45	1.3	—	251	7.4	420	12.4
3 Years	64	—	1291	203	436	.466	7	32	.219	178	263	.677	—	55	28	186	—	59	0.9	—	354	5.5	591	9.2

NBA

Year Tm	G	GS	Min	Md	Att	Pct	Md	Att	Pct	Md	Att	Pct	TO	Stl	Blk	PF	DQ	Ast	Avg	Off	Tot	Avg	Pts	Avg
91-92									Played in CBA															
92-93								Played in CBA, Played in France																
93-94								Played in CBA, Played in Italy																
94-95									Played in France															
95-96									Played in France															
96-97									Played in CBA															
97-98 Cha	27	2	169	17	53	.321	2	9	.222	31	39	.795	9	10	4	23	0	5	0.2	16	32	1.2	67	2.5
98-99									Played in Argentina															
99-00 GS	74	9	1199	127	312	.407	8	44	.182	203	265	.766	82	66	16	167	1	74	1.0	118	295	4.0	465	6.3
2 Years	101	11	1368	144	365	.395	10	53	.189	234	304	.770	91	76	20	190	1	79	0.8	134	327	3.2	532	5.3

Jamie Feick

(statistical profile on page 214)

Pos: F-C **College:** Michigan State **Drafted:** '96 2(48)—Phi   **Ht:** 6'8" **Wt:** 255 **Born:** 7/3/74 **Age:** 26

College			Field Goals			3-Pt FGs			Free Throws			Misc			Fouls		Assists		Rebounds			Points	
Year Tm	G	GS	Min	Md	Att	Pct	Md	Att	Pct	Md	Att	Pct	TO	Stl	Blk	PF	DQ	Ast	Avg	Off	Tot	Avg	Pts	Avg
92-93 MchSt	14	0	55	2	15	.133	0	1	.000	1	4	.250	4	2	1	7	0	1	0.1	8	20	1.4	5	0.4
93-94 MchSt	32	3	506	38	69	.551	0	2	.000	20	41	.488	22	12	11	57	2	23	0.7	36	104	3.3	96	3.0
94-95 MchSt	28	28	875	111	180	.617	0	0	—	54	93	.581	46	26	12	62	1	29	1.0	76	281	10.0	276	9.9
95-96 MchSt	32	31	986	116	268	.433	20	65	.308	71	115	.617	69	24	14	73	0	75	2.3	94	303	9.5	323	10.1
4 Years	106	62	2422	267	532	.502	20	68	.294	146	253	.577	141	64	38	199	3	128	1.2	214	708	6.7	700	6.6

NBA			Field Goals			3-Pt FGs			Free Throws			Misc			Fouls		Assists		Rebounds			Points	
Year Tm	G	GS	Min	Md	Att	Pct	Md	Att	Pct	Md	Att	Pct	TO	Stl	Blk	PF	DQ	Ast	Avg	Off	Tot	Avg	Pts	Avg
96-97 2Tm	41	0	624	56	157	.357	5	14	.357	34	67	.507	31	16	14	78	0	26	0.6	82	214	5.2	151	3.7
97-98 Mil	45	2	450	39	90	.433	4	13	.308	20	41	.488	21	25	15	67	0	16	0.4	45	124	2.8	102	2.3
98-99 2Tm	28	16	852	67	134	.500	0	0	—	43	60	.717	34	25	18	73	0	24	0.9	112	288	10.3	177	6.3
99-00 NJ	81	17	2241	181	423	.428	3	3	1.000	94	133	.707	59	43	38	206	2	68	0.8	264	755	9.3	459	5.7
96-97 Cha	3	0	10	2	4	.500	1	1	1.000	0	2	.000	0	0	1	3	0	0	0.0	1	3	1.0	5	1.7
SA	38	0	614	54	153	.353	4	13	.308	34	65	.523	31	16	13	75	0	26	0.7	81	211	5.6	146	3.8
98-99 Mil	2	0	3	0	1	.000	0	0	—	0	0	—	0	0	0	0	0	0	0.0	0	2	1.0	0	0.0
NJ	26	16	849	67	133	.504	0	0	—	43	60	.717	34	25	18	73	0	24	0.9	112	286	11.0	177	6.8
4 Years	195	35	4167	343	804	.427	12	30	.400	191	301	.635	145	109	87	424	2	134	0.7	503	1381	7.1	889	4.6

Danny Ferry

(statistical profile on page 214)

Pos: F **College:** Duke **Drafted:** '89 1(2)—LAC   **Ht:** 6'10" **Wt:** 235 **Born:** 10/17/66 **Age:** 34

College			Field Goals			3-Pt FGs			Free Throws			Misc			Fouls		Assists		Rebounds			Points	
Year Tm	G	GS	Min	Md	Att	Pct	Md	Att	Pct	Md	Att	Pct	TO	Stl	Blk	PF	DQ	Ast	Avg	Off	Tot	Avg	Pts	Avg
85-86 Duke	40	21	912	91	198	.460	—			54	86	.628	69	39	9	119	—	60	1.5	—	221	5.5	236	5.9
86-87 Duke	33	33	1094	172	383	.449	25	63	.397	92	109	.844	112	31	18	95	—	141	4.3	—	256	7.8	461	14.0
87-88 Duke	35	35	1138	247	519	.476	38	109	.349	135	163	.828	100	44	24	94	—	139	4.0	88	266	7.6	667	19.1
88-89 Duke	35	35	1163	300	575	.522	45	106	.425	146	193	.756	115	55	20	86	—	166	4.7	63	260	7.4	791	22.6
4 Years	143	124	4307	810	1675	.484	108	278	.388	427	551	.775	396	169	71	394	—	506	3.5	—	1003	7.0	2155	15.1

NBA			Field Goals			3-Pt FGs			Free Throws			Misc			Fouls		Assists		Rebounds			Points	
Year Tm	G	GS	Min	Md	Att	Pct	Md	Att	Pct	Md	Att	Pct	TO	Stl	Blk	PF	DQ	Ast	Avg	Off	Tot	Avg	Pts	Avg
89-90										Played in Italy														
90-91 Cle	81	2	1661	275	643	.428	23	77	.299	124	152	.816	120	43	25	230	1	142	1.8	99	286	3.5	697	8.6
91-92 Cle	68	1	937	134	328	.409	17	48	.354	61	73	.836	46	22	15	135	0	75	1.1	53	213	3.1	346	5.1
92-93 Cle	76	1	1461	220	459	.479	34	82	.415	99	113	.876	83	29	49	171	1	137	1.8	81	279	3.7	573	7.5
93-94 Cle	70	1	965	149	334	.446	14	51	.275	38	43	.884	41	28	22	113	0	74	1.1	47	141	2.0	350	5.0
94-95 Cle	82	6	1290	223	500	.446	94	233	.403	74	84	.881	59	27	22	131	0	96	1.2	30	143	1.7	614	7.5
95-96 Cle	82	79	2680	422	919	.459	143	363	.394	103	134	.769	122	57	37	233	3	191	2.3	71	309	3.8	1090	13.3
96-97 Cle	82	48	2633	341	794	.429	114	284	.401	74	87	.851	94	56	32	245	1	151	1.8	82	337	4.1	870	10.6
97-98 Cle	69	3	1034	113	286	.395	33	99	.333	32	40	.800	53	26	17	118	0	59	0.9	23	114	1.7	291	4.2
98-99 Cle	50	10	1058	141	296	.476	38	97	.392	29	33	.879	39	23	10	113	0	53	1.1	16	102	2.0	349	7.0
99-00 Cle	63	3	1326	189	380	.497	33	75	.440	52	57	.912	55	22	24	181	1	67	1.1	55	238	3.8	463	7.3
10 Years	723	154	15045	2207	4939	.447	543	1409	.385	686	816	.841	712	333	253	1670	7	1045	1.4	557	2162	3.0	5643	7.8

NBA Postseason			Field Goals			3-Pt FGs			Free Throws			Misc			Fouls		Assists		Rebounds			Points	
Year Tm	G	GS	Min	Md	Att	Pct	Md	Att	Pct	Md	Att	Pct	TO	Stl	Blk	PF	DQ	Ast	Avg	Off	Tot	Avg	Pts	Avg
91-92 Cle	9	0	55	7	15	.467	1	3	.333	4	4	1.000	2	1	1	7	0	1	0.1	7	16	1.8	19	2.1
92-93 Cle	8	0	118	13	34	.382	4	9	.444	9	10	.900	7	4	3	14	0	14	1.8	4	25	3.1	39	4.9
93-94 Cle	1	0	4	0	0	—	0	0	—	0	0	—	1	0	0	1	0	1	1.0	0	0	0.0	0	0.0
94-95 Cle	4	0	67	13	25	.520	8	15	.533	4	6	.667	0	2	0	9	0	6	1.5	0	3	0.8	38	9.5
95-96 Cle	3	3	117	14	41	.341	1	16	.063	0	0	—	4	3	2	13	1	9	3.0	1	15	5.0	29	9.7
97-98 Cle	3	0	10	0	2	.000	0	2	.000	0	0	—	0	0	0	1	0	0	0.0	0	1	0.3	0	0.0
6 Years	28	3	371	47	117	.402	14	45	.311	17	20	.850	14	10	6	45	1	31	1.1	12	60	2.1	125	4.5

Michael Finley

(statistical profile on page 215)

Pos: G-F **College:** Wisconsin **Drafted:** '95 1(21)—Pho   **Ht:** 6'7" **Wt:** 215 **Born:** 3/6/73 **Age:** 27

College			Field Goals			3-Pt FGs			Free Throws			Misc			Fouls		Assists		Rebounds			Points	
Year Tm	G	GS	Min	Md	Att	Pct	Md	Att	Pct	Md	Att	Pct	TO	Stl	Blk	PF	DQ	Ast	Avg	Off	Tot	Avg	Pts	Avg
91-92 Wisc	31	28	920	130	287	.453	26	72	.361	95	128	.742	87	27	24	73	3	85	2.7	—	152	4.9	381	12.3
92-93 Wisc	28	28	979	223	478	.467	63	173	.364	111	144	.771	76	49	18	79	3	86	3.1	—	161	5.8	620	22.1
93-94 Wisc	29	29	1046	208	446	.466	66	182	.363	110	140	.786	75	40	21	67	1	92	3.2	56	194	6.7	592	20.4
94-95 Wisc	27	27	1000	178	470	.379	58	204	.284	140	181	.773	80	52	15	73	1	108	4.0	39	141	5.2	554	20.5
4 Years	115	112	3945	739	1681	.440	213	631	.338	456	593	.769	318	168	78	292	8	371	3.2	—	648	5.6	2147	18.7

	NBA			Field Goals			3-Pt FGs			Free Throws			Misc			Fouls		Assists		Rebounds			Points	
Year Tm	G	GS	Min	Md	Att	Pct	Md	Att	Pct	Md	Att	Pct	TO	Stl	Blk	PF	DQ	Ast	Avg	Off	Tot	Avg	Pts	Avg
95-96 Pho	82	72	3212	465	976	.476	61	186	.328	242	323	.749	133	85	31	199	1	289	3.5	139	374	4.6	1233	15.0
96-97 2Tm	83	54	2790	475	1071	.444	101	280	.361	198	245	.808	164	68	24	138	0	224	2.7	88	372	4.5	1249	15.0
97-98 Dal	82	82	3394	675	1505	.449	87	244	.357	326	416	.784	219	132	30	163	0	405	4.9	149	438	5.3	1763	21.5
98-99 Dal	50	50	2051	389	876	.444	45	136	.331	186	226	.823	107	66	15	96	1	218	4.4	69	263	5.3	1009	20.2
99-00 Dal*	82	82	3464	748	1636	.457	99	247	.401	260	317	.820	196	109	32	171	1	438	5.3	122	518	6.3	1855	22.6
96-97 Pho	27	18	796	141	297	.475	14	55	.255	56	69	.812	44	18	4	42	0	68	2.5	34	120	4.4	352	13.0
Dal	56	36	1994	334	774	.432	87	225	.387	142	176	.807	120	50	20	96	0	156	2.8	54	252	4.5	897	16.0
5 Years	379	340	14911	2752	6064	.454	393	1093	.360	1212	1527	.794	819	460	132	767	3	1574	4.2	567	1965	5.2	7109	18.8

Derek Fisher

(statistical profile on page 215)

Pos: G **College:** Arkansas-Little Rock **Drafted:** '96 1(24)—LAL **Ht:** 6'1" **Wt:** 200 **Born:** 8/9/74 **Age:** 26

	College			Field Goals			3-Pt FGs			Free Throws			Misc			Fouls		Assists		Rebounds			Points	
Year Tm	G	GS	Min	Md	Att	Pct	Md	Att	Pct	Md	Att	Pct	TO	Stl	Blk	PF	DQ	Ast	Avg	Off	Tot	Avg	Pts	Avg
92-93 Ak-LR	27	—	749	57	138	.413	9	31	.290	71	92	.772	50	39	3	71	—	92	3.4	—	89	3.3	194	7.2
93-94 Ak-LR	28	—	888	94	212	.443	23	55	.418	72	93	.774	72	45	0	90	—	102	3.6	—	109	3.9	283	10.1
94-95 Ak-LR	27	—	938	153	386	.396	43	113	.381	130	180	.722	70	44	7	61	—	124	4.6	—	135	5.0	479	17.7
95-96 Ak-LR	30	30	1041	128	313	.409	50	130	.385	126	169	.746	81	56	2	64	0	154	5.1	29	155	5.2	432	14.4
4 Years	112	—	3616	432	1049	.412	125	329	.380	399	534	.747	273	184	12	286	—	472	4.2	—	488	4.4	1388	12.4

	NBA			Field Goals			3-Pt FGs			Free Throws			Misc			Fouls		Assists		Rebounds			Points	
Year Tm	G	GS	Min	Md	Att	Pct	Md	Att	Pct	Md	Att	Pct	TO	Stl	Blk	PF	DQ	Ast	Avg	Off	Tot	Avg	Pts	Avg
96-97 LAL	80	3	921	104	262	.397	22	73	.301	79	120	.658	71	41	5	87	0	119	1.5	25	97	1.2	309	3.9
97-98 LAL	82	36	1760	164	378	.434	31	81	.383	115	152	.757	119	75	5	126	1	333	4.1	38	193	2.4	474	5.8
98-99 LAL	50	21	1131	99	263	.376	38	97	.392	60	79	.759	77	61	1	95	0	197	3.9	21	91	1.8	296	5.9
99-00 LAL	78	22	1803	167	483	.346	52	166	.313	105	145	.724	75	80	3	150	1	216	2.8	22	143	1.8	491	6.3
4 Years	290	82	5615	534	1386	.385	143	417	.343	359	496	.724	342	257	14	458	2	865	3.0	106	524	1.8	1570	5.4

NBA Postseason

				Field Goals			3-Pt FGs			Free Throws			Misc			Fouls		Assists		Rebounds			Points	
Year Tm	G	GS	Min	Md	Att	Pct	Md	Att	Pct	Md	Att	Pct	TO	Stl	Blk	PF	DQ	Ast	Avg	Off	Tot	Avg	Pts	Avg
96-97 LAL	6	0	34	3	11	.273	0	5	.000	2	3	.667	6	1	0	4	0	6	1.0	0	3	0.5	8	1.3
97-98 LAL	13	13	278	27	68	.397	6	20	.300	18	29	.621	15	17	0	33	0	49	3.8	2	25	1.9	78	6.0
98-99 LAL	8	8	238	28	67	.418	10	29	.345	12	15	.800	11	8	0	20	1	39	4.9	6	29	3.6	78	9.8
99-00 LAL	21	0	322	34	79	.430	12	29	.414	19	25	.760	9	11	1	30	0	41	2.0	4	22	1.0	99	4.7
4 Years	48	21	872	92	225	.409	28	83	.337	51	72	.708	41	37	1	87	1	135	2.8	12	79	1.6	263	5.5

Danny Fortson

Pos: F-C **College:** Cincinnati **Drafted:** '97 1(10)—Mil **Ht:** 6'7" **Wt:** 260 **Born:** 3/27/76 **Age:** 24

	College			Field Goals			3-Pt FGs			Free Throws			Misc			Fouls		Assists		Rebounds			Points	
Year Tm	G	GS	Min	Md	Att	Pct	Md	Att	Pct	Md	Att	Pct	TO	Stl	Blk	PF	DQ	Ast	Avg	Off	Tot	Avg	Pts	Avg
94-95 Cin	34	25	797	190	355	.535	0	1	.000	134	196	.684	75	32	13	119	5	38	1.1	—	258	7.6	514	15.1
95-96 Cin	33	33	909	222	413	.538	0	1	.000	220	292	.753	83	40	13	118	4	45	1.4	149	316	9.6	664	20.1
96-97 Cin	33	33	986	243	392	.620	0	1	.000	217	281	.772	102	20	15	108	5	36	1.1	113	299	9.1	703	21.3
3 Years	100	91	2692	655	1160	.565	0	3	.000	571	769	.743	260	92	41	345	14	119	1.2	—	873	8.7	1881	18.8

	NBA			Field Goals			3-Pt FGs			Free Throws			Misc			Fouls		Assists		Rebounds			Points	
Year Tm	G	GS	Min	Md	Att	Pct	Md	Att	Pct	Md	Att	Pct	TO	Stl	Blk	PF	DQ	Ast	Avg	Off	Tot	Avg	Pts	Avg
97-98 Den	80	23	1811	276	611	.452	1	3	.333	263	339	.776	157	44	30	314	7	76	1.0	182	448	5.6	816	10.2
98-99 Den	50	38	1417	191	386	.495	0	3	.000	168	231	.727	77	31	22	212	9	32	0.6	210	581	11.6	550	11.0
99-00 Bos	55	5	856	140	265	.528	0	0	—	139	189	.735	67	20	5	180	4	29	0.5	141	366	6.7	419	7.6
3 Years	185	66	4084	607	1262	.481	1	6	.167	570	759	.751	301	95	57	706	20	137	0.7	533	1395	7.5	1785	9.6

Greg Foster

Pos: C **College:** UTEP **Drafted:** '90 2(35)—Was **Ht:** 6'11" **Wt:** 250 **Born:** 10/3/68 **Age:** 32

	College			Field Goals			3-Pt FGs			Free Throws			Misc			Fouls		Assists		Rebounds			Points	
Year Tm	G	GS	Min	Md	Att	Pct	Md	Att	Pct	Md	Att	Pct	TO	Stl	Blk	PF	DQ	Ast	Avg	Off	Tot	Avg	Pts	Avg
86-87 UCLA	31	0	441	44	88	.500	0	0	—	13	26	.500	25	5	24	61	1	25	0.8	—	76	2.5	101	3.3
87-88 UCLA	11	11	292	39	74	.527	0	0	—	16	37	.432	24	2	20	36	0	13	1.2	—	61	5.5	94	8.5
88-89 UTEP	26	—	728	117	242	.483	0	1	.000	54	83	.651	58	6	20	80	—	18	0.7	—	189	7.3	288	11.1
89-90 UTEP	32	—	837	133	286	.465	0	2	.000	73	90	.811	56	13	38	98	—	31	1.0	—	198	6.2	339	10.6
4 Years	100	—	2298	333	690	.483	0	3	.000	156	236	.661	163	26	102	275	—	87	0.9	—	524	5.2	822	8.2

	NBA			Field Goals			3-Pt FGs			Free Throws			Misc			Fouls		Assists		Rebounds			Points	
Year Tm	G	GS	Min	Md	Att	Pct	Md	Att	Pct	Md	Att	Pct	TO	Stl	Blk	PF	DQ	Ast	Avg	Off	Tot	Avg	Pts	Avg
90-91 Was	54	3	606	97	211	.460	0	5	.000	42	61	.689	45	12	22	112	1	37	0.7	52	151	2.8	236	4.4

NBA

Year Tm	G	GS	Min	FG Md	FG Att	FG Pct	3P Md	3P Att	3P Pct	FT Md	FT Att	FT Pct	TO	Stl	Blk	PF	DQ	Ast	Avg	Off	Tot	Avg	Pts	Avg
91-92 Was	49	3	548	89	193	.461	0	1	.000	35	49	.714	36	6	12	83	0	35	0.7	43	145	3.0	213	4.3
92-93 2Tm	43	0	298	55	120	.458	0	4	.000	15	21	.714	25	3	14	58	0	21	0.5	32	83	1.9	125	2.9
93-94 Mil	3	0	19	4	7	.571	0	0	—	2	2	1.000	1	0	1	3	0	0	0.0	0	3	1.0	10	3.3
94-95 2Tm	78	3	1144	150	318	.472	7	23	.304	78	111	.703	71	15	28	183	0	39	0.5	85	259	3.3	385	4.9
95-96 Uta	73	2	803	107	244	.439	1	8	.125	61	72	.847	58	7	22	120	0	25	0.3	53	178	2.4	276	3.8
96-97 Uta	79	12	920	111	245	.453	2	3	.667	54	65	.831	54	10	20	145	0	31	0.4	56	187	2.4	278	3.5
97-98 Uta	78	49	1446	186	418	.445	2	9	.222	67	87	.770	68	15	28	187	2	51	0.7	85	273	3.5	441	5.7
98-99 Uta	42	1	458	52	138	.377	1	4	.250	13	21	.619	24	6	8	63	1	25	0.6	28	83	2.0	118	2.8
99-00 Sea	60	5	718	91	224	.406	3	15	.200	18	28	.643	28	10	18	105	0	41	0.7	16	107	1.8	203	3.4
92-93 Was	10	0	93	11	25	.440	0	0	—	2	3	.667	9	0	5	17	0	11	1.1	8	27	2.7	24	2.4
Atl	33	0	205	44	95	.463	0	4	.000	13	18	.722	16	3	9	41	0	10	0.3	24	56	1.7	101	3.1
94-95 Chi	17	3	299	41	86	.477	0	0	—	22	31	.710	17	2	8	54	0	16	0.9	18	54	3.2	104	6.1
Min	61	0	845	109	232	.470	7	23	.304	56	80	.700	54	13	20	129	0	23	0.4	67	205	3.4	281	4.6
10 Years	559	78	6960	942	2118	.445	16	72	.222	385	517	.745	410	84	173	1059	4	305	0.5	450	1469	2.6	2285	4.1

NBA Postseason

Year Tm	G	GS	Min	FG Md	FG Att	FG Pct	3P Md	3P Att	3P Pct	FT Md	FT Att	FT Pct	TO	Stl	Blk	PF	DQ	Ast	Avg	Off	Tot	Avg	Pts	Avg
92-93 Atl	1	0	5	1	3	.333	0	0	—	3	4	.750	0	0	0	0	0	0	0.0	0	1	1.0	5	5.0
95-96 Uta	12	0	76	11	22	.500	0	0	—	6	10	.600	5	1	2	16	0	2	0.2	6	12	1.0	28	2.3
96-97 Uta	20	0	309	28	72	.389	2	8	.250	26	30	.867	11	4	7	53	0	11	0.6	15	56	2.8	84	4.2
97-98 Uta	20	16	335	39	86	.453	1	2	.500	3	5	.600	18	2	6	55	0	5	0.3	20	67	3.4	82	4.1
98-99 Uta	8	0	70	8	19	.421	0	0	—	0	0	—	3	1	0	11	0	1	0.1	1	8	1.0	16	2.0
99-00 Sea	5	0	68	7	19	.368	2	5	.400	2	2	1.000	3	0	1	14	0	1	0.2	1	11	2.2	18	3.6
6 Years	66	16	863	94	221	.425	5	15	.333	40	51	.784	40	8	16	149	0	20	0.3	43	155	2.3	233	3.5

Jeff Foster

Pos: C **College:** Southwest Texas St. **Drafted:** '99 1(21)—GS **Ht:** 6'11" **Wt:** 230 **Born:** 1/16/77 **Age:** 24

College

Year Tm	G	GS	Min	FG Md	FG Att	FG Pct	3P Md	3P Att	3P Pct	FT Md	FT Att	FT Pct	TO	Stl	Blk	PF	DQ	Ast	Avg	Off	Tot	Avg	Pts	Avg
95-96 SWTx	26	9	340	31	70	.443	1	1	1.000	19	39	.487	24	9	17	65	—	19	0.7	50	108	4.2	82	3.2
96-97 SWTx	29	25	637	87	170	.512	3	3	1.000	71	110	.645	54	23	38	88	4	25	0.9	79	222	7.7	248	8.6
97-98 SWTx	28	26	816	140	263	.532	0	0	—	77	126	.611	61	37	29	102	3	44	1.6	132	285	10.2	357	12.8
98-99 SWTx	28	28	787	142	285	.498	0	0	—	113	163	.693	56	30	27	84	4	43	1.5	142	316	11.3	397	14.2
4 Years	111	88	2580	400	788	.508	4	4	1.000	280	438	.639	195	99	111	339	—	131	1.2	403	931	8.4	1084	9.8

NBA

Year Tm	G	GS	Min	FG Md	FG Att	FG Pct	3P Md	3P Att	3P Pct	FT Md	FT Att	FT Pct	TO	Stl	Blk	PF	DQ	Ast	Avg	Off	Tot	Avg	Pts	Avg
99-00 Ind	19	0	86	13	23	.565	0	1	.000	17	25	.680	2	5	1	18	0	5	0.3	12	32	1.7	43	2.3

Rick Fox

(statistical profile on page 216)

Pos: G-F **College:** North Carolina **Drafted:** '91 1(24)—Bos **Ht:** 6'7" **Wt:** 242 **Born:** 7/24/69 **Age:** 31

College

Year Tm	G	GS	Min	FG Md	FG Att	FG Pct	3P Md	3P Att	3P Pct	FT Md	FT Att	FT Pct	TO	Stl	Blk	PF	DQ	Ast	Avg	Off	Tot	Avg	Pts	Avg
87-88 UNC	34	3	371	59	94	.628	3	9	.333	15	30	.500	41	26	5	68	—	32	0.9	—	63	1.9	136	4.0
88-89 UNC	37	17	829	165	283	.583	13	29	.448	83	105	.790	88	47	16	122	—	76	2.1	—	142	3.8	426	11.5
89-90 UNC	34	30	981	203	389	.522	70	160	.438	75	102	.735	108	54	6	112	—	84	2.5	—	157	4.6	551	16.2
90-91 UNC	35	32	999	206	455	.453	67	196	.342	111	138	.804	102	70	17	103	—	131	3.7	—	232	6.6	590	16.9
4 Years	140	82	3180	633	1221	.518	153	394	.388	284	375	.757	339	197	44	405	—	323	2.3	—	594	4.2	1703	12.2

NBA

Year Tm	G	GS	Min	FG Md	FG Att	FG Pct	3P Md	3P Att	3P Pct	FT Md	FT Att	FT Pct	TO	Stl	Blk	PF	DQ	Ast	Avg	Off	Tot	Avg	Pts	Avg
91-92 Bos	81	5	1535	241	525	.459	23	70	.329	139	184	.755	123	78	30	230	3	126	1.6	73	220	2.7	644	8.0
92-93 Bos	71	14	1082	184	380	.484	4	23	.174	81	101	.802	77	61	21	133	1	113	1.6	55	159	2.2	453	6.4
93-94 Bos	82	53	2096	340	728	.467	33	100	.330	174	230	.757	158	81	52	244	4	217	2.6	105	355	4.3	887	10.8
94-95 Bos	53	7	1039	169	351	.481	31	75	.413	95	123	.772	78	52	19	154	1	139	2.6	61	155	2.9	464	8.8
95-96 Bos	81	81	2588	421	928	.454	99	272	.364	196	254	.772	216	113	41	290	5	369	4.6	158	450	5.6	1137	14.0
96-97 Bos	76	75	2650	433	950	.456	101	278	.363	207	263	.787	178	167	40	279	4	286	3.8	114	394	5.2	1174	15.4
97-98 LAL	82	82	2709	363	771	.471	86	265	.325	171	230	.743	201	100	48	309	4	276	3.4	78	358	4.4	983	12.0
98-99 LAL	44	1	944	148	330	.448	32	95	.337	66	89	.742	56	28	10	114	1	89	2.0	26	89	2.0	394	9.0
99-00 LAL	82	1	1473	206	498	.414	59	181	.326	63	78	.808	87	52	26	203	1	138	1.7	63	198	2.4	534	6.5
9 Years	652	319	16116	2505	5461	.459	468	1359	.344	1192	1552	.768	1174	732	287	1956	24	1753	2.7	733	2378	3.6	6670	10.2

NBA Postseason

Year Tm	G	GS	Min	FG Md	FG Att	FG Pct	3P Md	3P Att	3P Pct	FT Md	FT Att	FT Pct	TO	Stl	Blk	PF	DQ	Ast	Avg	Off	Tot	Avg	Pts	Avg
91-92 Bos	8	0	67	11	23	.478	3	6	.500	4	4	1.000	2	2	2	11	0	4	0.5	3	6	0.8	29	3.6
92-93 Bos	4	0	71	7	25	.280	1	3	.333	2	2	1.000	4	2	1	7	0	5	1.3	8	19	4.8	19	4.3

NBA Postseason

Year Tm	G	GS	Min	Md	Att	Pct	Md	Att	Pct	Md	Att	Pct	TO	Stl	Blk	PF	DQ	Ast	Avg	Off	Tot	Avg	Pts	Avg
97-98 LAL	13	13	428	51	114	.447	21	53	.396	19	23	.826	21	11	3	47	2	51	3.9	18	58	4.5	142	10.9
98-99 LAL	8	1	181	24	60	.400	4	21	.190	1	1	1.000	14	4	5	26	1	12	1.5	9	22	2.8	53	6.6
99-00 LAL	23	0	331	33	73	.452	18	39	.462	16	21	.762	16	9	0	68	1	28	1.2	11	38	1.7	100	4.3
5 Years	56	14	1078	126	295	.427	47	122	.385	42	51	.824	57	28	11	159	4	100	1.8	49	143	2.6	341	6.1

Adonal Foyle

(statistical profile on page 216)

Pos: C **College:** Colgate **Drafted:** '97 1(8)—GS   **Ht:** 6'10" **Wt:** 250 **Born:** 3/9/75 **Age:** 25

College				Field Goals			3-Pt FGs			Free Throws			Misc			Fouls		Assists		Rebounds			Points	
Year Tm	G	GS	Min	Md	Att	Pct	Md	Att	Pct	Md	Att	Pct	TO	Stl	Blk	PF	DQ	Ast	Avg	Off	Tot	Avg	Pts	Avg
94-95 Colg	30	—	1063	207	370	.559	0	0	—	95	190	.500	98	21	147	76	2	36	1.2	—	371	12.4	509	17.0
95-96 Colg	29	—	1060	228	441	.517	0	3	.000	129	264	.489	114	21	165	77	2	44	1.5	—	364	12.6	585	20.2
96-97 Colg	28	28	1055	277	490	.565	1	7	.143	127	261	.487	117	19	180	60	1	54	1.9	112	368	13.1	682	24.4
3 Years	87	—	3178	712	1301	.547	1	10	.100	351	715	.491	329	61	492	213	5	134	1.5	—	1103	12.7	1776	20.4

NBA				Field Goals			3-Pt FGs			Free Throws			Misc			Fouls		Assists		Rebounds			Points	
Year Tm	G	GS	Min	Md	Att	Pct	Md	Att	Pct	Md	Att	Pct	TO	Stl	Blk	PF	DQ	Ast	Avg	Off	Tot	Avg	Pts	Avg
97-98 GS	55	1	656	69	170	.406	0	1	.000	27	62	.435	50	13	52	94	0	14	0.3	73	184	3.3	165	3.0
98-99 GS	44	0	614	52	121	.430	0	0	—	25	51	.490	31	15	43	90	0	18	0.4	79	194	4.4	129	2.9
99-00 GS	76	59	1654	193	380	.508	0	0	—	34	90	.378	71	26	136	218	2	42	0.6	174	424	5.6	420	5.5
3 Years	175	60	2924	314	671	.468	0	1	.000	86	203	.424	152	54	231	402	2	74	0.4	326	802	4.6	714	4.1

Steve Francis

(statistical profile on page 217)

Pos: G **College:** Maryland **Drafted:** '99 1(2)—Van   **Ht:** 6'3" **Wt:** 193 **Born:** 2/21/78 **Age:** 22

College				Field Goals			3-Pt FGs			Free Throws			Misc			Fouls		Assists		Rebounds			Points	
Year Tm	G	GS	Min	Md	Att	Pct	Md	Att	Pct	Md	Att	Pct	TO	Stl	Blk	PF	DQ	Ast	Avg	Off	Tot	Avg	Pts	Avg
98-99 Myld	34	33	1044	205	392	.523	45	116	.388	124	157	.790	102	91	6	95	2	152	4.5	57	154	4.5	579	17.0

NBA				Field Goals			3-Pt FGs			Free Throws			Misc			Fouls		Assists		Rebounds			Points	
Year Tm	G	GS	Min	Md	Att	Pct	Md	Att	Pct	Md	Att	Pct	TO	Stl	Blk	PF	DQ	Ast	Avg	Off	Tot	Avg	Pts	Avg
99-00 Hou	77	77	2776	497	1117	.445	107	310	.345	287	365	.786	306	118	29	231	2	507	6.6	152	409	5.3	1388	18.0

Todd Fuller

Pos: F-C **College:** North Carolina St. **Drafted:** '96 1(11)—GS   **Ht:** 6'11" **Wt:** 255 **Born:** 7/25/74 **Age:** 26

College				Field Goals			3-Pt FGs			Free Throws			Misc			Fouls		Assists		Rebounds			Points	
Year Tm	G	GS	Min	Md	Att	Pct	Md	Att	Pct	Md	Att	Pct	TO	Stl	Blk	PF	DQ	Ast	Avg	Off	Tot	Avg	Pts	Avg
92-93 NCSt	27	2	413	53	116	.457	1	2	.500	34	44	.773	15	1	8	35	—	6	0.2	38	97	3.6	141	5.2
93-94 NCSt	30	29	875	144	299	.482	0	4	.000	67	89	.753	42	11	38	61	—	33	1.1	94	253	8.4	355	11.8
94-95 NCSt	27	27	816	164	316	.519	0	6	.000	116	138	.841	41	7	45	53	—	35	1.3	100	229	8.5	444	16.4
95-96 NCSt	31	31	1044	225	445	.506	16	43	.372	183	229	.799	72	10	56	48	0	39	1.3	108	308	9.9	649	20.9
4 Years	115	89	3148	586	1176	.498	17	55	.309	400	500	.800	170	29	147	197	—	113	1.0	340	887	7.7	1589	13.8

NBA				Field Goals			3-Pt FGs			Free Throws			Misc			Fouls		Assists		Rebounds			Points	
Year Tm	G	GS	Min	Md	Att	Pct	Md	Att	Pct	Md	Att	Pct	TO	Stl	Blk	PF	DQ	Ast	Avg	Off	Tot	Avg	Pts	Avg
96-97 GS	75	18	949	114	266	.429	0	0	—	76	110	.691	52	10	20	146	0	24	0.3	108	249	3.3	304	4.1
97-98 GS	57	1	613	86	205	.420	0	4	.000	55	80	.688	37	6	16	89	0	10	0.2	61	196	3.4	227	4.0
98-99 Uta	42	2	462	56	124	.452	0	0	—	30	50	.600	27	6	14	60	0	6	0.1	28	101	2.4	142	3.4
99-00 Cha	41	2	399	51	122	.418	0	0	—	32	53	.604	27	9	8	46	0	5	0.1	36	110	2.7	134	3.3
4 Years	215	23	2423	307	717	.428	0	4	.000	193	293	.659	143	31	58	341	0	45	0.2	233	656	3.1	807	3.8

NBA Postseason

Year Tm	G	GS	Min	Md	Att	Pct	Md	Att	Pct	Md	Att	Pct	TO	Stl	Blk	PF	DQ	Ast	Avg	Off	Tot	Avg	Pts	Avg
98-99 Uta	10	0	105	10	26	.385	0	0	—	6	10	.600	5	0	2	21	0	0	0.0	8	28	2.8	26	2.6

Lawrence Funderburke

Pos: F **College:** Ohio State **Drafted:** '94 2(51)—Sac   **Ht:** 6'9" **Wt:** 230 **Born:** 12/15/70 **Age:** 30

College				Field Goals			3-Pt FGs			Free Throws			Misc			Fouls		Assists		Rebounds			Points	
Year Tm	G	GS	Min	Md	Att	Pct	Md	Att	Pct	Md	Att	Pct	TO	Stl	Blk	PF	DQ	Ast	Avg	Off	Tot	Avg	Pts	Avg
91-92 OhSt	23	13	668	115	210	.548	0	0	—	51	78	.654	33	15	55	40	0	18	0.8	63	149	6.5	281	12.2
92-93 OhSt	28	28	878	186	349	.533	1	3	.333	84	135	.622	56	21	54	49	0	34	1.2	62	190	6.8	457	16.3
93-94 OhSt	29	20	847	188	345	.545	2	7	.286	63	106	.594	50	11	22	51	0	28	1.0	68	190	6.6	441	15.2
3 Years	80	61	2393	489	904	.541	3	10	.300	198	319	.621	139	47	131	140	0	80	1.0	193	529	6.6	1179	14.7

NBA				Field Goals			3-Pt FGs			Free Throws			Misc			Fouls		Assists		Rebounds			Points	
Year Tm	G	GS	Min	Md	Att	Pct	Md	Att	Pct	Md	Att	Pct	TO	Stl	Blk	PF	DQ	Ast	Avg	Off	Tot	Avg	Pts	Avg
94-95										Played in Greece														
95-96										Played in Greece														
96-97										Played in France														
97-98 Sac	52	1	1094	191	390	.490	1	7	.143	110	162	.679	62	19	15	56	0	63	1.2	80	234	4.5	493	9.5
98-99 Sac	47	2	936	167	299	.559	1	5	.200	85	120	.708	52	22	23	77	0	30	0.6	101	222	4.7	420	8.9
99-00 Sac	75	1	1026	184	352	.523	0	2	.000	115	163	.706	40	32	20	91	0	33	0.4	98	234	3.1	483	6.4
3 Years	174	4	3056	542	1041	.521	2	14	.143	310	445	.697	154	73	58	224	0	126	0.7	279	690	4.0	1396	8.0
NBA Postseason																								
Year Tm	G	GS	Min	Md	Att	Pct	Md	Att	Pct	Md	Att	Pct	TO	Stl	Blk	PF	DQ	Ast	Avg	Off	Tot	Avg	Pts	Avg
98-99 Sac	3	0	31	5	12	.417	0	0	—	0	0	—	3	3	0	3	0	1	0.3	2	4	1.3	10	3.3
99-00 Sac	4	0	34	4	9	.444	0	0	—	2	4	.500	0	1	0	0	0	0	0.0	4	11	2.8	10	2.5
2 Years	7	0	65	9	21	.429	0	0	—	2	4	.500	3	4	0	3	0	1	0.1	6	15	2.1	20	2.9

Kevin Garnett

(statistical profile on page 217)

Pos: F **College:** None **Drafted:** '95 1(5)—Min **Ht:** 6'11" **Wt:** 220 **Born:** 5/19/76 **Age:** 24

NBA				Field Goals			3-Pt FGs			Free Throws			Misc			Fouls		Assists		Rebounds			Points	
Year Tm	G	GS	Min	Md	Att	Pct	Md	Att	Pct	Md	Att	Pct	TO	Stl	Blk	PF	DQ	Ast	Avg	Off	Tot	Avg	Pts	Avg
95-96 Min	80	43	2293	361	735	.491	8	28	.286	105	149	.705	110	86	131	189	2	145	1.8	175	501	6.3	835	10.4
96-97 Min*	77	77	2995	549	1100	.499	6	21	.286	205	272	.754	175	105	163	199	2	236	3.1	190	618	8.0	1309	17.0
97-98 Min*	82	82	3222	635	1293	.491	3	16	.188	245	332	.738	192	139	150	224	1	348	4.2	222	786	9.6	1518	18.5
98-99 Min	47	47	1780	414	900	.460	4	14	.286	145	206	.704	135	78	83	152	5	202	4.3	166	489	10.4	977	20.8
99-00 Min*	81	81	3243	759	1526	.497	30	81	.370	309	404	.765	268	120	126	205	1	401	5.0	223	956	11.8	1857	22.9
5 Years	367	330	13533	2718	5554	.489	51	160	.319	1009	1363	.740	880	528	653	969	11	1332	3.6	976	3350	9.1	6496	17.7
NBA Postseason																								
Year Tm	G	GS	Min	Md	Att	Pct	Md	Att	Pct	Md	Att	Pct	TO	Stl	Blk	PF	DQ	Ast	Avg	Off	Tot	Avg	Pts	Avg
96-97 Min	3	3	125	24	51	.471	1	1	1.000	3	3	1.000	4	4	3	6	0	11	3.7	14	28	9.3	52	17.3
97-98 Min	5	5	194	36	75	.480	0	0	—	7	9	.778	22	4	12	17	0	20	4.0	17	48	9.6	79	15.8
98-99 Min	4	4	170	35	79	.443	0	2	.000	17	23	.739	13	7	8	10	0	15	3.8	16	48	12.0	87	21.8
99-00 Min	4	4	171	30	78	.385	2	3	.667	13	16	.813	11	5	3	12	0	35	8.8	13	43	10.8	75	18.8
4 Years	16	16	660	125	283	.442	3	6	.500	40	51	.784	50	20	26	45	0	81	5.1	60	167	10.4	293	18.3

Dean Garrett

Pos: C **College:** Indiana **Drafted:** '88 2(38)—Pho **Ht:** 6'11" **Wt:** 250 **Born:** 11/27/66 **Age:** 34

College				Field Goals			3-Pt FGs			Free Throws			Misc			Fouls		Assists		Rebounds			Points	
Year Tm	G	GS	Min	Md	Att	Pct	Md	Att	Pct	Md	Att	Pct	TO	Stl	Blk	PF	DQ	Ast	Avg	Off	Tot	Avg	Pts	Avg
86-87 Ind	34	33	—	163	301	.542	0	0	—	61	96	.635	41	17	93	92	2	21	0.6	—	288	8.5	387	11.4
87-88 Ind	29	28	—	184	344	.535	0	0	—	99	142	.697	34	17	99	82	2	13	0.4	—	246	8.5	467	16.1
2 Years	63	61	—	347	645	.538	0	0	—	160	238	.672	75	34	192	174	4	34	0.5	—	534	8.5	854	13.6

NBA				Field Goals			3-Pt FGs			Free Throws			Misc			Fouls		Assists		Rebounds			Points	
Year Tm	G	GS	Min	Md	Att	Pct	Md	Att	Pct	Md	Att	Pct	TO	Stl	Blk	PF	DQ	Ast	Avg	Off	Tot	Avg	Pts	Avg
88-89										Did not play in NBA														
89-90										Played in Italy														
90-91										Played in Italy														
91-92										Played in Italy														
92-93										Played in Italy														
93-94										Played in Italy														
94-95										Played in Italy														
95-96										Played in Greece														
96-97 Min	68	47	1665	223	389	.573	0	0	—	96	138	.696	34	40	95	158	1	38	0.6	149	495	7.3	542	8.0
97-98 Den	82	82	2632	242	565	.428	0	0	—	114	176	.648	84	57	133	197	0	90	1.1	227	644	7.9	598	7.3
98-99 Min	49	37	1054	116	231	.502	0	0	—	38	51	.745	29	30	45	113	0	28	0.6	99	257	5.2	270	5.5
99-00 Min	56	23	604	48	108	.444	0	0	—	18	26	.692	21	8	40	94	1	19	0.3	41	140	2.5	114	2.0
4 Years	255	189	5955	629	1293	.486	0	0	—	266	391	.680	168	135	313	562	2	175	0.7	516	1536	6.0	1524	6.0
NBA Postseason																								
Year Tm	G	GS	Min	Md	Att	Pct	Md	Att	Pct	Md	Att	Pct	TO	Stl	Blk	PF	DQ	Ast	Avg	Off	Tot	Avg	Pts	Avg
96-97 Min	3	3	118	15	29	.517	0	0	—	8	10	.800	1	2	3	11	0	4	1.3	19	35	11.7	38	12.7
98-99 Min	4	4	92	10	18	.556	0	0	—	2	5	.400	2	2	3	16	1	5	1.3	9	16	4.0	22	5.5
99-00 Min	3	0	16	1	2	.500	0	0	—	1	2	.500	0	0	1	2	0	0	0.0	1	2	0.7	3	1.0
3 Years	10	6	226	26	49	.531	0	0	—	11	17	.647	3	4	7	29	1	9	0.9	29	53	5.3	63	6.3

Kiwane Garris

Pos: G **College:** Illinois **Drafted:** '97 FA—Den   **Ht:** 6'2" **Wt:** 183 **Born:** 9/24/74 **Age:** 26

College			Field Goals			3-Pt FGs			Free Throws			Misc			Fouls		Assists		Rebounds			Points	
Year Tm	G	GS	Min	Md	Att	Pct	Md	Att	Pct	Md	Att	Pct	TO	Stl	Blk	PF	DQ	Ast	Avg	Off	Tot	Avg	Pts	Avg
93-94 Ill	28	27	891	133	307	.433	29	87	.333	151	188	.803	78	33	1	59	0	107	3.8	23	98	3.5	446	15.9
94-95 Ill	31	30	1038	150	342	.439	46	119	.387	148	178	.831	75	36	0	74	0	117	3.8	17	88	2.8	494	15.9
95-96 Ill	25	22	785	118	316	.373	38	117	.325	112	130	.862	35	42	0	47	0	98	3.9	17	86	3.4	386	15.4
96-97 Ill	32	32	1089	171	428	.400	76	197	.386	204	245	.833	86	52	2	77	0	180	5.6	16	113	3.5	622	19.4
4 Years	116	111	3803	572	1393	.411	189	520	.363	615	741	.830	274	163	3	257	0	502	4.3	73	385	3.3	1948	16.8

NBA			Field Goals			3-Pt FGs			Free Throws			Misc			Fouls		Assists		Rebounds			Points	
Year Tm	G	GS	Min	Md	Att	Pct	Md	Att	Pct	Md	Att	Pct	TO	Stl	Blk	PF	DQ	Ast	Avg	Off	Tot	Avg	Pts	Avg
97-98 Den	28	0	225	22	65	.338	5	14	.357	19	25	.760	15	7	1	22	0	28	1.0	3	19	0.7	68	2.4
98-99										Played in Germany														
99-00 Orl	3	0	23	2	10	.200	0	1	.000	0	0	—	1	0	0	0	0	2	0.7	0	1	0.3	4	1.3
2 Years	31	0	248	24	75	.320	5	15	.333	19	25	.760	16	7	1	22	0	30	1.0	3	20	0.6	72	2.3

Pat Garrity

(statistical profile on page 218)

Pos: F **College:** Notre Dame **Drafted:** '98 1(19)—Mil   **Ht:** 6'9" **Wt:** 238 **Born:** 8/23/76 **Age:** 24

College			Field Goals			3-Pt FGs			Free Throws			Misc			Fouls		Assists		Rebounds			Points	
Year Tm	G	GS	Min	Md	Att	Pct	Md	Att	Pct	Md	Att	Pct	TO	Stl	Blk	PF	DQ	Ast	Avg	Off	Tot	Avg	Pts	Avg
94-95 ND	27	27	744	136	260	.523	7	18	.389	82	107	.766	70	18	17	77	3	34	1.3	43	137	5.1	361	13.4
95-96 ND	27	27	893	177	372	.476	14	51	.275	96	140	.686	72	24	14	79	3	38	1.4	66	193	7.1	464	17.2
96-97 ND	30	30	1056	221	457	.484	39	102	.382	152	196	.776	105	25	17	78	0	84	2.8	71	221	7.4	633	21.1
97-98 ND	27	27	956	214	445	.481	40	108	.370	159	212	.750	94	17	16	76	1	66	2.4	55	225	8.3	627	23.2
4 Years	111	111	3649	748	1534	.488	100	279	.358	489	655	.747	341	84	64	310	7	222	2.0	235	776	7.0	2085	18.8

NBA			Field Goals			3-Pt FGs			Free Throws			Misc			Fouls		Assists		Rebounds			Points	
Year Tm	G	GS	Min	Md	Att	Pct	Md	Att	Pct	Md	Att	Pct	TO	Stl	Blk	PF	DQ	Ast	Avg	Off	Tot	Avg	Pts	Avg
98-99 Pho	39	9	538	85	170	.500	7	18	.389	40	56	.714	20	8	3	62	0	18	0.5	26	75	1.9	217	5.6
99-00 Orl	82	1	1479	258	585	.441	79	197	.401	80	111	.721	85	31	19	197	1	58	0.7	44	210	2.6	675	8.2
2 Years	121	10	2017	343	755	.454	86	215	.400	120	167	.719	105	39	22	259	1	76	0.6	70	285	2.4	892	7.4

NBA Postseason																								
Year Tm	G	GS	Min	Md	Att	Pct	Md	Att	Pct	Md	Att	Pct	TO	Stl	Blk	PF	DQ	Ast	Avg	Off	Tot	Avg	Pts	Avg
98-99 Pho	3	0	52	9	17	.529	3	3	1.000	6	6	1.000	3	1	1	9	0	1	0.3	6	9	3.0	27	9.0

Chris Gatling

(statistical profile on page 218)

Pos: F-C **College:** Old Dominion **Drafted:** '91 1(16)—GS   **Ht:** 6'10" **Wt:** 230 **Born:** 9/3/67 **Age:** 33

College			Field Goals			3-Pt FGs			Free Throws			Misc			Fouls		Assists		Rebounds			Points	
Year Tm	G	GS	Min	Md	Att	Pct	Md	Att	Pct	Md	Att	Pct	TO	Stl	Blk	PF	DQ	Ast	Avg	Off	Tot	Avg	Pts	Avg
88-89 ODU	27	—	839	239	388	.616	0	0	—	126	179	.704	78	37	61	88	—	26	1.0	—	244	9.0	604	22.4
89-90 ODU	26	—	822	207	357	.580	0	0	—	120	179	.670	76	48	49	91	—	25	1.0	—	259	10.0	534	20.5
90-91 ODU	32	—	1002	251	405	.620	0	1	.000	171	247	.692	90	62	85	103	—	24	0.8	—	356	11.1	673	21.0
3 Years	85	—	2663	697	1150	.606	0	1	.000	417	605	.689	244	147	195	282	—	75	0.9	—	859	10.1	1811	21.3

NBA			Field Goals			3-Pt FGs			Free Throws			Misc			Fouls		Assists		Rebounds			Points	
Year Tm	G	GS	Min	Md	Att	Pct	Md	Att	Pct	Md	Att	Pct	TO	Stl	Blk	PF	DQ	Ast	Avg	Off	Tot	Avg	Pts	Avg
91-92 GS	54	1	612	117	206	.568	0	4	.000	72	109	.661	44	31	36	101	0	16	0.3	75	182	3.4	306	5.7
92-93 GS	70	11	1248	249	462	.539	0	6	.000	150	207	.725	102	44	53	197	2	40	0.6	129	320	4.6	648	9.3
93-94 GS	82	23	1296	271	461	.588	0	1	.000	129	208	.620	84	40	63	223	5	41	0.5	143	397	4.8	671	8.2
94-95 GS	58	22	1470	324	512	.633	0	1	.000	148	250	.592	117	39	52	184	4	51	0.9	144	443	7.6	796	13.7
95-96 2Tm	71	2	1427	326	567	.575	0	1	.000	139	207	.671	95	36	40	217	0	43	0.6	129	417	5.9	791	11.1
96-97 2Tm*	47	1	1283	327	623	.525	1	6	.167	236	329	.717	120	39	31	138	1	28	0.6	134	370	7.9	891	19.0
97-98 NJ	57	16	1359	248	545	.455	1	4	.250	159	265	.600	99	52	29	152	2	53	0.9	118	334	5.9	656	11.5
98-99 2Tm	48	3	775	117	265	.442	1	8	.125	37	93	.398	62	32	10	118	0	32	0.7	52	179	3.7	272	5.7
99-00 2Tm	85	0	1811	365	802	.455	18	70	.257	266	373	.713	169	82	23	246	2	71	0.8	154	502	5.9	1014	11.9
95-96 GS	47	2	862	171	308	.555	0	1	.000	84	132	.636	60	19	29	135	0	26	0.6	78	242	5.1	426	9.1
Mia	24	0	565	155	259	.598	0	0	—	55	75	.733	35	17	11	82	0	17	0.7	51	175	7.3	365	15.2
96-97 Dal	44	1	1191	309	580	.533	1	6	.167	221	313	.706	114	35	31	125	1	25	0.6	126	348	7.9	840	19.1
NJ	3	0	92	18	43	.419	0	0	—	15	16	.938	6	4	0	13	0	3	1.0	8	22	7.3	51	17.0
98-99 NJ	18	2	281	36	97	.371	0	1	.000	12	24	.500	29	8	4	40	0	12	0.7	21	65	3.6	84	4.7
Mil	30	1	494	81	168	.482	1	7	.143	25	69	.362	33	24	6	78	0	20	0.7	31	114	3.8	188	6.3
99-00 Orl	45	0	1041	210	462	.455	7	23	.304	171	245	.698	105	48	10	142	0	40	0.9	91	297	6.6	598	13.3
Den	40	0	770	155	340	.456	11	47	.234	95	128	.742	64	34	13	104	2	31	0.8	63	205	5.1	416	10.4
9 Years	572	79	11281	2344	4443	.528	21	101	.208	1336	2041	.655	892	395	337	1576	16	375	0.7	1078	3144	5.5	6045	10.6

NBA Postseason

Year Tm	G	GS	Min	Md	Att	Pct	Md	Att	Pct	Md	Att	Pct	TO	Stl	Blk	PF	DQ	Ast	Avg	Off	Tot	Avg	Pts	Avg
91-92 GS	4	0	81	18	29	.621	0	0	—	14	22	.636	1	2	10	14	0	0	0.0	9	25	6.3	50	12.5
93-94 GS	3	1	54	8	13	.615	0	0	—	10	13	.769	2	2	1	10	0	4	1.3	7	17	5.7	26	8.7
95-96 Mia	3	0	68	6	22	.273	0	0	—	6	12	.500	8	2	1	8	1	1	0.3	7	17	5.7	26	8.7
97-98 NJ	3	1	81	19	38	.500	0	0	—	8	12	.667	3	2	2	9	0	2	0.7	6	10	3.3	46	6.0
98-99 Mil	2	0	12	0	2	.000	0	0	—	0	2	.000	2	1	0	3	0	0	0.0	1	3	1.5	0	0.0
5 Years	15	2	296	51	104	.490	0	0	—	38	61	.623	16	9	13	44	1	7	0.5	33	79	5.3	140	9.3

Matt Geiger

Pos: C **College:** Georgia Tech **Drafted:** '92 2(42)—Mia   **Ht:** 7'1" **Wt:** 248 **Born:** 9/10/69 **Age:** 31

(statistical profile on page 219)

College

Year Tm	G	GS	Min	Md	Att	Pct	Md	Att	Pct	Md	Att	Pct	TO	Stl	Blk	PF	DQ	Ast	Avg	Off	Tot	Avg	Pts	Avg
87-88 Aub	30	—	597	80	156	.513	0	0	—	33	50	.660	63	11	9	75	—	24	0.8	—	124	4.1	193	6.4
88-89 Aub	28	—	807	170	337	.504	0	4	.000	106	154	.688	91	17	25	108	—	31	1.1	—	186	6.6	446	15.9
90-91 GTch	27	24	711	130	237	.549	0	3	.000	49	73	.671	54	5	29	79	—	26	1.0	66	172	6.4	309	11.4
91-92 GTch	35	35	952	165	270	.611	0	2	.000	84	119	.706	68	25	65	102	—	37	1.1	98	254	7.3	414	11.8
4 Years	120	—	3067	545	1000	.545	0	9	.000	272	396	.687	276	58	128	364	—	118	1.0	—	736	6.1	1362	11.4

NBA

Year Tm	G	GS	Min	Md	Att	Pct	Md	Att	Pct	Md	Att	Pct	TO	Stl	Blk	PF	DQ	Ast	Avg	Off	Tot	Avg	Pts	Avg
92-93 Mia	48	2	554	76	145	.524	0	4	.000	62	92	.674	36	15	18	123	6	14	0.3	46	120	2.5	214	4.5
93-94 Mia	72	0	1199	202	352	.574	1	5	.200	116	149	.779	61	36	29	201	2	32	0.4	119	303	4.2	521	7.2
94-95 Cha	74	43	1712	260	485	.536	4	10	.400	93	143	.650	113	41	51	245	5	55	0.7	146	413	5.6	617	8.3
95-96 Cha	77	50	2349	357	666	.536	3	8	.375	149	205	.727	137	46	63	290	11	60	0.8	201	649	8.4	866	11.2
96-97 Mia	49	13	1044	171	350	.489	6	20	.300	89	127	.701	67	20	27	153	1	38	0.8	100	258	5.3	437	8.9
97-98 Cha	78	42	1839	358	709	.505	1	11	.091	168	236	.712	111	68	87	191	1	78	1.0	196	521	6.7	885	11.3
98-99 Phi	50	40	1540	266	555	.479	1	5	.200	141	177	.797	101	39	40	157	2	58	1.2	137	362	7.2	674	13.5
99-00 Phi	65	20	1406	260	589	.441	0	4	.000	109	140	.779	91	29	22	194	1	39	0.6	154	387	6.0	629	9.7
8 Years	513	210	11643	1950	3851	.506	16	67	.239	927	1269	.730	717	294	337	1554	29	374	0.7	1099	3013	5.9	4843	9.4

NBA Postseason

Year Tm	G	GS	Min	Md	Att	Pct	Md	Att	Pct	Md	Att	Pct	TO	Stl	Blk	PF	DQ	Ast	Avg	Off	Tot	Avg	Pts	Avg
93-94 Mia	2	0	11	0	2	.000	0	0	—	1	2	.500	0	0	0	1	0	0	0.0	0	4	2.0	1	0.5
96-97 Cha	3	0	31	2	3	.667	0	0	—	2	2	1.000	2	2	1	5	0	2	0.7	4	8	2.7	6	2.0
97-98 Cha	4	0	22	1	6	.167	0	0	—	0	0	—	1	0	0	2	0	1	0.3	3	5	1.3	2	0.5
98-99 Phi	8	8	239	42	96	.438	0	1	.000	24	29	.828	13	9	6	29	0	6	0.8	23	61	7.6	108	13.5
99-00 Phi	8	0	128	25	50	.500	0	0	—	20	25	.800	5	5	2	23	0	2	0.3	17	40	5.0	70	8.8
5 Years	25	8	431	70	157	.446	0	1	.000	47	58	.810	21	16	9	60	0	11	0.4	47	118	4.7	187	7.5

Devean George

Pos: F **College:** Augsburg **Drafted:** '99 1(23)—LAL   **Ht:** 6'8" **Wt:** 220 **Born:** 8/29/77 **Age:** 23

College

Year Tm	G	GS	Min	Md	Att	Pct	Md	Att	Pct	Md	Att	Pct	TO	Stl	Blk	PF	DQ	Ast	Avg	Off	Tot	Avg	Pts	Avg
95-96 Aug	17	12	500	93	185	.503	17	40	.425	55	78	.705	24	28	19	45	—	28	1.6	—	111	6.5	258	15.2
96-97 Aug	25	25	766	207	419	.494	43	129	.333	109	152	.717	53	35	66	69	—	39	1.6	—	178	7.1	566	22.6
97-98 Aug	26	26	751	218	433	.503	43	134	.321	185	246	.752	52	38	61	68	—	31	1.2	—	262	10.1	664	25.5
98-99 Aug	28	28	969	281	542	.518	45	138	.326	163	213	.765	84	52	35	80	—	58	2.1	—	317	11.3	770	27.5
4 Years	96	91	2986	799	1579	.506	148	441	.336	512	689	.743	213	153	181	262	—	156	1.6	—	868	9.0	2258	23.5

NBA

Year Tm	G	GS	Min	Md	Att	Pct	Md	Att	Pct	Md	Att	Pct	TO	Stl	Blk	PF	DQ	Ast	Avg	Off	Tot	Avg	Pts	Avg
99-00 LAL	49	1	345	56	144	.389	16	47	.340	27	41	.659	21	10	4	54	0	12	0.2	29	75	1.5	155	3.2

NBA Postseason

Year Tm	G	GS	Min	Md	Att	Pct	Md	Att	Pct	Md	Att	Pct	TO	Stl	Blk	PF	DQ	Ast	Avg	Off	Tot	Avg	Pts	Avg
99-00 LAL	9	0	45	7	19	.368	2	10	.200	6	11	.545	3	1	0	5	0	2	0.2	4	10	1.1	22	2.4

Kendall Gill

Pos: G-F **College:** Illinois **Drafted:** '90 1(5)—Cha   **Ht:** 6'5" **Wt:** 216 **Born:** 5/25/68 **Age:** 32

(statistical profile on page 219)

College

Year Tm	G	GS	Min	Md	Att	Pct	Md	Att	Pct	Md	Att	Pct	TO	Stl	Blk	PF	DQ	Ast	Avg	Off	Tot	Avg	Pts	Avg
86-87 Ill	31	0	345	40	83	.482	0	1	.000	34	53	.642	23	39	8	27	0	27	0.9	—	42	1.4	114	3.7
87-88 Ill	33	23	946	128	272	.471	21	69	.304	67	89	.753	73	65	3	74	1	138	4.2	—	73	2.2	344	10.4
88-89 Ill	24	18	681	143	264	.542	38	83	.458	46	58	.793	43	51	6	37	0	91	3.8	—	70	2.9	370	15.4
89-90 Ill	29	29	1000	211	422	.500	23	66	.348	136	175	.777	72	63	16	66	0	96	3.3	—	143	4.9	581	20.0
4 Years	117	70	2972	522	1041	.501	82	219	.374	283	375	.755	211	218	33	204	1	352	3.0	—	328	2.8	1409	12.0

NBA			Field Goals			3-Pt FGs			Free Throws			Misc			Fouls		Assists		Rebounds			Points	
Year Tm	G	GS	Min	Md	Att	Pct	Md	Att	Pct	Md	Att	Pct	TO	Stl	Blk	PF	DQ	Ast	Avg	Off	Tot	Avg	Pts	Avg
90-91 Cha	82	36	1944	376	836	.450	2	14	.143	152	182	.835	163	104	39	186	0	303	3.7	105	263	3.2	906	11.0
91-92 Cha	79	79	2906	666	1427	.467	6	25	.240	284	381	.745	180	154	46	237	1	329	4.2	165	402	5.1	1622	20.5
92-93 Cha	69	67	2430	463	1032	.449	17	62	.274	224	290	.772	174	98	36	191	2	268	3.9	120	340	4.9	1167	16.9
93-94 Sea	79	77	2435	429	969	.443	38	120	.317	215	275	.782	143	151	32	194	1	275	3.5	91	268	3.4	1111	14.1
94-95 Sea	73	58	2125	392	858	.457	63	171	.368	155	209	.742	138	117	28	186	0	192	2.6	99	290	4.0	1002	13.7
95-96 2Tm	47	46	1683	246	524	.469	26	79	.329	138	176	.784	131	64	24	131	2	260	5.5	72	232	4.9	656	14.0
96-97 NJ	82	81	3199	644	1453	.443	74	220	.336	427	536	.797	218	154	46	225	2	326	4.0	183	499	6.1	1789	21.8
97-98 NJ	81	81	2733	418	974	.429	26	101	.257	225	327	.688	124	156	64	268	4	200	2.5	112	391	4.8	1087	13.4
98-99 NJ	50	47	1606	236	593	.398	2	17	.118	114	167	.683	71	134	26	162	4	123	2.5	61	244	4.9	588	11.8
99-00 NJ	76	75	2355	396	956	.414	20	78	.256	181	255	.710	89	139	41	211	3	210	2.8	82	283	3.7	993	13.1
95-96	36	36	1265	179	372	.481	17	54	.315	89	117	.761	110	42	22	201	2	225	6.3	56	189	5.3	464	12.9
NJ	11	10	418	67	152	.441	9	25	.360	49	59	.831	21	22	2	30	0	35	3.2	16	43	3.9	192	17.5
0 Years	718	647	23416	4266	9622	.443	274	887	.309	2115	2798	.756	1431	1271	382	1991	19	2486	3.5	1090	3212	4.5	10921	15.2

NBA Postseason

Year Tm	G	GS	Min	Md	Att	Pct	Md	Att	Pct	Md	Att	Pct	TO	Stl	Blk	PF	DQ	Ast	Avg	Off	Tot	Avg	Pts	Avg
92-93 Sea	9	9	353	65	162	.401	1	6	.167	25	35	.714	19	21	6	29	0	26	2.9	26	46	5.1	156	17.3
93-94 Sea	5	5	153	26	60	.433	2	9	.222	13	21	.619	6	6	1	12	0	10	2.0	7	24	4.8	67	13.4
94-95 Sea	4	0	72	9	25	.360	2	8	.250	5	8	.625	4	4	1	6	0	10	2.5	1	4	1.0	25	6.3
97-98 NJ	3	3	100	18	40	.450	0	0	—	7	8	.875	4	4	1	15	1	3	1.0	3	13	4.3	43	14.3
Years	21	17	678	118	287	.411	5	23	.217	50	72	.694	33	35	9	62	1	49	2.3	37	87	4.1	291	13.9

Armen Gilliam

Pos: F-C **College:** UNLV **Drafted:** '87 1(2)—Pho **Ht:** 6'9" **Wt:** 260 **Born:** 5/28/64 **Age:** 36

College			Field Goals			3-Pt FGs			Free Throws			Misc			Fouls		Assists		Rebounds			Points	
Year Tm	G	GS	Min	Md	Att	Pct	Md	Att	Pct	Md	Att	Pct	TO	Stl	Blk	PF	DQ	Ast	Avg	Off	Tot	Avg	Pts	Avg
84-85 UNLV	31	—	800	136	219	.621	—	—	—	98	150	.653	49	27	15	85	—	6	0.2	—	212	6.8	370	11.9
85-86 UNLV	37	—	1243	221	418	.529	—	—	—	140	190	.737	78	39	40	85	—	17	0.5	—	315	8.5	582	15.7
86-87 UNLV	39	—	1259	359	598	.600	0	0	—	185	254	.728	69	56	36	93	—	35	0.9	—	363	9.3	903	23.2
Years	107	—	3302	716	1235	.580	0	0	—	423	594	.712	196	122	91	263	—	58	0.5	—	890	8.3	1855	17.3

NBA			Field Goals			3-Pt FGs			Free Throws			Misc			Fouls		Assists		Rebounds			Points	
Year Tm	G	GS	Min	Md	Att	Pct	Md	Att	Pct	Md	Att	Pct	TO	Stl	Blk	PF	DQ	Ast	Avg	Off	Tot	Avg	Pts	Avg
87-88 Pho	55	53	1807	342	720	.475	0	0	—	131	193	.679	123	58	29	143	1	72	1.3	134	434	7.9	815	14.8
88-89 Pho	74	60	2120	468	930	.503	0	0	—	240	323	.743	140	54	27	176	2	52	0.7	165	541	7.3	1176	15.9
89-90 2Tm	76	66	2426	484	940	.515	0	2	.000	303	419	.723	183	69	51	212	4	99	1.3	211	599	7.9	1271	16.7
90-91 2Tm	75	75	2644	487	1001	.487	0	2	.000	268	329	.815	174	69	53	185	2	105	1.4	220	598	8.0	1242	16.6
91-92 Phi	81	81	2771	512	1001	.511	0	2	.000	343	425	.807	166	51	85	176	1	118	1.5	234	660	8.1	1367	16.9
92-93 Phi	80	26	1742	359	774	.464	0	1	.000	274	325	.843	157	37	54	123	0	116	1.5	136	472	5.9	992	12.4
93-94 NJ	82	5	1969	348	682	.510	0	1	.000	274	361	.759	106	38	61	129	0	69	0.8	197	500	6.1	970	11.8
94-95 NJ	82	30	2472	455	905	.503	0	2	.000	302	392	.770	152	67	89	171	0	99	1.2	192	613	7.5	1212	14.8
95-96 NJ	78	76	2856	576	1216	.474	0	1	.000	277	350	.791	177	73	53	180	1	140	1.8	241	713	9.1	1429	18.3
96-97 Mil	80	25	2050	246	522	.471	0	0	—	199	259	.768	105	61	40	206	0	53	0.7	136	497	6.2	691	8.6
97-98 Mil	82	25	2114	327	676	.484	0	4	.000	267	333	.802	148	65	37	177	1	104	1.3	146	439	5.4	921	11.2
98-99 Mil	34	5	668	101	223	.453	0	1	.000	79	101	.782	36	22	12	48	0	19	0.6	33	126	3.7	281	8.3
99-00 Uta	50	0	782	133	305	.436	0	1	.000	67	86	.779	55	12	16	83	0	42	0.8	72	209	4.2	333	6.7
89-90 Pho	16	7	267	52	121	.430	0	0	—	39	56	.696	17	6	5	28	0	8	0.5	26	70	4.4	143	8.9
Cha	60	59	2159	432	819	.527	0	2	.000	264	363	.727	166	63	46	184	4	91	1.5	185	529	8.8	1128	18.8
90-91 Cha	25	25	949	195	380	.513	0	0	—	104	128	.813	64	34	21	65	1	27	1.1	86	234	9.4	494	19.8
Phi	50	50	1695	292	621	.470	0	2	.000	164	201	.816	110	35	32	120	1	78	1.6	134	364	7.3	748	15.0
3 Years	929	527	26421	4838	9895	.489	0	17	.000	3024	3896	.776	1722	676	607	2009	12	1088	1.2	2117	6401	6.9	12700	13.7

NBA Postseason

Year Tm	G	GS	Min	Md	Att	Pct	Md	Att	Pct	Md	Att	Pct	TO	Stl	Blk	PF	DQ	Ast	Avg	Off	Tot	Avg	Pts	Avg
88-89 Pho	9	0	126	27	51	.529	0	0	—	19	22	.864	10	1	2	11	0	2	0.2	18	45	5.0	73	8.1
90-91 Phi	8	8	287	48	104	.462	0	0	—	39	46	.848	15	5	6	16	0	10	1.3	14	52	6.5	135	16.9
93-94 NJ	4	0	112	15	34	.441	0	1	.000	12	16	.750	3	2	7	7	0	1	0.3	1	25	6.3	42	10.5
98-99 Mil	3	0	35	6	15	.400	0	0	—	5	5	1.000	1	2	1	4	0	1	0.3	0	5	1.7	17	5.7
99-00 Uta	10	0	132	15	46	.326	0	0	—	5	13	.385	11	4	4	15	0	4	0.4	6	29	2.9	35	3.5
Years	34	8	692	111	250	.444	0	1	.000	80	102	.784	40	14	20	53	0	18	0.5	39	156	4.6	302	8.9

Dion Glover

Pos: G **College:** Georgia Tech **Drafted:** '99 1(20)—Atl   **Ht:** 6'5" **Wt:** 215 **Born:** 10/22/78 **Age:** 22

					Field Goals			3-Pt FGs			Free Throws			Misc			Fouls		Assists		Rebounds			Points	
College																									
Year	Tm	G	GS	Min	Md	Att	Pct	Md	Att	Pct	Md	Att	Pct	TO	Stl	Blk	PF	DQ	Ast	Avg	Off	Tot	Avg	Pts	Avg
97-98	GTch	33	33	1163	222	503	.441	45	166	.271	119	186	.640	119	70	8	66	1	86	2.6	73	166	5.0	608	18.4
NBA																									
Year	Tm	G	GS	Min	Md	Att	Pct	Md	Att	Pct	Md	Att	Pct	TO	Stl	Blk	PF	DQ	Ast	Avg	Off	Tot	Avg	Pts	Avg
99-00	Atl	30	1	446	66	171	.386	12	45	.267	51	70	.729	28	15	4	28	0	27	0.9	15	38	1.3	195	6.5

Brian Grant

(statistical profile on page 220)

Pos: F **College:** Xavier (OH) **Drafted:** '94 1(8)—Sac   **Ht:** 6'9" **Wt:** 260 **Born:** 3/5/72 **Age:** 28

					Field Goals			3-Pt FGs			Free Throws			Misc			Fouls		Assists		Rebounds			Points	
College																									
Year	Tm	G	GS	Min	Md	Att	Pct	Md	Att	Pct	Md	Att	Pct	TO	Stl	Blk	PF	DQ	Ast	Avg	Off	Tot	Avg	Pts	Avg
90-91	Xav	32	—	932	135	236	.572	0	0	—	100	144	.694	77	29	25	108	—	20	0.6	—	273	8.5	370	11.6
91-92	Xav	26	—	729	117	203	.576	0	0	—	74	127	.583	66	19	26	79	—	23	0.9	—	237	9.1	308	11.8
92-93	Xav	30	—	944	223	341	.654	0	0	—	110	159	.692	60	23	29	66	—	46	1.5	—	283	9.4	556	18.5
93-94	Xav	29	—	894	181	324	.559	1	3	.333	122	171	.713	67	27	47	74	—	47	1.6	—	287	9.9	485	16.7
4 Years		117	—	3499	656	1104	.594	1	3	.333	406	601	.676	270	98	127	327	—	136	1.2	—	1080	9.2	1719	14.7
NBA																									
Year	Tm	G	GS	Min	Md	Att	Pct	Md	Att	Pct	Md	Att	Pct	TO	Stl	Blk	PF	DQ	Ast	Avg	Off	Tot	Avg	Pts	Avg
94-95	Sac	80	59	2289	413	809	.511	0	4	.250	231	363	.636	163	49	116	276	4	99	1.2	207	598	7.5	1058	13.2
95-96	Sac	78	75	2398	427	842	.507	4	17	.235	262	358	.732	185	40	103	269	9	127	1.6	175	545	7.0	1120	14.4
96-97	Sac	24	15	607	91	207	.440	0	0	—	70	90	.778	44	19	25	75	0	28	1.2	49	142	5.9	252	10.5
97-98	Por	61	49	1921	283	557	.508	0	1	.000	171	228	.750	110	44	45	184	3	86	1.4	197	555	9.1	737	12.1
98-99	Por	48	46	1525	183	382	.479	0	0	—	184	226	.814	96	21	34	136	1	67	1.4	173	470	9.8	550	11.5
99-00	Por	63	14	1322	173	352	.491	1	2	.500	112	166	.675	84	32	28	166	2	64	1.0	121	344	5.5	459	7.3
6 Years		354	258	10062	1570	3149	.499	6	24	.250	1030	1431	.720	682	205	351	1106	19	471	1.3	922	2654	7.5	4176	11.8
NBA Postseason																									
Year	Tm	G	GS	Min	Md	Att	Pct	Md	Att	Pct	Md	Att	Pct	TO	Stl	Blk	PF	DQ	Ast	Avg	Off	Tot	Avg	Pts	Avg
95-96	Sac	4	4	124	16	42	.381	0	0	—	7	14	.500	13	2	7	14	1	4	1.0	7	20	5.0	39	9.8
97-98	Por	4	4	135	19	36	.528	0	0	—	15	18	.833	5	4	3	20	0	6	1.5	18	43	10.8	53	13.3
98-99	Por	13	13	482	63	119	.529	0	0	—	45	72	.625	21	10	16	48	1	14	1.1	34	119	9.2	171	13.2
99-00	Por	16	0	320	29	65	.446	0	0	—	29	39	.744	17	6	6	53	1	8	0.5	37	92	5.8	87	5.4
4 Years		37	21	1061	127	262	.485	0	0	—	96	143	.671	56	22	32	135	3	32	0.9	96	274	7.4	350	9.5

Gary Grant

Pos: G **College:** Michigan **Drafted:** '88 1(15)—Sea   **Ht:** 6'3" **Wt:** 185 **Born:** 4/21/65 **Age:** 35

					Field Goals			3-Pt FGs			Free Throws			Misc			Fouls		Assists		Rebounds			Points	
College																									
Year	Tm	G	GS	Min	Md	Att	Pct	Md	Att	Pct	Md	Att	Pct	TO	Stl	Blk	PF	DQ	Ast	Avg	Off	Tot	Avg	Pts	Avg
84-85	Mich	30	29	950	169	307	.550	—	—	—	49	60	.817	82	50	4	84	3	140	4.7	—	76	2.5	387	12.9
85-86	Mich	33	33	1010	172	348	.494	—	—	—	58	78	.744	95	84	9	85	4	185	5.6	—	104	3.2	402	12.2
86-87	Mich	32	32	1088	286	533	.537	33	68	.485	111	142	.782	103	86	11	93	3	172	5.4	—	159	5.0	716	22.4
87-88	Mich	34	34	1190	269	508	.530	44	99	.444	135	167	.808	150	80	5	105	2	234	6.9	—	116	3.4	717	21.1
4 Years		129	128	4238	896	1696	.528	77	167	.461	353	447	.790	430	300	29	367	12	731	5.7	—	455	3.5	2222	17.2
NBA																									
Year	Tm	G	GS	Min	Md	Att	Pct	Md	Att	Pct	Md	Att	Pct	TO	Stl	Blk	PF	DQ	Ast	Avg	Off	Tot	Avg	Pts	Avg
88-89	LAC	71	48	1924	361	830	.435	5	22	.227	119	162	.735	258	144	9	170	1	506	7.1	80	238	3.4	846	11.9
89-90	LAC	44	44	1529	241	517	.466	5	21	.238	88	113	.779	206	108	4	120	1	442	10.0	59	195	4.4	575	13.1
90-91	LAC	68	65	2105	265	587	.451	9	39	.231	51	74	.689	210	103	12	192	4	587	8.6	69	209	3.1	590	8.7
91-92	LAC	78	53	2049	275	595	.462	15	51	.294	44	54	.815	187	138	14	181	4	538	6.9	34	184	2.4	609	7.8
92-93	LAC	74	8	1624	210	476	.441	11	42	.262	55	74	.743	129	106	9	168	2	353	4.8	27	139	1.9	486	6.6
93-94	LAC	78	8	1533	253	563	.449	17	62	.274	65	76	.855	136	119	12	139	1	291	3.7	42	142	1.8	588	7.5
94-95	LAC	33	2	470	78	166	.470	4	16	.250	45	55	.818	44	29	3	66	0	93	2.8	8	35	1.1	205	6.2
95-96	NY	47	1	596	88	181	.486	8	24	.333	48	58	.828	45	39	3	91	0	69	1.5	12	52	1.1	232	4.9
96-97	Mia	28	0	365	39	110	.355	14	46	.304	18	22	.818	27	16	0	39	0	45	1.6	8	38	1.4	110	3.9
97-98	Por	22	2	359	43	93	.462	7	19	.368	12	14	.857	24	17	2	30	0	84	3.8	8	48	2.2	105	4.8
98-99	Por	2	0	7	0	1	.000	0	0	—	0	0	—	0	1	0	0	0	3	1.5	0	0	0.0	0	0.0
99-00	Por	3	0	24	6	14	.429	0	0	—	0	0	—	2	1	0	3	0	1	0.3	0	3	1.0	12	4.0
12 Years		548	231	12585	1859	4133	.450	95	342	.278	545	702	.776	1268	821	69	1199	13	3012	5.5	347	1283	2.3	4358	8.0
NBA Postseason																									
Year	Tm	G	GS	Min	Md	Att	Pct	Md	Att	Pct	Md	Att	Pct	TO	Stl	Blk	PF	DQ	Ast	Avg	Off	Tot	Avg	Pts	Avg
91-92	LAC	5	1	77	10	21	.476	0	2	.000	2	2	1.000	8	3	2	10	0	18	3.6	0	4	0.8	22	4.4
92-93	LAC	5	0	101	10	31	.323	0	0	—	1	2	.500	7	3	0	13	0	23	4.6	1	2	0.4	21	4.2

NBA Postseason

Year Tm	G	GS	Min	Md	Att	Pct	Md	Att	Pct	Md	Att	Pct	TO	Stl	Blk	PF	DQ	Ast	Avg	Off	Tot	Avg	Pts	Avg
95-96 NY	1	0	8	2	5	.400	2	3	.667	0	0	—	1	1	0	0	0	0	0.0	2	3	3.0	6	6.0
97-98 Por	4	0	27	2	7	.286	1	4	.250	0	0	—	2	1	1	2	0	7	1.8	2	5	1.3	5	1.3
99-00 Por	2	0	8	0	2	.000	0	0	—	1	2	.500	0	0	0	0	0	1	0.5	0	0	0.0	1	0.5
5 Years	17	1	221	24	66	.364	3	9	.333	4	6	.667	18	8	3	25	0	49	2.9	5	14	0.8	55	3.2

Horace Grant

(statistical profile on page 220)

Pos: F **College:** Clemson **Drafted:** '87 1(10)—Chi **Ht:** 6'10" **Wt:** 245 **Born:** 7/4/65 **Age:** 35

College Year Tm	G	GS	Min	Field Goals Md	Att	Pct	3-Pt FGs Md	Att	Pct	Free Throws Md	Att	Pct	Misc TO	Stl	Blk	Fouls PF	DQ	Assists Ast	Avg	Rebounds Off	Tot	Avg	Points Pts	Avg
83-84 Clem	28	9	551	64	120	.533	—	—		32	43	.744	34	21	12	65	—	49	1.8	42	129	4.6	160	5.7
84-85 Clem	29	26	703	132	238	.555	—	—		65	102	.637	52	19	21	83	—	32	1.1	76	196	6.8	329	11.3
85-86 Clem	34	31	1099	208	356	.584	—	—		140	193	.725	67	28	24	108	—	62	1.8	144	357	10.5	556	16.4
86-87 Clem	31	28	1010	256	390	.656	1	2	.500	138	195	.708	67	36	25	81	—	63	2.0	114	299	9.6	651	21.0
4 Years	122	94	3363	660	1104	.598	1	2	.500	375	533	.704	220	104	82	337	—	206	1.7	376	981	8.0	1696	13.9

NBA Year Tm	G	GS	Min	Field Goals Md	Att	Pct	3-Pt FGs Md	Att	Pct	Free Throws Md	Att	Pct	Misc TO	Stl	Blk	Fouls PF	DQ	Assists Ast	Avg	Rebounds Off	Tot	Avg	Points Pts	Avg
87-88 Chi	81	6	1827	254	507	.501	0	2	.000	114	182	.626	86	51	53	221	3	89	1.1	155	447	5.5	622	7.7
88-89 Chi	79	79	2809	405	781	.519	0	5	.000	140	199	.704	128	86	62	251	1	168	2.1	240	681	8.6	950	12.0
89-90 Chi	80	80	2753	446	853	.523	0	0	—	179	256	.699	110	92	84	230	1	227	2.8	236	629	7.9	1071	13.4
90-91 Chi	78	76	2641	401	733	.547	1	6	.167	197	277	.711	92	95	69	203	2	178	2.3	266	659	8.4	1000	12.8
91-92 Chi	81	81	2859	457	790	.578	0	2	.000	235	317	.741	98	100	131	196	0	217	2.7	344	807	10.0	1149	14.2
92-93 Chi	77	77	2745	421	829	.508	1	5	.200	174	281	.619	110	89	96	218	4	201	2.6	341	729	9.5	1017	13.2
93-94 Chi*	70	69	2570	460	878	.524	0	6	.000	137	230	.596	109	74	84	164	0	236	3.4	306	769	11.0	1057	15.1
94-95 Orl	74	74	2693	401	707	.567	0	8	.000	146	211	.692	85	76	88	203	2	173	2.3	223	715	9.7	948	12.8
95-96 Orl	63	62	2286	347	677	.513	1	6	.167	152	207	.734	64	62	74	144	1	170	2.7	178	580	9.2	847	13.4
96-97 Orl	67	67	2496	358	695	.515	1	6	.167	128	179	.715	99	101	65	157	1	163	2.4	206	600	9.0	845	12.6
97-98 Orl	76	76	2803	393	857	.459	0	7	.000	135	199	.678	88	81	79	180	2	172	2.3	228	618	8.1	921	12.1
98-99 Orl	**50**	50	1660	198	456	.434	0	2	.000	47	70	.671	44	46	60	99	0	90	1.8	117	351	7.0	443	8.9
99-00 Sea	76	76	2688	266	599	.444	0	4	.000	80	111	.721	61	55	60	192	0	188	2.5	167	591	7.8	612	8.1
13 Years	952	873	32830	4807	9362	.513	4	59	.068	1864	2719	.686	1174	1008	1005	2458	15	2272	2.4	3007	8176	8.6	11482	12.1

NBA Postseason

Year Tm	G	GS	Min	Md	Att	Pct	Md	Att	Pct	Md	Att	Pct	TO	Stl	Blk	PF	DQ	Ast	Avg	Off	Tot	Avg	Pts	Avg
87-88 Chi	10	10	299	46	81	.568	0	1	.000	9	15	.600	7	14	2	35	2	16	1.6	25	70	7.0	101	10.1
88-89 Chi	17	17	625	72	139	.518	0	0	—	40	50	.800	31	11	16	68	2	35	2.1	53	167	9.8	184	10.8
89-90 Chi	16	16	616	81	159	.509	0	2	.000	33	53	.623	26	18	18	51	1	40	2.5	73	159	9.9	195	12.2
90-91 Chi	17	17	666	91	156	.583	0	0	—	44	60	.733	20	15	6	45	0	38	2.2	56	138	8.1	226	13.3
91-92 Chi	22	22	856	99	183	.541	0	2	.000	51	76	.671	21	24	39	68	1	66	3.0	76	194	8.8	249	11.3
92-93 Chi	19	19	651	83	152	.546	0	0	—	37	54	.685	17	23	23	60	1	44	2.3	61	156	8.2	203	10.7
93-94 Chi	10	10	393	65	120	.542	1	1	1.000	31	42	.738	10	10	18	23	0	26	2.6	30	74	7.4	162	16.2
94-95 Orl	21	21	869	121	224	.540	0	2	.000	45	59	.763	26	21	24	68	1	39	1.9	74	219	10.4	287	13.7
95-96 Orl	9	9	334	61	94	.649	0	0	—	13	15	.867	6	7	6	23	0	13	1.4	31	94	10.4	135	15.0
98-99 Orl	4	4	128	11	30	.367	0	0	—	5	8	.625	2	2	2	12	0	5	1.3	14	28	7.0	27	6.8
99-00 Sea	5	5	185	11	27	.407	0	0	—	2	4	.500	1	8	5	12	0	10	2.0	8	31	6.2	24	4.8
11 Years	150	140	5622	741	1365	.543	1	8	.125	310	436	.711	167	153	159	465	8	332	2.2	501	1330	8.9	1793	12.0

Devin Gray

Pos: F **College:** Clemson **Drafted:** '96 FA—Sac **Ht:** 6'7" **Wt:** 240 **Born:** 3/10/72 **Age:** 28

College Year Tm	G	GS	Min	Field Goals Md	Att	Pct	3-Pt FGs Md	Att	Pct	Free Throws Md	Att	Pct	Misc TO	Stl	Blk	Fouls PF	DQ	Assists Ast	Avg	Rebounds Off	Tot	Avg	Points Pts	Avg
91-92 Clem	27	12	647	129	248	.520	1	3	.333	34	79	.430	48	40	6	81	—	20	0.7	60	138	5.1	293	10.9
92-93 Clem	30	25	950	197	372	.530	13	36	.361	93	146	.637	66	60	22	87	—	51	1.7	78	164	5.5	500	16.7
93-94 Clem	30	14	802	178	311	.572	1	10	.100	74	136	.544	51	37	15	85	—	30	1.0	74	180	6.0	431	14.4
94-95 Clem	7	7	162	38	62	.613	0	1	.000	22	36	.611	18	5	5	22	—	7	1.0	17	43	6.1	98	14.0
4 Years	94	58	2561	542	993	.546	15	50	.300	223	397	.562	183	142	48	275	—	108	1.1	229	525	5.6	1322	14.1

NBA Year Tm	G	GS	Min	Field Goals Md	Att	Pct	3-Pt FGs Md	Att	Pct	Free Throws Md	Att	Pct	Misc TO	Stl	Blk	Fouls PF	DQ	Assists Ast	Avg	Rebounds Off	Tot	Avg	Points Pts	Avg
95-96										Played in CBA														
96-97 2Tm	6	0	49	8	26	.308	0	0	—	2	5	.400	5	4	0	11	0	2	0.3	6	14	2.3	18	3.0
97-98										Played in Spain														
98-99										Played in CBA														
99-00 Hou	21	2	124	15	37	.405	0	0	—	19	29	.655	4	5	3	22	0	5	0.2	11	25	1.2	49	2.3
96-97 Sac	3	0	25	3	11	.273	0	0	—	2	4	.500	0	3	0	3	0	2	0.7	3	9	3.0	8	2.7
SA	3	0	24	5	15	.333	0	0	—	0	1	.000	5	1	0	8	0	0	0.0	3	5	1.7	10	3.3
2 Years	27	2	173	23	63	.365	0	0	—	21	34	.618	9	9	3	33	0	7	0.3	17	39	1.4	67	2.5

A.C. Green
(statistical profile on page 221)

Pos: F **College:** Oregon State **Drafted:** '85 1(23)—LAL **Ht:** 6'9" **Wt:** 225 **Born:** 10/4/63 **Age:** 37

College				Field Goals			3-Pt FGs			Free Throws			Misc			Fouls		Assists		Rebounds			Points	
Year Tm	G	GS	Min	Md	Att	Pct	Md	Att	Pct	Md	Att	Pct	TO	Stl	Blk	PF	DQ	Ast	Avg	Off	Tot	Avg	Pts	Avg
81-82 OreSt	30	—	895	99	161	.615	—	—	—	61	100	.610	72	27	7	74	1	32	1.1	—	158	5.3	259	8.6
82-83 OreSt	31	—	1113	162	290	.559	—	—	—	111	161	.689	83	27	11	73	2	53	1.7	—	235	7.6	435	14.0
83-84 OreSt	23	—	853	134	204	.657	—	—	—	141	183	.770	59	26	2	52	1	38	1.7	—	201	8.7	409	17.8
84-85 OreSt	31	31	1191	217	362	.599	—	—	—	157	231	.680	73	43	18	66	2	62	2.0	—	286	9.2	591	19.1
4 Years	115	—	4052	612	1017	.602	—	—	—	470	675	.696	287	123	38	265	6	185	1.6	—	880	7.7	1694	14.7

NBA				Field Goals			3-Pt FGs			Free Throws			Misc			Fouls		Assists		Rebounds			Points	
Year Tm	G	GS	Min	Md	Att	Pct	Md	Att	Pct	Md	Att	Pct	TO	Stl	Blk	PF	DQ	Ast	Avg	Off	Tot	Avg	Pts	Avg
85-86 LAL	82	1	1542	209	388	.539	1	6	.167	102	167	.611	99	49	49	229	2	54	0.7	160	381	4.6	521	6.4
86-87 LAL	79	72	2240	316	587	.538	0	5	.000	220	282	.780	102	70	80	171	0	84	1.1	210	615	7.8	852	10.8
87-88 LAL	82	64	2636	322	640	.503	0	2	.000	293	379	.773	120	87	45	204	0	93	1.1	245	710	8.7	937	11.4
88-89 LAL	82	82	2510	401	758	.529	4	17	.235	282	359	.786	119	94	55	172	0	103	1.3	258	739	9.0	1088	13.3
89-90 LAL*	82	82	2709	385	806	.478	13	46	.283	278	370	.751	116	66	50	207	0	90	1.1	262	712	8.7	1061	12.9
90-91 LAL	82	21	2164	258	542	.476	11	55	.200	223	302	.738	99	59	23	117	0	71	0.9	201	516	6.3	750	9.1
91-92 LAL	82	53	2902	382	803	.476	12	56	.214	340	457	.744	111	91	36	141	0	117	1.4	306	762	9.3	1116	13.6
92-93 LAL	82	55	2819	379	706	.537	16	46	.348	277	375	.739	116	88	39	149	0	116	1.4	287	711	8.7	1051	12.8
93-94 Pho	82	55	2825	465	926	.502	8	35	.229	266	362	.735	100	70	38	142	0	137	1.7	275	753	9.2	1204	14.7
94-95 Pho	82	52	2687	311	617	.504	43	127	.339	251	343	.732	114	55	31	146	0	127	1.5	194	669	8.2	916	11.2
95-96 Pho	82	36	2113	215	444	.484	14	52	.269	168	237	.709	79	45	23	141	1	72	0.9	166	554	6.8	612	7.5
96-97 2Tm	83	73	2492	234	484	.483	1	20	.050	128	197	.650	74	70	16	145	0	69	0.8	222	656	7.9	597	7.2
97-98 Dal	82	68	2649	242	534	.453	0	4	.000	116	162	.716	68	78	27	157	0	123	1.5	219	668	8.1	600	7.3
98-99 Dal	50	35	924	108	256	.422	0	8	.000	30	52	.577	19	28	8	69	0	25	0.5	82	228	4.6	246	4.9
99-00 LAL	82	82	1929	173	387	.447	1	4	.250	66	95	.695	53	53	18	127	0	80	1.0	160	486	5.9	413	5.0
96-97 Pho	27	19	548	61	128	.477	0	3	.000	31	48	.646	20	18	1	34	0	17	0.6	33	138	5.1	153	5.7
Dal	56	54	1944	173	356	.486	1	17	.059	97	149	.651	54	52	15	111	0	52	0.9	189	518	9.3	444	7.9
15 Years	1196	831	35141	4400	8878	.496	124	483	.257	3040	4139	.734	1389	1003	538	2317	3	1361	1.1	3247	9160	7.7	11964	10.0

NBA Postseason

Year Tm	G	GS	Min	Md	Att	Pct	Md	Att	Pct	Md	Att	Pct	TO	Stl	Blk	PF	DQ	Ast	Avg	Off	Tot	Avg	Pts	Avg
85-86 LAL	9	0	106	9	17	.529	0	0	—	4	9	.444	4	1	3	13	0	0	0.0	3	16	1.8	22	2.4
86-87 LAL	18	18	505	71	130	.546	0	0	—	65	87	.747	17	9	8	47	0	11	0.6	54	142	7.9	207	11.5
87-88 LAL	24	18	726	92	169	.544	0	0	—	55	73	.753	26	11	12	61	0	20	0.8	57	175	7.3	239	10.0
88-89 LAL	15	15	502	47	114	.412	0	3	.000	58	76	.763	23	16	6	37	1	18	1.2	38	137	9.1	152	10.1
89-90 LAL	9	9	252	41	79	.519	0	0	—	24	32	.750	14	5	4	22	0	9	1.0	34	81	9.0	106	11.8
90-91 LAL	19	1	400	41	97	.423	4	8	.500	38	54	.704	19	12	3	37	0	9	0.5	46	102	5.4	124	6.5
91-92 LAL	4	4	153	16	39	.410	0	0	—	19	23	.826	5	7	0	10	0	7	1.8	15	36	9.0	51	12.8
92-93 LAL	5	5	220	18	42	.429	0	5	.000	13	21	.619	9	7	3	14	1	13	2.6	26	73	14.6	49	9.8
93-94 Pho	10	2	350	40	83	.482	7	17	.412	38	62	.613	7	10	2	22	0	13	1.3	29	84	8.4	125	12.5
94-95 Pho	10	10	368	36	78	.462	1	12	.083	55	63	.873	10	6	2	22	0	13	1.3	38	120	12.0	128	12.8
95-96 Pho	4	4	87	6	17	.353	0	3	.000	7	8	.875	2	1	0	7	0	2	0.5	6	18	4.5	19	4.8
99-00 LAL	23	23	429	37	90	.411	0	0	—	16	23	.696	9	14	3	44	0	13	0.6	43	96	4.2	90	3.9
12 Years	150	109	4098	454	955	.475	12	48	.250	392	531	.738	145	99	46	336	2	128	0.9	389	1080	7.2	1312	8.7

Adrian Griffin
(statistical profile on page 221)

Pos: G-F **College:** Seton Hall **Drafted:** '99 FA—Bos **Ht:** 6'5" **Wt:** 215 **Born:** 7/4/74 **Age:** 26

College				Field Goals			3-Pt FGs			Free Throws			Misc			Fouls		Assists		Rebounds			Points	
Year Tm	G	GS	Min	Md	Att	Pct	Md	Att	Pct	Md	Att	Pct	TO	Stl	Blk	PF	DQ	Ast	Avg	Off	Tot	Avg	Pts	Avg
92-93 SetHl	35	1	465	44	87	.506	0	2	.000	31	53	.585	36	28	3	41	1	29	0.8	43	123	3.5	119	3.4
93-94 SetHl	30	30	893	106	224	.473	2	6	.333	76	126	.603	48	43	17	75	1	66	2.2	92	233	7.8	290	9.7
94-95 SetHl	30	29	949	184	332	.554	6	20	.300	86	119	.723	68	66	22	77	1	85	2.8	97	216	7.2	460	15.3
95-96 SetHl	28	28	983	213	438	.486	12	44	.273	107	161	.665	87	70	16	82	3	86	3.1	85	231	8.3	545	19.5
4 Years	123	88	3290	547	1081	.506	20	72	.278	300	459	.654	239	207	58	275	6	266	2.2	317	803	6.5	1414	11.5

NBA				Field Goals			3-Pt FGs			Free Throws			Misc			Fouls		Assists		Rebounds			Points	
Year Tm	G	GS	Min	Md	Att	Pct	Md	Att	Pct	Md	Att	Pct	TO	Stl	Blk	PF	DQ	Ast	Avg	Off	Tot	Avg	Pts	Avg
96-97	Played in CBA																							
97-98	Played in CBA, Played in USBL, Played in Italy																							
98-99	Played in CBA, Played in USBL																							
99-00 Bos	72	47	1927	175	413	.424	16	57	.281	119	158	.753	93	116	15	222	3	177	2.5	128	372	5.2	485	6.7

Tom Gugliotta

(statistical profile on page 222)

Pos: F **College:** North Carolina State **Drafted:** '92 1(6)—Was **Ht:** 6'10" **Wt:** 240 **Born:** 12/19/69 **Age:** 31

College

Year Tm	G	GS	Min	Md	Att	Pct	Md	Att	Pct	Md	Att	Pct	TO	Stl	Blk	PF	DQ	Ast	Avg	Off	Tot	Avg	Pts	Avg
				Field Goals			**3-Pt FGs**			**Free Throws**			**Misc**			**Fouls**		**Assists**		**Rebounds**			**Points**	
88-89 NCSt	21	0	171	18	42	.429	1	2	.500	19	29	.655	9	10	1	17	—	5	0.2	—	35	1.7	56	2.7
89-90 NCSt	30	29	886	135	268	.504	23	47	.489	41	61	.672	54	48	12	81	—	47	1.6	72	211	7.0	334	11.1
90-91 NCSt	31	31	1123	170	340	.500	66	166	.398	65	101	.644	67	53	34	73	—	87	2.8	83	281	9.1	471	15.2
91-92 NCSt	30	30	1107	240	534	.449	93	233	.399	102	149	.685	109	62	15	76	—	92	3.1	83	293	9.8	675	22.5
4 Years	112	90	3287	563	1184	.476	183	448	.408	227	340	.668	239	173	62	247	—	231	2.1	—	820	7.3	1536	13.7

NBA

Year Tm	G	GS	Min	Md	Att	Pct	Md	Att	Pct	Md	Att	Pct	TO	Stl	Blk	PF	DQ	Ast	Avg	Off	Tot	Avg	Pts	Avg
				Field Goals			**3-Pt FGs**			**Free Throws**			**Misc**			**Fouls**		**Assists**		**Rebounds**			**Points**	
92-93 Was	81	81	2795	484	1135	.426	38	135	.281	181	281	.644	230	134	35	195	0	306	3.8	219	781	9.6	1187	14.7
93-94 Was	78	78	2795	540	1159	.466	40	148	.270	213	311	.685	247	172	51	174	0	276	3.5	189	728	9.3	1333	17.1
94-95 3Tm	77	63	2568	371	837	.443	60	186	.323	174	252	.690	189	132	62	203	2	279	3.6	165	572	7.4	976	12.7
95-96 Min	78	78	2835	473	1004	.471	26	86	.302	289	374	.773	234	139	96	265	1	238	3.1	176	690	8.8	1261	16.2
96-97 Min*	81	81	3131	592	1339	.442	24	93	.258	464	566	.820	293	130	89	237	3	335	4.1	187	702	8.7	1672	20.6
97-98 Min	41	41	1582	319	635	.502	2	17	.118	183	223	.821	109	61	22	102	0	167	4.1	106	356	8.7	823	20.1
98-99 Pho	43	43	1563	277	573	.483	2	7	.286	173	218	.794	88	59	21	110	0	121	2.8	131	381	8.9	729	17.0
99-00 Pho	54	54	1767	310	645	.481	1	8	.125	117	151	.775	106	80	31	152	2	124	2.3	141	425	7.9	738	13.7
94-95 Was	6	6	226	33	83	.398	4	8	.500	26	33	.788	15	21	11	19	0	18	3.0	16	53	8.8	96	16.0
GS	40	40	1324	176	397	.443	28	90	.311	55	97	.567	93	50	23	98	2	122	3.1	100	297	7.4	435	10.9
Min	31	17	1018	162	357	.454	28	88	.318	93	122	.762	81	61	28	86	0	139	4.5	49	222	7.2	445	14.4
8 Years	533	519	19036	3366	7327	.459	193	680	.284	1794	2376	.755	1496	907	407	1438	8	1846	3.5	1314	4635	8.7	8719	16.4

NBA Postseason

Year Tm	G	GS	Min	Md	Att	Pct	Md	Att	Pct	Md	Att	Pct	TO	Stl	Blk	PF	DQ	Ast	Avg	Off	Tot	Avg	Pts	Avg
96-97 Min	3	3	121	23	52	.442	3	4	.750	6	10	.600	6	7	2	13	0	13	4.3	2	16	5.3	55	18.3
98-99 Pho	3	3	118	13	35	.371	0	0	—	6	8	.750	8	4	3	10	0	10	3.3	6	25	8.3	32	10.7
2 Years	6	6	239	36	87	.414	3	4	.750	12	18	.667	14	11	5	23	0	23	3.8	8	41	6.8	87	14.5

Darvin Ham

Pos: F **College:** Texas Tech **Drafted:** '96 FA—Den **Ht:** 6'7" **Wt:** 220 **Born:** 7/23/73 **Age:** 27

College

Year Tm	G	GS	Min	Md	Att	Pct	Md	Att	Pct	Md	Att	Pct	TO	Stl	Blk	PF	DQ	Ast	Avg	Off	Tot	Avg	Pts	Avg
				Field Goals			**3-Pt FGs**			**Free Throws**			**Misc**			**Fouls**		**Assists**		**Rebounds**			**Points**	
93-94 TxTch	28	28	668	97	157	.618	0	0	—	36	72	.500	44	21	5	94	5	34	1.2	79	152	5.4	230	8.2
94-95 TxTch	30	30	638	78	131	.595	0	0	—	50	85	.588	38	31	5	76	1	26	0.9	63	129	4.3	206	6.9
95-96 TxTch	32	32	750	115	198	.581	0	1	.000	61	138	.442	53	19	8	74	1	31	1.0	—	181	5.7	291	9.1
3 Years	90	90	2056	290	486	.597	0	1	.000	147	295	.498	135	71	18	244	7	91	1.0	—	462	5.1	727	8.1

NBA

Year Tm	G	GS	Min	Md	Att	Pct	Md	Att	Pct	Md	Att	Pct	TO	Stl	Blk	PF	DQ	Ast	Avg	Off	Tot	Avg	Pts	Avg
				Field Goals			**3-Pt FGs**			**Free Throws**			**Misc**			**Fouls**		**Assists**		**Rebounds**			**Points**	
96-97 2Tm	36	3	318	33	62	.532	0	0	—	17	35	.486	22	9	8	57	3	14	0.4	29	56	1.6	83	2.3
97-98 Was	71	3	635	55	104	.529	0	0	—	35	74	.473	37	21	25	118	1	16	0.2	72	131	1.8	145	2.0
98-99													Played in Spain											
99-00 Mil	35	21	792	71	128	.555	0	1	.000	35	78	.449	29	29	29	102	1	42	1.2	85	172	4.9	177	5.1
96-97 Den	35	3	313	32	61	.525	0	0	—	16	33	.485	21	8	8	57	3	14	0.4	29	56	1.6	80	2.3
Ind	1	0	5	1	1	1.000	0	0	—	1	2	.500	1	1	0	0	0	0	0.0	0	0	0.0	3	3.0
3 Years	142	27	1745	159	294	.541	0	1	.000	87	187	.465	88	59	62	277	5	72	0.5	186	359	2.5	405	2.9

NBA Postseason

Year Tm	G	GS	Min	Md	Att	Pct	Md	Att	Pct	Md	Att	Pct	TO	Stl	Blk	PF	DQ	Ast	Avg	Off	Tot	Avg	Pts	Avg
99-00 Mil	5	5	144	11	17	.647	0	1	.000	3	9	.333	7	1	8	22	0	7	1.4	17	29	5.8	25	5.0

Richard Hamilton

(statistical profile on page 222)

Pos: G-F **College:** Connecticut **Drafted:** '99 1(7)—Was **Ht:** 6'6" **Wt:** 185 **Born:** 2/14/78 **Age:** 22

College

Year Tm	G	GS	Min	Md	Att	Pct	Md	Att	Pct	Md	Att	Pct	TO	Stl	Blk	PF	DQ	Ast	Avg	Off	Tot	Avg	Pts	Avg
				Field Goals			**3-Pt FGs**			**Free Throws**			**Misc**			**Fouls**		**Assists**		**Rebounds**			**Points**	
96-97 Conn	32	32	980	174	451	.386	70	186	.376	91	116	.784	95	40	11	76	1	88	2.8	42	138	4.3	509	15.9
97-98 Conn	37	37	1203	270	614	.440	99	245	.404	156	185	.843	83	54	8	71	0	87	2.4	57	163	4.4	795	21.5
98-99 Conn	34	34	1091	247	557	.443	68	196	.347	170	204	.833	82	40	9	56	0	91	2.7	52	163	4.8	732	21.5
3 Years	103	103	3274	691	1622	.426	237	627	.378	417	505	.826	260	134	28	203	1	266	2.6	151	464	4.5	2036	19.8

NBA

Year Tm	G	GS	Min	Md	Att	Pct	Md	Att	Pct	Md	Att	Pct	TO	Stl	Blk	PF	DQ	Ast	Avg	Off	Tot	Avg	Pts	Avg
				Field Goals			**3-Pt FGs**			**Free Throws**			**Misc**			**Fouls**		**Assists**		**Rebounds**			**Points**	
99-00 Was	71	12	1373	254	605	.420	28	77	.364	103	133	.774	84	28	6	142	2	108	1.5	38	129	1.8	639	9.0

Thomas Hamilton

Pos: C **College:** None **Drafted:** '95 FA—Bos **Ht:** 7'2" **Wt:** 330 **Born:** 4/3/75 **Age:** 25

	NBA		Field Goals			3-Pt FGs			Free Throws			Misc			Fouls		Assists		Rebounds			Points	
Year Tm	G	GS	Min	Md	Att	Pct	Md	Att	Pct	Md	Att	Pct	TO	Stl	Blk	PF	DQ	Ast	Avg	Off	Tot	Avg	Pts	Avg
95-96 Bos	11	0	70	9	31	.290	0	0	—	7	18	.389	9	0	9	12	0	1	0.1	10	22	2.0	25	2.3
96-97 Chi							Did not play: injury — Abdominal Muscle																	
97-98							Did not play in NBA																	
98-99							Did not play in NBA																	
99-00 Hou	22	7	273	35	79	.443	0	0	—	12	23	.522	28	4	14	25	0	15	0.7	31	90	4.1	82	3.7
2 Years	33	7	343	44	110	.400	0	0	—	19	41	.463	37	4	23	37	0	16	0.5	41	112	3.4	107	3.2

Tom Hammonds

Pos: F **College:** Georgia Tech **Drafted:** '89 1(9)—Was **Ht:** 6'9" **Wt:** 225 **Born:** 3/27/67 **Age:** 33

	College		Field Goals			3-Pt FGs			Free Throws			Misc			Fouls		Assists		Rebounds			Points	
Year Tm	G	GS	Min	Md	Att	Pct	Md	Att	Pct	Md	Att	Pct	TO	Stl	Blk	PF	DQ	Ast	Avg	Off	Tot	Avg	Pts	Avg
85-86 GTch	34	33	1112	168	276	.609	—	—	—	80	98	.816	67	14	11	81	—	37	1.1	—	219	6.4	416	12.2
86-87 GTch	29	29	1088	206	362	.569	0	0	—	59	74	.797	72	12	15	62	—	41	1.4	62	208	7.2	471	16.2
87-88 GTch	30	30	1076	229	403	.568	0	0	—	109	132	.826	73	10	20	59	—	40	1.3	71	216	7.2	567	18.9
88-89 GTch	30	30	1111	250	465	.538	1	3	.333	126	163	.773	56	14	26	77	—	51	1.7	77	242	8.1	627	20.9
4 Years	123	122	4387	853	1506	.566	1	3	.333	374	467	.801	268	50	72	279	—	169	1.4	210	885	7.2	2081	16.9

	NBA		Field Goals			3-Pt FGs			Free Throws			Misc			Fouls		Assists		Rebounds			Points	
Year Tm	G	GS	Min	Md	Att	Pct	Md	Att	Pct	Md	Att	Pct	TO	Stl	Blk	PF	DQ	Ast	Avg	Off	Tot	Avg	Pts	Avg
89-90 Was	61	8	805	129	295	.437	0	1	.000	63	98	.643	46	11	14	98	0	51	0.8	61	168	2.8	321	5.3
90-91 Was	70	7	1023	155	336	.461	0	4	.000	57	79	.722	54	15	7	108	0	43	0.6	58	206	2.9	367	5.2
91-92 Was	37	19	984	195	400	.488	0	1	.000	50	82	.610	58	22	13	118	1	36	1.0	49	185	5.0	440	11.9
92-93 2Tm	54	5	713	105	221	.475	0	1	.000	38	62	.613	34	18	12	77	0	24	0.4	38	127	2.4	248	4.6
93-94 Den	74	2	877	115	230	.500	0	0	—	71	104	.683	41	20	12	91	0	34	0.5	62	199	2.7	301	4.1
94-95 Den	70	5	956	139	260	.535	0	1	.000	132	177	.746	56	11	14	132	1	36	0.5	55	222	3.2	410	5.9
95-96 Den	71	4	1045	127	268	.474	0	0	—	88	115	.765	48	23	13	137	0	23	0.3	85	223	3.1	342	4.8
96-97 Den	81	8	1758	191	398	.480	0	2	.000	124	172	.721	88	16	24	205	0	64	0.8	135	401	5.0	506	6.2
97-98 Min	57	2	1140	127	246	.516	0	1	.000	92	132	.697	48	15	17	127	1	36	0.6	100	271	4.8	346	6.1
98-99 Min	49	0	716	82	179	.458	0	0	—	48	75	.640	32	8	7	88	1	20	0.4	54	136	2.8	212	4.3
99-00 Min	56	0	372	42	97	.433	0	0	—	33	56	.589	21	8	3	55	0	10	0.2	34	101	1.8	117	2.1
92-93 Cha	19	5	142	19	45	.422	0	0	—	5	8	.625	3	0	4	20	0	8	0.4	5	31	1.6	43	2.3
Den	35	0	571	86	176	.489	0	1	.000	33	54	.611	31	18	8	57	0	16	0.5	33	96	2.7	205	5.9
11 Years	680	60	10389	1407	2930	.480	0	11	.000	796	1152	.691	526	167	136	1236	4	377	0.6	731	2239	3.3	3610	5.3

NBA Postseason

				Field Goals			3-Pt FGs			Free Throws			Misc			Fouls		Assists		Rebounds			Points	
Year Tm	G	GS	Min	Md	Att	Pct	Md	Att	Pct	Md	Att	Pct	TO	Stl	Blk	PF	DQ	Ast	Avg	Off	Tot	Avg	Pts	Avg
93-94 Den	8	0	49	2	9	.222	0	0	—	5	6	.833	1	0	0	6	0	2	0.3	5	13	1.6	9	1.1
94-95 Den	3	0	44	9	14	.643	0	0	—	2	6	.333	4	0	2	12	0	1	0.3	3	7	2.3	20	6.7
97-98 Min	5	1	113	12	28	.429	0	0	—	12	16	.750	4	0	1	18	0	2	0.4	10	22	4.4	36	7.2
98-99 Min	4	0	18	0	0	—	0	0	—	4	4	1.000	1	0	0	4	0	0	0.0	0	2	0.5	4	1.0
99-00 Min	1	0	2	0	0	—	0	0	—	0	0	—	0	0	0	0	0	0	0.0	0	0	0.0	0	0.0
5 Years	21	1	226	23	51	.451	0	0	—	23	32	.719	10	0	3	40	0	5	0.2	18	44	2.1	69	3.3

Anfernee Hardaway

(statistical profile on page 223)

Pos: G **College:** Memphis State **Drafted:** '93 1(3)—GS **Ht:** 6'7" **Wt:** 215 **Born:** 7/18/71 **Age:** 29

	College		Field Goals			3-Pt FGs			Free Throws			Misc			Fouls		Assists		Rebounds			Points	
Year Tm	G	GS	Min	Md	Att	Pct	Md	Att	Pct	Md	Att	Pct	TO	Stl	Blk	PF	DQ	Ast	Avg	Off	Tot	Avg	Pts	Avg
91-92 Mem	34	34	1224	209	483	.433	69	190	.363	103	158	.652	125	86	45	92	4	188	5.5	75	237	7.0	590	17.4
92-93 Mem	32	32	1196	249	522	.477	73	220	.332	158	206	.767	109	76	39	86	2	204	6.4	—	273	8.5	729	22.8
2 Years	66	66	2420	458	1005	.456	142	410	.346	261	364	.717	234	162	84	178	6	392	5.9	—	510	7.7	1319	20.0

	NBA		Field Goals			3-Pt FGs			Free Throws			Misc			Fouls		Assists		Rebounds			Points	
Year Tm	G	GS	Min	Md	Att	Pct	Md	Att	Pct	Md	Att	Pct	TO	Stl	Blk	PF	DQ	Ast	Avg	Off	Tot	Avg	Pts	Avg
93-94 Orl	82	82	3015	509	1092	.466	50	187	.267	245	330	.742	292	190	51	205	2	544	6.6	192	439	5.4	1313	16.0
94-95 Orl*	77	77	2901	585	1142	.512	87	249	.349	356	463	.769	258	130	26	158	1	551	7.2	139	336	4.4	1613	20.9
95-96 Orl*	82	82	3015	623	1215	.513	89	283	.314	445	580	.767	229	166	41	160	0	582	7.1	129	354	4.3	1780	21.7
96-97 Orl*	59	59	2221	421	941	.447	85	267	.318	283	345	.820	145	93	35	123	1	332	5.6	82	263	4.5	1210	20.5
97-98 Orl*	19	15	625	103	273	.377	15	50	.300	90	118	.763	46	28	15	45	0	68	3.6	8	76	4.0	311	16.4
98-99 Orl	50	50	1944	301	717	.420	40	140	.286	149	211	.706	150	111	23	111	0	266	5.3	74	284	5.7	791	15.8
99-00 Pho	60	60	2253	378	798	.474	33	102	.324	226	286	.790	153	94	38	164	1	315	5.3	91	347	5.8	1015	16.9
7 Years	429	425	15974	2920	6178	.473	399	1278	.312	1794	2333	.769	1273	812	229	966	5	2658	6.2	715	2099	4.9	8033	18.7

ear Tm	G	GS	Min	Md	Att	Pct	Md	Att	Pct	Md	Att	Pct	TO	Stl	Blk	PF	DQ	Ast	Avg	Off	Tot	Avg	Pts	Avg
3-94 Orl	3	3	133	22	50	.440	5	11	.455	7	10	.700	20	5	6	10	0	21	7.0	8	20	6.7	56	18.7
4-95 Orl	21	21	849	144	305	.472	40	99	.404	84	111	.757	73	40	15	70	0	162	7.7	30	79	3.8	412	19.6
5-96 Orl	12	12	473	101	217	.465	20	55	.364	58	78	.744	26	20	4	27	1	72	6.0	20	56	4.7	280	23.3
6-97 Orl	5	5	220	52	111	.468	11	30	.367	40	54	.741	9	12	7	14	0	17	3.4	7	30	6.0	155	31.0
8-99 Orl	4	4	167	20	57	.351	6	13	.462	30	39	.769	12	9	1	13	0	22	5.5	9	20	5.0	76	19.0
9-00 Pho	9	9	386	67	145	.462	5	19	.263	44	62	.710	25	14	9	29	0	51	5.7	14	44	4.9	183	20.3
Years	54	54	2228	406	885	.459	87	227	.383	263	354	.743	165	100	42	163	1	345	6.4	88	249	4.6	1162	21.5

Tim Hardaway

(statistical profile on page 223)

os: G **College:** UTEP **Drafted:** '89 1(14)—GS **Ht:** 6'0" **Wt:** 195 **Born:** 9/1/66 **Age:** 34

College				Field Goals			3-Pt FGs			Free Throws			Misc			Fouls		Assists		Rebounds			Points	
ear Tm	G	GS	Min	Md	Att	Pct	Md	Att	Pct	Md	Att	Pct	TO	Stl	Blk	PF	DQ	Ast	Avg	Off	Tot	Avg	Pts	Avg
5-86 UTEP	28	—	435	37	71	.521	—	—	—	41	63	.651	27	24	3	50	—	53	1.9	—	35	1.3	115	4.1
6-87 UTEP	31	—	922	120	245	.490	3	12	.250	67	101	.663	61	68	6	92	—	148	4.8	—	62	2.0	310	10.0
7-88 UTEP	32	—	1036	159	354	.449	18	53	.340	98	130	.754	72	77	8	76	—	183	5.7	—	93	2.9	434	13.6
8-89 UTEP	33	—	1182	255	509	.501	48	131	.366	169	228	.741	89	93	8	79	—	179	5.4	—	131	4.0	727	22.0
Years	124	—	3575	571	1179	.484	69	196	.352	375	522	.718	249	262	25	297	—	563	4.5	—	321	2.6	1586	12.8

NBA				Field Goals			3-Pt FGs			Free Throws			Misc			Fouls		Assists		Rebounds			Points	
ear Tm	G	GS	Min	Md	Att	Pct	Md	Att	Pct	Md	Att	Pct	TO	Stl	Blk	PF	DQ	Ast	Avg	Off	Tot	Avg	Pts	Avg
9-90 GS	79	78	2663	464	985	.471	23	84	.274	211	276	.764	260	165	12	232	6	689	8.7	57	310	3.9	1162	14.7
0-91 GS*	82	82	3215	739	1551	.476	97	252	.385	306	381	.803	270	214	12	228	7	793	9.7	87	332	4.0	1881	22.9
1-92 GS*	81	81	3332	734	1592	.461	127	376	.338	298	389	.766	267	164	13	208	1	807	10.0	81	310	3.8	1893	23.4
2-93 GS*	66	66	2609	522	1168	.447	102	309	.330	273	367	.744	220	116	12	152	0	699	10.6	60	263	4.0	1419	21.5
3-94 GS							Did not play: injury — Left Knee																	
4-95 GS	62	62	2321	430	1007	.427	168	444	.378	219	288	.760	214	88	12	155	1	578	9.3	46	190	3.1	1247	20.1
5-96 2Tm	80	46	2534	419	992	.422	138	379	.364	241	305	.790	235	132	17	201	3	640	8.0	35	229	2.9	1217	15.2
6-97 Mia*	81	81	3136	575	1384	.415	203	590	.344	291	364	.799	230	151	9	165	2	695	8.6	49	277	3.4	1644	20.3
7-98 Mia*	81	81	3031	558	1296	.431	155	442	.351	257	329	.781	224	136	16	200	2	672	8.3	48	299	3.7	1528	18.9
8-99 Mia	48	48	1772	301	752	.400	112	311	.360	121	149	.812	131	57	6	102	1	352	7.3	15	152	3.2	835	17.4
9-00 Mia	52	52	1672	246	638	.386	94	256	.367	110	133	.827	119	49	4	110	0	385	7.4	25	150	2.9	696	13.4
5-96 GS	52	18	1487	255	606	.421	85	232	.366	140	182	.769	125	74	11	131	3	360	6.9	22	131	2.5	735	14.1
Mia	28	28	1047	164	386	.425	53	147	.361	101	123	.821	110	58	6	70	0	280	10.0	13	98	3.5	482	17.2
0 Years	712	677	26285	4988	11365	.439	1219	3443	.354	2327	2981	.781	2170	1272	113	1755	23	6310	8.9	503	2512	3.5	13522	19.0

ear Tm	G	GS	Min	Md	Att	Pct	Md	Att	Pct	Md	Att	Pct	TO	Stl	Blk	PF	DQ	Ast	Avg	Off	Tot	Avg	Pts	Avg
0-91 GS	9	9	396	90	185	.486	17	48	.354	30	38	.789	25	28	7	22	0	101	11.2	5	33	3.7	227	25.2
1-92 GS	4	4	176	32	80	.400	10	29	.345	24	37	.649	14	13	0	14	0	29	7.3	6	15	3.8	98	24.5
5-96 Mia	3	3	110	20	43	.465	8	22	.364	5	7	.714	15	3	0	10	0	17	5.7	1	5	1.7	53	17.7
6-97 Mia	17	17	701	103	287	.359	42	134	.313	70	88	.795	53	27	1	37	0	119	7.0	13	69	4.1	318	18.7
7-98 Mia	5	5	222	42	94	.447	17	39	.436	29	37	.784	18	6	0	9	0	33	6.6	3	17	3.4	130	26.0
8-99 Mia	5	5	182	15	56	.268	5	25	.200	10	16	.625	18	5	1	14	0	32	6.4	3	14	2.8	45	9.0
9-00 Mia	7	7	182	20	68	.294	7	34	.206	7	10	.700	11	5	0	10	0	33	4.7	1	15	2.1	54	7.7
Years	50	50	1969	322	813	.396	106	331	.320	175	233	.751	154	87	9	116	0	364	7.3	32	168	3.4	925	18.5

Ron Harper

(statistical profile on page 224)

os: G **College:** Miami (OH) **Drafted:** '86 1(8)—Cle **Ht:** 6'6" **Wt:** 215 **Born:** 1/20/64 **Age:** 37

College				Field Goals			3-Pt FGs			Free Throws			Misc			Fouls		Assists		Rebounds			Points	
ear Tm	G	GS	Min	Md	Att	Pct	Md	Att	Pct	Md	Att	Pct	TO	Stl	Blk	PF	DQ	Ast	Avg	Off	Tot	Avg	Pts	Avg
2-83 Mia-O	28	—	887	148	298	.497	—	—	—	64	95	.674	84	62	29	70	—	62	2.2	—	195	7.0	360	12.9
3-84 Mia-O	30	—	989	197	367	.537	—	—	—	94	165	.570	66	42	30	85	—	64	2.1	—	229	7.6	488	16.3
4-85 Mia-O	31	—	1144	312	577	.541	—	—	—	148	224	.661	97	82	43	103	—	79	2.5	—	333	10.7	772	24.9
5-86 Mia-O	31	—	1144	312	572	.545	—	—	—	133	200	.665	88	101	71	84	—	133	4.3	—	362	11.7	757	24.4
Years	120	—	4164	969	1814	.534	—	—	—	439	684	.642	335	287	173	342	—	338	2.8	—	1119	9.3	2377	19.8

NBA				Field Goals			3-Pt FGs			Free Throws			Misc			Fouls		Assists		Rebounds			Points	
ear Tm	G	GS	Min	Md	Att	Pct	Md	Att	Pct	Md	Att	Pct	TO	Stl	Blk	PF	DQ	Ast	Avg	Off	Tot	Avg	Pts	Avg
6-87 Cle	82	82	3064	734	1614	.455	20	94	.213	386	564	.684	345	209	84	247	3	394	4.8	169	392	4.8	1874	22.9
7-88 Cle	57	52	1830	340	732	.464	3	20	.150	196	278	.705	158	122	52	157	3	281	4.9	64	223	3.9	879	15.4
8-89 Cle	82	82	2851	587	1149	.511	29	116	.250	323	430	.751	230	185	74	224	1	434	5.3	122	409	5.0	1526	18.6
9-90 2Tm	35	35	1367	301	637	.473	14	51	.275	182	231	.788	100	81	41	105	1	182	5.2	74	206	5.9	798	22.8
0-91 LAC	39	34	1383	285	729	.391	48	148	.324	145	217	.668	129	66	35	111	0	209	5.4	58	188	4.8	763	19.6
1-92 LAC	82	82	3144	569	1292	.440	64	211	.303	293	398	.736	252	152	72	199	0	417	5.1	120	447	5.5	1495	18.2
2-93 LAC	80	77	2970	542	1203	.451	52	186	.280	307	399	.769	222	177	73	212	1	360	4.5	117	425	5.3	1443	18.0

69

(continued)

NBA				Field Goals			3-Pt FGs			Free Throws			Misc			Fouls		Assists		Rebounds			Points	
Year Tm	G	GS	Min	Md	Att	Pct	Md	Att	Pct	Md	Att	Pct	TO	Stl	Blk	PF	DQ	Ast	Avg	Off	Tot	Avg	Pts	Avg
93-94 LAC	75	75	2856	569	1335	.426	71	236	.301	299	418	.715	242	144	54	167	0	344	4.6	129	460	6.1	1508	20.
94-95 Chi	77	53	1536	209	491	.426	31	110	.282	81	131	.618	100	97	27	132	1	157	2.0	51	180	2.3	530	6.
95-96 Chi	80	80	1886	234	501	.467	28	104	.269	98	139	.705	73	105	32	137	0	208	2.6	74	213	2.7	594	7.
96-97 Chi	76	74	1740	177	406	.436	68	188	.362	58	82	.707	50	86	38	138	0	191	2.5	46	193	2.5	480	6.
97-98 Chi	**82**	**82**	2284	293	665	.441	16	84	.190	162	216	.750	91	108	48	181	0	241	2.9	107	290	3.5	764	9.
98-99 Chi	35	35	1107	147	390	.377	27	85	.318	71	101	.703	65	60	35	80	0	115	3.3	49	180	5.1	392	11.
99-00 LAL	80	78	2042	212	531	.399	33	106	.311	100	147	.680	132	85	39	164	0	270	3.4	96	337	4.2	557	7.
89-90 Cle	7	7	262	61	138	.442	1	5	.200	31	41	.756	18	14	9	25	1	49	7.0	19	48	6.9	154	22.
LAC	28	28	1105	240	499	.481	13	46	.283	151	190	.795	82	67	32	80	0	133	4.8	55	158	5.6	644	23.
14 Years	962	921	30060	5199	11675	.445	504	1739	.290	2701	3751	.720	2189	1677	704	2254	10	3803	4.0	1276	4143	4.3	13603	14.

NBA Postseason

Year Tm	G	GS	Min	Md	Att	Pct	Md	Att	Pct	Md	Att	Pct	TO	Stl	Blk	PF	DQ	Ast	Avg	Off	Tot	Avg	Pts	Avg
87-88 Cle	4	4	134	30	63	.476	0	2	.000	11	16	.688	11	11	4	9	0	15	3.8	4	20	5.0	71	17.
88-89 Cle	5	5	189	39	69	.565	0	2	.000	20	26	.769	7	11	4	20	1	20	4.0	7	21	4.2	98	19.
91-92 LAC	5	5	206	39	87	.448	1	9	.111	11	14	.786	15	5	4	13	0	23	4.6	10	32	6.4	90	18.
92-93 LAC	5	5	174	37	78	.474	5	10	.500	11	17	.647	11	15	10	7	0	16	3.2	4	20	4.0	90	18.
94-95 Chi	6	0	40	6	14	.429	0	2	.000	0	0	—	1	3	1	6	0	4	0.7	2	6	1.0	12	2.
95-96 Chi	18	16	494	57	134	.425	15	47	.319	29	42	.690	18	25	7	38	0	45	2.5	26	67	3.7	158	8.
96-97 Chi	19	19	515	50	125	.400	21	61	.344	21	28	.750	11	24	14	43	1	57	3.0	20	81	4.3	142	7.
97-98 Chi	21	21	563	56	122	.459	5	19	.263	24	39	.615	18	20	18	42	0	48	2.3	22	77	3.7	141	6.
99-00 LAL	23	23	643	78	181	.431	9	39	.231	33	47	.702	28	23	13	63	0	73	3.2	30	85	3.7	198	8.
9 Years	106	98	2958	392	873	.449	56	191	.293	160	229	.699	120	137	75	241	2	301	2.8	125	409	3.9	1000	9.

Matt Harpring

Pos: F **College:** Georgia Tech **Drafted:** '98 1(15)—Orl   **Ht:** 6'7" **Wt:** 231 **Born:** 5/31/76 **Age:** 2

College				Field Goals			3-Pt FGs			Free Throws			Misc			Fouls		Assists		Rebounds			Points	
Year Tm	G	GS	Min	Md	Att	Pct	Md	Att	Pct	Md	Att	Pct	TO	Stl	Blk	PF	DQ	Ast	Avg	Off	Tot	Avg	Pts	Av
94-95 GTch	29	24	966	121	250	.484	28	73	.384	81	110	.736	62	39	7	66	—	68	2.3	85	180	6.2	351	12.
95-96 GTch	36	36	1328	233	457	.510	66	154	.429	138	181	.762	88	61	5	89	2	79	2.2	107	293	8.1	670	18.
96-97 GTch	27	27	1015	169	410	.412	65	190	.342	110	163	.675	97	32	10	70	0	60	2.2	83	222	8.2	513	19.
97-98 GTch	32	32	1163	230	504	.456	52	168	.310	179	221	.810	109	44	7	70	1	82	2.6	120	302	9.4	691	21.
4 Years	124	119	4472	753	1621	.465	211	585	.361	508	675	.753	356	176	29	295	—	289	2.3	395	997	8.0	2225	17.

NBA				Field Goals			3-Pt FGs			Free Throws			Misc			Fouls		Assists		Rebounds			Points	
Year Tm	G	GS	Min	Md	Att	Pct	Md	Att	Pct	Md	Att	Pct	TO	Stl	Blk	PF	DQ	Ast	Avg	Off	Tot	Avg	Pts	Av
98-99 Orl	**50**	22	1114	148	320	.463	10	25	.400	102	143	.713	73	30	6	112	0	45	0.9	88	214	4.3	408	8.
99-00 Orl	4	0	63	4	17	.235	2	2	1.000	6	7	.857	1	5	1	7	0	8	2.0	5	12	3.0	16	4.
2 Years	54	22	1177	152	337	.451	12	27	.444	108	150	.720	74	35	7	119	0	53	1.0	93	226	4.2	424	7

NBA Postseason

Year Tm	G	GS	Min	Md	Att	Pct	Md	Att	Pct	Md	Att	Pct	TO	Stl	Blk	PF	DQ	Ast	Avg	Off	Tot	Avg	Pts	Av
98-99 Orl	4	0	82	12	26	.462	1	5	.200	8	11	.727	5	1	0	9	0	7	1.8	7	20	5.0	33	8.

Al Harrington

Pos: F **College:** None **Drafted:** '98 1(25)—Ind   **Ht:** 6'9" **Wt:** 254 **Born:** 2/17/80 **Age:** 2

NBA				Field Goals			3-Pt FGs			Free Throws			Misc			Fouls		Assists		Rebounds			Points	
Year Tm	G	GS	Min	Md	Att	Pct	Md	Att	Pct	Md	Att	Pct	TO	Stl	Blk	PF	DQ	Ast	Avg	Off	Tot	Avg	Pts	Av
98-99 Ind	21	0	160	18	56	.321	0	5	.000	9	15	.600	11	4	2	26	0	5	0.2	20	39	1.9	45	2.
99-00 Ind	50	0	854	121	264	.458	8	34	.235	78	111	.703	65	25	9	130	0	38	0.8	47	159	3.2	328	6.
2 Years	71	0	1014	139	320	.434	8	39	.205	87	126	.690	76	29	11	156	0	43	0.6	67	198	2.8	373	5.

Othella Harrington

(statistical profile on page 22-)

Pos: F **College:** Georgetown **Drafted:** '96 2(30)—Hou   **Ht:** 6'9" **Wt:** 235 **Born:** 1/31/74 **Age:** 2

College				Field Goals			3-Pt FGs			Free Throws			Misc			Fouls		Assists		Rebounds			Points	
Year Tm	G	GS	Min	Md	Att	Pct	Md	Att	Pct	Md	Att	Pct	TO	Stl	Blk	PF	DQ	Ast	Avg	Off	Tot	Avg	Pts	Av
92-93 GTwn	33	33	1074	205	358	.573	0	0		144	193	.746	89	28	48	96	1	32	1.0	125	291	8.8	554	16.
93-94 GTwn	31	31	897	152	276	.551	0	1	.000	151	206	.733	92	22	51	100	4	36	1.2	83	248	8.0	455	14.
94-95 GTwn	31	31	769	132	236	.559	0	1	.000	115	163	.706	80	27	44	87	5	25	0.8	85	187	6.0	379	12.
95-96 GTwn	37	37	983	161	288	.559	0	2	.000	129	174	.741	65	29	58	91	4	44	1.2	100	257	6.9	451	12.
4 Years	132	132	3723	650	1158	.561	0	4	.000	539	736	.732	326	106	201	374	14	137	1.0	393	983	7.4	1839	13.

(continued)

Year Tm	G	GS	Min	Md	Att	Pct	Md	Att	Pct	Md	Att	Pct	TO	Stl	Blk	PF	DQ	Ast	Avg	Off	Tot	Avg	Pts	Avg
NBA				Field Goals			3-Pt FGs			Free Throws			Misc			Fouls		Assists		Rebounds			Points	
96-97 Hou	57	1	860	112	204	.549	0	3	.000	49	81	.605	57	12	22	112	2	18	0.3	75	198	3.5	273	4.8
97-98 Hou	58	3	903	129	266	.485	0	1	.000	92	122	.754	47	10	27	112	1	24	0.4	73	207	3.6	350	6.0
98-99 Hou	41	10	903	156	304	.513	0	0	—	88	122	.721	61	6	25	103	0	15	0.4	72	246	6.0	400	9.8
99-00 Van	82	82	2677	420	830	.506	0	2	.000	236	298	.792	217	36	58	287	3	97	1.2	196	563	6.9	1076	13.1
4 Years	238	96	5343	817	1604	.509	0	6	.000	465	623	.746	382	64	132	614	6	154	0.6	416	1214	5.1	2099	8.8
NBA Postseason																								
96-97 Hou	7	0	15	1	2	.500	0	0	—	7	10	.700	2	0	0	1	0	0	0.0	1	4	0.6	9	1.3
97-98 Hou	3	0	23	6	12	.500	0	1	.000	4	5	.800	0	0	1	1	0	0	0.0	3	7	2.3	16	5.3
98-99 Hou	4	0	42	9	14	.643	0	0	—	4	6	.667	3	0	1	2	0	1	0.3	5	14	3.5	22	5.5
3 Years	14	0	80	16	28	.571	0	1	.000	15	21	.714	5	0	2	4	0	1	0.1	9	25	1.8	47	3.4

Lucious Harris

(statistical profile on page 225)

Pos: G **College:** Long Beach State **Drafted:** '93 2(28)—Dal **Ht:** 6'5" **Wt:** 205 **Born:** 12/18/70 **Age:** 30

Year Tm	G	GS	Min	Md	Att	Pct	Md	Att	Pct	Md	Att	Pct	TO	Stl	Blk	PF	DQ	Ast	Avg	Off	Tot	Avg	Pts	Avg
College				Field Goals			3-Pt FGs			Free Throws			Misc			Fouls		Assists		Rebounds			Points	
89-90 LgBch	32	29	945	147	342	.430	45	136	.331	118	170	.694	52	49	5	63	—	52	1.6	82	152	4.8	457	14.3
90-91 LgBch	28	24	940	181	457	.396	50	153	.327	140	200	.700	79	47	2	63	2	69	2.5	59	131	4.7	552	19.7
91-92 LgBch	30	30	1132	197	418	.471	43	117	.368	127	173	.734	59	46	8	68	2	97	3.2	40	129	4.3	564	18.8
92-93 LgBch	32	32	1166	251	478	.525	73	177	.412	164	212	.774	66	58	7	49	—	79	2.5	45	169	5.3	739	23.1
4 Years	122	115	4183	776	1695	.458	211	583	.362	549	755	.727	256	200	22	243	—	297	2.4	226	581	4.8	2312	19.0
NBA				Field Goals			3-Pt FGs			Free Throws			Misc			Fouls		Assists		Rebounds			Points	
93-94 Dal	77	0	1165	162	385	.421	7	33	.212	87	119	.731	78	49	10	117	0	106	1.4	45	157	2.0	418	5.4
94-95 Dal	79	31	1695	280	610	.459	55	142	.387	136	170	.800	77	58	14	105	0	132	1.7	85	220	2.8	751	9.5
95-96 Dal	61	1	1016	183	397	.461	47	125	.376	68	87	.782	46	35	3	56	0	79	1.3	41	122	2.0	481	7.9
96-97 Phi	54	3	813	112	294	.381	36	99	.364	33	47	.702	34	41	3	45	0	50	0.9	27	71	1.3	293	5.4
97-98 NJ	50	0	671	69	177	.390	12	39	.308	41	55	.745	21	42	5	77	0	42	0.8	21	52	1.0	191	3.8
98-99 NJ	36	5	602	73	181	.403	11	50	.220	36	48	.750	18	18	7	52	1	31	0.9	21	67	1.9	193	5.4
99-00 NJ	77	11	1510	198	463	.428	38	115	.330	79	99	.798	42	65	6	98	0	100	1.3	53	187	2.4	513	6.7
7 Years	434	51	7472	1077	2507	.430	206	603	.342	480	625	.768	316	308	48	550	1	540	1.2	293	876	2.0	2840	6.5
NBA Postseason																								
97-98 NJ	3	0	52	2	6	.333	0	2	.000	5	6	.833	2	2	0	11	0	1	0.3	1	8	2.7	9	3.0

Antonio Harvey

Pos: F-C **College:** Pfeiffer **Drafted:** '93 FA—LAL **Ht:** 6'10" **Wt:** 245 **Born:** 7/6/70 **Age:** 30

Year Tm	G	GS	Min	Md	Att	Pct	Md	Att	Pct	Md	Att	Pct	TO	Stl	Blk	PF	DQ	Ast	Avg	Off	Tot	Avg	Pts	Avg
College				Field Goals			3-Pt FGs			Free Throws			Misc			Fouls		Assists		Rebounds			Points	
88-89 SIU	34	30	718	102	220	.464	0	0	—	31	64	.484	38	12	70	112	9	21	0.6	75	178	5.2	235	6.9
90-91 UGa	29	—	570	87	191	.455	0	4	.000	36	71	.507	46	17	60	78	—	21	0.7	—	125	4.3	210	7.2
91-92 Pfe	29	—	—	163	306	.533	4	8	.500	70	101	.693	—	—	140	—	—	21	0.7	—	234	8.1	400	13.8
92-93 Pfe	29	—	—	218	415	.525	5	12	.417	89	155	.574	—	—	154	—	—	36	1.2	—	294	10.1	530	18.3
4 Years	121	—	—	570	1132	.504	9	24	.375	226	391	.578	—	—	424	—	—	99	0.8	—	831	6.9	1375	11.4
NBA				Field Goals			3-Pt FGs			Free Throws			Misc			Fouls		Assists		Rebounds			Points	
93-94 LAL	27	6	247	29	79	.367	0	0	—	12	26	.462	17	8	19	39	0	5	0.2	26	59	2.2	70	2.6
94-95 LAL	59	8	572	77	176	.438	1	1	1.000	24	45	.533	25	15	41	87	0	23	0.4	39	102	1.7	179	3.0
95-96 2Tm	55	15	821	83	224	.371	0	2	.000	38	83	.458	44	27	47	76	0	15	0.3	69	200	3.6	204	3.7
96-97 Sea	6	0	26	5	11	.455	0	0	—	5	6	.833	1	0	4	8	0	1	0.2	2	10	1.7	15	2.5
97-98	Played in Greece																							
98-99	Played in Spain, Played in Greece																							
99-00 Por	19	0	137	17	30	.567	0	0	—	7	12	.583	12	1	6	20	0	5	0.3	8	33	1.7	41	2.2
95-96 Van	18	6	410	39	95	.411	0	2	.000	20	43	.465	18	14	21	38	0	9	0.5	27	94	5.2	98	5.4
LAC	37	9	411	44	129	.341	0	0	—	18	40	.450	26	13	26	38	0	6	0.2	42	106	2.9	106	2.9
5 Years	166	29	1803	211	520	.406	1	3	.333	86	172	.500	99	51	117	230	0	49	0.3	144	404	2.4	509	3.1
NBA Postseason																								
94-95 LAL	3	0	4	0	0	—	0	0	—	0	0	—	0	0	0	0	0	0	0.0	0	1	0.3	0	0.0

Hersey Hawkins

(statistical profile on page 225)

Pos: G **College:** Bradley **Drafted:** '88 1(6)—LAC **Ht:** 6'3" **Wt:** 200 **Born:** 9/29/66 **Age:** 34

	College			Field Goals			3-Pt FGs			Free Throws			Misc			Fouls		Assists		Rebounds			Points	
Year Tm	G	GS	Min	Md	Att	Pct	Md	Att	Pct	Md	Att	Pct	TO	Stl	Blk	PF	DQ	Ast	Avg	Off	Tot	Avg	Pts	Avg
84-85 Brad	30	30	1121	179	308	.581	—	—	—	81	105	.771	63	52	17	71	3	82	2.7	—	182	6.1	439	14.6
85-86 Brad	35	35	1291	250	461	.542	—	—	—	156	203	.768	70	66	23	83	3	104	3.0	—	200	5.7	656	18.7
86-87 Brad	29	29	1102	294	552	.533	31	108	.287	169	213	.793	99	59	12	77	1	103	3.6	—	195	6.7	788	27.2
87-88 Brad	31	31	1202	377	720	.524	87	221	.394	284	335	.848	66	82	24	79	1	111	3.6	—	241	7.8	1125	36.3
4 Years	125	125	4716	1100	2041	.539	118	329	.359	690	856	.806	298	259	76	310	8	400	3.2	—	818	6.5	3008	24.1

NBA				Field Goals			3-Pt FGs			Free Throws			Misc			Fouls		Assists		Rebounds			Points	
Year Tm	G	GS	Min	Md	Att	Pct	Md	Att	Pct	Md	Att	Pct	TO	Stl	Blk	PF	DQ	Ast	Avg	Off	Tot	Avg	Pts	Avg
88-89 Phi	79	79	2577	442	971	.455	71	166	.428	241	290	.831	158	120	37	184	0	239	3.0	51	225	2.8	1196	15.1
89-90 Phi	82	82	2856	522	1136	.460	84	200	.420	387	436	.888	185	130	28	217	2	261	3.2	85	304	3.7	1515	18.5
90-91 Phi*	80	80	3110	590	1251	.472	108	270	.400	479	550	.871	213	178	39	182	0	299	3.7	48	310	3.9	1767	22.1
91-92 Phi	81	81	3013	521	1127	.462	91	229	.397	403	461	.874	189	157	43	174	0	248	3.1	53	271	3.3	1536	19.0
92-93 Phi	81	81	2977	551	1172	.470	122	307	.397	419	487	.860	180	137	30	189	0	317	3.9	91	346	4.3	1643	20.3
93-94 Cha	82	82	2648	395	859	.460	78	235	.332	312	362	.862	158	135	22	167	2	216	2.6	89	377	4.6	1180	14.4
94-95 Cha	82	82	2731	390	809	.482	131	298	.440	261	301	.867	150	122	18	178	1	262	3.2	60	314	3.8	1172	14.3
95-96 Sea	82	82	2823	443	936	.473	146	380	.384	247	283	.873	164	149	14	172	1	218	2.7	86	297	3.6	1279	15.6
96-97 Sea	82	82	2755	369	795	.464	143	355	.403	258	295	.875	130	159	12	146	1	250	3.0	92	320	3.9	1139	13.9
97-98 Sea	82	82	2648	280	636	.440	125	301	.415	177	204	.868	102	148	17	153	0	221	2.7	71	334	4.1	862	10.5
98-99 Sea	50	34	1644	171	408	.419	55	180	.306	119	132	.902	80	80	18	90	1	123	2.5	51	201	4.0	516	10.3
99-00 Chi	61	49	1622	159	375	.424	55	141	.390	107	119	.899	100	74	15	146	1	134	2.2	31	175	2.9	480	7.9
12 Years	924	896	31353	4833	10475	.461	1209	3062	.395	3410	3920	.870	1809	1589	293	1998	8	2788	3.0	808	3474	3.8	14285	15.5

NBA Postseason				Field Goals			3-Pt FGs			Free Throws			Misc			Fouls		Assists		Rebounds			Points	
Year Tm	G	GS	Min	Md	Att	Pct	Md	Att	Pct	Md	Att	Pct	TO	Stl	Blk	PF	DQ	Ast	Avg	Off	Tot	Avg	Pts	Avg
88-89 Phi	3	3	72	3	24	.125	0	5	.000	2	2	1.000	3	3	1	6	0	4	1.3	1	5	1.7	8	2.7
89-90 Phi	10	10	415	81	163	.497	14	36	.389	59	63	.937	31	12	7	25	0	36	3.6	8	31	3.1	235	23.5
90-91 Phi	8	8	329	47	101	.465	14	26	.538	59	63	.937	16	20	10	29	1	27	3.4	8	46	5.8	167	20.9
94-95 Cha	4	4	130	13	32	.406	4	13	.308	15	17	.882	9	6	2	13	1	8	2.0	5	21	5.3	45	11.3
95-96 Sea	21	21	713	76	168	.452	22	64	.344	85	95	.895	33	27	4	55	0	46	2.2	17	63	3.0	259	12.3
96-97 Sea	12	12	483	62	132	.470	27	59	.458	32	35	.914	21	30	4	32	0	34	2.8	17	54	4.5	183	15.3
97-98 Sea	10	10	337	41	88	.466	17	43	.395	35	40	.875	9	18	1	24	0	36	3.6	17	57	5.7	134	13.4
7 Years	68	68	2479	323	708	.456	98	246	.398	287	315	.911	122	116	29	184	2	191	2.8	73	277	4.1	1031	15.2

Michael Hawkins

Pos: G **College:** Xavier (OH) **Drafted:** '96 FA—Bos **Ht:** 6'0" **Wt:** 180 **Born:** 10/28/72 **Age:** 28

	College			Field Goals			3-Pt FGs			Free Throws			Misc			Fouls		Assists		Rebounds			Points	
Year Tm	G	GS	Min	Md	Att	Pct	Md	Att	Pct	Md	Att	Pct	TO	Stl	Blk	PF	DQ	Ast	Avg	Off	Tot	Avg	Pts	Avg
91-92 Xav	27	—	743	76	185	.411	22	63	.349	35	54	.648	65	32	0	76	—	118	4.4	—	75	2.8	209	7.7
92-93 Xav	28	—	771	80	174	.460	36	88	.409	32	41	.780	65	23	0	64	—	104	3.7	—	71	2.5	228	8.1
93-94 Xav	29	—	570	68	182	.374	37	100	.370	23	36	.639	33	29	1	53	—	64	2.2	—	61	2.1	196	6.8
94-95 Xav	28	—	922	117	274	.427	59	152	.388	103	130	.792	84	45	2	54	—	162	5.8	—	93	3.3	396	14.1
4 Years	112	—	3006	341	815	.418	154	403	.382	193	261	.739	247	129	3	247	—	448	4.0	—	300	2.7	1029	9.2

NBA				Field Goals			3-Pt FGs			Free Throws			Misc			Fouls		Assists		Rebounds			Points	
Year Tm	G	GS	Min	Md	Att	Pct	Md	Att	Pct	Md	Att	Pct	TO	Stl	Blk	PF	DQ	Ast	Avg	Off	Tot	Avg	Pts	Avg
95-96										Played in CBA														
96-97 Bos	29	0	326	29	68	.426	10	31	.323	12	15	.800	28	16	1	40	0	64	2.2	9	31	1.1	80	2.8
97-98										Played in Greece														
98-99 Sac	24	0	203	14	40	.350	5	19	.263	3	3	1.000	13	3	1	14	0	27	1.1	10	25	1.0	36	1.5
99-00 Cha	12	0	36	3	13	.231	1	5	.200	1	2	.500	3	0	0	2	0	13	1.1	0	7	0.6	8	0.7
3 Years	65	0	565	46	121	.380	16	55	.291	16	20	.800	44	19	2	56	0	104	1.6	19	63	1.0	124	1.9

NBA Postseason				Field Goals			3-Pt FGs			Free Throws			Misc			Fouls		Assists		Rebounds			Points	
Year Tm	G	GS	Min	Md	Att	Pct	Md	Att	Pct	Md	Att	Pct	TO	Stl	Blk	PF	DQ	Ast	Avg	Off	Tot	Avg	Pts	Avg
98-99 Sac	2	0	10	0	1	.000	0	1	.000	2	2	1.000	0	0	0	1	0	0	0.0	0	0	0.0	2	1.0

Alan Henderson

(statistical profile on page 226)

Pos: F **College:** Indiana **Drafted:** '95 1(16)—Atl **Ht:** 6'9" **Wt:** 235 **Born:** 12/2/72 **Age:** 28

	College			Field Goals			3-Pt FGs			Free Throws			Misc			Fouls		Assists		Rebounds			Points	
Year Tm	G	GS	Min	Md	Att	Pct	Md	Att	Pct	Md	Att	Pct	TO	Stl	Blk	PF	DQ	Ast	Avg	Off	Tot	Avg	Pts	Avg
91-92 Ind	33	26	783	151	297	.508	1	4	.250	80	121	.661	32	32	50	84	2	17	0.5	86	238	7.2	383	11.6
92-93 Ind	30	25	737	130	267	.487	1	6	.167	72	113	.637	45	35	43	74	1	27	0.9	90	243	8.1	333	11.1
93-94 Ind	30	29	983	198	373	.531	2	6	.333	136	207	.657	60	39	56	90	1	36	1.2	100	308	10.3	534	17.8

(continued)

College	Year Tm	G	GS	Min	Md	Att	Pct	Md	Att	Pct	Md	Att	Pct	TO	Stl	Blk	PF	DQ	Ast	Avg	Off	Tot	Avg	Pts	Avg
					Field Goals			**3-Pt FGs**			**Free Throws**			**Misc**			**Fouls**		**Assists**		**Rebounds**			**Points**	
94-95 Ind		31	31	1093	284	476	.597	2	10	.200	159	251	.633	89	42	64	97	5	54	1.7	106	302	9.7	729	23.5
4 Years		124	111	3596	763	1413	.540	6	26	.231	447	692	.646	226	148	213	345	9	134	1.1	382	1091	8.8	1979	16.0

NBA	Year Tm	G	GS	Min	Md	Att	Pct	Md	Att	Pct	Md	Att	Pct	TO	Stl	Blk	PF	DQ	Ast	Avg	Off	Tot	Avg	Pts	Avg
95-96 Atl		79	4	1416	192	434	.442	0	3	.000	119	200	.595	87	44	43	217	5	51	0.6	164	356	4.5	503	6.4
96-97 Atl		30	0	501	77	162	.475	0	0	—	45	75	.600	29	21	6	73	1	23	0.8	47	116	3.9	199	6.6
97-98 Atl		69	33	2000	365	753	.485	3	6	.500	253	388	.652	110	42	36	175	1	73	1.1	199	442	6.4	986	14.3
98-99 Atl		38	37	1142	187	423	.442	0	1	.000	100	149	.671	58	33	19	96	1	28	0.7	100	250	6.6	474	12.5
99-00 Atl		82	82	2775	429	930	.461	1	10	.100	224	334	.671	139	81	54	233	3	77	0.9	265	571	7.0	1083	13.2
5 Years		298	156	7834	1250	2702	.463	4	20	.200	741	1146	.647	423	221	158	794	11	252	0.8	775	1735	5.8	3245	10.9

NBA Postseason

	Year Tm	G	GS	Min	Md	Att	Pct	Md	Att	Pct	Md	Att	Pct	TO	Stl	Blk	PF	DQ	Ast	Avg	Off	Tot	Avg	Pts	Avg
95-96 Atl		10	0	145	23	40	.575	0	0	—	7	10	.700	9	1	4	20	0	7	0.7	17	27	2.7	53	5.3
96-97 Atl		10	0	136	19	34	.559	0	0	—	20	26	.769	7	1	3	26	0	0	0.0	11	33	3.3	58	5.8
97-98 Atl		4	4	126	20	38	.526	0	1	.000	11	18	.611	6	3	1	13	0	4	1.0	10	22	5.5	51	12.8
98-99 Atl		1	0	4	0	0	—	0	0	—	0	0	—	0	0	0	1	0	0	0.0	0	0	0.0	0	0.0
4 Years		25	4	411	62	112	.554	0	1	.000	38	54	.704	22	5	8	60	0	11	0.4	38	82	3.3	162	6.5

Cedric Henderson

Pos: F **College:** Memphis **Drafted:** '97 2(45)—Cle **Ht:** 6'7" **Wt:** 225 **Born:** 3/11/75 **Age:** 25

College	Year Tm	G	GS	Min	Md	Att	Pct	Md	Att	Pct	Md	Att	Pct	TO	Stl	Blk	PF	DQ	Ast	Avg	Off	Tot	Avg	Pts	Avg
93-94 Mem		28	28	902	160	344	.465	18	67	.269	45	75	.600	77	30	29	76	1	52	1.9	56	142	5.1	383	13.7
94-95 Mem		34	33	1061	174	395	.441	23	77	.299	67	115	.583	81	40	37	84	2	48	1.4	—	172	5.1	438	12.9
95-96 Mem		30	30	877	146	297	.492	30	77	.390	57	93	.613	68	45	16	74	1	38	1.3	42	120	4.0	379	12.6
96-97 Mem		31	31	1069	184	441	.417	25	95	.263	104	151	.689	100	59	32	90	1	43	1.4	67	203	6.5	497	16.0
4 Years		123	122	3909	664	1477	.450	96	316	.304	273	434	.629	327	174	114	324	5	181	1.5	—	637	5.2	1697	13.8

NBA	Year Tm	G	GS	Min	Md	Att	Pct	Md	Att	Pct	Md	Att	Pct	TO	Stl	Blk	PF	DQ	Ast	Avg	Off	Tot	Avg	Pts	Avg
97-98 Cle		82	71	2527	348	725	.480	0	4	.000	136	190	.716	165	96	45	238	3	168	2.0	71	325	4.0	832	10.1
98-99 Cle		50	48	1517	189	453	.417	2	12	.167	74	91	.813	97	58	24	136	2	113	2.3	45	197	3.9	454	9.1
99-00 Cle		61	7	1107	129	326	.396	1	15	.067	69	104	.663	68	39	17	99	0	55	0.9	34	140	2.3	328	5.4
3 Years		193	126	5151	666	1504	.443	3	31	.097	279	385	.725	330	193	86	473	5	336	1.7	150	662	3.4	1614	8.4

NBA Postseason

	Year Tm	G	GS	Min	Md	Att	Pct	Md	Att	Pct	Md	Att	Pct	TO	Stl	Blk	PF	DQ	Ast	Avg	Off	Tot	Avg	Pts	Avg
97-98 Cle		4	4	157	11	28	.393	0	1	.000	8	13	.615	13	6	0	14	0	11	2.8	4	17	4.3	30	7.5

Mark Hendrickson

Pos: F **College:** Washington State **Drafted:** '96 2(31)—Phi **Ht:** 6'9" **Wt:** 220 **Born:** 6/23/74 **Age:** 26

College	Year Tm	G	GS	Min	Md	Att	Pct	Md	Att	Pct	Md	Att	Pct	TO	Stl	Blk	PF	DQ	Ast	Avg	Off	Tot	Avg	Pts	Avg
92-93 WshSt		27	27	927	119	214	.556	12	23	.522	89	125	.712	53	24	8	85	3	50	1.9	—	217	8.0	339	12.6
93-94 WshSt		28	28	889	96	198	.485	12	35	.343	90	126	.714	50	19	11	91	3	46	1.6	—	222	7.9	294	10.5
94-95 WshSt		30	30	991	183	292	.627	14	34	.412	104	131	.794	67	18	10	89	4	38	1.3	—	269	9.0	484	16.1
95-96 WshSt		23	23	763	127	222	.572	8	31	.258	117	165	.709	65	20	5	70	2	37	1.6	—	219	9.5	379	16.5
4 Years		108	108	3570	525	926	.567	46	123	.374	400	547	.731	235	81	34	335	12	171	1.6	—	927	8.6	1496	13.9

NBA	Year Tm	G	GS	Min	Md	Att	Pct	Md	Att	Pct	Md	Att	Pct	TO	Stl	Blk	PF	DQ	Ast	Avg	Off	Tot	Avg	Pts	Avg
96-97 Phi		29	1	301	32	77	.416	3	12	.250	18	26	.692	14	10	4	32	1	3	0.1	35	92	3.2	85	2.9
97-98 Sac		48	1	737	58	149	.389	0	5	.000	47	57	.825	31	26	9	60	0	41	0.9	33	143	3.0	163	3.4
98-99 NJ		22	6	399	39	88	.443	0	1	.000	42	50	.840	15	12	1	39	0	13	0.6	27	68	3.1	120	5.5
99-00 2Tm		15	0	71	5	8	.625	0	0	—	3	4	.750	3	2	1	8	0	6	0.4	3	13	0.9	13	0.9
99-00 Cle		10	0	47	5	7	.714	0	0	—	2	2	1.000	3	2	1	7	0	3	0.3	2	11	1.1	12	1.2
NJ		5	0	24	0	0	—	0	0	—	1	2	.500	0	0	0	1	0	3	0.6	1	2	0.4	1	0.2
4 Years		114	8	1508	134	322	.416	3	18	.167	110	137	.803	63	50	15	139	1	63	0.6	98	316	2.8	381	3.3

Chris Herren

Pos: G **College:** Fresno State **Drafted:** '99 2(33)—Den   **Ht:** 6'2" **Wt:** 185 **Born:** 9/27/75 **Age:** 25

College				Field Goals			3-Pt FGs			Free Throws			Misc			Fouls		Assists		Rebounds			Points	
Year Tm	G	GS	Min	Md	Att	Pct	Md	Att	Pct	Md	Att	Pct	TO	Stl	Blk	PF	DQ	Ast	Avg	Off	Tot	Avg	Pts	Avg
94-95 BC	1	0	21	3	4	.750	0	0	—	8	8	1.000	3	3	0	0	0	6	6.0	0	2	2.0	14	14.0
96-97 Fres	32	21	971	194	408	.475	68	188	.362	104	159	.654	93	61	4	103	8	146	4.6	15	74	2.3	560	17.5
97-98 Fres	29	25	953	162	347	.467	54	149	.362	75	133	.564	69	54	1	75	3	138	4.8	15	67	2.3	453	15.6
98-99 Fres	25	23	685	91	223	.408	44	115	.383	58	85	.682	69	25	1	64	2	181	7.2	10	41	1.6	284	11.4
4 Years	87	69	2630	450	982	.458	166	452	.367	245	385	.636	234	143	6	242	13	471	5.4	40	184	2.1	1311	15.1

NBA				Field Goals			3-Pt FGs			Free Throws			Misc			Fouls		Assists		Rebounds			Points	
Year Tm	G	GS	Min	Md	Att	Pct	Md	Att	Pct	Md	Att	Pct	TO	Stl	Blk	PF	DQ	Ast	Avg	Off	Tot	Avg	Pts	Avg
99-00 Den	45	1	597	45	124	.363	24	67	.358	27	40	.675	42	15	2	74	0	111	2.5	12	52	1.2	141	3.1

Grant Hill

(statistical profile on page 226)

Pos: F **College:** Duke **Drafted:** '94 1(3)—Det   **Ht:** 6'8" **Wt:** 225 **Born:** 10/5/72 **Age:** 28

College				Field Goals			3-Pt FGs			Free Throws			Misc			Fouls		Assists		Rebounds			Points	
Year Tm	G	GS	Min	Md	Att	Pct	Md	Att	Pct	Md	Att	Pct	TO	Stl	Blk	PF	DQ	Ast	Avg	Off	Tot	Avg	Pts	Avg
90-91 Duke	36	31	887	160	310	.516	1	2	.500	81	133	.609	74	51	30	79	—	79	2.2	63	183	5.1	402	11.2
91-92 Duke	33	24	1000	182	298	.611	0	1	.000	99	135	.733	80	39	27	91	—	134	4.1	49	187	5.7	463	14.0
92-93 Duke	26	26	822	185	320	.578	4	14	.286	94	126	.746	63	64	36	61	—	72	2.8	43	166	6.4	468	18.0
93-94 Duke	34	34	1213	218	472	.462	39	100	.390	116	165	.703	102	64	40	85	—	176	5.2	48	233	6.9	591	17.4
4 Years	129	115	3922	745	1400	.532	44	117	.376	390	559	.698	319	218	133	316	—	461	3.6	203	769	6.0	1924	14.9

NBA				Field Goals			3-Pt FGs			Free Throws			Misc			Fouls		Assists		Rebounds			Points	
Year Tm	G	GS	Min	Md	Att	Pct	Md	Att	Pct	Md	Att	Pct	TO	Stl	Blk	PF	DQ	Ast	Avg	Off	Tot	Avg	Pts	Avg
94-95 Det*	70	69	2678	508	1064	.477	4	27	.148	374	511	.732	202	124	62	203	1	353	5.0	125	445	6.4	1394	19.9
95-96 Det*	80	80	3260	564	1221	.462	5	26	.192	485	646	.751	263	100	48	242	1	548	6.9	127	783	9.8	1618	20.2
96-97 Det*	80	80	3147	625	1259	.496	10	33	.303	450	633	.711	259	144	48	186	0	583	7.3	123	721	9.0	1710	21.4
97-98 Det*	81	81	3294	615	1361	.452	3	21	.143	479	647	.740	285	143	53	196	1	551	6.8	93	623	7.7	1712	21.1
98-99 Det*	50	50	1852	384	802	.479	0	14	.000	285	379	.752	184	80	27	114	0	300	6.0	65	355	7.1	1053	21.1
99-00 Det*	74	74	2776	696	1422	.489	34	98	.347	480	604	.795	240	103	43	190	0	385	5.2	97	490	6.6	1906	25.8
6 Years	435	434	17007	3392	7129	.476	56	219	.256	2553	3420	.746	1433	694	281	1131	3	2720	6.3	630	3417	7.9	9393	21.6

NBA Postseason																								
Year Tm	G	GS	Min	Md	Att	Pct	Md	Att	Pct	Md	Att	Pct	TO	Stl	Blk	PF	DQ	Ast	Avg	Off	Tot	Avg	Pts	Avg
95-96 Det	3	3	115	22	39	.564	1	2	.500	12	14	.857	8	3	0	13	0	11	3.7	4	22	7.3	57	19.0
96-97 Det	5	5	203	45	103	.437	0	0	—	28	39	.718	19	4	5	14	0	27	5.4	13	34	6.8	118	23.6
98-99 Det	5	5	176	42	92	.457	0	1	.000	13	16	.813	12	10	2	12	0	37	7.4	7	36	7.2	97	19.4
99-00 Det	2	2	55	6	16	.375	1	2	.500	9	10	.900	10	1	0	7	0	9	4.5	0	11	5.5	22	11.0
4 Years	15	15	549	115	250	.460	2	5	.400	62	79	.785	49	18	7	46	0	84	5.6	24	103	6.9	294	19.6

Tyrone Hill

(statistical profile on page 227)

Pos: F **College:** Xavier (OH) **Drafted:** '90 1(11)—GS   **Ht:** 6'9" **Wt:** 250 **Born:** 3/19/68 **Age:** 32

College				Field Goals			3-Pt FGs			Free Throws			Misc			Fouls		Assists		Rebounds			Points	
Year Tm	G	GS	Min	Md	Att	Pct	Md	Att	Pct	Md	Att	Pct	TO	Stl	Blk	PF	DQ	Ast	Avg	Off	Tot	Avg	Pts	Avg
86-87 Xav	31	—	881	95	172	.552	0	0	—	84	125	.672	62	14	15	113	—	7	0.2	—	261	8.4	274	8.8
87-88 Xav	30	—	858	172	309	.557	0	0	—	114	153	.745	69	18	8	102	—	21	0.7	—	314	10.5	458	15.3
88-89 Xav	33	—	1094	235	388	.606	0	0	—	155	221	.701	112	44	24	105	—	45	1.4	—	403	12.2	625	18.9
89-90 Xav	32	—	1063	250	430	.581	0	2	.000	146	222	.658	98	31	21	99	—	49	1.5	—	402	12.6	646	20.2
4 Years	126	—	3896	752	1299	.579	0	2	.000	499	721	.692	341	107	68	419	—	122	1.0	—	1380	11.0	2003	15.9

NBA				Field Goals			3-Pt FGs			Free Throws			Misc			Fouls		Assists		Rebounds			Points	
Year Tm	G	GS	Min	Md	Att	Pct	Md	Att	Pct	Md	Att	Pct	TO	Stl	Blk	PF	DQ	Ast	Avg	Off	Tot	Avg	Pts	Avg
90-91 GS	74	22	1192	147	299	.492	0	0	—	96	152	.632	72	33	30	264	—	19	0.3	157	383	5.2	390	5.3
91-92 GS	82	75	1886	254	487	.522	0	1	.000	163	235	.694	106	73	43	315	7	47	0.6	182	593	7.2	671	8.2
92-93 GS	74	66	2070	251	494	.508	0	4	.000	138	221	.624	92	41	40	320	8	68	0.9	255	754	10.2	640	8.6
93-94 Cle*	57	20	1447	216	398	.543	0	2	.000	171	256	.668	78	53	35	193	5	46	0.8	184	499	8.8	603	10.6
94-95 Cle*	70	67	2397	350	694	.504	0	1	.000	263	397	.662	151	55	41	245	4	55	0.8	269	765	10.9	963	13.8
95-96 Cle	44	2	929	130	254	.512	0	0	—	81	135	.600	64	31	20	144	3	33	0.8	94	244	5.5	341	7.8
96-97 Cle	74	70	2582	357	595	.600	0	1	.000	241	381	.633	147	63	30	268	6	92	1.2	259	736	9.9	955	12.9
97-98 Mil	57	56	2064	208	418	.498	0	1	.000	155	255	.608	106	67	30	230	8	88	1.5	212	608	10.7	571	10.0
98-99 2Tm	38	23	1104	122	268	.455	0	0	—	81	150	.540	59	34	16	145	2	35	0.9	115	287	7.6	325	8.6
99-00 Phi	68	65	2155	318	656	.485	0	1	.000	179	259	.691	124	64	27	243	3	52	0.8	220	625	9.2	815	12.0
98-99 Mil	17	17	517	50	118	.424	0	0	—	46	81	.568	24	18	8	68	0	17	1.0	51	134	7.9	146	8.6
Phi	21	6	587	72	150	.480	0	0	—	35	69	.507	35	16	8	77	2	18	0.9	64	153	7.3	179	8.5
10 Years	638	466	17826	2353	4563	.516	0	11	.000	1568	2441	.642	999	514	312	2367	54	535	0.8	1947	5494	8.6	6274	9.8

NBA Postseason

Year Tm	G	GS	Min	Md	Att	Pct	Md	Att	Pct	Md	Att	Pct	TO	Stl	Blk	PF	DQ	Ast	Avg	Off	Tot	Avg	Pts	Avg
90-91 GS	9	0	80	9	14	.643	0	1	.000	4	6	.667	2	3	4	25	2	2	0.2	7	23	2.6	22	2.4
91-92 GS	4	1	47	3	7	.429	0	0	—	0	2	.000	3	2	0	12	0	1	0.3	3	8	2.0	6	1.5
93-94 Cle	3	3	123	11	27	.407	0	0	—	20	37	.541	8	1	1	14	1	4	1.3	14	31	10.3	42	14.0
94-95 Cle	4	4	139	9	29	.310	0	1	.000	16	25	.640	10	7	1	18	1	3	0.8	8	23	5.8	34	8.5
95-96 Cle	3	0	53	9	12	.750	0	0	—	7	9	.778	3	0	0	11	1	0	0.0	7	15	5.0	25	8.3
98-99 Phi	8	1	196	19	39	.487	0	0	—	7	19	.368	6	3	2	33	1	0	0.0	19	59	7.4	45	5.6
99-00 Phi	10	10	352	46	100	.460	0	1	.000	31	44	.705	12	9	1	38	0	9	0.9	36	97	9.7	123	12.3
7 Years	41	19	990	106	228	.465	0	3	.000	85	142	.599	44	25	9	151	6	19	0.5	94	256	6.2	297	7.2

Fred Hoiberg

Pos: G **College:** Iowa State **Drafted:** '95 2(52)—Ind   **Ht:** 6'4" **Wt:** 203 **Born:** 10/15/72 **Age:** 28

College				Field Goals			3-Pt FGs			Free Throws			Misc			Fouls		Assists		Rebounds			Points	
Year Tm	G	GS	Min	Md	Att	Pct	Md	Att	Pct	Md	Att	Pct	TO	Stl	Blk	PF	DQ	Ast	Avg	Off	Tot	Avg	Pts	Avg
91-92 IaSt	34	—	1037	161	281	.573	13	50	.260	75	93	.806	58	65	6	76	—	85	2.5	—	181	5.3	410	12.1
92-93 IaSt	31	—	1018	127	231	.550	22	60	.367	84	103	.816	52	56	1	48	—	93	3.0	—	194	6.3	360	11.6
93-94 IaSt	27	—	971	177	331	.535	59	131	.450	133	154	.864	58	47	3	46	—	97	3.6	—	181	6.7	546	20.2
94-95 IaSt	34	—	1252	207	473	.438	89	216	.412	174	202	.861	63	39	5	44	—	75	2.2	—	192	5.6	677	19.9
4 Years	126	—	4278	672	1316	.511	183	457	.400	466	552	.844	231	207	15	214	—	350	2.8	—	748	5.9	1993	15.8

NBA				Field Goals			3-Pt FGs			Free Throws			Misc			Fouls		Assists		Rebounds			Points	
Year Tm	G	GS	Min	Md	Att	Pct	Md	Att	Pct	Md	Att	Pct	TO	Stl	Blk	PF	DQ	Ast	Avg	Off	Tot	Avg	Pts	Avg
95-96 Ind	15	1	85	8	19	.421	1	3	.333	15	18	.833	7	6	1	12	0	8	0.5	4	9	0.6	32	2.1
96-97 Ind	47	0	572	67	156	.429	29	70	.414	61	77	.792	22	27	6	51	0	41	0.9	13	81	1.7	224	4.8
97-98 Ind	65	1	874	85	222	.383	32	85	.376	59	69	.855	22	40	3	101	0	45	0.7	14	123	1.9	261	4.0
98-99 Ind	12	0	87	6	21	.286	1	9	.111	6	6	1.000	3	0	0	11	0	4	0.3	2	11	0.9	19	1.6
99-00 Chi	31	11	845	89	230	.387	32	94	.340	69	76	.908	43	40	2	66	0	85	2.7	7	110	3.5	279	9.0
5 Years	170	13	2463	255	648	.394	95	261	.364	210	246	.854	97	113	12	241	0	183	1.1	40	334	2.0	815	4.8

NBA Postseason

Year Tm	G	GS	Min	Md	Att	Pct	Md	Att	Pct	Md	Att	Pct	TO	Stl	Blk	PF	DQ	Ast	Avg	Off	Tot	Avg	Pts	Avg
97-98 Ind	2	0	20	3	8	.375	1	2	.500	2	2	1.000	0	1	0	2	0	1	0.5	1	4	2.0	9	4.5
98-99 Ind	4	0	20	2	4	.500	0	0	—	0	0	—	0	3	0	1	0	2	0.5	0	3	0.8	4	1.0
2 Years	6	0	40	5	12	.417	1	2	.500	2	2	1.000	0	4	0	3	0	3	0.5	1	7	1.2	13	2.2

Derek Hood

Pos: F **College:** Arkansas **Drafted:** '99 FA—Cha   **Ht:** 6'8" **Wt:** 222 **Born:** 12/22/76 **Age:** 24

College				Field Goals			3-Pt FGs			Free Throws			Misc			Fouls		Assists		Rebounds			Points	
Year Tm	G	GS	Min	Md	Att	Pct	Md	Att	Pct	Md	Att	Pct	TO	Stl	Blk	PF	DQ	Ast	Avg	Off	Tot	Avg	Pts	Avg
95-96 Ark	33	28	717	105	222	.473	0	0	—	36	82	.439	75	32	22	103	7	36	1.1	98	200	6.1	246	7.5
96-97 Ark	32	31	872	130	269	.483	0	1	.000	50	79	.633	77	39	23	119	8	54	1.7	101	257	8.0	310	9.7
97-98 Ark	32	29	722	119	237	.502	0	0	—	32	60	.533	66	36	27	94	3	53	1.7	71	196	6.1	270	8.4
98-99 Ark	34	34	978	173	306	.565	0	2	.000	75	110	.682	66	41	31	115	5	61	1.8	144	349	10.3	421	12.4
4 Years	131	122	3289	527	1034	.510	0	3	.000	193	331	.583	284	148	103	431	23	204	1.6	414	1002	7.6	1247	9.5

NBA				Field Goals			3-Pt FGs			Free Throws			Misc			Fouls		Assists		Rebounds			Points	
Year Tm	G	GS	Min	Md	Att	Pct	Md	Att	Pct	Md	Att	Pct	TO	Stl	Blk	PF	DQ	Ast	Avg	Off	Tot	Avg	Pts	Avg
99-00 Cha	2	0	4	0	3	.000	0	0	—	0	0	—	0	0	0	0	0	0	0.0	0	1	0.5	0	0.0

Jeff Hornacek

(statistical profile on page 227)

Pos: G **College:** Iowa State **Drafted:** '86 2(46)—Pho   **Ht:** 6'4" **Wt:** 190 **Born:** 5/3/63 **Age:** 37

College				Field Goals			3-Pt FGs			Free Throws			Misc			Fouls		Assists		Rebounds			Points	
Year Tm	G	GS	Min	Md	Att	Pct	Md	Att	Pct	Md	Att	Pct	TO	Stl	Blk	PF	DQ	Ast	Avg	Off	Tot	Avg	Pts	Avg
82-83 IaSt	27	—	583	57	135	.422	—	—	—	32	45	.711	45	21	4	43	—	82	3.0	—	62	2.3	146	5.4
83-84 IaSt	29	—	1065	104	208	.500	—	—	—	83	105	.790	86	61	10	94	—	198	6.8	—	101	3.5	291	10.0
84-85 IaSt	34	—	1224	172	330	.521	—	—	—	81	96	.844	72	65	10	82	—	166	4.9	—	122	3.6	425	12.5
85-86 IaSt	33	—	1229	177	370	.478	—	—	—	97	125	.776	78	64	8	94	—	219	6.6	—	127	3.8	451	13.7
4 Years	123	—	4101	510	1043	.489	—	—	—	293	371	.790	281	211	32	313	—	665	5.4	—	412	3.3	1313	10.7

NBA				Field Goals			3-Pt FGs			Free Throws			Misc			Fouls		Assists		Rebounds			Points	
Year Tm	G	GS	Min	Md	Att	Pct	Md	Att	Pct	Md	Att	Pct	TO	Stl	Blk	PF	DQ	Ast	Avg	Off	Tot	Avg	Pts	Avg
86-87 Pho	80	3	1561	159	350	.454	12	43	.279	94	121	.777	153	70	5	130	0	361	4.5	41	184	2.3	424	5.3
87-88 Pho	82	49	2243	306	605	.506	17	58	.293	152	185	.822	156	107	10	151	0	540	6.6	71	262	3.2	781	9.5
88-89 Pho	78	73	2487	440	889	.495	27	81	.333	147	178	.826	111	129	8	188	0	465	6.0	75	266	3.4	1054	13.5
89-90 Pho	67	60	2278	483	901	.536	40	98	.408	173	202	.856	125	117	14	144	2	337	5.0	86	313	4.7	1179	17.6

NBA

Year Tm	G	GS	Min	Md	Att	Pct	Md	Att	Pct	Md	Att	Pct	TO	Stl	Blk	PF	DQ	Ast	Avg	Off	Tot	Avg	Pts	Avg
				Field Goals			3-Pt FGs			Free Throws			Misc			Fouls		Assists		Rebounds			Points	
90-91 Pho	80	77	2733	544	1051	.518	61	146	.418	201	224	.897	130	111	16	185	1	409	5.1	74	321	4.0	1350	16.9
91-92 Pho*	81	81	3078	635	1240	.512	83	189	.439	279	315	.886	170	158	31	218	1	411	5.1	106	407	5.0	1632	20.1
92-93 Phi	79	78	2860	582	1239	.470	97	249	.390	250	289	.865	222	131	21	203	2	548	6.9	84	342	4.3	1511	19.1
93-94 2Tm	80	62	2820	472	1004	.470	70	208	.337	260	296	.878	171	127	13	186	0	419	5.2	60	279	3.5	1274	15.9
94-95 Uta	81	81	2696	482	937	.514	89	219	.406	284	322	.882	145	129	17	181	1	347	4.3	53	210	2.6	1337	16.5
95-96 Uta	82	59	2588	442	880	.502	104	223	.466	259	290	.893	127	106	20	171	1	340	4.1	62	209	2.5	1247	15.2
96-97 Uta	82	82	2592	413	856	.482	72	195	.369	293	326	.899	134	124	26	188	1	361	4.4	60	241	2.9	1191	14.5
97-98 Uta	80	80	2460	399	828	.482	56	127	.441	285	322	.885	132	109	15	175	1	349	4.4	65	270	3.4	1139	14.2
98-99 Uta	48	48	1435	214	449	.477	34	81	.420	125	140	.893	82	52	14	95	0	192	4.0	33	160	3.3	587	12.2
99-00 Uta	77	77	2133	358	728	.492	66	138	.478	171	180	**.950**	113	66	16	149	1	202	2.6	49	182	2.4	953	12.4
93-94 Phi	53	53	1994	325	715	.455	52	166	.313	178	204	.873	138	95	10	115	0	315	5.9	41	214	4.0	880	16.6
Uta	27	9	826	147	289	.509	18	42	.429	82	92	.891	33	32	3	71	0	104	3.9	19	67	2.5	394	14.6
14 Years	1077	910	33964	5929	11957	.496	828	2055	.403	2973	3390	.877	1971	1536	226	2364	11	5281	4.9	919	3646	3.4	15659	14.5

NBA Postseason

Year Tm	G	GS	Min	Md	Att	Pct	Md	Att	Pct	Md	Att	Pct	TO	Stl	Blk	PF	DQ	Ast	Avg	Off	Tot	Avg	Pts	Avg
88-89 Pho	12	12	374	74	149	.497	0	7	.000	21	25	.840	18	16	3	34	0	62	5.2	25	69	5.8	169	14.1
89-90 Pho	16	16	583	112	219	.511	6	24	.250	68	73	.932	34	24	0	43	1	73	4.6	13	62	3.9	298	18.6
90-91 Pho	4	4	145	22	51	.431	3	6	.500	26	28	.929	3	3	2	13	0	8	2.0	3	25	6.3	73	18.3
91-92 Pho	8	8	343	62	128	.484	8	17	.471	31	34	.912	19	14	2	23	0	42	5.3	12	51	6.4	163	20.4
93-94 Uta	16	16	558	85	179	.475	15	34	.441	62	68	.912	28	24	6	45	0	64	4.0	11	39	2.4	247	15.4
94-95 Uta	5	5	178	26	51	.510	7	13	.538	11	14	.786	7	8	2	19	1	20	4.0	3	6	1.2	70	14.0
95-96 Uta	18	18	644	104	207	.502	34	58	.586	73	82	.890	27	19	3	41	1	60	3.3	22	65	3.6	315	17.5
96-97 Uta	20	20	704	90	208	.433	19	53	.358	92	105	.876	36	21	4	53	1	73	3.7	22	89	4.5	291	14.6
97-98 Uta	20	20	636	74	178	.416	14	30	.467	55	65	.846	32	20	4	51	1	64	3.2	7	50	2.5	217	10.9
98-99 Uta	11	11	304	49	106	.462	7	18	.389	29	33	.879	12	11	0	34	1	26	2.4	9	41	3.7	134	12.2
99-00 Uta	10	10	297	43	102	.422	9	22	.409	20	24	.833	15	10	0	28	0	33	3.3	9	30	3.0	115	11.5
11 Years	140	140	4766	741	1578	.470	122	282	.433	488	551	.886	231	170	26	384	6	525	3.8	136	527	3.8	2092	14.9

Robert Horry

(statistical profile on page 228)

Pos: F **College:** Alabama **Drafted:** '92 1(11)—Hou **Ht:** 6'10" **Wt:** 235 **Born:** 8/25/70 **Age:** 30

College

Year Tm	G	GS	Min	Md	Att	Pct	Md	Att	Pct	Md	Att	Pct	TO	Stl	Blk	PF	DQ	Ast	Avg	Off	Tot	Avg	Pts	Avg
88-89 Ala	31	—	590	79	185	.427	4	13	.308	38	59	.644	36	22	37	72	—	35	1.1	—	156	5.0	200	6.5
89-90 Ala	35	—	1022	164	351	.467	50	117	.427	79	104	.760	77	54	51	92	—	9	0.3	—	217	6.2	457	13.1
90-91 Ala	32	—	959	133	296	.449	33	98	.337	82	102	.804	74	54	77	104	—	56	1.8	—	260	8.1	381	11.9
91-92 Ala	35	—	1185	196	417	.470	42	120	.350	120	165	.727	102	54	121	100	—	88	2.5	—	296	8.5	554	15.8
4 Years	133	—	3756	572	1249	.458	129	348	.371	319	430	.742	289	184	286	368	—	188	1.4	—	929	7.0	1592	12.0

NBA

Year Tm	G	GS	Min	Md	Att	Pct	Md	Att	Pct	Md	Att	Pct	TO	Stl	Blk	PF	DQ	Ast	Avg	Off	Tot	Avg	Pts	Avg
92-93 Hou	79	79	2330	323	682	.474	12	47	.255	143	200	.715	156	80	83	210	1	191	2.4	113	392	5.0	801	10.1
93-94 Hou	81	81	2370	322	702	.459	44	136	.324	115	157	.732	137	119	75	186	0	231	2.9	128	440	5.4	803	9.9
94-95 Hou	64	61	2074	240	537	.447	86	227	.379	86	113	.761	122	94	76	161	0	216	3.4	81	324	5.1	652	10.2
95-96 Hou	71	71	2634	300	732	.410	142	388	.366	111	143	.776	160	116	109	197	3	281	4.0	97	412	5.8	853	12.0
96-97 2Tm	54	29	1395	157	360	.436	49	154	.318	60	90	.667	72	66	55	153	2	110	2.0	68	237	4.4	423	7.8
97-98 LAL	72	71	2192	200	420	.476	19	93	.204	117	169	.692	99	112	94	238	5	163	2.3	186	542	7.5	536	7.4
98-99 LAL	38	5	744	67	146	.459	20	45	.444	34	46	.739	49	36	39	103	2	56	1.5	56	152	4.0	188	4.9
99-00 LAL	76	0	1685	159	363	.438	29	94	.309	89	113	.788	73	84	80	189	0	118	1.6	133	361	4.8	436	5.7
96-97 Pho	32	15	719	82	195	.421	24	78	.308	32	50	.640	46	28	26	81	1	54	1.7	40	119	3.7	220	6.9
LAL	22	14	676	75	165	.455	25	76	.329	28	40	.700	26	38	29	72	1	56	2.5	28	118	5.4	203	9.2
8 Years	535	397	15424	1768	3942	.449	401	1184	.339	755	1031	.732	868	707	611	1437	13	1366	2.6	862	2860	5.3	4692	8.8

NBA Postseason

Year Tm	G	GS	Min	Md	Att	Pct	Md	Att	Pct	Md	Att	Pct	TO	Stl	Blk	PF	DQ	Ast	Avg	Off	Tot	Avg	Pts	Avg
92-93 Hou	12	12	374	47	101	.465	9	30	.300	20	27	.741	28	18	16	30	1	38	3.2	14	62	5.2	123	10.3
93-94 Hou	23	23	778	98	226	.434	34	89	.382	39	51	.765	27	35	20	68	0	82	3.6	40	141	6.1	269	11.7
94-95 Hou	22	22	841	93	209	.445	44	110	.400	58	78	.744	25	32	26	69	2	76	3.5	40	155	7.0	288	13.1
95-96 Hou	8	8	308	37	91	.407	21	53	.396	10	23	.435	15	21	13	29	1	24	3.0	15	57	7.1	105	13.1
96-97 LAL	9	9	279	17	38	.447	12	28	.429	14	18	.778	11	10	7	27	0	13	1.4	12	48	5.3	60	6.7
97-98 LAL	13	13	422	39	70	.557	6	17	.353	28	41	.683	18	14	14	45	0	40	3.1	34	84	6.5	112	8.6
98-99 LAL	8	0	177	12	26	.462	5	12	.417	11	14	.786	7	6	6	29	1	11	1.4	10	36	4.5	40	5.0
99-00 LAL	23	0	618	59	145	.407	17	59	.288	40	57	.702	30	20	19	88	3	58	2.5	38	123	5.3	175	7.6
8 Years	118	87	3797	402	906	.444	148	398	.372	220	309	.712	161	156	121	385	8	342	2.9	203	706	6.0	1172	9.9

Allan Houston

(statistical profile on page 228)

Pos: G **College:** Tennessee **Drafted:** '93 1(11)—Det **Ht:** 6'6" **Wt:** 200 **Born:** 4/20/71 **Age:** 29

College

Year Tm	G	GS	Min	Md	Att	Pct	Md	Att	Pct	Md	Att	Pct	TO	Stl	Blk	PF	DQ	Ast	Avg	Off	Tot	Avg	Pts	Avg
89-90 Tenn	30	—	1083	203	465	.437	83	192	.432	120	149	.805	101	36	11	70	—	127	4.2	—	88	2.9	609	20.3
90-91 Tenn	34	—	1212	265	550	.482	99	231	.429	177	205	.863	128	37	16	68	—	131	3.9	—	104	3.1	806	23.7
91-92 Tenn	34	—	1236	223	492	.453	82	196	.418	189	225	.840	94	32	15	69	—	110	3.2	—	180	5.3	717	21.1
92-93 Tenn	30	—	1075	211	454	.465	82	198	.414	165	188	.878	84	28	8	67	—	92	3.1	—	145	4.8	669	22.3
Years	128	—	4606	902	1961	.460	346	817	.424	651	767	.849	407	133	50	274	—	460	3.6	—	517	4.0	2801	21.9

NBA

Year Tm	G	GS	Min	Md	Att	Pct	Md	Att	Pct	Md	Att	Pct	TO	Stl	Blk	PF	DQ	Ast	Avg	Off	Tot	Avg	Pts	Avg
93-94 Det	79	20	1519	272	671	.405	35	117	.299	89	108	.824	99	34	13	165	2	100	1.3	19	120	1.5	668	8.5
94-95 Det	76	39	1996	398	859	.463	158	373	.424	147	171	.860	113	61	14	182	0	164	2.2	29	167	2.2	1101	14.5
95-96 Det	82	75	3072	564	1244	.453	191	447	.427	298	362	.823	233	61	16	233	—	250	3.0	54	300	3.7	1617	19.7
96-97 NY	81	81	2681	437	1032	.423	148	384	.385	175	218	.803	167	41	18	233	6	179	2.2	43	240	3.0	1197	14.8
97-98 NY	82	82	2848	571	1277	.447	82	213	.385	285	335	.851	200	63	24	207	2	212	2.6	43	274	3.3	1509	18.4
98-99 NY*	50	50	1815	294	703	.418	57	140	.407	168	195	.862	130	35	9	115	1	137	2.7	20	152	3.0	813	16.3
99-00 NY*	82	82	3169	614	1271	.483	106	243	.436	280	334	.838	186	65	14	219	1	224	2.7	38	271	3.3	1614	19.7
Years	532	429	17100	3150	7057	.446	777	1917	.405	1442	1723	.837	1128	360	108	1354	13	1266	2.4	246	1524	2.9	8519	16.0

NBA Postseason

Year Tm	G	GS	Min	Md	Att	Pct	Md	Att	Pct	Md	Att	Pct	TO	Stl	Blk	PF	DQ	Ast	Avg	Off	Tot	Avg	Pts	Avg
95-96 Det	3	3	136	25	58	.431	7	21	.333	18	20	.900	11	0	1	11	0	6	2.0	1	8	2.7	75	25.0
96-97 NY	9	9	360	58	133	.436	26	52	.500	31	35	.886	24	6	3	14	0	21	2.3	3	23	2.6	173	19.2
97-98 NY	10	10	403	76	175	.434	9	23	.391	50	58	.862	32	5	1	27	0	28	2.8	6	38	3.8	211	21.1
98-99 NY	20	20	783	135	305	.443	9	36	.250	91	103	.883	50	8	1	40	0	51	2.6	6	54	2.7	370	18.5
99-00 NY	16	16	654	103	235	.438	19	38	.500	56	65	.862	36	19	3	42	0	26	1.6	3	52	3.3	281	17.6
Years	58	58	2336	397	906	.438	70	170	.412	246	281	.875	153	38	9	134	0	132	2.3	19	175	3.0	1110	19.1

Juwan Howard

(statistical profile on page 229)

Pos: F **College:** Michigan **Drafted:** '94 1(5)—Was **Ht:** 6'9" **Wt:** 250 **Born:** 2/7/73 **Age:** 27

College

Year Tm	G	GS	Min	Md	Att	Pct	Md	Att	Pct	Md	Att	Pct	TO	Stl	Blk	PF	DQ	Ast	Avg	Off	Tot	Avg	Pts	Avg
91-92 Mich	34	31	956	150	333	.450	0	2	.000	77	112	.688	99	15	21	107	3	62	1.8	66	212	6.2	377	11.1
92-93 Mich	36	36	1095	206	407	.506	0	2	.000	112	160	.700	92	21	14	99	3	69	1.9	94	267	7.4	524	14.6
93-94 Mich	30	30	1020	261	469	.557	1	7	.143	102	151	.675	78	44	21	99	5	71	2.4	95	266	8.9	625	20.8
Years	100	97	3071	617	1209	.510	1	11	.091	291	423	.688	269	80	56	305	11	202	2.0	255	745	7.5	1526	15.3

NBA

Year Tm	G	GS	Min	Md	Att	Pct	Md	Att	Pct	Md	Att	Pct	TO	Stl	Blk	PF	DQ	Ast	Avg	Off	Tot	Avg	Pts	Avg
94-95 Was	65	52	2348	455	931	.489	0	7	.000	194	292	.664	166	52	15	236	2	165	2.5	184	545	8.4	1104	17.0
95-96 Was*	81	81	3294	733	1500	.489	4	13	.308	319	426	.749	303	67	39	269	3	360	4.4	188	660	8.1	1789	22.1
96-97 Was	82	82	3324	638	1313	.486	0	2	.000	294	389	.756	246	93	23	259	3	311	3.8	202	652	8.0	1570	19.1
97-98 Was	64	64	2559	463	991	.467	0	2	.000	258	358	.721	185	82	23	225	3	208	3.3	161	449	7.0	1184	18.5
98-99 Was	36	36	1430	286	604	.474	0	3	.000	110	146	.753	95	42	14	130	1	107	3.0	90	293	8.1	682	18.9
99-00 Was	82	82	2909	509	1108	.459	0	7	.000	202	275	.735	225	67	21	299	2	247	3.0	132	470	5.7	1220	14.9
Years	410	397	15864	3084	6447	.478	4	34	.118	1377	1886	.730	1220	403	135	1418	14	1398	3.4	957	3069	7.5	7549	18.4

NBA Postseason

Year Tm	G	GS	Min	Md	Att	Pct	Md	Att	Pct	Md	Att	Pct	TO	Stl	Blk	PF	DQ	Ast	Avg	Off	Tot	Avg	Pts	Avg
96-97 Was	3	3	129	20	44	.455	0	0	—	16	18	.889	3	2	2	9	0	5	1.7	10	18	6.0	56	18.7

Troy Hudson

(statistical profile on page 229)

Pos: G **College:** Southern Illinois **Drafted:** '97 FA—Uta **Ht:** 6'1" **Wt:** 170 **Born:** 3/13/76 **Age:** 24

College

Year Tm	G	GS	Min	Md	Att	Pct	Md	Att	Pct	Md	Att	Pct	TO	Stl	Blk	PF	DQ	Ast	Avg	Off	Tot	Avg	Pts	Avg
94-95 Misou	2	—	20	4	10	.400	1	6	.167	1	2	.500	1	1	0	1	—	4	2.0	—	2	1.0	10	5.0
95-96 SIU	25	20	812	179	459	.390	93	247	.377	82	103	.796	44	30	0	39	1	38	1.5	49	110	4.4	533	21.3
96-97 SIU	30	28	1075	209	534	.391	134	362	.370	79	96	.823	83	42	2	50	0	83	2.8	26	107	3.6	631	21.0
Years	57	—	1907	392	1003	.391	228	615	.371	162	201	.806	128	73	2	90	—	125	2.2	—	219	3.8	1174	20.6

NBA

Year Tm	G	GS	Min	Md	Att	Pct	Md	Att	Pct	Md	Att	Pct	TO	Stl	Blk	PF	DQ	Ast	Avg	Off	Tot	Avg	Pts	Avg
97-98 Uta	8	0	23	6	14	.429	0	3	.000	0	0	—	1	2	0	1	0	4	0.5	1	2	0.3	12	1.5
98-99 LAC	25	6	524	60	150	.400	15	47	.319	34	38	.895	38	11	2	28	1	92	3.7	15	55	2.2	169	6.8
99-00 LAC	62	38	1592	204	541	.377	60	193	.311	77	95	.811	108	43	0	65	0	242	3.9	28	148	2.4	545	8.8
Years	95	44	2139	270	705	.383	75	243	.309	111	133	.835	147	56	2	94	1	338	3.6	44	205	2.2	726	7.6

Larry Hughes

(statistical profile on page 230)

Pos: G **College:** Saint Louis **Drafted:** '98 1(8)—Phi   **Ht:** 6'5" **Wt:** 185 **Born:** 1/23/79 **Age:** 2?

College				Field Goals			3-Pt FGs			Free Throws			Misc			Fouls		Assists		Rebounds			Points	
Year Tm	G	GS	Min	Md	Att	Pct	Md	Att	Pct	Md	Att	Pct	TO	Stl	Blk	PF	DQ	Ast	Avg	Off	Tot	Avg	Pts	Avg
97-98 StL	32	32	1038	224	540	.415	42	145	.290	180	260	.692	122	69	13	76	2	77	2.4	62	162	5.1	670	20.9

NBA				Field Goals			3-Pt FGs			Free Throws			Misc			Fouls		Assists		Rebounds			Points	
Year Tm	G	GS	Min	Md	Att	Pct	Md	Att	Pct	Md	Att	Pct	TO	Stl	Blk	PF	DQ	Ast	Avg	Off	Tot	Avg	Pts	Avg
98-99 Phi	50	1	988	170	414	.411	8	52	.154	107	151	.709	68	44	14	97	0	77	1.5	83	189	3.8	455	9.?
99-00 2Tm	82	37	2324	459	1147	.400	29	125	.232	279	377	.740	195	115	28	191	2	205	2.5	113	349	4.3	1226	15.0
99-00 Phi	50	5	1018	192	461	.416	11	51	.216	106	142	.746	95	54	12	94	0	75	1.5	52	159	3.2	501	10.?
GS	32	32	1306	267	686	.389	18	74	.243	173	235	.736	100	61	16	97	2	130	4.1	61	190	5.9	725	22.?
2 Years	132	38	3312	629	1561	.403	37	177	.209	386	528	.731	263	159	42	288	2	282	2.1	196	538	4.1	1681	12.?

NBA Postseason				Field Goals			3-Pt FGs			Free Throws			Misc			Fouls		Assists		Rebounds			Points	
Year Tm	G	GS	Min	Md	Att	Pct	Md	Att	Pct	Md	Att	Pct	TO	Stl	Blk	PF	DQ	Ast	Avg	Off	Tot	Avg	Pts	Avg
98-99 Phi	8	2	198	31	77	.403	0	7	.000	20	24	.833	12	15	9	21	0	16	2.0	17	37	4.6	82	10.?

Rick Hughes

Pos: F **College:** Thomas More **Drafted:** '99 FA—Dal   **Ht:** 6'9" **Wt:** 235 **Born:** 8/22/73 **Age:** 2?

College				Field Goals			3-Pt FGs			Free Throws			Misc			Fouls		Assists		Rebounds			Points	
Year Tm	G	GS	Min	Md	Att	Pct	Md	Att	Pct	Md	Att	Pct	TO	Stl	Blk	PF	DQ	Ast	Avg	Off	Tot	Avg	Pts	Avg
92-93 ThMr	25	—	—	243	422	.576	0	0	—	114	150	.760	69	26	32	86	—	23	0.9	—	196	7.8	600	24.?
93-94 ThMr	26	—	—	286	477	.600	4	14	.286	111	160	.694	66	36	35	80	—	36	1.4	—	241	9.3	687	26.?
94-95 ThMr	24	—	—	257	407	.631	1	10	.100	143	193	.741	87	42	47	64	—	59	2.5	—	231	9.6	658	27.?
95-96 ThMr	26	—	—	253	394	.642	8	21	.381	146	192	.760	71	41	42	60	—	55	2.1	—	220	8.5	660	25.?
4 Years	101	—	—	1039	1700	.611	13	45	.289	514	695	.740	293	145	156	290	—	173	1.7	—	888	8.8	2605	25.?

NBA				Field Goals			3-Pt FGs			Free Throws			Misc			Fouls		Assists		Rebounds			Points	
Year Tm	G	GS	Min	Md	Att	Pct	Md	Att	Pct	Md	Att	Pct	TO	Stl	Blk	PF	DQ	Ast	Avg	Off	Tot	Avg	Pts	Avg
96-97										Played in IBA														
97-98										Played in Cyprus														
98-99										Played in Lebanon														
99-00 Dal	21	0	224	35	72	.486	0	1	.000	12	26	.462	14	3	1	30	0	9	0.4	24	49	2.3	82	3.?

Lindsey Hunter

(statistical profile on page 230)

Pos: G **College:** Jackson State **Drafted:** '93 1(10)—Det   **Ht:** 6'2" **Wt:** 195 **Born:** 12/3/70 **Age:** 3?

College				Field Goals			3-Pt FGs			Free Throws			Misc			Fouls		Assists		Rebounds			Points	
Year Tm	G	GS	Min	Md	Att	Pct	Md	Att	Pct	Md	Att	Pct	TO	Stl	Blk	PF	DQ	Ast	Avg	Off	Tot	Avg	Pts	Avg
88-89 Alc	27	—	624	70	178	.393	4	21	.190	23	32	.719	79	39	3	46	—	99	3.7	—	67	2.5	167	6.?
90-91 JkSt	30	—	1042	229	560	.409	86	235	.366	82	118	.695	91	69	9	67	—	105	3.5	—	100	3.3	626	20.?
91-92 JkSt	28	—	960	249	605	.412	95	257	.370	100	157	.637	110	60	5	57	—	121	4.3	—	96	3.4	693	24.?
92-93 JkSt	34	—	1152	320	777	.412	112	328	.341	155	201	.771	94	89	14	63	—	115	3.4	—	115	3.4	907	26.?
4 Years	119	—	3778	868	2120	.409	297	841	.353	360	508	.709	374	257	31	233	—	440	3.7	—	378	3.2	2393	20.?

NBA				Field Goals			3-Pt FGs			Free Throws			Misc			Fouls		Assists		Rebounds			Points	
Year Tm	G	GS	Min	Md	Att	Pct	Md	Att	Pct	Md	Att	Pct	TO	Stl	Blk	PF	DQ	Ast	Avg	Off	Tot	Avg	Pts	Avg
93-94 Det	82	26	2172	335	893	.375	69	207	.333	104	142	.732	184	121	10	174	1	390	4.8	47	189	2.3	843	10.?
94-95 Det	42	26	944	119	318	.374	36	108	.333	40	55	.727	79	51	7	94	1	159	3.8	24	75	1.8	314	7.?
95-96 Det	80	48	2138	239	628	.381	117	289	.405	84	120	.700	80	84	18	185	0	188	2.4	44	194	2.4	679	8.?
96-97 Det	82	76	3023	421	1042	.404	166	468	.355	158	203	.778	96	129	24	206	1	154	1.9	59	233	2.8	1166	14.?
97-98 Det	71	67	2505	316	826	.383	85	265	.321	145	196	.740	110	123	10	174	3	224	3.2	61	247	3.5	862	11.?
98-99 Det	49	49	1755	228	524	.435	59	153	.386	67	89	.753	92	86	8	126	2	193	3.9	26	168	3.4	582	11.?
99-00 Det	82	82	2919	379	892	.425	168	389	.432	117	154	.760	145	129	22	216	2	327	4.0	35	250	3.0	1043	12.?
7 Years	488	374	15456	2037	5123	.398	700	1879	.373	715	959	.746	786	723	99	1175	10	1635	3.4	296	1356	2.8	5489	11.?

NBA Postseason				Field Goals			3-Pt FGs			Free Throws			Misc			Fouls		Assists		Rebounds			Points	
Year Tm	G	GS	Min	Md	Att	Pct	Md	Att	Pct	Md	Att	Pct	TO	Stl	Blk	PF	DQ	Ast	Avg	Off	Tot	Avg	Pts	Avg
95-96 Det	2	0	36	2	8	.250	1	4	.250	1	2	.500	0	1	0	2	0	1	0.5	1	2	1.0	6	3.?
96-97 Det	5	5	201	29	66	.439	12	29	.414	5	7	.714	1	6	1	9	0	6	1.2	4	18	3.6	75	15.?
98-99 Det	5	5	180	14	53	.264	3	11	.273	5	5	1.000	7	7	0	11	0	12	2.4	5	15	3.0	36	7.?
99-00 Det	3	3	93	10	32	.313	1	9	.111	4	6	.667	5	5	1	4	0	5	1.7	0	7	2.3	25	8.?
4 Years	15	13	510	55	159	.346	17	53	.321	15	20	.750	13	19	2	26	0	24	1.6	10	42	2.8	142	9.?

Zydrunas Ilgauskas

Pos: C **College:** None **Drafted:** '96 1(20)—Cle   **Ht:** 7'3" **Wt:** 260 **Born:** 6/5/75 **Age:** 25

NBA

Year Tm	G	GS	Min	Md	Att	Pct	Md	Att	Pct	Md	Att	Pct	TO	Stl	Blk	PF	DQ	Ast	Avg	Off	Tot	Avg	Pts	Avg
				Field Goals			**3-Pt FGs**			**Free Throws**			**Misc**			**Fouls**		**Assists**		**Rebounds**			**Points**	
96-97 Cle				Did not play: injury — Right Foot																				
97-98 Cle	82	81	2379	454	876	.518	1	4	.250	230	302	.762	146	52	135	288	4	71	0.9	279	723	8.8	1139	13.9
98-99 Cle	5	5	171	29	57	.509	0	0	—	18	30	.600	9	4	7	24	1	4	0.8	17	44	8.8	76	15.2
99-00 Cle				Did not play: injury — Left Foot																				
2 Years	87	86	2550	483	933	.518	1	4	.250	248	332	.747	155	56	142	312	5	75	0.9	296	767	8.8	1215	14.0

NBA Postseason

Year Tm	G	GS	Min	Md	Att	Pct	Md	Att	Pct	Md	Att	Pct	TO	Stl	Blk	PF	DQ	Ast	Avg	Off	Tot	Avg	Pts	Avg
97-98 Cle	4	4	147	28	49	.571	0	0	—	13	25	.520	10	2	5	22	2	2	0.5	14	30	7.5	69	17.3

Allen Iverson

(statistical profile on page 231)

Pos: G **College:** Georgetown **Drafted:** '96 1(1)—Phi   **Ht:** 6'0" **Wt:** 165 **Born:** 6/7/75 **Age:** 25

College

Year Tm	G	GS	Min	Md	Att	Pct	Md	Att	Pct	Md	Att	Pct	TO	Stl	Blk	PF	DQ	Ast	Avg	Off	Tot	Avg	Pts	Avg
				Field Goals			**3-Pt FGs**			**Free Throws**			**Misc**			**Fouls**		**Assists**		**Rebounds**			**Points**	
94-95 GTwn	30	29	967	203	520	.390	35	151	.232	172	250	.688	133	89	5	78	4	134	4.5	45	99	3.3	613	20.4
95-96 GTwn	37	37	1213	312	650	.480	87	238	.366	215	317	.678	139	124	16	88	0	173	4.7	49	141	3.8	926	25.0
2 Years	67	66	2180	515	1170	.440	122	389	.314	387	567	.683	272	213	21	166	4	307	4.6	94	240	3.6	1539	23.0

NBA

Year Tm	G	GS	Min	Md	Att	Pct	Md	Att	Pct	Md	Att	Pct	TO	Stl	Blk	PF	DQ	Ast	Avg	Off	Tot	Avg	Pts	Avg
				Field Goals			**3-Pt FGs**			**Free Throws**			**Misc**			**Fouls**		**Assists**		**Rebounds**			**Points**	
96-97 Phi	76	74	3045	625	1504	.416	155	455	.341	382	544	.702	337	157	24	233	5	567	7.5	115	312	4.1	1787	23.5
97-98 Phi	80	80	3150	649	1407	.461	70	235	.298	390	535	.729	244	176	25	200	2	494	6.2	86	296	3.7	1758	22.0
98-99 Phi	48	48	1990	435	1056	.412	58	199	.291	356	474	.751	167	110	7	98	0	223	4.6	66	236	4.9	1284	26.8
99-00 Phi*	70	70	2853	729	1733	.421	89	261	.341	442	620	.713	230	144	5	162	1	328	4.7	71	267	3.8	1989	28.4
4 Years	274	272	11038	2438	5700	.428	372	1150	.323	1570	2173	.723	978	587	61	693	8	1612	5.9	338	1111	4.1	6818	24.9

NBA Postseason

Year Tm	G	GS	Min	Md	Att	Pct	Md	Att	Pct	Md	Att	Pct	TO	Stl	Blk	PF	DQ	Ast	Avg	Off	Tot	Avg	Pts	Avg
98-99 Phi	8	8	358	88	214	.411	15	53	.283	37	52	.712	24	20	2	19	0	39	4.9	14	33	4.1	228	28.5
99-00 Phi	10	10	444	91	237	.384	12	39	.308	68	92	.739	32	12	1	24	0	45	4.5	14	40	4.0	262	26.2
2 Years	18	18	802	179	451	.397	27	92	.293	105	144	.729	56	32	3	43	0	84	4.7	28	73	4.1	490	27.2

Bobby Jackson

Pos: G **College:** Minnesota **Drafted:** '97 1(23)—Sea   **Ht:** 6'1" **Wt:** 185 **Born:** 3/13/73 **Age:** 27

College

Year Tm	G	GS	Min	Md	Att	Pct	Md	Att	Pct	Md	Att	Pct	TO	Stl	Blk	PF	DQ	Ast	Avg	Off	Tot	Avg	Pts	Avg
				Field Goals			**3-Pt FGs**			**Free Throws**			**Misc**			**Fouls**		**Assists**		**Rebounds**			**Points**	
95-96 Minn	25	15	683	115	283	.406	28	95	.295	74	94	.787	56	34	7	63	1	68	2.7	44	119	4.8	332	13.3
96-97 Minn	35	35	1101	191	433	.441	31	97	.320	121	154	.786	81	74	8	88	1	139	4.0	51	213	6.1	534	15.3
2 Years	60	50	1784	306	716	.427	59	192	.307	195	248	.786	137	108	15	151	2	207	3.5	95	332	5.5	866	14.4

NBA

Year Tm	G	GS	Min	Md	Att	Pct	Md	Att	Pct	Md	Att	Pct	TO	Stl	Blk	PF	DQ	Ast	Avg	Off	Tot	Avg	Pts	Avg
				Field Goals			**3-Pt FGs**			**Free Throws**			**Misc**			**Fouls**		**Assists**		**Rebounds**			**Points**	
97-98 Den	68	53	2042	310	791	.392	21	81	.259	149	183	.814	184	105	11	160	0	317	4.7	78	302	4.4	790	11.6
98-99 Min	50	12	941	141	348	.405	10	27	.370	61	79	.772	75	39	3	75	1	167	3.3	43	135	2.7	353	7.1
99-00 Min	73	10	1034	140	346	.405	13	46	.283	76	98	.776	58	48	7	114	0	172	2.4	50	153	2.1	369	5.1
3 Years	191	75	4017	591	1485	.398	44	154	.286	286	360	.794	317	192	21	349	1	656	3.4	171	590	3.1	1512	7.9

NBA Postseason

Year Tm	G	GS	Min	Md	Att	Pct	Md	Att	Pct	Md	Att	Pct	TO	Stl	Blk	PF	DQ	Ast	Avg	Off	Tot	Avg	Pts	Avg
98-99 Min	4	0	27	2	10	.200	0	3	.000	0	0	—	1	0	0	3	0	2	0.5	1	4	1.0	4	1.0
99-00 Min	3	0	30	4	8	.500	1	3	.333	6	6	1.000	2	2	1	4	0	4	1.3	0	5	1.7	15	5.0
2 Years	7	0	57	6	18	.333	1	6	.167	6	6	1.000	3	2	1	7	0	6	0.9	1	9	1.3	19	2.7

Jaren Jackson

(statistical profile on page 231)

Pos: G **College:** Georgetown **Drafted:** '89 FA—NJ   **Ht:** 6'6" **Wt:** 225 **Born:** 10/27/67 **Age:** 33

College

Year Tm	G	GS	Min	Md	Att	Pct	Md	Att	Pct	Md	Att	Pct	TO	Stl	Blk	PF	DQ	Ast	Avg	Off	Tot	Avg	Pts	Avg
				Field Goals			**3-Pt FGs**			**Free Throws**			**Misc**			**Fouls**		**Assists**		**Rebounds**			**Points**	
85-86 GTwn	32	0	283	42	97	.433	—	—	—	18	22	.818	24	19	1	31	1	19	0.6		49	1.5	102	3.2
86-87 GTwn	34	0	387	68	148	.459	20	48	.417	37	52	.712	28	18	2	39	0	26	0.8	28	69	2.0	193	5.7
87-88 GTwn	30	6	558	100	243	.412	20	73	.274	42	56	.750	56	34	11	60	0	46	1.5	43	88	2.9	262	8.7
88-89 GTwn	34	34	923	161	357	.451	36	87	.414	59	90	.656	57	57	11	66	2	62	1.8	71	176	5.2	417	12.3
4 Years	130	40	2151	371	845	.439	76	208	.365	156	220	.709	165	128	25	196	3	153	1.2	142	382	2.9	974	7.5

NBA				Field Goals			3-Pt FGs			Free Throws			Misc			Fouls		Assists		Rebounds			Points	
Year Tm	G	GS	Min	Md	Att	Pct	Md	Att	Pct	Md	Att	Pct	TO	Stl	Blk	PF	DQ	Ast	Avg	Off	Tot	Avg	Pts	Avg
89-90 NJ	28	0	160	25	69	.362	0	3	.000	17	21	.810	18	13	1	16	0	13	0.5	16	24	0.9	67	2.4
90-91									Played in CBA, Played in WBL															
91-92 GS	5	0	54	11	23	.478	0	0	—	4	6	.667	4	2	0	7	1	3	0.6	5	10	2.0	26	5.2
92-93 LAC	34	0	350	53	128	.414	2	5	.400	23	27	.852	17	19	5	45	1	35	1.0	19	39	1.1	131	3.9
93-94 Por	29	0	187	34	87	.391	0	6	.000	12	14	.857	14	4	2	20	0	27	0.9	6	17	0.6	80	2.8
94-95 Phi	21	1	257	25	68	.368	4	15	.267	16	24	.667	17	9	5	33	0	19	0.9	18	42	2.0	70	3.3
95-96 Hou	4	0	33	4	8	.000	0	5	.000	8	10	.800	0	1	0	5	0	0	0.0	0	3	0.8	8	2.0
96-97 Was	75	0	1133	134	329	.407	53	158	.335	53	69	.768	60	45	16	131	0	65	0.9	31	132	1.8	374	5.0
97-98 SA	82	45	2226	258	654	.394	112	297	.377	94	118	.797	104	60	8	222	3	156	1.9	55	210	2.6	722	8.8
98-99 SA	47	13	861	108	284	.380	53	147	.361	32	39	.821	37	41	9	63	0	49	1.0	21	99	2.1	301	6.4
99-00 SA	81	12	1691	186	488	.381	108	306	.353	33	51	.647	66	54	7	157	1	118	1.5	34	181	2.2	513	6.3
10 Years	406	71	6952	834	2138	.390	332	942	.352	292	379	.770	337	248	53	699	6	485	1.2	205	757	1.9	2292	5.6

NBA Postseason

Year Tm	G	GS	Min	Md	Att	Pct	Md	Att	Pct	Md	Att	Pct	TO	Stl	Blk	PF	DQ	Ast	Avg	Off	Tot	Avg	Pts	Avg
92-93 LAC	4	0	28	5	13	.385	0	1	.000	0	0	—	3	2	0	6	0	2	0.5	4	5	1.3	10	2.5
93-94 Por	1	0	1	0	0	—	0	0	—	0	0	—	0	0	0	0	0	0	0.0	0	0	0.0	0	0.0
96-97 Was	3	0	11	0	0	—	0	0	—	0	2	.000	2	0	0	7	0	1	0.3	1	2	0.7	0	0.0
97-98 SA	9	8	319	30	88	.341	18	59	.305	14	19	.737	12	5	1	31	1	14	1.6	4	39	4.3	92	10.2
98-99 SA	17	0	345	50	131	.382	31	86	.360	9	13	.692	20	13	0	33	0	18	1.1	6	41	2.4	140	8.2
99-00 SA	2	0	19	0	3	.000	0	1	.000	2	4	.500	0	1	0	1	0	2	1.0	0	1	0.5	2	1.0
6 Years	36	8	723	85	235	.362	49	147	.333	25	38	.658	37	21	1	78	1	37	1.0	15	88	2.4	244	6.8

Jermaine Jackson

Pos: G **College:** Detroit Mercy **Drafted:** '99 FA—Det   **Ht:** 6'5" **Wt:** 204 **Born:** 6/7/76 **Age:** 24

College				Field Goals			3-Pt FGs			Free Throws			Misc			Fouls		Assists		Rebounds			Points	
Year Tm	G	GS	Min	Md	Att	Pct	Md	Att	Pct	Md	Att	Pct	TO	Stl	Blk	PF	DQ	Ast	Avg	Off	Tot	Avg	Pts	Avg
95-96 Det	27	—	955	83	200	.415	21	58	.362	53	82	.646	65	28	10	47	—	100	3.7	—	106	3.9	240	8.9
96-97 Det	29	29	993	90	218	.413	39	97	.402	76	108	.704	57	31	6	54	0	120	4.1	14	106	3.7	295	10.2
97-98 Det	31	31	993	124	275	.451	16	50	.320	110	156	.705	60	46	8	58	0	149	4.8	29	143	4.6	374	12.1
98-99 Det	31	31	1081	131	305	.430	24	75	.320	146	194	.753	91	37	7	54	1	140	4.5	45	198	6.4	432	13.9
4 Years	118	—	4022	428	998	.429	100	280	.357	385	540	.713	273	142	31	213	—	509	4.3	—	553	4.7	1341	11.4

NBA				Field Goals			3-Pt FGs			Free Throws			Misc			Fouls		Assists		Rebounds			Points	
Year Tm	G	GS	Min	Md	Att	Pct	Md	Att	Pct	Md	Att	Pct	TO	Stl	Blk	PF	DQ	Ast	Avg	Off	Tot	Avg	Pts	Avg
99-00 Det	7	0	73	1	11	.091	0	1	.000	5	8	.625	7	3	0	7	0	4	0.6	1	11	1.6	7	1.0

Jim Jackson

(statistical profile on page 232)

Pos: G **College:** Ohio State **Drafted:** '92 1(4)—Dal   **Ht:** 6'6" **Wt:** 220 **Born:** 10/14/70 **Age:** 30

College				Field Goals			3-Pt FGs			Free Throws			Misc			Fouls		Assists		Rebounds			Points	
Year Tm	G	GS	Min	Md	Att	Pct	Md	Att	Pct	Md	Att	Pct	TO	Stl	Blk	PF	DQ	Ast	Avg	Off	Tot	Avg	Pts	Avg
89-90 OhSt	30	30	1035	194	389	.499	21	59	.356	73	93	.785	96	39	14	110	3	110	3.7	83	166	5.5	482	16.1
90-91 OhSt	31	31	997	228	441	.517	17	51	.333	112	149	.752	100	55	24	69	0	133	4.3	63	169	5.5	585	18.9
91-92 OhSt	32	32	1133	264	535	.493	44	108	.407	146	180	.811	108	53	8	69	1	129	4.0	68	217	6.8	718	22.4
3 Years	93	93	3165	686	1365	.503	82	218	.376	331	422	.784	304	147	46	219	4	372	4.0	214	552	5.9	1785	19.2

NBA				Field Goals			3-Pt FGs			Free Throws			Misc			Fouls		Assists		Rebounds			Points	
Year Tm	G	GS	Min	Md	Att	Pct	Md	Att	Pct	Md	Att	Pct	TO	Stl	Blk	PF	DQ	Ast	Avg	Off	Tot	Avg	Pts	Avg
92-93 Dal	28	28	938	184	466	.395	21	73	.288	68	92	.739	115	40	11	80	0	131	4.7	42	122	4.4	457	16.3
93-94 Dal	82	82	3066	637	1432	.445	17	60	.283	285	347	.821	334	87	25	161	0	374	4.6	169	388	4.7	1576	19.2
94-95 Dal	51	51	1982	484	1026	.472	35	110	.318	306	380	.805	160	28	12	92	0	191	3.7	120	260	5.1	1309	25.7
95-96 Dal	82	82	2820	526	1308	.435	121	333	.363	345	418	.825	191	47	22	165	0	235	2.9	173	410	5.0	1604	19.6
96-97 2Tm	77	77	2831	444	1029	.431	86	247	.348	252	310	.813	208	86	32	194	0	316	4.1	132	411	5.3	1226	15.9
97-98 2Tm	79	78	3046	476	1107	.430	61	191	.319	229	282	.812	263	79	8	186	0	381	4.8	130	400	5.1	1242	15.7
98-99 Por	49	9	1175	152	370	.411	25	90	.278	85	101	.842	82	43	6	80	0	128	2.6	36	159	3.2	414	8.4
99-00 Atl	79	76	2767	507	1235	.411	117	303	.386	186	212	.877	185	57	10	167	0	230	2.9	101	394	5.0	1317	16.7
96-97 Dal	46	46	1676	260	588	.442	46	139	.331	148	188	.787	107	57	15	113	0	156	3.4	81	227	4.9	714	15.5
NJ	31	31	1155	184	441	.417	40	108	.370	104	122	.852	101	29	17	81	0	160	5.2	51	184	5.9	512	16.5
97-98 Phi	48	47	1788	246	535	.460	39	112	.348	126	154	.818	145	41	6	112	0	223	4.6	69	227	4.7	657	13.7
GS	31	31	1258	230	572	.402	22	79	.278	103	128	.805	118	38	2	74	0	158	5.1	61	173	5.6	585	18.9
8 Years	527	483	18625	3453	7973	.433	483	1407	.343	1756	2142	.820	1538	467	126	1125	0	1986	3.8	903	2544	4.8	9145	17.4

NBA Postseason

Year Tm	G	GS	Min	Md	Att	Pct	Md	Att	Pct	Md	Att	Pct	TO	Stl	Blk	PF	DQ	Ast	Avg	Off	Tot	Avg	Pts	Avg
98-99 Por	13	0	265	26	72	.361	5	18	.278	38	42	.905	18	7	1	26	0	19	1.5	8	30	2.3	95	7.3

Mark Jackson

Pos: G College: St. John's (NY) Drafted: '87 1(18)—NY Ht: 6'3" Wt: 205 Born: 4/1/65 Age: 35 (statistical profile on page 232)

College

Year Tm	G	GS	Min	Md	Att	Pct	Md	Att	Pct	Md	Att	Pct	TO	Stl	Blk	PF	DQ	Ast	Avg	Off	Tot	Avg	Pts	Avg
83-84 StJn	30	13	855	61	106	.575	—	—	—	53	77	.688	80	18	8	56	0	108	3.6	—	59	2.0	175	5.8
84-85 StJn	35	2	601	57	101	.564	—	—	—	66	91	.725	54	25	4	44	0	109	3.1	—	44	1.3	180	5.1
85-86 StJn	36	36	1340	151	316	.478	—	—	—	105	142	.739	84	68	8	60	0	328	9.1	—	125	3.5	407	11.3
86-87 StJn	30	30	1184	196	389	.504	49	117	.419	125	155	.806	81	61	6	59	0	193	6.4	29	110	3.7	566	18.9
4 Years	131	81	3980	465	912	.510	49	117	.419	349	465	.751	299	172	26	219	0	738	5.6	29	338	2.6	1328	10.1

NBA

Year Tm	G	GS	Min	Md	Att	Pct	Md	Att	Pct	Md	Att	Pct	TO	Stl	Blk	PF	DQ	Ast	Avg	Off	Tot	Avg	Pts	Avg
87-88 NY	82	80	3249	438	1013	.432	32	126	.254	206	266	.774	258	205	6	244	2	868	10.6	120	396	4.8	1114	13.6
88-89 NY*	72	72	2477	479	1025	.467	81	240	.338	180	258	.698	226	139	7	163	1	619	8.6	106	341	4.7	1219	16.9
89-90 NY	82	69	2428	327	749	.437	35	131	.267	120	165	.727	211	109	4	121	0	604	7.4	106	318	3.9	809	9.9
90-91 NY	72	21	1595	250	508	.492	13	51	.255	117	160	.731	135	60	9	81	0	452	6.3	62	197	2.7	630	8.8
91-92 NY	81	81	2461	367	747	.491	11	43	.256	171	222	.770	211	112	13	153	0	694	8.6	95	305	3.8	916	11.3
92-93 LAC	82	81	3117	459	945	.486	22	82	.268	241	300	.803	220	136	12	158	0	724	8.8	129	388	4.7	1181	14.4
93-94 LAC	79	79	2711	331	732	.452	36	127	.283	167	211	.791	232	120	6	115	0	678	8.6	107	348	4.4	865	10.9
94-95 Ind	82	67	2402	239	566	.422	27	87	.310	119	153	.778	210	105	16	148	0	616	7.5	73	306	3.7	624	7.6
95-96 Ind	81	81	2643	296	626	.473	64	149	.430	150	191	.785	201	100	5	153	0	635	7.8	66	307	3.8	806	10.0
96-97 2Tm	82	82	3054	289	679	.426	66	178	.371	168	213	.789	274	97	12	161	0	935	11.4	91	395	4.8	812	9.9
97-98 Ind	82	82	2413	249	598	.416	43	137	.314	137	180	.761	174	84	2	132	0	713	8.7	67	322	3.9	678	8.3
98-99 Ind	49	49	1382	138	329	.419	32	103	.311	65	79	.823	99	42	3	58	0	386	7.9	33	184	3.8	373	7.6
99-00 Ind	81	81	2190	246	570	.432	89	221	.403	79	98	.806	174	76	10	111	0	650	8.0	63	296	3.7	660	8.1
96-97 Den	52	52	2001	192	452	.425	48	121	.397	109	136	.801	172	51	9	104	0	641	12.3	71	271	5.2	541	10.4
Ind	30	30	1053	97	227	.427	18	57	.316	59	77	.766	102	46	3	57	0	294	9.8	20	124	4.1	271	9.0
13 Years	1007	925	32122	4108	9087	.452	551	1675	.329	1920	2496	.769	2625	1385	105	1798	3	8574	8.5	1118	4103	4.1	10687	10.6

NBA Postseason

Year Tm	G	GS	Min	Md	Att	Pct	Md	Att	Pct	Md	Att	Pct	TO	Stl	Blk	PF	DQ	Ast	Avg	Off	Tot	Avg	Pts	Avg
87-88 NY	4	4	171	22	60	.367	5	12	.417	8	11	.727	14	10	0	13	0	39	9.8	6	19	4.8	57	14.3
88-89 NY	9	9	336	51	100	.510	11	28	.393	19	28	.679	28	10	3	9	0	91	10.1	7	31	3.4	132	14.7
89-90 NY	9	0	81	13	31	.419	0	2	.000	8	11	.727	7	2	0	5	0	21	2.3	1	5	0.6	34	3.8
90-91 NY	3	0	36	1	3	.333	0	0	—	0	0	—	5	1	1	1	0	8	2.7	0	0	0.0	2	0.7
91-92 NY	12	12	368	37	92	.402	4	21	.190	22	27	.815	30	10	0	26	0	86	7.2	12	27	2.3	100	8.3
92-93 LAC	5	5	188	28	64	.438	1	2	.500	19	22	.864	13	8	1	8	0	38	7.6	8	29	5.8	76	15.2
94-95 Ind	17	17	553	59	130	.454	16	40	.400	34	46	.739	41	15	0	34	0	121	7.1	27	89	5.2	168	9.9
95-96 Ind	5	5	186	18	51	.353	4	18	.222	13	17	.765	13	6	0	9	0	30	6.0	3	25	5.0	53	10.6
97-98 Ind	16	16	494	53	127	.417	14	37	.378	27	34	.794	47	23	0	28	0	133	8.3	18	73	4.6	147	9.2
98-99 Ind	13	13	451	51	103	.495	14	34	.412	30	42	.714	35	14	1	32	0	112	8.6	14	59	4.5	146	11.2
99-00 Ind	23	23	634	69	176	.392	21	67	.313	28	31	.903	43	19	2	42	0	178	7.7	12	86	3.7	187	8.1
11 Years	116	104	3498	402	937	.429	90	261	.345	208	269	.773	276	118	8	207	0	857	7.4	108	443	3.8	1102	9.5

Randell Jackson

Pos: F College: Florida State Drafted: '98 FA—Was Ht: 6'11" Wt: 215 Born: 1/16/76 Age: 25

College

Year Tm	G	GS	Min	Md	Att	Pct	Md	Att	Pct	Md	Att	Pct	TO	Stl	Blk	PF	DQ	Ast	Avg	Off	Tot	Avg	Pts	Avg
95-96 FlaSt	24	15	630	90	180	.500	4	14	.286	43	68	.632	35	14	30	50	0	13	0.5	53	126	5.3	227	9.5
96-97 FlaSt	31	26	879	135	303	.446	7	18	.389	65	109	.596	52	23	46	69	2	18	0.6	80	194	6.3	342	11.0
97-98 FlaSt	31	28	868	153	314	.487	3	19	.158	85	118	.720	80	26	37	79	5	34	1.1	61	172	5.5	394	12.7
3 Years	86	69	2377	378	797	.474	14	51	.275	193	295	.654	167	63	113	198	7	65	0.8	194	492	5.7	963	11.2

NBA

Year Tm	G	GS	Min	Md	Att	Pct	Md	Att	Pct	Md	Att	Pct	TO	Stl	Blk	PF	DQ	Ast	Avg	Off	Tot	Avg	Pts	Avg
98-99 Was	27	8	271	46	108	.426	1	7	.143	21	32	.656	26	3	11	29	0	8	0.3	30	54	2.0	114	4.2
99-00 Dal	1	0	1	0	0	—	0	0	—	0	0	—	0	0	0	0	0	0	0.0	0	0	0.0	0	0.0
2 Years	28	8	272	46	108	.426	1	7	.143	21	32	.656	26	3	11	29	0	8	0.3	30	54	1.9	114	4.1

Sam Jacobson

Pos: G-F College: Minnesota Drafted: '98 1(26)—LAL Ht: 6'6" Wt: 215 Born: 7/22/75 Age: 25

College

Year Tm	G	GS	Min	Md	Att	Pct	Md	Att	Pct	Md	Att	Pct	TO	Stl	Blk	PF	DQ	Ast	Avg	Off	Tot	Avg	Pts	Avg
94-95 Minn	31	13	589	92	198	.465	17	53	.321	38	57	.667	44	20	3	86	6	37	1.2	72	149	4.8	239	7.7
95-96 Minn	32	32	853	143	347	.412	47	118	.398	75	95	.789	84	37	8	82	1	64	2.0	60	154	4.8	408	12.8
96-97 Minn	35	34	847	188	411	.457	61	155	.394	43	67	.642	77	32	6	104	6	58	1.7	55	158	4.5	480	13.7
97-98 Minn	32	32	995	215	505	.426	48	148	.324	104	143	.727	58	42	6	83	2	57	1.8	54	165	5.2	582	18.2
4 Years	130	111	3284	638	1461	.437	173	474	.365	260	362	.718	263	131	23	355	15	216	1.7	241	626	4.8	1709	13.1

NBA			Field Goals			3-Pt FGs			Free Throws			Misc			Fouls		Assists		Rebounds			Points	
Year Tm	G	GS	Min	Md	Att	Pct	Md	Att	Pct	Md	Att	Pct	TO	Stl	Blk	PF	DQ	Ast	Avg	Off	Tot	Avg	Pts	Avg
98-99 LAL	2	0	12	3	5	.600	0	1	.000	2	2	1.000	1	0	0	2	0	0	0.0	0	3	1.5	8	4.0
99-00 2Tm	52	5	681	108	212	.509	9	24	.375	30	41	.732	33	30	3	113	3	32	0.6	25	71	1.4	255	4.9
99-00 LAL	3	0	18	5	9	.556	0	0	—	0	2	.000	2	1	0	1	0	2	0.7	0	1	0.3	10	3.3
GS	49	5	663	103	203	.507	9	24	.375	30	39	.769	31	29	3	112	3	30	0.6	25	70	1.4	245	5.0
2 Years	54	5	693	111	217	.512	9	25	.360	32	43	.744	34	30	3	115	3	32	0.6	25	74	1.4	263	4.9

Tim James

Pos: G **College:** Miami (FL) **Drafted:** '99 1(25)—Mia **Ht:** 6'7" **Wt:** 212 **Born:** 12/25/76 **Age:** 24

College			Field Goals			3-Pt FGs			Free Throws			Misc			Fouls		Assists		Rebounds			Points	
Year Tm	G	GS	Min	Md	Att	Pct	Md	Att	Pct	Md	Att	Pct	TO	Stl	Blk	PF	DQ	Ast	Avg	Off	Tot	Avg	Pts	Avg
95-96 Mia-Fl	28	0	625	117	221	.529	2	6	.333	46	85	.541	48	22	50	50	0	12	0.4	71	151	5.4	282	10.1
96-97 Mia-Fl	29	26	900	165	380	.434	2	8	.250	73	120	.608	80	24	64	58	2	35	1.2	88	196	6.8	405	14.0
97-98 Mia-Fl	28	28	890	184	379	.485	4	17	.235	97	144	.674	88	41	45	64	1	12	0.4	90	263	9.4	469	16.8
98-99 Mia-Fl	30	30	956	215	451	.477	12	41	.293	115	165	.697	97	40	65	52	0	24	0.8	83	246	8.2	557	18.6
4 Years	115	84	3371	681	1431	.476	20	72	.278	331	514	.644	313	127	224	224	3	83	0.7	332	856	7.4	1713	14.9

NBA			Field Goals			3-Pt FGs			Free Throws			Misc			Fouls		Assists		Rebounds			Points	
Year Tm	G	GS	Min	Md	Att	Pct	Md	Att	Pct	Md	Att	Pct	TO	Stl	Blk	PF	DQ	Ast	Avg	Off	Tot	Avg	Pts	Avg
99-00 Mia	4	0	23	5	14	.357	0	0	—	1	3	.333	2	0	3	1	0	2	0.5	3	4	1.0	11	2.8

Antawn Jamison

(statistical profile on page 233)

Pos: F **College:** North Carolina **Drafted:** '98 1(4)—Tor **Ht:** 6'9" **Wt:** 223 **Born:** 6/12/76 **Age:** 24

College			Field Goals			3-Pt FGs			Free Throws			Misc			Fouls		Assists		Rebounds			Points	
Year Tm	G	GS	Min	Md	Att	Pct	Md	Att	Pct	Md	Att	Pct	TO	Stl	Blk	PF	DQ	Ast	Avg	Off	Tot	Avg	Pts	Avg
95-96 UNC	32	29	1052	201	322	.624	0	1	.000	82	156	.526	59	25	33	69	2	33	1.0	119	309	9.7	484	15.1
96-97 UNC	35	35	1199	270	496	.544	2	11	.182	126	203	.621	63	40	22	93	1	30	0.9	131	329	9.4	668	19.1
97-98 UNC	37	32	1227	316	546	.579	6	15	.400	184	276	.667	61	28	30	94	3	30	0.8	126	389	10.5	822	22.2
3 Years	104	96	3478	787	1364	.577	8	27	.296	392	635	.617	183	93	85	256	6	93	0.9	376	1027	9.9	1974	19.0

NBA			Field Goals			3-Pt FGs			Free Throws			Misc			Fouls		Assists		Rebounds			Points	
Year Tm	G	GS	Min	Md	Att	Pct	Md	Att	Pct	Md	Att	Pct	TO	Stl	Blk	PF	DQ	Ast	Avg	Off	Tot	Avg	Pts	Avg
98-99 GS	47	24	1058	178	394	.452	3	10	.300	90	153	.588	68	38	16	102	1	34	0.7	131	301	6.4	449	9.6
99-00 GS	43	41	1556	356	756	.471	2	7	.286	127	208	.611	113	30	15	115	0	90	2.1	172	359	8.3	841	19.6
2 Years	90	65	2614	534	1150	.464	5	17	.294	217	361	.601	181	68	31	217	1	124	1.4	303	660	7.3	1290	14.3

Harold Jamison

Pos: F **College:** Clemson **Drafted:** '99 FA—Mia **Ht:** 6'8" **Wt:** 260 **Born:** 11/20/76 **Age:** 24

College			Field Goals			3-Pt FGs			Free Throws			Misc			Fouls		Assists		Rebounds			Points	
Year Tm	G	GS	Min	Md	Att	Pct	Md	Att	Pct	Md	Att	Pct	TO	Stl	Blk	PF	DQ	Ast	Avg	Off	Tot	Avg	Pts	Avg
95-96 Clem	29	6	697	69	133	.519	0	0	—	83	135	.615	45	23	17	80	3	29	1.0	80	172	5.9	221	7.6
96-97 Clem	33	22	857	92	154	.597	0	0	—	68	120	.567	46	27	24	83	4	31	0.9	90	185	5.6	252	7.6
97-98 Clem	32	12	794	119	201	.592	0	0	—	74	154	.481	46	32	10	84	3	31	1.0	126	232	7.3	312	9.8
98-99 Clem	35	35	1017	174	258	.674	0	0	—	98	188	.521	76	19	15	88	1	34	1.0	123	346	9.9	446	12.7
4 Years	129	75	3365	454	746	.609	0	0	—	323	597	.541	213	101	66	335	11	125	1.0	419	935	7.2	1231	9.5

NBA			Field Goals			3-Pt FGs			Free Throws			Misc			Fouls		Assists		Rebounds			Points	
Year Tm	G	GS	Min	Md	Att	Pct	Md	Att	Pct	Md	Att	Pct	TO	Stl	Blk	PF	DQ	Ast	Avg	Off	Tot	Avg	Pts	Avg
99-00 Mia	12	0	74	7	20	.350	0	0	—	4	18	.222	4	2	1	17	0	4	0.3	16	21	1.8	18	1.5

Anthony Johnson

Pos: G **College:** Charleston **Drafted:** '97 2(40)—Sac **Ht:** 6'3" **Wt:** 190 **Born:** 10/2/74 **Age:** 26

College			Field Goals			3-Pt FGs			Free Throws			Misc			Fouls		Assists		Rebounds			Points	
Year Tm	G	GS	Min	Md	Att	Pct	Md	Att	Pct	Md	Att	Pct	TO	Stl	Blk	PF	DQ	Ast	Avg	Off	Tot	Avg	Pts	Avg
92-93 Char	27	—	273	23	58	.397	1	3	.333	37	52	.712	19	15	2	29	—	30	1.1	—	44	1.6	84	3.1
94-95 Char	29	—	492	34	87	.391	10	25	.400	22	34	.647	24	25	2	48	—	68	2.3	—	53	1.8	100	3.4
95-96 Char	29	29	946	119	259	.459	26	64	.406	65	97	.670	72	46	5	71	1	193	6.7	21	92	3.2	329	11.3
96-97 Char	32	32	1138	158	313	.505	30	74	.405	100	126	.794	90	50	10	75	2	229	7.2	21	113	3.5	446	13.9
4 Years	117	—	2849	334	717	.466	67	166	.404	224	309	.725	205	136	19	223	—	520	4.4	—	302	2.6	959	8.2

NBA			Field Goals			3-Pt FGs			Free Throws			Misc			Fouls		Assists		Rebounds			Points	
Year Tm	G	GS	Min	Md	Att	Pct	Md	Att	Pct	Md	Att	Pct	TO	Stl	Blk	PF	DQ	Ast	Avg	Off	Tot	Avg	Pts	Avg
97-98 Sac	77	62	2266	226	609	.371	42	128	.328	80	110	.727	120	64	6	188	1	329	4.3	51	171	2.2	574	7.5

NBA				Field Goals			3-Pt FGs			Free Throws			Misc			Fouls		Assists		Rebounds			Points	
Year Tm	G	GS	Min	Md	Att	Pct	Md	Att	Pct	Md	Att	Pct	TO	Stl	Blk	PF	DQ	Ast	Avg	Off	Tot	Avg	Pts	Avg
98-99 Atl	49	2	885	91	225	.404	5	19	.263	57	82	.695	65	35	7	67	0	107	2.2	16	75	1.5	244	5.0
99-00 2Tm	56	6	637	62	164	.378	2	11	.182	28	39	.718	32	33	4	58	0	72	1.3	21	51	0.9	154	2.8
99-00 Atl	38	2	423	36	103	.350	1	6	.167	19	24	.792	24	23	2	41	0	59	1.6	15	39	1.0	92	2.4
Orl	18	4	214	26	61	.426	1	5	.200	9	15	.600	8	10	2	17	0	13	0.7	6	12	0.7	62	3.4
3 Years	182	70	3788	379	998	.380	49	158	.310	165	231	.714	217	132	17	313	1	508	2.8	88	297	1.6	972	5.3

NBA Postseason																								
Year Tm	G	GS	Min	Md	Att	Pct	Md	Att	Pct	Md	Att	Pct	TO	Stl	Blk	PF	DQ	Ast	Avg	Off	Tot	Avg	Pts	Avg
98-99 Atl	9	0	111	8	29	.276	1	2	.500	7	10	.700	5	1	1	9	0	10	1.1	3	9	1.0	24	2.7

Avery Johnson

(statistical profile on page 233)

Pos: G **College:** Southern **Drafted:** '88 FA—Sea **Ht:** 5'11" **Wt:** 180 **Born:** 3/25/65 **Age:** 35

College				Field Goals			3-Pt FGs			Free Throws			Misc			Fouls		Assists		Rebounds			Points	
Year Tm	G	GS	Min	Md	Att	Pct	Md	Att	Pct	Md	Att	Pct	TO	Stl	Blk	PF	DQ	Ast	Avg	Off	Tot	Avg	Pts	Avg
84-85 Cam	33	—	—	54	106	.509	—	—	—	34	55	.618	—	—	—	—	—	111	3.4	—	31	0.9	142	4.3
86-87 Sou	31	—	1111	86	196	.439	7	24	.292	40	65	.615	—	—	—	—	—	333	10.7	—	73	2.4	219	7.1
87-88 Sou	30	—	1145	138	257	.537	22	47	.468	44	64	.688	—	—	—	—	—	399	13.3	—	84	2.8	342	11.4
3 Years	94	—		278	559	.497	29	71	.408	118	184	.641	—	—	—	—	—	843	9.0	—	188	2.0	703	7.5

NBA				Field Goals			3-Pt FGs			Free Throws			Misc			Fouls		Assists		Rebounds			Points	
Year Tm	G	GS	Min	Md	Att	Pct	Md	Att	Pct	Md	Att	Pct	TO	Stl	Blk	PF	DQ	Ast	Avg	Off	Tot	Avg	Pts	Avg
88-89 Sea	43	0	291	29	83	.349	1	9	.111	9	16	.563	18	21	3	34	0	73	1.7	11	24	0.6	68	1.6
89-90 Sea	53	10	575	55	142	.387	1	4	.250	29	40	.725	48	26	1	55	0	162	3.1	21	43	0.8	140	2.6
90-91 2Tm	68	14	959	130	277	.469	1	9	.111	59	87	.678	74	47	4	62	0	230	3.4	22	77	1.1	320	4.7
91-92 2Tm	69	15	1235	158	330	.479	4	15	.267	66	101	.653	110	61	9	89	1	266	3.9	13	80	1.2	386	5.6
92-93 SA	75	49	2030	256	510	.502	0	8	.000	144	182	.791	145	85	16	141	0	561	7.5	20	146	1.9	656	8.7
93-94 GS	82	70	2332	356	724	.492	0	12	.000	178	253	.704	172	113	8	160	0	433	5.3	41	176	2.1	890	10.9
94-95 SA	82	82	3011	448	863	.519	3	22	.136	202	295	.685	207	114	13	154	0	670	8.2	49	208	2.5	1101	13.4
95-96 SA	82	82	3084	438	887	.494	6	31	.194	189	262	.721	195	119	21	179	1	789	9.6	37	206	2.5	1071	13.1
96-97 SA	76	76	2472	327	685	.477	6	26	.231	140	203	.690	146	96	15	158	1	513	6.8	32	147	1.9	800	10.5
97-98 SA	75	73	2674	321	671	.478	2	13	.154	122	168	.726	165	84	18	140	0	591	7.9	30	150	2.0	766	10.2
98-99 SA	50	50	1672	218	461	.473	1	12	.083	50	88	.568	112	51	11	101	0	369	7.4	22	118	2.4	487	9.7
99-00 SA	82	82	2571	402	850	.473	1	9	.111	114	155	.735	140	76	18	150	0	491	6.0	33	158	1.9	919	11.2
90-91 Den	21	4	217	29	68	.426	0	4	.000	21	32	.656	27	14	2	22	0	77	3.7	9	21	1.0	79	3.8
SA	47	10	742	101	209	.483	1	5	.200	38	55	.691	47	33	2	40	0	153	3.3	13	56	1.2	241	5.1
91-92 SA	20	14	463	55	108	.509	1	5	.200	24	32	.750	45	21	3	43	1	100	5.0	5	35	1.8	135	6.8
Hou	49	1	772	103	222	.464	3	10	.300	42	69	.609	65	40	6	46	0	166	3.4	8	45	0.9	251	5.1
12 Years	837	603	22906	3138	6483	.484	26	170	.153	1302	1850	.704	1532	893	137	1423	3	5148	6.2	331	1533	1.8	7604	9.1

NBA Postseason																								
Year Tm	G	GS	Min	Md	Att	Pct	Md	Att	Pct	Md	Att	Pct	TO	Stl	Blk	PF	DQ	Ast	Avg	Off	Tot	Avg	Pts	Avg
88-89 Sea	6	0	31	5	12	.417	0	4	.000	1	2	.500	0	4	0	1	0	5	0.8	2	4	0.7	11	1.8
90-91 SA	3	0	19	0	5	.000	0	1	.000	2	2	1.000	0	1	0	3	0	4	1.3	0	0	0.0	2	0.7
92-93 SA	10	10	314	36	70	.514	0	1	.000	10	14	.714	23	10	1	27	0	81	8.1	8	31	3.1	82	8.2
93-94 GS	3	0	41	9	17	.529	0	1	.000	0	0	—	3	4	1	2	0	10	3.3	0	3	1.0	18	6.0
94-95 SA	15	15	575	91	176	.517	0	1	.000	36	58	.621	30	20	6	29	0	125	8.3	9	32	2.1	218	14.5
95-96 SA	10	10	407	52	121	.430	0	2	.000	19	27	.704	24	20	1	21	0	94	9.4	6	36	3.6	123	12.3
97-98 SA	9	9	342	61	101	.604	0	2	.000	34	51	.667	21	9	0	27	0	55	6.1	3	13	1.4	156	17.3
98-99 SA	17	17	653	91	187	.487	1	3	.333	32	47	.681	50	20	1	30	0	126	7.4	9	42	2.5	215	12.6
99-00 SA	4	4	144	19	42	.452	0	0	—	10	14	.714	10	4	0	10	0	21	5.3	2	9	2.3	48	12.0
9 Years	77	65	2526	364	731	.498	1	15	.067	144	215	.670	161	92	10	150	0	521	6.8	39	170	2.2	873	11.3

DeMarco Johnson

Pos: F **College:** UNC-Charlotte **Drafted:** '98 2(38)—NY **Ht:** 6'9" **Wt:** 245 **Born:** 10/6/75 **Age:** 25

College				Field Goals			3-Pt FGs			Free Throws			Misc			Fouls		Assists		Rebounds			Points	
Year Tm	G	GS	Min	Md	Att	Pct	Md	Att	Pct	Md	Att	Pct	TO	Stl	Blk	PF	DQ	Ast	Avg	Off	Tot	Avg	Pts	Avg
94-95 NC-Ch	28	0	495	97	193	.503	0	2	.000	48	67	.716	24	242	10	51	0	20	0.7	56	129	4.6	242	8.6
95-96 NC-Ch	29	29	963	206	413	.499	5	24	.208	109	164	.665	58	31	17	94	2	32	1.1	98	254	8.8	526	18.1
96-97 NC-Ch	31	30	1038	196	417	.470	11	36	.306	181	229	.790	75	39	18	86	1	44	1.4	97	263	8.5	584	18.8
97-98 NC-Ch	31	31	1103	238	475	.501	18	50	.360	159	204	.779	70	42	17	85	1	44	1.4	99	280	9.0	653	21.1
4 Years	119	90	3599	737	1498	.492	34	112	.304	497	664	.748	227	354	62	316	4	140	1.2	350	926	7.8	2005	16.8

NBA				Field Goals			3-Pt FGs			Free Throws			Misc			Fouls		Assists		Rebounds			Points	
Year Tm	G	GS	Min	Md	Att	Pct	Md	Att	Pct	Md	Att	Pct	TO	Stl	Blk	PF	DQ	Ast	Avg	Off	Tot	Avg	Pts	Avg
98-99										Played in Italy														
99-00 NY	5	0	37	3	9	.333	0	0	—	0	0	—	3	1	0	5	0	0	0.0	3	7	1.4	6	1.2

Ervin Johnson

(statistical profile on page 234)

Pos: C **College:** New Orleans **Drafted:** '93 1(23)—Sea   **Ht:** 6'11" **Wt:** 245 **Born:** 12/21/67 **Age:** 33

Year Tm	G	GS	Min	Md	Att	Pct	Md	Att	Pct	Md	Att	Pct	TO	Stl	Blk	PF	DQ	Ast	Avg	Off	Tot	Avg	Pts	Avg
	College			Field Goals			3-Pt FGs			Free Throws			Misc			Fouls		Assists		Rebounds			Points	
89-90 UNO	32	26	757	84	145	.579	0	0	—	32	57	.561	40	29	62	91	3	29	0.9	61	218	6.8	200	6.3
90-91 UNO	30	29	899	162	283	.572	0	0	—	58	108	.537	60	22	74	91	5	34	1.1	139	367	12.2	382	12.7
91-92 UNO	32	32	1073	185	317	.584	0	0	—	122	171	.713	79	31	81	111	5	56	1.8	144	356	11.1	492	15.4
92-93 UNO	29	29	965	208	336	.619	0	0	—	118	175	.674	74	27	77	87	1	16	0.6	136	346	11.9	534	18.4
4 Years	123	116	3694	639	1081	.591	0	0	—	330	511	.646	253	109	294	380	14	135	1.1	480	1287	10.5	1608	13.1

Year Tm	G	GS	Min	Md	Att	Pct	Md	Att	Pct	Md	Att	Pct	TO	Stl	Blk	PF	DQ	Ast	Avg	Off	Tot	Avg	Pts	Avg
	NBA			Field Goals			3-Pt FGs			Free Throws			Misc			Fouls		Assists		Rebounds			Points	
93-94 Sea	45	3	280	44	106	.415	0	0	—	29	46	.630	24	10	22	45	0	7	0.2	48	118	2.6	117	2.6
94-95 Sea	64	30	907	85	192	.443	0	1	.000	29	46	.630	54	17	67	163	1	16	0.3	101	289	4.5	199	3.1
95-96 Sea	81	60	1519	180	352	.511	1	3	.333	85	127	.669	98	40	129	245	3	48	0.6	129	433	5.3	446	5.5
96-97 Den	82	82	2599	243	467	.520	0	2	.000	96	156	.615	118	65	227	288	5	71	0.9	231	913	11.1	582	7.1
97-98 Mil	81	81	2261	253	471	.537	0	0	—	143	238	.601	117	79	158	321	7	59	0.7	242	685	8.5	649	8.0
98-99 Mil	50	7	1027	96	189	.508	0	0	—	64	105	.610	47	29	57	151	1	19	0.4	120	320	6.4	256	5.1
99-00 Mil	80	74	2129	144	279	.516	0	1	.000	95	157	.605	80	81	127	298	6	44	0.6	233	648	8.1	383	4.8
7 Years	483	337	10722	1045	2056	.508	1	7	.143	538	321	.618	1511	23	787	1511	23	264	0.5	1104	3406	7.1	2632	5.4

Year Tm	G	GS	Min	Md	Att	Pct	Md	Att	Pct	Md	Att	Pct	TO	Stl	Blk	PF	DQ	Ast	Avg	Off	Tot	Avg	Pts	Avg
	NBA Postseason																							
93-94 Sea	2	0	8	0	1	.000	0	0	—	0	0	—	1	0	0	1	0	0	0.0	0	4	2.0	0	0.0
94-95 Sea	4	2	54	4	14	.286	0	0	—	6	6	1.000	1	1	4	16	0	0	0.0	8	21	5.3	14	3.5
95-96 Sea	18	18	253	23	62	.371	0	0	—	9	11	.818	14	6	15	45	0	7	0.4	28	70	3.9	55	3.1
98-99 Mil	3	2	92	6	13	.462	0	0	—	1	2	.500	0	2	5	9	0	1	0.3	8	18	6.0	13	4.3
99-00 Mil	5	5	155	10	20	.500	0	0	—	11	18	.611	3	6	6	19	0	2	0.4	14	49	9.8	31	6.2
5 Years	32	27	562	43	110	.391	0	0	—	27	37	.730	19	15	30	90	0	10	0.3	58	162	5.1	113	3.5

Kevin Johnson

Pos: G **College:** California **Drafted:** '87 1(7)—Cle   **Ht:** 6'1" **Wt:** 190 **Born:** 3/4/66 **Age:** 34

Year Tm	G	GS	Min	Md	Att	Pct	Md	Att	Pct	Md	Att	Pct	TO	Stl	Blk	PF	DQ	Ast	Avg	Off	Tot	Avg	Pts	Avg
	College			Field Goals			3-Pt FGs			Free Throws			Misc			Fouls		Assists		Rebounds			Points	
83-84 Cal	28	—	773	98	192	.510	—	—	—	75	104	.721	—	23	12	62	—	65	2.3	—	83	3.0	271	9.7
84-85 Cal	27	25	902	127	282	.450	—	—	—	94	142	.662	—	49	—	64	—	111	4.1	—	104	3.9	348	12.9
85-86 Cal	29	29	1024	164	335	.490	—	—	—	123	151	.815	83	32	10	73	—	175	6.0	—	104	3.9	451	15.6
86-87 Cal	34	33	1115	212	450	.471	48	124	.387	113	138	.819	96	51	10	64	1	170	5.0	—	132	3.9	585	17.2
4 Years	118	—	3814	601	1259	.477	48	124	.387	405	535	.757	—	155	—	263	—	521	4.4	—	423	3.6	1655	14.0

Year Tm	G	GS	Min	Md	Att	Pct	Md	Att	Pct	Md	Att	Pct	TO	Stl	Blk	PF	DQ	Ast	Avg	Off	Tot	Avg	Pts	Avg
	NBA			Field Goals			3-Pt FGs			Free Throws			Misc			Fouls		Assists		Rebounds			Points	
87-88 2Tm	80	28	1917	275	596	.461	5	24	.208	177	211	.839	146	103	24	155	1	437	5.5	36	191	2.4	732	9.2
88-89 Pho	81	81	3179	570	1128	.505	2	22	.091	508	576	.882	322	135	24	226	1	991	12.2	46	340	4.2	1650	20.4
89-90 Pho	74	74	2782	578	1159	.499	8	41	.195	501	598	.838	269	95	14	143	0	846	11.4	42	270	3.6	1665	22.5
90-91 Pho*	77	76	2772	591	1145	.516	9	44	.205	519	616	.843	269	163	11	174	0	781	10.1	54	271	3.5	1710	22.2
91-92 Pho	78	78	2899	539	1125	.479	10	46	.217	448	555	.807	272	116	23	180	0	836	10.7	61	292	3.7	1536	19.7
92-93 Pho	49	47	1643	282	565	.499	1	8	.125	226	276	.819	151	85	19	100	0	384	7.8	30	104	2.1	791	16.1
93-94 Pho*	67	67	2449	477	980	.487	6	27	.222	380	464	.819	235	125	10	127	1	637	9.5	55	167	2.5	1340	20.0
94-95 Pho	47	35	1352	246	523	.470	4	26	.154	234	289	.810	105	47	18	88	0	360	7.7	32	115	2.4	730	15.5
95-96 Pho	56	55	2007	342	674	.507	21	57	.368	342	398	.859	170	82	13	144	0	517	9.2	42	221	3.9	1047	18.7
96-97 Pho	70	70	2658	441	890	.496	89	202	.441	439	515	.852	217	102	12	141	0	653	9.3	54	253	3.6	1410	20.1
97-98 Pho	50	12	1290	155	347	.447	4	26	.154	162	186	.871	101	27	8	57	0	245	4.9	35	164	3.3	476	9.5
98-99										Did not play basketball														
99-00 Pho	6	0	113	16	28	.571	1	1	1.000	7	7	1.000	7	2	0	6	0	24	4.0	0	16	2.7	40	6.7
87-88 Cle	52	3	1043	143	311	.460	2	9	.222	92	112	.821	82	60	17	96	1	193	3.7	10	72	1.4	380	7.3
Pho	28	25	874	132	285	.463	3	15	.200	85	99	.859	64	43	7	59	0	244	8.7	26	119	4.3	352	12.6
12 Years	735	623	25061	4512	9160	.493	160	524	.305	3943	4691	.841	2258	1082	176	1541	3	6711	9.1	487	2404	3.3	13127	17.9

Year Tm	G	GS	Min	Md	Att	Pct	Md	Att	Pct	Md	Att	Pct	TO	Stl	Blk	PF	DQ	Ast	Avg	Off	Tot	Avg	Pts	Avg
	NBA Postseason																							
88-89 Pho	12	12	494	90	182	.495	3	10	.300	102	110	.927	55	19	5	28	0	147	12.3	12	51	4.3	285	23.8
89-90 Pho	16	16	582	123	257	.479	2	11	.182	92	112	.821	62	25	0	28	0	170	10.6	9	53	3.3	340	21.3
90-91 Pho	4	4	146	16	53	.302	1	7	.143	18	30	.600	12	2	1	9	0	39	9.8	2	13	3.3	51	12.8
91-92 Pho	8	8	335	62	128	.484	3	6	.500	62	72	.861	25	12	2	24	1	93	11.6	8	33	4.1	189	23.6
92-93 Pho	23	23	914	143	298	.480	0	3	.000	124	156	.795	84	35	13	57	1	182	7.9	10	62	2.7	410	17.8
93-94 Pho	10	10	427	97	212	.458	3	10	.300	69	81	.852	34	10	1	23	0	96	9.6	10	35	3.5	266	26.6
94-95 Pho	10	10	371	86	150	.573	5	10	.500	71	84	.845	34	9	4	25	0	93	9.3	7	41	4.1	248	24.8
95-96 Pho	4	4	151	27	57	.474	1	4	.250	14	17	.824	11	2	2	8	0	43	10.8	2	17	4.3	69	17.3

Year Tm	G	GS	Min	Md	Att	Pct	Md	Att	Pct	Md	Att	Pct	TO	Stl	Blk	PF	DQ	Ast	Avg	Off	Tot	Avg	Pts	Avg
96-97 Pho	5	5	208	26	88	.295	3	22	.136	29	33	.879	18	13	0	15	1	30	6.0	8	22	4.4	84	16.8
97-98 Pho	4	1	122	23	42	.548	1	4	.250	8	12	.667	6	2	1	6	0	19	4.8	2	9	2.3	55	13.8
99-00 Pho	9	0	129	12	37	.324	0	3	.000	5	6	.833	13	3	1	10	0	23	2.6	0	13	1.4	29	3.2
11 Years	105	93	3879	705	1504	.469	22	90	.244	594	713	.833	354	132	30	233	3	935	8.9	70	349	3.3	2026	19.3

Larry Johnson

(statistical profile on page 234)

Pos: F **College:** UNLV **Drafted:** '91 1(1)—Cha   **Ht:** 6'7" **Wt:** 235 **Born:** 3/14/69 **Age:** 31

College				Field Goals			3-Pt FGs			Free Throws			Misc			Fouls		Assists		Rebounds			Points	
Year Tm	G	GS	Min	Md	Att	Pct	Md	Att	Pct	Md	Att	Pct	TO	Stl	Blk	PF	DQ	Ast	Avg	Off	Tot	Avg	Pts	Avg
89-90 UNLV	40	40	1259	304	487	.624	13	38	.342	201	262	.767	110	74	56	128	—	84	2.1	—	457	11.4	822	20.6
90-91 UNLV	35	35	1113	308	465	.662	17	48	.354	162	198	.818	78	74	36	79	—	104	3.0	—	380	10.9	795	22.7
2 Years	75	75	2372	612	952	.643	30	86	.349	363	460	.789	188	148	92	207	—	188	2.5	—	837	11.2	1617	21.6

NBA				Field Goals			3-Pt FGs			Free Throws			Misc			Fouls		Assists		Rebounds			Points	
Year Tm	G	GS	Min	Md	Att	Pct	Md	Att	Pct	Md	Att	Pct	TO	Stl	Blk	PF	DQ	Ast	Avg	Off	Tot	Avg	Pts	Avg
91-92 Cha	82	77	3047	616	1258	.490	5	22	.227	339	409	.829	160	81	51	225	3	292	3.6	323	899	11.0	1576	19.2
92-93 Cha*	82	82	3323	728	1385	.526	18	71	.254	336	438	.767	227	53	27	187	0	353	4.3	281	864	10.5	1810	22.1
93-94 Cha	51	51	1757	346	672	.515	5	21	.238	137	197	.695	116	29	14	131	0	184	3.6	143	448	8.8	834	16.4
94-95 Cha*	81	81	3234	585	1219	.480	81	210	.386	274	354	.774	207	78	28	174	2	369	4.6	190	585	7.2	1525	18.8
95-96 Cha	81	81	3274	583	1225	.476	67	183	.366	427	564	.757	182	55	43	173	0	355	4.4	249	683	8.4	1660	20.5
96-97 NY	76	76	2613	376	735	.512	34	105	.324	190	274	.693	136	64	36	249	2	174	2.3	165	393	5.2	976	12.8
97-98 NY	70	70	2412	429	884	.485	15	63	.238	214	283	.756	127	40	13	193	2	150	2.1	175	401	5.7	1087	15.5
98-99 NY	49	48	1639	210	458	.459	33	92	.359	134	164	.817	89	34	10	147	1	119	2.4	91	284	5.8	587	12.0
99-00 NY	70	68	2281	282	652	.433	58	174	.333	128	167	.766	94	42	7	205	1	175	2.5	87	380	5.4	750	10.7
9 Years	642	634	23580	4155	8488	.490	316	941	.336	2179	2850	.765	1338	476	229	1684	12	2171	3.4	1704	4937	7.7	10805	16.8

NBA Postseason																								
Year Tm	G	GS	Min	Md	Att	Pct	Md	Att	Pct	Md	Att	Pct	TO	Stl	Blk	PF	DQ	Ast	Avg	Off	Tot	Avg	Pts	Avg
92-93 Cha	9	9	348	68	122	.557	1	4	.250	41	52	.788	19	5	2	27	0	30	3.3	19	62	6.9	178	19.8
94-95 Cha	4	4	172	31	65	.477	1	9	.111	20	25	.800	6	4	2	7	0	11	2.8	10	23	5.8	83	20.8
96-97 NY	9	9	295	43	77	.558	6	17	.353	32	38	.842	15	7	1	27	0	23	2.6	11	36	4.0	124	13.8
97-98 NY	8	8	310	52	107	.486	2	10	.200	37	50	.740	25	10	3	30	0	13	1.6	25	53	6.6	143	17.9
98-99 NY	20	20	683	87	204	.426	24	82	.293	31	46	.674	33	21	1	64	2	31	1.6	22	97	4.9	229	11.5
99-00 NY	16	16	589	70	152	.461	13	33	.394	27	34	.794	23	8	2	47	1	26	1.6	15	80	5.0	180	11.3
6 Years	66	66	2397	351	727	.483	47	155	.303	188	245	.767	121	55	11	202	3	134	2.0	102	351	5.3	937	14.2

Charles Jones

Pos: G **College:** Long Island **Drafted:** '98 FA—Chi   **Ht:** 6'3" **Wt:** 185 **Born:** 7/15/75 **Age:** 25

College				Field Goals			3-Pt FGs			Free Throws			Misc			Fouls		Assists		Rebounds			Points	
Year Tm	G	GS	Min	Md	Att	Pct	Md	Att	Pct	Md	Att	Pct	TO	Stl	Blk	PF	DQ	Ast	Avg	Off	Tot	Avg	Pts	Avg
93-94 Rut	27	—	851	141	394	.358	67	180	.372	27	40	.675	50	44	11	38	—	75	2.8	—	77	2.9	376	13.9
94-95 Rut	21	—	627	107	263	.407	37	115	.322	29	46	.630	39	24	8	44	—	68	3.2	—	97	4.6	280	13.3
96-97 LIU	30	29	1118	338	750	.451	109	303	.360	118	186	.634	72	70	7	78	3	139	4.6	75	180	6.0	903	30.1
97-98 LIU	30	30	1106	326	720	.453	116	337	.344	101	158	.639	88	87	8	56	0	221	7.4	62	156	5.2	869	29.0
4 Years	108	—	3702	912	2127	.429	329	935	.352	275	430	.640	249	225	34	216		503	4.7	—	510	4.7	2428	22.5

NBA				Field Goals			3-Pt FGs			Free Throws			Misc			Fouls		Assists		Rebounds			Points	
Year Tm	G	GS	Min	Md	Att	Pct	Md	Att	Pct	Md	Att	Pct	TO	Stl	Blk	PF	DQ	Ast	Avg	Off	Tot	Avg	Pts	Avg
98-99 Chi	29	5	476	39	123	.317	19	61	.311	11	22	.500	29	18	5	30	0	41	1.4	9	42	1.4	108	3.7
99-00 LAC	56	0	662	66	201	.328	39	118	.331	17	23	.739	28	30	5	46	0	94	1.7	17	62	1.1	188	3.4
2 Years	85	5	1138	105	324	.324	58	179	.324	28	45	.622	57	48	10	76	0	135	1.6	26	104	1.2	296	3.5

Damon Jones

Pos: G **College:** Houston **Drafted:** '98 FA—NJ   **Ht:** 6'3" **Wt:** 185 **Born:** 8/25/76 **Age:** 24

College				Field Goals			3-Pt FGs			Free Throws			Misc			Fouls		Assists		Rebounds			Points	
Year Tm	G	GS	Min	Md	Att	Pct	Md	Att	Pct	Md	Att	Pct	TO	Stl	Blk	PF	DQ	Ast	Avg	Off	Tot	Avg	Pts	Avg
94-95 Hou	27	—	781	91	262	.347	55	168	.327	40	64	.625	59	25	0	40	—	77	2.9	—	92	3.4	277	10.3
95-96 Hou	27	27	857	115	266	.432	57	167	.341	34	51	.667	85	39	1	37	—	105	3.9	24	111	4.1	321	11.9
96-97 Hou	27	26	968	159	341	.466	70	186	.376	55	78	.705	117	38	3	49	1	132	4.9	14	120	4.4	443	16.4
3 Years	81	—	2606	365	869	.420	182	521	.349	129	193	.668	261	102	4	126		314	3.9	—	323	4.0	1041	12.9

NBA				Field Goals			3-Pt FGs			Free Throws			Misc			Fouls		Assists		Rebounds			Points	
Year Tm	G	GS	Min	Md	Att	Pct	Md	Att	Pct	Md	Att	Pct	TO	Stl	Blk	PF	DQ	Ast	Avg	Off	Tot	Avg	Pts	Avg
97-98								Played in IBA																	

85

NBA				Field Goals			3-Pt FGs			Free Throws			Misc			Fouls		Assists		Rebounds			Points	
Year Tm	G	GS	Min	Md	Att	Pct	Md	Att	Pct	Md	Att	Pct	TO	Stl	Blk	PF	DQ	Ast	Avg	Off	Tot	Avg	Pts	Avg
98-99 2Tm	24	0	344	43	119	.361	25	62	.403	14	17	.824	17	13	0	23	0	42	1.8	6	44	1.8	125	5.2
99-00 2Tm	55	1	612	80	208	.385	41	114	.360	32	48	.667	40	18	1	34	0	96	1.7	12	55	1.0	233	4.2
98-99 NJ	11	0	131	14	44	.318	10	29	.345	11	13	.846	5	7	0	7	0	13	1.2	2	13	1.2	49	4.5
Bos	13	0	213	29	75	.387	15	33	.455	3	4	.750	12	6	0	16	0	29	2.2	4	31	2.4	76	5.8
99-00 GS	13	1	196	25	54	.463	11	23	.478	7	9	.778	15	6	0	13	0	39	3.0	0	16	1.2	68	5.2
Dal	42	0	416	55	154	.357	30	91	.330	25	39	.641	25	12	1	21	0	57	1.4	12	39	0.9	165	3.9
2 Years	79	1	956	123	327	.376	66	176	.375	46	65	.708	57	31	1	57	0	138	1.7	18	99	1.3	358	4.5

Eddie Jones

(statistical profile on page 235)

Pos: G-F **College:** Temple **Drafted:** '94 1(10)—LAL **Ht:** 6'6" **Wt:** 200 **Born:** 10/20/71 **Age:** 29

College				Field Goals			3-Pt FGs			Free Throws			Misc			Fouls		Assists		Rebounds			Points	
Year Tm	G	GS	Min	Md	Att	Pct	Md	Att	Pct	Md	Att	Pct	TO	Stl	Blk	PF	DQ	Ast	Avg	Off	Tot	Avg	Pts	Avg
91-92 Tem	29	—	764	122	279	.437	47	134	.351	41	75	.547	29	57	19	90	—	30	1.0	—	122	4.2	332	11.4
92-93 Tem	32	—	1169	212	463	.458	49	141	.348	70	116	.603	55	70	42	75	—	56	1.8	—	225	7.0	543	17.0
93-94 Tem	31	—	1184	231	491	.470	45	128	.352	88	133	.662	53	70	46	69	—	58	1.9	—	210	6.8	595	19.2
3 Years	92	—	3117	565	1233	.458	141	403	.350	199	324	.614	137	197	107	234	—	144	1.6	—	557	6.1	1470	16.0

NBA				Field Goals			3-Pt FGs			Free Throws			Misc			Fouls		Assists		Rebounds			Points	
Year Tm	G	GS	Min	Md	Att	Pct	Md	Att	Pct	Md	Att	Pct	TO	Stl	Blk	PF	DQ	Ast	Avg	Off	Tot	Avg	Pts	Avg
94-95 LAL	64	58	1981	342	744	.460	91	246	.370	122	169	.722	75	131	41	175	1	128	2.0	79	249	3.9	897	14.0
95-96 LAL	70	66	2184	337	685	.492	83	227	.366	136	184	.739	99	129	45	162	0	246	3.5	45	233	3.3	893	12.8
96-97 LAL*	80	80	2998	473	1081	.438	152	389	.391	276	337	.819	169	189	49	226	3	270	3.4	90	326	4.1	1374	17.2
97-98 LAL*	80	80	2910	486	1005	.484	143	368	.389	234	306	.765	146	160	55	164	1	246	3.1	85	302	3.8	1349	16.9
98-99 2Tm	50	50	1881	260	595	.437	48	142	.338	212	271	.782	93	125	58	128	1	186	3.7	50	194	3.9	780	15.6
99-00 Cha*	72	72	2807	478	1119	.427	128	341	.375	362	419	.864	160	192	49	176	1	305	4.2	81	343	4.8	1446	20.1
98-99 LAL	20	20	724	96	227	.423	20	64	.313	59	80	.738	21	35	24	42	0	61	3.1	20	76	3.8	271	13.6
Cha	30	30	1157	164	368	.446	28	78	.359	153	191	.801	72	90	34	86	1	125	4.2	30	118	3.9	509	17.0
6 Years	416	406	14761	2376	5229	.454	645	1713	.377	1342	1686	.796	742	926	297	1031	6	1381	3.3	430	1647	4.0	6739	16.2

NBA Postseason																								
Year Tm	G	GS	Min	Md	Att	Pct	Md	Att	Pct	Md	Att	Pct	TO	Stl	Blk	PF	DQ	Ast	Avg	Off	Tot	Avg	Pts	Avg
94-95 LAL	10	0	286	30	80	.375	12	27	.444	15	21	.714	17	8	9	27	0	20	2.0	7	32	3.2	87	8.7
95-96 LAL	4	4	155	27	49	.551	10	19	.526	5	8	.625	4	8	1	16	0	6	1.5	7	21	5.3	69	17.3
96-97 LAL	9	9	283	33	72	.458	9	24	.375	26	35	.743	13	9	4	24	0	29	3.2	8	31	3.4	101	11.2
97-98 LAL	13	13	476	69	148	.466	20	48	.417	63	76	.829	17	26	21	37	0	32	2.5	12	51	3.9	221	17.0
99-00 Cha	4	4	171	22	58	.379	9	26	.346	15	16	.938	5	10	3	12	0	19	4.8	4	20	5.0	68	17.0
5 Years	40	30	1371	181	407	.445	60	144	.417	124	156	.795	56	61	38	116	0	106	2.7	38	155	3.9	546	13.7

Jumaine Jones

Pos: G **College:** Georgia **Drafted:** '99 1(27)—Atl **Ht:** 6'7" **Wt:** 210 **Born:** 2/10/79 **Age:** 21

College				Field Goals			3-Pt FGs			Free Throws			Misc			Fouls		Assists		Rebounds			Points	
Year Tm	G	GS	Min	Md	Att	Pct	Md	Att	Pct	Md	Att	Pct	TO	Stl	Blk	PF	DQ	Ast	Avg	Off	Tot	Avg	Pts	Avg
97-98 UGa	35	34	1031	188	415	.453	44	124	.355	95	121	.785	66	30	19	78	1	30	0.9	137	299	8.5	515	14.7
98-99 UGa	30	29	1032	197	443	.445	48	138	.348	122	168	.726	76	32	21	73	1	35	1.2	100	284	9.5	564	18.8
2 Years	65	63	2063	385	858	.449	92	262	.351	217	289	.751	142	62	40	151	2	65	1.0	237	583	9.0	1079	16.6

NBA				Field Goals			3-Pt FGs			Free Throws			Misc			Fouls		Assists		Rebounds			Points	
Year Tm	G	GS	Min	Md	Att	Pct	Md	Att	Pct	Md	Att	Pct	TO	Stl	Blk	PF	DQ	Ast	Avg	Off	Tot	Avg	Pts	Avg
99-00 Phi	33	0	138	22	58	.379	2	4	.500	11	18	.611	14	6	5	10	0	5	0.2	16	38	1.2	57	1.7

NBA Postseason																								
Year Tm	G	GS	Min	Md	Att	Pct	Md	Att	Pct	Md	Att	Pct	TO	Stl	Blk	PF	DQ	Ast	Avg	Off	Tot	Avg	Pts	Avg
99-00 Phi	4	0	8	1	3	.333	0	2	.000	0	0	—	0	0	0	0	0	0	0.0	0	0	0.0	2	0.5

Popeye Jones

Pos: F **College:** Murray State **Drafted:** '92 2(41)—Hou **Ht:** 6'8" **Wt:** 250 **Born:** 6/17/70 **Age:** 30

College				Field Goals			3-Pt FGs			Free Throws			Misc			Fouls		Assists		Rebounds			Points	
Year Tm	G	GS	Min	Md	Att	Pct	Md	Att	Pct	Md	Att	Pct	TO	Stl	Blk	PF	DQ	Ast	Avg	Off	Tot	Avg	Pts	Avg
88-89 Mur	30	—	518	65	133	.489	0	0	—	43	57	.754	30	19	5	65	—	21	0.7	—	138	4.6	173	5.8
89-90 Mur	30	—	1038	217	434	.500	15	34	.441	137	181	.757	71	57	17	81	—	59	2.0	—	336	11.2	586	19.5
90-91 Mur	33	—	1052	268	544	.493	7	32	.219	123	173	.711	84	36	32	80	—	69	2.1	—	469	14.2	666	20.2
91-92 Mur	30	—	994	232	475	.488	7	18	.389	161	207	.778	101	43	27	98	—	72	2.4	—	431	14.4	632	21.1
4 Years	123	—	3602	782	1586	.493	29	84	.345	464	618	.751	286	155	81	324	—	221	1.8	—	1374	11.2	2057	16.7

NBA Year Tm	G	GS	Min	Field Goals Md	Att	Pct	3-Pt FGs Md	Att	Pct	Free Throws Md	Att	Pct	Misc TO	Stl	Blk	Fouls PF	DQ	Assists Ast	Avg	Rebounds Off	Tot	Avg	Points Pts	Avg
92-93								Played in Italy																	
93-94 Dal	81	47	1773	195	407	.479	0	1	.000	78	107	.729	94	61	31	246	2	99	1.2	299	605	7.5	468	5.8
94-95 Dal	80	80	2385	372	839	.443	1	12	.083	80	124	.645	124	35	27	267	5	163	2.0	**329**	844	10.6	825	10.3
95-96 Dal	68	68	2322	327	733	.446	14	39	.359	102	133	.767	109	54	27	262	8	132	1.9	260	737	10.8	770	11.3
96-97 Tor	79	61	2421	258	537	.480	1	13	.077	99	121	.818	116	58	39	269	3	84	1.1	270	680	8.6	616	7.8
97-98 Tor	14	4	352	52	127	.409	2	3	.667	14	19	.737	16	10	3	39	0	18	1.3	50	102	7.3	120	8.6
98-99 Bos	18	2	206	20	51	.392	0	1	.000	14	17	.824	7	5	0	31	0	15	0.8	28	52	2.9	54	3.0
99-00 Den	40	1	330	44	104	.423	2	3	.667	14	19	.737	13	3	6	50	1	19	0.5	41	103	2.6	104	2.6
7 Years	380	263	9789	1268	2798	.453	20	72	.278	401	540	.743	479	226	133	1164	19	530	1.4	1277	3123	8.2	2957	7.8

Reggie Jordan

Pos: G **College:** New Mexico State **Drafted:** '93 FA—LAL **Ht:** 6'4" **Wt:** 195 **Born:** 1/26/68 **Age:** 33

College Year Tm	G	GS	Min	Field Goals Md	Att	Pct	3-Pt FGs Md	Att	Pct	Free Throws Md	Att	Pct	Misc TO	Stl	Blk	Fouls PF	DQ	Assists Ast	Avg	Rebounds Off	Tot	Avg	Points Pts	Avg
89-90 NMSt	31	—	802	137	307	.446	2	20	.100	52	82	.634	80	18	11	104	—	60	1.9	—	186	6.0	328	10.6
90-91 NMSt	29	—	844	162	384	.422	18	55	.327	82	136	.603	70	59	22	86	—	70	2.4	—	226	7.8	424	14.6
2 Years	60	—	1646	299	691	.433	20	75	.267	134	218	.615	150	113	44	190	—	130	2.2	—	412	6.9	752	12.5

NBA Year Tm	G	GS	Min	Field Goals Md	Att	Pct	3-Pt FGs Md	Att	Pct	Free Throws Md	Att	Pct	Misc TO	Stl	Blk	Fouls PF	DQ	Assists Ast	Avg	Rebounds Off	Tot	Avg	Points Pts	Avg
91-92								Played in CBA																
92-93								Played in CBA																
93-94 LAL	23	0	259	44	103	.427	2	4	.500	35	51	.686	14	14	5	26	0	26	1.1	46	67	2.9	125	5.4
94-95								Played in CBA, Played in Greece																
95-96 Atl	24	0	247	36	71	.507	0	0	—	22	38	.579	19	12	7	30	0	29	1.2	23	52	2.2	94	3.9
96-97 2Tm	19	0	130	16	26	.615	0	0	—	8	17	.471	8	7	3	15	0	12	0.6	11	27	1.4	40	2.1
97-98 Min	57	1	487	54	113	.478	0	1	.000	41	72	.569	30	35	9	63	0	50	0.9	57	97	1.7	149	2.6
98-99 Min	27	1	296	15	54	.278	0	0	—	21	38	.553	14	12	5	38	0	41	1.5	27	59	2.2	51	1.9
99-00 Was	36	0	243	17	53	.321	0	1	.000	7	13	.538	19	12	2	29	0	32	0.9	16	41	1.1	41	1.1
96-97 Por	9	0	99	8	16	.500	0	0	—	4	10	.400	6	5	3	13	0	11	1.2	11	23	2.6	20	2.2
Min	10	0	31	8	10	.800	0	0	—	4	7	.571	2	2	0	2	0	1	0.1	0	4	0.4	20	2.0
6 Years	186	2	1662	182	420	.433	2	6	.333	134	229	.585	104	92	31	201	0	190	1.0	180	343	1.8	500	2.7

NBA Postseason

Year Tm	G	GS	Min	Md	Att	Pct	Md	Att	Pct	Md	Att	Pct	TO	Stl	Blk	PF	DQ	Ast	Avg	Off	Tot	Avg	Pts	Avg
95-96 Atl	10	0	59	7	13	.538	0	0	—	3	7	.429	3	5	1	7	0	9	0.9	1	6	0.6	17	1.7
97-98 Min	2	0	29	5	8	.625	1	1	1.000	1	2	.500	0	1	0	5	0	3	1.5	3	9	4.5	12	6.0
2 Years	12	0	88	12	21	.571	1	1	1.000	4	9	.444	3	6	1	12	0	12	1.0	4	15	1.3	29	2.4

Adam Keefe

Pos: F **College:** Stanford **Drafted:** '92 1(10)—Atl **Ht:** 6'9" **Wt:** 230 **Born:** 2/22/70 **Age:** 30

College Year Tm	G	GS	Min	Field Goals Md	Att	Pct	3-Pt FGs Md	Att	Pct	Free Throws Md	Att	Pct	Misc TO	Stl	Blk	Fouls PF	DQ	Assists Ast	Avg	Rebounds Off	Tot	Avg	Points Pts	Avg
88-89 Stan	33	0	653	93	147	.633	0	0	—	91	132	.689	49	18	11	56	0	22	0.7	—	179	5.4	277	8.4
89-90 Stan	30	30	1065	210	335	.627	0	0	—	179	247	.725	71	23	18	72	1	41	1.4	—	272	9.1	599	20.0
90-91 Stan	33	33	1204	252	414	.609	2	4	.500	203	267	.760	93	51	12	75	2	61	1.8	—	313	9.5	709	21.5
91-92 Stan	29	29	1080	275	488	.564	5	11	.455	179	240	.746	96	49	14	63	0	86	3.0	—	355	12.2	734	25.3
4 Years	125	92	4002	830	1384	.600	7	15	.467	652	886	.736	309	141	55	266	3	210	1.7	—	1119	9.0	2319	18.6

NBA Year Tm	G	GS	Min	Field Goals Md	Att	Pct	3-Pt FGs Md	Att	Pct	Free Throws Md	Att	Pct	Misc TO	Stl	Blk	Fouls PF	DQ	Assists Ast	Avg	Rebounds Off	Tot	Avg	Points Pts	Avg
92-93 Atl	82	6	1549	188	376	.500	0	1	.000	166	237	.700	100	57	16	195	1	80	1.0	171	432	5.3	542	6.6
93-94 Atl	63	1	763	96	213	.451	0	0	—	81	111	.730	60	20	9	80	0	34	0.5	77	201	3.2	273	4.3
94-95 Uta	75	0	1270	172	298	.577	0	0	—	117	173	.676	62	36	25	141	0	30	0.4	135	327	4.4	461	6.1
95-96 Uta	82	0	1708	180	346	.520	0	4	.000	139	201	.692	88	51	41	174	0	64	0.8	176	455	5.5	499	6.1
96-97 Uta	62	0	915	82	160	.513	0	1	.000	71	103	.689	45	30	13	97	0	32	0.5	75	216	3.5	235	3.8
97-98 Uta	80	75	2047	229	424	.540	0	0	—	162	200	.810	72	52	24	172	0	89	1.1	179	438	5.5	620	7.8
98-99 Uta	44	0	642	56	124	.452	0	4	.000	62	89	.697	33	16	12	63	0	28	0.6	51	142	3.2	174	4.0
99-00 Uta	62	3	604	53	130	.408	0	1	.000	29	36	.806	46	17	13	90	0	34	0.5	45	136	2.2	135	2.2
8 Years	550	85	9498	1056	2071	.510	0	11	.000	827	1150	.719	505	279	153	1012	1	391	0.7	909	2347	4.3	2939	5.3

NBA Postseason

Year Tm	G	GS	Min	Md	Att	Pct	Md	Att	Pct	Md	Att	Pct	TO	Stl	Blk	PF	DQ	Ast	Avg	Off	Tot	Avg	Pts	Avg
92-93 Atl	3	0	53	7	13	.538	0	0	—	4	6	.667	3	1	0	7	0	6	2.0	4	13	4.3	18	6.0
93-94 Atl	7	0	62	6	10	.600	0	0	—	4	9	.444	4	1	1	9	0	2	0.3	3	13	1.9	16	2.3
94-95 Uta	4	0	69	7	12	.583	0	0	—	4	6	.667	0	5	1	4	0	2	0.5	8	17	4.3	18	4.5

NBA Postseason

Year Tm	G	GS	Min	Md	Att	Pct	Md	Att	Pct	Md	Att	Pct	TO	Stl	Blk	PF	DQ	Ast	Avg	Off	Tot	Avg	Pts	Avg
95-96 Uta	17	0	178	23	34	.676	1	2	.500	11	17	.647	8	3	1	23	0	2	0.1	9	33	1.9	58	3.4
96-97 Uta	8	0	59	2	6	.333	0	0	—	4	6	.667	2	2	1	5	0	2	0.3	3	16	2.0	8	1.0
97-98 Uta	15	10	154	10	29	.345	0	0	—	11	17	.647	3	4	2	18	0	2	0.1	13	34	2.3	31	2.1
98-99 Uta	10	0	101	18	30	.600	0	0	—	5	5	1.000	8	4	3	17	0	3	0.3	7	24	2.4	41	4.1
7 Years	64	10	676	73	134	.545	1	2	.500	43	66	.652	28	20	9	83	0	19	0.3	47	150	2.3	190	3.0

Shawn Kemp

(statistical profile on page 235)

Pos: F **College:** None **Drafted:** '89 1(17)—Sea **Ht:** 6'10" **Wt:** 280 **Born:** 11/26/69 **Age:** 31

NBA				Field Goals			3-Pt FGs			Free Throws			Misc			Fouls		Assists		Rebounds			Points	
Year Tm	G	GS	Min	Md	Att	Pct	Md	Att	Pct	Md	Att	Pct	TO	Stl	Blk	PF	DQ	Ast	Avg	Off	Tot	Avg	Pts	Avg
89-90 Sea	81	1	1120	203	424	.479	2	12	.167	117	159	.736	107	47	70	204	5	26	0.3	146	346	4.3	525	6.5
90-91 Sea	81	66	2442	462	909	.508	2	12	.167	288	436	.661	202	77	123	319	11	144	1.8	267	679	8.4	1214	15.0
91-92 Sea	64	23	1808	362	718	.504	0	3	.000	270	361	.748	156	70	124	261	13	86	1.3	264	665	10.4	994	15.5
92-93 Sea*	78	68	2582	515	1047	.492	0	4	.000	358	503	.712	217	119	146	327	13	155	2.0	287	833	10.7	1388	17.8
93-94 Sea*	79	73	2597	533	990	.538	1	4	.250	364	491	.741	259	142	166	312	11	207	2.6	312	851	10.8	1431	18.1
94-95 Sea*	82	79	2679	545	997	.547	2	7	.286	438	585	.749	259	102	122	337	9	149	1.8	318	893	10.9	1530	18.7
95-96 Sea*	79	76	2631	526	937	.561	5	12	.417	493	664	.742	315	93	127	299	6	173	2.2	276	904	11.4	1550	19.6
96-97 Sea*	81	75	2750	526	1032	.510	12	33	.364	452	609	.742	280	125	81	320	11	156	1.9	275	807	10.0	1516	18.7
97-98 Cle*	80	80	2769	518	1164	.445	2	8	.250	404	556	.727	271	108	90	310	15	197	2.5	219	745	9.3	1442	18.0
98-99 Cle	42	42	1475	277	575	.482	1	2	.500	307	389	.789	147	48	45	159	2	101	2.4	131	388	9.2	862	20.5
99-00 Cle	82	82	2492	484	1160	.417	2	6	.333	493	635	.776	291	100	96	371	13	138	1.7	231	725	8.8	1463	17.8
11 Years	829	665	25345	4951	9953	.497	29	103	.282	3984	5388	.739	2484	1031	1190	3219	109	1532	1.8	2726	7836	9.5	13915	16.8

NBA Postseason

Year Tm	G	GS	Min	Md	Att	Pct	Md	Att	Pct	Md	Att	Pct	TO	Stl	Blk	PF	DQ	Ast	Avg	Off	Tot	Avg	Pts	Avg
90-91 Sea	5	5	149	22	57	.386	0	1	.000	22	27	.815	16	3	4	20	1	6	1.2	13	36	7.2	66	13.2
91-92 Sea	9	9	338	48	101	.475	0	0	—	61	80	.763	27	5	14	41	0	4	0.4	47	110	12.2	157	17.4
92-93 Sea	19	19	663	110	215	.512	0	0	—	93	115	.809	54	29	40	78	2	49	2.6	80	190	10.0	313	16.5
93-94 Sea	5	5	206	26	70	.371	0	0	—	22	33	.667	14	10	12	18	0	17	3.4	20	49	9.8	74	14.8
94-95 Sea	4	4	160	33	57	.579	1	1	1.000	32	39	.821	15	8	7	17	0	11	2.8	17	48	12.0	99	24.8
95-96 Sea	20	20	720	147	258	.570	0	3	.000	124	156	.795	80	24	40	84	3	30	1.5	66	208	10.4	418	20.9
96-97 Sea	12	12	442	85	175	.486	2	10	.200	87	105	.829	47	14	16	55	2	36	3.0	52	148	12.3	259	21.6
97-98 Cle	4	4	152	33	71	.465	0	0	—	38	45	.844	16	5	4	12	0	8	2.0	16	41	10.3	104	26.0
8 Years	78	78	2830	504	1004	.502	3	15	.200	479	600	.798	269	98	137	325	8	161	2.1	311	830	10.6	1490	19.1

Steve Kerr

Pos: G **College:** Arizona **Drafted:** '88 2(50)—Pho **Ht:** 6'3" **Wt:** 180 **Born:** 9/27/65 **Age:** 35

College				Field Goals			3-Pt FGs			Free Throws			Misc			Fouls		Assists		Rebounds			Points	
Year Tm	G	GS	Min	Md	Att	Pct	Md	Att	Pct	Md	Att	Pct	TO	Stl	Blk	PF	DQ	Ast	Avg	Off	Tot	Avg	Pts	Avg
83-84 Ari	28	1	633	81	157	.516	—	—	—	36	52	.692	35	9	1	30	0	35	1.3	—	33	1.2	198	7.1
84-85 Ari	31	30	1036	126	222	.568	—	—	—	57	71	.803	46	19	4	43	1	123	4.0	—	73	2.4	309	10.0
85-86 Ari	32	32	1228	195	361	.540	—	—	—	71	79	.899	51	52	1	44	0	135	4.2	—	101	3.2	461	14.4
87-88 Ari	38	38	1239	151	270	.559	114	199	.573	61	74	.824	36	44	2	29	0	150	3.9	8	76	2.0	477	12.6
4 Years	129	101	4136	553	1010	.548	114	199	.573	225	276	.815	168	124	8	146	1	443	3.4	8	283	2.2	1445	11.2

NBA				Field Goals			3-Pt FGs			Free Throws			Misc			Fouls		Assists		Rebounds			Points	
Year Tm	G	GS	Min	Md	Att	Pct	Md	Att	Pct	Md	Att	Pct	TO	Stl	Blk	PF	DQ	Ast	Avg	Off	Tot	Avg	Pts	Avg
88-89 Pho	26	0	157	20	46	.435	8	17	.471	6	9	.667	6	7	0	12	0	24	0.9	3	17	0.7	54	2.1
89-90 Cle	78	5	1664	192	432	.444	73	144	.507	63	73	.863	74	45	7	59	0	248	3.2	12	98	1.3	520	6.7
90-91 Cle	57	4	905	99	223	.444	28	62	.452	45	53	.849	40	29	4	52	0	131	2.3	5	37	0.6	271	4.8
91-92 Cle	48	20	847	121	237	.511	32	74	.432	45	54	.833	31	27	10	29	0	110	2.3	14	78	1.6	319	6.6
92-93 2Tm	52	0	481	53	122	.434	6	26	.231	22	24	.917	27	10	1	36	0	70	1.3	5	45	0.9	134	2.6
93-94 Chi	82	0	2036	287	577	.497	52	124	.419	83	97	.856	57	75	3	97	0	210	2.6	26	131	1.6	709	8.6
94-95 Chi	82	0	1839	261	495	.527	89	170	.524	63	81	.778	48	44	3	114	0	151	1.8	20	119	1.5	674	8.2
95-96 Chi	82	0	1919	244	482	.506	122	237	.515	78	84	.929	42	63	2	109	0	192	2.3	25	110	1.3	688	8.4
96-97 Chi	82	0	1861	249	467	.533	110	237	.464	54	67	.806	43	67	3	98	0	175	2.1	29	130	1.6	662	8.1
97-98 Chi	50	0	1119	137	302	.454	57	130	.438	45	49	.918	27	26	5	71	0	96	1.9	14	77	1.5	376	7.5
98-99 SA	44	0	734	68	174	.391	25	80	.313	31	35	.886	22	23	3	28	0	49	1.1	6	44	1.0	192	4.4
99-00 SA	32	0	268	32	74	.432	16	31	.516	9	11	.818	7	4	0	14	0	12	0.4	3	19	0.6	89	2.8
92-93 Cle	5	0	41	5	10	.500	0	2	.000	2	2	1.000	2	2	0	2	0	11	2.2	0	7	1.4	12	2.4
Orl	47	0	440	48	112	.429	6	24	.250	20	22	.909	25	8	1	34	0	59	1.3	5	38	0.8	122	2.6
12 Years	715	29	13830	1763	3631	.486	618	1332	.464	544	637	.854	424	420	41	719	0	1468	2.1	162	905	1.3	4688	6.6

Year Tm	G	GS	Min	Md	Att	Pct	Md	Att	Pct	Md	Att	Pct	TO	Stl	Blk	PF	DQ	Ast	Avg	Off	Tot	Avg	Pts	Avg
89-90 Cle	5	0	73	4	14	.286	0	3	.000	0	0	—	2	4	0	6	0	10	2.0	1	6	1.2	8	1.6
91-92 Cle	12	3	149	18	41	.439	3	11	.273	5	5	1.000	4	5	0	12	0	10	0.8	1	6	0.5	44	3.7
93-94 Chi	10	0	186	13	36	.361	6	16	.375	3	3	1.000	1	7	0	13	0	10	1.0	2	14	1.4	35	3.5
94-95 Chi	10	0	193	19	40	.475	8	19	.421	5	5	1.000	0	1	0	14	0	15	1.5	1	6	0.6	51	5.1
95-96 Chi	18	0	357	39	87	.448	17	53	.321	27	31	.871	13	14	0	21	0	31	1.7	3	18	1.0	122	6.8
96-97 Chi	19	0	341	33	77	.429	16	42	.381	13	14	.929	8	17	2	25	0	20	1.1	4	18	0.9	95	5.0
97-98 Chi	21	0	415	33	76	.434	19	41	.463	18	22	.818	5	7	0	26	0	35	1.7	8	17	0.8	103	4.9
98-99 SA	11	0	97	8	30	.267	3	13	.231	5	6	.833	4	2	0	5	0	8	0.7	3	9	0.8	24	2.2
8 Years	106	3	1811	167	401	.416	72	198	.364	76	86	.884	37	57	2	122	0	139	1.3	23	94	0.9	482	4.5

Jerome Kersey
(statistical profile on page 236)

Pos: F **College:** Longwood College **Drafted:** '84 2(46)—Por **Ht:** 6'7" **Wt:** 245 **Born:** 6/26/62 **Age:** 38

College			Field Goals			3-Pt FGs			Free Throws			Misc			Fouls		Assists		Rebounds			Points	
Year Tm	G	GS	Min	Md	Att	Pct	Md	Att	Pct	Md	Att	Pct	TO	Stl	Blk	PF	DQ	Ast	Avg	Off	Tot	Avg	Pts	Avg
80-81 Lngwd	28	—	—	197	313	.629	—	—	—	78	133	.586	—	—	—	—	—	30	1.1	—	249	8.9	472	16.9
81-82 Lngwd	23	—	—	165	282	.585	—	—	—	62	98	.633	—	—	—	—	—	61	2.7	—	260	11.3	392	17.0
82-83 Lngwd	25	—	—	144	257	.560	—	—	—	76	125	.608	—	—	—	—	—	77	3.1	—	270	10.8	364	14.6
83-84 Lngwd	27	—	—	214	411	.521	—	—	—	100	165	.606	—	—	—	—	—	98	3.6	—	383	14.2	528	19.6
4 Years	103	—	—	720	1263	.570	—	—	—	316	521	.607	—	—	—	—	—	266	2.6	—	1162	11.3	1756	17.0

NBA			Field Goals			3-Pt FGs			Free Throws			Misc			Fouls		Assists		Rebounds			Points	
Year Tm	G	GS	Min	Md	Att	Pct	Md	Att	Pct	Md	Att	Pct	TO	Stl	Blk	PF	DQ	Ast	Avg	Off	Tot	Avg	Pts	Avg
84-85 Por	77	0	958	178	372	.478	0	3	.000	117	181	.646	66	49	29	147	1	63	0.8	95	206	2.7	473	6.1
85-86 Por	79	2	1217	258	470	.549	0	6	.000	156	229	.681	113	85	32	208	2	83	1.1	137	293	3.7	672	8.5
86-87 Por	82	8	2088	373	733	.509	1	23	.043	262	364	.720	149	122	77	328	5	194	2.4	201	496	6.0	1009	12.3
87-88 Por	79	75	2888	611	1225	.499	3	15	.200	291	396	.735	161	127	65	302	8	243	3.1	211	657	8.3	1516	19.2
88-89 Por	76	76	2716	533	1137	.469	6	21	.286	258	372	.694	167	137	84	277	6	243	3.2	246	629	8.3	1330	17.5
89-90 Por	82	82	2843	519	1085	.478	3	20	.150	269	390	.690	144	121	63	304	7	188	2.3	251	690	8.4	1310	16.0
90-91 Por	73	72	2359	424	887	.478	4	13	.308	232	327	.709	149	101	76	251	4	227	3.1	169	481	6.6	1084	14.8
91-92 Por	77	76	2553	398	852	.467	1	8	.125	174	262	.664	151	114	71	254	1	243	3.2	241	683	8.2	971	12.6
92-93 Por	65	50	1719	281	642	.438	8	28	.286	116	183	.634	84	80	41	181	2	121	1.9	126	406	6.2	686	10.6
93-94 Por	78	6	1276	203	469	.433	1	8	.125	101	135	.748	63	71	49	213	1	75	1.0	130	331	4.2	508	6.5
94-95 Por	63	0	1143	203	489	.415	7	27	.259	95	124	.766	64	52	35	173	1	82	1.3	93	263	4.1	508	8.1
95-96 GS	76	58	1620	205	500	.410	3	17	.176	97	147	.660	75	91	45	205	2	114	1.5	154	363	4.8	510	6.7
96-97 LAL	70	44	1766	194	449	.432	17	65	.262	71	118	.602	74	119	49	219	0	89	1.3	112	363	5.2	476	6.8
97-98 Sea	37	2	717	97	233	.416	1	10	.100	39	65	.600	36	52	14	104	1	44	1.2	56	135	3.6	234	6.3
98-99 SA	45	0	694	68	200	.340	3	14	.214	6	14	.429	30	37	14	92	1	41	0.9	42	130	2.9	145	3.2
99-00 SA	72	18	1310	146	354	.412	0	9	.000	29	41	.707	51	67	47	161	0	69	1.0	58	225	3.1	321	4.5
16 Years	1131	569	27872	4691	10097	.465	58	287	.202	2313	3348	.691	1577	1425	791	3419	42	2119	1.9	2322	6294	5.6	11753	10.4

NBA Postseason

Year Tm	G	GS	Min	Md	Att	Pct	Md	Att	Pct	Md	Att	Pct	TO	Stl	Blk	PF	DQ	Ast	Avg	Off	Tot	Avg	Pts	Avg
84-85 Por	8	0	60	16	31	.516	0	0	—	6	8	.750	2	7	2	11	0	6	0.8	5	9	1.1	38	4.8
85-86 Por	4	0	56	9	22	.409	0	1	.000	4	4	1.000	6	1	4	13	0	4	1.0	7	15	3.8	22	5.5
86-87 Por	4	0	60	10	25	.400	0	0	—	4	4	1.000	6	5	1	13	0	3	0.8	6	19	4.8	24	6.0
87-88 Por	4	4	127	32	65	.492	0	1	.000	15	21	.714	5	7	4	17	1	9	2.3	17	30	7.5	79	19.8
88-89 Por	3	3	117	23	47	.489	0	2	.000	15	19	.789	4	10	1	12	0	7	2.3	11	24	8.0	61	20.3
89-90 Por	21	21	831	166	361	.460	0	3	.000	103	144	.715	45	34	20	87	2	45	2.1	66	174	8.3	435	20.7
90-91 Por	16	16	588	105	226	.465	0	0	—	76	101	.752	17	28	7	68	2	49	3.1	52	111	6.9	286	17.9
91-92 Por	21	21	756	131	257	.510	0	3	.000	79	114	.693	53	41	19	85	2	75	3.6	59	162	7.7	341	16.2
92-93 Por	4	1	98	22	42	.524	1	1	1.000	12	17	.706	2	4	2	15	0	4	1.0	10	34	8.5	57	14.3
93-94 Por	3	0	38	5	16	.313	0	0	—	1	5	.200	0	1	1	5	0	0	0.0	5	9	3.0	11	3.7
94-95 Por	3	0	63	16	28	.571	0	2	.000	6	9	.667	0	3	1	11	1	3	1.0	2	8	2.7	38	12.7
96-97 LAL	9	0	210	17	35	.486	0	1	.000	15	19	.789	3	9	6	34	2	14	1.6	14	48	5.3	49	5.4
97-98 Sea	10	5	213	31	72	.431	0	3	.000	16	19	.842	13	10	10	32	0	9	0.9	17	40	4.0	78	7.8
98-99 SA	14	0	152	15	43	.349	1	4	.250	5	7	.714	6	6	1	19	0	4	0.3	10	30	2.1	36	2.6
99-00 SA	2	0	25	1	7	.143	0	0	—	0	0	—	1	2	1	5	0	1	0.5	2	4	2.0	2	1.0
15 Years	126	71	3394	599	1277	.469	2	21	.095	357	491	.727	163	168	80	427	10	233	1.8	283	717	5.7	1557	12.4

Lari Ketner

Pos: F **College:** Massachusetts **Drafted:** '99 2(49)—Chi **Ht:** 6'10" **Wt:** 285 **Born:** 2/1/77 **Age:** 23

College			Field Goals			3-Pt FGs			Free Throws			Misc			Fouls		Assists		Rebounds			Points	
Year Tm	G	GS	Min	Md	Att	Pct	Md	Att	Pct	Md	Att	Pct	TO	Stl	Blk	PF	DQ	Ast	Avg	Off	Tot	Avg	Pts	Avg
96-97 Mass	33	29	792	141	253	.557	0	1	.000	67	114	.588	61	8	73	103	7	23	0.7	70	175	5.3	349	10.6
97-98 Mass	32	31	968	195	373	.523	0	0	—	96	149	.644	59	14	67	98	3	16	0.5	85	238	7.4	486	15.2

	College			Field Goals			3-Pt FGs			Free Throws			Misc			Fouls		Assists		Rebounds			Points	
Year Tm	G	GS	Min	Md	Att	Pct	Md	Att	Pct	Md	Att	Pct	TO	Stl	Blk	PF	DQ	Ast	Avg	Off	Tot	Avg	Pts	Avg
98-99 Mass	29	28	879	128	303	.422	0	0	—	57	102	.559	50	11	64	90	4	35	1.2	70	242	8.3	313	10.8
3 Years	94	88	2639	464	929	.499	0	1	.000	220	365	.603	170	33	204	291	14	74	0.8	225	655	7.0	1148	12.2

	NBA			Field Goals			3-Pt FGs			Free Throws			Misc			Fouls		Assists		Rebounds			Points	
Year Tm	G	GS	Min	Md	Att	Pct	Md	Att	Pct	Md	Att	Pct	TO	Stl	Blk	PF	DQ	Ast	Avg	Off	Tot	Avg	Pts	Avg
99-00 2Tm	22	0	132	13	32	.406	0	0	—	8	12	.667	10	4	3	20	1	1	0.0	12	34	1.5	34	1.5
99-00 Chi	6	0	41	4	10	.400	0	0	—	2	2	1.000	3	1	1	8	1	1	0.2	0	7	1.2	10	1.7
Cle	16	0	91	9	22	.409	0	0	—	6	10	.600	7	3	2	12	0	0	0.0	12	27	1.7	24	1.5

Jason Kidd

(statistical profile on page 236)

Pos: G **College:** California **Drafted:** '94 1(2)—Dal **Ht:** 6'4" **Wt:** 212 **Born:** 3/23/73 **Age:** 27

	College			Field Goals			3-Pt FGs			Free Throws			Misc			Fouls		Assists		Rebounds			Points	
Year Tm	G	GS	Min	Md	Att	Pct	Md	Att	Pct	Md	Att	Pct	TO	Stl	Blk	PF	DQ	Ast	Avg	Off	Tot	Avg	Pts	Avg
92-93 Cal	29	29	922	133	287	.463	24	84	.286	88	134	.657	112	110	8	72	1	222	7.7	—	142	4.9	378	13.0
93-94 Cal	30	29	1053	166	352	.472	51	141	.362	117	169	.692	129	94	9	78	2	272	9.1	—	207	6.9	500	16.7
2 Years	59	58	1975	299	639	.468	75	225	.333	205	303	.677	241	204	17	150	3	494	8.4	—	349	5.9	878	14.9

	NBA			Field Goals			3-Pt FGs			Free Throws			Misc			Fouls		Assists		Rebounds			Points	
Year Tm	G	GS	Min	Md	Att	Pct	Md	Att	Pct	Md	Att	Pct	TO	Stl	Blk	PF	DQ	Ast	Avg	Off	Tot	Avg	Pts	Avg
94-95 Dal	79	79	2668	330	857	.385	70	257	.272	192	275	.698	250	151	24	146	0	607	7.7	152	430	5.4	922	11.7
95-96 Dal*	81	81	3034	493	1293	.381	133	396	.336	229	331	.692	328	175	26	155	0	783	9.7	203	553	6.8	1348	16.6
96-97 2Tm	55	45	1964	213	529	.403	61	165	.370	112	165	.679	142	124	20	114	0	496	9.0	64	249	4.5	599	10.9
97-98 Pho*	82	82	3118	357	859	.416	73	233	.313	167	209	.799	261	162	26	142	0	745	9.1	108	510	6.2	954	11.6
98-99 Pho	50	50	2060	310	698	.444	45	123	.366	181	239	.757	150	114	19	108	1	539	10.8	87	339	6.8	846	16.9
99-00 Pho*	67	67	2616	350	855	.409	56	166	.337	203	245	.829	226	134	28	148	2	678	10.1	96	483	7.2	959	14.3
96-97 Dal	22	22	791	75	203	.369	21	65	.323	46	69	.667	66	45	8	42	0	200	9.1	30	90	4.1	217	9.9
Pho	33	23	1173	138	326	.423	40	100	.400	66	96	.688	76	79	12	72	0	296	9.0	34	159	4.8	382	11.6
6 Years	414	404	15460	2053	5091	.403	438	1340	.327	1084	1464	.740	1357	860	143	813	3	3848	9.3	710	2564	6.2	5628	13.6

	NBA Postseason																							
Year Tm	G	GS	Min	Md	Att	Pct	Md	Att	Pct	Md	Att	Pct	TO	Stl	Blk	PF	DQ	Ast	Avg	Off	Tot	Avg	Pts	Avg
96-97 Pho	5	5	207	21	53	.396	8	22	.364	10	19	.526	13	11	2	11	0	49	9.8	4	30	6.0	60	12.0
97-98 Pho	4	4	171	22	58	.379	0	7	.000	13	16	.813	12	16	2	13	0	31	7.8	5	23	5.8	57	14.3
98-99 Pho	3	3	126	18	43	.419	4	16	.250	5	7	.714	9	5	1	12	0	31	10.3	1	7	2.3	45	15.0
99-00 Pho	6	6	229	22	55	.400	8	22	.364	7	9	.778	23	11	1	14	0	53	8.8	8	40	6.7	59	9.8
4 Years	18	18	733	83	209	.397	20	67	.299	35	51	.686	57	43	6	50	0	164	9.1	18	100	5.6	221	12.3

Gerard King

Pos: F **College:** Nicholls State **Drafted:** '98 FA—SA **Ht:** 6'9" **Wt:** 250 **Born:** 11/25/72 **Age:** 28

	College			Field Goals			3-Pt FGs			Free Throws			Misc			Fouls		Assists		Rebounds			Points	
Year Tm	G	GS	Min	Md	Att	Pct	Md	Att	Pct	Md	Att	Pct	TO	Stl	Blk	PF	DQ	Ast	Avg	Off	Tot	Avg	Pts	Avg
90-91 Nich	27	—	708	133	257	.518	0	4	.000	92	151	.609	78	40	35	101	—	23	0.9	—	182	6.7	358	13.3
91-92 Nich	28	—	708	137	274	.500	0	1	.000	98	153	.641	63	30	31	100	—	28	1.0	—	147	5.3	372	13.3
93-94 Nich	27	—	871	186	351	.530	0	0	—	127	205	.620	67	61	26	96	—	54	2.0	—	239	8.9	499	18.5
94-95 Nich	28	—	860	238	423	.563	1	1	1.000	128	182	.703	53	46	41	94	—	30	1.1	—	218	7.8	605	21.6
4 Years	110	—	3147	694	1305	.532	1	6	.167	445	691	.644	261	177	133	391	—	135	1.2	—	786	7.1	1834	16.7

	NBA			Field Goals			3-Pt FGs			Free Throws			Misc			Fouls		Assists		Rebounds			Points	
Year Tm	G	GS	Min	Md	Att	Pct	Md	Att	Pct	Md	Att	Pct	TO	Stl	Blk	PF	DQ	Ast	Avg	Off	Tot	Avg	Pts	Avg
95-96									Played in CBA, Played in USBL															
96-97									Played in Italy															
97-98									Played in Italy															
98-99 SA	19	0	63	6	14	.429	0	0	—	11	18	.611	4	2	1	12	0	4	0.2	6	14	0.7	23	1.2
99-00 Was	62	28	1060	139	277	.502	0	0	—	49	66	.742	41	34	15	132	1	49	0.8	84	250	4.0	327	5.3
2 Years	81	28	1123	145	291	.498	0	0	—	60	84	.714	45	36	16	144	1	53	0.7	90	264	3.3	350	4.3

	NBA Postseason																							
Year Tm	G	GS	Min	Md	Att	Pct	Md	Att	Pct	Md	Att	Pct	TO	Stl	Blk	PF	DQ	Ast	Avg	Off	Tot	Avg	Pts	Avg
98-99 SA	8	0	14	2	4	.500	0	0	—	0	0	—	1	0	1	2	0	1	0.1	0	4	0.5	4	0.5

Kerry Kittles

Pos: G **College:** Villanova **Drafted:** '96 1(8)—NJ **Ht:** 6'5" **Wt:** 190 **Born:** 6/12/74 **Age:** 26

(statistical profile on page 237)

College			Field Goals			3-Pt FGs			Free Throws			Misc			Fouls		Assists		Rebounds			Points	
Year Tm	G	GS	Min	Md	Att	Pct	Md	Att	Pct	Md	Att	Pct	TO	Stl	Blk	PF	DQ	Ast	Avg	Off	Tot	Avg	Pts	Avg
92-93 Vill	27	17	875	108	224	.482	41	95	.432	37	55	.673	53	47	11	43	0	79	2.9	31	94	3.5	294	10.9
93-94 Vill	32	31	1258	233	516	.452	73	209	.349	91	129	.705	71	87	13	41	0	109	3.4	68	207	6.5	630	19.7
94-95 Vill	33	33	1218	264	504	.524	86	209	.411	92	120	.767	70	71	13	55	1	115	3.5	65	201	6.1	706	21.4
95-96 Vill	30	29	1059	216	475	.455	78	193	.404	103	145	.710	55	72	11	45	0	105	3.5	65	213	7.1	613	20.4
4 Years	122	110	4410	821	1719	.478	278	706	.394	323	449	.719	249	277	48	184	1	408	3.3	229	715	5.9	2243	18.4

NBA			Field Goals			3-Pt FGs			Free Throws			Misc			Fouls		Assists		Rebounds			Points	
Year Tm	G	GS	Min	Md	Att	Pct	Md	Att	Pct	Md	Att	Pct	TO	Stl	Blk	PF	DQ	Ast	Avg	Off	Tot	Avg	Pts	Avg
96-97 NJ	82	57	3012	507	1189	.426	158	419	.377	175	227	.771	127	157	35	165	1	249	3.0	106	319	3.9	1347	16.4
97-98 NJ	77	76	2814	508	1154	.440	110	263	.418	202	250	.808	106	132	37	152	0	176	2.3	132	362	4.7	1328	17.2
98-99 NJ	46	40	1570	227	613	.370	50	158	.316	88	114	.772	66	79	26	82	0	116	2.5	52	191	4.2	592	12.9
99-00 NJ	62	61	1896	305	698	.437	96	240	.400	101	127	.795	56	79	19	120	0	142	2.3	46	225	3.6	807	13.0
4 Years	267	234	9292	1547	3654	.423	414	1080	.383	566	718	.788	355	447	117	519	1	683	2.6	336	1097	4.1	4074	15.3

NBA Postseason																								
Year Tm	G	GS	Min	Md	Att	Pct	Md	Att	Pct	Md	Att	Pct	TO	Stl	Blk	PF	DQ	Ast	Avg	Off	Tot	Avg	Pts	Avg
97-98 NJ	3	3	126	17	40	.425	5	13	.385	10	11	.909	7	4	2	12	1	8	2.7	0	15	5.0	49	16.3

Joe Kleine

Pos: C **College:** Arkansas **Drafted:** '85 1(6)—Sac **Ht:** 7'0" **Wt:** 271 **Born:** 1/4/62 **Age:** 39

College			Field Goals			3-Pt FGs			Free Throws			Misc			Fouls		Assists		Rebounds			Points	
Year Tm	G	GS	Min	Md	Att	Pct	Md	Att	Pct	Md	Att	Pct	TO	Stl	Blk	PF	DQ	Ast	Avg	Off	Tot	Avg	Pts	Avg
80-81 ND	29	—	291	32	50	.640	—	—	—	12	16	.750	—	—	—	—	—	11	0.4	—	71	2.4	76	2.6
82-83 Ark	30	—	950	165	307	.537	—	—	—	69	109	.633	—	—	—	—	—	18	0.6	—	219	7.3	399	13.3
83-84 Ark	32	—	1173	209	351	.595	—	—	—	163	211	.773	—	—	21	—	—	25	0.8	—	293	9.2	581	18.2
84-85 Ark	35	—	1289	294	484	.607	—	—	—	185	257	.720	—	—	—	—	—	23	0.7	—	294	8.4	773	22.1
4 Years	126	—	3703	700	1192	.587	—	—	—	429	593	.723	—	—	—	—	—	77	0.6	—	877	7.0	1829	14.5

NBA			Field Goals			3-Pt FGs			Free Throws			Misc			Fouls		Assists		Rebounds			Points	
Year Tm	G	GS	Min	Md	Att	Pct	Md	Att	Pct	Md	Att	Pct	TO	Stl	Blk	PF	DQ	Ast	Avg	Off	Tot	Avg	Pts	Avg
85-86 Sac	80	18	1180	160	344	.465	0	0	—	94	130	.723	107	24	34	224	1	46	0.6	113	373	4.7	414	5.2
86-87 Sac	79	31	1658	256	543	.471	0	1	.000	110	140	.786	90	35	30	213	2	71	0.9	173	483	6.1	622	7.9
87-88 Sac	82	60	1999	324	686	.472	0	0	—	153	188	.814	107	28	59	228	1	93	1.1	179	579	7.1	801	9.8
88-89 2Tm	75	13	1411	175	432	.405	0	2	.000	134	152	.882	104	33	23	192	2	67	0.9	124	378	5.0	484	6.5
89-90 Bos	81	4	1365	176	367	.480	0	4	.000	83	100	.830	64	15	27	170	0	46	0.6	117	355	4.4	435	5.4
90-91 Bos	72	1	850	102	218	.468	0	2	.000	54	69	.783	53	15	14	108	0	21	0.3	71	244	3.4	258	3.6
91-92 Bos	70	3	991	144	293	.491	4	8	.500	34	48	.708	27	23	14	99	0	32	0.5	94	296	4.2	326	4.7
92-93 Bos	78	3	1129	108	267	.404	0	6	.000	41	58	.707	37	17	17	123	0	39	0.5	113	346	4.4	257	3.3
93-94 Pho	74	4	848	125	256	.488	5	11	.455	30	39	.769	35	14	19	118	1	45	0.6	50	193	2.6	285	3.9
94-95 Pho	75	42	968	119	265	.449	0	2	.000	42	49	.857	35	14	18	174	2	39	0.5	82	259	3.5	280	3.7
95-96 Pho	56	9	663	71	169	.420	2	7	.286	20	25	.800	37	13	6	113	0	44	0.8	36	132	2.4	164	2.9
96-97 3Tm	59	10	848	69	170	.406	2	3	.667	28	38	.737	41	17	18	110	0	35	0.6	62	203	3.4	168	2.8
97-98 Chi	46	1	397	39	106	.368	0	0	—	15	18	.833	28	4	5	63	0	30	0.7	27	77	1.7	93	2.0
98-99 Pho	31	5	374	30	74	.405	0	2	.000	8	12	.667	10	8	1	46	0	12	0.4	27	67	2.2	68	2.2
99-00 Por	7	0	31	4	11	.364	0	0	—	3	3	1.000	2	1	0	7	0	2	0.3	0	6	0.9	11	1.6
88-89 Sac	47	11	913	116	303	.383	0	1	.000	81	88	.920	67	18	18	126	2	35	0.7	75	241	5.1	313	6.7
Bos	28	2	498	59	129	.457	0	1	.000	53	64	.828	37	15	5	66	0	32	1.1	49	137	4.9	171	6.1
96-97 3Tm	23	10	365	32	80	.400	1	1	1.000	13	18	.722	20	9	6	47	0	12	0.5	21	80	3.5	78	3.4
LAL	8	0	30	2	8	.250	0	0	—	2	2	1.000	0	0	0	6	0	0	0.0	2	9	1.1	6	0.8
NJ	28	0	453	35	82	.427	1	2	.500	13	18	.722	21	8	12	57	0	23	0.8	39	114	4.1	84	3.0
15 Years	965	204	14712	1902	4201	.453	13	48	.271	849	1069	.794	777	261	285	1988	9	622	0.6	1268	3991	4.1	4666	4.8

NBA Postseason																								
Year Tm	G	GS	Min	Md	Att	Pct	Md	Att	Pct	Md	Att	Pct	TO	Stl	Blk	PF	DQ	Ast	Avg	Off	Tot	Avg	Pts	Avg
85-86 Sac	3	0	45	5	13	.385	0	0	—	5	6	.833	2	1	1	8	0	1	0.3	8	14	4.7	15	5.0
88-89 Bos	3	0	65	6	11	.545	0	1	.000	7	9	.778	6	0	1	9	0	2	0.7	4	17	5.7	19	6.3
89-90 Bos	5	0	79	13	17	.765	0	1	.000	5	6	.833	4	2	3	12	0	2	0.4	3	14	2.8	31	6.2
90-91 Bos	5	1	31	4	9	.444	0	0	—	0	0	—	2	0	0	7	0	1	0.2	5	11	2.2	8	1.6
91-92 Bos	9	0	82	9	22	.409	0	1	.000	2	2	1.000	3	0	1	11	0	1	0.1	6	22	2.4	20	2.2
92-93 Bos	4	0	29	3	5	.600	0	0	—	0	0	—	0	0	1	4	0	0	0.0	0	5	1.3	6	1.5
93-94 Pho	8	0	81	12	28	.429	0	0	—	4	6	.667	2	1	4	15	0	3	0.4	5	17	2.1	28	3.5
94-95 Pho	10	10	167	31	54	.574	1	2	.500	0	0	—	6	5	3	35	0	8	0.8	8	31	3.1	63	6.3
95-96 Pho	2	0	8	0	2	.000	0	0	—	0	0	—	1	1	0	1	0	0	0.0	1	1	0.5	0	0.0
98-99 Pho	1	0	5	1	2	.500	0	0	—	0	0	—	0	1	1	1	0	0	0.0	1	1	1.0	2	2.0
10 Years	50	11	592	84	163	.515	1	5	.200	23	29	.793	26	11	15	103	0	18	0.4	40	133	2.7	192	3.8

Brevin Knight

(statistical profile on page 237)

Pos: G **College:** Stanford **Drafted:** '97 1(16)—Cle **Ht:** 5'10" **Wt:** 170 **Born:** 11/8/75 **Age:** 25

College

Year Tm	G	GS	Min	Md	Att	Pct	Md	Att	Pct	Md	Att	Pct	TO	Stl	Blk	PF	DQ	Ast	Avg	Off	Tot	Avg	Pts	Avg
93-94 Stan	28	28	916	90	254	.354	11	55	.200	121	160	.756	101	77	4	83	2	150	5.4	20	108	3.9	312	11.1
94-95 Stan	28	28	912	146	321	.455	19	51	.373	153	204	.750	95	78	1	79	3	184	6.6	23	109	3.9	464	16.6
95-96 Stan	29	29	915	140	323	.433	18	61	.295	151	178	.848	105	60	4	76	2	212	7.3	22	110	3.8	449	15.5
96-97 Stan	30	29	960	139	341	.408	45	110	.409	166	199	.834	105	83	4	85	1	234	7.8	26	111	3.7	489	16.3
4 Years	115	114	3703	515	1239	.416	93	277	.336	591	741	.798	406	298	13	323	8	780	6.8	91	438	3.8	1714	14.9

NBA

Year Tm	G	GS	Min	Md	Att	Pct	Md	Att	Pct	Md	Att	Pct	TO	Stl	Blk	PF	DQ	Ast	Avg	Off	Tot	Avg	Pts	Avg
97-98 Cle	80	76	2483	261	592	.441	0	7	.000	201	251	.801	194	196	18	271	5	656	8.2	67	253	3.2	723	9.0
98-99 Cle	39	38	1186	134	315	.425	0	5	.000	105	141	.745	105	70	7	115	1	302	7.7	16	131	3.4	373	9.6
99-00 Cle	65	46	1754	230	558	.412	2	10	.200	140	184	.761	157	107	21	185	2	458	7.0	38	193	3.0	602	9.3
3 Years	184	160	5423	625	1465	.427	2	22	.091	446	576	.774	456	373	46	571	8	1416	7.7	121	577	3.1	1698	9.2

NBA Postseason

Year Tm	G	GS	Min	Md	Att	Pct	Md	Att	Pct	Md	Att	Pct	TO	Stl	Blk	PF	DQ	Ast	Avg	Off	Tot	Avg	Pts	Avg
97-98 Cle	4	4	132	6	21	.286	0	0	—	6	10	.600	8	10	1	16	1	23	5.8	0	16	4.0	18	4.5

Travis Knight

Pos: F-C **College:** Connecticut **Drafted:** '96 1(29)—Chi **Ht:** 7'0" **Wt:** 235 **Born:** 9/13/74 **Age:** 26

College

Year Tm	G	GS	Min	Md	Att	Pct	Md	Att	Pct	Md	Att	Pct	TO	Stl	Blk	PF	DQ	Ast	Avg	Off	Tot	Avg	Pts	Avg
92-93 Conn	24	3	278	29	63	.460	0	5	.000	11	27	.407	27	6	23	44	—	9	0.4	—	61	2.5	69	2.9
93-94 Conn	33	8	390	36	82	.439	0	0	—	9	18	.500	21	13	32	77	3	24	0.7	40	97	2.9	81	2.5
94-95 Conn	33	32	768	129	231	.558	0	0	—	41	63	.651	54	29	56	105	—	38	1.2	—	272	8.2	299	9.1
95-96 Conn	34	33	854	126	242	.521	0	0	—	59	85	.694	77	24	68	81	2	71	2.1	116	317	9.3	311	9.1
4 Years	124	76	2290	320	618	.518	0	5	.000	120	193	.622	179	72	179	307	—	142	1.1	—	747	6.0	760	6.1

NBA

Year Tm	G	GS	Min	Md	Att	Pct	Md	Att	Pct	Md	Att	Pct	TO	Stl	Blk	PF	DQ	Ast	Avg	Off	Tot	Avg	Pts	Avg
96-97 LAL	71	14	1156	140	275	.509	0	0	—	62	100	.620	49	31	58	170	2	39	0.5	130	319	4.5	342	4.8
97-98 Bos	74	21	1503	193	438	.441	15	55	.273	81	103	.786	87	54	82	253	3	104	1.4	146	365	4.9	482	6.5
98-99 LAL	37	23	525	67	130	.515	0	1	.000	22	29	.759	35	21	27	108	2	31	0.8	34	128	3.5	156	4.2
99-00 LAL	63	0	410	46	118	.390	0	0	—	17	28	.607	26	6	23	88	1	23	0.4	46	129	2.0	109	1.7
4 Years	245	58	3594	446	961	.464	15	56	.268	182	260	.700	197	112	190	619	8	197	0.8	356	941	3.8	1089	4.4

NBA Postseason

Year Tm	G	GS	Min	Md	Att	Pct	Md	Att	Pct	Md	Att	Pct	TO	Stl	Blk	PF	DQ	Ast	Avg	Off	Tot	Avg	Pts	Avg
96-97 LAL	9	0	93	8	10	.800	0	0	—	3	4	.750	2	3	3	16	0	3	0.3	3	18	2.0	19	2.1
98-99 LAL	3	0	10	1	3	.333	0	0	—	1	2	.500	3	0	0	7	1	1	0.3	0	5	1.7	3	1.0
99-00 LAL	14	0	48	8	15	.533	0	0	—	2	6	.333	6	1	3	16	0	0	0.0	3	5	0.4	18	1.3
3 Years	26	0	151	17	28	.607	0	0	—	6	12	.500	11	4	6	39	1	4	0.2	6	28	1.1	40	1.5

Toni Kukoc

(statistical profile on page 238)

Pos: F **College:** None **Drafted:** '90 2(29)—Chi **Ht:** 6'11" **Wt:** 235 **Born:** 9/18/68 **Age:** 32

NBA

Year Tm	G	GS	Min	Md	Att	Pct	Md	Att	Pct	Md	Att	Pct	TO	Stl	Blk	PF	DQ	Ast	Avg	Off	Tot	Avg	Pts	Avg
90-91									Played in Yugoslavia															
91-92									Played in Italy															
92-93									Played in Italy															
93-94 Chi	75	8	1808	313	726	.431	32	118	.271	156	210	.743	167	81	33	122	0	252	3.4	98	297	4.0	814	10.9
94-95 Chi	81	55	2584	487	967	.504	62	198	.313	235	314	.748	165	102	16	163	1	372	4.6	155	440	5.4	1271	15.7
95-96 Chi	81	20	2103	386	787	.490	87	216	.403	206	267	.772	114	64	28	150	0	287	3.5	115	323	4.0	1065	13.1
96-97 Chi	57	15	1610	285	605	.471	50	151	.331	134	174	.770	91	60	29	97	1	256	4.5	94	261	4.6	754	13.2
97-98 Chi	74	52	2235	383	841	.455	63	174	.362	155	219	.708	154	76	37	149	0	314	4.2	121	327	4.4	984	13.3
98-99 Chi	44	44	1654	315	750	.420	39	137	.285	159	215	.740	121	49	11	82	0	235	5.3	65	310	7.0	828	18.8
99-00 2Tm	56	31	1784	297	728	.408	44	168	.262	192	265	.725	146	77	28	112	0	265	4.7	75	273	4.9	830	14.8
99-00 Chi	24	23	868	148	388	.381	18	78	.231	118	155	.761	75	44	19	51	0	124	5.2	37	130	5.4	432	18.0
Phi	32	8	916	149	340	.438	26	90	.289	74	110	.673	71	33	9	61	0	141	4.4	38	143	4.5	398	12.4
7 Years	468	225	13778	2466	5404	.456	377	1162	.324	1237	1664	.743	958	509	182	875	2	1981	4.2	723	2231	4.8	6546	14.0

NBA Postseason

Year Tm	G	GS	Min	Md	Att	Pct	Md	Att	Pct	Md	Att	Pct	TO	Stl	Blk	PF	DQ	Ast	Avg	Off	Tot	Avg	Pts	Avg
93-94 Chi	10	0	194	30	67	.448	8	19	.421	25	34	.735	17	5	3	15	0	36	3.6	11	40	4.0	93	9.3
94-95 Chi	10	10	372	53	111	.477	14	32	.438	18	26	.692	19	10	2	23	0	57	5.7	20	68	6.8	138	13.8

NBA Postseason

Year Tm	G	GS	Min	Md	Att	Pct	Md	Att	Pct	Md	Att	Pct	TO	Stl	Blk	PF	DQ	Ast	Avg	Off	Tot	Avg	Pts	Avg
95-96 Chi	15	5	439	59	151	.391	13	68	.191	31	37	.838	26	14	4	33	0	58	3.9	19	63	4.2	162	10.8
96-97 Chi	19	0	423	45	125	.360	19	53	.358	41	58	.707	17	13	4	30	0	54	2.8	13	54	2.8	150	7.9
97-98 Chi	21	17	637	106	218	.486	23	61	.377	40	62	.645	27	26	10	57	1	60	2.9	24	81	3.9	275	13.1
99-00 Phi	10	0	257	36	93	.387	11	34	.324	10	17	.588	15	10	3	26	0	17	1.7	7	37	3.7	93	9.3
5 Years	85	32	2322	329	765	.430	88	267	.330	165	234	.705	121	78	26	184	1	282	3.3	94	343	4.0	911	10.7

Christian Laettner

(statistical profile on page 238)

Pos: F **College:** Duke **Drafted:** '92 1(3)—Min   **Ht:** 6'11" **Wt:** 235 **Born:** 8/17/69 **Age:** 31

College				Field Goals			3-Pt FGs			Free Throws			Misc			Fouls		Assists		Rebounds			Points	
Year Tm	G	GS	Min	Md	Att	Pct	Md	Att	Pct	Md	Att	Pct	TO	Stl	Blk	PF	DQ	Ast	Avg	Off	Tot	Avg	Pts	Avg
88-89 Duke	36	16	607	115	159	.723	1	1	1.000	88	121	.727	58	35	28	104	—	44	1.2	58	170	4.7	319	8.9
89-90 Duke	38	38	1135	194	380	.511	6	12	.500	225	269	.836	101	59	41	120	—	84	2.2	129	364	9.6	619	16.3
90-91 Duke	39	39	1178	271	471	.575	18	53	.340	211	263	.802	121	75	44	111	—	76	1.9	102	340	8.7	771	19.8
91-92 Duke	35	35	1128	254	442	.575	54	97	.557	189	232	.815	116	74	32	90	—	69	2.0	82	275	7.9	751	21.5
4 Years	148	128	4048	834	1452	.574	79	163	.485	713	885	.806	396	243	145	425	—	273	1.8	371	1149	7.8	2460	16.6

NBA				Field Goals			3-Pt FGs			Free Throws			Misc			Fouls		Assists		Rebounds			Points	
Year Tm	G	GS	Min	Md	Att	Pct	Md	Att	Pct	Md	Att	Pct	TO	Stl	Blk	PF	DQ	Ast	Avg	Off	Tot	Avg	Pts	Avg
92-93 Min	81	81	2823	503	1061	.474	4	40	.100	462	553	.835	275	105	83	290	4	223	2.8	171	708	8.7	1472	18.2
93-94 Min	70	67	2428	396	883	.448	6	25	.240	375	479	.783	259	87	86	264	6	307	4.4	160	602	8.6	1173	16.8
94-95 Min	81	80	2770	450	920	.489	14	40	.325	409	500	.818	225	101	87	302	4	234	2.9	164	613	7.6	1322	16.3
95-96 2Tm	74	71	2495	442	907	.487	9	39	.231	324	396	.818	187	71	71	276	7	197	2.7	184	538	7.3	1217	16.4
96-97 Atl*	82	82	3140	548	1128	.486	31	88	.352	359	440	.816	218	102	64	277	8	223	2.7	212	720	8.8	1486	18.1
97-98 Atl	74	49	2282	354	730	.485	6	27	.222	306	354	.864	183	71	73	246	6	190	2.6	142	487	6.6	1020	13.8
98-99 Det	16	0	337	38	106	.358	1	3	.333	44	57	.772	19	15	12	30	0	24	1.5	21	54	3.4	121	7.6
99-00 Det	82	82	2443	379	801	.473	7	24	.292	237	292	.812	186	83	45	326	10	186	2.3	175	553	6.7	1002	12.2
95-96 Min	44	44	1518	283	582	.486	9	31	.290	217	266	.816	112	40	43	157	4	129	2.9	98	302	6.9	792	18.0
Atl	30	27	977	159	325	.489	0	8	.000	107	130	.823	75	31	28	119	3	68	2.3	86	236	7.9	425	14.2
8 Years	560	512	18718	3110	6536	.476	77	286	.269	2516	3071	.819	1552	635	521	2011	45	1584	2.8	1229	4275	7.6	8813	15.7

NBA Postseason

Year Tm	G	GS	Min	Md	Att	Pct	Md	Att	Pct	Md	Att	Pct	TO	Stl	Blk	PF	DQ	Ast	Avg	Off	Tot	Avg	Pts	Avg
95-96 Atl	10	10	334	59	122	.484	1	3	.333	38	54	.704	21	12	10	41	1	15	1.5	27	69	6.9	157	15.7
96-97 Atl	10	10	403	62	153	.405	4	21	.190	48	56	.857	31	10	8	32	0	26	2.6	19	72	7.2	176	17.6
97-98 Atl	4	0	87	12	35	.343	0	3	.000	15	17	.882	8	6	1	16	1	4	1.0	3	17	4.3	39	9.8
98-99 Det	5	0	123	20	47	.426	0	0	—	11	14	.786	3	4	1	14	0	11	2.2	6	14	2.8	51	10.2
99-00 Det	3	3	75	7	17	.412	0	0	—	6	8	.750	3	0	1	14	0	6	2.0	2	15	5.0	20	6.7
5 Years	32	23	1022	160	374	.428	5	27	.185	118	149	.792	66	32	21	117	2	62	1.9	57	187	5.8	443	13.8

Raef LaFrentz

(statistical profile on page 239)

Pos: F-C **College:** Kansas **Drafted:** '98 1(3)—Den   **Ht:** 6'11" **Wt:** 240 **Born:** 5/29/76 **Age:** 24

College				Field Goals			3-Pt FGs			Free Throws			Misc			Fouls		Assists		Rebounds			Points	
Year Tm	G	GS	Min	Md	Att	Pct	Md	Att	Pct	Md	Att	Pct	TO	Stl	Blk	PF	DQ	Ast	Avg	Off	Tot	Avg	Pts	Avg
94-95 Kan	31	31	732	143	268	.534	2	5	.400	65	102	.637	56	9	20	71	0	17	0.5	—	231	7.5	353	11.4
95-96 Kan	34	34	917	189	348	.543	2	7	.286	74	112	.661	62	29	27	86	1	14	0.4	93	278	8.2	454	13.4
96-97 Kan	36	36	1041	261	447	.584	1	6	.167	143	188	.761	64	33	46	96	0	25	0.7	126	335	9.3	666	18.5
97-98 Kan	30	30	906	232	423	.548	8	17	.471	121	164	.738	76	27	45	71	1	30	1.0	127	342	11.4	593	19.8
4 Years	131	131	3596	825	1486	.555	13	35	.371	403	566	.712	258	98	138	324	2	86	0.7	—	1186	9.1	2066	15.8

NBA				Field Goals			3-Pt FGs			Free Throws			Misc			Fouls		Assists		Rebounds			Points	
Year Tm	G	GS	Min	Md	Att	Pct	Md	Att	Pct	Md	Att	Pct	TO	Stl	Blk	PF	DQ	Ast	Avg	Off	Tot	Avg	Pts	Avg
98-99 Den	12	12	387	59	129	.457	12	31	.387	36	48	.750	9	9	17	38	2	8	0.7	33	91	7.6	166	13.8
99-00 Den	81	80	2435	392	879	.446	60	183	.328	162	236	.686	96	42	180	292	6	97	1.2	170	641	7.9	1006	12.4
2 Years	93	92	2822	451	1008	.447	72	214	.336	198	284	.697	105	51	197	330	8	105	1.1	203	732	7.9	1172	12.6

Andrew Lang

Pos: C **College:** Arkansas **Drafted:** '88 2(28)—Pho   **Ht:** 6'11" **Wt:** 275 **Born:** 6/28/66 **Age:** 34

College				Field Goals			3-Pt FGs			Free Throws			Misc			Fouls		Assists		Rebounds			Points	
Year Tm	G	GS	Min	Md	Att	Pct	Md	Att	Pct	Md	Att	Pct	TO	Stl	Blk	PF	DQ	Ast	Avg	Off	Tot	Avg	Pts	Avg
84-85 Ark	33	—	467	34	84	.405	—	—		18	32	.563	30	9	23	73	—	7	0.2	—	67	2.0	86	2.6
85-86 Ark	26	—	694	88	189	.466	—	—		37	61	.607	41	15	65	103	—	13	0.5	—	168	6.5	213	8.2
86-87 Ark	32	—	722	102	204	.500	0	0		56	87	.644	45	15	85	93	—	11	0.3	—	240	7.5	260	8.1
87-88 Ark	30	—	743	126	239	.527	0	0		27	60	.450	50	13	79	87	—	10	0.3	—	218	7.3	279	9.3
4 Years	121	—	2626	350	716	.489	0	0	—	138	240	.575	166	52	252	356	—	41	0.3	—	693	5.7	838	6.9

93

(continued)

Year Tm	G	GS	Min	Md	Att	Pct	Md	Att	Pct	Md	Att	Pct	TO	Stl	Blk	PF	DQ	Ast	Avg	Off	Tot	Avg	Pts	Avg
NBA				**Field Goals**			**3-Pt FGs**			**Free Throws**			**Misc**			**Fouls**		**Assists**		**Rebounds**			**Points**	
88-89 Pho	62	25	526	60	117	.513	0	0	—	39	60	.650	28	17	48	112	1	9	0.1	54	147	2.4	159	2.x
89-90 Pho	74	0	1011	97	174	.557	0	0	—	64	98	.653	41	22	133	171	1	21	0.3	83	271	3.7	258	3.5
90-91 Pho	63	18	1152	109	189	.577	0	1	.000	93	130	.715	45	17	127	168	2	27	0.4	113	303	4.8	311	4.9
91-92 Pho	81	71	1965	248	475	.522	0	1	.000	126	164	.768	87	48	201	306	8	43	0.5	170	546	6.7	622	7.7
92-93 Phi	73	59	1861	149	351	.425	1	5	.200	87	114	.763	89	46	141	261	4	79	1.1	136	436	6.0	386	5.x
93-94 Atl	82	0	1608	215	458	.469	1	4	.250	73	106	.689	81	38	87	192	2	51	0.6	126	313	3.8	504	6.1
94-95 Atl	82	63	2340	320	677	.473	2	3	.667	152	188	.809	108	45	144	271	4	72	0.9	154	456	5.6	794	9.7
95-96 2Tm	71	69	2365	353	790	.447	1	5	.200	125	156	.801	124	42	126	241	4	65	0.9	153	455	6.4	832	11.7
96-97 Mil	52	52	1194	115	248	.464	0	0	—	44	61	.721	39	26	47	140	4	25	0.5	94	278	5.3	274	5.x
97-98 Mil	57	0	692	54	143	.378	0	1	.000	44	57	.772	33	18	27	101	0	16	0.3	56	153	2.7	152	2.7
98-99 Chi	21	13	386	32	99	.323	0	0	—	16	23	.696	17	5	12	43	0	13	0.6	33	93	4.4	80	3.8
99-00 NY	19	10	244	28	64	.438	0	0	—	3	7	.429	5	8	6	31	0	3	0.2	16	60	3.2	59	3.1
95-96 Atl	51	51	1815	281	619	.454	0	3	.000	95	118	.805	94	35	85	178	4	62	1.2	111	334	6.5	657	12.9
Min	20	18	550	72	171	.421	1	2	.500	30	38	.789	30	7	41	63	0	3	0.2	42	121	6.1	175	8.x
12 Years	737	380	15344	1780	3785	.470	5	20	.250	866	1164	.744	697	332	1099	2037	30	424	0.6	1188	3511	4.8	4431	6.0

NBA Postseason

Year Tm	G	GS	Min	Md	Att	Pct	Md	Att	Pct	Md	Att	Pct	TO	Stl	Blk	PF	DQ	Ast	Avg	Off	Tot	Avg	Pts	Avg
88-89 Pho	4	0	8	0	2	.000	0	0	—	0	0	—	3	0	0	3	0	1	0.3	3	6	1.5	0	0.0
89-90 Pho	12	0	93	6	9	.667	0	0	—	4	7	.571	5	3	10	17	0	2	0.2	4	20	1.7	16	1.3
90-91 Pho	4	0	55	6	11	.545	0	0	—	14	17	.824	2	1	3	12	0	1	0.3	4	18	4.5	26	6.x
91-92 Pho	8	8	192	15	40	.375	0	0	—	15	19	.789	8	3	15	33	2	2	0.3	15	32	4.0	45	5.6
93-94 Atl	11	0	234	29	63	.460	0	1	.000	17	22	.773	15	6	20	35	1	5	0.5	15	47	4.3	75	6.8
94-95 Atl	3	3	101	12	28	.429	0	0	—	7	9	.778	6	2	2	12	0	1	0.3	3	12	4.0	31	10.3
6 Years	42	11	683	68	153	.444	0	1	.000	57	74	.770	39	15	50	112	3	12	0.3	44	135	3.2	193	4.6

Antonio Lang

Pos: F **College:** Duke **Drafted:** '94 2(29)—Pho   **Ht:** 6'8" **Wt:** 220 **Born:** 5/15/72 **Age:** 28

Year Tm	G	GS	Min	Md	Att	Pct	Md	Att	Pct	Md	Att	Pct	TO	Stl	Blk	PF	DQ	Ast	Avg	Off	Tot	Avg	Pts	Avg
College				**Field Goals**			**3-Pt FGs**			**Free Throws**			**Misc**			**Fouls**		**Assists**		**Rebounds**			**Points**	
90-91 Duke	36	0	426	57	94	.606	0	0	—	40	76	.526	25	14	28	55	—	7	0.2	47	82	2.3	154	4.3
91-92 Duke	34	18	763	77	137	.562	0	0	—	65	99	.657	43	20	10	87	—	23	0.7	74	139	4.1	219	6.4
92-93 Duke	31	27	808	80	153	.523	0	1	.000	55	84	.655	56	19	30	80	—	25	0.8	70	171	5.5	215	6.9
93-94 Duke	34	34	1023	153	260	.588	0	2	.000	118	163	.724	74	15	38	83	—	35	1.0	82	184	5.4	424	12.5
4 Years	135	79	3020	367	644	.570	0	3	.000	278	422	.659	198	68	106	305	—	90	0.7	273	576	4.3	1012	7.5

Year Tm	G	GS	Min	Md	Att	Pct	Md	Att	Pct	Md	Att	Pct	TO	Stl	Blk	PF	DQ	Ast	Avg	Off	Tot	Avg	Pts	Avg
NBA				**Field Goals**			**3-Pt FGs**			**Free Throws**			**Misc**			**Fouls**		**Assists**		**Rebounds**			**Points**	
94-95 Pho	12	0	53	4	10	.400	0	0	—	3	4	.750	5	0	2	11	0	1	0.1	3	4	0.3	11	0.9
95-96 Cle	41	0	367	41	77	.532	0	2	.000	34	47	.723	24	14	12	61	0	12	0.3	17	53	1.3	116	2.8
96-97 Cle	64	1	843	68	162	.420	0	6	.000	35	48	.729	50	33	30	111	0	33	0.5	52	127	2.0	171	2.7
97-98 Mia	6	0	29	3	5	.600	0	0	—	6	8	.750	4	2	0	3	0	1	0.2	2	5	0.8	12	2.0
98-99 Cle	10	0	65	4	6	.667	0	0	—	5	9	.556	4	2	1	13	0	1	0.1	6	16	1.6	13	1.3
99-00 2Tm	10	0	38	1	6	.167	0	0	—	4	5	.800	2	4	1	8	0	2	0.2	0	5	0.5	6	0.6
99-00 Tor	7	0	32	0	5	.000	0	0	—	3	4	.750	2	4	1	7	0	1	0.1	0	5	0.7	3	0.4
Phi	3	0	6	1	1	1.000	0	0	—	1	1	1.000	0	0	0	1	0	1	0.3	0	0	0.0	3	1.0
6 Years	143	1	1395	121	266	.455	0	8	.000	87	121	.719	89	55	46	207	0	50	0.3	80	210	1.5	329	2.3

NBA Postseason

Year Tm	G	GS	Min	Md	Att	Pct	Md	Att	Pct	Md	Att	Pct	TO	Stl	Blk	PF	DQ	Ast	Avg	Off	Tot	Avg	Pts	Avg
95-96 Cle	1	0	2	0	0	—	0	0	—	0	0	—	0	0	0	0	0	0	0.0	0	0	0.0	0	0.0

Trajan Langdon

Pos: G **College:** Duke **Drafted:** '99 1(11)—Cle   **Ht:** 6'3" **Wt:** 197 **Born:** 5/13/76 **Age:** 24

Year Tm	G	GS	Min	Md	Att	Pct	Md	Att	Pct	Md	Att	Pct	TO	Stl	Blk	PF	DQ	Ast	Avg	Off	Tot	Avg	Pts	Avg
College				**Field Goals**			**3-Pt FGs**			**Free Throws**			**Misc**			**Fouls**		**Assists**		**Rebounds**			**Points**	
94-95 Duke	31	24	797	124	274	.453	59	138	.428	44	56	.786	38	13	4	69	—	48	1.5	10	65	2.1	351	11.3
96-97 Duke	33	33	972	137	308	.445	86	195	.441	113	126	.897	50	33	10	56	0	68	2.1	29	97	2.9	473	14.3
97-98 Duke	36	36	1035	171	385	.444	85	215	.395	101	114	.886	58	22	8	77	0	70	1.9	28	104	2.9	528	14.7
98-99 Duke	36	36	1117	191	413	.462	112	254	.441	128	152	.842	64	52	3	84	0	69	1.9	30	123	3.4	622	17.3
4 Years	136	129	3921	623	1380	.451	342	802	.426	386	448	.862	210	120	25	286	—	255	1.9	97	389	2.9	1974	14.5

Year Tm	G	GS	Min	Md	Att	Pct	Md	Att	Pct	Md	Att	Pct	TO	Stl	Blk	PF	DQ	Ast	Avg	Off	Tot	Avg	Pts	Avg
NBA				**Field Goals**			**3-Pt FGs**			**Free Throws**			**Misc**			**Fouls**		**Assists**		**Rebounds**			**Points**	
99-00 Cle	10	0	145	15	40	.375	8	19	.421	11	11	1.000	6	5	0	16	0	11	1.1	4	15	1.5	49	4.9

Rusty LaRue

Pos: G **College:** Wake Forest **Drafted:** '97 FA—Chi **Ht:** 6'3" **Wt:** 185 **Born:** 12/10/73 **Age:** 27

	College			Field Goals			3-Pt FGs			Free Throws			Misc			Fouls		Assists		Rebounds			Points	
Year Tm	G	GS	Min	Md	Att	Pct	Md	Att	Pct	Md	Att	Pct	TO	Stl	Blk	PF	DQ	Ast	Avg	Off	Tot	Avg	Pts	Avg
92-93 Wake	15	0	52	6	14	.429	5	10	.500	4	5	.800	1	3	0	4	—	2	0.1	1	7	0.5	21	1.4
93-94 Wake	28	4	350	46	108	.426	36	80	.450	3	5	.600	16	15	1	35	—	10	0.4	8	41	1.5	131	4.7
94-95 Wake	32	0	634	67	159	.421	45	118	.381	13	14	.929	23	20	1	37	—	29	0.9	7	62	1.9	192	6.0
95-96 Wake	32	26	979	107	221	.484	65	140	.464	44	50	.880	51	28	3	51	1	62	1.9	18	96	3.0	323	10.1
4 Years	107	30	2015	226	502	.450	151	348	.434	64	74	.865	91	66	5	127	—	103	1.0	34	206	1.9	667	6.2

	NBA			Field Goals			3-Pt FGs			Free Throws			Misc			Fouls		Assists		Rebounds			Points	
Year Tm	G	GS	Min	Md	Att	Pct	Md	Att	Pct	Md	Att	Pct	TO	Stl	Blk	PF	DQ	Ast	Avg	Off	Tot	Avg	Pts	Avg
96-97										Played in CBA														
97-98 Chi	14	0	140	20	49	.408	4	16	.250	5	8	.625	6	3	1	12	0	5	0.4	1	8	0.6	49	3.5
98-99 Chi	43	6	732	78	217	.359	30	89	.337	17	17	1.000	34	33	3	66	0	63	1.5	9	56	1.3	203	4.7
99-00 Chi	4	1	129	15	43	.349	2	14	.143	5	7	.714	7	7	0	9	0	11	2.8	1	10	2.5	37	9.3
3 Years	61	7	1001	113	309	.366	36	119	.303	27	32	.844	47	43	4	87	0	79	1.3	11	74	1.2	289	4.7

Tim Legler

Pos: G **College:** LaSalle **Drafted:** '89 FA—Pho **Ht:** 6'4" **Wt:** 220 **Born:** 12/26/66 **Age:** 34

	College			Field Goals			3-Pt FGs			Free Throws			Misc			Fouls		Assists		Rebounds			Points	
Year Tm	G	GS	Min	Md	Att	Pct	Md	Att	Pct	Md	Att	Pct	TO	Stl	Blk	PF	DQ	Ast	Avg	Off	Tot	Avg	Pts	Avg
84-85 LaSal	26	—	494	69	147	.469	—	—	—	17	24	.708	—	—	—	—	—	51	2.0	—	72	2.8	155	6.0
85-86 LaSal	28	—	868	158	315	.502	—	—	—	45	54	.833	—	27	—	—	—	53	1.9	—	110	3.9	361	12.9
86-87 LaSal	33	—	1254	233	487	.478	57	141	.404	93	119	.782	—	—	—	—	—	68	2.1	—	147	4.5	616	18.7
87-88 LaSal	34	—	1292	203	414	.490	104	212	.491	57	71	.803	—	—	—	—	—	72	2.1	—	139	4.1	567	16.7
4 Years	121	—	3908	663	1363	.486	161	353	.456	212	268	.791	—	—	—	—	—	244	2.0	—	468	3.9	1699	14.0

	NBA			Field Goals			3-Pt FGs			Free Throws			Misc			Fouls		Assists		Rebounds			Points	
Year Tm	G	GS	Min	Md	Att	Pct	Md	Att	Pct	Md	Att	Pct	TO	Stl	Blk	PF	DQ	Ast	Avg	Off	Tot	Avg	Pts	Avg
88-89								Played in CBA, Played in WBL, Played in USBL																
89-90 Pho	11	0	83	11	29	.379	0	1	.000	6	6	1.000	4	2	0	12	0	6	0.5	4	8	0.7	28	2.5
90-91 Den	10	0	148	25	72	.347	3	12	.250	5	6	.833	4	2	0	20	0	12	1.2	8	18	1.8	58	5.8
91-92									Played in CBA, Played in USBL															
92-93 2Tm	33	0	635	105	241	.436	22	65	.338	57	71	.803	28	24	6	63	0	46	1.4	25	59	1.8	289	8.8
93-94 Dal	79	0	1322	231	528	.438	52	139	.374	142	169	.840	60	52	13	133	0	120	1.5	36	128	1.6	656	8.3
94-95 GS	24	0	371	60	115	.522	26	50	.520	30	34	.882	20	12	1	33	0	27	1.1	12	40	1.7	176	7.3
95-96 Was	77	0	1775	233	460	.507	128	245	**.522**	132	153	.863	45	45	12	141	0	136	1.8	29	140	1.8	726	9.4
96-97 Was	15	0	182	15	48	.313	8	29	.276	6	7	.857	9	3	5	21	0	7	0.5	0	21	1.4	44	2.9
97-98 Was	8	0	76	3	19	.158	0	6	.000	3	4	.750	4	1	0	11	0	3	0.4	2	4	0.5	9	1.1
98-99 Was	30	0	377	51	115	.443	14	35	.400	3	6	.500	14	4	3	42	0	21	0.7	8	40	1.3	119	4.0
99-00 GS	23	4	284	28	78	.359	7	21	.333	14	18	.778	6	4	1	33	0	24	1.0	4	23	1.0	77	3.3
92-93 Uta	3	0	5	1	3	.333	0	0	—	0	0	—	0	0	0	0	0	0	0.0	0	1	0.3	2	0.7
Dal	30	0	630	104	238	.437	22	65	.338	57	71	.803	28	24	6	63	0	46	1.5	25	58	1.9	287	9.6
10 Years	310	4	5253	762	1705	.447	260	603	.431	398	474	.840	194	149	41	509	0	402	1.3	128	481	1.6	2182	7.0

	NBA Postseason																							
Year Tm	G	GS	Min	Md	Att	Pct	Md	Att	Pct	Md	Att	Pct	TO	Stl	Blk	PF	DQ	Ast	Avg	Off	Tot	Avg	Pts	Avg
96-97 Was	3	0	19	0	2	.000	0	1	.000	1	2	.500	0	0	0	2	0	2	0.7	0	1	0.3	1	0.3

Voshon Lenard

(statistical profile on page 239)

Pos: G **College:** Minnesota **Drafted:** '94 2(46)—Mil **Ht:** 6'4" **Wt:** 205 **Born:** 5/14/73 **Age:** 27

	College			Field Goals			3-Pt FGs			Free Throws			Misc			Fouls		Assists		Rebounds			Points	
Year Tm	G	GS	Min	Md	Att	Pct	Md	Att	Pct	Md	Att	Pct	TO	Stl	Blk	PF	DQ	Ast	Avg	Off	Tot	Avg	Pts	Avg
91-92 Minn	32	32	868	139	330	.421	51	144	.354	82	101	.812	69	51	10	86	4	86	2.7	33	118	3.7	411	12.8
92-93 Minn	31	30	883	192	399	.481	58	158	.367	89	111	.802	55	49	9	75	3	82	2.6	38	113	3.6	531	17.1
93-94 Minn	33	33	1029	218	462	.472	86	209	.411	103	122	.844	66	43	12	95	5	74	2.2	33	123	3.7	625	18.9
94-95 Minn	31	31	992	174	422	.412	81	244	.332	107	141	.759	49	30	10	71	0	80	2.6	44	134	4.3	536	17.3
4 Years	127	126	3772	723	1613	.448	276	755	.366	381	475	.802	239	173	41	327	12	322	2.5	148	488	3.8	2103	16.6

	NBA			Field Goals			3-Pt FGs			Free Throws			Misc			Fouls		Assists		Rebounds			Points	
Year Tm	G	GS	Min	Md	Att	Pct	Md	Att	Pct	Md	Att	Pct	TO	Stl	Blk	PF	DQ	Ast	Avg	Off	Tot	Avg	Pts	Avg
94-95									Returned to College															
95-96 Mia	30	0	323	53	141	.376	36	101	.356	34	43	.791	23	6	1	31	0	31	1.0	12	52	1.7	176	5.9
96-97 Mia	73	47	2111	314	684	.459	183	442	.414	86	105	.819	109	50	18	168	1	161	2.2	38	217	3.0	897	12.3
97-98 Mia	81	81	2621	363	854	.425	153	378	.405	141	179	.788	99	58	16	219	0	180	2.2	72	292	3.6	1020	12.6
98-99 Mia	12	2	190	31	79	.392	12	35	.343	8	11	.727	7	3	1	18	0	10	0.8	4	16	1.3	82	6.8

NBA			Field Goals			3-Pt FGs			Free Throws			Misc			Fouls		Assists		Rebounds			Points	
Year Tm	G	GS	Min	Md	Att	Pct	Md	Att	Pct	Md	Att	Pct	TO	Stl	Blk	PF	DQ	Ast	Avg	Off	Tot	Avg	Pts	Avg
99-00 Mia	53	13	1434	228	560	.407	89	228	.390	84	106	.792	80	41	15	127	2	136	2.6	37	153	2.9	629	11.9
5 Years	249	143	6679	989	2318	.427	473	1184	.399	353	444	.795	318	158	51	563	3	518	2.1	163	730	2.9	2804	11.3

NBA Postseason

Year Tm	G	GS	Min	Md	Att	Pct	Md	Att	Pct	Md	Att	Pct	TO	Stl	Blk	PF	DQ	Ast	Avg	Off	Tot	Avg	Pts	Avg
96-97 Mia	17	17	548	63	155	.406	36	91	.396	32	37	.865	30	11	3	49	0	36	2.1	12	50	2.9	194	11.4
97-98 Mia	5	5	186	24	52	.462	9	26	.346	15	20	.750	11	1	2	20	0	7	1.4	1	19	3.8	72	14.4
98-99 Mia	4	0	57	12	22	.545	9	14	.643	4	4	1.000	1	0	1	4	0	3	0.8	0	1	0.3	37	9.3
3 Years	26	22	791	99	229	.432	54	131	.412	51	61	.836	42	12	6	73	0	46	1.8	13	70	2.7	303	11.7

Quincy Lewis

Pos: G **College:** Minnesota **Drafted:** '99 1(19)—Uta   **Ht:** 6'7" **Wt:** 215 **Born:** 6/26/77 **Age:** 23

College			Field Goals			3-Pt FGs			Free Throws			Misc			Fouls		Assists		Rebounds			Points	
Year Tm	G	GS	Min	Md	Att	Pct	Md	Att	Pct	Md	Att	Pct	TO	Stl	Blk	PF	DQ	Ast	Avg	Off	Tot	Avg	Pts	Avg
95-96 Minn	30	1	407	76	167	.455	26	71	.366	24	36	.667	42	17	11	68	2	35	1.2	15	56	1.9	202	6.7
96-97 Minn	35	0	618	110	230	.478	16	58	.276	45	70	.643	49	44	16	82	3	51	1.5	28	91	2.6	281	8.0
97-98 Minn	35	34	1044	197	431	.457	32	107	.299	80	118	.678	49	68	50	118	8	66	1.9	62	195	5.6	506	14.5
98-99 Minn	27	27	913	226	495	.457	53	133	.398	120	148	.811	56	50	16	78	1	38	1.4	48	160	5.9	625	23.1
4 Years	127	62	2982	609	1323	.460	127	369	.344	269	372	.723	196	179	93	346	14	190	1.5	153	502	4.0	1614	12.7

NBA			Field Goals			3-Pt FGs			Free Throws			Misc			Fouls		Assists		Rebounds			Points	
Year Tm	G	GS	Min	Md	Att	Pct	Md	Att	Pct	Md	Att	Pct	TO	Stl	Blk	PF	DQ	Ast	Avg	Off	Tot	Avg	Pts	Avg
99-00 Uta	74	0	896	111	298	.372	23	63	.365	38	52	.731	46	24	15	158	0	40	0.5	46	113	1.5	283	3.8

NBA Postseason

Year Tm	G	GS	Min	Md	Att	Pct	Md	Att	Pct	Md	Att	Pct	TO	Stl	Blk	PF	DQ	Ast	Avg	Off	Tot	Avg	Pts	Avg
99-00 Uta	8	0	106	10	27	.370	2	6	.333	4	5	.800	3	3	7	24	0	2	0.3	2	15	1.9	26	3.3

Rashard Lewis

(statistical profile on page 240)

Pos: G-F **College:** None **Drafted:** '98 2(32)—Sea   **Ht:** 6'10" **Wt:** 215 **Born:** 8/8/79 **Age:** 21

NBA			Field Goals			3-Pt FGs			Free Throws			Misc			Fouls		Assists		Rebounds			Points	
Year Tm	G	GS	Min	Md	Att	Pct	Md	Att	Pct	Md	Att	Pct	TO	Stl	Blk	PF	DQ	Ast	Avg	Off	Tot	Avg	Pts	Avg
98-99 Sea	20	7	145	19	52	.365	1	6	.167	8	14	.571	20	8	1	19	0	4	0.2	13	25	1.3	47	2.4
99-00 Sea	82	8	1575	275	566	.486	40	120	.333	84	123	.683	78	62	36	163	0	70	0.9	127	336	4.1	674	8.2
2 Years	102	15	1720	294	618	.476	41	126	.325	92	137	.672	98	70	37	182	0	74	0.7	140	361	3.5	721	7.1

NBA Postseason

Year Tm	G	GS	Min	Md	Att	Pct	Md	Att	Pct	Md	Att	Pct	TO	Stl	Blk	PF	DQ	Ast	Avg	Off	Tot	Avg	Pts	Avg
99-00 Sea	5	5	157	26	59	.441	9	19	.474	16	20	.800	10	5	3	11	0	3	0.6	12	31	6.2	77	15.4

Randy Livingston

Pos: G **College:** Louisiana State **Drafted:** '96 2(42)—Hou   **Ht:** 6'5" **Wt:** 209 **Born:** 4/2/75 **Age:** 25

College			Field Goals			3-Pt FGs			Free Throws			Misc			Fouls		Assists		Rebounds			Points	
Year Tm	G	GS	Min	Md	Att	Pct	Md	Att	Pct	Md	Att	Pct	TO	Stl	Blk	PF	DQ	Ast	Avg	Off	Tot	Avg	Pts	Avg
94-95 LSU	16	0	550	81	185	.438	20	65	.308	42	62	.677	86	40	3	39	—	151	9.4	—	64	4.0	224	14.0
95-96 LSU	13	12	318	24	83	.289	1	20	.050	30	38	.789	37	27	2	23	0	69	5.3	7	30	2.3	79	6.1
2 Years	29	12	868	105	268	.392	21	85	.247	72	100	.720	123	67	5	62	—	220	7.6	—	94	3.2	303	10.4

NBA			Field Goals			3-Pt FGs			Free Throws			Misc			Fouls		Assists		Rebounds			Points	
Year Tm	G	GS	Min	Md	Att	Pct	Md	Att	Pct	Md	Att	Pct	TO	Stl	Blk	PF	DQ	Ast	Avg	Off	Tot	Avg	Pts	Avg
96-97 Hou	64	0	981	100	229	.437	9	22	.409	42	65	.646	102	39	12	107	0	155	2.4	32	94	1.5	251	3.9
97-98 Atl	12	0	82	3	12	.250	0	0	—	4	5	.800	6	7	2	6	0	5	0.4	1	6	0.5	10	0.8
98-99 Pho	1	0	22	5	8	.625	0	0	—	2	2	1.000	1	2	0	1	0	3	3.0	0	2	2.0	12	12.0
99-00 Pho	79	15	1081	155	373	.416	19	55	.345	52	62	.839	92	49	13	129	1	170	2.2	25	130	1.6	381	4.2
4 Years	156	15	2166	263	622	.423	28	77	.364	100	134	.746	201	97	27	243	1	333	2.1	58	232	1.5	654	4.2

NBA Postseason

Year Tm	G	GS	Min	Md	Att	Pct	Md	Att	Pct	Md	Att	Pct	TO	Stl	Blk	PF	DQ	Ast	Avg	Off	Tot	Avg	Pts	Avg
96-97 Hou	2	0	15	1	4	.250	1	1	1.000	0	0	—	1	1	0	1	0	4	2.0	0	0	0.0	3	1.5
98-99 Pho	3	0	24	6	15	.400	0	1	.000	4	4	1.000	2	1	0	6	0	2	0.7	5	7	2.3	16	5.3
99-00 Pho	7	3	63	6	27	.222	2	6	.333	0	0	—	4	4	1	6	0	4	0.6	2	7	1.0	14	2.0
3 Years	12	3	102	13	46	.283	3	8	.375	4	4	1.000	7	6	1	13	0	10	0.8	7	14	1.2	33	2.8

Grant Long

Pos: F **College:** Eastern Michigan **Drafted:** '88 2(33)—Mia **Ht:** 6'9" **Wt:** 250 **Born:** 3/12/66 **Age:** 34

College

Year	Tm	G	GS	Min	Md	Att	Pct	Md	Att	Pct	Md	Att	Pct	TO	Stl	Blk	PF	DQ	Ast	Avg	Off	Tot	Avg	Pts	Avg
84-85	EstMi	28	—	551	44	78	.564	—	—	—	28	46	.609	22	17	9	79	—	10	0.4	—	112	4.0	116	4.1
85-86	EstMi	27	—	803	92	175	.526	—	—	—	47	73	.644	52	45	16	75	—	52	1.9	—	178	6.6	231	8.6
86-87	EstMi	29	—	879	169	308	.549	0	0	—	95	131	.725	74	50	30	101	—	83	2.9	—	260	9.0	433	14.9
87-88	EstMi	30	—	1026	237	427	.555	0	0	—	215	281	.765	73	59	10	85	—	66	2.2	—	313	10.4	689	23.0
4 Years		114	—	3259	542	988	.549	0	0	—	385	531	.725	221	171	65	340	—	211	1.9	—	863	7.6	1469	12.9

NBA

Year	Tm	G	GS	Min	Md	Att	Pct	Md	Att	Pct	Md	Att	Pct	TO	Stl	Blk	PF	DQ	Ast	Avg	Off	Tot	Avg	Pts	Avg
88-89	Mia	82	73	2435	336	692	.486	0	5	.000	304	406	.749	201	122	48	337	13	149	1.8	240	546	6.7	976	11.9
89-90	Mia	81	31	1856	257	532	.483	0	3	.000	172	241	.714	139	91	38	300	11	96	1.2	156	402	5.0	686	8.5
90-91	Mia	80	66	2514	276	561	.492	1	6	.167	181	230	.787	156	119	43	295	10	176	2.2	225	568	7.1	734	9.2
91-92	Mia	82	82	3063	440	890	.494	6	22	.273	326	404	.807	185	139	40	248	2	225	2.7	259	691	8.4	1212	14.8
92-93	Mia	76	62	2728	397	847	.469	6	26	.231	261	341	.765	133	104	31	264	8	182	2.4	197	568	7.5	1061	14.0
93-94	Mia	69	59	2201	300	672	.446	1	6	.167	187	238	.786	125	89	26	244	5	170	2.5	190	495	7.2	788	11.4
94-95	2Tm	81	79	2641	342	716	.478	11	31	.355	244	325	.751	155	109	34	243	3	131	1.6	191	606	7.5	939	11.6
95-96	Atl	82	82	3008	395	838	.471	31	86	.360	257	337	.763	157	108	34	233	3	183	2.2	248	788	9.6	1078	13.1
96-97	Det	65	24	1166	123	275	.447	17	47	.362	63	84	.750	48	43	6	106	0	39	0.6	88	222	3.4	326	5.0
97-98	Det	40	17	739	50	117	.427	0	4	.000	41	57	.719	22	29	12	91	2	25	0.6	57	150	3.8	141	3.5
98-99	Atl	50	13	1380	151	359	.421	3	18	.167	184	235	.783	74	57	16	143	0	53	1.1	100	296	5.9	489	9.8
99-00	Van	42	1	920	74	167	.443	0	4	.000	55	71	.775	49	45	10	108	1	43	1.0	86	234	5.6	203	4.8
94-95	Mia	2	2	62	5	12	.417	0	0	—	6	10	.600	4	2	0	11	1	4	2.0	1	11	5.5	16	8.0
	Atl	79	77	2579	337	704	.479	11	31	.355	238	315	.756	151	107	34	232	2	127	1.6	190	595	7.5	923	11.7
12 Years		830	589	24651	3141	6666	.471	76	258	.295	2275	2969	.766	1444	1055	338	2612	58	1472	1.8	2037	5566	6.7	8633	10.4

NBA Postseason

Year	Tm	G	GS	Min	Md	Att	Pct	Md	Att	Pct	Md	Att	Pct	TO	Stl	Blk	PF	DQ	Ast	Avg	Off	Tot	Avg	Pts	Avg
91-92	Mia	3	3	120	15	36	.417	0	4	.000	7	10	.700	5	5	0	11	0	8	2.7	7	15	5.0	37	12.3
93-94	Mia	4	2	110	14	36	.389	0	0	—	21	27	.778	10	3	2	16	1	7	1.8	10	18	4.5	49	12.3
94-95	Atl	3	3	110	14	28	.500	0	1	.000	13	18	.722	8	4	1	11	0	4	1.3	13	34	11.3	41	13.7
95-96	Atl	10	10	362	44	111	.396	6	24	.250	20	25	.800	19	7	3	27	1	28	2.8	30	86	8.6	114	11.4
96-97	Det	5	0	86	8	18	.444	0	2	.000	9	11	.818	0	4	0	11	0	3	0.6	4	11	2.2	25	5.0
98-99	Atl	9	9	358	36	88	.409	1	4	.250	32	44	.727	23	18	4	27	0	8	0.9	28	74	8.2	105	11.7
6 Years		34	27	1146	131	317	.413	7	35	.200	102	135	.756	65	41	10	103	2	58	1.7	92	238	7.0	371	10.9

Luc Longley

Pos: C **College:** New Mexico **Drafted:** '91 1(7)—Min **Ht:** 7'1" **Wt:** 260 **Born:** 1/19/69 **Age:** 32

(statistical profile on page 240)

College

Year	Tm	G	GS	Min	Md	Att	Pct	Md	Att	Pct	Md	Att	Pct	TO	Stl	Blk	PF	DQ	Ast	Avg	Off	Tot	Avg	Pts	Avg
87-88	NM	35	0	424	60	120	.500	0	0	—	20	51	.392	39	10	34	64	0	22	0.6	33	94	2.7	140	4.0
88-89	NM	33	30	966	174	301	.578	0	0	—	80	104	.769	79	25	90	92	0	78	2.4	48	223	6.8	428	13.0
89-90	NM	34	34	1192	233	417	.559	0	0	—	161	196	.821	112	31	117	90	2	108	3.2	61	330	9.7	627	18.4
90-91	NM	30	30	1067	229	349	.656	0	2	.000	116	162	.716	113	26	95	83	1	109	3.6	66	275	9.2	574	19.1
4 Years		132	94	3649	696	1187	.586	0	2	.000	377	513	.735	343	92	336	329	3	317	2.4	208	922	7.0	1769	13.4

NBA

Year	Tm	G	GS	Min	Md	Att	Pct	Md	Att	Pct	Md	Att	Pct	TO	Stl	Blk	PF	DQ	Ast	Avg	Off	Tot	Avg	Pts	Avg
91-92	Min	66	3	991	114	249	.458	0	0	—	53	80	.663	83	35	64	157	0	53	0.8	67	257	3.9	281	4.3
92-93	Min	55	25	1045	133	292	.455	0	0	—	53	74	.716	88	47	77	169	4	51	0.9	71	240	4.4	319	5.8
93-94	2Tm	76	46	1502	219	465	.471	0	1	.000	90	125	.720	119	45	79	216	3	109	1.4	129	433	5.7	528	6.9
94-95	Chi	55	0	1001	135	302	.447	0	2	.000	88	107	.822	86	24	45	177	5	73	1.3	82	263	4.8	358	6.5
95-96	Chi	62	62	1641	242	502	.482	0	0	—	80	103	.777	114	22	84	223	4	119	1.9	104	318	5.1	564	9.1
96-97	Chi	59	59	1472	221	485	.456	0	2	.000	95	120	.792	111	23	66	191	5	141	2.4	121	341	5.8	537	9.1
97-98	Chi	58	58	1703	277	609	.455	0	0	—	109	148	.736	130	34	62	206	7	161	2.8	113	341	5.9	663	11.4
98-99	Pho	39	39	933	140	290	.483	0	0	—	59	76	.776	53	23	21	119	0	45	1.2	59	221	5.7	339	8.7
99-00	Pho	72	68	1417	186	399	.466	0	0	—	80	97	.825	136	22	42	221	1	77	1.1	100	323	4.5	452	6.3
93-94	Min	49	29	989	134	289	.464	0	1	.000	56	80	.700	79	35	58	131	1	46	0.9	87	295	6.0	324	6.6
	Chi	27	17	513	85	176	.483	0	0	—	34	45	.756	40	10	21	85	2	63	2.3	42	138	5.1	204	7.6
9 Years		542	360	11705	1667	3593	.464	0	5	.000	707	930	.760	920	275	540	1679	29	829	1.5	846	2728	5.0	4041	7.5

NBA Postseason

Year	Tm	G	GS	Min	Md	Att	Pct	Md	Att	Pct	Md	Att	Pct	TO	Stl	Blk	PF	DQ	Ast	Avg	Off	Tot	Avg	Pts	Avg
93-94	Min	10	2	170	25	50	.500	0	0	—	13	18	.722	21	6	8	38	0	18	1.8	13	45	4.5	63	6.3
94-95	Chi	10	8	204	24	50	.480	0	0	—	8	10	.800	10	7	5	41	1	11	1.1	6	32	3.2	56	5.6
95-96	Chi	18	18	439	61	130	.469	0	0	—	28	37	.757	38	7	25	83	4	28	1.6	34	82	4.6	150	8.3
96-97	Chi	19	19	432	57	104	.548	0	0	—	10	26	.385	28	7	16	65	0	35	1.8	39	84	4.4	124	6.5

NBA Postseason

Year Tm	G	GS	Min	Md	Att	Pct	Md	Att	Pct	Md	Att	Pct	TO	Stl	Blk	PF	DQ	Ast	Avg	Off	Tot	Avg	Pts	Avg
97-98 Chi	18	16	456	54	120	.450	0	0	—	34	39	.872	36	12	15	73	2	35	1.9	34	90	5.0	142	7.9
98-99 Pho	3	2	51	2	12	.167	0	0	—	0	0	—	2	3	0	2	0	1	0.3	2	9	3.0	4	1.3
99-00 Pho	9	9	162	18	51	.353	0	0	—	2	3	.667	10	4	4	36	1	8	0.9	12	30	3.3	38	4.2
7 Years	87	74	1914	241	517	.466	0	0	—	95	133	.714	145	46	73	338	8	136	1.6	140	372	4.3	577	6.6

Felipe Lopez

Pos: G **College:** St. John's (NY) **Drafted:** '98 1(24)—SA **Ht:** 6'6" **Wt:** 195 **Born:** 12/19/74 **Age:** 26

College				Field Goals			3-Pt FGs			Free Throws			Misc			Fouls		Assists		Rebounds			Points	
Year Tm	G	GS	Min	Md	Att	Pct	Md	Att	Pct	Md	Att	Pct	TO	Stl	Blk	PF	DQ	Ast	Avg	Off	Tot	Avg	Pts	Avg
94-95 StJn	28	28	966	166	404	.411	35	114	.307	131	174	.753	90	41	13	75	0	77	2.8	75	160	5.7	498	17.8
95-96 StJn	27	27	905	156	384	.406	26	100	.260	99	145	.683	85	29	14	62	2	51	1.9	50	168	6.2	437	16.2
96-97 StJn	27	27	955	142	349	.407	27	108	.250	119	192	.620	97	28	12	80	3	61	2.3	79	183	6.8	430	15.9
97-98 StJn	32	32	1108	206	478	.431	60	178	.337	90	157	.573	73	37	24	96	3	85	2.7	62	152	4.8	562	17.6
4 Years	114	114	3934	670	1615	.415	148	500	.296	439	668	.657	345	135	63	313	8	274	2.4	266	663	5.8	1927	16.9

NBA				Field Goals			3-Pt FGs			Free Throws			Misc			Fouls		Assists		Rebounds			Points	
Year Tm	G	GS	Min	Md	Att	Pct	Md	Att	Pct	Md	Att	Pct	TO	Stl	Blk	PF	DQ	Ast	Avg	Off	Tot	Avg	Pts	Avg
98-99 Van	47	32	1218	169	379	.446	12	44	.273	87	135	.644	82	49	14	128	0	62	1.3	69	166	3.5	437	9.3
99-00 Van	65	0	781	111	261	.425	3	18	.167	67	109	.615	53	32	17	94	0	44	0.7	59	124	1.9	292	4.5
2 Years	112	32	1999	280	640	.438	15	62	.242	154	244	.631	135	81	31	222	0	106	0.9	128	290	2.6	729	6.5

Tyronn Lue

Pos: G **College:** Nebraska **Drafted:** '98 1(23)—Den **Ht:** 6'0" **Wt:** 175 **Born:** 5/3/77 **Age:** 23

College				Field Goals			3-Pt FGs			Free Throws			Misc			Fouls		Assists		Rebounds			Points	
Year Tm	G	GS	Min	Md	Att	Pct	Md	Att	Pct	Md	Att	Pct	TO	Stl	Blk	PF	DQ	Ast	Avg	Off	Tot	Avg	Pts	Avg
95-96 Neb	35	34	1033	105	232	.453	20	61	.328	66	96	.688	96	50	2	85	3	144	4.1	—	106	3.0	296	8.5
96-97 Neb	32	30	1150	215	476	.452	47	137	.343	126	155	.813	127	41	0	74	0	136	4.3	13	93	2.9	603	18.8
97-98 Neb	32	32	1149	240	547	.439	78	209	.373	120	145	.828	131	63	3	65	1	152	4.8	28	137	4.3	678	21.2
3 Years	99	96	3332	560	1255	.446	145	407	.356	312	396	.788	354	154	5	224	4	432	4.4	—	336	3.4	1577	15.9

NBA				Field Goals			3-Pt FGs			Free Throws			Misc			Fouls		Assists		Rebounds			Points	
Year Tm	G	GS	Min	Md	Att	Pct	Md	Att	Pct	Md	Att	Pct	TO	Stl	Blk	PF	DQ	Ast	Avg	Off	Tot	Avg	Pts	Avg
98-99 LAL	15	0	188	28	65	.431	7	16	.438	12	21	.571	11	5	0	28	0	25	1.7	2	6	0.4	75	5.0
99-00 LAL	8	0	146	19	39	.487	4	8	.500	6	8	.750	9	3	0	17	0	17	2.1	2	12	1.5	48	6.0
2 Years	23	0	334	47	104	.452	11	24	.458	18	29	.621	20	8	0	45	0	42	1.8	4	18	0.8	123	5.3

NBA Postseason

Year Tm	G	GS	Min	Md	Att	Pct	Md	Att	Pct	Md	Att	Pct	TO	Stl	Blk	PF	DQ	Ast	Avg	Off	Tot	Avg	Pts	Avg
98-99 LAL	3	0	33	7	17	.412	0	2	.000	0	0	—	4	2	0	4	0	6	2.0	0	2	0.7	14	4.7

George Lynch

(statistical profile on page 241)

Pos: F **College:** North Carolina **Drafted:** '93 1(12)—LAL **Ht:** 6'8" **Wt:** 228 **Born:** 9/3/70 **Age:** 30

College				Field Goals			3-Pt FGs			Free Throws			Misc			Fouls		Assists		Rebounds			Points	
Year Tm	G	GS	Min	Md	Att	Pct	Md	Att	Pct	Md	Att	Pct	TO	Stl	Blk	PF	DQ	Ast	Avg	Off	Tot	Avg	Pts	Avg
89-90 UNC	34	5	663	112	215	.521	1	3	.333	67	101	.663	66	37	14	105	—	34	1.0	77	183	5.4	292	8.6
90-91 UNC	35	28	912	172	329	.523	7	10	.700	85	135	.630	86	49	15	91	—	41	1.2	105	258	7.4	436	12.5
91-92 UNC	33	32	982	192	356	.539	1	8	.125	74	114	.649	77	66	10	105	—	86	2.6	111	291	8.8	459	13.9
92-93 UNC	38	37	1148	235	469	.501	2	11	.182	88	132	.667	89	89	21	85	—	72	1.9	138	365	9.6	560	14.7
4 Years	140	102	3705	711	1369	.519	11	32	.344	314	482	.651	318	241	60	386	—	233	1.7	431	1097	7.8	1747	12.5

NBA				Field Goals			3-Pt FGs			Free Throws			Misc			Fouls		Assists		Rebounds			Points	
Year Tm	G	GS	Min	Md	Att	Pct	Md	Att	Pct	Md	Att	Pct	TO	Stl	Blk	PF	DQ	Ast	Avg	Off	Tot	Avg	Pts	Avg
93-94 LAL	71	46	1762	291	573	.508	0	5	.000	99	166	.596	87	102	27	177	1	96	1.4	220	410	5.8	681	9.6
94-95 LAL	56	15	953	138	295	.468	3	21	.143	62	86	.721	73	51	10	86	0	62	1.1	75	184	3.3	341	6.1
95-96 LAL	76	6	1012	117	272	.430	4	13	.308	53	80	.663	40	47	10	106	0	51	0.7	82	209	2.8	291	3.8
96-97 Van	41	27	1059	137	291	.471	8	31	.258	60	97	.619	64	63	17	97	0	76	1.9	98	261	6.4	342	8.3
97-98 Van	82	0	1493	248	516	.481	9	30	.300	111	158	.703	104	65	41	161	0	122	1.5	147	362	4.4	616	7.5
98-99 Phi	43	43	1315	147	349	.421	9	23	.391	53	84	.631	79	85	22	142	2	76	1.8	110	279	6.5	356	8.3
99-00 Phi	75	75	2416	297	644	.461	15	36	.417	113	183	.617	120	119	38	231	2	136	1.8	216	582	7.8	722	9.6
7 Years	444	212	10010	1375	2940	.468	48	159	.302	551	854	.645	567	532	165	1000	6	619	1.4	948	2287	5.2	3349	7.5

NBA Postseason

Year Tm	G	GS	Min	Md	Att	Pct	Md	Att	Pct	Md	Att	Pct	TO	Stl	Blk	PF	DQ	Ast	Avg	Off	Tot	Avg	Pts	Avg
94-95 LAL	10	0	136	15	32	.469	1	5	.200	13	20	.650	9	8	0	22	0	7	0.7	13	30	3.0	44	4.4
95-96 LAL	2	0	15	2	4	.500	0	1	.000	0	0	—	2	0	0	4	0	1	0.5	0	3	1.5	4	2.0

Year Tm	G	GS	Min	Md	Att	Pct	Md	Att	Pct	Md	Att	Pct	TO	Stl	Blk	PF	DQ	Ast	Avg	Off	Tot	Avg	Pts	Avg
98-99 Phi	8	6	249	29	65	.446	2	6	.333	12	17	.706	13	18	2	30	1	16	2.0	28	53	6.6	72	9.0
99-00 Phi	10	10	293	22	65	.338	1	7	.143	14	18	.778	8	9	5	33	1	14	1.4	26	71	7.1	59	5.9
4 Years	30	16	693	68	166	.410	4	19	.211	39	55	.709	32	35	7	89	2	38	1.3	67	157	5.2	179	6.0

Todd MacCulloch

Pos: C **College:** Washington **Drafted:** '99 2(47)—Phi **Ht:** 7'0" **Wt:** 280 **Born:** 1/27/76 **Age:** 25

College				Field Goals			3-Pt FGs			Free Throws			Misc			Fouls		Assists		Rebounds			Points	
Year Tm	G	GS	Min	Md	Att	Pct	Md	Att	Pct	Md	Att	Pct	TO	Stl	Blk	PF	DQ	Ast	Avg	Off	Tot	Avg	Pts	Avg
95-96 Wash	28	15	419	104	154	.675	0	0	—	38	59	.644	26	10	32	77	6	4	0.1	55	134	4.8	246	8.8
96-97 Wash	28	24	614	163	241	.676	0	0	—	72	98	.735	48	17	25	88	4	12	0.4	80	204	7.3	398	14.2
97-98 Wash	30	30	848	225	346	.650	0	0	—	107	152	.704	46	13	38	66	0	11	0.4	94	292	9.7	557	18.6
98-99 Wash	29	29	904	210	317	.662	0	0	—	122	204	.598	42	29	47	74	2	24	0.8	85	345	11.9	542	18.7
4 Years	115	98	2785	702	1058	.664	0	0	—	339	513	.661	162	69	142	305	12	51	0.4	314	975	8.5	1743	15.2

NBA				Field Goals			3-Pt FGs			Free Throws			Misc			Fouls		Assists		Rebounds			Points	
Year Tm	G	GS	Min	Md	Att	Pct	Md	Att	Pct	Md	Att	Pct	TO	Stl	Blk	PF	DQ	Ast	Avg	Off	Tot	Avg	Pts	Avg
99-00 Phi	56	6	528	89	161	.553	0	0	—	28	54	.519	26	11	37	94	0	13	0.2	48	146	2.6	206	3.7

NBA Postseason

Year Tm	G	GS	Min	Md	Att	Pct	Md	Att	Pct	Md	Att	Pct	TO	Stl	Blk	PF	DQ	Ast	Avg	Off	Tot	Avg	Pts	Avg
99-00 Phi	5	0	24	2	3	.667	0	0	—	4	6	.667	0	0	0	2	0	0	0.0	3	9	1.8	8	1.6

Sam Mack

Pos: G-F **College:** Houston **Drafted:** '92 FA—SA **Ht:** 6'7" **Wt:** 220 **Born:** 5/26/70 **Age:** 30

College				Field Goals			3-Pt FGs			Free Throws			Misc			Fouls		Assists		Rebounds			Points	
Year Tm	G	GS	Min	Md	Att	Pct	Md	Att	Pct	Md	Att	Pct	TO	Stl	Blk	PF	DQ	Ast	Avg	Off	Tot	Avg	Pts	Avg
88-89 IaSt	29	—	726	126	273	.462	0	7	.000	89	124	.718	58	25	14	88	—	50	1.7	—	177	6.1	341	11.8
91-92 Hou	31	—	855	178	369	.482	53	134	.396	134	173	.775	67	32	11	82	—	43	1.4	—	181	5.8	543	17.5
2 Years	60	—	1581	304	642	.474	53	141	.376	223	297	.751	125	57	25	170	—	93	1.6	—	358	6.0	884	14.7

NBA				Field Goals			3-Pt FGs			Free Throws			Misc			Fouls		Assists		Rebounds			Points	
Year Tm	G	GS	Min	Md	Att	Pct	Md	Att	Pct	Md	Att	Pct	TO	Stl	Blk	PF	DQ	Ast	Avg	Off	Tot	Avg	Pts	Avg
92-93 SA	40	0	267	47	118	.398	3	22	.136	45	58	.776	22	14	5	44	0	15	0.4	18	48	1.2	142	3.6
93-94										Played in CBA														
94-95										Played in CBA														
95-96 Hou	31	20	868	121	287	.422	54	135	.400	39	46	.848	28	22	9	75	0	79	2.5	18	98	3.2	335	10.8
96-97 Hou	52	10	904	105	262	.401	47	142	.331	35	42	.833	42	29	6	67	0	58	1.1	20	106	2.0	292	5.6
97-98 Van	57	54	1414	222	559	.397	110	269	.409	62	77	.805	69	41	11	117	0	101	1.8	30	133	2.3	616	10.8
98-99 2Tm	44	15	1083	167	384	.435	87	219	.397	51	58	.879	33	35	4	94	1	55	1.3	14	95	2.2	472	10.7
99-00 Hou	23	5	333	37	122	.303	21	64	.328	19	20	.950	19	18	1	45	0	24	1.0	7	39	1.7	114	5.0
98-99 Van	19	15	577	86	212	.406	42	108	.389	28	30	.933	20	20	1	53	1	23	1.2	7	53	2.8	242	12.7
Hou	25	0	506	81	172	.471	45	111	.405	23	28	.821	13	15	3	41	0	32	1.3	7	42	1.7	230	9.2
6 Years	247	104	4869	699	1732	.404	322	851	.378	251	301	.834	213	159	36	442	1	332	1.3	107	519	2.1	1971	8.0

NBA Postseason

Year Tm	G	GS	Min	Md	Att	Pct	Md	Att	Pct	Md	Att	Pct	TO	Stl	Blk	PF	DQ	Ast	Avg	Off	Tot	Avg	Pts	Avg
95-96 Hou	6	0	47	5	15	.333	2	9	.222	0	3	.000	2	1	0	1	0	1	0.2	0	9	1.5	12	2.0
98-99 Hou	4	0	123	13	38	.342	10	26	.385	14	17	.824	5	4	0	11	0	7	1.8	1	9	2.3	50	12.5
2 Years	10	0	170	18	53	.340	12	35	.343	14	20	.700	7	5	0	12	0	8	0.8	1	18	1.8	62	6.2

Don MacLean

Pos: F **College:** UCLA **Drafted:** '92 1(19)—Det **Ht:** 6'10" **Wt:** 235 **Born:** 1/16/70 **Age:** 31

College				Field Goals			3-Pt FGs			Free Throws			Misc			Fouls		Assists		Rebounds			Points	
Year Tm	G	GS	Min	Md	Att	Pct	Md	Att	Pct	Md	Att	Pct	TO	Stl	Blk	PF	DQ	Ast	Avg	Off	Tot	Avg	Pts	Avg
88-89 UCLA	31	31	999	217	391	.555	1	3	.333	142	174	.816	71	16	7	97	5	37	1.2	—	231	7.5	577	18.6
89-90 UCLA	33	33	1111	238	461	.516	1	2	.500	179	211	.848	60	18	16	87	0	35	1.1	—	287	8.7	656	19.9
90-91 UCLA	31	31	1008	259	470	.551	3	13	.231	193	228	.846	79	16	8	60	0	62	2.0	—	226	7.3	714	23.0
91-92 UCLA	32	32	1033	229	454	.504	6	17	.353	197	214	.921	84	17	5	75	0	66	2.1	—	248	7.8	661	20.7
4 Years	127	127	4151	943	1776	.531	11	35	.314	711	827	.860	294	67	36	319	5	200	1.6	—	992	7.8	2608	20.5

NBA				Field Goals			3-Pt FGs			Free Throws			Misc			Fouls		Assists		Rebounds			Points	
Year Tm	G	GS	Min	Md	Att	Pct	Md	Att	Pct	Md	Att	Pct	TO	Stl	Blk	PF	DQ	Ast	Avg	Off	Tot	Avg	Pts	Avg
92-93 Was	62	4	674	157	361	.435	3	6	.500	90	111	.811	42	11	4	82	0	39	0.6	33	122	2.0	407	6.6
93-94 Was	75	69	2487	517	1030	.502	3	21	.143	328	398	.824	152	47	22	169	0	160	2.1	140	467	6.2	1365	18.2
94-95 Was	39	20	1052	158	361	.438	10	40	.250	104	136	.765	44	15	3	97	0	51	1.3	46	165	4.2	430	11.0

NBA			Field Goals			3-Pt FGs			Free Throws			Misc			Fouls		Assists		Rebounds			Points	
Year Tm	G	GS	Min	Md	Att	Pct	Md	Att	Pct	Md	Att	Pct	TO	Stl	Blk	PF	DQ	Ast	Avg	Off	Tot	Avg	Pts	Avg
95-96 Den	56	5	1107	233	547	.426	14	49	.286	145	198	.732	68	21	5	105	1	89	1.6	62	205	3.7	625	11.2
96-97 Phi	37	2	733	163	365	.447	12	38	.316	64	97	.660	47	12	10	71	0	37	1.0	41	140	3.8	402	10.9
97-98 NJ	9	0	42	1	10	.100	1	2	.500	0	0	—	2	0	0	7	0	0	0.0	3	5	0.6	3	0.3
98-99 Sea	17	10	365	63	159	.396	9	33	.273	50	80	.625	25	5	5	34	0	16	0.9	18	65	3.8	185	10.9
99-00 Pho	16	0	143	18	49	.367	2	6	.333	4	6	.667	8	2	1	24	0	8	0.5	6	23	1.4	42	2.6
8 Years	311	110	6603	1310	2882	.455	54	195	.277	785	1026	.765	388	113	50	589	1	400	1.3	349	1192	3.8	3459	11.1

Corey Maggette

(statistical profile on page 241)

Pos: G **College:** Duke **Drafted:** '99 1(13)—Sea   **Ht:** 6'6" **Wt:** 215 **Born:** 11/12/79 **Age:** 21

College			Field Goals			3-Pt FGs			Free Throws			Misc			Fouls		Assists		Rebounds			Points	
Year Tm	G	GS	Min	Md	Att	Pct	Md	Att	Pct	Md	Att	Pct	TO	Stl	Blk	PF	DQ	Ast	Avg	Off	Tot	Avg	Pts	Avg
98-99 Duke	39	3	691	137	261	.525	29	84	.345	111	155	.716	80	29	15	99	3	59	1.5	56	151	3.9	414	10.6

NBA			Field Goals			3-Pt FGs			Free Throws			Misc			Fouls		Assists		Rebounds			Points	
Year Tm	G	GS	Min	Md	Att	Pct	Md	Att	Pct	Md	Att	Pct	TO	Stl	Blk	PF	DQ	Ast	Avg	Off	Tot	Avg	Pts	Avg
99-00 Orl	77	5	1370	224	469	.478	2	11	.182	196	261	.751	138	24	26	169	1	61	0.8	123	303	3.9	646	8.4

Dan Majerle

(statistical profile on page 242)

Pos: G-F **College:** Central Michigan **Drafted:** '88 1(14)—Pho   **Ht:** 6'6" **Wt:** 222 **Born:** 9/9/65 **Age:** 35

College			Field Goals			3-Pt FGs			Free Throws			Misc			Fouls		Assists		Rebounds			Points	
Year Tm	G	GS	Min	Md	Att	Pct	Md	Att	Pct	Md	Att	Pct	TO	Stl	Blk	PF	DQ	Ast	Avg	Off	Tot	Avg	Pts	Avg
84-85 CenMi	12	—	360	92	162	.568	—	—	—	39	67	.582	—	24	9	27	—	24	2.0	—	80	6.7	223	18.6
85-86 CenMi	27	—	1002	228	433	.527	—	—	—	122	170	.718	62	50	22	63	—	51	1.9	—	212	7.9	578	21.4
86-87 CenMi	23	—	824	191	344	.555	2	8	.250	101	183	.552	44	48	35	59	—	53	2.3	—	196	8.5	485	21.1
87-88 CenMi	32	—	1197	279	535	.521	45	101	.446	156	242	.645	—	49	29	77	—	81	2.5	—	346	10.8	759	23.7
4 Years	94	—	3383	790	1474	.536	47	109	.431	418	662	.631	—	171	95	226	—	209	2.2	—	834	8.9	2045	21.8

NBA			Field Goals			3-Pt FGs			Free Throws			Misc			Fouls		Assists		Rebounds			Points	
Year Tm	G	GS	Min	Md	Att	Pct	Md	Att	Pct	Md	Att	Pct	TO	Stl	Blk	PF	DQ	Ast	Avg	Off	Tot	Avg	Pts	Avg
88-89 Pho	54	5	1354	181	432	.419	27	82	.329	78	127	.614	48	63	14	139	1	130	2.4	62	209	3.9	467	8.6
89-90 Pho	73	23	2244	296	698	.424	19	80	.238	198	260	.762	82	100	32	177	5	188	2.6	144	430	5.9	809	11.1
90-91 Pho	77	7	2281	397	821	.484	30	86	.349	227	298	.762	114	106	40	162	0	216	2.8	168	418	5.4	1051	13.6
91-92 Pho*	82	15	2853	551	1153	.478	87	228	.382	229	303	.756	102	131	43	158	0	274	3.3	148	483	5.9	1418	17.3
92-93 Pho*	82	82	3199	509	1096	.464	167	438	.381	203	261	.778	133	138	33	180	0	311	3.8	120	383	4.7	1388	16.9
93-94 Pho	80	76	3207	476	1138	.418	192	503	.382	176	238	.739	137	129	43	153	0	275	3.4	120	349	4.4	1320	16.5
94-95 Pho*	82	46	3091	438	1031	.425	199	548	.363	206	282	.730	105	96	38	155	0	340	4.1	104	375	4.6	1281	15.6
95-96 Cle	82	15	2367	303	748	.405	146	414	.353	120	169	.710	93	81	34	131	0	214	2.6	70	305	3.7	872	10.6
96-97 Mia	36	26	1264	141	347	.406	68	201	.338	40	59	.678	50	54	14	75	0	116	3.2	45	162	4.5	390	10.8
97-98 Mia	72	22	1928	184	439	.419	111	295	.376	40	51	.784	65	68	15	139	2	157	2.2	48	268	3.7	519	7.2
98-99 Mia	48	48	1624	118	298	.396	68	203	.335	33	46	.717	55	38	7	100	0	150	3.1	21	208	4.3	337	7.0
99-00 Mia	69	69	2308	170	422	.403	110	304	.362	56	69	.812	62	89	17	156	1	206	3.0	27	333	4.8	506	7.3
12 Years	837	434	27720	3764	8623	.437	1224	3382	.362	1606	2163	.742	1046	1093	330	1725	9	2577	3.1	1077	3923	4.7	10358	12.4

NBA Postseason																							
Year Tm	G	GS	Min	Md	Att	Pct	Md	Att	Pct	Md	Att	Pct	TO	Stl	Blk	PF	DQ	Ast	Avg	Off	Tot	Avg	Pts	Avg
88-89 Pho	12	0	352	63	144	.438	8	28	.286	38	48	.792	15	13	4	28	0	14	1.2	22	57	4.8	172	14.3
89-90 Pho	16	0	479	73	150	.487	4	12	.333	51	65	.785	18	20	2	34	0	34	2.1	30	81	5.1	201	12.6
90-91 Pho	4	0	110	12	32	.375	4	11	.364	14	19	.737	2	5	1	11	0	7	1.8	6	15	3.8	42	10.5
91-92 Pho	7	0	266	48	111	.432	9	33	.273	25	26	.962	9	10	0	11	0	20	2.9	13	44	6.3	130	18.6
92-93 Pho	24	24	1071	134	311	.431	54	137	.394	48	69	.696	32	33	28	57	0	88	3.7	29	140	5.8	370	15.4
93-94 Pho	10	10	410	46	127	.362	20	59	.339	11	16	.688	10	11	4	23	0	24	2.4	15	43	4.3	123	12.3
94-95 Pho	10	0	307	27	73	.370	16	44	.364	12	17	.706	9	14	3	24	0	17	1.7	8	31	3.1	82	8.2
95-96 Cle	3	0	91	16	36	.444	10	23	.435	8	9	.889	3	4	2	6	0	9	3.0	2	12	4.0	50	16.7
96-97 Mia	17	2	496	46	117	.393	25	74	.338	19	28	.679	13	21	4	31	0	43	2.5	16	72	4.2	136	8.0
97-98 Mia	2	2	62	3	8	.375	2	6	.333	1	2	.500	1	4	1	3	0	5	2.5	1	5	2.5	9	4.5
98-99 Mia	5	5	152	5	26	.192	5	22	.227	5	7	.714	3	5	2	15	0	6	1.2	3	29	5.8	20	4.0
99-00 Mia	10	10	372	30	71	.423	20	50	.400	10	14	.714	11	21	1	34	0	32	3.2	5	70	7.0	90	9.0
12 Years	120	53	4168	503	1206	.417	177	499	.355	242	320	.756	126	161	52	278	0	299	2.5	150	599	5.0	1425	11.9

Karl Malone

(statistical profile on page 242)

Pos: F **College:** Louisiana Tech **Drafted:** '85 1(13)—Uta **Ht:** 6'9" **Wt:** 256 **Born:** 7/24/63 **Age:** 37

College				Field Goals			3-Pt FGs			Free Throws			Misc			Fouls		Assists		Rebounds			Points	
Year Tm	G	GS	Min	Md	Att	Pct	Md	Att	Pct	Md	Att	Pct	TO	Stl	Blk	PF	DQ	Ast	Avg	Off	Tot	Avg	Pts	Avg
82-83 LaTch	28	—	—	217	373	.582	—	—	—	152	244	.623	—	53	—	—	—	10	0.4	—	289	10.3	586	20.9
83-84 LaTch	32	—	—	220	382	.576	—	—	—	161	236	.682	—	—	—	—	—	42	1.3	—	282	8.8	601	18.8
84-85 LaTch	32	—	—	216	399	.541	—	—	—	97	170	.571	—	—	—	—	—	73	2.3	—	288	9.0	529	16.5
3 Years	92	—	—	653	1154	.566	—	—	—	410	650	.631	—	—	—	—	—	125	1.4	—	859	9.3	1716	18.7

NBA				Field Goals			3-Pt FGs			Free Throws			Misc			Fouls		Assists		Rebounds			Points	
Year Tm	G	GS	Min	Md	Att	Pct	Md	Att	Pct	Md	Att	Pct	TO	Stl	Blk	PF	DQ	Ast	Avg	Off	Tot	Avg	Pts	Avg
85-86 Uta	81	76	2475	504	1016	.496	0	2	.000	195	405	.481	279	105	44	295	2	236	2.9	174	718	8.9	1203	14.9
86-87 Uta	82	82	2857	728	1422	.512	0	7	.000	323	540	.598	237	104	60	323	6	158	1.9	278	855	10.4	1779	21.7
87-88 Uta*	82	82	3198	858	1650	.520	0	5	.000	552	789	.700	325	117	50	296	2	199	2.4	277	986	12.0	2268	27.7
88-89 Uta*	80	80	3126	809	1559	.519	5	16	.313	703	918	.766	285	144	70	286	3	219	2.7	259	853	10.7	2326	29.1
89-90 Uta*	82	82	3122	914	1627	.562	16	43	.372	696	913	.762	304	121	50	259	1	226	2.8	232	911	11.1	2540	31.0
90-91 Uta*	82	82	3302	847	1608	.527	4	14	.286	684	888	.770	244	89	79	268	2	270	3.3	236	967	11.8	2382	29.0
91-92 Uta*	81	81	3054	798	1516	.526	3	17	.176	673	865	.778	248	108	51	226	2	241	3.0	225	909	11.2	2272	28.0
92-93 Uta*	82	82	3099	797	1443	.552	4	20	.200	619	836	.740	240	124	85	261	2	308	3.8	227	919	11.2	2217	27.0
93-94 Uta*	82	82	3329	772	1552	.497	8	32	.250	511	736	.694	234	125	126	268	2	328	4.0	235	940	11.5	2063	25.2
94-95 Uta*	82	82	3126	830	1548	.536	11	41	.268	516	695	.742	236	129	85	269	2	285	3.5	156	871	10.6	2187	26.7
95-96 Uta*	82	82	3113	789	1520	.519	16	40	.400	512	708	.723	199	138	56	245	1	345	4.2	175	804	9.8	2106	25.7
96-97 Uta*	82	82	2998	864	1571	.550	0	13	.000	521	690	.755	233	113	48	217	0	368	4.5	193	809	9.9	2249	27.4
97-98 Uta*	81	81	3030	780	1472	.530	2	6	.333	628	825	.761	247	96	70	237	0	316	3.9	189	834	10.3	2190	27.0
98-99 Uta	49	49	1832	393	797	.493	0	1	.000	378	480	.788	162	62	28	134	0	201	4.1	107	463	9.4	1164	23.8
99-00 Uta*	82	82	2947	752	1476	.509	2	8	.250	589	739	.797	231	79	71	229	1	304	3.7	169	779	9.5	2095	25.5
15 Years	1192	1187	44608	11435	21777	.525	71	265	.268	8100	11027	.735	3704	1654	973	3813	26	4004	3.4	3132	12618	10.6	31041	26.0

NBA Postseason

Year Tm	G	GS	Min	Md	Att	Pct	Md	Att	Pct	Md	Att	Pct	TO	Stl	Blk	PF	DQ	Ast	Avg	Off	Tot	Avg	Pts	Avg
85-86 Uta	4	4	144	38	72	.528	0	0	—	11	26	.423	6	8	0	18	1	4	1.0	6	30	7.5	87	21.8
86-87 Uta	5	5	200	37	88	.420	0	0	—	26	36	.722	17	11	4	20	1	6	1.2	15	48	9.6	100	20.0
87-88 Uta	11	11	494	123	255	.482	0	1	.000	81	112	.723	39	13	7	35	0	17	1.5	33	130	11.8	327	29.7
88-89 Uta	3	3	136	33	66	.500	0	0	—	26	32	.813	13	3	1	16	1	4	1.3	22	49	16.3	92	30.7
89-90 Uta	5	5	203	46	105	.438	0	1	.000	34	45	.756	12	11	5	22	1	11	2.2	16	51	10.2	126	25.2
90-91 Uta	9	9	383	95	209	.455	0	8	.000	77	91	.846	26	9	11	35	0	29	3.2	23	120	13.3	267	29.7
91-92 Uta	16	16	688	148	284	.521	0	2	.000	169	210	.805	46	22	19	57	0	42	2.6	43	181	11.3	465	29.1
92-93 Uta	5	5	216	44	97	.454	1	2	.500	31	38	.816	20	6	2	21	0	10	2.0	12	52	10.4	120	24.0
93-94 Uta	16	16	703	158	338	.467	0	4	.000	118	160	.738	34	23	13	59	2	54	3.4	52	198	12.4	434	27.1
94-95 Uta	5	5	216	48	103	.466	1	3	.333	54	78	.692	14	7	2	18	0	19	3.8	15	66	13.2	151	30.2
95-96 Uta	18	18	725	188	401	.469	0	3	.000	101	176	.574	45	34	10	61	0	79	4.4	47	186	10.3	477	26.5
96-97 Uta	20	20	816	187	430	.435	1	2	.500	144	200	.720	54	27	15	59	0	57	2.9	60	228	11.4	519	26.0
97-98 Uta	20	20	795	198	420	.471	0	3	.000	130	165	.788	60	22	20	69	0	68	3.4	47	217	10.9	526	26.3
98-99 Uta	11	11	451	86	206	.417	0	1	.000	68	86	.791	40	13	8	37	0	52	4.7	36	124	11.3	240	21.8
99-00 Uta	10	10	386	103	198	.520	2	2	1.000	64	79	.810	27	7	7	31	0	31	3.1	19	89	8.9	272	27.2
15 Years	158	158	6556	1532	3272	.468	5	32	.156	1134	1534	.739	453	216	124	558	6	483	3.1	446	1769	11.2	4203	26.6

Matt Maloney

Pos: G **College:** Pennsylvania **Drafted:** '96 FA—Hou **Ht:** 6'3" **Wt:** 200 **Born:** 12/6/71 **Age:** 29

College				Field Goals			3-Pt FGs			Free Throws			Misc			Fouls		Assists		Rebounds			Points	
Year Tm	G	GS	Min	Md	Att	Pct	Md	Att	Pct	Md	Att	Pct	TO	Stl	Blk	PF	DQ	Ast	Avg	Off	Tot	Avg	Pts	Avg
90-91 Van	30	—	557	41	100	.410	29	69	.420	11	14	.786	53	24	0	49	—	51	1.7	—	45	1.5	122	4.1
92-93 Penn	27	—	954	148	359	.412	91	205	.444	52	67	.776	61	45	0	57	—	96	3.6	—	88	3.3	439	16.3
93-94 Penn	28	—	918	133	338	.393	66	202	.327	61	68	.897	70	62	2	49	—	105	3.8	—	74	2.6	393	14.0
94-95 Penn	28	28	886	144	314	.459	87	198	.439	41	59	.695	57	50	1	36	0	121	4.3	14	78	2.8	416	14.9
4 Years	113	—	3315	466	1111	.419	273	674	.405	165	208	.793	241	181	3	191	—	373	3.3	—	285	2.5	1370	12.1

NBA				Field Goals			3-Pt FGs			Free Throws			Misc			Fouls		Assists		Rebounds			Points	
Year Tm	G	GS	Min	Md	Att	Pct	Md	Att	Pct	Md	Att	Pct	TO	Stl	Blk	PF	DQ	Ast	Avg	Off	Tot	Avg	Pts	Avg
95-96										Played in CBA														
96-97 Hou	82	82	2386	271	615	.441	154	381	.404	71	93	.763	122	82	1	125	0	303	3.7	19	160	2.0	767	9.4
97-98 Hou	78	78	2217	239	586	.408	126	346	.364	65	78	.833	107	62	5	99	0	219	2.8	16	142	1.8	669	8.6
98-99 Hou	15	7	186	5	28	.179	1	15	.067	10	11	.909	14	4	0	7	0	21	1.4	2	10	0.7	21	1.4
99-00 Chi	51	12	1175	114	318	.358	62	174	.356	37	45	.822	63	32	3	42	0	138	2.7	10	64	1.3	327	6.4
4 Years	226	179	5964	629	1547	.407	343	916	.374	183	227	.806	306	180	9	273	0	681	3.0	47	376	1.7	1784	7.9

NBA Postseason

Year Tm	G	GS	Min	Md	Att	Pct	Md	Att	Pct	Md	Att	Pct	TO	Stl	Blk	PF	DQ	Ast	Avg	Off	Tot	Avg	Pts	Avg
96-97 Hou	16	16	526	61	153	.399	43	108	.398	14	21	.667	38	10	3	31	0	50	3.1	1	19	1.2	179	11.2

NBA Postseason

Year Tm	G	GS	Min	Md	Att	Pct	Md	Att	Pct	Md	Att	Pct	TO	Stl	Blk	PF	DQ	Ast	Avg	Off	Tot	Avg	Pts	Avg
97-98 Hou	5	5	165	10	30	.333	5	20	.250	8	9	.889	4	2	2	11	0	18	3.6	0	8	1.6	33	6.6
2 Years	21	21	691	71	183	.388	48	128	.375	22	30	.733	42	12	5	42	0	68	3.2	1	27	1.3	212	10.1

Danny Manning

(statistical profile on page 243)

Pos: F-C **College:** Kansas **Drafted:** '88 1(1)—LAC **Ht:** 6'10" **Wt:** 244 **Born:** 5/17/66 **Age:** 34

College			Field Goals			3-Pt FGs			Free Throws			Misc			Fouls		Assists		Rebounds			Points	
Year Tm	G	GS	Min	Md	Att	Pct	Md	Att	Pct	Md	Att	Pct	TO	Stl	Blk	PF	DQ	Ast	Avg	Off	Tot	Avg	Pts	Avg
84-85 Kan	34	33	1120	209	369	.566	—	—		78	102	.765	88	58	34	122	7	108	3.2	—	258	7.6	496	14.6
85-86 Kan	39	39	1256	279	465	.600	—	—		95	127	.748	89	80	46	121	4	93	2.4	—	245	6.3	653	16.7
86-87 Kan	36	36	1249	347	562	.617	1	3	.333	165	226	.730	101	42	47	116	5	64	1.8	127	342	9.5	860	23.9
87-88 Kan	38	38	1336	381	653	.583	9	26	.346	171	233	.734	115	70	73	114	5	77	2.0	—	342	9.0	942	24.8
4 Years	147	146	4961	1216	2049	.593	10	29	.345	509	688	.740	393	250	200	473	21	342	2.3	—	1187	8.1	2951	20.1

NBA			Field Goals			3-Pt FGs			Free Throws			Misc			Fouls		Assists		Rebounds			Points	
Year Tm	G	GS	Min	Md	Att	Pct	Md	Att	Pct	Md	Att	Pct	TO	Stl	Blk	PF	DQ	Ast	Avg	Off	Tot	Avg	Pts	Avg
88-89 LAC	26	18	950	177	358	.494	1	5	.200	79	103	.767	93	44	25	89	1	81	3.1	70	171	6.6	434	16.7
89-90 LAC	71	42	2269	440	826	.533	0	5	.000	274	370	.741	188	91	39	261	4	187	2.6	142	422	5.9	1154	16.3
90-91 LAC	73	47	2197	470	905	.519	0	3	.000	219	306	.716	188	117	62	281	5	196	2.7	169	426	5.8	1159	15.9
91-92 LAC	82	82	2904	650	1199	.542	0	5	.000	279	385	.725	210	135	122	293	5	285	3.5	229	564	6.9	1579	19.3
92-93 LAC*	79	77	2761	702	1379	.509	8	30	.267	388	484	.802	230	108	101	323	8	207	2.6	198	520	6.6	1800	22.8
93-94 2Tm*	68	66	2520	586	1201	.488	3	17	.176	228	341	.669	233	99	82	260	2	261	3.8	131	465	6.8	1403	20.6
94-95 Pho	46	19	1510	340	622	.547	6	21	.286	136	202	.673	121	41	57	176	1	154	3.3	97	276	6.0	822	17.9
95-96 Pho	33	4	816	178	388	.459	3	14	.214	82	109	.752	77	38	24	121	2	65	2.0	30	143	4.3	441	13.4
96-97 Pho	77	17	2134	426	795	.536	7	36	.194	181	251	.721	161	81	74	268	7	173	2.2	137	469	6.1	1040	13.5
97-98 Pho	70	11	1794	390	756	.516	0	7	.000	167	226	.739	100	71	46	201	2	139	2.0	110	392	5.6	947	13.5
98-99 Pho	50	5	1184	187	386	.484	1	9	.111	78	112	.696	69	36	38	129	1	113	2.3	62	219	4.4	453	9.1
99-00 Mil	72	0	1217	149	339	.440	1	4	.250	34	52	.654	55	62	29	183	2	73	1.0	50	208	2.9	333	4.6
93-94 LAC	42	41	1595	409	829	.493	2	14	.143	174	258	.674	147	53	57	167	2	176	4.2	82	296	7.0	994	23.7
Atl	26	25	925	177	372	.476	1	3	.333	54	83	.651	86	46	25	93	0	85	3.3	49	169	6.5	409	15.7
12 Years	747	388	22256	4695	9154	.513	30	156	.192	2145	2941	.729	1725	923	699	2585	40	1934	2.6	1425	4275	5.7	11565	15.5

NBA Postseason

Year Tm	G	GS	Min	Md	Att	Pct	Md	Att	Pct	Md	Att	Pct	TO	Stl	Blk	PF	DQ	Ast	Avg	Off	Tot	Avg	Pts	Avg
91-92 LAC	5	5	194	46	81	.568	1	3	.333	20	31	.645	13	5	4	21	1	14	2.8	15	28	5.6	113	22.6
92-93 LAC	5	5	171	35	85	.412	0	2	.000	21	26	.808	13	7	5	19	0	8	1.6	12	36	7.2	91	18.2
93-94 Atl	11	11	426	84	172	.488	0	0	—	52	66	.788	26	15	9	39	0	37	3.4	28	77	7.0	220	20.0
95-96 Pho	4	0	90	22	48	.458	0	1	.000	5	8	.625	6	4	1	15	1	5	1.3	4	11	2.8	49	12.3
96-97 Pho	5	0	116	26	45	.578	0	3	.000	14	15	.933	8	4	7	21	1	7	1.4	4	30	6.0	66	13.2
98-99 Pho	3	1	79	14	24	.583	0	0	—	10	13	.769	3	4	0	12	0	6	2.0	0	5	1.7	38	12.7
99-00 Mil	1	0	5	0	1	.000	0	0	—	0	0	—	0	0	0	0	0	0	0.0	0	1	1.0	0	0.0
7 Years	34	22	1081	227	456	.498	1	9	.111	122	159	.767	69	39	26	127	3	77	2.3	63	188	5.5	577	17.0

Stephon Marbury

(statistical profile on page 243)

Pos: G **College:** Georgia Tech **Drafted:** '96 1(4)—Mil **Ht:** 6'2" **Wt:** 180 **Born:** 2/20/77 **Age:** 23

College			Field Goals			3-Pt FGs			Free Throws			Misc			Fouls		Assists		Rebounds			Points	
Year Tm	G	GS	Min	Md	Att	Pct	Md	Att	Pct	Md	Att	Pct	TO	Stl	Blk	PF	DQ	Ast	Avg	Off	Tot	Avg	Pts	Avg
95-96 GTch	36	35	1345	235	514	.457	88	238	.370	121	164	.738	115	63	4	83	0	161	4.5	34	113	3.1	679	18.9

NBA			Field Goals			3-Pt FGs			Free Throws			Misc			Fouls		Assists		Rebounds			Points	
Year Tm	G	GS	Min	Md	Att	Pct	Md	Att	Pct	Md	Att	Pct	TO	Stl	Blk	PF	DQ	Ast	Avg	Off	Tot	Avg	Pts	Avg
96-97 Min	67	64	2324	355	871	.408	102	288	.354	245	337	.727	210	67	19	159	2	522	7.8	54	184	2.7	1057	15.8
97-98 Min	82	81	3112	513	1237	.415	95	304	.313	329	450	.731	256	104	7	222	0	704	8.6	58	230	2.8	1450	17.7
98-99 2Tm	49	49	1895	378	883	.428	66	197	.335	222	278	.799	164	59	8	125	2	437	8.9	37	142	2.9	1044	21.3
99-00 NJ	74	74	2881	569	1317	.432	66	233	.283	436	536	.813	270	112	15	195	4	622	8.4	61	240	3.2	1640	22.2
98-99 Min	18	18	661	124	304	.408	8	39	.205	63	87	.724	55	29	5	44	0	167	9.3	17	62	3.4	319	17.7
NJ	31	31	1234	254	579	.439	58	158	.367	159	191	.832	109	30	3	81	0	270	8.7	20	80	2.6	725	23.4
4 Years	272	268	10212	1815	4308	.421	329	1022	.322	1232	1601	.770	900	342	49	701	6	2285	8.4	210	796	2.9	5191	19.1

NBA Postseason

Year Tm	G	GS	Min	Md	Att	Pct	Md	Att	Pct	Md	Att	Pct	TO	Stl	Blk	PF	DQ	Ast	Avg	Off	Tot	Avg	Pts	Avg
96-97 Min	3	3	117	26	65	.400	6	20	.300	6	10	.600	9	2	0	9	0	23	7.7	2	12	4.0	64	21.3
97-98 Min	5	5	209	22	72	.306	7	25	.280	18	23	.783	18	12	0	16	0	38	7.6	5	16	3.2	69	13.8
2 Years	8	8	326	48	137	.350	13	45	.289	24	33	.727	27	14	0	25	0	61	7.6	7	28	3.5	133	16.6

Shawn Marion

Pos: F **College:** UNLV **Drafted:** '99 1(9)—Pho   **Ht:** 6'7" **Wt:** 215 **Born:** 5/7/78 **Age:** 22   (statistical profile on page 244)

College			Field Goals			3-Pt FGs			Free Throws			Misc			Fouls		Assists		Rebounds			Points	
Year Tm	G	GS	Min	Md	Att	Pct	Md	Att	Pct	Md	Att	Pct	TO	Stl	Blk	PF	DQ	Ast	Avg	Off	Tot	Avg	Pts	Avg
98-99 UNLV	29	28	954	221	418	.529	20	67	.299	81	111	.730	41	73	54	60	1	36	1.2	97	269	9.3	543	18.7

NBA			Field Goals			3-Pt FGs			Free Throws			Misc			Fouls		Assists		Rebounds			Points	
Year Tm	G	GS	Min	Md	Att	Pct	Md	Att	Pct	Md	Att	Pct	TO	Stl	Blk	PF	DQ	Ast	Avg	Off	Tot	Avg	Pts	Avg
99-00 Pho	51	38	1260	222	471	.471	4	22	.182	72	85	.847	51	38	53	113	0	69	1.4	105	332	6.5	520	10.2

NBA Postseason																							
Year Tm	G	GS	Min	Md	Att	Pct	Md	Att	Pct	Md	Att	Pct	TO	Stl	Blk	PF	DQ	Ast	Avg	Off	Tot	Avg	Pts	Avg
99-00 Pho	9	9	281	36	86	.419	1	6	.167	9	11	.818	7	6	14	17	0	7	0.8	21	79	8.8	82	9.1

Sean Marks

Pos: F **College:** California **Drafted:** '98 2(44)—NY   **Ht:** 6'10" **Wt:** 250 **Born:** 8/23/75 **Age:** 25

College			Field Goals			3-Pt FGs			Free Throws			Misc			Fouls		Assists		Rebounds			Points	
Year Tm	G	GS	Min	Md	Att	Pct	Md	Att	Pct	Md	Att	Pct	TO	Stl	Blk	PF	DQ	Ast	Avg	Off	Tot	Avg	Pts	Avg
94-95 Cal	19	0	177	22	43	.512	0	0	—	13	24	.542	15	5	12	27	1	5	0.3		14	0.7	57	3.0
95-96 Cal	12	0	92	6	22	.273	0	0	—	1	1	1.000	7	1	5	17	0	3	0.3	6	24	2.0	13	1.1
96-97 Cal	29	15	513	90	173	.520	8	14	.571	43	63	.683	43	15	29	58	1	20	0.7	66	143	4.9	231	8.0
97-98 Cal	26	18	678	96	201	.478	2	11	.182	62	90	.689	60	27	24	73	2	19	0.7	64	197	7.6	256	9.8
4 Years	86	33	1460	214	439	.487	10	25	.400	119	178	.669	125	48	70	175	4	47	0.5		378	4.4	557	6.5

NBA			Field Goals			3-Pt FGs			Free Throws			Misc			Fouls		Assists		Rebounds			Points	
Year Tm	G	GS	Min	Md	Att	Pct	Md	Att	Pct	Md	Att	Pct	TO	Stl	Blk	PF	DQ	Ast	Avg	Off	Tot	Avg	Pts	Avg
98-99 Tor	8	0	28	5	8	.625	0	0	—	1	2	.500	3	1	0	3	0	0	0.0	0	1	0.1	11	1.4
99-00 Tor	5	0	12	2	6	.333	0	1	.000	4	4	1.000	3	1	1	3	0	0	0.0	0	2	0.4	8	1.6
2 Years	13	0	40	7	14	.500	0	1	.000	5	6	.833	6	2	1	6	0	0	0.0	0	3	0.2	19	1.5

Donny Marshall

Pos: F **College:** Connecticut **Drafted:** '95 2(39)—Cle   **Ht:** 6'7" **Wt:** 230 **Born:** 7/17/72 **Age:** 28

College			Field Goals			3-Pt FGs			Free Throws			Misc			Fouls		Assists		Rebounds			Points	
Year Tm	G	GS	Min	Md	Att	Pct	Md	Att	Pct	Md	Att	Pct	TO	Stl	Blk	PF	DQ	Ast	Avg	Off	Tot	Avg	Pts	Avg
91-92 Conn	27	1	241	17	46	.370	0	0	—	17	24	.708	12	10	0	38	—	10	0.4		43	1.6	51	1.9
92-93 Conn	28	22	677	81	174	.466	1	3	.333	54	71	.761	54	32	4	85	—	31	1.1		118	4.2	217	7.8
93-94 Conn	34	34	1001	152	294	.517	23	64	.359	96	124	.774	76	48	8	81	—	44	1.3	65	186	5.5	423	12.4
94-95 Conn	32	32	976	173	379	.456	24	92	.261	136	164	.829	72	37	5	72	—	44	1.4		187	5.8	506	15.8
4 Years	121	89	2895	423	893	.474	48	159	.302	303	383	.791	214	127	17	276	—	129	1.1		534	4.4	1197	9.9

NBA			Field Goals			3-Pt FGs			Free Throws			Misc			Fouls		Assists		Rebounds			Points	
Year Tm	G	GS	Min	Md	Att	Pct	Md	Att	Pct	Md	Att	Pct	TO	Stl	Blk	PF	DQ	Ast	Avg	Off	Tot	Avg	Pts	Avg
95-96 Cle	34	0	208	24	68	.353	7	30	.233	22	35	.629	7	8	2	26	0	7	0.2	9	26	0.8	77	2.3
96-97 Cle	56	0	548	52	160	.325	33	87	.379	38	54	.704	32	24	3	60	0	24	0.4	22	70	1.3	175	3.1
97-98							Did not play in NBA																	
98-99							Played in Italy																	
99-00 Cle	6	0	39	3	11	.273	0	3	.000	5	6	.833	3	2	0	7	0	0	0.0	0	1	0.2	11	1.8
3 Years	96	0	795	79	239	.331	40	120	.333	65	95	.684	42	34	5	93	0	31	0.3	31	97	1.0	263	2.7

NBA Postseason																							
Year Tm	G	GS	Min	Md	Att	Pct	Md	Att	Pct	Md	Att	Pct	TO	Stl	Blk	PF	DQ	Ast	Avg	Off	Tot	Avg	Pts	Avg
95-96 Cle	1	0	1	0	0	—	0	0	—	0	0	—	0	0	0	0	0	0	0.0	0	0	0.0	0	0.0

Donyell Marshall

Pos: F **College:** Connecticut **Drafted:** '94 1(4)—Min   **Ht:** 6'9" **Wt:** 230 **Born:** 5/18/73 **Age:** 27   (statistical profile on page 244)

College			Field Goals			3-Pt FGs			Free Throws			Misc			Fouls		Assists		Rebounds			Points	
Year Tm	G	GS	Min	Md	Att	Pct	Md	Att	Pct	Md	Att	Pct	TO	Stl	Blk	PF	DQ	Ast	Avg	Off	Tot	Avg	Pts	Avg
91-92 Conn	30	28	806	125	295	.424	15	62	.242	69	93	.742	84	31	78	93	—	45	1.5		183	6.1	334	11.1
92-93 Conn	27	26	854	166	332	.500	20	54	.370	107	129	.829	59	14	56	61	—	30	1.1		210	7.8	459	17.0
93-94 Conn	34	34	1157	306	599	.511	41	132	.311	200	266	.752	98	43	108	70	1	56	1.6	100	302	8.9	853	25.1
3 Years	91	88	2817	597	1226	.487	76	248	.306	376	488	.770	241	88	242	224	—	131	1.4		695	7.6	1646	18.1

NBA			Field Goals			3-Pt FGs			Free Throws			Misc			Fouls		Assists		Rebounds			Points	
Year Tm	G	GS	Min	Md	Att	Pct	Md	Att	Pct	Md	Att	Pct	TO	Stl	Blk	PF	DQ	Ast	Avg	Off	Tot	Avg	Pts	Avg
94-95 2Tm	72	31	2086	345	876	.394	69	243	.284	147	222	.662	115	45	88	157	1	105	1.5	137	405	5.6	906	12.6
95-96 GS	62	6	934	125	314	.398	28	94	.298	64	83	.771	48	22	31	83	0	49	0.8	65	213	3.4	342	5.5

(player name not shown)

	NBA			Field Goals			3-Pt FGs			Free Throws			Misc			Fouls		Assists		Rebounds			Points	
Year Tm	G	GS	Min	Md	Att	Pct	Md	Att	Pct	Md	Att	Pct	TO	Stl	Blk	PF	DQ	Ast	Avg	Off	Tot	Avg	Pts	Avg
96-97 GS	61	20	1022	174	421	.413	35	111	.315	61	98	.622	55	25	46	96	0	54	0.9	92	276	4.5	444	7.3
97-98 GS	73	73	2611	451	1091	.413	63	201	.313	158	216	.731	147	95	73	226	1	159	2.2	210	628	8.6	1123	15.4
98-99 GS	48	20	1250	208	494	.421	26	72	.361	88	121	.727	80	47	37	123	1	66	1.4	115	342	7.1	530	11.0
99-00 GS	64	51	2071	331	840	.394	49	138	.355	199	255	.780	123	68	68	180	1	167	2.6	189	637	10.0	910	14.2
94-95 Min	40	8	1036	158	423	.374	32	106	.302	83	122	.680	58	25	50	63	0	57	1.4	64	196	4.9	910	14.2
GS	32	23	1050	187	453	.413	37	137	.270	64	100	.640	57	20	38	94	1	48	1.5	73	209	6.5	475	14.8
6 Years	380	201	9974	1634	4036	.405	270	859	.314	717	995	.721	568	302	343	865	4	600	1.6	808	2501	6.6	4255	11.2

Darrick Martin

Pos: G **College:** UCLA **Drafted:** '94 FA—Min **Ht:** 5'11" **Wt:** 170 **Born:** 3/6/71 **Age:** 29

	College			Field Goals			3-Pt FGs			Free Throws			Misc			Fouls		Assists		Rebounds			Points	
Year Tm	G	GS	Min	Md	Att	Pct	Md	Att	Pct	Md	Att	Pct	TO	Stl	Blk	PF	DQ	Ast	Avg	Off	Tot	Avg	Pts	Avg
88-89 UCLA	31	22	929	92	203	.453	13	37	.351	68	91	.747	56	53	1	90	4	90	2.9	—	59	1.9	265	8.5
89-90 UCLA	33	33	1069	132	283	.466	20	63	.317	90	126	.714	82	46	1	96	3	199	6.0	—	71	2.2	374	11.3
90-91 UCLA	32	32	1030	129	278	.464	23	79	.291	90	120	.750	77	46	2	76	2	217	6.8	—	77	2.4	371	11.6
91-92 UCLA	33	9	642	52	120	.433	13	35	.371	68	82	.829	50	34	3	69	2	130	3.9	—	43	1.3	185	5.6
4 Years	129	96	3670	405	884	.458	69	214	.322	316	419	.754	265	179	7	331	11	636	4.9	—	250	1.9	1195	9.3

	NBA			Field Goals			3-Pt FGs			Free Throws			Misc			Fouls		Assists		Rebounds			Points	
Year Tm	G	GS	Min	Md	Att	Pct	Md	Att	Pct	Md	Att	Pct	TO	Stl	Blk	PF	DQ	Ast	Avg	Off	Tot	Avg	Pts	Avg
92-93							Played with Magic Johnson All-Stars																	
93-94							Played with Magic Johnson All-Stars																	
94-95 Min	34	9	803	95	233	.408	7	38	.184	57	65	.877	62	34	0	88	0	133	3.9	14	64	1.9	254	7.5
95-96 2Tm	59	16	1149	147	362	.406	20	69	.290	101	120	.842	107	53	3	123	0	217	3.7	16	82	1.4	415	7.0
96-97 LAC	82	64	1820	292	718	.407	91	234	.389	218	250	.872	127	57	2	165	1	339	4.1	26	113	1.4	893	10.9
97-98 LAC	82	63	2299	275	730	.377	107	293	.365	184	217	.848	154	82	10	198	2	331	4.0	19	164	2.0	841	10.3
98-99 LAC	37	25	941	102	278	.367	31	106	.292	61	76	.803	67	43	4	82	1	144	3.9	5	48	1.3	296	8.0
99-00 Sac	71	1	893	133	350	.380	38	124	.306	98	119	.824	62	28	2	89	0	122	1.7	7	44	0.6	402	5.7
95-96 Van	24	0	402	59	131	.450	5	22	.227	38	46	.826	37	27	1	47	0	61	2.5	13	38	1.6	161	6.7
Min	35	16	747	88	231	.381	15	47	.319	63	74	.851	70	26	2	76	0	156	4.5	3	44	1.3	254	7.3
6 Years	365	178	7905	1044	2671	.391	294	864	.340	719	847	.849	579	297	21	745	4	1286	3.5	87	515	1.4	3101	8.5

	NBA Postseason			Field Goals			3-Pt FGs			Free Throws			Misc			Fouls		Assists		Rebounds			Points	
Year Tm	G	GS	Min	Md	Att	Pct	Md	Att	Pct	Md	Att	Pct	TO	Stl	Blk	PF	DQ	Ast	Avg	Off	Tot	Avg	Pts	Avg
96-97 LAC	3	3	77	11	25	.440	5	9	.556	6	9	.667	2	0	0	9	0	13	4.3	1	2	0.7	33	11.0
99-00 Sac	2	0	21	3	9	.333	1	3	.333	3	4	.750	3	1	0	4	0	2	1.0	1	3	1.5	10	5.0
2 Years	5	3	98	14	34	.412	6	12	.500	9	13	.692	5	1	0	13	0	15	3.0	2	5	1.0	43	8.6

Jamal Mashburn

Pos: F **College:** Kentucky **Drafted:** '93 1(4)—Dal   (statistical profile on page 245) **Ht:** 6'8" **Wt:** 241 **Born:** 11/29/72 **Age:** 28

	College			Field Goals			3-Pt FGs			Free Throws			Misc			Fouls		Assists		Rebounds			Points	
Year Tm	G	GS	Min	Md	Att	Pct	Md	Att	Pct	Md	Att	Pct	TO	Stl	Blk	PF	DQ	Ast	Avg	Off	Tot	Avg	Pts	Avg
90-91 Kty	28	—	677	137	289	.474	24	82	.293	64	88	.727	56	37	15	91	—	42	1.5	—	195	7.0	362	12.9
91-92 Kty	36	—	1176	279	492	.567	58	132	.439	151	213	.709	84	65	23	123	—	52	1.4	—	281	7.8	767	21.3
92-93 Kty	34	34	1109	259	526	.492	66	180	.367	130	194	.670	103	51	15	92	—	124	3.6	—	284	8.4	714	21.0
3 Years		—	2962	675	1307	.516	148	394	.376	345	495	.697	243	153	53	306	—	218	2.2	—	760	7.8	1843	18.8

	NBA			Field Goals			3-Pt FGs			Free Throws			Misc			Fouls		Assists		Rebounds			Points	
Year Tm	G	GS	Min	Md	Att	Pct	Md	Att	Pct	Md	Att	Pct	TO	Stl	Blk	PF	DQ	Ast	Avg	Off	Tot	Avg	Pts	Avg
93-94 Dal	79	73	2896	561	1382	.406	85	299	.284	306	438	.699	245	89	14	205	0	266	3.4	107	353	4.5	1513	19.2
94-95 Dal	80	80	2980	683	1566	.436	113	344	.328	447	605	.739	235	82	8	190	0	298	3.7	116	331	4.1	1926	24.1
95-96 Dal	18	18	669	145	383	.379	35	102	.343	97	133	.729	55	14	3	39	0	50	2.8	37	97	5.4	422	23.4
96-97 2Tm	69	51	2164	286	743	.385	90	277	.325	160	228	.702	114	78	12	186	4	204	3.0	69	294	4.3	822	11.9
97-98 Mia	48	48	1729	251	577	.435	37	122	.303	184	231	.797	108	43	14	137	1	132	2.8	72	236	4.9	723	15.1
98-99 Mia	24	23	855	134	297	.451	13	30	.433	75	104	.721	60	20	3	58	0	75	3.1	24	146	6.1	356	14.8
99-00 Mia	76	76	2828	515	1158	.445	112	278	.403	186	239	.778	180	79	14	215	3	298	3.9	64	381	5.0	1328	17.5
96-97 Dal	37	21	975	140	376	.372	42	131	.321	72	111	.649	57	35	5	69	0	93	2.5	28	115	3.1	394	10.6
Mia	32	30	1189	146	367	.398	48	146	.329	88	117	.752	57	43	7	117	4	111	3.5	41	179	5.6	428	13.4
7 Years	394	369	14121	2575	6106	.422	485	1452	.334	1456	1978	.736	997	405	68	1030	8	1323	3.4	489	1838	4.7	7090	18.0

	NBA Postseason			Field Goals			3-Pt FGs			Free Throws			Misc			Fouls		Assists		Rebounds			Points	
Year Tm	G	GS	Min	Md	Att	Pct	Md	Att	Pct	Md	Att	Pct	TO	Stl	Blk	PF	DQ	Ast	Avg	Off	Tot	Avg	Pts	Avg
96-97 Mia	17	17	554	65	168	.387	22	62	.355	26	40	.650	30	17	2	58	2	35	2.1	22	84	4.9	178	10.5
97-98 Mia	5	3	129	12	45	.267	4	11	.364	3	4	.750	9	3	1	21	0	9	1.8	4	22	4.4	31	6.2
98-99 Mia	5	5	152	19	49	.388	6	14	.429	6	9	.667	12	2	0	11	0	10	2.0	4	22	4.4	50	10.0
99-00 Mia	10	10	423	63	157	.401	13	33	.394	36	42	.857	24	11	2	30	0	32	3.2	9	46	4.6	175	17.5
4 Years	37	35	1258	159	419	.379	45	120	.375	71	95	.747	73	33	5	120	4	86	2.3	39	165	4.5	434	11.7

(statistical profile on page 245)

Anthony Mason

Pos: F **College:** Tennessee State **Drafted:** '88 3(53)—Por   **Ht:** 6'8" **Wt:** 250 **Born:** 12/14/66 **Age:** 34

College

Year Tm	G	GS	Min	FG Md	Att	Pct	3P Md	Att	Pct	FT Md	Att	Pct	TO	Stl	Blk	PF	DQ	Ast	Avg	Off	Tot	Avg	Pts	Avg
84-85 TnSt	28	—	801	100	213	.469	—	—	—	79	122	.648	70	20	4	74	—	46	1.6	—	148	5.3	279	10.0
85-86 TnSt	28	—	913	206	427	.482	—	—	—	93	130	.715	81	30	4	58	—	69	2.5	—	192	6.9	505	18.0
86-87 TnSt	27	—	951	201	449	.448	17	49	.347	89	135	.659	74	34	13	70	—	68	2.5	—	262	9.7	508	18.8
87-88 TnSt	28	—	1064	276	608	.454	40	81	.494	191	247	.773	106	56	20	73	—	85	3.0	—	292	10.4	783	28.0
4 Years	111	—	3729	783	1697	.461	57	130	.438	452	634	.713	331	140	41	275	—	268	2.4	—	894	8.1	2075	18.7

NBA

Year Tm	G	GS	Min	FG Md	Att	Pct	3P Md	Att	Pct	FT Md	Att	Pct	TO	Stl	Blk	PF	DQ	Ast	Avg	Off	Tot	Avg	Pts	Avg
88-89	Played in Turkey																							
89-90 NJ	21	0	108	14	40	.350	0	0	—	9	15	.600	11	2	2	20	0	7	0.3	11	34	1.6	37	1.8
90-91 Den	3	0	21	2	4	.500	0	0	—	6	8	.750	0	1	0	6	0	0	0.0	3	5	1.7	10	3.3
91-92 NY	82	0	2198	203	399	.509	0	0	—	167	260	.642	101	46	20	229	0	106	1.3	216	573	7.0	573	7.0
92-93 NY	81	0	2482	316	629	.502	0	0	—	199	292	.682	137	43	19	240	2	170	2.1	231	640	7.9	831	10.3
93-94 NY	73	12	1903	206	433	.476	0	1	.000	116	161	.720	107	31	9	190	2	151	2.1	158	427	5.8	528	7.2
94-95 NY	77	11	2496	287	507	.566	0	1	.000	191	298	.641	123	69	21	253	0	240	3.1	182	650	8.4	765	9.9
95-96 NY	82	82	3457	449	798	.563	0	0	—	298	414	.720	211	69	34	246	3	363	4.4	220	764	9.3	1196	14.6
96-97 Cha	73	73	3143	433	825	.525	1	3	.333	319	428	.745	165	76	33	202	3	414	5.7	186	829	11.4	1186	16.2
97-98 Cha	81	80	3148	389	764	.509	0	4	.000	261	402	.649	146	68	18	182	1	342	4.2	177	826	10.2	1039	12.8
98-99	Did not play: injury — Right Biceps																							
99-00 Cha	82	81	3133	317	661	.480	0	1	.000	314	421	.746	160	74	29	220	0	367	4.5	145	699	8.5	948	11.6
10 Years	655	339	22089	2616	5060	.517	1	10	.100	1880	2699	.697	1161	479	185	1788	14	2160	3.3	1529	5447	8.3	7113	10.9

NBA Postseason

Year Tm	G	GS	Min	FG Md	Att	Pct	3P Md	Att	Pct	FT Md	Att	Pct	TO	Stl	Blk	PF	DQ	Ast	Avg	Off	Tot	Avg	Pts	Avg
91-92 NY	12	0	288	19	43	.442	0	0	—	22	28	.786	11	2	8	34	0	10	0.8	28	76	6.3	60	5.0
92-93 NY	15	0	510	72	122	.590	0	0	—	43	68	.632	23	10	6	50	2	41	2.7	55	109	7.3	187	12.5
93-94 NY	25	0	660	67	137	.489	0	0	—	55	77	.714	36	15	5	66	0	46	1.8	53	146	5.8	189	7.6
94-95 NY	11	0	352	31	51	.608	0	1	.000	43	69	.623	26	6	6	28	0	24	2.2	23	68	6.2	105	9.5
95-96 NY	8	8	350	41	78	.526	0	0	—	19	28	.679	20	4	1	20	0	26	3.3	17	62	7.8	101	12.6
96-97 Cha	3	3	131	16	38	.421	0	0	—	7	13	.538	9	1	1	6	0	9	3.0	8	36	12.0	39	13.0
97-98 Cha	9	9	367	57	99	.576	0	1	.000	25	42	.595	22	8	0	17	0	31	3.4	17	71	7.9	139	15.4
99-00 Cha	4	4	179	18	38	.474	0	1	.000	14	20	.700	13	4	0	13	0	22	5.5	16	39	9.8	50	12.5
8 Years	87	24	2837	321	606	.530	0	3	.000	228	345	.661	160	50	27	234	2	209	2.4	217	607	7.0	870	10.0

Tony Massenburg

Pos: F-C **College:** Maryland **Drafted:** '90 2(43)—SA   **Ht:** 6'9" **Wt:** 250 **Born:** 7/31/67 **Age:** 33

College

Year Tm	G	GS	Min	FG Md	Att	Pct	3P Md	Att	Pct	FT Md	Att	Pct	TO	Stl	Blk	PF	DQ	Ast	Avg	Off	Tot	Avg	Pts	Avg
85-86 Myld	29	8	349	28	56	.500	—	—	—	27	48	.563	13	9	11	49	—	0	0.0	—	60	2.1	83	2.9
87-88 Myld	23	16	616	93	179	.520	0	0	—	47	82	.573	40	9	22	67	—	10	0.4	65	122	5.3	233	10.1
88-89 Myld	29	29	1001	197	358	.550	0	1	.000	87	145	.600	69	15	27	90	—	21	0.7	85	226	7.8	481	16.6
89-90 Myld	31	30	973	206	408	.505	0	2	.000	145	201	.721	65	28	37	94	—	20	0.6	120	314	10.1	557	18.0
4 Years	112	83	2939	524	1001	.523	0	3	.000	306	476	.643	187	61	97	300	—	51	0.5	270	722	6.4	1354	12.1

NBA

Year Tm	G	GS	Min	FG Md	Att	Pct	3P Md	Att	Pct	FT Md	Att	Pct	TO	Stl	Blk	PF	DQ	Ast	Avg	Off	Tot	Avg	Pts	Avg
90-91 SA	35	0	161	27	60	.450	0	0	—	28	45	.622	13	4	9	26	0	4	0.1	23	58	1.7	82	2.3
91-92 4Tm	18	0	90	10	25	.400	0	0	—	9	15	.600	9	1	1	21	0	0	0.0	7	25	1.4	29	1.6
92-93	Played in Spain																							
93-94	Played in Spain																							
94-95 LAC	80	50	2127	282	601	.469	0	3	.000	177	235	.753	118	48	58	253	2	67	0.8	160	455	5.7	741	9.3
95-96 2Tm	54	28	1463	214	432	.495	0	3	.000	111	157	.707	73	28	20	140	0	30	0.6	127	352	6.5	539	10.0
96-97 NJ	79	49	1954	219	452	.485	0	1	.000	130	206	.631	91	38	50	217	2	23	0.3	222	517	6.5	568	7.2
97-98 Van	61	19	894	148	309	.479	0	0	—	100	137	.730	60	25	24	123	0	21	0.3	80	232	3.8	396	6.5
98-99 Van	43	35	1143	189	388	.487	0	2	.000	103	155	.665	64	26	39	108	0	23	0.5	83	257	6.0	481	11.2
99-00 Hou	10	0	109	16	36	.444	0	0	—	14	16	.875	9	2	5	13	0	3	0.3	7	27	2.7	46	4.6
91-92 SA	1	0	9	1	5	.200	0	0	—	0	0	—	0	0	0	2	0	0	0.0	1	4	1.3	2	2.0
Cha	3	0	13	0	3	.000				1	2	.500	4	1	0	7	0	0	0.0	2	9	1.3	1	0.3
Bos	7	0	46	4	9	.444				2	4	.500	2	0	1	7	0	0	0.0	4	12	1.7	10	1.4
GS	7	0	22	5	8	.625				6	9	.667	3	0	0	10	0	0	0.0	4	12	1.7	16	2.3
95-96 Tor	24	20	659	100	196	.510	0	3	.000	43	65	.662	35	13	9	67	0	18	0.8	52	166	6.9	243	10.1
Phi	30	8	804	114	236	.483	0	3	.000	68	92	.739	38	15	11	73	0	12	0.4	75	186	6.2	296	9.9
8 Years	380	175	7941	1105	2303	.480	0	9	.000	672	966	.696	437	172	206	901	4	171	0.5	709	1923	5.1	2882	7.6

NBA Postseason

Year Tm	G	GS	Min	FG Md	Att	Pct	3P Md	Att	Pct	FT Md	Att	Pct	TO	Stl	Blk	PF	DQ	Ast	Avg	Off	Tot	Avg	Pts	Avg
90-91 SA	1	0	1	0	0	—	0	0	—	0	0	—	0	0	0	0	0	0	0.0	0	0	0.0	0	0.0

Vernon Maxwell

Pos: G **College:** Florida **Drafted:** '88 2(47)—Den **Ht:** 6'4" **Wt:** 190 **Born:** 9/12/65 **Age:** 35

College				Field Goals			3-Pt FGs			Free Throws			Misc			Fouls		Assists		Rebounds			Points	
Year Tm	G	GS	Min	Md	Att	Pct	Md	Att	Pct	Md	Att	Pct	TO	Stl	Blk	PF	DQ	Ast	Avg	Off	Tot	Avg	Pts	Avg
84-85 Fla	30	—	752	163	366	.445	—	—	—	72	105	.686	49	29	1	68	—	40	1.3	—	72	2.4	398	13.3
85-86 Fla	33	—	1142	262	566	.463	—	—	—	124	177	.701	89	47	14	80	—	81	2.5	—	147	4.5	648	19.6
86-87 Fla	34	—	1086	266	548	.485	45	128	.352	161	217	.742	81	69	3	88	—	123	3.6	—	125	3.7	738	21.7
87-88 Fla	33	—	1214	230	515	.447	58	147	.395	148	207	.715	92	61	3	63	—	142	4.3	—	138	4.2	666	20.2
4 Years	130	—	4194	921	1995	.462	103	275	.375	505	706	.715	311	206	21	299	—	386	3.0	—	482	3.7	2450	18.8

NBA				Field Goals			3-Pt FGs			Free Throws			Misc			Fouls		Assists		Rebounds			Points	
Year Tm	G	GS	Min	Md	Att	Pct	Md	Att	Pct	Md	Att	Pct	TO	Stl	Blk	PF	DQ	Ast	Avg	Off	Tot	Avg	Pts	Avg
88-89 SA	79	36	2065	357	827	.432	32	129	.248	181	243	.745	178	86	8	136	0	301	3.8	49	202	2.6	927	11.7
89-90 2Tm	79	12	1987	275	627	.439	28	105	.267	136	211	.645	143	84	10	148	0	296	3.7	50	228	2.9	714	9.0
90-91 Hou	82	79	2870	504	1247	.404	172	510	.337	217	296	.733	171	127	15	179	2	303	3.7	41	238	2.9	1397	17.0
91-92 Hou	80	80	2700	502	1216	.413	162	473	.342	206	267	.772	178	104	28	200	3	326	4.1	37	243	3.0	1372	17.2
92-93 Hou	71	68	2251	349	858	.407	120	361	.332	164	228	.719	140	86	8	124	1	297	4.2	29	221	3.1	982	13.8
93-94 Hou	75	73	2571	380	976	.389	120	403	.298	143	191	.749	185	125	20	143	0	380	5.1	42	229	3.1	1023	13.6
94-95 Hou	64	54	2038	306	777	.394	143	441	.324	99	144	.688	137	75	13	157	1	274	4.3	18	164	2.6	854	13.3
95-96 Phi	75	57	2467	410	1052	.390	146	460	.317	251	332	.756	215	96	12	182	1	330	4.4	39	229	3.1	1217	16.2
96-97 SA	72	31	2068	340	906	.375	115	372	.309	134	180	.744	121	87	19	168	1	153	2.1	27	159	2.2	929	12.9
97-98 2Tm	42	0	636	103	258	.399	37	112	.330	48	60	.800	40	16	4	71	1	52	1.2	14	57	1.4	291	6.9
98-99 Sac	46	1	1007	164	421	.390	80	231	.346	84	114	.737	67	30	3	111	1	76	1.7	13	85	1.8	492	10.7
99-00 Sac	47	0	989	169	490	.345	67	223	.300	108	148	.730	53	38	9	83	0	75	1.6	15	79	1.7	513	10.9
89-90 SA	49	2	1118	133	306	.435	15	52	.288	59	95	.621	71	42	5	79	0	146	3.0	35	141	2.9	340	6.9
Hou	30	10	869	142	321	.442	13	53	.245	77	116	.664	72	42	5	69	0	150	5.0	15	87	2.9	374	12.5
97-98 Orl	11	0	169	26	78	.333	6	26	.231	23	26	.885	12	2	1	20	0	12	1.1	5	13	1.2	81	7.4
Cha	31	0	467	77	180	.428	31	86	.360	25	34	.735	28	14	3	51	1	40	1.3	9	44	1.4	210	6.8
12 Years	812	491	23649	3859	9655	.400	1222	3820	.320	1771	2414	.734	1628	954	149	1702	11	2863	3.5	374	2134	2.6	10711	13.2

NBA Postseason				Field Goals			3-Pt FGs			Free Throws			Misc			Fouls		Assists		Rebounds			Points	
Year Tm	G	GS	Min	Md	Att	Pct	Md	Att	Pct	Md	Att	Pct	TO	Stl	Blk	PF	DQ	Ast	Avg	Off	Tot	Avg	Pts	Avg
89-90 Hou	4	4	159	30	81	.370	8	26	.308	11	21	.524	6	5	0	12	0	17	4.3	5	12	3.0	79	19.8
90-91 Hou	3	3	113	23	56	.411	9	27	.333	1	2	.500	7	2	1	8	0	9	3.0	1	8	2.7	56	18.7
92-93 Hou	9	7	308	47	117	.402	11	46	.239	21	24	.875	17	11	2	17	0	32	3.6	3	22	2.4	126	14.0
93-94 Hou	23	23	880	118	314	.376	45	138	.326	37	54	.685	49	20	2	55	1	96	4.2	12	81	3.5	318	13.8
94-95 Hou	1	0	16	1	7	.143	0	2	.000	1	1	1.000	1	0	0	1	0	1	1.0	0	3	3.0	3	3.0
98-99 Sac	5	0	129	19	60	.317	11	35	.314	7	10	.700	6	6	0	12	0	5	1.0	4	11	2.2	56	11.2
6 Years	45	37	1605	238	635	.375	84	274	.307	78	112	.696	86	44	5	105	1	160	3.6	25	137	3.0	638	14.2

Walter McCarty

Pos: F **College:** Kentucky **Drafted:** '96 1(19)—NY **Ht:** 6'10" **Wt:** 230 **Born:** 2/1/74 **Age:** 26

College				Field Goals			3-Pt FGs			Free Throws			Misc			Fouls		Assists		Rebounds			Points	
Year Tm	G	GS	Min	Md	Att	Pct	Md	Att	Pct	Md	Att	Pct	TO	Stl	Blk	PF	DQ	Ast	Avg	Off	Tot	Avg	Pts	Avg
93-94 Kty	34	10	484	72	153	.471	19	50	.380	31	56	.554	49	20	19	60	—	39	1.1	—	131	3.9	194	5.7
94-95 Kty	33	27	744	128	251	.510	28	77	.364	61	84	.726	53	27	38	96	—	50	1.5	—	185	5.6	345	10.5
95-96 Kty	36	32	888	152	280	.543	28	60	.467	75	104	.721	81	44	51	117	3	92	2.6	87	206	5.7	407	11.3
3 Years	103	69	2116	352	684	.515	75	187	.401	167	244	.684	183	91	108	273	—	181	1.8	—	522	5.1	946	9.2

NBA				Field Goals			3-Pt FGs			Free Throws			Misc			Fouls		Assists		Rebounds			Points	
Year Tm	G	GS	Min	Md	Att	Pct	Md	Att	Pct	Md	Att	Pct	TO	Stl	Blk	PF	DQ	Ast	Avg	Off	Tot	Avg	Pts	Avg
96-97 NY	35	0	192	26	68	.382	4	14	.286	8	14	.571	17	7	9	38	0	13	0.4	8	23	0.7	64	1.8
97-98 Bos	82	64	2340	295	730	.404	54	175	.309	144	194	.742	141	110	44	274	6	177	2.2	141	364	4.4	788	9.6
98-99 Bos	32	4	659	64	177	.362	13	50	.260	40	57	.702	40	24	13	88	0	40	1.3	36	115	3.6	181	5.7
99-00 Bos	61	5	879	78	230	.339	34	110	.309	39	54	.722	67	24	23	83	1	70	1.1	33	110	1.8	229	3.8
4 Years	210	73	4070	463	1205	.384	105	349	.301	231	319	.724	265	165	89	483	7	300	1.4	218	612	2.9	1262	6.0

NBA Postseason				Field Goals			3-Pt FGs			Free Throws			Misc			Fouls		Assists		Rebounds			Points	
Year Tm	G	GS	Min	Md	Att	Pct	Md	Att	Pct	Md	Att	Pct	TO	Stl	Blk	PF	DQ	Ast	Avg	Off	Tot	Avg	Pts	Avg
96-97 NY	2	0	4	2	2	1.000	0	0	—	0	0	—	0	1	0	0	0	0	0.0	0	0	0.0	4	2.0

George McCloud

(statistical profile on page 246)

Pos: F **College:** Florida State **Drafted:** '89 1(7)—Ind **Ht:** 6'8" **Wt:** 225 **Born:** 5/27/67 **Age:** 33

College				Field Goals			3-Pt FGs			Free Throws			Misc			Fouls		Assists		Rebounds			Points	
Year Tm	G	GS	Min	Md	Att	Pct	Md	Att	Pct	Md	Att	Pct	TO	Stl	Blk	PF	DQ	Ast	Avg	Off	Tot	Avg	Pts	Avg
85-86 FlaSt	27	1	283	42	87	.483	—	—	—	31	49	.633	44	13	2	35	0	13	0.5	—	49	1.8	115	4.3
86-87 FlaSt	30	4	590	87	197	.442	14	47	.298	42	68	.618	53	4	2	57	0	18	0.6	—	126	4.2	230	7.7

College			Field Goals			3-Pt FGs			Free Throws			Misc			Fouls		Assists		Rebounds			Points	
Year Tm	G	GS	Min	Md	Att	Pct	Md	Att	Pct	Md	Att	Pct	TO	Stl	Blk	PF	DQ	Ast	Avg	Off	Tot	Avg	Pts	Avg
87-88 FlaSt	30	30	902	193	403	.479	72	159	.453	88	112	.786	85	34	6	69	3	48	1.6	—	111	3.7	546	18.2
88-89 FlaSt	30	28	1067	207	462	.448	115	262	.439	154	176	.875	97	53	6	70	1	125	4.2	—	109	3.6	683	22.8
4 Years	117	63	2842	529	1149	.460	201	468	.429	315	405	.778	279	104	16	231	4	204	1.7	—	395	3.4	1574	13.5

NBA			Field Goals			3-Pt FGs			Free Throws			Misc			Fouls		Assists		Rebounds			Points	
Year Tm	G	GS	Min	Md	Att	Pct	Md	Att	Pct	Md	Att	Pct	TO	Stl	Blk	PF	DQ	Ast	Avg	Off	Tot	Avg	Pts	Avg
89-90 Ind	44	0	413	45	144	.313	13	40	.325	15	19	.789	36	19	3	56	0	45	1.0	12	42	1.0	118	2.7
90-91 Ind	74	0	1070	131	351	.373	43	124	.347	38	49	.776	91	40	11	141	1	150	2.0	35	118	1.6	343	4.6
91-92 Ind	51	5	892	128	313	.409	32	94	.340	50	64	.781	62	26	11	95	1	116	2.3	45	132	2.6	338	6.6
92-93 Ind	78	21	1500	216	525	.411	58	181	.320	75	102	.735	107	53	11	165	0	192	2.5	60	205	2.6	565	7.2
93-94										Played in Italy														
94-95 Dal	42	3	802	144	328	.439	34	89	.382	80	96	.833	40	23	9	71	0	53	1.3	82	147	3.5	402	9.6
95-96 Dal	79	63	2846	530	1281	.414	257	678	.379	180	224	.804	166	113	38	212	1	212	2.7	116	379	4.8	1497	18.9
96-97 2Tm	64	28	1493	238	578	.412	99	254	.390	83	101	.822	61	61	8	126	1	109	1.7	36	179	2.8	658	10.3
97-98 Pho	63	13	1213	173	427	.405	71	208	.341	39	51	.765	63	54	13	132	1	84	1.3	45	218	3.5	456	7.2
98-99 Pho	48	16	1245	142	324	.438	69	166	.416	75	87	.862	49	45	14	127	0	79	1.6	34	162	3.4	428	8.9
99-00 Den	78	11	2118	266	638	.417	107	283	.378	148	181	.818	134	48	26	180	2	246	3.2	72	285	3.7	787	10.1
96-97 Dal	41	26	1207	204	482	.423	78	205	.380	77	92	.837	52	52	8	106	1	92	2.2	29	143	3.5	563	13.7
LAL	23	2	286	34	96	.354	21	49	.429	6	9	.667	9	9	0	20	0	17	0.7	7	36	1.6	95	4.1
10 Years	621	160	13592	2013	4909	.410	783	2117	.370	783	974	.804	809	482	144	1305	7	1286	2.1	537	1867	3.0	5592	9.0

NBA Postseason

Year Tm	G	GS	Min	Md	Att	Pct	Md	Att	Pct	Md	Att	Pct	TO	Stl	Blk	PF	DQ	Ast	Avg	Off	Tot	Avg	Pts	Avg
89-90 Ind	1	0	4	1	2	.500	0	0	—	0	0	—	1	0	0	2	0	0	0.0	1	1	1.0	2	2.0
91-92 Ind	2	2	53	6	12	.500	3	6	.500	8	11	.727	3	2	1	5	0	6	3.0	0	2	1.0	23	11.5
92-93 Ind	4	0	79	8	23	.348	2	12	.167	1	4	.250	5	4	1	14	0	14	3.5	3	11	2.8	19	4.8
97-98 Pho	4	3	126	21	41	.512	12	21	.571	3	4	.750	6	1	1	15	0	8	2.0	2	19	4.8	57	14.3
98-99 Pho	3	0	80	13	30	.433	9	20	.450	7	10	.700	3	5	0	13	0	2	0.7	2	13	4.3	42	14.0
5 Years	14	5	342	49	108	.454	26	59	.441	19	29	.655	18	12	3	49	0	30	2.1	8	46	3.3	143	10.2

Jelani McCoy

Pos: C **College:** UCLA **Drafted:** '98 2(33)—Sea   **Ht:** 6'10" **Wt:** 245 **Born:** 12/6/77 **Age:** 23

College			Field Goals			3-Pt FGs			Free Throws			Misc			Fouls		Assists		Rebounds			Points	
Year Tm	G	GS	Min	Md	Att	Pct	Md	Att	Pct	Md	Att	Pct	TO	Stl	Blk	PF	DQ	Ast	Avg	Off	Tot	Avg	Pts	Avg
95-96 UCLA	31	31	921	138	204	.676	0	0	—	40	92	.435	62	18	102	76	1	28	0.9	67	214	6.9	316	10.2
96-97 UCLA	32	28	846	152	201	.756	0	0	—	45	101	.446	86	19	61	85	0	48	1.5	62	207	6.5	349	10.9
97-98 UCLA	15	0	319	57	95	.600	0	0	—	35	67	.522	34	7	25	30	1	13	0.9	33	107	7.1	149	9.9
3 Years	78	59	2086	347	500	.694	0	0	—	120	260	.462	182	44	188	191	2	89	1.1	162	528	6.8	814	10.4

NBA			Field Goals			3-Pt FGs			Free Throws			Misc			Fouls		Assists		Rebounds			Points	
Year Tm	G	GS	Min	Md	Att	Pct	Md	Att	Pct	Md	Att	Pct	TO	Stl	Blk	PF	DQ	Ast	Avg	Off	Tot	Avg	Pts	Avg
98-99 Sea	26	0	331	56	76	.737	0	0	—	21	42	.500	10	11	20	42	0	4	0.2	27	79	3.0	133	5.1
99-00 Sea	58	2	746	102	177	.576	0	0	—	45	91	.495	45	15	46	127	0	24	0.4	54	179	3.1	249	4.3
2 Years	84	2	1077	158	253	.625	0	0	—	66	133	.496	55	26	66	169	0	28	0.3	81	258	3.1	382	4.5

NBA Postseason

Year Tm	G	GS	Min	Md	Att	Pct	Md	Att	Pct	Md	Att	Pct	TO	Stl	Blk	PF	DQ	Ast	Avg	Off	Tot	Avg	Pts	Avg
99-00 Sea	3	0	26	2	5	.400	0	0	—	0	3	.000	2	0	0	6	0	2	0.7	0	6	2.0	4	1.3

Antonio McDyess

Pos: F **College:** Alabama **Drafted:** '95 1(2)—LAC   (statistical profile on page 246)   **Ht:** 6'9" **Wt:** 240 **Born:** 9/7/74 **Age:** 26

College			Field Goals			3-Pt FGs			Free Throws			Misc			Fouls		Assists		Rebounds			Points	
Year Tm	G	GS	Min	Md	Att	Pct	Md	Att	Pct	Md	Att	Pct	TO	Stl	Blk	PF	DQ	Ast	Avg	Off	Tot	Avg	Pts	Avg
93-94 Ala	26	—	618	132	234	.564	0	0	—	32	60	.533	53	29	39	72	—	11	0.4	—	210	8.1	296	11.4
94-95 Ala	33	—	861	185	361	.512	0	1	.000	88	132	.667	78	28	66	109	—	21	0.6	—	337	10.2	458	13.9
2 Years	59	—	1479	317	595	.533	0	1	.000	120	192	.625	131	57	105	181	—	32	0.5	—	547	9.3	754	12.8

NBA			Field Goals			3-Pt FGs			Free Throws			Misc			Fouls		Assists		Rebounds			Points	
Year Tm	G	GS	Min	Md	Att	Pct	Md	Att	Pct	Md	Att	Pct	TO	Stl	Blk	PF	DQ	Ast	Avg	Off	Tot	Avg	Pts	Avg
95-96 Den	76	75	2280	427	881	.485	0	4	.000	166	243	.683	154	54	114	250	4	75	1.0	229	572	7.5	1020	13.4
96-97 Den	74	73	2565	536	1157	.463	6	35	.171	274	387	.708	199	62	126	276	9	106	1.4	155	537	7.3	1352	18.3
97-98 Pho	81	81	2441	497	927	.536	0	2	.000	231	329	.702	142	100	135	292	6	106	1.3	206	613	7.6	1225	15.1
98-99 Den	50	50	1937	415	882	.471	1	9	.111	230	338	.680	138	73	115	175	5	82	1.6	168	537	10.7	1061	21.2
99-00 Den	81	81	2698	614	1211	.507	0	2	.000	323	516	.626	230	69	139	316	12	159	2.0	234	685	8.5	1551	19.1
5 Years	362	360	11921	2489	5058	.492	7	52	.135	1224	1813	.675	863	358	629	1309	36	528	1.5	992	2944	8.1	6209	17.2

NBA Postseason

Year Tm	G	GS	Min	Md	Att	Pct	Md	Att	Pct	Md	Att	Pct	TO	Stl	Blk	PF	DQ	Ast	Avg	Off	Tot	Avg	Pts	Avg
97-98 Pho	4	4	147	31	65	.477	0	0	—	9	14	.643	5	2	6	12	0	4	1.0	18	53	13.3	71	17.8

Tracy McGrady

(statistical profile on page 247)

Pos: G-F **College:** None **Drafted:** '97 1(9)—Tor **Ht:** 6'8" **Wt:** 210 **Born:** 5/24/79 **Age:** 21

NBA Year Tm	G	GS	Min	Field Goals Md	Att	Pct	3-Pt FGs Md	Att	Pct	Free Throws Md	Att	Pct	Misc TO	Stl	Blk	Fouls PF	DQ	Assists Ast	Avg	Rebounds Off	Tot	Avg	Points Pts	Avg
97-98 Tor	64	17	1179	179	398	.450	14	41	.341	79	111	.712	66	49	61	86	0	98	1.5	105	269	4.2	451	7.0
98-99 Tor	49	2	1106	168	385	.436	8	35	.229	114	157	.726	80	52	66	94	1	113	2.3	120	278	5.7	458	9.3
99-00 Tor	79	34	2462	459	1018	.451	18	65	.277	277	392	.707	160	90	151	201	2	263	3.3	188	501	6.3	1213	15.4
3 Years	192	53	4747	806	1801	.448	40	141	.284	470	660	.712	306	191	278	381	3	474	2.5	413	1048	5.5	2122	11.1

NBA Postseason Year Tm	G	GS	Min	Md	Att	Pct	Md	Att	Pct	Md	Att	Pct	TO	Stl	Blk	PF	DQ	Ast	Avg	Off	Tot	Avg	Pts	Avg
99-00 Tor	3	3	111	17	44	.386	2	7	.286	14	16	.875	10	3	3	10	0	9	3.0	10	21	7.0	50	16.7

Jim McIlvaine

Pos: C **College:** Marquette **Drafted:** '94 2(32)—Was **Ht:** 7'1" **Wt:** 264 **Born:** 7/30/72 **Age:** 28

College Year Tm	G	GS	Min	Field Goals Md	Att	Pct	3-Pt FGs Md	Att	Pct	Free Throws Md	Att	Pct	Misc TO	Stl	Blk	Fouls PF	DQ	Assists Ast	Avg	Rebounds Off	Tot	Avg	Points Pts	Avg
90-91 Marq	28	2	540	84	145	.579	0	0	—	55	92	.598	37	7	92	58	2	14	0.5	32	132	4.7	223	8.0
91-92 Marq	29	27	701	102	187	.545	0	0	—	95	126	.754	50	7	86	75	4	16	0.6	46	134	4.6	299	10.3
92-93 Marq	28	4	532	111	192	.578	0	0	—	85	119	.714	49	6	79	74	2	21	0.8	47	134	4.8	307	11.0
93-94 Marq	33	33	946	170	322	.528	0	0	—	109	164	.665	51	9	142	88	2	43	1.3	76	273	8.3	449	13.6
4 Years	118	66	2719	467	846	.552	0	0	—	344	501	.687	187	29	399	295	10	94	0.8	201	673	5.7	1278	10.8

NBA Year Tm	G	GS	Min	Md	Att	Pct	Md	Att	Pct	Md	Att	Pct	TO	Stl	Blk	PF	DQ	Ast	Avg	Off	Tot	Avg	Pts	Avg
94-95 Was	55	0	534	34	71	.479	0	0	—	28	41	.683	19	10	60	95	0	10	0.2	40	105	1.9	96	1.7
95-96 Was	80	6	1195	62	145	.428	0	0	—	58	105	.552	36	21	166	171	0	11	0.1	66	230	2.9	182	2.3
96-97 Sea	82	79	1477	130	276	.471	1	7	.143	53	107	.495	62	39	164	247	4	23	0.3	132	330	4.0	314	3.8
97-98 Sea	78	72	1211	101	223	.453	0	3	.000	45	81	.556	54	24	137	240	3	19	0.2	96	259	3.3	247	3.2
98-99 NJ	22	1	269	22	51	.431	0	0	—	4	6	.667	13	9	32	59	1	2	0.1	31	54	2.5	48	2.2
99-00 NJ	66	53	1048	64	154	.416	0	0	—	29	56	.518	38	26	117	205	2	36	0.5	106	230	3.5	157	2.4
6 Years	383	211	5734	413	920	.449	1	10	.100	217	396	.548	222	129	676	1017	10	101	0.3	471	1208	3.2	1044	2.7

NBA Postseason Year Tm	G	GS	Min	Md	Att	Pct	Md	Att	Pct	Md	Att	Pct	TO	Stl	Blk	PF	DQ	Ast	Avg	Off	Tot	Avg	Pts	Avg
96-97 Sea	5	0	28	4	7	.571	0	0	—	1	2	.500	1	1	2	7	0	0	0.0	1	2	0.4	9	1.8
97-98 Sea	6	4	59	6	20	.300	0	1	.000	1	2	.500	1	2	6	22	1	1	0.2	7	10	1.7	13	2.2
2 Years	11	4	87	10	27	.370	0	1	.000	2	4	.500	2	3	8	29	1	1	0.1	8	12	1.1	22	2.0

Jeff McInnis

Pos: G **College:** North Carolina **Drafted:** '96 2(37)—Den **Ht:** 6'4" **Wt:** 190 **Born:** 10/22/74 **Age:** 26

College Year Tm	G	GS	Min	Field Goals Md	Att	Pct	3-Pt FGs Md	Att	Pct	Free Throws Md	Att	Pct	Misc TO	Stl	Blk	Fouls PF	DQ	Assists Ast	Avg	Rebounds Off	Tot	Avg	Points Pts	Avg
93-94 UNC	35	1	512	70	153	.458	27	65	.415	30	47	.638	50	26	0	31	—	85	2.4	16	58	1.7	197	5.6
94-95 UNC	34	32	981	155	316	.491	44	112	.393	66	99	.667	72	44	0	74	—	180	5.3	30	138	4.1	420	12.4
95-96 UNC	31	29	1067	178	409	.435	67	171	.392	88	110	.800	78	38	0	72	1	170	5.5	17	81	2.6	511	16.5
3 Years	100	62	2560	403	878	.459	138	348	.397	184	256	.719	200	108	0	177	—	435	4.4	63	277	2.8	1128	11.3

NBA Year Tm	G	GS	Min	Md	Att	Pct	Md	Att	Pct	Md	Att	Pct	TO	Stl	Blk	PF	DQ	Ast	Avg	Off	Tot	Avg	Pts	Avg
96-97 Den	13	0	117	23	49	.469	12	26	.462				13	2	1	16	0	18	1.4	2	6	0.5	65	5.0
97-98								Played in CBA																
98-99 Was	35	6	427	50	134	.373	9	35	.257	21	28	.750	30	19	1	36	0	73	2.1	9	21	0.6	130	3.7
99-00 LAC	25	10	597	80	186	.430	7	21	.333	13	17	.765	27	15	2	55	0	89	3.6	18	72	2.9	180	7.2
3 Years	73	16	1141	153	369	.415	28	82	.341	41	55	.745	70	36	4	107	0	180	2.5	29	99	1.4	375	5.1

Derrick McKey

Pos: F **College:** Alabama **Drafted:** '87 1(9)—Sea **Ht:** 6'10" **Wt:** 241 **Born:** 10/10/66 **Age:** 34

College Year Tm	G	GS	Min	Field Goals Md	Att	Pct	3-Pt FGs Md	Att	Pct	Free Throws Md	Att	Pct	Misc TO	Stl	Blk	Fouls PF	DQ	Assists Ast	Avg	Rebounds Off	Tot	Avg	Points Pts	Avg
84-85 Ala	33	—	728	74	155	.477	—	—		20	33	.606	7	10	37	86	—	44	1.3	—	134	4.1	168	5.1
85-86 Ala	33	—	1117	178	280	.636	—	—		92	117	.786	54	15	76	104	—	29	0.9	—	262	7.9	448	13.6
86-87 Ala	33	—	1199	247	425	.581	21	50	.420	100	116	.862	84	45	75	80	—	59	1.8	—	247	7.5	615	18.6
3 Years	99	—	3044	499	860	.580	21	50	.420	212	266	.797	177	73	188	270	—	132	1.3	—	643	6.5	1231	12.4

NBA

Year Tm	G	GS	Min	FG Md	FG Att	FG Pct	3P Md	3P Att	3P Pct	FT Md	FT Att	FT Pct	TO	Stl	Blk	PF	DQ	Ast	Avg	Off	Tot	Avg	Pts	Avg
87-88 Sea	82	4	1706	255	519	.491	11	30	.367	173	224	.772	108	70	63	237	3	107	1.3	115	328	4.0	694	8.5
88-89 Sea	82	82	2804	487	970	.502	30	89	.337	301	375	.803	188	105	70	264	4	219	2.7	167	464	5.7	1305	15.9
89-90 Sea	80	80	2748	468	949	.493	3	23	.130	315	403	.782	192	87	81	247	2	187	2.3	170	489	6.1	1254	15.7
90-91 Sea	73	55	2503	438	847	.517	4	19	.211	235	278	.845	158	91	56	220	2	169	2.3	172	423	5.8	1115	15.3
91-92 Sea	52	44	1757	285	604	.472	19	50	.380	188	222	.847	114	61	47	142	2	120	2.3	95	268	5.2	777	14.9
92-93 Sea	77	68	2439	387	780	.496	40	112	.357	220	297	.741	152	105	58	208	5	197	2.6	121	327	4.2	1034	13.4
93-94 Ind	76	76	2613	355	710	.500	9	31	.290	192	254	.756	228	111	49	248	1	327	4.3	129	402	5.3	911	12.0
94-95 Ind	81	81	2805	411	833	.493	32	89	.360	221	297	.744	168	125	49	260	5	276	3.4	125	394	4.9	1075	13.3
95-96 Ind	75	75	2440	346	712	.486	17	68	.250	170	221	.769	143	83	44	246	4	262	3.5	123	361	4.8	879	11.7
96-97 Ind	50	49	1449	148	379	.391	15	58	.259	89	123	.724	83	47	30	141	1	135	2.7	80	241	4.8	400	8.0
97-98 Ind	57	4	1316	150	327	.459	4	17	.235	55	77	.714	79	57	30	156	1	88	1.5	74	211	3.7	359	6.3
98-99 Ind	13	0	244	23	52	.442	0	1	.000	14	17	.824	12	12	4	24	0	13	1.0	18	41	3.2	60	4.6
99-00 Ind	32	0	634	43	108	.398	10	23	.435	43	56	.768	19	29	13	81	0	35	1.1	29	135	4.2	139	4.3
13 Years	830	618	25458	3796	7790	.487	194	610	.318	2216	2844	.779	1644	983	594	2474	30	2135	2.6	1418	4084	4.9	10002	12.1

NBA Postseason

Year Tm	G	GS	Min	FG Md	FG Att	FG Pct	3P Md	3P Att	3P Pct	FT Md	FT Att	FT Pct	TO	Stl	Blk	PF	DQ	Ast	Avg	Off	Tot	Avg	Pts	Avg
87-88 Sea	5	0	109	24	38	.632	2	6	.333	10	17	.588	5	3	5	12	0	8	1.6	7	20	4.0	60	12.0
88-89 Sea	8	8	286	44	89	.494	1	9	.111	17	21	.810	23	6	15	33	1	18	2.3	21	52	6.5	106	13.3
90-91 Sea	4	0	114	16	28	.571	0	1	.000	6	11	.545	6	3	0	13	0	8	2.0	7	23	5.8	38	9.5
91-92 Sea	9	9	315	52	99	.525	5	16	.313	38	45	.844	22	7	12	37	1	24	2.7	17	44	4.9	147	16.3
92-93 Sea	19	17	647	83	158	.525	2	5	.400	46	69	.667	36	12	17	51	0	71	3.7	51	98	5.2	214	11.3
93-94 Ind	16	16	587	58	142	.408	8	24	.333	31	47	.660	40	26	9	59	1	67	4.2	32	98	6.1	155	9.7
94-95 Ind	17	17	592	76	174	.437	11	35	.314	54	62	.871	36	17	11	65	2	64	3.8	29	81	4.8	217	12.8
95-96 Ind	5	5	180	24	57	.421	5	12	.417	11	13	.846	14	7	1	20	0	10	2.0	8	33	6.6	64	12.8
97-98 Ind	15	0	284	23	69	.333	3	10	.300	18	23	.783	11	9	8	50	0	11	0.7	8	40	2.7	67	4.5
98-99 Ind	13	0	245	15	40	.375	0	4	.000	17	26	.654	11	12	4	39	0	19	1.5	17	43	3.3	47	3.6
99-00 Ind	23	0	352	15	32	.469	1	6	.167	16	20	.800	19	7	4	45	0	14	0.6	25	79	3.4	47	2.0
11 Years	134	72	3711	430	926	.464	38	128	.297	264	354	.746	223	109	86	424	5	314	2.3	222	611	4.6	1162	8.7

Aaron McKie

Pos: G **College:** Temple **Drafted:** '94 1(17)—Por **Ht:** 6'5" **Wt:** 209 **Born:** 10/2/72 **Age:** 28

(statistical profile on page 247)

College

Year Tm	G	GS	Min	FG Md	FG Att	FG Pct	3P Md	3P Att	3P Pct	FT Md	FT Att	FT Pct	TO	Stl	Blk	PF	DQ	Ast	Avg	Off	Tot	Avg	Pts	Avg
91-92 Tem	28	—	1011	130	300	.433	42	131	.321	86	114	.754	46	62	6	67	—	94	3.4	—	167	6.0	388	13.9
92-93 Tem	33	—	1272	240	555	.432	77	196	.393	123	156	.788	78	76	7	71	—	109	3.3	—	195	5.9	680	20.6
93-94 Tem	31	—	1214	193	481	.401	59	159	.371	137	168	.815	52	58	10	54	—	98	3.2	—	224	7.2	582	18.8
3 Years	92	—	3497	563	1336	.421	178	486	.366	346	438	.790	176	196	23	192	—	301	3.3	—	586	6.4	1650	17.9

NBA

Year Tm	G	GS	Min	FG Md	FG Att	FG Pct	3P Md	3P Att	3P Pct	FT Md	FT Att	FT Pct	TO	Stl	Blk	PF	DQ	Ast	Avg	Off	Tot	Avg	Pts	Avg
94-95 Por	45	20	827	116	261	.444	11	28	.393	50	73	.685	39	36	16	97	1	89	2.0	35	129	2.9	293	6.5
95-96 Por	81	73	2259	337	722	.467	38	117	.325	152	199	.764	135	92	21	205	5	205	2.5	86	304	3.8	864	10.7
96-97 2Tm	83	11	1625	150	365	.411	41	103	.398	92	110	.836	90	77	22	130	1	161	1.9	40	221	2.7	433	5.2
97-98 2Tm	81	32	1813	139	381	.365	12	63	.190	42	55	.764	76	101	13	164	0	175	2.2	58	231	2.9	332	4.1
98-99 Phi	50	4	959	95	237	.401	6	31	.194	44	62	.710	57	63	3	90	1	100	2.0	27	140	2.8	240	4.8
99-00 Phi	82	14	1952	244	593	.411	44	121	.364	121	146	.829	113	108	18	194	3	240	2.9	47	246	3.0	653	8.0
96-97 Por	41	8	775	53	156	.340	23	55	.418	41	49	.837	48	34	15	61	1	84	2.0	13	93	2.3	170	4.1
Det	42	3	850	97	209	.464	18	48	.375	51	61	.836	42	43	7	69	0	77	1.8	27	128	3.0	263	6.3
97-98 Det	24	1	472	43	104	.413	3	17	.176	20	23	.870	24	23	1	47	0	38	1.6	24	68	2.8	109	4.5
Phi	57	31	1341	96	277	.347	9	46	.196	22	32	.688	52	78	12	117	0	137	2.4	34	163	2.9	223	3.9
6 Years	422	154	9435	1081	2559	.422	152	463	.328	501	645	.777	510	477	93	880	11	970	2.3	293	1271	3.0	2815	6.7

NBA Postseason

Year Tm	G	GS	Min	FG Md	FG Att	FG Pct	3P Md	3P Att	3P Pct	FT Md	FT Att	FT Pct	TO	Stl	Blk	PF	DQ	Ast	Avg	Off	Tot	Avg	Pts	Avg
94-95 Por	3	0	34	8	14	.571	1	2	.500	0	0	—	0	3	0	4	0	1	0.3	0	2	0.7	17	5.7
95-96 Por	5	4	134	11	30	.367	2	8	.250	7	9	.778	9	6	2	13	0	9	1.8	4	18	3.6	31	6.2
96-97 Det	5	0	97	7	20	.350	1	5	.200	0	0	—	3	6	2	12	0	10	2.0	1	10	2.0	15	3.0
98-99 Phi	6	0	97	7	23	.304	0	1	.000	6	7	.857	1	4	0	17	0	11	1.8	4	15	2.5	20	3.3
99-00 Phi	10	6	331	50	103	.485	12	35	.343	26	31	.839	16	4	2	26	0	46	4.6	4	36	3.6	138	13.8
5 Years	29	10	693	83	190	.437	16	51	.314	39	47	.830	29	23	6	72	0	77	2.7	13	81	2.8	221	7.6

Roshown McLeod

Pos: F **College:** Duke **Drafted:** '98 1(20)—Atl **Ht:** 6'8" **Wt:** 220 **Born:** 11/17/75 **Age:** 25

College			Field Goals			3-Pt FGs			Free Throws			Misc			Fouls		Assists		Rebounds			Points	
Year Tm	G	GS	Min	Md	Att	Pct	Md	Att	Pct	Md	Att	Pct	TO	Stl	Blk	PF	DQ	Ast	Avg	Off	Tot	Avg	Pts	Avg
93-94 StJn	29	5	542	77	179	.430	0	5	.000	39	53	.736	31	25	13	66	1	34	1.2	48	110	3.8	193	6.7
94-95 StJn	28	1	563	86	179	.480	3	9	.333	44	62	.710	30	17	20	85	3	27	1.0	50	119	4.3	219	7.8
96-97 Duke	33	30	797	142	290	.490	27	72	.375	81	102	.794	57	30	34	105	6	29	0.9	71	175	5.3	392	11.9
97-98 Duke	36	27	852	196	397	.494	44	107	.411	113	160	.706	68	42	26	102	2	49	1.4	64	201	5.6	549	15.3
4 Years	126	63	2754	501	1045	.479	74	193	.383	277	377	.735	186	114	93	358	12	139	1.1	233	605	4.8	1353	10.7

NBA			Field Goals			3-Pt FGs			Free Throws			Misc			Fouls		Assists		Rebounds			Points	
Year Tm	G	GS	Min	Md	Att	Pct	Md	Att	Pct	Md	Att	Pct	TO	Stl	Blk	PF	DQ	Ast	Avg	Off	Tot	Avg	Pts	Avg
98-99 Atl	34	0	348	62	163	.380	1	10	.100	37	45	.822	23	2	1	24	0	14	0.4	12	50	1.5	162	4.8
99-00 Atl	44	20	860	131	332	.395	2	13	.154	54	70	.771	59	16	5	84	0	52	1.2	41	138	3.1	318	7.2
2 Years	78	20	1208	193	495	.390	3	23	.130	91	115	.791	82	18	6	108	0	66	0.8	53	188	2.4	480	6.2

NBA Postseason																							
Year Tm	G	GS	Min	Md	Att	Pct	Md	Att	Pct	Md	Att	Pct	TO	Stl	Blk	PF	DQ	Ast	Avg	Off	Tot	Avg	Pts	Avg
98-99 Atl	6	0	49	11	21	.524	0	0	—	4	4	1.000	1	1	1	3	0	1	0.2	1	3	0.5	26	4.3

Ron Mercer

(statistical profile on page 248)

Pos: G **College:** Kentucky **Drafted:** '97 1(6)—Bos **Ht:** 6'7" **Wt:** 210 **Born:** 5/18/76 **Age:** 24

College			Field Goals			3-Pt FGs			Free Throws			Misc			Fouls		Assists		Rebounds			Points	
Year Tm	G	GS	Min	Md	Att	Pct	Md	Att	Pct	Md	Att	Pct	TO	Stl	Blk	PF	DQ	Ast	Avg	Off	Tot	Avg	Pts	Avg
95-96 Kty	36	12	677	107	234	.457	23	68	.338	51	65	.785	36	34	8	51	0	50	1.4	39	104	2.9	288	8.0
96-97 Kty	40	40	1299	297	603	.493	49	141	.348	82	105	.781	68	66	10	95	4	97	2.4	91	210	5.3	725	18.1
2 Years	76	52	1976	404	837	.483	72	209	.344	133	170	.782	104	100	18	146	4	147	1.9	130	314	4.1	1013	13.3

NBA			Field Goals			3-Pt FGs			Free Throws			Misc			Fouls		Assists		Rebounds			Points	
Year Tm	G	GS	Min	Md	Att	Pct	Md	Att	Pct	Md	Att	Pct	TO	Stl	Blk	PF	DQ	Ast	Avg	Off	Tot	Avg	Pts	Avg
97-98 Bos	80	62	2662	515	1145	.450	3	28	.107	188	224	.839	132	125	17	213	2	176	2.2	109	280	3.5	1221	15.3
98-99 Bos	41	40	1551	305	707	.431	5	30	.167	83	105	.790	89	67	12	81	1	104	2.5	37	155	3.8	698	17.0
99-00 2Tm	68	68	2377	460	1080	.426	15	48	.313	213	270	.789	151	75	23	151	2	158	2.3	64	250	3.7	1148	16.9
99-00 Den	37	37	1408	272	612	.444	15	39	.385	119	151	.788	87	33	15	75	0	104	2.8	29	152	4.1	678	18.3
Orl	31	31	969	188	468	.402	0	9	.000	94	119	.790	64	42	8	76	2	54	1.7	35	98	3.2	470	15.2
3 Years	189	170	6590	1280	2932	.437	23	106	.217	484	599	.808	372	267	52	445	5	438	2.3	210	685	3.6	3067	16.2

Andre Miller

(statistical profile on page 248)

Pos: G **College:** Utah **Drafted:** '99 1(8)—Cle **Ht:** 6'2" **Wt:** 200 **Born:** 3/19/76 **Age:** 24

College			Field Goals			3-Pt FGs			Free Throws			Misc			Fouls		Assists		Rebounds			Points	
Year Tm	G	GS	Min	Md	Att	Pct	Md	Att	Pct	Md	Att	Pct	TO	Stl	Blk	PF	DQ	Ast	Avg	Off	Tot	Avg	Pts	Avg
95-96 Utah	34	23	872	104	195	.533	6	19	.316	78	113	.690	90	38	21	67	1	157	4.6	33	126	3.7	292	8.6
96-97 Utah	33	32	974	121	249	.486	10	35	.286	71	122	.582	95	59	13	62	1	201	6.1	54	154	4.7	323	9.8
97-98 Utah	34	34	1075	173	315	.549	20	60	.333	117	162	.722	85	73	16	72	1	177	5.2	50	185	5.4	483	14.2
98-99 Utah	33	33	1092	190	387	.491	22	83	.265	118	171	.690	94	84	15	59	0	186	5.6	52	178	5.4	520	15.8
4 Years	134	122	4013	588	1146	.513	58	197	.294	384	568	.676	364	254	65	260	3	721	5.4	189	643	4.8	1618	12.1

NBA			Field Goals			3-Pt FGs			Free Throws			Misc			Fouls		Assists		Rebounds			Points	
Year Tm	G	GS	Min	Md	Att	Pct	Md	Att	Pct	Md	Att	Pct	TO	Stl	Blk	PF	DQ	Ast	Avg	Off	Tot	Avg	Pts	Avg
99-00 Cle	82	36	2093	339	755	.449	10	49	.204	226	292	.774	166	84	17	194	1	476	5.8	85	280	3.4	914	11.1

Anthony Miller

Pos: F **College:** Michigan State **Drafted:** '94 2(39)—GS **Ht:** 6'9" **Wt:** 255 **Born:** 10/27/71 **Age:** 29

College			Field Goals			3-Pt FGs			Free Throws			Misc			Fouls		Assists		Rebounds			Points	
Year Tm	G	GS	Min	Md	Att	Pct	Md	Att	Pct	Md	Att	Pct	TO	Stl	Blk	PF	DQ	Ast	Avg	Off	Tot	Avg	Pts	Avg
91-92 MchSt	30	3	555	83	154	.539	0	0	—	50	80	.625	53	14	12	61	1	24	0.8	59	156	5.2	216	7.2
92-93 MchSt	27	5	474	76	124	.613	1	1	1.000	26	48	.542	29	8	20	59	1	12	0.4	44	139	5.1	179	6.6
93-94 MchSt	32	32	910	162	249	.651	0	1	.000	78	136	.574	70	26	29	82	3	30	0.9	112	287	9.0	402	12.6
3 Years	89	40	1939	321	527	.609	1	2	.500	154	264	.583	152	48	61	202	5	66	0.7	215	582	6.5	797	9.0

NBA			Field Goals			3-Pt FGs			Free Throws			Misc			Fouls		Assists		Rebounds			Points	
Year Tm	G	GS	Min	Md	Att	Pct	Md	Att	Pct	Md	Att	Pct	TO	Stl	Blk	PF	DQ	Ast	Avg	Off	Tot	Avg	Pts	Avg
94-95 LAL	46	1	527	70	132	.530	2	5	.400	47	76	.618	38	20	7	77	2	35	0.8	67	152	3.3	189	4.1
95-96 LAL	27	0	123	15	35	.429	0	2	.000	6	10	.600	8	4	1	19	0	4	0.1	11	25	0.9	36	1.3
96-97 Atl	1	0	14	0	5	.000	0	0	—	0	0	—	0	0	0	2	0	0	0.0	2	7	7.0	0	0.0
97-98 Atl	37	0	228	29	52	.558	0	0	—	21	39	.538	14	15	3	41	0	3	0.1	30	70	1.9	79	2.1

NBA Year Tm	G	GS	Min	Field Goals Md	Att	Pct	3-Pt FGs Md	Att	Pct	Free Throws Md	Att	Pct	Misc TO	Stl	Blk	Fouls PF	DQ	Assists Ast	Avg	Rebounds Off	Tot	Avg	Points Pts	Avg
98-99 Hou	29	0	249	28	60	.467	0	1	.000	14	22	.636	9	7	5	34	0	7	0.2	26	67	2.3	70	2.4
99-00 Hou	35	14	476	52	97	.536	0	0	—	26	51	.510	19	11	10	68	1	16	0.5	49	164	4.7	130	3.7
6 Years	175	15	1617	194	381	.509	2	8	.250	114	198	.576	88	57	26	241	3	65	0.4	185	485	2.8	504	2.9

NBA Postseason

Year Tm	G	GS	Min	Md	Att	Pct	Md	Att	Pct	Md	Att	Pct	TO	Stl	Blk	PF	DQ	Ast	Avg	Off	Tot	Avg	Pts	Avg
94-95 LAL	4	0	15	0	2	.000	0	0	—	0	0	—	1	1	0	2	0	1	0.3	2	6	1.5	0	0.0
97-98 Atl	4	0	33	3	8	.375	0	0	—	2	2	1.000	3	2	1	5	0	1	0.3	5	9	2.3	8	2.0
2 Years	8	0	48	3	10	.300	0	0	—	2	2	1.000	4	3	1	7	0	2	0.3	7	15	1.9	8	1.0

Brad Miller

Pos: C College: Purdue Drafted: '98 FA—Cha Ht: 6'11" Wt: 250 Born: 4/12/76 Age: 24

College Year Tm	G	GS	Min	Field Goals Md	Att	Pct	3-Pt FGs Md	Att	Pct	Free Throws Md	Att	Pct	Misc TO	Stl	Blk	Fouls PF	DQ	Assists Ast	Avg	Rebounds Off	Tot	Avg	Points Pts	Avg
94-95 Pur	32	18	574	71	122	.582	0	0	—	66	100	.660	47	19	34	74	2	39	1.2	—	153	4.8	208	6.5
95-96 Pur	32	1	682	100	193	.518	1	6	.167	107	145	.738	60	31	27	86	2	46	1.4	50	158	4.9	308	9.6
96-97 Pur	30	29	934	128	239	.536	3	11	.273	171	220	.777	68	53	46	99	6	86	2.9	94	249	8.3	430	14.3
97-98 Pur	34	32	993	191	302	.632	3	10	.300	199	255	.780	101	42	56	92	3	86	2.5	100	302	8.9	584	17.2
4 Years	128	80	3183	490	856	.572	7	27	.259	543	720	.754	276	145	163	351	13	257	2.0	—	862	6.7	1530	12.0

NBA Year Tm	G	GS	Min	Md	Att	Pct	Md	Att	Pct	Md	Att	Pct	TO	Stl	Blk	PF	DQ	Ast	Avg	Off	Tot	Avg	Pts	Avg
98-99 Cha	38	0	469	78	138	.565	1	2	.500	81	102	.794	32	9	18	65	0	22	0.6	35	117	3.1	238	6.3
99-00 Cha	55	4	961	135	293	.461	0	2	.000	153	195	.785	48	23	35	111	1	45	0.8	113	293	5.3	423	7.7
2 Years	93	4	1430	213	431	.494	1	4	.250	234	297	.788	80	32	53	176	1	67	0.7	148	410	4.4	661	7.1

NBA Postseason

Year Tm	G	GS	Min	Md	Att	Pct	Md	Att	Pct	Md	Att	Pct	TO	Stl	Blk	PF	DQ	Ast	Avg	Off	Tot	Avg	Pts	Avg
99-00 Cha	4	0	62	9	17	.529	0	0	—	12	15	.800	9	0	3	11	0	3	0.8	8	13	3.3	30	7.5

Oliver Miller

Pos: C College: Arkansas Drafted: '92 1(22)—Pho Ht: 6'9" Wt: 315 Born: 4/6/70 Age: 30

College Year Tm	G	GS	Min	Field Goals Md	Att	Pct	3-Pt FGs Md	Att	Pct	Free Throws Md	Att	Pct	Misc TO	Stl	Blk	Fouls PF	DQ	Assists Ast	Avg	Rebounds Off	Tot	Avg	Points Pts	Avg
88-89 Ark	30	—	599	88	161	.547	4	12	.333	50	78	.641	65	20	60	95	—	41	1.4	—	112	3.7	230	7.7
89-90 Ark	35	13	757	152	238	.639	0	4	.000	86	132	.652	77	41	85	100	—	49	1.4	—	219	6.3	390	11.1
90-91 Ark	38	—	931	254	361	.704	1	3	.333	87	135	.644	109	55	112	114	—	103	2.7	—	294	7.7	596	15.7
91-92 Ark	34	—	956	186	306	.602	0	11	.000	87	133	.647	96	38	88	104	—	103	3.0	—	261	7.7	458	13.5
4 Years	137	—	3243	680	1069	.636	5	30	.167	309	478	.646	347	154	345	413		296	2.2	—	886	6.5	1674	12.2

NBA Year Tm	G	GS	Min	Field Goals Md	Att	Pct	3-Pt FGs Md	Att	Pct	Free Throws Md	Att	Pct	Misc TO	Stl	Blk	Fouls PF	DQ	Assists Ast	Avg	Rebounds Off	Tot	Avg	Points Pts	Avg
92-93 Pho	56	1	1069	121	255	.475	0	3	.000	71	100	.710	108	38	100	145	0	118	2.1	70	275	4.9	313	5.6
93-94 Pho	69	30	1786	277	455	.609	2	9	.222	80	137	.584	164	83	156	230	1	244	3.5	140	476	6.9	636	9.2
94-95 Det	64	22	1558	232	418	.555	3	13	.231	78	124	.629	115	60	116	217	1	93	1.5	162	475	7.4	545	8.5
95-96 Tor	76	72	2516	418	795	.526	0	11	.000	146	221	.661	202	108	143	277	4	219	2.9	177	562	7.4	982	12.9
96-97 2Tm	61	8	1152	123	238	.517	0	2	.000	48	79	.608	90	47	63	181	1	87	1.4	105	306	5.0	294	4.8
97-98 Tor	64	53	1628	170	369	.461	0	4	.000	61	101	.604	131	58	72	184	1	196	3.1	146	400	6.3	401	6.3
98-99 Sac	4	0	35	5	11	.455	0	0	—	0	0	—	4	0	2	3	0	0	0.0	7	8	2.0	10	2.5
99-00 Pho	51	9	1088	137	233	.588	0	0	—	49	73	.671	74	42	80	132	1	68	1.3	87	261	5.1	323	6.3
96-97 Dal	42	0	836	76	154	.494	0	1	.000	28	53	.528	70	34	50	133	1	58	1.4	82	233	5.5	180	4.3
Tor	19	8	316	47	84	.560	0	1	.000	20	26	.769	20	13	13	48	0	29	1.5	23	73	3.8	114	6.0
8 Years	445	195	10832	1483	2774	.535	5	42	.119	533	835	.638	888	436	732	1369	9	1025	2.3	894	2763	6.2	3504	7.9

NBA Postseason

Year Tm	G	GS	Min	Md	Att	Pct	Md	Att	Pct	Md	Att	Pct	TO	Stl	Blk	PF	DQ	Ast	Avg	Off	Tot	Avg	Pts	Avg
92-93 Pho	24	0	513	71	121	.587	0	2	.000	31	55	.564	42	21	59	76	0	51	2.1	33	124	5.2	173	7.2
93-94 Pho	10	4	146	16	27	.593	0	0	—	3	7	.429	13	6	12	22	0	13	1.3	14	44	4.4	35	3.5
99-00 Pho	7	0	37	2	9	.222	0	3	.000	2	4	.500	2	0	2	8	0	1	0.1	2	8	1.1	6	0.9
3 Years	41	4	696	89	157	.567	0	5	.000	36	66	.545	57	27	73	106	0	65	1.6	49	176	4.3	214	5.2

Reggie Miller

Pos: G **College:** UCLA **Drafted:** '87 1(11)—Ind   **Ht:** 6'7" **Wt:** 202 **Born:** 8/24/65 **Age:** 35

College			Field Goals			3-Pt FGs			Free Throws			Misc			Fouls		Assists		Rebounds			Points	
Year Tm	G	GS	Min	Md	Att	Pct	Md	Att	Pct	Md	Att	Pct	TO	Stl	Blk	PF	DQ	Ast	Avg	Off	Tot	Avg	Pts	Avg
83-84 UCLA	28	—	384	56	110	.509	—	—	—	18	28	.643	26	8	2	46	—	21	0.8	—	42	1.5	130	4.6
84-85 UCLA	33	33	1174	192	347	.553	—	—	—	119	148	.804	62	51	7	69	—	86	2.6	—	141	4.3	503	15.2
85-86 UCLA	29	29	1112	274	493	.556	—	—	—	202	229	.882	69	35	7	83	2	69	2.4	—	153	5.3	750	25.9
86-87 UCLA	32	32	1166	247	455	.543	69	157	.439	149	179	.832	61	64	6	64	3	71	2.2	—	173	5.4	712	22.3
4 Years	122	—	3836	769	1405	.547	69	157	.439	488	584	.836	218	158	22	262	—	247	2.0	—	509	4.2	2095	17.2

NBA			Field Goals			3-Pt FGs			Free Throws			Misc			Fouls		Assists		Rebounds			Points	
Year Tm	G	GS	Min	Md	Att	Pct	Md	Att	Pct	Md	Att	Pct	TO	Stl	Blk	PF	DQ	Ast	Avg	Off	Tot	Avg	Pts	Avg
87-88 Ind	82	1	1840	306	627	.488	61	172	.355	149	186	.801	101	53	19	157	0	132	1.6	95	190	2.3	822	10.0
88-89 Ind	74	70	2536	398	831	.479	98	244	.402	287	340	.844	143	93	29	170	2	227	3.1	73	292	3.9	1181	16.0
89-90 Ind*	82	82	3192	661	1287	.514	150	362	.414	544	627	.868	222	110	18	175	1	311	3.8	95	295	3.6	2016	24.6
90-91 Ind	82	82	2972	596	1164	.512	112	322	.348	551	600	.918	163	109	13	165	1	331	4.0	81	281	3.4	1855	22.6
91-92 Ind	82	82	3120	562	1121	.501	129	341	.378	442	515	.858	157	105	26	210	1	314	3.8	82	318	3.9	1695	20.7
92-93 Ind	82	82	2954	571	1193	.479	167	419	.399	427	485	.880	145	120	26	182	0	262	3.2	67	258	3.1	1736	21.2
93-94 Ind	79	79	2638	524	1042	.503	123	292	.421	403	444	.908	175	119	24	193	2	248	3.1	30	212	2.7	1574	19.9
94-95 Ind*	81	81	2665	505	1092	.462	195	470	.415	383	427	.897	151	98	16	157	0	242	3.0	30	210	2.6	1588	19.6
95-96 Ind*	76	76	2621	504	1066	.473	168	410	.410	430	498	.863	189	77	13	175	0	253	3.3	38	214	2.8	1606	21.1
96-97 Ind*	81	81	2966	552	1244	.444	229	536	.427	418	475	.880	166	75	25	172	1	273	3.4	53	286	3.5	1751	21.6
97-98 Ind*	81	81	2795	516	1081	.477	164	382	.429	382	440	.868	128	78	11	148	2	171	2.1	46	232	2.9	1578	19.5
98-99 Ind	50	50	1787	294	671	.438	106	275	.385	226	247	.915	76	37	9	101	1	112	2.2	25	135	2.7	920	18.4
99-00 Ind*	81	81	2987	466	1041	.448	165	404	.408	373	406	.919	129	85	25	126	0	187	2.3	50	239	3.0	1470	18.1
13 Years	1013	928	35073	6455	13460	.480	1867	4629	.403	5015	5690	.881	1945	1159	254	2131	11	3063	3.0	765	3162	3.1	19792	19.5

NBA Postseason																								
Year Tm	G	GS	Min	Md	Att	Pct	Md	Att	Pct	Md	Att	Pct	TO	Stl	Blk	PF	DQ	Ast	Avg	Off	Tot	Avg	Pts	Avg
89-90 Ind	3	3	125	20	35	.571	3	7	.429	19	21	.905	3	3	0	6	0	6	2.0	1	12	4.0	62	20.7
90-91 Ind	5	5	193	34	70	.486	8	19	.421	32	37	.865	12	8	2	14	0	14	2.8	5	16	3.2	108	21.6
91-92 Ind	3	3	130	25	43	.581	7	11	.636	24	30	.800	4	4	0	12	1	14	4.7	4	7	2.3	81	27.0
92-93 Ind	4	4	175	40	75	.533	10	19	.526	36	38	.947	10	3	0	11	0	11	2.8	4	12	3.0	126	31.5
93-94 Ind	16	16	576	121	270	.448	35	83	.422	94	112	.839	32	21	4	34	0	46	2.9	11	48	3.0	371	23.2
94-95 Ind	17	17	641	138	290	.476	54	128	.422	104	121	.860	39	15	4	35	0	36	2.1	9	61	3.6	434	25.5
95-96 Ind	1	1	31	7	17	.412	2	6	.333	13	15	.867	0	1	0	1	0	1	1.0	1	1	1.0	29	29.0
97-98 Ind	16	16	628	98	230	.426	38	95	.400	85	94	.904	27	19	3	26	0	32	2.0	5	28	1.8	319	19.9
98-99 Ind	13	13	481	79	199	.397	28	84	.333	77	86	.895	21	9	3	26	0	34	2.6	13	51	3.9	263	20.2
99-00 Ind	22	22	892	174	385	.452	58	147	.395	121	129	.938	28	23	10	37	0	60	2.7	9	53	2.4	527	24.0
10 Years	100	100	3872	736	1614	.456	243	599	.406	605	683	.886	176	106	26	202	1	254	2.5	62	289	2.9	2320	23.2

Chris Mills

Pos: F **College:** Arizona **Drafted:** '93 1(22)—Cle   **Ht:** 6'7" **Wt:** 216 **Born:** 1/25/70 **Age:** 31

College			Field Goals			3-Pt FGs			Free Throws			Misc			Fouls		Assists		Rebounds			Points	
Year Tm	G	GS	Min	Md	Att	Pct	Md	Att	Pct	Md	Att	Pct	TO	Stl	Blk	PF	DQ	Ast	Avg	Off	Tot	Avg	Pts	Avg
88-89 Kty	32	—	1124	180	372	.484	17	54	.315	82	115	.713	110	45	26	105	—	92	2.9	—	277	8.7	459	14.3
90-91 Ari	35	35	1025	206	397	.519	42	122	.344	91	122	.746	76	29	17	78	1	66	1.9	82	216	6.2	545	15.6
91-92 Ari	31	31	984	198	391	.506	28	89	.315	80	103	.777	60	36	8	80	1	73	2.4	83	244	7.9	504	16.3
92-93 Ari	28	28	870	211	406	.520	56	116	.483	92	110	.836	73	30	14	68	1	53	1.9	72	222	7.9	570	20.4
4 Years	126	—	4003	795	1566	.508	143	381	.375	345	450	.767	319	140	65	331	—	284	2.3	—	959	7.6	2078	16.5

NBA			Field Goals			3-Pt FGs			Free Throws			Misc			Fouls		Assists		Rebounds			Points	
Year Tm	G	GS	Min	Md	Att	Pct	Md	Att	Pct	Md	Att	Pct	TO	Stl	Blk	PF	DQ	Ast	Avg	Off	Tot	Avg	Pts	Avg
93-94 Cle	79	18	2022	284	677	.419	38	122	.311	137	176	.778	89	54	50	232	3	128	1.6	134	401	5.1	743	9.4
94-95 Cle	80	79	2814	359	855	.420	94	240	.392	174	213	.817	120	59	35	242	2	154	1.9	99	366	4.6	986	12.3
95-96 Cle	80	80	3060	454	971	.468	79	210	.376	218	263	.829	121	73	52	241	1	188	2.4	112	443	5.5	1205	15.1
96-97 Cle	80	79	3167	405	894	.453	86	220	.391	176	209	.842	120	86	41	222	1	198	2.5	118	497	6.2	1072	13.4
97-98 NY	80	29	2183	292	675	.433	40	137	.292	152	189	.804	107	45	30	218	3	133	1.7	120	408	5.1	776	9.7
98-99 GS	47	24	1395	186	453	.411	32	115	.278	79	96	.823	58	39	14	125	1	103	2.2	49	237	5.0	483	10.3
99-00 GS	20	11	649	123	292	.421	8	30	.267	68	84	.810	25	18	4	60	0	47	2.4	46	123	6.2	322	16.1
7 Years	466	320	15290	2103	4817	.437	377	1074	.351	1004	1230	.816	640	374	226	1340	11	951	2.0	678	2475	5.3	5587	12.0

NBA Postseason																								
Year Tm	G	GS	Min	Md	Att	Pct	Md	Att	Pct	Md	Att	Pct	TO	Stl	Blk	PF	DQ	Ast	Avg	Off	Tot	Avg	Pts	Avg
93-94 Cle	3	1	112	19	38	.500	4	5	.800	9	11	.818	5	7	1	9	0	8	2.7	10	23	7.7	51	17.0
94-95 Cle	4	4	139	20	37	.541	8	14	.571	5	5	1.000	6	3	2	18	1	11	2.8	2	16	4.0	53	13.3
95-96 Cle	3	3	105	11	33	.333	0	5	.000	1	1	1.000	3	2	2	10	0	5	1.7	6	16	5.3	23	7.7
97-98 NY	9	2	168	15	35	.429	4	10	.400	10	12	.833	6	8	2	21	0	5	0.6	8	27	3.0	44	4.9
4 Years	19	10	524	65	143	.455	16	34	.471	25	29	.862	20	20	7	58	1	29	1.5	25	82	4.3	171	9.0

Terry Mills

(statistical profile on page 249)

Pos: F **College:** Michigan **Drafted:** '90 1(16)—Mil **Ht:** 6'10" **Wt:** 250 **Born:** 12/21/67 **Age:** 33

College

Year Tm	G	GS	Min	Md	Att	Pct	Md	Att	Pct	Md	Att	Pct	TO	Stl	Blk	PF	DQ	Ast	Avg	Off	Tot	Avg	Pts	Avg
				Field Goals			3-Pt FGs			Free Throws			Misc			Fouls		Assists		Rebounds			Points	
87-88 Mich	34	33	884	181	341	.531	0	2	.000	51	70	.729	67	21	35	90	1	56	1.6	—	216	6.4	413	12.1
88-89 Mich	37	37	999	180	319	.564	0	2	.000	70	91	.769	77	20	49	95	3	104	2.8	—	218	5.9	430	11.6
89-90 Mich	31	31	961	237	405	.585	0	0	—	88	116	.759	75	37	27	81	5	68	2.2	—	247	8.0	562	18.1
3 Years	102	101	2844	598	1065	.562	0	4	.000	209	277	.755	219	78	111	266	9	228	2.2	—	681	6.7	1405	13.8

NBA

Year Tm	G	GS	Min	Md	Att	Pct	Md	Att	Pct	Md	Att	Pct	TO	Stl	Blk	PF	DQ	Ast	Avg	Off	Tot	Avg	Pts	Avg
				Field Goals			3-Pt FGs			Free Throws			Misc			Fouls		Assists		Rebounds			Points	
90-91 2Tm	55	2	819	134	288	.465	0	4	.000	47	66	.712	43	35	29	100	0	33	0.6	82	229	4.2	315	5.7
91-92 NJ	82	24	1714	310	670	.463	8	23	.348	114	152	.750	82	48	41	200	3	84	1.0	187	453	5.5	742	9.0
92-93 Det	81	46	2183	494	1072	.461	10	36	.278	201	254	.791	142	44	50	282	6	111	1.4	176	472	5.8	1199	14.8
93-94 Det	80	74	2773	588	1151	.511	24	73	.329	181	227	.797	153	64	62	309	6	177	2.2	193	672	8.4	1381	17.3
94-95 Det	72	69	2514	417	933	.447	109	285	.382	175	219	.799	144	68	33	253	5	160	2.2	124	558	7.8	1118	15.5
95-96 Det	82	5	1656	283	675	.419	82	207	.396	121	157	.771	98	42	20	197	0	98	1.2	108	352	4.3	769	9.4
96-97 Det	79	5	1997	312	702	.444	175	415	.422	58	70	.829	85	35	27	161	1	39	0.8	34	152	3.0	212	4.2
97-98 Mia	50	0	782	81	206	.393	25	81	.309	25	33	.758	45	19	9	129	1	39	0.8	34	152	3.0	212	4.2
98-99 Mia	1	0	29	3	8	.375	2	4	.500	1	2	.500	3	1	0	3	0	0	0.0	3	4	4.0	9	9.0
99-00 Det	82	78	1842	214	488	.439	95	242	.393	25	34	.735	46	38	24	242	4	85	1.0	50	390	4.8	548	6.7
90-91 Den	17	0	279	56	120	.467	0	2	.000	16	22	.727	18	16	9	44	0	16	0.9	31	88	5.2	128	7.5
NJ	38	2	540	78	168	.464	0	2	.000	31	44	.705	25	19	20	56	0	17	0.4	51	141	3.7	187	4.9
10 Years	664	303	16309	2836	6193	.458	530	1370	.387	948	1214	.781	841	394	295	1876	26	886	1.3	1025	3659	5.5	7150	10.8

NBA Postseason

Year Tm	G	GS	Min	Md	Att	Pct	Md	Att	Pct	Md	Att	Pct	TO	Stl	Blk	PF	DQ	Ast	Avg	Off	Tot	Avg	Pts	Avg
91-92 NJ	4	0	77	10	27	.370	0	1	.000	7	11	.636	7	1	2	18	0	8	2.0	9	24	6.0	27	6.8
95-96 Det	3	0	48	5	20	.250	1	8	.125	5	6	.833	1	1	0	6	0	4	1.3	3	5	1.7	16	5.3
96-97 Det	5	4	196	24	55	.436	9	26	.346	2	4	.500	4	6	0	14	0	7	1.4	4	35	7.0	59	11.8
97-98 Mia	2	0	11	1	5	.200	1	4	.250	1	2	.500	0	0	0	3	0	0	0.0	0	3	1.5	4	2.0
99-00 Det	3	3	77	9	15	.600	6	9	.667	1	2	.500	2	2	0	12	1	1	0.3	6	6	2.0	25	8.3
5 Years	17	7	409	49	122	.402	17	48	.354	16	25	.640	14	10	2	53	1	20	1.2	16	73	4.3	131	7.7

Jason Miskiri

Pos: G **College:** George Mason **Drafted:** '99 FA—Cha **Ht:** 6'2" **Wt:** 175 **Born:** 8/19/75 **Age:** 25

College

Year Tm	G	GS	Min	Md	Att	Pct	Md	Att	Pct	Md	Att	Pct	TO	Stl	Blk	PF	DQ	Ast	Avg	Off	Tot	Avg	Pts	Avg
				Field Goals			3-Pt FGs			Free Throws			Misc			Fouls		Assists		Rebounds			Points	
97-98 GMas	21	21	754	115	298	.386	31	115	.270	73	104	.702	83	40	6	69	3	92	4.4	23	93	4.4	334	15.9
98-99 GMas	29	28	996	157	393	.399	51	159	.321	93	152	.612	96	58	6	71	3	113	3.9	43	126	4.3	458	15.8
2 Years	50	49	1750	272	691	.394	82	274	.299	166	256	.648	179	98	12	140	6	205	4.1	66	219	4.4	792	15.8

NBA

Year Tm	G	GS	Min	Md	Att	Pct	Md	Att	Pct	Md	Att	Pct	TO	Stl	Blk	PF	DQ	Ast	Avg	Off	Tot	Avg	Pts	Avg
				Field Goals			3-Pt FGs			Free Throws			Misc			Fouls		Assists		Rebounds			Points	
99-00 Cha	1	0	3	0	1	.000	0	1	.000	0	0	—	0	0	0	2	0	1	1.0	0	0	0.0	0	0.0

Sam Mitchell

(statistical profile on page 250)

Pos: F **College:** Mercer **Drafted:** '85 3(54)—Hou **Ht:** 6'7" **Wt:** 210 **Born:** 9/2/63 **Age:** 37

College

Year Tm	G	GS	Min	Md	Att	Pct	Md	Att	Pct	Md	Att	Pct	TO	Stl	Blk	PF	DQ	Ast	Avg	Off	Tot	Avg	Pts	Avg
				Field Goals			3-Pt FGs			Free Throws			Misc			Fouls		Assists		Rebounds			Points	
81-82 Mer	27	—		77	155	.497	—	—	—	38	53	.717	—	—	—			13	0.5	—	100	3.7	192	7.1
82-83 Mer	28	—	964	178	343	.519	—	—	—	105	134	.784	—	—	—			47	1.7	—	164	5.9	461	16.5
83-84 Mer	26	—	935	219	432	.507	—	—	—	121	155	.781	—	—	—			46	1.8	—	184	7.1	559	21.5
84-85 Mer	31	—	1157	294	570	.516	—	—	—	186	248	.750	—	—	—			43	1.4	—	255	8.2	774	25.0
4 Years	112	—		768	1500	.512	—	—	—	450	590	.763	—	—	—			149	1.3	—	703	6.3	1986	17.7

NBA

Year Tm	G	GS	Min	Md	Att	Pct	Md	Att	Pct	Md	Att	Pct	TO	Stl	Blk	PF	DQ	Ast	Avg	Off	Tot	Avg	Pts	Avg
				Field Goals			3-Pt FGs			Free Throws			Misc			Fouls		Assists		Rebounds			Points	
85-86						Played in CBA, Played in USBL																		
86-87						Played in CBA																		
87-88						Played in France																		
88-89						Played in France																		
89-90 Min	80	30	2414	372	834	.446	0	9	.000	268	349	.768	96	66	54	301	7	89	1.1	180	462	5.8	1012	12.7
90-91 Min	82	60	3121	445	1010	.441	0	9	.000	307	396	.775	104	66	57	338	13	133	1.6	188	520	6.3	1197	14.6
91-92 Min	82	63	2151	307	725	.423	2	11	.182	209	266	.786	97	53	39	230	3	94	1.1	158	473	5.8	825	10.1
92-93 Ind	81	1	1402	215	483	.445	4	23	.174	150	185	.811	51	23	10	207	1	76	0.9	93	248	3.1	584	7.2
93-94 Ind	75	18	1084	140	306	.458	0	5	.000	82	110	.745	50	33	9	152	1	65	0.9	71	190	2.5	362	4.8

NBA			Field Goals			3-Pt FGs			Free Throws			Misc			Fouls		Assists		Rebounds			Points	
Year Tm	G	GS	Min	Md	Att	Pct	Md	Att	Pct	Md	Att	Pct	TO	Stl	Blk	PF	DQ	Ast	Avg	Off	Tot	Avg	Pts	Avg
94-95 Ind	81	12	1377	201	413	.487	1	10	.100	126	174	.724	54	43	20	206	0	61	0.8	95	243	3.0	529	6.5
95-96 Min	78	42	2145	303	618	.490	1	18	.056	237	291	.814	87	49	26	220	3	74	0.9	107	339	4.3	844	10.8
96-97 Min	82	5	2044	269	603	.446	4	25	.160	224	295	.759	93	51	20	232	1	79	1.0	112	326	4.0	766	9.3
97-98 Min	81	33	2239	371	800	.464	15	43	.349	243	292	.832	66	64	22	200	0	107	1.3	118	385	4.8	1000	12.3
98-99 Min	50	20	1344	213	522	.408	9	38	.237	126	165	.764	34	35	16	111	1	98	2.0	55	182	3.6	561	11.2
99-00 Min	66	24	1227	168	376	.447	10	23	.435	81	92	.880	44	27	14	116	0	111	1.7	28	138	2.1	427	6.5
11 Years	838	308	20548	3004	6690	.449	46	214	.215	2053	2615	.785	776	510	287	2313	30	987	1.2	1205	3506	4.2	8107	9.7

NBA Postseason																							
Year Tm	G	GS	Min	Md	Att	Pct	Md	Att	Pct	Md	Att	Pct	TO	Stl	Blk	PF	DQ	Ast	Avg	Off	Tot	Avg	Pts	Avg
92-93 Ind	4	0	25	5	8	.625	0	0	—	2	2	1.000	2	0	0	4	0	0	0.0	0	1	0.3	12	3.0
93-94 Ind	15	0	99	9	26	.346	0	1	.000	3	4	.750	4	2	2	22	0	5	0.3	5	17	1.1	21	1.4
94-95 Ind	17	0	223	23	64	.359	0	2	.000	22	28	.786	14	3	1	41	0	6	0.4	17	48	2.8	68	4.0
96-97 Min	3	0	47	6	13	.462	0	0	—	5	8	.625	1	1	1	9	0	1	0.3	2	7	2.3	17	5.7
97-98 Min	5	5	177	26	58	.448	3	14	.214	17	19	.895	5	1	1	18	0	8	1.6	7	27	5.4	72	14.4
98-99 Min	4	1	131	15	40	.375	1	6	.167	9	12	.750	8	1	2	13	0	6	1.5	5	14	3.5	40	10.0
99-00 Min	4	0	68	9	18	.500	2	5	.400	3	3	1.000	4	0	1	5	0	2	0.5	2	7	1.8	23	5.8
7 Years	52	6	770	93	227	.410	6	28	.214	61	76	.803	38	8	8	112	0	28	0.5	38	121	2.3	253	4.9

Cuttino Mobley

(statistical profile on page 250)

Pos: G **College:** Rhode Island **Drafted:** '98 2(41)—Hou   **Ht:** 6'4" **Wt:** 190 **Born:** 9/1/74 **Age:** 26

College			Field Goals			3-Pt FGs			Free Throws			Misc			Fouls		Assists		Rebounds			Points	
Year Tm	G	GS	Min	Md	Att	Pct	Md	Att	Pct	Md	Att	Pct	TO	Stl	Blk	PF	DQ	Ast	Avg	Off	Tot	Avg	Pts	Avg
94-95 RI	27	25	864	126	334	.377	43	142	.303	63	81	.778	60	43	14	87	—	39	1.4	—	129	4.8	358	13.3
95-96 RI	2	2	35	9	14	.643	5	7	.714	1	2	.500	4	4	0	6	0	5	2.5	0	0	0.0	24	12.0
96-97 RI	30	20	730	138	315	.438	29	97	.299	61	76	.803	48	39	9	82	1	44	1.5	36	117	3.9	366	12.2
97-98 RI	34	34	1133	193	402	.480	69	166	.416	131	153	.856	76	56	18	89	1	88	2.6	56	147	4.3	586	17.2
4 Years	93	81	2762	466	1065	.438	146	412	.354	256	312	.821	188	142	41	264	—	176	1.9	—	393	4.2	1334	14.3

NBA			Field Goals			3-Pt FGs			Free Throws			Misc			Fouls		Assists		Rebounds			Points	
Year Tm	G	GS	Min	Md	Att	Pct	Md	Att	Pct	Md	Att	Pct	TO	Stl	Blk	PF	DQ	Ast	Avg	Off	Tot	Avg	Pts	Avg
98-99 Hou	49	37	1456	172	405	.425	53	148	.358	90	110	.818	79	44	23	98	0	121	2.5	22	111	2.3	487	9.9
99-00 Hou	81	8	2496	437	1016	.430	104	292	.356	299	353	.847	186	87	32	171	0	208	2.6	59	288	3.6	1277	15.8
2 Years	130	45	3952	609	1421	.429	157	440	.357	389	463	.840	265	131	55	269	0	329	2.5	81	399	3.1	1764	13.6

NBA Postseason																							
Year Tm	G	GS	Min	Md	Att	Pct	Md	Att	Pct	Md	Att	Pct	TO	Stl	Blk	PF	DQ	Ast	Avg	Off	Tot	Avg	Pts	Avg
98-99 Hou	4	4	94	7	15	.467	4	7	.571	10	11	.909	5	2	0	11	0	11	2.8	0	4	1.0	28	7.0

Nazr Mohammed

Pos: C **College:** Kentucky **Drafted:** '98 1(29)—Uta   **Ht:** 6'10" **Wt:** 240 **Born:** 9/5/77 **Age:** 23

College			Field Goals			3-Pt FGs			Free Throws			Misc			Fouls		Assists		Rebounds			Points	
Year Tm	G	GS	Min	Md	Att	Pct	Md	Att	Pct	Md	Att	Pct	TO	Stl	Blk	PF	DQ	Ast	Avg	Off	Tot	Avg	Pts	Avg
95-96 Kty	16	0	88	13	29	.448	0	0	—	11	24	.458	18	4	8	18	0	3	0.2	6	24	1.5	37	2.3
96-97 Kty	39	12	667	132	259	.510	0	2	.000	45	89	.506	59	33	52	101	4	12	0.3	118	226	5.8	309	7.9
97-98 Kty	39	27	819	190	318	.597	0	0	—	88	135	.652	60	36	75	90	0	28	0.7	97	282	7.2	468	12.0
3 Years	94	39	1574	335	606	.553	0	2	.000	144	248	.581	137	73	135	209	4	43	0.5	221	532	5.7	814	8.7

NBA			Field Goals			3-Pt FGs			Free Throws			Misc			Fouls		Assists		Rebounds			Points	
Year Tm	G	GS	Min	Md	Att	Pct	Md	Att	Pct	Md	Att	Pct	TO	Stl	Blk	PF	DQ	Ast	Avg	Off	Tot	Avg	Pts	Avg
98-99 Phi	26	0	121	15	42	.357	0	0	—	12	21	.571	12	5	4	22	0	2	0.1	18	37	1.4	42	1.6
99-00 Phi	28	3	190	21	54	.389	0	0	—	12	22	.545	18	4	12	29	0	2	0.1	16	50	1.8	54	1.9
2 Years	54	3	311	36	96	.375	0	0	—	24	43	.558	30	9	16	51	0	4	0.1	34	87	1.6	96	1.8

NBA Postseason																							
Year Tm	G	GS	Min	Md	Att	Pct	Md	Att	Pct	Md	Att	Pct	TO	Stl	Blk	PF	DQ	Ast	Avg	Off	Tot	Avg	Pts	Avg
98-99 Phi	3	0	3	0	0	—	0	0	—	0	0	—	0	0	0	0	0	0	0.0	0	0	0.0	0	0.0

Eric Montross

Pos: C **College:** North Carolina **Drafted:** '94 1(9)—Bos   **Ht:** 7'0" **Wt:** 270 **Born:** 9/23/71 **Age:** 29

College			Field Goals			3-Pt FGs			Free Throws			Misc			Fouls		Assists		Rebounds			Points	
Year Tm	G	GS	Min	Md	Att	Pct	Md	Att	Pct	Md	Att	Pct	TO	Stl	Blk	PF	DQ	Ast	Avg	Off	Tot	Avg	Pts	Avg
90-91 UNC	35	9	531	81	138	.587	0	0	—	41	67	.612	32	6	30	79	—	11	0.3	47	148	4.2	203	5.8
91-92 UNC	31	25	784	140	244	.574	0	0	—	68	109	.624	47	17	30	112	—	18	0.6	92	218	7.0	348	11.2
92-93 UNC	38	36	1076	222	361	.615	0	0	—	156	228	.684	66	22	47	113	—	28	0.7	126	290	7.6	600	15.8

College			Field Goals			3-Pt FGs			Free Throws			Misc			Fouls		Assists		Rebounds			Points	
Year Tm	G	GS	Min	Md	Att	Pct	Md	Att	Pct	Md	Att	Pct	TO	Stl	Blk	PF	DQ	Ast	Avg	Off	Tot	Avg	Pts	Avg
93-94 UNC	35	35	1110	183	327	.560	0	0	—	110	197	.558	66	18	62	104	—	29	0.8	116	285	8.1	476	13.6
4 Years	139	105	3501	626	1070	.585	0	0	—	375	601	.624	211	63	169	408	—	86	0.6	381	941	6.8	1627	11.7

NBA			Field Goals			3-Pt FGs			Free Throws			Misc			Fouls		Assists		Rebounds			Points	
Year Tm	G	GS	Min	Md	Att	Pct	Md	Att	Pct	Md	Att	Pct	TO	Stl	Blk	PF	DQ	Ast	Avg	Off	Tot	Avg	Pts	Avg
94-95 Bos	78	75	2315	307	575	.534	0	1	.000	167	263	.635	112	29	61	299	10	36	0.5	196	566	7.3	781	10.0
95-96 Bos	61	59	1432	196	346	.566	0	0	—	50	133	.376	83	19	29	181	1	43	0.7	119	352	5.8	442	7.2
96-97 2Tm	78	77	1828	159	349	.456	0	0	—	21	62	.339	77	20	73	268	5	61	0.8	181	518	6.6	339	4.3
97-98 2Tm	48	30	691	61	144	.424	0	0	—	16	40	.400	29	13	27	127	1	11	0.2	69	199	4.1	138	2.9
98-99 Det	46	2	577	42	80	.525	0	1	.000	11	32	.344	16	12	27	107	1	14	0.3	45	139	3.0	95	2.1
99-00 Det	51	0	332	17	55	.309	0	0	—	6	12	.500	22	6	9	81	0	7	0.1	18	72	1.4	40	0.8
96-97 Dal	47	46	984	86	187	.460	0	0	—	10	34	.294	51	9	34	150	2	32	0.7	66	236	5.0	182	3.9
NJ	31	31	844	73	162	.451	0	0	—	11	28	.393	26	11	39	118	3	29	0.9	115	282	9.1	157	5.1
97-98 Phi	20	20	337	30	76	.395	0	0	—	7	19	.368	15	7	12	61	0	7	0.4	28	92	4.6	67	3.4
Det	28	10	354	31	68	.456	0	0	—	9	21	.429	14	6	15	66	1	4	0.1	41	107	3.8	71	2.5
6 Years	362	243	7175	782	1549	.505	0	2	.000	271	542	.500	339	99	226	1063	18	172	0.5	628	1846	5.1	1835	5.1

NBA Postseason

Year Tm	G	GS	Min	Md	Att	Pct	Md	Att	Pct	Md	Att	Pct	TO	Stl	Blk	PF	DQ	Ast	Avg	Off	Tot	Avg	Pts	Avg
94-95 Bos	4	4	62	5	11	.455	0	0	—	3	6	.500	8	0	0	13	0	0	0.0	7	9	2.3	13	3.3
98-99 Det	5	0	70	3	6	.500	0	0	—	1	2	.500	0	0	2	15	0	0	0.0	3	13	2.6	7	1.4
99-00 Det	2	0	5	0	0	—	0	0	—	0	0	—	0	0	0	2	0	0	0.0	0	2	1.0	0	0.0
3 Years	11	4	137	8	17	.471	0	0	—	4	8	.500	8	0	2	30	0	0	0.0	10	24	2.2	20	1.8

Mikki Moore

Pos: C **College:** Nebraska **Drafted:** '98 FA—Det   **Ht:** 7'0" **Wt:** 225 **Born:** 11/4/75 **Age:** 25

College			Field Goals			3-Pt FGs			Free Throws			Misc			Fouls		Assists		Rebounds			Points	
Year Tm	G	GS	Min	Md	Att	Pct	Md	Att	Pct	Md	Att	Pct	TO	Stl	Blk	PF	DQ	Ast	Avg	Off	Tot	Avg	Pts	Avg
93-94 Neb	14	0	87	10	22	.455	0	2	.000	11	18	.611	5	3	10	13	0	1	0.1	—	13	0.9	31	2.2
94-95 Neb	32	28	788	102	205	.498	2	8	.250	49	89	.551	42	15	67	94	4	25	0.8	—	198	6.2	255	8.0
95-96 Neb	35	27	968	118	202	.584	0	0	—	79	115	.687	65	26	71	112	5	36	1.0	—	205	5.9	315	9.0
96-97 Neb	33	32	1011	144	247	.583	1	2	.500	96	137	.701	82	35	88	105	5	43	1.3	99	245	7.4	385	11.7
4 Years	114	87	2854	374	676	.553	3	12	.250	235	359	.655	194	79	236	324	14	105	0.9	—	661	5.8	986	8.6

NBA			Field Goals			3-Pt FGs			Free Throws			Misc			Fouls		Assists		Rebounds			Points	
Year Tm	G	GS	Min	Md	Att	Pct	Md	Att	Pct	Md	Att	Pct	TO	Stl	Blk	PF	DQ	Ast	Avg	Off	Tot	Avg	Pts	Avg
97-98										Played in CBA														
98-99 Det	2	0	6	1	1	1.000	0	0	—	2	2	1.000	0	0	0	0	0	0	0.0	0	1	0.5	4	2.0
99-00 Det	29	0	488	87	140	.621	0	0	—	54	68	.794	23	9	31	104	5	17	0.6	44	112	3.9	228	7.9
2 Years	31	0	494	88	141	.624	0	0	—	56	70	.800	23	9	31	104	5	17	0.5	44	113	3.6	232	7.5

NBA Postseason

Year Tm	G	GS	Min	Md	Att	Pct	Md	Att	Pct	Md	Att	Pct	TO	Stl	Blk	PF	DQ	Ast	Avg	Off	Tot	Avg	Pts	Avg
99-00 Det	3	0	42	5	12	.417	0	0	—	8	8	1.000	4	1	0	9	0	3	1.0	7	12	4.0	18	6.0

Alonzo Mourning

(statistical profile on page 251)

Pos: C **College:** Georgetown **Drafted:** '92 1(2)—Cha   **Ht:** 6'10" **Wt:** 261 **Born:** 2/8/70 **Age:** 30

College			Field Goals			3-Pt FGs			Free Throws			Misc			Fouls		Assists		Rebounds			Points	
Year Tm	G	GS	Min	Md	Att	Pct	Md	Att	Pct	Md	Att	Pct	TO	Stl	Blk	PF	DQ	Ast	Avg	Off	Tot	Avg	Pts	Avg
88-89 GTwn	34	34	962	158	262	.603	1	4	.250	130	195	.667	67	15	169	102	6	24	0.7	89	248	7.3	447	13.1
89-90 GTwn	31	31	937	145	276	.525	0	2	.000	220	281	.783	88	15	69	112	10	36	1.2	91	265	8.5	510	16.5
90-91 GTwn	23	23	680	105	201	.522	4	13	.308	149	188	.793	58	10	55	74	1	25	1.1	64	176	7.7	363	15.8
91-92 GTwn	32	32	1051	204	343	.595	1	4	.250	272	359	.758	84	19	160	115	3	53	1.7	114	343	10.7	681	21.3
4 Years	120	120	3630	612	1082	.566	6	23	.261	771	1023	.754	297	59	453	403	20	138	1.2	358	1032	8.6	2001	16.7

NBA			Field Goals			3-Pt FGs			Free Throws			Misc			Fouls		Assists		Rebounds			Points	
Year Tm	G	GS	Min	Md	Att	Pct	Md	Att	Pct	Md	Att	Pct	TO	Stl	Blk	PF	DQ	Ast	Avg	Off	Tot	Avg	Pts	Avg
92-93 Cha	78	78	2644	572	1119	.511	0	3	.000	495	634	.781	236	27	271	286	6	76	1.0	263	805	10.3	1639	21.0
93-94 Cha*	60	59	2018	427	845	.505	0	2	.000	433	568	.762	199	27	188	207	3	86	1.4	177	610	10.2	1287	21.5
94-95 Cha*	77	77	2941	571	1101	.519	11	34	.324	490	644	.761	241	49	225	275	5	111	1.4	200	761	9.9	1643	21.3
95-96 Mia*	70	70	2671	563	1076	.523	9	30	.300	488	712	.685	262	70	189	245	5	159	2.3	218	727	10.4	1623	23.2
96-97 Mia*	66	65	2320	473	885	.534	1	9	.111	363	565	.642	226	56	189	272	9	104	1.6	189	656	9.9	1310	19.8
97-98 Mia	58	56	1939	403	732	.551	0	0	—	309	465	.665	179	40	130	208	4	52	0.9	193	558	9.6	1115	19.2
98-99 Mia	46	46	1753	324	634	.511	0	2	.000	276	423	.652	139	34	**180**	161	1	74	1.6	166	507	11.0	924	20.1
99-00 Mia*	79	78	2748	652	1184	.551	0	4	.000	414	582	.711	217	40	**294**	308	8	123	1.6	215	753	9.5	1718	21.7
8 Years	534	529	19034	3985	7576	.526	21	84	.250	3268	4593	.712	1699	343	1666	1962	41	785	1.5	1621	5377	10.1	11259	21.1

Year Tm	G	GS	Min	Md	Att	Pct	Md	Att	Pct	Md	Att	Pct	TO	Stl	Blk	PF	DQ	Ast	Avg	Off	Tot	Avg	Pts	Avg
92-93 Cha	9	9	367	71	148	.480	0	2	.000	72	93	.774	37	6	31	37	1	13	1.4	28	89	9.9	214	23.8
94-95 Cha	4	4	174	24	57	.421	4	8	.500	36	43	.837	14	3	13	17	0	11	2.8	14	53	13.3	88	22.0
95-96 Mia	3	3	92	17	35	.486	0	0	—	20	28	.714	16	2	3	13	1	4	1.3	3	18	6.0	54	18.0
96-97 Mia	17	17	630	107	218	.491	3	8	.375	86	155	.555	70	11	46	73	2	18	1.1	44	173	10.2	303	17.8
97-98 Mia	4	4	138	29	56	.518	0	0	—	19	29	.655	8	3	10	18	0	5	1.3	10	34	8.5	77	19.3
98-99 Mia	5	5	194	38	73	.521	0	0	—	32	49	.653	12	8	14	19	0	4	0.8	7	41	8.2	108	21.6
99-00 Mia	10	10	376	76	157	.484	0	1	.000	64	96	.667	24	2	33	40	1	14	1.4	31	100	10.0	216	21.6
7 Years	52	52	1971	362	744	.487	7	19	.368	329	493	.667	181	35	150	217	5	69	1.3	137	508	9.8	1060	20.4

Chris Mullin

Pos: F **College:** St. John's (NY) **Drafted:** '85 1(7)—GS   **Ht:** 6'7" **Wt:** 215 **Born:** 7/30/63 **Age:** 37

College

Year Tm	G	GS	Min	Md	Att	Pct	Md	Att	Pct	Md	Att	Pct	TO	Stl	Blk	PF	DQ	Ast	Avg	Off	Tot	Avg	Pts	Avg
81-82 StJn	30	30	1061	175	328	.534	—	—	—	148	187	.791	97	43	6	81	3	92	3.1	—	97	3.2	498	16.6
82-83 StJn	33	33	1210	228	395	.577	—	—	—	173	197	.878	94	39	8	69	1	101	3.1	—	123	3.7	629	19.1
83-84 StJn	27	27	1070	225	394	.571	—	—	—	169	187	.904	100	56	11	61	1	109	4.0	—	120	4.4	619	22.9
84-85 StJn	35	35	1327	251	482	.521	—	—	—	192	233	.824	90	73	17	68	0	151	4.3	—	169	4.8	694	19.8
4 Years	125	125	4668	879	1599	.550	—	—	—	682	804	.848	381	211	42	279	5	453	3.6	—	509	4.1	2440	19.5

NBA

Year Tm	G	GS	Min	Md	Att	Pct	Md	Att	Pct	Md	Att	Pct	TO	Stl	Blk	PF	DQ	Ast	Avg	Off	Tot	Avg	Pts	Avg
85-86 GS	55	30	1391	287	620	.463	5	27	.185	189	211	.896	75	70	23	130	1	105	1.9	42	115	2.1	768	14.0
86-87 GS	82	82	2377	477	928	.514	19	63	.302	269	326	.825	154	98	36	217	1	261	3.2	39	181	2.2	1242	15.1
87-88 GS	60	55	2033	470	926	.508	34	97	.351	239	270	.885	156	113	32	136	3	290	4.8	58	205	3.4	1213	20.2
88-89 GS*	82	82	3093	830	1630	.509	23	100	.230	493	553	.892	296	176	39	178	1	415	5.1	152	483	5.9	2176	26.5
89-90 GS*	78	78	2830	682	1272	.536	87	234	.372	505	568	.889	239	123	45	142	0	319	4.1	130	463	5.9	1956	25.1
90-91 GS*	82	82	3315	777	1449	.536	40	133	.301	513	580	.884	245	173	63	176	2	329	4.0	141	443	5.4	2107	25.7
91-92 GS*	81	81	3346	830	1584	.524	64	175	.366	350	420	.833	202	173	62	171	1	286	3.5	127	450	5.6	2074	25.6
92-93 GS*	46	46	1902	474	930	.510	60	133	.451	183	226	.810	139	68	41	76	0	166	3.6	42	232	5.0	1191	25.9
93-94 GS	62	39	2324	410	869	.472	55	151	.364	165	219	.753	178	107	53	114	0	315	5.1	42	345	5.6	1040	16.8
94-95 GS	25	23	890	170	348	.489	42	93	.452	94	107	.879	93	38	19	53	0	125	5.0	25	115	4.6	476	19.0
95-96 GS	55	19	1617	269	539	.499	59	150	.393	137	160	.856	122	75	32	127	0	194	3.5	44	159	2.9	734	13.3
96-97 GS	79	63	2733	438	792	.553	83	202	.411	184	213	.864	192	130	33	155	0	322	4.1	44	317	4.0	1143	14.5
97-98 Ind	82	82	2177	333	692	.481	107	243	.440	154	164	.939	117	95	39	186	0	186	2.3	38	249	3.0	927	11.3
98-99 Ind	50	50	1179	177	371	.477	73	157	.465	80	92	.870	60	47	13	101	0	81	1.6	25	160	3.2	507	10.1
99-00 Ind	47	2	582	80	187	.428	45	110	.409	37	41	.902	28	28	9	60	0	37	0.8	14	76	1.6	242	5.1
15 Years	966	814	31789	6704	13137	.510	796	2068	.385	3592	4150	.866	2296	1514	539	2022	10	3431	3.6	1016	3993	4.1	17796	18.4

NBA Postseason

Year Tm	G	GS	Min	Md	Att	Pct	Md	Att	Pct	Md	Att	Pct	TO	Stl	Blk	PF	DQ	Ast	Avg	Off	Tot	Avg	Pts	Avg
86-87 GS	10	10	262	49	98	.500	3	4	.750	12	16	.750	16	9	2	31	0	23	2.3	2	15	1.5	113	11.3
88-89 GS	8	8	341	88	163	.540	1	8	.125	58	67	.866	32	14	11	19	0	36	4.5	11	47	5.9	235	29.4
90-91 GS	8	8	366	69	131	.527	9	13	.692	43	50	.860	25	15	12	23	0	23	2.9	9	58	7.3	190	23.8
91-92 GS	4	4	168	27	63	.429	4	12	.333	13	14	.929	8	5	2	8	0	12	2.9	3	12	3.0	71	17.8
93-94 GS	3	3	135	30	51	.588	6	12	.500	10	11	.909	7	0	5	4	0	11	3.7	4	14	4.7	76	25.3
97-98 Ind	16	16	412	52	113	.460	20	52	.385	18	21	.857	24	15	9	32	0	23	1.4	13	57	3.6	142	8.9
98-99 Ind	13	13	283	41	100	.410	22	55	.400	20	23	.870	20	10	3	21	0	15	1.2	2	20	1.5	124	9.5
99-00 Ind	9	1	90	10	21	.476	2	8	.250	9	11	.818	4	6	1	7	0	5	0.6	2	14	1.6	31	3.4
8 Years	71	63	2057	366	740	.495	67	164	.409	183	213	.859	136	74	45	145	0	148	2.1	46	237	3.3	982	13.8

Eric Murdock

Pos: G **College:** Providence **Drafted:** '91 1(21)—Uta   **Ht:** 6'1" **Wt:** 200 **Born:** 6/14/68 **Age:** 32

College

Year Tm	G	GS	Min	Md	Att	Pct	Md	Att	Pct	Md	Att	Pct	TO	Stl	Blk	PF	DQ	Ast	Avg	Off	Tot	Avg	Pts	Avg
87-88 Prov	28	20	768	114	276	.413	27	76	.355	45	61	.738	66	90	3	84	5	106	3.8	26	85	3.0	300	10.7
88-89 Prov	29	29	936	164	359	.457	44	126	.349	99	130	.762	77	97	9	84	2	141	4.9	36	135	4.7	471	16.2
89-90 Prov	28	19	833	147	351	.419	42	115	.365	96	126	.762	68	78	15	78	0	92	3.3	34	116	4.1	432	15.4
90-91 Prov	32	32	1111	262	589	.445	56	160	.350	238	293	.812	119	111	5	98	2	148	4.6	59	168	5.3	818	25.6
4 Years	117	100	3648	687	1575	.436	169	477	.354	478	610	.784	330	376	32	344	9	487	4.2	155	504	4.3	2021	17.3

NBA

Year Tm	G	GS	Min	Md	Att	Pct	Md	Att	Pct	Md	Att	Pct	TO	Stl	Blk	PF	DQ	Ast	Avg	Off	Tot	Avg	Pts	Avg
91-92 Uta	50	0	478	76	183	.415	5	26	.192	46	61	.754	50	30	7	52	0	92	1.8	21	54	1.1	203	4.1
92-93 Mil	79	78	2437	438	936	.468	31	119	.261	231	296	.780	207	174	7	177	2	603	7.6	95	284	3.6	1138	14.4
93-94 Mil	82	76	2533	477	1019	.468	69	168	.411	234	288	.813	206	197	12	189	2	546	6.7	91	261	3.2	1257	15.3

NBA				Field Goals			3-Pt FGs			Free Throws			Misc			Fouls		Assists		Rebounds			Points	
Year Tm	G	GS	Min	Md	Att	Pct	Md	Att	Pct	Md	Att	Pct	TO	Stl	Blk	PF	DQ	Ast	Avg	Off	Tot	Avg	Pts	Avg
94-95 Mil	75	32	2158	338	814	.415	90	240	.375	211	267	.790	194	113	12	139	0	482	6.4	48	214	2.9	977	13.0
95-96 2Tm	73	14	1673	244	587	.416	45	145	.310	114	143	.797	132	135	9	140	0	327	4.5	26	169	2.3	647	8.9
96-97 Den	12	0	114	15	33	.455	4	10	.400	11	12	.917	11	9	2	9	0	24	2.0	1	11	0.9	45	3.8
97-98 Mia	82	1	1395	177	419	.422	28	91	.308	125	156	.801	104	103	13	173	1	219	2.7	39	156	1.9	507	6.2
98-99 NJ	15	8	401	45	114	.395	8	22	.364	21	26	.808	29	22	2	35	1	66	4.4	3	35	2.3	119	7.9
99-00 LAC	40	15	693	79	205	.385	16	42	.381	51	80	.638	58	47	5	67	0	108	2.7	15	77	1.9	225	5.6
95-96 Mil	9	0	193	24	66	.364	6	23	.261	8	12	.667	12	6	0	16	0	35	3.9	5	14	1.6	62	6.9
Van	64	14	1480	220	521	.422	39	122	.320	106	131	.809	120	129	9	124	0	292	4.6	21	155	2.4	585	9.1
9 Years	508	224	11882	1889	4310	.438	296	863	.343	1044	1329	.786	991	830	69	981	6	2467	4.9	339	1261	2.5	5118	10.1

NBA Postseason																								
Year Tm	G	GS	Min	Md	Att	Pct	Md	Att	Pct	Md	Att	Pct	TO	Stl	Blk	PF	DQ	Ast	Avg	Off	Tot	Avg	Pts	Avg
91-92 Uta	3	0	11	3	5	.600	0	1	.000	2	2	1.000	3	1	1	1	0	1	0.3	0	3	1.0	8	2.7
97-98 Mia	5	0	125	11	32	.344	2	9	.222	23	28	.821	4	7	0	11	0	15	3.0	3	20	4.0	47	9.4
2 Years	8	0	136	14	37	.378	2	10	.200	25	30	.833	7	8	1	12	0	16	2.0	3	23	2.9	55	6.9

Gheorghe Muresan

Pos: C **College:** Cluj (Romania) **Drafted:** '93 2(30)—Was **Ht:** 7'7" **Wt:** 303 **Born:** 2/14/71 **Age:** 29

NBA				Field Goals			3-Pt FGs			Free Throws			Misc			Fouls		Assists		Rebounds			Points	
Year Tm	G	GS	Min	Md	Att	Pct	Md	Att	Pct	Md	Att	Pct	TO	Stl	Blk	PF	DQ	Ast	Avg	Off	Tot	Avg	Pts	Avg
93-94 Was	54	2	650	128	235	.545	0	0	—	48	71	.676	54	28	48	120	1	18	0.3	66	192	3.6	304	5.6
94-95 Was	73	58	1720	303	541	.560	0	0	—	124	175	.709	115	48	127	259	6	38	0.5	179	488	6.7	730	10.0
95-96 Was	76	76	2242	466	798	.584	0	1	.000	172	278	.619	143	52	172	297	8	56	0.7	248	728	9.6	1104	14.5
96-97 Was	73	69	1849	327	541	.604	0	0	—	123	199	.618	117	43	96	230	3	29	0.4	141	481	6.6	777	10.6
97-98 Was										Did not play: injury — Left Knee														
98-99 NJ	1	0	1	0	1	.000	0	0	—	0	0	—	0	0	0	0	0	0	0.0	0	0	0.0	0	0.0
99-00 NJ	30	2	267	41	90	.456	0	0	—	23	38	.605	16	0	12	52	0	9	0.3	24	68	2.3	105	3.5
6 Years	307	207	6729	1265	2206	.573	0	1	.000	490	761	.644	446	171	455	958	18	150	0.5	658	1957	6.4	3020	9.8

NBA Postseason																								
Year Tm	G	GS	Min	Md	Att	Pct	Md	Att	Pct	Md	Att	Pct	TO	Stl	Blk	PF	DQ	Ast	Avg	Off	Tot	Avg	Pts	Avg
96-97 Was	3	3	70	4	9	.444	0	0	—	7	8	.875	11	0	4	6	0	0	0.0	2	18	6.0	15	5.0

Lamond Murray

(statistical profile on page 251)

Pos: F **College:** California **Drafted:** '94 1(7)—LAC **Ht:** 6'7" **Wt:** 236 **Born:** 4/20/73 **Age:** 27

College				Field Goals			3-Pt FGs			Free Throws			Misc			Fouls		Assists		Rebounds			Points	
Year Tm	G	GS	Min	Md	Att	Pct	Md	Att	Pct	Md	Att	Pct	TO	Stl	Blk	PF	DQ	Ast	Avg	Off	Tot	Avg	Pts	Avg
91-92 Cal	28	20	745	152	321	.474	17	56	.304	66	93	.710	64	34	19	66	2	56	2.0	—	171	6.1	387	13.8
92-93 Cal	30	28	897	230	445	.517	36	99	.364	76	121	.628	79	32	26	69	3	41	1.4	—	189	6.3	572	19.1
93-94 Cal	30	29	1047	262	550	.476	46	139	.331	159	208	.764	84	44	31	71	2	63	2.1	—	236	7.9	729	24.3
3 Years	88	77	2689	644	1316	.489	99	294	.337	301	422	.713	227	110	76	206	7	160	1.8	—	596	6.8	1688	19.2

NBA				Field Goals			3-Pt FGs			Free Throws			Misc			Fouls		Assists		Rebounds			Points	
Year Tm	G	GS	Min	Md	Att	Pct	Md	Att	Pct	Md	Att	Pct	TO	Stl	Blk	PF	DQ	Ast	Avg	Off	Tot	Avg	Pts	Avg
94-95 LAC	81	61	2556	439	1093	.402	65	218	.298	199	264	.754	163	72	55	180	3	133	1.6	132	354	4.4	1142	14.1
95-96 LAC	77	32	1816	257	575	.447	37	116	.319	99	132	.750	108	61	25	151	0	84	1.1	89	246	3.2	650	8.4
96-97 LAC	74	1	1295	181	435	.416	31	91	.341	156	211	.739	86	53	29	113	2	57	0.8	85	233	3.1	549	7.4
97-98 LAC	79	65	2579	473	984	.481	54	153	.353	220	294	.748	171	118	54	193	3	142	1.8	172	484	6.1	1220	15.4
98-99 LAC	50	13	1317	226	578	.391	34	103	.330	126	157	.803	99	58	20	107	1	61	1.2	59	195	3.9	612	12.2
99-00 Cle	74	72	2365	460	1019	.451	51	139	.367	204	268	.761	184	105	36	208	2	132	1.8	127	423	5.7	1175	15.9
6 Years	435	244	11928	2036	4684	.435	272	820	.332	1004	1326	.757	811	467	219	952	12	609	1.4	664	1935	4.4	5348	12.3

NBA Postseason																								
Year Tm	G	GS	Min	Md	Att	Pct	Md	Att	Pct	Md	Att	Pct	TO	Stl	Blk	PF	DQ	Ast	Avg	Off	Tot	Avg	Pts	Avg
96-97 LAC	3	0	65	6	20	.300	2	8	.250	7	7	1.000	4	2	3	7	0	3	1.0	2	11	3.7	21	7.0

Tracy Murray

(statistical profile on page 252)

Pos: F **College:** UCLA **Drafted:** '92 1(18)—SA **Ht:** 6'7" **Wt:** 228 **Born:** 7/25/71 **Age:** 29

College				Field Goals			3-Pt FGs			Free Throws			Misc			Fouls		Assists		Rebounds			Points	
Year Tm	G	GS	Min	Md	Att	Pct	Md	Att	Pct	Md	Att	Pct	TO	Stl	Blk	PF	DQ	Ast	Avg	Off	Tot	Avg	Pts	Avg
89-90 UCLA	33	18	863	146	330	.442	46	134	.343	69	90	.767	47	28	26	103	3	41	1.2	—	182	5.5	407	12.3
90-91 UCLA	32	32	1003	247	491	.503	73	189	.386	112	141	.794	62	41	35	88	3	43	1.3	—	213	6.7	679	21.2
91-92 UCLA	33	33	1083	240	446	.538	78	156	.500	148	185	.800	69	53	30	86	2	59	1.8	—	232	7.0	706	21.4
3 Years	98	83	2949	633	1267	.500	197	479	.411	329	416	.791	178	122	91	277	8	143	1.5	—	627	6.4	1792	18.3

117

NBA				Field Goals			3-Pt FGs			Free Throws			Misc			Fouls		Assists		Rebounds			Points	
Year Tm	G	GS	Min	Md	Att	Pct	Md	Att	Pct	Md	Att	Pct	TO	Stl	Blk	PF	DQ	Ast	Avg	Off	Tot	Avg	Pts	Avg
92-93 Por	48	14	495	108	260	.415	21	70	.300	35	40	.875	31	8	5	59	0	11	0.2	40	83	1.7	272	5.7
93-94 Por	66	1	820	167	355	.470	50	109	.459	50	72	.694	37	21	20	76	0	31	0.5	43	111	1.7	434	6.6
94-95 2Tm	54	3	516	95	233	.408	35	86	.407	33	42	.786	35	14	4	73	0	19	0.4	20	59	1.1	258	4.8
95-96 Tor	82	37	2458	496	1092	.454	151	358	.422	182	219	.831	132	87	40	208	2	131	1.6	114	352	4.3	1325	16.2
96-97 Was	82	1	1814	288	678	.425	106	300	.353	135	161	.839	86	69	19	150	1	78	1.0	84	253	3.1	817	10.0
97-98 Was	82	12	2227	449	1007	.446	158	403	.392	182	209	.871	102	67	25	167	0	84	1.0	75	277	3.4	1238	15.1
98-99 Was	36	0	653	83	237	.350	33	103	.320	34	42	.810	29	21	6	65	0	27	0.8	18	81	2.3	233	6.5
99-00 Was	80	8	1831	290	670	.433	113	263	.430	120	141	.851	84	45	24	185	2	72	0.9	63	271	3.4	813	10.2
94-95 Por	29	3	313	63	153	.412	16	41	.390	28	34	.824	20	7	1	42	0	14	0.5	18	37	1.3	170	5.9
Hou	25	0	203	32	80	.400	19	45	.422	5	8	.625	15	7	3	31	0	5	0.2	2	22	0.9	88	3.5
8 Years	530	76	10814	1976	4532	.436	667	1692	.394	771	926	.833	536	332	143	983	5	453	0.9	457	1487	2.8	5390	10.2

NBA Postseason

Year Tm	G	GS	Min	Md	Att	Pct	Md	Att	Pct	Md	Att	Pct	TO	Stl	Blk	PF	DQ	Ast	Avg	Off	Tot	Avg	Pts	Avg
93-94 Por	2	0	11	3	6	.500	0	1	.000	0	0	—	0	1	0	3	0	1	0.5	3	3	1.5	6	3.0
96-97 Was	3	0	87	17	30	.567	5	10	.500	16	17	.941	0	4	2	10	0	2	0.7	3	9	3.0	55	18.3
2 Years	5	0	98	20	36	.556	5	11	.455	16	17	.941	0	5	2	13	0	3	0.6	6	12	2.4	61	12.2

Dikembe Mutombo

Pos: C **College:** Georgetown **Drafted:** '91 1(4)—Den   (statistical profile on page 252)

Ht: 7'2" **Wt:** 261 **Born:** 6/25/66 **Age:** 34

College				Field Goals			3-Pt FGs			Free Throws			Misc			Fouls		Assists		Rebounds			Points	
Year Tm	G	GS	Min	Md	Att	Pct	Md	Att	Pct	Md	Att	Pct	TO	Stl	Blk	PF	DQ	Ast	Avg	Off	Tot	Avg	Pts	Avg
88-89 GTwn	33	0	374	53	75	.707	0	0	—	23	48	.479	30	11	75	61	2	5	0.2	38	109	3.3	129	3.9
89-90 GTwn	31	24	797	129	182	.709	0	0	—	73	122	.598	62	12	128	82	3	18	0.6	123	325	10.5	331	10.7
90-91 GTwn	32	32	1090	170	290	.586	0	0	—	147	209	.703	73	20	151	91	3	52	1.6	130	389	12.2	487	15.2
3 Years	96	56	2261	352	547	.644	0	0	—	243	379	.641	165	43	354	234	8	75	0.8	291	823	8.6	947	9.9

NBA				Field Goals			3-Pt FGs			Free Throws			Misc			Fouls		Assists		Rebounds			Points	
Year Tm	G	GS	Min	Md	Att	Pct	Md	Att	Pct	Md	Att	Pct	TO	Stl	Blk	PF	DQ	Ast	Avg	Off	Tot	Avg	Pts	Avg
91-92 Den*	71	71	2716	428	869	.493	0	0	—	321	500	.642	252	43	210	273	1	156	2.2	316	870	12.3	1177	16.6
92-93 Den	82	82	3029	398	781	.510	0	0	—	335	492	.681	216	43	287	284	5	147	1.8	344	1070	13.0	1131	13.8
93-94 Den	82	82	2853	365	642	.569	0	1	.000	256	439	.583	206	59	336	262	2	127	1.5	286	971	11.8	986	12.0
94-95 Den*	82	82	3100	349	628	.556	0	0	—	248	379	.654	192	40	321	284	2	113	1.4	319	1029	12.5	946	11.5
95-96 Den	74	74	2713	284	569	.499	0	1	.000	246	354	.695	150	38	332	258	4	108	1.5	249	814	11.0	814	11.0
96-97 Atl*	80	80	2973	380	721	.527	0	0	—	306	434	.705	186	49	264	249	3	110	1.4	268	929	11.6	1066	13.3
97-98 Atl*	82	82	2917	399	743	.537	0	0	—	303	452	.670	168	34	277	254		82	1.0	276	932	11.4	1101	13.4
98-99 Atl	50	50	1829	173	338	.512	0	0	—	195	285	.684	94	16	147	145	2	57	1.1	192	610	12.2	541	10.8
99-00 Atl*	82	82	2984	322	573	.562	0	0	—	298	421	.708	174	27	269	248	3	105	1.3	304	1157	14.1	942	11.5
9 Years	685	685	25114	3098	5864	.528	0	2	.000	2508	3756	.668	1638	349	2443	2257	23	1005	1.5	2554	8439	12.3	8704	12.7

NBA Postseason

Year Tm	G	GS	Min	Md	Att	Pct	Md	Att	Pct	Md	Att	Pct	TO	Stl	Blk	PF	DQ	Ast	Avg	Off	Tot	Avg	Pts	Avg
93-94 Den	12	12	511	50	108	.463	0	0	—	59	98	.602	30	8	69	42	0	21	1.8	40	144	12.0	159	13.3
94-95 Den	3	3	84	6	10	.600	0	0	—	6	9	.667	7	0	7	15	1	1	0.3	4	19	6.3	18	6.0
96-97 Atl	10	10	415	54	86	.628	0	0	—	46	64	.719	20	1	26	30	0	13	1.3	37	123	12.3	154	15.4
97-98 Atl	4	4	136	11	24	.458	0	0	—	10	16	.625	8	1	9	10	0	1	0.3	13	51	12.8	32	8.0
98-99 Atl	9	9	380	40	71	.563	0	0	—	33	47	.702	18	5	23	28	0	11	1.2	36	125	13.9	113	12.6
5 Years	38	38	1526	161	299	.538	0	0	—	154	234	.658	83	15	134	125	1	47	1.2	130	462	12.2	476	12.5

Steve Nash

Pos: G **College:** Santa Clara **Drafted:** '96 1(15)—Pho   (statistical profile on page 253)

Ht: 6'3" **Wt:** 195 **Born:** 2/7/74 **Age:** 26

College				Field Goals			3-Pt FGs			Free Throws			Misc			Fouls		Assists		Rebounds			Points	
Year Tm	G	GS	Min	Md	Att	Pct	Md	Att	Pct	Md	Att	Pct	TO	Stl	Blk	PF	DQ	Ast	Avg	Off	Tot	Avg	Pts	Avg
92-93 SanCl	31	5	743	78	184	.424	49	120	.408	47	57	.825	62	26	4	54	1	67	2.2	19	79	2.5	252	8.1
93-94 SanCl	26	23	778	122	295	.414	67	168	.399	69	83	.831	74	34	1	57	1	95	3.7	25	65	2.5	380	14.6
94-95 SanCl	27	27	902	164	369	.444	84	185	.454	153	174	.879	113	48	2	53	3	174	6.4	13	102	3.8	565	20.9
95-96 SanCl	29	29	979	164	381	.430	63	183	.344	101	113	.894	103	39	0	43	0	174	6.0	22	103	3.6	492	17.0
4 Years	113	84	3402	528	1229	.430	263	656	.401	370	427	.867	352	147	7	207	5	510	4.5	79	349	3.1	1689	14.9

NBA				Field Goals			3-Pt FGs			Free Throws			Misc			Fouls		Assists		Rebounds			Points	
Year Tm	G	GS	Min	Md	Att	Pct	Md	Att	Pct	Md	Att	Pct	TO	Stl	Blk	PF	DQ	Ast	Avg	Off	Tot	Avg	Pts	Avg
96-97 Pho	65	2	684	74	175	.423	23	55	.418	42	51	.824	63	20	0	92	1	138	2.1	16	63	1.0	213	3.3
97-98 Pho	76	9	1664	268	584	.459	81	195	.415	74	86	.860	98	63	4	145	1	262	3.4	32	160	2.1	691	9.1
98-99 Dal	40	19	1269	114	314	.363	49	131	.374	38	46	.826	83	37	2	98	2	219	5.5	32	160	2.9	315	7.9
99-00 Dal	56	27	1532	173	363	.477	60	149	.403	75	85	.882	102	37	3	122	1	272	4.9	34	121	2.2	481	8.6
4 Years	237	78	5149	629	1436	.438	213	530	.402	229	268	.854	346	157	9	457	5	891	3.8	114	458	1.9	1700	7.2

Year Tm	G	GS	Min	Md	Att	Pct	Md	Att	Pct	Md	Att	Pct	TO	Stl	Blk	PF	DQ	Ast	Avg	Off	Tot	Avg	Pts	Avg
96-97 Pho	4	0	15	2	9	.222	1	4	.250	0	0	—	2	1	1	5	0	1	0.3	1	1	0.3	5	1.3
97-98 Pho	4	1	51	8	18	.444	1	5	.200	5	8	.625	3	2	0	7	0	7	1.8	2	10	2.5	22	5.5
2 Years	8	1	66	10	27	.370	2	9	.222	5	8	.625	5	3	1	12	0	8	1.0	3	11	1.4	27	3.4

Tyrone Nesby

(statistical profile on page 253)

Pos: F **College:** UNLV **Drafted:** '98 FA—LAC **Ht:** 6'6" **Wt:** 225 **Born:** 1/31/76 **Age:** 25

College				Field Goals			3-Pt FGs			Free Throws			Misc			Fouls		Assists		Rebounds			Points	
Year Tm	G	GS	Min	Md	Att	Pct	Md	Att	Pct	Md	Att	Pct	TO	Stl	Blk	PF	DQ	Ast	Avg	Off	Tot	Avg	Pts	Avg
96-97 UNLV	32	31	1063	190	482	.394	41	147	.279	108	150	.720	67	48	24	87	2	60	1.9	73	228	7.1	529	16.5
97-98 UNLV	33	24	1082	187	486	.385	52	156	.333	95	134	.709	53	42	13	51	1	40	1.2	50	185	5.6	521	15.8
2 Years	65	55	2145	377	968	.389	93	303	.307	203	284	.715	120	90	37	138	3	100	1.5	123	413	6.4	1050	16.2

NBA				Field Goals			3-Pt FGs			Free Throws			Misc			Fouls		Assists		Rebounds			Points	
Year Tm	G	GS	Min	Md	Att	Pct	Md	Att	Pct	Md	Att	Pct	TO	Stl	Blk	PF	DQ	Ast	Avg	Off	Tot	Avg	Pts	Avg
98-99 LAC	50	36	1288	182	405	.449	35	96	.365	104	133	.782	53	77	20	143	2	82	1.6	57	175	3.5	503	10.1
99-00 LAC	73	39	2317	364	915	.398	94	281	.335	151	191	.791	102	75	31	205	5	121	1.7	82	275	3.8	973	13.3
2 Years	123	75	3605	546	1320	.414	129	377	.342	255	324	.787	155	152	51	348	7	203	1.7	139	450	3.7	1476	12.0

Radoslav Nesterovic

(statistical profile on page 254)

Pos: C **College:** None **Drafted:** '98 1(17)—Min **Ht:** 7'0" **Wt:** 248 **Born:** 5/30/76 **Age:** 24

NBA				Field Goals			3-Pt FGs			Free Throws			Misc			Fouls		Assists		Rebounds			Points	
Year Tm	G	GS	Min	Md	Att	Pct	Md	Att	Pct	Md	Att	Pct	TO	Stl	Blk	PF	DQ	Ast	Avg	Off	Tot	Avg	Pts	Avg
98-99 Min	2	0	30	3	12	.250	0	0	—	2	2	1.000	1	0	0	5	0	1	0.5	3	8	4.0	8	4.0
99-00 Min	82	55	1723	206	433	.476	0	2	.000	59	103	.573	71	21	85	262	9	93	1.1	135	379	4.6	471	5.7
2 Years	84	55	1753	209	445	.470	0	2	.000	61	105	.581	72	21	85	267	9	94	1.1	138	387	4.6	479	5.7

NBA Postseason																								
Year Tm	G	GS	Min	Md	Att	Pct	Md	Att	Pct	Md	Att	Pct	TO	Stl	Blk	PF	DQ	Ast	Avg	Off	Tot	Avg	Pts	Avg
98-99 Min	3	0	29	4	8	.500	0	0	—	0	0	—	1	0	0	4	0	3	1.0	4	7	2.3	8	2.7
99-00 Min	4	4	126	11	25	.440	0	0	—	3	6	.500	4	3	7	20	1	6	1.5	5	13	3.3	25	6.3
2 Years	7	4	155	15	33	.455	0	0	—	3	6	.500	5	3	7	24	1	9	1.3	9	20	2.9	33	4.7

Johnny Newman

(statistical profile on page 254)

Pos: F **College:** Richmond **Drafted:** '86 2(29)—Cle **Ht:** 6'7" **Wt:** 210 **Born:** 11/28/63 **Age:** 37

College				Field Goals			3-Pt FGs			Free Throws			Misc			Fouls		Assists		Rebounds			Points	
Year Tm	G	GS	Min	Md	Att	Pct	Md	Att	Pct	Md	Att	Pct	TO	Stl	Blk	PF	DQ	Ast	Avg	Off	Tot	Avg	Pts	Avg
82-83 Rich	28	—	763	137	259	.529	—	—	—	69	96	.719	55	24	5	69	—	24	0.9	—	87	3.1	343	12.3
83-84 Rich	32	—	1189	273	517	.528	—	—	—	155	197	.787	68	48	22	91	—	31	1.0	—	196	6.1	701	21.9
84-85 Rich	32	—	1128	270	490	.551	—	—	—	140	181	.773	84	37	28	98	—	38	1.2	—	166	5.2	680	21.3
85-86 Rich	30	—	1123	253	489	.517	—	—	—	153	172	.890	57	36	29	89	—	28	0.9	—	219	7.3	659	22.0
4 Years	122	—	4203	933	1755	.532	—	—	—	517	646	.800	264	145	84	347	—	121	1.0	—	668	5.5	2383	19.5

NBA				Field Goals			3-Pt FGs			Free Throws			Misc			Fouls		Assists		Rebounds			Points	
Year Tm	G	GS	Min	Md	Att	Pct	Md	Att	Pct	Md	Att	Pct	TO	Stl	Blk	PF	DQ	Ast	Avg	Off	Tot	Avg	Pts	Avg
86-87 Cle	59	0	630	113	275	.411	1	22	.045	66	76	.868	46	20	7	67	0	27	0.5	36	70	1.2	293	5.0
87-88 NY	77	25	1589	270	620	.435	26	93	.280	207	246	.841	103	72	11	204	5	62	0.8	87	159	2.1	773	10.0
88-89 NY	81	80	2336	455	957	.475	97	287	.338	286	351	.815	153	111	23	259	4	162	2.0	93	206	2.5	1293	16.0
89-90 NY	80	69	2277	374	786	.476	45	142	.317	239	299	.799	143	95	22	254	3	180	2.3	60	191	2.4	1032	12.9
90-91 Cha	81	81	2477	478	1017	.470	30	84	.357	385	476	.809	189	100	11	278	7	188	2.3	94	254	3.1	1371	16.9
91-92 Cha	55	55	1651	295	618	.477	13	46	.283	236	308	.766	129	70	14	181	4	146	2.7	71	179	3.3	839	15.3
92-93 Cha	64	27	1471	279	534	.522	12	45	.267	194	240	.808	90	45	19	154	1	72	0.9	86	180	2.2	832	10.3
93-94 2Tm	81	18	1697	313	664	.471	24	90	.267	182	225	.809	90	69	27	196	3	91	1.1	72	173	2.1	634	7.7
94-95 Mil	82	11	1896	226	488	.463	45	128	.352	137	171	.801	86	69	13	234	3	154	1.9	66	200	2.4	889	10.8
95-96 Mil	82	82	2690	321	649	.495	61	162	.377	186	232	.802	108	90	15	257	4	116	1.4	66	186	2.3	715	8.7
96-97 Mil	82	4	2060	246	547	.450	34	98	.347	189	247	.765	115	73	17	257	4	138	1.9	50	141	1.9	1089	14.7
97-98 Den	74	15	2176	344	799	.431	36	105	.343	365	445	.820	147	77	24	208	2	41	0.8	15	75	1.5	303	10.0
98-99 Cle	50	2	949	106	251	.422	23	61	.377	68	84	.810	41	28	12	126	2	65	0.8	39	154	1.9	820	10.0
99-00 NJ	82	9	1763	278	623	.446	72	190	.379	192	229	.838	89	53	11	207	0	65	0.8	—	—	—	234	13.0
93-94 Cha	18	18	429	91	174	.523	4	16	.250	48	59	.814	28	18	5	44	1	29	1.6	21	58	3.2	598	9.5
NJ	63	0	1268	222	490	.453	20	74	.270	134	166	.807	62	51	22	152	2	43	0.7	65	122	1.9	—	—
14 Years	1030	478	25662	4098	8828	.464	519	1553	.334	2932	3629	.808	1529	972	232	2882	42	1559	1.5	907	2311	2.2	11647	11.3

119

Year Tm	G	GS	Min	Md	Att	Pct	Md	Att	Pct	Md	Att	Pct	TO	Stl	Blk	PF	DQ	Ast	Avg	Off	Tot	Avg	Pts	Avg
87-88 NY	4	2	113	31	68	.456	0	9	.000	14	16	.875	6	6	1	16	0	7	1.8	8	11	2.8	76	19.0
88-89 NY	9	9	258	50	107	.467	7	28	.250	38	49	.776	18	8	1	27	1	17	1.9	13	25	2.8	145	16.1
89-90 NY	10	0	231	38	85	.447	4	10	.400	37	49	.755	17	9	3	41	1	10	1.0	11	21	2.1	117	11.7
92-93 Cha	9	9	173	28	55	.509	1	5	.200	11	16	.688	15	10	1	19	0	18	2.0	7	19	2.1	68	7.6
93-94 NJ	4	0	54	3	13	.231	1	4	.250	5	7	.714	3	2	2	11	0	2	0.5	2	5	1.3	12	3.0
5 Years	36	20	829	150	328	.457	13	56	.232	105	137	.766	59	35	8	114	2	54	1.5	41	81	2.3	418	11.6

Moochie Norris

Pos: G **College:** West Florida **Drafted:** '96 2(33)—Mil **Ht:** 6'1" **Wt:** 175 **Born:** 7/27/73 **Age:** 27

College				Field Goals			3-Pt FGs			Free Throws			Misc			Fouls		Assists		Rebounds			Points	
Year Tm	G	GS	Min	Md	Att	Pct	Md	Att	Pct	Md	Att	Pct	TO	Stl	Blk	PF	DQ	Ast	Avg	Off	Tot	Avg	Pts	Avg
94-95 Aub	29	—	1009	124	312	.397	57	161	.354	58	83	.699	74	51	1	55	—	143	4.9	—	116	4.0	363	12.5
95-96 WstFl	16	—	615	121	265	.457	50	118	.424	86	113	.761	50	47	1	23	—	143	8.9	—	92	5.8	378	23.6
2 Years	45	—	1624	245	577	.425	107	279	.384	144	196	.735	124	98	2	78	—	286	6.4	—	208	4.6	741	16.5

NBA				Field Goals			3-Pt FGs			Free Throws			Misc			Fouls		Assists		Rebounds			Points	
Year Tm	G	GS	Min	Md	Att	Pct	Md	Att	Pct	Md	Att	Pct	TO	Stl	Blk	PF	DQ	Ast	Avg	Off	Tot	Avg	Pts	Avg
96-97 Van	8	0	89	4	22	.182	2	10	.200	2	5	.400	5	4	0	5	0	23	2.9	3	12	1.5	12	1.5
97-98										Played in CBA														
98-99 Sea	12	0	140	13	40	.325	6	15	.400	6	16	.375	16	7	0	17	0	24	2.0	4	20	1.7	38	3.2
99-00 Hou	30	0	502	69	159	.434	12	29	.414	57	73	.781	30	23	1	32	0	94	3.1	16	68	2.3	207	6.9
3 Years	50	0	731	86	221	.389	20	54	.370	65	94	.691	51	34	1	54	0	141	2.8	23	100	2.0	257	5.1

Dirk Nowitzki

(statistical profile on page 255)

Pos: F **College:** None **Drafted:** '98 1(9)—Mil **Ht:** 7'0" **Wt:** 250 **Born:** 6/19/78 **Age:** 22

NBA				Field Goals			3-Pt FGs			Free Throws			Misc			Fouls		Assists		Rebounds			Points	
Year Tm	G	GS	Min	Md	Att	Pct	Md	Att	Pct	Md	Att	Pct	TO	Stl	Blk	PF	DQ	Ast	Avg	Off	Tot	Avg	Pts	Avg
98-99 Dal	47	24	958	136	336	.405	14	68	.206	99	128	.773	73	29	27	105	5	47	1.0	41	162	3.4	385	8.2
99-00 Dal	82	81	2938	515	1118	.461	116	306	.379	289	348	.830	141	63	68	256	4	203	2.5	102	532	6.5	1435	17.5
2 Years	129	105	3896	651	1454	.448	130	374	.348	388	476	.815	214	92	95	361	9	250	1.9	143	694	5.4	1820	14.1

Charles Oakley

(statistical profile on page 255)

Pos: F **College:** Virginia Union **Drafted:** '85 1(9)—Cle **Ht:** 6'9" **Wt:** 245 **Born:** 12/18/63 **Age:** 37

College				Field Goals			3-Pt FGs			Free Throws			Misc			Fouls		Assists		Rebounds			Points	
Year Tm	G	GS	Min	Md	Att	Pct	Md	Att	Pct	Md	Att	Pct	TO	Stl	Blk	PF	DQ	Ast	Avg	Off	Tot	Avg	Pts	Avg
81-82 VaUn	28	—	—	169	274	.617	—	—	—	106	174	.609	—	—	—	—	—			—	349	15.0	444	15.9
82-83 VaUn	28	—	—	220	378	.582	—	—	—	100	170	.588	—	—	—	—	—			—	365	13.0	540	19.3
83-84 VaUn	30	—	—	256	418	.612	—	—	—	139	224	.621	—	—	—	—	—	28	1.0	—	393	13.1	651	21.7
84-85 VaUn	31	—	—	283	453	.625	—	—	—	178	266	.669	—	—	—	—	—			—	535	17.3	744	24.0
4 Years	117	—	—	928	1523	.609	—	—	—	523	834	.627	—	—	—	—	—	66	2.1	—	1642	14.0	2379	20.3

NBA				Field Goals			3-Pt FGs			Free Throws			Misc			Fouls		Assists		Rebounds			Points	
Year Tm	G	GS	Min	Md	Att	Pct	Md	Att	Pct	Md	Att	Pct	TO	Stl	Blk	PF	DQ	Ast	Avg	Off	Tot	Avg	Pts	Avg
85-86 Chi	77	30	1772	281	541	.519	0	3	.000	178	269	.662	175	68	30	250	9	133	1.7	255	664	8.6	740	9.6
86-87 Chi	82	81	2980	468	1052	.445	11	30	.367	245	357	.686	299	85	36	315	4	296	3.6	299	1074	13.1	1192	14.5
87-88 Chi	82	82	2816	375	776	.483	3	12	.250	261	359	.727	241	68	28	272	2	248	3.0	326	1066	13.0	1014	12.4
88-89 NY	82	82	2604	426	835	.510	12	48	.250	197	255	.773	248	104	14	270	1	187	2.3	343	861	10.5	1061	12.9
89-90 NY	61	61	2196	336	641	.524	0	3	.000	217	285	.761	165	64	16	220	3	146	2.4	258	727	11.9	889	14.6
90-91 NY	76	74	2739	307	595	.516	0	2	.000	239	305	.784	215	62	17	288	4	204	2.7	305	920	12.1	853	11.2
91-92 NY	82	82	2309	210	402	.522	0	3	.000	86	117	.735	123	67	15	258	2	133	1.6	256	700	8.5	506	6.2
92-93 NY	82	82	2230	219	431	.508	0	1	.000	127	176	.722	124	85	15	289	5	126	1.5	288	708	8.6	565	6.9
93-94 NY*	82	82	2932	363	760	.478	0	3	.000	243	313	.776	193	110	18	293	4	218	2.7	349	965	11.8	969	11.8
94-95 NY	50	49	1567	192	393	.489	3	12	.250	119	150	.793	103	60	7	179	3	126	2.5	155	445	8.9	506	10.1
95-96 NY	53	51	1775	211	448	.471	7	26	.269	175	210	.833	104	58	14	195	6	137	2.6	162	460	8.7	604	11.4
96-97 NY	80	80	2873	339	694	.488	5	19	.263	181	224	.808	171	111	21	305	4	221	2.8	246	781	9.8	864	10.8
97-98 NY	79	79	2734	307	698	.440	0	6	.000	97	114	.851	126	123	22	280	4	201	2.5	218	724	9.2	711	9.0
98-99 Tor	50	50	1633	140	327	.428	1	5	.200	67	83	.807	96	46	21	182	6	168	3.4	96	374	7.5	348	7.0
99-00 Tor	80	80	2431	234	560	.418	14	41	.341	66	85	.776	154	102	45	294	6	253	3.2	117	540	6.8	548	6.9
15 Years	1098	1045	35591	4408	9153	.482	56	214	.262	2498	3302	.757	2537	1213	319	3890	61	2797	2.5	3673	11009	10.0	11370	10.4

NBA Postseason																								
Year Tm	G	GS	Min	Md	Att	Pct	Md	Att	Pct	Md	Att	Pct	TO	Stl	Blk	PF	DQ	Ast	Avg	Off	Tot	Avg	Pts	Avg
85-86 Chi	3	3	88	11	21	.524	0	0	—	8	13	.615	5	6	2	13	0	3	1.0	10	30	10.0	30	10.0

NBA Postseason

Year Tm	G	GS	Min	Md	Att	Pct	Md	Att	Pct	Md	Att	Pct	TO	Stl	Blk	PF	DQ	Ast	Avg	Off	Tot	Avg	Pts	Avg
86-87 Chi	3	3	129	19	50	.380	2	4	.500	20	24	.833	8	4	1	13	0	6	2.0	17	46	15.3	60	20.0
87-88 Chi	10	10	373	40	91	.440	0	2	.000	21	24	.875	18	6	4	33	0	32	3.2	39	128	12.8	101	10.1
88-89 NY	9	9	299	35	73	.479	1	2	.500	16	24	.667	22	12	1	31	1	11	1.2	43	101	11.2	87	9.7
89-90 NY	10	8	336	43	84	.512	1	1	1.000	34	52	.654	22	11	2	33	1	27	2.7	39	110	11.0	121	12.1
90-91 NY	3	3	100	10	21	.476	0	0	—	3	6	.500	7	2	1	13	0	3	1.0	15	31	10.3	23	7.7
91-92 NY	12	12	354	22	58	.379	0	0	—	20	27	.741	15	8	5	36	0	8	0.7	44	108	9.0	64	5.3
92-93 NY	15	15	507	63	131	.481	0	0	—	40	55	.727	36	16	2	51	1	17	1.1	71	165	11.0	166	11.1
93-94 NY	25	25	992	125	262	.477	0	0	—	79	102	.775	65	35	5	87	1	59	2.4	116	292	11.7	329	13.2
94-95 NY	11	11	421	49	109	.450	4	10	.400	42	51	.824	24	19	6	42	0	41	3.7	31	93	8.5	144	13.1
95-96 NY	8	8	308	39	78	.500	2	6	.333	25	36	.694	28	8	0	33	1	14	1.8	28	69	8.6	105	13.1
96-97 NY	10	10	358	38	86	.442	0	1	.000	22	29	.759	18	22	3	37	0	16	1.6	23	88	8.8	98	9.8
97-98 NY	10	10	342	29	71	.408	0	0	—	23	25	.920	13	11	2	38	1	14	1.4	21	85	8.5	81	8.1
99-00 Tor	3	3	110	14	29	.483	2	7	.286	0	1	.000	5	6	1	14	0	11	3.7	2	23	7.7	30	10.0
14 Years	132	130	4717	537	1164	.461	12	33	.364	353	469	.753	286	166	35	474	6	262	2.0	499	1369	10.4	1439	10.9

Lamar Odom

(statistical profile on page 256)

Pos: F **College:** Rhode Island **Drafted:** '99 1(4)—LAC **Ht:** 6'10" **Wt:** 220 **Born:** 11/6/79 **Age:** 21

College				Field Goals			3-Pt FGs			Free Throws			Misc			Fouls		Assists		Rebounds			Points	
Year Tm	G	GS	Min	Md	Att	Pct	Md	Att	Pct	Md	Att	Pct	TO	Stl	Blk	PF	DQ	Ast	Avg	Off	Tot	Avg	Pts	Avg
98-99 RI	32	32	1116	203	421	.482	33	100	.330	125	182	.687	111	27	49	92	4	122	3.8	82	302	9.4	564	17.6
NBA				Field Goals			3-Pt FGs			Free Throws			Misc			Fouls		Assists		Rebounds			Points	
Year Tm	G	GS	Min	Md	Att	Pct	Md	Att	Pct	Md	Att	Pct	TO	Stl	Blk	PF	DQ	Ast	Avg	Off	Tot	Avg	Pts	Avg
99-00 LAC	76	70	2767	449	1024	.438	59	164	.360	302	420	.719	258	91	95	291	13	317	4.2	159	595	7.8	1259	16.6

Hakeem Olajuwon

Pos: C **College:** Houston **Drafted:** '84 1(1)—Hou **Ht:** 7'0" **Wt:** 255 **Born:** 1/21/63 **Age:** 38

College				Field Goals			3-Pt FGs			Free Throws			Misc			Fouls		Assists		Rebounds			Points	
Year Tm	G	GS	Min	Md	Att	Pct	Md	Att	Pct	Md	Att	Pct	TO	Stl	Blk	PF	DQ	Ast	Avg	Off	Tot	Avg	Pts	Avg
81-82 Hou	29	6	529	91	150	.607	—	—		58	103	.563	41	26	72	85	—	11	0.4	—	179	6.2	240	8.3
82-83 Hou	34	34	932	192	314	.611	—	—		88	148	.595	79	47	175	112	—	29	0.9	—	388	11.4	472	13.9
83-84 Hou	37	37	1260	249	369	.675	—	—		122	232	.526	61	61	207	118	—	48	1.3	—	500	13.5	620	16.8
3 Years	100	77	2721	532	833	.639	—	—		268	483	.555	181	134	454	315	—	88	0.9	—	1067	10.7	1332	13.3
NBA				Field Goals			3-Pt FGs			Free Throws			Misc			Fouls		Assists		Rebounds			Points	
Year Tm	G	GS	Min	Md	Att	Pct	Md	Att	Pct	Md	Att	Pct	TO	Stl	Blk	PF	DQ	Ast	Avg	Off	Tot	Avg	Pts	Avg
84-85 Hou*	82	82	2914	677	1258	.538	0	0	—	338	551	.613	234	99	220	344	10	111	1.4	440	974	11.9	1692	20.6
85-86 Hou*	68	68	2467	625	1188	.526	0	0	—	347	538	.645	195	134	231	271	9	137	2.0	333	781	11.5	1597	23.5
86-87 Hou*	75	75	2760	677	1332	.508	1	5	.200	400	570	.702	228	140	254	294	8	220	2.9	315	858	11.4	1755	23.4
87-88 Hou*	79	79	2825	712	1385	.514	0	4	.000	381	548	.695	243	162	214	324	7	163	2.1	302	959	12.1	1805	22.8
88-89 Hou*	82	82	3024	790	1556	.508	0	10	.000	454	652	.696	275	213	282	329	10	149	1.8	338	1105	13.5	2034	24.8
89-90 Hou*	82	82	3124	806	1609	.501	1	6	.167	382	536	.713	316	174	376	314	6	234	2.9	299	1149	14.0	1995	24.3
90-91 Hou	56	50	2062	487	959	.508	0	4	.000	213	277	.769	174	121	221	221	5	131	2.3	219	770	13.8	1187	21.2
91-92 Hou*	70	69	2636	591	1177	.502	0	1	.000	328	428	.766	187	127	304	263	7	157	2.2	246	845	12.1	1510	21.6
92-93 Hou*	82	82	3242	848	1603	.529	0	8	.000	444	570	.779	262	150	342	305	5	291	3.5	283	1068	13.0	2140	26.1
93-94 Hou*	80	80	3277	894	1694	.528	8	19	.421	388	542	.716	271	128	297	289	4	287	3.6	229	955	11.9	2184	27.3
94-95 Hou*	72	72	2853	798	1545	.517	3	16	.188	406	537	.756	237	133	242	250	3	255	3.5	172	775	10.8	2005	27.8
95-96 Hou*	72	72	2797	768	1494	.514	3	14	.214	397	548	.724	247	113	207	242	0	257	3.6	176	784	10.9	1936	26.9
96-97 Hou*	78	78	2852	727	1426	.510	5	16	.313	351	446	.787	281	117	173	249	3	236	3.0	173	716	9.2	1810	23.2
97-98 Hou	47	45	1633	306	633	.483	0	3	.000	160	212	.755	126	84	96	152	0	143	3.0	116	460	9.8	772	16.4
98-99 Hou	50	50	1784	373	725	.514	4	13	.308	195	272	.717	139	82	123	160	3	88	1.8	106	477	9.5	945	18.9
99-00 Hou	44	28	1049	193	421	.458	0	2	.000	69	112	.616	73	41	70	88	0	61	1.4	65	274	6.2	455	10.3
16 Years	1119	1094	41299	10272	20005	.513	25	121	.207	5253	7339	.716	3488	2018	3652	4095	80	2920	2.6	3812	12950	11.6	25822	23.1

NBA Postseason

Year Tm	G	GS	Min	Md	Att	Pct	Md	Att	Pct	Md	Att	Pct	TO	Stl	Blk	PF	DQ	Ast	Avg	Off	Tot	Avg	Pts	Avg
84-85 Hou	5	5	187	42	88	.477	0	0	—	22	46	.478	11	7	13	22	0	7	1.4	33	65	13.0	106	21.2
85-86 Hou	20	20	766	205	387	.530	0	1	.000	127	199	.638	43	40	69	87	3	39	2.0	101	236	11.8	537	26.9
86-87 Hou	10	10	389	110	179	.615	0	1	.000	72	97	.742	36	13	43	44	1	25	2.5	39	113	11.3	292	29.2
87-88 Hou	4	4	162	56	98	.571	0	1	.000	38	43	.884	9	9	11	14	0	7	1.8	20	67	16.8	150	37.5
88-89 Hou	4	4	162	42	81	.519	0	0	—	17	25	.680	10	10	11	17	0	12	3.0	14	52	13.0	101	25.3
89-90 Hou	4	4	161	31	70	.443	0	0	—	12	17	.706	11	10	23	19	0	8	2.0	15	46	11.5	74	18.5
90-91 Hou	3	3	129	26	45	.578	0	1	.000	14	17	.824	8	4	8	11	0	6	2.0	12	44	14.7	66	22.0
92-93 Hou	12	12	518	123	238	.517	0	1	.000	62	75	.827	45	21	59	37	0	57	4.8	52	168	14.0	308	25.7
93-94 Hou	23	23	989	267	514	.519	2	4	.500	128	161	.795	83	40	92	82	0	98	4.3	55	254	11.0	664	28.9

Year Tm	G	GS	Min	Md	Att	Pct	Md	Att	Pct	Md	Att	Pct	TO	Stl	Blk	PF	DQ	Ast	Avg	Off	Tot	Avg	Pts	Avg
94-95 Hou	22	22	929	306	576	.531	2	4	.500	111	163	.681	69	26	62	95	0	98	4.5	44	227	10.3	725	33.0
95-96 Hou	8	8	329	75	147	.510	0	1	.000	29	40	.725	29	15	17	28	1	31	3.9	17	73	9.1	179	22.4
96-97 Hou	16	16	629	147	249	.590	0	3	.000	76	104	.731	46	33	41	61	0	54	3.4	46	174	10.9	370	23.1
97-98 Hou	5	5	190	39	99	.394	0	1	.000	24	33	.727	13	5	16	18	0	12	2.4	9	54	10.8	102	20.4
98-99 Hou	4	4	123	23	54	.426	0	0	—	7	8	.875	5	5	3	18	0	2	0.5	5	29	7.3	53	13.3
14 Years	140	140	5663	1492	2825	.528	4	18	.222	739	1028	.719	418	238	468	553	5	456	3.3	462	1602	11.4	3727	26.6

Kevin Ollie

Pos: G **College:** Connecticut **Drafted:** '97 FA—Dal **Ht:** 6'4" **Wt:** 195 **Born:** 12/27/72 **Age:** 28

College				Field Goals			3-Pt FGs			Free Throws			Misc			Fouls		Assists		Rebounds			Points	
Year Tm	G	GS	Min	Md	Att	Pct	Md	Att	Pct	Md	Att	Pct	TO	Stl	Blk	PF	DQ	Ast	Avg	Off	Tot	Avg	Pts	Avg
91-92 Conn	29	0	294	17	45	.378	0	0	—	28	39	.718	31	13	2	30	—	40	1.4	—	23	0.8	62	2.1
92-93 Conn	28	28	864	69	176	.392	1	9	.111	81	109	.743	69	27	2	69	—	158	5.6	—	64	2.3	220	7.9
93-94 Conn	34	34	973	73	155	.471	2	10	.200	71	97	.732	85	23	1	50	2	209	6.1	17	83	2.4	219	6.4
94-95 Conn	33	33	1025	112	222	.505	13	42	.310	87	108	.806	84	44	2	40	—	212	6.4	—	82	2.5	324	9.8
4 Years	124	95	3156	271	598	.453	16	61	.262	267	353	.756	269	107	7	189	—	619	5.0	—	252	2.0	825	6.7

NBA				Field Goals			3-Pt FGs			Free Throws			Misc			Fouls		Assists		Rebounds			Points	
Year Tm	G	GS	Min	Md	Att	Pct	Md	Att	Pct	Md	Att	Pct	TO	Stl	Blk	PF	DQ	Ast	Avg	Off	Tot	Avg	Pts	Avg
95-96										Played in CBA														
96-97										Played in CBA														
97-98 2Tm	35	0	430	37	98	.378	0	1	.000	49	70	.700	44	13	0	31	0	65	1.9	9	39	1.1	123	3.5
98-99 2Tm	8	0	72	4	14	.286	0	0	—	5	7	.714	3	3	1	9	0	3	0.4	0	7	0.9	13	1.6
99-00 Phi	40	0	290	22	49	.449	0	0	—	28	37	.757	10	10	0	27	0	46	1.2	4	31	0.8	72	1.8
97-98 Dal	16	0	214	14	42	.333	0	0	—	18	25	.720	16	6	0	16	0	32	2.0	6	21	1.3	46	2.9
Orl	19	0	216	23	56	.411	0	1	.000	31	45	.689	28	7	0	15	0	33	1.7	3	18	0.9	77	4.1
98-99 Sac	7	0	68	4	13	.308	0	0	—	4	5	.800	3	3	1	8	0	3	0.4	0	6	0.9	12	1.7
Orl	1	0	4	0	1	.000	0	0	—	1	2	.500	0	0	0	1	0	0	0.0	0	1	1.0	1	1.0
3 Years	83	0	792	63	161	.391	0	1	.000	82	114	.719	57	26	1	67	0	114	1.4	13	77	0.9	208	2.5

NBA Postseason																								
Year Tm	G	GS	Min	Md	Att	Pct	Md	Att	Pct	Md	Att	Pct	TO	Stl	Blk	PF	DQ	Ast	Avg	Off	Tot	Avg	Pts	Avg
99-00 Phi	10	0	65	6	12	.500	0	0	—	8	9	.889	3	2	0	5	0	12	1.2	0	5	0.5	20	2.0

Michael Olowokandi

(statistical profile on page 256)

Pos: C **College:** Pacific **Drafted:** '98 1(1)—LAC **Ht:** 7'0" **Wt:** 269 **Born:** 4/3/75 **Age:** 25

College				Field Goals			3-Pt FGs			Free Throws			Misc			Fouls		Assists		Rebounds			Points	
Year Tm	G	GS	Min	Md	Att	Pct	Md	Att	Pct	Md	Att	Pct	TO	Stl	Blk	PF	DQ	Ast	Avg	Off	Tot	Avg	Pts	Avg
95-96 Pac	25	0	257	40	76	.526	0	0	—	20	36	.556	19	2	33	48	1	4	0.2	27	84	3.4	100	4.0
96-97 Pac	19	14	433	94	165	.570	0	0	—	19	57	.333	42	8	32	48	3	8	0.4	35	126	6.6	207	10.9
97-98 Pac	33	33	1046	309	508	.608	0	0	—	114	235	.485	92	9	95	83	3	26	0.8	98	369	11.2	732	22.2
3 Years	77	47	1736	443	749	.591	0	0	—	153	328	.466	153	19	160	179	7	38	0.5	160	579	7.5	1039	13.5

NBA				Field Goals			3-Pt FGs			Free Throws			Misc			Fouls		Assists		Rebounds			Points	
Year Tm	G	GS	Min	Md	Att	Pct	Md	Att	Pct	Md	Att	Pct	TO	Stl	Blk	PF	DQ	Ast	Avg	Off	Tot	Avg	Pts	Avg
98-99 LAC	45	36	1279	172	399	.431	0	0	—	57	118	.483	85	27	55	137	2	25	0.6	120	357	7.9	401	8.9
99-00 LAC	80	77	2493	330	756	.437	0	0	—	123	189	.651	177	35	140	304	10	38	0.5	194	656	8.2	783	9.8
2 Years	125	113	3772	502	1155	.435	0	0	—	180	307	.586	262	62	195	441	12	63	0.5	314	1013	8.1	1184	9.5

Jermaine O'Neal

Pos: F **College:** None **Drafted:** '96 1(17)—Por **Ht:** 6'11" **Wt:** 248 **Born:** 10/13/78 **Age:** 22

NBA				Field Goals			3-Pt FGs			Free Throws			Misc			Fouls		Assists		Rebounds			Points	
Year Tm	G	GS	Min	Md	Att	Pct	Md	Att	Pct	Md	Att	Pct	TO	Stl	Blk	PF	DQ	Ast	Avg	Off	Tot	Avg	Pts	Avg
96-97 Por	45	0	458	69	153	.451	0	1	.000	47	78	.603	27	2	46	46	0	8	0.2	39	124	2.8	185	4.1
97-98 Por	60	9	808	112	231	.485	0	2	.000	45	89	.506	55	15	58	101	0	17	0.3	80	201	3.4	269	4.5
98-99 Por	35	1	310	36	83	.434	0	1	.000	18	35	.514	14	4	14	41	0	13	0.4	42	97	2.8	90	2.6
99-00 Por	70	8	859	108	222	.486	0	1	.000	57	98	.582	47	11	55	127	1	18	0.3	97	229	3.3	273	3.9
4 Years	210	18	2435	325	689	.472	0	5	.000	167	300	.557	143	32	153	315	1	56	0.3	258	651	3.1	817	3.9

NBA Postseason																								
Year Tm	G	GS	Min	Md	Att	Pct	Md	Att	Pct	Md	Att	Pct	TO	Stl	Blk	PF	DQ	Ast	Avg	Off	Tot	Avg	Pts	Avg
96-97 Por	2	0	4	0	2	.000	0	1	.000	0	2	.000	0	0	1	0	0	0	0.0	0	1	0.5	0	0.0
97-98 Por	1	0	3	0	3	.000	0	1	.000	0	0	—	0	0	2	1	0	0	0.0	1	1	1.0	0	0.0
98-99 Por	9	0	55	4	10	.400	0	0	—	6	12	.500	2	0	3	11	0	1	0.1	8	17	1.9	14	1.6

NBA Postseason

Year Tm	G	GS	Min	Md	Att	Pct	Md	Att	Pct	Md	Att	Pct	TO	Stl	Blk	PF	DQ	Ast	Avg	Off	Tot	Avg	Pts	Avg
99-00 Por	8	0	38	3	11	.273	0	0	—	6	9	.667	0	0	3	9	0	1	0.1	2	7	0.9	12	1.5
4 Years	20	0	100	7	26	.269	0	2	.000	12	23	.522	2	0	9	21	0	2	0.1	11	26	1.3	26	1.3

Shaquille O'Neal

(statistical profile on page 257)

Pos: C **College:** Louisiana State **Drafted:** '92 1(1)—Orl **Ht:** 7'1" **Wt:** 315 **Born:** 3/6/72 **Age:** 28

College

Year Tm	G	GS	Min	Md	Att	Pct	Md	Att	Pct	Md	Att	Pct	TO	Stl	Blk	PF	DQ	Ast	Avg	Off	Tot	Avg	Pts	Avg
89-90 LSU	32	28	901	180	314	.573	0	0	—	85	153	.556	93	38	115	122	9	61	1.9	—	385	12.0	445	13.9
90-91 LSU	28	28	881	312	497	.628	0	0	—	150	235	.638	99	41	41	79	1	45	1.6	—	411	14.7	774	27.6
91-92 LSU	30	30	959	294	478	.615	0	0	—	134	254	.528	103	29	157	86	5	46	1.5	—	421	14.0	722	24.1
3 Years	90	86	2741	786	1289	.610	0	0	—	369	642	.575	295	108	313	287	15	152	1.7	—	1217	13.5	1941	21.6

NBA

Year Tm	G	GS	Min	Md	Att	Pct	Md	Att	Pct	Md	Att	Pct	TO	Stl	Blk	PF	DQ	Ast	Avg	Off	Tot	Avg	Pts	Avg
92-93 Orl*	81	81	3071	733	1304	.562	0	2	.000	427	721	.592	307	60	286	321	8	152	1.9	342	1122	13.9	1893	23.4
93-94 Orl*	81	81	3224	953	1591	.599	0	2	.000	471	850	.554	222	76	231	281	3	195	2.4	384	1072	13.2	2377	29.3
94-95 Orl*	79	79	2923	930	1594	.583	0	5	.000	455	854	.533	204	73	192	258	1	214	2.7	328	901	11.4	2315	29.3
95-96 Orl*	54	52	1946	592	1033	.573	1	2	.500	249	511	.487	155	34	115	193	1	155	2.9	182	596	11.0	1434	26.6
96-97 LAL*	51	51	1941	552	991	.557	0	4	.000	232	479	.484	146	46	147	180	2	159	3.1	195	640	12.5	1336	26.2
97-98 LAL*	60	57	2175	670	1147	.584	0	1	.000	359	681	.527	175	39	144	193	1	142	2.4	208	681	11.4	1699	28.3
98-99 LAL	49	49	1705	510	885	.576	0	1	.000	269	498	.540	122	36	82	155	4	114	2.3	187	525	10.7	1289	26.3
99-00 LAL*	79	79	3163	956	1665	.574	0	1	.000	432	824	.524	223	36	239	255	2	299	3.8	336	1078	13.6	2344	29.7
8 Years	534	529	20148	5896	10210	.577	1	17	.059	2894	5418	.534	1554	400	1436	1836	22	1430	2.7	2162	6615	12.4	14687	27.5

NBA Postseason

Year Tm	G	GS	Min	Md	Att	Pct	Md	Att	Pct	Md	Att	Pct	TO	Stl	Blk	PF	DQ	Ast	Avg	Off	Tot	Avg	Pts	Avg
93-94 Orl	3	3	126	23	45	.511	0	0	—	16	34	.471	10	2	9	13	0	7	2.3	17	40	13.3	62	20.7
94-95 Orl	21	21	805	195	338	.577	0	0	—	149	261	.571	73	18	40	84	1	70	3.3	95	250	11.9	539	25.7
95-96 Orl	12	12	459	131	216	.606	0	0	—	48	122	.393	44	9	15	40	0	55	4.6	49	120	10.0	310	25.8
96-97 LAL	9	9	326	89	173	.514	0	0	—	64	105	.610	22	5	17	37	1	29	3.2	38	95	10.6	242	26.9
97-98 LAL	13	13	501	158	258	.612	0	0	—	80	159	.503	43	7	34	41	1	38	2.9	48	132	10.2	396	30.5
98-99 LAL	8	8	315	79	155	.510	0	0	—	55	118	.466	18	7	23	29	0	18	2.3	44	93	11.6	213	26.6
99-00 LAL	23	23	1000	286	505	.566	0	0	—	135	296	.456	56	13	55	67	1	71	3.1	119	355	15.4	707	30.7
Years	89	89	3532	961	1690	.569	0	0	—	547	1095	.500	266	61	193	311	4	288	3.2	410	1085	12.2	2469	27.7

Greg Ostertag

(statistical profile on page 257)

Pos: C **College:** Kansas **Drafted:** '95 1(28)—Uta **Ht:** 7'2" **Wt:** 280 **Born:** 3/6/73 **Age:** 27

College

Year Tm	G	GS	Min	Md	Att	Pct	Md	Att	Pct	Md	Att	Pct	TO	Stl	Blk	PF	DQ	Ast	Avg	Off	Tot	Avg	Pts	Avg
91-92 Kan	32	1	311	61	112	.545	0	1	.000	32	49	.653	30	7	34	50	0	5	0.2	—	112	3.5	154	4.8
92-93 Kan	29	1	389	61	118	.517	0	0	—	33	55	.600	36	8	36	59	1	11	0.4	—	118	4.1	155	5.3
93-94 Kan	35	34	739	145	272	.533	0	2	.000	70	111	.631	60	15	97	81	1	12	0.3	—	307	8.8	360	10.3
94-95 Kan	31	28	604	121	203	.596	0	0	—	57	103	.553	50	11	91	73	2	13	0.4	—	233	7.5	299	9.6
Years	127	64	2043	388	705	.550	0	3	.000	192	318	.604	176	41	258	263	4	41	0.3	—	770	6.1	968	7.6

NBA

Year Tm	G	GS	Min	Md	Att	Pct	Md	Att	Pct	Md	Att	Pct	TO	Stl	Blk	PF	DQ	Ast	Avg	Off	Tot	Avg	Pts	Avg
95-96 Uta	57	10	661	86	182	.473	0	0	—	36	54	.667	25	5	63	91	1	5	0.1	57	175	3.1	208	3.6
96-97 Uta	77	70	1818	210	408	.515	0	4	.000	139	205	.678	74	24	152	233	2	27	0.4	180	565	7.3	559	7.3
97-98 Uta	63	23	1288	115	239	.481	0	0	—	67	140	.479	74	28	132	166	1	25	0.4	134	374	5.9	297	4.7
98-99 Uta	48	48	1340	99	208	.476	0	0	—	75	121	.620	45	12	131	140	2	23	0.5	105	348	7.3	273	5.7
99-00 Uta	81	3	1606	124	267	.464	0	1	.000	119	187	.636	79	20	172	196	2	18	0.2	172	482	6.0	367	4.5
Years	326	154	6713	634	1304	.486	0	5	.000	436	707	.617	297	89	650	826	8	98	0.3	648	1944	6.0	1704	5.2

NBA Postseason

Year Tm	G	GS	Min	Md	Att	Pct	Md	Att	Pct	Md	Att	Pct	TO	Stl	Blk	PF	DQ	Ast	Avg	Off	Tot	Avg	Pts	Avg
95-96 Uta	15	0	212	20	45	.444	0	0	—	13	21	.619	4	2	21	28	0	1	0.1	18	50	3.3	53	3.5
96-97 Uta	20	20	459	34	83	.410	0	0	—	26	35	.743	18	10	47	76	3	6	0.3	52	137	6.9	94	4.7
97-98 Uta	19	1	336	26	46	.565	0	0	—	12	25	.480	12	7	37	51	0	5	0.3	25	81	4.3	64	3.4
98-99 Uta	11	11	261	13	35	.371	0	0	—	18	28	.643	8	2	24	27	0	6	0.5	18	65	5.9	44	4.0
99-00 Uta	8	0	172	10	19	.526	0	0	—	10	22	.455	8	2	17	20	0	2	0.3	19	45	5.6	30	3.8
Years	73	32	1440	103	228	.452	0	0	—	79	131	.603	50	23	146	202	3	20	0.3	132	378	5.2	285	3.9

Bo Outlaw

(statistical profile on page 258)

Pos: F-C **College:** Houston **Drafted:** '93 FA—LAC   **Ht:** 6'8" **Wt:** 210 **Born:** 4/13/71 **Age:** 29

College				Field Goals			3-Pt FGs			Free Throws			Misc			Fouls		Assists		Rebounds			Points	
Year Tm	G	GS	Min	Md	Att	Pct	Md	Att	Pct	Md	Att	Pct	TO	Stl	Blk	PF	DQ	Ast	Avg	Off	Tot	Avg	Pts	Avg
91-92 Hou	31	—	970	156	228	.684	0	0	—	57	129	.442	77	54	97	87	—	81	2.6	—	254	8.2	369	11.9
92-93 Hou	30	—	1055	196	298	.658	0	0	—	95	192	.495	68	68	114	88	—	99	3.3	—	301	10.0	487	16.2
2 Years	61	—	2025	352	526	.669	0	0	—	152	321	.474	145	122	211	175	—	180	3.0	—	555	9.1	856	14.0

NBA				Field Goals			3-Pt FGs			Free Throws			Misc			Fouls		Assists		Rebounds			Points	
Year Tm	G	GS	Min	Md	Att	Pct	Md	Att	Pct	Md	Att	Pct	TO	Stl	Blk	PF	DQ	Ast	Avg	Off	Tot	Avg	Pts	Avg
93-94 LAC	37	14	871	98	167	.587	0	2	.000	61	103	.592	31	36	37	94	1	36	1.0	81	212	5.7	257	6.9
94-95 LAC	81	31	1655	170	325	.523	0	5	.000	82	186	.441	78	90	151	227	4	84	1.0	121	313	3.9	422	5.2
95-96 LAC	80	3	985	107	186	.575	0	3	.000	72	162	.444	45	44	91	127	0	50	0.6	87	200	2.5	286	3.6
96-97 LAC	82	25	2195	254	417	.609	0	8	.000	117	232	.504	107	94	142	227	5	157	1.9	174	454	5.5	625	7.6
97-98 Orl	82	76	2953	301	543	.554	1	4	.250	180	313	.575	175	107	181	260	1	216	2.6	255	637	7.8	783	9.5
98-99 Orl	31	22	851	84	154	.545	0	3	.000	35	81	.432	58	40	43	79	1	56	1.8	54	167	5.4	203	6.5
99-00 Orl	82	55	2326	204	339	.602	0	3	.000	82	162	.506	133	113	148	203	0	245	3.0	202	525	6.4	490	6.0
7 Years	475	226	11836	1218	2131	.572	1	28	.036	629	1239	.508	627	524	793	1217	12	844	1.8	974	2508	5.3	3066	6.5

NBA Postseason																								
Year Tm	G	GS	Min	Md	Att	Pct	Md	Att	Pct	Md	Att	Pct	TO	Stl	Blk	PF	DQ	Ast	Avg	Off	Tot	Avg	Pts	Avg
96-97 LAC	3	0	66	6	11	.545	0	1	.000	3	10	.300	3	1	2	5	0	4	1.3	6	14	4.7	15	5.0
98-99 Orl	4	0	83	6	10	.600	0	0	—	6	13	.462	6	1	8	9	0	2	0.5	3	15	3.8	18	4.5
2 Years	7	0	149	12	21	.571	0	1	.000	9	23	.391	9	2	10	14	0	6	0.9	9	29	4.1	33	4.7

Doug Overton

Pos: G **College:** LaSalle **Drafted:** '91 2(40)—Det   **Ht:** 6'3" **Wt:** 190 **Born:** 8/3/69 **Age:** 31

College				Field Goals			3-Pt FGs			Free Throws			Misc			Fouls		Assists		Rebounds			Points	
Year Tm	G	GS	Min	Md	Att	Pct	Md	Att	Pct	Md	Att	Pct	TO	Stl	Blk	PF	DQ	Ast	Avg	Off	Tot	Avg	Pts	Avg
87-88 LaSal	34	—	918	110	221	.498	8	27	.296	37	44	.841	43	45	1	55	—	91	2.7	—	81	2.4	265	7.8
88-89 LaSal	32	—	1221	174	352	.494	26	65	.400	47	59	.797	104	98	1	49	—	244	7.6	—	101	3.2	421	13.2
89-90 LaSal	32	—	1202	201	387	.519	54	124	.435	95	119	.798	96	85	3	58	—	212	6.6	—	133	4.2	551	17.2
90-91 LaSal	25	—	959	199	447	.445	54	160	.338	106	128	.828	91	49	0	62	—	124	5.0	—	103	4.1	558	22.3
4 Years	123	—	4300	684	1407	.486	142	376	.378	285	350	.814	334	277	5	224	—	671	5.5	—	418	3.4	1795	14.6

NBA				Field Goals			3-Pt FGs			Free Throws			Misc			Fouls		Assists		Rebounds			Points	
Year Tm	G	GS	Min	Md	Att	Pct	Md	Att	Pct	Md	Att	Pct	TO	Stl	Blk	PF	DQ	Ast	Avg	Off	Tot	Avg	Pts	Avg
91-92										Played in CBA														
92-93 Was	45	13	990	152	323	.471	3	13	.231	59	81	.728	72	31	6	81	0	157	3.5	25	106	2.4	366	8.1
93-94 Was	61	1	749	87	216	.403	1	11	.091	43	52	.827	54	21	1	48	0	92	1.5	19	69	1.1	218	3.6
94-95 Was	82	20	1704	207	498	.416	53	125	.424	109	125	.872	104	53	2	126	1	246	3.0	26	143	1.7	576	7.0
95-96 Den	55	0	607	67	178	.376	8	26	.308	40	55	.727	40	13	5	49	0	106	1.9	8	63	1.1	182	3.3
96-97 Phi	61	4	634	81	190	.426	10	40	.250	45	48	.938	39	24	0	44	0	101	1.7	18	68	1.1	217	3.6
97-98 Phi	23	2	277	24	63	.381	0	3	.000	14	16	.875	23	8	1	34	0	37	1.6	2	14	0.6	62	2.7
98-99 3Tm	24	1	244	36	84	.429	2	7	.286	18	20	.900	20	5	1	18	0	23	1.0	7	21	0.9	92	3.8
99-00 Bos	48	0	432	61	154	.396	10	28	.357	20	21	.952	20	10	0	46	0	53	1.1	14	33	0.7	152	3.2
98-99 Orl	6	0	33	6	12	.500	0	2	.000	6	6	1.000	3	1	0	2	0	3	0.5	1	2	0.3	18	3.0
NJ	8	1	174	25	57	.439	2	4	.500	12	14	.857	15	3	1	14	0	16	2.0	6	17	2.1	64	8.0
Phi	10	0	37	5	15	.333	0	1	.000	0	0	—	2	1	0	2	0	4	0.4	0	2	0.2	10	1.0
8 Years	399	41	5637	715	1706	.419	87	253	.344	348	418	.833	372	165	16	446	1	815	2.0	119	517	1.3	1865	4.7

Billy Owens

(statistical profile on page 258)

Pos: F **College:** Syracuse **Drafted:** '91 1(3)—Sac   **Ht:** 6'9" **Wt:** 225 **Born:** 5/1/69 **Age:** 31

College				Field Goals			3-Pt FGs			Free Throws			Misc			Fouls		Assists		Rebounds			Points	
Year Tm	G	GS	Min	Md	Att	Pct	Md	Att	Pct	Md	Att	Pct	TO	Stl	Blk	PF	DQ	Ast	Avg	Off	Tot	Avg	Pts	Avg
88-89 Syr	38	38	1215	196	376	.521	8	36	.222	94	145	.648	76	64	35	110	2	119	3.1	114	263	6.9	494	13.0
89-90 Syr	33	33	1188	228	469	.486	19	60	.317	127	176	.722	79	74	25	99	2	151	4.6	124	276	8.4	602	18.2
90-91 Syr	32	32	1215	282	554	.509	23	58	.397	157	233	.674	113	78	37	86	0	111	3.5	134	371	11.6	744	23.3
3 Years	103	103	3618	706	1399	.505	50	154	.325	378	554	.682	268	216	97	295	4	381	3.7	372	910	8.8	1840	17.9

NBA				Field Goals			3-Pt FGs			Free Throws			Misc			Fouls		Assists		Rebounds			Points	
Year Tm	G	GS	Min	Md	Att	Pct	Md	Att	Pct	Md	Att	Pct	TO	Stl	Blk	PF	DQ	Ast	Avg	Off	Tot	Avg	Pts	Avg
91-92 GS	80	77	2510	468	891	.525	1	9	.111	204	312	.654	179	90	65	276	1	188	2.4	243	639	8.0	1141	14.3
92-93 GS	37	37	1201	247	493	.501	1	11	.091	117	183	.639	106	35	28	105	1	144	3.9	108	264	7.1	612	16.5
93-94 GS	79	72	2738	492	971	.507	3	15	.200	199	326	.610	214	83	60	269	5	326	4.1	230	640	8.1	1186	15.0
94-95 Mia	70	60	2296	403	820	.491	2	22	.091	194	313	.620	204	80	30	205	6	246	3.5	203	502	7.2	1002	14.3
95-96 2Tm	62	51	1982	323	673	.480	5	18	.278	157	247	.636	164	49	38	192	2	204	3.3	143	411	6.6	808	13.0

NBA			Field Goals			3-Pt FGs			Free Throws			Misc			Fouls		Assists		Rebounds			Points	
Year Tm	G	GS	Min	Md	Att	Pct	Md	Att	Pct	Md	Att	Pct	TO	Stl	Blk	PF	DQ	Ast	Avg	Off	Tot	Avg	Pts	Avg
96-97 Sac	66	56	1995	299	640	.467	25	72	.347	101	145	.697	133	62	25	187	4	187	2.8	134	392	5.9	724	11.0
97-98 Sac	78	78	2348	338	728	.464	26	70	.371	116	197	.589	153	93	38	231	5	219	2.8	170	582	7.5	818	10.5
98-99 Sea	21	19	451	65	165	.394	5	11	.455	28	35	.800	33	12	4	37	0	38	1.8	35	80	3.8	163	7.8
99-00 2Tm	62	11	1305	150	358	.419	11	34	.324	63	106	.594	85	33	21	166	1	97	1.6	99	301	4.9	374	6.0
95-96 Mia	40	40	1388	239	473	.505	0	6	.000	112	177	.633	113	30	22	132	1	134	3.4	94	286	7.2	590	14.8
Sac	22	11	594	84	200	.420	5	12	.417	45	70	.643	51	19	16	60	1	70	3.2	49	125	5.7	218	9.9
99-00 Phi	46	7	919	112	258	.434	9	27	.333	38	64	.594	61	26	16	119	1	59	1.3	63	192	4.2	271	5.9
GS	16	4	386	38	100	.380	2	7	.286	25	42	.595	24	7	5	47	0	38	2.4	36	109	6.8	103	6.4
9 Years	555	461	16826	2785	5739	.485	79	262	.302	1179	1864	.633	1271	537	309	1668	28	1649	3.0	1365	3811	6.9	6828	12.3

NBA Postseason

Year Tm	G	GS	Min	Md	Att	Pct	Md	Att	Pct	Md	Att	Pct	TO	Stl	Blk	PF	DQ	Ast	Avg	Off	Tot	Avg	Pts	Avg
91-92 GS	4	4	157	30	57	.526	0	0	—	17	27	.630	6	8	2	14	0	13	3.3	13	33	8.3	77	19.3
93-94 GS	3	3	127	25	50	.500	0	1	.000	9	12	.750	7	4	2	11	0	13	4.3	12	30	10.0	59	19.7
95-96 Sac	4	4	131	15	34	.441	0	4	.000	3	6	.500	11	4	1	17	1	14	3.5	5	26	6.5	33	8.3
3 Years	11	11	415	70	141	.496	0	5	.000	29	45	.644	24	16	5	42	1	40	3.6	30	89	8.1	169	15.4

Robert Pack

Pos: G **College:** Southern California **Drafted:** '91 FA—Por **Ht:** 6'2" **Wt:** 190 **Born:** 2/3/69 **Age:** 31

College			Field Goals			3-Pt FGs			Free Throws			Misc			Fouls		Assists		Rebounds			Points	
Year Tm	G	GS	Min	Md	Att	Pct	Md	Att	Pct	Md	Att	Pct	TO	Stl	Blk	PF	DQ	Ast	Avg	Off	Tot	Avg	Pts	Avg
89-90 USC	28	26	883	118	250	.472	19	57	.333	84	124	.677	102	43	0	70	4	165	5.9	—	67	2.4	339	12.1
90-91 USC	29	29	941	145	302	.480	14	55	.255	123	155	.794	93	46	1	84	3	154	5.3	—	93	3.2	427	14.7
2 Years	57	55	1824	263	552	.476	33	112	.295	207	279	.742	195	89	1	154	7	319	5.6	—	160	2.8	766	13.4

NBA			Field Goals			3-Pt FGs			Free Throws			Misc			Fouls		Assists		Rebounds			Points	
Year Tm	G	GS	Min	Md	Att	Pct	Md	Att	Pct	Md	Att	Pct	TO	Stl	Blk	PF	DQ	Ast	Avg	Off	Tot	Avg	Pts	Avg
91-92 Por	72	0	894	115	272	.423	0	10	.000	102	127	.803	92	40	4	101	0	140	1.9	32	97	1.3	332	4.6
92-93 Den	77	1	1579	285	606	.470	1	8	.125	239	311	.768	185	81	10	182	1	335	4.4	52	160	2.1	810	10.5
93-94 Den	66	4	1382	223	503	.443	6	29	.207	179	236	.758	204	81	9	147	1	356	5.4	25	123	1.9	631	9.6
94-95 Den	42	32	1144	170	395	.430	30	72	.417	137	175	.783	134	61	6	101	1	290	6.9	19	113	2.7	507	12.1
95-96 Was	31	31	1084	190	444	.428	26	98	.265	154	182	.846	114	62	1	68	0	242	7.8	29	132	4.3	560	18.1
96-97 2Tm	54	42	1782	272	693	.392	31	112	.277	196	243	.807	217	94	6	139	0	452	8.4	28	146	2.7	771	14.3
97-98 Dal	12	10	292	33	98	.337	3	6	.500	25	36	.694	38	20	1	17	0	42	3.5	8	34	2.8	94	7.8
98-99 Dal	25	0	468	75	174	.431	0	4	.000	72	88	.818	49	20	1	41	0	81	3.2	9	36	1.4	222	8.9
99-00 Dal	29	22	665	96	230	.417	4	11	.364	63	78	.808	76	31	3	44	0	168	5.8	7	42	1.4	259	8.9
96-97 NJ	34	31	1185	193	474	.407	22	74	.297	134	170	.788	150	59	3	83	0	325	9.6	15	86	2.5	542	15.9
Dal	20	11	597	79	219	.361	9	38	.237	62	73	.849	67	35	3	56	0	127	6.4	13	60	3.0	229	11.5
9 Years	408	142	9290	1459	3415	.427	101	350	.289	1167	1476	.791	1109	490	41	840	3	2106	5.2	209	883	2.2	4186	10.3

NBA Postseason

Year Tm	G	GS	Min	Md	Att	Pct	Md	Att	Pct	Md	Att	Pct	TO	Stl	Blk	PF	DQ	Ast	Avg	Off	Tot	Avg	Pts	Avg
91-92 Por	14	0	52	4	18	.222	0	0	—	3	4	.750	3	5	1	10	0	7	0.5	2	6	0.4	11	0.8
93-94 Den	12	0	332	48	118	.407	6	20	.300	39	55	.709	46	18	6	41	0	51	4.3	5	28	2.3	141	11.8
2 Years	26	0	384	52	136	.382	6	20	.300	42	59	.712	49	23	7	51	0	58	2.2	7	34	1.3	152	5.8

Scott Padgett

Pos: G **College:** Kentucky **Drafted:** '99 1(28)—Uta **Ht:** 6'9" **Wt:** 240 **Born:** 4/19/76 **Age:** 24

College			Field Goals			3-Pt FGs			Free Throws			Misc			Fouls		Assists		Rebounds			Points	
Year Tm	G	GS	Min	Md	Att	Pct	Md	Att	Pct	Md	Att	Pct	TO	Stl	Blk	PF	DQ	Ast	Avg	Off	Tot	Avg	Pts	Avg
94-95 Kty	14	0	57	7	27	.259	4	13	.308	10	12	.833	3	3	1	12	0	4	0.3	6	17	1.2	28	2.0
96-97 Kty	32	24	759	100	244	.410	47	138	.341	61	80	.763	57	48	16	91	6	56	1.8	72	162	5.1	308	9.6
97-98 Kty	39	37	1089	161	338	.476	40	107	.374	87	102	.853	84	49	27	93	0	82	2.1	103	255	6.5	449	11.5
98-99 Kty	37	37	1075	156	335	.466	61	160	.381	94	138	.681	66	47	24	84	1	96	2.6	71	217	5.9	467	12.6
4 Years	122	98	2980	424	944	.449	152	418	.364	252	332	.759	210	147	68	280	7	238	2.0	252	651	5.3	1252	10.3

NBA			Field Goals			3-Pt FGs			Free Throws			Misc			Fouls		Assists		Rebounds			Points	
Year Tm	G	GS	Min	Md	Att	Pct	Md	Att	Pct	Md	Att	Pct	TO	Stl	Blk	PF	DQ	Ast	Avg	Off	Tot	Avg	Pts	Avg
99-00 Uta	47	9	432	44	140	.314	13	44	.295	19	27	.704	22	14	8	55	1	25	0.5	24	88	1.9	120	2.6

NBA Postseason

Year Tm	G	GS	Min	Md	Att	Pct	Md	Att	Pct	Md	Att	Pct	TO	Stl	Blk	PF	DQ	Ast	Avg	Off	Tot	Avg	Pts	Avg
99-00 Uta	8	0	59	6	16	.375	3	9	.333	0	0	—	4	1	2	10	0	5	0.6	3	17	2.1	15	1.9

Milt Palacio

Pos: G **College:** Colorado State **Drafted:** '99 FA—Van   **Ht:** 6'3" **Wt:** 195 **Born:** 2/17/78 **Age:** 22

College				Field Goals			3-Pt FGs			Free Throws			Misc			Fouls		Assists		Rebounds			Points	
Year Tm	G	GS	Min	Md	Att	Pct	Md	Att	Pct	Md	Att	Pct	TO	Stl	Blk	PF	DQ	Ast	Avg	Off	Tot	Avg	Pts	Avg
96-97 ColSt	29	29	898	75	151	.497	18	47	.383	62	89	.697	85	43	3	62	2	147	5.1	12	111	3.8	230	7.9
97-98 ColSt	29	29	957	98	205	.478	23	61	.377	64	97	.660	67	49	1	67	0	148	5.1	13	103	3.6	283	9.8
98-99 ColSt	30	30	1073	188	419	.449	41	119	.345	135	179	.754	118	60	4	72	2	130	4.3	48	155	5.2	552	18.4
3 Years	88	88	2928	361	775	.466	82	227	.361	261	365	.715	270	152	8	201	4	425	4.8	73	369	4.2	1065	12.1

NBA				Field Goals			3-Pt FGs			Free Throws			Misc			Fouls		Assists		Rebounds			Points	
Year Tm	G	GS	Min	Md	Att	Pct	Md	Att	Pct	Md	Att	Pct	TO	Stl	Blk	PF	DQ	Ast	Avg	Off	Tot	Avg	Pts	Avg
99-00 Van	53	0	394	43	98	.439	0	2	.000	22	37	.595	44	20	0	32	0	48	0.9	17	51	1.0	108	2.0

Anthony Parker

Pos: G **College:** Bradley **Drafted:** '97 1(21)—NJ   **Ht:** 6'6" **Wt:** 215 **Born:** 6/19/75 **Age:** 25

College				Field Goals			3-Pt FGs			Free Throws			Misc			Fouls		Assists		Rebounds			Points	
Year Tm	G	GS	Min	Md	Att	Pct	Md	Att	Pct	Md	Att	Pct	TO	Stl	Blk	PF	DQ	Ast	Avg	Off	Tot	Avg	Pts	Avg
93-94 Brad	31	28	905	106	231	.459	47	114	.412	84	120	.700	73	37	16	60	3	79	2.5	32	137	4.4	343	11.1
94-95 Brad	30	30	1021	131	308	.425	46	128	.359	118	155	.761	70	39	19	64	3	99	3.3	31	198	6.6	426	14.2
95-96 Brad	30	29	963	178	377	.472	73	173	.422	137	172	.797	77	46	33	61	0	105	3.5	32	196	6.5	566	18.9
96-97 Brad	21	20	715	109	257	.424	29	100	.290	101	140	.721	57	37	10	36	0	72	3.4	15	112	5.3	348	16.6
4 Years	112	107	3604	524	1173	.447	195	515	.379	440	587	.750	277	159	78	221	6	355	3.2	110	643	5.7	1683	15.0

NBA				Field Goals			3-Pt FGs			Free Throws			Misc			Fouls		Assists		Rebounds			Points	
Year Tm	G	GS	Min	Md	Att	Pct	Md	Att	Pct	Md	Att	Pct	TO	Stl	Blk	PF	DQ	Ast	Avg	Off	Tot	Avg	Pts	Avg
97-98 Phi	37	0	196	25	63	.397	9	28	.321	13	20	.650	11	11	3	17	0	19	0.5	8	26	0.7	72	1.9
98-99 Phi	2	0	3	1	1	1.000	0	0	—	0	0	—	0	0	0	0	0	0	0.0	0	0	0.0	2	1.0
99-00 Orl	16	0	185	24	57	.421	1	14	.071	8	11	.727	11	8	4	13	0	10	0.6	5	27	1.7	57	3.6
3 Years	55	0	384	50	121	.413	10	42	.238	21	31	.677	22	19	7	30	0	29	0.5	13	53	1.0	131	2.4

Cherokee Parks

Pos: F-C **College:** Duke **Drafted:** '95 1(12)—Dal   **Ht:** 6'11" **Wt:** 240 **Born:** 10/11/72 **Age:** 28

College				Field Goals			3-Pt FGs			Free Throws			Misc			Fouls		Assists		Rebounds			Points	
Year Tm	G	GS	Min	Md	Att	Pct	Md	Att	Pct	Md	Att	Pct	TO	Stl	Blk	PF	DQ	Ast	Avg	Off	Tot	Avg	Pts	Avg
91-92 Duke	34	3	435	60	105	.571	0	0	—	50	69	.725	30	5	35	57	—	13	0.4	30	81	2.4	170	5.0
92-93 Duke	32	31	899	161	247	.652	0	0	—	72	100	.720	56	25	65	68	—	14	0.4	65	220	6.9	394	12.3
93-94 Duke	34	34	1038	186	347	.536	3	17	.176	115	149	.772	57	37	76	77	—	31	0.9	100	284	8.4	490	14.4
94-95 Duke	31	31	1091	222	443	.501	31	85	.365	114	147	.776	63	26	55	68	—	45	1.5	68	289	9.3	589	19.0
4 Years	131	99	3463	629	1142	.551	34	102	.333	351	465	.755	206	93	231	270		103	0.8	263	874	6.7	1643	12.5

NBA				Field Goals			3-Pt FGs			Free Throws			Misc			Fouls		Assists		Rebounds			Points	
Year Tm	G	GS	Min	Md	Att	Pct	Md	Att	Pct	Md	Att	Pct	TO	Stl	Blk	PF	DQ	Ast	Avg	Off	Tot	Avg	Pts	Avg
95-96 Dal	64	3	869	101	247	.409	7	26	.269	41	62	.661	31	25	32	100	0	29	0.5	66	216	3.4	250	3.9
96-97 Min	76	0	961	103	202	.510	0	1	.000	46	76	.605	32	41	48	150	2	34	0.4	83	195	2.6	252	3.3
97-98 Min	79	43	1703	224	449	.499	0	1	.000	110	169	.651	66	36	86	237	4	53	0.7	140	437	5.5	558	7.1
98-99 Van	48	41	1118	118	275	.429	0	1	.000	30	55	.545	49	28	28	114	0	36	0.8	75	243	5.1	266	5.5
99-00 Van	56	14	808	72	145	.497	0	1	.000	24	37	.649	28	29	45	115	2	35	0.6	55	183	3.3	168	3.0
5 Years	323	101	5459	618	1318	.469	7	30	.233	251	399	.629	206	159	239	716	8	187	0.6	419	1274	3.9	1494	4.6

NBA Postseason				Field Goals			3-Pt FGs			Free Throws			Misc			Fouls		Assists		Rebounds			Points	
Year Tm	G	GS	Min	Md	Att	Pct	Md	Att	Pct	Md	Att	Pct	TO	Stl	Blk	PF	DQ	Ast	Avg	Off	Tot	Avg	Pts	Avg
96-97 Min	1	0	11	2	3	.667	0	0	—	0	0	—	0	1	0	5	0	0	0.0	0	5	5.0	4	4.0
97-98 Min	1	0	1	0	0	—	0	0	—	0	0	—	0	0	0	0	0	0	0.0	0	0	0.0	0	0.0
2 Years	2	0	12	2	3	.667	0	0	—	0	0	—	0	1	0	5	0	0	0.0	0	5	2.5	4	2.0

Andrae Patterson

Pos: F **College:** Indiana **Drafted:** '98 2(46)—Min   **Ht:** 6'9" **Wt:** 240 **Born:** 11/12/75 **Age:** 25

College				Field Goals			3-Pt FGs			Free Throws			Misc			Fouls		Assists		Rebounds			Points	
Year Tm	G	GS	Min	Md	Att	Pct	Md	Att	Pct	Md	Att	Pct	TO	Stl	Blk	PF	DQ	Ast	Avg	Off	Tot	Avg	Pts	Avg
94-95 Ind	28	0	540	84	170	.494	4	8	.500	31	45	.689	49	16	16	80	5	21	0.8	39	108	3.9	203	7.3
95-96 Ind	31	29	803	130	282	.461	20	57	.351	70	95	.737	73	28	42	103	5	46	1.5	65	191	6.2	350	11.3
96-97 Ind	30	25	829	151	321	.470	11	43	.256	97	128	.758	77	32	38	91	3	43	1.4	75	201	6.7	410	13.7
97-98 Ind	32	27	815	152	307	.495	10	36	.278	88	111	.793	68	29	30	95	2	46	1.4	50	187	5.8	402	12.6
4 Years	121	81	2987	517	1080	.479	45	144	.313	286	379	.755	267	105	126	369	15	156	1.3	229	687	5.7	1365	11.3

NBA				Field Goals			3-Pt FGs			Free Throws			Misc			Fouls		Assists		Rebounds			Points	
Year Tm	G	GS	Min	Md	Att	Pct	Md	Att	Pct	Md	Att	Pct	TO	Stl	Blk	PF	DQ	Ast	Avg	Off	Tot	Avg	Pts	Avg
98-99 Min	35	0	284	43	97	.443	0	5	.000	28	36	.778	22	19	7	62	1	15	0.4	30	65	1.9	114	3.3
99-00 Min	5	0	20	3	4	.750	0	0	—	0	0	—	1	1	0	4	0	1	0.2	1	2	0.4	6	1.2
2 Years	40	0	304	46	101	.455	0	5	.000	28	36	.778	23	20	7	66	1	16	0.4	31	67	1.7	120	3.0

NBA Postseason																								
Year Tm	G	GS	Min	Md	Att	Pct	Md	Att	Pct	Md	Att	Pct	TO	Stl	Blk	PF	DQ	Ast	Avg	Off	Tot	Avg	Pts	Avg
98-99 Min	2	0	7	0	0	—	0	0	—	0	0	—	1	0	0	1	0	2	1.0	1	4	2.0	0	0.0

Ruben Patterson

(statistical profile on page 259)

Pos: F **College:** Cincinnati **Drafted:** '98 2(31)—LAL   **Ht:** 6'5" **Wt:** 224 **Born:** 7/31/75 **Age:** 25

College				Field Goals			3-Pt FGs			Free Throws			Misc			Fouls		Assists		Rebounds			Points	
Year Tm	G	GS	Min	Md	Att	Pct	Md	Att	Pct	Md	Att	Pct	TO	Stl	Blk	PF	DQ	Ast	Avg	Off	Tot	Avg	Pts	Avg
96-97 Cin	31	26	723	164	299	.548	11	39	.282	87	144	.604	73	35	10	62	0	44	1.4	81	174	5.6	426	13.7
97-98 Cin	19	14	530	109	231	.472	18	67	.269	77	126	.611	67	22	12	48	2	41	2.2	44	119	6.3	313	16.5
2 Years	50	40	1253	273	530	.515	29	106	.274	164	270	.607	140	57	22	110	2	85	1.7	125	293	5.9	739	14.8

NBA				Field Goals			3-Pt FGs			Free Throws			Misc			Fouls		Assists		Rebounds			Points	
Year Tm	G	GS	Min	Md	Att	Pct	Md	Att	Pct	Md	Att	Pct	TO	Stl	Blk	PF	DQ	Ast	Avg	Off	Tot	Avg	Pts	Avg
98-99 LAL	24	2	144	21	51	.412	1	6	.167	22	31	.710	12	5	3	16	0	2	0.1	17	30	1.3	65	2.7
99-00 Sea	81	74	2097	354	661	.536	12	27	.444	222	321	.692	144	94	40	190	0	126	1.6	218	434	5.4	942	11.6
2 Years	105	76	2241	375	712	.527	13	33	.394	244	352	.693	156	99	43	206	0	128	1.2	235	464	4.4	1007	9.6

NBA Postseason																								
Year Tm	G	GS	Min	Md	Att	Pct	Md	Att	Pct	Md	Att	Pct	TO	Stl	Blk	PF	DQ	Ast	Avg	Off	Tot	Avg	Pts	Avg
98-99 LAL	3	0	5	0	1	.000	0	0	—	0	0	—	1	0	0	0	0	0	0.0	0	0	0.0	0	0.0
99-00 Sea	5	0	84	14	26	.538	0	2	.000	13	15	.867	8	3	2	6	0	2	0.4	9	15	3.0	41	8.2
2 Years	8	0	89	14	27	.519	0	2	.000	13	15	.867	9	3	2	6	0	2	0.3	9	15	1.9	41	5.1

Gary Payton

(statistical profile on page 259)

Pos: G **College:** Oregon State **Drafted:** '90 1(2)—Sea   **Ht:** 6'4" **Wt:** 180 **Born:** 7/23/68 **Age:** 32

College				Field Goals			3-Pt FGs			Free Throws			Misc			Fouls		Assists		Rebounds			Points	
Year Tm	G	GS	Min	Md	Att	Pct	Md	Att	Pct	Md	Att	Pct	TO	Stl	Blk	PF	DQ	Ast	Avg	Off	Tot	Avg	Pts	Avg
86-87 OreSt	30	30	1115	153	333	.459	13	35	.371	55	82	.671	93	58	20	98	3	229	7.6	—	120	4.0	374	12.5
87-88 OreSt	31	31	1178	180	368	.489	31	78	.397	58	83	.699	106	72	11	106	3	230	7.4	—	103	3.3	449	14.5
88-89 OreSt	30	30	1140	208	438	.475	82	213	.385	105	155	.677	91	91	17	108	1	244	8.1	—	122	4.1	603	20.1
89-90 OreSt	29	29	1095	288	571	.504	52	156	.333	118	171	.690	106	100	15	103	4	235	8.1	—	135	4.7	746	25.7
4 Years	120	120	4528	829	1710	.485	178	482	.369	336	491	.684	396	321	63	415	13	938	7.8	—	480	4.0	2172	18.1

NBA				Field Goals			3-Pt FGs			Free Throws			Misc			Fouls		Assists		Rebounds			Points	
Year Tm	G	GS	Min	Md	Att	Pct	Md	Att	Pct	Md	Att	Pct	TO	Stl	Blk	PF	DQ	Ast	Avg	Off	Tot	Avg	Pts	Avg
90-91 Sea	82	82	2244	259	575	.450	1	13	.077	69	97	.711	180	165	15	249	3	528	6.4	108	243	3.0	588	7.2
91-92 Sea	81	79	2549	331	734	.451	3	23	.130	99	148	.669	174	147	21	248	0	506	6.2	123	295	3.6	764	9.4
92-93 Sea	82	78	2548	476	963	.494	7	34	.206	151	196	.770	148	177	21	250	1	399	4.9	95	281	3.4	1110	13.5
93-94 Sea*	82	82	2881	584	1159	.504	15	54	.278	166	279	.595	173	188	19	227	0	494	6.0	105	269	3.3	1349	16.5
94-95 Sea*	82	82	3015	685	1345	.509	70	232	.302	249	348	.716	201	204	13	206	1	583	7.1	108	281	3.4	1689	20.6
95-96 Sea*	81	81	3162	618	1276	.484	98	299	.328	229	306	.748	260	231	19	221	1	608	7.5	104	339	4.2	1563	19.3
96-97 Sea*	82	82	3213	706	1482	.476	119	380	.313	254	355	.715	215	197	13	208	1	583	7.1	106	378	4.6	1785	21.8
97-98 Sea*	82	82	3145	579	1278	.453	134	397	.338	279	375	.744	229	185	18	195	0	679	8.3	77	376	4.6	1571	19.2
98-99 Sea	50	50	2008	401	923	.434	83	281	.295	199	276	.721	154	109	12	115	0	436	8.7	62	244	4.9	1084	21.7
99-00 Sea*	82	82	3425	747	1666	.448	177	520	.340	311	423	.735	224	153	18	178	0	732	8.9	100	529	6.5	1982	24.2
10 Years	786	780	28190	5386	11401	.472	707	2233	.317	2006	2803	.716	1958	1756	169	2097	7	5548	7.1	988	3235	4.1	13485	17.2

NBA Postseason																								
Year Tm	G	GS	Min	Md	Att	Pct	Md	Att	Pct	Md	Att	Pct	TO	Stl	Blk	PF	DQ	Ast	Avg	Off	Tot	Avg	Pts	Avg
90-91 Sea	5	5	135	11	27	.407	0	1	.000	2	2	1.000	9	8	1	16	0	32	6.4	5	13	2.6	24	4.8
91-92 Sea	8	8	221	27	58	.466	0	2	.000	7	12	.583	10	8	2	26	1	38	4.8	6	21	2.6	61	7.6
92-93 Sea	19	19	605	104	235	.443	1	6	.167	25	37	.676	34	34	3	64	1	70	3.7	22	63	3.3	234	12.3
93-94 Sea	5	5	181	34	69	.493	3	9	.333	8	19	.421	8	8	2	15	0	28	5.6	6	17	3.4	79	15.8
94-95 Sea	4	4	172	32	67	.478	2	10	.200	5	12	.417	8	5	0	13	0	21	5.3	6	10	2.5	71	17.8
95-96 Sea	21	21	911	162	334	.485	41	100	.410	69	109	.633	62	37	7	69	0	143	6.8	19	108	5.1	434	20.7
96-97 Sea	12	12	546	105	255	.412	25	75	.333	50	61	.820	35	26	4	26	0	104	8.7	20	65	5.4	285	23.8
97-98 Sea	10	10	428	87	183	.475	19	50	.380	47	50	.940	26	18	1	31	1	70	7.0	9	34	3.4	240	24.0
99-00 Sea	5	5	221	50	113	.442	9	23	.391	20	26	.769	18	9	1	16	0	37	7.4	8	38	7.6	129	25.8
9 Years	89	89	3420	612	1341	.456	100	276	.362	233	328	.710	210	153	21	276	3	543	6.1	101	369	4.1	1557	17.5

127

(statistical profile on page 260)

Anthony Peeler

Pos: G **College:** Missouri **Drafted:** '92 1(15)—LAL   **Ht:** 6'4" **Wt:** 210 **Born:** 11/25/69 **Age:** 31

College				Field Goals			3-Pt FGs			Free Throws			Misc			Fouls		Assists		Rebounds			Points	
Year Tm	G	GS	Min	Md	Att	Pct	Md	Att	Pct	Md	Att	Pct	TO	Stl	Blk	PF	DQ	Ast	Avg	Off	Tot	Avg	Pts	Avg
88-89 Misou	36	9	801	130	258	.504	13	37	.351	89	118	.754	95	34	8	79	0	102	2.8	—	134	3.7	362	10.1
89-90 Misou	31	30	1031	184	413	.446	24	68	.353	130	169	.769	90	63	15	76	0	179	5.8	—	168	5.4	522	16.8
90-91 Misou	21	17	725	134	282	.475	24	58	.414	116	151	.768	74	37	3	51	0	104	5.0	—	131	6.2	408	19.4
91-92 Misou	29	28	1026	218	475	.459	55	132	.417	187	232	.806	101	62	10	72	1	112	3.9	—	160	5.5	678	23.4
4 Years	117	84	3583	666	1428	.466	116	295	.393	522	670	.779	360	196	36	278	1	497	4.2	—	593	5.1	1970	16.8

NBA				Field Goals			3-Pt FGs			Free Throws			Misc			Fouls		Assists		Rebounds			Points	
Year Tm	G	GS	Min	Md	Att	Pct	Md	Att	Pct	Md	Att	Pct	TO	Stl	Blk	PF	DQ	Ast	Avg	Off	Tot	Avg	Pts	Avg
92-93 LAL	77	11	1656	297	634	.468	46	118	.390	162	206	.786	123	60	14	193	0	166	2.2	64	179	2.3	802	10.4
93-94 LAL	30	30	923	176	409	.430	14	63	.222	57	71	.803	59	43	8	93	0	94	3.1	48	109	3.6	423	14.1
94-95 LAL	73	24	1559	285	659	.432	84	216	.389	102	128	.797	82	52	13	143	1	122	1.7	62	168	2.3	756	10.4
95-96 LAL	73	12	1608	272	602	.452	105	254	.413	61	86	.709	56	59	10	139	0	118	1.6	45	137	1.9	710	9.7
96-97 Van	72	57	2291	402	1011	.398	128	343	.373	109	133	.820	157	105	17	168	0	256	3.6	54	247	3.4	1041	14.5
97-98 2Tm	38	32	1193	190	420	.452	53	125	.424	36	47	.766	51	61	6	97	0	137	3.6	37	123	3.2	469	12.3
98-99 Min	28	28	810	103	272	.379	34	114	.298	30	41	.732	38	35	6	60	0	78	2.8	30	84	3.0	270	9.6
99-00 Min	82	22	2073	316	725	.436	85	255	.333	87	109	.798	85	62	10	171	1	195	2.4	58	232	2.8	804	9.8
97-98 Van	8	8	202	35	72	.486	5	19	.263	4	6	.667	6	9	0	16	0	23	2.9	6	20	2.5	79	9.9
Min	30	24	991	155	348	.445	48	106	.453	32	41	.780	45	52	6	81	0	114	3.8	31	103	3.4	390	13.0
8 Years	473	216	12113	2041	4732	.431	549	1488	.369	644	821	.784	651	477	84	1064	2	1166	2.5	398	1279	2.7	5275	11.2

NBA Postseason																								
Year Tm	G	GS	Min	Md	Att	Pct	Md	Att	Pct	Md	Att	Pct	TO	Stl	Blk	PF	DQ	Ast	Avg	Off	Tot	Avg	Pts	Avg
94-95 LAL	10	10	268	32	79	.405	8	31	.258	17	22	.773	12	10	2	23	0	25	2.5	8	28	2.8	89	8.9
95-96 LAL	3	0	72	9	27	.333	6	14	.429	4	4	1.000	3	6	0	6	0	3	1.0	2	8	2.7	28	9.3
97-98 Min	5	5	213	31	77	.403	15	31	.484	4	4	1.000	8	10	3	15	0	18	3.6	16	38	7.6	81	16.2
98-99 Min	4	4	125	11	35	.314	5	13	.385	0	0	—	4	4	0	12	1	6	1.5	7	16	4.0	27	6.8
99-00 Min	4	0	90	11	24	.458	2	10	.200	6	8	.750	1	3	1	9	0	5	1.3	2	9	2.3	30	7.5
5 Years	26	19	768	94	242	.388	36	99	.364	31	38	.816	28	33	6	65	1	57	2.2	35	99	3.8	255	9.8

Will Perdue

Pos: C **College:** Vanderbilt **Drafted:** '88 1(11)—Chi   **Ht:** 7'0" **Wt:** 240 **Born:** 8/29/65 **Age:** 35

College				Field Goals			3-Pt FGs			Free Throws			Misc			Fouls		Assists		Rebounds			Points	
Year Tm	G	GS	Min	Md	Att	Pct	Md	Att	Pct	Md	Att	Pct	TO	Stl	Blk	PF	DQ	Ast	Avg	Off	Tot	Avg	Pts	Avg
83-84 Van	17	—	111	21	45	.467	—	—	—	4	9	.444	10	2	4	16	—	2	0.1	—	38	2.2	46	2.7
85-86 Van	22	—	181	31	53	.585	—	—	—	14	32	.438	13	2	13	22	—	4	0.2	—	61	2.8	76	3.5
86-87 Van	34	—	1033	233	389	.599	0	0	—	126	204	.618	70	15	72	95	—	50	1.5	—	295	8.7	592	17.4
87-88 Van	31	—	1013	234	369	.634	0	0	—	99	147	.673	65	13	74	105	—	81	2.6	—	314	10.1	567	18.3
4 Years	104	—	2338	519	856	.606	0	0	—	243	392	.620	158	32	163	238	—	137	1.3	—	708	6.8	1281	12.3

NBA				Field Goals			3-Pt FGs			Free Throws			Misc			Fouls		Assists		Rebounds			Points	
Year Tm	G	GS	Min	Md	Att	Pct	Md	Att	Pct	Md	Att	Pct	TO	Stl	Blk	PF	DQ	Ast	Avg	Off	Tot	Avg	Pts	Avg
88-89 Chi	30	0	190	29	72	.403	0	0	—	8	14	.571	15	4	6	38	0	11	0.4	18	45	1.5	66	2.2
89-90 Chi	77	11	884	111	268	.414	0	5	.000	72	104	.692	65	19	26	150	0	46	0.6	88	214	2.8	294	3.8
90-91 Chi	74	3	972	116	235	.494	0	3	.000	75	112	.670	75	23	57	147	1	47	0.6	122	336	4.5	307	4.1
91-92 Chi	77	7	1007	152	278	.547	1	2	.500	45	91	.495	72	16	43	133	1	80	1.0	108	312	4.1	350	4.5
92-93 Chi	72	16	998	137	246	.557	0	1	.000	67	111	.604	74	22	47	139	2	74	1.0	103	287	4.0	341	4.7
93-94 Chi	43	6	497	47	112	.420	0	1	.000	23	32	.719	42	8	11	61	0	34	0.8	40	126	2.9	117	2.7
94-95 Chi	78	78	1592	254	459	.553	0	1	.000	113	194	.582	116	26	56	220	3	90	1.2	211	522	6.7	621	8.0
95-96 SA	80	22	1396	173	331	.523	0	1	.000	67	125	.536	86	28	74	183	0	33	0.4	175	485	6.1	413	5.2
96-97 SA	65	34	1918	233	410	.568	0	0	—	99	171	.579	87	32	102	184	2	38	0.6	251	638	9.8	565	8.7
97-98 SA	79	30	1491	162	295	.549	0	1	.000	70	133	.526	81	22	50	137	0	57	0.7	177	535	6.8	394	5.0
98-99 SA	37	1	445	38	60	.633	0	0	—	14	26	.538	22	9	10	63	0	18	0.5	33	138	3.7	90	2.4
99-00 Chi	67	15	1012	59	168	.351	0	0	—	50	105	.476	78	14	42	126	1	65	1.0	88	262	3.9	168	2.5
12 Years	779	223	12302	1511	2934	.515	1	15	.067	703	1218	.577	813	223	524	1581	10	593	0.8	1414	3900	5.0	3726	4.8

NBA Postseason																								
Year Tm	G	GS	Min	Md	Att	Pct	Md	Att	Pct	Md	Att	Pct	TO	Stl	Blk	PF	DQ	Ast	Avg	Off	Tot	Avg	Pts	Avg
88-89 Chi	3	0	22	6	9	.667	0	1	.000	2	3	.667	0	0	0	4	0	2	0.7	3	6	2.0	14	4.7
89-90 Chi	13	0	78	13	28	.464	1	2	.500	13	18	.722	4	0	5	13	0	2	0.2	7	19	1.5	40	3.1
90-91 Chi	17	0	198	29	53	.547	0	0	—	12	20	.545	14	2	8	41	1	4	0.2	32	65	3.8	70	4.1
91-92 Chi	18	0	157	18	37	.486	0	1	.000	9	20	.450	12	3	10	34	1	9	0.5	18	40	2.2	45	2.5
92-93 Chi	13	0	101	10	20	.500	0	0	—	5	10	.500	8	1	2	18	0	5	0.4	15	30	2.3	25	1.9
94-95 Chi	10	2	176	19	37	.514	0	0	—	12	21	.571	10	1	3	27	0	6	0.6	18	48	4.8	50	5.0
95-96 SA	10	2	242	29	42	.690	0	0	—	16	20	.800	11	2	4	24	0	5	0.5	26	79	7.9	74	7.4
97-98 SA	9	7	191	9	27	.333	0	0	—	18	21	.857	11	6	9	26	0	1	0.1	24	60	6.7	36	4.0

NBA Postseason

Year Tm	G	GS	Min	Md	Att	Pct	Md	Att	Pct	Md	Att	Pct	TO	Stl	Blk	PF	DQ	Ast	Avg	Off	Tot	Avg	Pts	Avg
8-99 SA	12	0	86	6	11	.545	0	0	—	1	2	.500	3	0	1	19	0	0	0.0	9	28	2.3	13	1.1
Years	105	11	1251	139	264	.527	1	4	.250	88	137	.642	73	15	42	206	2	34	0.3	152	375	3.6	367	3.5

Sam Perkins

(statistical profile on page 260)

Pos: C **College:** North Carolina **Drafted:** '84 1(4)—Dal **Ht:** 6'9" **Wt:** 270 **Born:** 6/14/61 **Age:** 39

College				Field Goals			3-Pt FGs			Free Throws			Misc			Fouls		Assists		Rebounds			Points	
Year Tm	G	GS	Min	Md	Att	Pct	Md	Att	Pct	Md	Att	Pct	TO	Stl	Blk	PF	DQ	Ast	Avg	Off	Tot	Avg	Pts	Avg
0-81 UNC	37	21	1115	199	318	.626	—	—	—	152	205	.741	—	23	67	115	—	27	0.7	—	289	7.8	550	14.9
1-82 UNC	32	—	1141	174	301	.578	—	—	—	109	142	.768	53	33	53	74	—	35	1.1	—	250	7.8	457	14.3
2-83 UNC	35	—	1174	218	414	.527	12	28	.429	145	177	.819	—	47	65	—	—	47	1.3	—	330	9.4	593	16.9
3-84 UNC	31	—	1029	195	331	.589	—	—	—	155	181	.856	—	28	60	—	—	51	1.6	—	298	9.6	545	17.6
Years	135	—	4459	786	1364	.576	12	28	.429	561	705	.796	—	131	245	—	—	160	1.2	—	1167	8.6	2145	15.9

NBA				Field Goals			3-Pt FGs			Free Throws			Misc			Fouls		Assists		Rebounds			Points	
Year Tm	G	GS	Min	Md	Att	Pct	Md	Att	Pct	Md	Att	Pct	TO	Stl	Blk	PF	DQ	Ast	Avg	Off	Tot	Avg	Pts	Avg
4-85 Dal	82	42	2317	347	736	.471	9	36	.250	200	244	.820	102	63	63	236	1	135	1.6	189	605	7.4	903	11.0
5-86 Dal	80	79	2626	458	910	.503	11	33	.333	307	377	.814	145	75	94	212	2	153	1.9	195	685	8.6	1234	15.4
6-87 Dal	80	80	2687	461	957	.482	19	54	.352	245	296	.828	132	109	77	269	6	146	1.8	197	616	7.7	1186	14.8
7-88 Dal	75	75	2499	394	876	.450	5	30	.167	273	332	.822	119	74	54	227	2	118	1.6	201	601	8.0	1066	14.2
8-89 Dal	78	77	2860	445	959	.464	7	38	.184	274	329	.833	141	76	92	224	1	127	1.6	235	688	8.8	1171	15.0
9-90 Dal	76	70	2668	435	883	.493	6	28	.214	330	424	.778	148	88	64	225	4	175	2.3	209	572	7.5	1206	15.9
0-91 LAL	73	66	2504	368	744	.495	18	64	.281	229	279	.821	103	64	78	247	2	108	1.5	167	538	7.4	983	13.5
1-92 LAL	63	63	2332	361	803	.450	15	69	.217	304	372	.817	83	64	62	192	1	141	2.2	192	556	8.8	1041	16.5
2-93 2Tm	79	62	2351	381	799	.477	24	71	.338	250	305	.820	108	60	82	225	0	156	2.0	163	524	6.6	1036	13.1
3-94 Sea	81	41	2170	341	779	.438	99	270	.367	218	272	.801	103	67	31	197	0	111	1.4	120	366	4.5	999	12.3
4-95 Sea	82	37	2356	346	742	.466	136	343	.397	215	269	.799	77	72	45	186	0	135	1.6	96	398	4.9	1043	12.7
5-96 Sea	82	20	2169	325	797	.408	129	363	.355	191	241	.793	82	83	48	174	1	120	1.5	101	367	4.5	970	11.8
6-97 Sea	81	4	1976	290	661	.439	122	309	.395	187	229	.817	77	69	49	134	0	103	1.3	74	300	3.7	889	11.0
7-98 Sea	81	0	1675	196	471	.416	87	222	.392	101	128	.789	62	62	29	158	0	113	1.4	53	255	3.1	580	7.2
8-99 Ind	48	0	789	80	200	.400	35	90	.389	43	60	.717	22	15	14	74	0	25	0.5	36	138	2.9	238	5.0
9-00 Ind	81	0	1620	184	441	.417	89	218	.408	80	97	.825	63	31	33	136	0	68	0.8	64	289	3.6	537	6.6
2-93 LAL	49	49	1589	242	527	.459	5	29	.172	184	222	.829	76	40	51	139	0	128	2.6	111	379	7.7	673	13.7
Sea	30	13	762	139	272	.511	19	42	.452	66	83	.795	32	20	31	86	0	28	0.9	52	145	4.8	363	12.1
6 Years	1222	716	35599	5412	11758	.460	811	2238	.362	3447	4254	.810	1567	1072	915	3116	20	1934	1.6	2292	7498	6.1	15082	12.3

NBA Postseason

Year Tm	G	GS	Min	Md	Att	Pct	Md	Att	Pct	Md	Att	Pct	TO	Stl	Blk	PF	DQ	Ast	Avg	Off	Tot	Avg	Pts	Avg
4-85 Dal	4	4	169	24	49	.490	1	4	.250	26	34	.765	3	2	1	13	1	11	2.8	16	51	12.8	75	18.8
5-86 Dal	10	10	347	57	133	.429	2	8	.250	33	43	.767	16	9	14	32	0	24	2.4	30	83	8.3	149	14.9
6-87 Dal	4	4	133	26	52	.500	0	4	.000	16	23	.696	9	4	1	16	0	5	1.3	12	34	8.5	68	17.0
7-88 Dal	17	17	572	88	195	.451	1	7	.143	53	66	.803	30	25	17	51	1	31	1.8	39	112	6.6	230	13.5
9-90 Dal	3	3	118	16	36	.444	0	1	.000	13	17	.765	7	3	2	17	2	8	2.7	10	22	7.3	45	15.0
0-91 LAL	19	19	752	121	221	.548	11	30	.367	83	109	.761	37	15	27	69	0	33	1.7	41	157	8.3	336	17.7
2-93 Sea	19	17	626	98	225	.436	30	79	.380	48	55	.873	21	19	25	55	0	37	1.9	33	133	7.0	274	14.4
3-94 Sea	5	0	141	14	42	.333	6	14	.429	15	17	.882	6	4	2	15	0	4	0.8	6	36	7.2	49	9.8
4-95 Sea	4	2	141	21	48	.438	10	22	.455	2	2	1.000	9	3	5	12	0	13	3.3	6	31	7.8	54	13.5
5-96 Sea	21	1	654	90	196	.459	32	87	.368	46	61	.754	30	15	6	44	0	35	1.7	21	90	4.3	258	12.3
6-97 Sea	12	6	340	31	92	.337	14	45	.311	25	29	.862	13	12	12	34	1	15	1.3	15	53	4.4	101	8.4
7-98 Sea	10	1	210	16	42	.381	10	24	.417	12	20	.600	11	3	5	22	0	14	1.4	6	32	3.2	54	5.4
8-99 Ind	13	0	146	18	35	.514	11	24	.458	6	9	.667	7	0	3	13	0	6	0.5	2	25	1.9	53	4.1
9-00 Ind	23	0	417	34	105	.324	23	66	.348	19	21	.905	8	4	6	45	1	10	0.4	17	73	3.2	110	4.8
4 Years	164	84	4766	654	1471	.445	151	415	.364	397	506	.785	207	118	126	438	6	246	1.5	254	932	5.7	1856	11.3

Elliot Perry

Pos: G **College:** Memphis **Drafted:** '91 2(37)—LAC **Ht:** 6'0" **Wt:** 152 **Born:** 3/28/69 **Age:** 31

College				Field Goals			3-Pt FGs			Free Throws			Misc			Fouls		Assists		Rebounds			Points	
Year Tm	G	GS	Min	Md	Att	Pct	Md	Att	Pct	Md	Att	Pct	TO	Stl	Blk	PF	DQ	Ast	Avg	Off	Tot	Avg	Pts	Avg
7-88 Mem	32	32	968	140	336	.417	53	136	.390	87	108	.806	104	71	7	65	0	130	4.1	33	113	3.5	420	13.1
8-89 Mem	32	32	1017	202	437	.462	24	76	.316	192	234	.821	99	66	1	88	3	118	3.7	33	109	3.4	620	19.4
9-90 Mem	30	30	970	175	419	.418	17	66	.258	137	182	.753	93	82	6	70	2	150	5.0	39	110	3.7	504	16.8
0-91 Mem	32	32	1169	235	507	.464	49	136	.360	146	184	.793	108	85	1	57	0	148	4.6	30	111	3.5	665	20.8
Years	126	126	4124	752	1699	.443	143	414	.345	562	708	.794	404	304	15	280	5	546	4.3	135	443	3.5	2209	17.5

129

NBA Year Tm	G	GS	Min	Field Goals Md	Att	Pct	3-Pt FGs Md	Att	Pct	Free Throws Md	Att	Pct	Misc TO	Stl	Blk	Fouls PF	DQ	Assists Ast	Avg	Rebounds Off	Tot	Avg	Points Pts	Avg
91-92 2Tm	50	0	437	49	129	.380	1	7	.143	27	41	.659	50	34	3	36	0	78	1.6	14	39	0.8	126	2.5
92-93									Played in CBA															
93-94 Pho	27	9	432	42	113	.372	0	3	.000	21	28	.750	43	25	1	36	0	125	4.6	12	39	1.4	105	3.9
94-95 Pho	82	51	1977	306	588	.520	25	60	.417	158	195	.810	163	156	4	142	0	394	4.8	51	151	1.8	795	9.7
95-96 Mil	81	26	1668	261	549	.475	24	59	.407	151	194	.778	146	87	5	140	1	353	4.4	34	136	1.7	697	8.6
96-97 Mil	82	3	1595	217	458	.474	49	137	.358	79	106	.745	111	98	3	117	0	247	3.0	24	124	1.5	562	6.9
97-98 Mil	81	33	1752	241	561	.430	17	50	.340	92	109	.844	128	90	2	129	1	230	2.8	21	108	1.3	591	7.3
98-99 2Tm	35	0	290	39	103	.379	10	24	.417	10	14	.714	34	20	0	25	0	47	1.3	7	34	1.0	98	2.8
99-00 NJ	60	5	803	128	294	.435	11	39	.282	50	62	.806	60	39	1	47	0	139	2.3	13	61	1.0	317	5.x
91-92 LAC	10	0	66	6	15	.400	0	2	.000	1	2	.500	13	9	1	10	0	14	1.4	2	7	0.7	13	1.x
Cha	40	0	371	43	114	.377	1	5	.200	26	39	.667	37	25	2	26	0	64	1.6	12	32	0.8	113	2.x
98-99 Mil	5	0	47	9	17	.529	1	1	1.000	1	2	.500	2	4	0	3	0	12	2.4	1	8	1.6	20	4.x
NJ	30	0	243	30	86	.349	9	23	.391	9	12	.750	32	16	0	22	0	35	1.2	6	26	0.9	78	2.x
8 Years	498	127	8954	1283	2795	.459	137	379	.361	588	749	.785	735	549	19	672	2	1613	3.2	176	692	1.4	3291	6.x

NBA Postseason

Year Tm	G	GS	Min	Md	Att	Pct	Md	Att	Pct	Md	Att	Pct	TO	Stl	Blk	PF	DQ	Ast	Avg	Off	Tot	Avg	Pts	Avg
93-94 Pho	4	0	13	1	7	.143	0	0	—	0	0	—	1	1	0	2	0	1	0.3	0	0	0.0	2	0.5
94-95 Pho	9	0	106	20	42	.476	2	5	.400	20	25	.800	9	5	1	8	0	12	1.3	3	10	1.1	62	6.x
95-96 Pho	4	0	51	7	14	.500	0	0	—	0	1	.000	0	2	0	3	0	12	3.0	0	2	0.5	14	3.5
3 Years	17	0	170	28	63	.444	2	5	.400	20	26	.769	10	8	1	13	0	25	1.5	3	12	0.7	78	4.x

Chuck Person

Pos: F **College:** Auburn **Drafted:** '86 1(4)—Ind   **Ht:** 6'8" **Wt:** 235 **Born:** 6/27/64 **Age:** 3x

College Year Tm	G	GS	Min	Field Goals Md	Att	Pct	3-Pt FGs Md	Att	Pct	Free Throws Md	Att	Pct	Misc TO	Stl	Blk	Fouls PF	DQ	Assists Ast	Avg	Rebounds Off	Tot	Avg	Points Pts	Avg
82-83 Aub	28	—	636	118	218	.541	—	—	—	25	33	.758	37	13	6	57	1	37	1.3	—	128	4.6	261	9.x
83-84 Aub	31	—	1079	255	470	.543	—	—	—	83	114	.728	78	38	8	62	3	38	1.2	—	249	8.0	593	19.x
84-85 Aub	34	—	1240	334	614	.544	—	—	—	79	107	.738	80	42	18	78	0	69	2.0	—	303	8.9	747	22.x
85-86 Aub	33	—	1178	310	597	.519	—	—	—	90	112	.804	74	31	12	83	3	30	0.9	—	260	7.9	710	21.x
4 Years	126	—	4133	1017	1899	.536	—	—	—	277	366	.757	269	124	44	280	7	174	1.4	—	940	7.5	2311	18.x

NBA Year Tm	G	GS	Min	Field Goals Md	Att	Pct	3-Pt FGs Md	Att	Pct	Free Throws Md	Att	Pct	Misc TO	Stl	Blk	Fouls PF	DQ	Assists Ast	Avg	Rebounds Off	Tot	Avg	Points Pts	Avg
86-87 Ind	82	78	2956	635	1358	.468	49	138	.355	222	297	.747	211	90	16	310	4	295	3.6	168	677	8.3	1541	18.x
87-88 Ind	79	71	2807	575	1252	.459	59	177	.333	132	197	.670	210	73	9	266	4	309	3.9	171	536	6.8	1341	17.x
88-89 Ind	80	79	3012	711	1453	.489	63	205	.307	243	307	.792	308	83	18	280	12	289	3.6	144	516	6.5	1728	21.x
89-90 Ind	77	73	2714	605	1242	.487	94	253	.372	211	270	.781	170	53	20	217	1	230	3.0	126	445	5.8	1515	19.x
90-91 Ind	80	79	2566	620	1231	.504	69	203	.340	165	229	.721	184	56	17	221	1	238	3.0	121	417	5.2	1474	18.x
91-92 Ind	81	81	2923	616	1284	.480	132	354	.373	133	197	.675	216	68	18	247	5	382	4.7	114	426	5.3	1497	18.x
92-93 Min	78	75	2985	541	1248	.433	118	332	.355	109	168	.649	219	67	30	198	2	343	4.4	98	433	5.6	1309	16.x
93-94 Min	77	38	2029	356	843	.422	100	272	.368	82	108	.759	121	45	12	164	0	185	2.4	55	253	3.3	894	11.x
94-95 SA	81	1	2033	317	750	.423	172	445	.387	66	102	.647	102	45	12	198	0	106	1.3	49	258	3.2	872	10.x
95-96 SA	80	16	2131	308	705	.437	190	463	.410	67	104	.644	91	49	26	197	2	100	1.3	76	413	5.2	873	10.x
96-97 SA								Did not play: injury — Back																
97-98 SA	61	11	1455	143	398	.359	95	276	.344	28	37	.757	67	29	10	121	1	86	1.4	17	204	3.3	409	6.x
98-99 Cha	50	21	990	112	289	.388	55	157	.350	24	32	.750	41	20	8	90	0	60	1.2	17	132	2.6	303	6.x
99-00 Sea	37	0	340	37	123	.301	24	95	.253	4	8	.500	12	5	2	56	1	22	0.6	6	53	1.4	102	2.x
13 Years	943	623	28941	5576	12176	.458	1220	3370	.362	1486	2056	.723	1952	683	198	2565	33	2645	2.8	1162	4763	5.1	13858	14.x

NBA Postseason

Year Tm	G	GS	Min	Md	Att	Pct	Md	Att	Pct	Md	Att	Pct	TO	Stl	Blk	PF	DQ	Ast	Avg	Off	Tot	Avg	Pts	Avg
86-87 Ind	4	4	159	38	74	.514	2	8	.250	30	39	.769	15	5	2	14	0	20	5.0	6	33	8.3	108	27.x
89-90 Ind	3	3	123	17	45	.378	1	10	.100	5	12	.417	4	1	0	11	0	12	4.0	6	20	6.7	40	13.x
90-91 Ind	5	5	192	48	90	.533	17	31	.548	17	21	.810	12	5	0	15	1	16	3.2	3	28	5.6	130	26.x
91-92 Ind	3	3	118	19	47	.404	5	15	.333	8	12	.667	6	2	0	11	0	7	2.3	1	9	3.0	51	17.x
94-95 SA	15	0	258	27	77	.351	13	45	.289	8	11	.727	6	4	7	22	0	8	0.5	2	27	1.8	75	5.x
95-96 SA	10	0	284	41	77	.532	25	47	.532	14	17	.824	11	2	3	32	0	16	1.6	5	40	4.0	121	12.x
97-98 SA	9	0	196	18	53	.340	14	40	.350	2	2	1.000	6	4	0	15	1	7	0.8	0	27	3.0	52	5.x
99-00 Sea	2	0	2	0	1	.000	0	1	.000	0	0	—	0	0	0	0	0	0	0.0	0	0	0.0	0	0.x
8 Years	51	15	1332	208	464	.448	77	197	.391	84	114	.737	60	23	12	120	2	86	1.7	23	184	3.6	577	11.x

Wesley Person

(statistical profile on page 261)

Pos: G **College:** Auburn **Drafted:** '94 1(23)—Pho   **Ht:** 6'6" **Wt:** 200 **Born:** 3/28/71 **Age:** 29

College				Field Goals			3-Pt FGs			Free Throws			Misc			Fouls		Assists		Rebounds			Points	
Year Tm	G	GS	Min	Md	Att	Pct	Md	Att	Pct	Md	Att	Pct	TO	Stl	Blk	PF	DQ	Ast	Avg	Off	Tot	Avg	Pts	Avg
90-91 Aub	26	—	857	153	325	.471	42	118	.356	52	68	.765	49	35	31	49	0	48	1.8	—	147	5.7	400	15.4
91-92 Aub	27	—	955	208	411	.506	69	141	.489	53	73	.726	60	28	29	45	1	55	2.0	—	183	6.8	538	19.9
92-93 Aub	27	—	957	194	349	.556	58	125	.464	61	79	.772	69	21	11	46	0	102	3.8	—	192	7.1	507	18.8
93-94 Aub	28	—	1006	217	448	.484	93	210	.443	94	128	.734	84	28	11	45	1	79	2.8	—	179	6.4	621	22.2
4 Years	108	—	3775	772	1533	.504	262	594	.441	260	348	.747	262	112	82	185	2	284	2.6	—	701	6.5	2066	19.1

NBA				Field Goals			3-Pt FGs			Free Throws			Misc			Fouls		Assists		Rebounds			Points	
Year Tm	G	GS	Min	Md	Att	Pct	Md	Att	Pct	Md	Att	Pct	TO	Stl	Blk	PF	DQ	Ast	Avg	Off	Tot	Avg	Pts	Avg
94-95 Pho	78	56	1800	309	638	.484	116	266	.436	80	101	.792	79	48	24	149	0	105	1.3	67	201	2.6	814	10.4
95-96 Pho	82	47	2609	390	877	.445	117	313	.374	148	192	.771	89	55	22	148	0	138	1.7	56	321	3.9	1045	12.7
96-97 Pho	80	42	2326	409	903	.453	171	414	.413	91	114	.798	76	86	20	102	0	123	1.5	68	292	3.7	1080	13.5
97-98 Cle	82	82	3198	440	957	.460	192	447	.430	132	170	.776	110	129	49	108	0	188	2.3	65	363	4.4	1204	14.7
98-99 Cle	45	42	1342	198	437	.453	75	200	.375	32	53	.604	41	37	16	52	0	80	1.8	19	142	3.2	503	11.2
99-00 Cle	79	38	2056	280	654	.428	106	250	.424	61	77	.792	60	40	19	119	1	146	1.8	44	267	3.4	727	9.2
6 Years	446	307	13331	2026	4466	.454	777	1890	.411	544	707	.769	455	395	150	678	1	780	1.7	319	1586	3.6	5373	12.0

NBA Postseason				Field Goals			3-Pt FGs			Free Throws			Misc			Fouls		Assists		Rebounds			Points	
Year Tm	G	GS	Min	Md	Att	Pct	Md	Att	Pct	Md	Att	Pct	TO	Stl	Blk	PF	DQ	Ast	Avg	Off	Tot	Avg	Pts	Avg
94-95 Pho	10	10	247	34	83	.410	17	45	.378	11	12	.917	9	3	1	19	0	11	1.1	9	21	2.1	96	9.6
95-96 Pho	4	4	183	22	56	.393	9	29	.310	4	5	.800	5	3	1	7	0	3	0.8	8	23	5.8	57	14.3
96-97 Pho	5	1	163	25	53	.472	14	33	.424	14	18	.778	4	4	3	5	0	6	1.2	5	33	6.6	78	15.6
97-98 Cle	4	4	136	11	29	.379	7	19	.368	3	4	.750	1	3	0	5	0	10	2.5	2	9	2.3	32	8.0
4 Years	23	19	729	92	221	.416	47	126	.373	32	39	.821	19	13	5	36	0	30	1.3	24	86	3.7	263	11.4

Bobby Phills

In Memoriam
Pos: G-F **College:** Southern **Drafted:** '91 2(45)—Mil   **Ht:** 6'5" **Wt:** 226 **Born:** 12/20/69 **Died:** 1/12/00

College				Field Goals			3-Pt FGs			Free Throws			Misc			Fouls		Assists		Rebounds			Points	
Year Tm	G	GS	Min	Md	Att	Pct	Md	Att	Pct	Md	Att	Pct	TO	Stl	Blk	PF	DQ	Ast	Avg	Off	Tot	Avg	Pts	Avg
87-88 Sou	23	—	158	26	53	.491	3	7	.429	30	42	.714	13	6	2	13	—	8	0.3	—	41	1.8	85	3.7
88-89 Sou	31	—	923	166	385	.431	44	128	.344	44	60	.733	49	56	3	52	—	55	1.8	—	142	4.6	420	13.5
89-90 Sou	31	—	937	232	574	.404	112	300	.373	46	70	.657	57	66	9	—	—	89	2.9	—	132	4.3	622	20.1
90-91 Sou	28	—	986	260	641	.406	123	353	.348	152	211	.720	63	90	13	—	—	52	1.9	—	132	4.7	795	28.4
4 Years	113	—	3004	684	1653	.414	282	788	.358	272	383	.710	182	218	27	—	—	204	1.8	—	447	4.0	1922	17.0

NBA				Field Goals			3-Pt FGs			Free Throws			Misc			Fouls		Assists		Rebounds			Points	
Year Tm	G	GS	Min	Md	Att	Pct	Md	Att	Pct	Md	Att	Pct	TO	Stl	Blk	PF	DQ	Ast	Avg	Off	Tot	Avg	Pts	Avg
91-92 Cle	10	0	65	12	28	.429	0	2	.000	7	11	.636	8	3	1	3	0	4	0.4	4	8	0.8	31	3.1
92-93 Cle	31	0	139	38	82	.463	2	5	.400	15	25	.600	18	10	2	19	0	10	0.3	6	17	0.5	93	3.0
93-94 Cle	72	53	1531	242	514	.471	1	12	.083	113	157	.720	63	67	12	135	1	133	1.8	71	212	2.9	598	8.3
94-95 Cle	80	79	2500	338	816	.414	19	55	.345	183	235	.779	113	115	25	206	0	180	2.3	90	265	3.3	878	11.0
95-96 Cle	72	69	2530	386	826	.467	93	211	.441	186	240	.775	126	102	27	192	3	271	3.8	62	261	3.6	1051	14.6
96-97 Cle	69	65	2375	328	766	.428	85	216	.394	125	174	.718	135	113	21	174	1	233	3.4	63	245	3.6	866	12.6
97-98 Cha	62	61	1887	246	552	.446	44	114	.386	106	140	.757	108	81	18	181	2	187	3.0	59	216	3.5	642	10.4
98-99 Cha	43	43	1574	215	497	.433	68	172	.395	115	168	.685	92	60	25	124	1	149	3.5	39	174	4.0	613	14.3
99-00 Cha	28	9	825	152	335	.454	30	91	.330	47	65	.723	48	41	8	72	2	79	2.8	17	71	2.5	381	13.6
9 Years	467	379	13426	1957	4416	.443	342	878	.390	897	1215	.738	711	592	139	1106	10	1246	2.7	411	1469	3.1	5153	11.0

NBA Postseason				Field Goals			3-Pt FGs			Free Throws			Misc			Fouls		Assists		Rebounds			Points	
Year Tm	G	GS	Min	Md	Att	Pct	Md	Att	Pct	Md	Att	Pct	TO	Stl	Blk	PF	DQ	Ast	Avg	Off	Tot	Avg	Pts	Avg
91-92 Cle	5	0	12	4	9	.444	0	1	.000	3	4	.750	2	1	0	1	0	5	1.0	2	6	1.2	11	2.2
92-93 Cle	2	0	9	1	3	.333	0	0	—	2	2	1.000	1	0	0	0	0	0	0.0	0	0	0.0	4	2.0
93-94 Cle	3	2	68	9	24	.375	1	1	1.000	1	2	.500	5	2	0	11	0	7	2.3	5	14	4.7	20	6.7
94-95 Cle	4	4	146	19	43	.442	4	7	.571	15	20	.750	9	9	0	8	0	6	1.5	3	12	3.0	57	14.3
95-96 Cle	3	3	96	13	35	.371	2	10	.200	1	4	.250	5	2	1	4	0	6	2.0	5	14	4.7	29	9.7
97-98 Cha	9	9	269	25	64	.391	5	17	.294	2	8	.250	13	10	2	24	0	24	2.7	4	23	2.6	57	6.3
6 Years	26	18	600	71	178	.399	12	36	.333	24	40	.600	35	24	3	48	0	48	1.8	19	69	2.7	178	6.8

Eric Piatkowski

(statistical profile on page 261)

Pos: G **College:** Nebraska **Drafted:** '94 1(15)—Ind   **Ht:** 6'7" **Wt:** 215 **Born:** 9/30/70 **Age:** 30

College				Field Goals			3-Pt FGs			Free Throws			Misc			Fouls		Assists		Rebounds			Points	
Year Tm	G	GS	Min	Md	Att	Pct	Md	Att	Pct	Md	Att	Pct	TO	Stl	Blk	PF	DQ	Ast	Avg	Off	Tot	Avg	Pts	Avg
90-91 Neb	34	1	679	128	275	.465	44	127	.346	72	86	.837	48	22	18	61	1	68	2.0	—	125	3.7	372	10.9

College			Field Goals			3-Pt FGs			Free Throws			Misc			Fouls		Assists		Rebounds			Points	
Year Tm	G	GS	Min	Md	Att	Pct	Md	Att	Pct	Md	Att	Pct	TO	Stl	Blk	PF	DQ	Ast	Avg	Off	Tot	Avg	Pts	Avg
91-92 Neb	29	28	873	144	338	.426	47	136	.346	79	109	.725	74	21	18	71	2	97	3.3	—	184	6.3	414	14.3
92-93 Neb	30	30	892	178	367	.485	48	129	.372	98	129	.760	67	33	8	63	0	75	2.5	—	171	5.7	502	16.7
93-94 Neb	30	30	972	226	456	.496	63	172	.366	131	165	.794	72	46	20	64	1	82	2.7	—	189	6.3	646	21.5
4 Years	123	89	3416	676	1436	.471	202	564	.358	380	489	.777	261	122	64	259	4	322	2.6	—	669	5.4	1934	15.7

NBA			Field Goals			3-Pt FGs			Free Throws			Misc			Fouls		Assists		Rebounds			Points	
Year Tm	G	GS	Min	Md	Att	Pct	Md	Att	Pct	Md	Att	Pct	TO	Stl	Blk	PF	DQ	Ast	Avg	Off	Tot	Avg	Pts	Avg
94-95 LAC	81	11	1208	201	456	.441	74	198	.374	90	115	.783	63	37	15	150	1	77	1.0	63	133	1.6	566	7.0
95-96 LAC	65	1	784	98	242	.405	38	114	.333	67	82	.817	45	24	10	83	0	48	0.7	40	103	1.6	301	4.6
96-97 LAC	65	0	747	134	298	.450	51	120	.425	69	84	.821	46	33	10	85	0	52	0.8	49	105	1.6	388	6.0
97-98 LAC	67	35	1740	257	568	.452	106	259	.409	140	170	.824	80	51	12	137	0	85	1.3	70	236	3.5	760	11.3
98-99 LAC	49	38	1242	180	417	.432	65	165	.394	88	102	.863	53	44	6	86	0	53	1.1	39	140	2.9	513	10.5
99-00 LAC	75	23	1712	238	573	.415	93	243	.383	85	100	.850	57	44	13	140	0	81	1.1	74	222	3.0	654	8.7
6 Years	402	108	7433	1108	2554	.434	427	1099	.389	539	653	.825	344	233	66	681	1	396	1.0	335	939	2.3	3182	7.9

NBA Postseason																							
Year Tm	G	GS	Min	Md	Att	Pct	Md	Att	Pct	Md	Att	Pct	TO	Stl	Blk	PF	DQ	Ast	Avg	Off	Tot	Avg	Pts	Avg
96-97 LAC	3	0	38	4	11	.364	2	5	.400	6	7	.857	0	1	0	5	0	0	0.0	1	2	0.7	16	5.3

Paul Pierce

(statistical profile on page 262)

Pos: F **College:** Kansas **Drafted:** '98 1(10)—Bos   **Ht:** 6'7" **Wt:** 220 **Born:** 10/13/77 **Age:** 23

College			Field Goals			3-Pt FGs			Free Throws			Misc			Fouls		Assists		Rebounds			Points	
Year Tm	G	GS	Min	Md	Att	Pct	Md	Att	Pct	Md	Att	Pct	TO	Stl	Blk	PF	DQ	Ast	Avg	Off	Tot	Avg	Pts	Avg
95-96 Kan	34	33	862	143	341	.419	35	115	.304	83	137	.606	80	44	27	82	1	61	1.8	81	180	5.3	404	11.9
96-97 Kan	36	35	1013	215	441	.488	33	71	.465	124	173	.717	108	61	28	98	2	77	2.1	83	243	6.8	587	16.3
97-98 Kan	38	38	1155	287	559	.513	40	116	.345	163	221	.738	110	42	43	89	2	98	2.6	101	253	6.7	777	20.4
3 Years	108	106	3030	645	1341	.481	108	302	.358	370	531	.697	298	147	98	269	5	236	2.2	265	676	6.3	1768	16.4

NBA			Field Goals			3-Pt FGs			Free Throws			Misc			Fouls		Assists		Rebounds			Points	
Year Tm	G	GS	Min	Md	Att	Pct	Md	Att	Pct	Md	Att	Pct	TO	Stl	Blk	PF	DQ	Ast	Avg	Off	Tot	Avg	Pts	Avg
98-99 Bos	48	47	1632	284	647	.439	84	204	.412	139	195	.713	113	82	50	139	1	115	2.4	117	309	6.4	791	16.5
99-00 Bos	73	72	2583	486	1099	.442	96	280	.343	359	450	.798	178	152	62	237	5	221	3.0	83	396	5.4	1427	19.5
2 Years	121	119	4215	770	1746	.441	180	484	.372	498	645	.772	291	234	112	376	6	336	2.8	200	705	5.8	2218	18.3

Scottie Pippen

(statistical profile on page 262)

Pos: F **College:** Central Arkansas **Drafted:** '87 1(5)—Sea   **Ht:** 6'7" **Wt:** 228 **Born:** 9/25/65 **Age:** 35

College			Field Goals			3-Pt FGs			Free Throws			Misc			Fouls		Assists		Rebounds			Points	
Year Tm	G	GS	Min	Md	Att	Pct	Md	Att	Pct	Md	Att	Pct	TO	Stl	Blk	PF	DQ	Ast	Avg	Off	Tot	Avg	Pts	Avg
83-84 CnAk	20	—	—	36	79	.456	—	—	—	13	19	.684	26	10	—	36	—	14	0.7	—	59	3.0	85	4.3
84-85 CnAk	19	—	—	141	250	.564	—	—	—	69	102	.676	60	35	—	61	—	30	1.6	—	175	9.2	351	18.5
85-86 CnAk	29	—	—	229	412	.556	—	—	—	116	169	.686	111	70	—	87	—	102	3.5	—	266	9.2	574	19.8
86-87 CnAk	25	—	—	231	390	.592	23	40	.575	105	146	.719	94	78	—	77	—	107	4.3	—	249	10.0	590	23.6
4 Years	93	—	—	637	1131	.563	23	40	.575	303	436	.695	291	193	—	261	—	253	2.7	—	749	8.1	1600	17.2

NBA			Field Goals			3-Pt FGs			Free Throws			Misc			Fouls		Assists		Rebounds			Points	
Year Tm	G	GS	Min	Md	Att	Pct	Md	Att	Pct	Md	Att	Pct	TO	Stl	Blk	PF	DQ	Ast	Avg	Off	Tot	Avg	Pts	Avg
87-88 Chi	79	0	1650	261	564	.463	4	23	.174	99	172	.576	131	91	52	214	3	169	2.1	115	298	3.8	625	7.9
88-89 Chi	73	56	2413	413	867	.476	21	77	.273	201	301	.668	199	139	61	261	8	256	3.5	138	445	6.1	1048	14.4
89-90 Chi*	82	82	3148	562	1150	.489	28	112	.250	199	295	.675	278	211	101	298	6	444	5.4	150	547	6.7	1351	16.5
90-91 Chi*	82	82	3014	600	1153	.520	21	68	.309	240	340	.706	232	193	93	270	3	511	6.2	163	595	7.3	1461	17.8
91-92 Chi*	82	82	3164	687	1359	.506	16	80	.200	330	434	.760	253	155	93	242	2	572	7.0	185	630	7.7	1720	21.0
92-93 Chi*	81	81	3123	628	1327	.473	22	93	.237	232	350	.663	246	173	73	219	3	507	6.3	203	621	7.7	1510	18.6
93-94 Chi*	72	72	2759	627	1278	.491	63	197	.320	270	409	.660	232	211	58	227	1	403	5.6	173	629	8.7	1587	22.0
94-95 Chi*	79	79	3014	634	1320	.480	109	316	.345	315	440	.716	271	232	89	238	4	409	5.2	175	639	8.1	1692	21.4
95-96 Chi*	77	77	2825	563	1216	.463	150	401	.374	220	324	.679	207	133	57	198	0	452	5.9	152	496	6.4	1496	19.4
96-97 Chi*	82	82	3095	648	1366	.474	156	424	.368	204	291	.701	214	154	45	213	2	467	5.7	160	531	6.5	1656	20.2
97-98 Chi*	44	44	1652	315	704	.447	61	192	.368	150	193	.777	109	79	43	116	0	254	5.8	53	227	5.2	841	19.1
98-99 Hou	50	50	2011	261	604	.432	72	212	.340	132	183	.721	159	98	37	118	0	293	5.9	63	323	6.5	726	14.5
99-00 Por	82	82	2749	388	860	.451	86	263	.327	160	223	.717	208	117	41	208	0	406	5.0	114	513	6.3	1022	12.5
13 Years	965	869	34617	6587	13768	.478	809	2458	.329	2752	3955	.696	2739	1986	843	2822	32	5143	5.3	1844	6494	6.7	16735	17.3

NBA Postseason																							
Year Tm	G	GS	Min	Md	Att	Pct	Md	Att	Pct	Md	Att	Pct	TO	Stl	Blk	PF	DQ	Ast	Avg	Off	Tot	Avg	Pts	Avg
87-88 Chi	10	6	294	46	99	.465	3	6	.500	5	7	.714	26	8	8	33	1	24	2.4	24	52	5.2	100	10.0
88-89 Chi	17	17	619	84	182	.462	22	56	.393	32	50	.640	41	23	16	63	2	67	3.9	34	129	7.6	222	13.1
89-90 Chi	15	14	612	104	210	.495	10	31	.323	71	100	.710	49	31	19	62	0	83	5.5	33	108	7.2	289	19.3

Year Tm	G	GS	Min	Md	Att	Pct	Md	Att	Pct	Md	Att	Pct	TO	Stl	Blk	PF	DQ	Ast	Avg	Off	Tot	Avg	Pts	Avg
90-91 Chi	17	17	704	142	282	.504	4	17	.235	80	101	.792	55	42	19	58	1	99	5.8	37	151	8.9	368	21.6
91-92 Chi	22	22	899	152	325	.468	6	24	.250	118	155	.761	70	41	25	72	1	147	6.7	59	193	8.8	428	19.5
92-93 Chi	19	19	789	152	327	.465	3	17	.176	74	116	.638	71	41	13	62	0	107	5.6	37	132	6.9	381	20.1
93-94 Chi	10	10	384	85	196	.434	12	45	.267	46	52	.885	37	24	7	33	1	46	4.6	17	83	8.3	228	22.8
94-95 Chi	10	10	396	58	131	.443	14	38	.368	48	71	.676	27	14	10	40	1	58	5.8	24	86	8.6	178	17.8
95-96 Chi	18	18	742	112	287	.390	30	105	.286	51	80	.638	41	47	16	51	0	107	5.9	62	153	8.5	305	16.9
96-97 Chi	19	19	753	129	309	.417	39	113	.345	68	86	.791	55	28	18	49	0	72	3.8	36	129	6.8	365	19.2
97-98 Chi	21	21	836	122	294	.415	18	79	.228	91	134	.679	51	45	20	66	1	110	5.2	49	150	7.1	353	16.8
98-99 Hou	4	4	172	23	70	.329	6	22	.273	21	26	.808	13	7	3	12	0	22	5.5	20	47	11.8	73	18.3
99-00 Por	16	16	614	83	198	.419	21	70	.300	52	70	.743	37	32	7	49	1	69	4.3	22	114	7.1	239	14.9
13 Years	198	193	7814	1292	2910	.444	188	623	.302	757	1048	.722	573	383	181	650	9	1011	5.1	454	1527	7.7	3529	17.8

Scot Pollard

(statistical profile on page 263)

Pos: F-C **College:** Kansas **Drafted:** '97 1(19)—Det **Ht:** 6'11" **Wt:** 265 **Born:** 2/12/75 **Age:** 25

College				Field Goals			3-Pt FGs			Free Throws			Misc			Fouls		Assists		Rebounds			Points	
Year Tm	G	GS	Min	Md	Att	Pct	Md	Att	Pct	Md	Att	Pct	TO	Stl	Blk	PF	DQ	Ast	Avg	Off	Tot	Avg	Pts	Avg
93-94 Kan	35	0	597	95	175	.543	0	0	—	74	108	.685	32	22	27	89	3	13	0.4	—	173	4.9	264	7.5
94-95 Kan	31	3	620	113	203	.557	0	0	—	89	136	.654	47	20	34	79	2	17	0.5	—	192	6.2	315	10.2
95-96 Kan	34	33	835	123	218	.564	0	0	—	96	151	.636	72	26	84	103	3	10	0.3	84	253	7.4	342	10.1
96-97 Kan	28	26	702	94	178	.528	1	1	1.000	99	140	.707	42	35	73	68	2	19	0.7	80	232	8.3	288	10.3
4 Years	128	62	2754	425	774	.549	1	1	1.000	358	535	.669	193	103	218	339	10	59	0.5	—	850	6.6	1209	9.4

NBA				Field Goals			3-Pt FGs			Free Throws			Misc			Fouls		Assists		Rebounds			Points	
Year Tm	G	GS	Min	Md	Att	Pct	Md	Att	Pct	Md	Att	Pct	TO	Stl	Blk	PF	DQ	Ast	Avg	Off	Tot	Avg	Pts	Avg
97-98 Det	33	0	317	35	70	.500	0	0	—	19	23	.826	12	8	10	48	0	9	0.3	34	74	2.2	89	2.7
98-99 Sac	16	5	259	33	61	.541	0	0	—	16	23	.696	5	8	18	41	0	4	0.3	38	82	5.1	82	5.1
99-00 Sac	76	5	1336	149	283	.527	0	0	—	114	159	.717	50	55	59	213	3	43	0.6	168	404	5.3	412	5.4
3 Years	125	10	1912	217	414	.524	0	0	—	149	205	.727	67	71	87	302	3	56	0.4	240	560	4.5	583	4.7

NBA Postseason																								
Year Tm	G	GS	Min	Md	Att	Pct	Md	Att	Pct	Md	Att	Pct	TO	Stl	Blk	PF	DQ	Ast	Avg	Off	Tot	Avg	Pts	Avg
98-99 Sac	5	0	74	6	9	.667	0	0	—	3	5	.600	2	4	6	13	0	1	0.2	5	11	2.2	15	3.0
99-00 Sac	5	0	70	9	16	.563	0	0	—	2	6	.333	3	2	1	18	1	1	0.2	6	16	3.2	20	4.0
2 Years	10	0	144	15	25	.600	0	0	—	5	11	.455	5	6	7	31	1	2	0.2	11	27	2.7	35	3.5

Olden Polynice

(statistical profile on page 263)

Pos: C **College:** Virginia **Drafted:** '87 1(8)—Chi **Ht:** 7'0" **Wt:** 250 **Born:** 11/21/64 **Age:** 36

College				Field Goals			3-Pt FGs			Free Throws			Misc			Fouls		Assists		Rebounds			Points	
Year Tm	G	GS	Min	Md	Att	Pct	Md	Att	Pct	Md	Att	Pct	TO	Stl	Blk	PF	DQ	Ast	Avg	Off	Tot	Avg	Pts	Avg
83-84 UVa	33	25	866	98	178	.551	—	—	—	57	97	.588	37	3	17	62	—	20	0.6	—	184	5.6	253	7.7
84-85 UVa	32	29	1095	161	267	.603	—	—	—	94	157	.599	96	12	35	74	—	16	0.5	—	243	7.6	416	13.0
85-86 UVa	30	30	1074	183	320	.572	—	—	—	116	182	.637	87	10	34	87	—	16	0.5	—	240	8.0	482	16.1
3 Years	95	84	3035	442	765	.578	—	—	—	267	436	.612	220	25	86	223	—	52	0.5	—	667	7.0	1151	12.1

NBA				Field Goals			3-Pt FGs			Free Throws			Misc			Fouls		Assists		Rebounds			Points	
Year Tm	G	GS	Min	Md	Att	Pct	Md	Att	Pct	Md	Att	Pct	TO	Stl	Blk	PF	DQ	Ast	Avg	Off	Tot	Avg	Pts	Avg
87-88 Sea	82	0	1080	118	254	.465	0	2	.000	101	158	.639	81	32	26	215	1	33	0.4	122	330	4.0	337	4.1
88-89 Sea	80	0	835	91	180	.506	0	2	.000	51	86	.593	46	37	30	164	0	21	0.3	98	206	2.6	233	2.9
89-90 Sea	79	7	1085	156	289	.540	1	2	.500	47	99	.475	35	25	21	187	0	15	0.2	128	300	3.8	360	4.6
90-91 2Tm	79	30	2092	316	564	.560	0	1	.000	146	252	.579	88	42	32	192	1	42	0.5	195	536	7.0	778	9.8
91-92 LAC	76	65	1834	244	470	.519	0	1	.000	125	201	.622	83	45	20	165	0	46	0.6	181	418	6.2	486	7.3
92-93 Det	67	18	1299	210	429	.490	0	2	.000	66	142	.465	54	31	21	126	0	29	0.4	299	809	11.9	789	11.6
93-94 2Tm	68	65	2402	346	662	.523	0	2	.000	97	191	.508	78	42	67	189	2	41	0.6	277	725	9.0	877	10.8
94-95 Sac	81	81	2534	376	691	.544	1	1	1.000	124	194	.639	113	48	52	238	0	62	0.8	257	764	9.4	985	12.2
95-96 Sac	81	80	2441	431	818	.527	0	3	.333	122	203	.601	127	52	66	250	3	58	0.7	257	764	9.4	985	12.2
96-97 Sac	82	82	2893	442	967	.457	0	6	.000	141	251	.562	166	46	80	298	4	178	2.2	272	772	9.4	1025	12.5
97-98 Sac	70	25	1458	249	542	.459	0	1	.000	52	115	.452	98	37	45	158	0	107	1.5	173	439	6.3	550	7.9
98-99 Sea	48	47	1481	169	358	.472	1	1	1.000	29	94	.309	49	20	30	150	0	43	0.9	184	425	8.9	368	7.7
99-00 Uta	82	79	1819	203	398	.510	1	2	.500	28	90	.311	70	30	84	260	1	37	0.5	166	453	5.5	435	5.3
90-91 Sea	48	0	960	165	303	.545	0	0	—	67	114	.588	53	26	19	94	0	16	0.3	114	270	5.6	397	8.3
LAC	31	30	1132	151	261	.579	0	1	.000	79	138	.572	35	17	13	98	1	26	0.8	106	283	9.1	381	12.3
93-94 Det	37	36	1350	222	406	.547	0	1	.000	42	92	.457	49	24	36	108	1	22	0.6	148	456	12.3	486	13.1
Sac	31	29	1052	124	256	.484	0	1	.000	55	99	.556	29	18	31	81	1	19	0.6	151	353	11.4	303	9.8
13 Years	975	579	23253	3351	6622	.506	5	25	.200	1129	2076	.544	1088	488	574	2592	12	712	0.7	2572	6730	6.9	7836	8.0

133

NBA Postseason

Year Tm	G	GS	Min	Md	Att	Pct	Md	Att	Pct	Md	Att	Pct	TO	Stl	Blk	PF	DQ	Ast	Avg	Off	Tot	Avg	Pts	Avg
87-88 Sea	5	0	44	5	11	.455	0	0	—	0	2	.000	1	3	0	6	0	0	0.0	2	8	1.6	10	2.0
88-89 Sea	8	0	162	25	41	.610	0	0	—	7	13	.538	5	6	4	32	1	1	0.1	27	62	7.8	57	7.1
91-92 LAC	5	0	63	7	12	.583	0	0	—	2	6	.333	1	1	1	11	0	2	0.4	2	18	3.6	16	3.2
95-96 Sac	4	4	141	24	46	.522	1	1	1.000	6	9	.667	3	1	7	15	0	3	0.8	16	48	12.0	55	13.8
99-00 Uta	10	10	260	28	52	.538	0	0	—	3	6	.500	13	3	8	36	1	5	0.5	24	66	6.6	59	5.9
5 Years	32	14	670	89	162	.549	1	1	1.000	18	36	.500	23	14	20	100	2	11	0.3	71	202	6.3	197	6.2

Terry Porter

(statistical profile on page 264)

Pos: G **College:** Wis.-Stevens Point **Drafted:** '85 1(24)—Por   **Ht:** 6'3" **Wt:** 205 **Born:** 4/8/63 **Age:** 37

College Year Tm	G	GS	Min	Field Goals Md	Att	Pct	3-Pt FGs Md	Att	Pct	Free Throws Md	Att	Pct	Misc TO	Stl	Blk	Fouls PF	DQ	Assists Ast	Avg	Rebounds Off	Tot	Avg	Points Pts	Avg
81-82 Wis-SP	25	—	273	21	57	.368	—	—	—	9	13	.692	—	—	—	—	—	21	0.8	—	13	0.5	51	2.0
82-83 Wis-SP	30	—	949	140	229	.611	—	—	—	62	89	.697	—	—	—	—	—	157	5.2	—	117	3.9	342	11.4
83-84 Wis-SP	32	—	1040	244	392	.622	—	—	—	112	135	.830	—	—	—	—	—	133	4.2	—	165	5.2	600	18.8
84-85 Wis-SP	30	—	1042	233	405	.575	—	—	—	126	151	.834	—	—	—	—	—	129	4.3	—	155	5.2	592	19.7
4 Years	117	—	3304	638	1083	.589	—	—	—	309	388	.796	—	—	—	—	—	440	3.8	—	450	3.8	1585	13.5

NBA Year Tm	G	GS	Min	Field Goals Md	Att	Pct	3-Pt FGs Md	Att	Pct	Free Throws Md	Att	Pct	Misc TO	Stl	Blk	Fouls PF	DQ	Assists Ast	Avg	Rebounds Off	Tot	Avg	Points Pts	Avg
85-86 Por	79	3	1214	212	447	.474	13	42	.310	125	155	.806	106	81	1	136	0	198	2.5	35	117	1.5	562	7.1
86-87 Por	80	80	2714	376	770	.488	13	60	.217	280	334	.838	255	159	9	192	0	715	8.9	70	337	4.2	1045	13.1
87-88 Por	82	82	2991	462	890	.519	24	69	.348	274	324	.846	244	150	16	204	1	831	10.1	65	378	4.6	1222	14.9
88-89 Por	81	81	3102	540	1146	.471	79	219	.361	272	324	.840	248	146	8	187	1	770	9.5	85	367	4.5	1431	17.7
89-90 Por	80	80	2781	448	969	.462	89	238	.374	421	472	.892	245	151	4	150	0	726	9.1	59	272	3.4	1406	17.6
90-91 Por*	81	81	2665	486	944	.515	130	313	.415	279	339	.823	189	158	12	151	0	649	8.0	52	282	3.5	1381	17.0
91-92 Por	82	82	2784	521	1129	.461	128	324	.395	315	368	.856	188	127	12	155	2	477	5.8	51	255	3.1	1485	18.1
92-93 Por*	81	81	2883	503	1108	.454	143	345	.414	327	388	.843	199	101	10	122	0	419	5.2	58	316	3.9	1476	18.2
93-94 Por	77	34	2074	348	836	.416	110	282	.390	204	234	.872	166	79	18	132	0	401	5.2	45	215	2.8	1010	13.1
94-95 Por	35	9	770	105	267	.393	44	114	.386	58	82	.707	58	30	2	60	0	133	3.8	18	81	2.3	312	8.9
95-96 Min	82	40	2072	269	608	.442	71	226	.314	164	209	.785	173	89	15	154	0	452	5.5	36	212	2.6	773	9.4
96-97 Min	82	20	1568	187	449	.416	67	200	.335	127	166	.765	128	54	11	104	0	295	3.6	31	176	2.1	568	6.9
97-98 Min	82	8	1786	259	577	.449	92	233	.395	167	195	.856	104	63	16	103	0	271	3.3	37	168	2.0	777	9.5
98-99 Mia	50	1	1365	172	370	.465	58	141	.411	123	148	.831	74	48	11	97	0	146	2.9	13	140	2.8	525	10.5
99-00 SA	68	8	1613	207	463	.447	90	207	.435	137	170	.806	100	50	9	79	0	221	3.3	24	191	2.8	641	9.4
15 Years	1122	690	32382	5095	10973	.464	1151	3013	.382	3273	3908	.838	2477	1486	154	2026	5	6704	6.0	679	3507	3.1	14614	13.0

NBA Postseason

Year Tm	G	GS	Min	Md	Att	Pct	Md	Att	Pct	Md	Att	Pct	TO	Stl	Blk	PF	DQ	Ast	Avg	Off	Tot	Avg	Pts	Avg
85-86 Por	4	0	68	12	27	.444	1	6	.167	2	4	.500	6	3	2	10	0	12	3.0	1	5	1.3	27	6.8
86-87 Por	4	4	150	24	50	.480	2	5	.400	18	20	.900	13	10	2	14	0	40	10.0	1	19	4.8	68	17.0
87-88 Por	4	4	149	29	52	.558	1	3	.333	9	13	.692	13	10	0	13	0	28	7.0	1	14	3.5	68	17.0
88-89 Por	3	3	124	26	52	.500	4	11	.364	10	12	.833	7	1	1	8	0	25	8.3	6	16	5.3	66	22.0
89-90 Por	21	21	815	127	274	.464	40	102	.392	139	165	.842	62	28	3	51	1	155	7.4	9	61	2.9	433	20.6
90-91 Por	16	16	595	102	204	.500	17	47	.362	68	79	.861	32	24	1	32	0	105	6.6	8	44	2.8	289	18.1
91-92 Por	21	21	870	147	285	.516	37	78	.474	119	143	.832	46	22	3	49	0	141	6.7	25	97	4.6	450	21.4
92-93 Por	4	4	152	27	68	.397	3	19	.158	9	11	.818	6	4	0	10	0	8	2.0	4	20	5.0	66	16.5
93-94 Por	4	0	76	12	35	.343	6	14	.429	11	14	.786	2	4	0	3	0	9	2.3	1	12	3.0	41	10.3
94-95 Por	3	0	21	7	13	.538	2	5	.400	3	5	.600	1	0	0	6	0	4	1.3	1	2	0.7	19	6.3
96-97 Min	3	0	46	5	13	.385	3	9	.333	3	4	.750	2	2	2	2	0	9	3.0	1	3	1.0	16	5.3
97-98 Min	5	4	188	27	63	.429	10	25	.400	15	18	.833	4	5	0	10	0	16	3.2	7	25	5.0	79	15.8
98-99 Mia	5	0	139	15	32	.469	3	12	.250	12	15	.800	8	3	0	8	0	15	3.0	3	19	3.8	45	9.0
99-00 SA	4	0	89	8	31	.258	4	14	.286	0	0	—	7	6	0	4	0	5	1.3	0	1	0.3	20	5.0
14 Years	101	77	3482	568	1199	.474	133	350	.380	418	503	.831	209	122	14	220	1	572	5.7	71	338	3.3	1687	16.7

James Posey

(statistical profile on page 264)

Pos: F **College:** Xavier (OH) **Drafted:** '99 1(18)—Den   **Ht:** 6'8" **Wt:** 215 **Born:** 1/13/77 **Age:** 24

College Year Tm	G	GS	Min	Field Goals Md	Att	Pct	3-Pt FGs Md	Att	Pct	Free Throws Md	Att	Pct	Misc TO	Stl	Blk	Fouls PF	DQ	Assists Ast	Avg	Rebounds Off	Tot	Avg	Points Pts	Avg
96-97 Xav	29	3	780	130	232	.560	6	32	.188	121	155	.781	60	49	15	75	3	40	1.4	96	226	7.8	387	13.3
97-98 Xav	30	2	864	145	261	.556	19	59	.322	150	182	.824	70	63	16	88	2	39	1.3	94	253	8.4	459	15.3
98-99 Xav	36	36	1268	191	391	.488	48	131	.366	179	220	.814	118	102	34	123	4	84	2.3	108	322	8.9	609	16.9
3 Years	95	41	2912	466	884	.527	73	222	.329	450	557	.808	248	214	65	286	9	163	1.7	298	801	8.4	1455	15.3

NBA Year Tm	G	GS	Min	Field Goals Md	Att	Pct	3-Pt FGs Md	Att	Pct	Free Throws Md	Att	Pct	Misc TO	Stl	Blk	Fouls PF	DQ	Assists Ast	Avg	Rebounds Off	Tot	Avg	Points Pts	Avg
99-00 Den	81	77	2052	230	536	.429	82	220	.373	120	150	.800	95	98	33	207	1	146	1.8	85	317	3.9	662	8.2

Vitaly Potapenko
(statistical profile on page 265)

Pos: F-C **College:** Wright State **Drafted:** '96 1(12)—Cle **Ht:** 6'10" **Wt:** 285 **Born:** 3/21/75 **Age:** 25

College				Field Goals			3-Pt FGs			Free Throws			Misc			Fouls		Assists		Rebounds			Points	
Year Tm	G	GS	Min	Md	Att	Pct	Md	Att	Pct	Md	Att	Pct	TO	Stl	Blk	PF	DQ	Ast	Avg	Off	Tot	Avg	Pts	Avg
94-95 Wri	30	—	900	212	352	.602	0	0	—	151	206	.733	133	17	39	110	—	41	1.4	—	193	6.4	575	19.2
95-96 Wri	26	26	807	198	328	.604	1	6	.167	141	197	.716	102	11	17	97	4	36	1.4	75	193	7.4	538	20.7
2 Years	56	—	1707	410	680	.603	1	6	.167	292	403	.725	235	28	56	207	—	77	1.4	—	386	6.9	1113	19.9

NBA				Field Goals			3-Pt FGs			Free Throws			Misc			Fouls		Assists		Rebounds			Points	
Year Tm	G	GS	Min	Md	Att	Pct	Md	Att	Pct	Md	Att	Pct	TO	Stl	Blk	PF	DQ	Ast	Avg	Off	Tot	Avg	Pts	Avg
96-97 Cle	80	3	1238	186	423	.440	1	2	.500	92	125	.736	109	26	34	216	3	40	0.5	105	217	2.7	465	5.8
97-98 Cle	80	0	1412	234	488	.480	0	1	.000	102	144	.708	132	27	28	198	2	57	0.7	110	313	3.9	570	7.1
98-99 2Tm	50	44	1394	204	412	.495	0	1	.000	91	155	.587	100	35	36	169	4	75	1.5	114	332	6.6	499	10.0
99-00 Bos	79	72	1797	307	615	.499	0	1	.000	109	160	.681	145	41	29	239	4	77	1.0	182	499	6.3	723	9.2
98-99 Cle	17	12	467	55	126	.437	0	1	.000	33	49	.673	28	11	16	53	2	16	0.9	23	94	5.5	143	8.4
Bos	33	32	927	149	286	.521	0	0	—	58	106	.547	72	24	20	116	2	59	1.8	91	238	7.2	356	10.8
4 Years	289	119	5841	931	1938	.480	1	5	.200	394	584	.675	486	129	127	822	13	249	0.9	511	1361	4.7	2257	7.8

NBA Postseason																								
Year Tm	G	GS	Min	Md	Att	Pct	Md	Att	Pct	Md	Att	Pct	TO	Stl	Blk	PF	DQ	Ast	Avg	Off	Tot	Avg	Pts	Avg
97-98 Cle	4	0	70	6	15	.400	0	0	—	5	10	.500	6	2	0	8	0	3	0.8	3	11	2.8	17	4.3

Brent Price

Pos: G **College:** Oklahoma **Drafted:** '92 2(32)—Was **Ht:** 6'1" **Wt:** 185 **Born:** 12/9/68 **Age:** 32

College				Field Goals			3-Pt FGs			Free Throws			Misc			Fouls		Assists		Rebounds			Points	
Year Tm	G	GS	Min	Md	Att	Pct	Md	Att	Pct	Md	Att	Pct	TO	Stl	Blk	PF	DQ	Ast	Avg	Off	Tot	Avg	Pts	Avg
87-88 SCar	29	—	643	98	213	.460	49	112	.438	66	77	.857	64	41	0	69	—	78	2.7	—	47	1.6	311	10.7
88-89 SCar	30	—	952	144	294	.490	68	139	.489	76	90	.844	76	52	4	80	—	128	4.3	—	75	2.5	432	14.4
90-91 Okla	35	34	1197	178	428	.416	91	244	.373	166	198	.838	117	97	8	107	5	192	5.5	60	127	3.6	613	17.5
91-92 Okla	30	30	1064	182	391	.465	76	194	.392	120	152	.789	70	80	6	94	2	185	6.2	45	111	3.7	560	18.7
4 Years	124	—	3856	602	1326	.454	284	689	.412	428	517	.828	327	270	18	350	—	583	4.7	—	360	2.9	1916	15.5

NBA				Field Goals			3-Pt FGs			Free Throws			Misc			Fouls		Assists		Rebounds			Points	
Year Tm	G	GS	Min	Md	Att	Pct	Md	Att	Pct	Md	Att	Pct	TO	Stl	Blk	PF	DQ	Ast	Avg	Off	Tot	Avg	Pts	Avg
92-93 Was	68	9	859	100	279	.358	8	48	.167	54	68	.794	85	56	3	90	0	154	2.3	28	103	1.5	262	3.9
93-94 Was	65	13	1035	141	326	.433	50	150	.333	68	87	.782	119	55	2	114	1	213	3.3	31	90	1.4	400	6.2
94-95 Was								Did not play: injury — Left Knee																
95-96 Was	81	50	2042	252	534	.472	139	301	.462	167	191	.874	153	78	4	184	3	416	5.1	38	228	2.8	810	10.0
96-97 Hou	25	0	390	44	105	.419	17	53	.321	21	21	1.000	32	17	0	34	0	65	2.6	10	29	1.2	126	5.0
97-98 Hou	72	2	1332	128	310	.413	73	187	.390	77	98	.786	111	52	4	163	3	192	2.7	37	107	1.5	406	5.6
98-99 Hou	40	6	806	100	207	.483	46	112	.411	46	61	.754	65	33	1	90	0	113	2.8	18	78	2.0	292	7.3
99-00 Van	41	0	424	41	119	.345	25	68	.368	34	39	.872	47	17	1	63	0	69	1.7	8	37	0.9	141	3.4
7 Years	392	80	6888	806	1880	.429	358	919	.390	467	565	.827	612	308	15	738	7	1222	3.1	170	672	1.7	2437	6.2

NBA Postseason																								
Year Tm	G	GS	Min	Md	Att	Pct	Md	Att	Pct	Md	Att	Pct	TO	Stl	Blk	PF	DQ	Ast	Avg	Off	Tot	Avg	Pts	Avg
97-98 Hou	5	0	75	6	15	.400	5	13	.385	2	3	.667	6	4	0	12	1	6	1.2	1	9	1.8	19	3.8
98-99 Hou	4	0	98	11	24	.458	5	14	.357	6	6	1.000	6	4	1	5	0	14	3.5	3	8	2.0	33	8.3
2 Years	9	0	173	17	39	.436	10	27	.370	8	9	.889	12	8	1	17	1	20	2.2	4	17	1.9	52	5.8

Laron Profit

Pos: G **College:** Maryland **Drafted:** '99 2(38)—Orl **Ht:** 6'5" **Wt:** 204 **Born:** 8/5/77 **Age:** 23

College				Field Goals			3-Pt FGs			Free Throws			Misc			Fouls		Assists		Rebounds			Points	
Year Tm	G	GS	Min	Md	Att	Pct	Md	Att	Pct	Md	Att	Pct	TO	Stl	Blk	PF	DQ	Ast	Avg	Off	Tot	Avg	Pts	Avg
95-96 Mlyd	27	0	366	54	112	.482	12	33	.364	34	45	.756	56	40	2	42	0	32	1.2	33	74	2.7	154	5.7
96-97 Mlyd	32	30	1033	160	337	.475	35	99	.354	57	91	.626	87	63	21	70	3	78	2.4	40	171	5.3	412	12.9
97-98 Mlyd	32	32	1008	184	412	.447	34	117	.291	104	147	.707	89	87	36	87	3	104	3.3	66	165	5.2	506	15.8
98-99 Mlyd	34	34	982	185	368	.503	24	77	.312	100	148	.676	86	66	13	77	1	73	2.1	42	162	4.8	494	14.5
4 Years	125	96	3389	583	1229	.474	105	326	.322	295	431	.684	318	256	72	276	7	287	2.3	181	572	4.6	1566	12.5

NBA				Field Goals			3-Pt FGs			Free Throws			Misc			Fouls		Assists		Rebounds			Points	
Year Tm	G	GS	Min	Md	Att	Pct	Md	Att	Pct	Md	Att	Pct	TO	Stl	Blk	PF	DQ	Ast	Avg	Off	Tot	Avg	Pts	Avg
99-00 Was	33	1	225	21	59	.356	3	17	.176	4	10	.400	19	7	4	26	0	25	0.8	2	26	0.8	49	1.5

Aleksandar Radojevic

Pos: C **College:** Barton County CC (KS) **Drafted:** '99 1(12)—Tor **Ht:** 7'3" **Wt:** 250 **Born:** 8/8/76 **Age:** 24

	NBA			Field Goals			3-Pt FGs			Free Throws			Misc			Fouls		Assists		Rebounds			Points	
Year Tm	G	GS	Min	Md	Att	Pct	Md	Att	Pct	Md	Att	Pct	TO	Stl	Blk	PF	DQ	Ast	Avg	Off	Tot	Avg	Pts	Avg
99-00 Tor	3	0	24	2	7	.286	0	0	—	3	6	.500	5	2	1	5	0	1	0.3	2	8	2.7	7	2.3

Theo Ratliff

(statistical profile on page 265)

Pos: F-C **College:** Wyoming **Drafted:** '95 1(18)—Det   **Ht:** 6'10" **Wt:** 225 **Born:** 4/17/73 **Age:** 27

	College			Field Goals			3-Pt FGs			Free Throws			Misc			Fouls		Assists		Rebounds			Points	
Year Tm	G	GS	Min	Md	Att	Pct	Md	Att	Pct	Md	Att	Pct	TO	Stl	Blk	PF	DQ	Ast	Avg	Off	Tot	Avg	Pts	Avg
91-92 Wyo	27	—	298	14	32	.438	0	0	—	21	36	.583	11	7	43	40	—	8	0.3	—	54	2.0	49	1.8
92-93 Wyo	28	—	824	99	184	.538	0	1	.000	60	116	.517	56	14	124	89	—	8	0.3	—	173	6.2	258	9.2
93-94 Wyo	28	—	892	160	281	.569	0	1	.000	111	171	.649	71	25	114	98	—	27	1.0	—	217	7.8	431	15.4
94-95 Wyo	28	—	912	148	272	.544	1	5	.200	107	169	.633	69	16	144	95	—	31	1.1	—	211	7.5	404	14.4
4 Years	111	—	2926	421	769	.547	1	7	.143	299	492	.608	207	62	425	322	—	74	0.7	—	655	5.9	1142	10.3

	NBA			Field Goals			3-Pt FGs			Free Throws			Misc			Fouls		Assists		Rebounds			Points	
Year Tm	G	GS	Min	Md	Att	Pct	Md	Att	Pct	Md	Att	Pct	TO	Stl	Blk	PF	DQ	Ast	Avg	Off	Tot	Avg	Pts	Avg
95-96 Det	75	2	1305	128	230	.557	0	1	.000	85	120	.708	56	16	116	144	1	13	0.2	110	297	4.0	341	4.5
96-97 Det	76	38	1292	179	337	.531	0	0	—	81	116	.698	56	29	111	181	2	13	0.2	109	256	3.4	439	5.8
97-98 2Tm	82	67	2447	306	597	.513	0	0	—	197	281	.701	116	50	258	292	8	57	0.7	221	547	6.7	809	9.9
98-99 Phi	50	50	1627	197	419	.470	0	0	—	166	229	.725	92	45	149	180	8	30	0.6	139	407	8.1	560	11.2
99-00 Phi	57	56	1795	247	491	.503	0	0	—	182	236	.771	108	32	171	185	4	36	0.6	140	435	7.6	676	11.9
97-98 Det	24	12	586	57	111	.514	0	0	—	43	63	.683	34	12	55	83	2	15	0.6	46	121	5.0	157	6.5
Phi	58	55	1861	249	486	.512	0	0	—	154	218	.706	82	38	203	209	6	42	0.7	175	426	7.3	652	11.2
5 Years	340	213	8466	1057	2074	.510	0	1	.000	711	982	.724	428	172	805	982	23	149	0.4	719	1942	5.7	2825	8.3

NBA Postseason																								
Year Tm	G	GS	Min	Md	Att	Pct	Md	Att	Pct	Md	Att	Pct	TO	Stl	Blk	PF	DQ	Ast	Avg	Off	Tot	Avg	Pts	Avg
95-96 Det	1	0	4	0	0	—	0	0	—	0	0	—	0	0	0	0	0	0	0.0	0	0	0.0	0	0.0
96-97 Det	3	0	18	3	4	.750	0	0	—	2	4	.500	3	1	4	5	0	1	0.3	2	4	1.3	8	2.7
98-99 Phi	7	7	204	20	43	.465	0	0	—	11	19	.579	7	5	18	19	0	6	0.9	23	51	7.3	51	7.3
99-00 Phi	10	10	374	48	101	.475	0	0	—	34	47	.723	17	10	30	35	1	9	0.9	28	79	7.9	130	13.0
4 Years	21	17	600	71	148	.480	0	0	—	47	70	.671	27	16	52	59	1	16	0.8	53	134	6.4	189	9.0

Eldridge Recasner

Pos: G **College:** Washington **Drafted:** '94 FA—Den   **Ht:** 6'3" **Wt:** 190 **Born:** 12/14/67 **Age:** 33

	College			Field Goals			3-Pt FGs			Free Throws			Misc			Fouls		Assists		Rebounds			Points	
Year Tm	G	GS	Min	Md	Att	Pct	Md	Att	Pct	Md	Att	Pct	TO	Stl	Blk	PF	DQ	Ast	Avg	Off	Tot	Avg	Pts	Avg
86-87 Wash	35	33	1124	111	234	.474	3	14	.214	69	99	.697	78	31	9	76	0	103	2.9	—	131	3.7	294	8.4
87-88 Wash	28	27	1061	173	338	.512	26	67	.388	105	128	.820	68	35	5	71	1	78	2.8	—	107	3.7	477	17.0
88-89 Wash	28	26	1011	175	352	.497	52	116	.448	106	128	.828	83	28	11	78	2	107	3.8	—	95	3.4	508	18.1
89-90 Wash	26	26	981	142	326	.446	38	103	.369	99	112	.884	78	24	3	60	0	88	3.4	—	101	3.9	421	16.2
4 Years	117	112	4177	601	1250	.481	119	300	.397	379	467	.812	307	118	28	285	3	376	3.2	—	434	3.7	1700	14.5

	NBA			Field Goals			3-Pt FGs			Free Throws			Misc			Fouls		Assists		Rebounds			Points	
Year Tm	G	GS	Min	Md	Att	Pct	Md	Att	Pct	Md	Att	Pct	TO	Stl	Blk	PF	DQ	Ast	Avg	Off	Tot	Avg	Pts	Avg
90-91										Played in Germany														
91-92										Played in GBA														
92-93										Played in CBA														
93-94										Played in CBA														
94-95 Den	3	0	13	1	6	.167	0	1	.000	4	4	1.000	2	3	0	0	0	1	0.3	0	2	0.7	6	2.0
95-96 Hou	63	27	1275	149	359	.415	81	191	.424	57	66	.864	61	23	5	111	1	170	2.7	31	144	2.3	436	6.9
96-97 Atl	71	4	1207	148	350	.423	58	140	.414	51	58	.879	65	38	4	97	0	94	1.3	35	115	1.6	405	5.7
97-98 Atl	59	14	1454	206	452	.456	62	148	.419	74	79	.937	91	41	1	94	0	117	2.0	32	142	2.4	548	9.3
98-99 Cha	44	2	708	82	184	.446	24	60	.400	34	39	.872	58	17	1	66	0	91	2.1	20	77	1.8	222	5.0
99-00 Cha	7	0	28	3	7	.429	1	4	.250	0	0	—	0	0	0	1	0	5	0.7	0	4	0.6	7	1.0
6 Years	247	47	4685	589	1358	.434	226	544	.415	220	246	.894	277	122	11	369	1	478	1.9	118	484	2.0	1624	6.6

NBA Postseason																								
Year Tm	G	GS	Min	Md	Att	Pct	Md	Att	Pct	Md	Att	Pct	TO	Stl	Blk	PF	DQ	Ast	Avg	Off	Tot	Avg	Pts	Avg
95-96 Hou	1	0	8	0	3	.000	0	1	.000	0	0	—	1	0	0	0	0	2	2.0	0	1	1.0	0	0.0
96-97 Atl	10	0	121	11	26	.423	4	11	.364	5	8	.625	7	2	0	9	0	9	0.9	3	11	1.1	31	3.1
97-98 Atl	4	0	89	10	25	.400	7	12	.583	2	2	1.000	2	2	0	7	0	8	2.0	0	4	1.0	29	7.3
3 Years	15	0	218	21	54	.389	11	24	.458	7	10	.700	10	4	0	16	0	19	1.3	3	16	1.1	60	4.0

Bryant Reeves

(statistical profile on page 266)

Pos: C **College:** Oklahoma State **Drafted:** '95 1(6)—Van   **Ht:** 7'0" **Wt:** 280 **Born:** 6/8/73 **Age:** 27

College			Field Goals			3-Pt FGs			Free Throws			Misc			Fouls		Assists		Rebounds			Points	
Year Tm	G	GS	Min	Md	Att	Pct	Md	Att	Pct	Md	Att	Pct	TO	Stl	Blk	PF	DQ	Ast	Avg	Off	Tot	Avg	Pts	Avg
91-92 OkSt	36	34	763	111	213	.521	0	0	—	69	109	.633	55	7	26	116	2	24	0.7	68	182	5.1	291	8.1
92-93 OkSt	29	28	944	210	338	.621	1	2	.500	145	223	.650	71	14	38	91	3	36	1.2	85	291	10.0	566	19.5
93-94 OkSt	34	34	1170	264	451	.585	0	1	.000	185	311	.595	90	27	70	105	3	52	1.5	104	329	9.7	713	21.0
94-95 OkSt	37	37	1288	289	493	.586	0	5	.000	219	310	.706	109	18	60	118	2	30	0.8	106	350	9.5	797	21.5
4 Years	136	133	4165	874	1495	.585	1	8	.125	618	953	.648	325	66	194	430	10	142	1.0	363	1152	8.5	2367	17.4

NBA			Field Goals			3-Pt FGs			Free Throws			Misc			Fouls		Assists		Rebounds			Points	
Year Tm	G	GS	Min	Md	Att	Pct	Md	Att	Pct	Md	Att	Pct	TO	Stl	Blk	PF	DQ	Ast	Avg	Off	Tot	Avg	Pts	Avg
95-96 Van	77	63	2460	401	877	.457	0	3	.000	219	299	.732	157	43	55	226	2	109	1.4	178	570	7.4	1021	13.3
96-97 Van	75	75	2777	498	1025	.486	1	11	.091	216	307	.704	175	29	67	270	3	160	2.1	174	610	8.1	1213	16.2
97-98 Van	74	74	2527	492	941	.523	0	4	.000	223	316	.706	156	39	80	278	6	155	2.1	196	585	7.9	1207	16.3
98-99 Van	25	14	702	102	251	.406	0	1	.000	67	116	.578	47	13	8	103	3	37	1.5	50	138	5.5	271	10.8
99-00 Van	69	67	1773	252	562	.448	0	4	.000	107	165	.648	119	33	38	245	8	82	1.2	126	390	5.7	611	8.9
5 Years	320	293	10239	1745	3656	.477	1	23	.043	832	1203	.692	654	157	248	1122	22	543	1.7	724	2293	7.2	4323	13.5

Khalid Reeves

Pos: G **College:** Arizona **Drafted:** '94 1(12)—Mia   **Ht:** 6'3" **Wt:** 201 **Born:** 7/15/72 **Age:** 28

College			Field Goals			3-Pt FGs			Free Throws			Misc			Fouls		Assists		Rebounds			Points	
Year Tm	G	GS	Min	Md	Att	Pct	Md	Att	Pct	Md	Att	Pct	TO	Stl	Blk	PF	DQ	Ast	Avg	Off	Tot	Avg	Pts	Avg
90-91 Ari	35	0	657	104	229	.454	31	67	.463	78	113	.690	70	36	6	74	3	103	2.9	12	82	2.3	317	9.1
91-92 Ari	30	28	921	148	311	.476	44	119	.370	78	99	.788	71	50	2	69	1	110	3.7	29	95	3.2	418	13.9
92-93 Ari	28	26	754	118	237	.498	26	79	.329	80	110	.727	54	37	1	64	3	80	2.9	19	97	3.5	342	12.2
93-94 Ari	35	35	1113	276	572	.483	85	224	.379	211	264	.799	85	64	4	88	1	103	2.9	47	150	4.3	848	24.2
4 Years	128	89	3445	646	1349	.479	186	489	.380	447	586	.763	280	187	13	295	8	396	3.1	107	424	3.3	1925	15.0

NBA			Field Goals			3-Pt FGs			Free Throws			Misc			Fouls		Assists		Rebounds			Points	
Year Tm	G	GS	Min	Md	Att	Pct	Md	Att	Pct	Md	Att	Pct	TO	Stl	Blk	PF	DQ	Ast	Avg	Off	Tot	Avg	Pts	Avg
94-95 Mia	67	17	1462	206	465	.443	67	171	.392	140	196	.714	132	77	10	139	1	288	4.3	52	186	2.8	619	9.2
95-96 2Tm	51	12	833	95	227	.419	28	91	.308	61	82	.744	63	37	3	115	2	118	2.3	18	79	1.5	279	5.5
96-97 2Tm	63	30	1432	184	470	.391	83	227	.366	65	87	.747	108	34	9	159	3	226	3.6	34	119	1.9	516	8.2
97-98 Dal	82	54	1950	248	593	.418	56	152	.368	165	213	.775	130	80	10	195	3	230	2.8	54	185	2.3	717	8.7
98-99 Det	11	0	112	8	21	.381	1	3	.333	8	14	.571	7	4	0	13	0	11	1.0	3	7	0.6	25	2.3
99-00 Chi	3	0	48	3	12	.250	0	3	.000	5	5	1.000	6	2	0	8	0	13	4.3	2	4	1.3	11	3.7
95-96 Cha	20	5	418	54	118	.458	11	36	.306	43	51	.843	30	16	1	46	0	72	3.6	11	40	2.0	162	8.1
NJ	31	7	415	41	109	.376	17	55	.309	18	31	.581	33	21	2	69	2	46	1.5	7	39	1.3	117	3.8
96-97 NJ	50	18	1048	141	359	.393	76	192	.396	56	75	.747	82	23	7	119	3	170	3.4	22	88	1.8	414	8.3
Dal	13	12	384	43	111	.387	7	35	.200	9	12	.750	26	11	2	40	0	56	4.3	12	31	2.4	102	7.8
6 Years	277	113	5837	744	1788	.416	235	647	.363	444	597	.744	446	234	32	629	9	886	3.2	163	580	2.1	2167	7.8

Don Reid

Pos: F **College:** Georgetown **Drafted:** '95 2(58)—Det   **Ht:** 6'8" **Wt:** 250 **Born:** 12/30/73 **Age:** 27

College			Field Goals			3-Pt FGs			Free Throws			Misc			Fouls		Assists		Rebounds			Points	
Year Tm	G	GS	Min	Md	Att	Pct	Md	Att	Pct	Md	Att	Pct	TO	Stl	Blk	PF	DQ	Ast	Avg	Off	Tot	Avg	Pts	Avg
91-92 GTwn	28	10	215	13	30	.433	0	0	—	18	30	.600	22	10	10	55	1	7	0.3	29	59	2.1	44	1.6
92-93 GTwn	32	0	278	18	43	.419	0	0	—	14	31	.452	26	11	13	62	2	4	0.1	27	68	2.1	50	1.6
93-94 GTwn	31	31	713	90	140	.643	0	0	—	58	92	.630	50	37	39	117	10	27	0.9	73	182	5.9	238	7.7
94-95 GTwn	31	31	731	88	148	.595	0	0	—	47	91	.516	44	31	60	113	9	26	0.8	62	178	5.7	223	7.2
4 Years	122	72	1937	209	361	.579	0	0	—	137	244	.561	142	89	122	347	22	64	0.5	191	487	4.0	555	4.5

NBA			Field Goals			3-Pt FGs			Free Throws			Misc			Fouls		Assists		Rebounds			Points	
Year Tm	G	GS	Min	Md	Att	Pct	Md	Att	Pct	Md	Att	Pct	TO	Stl	Blk	PF	DQ	Ast	Avg	Off	Tot	Avg	Pts	Avg
95-96 Det	69	46	997	106	187	.567	0	0	—	51	77	.662	41	47	40	199	2	11	0.2	78	203	2.9	263	3.8
96-97 Det	47	14	462	54	112	.482	0	1	.000	24	32	.750	23	16	15	105	1	14	0.3	36	101	2.1	132	2.8
97-98 Det	68	44	994	94	176	.534	0	0	—	50	71	.704	28	25	55	183	2	26	0.4	77	175	2.6	238	3.5
98-99 Det	47	30	935	97	174	.557	0	0	—	48	79	.608	36	27	43	156	2	33	0.7	66	170	3.6	242	5.1
99-00 2Tm	38	3	498	60	112	.536	0	0	—	24	34	.706	23	24	31	118	5	11	0.3	31	102	2.7	144	3.8
99-00 Det	21	3	165	16	34	.471	0	0	—	3	6	.500	11	5	12	45	1	1	0.0	5	25	1.2	35	1.7
Was	17	0	333	44	78	.564	0	0	—	21	28	.750	12	19	19	73	4	10	0.6	26	77	4.5	109	6.4
5 Years	269	137	3886	411	761	.540	0	1	.000	197	293	.672	151	139	184	761	12	95	0.4	288	751	2.8	1019	3.8

NBA Postseason																							
Year Tm	G	GS	Min	Md	Att	Pct	Md	Att	Pct	Md	Att	Pct	TO	Stl	Blk	PF	DQ	Ast	Avg	Off	Tot	Avg	Pts	Avg
95-96 Det	3	0	26	1	3	.333	0	0	—	1	3	.333	1	0	2	8	0	1	0.3	0	1	0.3	3	1.0

NBA Postseason

Year Tm	G	GS	Min	Md	Att	Pct	Md	Att	Pct	Md	Att	Pct	TO	Stl	Blk	PF	DQ	Ast	Avg	Off	Tot	Avg	Pts	Avg
96-97 Det	1	0	3	0	0	—	0	0	—	4	4	1.000	0	0	0	0	0	0	0.0	0	1	1.0	4	4.0
98-99 Det	4	0	21	2	3	.667	0	0	—	0	0	—	0	0	0	2	0	1	0.3	2	4	1.0	4	1.0
3 Years	8	0	50	3	6	.500	0	0	—	5	7	.714	1	0	2	10	0	2	0.3	2	6	0.8	11	1.4

J.R. Reid

Pos: F-C **College:** North Carolina **Drafted:** '89 1(5)—Cha **Ht:** 6'10" **Wt:** 247 **Born:** 3/31/68 **Age:** 32

College			Field Goals			3-Pt FGs			Free Throws			Misc			Fouls		Assists		Rebounds			Points	
Year Tm	G	GS	Min	Md	Att	Pct	Md	Att	Pct	Md	Att	Pct	TO	Stl	Blk	PF	DQ	Ast	Avg	Off	Tot	Avg	Pts	Avg
86-87 UNC	36	31	1030	198	339	.584	0	0	—	132	202	.653	94	47	27	110	—	66	1.8	—	268	7.4	528	14.7
87-88 UNC	33	33	1042	222	366	.607	0	0	—	151	222	.680	127	39	38	113	—	57	1.7	—	293	8.9	595	18.0
88-89 UNC	27	16	716	164	267	.614	0	0	—	101	151	.669	71	23	21	81	—	36	1.3	—	170	6.3	429	15.9
3 Years	96	80	2788	584	972	.601	0	0	—	384	575	.668	292	109	86	304	—	159	1.7	—	731	7.6	1552	16.2

NBA			Field Goals			3-Pt FGs			Free Throws			Misc			Fouls		Assists		Rebounds			Points	
Year Tm	G	GS	Min	Md	Att	Pct	Md	Att	Pct	Md	Att	Pct	TO	Stl	Blk	PF	DQ	Ast	Avg	Off	Tot	Avg	Pts	Avg
89-90 Cha	82	82	2757	358	814	.440	0	5	.000	192	289	.664	172	92	54	292	7	101	1.2	199	691	8.4	908	11.1
90-91 Cha	80	80	2467	360	773	.466	0	2	.000	182	259	.703	153	87	47	286	6	89	1.1	154	502	6.3	902	11.3
91-92 Cha	51	7	1257	213	435	.490	0	3	.000	134	190	.705	84	49	23	159	0	81	1.6	96	317	6.2	560	11.0
92-93 2Tm	83	25	1887	283	595	.476	0	5	.000	214	280	.764	125	47	31	266	3	80	1.0	120	456	5.5	780	9.4
93-94 SA	70	11	1344	260	530	.491	0	3	.000	107	153	.699	84	43	25	165	1	73	1.0	91	220	3.1	627	9.0
94-95 SA	81	37	1566	201	396	.508	1	2	.500	160	233	.687	113	60	32	230	2	55	0.7	120	393	4.9	563	7.0
95-96 2Tm	65	21	1313	160	324	.494	0	1	.000	107	142	.754	79	43	17	187	0	42	0.6	73	255	3.9	427	6.6
96-97										Played in France														
97-98 Cha	79	1	1109	146	318	.459	3	8	.375	89	122	.730	65	35	19	172	1	51	0.6	72	210	2.7	384	4.9
98-99 Cha	41	26	1029	132	277	.477	0	1	.000	105	137	.766	51	37	10	135	3	48	1.2	45	212	5.2	369	9.0
99-00 Mil	34	7	602	53	127	.417	1	7	.143	43	56	.768	20	19	5	81	2	18	0.5	29	117	3.4	150	4.4
92-93 Cha	17	1	295	42	98	.429	0	1	.000	43	58	.741	24	11	5	49	1	24	1.4	20	70	4.1	127	7.5
SA	66	24	1592	241	497	.485	0	4	.000	171	222	.770	101	36	26	217	2	56	0.8	100	386	5.8	653	9.9
95-96 NY	32	5	643	72	164	.439	0	1	.000	64	87	.736	49	25	10	98	0	14	0.4	35	123	3.8	208	6.5
NY	33	16	670	88	160	.550	0	0	—	43	55	.782	30	18	7	89	0	28	0.8	38	132	4.0	219	6.6
98-99 Cha	16	16	556	88	169	.521	0	0	—	67	84	.798	28	22	10	63	2	25	1.6	21	113	7.1	243	15.2
LAL	25	10	473	44	108	.407	0	1	.000	38	53	.717	23	15	0	72	1	23	0.9	24	99	4.0	126	5.0
10 Years	666	297	15331	2166	4589	.472	5	37	.135	1333	1861	.716	946	512	263	1973	24	638	1.0	999	3373	5.1	5670	8.5

NBA Postseason

Year Tm	G	GS	Min	Md	Att	Pct	Md	Att	Pct	Md	Att	Pct	TO	Stl	Blk	PF	DQ	Ast	Avg	Off	Tot	Avg	Pts	Avg
92-93 SA	10	2	220	29	60	.483	0	2	.000	27	35	.771	13	8	8	31	0	15	1.5	16	50	5.0	85	8.5
93-94 SA	4	0	56	6	21	.286	0	0	—	3	5	.600	1	1	2	10	0	3	0.8	3	12	3.0	15	3.8
94-95 SA	15	1	209	29	59	.492	0	0	—	33	39	.846	15	7	4	36	0	9	0.6	14	42	2.8	91	6.1
95-96 NY	1	0	7	1	1	1.000	0	0	—	0	0	—	1	0	0	2	0	1	1.0	0	1	1.0	2	2.0
97-98 Cha	9	0	114	11	28	.393	0	1	.000	8	10	.800	11	3	2	23	0	2	0.2	7	20	2.2	30	3.3
98-99 LAL	8	8	178	10	28	.357	0	0	—	6	8	.750	2	4	5	33	1	3	0.4	9	42	5.3	26	3.3
6 Years	47	11	784	86	197	.437	0	3	.000	77	97	.794	43	23	21	135	1	33	0.7	49	167	3.6	249	5.3

Rodrick Rhodes

Pos: F **College:** Southern California **Drafted:** '97 1(24)—Hou **Ht:** 6'6" **Wt:** 225 **Born:** 9/24/73 **Age:** 27

College			Field Goals			3-Pt FGs			Free Throws			Misc			Fouls		Assists		Rebounds			Points	
Year Tm	G	GS	Min	Md	Att	Pct	Md	Att	Pct	Md	Att	Pct	TO	Stl	Blk	PF	DQ	Ast	Avg	Off	Tot	Avg	Pts	Avg
92-93 Kty	33	19	661	101	224	.451	27	70	.386	70	101	.693	72	36	13	73	0	59	1.8	—	80	2.4	299	9.1
93-94 Kty	33	29	848	142	326	.436	32	117	.274	167	215	.777	74	76	18	104	5	91	2.8	—	136	4.1	483	14.6
94-95 Kty	33	32	902	130	333	.390	39	110	.355	128	164	.780	90	51	11	93	2	125	3.8	—	120	3.6	427	12.9
96-97 USC	25	16	716	114	255	.447	30	81	.370	92	154	.597	95	41	7	66	2	104	4.2	38	122	4.9	350	14.0
4 Years	124	96	3127	487	1138	.428	128	378	.339	457	634	.721	331	204	49	336	9	379	3.1	—	458	3.7	1559	12.6

NBA			Field Goals			3-Pt FGs			Free Throws			Misc			Fouls		Assists		Rebounds			Points	
Year Tm	G	GS	Min	Md	Att	Pct	Md	Att	Pct	Md	Att	Pct	TO	Stl	Blk	PF	DQ	Ast	Avg	Off	Tot	Avg	Pts	Avg
97-98 Hou	58	13	1070	112	305	.367	2	8	.250	111	180	.617	97	62	10	125	0	110	1.9	28	70	1.2	337	5.8
98-99 2Tm	13	1	156	13	52	.250	1	7	.143	16	25	.640	20	5	2	21	0	11	0.8	9	17	1.3	43	3.3
99-00 Dal	1	0	8	0	3	.000	0	0	—	0	0	—	2	2	0	0	0	0	0.0	1	1	1.0	0	0.0
98-99 Hou	3	0	33	2	8	.250	0	0	—	5	6	.833	5	1	0	5	0	1	0.3	2	4	1.3	9	3.0
Van	10	1	123	11	44	.250	1	7	.143	11	19	.579	15	4	2	16	0	10	1.0	7	13	1.3	34	3.4
3 Years	72	14	1234	125	360	.347	3	15	.200	127	205	.620	119	69	12	146	0	121	1.7	38	88	1.2	380	5.3

NBA Postseason

Year Tm	G	GS	Min	Md	Att	Pct	Md	Att	Pct	Md	Att	Pct	TO	Stl	Blk	PF	DQ	Ast	Avg	Off	Tot	Avg	Pts	Avg
97-98 Hou	3	0	7	2	3	.667	0	0	—	2	4	.500	1	1	0	0	0	0	0.0	0	1	0.3	6	2.0

Glen Rice

(statistical profile on page 266)

Pos: G-F **College:** Michigan **Drafted:** '89 1(4)—Mia   **Ht:** 6'8" **Wt:** 220 **Born:** 5/28/67 **Age:** 33

College			Field Goals			3-Pt FGs			Free Throws			Misc			Fouls		Assists		Rebounds			Points	
Year Tm	G	GS	Min	Md	Att	Pct	Md	Att	Pct	Md	Att	Pct	TO	Stl	Blk	PF	DQ	Ast	Avg	Off	Tot	Avg	Pts	Avg
85-86 Mich	32	0	520	105	191	.550	—	—	—	15	25	.600	29	13	5	43	0	21	0.7	—	97	3.0	225	7.0
86-87 Mich	32	31	1056	226	402	.562	3	12	.250	85	108	.787	66	14	15	74	1	76	2.4	—	294	9.2	540	16.9
87-88 Mich	33	33	1155	308	539	.571	33	77	.429	79	98	.806	70	36	9	62	0	92	2.8	—	236	7.2	728	22.1
88-89 Mich	37	37	1258	363	629	.577	99	192	.516	124	149	.832	81	39	11	75	1	85	2.3	—	232	6.3	949	25.6
4 Years	134	101	3989	1002	1761	.569	135	281	.480	303	380	.797	246	102	40	254	2	274	2.0	—	859	6.4	2442	18.2

NBA			Field Goals			3-Pt FGs			Free Throws			Misc			Fouls		Assists		Rebounds			Points	
Year Tm	G	GS	Min	Md	Att	Pct	Md	Att	Pct	Md	Att	Pct	TO	Stl	Blk	PF	DQ	Ast	Avg	Off	Tot	Avg	Pts	Avg
89-90 Mia	77	60	2311	470	1071	.439	17	69	.246	91	124	.734	113	67	27	198	1	138	1.8	100	352	4.6	1048	13.6
90-91 Mia	77	77	2646	550	1193	.461	71	184	.386	171	209	.818	166	101	26	216	0	189	2.5	85	381	4.9	1342	17.4
91-92 Mia	79	79	3007	672	1432	.469	155	396	.391	266	318	.836	145	90	35	170	0	184	2.3	84	394	5.0	1765	22.3
92-93 Mia	82	82	3082	582	1324	.440	148	386	.383	242	295	.820	157	92	25	201	0	180	2.2	92	424	5.2	1554	19.0
93-94 Mia	81	81	2999	663	1421	.467	132	346	.382	250	284	.880	130	110	32	186	0	184	2.3	76	434	5.4	1708	21.1
94-95 Mia	82	82	3014	667	1403	.475	185	451	.410	312	365	.855	153	112	14	203	1	192	2.3	99	378	4.6	1831	22.3
95-96 Cha*	79	79	3142	610	1296	.471	171	403	.424	319	381	.837	163	91	19	217	1	232	2.9	86	378	4.8	1710	21.6
96-97 Cha*	79	78	3362	722	1513	.477	207	440	.470	464	535	.867	177	72	26	190	0	160	2.0	67	318	4.0	2115	26.8
97-98 Cha*	82	82	3295	634	1386	.457	130	300	.433	428	504	.849	182	77	22	200	0	182	2.2	89	353	4.3	1826	22.3
98-99 LAL	27	25	985	171	396	.432	53	135	.393	77	90	.856	45	17	6	67	1	71	2.6	9	99	3.7	472	17.5
99-00 LAL	80	80	2530	421	980	.430	84	229	.367	346	396	.874	114	47	12	179	0	176	2.2	56	327	4.1	1272	15.9
11 Years	825	805	30373	6162	13415	.459	1353	3339	.405	2966	3501	.847	1545	876	244	2027	4	1888	2.3	843	3838	4.7	16643	20.2

NBA Postseason																							
Year Tm	G	GS	Min	Md	Att	Pct	Md	Att	Pct	Md	Att	Pct	TO	Stl	Blk	PF	DQ	Ast	Avg	Off	Tot	Avg	Pts	Avg
91-92 Mia	3	3	119	24	64	.375	3	12	.250	6	7	.857	6	2	0	7	0	5	1.7	3	10	3.3	57	19.0
93-94 Mia	5	5	195	26	68	.382	7	23	.304	6	8	.750	14	11	2	14	0	10	2.0	6	36	7.2	65	13.0
96-97 Cha	3	3	137	28	57	.491	6	16	.375	21	23	.913	4	4	1	11	0	11	3.7	1	11	3.7	83	27.7
97-98 Cha	9	9	306	82	173	.474	11	36	.306	30	36	.833	13	5	3	26	0	13	1.4	11	51	5.7	205	22.8
98-99 LAL	7	7	307	45	101	.446	10	28	.357	28	29	.966	9	5	1	15	0	11	1.6	4	27	3.9	128	18.3
99-00 LAL	23	23	766	93	228	.408	28	67	.418	71	89	.798	36	15	4	50	0	48	2.1	10	92	4.0	285	12.4
6 Years	50	50	1893	298	691	.431	65	182	.357	162	192	.844	82	42	11	123	0	98	2.0	35	227	4.5	823	16.5

Mitch Richmond

(statistical profile on page 267)

Pos: G **College:** Kansas State **Drafted:** '88 1(5)—GS   **Ht:** 6'5" **Wt:** 220 **Born:** 6/30/65 **Age:** 35

College			Field Goals			3-Pt FGs			Free Throws			Misc			Fouls		Assists		Rebounds			Points	
Year Tm	G	GS	Min	Md	Att	Pct	Md	Att	Pct	Md	Att	Pct	TO	Stl	Blk	PF	DQ	Ast	Avg	Off	Tot	Avg	Pts	Avg
86-87 KanSt	30	28	964	201	450	.447	39	108	.361	118	155	.761	82	38	13	79	2	80	2.7	72	170	5.7	559	18.6
87-88 KanSt	34	34	1200	268	521	.514	46	98	.469	186	240	.775	115	23	13	77	3	125	3.7	69	213	6.3	768	22.6
2 Years	64	62	2164	469	971	.483	85	206	.413	304	395	.770	197	61	26	156	5	205	3.2	141	383	6.0	1327	20.7

NBA			Field Goals			3-Pt FGs			Free Throws			Misc			Fouls		Assists		Rebounds			Points	
Year Tm	G	GS	Min	Md	Att	Pct	Md	Att	Pct	Md	Att	Pct	TO	Stl	Blk	PF	DQ	Ast	Avg	Off	Tot	Avg	Pts	Avg
88-89 GS	79	79	2717	649	1386	.468	33	90	.367	410	506	.810	269	82	13	223	5	334	4.2	158	468	5.9	1741	22.0
89-90 GS	78	78	2799	640	1287	.497	34	95	.358	406	469	.866	201	98	24	210	3	223	2.9	98	360	4.6	1720	22.1
90-91 GS	77	77	3027	703	1424	.494	40	115	.348	394	465	.847	230	126	34	207	0	238	3.1	147	452	5.9	1840	23.9
91-92 Sac	80	80	3095	685	1465	.468	103	268	.384	330	406	.813	247	92	34	231	1	411	5.1	62	319	4.0	1803	22.5
92-93 Sac*	45	45	1728	371	782	.474	48	130	.369	197	233	.845	130	53	9	137	3	221	4.9	18	154	3.4	987	21.9
93-94 Sac*	78	78	2897	635	1428	.445	127	312	.407	426	511	.834	216	103	17	211	3	313	4.0	70	286	3.7	1823	23.4
94-95 Sac*	82	82	3172	668	1497	.446	156	424	.368	375	445	.843	234	91	29	227	2	311	3.8	69	357	4.4	1867	22.8
95-96 Sac*	81	81	2946	611	1368	.447	225	515	.437	425	491	.866	220	125	19	233	6	255	3.1	54	269	3.3	1872	23.1
96-97 Sac*	81	81	3125	717	1578	.454	204	477	.428	457	531	.861	237	118	24	211	1	338	4.2	59	353	3.9	2095	25.9
97-98 Sac*	70	70	2569	543	1220	.445	130	334	.389	407	471	.864	181	88	15	154	0	279	4.0	50	229	3.3	1623	23.2
98-99 Was	50	50	1912	331	803	.412	70	221	.317	251	293	.857	136	64	10	121	1	122	2.4	30	172	3.4	983	19.7
99-00 Was	74	69	2397	447	1049	.426	93	241	.386	298	340	.876	154	110	13	191	2	185	2.5	37	213	2.9	1285	17.4
12 Years	875	870	32384	7000	15287	.458	1263	3222	.392	4376	5161	.848	2455	1150	241	2356	27	3230	3.7	852	3598	4.1	19639	22.4

NBA Postseason																							
Year Tm	G	GS	Min	Md	Att	Pct	Md	Att	Pct	Md	Att	Pct	TO	Stl	Blk	PF	DQ	Ast	Avg	Off	Tot	Avg	Pts	Avg
88-89 GS	8	8	314	62	135	.459	3	16	.188	34	38	.895	24	14	1	25	0	35	4.4	10	58	7.3	161	20.1
90-91 GS	9	9	372	85	169	.503	8	24	.333	23	24	.958	17	5	6	28	1	22	2.4	10	47	5.2	201	22.3
95-96 Sac	4	4	146	24	54	.444	8	23	.348	28	35	.800	15	3	0	11	0	12	3.0	3	17	4.3	84	21.0
3 Years	21	21	832	171	358	.478	19	63	.302	85	97	.876	56	22	7	64	1	69	3.3	23	122	5.8	446	21.2

Isaiah Rider

(statistical profile on page 267)

Pos: G **College:** UNLV **Drafted:** '93 1(5)—Min **Ht:** 6'5" **Wt:** 215 **Born:** 3/12/71 **Age:** 29

College			Field Goals			3-Pt FGs			Free Throws			Misc			Fouls		Assists		Rebounds			Points	
Year Tm	G	GS	Min	Md	Att	Pct	Md	Att	Pct	Md	Att	Pct	TO	Stl	Blk	PF	DQ	Ast	Avg	Off	Tot	Avg	Pts	Avg
91-92 UNLV	27	—	922	206	420	.490	81	202	.401	65	87	.747	80	19	11	51	—	87	3.2	—	141	5.2	558	20.7
92-93 UNLV	28	—	992	282	548	.515	55	137	.401	195	236	.826	107	41	18	83	—	71	2.5	—	250	8.9	814	29.1
2 Years	55	—	1914	488	968	.504	136	339	.401	260	323	.805	187	60	29	134	—	158	2.9	—	391	7.1	1372	24.9

NBA			Field Goals			3-Pt FGs			Free Throws			Misc			Fouls		Assists		Rebounds			Points	
Year Tm	G	GS	Min	Md	Att	Pct	Md	Att	Pct	Md	Att	Pct	TO	Stl	Blk	PF	DQ	Ast	Avg	Off	Tot	Avg	Pts	Avg
93-94 Min	79	60	2415	522	1115	.468	54	150	.360	215	265	.811	218	54	28	194	0	202	2.6	118	315	4.0	1313	16.6
94-95 Min	75	67	2645	558	1249	.447	139	396	.351	277	339	.817	232	69	23	194	3	245	3.3	90	249	3.3	1532	20.4
95-96 Min	75	68	2594	560	1206	.464	102	275	.371	248	296	.838	201	48	23	204	2	213	2.8	99	309	4.1	1470	19.6
96-97 Por	76	68	2563	456	983	.464	99	257	.385	212	261	.812	212	45	19	199	2	198	2.6	94	304	4.0	1223	16.1
97-98 Por	74	66	2786	551	1302	.423	135	420	.321	221	267	.828	187	55	17	188	1	231	3.1	99	346	4.7	1458	19.7
98-99 Por	47	41	1385	249	605	.412	42	111	.378	111	147	.755	95	25	9	100	0	104	2.2	59	196	4.2	651	13.9
99-00 Atl	60	47	2084	449	1072	.419	56	180	.311	204	260	.785	168	41	6	132	3	219	3.7	63	258	4.3	1158	19.3
7 Years	486	417	16472	3345	7532	.444	627	1789	.350	1488	1835	.811	1313	337	127	1211	11	1412	2.9	622	1977	4.1	8805	18.1

NBA Postseason																							
Year Tm	G	GS	Min	Md	Att	Pct	Md	Att	Pct	Md	Att	Pct	TO	Stl	Blk	PF	DQ	Ast	Avg	Off	Tot	Avg	Pts	Avg
96-97 Por	4	4	161	16	43	.372	6	16	.375	15	17	.882	12	3	0	11	0	17	4.3	1	8	2.0	53	13.3
97-98 Por	4	4	166	28	67	.418	1	11	.091	20	26	.769	16	5	0	11	0	17	4.3	7	20	5.0	77	19.3
98-99 Por	13	13	426	70	163	.429	11	26	.423	63	71	.887	33	11	0	30	0	31	2.4	17	50	3.8	214	16.5
3 Years	21	21	753	114	273	.418	18	53	.340	98	114	.860	61	19	0	52	0	65	3.1	25	78	3.7	344	16.4

Eric Riley

Pos: C **College:** Michigan **Drafted:** '93 2(33)—Dal **Ht:** 7'0" **Wt:** 245 **Born:** 6/2/70 **Age:** 30

College			Field Goals			3-Pt FGs			Free Throws			Misc			Fouls		Assists		Rebounds			Points	
Year Tm	G	GS	Min	Md	Att	Pct	Md	Att	Pct	Md	Att	Pct	TO	Stl	Blk	PF	DQ	Ast	Avg	Off	Tot	Avg	Pts	Avg
89-90 Mich	31	0	403	34	56	.607	0	0	—	16	35	.457	27	9	40	84	1	15	0.5	—	102	3.3	84	2.7
90-91 Mich	28	26	855	105	235	.447	0	1	.000	87	115	.757	76	20	78	108	8	29	1.0	—	242	8.6	297	10.6
91-92 Mich	32	2	497	82	139	.590	0	0	—	37	64	.578	50	7	19	84	4	21	0.7	54	139	4.3	201	6.3
92-93 Mich	35	0	528	78	133	.586	0	1	.000	39	53	.736	37	15	31	82	2	14	0.4	63	169	4.8	195	5.6
4 Years	126	28	2283	299	563	.531	0	2	.000	179	267	.670	190	51	168	358	15	79	0.6	—	652	5.2	777	6.2

NBA			Field Goals			3-Pt FGs			Free Throws			Misc			Fouls		Assists		Rebounds			Points	
Year Tm	G	GS	Min	Md	Att	Pct	Md	Att	Pct	Md	Att	Pct	TO	Stl	Blk	PF	DQ	Ast	Avg	Off	Tot	Avg	Pts	Avg
93-94 Hou	47	2	219	34	70	.486	0	1	.000	20	37	.541	15	5	9	30	0	9	0.2	24	59	1.3	88	1.9
94-95 LAC	40	4	434	65	145	.448	0	1	.000	47	64	.734	31	17	35	78	1	11	0.3	45	112	2.8	177	4.4
95-96 Min	25	10	310	35	74	.473	0	1	.000	22	28	.786	17	8	16	42	0	5	0.2	32	76	3.0	92	3.7
96-97										Played in Greece														
97-98 Dal	39	14	544	56	135	.415	0	1	.000	27	36	.750	37	15	46	80	0	22	0.6	43	133	3.4	139	3.6
98-99 Bos	35	11	337	28	54	.519	0	0	—	22	31	.710	26	9	26	73	2	13	0.4	36	99	2.8	78	2.2
99-00 Min										Active but did not play														
5 Years	186	41	1844	218	478	.456	0	4	.000	138	196	.704	126	54	132	303	3	60	0.3	180	479	2.6	574	3.1

Stanley Roberts

Pos: C **College:** Louisiana State **Drafted:** '91 1(23)—Orl **Ht:** 7'0" **Wt:** 290 **Born:** 2/7/70 **Age:** 30

College			Field Goals			3-Pt FGs			Free Throws			Misc			Fouls		Assists		Rebounds			Points	
Year Tm	G	GS	Min	Md	Att	Pct	Md	Att	Pct	Md	Att	Pct	TO	Stl	Blk	PF	DQ	Ast	Avg	Off	Tot	Avg	Pts	Avg
89-90 LSU	32	—	859	200	347	.576	0	1	.000	51	111	.459	56	20	60	122	—	40	1.3	—	315	9.8	451	14.1

NBA			Field Goals			3-Pt FGs			Free Throws			Misc			Fouls		Assists		Rebounds			Points	
Year Tm	G	GS	Min	Md	Att	Pct	Md	Att	Pct	Md	Att	Pct	TO	Stl	Blk	PF	DQ	Ast	Avg	Off	Tot	Avg	Pts	Avg
91-92 Orl	55	34	1118	236	446	.529	0	1	.000	101	196	.515	78	22	83	221	7	39	0.7	113	336	6.1	573	10.4
92-93 LAC	77	76	1816	375	711	.527	0	0	—	120	246	.488	121	34	141	332	15	59	0.8	181	478	6.2	870	11.3
93-94 LAC	14	14	350	43	100	.430	0	0	—	18	44	.409	24	6	25	54	2	11	0.8	27	93	6.6	104	7.4
94-95 LAC										Did not play: injury — Achilles Tendon														
95-96 LAC	51	7	795	141	304	.464	0	0	—	74	133	.556	48	15	39	153	3	41	0.8	42	162	3.2	356	7.0
96-97 LAC	18	2	378	63	148	.426	0	0	—	45	64	.703	23	8	23	57	2	9	0.5	24	91	5.1	171	9.5
97-98 Min	74	44	1328	191	386	.495	0	0	—	75	156	.481	70	24	72	226	5	27	0.4	109	363	4.9	457	6.2
98-99 Hou	6	0	33	5	13	.385	0	0	—	4	8	.500	4	0	1	2	0	0	0.0	4	11	1.8	14	2.3
99-00 Phi	5	1	51	5	16	.313	0	1	.000	0	3	.000	2	1	1	15	0	3	0.6	6	15	3.0	10	2.0
8 Years	300	178	5869	1059	2124	.499	0	2	.000	437	850	.514	370	110	385	1060	34	189	0.6	506	1549	5.2	2555	8.5

140

NBA Postseason

Year Tm	G	GS	Min	Md	Att	Pct	Md	Att	Pct	Md	Att	Pct	TO	Stl	Blk	PF	DQ	Ast	Avg	Off	Tot	Avg	Pts	Avg
92-93 LAC	5	5	149	26	50	.520	0	1	.000	5	18	.278	10	3	3	24	2	1	0.2	17	41	8.2	57	11.4
97-98 Min	1	0	8	0	1	.000	0	0	—	1	2	.500	1	0	0	0	0	0	0.0	1	2	2.0	1	1.0
98-99 Hou	3	0	20	0	6	.000	0	0	—	1	2	.500	0	0	4	5	0	0	0.0	0	3	1.0	1	0.3
3 Years	9	5	177	26	57	.456	0	1	.000	7	22	.318	11	3	7	29	2	1	0.1	18	46	5.1	59	6.6

Ryan Robertson

Pos: G **College:** Kansas **Drafted:** '99 2(45)—Sac **Ht:** 6'5" **Wt:** 190 **Born:** 10/2/76 **Age:** 24

College			Field Goals			3-Pt FGs			Free Throws			Misc			Fouls		Assists		Rebounds			Points	
Year Tm	G	GS	Min	Md	Att	Pct	Md	Att	Pct	Md	Att	Pct	TO	Stl	Blk	PF	DQ	Ast	Avg	Off	Tot	Avg	Pts	Avg
95-96 Kan	34	0	303	40	82	.488	19	42	.452	47	61	.770	11	16	1	32	0	32	0.9	16	43	1.3	146	4.3
96-97 Kan	36	11	654	50	120	.417	24	58	.414	37	46	.804	46	16	7	63	2	99	2.8	17	54	1.5	161	4.5
97-98 Kan	39	38	1223	104	229	.454	50	116	.431	66	90	.733	93	55	12	88	2	248	6.4	11	109	2.8	324	8.3
98-99 Kan	33	33	1165	136	310	.439	51	138	.370	101	116	.871	48	56	13	77	0	106	3.2	21	132	4.0	424	12.8
4 Years	142	82	3345	330	741	.445	144	354	.407	251	313	.802	198	143	33	260	4	485	3.4	65	338	2.4	1055	7.4

NBA			Field Goals			3-Pt FGs			Free Throws			Misc			Fouls		Assists		Rebounds			Points	
Year Tm	G	GS	Min	Md	Att	Pct	Md	Att	Pct	Md	Att	Pct	TO	Stl	Blk	PF	DQ	Ast	Avg	Off	Tot	Avg	Pts	Avg
99-00 Sac	1	0	25	2	6	.333	0	2	.000	1	1	1.000	0	0	0	0	0	0	0.0	0	0	0.0	5	5.0

Clifford Robinson

(statistical profile on page 268)

Pos: F **College:** Connecticut **Drafted:** '89 2(36)—Por **Ht:** 6'10" **Wt:** 225 **Born:** 12/16/66 **Age:** 34

College			Field Goals			3-Pt FGs			Free Throws			Misc			Fouls		Assists		Rebounds			Points	
Year Tm	G	GS	Min	Md	Att	Pct	Md	Att	Pct	Md	Att	Pct	TO	Stl	Blk	PF	DQ	Ast	Avg	Off	Tot	Avg	Pts	Avg
85-86 Conn	28	2	442	60	164	.366	—	—	—	36	59	.610	33	10	12	74	—	14	0.5	—	88	3.1	156	5.6
86-87 Conn	16	16	556	107	255	.420	6	18	.333	69	121	.570	57	11	11	54	—	32	2.0	—	119	7.4	289	18.1
87-88 Conn	34	34	1079	222	463	.479	0	0	—	156	238	.655	92	34	49	114	—	44	1.3	—	233	6.9	600	17.6
88-89 Conn	31	30	974	235	500	.470	4	12	.333	145	212	.684	75	55	44	104	—	46	1.5	—	228	7.4	619	20.0
4 Years	109	82	3051	624	1382	.452	10	30	.333	406	630	.644	257	110	116	346	—	136	1.2	—	668	6.1	1664	15.3

NBA			Field Goals			3-Pt FGs			Free Throws			Misc			Fouls		Assists		Rebounds			Points	
Year Tm	G	GS	Min	Md	Att	Pct	Md	Att	Pct	Md	Att	Pct	TO	Stl	Blk	PF	DQ	Ast	Avg	Off	Tot	Avg	Pts	Avg
89-90 Por	82	0	1565	298	751	.397	12	44	.273	138	251	.550	129	53	53	226	4	72	0.9	110	308	3.8	746	9.1
90-91 Por	82	11	1940	373	806	.463	6	19	.316	205	314	.653	133	78	76	263	2	151	1.8	123	349	4.3	957	11.7
91-92 Por	82	7	2124	398	854	.466	1	11	.091	219	330	.664	154	85	107	274	11	137	1.7	140	416	5.1	1016	12.4
92-93 Por	82	12	2575	632	1336	.473	19	77	.247	287	416	.690	173	98	163	287	8	182	2.2	165	542	6.6	1570	19.1
93-94 Por*	82	64	2853	641	1404	.457	13	53	.245	352	460	.765	169	118	111	263	0	159	1.9	164	550	6.7	1647	20.1
94-95 Por	75	73	2725	597	1320	.452	142	383	.371	265	382	.694	158	79	82	240	3	198	2.6	152	423	5.6	1601	21.3
95-96 Por	78	76	2980	553	1306	.423	178	471	.378	360	542	.664	194	86	68	248	3	190	2.4	123	443	5.7	1644	21.1
96-97 Por	81	79	3077	444	1043	.426	121	350	.346	215	309	.696	172	99	66	251	6	261	3.2	90	321	4.0	1224	15.1
97-98 Pho	80	64	2359	429	895	.479	27	84	.321	248	360	.689	140	92	90	249	5	170	2.1	152	410	5.1	1133	14.2
98-99 Pho	50	35	1740	299	629	.475	58	139	.417	163	234	.697	88	75	59	154	2	128	2.6	69	227	4.5	819	16.4
99-00 Pho	80	67	2839	530	1142	.464	120	324	.370	298	381	.782	166	90	61	239	3	224	2.8	105	359	4.5	1478	18.5
11 Years	854	488	26777	5194	11486	.452	697	1955	.357	2750	3979	.691	1676	953	936	2694	47	1872	2.2	1393	4348	5.1	13835	16.2

NBA Postseason

Year Tm	G	GS	Min	Md	Att	Pct	Md	Att	Pct	Md	Att	Pct	TO	Stl	Blk	PF	DQ	Ast	Avg	Off	Tot	Avg	Pts	Avg
89-90 Por	21	6	391	54	151	.358	0	4	.000	29	52	.558	25	19	24	71	1	23	1.1	32	87	4.1	137	6.5
90-91 Por	16	0	354	63	117	.538	1	3	.333	38	69	.551	25	7	16	47	1	18	1.1	24	63	3.9	165	10.3
91-92 Por	21	0	522	91	197	.462	1	6	.167	44	77	.571	28	22	21	84	3	43	2.0	25	88	4.2	227	10.8
92-93 Por	4	0	131	16	61	.262	0	1	.000	9	22	.409	8	6	7	17	1	6	1.5	10	17	4.3	41	10.3
93-94 Por	4	4	149	28	68	.412	2	9	.222	7	8	.875	11	3	6	13	0	10	2.5	11	25	6.3	65	16.3
94-95 Por	3	3	119	17	47	.362	4	17	.235	9	16	.563	8	2	1	13	0	8	2.7	7	19	6.3	47	15.7
95-96 Por	5	5	181	21	61	.344	6	23	.261	28	37	.757	16	7	5	19	0	8	1.6	4	18	3.6	76	15.2
96-97 Por	4	4	161	17	47	.362	3	16	.188	11	16	.688	10	2	4	13	0	12	3.0	12	27	6.8	48	12.0
97-98 Pho	4	4	92	9	33	.273	0	1	.000	7	9	.778	5	3	2	19	1	3	0.8	6	12	3.0	25	6.3
98-99 Pho	3	3	117	19	40	.475	2	9	.222	7	11	.636	7	6	1	12	1	8	2.7	7	16	5.3	47	15.7
99-00 Pho	9	9	333	56	145	.386	13	40	.325	33	45	.733	18	11	7	35	0	19	2.1	18	54	6.0	158	17.6
11 Years	94	38	2550	391	967	.404	32	129	.248	222	362	.613	161	88	94	343	8	158	1.7	156	426	4.5	1036	11.0

David Robinson

(statistical profile on page 268)

Pos: C **College:** Navy **Drafted:** '87 1(1)—SA   **Ht:** 7'1" **Wt:** 250 **Born:** 8/6/65 **Age:** 35

College			Field Goals			3-Pt FGs			Free Throws			Misc			Fouls		Assists		Rebounds			Points	
Year Tm	G	GS	Min	Md	Att	Pct	Md	Att	Pct	Md	Att	Pct	TO	Stl	Blk	PF	DQ	Ast	Avg	Off	Tot	Avg	Pts	Avg
83-84 Navy	28	0	372	86	138	.623	—	—	—	42	73	.575	31	6	37	81	—	6	0.2	—	111	4.0	214	7.6
84-85 Navy	32	32	1075	302	469	.644	—	—	—	152	243	.626	73	27	128	82	—	19	0.6	—	370	11.6	756	23.6
85-86 Navy	35	35	1187	294	484	.607	—	—	—	208	331	.628	86	59	207	100	—	24	0.7	—	455	13.0	796	22.7
86-87 Navy	32	32	1107	350	592	.591	1	1	1.000	202	317	.637	71	66	144	87	—	33	1.0	—	378	11.8	903	28.2
4 Years	127	99	3741	1032	1683	.613	1	1	1.000	604	964	.627	261	158	516	350	—	82	0.6	—	1314	10.3	2669	21.0

NBA			Field Goals			3-Pt FGs			Free Throws			Misc			Fouls		Assists		Rebounds			Points	
Year Tm	G	GS	Min	Md	Att	Pct	Md	Att	Pct	Md	Att	Pct	TO	Stl	Blk	PF	DQ	Ast	Avg	Off	Tot	Avg	Pts	Avg
87-88 SA							Did not play basketball — Served in Navy																	
88-89 SA							Did not play basketball — Served in Navy																	
89-90 SA*	82	81	3002	690	1300	.531	0	2	.000	613	837	.732	257	138	319	259	3	164	2.0	303	983	12.0	1993	24.3
90-91 SA*	82	81	3095	754	1366	.552	1	7	.143	592	777	.762	270	127	320	264	5	208	2.5	335	1063	13.0	2101	25.6
91-92 SA*	68	68	2564	592	1074	.551	1	8	.125	393	561	.701	182	158	305	219	2	181	2.7	261	829	12.2	1578	23.2
92-93 SA*	82	82	3211	676	1348	.501	3	17	.176	561	766	.732	241	127	264	239	5	301	3.7	229	956	11.7	1916	23.4
93-94 SA*	80	80	3241	840	1658	.507	10	29	.345	693	925	.749	253	139	265	228	3	381	4.8	241	855	10.7	2383	29.8
94-95 SA*	81	81	3074	788	1487	.530	6	20	.300	656	847	.774	233	134	262	230	2	236	2.9	234	877	10.8	2238	27.6
95-96 SA*	82	82	3019	711	1378	.516	3	9	.333	626	823	.761	190	111	271	262	1	247	3.0	319	1000	12.0	2051	25.0
96-97 SA	6	6	147	36	72	.500	0	0	—	34	52	.654	8	6	6	9	0	8	1.3	19	51	8.5	106	17.7
97-98 SA*	73	73	2457	544	1065	.511	1	4	.250	485	660	.735	202	64	192	204	2	199	2.7	239	775	10.6	1574	21.6
98-99 SA	49	49	1554	268	527	.509	0	1	.000	239	363	.658	108	69	119	143	0	103	2.1	148	492	10.0	775	15.8
99-00 SA*	80	80	2557	528	1031	.512	0	2	.000	371	511	.726	164	97	183	247	1	142	1.8	193	770	9.6	1427	17.8
11 Years	765	763	27921	6427	12306	.522	25	99	.253	5263	7122	.739	2108	1170	2506	2304	24	2170	2.8	2521	8651	11.3	18142	23.7

NBA Postseason																								
Year Tm	G	GS	Min	Md	Att	Pct	Md	Att	Pct	Md	Att	Pct	TO	Stl	Blk	PF	DQ	Ast	Avg	Off	Tot	Avg	Pts	Avg
89-90 SA	10	10	375	89	167	.533	0	0	—	65	96	.677	24	11	40	35	1	23	2.3	36	120	12.0	243	24.3
90-91 SA	4	4	166	35	51	.686	0	1	.000	33	38	.868	15	6	15	11	0	8	2.0	11	54	13.5	103	25.8
92-93 SA	10	10	421	79	170	.465	0	1	.000	73	110	.664	25	10	36	39	0	40	4.0	29	126	12.6	231	23.1
93-94 SA	4	4	146	30	73	.411	0	1	.000	20	27	.741	9	3	10	14	0	14	3.5	13	40	10.0	80	20.0
94-95 SA	15	15	623	129	289	.446	1	5	.200	121	149	.812	56	22	39	63	1	47	3.1	57	182	12.1	380	25.3
95-96 SA	10	10	353	83	161	.516	0	0	—	70	105	.667	24	15	25	38	2	24	2.4	37	101	10.1	236	23.6
97-98 SA	9	9	353	57	134	.425	0	0	—	61	96	.635	25	11	30	28	1	23	2.6	41	127	14.1	175	19.4
98-99 SA	17	17	600	87	180	.483	0	0	—	91	126	.722	40	28	40	61	1	43	2.5	36	168	9.9	265	15.6
99-00 SA	4	4	155	31	83	.373	0	1	.000	32	42	.762	8	7	12	15	0	10	2.5	17	55	13.8	94	23.5
9 Years	83	83	3192	620	1308	.474	1	9	.111	566	789	.717	226	113	247	304	6	232	2.8	277	973	11.7	1807	21.8

Eddie Robinson

Pos: F **College:** Central Oklahoma **Drafted:** '99 FA—Cha   **Ht:** 6'9" **Wt:** 210 **Born:** 4/19/76 **Age:** 24

College			Field Goals			3-Pt FGs			Free Throws			Misc			Fouls		Assists		Rebounds			Points	
Year Tm	G	GS	Min	Md	Att	Pct	Md	Att	Pct	Md	Att	Pct	TO	Stl	Blk	PF	DQ	Ast	Avg	Off	Tot	Avg	Pts	Avg
97-98 CnOk	27	—	690	170	331	.514	27	101	.267	33	49	.673	49	48	35	41	—	21	0.8	—	200	7.4	400	14.8
98-99 CnOk	26	—	872	305	550	.555	24	74	.324	95	123	.772	50	56	58	32	—	40	1.5	—	246	9.5	729	28.0
2 Years	53	—	1562	475	881	.539	51	175	.291	128	172	.744	99	104	93	73	—	61	1.2	—	446	8.4	1129	21.3

NBA			Field Goals			3-Pt FGs			Free Throws			Misc			Fouls		Assists		Rebounds			Points	
Year Tm	G	GS	Min	Md	Att	Pct	Md	Att	Pct	Md	Att	Pct	TO	Stl	Blk	PF	DQ	Ast	Avg	Off	Tot	Avg	Pts	Avg
99-00 Cha	67	8	1112	212	386	.549	0	4	.000	47	64	.734	39	48	25	67	0	32	0.5	54	184	2.7	471	7.0

NBA Postseason																								
Year Tm	G	GS	Min	Md	Att	Pct	Md	Att	Pct	Md	Att	Pct	TO	Stl	Blk	PF	DQ	Ast	Avg	Off	Tot	Avg	Pts	Avg
99-00 Cha	4	0	45	5	12	.417	0	0	—	2	2	1.000	1	2	1	2	0	4	1.0	1	3	0.8	12	3.0

Glenn Robinson

(statistical profile on page 269)

Pos: F **College:** Purdue **Drafted:** '94 1(1)—Mil   **Ht:** 6'7" **Wt:** 230 **Born:** 1/10/73 **Age:** 28

College			Field Goals			3-Pt FGs			Free Throws			Misc			Fouls		Assists		Rebounds			Points	
Year Tm	G	GS	Min	Md	Att	Pct	Md	Att	Pct	Md	Att	Pct	TO	Stl	Blk	PF	DQ	Ast	Avg	Off	Tot	Avg	Pts	Avg
92-93 Pur	28	28	1010	246	519	.474	32	80	.400	152	205	.741	103	54	82	82	3	49	1.8	77	258	9.2	676	24.1
93-94 Pur	34	34	1166	368	762	.483	79	208	.380	215	270	.796	139	56	31	88	2	66	1.9	102	344	10.1	1030	30.3
2 Years	62	62	2176	614	1281	.479	111	288	.385	367	475	.773	242	113	65	170	5	115	1.9	179	602	9.7	1706	27.5

NBA			Field Goals			3-Pt FGs			Free Throws			Misc			Fouls		Assists		Rebounds			Points	
Year Tm	G	GS	Min	Md	Att	Pct	Md	Att	Pct	Md	Att	Pct	TO	Stl	Blk	PF	DQ	Ast	Avg	Off	Tot	Avg	Pts	Avg
94-95 Mil	80	76	2958	636	1410	.451	86	268	.321	397	499	.796	313	115	22	234	2	197	2.5	169	513	6.4	1755	21.9
95-96 Mil	82	82	3249	627	1382	.454	90	263	.342	316	389	.812	282	95	42	236	2	293	3.6	136	504	6.1	1660	20.2

NBA				Field Goals			3-Pt FGs			Free Throws			Misc			Fouls		Assists		Rebounds			Points	
Year Tm	G	GS	Min	Md	Att	Pct	Md	Att	Pct	Md	Att	Pct	TO	Stl	Blk	PF	DQ	Ast	Avg	Off	Tot	Avg	Pts	Avg
96-97 Mil	80	79	3114	669	1438	.465	63	180	.350	288	364	.791	269	103	68	225	5	248	3.1	130	502	6.3	1689	21.1
97-98 Mil	56	56	2294	534	1136	.470	25	65	.385	215	266	.808	200	69	34	164	2	158	2.8	82	307	5.5	1308	23.4
98-99 Mil	47	47	1579	347	756	.459	31	79	.392	140	161	.870	106	46	41	114	1	100	2.1	73	276	5.9	865	18.4
99-00 Mil*	81	81	2909	690	1461	.472	86	237	.363	227	283	.802	223	78	41	212	3	193	2.4	107	485	6.0	1693	20.9
6 Years	426	421	16103	3503	7583	.462	381	1092	.349	1583	1962	.807	1393	506	248	1185	15	1189	2.8	697	2587	6.1	8970	21.1

NBA Postseason																								
Year Tm	G	GS	Min	Md	Att	Pct	Md	Att	Pct	Md	Att	Pct	TO	Stl	Blk	PF	DQ	Ast	Avg	Off	Tot	Avg	Pts	Avg
98-99 Mil	3	3	118	21	51	.412	4	8	.500	16	18	.889	10	3	2	5	0	5	1.7	4	25	8.3	62	20.7
99-00 Mil	5	5	174	32	79	.405	2	7	.286	11	13	.846	15	8	4	18	0	13	2.6	0	21	4.2	77	15.4
2 Years	8	8	292	53	130	.408	6	15	.400	27	31	.871	25	11	6	23	0	18	2.3	4	46	5.8	139	17.4

Dennis Rodman

Pos: F **College:** Southeastern Okla. St. **Drafted:** '86 2(27)—Det **Ht:** 6'6" **Wt:** 220 **Born:** 5/13/61 **Age:** 39

College				Field Goals			3-Pt FGs			Free Throws			Misc			Fouls		Assists		Rebounds			Points	
Year Tm	G	GS	Min	Md	Att	Pct	Md	Att	Pct	Md	Att	Pct	TO	Stl	Blk	PF	DQ	Ast	Avg	Off	Tot	Avg	Pts	Avg
83-84 SEOk	30	—	—	303	490	.618	—	—	—	173	264	.655	76	31	30	88	—	23	0.8	—	392	13.1	779	26.0
84-85 SEOk	32	—	—	353	545	.648	—	—	—	151	267	.566	91	39	40	109	—	12	0.4	—	510	15.9	857	26.8
85-86 SEOk	34	—	—	332	515	.645	—	—	—	165	252	.655	116	61	53	107	—	26	0.8	—	605	17.8	829	24.4
3 Years	96	—	—	988	1550	.637	—	—	—	489	783	.625	283	131	123	304	—	61	0.6	—	1507	15.7	2465	25.7

NBA				Field Goals			3-Pt FGs			Free Throws			Misc			Fouls		Assists		Rebounds			Points	
Year Tm	G	GS	Min	Md	Att	Pct	Md	Att	Pct	Md	Att	Pct	TO	Stl	Blk	PF	DQ	Ast	Avg	Off	Tot	Avg	Pts	Avg
86-87 Det	77	1	1155	213	391	.545	0	1	.000	74	126	.587	93	38	48	166	1	56	0.7	163	332	4.3	500	6.5
87-88 Det	82	32	2147	398	709	.561	5	17	.294	152	284	.535	156	75	45	273	5	110	1.3	318	715	8.7	953	11.6
88-89 Det	82	8	2208	316	531	.595	6	26	.231	97	155	.626	126	55	76	292	4	99	1.2	327	772	9.4	735	9.0
89-90 Det*	82	43	2377	288	496	.581	1	9	.111	142	217	.654	90	52	60	276	2	72	0.9	336	792	9.7	719	8.8
90-91 Det*	82	77	2747	276	560	.493	6	30	.200	111	176	.631	94	65	55	281	7	85	1.0	361	1026	12.5	669	8.2
91-92 Det*	82	80	3301	342	635	.539	32	101	.317	84	140	.600	140	68	70	248	0	191	2.3	523	1530	18.7	800	9.8
92-93 Det	62	55	2410	183	429	.427	15	73	.205	87	163	.534	103	48	45	201	0	102	1.6	367	1132	18.3	468	7.5
93-94 SA	79	51	2989	156	292	.534	5	24	.208	53	102	.520	138	52	32	229	0	184	2.3	453	1367	17.3	370	4.7
94-95 SA	49	26	1568	137	240	.571	0	2	.000	75	111	.676	98	31	23	159	1	97	2.0	274	823	16.8	349	7.1
95-96 Chi	64	57	2088	146	304	.480	3	27	.111	56	106	.528	138	36	27	196	1	160	2.5	356	952	14.9	351	5.5
96-97 Chi	55	54	1947	128	286	.448	5	19	.263	50	88	.568	111	32	19	172	1	170	3.1	320	883	16.1	311	5.7
97-98 Chi	80	66	2856	155	360	.431	4	23	.174	61	111	.550	147	47	18	238	2	230	2.9	421	1201	15.0	375	4.7
98-99 LAL	23	11	657	16	46	.348	0	2	.000	17	39	.436	31	10	12	71	0	30	1.3	62	258	11.2	49	2.1
99-00 Dal	12	12	389	12	31	.387	0	1	.000	10	14	.714	19	2	1	41	2	14	1.2	48	171	14.3	34	2.8
14 Years	911	573	28839	2766	5310	.521	82	355	.231	1069	1832	.584	1484	611	531	2843	26	1600	1.8	4329	11954	13.1	6683	7.3

NBA Postseason																								
Year Tm	G	GS	Min	Md	Att	Pct	Md	Att	Pct	Md	Att	Pct	TO	Stl	Blk	PF	DQ	Ast	Avg	Off	Tot	Avg	Pts	Avg
86-87 Det	15	0	245	40	74	.541	0	0	—	18	32	.563	17	6	17	48	0	3	0.2	32	71	4.7	98	6.5
87-88 Det	23	0	474	71	136	.522	0	2	.000	22	54	.407	31	14	14	87	1	21	0.9	51	136	5.9	164	7.1
88-89 Det	17	0	409	37	70	.529	0	4	.000	24	35	.686	24	6	12	58	0	16	0.9	56	170	10.0	98	5.8
89-90 Det	19	17	560	54	95	.568	0	0	—	18	35	.514	31	9	13	62	1	17	0.9	55	161	8.5	126	6.6
90-91 Det	15	14	495	41	91	.451	2	9	.222	10	24	.417	13	11	10	55	1	14	0.9	67	177	11.8	94	6.3
91-92 Det	5	5	156	16	27	.593	0	2	.000	4	8	.500	7	4	2	17	0	9	1.8	16	51	10.2	36	7.2
93-94 SA	3	3	114	12	24	.500	0	5	.000	1	6	.167	6	6	4	14	0	2	0.7	24	48	16.0	25	8.3
94-95 SA	14	12	459	52	96	.542	0	5	.000	20	35	.571	25	12	1	51	1	18	1.3	69	207	14.8	124	8.9
95-96 Chi	18	15	620	50	103	.485	0	0	—	35	59	.593	41	14	8	76	1	37	2.1	98	247	13.7	135	7.5
96-97 Chi	19	14	535	30	81	.370	4	16	.250	15	26	.577	28	10	4	74	3	27	1.4	59	160	8.4	79	4.2
97-98 Chi	21	9	722	39	105	.371	1	4	.250	23	38	.605	35	14	13	88	4	41	2.0	99	248	11.8	102	4.9
11 Years	169	89	4789	442	902	.490	7	47	.149	190	352	.540	258	106	98	630	12	205	1.2	626	1676	9.9	1081	6.4

Carlos Rogers

Pos: F-C **College:** Tennessee State **Drafted:** '94 1(11)—Sea **Ht:** 6'10" **Wt:** 232 **Born:** 2/6/71 **Age:** 29

College				Field Goals			3-Pt FGs			Free Throws			Misc			Fouls		Assists		Rebounds			Points	
Year Tm	G	GS	Min	Md	Att	Pct	Md	Att	Pct	Md	Att	Pct	TO	Stl	Blk	PF	DQ	Ast	Avg	Off	Tot	Avg	Pts	Avg
90-91 Ak-LR	19	—	393	64	126	.508	0	0	—	31	56	.554	30	11	38	127	—	22	1.2	—	132	6.9	159	8.4
92-93 TnSt	29	—	918	239	385	.621	0	3	.000	111	178	.624	63	19	93	103	—	30	1.0	—	339	11.7	589	20.3
93-94 TnSt	31	—	1052	288	469	.614	4	13	.308	179	276	.649	122	21	93	89	—	47	1.5	—	358	11.5	759	24.5
3 Years	79	—	2363	591	980	.603	4	16	.250	321	510	.629	215	51	224	319	—	99	1.3	—	829	10.5	1507	19.1

NBA				Field Goals			3-Pt FGs			Free Throws			Misc			Fouls		Assists		Rebounds			Points	
Year Tm	G	GS	Min	Md	Att	Pct	Md	Att	Pct	Md	Att	Pct	TO	Stl	Blk	PF	DQ	Ast	Avg	Off	Tot	Avg	Pts	Avg
94-95 GS	49	18	1017	180	340	.529	2	14	.143	76	146	.521	84	22	52	124	2	37	0.8	108	278	5.7	438	8.9

NBA				Field Goals			3-Pt FGs			Free Throws			Misc			Fouls		Assists		Rebounds			Points	
Year Tm	G	GS	Min	Md	Att	Pct	Md	Att	Pct	Md	Att	Pct	TO	Stl	Blk	PF	DQ	Ast	Avg	Off	Tot	Avg	Pts	Avg
95-96 Tor	56	18	1043	178	344	.517	3	21	.143	71	130	.546	61	25	48	87	0	35	0.6	80	170	3.0	430	7.7
96-97 Tor	56	3	1397	212	404	.525	25	66	.379	102	170	.600	53	42	69	140	1	37	0.7	120	304	5.4	551	9.8
97-98 2Tm	21	0	376	47	91	.516	0	2	.000	18	32	.563	14	10	8	35	0	18	0.9	35	67	3.2	112	5.3
98-99 Por	2	0	8	2	2	1.000	0	0	—	1	4	.250	0	0	0	2	0	1	0.5	0	1	0.5	5	2.5
99-00 Hou	53	15	1101	170	324	.525	1	14	.071	81	137	.591	63	14	34	77	0	42	0.8	98	275	5.2	422	8.0
97-98 Tor	18	0	351	45	87	.517	0	1	.000	18	32	.563	13	9	8	34	0	16	0.9	34	65	3.6	108	6.0
Por	3	0	25	2	4	.500	0	1	.000	0	0	—	1	1	0	1	0	2	0.7	1	2	0.7	4	1.3
6 Years	237	54	4942	789	1505	.524	31	117	.265	349	619	.564	275	113	211	465	3	170	0.7	441	1095	4.6	1958	8.3

Rodney Rogers

Pos: F **College:** Wake Forest **Drafted:** '93 1(9)—Den   (statistical profile on page 269)

Ht: 6'7" **Wt:** 255 **Born:** 6/20/71 **Age:** 29

College				Field Goals			3-Pt FGs			Free Throws			Misc			Fouls		Assists		Rebounds			Points	
Year Tm	G	GS	Min	Md	Att	Pct	Md	Att	Pct	Md	Att	Pct	TO	Stl	Blk	PF	DQ	Ast	Avg	Off	Tot	Avg	Pts	Avg
90-91 Wake	30	29	895	199	349	.570	10	35	.286	81	121	.669	81	53	19	83	—	46	1.5	89	237	7.9	489	16.3
91-92 Wake	29	28	945	245	399	.614	19	50	.380	86	126	.683	69	39	27	86	—	81	2.8	98	247	8.5	595	20.5
92-93 Wake	30	29	981	239	431	.555	24	67	.358	134	187	.717	97	54	28	80	—	68	2.3	79	221	7.4	636	21.2
3 Years	89	86	2821	683	1179	.579	53	152	.349	301	434	.694	247	146	74	249		195	2.2	266	705	7.9	1720	19.3

NBA				Field Goals			3-Pt FGs			Free Throws			Misc			Fouls		Assists		Rebounds			Points	
Year Tm	G	GS	Min	Md	Att	Pct	Md	Att	Pct	Md	Att	Pct	TO	Stl	Blk	PF	DQ	Ast	Avg	Off	Tot	Avg	Pts	Avg
93-94 Den	79	14	1406	239	545	.439	35	92	.380	127	189	.672	131	63	48	195	3	101	1.3	90	226	2.9	640	8.1
94-95 Den	80	77	2142	375	769	.488	50	148	.338	179	275	.651	173	95	46	281	7	161	2.0	132	385	4.8	979	12.2
95-96 LAC	67	51	1950	306	641	.477	49	153	.320	113	180	.628	144	75	35	216	2	167	2.5	113	286	4.3	774	11.6
96-97 LAC	81	62	2480	408	884	.462	65	180	.361	191	288	.663	221	88	61	272	5	222	2.7	137	411	5.1	1072	13.2
97-98 LAC	76	70	2499	426	935	.456	72	212	.340	225	328	.686	193	93	38	242	5	202	2.7	155	424	5.6	1149	15.1
98-99 LAC	47	7	967	131	297	.441	18	63	.286	68	101	.673	66	47	22	140	2	77	1.6	65	179	3.8	348	7.4
99-00 Pho	82	7	2286	428	881	.486	115	262	.439	159	249	.639	163	94	47	290	5	170	2.1	138	447	5.5	1130	13.8
7 Years	512	288	13730	2313	4952	.467	404	1110	.364	1062	1610	.660	1091	555	297	1636	29	1100	2.1	830	2358	4.6	6092	11.9

NBA Postseason																								
Year Tm	G	GS	Min	Md	Att	Pct	Md	Att	Pct	Md	Att	Pct	TO	Stl	Blk	PF	DQ	Ast	Avg	Off	Tot	Avg	Pts	Avg
93-94 Den	12	0	190	19	49	.388	6	19	.316	17	27	.630	8	7	6	25	0	16	1.3	8	21	1.8	61	5.1
94-95 Den	3	3	76	12	22	.545	1	4	.250	1	4	.250	5	3	4	13	1	5	1.7	1	12	4.0	26	8.7
96-97 LAC	3	3	85	12	29	.414	2	10	.200	6	8	.750	7	4	3	13	0	6	2.0	3	7	2.3	32	10.7
99-00 Pho	9	0	263	48	115	.417	8	36	.222	23	31	.742	15	10	10	31	1	14	1.6	16	61	6.8	127	14.1
4 Years	27	6	614	91	215	.423	17	69	.246	47	70	.671	35	24	23	82	2	41	1.5	28	101	3.7	246	9.1

Roy Rogers

Pos: F **College:** Alabama **Drafted:** '96 FA—Van

Ht: 6'10" **Wt:** 235 **Born:** 8/19/73 **Age:** 27

College				Field Goals			3-Pt FGs			Free Throws			Misc			Fouls		Assists		Rebounds			Points	
Year Tm	G	GS	Min	Md	Att	Pct	Md	Att	Pct	Md	Att	Pct	TO	Stl	Blk	PF	DQ	Ast	Avg	Off	Tot	Avg	Pts	Avg
92-93 Ala	14	—	155	16	31	.516	0	1	.000	3	6	.500	9	1	14	20	—	4	0.3	—	32	2.3	35	2.5
93-94 Ala	23	—	275	27	55	.491	0	0	—	15	22	.682	19	9	28	30	—	2	0.1	—	63	2.7	69	3.0
94-95 Ala	33	—	479	47	93	.505	0	0	—	21	38	.553	36	10	68	52	—	19	0.6	—	120	3.6	115	3.5
95-96 Ala	32	32	1173	186	355	.524	0	1	.000	61	98	.622	61	21	156	74	0	30	0.9	92	299	9.3	433	13.5
4 Years	102	—	2082	276	534	.517	0	2	.000	100	164	.610	125	41	266	176		55	0.5		514	5.0	652	6.4

NBA				Field Goals			3-Pt FGs			Free Throws			Misc			Fouls		Assists		Rebounds			Points	
Year Tm	G	GS	Min	Md	Att	Pct	Md	Att	Pct	Md	Att	Pct	TO	Stl	Blk	PF	DQ	Ast	Avg	Off	Tot	Avg	Pts	Avg
96-97 Van	82	50	1848	244	483	.505	1	1	1.000	54	94	.574	86	21	161	214	1	46	0.6	139	386	4.7	543	6.6
97-98 2Tm	15	0	106	9	25	.360	0	0	—	2	6	.333	5	3	8	18	0	2	0.1	8	17	1.1	20	1.3
98-99 Hou										Active but did not play														
99-00 Den	40	0	355	35	88	.398	0	1	.000	19	41	.463	10	2	38	36	0	9	0.2	33	80	2.0	89	2.2
97-98 Bos	9	0	37	3	8	.375	0	0	—	1	2	.500	1	2	4	6	0	1	0.1	0	5	0.6	7	0.8
Tor	6	0	69	6	17	.353	0	0	—	1	4	.250	4	1	4	12	0	1	0.2	8	12	2.0	13	2.2
3 Years	137	50	2309	288	596	.483	1	2	.500	75	141	.532	101	26	207	268	1	57	0.4	180	483	3.5	652	4.8

Sean Rooks

Pos: C **College:** Arizona **Drafted:** '92 2(30)—Dal

Ht: 6'10" **Wt:** 260 **Born:** 9/9/69 **Age:** 31

College				Field Goals			3-Pt FGs			Free Throws			Misc			Fouls		Assists		Rebounds			Points	
Year Tm	G	GS	Min	Md	Att	Pct	Md	Att	Pct	Md	Att	Pct	TO	Stl	Blk	PF	DQ	Ast	Avg	Off	Tot	Avg	Pts	Avg
88-89 Ari	32	1	362	70	117	.598	0	0	—	40	65	.615	30	6	18	53	1	18	0.6	33	88	2.8	180	5.6
89-90 Ari	31	6	684	140	263	.532	0	0	—	114	161	.708	57	14	49	80	2	31	1.0	51	151	4.9	394	12.7

College				Field Goals			3-Pt FGs			Free Throws			Misc			Fouls		Assists		Rebounds			Points	
Year Tm	G	GS	Min	Md	Att	Pct	Md	Att	Pct	Md	Att	Pct	TO	Stl	Blk	PF	DQ	Ast	Avg	Off	Tot	Avg	Pts	Avg
90-91 Ari	35	26	800	159	283	.562	2	4	.500	98	149	.658	75	16	43	81	1	43	1.2	67	198	5.7	418	11.9
91-92 Ari	31	29	878	181	323	.560	3	5	.600	140	215	.651	68	27	32	83	2	54	1.7	74	214	6.9	505	16.3
4 Years	129	62	2724	550	986	.558	5	9	.556	392	590	.664	230	63	142	297	6	146	1.1	225	651	5.0	1497	11.6

NBA				Field Goals			3-Pt FGs			Free Throws			Misc			Fouls		Assists		Rebounds			Points	
Year Tm	G	GS	Min	Md	Att	Pct	Md	Att	Pct	Md	Att	Pct	TO	Stl	Blk	PF	DQ	Ast	Avg	Off	Tot	Avg	Pts	Avg
92-93 Dal	72	68	2087	368	747	.493	0	2	.000	234	389	.602	160	38	81	204	2	95	1.3	196	536	7.4	970	13.5
93-94 Dal	47	28	1255	193	393	.491	0	1	.000	150	210	.714	80	21	44	109	0	49	1.0	84	259	5.5	536	11.4
94-95 Min	80	70	2405	289	615	.470	0	5	.000	290	381	.761	142	29	71	208	1	97	1.2	165	486	6.1	868	10.9
95-96 2Tm	65	7	1117	144	285	.505	1	7	.143	135	202	.668	80	23	42	141	0	47	0.7	81	255	3.9	424	6.5
96-97 LAL	69	3	735	87	185	.470	0	1	.000	91	130	.700	51	17	38	123	1	42	0.6	56	163	2.4	265	3.8
97-98 LAL	41	1	425	46	101	.455	0	0	—	47	79	.595	19	2	23	68	0	24	0.6	46	118	2.9	139	3.4
98-99 LAL	36	0	315	32	79	.405	0	2	.000	34	48	.708	21	2	9	61	0	9	0.3	33	72	2.0	98	2.7
99-00 Dal	71	13	1001	122	283	.431	0	0	—	65	89	.730	70	29	52	169	0	68	1.0	82	248	3.5	309	4.4
95-96 Min	49	7	902	112	227	.493	1	6	.167	106	159	.667	49	19	28	106	0	38	0.8	60	204	4.2	331	6.8
Atl	16	0	215	32	58	.552	0	1	.000	29	43	.674	31	4	14	35	0	9	0.6	21	51	3.2	93	5.8
8 Years	481	190	9340	1281	2688	.477	1	18	.056	1046	1528	.685	623	161	360	1083	4	431	0.9	743	2137	4.4	3609	7.5

NBA Postseason

Year Tm	G	GS	Min	Md	Att	Pct	Md	Att	Pct	Md	Att	Pct	TO	Stl	Blk	PF	DQ	Ast	Avg	Off	Tot	Avg	Pts	Avg
95-96 Atl	10	0	140	16	28	.571	0	0	—	13	21	.619	9	4	4	35	0	7	0.7	13	27	2.7	45	4.5
96-97 LAL	8	0	54	4	9	.444	0	0	—	6	8	.750	3	3	3	10	0	1	0.1	5	12	1.5	14	1.8
97-98 LAL	4	0	11	2	6	.333	0	0	—	0	0	—	0	0	3	2	0	0	0.0	1	1	0.3	4	1.0
98-99 LAL	7	0	48	2	6	.333	0	0	—	5	6	.833	1	0	1	13	0	3	0.4	1	2	0.3	9	1.3
4 Years	29	0	253	24	49	.490	0	0	—	24	35	.686	13	7	11	60	0	11	0.4	20	42	1.4	72	2.5

Jalen Rose
(statistical profile on page 270)

Pos: G-F **College:** Michigan **Drafted:** '94 1(13)—Den **Ht:** 6'8" **Wt:** 225 **Born:** 1/30/73 **Age:** 28

College				Field Goals			3-Pt FGs			Free Throws			Misc			Fouls		Assists		Rebounds			Points	
Year Tm	G	GS	Min	Md	Att	Pct	Md	Att	Pct	Md	Att	Pct	TO	Stl	Blk	PF	DQ	Ast	Avg	Off	Tot	Avg	Pts	Avg
91-92 Mich	34	33	1126	206	424	.486	36	111	.324	149	197	.756	114	38	8	75	0	135	4.0	52	146	4.3	597	17.6
92-93 Mich	36	36	1232	203	455	.446	33	103	.320	116	161	.720	113	43	15	82	1	140	3.9	37	150	4.2	555	15.4
93-94 Mich	32	32	1152	220	477	.461	55	155	.355	141	192	.734	85	38	6	84	2	126	3.9	53	181	5.7	636	19.9
3 Years	102	101	3510	629	1356	.464	124	369	.336	406	550	.738	312	119	29	241	3	401	3.9	142	477	4.7	1788	17.5

NBA				Field Goals			3-Pt FGs			Free Throws			Misc			Fouls		Assists		Rebounds			Points	
Year Tm	G	GS	Min	Md	Att	Pct	Md	Att	Pct	Md	Att	Pct	TO	Stl	Blk	PF	DQ	Ast	Avg	Off	Tot	Avg	Pts	Avg
94-95 Den	81	37	1798	227	500	.454	36	114	.316	173	234	.739	160	65	22	206	0	389	4.8	57	217	2.7	663	8.2
95-96 Den	80	37	2134	290	604	.480	32	108	.296	191	277	.690	234	53	39	229	3	495	6.2	46	260	3.3	803	10.0
96-97 Ind	66	6	1188	172	377	.456	21	72	.292	117	156	.750	107	57	18	136	1	155	2.3	27	121	1.8	482	7.3
97-98 Ind	82	0	1706	290	607	.478	25	73	.342	166	228	.728	132	56	14	171	0	155	1.9	28	195	2.4	771	9.4
98-99 Ind	49	1	1238	200	496	.403	17	65	.262	125	158	.791	72	50	15	128	0	93	1.9	34	154	3.1	542	11.1
99-00 Ind	80	80	2978	563	1196	.471	77	196	.393	254	307	.827	188	84	49	234	1	320	4.0	42	387	4.8	1457	18.2
6 Years	438	161	11042	1742	3780	.461	208	628	.331	1026	1360	.754	893	365	157	1104	5	1607	3.7	234	1334	3.0	4718	10.8

NBA Postseason

Year Tm	G	GS	Min	Md	Att	Pct	Md	Att	Pct	Md	Att	Pct	TO	Stl	Blk	PF	DQ	Ast	Avg	Off	Tot	Avg	Pts	Avg
94-95 Den	3	3	99	13	28	.464	1	4	.250	3	5	.600	9	3	2	9	0	18	6.0	4	11	3.7	30	10.0
97-98 Ind	15	0	293	48	100	.480	6	16	.375	20	27	.741	25	11	6	37	0	28	1.9	1	27	1.8	122	8.1
98-99 Ind	13	0	355	61	138	.442	8	23	.348	28	34	.824	25	13	5	39	0	32	2.5	11	31	2.4	158	12.2
99-00 Ind	23	23	964	171	391	.437	30	70	.429	107	133	.805	50	16	11	71	0	78	3.4	10	101	4.4	479	20.8
4 Years	54	26	1711	293	657	.446	45	113	.398	158	199	.794	109	43	24	156	0	156	2.9	26	170	3.1	789	14.6

Malik Rose
(statistical profile on page 270)

Pos: F **College:** Drexel **Drafted:** '96 2(44)—Cha **Ht:** 6'7" **Wt:** 255 **Born:** 11/23/74 **Age:** 26

College				Field Goals			3-Pt FGs			Free Throws			Misc			Fouls		Assists		Rebounds			Points	
Year Tm	G	GS	Min	Md	Att	Pct	Md	Att	Pct	Md	Att	Pct	TO	Stl	Blk	PF	DQ	Ast	Avg	Off	Tot	Avg	Pts	Avg
92-93 Drex	29	—	820	144	287	.502	0	0	—	107	190	.563	75	13	24	111	—	10	0.3	—	330	11.4	395	13.6
93-94 Drex	30	—	875	154	296	.520	0	0	—	110	202	.545	76	10	29	103	—	20	0.7	—	371	12.4	418	13.9
94-95 Drex	30	—	984	216	384	.563	0	3	.000	152	213	.714	102	34	38	103	—	36	1.2	—	404	13.5	584	19.5
95-96 Drex	31	31	972	219	368	.595	7	21	.333	182	255	.714	87	35	30	85	1	53	1.7	100	409	13.2	627	20.2
4 Years	120	—	3651	733	1335	.549	7	24	.292	551	860	.641	340	92	121	402	—	119	1.0	—	1514	12.6	2024	16.9

NBA				Field Goals			3-Pt FGs			Free Throws			Misc			Fouls		Assists		Rebounds			Points	
Year Tm	G	GS	Min	Md	Att	Pct	Md	Att	Pct	Md	Att	Pct	TO	Stl	Blk	PF	DQ	Ast	Avg	Off	Tot	Avg	Pts	Avg
96-97 Cha	54	1	525	61	128	.477	0	2	.000	38	62	.613	41	28	17	114	3	32	0.6	70	164	3.0	160	3.0

	NBA			Field Goals			3-Pt FGs			Free Throws			Misc			Fouls		Assists		Rebounds			Points	
Year Tm	G	GS	Min	Md	Att	Pct	Md	Att	Pct	Md	Att	Pct	TO	Stl	Blk	PF	DQ	Ast	Avg	Off	Tot	Avg	Pts	Avg
97-98 SA	53	0	429	59	136	.434	1	3	.333	39	61	.639	44	21	7	79	1	19	0.4	40	90	1.7	158	3.0
98-99 SA	47	0	608	93	201	.463	0	1	.000	98	146	.671	56	40	22	120	0	29	0.6	90	182	3.9	284	6.0
99-00 SA	74	3	1341	176	385	.457	1	3	.333	143	198	.722	99	35	52	232	2	47	0.6	133	335	4.5	496	6.7
4 Years	228	4	2903	389	850	.458	2	9	.222	318	467	.681	240	124	98	545	6	127	0.6	333	771	3.4	1098	4.8

NBA Postseason																								
Year Tm	G	GS	Min	Md	Att	Pct	Md	Att	Pct	Md	Att	Pct	TO	Stl	Blk	PF	DQ	Ast	Avg	Off	Tot	Avg	Pts	Avg
96-97 Cha	2	0	12	2	4	.500	0	0	—	0	0	—	2	0	0	2	0	1	0.5	4	5	2.5	4	2.0
97-98 SA	5	0	18	4	6	.667	0	0	—	2	4	.500	4	1	0	2	0	1	0.2	3	7	1.4	10	2.0
98-99 SA	17	0	194	14	38	.368	0	0	—	18	26	.692	10	7	4	52	0	3	0.2	17	39	2.3	46	2.7
99-00 SA	4	0	83	8	18	.444	0	0	—	5	9	.556	7	2	3	12	0	1	0.3	5	19	4.8	21	5.3
4 Years	28	0	307	28	66	.424	0	0	—	25	39	.641	23	10	7	68	0	6	0.2	29	70	2.5	81	2.9

Michael Ruffin

Pos: F **College:** Tulsa **Drafted:** '99 2(32)—Chi **Ht:** 6'8" **Wt:** 248 **Born:** 1/21/77 **Age:** 24

College				Field Goals			3-Pt FGs			Free Throws			Misc			Fouls		Assists		Rebounds			Points	
Year Tm	G	GS	Min	Md	Att	Pct	Md	Att	Pct	Md	Att	Pct	TO	Stl	Blk	PF	DQ	Ast	Avg	Off	Tot	Avg	Pts	Avg
95-96 Tuls	30	17	689	78	146	.534	0	1	.000	57	123	.463	49	25	46	77	2	22	0.7	89	232	7.7	213	7.1
96-97 Tuls	34	34	965	98	174	.563	0	1	.000	95	150	.633	74	31	56	92	1	37	1.1	117	341	10.0	291	8.6
97-98 Tuls	31	31	1030	109	217	.502	0	2	.000	104	154	.675	113	36	78	88	2	46	1.5	105	296	9.5	322	10.4
98-99 Tuls	33	33	1063	117	222	.527	0	0	—	149	247	.603	88	61	86	98	3	45	1.4	115	342	10.4	383	11.6
4 Years	128	115	3747	402	759	.530	0	4	.000	405	674	.601	324	153	266	355	8	150	1.2	426	1211	9.5	1209	9.4

NBA				Field Goals			3-Pt FGs			Free Throws			Misc			Fouls		Assists		Rebounds			Points	
Year Tm	G	GS	Min	Md	Att	Pct	Md	Att	Pct	Md	Att	Pct	TO	Stl	Blk	PF	DQ	Ast	Avg	Off	Tot	Avg	Pts	Avg
99-00 Chi	71	6	975	58	138	.420	0	0	—	43	88	.489	59	26	26	170	1	44	0.6	117	250	3.5	159	2.2

Bryon Russell

Pos: F **College:** Long Beach State **Drafted:** '93 2(45)—Uta **Ht:** 6'7" **Wt:** 225 **Born:** 12/31/70 **Age:** 30

(statistical profile on page 271)

College				Field Goals			3-Pt FGs			Free Throws			Misc			Fouls		Assists		Rebounds			Points	
Year Tm	G	GS	Min	Md	Att	Pct	Md	Att	Pct	Md	Att	Pct	TO	Stl	Blk	PF	DQ	Ast	Avg	Off	Tot	Avg	Pts	Avg
90-91 LgBch	28	14	552	83	193	.430	9	28	.321	45	69	.652	62	16	8	87	4	41	1.5	72	162	5.8	220	7.9
91-92 LgBch	26	24	776	126	227	.555	11	28	.393	99	151	.656	57	55	26	96	7	30	1.2	62	192	7.4	362	13.9
92-93 LgBch	32	32	1006	153	285	.537	11	34	.324	104	143	.727	65	54	14	95	2	66	2.1	76	213	6.7	421	13.2
3 Years	86	70	2334	362	705	.513	31	90	.344	248	363	.683	184	125	48	278	13	137	1.6	210	567	6.6	1003	11.7

NBA				Field Goals			3-Pt FGs			Free Throws			Misc			Fouls		Assists		Rebounds			Points	
Year Tm	G	GS	Min	Md	Att	Pct	Md	Att	Pct	Md	Att	Pct	TO	Stl	Blk	PF	DQ	Ast	Avg	Off	Tot	Avg	Pts	Avg
93-94 Uta	67	48	1121	135	279	.484	2	22	.091	62	101	.614	55	68	19	138	0	54	0.8	61	181	2.7	334	5.0
94-95 Uta	63	15	860	104	238	.437	13	44	.295	62	93	.667	42	48	11	101	0	34	0.5	44	141	2.2	283	4.5
95-96 Uta	59	9	577	56	142	.394	14	40	.350	48	67	.716	36	29	8	66	0	29	0.5	28	90	1.5	174	2.9
96-97 Uta	81	81	2525	297	620	.479	108	264	.409	171	244	.701	94	129	27	237	2	123	1.5	79	331	4.1	873	10.8
97-98 Uta	**82**	7	2219	226	525	.430	73	214	.341	213	278	.766	81	90	31	229	2	101	1.2	78	326	4.0	738	9.0
98-99 Uta	50	50	1770	217	468	.464	52	147	.354	136	171	.795	76	76	15	154	3	74	1.5	65	266	5.3	622	12.4
99-00 Uta	82	70	2900	408	914	.446	106	268	.396	237	316	.750	101	128	23	255	3	158	1.9	99	427	5.2	1159	14.1
7 Years	484	280	11972	1443	3186	.453	368	999	.368	929	1270	.731	485	568	134	1180	10	573	1.2	454	1762	3.6	4183	8.6

NBA Postseason																								
Year Tm	G	GS	Min	Md	Att	Pct	Md	Att	Pct	Md	Att	Pct	TO	Stl	Blk	PF	DQ	Ast	Avg	Off	Tot	Avg	Pts	Avg
93-94 Uta	6	0	36	4	10	.400	2	3	.667	6	6	1.000	1	0	0	3	0	3	0.5	4	9	1.5	16	2.7
94-95 Uta	2	0	13	4	7	.571	2	4	.500	1	2	.500	0	1	0	2	0	3	1.5	1	2	1.0	11	5.5
95-96 Uta	18	0	459	58	124	.468	25	53	.472	31	38	.816	10	23	9	42	0	22	1.2	17	75	4.2	172	9.6
96-97 Uta	20	20	758	89	193	.461	36	101	.356	31	43	.721	20	21	6	59	1	27	1.4	18	92	4.6	245	12.3
97-98 Uta	20	13	698	69	147	.469	23	63	.365	58	81	.716	17	21	5	49	0	22	1.1	12	93	4.7	219	11.0
98-99 Uta	11	11	387	49	115	.426	9	36	.250	26	36	.722	11	20	2	37	0	13	1.2	17	67	6.1	133	12.1
99-00 Uta	10	10	371	48	114	.421	13	45	.289	31	41	.756	15	16	5	27	0	21	2.1	9	52	5.2	140	14.0
7 Years	87	54	2722	321	710	.452	110	305	.361	184	247	.745	74	102	27	219	1	111	1.3	78	390	4.5	936	10.8

Arvydas Sabonis

Pos: C **College:** None **Drafted:** '86 1(24)—Por **Ht:** 7'3" **Wt:** 292 **Born:** 12/19/64 **Age:** 36

(statistical profile on page 271)

NBA				Field Goals			3-Pt FGs			Free Throws			Misc			Fouls		Assists		Rebounds		Points	
Year Tm	G	GS	Min	Md	Att	Pct	Md	Att	Pct	Md	Att	Pct	TO	Stl	Blk	PF	DQ	Ast	Avg	Off	Tot	Avg	Pts	Avg
86-87										Played in USSR														
87-88										Did not play: injury — Achilles Tendon														

146

NBA

Year Tm	G	GS	Min	Md	Att	Pct	Md	Att	Pct	Md	Att	Pct	TO	Stl	Blk	PF	DQ	Ast	Avg	Off	Tot	Avg	Pts	Avg
				Field Goals			3-Pt FGs			Free Throws			Misc			Fouls		Assists		Rebounds			Points	
88-89										Played in USSR														
89-90										Played in Spain														
90-91										Played in Spain														
91-92										Played in Spain														
92-93										Played in Spain														
93-94										Played in Spain														
94-95										Played in Spain														
95-96 Por	73	21	1735	394	723	.545	39	104	.375	231	305	.757	154	64	78	211	2	130	1.8	147	588	8.1	1058	14.5
96-97 Por	69	68	1762	328	658	.498	49	132	.371	223	287	.777	151	63	84	203	4	146	2.1	114	547	7.9	928	13.4
97-98 Por	73	73	2333	407	826	.493	30	115	.261	323	405	.798	190	65	80	267	7	218	3.0	149	729	10.0	1167	16.0
98-99 Por	50	48	1349	232	478	.485	7	24	.292	135	175	.771	85	34	63	147	2	119	2.4	88	393	7.9	606	12.1
99-00 Por	66	61	1688	302	598	.505	7	19	.368	167	198	.843	97	43	78	184	3	118	1.8	97	513	7.8	778	11.8
5 Years	331	271	8867	1663	3283	.507	132	394	.335	1079	1370	.788	677	269	383	1012	18	731	2.2	595	2770	8.4	4537	13.7

NBA Postseason

Year Tm	G	GS	Min	Md	Att	Pct	Md	Att	Pct	Md	Att	Pct	TO	Stl	Blk	PF	DQ	Ast	Avg	Off	Tot	Avg	Pts	Avg
95-96 Por	5	5	177	35	81	.432	5	9	.556	43	60	.717	10	4	3	17	0	9	1.8	12	51	10.2	118	23.6
96-97 Por	4	4	108	18	42	.429	2	8	.250	7	8	.875	9	3	3	19	1	9	2.3	8	26	6.5	45	11.3
97-98 Por	4	4	107	18	40	.450	1	2	.500	12	14	.857	10	7	3	19	1	6	1.5	7	31	7.8	49	12.3
98-99 Por	13	13	392	45	113	.398	1	5	.200	39	43	.907	19	15	15	35	0	29	2.2	12	114	8.8	130	10.0
99-00 Por	16	16	493	68	150	.453	6	21	.286	39	49	.796	26	14	13	59	2	31	1.9	19	107	6.7	181	11.3
5 Years	42	42	1277	184	426	.432	15	45	.333	140	174	.805	74	43	37	149	4	84	2.0	58	329	7.8	523	12.5

John Salley

Pos: F-C **College:** Georgia Tech **Drafted:** '86 1(11)—Det **Ht:** 6'11" **Wt:** 255 **Born:** 5/16/64 **Age:** 36

College

Year Tm	G	GS	Min	Md	Att	Pct	Md	Att	Pct	Md	Att	Pct	TO	Stl	Blk	PF	DQ	Ast	Avg	Off	Tot	Avg	Pts	Avg
				Field Goals			3-Pt FGs			Free Throws			Misc			Fouls		Assists		Rebounds			Points	
82-83 GTch	27	27	829	104	207	.502	—	—	—	102	160	.638	69	18	35	97	—	36	1.3	—	153	5.7	310	11.5
83-84 GTch	29	29	992	126	214	.589	—	—	—	89	132	.674	81	22	67	89	—	73	2.5	—	167	5.8	341	11.8
84-85 GTch	35	35	1231	193	308	.627	—	—	—	105	165	.636	97	29	82	103	—	93	2.7	—	250	7.1	491	14.0
85-86 GTch	34	34	1145	172	284	.606	—	—	—	101	170	.594	95	28	59	108	—	117	3.4	—	228	6.7	445	13.1
4 Years	125	125	4197	595	1013	.587	—	—	—	397	627	.633	342	97	243	397	—	319	2.6	—	798	6.4	1587	12.7

NBA

Year Tm	G	GS	Min	Md	Att	Pct	Md	Att	Pct	Md	Att	Pct	TO	Stl	Blk	PF	DQ	Ast	Avg	Off	Tot	Avg	Pts	Avg
				Field Goals			3-Pt FGs			Free Throws			Misc			Fouls		Assists		Rebounds			Points	
86-87 Det	82	2	1463	163	290	.562	0	1	.000	105	171	.614	74	44	125	256	5	54	0.7	108	296	3.6	431	5.3
87-88 Det	82	16	2003	258	456	.566	0	0	—	185	261	.709	120	53	137	294	4	113	1.4	166	402	4.9	701	8.5
88-89 Det	67	21	1458	166	333	.498	0	2	.000	135	195	.692	100	40	72	197	3	75	1.1	134	335	5.0	467	7.0
89-90 Det	82	12	1914	209	408	.512	1	4	.250	174	244	.713	97	51	112	282	7	67	0.8	154	439	5.4	593	7.2
90-91 Det	74	1	1649	179	377	.475	0	1	.000	186	256	.727	91	52	112	240	7	70	0.9	137	327	4.4	544	7.4
91-92 Det	72	38	1774	249	486	.512	0	3	.000	186	260	.715	102	49	110	222	1	116	1.6	106	296	4.1	684	9.5
92-93 Mia	51	34	1422	154	307	.502	0	0	—	115	144	.799	101	32	70	192	7	83	1.6	113	313	6.1	423	8.3
93-94 Mia	76	45	1910	208	436	.477	2	3	.667	164	225	.729	94	56	78	260	4	135	1.8	132	407	5.4	582	7.7
94-95 Mia	75	50	1955	197	395	.499	0	0	—	153	207	.739	97	47	85	279	5	123	1.6	110	336	4.5	547	7.3
95-96 2Tm	42	6	673	63	140	.450	0	0	—	59	85	.694	55	19	27	110	3	54	1.3	46	140	3.3	185	4.4
96-97										Did not play basketball														
97-98										Did not play basketball														
98-99										Did not play basketball														
99-00 LAL	45	3	303	25	69	.362	0	0	—	21	28	.750	18	8	14	67	1	26	0.6	20	65	1.4	71	1.6
95-96 Tor	25	6	482	51	105	.486	0	0	—	47	65	.723	39	11	12	72	3	39	1.6	26	97	3.9	149	6.0
Chi	17	0	191	12	35	.343	0	0	—	12	20	.600	16	8	15	38	0	15	0.9	20	43	2.5	36	2.1
11 Years	748	228	16524	1871	3697	.506	3	14	.214	1483	2076	.714	949	451	983	2399	47	916	1.2	1226	3356	4.5	5228	7.0

NBA Postseason

Year Tm	G	GS	Min	Md	Att	Pct	Md	Att	Pct	Md	Att	Pct	TO	Stl	Blk	PF	DQ	Ast	Avg	Off	Tot	Avg	Pts	Avg
86-87 Det	15	0	311	33	66	.500	0	0	—	27	42	.643	14	3	17	60	1	11	0.7	30	72	4.8	93	6.2
87-88 Det	23	0	623	56	104	.538	0	1	.000	49	69	.710	23	15	37	88	2	21	0.9	64	155	6.7	161	7.0
88-89 Det	17	0	392	58	99	.586	0	0	—	36	54	.667	12	9	25	58	0	9	0.5	34	79	4.6	152	8.9
89-90 Det	20	0	547	58	122	.475	0	0	—	74	98	.755	29	9	33	76	2	20	1.0	57	117	5.9	190	9.5
90-91 Det	15	0	308	38	70	.543	0	0	—	36	60	.600	13	6	20	58	1	11	0.7	20	62	4.1	112	7.5
91-92 Det	5	1	149	20	44	.455	0	1	.000	23	28	.821	9	3	14	18	0	14	2.8	10	30	6.0	63	12.6
93-94 Mia	5	5	201	22	57	.386	0	0	—	11	16	.688	6	2	5	21	1	8	1.6	16	40	8.0	55	11.0
95-96 Chi	16	0	85	6	11	.545	0	0	—	2	7	.286	4	1	2	25	0	6	0.4	4	11	0.7	14	0.9
99-00 LAL	18	0	78	5	13	.385	0	0	—	7	10	.700	4	1	6	16	0	4	0.2	9	22	1.2	17	0.9
9 Years	134	6	2694	296	586	.505	0	2	.000	265	384	.690	107	49	159	420	7	104	0.8	244	588	4.4	857	6.4

Detlef Schrempf

(statistical profile on page 272)

Pos: F **College:** Washington **Drafted:** '85 1(8)—Dal   **Ht:** 6'10" **Wt:** 235 **Born:** 1/21/63 **Age:** 38

College

Year Tm	G	GS	Min	Md	Att	Pct	Md	Att	Pct	Md	Att	Pct	TO	Stl	Blk	PF	DQ	Ast	Avg	Off	Tot	Avg	Pts	Avg
				Field Goals			**3-Pt FGs**			**Free Throws**			**Misc**			**Fouls**		**Assists**		**Rebounds**			**Points**	
81-82 Wash	28	—	314	33	73	.452	—	—	—	26	47	.553	22	3	2	54	1	13	0.5	—	56	2.0	92	3.3
82-83 Wash	31	—	958	124	266	.466	—	—	—	81	113	.717	76	17	8	115	8	44	1.4	—	211	6.8	329	10.6
83-84 Wash	31	—	1186	195	362	.539	—	—	—	131	178	.736	—	32	12	—	—	93	3.0	—	230	7.4	521	16.8
84-85 Wash	32	31	1180	191	342	.558	—	—	—	125	175	.714	—	17	20	—	—	134	4.2	—	255	8.0	507	15.8
4 Years	122	—	3638	543	1043	.521	—	—	—	363	513	.708	—	69	42	—	—	284	2.3	—	752	6.2	1449	11.9

NBA

Year Tm	G	GS	Min	Md	Att	Pct	Md	Att	Pct	Md	Att	Pct	TO	Stl	Blk	PF	DQ	Ast	Avg	Off	Tot	Avg	Pts	Avg
				Field Goals			**3-Pt FGs**			**Free Throws**			**Misc**			**Fouls**		**Assists**		**Rebounds**			**Points**	
85-86 Dal	64	12	969	142	315	.451	3	7	.429	110	152	.724	84	23	10	166	1	88	1.4	70	198	3.1	397	6.2
86-87 Dal	81	5	1711	265	561	.472	33	69	.478	193	260	.742	110	50	16	224	2	161	2.0	87	303	3.7	756	9.3
87-88 Dal	82	4	1587	246	539	.456	5	32	.156	201	266	.756	108	42	32	189	0	159	1.9	102	279	3.4	698	8.5
88-89 2Tm	69	13	1850	274	578	.474	7	35	.200	273	350	.780	133	53	19	220	3	179	2.6	126	395	5.7	828	12.0
89-90 Ind	78	18	2573	424	822	.516	17	48	.354	402	490	.820	180	59	16	271	6	247	3.2	149	620	7.9	1267	16.2
90-91 Ind	82	3	2632	432	831	.520	15	40	.375	441	539	.818	175	58	22	262	3	301	3.7	178	660	8.0	1320	16.1
91-92 Ind	80	4	2605	496	925	.536	23	71	.324	365	441	.828	191	62	37	286	4	312	3.9	202	770	9.6	1380	17.3
92-93 Ind*	82	60	3098	517	1085	.476	8	52	.154	525	653	.804	243	79	27	305	3	493	6.0	210	780	9.5	1567	19.1
93-94 Sea	81	80	2728	445	903	.493	22	68	.324	300	390	.769	173	73	9	273	3	275	3.4	144	454	5.6	1212	15.0
94-95 Sea*	82	82	2886	521	997	.523	93	181	.514	437	521	.839	176	93	35	252	0	310	3.8	135	508	6.2	1572	19.2
95-96 Sea	63	60	2200	360	740	.486	73	179	.408	287	370	.776	146	56	8	179	0	276	4.4	73	328	5.2	1080	17.1
96-97 Sea*	61	60	2192	356	724	.492	57	161	.354	253	316	.801	150	63	16	151	0	266	4.4	87	394	6.5	1022	16.8
97-98 Sea	78	78	2742	437	898	.487	61	147	.415	297	352	.844	168	60	19	205	0	341	4.4	135	554	7.1	1232	15.8
98-99 Sea	50	39	1765	259	549	.472	34	86	.395	200	243	.823	103	41	26	152	0	184	3.7	77	370	7.4	752	15.0
99-00 Por	77	6	1662	187	433	.432	21	52	.404	179	215	.833	100	37	17	182	0	197	2.6	79	332	4.3	574	7.5
88-89 Dal	37	1	845	112	263	.426	2	16	.125	127	161	.789	56	24	9	118	3	86	2.3	56	166	4.5	353	9.5
Ind	32	12	1005	162	315	.514	5	19	.263	146	189	.772	77	29	10	102	0	93	2.9	70	229	7.2	475	14.8
15 Years	1110	524	33200	5361	10900	.492	472	1228	.384	4463	5558	.803	2240	849	309	3317	25	3789	3.4	1854	6945	6.3	15657	14.1

NBA Postseason

Year Tm	G	GS	Min	Md	Att	Pct	Md	Att	Pct	Md	Att	Pct	TO	Stl	Blk	PF	DQ	Ast	Avg	Off	Tot	Avg	Pts	Avg
85-86 Dal	10	0	120	13	28	.464	0	1	.000	11	17	.647	10	2	1	24	0	14	1.4	7	23	2.3	37	3.7
86-87 Dal	4	0	97	13	35	.371	0	3	.000	5	11	.455	6	3	2	13	0	6	1.5	4	12	3.0	31	7.8
87-88 Dal	15	0	274	40	86	.465	1	3	.333	36	51	.706	21	8	7	29	0	24	1.6	25	55	3.7	117	7.8
89-90 Ind	3	3	125	23	47	.489	0	3	.000	15	16	.938	10	2	1	13	0	5	1.7	5	22	7.3	61	20.3
90-91 Ind	5	0	179	27	57	.474	0	4	.000	25	30	.833	11	2	0	17	0	11	2.2	10	36	7.2	79	15.8
91-92 Ind	3	0	120	18	47	.383	2	4	.500	25	28	.893	7	2	1	10	0	7	2.3	12	39	13.0	63	21.0
92-93 Ind	4	4	165	25	54	.463	0	2	.000	28	36	.778	17	1	2	14	0	29	7.3	3	23	5.8	78	19.5
93-94 Sea	5	5	174	26	50	.520	2	6	.333	39	45	.867	8	1	3	21	1	10	2.0	8	27	5.4	93	18.6
94-95 Sea	4	4	153	23	57	.404	10	18	.556	19	24	.792	11	3	2	12	0	12	3.0	2	19	4.8	75	18.8
95-96 Sea	21	21	789	123	259	.475	21	57	.368	69	92	.750	67	14	5	63	1	67	3.2	19	105	5.0	336	16.0
96-97 Sea	12	12	459	67	142	.472	16	29	.552	53	65	.815	18	13	1	40	0	41	3.4	20	69	5.8	203	16.9
97-98 Sea	10	10	375	64	125	.512	2	14	.143	31	38	.816	22	7	1	21	0	39	3.9	18	77	7.7	161	16.1
99-00 Por	15	0	276	22	56	.393	1	6	.167	39	47	.830	15	4	0	29	0	30	2.0	10	53	3.5	84	5.6
13 Years	111	59	3306	484	1043	.464	55	150	.367	395	500	.790	223	62	26	306	2	295	2.7	143	560	5.0	1418	12.8

Dennis Scott

(statistical profile on page 272)

Pos: G-F **College:** Georgia Tech **Drafted:** '90 1(4)—Orl   **Ht:** 6'8" **Wt:** 230 **Born:** 9/5/68 **Age:** 32

College

Year Tm	G	GS	Min	Md	Att	Pct	Md	Att	Pct	Md	Att	Pct	TO	Stl	Blk	PF	DQ	Ast	Avg	Off	Tot	Avg	Pts	Avg
				Field Goals			**3-Pt FGs**			**Free Throws**			**Misc**			**Fouls**		**Assists**		**Rebounds**			**Points**	
87-88 GTch	32	31	1113	181	411	.440	98	208	.471	36	55	.655	63	43	11	70	—	116	3.6	37	161	5.0	496	15.5
88-89 GTch	32	32	1205	227	512	.443	116	292	.397	79	97	.814	73	45	7	64	—	98	3.1	37	131	4.1	649	20.3
89-90 GTch	35	35	1368	336	722	.465	137	331	.414	161	203	.793	90	62	33	73	—	71	2.0	65	231	6.6	970	27.7
3 Years	99	98	3686	744	1645	.452	351	831	.422	276	355	.777	226	150	51	207	—	285	2.9	139	523	5.3	2115	21.4

NBA

Year Tm	G	GS	Min	Md	Att	Pct	Md	Att	Pct	Md	Att	Pct	TO	Stl	Blk	PF	DQ	Ast	Avg	Off	Tot	Avg	Pts	Avg
				Field Goals			**3-Pt FGs**			**Free Throws**			**Misc**			**Fouls**		**Assists**		**Rebounds**			**Points**	
90-91 Orl	82	73	2336	503	1183	.425	125	334	.374	153	204	.750	127	62	25	203	1	134	1.6	62	235	2.9	1284	15.7
91-92 Orl	18	15	608	133	331	.402	29	89	.326	64	71	.901	31	20	9	49	1	35	1.9	14	66	3.7	359	19.9
92-93 Orl	54	43	1759	329	763	.431	108	268	.403	92	117	.786	104	57	18	131	3	136	2.5	38	186	3.4	858	15.9
93-94 Orl	82	37	2283	384	949	.405	155	388	.399	123	159	.774	93	81	32	161	0	216	2.6	54	218	2.7	1046	12.8
94-95 Orl	62	10	1499	283	645	.439	150	352	.426	86	114	.754	57	45	14	119	1	131	2.1	25	146	2.4	802	12.9
95-96 Orl	82	82	3041	491	1117	.440	267	628	.425	182	222	.820	122	90	29	169	1	243	3.0	63	309	3.8	1431	17.5
96-97 Orl	66	62	2166	298	749	.398	147	373	.394	80	101	.792	81	74	19	138	2	139	2.1	40	203	3.1	823	12.5
97-98 2Tm	81	45	2290	329	828	.397	125	342	.365	105	130	.808	104	53	39	152	1	153	1.9	47	247	3.0	888	11.0
98-99 2Tm	36	9	738	87	213	.408	37	97	.381	23	31	.742	19	15	3	49	0	40	1.1	8	58	1.6	234	6.5

NBA			Field Goals			3-Pt FGs			Free Throws			Misc			Fouls		Assists		Rebounds			Points	
Year Tm	G	GS	Min	Md	Att	Pct	Md	Att	Pct	Md	Att	Pct	TO	Stl	Blk	PF	DQ	Ast	Avg	Off	Tot	Avg	Pts	Avg
99-00 Van	66	0	1263	125	333	.375	71	189	.376	48	57	.842	30	28	9	104	0	69	1.0	16	106	1.6	369	5.6
97-98 Dal	52	42	1797	258	666	.387	94	273	.344	97	118	.822	92	43	32	121	1	129	2.5	39	197	3.8	707	13.6
Pho	29	3	493	71	162	.438	31	69	.449	8	12	.667	12	10	7	31	0	24	0.8	8	50	1.7	181	6.2
98-99 NY	15	0	206	17	56	.304	8	29	.276	1	4	.250	5	3	1	17	0	8	0.5	3	20	1.3	43	2.9
Min	21	9	532	70	157	.446	29	68	.426	22	27	.815	14	12	2	32	0	32	1.5	5	38	1.8	191	9.1
10 Years	629	376	17983	2962	7111	.417	1214	3060	.397	956	1206	.793	768	525	197	1275	10	1296	2.1	367	1774	2.8	8094	12.9

NBA Postseason																							
Year Tm	G	GS	Min	Md	Att	Pct	Md	Att	Pct	Md	Att	Pct	TO	Stl	Blk	PF	DQ	Ast	Avg	Off	Tot	Avg	Pts	Avg
93-94 Orl	3	3	99	14	41	.341	7	22	.318	8	10	.800	8	2	3	7	0	3	1.0	1	6	2.0	43	14.3
94-95 Orl	21	15	746	109	264	.413	56	151	.371	34	40	.850	33	22	5	62	0	45	2.1	9	63	3.0	308	14.7
95-96 Orl	12	12	446	48	116	.414	26	69	.377	14	22	.636	15	9	1	37	0	23	1.9	9	43	3.6	136	11.3
96-97 Orl	5	1	94	6	23	.261	3	11	.273	0	0	—	2	2	0	8	0	5	1.0	2	9	1.8	15	3.0
97-98 Pho	4	0	62	7	17	.412	3	8	.375	0	0	—	2	1	0	2	0	1	0.3	2	8	2.0	17	4.3
5 Years	45	31	1447	184	461	.399	95	261	.364	56	72	.778	60	36	9	116	0	77	1.7	23	129	2.9	519	11.5

In Memoriam **Malik Sealy** (statistical profile on page 273)

Pos: G **College:** St. John's (NY) **Drafted:** '92 1(14)—Ind **Ht:** 6'8" **Wt:** 200 **Born:** 2/1/70 **Died:** 5/20/00

College			Field Goals			3-Pt FGs			Free Throws			Misc			Fouls		Assists		Rebounds			Points	
Year Tm	G	GS	Min	Md	Att	Pct	Md	Att	Pct	Md	Att	Pct	TO	Stl	Blk	PF	DQ	Ast	Avg	Off	Tot	Avg	Pts	Avg
88-89 StJn	31	31	1172	163	333	.489	7	33	.212	67	120	.558	82	36	21	72	0	67	2.2	—	197	6.4	400	12.9
89-90 StJn	34	34	1304	227	432	.525	2	27	.074	159	213	.746	62	75	33	98	0	58	1.7	96	233	6.9	615	18.1
90-91 StJn	32	32	1203	263	535	.492	16	53	.302	165	222	.743	78	66	41	95	2	54	1.7	113	247	7.7	707	22.1
91-92 StJn	30	30	1162	247	523	.472	16	53	.302	169	213	.793	69	61	19	81	3	50	1.7	87	203	6.8	679	22.6
4 Years	127	127	4841	900	1823	.494	41	166	.247	560	768	.729	291	238	114	346	5	229	1.8	—	880	6.9	2401	18.9

NBA			Field Goals			3-Pt FGs			Free Throws			Misc			Fouls		Assists		Rebounds			Points	
Year Tm	G	GS	Min	Md	Att	Pct	Md	Att	Pct	Md	Att	Pct	TO	Stl	Blk	PF	DQ	Ast	Avg	Off	Tot	Avg	Pts	Avg
92-93 Ind	58	2	672	136	319	.426	7	31	.226	51	74	.689	58	36	7	74	0	47	0.8	60	112	1.9	330	5.7
93-94 Ind	43	5	623	111	274	.405	4	16	.250	59	87	.678	51	31	8	84	0	48	1.1	43	118	2.7	285	6.6
94-95 LAC	60	41	1604	291	669	.435	22	73	.301	174	223	.780	83	72	25	173	2	107	1.8	77	214	3.6	778	13.0
95-96 LAC	62	48	1601	272	655	.415	21	100	.210	147	184	.799	113	84	28	150	2	116	1.9	76	240	3.9	712	11.5
96-97 LAC	80	79	2456	373	942	.396	79	222	.356	254	290	.876	154	124	45	185	4	165	2.1	59	238	3.0	1079	13.5
97-98 Det	77	10	1641	216	505	.428	9	41	.220	150	182	.824	79	65	20	156	2	100	1.3	48	219	2.8	591	7.7
98-99 Min	31	7	731	95	231	.411	6	23	.261	55	61	.902	33	30	5	68	0	36	1.2	23	92	3.0	251	8.1
99-00 Min	82	61	2392	371	780	.476	10	35	.286	177	218	.812	110	76	19	197	1	197	2.4	119	352	4.3	929	11.3
8 Years	493	253	11720	1865	4375	.426	158	541	.292	1067	1319	.809	681	518	157	1087	11	816	1.7	505	1585	3.2	4955	10.1

NBA Postseason																							
Year Tm	G	GS	Min	Md	Att	Pct	Md	Att	Pct	Md	Att	Pct	TO	Stl	Blk	PF	DQ	Ast	Avg	Off	Tot	Avg	Pts	Avg
92-93 Ind	3	0	18	0	5	.000	0	1	.000	2	2	1.000	1	0	0	1	0	0	0.0	2	2	0.7	2	0.7
96-97 LAC	3	3	79	12	25	.480	1	5	.200	11	15	.733	5	0	0	10	1	5	1.7	1	3	1.0	36	12.0
98-99 Min	4	0	70	8	23	.348	0	0	—	4	5	.800	2	1	1	4	0	3	0.8	2	6	1.5	20	5.0
99-00 Min	4	4	122	19	41	.463	1	3	.333	11	16	.688	8	2	0	10	0	5	1.3	5	18	4.5	50	12.5
4 Years	14	7	289	39	94	.415	2	9	.222	28	38	.737	16	3	1	25	1	13	0.9	10	29	2.1	108	7.7

Rony Seikaly

Pos: C **College:** Syracuse **Drafted:** '88 1(9)—Mia **Ht:** 6'11" **Wt:** 245 **Born:** 5/10/65 **Age:** 35

College			Field Goals			3-Pt FGs			Free Throws			Misc			Fouls		Assists		Rebounds			Points	
Year Tm	G	GS	Min	Md	Att	Pct	Md	Att	Pct	Md	Att	Pct	TO	Stl	Blk	PF	DQ	Ast	Avg	Off	Tot	Avg	Pts	Avg
84-85 Syr	31	—	775	96	177	.542	—	—	—	58	104	.558	51	12	59	117	—	13	0.4	—	198	6.4	250	8.1
85-86 Syr	32	—	875	122	223	.547	—	—	—	80	142	.563	62	25	97	114	8	15	0.5	—	250	7.8	324	10.1
86-87 Syr	38	35	1032	216	380	.568	0	1	.000	141	235	.600	75	28	78	112	3	36	0.9	118	311	8.2	573	15.1
87-88 Syr	35	35	1084	218	385	.566	0	0	—	133	234	.568	87	23	85	105	1	22	0.6	114	335	9.6	569	16.3
4 Years	136	—	3766	652	1165	.560	0	1	.000	412	715	.576	275	88	319	448	—	86	0.6	232	1094	8.0	1716	12.6

NBA			Field Goals			3-Pt FGs			Free Throws			Misc			Fouls		Assists		Rebounds			Points	
Year Tm	G	GS	Min	Md	Att	Pct	Md	Att	Pct	Md	Att	Pct	TO	Stl	Blk	PF	DQ	Ast	Avg	Off	Tot	Avg	Pts	Avg
88-89 Mia	78	62	1962	333	744	.448	1	4	.250	181	354	.511	200	46	96	258	8	55	0.7	204	549	7.0	848	10.9
89-90 Mia	74	72	2409	486	968	.502	0	1	.000	256	431	.594	236	78	124	258	8	78	1.1	253	766	10.4	1228	16.6
90-91 Mia	64	59	2171	395	822	.481	2	6	.333	258	417	.619	205	51	86	213	2	95	1.5	207	709	11.1	1050	16.4
91-92 Mia	79	78	2800	463	947	.489	0	3	.000	370	505	.733	216	40	121	278	2	109	1.4	307	934	11.8	1296	16.4
92-93 Mia	72	64	2456	417	868	.480	1	8	.125	397	540	.735	203	38	83	260	3	100	1.4	259	846	11.8	1232	17.1
93-94 Mia	72	60	2410	392	803	.488	0	0	.000	304	422	.720	195	59	100	279	8	136	1.9	244	740	10.3	1088	15.1

	NBA			Field Goals			3-Pt FGs			Free Throws			Misc			Fouls		Assists		Rebounds			Points	
Year	Tm	G	GS	Min	Md	Att	Pct	Md	Att	Pct	Md	Att	Pct	TO	Stl	Blk	PF	DQ	Ast	Avg	Off	Tot	Avg	Pts	Avg
94-95	GS	36	35	1035	162	314	.516	0	0	—	111	160	.694	104	20	37	122	1	45	1.3	77	266	7.4	435	12.1
95-96	GS	64	60	1813	285	568	.502	2	3	.667	204	282	.723	180	40	69	219	5	71	1.1	166	499	7.8	776	12.1
96-97	Orl	74	68	2615	460	907	.507	0	3	.000	357	500	.714	218	49	107	275	4	92	1.2	274	701	9.5	1277	17.3
97-98	2Tm	56	49	1636	250	579	.432	0	2	.000	246	332	.741	146	28	43	164	2	77	1.4	146	393	7.0	746	13.3
98-99	NJ	9	0	88	4	20	.200	0	0	—	7	18	.389	10	4	6	15	0	2	0.2	5	21	2.3	15	1.7
99-00	NJ							Did not play: injury — Left Foot																	
97-98	Orl	47	47	1484	237	538	.441	0	2	.000	230	305	.754	134	25	39	137	2	69	1.5	130	357	7.6	704	15.0
	NJ	9	2	152	13	41	.317	0	0	—	16	27	.593	12	3	4	27	0	8	0.9	16	36	4.0	42	4.7
11 Years		678	607	21395	3647	7540	.484	6	32	.188	2691	3961	.679	1913	453	872	2341	43	860	1.3	2142	6424	9.5	9991	14.7

	NBA Postseason																								
Year	Tm	G	GS	Min	Md	Att	Pct	Md	Att	Pct	Md	Att	Pct	TO	Stl	Blk	PF	DQ	Ast	Avg	Off	Tot	Avg	Pts	Avg
91-92	Mia	3	3	117	19	35	.543	0	0	—	24	32	.750	9	1	5	15	1	4	1.3	11	30	10.0	62	20.7
93-94	Mia	5	5	165	14	32	.438	0	0	—	13	23	.565	11	4	7	22	0	8	1.6	19	47	9.4	41	8.2
96-97	Orl	3	3	86	7	22	.318	0	0	—	5	7	.714	4	1	3	10	0	0	0.0	5	16	5.3	19	6.3
97-98	NJ	3	0	37	7	9	.778	0	0	—	4	6	.667	4	1	0	4	0	0	0.0	3	9	3.0	18	6.0
4 Years		14	9	405	47	98	.480	0	0	—	46	68	.676	28	7	15	51	1	12	0.9	38	102	7.3	140	10.0

Brian Shaw

(statistical profile on page 273)

Pos: G **College:** Cal.-Santa Barbara **Drafted:** '88 1(24)—Bos **Ht:** 6'6" **Wt:** 200 **Born:** 3/22/66 **Age:** 34

	College			Field Goals			3-Pt FGs			Free Throws			Misc			Fouls		Assists		Rebounds			Points	
Year	Tm	G	GS	Min	Md	Att	Pct	Md	Att	Pct	Md	Att	Pct	TO	Stl	Blk	PF	DQ	Ast	Avg	Off	Tot	Avg	Pts	Avg
83-84	StMry	14	—	129	13	36	.361	—	—	—	14	19	.737	—	—	—	20	—	23	1.6	—	12	0.9	40	2.9
84-85	StMry	27	—	976	99	246	.402	—	—	—	55	76	.724	95	37	9	75	—	142	5.3	—	144	5.3	253	9.4
86-87	UCSB	29	—	1013	125	288	.434	18	42	.429	47	66	.712	112	41	9	86	—	193	6.7	—	224	7.7	315	10.9
87-88	UCSB	30	—	1073	151	324	.466	26	74	.351	71	96	.740	95	49	8	76	—	182	6.1	—	260	8.7	399	13.3
4 Years		100	—	3191	388	894	.434	44	116	.379	187	257	.728	—	—	—	257	—	540	5.4	—	640	6.4	1007	10.1

	NBA			Field Goals			3-Pt FGs			Free Throws			Misc			Fouls		Assists		Rebounds			Points	
Year	Tm	G	GS	Min	Md	Att	Pct	Md	Att	Pct	Md	Att	Pct	TO	Stl	Blk	PF	DQ	Ast	Avg	Off	Tot	Avg	Pts	Avg
88-89	Bos	82	54	2301	297	686	.433	0	13	.000	109	132	.826	188	78	27	211	1	472	5.8	119	376	4.6	703	8.6
89-90								Played in Italy																		
90-91	Bos	79	79	2772	442	942	.469	3	27	.111	204	249	.819	223	105	34	206	1	602	7.6	104	370	4.7	1091	13.8
91-92	2Tm	63	26	1423	209	513	.407	5	23	.217	72	91	.791	99	57	22	115	0	250	4.0	50	204	3.2	495	7.9
92-93	Mia	68	45	1603	197	501	.393	43	130	.331	61	78	.782	96	48	19	163	2	235	3.5	70	257	3.8	498	7.3
93-94	Mia	77	52	2037	278	667	.417	73	216	.338	64	89	.719	173	71	21	195	1	385	5.0	104	350	4.5	693	9.0
94-95	Orl	78	9	1836	192	494	.389	48	184	.261	70	95	.737	184	73	18	184	1	406	5.2	52	241	3.1	502	6.4
95-96	Orl	75	1	1679	182	486	.374	41	144	.285	91	114	.798	173	58	11	160	1	336	4.5	58	224	3.0	496	6.6
96-97	Orl	77	31	1867	189	516	.366	63	194	.325	111	140	.793	170	67	26	197	3	319	4.1	47	194	2.5	552	7.2
97-98	2Tm	59	34	1530	154	446	.345	28	95	.295	36	52	.692	99	49	17	148	4	261	4.4	37	215	3.6	372	6.3
98-99	Por	1	0	5	0	1	.000	0	0	—	0	0	—	1	0	1	1	0	1	1.0	0	1	1.0	0	0.0
99-00	LAL	74	2	1249	123	322	.382	18	58	.310	41	54	.759	75	35	14	105	0	201	2.7	45	216	2.9	305	4.1
91-92	Bos	17	3	436	70	164	.427	0	7	.000	35	40	.875	32	12	10	29	0	89	5.2	11	69	4.1	175	10.3
	Mia	46	23	987	139	349	.398	5	16	.313	37	51	.725	67	45	12	86	0	161	3.5	39	135	2.9	320	7.0
97-98	GS	39	32	1028	103	307	.336	21	67	.313	24	33	.727	75	35	14	93	3	173	4.4	20	151	3.9	251	6.4
	Phi	20	2	502	51	139	.367	7	28	.250	12	19	.632	24	14	3	55	1	88	4.4	17	64	3.2	121	6.1
11 Years		733	333	18302	2263	5574	.406	322	1084	.297	859	1094	.785	1481	641	209	1685	14	3468	4.7	686	2648	3.6	5707	7.8

	NBA Postseason																								
Year	Tm	G	GS	Min	Md	Att	Pct	Md	Att	Pct	Md	Att	Pct	TO	Stl	Blk	PF	DQ	Ast	Avg	Off	Tot	Avg	Pts	Avg
88-89	Bos	3	3	124	22	43	.512	0	1	.000	7	9	.778	6	3	0	11	0	19	6.3	2	17	5.7	51	17.0
90-91	Bos	11	11	316	47	100	.470	1	3	.333	26	30	.867	25	10	1	34	0	51	4.6	8	38	3.5	121	11.0
91-92	Mia	3	3	85	14	30	.467	3	5	.600	5	8	.625	7	2	0	13	0	12	4.0	2	13	4.3	36	12.0
93-94	Mia	5	5	112	16	41	.390	0	13	.000	7	12	.583	13	4	1	8	0	9	1.8	3	20	4.0	39	7.8
94-95	Orl	21	0	355	48	123	.390	22	57	.386	20	32	.625	26	11	4	49	0	66	3.1	17	62	3.0	138	6.6
95-96	Orl	10	0	217	18	52	.346	8	22	.364	3	4	.750	19	5	0	27	0	46	4.6	6	21	2.1	47	4.7
96-97	Orl	5	4	82	3	19	.158	2	6	.333	2	4	.500	8	1	1	5	0	8	1.6	1	9	1.8	10	2.0
99-00	LAL	22	1	408	45	107	.421	16	48	.333	13	16	.813	17	11	4	46	1	67	3.0	7	51	2.3	119	5.4
8 Years		80	27	1699	213	515	.414	52	155	.335	83	115	.722	121	47	11	193	1	278	3.5	46	231	2.9	561	7.0

Dickey Simpkins

(statistical profile on page 274)

Pos: F-C **College:** Providence **Drafted:** '94 1(21)—Chi **Ht:** 6'9" **Wt:** 255 **Born:** 4/6/72 **Age:** 28

	College			Field Goals			3-Pt FGs			Free Throws			Misc			Fouls		Assists		Rebounds			Points	
Year	Tm	G	GS	Min	Md	Att	Pct	Md	Att	Pct	Md	Att	Pct	TO	Stl	Blk	PF	DQ	Ast	Avg	Off	Tot	Avg	Pts	Avg
90-91	Prov	32	7	697	90	183	.492	4	10	.400	67	110	.609	48	24	31	77	1	33	1.0	82	211	6.6	251	7.8

College				Field Goals			3-Pt FGs			Free Throws			Misc			Fouls		Assists		Rebounds			Points	
Year Tm	G	GS	Min	Md	Att	Pct	Md	Att	Pct	Md	Att	Pct	TO	Stl	Blk	PF	DQ	Ast	Avg	Off	Tot	Avg	Pts	Avg
91-92 Prov	30	24	793	89	181	.492	1	4	.250	90	128	.703	81	14	27	83	1	36	1.2	67	174	5.8	269	9.0
92-93 Prov	33	33	976	122	271	.450	1	3	.333	106	178	.596	82	25	18	84	4	41	1.2	94	216	6.5	351	10.6
93-94 Prov	30	30	877	129	250	.516	3	9	.333	94	137	.686	57	22	21	63	0	38	1.3	69	189	6.3	355	11.8
4 Years	125	94	3343	430	885	.486	9	26	.346	357	553	.646	268	85	97	307	6	148	1.2	312	790	6.3	1226	9.8

NBA				Field Goals			3-Pt FGs			Free Throws			Misc			Fouls		Assists		Rebounds			Points	
Year Tm	G	GS	Min	Md	Att	Pct	Md	Att	Pct	Md	Att	Pct	TO	Stl	Blk	PF	DQ	Ast	Avg	Off	Tot	Avg	Pts	Avg
94-95 Chi	59	5	586	78	184	.424	0	0	—	50	72	.694	45	10	7	72	0	37	0.6	60	151	2.6	206	3.5
95-96 Chi	60	12	685	77	160	.481	1	1	1.000	61	97	.629	56	9	8	78	0	38	0.6	66	156	2.6	216	3.6
96-97 Chi	48	0	395	31	93	.333	1	4	.250	28	40	.700	35	5	5	44	0	31	0.6	36	92	1.9	91	1.9
97-98 2Tm	40	0	433	48	89	.539	0	2	.000	36	70	.514	32	9	5	54	0	33	0.8	27	77	1.9	132	3.3
98-99 Chi	50	35	1448	150	324	.463	0	1	.000	156	242	.645	72	36	13	128	1	65	1.3	110	339	6.8	456	9.1
99-00 Chi	69	48	1651	111	274	.405	0	1	.000	65	120	.542	128	22	22	217	4	100	1.4	124	372	5.4	287	4.2
97-98 GS	19	0	196	22	48	.458	0	1	.000	10	26	.385	19	5	2	19	0	16	0.8	19	46	2.4	54	2.8
Chi	21	0	237	26	41	.634	0	1	.000	26	44	.591	13	4	3	35	0	17	0.8	8	31	1.5	78	3.7
6 Years	326	100	5198	495	1124	.440	2	9	.222	396	641	.618	368	91	60	593	5	304	0.9	423	1187	3.6	1388	4.3

NBA Postseason																								
Year Tm	G	GS	Min	Md	Att	Pct	Md	Att	Pct	Md	Att	Pct	TO	Stl	Blk	PF	DQ	Ast	Avg	Off	Tot	Avg	Pts	Avg
97-98 Chi	13	0	74	6	16	.375	0	0	—	4	9	.444	3	2	1	10	0	3	0.2	4	13	1.0	16	1.2

Brian Skinner

Pos: F **College:** Baylor **Drafted:** '98 1(22)—LAC **Ht:** 6'9" **Wt:** 255 **Born:** 5/19/76 **Age:** 24

College				Field Goals			3-Pt FGs			Free Throws			Misc			Fouls		Assists		Rebounds			Points	
Year Tm	G	GS	Min	Md	Att	Pct	Md	Att	Pct	Md	Att	Pct	TO	Stl	Blk	PF	DQ	Ast	Avg	Off	Tot	Avg	Pts	Avg
94-95 Bay	18	17	501	98	164	.598	0	0	—	40	95	.421	43	15	69	56	—	9	0.5	—	147	8.2	236	13.1
95-96 Bay	27	27	900	187	311	.601	0	0	—	101	163	.620	83	26	82	79	—	16	0.6	—	250	9.3	475	17.6
96-97 Bay	30	30	929	196	349	.562	0	0	—	92	172	.535	72	37	97	88	3	26	0.9	85	253	8.4	484	16.1
97-98 Bay	28	28	976	192	347	.553	0	0	—	123	208	.591	74	38	98	84	3	15	0.5	78	265	9.5	507	18.1
4 Years	103	102	3306	673	1171	.575	0	0	—	356	638	.558	272	116	346	307	—	66	0.6	—	915	8.9	1702	16.5

NBA				Field Goals			3-Pt FGs			Free Throws			Misc			Fouls		Assists		Rebounds			Points	
Year Tm	G	GS	Min	Md	Att	Pct	Md	Att	Pct	Md	Att	Pct	TO	Stl	Blk	PF	DQ	Ast	Avg	Off	Tot	Avg	Pts	Avg
98-99 LAC	21	0	258	33	71	.465	0	0	—	20	33	.606	19	10	13	20	0	1	0.0	20	53	2.5	86	4.1
99-00 LAC	33	9	775	68	134	.507	0	0	—	43	65	.662	37	16	44	75	0	11	0.3	63	201	6.1	179	5.4
2 Years	54	9	1033	101	205	.493	0	0	—	63	98	.643	56	26	57	95	0	12	0.2	83	254	4.7	265	4.9

Joe Smith

(statistical profile on page 274)

Pos: F **College:** Maryland **Drafted:** '95 1(1)—GS **Ht:** 6'10" **Wt:** 225 **Born:** 7/26/75 **Age:** 25

College				Field Goals			3-Pt FGs			Free Throws			Misc			Fouls		Assists		Rebounds			Points	
Year Tm	G	GS	Min	Md	Att	Pct	Md	Att	Pct	Md	Att	Pct	TO	Stl	Blk	PF	DQ	Ast	Avg	Off	Tot	Avg	Pts	Avg
93-94 Myld	30	30	988	206	395	.522	2	5	.400	168	229	.734	59	42	93	104	7	25	0.8	109	321	10.7	582	19.4
94-95 Myld	34	34	1110	245	424	.578	9	21	.429	209	282	.741	72	51	97	87	3	40	1.2	135	362	10.6	708	20.8
2 Years	64	64	2098	451	819	.551	11	26	.423	377	511	.738	131	93	190	191	10	65	1.0	244	683	10.7	1290	20.2

NBA				Field Goals			3-Pt FGs			Free Throws			Misc			Fouls		Assists		Rebounds			Points	
Year Tm	G	GS	Min	Md	Att	Pct	Md	Att	Pct	Md	Att	Pct	TO	Stl	Blk	PF	DQ	Ast	Avg	Off	Tot	Avg	Pts	Avg
95-96 GS	82	82	2821	469	1024	.458	10	28	.357	303	392	.773	138	85	134	224	5	79	1.0	300	717	8.7	1251	15.3
96-97 GS	80	80	3086	587	1293	.454	12	46	.261	307	377	.814	192	74	86	244	3	125	1.6	261	679	8.5	1493	18.7
97-98 2Tm	79	55	2344	464	1070	.434	0	8	.000	227	293	.775	158	62	51	263	2	94	1.2	199	471	6.0	1155	14.6
98-99 Min	43	42	1418	223	522	.427	0	3	.000	142	188	.755	66	32	66	147	3	68	1.6	154	354	8.2	588	13.7
99-00 Min	78	9	1975	289	623	.464	1	1	1.000	195	258	.756	119	45	85	302	8	88	1.1	186	484	6.2	774	9.9
97-98 Min	49	49	1645	343	800	.429	0	7	.000	160	208	.769	106	44	38	169	2	67	1.4	141	338	6.9	846	17.3
Phi	30	6	699	121	270	.448	0	1	.000	67	85	.788	52	18	13	94	0	27	0.9	58	133	4.4	309	10.3
5 Years	362	268	11644	2032	4532	.448	23	86	.267	1174	1508	.779	673	298	422	1180	21	454	1.3	1100	2705	7.5	5261	14.5

NBA Postseason																								
Year Tm	G	GS	Min	Md	Att	Pct	Md	Att	Pct	Md	Att	Pct	TO	Stl	Blk	PF	DQ	Ast	Avg	Off	Tot	Avg	Pts	Avg
98-99 Min	4	4	120	11	37	.297	0	0	—	8	11	.727	5	2	8	15	0	5	1.3	10	26	6.5	30	7.5
99-00 Min	4	0	79	8	17	.471	0	1	.000	2	2	1.000	4	3	1	15	0	1	0.3	7	12	3.0	18	4.5
2 Years	8	4	199	19	54	.352	0	1	.000	10	13	.769	9	5	9	30	0	6	0.8	17	38	4.8	48	6.0

Leon Smith

Pos: F **College:** None **Drafted:** '99 1(29)—SA　　**Ht:** 6'10" **Wt:** 235 **Born:** 11/2/80 **Age:** 20

NBA			Field Goals			3-Pt FGs			Free Throws			Misc			Fouls		Assists		Rebounds			Points	
Year Tm	G	GS	Min	Md	Att	Pct	Md	Att	Pct	Md	Att	Pct	TO	Stl	Blk	PF	DQ	Ast	Avg	Off	Tot	Avg	Pts	Avg
99-00 Dal							Active but did not play																	

Michael Smith

Pos: G-F **College:** Providence **Drafted:** '94 2(35)—Sac　　**Ht:** 6'8" **Wt:** 240 **Born:** 3/28/72 **Age:** 28

College			Field Goals			3-Pt FGs			Free Throws			Misc			Fouls		Assists		Rebounds			Points	
Year Tm	G	GS	Min	Md	Att	Pct	Md	Att	Pct	Md	Att	Pct	TO	Stl	Blk	PF	DQ	Ast	Avg	Off	Tot	Avg	Pts	Avg
91-92 Prov	31	28	876	108	218	.495	0	1	.000	117	202	.579	70	32	51	90	2	41	1.3	121	319	10.3	333	10.7
92-93 Prov	33	33	976	135	243	.556	0	0	—	119	218	.546	73	40	31	92	2	38	1.2	143	375	11.4	389	11.8
93-94 Prov	30	30	872	144	238	.605	0	1	.000	100	140	.714	44	33	23	89	2	25	0.8	118	344	11.5	388	12.9
3 Years	94	91	2724	387	699	.554	0	2	.000	336	560	.600	187	105	105	271	6	104	1.1	382	1038	11.0	1110	11.8

NBA			Field Goals			3-Pt FGs			Free Throws			Misc			Fouls		Assists		Rebounds			Points	
Year Tm	G	GS	Min	Md	Att	Pct	Md	Att	Pct	Md	Att	Pct	TO	Stl	Blk	PF	DQ	Ast	Avg	Off	Tot	Avg	Pts	Avg
94-95 Sac	82	0	1736	220	406	.542	0	2	.000	127	262	.485	106	61	49	235	1	67	0.8	174	486	5.9	567	6.9
95-96 Sac	65	0	1384	144	238	.605	1	1	1.000	68	177	.384	72	47	46	166	0	110	1.7	143	389	6.0	357	5.5
96-97 Sac	81	52	2526	202	375	.539	0	0	—	128	258	.496	130	82	60	251	3	191	2.4	257	769	9.5	532	6.6
97-98 2Tm	48	33	1053	93	194	.479	0	1	.000	65	103	.631	51	41	15	95	0	88	1.8	120	306	6.4	251	5.2
98-99 Van	48	10	1098	77	144	.535	0	1	.000	76	128	.594	60	46	18	107	0	48	1.0	135	350	7.3	230	4.8
99-00 Was	46	46	1145	108	192	.563	0	1	.000	73	101	.723	45	27	23	127	0	56	1.2	121	331	7.2	289	6.3
97-98 Sac	18	4	347	26	61	.426	0	0	—	17	30	.567	15	15	9	35	0	29	1.6	35	100	5.6	69	3.8
Van	30	29	706	67	133	.504	0	1	.000	48	73	.658	36	26	6	60	0	59	2.0	85	206	6.9	182	6.1
6 Years	370	141	8942	844	1549	.545	1	6	.167	537	1029	.522	464	304	211	981	4	560	1.5	950	2631	7.1	2226	6.0

NBA Postseason			Field Goals			3-Pt FGs			Free Throws			Misc			Fouls		Assists		Rebounds			Points	
Year Tm	G	GS	Min	Md	Att	Pct	Md	Att	Pct	Md	Att	Pct	TO	Stl	Blk	PF	DQ	Ast	Avg	Off	Tot	Avg	Pts	Avg
95-96 Sac	4	0	87	7	12	.583	0	0	—	5	11	.455	2	1	2	14	0	8	2.0	7	22	5.5	19	4.8

Steve Smith

(statistical profile on page 275)

Pos: G **College:** Michigan State **Drafted:** '91 1(5)—Mia　　**Ht:** 6'8" **Wt:** 221 **Born:** 3/31/69 **Age:** 31

College			Field Goals			3-Pt FGs			Free Throws			Misc			Fouls		Assists		Rebounds			Points	
Year Tm	G	GS	Min	Md	Att	Pct	Md	Att	Pct	Md	Att	Pct	TO	Stl	Blk	PF	DQ	Ast	Avg	Off	Tot	Avg	Pts	Avg
87-88 MchSt	28	26	812	108	232	.466	14	30	.467	69	91	.758	74	27	2	72	3	82	2.9	—	112	4.0	299	10.7
88-89 MchSt	33	32	1168	217	454	.478	22	63	.349	129	169	.763	98	43	12	90	2	112	3.4	—	229	6.9	585	17.7
89-90 MchSt	31	29	1081	233	443	.526	45	98	.459	116	167	.695	112	25	17	81	2	150	4.8	60	216	7.0	627	20.2
90-91 MchSt	30	30	1134	268	566	.473	66	162	.407	150	187	.802	100	16	5	75	0	109	3.6	47	183	6.1	752	25.1
4 Years	122	117	4195	826	1695	.487	147	353	.416	464	614	.756	384	111	36	318	7	453	3.7	—	740	6.1	2263	18.5

NBA			Field Goals			3-Pt FGs			Free Throws			Misc			Fouls		Assists		Rebounds			Points	
Year Tm	G	GS	Min	Md	Att	Pct	Md	Att	Pct	Md	Att	Pct	TO	Stl	Blk	PF	DQ	Ast	Avg	Off	Tot	Avg	Pts	Avg
91-92 Mia	61	59	1806	297	654	.454	40	125	.320	95	127	.748	152	59	19	162	1	278	4.6	81	188	3.1	729	12.0
92-93 Mia	48	43	1610	279	619	.451	53	132	.402	155	197	.787	129	50	16	148	3	267	5.6	56	197	4.1	766	16.0
93-94 Mia	78	77	2776	491	1076	.456	91	262	.347	273	327	.835	202	84	35	217	6	394	5.1	156	352	4.5	1346	17.3
94-95 2Tm	80	61	2665	428	1005	.426	137	416	.329	312	371	.841	155	62	33	225	2	274	3.4	104	276	3.5	1305	16.3
95-96 Atl	80	80	2856	494	1143	.432	140	423	.331	318	385	.826	151	68	17	207	1	224	2.8	124	326	4.1	1446	18.1
96-97 Atl	72	72	2818	491	1145	.429	130	388	.335	333	393	.847	176	62	23	173	2	305	4.2	90	238	3.3	1445	20.1
97-98 Atl*	73	73	2857	489	1101	.444	97	276	.351	389	455	.855	176	75	29	219	4	292	4.0	133	309	4.2	1464	20.1
98-99 Atl	36	36	1314	217	540	.402	47	139	.338	191	225	.849	99	36	11	100	2	118	3.3	50	151	4.2	672	18.7
99-00 Por	82	81	2689	420	900	.467	96	241	.398	289	340	.850	117	71	31	214	0	209	2.5	123	313	3.8	1225	14.9
94-95 Mia	2	2	62	11	29	.379	2	12	.167	17	22	.773	4	2	1	9	0	7	3.5	4	6	3.0	41	20.5
Atl	78	59	2603	417	976	.427	135	404	.334	295	349	.845	151	60	32	216	2	267	3.4	100	270	3.5	1264	16.2
9 Years	610	582	21391	3606	8183	.441	831	2402	.346	2355	2820	.835	1357	567	214	1665	21	2361	3.9	917	2350	3.9	10398	17.0

NBA Postseason			Field Goals			3-Pt FGs			Free Throws			Misc			Fouls		Assists		Rebounds			Points	
Year Tm	G	GS	Min	Md	Att	Pct	Md	Att	Pct	Md	Att	Pct	TO	Stl	Blk	PF	DQ	Ast	Avg	Off	Tot	Avg	Pts	Avg
91-92 Mia	3	3	100	18	34	.529	7	11	.636	5	6	.833	3	4	1	2	0	15	5.0	3	6	2.0	48	16.0
93-94 Mia	5	5	192	33	80	.413	9	22	.409	21	25	.840	10	4	2	12	0	11	2.2	17	30	6.0	96	19.2
94-95 Atl	3	3	108	17	43	.395	7	18	.389	16	19	.842	3	6	1	14	0	6	2.0	1	8	2.7	57	19.0
95-96 Atl	10	10	421	75	171	.439	25	61	.410	42	52	.808	16	13	13	31	0	32	3.2	15	41	4.1	217	21.7
96-97 Atl	10	10	421	55	139	.396	18	55	.327	61	74	.824	28	4	1	38	0	17	1.7	12	39	3.9	189	18.9
97-98 Atl	4	4	160	39	68	.574	10	20	.500	11	16	.688	5	2	3	17	1	9	2.3	2	11	2.8	99	24.8
98-99 Atl	9	9	356	54	153	.353	9	33	.273	39	43	.907	21	14	2	32	0	30	3.3	14	31	3.4	156	17.3
99-00 Por	16	16	604	88	181	.486	29	53	.547	69	78	.885	27	19	4	44	0	44	2.8	13	40	2.5	274	17.1
8 Years	60	60	2362	379	869	.436	114	273	.418	264	313	.843	113	66	27	190	1	164	2.7	77	206	3.4	1136	18.9

Rik Smits

(statistical profile on page 275)

Pos: C **College:** Marist **Drafted:** '88 1(2)—Ind **Ht:** 7'4" **Wt:** 265 **Born:** 8/23/66 **Age:** 34

College

Year Tm	G	GS	Min	Md	Att	Pct	Md	Att	Pct	Md	Att	Pct	TO	Stl	Blk	PF	DQ	Ast	Avg	Off	Tot	Avg	Pts	Avg
				Field Goals			**3-Pt FGs**			**Free Throws**			**Misc**			**Fouls**		**Assists**		**Rebounds**			**Points**	
84-85 Mar	29	—	776	132	233	.567	—	—	—	60	104	.577	—	—	75	—	—	5	0.2	—	162	5.6	324	11.2
85-86 Mar	30	—	870	216	347	.622	—	—	—	98	144	.681	—	—	82	—	—	8	0.3	—	242	8.1	530	17.7
86-87 Mar	21	—	634	157	258	.609	0	0	—	109	151	.722	46	13	83	71	—	16	0.8	—	171	8.1	423	20.1
87-88 Mar	27	—	861	251	403	.623	0	2	.000	166	226	.735	80	9	105	87	—	17	0.6	—	236	8.7	668	24.7
4 Years	107	—	3141	756	1241	.609	0	2	.000	433	625	.693	—	—	345	—	—	46	0.4	—	811	7.6	1945	18.2

NBA

Year Tm	G	GS	Min	Md	Att	Pct	Md	Att	Pct	Md	Att	Pct	TO	Stl	Blk	PF	DQ	Ast	Avg	Off	Tot	Avg	Pts	Avg
				Field Goals			**3-Pt FGs**			**Free Throws**			**Misc**			**Fouls**		**Assists**		**Rebounds**			**Points**	
88-89 Ind	82	71	2041	386	746	.517	0	1	.000	184	255	.722	130	37	151	310	14	70	0.9	185	500	6.1	956	11.7
89-90 Ind	82	82	2404	515	967	.533	0	1	.000	241	297	.811	143	45	169	**328**	11	142	1.7	135	512	6.2	1271	15.5
90-91 Ind	76	38	1690	342	705	.485	0	0	—	144	189	.762	86	24	111	246	3	84	1.1	116	357	4.7	828	10.9
91-92 Ind	74	55	1772	436	855	.510	0	2	.000	152	193	.788	130	29	100	231	4	116	1.6	124	417	5.6	1024	13.8
92-93 Ind	81	81	2072	494	1017	.486	0	0	—	167	228	.732	147	27	75	285	5	121	1.5	126	432	5.3	1155	14.3
93-94 Ind	78	75	2113	493	923	.534	0	1	.000	238	300	.793	151	49	82	281	11	156	2.0	135	483	6.2	1224	15.7
94-95 Ind	78	78	2381	558	1060	.526	0	2	.000	284	377	.753	189	40	79	278	6	111	1.4	192	601	7.7	1400	17.9
95-96 Ind	63	63	1901	466	894	.521	1	5	.200	231	293	.788	160	21	45	226	5	110	1.7	119	433	6.9	1164	18.5
96-97 Ind	52	52	1518	356	733	.486	2	8	.250	173	217	.797	126	22	59	175	3	67	1.3	105	361	6.9	887	17.1
97-98 Ind*	73	69	2085	514	1038	.495	0	3	.000	188	240	.783	134	40	88	243	9	101	1.4	127	505	6.9	1216	16.7
98-99 Ind	49	49	1271	310	633	.490	0	2	.000	108	132	.818	75	18	52	159	1	52	1.1	73	275	5.6	728	14.9
99-00 Ind	79	79	1852	431	890	.484	0	1	.000	156	211	.739	108	20	100	249	1	85	1.1	94	401	5.1	1018	12.9
12 Years	867	792	23100	5301	10461	.507	3	26	.115	2266	2932	.773	1579	372	1111	3011	73	1215	1.4	1531	5277	6.1	12871	14.8

NBA Postseason

Year Tm	G	GS	Min	Md	Att	Pct	Md	Att	Pct	Md	Att	Pct	TO	Stl	Blk	PF	DQ	Ast	Avg	Off	Tot	Avg	Pts	Avg
89-90 Ind	3	3	96	14	28	.500	0	0	—	9	11	.818	5	2	4	12	0	3	1.0	4	16	5.3	37	12.3
90-91 Ind	5	0	88	21	37	.568	0	0	—	7	8	.875	5	1	7	23	1	2	0.4	4	18	3.6	49	9.8
91-92 Ind	3	1	28	4	11	.364	0	0	—	2	2	1.000	3	2	1	7	0	0	0.0	3	6	2.0	10	3.3
92-93 Ind	4	4	143	37	64	.578	0	1	.000	16	22	.727	8	5	4	18	1	7	1.8	13	32	8.0	90	22.5
93-94 Ind	16	16	450	103	218	.472	0	0	—	50	62	.806	43	10	9	64	1	31	1.9	23	84	5.3	256	16.0
94-95 Ind	17	17	546	127	232	.547	1	1	1.000	86	107	.804	34	5	14	73	2	34	2.0	32	119	7.0	341	20.1
95-96 Ind	5	5	166	42	77	.545	0	0	—	11	14	.786	14	2	2	20	1	8	1.6	13	37	7.4	95	19.0
97-98 Ind	16	16	476	105	209	.502	0	1	.000	55	64	.859	21	8	14	67	3	20	1.3	17	85	5.3	265	16.6
98-99 Ind	13	13	293	67	147	.456	0	0	—	19	20	.950	25	6	15	51	3	9	0.7	16	65	5.0	153	11.8
99-00 Ind	22	21	461	103	207	.498	0	1	.000	35	40	.875	27	10	20	84	1	21	1.0	24	78	3.5	241	11.0
10 Years	104	96	2747	623	1230	.507	1	4	.250	290	350	.829	185	51	90	419	13	135	1.3	149	540	5.2	1537	14.8

Eric Snow

(statistical profile on page 276)

Pos: G **College:** Michigan State **Drafted:** '95 2(43)—Mil **Ht:** 6'3" **Wt:** 204 **Born:** 4/24/73 **Age:** 27

College

Year Tm	G	GS	Min	Md	Att	Pct	Md	Att	Pct	Md	Att	Pct	TO	Stl	Blk	PF	DQ	Ast	Avg	Off	Tot	Avg	Pts	Avg
				Field Goals			**3-Pt FGs**			**Free Throws**			**Misc**			**Fouls**		**Assists**		**Rebounds**			**Points**	
91-92 MchSt	25	0	144	12	25	.480	0	2	.000	3	15	.200	20	6	0	10	0	24	1.0	3	15	0.6	27	1.1
92-93 MchSt	28	27	798	53	97	.546	0	5	.000	15	56	.268	69	27	5	82	5	145	5.2	8	73	2.6	121	4.3
93-94 MchSt	32	31	992	91	177	.514	13	45	.289	22	49	.449	86	57	5	77	3	213	6.7	10	111	3.5	217	6.8
94-95 MchSt	28	28	916	117	225	.520	7	24	.292	62	102	.608	86	52	4	77	3	217	7.8	15	92	3.3	303	10.8
4 Years	113	86	2850	273	524	.521	20	76	.263	102	222	.459	261	142	14	246	11	599	5.3	36	291	2.6	668	5.9

NBA

Year Tm	G	GS	Min	Md	Att	Pct	Md	Att	Pct	Md	Att	Pct	TO	Stl	Blk	PF	DQ	Ast	Avg	Off	Tot	Avg	Pts	Avg
				Field Goals			**3-Pt FGs**			**Free Throws**			**Misc**			**Fouls**		**Assists**		**Rebounds**			**Points**	
95-96 Sea	43	1	389	42	100	.420	2	10	.200	29	49	.592	38	28	0	53	0	73	1.7	9	43	1.0	115	2.7
96-97 Sea	67	0	775	74	164	.451	4	15	.267	47	66	.712	48	37	3	94	0	159	2.4	17	70	1.0	199	3.0
97-98 2Tm	64	0	918	79	184	.429	2	17	.118	49	71	.690	63	60	5	114	0	177	2.8	19	81	1.3	209	3.3
98-99 Phi	48	48	1716	149	348	.428	5	21	.238	110	150	.733	111	100	1	149	2	301	6.3	25	162	3.4	413	8.6
99-00 Phi	82	80	2866	257	597	.430	11	45	.244	126	177	.712	162	140	8	243	2	624	7.6	42	261	3.2	651	7.9
97-98 Sea	17	0	74	10	23	.435	0	1	.000	5	10	.500	12	0	1	15	0	13	0.8	0	4	0.2	25	1.5
Phi	47	0	844	69	161	.429	2	16	.125	44	61	.721	51	60	4	99	0	164	3.5	19	77	1.6	184	3.9
5 Years	304	129	6664	601	1393	.431	24	108	.222	361	513	.704	422	365	17	653	4	1334	4.4	112	617	2.0	1587	5.2

NBA Postseason

Year Tm	G	GS	Min	Md	Att	Pct	Md	Att	Pct	Md	Att	Pct	TO	Stl	Blk	PF	DQ	Ast	Avg	Off	Tot	Avg	Pts	Avg
95-96 Sea	10	0	24	1	7	.143	0	2	.000	0	0	—	4	2	0	3	0	6	0.6	0	4	0.4	2	0.2
96-97 Sea	8	0	48	5	11	.455	2	4	.500	1	2	.500	0	4	0	7	0	12	1.5	0	2	0.3	13	1.6
98-99 Phi	8	8	306	37	88	.420	3	13	.231	22	27	.815	25	8	1	26	0	57	7.1	3	33	4.1	99	12.4
99-00 Phi	5	4	138	15	31	.484	3	4	.750	4	4	1.000	7	4	1	14	0	35	7.0	0	10	2.0	37	7.4
4 Years	31	12	516	58	137	.423	8	23	.348	27	33	.818	36	18	2	50	0	110	3.5	3	49	1.6	151	4.9

Felton Spencer

Pos: C **College:** Louisville **Drafted:** '90 1(6)—Min   **Ht:** 7'0" **Wt:** 280 **Born:** 1/5/68 **Age:** 33

College			Field Goals			3-Pt FGs			Free Throws			Misc			Fouls		Assists		Rebounds			Points	
Year Tm	G	GS	Min	Md	Att	Pct	Md	Att	Pct	Md	Att	Pct	TO	Stl	Blk	PF	DQ	Ast	Avg	Off	Tot	Avg	Pts	Avg
86-87 Lou	31	1	356	43	78	.551	0	0	—	32	65	.492	35	3	18	60	0	12	0.4	—	83	2.7	118	3.8
87-88 Lou	35	1	532	93	157	.592	0	0	—	73	114	.640	38	8	17	101	6	18	0.5	—	146	4.2	259	7.4
88-89 Lou	33	4	581	85	140	.607	0	0	—	99	135	.733	48	14	29	100	7	20	0.6	—	169	5.1	269	8.2
89-90 Lou	35	35	995	188	276	.681	0	0	—	146	204	.716	81	24	69	126	4	45	1.3	—	296	8.5	522	14.9
4 Years	134	41	2464	409	651	.628	0	0	—	350	518	.676	202	49	133	387	17	95	0.7	—	694	5.2	1168	8.7

NBA			Field Goals			3-Pt FGs			Free Throws			Misc			Fouls		Assists		Rebounds			Points	
Year Tm	G	GS	Min	Md	Att	Pct	Md	Att	Pct	Md	Att	Pct	TO	Stl	Blk	PF	DQ	Ast	Avg	Off	Tot	Avg	Pts	Avg
90-91 Min	81	46	2099	195	381	.512	0	1	.000	182	252	.722	77	48	121	337	14	25	0.3	272	641	7.9	572	7.1
91-92 Min	61	54	1481	141	331	.426	0	0	—	123	178	.691	70	27	79	241	7	53	0.9	167	435	7.1	405	6.6
92-93 Min	71	48	1296	105	226	.465	0	0	—	83	127	.654	70	23	66	243	10	17	0.2	134	324	4.6	293	4.1
93-94 Uta	79	79	2210	256	507	.505	0	0	—	165	272	.607	127	41	67	304	5	43	0.5	235	658	8.3	677	8.6
94-95 Uta	34	34	905	105	215	.488	0	0	—	107	135	.793	68	12	32	131	3	17	0.5	90	260	7.6	317	9.3
95-96 Uta	71	70	1267	146	281	.520	0	0	—	104	151	.689	77	20	54	240	1	11	0.2	100	306	4.3	396	5.6
96-97 2Tm	73	65	1558	139	284	.489	0	0	—	94	161	.584	88	34	50	275	7	22	0.3	157	416	5.7	372	5.1
97-98 GS	68	0	813	59	129	.457	0	0	—	44	79	.557	49	23	37	175	3	17	0.3	93	226	3.3	162	2.4
98-99 GS	26	0	159	15	33	.455	0	0	—	12	26	.462	9	5	10	41	0	0	0.0	18	46	1.8	42	1.6
99-00 SA	26	0	149	15	33	.455	0	0	—	20	30	.667	9	6	8	32	0	3	0.1	15	39	1.5	50	1.9
96-97 Orl	1	1	19	2	2	1.000	0	0	—	0	0	—	1	0	0	2	0	1	1.0	5	6	6.0	4	4.0
GS	72	64	1539	137	282	.486	0	0	—	94	161	.584	87	34	50	273	7	21	0.3	152	410	5.7	368	5.1
10 Years	590	396	11937	1176	2420	.486	0	1	.000	934	1411	.662	644	239	524	2019	50	208	0.4	1281	3351	5.7	3286	5.6

NBA Postseason																							
Year Tm	G	GS	Min	Md	Att	Pct	Md	Att	Pct	Md	Att	Pct	TO	Stl	Blk	PF	DQ	Ast	Avg	Off	Tot	Avg	Pts	Avg
93-94 Uta	16	16	492	47	105	.448	0	0	—	33	50	.660	24	3	20	73	3	7	0.4	61	135	8.4	127	7.9
95-96 Uta	18	18	276	23	53	.434	0	1	.000	5	9	.556	19	5	22	58	0	2	0.1	26	54	3.0	51	2.8
2 Years	34	34	768	70	158	.443	0	1	.000	38	59	.644	43	8	42	131	3	9	0.3	87	189	5.6	178	5.2

Latrell Sprewell

(statistical profile on page 276)

Pos: G-F **College:** Alabama **Drafted:** '92 1(24)—GS   **Ht:** 6'5" **Wt:** 190 **Born:** 9/8/70 **Age:** 30

College			Field Goals			3-Pt FGs			Free Throws			Misc			Fouls		Assists		Rebounds			Points	
Year Tm	G	GS	Min	Md	Att	Pct	Md	Att	Pct	Md	Att	Pct	TO	Stl	Blk	PF	DQ	Ast	Avg	Off	Tot	Avg	Pts	Avg
90-91 Ala	33	—	865	116	217	.535	5	12	.417	58	84	.690	54	35	16	53	—	62	1.9	—	165	5.0	295	8.9
91-92 Ala	35	—	1266	227	460	.493	68	171	.398	101	131	.771	92	63	23	64	—	74	2.1	—	183	5.2	623	17.8
2 Years	68	—	2131	343	677	.507	73	183	.399	159	215	.740	146	98	39	117	—	136	2.0	—	348	5.1	918	13.5

NBA			Field Goals			3-Pt FGs			Free Throws			Misc			Fouls		Assists		Rebounds			Points	
Year Tm	G	GS	Min	Md	Att	Pct	Md	Att	Pct	Md	Att	Pct	TO	Stl	Blk	PF	DQ	Ast	Avg	Off	Tot	Avg	Pts	Avg
92-93 GS	77	69	2741	449	968	.464	73	198	.369	211	283	.746	203	126	52	166	2	295	3.8	79	271	3.5	1182	15.4
93-94 GS*	82	82	3533	613	1417	.433	141	391	.361	353	456	.774	226	180	76	158	0	385	4.7	80	401	4.9	1720	21.0
94-95 GS*	69	69	2771	490	1171	.418	90	326	.276	350	448	.781	230	112	46	108	0	279	4.0	58	256	3.7	1420	20.6
95-96 GS	78	78	3064	515	1202	.428	91	282	.323	352	446	.789	222	127	45	150	1	328	4.2	124	380	4.9	1473	18.9
96-97 GS*	80	79	3353	649	1444	.449	147	415	.354	493	585	.843	322	132	45	153	0	507	6.3	58	366	4.6	1938	24.2
97-98 GS	14	13	547	110	277	.397	9	48	.188	70	94	.745	44	19	5	26	0	68	4.9	7	51	3.6	299	21.4
98-99 NY	37	4	1233	215	518	.415	21	77	.273	155	191	.812	79	46	2	65	0	91	2.5	41	156	4.2	606	16.4
99-00 NY	82	82	3276	568	1305	.435	44	127	.346	344	397	.866	226	109	22	184	0	332	4.0	49	349	4.3	1524	18.6
8 Years	519	476	20518	3609	8302	.435	616	1864	.330	2328	2900	.803	1552	851	293	1010	3	2285	4.4	496	2230	4.3	10162	19.6

NBA Postseason																							
Year Tm	G	GS	Min	Md	Att	Pct	Md	Att	Pct	Md	Att	Pct	TO	Stl	Blk	PF	DQ	Ast	Avg	Off	Tot	Avg	Pts	Avg
93-94 GS	3	3	122	26	60	.433	8	23	.348	8	12	.667	9	2	3	15	0	21	7.0	1	9	3.0	68	22.7
98-99 NY	20	8	743	145	346	.419	4	25	.160	113	133	.850	58	19	6	40	1	43	2.2	24	96	4.8	407	20.4
99-00 NY	16	16	700	110	266	.414	10	30	.333	69	88	.784	37	18	5	28	0	58	3.6	12	70	4.4	299	18.7
3 Years	39	27	1565	281	672	.418	22	78	.282	190	233	.815	104	39	14	83	1	122	3.1	37	175	4.5	774	19.8

Ryan Stack

Pos: F **College:** South Carolina **Drafted:** '98 2(48)—Cle   **Ht:** 6'11" **Wt:** 221 **Born:** 7/24/75 **Age:** 25

College			Field Goals			3-Pt FGs			Free Throws			Misc			Fouls		Assists		Rebounds			Points	
Year Tm	G	GS	Min	Md	Att	Pct	Md	Att	Pct	Md	Att	Pct	TO	Stl	Blk	PF	DQ	Ast	Avg	Off	Tot	Avg	Pts	Avg
94-95 SCar	27	0	472	59	139	.424	17	43	.395	27	46	.587	41	13	29	52	2	18	0.7	41	100	3.7	162	6.0
95-96 SCar	31	4	427	45	89	.506	7	20	.350	34	44	.773	38	5	12	37	0	15	0.5	31	83	2.7	131	4.2
96-97 SCar	31	28	725	61	132	.462	20	53	.377	49	72	.681	52	19	28	72	3	27	0.9	48	132	4.3	191	6.2
97-98 SCar	31	31	925	107	215	.498	15	47	.319	68	96	.708	69	22	55	75	4	32	1.0	53	186	6.0	297	9.6
4 Years	120	63	2549	272	575	.473	59	163	.362	178	258	.690	200	59	124	236	9	92	0.8	173	501	4.2	781	6.5

NBA			Field Goals			3-Pt FGs			Free Throws			Misc			Fouls		Assists		Rebounds			Points	
Year Tm	G	GS	Min	Md	Att	Pct	Md	Att	Pct	Md	Att	Pct	TO	Stl	Blk	PF	DQ	Ast	Avg	Off	Tot	Avg	Pts	Avg
98-99 Cle	18	0	199	14	37	.378	0	0	—	19	20	.950	9	2	11	31	0	5	0.3	19	34	1.9	47	2.6
99-00 Cle	25	0	198	17	51	.333	0	1	.000	18	27	.667	17	4	11	47	3	5	0.2	15	45	1.8	52	2.1
2 Years	43	0	397	31	88	.352	0	1	.000	37	47	.787	26	6	22	78	3	10	0.2	34	79	1.8	99	2.3

Jerry Stackhouse

(statistical profile on page 277)

Pos: G-F **College:** North Carolina **Drafted:** '95 1(3)—Phi **Ht:** 6'6" **Wt:** 218 **Born:** 11/5/74 **Age:** 26

College			Field Goals			3-Pt FGs			Free Throws			Misc			Fouls		Assists		Rebounds			Points	
Year Tm	G	GS	Min	Md	Att	Pct	Md	Att	Pct	Md	Att	Pct	TO	Stl	Blk	PF	DQ	Ast	Avg	Off	Tot	Avg	Pts	Avg
93-94 UNC	35	1	734	138	296	.466	2	20	.100	150	205	.732	87	42	17	55	—	69	2.0	76	176	5.0	428	12.2
94-95 UNC	34	33	1170	215	416	.517	37	90	.411	185	260	.712	111	50	59	74	—	93	2.7	95	280	8.2	652	19.2
2 Years	69	34	1904	353	712	.496	39	110	.355	335	465	.720	198	92	76	129	—	162	2.3	171	456	6.6	1080	15.7

NBA			Field Goals			3-Pt FGs			Free Throws			Misc			Fouls		Assists		Rebounds			Points	
Year Tm	G	GS	Min	Md	Att	Pct	Md	Att	Pct	Md	Att	Pct	TO	Stl	Blk	PF	DQ	Ast	Avg	Off	Tot	Avg	Pts	Avg
95-96 Phi	72	71	2701	452	1091	.414	93	292	.318	387	518	.747	252	76	79	179	0	278	3.9	90	265	3.7	1384	19.2
96-97 Phi	81	81	3166	533	1308	.407	102	342	.298	511	667	.766	316	93	63	219	2	253	3.1	156	338	4.2	1679	20.7
97-98 2Tm	79	37	2545	424	975	.435	47	195	.241	354	450	.787	224	89	59	175	2	241	3.1	105	266	3.4	1249	15.8
98-99 Det	42	9	1188	181	488	.371	35	126	.278	210	247	.850	121	34	19	79	0	118	2.8	26	107	2.5	607	14.5
99-00 Det*	82	82	3148	619	1447	.428	83	288	.288	618	758	.815	311	103	36	188	2	365	4.5	118	315	3.8	1939	23.6
97-98 Phi	22	22	748	128	283	.452	16	46	.348	81	101	.802	74	31	21	56	1	67	3.0	28	76	3.5	353	16.0
Det	57	15	1797	296	692	.428	31	149	.208	273	349	.782	150	58	38	119	1	174	3.1	77	190	3.3	896	15.7
5 Years	356	280	12748	2209	5309	.416	360	1243	.290	2080	2640	.788	1224	395	256	840	5	1255	3.5	495	1291	3.6	6858	19.3

NBA Postseason			Field Goals			3-Pt FGs			Free Throws			Misc			Fouls		Assists		Rebounds			Points	
Year Tm	G	GS	Min	Md	Att	Pct	Md	Att	Pct	Md	Att	Pct	TO	Stl	Blk	PF	DQ	Ast	Avg	Off	Tot	Avg	Pts	Avg
98-99 Det	5	0	124	18	46	.391	2	8	.250	12	14	.857	10	2	1	11	0	6	1.2	3	8	1.6	50	10.0
99-00 Det	3	3	120	24	59	.407	3	7	.429	23	31	.742	14	2	0	4	0	10	3.3	1	12	4.0	74	24.7
2 Years	8	3	244	42	105	.400	5	15	.333	35	45	.778	24	4	1	15	0	16	2.0	4	20	2.5	124	15.5

John Starks

Pos: G **College:** Oklahoma State **Drafted:** '88 FA—GS **Ht:** 6'5" **Wt:** 185 **Born:** 8/10/65 **Age:** 35

College			Field Goals			3-Pt FGs			Free Throws			Misc			Fouls		Assists		Rebounds			Points	
Year Tm	G	GS	Min	Md	Att	Pct	Md	Att	Pct	Md	Att	Pct	TO	Stl	Blk	PF	DQ	Ast	Avg	Off	Tot	Avg	Pts	Avg
87-88 OkSt	30	28	982	154	310	.497	41	108	.380	114	136	.838	94	66	10	100	6	137	4.6	37	141	4.7	463	15.4

NBA			Field Goals			3-Pt FGs			Free Throws			Misc			Fouls		Assists		Rebounds			Points	
Year Tm	G	GS	Min	Md	Att	Pct	Md	Att	Pct	Md	Att	Pct	TO	Stl	Blk	PF	DQ	Ast	Avg	Off	Tot	Avg	Pts	Avg
88-89 GS	36	0	316	51	125	.408	10	26	.385	34	52	.654	39	23	3	36	0	27	0.8	15	41	1.1	146	4.1
89-90							Played in CBA, Played in WBL																	
90-91 NY	61	10	1173	180	410	.439	27	93	.290	79	105	.752	74	59	17	137	1	204	3.3	30	131	2.1	466	7.6
91-92 NY	82	0	2118	405	902	.449	94	270	.348	235	302	.778	150	103	18	231	4	276	3.4	45	191	2.3	1139	13.9
92-93 NY	80	51	2477	513	1199	.428	108	336	.321	263	331	.795	173	91	12	234	2	404	5.1	54	204	2.6	1397	17.5
93-94 NY*	59	54	2057	410	977	.420	113	337	.335	187	248	.754	184	95	6	191	4	348	5.9	37	185	3.1	1120	19.0
94-95 NY	80	78	2725	419	1062	.395	217	611	.355	168	228	.737	160	92	4	257	3	411	5.1	34	219	2.7	1223	15.3
95-96 NY	81	71	2491	375	846	.443	143	396	.361	131	174	.753	156	103	11	226	2	315	3.9	31	237	2.9	1024	12.6
96-97 NY	77	1	2042	369	856	.431	150	407	.369	173	225	.769	158	90	11	196	2	217	2.8	36	205	2.7	1061	13.8
97-98 NY	82	10	2188	372	947	.393	130	398	.327	185	235	.787	143	78	5	205	2	219	2.7	48	230	2.8	1059	12.9
98-99 GS	50	50	1686	269	728	.370	78	269	.290	74	100	.740	83	69	5	135	3	235	4.7	33	163	3.3	690	13.8
99-00 2Tm	37	30	1190	203	542	.375	59	171	.345	50	59	.847	67	42	4	102	1	181	4.9	10	101	2.7	515	13.9
99-00 GS	33	30	1108	192	508	.378	56	161	.348	45	54	.833	64	37	3	93	1	170	5.2	10	91	2.8	485	14.7
Chi	4	0	82	11	34	.324	3	10	.300	5	5	1.000	3	5	1	9	0	11	2.8	0	10	2.5	30	7.5
11 Years	725	355	20463	3566	8594	.415	1129	3314	.341	1579	2059	.767	1387	845	96	1950	25	2837	3.9	373	1907	2.6	9840	13.6

NBA Postseason			Field Goals			3-Pt FGs			Free Throws			Misc			Fouls		Assists		Rebounds			Points	
Year Tm	G	GS	Min	Md	Att	Pct	Md	Att	Pct	Md	Att	Pct	TO	Stl	Blk	PF	DQ	Ast	Avg	Off	Tot	Avg	Pts	Avg
90-91 NY	3	0	28	2	5	.400	0	0	—	2	2	1.000	6	0	0	4	0	6	2.0	1	3	1.0	6	2.0
91-92 NY	12	0	295	46	123	.374	11	46	.239	42	52	.808	22	17	0	45	1	38	3.2	7	30	2.5	145	12.1
92-93 NY	15	15	575	88	200	.440	28	75	.373	43	60	.717	55	15	3	57	0	96	6.4	4	52	3.5	247	16.5
93-94 NY	25	18	840	110	289	.381	47	132	.356	97	126	.770	57	35	2	86	1	114	4.6	9	58	2.3	364	14.6
94-95 NY	11	11	380	58	129	.450	30	73	.411	26	42	.619	26	13	1	40	0	56	5.1	2	25	2.3	172	15.6
95-96 NY	8	8	314	39	87	.448	21	45	.467	29	39	.744	25	13	1	26	0	33	4.1	3	29	3.6	128	16.0
96-97 NY	9	1	253	44	99	.444	13	41	.317	25	31	.806	20	10	0	25	1	25	2.8	7	31	3.4	126	14.0
97-98 NY	10	2	314	59	125	.472	25	59	.424	21	24	.875	11	16	1	35	1	23	2.3	4	40	4.0	164	16.4
8 Years	93	55	2999	446	1057	.422	175	471	.372	285	376	.758	222	119	8	318	4	391	4.2	37	268	2.9	1352	14.5

Vladimir Stepania

Pos: C **College:** None **Drafted:** '98 1(27)—Sea **Ht:** 7'0" **Wt:** 236 **Born:** 8/5/76 **Age:** 24

Year Tm	G	GS	Min	Md	Att	Pct	Md	Att	Pct	Md	Att	Pct	TO	Stl	Blk	PF	DQ	Ast	Avg	Off	Tot	Avg	Pts	Avg
	NBA			Field Goals			3-Pt FGs			Free Throws			Misc			Fouls		Assists		Rebounds			Points	
98-99 Sea	23	6	313	53	125	.424	0	3	.000	21	40	.525	32	10	23	58	0	12	0.5	27	75	3.3	127	5.5
99-00 Sea	30	1	202	29	79	.367	0	6	.000	17	36	.472	22	10	11	44	0	3	0.1	21	47	1.6	75	2.5
2 Years	53	7	515	82	204	.402	0	9	.000	38	76	.500	54	20	34	102	0	15	0.3	48	122	2.3	202	3.8

Joe Stephens

Pos: F **College:** Arkansas-Little Rock **Drafted:** '96 FA—Hou **Ht:** 6'7" **Wt:** 210 **Born:** 1/28/73 **Age:** 28

Year Tm	G	GS	Min	Md	Att	Pct	Md	Att	Pct	Md	Att	Pct	TO	Stl	Blk	PF	DQ	Ast	Avg	Off	Tot	Avg	Pts	Avg
	College			Field Goals			3-Pt FGs			Free Throws			Misc			Fouls		Assists		Rebounds			Points	
91-92 Colo	19	—	90	12	37	.324	5	19	.263	7	11	.636	—	—	—	—	—	1	0.1	—	8	0.4	36	1.9
92-93 Colo	11	—	65	10	27	.370	3	11	.273	4	8	.500	—	—	—	—	—	2	0.2	—	11	1.0	27	2.5
94-95 Ak-LR	25	—	705	80	218	.367	15	46	.326	36	61	.590	—	—	—	—	—	27	1.1	—	145	5.8	211	8.4
95-96 Ak-LR	30	30	1003	143	309	.463	6	20	.300	79	106	.745	49	36	12	59	1	34	1.1	80	212	7.1	371	12.4
4 Years	85	—	1863	245	591	.415	29	96	.302	126	186	.677	—	—	—	—	—	64	0.8	—	376	4.4	645	7.6
	NBA			Field Goals			3-Pt FGs			Free Throws			Misc			Fouls		Assists		Rebounds			Points	
96-97 Hou	2	0	9	1	5	.200	1	3	.333	0	0	—	3	3	0	3	0	0	0.0	2	3	1.5	3	1.5
97-98 Hou	7	0	37	10	28	.357	3	10	.300	4	6	.667	2	2	0	2	0	1	0.1	3	6	0.9	27	3.9
98-99										Played in CBA														
99-00 Van	13	0	181	19	51	.373	0	8	.000	3	4	.750	6	7	3	9	0	11	0.8	13	36	2.8	41	3.2
3 Years	22	0	227	30	84	.357	4	21	.190	7	10	.700	11	12	3	14	0	12	0.5	18	45	2.0	71	3.2

Kebu Stewart

Pos: F **College:** Cal State-Bakersfield **Drafted:** '97 2(36)—Phi **Ht:** 6'8" **Wt:** 239 **Born:** 12/19/73 **Age:** 27

Year Tm	G	GS	Min	Md	Att	Pct	Md	Att	Pct	Md	Att	Pct	TO	Stl	Blk	PF	DQ	Ast	Avg	Off	Tot	Avg	Pts	Avg
	College			Field Goals			3-Pt FGs			Free Throws			Misc			Fouls		Assists		Rebounds			Points	
93-94 UNLV	22	—	738	140	284	.493	0	1	.000	135	220	.614	61	26	26	73	—	10	0.5	—	256	11.6	415	18.9
94-95 UNLV	21	—	737	116	238	.487	1	4	.250	124	186	.667	76	18	10	60	—	26	1.2	—	209	10.0	357	17.0
95-96 CS-Bk	30	—	998	201	342	.588	0	1	.000	180	262	.687	101	27	33	83	—	17	0.6	—	324	10.8	582	19.4
96-97 CS-Bk	33	—	1097	228	398	.573	0	1	.000	252	354	.712	84	32	34	89	—	15	0.5	—	442	13.4	708	21.5
4 Years	106	—	3570	685	1262	.543	1	7	.143	691	1022	.676	322	103	103	305	—	68	0.6	—	1231	11.6	2062	19.5
	NBA			Field Goals			3-Pt FGs			Free Throws			Misc			Fouls		Assists		Rebounds			Points	
97-98 Phi	15	0	110	12	26	.462	0	0	—	16	25	.640	8	5	2	13	0	2	0.1	9	31	2.1	40	2.7
98-99										Did not play in NBA														
99-00 Dal										Active but did not play														

Michael Stewart

Pos: C **College:** California **Drafted:** '97 FA—Sac **Ht:** 6'10" **Wt:** 230 **Born:** 4/24/75 **Age:** 25

Year Tm	G	GS	Min	Md	Att	Pct	Md	Att	Pct	Md	Att	Pct	TO	Stl	Blk	PF	DQ	Ast	Avg	Off	Tot	Avg	Pts	Avg
	College			Field Goals			3-Pt FGs			Free Throws			Misc			Fouls		Assists		Rebounds			Points	
93-94 Cal	30	18	696	40	85	.471	0	0	—	31	65	.477	23	13	59	86	4	9	0.3	—	152	5.1	111	3.7
94-95 Cal	27	22	470	43	85	.506	0	0	—	18	39	.462	17	12	49	73	2	7	0.3	—	116	4.3	104	3.9
95-96 Cal	28	22	440	35	65	.538	0	0	—	12	27	.444	19	7	43	73	4	8	0.3	47	121	4.3	82	2.9
96-97 Cal	32	32	659	83	159	.522	0	0	—	36	68	.529	36	11	56	82	1	8	0.3	60	160	5.0	202	6.3
4 Years	117	94	2265	201	394	.510	0	0	—	97	199	.487	95	43	207	314	11	32	0.3	—	549	4.7	499	4.3
	NBA			Field Goals			3-Pt FGs			Free Throws			Misc			Fouls		Assists		Rebounds			Points	
97-98 Sac	81	37	1761	155	323	.480	0	0	—	65	142	.458	85	29	195	251	6	61	0.8	197	536	6.6	375	4.6
98-99 Tor	42	2	394	22	53	.415	0	0	—	17	25	.680	12	4	28	76	0	5	0.1	43	99	2.4	61	1.5
99-00 Tor	42	1	389	20	53	.377	0	0	—	18	32	.563	17	5	19	81	3	6	0.1	33	94	2.2	58	1.4
3 Years	165	40	2544	197	429	.459	0	0	—	100	199	.503	114	38	242	408	9	72	0.4	273	729	4.4	494	3.0

Bryant Stith

Pos: G-F **College:** Virginia **Drafted:** '92 1(13)—Den   **Ht:** 6'5" **Wt:** 210 **Born:** 12/10/70 **Age:** 30

College			Field Goals			3-Pt FGs			Free Throws			Misc			Fouls		Assists		Rebounds			Points	
Year Tm	G	GS	Min	Md	Att	Pct	Md	Att	Pct	Md	Att	Pct	TO	Stl	Blk	PF	DQ	Ast	Avg	Off	Tot	Avg	Pts	Avg
88-89 UVa	33	32	942	181	330	.548	1	1	1.000	150	195	.769	71	45	5	83	—	50	1.5	121	216	6.5	513	15.5
89-90 UVa	32	31	1127	217	451	.481	40	102	.392	192	247	.777	61	41	9	63	—	53	1.7	80	221	6.9	666	20.8
90-91 UVa	33	32	1120	228	484	.471	38	125	.304	159	201	.791	82	51	19	84	—	41	1.2	68	203	6.2	653	19.8
91-92 UVa	33	33	1202	230	509	.452	35	95	.368	189	232	.815	66	40	13	78	—	72	2.2	73	219	6.6	684	20.7
4 Years	131	128	4391	856	1774	.483	114	323	.353	690	875	.789	280	177	46	308	—	216	1.6	342	859	6.6	2516	19.2

NBA			Field Goals			3-Pt FGs			Free Throws			Misc			Fouls		Assists		Rebounds			Points	
Year Tm	G	GS	Min	Md	Att	Pct	Md	Att	Pct	Md	Att	Pct	TO	Stl	Blk	PF	DQ	Ast	Avg	Off	Tot	Avg	Pts	Avg
92-93 Den	39	12	865	124	278	.446	0	4	.000	99	119	.832	44	24	5	82	0	49	1.3	39	124	3.2	347	8.9
93-94 Den	82	82	2853	365	811	.450	2	9	.222	291	351	.829	131	116	16	165	0	199	2.4	119	349	4.3	1023	12.5
94-95 Den	81	51	2329	312	661	.472	20	68	.294	267	324	.824	110	91	18	142	0	153	1.9	95	268	3.3	911	11.2
95-96 Den	82	77	2810	379	911	.416	41	148	.277	320	379	.844	157	114	16	187	3	241	2.9	125	400	4.9	1119	13.6
96-97 Den	52	52	1788	251	603	.416	70	182	.385	202	234	.863	101	60	20	119	1	133	2.6	74	217	4.2	774	14.9
97-98 Den	31	15	718	75	225	.333	10	48	.208	75	86	.872	35	21	8	52	0	50	1.6	15	65	2.1	235	7.6
98-99 Den	46	32	1194	114	290	.393	31	106	.292	61	71	.859	45	28	15	65	0	82	1.8	30	107	2.3	320	7.0
99-00 Den	45	6	691	86	189	.455	17	56	.304	64	77	.831	33	18	12	56	0	61	1.4	23	84	1.9	253	5.6
8 Years	458	327	13248	1706	3968	.430	191	621	.308	1379	1641	.840	656	472	110	868	4	968	2.1	520	1614	3.5	4982	10.9

NBA Postseason																							
Year Tm	G	GS	Min	Md	Att	Pct	Md	Att	Pct	Md	Att	Pct	TO	Stl	Blk	PF	DQ	Ast	Avg	Off	Tot	Avg	Pts	Avg
93-94 Den	12	12	413	43	102	.422	0	1	.000	50	60	.833	14	11	2	23	0	26	2.2	23	56	4.7	136	11.3
94-95 Den	3	1	85	17	32	.531	1	6	.167	15	19	.789	0	1	1	7	0	7	2.3	3	9	3.0	50	16.7
2 Years	15	13	498	60	134	.448	1	7	.143	65	79	.823	14	12	3	30	0	33	2.2	26	65	4.3	186	12.4

John Stockton

(statistical profile on page 277)

Pos: G **College:** Gonzaga **Drafted:** '84 1(16)—Uta   **Ht:** 6'1" **Wt:** 175 **Born:** 3/26/62 **Age:** 38

College			Field Goals			3-Pt FGs			Free Throws			Misc			Fouls		Assists		Rebounds			Points	
Year Tm	G	GS	Min	Md	Att	Pct	Md	Att	Pct	Md	Att	Pct	TO	Stl	Blk	PF	DQ	Ast	Avg	Off	Tot	Avg	Pts	Avg
80-81 Gonz	25	—	235	26	45	.578	—	—		26	35	.743	23	17	1	25	0	34	1.4	—	11	0.4	78	3.1
81-82 Gonz	27	—	1054	117	203	.576	—	—		69	102	.676	85	68	1	76	2	135	5.0	—	67	2.5	303	11.2
82-83 Gonz	27	—	1036	142	274	.518	—	—		91	115	.791	95	68	8	72	1	184	6.8	—	87	3.2	375	13.9
83-84 Gonz	28	—	1053	229	397	.577	—	—		126	182	.692	93	109	4	82	3	201	7.2	—	66	2.4	584	20.9
4 Years	107	—	3378	514	919	.559	—	—		312	434	.719	296	262	14	255	6	554	5.2	—	231	2.2	1340	12.5

NBA			Field Goals			3-Pt FGs			Free Throws			Misc			Fouls		Assists		Rebounds			Points	
Year Tm	G	GS	Min	Md	Att	Pct	Md	Att	Pct	Md	Att	Pct	TO	Stl	Blk	PF	DQ	Ast	Avg	Off	Tot	Avg	Pts	Avg
84-85 Uta	82	5	1490	157	333	.471	2	11	.182	142	193	.736	150	109	11	203	3	415	5.1	26	105	1.3	458	5.6
85-86 Uta	82	38	1935	228	466	.489	2	15	.133	172	205	.839	168	157	10	227	2	610	7.4	33	179	2.2	630	7.7
86-87 Uta	82	2	1858	231	463	.499	7	39	.179	179	229	.782	164	177	14	224	1	670	8.2	32	151	1.8	648	7.9
87-88 Uta	82	79	2842	454	791	.574	24	67	.358	272	324	.840	262	242	16	247	5	1128	13.8	54	237	2.9	1204	14.7
88-89 Uta*	82	82	3171	497	923	.538	16	66	.242	390	452	.863	308	263	14	241	3	1118	13.6	83	248	3.0	1400	17.1
89-90 Uta*	78	78	2915	472	918	.514	47	113	.416	354	432	.819	272	207	18	233	3	1134	14.5	57	206	2.6	1345	17.2
90-91 Uta*	82	82	3103	496	978	.507	58	168	.345	363	434	.836	298	234	16	233	1	1164	14.2	46	237	2.9	1413	17.2
91-92 Uta*	82	82	3002	453	939	.482	83	204	.407	308	366	.842	286	244	22	234	3	1126	13.7	68	270	3.3	1297	15.8
92-93 Uta*	82	82	2863	437	899	.486	72	187	.385	293	367	.798	266	199	21	224	2	987	12.0	64	237	2.9	1239	15.1
93-94 Uta*	82	82	2969	458	868	.528	48	149	.322	272	338	.805	266	199	22	236	3	1031	12.6	72	258	3.1	1236	15.1
94-95 Uta*	82	82	2867	429	791	.542	102	227	.449	246	306	.804	267	194	22	215	3	1011	12.3	57	251	3.1	1206	14.7
95-96 Uta*	82	82	2915	440	818	.538	95	225	.422	234	282	.830	246	140	15	207	1	916	11.2	54	226	2.8	1209	14.7
96-97 Uta*	82	82	2896	416	759	.548	76	180	.422	275	325	.846	248	166	15	194	2	860	10.5	45	228	2.8	1183	14.4
97-98 Uta	64	64	1858	270	511	.528	39	91	.429	191	231	.827	161	89	10	138	0	543	8.5	35	166	2.6	770	12.0
98-99 Uta	50	50	1410	200	410	.488	16	50	.320	137	169	.811	110	81	13	107	0	374	7.5	31	146	2.9	553	11.1
99-00 Uta*	82	82	2432	363	725	.501	43	121	.355	221	257	.860	179	143	15	192	0	703	8.6	45	215	2.6	990	12.1
16 Years	1258	1054	40526	6001	11592	.518	730	1913	.382	4049	4910	.825	3651	2844	254	3355	32	13790	11.0	802	3360	2.7	16781	13.3

NBA Postseason																							
Year Tm	G	GS	Min	Md	Att	Pct	Md	Att	Pct	Md	Att	Pct	TO	Stl	Blk	PF	DQ	Ast	Avg	Off	Tot	Avg	Pts	Avg
84-85 Uta	10	0	186	21	45	.467	0	2	.000	26	35	.743	16	11	2	30	0	43	4.3	7	28	2.8	68	6.8
85-86 Uta	4	0	73	9	17	.529	1	1	1.000	8	9	.889	4	5	0	10	0	14	3.5	3	6	1.5	27	6.8
86-87 Uta	5	2	157	18	29	.621	4	5	.800	10	13	.769	11	15	1	18	0	40	8.0	2	11	2.2	50	10.0
87-88 Uta	11	11	478	68	134	.507	4	14	.286	75	91	.824	48	37	3	36	0	163	14.8	14	45	4.1	215	19.5
88-89 Uta	3	3	139	30	59	.508	3	4	.750	19	21	.905	11	11	5	15	0	41	13.7	2	10	3.3	82	27.3
89-90 Uta	5	5	194	29	69	.420	1	13	.077	16	20	.800	14	6	0	20	0	75	15.0	4	16	3.2	75	15.0
90-91 Uta	9	9	373	58	108	.537	11	27	.407	37	44	.841	32	20	2	33	0	124	13.8	10	42	4.7	164	18.2
91-92 Uta	16	16	623	77	182	.423	18	58	.310	65	78	.833	58	34	5	38	0	217	13.6	10	47	2.9	237	14.8
92-93 Uta	5	5	193	23	51	.451	5	13	.385	15	18	.833	15	12	0	16	0	55	11.0	5	12	2.4	66	13.2

Year Tm	G	GS	Min	Md	Att	Pct	Md	Att	Pct	Md	Att	Pct	TO	Stl	Blk	PF	DQ	Ast	Avg	Off	Tot	Avg	Pts	Avg
93-94 Uta	16	16	597	88	193	.456	4	24	.167	51	63	.810	40	27	8	44	0	157	9.8	14	52	3.3	231	14.4
94-95 Uta	5	5	193	34	74	.459	8	20	.400	13	17	.765	14	7	1	13	0	51	10.2	6	17	3.4	89	17.8
95-96 Uta	18	18	679	70	157	.446	11	38	.289	48	59	.814	58	29	7	50	0	195	10.8	14	58	3.2	199	11.1
96-97 Uta	20	20	739	113	217	.521	19	50	.380	77	90	.856	62	33	5	52	0	191	9.6	18	78	3.9	322	16.1
97-98 Uta	20	20	596	81	164	.494	9	26	.346	51	71	.718	48	31	3	54	0	155	7.8	16	60	3.0	222	11.1
98-99 Uta	11	11	352	42	105	.400	4	12	.333	34	46	.739	31	18	1	32	0	92	8.4	11	36	3.3	122	11.1
99-00 Uta	10	10	350	41	89	.461	7	18	.389	23	30	.767	26	13	2	30	0	103	10.3	7	30	3.0	112	11.2
16 Years	168	151	5922	802	1693	.474	109	325	.335	568	705	.806	488	309	45	491	0	1716	10.2	143	548	3.3	2281	13.6

Predrag Stojakovic

(statistical profile on page 278)

Pos: G-F **College:** None **Drafted:** '96 1(14)—Sac **Ht:** 6'9" **Wt:** 229 **Born:** 6/9/77 **Age:** 23

NBA			Field Goals			3-Pt FGs			Free Throws			Misc			Fouls		Assists		Rebounds			Points	
Year Tm	G	GS	Min	Md	Att	Pct	Md	Att	Pct	Md	Att	Pct	TO	Stl	Blk	PF	DQ	Ast	Avg	Off	Tot	Avg	Pts	Avg
96-97										Played in Greece														
97-98										Played in Greece														
98-99 Sac	48	1	1025	141	373	.378	57	178	.320	63	74	.851	53	41	7	43	0	72	1.5	43	143	3.0	402	8.4
99-00 Sac	74	11	1749	321	717	.448	100	267	.375	135	153	.882	88	52	7	97	0	106	1.4	74	276	3.7	877	11.9
2 Years	122	12	2774	462	1090	.424	157	445	.353	198	227	.872	141	93	14	140	0	178	1.5	117	419	3.4	1279	10.5

NBA Postseason																								
Year Tm	G	GS	Min	Md	Att	Pct	Md	Att	Pct	Md	Att	Pct	TO	Stl	Blk	PF	DQ	Ast	Avg	Off	Tot	Avg	Pts	Avg
98-99 Sac	5	0	108	9	26	.346	3	14	.214	3	3	1.000	6	3	0	7	0	2	0.4	12	19	3.8	24	4.8
99-00 Sac	5	0	129	16	40	.400	6	13	.462	6	9	.667	5	4	0	7	0	3	0.6	2	17	3.4	44	8.8
2 Years	10	0	237	25	66	.379	9	27	.333	9	12	.750	11	7	0	14	0	5	0.5	14	36	3.6	68	6.8

Damon Stoudamire

(statistical profile on page 278)

Pos: G **College:** Arizona **Drafted:** '95 1(7)—Tor **Ht:** 5'10" **Wt:** 171 **Born:** 9/3/73 **Age:** 27

College			Field Goals			3-Pt FGs			Free Throws			Misc			Fouls		Assists		Rebounds			Points	
Year Tm	G	GS	Min	Md	Att	Pct	Md	Att	Pct	Md	Att	Pct	TO	Stl	Blk	PF	DQ	Ast	Avg	Off	Tot	Avg	Pts	Avg
91-92 Ari	30	0	540	76	167	.455	28	69	.406	37	48	.771	44	22	3	43	0	76	2.5	13	65	2.2	217	7.2
92-93 Ari	28	27	870	99	226	.438	39	102	.382	72	91	.791	82	45	6	62	1	159	5.7	26	116	4.1	309	11.0
93-94 Ari	35	35	1164	217	484	.448	93	265	.351	112	140	.800	113	55	3	81	1	208	5.9	30	157	4.5	639	18.3
94-95 Ari	30	30	1092	222	466	.476	112	241	.465	128	155	.826	139	52	1	61	1	220	7.3	17	128	4.3	684	22.8
4 Years	123	92	3666	614	1343	.457	272	677	.402	349	434	.804	378	174	13	247	3	663	5.4	86	466	3.8	1849	15.0

NBA			Field Goals			3-Pt FGs			Free Throws			Misc			Fouls		Assists		Rebounds			Points	
Year Tm	G	GS	Min	Md	Att	Pct	Md	Att	Pct	Md	Att	Pct	TO	Stl	Blk	PF	DQ	Ast	Avg	Off	Tot	Avg	Pts	Avg
95-96 Tor	70	70	2865	481	1129	.426	133	337	.395	236	296	.797	267	98	19	166	0	653	9.3	59	281	4.0	1331	19.0
96-97 Tor	81	81	3311	564	1407	.401	176	496	.355	330	401	.823	288	123	13	162	1	709	8.8	86	330	4.1	1634	20.2
97-98 2Tm	71	71	2839	448	1091	.411	91	304	.299	238	287	.829	223	113	7	150	0	580	8.2	87	298	4.2	1225	17.3
98-99 Por	50	50	1673	249	629	.396	44	142	.310	89	122	.730	110	49	4	81	0	312	6.2	41	167	3.3	631	12.6
99-00 Por	78	78	2372	386	894	.432	80	212	.377	122	145	.841	149	77	1	173	0	405	5.2	61	243	3.1	974	12.5
97-98 Tor	49	49	2033	354	833	.425	65	205	.317	179	212	.844	159	80	5	112	0	399	8.1	63	217	4.4	952	19.4
Por	22	22	806	94	258	.364	26	99	.263	59	75	.787	64	33	2	38	0	181	8.2	24	81	3.7	273	12.4
5 Years	350	350	13060	2128	5150	.413	524	1491	.351	1015	1251	.811	1037	460	44	732	1	2659	7.6	334	1319	3.8	5795	16.6

NBA Postseason																								
Year Tm	G	GS	Min	Md	Att	Pct	Md	Att	Pct	Md	Att	Pct	TO	Stl	Blk	PF	DQ	Ast	Avg	Off	Tot	Avg	Pts	Avg
97-98 Por	4	4	166	25	63	.397	8	22	.364	13	13	1.000	16	5	1	13	0	38	9.5	6	17	4.3	71	17.8
98-99 Por	13	13	403	49	129	.380	10	22	.455	24	34	.706	38	8	4	31	0	73	5.6	7	41	3.2	132	10.2
99-00 Por	16	16	447	56	135	.415	10	30	.333	20	24	.833	19	8	1	43	1	58	3.6	8	42	2.6	142	8.9
3 Years	33	33	1016	130	327	.398	28	74	.378	57	71	.803	73	21	6	87	1	169	5.1	21	100	3.0	345	10.5

Erick Strickland

(statistical profile on page 279)

Pos: G **College:** Nebraska **Drafted:** '96 FA—Dal **Ht:** 6'3" **Wt:** 222 **Born:** 11/25/73 **Age:** 27

College			Field Goals			3-Pt FGs			Free Throws			Misc			Fouls		Assists		Rebounds			Points	
Year Tm	G	GS	Min	Md	Att	Pct	Md	Att	Pct	Md	Att	Pct	TO	Stl	Blk	PF	DQ	Ast	Avg	Off	Tot	Avg	Pts	Avg
92-93 Neb	31	6	534	84	185	.454	32	88	.364	43	59	.729	61	47	4	78	2	66	2.1	—	63	2.0	243	7.8
93-94 Neb	30	13	671	102	241	.423	41	117	.350	77	95	.811	71	60	11	86	5	96	3.2	—	103	3.4	322	10.7
94-95 Neb	31	31	942	175	394	.444	54	160	.338	101	139	.727	96	89	7	96	5	133	4.3	—	167	5.4	505	16.3
95-96 Neb	35	34	1087	174	399	.436	52	148	.351	116	141	.823	100	61	10	101	5	119	3.4	—	170	4.9	516	14.7
4 Years	127	84	3234	535	1219	.439	179	513	.349	337	434	.776	328	257	32	361	17	414	3.3	—	503	4.0	1586	12.5

NBA			Field Goals			3-Pt FGs			Free Throws			Misc			Fouls		Assists		Rebounds			Points	
Year Tm	G	GS	Min	Md	Att	Pct	Md	Att	Pct	Md	Att	Pct	TO	Stl	Blk	PF	DQ	Ast	Avg	Off	Tot	Avg	Pts	Avg
96-97 Dal	28	15	759	102	256	.398	28	92	.304	65	80	.813	66	27	5	75	3	68	2.4	21	90	3.2	297	10.6
97-98 Dal	67	19	1505	199	558	.357	48	163	.294	65	84	.774	106	56	8	140	1	167	2.5	35	161	2.4	511	7.6
98-99 Dal	33	2	567	89	221	.403	18	59	.305	53	65	.815	36	40	2	44	0	64	1.9	12	83	2.5	249	7.5
99-00 Dal	68	67	2025	316	730	.433	73	186	.392	162	195	.831	102	105	13	190	3	211	3.1	69	323	4.8	867	12.8
4 Years	196	103	4856	706	1765	.400	167	500	.334	345	424	.814	310	228	28	449	7	510	2.6	137	657	3.4	1924	9.8

Mark Strickland

Pos: F **College:** Temple **Drafted:** '94 FA—Ind **Ht:** 6'10" **Wt:** 215 **Born:** 7/14/70 **Age:** 30

College			Field Goals			3-Pt FGs			Free Throws			Misc			Fouls		Assists		Rebounds			Points	
Year Tm	G	GS	Min	Md	Att	Pct	Md	Att	Pct	Md	Att	Pct	TO	Stl	Blk	PF	DQ	Ast	Avg	Off	Tot	Avg	Pts	Avg
89-90 Tem	31	—	679	68	127	.535	0	3	.000	18	49	.367	—	—	32	—	—	6	0.2	—	161	5.2	154	5.0
90-91 Tem	34	—	1143	113	229	.493	—	—	—	35	82	.427	—	—	72	—	—	10	0.3	—	236	6.9	261	7.7
91-92 Tem	30	—	988	127	239	.531	—	—	—	39	91	.429	—	—	73	—	—	6	0.2	—	179	6.0	293	9.8
3 Years	95	—	2810	308	595	.518	—	—	—	92	222	.414	—	—	177	—	—	22	0.2	—	576	6.1	708	7.5

NBA			Field Goals			3-Pt FGs			Free Throws			Misc			Fouls		Assists		Rebounds			Points	
Year Tm	G	GS	Min	Md	Att	Pct	Md	Att	Pct	Md	Att	Pct	TO	Stl	Blk	PF	DQ	Ast	Avg	Off	Tot	Avg	Pts	Avg
92-93										Played in USBL														
93-94										Played in USBL														
94-95 Ind	4	0	9	1	3	.333	0	0	—	1	2	.500	1	0	1	0	0	0	0.0	2	4	1.0	3	0.8
95-96										Played in CBA														
96-97 Mia	31	0	153	25	60	.417	0	1	.000	12	21	.571	15	4	10	17	0	1	0.0	16	37	1.2	62	2.0
97-98 Mia	51	8	847	145	269	.539	0	1	.000	59	82	.720	47	18	34	87	0	26	0.5	80	213	4.2	349	6.8
98-99 Mia	32	1	357	50	101	.495	0	1	.000	19	26	.731	13	7	8	28	0	9	0.3	26	78	2.4	119	3.7
99-00 Mia	58	5	663	122	224	.545	0	0	—	40	56	.714	24	15	18	68	0	22	0.4	44	140	2.4	284	4.9
5 Years	176	14	2029	343	657	.522	0	3	.000	131	187	.701	100	44	71	200	0	58	0.3	168	472	2.7	817	4.6

NBA Postseason																								
Year Tm	G	GS	Min	Md	Att	Pct	Md	Att	Pct	Md	Att	Pct	TO	Stl	Blk	PF	DQ	Ast	Avg	Off	Tot	Avg	Pts	Avg
96-97 Mia	4	0	16	4	8	.500	0	0	—	0	2	.000	2	1	0	0	0	1	0.3	0	3	0.8	8	2.0
97-98 Mia	3	0	28	4	5	.800	0	0	—	1	2	.500	0	0	1	4	0	0	0.0	2	7	2.3	9	3.0
98-99 Mia	2	0	8	1	2	.500	0	0	—	2	2	1.000	1	1	0	0	0	0	0.0	1	3	1.5	4	2.0
99-00 Mia	1	0	10	1	3	.333	0	0	—	0	2	.000	1	2	0	0	0	0	0.0	0	0	0.0	2	2.0
4 Years	10	0	62	10	18	.556	0	0	—	3	8	.375	4	4	1	4	0	1	0.1	3	13	1.3	23	2.3

Rod Strickland

(statistical profile on page 279)

Pos: G **College:** DePaul **Drafted:** '88 1(19)—NY **Ht:** 6'3" **Wt:** 185 **Born:** 7/11/66 **Age:** 34

College			Field Goals			3-Pt FGs			Free Throws			Misc			Fouls		Assists		Rebounds			Points	
Year Tm	G	GS	Min	Md	Att	Pct	Md	Att	Pct	Md	Att	Pct	TO	Stl	Blk	PF	DQ	Ast	Avg	Off	Tot	Avg	Pts	Avg
85-86 DeP	31	23	1063	176	354	.497	—	—	—	85	126	.675	84	69	5	74	2	159	5.1	—	84	2.7	437	14.1
86-87 DeP	30	27	980	188	323	.582	8	15	.533	106	175	.606	86	60	5	56	1	196	6.5	—	113	3.8	490	16.3
87-88 DeP	26	21	837	207	392	.528	24	54	.444	83	137	.606	81	75	4	53	0	202	7.8	39	98	3.8	521	20.0
3 Years	87	71	2880	571	1069	.534	32	69	.464	274	438	.626	251	204	14	183	3	557	6.4	—	295	3.4	1448	16.6

NBA			Field Goals			3-Pt FGs			Free Throws			Misc			Fouls		Assists		Rebounds			Points	
Year Tm	G	GS	Min	Md	Att	Pct	Md	Att	Pct	Md	Att	Pct	TO	Stl	Blk	PF	DQ	Ast	Avg	Off	Tot	Avg	Pts	Avg
88-89 NY	81	10	1358	265	567	.467	19	59	.322	172	231	.745	148	98	3	142	2	319	3.9	51	160	2.0	721	8.9
89-90 2Tm	82	24	2140	343	756	.454	8	30	.267	174	278	.626	170	127	14	160	3	468	5.7	90	259	3.2	868	10.6
90-91 SA	58	56	2076	314	651	.482	11	33	.333	161	211	.763	156	117	11	125	0	463	8.0	57	219	3.8	800	13.8
91-92 SA	57	54	2053	300	659	.455	5	15	.333	182	265	.687	160	118	17	122	0	491	8.6	92	265	4.6	787	13.8
92-93 Por	78	35	2474	396	816	.485	4	30	.133	273	381	.717	199	131	24	153	1	559	7.2	120	337	4.3	1069	13.7
93-94 Por	82	58	2889	528	1093	.483	2	10	.200	353	471	.749	257	147	24	171	0	740	9.0	122	370	4.5	1411	17.2
94-95 Por	64	61	2267	441	946	.466	46	123	.374	283	380	.745	209	123	9	118	0	562	8.8	73	317	5.0	1211	18.9
95-96 Por	67	63	2526	471	1023	.460	38	111	.342	276	423	.652	255	97	16	135	2	640	9.6	89	297	4.4	1256	18.7
96-97 Was	82	81	2997	515	1105	.466	13	77	.169	367	497	.738	270	143	14	166	2	727	8.9	95	335	4.1	1410	17.2
97-98 Was	76	76	3020	490	1130	.434	12	48	.250	357	492	.726	266	126	25	182	2	801	10.5	112	405	5.3	1349	17.8
98-99 Was	44	43	1632	251	603	.416	12	42	.286	176	236	.746	142	76	5	91	0	434	9.9	56	212	4.8	690	15.7
99-00 Was	69	67	2188	327	762	.429	1	21	.048	214	305	.702	187	94	18	147	1	519	7.5	73	259	3.8	869	12.6
89-90 NY	51	0	1019	170	386	.440	6	21	.286	83	130	.638	85	70	8	71	0	219	4.3	43	126	2.5	429	8.4
SA	31	24	1121	173	370	.468	2	9	.222	91	148	.615	85	57	6	89	3	249	8.0	47	133	4.3	439	14.2
12 Years	840	628	27620	4641	10111	.459	171	599	.285	2988	4170	.717	2419	1397	180	1712	13	6723	8.0	1030	3435	4.1	12441	14.8

NBA Postseason																								
Year Tm	G	GS	Min	Md	Att	Pct	Md	Att	Pct	Md	Att	Pct	TO	Stl	Blk	PF	DQ	Ast	Avg	Off	Tot	Avg	Pts	Avg
88-89 NY	9	0	111	22	49	.449	1	1	1.000	9	17	.529	13	4	1	21	0	25	2.8	6	13	1.4	54	6.0
89-90 SA	10	10	384	54	127	.425	0	7	.000	15	27	.556	34	14	0	30	2	112	11.2	22	53	5.3	123	12.3

159

			Field Goals			3-Pt FGs			Free Throws			Misc			Fouls		Assists		Rebounds			Points	

NBA Postseason

Year Tm	G	GS	Min	Md	Att	Pct	Md	Att	Pct	Md	Att	Pct	TO	Stl	Blk	PF	DQ	Ast	Avg	Off	Tot	Avg	Pts	Avg
90-91 SA	4	4	168	29	67	.433	0	6	.000	17	21	.810	13	9	0	14	0	35	8.8	5	21	5.3	75	18.8
91-92 SA	2	2	80	13	22	.591	0	0	—	5	8	.625	6	3	2	8	0	19	9.5	0	7	3.5	31	15.5
92-93 Por	4	4	156	22	52	.423	0	1	.000	10	12	.833	7	5	2	10	0	37	9.3	9	26	6.5	54	13.5
93-94 Por	4	4	154	36	72	.500	0	1	.000	22	27	.815	10	4	2	13	0	39	9.8	3	16	4.0	94	23.5
94-95 Por	3	3	126	27	65	.415	2	5	.400	14	18	.778	10	3	2	11	0	37	12.3	1	12	4.0	70	23.3
95-96 Por	5	5	202	37	84	.440	6	12	.500	23	36	.639	12	5	0	14	0	42	8.4	12	31	6.2	103	20.6
96-97 Was	3	3	124	22	52	.423	1	2	.500	14	19	.737	11	3	0	8	0	25	8.3	5	18	6.0	59	19.7
9 Years	44	35	1505	262	590	.444	10	35	.286	129	185	.697	116	50	9	129	2	371	8.4	63	197	4.5	663	15.1

Derek Strong

Pos: F **College:** Xavier (OH) **Drafted:** '90 2(47)—Phi **Ht:** 6'9" **Wt:** 240 **Born:** 2/9/68 **Age:** 32

College			Field Goals			3-Pt FGs			Free Throws			Misc			Fouls		Assists		Rebounds			Points	
Year Tm	G	GS	Min	Md	Att	Pct	Md	Att	Pct	Md	Att	Pct	TO	Stl	Blk	PF	DQ	Ast	Avg	Off	Tot	Avg	Pts	Avg
87-88 Xav	30	—	668	112	197	.569	0	0	—	94	131	.718	61	20	11	91	—	23	0.8	—	213	7.1	318	10.6
88-89 Xav	33	—	983	163	264	.617	0	0	—	178	218	.817	69	27	16	102	—	17	0.5	—	264	8.0	504	15.3
89-90 Xav	33	—	981	146	274	.533	0	0	—	177	211	.839	79	26	26	111	—	31	0.9	—	328	9.9	469	14.2
3 Years	96	—	2632	421	735	.573	0	0	—	449	560	.802	209	73	53	304	—	71	0.7	—	805	8.4	1291	13.4

NBA			Field Goals			3-Pt FGs			Free Throws			Misc			Fouls		Assists		Rebounds			Points	
Year Tm	G	GS	Min	Md	Att	Pct	Md	Att	Pct	Md	Att	Pct	TO	Stl	Blk	PF	DQ	Ast	Avg	Off	Tot	Avg	Pts	Avg
90-91									Played in Spain, Played in USBL															
91-92 Was	1	0	12	0	4	.000	0	0	—	3	4	.750	1	0	0	1	0	1	1.0	1	5	5.0	3	3.0
92-93 Mil	23	0	339	42	92	.457	4	8	.500	68	85	.800	13	11	1	20	0	14	0.6	40	115	5.0	156	6.8
93-94 Mil	67	11	1131	141	341	.413	3	13	.231	159	206	.772	61	38	14	69	1	48	0.7	109	281	4.2	444	6.6
94-95 Bos	70	24	1344	149	329	.453	2	7	.286	141	172	.820	79	24	13	143	0	44	0.6	136	375	5.4	441	6.3
95-96 LAL	63	0	746	72	169	.426	1	9	.111	69	85	.812	20	18	12	80	1	32	0.5	60	178	2.8	214	3.4
96-97 Orl	82	21	2004	262	586	.447	0	13	.000	175	218	.803	102	47	20	196	2	73	0.9	174	519	6.3	699	8.5
97-98 Orl	58	8	1638	259	617	.420	0	4	.000	218	279	.781	74	31	24	122	0	51	0.9	152	427	7.4	736	12.7
98-99 Orl	44	0	695	76	180	.422	0	2	.000	71	99	.717	37	15	7	64	0	17	0.4	66	161	3.7	223	5.1
99-00 Orl	20	0	148	21	48	.438	1	4	.250	11	14	.786	12	5	2	15	0	4	0.2	11	44	2.2	54	2.7
9 Years	428	64	8057	1022	2366	.432	11	60	.183	915	1162	.787	399	189	93	710	4	284	0.7	749	2105	4.9	2970	6.9

NBA Postseason

Year Tm	G	GS	Min	Md	Att	Pct	Md	Att	Pct	Md	Att	Pct	TO	Stl	Blk	PF	DQ	Ast	Avg	Off	Tot	Avg	Pts	Avg
94-95 Bos	4	1	81	4	12	.333	0	0	—	3	6	.500	5	3	1	7	0	3	0.8	13	24	6.0	11	2.8
96-97 Orl	5	5	195	21	40	.525	0	1	.000	19	25	.760	14	2	2	20	1	4	0.8	20	50	10.0	61	12.2
98-99 Orl	1	0	16	1	2	.500	0	0	—	2	2	1.000	1	1	0	2	0	0	0.0	0	0	0.0	4	4.0
3 Years	10	6	292	26	54	.481	0	1	.000	24	33	.727	20	6	3	29	1	7	0.7	33	74	7.4	76	7.6

Bruno Sundov

Pos: C **College:** None **Drafted:** '98 2(35)—Dal **Ht:** 7'2" **Wt:** 220 **Born:** 2/10/80 **Age:** 20

NBA			Field Goals			3-Pt FGs			Free Throws			Misc			Fouls		Assists		Rebounds			Points	
Year Tm	G	GS	Min	Md	Att	Pct	Md	Att	Pct	Md	Att	Pct	TO	Stl	Blk	PF	DQ	Ast	Avg	Off	Tot	Avg	Pts	Avg
98-99 Dal	3	0	11	2	7	.286	0	0	—	0	0	—	1	0	0	4	0	1	0.3	0	0	0.0	4	1.3
99-00 Dal	14	0	61	12	31	.387	0	0	—	2	2	1.000	4	2	2	16	0	2	0.1	5	12	0.9	26	1.9
2 Years	17	0	72	14	38	.368	0	0	—	2	2	1.000	5	2	2	20	0	3	0.2	5	12	0.7	30	1.8

Bob Sura

(statistical profile on page 280)

Pos: G **College:** Florida State **Drafted:** '95 1(17)—Cle **Ht:** 6'5" **Wt:** 200 **Born:** 3/25/73 **Age:** 27

College			Field Goals			3-Pt FGs			Free Throws			Misc			Fouls		Assists		Rebounds			Points	
Year Tm	G	GS	Min	Md	Att	Pct	Md	Att	Pct	Md	Att	Pct	TO	Stl	Blk	PF	DQ	Ast	Avg	Off	Tot	Avg	Pts	Avg
91-92 FlaSt	31	12	872	124	269	.461	38	98	.388	94	150	.627	72	41	5	67	0	76	2.5	39	107	3.5	380	12.3
92-93 FlaSt	34	34	1213	241	533	.452	73	220	.332	120	188	.638	129	54	7	87	2	92	2.7	81	209	6.1	675	19.9
93-94 FlaSt	27	26	932	202	431	.469	52	164	.317	117	179	.654	112	65	19	67	2	121	4.5	79	213	7.9	573	21.2
94-95 FlaSt	27	26	981	164	393	.417	51	158	.323	123	179	.687	92	49	5	76	3	146	5.4	55	185	6.9	502	18.6
4 Years	119	98	3998	731	1626	.450	214	640	.334	454	696	.652	405	209	36	297	7	435	3.7	254	714	6.0	2130	17.9

NBA			Field Goals			3-Pt FGs			Free Throws			Misc			Fouls		Assists		Rebounds			Points	
Year Tm	G	GS	Min	Md	Att	Pct	Md	Att	Pct	Md	Att	Pct	TO	Stl	Blk	PF	DQ	Ast	Avg	Off	Tot	Avg	Pts	Avg
95-96 Cle	79	3	1150	148	360	.411	27	78	.346	99	141	.702	115	56	21	126	1	233	2.9	34	135	1.7	422	5.3
96-97 Cle	82	23	2269	253	587	.431	53	164	.323	196	319	.614	181	90	33	218	3	390	4.8	76	308	3.8	755	9.2
97-98 Cle	46	4	942	87	231	.377	19	60	.317	74	131	.565	93	44	7	113	0	171	3.7	25	94	2.0	267	5.8
98-99 Cle	50	6	841	70	210	.333	9	45	.200	65	103	.631	67	46	14	98	1	152	3.0	21	102	2.0	214	4.3

NBA				Field Goals			3-Pt FGs			Free Throws			Misc			Fouls		Assists		Rebounds			Points	
Year Tm	G	GS	Min	Md	Att	Pct	Md	Att	Pct	Md	Att	Pct	TO	Stl	Blk	PF	DQ	Ast	Avg	Off	Tot	Avg	Pts	Avg
'99-00 Cle	73	45	2216	356	815	.437	122	332	.367	175	251	.697	148	91	19	201	0	284	3.9	50	288	3.9	1009	13.8
Years	330	81	7418	914	2203	.415	230	679	.339	609	945	.644	604	327	94	756	5	1230	3.7	206	927	2.8	2667	8.1

NBA Postseason

Year Tm	G	GS	Min	Md	Att	Pct	Md	Att	Pct	Md	Att	Pct	TO	Stl	Blk	PF	DQ	Ast	Avg	Off	Tot	Avg	Pts	Avg
'95-96 Cle	3	0	18	2	3	.667	0	0	—	0	0	—	4	1	0	4	0	3	1.0	0	1	0.3	4	1.3
'97-98 Cle	3	0	31	1	5	.200	0	2	.000	2	3	.667	2	1	0	4	0	4	1.3	0	3	1.0	4	1.3
Years	6	0	49	3	8	.375	0	2	.000	2	3	.667	6	2	0	8	0	7	1.2	0	4	0.7	8	1.3

Wally Szczerbiak

(statistical profile on page 280)

Pos: F **College:** Miami (OH) **Drafted:** '99 1(6)—Min   **Ht:** 6'8" **Wt:** 245 **Born:** 3/5/77 **Age:** 23

College				Field Goals			3-Pt FGs			Free Throws			Misc			Fouls		Assists		Rebounds			Points	
Year Tm	G	GS	Min	Md	Att	Pct	Md	Att	Pct	Md	Att	Pct	TO	Stl	Blk	PF	DQ	Ast	Avg	Off	Tot	Avg	Pts	Avg
'95-96 Mia-O	22	4	382	66	127	.520	22	47	.468	22	28	.786	27	6	11	44	1	23	1.0	28	72	3.3	176	8.0
'96-97 Mia-O	30	23	925	150	316	.475	56	121	.463	28	39	.718	54	22	12	81	2	63	2.1	42	162	5.4	384	12.8
'97-98 Mia-O	21	21	802	185	350	.529	63	128	.492	79	98	.806	72	18	24	60	2	52	2.5	40	160	7.6	512	24.4
'98-99 Mia-O	32	32	1181	270	517	.522	63	177	.356	172	207	.831	101	39	32	98	2	93	2.9	75	272	8.5	775	24.2
Years	105	80	3290	671	1310	.512	204	473	.431	301	372	.809	254	85	79	283	7	231	2.2	185	666	6.3	1847	17.6

NBA				Field Goals			3-Pt FGs			Free Throws			Misc			Fouls		Assists		Rebounds			Points	
Year Tm	G	GS	Min	Md	Att	Pct	Md	Att	Pct	Md	Att	Pct	TO	Stl	Blk	PF	DQ	Ast	Avg	Off	Tot	Avg	Pts	Avg
'99-00 Min	73	53	2171	342	669	.511	28	78	.359	133	161	.826	83	58	23	175	3	201	2.8	89	272	3.7	845	11.6

NBA Postseason

Year Tm	G	GS	Min	Md	Att	Pct	Md	Att	Pct	Md	Att	Pct	TO	Stl	Blk	PF	DQ	Ast	Avg	Off	Tot	Avg	Pts	Avg
'99-00 Min	4	4	94	12	30	.400	0	3	.000	0	0	—	1	3	1	7	0	2	0.5	2	8	2.0	24	6.0

Zan Tabak

Pos: C **College:** None **Drafted:** '91 2(51)—Hou   **Ht:** 7'0" **Wt:** 257 **Born:** 6/15/70 **Age:** 30

NBA				Field Goals			3-Pt FGs			Free Throws			Misc			Fouls		Assists		Rebounds			Points	
Year Tm	G	GS	Min	Md	Att	Pct	Md	Att	Pct	Md	Att	Pct	TO	Stl	Blk	PF	DQ	Ast	Avg	Off	Tot	Avg	Pts	Avg
'91-92										Played in Croatia														
'92-93										Played in Croatia														
'93-94										Played in Italy														
'94-95 Hou	37	0	182	24	53	.453	0	1	.000	27	44	.614	18	2	7	37	0	4	0.1	23	57	1.5	75	2.0
'95-96 Tor	67	18	1332	225	414	.543	0	1	.000	64	114	.561	101	24	31	204	2	62	0.9	117	320	4.8	514	7.7
'96-97 Tor	13	4	218	32	71	.451	0	0	—	20	29	.690	21	6	11	35	0	14	1.1	20	49	3.8	84	6.5
'97-98 2Tm	57	34	984	142	304	.467	0	1	.000	23	61	.377	61	20	38	163	2	48	0.8	84	212	3.7	307	5.4
'98-99										Played in Turkey														
'99-00 Ind	18	0	114	16	34	.471	0	0	—	5	8	.625	11	3	9	13	0	4	0.2	16	32	1.8	37	2.1
'97-98 Tor	39	29	752	116	249	.466	0	1	.000	16	48	.333	44	15	27	117	1	36	0.9	59	154	3.9	248	6.4
Bos	18	5	232	26	55	.473	0	0	—	7	13	.538	17	5	11	46	1	12	0.7	25	58	3.2	59	3.3
Years	192	56	2830	439	876	.501	0	3	.000	139	256	.543	212	55	96	452	4	132	0.7	260	670	3.5	1017	5.3

NBA Postseason

Year Tm	G	GS	Min	Md	Att	Pct	Md	Att	Pct	Md	Att	Pct	TO	Stl	Blk	PF	DQ	Ast	Avg	Off	Tot	Avg	Pts	Avg
'94-95 Hou	8	0	31	2	5	.400	0	0	—	2	2	1.000	2	1	3	5	0	1	0.1	1	1	0.1	6	0.8
'99-00 Ind	10	0	47	4	8	.500	0	0	—	4	4	1.000	1	0	2	10	0	0	0.0	4	16	1.6	12	1.2
Years	18	0	78	6	13	.462	0	0	—	6	6	1.000	3	1	5	15	0	1	0.1	5	17	0.9	18	1.0

Johnny Taylor

Pos: F **College:** Chattanooga **Drafted:** '97 1(17)—Orl   **Ht:** 6'9" **Wt:** 220 **Born:** 6/4/74 **Age:** 26

College				Field Goals			3-Pt FGs			Free Throws			Misc			Fouls		Assists		Rebounds			Points	
Year Tm	G	GS	Min	Md	Att	Pct	Md	Att	Pct	Md	Att	Pct	TO	Stl	Blk	PF	DQ	Ast	Avg	Off	Tot	Avg	Pts	Avg
'95-96 Chat	27	—	799	181	355	.510	39	102	.382	90	123	.732	78	21	19	84	2	49	1.8	—	192	7.1	491	18.2
'96-97 Chat	35	35	1072	214	440	.486	28	97	.289	123	185	.665	72	43	29	102	1	74	2.1	101	255	7.3	579	16.5
Years	62	—	1871	395	795	.497	67	199	.337	213	308	.692	150	64	48	186	3	123	2.0	—	447	7.2	1070	17.3

NBA				Field Goals			3-Pt FGs			Free Throws			Misc			Fouls		Assists		Rebounds			Points	
Year Tm	G	GS	Min	Md	Att	Pct	Md	Att	Pct	Md	Att	Pct	TO	Stl	Blk	PF	DQ	Ast	Avg	Off	Tot	Avg	Pts	Avg
'97-98 Orl	12	0	108	13	37	.351	1	2	.500	11	16	.688	8	3	2	22	0	1	0.1	4	13	1.1	38	3.2
'98-99 Den	36	9	724	82	198	.414	26	68	.382	17	23	.739	34	28	17	97	1	24	0.7	30	101	2.8	207	5.8
'99-00 2Tm	6	0	34	5	14	.357	1	1	1.000	0	0	—	2	1	1	5	0	1	0.2	2	6	1.0	11	1.8
'99-00 Den	1	0	5	0	2	.000	0	0	—	0	0	—	0	0	0	1	0	0	0.0	0	1	1.0	0	0.0
Orl	5	0	29	5	12	.417	1	1	1.000	0	0	—	2	1	1	4	0	1	0.2	2	5	1.0	11	2.2
Years	54	9	866	100	249	.402	28	71	.394	28	39	.718	44	32	20	124	1	26	0.5	36	120	2.2	256	4.7

Maurice Taylor

(statistical profile on page 28

Pos: F **College:** Michigan **Drafted:** '97 1(14)—LAC **Ht:** 6'9" **Wt:** 260 **Born:** 10/30/76 **Age:** 2

College

Year Tm	G	GS	Min	Md	Att	Pct	Md	Att	Pct	Md	Att	Pct	TO	Stl	Blk	PF	DQ	Ast	Avg	Off	Tot	Avg	Pts	Av
				Field Goals			3-Pt FGs			Free Throws			Misc			Fouls		Assists		Rebounds			Points	
94-95 Mich	31	29	806	161	342	.471	3	7	.429	59	98	.602	64	14	34	102	5	36	1.2	65	158	5.1	384	12
95-96 Mich	32	32	896	194	380	.511	1	4	.250	58	98	.592	66	21	25	92	1	42	1.3	89	223	7.0	447	14
96-97 Mich	35	33	1050	173	341	.507	1	5	.200	84	117	.718	70	26	31	95	4	40	1.1	84	218	6.2	431	12
3 Years	98	94	2752	528	1063	.497	5	16	.313	201	313	.642	200	61	90	289	10	118	1.2	238	599	6.1	1262	12

NBA

Year Tm	G	GS	Min	Md	Att	Pct	Md	Att	Pct	Md	Att	Pct	TO	Stl	Blk	PF	DQ	Ast	Avg	Off	Tot	Avg	Pts	Av
97-98 LAC	71	3	1513	321	675	.476	0	1	.000	173	244	.709	107	34	40	222	7	53	0.7	118	296	4.2	815	11
98-99 LAC	46	45	1505	311	675	.461	1	6	.167	150	206	.728	120	16	29	179	5	67	1.5	100	242	5.3	773	16
99-00 LAC	62	60	2227	458	988	.464	1	8	.125	143	201	.711	169	51	48	217	4	101	1.6	96	400	6.5	1060	17
3 Years	179	108	5245	1090	2338	.466	2	15	.133	466	651	.716	396	101	117	618	16	221	1.2	314	938	5.2	2648	14

Jason Terry

(statistical profile on page 28

Pos: G **College:** Arizona **Drafted:** '99 1(10)—Atl **Ht:** 6'2" **Wt:** 172 **Born:** 9/15/77 **Age:** 2

College

Year Tm	G	GS	Min	Md	Att	Pct	Md	Att	Pct	Md	Att	Pct	TO	Stl	Blk	PF	DQ	Ast	Avg	Off	Tot	Avg	Pts	Av
95-96 Ari	31	0	303	32	59	.542	15	26	.577	16	27	.593	35	19	0	28	0	35	1.1	6	23	0.7	95	3
96-97 Ari	34	18	1037	124	280	.443	40	121	.331	72	101	.713	73	85	3	66	1	150	4.4	19	91	2.7	360	10
97-98 Ari	35	0	797	124	294	.422	61	176	.347	62	75	.827	76	61	8	55	0	149	4.3	14	84	2.4	371	10
98-99 Ari	29	29	1107	209	472	.443	76	191	.398	141	168	.839	123	79	6	40	0	159	5.5	11	97	3.3	635	21
4 Years	129	47	3244	489	1105	.443	192	514	.374	291	371	.784	307	244	17	189	1	493	3.8	50	295	2.3	1461	11

NBA

Year Tm	G	GS	Min	Md	Att	Pct	Md	Att	Pct	Md	Att	Pct	TO	Stl	Blk	PF	DQ	Ast	Avg	Off	Tot	Avg	Pts	Av
99-00 Atl	81	27	1888	249	600	.415	46	157	.293	113	140	.807	156	90	10	133	0	346	4.3	24	166	2.0	657	8

Jamel Thomas

Pos: F **College:** Providence **Drafted:** '99 FA—Bos **Ht:** 6'6" **Wt:** 219 **Born:** 7/19/76 **Age:** 2

College

Year Tm	G	GS	Min	Md	Att	Pct	Md	Att	Pct	Md	Att	Pct	TO	Stl	Blk	PF	DQ	Ast	Avg	Off	Tot	Avg	Pts	Av
95-96 Prov	29	0	606	105	232	.453	24	64	.375	36	58	.621	57	41	2	67	0	44	1.5	58	132	4.6	270	9
96-97 Prov	36	33	1103	187	429	.436	65	162	.401	65	96	.677	91	37	16	98	6	76	2.1	63	184	5.1	504	14
97-98 Prov	29	29	1019	163	455	.358	54	178	.303	156	200	.780	106	44	12	91	3	59	2.0	60	200	6.9	536	18
98-99 Prov	30	30	985	225	532	.423	58	183	.317	153	203	.754	124	39	11	79	1	63	2.1	65	217	7.2	661	22
4 Years	124	92	3713	680	1648	.413	201	587	.342	410	557	.736	378	161	41	335	10	242	2.0	246	733	5.9	1971	15

NBA

Year Tm	G	GS	Min	Md	Att	Pct	Md	Att	Pct	Md	Att	Pct	TO	Stl	Blk	PF	DQ	Ast	Avg	Off	Tot	Avg	Pts	Av
99-00 2Tm	7	0	46	8	18	.444	0	3	.000	1	1	1.000	5	1	0	2	0	6	0.9	1	5	0.7	17	2
99-00 Bos	3	0	19	5	10	.500	0	1	.000	1	1	1.000	1	0	0	0	0	2	0.7	0	2	0.7	11	3
GS	4	0	27	3	8	.375	0	2	.000	0	0	—	4	1	0	2	0	4	1.0	1	3	0.8	6	1

John Thomas

Pos: F **College:** Minnesota **Drafted:** '97 1(25)—NY **Ht:** 6'9" **Wt:** 265 **Born:** 9/8/75 **Age:** 2

College

Year Tm	G	GS	Min	Md	Att	Pct	Md	Att	Pct	Md	Att	Pct	TO	Stl	Blk	PF	DQ	Ast	Avg	Off	Tot	Avg	Pts	Av
93-94 Minn	26	2	254	27	70	.386	0	0	—	10	23	.435	13	2	5	37	1	3	0.1	39	65	2.5	64	2
94-95 Minn	31	30	639	91	195	.467	0	0	—	45	84	.536	62	19	11	81	3	23	0.7	68	144	4.6	227	7
95-96 Minn	32	32	845	106	221	.480	0	0	—	66	127	.520	61	24	24	97	2	25	0.8	74	206	6.4	278	8
96-97 Minn	35	35	834	125	217	.576	0	1	.000	66	115	.574	54	30	25	86	3	40	1.1	81	221	6.3	316	9
4 Years	124	99	2572	349	703	.496	0	1	.000	187	349	.536	190	75	65	301	9	91	0.7	262	636	5.1	885	7

NBA

Year Tm	G	GS	Min	Md	Att	Pct	Md	Att	Pct	Md	Att	Pct	TO	Stl	Blk	PF	DQ	Ast	Avg	Off	Tot	Avg	Pts	Av
97-98 2Tm	54	2	535	55	113	.487	0	0	—	41	54	.759	46	22	12	97	0	17	0.3	48	106	2.0	151	2
98-99 Tor	39	11	593	71	123	.577	0	1	.000	27	48	.563	21	17	9	82	0	15	0.4	65	134	3.4	169	4
99-00 Tor	55	6	477	49	107	.458	0	1	.000	16	41	.390	14	12	14	106	1	9	0.2	37	75	1.4	114	2
97-98 Bos	33	2	368	41	80	.513	0	0	—	26	33	.788	33	19	9	65	0	13	0.4	32	70	2.1	108	3
Tor	21	0	167	14	33	.424	0	0	—	15	21	.714	13	3	3	32	0	4	0.2	16	36	1.7	43	2
3 Years	148	19	1605	175	343	.510	0	2	.000	84	143	.587	81	51	35	285	1	41	0.3	150	315	2.1	434	2

NBA Postseason

Year Tm	G	GS	Min	Md	Att	Pct	Md	Att	Pct	Md	Att	Pct	TO	Stl	Blk	PF	DQ	Ast	Avg	Off	Tot	Avg	Pts	Av
99-00 Tor	1	0	1	0	0		0	0		0	0	—	0	0	0	0	0	0	0.0	0	0	0.0	0	2

Kenny Thomas

(statistical profile on page 282)

Pos: F **College:** New Mexico **Drafted:** '99 1(22)—Hou   **Ht:** 6'7" **Wt:** 261 **Born:** 7/25/77 **Age:** 23

College				Field Goals			3-Pt FGs			Free Throws			Misc			Fouls		Assists		Rebounds			Points	
Year Tm	G	GS	Min	Md	Att	Pct	Md	Att	Pct	Md	Att	Pct	TO	Stl	Blk	PF	DQ	Ast	Avg	Off	Tot	Avg	Pts	Avg
5-96 NM	33	29	981	170	294	.578	0	3	.000	144	203	.709	98	21	50	118	4	53	1.6	95	256	7.8	484	14.7
6-97 NM	32	31	1000	139	264	.527	11	36	.306	155	206	.752	98	22	48	98	3	63	2.0	74	220	6.9	444	13.9
7-98 NM	32	32	1047	195	385	.506	27	72	.375	122	159	.767	97	28	79	101	4	95	3.0	102	297	9.3	539	16.8
8-99 NM	26	26	903	162	297	.545	27	73	.370	113	154	.734	68	41	62	66	1	51	2.0	61	259	10.0	464	17.8
Years	123	118	3931	666	1240	.537	65	184	.353	534	722	.740	361	112	239	383	12	262	2.1	332	1032	8.4	1931	15.7

NBA				Field Goals			3-Pt FGs			Free Throws			Misc			Fouls		Assists		Rebounds			Points	
Year Tm	G	GS	Min	Md	Att	Pct	Md	Att	Pct	Md	Att	Pct	TO	Stl	Blk	PF	DQ	Ast	Avg	Off	Tot	Avg	Pts	Avg
9-00 Hou	72	29	1797	212	531	.399	32	122	.262	138	209	.660	112	54	22	167	0	113	1.6	147	437	6.1	594	8.3

Kurt Thomas

(statistical profile on page 282)

Pos: F **College:** Texas Christian **Drafted:** '95 1(10)—Mia   **Ht:** 6'9" **Wt:** 230 **Born:** 10/4/72 **Age:** 28

College				Field Goals			3-Pt FGs			Free Throws			Misc			Fouls		Assists		Rebounds			Points	
Year Tm	G	GS	Min	Md	Att	Pct	Md	Att	Pct	Md	Att	Pct	TO	Stl	Blk	PF	DQ	Ast	Avg	Off	Tot	Avg	Pts	Avg
0-91 TCU	28	—	42	8	18	.444	0	2	.000	7	14	.500	7	1	2	11	—	2	0.1	7	13	0.5	23	0.8
1-92 TCU	21	—	347	58	119	.487	0	0	—	34	51	.667	37	9	29	58	—	24	1.1	33	114	5.4	150	7.1
3-94 TCU	27	—	805	224	440	.509	12	46	.261	98	152	.645	73	26	69	108	—	50	1.9	50	262	9.7	558	20.7
4-95 TCU	27	—	872	288	526	.548	3	12	.250	202	283	.714	77	51	66	106	—	32	1.2	131	393	14.6	781	28.9
Years	103	—	2066	578	1103	.524	15	60	.250	341	500	.682	194	87	166	283	—	108	1.0	221	782	7.6	1512	14.7

NBA				Field Goals			3-Pt FGs			Free Throws			Misc			Fouls		Assists		Rebounds			Points	
Year Tm	G	GS	Min	Md	Att	Pct	Md	Att	Pct	Md	Att	Pct	TO	Stl	Blk	PF	DQ	Ast	Avg	Off	Tot	Avg	Pts	Avg
5-96 Mia	74	42	1655	274	547	.501	0	2	.000	118	178	.663	98	47	36	271	7	46	0.6	122	439	5.9	666	9.0
6-97 Mia	18	9	374	39	105	.371	0	1	.000	35	46	.761	25	12	9	67	3	9	0.5	31	107	5.9	113	6.3
7-98 Dal	5	0	73	17	45	.378	0	0	—	3	3	1.000	10	1	0	19	1	3	0.6	8	24	4.8	37	7.4
8-99 NY	50	44	1182	170	368	.462	0	1	.000	66	108	.611	73	45	17	159	3	55	1.1	82	286	5.7	406	8.1
9-00 NY	80	21	1971	270	535	.505	1	3	.333	100	128	.781	105	51	42	278	6	82	1.0	144	505	6.3	641	8.0
Years	227	116	5255	770	1600	.481	1	7	.143	322	463	.695	311	156	104	794	20	195	0.9	387	1361	6.0	1863	8.2

NBA Postseason																								
Year Tm	G	GS	Min	Md	Att	Pct	Md	Att	Pct	Md	Att	Pct	TO	Stl	Blk	PF	DQ	Ast	Avg	Off	Tot	Avg	Pts	Avg
5-96 Mia	3	3	60	4	10	.400	0	0	—	4	4	1.000	5	2	1	13	1	3	1.0	4	16	5.3	12	4.0
8-99 NY	20	12	419	45	118	.381	0	0	—	16	23	.696	19	15	12	76	0	7	0.4	38	110	5.5	106	5.3
9-00 NY	16	0	251	31	61	.508	0	0	—	7	10	.700	14	3	6	44	1	5	0.3	19	51	3.2	69	4.3
Years	39	15	730	80	189	.423	0	0	—	27	37	.730	38	20	19	133	2	15	0.4	61	177	4.5	187	4.8

Tim Thomas

(statistical profile on page 283)

Pos: F **College:** Villanova **Drafted:** '97 1(7)—NJ   **Ht:** 6'10" **Wt:** 230 **Born:** 2/26/77 **Age:** 23

College				Field Goals			3-Pt FGs			Free Throws			Misc			Fouls		Assists		Rebounds			Points	
Year Tm	G	GS	Min	Md	Att	Pct	Md	Att	Pct	Md	Att	Pct	TO	Stl	Blk	PF	DQ	Ast	Avg	Off	Tot	Avg	Pts	Avg
6-97 Vill	32	31	1005	187	416	.450	47	140	.336	121	152	.796	91	56	33	88	4	66	2.1	66	193	6.0	542	16.9

NBA				Field Goals			3-Pt FGs			Free Throws			Misc			Fouls		Assists		Rebounds			Points	
Year Tm	G	GS	Min	Md	Att	Pct	Md	Att	Pct	Md	Att	Pct	TO	Stl	Blk	PF	DQ	Ast	Avg	Off	Tot	Avg	Pts	Avg
7-98 Phi	77	48	1779	306	684	.447	62	171	.363	171	231	.740	118	54	17	185	2	90	1.2	107	288	3.7	845	11.0
8-99 2Tm	50	26	812	132	279	.473	21	68	.309	73	112	.652	46	26	12	107	2	46	0.9	49	126	2.5	358	7.2
9-00 Mil	80	1	2093	347	753	.461	63	182	.346	188	243	.774	129	59	31	227	3	113	1.4	100	332	4.2	945	11.8
8-99 Phi	17	0	188	27	67	.403	5	19	.263	19	24	.792	15	3		21	0	15	0.9	7	33	1.9	78	4.6
Mil	33	26	624	105	212	.495	16	49	.327	54	88	.614	31	23	9	86	2	31	0.9	42	93	2.8	280	8.5
Years	207	75	4684	785	1716	.457	146	421	.347	432	586	.737	293	139	60	519	7	249	1.2	256	746	3.6	2148	10.4

NBA Postseason																								
Year Tm	G	GS	Min	Md	Att	Pct	Md	Att	Pct	Md	Att	Pct	TO	Stl	Blk	PF	DQ	Ast	Avg	Off	Tot	Avg	Pts	Avg
4-99 Mil	3	3	60	8	18	.444	0	2	.000	7	12	.583	5	1	1	11	0	1	0.3	4	12	4.0	23	7.7
9-00 Mil	5	0	142	29	59	.492	5	15	.333	14	17	.824	1	1	4	14	0	10	2.0	6	24	4.8	77	15.4
Years	8	3	202	37	77	.481	5	17	.294	21	29	.724	6	2	5	25	0	11	1.4	10	36	4.5	100	12.5

Otis Thorpe

Pos: F-C **College:** Providence **Drafted:** '84 1(9)—KC   **Ht:** 6'10" **Wt:** 246 **Born:** 8/5/62 **Age:** 3(cut)

Year Tm	G	GS	Min	Md	Att	Pct	Md	Att	Pct	Md	Att	Pct	TO	Stl	Blk	PF	DQ	Ast	Avg	Off	Tot	Avg	Pts	Avg
College				**Field Goals**			**3-Pt FGs**			**Free Throws**			**Misc**			**Fouls**		**Assists**		**Rebounds**			**Points**	
80-81 Prov	26	12	668	100	194	.515	—	—	—	50	76	.658	42	16	12	69	4	11	0.4	—	137	5.3	250	9.(
81-82 Prov	27	27	942	153	283	.541	—	—	—	74	115	.643	74	11	26	93	7	36	1.3	—	216	8.0	380	14.
82-83 Prov	31	31	1041	204	321	.636	—	—	—	91	138	.659	83	21	26	113	9	24	0.8	—	249	8.0	499	16.
83-84 Prov	29	29	1051	167	288	.580	—	—	—	162	248	.653	67	29	43	92	3	36	1.2	—	300	10.3	496	17.
4 Years	113	99	3702	624	1086	.575	—	—	—	377	577	.653	266	77	107	367	23	107	0.9	—	902	8.0	1625	14.
NBA				**Field Goals**			**3-Pt FGs**			**Free Throws**			**Misc**			**Fouls**		**Assists**		**Rebounds**			**Points**	
84-85 KC	82	23	1918	411	685	.600	0	2	.000	230	371	.620	187	34	37	256	2	111	1.4	187	556	6.8	1052	12.
85-86 Sac	75	18	1675	289	492	.587	0	0	—	164	248	.661	123	35	34	233	3	84	1.1	137	420	5.6	742	9.
86-87 Sac	82	82	2956	567	1050	.540	0	3	.000	413	543	.761	189	46	60	292	11	201	2.5	259	819	10.0	1547	18.
87-88 Sac	82	82	3072	622	1226	.507	0	6	.000	460	609	.755	228	62	56	264	3	266	3.2	279	837	10.2	1704	20.
88-89 Hou	82	82	3135	521	961	.542	0	2	.000	328	450	.729	225	82	37	259	6	202	2.5	272	787	9.6	1370	16.
89-90 Hou	82	82	2947	547	998	.548	0	10	.000	307	446	.688	229	66	24	270	5	261	3.2	258	734	9.0	1401	17.
90-91 Hou	82	82	3039	549	988	.556	3	7	.429	334	480	.696	217	73	20	278	10	197	2.4	287	846	10.3	1435	17.
91-92 Hou*	82	82	3056	558	943	.592	0	7	.000	304	463	.657	237	52	37	307	7	250	3.0	285	862	10.5	1420	17.
92-93 Hou	72	69	2357	385	690	.558	0	2	.000	153	256	.598	151	43	19	234	3	181	2.5	219	589	8.2	923	12.
93-94 Hou	82	82	2909	449	801	.561	0	2	.000	251	382	.657	185	66	28	253	1	189	2.3	271	870	10.6	1149	14.
94-95 2Tm	70	35	2096	385	681	.565	0	7	.000	167	281	.594	132	41	28	224	3	112	1.6	202	558	8.0	937	13.
95-96 Det	82	82	2841	452	853	.530	0	2	.000	257	362	.710	195	53	39	300	7	158	1.9	211	688	8.4	1161	14.
96-97 Det	79	79	2661	419	787	.532	0	2	.000	198	303	.653	145	59	17	298	7	133	1.7	226	622	7.9	1036	13.
97-98 2Tm	74	66	2197	294	624	.471	0	5	.000	164	240	.683	152	48	30	238	4	222	3.0	151	537	7.3	752	10.
98-99 Was	49	38	1539	240	440	.545	0	2	.000	74	106	.698	88	42	19	196	9	101	2.1	96	334	6.8	554	11.
99-00 Mia	51	1	777	125	243	.514	0	3	.000	29	48	.604	59	26	9	136	4	33	0.6	56	166	3.3	279	5.
94-95	36	35	1188	206	366	.563	0	3	.000	67	127	.528	76	22	13	102	1	58	1.6	113	322	8.9	479	13.
Por	34	0	908	179	315	.568	0	4	.000	100	154	.649	56	19	15	122	2	54	1.6	89	236	6.9	458	13.
97-98 Van	47	46	1574	205	430	.477	0	4	.000	118	170	.694	115	30	23	158	3	161	3.4	100	371	7.9	528	11.
Sac	27	20	623	89	194	.459	0	1	.000	46	70	.657	37	18	7	80	1	61	2.3	51	166	6.1	224	8.
16 Years	1208	985	39175	6813	12462	.547	3	64	.047	3833	5588	.686	2742	828	494	4038	85	2701	2.2	3396	10225	8.5	17462	14.

NBA Postseason

Year Tm	G	GS	Min	Md	Att	Pct	Md	Att	Pct	Md	Att	Pct	TO	Stl	Blk	PF	DQ	Ast	Avg	Off	Tot	Avg	Pts	Avg
85-86 Sac	3	0	35	3	13	.231	0	0	—	6	13	.462	1	0	1	4	0	0	0.0	8	12	4.0	12	4.
88-89 Hou	4	4	152	24	37	.649	0	0	—	16	21	.762	15	5	1	17	1	12	3.0	6	20	5.0	64	16.
89-90 Hou	4	4	164	27	45	.600	0	0	—	26	38	.684	9	5	0	12	0	7	1.8	14	33	8.3	80	20.
90-91 Hou	3	3	116	22	38	.579	0	0	—	3	6	.500	6	2	0	8	0	8	2.7	7	25	8.3	47	15.
92-93 Hou	12	12	419	73	115	.635	0	0	—	28	43	.651	17	6	1	35	0	31	2.6	36	103	8.6	174	14.
93-94 Hou	23	23	854	111	194	.572	1	2	.500	38	67	.567	37	13	10	86	2	54	2.3	68	228	9.9	261	11.
94-95 Por	3	0	66	12	21	.571	0	0	—	7	10	.700	3	0	0	12	1	2	0.7	5	13	4.3	31	10.
95-96 Det	3	3	101	13	24	.542	0	0	—	9	12	.750	7	0	0	9	0	7	2.3	14	35	11.7	35	11.
96-97 Det	5	5	152	21	41	.512	0	0	—	7	9	.778	9	2	0	21	0	4	0.8	12	32	6.4	49	9.
99-00 Mia	10	0	136	13	27	.481	0	1	.000	7	14	.500	11	0	2	29	0	3	0.3	6	29	2.9	33	3.
10 Years	70	54	2195	319	555	.575	1	3	.333	147	233	.631	115	33	15	233	4	128	1.8	176	530	7.6	786	11.

Robert Traylor

Pos: F-C **College:** Michigan **Drafted:** '98 1(6)—Dal   **Ht:** 6'8" **Wt:** 284 **Born:** 2/1/77 **Age:** 2(cut)

Year Tm	G	GS	Min	Md	Att	Pct	Md	Att	Pct	Md	Att	Pct	TO	Stl	Blk	PF	DQ	Ast	Avg	Off	Tot	Avg	Pts	Avg
College				**Field Goals**			**3-Pt FGs**			**Free Throws**			**Misc**			**Fouls**		**Assists**		**Rebounds**			**Points**	
95-96 Mich	22	4	438	82	148	.554	0	0	—	34	62	.548	53	19	15	68	3	12	0.5	61	130	5.9	198	9.
96-97 Mich	35	35	955	190	342	.556	0	0	—	80	176	.455	99	40	36	117	5	33	0.9	121	271	7.7	460	13.
97-98 Mich	34	34	1090	224	387	.579	0	1	.000	104	162	.642	110	44	46	108	2	88	2.6	125	344	10.1	552	16.
3 Years	91	73	2483	496	877	.566	0	1	.000	218	400	.545	262	103	97	293	10	133	1.5	307	745	8.2	1210	13.
NBA				**Field Goals**			**3-Pt FGs**			**Free Throws**			**Misc**			**Fouls**		**Assists**		**Rebounds**			**Points**	
98-99 Mil	49	43	786	108	201	.537	0	1	.000	43	80	.538	42	44	44	140	4	38	0.8	80	182	3.7	259	5.
99-00 Mil	44	16	447	58	122	.475	0	4	.000	41	68	.603	27	25	25	79	0	20	0.5	50	115	2.6	157	3.
2 Years	93	59	1233	166	323	.514	0	5	.000	84	148	.568	69	69	69	219	4	58	0.6	130	297	3.2	416	4.

NBA Postseason

Year Tm	G	GS	Min	Md	Att	Pct	Md	Att	Pct	Md	Att	Pct	TO	Stl	Blk	PF	DQ	Ast	Avg	Off	Tot	Avg	Pts	Avg
98-99 Mil	3	1	45	7	9	.778	0	0	—	2	4	.500	4	2	4	15	1	2	0.7	6	12	4.0	16	5.
99-00 Mil	1	0	4	0	1	.000	0	0	—	0	0	—	0	0	1	2	0	1	1.0	1	2	2.0	0	0.
2 Years	4	1	49	7	10	.700	0	0	—	2	4	.500	4	2	5	17	1	3	0.8	7	14	3.5	16	4.

Gary Trent

Pos: F **College:** Ohio **Drafted:** '95 1(11)—Mil **Ht:** 6'8" **Wt:** 250 **Born:** 9/22/74 **Age:** 26

College

Year Tm	G	GS	Min	Md	Att	Pct	Md	Att	Pct	Md	Att	Pct	TO	Stl	Blk	PF	DQ	Ast	Avg	Off	Tot	Avg	Pts	Avg
				Field Goals			3-Pt FGs			Free Throws			Misc			Fouls		Assists		Rebounds			Points	
92-93 Ohio	27	—	892	194	298	.651	0	1	.000	126	181	.696	69	12	26	52	—	42	1.6	—	250	9.3	514	19.0
93-94 Ohio	33	—	1119	309	536	.576	9	33	.273	210	291	.722	125	28	53	78	—	65	2.0	—	377	11.4	837	25.4
94-95 Ohio	33	—	1134	293	556	.527	8	35	.229	163	254	.642	115	20	26	75	—	79	2.4	—	423	12.8	757	22.9
3 Years	93	—	3145	796	1390	.573	17	69	.246	499	726	.687	309	60	105	205	—	186	2.0	—	1050	11.3	2108	22.7

NBA

Year Tm	G	GS	Min	Md	Att	Pct	Md	Att	Pct	Md	Att	Pct	TO	Stl	Blk	PF	DQ	Ast	Avg	Off	Tot	Avg	Pts	Avg
				Field Goals			3-Pt FGs			Free Throws			Misc			Fouls		Assists		Rebounds			Points	
95-96 Por	69	10	1219	220	429	.513	0	9	.000	78	141	.553	92	25	11	116	0	50	0.7	84	238	3.4	518	7.5
96-97 Por	82	28	1918	361	674	.536	0	11	.000	160	229	.699	129	48	35	186	2	87	1.1	156	428	5.2	882	10.8
97-98 2Tm	54	20	1360	241	505	.477	4	12	.333	144	212	.679	94	35	27	161	3	72	1.3	123	338	6.3	630	11.7
98-99 Dal	45	23	1362	287	602	.477	0	5	.000	145	235	.617	66	29	23	122	1	77	1.7	127	351	7.8	719	16.0
99-00 Dal	11	11	301	70	142	.493	0	2	.000	11	21	.524	25	8	3	28	0	22	2.0	20	52	4.7	151	13.7
97-98 Por	41	13	1005	177	359	.493	4	9	.444	113	163	.693	72	27	19	115	2	58	1.4	80	234	5.7	471	11.5
Tor	13	7	355	64	146	.438	0	3	.000	31	49	.633	22	8	8	46	1	14	1.1	43	104	8.0	159	12.2
5 Years	261	92	6160	1179	2352	.501	4	39	.103	538	838	.642	406	145	99	613	6	308	1.2	510	1407	5.4	2900	11.1

NBA Postseason

Year Tm	G	GS	Min	Md	Att	Pct	Md	Att	Pct	Md	Att	Pct	TO	Stl	Blk	PF	DQ	Ast	Avg	Off	Tot	Avg	Pts	Avg
95-96 Por	2	0	10	1	4	.250	0	0	—	0	0	—	0	1	0	3	0	0	0.0	0	1	0.5	2	1.0
96-97 Por	4	0	61	13	29	.448	0	1	.000	6	11	.545	6	0	1	11	0	4	1.0	5	12	3.0	32	8.0
2 Years	6	0	71	14	33	.424	0	1	.000	6	11	.545	6	1	1	14	0	4	0.7	5	13	2.2	34	5.7

Mirsad Turkcan

Pos: F **College:** None **Drafted:** '98 1(18)—Hou **Ht:** 6'9" **Wt:** 216 **Born:** 6/7/76 **Age:** 24

NBA

Year Tm	G	GS	Min	Md	Att	Pct	Md	Att	Pct	Md	Att	Pct	TO	Stl	Blk	PF	DQ	Ast	Avg	Off	Tot	Avg	Pts	Avg
				Field Goals			3-Pt FGs			Free Throws			Misc			Fouls		Assists		Rebounds			Points	
98-99										Played in Turkey														
99-00 2Tm	17	0	90	14	38	.368	0	6	.000	5	8	.625	8	3	1	14	0	5	0.3	13	33	1.9	33	1.9
99-00 NY	7	0	25	2	10	.200	0	2	.000	0	0	—	1	2	0	4	0	1	0.1	2	10	1.4	4	0.6
Mil	10	0	65	12	28	.429	0	4	.000	5	8	.625	7	1	1	10	0	4	0.4	11	23	2.3	29	2.9

NBA Postseason

Year Tm	G	GS	Min	Md	Att	Pct	Md	Att	Pct	Md	Att	Pct	TO	Stl	Blk	PF	DQ	Ast	Avg	Off	Tot	Avg	Pts	Avg
99-00 Mil	2	0	10	1	5	.200	0	1	.000	2	2	1.000	3	0	0	1	0	0	0.0	0	2	1.0	4	2.0

Wayne Turner

Pos: G **College:** Kentucky **Drafted:** '99 FA—Bos **Ht:** 6'2" **Wt:** 190 **Born:** 3/22/76 **Age:** 24

College

Year Tm	G	GS	Min	Md	Att	Pct	Md	Att	Pct	Md	Att	Pct	TO	Stl	Blk	PF	DQ	Ast	Avg	Off	Tot	Avg	Pts	Avg
				Field Goals			3-Pt FGs			Free Throws			Misc			Fouls		Assists		Rebounds			Points	
95-96 Kty	35	8	459	65	122	.533	1	4	.250	25	40	.625	37	40	4	54	1	56	1.6	15	52	1.5	156	4.5
96-97 Kty	40	10	908	112	240	.467	4	15	.267	36	68	.529	72	79	9	85	1	120	3.0	15	107	2.7	264	6.6
97-98 Kty	39	39	1098	137	285	.481	21	57	.368	67	108	.620	93	62	18	85	1	173	4.4	20	119	3.1	362	9.3
98-99 Kty	37	36	1063	141	284	.496	12	43	.279	94	137	.686	91	57	6	67	0	145	3.9	26	103	2.8	388	10.5
4 Years	151	93	3528	455	931	.489	38	119	.319	222	353	.629	293	238	37	291	3	494	3.3	76	381	2.5	1170	7.7

NBA

Year Tm	G	GS	Min	Md	Att	Pct	Md	Att	Pct	Md	Att	Pct	TO	Stl	Blk	PF	DQ	Ast	Avg	Off	Tot	Avg	Pts	Avg
99-00 Bos	3	0	41	1	6	.167	0	0	—	2	6	.333	3	0	0	4	0	5	1.7	1	3	1.0	4	1.3

Nick Van Exel

(statistical profile on page 283)

Pos: G **College:** Cincinnati **Drafted:** '93 2(37)—LAL **Ht:** 6'1" **Wt:** 190 **Born:** 11/27/71 **Age:** 29

College

Year Tm	G	GS	Min	Md	Att	Pct	Md	Att	Pct	Md	Att	Pct	TO	Stl	Blk	PF	DQ	Ast	Avg	Off	Tot	Avg	Pts	Avg
				Field Goals			3-Pt FGs			Free Throws			Misc			Fouls		Assists		Rebounds			Points	
91-92 Cin	34	17	834	144	323	.446	62	163	.380	68	101	.673	51	43	6	61	—	99	2.9	—	87	2.6	418	12.3
92-93 Cin	31	—	1049	198	513	.386	85	248	.343	87	120	.725	82	55	6	45	—	138	4.5	—	75	2.4	568	18.3
2 Years	65	—	1883	342	836	.409	147	411	.358	155	221	.701	133	98	12	106	—	237	3.6	—	162	2.5	986	15.2

NBA

Year Tm	G	GS	Min	Md	Att	Pct	Md	Att	Pct	Md	Att	Pct	TO	Stl	Blk	PF	DQ	Ast	Avg	Off	Tot	Avg	Pts	Avg
93-94 LAL	81	80	2700	413	1049	.394	123	364	.338	150	192	.781	145	85	8	154	1	466	5.8	47	238	2.9	1099	13.6
94-95 LAL	80	80	2944	465	1107	.420	183	511	.358	235	300	.783	220	97	6	157	0	660	8.3	27	223	2.8	1348	16.9
95-96 LAL	74	74	2513	396	950	.417	144	403	.357	163	204	.799	156	70	10	115	0	509	6.9	29	181	2.4	1099	14.9

NBA			Field Goals			3-Pt FGs			Free Throws			Misc			Fouls		Assists		Rebounds			Points	
Year Tm	G	GS	Min	Md	Att	Pct	Md	Att	Pct	Md	Att	Pct	TO	Stl	Blk	PF	DQ	Ast	Avg	Off	Tot	Avg	Pts	Avg
96-97 LAL	79	79	2937	432	1075	.402	177	468	.378	165	200	.825	212	75	10	110	0	672	8.5	44	226	2.9	1206	15.3
97-98 LAL*	64	46	2053	311	743	.419	123	316	.389	136	172	.791	104	64	6	120	0	442	6.9	31	194	3.0	881	13.8
98-99 Den	50	50	1802	306	769	.398	72	234	.308	142	175	.811	121	40	3	90	0	368	7.4	14	113	2.3	826	16.5
99-00 Den	79	79	2950	473	1213	.390	133	401	.332	196	240	.817	221	68	0	148	0	714	9.0	34	311	3.9	1275	16.1
7 Years	507	488	17899	2796	6906	.405	955	2697	.354	1187	1483	.800	1179	499	54	894	1	3831	7.6	226	1486	2.9	7734	15.3

NBA Postseason

Year Tm	G	GS	Min	Md	Att	Pct	Md	Att	Pct	Md	Att	Pct	TO	Stl	Blk	PF	DQ	Ast	Avg	Off	Tot	Avg	Pts	Avg
94-95 LAL	10	10	464	67	162	.414	21	66	.318	45	59	.763	22	21	3	33	0	73	7.3	9	38	3.8	200	20.0
95-96 LAL	4	4	137	16	54	.296	5	16	.313	10	13	.769	11	2	0	10	0	27	6.8	4	16	4.0	47	11.8
96-97 LAL	9	9	353	45	119	.378	12	44	.273	28	34	.824	18	10	0	19	0	58	6.4	6	31	3.4	130	14.4
97-98 LAL	13	0	367	50	151	.331	22	70	.314	29	40	.725	22	8	1	30	0	54	4.2	9	32	2.5	151	11.6
4 Years	36	23	1321	178	486	.366	60	196	.306	112	146	.767	73	41	4	92	0	212	5.9	28	117	3.3	528	14.7

Keith Van Horn

Pos: F **College:** Utah **Drafted:** '97 1(2)—Phi   **Ht:** 6'10" **Wt:** 255 **Born:** 10/23/75 **Age:** 25 (statistical profile on page 284)

College			Field Goals			3-Pt FGs			Free Throws			Misc			Fouls		Assists		Rebounds			Points	
Year Tm	G	GS	Min	Md	Att	Pct	Md	Att	Pct	Md	Att	Pct	TO	Stl	Blk	PF	DQ	Ast	Avg	Off	Tot	Avg	Pts	Avg
93-94 Utah	25	24	740	161	312	.516	35	79	.443	100	129	.775	54	19	41	60	2	21	0.8	—	208	8.3	457	18.3
94-95 Utah	33	33	994	246	451	.545	59	153	.386	143	167	.856	77	25	25	69	1	45	1.4	—	280	8.5	694	21.0
95-96 Utah	32	32	990	236	439	.538	54	132	.409	160	188	.851	72	21	23	63	1	31	1.0	69	283	8.8	686	21.4
96-97 Utah	32	32	1008	248	504	.492	58	150	.387	151	167	.904	79	22	37	61	1	45	1.4	53	303	9.5	705	22.0
4 Years	122	121	3732	891	1706	.522	206	514	.401	554	651	.851	282	87	126	253	5	142	1.2	—	1074	8.8	2542	20.8

NBA			Field Goals			3-Pt FGs			Free Throws			Misc			Fouls		Assists		Rebounds			Points	
Year Tm	G	GS	Min	Md	Att	Pct	Md	Att	Pct	Md	Att	Pct	TO	Stl	Blk	PF	DQ	Ast	Avg	Off	Tot	Avg	Pts	Avg
97-98 NJ	62	62	2325	446	1047	.426	69	224	.308	258	305	.846	164	64	25	216	0	106	1.7	142	408	6.6	1219	19.7
98-99 NJ	42	42	1576	322	752	.428	16	53	.302	256	298	.859	133	43	53	134	2	65	1.5	114	358	8.5	916	21.8
99-00 NJ	80	80	2782	559	1257	.445	84	228	.368	333	393	.847	245	64	60	258	5	158	2.0	200	676	8.5	1535	19.2
3 Years	184	184	6683	1327	3056	.434	169	505	.335	847	996	.850	542	171	138	608	7	329	1.8	456	1442	7.8	3670	19.9

NBA Postseason

Year Tm	G	GS	Min	Md	Att	Pct	Md	Att	Pct	Md	Att	Pct	TO	Stl	Blk	PF	DQ	Ast	Avg	Off	Tot	Avg	Pts	Avg
97-98 NJ	3	3	77	13	29	.448	0	2	.000	12	15	.800	2	0	0	7	0	1	0.3	2	9	3.0	38	12.7

Jacque Vaughn

Pos: G **College:** Kansas **Drafted:** '97 1(27)—Uta   **Ht:** 6'1" **Wt:** 190 **Born:** 2/11/75 **Age:** 25

College			Field Goals			3-Pt FGs			Free Throws			Misc			Fouls		Assists		Rebounds			Points	
Year Tm	G	GS	Min	Md	Att	Pct	Md	Att	Pct	Md	Att	Pct	TO	Stl	Blk	PF	DQ	Ast	Avg	Off	Tot	Avg	Pts	Avg
93-94 Kan	35	35	896	91	195	.467	28	70	.400	63	94	.670	98	38	1	74	1	181	5.2	—	89	2.5	273	7.8
94-95 Kan	31	31	1046	94	208	.452	20	58	.345	92	134	.687	94	31	4	74	0	238	7.7	—	116	3.7	300	9.7
95-96 Kan	34	34	1045	120	249	.482	39	92	.424	91	131	.695	95	45	6	72	0	223	6.6	13	106	3.1	370	10.9
96-97 Kan	26	25	820	79	185	.427	18	54	.333	88	113	.779	64	46	4	60	1	162	6.2	6	62	2.4	264	10.2
4 Years	126	125	3807	384	837	.459	105	274	.383	334	472	.708	351	160	15	280	2	804	6.4	—	373	3.0	1207	9.6

NBA			Field Goals			3-Pt FGs			Free Throws			Misc			Fouls		Assists		Rebounds			Points	
Year Tm	G	GS	Min	Md	Att	Pct	Md	Att	Pct	Md	Att	Pct	TO	Stl	Blk	PF	DQ	Ast	Avg	Off	Tot	Avg	Pts	Avg
97-98 Uta	45	0	419	44	122	.361	3	8	.375	48	68	.706	56	9	1	63	1	84	1.9	4	38	0.8	139	3.1
98-99 Uta	19	0	87	11	30	.367	2	8	.250	20	24	.833	14	5	0	14	0	12	0.6	1	11	0.6	44	2.3
99-00 Uta	78	0	884	109	262	.416	14	34	.412	57	76	.750	77	32	0	92	0	121	1.6	11	65	0.8	289	3.7
3 Years	142	0	1390	164	414	.396	19	50	.380	125	168	.744	147	46	1	169	1	217	1.5	16	114	0.8	472	3.3

NBA Postseason

Year Tm	G	GS	Min	Md	Att	Pct	Md	Att	Pct	Md	Att	Pct	TO	Stl	Blk	PF	DQ	Ast	Avg	Off	Tot	Avg	Pts	Avg
97-98 Uta	7	0	24	2	10	.200	1	2	.500	2	2	1.000	4	0	0	0	0	4	0.6	0	3	0.4	7	1.0
98-99 Uta	2	0	6	1	2	.500	1	1	1.000	0	0	—	0	0	0	2	0	2	1.0	0	0	0.0	3	1.5
99-00 Uta	7	0	67	10	28	.357	1	2	.500	7	8	.875	9	4	1	5	0	11	1.6	4	12	1.7	28	4.0
3 Years	16	0	97	13	40	.325	3	5	.600	9	10	.900	13	4	1	7	0	17	1.1	4	15	0.9	38	2.4

Loy Vaught

Pos: F **College:** Michigan **Drafted:** '90 1(13)—LAC   **Ht:** 6'9" **Wt:** 240 **Born:** 2/27/68 **Age:** 32

College			Field Goals			3-Pt FGs			Free Throws			Misc			Fouls		Assists		Rebounds			Points	
Year Tm	G	GS	Min	Md	Att	Pct	Md	Att	Pct	Md	Att	Pct	TO	Stl	Blk	PF	DQ	Ast	Avg	Off	Tot	Avg	Pts	Avg
86-87 Mich	32	1	416	68	122	.557	0	0	—	11	22	.500	32	11	31	73	1	12	0.4	—	125	3.9	147	4.6
87-88 Mich	34	20	748	151	243	.621	0	0	—	55	76	.724	50	19	10	96	4	22	0.6	—	150	4.4	357	10.5

Year Tm	G	GS	Min	Field Goals Md	Att	Pct	3-Pt FGs Md	Att	Pct	Free Throws Md	Att	Pct	Misc TO	Stl	Blk	Fouls PF	DQ	Assists Ast	Avg	Rebounds Off	Tot	Avg	Points Pts	Avg
				College																				
8-89 Mich	37	21	851	201	304	.661	2	5	.400	63	81	.778	50	19	11	94	3	36	1.0	—	296	8.0	467	12.6
9-90 Mich	31	31	930	197	331	.595	0	1	.000	86	107	.804	47	15	26	100	7	30	1.0	—	346	11.2	480	15.5
Years	134	73	2945	617	1000	.617	2	6	.333	215	286	.752	179	64	78	363	15	100	0.7	—	917	6.8	1451	10.8

Year Tm	G	GS	Min	Field Goals Md	Att	Pct	3-Pt FGs Md	Att	Pct	Free Throws Md	Att	Pct	Misc TO	Stl	Blk	Fouls PF	DQ	Assists Ast	Avg	Rebounds Off	Tot	Avg	Points Pts	Avg
				NBA																				
0-91 LAC	73	0	1178	175	359	.487	0	2	.000	49	74	.662	49	20	23	135	2	40	0.5	124	349	4.8	399	5.5
1-92 LAC	79	38	1687	271	551	.492	4	5	.800	55	69	.797	66	37	31	165	1	71	0.9	160	512	6.5	601	7.6
2-93 LAC	79	4	1653	313	616	.508	1	4	.250	116	155	.748	83	55	39	172	2	54	0.7	164	492	6.2	743	9.4
3-94 LAC	75	56	2118	373	695	.537	0	5	.000	131	182	.720	96	76	22	221	5	74	1.0	218	656	8.7	877	11.7
4-95 LAC	80	79	2966	609	1185	.514	7	33	.212	176	248	.710	166	104	29	243	4	139	1.7	261	772	9.7	1401	17.5
5-96 LAC	80	78	2966	571	1087	.525	7	19	.368	149	205	.727	158	87	40	241	4	112	1.4	204	808	10.1	1298	16.2
6-97 LAC	82	82	2838	542	1084	.500	2	12	.167	134	191	.702	137	85	25	241	3	110	1.3	222	817	10.0	1220	14.9
7-98 LAC	10	6	265	36	84	.429	0	2	.000	3	8	.375	13	4	2	33	0	7	0.7	16	65	6.5	75	7.5
8-99 Det	37	10	481	59	155	.381	0	1	.000	9	14	.643	17	15	6	54	0	11	0.3	36	146	3.9	127	3.4
9-00 Det	43	0	292	32	89	.360	0	3	.000	11	16	.688	11	6	4	45	0	11	0.3	26	91	2.1	75	1.7
0 Years	638	353	16444	2981	5905	.505	21	86	.244	833	1162	.717	796	489	221	1550	21	629	1.0	1431	4708	7.4	6816	10.7

NBA Postseason

Year Tm	G	GS	Min	Field Goals Md	Att	Pct	3-Pt FGs Md	Att	Pct	Free Throws Md	Att	Pct	Misc TO	Stl	Blk	Fouls PF	DQ	Assists Ast	Avg	Rebounds Off	Tot	Avg	Points Pts	Avg
1-92 LAC	5	0	36	7	11	.636	1	1	1.000	2	2	1.000	1	1	1	3	0	4	0.8	2	12	2.4	17	3.4
2-93 LAC	3	0	50	6	15	.400	0	0	—	4	5	.800	3	4	1	7	0	0	0.0	4	18	6.0	16	5.3
6-97 LAC	3	3	90	19	31	.613	1	3	.333	6	9	.667	6	3	2	12	1	2	0.7	5	27	9.0	45	15.0
8-99 Det	2	0	15	2	4	.500	0	0	—	0	0	—	0	1	0	1	0	0	0.0	0	1	0.5	4	2.0
9-00 Det	2	0	16	0	3	.000	0	0	—	0	0	—	1	2	0	1	0	0	0.0	1	6	3.0	0	0.0
Years	15	3	207	34	64	.531	2	4	.500	12	16	.750	11	11	4	24	1	6	0.4	12	64	4.3	82	5.5

Fred Vinson

Pos: G **College:** Georgia Tech **Drafted:** '94 FA—Atl   **Ht:** 6'4" **Wt:** 200 **Born:** 1/28/71 **Age:** 30

Year Tm	G	GS	Min	Field Goals Md	Att	Pct	3-Pt FGs Md	Att	Pct	Free Throws Md	Att	Pct	Misc TO	Stl	Blk	Fouls PF	DQ	Assists Ast	Avg	Rebounds Off	Tot	Avg	Points Pts	Avg
				College																				
1-92 GTch	32	0	251	28	80	.350	20	59	.339	7	10	.700	20	12	2	26	—	14	0.4	16	39	1.2	83	2.6
3-94 GTch	29	17	892	122	285	.428	72	181	.398	28	34	.824	48	31	7	40	—	37	1.3	46	113	3.9	344	11.9
Years	61	17	1143	150	365	.411	92	240	.383	35	44	.795	68	43	9	66	—	51	0.8	62	152	2.5	427	7.0

Year Tm	G	GS	Min	Field Goals Md	Att	Pct	3-Pt FGs Md	Att	Pct	Free Throws Md	Att	Pct	Misc TO	Stl	Blk	Fouls PF	DQ	Assists Ast	Avg	Rebounds Off	Tot	Avg	Points Pts	Avg
				NBA																				
4-95 Atl	5	0	27	1	7	.143	1	6	.167	1	1	1.000	2	0	0	4	0	1	0.2	0	0	0.0	4	0.8
5-96									Played in CBA															
6-97									Did not play in NBA															
7-98									Did not play in NBA															
8-99									Played in Dominican Republic															
9-00 Sea	8	0	40	5	17	.294	2	7	.286	1	2	.500	4	3	0	2	0	0	0.0	0	1	0.1	13	1.6
Years	13	0	67	6	24	.250	3	13	.231	2	3	.667	6	3	0	6	0	1	0.1	0	1	0.1	17	1.3

Antoine Walker

(statistical profile on page 284)

Pos: F **College:** Kentucky **Drafted:** '96 1(6)—Bos   **Ht:** 6'9" **Wt:** 245 **Born:** 8/12/76 **Age:** 24

Year Tm	G	GS	Min	Field Goals Md	Att	Pct	3-Pt FGs Md	Att	Pct	Free Throws Md	Att	Pct	Misc TO	Stl	Blk	Fouls PF	DQ	Assists Ast	Avg	Rebounds Off	Tot	Avg	Points Pts	Avg
				College																				
4-95 Kty	33	2	479	95	227	.419	17	55	.309	52	73	.712	59	28	8	62	—	47	1.4	—	148	4.5	259	7.8
5-96 Kty	36	35	971	228	492	.463	9	48	.188	82	130	.631	89	61	25	85	1	104	2.9	110	302	8.4	547	15.2
Years	69	37	1450	323	719	.449	26	103	.252	134	203	.660	148	89	33	147	—	151	2.2	—	450	6.5	806	11.7

Year Tm	G	GS	Min	Field Goals Md	Att	Pct	3-Pt FGs Md	Att	Pct	Free Throws Md	Att	Pct	Misc TO	Stl	Blk	Fouls PF	DQ	Assists Ast	Avg	Rebounds Off	Tot	Avg	Points Pts	Avg
				NBA																				
6-97 Bos	82	68	2970	576	1354	.425	52	159	.327	231	366	.631	230	105	53	271	1	262	3.2	288	741	9.0	1435	17.5
7-98 Bos*	82	82	3268	722	1705	.423	91	292	.312	305	473	.645	292	142	60	262	2	273	3.3	270	836	10.2	1840	22.4
8-99 Bos	42	41	1549	303	735	.412	65	176	.369	113	202	.559	119	63	28	142	2	130	3.1	106	359	8.5	784	18.7
9-00 Bos	82	82	3003	648	1506	.430	73	285	.256	311	445	.699	259	117	32	263	4	305	3.7	199	652	8.0	1680	20.5
Years	288	273	10790	2249	5300	.424	281	912	.308	960	1486	.646	900	427	173	938	9	970	3.4	863	2588	9.0	5739	19.9

Samaki Walker

Pos: F **College:** Louisville **Drafted:** '96 1(9)—Dal　　　**Ht:** 6'9" **Wt:** 250 **Born:** 2/25/76 **Age:** 24

College			Field Goals			3-Pt FGs			Free Throws			Misc			Fouls		Assists		Rebounds		Points	
Year Tm	G	GS	Min	Md	Att	Pct	Md	Att	Pct	Md	Att	Pct	TO	Stl	Blk	PF	DQ	Ast	Avg	Off	Tot Avg	Pts Avg
94-95 Lou	29	29	841	153	279	.548	2	6	.333	88	164	.537	45	17	78	60	1	37	1.3	—	210 7.2	396 13.7
95-96 Lou	21	13	634	124	207	.599	0	1	.000	70	114	.614	49	17	43	53	1	23	1.1	44	157 7.5	318 15.1
2 Years	50	42	1475	277	486	.570	2	7	.286	158	278	.568	94	34	121	113	2	60	1.2	—	367 7.3	714 14.3

NBA			Field Goals			3-Pt FGs			Free Throws			Misc			Fouls		Assists		Rebounds		Points	
Year Tm	G	GS	Min	Md	Att	Pct	Md	Att	Pct	Md	Att	Pct	TO	Stl	Blk	PF	DQ	Ast	Avg	Off	Tot Avg	Pts Avg
96-97 Dal	43	12	602	83	187	.444	0	1	.000	48	74	.649	39	15	22	71	0	17	0.4	47	147 3.4	214 5.0
97-98 Dal	41	19	1027	156	321	.486	0	1	.000	53	97	.546	61	30	40	127	2	24	0.6	96	302 7.4	365 8.9
98-99 Dal	39	2	568	88	190	.463	0	1	.000	53	98	.541	37	9	16	87	3	6	0.2	46	143 3.7	229 5.9
99-00 SA	71	7	980	137	305	.449	0	0	—	86	126	.683	64	10	35	108	1	38	0.5	77	272 3.8	360 5.1
4 Years	194	40	3177	464	1003	.463	0	3	.000	240	395	.608	201	64	113	393	6	85	0.4	266	864 4.5	1168 6.0

NBA Postseason																						
Year Tm	G	GS	Min	Md	Att	Pct	Md	Att	Pct	Md	Att	Pct	TO	Stl	Blk	PF	DQ	Ast	Avg	Off	Tot Avg	Pts Avg
99-00 SA	4	4	121	14	31	.452	0	0	—	8	12	.667	8	1	12	13	0	2	0.5	13	45 11.3	36 9.0

Ben Wallace

(statistical profile on page 285)

Pos: F-C **College:** Virginia Union **Drafted:** '96 FA—Was　　　**Ht:** 6'9" **Wt:** 240 **Born:** 9/10/74 **Age:** 26

College			Field Goals			3-Pt FGs			Free Throws			Misc			Fouls		Assists		Rebounds		Points	
Year Tm	G	GS	Min	Md	Att	Pct	Md	Att	Pct	Md	Att	Pct	TO	Stl	Blk	PF	DQ	Ast	Avg	Off	Tot Avg	Pts Avg
94-95 VaUn	31	—	—	180	330	.545	0	1	.000	85	209	.407	—	36	111	—	—	27	0.9	—	295 9.5	445 14.4
95-96 VaUn	31	—	902	159	318	.500	0	1	.000	70	187	.374	58	31	114	56	—	18	0.6	—	325 10.5	388 12.5
2 Years	62	—	—	339	648	.523	0	2	.000	155	396	.391	—	67	225	—	—	45	0.7	—	620 10.0	833 13.4

NBA			Field Goals			3-Pt FGs			Free Throws			Misc			Fouls		Assists		Rebounds		Points	
Year Tm	G	GS	Min	Md	Att	Pct	Md	Att	Pct	Md	Att	Pct	TO	Stl	Blk	PF	DQ	Ast	Avg	Off	Tot Avg	Pts Avg
96-97 Was	34	0	197	16	46	.348	0	0	—	6	20	.300	18	8	11	27	0	2	0.1	25	58 1.7	38 1.1
97-98 Was	67	16	1124	85	164	.518	0	0	—	35	98	.357	28	61	72	116	1	18	0.4	112	324 4.8	205 3.1
98-99 Was	46	16	1231	115	199	.578	0	0	—	47	132	.356	36	50	90	111	0	18	0.4	137	384 8.3	277 6.0
99-00 Orl	81	81	1959	168	334	.503	0	0	—	54	114	.474	67	72	130	162	0	67	0.8	211	665 8.2	390 4.8
4 Years	228	113	4511	384	743	.517	0	0	—	142	364	.390	149	191	303	416	1	105	0.5	485	1431 6.3	910 4.0

John Wallace

Pos: F **College:** Syracuse **Drafted:** '96 1(18)—NY　　　**Ht:** 6'9" **Wt:** 255 **Born:** 2/9/74 **Age:** 26

College			Field Goals			3-Pt FGs			Free Throws			Misc			Fouls		Assists		Rebounds		Points	
Year Tm	G	GS	Min	Md	Att	Pct	Md	Att	Pct	Md	Att	Pct	TO	Stl	Blk	PF	DQ	Ast	Avg	Off	Tot Avg	Pts Avg
92-93 Syr	29	29	863	130	247	.526	0	1	.000	61	85	.718	92	34	39	75	2	38	1.3	76	221 7.6	321 11.1
93-94 Syr	30	30	984	164	290	.566	0	2	.000	121	159	.761	93	28	52	90	4	50	1.7	77	270 9.0	449 15.0
94-95 Syr	30	30	990	197	335	.588	4	14	.286	106	156	.679	91	39	55	80	4	77	2.6	86	245 8.2	504 16.8
95-96 Syr	38	38	1379	293	599	.489	37	88	.420	222	291	.763	122	44	63	94	1	90	2.4	88	329 8.7	845 22.2
4 Years	127	127	4216	784	1471	.533	41	105	.390	510	691	.738	398	145	209	339	11	255	2.0	327	1065 8.4	2119 16.7

NBA			Field Goals			3-Pt FGs			Free Throws			Misc			Fouls		Assists		Rebounds		Points	
Year Tm	G	GS	Min	Md	Att	Pct	Md	Att	Pct	Md	Att	Pct	TO	Stl	Blk	PF	DQ	Ast	Avg	Off	Tot Avg	Pts Avg
96-97 NY	68	6	787	122	236	.517	2	4	.500	79	110	.718	76	21	25	102	0	37	0.5	51	155 2.3	325 4.8
97-98 Tor	82	36	2361	468	979	.478	1	2	.500	210	293	.717	172	62	101	239	7	110	1.3	117	373 4.5	1147 14.0
98-99 Tor	48	3	812	153	354	.432	0	0	—	105	150	.700	70	12	43	92	0	46	1.0	54	171 3.6	411 8.6
99-00 NY	60	0	798	155	332	.467	0	3	.000	82	102	.804	63	10	14	103	0	22	0.4	42	135 2.3	392 6.6
4 Years	258	45	4758	898	1901	.472	3	9	.333	476	655	.727	381	105	183	536	7	215	0.8	264	834 3.2	2275 8.8

NBA Postseason																						
Year Tm	G	GS	Min	Md	Att	Pct	Md	Att	Pct	Md	Att	Pct	TO	Stl	Blk	PF	DQ	Ast	Avg	Off	Tot Avg	Pts Avg
96-97 NY	4	1	40	4	15	.267	0	1	.000	2	2	1.000	2	1	2	6	0	5	1.3	2	7 1.8	10 2.5
99-00 NY	1	0	4	0	2	.000	0	0	—	0	0	—	1	1	0	1	0	0	0.0	0	1 1.0	0 0.0
2 Years	5	1	44	4	17	.235	0	1	.000	2	2	1.000	3	2	2	7	0	5	1.0	2	8 1.6	10 2.0

Rasheed Wallace

(statistical profile on page 285)

Pos: F-C **College:** North Carolina **Drafted:** '95 1(4)—Was　　　**Ht:** 6'11" **Wt:** 230 **Born:** 9/17/74 **Age:** 26

College			Field Goals			3-Pt FGs			Free Throws			Misc			Fouls		Assists		Rebounds		Points	
Year Tm	G	GS	Min	Md	Att	Pct	Md	Att	Pct	Md	Att	Pct	TO	Stl	Blk	PF	DQ	Ast	Avg	Off	Tot Avg	Pts Avg
93-94 UNC	35	7	732	139	230	.604	0	1	.000	55	91	.604	49	24	63	81	—	18	0.5	86	232 6.6	333 9.5

(continued)

Year Tm	G	GS	Min	Md	Att	Pct	Md	Att	Pct	Md	Att	Pct	TO	Stl	Blk	PF	DQ	Ast	Avg	Off	Tot	Avg	Pts	Avg
				Field Goals			3-Pt FGs			Free Throws			Misc			Fouls		Assists		Rebounds			Points	
College																								
4-95 UNC	34	34	1030	238	364	.654	1	3	.333	89	141	.631	52	17	93	95		35	1.0	102	279	8.2	566	16.6
Years	69	41	1762	377	594	.635	1	4	.250	144	232	.621	101	41	156	176	—	53	0.8	188	511	7.4	899	13.0
NBA																								
5-96 Was	65	51	1788	275	565	.487	27	82	.329	78	120	.650	103	42	54	206	4	85	1.3	93	303	4.7	655	10.1
6-97 Por	62	56	1892	380	681	.558	9	33	.273	169	265	.638	114	48	59	198	1	74	1.2	122	419	6.8	938	15.1
7-98 Por	77	77	2896	466	875	.533	8	39	.205	184	278	.662	167	75	88	268	6	195	2.5	132	478	6.2	1124	14.6
8-99 Por	49	18	1414	242	476	.508	13	31	.419	131	179	.732	80	48	54	175	6	60	1.2	57	241	4.9	628	12.8
9-00 Por*	81	77	2845	542	1045	.519	8	50	.160	233	331	.704	157	87	107	216	2	142	1.8	129	566	7.0	1325	16.4
Years	334	279	10835	1905	3642	.523	65	235	.277	795	1173	.678	621	300	362	1063	19	556	1.7	533	2007	6.0	4670	14.0
NBA Postseason																								
6-97 Por	4	4	148	33	56	.589	2	5	.400	11	20	.550	6	2	2	17	1	6	1.5	8	24	6.0	79	19.8
7-98 Por	4	4	157	23	47	.489	4	5	.800	8	16	.500	5	2	2	16	0	11	2.8	7	19	4.8	58	14.5
8-99 Por	13	13	468	75	146	.514	1	9	.111	42	58	.724	16	20	11	50	1	20	1.5	17	63	4.8	193	14.8
9-00 Por	16	16	605	110	225	.489	8	13	.615	58	75	.773	23	15	20	52	0	28	1.8	31	103	6.4	286	17.9
Years	37	37	1378	241	474	.508	15	32	.469	119	169	.704	50	39	35	135	2	65	1.8	63	209	5.6	616	16.6

Rex Walters

os: G **College:** Kansas **Drafted:** '93 1(16)—NJ **Ht:** 6'4" **Wt:** 195 **Born:** 3/12/70 **Age:** 30

Year Tm	G	GS	Min	Md	Att	Pct	Md	Att	Pct	Md	Att	Pct	TO	Stl	Blk	PF	DQ	Ast	Avg	Off	Tot	Avg	Pts	Avg
				Field Goals			3-Pt FGs			Free Throws			Misc			Fouls		Assists		Rebounds			Points	
College																								
3-89 NW	24	0	165	17	45	.378	5	18	.278	11	12	.917	22	4	0	17	0	33	1.4	—	17	0.7	50	2.1
9-90 NW	28	28	892	181	360	.503	53	112	.473	77	97	.794	81	34	7	80	3	125	4.5	—	75	2.7	492	17.6
1-92 Kan	32	32	918	165	314	.525	68	168	.405	115	139	.827	75	53	10	89	2	124	3.9	—	105	3.3	513	16.0
2-93 Kan	36	36	1028	179	365	.490	83	193	.430	110	126	.873	96	40	7	83	0	154	4.3	—	96	2.7	551	15.3
Years	120	96	3003	542	1084	.500	209	491	.426	313	374	.837	274	131	24	269	5	436	3.6	—	293	2.4	1606	13.4
NBA																								
3-94 NJ	48	0	386	60	115	.522	14	28	.500	28	34	.824	30	15	3	41	0	71	1.5	6	38	0.8	162	3.4
4-95 NJ	80	30	1435	206	469	.439	71	196	.362	40	52	.769	71	37	16	135	0	121	1.5	18	93	1.2	523	6.5
5-96 2Tm	44	8	610	61	148	.412	22	66	.333	42	52	.808	41	25	4	53	0	106	2.4	13	55	1.3	186	4.2
6-97 Phi	59	16	1041	148	325	.455	57	148	.385	49	62	.790	61	28	3	75	1	113	1.9	21	107	1.8	402	6.8
7-98 2Tm	38	0	235	24	53	.453	6	22	.273	26	28	.929	27	8	1	28	0	35	0.9	5	24	0.6	80	2.1
8-99 Mia	33	13	506	35	95	.368	12	38	.316	19	23	.826	32	10	3	63	0	58	1.8	10	50	1.5	101	3.1
9-00 Mia	33	0	389	38	91	.418	5	20	.250	12	16	.750	29	6	0	44	0	65	2.0	8	36	1.1	93	2.8
5-96 NJ	11	0	87	12	33	.364	3	12	.250	6	6	1.000	7	3	0	4	0	11	1.0	2	7	0.6	33	3.0
Phi	33	8	523	49	115	.426	19	54	.352	36	46	.783	34	22	4	49	0	95	2.9	11	48	1.5	153	4.6
7-98 Phi	19	0	127	11	29	.379	3	14	.214	17	17	1.000	17	5	0	17	0	21	1.1	3	9	0.5	42	2.2
Mia	19	0	108	13	24	.542	3	8	.375	9	11	.818	10	3	1	11	0	14	0.7	2	15	0.8	38	2.0
Years	335	67	4602	572	1296	.441	187	518	.361	216	267	.809	291	129	30	439	1	569	1.7	81	403	1.2	1547	4.6
NBA Postseason																								
3-94 NJ	1	0	1	1	1	1.000	0	0	—	0	0	—	0	0	0	0	0	0	0.0	0	0	0.0	2	2.0
8-99 Mia	3	0	13	0	3	.000	0	2	.000	0	0	—	0	0	0	0	0	4	1.3	0	0	0.0	0	0.0
Years	4	0	14	1	4	.250	0	2	.000	0	0	—	0	0	0	0	0	4	1.0	0	0	0.0	2	0.5

Charlie Ward

(statistical profile on page 286)

os: G **College:** Florida State **Drafted:** '94 1(26)—NY **Ht:** 6'2" **Wt:** 190 **Born:** 10/12/70 **Age:** 30

Year Tm	G	GS	Min	Md	Att	Pct	Md	Att	Pct	Md	Att	Pct	TO	Stl	Blk	PF	DQ	Ast	Avg	Off	Tot	Avg	Pts	Avg
				Field Goals			3-Pt FGs			Free Throws			Misc			Fouls		Assists		Rebounds			Points	
College																								
0-91 FlaSt	30	21	715	81	178	.455	15	48	.313	62	87	.713	60	71	8	53	1	103	3.4	23	89	3.0	239	8.0
1-92 FlaSt	28	22	841	72	145	.497	22	48	.458	35	66	.530	74	75	6	67	2	122	4.4	19	90	3.2	201	7.2
2-93 FlaSt	17	14	557	49	106	.462	16	50	.320	18	27	.667	36	48	5	32	0	93	5.5	9	45	2.6	132	7.8
3-94 FlaSt	16	16	574	61	167	.365	21	83	.253	25	40	.625	42	44	2	36	2	78	4.9	23	62	3.9	168	10.5
Years	91	73	2687	263	596	.441	74	229	.323	140	220	.636	212	238	21	188	5	396	4.4	74	286	3.1	740	8.1
NBA																								
4-95 NY	10	0	44	4	19	.211	1	10	.100	7	10	.700	8	2	0	7	0	4	0.4	1	6	0.6	16	1.6
5-96 NY	62	1	787	87	218	.399	33	99	.333	37	54	.685	79	54	6	98	0	132	2.1	29	102	1.6	244	3.9
6-97 NY	79	21	1763	133	337	.395	48	154	.312	95	125	.760	147	83	15	188	2	326	4.1	45	220	2.8	409	5.2
7-98 NY	82	82	2317	235	516	.455	81	215	.377	91	113	.805	175	144	37	195	3	466	5.7	32	274	3.3	642	7.8

NBA				Field Goals			3-Pt FGs			Free Throws			Misc			Fouls		Assists		Rebounds			Points	
Year Tm	G	GS	Min	Md	Att	Pct	Md	Att	Pct	Md	Att	Pct	TO	Stl	Blk	PF	DQ	Ast	Avg	Off	Tot	Avg	Pts	Av
98-99 NY	50	50	1556	135	334	.404	53	149	.356	55	78	.705	131	103	8	105	0	271	5.4	23	172	3.4	378	7
99-00 NY	72	69	1986	189	447	.423	102	264	.386	48	58	.828	102	95	16	176	3	300	4.2	22	228	3.2	528	7.
6 Years	355	223	8453	783	1871	.418	318	891	.357	333	438	.760	642	481	82	769	8	1499	4.2	152	1002	2.8	2217	6.

NBA Postseason

Year Tm	G	GS	Min	Md	Att	Pct	Md	Att	Pct	Md	Att	Pct	TO	Stl	Blk	PF	DQ	Ast	Avg	Off	Tot	Avg	Pts	Av
95-96 NY	7	0	92	13	27	.481	3	12	.250	3	7	.429	6	11	0	9	0	17	2.4	2	9	1.3	32	4.
96-97 NY	9	0	182	8	27	.296	1	9	.111	3	4	.750	15	13	0	18	1	39	4.3	3	25	2.8	20	2
97-98 NY	10	10	261	23	55	.418	9	21	.429	11	16	.688	17	20	2	24	0	60	6.0	3	28	2.8	66	6
98-99 NY	20	20	494	34	93	.366	18	56	.321	6	8	.750	24	35	3	45	0	75	3.8	12	46	2.3	92	4
99-00 NY	16	16	439	57	113	.504	21	53	.396	15	21	.714	20	22	5	40	1	65	4.1	11	68	4.3	150	9.
5 Years	62	46	1468	135	315	.429	52	151	.344	38	56	.679	82	101	10	136	2	256	4.1	31	176	2.8	360	5

Clarence Weatherspoon

(statistical profile on page 28•)

Pos: F **College:** Southern Mississippi **Drafted:** '92 1(9)—Phi **Ht:** 6'7" **Wt:** 265 **Born:** 9/8/70 **Age:** 3

College				Field Goals			3-Pt FGs			Free Throws			Misc			Fouls		Assists		Rebounds			Points	
Year Tm	G	GS	Min	Md	Att	Pct	Md	Att	Pct	Md	Att	Pct	TO	Stl	Blk	PF	DQ	Ast	Avg	Off	Tot	Avg	Pts	Av
88-89 SoMs	27	27	915	152	279	.545	1	3	.333	92	156	.590	65	31	44	78	2	30	1.1	102	289	10.7	397	14.7
89-90 SoMs	32	32	1166	205	339	.605	0	2	.000	159	230	.691	73	35	45	89	0	28	0.9	145	371	11.6	569	17
90-91 SoMs	29	29	1019	195	331	.589	7	14	.500	120	161	.745	74	42	60	75	0	66	2.3	110	355	12.2	517	17
91-92 SoMs	29	29	1057	246	437	.563	24	53	.453	131	194	.675	76	47	78	57	0	47	1.6	105	305	10.5	647	22
4 Years	117	117	4157	798	1386	.576	32	72	.444	502	741	.677	288	155	227	299	2	171	1.5	462	1320	11.3	2130	18

NBA				Field Goals			3-Pt FGs			Free Throws			Misc			Fouls		Assists		Rebounds			Points	
Year Tm	G	GS	Min	Md	Att	Pct	Md	Att	Pct	Md	Att	Pct	TO	Stl	Blk	PF	DQ	Ast	Avg	Off	Tot	Avg	Pts	Av
92-93 Phi	82	82	2654	494	1053	.469	1	4	.250	291	408	.713	176	85	67	188	1	147	1.8	179	589	7.2	1280	15
93-94 Phi	82	82	3147	602	1246	.483	4	17	.235	298	430	.693	195	100	116	152	0	192	2.3	254	832	10.1	1506	18
94-95 Phi	76	76	2991	543	1238	.439	4	21	.190	283	377	.751	191	115	67	195	1	215	2.8	144	526	6.9	1373	18
95-96 Phi	78	75	3096	491	1015	.484	0	2	.000	318	426	.746	179	112	108	214	3	158	2.0	237	753	9.7	1300	16
96-97 Phi	82	82	2949	398	811	.491	1	6	.167	206	279	.738	137	74	86	187	1	140	1.7	219	679	8.3	1003	12
97-98 2Tm	79	49	2325	268	608	.441	0	0	—	200	277	.722	119	85	74	194	2	89	1.1	198	594	7.5	736	9
98-99 Mia	49	3	1040	141	264	.534	0	0	—	115	143	.804	61	28	17	107	0	34	0.7	72	243	5.0	397	8
99-00 Mia	78	2	1615	215	419	.513	0	0	—	135	183	.738	100	51	49	165	1	93	1.2	128	449	5.8	565	7
97-98 Phi	48	18	1290	141	331	.426	0	0	—	123	174	.707	69	43	52	108	1	40	0.8	109	336	7.0	405	8
GS	31	31	1035	127	277	.458	0	0	—	77	103	.748	50	42	22	86	1	49	1.6	89	258	8.3	331	10
8 Years	606	451	19817	3152	6654	.474	10	50	.200	1846	2523	.732	1158	650	584	1402	8	1068	1.8	1431	4665	7.7	8160	13

NBA Postseason

Year Tm	G	GS	Min	Md	Att	Pct	Md	Att	Pct	Md	Att	Pct	TO	Stl	Blk	PF	DQ	Ast	Avg	Off	Tot	Avg	Pts	Av
98-99 Mia	5	0	112	9	26	.346	0	0	—	11	17	.647	3	7	1	8	0	2	0.4	4	21	4.2	29	5
99-00 Mia	10	0	170	25	60	.417	0	0	—	14	24	.583	8	4	3	23	0	1	0.1	18	41	4.1	64	6
2 Years	15	0	282	34	86	.395	0	0	—	25	41	.610	11	11	4	31	0	3	0.2	22	62	4.1	93	6

Chris Webber

(statistical profile on page 28•)

Pos: F **College:** Michigan **Drafted:** '93 1(1)—Orl **Ht:** 6'10" **Wt:** 245 **Born:** 3/1/73 **Age:** 2

College				Field Goals			3-Pt FGs			Free Throws			Misc			Fouls		Assists		Rebounds			Points	
Year Tm	G	GS	Min	Md	Att	Pct	Md	Att	Pct	Md	Att	Pct	TO	Stl	Blk	PF	DQ	Ast	Avg	Off	Tot	Avg	Pts	Av
91-92 Mich	34	34	1089	229	412	.556	14	54	.259	56	113	.496	95	54	84	99	5	76	2.2	128	340	10.0	528	15
92-93 Mich	36	36	1143	281	454	.619	27	80	.338	101	183	.552	105	49	91	102	8	90	2.5	155	362	10.1	690	19
2 Years	70	70	2232	510	866	.589	41	134	.306	157	296	.530	200	103	175	201	13	166	2.4	283	702	10.0	1218	17

NBA				Field Goals			3-Pt FGs			Free Throws			Misc			Fouls		Assists		Rebounds			Points	
Year Tm	G	GS	Min	Md	Att	Pct	Md	Att	Pct	Md	Att	Pct	TO	Stl	Blk	PF	DQ	Ast	Avg	Off	Tot	Avg	Pts	Av
93-94 GS	76	76	2438	572	1037	.552	0	14	.000	189	355	.532	206	93	164	247	4	272	3.6	305	694	9.1	1333	17
94-95 Was	54	52	2067	464	938	.495	40	145	.276	117	233	.502	167	83	85	186	2	256	4.7	200	518	9.6	1085	20
95-96 Was	15	15	558	150	276	.543	15	34	.441	41	69	.594	49	27	9	51	1	75	5.0	37	114	7.6	356	23
96-97 Was*	72	72	2806	604	1167	.518	60	151	.397	177	313	.565	230	122	137	258	6	331	4.6	238	743	10.3	1445	20
97-98 Was	71	71	2809	647	1341	.482	65	205	.317	196	333	.589	185	111	124	269	4	273	3.8	176	674	9.5	1555	21
98-99 Sac	42	42	1719	378	778	.486	4	34	.118	79	174	.454	148	60	89	145	1	173	4.1	149	545	**13.0**	839	20
99-00 Sac*	75	75	2880	748	1548	.483	27	95	.284	311	414	.751	212	120	128	264	7	345	4.6	189	787	10.5	1834	24
7 Years	405	403	15277	3563	7085	.503	211	678	.311	1110	1891	.587	1203	616	736	1420	25	1725	4.3	1294	4075	10.1	8447	20

NBA Postseason

Year Tm	G	GS	Min	Md	Att	Pct	Md	Att	Pct	Md	Att	Pct	TO	Stl	Blk	PF	DQ	Ast	Avg	Off	Tot	Avg	Pts	Av
93-94 GS	3	3	109	22	40	.550	0	2	.000	3	10	.300	9	3	9	11	0	27	9.0	13	26	8.7	47	15
96-97 Was	3	3	106	19	30	.633	5	11	.455	4	8	.500	16	2	7	18	3	10	3.3	7	24	8.0	47	15

NBA Postseason

Year Tm	G	GS	Min	Md	Att	Pct	Md	Att	Pct	Md	Att	Pct	TO	Stl	Blk	PF	DQ	Ast	Avg	Off	Tot	Avg	Pts	Avg
98-99 Sac	5	5	192	31	80	.388	2	7	.286	10	25	.400	20	9	5	20	1	20	4.0	13	47	9.4	74	14.8
99-00 Sac	5	5	196	47	110	.427	1	5	.200	27	34	.794	8	8	10	14	1	27	5.4	14	48	9.6	122	24.4
4 Years	16	16	603	119	260	.458	8	25	.320	44	77	.571	53	22	31	63	5	84	5.3	47	145	9.1	290	18.1

Bonzi Wells

Pos: G-F **College:** Ball State **Drafted:** '98 1(11)—Det   **Ht:** 6'5" **Wt:** 210 **Born:** 9/20/76 **Age:** 24

College				Field Goals			3-Pt FGs			Free Throws			Misc			Fouls		Assists		Rebounds			Points	
Year Tm	G	GS	Min	Md	Att	Pct	Md	Att	Pct	Md	Att	Pct	TO	Stl	Blk	PF	DQ	Ast	Avg	Off	Tot	Avg	Pts	Avg
94-95 BlSt	30	30	887	177	380	.466	33	99	.333	87	141	.617	80	84	18	78	1	84	2.8	63	183	6.1	474	15.8
95-96 BlSt	28	28	910	269	544	.494	31	92	.337	143	202	.708	106	87	34	86	3	80	2.9	70	246	8.8	712	25.4
96-97 BlSt	29	28	900	229	492	.465	25	104	.240	154	223	.691	124	73	20	85	3	127	4.4	67	230	7.9	637	22.0
97-98 BlSt	29	28	843	238	486	.490	53	142	.373	133	193	.689	100	103	20	90	3	95	3.3	48	184	6.3	662	22.8
4 Years	116	114	3540	913	1902	.480	142	437	.325	517	759	.681	410	347	92	339	10	386	3.3	248	843	7.3	2485	21.4

NBA				Field Goals			3-Pt FGs			Free Throws			Misc			Fouls		Assists		Rebounds			Points	
Year Tm	G	GS	Min	Md	Att	Pct	Md	Att	Pct	Md	Att	Pct	TO	Stl	Blk	PF	DQ	Ast	Avg	Off	Tot	Avg	Pts	Avg
98-99 Por	7	0	35	11	20	.550	1	3	.333	8	18	.444	6	1	1	5	0	3	0.4	4	9	1.3	31	4.4
99-00 Por	66	0	1162	236	480	.492	20	53	.377	88	129	.682	97	69	12	153	3	97	1.5	78	182	2.8	580	8.8
2 Years	73	0	1197	247	500	.494	21	56	.375	96	147	.653	103	70	13	158	3	100	1.4	82	191	2.6	611	8.4

NBA Postseason

Year Tm	G	GS	Min	Md	Att	Pct	Md	Att	Pct	Md	Att	Pct	TO	Stl	Blk	PF	DQ	Ast	Avg	Off	Tot	Avg	Pts	Avg
99-00 Por	14	0	188	37	83	.446	2	10	.200	29	41	.707	16	7	0	33	0	13	0.9	12	35	2.5	105	7.5

Bill Wennington

Pos: C **College:** St. John's (NY) **Drafted:** '85 1(16)—Dal   **Ht:** 7'0" **Wt:** 277 **Born:** 4/26/63 **Age:** 37

College				Field Goals			3-Pt FGs			Free Throws			Misc			Fouls		Assists		Rebounds			Points	
Year Tm	G	GS	Min	Md	Att	Pct	Md	Att	Pct	Md	Att	Pct	TO	Stl	Blk	PF	DQ	Ast	Avg	Off	Tot	Avg	Pts	Avg
81-82 StJn	30	0	505	37	85	.435	—	—		23	34	.676	20	8	35	86	6	4	0.1	—	126	4.2	97	3.2
82-83 StJn	33	6	656	69	114	.605	—	—		44	63	.698	29	9	31	92	6	9	0.3	—	146	4.4	182	5.5
83-84 StJn	26	26	735	124	209	.593	—	—		56	83	.675	43	16	34	82	6	32	1.2	—	148	5.7	304	11.7
84-85 StJn	35	35	1099	168	279	.602	—	—		102	125	.816	57	21	51	113	4	55	1.6	—	224	6.4	438	12.5
4 Years	124	67	2995	398	687	.579	—	—		225	305	.738	149	54	151	373	22	100	0.8	—	644	5.2	1021	8.2

NBA				Field Goals			3-Pt FGs			Free Throws			Misc			Fouls		Assists		Rebounds			Points	
Year Tm	G	GS	Min	Md	Att	Pct	Md	Att	Pct	Md	Att	Pct	TO	Stl	Blk	PF	DQ	Ast	Avg	Off	Tot	Avg	Pts	Avg
85-86 Dal	56	3	562	72	153	.471	0	4	.000	45	62	.726	21	11	22	83	0	21	0.4	32	132	2.4	189	3.4
86-87 Dal	58	0	560	56	132	.424	0	2	.000	45	60	.750	39	13	10	95	0	24	0.4	53	129	2.2	157	2.7
87-88 Dal	30	0	125	25	49	.510	1	2	.500	12	19	.632	9	5	9	33	0	4	0.1	14	39	1.3	63	2.1
88-89 Dal	65	9	1074	119	275	.433	1	9	.111	61	82	.744	54	16	35	211	3	46	0.7	82	286	4.4	300	4.6
89-90 Dal	60	2	814	105	234	.449	0	4	.000	60	75	.800	50	20	21	144	2	41	0.7	64	198	3.3	270	4.5
90-91 Sac	77	23	1455	181	415	.436	1	5	.200	74	94	.787	51	46	59	230	4	69	0.9	101	340	4.4	437	5.7
91-92										Played in Italy														
92-93										Played in Italy														
93-94 Chi	76	0	1371	235	482	.488	0	2	.000	72	88	.818	75	43	29	214	4	70	0.9	117	353	4.6	542	7.1
94-95 Chi	73	1	956	156	317	.492	0	4	.000	51	63	.810	39	22	17	198	5	40	0.5	64	190	2.6	363	5.0
95-96 Chi	71	0	1065	169	343	.493	1	1	1.000	37	43	.860	37	21	16	171	1	46	0.6	58	174	2.5	376	5.3
96-97 Chi	61	19	783	118	237	.498	0	2	.000	44	53	.830	31	10	11	132	1	41	0.7	46	129	2.1	280	4.6
97-98 Chi	48	8	467	75	172	.436	0	0	—	17	21	.810	16	4	5	77	1	19	0.4	32	80	1.7	167	3.5
98-99 Chi	38	3	451	62	178	.348	1	1	1.000	18	22	.818	17	13	12	79	1	18	0.5	20	79	2.1	143	3.8
99-00 Sac	7	0	57	6	19	.316	0	0	—	2	2	1.000	2	1	2	13	0	1	0.1	5	19	2.7	14	2.0
13 Years	720	88	9740	1379	3006	.459	5	36	.139	538	684	.787	440	226	248	1680	22	440	0.6	688	2148	3.0	3301	4.6

NBA Postseason

Year Tm	G	GS	Min	Md	Att	Pct	Md	Att	Pct	Md	Att	Pct	TO	Stl	Blk	PF	DQ	Ast	Avg	Off	Tot	Avg	Pts	Avg
85-86 Dal	6	0	18	2	6	.333	1	1	1.000	2	2	1.000	0	0	0	4	0	0	0.0	4	5	0.8	7	1.2
86-87 Dal	4	0	47	6	12	.500	0	0	—	3	5	.600	3	0	3	9	0	4	1.0	4	10	2.5	15	3.8
87-88 Dal	6	0	14	0	4	.000	0	0	—	0	0	—	1	1	0	5	0	1	0.2	3	4	0.7	0	0.0
89-90 Dal	3	0	25	1	5	.200	0	0	—	0	0	—	2	0	1	5	0	1	0.3	0	3	1.0	2	0.7
93-94 Chi	7	0	47	3	6	.500	0	0	—	2	3	.667	1	0	1	14	0	4	0.6	4	7	1.0	8	1.1
94-95 Chi	10	0	133	21	51	.412	0	0	—	6	6	1.000	8	3	3	32	0	3	0.3	12	28	2.8	48	4.8
95-96 Chi	18	0	169	26	50	.520	0	1	.000	2	4	.500	5	4	1	30	0	9	0.5	11	30	1.7	54	3.0
97-98 Chi	16	0	119	20	38	.526	0	0	—	4	8	.500	8	6	2	23	0	3	0.2	3	14	0.9	44	2.8
8 Years	70	0	572	79	172	.459	1	2	.500	19	28	.679	28	14	11	122	1	25	0.4	41	101	1.4	178	2.5

David Wesley

(statistical profile on page 287)

Pos: G **College:** Baylor **Drafted:** '93 FA—NJ   **Ht:** 6'1" **Wt:** 202 **Born:** 11/14/70 **Age:** 30

College			Field Goals			3-Pt FGs			Free Throws			Misc			Fouls		Assists		Rebounds			Points	
Year Tm	G	GS	Min	Md	Att	Pct	Md	Att	Pct	Md	Att	Pct	TO	Stl	Blk	PF	DQ	Ast	Avg	Off	Tot	Avg	Pts	Avg
89-90 Bay	18	—	394	61	134	.455	25	56	.446	61	73	.836	44	30	2	35	—	37	2.1	—	39	2.2	208	11.6
90-91 Bay	26	—	837	133	314	.424	39	114	.342	125	149	.839	105	59	4	84	—	148	5.7	—	76	2.9	430	16.5
91-92 Bay	28	—	1020	174	387	.450	59	156	.378	179	219	.817	101	56	10	83	—	131	4.7	—	136	4.9	586	20.9
3 Years	72	—	2251	368	835	.441	123	326	.377	365	441	.828	250	145	16	202	—	316	4.4	—	251	3.5	1224	17.0

NBA			Field Goals			3-Pt FGs			Free Throws			Misc			Fouls		Assists		Rebounds			Points	
Year Tm	G	GS	Min	Md	Att	Pct	Md	Att	Pct	Md	Att	Pct	TO	Stl	Blk	PF	DQ	Ast	Avg	Off	Tot	Avg	Pts	Avg
92-93									Played in CBA															
93-94 NJ	60	0	542	64	174	.368	11	47	.234	44	53	.830	52	38	4	47	0	123	2.1	10	44	0.7	183	3.1
94-95 Bos	51	36	1380	128	313	.409	51	119	.429	71	94	.755	87	82	9	144	0	266	5.2	31	117	2.3	378	7.4
95-96 Bos	82	53	2104	338	736	.459	116	272	.426	217	288	.753	159	100	11	207	0	390	4.8	68	264	3.2	1009	12.3
96-97 Bos	74	73	2991	456	974	.468	103	286	.360	225	288	.781	211	162	13	221	1	537	7.3	67	264	3.6	1240	16.8
97-98 Cha	81	81	2845	383	864	.443	59	170	.347	229	288	.795	226	140	30	229	3	529	6.5	49	213	2.6	1054	13.0
98-99 Cha	50	50	1848	243	545	.446	61	170	.359	159	191	.832	142	100	10	130	2	322	6.4	23	161	3.2	706	14.1
99-00 Cha	82	82	2760	407	955	.426	88	248	.355	214	275	.778	159	109	11	186	2	463	5.6	39	225	2.7	1116	13.6
7 Years	480	375	14470	2019	4561	.443	489	1312	.373	1159	1477	.785	1036	731	88	1164	8	2630	5.5	287	1288	2.7	5686	11.8

NBA Postseason																								
Year Tm	G	GS	Min	Md	Att	Pct	Md	Att	Pct	Md	Att	Pct	TO	Stl	Blk	PF	DQ	Ast	Avg	Off	Tot	Avg	Pts	Avg
93-94 NJ	3	0	18	3	7	.429	1	4	.250	2	2	1.000	4	2	0	0	0	3	1.0	0	0	0.0	9	3.0
97-98 Cha	9	9	285	33	83	.398	9	21	.429	15	21	.714	19	7	0	25	0	60	6.7	5	18	2.0	90	10.0
99-00 Cha	4	4	152	16	48	.333	3	10	.300	9	9	1.000	6	8	0	17	0	19	4.8	3	12	3.0	44	11.0
3 Years	16	13	455	52	138	.377	13	35	.371	26	32	.813	29	17	0	42	0	82	5.1	8	30	1.9	143	8.9

Doug West

Pos: G **College:** Villanova **Drafted:** '89 2(38)—Min   **Ht:** 6'6" **Wt:** 220 **Born:** 5/27/67 **Age:** 33

College			Field Goals			3-Pt FGs			Free Throws			Misc			Fouls		Assists		Rebounds			Points	
Year Tm	G	GS	Min	Md	Att	Pct	Md	Att	Pct	Md	Att	Pct	TO	Stl	Blk	PF	DQ	Ast	Avg	Off	Tot	Avg	Pts	Avg
85-86 Vill	37	—	995	158	307	.515	—	—	—	60	88	.682	78	25	16	125	—	16	0.4	—	136	3.7	376	10.2
86-87 Vill	31	—	1022	180	376	.479	16	43	.372	94	129	.729	59	19	9	89	—	9	0.3	—	151	4.9	470	15.2
87-88 Vill	37	—	1281	215	433	.497	61	143	.427	92	127	.724	81	36	10	100	—	82	2.2	—	181	4.9	583	15.8
88-89 Vill	33	—	1137	226	488	.463	66	177	.373	90	125	.720	80	47	16	99	—	92	2.8	—	162	4.9	608	18.4
4 Years	138	—	4435	779	1604	.486	143	363	.394	336	469	.716	298	127	51	413	—	199	1.4	—	630	4.6	2037	14.8

NBA			Field Goals			3-Pt FGs			Free Throws			Misc			Fouls		Assists		Rebounds			Points	
Year Tm	G	GS	Min	Md	Att	Pct	Md	Att	Pct	Md	Att	Pct	TO	Stl	Blk	PF	DQ	Ast	Avg	Off	Tot	Avg	Pts	Avg
89-90 Min	52	0	378	53	135	.393	3	11	.273	26	32	.813	31	10	6	61	0	18	0.3	24	70	1.3	135	2.6
90-91 Min	75	1	824	118	246	.480	0	1	.000	58	84	.690	41	35	23	115	—	48	0.6	56	136	1.8	294	3.9
91-92 Min	80	72	2540	463	894	.518	4	23	.174	186	231	.805	120	66	26	239	1	281	3.5	107	257	3.2	1116	14.0
92-93 Min	80	80	3104	646	1249	.517	2	23	.087	249	296	.841	165	85	21	279	1	235	2.9	89	247	3.1	1543	19.3
93-94 Min	72	61	2182	434	891	.487	1	8	.125	187	231	.810	137	65	24	236	3	172	2.4	61	231	3.2	1056	14.7
94-95 Min	71	65	2328	351	762	.461	11	61	.180	206	246	.837	126	65	24	250	4	185	2.6	60	227	3.2	919	12.9
95-96 Min	73	16	1639	175	393	.445	1	13	.077	114	144	.792	81	30	17	228	2	119	1.6	48	161	2.2	465	6.4
96-97 Min	68	66	1920	226	484	.467	15	45	.333	64	94	.681	66	61	24	218	3	113	1.7	37	148	2.2	531	7.8
97-98 Min	38	10	688	64	171	.374	0	2	.000	29	40	.725	21	11	5	97	1	45	1.2	23	82	2.2	157	4.1
98-99 Van	14	2	294	31	65	.477	0	2	.000	19	25	.760	12	16	7	38	1	19	1.4	5	25	1.8	81	5.8
99-00 Van	38	0	581	59	145	.407	0	3	.000	34	40	.850	19	12	8	80	1	43	1.1	18	71	1.9	152	4.0
11 Years	661	373	16478	2620	5435	.482	37	192	.193	1172	1463	.801	819	456	185	1841	17	1278	1.9	528	1655	2.5	6449	9.8

NBA Postseason																								
Year Tm	G	GS	Min	Md	Att	Pct	Md	Att	Pct	Md	Att	Pct	TO	Stl	Blk	PF	DQ	Ast	Avg	Off	Tot	Avg	Pts	Avg
96-97 Min	3	3	87	12	22	.545	0	2	.000	9	9	1.000	1	2	1	11	0	6	2.0	0	4	1.3	33	11.0

Mark West

Pos: C **College:** Old Dominion **Drafted:** '83 2(30)—Dal   **Ht:** 6'10" **Wt:** 246 **Born:** 11/5/60 **Age:** 40

College			Field Goals			3-Pt FGs			Free Throws			Misc			Fouls		Assists		Rebounds			Points	
Year Tm	G	GS	Min	Md	Att	Pct	Md	Att	Pct	Md	Att	Pct	TO	Stl	Blk	PF	DQ	Ast	Avg	Off	Tot	Avg	Pts	Avg
79-80 ODU	30	—	679	67	141	.475	—	—	—	10	27	.370	—	—	117	—	—	29	1.0	—	212	7.1	144	4.8
80-81 ODU	28	—	845	128	243	.527	—	—	—	48	83	.578	—	—	113	—	—	15	0.5	—	287	10.3	304	10.9
81-82 ODU	30	—	1007	197	323	.610	—	—	—	78	147	.531	—	—	123	—	—	10	0.3	—	300	10.0	472	15.7
82-83 ODU	29	—	1005	169	297	.569	—	—	—	80	163	.491	—	—	93	—	—	17	0.6	—	314	10.8	418	14.4
4 Years	117	—	3536	561	1004	.559	—	—	—	216	420	.514	—	—	446	—	—	71	0.6	—	1113	9.5	1338	11.4

NBA

Year Tm	G	GS	Min	Md	Att	Pct	Md	Att	Pct	Md	Att	Pct	TO	Stl	Blk	PF	DQ	Ast	Avg	Off	Tot	Avg	Pts	Avg
				Field Goals			**3-Pt FGs**			**Free Throws**			**Misc**			**Fouls**		**Assists**		**Rebounds**			**Points**	
3-84 Dal	34	0	202	15	42	.357	0	0	—	7	22	.318	12	1	15	55	0	13	0.4	19	46	1.4	37	1.1
4-85 2Tm	66	25	888	106	194	.546	0	1	.000	43	87	.494	59	13	49	197	7	15	0.2	90	251	3.8	255	3.9
6-86 Cle	67	26	1172	113	209	.541	0	0	—	54	103	.524	91	27	62	235	6	20	0.3	97	322	4.8	280	4.2
6-87 Cle	78	13	1333	209	385	.543	0	2	.000	89	173	.514	106	22	81	229	5	41	0.5	126	339	4.3	507	6.5
7-88 2Tm	83	41	2098	316	573	.551	0	1	.000	170	285	.596	173	47	147	265	4	74	0.9	165	523	6.3	802	9.7
8-89 Pho	82	32	2019	243	372	.653	0	0	—	108	202	.535	103	35	187	273	4	39	0.5	167	551	6.7	594	7.2
9-90 Pho	82	79	2399	331	530	**.625**	0	0	—	199	288	.691	126	36	184	277	5	45	0.5	212	728	8.9	861	10.5
0-91 Pho	82	64	1957	247	382	.647	0	0	—	135	206	.655	86	32	161	266	2	37	0.5	171	564	6.9	629	7.7
1-92 Pho	82	11	1436	196	310	.632	0	0	—	109	171	.637	82	14	81	239	2	22	0.3	134	372	4.5	501	6.1
2-93 Pho	82	82	1558	175	285	.614	0	0	—	86	166	.518	93	16	103	243	3	29	0.4	153	458	5.6	436	5.3
3-94 Pho	82	50	1236	162	286	.566	0	0	—	58	116	.500	74	31	100	214	4	33	0.4	112	295	3.6	382	4.7
4-95 Det	67	58	1543	217	390	.556	0	0	—	66	138	.478	85	27	102	247	8	18	0.3	160	408	6.1	500	7.5
5-96 Det	47	21	682	61	126	.484	0	0	—	28	45	.622	35	6	37	135	2	6	0.1	49	133	2.8	150	3.2
6-97 Cle	70	43	959	100	180	.556	0	0	—	27	56	.482	52	11	55	142	0	19	0.3	69	186	2.7	227	3.2
7-98 Ind	15	1	105	10	21	.476	0	0	—	3	6	.500	8	2	4	15	0	2	0.1	6	15	1.0	23	1.5
8-99 Atl	49	0	499	22	59	.373	0	0	—	16	45	.356	17	4	22	81	0	13	0.3	49	125	2.6	60	1.2
9-00 Pho	22	2	127	5	12	.417	0	0	—	5	8	.625	6	2	4	23	0	2	0.1	6	31	1.4	15	0.7
4-85 Mil	1	0	6	0	0	1.000	0	0	—	2	2	1.000	2	0	1	4	0	1	0.0	1	1	1.0	2	2.0
Cle	65	25	882	106	193	.549	0	1	.000	41	85	.482	57	13	48	193	7	15	0.2	89	250	3.8	253	3.9
7-88 Cle	54	12	1183	182	316	.576	0	0	—	95	153	.621	91	25	79	158	2	50	0.9	83	281	5.2	459	8.5
Pho	29	29	915	134	257	.521	0	1	.000	75	132	.568	82	22	68	107	2	24	0.8	82	242	8.3	343	11.8
7 Years	1090	548	20213	2528	4356	.580	0	4	.000	1203	2117	.568	1208	326	1403	3136	52	428	0.4	1785	5347	4.9	6259	5.7

NBA Postseason

Year Tm	G	GS	Min	Md	Att	Pct	Md	Att	Pct	Md	Att	Pct	TO	Stl	Blk	PF	DQ	Ast	Avg	Off	Tot	Avg	Pts	Avg
3-84 Dal	4	0	32	5	9	.556	0	0	—	2	3	.667	3	0	3	11	1	3	0.8	0	7	1.8	12	3.0
4-85 Cle	4	4	68	3	5	.600	0	0	—	2	5	.400	5	2	0	19	0	4	1.0	5	18	4.5	8	2.0
8-89 Pho	12	12	227	32	50	.640	0	0	—	10	14	.714	13	7	19	36	1	6	0.5	21	53	4.4	74	6.2
9-90 Pho	16	16	544	75	130	.577	0	0	—	27	50	.540	26	4	41	73	3	5	0.3	53	164	10.3	177	11.1
0-91 Pho	4	4	93	9	15	.600	0	0	—	5	7	.714	3	2	10	15	0	2	0.5	8	18	4.5	23	5.8
1-92 Pho	8	0	96	14	19	.737	0	0	—	4	8	.500	2	2	4	21	1	2	0.3	8	17	2.1	32	4.0
2-93 Pho	24	24	469	43	79	.544	0	0	—	28	46	.609	17	4	33	69	2	11	0.5	36	99	4.1	114	4.8
3-94 Pho	7	6	69	5	15	.333	0	0	—	7	10	.700	4	0	7	19	0	0	0.0	11	20	2.9	17	2.4
5-96 Det	3	3	78	11	21	.524	0	0	—	6	13	.462	2	1	1	12	0	1	0.3	6	16	5.3	28	9.3
7-98 Ind	4	0	11	1	2	.500	0	0	—	1	3	.333	0	0	0	4	0	0	0.0	1	1	0.3	3	0.8
8-99 Atl	9	0	68	3	10	.300	0	0	—	2	4	.500	6	2	1	14	0	2	0.2	3	9	1.0	8	0.9
1 Years	95	69	1755	201	355	.566	0	0	—	94	163	.577	81	24	119	293	8	36	0.4	152	422	4.4	496	5.2

Jahidi White

(statistical profile on page 288)

Pos: F-C **College:** Georgetown **Drafted:** '98 2(43)—Was   **Ht:** 6'9" **Wt:** 290 **Born:** 2/19/76 **Age:** 24

College

Year Tm	G	GS	Min	Md	Att	Pct	Md	Att	Pct	Md	Att	Pct	TO	Stl	Blk	PF	DQ	Ast	Avg	Off	Tot	Avg	Pts	Avg
4-95 GTwn	26	0	201	24	56	.429	0	0	—	13	35	.371	22	8	23	28	1	2	0.1	19	46	1.8	61	2.3
5-96 GTwn	37	0	409	70	125	.560	0	0	—	43	89	.483	53	18	44	87	7	5	0.1	67	138	3.7	183	4.9
6-97 GTwn	30	29	607	84	164	.512	0	0	—	50	103	.485	66	15	59	99	5	14	0.5	86	193	6.4	218	7.3
7-98 GTwn	12	12	259	52	82	.634	0	0	—	22	50	.440	19	12	26	39	3	2	0.2	54	100	8.3	126	10.5
Years	105	41	1476	230	427	.539	0	0	—	128	277	.462	160	53	152	253	16	23	0.2	226	477	4.5	588	5.6

NBA

Year Tm	G	GS	Min	Md	Att	Pct	Md	Att	Pct	Md	Att	Pct	TO	Stl	Blk	PF	DQ	Ast	Avg	Off	Tot	Avg	Pts	Avg
8-99 Was	20	0	191	17	32	.531	0	0	—	15	35	.429	16	3	11	39	1	1	0.1	23	58	2.9	49	2.5
9-00 Was	80	59	1537	228	450	.507	0	0	—	113	211	.536	94	31	83	234	2	15	0.2	202	553	6.9	569	7.1
Years	100	59	1728	245	482	.508	0	0	—	128	246	.520	110	34	94	273	3	16	0.2	225	611	6.1	618	6.2

Chris Whitney

(statistical profile on page 288)

Pos: G **College:** Clemson **Drafted:** '93 2(47)—SA   **Ht:** 6'0" **Wt:** 175 **Born:** 10/5/71 **Age:** 29

College

Year Tm	G	GS	Min	Md	Att	Pct	Md	Att	Pct	Md	Att	Pct	TO	Stl	Blk	PF	DQ	Ast	Avg	Off	Tot	Avg	Pts	Avg
1-92 Clem	28	27	982	119	290	.410	80	191	.419	56	73	.767	94	41	0	95	—	161	5.8	16	92	3.3	374	13.4
2-93 Clem	30	29	1126	149	338	.441	87	213	.408	85	106	.802	110	73	2	87	—	193	6.4	20	122	4.1	470	15.7
Years	58	56	2108	268	628	.427	167	404	.413	141	179	.788	204	114	2	182	—	354	6.1	36	214	3.7	844	14.6

NBA

Year Tm	G	GS	Min	Md	Att	Pct	Md	Att	Pct	Md	Att	Pct	TO	Stl	Blk	PF	DQ	Ast	Avg	Off	Tot	Avg	Pts	Avg
3-94 SA	40	4	339	25	82	.305	10	30	.333	12	15	.800	37	11	1	53	0	53	1.3	5	29	0.7	72	1.8

NBA			Field Goals			3-Pt FGs			Free Throws			Misc			Fouls		Assists		Rebounds			Points	
Year Tm	G	GS	Min	Md	Att	Pct	Md	Att	Pct	Md	Att	Pct	TO	Stl	Blk	PF	DQ	Ast	Avg	Off	Tot	Avg	Pts	Av
94-95 SA	25	0	179	14	47	.298	3	19	.158	11	11	1.000	18	4	0	34	1	28	1.1	4	13	0.5	42	1.
95-96 Was	21	0	335	45	99	.455	19	44	.432	41	44	.932	23	18	1	46	0	51	2.4	2	33	1.6	150	7.
96-97 Was	82	1	1117	139	330	.421	58	163	.356	94	113	.832	68	49	4	100	0	182	2.2	13	104	1.3	430	5.
97-98 Was	82	6	1073	126	355	.355	52	169	.308	118	129	.915	65	34	6	106	0	196	2.4	16	115	1.4	422	5.
98-99 Was	39	1	441	64	156	.410	32	95	.337	27	31	.871	36	18	2	49	0	69	1.8	8	47	1.2	187	4.
99-00 Was	82	15	1627	217	521	.417	96	255	.376	112	132	.848	107	55	5	166	1	313	3.8	20	134	1.6	642	7.
7 Years	371	27	5111	630	1590	.396	270	775	.348	415	475	.874	354	189	19	554	2	892	2.4	68	475	1.3	1945	5.

NBA Postseason

Year Tm	G	GS	Min	Md	Att	Pct	Md	Att	Pct	Md	Att	Pct	TO	Stl	Blk	PF	DQ	Ast	Avg	Off	Tot	Avg	Pts	Av
96-97 Was	3	0	20	2	5	.400	2	4	.500	1	1	1.000	5	0	0	1	0	2	0.7	0	2	0.7	7	2.

Aaron Williams

(statistical profile on page 289

Pos: F-C **College:** Xavier (OH) **Drafted:** '93 FA—Uta   **Ht:** 6'9" **Wt:** 225 **Born:** 10/2/71 **Age:** 2

College			Field Goals			3-Pt FGs			Free Throws			Misc			Fouls		Assists		Rebounds			Points	
Year Tm	G	GS	Min	Md	Att	Pct	Md	Att	Pct	Md	Att	Pct	TO	Stl	Blk	PF	DQ	Ast	Avg	Off	Tot	Avg	Pts	Av
89-90 Xav	28	—	278	27	47	.574	0	0	—	8	20	.400	15	6	28	38	—	6	0.2	—	76	2.7	62	2.
90-91 Xav	32	—	858	127	237	.536	0	0	—	55	77	.714	87	25	57	115	—	33	1.0	—	209	6.5	309	9.
91-92 Xav	27	—	786	148	253	.585	0	0	—	79	113	.699	68	15	57	95	—	31	1.1	—	215	8.0	375	13.
92-93 Xav	30	—	843	127	247	.514	0	0	—	73	94	.777	67	21	55	93	—	54	1.8	—	213	7.1	327	10.
4 Years	117	—	2765	429	784	.547	0	0	—	215	304	.707	237	67	197	341	—	124	1.1	—	713	6.1	1073	9.

NBA			Field Goals			3-Pt FGs			Free Throws			Misc			Fouls		Assists		Rebounds			Points	
Year Tm	G	GS	Min	Md	Att	Pct	Md	Att	Pct	Md	Att	Pct	TO	Stl	Blk	PF	DQ	Ast	Avg	Off	Tot	Avg	Pts	Av
93-94 Uta	6	0	12	2	8	.250	0	0	—	0	1	.000	1	0	0	4	0	1	0.2	1	3	0.5	4	0.
94-95 Mil	15	0	72	8	24	.333	0	1	.000	8	12	.667	7	2	6	14	0	0	0.0	5	19	1.3	24	1.
95-96							Played in CBA																	
96-97 2Tm	33	1	563	85	148	.574	0	1	.000	33	49	.673	32	16	29	72	1	15	0.5	62	143	4.3	203	6.
97-98 Sea	65	9	757	115	220	.523	0	1	.000	66	85	.776	50	19	38	119	0	14	0.2	48	147	2.3	296	4.
98-99 Sea	40	2	458	52	123	.423	0	1	.000	54	74	.730	30	14	24	75	1	22	0.6	54	128	3.2	158	4.
99-00 Was	81	0	1545	235	450	.522	0	3	.000	146	201	.726	80	41	92	234	3	58	0.7	159	409	5.0	616	7.
96-97 Den	1	0	10	3	5	.600	0	0	—	0	0	—	4	0	3	0	0	0	0.0	2	5	5.0	6	6.
Van	32	1	553	82	143	.573	0	1	.000	33	49	.673	28	16	26	72	1	15	0.5	60	138	4.3	197	6.
6 Years	240	12	3407	497	973	.511	0	7	.000	307	422	.727	200	92	189	518	5	110	0.5	329	849	3.5	1301	5.

NBA Postseason

Year Tm	G	GS	Min	Md	Att	Pct	Md	Att	Pct	Md	Att	Pct	TO	Stl	Blk	PF	DQ	Ast	Avg	Off	Tot	Avg	Pts	Av
97-98 Sea	3	0	7	0	3	.000	0	0	—	2	2	1.000	1	0	1	0	0	0	0.0	1	1	0.3	2	0.

Alvin Williams

Pos: G **College:** Villanova **Drafted:** '97 2(48)—Por   **Ht:** 6'5" **Wt:** 185 **Born:** 8/6/74 **Age:** 2

College			Field Goals			3-Pt FGs			Free Throws			Misc			Fouls		Assists		Rebounds			Points	
Year Tm	G	GS	Min	Md	Att	Pct	Md	Att	Pct	Md	Att	Pct	TO	Stl	Blk	PF	DQ	Ast	Avg	Off	Tot	Avg	Pts	Av
93-94 Vill	31	0	720	79	203	.389	20	51	.392	67	96	.698	57	41	3	82	2	88	2.8	20	87	2.8	245	7.
94-95 Vill	33	18	963	79	195	.405	15	57	.263	61	82	.744	75	53	5	84	3	159	4.8	24	116	3.5	234	7.
95-96 Vill	33	33	1078	129	284	.454	35	101	.347	71	100	.710	80	46	18	89	3	177	5.4	22	117	3.5	364	11.
96-97 Vill	34	34	1163	198	412	.481	63	171	.368	121	163	.742	91	60	12	86	2	129	3.8	45	169	5.0	580	17.
4 Years	131	85	3924	485	1094	.443	133	380	.350	320	441	.726	303	200	38	341	10	553	4.2	111	489	3.7	1423	10.

NBA			Field Goals			3-Pt FGs			Free Throws			Misc			Fouls		Assists		Rebounds			Points	
Year Tm	G	GS	Min	Md	Att	Pct	Md	Att	Pct	Md	Att	Pct	TO	Stl	Blk	PF	DQ	Ast	Avg	Off	Tot	Avg	Pts	Av
97-98 2Tm	54	13	1071	125	282	.443	9	28	.321	65	90	.722	58	38	3	79	0	103	1.9	24	81	1.5	324	6.
98-99 Tor	50	45	1051	95	237	.401	14	42	.333	44	52	.846	56	51	12	94	1	130	2.6	19	82	1.6	248	5.
99-00 Tor	55	28	779	114	287	.397	16	55	.291	48	65	.738	47	34	11	78	0	126	2.3	27	85	1.5	292	5.
97-98 Por	41	10	864	109	238	.458	7	24	.292	58	79	.734	50	30	2	60	0	83	2.0	19	60	1.5	283	6.
Tor	13	3	207	16	44	.364	2	4	.500	7	11	.636	8	8	1	19	0	20	1.5	5	21	1.6	41	3.
3 Years	159	86	2901	334	806	.414	39	125	.312	157	207	.758	161	123	26	251	1	359	2.3	70	248	1.6	864	5.

NBA Postseason

Year Tm	G	GS	Min	Md	Att	Pct	Md	Att	Pct	Md	Att	Pct	TO	Stl	Blk	PF	DQ	Ast	Avg	Off	Tot	Avg	Pts	Av
99-00 Tor	1	0	1	0	0	—	0	0	—	0	0	—	0	0	0	0	0	0	0.0	0	0	0.0	0	0.

Brandon Williams

Pos: F **College:** Davidson **Drafted:** '97 FA—GS   **Ht:** 6'6" **Wt:** 215 **Born:** 2/27/75 **Age:** 25

College

Year Tm	G	GS	Min	FG Md	FG Att	FG Pct	3P Md	3P Att	3P Pct	FT Md	FT Att	FT Pct	TO	Stl	Blk	PF	DQ	Ast	Avg	Off	Tot	Avg	Pts	Avg
92-93 Dav	28	—	—	68	160	.425	13	36	.361	38	62	.613	—	—	—	—	—	19	0.7	—	99	3.5	187	6.7
93-94 Dav	30	—	887	151	335	.451	34	96	.354	97	125	.776	—			—		28	0.9	—	188	6.3	433	14.4
94-95 Dav	24	—	764	116	292	.397	34	115	.296	74	96	.771	—			—		26	1.1	—	125	5.2	340	14.2
95-96 Dav	30	—	835	194	391	.496	50	123	.407	107	138	.775	—			—		39	1.3	—	179	6.0	545	18.2
4 Years	112	—	—	529	1178	.449	131	370	.354	316	421	.751	—			—		112	1.0	—	591	5.3	1505	13.4

NBA

Year Tm	G	GS	Min	FG Md	FG Att	FG Pct	3P Md	3P Att	3P Pct	FT Md	FT Att	FT Pct	TO	Stl	Blk	PF	DQ	Ast	Avg	Off	Tot	Avg	Pts	Avg
96-97										Played in France														
97-98 GS	9	2	140	16	50	.320	3	9	.333	2	4	.500	9	6	3	18	0	3	0.3	4	15	1.7	37	4.1
98-99 SA	3	0	4	0	0	—	0	0	—	2	4	.500	0	0	0	0	0	0	0.0	1	1	0.3	2	0.7
99-00 NY										Active but did not play														
2 Years	12	2	144	16	50	.320	3	9	.333	4	8	.500	9	6	3	18	0	3	0.3	5	16	1.3	39	3.3

Eric Williams

(statistical profile on page 289)

Pos: F **College:** Providence **Drafted:** '95 1(14)—Bos   **Ht:** 6'8" **Wt:** 220 **Born:** 7/17/72 **Age:** 28

College

Year Tm	G	GS	Min	FG Md	FG Att	FG Pct	3P Md	3P Att	3P Pct	FT Md	FT Att	FT Pct	TO	Stl	Blk	PF	DQ	Ast	Avg	Off	Tot	Avg	Pts	Avg
93-94 Prov	30	13	781	166	327	.508	0	5	.000	138	209	.660	53	36	13	68	2	37	1.2	78	151	5.0	470	15.7
94-95 Prov	30	30	1041	184	445	.413	29	78	.372	134	195	.687	79	60	10	95	4	75	2.5	72	201	6.7	531	17.7
2 Years	60	43	1822	350	772	.453	29	83	.349	272	404	.673	132	96	23	163	6	112	1.9	150	352	5.9	1001	16.7

NBA

Year Tm	G	GS	Min	FG Md	FG Att	FG Pct	3P Md	3P Att	3P Pct	FT Md	FT Att	FT Pct	TO	Stl	Blk	PF	DQ	Ast	Avg	Off	Tot	Avg	Pts	Avg
95-96 Bos	64	6	1470	241	546	.441	3	10	.300	200	298	.671	88	56	11	147	1	70	1.1	92	217	3.4	685	10.7
96-97 Bos	72	67	2435	374	820	.456	2	8	.250	328	436	.752	139	72	13	213	0	129	1.8	126	329	4.6	1078	15.0
97-98 Den	4	4	145	24	61	.393	0	0	—	31	45	.689	9	4	0	9	0	12	3.0	10	21	5.3	79	19.8
98-99 Den	38	8	780	80	219	.365	6	26	.231	111	139	.799	49	27	8	76	0	37	1.0	34	81	2.1	277	7.3
99-00 Den	68	17	1378	165	386	.427	25	72	.347	134	169	.793	66	44	16	165	3	93	1.4	55	156	2.3	489	7.2
5 Years	246	102	6208	884	2032	.435	36	116	.310	804	1087	.740	351	203	48	610	4	341	1.4	317	804	3.3	2608	10.6

Hot Rod Williams

Pos: C **College:** Tulane **Drafted:** '85 2(45)—Cle   **Ht:** 6'11" **Wt:** 245 **Born:** 8/9/62 **Age:** 38

College

Year Tm	G	GS	Min	FG Md	FG Att	FG Pct	3P Md	3P Att	3P Pct	FT Md	FT Att	FT Pct	TO	Stl	Blk	PF	DQ	Ast	Avg	Off	Tot	Avg	Pts	Avg
81-82 Tula	28	—	932	163	279	.584	—	—		88	133	.662	—			—		32	1.1	—	202	7.2	414	14.8
82-83 Tula	31	—	996	151	317	.476	—	—		83	118	.703	—			—		40	1.3	—	166	5.4	385	12.4
83-84 Tula	28	—	1038	202	355	.569	—	—		140	184	.761	—			—		61	2.2	—	222	7.9	544	19.4
84-85 Tula	28	—	1006	189	334	.566	—	—		120	155	.774	—			—		65	2.3	—	219	7.8	498	17.8
4 Years	115	—	3972	705	1285	.549	—	—		431	590	.731	—			—		198	1.7	—	809	7.0	1841	16.0

NBA

Year Tm	G	GS	Min	FG Md	FG Att	FG Pct	3P Md	3P Att	3P Pct	FT Md	FT Att	FT Pct	TO	Stl	Blk	PF	DQ	Ast	Avg	Off	Tot	Avg	Pts	Avg
85-86										Played in USBL														
86-87 Cle	80	80	2714	435	897	.485	0	1	.000	298	400	.745	139	58	167	197	0	154	1.9	222	629	7.9	1168	14.6
87-88 Cle	77	50	2106	316	663	.477	0	1	.000	211	279	.756	104	61	145	203	2	103	1.3	159	506	6.6	843	10.9
88-89 Cle	82	10	2125	356	700	.509	1	4	.250	235	314	.748	102	77	134	188	1	108	1.3	173	477	5.8	948	11.6
89-90 Cle	82	29	2776	528	1070	.493	0	0	—	325	440	.739	143	86	167	214	2	168	2.0	220	663	8.1	1381	16.8
90-91 Cle	43	14	1293	199	430	.463	0	1	.000	107	164	.652	63	36	69	126	2	100	2.3	111	290	6.7	505	11.7
91-92 Cle	80	12	2432	341	678	.503	0	4	.000	270	359	.752	83	60	182	191	2	196	2.5	228	607	7.6	952	11.9
92-93 Cle	67	13	2055	263	560	.470	0	0	—	212	296	.716	116	48	105	171	2	152	2.3	127	415	6.2	738	11.0
93-94 Cle	76	72	2660	394	825	.478	0	0	—	252	346	.728	149	78	101	219	3	193	2.5	207	575	7.6	1040	13.7
94-95 Cle	74	73	2641	366	810	.452	1	5	.200	196	286	.685	149	83	101	211	2	192	2.6	173	507	6.9	929	12.6
95-96 Pho	62	58	1652	180	397	.453	0	1	.000	95	130	.731	62	46	90	170	2	62	1.0	129	372	6.0	455	7.3
96-97 Pho	68	66	2137	204	416	.490	0	2	.000	133	198	.672	66	67	88	176	1	100	1.5	178	562	8.3	541	8.0
97-98 Pho	71	30	1333	95	202	.470	0	0	—	65	93	.699	29	33	60	138	2	49	0.7	107	312	4.4	255	3.6
98-99 Dal	25	11	403	11	33	.333	0	0	—	7	10	.700	13	13	18	49	0	15	0.6	36	83	3.3	29	1.2
99-00 Dal										Did not play: injury — Back														
13 Years	887	518	26327	3688	7681	.480	2	19	.105	2406	3315	.726	1208	746	1456	2253	21	1592	1.8	2070	5998	6.8	9784	11.0

NBA Postseason

Year Tm	G	GS	Min	FG Md	FG Att	FG Pct	3P Md	3P Att	3P Pct	FT Md	FT Att	FT Pct	TO	Stl	Blk	PF	DQ	Ast	Avg	Off	Tot	Avg	Pts	Avg
87-88 Cle	5	0	133	20	40	.500	0	0	—	6	13	.462	4	3	13	13	0	4	0.8	13	29	5.8	46	9.2

Year Tm	G	GS	Min	Md	Att	Pct	Md	Att	Pct	Md	Att	Pct	TO	Stl	Blk	PF	DQ	Ast	Avg	Off	Tot	Avg	Pts	Avg
88-89 Cle	5	2	161	21	45	.467	0	0	—	13	18	.722	11	2	7	12	0	10	2.0	7	34	6.8	55	11.0
89-90 Cle	5	0	174	39	70	.557	0	0	—	17	22	.773	7	2	5	23	1	11	2.2	14	46	9.2	95	19.0
91-92 Cle	17	0	567	84	154	.545	0	0	—	87	109	.798	31	24	17	58	2	42	2.5	50	130	7.6	255	15.0
92-93 Cle	9	0	237	30	75	.400	0	0	—	21	28	.750	11	5	14	26	1	17	1.9	12	41	4.6	81	9.0
94-95 Cle	4	4	144	12	42	.286	0	1	.000	3	8	.375	10	9	3	11	0	11	2.8	3	25	6.3	27	6.8
95-96 Pho	4	4	115	14	32	.438	0	0	—	8	12	.667	6	0	7	17	1	1	0.3	11	26	6.5	36	9.0
96-97 Pho	5	5	105	8	15	.533	0	0	—	4	10	.400	5	2	8	12	0	3	0.6	10	23	4.6	20	4.0
97-98 Pho	3	0	33	2	7	.286	0	0	—	2	3	.667	0	0	2	8	0	1	0.3	2	4	1.3	6	2.0
9 Years	57	15	1669	230	480	.479	0	1	.000	161	223	.722	85	47	70	180	5	100	1.8	122	358	6.3	621	10.9

Jason Williams

Pos: G **College:** Florida **Drafted:** '98 1(7)—Sac

(statistical profile on page 290)

Ht: 6'1" **Wt:** 190 **Born:** 11/18/75 **Age:** 25

College

Year Tm	G	GS	Min	Field Goals			3-Pt FGs			Free Throws			Misc			Fouls		Assists		Rebounds			Points	
				Md	Att	Pct	Md	Att	Pct	Md	Att	Pct	TO	Stl	Blk	PF	DQ	Ast	Avg	Off	Tot	Avg	Pts	Avg
95-96 Mrsh	28	—	816	144	276	.522	35	92	.380	52	70	.743	75	50	9	49	—	178	6.4	—	99	3.5	375	13.4
97-98 Fla	20	17	635	112	254	.441	54	134	.403	63	75	.840	87	53	4	30	0	134	6.7	6	59	3.0	341	17.1
2 Years	48	—	1451	256	530	.483	89	226	.394	115	145	.793	162	103	13	79		312	6.5		158	3.3	716	14.9

NBA

Year Tm	G	GS	Min	Field Goals			3-Pt FGs			Free Throws			Misc			Fouls		Assists		Rebounds			Points	
				Md	Att	Pct	Md	Att	Pct	Md	Att	Pct	TO	Stl	Blk	PF	DQ	Ast	Avg	Off	Tot	Avg	Pts	Avg
98-99 Sac	50	50	1805	231	617	.374	100	323	.310	79	105	.752	143	95	1	91	0	299	6.0	14	153	3.1	641	12.8
99-00 Sac	81	81	2760	363	973	.373	145	505	.287	128	170	.753	296	117	8	140	0	589	7.3	22	230	2.8	999	12.3
2 Years	131	131	4565	594	1590	.374	245	828	.296	207	275	.753	439	212	9	231	0	888	6.8	36	383	2.9	1640	12.5

NBA Postseason

Year Tm	G	GS	Min	Field Goals			3-Pt FGs			Free Throws			Misc			Fouls		Assists		Rebounds			Points	
				Md	Att	Pct	Md	Att	Pct	Md	Att	Pct	TO	Stl	Blk	PF	DQ	Ast	Avg	Off	Tot	Avg	Pts	Avg
98-99 Sac	5	5	163	16	45	.356	9	29	.310	9	9	1.000	13	8	1	15	0	20	4.0	2	18	3.6	50	10.0
99-00 Sac	5	5	145	18	48	.375	8	25	.320	8	10	.800	8	3	0	8	0	12	2.4	1	8	1.6	52	10.4
2 Years	10	10	308	34	93	.366	17	54	.315	17	19	.895	21	11	1	23	0	32	3.2	3	26	2.6	102	10.2

Jayson Williams

Pos: C **College:** St. John's (NY) **Drafted:** '90 1(21)—Pho

Ht: 6'10" **Wt:** 245 **Born:** 2/22/68 **Age:** 32

College

Year Tm	G	GS	Min	Field Goals			3-Pt FGs			Free Throws			Misc			Fouls		Assists		Rebounds			Points	
				Md	Att	Pct	Md	Att	Pct	Md	Att	Pct	TO	Stl	Blk	PF	DQ	Ast	Avg	Off	Tot	Avg	Pts	Avg
87-88 StJn	28	13	662	102	199	.513	0	0	—	72	120	.600	45	12	14	100	7	12	0.4	69	143	5.1	276	9.9
88-89 StJn	31	31	1036	236	412	.573	0	2	.000	134	191	.702	85	17	30	90	2	18	0.6	—	246	7.9	606	19.5
89-90 StJn	13	13	377	70	131	.534	1	2	.500	49	80	.613	31	3	12	46	1	7	0.5	35	101	7.8	190	14.6
3 Years	72	57	2075	408	742	.550	1	4	.250	255	391	.652	161	32	56	236	10	37	0.5	—	490	6.8	1072	14.9

NBA

Year Tm	G	GS	Min	Field Goals			3-Pt FGs			Free Throws			Misc			Fouls		Assists		Rebounds			Points	
				Md	Att	Pct	Md	Att	Pct	Md	Att	Pct	TO	Stl	Blk	PF	DQ	Ast	Avg	Off	Tot	Avg	Pts	Avg
90-91 Phi	52	1	508	72	161	.447	1	2	.500	37	56	.661	40	9	6	92	1	16	0.3	41	111	2.1	182	3.5
91-92 Phi	50	8	646	75	206	.364	0	0	—	56	88	.636	44	20	20	110	1	12	0.2	62	145	2.9	206	4.1
92-93 NJ	12	2	139	21	46	.457	0	0	—	7	18	.389	8	4	4	24	0	0	0.0	22	41	3.4	49	4.1
93-94 NJ	70	0	877	125	293	.427	0	0	—	72	119	.605	35	17	36	140	1	26	0.4	109	263	3.8	322	4.6
94-95 NJ	75	6	982	149	323	.461	0	5	.000	65	122	.533	59	26	33	160	2	35	0.5	179	425	5.7	363	4.8
95-96 NJ	80	6	1858	279	660	.423	2	7	.286	161	272	.592	106	35	57	238	4	47	0.6	342	803	10.0	721	9.0
96-97 NJ	41	40	1432	221	540	.409	0	4	.000	108	183	.590	82	24	36	158	5	51	1.2	242	553	13.5	550	13.4
97-98 NJ*	65	65	2343	321	645	.498	0	4	.000	195	293	.666	95	45	49	236	7	67	1.0	443	883	13.6	837	12.9
98-99 NJ	30	30	1020	97	218	.445	0	2	.000	48	85	.565	46	24	60	126	3	33	1.1	147	360	12.0	242	8.1
99-00 NJ							Did not play: injury — Right Leg, Left Foot																	
9 Years	475	158	9805	1360	3092	.440	3	24	.125	749	1236	.606	515	204	301	1284	24	287	0.6	1587	3584	7.5	3472	7.3

NBA Postseason

Year Tm	G	GS	Min	Field Goals			3-Pt FGs			Free Throws			Misc			Fouls		Assists		Rebounds			Points	
				Md	Att	Pct	Md	Att	Pct	Md	Att	Pct	TO	Stl	Blk	PF	DQ	Ast	Avg	Off	Tot	Avg	Pts	Avg
90-91 Phi	4	0	10	4	5	.800	0	0	—	0	0	—	1	0	0	1	0	0	0.0	2	4	1.0	8	2.0
93-94 NJ	2	0	17	0	3	.000	0	0	—	1	2	.500	2	0	0	5	0	0	0.0	3	3	1.5	1	0.5
97-98 NJ	3	2	116	9	21	.429	0	0	—	3	6	.500	2	2	3	8	0	5	1.7	20	42	14.0	21	7.0
3 Years	9	2	143	13	29	.448	0	0	—	4	8	.500	5	2	3	14	0	5	0.6	25	49	5.4	30	3.3

Jerome Williams

(statistical profile on page 290)

Pos: F **College:** Georgetown **Drafted:** '96 1(26)—Det **Ht:** 6'9" **Wt:** 206 **Born:** 5/10/73 **Age:** 27

College

Year Tm	G	GS	Min	Md	Att	Pct	Md	Att	Pct	Md	Att	Pct	TO	Stl	Blk	PF	DQ	Ast	Avg	Off	Tot	Avg	Pts	Avg
				Field Goals			3-Pt FGs			Free Throws			Misc			Fouls		Assists		Rebounds			Points	
94-95 GTwn	31	31	938	126	252	.500	2	11	.182	83	132	.629	83	38	11	54	0	45	1.5	138	310	10.0	337	10.9
95-96 GTwn	37	37	1016	147	250	.588	1	7	.143	85	133	.639	72	70	16	67	0	51	1.4	130	324	8.8	380	10.3
2 Years	68	68	1954	273	502	.544	3	18	.167	168	265	.634	155	108	27	121	0	96	1.4	268	634	9.3	717	10.5

NBA

Year Tm	G	GS	Min	Md	Att	Pct	Md	Att	Pct	Md	Att	Pct	TO	Stl	Blk	PF	DQ	Ast	Avg	Off	Tot	Avg	Pts	Avg
96-97 Det	33	0	177	20	51	.392	0	0	—	9	17	.529	13	13	1	18	0	7	0.2	22	50	1.5	49	1.5
97-98 Det	77	3	1305	151	288	.524	0	1	.000	108	166	.651	60	51	10	144	1	48	0.6	170	379	4.9	410	5.3
98-99 Det	50	10	1154	124	248	.500	0	0	—	107	159	.673	41	63	7	108	0	23	0.5	158	349	7.0	355	7.1
99-00 Det	82	1	2102	257	456	.564	0	3	.000	175	284	.616	105	95	21	196	0	68	0.8	277	789	9.6	689	8.4
4 Years	242	14	4738	552	1043	.529	0	4	.000	399	626	.637	219	222	39	466	1	146	0.6	627	1567	6.5	1503	6.2

NBA Postseason

Year Tm	G	GS	Min	Md	Att	Pct	Md	Att	Pct	Md	Att	Pct	TO	Stl	Blk	PF	DQ	Ast	Avg	Off	Tot	Avg	Pts	Avg
96-97 Det	1	0	5	2	2	1.000	0	0	—	0	0	—	1	1	0	0	0	0	0.0	0	3	3.0	4	4.0
98-99 Det	5	5	123	12	27	.444	0	0	—	7	9	.778	4	4	0	7	0	4	0.8	12	32	6.4	31	6.2
99-00 Det	3	0	73	7	14	.500	0	0	—	1	8	.125	3	3	0	8	0	2	0.7	7	21	7.0	15	5.0
3 Years	9	5	201	21	43	.488	0	0	—	8	17	.471	8	8	0	15	0	6	0.7	19	56	6.2	50	5.6

Lorenzo Williams

Pos: F-C **College:** Stetson **Drafted:** '92 FA—Cha **Ht:** 6'9" **Wt:** 230 **Born:** 7/15/69 **Age:** 31

College

Year Tm	G	GS	Min	Md	Att	Pct	Md	Att	Pct	Md	Att	Pct	TO	Stl	Blk	PF	DQ	Ast	Avg	Off	Tot	Avg	Pts	Avg
				Field Goals			3-Pt FGs			Free Throws			Misc			Fouls		Assists		Rebounds			Points	
89-90 Stet	32	31	—	116	223	.520	—	—	—	18	61	.295	—	15	121	—	—	51	1.6	—	269	8.4	250	7.8
90-91 Stet	31	31	—	121	224	.540	—	—	—	42	63	.667	—	14	113	—	—	49	1.6	—	312	10.1	284	9.2
2 Years	63	62	—	237	447	.530	—	—	—	60	124	.484	—	29	234	—	—	100	1.6	—	581	9.2	534	8.5

NBA

Year Tm	G	GS	Min	Md	Att	Pct	Md	Att	Pct	Md	Att	Pct	TO	Stl	Blk	PF	DQ	Ast	Avg	Off	Tot	Avg	Pts	Avg
91-92									Played in USBL, Played in GBA															
92-93 3Tm	27	7	179	17	36	.472	0	0	—	2	7	.286	8	5	17	29	0	5	0.2	17	55	2.0	36	1.3
93-94 3Tm	38	11	716	49	110	.445	0	1	.000	12	28	.429	22	18	46	92	0	25	0.7	95	217	5.7	110	2.9
94-95 Dal	82	81	2383	145	304	.477	0	0	—	38	101	.376	105	52	148	306	6	124	1.5	291	690	8.4	328	4.0
95-96 Dal	65	61	1806	87	214	.407	0	1	.000	24	70	.343	78	48	122	226	9	85	1.3	234	521	8.0	198	3.0
96-97 Was	19	0	264	20	31	.645	0	0	—	5	7	.714	18	6	8	49	0	4	0.2	28	69	3.6	45	2.4
97-98 Was	14	6	111	13	17	.765	0	0	—	0	2	.000	2	2	3	17	0	3	0.2	16	26	1.9	26	1.9
98-99									Did not play: injury — Feet															
99-00 Was	8	0	76	7	9	.778	0	0	—	0	0	—	3	3	6	13	0	1	0.1	12	25	3.1	14	1.8
92-93 Cha	2	0	18	1	3	.333	0	0	—	0	0	—	2	0	2	4	0	0	0.0	3	9	4.5	2	1.0
Orl	3	0	10	0	2	.000	0	0	—	0	0	—	0	1	1	2	0	0	0.0	1	2	0.7	0	0.0
Bos	22	7	151	16	31	.516	0	0	—	2	7	.286	6	4	14	23	0	5	0.2	13	44	2.0	34	1.5
93-94 Orl	3	0	19	1	6	.167	0	1	.000	0	0	—	0	2	3	3	0	2	0.7	3	4	1.3	2	0.7
Cha	1	0	19	0	1	.000	0	0	—	0	0	—	1	1	2	1	0	0	0.0	0	4	4.0	0	0.0
Dal	34	11	678	48	103	.466	0	0	—	12	28	.429	21	15	41	87	0	23	0.7	92	209	6.1	108	3.2
7 Years	253	166	5535	338	721	.469	0	2	.000	81	215	.377	236	134	350	732	15	247	1.0	693	1603	6.3	757	3.0

NBA Postseason

Year Tm	G	GS	Min	Md	Att	Pct	Md	Att	Pct	Md	Att	Pct	TO	Stl	Blk	PF	DQ	Ast	Avg	Off	Tot	Avg	Pts	Avg
92-93 Bos	1	0	3	1	1	1.000	0	0	—	0	0	—	0	0	0	0	0	0	0.0	1	1	1.0	2	2.0
96-97 Was	2	0	5	0	0	—	0	0	—	0	0	—	0	0	0	1	0	0	0.0	0	0	0.0	0	0.0
2 Years	3	0	8	1	1	1.000	0	0	—	0	0	—	0	0	0	1	0	0	0.0	1	1	0.3	2	0.7

Monty Williams

(statistical profile on page 291)

Pos: F **College:** Notre Dame **Drafted:** '94 1(24)—NY **Ht:** 6'8" **Wt:** 225 **Born:** 10/8/71 **Age:** 29

College

Year Tm	G	GS	Min	Md	Att	Pct	Md	Att	Pct	Md	Att	Pct	TO	Stl	Blk	PF	DQ	Ast	Avg	Off	Tot	Avg	Pts	Avg
				Field Goals			3-Pt FGs			Free Throws			Misc			Fouls		Assists		Rebounds			Points	
89-90 ND	29	—	588	83	172	.483	2	10	.200	54	73	.740	49	15	16	63	—	31	1.1	—	108	3.7	222	7.7
92-93 ND	27	—	942	177	384	.461	25	74	.338	121	153	.791	86	31	19	65	—	39	1.4	—	251	9.3	500	18.5
93-94 ND	29	—	1000	237	464	.511	32	78	.410	143	205	.698	101	41	15	74	—	68	2.3	—	239	8.2	649	22.4
3 Years	85	—	2530	497	1020	.487	59	162	.364	318	431	.738	236	87	50	202	—	138	1.6	—	598	7.0	1371	16.1

NBA

Year Tm	G	GS	Min	Md	Att	Pct	Md	Att	Pct	Md	Att	Pct	TO	Stl	Blk	PF	DQ	Ast	Avg	Off	Tot	Avg	Pts	Avg
94-95 NY	41	23	503	60	133	.451	0	8	.000	17	38	.447	41	20	4	87	0	49	1.2	42	98	2.4	137	3.3

NBA

Year Tm	G	GS	Min	Field Goals			3-Pt FGs			Free Throws			Misc			Fouls		Assists		Rebounds			Points	
				Md	Att	Pct	Md	Att	Pct	Md	Att	Pct	TO	Stl	Blk	PF	DQ	Ast	Avg	Off	Tot	Avg	Pts	Avg
95-96 2Tm	31	0	184	27	68	.397	0	1	.000	14	20	.700	18	6	2	26	0	8	0.3	20	40	1.3	68	2.2
96-97 SA	65	26	1345	234	460	.509	0	1	.000	120	186	.645	116	55	52	161	1	91	1.4	98	206	3.2	588	9.0
97-98 SA	72	16	1314	165	368	.448	1	2	.500	122	182	.670	82	34	24	133	1	89	1.2	67	179	2.5	453	6.3
98-99 Den	1	0	6	0	2	.000	0	0	—	1	2	.500	0	0	0	0	0	0	0.0	0	0	0.0	1	1.0
99-00 Orl	75	23	1501	263	538	.489	2	5	.400	123	166	.741	109	46	17	187	1	106	1.4	96	250	3.3	651	8.7
95-96 NY	14	0	62	7	22	.318	0	0	—	5	8	.625	5	2	0	9	0	4	0.3	9	17	1.2	19	1.4
SA	17	0	122	20	46	.435	0	1	.000	9	12	.750	13	4	2	17	0	4	0.2	11	23	1.4	49	2.9
6 Years	285	88	4853	749	1569	.477	3	17	.176	397	594	.668	366	161	99	594	3	343	1.2	323	773	2.7	1898	6.7

NBA Postseason

Year Tm	G	GS	Min	Field Goals			3-Pt FGs			Free Throws			Misc			Fouls		Assists		Rebounds			Points	
				Md	Att	Pct	Md	Att	Pct	Md	Att	Pct	TO	Stl	Blk	PF	DQ	Ast	Avg	Off	Tot	Avg	Pts	Avg
94-95 NY	1	0	4	2	2	1.000	0	0	—	0	0	—	0	0	0	0	0	0	0.0	0	0	0.0	4	4.0
95-96 SA	7	0	29	2	9	.222	0	0	—	3	6	.500	4	0	0	4	0	0	0.0	0	0	0.0	7	1.0
97-98 SA	5	0	28	5	8	.625	0	0	—	2	3	.667	4	0	0	2	0	1	0.2	3	7	1.4	12	2.4
3 Years	13	0	61	9	19	.474	0	0	—	5	9	.556	8	0	0	7	0	1	0.1	5	13	1.0	23	1.8

Scott Williams

Pos: F-C **College:** North Carolina **Drafted:** '90 FA—Chi **Ht:** 6'10" **Wt:** 230 **Born:** 3/21/68 **Age:** 32 (statistical profile on page 291)

College

Year Tm	G	GS	Min	Field Goals			3-Pt FGs			Free Throws			Misc			Fouls		Assists		Rebounds			Points	
				Md	Att	Pct	Md	Att	Pct	Md	Att	Pct	TO	Stl	Blk	PF	DQ	Ast	Avg	Off	Tot	Avg	Pts	Avg
86-87 UNC	36	1	540	78	157	.497	0	1	.000	43	77	.558	49	29	27	94	—	31	0.9	—	150	4.2	199	5.5
87-88 UNC	34	33	900	162	283	.572	3	7	.429	107	159	.673	80	45	43	122	—	42	1.2	—	217	6.4	434	12.8
88-89 UNC	35	30	802	165	297	.556	0	2	.000	68	104	.654	65	30	50	113	—	26	0.7	—	254	7.3	398	11.4
89-90 UNC	33	30	813	190	343	.554	1	7	.143	96	156	.615	72	36	41	114	—	25	0.8	—	240	7.3	477	14.5
4 Years	138	94	3055	595	1080	.551	4	17	.235	314	496	.633	266	140	161	443	—	124	0.9	—	861	6.2	1508	10.9

NBA

Year Tm	G	GS	Min	Field Goals			3-Pt FGs			Free Throws			Misc			Fouls		Assists		Rebounds			Points	
				Md	Att	Pct	Md	Att	Pct	Md	Att	Pct	TO	Stl	Blk	PF	DQ	Ast	Avg	Off	Tot	Avg	Pts	Avg
90-91 Chi	51	0	337	53	104	.510	1	2	.500	20	28	.714	23	12	13	51	0	16	0.3	42	98	1.9	127	2.5
91-92 Chi	63	0	690	83	172	.483	0	3	.000	48	74	.649	35	13	36	122	0	50	0.8	90	247	3.9	214	3.4
92-93 Chi	71	5	1369	166	356	.466	0	7	.000	90	126	.714	73	55	66	230	3	68	1.0	168	451	6.4	422	5.9
93-94 Chi	38	11	638	114	236	.483	0	2	.200	60	98	.612	44	16	21	112	1	39	1.0	69	181	4.8	289	6.4
94-95 Phi	77	43	1781	206	434	.475	0	7	.000	79	107	.738	84	71	40	237	4	59	0.8	173	485	6.3	491	6.4
95-96 Phi	13	1	193	15	29	.517	0	2	.000	10	12	.833	8	6	7	27	0	5	0.4	13	46	3.5	40	3.1
96-97 Phi	62	52	1317	162	318	.509	0	2	.000	38	55	.691	50	44	41	206	5	41	0.7	155	397	6.4	362	5.8
97-98 Phi	58	7	801	93	213	.437	0	5	.000	51	63	.810	30	17	21	132	0	29	0.5	87	211	3.6	237	4.1
98-99 2Tm	7	0	46	5	17	.294	0	0	—	4	7	.571	4	3	2	9	0	1	0.1	3	14	2.0	14	2.0
99-00 Mil	68	46	1488	213	426	.500	0	0	—	94	129	.729	65	40	66	230	3	28	0.4	177	448	6.6	520	7.6
98-99 2Tm	2	0	17	0	2	.000	0	0	—	0	0	—	2	2	1	4	0	1	0.5	1	2	1.0	0	0.0
Mil	5	0	29	5	15	.333	0	0	—	4	7	.571	2	1	1	5	0	0	0.0	2	12	2.4	14	2.8
10 Years	508	165	8660	1110	2305	.482	2	33	.061	494	699	.707	416	277	313	1356	16	336	0.7	977	2578	5.1	2716	5.3

NBA Postseason

Year Tm	G	GS	Min	Field Goals			3-Pt FGs			Free Throws			Misc			Fouls		Assists		Rebounds			Points	
				Md	Att	Pct	Md	Att	Pct	Md	Att	Pct	TO	Stl	Blk	PF	DQ	Ast	Avg	Off	Tot	Avg	Pts	Avg
90-91 Chi	12	0	72	6	13	.462	0	1	.000	11	20	.550	4	1	3	15	0	3	0.3	4	20	1.7	23	1.9
91-92 Chi	22	0	321	34	70	.486	0	1	.000	20	28	.714	15	6	18	65	0	7	0.3	33	95	4.3	88	4.0
92-93 Chi	19	0	395	44	87	.506	0	2	.000	16	29	.552	24	7	17	58	2	26	1.4	40	111	5.8	104	5.5
93-94 Chi	10	0	151	24	57	.421	0	0	—	15	21	.714	9	7	3	23	0	7	0.7	15	39	3.9	63	6.3
99-00 Mil	5	0	93	23	36	.639	0	0	—	5	6	.833	4	2	5	16	0	2	0.4	9	28	5.6	51	10.2
5 Years	68	0	1032	131	263	.498	0	4	.000	67	104	.644	56	23	46	177	2	45	0.7	101	293	4.3	329	4.8

Shammond Williams

Pos: G **College:** North Carolina **Drafted:** '98 2(34)—Chi **Ht:** 6'1" **Wt:** 201 **Born:** 4/5/75 **Age:** 25

College

Year Tm	G	GS	Min	Field Goals			3-Pt FGs			Free Throws			Misc			Fouls		Assists		Rebounds			Points	
				Md	Att	Pct	Md	Att	Pct	Md	Att	Pct	TO	Stl	Blk	PF	DQ	Ast	Avg	Off	Tot	Avg	Pts	Avg
94-95 UNC	29	0	132	12	31	.387	6	20	.300	18	21	.857	22	7	0	9	0	20	0.7	2	12	0.4	48	1.7
95-96 UNC	32	3	663	84	186	.452	46	116	.397	53	69	.768	57	15	0	44	0	65	2.0	9	82	2.6	267	8.3
96-97 UNC	35	31	1146	155	367	.422	95	227	.419	88	108	.815	94	31	0	66	0	153	4.4	24	115	3.3	493	14.1
97-98 UNC	38	32	1250	209	428	.488	86	215	.400	133	146	.911	98	39	2	45	0	161	4.2	20	123	3.2	637	16.8
4 Years	134	66	3191	460	1012	.455	233	578	.403	292	344	.849	271	92	2	164	0	399	3.0	55	332	2.5	1445	10.8

NBA

Year Tm	G	GS	Min	Field Goals			3-Pt FGs			Free Throws			Misc			Fouls		Assists		Rebounds			Points	
				Md	Att	Pct	Md	Att	Pct	Md	Att	Pct	TO	Stl	Blk	PF	DQ	Ast	Avg	Off	Tot	Avg	Pts	Avg
98-99 Atl	2	0	4	0	1	.000	0	0	—	3	4	.750	0	0	0	0	0	1	0.5	0	0	0.0	3	1.5
99-00 Sea	43	5	517	84	225	.373	24	81	.296	33	51	.647	40	18	0	39	0	78	1.8	12	52	1.2	225	5.2
2 Years	45	5	521	84	226	.372	24	81	.296	36	55	.655	40	18	0	39	0	79	1.8	12	52	1.2	228	5.1

NBA Postseason

Year Tm	G	GS	Min	Md	Att	Pct	Md	Att	Pct	Md	Att	Pct	TO	Stl	Blk	PF	DQ	Ast	Avg	Off	Tot	Avg	Pts	Avg
99-00 Sea	5	2	99	18	33	.545	7	11	.636	8	11	.727	6	8	0	3	0	18	3.6	2	11	2.2	51	10.2

Walt Williams

(statistical profile on page 292)

Pos: G-F **College:** Maryland **Drafted:** '92 1(7)—Sac   **Ht:** 6'8" **Wt:** 230 **Born:** 4/16/70 **Age:** 30

College

Year Tm	G	GS	Min	Md	Att	Pct	Md	Att	Pct	Md	Att	Pct	TO	Stl	Blk	PF	DQ	Ast	Avg	Off	Tot	Avg	Pts	Avg
88-89 Myld	26	12	617	75	170	.441	7	27	.259	33	53	.623	71	33	13	76	7	66	2.5	31	92	3.5	190	7.3
89-90 Myld	33	31	993	143	296	.483	30	67	.448	104	134	.776	125	67	34	115	7	149	4.5	41	138	4.2	420	12.7
90-91 Myld	17	14	537	109	243	.449	28	95	.295	72	86	.837	70	15	6	51	2	91	5.4	23	86	5.1	318	18.7
91-92 Myld	29	29	1042	256	542	.472	89	240	.371	175	231	.758	111	60	28	98	6	104	3.6	65	162	5.6	776	26.8
4 Years	105	86	3189	583	1251	.466	154	429	.359	384	504	.762	377	175	81	340	22	410	3.9	160	478	4.6	1704	16.2

NBA

Year Tm	G	GS	Min	Md	Att	Pct	Md	Att	Pct	Md	Att	Pct	TO	Stl	Blk	PF	DQ	Ast	Avg	Off	Tot	Avg	Pts	Avg
92-93 Sac	59	26	1673	358	823	.435	61	191	.319	224	302	.742	179	66	29	209	6	178	3.0	115	265	4.5	1001	17.0
93-94 Sac	57	4	1356	226	580	.390	38	132	.288	148	233	.635	145	52	23	200	6	132	2.3	71	235	4.1	638	11.2
94-95 Sac	77	77	2739	445	998	.446	103	296	.348	266	364	.731	243	123	63	265	3	316	4.1	100	345	4.5	1259	16.4
95-96 2Tm	73	73	2169	359	808	.444	114	293	.389	163	232	.703	151	85	58	238	0	230	3.2	99	319	4.4	995	13.6
96-97 Tor	73	73	2647	419	982	.427	175	437	.400	186	243	.765	174	97	62	282	11	197	2.7	103	367	5.0	1199	16.4
97-98 2Tm	59	17	1470	210	544	.386	80	219	.365	108	125	.864	92	59	35	161	2	122	2.1	50	200	3.4	608	10.3
98-99 Por	48	16	1044	147	347	.424	63	144	.438	89	107	.832	63	37	28	101	2	80	1.7	36	143	3.0	446	9.3
99-00 Hou	76	66	1859	312	681	.458	102	261	.391	101	123	.821	113	49	44	190	2	157	2.1	69	306	4.0	827	10.9
95-96 Sac	45	45	1381	235	540	.435	58	170	.341	130	172	.756	103	53	42	151	0	165	3.7	62	207	4.6	658	14.6
Mia	28	28	788	124	268	.463	56	123	.455	33	60	.550	48	32	16	87	0	65	2.3	37	112	4.0	337	12.0
97-98 Tor	28	16	876	125	319	.392	49	129	.380	49	60	.817	52	40	23	100	2	69	2.5	27	118	4.2	348	12.4
Por	31	1	594	85	225	.378	31	90	.344	59	65	.908	40	19	12	61	0	53	1.7	23	82	2.6	260	8.4
8 Years	522	352	14957	2476	5763	.430	736	1973	.373	1285	1729	.743	1160	568	342	1646	32	1412	2.7	643	2180	4.2	6973	13.4

NBA Postseason

Year Tm	G	GS	Min	Md	Att	Pct	Md	Att	Pct	Md	Att	Pct	TO	Stl	Blk	PF	DQ	Ast	Avg	Off	Tot	Avg	Pts	Avg
95-96 Mia	3	3	70	6	18	.333	1	9	.111	1	2	.500	3	1	1	4	0	5	1.7	3	12	4.0	14	4.7
97-98 Por	4	0	102	17	31	.548	8	15	.533	11	14	.786	1	1	0	18	2	9	2.3	3	14	3.5	53	13.3
98-99 Por	13	0	185	21	58	.362	13	32	.406	8	14	.571	11	7	3	27	0	11	0.8	5	16	1.2	63	4.8
3 Years	20	3	357	44	107	.411	22	56	.393	20	30	.667	15	9	4	49	2	25	1.3	11	42	2.1	130	6.5

Corliss Williamson

(statistical profile on page 292)

Pos: F **College:** Arkansas **Drafted:** '95 1(13)—Sac   **Ht:** 6'7" **Wt:** 245 **Born:** 12/4/73 **Age:** 27

College

Year Tm	G	GS	Min	Md	Att	Pct	Md	Att	Pct	Md	Att	Pct	TO	Stl	Blk	PF	DQ	Ast	Avg	Off	Tot	Avg	Pts	Avg
92-93 Ark	18	—	454	101	176	.574	0	0	—	61	98	.622	40	7	22	45	—	30	1.7	—	92	5.1	263	14.6
93-94 Ark	34	34	989	273	436	.626	0	0	—	149	213	.700	90	39	39	78	—	74	2.2	—	262	7.7	695	20.4
94-95 Ark	39	39	1208	283	515	.550	1	6	.167	203	304	.668	92	67	33	106	—	89	2.3	—	293	7.5	770	19.7
3 Years	91	—	2651	657	1127	.583	1	6	.167	413	615	.672	222	113	94	229	—	193	2.1	—	647	7.1	1728	19.0

NBA

Year Tm	G	GS	Min	Md	Att	Pct	Md	Att	Pct	Md	Att	Pct	TO	Stl	Blk	PF	DQ	Ast	Avg	Off	Tot	Avg	Pts	Avg
95-96 Sac	53	3	609	125	268	.466	0	3	.000	47	84	.560	76	11	9	115	2	23	0.4	56	114	2.2	297	5.6
96-97 Sac	79	31	1992	371	745	.498	0	3	.000	173	251	.689	157	60	49	263	4	124	1.6	139	326	4.1	915	11.6
97-98 Sac	79	75	2819	561	1134	.495	0	9	.000	279	443	.630	199	76	48	252	4	230	2.9	162	446	5.6	1401	17.7
98-99 Sac	50	50	1374	269	555	.485	1	5	.200	120	188	.638	75	30	8	118	1	66	1.3	85	206	4.1	659	13.2
99-00 Sac	76	76	1707	311	622	.500	0	0	—	163	212	.769	110	38	19	192	0	82	1.1	122	290	3.8	785	10.3
5 Years	337	235	8501	1637	3324	.492	1	20	.050	782	1178	.664	617	215	133	940	11	525	1.6	564	1382	4.1	4057	12.0

NBA Postseason

Year Tm	G	GS	Min	Md	Att	Pct	Md	Att	Pct	Md	Att	Pct	TO	Stl	Blk	PF	DQ	Ast	Avg	Off	Tot	Avg	Pts	Avg
95-96 Sac	1	0	2	0	1	.000	0	0	—	1	1	1.000	0	0	0	0	0	0	0.0	0	0	0.0	1	1.0
98-99 Sac	5	5	130	23	40	.575	0	0	—	7	10	.700	6	2	1	13	0	6	1.2	7	16	3.2	53	10.6
99-00 Sac	5	5	87	11	16	.688	0	0	—	11	12	.917	5	1	0	8	0	1	0.2	4	15	3.0	33	6.6
3 Years	11	10	219	34	57	.596	0	0	—	19	23	.826	11	3	1	21	0	7	0.6	11	31	2.8	87	7.9

Kevin Willis

(statistical profile on page 293)

Pos: F-C **College:** Michigan State **Drafted:** '84 1(11)—Atl   **Ht:** 7'0" **Wt:** 245 **Born:** 9/6/62 **Age:** 38

	College			Field Goals			3-Pt FGs			Free Throws			Misc			Fouls		Assists		Rebounds			Points	
Year Tm	G	GS	Min	Md	Att	Pct	Md	Att	Pct	Md	Att	Pct	TO	Stl	Blk	PF	DQ	Ast	Avg	Off	Tot	Avg	Pts	Avg
81-82 MchSt	27	14	518	73	154	.474	—	—	—	17	30	.567	—	10	12	64	3	2	0.1	—	113	4.2	163	6.0
82-83 MchSt	27	25	865	162	272	.596	0	1	.000	36	70	.514	—	22	35	83	4	8	0.3	—	258	9.6	360	13.3
83-84 MchSt	25	23	738	118	240	.492	—	—	—	39	59	.661	—	10	24	88	4	7	0.3	—	192	7.7	275	11.0
3 Years	79	62	2121	353	666	.530	0	1	.000	92	159	.579	—	42	71	235	11	17	0.2	—	563	7.1	798	10.1

	NBA			Field Goals			3-Pt FGs			Free Throws			Misc			Fouls		Assists		Rebounds			Points	
Year Tm	G	GS	Min	Md	Att	Pct	Md	Att	Pct	Md	Att	Pct	TO	Stl	Blk	PF	DQ	Ast	Avg	Off	Tot	Avg	Pts	Avg
84-85 Atl	82	19	1785	322	690	.467	2	9	.222	119	181	.657	104	31	49	226	4	36	0.4	177	522	6.4	765	9.3
85-86 Atl	82	59	2300	419	811	.517	0	6	.000	172	263	.654	177	66	44	294	6	45	0.5	243	704	8.6	1010	12.3
86-87 Atl	81	81	2626	538	1003	.536	1	4	.250	227	320	.709	173	65	61	313	4	62	0.8	321	849	10.5	1304	16.1
87-88 Atl	75	55	2091	356	687	.518	0	2	.000	159	245	.649	138	68	41	240	2	28	0.4	233	547	7.3	871	11.6
88-89 Atl							Did not play: injury — Left Foot																	
89-90 Atl	81	51	2273	418	805	.519	2	7	.286	168	246	.683	144	63	47	259	4	57	0.7	253	645	8.0	1006	12.4
90-91 Atl	80	80	2373	444	881	.504	4	10	.400	159	238	.668	153	60	40	235	2	99	1.2	259	704	8.8	1051	13.1
91-92 Atl*	81	80	2962	591	1224	.483	6	37	.162	292	363	.804	197	72	54	223	0	173	2.1	418	1258	15.5	1480	18.3
92-93 Atl	80	80	2878	616	1218	.506	7	29	.241	196	300	.653	213	68	41	264	1	165	2.1	335	1028	12.9	1435	17.9
93-94 Atl	80	80	2867	627	1257	.499	9	24	.375	268	376	.713	188	79	38	250	2	150	1.9	335	963	12.0	1531	19.1
94-95 2Tm	67	63	2390	473	1015	.466	3	15	.200	205	297	.690	162	60	36	215	3	86	1.3	227	732	10.9	1154	17.2
95-96 2Tm	75	60	2135	325	712	.456	1	9	.111	143	202	.708	161	32	41	253	4	53	0.7	208	638	8.5	794	10.6
96-97 Hou	75	32	1964	350	728	.481	2	14	.143	140	202	.693	119	42	32	216	1	71	0.9	146	561	7.5	842	11.2
97-98 Hou	81	74	2528	531	1041	.510	1	7	.143	242	305	.793	150	55	38	235	1	78	1.0	232	679	8.4	1305	16.1
98-99 Tor	42	38	1216	187	447	.418	0	2	.000	130	155	.839	86	28	28	134	1	67	1.6	109	350	8.3	504	12.0
99-00 Tor	79	1	1679	236	569	.415	1	3	.333	131	164	.799	98	36	48	256	3	49	0.6	201	482	6.1	604	7.6
94-95 Atl	2	2	89	16	41	.390	0	1	.000	10	15	.667	7	1	3	7	0	3	1.5	10	36	18.0	42	21.0
Mia	65	61	2301	457	974	.469	3	14	.214	195	282	.691	155	59	33	208	3	83	1.3	217	696	10.7	1112	17.1
95-96 Mia	47	42	1357	195	412	.473	0	5	.000	89	125	.712	99	19	25	158	4	34	0.7	134	420	8.9	479	10.2
GS	28	18	778	130	300	.433	1	4	.250	54	77	.701	62	13	16	95	0	19	0.7	74	218	7.8	315	11.3
15 Years	1141	853	34067	6433	13088	.492	39	178	.219	2751	3857	.713	2283	825	638	3613	38	1219	1.1	3699	10662	9.3	15656	13.7

NBA Postseason

Year Tm	G	GS	Min	Md	Att	Pct	Md	Att	Pct	Md	Att	Pct	TO	Stl	Blk	PF	DQ	Ast	Avg	Off	Tot	Avg	Pts	Avg
85-86 Atl	9	9	280	55	98	.561	0	0	—	15	23	.652	15	7	8	38	2	5	0.6	31	65	7.2	125	13.9
86-87 Atl	9	9	356	60	115	.522	0	0	—	21	31	.677	17	9	7	33	0	6	0.7	33	83	9.2	141	15.7
87-88 Atl	12	12	462	80	138	.580	0	1	.000	34	50	.680	25	10	10	51	1	11	0.9	36	108	9.0	194	16.2
90-91 Atl	5	5	159	27	67	.403	2	3	.667	21	30	.700	2	3	1	22	0	5	1.0	18	45	9.0	77	15.4
92-93 Atl	3	3	103	21	45	.467	0	1	.000	8	14	.571	7	2	0	13	0	3	1.0	13	26	8.7	50	16.7
93-94 Atl	11	11	362	59	129	.457	0	5	.000	16	21	.762	19	8	5	37	0	11	1.0	38	119	10.8	134	12.2
96-97 Hou	16	0	295	38	95	.400	0	1	.000	26	38	.684	22	9	4	47	0	11	0.7	22	75	4.7	102	6.4
97-98 Hou	5	5	168	22	55	.400	0	1	.000	12	16	.750	12	8	3	21	0	1	0.2	18	53	10.6	56	11.2
99-00 Tor	3	0	76	12	33	.364	0	0	—	15	20	.750	2	2	0	11	0	1	0.3	6	26	8.7	39	13.0
9 Years	73	54	2261	374	775	.483	2	12	.167	168	243	.691	121	58	38	273	3	58	0.8	215	600	8.2	918	12.6

Dedric Willoughby

Pos: G **College:** Iowa State **Drafted:** '99 FA—Chi   **Ht:** 6'3" **Wt:** 191 **Born:** 4/6/72 **Age:** 28

	College			Field Goals			3-Pt FGs			Free Throws			Misc			Fouls		Assists		Rebounds			Points	
Year Tm	G	GS	Min	Md	Att	Pct	Md	Att	Pct	Md	Att	Pct	TO	Stl	Blk	PF	DQ	Ast	Avg	Off	Tot	Avg	Pts	Avg
92-93 UNO	5	4	95	7	24	.292	7	22	.318	5	9	.556	3	1	0	1	0	12	2.4	2	13	2.6	26	5.2
93-94 UNO	28	4	594	76	176	.432	44	110	.400	55	69	.797	28	13	1	20	0	20	0.7	14	58	2.1	251	9.0
95-96 IaSt	33	33	1262	204	492	.415	88	261	.337	180	227	.793	79	42	3	55	0	82	2.5	33	137	4.2	676	20.5
96-97 IaSt	27	26	969	158	365	.433	102	226	.451	92	112	.821	56	22	2	26	0	53	2.0	11	91	3.4	510	18.9
4 Years	93	67	2920	445	1057	.421	241	619	.389	332	417	.796	166	78	6	102	0	167	1.8	60	299	3.2	1463	15.7

	NBA			Field Goals			3-Pt FGs			Free Throws			Misc			Fouls		Assists		Rebounds			Points	
Year Tm	G	GS	Min	Md	Att	Pct	Md	Att	Pct	Md	Att	Pct	TO	Stl	Blk	PF	DQ	Ast	Avg	Off	Tot	Avg	Pts	Avg
97-98										Played in Italy														
98-99										Played in Italy														
99-00 Chi	25	1	508	61	179	.341	29	98	.296	39	51	.765	37	23	2	32	0	66	2.6	11	51	2.0	190	7.6

David Wingate

Pos: G-F **College:** Georgetown **Drafted:** '86 2(44)—Phi   **Ht:** 6'5" **Wt:** 187 **Born:** 12/15/63 **Age:** 37

	College			Field Goals			3-Pt FGs			Free Throws			Misc			Fouls		Assists		Rebounds			Points	
Year Tm	G	GS	Min	Md	Att	Pct	Md	Att	Pct	Md	Att	Pct	TO	Stl	Blk	PF	DQ	Ast	Avg	Off	Tot	Avg	Pts	Avg
82-83 GTwn	32	31	855	149	335	.445	—	—	—	87	124	.702	75	43	10	90	3	69	2.2	—	95	3.0	385	12.0

180

College

Year	Tm	G	GS	Min	Md	Att	Pct	Md	Att	Pct	Md	Att	Pct	TO	Stl	Blk	PF	DQ	Ast	Avg	Off	Tot	Avg	Pts	Avg
					Field Goals			**3-Pt FGs**			**Free Throws**			**Misc**			**Fouls**		**Assists**		**Rebounds**			**Points**	
83-84	GTwn	37	37	1005	161	370	.435	—	—	—	93	129	.721	75	50	4	65	2	99	2.7	—	135	3.6	415	11.2
84-85	GTwn	38	38	1128	191	395	.484	—	—	—	91	132	.689	99	62	5	90	2	121	3.2	—	135	3.6	473	12.4
85-86	GTwn	32	31	956	196	394	.497	—	—	—	117	155	.755	66	54	5	81	0	75	2.3	—	129	4.0	509	15.9
4 Years		139	137	3944	697	1494	.467	—	—	—	388	540	.719	315	209	24	326	7	364	2.6	—	494	3.6	1782	12.8

NBA

Year	Tm	G	GS	Min	Md	Att	Pct	Md	Att	Pct	Md	Att	Pct	TO	Stl	Blk	PF	DQ	Ast	Avg	Off	Tot	Avg	Pts	Avg
					Field Goals			**3-Pt FGs**			**Free Throws**			**Misc**			**Fouls**		**Assists**		**Rebounds**			**Points**	
86-87	Phi	77	9	1612	259	602	.430	13	52	.250	149	201	.741	128	93	19	169	1	155	2.0	70	156	2.0	680	8.8
87-88	Phi	61	22	1419	218	545	.400	10	40	.250	99	132	.750	104	47	22	125	0	119	2.0	44	101	1.7	545	8.9
88-89	Phi	33	6	372	54	115	.470	2	6	.333	27	34	.794	35	9	2	43	0	73	2.2	12	37	1.1	137	4.2
89-90	SA	78	2	1856	220	491	.448	0	13	.000	87	112	.777	127	89	18	154	2	208	2.7	62	195	2.5	527	6.8
90-91	SA	25	0	563	53	138	.384	1	9	.111	29	41	.707	42	19	5	66	0	46	1.8	24	75	3.0	136	5.4
91-92	Was	81	72	2127	266	572	.465	1	18	.056	105	146	.719	124	123	21	162	1	247	3.0	80	269	3.3	638	7.9
92-93	Cha	72	55	1471	180	336	.536	1	6	.167	79	107	.738	89	66	9	135	1	183	2.5	49	174	2.4	440	6.1
93-94	Cha	50	36	1005	136	283	.481	4	12	.333	34	51	.667	53	42	6	85	0	104	2.1	30	134	2.7	310	6.2
94-95	Cha	52	9	515	50	122	.410	4	22	.182	18	24	.750	27	19	6	60	0	56	1.1	11	60	1.2	122	2.3
95-96	Sea	60	3	695	88	212	.415	15	34	.441	32	41	.780	42	20	4	66	0	58	1.0	17	56	0.9	223	3.7
96-97	Sea	65	2	929	89	214	.416	25	71	.352	33	40	.825	37	44	5	108	0	80	1.2	23	74	1.1	236	3.6
97-98	Sea	58	2	546	66	140	.471	3	7	.429	15	29	.517	37	21	3	58	0	37	0.6	19	79	1.4	150	2.6
98-99	NY	20	0	92	7	16	.438	0	0	—	0	0	—	6	4	0	10	0	5	0.3	3	8	0.4	14	0.7
99-00	NY	7	0	32	1	9	.111	0	0	—	0	0	—	2	1	2	7	0	3	0.4	1	2	0.3	2	0.3
14 Years		739	218	13234	1687	3795	.445	79	290	.272	707	958	.738	853	597	122	1248	5	1374	1.9	445	1420	1.9	4160	5.6

NBA Postseason

Year	Tm	G	GS	Min	Md	Att	Pct	Md	Att	Pct	Md	Att	Pct	TO	Stl	Blk	PF	DQ	Ast	Avg	Off	Tot	Avg	Pts	Avg
86-87	Phi	5	0	90	15	37	.405	2	2	1.000	9	14	.643	9	5	1	11	1	9	1.8	5	12	2.4	41	8.2
89-90	SA	10	0	293	40	77	.519	2	3	.667	9	12	.750	14	18	3	34	1	38	3.8	9	37	3.7	91	9.1
90-91	SA	3	0	38	6	12	.500	0	0	—	2	3	.667	1	1	0	8	1	1	0.3	1	3	1.0	14	4.7
92-93	Cha	9	0	117	8	22	.364	0	0	—	3	8	.375	1	4	1	9	0	15	1.7	4	12	1.3	19	2.1
94-95	Cha	4	4	73	13	27	.481	2	6	.333	4	6	.667	4	4	0	14	0	15	3.8	3	6	1.5	32	8.0
95-96	Sea	13	0	68	7	16	.438	1	2	.500	4	4	1.000	4	0	0	16	0	0	0.0	1	3	0.2	19	1.5
96-97	Sea	12	0	192	28	66	.424	12	31	.387	9	13	.692	9	5	3	22	0	14	1.2	13	37	3.1	77	6.4
97-98	Sea	3	0	13	2	5	.400	0	0	—	4	6	.667	1	1	0	1	0	2	0.7	2	4	1.3	8	2.7
8 Years		59	4	884	119	262	.454	19	44	.432	44	66	.667	43	38	8	115	3	94	1.6	38	114	1.9	301	5.1

Haywoode Workman

Pos: G **College:** Oral Roberts **Drafted:** '89 2(49)—Atl **Ht:** 6'3" **Wt:** 200 **Born:** 1/23/66 **Age:** 35

College

Year	Tm	G	GS	Min	Md	Att	Pct	Md	Att	Pct	Md	Att	Pct	TO	Stl	Blk	PF	DQ	Ast	Avg	Off	Tot	Avg	Pts	Avg
					Field Goals			**3-Pt FGs**			**Free Throws**			**Misc**			**Fouls**		**Assists**		**Rebounds**			**Points**	
84-85	W-Sal	25	—		102	223	.457	—	—	—	53	90	.589	—	—	—	—	—	53	2.1	—	75	3.0	257	10.3
86-87	OrRob	28	—	1086	125	342	.365	16	56	.286	121	152	.796	98	54	2	88	—	188	6.7	—	93	3.3	387	13.8
87-88	OrRob	29	—	988	206	496	.415	42	149	.282	108	143	.755	62	103	4	88	—	78	2.7	—	174	6.0	562	19.4
88-89	OrRob	28	—	980	205	424	.483	37	101	.366	110	135	.815	72	93	3	81	—	110	3.9	—	171	6.1	557	19.9
4 Years		110	—		638	1485	.430	95	306	.310	392	520	.754	—	—	—	—	—	429	3.9	—	513	4.7	1763	16.0

NBA

Year	Tm	G	GS	Min	Md	Att	Pct	Md	Att	Pct	Md	Att	Pct	TO	Stl	Blk	PF	DQ	Ast	Avg	Off	Tot	Avg	Pts	Avg
					Field Goals			**3-Pt FGs**			**Free Throws**			**Misc**			**Fouls**		**Assists**		**Rebounds**			**Points**	
89-90	Atl	6	0	16	2	3	.667	0	0	—	2	2	1.000	0	3	0	3	0	2	0.3	0	3	0.5	6	1.0
90-91	Was	73	56	2034	234	515	.454	12	50	.240	101	133	.759	135	87	7	162	1	353	4.8	51	242	3.3	581	8.0
91-92								Played in Italy																	
92-93								Played in Italy																	
93-94	Ind	65	52	1714	195	460	.424	18	56	.321	93	116	.802	151	85	4	152	0	404	6.2	32	204	3.1	501	7.7
94-95	Ind	69	14	1028	101	269	.375	35	98	.357	55	74	.743	73	59	5	115	0	194	2.8	21	111	1.6	292	4.2
95-96	Ind	77	4	1164	101	259	.390	23	71	.324	54	73	.740	93	65	4	152	0	213	2.8	27	124	1.6	279	3.6
96-97	Ind	4	2	81	11	20	.550	0	3	.000	5	5	1.000	5	3	0	10	0	11	2.8	4	7	1.8	22	5.5
97-98	Ind							Did not play: injury — Left Knee																	
98-99	Mil	29	29	815	73	170	.429	17	47	.362	37	47	.787	63	32	1	53	0	172	5.9	14	102	3.5	200	6.9
99-00	2Tm	36	2	350	31	90	.344	14	43	.326	10	15	.667	18	20	0	37	1	61	1.7	1	26	0.7	86	2.4
99-00	Phi	23	1	248	23	62	.371	11	29	.379	9	13	.692	14	11	0	23	0	44	1.9	1	17	0.7	66	2.9
	Tor	13	1	102	8	28	.286	3	14	.214	1	2	.500	4	9	0	14	1	17	1.3	0	9	0.7	20	1.5
8 Years		359	159	7202	748	1786	.419	119	368	.323	352	461	.764	538	354	21	684	2	1410	3.9	150	819	2.3	1967	5.5

NBA Postseason

Year	Tm	G	GS	Min	Md	Att	Pct	Md	Att	Pct	Md	Att	Pct	TO	Stl	Blk	PF	DQ	Ast	Avg	Off	Tot	Avg	Pts	Avg
93-94	Ind	16	15	511	45	131	.344	6	21	.286	32	38	.842	38	28	1	40	0	112	7.0	11	51	3.2	128	8.0
94-95	Ind	17	0	275	24	67	.358	2	18	.111	27	32	.844	16	11	0	45	0	46	2.7	5	28	1.6	77	4.5
95-96	Ind	5	0	53	7	16	.438	3	5	.600	2	2	1.000	2	2	0	5	0	2	0.4	1	3	0.6	19	3.8
98-99	Mil	3	0	53	4	11	.364	0	3	.000	5	6	.833	7	3	0	7	0	7	2.3	1	3	1.0	13	4.3
4 Years		41	15	892	80	225	.356	11	47	.234	66	78	.846	63	44	1	97	0	167	4.1	18	85	2.1	237	5.8

Lorenzen Wright

(statistical profile on page 293)

Pos: F-C **College:** Memphis **Drafted:** '96 1(7)—LAC **Ht:** 6'11" **Wt:** 240 **Born:** 11/4/75 **Age:** 25

College				Field Goals			3-Pt FGs			Free Throws			Misc			Fouls		Assists		Rebounds			Points	
Year Tm	G	GS	Min	Md	Att	Pct	Md	Att	Pct	Md	Att	Pct	TO	Stl	Blk	PF	DQ	Ast	Avg	Off	Tot	Avg	Pts	Avg
94-95 Mem	34	—	1170	198	353	.561	0	1	.000	107	171	.626	75	26	71	90	—	50	1.5	—	345	10.1	503	14.8
95-96 Mem	30	30	1058	207	382	.542	0	1	.000	109	169	.645	56	40	59	78	3	35	1.2	104	313	10.4	523	17.4
2 Years	64	—	2228	405	735	.551	0	2	.000	216	340	.635	131	66	130	168	—	85	1.3	—	658	10.3	1026	16.0

NBA				Field Goals			3-Pt FGs			Free Throws			Misc			Fouls		Assists		Rebounds			Points	
Year Tm	G	GS	Min	Md	Att	Pct	Md	Att	Pct	Md	Att	Pct	TO	Stl	Blk	PF	DQ	Ast	Avg	Off	Tot	Avg	Pts	Avg
96-97 LAC	77	51	1936	236	491	.481	1	4	.250	88	150	.587	79	48	60	211	2	49	0.6	206	471	6.1	561	7.3
97-98 LAC	69	38	2067	241	542	.445	0	2	.000	141	214	.659	81	55	87	237	2	55	0.8	180	606	8.8	623	9.0
98-99 LAC	48	15	1135	119	260	.458	0	1	.000	81	117	.692	48	26	36	162	2	33	0.7	142	361	7.5	319	6.6
99-00 Atl	75	0	1205	180	361	.499	1	3	.333	87	135	.644	66	29	40	203	3	21	0.3	117	305	4.1	448	6.0
4 Years	269	104	6343	776	1654	.469	2	10	.200	397	616	.644	274	158	223	813	9	158	0.6	645	1743	6.5	1951	7.3

NBA Postseason																								
Year Tm	G	GS	Min	Md	Att	Pct	Md	Att	Pct	Md	Att	Pct	TO	Stl	Blk	PF	DQ	Ast	Avg	Off	Tot	Avg	Pts	Avg
96-97 LAC	3	3	92	13	32	.406	0	0	—	5	5	1.000	1	3	2	6	0	2	0.7	7	22	7.3	31	10.3

Tim Young

Pos: C **College:** Stanford **Drafted:** '99 2(56)—GS **Ht:** 7'2" **Wt:** 270 **Born:** 2/6/76 **Age:** 24

College				Field Goals			3-Pt FGs			Free Throws			Misc			Fouls		Assists		Rebounds			Points	
Year Tm	G	GS	Min	Md	Att	Pct	Md	Att	Pct	Md	Att	Pct	TO	Stl	Blk	PF	DQ	Ast	Avg	Off	Tot	Avg	Pts	Avg
94-95 Stan	29	22	733	137	274	.500	0	0	—	83	120	.692	44	14	43	85	4	11	0.4	93	249	8.6	357	12.3
95-96 Stan	5	5	137	16	38	.421	0	0	—	18	25	.720	12	4	2	14	0	8	1.6	15	45	9.0	50	10.0
96-97 Stan	30	30	782	140	278	.504	0	0	—	131	165	.794	67	20	50	86	4	42	1.4	82	253	8.4	411	13.7
97-98 Stan	35	35	947	148	288	.514	0	0	—	100	131	.763	64	8	41	106	4	59	1.7	88	284	8.1	396	11.3
98-99 Stan	33	33	821	118	233	.506	0	0	—	94	114	.825	60	12	31	84	5	67	2.0	71	239	7.2	330	10.0
5 Years	132	125	3420	559	1111	.503	0	0	—	426	555	.768	247	58	167	375	17	187	1.4	349	1070	8.1	1544	11.7

NBA				Field Goals			3-Pt FGs			Free Throws			Misc			Fouls		Assists		Rebounds			Points	
Year Tm	G	GS	Min	Md	Att	Pct	Md	Att	Pct	Md	Att	Pct	TO	Stl	Blk	PF	DQ	Ast	Avg	Off	Tot	Avg	Pts	Avg
99-00 GS	25	0	137	13	39	.333	0	0	—	28	36	.778	9	2	1	18	0	5	0.2	13	35	1.4	54	2.2

Player Profiles

The following section contains statistical breakdowns for everyone who played at least 1,200 minutes in the NBA last season.

For rookies like Elton Brand and Steve Francis, obviously we can list only their 1999-2000 breakdowns. But for veterans, you'll also find their combined stats over the last five seasons (1995-96 through 1999-2000). For players who have been in the league less than five years, their breakdowns will encompass their entire careers.

Pre and Post All-Star splits which appear in the Last Five Seasons section do not include the 1998-99 season, as there was no All-Star Game played that year.

For an explanation of any abbreviation, please see the Abbreviations page in the back of this book.

Tariq Abdul-Wahad
Denver Nuggets — Guard

1999-2000 Per Game Averages

	G	Min	FGA	FG%	3PA	3P%	FTA	FT%	Blk	Stl	Ast	Reb	Pts
Total	61	25.9	10.6	.424	0.4	.130	3.2	.756	0.46	0.97	1.6	4.8	11.4
Home	29	23.9	10.4	.430	0.4	.231	3.1	.700	0.45	0.97	1.8	4.7	11.2
Road	32	27.6	10.8	.419	0.3	.000	3.2	.806	0.47	0.97	1.5	4.8	11.6
vs. Playoff	35	25.7	11.0	.400	0.5	.118	3.0	.752	0.34	0.97	1.5	4.9	11.1
vs. Non-Playoff	26	26.2	10.0	.460	0.4	.167	3.4	.761	0.62	0.96	1.7	4.6	11.8
vs. East	33	26.9	11.2	.419	0.5	.059	3.3	.787	0.39	0.79	1.8	5.5	12.0
vs. West	28	24.6	9.9	.431	0.2	.333	3.0	.718	0.54	1.18	1.4	3.9	10.8
vs. Div.	14	29.5	12.4	.434	0.6	.125	3.5	.735	0.57	0.79	1.6	6.5	13.4
As Starter	56	26.5	11.1	.425	0.4	.136	3.2	.754	0.43	1.04	1.6	5.0	11.9
Off Bench	5	19.2	5.0	.400	0.2	.000	2.8	.786	0.80	0.20	1.8	2.0	6.2
In wins	27	25.1	9.6	.446	0.3	.000	3.1	.765	0.44	0.96	2.0	4.6	10.9
In losses	34	26.4	11.4	.410	0.4	.214	3.2	.750	0.47	0.97	1.3	4.9	11.8

	G	Min	FGA	FG%	3PA	3P%	FTA	FT%	Blk	Stl	Ast	Reb	Pts
Pre All-Star	51	25.9	10.8	.434	0.5	.130	3.2	.764	0.41	1.08	1.6	5.0	11.9
Post All-Star	10	25.6	9.5	.368	0.0	—	2.8	.714	0.70	0.40	1.5	3.7	9.0
November	15	28.5	11.9	.438	1.2	.111	1.9	.724	0.33	1.13	1.4	5.7	11.9
December	14	24.4	9.4	.424	0.1	.000	3.9	.727	0.29	1.21	1.6	5.4	10.9
January	17	25.7	12.1	.434	0.1	.000	3.9	.806	0.41	1.12	1.7	4.6	13.6
February	11	26.3	9.0	.424	0.2	.500	3.0	.758	0.64	0.45	1.8	3.5	10.0
March	4	21.0	8.0	.281	0.0	—	2.3	.667	1.25	0.25	1.5	3.3	6.0
April	0	—	—	—	—	—	—	—	—	—	—	—	—
0 Days Rest	17	27.8	10.7	.412	0.4	.000	3.4	.719	0.53	1.06	1.7	6.0	11.2
1 Days Rest	30	25.1	10.3	.447	0.3	.222	3.2	.747	0.53	0.80	1.7	5.3	11.6
2 Days Rest	5	26.4	13.0	.354	0.8	.000	3.0	1.000	0.00	1.20	1.0	5.8	12.2
3+ Days Rest	9	24.3	10.0	.422	0.3	.333	2.9	.731	0.33	1.22	1.3	4.8	10.7

Career (1997-98 thru 1999-2000)

	G	Min	FGA	FG%	3PA	3P%	FTA	FT%	Blk	Stl	Ast	Reb	Pts
Total	169	22.1	8.3	.422	0.4	.206	2.7	.714	0.34	0.85	1.2	3.5	9.0
Home	81	21.4	8.4	.423	0.4	.233	2.9	.697	0.33	0.93	1.1	3.6	9.2
Road	88	22.8	8.3	.421	0.4	.182	2.5	.731	0.34	0.78	1.2	3.4	8.9
vs. Playoff	98	21.7	8.1	.397	0.4	.222	2.5	.693	0.33	0.91	1.1	3.4	8.3
vs. Non-Playoff	71	22.8	8.6	.454	0.4	.185	3.0	.738	0.35	0.77	1.2	3.6	10.1
vs. East	59	21.7	8.9	.418	0.4	.043	2.8	.739	0.34	0.68	1.3	3.9	9.5
vs. West	110	22.4	8.0	.424	0.4	.300	2.6	.699	0.34	0.95	1.1	3.3	8.8
vs. Div.	49	25.8	9.2	.434	0.4	.263	3.1	.693	0.47	0.96	1.2	4.4	10.3
As Starter	121	26.1	9.9	.431	0.5	.211	3.1	.729	0.39	1.03	1.4	4.4	11.0
Off Bench	48	12.1	4.3	.367	0.1	.167	1.6	.636	0.21	0.40	0.7	1.4	4.2
In wins	71	21.9	8.4	.439	0.4	.040	3.0	.703	0.32	0.90	1.3	3.6	9.5
In losses	98	22.3	8.3	.409	0.4	.316	2.5	.723	0.35	0.82	1.1	3.4	8.7

	G	Min	FGA	FG%	3PA	3P%	FTA	FT%	Blk	Stl	Ast	Reb	Pts
Pre All-Star	82	20.9	8.7	.428	0.4	.103	2.5	.739	0.30	0.85	1.2	3.6	9.3
Post All-Star	38	21.8	7.7	.390	0.3	.308	2.9	.694	0.42	0.63	1.3	2.9	8.1
Oct/Nov	24	21.0	8.7	.438	0.8	.111	1.5	.667	0.25	0.79	1.0	3.8	8.7
December	22	20.6	8.2	.417	0.3	.000	2.7	.750	0.23	0.95	1.1	4.0	8.9
January	28	21.7	9.8	.429	0.1	.000	3.4	.747	0.32	0.96	1.4	3.6	10.9
February	32	21.2	7.4	.418	0.3	.300	2.5	.741	0.34	0.56	1.3	2.9	8.2
March	37	22.9	7.4	.392	0.4	.231	2.9	.679	0.41	0.95	0.9	3.6	7.9
Apr/May	26	25.2	9.2	.444	0.5	.385	2.8	.685	0.42	0.92	1.3	3.4	10.3
0 Days Rest	44	23.7	8.7	.395	0.4	.158	3.1	.711	0.39	0.95	1.3	4.0	9.1
1 Days Rest	83	22.7	8.6	.442	0.4	.267	2.8	.696	0.39	0.86	1.3	3.3	9.6
2 Days Rest	16	21.3	8.3	.398	0.4	.000	2.9	.804	0.06	0.69	0.7	3.9	8.9
3+ Days Rest	26	18.3	7.0	.418	0.3	.250	1.7	.721	0.27	0.77	0.8	2.9	7.1

Shareef Abdur-Rahim
Vancouver Grizzlies — Forward

1999-2000 Per Game Averages

	G	Min	FGA	FG%	3PA	3P%	FTA	FT%	Blk	Stl	Ast	Reb	Pts
Total	82	39.3	15.6	.465	1.2	.302	6.7	.809	1.06	1.09	3.3	10.1	20.3
Home	41	39.9	16.4	.467	1.3	.352	5.8	.816	1.29	1.27	3.8	10.6	20.6
Road	41	38.7	14.7	.463	1.0	.238	7.6	.804	0.83	0.90	2.8	9.6	20.0
vs. Playoff	48	39.6	15.6	.465	1.1	.373	6.7	.804	1.10	0.92	3.1	9.6	20.3
vs. Non-Playoff	34	38.9	15.6	.466	1.3	.222	6.7	.817	1.00	1.32	3.5	10.7	20.3
vs. East	30	38.3	14.2	.450	1.0	.207	6.9	.817	1.33	0.93	3.3	9.0	18.7
vs. West	52	39.9	16.3	.473	1.3	.343	6.6	.805	0.90	1.17	3.3	10.7	21.2
vs. Div.	24	40.0	17.0	.479	1.7	.425	6.4	.825	0.46	1.04	2.5	10.5	22.3
As Starter	82	39.3	15.6	.465	1.2	.302	6.7	.809	1.06	1.09	3.3	10.1	20.3
Off Bench	0	—	—	—	—	—	—	—	—	—	—	—	—
In wins	22	39.7	14.6	.488	0.7	.438	7.0	.864	1.27	1.45	4.1	10.0	20.6
In losses	60	39.2	15.9	.458	1.3	.275	6.6	.788	0.98	0.95	3.0	10.1	20.2

	G	Min	FGA	FG%	3PA	3P%	FTA	FT%	Blk	Stl	Ast	Reb	Pts
Pre All-Star	48	38.1	16.1	.458	1.2	.263	7.3	.804	1.19	1.17	3.3	10.0	21.0
Post All-Star	34	40.9	14.8	.476	1.1	.359	5.9	.819	0.88	0.97	3.3	10.1	19.3
November	14	38.9	14.9	.469	1.2	.235	7.9	.782	1.07	1.07	4.2	11.4	20.4
December	15	38.5	18.0	.456	1.1	.375	7.7	.774	0.93	1.53	3.2	9.6	22.7
January	14	37.4	15.4	.417	1.2	.176	7.5	.838	1.64	0.93	2.6	8.4	19.4
February	13	39.1	15.2	.490	0.8	.300	5.2	.809	0.77	1.00	3.5	10.5	19.4
March	15	39.3	14.3	.463	1.3	.316	6.1	.826	1.07	1.07	3.5	9.3	18.7
April	11	43.6	15.5	.512	1.4	.412	5.5	.852	0.82	0.82	2.8	11.5	21.2
0 Days Rest	19	39.1	14.3	.441	1.1	.381	6.7	.811	1.11	1.21	2.5	9.9	18.5
1 Days Rest	47	39.3	15.8	.473	1.3	.317	6.6	.822	1.02	0.91	3.5	10.0	20.7
2 Days Rest	7	38.0	15.7	.491	1.0	.286	8.0	.750	0.86	1.43	3.7	9.0	21.7
3+ Days Rest	9	41.1	17.0	.451	0.9	.000	6.6	.797	1.33	1.44	3.4	11.3	20.6

Career (1996-97 thru 1999-2000)

	G	Min	FGA	FG%	3PA	3P%	FTA	FT%	Blk	Stl	Ast	Reb	Pts
Total	294	37.4	16.1	.461	0.7	.324	7.3	.793	1.01	1.11	2.8	7.9	20.9
Home	147	38.2	16.7	.467	0.7	.382	7.4	.800	1.34	1.29	3.1	8.7	21.8
Road	147	36.6	15.5	.456	0.7	.260	7.2	.785	0.68	0.93	2.6	7.2	20.0
vs. Playoff	172	37.0	16.0	.446	0.7	.397	7.2	.788	0.97	1.11	2.8	7.7	20.2
vs. Non-Playoff	122	38.0	16.3	.483	0.7	.225	7.5	.800	1.07	1.11	2.9	8.3	21.9
vs. East	96	37.1	15.1	.465	0.6	.200	7.1	.799	1.17	0.92	2.8	7.4	20.3
vs. West	198	37.5	16.6	.460	0.7	.373	7.4	.790	0.93	1.20	2.8	8.2	21.4
vs. Div.	92	37.2	16.6	.465	0.8	.478	6.8	.792	0.77	1.05	2.8	8.1	21.2
As Starter	285	37.8	16.4	.462	0.7	.325	7.4	.793	1.02	1.11	2.8	8.0	21.2
Off Bench	9	25.2	7.6	.397	0.1	.000	5.2	.787	0.56	1.11	2.1	4.8	10.1
In wins	62	38.9	16.2	.484	0.6	.400	8.6	.820	1.24	1.29	3.3	8.9	23.0
In losses	232	37.0	16.1	.455	0.7	.306	7.0	.784	0.95	1.06	2.7	7.7	20.3

	G	Min	FGA	FG%	3PA	3P%	FTA	FT%	Blk	Stl	Ast	Reb	Pts
Pre All-Star	147	35.9	15.6	.463	0.6	.276	7.2	.770	1.02	1.14	2.6	7.8	20.2
Post All-Star	97	38.2	15.9	.476	0.9	.379	6.8	.798	0.95	0.92	2.9	8.4	20.8
Oct/Nov	48	34.1	14.1	.442	0.5	.182	6.6	.771	0.77	0.98	2.6	7.7	17.7
December	41	37.4	16.8	.469	0.8	.385	7.9	.763	0.95	1.32	3.1	8.4	22.0
January	47	36.2	16.3	.460	0.6	.207	7.5	.767	1.43	1.19	2.1	7.3	20.9
February	48	38.4	16.8	.473	0.6	.357	7.3	.788	0.96	1.21	3.0	8.8	21.9
March	62	37.8	15.6	.456	0.8	.429	7.2	.821	0.84	0.94	2.8	7.4	20.5
Apr/May	48	40.3	17.3	.467	1.2	.304	7.4	.825	1.17	1.10	3.3	8.2	22.6
0 Days Rest	71	36.4	15.5	.436	0.5	.432	7.1	.808	0.90	1.01	2.4	7.1	19.5
1 Days Rest	167	38.0	16.5	.465	0.8	.326	7.4	.786	1.02	1.07	2.8	8.3	21.4
2 Days Rest	28	36.1	15.8	.489	0.7	.300	7.5	.825	1.07	1.39	3.3	7.0	21.9
3+ Days Rest	28	37.9	15.8	.475	0.5	.067	6.9	.766	1.14	1.32	3.4	8.5	20.3

Ray Allen

1999-2000 Per Game Averages

	G	Min	FGA	FG%	3PA	3P%	FTA	FT%	Blk	Stl	Ast	Reb	Pts
Total	82	37.4	17.2	.455	5.0	.423	4.9	.887	0.23	1.34	3.8	4.4	22.1
Home	41	36.7	17.1	.454	4.9	.396	5.5	.879	0.22	1.07	4.3	4.7	22.3
Road	41	38.2	17.3	.456	5.0	.449	4.2	.897	0.24	1.61	3.2	4.1	21.8
vs. Playoff	43	38.0	17.9	.439	5.3	.430	4.7	.901	0.26	1.35	3.8	4.6	22.2
vs. Non-Playoff	39	36.9	16.5	.474	4.6	.413	5.0	.872	0.21	1.33	3.7	4.1	21.9
vs. East	54	37.2	17.0	.467	4.9	.427	4.6	.879	0.23	1.37	3.7	4.3	22.0
vs. West	28	37.8	17.6	.433	5.2	.414	5.4	.901	0.25	1.29	3.9	4.6	22.2
vs. Div.	28	36.6	16.9	.466	4.5	.384	4.8	.867	0.11	1.50	3.8	4.3	21.7
As Starter	82	37.4	17.2	.455	5.0	.423	4.9	.887	0.23	1.34	3.8	4.4	22.1
Off Bench	0	—											
In wins	42	36.5	16.9	.484	4.7	.444	4.9	.865	0.26	1.36	3.8	4.4	22.7
In losses	40	38.4	17.6	.426	5.3	.403	4.8	.911	0.20	1.33	3.7	4.3	21.4

	G	Min	FGA	FG%	3PA	3P%	FTA	FT%	Blk	Stl	Ast	Reb	Pts
Pre All-Star	50	37.4	17.4	.438	5.0	.405	5.1	.894	0.22	1.32	4.0	4.4	21.9
Post All-Star	32	37.6	16.8	.482	4.8	.452	4.5	.874	0.25	1.38	3.3	4.4	22.3
November	14	36.1	17.1	.458	4.6	.422	5.9	.880	0.29	1.29	4.1	4.4	22.9
December	16	38.2	17.7	.410	4.8	.442	4.6	.918	0.19	1.13	3.9	3.9	20.8
January	15	37.3	17.3	.452	5.0	.360	4.5	.896	0.07	1.27	4.3	4.1	21.4
February	12	37.1	17.6	.450	5.3	.391	5.8	.914	0.42	1.17	3.3	5.8	23.3
March	14	39.1	17.4	.508	5.6	.462	3.5	.857	0.14	1.79	3.4	4.8	23.3
April	11	36.5	15.8	.460	4.5	.469	5.1	.839	0.36	1.45	3.3	3.4	20.9
0 Days Rest	19	38.4	18.3	.455	5.8	.464	4.3	.902	0.21	1.21	4.5	4.1	23.2
1 Days Rest	49	37.0	16.7	.442	4.6	.402	5.1	.879	0.26	1.37	3.4	4.4	21.0
2 Days Rest	5	37.4	16.2	.481	4.8	.375	4.0	.850	0.00	1.00	4.6	4.0	20.8
3+ Days Rest	9	37.8	18.4	.506	5.4	.449	5.1	.935	0.11	1.67	3.8	4.8	25.9

Career (1996-97 thru 1999-2000)

	G	Min	FGA	FG%	3PA	3P%	FTA	FT%	Blk	Stl	Ast	Reb	Pts
Total	296	35.8	14.6	.441	4.3	.388	4.2	.873	0.16	1.18	3.6	4.4	18.1
Home	148	35.4	14.3	.454	4.4	.389	4.4	.875	0.16	1.14	3.8	4.4	18.5
Road	148	36.3	14.8	.428	4.3	.387	4.0	.870	0.16	1.22	3.3	4.4	17.7
vs. Playoff	161	36.3	15.0	.425	4.5	.393	4.4	.876	0.15	1.15	3.5	4.6	18.0
vs. Non-Playoff	135	35.3	14.0	.461	4.1	.382	4.3	.869	0.18	1.21	3.6	4.1	18.3
vs. East	207	35.7	14.3	.445	4.4	.391	4.1	.870	0.15	1.16	3.6	4.4	18.0
vs. West	89	36.1	15.1	.432	4.3	.380	4.3	.879	0.18	1.21	3.5	4.4	18.4
vs. Div.	108	35.2	13.9	.437	4.2	.379	4.1	.868	0.15	1.10	3.5	4.3	17.3
As Starter	295	35.9	14.6	.441	4.3	.388	4.2	.873	0.16	1.18	3.6	4.4	18.1
Off Bench	1	16.0	7.0	.286	0.0	—	0.0	—	0.00	0.00	1.0	4.0	4.0
In wins	139	35.1	14.0	.482	4.2	.426	4.6	.863	0.19	1.31	3.5	4.3	19.2
In losses	157	36.5	15.0	.407	4.5	.357	3.8	.883	0.13	1.06	3.6	4.5	17.2

	G	Min	FGA	FG%	3PA	3P%	FTA	FT%	Blk	Stl	Ast	Reb	Pts
Pre All-Star	144	35.5	14.3	.433	4.2	.402	4.1	.864	0.13	1.25	3.4	4.1	17.6
Post All-Star	102	37.1	15.4	.447	4.6	.384	4.4	.871	0.22	1.14	3.7	4.9	19.4
Oct/Nov	44	33.4	14.1	.453	3.8	.402	4.5	.859	0.16	1.20	3.2	3.9	18.2
December	44	36.6	14.1	.426	4.0	.421	3.8	.888	0.11	1.18	3.6	4.2	17.2
January	45	36.1	14.4	.425	4.2	.387	3.7	.837	0.09	1.31	3.5	3.9	17.0
February	47	35.8	14.3	.442	4.7	.391	4.2	.893	0.26	1.15	4.0	4.7	18.3
March	64	35.8	15.2	.437	4.5	.371	3.9	.900	0.13	1.20	3.3	4.7	18.5
Apr/May	52	37.0	14.7	.460	4.5	.371	4.9	.854	0.23	1.04	3.8	4.7	19.3
0 Days Rest	78	36.5	14.7	.455	4.5	.433	4.0	.846	0.14	1.03	3.5	4.0	18.7
1 Days Rest	156	35.4	14.4	.437	4.1	.378	4.1	.880	0.18	1.21	3.6	4.6	17.7
2 Days Rest	38	35.9	14.4	.410	4.4	.325	4.2	.870	0.13	1.21	3.5	4.4	16.9
3+ Days Rest	24	36.6	15.5	.464	4.8	.395	5.0	.909	0.17	1.46	3.7	4.5	20.9

John Amaechi

1999-2000 Per Game Averages

	G	Min	FGA	FG%	3PA	3P%	FTA	FT%	Blk	Stl	Ast	Reb	Pts
Total	80	21.1	8.8	.437	0.1	.167	3.6	.766	0.46	0.44	1.2	3.3	10.5
Home	40	21.2	9.5	.432	0.1	.000	3.7	.748	0.43	0.43	1.2	3.3	11.0
Road	40	21.0	8.0	.444	0.1	.250	3.6	.785	0.50	0.45	1.2	3.4	10.0
vs. Playoff	45	20.6	8.4	.392	0.1	.000	3.9	.736	0.40	0.31	1.1	3.4	9.4
vs. Non-Playoff	35	21.6	9.2	.491	0.1	.500	3.3	.812	0.54	0.60	1.3	3.3	11.8
vs. East	52	21.3	8.4	.428	0.1	.167	3.6	.762	0.46	0.35	1.2	3.4	9.9
vs. West	28	20.7	9.4	.452	0.0	—	3.8	.764	0.46	0.61	1.1	3.1	11.4
vs. Div.	25	22.5	9.2	.455	0.2	.250	3.2	.785	0.44	0.40	1.1	3.5	10.9
As Starter	53	22.7	9.8	.443	0.1	.200	3.6	.751	0.55	0.53	1.2	3.3	11.3
Off Bench	27	17.7	6.8	.421	0.0	.000	3.8	.794	0.30	0.26	1.1	3.4	8.7
In wins	39	22.8	9.6	.456	0.1	.500	4.3	.762	0.64	0.64	1.4	3.7	12.0
In losses	41	19.4	8.0	.416	0.1	.000	3.0	.772	0.29	0.24	1.0	3.0	9.0

	G	Min	FGA	FG%	3PA	3P%	FTA	FT%	Blk	Stl	Ast	Reb	Pts
Pre All-Star	48	18.7	7.7	.418	0.0	.000	3.4	.756	0.44	0.40	1.1	3.2	9.0
Post All-Star	32	24.6	10.3	.459	0.2	.200	4.0	.780	0.50	0.50	1.3	3.5	12.6
November	13	16.3	6.6	.395	0.1	.000	3.8	.820	0.15	0.23	1.2	3.2	8.4
December	14	19.1	6.9	.443	0.0	—	3.7	.769	0.43	0.29	0.9	3.6	9.0
January	17	18.2	8.2	.386	0.0	—	2.1	.750	0.53	0.59	1.1	2.6	7.9
February	11	24.7	11.1	.484	0.1	.000	4.9	.685	0.64	0.55	1.1	3.5	14.1
March	16	24.0	9.7	.510	0.1	.500	3.8	.783	0.56	0.50	1.5	2.9	12.9
April	9	26.7	11.1	.370	0.2	.000	4.3	.795	0.44	0.44	1.2	5.0	11.7
0 Days Rest	20	20.9	8.4	.419	0.1	1.000	4.3	.753	0.50	0.55	1.1	3.0	10.3
1 Days Rest	40	20.7	8.5	.422	0.1	.000	3.1	.792	0.55	0.43	1.2	3.4	9.7
2 Days Rest	10	24.0	10.3	.495	0.1	.000	3.7	.838	0.40	0.30	1.0	3.3	13.3
3+ Days Rest	10	20.0	8.9	.461	0.0	—	4.4	.659	0.10	0.40	1.4	3.9	11.1

Career (1995-96 thru 1999-2000)

	G	Min	FGA	FG%	3PA	3P%	FTA	FT%	Blk	Stl	Ast	Reb	Pts
Total	108	18.9	7.1	.435	0.1	.167	3.0	.747	0.44	0.38	1.0	2.9	8.5
Home	55	18.2	7.5	.433	0.0	.000	2.9	.741	0.42	0.38	1.0	2.9	8.6
Road	53	19.6	6.8	.437	0.1	.250	3.1	.753	0.47	0.38	1.0	2.9	8.3
vs. Playoff	58	19.2	7.3	.396	0.1	.000	3.3	.724	0.41	0.24	0.9	3.1	8.2
vs. Non-Playoff	50	18.5	6.9	.483	0.0	.500	2.6	.780	0.48	0.54	1.0	2.8	8.8
vs. East	74	19.1	6.8	.428	0.1	.167	3.0	.738	0.45	0.32	1.0	3.0	8.0
vs. West	34	18.4	7.9	.448	0.0	—	3.2	.764	0.44	0.50	0.9	2.8	9.5
vs. Div.	35	20.4	7.5	.462	0.1	.250	2.8	.753	0.43	0.31	0.9	3.1	9.0
As Starter	56	22.6	9.6	.439	0.1	.200	3.4	.754	0.55	0.50	1.2	3.2	11.0
Off Bench	52	14.9	4.5	.426	0.0	.000	2.6	.737	0.33	0.25	0.7	2.6	5.7
In wins	54	19.5	7.4	.454	0.0	.500	3.4	.738	0.57	0.56	1.1	3.1	9.2
In losses	54	18.3	6.9	.415	0.1	.000	2.6	.759	0.31	0.20	0.8	2.8	7.7

	G	Min	FGA	FG%	3PA	3P%	FTA	FT%	Blk	Stl	Ast	Reb	Pts
Pre All-Star	74	16.7	5.9	.415	0.0	.000	2.6	.724	0.42	0.34	0.9	2.8	6.8
Post All-Star	34	23.6	9.8	.461	0.1	.200	3.8	.781	0.50	0.47	1.2	3.3	12.0
Oct/Nov	27	16.7	5.1	.399	0.0	.000	2.7	.730	0.33	0.22	0.8	2.8	6.1
December	23	16.0	4.8	.436	0.0	—	2.6	.750	0.39	0.30	0.7	2.9	6.1
January	20	15.7	7.0	.386	0.0	—	1.8	.750	0.45	0.50	1.0	2.2	6.8
February	11	24.7	11.1	.484	0.1	.000	4.9	.685	0.64	0.55	1.1	3.5	14.1
March	16	24.0	9.7	.510	0.1	.500	3.8	.783	0.56	0.50	1.5	2.9	12.9
Apr/May	11	23.2	9.5	.381	0.2	.000	3.6	.800	0.45	0.36	1.1	4.2	10.2
0 Days Rest	26	19.9	7.4	.401	0.0	1.000	3.7	.711	0.50	0.50	1.0	3.0	8.6
1 Days Rest	48	19.7	7.6	.427	0.1	.000	2.9	.774	0.52	0.44	1.1	3.2	8.7
2 Days Rest	20	16.7	5.7	.496	0.1	.000	2.3	.826	0.35	0.15	0.7	2.1	7.5
3+ Days Rest	14	17.4	7.1	.460	0.0	—	3.1	.659	0.21	0.29	1.0	3.3	8.6

Derek Anderson
Los Angeles Clippers — Guard

1999-2000 Per Game Averages

	G	Min	FGA	FG%	3PA	3P%	FTA	FT%	Blk	Stl	Ast	Reb	Pts		G	Min	FGA	FG%	3PA	3P%	FTA	FT%	Blk	Stl	Ast	Reb	Pts
Total	64	34.4	13.4	.438	2.8	.309	4.8	.877	0.17	1.41	3.4	4.0	16.9	Pre All-Star	38	35.4	13.4	.454	3.0	.289	4.7	.865	0.24	1.18	3.4	4.3	17.1
Home	38	35.1	13.8	.442	2.7	.298	5.6	.868	0.13	1.47	3.5	4.3	17.8	Post All-Star	26	32.9	13.5	.416	2.5	.344	5.0	.893	0.08	1.73	3.5	3.6	16.6
Road	26	33.3	13.0	.433	2.8	.324	3.7	.897	0.23	1.31	3.3	3.7	15.5	November	11	37.5	14.7	.426	3.4	.324	6.9	.895	0.18	0.73	3.3	6.0	19.8
vs. Playoff	40	33.4	13.0	.439	2.6	.350	4.4	.903	0.15	1.23	3.6	4.2	16.3	December	7	35.4	13.0	.418	3.0	.286	3.6	.800	0.14	1.29	5.4	4.4	14.6
vs. Non-Playoff	24	36.0	14.2	.437	3.1	.253	5.5	.842	0.21	1.71	3.2	3.8	17.9	January	14	33.6	12.8	.514	2.6	.433	4.1	.842	0.36	1.14	3.0	2.9	17.4
vs. East	25	35.2	13.1	.409	2.4	.311	5.2	.907	0.20	1.64	3.9	3.9	16.2	February	13	32.5	12.0	.385	2.4	.290	3.5	.911	0.15	1.77	2.4	4.5	13.1
vs. West	39	33.8	13.6	.457	3.0	.308	4.6	.856	0.15	1.26	3.1	4.1	17.3	March	14	35.7	13.7	.417	2.7	.263	5.8	.877	0.07	1.93	4.1	3.4	17.2
vs. Div.	17	32.4	12.6	.444	2.7	.283	4.5	.883	0.06	1.24	2.9	3.8	15.9	April	5	29.8	16.0	.475	3.0	.400	5.0	.920	0.00	1.40	3.0	2.8	21.0
As Starter	58	35.3	13.7	.436	2.8	.301	4.8	.884	0.17	1.50	3.6	4.1	17.0	0 Days Rest	14	32.0	11.4	.444	2.9	.300	2.6	.892	0.21	1.71	2.4	3.4	13.4
Off Bench	6	25.2	10.7	.469	2.5	.400	5.5	.818	0.17	0.50	2.0	3.2	15.5	1 Days Rest	29	35.7	14.0	.457	2.7	.321	5.8	.893	0.24	1.31	4.1	4.8	18.4
In wins	7	38.7	13.1	.424	2.4	.471	7.3	.784	0.29	1.57	4.3	4.0	18.0	2 Days Rest	10	36.0	14.2	.415	2.7	.259	4.4	.795	0.10	1.70	2.5	5.1	16.0
In losses	57	33.9	13.5	.440	2.8	.292	4.5	.895	0.16	1.39	3.3	4.0	16.7	3+ Days Rest	11	32.5	13.9	.405	3.0	.333	5.4	.881	0.00	1.00	2.8	3.6	17.0

Career (1997-98 thru 1999-2000)

	G	Min	FGA	FG%	3PA	3P%	FTA	FT%	Blk	Stl	Ast	Reb	Pts		G	Min	FGA	FG%	3PA	3P%	FTA	FT%	Blk	Stl	Ast	Reb	Pts
Total	168	29.9	10.5	.421	2.0	.281	4.7	.867	0.17	1.33	3.5	3.3	13.4	Pre All-Star	81	32.5	11.1	.430	2.1	.246	5.0	.876	0.25	1.30	3.6	3.7	14.4
Home	90	31.0	10.8	.448	1.9	.302	5.1	.868	0.20	1.30	3.9	3.5	14.7	Post All-Star	49	28.8	11.2	.420	1.9	.330	4.5	.874	0.08	1.45	3.2	3.0	14.0
Road	78	28.6	10.1	.387	2.0	.258	4.2	.865	0.13	1.37	3.1	3.1	12.0	Oct/Nov	26	35.0	10.9	.398	2.1	.255	5.6	.883	0.19	1.00	3.7	4.6	14.2
vs. Playoff	100	30.2	10.8	.424	2.0	.308	4.4	.889	0.16	1.22	3.7	3.3	13.7	December	20	31.9	10.8	.442	2.0	.256	4.8	.896	0.15	1.35	4.1	3.8	14.3
vs. Non-Playoff	68	29.3	10.0	.416	2.0	.243	5.1	.839	0.18	1.50	3.3	3.3	13.1	January	29	29.9	11.1	.453	2.0	.263	4.9	.851	0.38	1.38	3.3	2.8	14.7
vs. East	98	29.5	9.6	.405	1.7	.247	4.7	.862	0.16	1.36	3.8	3.2	12.2	February	24	31.5	10.3	.415	1.5	.297	4.5	.852	0.13	1.63	3.2	4.0	12.9
vs. West	70	30.3	11.7	.439	2.4	.315	4.7	.873	0.17	1.30	3.2	3.5	15.2	March	42	28.5	10.4	.402	2.2	.283	4.5	.862	0.10	1.60	3.6	2.7	12.8
vs. Div.	52	28.8	9.7	.414	1.9	.247	3.9	.832	0.12	1.15	3.4	3.2	11.7	Apr/May	27	24.2	9.5	.426	1.9	.333	4.1	.864	0.07	0.93	3.4	2.6	12.2
As Starter	84	35.1	12.3	.423	2.5	.267	5.1	.875	0.18	1.52	4.1	4.2	15.5	0 Days Rest	41	30.0	9.7	.409	2.0	.268	3.8	.885	0.17	1.44	3.5	3.3	11.8
Off Bench	84	24.6	8.6	.419	1.4	.306	4.3	.857	0.15	1.14	3.0	2.4	11.4	1 Days Rest	76	30.2	10.8	.430	1.9	.266	5.1	.871	0.17	1.26	3.9	3.4	14.2
In wins	63	27.4	8.5	.422	1.3	.345	5.2	.835	0.19	1.33	3.8	2.8	12.0	2 Days Rest	29	30.1	10.5	.421	2.1	.283	4.5	.809	0.21	1.38	2.8	3.2	13.1
In losses	105	31.3	11.6	.421	2.4	.259	4.4	.889	0.15	1.33	3.4	3.6	14.3	3+ Days Rest	22	28.3	11.0	.412	2.1	.348	5.1	.894	0.09	1.32	3.2	3.0	14.4

Kenny Anderson
Boston Celtics — Guard

1999-2000 Per Game Averages

	G	Min	FGA	FG%	3PA	3P%	FTA	FT%	Blk	Stl	Ast	Reb	Pts		G	Min	FGA	FG%	3PA	3P%	FTA	FT%	Blk	Stl	Ast	Reb	Pts
Total	82	31.6	12.0	.440	2.7	.386	3.1	.775	0.10	1.70	5.1	2.7	14.0	Pre All-Star	49	31.8	12.3	.436	2.3	.339	3.3	.775	0.10	1.53	5.1	2.7	14.1
Home	41	31.5	12.2	.438	3.0	.413	3.1	.767	0.10	1.80	5.4	3.0	14.3	Post All-Star	33	31.3	11.6	.446	3.2	.438	2.8	.774	0.09	1.94	5.2	2.8	13.9
Road	41	31.8	11.9	.442	2.4	.354	3.0	.782	0.10	1.59	4.8	2.5	13.7	November	14	29.0	11.4	.438	2.2	.419	4.1	.772	0.00	1.43	4.1	2.0	14.1
vs. Playoff	46	31.9	12.3	.444	2.8	.417	3.4	.753	0.11	1.52	5.1	2.8	14.7	December	14	33.0	13.2	.476	2.1	.267	2.8	.795	0.36	1.43	5.3	2.6	15.4
vs. Non-Playoff	36	31.2	11.6	.434	2.6	.344	2.6	.811	0.08	1.92	5.2	2.7	13.1	January	15	33.0	11.6	.402	2.6	.333	3.0	.711	0.00	1.73	5.3	3.7	12.3
vs. East	54	30.6	11.9	.432	3.1	.386	3.1	.766	0.02	1.59	4.7	2.7	13.8	February	13	33.2	13.4	.431	2.2	.393	4.1	.792	0.15	1.92	6.2	2.0	15.6
vs. West	28	33.5	12.3	.455	1.9	.389	3.1	.791	0.25	1.89	6.0	2.9	14.4	March	16	30.8	10.5	.405	2.4	.421	1.9	.710	0.06	1.75	5.4	3.1	10.9
vs. Div.	24	30.6	11.3	.433	3.2	.408	2.4	.793	0.00	1.63	4.8	2.3	13.0	April	10	30.7	12.5	.504	5.4	.444	2.8	.893	0.00	2.00	4.2	3.1	17.5
As Starter	82	31.6	12.0	.440	2.7	.386	3.1	.775	0.10	1.70	5.1	2.7	14.0	0 Days Rest	22	33.3	12.9	.442	3.0	.292	3.8	.762	0.14	1.64	5.2	2.4	15.1
Off Bench	0	—	—	—	—	—	—	—	—	—	—	—	—	1 Days Rest	42	31.0	11.4	.434	2.7	.411	2.9	.750	0.12	1.71	5.2	3.0	13.1
In wins	35	30.5	11.5	.460	2.9	.436	3.0	.755	0.03	1.86	5.2	3.1	14.1	2 Days Rest	9	31.8	13.2	.395	2.9	.500	1.8	.875	0.00	2.22	5.1	2.8	13.4
In losses	47	32.4	12.4	.426	2.5	.345	3.1	.789	0.15	1.57	5.1	2.4	13.9	3+ Days Rest	9	30.3	11.9	.514	1.9	.412	3.7	.848	0.00	1.22	4.4	2.7	16.1

Last Five Seasons

	G	Min	FGA	FG%	3PA	3P%	FTA	FT%	Blk	Stl	Ast	Reb	Pts		G	Min	FGA	FG%	3PA	3P%	FTA	FT%	Blk	Stl	Ast	Reb	Pts
Total	328	33.2	12.2	.426	3.1	.363	4.0	.777	0.12	1.62	6.5	3.3	14.6	Pre All-Star	179	34.2	12.6	.410	3.2	.361	4.4	.778	0.15	1.55	6.4	3.3	14.9
Home	162	33.0	11.9	.429	3.2	.379	4.0	.792	0.10	1.58	6.7	3.3	14.5	Post All-Star	115	32.7	12.0	.444	3.7	.371	3.7	.764	0.10	1.92	6.8	3.2	14.9
Road	166	33.4	12.4	.422	3.1	.346	4.1	.764	0.14	1.66	6.3	3.2	14.7	Oct/Nov	53	32.2	12.2	.410	3.5	.393	5.1	.770	0.08	1.70	5.6	3.1	15.2
vs. Playoff	184	33.5	12.3	.418	3.2	.371	4.0	.773	0.09	1.46	6.3	3.1	14.6	December	53	33.1	13.0	.420	3.4	.300	4.3	.827	0.21	1.42	6.2	3.3	15.5
vs. Non-Playoff	144	32.9	11.9	.435	3.1	.353	4.0	.784	0.16	1.83	6.7	3.5	14.6	January	58	37.0	12.4	.400	2.8	.366	4.1	.759	0.17	1.57	7.2	3.7	14.1
vs. East	187	32.5	11.7	.420	2.9	.351	3.9	.767	0.12	1.43	6.3	3.2	13.9	February	58	34.0	13.0	.430	3.2	.386	4.4	.744	0.14	1.90	7.5	3.2	15.7
vs. West	141	34.1	12.8	.432	3.4	.376	4.1	.791	0.13	1.88	6.6	3.3	15.6	March	68	31.4	10.7	.453	2.5	.333	3.3	.755	0.06	1.47	6.2	3.0	12.9
vs. Div.	100	32.5	11.8	.420	3.3	.383	3.9	.791	0.07	1.62	5.6	3.3	14.3	Apr/May	38	31.0	11.9	.443	3.9	.400	3.3	.843	0.08	1.74	5.8	3.3	14.9
As Starter	316	33.6	12.3	.427	3.2	.365	4.0	.781	0.13	1.65	6.6	3.3	14.8	0 Days Rest	82	34.1	12.6	.431	3.0	.316	4.6	.797	0.12	1.60	6.4	3.4	15.5
Off Bench	12	22.3	8.8	.358	2.9	.255	4.5	.704	0.00	0.83	3.0	2.3	10.1	1 Days Rest	162	33.4	12.0	.423	3.2	.362	4.0	.753	0.12	1.59	6.6	3.2	14.2
In wins	161	33.3	12.1	.447	3.5	.397	4.3	.795	0.11	1.76	6.9	3.5	15.6	2 Days Rest	45	32.9	12.5	.438	3.4	.450	3.3	.860	0.16	1.71	5.9	3.1	15.3
In losses	167	33.1	12.2	.405	2.8	.321	3.7	.758	0.13	1.49	6.0	3.0	13.6	3+ Days Rest	39	30.9	11.6	.408	2.8	.352	4.0	.752	0.10	1.69	6.4	3.2	13.5

Nick Anderson
Sacramento Kings — Guard-Forward

1999-2000 Per Game Averages

	G	Min	FGA	FG%	3PA	3P%	FTA	FT%	Blk	Stl	Ast	Reb	Pts		G	Min	FGA	FG%	3PA	3P%	FTA	FT%	Blk	Stl	Ast	Reb	Pts
Total	72	29.1	10.9	.391	5.5	.332	1.1	.487	0.22	1.31	1.7	4.7	10.8	Pre All-Star	47	29.2	10.9	.389	5.7	.337	0.8	.486	0.23	1.45	1.7	4.7	10.8
Home	37	29.3	11.4	.408	6.0	.359	1.2	.442	0.24	1.19	1.8	4.9	12.0	Post All-Star	25	28.9	10.8	.396	5.2	.323	1.6	.487	0.20	1.04	1.7	4.8	11.0
Road	35	28.8	10.3	.372	5.0	.299	0.9	.545	0.20	1.43	1.7	4.5	9.7	November	12	29.5	11.1	.346	6.3	.355	0.3	.250	0.33	1.25	2.0	5.6	10.0
vs. Playoff	37	30.3	11.6	.383	5.3	.333	1.4	.480	0.22	1.16	1.6	5.1	11.3	December	14	28.1	8.4	.356	4.7	.242	0.6	.333	0.14	1.64	1.1	4.2	7.4
vs. Non-Playoff	35	27.8	10.1	.401	5.8	.332	0.7	.500	0.23	1.46	1.8	4.3	10.4	January	16	30.6	12.4	.442	7.0	.400	1.4	.591	0.25	1.63	1.7	4.8	14.2
vs. East	29	28.9	10.9	.444	5.7	.361	0.8	.583	0.21	1.52	1.8	4.5	12.2	February	11	26.7	11.1	.426	5.5	.333	1.0	.545	0.27	0.82	2.2	3.4	11.8
vs. West	43	29.2	10.9	.355	5.4	.312	1.2	.442	0.23	1.16	1.7	4.8	9.9	March	11	29.5	11.3	.371	5.6	.306	0.7	.125	0.09	0.73	1.5	5.3	10.2
vs. Div.	19	28.7	11.0	.349	5.5	.260	1.7	.438	0.26	1.11	1.5	4.8	9.8	April	8	29.8	10.8	.372	4.8	.316	2.8	.591	0.25	1.63	1.9	5.3	11.1
As Starter	72	29.1	10.9	.391	5.5	.332	1.1	.487	0.22	1.31	1.7	4.7	10.8	0 Days Rest	13	29.1	11.8	.377	6.3	.329	1.0	.692	0.46	1.23	1.5	4.9	11.7
Off Bench	0	—												1 Days Rest	42	29.8	11.3	.389	5.6	.321	1.2	.388	0.17	1.31	1.6	5.1	11.1
In wins	41	28.8	11.0	.406	5.9	.342	1.1	.523	0.20	1.32	1.9	4.7	11.5	2 Days Rest	9	27.8	9.3	.440	4.4	.400	0.9	.750	0.22	2.00	1.8	2.6	10.7
In losses	31	29.5	10.6	.371	5.1	.318	1.0	.438	0.26	1.29	1.5	4.8	9.9	3+ Days Rest	8	26.6	8.6	.377	4.8	.342	0.8	.500	0.13	0.63	2.3	4.6	8.5

Last Five Seasons

	G	Min	FGA	FG%	3PA	3P%	FTA	FT%	Blk	Stl	Ast	Reb	Pts		G	Min	FGA	FG%	3PA	3P%	FTA	FT%	Blk	Stl	Ast	Reb	Pts
Total	317	32.4	12.0	.418	5.4	.358	2.4	.606	0.42	1.49	2.5	5.1	13.4	Pre All-Star	154	31.2	11.0	.409	5.3	.358	1.9	.573	0.51	1.44	2.4	5.1	11.9
Home	163	33.1	12.6	.431	5.7	.365	2.8	.639	0.44	1.51	2.5	5.5	14.7	Post All-Star	116	33.3	12.7	.438	5.5	.361	2.8	.632	0.33	1.59	2.8	4.9	14.9
Road	154	31.5	11.4	.403	5.1	.348	2.1	.559	0.39	1.46	2.5	4.8	12.1	Oct/Nov	54	31.9	12.0	.402	5.2	.346	2.4	.589	0.59	1.37	2.1	5.6	12.9
vs. Playoff	167	33.6	12.5	.408	5.6	.349	2.6	.631	0.42	1.40	2.2	5.2	13.8	December	34	28.7	9.3	.401	4.6	.304	1.9	.587	0.29	1.68	2.0	4.2	10.0
vs. Non-Playoff	150	30.9	11.4	.430	5.2	.368	2.2	.573	0.41	1.59	2.8	5.1	13.0	January	51	32.0	10.4	.408	5.2	.375	1.5	.532	0.59	1.39	2.9	5.2	11.3
vs. East	199	33.3	12.5	.421	5.5	.356	2.7	.627	0.47	1.49	2.6	5.4	14.2	February	62	34.5	13.6	.457	6.1	.401	2.7	.661	0.40	1.52	2.9	4.9	16.6
vs. West	118	30.7	11.2	.412	5.3	.359	1.9	.554	0.33	1.47	2.4	4.7	12.2	March	63	32.7	12.9	.408	5.8	.342	2.7	.581	0.21	1.46	2.5	5.0	14.0
vs. Div.	98	33.1	12.8	.414	5.7	.347	2.9	.589	0.52	1.65	2.8	5.7	14.3	Apr/May	53	32.6	12.3	.413	5.2	.344	3.2	.620	0.42	1.57	2.4	5.7	14.0
As Starter	293	33.4	12.4	.421	5.6	.359	2.5	.603	0.42	1.55	2.6	5.3	14.0	0 Days Rest	70	32.1	12.1	.390	5.7	.349	2.4	.588	0.47	1.33	2.3	5.2	12.8
Off Bench	24	19.2	7.0	.355	3.5	.321	1.0	.320	0.38	0.71	1.2	3.7	6.5	1 Days Rest	174	32.9	12.3	.422	5.6	.361	2.3	.597	0.39	1.49	2.5	5.4	13.8
In wins	197	32.4	12.0	.434	5.5	.371	2.6	.631	0.37	1.59	2.9	5.3	14.1	2 Days Rest	37	31.9	10.1	.444	4.3	.390	2.8	.648	0.46	1.81	3.4	4.0	12.4
In losses	120	32.3	12.0	.392	5.4	.335	2.1	.554	0.49	1.32	1.8	4.8	12.3	3+ Days Rest	36	31.0	12.4	.427	5.5	.333	2.5	.629	0.42	1.44	2.2	4.8	14.0

Shandon Anderson
Houston Rockets — Forward

1999-2000 Per Game Averages

	G	Min	FGA	FG%	3PA	3P%	FTA	FT%	Blk	Stl	Ast	Reb	Pts		G	Min	FGA	FG%	3PA	3P%	FTA	FT%	Blk	Stl	Ast	Reb	Pts
Total	82	32.9	9.5	.473	2.7	.351	3.1	.767	0.39	1.17	2.9	4.7	12.3	Pre All-Star	50	31.2	8.8	.455	2.2	.339	2.4	.731	0.44	1.22	2.9	4.6	10.5
Home	41	33.2	9.9	.466	2.9	.367	2.5	.777	0.37	1.15	3.2	5.0	12.2	Post All-Star	32	35.7	10.5	.497	3.5	.363	4.2	.799	0.31	1.09	2.9	4.8	15.1
Road	41	32.6	9.1	.481	2.6	.333	3.7	.760	0.41	1.20	2.7	4.4	12.4	November	15	26.4	7.4	.459	1.9	.321	0.9	.692	0.33	1.07	2.6	3.0	8.0
vs. Playoff	48	33.1	9.4	.480	2.8	.346	3.5	.777	0.38	1.13	2.8	4.7	12.7	December	15	31.5	8.4	.476	2.7	.366	2.2	.697	0.53	0.93	3.1	4.3	10.5
vs. Non-Playoff	34	32.6	9.6	.463	2.6	.360	2.6	.747	0.41	1.24	3.1	4.6	11.8	January	14	35.1	9.5	.451	2.3	.375	3.0	.762	0.57	1.50	3.1	6.6	11.7
vs. East	30	32.0	9.3	.464	2.7	.370	3.0	.747	0.30	0.97	3.1	4.2	11.9	February	13	32.5	10.5	.416	2.1	.148	4.4	.789	0.15	1.46	2.9	4.5	12.5
vs. West	52	33.5	9.6	.478	2.8	.340	3.1	.778	0.44	1.29	2.8	4.9	12.6	March	15	35.1	9.8	.524	3.5	.453	3.9	.810	0.27	1.13	3.3	4.4	15.0
vs. Div.	24	32.5	8.4	.413	2.6	.306	3.8	.744	0.46	1.00	2.7	5.2	10.5	April	10	39.1	12.4	.508	4.4	.341	5.0	.760	0.50	0.90	2.3	5.8	17.9
As Starter	82	32.9	9.5	.473	2.7	.351	3.1	.767	0.39	1.17	2.9	4.7	12.3	0 Days Rest	17	32.8	9.6	.470	2.6	.400	3.4	.789	0.41	1.00	2.8	4.3	12.8
Off Bench	0	—												1 Days Rest	45	33.6	9.6	.482	2.7	.344	3.5	.753	0.40	1.33	3.0	5.1	12.9
In wins	34	35.5	11.1	.507	3.1	.383	3.3	.779	0.38	1.50	3.4	5.6	15.0	2 Days Rest	17	31.5	8.4	.462	2.7	.304	1.6	.750	0.35	0.88	2.6	4.2	9.8
In losses	48	31.1	8.4	.441	2.5	.322	2.9	.757	0.40	0.94	2.5	4.0	10.4	3+ Days Rest	3	32.0	12.3	.432	4.0	.417	3.3	.900	0.33	1.33	3.7	3.7	15.3

Career (1996-97 thru 1999-2000)

	G	Min	FGA	FG%	3PA	3P%	FTA	FT%	Blk	Stl	Ast	Reb	Pts		G	Min	FGA	FG%	3PA	3P%	FTA	FT%	Blk	Stl	Ast	Reb	Pts
Total	279	23.1	7.0	.483	1.2	.359	2.4	.736	0.24	0.82	1.6	3.3	9.0	Pre All-Star	126	22.8	6.7	.492	1.1	.357	2.2	.715	0.25	0.90	1.7	3.4	8.6
Home	143	22.8	6.9	.489	1.3	.380	2.2	.759	0.25	0.76	1.6	3.4	9.0	Post All-Star	103	24.2	7.2	.491	1.6	.366	2.5	.769	0.25	0.74	1.6	3.5	9.6
Road	136	23.4	7.1	.476	1.2	.337	2.5	.714	0.24	0.88	1.5	3.2	9.0	Oct/Nov	41	20.7	6.4	.451	1.0	.381	1.7	.623	0.20	0.71	1.5	3.4	7.2
vs. Playoff	151	22.8	6.8	.462	1.2	.335	2.4	.744	0.22	0.76	1.5	3.1	8.5	December	45	21.7	6.0	.520	1.0	.348	1.8	.688	0.29	0.71	1.5	3.0	7.8
vs. Non-Playoff	128	23.5	7.3	.505	1.3	.388	2.3	.725	0.27	0.88	1.7	3.5	9.5	January	28	27.0	7.7	.516	1.4	.385	2.8	.782	0.36	1.29	2.1	4.3	10.6
vs. East	89	22.8	6.7	.509	1.3	.366	2.3	.749	0.20	0.81	1.6	3.1	9.0	February	49	22.8	7.6	.468	1.2	.310	3.1	.781	0.20	1.00	1.5	3.2	9.8
vs. West	190	23.2	7.2	.471	1.2	.356	2.4	.730	0.26	0.82	1.5	3.4	8.9	March	63	23.3	6.8	.497	1.4	.395	2.3	.733	0.25	0.67	1.6	3.3	9.0
vs. Div.	84	22.8	6.9	.441	1.2	.354	2.7	.731	0.30	0.71	1.6	3.5	8.4	Apr/May	53	24.0	7.7	.461	1.4	.338	2.6	.746	0.21	0.75	1.3	3.2	9.5
As Starter	86	32.7	9.5	.470	2.7	.349	3.1	.764	0.41	1.15	2.9	4.6	12.2	0 Days Rest	67	22.8	7.1	.456	1.1	.408	2.5	.712	0.16	0.81	1.5	3.2	8.7
Off Bench	193	18.8	5.9	.492	0.6	.379	2.1	.717	0.17	0.67	0.9	2.7	7.5	1 Days Rest	152	23.2	6.9	.484	1.2	.360	2.4	.743	0.26	0.84	1.7	3.2	8.8
In wins	189	21.9	6.8	.500	1.1	.395	2.3	.741	0.21	0.81	1.5	3.2	8.9	2 Days Rest	42	24.1	7.1	.507	1.3	.255	2.0	.762	0.40	0.76	1.5	3.5	9.0
In losses	90	25.6	7.4	.451	1.6	.310	2.6	.725	0.31	0.83	1.7	3.5	9.1	3+ Days Rest	18	20.7	7.7	.518	1.6	.429	2.8	.720	0.06	0.78	1.1	3.7	10.7

Greg Anthony

1999-2000 Per Game Averages

	G	Min	FGA	FG%	3PA	3P%	FTA	FT%	Blk	Stl	Ast	Reb	Pts
Total	82	18.9	5.1	.406	2.8	.378	1.4	.772	0.11	0.72	2.5	1.6	6.3
Home	41	19.8	5.2	.387	3.0	.358	1.5	.742	0.10	0.59	2.9	1.7	6.2
Road	41	18.0	5.0	.426	2.7	.400	1.3	.808	0.12	0.85	2.2	1.5	6.3
vs. Playoff	44	18.0	4.6	.401	2.5	.396	1.9	.747	0.05	0.75	2.3	1.5	6.1
vs. Non-Playoff	38	19.8	5.6	.411	3.2	.361	0.8	.839	0.18	0.68	2.8	1.8	6.5
vs. East	30	19.5	5.7	.409	3.2	.354	1.6	.750	0.07	0.83	2.9	1.7	7.0
vs. West	52	18.5	4.7	.404	2.6	.394	1.3	.788	0.13	0.65	2.3	1.6	5.8
vs. Div.	24	16.9	4.1	.414	2.3	.407	1.0	.917	0.04	0.71	2.1	1.2	5.3
As Starter	3	35.0	11.7	.371	5.7	.412	2.7	.875	0.00	2.33	5.7	5.0	13.3
Off Bench	79	18.3	4.8	.409	2.7	.375	1.3	.764	0.11	0.66	2.4	1.5	6.0
In wins	59	18.9	4.9	.441	2.7	.413	1.4	.800	0.10	0.80	2.7	1.6	6.6
In losses	23	18.7	5.6	.328	3.2	.301	1.3	.690	0.13	0.52	2.0	1.6	5.5

	G	Min	FGA	FG%	3PA	3P%	FTA	FT%	Blk	Stl	Ast	Reb	Pts
Pre All-Star	49	19.3	5.7	.411	3.1	.347	1.7	.776	0.08	0.86	2.8	1.7	7.1
Post All-Star	33	18.3	4.1	.397	2.5	.434	0.9	.759	0.15	0.52	2.2	1.5	5.0
November	16	18.1	5.5	.455	2.8	.318	2.3	.919	0.13	0.88	2.7	1.3	8.0
December	13	21.7	7.1	.391	4.3	.375	2.2	.714	0.00	1.15	3.6	1.6	8.7
January	14	17.8	4.6	.354	2.4	.382	1.4	.579	0.07	0.64	2.1	2.1	5.0
February	14	18.5	4.7	.424	2.1	.333	0.8	.818	0.14	0.71	2.2	2.1	5.4
March	14	18.3	4.1	.431	2.6	.528	0.7	.600	0.14	0.29	1.9	1.3	5.4
April	11	19.3	4.3	.362	3.0	.333	0.8	.889	0.18	0.64	2.7	1.5	4.8
0 Days Rest	22	20.0	6.0	.450	3.2	.386	2.0	.884	0.05	0.77	2.7	1.8	8.3
1 Days Rest	39	17.7	4.3	.383	2.5	.398	1.2	.766	0.13	0.62	2.3	1.3	5.2
2 Days Rest	15	20.1	6.1	.370	3.2	.333	1.5	.591	0.13	0.67	2.3	2.2	6.5
3+ Days Rest	6	19.7	4.3	.462	2.8	.353	0.3	.500	0.17	1.33	4.3	2.0	5.2

Last Five Seasons

	G	Min	FGA	FG%	3PA	3P%	FTA	FT%	Blk	Stl	Ast	Reb	Pts
Total	346	21.2	6.7	.411	3.0	.371	2.2	.741	0.09	1.25	4.0	1.9	8.2
Home	172	21.2	6.8	.405	3.0	.373	2.4	.731	0.09	1.30	4.3	1.8	8.4
Road	174	21.2	6.5	.416	2.9	.370	2.0	.754	0.08	1.21	3.7	2.1	8.0
vs. Playoff	187	21.1	6.4	.417	2.8	.381	2.2	.741	0.04	1.26	3.9	1.9	8.1
vs. Non-Playoff	159	21.3	6.9	.403	3.2	.361	2.2	.742	0.14	1.25	4.2	2.0	8.3
vs. East	120	22.5	7.3	.415	3.1	.363	2.5	.728	0.08	1.28	4.5	1.9	9.0
vs. West	226	20.5	6.3	.408	2.9	.376	2.0	.750	0.09	1.24	3.8	1.9	7.8
vs. Div.	106	19.4	6.1	.392	2.8	.339	1.8	.758	0.08	1.26	3.4	1.9	7.0
As Starter	115	31.4	10.4	.406	4.0	.348	3.8	.766	0.13	1.90	6.9	2.9	12.7
Off Bench	231	16.1	4.8	.416	2.4	.391	1.4	.709	0.06	0.94	2.6	1.4	5.9
In wins	176	17.6	5.3	.439	2.5	.416	1.9	.740	0.08	1.14	3.1	1.6	7.1
In losses	170	24.9	8.1	.391	3.5	.338	2.5	.742	0.09	1.38	5.0	2.2	9.3

	G	Min	FGA	FG%	3PA	3P%	FTA	FT%	Blk	Stl	Ast	Reb	Pts
Pre All-Star	175	22.0	7.3	.417	3.0	.358	2.6	.747	0.09	1.22	4.5	2.0	9.1
Post All-Star	121	22.2	6.5	.399	3.2	.383	1.8	.748	0.09	1.28	4.2	2.0	7.7
Oct/Nov	64	22.8	7.4	.435	2.7	.339	3.0	.764	0.08	1.44	4.5	2.2	9.6
December	38	19.3	6.8	.411	2.8	.358	2.3	.685	0.08	0.74	3.9	1.6	8.2
January	59	22.8	7.5	.405	3.3	.381	2.7	.758	0.08	1.29	4.9	2.2	9.4
February	58	21.9	6.6	.416	3.0	.362	1.8	.804	0.10	1.47	4.1	1.9	8.1
March	71	20.6	6.0	.399	2.8	.412	1.7	.702	0.07	1.25	3.6	1.7	7.2
Apr/May	56	18.9	5.7	.392	3.2	.363	1.6	.700	0.11	1.14	3.1	1.9	6.8
0 Days Rest	84	21.5	7.1	.447	3.2	.368	2.3	.777	0.05	1.36	3.8	1.8	9.3
1 Days Rest	177	21.4	6.7	.409	3.0	.385	2.2	.731	0.10	1.26	4.2	2.1	8.2
2 Days Rest	50	20.3	6.2	.345	2.5	.323	2.0	.710	0.10	1.06	3.8	2.0	6.5
3+ Days Rest	35	20.5	6.1	.413	2.9	.369	2.1	.747	0.09	1.26	4.1	1.4	7.7

Darrell Armstrong

1999-2000 Per Game Averages

	G	Min	FGA	FG%	3PA	3P%	FTA	FT%	Blk	Stl	Ast	Reb	Pts
Total	82	31.6	13.6	.433	4.9	.340	3.0	.911	0.11	2.06	6.1	3.3	16.2
Home	41	31.0	13.9	.454	5.1	.359	3.1	.922	0.12	2.34	6.6	3.3	17.3
Road	41	32.2	13.4	.410	4.7	.320	2.9	.899	0.10	1.78	5.6	3.3	15.1
vs. Playoff	47	31.9	13.6	.412	5.0	.300	2.9	.920	0.09	2.21	5.9	3.3	15.4
vs. Non-Playoff	35	31.2	13.7	.459	4.7	.398	3.1	.899	0.14	1.86	6.4	3.3	17.3
vs. East	54	31.1	13.0	.420	4.7	.312	3.2	.914	0.15	1.96	5.9	3.4	15.3
vs. West	28	32.5	14.9	.454	5.4	.387	2.6	.904	0.04	2.25	6.4	3.1	17.9
vs. Div.	25	32.0	13.6	.408	5.0	.288	2.8	.930	0.20	1.72	6.0	3.8	15.2
As Starter	82	31.6	13.6	.433	4.9	.340	3.0	.911	0.11	2.06	6.1	3.3	16.2
Off Bench	0	—	—	—	—	—	—	—	—	—	—	—	—
In wins	41	31.0	12.9	.446	4.7	.351	3.5	.910	0.10	2.22	6.9	3.1	16.3
In losses	41	32.2	14.4	.421	5.1	.330	2.5	.913	0.12	1.90	5.4	3.5	16.1

	G	Min	FGA	FG%	3PA	3P%	FTA	FT%	Blk	Stl	Ast	Reb	Pts
Pre All-Star	50	31.9	13.7	.428	4.8	.324	3.2	.906	0.10	2.04	6.7	3.3	16.2
Post All-Star	32	31.2	13.6	.439	5.1	.364	2.8	.920	0.13	2.09	5.2	3.2	16.3
November	15	33.3	16.0	.450	5.7	.329	4.1	.902	0.07	2.13	7.5	4.3	19.9
December	14	31.3	13.8	.383	5.6	.295	3.1	.864	0.00	1.93	6.9	2.6	14.9
January	17	31.8	12.8	.454	3.9	.379	2.2	.974	0.24	2.00	5.5	3.2	15.3
February	11	30.8	11.6	.461	4.7	.346	2.4	.885	0.00	2.09	6.0	2.5	14.5
March	16	29.8	12.9	.435	4.7	.387	2.9	.872	0.19	2.25	5.3	2.9	15.6
April	9	32.9	14.8	.406	5.2	.298	3.4	1.000	0.11	1.89	5.2	4.4	17.0
0 Days Rest	22	31.7	12.7	.441	4.3	.340	3.0	.954	0.09	1.86	6.0	3.4	15.6
1 Days Rest	42	31.5	14.2	.425	5.1	.329	3.2	.902	0.14	2.12	6.3	3.3	16.6
2 Days Rest	8	34.1	13.3	.453	4.8	.289	2.4	.947	0.13	1.75	5.8	3.6	15.6
3+ Days Rest	10	29.4	13.6	.434	5.8	.414	3.0	.833	0.00	2.50	5.9	2.9	16.7

Last Five Seasons

	G	Min	FGA	FG%	3PA	3P%	FTA	FT%	Blk	Stl	Ast	Reb	Pts
Total	260	24.5	9.2	.425	3.3	.342	2.5	.892	0.10	1.55	4.8	2.6	11.2
Home	128	24.0	9.3	.447	3.4	.370	2.8	.910	0.12	1.57	4.8	2.6	12.1
Road	132	25.1	9.2	.403	3.1	.313	2.3	.870	0.09	1.52	4.8	2.7	10.3
vs. Playoff	137	25.3	9.7	.403	3.5	.322	2.6	.895	0.07	1.61	4.8	2.7	11.3
vs. Non-Playoff	123	23.7	8.7	.451	3.0	.369	2.5	.888	0.15	1.47	4.9	2.6	11.2
vs. East	180	25.0	9.1	.426	3.3	.339	2.7	.904	0.13	1.58	5.0	2.7	11.3
vs. West	80	23.4	9.6	.422	3.2	.349	2.2	.860	0.04	1.46	4.5	2.5	11.1
vs. Div.	78	25.6	9.4	.412	3.5	.326	2.9	.917	0.18	1.50	5.3	2.8	11.6
As Starter	114	32.2	13.0	.427	4.5	.346	3.1	.903	0.12	2.06	6.3	3.7	15.5
Off Bench	146	18.5	6.2	.420	2.3	.336	2.1	.879	0.09	1.14	3.6	1.8	7.9
In wins	141	23.3	8.6	.450	3.0	.372	2.8	.897	0.12	1.67	5.2	2.5	11.4
In losses	119	26.0	9.9	.398	3.6	.312	2.2	.885	0.08	1.39	4.4	2.8	10.9

	G	Min	FGA	FG%	3PA	3P%	FTA	FT%	Blk	Stl	Ast	Reb	Pts
Pre All-Star	148	24.1	8.9	.417	2.9	.342	2.4	.878	0.11	1.36	4.7	2.6	10.8
Post All-Star	62	21.1	9.1	.427	3.7	.325	1.9	.915	0.11	1.50	3.6	2.1	10.7
Oct/Nov	45	24.7	9.6	.463	3.3	.381	2.7	.861	0.11	1.42	5.3	2.6	12.4
December	45	24.2	8.6	.370	3.5	.299	2.4	.869	0.07	1.31	4.4	2.1	9.5
January	49	24.4	8.9	.422	3.2	.358	2.4	.906	0.16	1.41	4.5	2.9	10.5
February	38	20.6	7.6	.455	2.7	.386	2.1	.885	0.00	1.47	4.5	1.9	9.8
March	45	24.6	10.0	.428	3.6	.350	2.8	.891	0.11	1.73	4.8	2.6	12.4
Apr/May	38	28.7	10.6	.413	4.6	.307	2.8	.943	0.16	2.00	5.5	3.7	12.8
0 Days Rest	63	27.8	10.2	.407	3.4	.308	3.1	.907	0.13	1.76	5.3	3.0	12.1
1 Days Rest	130	25.8	9.8	.427	3.5	.342	2.6	.892	0.12	1.59	5.1	2.9	11.9
2 Days Rest	24	23.5	8.2	.398	2.9	.290	2.4	.877	0.08	1.17	4.5	2.3	9.4
3+ Days Rest	43	16.6	6.6	.473	2.7	.436	1.5	.864	0.02	1.30	3.4	1.6	8.7

Ron Artest

1999-2000 Per Game Averages

	G	Min	FGA	FG%	3PA	3P%	FTA	FT%	Blk	Stl	Ast	Reb	Pts		G	Min	FGA	FG%	3PA	3P%	FTA	FT%	Blk	Stl	Ast	Reb	Pts
Total	72	31.1	10.5	.407	2.7	.314	3.9	.674	0.54	1.65	2.8	4.3	12.0	Pre All-Star	47	32.5	11.1	.398	3.0	.282	4.1	.725	0.55	1.87	3.0	4.4	12.7
Home	37	31.6	10.9	.408	2.8	.352	3.7	.630	0.59	1.62	3.3	4.5	12.3	Post All-Star	25	28.4	9.5	.426	2.0	.408	3.4	.558	0.52	1.24	2.4	4.1	10.8
Road	35	30.5	10.1	.406	2.5	.267	4.0	.716	0.49	1.69	2.3	4.1	11.8	November	13	22.7	9.0	.376	2.0	.308	3.3	.698	0.38	1.38	1.9	3.4	9.7
vs. Playoff	42	30.9	10.5	.398	2.6	.324	4.0	.698	0.55	1.98	2.8	4.0	12.0	December	14	37.7	13.1	.375	3.6	.294	3.6	.725	0.36	1.71	3.9	6.0	13.6
vs. Non-Playoff	30	31.4	10.6	.420	2.8	.301	3.7	.636	0.53	1.20	2.8	4.7	12.0	January	14	38.1	11.9	.452	3.1	.273	5.3	.716	1.00	2.36	3.6	4.4	15.4
vs. East	45	31.8	10.7	.418	2.6	.322	4.2	.665	0.58	1.67	3.0	4.2	12.6	February	14	27.6	8.5	.345	2.5	.343	3.4	.688	0.64	1.36	2.7	3.5	9.1
vs. West	27	30.0	10.2	.388	2.7	.301	3.3	.693	0.48	1.63	2.6	4.3	11.0	March	11	28.5	9.1	.460	2.0	.318	2.5	.519	0.36	1.64	1.9	4.2	10.3
vs. Div.	24	32.2	11.6	.419	2.8	.348	4.2	.693	0.63	1.58	3.0	3.9	13.6	April	6	30.2	12.2	.466	2.2	.462	6.0	.583	0.33	1.17	2.2	3.8	15.8
As Starter	63	32.3	10.7	.402	2.8	.303	3.9	.675	0.57	1.71	2.8	4.4	12.0	0 Days Rest	20	30.8	10.3	.398	2.8	.339	4.6	.772	0.40	1.70	2.6	4.2	12.7
Off Bench	9	22.3	9.8	.443	1.8	.438	3.7	.667	0.33	1.22	2.4	3.6	11.9	1 Days Rest	31	31.5	10.8	.434	2.8	.345	3.5	.607	0.71	1.65	2.9	4.5	12.4
In wins	16	33.0	10.4	.470	3.0	.333	4.9	.633	0.69	1.69	3.6	4.1	13.9	2 Days Rest	12	31.4	9.8	.385	1.9	.217	4.6	.655	0.50	1.67	2.9	3.8	10.9
In losses	56	30.5	10.6	.390	2.6	.308	3.6	.690	0.50	1.64	2.6	4.3	11.5	3+ Days Rest	9	30.0	11.3	.363	2.8	.240	2.8	.640	0.33	1.56	2.9	4.6	10.7

Chucky Atkins

1999-2000 Per Game Averages

	G	Min	FGA	FG%	3PA	3P%	FTA	FT%	Blk	Stl	Ast	Reb	Pts		G	Min	FGA	FG%	3PA	3P%	FTA	FT%	Blk	Stl	Ast	Reb	Pts
Total	82	19.8	9.0	.424	2.0	.350	1.6	.729	0.04	0.63	3.7	1.5	9.5	Pre All-Star	50	18.8	8.1	.435	1.5	.342	1.7	.744	0.04	0.52	3.7	1.4	8.8
Home	41	19.4	8.7	.423	1.8	.360	1.6	.738	0.05	0.46	3.8	1.7	9.1	Post All-Star	32	21.4	10.5	.411	2.8	.356	1.5	.702	0.03	0.81	3.8	1.8	10.7
Road	41	20.2	9.4	.425	2.1	.341	1.7	.721	0.02	0.80	3.6	1.3	9.9	November	15	15.8	7.3	.385	1.5	.174	1.1	.688	0.07	0.40	2.7	1.0	6.6
vs. Playoff	47	20.1	9.3	.437	2.2	.381	1.6	.712	0.02	0.68	3.7	1.6	10.1	December	14	19.3	9.3	.454	1.4	.400	2.2	.839	0.07	0.71	3.4	1.4	10.9
vs. Non-Playoff	35	19.5	8.7	.405	1.7	.293	1.7	.750	0.06	0.57	3.8	1.4	8.8	January	17	20.3	7.5	.417	1.5	.440	1.6	.667	0.00	0.35	3.5	1.5	7.9
vs. East	54	20.1	9.0	.401	2.1	.360	1.8	.758	0.04	0.63	3.7	1.7	9.3	February	11	22.5	11.2	.504	2.2	.333	1.6	.667	0.00	1.18	5.7	2.5	13.1
vs. West	28	19.3	9.1	.467	1.8	.327	1.4	.658	0.04	0.64	3.7	1.3	10.0	March	16	21.0	10.1	.414	2.4	.385	1.6	.800	0.06	0.56	3.5	1.4	10.6
vs. Div.	25	19.6	8.8	.430	2.3	.345	1.7	.767	0.04	0.56	3.4	1.2	9.7	April	9	21.1	10.0	.344	3.6	.344	1.8	.625	0.00	0.89	4.3	2.0	9.2
As Starter	0	—	—	—	—	—	—	—	—	—	—	—	—	0 Days Rest	22	20.6	9.0	.399	2.0	.356	1.6	.714	0.05	0.86	3.9	1.4	9.0
Off Bench	82	19.8	9.0	.424	2.0	.350	1.6	.729	0.04	0.63	3.7	1.5	9.5	1 Days Rest	42	19.7	8.9	.406	1.8	.351	1.6	.706	0.02	0.50	3.8	1.5	9.0
In wins	41	19.4	8.8	.450	1.6	.406	2.0	.756	0.05	0.61	4.2	1.6	10.0	2 Days Rest	8	17.9	8.5	.485	2.8	.318	1.6	.769	0.00	0.38	2.6	1.4	10.4
In losses	41	20.2	9.3	.399	2.4	.313	1.2	.686	0.02	0.66	3.3	1.4	9.0	3+ Days Rest	10	20.3	10.1	.495	1.9	.368	1.7	.824	0.10	0.90	3.9	2.1	12.1

Vin Baker

Seattle SuperSonics — Forward

1999-2000 Per Game Averages

	G	Min	FGA	FG%	3PA	3P%	FTA	FT%	Blk	Stl	Ast	Reb	Pts		G	Min	FGA	FG%	3PA	3P%	FTA	FT%	Blk	Stl	Ast	Reb	Pts
Total	79	36.1	14.3	.455	0.1	.250	5.2	.682	0.84	0.59	1.9	7.7	16.6	Pre All-Star	50	38.0	15.2	.459	0.1	.000	5.4	.706	0.94	0.58	2.2	8.2	17.7
Home	39	35.3	13.8	.461	0.1	.000	4.9	.689	0.85	0.69	1.9	7.3	16.1	Post All-Star	29	32.8	12.8	.447	0.2	.400	4.9	.636	0.66	0.62	1.3	6.7	14.7
Road	40	36.8	14.8	.450	0.1	.400	5.6	.676	0.83	0.50	1.9	8.0	17.1	November	14	36.7	14.9	.483	0.1	.000	4.1	.603	0.79	0.71	1.8	8.4	16.9
vs. Playoff	43	37.3	14.3	.435	0.1	.167	5.3	.691	0.86	0.63	1.8	7.7	16.2	December	15	37.6	14.7	.448	0.0	—	5.2	.769	0.93	0.47	2.2	7.3	17.2
vs. Non-Playoff	36	34.6	14.3	.480	0.1	.500	5.1	.670	0.81	0.56	2.0	7.6	17.1	January	15	39.3	15.7	.438	0.1	.000	7.0	.695	1.00	0.60	2.5	9.5	18.6
vs. East	29	36.5	14.1	.474	0.1	.333	5.8	.685	0.86	0.38	1.9	7.2	17.4	February	13	36.2	13.9	.475	0.1	1.000	4.3	.679	0.85	0.62	1.9	6.8	16.2
vs. West	50	35.8	14.4	.444	0.1	.200	4.9	.680	0.82	0.72	1.9	7.9	16.1	March	12	35.3	13.7	.470	0.2	.500	6.2	.635	0.42	0.42	1.2	7.3	16.8
vs. Div.	24	36.7	14.2	.441	0.0	.000	5.5	.639	0.92	0.75	1.8	8.5	16.0	April	10	28.7	11.9	.403	0.2	.000	4.1	.683	1.00	0.80	1.4	5.7	12.4
As Starter	75	36.5	14.3	.454	0.1	.250	5.3	.676	0.83	0.57	1.9	7.8	16.6	0 Days Rest	19	36.9	15.2	.484	0.2	.500	5.2	.657	1.11	0.21	1.7	7.5	18.3
Off Bench	4	28.3	14.0	.482	0.0	—	4.3	.824	1.00	1.00	1.5	5.3	17.0	1 Days Rest	38	35.5	13.9	.448	0.1	.000	5.0	.733	0.84	0.63	1.8	7.4	15.8
In wins	43	36.1	14.5	.464	0.0	.000	5.4	.706	0.65	0.60	2.1	8.1	17.2	2 Days Rest	17	37.0	14.4	.426	0.1	.000	5.7	.639	0.53	0.71	2.2	7.8	15.9
In losses	36	36.1	14.1	.445	0.2	.333	5.0	.652	1.06	0.58	1.6	7.2	15.8	3+ Days Rest	5	34.2	13.6	.574	0.0	—	5.0	.560	0.80	1.40	2.2	10.2	18.4

Last Five Seasons

	G	Min	FGA	FG%	3PA	3P%	FTA	FT%	Blk	Stl	Ast	Reb	Pts		G	Min	FGA	FG%	3PA	3P%	FTA	FT%	Blk	Stl	Ast	Reb	Pts
Total	355	37.8	15.2	.494	0.3	.233	5.9	.640	1.10	0.90	2.2	8.7	18.9	Pre All-Star	185	38.6	16.0	.500	0.3	.190	6.3	.681	1.14	0.94	2.3	9.2	20.3
Home	177	37.5	14.7	.508	0.3	.208	5.5	.646	1.16	0.95	2.2	8.6	18.6	Post All-Star	136	37.8	14.8	.495	0.4	.288	5.7	.618	1.07	0.83	2.2	8.6	18.3
Road	178	38.2	15.7	.482	0.4	.254	6.3	.635	1.03	0.85	2.2	8.8	19.3	Oct/Nov	55	37.4	15.7	.494	0.3	.267	5.3	.683	1.16	0.96	2.1	9.5	19.2
vs. Playoff	199	38.5	15.1	.488	0.4	.265	6.0	.642	1.08	0.90	2.1	8.5	18.7	December	57	38.9	15.8	.513	0.2	.250	6.1	.671	0.91	0.91	2.5	9.1	20.4
vs. Non-Playoff	156	37.0	15.4	.503	0.2	.162	5.8	.637	1.12	0.89	2.3	8.9	19.2	January	58	39.0	16.4	.489	0.5	.138	7.1	.676	1.28	0.95	2.1	9.3	20.9
vs. East	169	39.0	15.8	.509	0.4	.222	6.1	.657	1.14	0.78	2.2	9.0	20.2	February	62	38.5	15.4	.491	0.3	.333	5.5	.583	1.31	0.95	2.4	8.1	18.4
vs. West	186	36.8	14.7	.480	0.3	.250	5.8	.624	1.05	1.01	2.2	8.4	17.8	March	70	37.8	14.7	.486	0.4	.323	6.1	.621	0.89	0.77	2.0	8.3	18.2
vs. Div.	120	38.7	15.0	.486	0.4	.209	6.1	.603	1.03	0.91	2.3	8.7	18.6	Apr/May	53	35.2	13.4	.495	0.2	.000	5.3	.604	1.06	0.87	2.1	7.9	16.4
As Starter	348	38.0	15.3	.494	0.3	.233	5.9	.641	1.09	0.91	2.2	8.7	19.0	0 Days Rest	90	37.5	14.8	.473	0.4	.256	5.9	.642	1.10	0.87	2.0	8.7	18.0
Off Bench	7	27.9	12.1	.506	0.0	—	4.4	.581	1.29	0.57	1.1	5.7	14.9	1 Days Rest	168	37.5	15.2	.508	0.3	.213	5.7	.642	1.05	0.85	2.3	8.1	19.2
In wins	178	37.3	15.2	.512	0.2	.207	6.0	.646	1.10	0.94	2.2	8.5	19.5	2 Days Rest	68	39.3	15.5	.491	0.3	.318	6.0	.627	1.12	1.09	2.2	9.3	19.1
In losses	177	38.4	15.2	.476	0.5	.242	5.8	.634	1.10	0.85	2.1	8.8	18.3	3+ Days Rest	29	37.7	16.0	.489	0.4	.083	6.7	.651	1.28	0.83	2.3	10.3	20.1

Brent Barry

Seattle SuperSonics — Guard

1999-2000 Per Game Averages

	G	Min	FGA	FG%	3PA	3P%	FTA	FT%	Blk	Stl	Ast	Reb	Pts		G	Min	FGA	FG%	3PA	3P%	FTA	FT%	Blk	Stl	Ast	Reb	Pts
Total	80	34.1	8.8	.463	5.0	.411	2.0	.809	0.39	1.29	3.6	4.7	11.8	Pre All-Star	49	34.3	9.0	.472	5.0	.418	2.0	.800	0.37	1.43	3.7	5.0	12.2
Home	40	32.8	8.2	.466	4.6	.408	2.0	.850	0.38	1.33	4.2	4.7	11.2	Post All-Star	31	33.6	8.5	.447	5.0	.400	1.8	.825	0.42	1.06	3.5	4.2	11.1
Road	40	35.3	9.5	.459	5.4	.414	1.9	.766	0.40	1.25	3.1	4.7	12.5	November	14	30.9	7.6	.481	4.6	.338	1.9	.769	0.29	1.50	4.1	4.1	10.3
vs. Playoff	43	34.7	9.1	.435	5.3	.385	2.0	.788	0.49	1.21	3.3	4.8	11.5	December	15	32.7	9.0	.467	4.4	.394	2.3	.794	0.33	1.60	3.7	5.2	11.9
vs. Non-Playoff	37	33.4	8.5	.497	4.7	.445	1.9	.833	0.27	1.38	4.1	4.5	12.1	January	14	37.9	10.0	.479	5.2	.452	2.6	.806	0.50	1.07	3.4	5.4	14.0
vs. East	29	34.2	9.1	.438	5.2	.360	2.2	.746	0.38	1.10	3.4	4.8	11.5	February	13	36.5	9.4	.467	6.2	.463	1.5	.800	0.38	1.54	3.6	5.0	12.8
vs. West	51	34.0	8.7	.477	4.9	.442	1.8	.851	0.39	1.39	3.7	4.6	12.0	March	14	35.1	9.2	.426	5.1	.380	2.1	.862	0.50	1.07	3.9	4.6	11.6
vs. Div.	23	33.8	9.0	.473	5.0	.430	1.9	.864	0.39	1.74	3.7	4.7	12.3	April	10	30.6	7.5	.453	4.4	.422	1.2	.833	0.30	0.80	3.1	3.1	9.7
As Starter	74	34.6	8.9	.466	5.0	.410	2.0	.815	0.41	1.30	3.7	4.8	12.1	0 Days Rest	20	37.9	10.5	.476	5.3	.457	2.3	.804	0.40	1.20	4.2	5.2	14.3
Off Bench	6	27.3	7.7	.413	4.3	.423	1.0	.667	0.17	1.17	2.3	2.8	8.8	1 Days Rest	39	32.6	8.2	.469	4.6	.397	1.7	.769	0.31	1.28	3.6	4.2	10.8
In wins	44	34.0	8.5	.504	5.0	.434	1.8	.852	0.34	1.61	4.4	4.7	12.3	2 Days Rest	16	33.3	8.7	.432	5.6	.378	2.1	.912	0.63	1.31	3.0	5.2	11.6
In losses	36	34.2	9.2	.416	5.0	.383	2.1	.763	0.44	0.89	2.7	4.6	11.2	3+ Days Rest	5	32.6	7.6	.447	5.0	.440	2.4	.750	0.20	1.60	3.6	4.6	10.8

Career (1995-96 thru 1999-2000)

	G	Min	FGA	FG%	3PA	3P%	FTA	FT%	Blk	Stl	Ast	Reb	Pts		G	Min	FGA	FG%	3PA	3P%	FTA	FT%	Blk	Stl	Ast	Reb	Pts
Total	313	27.2	8.1	.440	4.1	.382	2.0	.815	0.34	1.13	3.0	3.1	10.3	Pre All-Star	158	28.2	8.6	.457	4.2	.414	2.1	.813	0.37	1.20	3.2	3.3	11.3
Home	156	27.6	8.3	.447	4.1	.387	2.2	.825	0.36	1.23	3.0	3.1	10.8	Post All-Star	118	24.2	7.1	.430	3.6	.365	1.6	.843	0.31	1.04	2.7	2.5	8.7
Road	157	26.7	8.0	.433	4.0	.377	1.8	.803	0.32	1.04	3.0	3.1	9.9	Oct/Nov	46	28.5	8.7	.468	4.2	.390	2.4	.782	0.39	1.30	3.5	3.5	11.7
vs. Playoff	174	27.4	8.2	.433	4.1	.377	2.1	.811	0.37	1.11	2.9	3.0	10.3	December	53	23.8	7.4	.428	3.5	.388	2.0	.830	0.34	1.08	2.5	2.9	9.3
vs. Non-Playoff	139	26.8	8.1	.448	4.0	.389	1.9	.821	0.29	1.16	3.2	3.2	10.4	January	48	31.5	9.3	.476	4.4	.433	2.2	.817	0.44	1.17	3.5	3.5	12.5
vs. East	142	26.9	8.0	.406	4.0	.329	2.1	.803	0.30	1.04	2.7	3.0	9.5	February	53	28.1	8.9	.426	4.8	.405	2.2	.798	0.26	1.32	2.9	3.3	11.3
vs. West	171	27.4	8.2	.467	4.1	.425	1.9	.826	0.37	1.21	3.3	3.2	11.0	March	72	26.2	7.4	.426	3.8	.344	1.8	.855	0.32	0.97	2.7	2.9	9.2
vs. Div.	98	28.3	8.6	.451	4.2	.397	2.1	.788	0.33	1.10	3.2	3.4	11.1	Apr/May	41	25.3	7.4	.410	3.6	.322	1.4	.789	0.29	1.02	3.4	2.4	8.4
As Starter	184	32.9	9.7	.454	4.8	.398	2.3	.812	0.40	1.29	3.5	4.0	12.6	0 Days Rest	80	29.2	9.2	.430	4.3	.395	2.6	.812	0.34	1.04	3.2	3.3	11.7
Off Bench	129	19.0	5.9	.407	3.0	.346	1.5	.822	0.26	0.91	2.3	1.8	7.1	1 Days Rest	151	26.7	7.8	.449	3.9	.387	1.8	.789	0.35	1.13	2.9	2.9	9.9
In wins	126	27.0	7.8	.466	3.9	.402	1.8	.848	0.31	1.24	3.5	3.3	10.4	2 Days Rest	49	27.8	8.0	.432	4.2	.362	2.0	.866	0.43	1.16	2.9	3.6	10.1
In losses	187	27.3	8.4	.423	4.2	.369	2.1	.796	0.36	1.06	2.7	3.0	10.3	3+ Days Rest	33	23.2	7.3	.436	3.8	.357	1.6	.868	0.15	1.36	3.1	2.8	9.1

Jon Barry

1999-2000 Per Game Averages

	G	Min	FGA	FG%	3PA	3P%	FTA	FT%	Blk	Stl	Ast	Reb	Pts		G	Min	FGA	FG%	3PA	3P%	FTA	FT%	Blk	Stl	Ast	Reb	Pts
Total	62	20.7	5.6	.465	2.5	.429	1.9	.922	0.11	1.21	2.4	2.6	8.0	Pre All-Star	39	20.2	5.6	.466	2.4	.426	2.0	.909	0.13	1.38	2.3	2.5	8.1
Home	31	20.2	5.4	.458	2.5	.423	1.6	.939	0.13	1.16	2.5	2.7	7.5	Post All-Star	23	21.5	5.5	.465	2.6	.433	1.7	.949	0.09	0.91	2.7	2.7	7.9
Road	31	21.2	5.8	.472	2.5	.434	2.2	.910	0.10	1.26	2.3	2.4	8.5	November	12	19.5	5.9	.521	2.3	.481	2.4	.897	0.17	1.58	2.2	2.8	9.4
vs. Playoff	31	20.0	5.6	.463	2.5	.430	1.6	.902	0.19	1.06	2.1	2.1	7.8	December	6	23.2	6.0	.500	2.2	.385	2.0	.833	0.17	1.67	3.3	3.5	8.5
vs. Non-Playoff	31	21.3	5.5	.468	2.4	.427	2.1	.938	0.03	1.35	2.7	3.1	8.2	January	16	19.5	5.6	.393	2.3	.378	1.9	.967	0.06	1.06	2.1	1.6	7.1
vs. East	23	20.3	5.3	.410	2.5	.404	2.1	.896	0.04	1.00	2.1	2.1	7.2	February	13	23.2	5.5	.486	3.3	.465	1.7	.909	0.23	1.31	2.7	3.0	8.5
vs. West	39	20.8	5.7	.496	2.5	.443	1.7	.941	0.15	1.33	2.6	2.8	8.4	March	10	21.7	5.7	.509	2.4	.458	2.3	.957	0.00	0.80	2.8	3.0	9.1
vs. Div.	16	19.3	4.4	.414	2.0	.406	1.6	1.000	0.19	0.94	2.5	2.0	6.0	April	5	15.6	4.2	.333	2.0	.300	0.0	—	0.00	0.80	1.6	1.8	3.4
As Starter	1	21.0	7.0	.714	2.0	1.000	0.0	—	0.00	1.00	2.0	3.0	12.0	0 Days Rest	12	21.6	5.6	.433	2.4	.483	2.3	.926	0.17	1.67	2.1	2.5	8.1
Off Bench	61	20.7	5.6	.460	2.5	.421	1.9	.922	0.11	1.21	2.4	2.6	7.9	1 Days Rest	35	21.5	5.6	.492	2.5	.442	1.9	.938	0.09	1.14	2.3	2.7	8.3
In wins	36	20.5	5.6	.495	2.4	.460	1.9	.942	0.08	1.42	2.6	2.7	8.9	2 Days Rest	8	19.6	6.5	.481	2.8	.409	1.9	.800	0.00	1.00	3.6	3.1	8.9
In losses	26	20.9	5.6	.425	2.6	.388	1.8	.894	0.15	0.92	2.2	2.3	7.4	3+ Days Rest	7	16.3	4.6	.344	2.4	.294	1.3	1.000	0.29	1.00	2.0	1.4	5.1

Last Five Seasons

	G	Min	FGA	FG%	3PA	3P%	FTA	FT%	Blk	Stl	Ast	Reb	Pts		G	Min	FGA	FG%	3PA	3P%	FTA	FT%	Blk	Stl	Ast	Reb	Pts
Total	280	14.5	3.6	.441	1.8	.391	1.1	.875	0.10	0.86	1.8	1.6	4.9	Pre All-Star	138	14.8	4.0	.448	1.8	.418	1.1	.878	0.12	0.91	1.7	1.6	5.2
Home	135	14.0	3.5	.438	1.9	.371	1.1	.877	0.11	0.79	1.8	1.6	4.7	Post All-Star	99	13.0	3.4	.434	1.8	.392	0.8	.901	0.07	0.63	1.6	1.3	4.4
Road	145	15.0	3.7	.443	1.8	.412	1.1	.873	0.10	0.92	1.8	1.6	5.0	Oct/Nov	52	17.2	4.4	.456	2.0	.408	1.0	.815	0.12	1.04	1.9	1.8	5.7
vs. Playoff	142	14.4	3.7	.448	1.9	.404	1.2	.864	0.12	0.84	1.6	1.5	5.1	December	31	14.0	3.6	.469	1.6	.388	1.1	.886	0.23	0.90	2.4	1.7	5.0
vs. Non-Playoff	138	14.6	3.6	.433	1.7	.378	1.0	.888	0.09	0.88	2.0	1.7	4.7	January	41	13.0	3.9	.405	1.6	.433	1.1	.956	0.05	0.73	1.3	1.2	4.9
vs. East	116	14.7	3.7	.413	1.9	.391	0.9	.837	0.09	0.79	1.7	1.4	4.5	February	56	16.7	4.1	.441	2.4	.400	1.3	.845	0.16	1.04	2.2	2.0	5.6
vs. West	164	14.4	3.6	.461	1.8	.392	1.3	.894	0.12	0.90	1.9	1.7	5.1	March	62	12.7	3.1	.459	1.7	.359	1.2	.920	0.06	0.61	1.6	1.6	4.6
vs. Div.	87	14.9	3.4	.449	1.7	.386	0.8	.864	0.10	0.83	1.9	1.4	4.3	Apr/May	38	12.8	2.6	.394	1.4	.352	0.8	.813	0.03	0.84	1.7	1.3	3.2
As Starter	10	31.9	6.5	.415	2.2	.273	1.6	.750	0.00	1.60	2.9	3.9	7.2	0 Days Rest	66	15.6	3.9	.440	2.0	.429	1.3	.898	0.09	1.06	1.9	1.8	5.5
Off Bench	270	13.9	3.5	.442	1.8	.397	1.1	.882	0.11	0.83	1.8	1.5	4.8	1 Days Rest	118	15.5	3.7	.453	1.9	.369	1.2	.853	0.10	0.89	1.9	1.7	5.1
In wins	162	13.7	3.4	.448	1.6	.384	1.0	.890	0.09	0.87	1.9	1.6	4.5	2 Days Rest	40	13.9	3.9	.471	1.7	.409	0.8	.839	0.08	0.68	1.9	1.8	5.0
In losses	118	15.6	4.0	.433	2.1	.399	1.3	.858	0.13	0.84	1.7	1.6	5.4	3+ Days Rest	56	11.7	3.0	.381	1.6	.378	0.9	.920	0.14	0.68	1.6	1.1	3.7

Tony Battie

1999-2000 Per Game Averages

	G	Min	FGA	FG%	3PA	3P%	FTA	FT%	Blk	Stl	Ast	Reb	Pts		G	Min	FGA	FG%	3PA	3P%	FTA	FT%	Blk	Stl	Ast	Reb	Pts
Total	82	18.4	5.6	.477	0.1	.125	1.8	.675	0.85	0.57	0.8	5.0	6.6	Pre All-Star	49	18.4	5.7	.478	0.1	.333	2.1	.680	0.92	0.67	0.9	4.9	6.9
Home	41	18.6	6.0	.500	0.1	.167	1.8	.730	1.12	0.56	0.9	5.7	7.3	Post All-Star	33	18.3	5.5	.475	0.2	.000	1.5	.667	0.76	0.42	0.6	5.2	6.2
Road	41	18.1	5.2	.451	0.0	.000	1.9	.623	0.59	0.59	0.7	4.3	5.9	November	14	17.8	5.2	.493	0.0	—	1.6	.870	1.07	0.50	1.1	4.0	6.6
vs. Playoff	46	18.4	5.6	.463	0.1	.000	1.8	.679	0.87	0.63	0.6	5.0	6.5	December	14	22.1	7.1	.450	0.1	.000	3.5	.551	1.07	0.93	1.1	6.6	8.4
vs. Non-Playoff	36	18.3	5.6	.495	0.1	.200	1.9	.672	0.83	0.50	0.9	5.0	6.8	January	15	16.0	4.9	.493	0.1	.500	1.3	.650	0.60	0.67	0.6	4.1	5.7
vs. East	54	17.8	5.5	.478	0.1	.000	1.7	.699	0.98	0.56	0.7	4.9	6.5	February	13	17.8	4.8	.435	0.0	—	1.3	.882	0.69	0.62	0.5	4.8	5.3
vs. West	28	19.5	5.8	.475	0.1	.333	2.1	.638	0.61	0.61	0.9	5.3	6.9	March	16	19.5	5.9	.479	0.3	.000	1.5	.625	0.94	0.31	0.8	6.0	6.6
vs. Div.	24	18.1	5.4	.538	0.1	.000	2.0	.667	1.54	0.50	0.7	5.7	7.2	April	10	16.3	5.7	.526	0.1	.000	1.8	.667	0.70	0.40	0.3	4.2	7.2
As Starter	4	20.0	6.5	.385	0.3	.000	5.0	.450	0.25	1.00	0.8	4.5	7.3	0 Days Rest	22	17.8	5.1	.438	0.1	.000	2.0	.636	0.68	0.64	0.6	4.3	5.7
Off Bench	78	18.3	5.6	.483	0.1	.143	1.7	.710	0.88	0.55	0.8	5.0	6.6	1 Days Rest	42	18.4	6.0	.510	0.1	.200	1.7	.676	0.88	0.64	0.9	5.0	7.3
In wins	35	19.4	6.3	.525	0.1	.000	1.8	.726	1.23	0.71	0.9	5.7	7.9	2 Days Rest	9	19.2	5.4	.449	0.0	—	1.6	.714	1.00	0.33	0.4	5.7	6.0
In losses	47	17.6	5.1	.433	0.1	.333	1.9	.640	0.57	0.47	0.7	4.4	5.6	3+ Days Rest	9	18.4	5.0	.422	0.1	.000	2.4	.727	1.00	0.33	1.1	5.9	6.0

Career (1997-98 thru 1999-2000)

	G	Min	FGA	FG%	3PA	3P%	FTA	FT%	Blk	Stl	Ast	Reb	Pts		G	Min	FGA	FG%	3PA	3P%	FTA	FT%	Blk	Stl	Ast	Reb	Pts
Total	197	21.0	6.4	.474	0.1	.160	1.6	.684	1.07	0.66	0.9	5.4	7.2	Pre All-Star	86	21.7	7.2	.464	0.1	.273	2.2	.690	0.98	0.83	1.0	5.3	8.2
Home	97	21.2	6.4	.468	0.1	.214	1.6	.734	1.24	0.64	0.9	5.8	7.2	Post All-Star	61	18.8	6.0	.455	0.2	.091	1.1	.676	0.90	0.49	0.6	5.0	6.2
Road	100	20.8	6.5	.479	0.1	.091	1.6	.636	0.90	0.68	0.9	4.9	7.2	Oct/Nov	20	21.1	6.8	.515	0.0	.000	1.7	.824	0.95	0.60	1.3	4.8	8.4
vs. Playoff	109	21.2	6.6	.444	0.2	.118	1.5	.693	1.04	0.70	0.8	5.4	6.9	December	28	23.5	8.0	.420	0.1	.333	3.3	.634	0.93	1.11	1.0	6.5	8.9
vs. Non-Playoff	88	20.7	6.2	.513	0.1	.250	1.7	.673	1.10	0.61	1.0	5.3	7.5	January	30	21.1	6.9	.471	0.2	.200	1.6	.653	1.10	0.77	1.0	4.6	7.6
vs. East	125	20.5	6.0	.463	0.1	.071	1.4	.709	1.14	0.54	0.9	5.4	6.6	February	37	21.9	6.4	.440	0.2	.333	1.1	.795	1.08	0.68	0.8	5.2	6.4
vs. West	72	21.8	7.2	.489	0.2	.273	2.0	.653	0.93	0.88	0.9	5.3	8.3	March	47	19.6	5.7	.500	0.1	.000	1.1	.630	1.00	0.43	0.7	5.5	6.4
vs. Div.	59	21.1	6.4	.491	0.1	.250	1.7	.636	1.53	0.69	0.9	5.7	7.4	Apr/May	35	19.7	5.7	.513	0.1	.000	1.3	.681	1.29	0.54	0.9	5.6	6.7
As Starter	68	25.7	8.0	.462	0.2	.231	1.9	.690	1.34	0.88	1.1	5.8	8.8	0 Days Rest	54	20.6	6.1	.461	0.1	.000	1.5	.663	1.11	0.70	0.9	5.0	6.2
Off Bench	129	18.5	5.6	.482	0.1	.083	1.4	.679	0.92	0.54	0.8	5.2	6.4	1 Days Rest	101	21.4	6.8	.488	0.1	.200	1.5	.673	1.06	0.68	1.0	5.6	7.7
In wins	62	19.7	5.8	.550	0.1	.000	1.7	.679	1.37	0.76	1.0	5.6	7.5	2 Days Rest	20	21.8	6.7	.403	0.1	1.000	1.6	.719	1.05	0.80	0.9	5.6	6.6
In losses	135	21.5	6.7	.443	0.1	.222	1.6	.686	0.93	0.61	0.9	5.3	7.1	3+ Days Rest	22	19.2	5.4	.508	0.1	.000	2.0	.733	1.00	0.32	0.7	5.2	7.0

Travis Best

1999-2000 Per Game Averages

	G	Min	FGA	FG%	3PA	3P%	FTA	FT%	Blk	Stl	Ast	Reb	Pts		G	Min	FGA	FG%	3PA	3P%	FTA	FT%	Blk	Stl	Ast	Reb	Pts
Total	82	20.6	6.8	.483	1.1	.376	2.3	.821	0.06	0.93	3.3	1.7	8.9	Pre All-Star	48	19.6	6.5	.465	1.1	.315	2.0	.823	0.08	1.02	3.4	1.7	8.0
Home	41	21.1	7.0	.481	1.2	.420	2.4	.857	0.07	1.07	3.3	1.7	9.3	Post All-Star	34	22.0	7.3	.506	1.1	.462	2.8	.819	0.03	0.79	3.2	1.8	10.2
Road	41	20.1	6.6	.485	1.0	.326	2.2	.783	0.05	0.78	3.3	1.8	8.5	November	15	19.3	7.0	.467	1.2	.278	0.9	.786	0.07	0.67	2.9	1.6	7.6
vs. Playoff	44	20.2	6.7	.447	1.2	.373	2.6	.788	0.11	0.70	3.4	1.8	8.4	December	14	19.1	5.9	.434	1.2	.353	2.2	.806	0.07	1.50	3.8	1.6	7.4
vs. Non-Playoff	38	21.1	7.1	.522	1.1	.381	2.0	.870	0.00	1.18	3.2	1.7	9.6	January	14	20.4	7.1	.470	1.0	.286	2.4	.909	0.07	1.07	3.6	1.6	9.1
vs. East	54	20.4	6.5	.466	1.2	.369	1.8	.776	0.07	0.72	3.0	1.5	7.9	February	13	19.3	5.5	.437	0.9	.333	3.1	.800	0.08	0.62	2.9	1.7	7.5
vs. West	28	21.1	7.5	.512	1.0	.393	3.3	.870	0.04	1.32	3.9	2.2	10.9	March	16	22.7	7.5	.575	1.0	.438	3.1	.837	0.06	1.00	3.3	2.0	11.6
vs. Div.	28	20.2	6.7	.473	1.4	.350	1.9	.755	0.07	0.75	3.2	1.4	8.3	April	10	23.4	8.2	.476	1.6	.563	2.3	.739	0.00	0.60	3.4	1.8	10.4
As Starter	0	—	—	—	—	—	—	—	—	—	—	—	—	0 Days Rest	21	20.7	7.0	.486	1.1	.167	2.2	.739	0.05	0.76	3.1	1.8	8.7
Off Bench	82	20.6	6.8	.483	1.1	.376	2.3	.821	0.06	0.93	3.3	1.7	8.9	1 Days Rest	41	21.1	7.2	.481	1.1	.435	2.5	.864	0.05	0.93	3.4	1.7	9.6
In wins	56	20.8	6.9	.491	1.1	.407	2.4	.818	0.05	1.07	3.4	1.8	9.1	2 Days Rest	14	20.6	6.4	.539	1.2	.300	2.4	.818	0.14	1.29	3.9	1.7	9.4
In losses	26	20.2	6.8	.466	1.3	.324	2.2	.828	0.08	0.62	3.2	1.7	8.6	3+ Days Rest	6	17.3	4.5	.296	0.8	.400	1.3	.750	0.00	0.67	2.2	1.8	4.0

Career (1995-96 thru 1999-2000)

	G	Min	FGA	FG%	3PA	3P%	FTA	FT%	Blk	Stl	Ast	Reb	Pts		G	Min	FGA	FG%	3PA	3P%	FTA	FT%	Blk	Stl	Ast	Reb	Pts
Total	348	19.9	6.1	.442	1.2	.356	2.0	.813	0.06	0.92	3.3	1.6	7.4	Pre All-Star	163	20.3	6.5	.449	1.2	.307	2.0	.791	0.09	0.99	3.5	1.8	7.7
Home	178	19.7	6.0	.439	1.1	.352	1.8	.811	0.07	0.89	3.1	1.6	7.1	Post All-Star	136	18.8	5.7	.444	1.1	.409	2.1	.830	0.02	0.87	2.9	1.4	7.2
Road	170	20.1	6.3	.446	1.2	.359	2.1	.815	0.05	0.95	3.5	1.6	7.6	Oct/Nov	52	20.3	6.6	.456	1.3	.309	1.6	.765	0.10	0.87	3.2	1.7	7.6
vs. Playoff	186	20.2	6.3	.434	1.3	.363	2.0	.830	0.06	0.98	3.3	1.7	7.5	December	55	19.3	6.2	.452	1.0	.298	2.0	.809	0.05	0.95	3.3	1.7	7.5
vs. Non-Playoff	162	19.6	5.9	.453	1.0	.345	2.0	.794	0.06	1.08	3.3	1.5	7.3	January	44	22.0	6.9	.447	1.1	.354	2.5	.811	0.14	1.27	4.0	1.9	8.6
vs. East	242	19.6	5.8	.443	1.2	.365	1.9	.804	0.06	0.83	3.2	1.5	7.1	February	63	19.1	5.3	.389	1.1	.412	1.8	.826	0.05	0.76	3.0	1.5	6.1
vs. West	106	20.5	6.8	.442	1.1	.333	2.2	.832	0.08	1.13	3.4	1.7	8.2	March	76	18.9	5.8	.459	1.2	.364	2.1	.829	0.05	0.92	3.1	1.4	7.5
vs. Div.	122	19.7	6.0	.438	1.2	.336	1.8	.819	0.07	0.82	3.3	1.4	7.1	Apr/May	58	20.5	6.2	.446	1.3	.438	2.0	.819	0.02	0.86	3.1	1.5	7.7
As Starter	47	31.3	9.2	.433	2.1	.340	3.0	.773	0.09	1.55	5.1	2.6	11.0	0 Days Rest	92	20.8	6.4	.440	1.2	.298	2.4	.824	0.03	0.89	3.3	1.7	8.0
Off Bench	301	18.1	5.6	.445	1.0	.361	1.8	.824	0.06	0.82	3.0	1.4	6.9	1 Days Rest	169	19.6	6.0	.439	1.1	.380	1.8	.821	0.06	0.89	3.2	1.6	7.2
In wins	217	19.4	6.0	.461	1.0	.379	1.9	.819	0.06	0.96	3.3	1.6	7.5	2 Days Rest	48	19.9	6.4	.489	1.2	.464	2.0	.776	0.13	1.17	3.4	1.5	8.3
In losses	131	20.6	6.3	.413	1.4	.326	2.1	.804	0.06	0.85	3.3	1.6	7.3	3+ Days Rest	39	19.0	5.5	.402	1.2	.267	1.7	.800	0.08	0.85	3.2	1.6	6.1

Mike Bibby

1999-2000 Per Game Averages

	G	Min	FGA	FG%	3PA	3P%	FTA	FT%	Blk	Stl	Ast	Reb	Pts		G	Min	FGA	FG%	3PA	3P%	FTA	FT%	Blk	Stl	Ast	Reb	Pts
Total	82	38.5	12.6	.445	2.6	.363	3.0	.780	0.18	1.61	8.1	3.7	14.5	Pre All-Star	48	36.7	12.1	.438	2.1	.382	3.2	.796	0.17	1.58	7.3	3.7	14.0
Home	41	38.8	12.8	.438	2.7	.321	2.8	.807	0.27	1.93	8.6	3.7	14.3	Post All-Star	34	40.9	13.2	.454	3.2	.345	2.9	.755	0.21	1.65	9.3	3.8	15.3
Road	41	38.2	12.3	.453	2.4	.410	3.3	.757	0.10	1.29	7.6	3.8	14.7	November	14	34.0	10.0	.429	1.0	.357	3.1	.721	0.07	1.50	6.1	3.2	11.1
vs. Playoff	48	39.0	12.5	.442	2.7	.359	3.1	.779	0.21	1.46	8.5	3.5	14.4	December	15	37.4	12.5	.463	1.9	.393	2.7	.825	0.20	1.13	8.1	3.6	14.5
vs. Non-Playoff	34	37.7	12.7	.449	2.4	.370	3.0	.782	0.15	1.82	7.6	4.1	14.6	January	14	39.1	13.5	.434	3.1	.419	4.1	.810	0.21	2.36	7.9	4.4	16.4
vs. East	30	38.2	12.1	.428	2.7	.415	3.4	.735	0.23	1.93	7.8	3.4	14.0	February	13	38.9	13.8	.436	3.1	.325	3.2	.810	0.08	1.69	8.5	3.5	15.6
vs. West	52	38.6	12.9	.454	2.5	.331	2.8	.811	0.15	1.42	8.3	3.9	14.8	March	15	39.2	11.9	.455	3.2	.292	2.8	.714	0.47	1.07	8.9	3.4	13.7
vs. Div.	24	38.9	13.9	.477	2.1	.314	3.0	.806	0.17	1.83	8.4	4.5	16.3	April	11	43.4	14.3	.452	3.5	.410	2.3	.800	0.00	2.09	9.4	4.5	16.2
As Starter	82	38.5	12.6	.445	2.6	.363	3.0	.780	0.18	1.61	8.1	3.7	14.5	0 Days Rest	19	38.1	12.5	.439	2.7	.462	3.2	.683	0.11	1.53	7.8	3.0	14.4
Off Bench	0	—	—	—	—	—	—	—	—	—	—	—	—	1 Days Rest	47	38.4	12.6	.432	2.7	.333	2.9	.810	0.23	1.68	7.9	4.1	14.1
In wins	22	38.8	13.1	.490	2.6	.431	3.8	.771	0.05	2.00	8.6	4.4	16.9	2 Days Rest	7	36.7	12.1	.494	1.4	.400	3.4	.833	0.00	1.00	9.0	3.3	15.4
In losses	60	38.4	12.4	.428	2.6	.338	2.8	.784	0.21	1.47	7.9	3.5	13.7	3+ Days Rest	9	41.1	13.0	.487	2.7	.292	3.2	.793	0.22	1.89	8.9	3.7	16.0

Career (1998-99 thru 1999-2000)

	G	Min	FGA	FG%	3PA	3P%	FTA	FT%	Blk	Stl	Ast	Reb	Pts		G	Min	FGA	FG%	3PA	3P%	FTA	FT%	Blk	Stl	Ast	Reb	Pts
Total	132	37.2	12.4	.439	2.2	.322	3.2	.768	0.15	1.59	7.5	3.3	14.0	Pre All-Star	48	36.7	12.1	.438	2.1	.382	3.2	.796	0.17	1.58	7.3	3.7	14.0
Home	66	37.7	12.4	.441	2.4	.295	2.7	.790	0.23	1.82	8.2	3.5	13.8	Post All-Star	34	40.9	13.2	.454	3.2	.345	2.9	.755	0.21	1.65	9.3	3.8	15.3
Road	66	36.7	12.4	.438	2.0	.354	3.6	.752	0.08	1.36	6.8	3.2	14.3	Oct/Nov	14	34.0	10.0	.429	1.0	.357	3.1	.721	0.07	1.50	6.1	3.2	11.1
vs. Playoff	78	37.3	12.5	.438	2.3	.328	2.9	.765	0.15	1.47	7.6	3.1	13.9	December	15	37.4	12.5	.463	1.9	.393	2.7	.825	0.20	1.13	8.1	3.6	14.5
vs. Non-Playoff	54	37.1	12.3	.441	2.0	.312	3.5	.772	0.15	1.76	7.3	3.7	14.2	January	14	39.1	13.5	.434	3.1	.419	4.1	.810	0.21	2.36	7.9	4.4	16.4
vs. East	36	38.5	12.0	.443	2.5	.404	3.8	.772	0.22	1.75	7.7	3.2	14.6	February	26	38.6	12.5	.425	2.3	.295	3.5	.855	0.04	1.62	8.1	3.2	14.2
vs. West	96	36.7	12.5	.438	2.1	.284	2.9	.767	0.13	1.53	7.4	3.4	13.8	March	32	36.3	12.0	.465	2.4	.286	2.8	.711	0.31	1.31	7.5	3.2	13.9
vs. Div.	45	36.4	13.1	.457	1.8	.263	3.1	.739	0.13	1.64	7.2	3.9	14.7	Apr/May	31	37.5	13.2	.423	2.0	.286	3.1	.732	0.06	1.77	7.2	3.2	14.0
As Starter	132	37.2	12.4	.439	2.2	.322	3.2	.768	0.15	1.59	7.5	3.3	14.0	0 Days Rest	33	37.2	11.9	.444	2.2	.375	3.4	.714	0.06	1.30	7.3	3.1	13.8
Off Bench	0	—	—	—	—	—	—	—	—	—	—	—	—	1 Days Rest	79	36.9	12.5	.431	2.2	.309	2.9	.789	0.20	1.71	7.3	3.5	13.8
In wins	30	38.2	12.6	.481	2.3	.382	3.7	.768	0.03	2.07	8.4	4.3	15.9	2 Days Rest	10	36.1	12.6	.468	1.5	.267	3.9	.795	0.00	1.30	8.2	3.2	15.3
In losses	102	36.9	12.3	.427	2.1	.303	3.0	.769	0.19	1.45	7.2	3.1	13.5	3+ Days Rest	10	40.6	13.1	.458	2.4	.292	3.6	.778	0.20	1.90	8.9	3.4	15.6

Mookie Blaylock

1999-2000 Per Game Averages

	G	Min	FGA	FG%	3PA	3P%	FTA	FT%	Blk	Stl	Ast	Reb	Pts
Total	73	33.7	11.5	.391	4.1	.336	1.3	.705	0.30	2.00	6.7	3.7	11.3
Home	36	34.0	12.1	.406	3.8	.311	1.8	.646	0.31	2.19	6.9	3.7	12.2
Road	37	33.4	10.8	.374	4.5	.355	0.8	.833	0.30	1.81	6.5	3.7	10.4
vs. Playoff	43	33.6	11.6	.361	4.0	.299	1.3	.667	0.30	1.91	6.1	3.7	10.4
vs. Non-Playoff	30	33.9	11.3	.434	4.2	.386	1.4	.756	0.30	2.13	7.5	3.7	12.5
vs. East	29	33.3	10.5	.387	4.6	.333	1.3	.641	0.21	1.93	6.8	4.1	10.5
vs. West	44	33.9	12.1	.393	3.8	.337	1.3	.750	0.36	2.05	6.6	3.5	11.8
vs. Div.	19	34.7	13.1	.367	4.1	.333	1.1	.714	0.53	2.47	6.7	3.8	11.7
As Starter	72	33.8	11.6	.391	4.1	.336	1.3	.705	0.31	2.03	6.7	3.7	11.3
Off Bench	1	23.0	5.0	.400	3.0	.333	0.0	—	0.00	0.00	3.0	0.0	
In wins	18	36.9	11.7	.412	4.3	.397	1.8	.697	0.28	2.44	8.9	4.2	12.7
In losses	55	32.6	11.4	.383	4.1	.314	1.1	.710	0.31	1.85	6.0	3.5	10.8

	G	Min	FGA	FG%	3PA	3P%	FTA	FT%	Blk	Stl	Ast	Reb	Pts
Pre All-Star	38	33.5	10.8	.415	4.2	.390	1.2	.696	0.16	2.11	7.4	3.3	11.4
Post All-Star	35	33.9	12.2	.368	4.1	.275	1.4	.714	0.46	1.89	5.9	4.2	11.1
November	11	31.4	8.6	.379	2.9	.313	0.5	.400	0.27	1.64	6.6	2.5	7.6
December	9	34.6	10.9	.316	4.8	.326	0.7	.667	0.11	2.78	7.7	4.2	8.9
January	12	35.3	12.5	.467	4.7	.464	2.1	.760	0.17	2.25	8.4	3.2	15.4
February	15	34.3	11.5	.405	4.6	.348	1.7	.720	0.21	1.93	6.2	3.9	12.1
March	17	32.2	11.2	.377	3.5	.267	0.9	.733	0.53	1.71	5.6	3.4	10.1
April	9	35.1	14.4	.369	4.6	.268	2.1	.684	0.33	2.00	6.4	5.4	13.3
0 Days Rest	16	35.1	11.7	.390	4.8	.342	0.9	.857	0.31	1.44	6.6	4.1	11.5
1 Days Rest	41	33.2	11.4	.400	4.0	.352	1.4	.724	0.37	2.20	7.0	3.5	11.6
2 Days Rest	8	37.9	13.8	.318	4.5	.278	2.1	.471	0.00	2.13	5.6	4.3	11.0
3+ Days Rest	8	29.3	9.1	.425	3.4	.296	0.8	.833	0.25	2.00	6.6	3.3	9.4

Last Five Seasons

	G	Min	FGA	FG%	3PA	3P%	FTA	FT%	Blk	Stl	Ast	Reb	Pts
Total	350	36.8	13.5	.403	6.0	.341	1.9	.736	0.25	2.43	6.2	4.5	14.3
Home	177	37.4	13.7	.415	6.1	.347	2.0	.723	0.28	2.53	6.3	4.7	14.9
Road	173	36.2	13.2	.391	6.0	.335	1.8	.752	0.23	2.34	6.2	4.3	13.7
vs. Playoff	185	36.9	13.7	.385	6.2	.332	1.7	.709	0.26	2.31	6.0	4.5	13.8
vs. Non-Playoff	165	36.6	13.2	.424	5.9	.351	2.1	.762	0.25	2.58	6.5	4.5	14.8
vs. East	221	37.5	13.5	.402	6.2	.336	2.1	.726	0.23	2.43	6.2	4.6	14.5
vs. West	129	35.5	13.3	.405	5.8	.349	1.6	.758	0.29	2.45	6.2	4.3	14.0
vs. Div.	118	38.1	14.0	.400	6.3	.349	1.9	.741	0.27	2.31	6.4	4.6	14.8
As Starter	348	36.8	13.5	.403	6.1	.341	1.9	.736	0.25	2.44	6.2	4.5	14.4
Off Bench	2	28.5	9.5	.368	3.0	.167	0.5	1.000	0.50	2.00	5.5	3.0	8.0
In wins	191	38.2	13.9	.432	6.3	.376	2.4	.740	0.28	2.64	6.9	5.0	16.1
In losses	159	35.0	12.9	.366	5.8	.294	1.3	.729	0.23	2.18	5.4	3.9	12.1

	G	Min	FGA	FG%	3PA	3P%	FTA	FT%	Blk	Stl	Ast	Reb	Pts
Pre All-Star	167	35.9	13.2	.407	6.2	.360	1.9	.708	0.25	2.31	6.2	4.2	14.3
Post All-Star	135	37.9	13.7	.407	6.2	.327	1.8	.766	0.29	2.72	6.4	4.9	14.6
Oct/Nov	53	36.2	12.5	.391	5.7	.361	1.9	.650	0.23	2.30	6.6	4.0	13.1
December	45	34.3	13.2	.387	6.4	.325	1.7	.724	0.20	2.18	5.5	4.2	13.5
January	53	37.1	13.9	.433	6.4	.391	2.3	.750	0.28	2.47	6.5	4.2	16.3
February	64	37.7	13.8	.403	5.9	.332	1.8	.735	0.34	2.67	6.4	4.6	14.4
March	75	36.7	12.9	.393	5.9	.309	1.8	.733	0.25	2.51	6.1	4.4	13.3
Apr/May	60	37.9	14.3	.409	6.0	.338	2.0	.808	0.20	2.37	6.2	5.5	15.3
0 Days Rest	90	35.8	12.9	.380	5.9	.323	1.7	.765	0.28	2.13	5.9	4.6	12.9
1 Days Rest	177	37.3	13.6	.412	6.1	.352	2.1	.745	0.27	2.56	6.4	4.6	14.9
2 Days Rest	44	38.2	14.6	.415	6.8	.375	1.6	.583	0.11	2.39	6.0	4.2	15.6
3+ Days Rest	39	35.1	12.7	.400	5.3	.280	1.8	.786	0.28	2.59	6.4	4.2	13.1

Muggsy Bogues

1999-2000 Per Game Averages

	G	Min	FGA	FG%	3PA	3P%	FTA	FT%	Blk	Stl	Ast	Reb	Pts
Total	80	21.6	4.5	.439	0.6	.333	1.1	.908	0.05	0.81	3.7	1.7	5.1
Home	41	21.9	4.7	.430	0.7	.296	1.1	.936	0.07	0.83	3.8	1.5	5.3
Road	39	21.4	4.2	.448	0.6	.375	1.0	.875	0.03	0.79	3.7	1.9	4.9
vs. Playoff	41	20.9	4.1	.379	0.6	.174	0.9	.947	0.02	0.88	3.4	1.7	4.1
vs. Non-Playoff	39	22.4	4.8	.492	0.7	.464	1.3	.878	0.08	0.74	4.1	1.7	6.2
vs. East	52	22.6	4.7	.447	0.7	.405	1.3	.912	0.06	0.85	4.0	1.7	5.7
vs. West	28	19.8	4.0	.420	0.5	.143	0.7	.895	0.04	0.75	3.3	1.7	4.0
vs. Div.	28	22.7	4.8	.481	0.8	.435	1.1	.967	0.00	0.86	4.6	1.6	6.0
As Starter	5	30.4	4.2	.619	1.4	.571	0.6	.667	0.00	1.00	4.8	2.6	4.7
Off Bench	75	21.1	4.5	.427	0.6	.295	1.1	.917	0.05	0.80	3.7	1.6	5.0
In wins	45	21.2	4.2	.471	0.6	.480	1.6	.915	0.07	0.89	4.0	1.7	5.7
In losses	35	22.3	4.8	.402	0.7	.192	0.5	.875	0.03	0.71	3.3	1.7	4.4

	G	Min	FGA	FG%	3PA	3P%	FTA	FT%	Blk	Stl	Ast	Reb	Pts
Pre All-Star	47	21.6	4.2	.455	0.3	.333	1.3	.935	0.06	0.81	3.8	1.6	5.1
Post All-Star	33	21.7	4.8	.419	1.2	.333	0.8	.840	0.03	0.82	3.6	1.8	5.1
November	15	20.5	2.9	.455	0.1	.000	1.1	1.000	0.00	0.87	3.9	2.3	3.8
December	14	21.4	4.6	.406	0.3	.250	1.0	.929	0.07	1.00	3.2	0.9	4.7
January	14	23.5	5.1	.521	0.4	.400	1.8	.880	0.14	0.64	4.1	1.4	7.0
February	12	19.8	5.0	.400	0.8	.222	0.7	1.000	0.00	0.42	3.5	2.2	4.8
March	17	19.3	4.8	.420	1.2	.400	1.1	.833	0.06	0.88	3.8	1.6	5.4
April	8	28.6	4.8	.421	1.5	.333	0.6	.800	0.00	1.13	4.0	2.0	5.0
0 Days Rest	17	19.9	4.1	.449	0.5	.444	1.0	.824	0.06	1.00	3.6	1.9	4.7
1 Days Rest	47	22.2	4.8	.429	0.7	.294	1.1	.925	0.04	0.81	3.8	1.7	5.3
2 Days Rest	9	20.9	3.6	.531	0.7	.500	1.0	.889	0.00	0.56	3.8	1.2	5.0
3+ Days Rest	7	23.3	4.7	.394	0.3	.000	1.1	1.000	0.14	0.71	3.6	1.9	4.9

Last Five Seasons

	G	Min	FGA	FG%	3PA	3P%	FTA	FT%	Blk	Stl	Ast	Reb	Pts
Total	248	24.1	5.2	.451	0.9	.372	1.0	.883	0.04	1.04	5.0	2.0	6.0
Home	133	24.8	5.4	.452	0.9	.392	1.1	.878	0.04	1.12	5.4	1.9	6.2
Road	115	23.3	5.0	.450	0.9	.347	1.0	.891	0.04	0.96	4.6	2.0	5.7
vs. Playoff	129	24.1	5.2	.436	0.8	.356	0.9	.906	0.02	1.14	5.0	1.9	5.6
vs. Non-Playoff	119	24.1	5.3	.468	1.0	.386	1.2	.864	0.06	0.94	5.1	2.1	6.3
vs. East	118	25.3	5.5	.449	1.1	.378	1.1	.859	0.04	1.00	5.3	2.0	6.3
vs. West	130	22.9	5.0	.454	0.7	.363	1.0	.907	0.04	1.08	4.9	1.9	5.7
vs. Div.	80	23.6	5.1	.473	0.8	.343	1.0	.901	0.01	1.05	5.0	1.9	6.0
As Starter	106	29.8	6.4	.462	1.5	.415	1.1	.832	0.04	1.25	6.7	2.3	7.4
Off Bench	142	19.8	4.4	.440	0.4	.254	1.0	.924	0.04	0.89	3.8	1.7	4.9
In wins	129	24.8	5.4	.466	1.1	.419	1.4	.885	0.03	1.14	5.7	2.1	6.8
In losses	119	23.3	5.0	.433	0.6	.271	0.6	.880	0.05	0.94	4.4	1.8	5.0

	G	Min	FGA	FG%	3PA	3P%	FTA	FT%	Blk	Stl	Ast	Reb	Pts
Pre All-Star	111	22.9	5.1	.453	0.5	.379	1.1	.909	0.04	0.95	5.0	1.7	5.8
Post All-Star	101	26.9	5.7	.438	1.5	.383	1.0	.860	0.05	1.10	5.6	2.2	6.4
Oct/Nov	35	21.1	4.4	.448	0.3	.182	0.9	.969	0.03	1.03	4.6	1.7	4.9
December	40	23.1	5.1	.446	0.4	.313	1.1	.905	0.03	0.90	5.0	1.7	5.6
January	29	24.1	5.6	.463	0.7	.421	1.2	.882	0.07	0.97	5.2	1.5	6.5
February	45	24.0	5.7	.430	1.4	.375	0.9	.833	0.02	1.09	5.8	2.4	6.2
March	57	25.6	5.3	.457	1.1	.431	1.0	.828	0.05	1.11	4.9	2.2	6.2
Apr/May	42	25.5	5.1	.467	1.0	.326	1.2	.918	0.05	1.12	4.8	2.0	6.2
0 Days Rest	58	22.4	5.2	.427	0.9	.278	0.8	.875	0.07	1.09	5.0	2.0	5.4
1 Days Rest	126	24.8	5.2	.459	0.8	.380	1.2	.868	0.03	1.06	5.1	2.0	6.1
2 Days Rest	33	24.8	5.6	.459	1.1	.459	0.8	.889	0.03	1.00	5.3	1.6	6.4
3+ Days Rest	31	23.7	5.0	.455	0.9	.407	1.0	.967	0.03	0.94	4.7	2.1	5.9

Shawn Bradley

Dallas Mavericks — Center

1999-2000 Per Game Averages

	G	Min	FGA	FG%	3PA	3P%	FTA	FT%	Blk	Stl	Ast	Reb	Pts
Total	77	24.7	7.2	.479	0.1	.200	1.9	.765	2.47	0.92	0.8	6.5	8.4
Home	39	24.8	7.3	.486	0.1	.000	2.1	.793	3.00	1.21	0.7	7.2	8.7
Road	38	24.5	7.1	.472	0.1	.333	1.8	.731	1.92	0.63	0.8	5.7	8.1
vs. Playoff	44	25.0	7.7	.451	0.1	.333	1.8	.763	2.32	0.84	0.9	6.4	8.3
vs. Non-Playoff	33	24.3	6.6	.523	0.1	.000	2.1	.768	2.67	1.03	0.6	6.5	8.5
vs. East	26	24.7	7.0	.497	0.1	.500	2.2	.759	3.19	0.77	0.6	6.3	8.7
vs. West	51	24.7	7.3	.470	0.1	.000	1.8	.769	2.10	1.00	0.9	6.5	8.2
vs. Div.	24	27.2	7.3	.534	0.0	.000	1.7	.707	2.17	1.08	0.9	6.7	9.0
As Starter	54	26.7	7.8	.498	0.1	.000	2.2	.783	2.52	0.98	0.9	6.9	9.5
Off Bench	23	20.0	5.8	.421	0.1	.500	1.3	.690	2.35	0.78	0.6	5.4	5.8
In wins	38	24.4	6.9	.515	0.0	.000	2.1	.763	2.74	1.05	0.8	6.6	8.7
In losses	39	24.9	7.5	.447	0.1	.250	1.8	.768	2.21	0.79	0.7	6.3	8.1

	G	Min	FGA	FG%	3PA	3P%	FTA	FT%	Blk	Stl	Ast	Reb	Pts
Pre All-Star	48	25.2	7.1	.482	0.1	.333	1.9	.750	2.77	0.88	0.9	6.5	8.3
Post All-Star	29	23.9	7.4	.474	0.1	.000	2.0	.789	1.97	1.00	0.6	6.4	8.6
November	16	25.3	7.6	.484	0.1	1.000	1.5	.792	2.88	1.00	0.9	5.0	8.6
December	14	25.0	6.3	.420	0.0	—	1.4	.750	3.21	0.57	1.0	6.7	6.4
January	13	25.8	7.8	.490	0.2	.000							
February	10	21.8	7.0	.529	0.0	—	2.4	.667	2.30	1.40	0.6	4.7	9.0
March	15	23.9	7.3	.450	0.1	.000	2.1	.806	1.93	0.93	0.5	6.8	8.2
April	9	26.0	7.1	.531	0.0	—	2.3	.810	1.78	1.11	0.8	7.0	9.4
0 Days Rest	15	25.3	8.3	.432	0.1	.000	1.8	.778	1.67	0.73	0.7	5.5	8.6
1 Days Rest	41	24.5	7.0	.488	0.1	.250	2.1	.728	2.61	0.93	0.8	6.9	8.3
2 Days Rest	15	24.8	6.1	.522	0.0	—	2.1	.871	3.13	0.80	0.8	6.7	8.2
3+ Days Rest	6	24.5	8.2	.469	0.0	—	1.7	.700	1.83	1.67	1.0	5.3	8.8

Last Five Seasons

	G	Min	FGA	FG%	3PA	3P%	FTA	FT%	Blk	Stl	Ast	Reb	Pts
Total	342	28.2	9.9	.450	0.1	.125	2.7	.706	3.21	0.72	0.8	7.8	10.8
Home	174	28.6	10.6	.452	0.1	.111	3.0	.710	3.71	0.84	0.9	8.6	11.7
Road	168	27.7	9.2	.447	0.1	.133	2.3	.701	2.70	0.59	0.8	6.9	9.9
vs. Playoff	202	27.4	9.8	.445	0.1	.125	2.7	.692	2.76	0.70	0.8	7.2	10.6
vs. Non-Playoff	140	29.3	10.1	.457	0.1	.125	2.6	.727	3.87	0.75	0.9	8.6	11.1
vs. East	149	28.9	10.4	.450	0.1	.100	2.9	.705	3.39	0.64	0.7	7.8	11.4
vs. West	193	27.6	9.5	.450	0.1	.143	2.5	.706	3.08	0.78	0.9	7.4	10.5
vs. Div.	105	28.9	9.9	.471	0.0	.000	2.7	.699	3.33	0.82	0.8	8.2	11.1
As Starter	271	29.9	10.6	.454	0.1	.100	2.8	.710	3.29	0.70	0.9	8.1	11.7
Off Bench	71	21.7	7.3	.425	0.1	.250	2.2	.684	2.92	0.77	0.6	6.5	7.7
In wins	119	28.2	9.5	.461	0.0	.000	2.6	.739	3.62	0.80	0.9	8.1	10.6
In losses	223	28.2	10.2	.444	0.1	.143	2.7	.689	3.00	0.68	0.7	7.6	10.9

	G	Min	FGA	FG%	3PA	3P%	FTA	FT%	Blk	Stl	Ast	Reb	Pts
Pre All-Star	160	28.1	9.7	.439	0.1	.250	2.6	.694	3.31	0.69	0.8	7.6	10.3
Post All-Star	133	28.9	11.2	.454	0.1	.000	3.0	.706	3.09	0.76	0.8	7.8	12.3
Oct/Nov	54	28.7	9.8	.446	0.1	.500	2.6	.719	3.46	0.70	0.8	7.8	10.6
December	41	26.4	8.4	.422	0.0	.000	2.2	.644	3.37	0.59	0.7	6.8	8.5
January	49	28.0	10.3	.425	0.1	.000	2.8	.705	2.82	0.67	0.8	7.9	10.7
February	65	27.8	9.1	.473	0.1	.250	2.7	.711	3.46	0.77	0.7	7.4	10.5
March	76	28.4	10.7	.457	0.1	.000	2.9	.687	3.08	0.78	0.8	7.7	11.7
Apr/May	57	29.1	10.8	.459	0.1	.000	2.8	.750	3.11	0.74	1.0	8.8	12.0
0 Days Rest	87	28.7	10.3	.454	0.1	.000	2.4	.689	3.15	0.57	0.9	7.6	11.0
1 Days Rest	166	27.9	9.8	.448	0.1	.154	2.7	.707	3.30	0.74	0.8		10.7
2 Days Rest	57	28.6	10.5	.438	0.1	.200	2.9	.713	3.32	0.79	0.9	8.1	11.3
3+ Days Rest	32	27.5	8.8	.470	0.0	.000	2.8	.727	2.78	0.88	0.5	6.5	10.3

Elton Brand

Chicago Bulls — Forward

1999-2000 Per Game Averages

	G	Min	FGA	FG%	3PA	3P%	FTA	FT%	Blk	Stl	Ast	Reb	Pts
Total	81	37.0	16.1	.482	0.0	.000	6.6	.685	1.63	0.81	1.9	10.0	20.1
Home	41	37.9	16.3	.471	0.0	.000	7.0	.668	2.10	0.66	2.0	11.1	20.1
Road	40	36.2	15.9	.495	0.0	.000	6.2	.704	1.15	0.98	1.8	8.9	20.1
vs. Playoff	47	37.1	15.7	.489	0.0	—	6.6	.663	1.70	0.94	2.0	9.4	19.7
vs. Non-Playoff	34	37.0	16.8	.474	0.0	.000	6.7	.714	1.53	0.65	1.8	10.8	20.6
vs. East	53	37.5	16.2	.492	0.0	.000	6.9	.699	1.75	0.79	1.9	10.4	20.8
vs. West	28	36.0	16.0	.464	0.0	.000	6.1	.653	1.39	0.86	2.0	9.2	18.8
vs. Div.	27	38.4	17.6	.508	0.0	.000	6.7	.703	1.44	0.63	2.0	10.5	22.7
As Starter	80	37.2	16.3	.482	0.0	.000	6.6	.688	1.64	0.80	1.9	10.1	20.2
Off Bench	1	21.0	6.0	.667	0.0	—	10.0	.500	1.00	2.00	1.0	3.0	13.0
In wins	17	36.6	16.7	.475	0.0	—	6.5	.700	1.53	0.59	1.9	12.0	20.4
In losses	64	37.1	16.0	.484	0.0	.000	6.7	.681	1.66	0.88	1.9	9.5	20.0

	G	Min	FGA	FG%	3PA	3P%	FTA	FT%	Blk	Stl	Ast	Reb	Pts
Pre All-Star	46	35.2	14.7	.486	0.0	.000	6.0	.656	1.46	0.98	1.7	9.7	18.2
Post All-Star	35	39.4	18.0	.479	0.0	.000	7.4	.715	1.86	0.60	2.3	10.4	22.5
November	13	32.1	13.9	.442	0.0	—	6.0	.654	1.23	0.77	1.7	8.2	16.2
December	13	35.8	14.2	.446	0.0	—	6.2	.630	2.15	1.15	1.9	10.2	16.5
January	14	38.9	17.1	.515	0.0	—	5.9	.659	1.29	1.07	1.6	12.0	21.4
February	14	36.3	16.0	.518	0.1	.000	5.3	.743	1.43	0.64	2.3	8.6	20.5
March	16	39.3	18.2	.460	0.1	.000	7.3	.681	1.81	0.75	1.6	10.1	21.7
April	11	39.5	17.0	.508	0.0	—	9.5	.733	1.91	0.45	2.5	10.9	24.3
0 Days Rest	24	34.9	14.8	.480	0.0	—	5.7	.686	1.29	0.58	2.3	9.1	18.1
1 Days Rest	36	38.9	17.2	.490	0.0	.000	7.2	.696	1.89	0.86	2.0	10.5	21.9
2 Days Rest	13	37.6	16.5	.502	0.1	.000	7.2	.649	1.69	0.92	1.5	10.7	21.3
3+ Days Rest	8	34.0	14.9	.412	0.0	—	5.6	.689	1.38	1.13	1.4	9.4	16.1

Terrell Brandon

1999-2000 Per Game Averages

	G	Min	FGA	FG%	3PA	3P%	FTA	FT%	Blk	Stl	Ast	Reb	Pts
Total	71	36.4	14.7	.466	1.9	.402	2.9	.899	0.42	1.89	8.9	3.4	17.1
Home	36	35.8	13.9	.479	1.9	.333	2.5	.879	0.64	1.61	9.2	3.5	16.2
Road	35	37.1	15.5	.455	1.8	.476	3.3	.915	0.20	2.17	8.5	3.2	18.0
vs. Playoff	39	37.7	15.1	.478	1.8	.437	3.3	.876	0.49	1.92	8.8	3.4	18.1
vs. Non-Playoff	32	34.9	14.2	.452	1.9	.361	2.5	.937	0.34	1.84	8.9	3.1	15.8
vs. East	27	37.6	14.6	.444	1.8	.375	3.3	.922	0.33	2.07	9.5	3.7	16.7
vs. West	44	35.8	14.7	.480	1.9	.417	2.7	.881	0.48	1.77	8.5	3.1	17.3
vs. Div.	20	35.3	14.3	.476	1.9	.405	2.8	.946	0.60	1.85	7.7	3.3	17.0
As Starter	71	36.4	14.7	.466	1.9	.402	2.9	.899	0.42	1.89	8.9	3.4	17.1
Off Bench	0	—											
In wins	43	36.8	14.7	.512	1.8	.481	3.3	.910	0.53	2.05	9.3	3.9	19.0
In losses	28	35.9	14.6	.396	1.9	.283	2.3	.875	0.25	1.64	8.2	2.6	14.1

	G	Min	FGA	FG%	3PA	3P%	FTA	FT%	Blk	Stl	Ast	Reb	Pts
Pre All-Star	38	36.3	14.8	.442	1.6	.356	3.5	.910	0.47	1.66	8.8	3.2	16.8
Post All-Star	33	36.6	14.5	.495	2.2	.438	2.3	.880	0.36	2.15	9.0	3.5	17.3
November	12	33.5	15.1	.453	1.2	.357	2.0	.917	0.42	2.08	8.3	2.8	15.9
December	15	36.7	14.9	.420	1.7	.269	3.5	.885	0.47	1.60	8.5	2.9	16.1
January	11	38.6	14.4	.462	1.7	.474	5.2	.930	0.55	1.27	9.7	4.3	18.9
February	9	34.6	11.4	.563	2.0	.333	2.0	.778	0.78	1.33	7.9	3.6	15.1
March	16	38.1	15.4	.504	2.2	.457	2.8	.909	0.19	2.81	9.4	3.9	19.0
April	8	36.1	16.3	.423	2.5	.500	1.6	.923	0.25	1.75	9.3	2.6	16.5
0 Days Rest	16	36.6	14.4	.517	2.3	.622	3.3	.887	0.31	1.81	8.7	3.3	19.3
1 Days Rest	41	36.2	14.6	.458	1.8	.278	3.1	.921	0.37	1.83	8.3	3.4	16.7
2 Days Rest	5	36.6	15.6	.513	2.0	.600	2.2	.909	0.20	2.40	8.8	3.8	19.2
3+ Days Rest	9	37.1	14.9	.388	1.4	.308	2.0	.778	1.00	2.00	11.8	3.0	13.6

Last Five Seasons

	G	Min	FGA	FG%	3PA	3P%	FTA	FT%	Blk	Stl	Ast	Reb	Pts
Total	310	35.6	15.1	.453	2.5	.370	3.6	.884	0.39	1.86	7.4	3.5	17.8
Home	157	35.5	15.1	.455	2.6	.381	3.4	.885	0.48	1.69	7.4	3.5	17.8
Road	153	35.6	15.1	.450	2.4	.358	3.8	.883	0.29	2.05	7.0	3.6	17.9
vs. Playoff	166	36.3	15.5	.455	2.6	.376	3.7	.886	0.39	1.87	7.2	3.4	18.3
vs. Non-Playoff	144	34.8	14.7	.450	2.4	.363	3.5	.882	0.39	1.86	7.6	3.7	17.2
vs. East	172	35.7	15.2	.455	2.7	.370	3.7	.877	0.33	1.83	7.1	3.7	18.1
vs. West	138	35.4	15.0	.450	2.3	.370	3.5	.893	0.46	1.91	7.8	3.3	17.5
vs. Div.	100	35.2	15.1	.462	2.4	.346	3.5	.872	0.40	1.83	7.3	3.6	17.8
As Starter	306	35.7	15.2	.453	2.5	.370	3.6	.884	0.38	1.87	7.5	3.5	17.9
Off Bench	4	26.8	9.3	.432	1.5	.333	3.5	.857	0.75	1.50	4.3	2.8	11.5
In wins	175	35.4	14.9	.471	2.4	.415	4.1	.903	0.46	1.91	8.1	3.9	18.7
In losses	135	35.8	15.5	.429	2.6	.317	3.0	.851	0.29	1.80	6.5	3.0	16.7

	G	Min	FGA	FG%	3PA	3P%	FTA	FT%	Blk	Stl	Ast	Reb	Pts
Pre All-Star	171	36.0	15.6	.453	2.6	.388	3.9	.890	0.46	1.91	7.3	3.5	18.6
Post All-Star	103	35.4	14.8	.463	2.7	.362	3.6	.883	0.30	1.83	7.2	3.5	17.8
Oct/Nov	55	33.8	15.0	.457	2.4	.368	3.0	.859	0.33	2.24	7.0	3.2	17.1
December	50	37.2	15.4	.454	2.7	.391	4.6	.926	0.50	1.66	7.3	3.4	19.3
January	56	38.0	16.4	.444	2.8	.386	4.5	.874	0.57	1.86	8.0	3.9	19.6
February	47	32.9	13.5	.461	2.6	.336	3.0	.895	0.38	1.47	6.3	3.3	16.0
March	52	35.5	14.9	.457	2.1	.393	3.3	.855	0.33	2.12	7.6	3.8	17.2
Apr/May	50	35.8	15.4	.445	2.5	.344	3.2	.886	0.20	1.78	8.3	3.6	17.3
0 Days Rest	75	34.8	14.6	.460	2.7	.414	3.7	.884	0.33	1.83	7.0	3.5	17.9
1 Days Rest	151	36.1	15.2	.448	2.4	.351	3.9	.892	0.41	1.89	7.5	3.5	17.9
2 Days Rest	55	35.8	15.7	.461	2.6	.364	3.2	.876	0.31	1.89	7.3	3.6	18.3
3+ Days Rest	29	34.4	14.8	.441	2.3	.358	2.8	.841	0.55	1.76	8.0	3.3	16.2

P.J. Brown

1999-2000 Per Game Averages

	G	Min	FGA	FG%	3PA	3P%	FTA	FT%	Blk	Stl	Ast	Reb	Pts
Total	80	28.8	8.4	.480	0.0	.000	2.0	.755	0.76	0.81	1.8	7.5	9.6
Home	40	29.6	8.2	.483	0.0	—	1.9	.733	0.83	0.78	1.7	7.8	9.3
Road	40	27.9	8.6	.477	0.0	.000	2.1	.774	0.70	0.85	1.9	7.3	9.8
vs. Playoff	42	29.6	8.5	.457	0.0	—	2.0	.779	0.79	0.74	1.9	7.4	9.4
vs. Non-Playoff	38	27.9	8.2	.506	0.0	.000	1.9	.726	0.74	0.89	1.7	7.6	9.7
vs. East	53	27.9	7.7	.457	0.0	.000	1.9	.727	0.68	0.83	1.6	6.9	8.4
vs. West	27	30.4	9.8	.515	0.0	—	2.2	.800	0.93	0.78	2.3	8.7	11.9
vs. Div.	24	30.4	8.3	.460	0.0	—	2.3	.648	0.75	0.83	1.6	7.8	9.0
As Starter	80	28.8	8.4	.480	0.0	.000	2.0	.755	0.76	0.81	1.8	7.5	9.6
Off Bench	0	—											
In wins	52	28.8	8.3	.500	0.0	.000	2.2	.730	0.79	0.73	1.8	7.8	9.9
In losses	28	28.8	8.5	.444	0.0	—	1.6	.818	0.71	0.96	1.8	6.9	8.9

	G	Min	FGA	FG%	3PA	3P%	FTA	FT%	Blk	Stl	Ast	Reb	Pts
Pre All-Star	47	30.2	9.0	.480	0.0	.000	2.3	.783	0.74	0.87	2.1	8.1	10.4
Post All-Star	33	26.8	7.5	.480	0.0	—	1.6	.698	0.79	0.73	1.5	6.6	8.3
November	14	31.4	8.9	.516	0.1	.000	3.6	.824	0.64	0.93	1.8	7.9	12.1
December	14	31.6	10.3	.493	0.0	—	2.3	.813	0.57	0.64	2.5	8.4	10.2
January	15	28.8	8.7	.473	0.0	—	0.9	.615	0.87	1.07	2.1	7.8	8.8
February	14	28.0	8.0	.438	0.0	—	1.7	.750	0.93	0.93	1.1	7.9	8.3
March	12	26.3	8.1	.515	0.0	—	1.1	.846	0.67	0.67	1.4	6.0	9.3
April	11	25.5	5.7	.413	0.0	—	2.4	.577	0.91	0.55	1.8	6.6	6.1
0 Days Rest	17	27.9	7.7	.519	0.1	.000	1.8	.733	0.65	0.53	1.5	8.1	9.3
1 Days Rest	44	29.0	8.5	.458	0.0	—	1.8	.738	0.68	0.68	1.9	7.4	9.1
2 Days Rest	12	28.7	8.7	.481	0.0	—	2.6	.774	1.42	1.25	2.2	7.7	10.3
3+ Days Rest	7	29.7	9.0	.524	0.0	—	2.6	.833	0.43	1.57	1.6	6.7	11.6

Last Five Seasons

	G	Min	FGA	FG%	3PA	3P%	FTA	FT%	Blk	Stl	Ast	Reb	Pts
Total	365	32.4	8.7	.465	0.0	.167	2.7	.759	1.11	0.93	1.6	7.7	10.2
Home	180	32.7	8.9	.458	0.1	.154	2.5	.757	1.21	0.84	1.5	7.8	10.1
Road	185	32.0	8.6	.471	0.0	.200	2.9	.761	1.01	1.02	1.6	7.6	10.3
vs. Playoff	193	32.3	8.5	.466	0.0	.111	2.7	.764	1.03	0.90	1.5	7.4	10.0
vs. Non-Playoff	172	32.4	9.0	.463	0.1	.222	2.7	.762	1.20	0.97	1.6	8.0	10.4
vs. East	254	32.1	8.6	.462	0.1	.143	2.7	.756	1.02	0.91	1.5	7.4	10.0
vs. West	111	33.0	9.0	.471	0.0	.250	2.7	.765	1.32	0.98	1.8	8.4	10.5
vs. Div.	115	33.1	8.9	.470	0.1	.111	3.0	.745	1.11	0.96	1.5	8.0	10.6
As Starter	356	32.6	8.8	.464	0.1	.167	2.7	.760	1.12	0.95	1.6	7.8	10.3
Off Bench	9	21.3	5.2	.489	0.0	—	2.0	.722	0.89	0.44	0.8	4.8	6.6
In wins	222	32.3	8.8	.474	0.0	.091	2.8	.764	1.17	0.90	1.6	8.1	10.5
In losses	143	32.5	8.6	.450	0.0	.286	2.5	.749	1.02	0.99	1.6	7.1	9.7

	G	Min	FGA	FG%	3PA	3P%	FTA	FT%	Blk	Stl	Ast	Reb	Pts
Pre All-Star	186	32.4	8.4	.458	0.1	.083	2.7	.754	1.15	0.86	1.5	7.7	9.7
Post All-Star	129	32.4	8.9	.468	0.0	.333	2.7	.765	1.11	1.05	1.7	7.8	10.4
Oct/Nov	57	30.7	8.1	.465	0.1	.167	2.8	.790	1.16	0.88	1.2	7.7	9.8
December	55	32.5	8.6	.499	0.0	.000	2.7	.720	1.18	0.75	1.8	7.5	10.5
January	59	34.1	9.1	.446	0.1	.000	2.5	.750	1.12	1.00	1.6	7.9	9.9
February	67	32.8	8.7	.443	0.0	.000	2.6	.785	1.16	1.09	1.7	8.2	9.8
March	65	33.1	9.3	.478	0.0	—	2.8	.761	1.15	1.00	1.7	8.0	11.0
Apr/May	62	30.8	8.6	.461	0.0	.667	2.7	.741	0.89	0.85	1.4	7.2	10.0
0 Days Rest	95	31.3	8.2	.449	0.0	.000	2.6	.773	1.03	0.81	1.7	7.4	9.4
1 Days Rest	174	32.4	9.0	.473	0.0	.429	2.7	.768	1.10	0.90	1.5	7.9	10.6
2 Days Rest	65	34.1	9.1	.460	0.0	—	2.9	.731	1.43	1.22	1.6	8.0	10.5
3+ Days Rest	31	31.9	7.9	.471	0.1	.000	2.7	.729	0.71	0.90	1.3	7.1	9.4

Randy Brown

Chicago Bulls — Guard

1999-2000 Per Game Averages

	G	Min	FGA	FG%	3PA	3P%	FTA	FT%	Blk	Stl	Ast	Reb	Pts
Total	59	27.5	7.4	.361	0.1	.500	1.4	.738	0.25	1.03	3.4	2.4	6.4
Home	28	25.8	7.3	.358	0.1	1.000	1.4	.711	0.07	1.07	3.6	2.5	6.3
Road	31	29.1	7.5	.364	0.1	.250	1.5	.761	0.42	1.00	3.3	2.4	6.6
vs. Playoff	35	26.5	6.8	.332	0.1	.333	1.1	.676	0.17	0.94	3.3	2.5	5.3
vs. Non-Playoff	24	29.0	8.2	.396	0.1	.667	2.0	.787	0.38	1.17	3.6	2.4	8.1
vs. East	35	25.9	6.9	.325	0.1	.600	1.1	.775	0.26	1.06	2.8	2.4	5.5
vs. West	24	29.9	8.0	.406	0.0	.000	1.8	.705	0.25	1.00	4.3	2.5	7.8
vs. Div.	21	26.0	7.1	.327	0.1	.500	0.9	.737	0.33	1.24	3.3	2.7	5.4
As Starter	55	28.3	7.6	.365	0.1	.500	1.5	.744	0.27	1.00	3.5	2.5	6.7
Off Bench	4	17.3	4.0	.250	0.0	—	0.5	.500	0.00	1.50	2.0	1.8	2.3
In wins	12	27.8	6.4	.299	0.2	1.000	1.9	.739	0.17	0.92	3.9	2.4	5.4
In losses	47	27.5	7.6	.374	0.1	.250	1.3	.738	0.28	1.06	3.3	2.4	6.7

	G	Min	FGA	FG%	3PA	3P%	FTA	FT%	Blk	Stl	Ast	Reb	Pts
Pre All-Star	32	28.8	7.7	.386	0.1	.500	0.9	.690	0.31	1.06	3.4	2.1	6.6
Post All-Star	27	26.0	7.0	.328	0.1	.500	2.0	.764	0.19	1.00	3.5	2.8	6.2
November	13	33.2	10.1	.389	0.3	.500	1.0	.692	0.54	0.92	3.8	2.5	8.7
December	5	26.6	7.2	.417	0.0	—	1.0	.800	0.20	0.80	2.6	1.6	6.8
January	8	22.4	4.8	.316	0.0	—	0.3	.500	0.00	1.50	2.8	2.0	3.1
February	14	28.2	7.5	.400	0.0	—	1.6	.696	0.14	0.79	3.4	2.5	7.1
March	15	27.1	7.1	.292	0.1	.500	2.5	.811	0.27	1.27	3.9	2.8	6.2
April	4	20.3	4.8	.316	0.0	—	1.0	.500	0.25	0.75	2.8	2.8	3.5
0 Days Rest	16	30.3	7.7	.431	0.2	.333	1.9	.710	0.63	0.94	3.6	2.6	8.1
1 Days Rest	24	27.2	7.3	.309	0.0	1.000	1.5	.838	0.04	1.04	3.3	2.9	5.8
2 Days Rest	9	26.6	8.8	.367	0.2	.500	1.0	.444	0.33	1.11	3.6	2.4	7.0
3+ Days Rest	10	25.0	5.8	.362	0.0	—	0.7	.714	0.10	1.10	3.5	1.2	4.7

Last Five Seasons

	G	Min	FGA	FG%	3PA	3P%	FTA	FT%	Blk	Stl	Ast	Reb	Pts
Total	309	18.2	5.1	.394	0.2	.148	1.3	.711	0.21	1.09	2.3	1.8	5.0
Home	158	18.2	5.2	.412	0.2	.208	1.4	.729	0.19	1.18	2.5	1.8	5.3
Road	151	18.3	5.1	.375	0.2	.100	1.2	.689	0.23	1.00	2.0	1.7	4.6
vs. Playoff	162	17.9	4.9	.391	0.2	.061	1.1	.712	0.17	1.04	2.3	1.7	4.7
vs. Non-Playoff	147	18.7	5.3	.397	0.1	.286	1.4	.711	0.25	1.15	2.3	1.8	5.3
vs. East	209	18.5	5.2	.380	0.2	.200	1.4	.730	0.20	1.14	2.3	1.9	5.0
vs. West	100	17.7	5.0	.423	0.2	.053	1.1	.664	0.22	1.00	2.3	1.5	5.0
vs. Div.	110	18.6	5.2	.392	0.1	.133	1.4	.722	0.21	1.17	2.4	1.9	5.1
As Starter	96	28.7	7.8	.385	0.2	.188	1.9	.754	0.23	1.30	3.7	2.9	7.5
Off Bench	213	13.6	3.9	.403	0.2	.132	1.0	.673	0.20	1.00	1.6	1.3	3.8
In wins	196	15.6	4.4	.404	0.2	.182	1.2	.703	0.19	1.08	2.0	1.6	4.4
In losses	113	22.8	6.4	.382	0.2	.095	1.4	.724	0.23	1.12	2.8	2.0	5.9

	G	Min	FGA	FG%	3PA	3P%	FTA	FT%	Blk	Stl	Ast	Reb	Pts
Pre All-Star	164	16.8	4.8	.406	0.2	.214	0.9	.665	0.23	1.04	2.0	1.4	4.6
Post All-Star	106	16.4	4.5	.361	0.2	.125	1.3	.730	0.18	0.94	2.2	1.7	4.2
Oct/Nov	57	18.9	5.8	.396	0.3	.333	0.8	.581	0.25	0.84	2.2	1.5	5.1
December	44	15.2	4.1	.400	0.1	.167	1.5	.716	0.20	1.11	1.8	1.3	4.4
January	48	15.0	4.1	.414	0.0	.000	0.6	.733	0.21	1.27	1.6	1.4	3.9
February	52	20.7	5.5	.411	0.1	.000	1.1	.712	0.17	1.08	2.7	2.2	5.3
March	64	20.1	5.7	.397	0.2	.083	2.1	.773	0.20	1.03	2.7	2.1	6.1
Apr/May	44	18.5	5.1	.344	0.3	.091	1.5	.656	0.20	1.32	2.6	2.1	4.5
0 Days Rest	81	20.8	5.8	.433	0.2	.250	1.4	.681	0.36	1.21	2.3	2.1	6.0
1 Days Rest	132	18.1	5.0	.364	0.2	.048	1.4	.754	0.14	1.05	2.4	1.9	4.7
2 Days Rest	52	15.7	4.7	.373	0.2	.333	1.0	.660	0.21	0.79	2.0	1.5	4.2
3+ Days Rest	44	17.2	4.9	.423	0.2	.000	0.9	.658	0.14	1.36	2.3	1.1	4.7

Kobe Bryant

Los Angeles Lakers — Guard

1999-2000 Per Game Averages

	G	Min	FGA	FG%	3PA	3P%	FTA	FT%	Blk	Stl	Ast	Reb	Pts
Total	66	38.2	17.9	.468	2.2	.319	6.1	.821	0.94	1.61	4.9	6.3	22.5
Home	33	36.1	17.5	.479	2.4	.325	6.3	.816	0.88	1.58	4.8	6.5	22.7
Road	33	40.4	18.3	.458	1.9	.313	5.9	.827	1.00	1.64	4.9	6.1	22.3
vs. Playoff	37	38.7	18.5	.470	2.2	.288	6.1	.815	0.92	1.51	5.0	6.5	23.0
vs. Non-Playoff	29	37.6	17.2	.466	2.2	.359	6.1	.830	0.97	1.72	4.8	6.0	21.8
vs. East	26	37.7	16.7	.447	1.7	.256	5.8	.833	1.04	1.65	4.7	5.6	20.2
vs. West	40	38.6	18.7	.481	2.5	.347	6.3	.814	0.88	1.58	5.1	6.8	24.0
vs. Div.	20	37.6	18.1	.510	2.4	.340	7.0	.814	0.75	1.55	4.4	7.0	24.9
As Starter	62	38.8	18.1	.471	2.2	.324	5.9	.825	0.97	1.63	5.1	6.4	22.7
Off Bench	4	30.3	14.5	.414	2.0	.250	8.8	.800	1.00	0.25	2.0	4.5	19.5
In wins	55	37.8	17.6	.481	2.1	.345	6.5	.825	1.00	1.64	5.1	6.7	23.1
In losses	11	40.4	19.6	.412	2.5	.214	4.4	.792	0.64	1.45	4.1	7.4	20.2

	G	Min	FGA	FG%	3PA	3P%	FTA	FT%	Blk	Stl	Ast	Reb	Pts
Pre All-Star	33	37.8	18.0	.462	2.1	.362	6.2	.843	0.97	1.58	4.3	6.2	22.6
Post All-Star	33	38.7	17.9	.475	2.3	.280	6.0	.799	0.91	1.64	5.5	6.4	22.4
November	0	—											
December	15	37.1	17.4	.456	1.3	.263	7.2	.852	0.73	1.40	4.3	5.3	22.3
January	14	39.3	19.4	.456	2.9	.366	5.2	.849	1.07	1.64	3.2	7.1	23.2
February	13	37.1	15.4	.510	1.9	.400	5.5	.819	1.46	1.85	6.1	5.5	21.0
March	16	38.4	17.9	.481	2.3	.306	6.4	.765	0.69	1.63	5.1	6.8	22.8
April	8	40.3	20.4	.436	2.9	.217	6.0	.833	0.75	1.50	6.5	7.3	23.4
0 Days Rest	15	39.4	20.2	.485	2.5	.378	5.7	.791	0.60	1.40	5.1	6.1	25.1
1 Days Rest	35	38.1	16.9	.446	2.1	.280	6.5	.837	1.03	1.71	4.6	6.7	21.1
2 Days Rest	10	38.3	17.7	.503	2.0	.400	5.6	.804	1.10	1.30	6.7	5.9	23.1
3+ Days Rest	6	36.2	18.8	.487	2.0	.250	5.7	.824	1.00	2.00	3.3	5.3	23.5

Career (1996-97 thru 1999-2000)

	G	Min	FGA	FG%	3PA	3P%	FTA	FT%	Blk	Stl	Ast	Reb	Pts
Total	266	28.5	12.4	.450	2.3	.331	5.0	.816	0.66	1.13	3.0	4.0	15.9
Home	131	28.6	12.6	.461	2.3	.316	5.4	.836	0.70	1.20	3.2	4.0	16.8
Road	135	28.4	12.2	.439	2.2	.347	4.6	.792	0.61	1.07	2.8	3.9	15.1
vs. Playoff	143	29.0	12.9	.444	2.3	.312	5.1	.811	0.69	1.10	3.0	4.0	16.3
vs. Non-Playoff	123	27.9	11.8	.458	2.2	.354	4.8	.822	0.62	1.17	3.1	4.0	15.6
vs. East	88	26.5	11.7	.433	2.1	.326	4.5	.797	0.59	1.05	2.5	3.5	14.4
vs. West	178	29.5	12.7	.459	2.4	.333	5.2	.824	0.69	1.17	3.3	4.2	16.7
vs. Div.	86	29.2	12.5	.466	2.2	.344	5.5	.808	0.67	1.26	3.0	4.1	16.9
As Starter	119	38.0	16.7	.468	2.2	.309	5.8	.831	0.97	1.55	4.4	5.8	21.1
Off Bench	147	20.8	8.9	.423	2.3	.348	4.3	.799	0.40	0.80	1.9	2.5	11.8
In wins	192	28.3	12.3	.465	2.1	.353	5.2	.829	0.72	1.22	3.2	4.0	16.4
In losses	74	28.9	12.7	.413	2.8	.289	4.3	.775	0.49	0.89	2.5	3.8	14.6

	G	Min	FGA	FG%	3PA	3P%	FTA	FT%	Blk	Stl	Ast	Reb	Pts
Pre All-Star	114	25.7	11.9	.449	2.4	.359	4.9	.809	0.58	1.09	2.5	3.7	15.5
Post All-Star	102	27.0	11.4	.441	2.3	.326	4.6	.809	0.58	1.03	3.2	3.6	14.5
Oct/Nov	26	17.4	8.2	.404	2.3	.361	3.4	.742	0.38	0.73	1.5	2.2	10.0
December	39	26.9	12.9	.450	2.3	.346	5.6	.804	0.56	1.00	2.6	3.7	16.9
January	40	29.3	13.3	.466	2.7	.358	5.0	.833	0.65	1.28	2.5	4.4	17.4
February	50	30.6	12.7	.446	2.1	.311	4.7	.843	0.86	1.16	3.4	4.2	16.7
March	64	29.4	12.6	.457	2.1	.314	5.3	.819	0.66	1.28	3.1	3.9	16.5
Apr/May	47	31.7	12.9	.447	2.4	.319	5.1	.808	0.68	1.11	4.1	3.6	16.4
0 Days Rest	66	39.3	13.0	.456	2.1	.362	4.6	.814	0.56	1.11	3.0	4.0	16.4
1 Days Rest	134	29.1	12.6	.448	2.3	.315	5.4	.816	0.66	1.17	3.0	4.2	16.4
2 Days Rest	35	28.6	11.5	.468	2.4	.361	4.7	.807	0.89	1.11	3.8	3.7	15.5
3+ Days Rest	31	24.0	11.3	.421	2.1	.303	4.2	.829	0.61	1.03	2.3	3.1	13.6

Mark Bryant
Cleveland Cavaliers — Forward

1999-2000 Per Game Averages

	G	Min	FGA	FG%	3PA	3P%	FTA	FT%	Blk	Stl	Ast	Reb	Pts
Total	75	22.8	4.6	.503	0.0	—	1.3	.809	0.41	0.41	0.8	4.7	5.7
Home	36	22.7	4.4	.484	0.0	—	1.4	.824	0.42	0.39	0.9	4.8	5.4
Road	39	22.9	4.8	.519	0.0	—	1.1	.791	0.41	0.44	0.7	4.6	5.8
vs. Playoff	42	23.2	4.6	.482	0.0	—	1.6	.791	0.33	0.48	1.0	4.8	5.7
vs. Non-Playoff	33	22.3	4.6	.530	0.0	—	0.8	.852	0.52	0.33	0.6	4.5	5.5
vs. East	48	22.1	4.4	.512	0.0	—	1.3	.833	0.40	0.31	0.9	4.5	5.5
vs. West	27	24.1	5.0	.489	0.0	—	1.3	.765	0.44	0.59	0.6	5.0	5.9
vs. Div.	24	22.2	4.0	.484	0.0	—	1.2	.828	0.46	0.33	0.9	4.5	4.8
As Starter	50	25.3	5.0	.478	0.0	—	1.3	.781	0.42	0.50	1.0	4.6	5.8
Off Bench	25	17.8	3.8	.568	0.0	—	1.2	.867	0.40	0.24	0.5	4.0	5.4
In wins	29	23.6	5.0	.500	0.0	—	1.5	.818	0.48	0.59	1.0	4.8	6.2
In losses	46	22.3	4.4	.505	0.0	—	1.1	.800	0.37	0.30	0.7	4.6	5.3
Pre All-Star	42	21.2	4.3	.527	0.0	—	1.3	.870	0.38	0.43	0.8	4.4	5.7
Post All-Star	33	24.9	5.0	.476	0.0	—	1.2	.725	0.45	0.39	0.8	5.1	5.6
November	9	11.3	2.1	.632	0.0	—	1.6	.786	0.33	0.11	0.3	2.9	3.9
December	13	22.9	4.8	.571	0.0	—	0.9	.917	0.15	0.38	0.8	4.5	6.4
January	15	24.9	5.1	.474	0.0	—	1.6	.875	0.47	0.67	1.3	4.9	6.2
February	12	26.6	5.5	.409	0.0	—	0.9	.818	0.58	0.50	0.7	5.9	5.3
March	15	24.8	4.5	.478	0.0	—	1.3	.700	0.53	0.60	0.7	5.2	5.2
April	11	22.5	5.0	.564	0.0	—	1.2	.769	0.36	0.00	1.0	4.1	6.5
0 Days Rest	20	23.5	5.1	.588	0.0	—	1.2	.826	0.25	0.30	1.0	4.6	7.0
1 Days Rest	32	23.7	4.8	.408	0.0	—	1.3	.786	0.44	0.53	0.7	5.1	4.9
2 Days Rest	14	21.9	3.9	.574	0.0	—	1.1	.867	0.64	0.36	0.9	4.4	5.4
3+ Days Rest	9	19.6	4.2	.553	0.0	—	1.6	.786	0.33	0.33	0.9	4.1	5.9

Last Five Seasons

	G	Min	FGA	FG%	3PA	3P%	FTA	FT%	Blk	Stl	Ast	Reb	Pts
Total	302	22.0	5.4	.515	0.0	.000	1.9	.724	0.28	0.51	0.8	4.6	7.0
Home	146	21.2	5.3	.506	0.0	.000	1.8	.702	0.30	0.49	0.8	4.4	6.6
Road	156	22.6	5.5	.524	0.0	.000	2.1	.742	0.27	0.53	0.9	4.8	7.3
vs. Playoff	171	21.7	5.2	.513	0.0	.000	1.8	.768	0.21	0.51	0.8	4.4	6.7
vs. Non-Playoff	131	22.3	5.7	.518	0.0	—	2.1	.676	0.38	0.51	0.9	4.8	7.4
vs. East	158	22.6	5.5	.504	0.0	.000	2.0	.726	0.31	0.51	1.0	4.7	7.0
vs. West	144	21.2	5.4	.528	0.0	.000	1.8	.722	0.26	0.51	0.7	4.5	7.0
vs. Div.	96	22.8	5.7	.509	0.0	.000	2.1	.717	0.30	0.42	0.9	4.7	7.3
As Starter	128	26.1	6.7	.507	0.0	.000	2.0	.709	0.33	0.62	1.0	5.4	8.2
Off Bench	174	18.9	4.5	.524	0.0	.000	1.9	.736	0.25	0.43	0.7	4.1	6.1
In wins	147	21.0	5.2	.538	0.0	.000	2.0	.736	0.30	0.55	0.8	4.4	7.1
In losses	155	22.9	5.6	.495	0.0	.000	1.9	.712	0.27	0.47	0.8	4.8	6.9
Pre All-Star	149	20.3	4.6	.529	0.0	.000	1.8	.751	0.26	0.50	0.8	4.4	6.3
Post All-Star	108	22.3	5.6	.518	0.0	.000	1.9	.731	0.29	0.43	0.9	4.6	7.1
Oct/Nov	25	14.6	2.9	.500	0.0	—	1.9	.792	0.24	0.04	0.4	3.6	4.4
December	51	19.4	4.6	.536	0.0	.000	1.6	.732	0.31	0.39	0.7	4.1	6.1
January	58	22.8	5.5	.530	0.0	—	2.1	.736	0.19	0.76	0.9	4.8	7.3
February	63	24.6	5.7	.508	0.0	.000	1.7	.736	0.33	0.57	0.8	5.5	7.1
March	57	22.2	5.8	.500	0.0	.000	1.9	.691	0.32	0.58	0.7	4.4	7.1
Apr/May	48	23.8	6.8	.512	0.0	.000	2.4	.699	0.29	0.42	1.3	4.5	8.6
0 Days Rest	74	22.1	5.8	.544	0.0	—	2.1	.748	0.30	0.51	0.9	4.8	7.9
1 Days Rest	146	22.3	5.6	.486	0.0	.000	1.7	.721	0.31	0.51	0.9	4.7	6.7
2 Days Rest	48	22.0	5.2	.548	0.0	—	2.0	.673	0.21	0.46	0.9	4.5	7.0
3+ Days Rest	34	20.2	4.5	.533	0.0	.000	2.2	.750	0.26	0.59	0.6	3.9	6.4

Scott Burrell
New Jersey Nets — Forward

1999-2000 Per Game Averages

	G	Min	FGA	FG%	3PA	3P%	FTA	FT%	Blk	Stl	Ast	Reb	Pts
Total	74	18.1	5.7	.394	3.1	.353	0.7	.780	0.59	0.91	1.0	3.5	6.1
Home	37	18.1	5.8	.366	3.1	.336	0.9	.750	0.57	0.81	0.9	3.7	6.0
Road	37	18.0	5.5	.424	3.1	.371	0.5	.833	0.62	1.00	1.1	3.2	6.1
vs. Playoff	41	19.0	6.1	.371	3.4	.333	0.9	.811	0.66	0.83	1.1	3.7	6.4
vs. Non-Playoff	33	16.8	5.1	.429	2.8	.385	0.4	.692	0.52	1.00	0.8	3.2	5.7
vs. East	49	18.8	6.0	.432	3.3	.372	0.7	.722	0.63	0.92	1.0	3.4	7.0
vs. West	25	16.5	4.9	.301	2.7	.309	0.6	.929	0.52	0.88	0.8	3.5	4.3
vs. Div.	22	17.6	5.7	.468	3.5	.462	0.9	.684	0.50	0.82	0.6	3.4	7.6
As Starter	9	25.9	6.8	.393	3.1	.429	1.4	.923	0.44	1.67	1.2	5.3	8.0
Off Bench	65	17.0	5.5	.394	3.1	.343	0.6	.730	0.62	0.80	0.9	3.2	5.8
In wins	31	18.2	5.5	.394	3.1	.347	0.7	.727	0.77	1.10	0.9	3.7	5.9
In losses	43	18.0	5.8	.394	3.2	.358	0.7	.821	0.47	0.77	1.0	3.3	6.2
Pre All-Star	43	18.2	5.3	.438	3.0	.395	0.7	.742	0.58	1.02	0.9	2.9	6.3
Post All-Star	31	17.9	6.2	.342	3.3	.301	0.6	.842	0.61	0.74	1.1	4.3	5.8
November	11	18.2	4.8	.434	2.7	.467	1.0	.909	0.36	0.91	0.8	3.6	6.4
December	14	18.6	5.0	.414	2.6	.297	0.5	.714	0.64	0.79	1.0	2.4	5.3
January	13	17.3	4.9	.438	3.0	.410	0.9	.667	0.62	1.23	0.8	2.6	6.2
February	12	17.8	6.2	.392	3.8	.348	0.3	.667	0.58	0.92	0.9	3.7	6.3
March	16	17.8	6.4	.353	3.9	.371	0.8	.846	0.88	0.88	0.3	4.3	6.6
April	8	19.1	7.0	.357	2.3	.111	0.5	.750	0.25	0.63	1.5	4.6	5.6
0 Days Rest	16	18.3	5.4	.460	3.0	.417	0.8	.692	0.56	1.06	1.1	2.8	6.8
1 Days Rest	40	18.2	5.8	.397	3.4	.343	0.6	.800	0.65	0.85	0.9	4.0	6.3
2 Days Rest	8	17.9	5.3	.262	2.1	.176	0.5	.750	0.50	0.63	0.8	3.9	3.5
3+ Days Rest	10	17.1	5.8	.379	3.3	.394	0.8	.875	0.50	1.10	1.3	2.1	6.4

Last Five Seasons

	G	Min	FGA	FG%	3PA	3P%	FTA	FT%	Blk	Stl	Ast	Reb	Pts
Total	263	18.1	5.6	.398	2.5	.361	1.1	.760	0.47	0.86	1.2	3.2	6.2
Home	127	18.9	5.9	.395	2.6	.343	1.2	.795	0.50	0.76	1.3	3.4	6.5
Road	136	17.5	5.4	.401	2.5	.379	1.0	.720	0.45	0.95	1.0	2.9	5.9
vs. Playoff	150	17.5	5.5	.385	2.4	.357	1.1	.745	0.42	0.72	1.1	3.0	5.9
vs. Non-Playoff	113	19.0	5.8	.415	2.6	.366	1.1	.780	0.54	1.04	1.2	3.3	6.6
vs. East	167	18.2	5.6	.398	2.5	.348	1.1	.726	0.44	0.86	1.1	3.1	6.1
vs. West	96	18.1	5.7	.399	2.6	.383	1.1	.817	0.53	0.85	1.3	3.2	6.4
vs. Div.	82	17.2	5.7	.412	2.5	.389	1.1	.777	0.39	0.80	1.1	3.1	6.5
As Starter	44	30.2	8.5	.444	4.0	.423	2.0	.753	0.55	1.55	1.8	4.8	10.8
Off Bench	219	15.7	5.0	.383	2.2	.339	0.9	.764	0.46	0.72	1.0	2.8	5.3
In wins	134	17.9	5.4	.413	2.5	.351	1.3	.763	0.54	0.97	1.2	3.1	6.4
In losses	129	18.4	5.8	.384	2.5	.371	0.9	.757	0.40	0.74	1.1	3.2	6.1
Pre All-Star	136	18.3	5.4	.416	2.4	.375	1.3	.760	0.50	0.86	1.1	2.9	6.4
Post All-Star	95	16.5	5.7	.388	2.7	.335	0.7	.730	0.47	0.73	1.1	3.3	5.8
Oct/Nov	44	17.6	5.2	.346	2.1	.312	1.3	.800	0.45	0.70	1.2	2.8	5.3
December	55	21.2	5.9	.429	2.6	.375	1.6	.770	0.56	0.76	1.2	3.4	7.2
January	29	13.5	3.9	.478	2.1	.417	1.2	.686	0.38	1.21	0.9	1.9	5.4
February	44	18.4	6.3	.406	2.9	.365	0.9	.795	0.45	0.80	1.1	3.1	6.8
March	57	16.7	5.6	.353	2.5	.352	0.9	.700	0.51	0.70	1.0	3.5	5.4
Apr/May	34	19.9	6.6	.422	2.8	.362	0.6	.818	0.38	1.26	1.5	3.8	7.1
0 Days Rest	64	18.3	5.3	.436	2.4	.396	1.0	.716	0.45	0.84	1.0	2.8	6.4
1 Days Rest	132	18.5	5.9	.402	2.7	.358	1.1	.767	0.51	0.98	1.2	3.4	6.5
2 Days Rest	40	17.5	5.4	.335	2.2	.345	1.0	.821	0.40	0.70	1.3	3.1	5.2
3+ Days Rest	27	17.0	5.3	.382	2.6	.319	1.3	.750	0.44	0.56	1.3	2.7	5.9

Jason Caffey

Golden State Warriors — Forward

1999-2000 Per Game Averages

	G	Min	FGA	FG%	3PA	3P%	FTA	FT%	Blk	Stl	Ast	Reb	Pts		G	Min	FGA	FG%	3PA	3P%	FTA	FT%	Blk	Stl	Ast	Reb	Pts
Total	71	30.4	9.5	.479	0.0	.000	4.9	.597	0.28	0.87	1.7	6.8	12.0	Pre All-Star	38	27.8	9.5	.465	0.0	.000	4.3	.580	0.18	0.74	1.7	6.7	11.3
Home	34	33.0	10.8	.489	0.0	.000	5.6	.586	0.21	0.88	2.1	7.6	13.9	Post All-Star	33	33.4	9.5	.494	0.0	.000	5.5	.612	0.39	1.03	1.7	6.8	12.8
Road	37	28.1	8.3	.466	0.0	.000	4.2	.610	0.35	0.86	1.2	6.0	10.3	November	5	18.0	6.6	.424	0.0	—	2.6	.692	0.20	0.60	0.2	4.2	7.4
vs. Playoff	42	31.5	9.6	.468	0.0	.000	4.5	.619	0.29	1.00	1.5	7.3	11.8	December	16	29.8	10.9	.454	0.1	.000	4.2	.582	0.19	0.94	1.8	9.1	12.3
vs. Non-Playoff	29	28.8	9.3	.494	0.0	—	5.4	.571	0.28	0.69	1.9	6.0	12.3	January	12	31.7	10.2	.443	0.0	—	4.7	.571	0.25	0.58	2.1	5.7	11.7
vs. East	26	30.0	8.9	.511	0.0	.000	5.6	.566	0.27	0.96	1.8	6.9	12.2	February	14	29.2	8.2	.600	0.0	—	5.0	.571	0.14	0.64	1.6	6.0	12.7
vs. West	45	30.7	9.9	.462	0.0	.000	4.4	.620	0.29	0.82	1.6	6.7	11.9	March	17	31.5	8.9	.480	0.1	.000	4.2	.583	0.53	0.94	1.5	6.1	11.1
vs. Div.	20	33.6	11.0	.452	0.1	.000	4.1	.580	0.15	0.95	1.7	7.7	12.3	April	7	38.1	11.3	.430	0.0	—	9.6	.657	0.29	1.71	2.1	8.7	16.0
As Starter	56	32.4	9.9	.474	0.0	.000	4.7	.602	0.29	0.86	1.8	7.3	12.3	0 Days Rest	16	29.8	9.1	.407	0.1	.000	4.4	.629	0.38	0.88	1.4	7.1	10.1
Off Bench	15	23.1	7.9	.500	0.0	—	5.4	.580	0.27	0.93	1.3	4.9	11.0	1 Days Rest	41	30.9	9.7	.495	0.0	.000	5.2	.594	0.32	0.98	1.9	6.6	12.6
In wins	16	31.1	9.6	.556	0.0	—	5.7	.560	0.19	0.75	2.4	7.8	13.8	2 Days Rest	7	34.7	12.1	.506	0.0	—	5.0	.600	0.14	0.57	1.9	9.1	15.3
In losses	55	30.2	9.5	.456	0.0	.000	4.6	.610	0.31	0.91	1.5	6.5	11.5	3+ Days Rest	7	24.4	7.0	.510	0.0	—	4.0	.536	0.00	0.57	1.0	5.1	9.3

Career (1995-96 thru 1999-2000)

	G	Min	FGA	FG%	3PA	3P%	FTA	FT%	Blk	Stl	Ast	Reb	Pts		G	Min	FGA	FG%	3PA	3P%	FTA	FT%	Blk	Stl	Ast	Reb	Pts
Total	318	20.2	6.2	.482	0.0	.000	2.9	.627	0.20	0.47	1.0	4.5	7.8	Pre All-Star	162	16.6	5.1	.489	0.0	.000	2.4	.591	0.19	0.35	0.9	3.7	6.4
Home	160	20.8	6.5	.474	0.0	.000	3.1	.630	0.22	0.49	1.2	4.7	8.2	Post All-Star	121	23.5	7.1	.489	0.0	.000	3.6	.657	0.21	0.55	1.2	5.2	9.3
Road	158	19.5	5.8	.492	0.0	.000	2.7	.623	0.19	0.44	0.8	4.4	7.4	Oct/Nov	44	13.7	4.2	.459	0.0	—	2.2	.567	0.11	0.39	0.6	3.3	5.1
vs. Playoff	182	20.1	6.1	.471	0.0	.000	2.6	.635	0.20	0.45	0.9	4.6	7.4	December	51	16.7	5.7	.467	0.0	.000	2.2	.607	0.22	0.39	0.4	4.4	6.6
vs. Non-Playoff	136	20.3	6.3	.497	0.0	.000	3.2	.618	0.21	0.49	1.1	4.5	8.3	January	51	19.4	5.7	.500	0.0	—	2.5	.585	0.27	0.33	1.1	3.7	7.2
vs. East	155	18.2	5.1	.502	0.0	.000	2.7	.634	0.17	0.38	1.0	4.1	6.9	February	63	19.6	5.4	.538	0.0	—	3.0	.624	0.11	0.44	0.8	4.1	7.4
vs. West	163	22.0	7.2	.469	0.0	.000	3.1	.621	0.24	0.55	1.0	5.0	8.6	March	65	24.0	7.6	.462	0.0	.000	3.2	.652	0.28	0.55	1.2	5.4	9.1
vs. Div.	104	20.6	6.6	.468	0.0	.000	2.9	.639	0.13	0.46	0.8	4.9	8.0	Apr/May	44	26.7	8.3	.467	0.0	.000	4.2	.674	0.23	0.68	1.3	6.2	10.6
As Starter	121	29.5	8.9	.474	0.0	.000	3.8	.611	0.26	0.73	1.5	6.7	10.7	0 Days Rest	76	20.0	6.0	.468	0.1	.000	2.8	.619	0.21	0.45	0.9	4.6	7.4
Off Bench	197	14.4	4.5	.493	0.0	.000	2.3	.643	0.17	0.30	0.7	3.2	6.0	1 Days Rest	158	21.2	6.5	.486	0.0	.000	3.1	.645	0.23	0.51	1.1	4.8	8.3
In wins	186	17.4	5.2	.517	0.0	.000	2.6	.631	0.19	0.38	0.9	3.9	7.0	2 Days Rest	48	19.3	6.0	.503	0.0	—	2.7	.664	0.15	0.46	1.1	4.1	7.8
In losses	132	24.1	7.6	.450	0.0	.000	3.4	.622	0.22	0.59	1.1	5.4	8.9	3+ Days Rest	36	16.8	5.4	.464	0.0	—	2.6	.500	0.17	0.33	0.7	4.0	6.4

Marcus Camby

New York Knicks — Forward-Center

1999-2000 Per Game Averages

	G	Min	FGA	FG%	3PA	3P%	FTA	FT%	Blk	Stl	Ast	Reb	Pts		G	Min	FGA	FG%	3PA	3P%	FTA	FT%	Blk	Stl	Ast	Reb	Pts
Total	59	26.2	8.0	.480	0.0	.500	3.7	.670	1.97	0.73	0.8	7.8	10.2	Pre All-Star	41	26.8	8.3	.484	0.0	.500	3.8	.647	2.12	0.83	0.7	7.7	10.5
Home	29	27.3	8.1	.453	0.0	1.000	4.3	.742	2.14	0.90	0.9	8.2	10.6	Post All-Star	18	25.0	7.3	.470	0.0	—	3.6	.723	1.61	0.50	1.2	8.1	9.5
Road	30	25.2	7.8	.506	0.0	.000	3.2	.577	1.80	0.57	0.7	7.4	9.8	November	13	26.4	8.6	.509	0.0	—	4.8	.667	2.23	0.92	0.5	8.0	12.0
vs. Playoff	29	28.8	8.9	.494	0.1	.500	4.2	.620	1.83	0.55	1.0	8.8	11.4	December	13	28.4	7.9	.437	0.0	—	3.6	.596	2.77	0.92	0.8	8.4	9.1
vs. Non-Playoff	30	23.8	7.1	.463	0.0	—	3.3	.730	2.10	0.90	0.6	6.9	9.0	January	12	25.3	7.9	.516	0.2	.500	2.3	.704	1.67	0.83	0.6	7.0	9.8
vs. East	38	27.1	7.7	.512	0.0	.000	4.1	.669	2.32	0.76	0.8	8.2	10.6	February	3	27.7	9.7	.448	0.0	—	6.3	.632	0.67	0.00	1.0	6.3	12.7
vs. West	21	24.7	8.6	.428	0.0	1.000	3.2	.672	1.33	0.67	0.9	7.0	9.5	March	10	23.7	8.1	.506	0.0	—	2.3	.696	1.00	0.40	1.0	8.6	9.8
vs. Div.	16	25.0	6.9	.450	0.0	—	4.6	.630	2.06	0.75	0.7	6.8	9.1	April	8	26.6	6.4	.412	0.0	—	5.3	.738	2.38	0.63	1.5	7.4	9.1
As Starter	11	28.1	7.3	.525	0.0	—	4.0	.659	2.91	0.82	0.9	8.6	10.3	0 Days Rest	13	25.6	7.5	.464	0.1	.000	3.3	.698	2.23	0.69	0.6	6.6	9.2
Off Bench	48	25.8	8.1	.471	0.0	.500	3.7	.672	1.75	0.71	0.8	7.6	10.2	1 Days Rest	29	27.7	8.8	.478	0.0	1.000	3.6	.683	2.07	0.69	1.1	8.1	10.9
In wins	38	26.3	7.8	.498	0.0	1.000	3.1	.678	2.29	0.76	0.9	8.4	9.9	2 Days Rest	10	27.1	8.8	.523	0.0	—	3.9	.487	1.70	0.50	0.4	8.6	11.1
In losses	21	26.1	8.4	.449	0.0	.000	4.9	.660	1.38	0.67	0.6	6.7	10.8	3+ Days Rest	7	20.3	4.4	.419	0.0	—	5.0	.800	1.43	1.29	0.7	7.7	7.7

Career (1996-97 thru 1999-2000)

	G	Min	FGA	FG%	3PA	3P%	FTA	FT%	Blk	Stl	Ast	Reb	Pts		G	Min	FGA	FG%	3PA	3P%	FTA	FT%	Blk	Stl	Ast	Reb	Pts
Total	231	27.7	9.8	.463	0.1	.167	3.6	.645	2.38	0.89	1.2	6.8	11.4	Pre All-Star	106	29.0	10.2	.452	0.1	.167	3.6	.665	2.52	1.04	1.4	6.8	11.6
Home	116	28.3	10.3	.458	0.1	.182	3.7	.658	2.76	0.84	1.3	7.2	11.9	Post All-Star	79	30.1	11.6	.460	0.1	.167	4.4	.651	2.65	0.85	1.4	7.6	13.5
Road	115	27.1	9.3	.468	0.1	.143	3.5	.632	2.00	0.95	1.0	6.5	10.9	Oct/Nov	35	28.5	10.3	.475	0.1	.250	4.2	.687	2.34	1.23	1.1	6.1	12.7
vs. Playoff	128	27.8	10.0	.447	0.1	.214	3.7	.635	2.29	0.77	1.1	6.6	11.3	December	28	27.8	9.0	.415	0.1	.000	3.0	.694	2.71	0.96	1.1	7.0	9.6
vs. Non-Playoff	103	27.5	9.5	.484	0.0	.000	3.5	.659	2.50	1.04	1.2	7.1	11.5	January	34	29.4	10.7	.459	0.1	.250	3.3	.611	2.47	1.06	1.6	7.1	11.9
vs. East	161	27.5	9.6	.468	0.1	.100	3.5	.650	2.44	0.89	1.0	6.7	11.2	February	39	25.4	8.1	.438	0.1	.000	3.7	.618	2.21	0.67	1.0	6.1	9.4
vs. West	70	28.1	10.2	.453	0.1	.250	3.9	.636	2.24	0.90	1.4	7.0	11.7	March	56	27.3	10.6	.496	0.1	.200	3.8	.645	2.14	0.79	1.0	7.6	12.9
vs. Div.	76	26.9	9.9	.454	0.1	.250	3.8	.664	2.13	0.83	0.9	6.2	11.5	Apr/May	39	28.1	9.5	.457	0.0	—	3.4	.629	2.62	0.77	1.1	6.8	10.8
As Starter	107	32.8	12.7	.450	0.1	.091	4.2	.657	3.12	1.12	1.7	7.4	14.2	0 Days Rest	51	26.6	8.5	.451	0.1	.200	3.4	.694	2.08	0.94	0.9	6.1	10.1
Off Bench	124	23.3	7.2	.483	0.1	.286	3.1	.632	1.74	0.69	0.7	6.3	9.0	1 Days Rest	119	29.0	10.7	.475	0.1	.143	3.6	.637	2.62	0.88	1.3	7.4	12.4
In wins	105	27.7	9.1	.495	0.1	.333	3.5	.642	2.55	0.83	1.3	7.7	11.2	2 Days Rest	30	28.3	9.7	.483	0.2	.200	3.7	.609	2.20	0.73	1.1	6.3	11.7
In losses	126	27.6	10.4	.440	0.1	.000	3.7	.648	2.24	0.94	1.0	6.1	11.5	3+ Days Rest	31	23.8	8.4	.402	0.0	.000	3.9	.639	2.13	1.00	1.1	6.1	9.2

198

Elden Campbell

1999-2000 Per Game Averages

	G	Min	FGA	FG%	3PA	3P%	FTA	FT%	Blk	Stl	Ast	Reb	Pts
Total	78	32.5	10.6	.446	0.1	.000	4.6	.690	1.92	0.72	1.7	7.6	12.7
Home	39	32.9	10.0	.458	0.1	.000	4.2	.617	1.97	0.62	1.7	7.6	11.7
Road	39	32.2	11.3	.436	0.1	.000	5.0	.750	1.87	0.82	1.6	7.5	13.6
vs. Playoff	43	34.4	10.8	.458	0.0	.000	4.5	.703	1.79	0.77	1.7	7.9	13.0
vs. Non-Playoff	35	30.3	10.5	.432	0.1	.000	4.7	.675	2.09	0.66	1.7	7.2	12.2
vs. East	52	32.0	10.3	.442	0.1	.000	4.6	.700	1.88	0.67	1.7	6.9	12.4
vs. West	26	33.6	11.2	.454	0.1	.000	4.5	.669	2.00	0.81	1.6	8.8	13.2
vs. Div.	27	32.6	10.0	.439	0.0	—	4.7	.754	1.74	0.67	2.1	7.7	12.3
As Starter	77	32.9	10.8	.446	0.1	.000	4.6	.690	1.92	0.73	1.7	7.6	12.7
Off Bench	1	7.0	1.0	1.000	0.0	—	6.0	.667	2.00	0.00	1.0	3.0	6.0
In wins	45	32.9	10.5	.466	0.0	.000	4.6	.668	2.13	0.60	2.0	7.4	12.8
In losses	33	32.1	10.8	.420	0.1	.000	4.6	.719	1.64	0.88	1.2	7.8	12.4

	G	Min	FGA	FG%	3PA	3P%	FTA	FT%	Blk	Stl	Ast	Reb	Pts
Pre All-Star	44	31.2	10.3	.429	0.1	.000	4.9	.706	1.98	0.98	1.5	7.2	12.3
Post All-Star	34	34.3	11.0	.468	0.1	.000	4.2	.667	1.85	0.38	1.8	8.0	13.1
November	14	31.1	12.3	.366	0.1	.000	5.1	.592	1.79	1.07	1.5	7.2	12.0
December	12	29.8	9.8	.504	0.0	—	3.8	.739	1.58	1.25	1.3	7.4	12.7
January	13	32.1	9.3	.446	0.2	.000	5.1	.758	2.23	0.85	2.1	6.6	12.2
February	14	34.3	11.1	.458	0.1	.000	4.1	.754	1.79	0.29	0.9	8.7	13.2
March	14	34.6	11.3	.487	0.1	.000	4.5	.698	2.36	0.57	2.1	9.1	14.1
April	11	33.0	9.6	.434	0.1	.000	5.0	.618	1.73	0.27	2.1	5.8	11.5
0 Days Rest	20	31.3	11.5	.417	0.2	.000	5.0	.667	2.10	0.65	1.5	7.5	12.9
1 Days Rest	42	33.3	10.5	.482	0.0	.000	4.3	.729	1.88	0.71	2.0	7.5	13.3
2 Days Rest	7	29.6	7.7	.352	0.0	—	3.9	.704	1.57	0.57	1.4	5.9	8.1
3+ Days Rest	9	34.0	11.4	.408	0.0	—	5.7	.588	2.00	1.00	0.9	9.7	12.7

Last Five Seasons

	G	Min	FGA	FG%	3PA	3P%	FTA	FT%	Blk	Stl	Ast	Reb	Pts
Total	367	30.0	10.2	.472	0.0	.111	4.6	.692	1.78	0.72	1.6	7.3	12.4
Home	181	29.7	9.8	.478	0.0	.250	4.5	.677	1.72	0.67	1.7	7.4	12.4
Road	186	30.2	10.6	.467	0.1	.000	4.7	.706	1.84	0.77	1.5	7.2	13.2
vs. Playoff	200	31.0	10.2	.475	0.1	.182	4.6	.702	1.72	0.69	1.5	7.5	12.9
vs. Non-Playoff	167	28.8	10.2	.469	0.0	.000	4.6	.680	1.86	0.76	1.7	7.0	12.7
vs. East	174	31.5	10.8	.467	0.0	.125	4.9	.682	1.77	0.76	1.6	7.5	13.4
vs. West	193	28.5	9.7	.478	0.1	.100	4.3	.702	1.79	0.68	1.6	7.2	12.3
vs. Div.	120	29.4	10.4	.467	0.0	.200	4.6	.702	1.74	0.63	1.7	7.3	12.7
As Starter	297	32.8	11.3	.475	0.1	.059	4.9	.696	1.98	0.82	1.8	7.8	14.1
Off Bench	70	17.7	5.7	.452	0.0	1.000	3.2	.664	0.94	0.29	0.7	5.0	7.3
In wins	241	29.2	9.8	.487	0.0	.125	4.6	.695	1.85	0.68	1.7	7.3	12.8
In losses	126	31.3	10.9	.446	0.1	.100	4.6	.686	1.64	0.80	1.4	7.4	12.9

	G	Min	FGA	FG%	3PA	3P%	FTA	FT%	Blk	Stl	Ast	Reb	Pts
Pre All-Star	183	30.3	9.9	.470	0.0	.000	4.5	.692	1.77	0.82	1.5	7.2	12.4
Post All-Star	135	29.6	10.9	.473	0.1	.200	4.5	.716	1.90	0.56	1.8	7.2	13.5
Oct/Nov	59	29.8	9.9	.442	0.1	.000	4.4	.689	1.58	1.02	1.4	6.7	11.8
December	58	32.6	11.2	.499	0.0	.000	4.8	.662	1.84	0.83	1.5	8.0	14.4
January	52	27.8	8.3	.456	0.0	.000	4.6	.692	1.77	0.63	1.6	6.6	10.3
February	64	29.1	10.2	.475	0.1	.250	4.7	.728	1.75	0.56	1.5	7.6	13.1
March	74	30.9	10.9	.477	0.1	.250	4.7	.692	2.05	0.61	1.7	7.9	13.7
Apr/May	60	29.2	10.3	.475	0.1	.000	5.0	.687	1.63	0.70	1.8	6.8	13.2
0 Days Rest	94	29.6	10.4	.438	0.0	.000	4.2	.649	1.91	0.63	1.4	7.4	11.9
1 Days Rest	197	30.4	10.2	.487	0.1	.167	4.7	.722	1.76	0.81	1.8	7.2	13.4
2 Days Rest	40	28.8	9.4	.471	0.0	.000	4.2	.695	1.53	0.63	1.5	7.2	11.8
3+ Days Rest	36	30.1	10.6	.482	0.0	.000	5.4	.634	1.86	0.58	1.2	7.7	13.6

Anthony Carter

1999-2000 Per Game Averages

	G	Min	FGA	FG%	3PA	3P%	FTA	FT%	Blk	Stl	Ast	Reb	Pts
Total	79	23.5	6.4	.395	0.3	.130	1.6	.750	0.06	1.18	4.8	2.5	6.3
Home	40	23.5	6.7	.424	0.3	.091	1.5	.712	0.03	1.33	5.4	2.5	6.8
Road	39	23.6	6.2	.363	0.3	.167	1.7	.785	0.10	1.03	4.2	2.5	5.8
vs. Playoff	40	22.7	6.5	.380	0.3	.167	1.5	.729	0.08	1.08	4.5	2.5	6.0
vs. Non-Playoff	39	24.4	6.4	.410	0.3	.091	1.7	.769	0.05	1.28	5.1	2.5	6.6
vs. East	52	21.9	6.2	.401	0.3	.125	1.6	.759	0.06	1.25	4.2	2.3	6.2
vs. West	27	26.6	6.9	.385	0.3	.143	1.5	.732	0.07	1.04	5.9	2.9	6.5
vs. Div.	22	21.0	5.8	.370	0.3	.143	1.6	.829	0.05	1.23	4.0	2.4	5.6
As Starter	30	32.2	9.0	.446	0.3	.100	2.1	.813	0.07	1.13	6.4	3.1	9.8
Off Bench	49	18.2	4.9	.338	0.3	.154	1.2	.683	0.06	1.20	3.8	2.2	4.2
In wins	50	22.3	6.1	.388	0.3	.071	1.5	.757	0.04	1.06	5.2	2.6	5.9
In losses	29	25.7	7.0	.406	0.3	.222	1.7	.740	0.10	1.38	4.0	2.3	7.0

	G	Min	FGA	FG%	3PA	3P%	FTA	FT%	Blk	Stl	Ast	Reb	Pts
Pre All-Star	44	25.9	7.4	.412	0.3	.154	1.7	.789	0.05	1.09	5.3	2.6	7.5
Post All-Star	35	20.5	5.3	.364	0.3	.100	1.4	.688	0.09	1.29	4.1	2.4	4.8
November	11	15.5	4.6	.255	0.1	.000	1.1	.917	0.00	1.09	3.6	1.5	3.4
December	14	31.2	9.1	.465	0.4	.000	2.6	.833	0.07	0.57	6.4	3.1	10.6
January	15	30.4	8.1	.426	0.3	.500	1.5	.696	0.07	1.40	6.5	3.1	8.1
February	14	18.7	5.0	.314	0.4	.000	1.2	.824	0.14	1.50	2.9	2.4	4.1
March	14	16.7	3.4	.255	0.2	.333	1.4	.579	0.00	0.79	4.1	1.9	2.6
April	11	27.2	8.4	.467	0.4	.000	1.5	.647	0.09	1.82	4.8	2.9	8.8
0 Days Rest	17	22.5	6.4	.413	0.3	.200	2.1	.886	0.12	0.82	3.8	1.9	7.2
1 Days Rest	43	23.3	6.6	.385	0.2	.000	1.2	.660	0.05	1.26	4.8	2.4	5.8
2 Days Rest	12	25.6	6.3	.400	0.3	.250	1.9	.739	0.00	1.08	5.3	3.7	6.5
3+ Days Rest	7	23.7	6.0	.405	0.6	.250	2.3	.750	0.14	1.71	6.0	2.7	6.7

Vince Carter

1999-2000 Per Game Averages

	G	Min	FGA	FG%	3PA	3P%	FTA	FT%	Blk	Stl	Ast	Reb	Pts		G	Min	FGA	FG%	3PA	3P%	FTA	FT%	Blk	Stl	Ast	Reb	Pts
Total	82	38.1	20.7	.465	2.9	.403	6.7	.791	1.12	1.34	3.9	5.8	25.7	Pre All-Star	47	37.4	20.8	.452	2.0	.359	6.3	.797	1.11	1.43	3.9	6.1	24.5
Home	41	38.0	20.4	.478	3.2	.455	5.9	.808	1.54	1.56	3.8	5.1	25.7	Post All-Star	35	39.1	20.5	.482	4.1	.431	7.3	.784	1.14	1.23	4.0	5.5	27.3
Road	41	38.3	21.0	.452	2.5	.337	7.6	.778	0.71	1.12	4.1	6.5	25.7	November	15	35.2	18.5	.446	1.8	.296	5.9	.750	1.20	0.93	3.4	6.4	21.5
vs. Playoff	42	38.0	21.7	.461	2.8	.403	6.4	.805	1.14	1.31	3.7	5.8	26.3	December	14	39.1	22.4	.463	1.6	.364	7.6	.794	1.14	1.36	3.6	6.0	27.4
vs. Non-Playoff	40	38.2	19.6	.469	2.9	.402	7.1	.778	1.10	1.38	4.2	5.9	25.1	January	14	37.3	21.1	.447	2.1	.414	4.6	.815	1.07	1.50	4.4	5.2	23.5
vs. East	54	38.2	20.3	.465	3.0	.415	7.0	.791	1.30	1.39	4.1	5.7	25.7	February	12	39.9	22.2	.496	3.6	.419	7.1	.882	0.83	2.17	3.8	6.3	29.8
vs. West	28	38.0	21.4	.464	2.6	.375	6.2	.792	0.79	1.25	3.6	6.0	25.7	March	17	40.7	22.4	.447	4.5	.408	8.8	.773	0.94	1.00	3.9	5.7	28.6
vs. Div.	28	39.0	19.9	.482	3.1	.442	6.7	.819	1.39	1.32	4.3	5.6	26.1	April	10	35.7	16.4	.518	3.9	.462	5.6	.732	1.70	1.30	4.5	5.1	22.9
As Starter	82	38.1	20.7	.465	2.9	.403	6.7	.791	1.12	1.34	3.9	5.8	25.7	0 Days Rest	18	37.2	19.4	.483	2.6	.413	6.8	.787	0.44	1.50	3.5	5.6	25.2
Off Bench	0	—	—	—	—	—	—	—	—	—	—	—	—	1 Days Rest	48	38.6	21.9	.461	3.0	.408	6.5	.783	1.21	1.33	4.0	5.9	26.5
In wins	45	39.0	20.8	.504	3.0	.471	6.5	.806	1.31	1.49	4.3	5.9	27.6	2 Days Rest	9	38.6	20.0	.461	2.8	.400	8.2	.824	2.00	1.33	5.0	6.6	26.3
In losses	37	37.1	20.6	.416	2.7	.310	6.9	.774	0.89	1.16	3.5	5.7	23.4	3+ Days Rest	7	36.6	16.4	.443	3.3	.348	6.0	.810	1.14	1.00	3.0	4.7	20.6

Career (1998-99 thru 1999-2000)

	G	Min	FGA	FG%	3PA	3P%	FTA	FT%	Blk	Stl	Ast	Reb	Pts		G	Min	FGA	FG%	3PA	3P%	FTA	FT%	Blk	Stl	Ast	Reb	Pts
Total	132	37.0	18.7	.460	2.3	.377	6.2	.781	1.28	1.25	3.6	5.8	22.9	Pre All-Star	47	37.4	20.8	.452	2.0	.359	6.3	.797	1.11	1.43	3.9	6.1	24.5
Home	66	36.9	18.7	.474	2.5	.433	5.7	.788	1.79	1.38	3.6	5.4	23.3	Post All-Star	35	39.1	20.5	.482	4.1	.431	7.3	.784	1.14	1.23	4.0	5.5	27.3
Road	66	37.2	18.6	.446	2.1	.312	6.8	.776	0.77	1.12	3.5	6.1	22.5	Oct/Nov	15	35.2	18.5	.446	1.8	.296	5.9	.750	1.20	0.93	3.4	6.4	21.5
vs. Playoff	70	36.8	19.3	.454	2.3	.350	6.1	.795	1.36	1.27	3.3	5.7	23.2	December	14	39.1	22.4	.463	1.6	.364	7.6	.794	1.14	1.36	3.6	6.0	27.4
vs. Non-Playoff	62	37.2	18.0	.467	2.2	.410	6.3	.766	1.19	1.23	3.9	5.9	22.5	January	14	37.3	21.1	.447	2.1	.414	4.6	.815	1.07	1.50	4.4	5.2	23.5
vs. East	99	36.7	18.0	.453	2.2	.361	6.3	.777	1.38	1.23	3.6	5.7	22.0	February	24	37.5	17.2	.488	2.4	.397	5.9	.824	1.33	1.71	2.9	5.9	22.6
vs. West	33	37.8	20.6	.479	2.5	.422	5.9	.765	0.97	1.30	3.6	5.8	25.5	March	31	39.1	20.5	.450	2.9	.370	6.8	.774	1.15	0.94	3.3	5.9	23.5
vs. Div.	51	37.3	18.1	.467	2.3	.356	6.1	.801	1.51	1.06	3.8	5.9	22.6	Apr/May	31	35.4	16.6	.464	2.1	.394	6.0	.754	1.58	1.23	4.1	5.4	20.8
As Starter	131	37.0	18.6	.462	2.3	.379	6.2	.781	1.28	1.25	3.5	5.7	22.9	0 Days Rest	36	35.8	17.1	.462	1.9	.403	5.8	.805	0.78	1.22	3.1	6.0	21.3
Off Bench	1	40.0	20.0	.300	1.0	.000	6.0	.833	1.00	1.00	8.0	12.0	17.0	1 Days Rest	73	37.5	19.7	.459	2.4	.394	6.2	.762	1.40	1.27	3.8	5.8	23.7
In wins	68	37.3	18.9	.497	2.4	.463	6.1	.799	1.44	1.38	3.9	5.8	24.8	2 Days Rest	13	38.2	19.5	.472	2.5	.313	7.5	.804	2.00	1.15	4.5	5.8	25.2
In losses	64	36.7	18.4	.420	2.2	.275	6.3	.763	1.11	1.11	3.2	5.7	20.9	3+ Days Rest	10	36.3	15.4	.448	2.8	.286	5.8	.810	1.30	1.30	2.6	4.3	19.3

Sam Cassell

1999-2000 Per Game Averages

	G	Min	FGA	FG%	3PA	3P%	FTA	FT%	Blk	Stl	Ast	Reb	Pts		G	Min	FGA	FG%	3PA	3P%	FTA	FT%	Blk	Stl	Ast	Reb	Pts
Total	81	35.8	14.4	.466	1.1	.289	5.5	.876	0.10	1.26	9.0	3.7	18.6	Pre All-Star	49	35.2	14.3	.456	1.3	.303	5.6	.876	0.12	1.27	9.3	3.8	18.4
Home	41	35.6	13.4	.456	0.9	.342	5.1	.899	0.05	1.41	9.3	3.7	17.1	Post All-Star	32	36.6	14.6	.481	0.8	.250	5.3	.877	0.06	1.25	8.5	3.6	18.9
Road	40	36.0	15.6	.474	1.3	.250	5.9	.857	0.15	1.10	8.7	3.7	20.2	November	14	34.1	15.4	.470	0.9	.231	5.3	.905	0.07	1.36	8.4	3.4	19.4
vs. Playoff	42	35.5	13.9	.453	1.4	.293	5.2	.868	0.10	0.98	9.0	3.4	17.6	December	16	34.6	13.2	.455	0.8	.333	5.1	.815	0.13	1.44	9.6	4.3	16.4
vs. Non-Playoff	39	36.1	15.0	.479	0.8	.281	5.8	.884	0.10	1.56	9.1	4.1	19.7	January	14	36.4	14.5	.433	2.6	.361	6.9	.917	0.14	0.79	10.3	3.9	19.8
vs. East	53	35.7	14.3	.455	1.1	.310	5.4	.888	0.13	1.32	8.8	3.6	18.1	February	12	36.3	14.1	.485	1.1	.308	4.2	.880	0.17	1.42	8.4	3.3	17.7
vs. West	28	35.9	14.8	.486	1.1	.250	5.7	.856	0.04	1.14	9.4	3.9	19.5	March	14	36.4	14.6	.478	0.6	.111	3.9	.855	0.00	1.00	8.7	3.1	17.4
vs. Div.	27	35.2	14.6	.476	1.3	.514	5.7	.915	0.15	1.48	9.6	3.5	19.8	April	11	37.5	15.2	.479	0.6	.143	8.1	.876	0.09	1.64	8.4	4.3	21.7
As Starter	81	35.8	14.4	.466	1.1	.289	5.5	.876	0.10	1.26	9.0	3.7	18.6	0 Days Rest	19	35.9	13.6	.446	1.0	.158	6.4	.861	0.11	1.74	8.4	4.4	17.8
Off Bench	0	—	—	—	—	—	—	—	—	—	—	—	—	1 Days Rest	47	36.1	15.2	.477	1.4	.328	5.1	.880	0.09	1.23	8.9	3.6	19.4
In wins	42	35.3	14.8	.483	1.0	.415	6.7	.883	0.07	1.50	9.5	4.1	20.7	2 Days Rest	5	33.4	10.8	.370	0.4	.000	3.0	.933	0.20	1.00	10.2	3.0	10.8
In losses	39	36.3	14.0	.446	1.3	.184	4.2	.865	0.13	1.00	8.4	3.3	16.4	3+ Days Rest	10	35.5	14.5	.483	0.5	.400	6.7	.881	0.10	0.60	10.0	3.5	20.1

Last Five Seasons

	G	Min	FGA	FG%	3PA	3P%	FTA	FT%	Blk	Stl	Ast	Reb	Pts		G	Min	FGA	FG%	3PA	3P%	FTA	FT%	Blk	Stl	Ast	Reb	Pts
Total	286	31.8	13.5	.446	2.2	.317	5.4	.858	0.18	1.27	6.8	3.2	17.3	Pre All-Star	174	30.3	12.8	.431	2.2	.305	5.4	.845	0.19	1.21	6.5	3.1	16.3
Home	143	31.5	12.5	.447	1.9	.351	4.7	.859	0.19	1.22	6.8	3.3	16.0	Post All-Star	104	34.8	14.8	.469	2.2	.344	5.3	.874	0.17	1.38	7.5	3.5	19.3
Road	143	32.1	14.5	.444	2.4	.290	6.0	.858	0.17	1.31	6.8	3.1	18.7	Oct/Nov	54	31.0	14.1	.418	2.0	.266	6.4	.857	0.17	1.44	6.4	2.9	17.8
vs. Playoff	155	32.2	13.7	.421	2.7	.311	5.3	.863	0.17	1.15	6.7	3.2	16.9	December	58	29.7	12.2	.445	1.9	.327	5.2	.829	0.22	1.19	6.7	3.2	15.8
vs. Non-Playoff	131	31.4	13.3	.476	1.5	.330	5.5	.853	0.18	1.40	7.0	3.2	17.8	January	49	30.1	12.4	.421	2.8	.326	4.8	.856	0.18	0.90	6.3	3.0	15.4
vs. East	155	32.5	13.6	.440	1.8	.306	5.6	.858	0.16	1.22	7.0	3.1	17.3	February	49	31.9	12.9	.484	2.0	.347	4.7	.857	0.18	1.39	6.6	3.2	17.2
vs. West	131	31.0	13.4	.452	2.6	.327	5.1	.858	0.20	1.32	6.6	3.3	17.3	March	44	36.2	15.9	.440	2.5	.330	4.6	.856	0.11	1.27	8.0	3.4	18.8
vs. Div.	88	32.1	13.6	.446	2.1	.308	6.0	.868	0.20	1.36	7.0	3.2	18.0	Apr/May	32	33.6	14.2	.480	1.6	.327	7.1	.904	0.19	1.47	7.3	3.6	20.6
As Starter	200	34.5	14.9	.451	1.8	.299	5.7	.870	0.21	1.46	7.9	3.4	18.9	0 Days Rest	66	32.0	13.4	.422	2.2	.296	5.8	.857	0.14	1.48	6.8	3.3	16.9
Off Bench	86	25.5	10.3	.427	3.0	.342	4.6	.825	0.12	0.83	4.3	2.8	13.6	1 Days Rest	137	32.4	13.9	.450	2.1	.319	5.5	.857	0.15	1.24	7.0	3.3	17.8
In wins	142	31.1	13.0	.468	1.9	.368	5.7	.853	0.14	1.37	7.3	3.4	17.7	2 Days Rest	43	29.3	12.0	.444	2.4	.295	4.2	.883	0.21	1.26	6.1	3.0	15.0
In losses	144	32.5	13.9	.425	2.5	.279	5.1	.865	0.22	1.16	6.4	3.0	16.9	3+ Days Rest	40	32.1	14.1	.468	2.2	.372	5.7	.845	0.30	1.00	6.8	3.0	18.8

Kelvin Cato
Houston Rockets — Center

1999-2000 Per Game Averages

	G	Min	FGA	FG%	3PA	3P%	FTA	FT%	Blk	Stl	Ast	Reb	Pts
Total	65	24.3	6.2	.537	0.1	.000	3.2	.649	1.91	0.51	0.4	6.0	8.7
Home	33	23.4	6.3	.567	0.0	.000	3.2	.638	1.97	0.48	0.2	6.0	9.2
Road	32	25.3	6.1	.505	0.1	.000	3.2	.660	1.84	0.53	0.6	5.9	8.3
vs. Playoff	38	23.6	5.5	.500	0.1	.000	3.2	.683	1.58	0.66	0.4	5.6	7.7
vs. Non-Playoff	27	25.3	7.1	.578	0.0	—	3.3	.602	2.37	0.30	0.3	6.6	10.2
vs. East	27	23.4	6.2	.506	0.0	.000	3.2	.678	2.04	0.37	0.5	6.3	8.5
vs. West	38	25.0	6.2	.560	0.1	.000	3.2	.628	1.82	0.61	0.3	5.7	8.9
vs. Div.	18	23.6	6.2	.563	0.1	.000	3.3	.610	1.94	0.44	0.3	5.3	9.0
As Starter	32	27.6	7.0	.558	0.1	.000	3.1	.667	1.91	0.44	0.6	6.5	9.9
Off Bench	33	21.1	5.4	.511	0.0	—	3.3	.633	1.91	0.58	0.2	5.5	7.6
In wins	28	26.1	6.9	.572	0.0	.000	3.5	.639	2.04	0.50	0.4	6.6	10.1
In losses	37	23.0	5.6	.505	0.1	.000	3.0	.658	1.81	0.51	0.4	5.5	7.6
Pre All-Star	38	22.6	6.2	.532	0.1	.000	3.7	.619	1.92	0.53	0.3	5.8	8.9
Post All-Star	27	26.8	6.1	.545	0.1	.000	2.6	.710	1.89	0.48	0.5	6.2	8.5
November	14	18.5	4.8	.463	0.0	—	2.9	.600	1.43	0.43	0.1	5.1	6.1
December	15	27.4	7.6	.570	0.1	.000	4.0	.600	2.27	0.67	0.3	6.1	11.1
January	3	13.7	3.0	.667	0.0	—	3.7	.545	2.33	0.33	0.3	4.3	6.0
February	8	23.9	7.5	.517	0.3	.000	3.9	.677	1.88	0.50	0.8	8.1	10.4
March	15	23.9	5.8	.494	0.0	—	2.5	.649	1.80	0.53	0.3	5.3	7.3
April	10	32.1	6.5	.615	0.1	.000	2.9	.828	2.10	0.40	0.8	6.8	10.4
0 Days Rest	13	24.2	6.0	.500	0.0	—	2.0	.615	1.85	0.54	0.4	5.2	7.2
1 Days Rest	34	24.9	6.5	.549	0.1	.000	3.8	.693	1.76	0.55	0.4	5.9	9.8
2 Days Rest	14	24.9	6.1	.558	0.0	.000	3.1	.605	2.57	0.43	0.4	6.3	8.7
3+ Days Rest	5	19.4	5.0	.480	0.0	—	2.4	.417	1.20	0.40	0.4	7.4	5.8

Career (1997-98 thru 1999-2000)

	G	Min	FGA	FG%	3PA	3P%	FTA	FT%	Blk	Stl	Ast	Reb	Pts
Total	182	17.2	4.2	.489	0.0	.125	2.2	.638	1.51	0.47	0.4	4.3	5.5
Home	90	17.3	4.1	.523	0.0	.333	2.4	.637	1.57	0.46	0.3	4.5	5.9
Road	92	17.2	4.2	.457	0.1	.000	2.0	.638	1.45	0.48	0.4	4.2	5.1
vs. Playoff	101	16.5	3.6	.462	0.1	.167	2.1	.664	1.37	0.52	0.3	4.1	4.8
vs. Non-Playoff	81	18.1	4.8	.515	0.0	.000	2.3	.607	1.68	0.40	0.4	4.6	6.4
vs. East	59	17.1	4.0	.464	0.1	.000	2.3	.696	1.46	0.27	0.4	4.6	5.3
vs. West	123	17.3	4.3	.501	0.0	.200	2.2	.608	1.53	0.56	0.3	4.2	5.6
vs. Div.	56	17.5	4.4	.470	0.0	.000	2.3	.638	1.61	0.57	0.3	4.4	5.7
As Starter	40	26.6	6.7	.535	0.1	.000	3.0	.667	2.13	0.58	0.5	6.4	9.3
Off Bench	142	14.6	3.5	.464	0.0	.250	2.0	.625	1.33	0.44	0.3	3.8	4.5
In wins	98	16.9	4.3	.508	0.0	.250	2.2	.618	1.64	0.49	0.4	4.3	5.7
In losses	84	17.6	4.1	.466	0.0	.000	2.1	.661	1.35	0.44	0.4	4.4	5.2
Pre All-Star	80	18.1	4.4	.496	0.1	.000	2.6	.663	1.73	0.40	0.3	4.8	6.1
Post All-Star	59	19.3	4.7	.500	0.1	.000	2.1	.664	1.36	0.51	0.4	4.4	6.2
Oct/Nov	29	15.4	3.7	.443	0.0	.000	2.0	.655	1.21	0.34	0.3	4.4	4.6
December	25	22.8	5.8	.556	0.0	.000	3.4	.663	2.36	0.52	0.3	5.4	8.7
January	17	15.4	2.6	.409	0.1	.000	1.9	.625	1.82	0.35	0.3	4.0	3.3
February	31	14.4	4.2	.500	0.1	.000	2.4	.600	1.16	0.39	0.5	4.2	5.6
March	41	15.6	3.7	.447	0.0	1.000	1.8	.616	1.10	0.49	0.3	3.3	4.4
Apr/May	39	19.8	4.7	.511	0.0	.000	1.9	.658	1.74	0.62	0.5	4.9	6.1
0 Days Rest	48	17.3	4.2	.450	0.0	.000	1.7	.613	1.56	0.52	0.4	4.3	4.8
1 Days Rest	84	17.3	4.3	.506	0.1	.167	2.6	.683	1.35	0.49	0.4	4.2	6.1
2 Days Rest	32	18.9	4.3	.544	0.0	.000	2.3	.611	2.09	0.44	0.3	4.6	6.0
3+ Days Rest	18	13.6	3.3	.400	0.0	—	1.7	.433	1.06	0.28	0.3	4.5	3.4

Cedric Ceballos
Dallas Mavericks — Forward

1999-2000 Per Game Averages

	G	Min	FGA	FG%	3PA	3P%	FTA	FT%	Blk	Stl	Ast	Reb	Pts
Total	69	29.9	14.5	.446	1.9	.328	3.6	.843	0.35	0.81	1.3	6.7	16.6
Home	36	30.3	14.9	.432	2.0	.329	4.1	.863	0.56	0.64	1.3	7.4	17.1
Road	33	29.5	14.1	.462	1.8	.328	3.1	.814	0.12	1.00	1.3	6.0	16.2
vs. Playoff	43	30.3	14.7	.438	2.1	.370	3.4	.828	0.40	0.74	1.2	6.6	16.4
vs. Non-Playoff	26	29.3	14.3	.460	1.6	.238	4.0	.864	0.27	0.92	1.5	6.8	17.0
vs. East	28	29.3	14.3	.401	1.8	.265	2.7	.855	0.21	0.68	1.3	6.4	14.2
vs. West	41	30.4	14.7	.476	2.1	.365	4.2	.837	0.44	0.90	1.3	6.9	18.3
vs. Div.	17	30.2	15.1	.471	2.2	.432	3.8	.862	0.53	0.94	0.9	6.9	18.5
As Starter	25	35.8	15.7	.462	2.2	.400	5.0	.855	0.44	1.04	2.2	8.6	19.6
Off Bench	44	26.6	13.9	.436	1.8	.278	2.8	.831	0.30	0.68	0.8	5.6	14.9
In wins	33	29.9	14.2	.458	2.0	.343	3.5	.887	0.33	0.88	1.6	6.7	16.8
In losses	36	29.9	14.9	.436	1.9	.313	3.7	.805	0.36	0.75	1.0	6.7	16.5
Pre All-Star	45	33.2	15.7	.447	2.0	.341	4.2	.843	0.40	0.98	1.6	7.9	18.3
Post All-Star	24	23.7	12.4	.444	1.8	.302	2.4	.842	0.25	0.50	0.7	4.4	13.5
November	13	30.0	15.6	.399	1.5	.250	3.9	.804	0.31	1.08	0.8	8.2	16.0
December	14	35.1	15.1	.472	2.0	.429	3.0	.762	0.50	1.14	1.5	6.7	17.4
January	13	34.6	16.2	.483	2.4	.290	6.2	.889	0.23	0.77	2.8	9.3	21.9
February	13	31.5	16.0	.452	2.3	.367	2.5	.879	0.54	0.46	1.2	6.2	17.5
March	12	20.8	10.6	.394	1.4	.118	2.0	.833	0.00	0.33	0.3	3.6	10.2
April	4	18.5	10.3	.488	2.0	.625	4.3	.882	0.75	1.50	0.5	4.5	15.0
0 Days Rest	14	29.5	12.4	.387	1.9	.346	2.9	.805	0.00	1.14	1.5	6.2	12.6
1 Days Rest	35	29.3	14.3	.449	1.8	.250	4.1	.838	0.26	0.91	1.1	6.7	16.7
2 Days Rest	12	34.1	18.8	.493	2.8	.485	3.3	.872	1.00	0.58	1.6	7.3	22.7
3+ Days Rest	8	27.1	12.9	.427	1.4	.273	3.3	.885	0.38	0.13	1.3	6.6	14.3

Last Five Seasons

	G	Min	FGA	FG%	3PA	3P%	FTA	FT%	Blk	Stl	Ast	Reb	Pts
Total	257	29.0	13.1	.483	2.0	.295	4.0	.789	0.35	0.87	1.3	6.6	15.9
Home	128	28.8	13.1	.486	1.8	.305	4.2	.812	0.40	0.86	1.3	6.5	16.8
Road	129	29.2	13.1	.479	2.2	.287	3.8	.763	0.30	0.88	1.4	6.2	16.1
vs. Playoff	144	29.6	13.4	.465	2.2	.297	4.1	.773	0.33	0.88	1.2	6.3	16.3
vs. Non-Playoff	113	28.3	12.8	.506	1.8	.294	4.0	.809	0.37	0.86	1.5	6.9	16.7
vs. East	101	29.3	13.0	.456	1.9	.306	3.5	.813	0.30	0.81	1.4	5.9	15.9
vs. West	156	28.9	13.3	.500	2.1	.289	4.4	.776	0.30	1.13	1.3	6.7	17.2
vs. Div.	67	29.7	13.4	.496	2.1	.286	4.5	.765	0.36	0.93	1.1	7.1	17.4
As Starter	166	33.1	14.7	.494	2.3	.290	4.7	.787	0.39	1.05	1.7	7.3	18.9
Off Bench	91	21.6	10.4	.454	1.5	.309	2.8	.794	0.29	0.54	0.8	4.7	12.1
In wins	143	28.9	13.0	.507	2.0	.313	3.8	.810	0.37	0.97	1.5	6.2	16.9
In losses	114	29.2	13.3	.453	2.1	.274	4.3	.765	0.32	0.75	1.2	6.5	15.9
Pre All-Star	144	31.0	13.9	.481	2.0	.277	4.6	.804	0.34	0.99	1.5	6.8	17.6
Post All-Star	100	26.4	12.4	.493	2.1	.307	3.3	.772	0.36	0.73	1.2	5.7	15.4
Oct/Nov	42	30.9	13.2	.459	1.9	.203	5.1	.836	0.40	1.05	1.5	7.2	16.8
December	45	30.8	13.8	.495	2.0	.348	4.6	.726	0.29	1.16	1.2	6.3	17.8
January	45	30.8	14.2	.495	1.9	.235	4.3	.833	0.29	0.73	1.8	7.1	18.0
February	56	30.4	13.8	.474	2.4	.364	3.6	.762	0.52	0.77	1.3	6.4	16.7
March	45	24.9	11.4	.469	1.9	.226	2.9	.795	0.27	0.76	1.1	5.6	13.4
Apr/May	24	23.6	11.6	.523	1.9	.391	3.8	.778	0.25	0.71	0.9	5.0	15.8
0 Days Rest	58	29.4	12.4	.450	2.0	.217	4.1	.773	0.26	0.98	1.4	6.4	14.8
1 Days Rest	133	29.6	13.8	.483	2.0	.290	4.3	.776	0.35	0.92	1.3	6.7	17.2
2 Days Rest	31	31.4	14.9	.525	2.4	.486	3.9	.826	0.61	0.77	1.6	6.1	20.0
3+ Days Rest	35	23.9	10.4	.490	1.7	.233	2.9	.854	0.29	0.57	1.2	5.4	13.1

Calbert Cheaney

1999-2000 Per Game Averages

	G	Min	FGA	FG%	3PA	3P%	FTA	FT%	Blk	Stl	Ast	Reb	Pts
Total	67	19.5	4.1	.440	0.8	.333	0.3	.429	0.21	0.66	1.2	2.1	4.0
Home	35	20.1	4.4	.426	0.9	.344	0.4	.385	0.31	0.74	1.3	2.0	4.2
Road	32	18.9	3.7	.458	0.7	.318	0.3	.500	0.09	0.56	1.0	2.2	3.7
vs. Playoff	37	19.5	3.9	.417	0.8	.345	0.4	.462	0.19	0.51	1.0	1.9	3.7
vs. Non-Playoff	30	19.5	4.3	.465	0.8	.320	0.3	.375	0.23	0.83	1.4	2.0	3.5
vs. East	47	19.4	4.0	.432	0.8	.361	0.2	.375	0.21	0.64	1.1	2.1	3.8
vs. West	20	19.9	4.2	.458	0.9	.278	0.7	.462	0.20	0.70	1.3	2.1	4.4
vs. Div.	21	19.8	4.1	.379	0.7	.200	0.3	.500	0.24	0.48	1.1	2.8	3.4
As Starter	19	25.3	5.5	.452	1.3	.333	0.4	.375	0.32	0.68	1.7	2.6	5.5
Off Bench	48	17.3	3.5	.432	0.6	.333	0.3	.462	0.17	0.65	1.0	1.9	3.4
In wins	29	20.8	4.5	.415	0.9	.308	0.5	.286	0.28	0.90	1.3	2.1	4.1
In losses	38	18.6	3.8	.462	0.7	.357	0.2	.714	0.16	0.47	1.1	2.0	3.9

	G	Min	FGA	FG%	3PA	3P%	FTA	FT%	Blk	Stl	Ast	Reb	Pts
Pre All-Star	41	20.8	4.4	.425	0.8	.375	0.3	.462	0.17	0.71	1.2	2.3	4.1
Post All-Star	26	17.5	3.6	.468	0.8	.273	0.3	.375	0.27	0.58	1.1	1.6	3.7
November	8	20.1	4.4	.400	0.1	.000	0.3	.000	0.25	1.13	0.8	2.4	3.7
December	14	19.6	4.6	.438	0.9	.417	0.4	.667	0.21	0.79	1.3	2.5	4.6
January	13	21.7	3.8	.408	1.0	.308	0.3	.250	0.00	0.54	1.3	2.0	3.5
February	6	22.7	5.2	.452	1.0	.500	0.2	1.000	0.33	0.33	1.7	2.7	5.3
March	16	16.6	3.4	.481	0.8	.231	0.4	.500	0.31	0.44	1.0	1.6	3.6
April	10	18.9	4.0	.450	0.9	.333	0.2	.000	0.20	0.80	1.3	1.7	3.9
0 Days Rest	17	18.2	4.0	.485	0.9	.400	0.2	.667	0.18	0.41	1.1	1.6	4.4
1 Days Rest	36	20.8	4.3	.439	0.9	.323	0.4	.429	0.19	0.67	1.3	2.1	4.2
2 Days Rest	5	17.8	3.2	.375	0.8	.250	0.4	.500	0.60	0.40	1.6	2.8	2.8
3+ Days Rest	9	18.0	3.8	.382	0.4	.250	0.2	.000	0.11	1.22	0.6	2.4	3.0

Last Five Seasons

	G	Min	FGA	FG%	3PA	3P%	FTA	FT%	Blk	Stl	Ast	Reb	Pts
Total	348	29.2	9.5	.465	0.9	.296	1.9	.653	0.29	0.93	1.7	3.2	10.3
Home	177	29.8	9.9	.471	1.1	.312	2.1	.659	0.32	0.95	1.7	3.1	11.0
Road	171	28.6	9.1	.458	0.8	.273	1.6	.645	0.27	0.91	1.7	3.2	9.6
vs. Playoff	190	28.9	9.3	.451	1.0	.286	1.8	.659	0.23	0.84	1.6	3.2	9.8
vs. Non-Playoff	158	29.5	9.7	.481	0.9	.308	1.9	.646	0.37	1.04	1.8	3.2	10.9
vs. East	244	28.8	9.2	.463	0.8	.304	1.9	.669	0.30	0.86	1.7	3.2	10.0
vs. West	104	30.0	10.3	.468	1.2	.282	1.9	.616	0.29	1.09	1.8	3.3	11.1
vs. Div.	111	29.4	9.3	.463	0.9	.311	2.1	.638	0.34	0.83	1.7	3.4	10.3
As Starter	268	32.1	10.8	.470	1.0	.302	2.2	.670	0.31	1.00	1.9	3.5	12.0
Off Bench	80	19.2	5.0	.427	0.7	.264	0.7	.463	0.25	0.69	1.1	2.1	4.7
In wins	164	30.1	9.9	.491	0.8	.268	2.2	.660	0.40	1.04	1.9	3.3	11.4
In losses	184	28.3	9.1	.439	1.1	.313	1.6	.644	0.20	0.83	1.6	3.1	9.4

	G	Min	FGA	FG%	3PA	3P%	FTA	FT%	Blk	Stl	Ast	Reb	Pts
Pre All-Star	168	29.0	9.0	.476	0.9	.322	1.8	.686	0.26	0.99	1.5	3.1	10.1
Post All-Star	130	30.9	10.6	.467	1.1	.289	2.2	.655	0.32	0.91	2.0	3.5	11.6
Oct/Nov	52	30.3	10.0	.439	1.2	.306	2.1	.615	0.21	1.10	1.5	3.3	10.5
December	53	27.3	8.0	.486	0.6	.303	1.9	.755	0.32	1.21	1.5	2.8	9.5
January	47	29.2	8.4	.519	0.7	.323	1.5	.681	0.21	0.79	1.5	3.1	9.9
February	55	31.6	11.8	.447	1.3	.405	2.3	.661	0.29	0.76	1.9	3.4	12.6
March	80	28.3	9.0	.462	1.0	.207	1.8	.599	0.34	0.85	1.9	3.3	9.6
Apr/May	61	28.7	9.7	.459	0.8	.239	1.7	.641	0.34	0.90	1.8	3.2	10.1
0 Days Rest	94	29.7	9.5	.458	1.0	.302	1.9	.714	0.22	0.74	1.8	3.4	10.4
1 Days Rest	175	28.5	9.1	.468	0.9	.293	1.8	.640	0.34	0.97	1.7	2.9	9.9
2 Days Rest	45	32.7	11.6	.477	0.9	.381	2.3	.657	0.29	1.16	1.8	3.9	12.9
3+ Days Rest	34	26.5	8.9	.444	1.0	.182	1.6	.527	0.26	0.91	1.3	3.2	8.9

Chris Childs

1999-2000 Per Game Averages

	G	Min	FGA	FG%	3PA	3P%	FTA	FT%	Blk	Stl	Ast	Reb	Pts
Total	71	23.6	5.0	.409	1.5	.356	0.8	.797	0.06	0.51	4.0	2.1	5.3
Home	35	24.5	4.7	.448	1.3	.364	1.0	.857	0.06	0.49	4.7	1.9	5.5
Road	36	22.7	5.4	.376	1.7	.350	0.7	.708	0.06	0.53	3.4	2.2	5.1
vs. Playoff	37	24.5	5.5	.422	1.6	.407	0.8	.833	0.05	0.46	4.5	2.1	6.0
vs. Non-Playoff	34	22.6	4.5	.392	1.3	.289	0.9	.759	0.06	0.56	3.5	2.1	4.6
vs. East	45	23.8	5.0	.411	1.5	.379	0.7	.750	0.09	0.53	4.2	2.3	5.2
vs. West	26	23.3	5.1	.406	1.5	.316	1.0	.852	0.00	0.46	3.7	1.7	5.5
vs. Div.	20	22.4	4.8	.427	1.5	.414	0.9	.611	0.10	0.60	3.1	1.5	5.3
As Starter	2	32.0	8.0	.500	1.0	.500	2.0	.750	0.00	2.00	3.0	2.5	10.0
Off Bench	69	23.3	4.9	.405	1.5	.353	0.8	.800	0.06	0.46	4.0	2.1	5.2
In wins	42	22.8	4.5	.424	1.2	.360	0.7	.897	0.05	0.40	4.4	2.0	4.9
In losses	29	24.7	5.7	.392	1.9	.352	1.0	.700	0.07	0.66	3.5	2.1	5.9

	G	Min	FGA	FG%	3PA	3P%	FTA	FT%	Blk	Stl	Ast	Reb	Pts
Pre All-Star	39	22.9	5.0	.405	1.5	.328	0.7	.857	0.05	0.41	3.9	1.9	5.2
Post All-Star	32	24.4	5.1	.414	1.4	.391	1.0	.742	0.06	0.63	4.1	2.3	5.5
November	16	23.9	5.1	.402	1.9	.367	0.9	.857	0.06	0.44	4.2	2.1	5.6
December	12	22.8	4.8	.368	1.3	.313	1.0	.833	0.08	0.33	3.4	1.9	4.8
January	10	21.6	5.3	.472	1.2	.250	0.2	1.000	0.00	0.50	3.9	1.4	5.5
February	9	25.4	4.6	.341	1.2	.364	0.7	.833	0.00	0.33	5.0	2.3	4.1
March	17	24.5	5.1	.442	1.5	.360	1.2	.714	0.06	0.71	3.7	2.1	5.9
April	7	22.6	5.4	.395	1.4	.500	0.6	.750	0.14	0.71	4.3	2.7	5.4
0 Days Rest	17	24.2	5.1	.402	2.0	.265	0.7	.500	0.00	0.65	4.1	2.7	5.0
1 Days Rest	35	22.9	4.6	.404	1.1	.375	1.1	.865	0.11	0.49	3.6	1.7	5.1
2 Days Rest	12	24.7	6.3	.413	1.7	.350	0.5	1.000	0.00	0.50	5.1	2.1	6.3
3+ Days Rest	7	23.9	4.9	.441	1.4	.600	0.6	.750	0.00	0.29	4.1	2.3	5.6

Last Five Seasons

	G	Min	FGA	FG%	3PA	3P%	FTA	FT%	Blk	Stl	Ast	Reb	Pts
Total	330	27.4	6.9	.417	2.2	.366	2.2	.820	0.09	0.98	5.1	2.7	8.3
Home	159	27.6	6.6	.422	2.2	.372	2.3	.838	0.07	1.00	5.7	2.6	8.4
Road	171	27.3	7.1	.412	2.2	.359	2.0	.800	0.11	0.97	4.6	2.7	8.2
vs. Playoff	181	27.7	7.1	.419	2.3	.370	2.2	.831	0.08	0.96	5.2	2.6	8.6
vs. Non-Playoff	149	27.2	6.6	.413	2.0	.360	2.1	.806	0.11	1.01	5.1	2.7	7.9
vs. East	227	27.6	6.8	.408	2.2	.361	2.1	.806	0.11	1.05	5.0	2.8	8.4
vs. West	103	27.1	7.0	.434	2.2	.377	2.2	.848	0.04	0.84	5.4	2.4	8.8
vs. Div.	103	27.3	6.6	.415	2.2	.365	2.3	.791	0.13	1.12	4.9	2.7	8.1
As Starter	117	34.3	9.8	.415	3.3	.365	3.3	.815	0.14	1.48	7.2	3.3	12.0
Off Bench	213	23.7	5.3	.418	1.6	.366	1.6	.825	0.07	0.71	4.0	2.3	6.3
In wins	176	27.1	6.4	.437	2.0	.400	2.1	.811	0.07	1.03	5.4	2.6	8.1
In losses	154	27.9	7.4	.397	2.4	.333	2.2	.830	0.11	0.93	4.9	2.7	8.6

	G	Min	FGA	FG%	3PA	3P%	FTA	FT%	Blk	Stl	Ast	Reb	Pts
Pre All-Star	163	25.8	6.9	.415	2.2	.376	2.0	.849	0.09	0.82	4.9	2.6	8.3
Post All-Star	119	29.9	7.3	.416	2.4	.346	2.6	.788	0.13	1.24	5.9	2.8	8.9
Oct/Nov	48	24.4	6.0	.426	2.1	.353	1.9	.826	0.06	0.75	4.7	2.1	7.5
December	55	24.8	6.8	.413	1.9	.433	1.9	.857	0.11	0.80	4.5	2.5	8.1
January	49	26.5	7.5	.410	2.3	.315	1.9	.880	0.06	0.86	4.8	2.6	8.5
February	57	30.6	7.4	.431	2.3	.398	2.8	.803	0.07	1.67	6.1	3.1	9.5
March	68	29.3	6.8	.406	2.2	.358	2.4	.741	0.13	0.91	5.4	2.8	8.1
Apr/May	53	28.0	6.7	.416	2.4	.339	2.0	.875	0.09	0.87	5.1	2.7	8.1
0 Days Rest	83	28.0	7.0	.415	2.3	.359	2.3	.840	0.10	0.95	4.9	2.8	8.6
1 Days Rest	160	27.4	6.7	.424	2.1	.367	2.2	.817	0.11	0.97	5.2	2.7	8.3
2 Days Rest	53	28.2	7.9	.422	2.5	.374	2.1	.836	0.02	1.17	5.5	2.9	9.3
3+ Days Rest	34	25.0	5.6	.366	1.8	.361	1.9	.746	0.09	0.85	4.9	1.8	6.1

Doug Christie

1999-2000 Per Game Averages

	G	Min	FGA	FG%	3PA	3P%	FTA	FT%	Blk	Stl	Ast	Reb	Pts
Total	73	31.0	10.5	.407	3.8	.360	3.0	.843	0.59	1.40	4.4	3.9	12.4
Home	37	30.6	10.6	.413	4.1	.349	2.5	.839	0.92	1.41	5.0	3.9	12.3
Road	36	31.4	10.3	.401	3.4	.374	3.4	.846	0.25	1.39	3.8	3.9	12.4
vs. Playoff	37	31.9	10.9	.412	4.0	.389	3.7	.816	0.49	1.16	4.3	4.0	13.5
vs. Non-Playoff	36	30.1	10.0	.402	3.5	.325	2.2	.888	0.69	1.64	4.5	3.8	11.2
vs. East	46	31.0	10.8	.419	4.1	.356	3.0	.886	0.63	1.52	4.5	3.9	12.4
vs. West	27	31.1	9.8	.385	3.2	.368	2.8	.763	0.52	1.19	4.1	3.9	10.9
vs. Div.	23	31.3	11.2	.380	4.3	.330	3.0	.899	0.70	1.35	4.3	4.0	12.7
As Starter	73	31.0	10.5	.407	3.8	.360	3.0	.843	0.59	1.40	4.4	3.9	12.4
Off Bench	0	—	—	—	—	—	—	—	—	—	—	—	—
In wins	40	31.3	10.9	.417	4.3	.395	3.1	.887	0.88	1.85	4.7	4.0	16.1
In losses	33	30.7	9.9	.393	3.1	.301	2.8	.783	0.24	0.85	4.1	3.8	10.9

	G	Min	FGA	FG%	3PA	3P%	FTA	FT%	Blk	Stl	Ast	Reb	Pts
Pre All-Star	43	31.1	11.4	.400	4.2	.348	3.4	.810	0.47	1.30	4.0	3.8	13.4
Post All-Star	30	30.8	9.1	.419	3.1	.383	2.3	.913	0.77	1.53	5.0	4.1	10.9
November	15	30.8	11.5	.465	3.7	.411	2.9	.750	0.60	1.27	3.1	4.0	14.4
December	10	27.5	10.7	.355	4.8	.292	2.5	.880	0.10	1.40	4.6	2.4	11.2
January	14	33.8	12.3	.378	4.8	.373	4.4	.820	0.57	1.43	4.9	4.1	14.6
February	12	32.1	8.7	.433	3.3	.282	2.6	.806	1.08	1.33	5.1	4.4	10.5
March	17	32.2	10.3	.400	3.1	.415	2.9	.939	0.59	1.59	4.6	4.4	12.2
April	5	24.4	6.8	.382	2.4	.333	1.2	1.000	0.40	1.20	4.2	3.4	7.2
0 Days Rest	16	31.6	10.8	.422	3.4	.389	3.3	.885	0.31	1.63	4.6	4.0	13.3
1 Days Rest	40	30.6	9.9	.373	3.7	.342	2.5	.810	0.80	1.30	4.1	3.9	10.7
2 Days Rest	8	31.8	11.9	.495	3.9	.355	3.1	.960	0.25	1.63	4.3	2.6	16.1
3+ Days Rest	9	31.2	11.0	.434	4.6	.390	4.3	.795	0.44	1.22	5.4	4.8	14.8

Last Five Seasons

	G	Min	FGA	FG%	3PA	3P%	FTA	FT%	Blk	Stl	Ast	Reb	Pts
Total	337	33.0	11.2	.416	3.7	.358	3.5	.813	0.56	2.01	3.6	4.4	13.5
Home	168	33.2	11.2	.409	3.7	.371	3.5	.834	0.73	2.11	4.1	4.6	13.5
Road	169	32.9	11.1	.422	3.6	.344	3.5	.792	0.40	1.91	3.1	4.1	13.4
vs. Playoff	182	33.9	11.3	.413	3.8	.358	3.7	.794	0.58	1.97	3.6	4.5	13.7
vs. Non-Playoff	155	32.0	11.0	.418	3.5	.358	3.3	.839	0.55	2.05	3.7	4.3	13.3
vs. East	229	33.2	11.4	.411	3.7	.362	3.7	.824	0.56	2.04	3.6	4.4	13.8
vs. West	108	32.8	10.8	.425	3.5	.348	3.1	.787	0.56	1.93	3.8	4.4	12.9
vs. Div.	118	32.8	10.8	.396	3.5	.340	3.5	.820	0.61	1.89	3.4	4.1	12.6
As Starter	299	35.5	12.1	.416	3.9	.353	3.8	.818	0.60	2.13	3.9	4.7	14.6
Off Bench	38	13.6	4.2	.404	1.3	.471	1.3	.708	0.26	1.00	1.4	2.3	4.9
In wins	127	33.0	11.2	.439	4.0	.415	3.5	.836	0.66	2.21	4.2	4.5	14.5
In losses	210	33.0	11.2	.401	3.4	.317	3.5	.800	0.50	1.88	3.3	4.3	12.9

	G	Min	FGA	FG%	3PA	3P%	FTA	FT%	Blk	Stl	Ast	Reb	Pts
Pre All-Star	152	32.0	10.5	.416	3.6	.356	3.2	.788	0.59	1.72	3.4	4.4	12.6
Post All-Star	135	33.3	11.3	.427	3.9	.377	3.3	.825	0.55	2.24	3.8	4.5	13.9
Oct/Nov	50	31.8	10.8	.426	3.3	.348	2.9	.782	0.56	1.58	2.8	4.2	12.6
December	39	33.2	10.4	.384	3.7	.336	3.7	.790	0.62	1.79	3.7	4.6	12.2
January	54	31.3	10.1	.432	3.8	.382	3.3	.790	0.59	1.81	3.8	4.3	13.1
February	57	33.3	11.5	.412	3.8	.339	3.5	.822	0.53	2.02	3.8	4.5	13.7
March	81	34.1	11.3	.409	3.3	.374	3.8	.833	0.52	2.28	3.9	4.7	13.7
Apr/May	56	34.0	12.5	.425	4.1	.358	3.8	.832	0.61	2.30	3.7	4.0	15.3
0 Days Rest	79	31.8	10.7	.433	3.3	.385	3.4	.801	0.38	1.92	3.4	3.8	13.3
1 Days Rest	181	34.2	11.5	.405	3.7	.350	3.5	.815	0.65	2.01	3.7	4.7	13.6
2 Days Rest	44	34.4	11.8	.431	4.2	.314	4.1	.822	0.66	2.68	3.9	4.7	14.9
3+ Days Rest	33	27.6	10.0	.417	3.6	.408	3.5	.817	0.39	1.27	3.4	3.7	12.7

Keon Clark

1999-2000 Per Game Averages

	G	Min	FGA	FG%	3PA	3P%	FTA	FT%	Blk	Stl	Ast	Reb	Pts
Total	81	22.8	6.5	.542	0.1	.125	2.2	.688	1.41	0.56	0.9	6.2	8.6
Home	40	21.6	6.5	.529	0.2	.167	1.8	.722	1.90	0.45	0.9	6.3	8.2
Road	41	24.1	6.6	.554	0.0	.000	2.5	.663	0.93	0.66	0.9	6.2	9.0
vs. Playoff	48	22.6	6.1	.536	0.1	.250	1.7	.650	1.33	0.52	0.8	6.2	7.6
vs. Non-Playoff	33	23.2	7.1	.549	0.1	.000	2.9	.719	1.52	0.61	1.1	6.3	9.9
vs. East	29	23.4	7.1	.544	0.1	.250	2.7	.646	1.21	0.48	0.7	6.1	9.5
vs. West	52	22.5	6.2	.540	0.1	.000	1.9	.722	1.52	0.60	1.0	6.3	8.0
vs. Div.	24	23.5	6.3	.533	0.1	.000	1.9	.689	1.29	0.54	1.0	6.5	8.0
As Starter	20	27.9	7.6	.530	0.1	.000	2.6	.745	1.50	0.60	1.0	7.5	9.9
Off Bench	61	21.2	6.2	.546	0.1	.167	2.0	.664	1.38	0.54	0.9	5.8	8.1
In wins	35	21.6	6.0	.507	0.1	.000	1.4	.750	1.86	0.51	1.0	6.4	7.1
In losses	46	23.8	6.9	.564	0.1	.200	2.8	.664	1.07	0.59	0.8	6.1	9.7

	G	Min	FGA	FG%	3PA	3P%	FTA	FT%	Blk	Stl	Ast	Reb	Pts
Pre All-Star	48	20.3	5.8	.536	0.1	.167	1.8	.667	1.40	0.52	0.8	6.1	7.4
Post All-Star	33	26.5	7.6	.548	0.1	.000	2.8	.707	1.42	0.61	1.0	6.4	10.3
November	13	17.2	4.5	.525	0.0	—	1.2	.600	1.23	0.46	0.4	5.4	5.5
December	15	21.9	7.1	.533	0.1	.000	2.7	.725	1.87	0.73	0.7	6.7	9.5
January	14	22.6	5.6	.519	0.3	.250	1.6	.591	1.07	0.50	1.1	6.4	6.9
February	13	22.6	6.5	.571	0.1	.000	2.4	.677	1.38	0.38	1.2	6.9	9.0
March	16	29.6	9.0	.549	0.1	.000	3.2	.765	1.63	0.50	1.1	7.1	12.3
April	10	21.4	5.5	.545	0.1	.000	1.7	.588	1.50	0.60	0.7	4.2	7.0
0 Days Rest	21	22.5	5.8	.512	0.0	.000	2.1	.689	1.24	0.57	1.0	5.5	7.4
1 Days Rest	39	22.5	6.9	.546	0.1	.200	2.2	.644	1.31	0.46	0.8	6.7	9.0
2 Days Rest	13	24.2	5.8	.539	0.1	.000	2.8	.757	1.46	0.92	0.8	5.7	8.5
3+ Days Rest	8	23.0	7.8	.581	0.1	.000	0.9	.857	2.25	0.38	1.3	6.8	9.8

Career (1998-99 thru 1999-2000)

	G	Min	FGA	FG%	3PA	3P%	FTA	FT%	Blk	Stl	Ast	Reb	Pts
Total	109	20.7	5.6	.530	0.1	.111	2.0	.667	1.33	0.50	0.7	5.5	7.2
Home	54	19.8	5.6	.523	0.1	.167	1.7	.703	1.76	0.46	0.7	5.5	7.0
Road	55	21.7	5.6	.536	0.1	.000	2.2	.639	0.91	0.55	0.7	5.5	7.4
vs. Playoff	66	20.8	5.2	.513	0.1	.250	1.6	.629	1.27	0.50	0.7	5.5	6.3
vs. Non-Playoff	43	20.5	6.2	.551	0.1	.000	2.5	.704	1.42	0.51	0.9	5.5	8.6
vs. East	34	22.6	6.4	.548	0.1	.250	2.4	.634	1.24	0.50	0.6	6.0	8.6
vs. West	75	19.9	5.2	.519	0.1	.000	1.7	.687	1.37	0.51	0.8	5.3	6.6
vs. Div.	41	20.3	5.1	.495	0.1	.000	1.6	.677	1.32	0.41	0.8	5.2	6.1
As Starter	20	27.9	7.6	.530	0.1	.000	2.6	.745	1.50	0.60	1.0	7.5	9.9
Off Bench	89	19.1	5.1	.530	0.1	.143	1.8	.642	1.29	0.48	0.7	5.1	6.6
In wins	43	19.9	5.3	.522	0.1	.000	1.5	.714	1.72	0.51	0.9	5.7	6.6
In losses	66	21.3	5.7	.534	0.1	.167	2.3	.647	1.08	0.50	0.7	5.4	7.6

	G	Min	FGA	FG%	3PA	3P%	FTA	FT%	Blk	Stl	Ast	Reb	Pts
Pre All-Star	48	20.3	5.8	.536	0.1	.167	1.8	.667	1.42	0.52	0.8	6.1	7.4
Post All-Star	33	26.5	7.6	.548	0.1	.000	2.8	.707	1.42	0.61	1.0	6.4	10.3
Oct/Nov	13	17.2	4.5	.525	0.0	—	1.2	.600	1.23	0.46	0.4	5.4	5.5
December	15	21.9	7.1	.533	0.1	.000	2.7	.725	1.87	0.73	0.7	6.7	9.5
January	14	22.6	5.6	.519	0.3	.250	1.6	.591	1.07	0.50	1.1	6.4	6.9
February	25	17.2	4.6	.552	0.1	.000	1.9	.625	1.08	0.44	0.8	4.6	6.3
March	32	23.3	6.0	.516	0.0	.000	2.2	.718	1.50	0.38	0.8	5.8	7.8
Apr/May	10	21.4	5.5	.545	0.1	.000	1.7	.588	1.10	0.80	0.7	4.2	7.0
0 Days Rest	29	19.5	5.0	.514	0.1	.000	1.8	.647	1.17	0.52	0.7	4.8	6.2
1 Days Rest	55	20.8	5.7	.530	0.1	.200	2.0	.657	1.31	0.40	0.7	5.9	7.3
2 Days Rest	13	24.2	5.8	.539	0.1	.000	2.8	.757	1.46	0.92	0.8	5.7	8.5
3+ Days Rest	12	19.4	6.3	.547	0.1	.000	1.4	.588	1.67	0.50	0.9	5.3	7.7

Derrick Coleman

1999-2000 Per Game Averages

	G	Min	FGA	FG%	3PA	3P%	FTA	FT%	Blk	Stl	Ast	Reb	Pts		G	Min	FGA	FG%	3PA	3P%	FTA	FT%	Blk	Stl	Ast	Reb	Pts
Total	74	31.7	13.2	.456	1.9	.362	5.1	.785	1.76	0.46	2.4	8.5	16.7	Pre All-Star	44	30.0	12.2	.470	1.5	.338	4.9	.811	2.02	0.50	1.9	7.8	16.0
Home	38	31.1	12.9	.480	2.1	.363	5.2	.802	2.21	0.39	2.4	8.1	17.3	Post All-Star	30	34.2	14.8	.438	2.4	.384	5.3	.750	1.37	0.40	3.1	9.6	17.9
Road	36	32.3	13.5	.431	1.7	.361	5.0	.767	1.28	0.53	2.3	9.0	16.1	November	13	20.7	7.6	.424	0.5	.429	2.8	.838	1.69	0.31	1.0	6.2	9.1
vs. Playoff	40	31.5	13.7	.429	2.1	.317	4.7	.775	1.53	0.58	2.5	8.0	16.0	December	13	33.2	13.8	.475	1.5	.263	5.7	.811	2.38	0.54	2.2	7.2	18.1
vs. Non-Playoff	34	32.0	12.7	.490	1.7	.424	5.6	.795	2.03	0.32	2.2	9.2	17.6	January	13	34.4	14.2	.478	2.5	.375	5.5	.819	1.85	0.77	2.2	9.5	19.0
vs. East	49	31.1	12.6	.437	1.9	.355	5.0	.789	1.65	0.45	2.4	7.9	15.7	February	13	34.9	15.5	.483	2.3	.400	5.2	.765	1.85	0.38	2.7	10.2	19.8
vs. West	25	32.8	14.4	.488	1.9	.375	5.2	.779	1.96	0.48	2.2	9.8	18.9	March	12	34.8	15.3	.448	2.4	.241	7.5	.756	1.50	0.17	3.3	8.6	19.9
vs. Div.	26	31.4	12.3	.452	1.9	.347	5.2	.769	1.69	0.50	2.7	7.2	15.8	April	10	32.9	13.3	.391	2.4	.500	3.6	.722	1.10	0.60	3.0	10.1	14.2
As Starter	64	33.4	14.0	.457	2.1	.363	5.5	.780	1.72	0.50	2.5	8.9	17.8	0 Days Rest	17	31.9	13.0	.434	1.6	.407	5.3	.800	1.82	0.65	2.3	9.1	16.2
Off Bench	10	21.2	8.6	.442	0.6	.333	2.7	.852	2.00	0.20	1.2	6.5	10.1	1 Days Rest	38	31.6	13.5	.476	2.2	.398	4.9	.801	1.55	0.39	2.7	8.6	17.6
In wins	43	32.8	13.3	.497	2.0	.407	5.5	.807	2.00	0.35	2.8	9.8	18.5	2 Days Rest	8	28.4	13.5	.435	1.3	.100	3.1	.920	2.75	0.63	1.8	6.4	14.8
In losses	31	30.3	13.1	.397	1.8	.291	4.5	.748	1.42	0.61	1.7	8.1	14.3	3+ Days Rest	11	34.2	12.5	.431	1.9	.286	6.9	.684	1.64	0.27	1.9	9.0	16.0

Last Five Seasons

	G	Min	FGA	FG%	3PA	3P%	FTA	FT%	Blk	Stl	Ast	Reb	Pts		G	Min	FGA	FG%	3PA	3P%	FTA	FT%	Blk	Stl	Ast	Reb	Pts
Total	238	33.8	13.5	.431	1.7	.299	5.7	.762	1.37	0.66	2.6	9.2	16.5	Pre All-Star	114	33.1	12.8	.440	1.7	.303	5.6	.766	1.60	0.65	2.6	8.6	16.1
Home	120	33.6	12.9	.454	1.8	.301	5.7	.773	1.51	0.64	2.7	9.1	16.7	Post All-Star	87	35.7	15.4	.427	2.1	.309	6.1	.762	1.16	0.69	2.9	10.2	18.4
Road	118	34.1	14.1	.409	1.7	.296	5.7	.751	1.22	0.69	2.5	9.3	16.3	Oct/Nov	37	30.9	10.6	.445	1.4	.321	4.8	.785	1.41	0.57	2.6	7.9	13.7
vs. Playoff	143	34.5	13.9	.417	1.9	.293	5.4	.751	1.27	0.73	2.5	9.2	16.2	December	35	34.2	13.9	.438	2.0	.261	6.5	.754	1.60	0.71	2.7	8.1	17.6
vs. Non-Playoff	95	32.9	12.9	.453	1.5	.310	6.1	.778	1.51	0.56	2.7	9.2	16.9	January	35	33.8	14.1	.431	1.8	.328	5.3	.763	1.71	0.74	2.3	9.9	16.8
vs. East	158	33.7	13.0	.426	1.7	.290	5.6	.765	1.27	0.66	2.7	8.9	15.9	February	50	35.6	14.4	.424	2.0	.316	5.7	.741	1.32	0.60	2.4	10.0	17.1
vs. West	80	34.2	14.3	.441	1.8	.314	5.9	.757	1.56	0.68	2.5	9.8	17.6	March	48	36.0	14.4	.432	1.6	.237	6.9	.759	1.21	0.81	3.1	9.9	18.1
vs. Div.	77	33.1	12.3	.451	1.7	.298	5.6	.740	1.22	0.60	2.9	8.5	15.8	Apr/May	33	31.1	12.8	.420	1.6	.346	4.4	.795	1.00	0.52	2.4	8.9	14.8
As Starter	216	35.0	14.0	.431	1.8	.302	6.0	.757	1.36	0.71	2.8	9.5	17.1	0 Days Rest	61	33.9	13.5	.427	1.8	.299	5.5	.754	1.39	0.84	2.4	8.7	16.2
Off Bench	22	22.3	8.5	.433	0.6	.214	3.0	.877	1.45	0.23	1.0	6.5	10.1	1 Days Rest	114	34.0	13.6	.448	1.8	.337	5.8	.767	1.29	0.66	2.8	9.5	17.2
In wins	100	34.2	13.0	.466	1.7	.363	6.2	.783	1.60	0.62	2.9	9.5	17.5	2 Days Rest	24	34.0	14.1	.451	1.9	.244	4.7	.786	1.71	0.71	2.5	8.5	16.9
In losses	138	33.6	13.8	.407	1.7	.253	5.3	.745	1.20	0.70	2.4	9.0	15.7	3+ Days Rest	39	33.3	12.7	.372	1.5	.207	6.3	.750	1.33	0.38	2.4	9.7	14.4

Bimbo Coles

1999-2000 Per Game Averages

	G	Min	FGA	FG%	3PA	3P%	FTA	FT%	Blk	Stl	Ast	Reb	Pts		G	Min	FGA	FG%	3PA	3P%	FTA	FT%	Blk	Stl	Ast	Reb	Pts
Total	80	24.1	7.6	.455	0.5	.205	1.3	.817	0.14	0.73	3.6	2.2	8.1	Pre All-Star	45	26.6	8.6	.476	0.5	.167	1.2	.836	0.20	0.87	4.0	2.5	9.3
Home	39	23.1	6.6	.463	0.5	.056	1.6	.859	0.10	0.79	3.4	2.3	7.5	Post All-Star	35	20.8	6.2	.417	0.4	.267	1.4	.796	0.06	0.54	3.1	1.7	6.4
Road	41	25.0	8.5	.449	0.5	.333	1.0	.750	0.17	0.66	3.9	2.0	8.6	November	15	26.1	9.1	.515	0.5	.125	1.5	.783	0.13	1.07	4.3	2.3	10.6
vs. Playoff	45	23.3	6.8	.454	0.4	.118	1.3	.842	0.22	0.71	3.4	1.9	7.3	December	14	25.9	7.9	.436	0.4	.167	0.9	.923	0.21	0.64	3.9	2.4	7.3
vs. Non-Playoff	35	25.1	8.6	.455	0.6	.273	1.3	.787	0.03	0.74	3.9	2.5	9.1	January	11	27.4	8.6	.484	0.5	.333	1.2	.769	0.18	0.82	4.1	2.3	9.5
vs. East	52	23.2	7.3	.489	0.5	.208	1.3	.826	0.17	0.67	3.5	1.9	8.3	February	12	32.0	10.3	.423	0.5	.000	1.5	.778	0.17	0.67	4.7	3.3	9.8
vs. West	28	25.6	8.2	.397	0.5	.200	1.3	.800	0.07	0.82	3.9	2.7	7.6	March	17	16.9	4.4	.400	0.4	.333	1.3	.818	0.06	0.35	2.2	1.9	4.7
vs. Div.	27	23.0	7.3	.515	0.5	.231	1.2	.909	0.26	0.56	3.5	1.9	8.7	April	11	18.0	6.2	.441	0.6	.286	1.4	.867	0.09	0.91	2.9	0.5	6.8
As Starter	54	27.5	8.9	.471	0.5	.154	1.3	.797	0.19	0.80	4.2	2.5	9.4	0 Days Rest	23	25.0	8.6	.490	0.5	.583	1.2	.778	0.13	0.83	4.1	2.8	9.7
Off Bench	26	16.8	5.0	.395	0.5	.308	1.3	.857	0.04	0.58	2.4	1.4	5.2	1 Days Rest	35	23.1	6.6	.422	0.5	.059	1.3	.894	0.11	0.63	3.3	1.7	6.8
In wins	28	24.1	8.2	.450	0.4	.000	1.7	.809	0.11	1.04	4.0	2.1	8.7	2 Days Rest	14	23.6	7.7	.463	0.4	.000	1.7	.667	0.21	0.86	3.3	2.1	8.3
In losses	52	24.0	7.3	.458	0.5	.296	1.1	.825	0.15	0.56	3.4	2.2	7.7	3+ Days Rest	8	26.3	8.6	.449	0.6	.000	0.8	1.000	0.13	0.63	4.1	2.0	8.5

Last Five Seasons

	G	Min	FGA	FG%	3PA	3P%	FTA	FT%	Blk	Stl	Ast	Reb	Pts		G	Min	FGA	FG%	3PA	3P%	FTA	FT%	Blk	Stl	Ast	Reb	Pts
Total	313	27.0	8.1	.418	1.5	.304	1.8	.816	0.19	0.90	4.3	2.5	8.7	Pre All-Star	172	29.0	8.6	.422	1.7	.304	1.8	.835	0.22	0.91	4.4	2.7	9.2
Home	150	26.7	7.8	.418	1.6	.281	2.1	.804	0.18	0.95	4.5	2.7	8.7	Post All-Star	93	23.7	7.1	.392	1.8	.313	1.6	.772	0.12	0.87	3.7	2.2	7.3
Road	163	27.4	8.4	.417	1.5	.326	1.5	.831	0.20	0.87	4.0	2.4	8.7	Oct/Nov	51	27.3	8.3	.454	1.5	.333	1.7	.852	0.27	1.04	4.3	2.5	9.5
vs. Playoff	183	27.0	8.1	.408	1.6	.290	1.6	.808	0.22	0.92	4.2	2.4	8.4	December	54	29.3	8.7	.405	1.8	.295	1.9	.840	0.17	0.80	4.4	2.6	9.1
vs. Non-Playoff	130	27.2	8.1	.431	1.5	.325	2.0	.824	0.15	0.88	4.3	2.8	9.2	January	55	30.1	8.8	.402	1.7	.290	1.7	.824	0.16	0.89	4.5	2.9	8.9
vs. East	138	26.8	7.8	.432	1.4	.327	1.6	.821	0.15	0.91	4.1	2.6	8.8	February	54	26.4	7.6	.399	1.5	.301	2.0	.745	0.17	0.94	4.6	3.0	8.0
vs. West	175	27.2	8.4	.407	1.6	.288	1.6	.811	0.22	0.90	4.4	2.5	8.6	March	58	23.9	7.1	.427	1.3	.273	1.8	.794	0.21	0.97	3.5	2.5	7.8
vs. Div.	98	27.3	8.5	.440	1.5	.327	1.6	.836	0.22	0.89	4.3	2.6	9.3	Apr/May	41	25.0	8.6	.423	1.2	.353	1.5	.871	0.15	0.76	4.3	1.5	9.0
As Starter	198	30.6	9.6	.428	1.5	.314	2.0	.822	0.24	1.00	4.8	2.9	10.4	0 Days Rest	82	27.4	8.3	.446	1.2	.396	1.7	.831	0.21	0.90	4.4	2.8	9.3
Off Bench	115	20.9	5.6	.388	1.5	.287	1.3	.797	0.10	0.74	3.3	1.9	5.8	1 Days Rest	150	27.1	8.0	.400	1.7	.304	1.7	.819	0.15	0.86	4.2	2.6	8.3
In wins	113	27.4	8.4	.451	1.5	.343	2.6	.818	0.19	0.97	4.8	2.8	10.2	2 Days Rest	52	26.3	8.2	.423	1.5	.218	2.0	.769	0.23	0.94	3.9	2.1	8.8
In losses	200	26.9	8.0	.398	1.5	.282	1.3	.812	0.19	0.87	3.9	2.4	7.8	3+ Days Rest	29	26.8	8.0	.418	1.3	.237	2.0	.847	0.24	1.07	4.7	2.4	8.7

Austin Croshere
Indiana Pacers — Forward

1999-2000 Per Game Averages

	G	Min	FGA	FG%	3PA	3P%	FTA	FT%	Blk	Stl	Ast	Reb	Pts		G	Min	FGA	FG%	3PA	3P%	FTA	FT%	Blk	Stl	Ast	Reb	Pts
Total	81	23.3	8.1	.441	2.1	.362	2.9	.848	0.74	0.54	1.1	6.4	10.3	Pre All-Star	47	21.2	7.6	.410	2.2	.327	3.0	.810	0.83	0.55	1.1	5.9	9.4
Home	40	22.6	7.6	.460	2.0	.388	3.2	.867	0.55	0.65	0.9	6.5	10.5	Post All-Star	34	26.1	8.7	.478	2.1	.414	2.6	.910	0.62	0.53	1.1	7.0	11.6
Road	41	24.0	8.6	.425	2.3	.340	2.5	.825	0.93	0.44	1.3	6.2	10.1	November	15	19.6	8.1	.364	2.3	.294	2.2	.818	1.47	0.60	0.8	6.1	8.3
vs. Playoff	43	24.0	8.2	.432	2.3	.354	3.0	.884	0.67	0.53	1.0	6.6	10.6	December	14	21.1	7.0	.429	2.3	.313	3.4	.854	0.43	0.93	0.9	5.6	9.6
vs. Non-Playoff	38	22.4	7.9	.452	2.0	.373	2.7	.804	0.82	0.55	1.2	6.1	10.0	January	14	23.6	8.0	.438	2.4	.394	3.9	.782	0.64	0.29	1.7	6.6	11.0
vs. East	54	23.6	8.1	.442	2.1	.342	3.0	.845	0.74	0.50	1.2	6.1	10.4	February	12	24.7	7.8	.511	1.9	.348	2.2	.846	0.75	0.42	0.8	5.7	10.5
vs. West	27	22.5	8.0	.440	2.2	.400	2.6	.857	0.74	0.63	1.0	6.8	10.1	March	16	27.9	9.3	.490	2.4	.500	2.2	.886	0.56	0.50	1.2	8.1	12.3
vs. Div.	28	24.5	8.2	.457	2.3	.323	2.9	.927	0.79	0.71	1.2	6.3	11.0	April	10	22.3	7.9	.405	1.4	.214	3.4	.941	0.50	0.50	1.2	5.7	9.9
As Starter	14	31.2	9.7	.463	2.1	.345	2.7	.921	0.50	0.50	1.1	8.9	12.2	0 Days Rest	20	24.8	8.0	.472	1.9	.324	3.2	.857	1.20	0.85	1.4	6.1	10.8
Off Bench	67	21.6	7.7	.435	2.2	.366	2.9	.834	0.79	0.55	1.2	5.9	9.9	1 Days Rest	41	23.6	8.5	.430	2.3	.372	2.9	.863	0.68	0.51	1.3	6.8	10.6
In wins	55	23.4	7.7	.469	1.9	.377	3.0	.841	0.71	0.60	1.2	6.5	10.0	3+ Days Rest	7	21.4	7.7	.426	2.0	.214	3.1	.773	0.29	0.43	0.9	6.3	9.4
In losses	26	23.1	8.9	.390	2.6	.338	2.6	.866	0.81	0.42	0.9	6.1	10.0														

Career (1997-98 thru 1999-2000)

	G	Min	FGA	FG%	3PA	3P%	FTA	FT%	Blk	Stl	Ast	Reb	Pts		G	Min	FGA	FG%	3PA	3P%	FTA	FT%	Blk	Stl	Ast	Reb	Pts
Total	134	17.7	6.1	.432	1.6	.347	2.0	.836	0.54	0.45	0.8	4.5	7.5	Pre All-Star	59	18.7	6.6	.395	1.8	.327	2.5	.793	0.73	0.47	0.9	5.1	7.8
Home	75	16.4	5.6	.443	1.4	.370	2.0	.856	0.40	0.48	0.5	4.4	7.2	Post All-Star	48	21.3	7.2	.476	1.7	.398	2.0	.895	0.46	0.52	0.9	5.4	9.3
Road	59	19.4	6.7	.421	1.8	.324	1.9	.809	0.73	0.41	1.1	4.7	7.8	Oct/Nov	17	18.3	7.4	.349	2.0	.294	1.9	.818	1.35	0.59	0.8	5.4	7.4
vs. Playoff	65	19.4	6.4	.439	1.8	.359	2.2	.882	0.54	0.46	0.8	5.0	8.2	December	17	18.1	6.1	.408	1.9	.313	2.8	.854	0.35	0.76	0.7	4.6	7.9
vs. Non-Playoff	69	16.2	5.8	.426	1.4	.333	1.8	.782	0.55	0.43	0.8	4.1	6.8	January	19	21.1	7.2	.412	1.7	.394	3.3	.746	0.63	0.26	1.4	6.1	9.1
vs. East	93	17.3	5.8	.438	1.5	.338	2.0	.823	0.53	0.43	0.8	4.2	7.2	February	26	16.6	5.1	.515	1.5	.368	1.4	.861	0.46	0.42	0.6	3.4	7.0
vs. West	41	18.8	6.8	.421	1.8	.365	2.0	.866	0.59	0.49	0.7	5.3	8.1	March	34	18.4	6.4	.461	1.8	.393	1.5	.860	0.38	0.38	0.7	4.8	7.9
vs. Div.	46	18.4	6.1	.448	1.7	.316	2.0	.903	0.63	0.57	0.9	4.5	7.8	Apr/May	21	14.3	4.8	.420	0.9	.222	1.8	.921	0.33	0.38	0.7	3.2	5.9
As Starter	14	31.2	9.7	.463	2.1	.345	2.7	.921	0.50	0.50	1.1	8.9	12.2	0 Days Rest	30	19.7	6.1	.484	1.5	.326	2.4	.817	0.83	0.67	1.2	4.2	8.4
Off Bench	120	16.2	5.7	.426	1.6	.348	1.9	.822	0.55	0.44	0.8	4.0	6.9	1 Days Rest	61	19.3	6.8	.424	1.8	.366	2.1	.857	0.56	0.44	0.9	5.2	8.2
In wins	97	17.2	5.7	.443	1.4	.350	2.0	.827	0.52	0.47	0.8	4.4	7.2	2 Days Rest	17	19.9	6.5	.414	1.9	.424	2.4	.829	0.41	0.24	0.2	5.5	8.2
In losses	37	19.2	6.9	.409	2.1	.342	2.1	.857	0.62	0.38	0.7	4.8	8.2	3+ Days Rest	26	10.4	4.1	.396	1.0	.200	1.2	.800	0.27	0.35	0.4	2.6	4.3

Vonteego Cummings
Golden State Warriors — Guard

1999-2000 Per Game Averages

	G	Min	FGA	FG%	3PA	3P%	FTA	FT%	Blk	Stl	Ast	Reb	Pts		G	Min	FGA	FG%	3PA	3P%	FTA	FT%	Blk	Stl	Ast	Reb	Pts
Total	75	23.9	8.7	.405	2.0	.325	2.3	.751	0.17	1.21	3.3	2.5	9.4	Pre All-Star	44	24.2	8.6	.405	2.1	.326	2.0	.736	0.27	1.27	3.5	2.5	9.1
Home	38	24.1	8.7	.413	2.5	.344	2.2	.683	0.11	1.13	3.7	2.6	9.5	Post All-Star	31	23.5	8.9	.404	1.9	.322	2.6	.768	0.03	1.13	3.0	2.3	9.8
Road	37	23.8	8.8	.396	1.5	.291	2.4	.816	0.24	1.30	2.8	2.3	9.3	November	10	15.7	4.7	.362	1.3	.308	2.0	.750	0.30	0.60	2.5	2.4	5.3
vs. Playoff	43	23.0	8.7	.391	2.0	.318	1.9	.750	0.12	1.16	3.1	2.1	8.8	December	16	25.6	8.8	.436	2.2	.343	1.6	.640	0.31	1.50	4.2	2.0	9.4
vs. Non-Playoff	32	25.2	8.8	.422	2.0	.333	2.8	.753	0.25	1.28	3.5	3.0	10.2	January	12	29.1	11.1	.376	2.3	.321	2.4	.793	0.17	1.58	3.5	3.7	11.0
vs. East	27	24.9	8.7	.413	2.3	.306	3.1	.765	0.11	1.37	3.2	2.5	10.3	February	15	24.7	9.5	.378	2.5	.297	2.3	.765	0.13	1.47	3.6	2.3	9.7
vs. West	48	23.4	8.8	.400	1.9	.337	1.8	.738	0.21	1.13	3.4	2.4	8.9	March	15	25.1	9.4	.440	1.7	.280	3.7	.764	0.07	1.07	2.5	2.5	11.5
vs. Div.	22	24.8	9.6	.368	1.9	.262	1.8	.718	0.18	0.95	4.0	2.1	8.9	April	7	18.7	7.3	.412	1.9	.462	0.9	.833	0.00	0.57	3.1	1.9	7.6
As Starter	11	37.3	12.0	.386	3.3	.389	1.9	.762	0.55	2.27	5.1	3.8	12.0	0 Days Rest	16	26.3	8.9	.437	1.4	.400	3.0	.833	0.19	1.63	4.2	2.7	10.9
Off Bench	64	21.6	8.2	.409	1.8	.304	2.3	.750	0.11	1.03	3.0	2.2	9.0	1 Days Rest	41	24.1	9.0	.403	2.0	.333	2.2	.753	0.12	1.07	3.1	2.6	9.6
In wins	19	21.8	7.6	.431	1.8	.294	2.6	.700	0.21	1.16	3.3	2.5	8.9	2 Days Rest	9	18.4	6.7	.317	2.0	.111	1.8	.625	0.22	1.00	2.2	1.9	5.6
In losses	56	24.6	9.1	.397	2.1	.333	2.1	.773	0.16	1.23	3.3	2.4	9.6	3+ Days Rest	9	24.0	9.2	.422	2.7	.375	1.8	.625	0.33	1.33	3.6	2.0	9.9

Michael Curry
Detroit Pistons — Forward

1999-2000 Per Game Averages

	G	Min	FGA	FG%	3PA	3P%	FTA	FT%	Blk	Stl	Ast	Reb	Pts		G	Min	FGA	FG%	3PA	3P%	FTA	FT%	Blk	Stl	Ast	Reb	Pts
Total	82	19.6	4.6	.480	0.1	.200	2.0	.839	0.06	0.40	1.1	1.3	6.2	Pre All-Star	48	20.0	4.9	.477	0.1	.333	2.2	.822	0.06	0.33	1.0	1.3	6.5
Home	41	19.2	4.8	.451	0.1	.000	1.9	.821	0.05	0.46	1.2	1.7	5.9	Post All-Star	34	19.2	4.2	.486	0.1	.000	1.8	.869	0.06	0.50	1.2	1.3	5.7
Road	41	20.1	4.5	.511	0.0	1.000	2.2	.856	0.07	0.34	0.9	0.8	6.5	November	15	17.0	4.3	.438	0.0	—	2.0	.833	0.07	0.20	0.8	1.4	5.4
vs. Playoff	44	19.3	4.5	.421	0.1	.000	2.3	.800	0.07	0.41	0.9	1.3	5.6	December	14	19.1	4.1	.466	0.0	—	2.0	.750	0.14	0.21	0.7	1.0	5.4
vs. Non-Playoff	38	20.0	4.8	.544	0.1	.500	1.8	.897	0.05	0.39	1.2	1.2	6.8	January	15	22.5	5.7	.488	0.2	.333	2.5	.865	0.00	0.60	0.9	1.2	7.8
vs. East	54	19.4	4.8	.500	0.0	.500	2.0	.853	0.06	0.43	0.9	1.4	6.6	February	12	20.5	4.6	.509	0.0	—	1.8	.905	0.08	0.33	2.2	1.4	6.3
vs. West	28	20.2	4.3	.437	0.1	.000	2.1	.814	0.07	0.36	1.3	1.1	5.4	March	15	17.9	4.2	.444	0.1	.000	1.9	.793	0.00	0.53	0.9	1.1	5.3
vs. Div.	28	19.9	5.0	.518	0.0	1.000	2.0	.782	0.11	0.46	1.1	1.4	6.8	April	11	21.5	4.8	.547	0.1	.000	2.1	.913	0.09	0.55	1.1	1.5	7.2
As Starter	3	28.3	7.0	.714	0.0	—	3.0	.889	0.00	0.67	1.3	2.3	12.7	0 Days Rest	20	19.6	4.8	.531	0.1	.000	2.4	.750	0.10	0.30	0.9	1.3	6.9
Off Bench	79	18.6	4.5	.466	0.1	.200	2.0	.836	0.06	0.39	1.1	1.2	5.9	1 Days Rest	45	19.8	4.8	.463	0.1	.250	2.0	.880	0.04	0.51	1.1	1.3	6.2
In wins	42	18.6	4.4	.484	0.0	.000	1.9	.833	0.05	0.52	1.1	1.3	6.3	2 Days Rest	8	19.1	4.4	.514	0.0	—	2.3	.778	0.00	0.13	1.0	1.3	6.3
In losses	40	20.7	4.8	.477	0.1	.250	2.3	.844	0.08	0.28	1.0	1.2	6.5	3+ Days Rest	9	19.7	3.8	.412	0.0	—	1.1	1.000	0.11	0.33	1.1	1.0	4.2

Last Five Seasons

	G	Min	FGA	FG%	3PA	3P%	FTA	FT%	Blk	Stl	Ast	Reb	Pts		G	Min	FGA	FG%	3PA	3P%	FTA	FT%	Blk	Stl	Ast	Reb	Pts
Total	341	19.8	4.1	.462	0.5	.308	1.7	.831	0.12	0.55	1.1	1.5	5.3	Pre All-Star	149	17.8	3.6	.439	0.5	.338	1.8	.840	0.11	0.46	0.9	1.2	4.9
Home	172	18.7	4.0	.445	0.5	.358	1.8	.829	0.09	0.56	1.1	1.6	5.2	Post All-Star	142	20.7	4.5	.489	0.5	.329	1.7	.833	0.12	0.53	1.2	1.6	6.0
Road	169	20.8	4.2	.479	0.5	.256	1.7	.834	0.15	0.53	1.1	1.4	5.5	Oct/Nov	43	16.9	3.3	.399	0.3	.133	2.0	.821	0.07	0.40	0.7	1.2	4.3
vs. Playoff	182	19.1	3.9	.430	0.4	.231	1.8	.840	0.09	0.51	1.1	1.3	4.9	December	43	18.3	3.7	.456	0.5	.524	1.6	.779	0.12	0.37	0.7	1.2	4.8
vs. Non-Playoff	159	20.5	4.3	.496	0.6	.362	1.7	.821	0.14	0.59	1.1	1.7	5.8	January	49	18.0	3.6	.432	0.5	.240	2.0	.887	0.16	0.59	0.7	1.1	5.0
vs. East	238	20.0	4.2	.472	0.5	.313	1.6	.826	0.09	0.58	1.1	1.5	5.4	February	61	19.8	4.0	.481	0.5	.290	1.7	.817	0.11	0.54	1.5	1.7	5.4
vs. West	103	19.1	3.8	.436	0.4	.295	2.0	.842	0.17	0.46	1.1	1.5	5.1	March	81	20.0	4.3	.460	0.4	.333	1.5	.858	0.07	0.57	1.0	1.7	5.4
vs. Div.	125	20.5	4.2	.499	0.4	.339	1.6	.786	0.10	0.58	1.1	1.4	5.7	Apr/May	64	23.7	4.9	.498	0.5	.294	1.9	.808	0.17	0.70	1.5	1.8	6.5
As Starter	37	33.2	7.8	.510	0.4	.286	2.1	.886	0.22	0.95	2.2	1.8	9.9	0 Days Rest	91	21.3	4.2	.465	0.6	.278	2.2	.828	0.13	0.57	1.2	1.7	5.9
Off Bench	304	18.1	3.6	.449	0.5	.310	1.7	.823	0.11	0.50	1.1	1.5	4.8	1 Days Rest	174	19.9	4.3	.470	0.4	.356	1.6	.833	0.13	0.51	1.1	1.5	5.5
In wins	186	18.6	3.8	.468	0.5	.330	1.7	.822	0.12	0.53	1.1	1.6	5.5	2 Days Rest	47	18.1	3.4	.451	0.4	.400	1.5	.873	0.11	0.70	1.1	1.4	4.6
In losses	155	21.1	4.4	.456	0.4	.279	1.8	.842	0.12	0.57	1.1	1.4	5.7	3+ Days Rest	29	16.5	3.3	.411	0.4	.000	1.4	.762	0.03	0.41	0.8	1.3	3.8

Antonio Davis
Toronto Raptors — Forward-Center

1999-2000 Per Game Averages

	G	Min	FGA	FG%	3PA	3P%	FTA	FT%	Blk	Stl	Ast	Reb	Pts		G	Min	FGA	FG%	3PA	3P%	FTA	FT%	Blk	Stl	Ast	Reb	Pts
Total	79	31.4	9.0	.440	0.0	—	4.7	.765	1.27	0.48	1.3	8.8	11.5	Pre All-Star	46	31.2	9.5	.451	0.0	—	4.8	.821	1.37	0.46	1.2	9.2	12.5
Home	39	31.2	9.1	.430	0.0	—	4.6	.783	1.77	0.41	1.4	8.8	11.5	Post All-Star	33	31.7	8.3	.422	0.0	—	4.5	.682	1.12	0.52	1.5	8.3	10.1
Road	40	31.6	8.9	.449	0.0	—	4.8	.749	0.78	0.55	1.2	8.8	11.6	November	15	32.0	9.1	.453	0.0	—	4.4	.864	1.00	0.73	1.5	8.7	12.1
vs. Playoff	42	32.9	9.4	.390	0.0	—	4.3	.749	1.31	0.55	1.3	9.5	10.5	December	14	32.6	10.4	.455	0.0	—	5.1	.764	1.50	0.29	1.2	11.1	13.4
vs. Non-Playoff	37	29.7	8.6	.502	0.0	—	5.2	.781	1.22	0.41	1.4	8.0	12.6	January	13	28.6	8.5	.450	0.0	—	5.0	.862	1.62	0.31	0.8	7.9	12.0
vs. East	52	31.5	8.8	.437	0.0	—	4.5	.765	1.29	0.48	1.4	9.1	11.2	February	12	33.3	10.0	.392	0.0	—	5.3	.672	1.25	0.58	1.5	9.1	11.4
vs. West	27	31.1	9.3	.444	0.0	—	5.1	.766	1.22	0.48	1.3	8.3	12.2	March	15	30.4	7.3	.427	0.0	—	4.4	.667	1.00	0.60	1.3	7.7	9.2
vs. Div.	27	32.0	9.0	.463	0.0	—	4.2	.763	1.26	0.48	1.4	9.1	11.2	April	10	31.6	8.9	.461	0.0	—	3.8	.763	1.30	0.30	1.9	8.3	11.1
As Starter	78	31.6	9.1	.439	0.0	—	4.7	.764	1.28	0.49	1.3	8.9	11.6	0 Days Rest	17	31.2	9.9	.440	0.0	—	5.1	.690	0.76	0.59	1.3	8.3	12.2
Off Bench	1	15.0	3.0	.667	0.0	—	6.0	.833	0.00	0.00	0.0	3.0	9.0	1 Days Rest	45	32.4	9.0	.442	0.0	—	4.6	.767	1.40	0.42	1.3	9.4	11.5
In wins	43	30.4	8.3	.475	0.0	—	4.6	.782	1.28	0.42	1.3	8.3	11.4	2 Days Rest	9	30.7	7.8	.471	0.0	—	4.8	.791	1.56	0.89	1.6	7.3	11.1
In losses	36	32.5	9.9	.404	0.0	—	4.8	.747	1.25	0.56	1.4	9.4	11.6	3+ Days Rest	8	26.8	8.4	.388	0.0	—	4.4	.914	1.25	0.13	1.1	8.4	10.5

Last Five Seasons

	G	Min	FGA	FG%	3PA	3P%	FTA	FT%	Blk	Stl	Ast	Reb	Pts		G	Min	FGA	FG%	3PA	3P%	FTA	FT%	Blk	Stl	Ast	Reb	Pts
Total	374	27.7	7.2	.470	0.1	.105	4.5	.709	0.97	0.48	0.8	7.2	10.2	Pre All-Star	185	27.7	7.3	.474	0.0	.111	4.7	.708	1.03	0.45	0.8	7.3	10.2
Home	187	27.5	7.3	.461	0.0	.000	4.4	.736	1.12	0.41	0.9	7.4	10.0	Post All-Star	140	28.3	7.2	.464	0.1	.100	4.4	.713	0.94	0.53	0.9	7.2	10.1
Road	187	27.9	7.2	.480	0.0	.222	4.6	.683	0.82	0.56	0.8	7.0	10.0	Oct/Nov	54	29.4	7.4	.445	0.0	.000	4.5	.717	0.91	0.69	0.9	7.5	9.8
vs. Playoff	199	28.7	7.6	.457	0.0	.111	4.3	.693	0.92	0.48	0.8	7.4	9.9	December	59	27.7	7.3	.478	0.1	.333	5.2	.695	1.14	0.41	0.8	7.5	10.7
vs. Non-Playoff	175	26.7	6.9	.488	0.1	.100	4.6	.727	1.03	0.48	0.8	7.0	10.1	January	58	26.3	6.9	.494	0.1	.000	4.6	.707	1.07	0.34	0.7	7.1	10.0
vs. East	258	27.8	7.1	.476	0.1	.133	4.4	.714	0.99	0.47	0.8	7.2	9.9	February	65	27.3	7.4	.440	0.0	.000	4.3	.700	0.82	0.52	0.8	7.0	9.5
vs. West	116	27.8	7.6	.459	0.0	.000	4.7	.699	0.94	0.52	0.8	7.1	10.3	March	77	27.3	6.8	.490	0.0	.000	3.9	.719	0.86	0.49	0.7	6.8	9.5
vs. Div.	133	27.2	7.0	.491	0.0	.000	4.2	.714	0.95	0.44	0.8	6.8	9.9	Apr/May	61	28.5	7.8	.474	0.0	.500	4.4	.720	1.10	0.44	1.0	7.6	10.6
As Starter	133	32.4	9.5	.461	0.0	.000	4.8	.736	1.17	0.55	1.2	8.8	12.3	0 Days Rest	98	28.0	7.2	.470	0.1	.200	4.3	.693	0.94	0.51	0.8	7.0	9.8
Off Bench	241	25.2	6.0	.478	0.1	.154	4.3	.693	0.87	0.44	0.6	6.3	8.7	1 Days Rest	193	28.2	7.4	.469	0.0	.000	4.6	.713	1.03	0.45	0.8	7.6	10.3
In wins	225	27.3	6.9	.499	0.0	.182	4.6	.719	1.02	0.50	0.8	7.2	10.2	2 Days Rest	49	26.1	6.5	.498	0.0	.000	4.4	.712	0.84	0.67	0.8	6.2	9.6
In losses	149	28.4	7.8	.432	0.1	.000	4.3	.694	0.91	0.45	0.8	7.2	9.7	3+ Days Rest	34	26.4	7.4	.442	0.1	.200	3.9	.731	0.94	0.32	0.8	7.2	9.4

Baron Davis

1999-2000 Per Game Averages

	G	Min	FGA	FG%	3PA	3P%	FTA	FT%	Blk	Stl	Ast	Reb	Pts		G	Min	FGA	FG%	3PA	3P%	FTA	FT%	Blk	Stl	Ast	Reb	Pts
Total	82	18.6	5.3	.420	1.4	.225	1.9	.634	0.23	1.18	3.8	2.0	5.9	Pre All-Star	47	19.5	5.7	.405	1.3	.206	2.0	.617	0.23	1.26	3.9	2.1	6.1
Home	41	19.2	5.5	.446	1.5	.295	2.1	.659	0.24	1.39	4.1	2.3	6.7	Post All-Star	35	17.4	4.7	.445	1.4	.250	1.7	.661	0.23	1.09	3.6	1.9	5.6
Road	41	17.9	5.1	.392	1.2	.140	1.6	.600	0.22	0.98	3.4	1.7	5.1	November	14	19.4	5.5	.429	1.6	.174	1.5	.619	0.07	1.64	3.4	2.2	5.9
vs. Playoff	44	17.9	5.0	.416	1.1	.255	2.2	.642	0.30	1.09	3.5	2.0	5.8	December	15	19.6	5.9	.404	1.1	.176	2.4	.583	0.27	1.40	4.6	2.1	6.4
vs. Non-Playoff	38	19.3	5.6	.425	1.7	.203	1.5	.621	0.16	1.29	4.1	2.1	6.1	January	13	19.9	6.2	.400	0.9	.333	2.2	.643	0.31	0.77	3.6	1.8	6.6
vs. East	54	18.3	5.0	.391	1.3	.188	1.7	.615	0.22	1.26	3.7	2.1	5.2	February	14	15.2	4.3	.300	1.7	.208	1.6	.727	0.21	0.64	3.1	1.9	4.1
vs. West	28	19.1	5.8	.469	1.5	.286	2.2	.661	0.25	1.04	3.9	1.8	7.3	March	15	18.4	5.3	.500	1.4	.238	1.1	.588	0.27	1.40	3.9	2.1	6.3
vs. Div.	28	18.3	5.0	.393	1.3	.229	1.6	.600	0.25	1.29	3.6	2.3	5.2	April	11	19.0	4.3	.489	1.3	.286	2.6	.655	0.27	1.18	3.9	1.9	6.3
As Starter	0	—	—	—	—	—	—	—	—	—	—	—	—	0 Days Rest	22	19.0	5.6	.379	1.2	.222	2.3	.686	0.18	1.18	3.6	1.7	6.1
Off Bench	82	18.6	5.3	.420	1.4	.225	1.9	.634	0.23	1.18	3.8	2.0	5.9	1 Days Rest	43	18.0	5.0	.409	1.4	.213	1.4	.689	0.30	1.21	4.0	2.2	5.4
In wins	49	18.4	5.2	.434	1.3	.231	1.8	.622	0.22	1.29	3.8	2.2	6.0	2 Days Rest	8	19.9	6.8	.519	1.6	.308	1.9	.400	0.00	1.00	4.8	1.9	8.3
In losses	33	18.8	5.4	.401	1.4	.217	1.9	.651	0.24	1.03	3.8	1.7	5.8	3+ Days Rest	9	19.0	4.4	.475	1.1	.200	2.9	.538	0.22	1.22	2.1	2.1	6.0

Dale Davis

1999-2000 Per Game Averages

	G	Min	FGA	FG%	3PA	3P%	FTA	FT%	Blk	Stl	Ast	Reb	Pts		G	Min	FGA	FG%	3PA	3P%	FTA	FT%	Blk	Stl	Ast	Reb	Pts
Total	74	28.7	8.1	.502	0.0	—	2.7	.685	1.27	0.70	0.9	9.9	10.0	Pre All-Star	48	29.7	8.7	.519	0.0	—	3.2	.704	1.35	0.60	0.9	10.1	11.2
Home	35	28.3	7.5	.494	0.0	—	2.3	.646	1.29	0.66	0.8	9.6	8.9	Post All-Star	26	27.0	7.2	.462	0.0	—	2.0	.627	1.12	0.88	0.8	9.3	7.8
Road	39	29.2	8.7	.507	0.0	—	3.1	.711	1.26	0.74	0.9	10.1	11.0	November	15	29.7	8.7	.595	0.0	—	4.0	.617	1.80	0.60	0.7	9.2	12.9
vs. Playoff	40	29.7	7.8	.490	0.0	—	1.8	.743	1.15	0.73	0.9	10.2	9.0	December	14	31.1	10.3	.486	0.0	—	3.1	.841	0.93	0.50	1.4	11.4	12.6
vs. Non-Playoff	34	27.6	8.5	.514	0.0	—	3.9	.654	1.41	0.68	0.9	9.4	11.3	January	14	28.7	7.6	.458	0.0	—	2.4	.667	1.00	0.79	0.6	9.4	8.6
vs. East	48	29.3	8.1	.518	0.0	—	2.8	.699	1.42	0.67	0.9	9.8	10.4	February	12	27.9	7.1	.482	0.0	—	2.0	.667	1.67	0.75	0.9	9.6	8.2
vs. West	26	27.7	8.2	.472	0.0	—	2.6	.657	1.00	0.77	0.7	9.9	9.5	March	10	24.2	6.6	.394	0.0	—	2.6	.615	0.70	0.90	0.7	8.9	6.8
vs. Div.	23	30.6	8.6	.540	0.0	—	2.5	.776	1.48	0.78	1.0	9.8	11.3	April	9	29.8	7.7	.551	0.0	—	1.8	.688	1.44	0.78	0.8	10.7	9.7
As Starter	72	29.2	8.3	.501	0.0	—	2.8	.687	1.29	0.72	0.9	10.0	10.2	0 Days Rest	19	31.0	8.4	.497	0.0	—	2.4	.717	1.11	0.58	1.2	10.3	10.1
Off Bench	2	14.0	3.5	.571	0.0	—	1.0	.500	0.50	0.00	0.5	5.5	4.5	1 Days Rest	35	27.7	7.9	.489	0.0	—	2.9	.683	1.14	0.77	0.8	9.3	9.7
In wins	51	28.2	8.1	.509	0.0	—	2.8	.662	1.33	0.76	0.9	9.5	10.1	2 Days Rest	11	30.4	9.3	.520	0.0	—	2.9	.781	1.91	0.82	0.7	11.2	11.9
In losses	23	30.0	8.3	.487	0.0	—	2.5	.741	1.13	0.57	0.8	10.5	10.0	3+ Days Rest	9	26.2	7.0	.540	0.0	—	2.7	.500	1.33	0.56	0.6	9.2	8.9

Last Five Seasons

	G	Min	FGA	FG%	3PA	3P%	FTA	FT%	Blk	Stl	Ast	Reb	Pts		G	Min	FGA	FG%	3PA	3P%	FTA	FT%	Blk	Stl	Ast	Reb	Pts
Total	360	30.2	7.5	.536	0.0	—	2.8	.521	1.19	0.66	0.8	9.0	9.5	Pre All-Star	178	31.1	7.6	.532	0.0	—	3.0	.535	1.29	0.68	1.0	9.3	9.7
Home	179	30.1	7.5	.538	0.0	—	2.7	.508	1.16	0.68	0.8	9.2	9.4	Post All-Star	132	30.1	7.8	.541	0.0	—	2.6	.465	1.06	0.74	0.7	8.8	9.7
Road	181	30.3	7.5	.533	0.0	—	2.9	.533	1.21	0.65	0.8	8.8	9.5	Oct/Nov	52	32.3	7.7	.532	0.0	—	3.4	.520	1.44	0.75	0.8	9.8	10.0
vs. Playoff	193	30.7	7.2	.516	0.0	—	2.4	.528	1.11	0.67	0.8	9.3	8.7	December	59	31.5	7.8	.516	0.0	—	2.7	.591	1.03	0.69	1.3	9.4	9.6
vs. Non-Playoff	167	29.6	7.8	.556	0.0	—	3.2	.515	1.27	0.66	0.9	8.7	10.3	January	53	29.8	7.5	.538	0.0	—	2.9	.484	1.32	0.58	0.8	8.6	9.5
vs. East	250	30.3	7.3	.542	0.0	—	2.7	.528	1.24	0.64	0.8	8.8	9.4	February	63	28.9	7.1	.520	0.0	—	2.2	.557	1.08	0.70	0.6	8.4	8.6
vs. West	110	30.1	7.8	.522	0.0	—	2.9	.505	1.06	0.71	0.9	9.4	9.6	March	73	29.1	7.2	.552	0.0	—	2.7	.415	1.08	0.66	0.7	8.5	9.1
vs. Div.	128	30.9	7.4	.544	0.0	—	2.7	.526	1.29	0.66	0.8	8.7	9.5	Apr/May	60	30.3	7.6	.551	0.0	—	2.9	.584	1.23	0.60	0.7	9.3	10.1
As Starter	353	30.4	7.5	.534	0.0	—	2.8	.525	1.20	0.67	0.8	9.0	9.5	0 Days Rest	96	30.8	7.6	.511	0.0	—	2.4	.585	1.06	0.50	0.8	8.8	9.1
Off Bench	7	21.7	5.1	.639	0.0	—	2.3	.250	0.71	0.43	0.4	6.1	7.1	1 Days Rest	179	29.7	7.5	.550	0.0	—	3.0	.512	1.11	0.69	0.8	8.9	9.8
In wins	227	29.4	7.4	.551	0.0	—	2.8	.539	1.27	0.62	0.9	8.8	9.7	2 Days Rest	47	30.9	7.4	.534	0.0	—	3.0	.521	1.66	0.79	0.8	9.4	9.5
In losses	133	31.6	7.6	.509	0.0	—	2.7	.489	1.04	0.74	0.7	9.3	9.1	3+ Days Rest	38	30.3	7.1	.531	0.0	—	2.7	.422	1.26	0.82	0.9	9.2	8.7

Hubert Davis

1999-2000 Per Game Averages

	G	Min	FGA	FG%	3PA	3P%	FTA	FT%	Blk	Stl	Ast	Reb	Pts		G	Min	FGA	FG%	3PA	3P%	FTA	FT%	Blk	Stl	Ast	Reb	Pts
Total	79	23.0	5.9	.468	2.1	.491	1.0	.870	0.04	0.30	1.8	1.7	7.4	Pre All-Star	48	26.2	6.2	.486	2.7	.527	1.0	.860	0.00	0.44	2.0	1.8	8.3
Home	40	21.9	4.9	.462	1.9	.526	1.0	.895	0.05	0.23	1.5	1.7	6.4	Post All-Star	31	18.1	5.4	.435	1.2	.361	0.9	.889	0.10	0.10	1.4	1.5	5.9
Road	39	24.2	6.9	.472	2.3	.462	1.0	.846	0.03	0.38	2.1	1.7	8.4	November	16	22.7	6.2	.444	2.8	.444	1.0	.938	0.00	0.38	2.6	1.8	7.7
vs. Playoff	46	23.0	5.5	.464	1.8	.500	0.7	.941	0.04	0.35	1.6	1.7	6.7	December	14	34.7	7.8	.495	3.1	.545	1.3	.778	0.00	0.64	1.7	2.0	10.4
vs. Non-Playoff	33	23.0	6.4	.472	2.5	.482	1.3	.814	0.03	0.24	2.0	1.8	8.3	January	13	26.2	5.7	.541	2.8	.639	1.2	.875	0.00	0.46	1.9	1.8	9.0
vs. East	29	21.9	5.7	.452	2.4	.514	1.2	.765	0.03	0.24	1.8	1.5	7.3	February	13	13.1	3.1	.375	0.9	.333	0.5	.714	0.08	0.15	1.2	1.1	3.0
vs. West	50	23.6	6.0	.477	1.9	.474	0.9	.953	0.04	0.34	1.8	1.8	7.4	March	13	16.0	4.8	.492	1.2	.467	0.5	1.000	0.00	0.08	1.2	1.5	5.8
vs. Div.	23	25.3	6.5	.416	1.6	.361	1.0	.957	0.04	0.35	2.1	1.9	6.9	April	10	24.9	7.9	.418	1.5	.267	1.3	.923	0.20	0.00	1.9	2.1	8.2
As Starter	15	35.7	8.3	.460	3.1	.468	1.6	.792	0.00	0.53	2.3	2.2	10.3	0 Days Rest	17	22.6	6.6	.473	2.8	.447	1.1	.947	0.00	0.41	2.2	1.3	8.5
Off Bench	64	20.0	5.3	.471	1.9	.500	0.8	.906	0.05	0.25	1.7	1.6	6.7	1 Days Rest	40	22.9	5.7	.434	1.9	.487	1.0	.850	0.08	0.23	1.5	1.7	6.7
In wins	39	21.2	5.4	.500	1.9	.553	0.9	.824	0.05	0.21	1.7	1.8	7.5	2 Days Rest	16	24.6	5.8	.522	2.1	.515	0.6	.778	0.00	0.38	2.1	2.1	7.5
In losses	40	24.8	6.3	.440	2.3	.440	1.1	.907	0.03	0.40	1.9	1.6	7.5	3+ Days Rest	6	21.0	5.3	.531	1.8	.636	1.5	.889	0.00	0.33	1.5	2.0	8.2

Last Five Seasons

	G	Min	FGA	FG%	3PA	3P%	FTA	FT%	Blk	Stl	Ast	Reb	Pts		G	Min	FGA	FG%	3PA	3P%	FTA	FT%	Blk	Stl	Ast	Reb	Pts
Total	320	24.9	7.4	.458	2.7	.445	1.2	.853	0.07	0.41	1.6	1.7	9.1	Pre All-Star	163	24.4	6.9	.467	2.7	.456	1.2	.813	0.01	0.45	1.5	1.7	8.7
Home	165	24.3	7.0	.467	2.7	.474	1.3	.868	0.07	0.38	1.5	1.7	9.0	Post All-Star	107	24.4	7.9	.456	2.7	.427	1.4	.898	0.15	0.34	1.8	1.8	9.6
Road	155	25.5	7.9	.450	2.8	.417	1.1	.835	0.06	0.43	1.8	1.8	9.2	Oct/Nov	59	21.2	6.7	.415	2.5	.363	1.0	.767	0.00	0.36	1.4	1.4	7.2
vs. Playoff	182	25.4	7.3	.448	2.6	.430	1.2	.879	0.05	0.43	1.6	1.7	8.7	December	49	27.4	7.3	.482	3.0	.497	1.1	.821	0.02	0.47	1.4	1.9	9.9
vs. Non-Playoff	138	24.2	7.6	.471	2.9	.464	1.3	.822	0.08	0.37	1.7	1.8	9.6	January	41	26.1	7.0	.507	2.8	.509	1.6	.848	0.02	0.59	1.8	1.9	9.9
vs. East	134	23.6	6.9	.462	2.8	.458	1.3	.829	0.10	0.34	1.4	1.7	8.7	February	62	21.8	6.4	.444	2.2	.415	0.9	.845	0.08	0.29	1.6	1.5	7.4
vs. West	186	25.9	7.8	.456	2.7	.436	1.2	.873	0.04	0.46	1.8	1.8	9.4	March	60	24.5	8.2	.460	2.8	.450	1.4	.877	0.12	0.40	1.5	1.9	10.0
vs. Div.	100	25.6	7.5	.447	2.5	.437	1.2	.896	0.07	0.37	1.8	1.7	8.8	Apr/May	49	30.3	9.1	.457	3.4	.449	1.5	.932	0.14	0.41	2.2	1.9	11.3
As Starter	80	36.2	10.6	.457	3.8	.424	1.6	.836	0.09	0.61	2.5	2.4	12.6	0 Days Rest	79	25.6	8.2	.456	3.3	.441	1.1	.911	0.06	0.42	1.7	1.6	10.0
Off Bench	240	21.1	6.4	.459	2.4	.456	1.1	.861	0.06	0.34	1.4	1.5	7.9	1 Days Rest	154	25.3	7.5	.453	2.7	.442	1.3	.868	0.07	0.41	1.6	1.7	9.1
In wins	130	23.4	7.0	.499	2.6	.503	1.4	.860	0.06	0.31	1.7	1.8	9.5	2 Days Rest	61	24.7	7.0	.457	2.4	.434	1.0	.806	0.05	0.41	1.8	2.0	8.2
In losses	190	26.0	7.7	.433	2.8	.408	1.1	.847	0.07	0.47	1.6	1.7	8.8	3+ Days Rest	26	20.5	5.6	.514	2.3	.517	1.5	.718	0.08	0.35	1.4	1.4	8.0

Andrew DeClercq

1999-2000 Per Game Averages

	G	Min	FGA	FG%	3PA	3P%	FTA	FT%	Blk	Stl	Ast	Reb	Pts		G	Min	FGA	FG%	3PA	3P%	FTA	FT%	Blk	Stl	Ast	Reb	Pts
Total	82	22.3	5.4	.508	0.0	—	2.0	.588	0.80	0.77	0.7	5.4	6.6	Pre All-Star	49	25.4	6.0	.517	0.0	—	2.3	.616	0.92	0.96	0.8	6.3	7.6
Home	41	23.4	5.7	.543	0.0	—	2.3	.602	0.98	0.71	0.8	6.0	7.6	Post All-Star	33	17.8	4.6	.490	0.0	—	1.5	.521	0.64	0.48	0.6	4.0	5.2
Road	41	21.3	5.1	.469	0.0	—	1.6	.567	0.63	0.83	0.6	4.7	5.7	November	13	28.9	7.6	.566	0.0	—	2.6	.647	1.00	1.15	0.8	7.0	10.3
vs. Playoff	47	22.7	5.5	.504	0.0	—	2.0	.552	0.66	0.83	0.8	5.6	6.7	December	16	29.0	6.5	.481	0.0	—	3.2	.588	0.94	0.94	0.9	6.8	8.1
vs. Non-Playoff	35	21.8	5.2	.514	0.0	—	1.8	.641	1.00	0.69	0.5	5.0	6.5	January	15	22.6	4.5	.485	0.0	—	1.5	.609	0.87	1.07	0.8	6.0	5.3
vs. East	54	22.4	5.3	.493	0.0	—	2.5	.586	0.74	0.76	0.8	5.1	6.7	February	12	15.4	3.8	.543	0.0	—	0.7	.625	0.75	0.17	0.6	4.0	4.6
vs. West	28	22.3	5.6	.535	0.0	—	1.0	.593	0.93	0.79	0.5	5.8	6.6	March	15	17.7	4.7	.557	0.0	—	1.1	.500	0.67	0.40	0.3	3.4	5.7
vs. Div.	28	22.9	5.3	.544	0.0	—	2.6	.589	0.68	0.75	0.9	5.0	7.3	April	11	18.3	5.1	.393	0.0	—	2.5	.536	0.55	0.82	0.9	4.6	5.4
As Starter	31	27.0	6.5	.500	0.0	—	2.6	.610	0.97	0.90	0.8	6.1	8.1	0 Days Rest	24	22.8	5.0	.555	0.0	—	2.6	.613	0.67	0.71	0.7	5.2	7.1
Off Bench	51	19.5	4.7	.515	0.0	—	1.5	.564	0.71	0.69	0.7	4.9	5.7	1 Days Rest	35	21.9	5.6	.487	0.0	—	1.7	.569	0.74	0.91	0.8	5.0	6.4
In wins	32	22.0	5.3	.535	0.0	—	1.9	.548	1.09	0.66	0.8	5.7	6.8	2 Days Rest	16	22.1	5.3	.494	0.0	—	1.4	.636	1.00	0.38	0.8	6.1	6.1
In losses	50	22.5	5.5	.491	0.0	—	2.0	.612	0.62	0.84	0.6	5.1	6.6	3+ Days Rest	7	23.3	6.3	.500	0.0	—	2.6	.500	1.14	1.14	0.4	6.0	7.6

Career (1995-96 thru 1999-2000)

	G	Min	FGA	FG%	3PA	3P%	FTA	FT%	Blk	Stl	Ast	Reb	Pts		G	Min	FGA	FG%	3PA	3P%	FTA	FT%	Blk	Stl	Ast	Reb	Pts
Total	303	18.9	4.6	.505	0.0	.000	2.1	.613	0.58	0.79	0.6	4.7	5.9	Pre All-Star	132	18.3	4.2	.501	0.0	—	1.8	.608	0.63	0.77	0.6	4.6	5.3
Home	145	18.8	4.8	.519	0.0	—	2.2	.628	0.64	0.81	0.7	5.0	6.4	Post All-Star	124	17.8	4.5	.512	0.0	.000	2.1	.586	0.52	0.69	0.6	4.5	5.8
Road	158	19.0	4.3	.491	0.0	.000	2.0	.599	0.53	0.77	0.5	4.4	5.4	Oct/Nov	38	17.9	4.7	.503	0.0	—	1.7	.625	0.53	0.66	0.6	4.4	5.7
vs. Playoff	175	18.5	4.4	.499	0.0	.000	2.2	.608	0.47	0.82	0.6	4.5	5.7	December	41	21.0	4.5	.457	0.0	—	2.2	.533	0.78	0.95	0.6	5.1	5.3
vs. Non-Playoff	128	19.5	4.8	.512	0.0	—	2.0	.622	0.73	0.73	0.6	4.9	6.1	January	43	16.9	3.5	.530	0.0	—	1.6	.672	0.58	0.79	0.6	4.5	4.7
vs. East	179	20.0	4.9	.502	0.0	—	2.4	.606	0.63	0.83	0.6	4.9	6.3	February	48	16.4	4.1	.543	0.0	.000	1.4	.662	0.52	0.56	0.6	4.4	5.3
vs. West	124	17.2	4.1	.511	0.0	.000	1.7	.630	0.52	0.73	0.6	4.4	5.3	March	71	18.8	4.4	.546	0.0	—	2.2	.579	0.59	0.73	0.6	4.5	6.1
vs. Div.	106	20.0	4.5	.505	0.0	.000	2.5	.600	0.60	0.91	0.7	4.7	6.0	Apr/May	62	21.5	5.8	.464	0.0	—	3.0	.640	0.52	0.98	0.7	5.1	7.3
As Starter	114	24.7	5.9	.506	0.0	—	2.9	.643	0.75	1.13	0.8	5.9	7.9	0 Days Rest	75	20.1	4.5	.519	0.0	—	2.5	.639	0.51	0.76	0.6	4.9	6.3
Off Bench	189	15.4	3.7	.504	0.0	.000	1.6	.582	0.48	0.58	0.5	4.0	4.7	1 Days Rest	151	19.5	4.8	.514	0.0	.000	2.1	.577	0.58	0.85	0.6	4.9	6.2
In wins	119	19.7	4.9	.529	0.0	—	2.0	.611	0.72	0.71	0.7	5.2	6.3	2 Days Rest	44	18.3	4.7	.466	0.0	.000	1.8	.714	0.77	0.75	0.6	4.3	5.7
In losses	184	18.4	4.4	.488	0.0	.000	2.2	.615	0.49	0.83	0.6	4.3	5.6	3+ Days Rest	33	14.2	3.3	.473	0.0	—	1.6	.593	0.48	0.58	0.6	3.7	4.1

Vinny Del Negro

1999-2000 Per Game Averages

	G	Min	FGA	FG%	3PA	3P%	FTA	FT%	Blk	Stl	Ast	Reb	Pts
Total	67	18.1	4.9	.471	0.4	.333	0.6	.897	0.00	0.54	2.4	1.6	5.2
Home	37	17.9	4.6	.476	0.3	.100	0.6	.826	0.00	0.54	2.3	1.5	4.9
Road	30	18.3	5.2	.465	0.5	.500	0.5	1.000	0.00	0.53	2.5	1.7	5.6
vs. Playoff	37	17.4	4.7	.451	0.3	.182	0.6	.909	0.00	0.38	2.1	1.4	4.8
vs. Non-Playoff	30	18.9	5.1	.493	0.4	.462	0.6	.882	0.00	0.73	2.8	1.8	5.7
vs. East	44	17.5	4.7	.490	0.4	.471	0.6	.926	0.00	0.48	2.5	1.5	5.4
vs. West	23	19.3	5.1	.436	0.3	.000	0.5	.833	0.00	0.65	2.2	1.8	4.9
vs. Div.	26	16.5	4.4	.470	0.3	.500	0.5	.929	0.00	0.38	2.3	1.4	4.8
As Starter	0	—	—	—	—	—	—	—	—	—	—	—	—
Off Bench	67	18.1	4.9	.471	0.4	.333	0.6	.897	0.00	0.54	2.4	1.6	5.2
In wins	33	19.4	5.0	.497	0.3	.444	0.7	.870	0.00	0.73	2.7	1.7	5.7
In losses	34	16.8	4.7	.444	0.4	.267	0.5	.938	0.00	0.35	2.1	1.5	4.7
Pre All-Star	50	18.1	4.9	.480	0.3	.267	0.6	.938	0.00	0.54	2.4	1.6	5.4
Post All-Star	17	17.9	4.6	.443	0.5	.444	0.4	.714	0.00	0.53	2.4	1.6	4.6
November	14	13.5	3.2	.378	0.3	.000	0.6	1.000	0.00	0.50	1.7	1.2	3.1
December	16	19.9	5.6	.500	0.4	.429	0.5	1.000	0.00	0.75	2.7	2.0	6.3
January	15	19.6	5.6	.512	0.2	.333	0.6	.778	0.00	0.47	2.7	1.6	6.3
February	12	18.8	4.8	.431	0.3	.250	0.6	1.000	0.00	0.25	2.1	1.3	4.8
March	5	17.2	5.2	.423	0.6	.667	0.4	.500	0.00	0.80	3.2	2.2	5.0
April	5	19.6	4.4	.545	0.6	.333	0.8	.750	0.00	0.60	2.4	1.6	5.6
0 Days Rest	15	17.8	5.5	.500	0.4	.167	0.5	1.000	0.00	0.33	2.1	1.7	6.1
1 Days Rest	37	17.6	4.5	.448	0.3	.500	0.5	.944	0.00	0.57	2.6	1.6	4.6
2 Days Rest	5	16.6	5.6	.500	0.6	.333	0.6	1.000	0.00	0.60	2.0	1.4	6.4
3+ Days Rest	10	20.8	5.0	.480	0.5	.200	1.0	.700	0.00	0.70	2.2	1.6	5.6

Last Five Seasons

	G	Min	FGA	FG%	3PA	3P%	FTA	FT%	Blk	Stl	Ast	Reb	Pts
Total	323	28.0	8.7	.469	1.2	.363	1.6	.836	0.07	0.78	3.3	2.6	10.0
Home	166	27.8	8.7	.475	1.0	.331	1.8	.858	0.05	0.81	3.3	2.6	10.2
Road	157	28.1	8.8	.463	1.4	.388	1.4	.807	0.08	0.75	3.3	2.7	9.8
vs. Playoff	178	28.1	8.6	.451	1.2	.330	1.6	.821	0.06	0.80	3.1	2.5	9.5
vs. Non-Playoff	145	27.8	8.8	.490	1.2	.401	1.7	.854	0.08	0.76	3.6	2.7	10.6
vs. East	165	25.9	7.7	.473	1.0	.385	1.3	.829	0.07	0.70	3.2	2.4	8.8
vs. West	158	30.2	9.8	.466	1.4	.346	2.0	.841	0.06	0.86	3.4	2.9	11.2
vs. Div.	106	26.8	8.5	.464	1.0	.419	1.8	.807	0.08	0.67	3.4	2.5	9.7
As Starter	180	33.5	11.0	.484	1.6	.377	2.0	.837	0.08	0.83	3.7	3.1	12.9
Off Bench	143	21.0	5.9	.435	0.7	.323	1.1	.835	0.05	0.59	2.8	2.0	6.3
In wins	170	28.5	8.9	.486	1.0	.446	2.0	.840	0.09	0.84	3.7	2.8	10.8
In losses	153	27.3	8.5	.449	1.4	.293	1.2	.829	0.05	0.72	2.9	2.4	9.0
Pre All-Star	153	25.2	8.0	.465	1.2	.303	1.5	.864	0.06	0.69	2.9	2.3	9.2
Post All-Star	122	33.5	10.8	.482	1.4	.417	2.0	.817	0.08	0.93	3.7	3.1	12.6
Oct/Nov	44	23.6	7.2	.461	1.4	.279	1.2	.849	0.07	0.66	2.8	2.0	8.0
December	47	25.8	8.6	.457	1.3	.339	1.4	.908	0.02	0.81	2.8	2.5	9.6
January	48	26.0	8.3	.470	1.0	.292	2.0	.814	0.10	0.69	2.9	2.5	9.8
February	62	29.1	9.2	.496	1.3	.392	1.8	.841	0.05	0.77	3.5	2.5	11.2
March	70	31.8	9.6	.475	1.1	.468	1.8	.832	0.11	0.74	4.0	3.1	11.1
Apr/May	52	28.8	8.8	.441	1.1	.351	1.4	.792	0.04	1.00	3.4	2.7	9.2
0 Days Rest	70	28.0	8.9	.491	1.2	.369	1.4	.896	0.09	0.79	3.1	2.5	10.4
1 Days Rest	187	28.6	8.8	.465	1.2	.360	1.7	.839	0.05	0.78	3.5	2.6	10.1
2 Days Rest	32	26.9	8.8	.465	1.1	.294	1.6	.808	0.00	1.00	3.2	2.8	9.8
3+ Days Rest	34	25.6	7.8	.449	1.1	.432	1.8	.750	0.21	0.59	2.7	2.6	8.8

Michael Dickerson

1999-2000 Per Game Averages

	G	Min	FGA	FG%	3PA	3P%	FTA	FT%	Blk	Stl	Ast	Reb	Pts
Total	82	37.8	15.5	.436	3.5	.409	4.0	.830	0.55	1.41	2.5	3.4	18.2
Home	41	38.2	15.6	.437	3.5	.421	3.4	.851	0.66	1.39	2.5	3.4	18.1
Road	41	37.4	15.3	.436	3.6	.397	4.5	.814	0.44	1.44	2.6	3.2	18.4
vs. Playoff	48	37.6	14.9	.431	3.6	.408	3.8	.811	0.46	1.19	2.6	3.2	17.4
vs. Non-Playoff	34	38.2	16.3	.443	3.4	.410	4.2	.854	0.68	1.74	2.5	3.7	19.4
vs. East	30	37.4	15.3	.446	3.5	.433	4.0	.851	0.57	1.67	2.5	3.4	18.6
vs. West	52	38.1	15.6	.431	3.6	.396	3.9	.818	0.54	1.27	2.6	3.4	18.0
vs. Div.	24	38.2	15.7	.372	3.3	.338	4.0	.895	0.54	1.38	3.0	3.1	16.3
As Starter	82	37.8	15.5	.436	3.5	.409	4.0	.830	0.55	1.41	2.5	3.4	18.2
Off Bench	0	—	—	—	—	—	—	—	—	—	—	—	—
In wins	22	39.5	16.3	.490	3.7	.531	4.8	.811	0.55	1.77	2.5	3.6	21.9
In losses	60	37.3	15.2	.415	3.5	.362	3.6	.839	0.55	1.28	2.6	3.3	16.9
Pre All-Star	48	37.0	15.1	.431	3.1	.407	3.2	.845	0.35	1.25	2.3	3.2	17.0
Post All-Star	34	39.1	16.0	.444	4.1	.411	5.0	.817	0.82	1.65	2.9	3.7	19.9
November	14	36.1	12.9	.381	2.7	.316	1.6	.818	0.36	1.21	2.1	3.4	12.0
December	15	36.7	14.6	.461	3.0	.400	3.5	.925	0.33	0.93	2.1	2.5	17.9
January	14	38.6	16.7	.432	3.8	.472	3.9	.778	0.43	1.71	2.6	3.6	19.2
February	13	38.1	16.3	.472	3.8	.460	5.5	.847	0.69	1.92	2.8	4.3	21.8
March	15	35.7	14.3	.453	3.5	.343	3.5	.811	0.60	1.20	2.3	2.9	17.3
April	11	43.2	19.1	.410	3.5	.474	6.4	.800	1.00	1.64	3.5	4.0	22.4
0 Days Rest	19	38.3	16.2	.430	3.8	.397	4.5	.894	0.58	1.42	3.1	3.2	19.4
1 Days Rest	47	37.7	15.6	.446	3.4	.432	4.0	.814	0.64	1.49	2.5	3.6	18.6
2 Days Rest	7	35.7	13.0	.407	2.7	.263	3.4	.792	0.14	1.29	2.1	2.0	14.0
3+ Days Rest	9	39.2	15.7	.418	4.1	.405	3.0	.778	0.33	1.11	2.0	4.1	17.1

Career (1998-99 thru 1999-2000)

	G	Min	FGA	FG%	3PA	3P%	FTA	FT%	Blk	Stl	Ast	Reb	Pts
Total	132	35.3	13.1	.444	3.4	.418	3.0	.795	0.42	1.08	2.3	2.7	15.5
Home	66	35.1	13.3	.449	3.5	.419	2.7	.818	0.53	1.11	2.4	2.8	15.7
Road	66	35.5	12.9	.439	3.3	.416	3.3	.777	0.32	1.06	2.2	2.7	15.3
vs. Playoff	73	35.0	12.7	.430	3.3	.416	3.0	.794	0.42	0.96	2.3	2.6	14.6
vs. Non-Playoff	59	35.7	13.7	.460	3.6	.420	3.0	.798	0.42	1.24	2.3	2.9	16.5
vs. East	36	37.7	14.8	.443	3.6	.446	3.5	.843	0.50	1.61	2.5	3.3	17.7
vs. West	96	34.4	12.5	.445	3.4	.406	2.8	.773	0.40	0.89	2.2	2.6	14.6
vs. Div.	45	34.7	12.5	.416	3.2	.418	3.0	.828	0.40	0.96	2.4	2.4	14.2
As Starter	132	35.3	13.1	.444	3.4	.418	3.0	.795	0.42	1.08	2.3	2.7	15.5
Off Bench	0	—	—	—	—	—	—	—	—	—	—	—	—
In wins	53	35.1	12.6	.497	3.7	.495	3.0	.747	0.36	1.13	2.3	2.5	16.6
In losses	79	35.4	13.4	.411	3.3	.358	3.0	.828	0.47	1.05	2.3	2.9	14.7
Pre All-Star	48	37.0	15.1	.431	3.1	.407	3.2	.845	0.35	1.25	2.3	3.2	17.0
Post All-Star	34	39.1	16.0	.444	4.1	.411	5.0	.817	0.82	1.65	2.9	3.7	19.9
Oct/Nov	14	36.1	12.9	.381	2.7	.316	1.6	.818	0.36	1.21	2.1	3.4	12.0
December	15	36.7	14.6	.461	3.0	.400	3.5	.925	0.33	0.93	2.1	2.5	17.9
January	14	38.6	16.7	.432	3.8	.472	3.9	.778	0.43	1.71	2.6	3.6	19.2
February	27	34.7	12.7	.449	3.3	.438	3.2	.805	0.37	1.22	2.2	3.0	15.4
March	32	35.1	11.9	.476	4.2	.407	2.6	.720	0.44	0.94	2.1	2.4	14.9
Apr/May	30	33.4	12.4	.434	3.2	.432	3.3	.786	0.53	0.83	2.7	2.4	14.7
0 Days Rest	36	34.5	12.3	.441	3.5	.448	3.0	.833	0.33	1.08	2.6	2.5	14.9
1 Days Rest	73	36.0	13.7	.455	3.4	.426	3.1	.789	0.53	1.15	2.2	2.8	16.4
2 Days Rest	12	31.2	10.4	.376	2.9	.286	2.7	.719	0.08	0.83	2.2	2.2	10.6
3+ Days Rest	11	38.2	15.1	.434	4.0	.386	2.6	.793	0.36	0.91	1.9	3.6	16.7

Vlade Divac

1999-2000 Per Game Averages

	G	Min	FGA	FG%	3PA	3P%	FTA	FT%	Blk	Stl	Ast	Reb	Pts
Total	82	29.0	9.3	.503	0.3	.269	4.1	.691	1.26	1.26	3.0	8.0	12.3
Home	41	29.7	9.0	.514	0.3	.273	4.4	.698	1.39	1.24	3.0	8.6	12.4
Road	41	28.2	9.7	.492	0.4	.267	3.7	.682	1.12	1.27	3.0	7.4	12.1
vs. Playoff	44	29.1	8.9	.505	0.4	.333	3.8	.697	1.02	1.23	2.9	7.8	11.7
vs. Non-Playoff	38	28.7	9.8	.500	0.3	.125	4.4	.685	1.53	1.29	3.0	8.3	12.9
vs. East	30	30.3	10.2	.511	0.3	.200	4.8	.713	1.40	1.10	3.1	8.2	13.9
vs. West	52	28.2	8.8	.497	0.3	.313	3.7	.674	1.17	1.35	2.9	7.9	11.3
vs. Div.	24	29.0	8.3	.503	0.4	.333	4.2	.630	1.04	1.25	2.7	7.9	11.1
As Starter	81	29.1	9.4	.502	0.3	.269	4.1	.689	1.26	1.27	3.0	8.0	12.3
Off Bench	1	19.0	3.0	.667	0.0	—	2.0	1.000	1.00	0.00	0.0	7.0	6.0
In wins	44	29.4	9.0	.535	0.2	.200	4.3	.702	1.61	1.25	3.2	8.4	12.8
In losses	38	28.4	9.6	.467	0.4	.313	3.7	.676	0.84	1.26	2.8	7.5	11.7

	G	Min	FGA	FG%	3PA	3P%	FTA	FT%	Blk	Stl	Ast	Reb	Pts
Pre All-Star	48	29.3	9.1	.510	0.3	.250	4.0	.705	1.46	1.25	2.8	8.0	12.2
Post All-Star	34	28.5	9.7	.492	0.3	.300	4.1	.671	0.97	1.26	3.2	8.0	12.4
November	12	27.8	8.6	.573	0.4	.400	2.8	.758	1.25	1.08	2.3	7.2	12.1
December	15	28.0	9.7	.445	0.3	.200	4.7	.643	1.33	0.93	3.4	7.7	11.7
January	16	31.8	9.4	.520	0.3	.167	4.4	.676	1.63	1.69	2.8	8.8	12.8
February	13	27.6	8.2	.439	0.1	.000	3.3	.837	1.54	1.15	2.8	7.5	10.0
March	15	28.0	9.7	.531	0.1	.500	4.6	.623	0.93	1.07	2.7	7.5	13.2
April	11	30.3	10.3	.513	0.6	.286	4.3	.702	0.73	1.64	4.1	9.5	13.7
0 Days Rest	18	27.0	9.3	.524	0.3	.400	2.7	.667	1.17	1.22	3.1	7.7	11.7
1 Days Rest	50	29.6	9.5	.506	0.4	.263	4.2	.720	1.30	1.26	2.8	8.1	12.7
2 Days Rest	9	28.9	8.6	.468	0.2	.000	5.6	.620	1.22	0.78	3.9	8.0	11.4
3+ Days Rest	5	29.2	9.0	.444	0.0	—	4.8	.625	1.20	2.20	2.6	8.2	11.0

Last Five Seasons

	G	Min	FGA	FG%	3PA	3P%	FTA	FT%	Blk	Stl	Ast	Reb	Pts
Total	356	31.6	9.9	.497	0.4	.236	3.7	.680	1.57	1.15	3.4	8.6	12.4
Home	177	32.0	10.0	.507	0.4	.257	4.1	.678	1.86	1.17	3.7	9.1	13.0
Road	179	31.2	9.7	.487	0.4	.218	3.4	.684	1.28	1.13	3.1	8.2	11.9
vs. Playoff	192	31.1	9.5	.494	0.5	.287	3.8	.684	1.38	1.10	3.2	8.0	12.1
vs. Non-Playoff	164	32.2	10.3	.500	0.3	.148	3.7	.677	1.79	1.20	3.6	9.4	12.8
vs. East	163	31.1	9.7	.499	0.3	.255	3.4	.685	1.79	1.13	3.3	8.5	12.1
vs. West	193	32.1	10.0	.495	0.5	.226	4.0	.677	1.39	1.16	3.4	8.8	12.7
vs. Div.	119	32.1	9.7	.479	0.4	.226	4.0	.665	1.46	1.25	3.3	8.5	12.1
As Starter	331	32.3	10.1	.500	0.4	.245	3.8	.682	1.60	1.15	3.4	8.7	12.8
Off Bench	25	22.5	6.8	.438	0.2	.000	3.2	.663	1.16	1.16	2.7	7.6	8.0
In wins	215	32.5	10.0	.514	0.4	.250	3.8	.693	1.78	1.20	3.6	9.1	13.0
In losses	141	30.3	9.7	.470	0.5	.221	3.7	.661	1.26	1.06	3.0	8.0	11.7

	G	Min	FGA	FG%	3PA	3P%	FTA	FT%	Blk	Stl	Ast	Reb	Pts
Pre All-Star	179	31.4	9.7	.502	0.4	.242	3.7	.671	1.71	1.16	3.1	8.5	12.3
Post All-Star	127	30.5	9.6	.502	0.3	.205	3.8	.682	1.59	1.24	3.4	8.4	12.0
Oct/Nov	54	28.8	8.9	.523	0.4	.308	3.2	.690	1.61	1.11	2.6	8.0	11.5
December	60	30.1	10.1	.469	0.3	.167	3.8	.632	1.62	1.12	3.2	8.3	11.9
January	53	35.0	10.3	.512	0.4	.211	4.1	.676	1.85	1.28	3.3	9.3	13.4
February	52	32.7	9.7	.512	0.4	.263	3.0	.728	1.94	1.21	3.8	9.0	12.1
March	76	30.6	9.6	.476	0.5	.263	4.1	.696	1.37	1.11	3.3	8.3	12.1
Apr/May	61	32.9	10.7	.503	0.5	.179	4.0	.673	1.18	1.10	3.9	9.1	13.5
0 Days Rest	92	31.4	10.2	.495	0.5	.214	3.5	.678	1.55	1.08	3.2	8.6	12.5
1 Days Rest	186	31.4	9.7	.501	0.4	.244	3.8	.688	1.49	1.17	3.4	8.6	12.5
2 Days Rest	47	32.9	9.5	.513	0.4	.286	3.9	.683	1.96	1.11	3.5	9.0	12.5
3+ Days Rest	31	31.7	10.3	.459	0.2	.143	3.8	.636	1.52	1.32	3.4	8.6	11.9

Michael Doleac

1999-2000 Per Game Averages

	G	Min	FGA	FG%	3PA	3P%	FTA	FT%	Blk	Stl	Ast	Reb	Pts
Total	81	16.5	6.6	.452	0.0	.500	1.2	.842	0.42	0.36	0.8	4.1	7.0
Home	41	16.2	6.0	.453	0.0	—	0.8	.788	0.32	0.51	0.6	3.9	6.0
Road	40	16.8	7.3	.452	0.1	.500	1.6	.871	0.53	0.20	1.0	4.4	7.9
vs. Playoff	47	17.2	7.0	.453	0.0	.500	1.6	.840	0.49	0.32	0.7	4.2	7.7
vs. Non-Playoff	34	15.5	6.1	.452	0.0	—	0.6	.850	0.32	0.41	0.9	4.0	6.0
vs. East	54	16.4	6.2	.451	0.0	1.000	1.2	.815	0.50	0.28	0.8	4.2	6.6
vs. West	27	16.6	7.3	.455	0.0	.000	1.1	.900	0.26	0.52	0.7	3.9	7.7
vs. Div.	25	16.5	6.2	.452	0.0	—	0.7	.833	0.40	0.32	0.9	3.6	6.2
As Starter	29	16.6	7.7	.410	0.0	—	1.5	.884	0.48	0.45	0.8	3.9	7.6
Off Bench	52	16.4	6.0	.482	0.0	.500	1.0	.808	0.38	0.31	0.8	4.3	6.6
In wins	40	17.6	6.9	.480	0.0	—	0.9	.806	0.45	0.38	0.8	4.5	7.4
In losses	41	15.4	6.3	.422	0.0	.500	1.4	.864	0.34	0.34	0.7	3.8	6.5

	G	Min	FGA	FG%	3PA	3P%	FTA	FT%	Blk	Stl	Ast	Reb	Pts
Pre All-Star	49	16.8	7.6	.454	0.0	.000	1.5	.865	0.49	0.41	0.9	4.0	8.2
Post All-Star	32	16.0	5.2	.448	0.0	1.000	0.7	.762	0.31	0.28	0.7	4.3	5.2
November	15	17.5	8.2	.390	0.0	—	1.5	.826	0.40	0.27	0.8	4.1	7.7
December	14	15.6	7.1	.434	0.0	—	1.4	.950	0.57	0.64	0.8	3.6	7.5
January	16	16.3	7.1	.478	0.1	.000	1.5	.875	0.63	0.25	1.1	4.6	8.1
February	11	19.7	7.9	.517	0.1	1.000	1.1	.750	0.36	0.55	0.7	3.6	9.1
March	16	16.3	4.8	.403	0.0	—	0.8	.833	0.19	0.31	0.4	4.8	4.5
April	9	12.8	4.0	.583	0.0	—	0.4	.500	0.33	0.11	1.0	3.4	4.9
0 Days Rest	21	15.1	6.9	.465	0.0	—	1.1	.750	0.48	0.24	0.9	4.4	7.2
1 Days Rest	42	17.4	6.9	.454	0.0	1.000	0.8	.824	0.45	0.45	0.8	4.3	7.0
2 Days Rest	7	17.1	5.1	.444	0.1	.000	2.4	1.000	0.57	0.29	0.7	4.1	7.0
3+ Days Rest	11	15.4	5.8	.422	0.0	—	1.8	.850	0.09	0.27	0.5	3.0	6.5

Career (1998-99 thru 1999-2000)

	G	Min	FGA	FG%	3PA	3P%	FTA	FT%	Blk	Stl	Ast	Reb	Pts
Total	130	16.3	6.2	.458	0.0	.500	1.3	.766	0.39	0.37	0.6	3.7	6.7
Home	66	16.5	6.1	.470	0.0	—	1.3	.675	0.32	0.53	0.5	3.8	6.5
Road	64	16.1	6.3	.445	0.0	.500	1.4	.848	0.47	0.20	0.7	3.6	6.8
vs. Playoff	74	16.6	6.4	.462	0.0	.500	1.2	.823	0.43	0.36	0.6	3.6	7.1
vs. Non-Playoff	56	15.8	5.9	.452	0.0	—	1.1	.661	0.34	0.38	0.6	3.8	6.1
vs. East	97	16.0	5.7	.458	0.0	1.000	1.4	.741	0.45	0.31	0.6	3.7	6.3
vs. West	33	17.2	7.4	.457	0.0	.000	1.1	.861	0.21	0.55	0.7	3.7	7.7
vs. Div.	43	15.5	5.4	.468	0.0	—	1.2	.717	0.35	0.26	0.7	3.3	5.9
As Starter	29	16.6	7.7	.410	0.0	—	1.5	.884	0.48	0.45	0.8	3.9	7.6
Off Bench	101	16.2	5.7	.476	0.0	.500	1.3	.727	0.37	0.35	0.6	3.7	6.4
In wins	72	17.0	6.2	.481	0.0	—	1.3	.711	0.38	0.40	0.7	3.9	6.9
In losses	58	15.4	6.1	.428	0.0	.500	1.5	.824	0.41	0.33	0.6	3.4	6.5

	G	Min	FGA	FG%	3PA	3P%	FTA	FT%	Blk	Stl	Ast	Reb	Pts
Pre All-Star	49	16.8	7.6	.454	0.0	.000	1.5	.865	0.49	0.41	0.9	4.0	8.2
Post All-Star	32	16.0	5.2	.448	0.0	1.000	0.7	.762	0.31	0.28	0.7	4.3	5.2
Oct/Nov	15	17.5	8.2	.390	0.0	—	1.5	.826	0.40	0.27	0.8	4.1	7.7
December	14	15.6	7.1	.434	0.0	—	1.4	.950	0.57	0.64	0.8	3.6	7.5
January	16	16.3	7.1	.478	0.1	.000	1.5	.875	0.63	0.25	1.1	4.6	8.1
February	25	16.2	5.9	.503	0.0	1.000	0.9	.773	0.28	0.56	0.6	2.9	6.6
March	33	17.0	5.4	.480	0.0	—	1.4	.723	0.21	0.24	0.3	4.2	6.6
Apr/May	27	15.1	5.3	.441	0.0	—	1.4	.615	0.48	0.33	0.7	3.1	5.6
0 Days Rest	37	15.9	6.2	.476	0.0	—	1.7	.742	0.46	0.27	0.6	3.9	7.1
1 Days Rest	69	16.6	6.3	.450	0.0	1.000	0.9	.708	0.41	0.39	0.7	3.8	6.3
2 Days Rest	10	17.9	6.4	.484	0.1	.000	2.6	.923	0.50	0.70	0.6	3.6	8.6
3+ Days Rest	14	14.6	5.4	.421	0.0	—	1.6	.818	0.07	0.29	0.4	2.9	5.9

Bryce Drew
Houston Rockets — Guard

1999-2000 Per Game Averages

	G	Min	FGA	FG%	3PA	3P%	FTA	FT%	Blk	Stl	Ast	Reb	Pts
Total	72	18.0	5.7	.383	2.3	.362	0.7	.849	0.01	0.57	2.3	1.4	5.8
Home	37	17.1	5.4	.338	2.2	.346	0.5	.842	0.03	0.38	2.2	1.4	4.8
Road	35	18.8	6.1	.423	2.3	.378	1.0	.853	0.00	0.77	2.3	1.4	6.9
vs. Playoff	41	17.5	5.5	.376	2.1	.310	0.8	.839	0.00	0.66	2.1	1.4	5.4
vs. Non-Playoff	31	18.6	6.0	.390	2.5	.421	0.7	.864	0.03	0.45	2.5	1.5	6.4
vs. East	28	16.7	5.1	.387	2.0	.327	0.7	.842	0.00	0.79	2.4	1.4	5.1
vs. West	44	18.8	6.2	.380	2.5	.380	0.8	.853	0.02	0.43	2.2	1.5	6.3
vs. Div.	20	21.7	7.4	.361	3.0	.322	1.3	.880	0.05	0.45	2.4	1.6	7.4
As Starter	5	42.8	15.2	.447	6.2	.387	1.2	1.000	0.20	1.00	6.6	2.8	17.2
Off Bench	67	16.1	5.0	.368	2.0	.356	0.7	.830	0.00	0.54	1.9	1.3	5.0
In wins	28	17.9	5.7	.406	2.4	.418	0.5	.923	0.04	0.32	2.6	1.3	6.1
In losses	44	18.0	5.8	.368	2.2	.323	0.9	.825	0.00	0.73	2.0	1.5	5.7

	G	Min	FGA	FG%	3PA	3P%	FTA	FT%	Blk	Stl	Ast	Reb	Pts
Pre All-Star	50	20.0	6.8	.391	2.8	.376	0.8	.875	0.02	0.62	2.4	1.4	7.0
Post All-Star	22	13.3	3.4	.347	1.0	.273	0.6	.769	0.00	0.45	1.8	1.4	3.1
November	15	17.2	6.1	.429	2.4	.361	0.9	.769	0.00	0.47	1.2	1.1	6.7
December	15	23.3	7.5	.393	3.2	.521	0.7	.900	0.07	0.80	3.0	2.2	8.1
January	14	16.4	5.8	.333	2.6	.306	0.7	.900	0.00	0.36	2.2	1.0	5.3
February	13	21.4	6.6	.372	2.5	.212	1.2	.800	0.00	0.92	3.7	1.5	6.4
March	13	12.7	3.1	.400	0.8	.300	0.4	1.000	0.00	0.38	1.5	1.4	3.1
April	2	7.0	1.5	.000	0.0	—	0.0	—	0.00	0.00	0.5	1.5	0.0
0 Days Rest	14	21.1	7.1	.380	2.4	.382	1.2	.824	0.00	0.71	2.5	1.2	7.4
1 Days Rest	38	19.3	6.2	.377	2.6	.374	0.7	.821	0.03	0.42	2.5	1.6	6.3
2 Days Rest	16	12.3	3.8	.383	1.2	.263	0.4	1.000	0.00	0.69	1.2	1.3	3.6
3+ Days Rest	4	17.0	4.3	.471	2.8	.364	0.5	1.000	0.00	1.00	3.0	1.0	5.5

Career (1998-99 thru 1999-2000)

	G	Min	FGA	FG%	3PA	3P%	FTA	FT%	Blk	Stl	Ast	Reb	Pts
Total	106	16.4	5.1	.378	2.0	.354	0.6	.869	0.05	0.50	2.0	1.3	5.1
Home	55	15.2	4.8	.332	1.9	.349	0.4	.870	0.04	0.38	2.1	1.3	4.8
Road	51	17.6	5.4	.422	2.1	.358	0.7	.868	0.06	0.63	2.0	1.3	6.0
vs. Playoff	60	15.5	4.9	.369	1.9	.310	0.6	.848	0.02	0.53	1.8	1.2	4.7
vs. Non-Playoff	46	17.4	5.4	.389	2.2	.404	0.6	.893	0.09	0.46	2.3	1.4	5.6
vs. East	30	16.2	4.9	.388	1.9	.333	0.6	.842	0.03	0.73	2.3	1.3	5.0
vs. West	76	16.4	5.2	.375	2.0	.361	0.6	.881	0.05	0.41	1.9	1.3	5.1
vs. Div.	36	18.9	6.1	.379	2.4	.318	0.8	.900	0.11	0.39	2.2	1.4	6.1
As Starter	5	42.8	15.2	.447	6.2	.387	1.2	1.000	0.20	1.00	6.6	2.8	17.2
Off Bench	101	15.0	4.6	.367	1.8	.348	0.5	.855	0.04	0.48	1.8	1.2	4.5
In wins	47	15.7	5.0	.395	2.0	.396	0.4	.947	0.06	0.40	2.3	1.2	5.1
In losses	59	16.9	5.2	.366	2.0	.319	0.7	.833	0.03	0.58	1.8	1.3	5.1

	G	Min	FGA	FG%	3PA	3P%	FTA	FT%	Blk	Stl	Ast	Reb	Pts
Pre All-Star	50	20.0	6.8	.391	2.8	.376	0.8	.875	0.02	0.62	2.4	1.4	7.0
Post All-Star	22	13.3	3.4	.347	1.0	.273	0.6	.769	0.00	0.45	1.8	1.4	3.1
Oct/Nov	15	17.2	6.1	.429	2.4	.361	0.9	.769	0.00	0.47	1.2	1.1	6.7
December	15	23.3	7.5	.393	3.2	.521	0.7	.900	0.07	0.80	3.0	2.2	8.1
January	14	16.4	5.8	.333	2.6	.306	0.7	.900	0.00	0.36	2.2	1.0	5.3
February	25	17.0	5.2	.364	1.9	.229	0.8	.857	0.12	0.72	2.8	1.2	4.9
March	19	11.2	2.6	.327	0.8	.200	0.4	1.000	0.00	0.32	1.3	1.3	2.2
Apr/May	18	14.4	4.4	.400	1.6	.410	0.0	—	0.06	0.28	1.4	1.0	4.2
0 Days Rest	24	18.0	6.0	.396	2.3	.407	0.9	.857	0.08	0.71	2.0	1.0	6.4
1 Days Rest	51	17.8	5.6	.365	2.3	.361	0.6	.844	0.04	0.39	2.3	1.5	5.5
2 Days Rest	21	12.8	3.9	.402	1.2	.231	0.3	1.000	0.00	0.52	1.0	1.1	3.7
3+ Days Rest	10	12.4	3.1	.355	1.3	.308	0.2	1.000	0.10	0.50	2.6	1.1	2.8

Tim Duncan
San Antonio Spurs — Forward-Center

1999-2000 Per Game Averages

	G	Min	FGA	FG%	3PA	3P%	FTA	FT%	Blk	Stl	Ast	Reb	Pts
Total	74	38.9	17.3	.490	0.1	.091	8.1	.761	2.23	0.89	3.2	12.4	23.2
Home	35	37.3	16.6	.486	0.1	.000	7.8	.784	2.60	0.71	3.1	12.5	22.3
Road	39	40.3	17.9	.494	0.2	.167	8.5	.742	1.90	1.05	3.3	12.3	24.0
vs. Playoff	38	39.8	18.4	.480	0.2	.111	8.6	.758	2.05	0.79	2.7	13.1	24.2
vs. Non-Playoff	36	37.8	16.2	.503	0.1	.000	7.7	.764	2.42	1.00	3.7	11.7	22.1
vs. East	28	39.4	17.2	.484	0.0	—	7.9	.739	2.71	0.68	3.3	12.4	22.5
vs. West	46	38.5	17.4	.494	0.2	.091	8.3	.774	1.93	1.02	3.1	12.4	23.6
vs. Div.	20	39.6	18.0	.511	0.2	.000	8.7	.798	1.75	1.25	3.7	11.9	25.3
As Starter	74	38.9	17.3	.490	0.1	.091	8.1	.761	2.23	0.89	3.2	12.4	23.2
Off Bench	0	—	—	—	—	—	—	—	—	—	—	—	—
In wins	48	38.6	17.5	.504	0.0	.000	8.0	.766	2.52	1.02	3.5	13.2	23.8
In losses	26	39.3	17.0	.464	0.3	.111	8.4	.753	1.69	0.65	2.5	11.0	22.2

	G	Min	FGA	FG%	3PA	3P%	FTA	FT%	Blk	Stl	Ast	Reb	Pts
Pre All-Star	49	39.6	17.9	.499	0.2	.111	8.8	.763	2.22	1.00	3.0	13.1	24.6
Post All-Star	25	37.4	16.1	.471	0.1	.000	6.9	.757	2.24	0.68	3.5	11.0	20.4
November	16	38.4	16.9	.494	0.1	.000	7.7	.659	2.50	0.50	3.2	13.8	21.8
December	15	41.4	18.9	.491	0.1	.000	9.5	.804	2.40	1.20	2.7	12.5	26.2
January	13	38.8	17.1	.514	0.3	.250	9.4	.779	2.00	0.85	2.6	12.8	24.9
February	10	36.4	18.6	.457	0.2	.000	6.4	.828	1.60	1.60	3.0	10.7	22.3
March	14	37.3	15.4	.498	0.1	.000	7.1	.788	2.36	0.71	4.1	12.1	20.9
April	6	41.7	17.3	.471	0.2	.000	8.7	.712	2.33	0.50	3.5	11.2	22.5
0 Days Rest	17	39.4	17.1	.512	0.2	.000	7.1	.817	2.24	1.29	2.6	11.5	23.3
1 Days Rest	35	38.6	17.4	.475	0.1	.000	7.7	.770	2.17	0.80	3.4	12.3	22.4
2 Days Rest	18	39.0	17.5	.502	0.2	.333	10.0	.711	2.39	0.72	3.4	13.1	24.7
3+ Days Rest	4	38.0	16.5	.485	0.3	.000	8.5	.765	2.00	0.75	2.3	13.8	22.5

Career (1997-98 thru 1999-2000)

	G	Min	FGA	FG%	3PA	3P%	FTA	FT%	Blk	Stl	Ast	Reb	Pts
Total	206	39.0	16.6	.513	0.1	.071	7.0	.710	2.41	0.81	2.8	12.0	22.0
Home	101	38.7	16.2	.513	0.1	.000	6.8	.705	2.62	0.74	2.9	12.5	21.4
Road	105	39.4	17.0	.513	0.2	.125	7.2	.715	2.21	0.87	2.7	11.5	22.6
vs. Playoff	109	39.7	16.8	.495	0.2	.100	7.2	.692	2.08	0.77	2.6	12.3	21.7
vs. Non-Playoff	97	38.3	16.3	.535	0.1	.000	6.8	.733	2.78	0.85	3.0	11.6	22.4
vs. East	64	39.5	16.3	.529	0.0	.000	5.9	.712	2.69	0.70	3.1	12.3	21.5
vs. West	142	38.9	16.7	.506	0.2	.080	7.5	.710	2.29	0.85	2.7	11.8	22.2
vs. Div.	65	38.5	16.4	.521	0.1	.000	7.2	.693	2.45	0.78	3.0	11.3	22.1
As Starter	206	39.0	16.6	.513	0.1	.071	7.0	.710	2.41	0.81	2.8	12.0	22.0
Off Bench	0	—	—	—	—	—	—	—	—	—	—	—	—
In wins	141	38.7	16.6	.529	0.1	.091	6.8	.711	2.62	0.89	3.1	12.2	22.4
In losses	65	39.8	16.5	.479	0.3	.059	7.5	.709	1.97	0.62	2.2	11.6	21.1

	G	Min	FGA	FG%	3PA	3P%	FTA	FT%	Blk	Stl	Ast	Reb	Pts
Pre All-Star	97	38.7	15.8	.524	0.2	.067	6.9	.699	2.31	0.82	2.8	12.3	21.4
Post All-Star	59	39.5	17.5	.513	0.1	.000	7.1	.746	2.49	0.69	3.2	11.8	23.2
Oct/Nov	32	36.9	14.3	.524	0.1	.000	6.0	.583	2.53	0.50	2.5	13.8	18.5
December	28	40.2	16.6	.524	0.0	.000	7.6	.745	2.57	0.96	2.5	12.2	23.0
January	30	39.1	15.8	.528	0.2	.143	7.0	.724	2.03	0.77	3.0	12.1	21.8
February	35	38.1	17.8	.469	0.1	.000	5.7	.707	2.26	0.89	2.9	12.1	22.0
March	46	38.8	16.8	.526	0.1	.167	6.7	.753	2.52	0.93	2.7	11.9	22.8
Apr/May	35	41.3	17.7	.515	0.2	.000	7.4	.717	2.51	0.74	3.1	11.3	23.5
0 Days Rest	48	39.3	16.5	.499	0.1	.000	6.7	.724	2.38	0.96	2.5	11.4	21.3
1 Days Rest	111	39.3	16.8	.512	0.1	.000	7.0	.729	2.43	0.74	2.9	12.1	22.3
2 Days Rest	38	38.6	16.5	.534	0.2	.333	7.5	.644	2.61	0.84	3.1	12.3	22.5
3+ Days Rest	9	36.1	14.6	.527	0.1	.000	6.9	.710	1.56	0.67	2.3	12.1	20.2

Howard Eisley

1999-2000 Per Game Averages

	G	Min	FGA	FG%	3PA	3P%	FTA	FT%	Blk	Stl	Ast	Reb	Pts		G	Min	FGA	FG%	3PA	3P%	FTA	FT%	Blk	Stl	Ast	Reb	Pts
Total	82	25.6	8.2	.418	2.0	.368	1.2	.824	0.11	0.72	4.2	2.1	8.6	Pre All-Star	47	25.4	8.3	.404	1.9	.386	1.5	.806	0.13	0.79	4.1	2.1	8.6
Home	41	25.5	8.3	.440	2.2	.411	1.0	.878	0.15	0.71	4.5	2.0	9.1	Post All-Star	35	25.8	8.2	.437	2.1	.347	0.9	.867	0.09	0.63	4.4	2.1	8.6
Road	41	25.6	8.1	.395	1.8	.315	1.5	.787	0.07	0.73	3.9	2.1	8.2	November	14	22.6	7.4	.404	2.0	.464	1.1	.933	0.00	0.43	3.6	1.9	7.9
vs. Playoff	44	24.2	7.8	.379	2.0	.315	1.1	.809	0.09	0.50	3.9	2.0	7.4	December	14	24.8	8.1	.395	1.9	.308	2.1	.793	0.07	0.93	4.1	1.8	8.6
vs. Non-Playoff	38	27.1	8.7	.458	1.9	.432	1.4	.836	0.13	0.97	4.6	2.1	10.1	January	14	27.9	9.5	.421	1.6	.348	1.9	.741	0.36	1.07	4.4	2.5	10.0
vs. East	30	24.9	8.0	.433	2.3	.362	1.3	.816	0.10	0.60	4.0	1.7	8.8	February	13	25.3	7.8	.412	2.7	.371	0.6	.750	0.08	0.69	4.6	2.0	7.9
vs. West	52	25.9	8.4	.409	1.8	.372	1.2	.828	0.12	0.79	4.3	2.3	8.5	March	16	25.4	8.3	.470	1.8	.429	0.9	.857	0.13	0.38	4.1	2.1	9.3
vs. Div.	24	27.6	8.9	.407	1.8	.395	1.3	.800	0.17	1.00	4.6	2.3	9.0	April	11	27.8	8.2	.389	2.1	.261	0.8	1.000	0.00	0.91	4.8	2.2	7.7
As Starter	5	33.6	8.0	.475	1.6	.250	2.0	.600	0.00	1.20	3.6	1.8	9.2	0 Days Rest	19	24.5	7.6	.410	2.3	.302	1.6	.806	0.11	0.58	3.3	2.1	8.2
Off Bench	77	25.0	8.2	.414	2.0	.374	1.2	.848	0.12	0.69	4.3	2.1	8.6	1 Days Rest	45	25.8	8.0	.432	1.7	.400	1.1	.800	0.11	0.78	4.4	2.0	8.5
In wins	55	25.5	8.1	.444	1.8	.416	1.3	.812	0.15	0.80	4.5	2.1	8.9	2 Days Rest	12	26.2	9.4	.407	2.5	.433	1.0	.917	0.17	0.83	5.1	2.4	9.7
In losses	27	25.7	8.6	.368	2.3	.290	1.2	.848	0.04	0.56	3.6	2.0	8.0	3+ Days Rest	6	25.8	9.5	.368	2.5	.267	1.5	.889	0.00	0.50	4.2	1.8	9.0

Last Five Seasons

	G	Min	FGA	FG%	3PA	3P%	FTA	FT%	Blk	Stl	Ast	Reb	Pts		G	Min	FGA	FG%	3PA	3P%	FTA	FT%	Blk	Stl	Ast	Reb	Pts
Total	361	19.1	5.7	.434	1.3	.351	1.4	.831	0.10	0.60	3.4	1.6	6.5	Pre All-Star	171	19.5	5.8	.431	1.3	.339	1.5	.815	0.12	0.57	3.3	1.6	6.6
Home	181	19.4	5.6	.440	1.4	.352	1.3	.840	0.16	0.60	3.6	1.6	6.5	Post All-Star	140	18.1	5.4	.434	1.3	.346	1.2	.851	0.11	0.64	3.3	1.6	6.1
Road	180	18.9	5.8	.429	1.2	.349	1.5	.823	0.04	0.59	3.2	1.7	6.6	Oct/Nov	42	21.9	6.7	.443	1.5	.500	1.4	.828	0.17	0.50	3.7	1.8	7.8
vs. Playoff	190	18.4	5.7	.426	1.4	.360	1.2	.828	0.08	0.48	3.2	1.5	6.3	December	57	17.8	5.2	.428	1.3	.250	1.8	.812	0.07	0.67	3.0	1.5	6.3
vs. Non-Playoff	171	20.0	5.7	.444	1.2	.338	1.6	.833	0.12	0.73	3.6	1.8	6.8	January	56	18.9	5.8	.423	1.2	.262	1.3	.803	0.14	0.59	3.4	1.7	6.2
vs. East	119	17.9	5.2	.443	1.3	.327	1.4	.857	0.11	0.61	3.1	1.5	6.3	February	61	19.5	5.6	.430	1.4	.345	1.2	.882	0.05	0.64	3.6	1.7	6.4
vs. West	242	19.7	5.9	.431	1.3	.362	1.4	.818	0.10	0.60	3.5	1.7	6.7	March	80	17.8	5.7	.453	1.2	.424	1.5	.830	0.10	0.55	3.0	1.6	6.9
vs. Div.	109	19.9	6.0	.434	1.2	.371	1.5	.816	0.17	0.64	3.5	1.7	6.9	Apr/May	65	20.0	5.5	.425	1.3	.321	1.1	.829	0.11	0.63	3.8	1.7	6.0
As Starter	23	30.4	8.4	.474	1.7	.462	2.2	.780	0.17	0.83	5.3	2.0	10.5	0 Days Rest	87	19.3	5.7	.427	1.3	.325	1.7	.837	0.08	0.61	2.9	1.8	6.7
Off Bench	338	18.4	5.5	.430	1.3	.340	1.3	.837	0.10	0.58	3.3	1.6	6.3	1 Days Rest	197	19.1	5.7	.449	1.2	.363	1.3	.826	0.11	0.58	3.5	1.5	6.6
In wins	261	19.3	5.7	.440	1.3	.349	1.3	.837	0.12	0.67	3.6	1.7	6.6	2 Days Rest	49	19.7	6.2	.414	1.5	.387	1.1	.811	0.12	0.57	3.9	1.8	6.6
In losses	100	18.7	5.7	.419	1.3	.353	1.5	.816	0.06	0.41	2.8	1.5	6.5	3+ Days Rest	28	18.0	5.1	.389	1.3	.278	1.4	.872	0.07	0.75	3.2	1.5	5.6

Mario Elie

1999-2000 Per Game Averages

	G	Min	FGA	FG%	3PA	3P%	FTA	FT%	Blk	Stl	Ast	Reb	Pts		G	Min	FGA	FG%	3PA	3P%	FTA	FT%	Blk	Stl	Ast	Reb	Pts
Total	79	28.1	5.8	.427	2.4	.398	1.9	.846	0.11	0.92	2.4	3.2	7.5	Pre All-Star	49	28.9	6.1	.445	2.4	.381	2.2	.858	0.10	1.12	2.6	3.3	8.2
Home	40	27.2	5.9	.434	2.5	.388	1.9	.831	0.13	1.00	2.4	3.7	7.7	Post All-Star	30	26.6	5.3	.392	2.3	.426	1.4	.814	0.13	0.60	2.1	2.9	6.3
Road	39	29.0	5.7	.419	2.3	.409	1.8	.861	0.10	0.85	2.5	2.6	7.3	November	16	28.6	6.9	.509	2.3	.472	1.8	.897	0.06	1.44	2.7	3.2	9.7
vs. Playoff	42	28.7	5.8	.408	2.2	.340	1.5	.862	0.05	1.05	2.4	3.0	6.9	December	15	30.7	6.1	.413	2.9	.395	2.7	.800	0.13	0.67	2.4	3.1	8.3
vs. Non-Playoff	37	27.4	5.7	.448	2.5	.457	2.3	.833	0.19	0.78	2.5	3.4	8.2	January	13	27.5	5.5	.408	2.0	.308	2.2	.862	0.08	1.31	2.6	3.5	7.0
vs. East	30	30.1	6.0	.459	2.5	.387	2.0	.767	0.17	1.00	2.5	3.1	8.0	February	13	28.7	5.6	.370	2.2	.379	1.7	.955	0.23	1.00	2.8	3.4	6.6
vs. West	49	26.8	5.6	.406	2.3	.405	1.8	.899	0.08	0.88	2.4	3.2	7.1	March	15	28.7	5.3	.438	2.6	.410	1.7	.760	0.13	0.60	2.0	2.9	7.0
vs. Div.	23	27.8	5.9	.378	2.4	.429	2.3	.887	0.17	1.26	2.6	3.4	7.5	April	7	19.9	4.4	.323	1.9	.385	0.6	.750	0.00	0.14	2.0	2.7	4.0
As Starter	79	28.1	5.8	.427	2.4	.398	1.9	.846	0.11	0.92	2.4	3.2	7.5	0 Days Rest	16	30.3	5.9	.319	2.6	.317	2.7	.884	0.19	1.06	2.8	3.4	6.9
Off Bench	0	—	—	—	—	—	—	—	—	—	—	—	—	1 Days Rest	42	26.7	5.8	.451	2.5	.457	1.7	.808	0.12	0.93	2.4	3.2	7.8
In wins	51	28.3	5.9	.460	2.5	.405	2.0	.832	0.14	1.04	2.5	3.5	8.1	2 Days Rest	17	29.8	5.5	.479	2.0	.294	1.8	.867	0.06	0.82	2.5	2.7	7.4
In losses	28	27.6	5.6	.363	2.1	.383	1.7	.875	0.07	0.71	2.4	2.6	6.4	3+ Days Rest	4	25.8	6.3	.400	1.5	.500	0.8	1.000	0.00	0.75	1.8	3.3	6.5

Last Five Seasons

	G	Min	FGA	FG%	3PA	3P%	FTA	FT%	Blk	Stl	Ast	Reb	Pts		G	Min	FGA	FG%	3PA	3P%	FTA	FT%	Blk	Stl	Ast	Reb	Pts
Total	322	29.7	6.8	.470	2.8	.369	2.4	.862	0.16	1.05	3.0	2.9	9.5	Pre All-Star	174	30.6	7.0	.474	2.8	.346	2.6	.862	0.16	1.14	3.0	2.8	9.8
Home	162	29.7	7.0	.460	2.9	.368	2.5	.863	0.17	1.12	3.1	3.2	9.6	Post All-Star	101	29.1	6.3	.463	3.0	.404	2.2	.858	0.13	0.92	3.4	3.0	8.9
Road	160	29.7	6.6	.481	2.7	.370	2.4	.860	0.15	0.97	2.8	2.6	9.4	Oct/Nov	59	30.1	7.3	.501	2.8	.354	2.6	.853	0.10	1.24	3.2	2.7	10.6
vs. Playoff	175	30.0	6.9	.471	2.8	.374	2.2	.864	0.15	1.01	2.8	2.9	9.4	December	55	32.7	7.5	.449	3.0	.352	2.5	.837	0.18	0.98	2.7	2.7	9.9
vs. Non-Playoff	147	29.4	6.7	.469	2.8	.363	2.8	.859	0.18	1.10	3.1	2.9	9.7	January	49	29.0	6.3	.473	2.6	.325	2.7	.896	0.18	1.18	2.8	3.0	9.3
vs. East	107	30.6	6.4	.470	2.6	.364	2.5	.850	0.16	1.07	2.9	2.8	9.1	February	48	28.4	6.8	.438	2.7	.354	2.3	.899	0.23	0.88	3.0	3.3	8.9
vs. West	215	29.3	7.0	.470	2.9	.371	2.4	.868	0.16	1.04	3.0	3.0	9.7	March	56	29.6	6.2	.484	2.9	.454	2.1	.807	0.07	0.98	3.0	2.9	9.0
vs. Div.	99	29.9	7.0	.475	2.9	.370	2.6	.869	0.21	1.27	3.1	3.1	10.0	Apr/May	55	28.1	6.5	.471	2.7	.361	2.5	.881	0.22	1.00	2.9	2.9	9.3
As Starter	268	30.8	6.9	.472	2.9	.381	2.6	.870	0.16	1.12	3.1	3.0	9.8	0 Days Rest	64	30.0	6.8	.467	2.8	.335	2.9	.876	0.20	0.98	2.7	2.8	9.8
Off Bench	54	24.6	6.3	.463	2.3	.293	1.8	.806	0.19	0.70	2.3	2.6	7.9	1 Days Rest	179	29.5	6.7	.468	2.8	.385	2.4	.851	0.16	1.07	3.0	2.9	9.4
In wins	204	29.6	6.7	.495	2.8	.396	2.7	.875	0.17	1.17	3.1	3.0	10.1	2 Days Rest	54	31.1	7.1	.501	2.9	.372	2.1	.868	0.06	0.93	3.1	2.9	10.0
In losses	118	29.8	6.9	.428	2.8	.320	2.0	.831	0.15	0.83	2.8	2.8	8.5	3+ Days Rest	25	27.6	6.4	.422	2.7	.328	2.4	.881	0.28	1.28	2.9	2.8	6.4

LaPhonso Ellis

1999-2000 Per Game Averages

	G	Min	FGA	FG%	3PA	3P%	FTA	FT%	Blk	Stl	Ast	Reb	Pts		G	Min	FGA	FG%	3PA	3P%	FTA	FT%	Blk	Stl	Ast	Reb	Pts
Total	58	22.6	8.0	.450	0.4	.143	1.6	.695	0.43	0.55	1.0	5.0	8.4	Pre All-Star	23	20.4	7.5	.453	0.3	.125	1.9	.791	0.43	0.39	1.0	4.7	8.3
Home	28	22.0	8.3	.446	0.4	.182	2.2	.656	0.21	0.54	1.1	5.2	8.9	Post All-Star	35	24.0	8.3	.449	0.4	.154	1.5	.615	0.43	0.66	1.0	5.2	8.5
Road	30	23.1	7.8	.455	0.3	.100	1.1	.765	0.63	0.57	1.0	4.8	8.0	November	0	—	—	—	—	—	—	—	—	—	—	—	—
vs. Playoff	33	22.4	8.0	.418	0.4	.154	1.3	.698	0.33	0.42	1.1	5.1	7.6	December	5	19.6	10.6	.453	0.6	.000	2.2	.909	0.20	0.20	0.4	4.4	11.6
vs. Non-Playoff	25	22.8	8.0	.493	0.3	.125	2.1	.692	0.56	0.72	0.9	4.8	9.4	January	13	20.5	6.6	.419	0.2	.333	1.7	.682	0.38	0.54	1.2	4.9	6.8
vs. East	40	22.5	8.1	.466	0.4	.200	1.8	.714	0.43	0.53	1.0	4.9	8.8	February	12	20.3	6.2	.554	0.2	.000	1.2	.786	0.67	0.75	0.9	4.8	7.8
vs. West	18	22.7	7.9	.415	0.3	.000	1.4	.640	0.44	0.61	1.1	5.3	7.4	March	17	20.6	7.8	.444	0.3	.000	1.8	.613	0.29	0.47	1.0	4.7	8.1
vs. Div.	20	21.9	8.7	.434	0.3	.000	1.7	.697	0.45	0.30	0.8	5.0	8.7	April	11	31.7	10.7	.415	0.7	.250	1.5	.647	0.55	0.64	1.2	6.0	10.1
As Starter	8	32.5	10.5	.440	0.8	.333	1.6	.692	0.75	0.50	1.1	6.1	10.6	0 Days Rest	18	22.4	7.8	.407	0.4	.000	2.1	.737	0.33	0.56	1.2	5.7	7.9
Off Bench	50	21.0	7.6	.453	0.3	.067	1.6	.695	0.38	0.56	1.0	4.8	8.0	1 Days Rest	26	23.1	8.1	.455	0.3	.222	1.7	.614	0.46	0.50	0.8	4.9	8.5
In wins	18	20.9	7.6	.504	0.3	.167	1.4	.760	0.44	0.61	1.2	4.3	8.8	2 Days Rest	8	23.3	8.6	.435	0.5	.250	0.9	.857	0.50	0.63	1.3	4.8	8.4
In losses	40	23.3	8.2	.428	0.4	.133	1.8	.671	0.43	0.53	0.9	5.3	8.2	3+ Days Rest	6	19.8	7.3	.591	0.2	.000	1.0	.833	0.50	0.67	1.2	3.8	9.5

Last Five Seasons

	G	Min	FGA	FG%	3PA	3P%	FTA	FT%	Blk	Stl	Ast	Reb	Pts		G	Min	FGA	FG%	3PA	3P%	FTA	FT%	Blk	Stl	Ast	Reb	Pts
Total	254	30.3	12.2	.429	2.0	.315	3.3	.739	0.61	0.73	1.9	6.5	13.6	Pre All-Star	107	28.3	12.4	.423	2.2	.329	3.2	.761	0.54	0.68	1.9	5.8	13.6
Home	129	30.4	12.6	.442	2.0	.351	3.9	.741	0.58	0.73	2.0	6.9	14.7	Post All-Star	127	32.5	12.6	.435	2.1	.305	3.4	.726	0.71	0.82	2.1	7.2	14.1
Road	125	30.1	11.9	.415	2.0	.276	2.7	.736	0.64	0.73	1.9	6.0	12.4	Oct/Nov	11	27.6	11.3	.371	2.1	.261	3.0	.636	0.27	0.55	2.0	5.1	10.8
vs. Playoff	140	30.4	12.4	.415	2.1	.300	3.2	.752	0.57	0.71	2.0	6.4	13.3	December	28	28.2	12.5	.399	2.1	.276	2.8	.833	0.54	0.46	1.9	5.2	12.9
vs. Non-Playoff	114	30.2	12.0	.447	1.9	.335	3.4	.724	0.66	0.75	1.9	6.6	13.9	January	55	28.9	12.7	.439	2.5	.362	3.6	.747	0.60	0.82	2.1	6.1	14.8
vs. East	123	28.7	11.5	.434	1.6	.330	2.8	.760	0.48	0.66	1.6	6.0	12.7	February	57	29.9	12.2	.448	1.8	.297	3.4	.777	0.44	0.82	1.8	6.6	14.1
vs. West	131	31.8	12.9	.425	2.4	.305	3.8	.724	0.73	0.79	2.3	7.0	14.4	March	68	31.2	11.8	.416	1.9	.325	3.5	.719	0.63	0.63	2.0	6.5	12.9
vs. Div.	81	29.9	12.5	.418	2.1	.287	3.5	.754	0.63	0.72	1.9	6.5	13.6	Apr/May	35	33.9	12.4	.448	1.8	.274	3.0	.657	1.03	0.89	1.9	8.5	13.5
As Starter	176	33.7	13.7	.427	2.6	.322	3.7	.754	0.68	0.77	2.3	7.1	15.3	0 Days Rest	64	30.0	12.1	.429	1.9	.295	3.3	.703	0.62	0.63	2.0	7.1	13.2
Off Bench	78	22.7	8.9	.438	0.7	.255	2.4	.684	0.46	0.63	1.2	5.2	9.6	1 Days Rest	124	31.0	12.4	.428	2.1	.320	3.2	.769	0.65	0.73	2.0	6.5	13.8
In wins	73	28.5	11.4	.467	1.8	.398	3.2	.735	0.79	0.71	1.9	6.7	13.6	2 Days Rest	43	30.6	12.8	.403	2.1	.333	3.2	.699	0.58	0.79	1.8	6.2	13.2
In losses	181	31.0	12.6	.415	2.1	.287	3.4	.740	0.54	0.73	2.0	6.4	13.5	3+ Days Rest	23	26.7	10.7	.494	1.7	.300	3.8	.747	0.74	0.91	2.0	5.4	13.9

Patrick Ewing

1999-2000 Per Game Averages

	G	Min	FGA	FG%	3PA	3P%	FTA	FT%	Blk	Stl	Ast	Reb	Pts		G	Min	FGA	FG%	3PA	3P%	FTA	FT%	Blk	Stl	Ast	Reb	Pts
Total	62	32.8	12.5	.466	0.0	.000	4.6	.731	1.35	0.58	0.9	9.7	15.0	Pre All-Star	27	31.9	11.5	.442	0.1	.000	5.0	.701	1.56	0.70	0.8	10.0	13.6
Home	34	32.6	12.2	.473	0.0	—	4.6	.755	1.38	0.56	1.0	9.6	15.0	Post All-Star	35	33.6	13.3	.482	0.0	—	4.3	.758	1.20	0.49	1.1	9.5	16.0
Road	28	33.1	12.9	.457	0.1	.000	4.6	.703	1.32	0.61	0.9	9.9	15.0	November	0	—	—	—	—	—	—	—	—	—	—	—	—
vs. Playoff	36	33.8	13.3	.460	0.1	.000	4.1	.698	1.28	0.56	1.0	10.0	15.1	December	10	31.1	10.0	.410	0.0	—	6.2	.677	2.00	0.40	0.6	9.7	12.4
vs. Non-Playoff	26	31.5	11.4	.475	0.0	—	5.2	.769	1.46	0.62	0.8	9.4	14.8	January	12	30.7	11.6	.453	0.0	—	3.2	.816	1.33	0.92	0.9	9.9	13.1
vs. East	43	32.6	12.2	.458	0.0	.000	4.5	.718	1.37	0.58	0.9	10.2	14.4	February	13	35.8	13.9	.464	0.2	.000	5.3	.681	1.54	0.77	0.9	10.1	16.5
vs. West	19	33.4	13.2	.482	0.0	—	4.6	.761	1.32	0.58	1.1	8.8	16.3	March	17	33.8	12.9	.477	0.0	—	3.5	.767	0.94	0.53	1.4	9.8	15.1
vs. Div.	19	33.2	12.9	.459	0.0	—	5.8	.709	1.63	0.74	0.8	11.3	16.0	April	10	31.5	13.5	.504	0.0	—	5.4	.759	1.20	0.20	0.6	9.1	17.7
As Starter	62	32.8	12.5	.466	0.0	.000	4.6	.731	1.35	0.58	0.9	9.7	15.0	0 Days Rest	13	33.0	12.8	.503	0.0	—	3.7	.729	0.62	0.69	0.9	9.0	15.6
Off Bench	0	—	—	—	—	—	—	—	—	—	—	—	—	1 Days Rest	33	33.2	13.1	.460	0.1	.000	4.9	.722	1.42	0.36	1.2	9.8	15.6
In wins	39	33.1	12.1	.485	0.1	.000	5.3	.749	1.49	0.56	1.0	10.0	15.7	2 Days Rest	11	31.9	10.7	.483	0.0	—	4.0	.659	1.73	0.91	0.6	9.8	13.0
In losses	23	32.4	13.3	.436	0.0	—	3.3	.684	1.13	0.61	0.8	9.3	13.8	3+ Days Rest	5	32.2	11.4	.368	0.0	—	5.8	.897	2.00	1.00	0.0	11.0	13.6

Last Five Seasons

	G	Min	FGA	FG%	3PA	3P%	FTA	FT%	Blk	Stl	Ast	Reb	Pts		G	Min	FGA	FG%	3PA	3P%	FTA	FT%	Blk	Stl	Ast	Reb	Pts
Total	280	35.2	16.2	.472	0.2	.140	6.2	.742	2.20	0.78	1.6	10.3	20.0	Pre All-Star	140	34.9	16.4	.477	0.2	.115	6.1	.739	2.39	0.83	1.5	10.3	20.2
Home	140	34.9	16.0	.472	0.1	.118	6.1	.751	2.10	0.78	1.6	10.1	19.7	Post All-Star	102	36.0	16.5	.477	0.1	.200	6.5	.760	1.77	0.72	1.9	10.4	20.7
Road	140	35.5	16.5	.472	0.2	.154	6.4	.734	2.29	0.79	1.6	10.5	20.3	Oct/Nov	43	34.8	16.0	.498	0.3	.182	7.1	.747	2.35	0.86	1.6	10.1	21.3
vs. Playoff	149	36.0	16.7	.459	0.2	.167	6.1	.737	2.07	0.75	1.4	10.4	19.8	December	49	34.2	16.0	.452	0.1	.000	5.9	.715	2.47	0.78	1.5	9.9	18.7
vs. Non-Playoff	131	34.2	15.7	.487	0.1	.105	6.4	.748	2.34	0.82	1.8	10.2	20.1	January	39	35.1	16.9	.489	0.1	.200	5.2	.779	2.46	0.82	1.6	10.7	20.6
vs. East	195	34.8	15.9	.471	0.1	.103	6.2	.743	2.22	0.72	1.7	10.0	19.6	February	46	37.2	16.8	.441	0.2	.111	6.7	.686	2.37	0.78	1.6	11.0	19.4
vs. West	85	36.0	17.0	.474	0.2	.214	6.3	.741	2.14	0.93	1.4	11.0	20.9	March	58	35.3	16.4	.494	0.1	.200	6.0	.744	1.69	0.72	1.5	10.2	20.6
vs. Div.	85	34.8	16.3	.473	0.1	.200	6.3	.745	2.41	0.87	1.6	10.5	20.1	Apr/May	45	34.6	15.4	.456	0.2	.143	6.5	.797	2.00	0.76	1.8	10.1	19.2
As Starter	280	35.2	16.2	.472	0.2	.140	6.2	.742	2.20	0.78	1.6	10.3	20.0	0 Days Rest	71	35.8	16.6	.453	0.3	.222	7.0	.741	1.96	0.69	1.9	10.4	20.3
Off Bench	0	—	—	—	—	—	—	—	—	—	—	—	—	1 Days Rest	135	35.3	16.3	.483	0.1	.000	6.0	.736	2.25	0.83	1.6	10.6	20.2
In wins	174	35.2	16.0	.497	0.1	.111	6.6	.754	2.39	0.87	1.8	10.4	20.9	2 Days Rest	51	35.5	16.7	.469	0.2	.182	5.6	.761	2.49	0.78	1.3	10.3	20.0
In losses	106	35.1	16.5	.432	0.2	.160	5.6	.720	1.88	0.64	1.3	10.2	18.3	3+ Days Rest	23	32.0	13.3	.472	0.1	.000	6.5	.747	1.96	0.78	1.2	8.5	17.4

Jamie Feick

1999-2000 Per Game Averages

	G	Min	FGA	FG%	3PA	3P%	FTA	FT%	Blk	Stl	Ast	Reb	Pts
Total	81	27.7	5.2	.428	0.0	1.000	1.6	.707	0.47	0.53	0.8	9.3	5.7
Home	41	29.3	6.2	.449	0.1	1.000	2.0	.726	0.56	0.41	0.9	11.0	7.2
Road	40	26.0	4.2	.395	0.0	—	1.2	.673	0.38	0.65	0.8	7.6	4.1
vs. Playoff	45	26.7	5.0	.403	0.1	1.000	1.7	.800	0.51	0.53	0.8	9.0	5.4
vs. Non-Playoff	36	28.9	5.5	.457	0.0	—	1.6	.586	0.42	0.53	0.9	9.7	5.9
vs. East	53	28.1	5.1	.411	0.0	1.000	1.8	.677	0.49	0.55	0.7	9.9	5.4
vs. West	28	26.9	5.5	.458	0.1	1.000	1.3	.784	0.43	0.50	1.2	8.1	6.1
vs. Div.	24	26.1	5.2	.427	0.0	1.000	1.5	.500	0.63	0.42	0.6	9.7	5.2
As Starter	17	34.9	5.8	.384	0.1	1.000	1.9	.818	0.35	0.76	1.6	11.5	6.1
Off Bench	64	25.8	5.1	.441	0.0	1.000	1.6	.670	0.50	0.47	0.6	8.7	5.5
In wins	30	27.4	6.0	.456	0.1	1.000	1.6	.809	0.73	0.43	1.0	10.5	6.8
In losses	51	27.8	4.8	.407	0.0	1.000	1.7	.651	0.31	0.59	0.8	8.6	5.0

	G	Min	FGA	FG%	3PA	3P%	FTA	FT%	Blk	Stl	Ast	Reb	Pts
Pre All-Star	48	31.1	6.3	.423	0.0	—	2.0	.740	0.54	0.56	1.0	10.8	6.8
Post All-Star	33	22.7	3.7	.439	0.1	1.000	1.1	.622	0.36	0.48	0.6	7.2	4.1
November	15	34.7	6.0	.433	0.0	—	2.9	.651	0.47	0.60	1.1	11.3	7.1
December	15	32.6	8.4	.429	0.0	—	1.9	.821	0.93	0.67	1.0	13.2	8.7
January	13	28.2	5.2	.388	0.0	—	1.8	.792	0.38	0.54	1.0	9.0	5.5
February	12	16.8	2.8	.424	0.0	—	0.5	1.000	0.17	0.25	0.4	4.4	2.8
March	16	24.5	4.3	.478	0.1	1.000	1.3	.619	0.50	0.50	0.6	8.1	5.1
April	10	27.2	3.8	.395	0.1	1.000	1.1	.455	0.20	0.60	0.9	8.9	3.6
0 Days Rest	19	28.9	5.7	.459	0.0	—	1.5	.571	0.37	0.42	0.5	9.7	6.1
1 Days Rest	44	26.5	5.0	.414	0.1	1.000	1.6	.750	0.52	0.55	1.0	8.9	5.4
2 Days Rest	11	28.4	5.9	.446	0.0	—	1.7	.737	0.64	0.73	1.2	9.8	6.5
3+ Days Rest	7	30.9	4.1	.379	0.0	—	2.0	.714	0.14	0.43	0.1	10.1	4.6

Career (1996-97 thru 1999-2000)

	G	Min	FGA	FG%	3PA	3P%	FTA	FT%	Blk	Stl	Ast	Reb	Pts
Total	195	21.4	4.1	.427	0.2	.400	1.5	.635	0.45	0.56	0.7	7.1	4.6
Home	100	22.2	4.5	.436	0.2	.467	1.8	.621	0.57	0.48	0.7	7.8	5.2
Road	95	20.5	3.7	.414	0.2	.333	1.3	.655	0.32	0.64	0.6	6.3	3.9
vs. Playoff	109	20.4	3.9	.407	0.2	.455	1.5	.687	0.40	0.51	0.7	6.6	4.3
vs. Non-Playoff	86	22.5	4.4	.449	0.1	.250	1.6	.570	0.50	0.62	0.7	7.7	4.9
vs. East	121	23.0	4.2	.415	0.1	.300	1.6	.658	0.47	0.60	0.7	7.9	4.6
vs. West	74	18.7	4.0	.447	0.3	.450	1.5	.593	0.41	0.49	0.7	5.7	4.6
vs. Div.	60	21.3	4.2	.376	0.1	.500	1.8	.585	0.50	0.52	0.6	7.3	4.2
As Starter	35	35.4	5.9	.452	0.0	1.000	2.4	.711	0.60	1.06	1.3	11.8	7.1
Off Bench	160	18.3	3.7	.418	0.2	.379	1.4	.606	0.41	0.45	0.5	6.1	4.0
In wins	74	20.8	4.2	.450	0.1	.429	1.3	.758	0.61	0.50	0.7	7.5	4.8
In losses	121	21.7	4.1	.411	0.2	.391	1.7	.578	0.35	0.60	0.7	6.8	4.4

	G	Min	FGA	FG%	3PA	3P%	FTA	FT%	Blk	Stl	Ast	Reb	Pts
Pre All-Star	76	23.0	4.7	.419	0.0	.500	1.5	.675	0.50	0.50	0.8	8.0	5.0
Post All-Star	91	17.2	3.5	.404	0.3	.393	1.4	.556	0.34	0.51	0.6	5.3	3.7
Oct/Nov	27	24.7	4.2	.465	0.0	—	2.1	.589	0.52	0.74	0.9	7.9	5.1
December	20	25.4	6.5	.423	0.0	—	1.4	.821	0.70	0.50	0.8	10.3	6.7
January	22	18.9	3.5	.377	0.0	1.000	1.4	.700	0.41	0.32	0.6	5.9	3.6
February	27	15.3	3.4	.330	0.2	.400	0.8	.682	0.26	0.30	0.6	4.6	2.9
March	51	16.9	3.0	.458	0.3	.429	1.3	.600	0.39	0.47	0.5	5.4	3.7
Apr/May	48	27.1	4.9	.443	0.2	.300	2.1	.600	0.48	0.83	0.9	9.0	5.7
0 Days Rest	48	25.5	5.1	.435	0.2	.111	1.8	.607	0.50	0.81	0.7	8.5	7.1
1 Days Rest	93	21.9	4.0	.433	0.1	.636	1.5	.671	0.46	0.51	0.8	7.2	4.6
2 Days Rest	26	19.6	4.3	.416	0.3	.429	1.6	.643	0.50	0.62	0.8	6.6	4.8
3+ Days Rest	28	14.2	2.5	.380	0.1	.333	1.1	.531	0.25	0.25	0.4	4.6	2.6

Danny Ferry

1999-2000 Per Game Averages

	G	Min	FGA	FG%	3PA	3P%	FTA	FT%	Blk	Stl	Ast	Reb	Pts
Total	63	21.0	6.0	.497	1.2	.440	0.9	.912	0.38	0.35	1.1	3.8	7.3
Home	31	20.9	6.3	.541	1.3	.610	1.1	.909	0.45	0.42	1.2	3.6	8.5
Road	32	21.2	5.8	.452	1.1	.235	0.8	.917	0.31	0.28	1.0	4.0	6.2
vs. Playoff	37	20.8	5.7	.472	1.0	.447	0.8	.893	0.46	0.30	0.9	3.5	6.5
vs. Non-Playoff	26	21.5	6.5	.530	1.4	.432	1.1	.931	0.27	0.42	1.3	4.2	8.5
vs. East	43	20.2	6.0	.479	1.1	.429	0.9	.925	0.35	0.35	1.2	3.5	7.1
vs. West	20	22.9	6.2	.537	1.3	.462	0.9	.882	0.45	0.35	0.7	4.4	8.0
vs. Div.	23	19.2	5.4	.492	1.0	.458	1.0	.955	0.22	0.30	1.2	3.1	6.7
As Starter	3	30.7	6.0	.389	1.3	.000	1.3	.750	0.67	1.00	2.3	6.3	5.7
Off Bench	60	20.6	6.0	.503	1.2	.465	0.9	.925	0.37	0.32	1.0	3.7	7.4
In wins	25	21.2	6.4	.547	1.1	.536	0.9	.909	0.32	0.40	1.4	4.1	8.4
In losses	38	20.9	5.8	.461	1.2	.383	0.9	.914	0.42	0.32	0.9	3.6	6.6

	G	Min	FGA	FG%	3PA	3P%	FTA	FT%	Blk	Stl	Ast	Reb	Pts
Pre All-Star	30	20.5	5.9	.477	1.1	.324	1.2	.889	0.47	0.50	1.0	4.0	7.0
Post All-Star	33	21.6	6.2	.515	1.2	.537	0.6	.952	0.30	0.21	1.1	3.5	7.6
November	11	21.6	6.9	.395	1.1	.167	1.4	.867	0.91	0.82	1.3	4.2	6.8
December	7	12.1	3.6	.560	0.4	.667	0.6	.750	0.00	0.29	0.6	2.9	4.7
January	7	21.9	6.1	.465	1.7	.333	0.9	.833	0.14	0.14	0.9	4.6	7.0
February	12	24.8	6.8	.585	1.3	.533	1.3	.938	0.50	0.33	1.1	3.7	9.9
March	15	22.1	6.1	.505	1.3	.421	0.9	1.000	0.33	0.33	1.2	3.9	7.5
April	11	20.1	5.7	.492	1.3	.643	0.3	1.000	0.18	0.09	1.1	3.4	6.7
0 Days Rest	18	20.4	6.0	.481	0.8	.400	0.9	1.000	0.28	0.28	1.1	3.3	7.1
1 Days Rest	25	21.0	6.0	.503	1.4	.457	1.1	.852	0.40	0.28	0.9	3.9	7.6
2 Days Rest	11	24.0	6.7	.527	1.4	.600	0.5	1.000	0.27	0.64	1.5	4.1	8.4
3+ Days Rest	9	19.0	5.2	.468	1.1	.200	0.9	.875	0.67	0.33	0.9	4.0	5.9

Last Five Seasons

	G	Min	FGA	FG%	3PA	3P%	FTA	FT%	Blk	Stl	Ast	Reb	Pts
Total	346	25.2	7.7	.451	2.7	.393	1.0	.826	0.35	0.53	1.5	3.2	8.9
Home	174	25.1	7.9	.457	2.9	.414	1.0	.840	0.44	0.55	1.7	3.0	9.2
Road	172	25.4	7.6	.445	2.4	.368	1.1	.813	0.26	0.51	1.3	3.3	8.5
vs. Playoff	196	25.2	7.6	.423	2.6	.367	0.9	.812	0.37	0.48	1.4	3.0	8.2
vs. Non-Playoff	150	25.3	7.8	.487	2.7	.426	1.1	.842	0.31	0.59	1.6	3.4	9.7
vs. East	241	24.9	7.6	.447	2.6	.377	1.0	.813	0.35	0.49	1.5	3.0	8.6
vs. West	105	26.1	8.1	.459	2.9	.427	0.9	.859	0.33	0.62	1.5	3.5	9.4
vs. Div.	125	24.3	7.3	.433	2.5	.355	1.0	.810	0.31	0.41	1.5	3.0	8.0
As Starter	143	33.4	10.7	.454	4.0	.387	1.4	.807	0.46	0.74	2.1	3.9	12.4
Off Bench	203	19.5	5.7	.447	1.7	.403	0.7	.852	0.27	0.38	1.1	2.7	6.4
In wins	175	24.9	7.8	.479	2.6	.456	1.1	.833	0.32	0.59	1.7	3.2	9.6
In losses	171	25.6	7.6	.421	2.7	.330	1.0	.818	0.37	0.47	1.3	3.1	8.1

	G	Min	FGA	FG%	3PA	3P%	FTA	FT%	Blk	Stl	Ast	Reb	Pts
Pre All-Star	170	24.8	7.7	.436	2.7	.366	1.1	.828	0.36	0.61	1.7	3.4	8.6
Post All-Star	126	27.4	8.5	.461	2.9	.427	1.0	.811	0.39	0.46	1.5	3.3	10.1
Oct/Nov	54	24.6	7.8	.437	2.6	.378	1.2	.781	0.44	0.57	1.4	3.6	8.1
December	48	24.7	7.6	.425	2.7	.382	1.1	.870	0.29	0.60	1.8	3.0	8.5
January	53	25.2	7.8	.426	2.6	.331	1.0	.796	0.32	0.55	1.6	3.6	8.3
February	57	23.7	7.4	.475	2.5	.393	0.8	.864	0.35	0.49	1.5	2.9	8.1
March	70	27.1	7.9	.482	2.6	.465	1.1	.813	0.27	0.56	1.3	3.0	9.1
Apr/May	64	25.6	7.8	.447	2.7	.389	0.9	.850	0.41	0.44	1.3	2.9	8.9
0 Days Rest	96	24.5	7.1	.470	2.6	.391	1.0	.876	0.34	0.56	1.3	2.9	8.4
1 Days Rest	160	25.3	7.9	.446	2.8	.374	0.9	.828	0.31	0.55	1.6	3.1	8.8
2 Days Rest	60	27.1	8.5	.447	2.6	.438	1.3	.818	0.38	0.52	1.4	3.7	9.1
3+ Days Rest	30	23.3	7.5	.431	2.4	.423	1.1	.688	0.47	0.37	1.6	3.3	8.4

Michael Finley

1999-2000 Per Game Averages

	G	Min	FGA	FG%	3PA	3P%	FTA	FT%	Blk	Stl	Ast	Reb	Pts		G	Min	FGA	FG%	3PA	3P%	FTA	FT%	Blk	Stl	Ast	Reb	Pts
Total	82	42.2	20.0	.457	3.0	.401	3.9	.820	0.39	1.33	5.3	6.3	22.6	Pre All-Star	48	42.4	20.7	.445	2.7	.359	4.1	.829	0.31	1.31	6.0	7.1	22.8
Home	41	43.1	19.4	.482	2.9	.433	3.4	.804	0.59	1.27	5.3	6.3	22.7	Post All-Star	34	42.0	18.9	.476	3.5	.445	3.5	.805	0.50	1.35	4.4	5.2	22.4
Road	41	41.4	20.5	.434	3.1	.370	4.4	.832	0.20	1.39	5.4	6.3	22.6	November	16	40.0	20.3	.437	3.0	.292	4.3	.794	0.31	1.38	4.6	7.2	22.0
vs. Playoff	48	41.6	19.5	.459	3.1	.401	3.6	.776	0.29	1.42	5.0	5.8	22.0	December	14	44.2	21.1	.429	2.6	.378	4.4	.839	0.29	1.50	5.9	8.1	22.9
vs. Non-Playoff	34	43.2	20.5	.454	2.9	.400	4.2	.874	0.53	1.21	5.8	7.0	23.5	January	13	42.4	20.3	.462	2.1	.407	3.5	.800	0.38	0.85	7.7	5.9	22.4
vs. East	30	40.9	19.5	.441	2.9	.372	3.5	.846	0.43	1.27	4.9	6.4	21.2	February	13	40.8	19.3	.446	2.6	.382	3.5	.844	0.38	1.54	4.5	5.2	21.2
vs. West	52	43.0	20.2	.466	3.1	.416	4.1	.808	0.37	1.37	5.6	6.3	23.4	March	16	42.3	19.1	.503	3.1	.400	3.7	.780	0.25	1.25	4.5	6.1	23.4
vs. Div.	24	43.8	20.2	.450	2.9	.406	4.2	.800	0.38	1.17	5.0	6.5	22.7	April	10	44.8	19.4	.469	5.1	.529	3.8	.895	0.90	1.50	5.1	4.9	24.3
As Starter	82	42.2	20.0	.457	3.0	.401	3.9	.820	0.39	1.33	5.3	6.3	22.6	0 Days Rest	18	42.5	21.2	.425	3.4	.355	4.1	.808	0.22	1.78	5.7	6.4	22.5
Off Bench	0	—	—	—	—	—	—	—	—	—	—	—	—	1 Days Rest	44	42.0	19.2	.470	3.0	.412	4.0	.818	0.39	1.14	4.7	6.1	22.6
In wins	40	43.1	19.5	.486	2.8	.513	4.5	.855	0.53	1.40	5.6	6.8	24.2	2 Days Rest	16	41.8	20.1	.449	2.5	.450	3.4	.818	0.44	1.69	6.3	6.8	21.9
In losses	42	41.5	20.4	.431	3.2	.306	3.3	.775	0.26	1.26	5.1	5.9	21.1	3+ Days Rest	4	45.3	22.0	.500	3.5	.357	3.3	.923	1.00	0.00	7.0	6.0	26.3

Career (1995-96 thru 1999-2000)

	G	Min	FGA	FG%	3PA	3P%	FTA	FT%	Blk	Stl	Ast	Reb	Pts		G	Min	FGA	FG%	3PA	3P%	FTA	FT%	Blk	Stl	Ast	Reb	Pts
Total	379	39.3	16.0	.454	2.9	.360	4.0	.794	0.35	1.21	4.2	5.2	18.8	Pre All-Star	186	37.2	15.1	.453	2.7	.335	4.0	.803	0.36	1.13	4.0	5.3	17.8
Home	192	39.9	16.0	.464	2.8	.385	4.2	.797	0.44	1.20	4.3	5.4	19.3	Post All-Star	143	41.5	16.6	.458	3.1	.396	3.9	.770	0.35	1.29	4.3	5.0	19.5
Road	187	38.7	16.0	.443	3.0	.336	3.9	.790	0.25	1.23	4.1	5.0	18.3	Oct/Nov	59	35.1	14.4	.442	3.4	.338	4.1	.763	0.41	1.10	3.4	5.2	17.0
vs. Playoff	223	39.2	16.1	.448	3.0	.362	4.0	.794	0.34	1.23	4.0	4.9	18.7	December	56	38.2	15.6	.450	2.6	.329	3.7	.832	0.25	1.09	4.3	5.6	18.0
vs. Non-Playoff	156	39.5	15.8	.463	2.7	.355	4.1	.794	0.37	1.19	4.4	5.6	18.8	January	57	37.7	15.1	.463	2.3	.315	4.0	.789	0.39	1.23	4.2	4.8	17.9
vs. East	122	40.3	16.2	.455	2.9	.370	4.1	.806	0.46	1.14	4.0	5.2	19.0	February	66	39.8	16.0	.450	2.5	.424	4.2	.798	0.38	1.47	3.7	5.0	18.8
vs. West	257	38.9	15.9	.453	2.9	.354	4.0	.788	0.30	1.25	4.2	5.2	18.6	March	82	41.7	17.0	.454	3.0	.356	4.0	.765	0.33	1.13	4.7	5.2	19.6
vs. Div.	117	38.5	15.5	.452	3.0	.379	4.1	.811	0.32	1.21	3.9	5.2	20.8	Apr/May	59	42.6	17.4	.462	3.4	.383	4.1	.831	0.34	1.25	4.5	5.5	20.8
As Starter	340	40.8	16.8	.454	2.9	.361	4.2	.794	0.36	1.29	4.4	5.4	19.6	0 Days Rest	90	39.3	16.3	.443	3.1	.371	4.3	.802	0.29	1.27	4.2	5.1	18.9
Off Bench	39	26.4	9.2	.447	3.0	.345	2.9	.786	0.23	0.59	1.7	3.6	11.5	1 Days Rest	205	39.9	16.0	.455	2.9	.342	4.0	.788	0.38	1.18	4.1	5.2	18.7
In wins	143	40.3	16.0	.494	2.4	.437	4.4	.817	0.44	1.17	4.3	5.8	20.5	2 Days Rest	63	38.5	16.4	.461	2.9	.387	4.0	.787	0.35	1.35	4.5	5.4	19.4
In losses	236	38.8	16.0	.429	3.2	.323	3.8	.777	0.29	1.24	4.1	4.8	17.7	3+ Days Rest	21	36.9	13.6	.476	2.4	.400	3.0	.841	0.33	0.90	3.7	4.8	16.4

Derek Fisher

1999-2000 Per Game Averages

	G	Min	FGA	FG%	3PA	3P%	FTA	FT%	Blk	Stl	Ast	Reb	Pts		G	Min	FGA	FG%	3PA	3P%	FTA	FT%	Blk	Stl	Ast	Reb	Pts
Total	78	23.1	6.2	.346	2.1	.313	1.9	.724	0.04	1.03	2.8	1.8	6.3	Pre All-Star	48	25.7	7.7	.351	2.8	.311	2.3	.685	0.06	1.33	3.1	2.1	7.9
Home	39	22.5	5.9	.358	2.1	.284	2.3	.705	0.05	1.15	2.7	1.7	6.4	Post All-Star	30	19.0	3.8	.327	1.0	.323	1.1	.853	0.00	0.53	2.3	1.5	3.8
Road	39	23.8	6.4	.335	2.2	.341	1.5	.754	0.03	0.90	2.8	1.9	6.2	November	15	30.6	9.3	.400	3.2	.375	3.4	.627	0.07	1.47	4.1	2.5	10.8
vs. Playoff	41	22.6	5.7	.357	2.1	.282	1.6	.738	0.00	0.95	2.6	1.7	5.9	December	15	24.2	6.1	.326	2.6	.256	2.3	.706	0.00	1.40	2.6	1.8	6.3
vs. Non-Playoff	37	23.6	6.7	.335	2.2	.346	2.2	.713	0.08	1.11	3.0	2.0	6.8	January	14	22.6	7.7	.333	2.8	.359	1.4	.800	0.14	1.07	2.6	1.9	7.3
vs. East	30	22.3	5.0	.400	1.7	.412	2.2	.754	0.00	0.83	2.8	1.8	6.3	February	13	22.9	5.2	.309	1.9	.200	1.2	.750	0.00	1.23	3.3	2.0	4.5
vs. West	48	23.6	6.9	.321	2.4	.270	1.7	.700	0.06	1.15	2.8	1.9	6.3	March	16	17.3	3.1	.340	0.3	.400	1.1	.889	0.00	0.25	1.9	1.3	3.3
vs. Div.	23	21.7	5.9	.274	2.0	.222	1.7	.763	0.04	0.83	2.3	1.6	4.9	April	5	18.0	5.0	.280	2.0	.222	1.2	.833	0.00	0.40	1.4	1.4	4.4
As Starter	22	29.5	8.6	.360	3.0	.328	3.0	.672	0.05	1.41	3.9	2.5	9.2	0 Days Rest	21	24.1	6.4	.351	2.6	.345	2.0	.714	0.05	1.29	3.0	1.5	6.8
Off Bench	56	20.6	5.3	.337	1.8	.303	1.4	.769	0.04	0.88	2.3	1.6	5.1	1 Days Rest	39	21.8	5.8	.352	1.8	.324	1.9	.767	0.05	0.90	2.4	1.8	6.1
In wins	65	23.1	5.9	.348	2.0	.333	1.9	.711	0.05	1.11	2.9	1.9	6.1	2 Days Rest	12	22.7	6.4	.390	1.8	.318	1.8	.636	0.00	0.83	2.6	1.8	6.8
In losses	13	23.2	7.5	.337	2.6	.235	1.8	.792	0.00	0.62	2.2	1.3	7.2	3+ Days Rest	6	29.0	7.5	.222	3.0	.167	1.3	.625	0.00	1.33	5.2	3.3	4.7

Career (1996-97 thru 1999-2000)

	G	Min	FGA	FG%	3PA	3P%	FTA	FT%	Blk	Stl	Ast	Reb	Pts		G	Min	FGA	FG%	3PA	3P%	FTA	FT%	Blk	Stl	Ast	Reb	Pts
Total	290	19.4	4.8	.385	1.4	.343	1.7	.724	0.05	0.89	3.0	1.8	5.4	Pre All-Star	139	17.6	4.7	.378	1.4	.304	1.8	.690	0.04	0.91	2.6	1.6	5.2
Home	144	18.9	4.6	.393	1.4	.333	1.8	.709	0.04	0.92	3.1	1.7	5.4	Post All-Star	101	20.2	4.7	.401	1.2	.365	1.6	.758	0.08	0.68	3.1	2.1	5.5
Road	146	19.8	4.9	.378	1.5	.352	1.6	.740	0.05	0.85	2.8	1.9	5.4	Oct/Nov	47	19.4	5.5	.386	1.7	.305	2.5	.672	0.02	0.70	2.9	1.9	6.4
vs. Playoff	156	18.7	4.6	.393	1.4	.344	1.6	.734	0.03	0.84	2.8	1.6	5.3	December	44	16.7	4.1	.394	1.3	.327	1.9	.659	0.00	1.05	2.4	1.3	4.9
vs. Non-Playoff	134	20.1	5.0	.377	1.4	.342	1.9	.714	0.07	0.94	3.2	2.0	5.6	January	39	15.9	4.2	.348	1.2	.326	1.0	.821	0.05	0.85	2.2	1.4	4.1
vs. East	95	18.8	4.2	.421	1.1	.383	2.0	.714	0.02	0.75	2.7	1.8	5.3	February	52	21.4	5.0	.363	1.6	.247	1.6	.765	0.10	1.10	3.4	2.0	5.3
vs. West	195	19.6	5.1	.371	1.6	.329	1.6	.730	0.05	0.95	3.1	1.8	5.4	March	64	20.5	4.6	.428	1.1	.472	1.6	.705	0.06	0.83	3.2	2.1	5.6
vs. Div.	93	18.9	4.5	.371	1.5	.377	1.4	.732	0.04	0.88	2.7	1.7	4.9	Apr/May	44	21.0	5.2	.376	1.8	.383	1.5	.818	0.05	0.80	3.5	1.9	5.8
As Starter	82	28.9	6.8	.398	2.2	.363	2.4	.727	0.10	1.27	4.9	2.8	8.0	0 Days Rest	76	21.1	5.3	.374	1.8	.350	1.8	.761	0.09	1.00	3.1	2.1	5.9
Off Bench	208	15.6	4.0	.377	1.1	.328	1.5	.722	0.03	0.74	2.2	1.4	4.4	1 Days Rest	153	18.3	4.5	.394	1.2	.361	1.7	.716	0.04	0.84	2.9	1.7	5.2
In wins	212	19.8	4.7	.396	1.4	.363	1.7	.730	0.05	0.92	3.2	1.9	5.5	2 Days Rest	36	21.1	5.0	.391	1.5	.340	1.6	.724	0.03	0.92	3.5	1.6	5.6
In losses	78	18.1	4.9	.358	1.6	.297	1.7	.708	0.05	0.78	2.5	1.5	5.2	3+ Days Rest	25	18.0	4.8	.364	1.4	.222	1.6	.650	0.00	0.80	2.7	1.8	4.9

Rick Fox

1999-2000 Per Game Averages

	G	Min	FGA	FG%	3PA	3P%	FTA	FT%	Blk	Stl	Ast	Reb	Pts		G	Min	FGA	FG%	3PA	3P%	FTA	FT%	Blk	Stl	Ast	Reb	Pts
Total	82	18.0	6.1	.414	2.2	.326	1.0	.808	0.32	0.63	1.7	2.4	6.5	Pre All-Star	48	18.1	6.5	.437	2.2	.317	1.0	.766	0.42	0.65	1.5	2.5	7.1
Home	41	18.6	6.7	.418	2.3	.323	1.2	.755	0.39	0.56	1.6	2.5	7.3	Post All-Star	34	17.8	5.5	.374	2.3	.338	0.9	.871	0.18	0.62	1.9	2.3	5.7
Road	41	17.3	5.4	.408	2.1	.329	0.7	.897	0.24	0.71	1.8	2.4	5.8	November	15	19.3	7.5	.451	1.9	.179	1.1	.824	0.67	0.93	1.5	3.3	8.1
vs. Playoff	44	17.0	5.5	.365	2.3	.243	0.8	.818	0.20	0.61	1.5	2.4	5.2	December	15	19.3	6.5	.433	1.3	.400	1.5	.739	0.27	0.47	1.7	2.9	7.3
vs. Non-Playoff	38	19.1	6.7	.461	2.1	.436	1.2	.800	0.45	0.66	1.9	2.4	8.0	January	14	15.3	5.4	.395	3.1	.341	0.4	.600	0.29	0.50	1.2	1.4	5.6
vs. East	30	18.4	6.1	.407	2.2	.284	0.8	.750	0.37	0.57	1.8	2.3	6.2	February	13	18.1	6.2	.425	2.7	.371	0.5	1.000	0.46	0.62	1.8	1.8	6.8
vs. West	52	17.7	6.1	.418	2.2	.351	1.0	.833	0.29	0.67	1.6	2.5	6.7	March	16	17.6	4.4	.380	1.9	.355	1.0	.750	0.13	0.56	2.3	2.1	4.8
vs. Div.	24	17.4	5.2	.368	1.9	.370	1.1	.692	0.25	0.67	1.8	2.5	5.3	April	9	18.1	6.8	.361	2.6	.304	1.1	1.000	0.00	0.78	1.3	3.1	6.8
As Starter	1	31.0	7.0	.571	4.0	.500	2.0	1.000	0.00	1.00	6.0	6.0	12.0	0 Days Rest	22	19.7	6.8	.396	2.1	.277	1.0	.952	0.32	0.55	2.5	2.9	6.9
Off Bench	81	17.8	6.1	.411	2.2	.322	0.9	.803	0.32	0.63	1.6	2.4	6.4	1 Days Rest	41	17.7	6.0	.411	2.1	.353	1.0	.707	0.29	0.54	1.4	2.2	6.4
In wins	67	18.2	6.1	.427	2.2	.354	1.0	.794	0.34	0.66	1.7	2.5	6.9	2 Days Rest	12	17.6	5.8	.443	2.7	.313	1.0	.917	0.42	0.75	1.8	2.5	6.9
In losses	15	16.7	5.7	.349	2.3	.206	0.7	.900	0.20	0.53	1.5	2.1	5.1	3+ Days Rest	7	14.9	4.7	.455	2.4	.353	0.6	.750	0.29	1.29	0.9	1.9	5.6

Last Five Seasons

	G	Min	FGA	FG%	3PA	3P%	FTA	FT%	Blk	Stl	Ast	Reb	Pts		G	Min	FGA	FG%	3PA	3P%	FTA	FT%	Blk	Stl	Ast	Reb	Pts
Total	365	28.4	9.5	.452	3.0	.346	2.5	.769	0.45	1.26	3.2	4.1	11.6	Pre All-Star	186	28.7	9.8	.463	2.7	.330	2.7	.783	0.50	1.38	3.2	4.6	12.1
Home	182	28.9	10.1	.469	3.1	.360	2.9	.782	0.52	1.35	3.3	4.4	12.8	Post All-Star	135	30.3	9.7	.437	3.7	.363	2.5	.755	0.46	1.30	3.6	4.1	11.7
Road	183	27.9	9.0	.433	2.8	.330	2.1	.753	0.39	1.17	3.1	3.8	10.3	Oct/Nov	56	28.2	8.8	.465	2.4	.287	2.6	.783	0.39	1.50	3.0	4.2	10.9
vs. Playoff	202	28.2	9.5	.446	3.1	.352	2.2	.776	0.38	1.23	3.1	4.2	11.3	December	59	28.4	10.2	.463	2.5	.345	2.7	.759	0.49	1.03	2.9	4.6	12.3
vs. Non-Playoff	163	28.7	9.5	.459	2.9	.338	2.9	.763	0.55	1.29	3.3	3.9	11.9	January	57	29.2	10.2	.459	2.8	.323	2.5	.804	0.63	1.53	3.6	5.1	12.3
vs. East	168	30.4	10.3	.455	3.1	.340	2.8	.762	0.46	1.43	3.3	4.5	12.6	February	64	28.8	9.8	.444	3.9	.401	2.6	.784	0.42	1.20	3.4	3.4	12.3
vs. West	197	26.7	8.9	.448	2.9	.351	2.2	.777	0.45	1.12	3.0	3.7	10.7	March	81	28.7	9.4	.447	3.6	.346	2.4	.746	0.42	1.14	3.3	3.4	11.4
vs. Div.	113	28.4	9.4	.456	2.8	.350	2.7	.763	0.46	1.29	3.0	4.2	11.7	Apr/May	48	26.6	8.5	.432	2.4	.327	2.1	.735	0.35	1.23	2.7	4.2	9.7
As Starter	240	33.3	11.1	.460	3.4	.352	3.1	.774	0.54	1.59	3.9	5.0	13.8	0 Days Rest	98	28.3	9.6	.427	2.9	.297	2.4	.796	0.46	1.28	3.2	3.9	10.9
Off Bench	125	19.0	6.6	.426	2.2	.327	1.3	.747	0.29	0.63	1.7	2.2	7.3	1 Days Rest	181	28.3	9.7	.460	3.1	.374	2.6	.761	0.46	1.14	3.0	4.1	12.1
In wins	201	26.8	8.5	.471	2.8	.361	2.4	.765	0.45	1.10	3.0	3.7	10.9	2 Days Rest	49	29.3	8.8	.483	2.9	.361	2.8	.787	0.51	1.29	3.8	4.6	11.7
In losses	164	30.4	10.8	.433	3.3	.330	2.7	.774	0.46	1.46	3.4	4.5	12.4	3+ Days Rest	37	27.8	9.7	.439	2.8	.304	1.8	.701	0.32	1.78	2.9	4.1	10.6

Adonal Foyle

1999-2000 Per Game Averages

	G	Min	FGA	FG%	3PA	3P%	FTA	FT%	Blk	Stl	Ast	Reb	Pts		G	Min	FGA	FG%	3PA	3P%	FTA	FT%	Blk	Stl	Ast	Reb	Pts
Total	76	21.8	5.0	.508	0.0	—	1.2	.378	1.79	0.34	0.6	5.6	5.5	Pre All-Star	42	21.6	5.3	.498	0.0	—	1.2	.442	1.83	0.31	0.4	5.9	5.8
Home	38	21.6	5.0	.532	0.0	—	1.1	.372	1.71	0.37	0.7	5.8	5.7	Post All-Star	34	21.9	4.6	.522	0.0	—	1.1	.289	1.74	0.38	0.8	5.2	5.1
Road	38	21.9	5.0	.484	0.0	—	1.2	.383	1.87	0.32	0.4	5.3	5.3	November	13	24.8	7.2	.468	0.0	—	0.8	.600	2.62	0.31	0.4	8.2	7.2
vs. Playoff	46	22.0	4.8	.514	0.0	—	1.3	.367	1.65	0.33	0.5	5.2	5.4	December	14	20.8	5.3	.568	0.0	—	1.5	.238	1.57	0.36	0.4	4.6	6.4
vs. Non-Playoff	30	21.4	5.3	.500	0.0	—	1.0	.400	2.00	0.37	0.6	6.1	5.7	January	9	18.8	3.4	.419	0.0	—	1.3	.500	1.33	0.22	0.2	5.2	3.6
vs. East	26	19.5	4.3	.460	0.0	—	1.4	.378	1.92	0.50	0.5	5.4	4.5	February	14	13.9	2.8	.538	0.0	—	0.9	.500	1.00	0.29	0.3	2.9	3.4
vs. West	50	22.9	5.3	.528	0.0	—	1.1	.377	1.72	0.26	0.6	5.7	6.0	March	17	23.8	4.4	.453	0.0	—	1.7	.276	2.24	0.35	0.9	5.5	4.5
vs. Div.	23	23.4	4.7	.593	0.0	—	1.7	.359	1.57	0.30	0.6	5.7	6.2	April	9	30.2	7.4	.582	0.0	—	0.7	.500	1.78	0.56	1.1	7.8	9.0
As Starter	59	24.7	5.7	.493	0.0	—	1.2	.425	1.98	0.37	0.7	6.6	6.2	0 Days Rest	18	23.8	6.2	.563	0.0	—	1.5	.407	2.06	0.39	0.3	6.8	7.6
Off Bench	17	11.5	2.5	.628	0.0	—	1.0	.176	1.12	0.24	0.2	2.1	3.4	1 Days Rest	38	21.1	4.6	.477	0.0	—	1.0	.395	1.97	0.29	0.7	5.0	4.8
In wins	16	21.3	5.6	.600	0.0	—	1.1	.389	1.75	0.31	0.5	5.4	7.2	2 Days Rest	11	21.1	4.9	.426	0.0	—	1.1	.250	0.91	0.27	0.5	6.3	4.5
In losses	60	21.9	4.8	.479	0.0	—	1.2	.375	1.80	0.36	0.6	5.6	5.1	3+ Days Rest	9	21.4	4.2	.605	0.0	—	1.4	.385	1.56	0.56	0.4	4.7	5.7

Career (1997-98 thru 1999-2000)

	G	Min	FGA	FG%	3PA	3P%	FTA	FT%	Blk	Stl	Ast	Reb	Pts		G	Min	FGA	FG%	3PA	3P%	FTA	FT%	Blk	Stl	Ast	Reb	Pts
Total	175	16.7	3.8	.468	0.0	.000	1.2	.424	1.32	0.31	0.4	4.6	4.1	Pre All-Star	78	18.2	4.5	.470	0.0	.000	1.2	.438	1.55	0.31	0.3	4.9	4.7
Home	85	16.7	3.9	.488	0.0	.000	1.0	.444	1.36	0.31	0.4	4.7	4.3	Post All-Star	53	16.9	3.8	.488	0.0	—	1.1	.339	1.26	0.28	0.6	4.3	4.1
Road	90	16.7	3.7	.448	0.0	—	1.4	.410	1.28	0.31	0.4	4.4	3.9	Oct/Nov	24	18.6	5.6	.418	0.0	—	1.0	.542	1.79	0.42	0.3	6.0	5.2
vs. Playoff	106	17.2	3.9	.463	0.0	—	1.2	.434	1.35	0.32	0.4	4.5	4.2	December	24	17.5	4.7	.545	0.0	—	1.3	.258	1.33	0.21	0.3	4.1	5.4
vs. Non-Playoff	69	15.9	3.7	.477	0.0	.000	1.1	.405	1.28	0.29	0.5	4.7	4.0	January	22	17.7	3.4	.453	0.0	.000	1.5	.469	1.50	0.32	0.3	5.0	3.8
vs. East	51	14.9	3.5	.449	0.0	—	1.2	.367	1.25	0.33	0.4	4.1	3.5	February	31	12.6	2.7	.429	0.0	—	0.8	.500	0.94	0.19	0.3	3.0	2.7
vs. West	124	17.5	4.0	.475	0.0	.000	1.2	.448	1.35	0.30	0.4	4.8	4.3	March	40	16.4	3.4	.459	0.0	—	1.3	.327	1.43	0.30	0.6	4.6	3.5
vs. Div.	57	17.6	3.9	.518	0.0	—	1.3	.395	1.18	0.32	0.4	4.6	4.6	Apr/May	34	18.3	3.9	.496	0.0	—	1.1	.526	1.09	0.41	0.6	5.1	4.4
As Starter	60	24.6	5.7	.487	0.0	—	1.3	.413	1.95	0.37	0.7	6.5	6.1	0 Days Rest	48	17.3	4.4	.479	0.0	—	1.4	.409	1.31	0.31	0.3	5.5	4.8
Off Bench	115	12.6	2.9	.448	0.0	.000	1.1	.430	0.99	0.28	0.3	3.6	3.1	1 Days Rest	76	17.3	3.8	.450	0.0	.000	1.1	.463	1.53	0.29	0.6	4.3	3.9
In wins	41	16.0	3.7	.572	0.0	—	0.9	.395	1.22	0.24	0.4	4.5	4.6	2 Days Rest	25	17.5	3.9	.469	0.0	—	1.4	.324	1.08	0.28	0.4	5.0	4.1
In losses	134	16.9	3.9	.437	0.0	.000	1.2	.430	1.35	0.33	0.4	4.6	3.9	3+ Days Rest	26	13.0	2.8	.507	0.0	—	0.9	.478	0.96	0.38	0.2	3.3	3.3

Steve Francis
Houston Rockets — Guard

1999-2000 Per Game Averages

	G	Min	FGA	FG%	3PA	3P%	FTA	FT%	Blk	Stl	Ast	Reb	Pts		G	Min	FGA	FG%	3PA	3P%	FTA	FT%	Blk	Stl	Ast	Reb	Pts
Total	77	36.1	14.5	.445	4.0	.345	4.7	.786	0.38	1.53	6.6	5.3	18.0	Pre All-Star	45	35.2	14.8	.429	3.7	.301	5.2	.775	0.38	1.49	7.0	5.2	17.8
Home	39	36.2	14.2	.435	3.6	.345	4.6	.765	0.31	1.56	7.1	5.8	17.1	Post All-Star	32	37.3	14.1	.469	4.5	.396	4.0	.806	0.38	1.59	6.1	5.5	18.3
Road	38	35.9	14.9	.455	4.5	.345	4.9	.806	0.45	1.50	6.1	4.8	19.0	November	15	35.3	14.3	.425	5.1	.303	4.7	.743	0.33	1.67	6.3	5.2	17.1
vs. Playoff	45	37.6	14.6	.451	4.6	.353	4.8	.797	0.20	1.47	6.4	5.2	18.7	December	12	34.8	13.7	.457	2.6	.290	4.7	.714	0.33	1.42	6.9	4.3	16.6
vs. Non-Playoff	32	33.9	14.3	.436	3.2	.330	4.6	.770	0.63	1.63	6.8	5.5	17.1	January	14	36.6	16.1	.447	3.1	.318	7.1	.828	0.29	1.21	8.1	6.1	21.3
vs. East	29	35.2	13.5	.429	4.1	.331	3.9	.770	0.55	1.59	5.9	4.4	15.9	February	11	33.5	13.3	.329	4.3	.298	2.6	.828	0.36	1.64	5.7	4.8	12.2
vs. West	48	36.6	15.1	.454	4.0	.354	5.3	.794	0.27	1.50	7.0	5.9	19.3	March	15	36.9	13.9	.495	5.3	.392	4.3	.846	0.33	1.87	5.6	5.1	19.5
vs. Div.	22	35.1	14.8	.409	3.4	.307	5.4	.788	0.32	1.14	6.4	5.4	17.4	April	10	39.6	15.9	.497	3.3	.485	4.6	.739	0.70	1.30	6.9	6.5	20.8
As Starter	77	36.1	14.5	.445	4.0	.345	4.7	.786	0.38	1.53	6.6	5.3	18.0	0 Days Rest	15	33.2	13.5	.424	3.9	.259	4.8	.833	0.53	1.33	5.1	4.8	16.5
Off Bench	0	—												1 Days Rest	40	36.9	15.0	.445	4.3	.368	4.6	.792	0.33	1.45	7.2	5.7	18.5
In wins	31	36.3	14.6	.480	3.6	.414	4.4	.825	0.42	1.55	7.5	5.8	19.1	2 Days Rest	17	37.3	14.9	.472	3.6	.387	4.9	.762	0.41	2.00	6.5	5.1	19.3
In losses	46	35.9	14.5	.421	4.3	.307	5.0	.763	0.35	1.52	6.0	5.0	17.3	3+ Days Rest	5	33.4	12.4	.403	3.8	.263	5.2	.692	0.20	1.20	6.0	4.8	14.6

Kevin Garnett
Minnesota Timberwolves — Forward

1999-2000 Per Game Averages

	G	Min	FGA	FG%	3PA	3P%	FTA	FT%	Blk	Stl	Ast	Reb	Pts		G	Min	FGA	FG%	3PA	3P%	FTA	FT%	Blk	Stl	Ast	Reb	Pts
Total	81	40.0	18.8	.497	1.0	.370	5.0	.765	1.56	1.48	5.0	11.8	22.9	Pre All-Star	47	39.8	19.1	.505	1.2	.439	4.4	.751	1.89	1.62	4.7	12.0	23.2
Home	40	40.4	19.5	.488	1.1	.372	5.4	.758	1.65	1.33	5.0	11.8	23.5	Post All-Star	34	40.3	18.4	.486	0.7	.208	5.7	.779	1.09	1.29	5.3	11.5	22.6
Road	41	39.7	18.2	.507	0.9	.368	4.6	.772	1.46	1.63	5.0	11.8	22.4	November	12	37.6	18.8	.476	1.7	.350	4.8	.759	2.00	1.67	4.2	11.9	22.1
vs. Playoff	44	40.7	19.6	.490	1.2	.333	5.1	.774	1.52	1.20	4.7	11.8	23.6	December	15	41.5	18.4	.486	1.3	.421	4.3	.750	2.13	1.87	5.0	13.5	21.6
vs. Non-Playoff	37	39.2	18.0	.507	0.7	.444	4.8	.753	1.59	1.81	5.2	11.9	22.2	January	15	40.7	19.9	.559	0.9	.615	3.9	.776	1.73	1.33	4.9	10.5	25.8
vs. East	30	41.6	19.4	.511	1.1	.406	5.9	.761	1.80	1.50	4.8	12.2	24.9	February	14	39.3	18.7	.466	1.1	.188	6.6	.761	1.29	1.21	5.7	12.4	22.6
vs. West	51	39.1	18.5	.489	1.0	.347	4.4	.752	1.41	1.47	5.0	11.5	21.7	March	16	40.3	18.9	.531	0.5	.375	5.5	.761	1.06	1.31	4.5	11.1	24.5
vs. Div.	23	38.3	18.5	.522	0.7	.438	4.3	.758	1.48	1.61	5.1	11.0	22.9	April	9	40.6	17.9	.422	0.6	.200	4.9	.795	1.00	1.56	5.6	11.3	19.1
As Starter	81	40.0	18.8	.497	1.0	.370	5.0	.765	1.56	1.48	5.0	11.8	22.9	0 Days Rest	18	39.4	18.7	.475	1.2	.182	5.4	.776	1.33	1.28	4.8	11.4	22.2
Off Bench	0	—												1 Days Rest	50	40.0	18.9	.507	0.8	.415	4.7	.734	1.58	1.50	5.0	11.8	22.9
In wins	50	39.8	18.4	.543	0.8	.415	4.8	.759	1.44	1.60	5.2	11.8	24.0	2 Days Rest	5	38.4	15.4	.481	0.4	.500	5.2	.846	1.20	2.20	5.8	9.8	19.4
In losses	31	40.5	19.5	.428	1.3	.325	5.3	.773	1.74	1.29	4.5	11.9	21.2	3+ Days Rest	8	42.4	20.9	.497	2.0	.500	5.9	.851	2.13	1.38	4.3	14.3	26.8

Career (1995-96 thru 1999-2000)

	G	Min	FGA	FG%	3PA	3P%	FTA	FT%	Blk	Stl	Ast	Reb	Pts		G	Min	FGA	FG%	3PA	3P%	FTA	FT%	Blk	Stl	Ast	Reb	Pts
Total	367	36.9	15.1	.489	0.4	.319	3.7	.740	1.78	1.44	3.6	9.1	17.7	Pre All-Star	179	34.9	13.6	.490	0.5	.427	3.4	.757	1.89	1.43	3.3	8.5	16.1
Home	186	37.4	15.3	.495	0.4	.316	3.8	.735	1.99	1.45	3.8	9.6	18.1	Post All-Star	141	39.0	15.8	.500	0.4	.158	4.0	.736	1.65	1.38	3.8	9.6	18.7
Road	181	36.3	14.9	.484	0.5	.321	3.6	.746	1.56	1.43	3.4	8.7	17.3	Oct/Nov	54	34.9	13.7	.459	0.7	.417	3.7	.741	2.11	1.61	3.3	8.5	15.6
vs. Playoff	200	37.0	15.3	.473	0.5	.340	3.6	.743	1.69	1.35	3.4	9.1	17.3	December	54	33.2	12.6	.487	0.5	.320	3.5	.750	1.76	1.43	3.2	8.6	14.9
vs. Non-Playoff	167	36.8	15.0	.509	0.4	.288	4.0	.737	1.89	1.55	3.9	9.1	18.2	January	56	36.4	14.3	.528	0.4	.565	2.9	.782	1.86	1.23	3.3	8.1	17.6
vs. East	124	37.2	15.1	.506	0.5	.311	3.8	.754	1.69	1.29	3.5	9.2	18.3	February	65	37.6	16.1	.468	0.3	.182	4.0	.757	1.77	1.63	3.9	10.0	18.2
vs. West	243	36.7	15.1	.481	0.4	.323	3.7	.733	1.82	1.51	3.7	9.1	17.4	March	81	39.2	16.6	.505	0.3	.192	3.9	.707	1.62	1.36	4.0	9.6	19.6
vs. Div.	110	36.5	15.3	.476	0.3	.270	3.3	.756	1.85	1.57	3.8	8.8	17.1	Apr/May	57	38.5	16.6	.484	0.3	.235	4.2	.730	1.65	1.39	3.8	9.6	19.2
As Starter	330	38.8	16.1	.493	0.4	.310	4.0	.740	1.88	1.51	3.9	9.7	19.0	0 Days Rest	86	36.3	15.1	.468	0.5	.217	3.8	.746	1.60	1.35	3.9	8.9	17.2
Off Bench	37	19.5	6.4	.407	0.5	.389	1.2	.750	0.92	0.84	1.2	3.8	6.3	1 Days Rest	201	37.5	15.4	.493	0.4	.367	3.7	.730	1.77	1.50	3.6	9.4	18.0
In wins	185	37.5	15.7	.517	0.4	.314	3.9	.759	2.01	1.66	4.1	9.6	19.4	2 Days Rest	49	36.2	14.0	.500	0.2	.182	3.6	.744	1.80	1.45	3.6	8.5	16.7
In losses	182	36.3	14.6	.459	0.5	.322	3.5	.719	1.54	1.21	3.2	8.7	16.0	3+ Days Rest	31	35.5	15.3	.505	0.8	.417	3.7	.783	2.32	1.29	3.2	8.8	18.7

Pat Garrity

Orlando Magic — Forward

1999-2000 Per Game Averages

	G	Min	FGA	FG%	3PA	3P%	FTA	FT%	Blk	Stl	Ast	Reb	Pts		G	Min	FGA	FG%	3PA	3P%	FTA	FT%	Blk	Stl	Ast	Reb	Pts
Total	82	18.0	7.1	.441	2.4	.401	1.4	.721	0.23	0.38	0.7	2.6	8.2	Pre All-Star	50	15.4	6.7	.473	1.9	.402	1.5	.730	0.20	0.30	0.6	2.1	8.2
Home	41	19.6	7.9	.460	2.9	.398	1.3	.691	0.29	0.24	0.7	3.0	9.3	Post All-Star	32	22.1	7.8	.398	3.1	.400	1.2	.703	0.28	0.50	0.9	3.2	8.3
Road	41	16.4	6.4	.418	1.9	.405	1.4	.750	0.17	0.51	0.7	2.2	7.2	November	15	15.9	6.5	.531	1.2	.333	1.7	.760	0.07	0.47	0.8	1.7	8.6
vs. Playoff	47	19.0	7.7	.456	2.6	.385	1.6	.724	0.19	0.38	0.7	2.7	9.2	December	14	15.6	7.1	.434	2.5	.400	1.9	.731	0.14	0.21	0.4	2.2	8.5
vs. Non-Playoff	35	16.8	6.4	.417	2.1	.427	1.0	.714	0.29	0.37	0.7	2.4	6.9	January	17	13.6	6.1	.442	1.6	.393	1.2	.667	0.35	0.29	0.5	2.1	6.9
vs. East	54	19.1	7.7	.434	2.5	.422	1.4	.688	0.30	0.41	0.8	2.6	8.7	February	11	23.6	9.4	.485	4.3	.426	1.4	.733	0.18	0.27	1.1	4.0	11.9
vs. West	28	16.1	6.1	.459	2.2	.355	1.2	.794	0.11	0.32	0.6	2.5	7.3	March	16	21.1	7.1	.372	2.5	.475	0.6	.700	0.25	0.38	0.9	2.8	6.9
vs. Div.	25	17.8	6.3	.449	2.3	.491	0.8	.700	0.52	0.56	0.8	2.4	7.4	April	9	21.4	7.6	.368	3.2	.310	1.6	.714	0.44	0.78	0.7	3.2	7.7
As Starter	1	26.0	9.0	.111	4.0	.000	0.0	—	0.00	0.00	2.0	4.0	2.0	0 Days Rest	22	17.8	7.7	.438	1.9	.405	1.4	.677	0.18	0.36	0.6	2.1	8.5
Off Bench	81	17.9	7.1	.446	2.4	.409	1.4	.721	0.23	0.38	0.7	2.5	8.3	1 Days Rest	42	18.5	7.0	.451	2.7	.400	1.3	.786	0.26	0.43	0.8	2.8	8.5
In wins	41	17.7	7.0	.467	2.4	.423	1.1	.652	0.22	0.22	0.6	2.4	8.2	2 Days Rest	8	14.4	4.8	.342	1.3	.300	1.0	.500	0.38	0.13	0.8	2.0	4.1
In losses	41	18.4	7.3	.417	2.4	.380	1.6	.769	0.24	0.54	0.8	2.7	8.2	3+ Days Rest	10	19.6	8.3	.458	3.3	.364	1.6	.688	0.10	0.40	0.6	3.1	9.9

Career (1998-99 thru 1999-2000)

	G	Min	FGA	FG%	3PA	3P%	FTA	FT%	Blk	Stl	Ast	Reb	Pts		G	Min	FGA	FG%	3PA	3P%	FTA	FT%	Blk	Stl	Ast	Reb	Pts
Total	121	16.7	6.2	.454	1.8	.400	1.4	.719	0.18	0.32	0.6	2.4	7.4	Pre All-Star	50	15.4	6.7	.473	1.9	.402	1.5	.730	0.20	0.30	0.6	2.1	8.2
Home	60	17.3	6.6	.489	2.1	.408	1.4	.694	0.22	0.20	0.6	2.6	8.3	Post All-Star	32	22.1	7.8	.398	3.1	.400	1.2	.703	0.28	0.50	0.9	3.2	8.3
Road	61	16.1	5.9	.416	1.5	.389	1.3	.744	0.15	0.44	0.7	2.1	6.5	Oct/Nov	15	15.9	6.5	.531	1.2	.333	1.7	.760	0.07	0.47	0.8	1.7	8.6
vs. Playoff	69	17.6	6.7	.466	1.9	.396	1.6	.743	0.14	0.32	0.7	2.5	8.1	December	14	15.6	7.1	.434	2.5	.400	1.9	.731	0.14	0.21	0.4	2.2	8.5
vs. Non-Playoff	52	15.5	5.7	.436	1.6	.407	1.1	.672	0.23	0.33	0.6	2.2	6.3	January	17	13.6	6.1	.442	1.6	.393	1.2	.667	0.35	0.29	0.5	2.1	6.9
vs. East	57	18.3	7.4	.433	2.4	.422	1.4	.692	0.20	0.39	0.8	2.5	8.5	February	21	16.8	6.4	.493	2.5	.385	1.4	.655	0.19	0.24	0.6	2.4	8.1
vs. West	64	15.2	5.2	.481	1.3	.363	1.4	.742	0.09	0.27	0.5	2.2	6.5	March	26	15.6	5.5	.359	1.6	.488	0.7	.706	0.15	0.27	0.7	1.9	5.2
vs. Div.	40	15.6	5.2	.438	1.6	.492	0.9	.676	0.35	0.43	0.7	2.0	6.0	Apr/May	28	20.4	6.4	.478	1.5	.366	1.8	.755	0.18	0.43	0.7	3.3	7.9
As Starter	10	30.6	9.9	.535	1.2	.333	2.5	.760	0.00	0.40	1.2	5.1	12.9	0 Days Rest	33	17.7	7.1	.457	1.6	.423	1.6	.717	0.15	0.33	0.7	2.3	8.3
Off Bench	111	15.4	5.9	.442	1.8	.404	1.3	.711	0.20	0.32	0.6	2.1	6.9	1 Days Rest	56	17.9	6.4	.474	2.1	.415	1.4	.772	0.23	0.38	0.7	2.6	8.1
In wins	65	16.1	6.1	.477	1.7	.409	1.2	.654	0.17	0.20	0.5	2.3	7.3	2 Days Rest	16	11.9	3.9	.323	0.6	.300	1.0	.500	0.19	0.19	0.4	1.6	3.2
In losses	56	17.3	6.4	.429	1.9	.390	1.6	.775	0.20	0.46	0.8	2.4	7.5	3+ Days Rest	16	15.0	6.1	.459	2.2	.343	1.2	.684	0.06	0.25	0.4	2.4	7.2

Chris Gatling

Denver Nuggets — Forward-Center

1999-2000 Per Game Averages

	G	Min	FGA	FG%	3PA	3P%	FTA	FT%	Blk	Stl	Ast	Reb	Pts		G	Min	FGA	FG%	3PA	3P%	FTA	FT%	Blk	Stl	Ast	Reb	Pts
Total	85	21.3	9.4	.455	0.8	.257	4.4	.713	0.27	0.96	0.8	5.9	11.9	Pre All-Star	51	22.6	10.1	.458	0.6	.310	5.0	.694	0.31	1.02	0.9	6.4	12.9
Home	36	21.8	9.5	.464	0.8	.310	4.7	.712	0.28	0.94	0.8	6.4	12.4	Post All-Star	34	19.4	8.4	.449	1.2	.220	3.5	.754	0.21	0.88	0.8	5.2	10.4
Road	49	20.9	9.4	.449	0.8	.220	4.1	.714	0.27	0.98	0.8	5.5	11.6	November	15	23.1	10.9	.528	0.4	.500	5.9	.674	0.13	1.40	0.9	7.8	15.7
vs. Playoff	47	20.7	9.4	.461	0.7	.314	4.1	.696	0.26	0.81	0.8	5.6	11.7	December	13	22.5	10.1	.435	0.8	.300	3.9	.647	0.31	1.00	1.2	5.5	11.5
vs. Non-Playoff	38	22.0	9.5	.448	0.9	.200	4.7	.732	0.29	1.16	0.9	6.2	12.2	January	17	23.6	9.9	.399	0.4	.143	6.2	.743	0.24	0.82	0.7	6.4	12.5
vs. East	41	21.7	9.3	.441	0.5	.227	4.9	.719	0.10	0.98	1.0	6.1	11.8	February	13	17.8	8.2	.467	1.5	.300	2.3	.700	0.62	0.77	0.8	4.5	9.8
vs. West	44	21.0	9.6	.468	1.1	.271	4.0	.707	0.43	0.95	0.7	5.7	12.0	March	17	23.2	10.2	.451	1.0	.235	4.5	.805	0.12	1.18	1.0	6.2	13.1
vs. Div.	21	21.3	9.6	.396	0.8	.063	4.0	.667	0.29	0.76	0.7	6.0	10.3	April	10	14.4	6.0	.450	1.0	.100	2.1	.571	0.30	0.40	0.4	4.1	6.7
As Starter	0	—	—	—	—	—	—	—	—	—	—	—	—	0 Days Rest	27	20.5	9.4	.465	0.7	.211	3.4	.717	0.19	1.00	0.9	5.4	11.3
Off Bench	85	21.3	9.4	.455	0.8	.257	4.4	.713	0.27	0.96	0.8	5.9	11.9	1 Days Rest	40	21.8	9.8	.442	1.0	.237	4.8	.774	0.20	1.03	0.9	6.4	12.6
In wins	34	19.8	8.9	.493	0.9	.367	4.0	.644	0.38	1.15	0.7	5.6	11.7	2 Days Rest	11	20.0	7.7	.459	1.0	.364	5.1	.554	0.64	0.82	0.5	4.9	10.3
In losses	51	22.4	9.8	.432	0.8	.175	4.7	.752	0.20	0.84	0.9	6.1	12.1	3+ Days Rest	7	24.0	10.3	.486	0.3	.500	5.0	.629	0.43	0.71	0.9	6.6	13.3

Last Five Seasons

	G	Min	FGA	FG%	3PA	3P%	FTA	FT%	Blk	Stl	Ast	Reb	Pts		G	Min	FGA	FG%	3PA	3P%	FTA	FT%	Blk	Stl	Ast	Reb	Pts
Total	308	21.6	9.1	.494	0.3	.236	4.1	.661	0.43	0.78	0.7	5.9	11.8	Pre All-Star	159	23.1	10.1	.492	0.2	.263	5.1	.663	0.55	0.79	0.7	6.3	13.4
Home	145	21.6	9.0	.499	0.3	.256	4.2	.636	0.49	0.70	0.8	6.1	11.8	Post All-Star	101	21.9	9.2	.511	0.4	.233	3.6	.723	0.35	0.82	0.8	6.2	12.1
Road	163	21.7	9.2	.489	0.3	.217	4.0	.683	0.38	0.85	0.7	5.7	11.8	Oct/Nov	54	24.6	11.1	.497	0.2	.333	5.8	.590	0.56	1.06	0.7	6.9	14.5
vs. Playoff	163	21.8	9.3	.486	0.3	.236	4.1	.647	0.39	0.77	0.7	5.9	11.8	December	41	22.9	9.8	.476	0.3	.250	4.5	.727	0.63	0.78	0.9	6.1	12.4
vs. Non-Playoff	145	21.4	8.9	.502	0.3	.191	4.1	.676	0.48	0.79	0.7	5.7	11.8	January	49	22.3	9.9	.492	0.2	.222	5.5	.701	0.45	0.57	0.6	6.1	13.6
vs. East	178	21.0	8.7	.491	0.2	.212	3.7	.636	0.35	0.81	0.8	5.7	10.9	February	57	19.3	7.9	.491	0.4	.250	2.8	.671	0.40	0.67	0.7	5.4	9.7
vs. West	130	22.5	9.7	.496	0.4	.250	4.7	.687	0.54	0.75	0.6	6.1	12.9	March	58	21.9	8.9	.505	0.3	.263	3.6	.657	0.31	0.88	0.8	5.7	11.5
vs. Div.	94	21.2	9.0	.512	0.2	.045	3.7	.610	0.49	0.76	0.8	5.8	11.5	Apr/May	49	18.9	7.1	.497	0.3	.125	2.8	.647	0.29	0.71	0.6	4.9	8.9
As Starter	22	30.1	12.3	.463	0.1	.000	6.4	.543	0.68	0.95	1.0	7.4	14.8	0 Days Rest	82	21.5	8.9	.469	0.3	.231	3.6	.662	0.43	0.78	0.6	5.5	10.8
Off Bench	286	21.0	8.9	.497	0.3	.244	3.9	.675	0.41	0.77	0.7	5.7	11.5	1 Days Rest	143	21.5	9.0	.492	0.3	.196	4.0	.687	0.45	0.78	0.8	5.5	11.7
In wins	137	20.9	8.9	.520	0.3	.310	4.2	.627	0.53	0.79	0.7	5.9	12.0	2 Days Rest	48	21.1	8.7	.550	0.3	.308	4.7	.638	0.44	0.77	0.6	5.4	12.6
In losses	171	22.2	9.3	.473	0.3	.170	4.0	.688	0.35	0.78	0.7	5.8	11.6	3+ Days Rest	35	22.9	10.5	.484	0.1	.500	5.2	.604	0.34	0.80	0.6	7.0	13.3

Matt Geiger

Philadelphia 76ers — Center

1999-2000 Per Game Averages

	G	Min	FGA	FG%	3PA	3P%	FTA	FT%	Blk	Stl	Ast	Reb	Pts		G	Min	FGA	FG%	3PA	3P%	FTA	FT%	Blk	Stl	Ast	Reb	Pts
Total	65	21.6	9.1	.441	0.1	.000	2.2	.779	0.34	0.45	0.6	6.0	9.7	Pre All-Star	32	23.5	9.8	.412	0.1	.000	1.9	.774	0.41	0.44	0.8	6.1	9.6
Home	33	21.4	8.7	.443	0.0	.000	2.3	.787	0.33	0.39	0.7	6.1	9.5	Post All-Star	33	19.8	8.4	.475	0.0	.000	2.4	.782	0.27	0.45	0.4	5.8	9.8
Road	32	21.9	9.4	.440	0.1	.000	2.0	.769	0.34	0.50	0.5	5.8	9.9	November	0	—											
vs. Playoff	32	21.9	8.7	.437	0.1	.000	2.0	.703	0.41	0.44	0.6	5.9	9.0	December	15	26.3	12.1	.385	0.2	.000	1.4	.762	0.60	0.60	0.9	5.7	10.4
vs. Non-Playoff	33	21.4	9.5	.446	0.1	.000	2.3	.842	0.27	0.45	0.6	6.0	10.4	January	12	23.3	8.3	.470	0.0	—	3.1	.757	0.17	0.33	0.8	7.6	10.2
vs. East	43	20.8	8.4	.439	0.0	.000	2.3	.828	0.30	0.42	0.5	6.1	9.3	February	12	17.0	7.5	.400	0.0	—	1.8	.810	0.25	0.42	0.5	4.4	7.4
vs. West	22	23.2	10.3	.445	0.1	.000	1.9	.659	0.41	0.50	0.8	5.6	10.4	March	16	20.9	8.9	.455	0.1	.000	2.3	.806	0.31	0.31	0.3	6.2	9.9
vs. Div.	17	20.2	7.2	.472	0.1	.000	2.5	.907	0.41	0.41	0.5	5.5	9.1	April	10	19.3	7.4	.568	0.0	—	2.5	.760	0.30	0.60	0.4	5.8	10.3
As Starter	20	27.7	11.7	.412	0.2	.000	2.1	.683	0.65	0.55	0.9	6.6	11.0	0 Days Rest	15	22.3	9.5	.521	0.1	.000	1.6	.792	0.60	0.53	0.7	5.7	11.1
Off Bench	45	18.9	7.9	.461	0.0	—	2.2	.818	0.20	0.40	0.5	5.7	9.1	1 Days Rest	35	20.9	8.8	.427	0.1	.000	2.4	.812	0.23	0.37	0.4	6.0	9.5
In wins	41	21.3	9.1	.469	0.0	.000	2.4	.784	0.29	0.46	0.5	6.0	10.1	2 Days Rest	7	17.6	7.4	.385	0.0	—	1.7	.833	0.14	0.57	0.9	5.1	7.1
In losses	24	22.2	9.0	.394	0.1	.000	1.8	.767	0.42	0.42	0.8	5.9	8.5	3+ Days Rest	8	27.1	11.0	.398	0.0	—	2.4	.579	0.50	0.50	0.9	6.8	10.1

Last Five Seasons

	G	Min	FGA	FG%	3PA	3P%	FTA	FT%	Blk	Stl	Ast	Reb	Pts		G	Min	FGA	FG%	3PA	3P%	FTA	FT%	Blk	Stl	Ast	Reb	Pts
Total	319	25.6	9.0	.492	0.2	.229	2.8	.741	0.75	0.63	0.9	6.8	10.9	Pre All-Star	149	23.6	8.1	.484	0.2	.226	2.5	.728	0.72	0.60	0.8	6.4	9.7
Home	162	25.6	9.0	.491	0.1	.208	2.9	.752	0.88	0.75	1.0	7.2	11.0	Post All-Star	120	26.1	9.2	.508	0.1	.250	2.8	.727	0.76	0.61	0.8	7.2	11.4
Road	157	25.6	9.0	.493	0.2	.250	2.6	.729	0.61	0.51	0.8	6.5	10.8	Oct/Nov	42	21.5	6.9	.500	0.4	.313	3.0	.742	0.64	0.62	0.7	5.7	9.2
vs. Playoff	167	25.7	9.0	.466	0.2	.250	2.7	.718	0.71	0.67	0.9	6.6	10.4	December	56	22.5	8.0	.455	0.2	.182	2.0	.766	0.68	0.64	0.6	5.4	8.8
vs. Non-Playoff	152	25.6	9.0	.522	0.1	.167	2.9	.765	0.80	0.59	0.8	7.0	11.5	January	40	27.0	9.3	.484	0.1	.000	2.7	.679	0.80	0.48	0.9	8.4	10.9
vs. East	223	25.6	8.7	.491	0.1	.194	2.9	.758	0.74	0.68	0.9	6.7	10.7	February	50	28.0	10.1	.490	0.0	.000	2.8	.755	1.08	0.70	0.9	7.1	12.0
vs. West	96	25.8	9.7	.495	0.2	.294	2.6	.699	0.76	0.53	0.8	7.0	11.5	March	76	26.1	9.5	.502	0.1	.200	3.1	.766	0.70	0.68	0.8	7.0	11.9
vs. Div.	106	25.2	8.6	.496	0.2	.176	2.9	.758	0.85	0.68	0.8	6.5	10.7	Apr/May	55	28.2	9.7	.513	0.1	.400	3.0	.718	0.64	0.62	1.2	7.4	12.1
As Starter	165	30.9	10.9	.493	0.2	.276	3.1	.725	0.99	0.76	1.1	8.1	13.0	0 Days Rest	80	25.4	8.9	.483	0.1	.111	2.6	.771	0.73	0.68	0.9	6.5	10.6
Off Bench	154	20.0	7.0	.491	0.1	.158	2.5	.763	0.49	0.49	0.6	5.4	8.7	1 Days Rest	163	25.8	9.0	.497	0.2	.231	2.9	.747	0.65	0.61	0.8	7.1	11.2
In wins	190	25.4	9.0	.510	0.2	.258	2.9	.740	0.79	0.68	0.8	7.1	11.4	2 Days Rest	43	26.0	9.3	.507	0.3	.333	2.4	.641	1.09	0.81	0.9	7.0	11.1
In losses	129	26.0	8.9	.465	0.1	.176	2.6	.743	0.69	0.57	0.9	6.5	10.3	3+ Days Rest	33	25.1	8.7	.467	0.0	.000	3.0	.755	0.85	0.39	0.9	6.2	10.4

Kendall Gill

New Jersey Nets — Guard-Forward

1999-2000 Per Game Averages

	G	Min	FGA	FG%	3PA	3P%	FTA	FT%	Blk	Stl	Ast	Reb	Pts		G	Min	FGA	FG%	3PA	3P%	FTA	FT%	Blk	Stl	Ast	Reb	Pts
Total	76	31.0	12.6	.414	1.0	.256	3.4	.710	0.54	1.83	2.8	3.7	13.1	Pre All-Star	43	30.3	12.3	.416	1.3	.263	3.0	.729	0.56	1.95	2.5	3.7	12.8
Home	39	31.1	12.2	.432	1.1	.302	4.0	.745	0.62	2.18	3.0	3.8	13.8	Post All-Star	33	31.9	12.9	.412	0.6	.238	3.8	.690	0.52	1.67	3.1	3.8	13.4
Road	37	30.9	13.0	.396	0.9	.200	2.6	.653	0.46	1.46	2.5	3.7	12.2	November	11	29.2	10.4	.377	0.6	.000	2.9	.656	0.45	2.27	2.2	3.5	9.7
vs. Playoff	42	31.0	12.0	.412	0.9	.189	3.6	.671	0.57	1.71	2.4	3.7	12.5	December	14	28.8	12.8	.419	2.0	.357	1.6	.739	0.79	1.93	2.3	3.7	12.6
vs. Non-Playoff	34	31.0	13.3	.417	1.2	.317	3.0	.767	0.50	1.97	3.2	3.8	13.8	January	13	30.7	12.6	.396	1.1	.286	4.5	.712	0.46	1.77	2.8	4.2	13.5
vs. East	52	31.5	13.2	.418	1.2	.283	3.1	.687	0.62	1.85	2.9	3.8	13.5	February	12	35.1	14.6	.440	1.3	.125	3.6	.791	0.83	2.00	2.8	4.0	15.8
vs. West	24	29.9	11.3	.406	0.8	.167	3.8	.750	0.38	1.79	2.5	3.5	12.2	March	16	29.3	11.1	.427	0.5	.250	3.4	.673	0.31	1.44	2.5	2.6	11.9
vs. Div.	24	33.4	14.2	.415	1.3	.375	3.5	.714	0.54	2.00	3.0	4.0	14.8	April	10	34.2	14.6	.411	0.5	.400	4.3	.698	0.40	1.70	4.4	4.9	15.2
As Starter	75	31.1	12.6	.414	1.0	.256	3.3	.705	0.52	1.83	2.8	3.7	13.1	0 Days Rest	18	31.2	13.7	.467	1.6	.286	2.7	.688	0.39	1.67	2.7	3.4	15.1
Off Bench	1	26.0	11.0	.455	0.0		4.0	1.000	2.00	2.00	0.0	2.0	14.0	1 Days Rest	42	30.0	12.0	.388	0.9	.306	3.5	.728	0.48	1.64	2.7	3.6	12.1
In wins	30	30.6	12.9	.455	1.0	.323	3.5	.755	0.57	2.30	3.2	4.0	14.7	2 Days Rest	8	32.9	13.3	.453	0.4	.000	4.0	.688	0.75	3.25	3.6	3.8	14.8
In losses	46	31.3	12.4	.387	1.0	.213	3.2	.678	0.52	1.52	2.5	3.6	12.0	3+ Days Rest	8	34.0	12.8	.373	1.4	.091	3.5	.679	1.00	1.75	2.5	5.0	12.0

Last Five Seasons

	G	Min	FGA	FG%	3PA	3P%	FTA	FT%	Blk	Stl	Ast	Reb	Pts		G	Min	FGA	FG%	3PA	3P%	FTA	FT%	Blk	Stl	Ast	Reb	Pts
Total	336	34.5	13.4	.431	1.5	.299	4.3	.743	0.60	1.93	3.3	4.9	15.2	Pre All-Star	182	35.2	13.6	.438	1.8	.300	4.4	.764	0.64	1.79	3.7	5.2	15.8
Home	166	34.0	13.0	.441	1.4	.328	4.8	.753	0.72	2.10	3.4	5.0	15.5	Post All-Star	104	34.2	13.8	.433	1.4	.317	4.7	.758	0.50	1.80	3.0	4.4	15.9
Road	170	34.9	13.8	.422	1.5	.272	3.9	.730	0.48	1.76	3.3	4.8	14.9	Oct/Nov	53	34.2	12.8	.422	1.4	.267	4.3	.758	0.60	1.79	4.0	5.1	14.4
vs. Playoff	186	34.8	13.5	.415	1.5	.267	4.4	.751	0.59	1.78	3.2	5.0	14.9	December	58	34.2	13.1	.440	1.8	.274	4.1	.748	0.81	1.81	3.8	5.3	15.1
vs. Non-Playoff	150	34.0	13.2	.451	1.4	.341	4.3	.732	0.61	2.11	3.5	4.8	15.6	January	55	36.5	14.1	.447	2.1	.372	4.9	.776	0.58	1.73	3.4	5.3	17.2
vs. East	231	34.5	13.4	.429	1.4	.310	4.2	.736	0.57	1.99	3.2	4.9	15.0	February	56	34.7	14.3	.428	1.7	.274	4.3	.785	0.57	1.84	3.2	4.8	16.1
vs. West	105	34.4	13.5	.436	1.6	.278	4.8	.756	0.66	1.78	3.6	5.0	15.7	March	62	32.4	12.0	.404	1.0	.203	4.4	.696	0.45	1.85	2.6	4.2	12.9
vs. Div.	102	35.1	13.7	.429	1.5	.323	4.1	.730	0.60	2.18	3.3	5.0	15.3	Apr/May	52	35.1	14.2	.444	0.9	.404	4.1	.689	0.58	2.58	3.1	4.8	15.8
As Starter	330	34.6	13.5	.431	1.5	.303	4.4	.743	0.60	1.94	3.4	4.9	15.3	0 Days Rest	94	35.1	13.5	.428	1.5	.299	4.6	.754	0.40	1.82	3.4	5.2	15.4
Off Bench	6	24.2	9.7	.414	1.0	.000	2.5	.733	0.33	1.00	2.2	3.5	9.8	1 Days Rest	163	34.0	13.4	.437	1.4	.330	4.2	.740	0.71	2.00	3.1	4.7	15.3
In wins	135	34.4	13.0	.464	1.4	.339	4.9	.740	0.71	2.18	3.6	4.9	16.2	2 Days Rest	43	34.3	13.2	.440	1.5	.288	4.3	.707	0.65	2.07	3.7	4.9	15.1
In losses	201	34.5	13.6	.410	1.6	.276	4.0	.745	0.52	1.76	3.2	4.9	14.6	3+ Days Rest	36	34.9	13.3	.402	1.6	.186	4.3	.766	0.56	1.69	3.5	5.3	14.3

Brian Grant

Portland Trail Blazers — Forward

1999-2000 Per Game Averages

	G	Min	FGA	FG%	3PA	3P%	FTA	FT%	Blk	Stl	Ast	Reb	Pts
Total	63	21.0	5.6	.491	0.0	.500	2.6	.675	0.44	0.51	1.0	5.5	7.3
Home	32	21.4	5.6	.511	0.0	.000	2.7	.678	0.41	0.50	1.2	5.6	7.6
Road	31	20.6	5.5	.471	0.0	1.000	2.5	.671	0.48	0.52	0.9	5.3	7.0
vs. Playoff	34	20.6	5.5	.495	0.0	—	2.4	.659	0.32	0.38	1.0	5.5	7.1
vs. Non-Playoff	29	21.5	5.7	.488	0.1	.500	2.9	.690	0.59	0.66	1.0	5.4	7.6
vs. East	23	18.0	4.6	.453	0.0	.000	2.2	.765	0.35	0.48	1.0	4.6	5.9
vs. West	40	22.7	6.2	.508	0.0	1.000	2.9	.635	0.50	0.53	1.1	6.0	8.1
vs. Div.	18	21.2	5.6	.510	0.0	—	2.8	.647	0.28	0.50	0.8	5.2	7.5
As Starter	14	27.3	7.9	.573	0.1	1.000	4.1	.667	0.43	0.79	1.1	6.5	11.8
Off Bench	49	19.2	4.9	.455	0.0	.000	2.2	.679	0.45	0.43	1.0	5.2	6.0
In wins	46	20.7	5.2	.532	0.0	.680	2.8	.680	0.37	0.50	0.9	5.9	7.4
In losses	17	21.8	6.8	.409	0.1	1.000	2.2	.658	0.65	0.53	1.4	6.1	7.1

	G	Min	FGA	FG%	3PA	3P%	FTA	FT%	Blk	Stl	Ast	Reb	Pts
Pre All-Star	41	20.6	5.6	.472	0.0	—	2.6	.682	0.44	0.44	0.9	5.5	7.1
Post All-Star	22	21.7	5.5	.529	0.1	.500	2.7	.661	0.45	0.64	1.2	5.4	7.6
November	8	13.6	4.4	.429	0.0	—	1.9	.733	0.13	0.50	0.4	4.4	5.1
December	13	21.6	6.6	.442	0.0	—	2.4	.581	0.69	0.46	0.8	5.7	7.2
January	14	23.0	5.4	.507	0.0	—	2.9	.683	0.57	0.43	1.2	5.5	7.4
February	13	20.6	4.7	.459	0.1	.000	3.2	.786	0.15	0.62	0.5	5.4	6.8
March	4	18.5	4.5	.611	0.0	—	1.5	.500	0.00	0.00	2.3	4.0	6.3
April	11	24.4	7.0	.558	0.1	1.000	2.8	.613	0.73	0.73	1.5	6.5	9.6
0 Days Rest	16	20.9	5.4	.368	0.1	.500	2.7	.721	0.44	0.56	0.8	5.2	6.0
1 Days Rest	30	21.7	6.0	.544	0.0	—	3.0	.633	0.37	0.53	1.0	5.6	8.4
2 Days Rest	10	21.7	5.5	.509	0.0	—	2.3	.783	0.80	0.40	1.1	5.9	7.4
3+ Days Rest	7	16.9	4.3	.500	0.0	—	1.4	.600	0.29	0.43	1.4	4.9	5.1

Last Five Seasons

	G	Min	FGA	FG%	3PA	3P%	FTA	FT%	Blk	Stl	Ast	Reb	Pts
Total	274	28.4	8.5	.494	0.1	.250	3.9	.748	0.86	0.57	1.4	7.5	11.4
Home	135	29.1	8.8	.503	0.0	.500	4.2	.741	0.90	0.59	1.4	7.9	12.0
Road	139	27.6	8.3	.486	0.1	.188	3.6	.756	0.82	0.55	1.3	7.2	10.7
vs. Playoff	147	28.2	8.2	.492	0.1	.111	3.9	.738	0.78	0.49	1.4	7.3	10.9
vs. Non-Playoff	127	28.6	9.0	.497	0.1	.364	3.8	.760	0.95	0.66	1.3	7.8	11.9
vs. East	79	26.3	7.6	.508	0.1	.125	4.0	.763	0.95	0.52	1.3	6.4	10.8
vs. West	195	29.2	8.9	.490	0.1	.333	3.9	.742	0.82	0.59	1.4	8.0	11.6
vs. Div.	91	28.8	8.8	.488	0.1	.500	4.0	.736	0.78	0.46	1.4	7.8	11.6
As Starter	199	31.9	9.8	.504	0.1	.278	4.4	.759	0.99	0.61	1.5	8.4	13.3
Off Bench	75	19.1	5.1	.445	0.0	.200	2.5	.699	0.49	0.47	0.9	5.0	6.3
In wins	161	28.0	8.5	.511	0.0	.200	4.2	.745	0.78	0.57	1.2	7.7	11.8
In losses	113	29.0	8.6	.471	0.1	.267	3.5	.754	0.96	0.57	1.5	7.2	10.8

	G	Min	FGA	FG%	3PA	3P%	FTA	FT%	Blk	Stl	Ast	Reb	Pts
Pre All-Star	114	26.7	8.4	.497	0.0	.000	3.7	.724	0.87	0.56	1.4	7.0	11.1
Post All-Star	112	28.6	8.9	.497	0.2	.294	3.8	.737	0.91	0.63	1.3	7.0	11.7
Oct/Nov	43	28.7	9.3	.477	0.0	.000	4.2	.722	1.02	0.65	1.3	7.9	11.9
December	34	26.1	7.9	.500	0.0	—	3.4	.704	0.82	0.74	1.2	6.7	10.3
January	28	25.8	8.1	.527	0.0	—	3.4	.740	0.79	0.32	1.7	6.3	11.0
February	46	26.1	7.1	.479	0.1	.400	3.9	.742	0.85	0.48	1.0	7.3	9.7
March	62	29.6	9.0	.488	0.1	.250	4.3	.781	0.77	0.55	1.5	7.7	12.2
Apr/May	61	31.0	9.2	.506	0.1	.200	3.8	.761	0.89	0.62	1.5	8.2	12.2
0 Days Rest	71	27.8	8.6	.452	0.2	.273	4.1	.791	0.76	0.62	1.3	7.9	11.0
1 Days Rest	131	29.1	8.9	.518	0.1	.250	4.1	.738	0.93	0.47	1.3	7.6	12.3
2 Days Rest	40	29.0	8.1	.512	0.0	—	3.2	.693	0.83	0.63	1.6	7.3	10.5
3+ Days Rest	32	26.0	7.4	.464	0.0	—	3.4	.745	0.81	0.81	1.5	6.7	9.4

Horace Grant

Seattle SuperSonics — Forward

1999-2000 Per Game Averages

	G	Min	FGA	FG%	3PA	3P%	FTA	FT%	Blk	Stl	Ast	Reb	Pts
Total	76	35.4	7.9	.444	0.1	.000	1.5	.721	0.79	0.72	2.5	7.8	8.1
Home	35	34.7	7.6	.475	0.1	.000	1.8	.683	0.63	0.66	2.3	8.1	8.4
Road	41	36.0	8.1	.419	0.0	.000	1.2	.771	0.93	0.78	2.6	7.5	7.7
vs. Playoff	39	36.2	7.7	.395	0.1	.000	1.7	.662	0.82	0.67	2.4	7.9	7.2
vs. Non-Playoff	37	34.5	8.1	.493	0.0	.000	1.2	.804	0.76	0.78	2.6	7.6	9.0
vs. East	27	34.5	7.3	.413	0.1	.000	1.6	.773	0.70	0.44	2.2	7.6	7.3
vs. West	49	35.9	8.2	.459	0.0	.000	1.4	.687	0.84	0.88	2.6	7.9	8.5
vs. Div.	23	36.9	8.3	.395	0.0	.000	1.3	.700	0.74	0.87	2.2	8.3	7.4
As Starter	76	35.4	7.9	.444	0.1	.000	1.5	.721	0.79	0.72	2.5	7.8	8.1
Off Bench	0	—	—	—	—	—	—	—	—	—	—	—	—
In wins	43	35.8	8.3	.479	0.0	.000	1.4	.710	0.77	0.84	2.6	8.0	9.0
In losses	33	34.8	7.3	.392	0.1	.000	1.5	.735	0.82	0.58	2.3	7.5	6.8

	G	Min	FGA	FG%	3PA	3P%	FTA	FT%	Blk	Stl	Ast	Reb	Pts
Pre All-Star	47	35.6	8.0	.439	0.1	.000	1.4	.703	0.77	0.74	2.6	7.8	8.0
Post All-Star	29	35.0	7.7	.453	0.0	.000	1.6	.745	0.83	0.69	2.2	7.8	8.2
November	15	37.6	10.0	.487	0.1	.000	1.5	.739	0.60	1.00	2.5	8.3	10.9
December	12	34.7	7.6	.352	0.0	—	1.5	.778	0.83	0.42	2.6	9.1	6.5
January	14	33.8	6.5	.484	0.1	.000	1.5	.619	0.86	0.93	2.6	7.1	7.2
February	13	34.6	6.7	.356	0.0	—	0.7	.778	0.85	0.38	2.5	6.5	5.3
March	13	36.0	8.2	.472	0.1	.000	2.0	.846	0.54	0.92	1.5	7.3	9.4
April	9	35.2	8.2	.486	0.0	—	1.6	.500	1.22	0.56	3.4	8.7	8.8
0 Days Rest	18	38.1	7.8	.475	0.1	.000	1.6	.724	0.89	1.06	2.5	7.9	8.6
1 Days Rest	38	34.9	8.4	.443	0.0	—	1.5	.719	0.76	0.58	2.5	7.9	8.5
2 Days Rest	12	35.8	7.8	.398	0.2	.000	1.4	.765	0.75	0.92	2.1	8.7	7.3
3+ Days Rest	8	30.6	5.9	.447	0.1	.000	1.0	.625	0.75	0.38	2.0	5.6	5.9

Last Five Seasons

	G	Min	FGA	FG%	3PA	3P%	FTA	FT%	Blk	Stl	Ast	Reb	Pts
Total	332	35.9	9.9	.476	0.1	.080	2.3	.708	1.02	1.04	2.3	8.4	11.0
Home	164	36.4	9.5	.484	0.1	.000	2.5	.697	1.11	1.13	2.4	8.7	11.0
Road	168	35.5	10.3	.468	0.1	.125	2.1	.720	0.93	0.95	2.3	7.9	11.1
vs. Playoff	176	36.5	9.5	.449	0.1	.000	2.3	.686	0.95	0.93	2.2	8.3	10.1
vs. Non-Playoff	156	35.3	10.3	.503	0.1	.133	2.3	.733	1.10	1.17	2.5	8.2	12.1
vs. East	210	35.4	10.1	.474	0.1	.067	2.3	.722	1.00	0.95	2.2	8.1	11.2
vs. West	122	36.8	9.6	.479	0.1	.100	2.3	.682	1.05	1.20	2.6	8.5	10.8
vs. Div.	103	35.7	10.4	.475	0.0	.000	2.3	.705	0.92	1.11	2.2	8.6	11.5
As Starter	331	36.0	9.9	.476	0.1	.080	2.3	.708	1.02	1.04	2.4	8.3	11.1
Off Bench	1	25.0	8.0	.500	0.0	—	3.0	.667	1.00	2.00	2.0	6.0	10.0
In wins	199	36.1	10.1	.497	0.1	.000	2.5	.723	1.10	1.15	2.5	8.6	11.8
In losses	133	35.8	9.5	.443	0.1	.167	2.1	.680	0.90	0.88	2.2	7.7	9.9

	G	Min	FGA	FG%	3PA	3P%	FTA	FT%	Blk	Stl	Ast	Reb	Pts
Pre All-Star	157	36.4	10.0	.463	0.1	.077	2.6	.689	1.04	1.06	2.6	8.4	11.0
Post All-Star	125	36.4	10.1	.507	0.1	.000	2.3	.742	0.91	1.06	2.3	8.6	12.0
Oct/Nov	53	36.0	10.2	.469	0.1	.000	2.9	.691	0.89	1.11	2.2	8.7	11.5
December	47	37.7	9.8	.415	0.2	.125	2.5	.716	1.21	0.96	2.7	8.7	9.9
January	42	35.5	9.7	.506	0.0	.000	2.5	.663	1.00	1.19	2.8	7.8	11.5
February	65	36.0	9.9	.474	0.1	.000	1.7	.743	1.00	1.05	2.4	8.3	10.7
March	74	35.9	9.8	.488	0.1	.000	2.2	.739	0.95	1.12	1.9	8.2	11.1
Apr/May	51	34.5	10.0	.497	0.1	.333	2.4	.683	1.12	0.78	2.4	7.7	11.5
0 Days Rest	82	36.1	9.7	.469	0.0	.000	2.3	.693	0.94	1.00	2.2	8.3	10.7
1 Days Rest	167	36.3	10.0	.474	0.1	.077	2.3	.705	1.06	1.07	2.5	8.1	11.1
2 Days Rest	40	36.2	9.9	.501	0.1	.000	2.2	.739	1.03	1.20	2.2	8.8	11.6
3+ Days Rest	43	33.8	9.7	.472	0.1	.333	2.4	.718	1.00	0.84	2.3	8.5	10.9

A.C. Green
Los Angeles Lakers — Forward

1999-2000 Per Game Averages

	G	Min	FGA	FG%	3PA	3P%	FTA	FT%	Blk	Stl	Ast	Reb	Pts		G	Min	FGA	FG%	3PA	3P%	FTA	FT%	Blk	Stl	Ast	Reb	Pts
Total	82	23.5	4.7	.447	0.0	.250	1.2	.695	0.22	0.65	1.0	5.9	5.0	Pre All-Star	48	24.4	4.8	.470	0.1	.250	1.3	.719	0.19	0.75	0.8	6.3	5.5
Home	41	23.0	4.7	.459	0.0	.000	1.3	.722	0.24	0.68	1.2	6.2	5.3	Post All-Star	34	22.3	4.6	.414	0.0	—	0.9	.645	0.26	0.50	1.2	5.5	4.4
Road	41	24.0	4.7	.435	0.0	.500	1.0	.659	0.20	0.61	0.8	5.7	4.8	November	15	27.6	5.5	.434	0.1	1.000	2.2	.727	0.07	1.00	1.1	7.7	6.5
vs. Playoff	44	23.5	4.6	.412	0.0	.000	0.9	.634	0.25	0.73	0.9	5.9	4.4	December	15	24.3	4.5	.515	0.1	.000	1.4	.762	0.33	0.47	0.7	6.1	5.7
vs. Non-Playoff	38	23.5	4.8	.486	0.1	.500	1.4	.741	0.18	0.55	1.1	6.0	5.8	January	14	21.4	4.1	.431	0.1	.000	0.6	.625	0.21	0.93	0.9	4.6	3.9
vs. East	30	22.4	4.8	.407	0.0	.000	0.6	.611	0.27	0.63	1.2	5.2	4.3	February	13	25.2	5.9	.455	0.0	—	0.5	.333	0.15	0.46	0.9	6.2	5.5
vs. West	52	24.2	4.7	.471	0.1	.333	1.5	.714	0.19	0.65	0.8	6.3	5.5	March	16	19.9	4.1	.409	0.0	—	0.9	.800	0.44	0.50	1.0	5.0	4.1
vs. Div.	24	23.4	4.3	.442	0.1	.000	1.9	.739	0.25	0.67	0.7	6.3	5.3	April	9	22.9	3.9	.429	0.0	—	1.3	.583	0.00	0.44	1.4	6.1	4.1
As Starter	82	23.5	4.7	.447	0.0	.250	1.2	.695	0.22	0.65	1.0	5.9	5.0	0 Days Rest	22	24.6	5.3	.419	0.1	.500	1.9	.714	0.32	0.64	1.0	6.0	5.9
Off Bench	0	—	—	—	—	—	—	—	—	—	—	—	—	1 Days Rest	41	22.1	4.3	.444	0.0	.000	0.7	.724	0.17	0.56	0.9	5.6	4.4
In wins	67	23.2	4.7	.447	0.0	.500	1.1	.716	0.24	0.60	0.9	6.1	5.0	2 Days Rest	12	24.7	4.6	.491	0.0	—	1.8	.619	0.17	1.08	0.9	6.8	5.6
In losses	15	24.9	4.9	.446	0.1	.000	1.4	.619	0.13	0.87	1.2	5.3	5.4	3+ Days Rest	7	26.1	5.3	.486	0.0	—	0.4	.667	0.29	0.43	1.3	6.6	5.4

Last Five Seasons

	G	Min	FGA	FG%	3PA	3P%	FTA	FT%	Blk	Stl	Ast	Reb	Pts		G	Min	FGA	FG%	3PA	3P%	FTA	FT%	Blk	Stl	Ast	Reb	Pts
Total	379	26.7	5.6	.462	0.2	.182	2.0	.684	0.24	0.72	1.0	6.8	6.5	Pre All-Star	186	28.0	5.6	.475	0.3	.291	2.3	.678	0.18	0.70	1.1	7.3	7.0
Home	192	27.0	5.7	.452	0.3	.146	2.2	.685	0.26	0.71	1.0	7.3	6.6	Post All-Star	143	27.7	5.6	.457	0.2	.000	1.9	.713	0.35	0.80	1.0	7.0	6.4
Road	187	26.4	5.4	.472	0.2	.225	1.7	.682	0.22	0.73	0.9	6.4	6.4	Oct/Nov	58	29.1	6.2	.457	0.3	.150	2.7	.726	0.12	0.72	1.4	7.9	7.6
vs. Playoff	219	26.2	5.3	.452	0.2	.102	1.7	.673	0.25	0.71	0.9	6.6	5.9	December	57	28.1	5.9	.478	0.3	.375	2.1	.730	0.18	0.61	1.0	7.0	7.3
vs. Non-Playoff	160	27.3	5.9	.474	0.2	.282	2.3	.695	0.23	0.74	1.0	7.1	7.3	January	58	28.4	5.3	.476	0.3	.368	2.2	.576	0.22	0.81	1.1	7.1	6.4
vs. East	122	26.2	5.4	.471	0.2	.130	1.7	.673	0.28	0.64	1.0	6.5	6.2	February	66	25.3	5.3	.442	0.1	.000	1.7	.624	0.24	0.61	0.8	6.6	5.8
vs. West	257	26.9	5.6	.457	0.3	.200	2.1	.688	0.23	0.76	1.0	7.0	6.6	March	82	25.4	5.8	.456	0.2	.000	1.7	.752	0.34	0.74	0.8	6.4	6.5
vs. Div.	117	26.9	5.2	.465	0.2	.174	2.2	.725	0.21	0.78	0.8	7.0	6.5	Apr/May	58	24.6	4.7	.469	0.1	.000	1.6	.667	0.31	0.84	0.8	6.2	5.5
As Starter	294	29.3	6.2	.468	0.2	.206	2.0	.700	0.27	0.79	1.1	7.6	7.3	0 Days Rest	94	26.4	5.3	.452	0.2	.136	1.9	.669	0.24	0.74	1.1	6.6	6.1
Off Bench	85	17.5	3.4	.420	0.2	.100	1.7	.615	0.14	0.51	0.6	4.4	3.9	1 Days Rest	202	26.1	5.5	.463	0.2	.130	1.7	.689	0.23	0.71	0.8	6.7	6.3
In wins	170	24.9	5.3	.472	0.2	.276	1.9	.707	0.22	0.69	1.0	6.6	6.4	2 Days Rest	59	27.7	5.6	.446	0.2	.200	2.3	.677	0.15	0.78	1.2	7.2	6.6
In losses	209	28.1	5.8	.454	0.3	.136	2.0	.665	0.26	0.75	1.0	7.0	6.6	3+ Days Rest	24	29.6	6.6	.519	0.4	.500	3.4	.707	0.54	0.58	1.0	8.0	9.5

Adrian Griffin
Boston Celtics — Guard-Forward

1999-2000 Per Game Averages

	G	Min	FGA	FG%	3PA	3P%	FTA	FT%	Blk	Stl	Ast	Reb	Pts		G	Min	FGA	FG%	3PA	3P%	FTA	FT%	Blk	Stl	Ast	Reb	Pts
Total	72	26.8	5.7	.424	0.8	.281	2.2	.753	0.21	1.61	2.5	5.2	6.7	Pre All-Star	40	31.7	6.9	.462	1.2	.319	2.6	.760	0.23	1.78	3.2	6.6	8.8
Home	36	27.4	5.8	.401	0.9	.265	2.5	.725	0.22	1.78	2.8	6.0	6.7	Post All-Star	32	20.7	4.3	.346	0.3	.100	1.7	.741	0.19	1.41	1.5	3.4	4.2
Road	36	26.1	5.7	.447	0.6	.304	1.9	.791	0.19	1.44	2.1	4.3	6.8	November	14	35.2	7.8	.541	1.5	.429	3.4	.681	0.29	2.43	3.9	7.9	11.4
vs. Playoff	41	25.6	5.5	.411	0.8	.313	1.4	.746	0.10	1.66	2.5	4.8	5.8	December	14	31.1	7.8	.450	1.3	.222	1.9	.769	0.14	1.64	3.3	7.6	8.7
vs. Non-Playoff	31	28.4	6.1	.439	0.8	.240	3.2	.758	0.35	1.55	2.4	5.6	8.0	January	6	30.2	5.3	.375	0.8	.400	2.3	.929	0.50	1.00	3.0	4.0	6.5
vs. East	48	25.9	5.4	.446	0.8	.325	2.1	.762	0.23	1.63	2.5	4.9	6.7	February	13	28.9	5.4	.343	0.5	.000	2.5	.788	0.15	1.62	1.8	4.5	5.7
vs. West	24	28.6	6.4	.386	0.7	.176	2.4	.737	0.17	1.58	2.4	5.6	6.8	March	16	19.9	5.2	.337	0.4	.167	1.9	.733	0.19	1.63	1.6	3.5	4.9
vs. Div.	21	26.8	6.1	.395	0.6	.333	2.0	.698	0.19	1.67	2.8	5.4	6.5	April	9	13.6	1.1	.300	0.1	.000	0.9	.750	0.11	0.67	1.0	1.8	1.3
As Starter	47	31.9	7.1	.447	1.1	.294	2.6	.775	0.30	1.89	3.0	6.5	8.6	0 Days Rest	19	26.4	5.4	.412	0.6	.250	1.4	.741	0.11	1.89	1.9	4.3	5.6
Off Bench	25	17.2	3.2	.325	0.2	.167	1.5	.684	0.04	1.08	1.4	2.6	3.2	1 Days Rest	34	25.7	6.1	.403	0.9	.290	2.4	.704	0.15	1.68	2.8	5.9	6.8
In wins	29	28.4	5.7	.428	0.8	.167	2.8	.741	0.34	1.66	2.8	6.2	7.1	2 Days Rest	8	25.5	4.9	.436	0.4	.333	2.6	.762	0.25	1.00	1.8	3.6	6.4
In losses	43	25.7	5.7	.421	0.8	.364	1.8	.766	0.12	1.58	2.2	4.4	6.5	3+ Days Rest	11	31.5	6.0	.500	1.0	.273	2.6	.897	0.55	1.36	3.0	5.7	8.6

221

Tom Gugliotta
Phoenix Suns — Forward

1999-2000 Per Game Averages

	G	Min	FGA	FG%	3PA	3P%	FTA	FT%	Blk	Stl	Ast	Reb	Pts
Total	54	32.7	11.9	.481	0.1	.125	2.8	.775	0.57	1.48	2.3	7.9	13.7
Home	28	31.3	10.7	.508	0.0	—	2.1	.800	0.43	1.46	2.1	6.9	12.6
Road	26	34.3	13.3	.457	0.3	.125	3.5	.758	0.73	1.50	2.5	8.9	14.8
vs. Playoff	29	33.5	11.9	.449	0.2	.000	2.8	.765	0.62	1.17	2.1	7.5	12.8
vs. Non-Playoff	25	31.8	12.0	.517	0.1	.333	2.8	.786	0.52	1.84	2.5	8.3	14.6
vs. East	25	32.8	11.5	.479	0.1	.000	3.0	.787	0.64	1.64	2.2	7.5	13.4
vs. West	29	32.7	12.3	.482	0.2	.200	2.6	.763	0.52	1.34	2.3	8.2	13.9
vs. Div.	12	33.1	12.1	.497	0.3	.000	2.5	.733	0.42	1.17	2.3	8.3	13.8
As Starter	54	32.7	11.9	.481	0.1	.125	2.8	.775	0.57	1.48	2.3	7.9	13.7
Off Bench	0	—											
In wins	36	32.5	11.4	.534	0.1	.333	3.2	.826	0.53	1.89	2.3	7.9	14.8
In losses	18	33.2	13.1	.387	0.3	.000	2.0	.611	0.67	0.67	2.3	7.8	11.3
Pre All-Star	41	31.6	12.0	.473	0.2	.125	2.4	.717	0.54	1.32	2.1	8.0	13.1
Post All-Star	13	36.2	11.8	.506	0.0	—	4.0	.885	0.69	2.00	2.9	7.5	15.5
November	14	32.3	11.5	.516	0.1	.000	3.1	.628	0.71	1.43	2.5	8.3	13.8
December	8	33.5	12.8	.500	0.1	.000	2.8	.727	0.38	0.88	1.6	7.8	14.8
January	14	30.1	12.4	.402	0.4	.200	2.0	.786	0.57	1.00	1.7	8.2	11.6
February	13	34.3	11.8	.481	0.1	.000	3.1	.900	0.54	2.15	3.0	7.3	14.2
March	5	36.0	10.8	.593	0.0	—	3.6	.889	0.60	2.20	2.6	7.4	16.0
April	0	—											
0 Days Rest	12	35.3	13.0	.494	0.2	.000	3.4	.854	0.83	1.58	2.1	7.3	15.8
1 Days Rest	26	31.0	11.0	.498	0.1	.000	2.7	.783	0.54	1.54	2.5	7.2	13.1
2 Days Rest	11	33.8	13.1	.438	0.2	.000	2.0	.682	0.64	1.36	1.9	8.6	12.8
3+ Days Rest	5	32.8	11.6	.466	0.4	.500	3.8	.684	0.00	1.20	2.6	11.0	13.6

Last Five Seasons

	G	Min	FGA	FG%	3PA	3P%	FTA	FT%	Blk	Stl	Ast	Reb	Pts
Total	297	36.6	14.1	.470	0.7	.261	5.2	.800	0.87	1.58	3.3	8.6	17.6
Home	152	36.3	13.8	.475	0.7	.293	5.0	.788	0.97	1.56	3.4	8.3	17.2
Road	145	37.0	14.5	.465	0.8	.232	5.4	.812	0.77	1.60	3.2	8.9	18.0
vs. Playoff	164	36.4	13.8	.455	0.7	.237	5.0	.793	0.89	1.55	3.3	8.3	16.7
vs. Non-Playoff	133	36.9	14.5	.487	0.7	.290	5.4	.809	0.85	1.61	3.4	9.0	18.7
vs. East	103	36.6	13.5	.458	0.7	.229	4.7	.820	0.81	1.50	3.3	8.1	16.4
vs. West	194	36.6	14.4	.476	0.7	.277	5.4	.791	0.91	1.62	3.3	8.9	18.2
vs. Div.	84	36.8	14.3	.475	0.7	.246	5.8	.792	0.86	1.54	3.2	9.1	18.3
As Starter	297	36.6	14.1	.470	0.7	.261	5.2	.800	0.87	1.58	3.3	8.6	17.6
Off Bench	0	—											
In wins	148	36.8	14.1	.508	0.5	.257	5.3	.799	0.94	1.74	3.6	8.9	18.7
In losses	149	36.5	14.2	.431	0.9	.263	5.0	.802	0.81	1.42	3.1	8.3	16.4
Pre All-Star	174	36.4	14.6	.470	0.8	.279	5.3	.793	0.94	1.59	3.3	8.9	18.1
Post All-Star	80	37.2	13.5	.463	0.9	.221	5.0	.820	0.94	1.66	3.7	7.9	16.8
Oct/Nov	56	36.9	14.8	.464	0.9	.280	6.0	.771	0.88	1.61	3.5	8.8	18.6
December	52	37.0	14.2	.483	0.7	.378	4.7	.812	0.90	1.50	3.1	9.4	18.1
January	54	35.6	15.0	.456	0.8	.244	5.2	.805	1.07	1.54	3.1	9.4	18.1
February	51	36.8	13.2	.483	0.4	.150	5.2	.818	0.78	1.51	3.1	8.2	17.0
March	53	37.4	13.8	.478	0.6	.290	5.1	.790	0.79	1.79	3.7	8.2	17.4
Apr/May	31	35.7	13.5	.447	1.0	.156	4.3	.827	0.74	1.48	3.5	8.2	15.8
0 Days Rest	67	37.1	14.9	.481	0.8	.176	4.8	.828	0.64	1.66	3.0	7.7	18.4
1 Days Rest	152	36.2	13.5	.469	0.7	.275	5.5	.787	0.97	1.60	3.4	8.6	17.2
2 Days Rest	48	36.5	14.6	.457	0.6	.300	4.6	.812	0.98	1.44	3.5	9.2	17.3
3+ Days Rest	30	37.9	14.7	.468	0.9	.321	5.0	.801	0.73	1.53	3.3	9.9	18.1

Richard Hamilton
Washington Wizards — Guard-Forward

1999-2000 Per Game Averages

	G	Min	FGA	FG%	3PA	3P%	FTA	FT%	Blk	Stl	Ast	Reb	Pts
Total	71	19.3	8.5	.420	1.1	.364	1.9	.774	0.08	0.39	1.5	1.8	9.0
Home	36	19.9	8.8	.429	1.1	.359	1.9	.776	0.06	0.39	1.5	1.7	9.3
Road	35	18.7	8.3	.410	1.1	.368	1.9	.773	0.11	0.40	1.5	1.9	8.7
vs. Playoff	39	17.9	7.3	.393	1.1	.317	1.6	.758	0.00	0.41	1.4	1.9	7.3
vs. Non-Playoff	32	21.1	10.0	.444	1.1	.417	2.2	.789	0.19	0.38	1.7	1.7	11.1
vs. East	49	21.5	9.8	.415	1.3	.338	2.4	.773	0.08	0.51	1.7	2.0	10.4
vs. West	22	14.5	5.7	.440	0.5	.500	0.6	.786	0.09	0.14	1.0	1.5	5.8
vs. Div.	22	20.7	9.8	.400	1.5	.412	2.0	.818	0.09	0.59	1.5	2.1	10.1
As Starter	12	28.9	12.6	.404	1.8	.238	3.2	.816	0.17	0.58	1.8	3.1	13.2
Off Bench	59	17.4	7.7	.425	0.9	.411	1.6	.758	0.07	0.36	1.5	1.6	8.2
In wins	24	20.5	8.3	.495	1.0	.435	1.8	.818	0.13	0.42	1.9	1.8	10.2
In losses	47	18.8	8.6	.383	1.1	.333	1.9	.753	0.06	0.38	1.3	1.8	8.4
Pre All-Star	38	20.0	8.5	.392	1.2	.273	2.1	.800	0.11	0.39	1.2	1.9	8.7
Post All-Star	33	18.6	8.5	.452	1.0	.485	1.6	.736	0.06	0.39	1.9	1.8	9.4
November	15	21.7	10.3	.409	1.6	.333	2.0	.833	0.07	0.53	1.0	2.9	10.6
December	7	13.3	4.9	.353	0.3	.000	1.0	.857	0.00	0.07	0.4		4.3
January	11	23.3	9.1	.390	1.3	.143	3.1	.735	0.27	0.55	1.8	1.8	9.5
February	12	14.1	5.6	.388	0.5	.500	1.3	.867	0.00	0.25	0.7	1.1	5.7
March	17	15.8	6.7	.474	0.6	.400	0.8	.786	0.12	0.24	1.6	1.0	7.2
April	9	29.0	15.1	.441	2.3	.524	3.7	.697	0.00	0.78	3.6	3.6	17.1
0 Days Rest	21	17.0	7.1	.403	0.9	.263	1.7	.829	0.05	0.29	1.2	1.6	7.3
1 Days Rest	30	18.4	8.8	.414	1.1	.394	1.8	.717	0.10	0.40	1.7	1.9	9.0
2 Days Rest	9	27.3	12.3	.468	1.6	.429	2.4	.818	0.11	0.44	1.6	2.4	14.2
3+ Days Rest	11	19.9	7.5	.402	1.0	.364	2.1	.783	0.09	0.55	1.6	1.4	8.0

Anfernee Hardaway

1999-2000 Per Game Averages

	G	Min	FGA	FG%	3PA	3P%	FTA	FT%	Blk	Stl	Ast	Reb	Pts
Total	60	37.6	13.3	.474	1.7	.324	4.8	.790	0.63	1.57	5.3	5.8	16.9
Home	29	36.7	12.7	.460	1.5	.302	4.6	.850	0.72	1.52	5.1	5.9	16.0
Road	31	38.4	13.9	.485	1.9	.339	4.9	.739	0.55	1.61	5.4	5.7	17.8
vs. Playoff	31	38.7	14.1	.473	2.0	.333	5.0	.795	0.58	1.52	4.8	6.0	18.0
vs. Non-Playoff	29	36.3	12.4	.475	1.3	.308	4.5	.785	0.69	1.62	5.7	5.6	15.7
vs. East	25	37.2	12.9	.500	2.0	.367	4.8	.775	0.72	1.64	4.7	5.1	17.3
vs. West	35	37.8	13.6	.456	1.5	.283	4.7	.801	0.57	1.51	5.7	6.3	16.6
vs. Div.	16	38.5	13.4	.472	1.1	.353	4.9	.795	0.56	1.56	6.1	6.5	16.9
As Starter	60	37.6	13.3	.474	1.7	.324	4.8	.790	0.63	1.57	5.3	5.8	16.9
Off Bench	0	—											
In wins	42	36.7	13.0	.472	1.4	.288	4.4	.804	0.76	1.69	5.5	5.5	16.2
In losses	18	39.4	14.1	.478	2.4	.372	5.7	.765	0.33	1.28	4.7	6.5	18.7

	G	Min	FGA	FG%	3PA	3P%	FTA	FT%	Blk	Stl	Ast	Reb	Pts
Pre All-Star	26	36.4	12.5	.500	1.9	.347	4.5	.802	0.81	1.23	4.2	5.8	16.7
Post All-Star	34	38.4	13.9	.456	1.6	.302	5.0	.782	0.50	1.82	6.0	5.8	17.1
November	13	36.1	12.2	.468	2.2	.345	4.5	.776	0.85	1.62	4.3	5.7	15.6
December	2	42.5	17.0	.471	1.5	.333	6.0	.750	0.00	1.50	5.5	8.5	21.0
January	6	35.8	13.3	.513	2.0	.417	5.7	.853	1.17	0.33	3.3	4.8	19.3
February	13	37.0	11.5	.493	1.2	.375	3.9	.765	0.62	1.69	4.3	5.6	14.8
March	16	38.7	14.4	.472	1.4	.227	5.1	.753	0.56	1.81	6.6	5.4	17.8
April	10	38.4	14.5	.441	2.0	.300	5.0	.860	0.30	1.70	6.6	6.7	17.7
0 Days Rest	13	38.2	15.5	.480	2.4	.387	3.5	.689	0.54	1.62	5.4	5.7	18.2
1 Days Rest	33	37.7	12.8	.488	1.6	.358	4.9	.789	0.58	1.48	5.6	5.8	17.0
2 Days Rest	10	37.3	12.7	.441	1.2	.083	6.0	.800	0.70	1.70	4.1	6.0	16.1
3+ Days Rest	4	34.8	11.3	.400	1.5	.167	5.5	.909	1.25	1.75	4.5	5.5	14.3

Last Five Seasons

	G	Min	FGA	FG%	3PA	3P%	FTA	FT%	Blk	Stl	Ast	Reb	Pts
Total	270	37.3	14.6	.463	3.1	.311	5.7	.775	0.56	1.82	5.8	4.9	18.9
Home	135	37.1	14.3	.466	3.0	.299	5.8	.795	0.54	1.80	5.9	5.0	18.8
Road	135	37.4	15.0	.460	3.2	.323	5.6	.754	0.59	1.84	5.6	4.8	19.0
vs. Playoff	143	38.1	15.4	.447	3.6	.318	5.3	.780	0.54	1.84	5.6	4.9	19.1
vs. Non-Playoff	127	36.3	13.7	.484	2.6	.300	6.1	.769	0.59	1.80	6.0	4.9	18.7
vs. East	174	37.0	14.4	.462	3.3	.327	5.4	.770	0.57	1.85	5.4	4.7	18.6
vs. West	96	37.6	14.9	.465	2.8	.278	6.2	.783	0.55	1.77	6.4	5.3	19.5
vs. Div.	83	37.3	14.6	.463	3.0	.305	5.4	.771	0.54	1.84	5.9	5.0	18.6
As Starter	266	37.4	14.7	.465	3.1	.309	5.7	.773	0.55	1.83	5.8	4.9	19.0
Off Bench	4	30.3	11.8	.277	2.5	.500	3.5	.929	1.25	1.25	5.8	3.3	11.0
In wins	183	37.5	14.6	.490	2.8	.321	5.9	.778	0.66	1.98	6.3	5.1	19.8
In losses	87	36.8	14.6	.407	3.7	.295	5.4	.766	0.36	1.48	4.8	4.6	17.1

	G	Min	FGA	FG%	3PA	3P%	FTA	FT%	Blk	Stl	Ast	Reb	Pts
Pre All-Star	112	36.9	15.0	.470	3.1	.330	6.8	.783	0.70	1.69	5.6	4.9	20.4
Post All-Star	108	36.8	14.3	.476	3.3	.302	5.3	.788	0.47	1.78	6.2	4.6	18.8
Oct/Nov	43	36.9	15.3	.456	3.0	.298	8.0	.771	0.79	1.72	4.8	5.5	21.0
December	19	37.8	16.5	.475	3.6	.338	7.5	.754	0.53	1.79	6.6	4.9	22.5
January	35	37.0	15.0	.483	3.3	.386	5.9	.836	0.80	1.46	5.3	4.4	20.7
February	59	36.1	13.3	.448	2.9	.302	5.0	.713	0.46	1.97	5.9	5.0	16.4
March	65	38.9	15.0	.472	3.1	.286	5.2	.779	0.45	1.74	6.3	4.9	19.0
Apr/May	49	36.8	14.0	.453	3.2	.297	4.4	.812	0.49	2.12	5.9	4.8	17.3
0 Days Rest	67	37.5	15.2	.473	3.4	.350	5.6	.753	0.52	1.81	5.3	4.8	19.8
1 Days Rest	145	37.5	14.5	.461	3.1	.287	5.8	.776	0.60	1.86	6.1	4.9	18.8
2 Days Rest	33	37.3	14.6	.465	3.2	.343	5.3	.823	0.45	2.18	5.6	5.0	19.0
3+ Days Rest	25	34.9	13.7	.442	2.6	.292	5.6	.764	0.60	1.20	5.4	5.2	17.1

Tim Hardaway

1999-2000 Per Game Averages

	G	Min	FGA	FG%	3PA	3P%	FTA	FT%	Blk	Stl	Ast	Reb	Pts
Total	52	32.2	12.3	.386	4.9	.367	2.6	.827	0.08	0.94	7.4	2.9	13.4
Home	26	30.6	11.7	.365	5.0	.338	2.7	.873	0.08	1.00	7.6	2.7	12.6
Road	26	33.7	12.8	.404	4.8	.397	2.4	.774	0.08	0.88	7.2	3.1	14.2
vs. Playoff	27	34.9	12.8	.409	5.0	.368	2.7	.811	0.07	1.00	7.8	3.4	14.5
vs. Non-Playoff	25	29.2	11.7	.358	4.8	.367	2.4	.847	0.08	0.88	7.0	2.4	12.2
vs. East	39	32.6	12.9	.390	5.1	.370	2.8	.824	0.10	1.10	7.6	2.9	14.3
vs. West	13	30.8	10.2	.368	4.3	.357	1.9	.810	0.00	0.46	6.9	2.7	10.7
vs. Div.	18	32.2	12.9	.388	5.1	.380	2.7	.771	0.00	1.06	7.3	3.6	14.0
As Starter	52	32.2	12.3	.386	4.9	.367	2.6	.827	0.08	0.94	7.4	2.9	13.4
Off Bench	0	—											
In wins	35	31.8	12.3	.390	5.1	.395	3.0	.848	0.09	1.20	7.8	2.8	14.1
In losses	17	32.9	12.2	.377	4.6	.304	1.6	.750	0.06	0.41	6.5	3.1	11.8

	G	Min	FGA	FG%	3PA	3P%	FTA	FT%	Blk	Stl	Ast	Reb	Pts
Pre All-Star	21	32.5	12.1	.408	4.9	.392	3.0	.781	0.05	0.90	7.1	3.3	14.2
Post All-Star	31	31.9	12.4	.371	5.0	.351	2.2	.870	0.10	0.97	7.6	2.6	12.8
November	11	35.6	13.6	.420	5.6	.387	4.7	.750	0.00	1.27	7.7	3.8	17.2
December	0	—											
January	6	26.7	8.0	.333	3.3	.350	1.3	.875	0.17	0.17	6.7	2.5	7.7
February	14	31.9	12.4	.382	4.9	.420	1.4	.950	0.07	0.93	7.0	2.7	12.9
March	14	34.3	13.6	.405	4.9	.338	2.9	.825	0.07	1.00	8.3	2.5	15.0
April	7	27.6	11.0	.312	5.3	.297	1.9	.923	0.14	1.00	6.6	2.9	10.1
0 Days Rest	12	33.7	13.0	.346	5.0	.333	2.8	.824	0.00	0.92	7.6	3.5	13.0
1 Days Rest	27	32.9	13.0	.398	5.5	.389	2.5	.809	0.11	1.07	7.8	3.0	14.6
2 Days Rest	7	29.9	10.0	.457	3.9	.407	2.0	.786	0.14	0.71	5.7	2.0	12.3
3+ Days Rest	6	28.7	10.0	.333	3.3	.250	2.8	.941	0.00	0.67	7.3	2.3	10.2

Last Five Seasons

	G	Min	FGA	FG%	3PA	3P%	FTA	FT%	Blk	Stl	Ast	Reb	Pts
Total	342	35.5	14.8	.415	5.8	.355	3.7	.797	0.15	1.54	8.0	3.2	17.3
Home	170	34.8	14.5	.423	5.8	.360	3.7	.800	0.17	1.54	8.3	3.1	17.3
Road	172	36.2	15.1	.407	5.8	.350	3.8	.794	0.13	1.53	7.7	3.4	17.3
vs. Playoff	174	36.7	15.3	.409	6.1	.358	3.8	.802	0.12	1.48	8.0	3.5	17.7
vs. Non-Playoff	168	34.3	14.3	.421	5.5	.351	3.7	.791	0.18	1.60	8.1	2.9	16.9
vs. East	233	36.1	14.9	.415	5.8	.358	3.9	.801	0.12	1.62	8.1	3.3	17.5
vs. West	109	34.3	14.7	.415	5.7	.348	3.5	.786	0.22	1.36	7.8	3.1	16.9
vs. Div.	104	36.1	15.0	.403	5.7	.340	4.0	.796	0.09	1.62	8.1	3.5	17.1
As Starter	308	36.7	15.3	.417	6.0	.355	3.8	.805	0.15	1.58	8.2	3.4	18.0
Off Bench	34	24.7	10.3	.383	4.1	.360	2.8	.698	0.15	1.15	6.6	2.2	11.3
In wins	224	35.4	14.8	.428	5.8	.370	3.8	.786	0.16	1.64	8.5	3.3	17.8
In losses	118	35.7	14.8	.390	5.8	.326	3.6	.819	0.14	1.34	7.0	3.2	16.3

	G	Min	FGA	FG%	3PA	3P%	FTA	FT%	Blk	Stl	Ast	Reb	Pts
Pre All-Star	163	34.7	14.4	.425	5.3	.353	3.9	.782	0.17	1.64	7.8	3.4	17.1
Post All-Star	131	36.0	15.0	.408	6.1	.355	3.8	.811	0.14	1.53	8.6	3.0	17.5
Oct/Nov	57	36.7	14.8	.444	5.4	.357	4.2	.803	0.18	1.81	8.2	3.8	18.4
December	42	34.3	14.5	.434	5.1	.362	4.4	.768	0.26	1.81	7.8	3.5	17.8
January	48	33.5	14.0	.403	5.5	.346	3.0	.792	0.13	1.35	7.6	3.3	15.6
February	66	33.8	13.9	.408	5.8	.399	3.9	.789	0.11	1.42	7.4	2.6	16.7
March	72	37.7	16.3	.406	6.7	.347	3.7	.834	0.14	1.46	9.0	3.3	18.6
Apr/May	57	36.4	14.8	.400	5.7	.315	3.4	.781	0.14	1.44	7.9	3.2	16.3
0 Days Rest	85	35.6	14.9	.404	5.6	.349	3.9	.785	0.21	1.49	7.9	3.5	17.0
1 Days Rest	168	35.9	14.8	.417	5.9	.353	3.7	.789	0.15	1.55	8.2	3.3	17.3
2 Days Rest	61	34.9	15.4	.417	6.1	.345	3.7	.815	0.13	1.57	7.8	3.1	18.0
3+ Days Rest	28	34.0	13.2	.428	5.2	.414	3.6	.843	0.04	1.50	8.0	2.7	16.5

Ron Harper
Los Angeles Lakers — Guard

1999-2000 Per Game Averages

	G	Min	FGA	FG%	3PA	3P%	FTA	FT%	Blk	Stl	Ast	Reb	Pts		G	Min	FGA	FG%	3PA	3P%	FTA	FT%	Blk	Stl	Ast	Reb	Pts
Total	80	25.5	6.6	.399	1.3	.311	1.8	.680	0.49	1.06	3.4	4.2	7.0	Pre All-Star	48	27.1	7.2	.372	1.4	.303	1.9	.681	0.56	1.06	3.6	4.3	7.0
Home	41	25.8	7.0	.421	1.4	.339	1.8	.689	0.51	1.17	3.6	3.9	7.6	Post All-Star	32	23.1	5.8	.449	1.3	.325	1.8	.679	0.38	1.06	3.0	4.2	6.8
Road	39	25.3	6.3	.374	1.2	.277	1.9	.671	0.46	0.95	3.2	4.5	6.3	November	15	28.7	7.8	.402	1.2	.278	1.7	.692	0.47	0.93	3.4	3.9	7.8
vs. Playoff	44	27.6	7.4	.410	1.5	.333	1.8	.679	0.64	1.16	3.3	4.8	7.8	December	15	27.5	7.2	.333	1.7	.423	2.1	.677	0.73	1.00	3.2	4.7	6.9
vs. Non-Playoff	36	23.0	5.8	.382	1.1	.275	1.9	.681	0.31	0.94	3.4	3.5	6.0	January	14	26.6	7.1	.390	1.8	.182	2.0	.714	0.57	1.29	4.7	4.4	7.3
vs. East	30	24.5	6.7	.421	1.3	.368	2.4	.690	0.47	0.97	3.2	4.1	7.8	February	13	21.4	5.0	.323	0.5	.333	1.5	.550	0.31	0.85	3.1	3.9	4.2
vs. West	50	26.1	6.6	.386	1.4	.279	1.5	.671	0.50	1.12	3.5	4.3	6.5	March	16	22.6	5.8	.489	1.6	.400	1.9	.767	0.38	1.06	2.6	3.6	7.7
vs. Div.	23	28.2	7.3	.373	1.8	.310	1.2	.607	0.78	1.13	3.9	4.3	6.8	April	7	26.7	7.0	.490	1.3	.111	1.7	.583	0.43	1.43	3.3	5.4	8.0
As Starter	78	25.9	6.8	.400	1.4	.311	1.9	.680	0.50	1.09	3.4	4.2	7.1	0 Days Rest	20	24.1	6.3	.304	1.3	.231	1.7	.706	0.35	0.95	3.1	3.6	5.3
Off Bench	2	11.0	0.5	.000	0.0	—	0.0	—	0.00	0.00	1.5	3.5	0.0	1 Days Rest	40	26.0	7.0	.459	1.5	.345	2.0	.654	0.53	1.13	3.4	4.5	8.3
In wins	66	25.2	6.6	.404	1.3	.330	1.8	.678	0.47	1.03	3.4	4.2	7.0	2 Days Rest	12	24.5	5.3	.444	1.1	.308	1.5	.722	0.42	1.00	2.9	3.4	6.1
In losses	14	27.1	6.8	.379	1.3	.222	1.9	.692	0.57	1.21	3.1	4.4	6.7	3+ Days Rest	8	28.3	7.8	.274	1.1	.333	1.8	.714	0.75	1.13	5.0	5.6	5.9

Last Five Seasons

	G	Min	FGA	FG%	3PA	3P%	FTA	FT%	Blk	Stl	Ast	Reb	Pts		G	Min	FGA	FG%	3PA	3P%	FTA	FT%	Blk	Stl	Ast	Reb	Pts
Total	353	25.7	7.1	.426	1.6	.303	1.9	.714	0.54	1.26	2.9	3.4	7.9	Pre All-Star	186	25.4	6.8	.429	1.5	.295	1.8	.725	0.52	1.19	2.7	3.3	7.6
Home	177	25.6	7.4	.429	1.7	.299	2.0	.720	0.57	1.32	3.1	3.4	8.2	Post All-Star	132	24.5	6.4	.445	1.6	.308	1.8	.702	0.45	1.23	3.0	3.1	7.5
Road	176	25.7	6.8	.424	1.5	.308	1.9	.708	0.52	1.19	2.7	3.4	7.6	Oct/Nov	61	25.7	6.8	.434	1.2	.278	1.6	.649	0.57	1.16	2.8	3.2	7.3
vs. Playoff	188	26.4	7.1	.416	1.6	.311	1.7	.707	0.51	1.21	2.8	3.6	7.7	December	57	25.4	6.9	.429	1.5	.364	2.5	.750	0.58	1.11	2.4	3.6	8.4
vs. Non-Playoff	165	24.9	7.0	.438	1.6	.294	2.2	.720	0.59	1.32	3.1	3.3	8.2	January	53	25.5	7.0	.434	1.9	.253	1.6	.782	0.45	1.40	3.1	3.3	7.7
vs. East	217	25.7	7.3	.442	1.7	.320	2.0	.694	0.55	1.29	2.9	3.4	8.3	February	65	26.1	7.3	.394	1.4	.326	1.8	.737	0.52	1.20	2.7	3.4	7.6
vs. West	136	25.7	6.8	.400	1.4	.271	1.9	.748	0.54	1.20	2.9	3.5	7.2	March	69	25.6	6.8	.447	1.7	.277	2.1	.690	0.59	1.30	3.2	3.2	8.0
vs. Div.	119	26.2	7.3	.415	1.8	.294	1.6	.675	0.58	1.25	2.9	3.5	7.7	Apr/May	48	25.7	7.6	.423	2.0	.330	2.2	.679	0.52	1.42	3.2	4.0	8.6
As Starter	349	25.7	7.1	.426	1.6	.302	2.0	.714	0.55	1.27	2.9	3.4	7.9	0 Days Rest	94	25.7	7.1	.429	1.7	.308	2.1	.701	0.60	1.35	3.2	3.4	8.0
Off Bench	4	18.3	3.8	.467	1.0	.500	0.0	—	0.00	0.50	2.0	2.8	4.0	1 Days Rest	166	25.4	7.0	.446	1.7	.314	2.1	.708	0.45	1.18	2.8	3.5	8.2
In wins	272	25.2	6.8	.453	1.6	.320	1.9	.712	0.53	1.21	2.8	3.3	8.1	2 Days Rest	58	25.8	6.6	.422	1.4	.268	1.6	.750	0.69	1.24	2.7	3.1	7.2
In losses	81	27.4	7.9	.348	1.6	.246	1.9	.720	0.60	1.41	3.1	3.8	7.3	3+ Days Rest	35	26.5	8.2	.350	1.5	.288	1.6	.737	0.63	1.40	3.2	4.0	7.3

Othella Harrington
Vancouver Grizzlies — Forward

1999-2000 Per Game Averages

	G	Min	FGA	FG%	3PA	3P%	FTA	FT%	Blk	Stl	Ast	Reb	Pts		G	Min	FGA	FG%	3PA	3P%	FTA	FT%	Blk	Stl	Ast	Reb	Pts
Total	82	32.6	10.1	.506	0.0	.000	3.6	.792	0.71	0.44	1.2	6.9	13.1	Pre All-Star	48	32.6	10.3	.497	0.0	.000	3.6	.780	0.63	0.44	1.3	6.8	13.0
Home	41	32.1	9.9	.495	0.0	.000	3.3	.813	0.85	0.32	1.1	7.4	12.4	Post All-Star	34	32.7	9.9	.519	0.0	.000	3.7	.808	0.82	0.44	1.1	6.9	13.3
Road	41	33.2	10.4	.516	0.0	.000	4.0	.774	0.56	0.56	1.2	6.3	13.8	November	14	35.1	12.6	.554	0.0	—	3.7	.769	0.57	0.36	1.8	7.9	16.9
vs. Playoff	48	33.0	10.0	.496	0.0	.000	3.9	.789	0.52	0.42	1.2	6.6	13.0	December	15	30.9	8.9	.448	0.0	—	3.5	.673	0.60	0.33	0.9	6.3	10.3
vs. Non-Playoff	34	32.1	10.3	.520	0.0	.000	3.3	.796	0.97	0.47	1.1	7.2	13.4	January	14	33.9	9.6	.515	0.1	.000	4.3	.900	0.64	0.64	1.4	7.2	13.7
vs. East	30	32.5	9.9	.503	0.0	—	3.2	.866	0.73	0.57	1.3	7.2	12.7	February	13	29.2	9.1	.483	0.0	—	2.2	.793	1.00	0.38	0.9	5.2	10.5
vs. West	52	32.7	10.3	.507	0.0	.000	3.9	.756	0.69	0.37	1.1	6.7	13.3	March	15	31.9	9.9	.477	0.0	—	3.5	.750	0.60	0.60	1.2	7.4	12.1
vs. Div.	24	32.4	10.1	.533	0.1	.000	3.8	.791	0.79	0.21	1.0	6.3	13.8	April	11	35.3	10.7	.551	0.1	.000	4.8	.849	0.27		0.9	7.1	15.9
As Starter	82	32.6	10.1	.506	0.0	.000	3.6	.792	0.71	0.44	1.2	6.9	13.1	0 Days Rest	19	32.5	9.5	.552	0.0	—	3.3	.823	0.37	0.53	1.2	6.5	13.2
Off Bench	0	—	—	—	—	—	—	—	—	—	—	—	—	1 Days Rest	47	32.5	10.3	.490	0.0	.000	3.9	.791	0.81	0.47	1.1	6.8	13.1
In wins	22	30.9	10.1	.509	0.0	—	3.5	.885	0.86	0.27	1.1	7.7	13.4	2 Days Rest	7	33.6	10.4	.548	0.0	—	4.0	.643	0.71	0.43	1.3	6.7	14.0
In losses	60	33.3	10.1	.505	0.0	.000	3.7	.759	0.65	0.50	1.2	6.6	13.0	3+ Days Rest	9	32.9	10.2	.467	0.1	.000	2.9	.885	0.89	0.11	1.4	8.0	12.1

Career (1996-97 thru 1999-2000)

	G	Min	FGA	FG%	3PA	3P%	FTA	FT%	Blk	Stl	Ast	Reb	Pts		G	Min	FGA	FG%	3PA	3P%	FTA	FT%	Blk	Stl	Ast	Reb	Pts
Total	238	22.4	6.7	.509	0.0	.000	2.6	.746	0.55	0.27	0.6	5.1	8.8	Pre All-Star	114	22.4	6.8	.507	0.0	.000	2.3	.745	0.50	0.32	0.7	5.0	8.7
Home	114	22.1	6.7	.510	0.0	.000	2.5	.743	0.64	0.23	0.6	5.3	8.6	Post All-Star	83	22.7	6.3	.511	0.0	.000	2.8	.761	0.60	0.25	0.7	4.8	8.6
Road	124	22.8	6.8	.509	0.0	.000	2.7	.749	0.48	0.31	0.7	4.9	9.0	Oct/Nov	29	22.3	8.1	.543	0.0	—	2.3	.712	0.48	0.38	1.0	5.1	10.4
vs. Playoff	129	22.9	6.8	.484	0.0	.000	2.8	.773	0.47	0.26	0.7	5.2	8.7	December	34	19.6	5.6	.458	0.0	.000	2.1	.667	0.44	0.18	0.5	4.3	6.6
vs. Non-Playoff	109	21.9	6.6	.540	0.0	.000	2.4	.711	0.66	0.28	0.5	5.0	8.9	January	41	25.0	7.0	.517	0.0	.000	2.8	.807	0.59	0.44	0.8	5.7	9.5
vs. East	68	22.6	6.8	.516	0.0	.000	2.3	.809	0.56	0.30	0.7	5.3	8.9	February	41	22.3	7.0	.542	0.0	—	2.3	.809	0.54	0.20	0.5	5.2	9.4
vs. West	156	22.2	6.7	.506	0.0	.000	2.8	.720	0.55	0.25	0.6	5.0	8.8	March	55	23.4	7.0	.492	0.0	.000	2.8	.708	0.64	0.29	0.7	5.5	9.8
vs. Div.	72	22.8	6.8	.494	0.1	.000	2.8	.751	0.60	0.17	0.6	4.8	8.9	Apr/May	38	21.1	5.8	.495	0.0	.000	3.2	.756	0.58	0.13	0.5	4.5	8.2
As Starter	96	32.3	10.1	.510	0.0	.000	3.7	.783	0.74	0.40	1.1	7.0	13.2	0 Days Rest	52	23.8	7.3	.544	0.0	—	2.5	.822	0.38	0.31	0.7	5.5	9.9
Off Bench	142	15.8	4.5	.508	0.0	.000	1.9	.699	0.43	0.18	0.3	3.8	5.9	1 Days Rest	119	24.6	7.4	.499	0.0	.000	3.0	.747	0.69	0.30	0.6	5.5	9.7
In wins	114	19.1	5.8	.524	0.0	.000	2.2	.736	0.58	0.20	0.5	4.7	7.7	2 Days Rest	30	18.2	4.9	.510	0.0	—	2.4	.625	0.43	0.17	0.6	3.7	6.5
In losses	124	25.6	7.6	.499	0.0	.000	3.0	.753	0.53	0.33	0.8	5.5	9.8	3+ Days Rest	37	17.2	5.3	.490	0.1	.000	1.7	.730	0.46	0.19	0.6	4.3	6.4

Lucious Harris

1999-2000 Per Game Averages

	G	Min	FGA	FG%	3PA	3P%	FTA	FT%	Blk	Stl	Ast	Reb	Pts		G	Min	FGA	FG%	3PA	3P%	FTA	FT%	Blk	Stl	Ast	Reb	Pts
Total	77	19.6	6.0	.428	1.5	.330	1.3	.798	0.08	0.84	1.3	2.4	6.7	Pre All-Star	45	17.6	5.8	.435	1.4	.355	1.0	.814	0.11	0.80	0.9	2.2	6.3
Home	38	18.7	5.4	.412	1.3	.271	1.2	.886	0.08	0.82	1.2	2.6	5.8	Post All-Star	32	22.5	6.3	.419	1.7	.302	1.8	.786	0.03	0.91	1.8	2.8	7.2
Road	39	20.5	6.6	.440	1.7	.373	1.4	.727	0.08	0.87	1.4	2.3	7.5	November	14	20.1	6.6	.473	0.9	.250	1.0	.786	0.21	0.86	1.3	2.2	7.3
vs. Playoff	43	20.0	6.0	.467	1.5	.302	1.3	.833	0.09	0.86	1.2	2.6	7.1	December	15	17.2	5.3	.380	1.4	.333	1.1	.875	0.07	0.53	0.8	2.8	5.4
vs. Non-Playoff	34	19.1	6.1	.379	1.5	.365	1.3	.756	0.06	0.82	1.4	2.2	6.1	January	14	15.4	5.4	.434	1.7	.375	0.8	.727	0.07	1.14	1.8	1.6	5.9
vs. East	51	19.7	6.0	.411	1.5	.307	1.5	.773	0.12	0.90	1.3	2.4	6.5	February	8	16.8	5.1	.463	1.6	.462	1.5	.833	0.00	0.38	1.0	2.0	6.8
vs. West	26	19.5	6.1	.459	1.5	.375	0.9	.875	0.00	0.73	1.3	2.5	7.0	March	16	19.9	5.6	.456	1.5	.292	1.9	.833	0.06	0.81	1.4	2.9	7.1
vs. Div.	22	19.3	6.1	.378	1.5	.265	1.9	.732	0.00	1.05	1.2	2.0	6.4	April	10	30.1	8.4	.369	2.1	.286	1.6	.688	0.00	1.30	2.8	2.9	7.9
As Starter	11	33.4	10.4	.412	2.2	.333	1.7	.684	0.00	1.55	3.0	3.3	10.5	0 Days Rest	18	21.6	5.6	.420	1.3	.333	1.2	.802	0.11	0.83	1.8	2.0	5.9
Off Bench	66	17.3	5.3	.433	1.4	.330	1.2	.825	0.09	0.73	1.0	2.3	6.0	1 Days Rest	41	19.4	6.4	.420	1.4	.322	1.4	.821	0.07	0.83	1.2	2.7	7.0
In wins	29	18.8	5.3	.435	1.4	.325	1.6	.783	0.07	0.86	1.1	3.0	6.3	2 Days Rest	9	13.9	4.8	.372	1.4	.077	0.2	1.000	0.00	0.67	0.8	1.7	3.9
In losses	48	20.1	6.4	.424	1.6	.333	1.1	.811	0.08	0.83	1.4	2.1	6.9	3+ Days Rest	9	22.3	6.2	.518	2.1	.526	2.1	.842	0.11	1.11	1.4	2.9	9.3

Last Five Seasons

	G	Min	FGA	FG%	3PA	3P%	FTA	FT%	Blk	Stl	Ast	Reb	Pts		G	Min	FGA	FG%	3PA	3P%	FTA	FT%	Blk	Stl	Ast	Reb	Pts
Total	278	16.6	5.4	.420	1.5	.336	1.2	.765	0.09	0.72	1.1	1.8	6.0	Pre All-Star	126	16.1	5.4	.423	1.6	.345	1.0	.809	0.09	0.76	0.9	1.7	5.9
Home	133	16.0	5.2	.417	1.5	.342	1.1	.780	0.11	0.65	1.0	1.8	5.7	Post All-Star	116	17.1	5.6	.421	1.5	.360	1.4	.732	0.05	0.75	1.3	1.9	6.3
Road	145	17.1	5.6	.422	1.6	.332	1.3	.753	0.07	0.79	1.1	1.8	6.3	Oct/Nov	42	17.7	6.1	.422	1.7	.314	1.2	.808	0.10	0.74	1.1	1.7	6.7
vs. Playoff	155	17.2	5.5	.434	1.6	.357	1.3	.789	0.10	0.79	1.1	1.8	5.4	December	36	16.2	5.2	.388	1.5	.358	1.0	.806	0.06	0.61	0.8	1.9	5.4
vs. Non-Playoff	123	15.8	5.4	.402	1.5	.310	1.1	.730	0.09	0.64	1.1	1.8	5.6	January	40	14.8	4.8	.427	1.6	.355	0.8	.788	0.13	0.90	0.9	1.6	5.3
vs. East	167	17.0	5.3	.406	1.4	.318	1.3	.749	0.10	0.72	1.1	1.8	5.7	February	42	13.8	4.3	.419	1.2	.314	1.4	.667	0.07	0.60	0.8	1.4	4.9
vs. West	111	15.9	5.6	.440	1.7	.360	1.1	.793	0.06	0.72	1.1	1.7	6.4	March	66	17.4	6.0	.442	1.7	.339	1.5	.810	0.08	0.67	1.2	2.0	7.1
vs. Div.	85	16.5	5.5	.419	1.7	.361	1.3	.696	0.08	0.81	1.1	2.0	6.2	Apr/May	52	18.6	5.8	.405	1.6	.337	1.1	.709	0.10	0.83	1.5	2.0	6.0
As Starter	20	28.6	9.0	.406	2.3	.356	1.3	.720	0.10	1.00	2.3	2.7	9.0	0 Days Rest	65	17.9	5.3	.424	1.6	.304	1.0	.701	0.08	0.74	1.2	1.9	5.7
Off Bench	258	15.7	5.2	.422	1.5	.334	1.2	.768	0.09	0.70	1.0	1.7	5.8	1 Days Rest	132	16.8	5.7	.423	1.6	.364	1.3	.787	0.10	0.73	1.1	1.9	6.4
In wins	98	16.0	5.0	.445	1.4	.358	1.2	.785	0.13	0.82	1.1	2.1	5.9	2 Days Rest	45	14.0	5.0	.377	1.5	.242	0.8	.800	0.04	0.62	0.9	1.4	4.7
In losses	180	16.9	5.7	.408	1.6	.326	1.2	.753	0.06	0.67	1.1	1.6	6.1	3+ Days Rest	36	16.6	5.3	.453	1.4	.412	1.6	.750	0.11	0.78	1.0	1.9	6.6

Hersey Hawkins

1999-2000 Per Game Averages

	G	Min	FGA	FG%	3PA	3P%	FTA	FT%	Blk	Stl	Ast	Reb	Pts		G	Min	FGA	FG%	3PA	3P%	FTA	FT%	Blk	Stl	Ast	Reb	Pts
Total	61	26.6	6.1	.424	2.3	.390	2.0	.899	0.25	1.21	2.2	2.9	7.9	Pre All-Star	27	24.0	5.7	.444	2.1	.393	1.5	.902	0.15	1.15	1.9	2.7	7.2
Home	29	27.0	6.4	.412	2.4	.391	2.1	.869	0.31	1.28	2.6	2.9	8.1	Post All-Star	34	28.7	6.5	.410	2.5	.388	2.3	.897	0.32	1.26	2.4	3.0	8.4
Road	32	26.2	5.9	.436	2.3	.389	1.8	.931	0.19	1.16	1.8	2.9	7.7	November	13	30.8	7.0	.484	2.5	.406	2.2	.893	0.15	1.69	2.3	2.9	9.7
vs. Playoff	35	26.3	6.5	.465	2.5	.430	1.6	.982	0.23	1.26	2.3	2.9	8.6	December	3	25.0	5.7	.294	1.3	.000	1.7	.800	0.33	1.00	2.0	3.0	4.7
vs. Non-Playoff	26	27.0	5.7	.362	2.1	.327	2.4	.825	0.27	1.15	2.1	2.9	6.8	January	5	11.4	2.4	.167	0.8	.000	0.4	1.000	0.20	0.40	1.2	1.8	1.2
vs. East	38	27.7	6.5	.444	2.4	.398	1.9	.958	0.34	1.13	2.4	3.0	8.6	February	14	24.4	6.4	.433	2.9	.500	1.6	.818	0.07	0.50	1.7	3.1	8.3
vs. West	23	24.7	5.5	.386	2.1	.375	2.0	.809	0.09	1.35	1.8	2.7	6.7	March	16	28.3	6.4	.412	2.5	.375	2.1	.941	0.31	1.63	2.6	2.4	8.2
vs. Div.	22	25.3	5.6	.398	2.2	.367	1.9	.976	0.50	0.82	2.5	2.8	7.1	April	10	29.6	6.3	.429	2.1	.333	2.8	.929	0.50	1.40	2.7	3.8	8.7
As Starter	49	29.4	6.9	.436	2.6	.384	2.2	.890	0.29	1.37	2.4	3.0	9.0	0 Days Rest	16	25.8	5.4	.356	1.8	.172	2.1	.941	0.19	1.31	1.7	2.9	6.2
Off Bench	12	14.9	3.2	.316	1.3	.438	0.8	1.000	0.08	0.58	1.2	2.3	3.4	1 Days Rest	30	28.3	6.9	.427	2.7	.407	2.1	.921	0.37	1.23	2.3	3.2	8.9
In wins	12	26.2	6.2	.419	2.6	.516	2.6	.871	0.17	0.83	1.7	3.8	8.8	2 Days Rest	9	25.4	6.7	.517	2.7	.583	2.2	.800	0.11	1.56	3.3	2.2	10.2
In losses	49	26.7	6.1	.425	2.2	.355	1.8	.909	0.27	1.31	2.3	2.6	7.7	3+ Days Rest	6	22.0	3.7	.409	1.2	.429	0.3	.500	0.00	0.33	1.2	2.0	3.7

Last Five Seasons

	G	Min	FGA	FG%	3PA	3P%	FTA	FT%	Blk	Stl	Ast	Reb	Pts		G	Min	FGA	FG%	3PA	3P%	FTA	FT%	Blk	Stl	Ast	Reb	Pts
Total	357	32.0	8.8	.451	3.8	.386	2.9	.879	0.21	1.71	2.6	3.7	12.0	Pre All-Star	167	31.2	8.9	.448	4.0	.382	2.8	.868	0.17	1.71	2.6	3.7	11.9
Home	177	32.1	8.8	.464	3.7	.380	3.0	.873	0.23	1.82	2.9	3.9	12.1	Post All-Star	140	32.7	8.9	.466	3.7	.420	3.1	.884	0.21	1.74	2.8	3.6	12.6
Road	180	32.0	8.9	.439	3.9	.392	2.8	.885	0.20	1.59	2.4	3.5	11.8	Oct/Nov	61	31.6	8.8	.445	4.0	.365	2.5	.829	0.18	1.82	2.6	3.7	11.3
vs. Playoff	198	32.4	9.0	.446	3.8	.374	2.7	.886	0.22	1.55	2.6	3.6	11.8	December	45	31.9	9.4	.454	4.0	.397	3.3	.893	0.13	1.56	2.6	3.6	13.0
vs. Non-Playoff	159	31.6	8.6	.459	3.8	.402	3.1	.872	0.20	1.91	2.8	3.9	12.2	January	48	31.0	9.1	.456	4.1	.388	2.9	.869	0.21	1.79	2.6	3.6	12.4
vs. East	134	31.7	8.6	.446	3.7	.382	2.9	.893	0.19	1.62	2.8	3.7	11.7	February	60	31.4	8.1	.420	3.7	.362	2.9	.918	0.12	1.58	2.7	3.9	10.8
vs. West	223	32.3	9.0	.455	3.9	.389	2.9	.871	0.22	1.76	2.5	3.6	12.2	March	81	33.2	8.7	.483	3.7	.426	3.0	.858	0.25	1.88	2.8	3.6	12.6
vs. Div.	115	31.4	8.6	.465	3.7	.396	2.8	.886	0.28	1.67	2.7	3.7	11.9	Apr/May	62	32.7	9.0	.440	3.6	.369	2.9	.910	0.35	1.55	2.5	3.8	11.9
As Starter	329	32.8	9.1	.455	3.9	.391	3.0	.877	0.22	1.74	2.7	3.8	12.4	0 Days Rest	92	31.2	8.8	.433	3.7	.358	2.6	.896	0.21	1.57	2.3	3.3	11.3
Off Bench	28	23.8	5.5	.381	2.4	.294	2.0	.909	0.18	1.32	1.6	3.0	6.7	1 Days Rest	179	32.7	8.9	.455	3.8	.387	3.0	.886	0.21	1.77	2.8	3.8	12.3
In wins	219	32.5	9.3	.471	4.1	.416	3.3	.873	0.22	1.84	2.8	4.0	13.3	2 Days Rest	60	32.4	9.2	.467	4.1	.427	2.9	.822	0.25	1.90	3.1	4.0	12.8
In losses	138	31.3	8.1	.416	3.4	.330	2.3	.893	0.20	1.50	2.4	3.3	9.9	3+ Days Rest	26	30.0	7.7	.455	3.3	.372	2.8	.904	0.15	1.38	1.9	3.8	10.8

Alan Henderson
Atlanta Hawks — Forward

1999-2000 Per Game Averages

	G	Min	FGA	FG%	3PA	3P%	FTA	FT%	Blk	Stl	Ast	Reb	Pts		G	Min	FGA	FG%	3PA	3P%	FTA	FT%	Blk	Stl	Ast	Reb	Pts
Total	82	33.8	11.3	.461	0.1	.100	4.1	.671	0.66	0.99	0.9	7.0	13.2	Pre All-Star	47	35.5	11.4	.455	0.1	.200	4.6	.671	0.79	0.89	1.0	7.8	13.5
Home	41	34.0	11.1	.486	0.1	.000	4.2	.699	0.63	1.00	1.0	6.8	13.7	Post All-Star	35	31.7	11.3	.470	0.1	.000	3.4	.669	0.49	1.11	0.8	5.9	12.8
Road	41	33.6	11.6	.438	0.1	.167	3.9	.640	0.68	0.98	0.9	7.1	12.7	November	15	36.6	12.1	.434	0.1	.000	4.4	.561	0.40	0.73	1.0	9.8	13.0
vs. Playoff	47	34.5	11.5	.455	0.1	.000	3.6	.665	0.60	1.04	1.0	7.0	12.8	December	14	35.4	10.1	.423	0.1	.000	4.9	.681	0.93	0.71	1.2	7.3	11.9
vs. Non-Playoff	35	33.0	11.2	.471	0.1	.200	4.7	.677	0.74	0.91	0.9	6.9	13.7	January	13	35.2	10.9	.514	0.2	.500	5.2	.761	1.08	1.31	0.8	6.6	15.2
vs. East	54	33.1	10.8	.475	0.1	.167	4.4	.720	0.78	0.91	0.9	6.8	13.4	February	12	33.5	12.3	.449	0.0	—	2.8	.706	0.75	1.33	0.9	7.1	13.0
vs. West	28	35.2	12.5	.438	0.1	.000	3.5	.551	0.43	1.14	1.0	7.3	12.9	March	17	32.3	11.1	.479	0.1	.000	3.5	.678	0.47	0.59	1.0	6.1	12.9
vs. Div.	28	33.5	10.5	.492	0.1	.000	4.9	.713	0.64	1.14	1.0	7.0	13.8	April	11	29.2	11.7	.473	0.4	.000	3.5	.641	0.36	1.55	0.6	4.3	13.4
As Starter	82	33.8	11.3	.461	0.1	.100	4.1	.671	0.66	0.99	0.9	7.0	13.2	0 Days Rest	24	33.2	10.9	.454	0.1	.333	4.2	.683	0.79	0.75	1.0	7.0	12.8
Off Bench	0	—												1 Days Rest	37	33.9	11.4	.451	0.1	.000	4.2	.675	0.54	1.27	0.6	6.7	13.1
In wins	28	34.1	11.6	.491	0.1	.000	4.6	.688	0.82	1.11	1.0	7.2	14.6	2 Days Rest	14	35.1	12.4	.471	0.1	.000	2.9	.600	0.57	0.57	0.6	6.6	13.4
In losses	54	33.7	11.2	.445	0.1	.143	3.8	.660	0.57	0.93	0.9	6.9	12.5	3+ Days Rest	7	33.3	10.4	.521	0.0	—	5.6	.692	1.00	1.14	1.4	9.0	14.7

Career (1995-96 thru 1999-2000)

	G	Min	FGA	FG%	3PA	3P%	FTA	FT%	Blk	Stl	Ast	Reb	Pts		G	Min	FGA	FG%	3PA	3P%	FTA	FT%	Blk	Stl	Ast	Reb	Pts
Total	298	26.3	9.1	.463	0.1	.200	3.8	.647	0.53	0.74	0.8	5.8	10.9	Pre All-Star	127	25.9	8.4	.450	0.1	.200	3.9	.647	0.62	0.66	0.8	6.1	10.1
Home	152	26.7	9.1	.483	0.1	.200	4.0	.651	0.54	0.74	0.9	5.8	11.3	Post All-Star	133	25.6	9.1	.481	0.1	.222	3.8	.639	0.45	0.78	1.0	5.3	11.2
Road	146	25.9	9.1	.442	0.1	.200	3.7	.642	0.52	0.75	0.8	5.9	10.4	Oct/Nov	39	26.1	8.3	.468	0.1	.250	3.9	.583	0.46	0.59	0.7	7.2	10.1
vs. Playoff	158	26.7	8.9	.433	0.1	.000	3.6	.638	0.46	0.70	0.8	5.8	10.0	December	31	25.9	8.3	.436	0.0	.000	3.5	.645	0.61	0.55	0.9	5.9	9.5
vs. Non-Playoff	140	25.8	9.2	.495	0.1	.364	4.2	.655	0.61	0.79	0.9	5.8	11.9	January	45	26.0	8.3	.445	0.1	.250	4.4	.680	0.71	0.87	0.8	5.6	10.4
vs. East	207	26.9	9.2	.474	0.1	.250	4.0	.667	0.62	0.76	0.8	6.0	11.4	February	54	27.4	9.7	.458	0.0	.500	3.5	.676	0.43	0.76	0.8	6.0	11.3
vs. West	91	24.8	8.8	.436	0.1	.125	3.6	.596	0.33	0.69	0.9	5.4	9.8	March	76	26.3	9.3	.455	0.1	.000	3.7	.645	0.59	0.68	0.9	5.8	10.8
vs. Div.	111	27.2	9.1	.474	0.1	.143	3.9	.654	0.55	0.86	0.8	6.3	11.2	Apr/May	53	25.6	9.8	.500	0.1	.200	4.2	.638	0.40	0.92	0.8	4.8	12.5
As Starter	156	33.0	11.6	.469	0.1	.231	4.4	.669	0.56	0.92	1.0	6.9	13.9	0 Days Rest	82	26.2	9.2	.438	0.1	.167	3.4	.667	0.65	0.65	1.0	5.1	10.8
Off Bench	142	18.9	6.3	.449	0.0	.143	3.2	.612	0.50	0.55	0.7	4.7	7.6	1 Days Rest	145	26.6	9.1	.459	0.1	.125	4.0	.640	0.52	0.77	0.8	5.9	10.9
In wins	158	25.2	8.7	.498	0.1	.273	4.1	.654	0.59	0.78	0.9	5.8	11.3	2 Days Rest	40	26.4	8.9	.476	0.1	.200	3.8	.627	0.43	0.60	0.7	5.6	10.9
In losses	140	27.5	9.5	.426	0.1	.111	3.6	.637	0.46	0.69	0.8	5.9	10.4	3+ Days Rest	31	25.1	8.9	.529	0.0	1.000	4.3	.657	0.42	1.03	1.0	6.3	12.3

Grant Hill
Detroit Pistons — Forward

1999-2000 Per Game Averages

	G	Min	FGA	FG%	3PA	3P%	FTA	FT%	Blk	Stl	Ast	Reb	Pts		G	Min	FGA	FG%	3PA	3P%	FTA	FT%	Blk	Stl	Ast	Reb	Pts
Total	74	37.5	19.2	.489	1.3	.347	8.2	.795	0.58	1.39	5.2	6.6	25.8	Pre All-Star	43	38.6	19.8	.490	1.4	.377	8.8	.821	0.58	1.42	5.5	6.4	27.2
Home	36	38.0	18.9	.486	1.0	.297	9.3	.799	0.44	1.39	4.8	6.5	26.0	Post All-Star	31	36.1	18.4	.489	1.2	.297	7.3	.751	0.58	1.35	4.8	6.9	23.7
Road	38	37.1	19.6	.493	1.6	.377	7.1	.790	0.71	1.39	5.6	6.8	25.5	November	15	38.9	19.9	.470	0.9	.214	8.9	.820	0.33	1.07	5.5	6.4	26.1
vs. Playoff	40	37.5	18.9	.482	1.4	.327	8.0	.821	0.38	1.30	5.2	6.1	25.2	December	14	38.2	19.9	.473	1.1	.438	8.9	.831	0.43	1.64	5.7	7.1	26.6
vs. Non-Playoff	34	37.6	19.6	.498	1.3	.372	8.4	.766	0.82	1.50	5.2	7.2	26.4	January	12	37.3	19.1	.524	2.3	.464	8.9	.813	1.08	1.83	5.4	5.0	28.3
vs. East	48	38.0	18.9	.475	1.4	.358	8.0	.803	0.54	1.48	5.3	6.4	24.9	February	10	40.5	21.1	.498	1.5	.267	5.6	.732	0.90	1.20	5.1	7.7	25.5
vs. West	26	36.7	19.8	.516	1.2	.323	8.4	.780	0.65	1.23	5.0	7.1	27.4	March	15	36.7	19.1	.495	1.1	.188	8.1	.769	0.27	1.33	4.9	6.7	25.3
vs. Div.	24	37.8	19.5	.454	1.2	.379	8.0	.839	0.42	1.54	5.5	6.1	24.9	April	8	31.9	15.0	.483	1.1	.444	7.9	.746	0.75	1.25	4.1	7.3	20.9
As Starter	74	37.5	19.2	.489	1.3	.347	8.2	.795	0.58	1.39	5.2	6.6	25.8	0 Days Rest	17	38.0	19.8	.490	1.4	.375	10.0	.735	0.59	0.65	5.1	6.6	27.3
Off Bench	0	—												1 Days Rest	38	36.8	18.8	.496	1.3	.313	7.6	.800	0.66	1.68	4.8	6.7	25.1
In wins	40	37.6	18.9	.523	1.2	.383	8.3	.804	0.50	1.53	5.3	6.7	26.9	2 Days Rest	8	37.9	17.5	.421	1.0	.375	6.6	.868	0.38	1.25	6.9	6.3	20.9
In losses	34	37.4	19.6	.451	1.5	.314	8.0	.783	0.68	1.24	5.1	6.5	24.4	3+ Days Rest	11	39.1	21.1	.509	1.6	.389	8.3	.846	0.45	1.64	5.5	6.5	29.1

Last Five Seasons

	G	Min	FGA	FG%	3PA	3P%	FTA	FT%	Blk	Stl	Ast	Reb	Pts		G	Min	FGA	FG%	3PA	3P%	FTA	FT%	Blk	Stl	Ast	Reb	Pts
Total	365	39.3	16.6	.476	0.5	.271	8.0	.749	0.60	1.56	6.5	8.1	21.9	Pre All-Star	178	39.8	17.2	.472	0.6	.337	8.3	.757	0.72	1.64	6.4	7.9	22.7
Home	180	39.5	16.3	.485	0.4	.227	8.3	.741	0.61	1.52	6.9	8.3	22.1	Post All-Star	137	39.4	16.0	.480	0.6	.234	7.7	.736	0.46	1.45	6.8	8.8	21.2
Road	185	39.0	16.9	.467	0.6	.299	7.6	.757	0.59	1.60	6.1	8.0	21.8	Oct/Nov	58	38.8	17.1	.442	0.5	.258	8.8	.775	0.52	1.40	6.2	7.3	22.1
vs. Playoff	198	39.7	16.8	.463	0.5	.265	7.9	.759	0.48	1.57	6.4	7.8	21.7	December	58	40.1	17.0	.476	0.5	.333	7.9	.755	0.76	1.74	6.3	8.1	22.3
vs. Non-Playoff	167	38.8	16.4	.491	0.5	.278	8.0	.737	0.74	1.56	6.6	8.5	22.2	January	52	40.4	17.8	.494	0.7	.444	8.4	.741	0.92	1.85	6.8	8.2	24.1
vs. East	250	39.2	16.3	.477	0.5	.274	8.0	.742	0.57	1.57	6.5	8.1	21.6	February	60	39.0	16.4	.484	0.5	.148	7.5	.741	0.58	1.47	6.5	7.8	21.5
vs. West	115	39.5	17.4	.472	0.5	.263	7.9	.764	0.67	1.54	6.5	8.2	22.5	March	80	39.0	16.2	.484	0.6	.180	8.0	.754	0.41	1.54	6.2	8.8	21.8
vs. Div.	126	39.3	16.5	.473	0.5	.279	7.6	.741	0.53	1.71	6.6	8.0	21.5	Apr/May	57	38.3	15.4	.473	0.3	.278	7.3	.720	0.51	1.42	7.1	8.4	19.9
As Starter	365	39.3	16.6	.476	0.5	.271	8.0	.749	0.60	1.56	6.5	8.1	21.9	0 Days Rest	90	39.4	16.3	.481	0.6	.308	8.6	.756	0.52	1.56	6.2	8.3	22.4
Off Bench	0	—												1 Days Rest	187	38.9	16.5	.480	0.5	.237	7.7	.749	0.64	1.60	6.6	8.2	21.8
In wins	202	39.2	16.1	.513	0.5	.330	8.0	.749	0.65	1.63	6.8	8.5	22.7	2 Days Rest	52	40.9	16.8	.456	0.4	.263	7.5	.740	0.65	1.50	7.0	8.8	21.0
In losses	163	39.3	17.2	.432	0.6	.214	7.9	.749	0.53	1.47	6.1	7.7	20.9	3+ Days Rest	36	38.4	17.8	.467	0.8	.321	8.2	.740	0.53	1.44	5.6	6.8	22.9

Tyrone Hill

1999-2000 Per Game Averages

	G	Min	FGA	FG%	3PA	3P%	FTA	FT%	Blk	Stl	Ast	Reb	Pts		G	Min	FGA	FG%	3PA	3P%	FTA	FT%	Blk	Stl	Ast	Reb	Pts
Total	68	31.7	9.6	.485	0.0	.000	3.8	.691	0.40	0.94	0.8	9.2	12.0	Pre All-Star	40	31.3	9.3	.442	0.0	—	3.7	.723	0.45	0.93	0.8	8.8	10.9
Home	35	30.3	8.9	.503	0.0	.000	4.0	.719	0.37	0.86	0.6	8.7	11.8	Post All-Star	28	32.3	10.1	.541	0.0	.000	4.0	.649	0.32	0.96	0.7	9.7	13.5
Road	33	33.1	10.5	.468	0.0	—	3.6	.658	0.42	1.03	0.9	9.7	12.2	November	9	28.2	8.2	.419	0.0	—	2.1	.789	1.00	0.56	0.7	8.1	8.6
vs. Playoff	36	31.4	9.4	.496	0.0	.000	3.6	.680	0.47	0.78	0.8	9.1	11.8	December	14	33.0	10.7	.453	0.0	—	4.1	.754	0.36	1.29	1.1	9.5	12.8
vs. Non-Playoff	32	32.0	9.9	.473	0.0	—	4.1	.702	0.31	1.13	0.8	9.3	12.3	January	12	32.8	8.7	.462	0.0	—	5.2	.677	0.17	1.08	0.8	8.3	11.5
vs. East	43	32.7	10.3	.510	0.0	.000	4.4	.712	0.33	1.00	0.8	9.7	13.7	February	12	29.4	8.5	.520	0.0	—	3.3	.725	0.50	1.17	0.6	9.5	11.3
vs. West	25	30.0	8.4	.431	0.0	—	2.7	.632	0.52	0.84	0.8	8.2	9.0	March	11	32.3	10.4	.518	0.0	—	4.0	.614	0.27	0.36	0.6	10.1	13.2
vs. Div.	17	32.2	9.9	.491	0.1	.000	4.4	.747	0.29	0.88	0.7	9.7	13.1	April	10	33.7	11.2	.527	0.1	.000	3.7	.622	0.20	1.00	0.7	9.4	14.1
As Starter	65	32.2	9.8	.494	0.0	.000	3.8	.698	0.37	0.98	0.8	9.3	12.4	0 Days Rest	17	32.1	9.8	.434	0.1	.000	2.8	.596	0.35	0.76	0.6	8.8	10.1
Off Bench	3	21.0	6.0	.167	0.0	—	3.7	.545	1.00	0.00	0.7	7.3	4.0	1 Days Rest	33	31.8	10.5	.511	0.0	—	4.1	.728	0.27	1.03	0.7	9.8	13.8
In wins	41	32.0	9.5	.526	0.0	.000	3.8	.707	0.20	1.07	0.8	9.4	12.7	2 Days Rest	9	30.6	7.3	.530	0.0	—	4.4	.750	0.67	1.22	1.0	8.3	11.1
In losses	27	31.3	9.9	.425	0.0	—	3.8	.667	0.70	0.74	0.8	8.9	11.0	3+ Days Rest	9	31.6	8.4	.434	0.0	—	4.0	.611	0.67	0.67	1.1	8.7	9.8

Last Five Seasons

	G	Min	FGA	FG%	3PA	3P%	FTA	FT%	Blk	Stl	Ast	Reb	Pts		G	Min	FGA	FG%	3PA	3P%	FTA	FT%	Blk	Stl	Ast	Reb	Pts
Total	281	31.4	7.8	.518	0.0	.000	4.2	.625	0.44	0.92	1.1	8.9	10.7	Pre All-Star	131	33.1	8.0	.505	0.0	.000	4.1	.659	0.47	0.97	1.2	9.3	10.8
Home	143	30.8	7.8	.521	0.0	.000	4.2	.628	0.45	0.90	1.1	8.8	10.7	Post All-Star	112	30.3	7.8	.553	0.0	.000	4.4	.612	0.40	0.88	1.0	8.9	11.3
Road	138	32.1	7.8	.515	0.0	.000	4.2	.621	0.42	0.95	1.1	9.0	10.7	Oct/Nov	39	32.7	7.8	.487	0.1	.000	4.1	.620	0.62	0.85	1.4	9.0	10.2
vs. Playoff	149	31.9	7.9	.518	0.0	.000	4.1	.617	0.36	0.84	1.0	8.9	10.7	December	41	35.3	8.7	.522	0.0	—	4.3	.731	0.59	1.02	1.4	10.4	12.2
vs. Non-Playoff	132	30.9	7.7	.518	0.0	—	4.3	.632	0.53	1.02	1.1	8.9	10.7	January	36	32.5	7.8	.520	0.0	—	4.1	.626	0.19	1.08	0.8	8.4	10.6
vs. East	198	31.9	7.9	.519	0.0	.000	4.4	.622	0.43	0.92	1.1	9.0	11.0	February	58	30.6	7.3	.505	0.0	—	4.0	.662	0.50	0.97	1.1	9.3	10.1
vs. West	83	30.4	7.5	.516	0.0	—	3.6	.631	0.45	0.93	1.1	8.7	10.0	March	62	30.1	7.9	.543	0.0	—	4.8	.591	0.40	0.79	1.0	8.6	11.4
vs. Div.	95	31.7	7.7	.521	0.0	.000	4.3	.621	0.43	0.89	0.9	9.0	10.6	Apr/May	45	29.0	7.5	.521	0.0	.000	3.8	.524	0.31	0.89	0.8	7.8	9.8
As Starter	216	31.4	8.4	.527	0.0	.000	4.5	.639	0.43	1.00	1.2	9.7	11.7	0 Days Rest	69	31.3	7.6	.501	0.0	—	3.8	.598	0.36	0.96	0.9	8.6	9.9
Off Bench	65	22.6	5.9	.478	0.0	—	3.3	.557	0.46	0.68	0.7	6.2	7.4	1 Days Rest	125	31.1	8.2	.524	0.0	.000	4.2	.628	0.38	0.86	1.0	8.9	11.2
In wins	153	31.0	7.9	.539	0.0	.000	4.2	.631	0.42	0.99	1.1	8.9	11.1	2 Days Rest	45	31.5	7.2	.528	0.0	—	3.9	.665	0.58	1.09	1.2	8.6	10.2
In losses	128	32.0	7.7	.492	0.0	.000	4.2	.617	0.46	0.84	1.1	8.9	10.2	3+ Days Rest	42	32.7	7.7	.519	0.0	—	5.1	.616	0.60	0.86	1.3	9.7	11.1

Jeff Hornacek

1999-2000 Per Game Averages

	G	Min	FGA	FG%	3PA	3P%	FTA	FT%	Blk	Stl	Ast	Reb	Pts		G	Min	FGA	FG%	3PA	3P%	FTA	FT%	Blk	Stl	Ast	Reb	Pts
Total	77	27.7	9.5	.492	1.8	.478	2.3	.950	0.21	0.86	2.6	2.4	12.4	Pre All-Star	44	28.9	9.9	.491	1.6	.380	2.7	.966	0.27	0.93	2.7	2.5	12.9
Home	40	26.9	9.6	.527	2.0	.519	2.5	.970	0.18	0.85	2.8	2.1	13.5	Post All-Star	33	26.1	8.9	.493	2.0	.582	1.9	.919	0.12	0.76	2.5	2.2	11.7
Road	37	28.5	9.3	.452	1.6	.424	2.2	.926	0.24	0.86	2.5	2.6	11.1	November	14	30.6	10.7	.480	1.5	.333	3.2	.956	0.43	0.79	2.5	2.6	13.9
vs. Playoff	42	28.6	10.0	.461	1.9	.475	2.3	.949	0.19	0.95	2.3	2.4	12.4	December	14	29.5	9.8	.504	1.6	.455	2.9	1.000	0.14	0.86	3.1	2.6	13.5
vs. Non-Playoff	35	26.6	8.8	.534	1.7	.483	2.3	.951	0.23	0.74	3.0	2.3	12.4	January	11	26.6	8.9	.459	1.7	.316	2.1	.913	0.18	1.09	2.1	2.3	10.6
vs. East	30	28.6	9.7	.507	1.9	.569	2.1	.969	0.13	0.90	2.4	2.3	13.0	February	13	29.2	10.2	.519	2.3	.633	2.3	.933	0.31	0.77	2.8	2.4	14.2
vs. West	47	27.1	9.3	.482	1.7	.413	2.5	.940	0.26	0.83	2.8	2.4	12.0	March	16	25.9	8.3	.485	1.9	.567	2.1	.940	0.06	1.06	2.8	2.2	11.1
vs. Div.	21	27.4	9.0	.497	1.6	.303	2.2	.936	0.43	0.81	2.3	2.7	11.5	April	9	22.7	8.7	.500	1.8	.438	0.8	.857	0.11	0.44	2.3	2.0	10.1
As Starter	77	27.7	9.5	.492	1.8	.478	2.3	.950	0.21	0.86	2.6	2.4	12.4	0 Days Rest	16	27.9	8.6	.486	1.7	.593	2.8	.956	0.19	0.75	2.9	2.4	12.1
Off Bench	0	—	—	—	—	—	—	—	—	—	—	—	—	1 Days Rest	42	27.8	9.8	.512	1.8	.527	2.0	.952	0.21	0.90	2.7	2.4	12.9
In wins	52	27.8	9.3	.512	1.8	.484	2.4	.960	0.17	0.96	2.9	2.5	12.8	2 Days Rest	12	27.8	9.7	.483	2.0	.250	2.9	.914	0.25	0.92	2.3	3.1	12.5
In losses	25	27.5	9.7	.450	1.7	.465	2.2	.929	0.28	0.64	2.1	2.1	11.6	3+ Days Rest	7	26.4	8.9	.387	1.9	.385	2.4	1.000	0.14	0.71	1.9	0.9	10.0

Last Five Seasons

	G	Min	FGA	FG%	3PA	3P%	FTA	FT%	Blk	Stl	Ast	Reb	Pts		G	Min	FGA	FG%	3PA	3P%	FTA	FT%	Blk	Stl	Ast	Reb	Pts
Total	369	30.4	10.1	.488	2.1	.435	3.4	.901	0.25	1.24	3.9	2.9	13.9	Pre All-Star	185	31.1	10.6	.482	2.2	.410	3.6	.905	0.27	1.30	3.8	3.0	14.3
Home	185	29.3	10.2	.512	2.2	.468	3.5	.902	0.29	1.15	4.1	3.0	14.6	Post All-Star	136	29.6	9.8	.502	2.0	.475	3.4	.897	0.20	1.21	4.0	2.6	13.8
Road	184	31.4	10.1	.464	1.9	.395	3.3	.899	0.20	1.33	3.8	2.8	13.2	Oct/Nov	58	30.8	10.8	.470	2.1	.412	4.5	.900	0.34	1.31	3.9	3.2	15.0
vs. Playoff	199	31.3	10.2	.468	2.1	.426	3.5	.910	0.20	1.15	3.7	2.9	13.7	December	58	31.2	10.4	.458	2.2	.384	3.6	.923	0.19	1.26	3.9	2.8	13.6
vs. Non-Playoff	170	29.3	10.0	.512	2.0	.445	3.3	.889	0.30	1.34	4.1	2.8	14.1	January	53	31.2	10.6	.512	2.4	.440	2.8	.887	0.23	1.25	3.8	3.0	14.4
vs. East	126	31.1	10.3	.483	2.1	.419	3.8	.899	0.21	1.11	3.7	2.8	14.2	February	59	30.0	10.0	.502	2.0	.415	3.2	.877	0.37	1.29	3.9	2.7	13.7
vs. West	243	30.0	10.0	.491	2.1	.443	3.2	.902	0.27	1.30	4.0	2.9	13.7	March	78	30.3	9.7	.497	1.9	.503	3.6	.906	0.18	1.19	4.1	2.5	13.8
vs. Div.	109	30.1	10.1	.485	1.9	.430	3.2	.899	0.33	1.32	4.0	3.1	13.5	Apr/May	63	28.9	9.6	.490	2.0	.437	2.8	.904	0.19	1.16	3.9	3.1	12.8
As Starter	346	30.4	10.1	.490	2.1	.432	3.3	.900	0.24	1.24	3.9	2.9	13.8	0 Days Rest	87	30.5	9.7	.471	2.0	.434	3.3	.913	0.21	1.24	3.8	2.9	13.0
Off Bench	23	29.6	10.0	.459	2.3	.463	4.3	.909	0.30	1.26	3.7	2.3	14.2	1 Days Rest	199	30.2	10.2	.497	2.1	.443	3.5	.897	0.27	1.28	4.0	2.8	14.2
In wins	267	29.9	9.9	.503	1.9	.462	3.5	.899	0.26	1.28	4.1	3.0	14.1	2 Days Rest	51	31.5	10.6	.492	2.1	.402	3.4	.878	0.27	1.18	3.7	3.2	14.2
In losses	102	31.6	10.7	.451	2.4	.377	3.1	.907	0.22	1.13	3.4	2.6	13.4	3+ Days Rest	32	29.7	10.1	.471	2.2	.437	3.5	.929	0.16	1.09	4.1	2.6	13.8

Robert Horry
Los Angeles Lakers — Forward

1999-2000 Per Game Averages

	G	Min	FGA	FG%	3PA	3P%	FTA	FT%	Blk	Stl	Ast	Reb	Pts
Total	76	22.2	4.8	.438	1.2	.309	1.5	.788	1.05	1.11	1.6	4.8	5.7
Home	39	22.3	4.8	.420	1.1	.302	1.6	.806	1.23	1.28	1.7	5.3	5.7
Road	37	22.0	4.7	.457	1.4	.314	1.4	.765	0.86	0.92	1.4	4.2	5.8
vs. Playoff	42	22.9	4.6	.420	1.3	.236	1.5	.766	1.21	0.98	1.4	4.5	5.3
vs. Non-Playoff	34	21.3	5.0	.459	1.1	.410	1.4	.816	0.85	1.24	1.8	5.1	6.2
vs. East	30	22.3	4.5	.478	1.2	.432	1.7	.745	1.13	1.00	1.4	4.5	6.1
vs. West	46	22.1	4.9	.414	1.2	.228	1.3	.823	1.00	1.17	1.7	4.9	5.5
vs. Div.	23	23.2	5.0	.426	1.3	.267	1.2	.852	1.09	1.09	1.7	5.3	5.6
As Starter	0	—	—	—	—	—	—	—	—	—	—	—	—
Off Bench	76	22.2	4.8	.438	1.2	.309	1.5	.788	1.05	1.11	1.6	4.8	5.7
In wins	62	22.8	4.9	.464	1.3	.325	1.5	.824	1.03	1.06	1.6	5.0	6.1
In losses	14	19.6	4.4	.311	1.0	.214	1.6	.636	1.14	1.29	1.5	3.6	3.9

	G	Min	FGA	FG%	3PA	3P%	FTA	FT%	Blk	Stl	Ast	Reb	Pts
Pre All-Star	42	20.8	4.5	.423	0.7	.200	1.3	.741	1.05	1.21	1.6	5.2	4.9
Post All-Star	34	23.9	5.1	.454	1.9	.359	1.7	.831	1.06	0.97	1.5	4.2	6.8
November	9	15.2	4.6	.366	0.4	.000	0.8	.714	0.78	1.44	1.7	4.1	3.9
December	15	22.3	4.7	.429	0.8	.167	1.4	.857	1.20	1.60	1.7	6.2	5.3
January	14	23.6	4.6	.438	0.9	.308	1.3	.667	1.00	1.00	1.5	5.4	5.1
February	13	19.7	4.5	.483	1.2	.400	1.5	.750	1.23	0.46	1.3	2.8	5.9
March	16	26.9	5.6	.489	2.6	.415	1.7	.852	0.94	1.19	2.0	5.1	8.0
April	9	21.9	4.4	.350	1.0	.000	2.2	.800	1.11	0.89	0.8	4.2	4.9
0 Days Rest	19	21.3	4.4	.482	1.6	.300	0.7	.857	0.74	0.84	1.5	4.6	5.3
1 Days Rest	39	22.9	4.5	.437	1.0	.350	1.8	.736	1.13	1.08	1.5	5.1	5.6
2 Days Rest	11	21.5	5.7	.365	1.6	.333	1.8	.857	1.00	1.18	1.5	4.5	6.4
3+ Days Rest	7	21.4	6.1	.465	0.9	.000	0.9	1.000	1.57	1.86	1.9	3.6	6.6

Last Five Seasons

	G	Min	FGA	FG%	3PA	3P%	FTA	FT%	Blk	Stl	Ast	Reb	Pts
Total	311	27.8	6.5	.437	2.5	.335	1.8	.733	1.21	1.33	2.3	5.5	7.8
Home	155	27.3	6.4	.433	2.4	.339	1.9	.739	1.30	1.41	2.6	5.5	7.7
Road	156	28.3	6.6	.440	2.6	.331	1.8	.726	1.13	1.26	2.1	5.5	7.9
vs. Playoff	169	28.3	6.3	.412	2.6	.302	1.8	.730	1.27	1.28	2.2	5.3	7.4
vs. Non-Playoff	142	27.2	6.7	.465	2.4	.377	1.8	.736	1.15	1.39	2.5	5.7	8.4
vs. East	103	29.1	6.6	.442	2.6	.342	2.1	.705	1.33	1.35	2.3	5.6	8.2
vs. West	208	27.2	6.4	.434	2.4	.331	1.7	.750	1.15	1.32	2.4	5.4	7.6
vs. Div.	103	26.9	6.1	.432	2.4	.355	1.7	.749	1.10	1.35	2.2	5.3	7.2
As Starter	176	33.0	7.9	.435	3.3	.333	2.2	.724	1.36	1.53	3.0	6.4	9.6
Off Bench	135	21.1	4.6	.441	1.4	.338	1.3	.751	1.01	1.07	1.4	4.3	5.6
In wins	205	27.7	6.4	.473	2.3	.378	1.9	.761	1.22	1.33	2.5	5.8	8.4
In losses	106	28.0	6.6	.368	2.8	.267	1.6	.667	1.19	1.33	2.1	4.9	6.7

	G	Min	FGA	FG%	3PA	3P%	FTA	FT%	Blk	Stl	Ast	Reb	Pts
Pre All-Star	166	28.1	6.8	.421	2.6	.315	1.9	.722	1.23	1.37	2.3	5.5	7.9
Post All-Star	107	30.3	6.9	.457	2.7	.347	1.9	.748	1.24	1.41	2.7	6.0	8.7
Oct/Nov	52	28.6	7.6	.455	2.6	.381	1.7	.663	1.29	1.50	2.8	5.7	9.0
December	58	27.2	6.6	.426	2.4	.313	1.9	.757	1.16	1.26	2.0	5.5	7.8
January	45	28.6	6.2	.361	2.5	.219	1.9	.736	1.27	1.36	2.2	5.4	6.4
February	48	28.5	6.5	.465	2.9	.380	1.9	.710	1.31	1.21	2.5	4.8	8.5
March	57	27.7	6.2	.459	2.3	.368	1.7	.786	1.07	1.32	2.5	5.8	7.9
Apr/May	51	26.5	6.0	.443	2.1	.330	1.6	.735	1.22	1.35	2.1	5.5	7.2
0 Days Rest	72	27.5	6.3	.470	2.3	.385	1.5	.769	1.13	1.14	2.0	5.4	7.8
1 Days Rest	156	28.3	6.5	.428	2.4	.304	2.0	.705	1.23	1.31	2.3	5.6	7.7
2 Days Rest	45	28.5	7.5	.396	3.1	.312	1.9	.770	1.18	1.40	2.5	5.6	8.4
3+ Days Rest	38	25.5	5.9	.473	2.2	.410	1.3	.765	1.34	1.68	2.9	4.7	7.5

Allan Houston
New York Knicks — Guard

1999-2000 Per Game Averages

	G	Min	FGA	FG%	3PA	3P%	FTA	FT%	Blk	Stl	Ast	Reb	Pts
Total	82	38.6	15.5	.483	3.0	.436	4.1	.838	0.17	0.79	2.7	3.3	19.7
Home	41	38.2	15.3	.478	2.9	.419	4.4	.813	0.24	0.68	2.9	3.7	19.4
Road	41	39.0	15.7	.488	3.1	.452	3.7	.868	0.10	0.90	2.5	2.9	19.9
vs. Playoff	44	38.8	15.4	.481	3.2	.468	4.1	.862	0.09	0.73	3.0	3.3	19.9
vs. Non-Playoff	38	38.5	15.6	.486	2.7	.392	4.0	.810	0.26	0.87	2.4	3.3	19.5
vs. East	54	39.4	15.4	.477	3.1	.465	3.9	.863	0.17	0.87	2.6	3.1	19.6
vs. West	28	37.3	15.6	.494	2.6	.370	4.4	.797	0.18	0.64	2.9	3.6	19.9
vs. Div.	24	40.2	15.3	.444	2.9	.400	4.8	.842	0.21	1.04	2.4	2.8	18.8
As Starter	82	38.6	15.5	.483	3.0	.436	4.1	.838	0.17	0.79	2.7	3.3	19.7
Off Bench	0	—	—	—	—	—	—	—	—	—	—	—	—
In wins	50	38.2	15.7	.501	3.2	.459	4.1	.820	0.18	0.84	2.8	3.5	20.6
In losses	32	39.4	15.2	.454	2.6	.393	4.0	.867	0.16	0.72	2.7	2.9	18.3

	G	Min	FGA	FG%	3PA	3P%	FTA	FT%	Blk	Stl	Ast	Reb	Pts
Pre All-Star	47	39.4	16.2	.491	3.2	.450	4.4	.829	0.28	0.81	2.9	3.7	20.9
Post All-Star	35	37.6	14.6	.472	2.7	.415	3.7	.853	0.03	0.77	2.5	2.8	18.0
November	16	39.1	14.8	.511	2.9	.511	5.4	.860	0.44	0.56	2.9	3.6	21.3
December	14	38.7	16.8	.455	3.4	.298	4.8	.761	0.21	1.21	2.4	2.9	19.9
January	12	40.8	17.3	.500	3.3	.538	2.8	.848	0.25	0.83	3.3	4.8	21.4
February	13	38.5	15.2	.477	2.7	.400	3.8	.857	0.00	0.62	3.1	2.8	18.8
March	17	38.3	14.9	.504	2.9	.460	4.2	.875	0.06	0.94	2.6	2.8	20.1
April	10	36.0	14.0	.429	2.5	.400	2.7	.815	0.00	2.00	2.0	3.2	15.2
0 Days Rest	20	38.8	16.2	.433	2.7	.352	5.3	.884	0.15	1.05	2.5	3.2	18.0
1 Days Rest	42	38.7	15.4	.499	2.9	.405	4.5	.824	0.14	0.71	2.5	3.1	20.2
2 Days Rest	14	37.6	14.7	.490	3.4	.521	3.3	.870	0.14	0.71	2.6	3.9	19.1
3+ Days Rest	6	40.0	15.8	.526	3.3	.650	5.2	.774	0.50	0.67	2.5	3.8	22.8

Last Five Seasons

	G	Min	FGA	FG%	3PA	3P%	FTA	FT%	Blk	Stl	Ast	Reb	Pts
Total	377	36.0	14.7	.449	3.8	.409	3.8	.835	0.21	0.70	2.7	3.3	17.9
Home	189	35.9	14.8	.457	3.8	.417	4.1	.828	0.23	0.71	2.8	3.4	18.5
Road	188	36.1	14.5	.440	3.7	.401	3.6	.844	0.20	0.69	2.5	3.1	17.3
vs. Playoff	200	36.2	14.8	.442	3.9	.407	4.1	.830	0.21	0.67	2.6	3.3	18.0
vs. Non-Playoff	177	35.8	14.5	.456	3.7	.412	3.5	.842	0.22	0.75	2.7	3.2	17.8
vs. East	260	36.2	14.6	.451	3.6	.423	3.8	.831	0.18	0.73	2.6	3.3	17.8
vs. West	117	35.7	14.8	.444	4.1	.383	3.9	.843	0.29	0.64	2.9	3.3	18.0
vs. Div.	120	36.9	14.7	.453	4.0	.435	4.0	.817	0.14	0.81	2.6	3.3	18.3
As Starter	370	36.3	14.7	.450	3.8	.412	3.8	.837	0.21	0.70	2.7	3.3	18.0
Off Bench	7	22.4	11.1	.346	4.6	.281	3.0	.714	0.43	1.00	2.6	2.0	11.1
In wins	222	35.8	14.5	.469	3.8	.447	3.8	.832	0.24	0.74	2.8	3.4	18.5
In losses	155	36.4	14.8	.420	3.8	.357	3.8	.840	0.18	0.65	2.4	3.1	17.1

	G	Min	FGA	FG%	3PA	3P%	FTA	FT%	Blk	Stl	Ast	Reb	Pts
Pre All-Star	186	35.3	14.6	.445	3.7	.402	3.6	.819	0.25	0.70	2.6	3.2	17.5
Post All-Star	141	37.0	14.9	.464	4.3	.418	4.0	.846	0.18	0.71	2.7	3.5	19.1
Oct/Nov	59	32.3	12.7	.434	3.3	.371	3.8	.806	0.37	0.80	2.8	2.6	15.3
December	58	35.4	14.7	.439	4.0	.403	3.7	.804	0.21	0.69	2.2	3.4	17.5
January	54	37.4	15.9	.452	3.6	.415	3.2	.822	0.22	0.67	2.6	3.3	18.5
February	64	37.2	15.4	.451	4.2	.424	4.5	.860	0.19	0.66	3.0	3.9	19.5
March	82	37.5	15.0	.454	4.1	.420	4.0	.854	0.20	0.70	2.8	3.1	18.8
Apr/May	60	35.9	14.2	.457	3.3	.410	3.7	.845	0.12	0.72	2.6	3.3	17.4
0 Days Rest	97	36.1	14.8	.418	3.8	.375	3.7	.842	0.19	0.74	2.4	3.4	16.9
1 Days Rest	195	36.2	14.7	.469	3.9	.429	3.9	.839	0.22	0.73	2.7	3.2	18.7
2 Days Rest	57	35.6	14.3	.442	3.6	.405	3.4	.831	0.16	0.53	2.9	3.4	17.0
3+ Days Rest	28	35.7	14.7	.430	3.6	.390	4.4	.797	0.43	0.71	2.6	3.3	17.5

Juwan Howard
Washington Wizards — Forward

1999-2000 Per Game Averages

	G	Min	FGA	FG%	3PA	3P%	FTA	FT%	Blk	Stl	Ast	Reb	Pts
Total	82	35.5	13.5	.459	0.1	.000	3.4	.735	0.26	0.82	3.0	5.7	14.9
Home	41	35.3	13.3	.479	0.1	.000	4.0	.761	0.27	0.93	2.7	5.8	15.8
Road	41	35.6	13.7	.440	0.1	.000	2.7	.696	0.24	0.71	3.3	5.7	14.0
vs. Playoff	46	35.8	13.5	.467	0.1	.000	3.0	.719	0.24	0.65	3.0	5.8	14.8
vs. Non-Playoff	36	35.0	13.5	.450	0.1	.000	3.8	.750	0.28	1.03	3.0	5.6	15.0
vs. East	54	35.2	13.3	.485	0.1	.000	3.4	.757	0.22	0.89	3.3	5.5	15.5
vs. West	28	36.1	14.0	.412	0.1	.000	3.2	.689	0.32	0.68	2.5	6.1	13.7
vs. Div.	24	36.2	13.1	.502	0.1	.000	3.6	.759	0.25	1.04	3.1	5.7	15.9
As Starter	82	35.5	13.5	.459	0.1	.000	3.4	.735	0.26	0.82	3.0	5.7	14.9
Off Bench	0	—	—	—	—	—	—	—	—	—	—	—	—
In wins	29	34.4	13.6	.456	0.1	.000	3.2	.731	0.21	0.93	3.1	5.5	14.8
In losses	53	36.1	13.5	.461	0.1	.000	3.4	.736	0.28	0.75	2.9	5.8	14.9

	G	Min	FGA	FG%	3PA	3P%	FTA	FT%	Blk	Stl	Ast	Reb	Pts
Pre All-Star	49	34.7	13.4	.472	0.1	.000	3.4	.753	0.31	0.90	2.6	5.3	15.2
Post All-Star	33	36.6	13.6	.441	0.1	.000	3.3	.706	0.18	0.70	3.6	6.4	14.3
November	15	31.5	12.7	.468	0.0	—	2.6	.718	0.40	1.07	1.8	4.7	13.7
December	15	33.5	12.9	.428	0.0	—	3.3	.673	0.27	0.67	2.7	4.4	13.3
January	14	36.8	14.4	.520	0.2	.000	4.6	.815	0.21	0.79	3.0	5.6	18.8
February	12	38.3	14.0	.417	0.0	—	3.8	.733	0.42	0.67	3.3	7.7	14.4
March	17	37.4	14.5	.447	0.2	.000	2.8	.723	0.12	0.82	3.1	6.6	14.9
April	9	36.2	12.0	.481	0.1	.000	3.3	.700	0.11	0.89	5.0	5.6	13.9
0 Days Rest	22	36.1	13.0	.425	0.1	.000	3.5	.654	0.27	0.82	3.0	6.0	13.4
1 Days Rest	39	35.7	14.2	.468	0.1	.000	3.2	.736	0.21	0.72	3.2	6.0	15.6
2 Days Rest	13	33.2	12.2	.472	0.0	—	3.3	.791	0.38	1.23	2.4	5.3	14.2
3+ Days Rest	8	36.5	13.5	.491	0.1	.000	3.6	.862	0.25	0.63	3.4	4.5	16.4

Last Five Seasons

	G	Min	FGA	FG%	3PA	3P%	FTA	FT%	Blk	Stl	Ast	Reb	Pts
Total	345	39.2	16.0	.477	0.1	.148	4.6	.742	0.35	1.02	3.6	7.3	18.7
Home	172	39.2	16.0	.485	0.1	.083	4.9	.762	0.40	1.15	3.6	7.3	19.3
Road	173	39.1	16.0	.469	0.1	.200	4.3	.720	0.30	0.88	3.5	7.3	18.1
vs. Playoff	197	39.5	16.0	.473	0.1	.071	4.4	.744	0.34	0.94	3.4	7.1	18.4
vs. Non-Playoff	148	38.8	16.0	.482	0.1	.231	4.9	.740	0.36	1.11	3.7	7.6	19.1
vs. East	236	39.1	16.0	.475	0.1	.111	4.6	.741	0.32	1.00	3.6	7.4	18.6
vs. West	109	39.4	16.1	.479	0.1	.222	4.7	.744	0.40	1.06	3.6	7.1	18.9
vs. Div.	104	38.9	15.5	.493	0.1	.143	5.0	.749	0.38	1.07	3.5	7.5	19.0
As Starter	345	39.2	16.0	.477	0.1	.148	4.6	.742	0.35	1.02	3.6	7.3	18.7
Off Bench	0	—	—	—	—	—	—	—	—	—	—	—	—
In wins	157	39.4	16.2	.497	0.1	.083	4.8	.761	0.38	1.18	3.9	7.6	19.8
In losses	188	39.0	15.8	.459	0.1	.200	4.5	.726	0.32	0.88	3.3	7.1	17.8

	G	Min	FGA	FG%	3PA	3P%	FTA	FT%	Blk	Stl	Ast	Reb	Pts
Pre All-Star	188	38.7	15.7	.475	0.1	.188	4.5	.739	0.34	1.06	3.5	7.0	18.3
Post All-Star	121	39.7	16.2	.479	0.1	.125	4.9	.744	0.36	0.91	3.9	7.6	19.2
Oct/Nov	57	37.7	15.5	.473	0.1	.167	4.1	.722	0.42	1.02	3.0	7.2	17.6
December	60	38.3	15.3	.476	0.1	.400	4.8	.716	0.37	1.20	3.6	6.6	18.0
January	56	40.0	16.2	.481	0.1	.000	5.0	.780	0.21	0.88	3.7	6.8	19.5
February	52	39.4	16.9	.451	0.1	.000	4.9	.711	0.38	0.77	3.8	8.5	18.7
March	74	39.9	16.5	.467	0.1	.000	4.0	.773	0.35	1.09	3.5	7.5	18.5
Apr/May	46	39.7	15.5	.523	0.0	.500	5.1	.744	0.35	1.11	4.0	7.5	20.1
0 Days Rest	94	38.7	15.8	.472	0.1	.111	4.9	.733	0.40	0.96	3.5	7.3	18.5
1 Days Rest	169	39.7	16.5	.484	0.1	.154	4.6	.722	0.35	1.07	3.7	7.3	19.3
2 Days Rest	48	38.0	15.4	.463	0.0	.000	3.9	.787	0.25	1.13	3.4	7.1	17.3
3+ Days Rest	34	39.6	15.0	.468	0.1	.250	4.7	.813	0.32	0.79	3.6	7.7	17.9

Troy Hudson
Los Angeles Clippers — Guard

1999-2000 Per Game Averages

	G	Min	FGA	FG%	3PA	3P%	FTA	FT%	Blk	Stl	Ast	Reb	Pts
Total	62	25.7	8.7	.377	3.1	.311	1.5	.811	0.00	0.69	3.9	2.4	8.8
Home	28	25.3	8.4	.373	3.0	.262	1.3	.829	0.00	0.57	3.8	2.4	8.1
Road	34	26.0	9.0	.380	3.2	.349	1.8	.800	0.00	0.79	4.0	2.4	9.4
vs. Playoff	36	26.2	8.7	.373	3.1	.304	1.5	.818	0.00	0.72	3.5	2.2	8.7
vs. Non-Playoff	26	24.9	8.7	.383	3.1	.321	1.5	.800	0.00	0.65	4.4	2.6	8.9
vs. East	25	26.5	9.6	.408	3.6	.344	1.6	.805	0.00	0.64	3.9	2.3	10.4
vs. West	37	25.1	8.1	.352	2.8	.282	1.5	.815	0.00	0.73	3.9	2.4	7.7
vs. Div.	16	27.1	8.8	.340	2.9	.239	1.9	.806	0.00	1.00	4.3	3.1	8.3
As Starter	38	32.1	10.9	.386	3.7	.345	2.0	.803	0.00	0.92	4.9	3.3	11.3
Off Bench	24	15.5	5.3	.346	2.1	.216	0.8	.842	0.00	0.33	2.3	1.0	4.8
In wins	12	31.3	11.3	.415	4.3	.353	2.2	.885	0.00	1.00	5.2	3.4	12.8
In losses	50	24.3	8.1	.365	2.8	.296	1.4	.783	0.00	0.62	3.6	2.1	7.8

	G	Min	FGA	FG%	3PA	3P%	FTA	FT%	Blk	Stl	Ast	Reb	Pts
Pre All-Star	48	27.8	9.2	.377	3.1	.305	1.7	.817	0.00	0.83	4.3	2.7	9.3
Post All-Star	14	18.5	7.3	.378	3.0	.333	0.9	.769	0.00	0.21	2.6	1.4	7.0
November	14	29.4	9.6	.356	3.6	.300	1.6	.783	0.00	1.21	2.4	2.4	9.2
December	14	29.4	10.0	.393	2.8	.308	2.2	.774	0.00	0.64	5.5	3.5	10.4
January	14	26.2	7.6	.387	2.4	.273	1.2	.941	0.00	0.64	3.9	2.6	7.6
February	15	25.5	9.5	.378	4.2	.365	1.3	.789	0.00	0.47	4.3	1.9	9.7
March	5	6.8	3.4	.353	1.6	.125	1.0	.800	0.00	0.20	0.4	0.2	3.4
April	0	—	—	—	—	—	—	—	—	—	—	—	—
0 Days Rest	17	27.2	10.5	.404	3.6	.339	2.1	.771	0.00	0.88	4.6	2.9	11.3
1 Days Rest	25	24.3	7.6	.376	2.4	.361	1.3	.813	0.00	0.44	3.6	2.2	7.6
2 Days Rest	12	30.9	10.0	.367	4.3	.269	1.9	.870	0.00	0.83	4.0	2.8	10.2
3+ Days Rest	8	18.9	6.8	.315	2.3	.167	0.6	.800	0.00	0.88	3.0	1.4	5.1

Career (1997-98 thru 1999-2000)

	G	Min	FGA	FG%	3PA	3P%	FTA	FT%	Blk	Stl	Ast	Reb	Pts
Total	95	22.5	7.4	.383	2.6	.309	1.4	.835	0.02	0.59	3.6	2.2	7.6
Home	47	20.1	6.7	.369	2.2	.248	1.0	.833	0.00	0.51	3.1	2.1	6.3
Road	48	24.9	8.1	.394	2.9	.355	1.8	.835	0.04	0.67	4.0	2.3	8.9
vs. Playoff	54	23.8	7.7	.379	2.6	.303	1.5	.838	0.02	0.65	3.5	2.1	7.9
vs. Non-Playoff	41	20.9	7.0	.389	2.5	.317	1.3	.830	0.02	0.51	3.7	2.2	7.3
vs. East	28	24.0	8.7	.402	3.3	.341	1.5	.805	0.00	0.57	3.5	2.1	9.3
vs. West	67	21.9	6.9	.373	2.3	.289	1.4	.848	0.03	0.60	3.6	2.2	7.0
vs. Div.	26	23.0	7.7	.358	2.3	.250	1.7	.860	0.00	0.88	4.0	2.6	7.5
As Starter	44	34.0	11.2	.385	3.8	.339	2.3	.842	0.02	0.93	5.5	3.5	11.8
Off Bench	51	12.6	4.1	.379	1.5	.244	0.6	.813	0.02	0.29	1.8	1.0	4.0
In wins	22	21.0	7.6	.417	2.7	.317	1.4	.867	0.00	0.68	3.5	2.4	8.4
In losses	73	23.0	7.4	.372	2.5	.306	1.4	.825	0.03	0.56	3.6	2.1	7.4

	G	Min	FGA	FG%	3PA	3P%	FTA	FT%	Blk	Stl	Ast	Reb	Pts
Pre All-Star	56	24.2	8.2	.379	2.8	.299	1.5	.817	0.00	0.75	3.7	2.3	8.2
Post All-Star	14	18.5	7.0	.378	3.0	.333	0.9	.769	0.00	0.21	2.6	1.4	7.0
Oct/Nov	20	21.4	7.3	.372	2.6	.294	1.2	.783	0.00	0.95	2.5	1.8	7.1
December	16	25.2	9.0	.382	2.6	.293	1.9	.774	0.00	0.56	4.8	3.1	9.1
January	14	26.2	7.6	.387	2.4	.273	1.2	.941	0.00	0.64	3.9	2.6	7.6
February	15	25.5	9.5	.378	4.2	.365	1.3	.789	0.00	0.47	4.3	1.9	9.7
March	10	11.1	3.4	.529	1.3	.308	1.1	.818	0.00	0.30	1.2	1.2	4.9
Apr/May	20	22.4	6.7	.361	2.1	.286	1.6	.906	0.10	0.45	4.1	2.2	6.9
0 Days Rest	27	23.6	8.6	.424	2.9	.325	1.6	.814	0.04	0.74	3.9	2.5	9.5
1 Days Rest	41	22.2	6.6	.367	2.2	.344	1.4	.821	0.02	0.37	3.5	2.0	6.7
2 Days Rest	14	30.1	9.8	.365	4.0	.286	2.1	.897	0.00	0.86	4.4	2.8	10.1
3+ Days Rest	13	13.1	5.2	.343	1.5	.150	0.4	.800	0.00	0.69	2.1	1.2	4.1

Larry Hughes

1999-2000 Per Game Averages

	G	Min	FGA	FG%	3PA	3P%	FTA	FT%	Blk	Stl	Ast	Reb	Pts		G	Min	FGA	FG%	3PA	3P%	FTA	FT%	Blk	Stl	Ast	Reb	Pts
Total	82	28.3	14.0	.400	1.5	.232	4.6	.740	0.34	1.40	2.5	4.3	15.0	Pre All-Star	49	20.5	9.3	.417	1.0	.216	2.9	.746	0.24	1.10	1.5	3.2	10.1
Home	42	29.9	15.0	.433	1.7	.243	4.7	.756	0.40	1.55	2.9	5.0	16.9	Post All-Star	33	39.9	20.9	.389	2.2	.243	7.1	.736	0.48	1.85	4.0	5.8	22.1
Road	40	26.7	13.0	.360	1.4	.218	4.5	.722	0.28	1.25	2.1	3.4	12.9	November	16	23.6	11.4	.432	1.1	.278	3.7	.695	0.25	1.50	1.8	3.2	12.8
vs. Playoff	46	30.3	15.1	.405	1.8	.244	5.2	.718	0.33	1.57	2.5	4.2	16.4	December	16	21.2	9.1	.384	1.2	.158	2.8	.773	0.31	0.88	1.6	2.8	9.3
vs. Non-Playoff	36	25.9	12.6	.392	1.2	.209	3.9	.777	0.36	1.19	2.5	4.4	13.1	January	12	17.8	8.3	.470	0.8	.200	2.3	.750	0.25	0.83	1.3	4.0	9.8
vs. East	42	25.2	12.4	.420	1.3	.278	3.7	.753	0.36	1.00	2.1	4.0	13.5	February	12	25.9	12.8	.340	1.7	.350	4.2	.840	0.25	1.25	2.6	4.7	12.8
vs. West	40	31.7	15.7	.384	1.8	.197	5.6	.731	0.33	1.83	2.9	4.5	16.5	March	17	40.8	20.6	.391	2.3	.179	7.1	.702	0.47	2.06	3.2	5.1	21.5
vs. Div.	23	30.7	15.4	.411	1.7	.205	5.7	.695	0.48	1.48	2.3	4.3	17.0	April	9	43.3	23.9	.409	2.1	.263	8.3	.747	0.56	1.89	5.6	7.1	26.3
As Starter	37	38.8	20.4	.393	2.2	.244	6.9	.737	0.51	1.86	3.9	5.7	21.6	0 Days Rest	20	26.1	12.2	.389	1.3	.200	5.3	.733	0.20	1.25	2.3	3.1	13.6
Off Bench	45	19.8	8.7	.415	1.0	.209	2.7	.746	0.20	1.02	1.3	3.0	9.5	1 Days Rest	44	30.6	15.3	.398	1.6	.214	4.8	.748	0.43	1.43	2.7	4.9	16.0
In wins	33	23.5	11.4	.451	1.2	.341	3.4	.768	0.36	1.18	2.0	4.2	13.3	2 Days Rest	10	30.2	16.0	.431	2.2	.364	4.8	.688	0.50	1.50	2.8	4.4	17.9
In losses	49	31.6	15.7	.375	1.7	.179	5.4	.728	0.33	1.55	2.8	4.3	16.0	3+ Days Rest	8	19.3	9.0	.389	1.0	.125	1.8	.857	0.00	1.00	1.5	3.8	8.6

Career (1998-99 thru 1999-2000)

	G	Min	FGA	FG%	3PA	3P%	FTA	FT%	Blk	Stl	Ast	Reb	Pts		G	Min	FGA	FG%	3PA	3P%	FTA	FT%	Blk	Stl	Ast	Reb	Pts
Total	132	25.1	11.8	.403	1.3	.209	4.0	.731	0.32	1.20	2.1	4.1	12.7	Pre All-Star	49	20.5	9.3	.417	1.0	.216	2.9	.746	0.24	1.10	1.5	3.2	10.1
Home	67	26.3	12.6	.416	1.5	.210	4.2	.730	0.39	1.24	2.5	4.5	13.9	Post All-Star	33	39.9	20.9	.389	2.2	.243	7.1	.736	0.48	1.85	4.0	5.8	22.1
Road	65	23.8	11.0	.388	1.2	.208	3.8	.733	0.25	1.17	1.8	3.6	11.6	Oct/Nov	16	23.6	11.4	.432	1.1	.278	3.7	.695	0.25	1.50	1.8	3.2	12.8
vs. Playoff	73	25.9	12.1	.405	1.5	.208	4.3	.722	0.29	1.27	2.1	3.7	13.2	December	16	21.2	9.1	.384	1.2	.158	2.8	.773	0.31	0.88	1.6	2.8	9.3
vs. Non-Playoff	59	24.1	11.5	.401	1.2	.211	3.6	.745	0.36	1.12	2.2	4.5	12.1	January	12	17.8	8.3	.470	0.8	.200	2.3	.750	0.25	0.83	1.3	4.0	9.8
vs. East	86	22.6	10.2	.414	1.2	.232	3.3	.728	0.33	0.97	1.8	4.0	11.1	February	25	21.9	10.2	.387	1.4	.265	3.8	.734	0.28	0.92	1.9	4.0	11.0
vs. West	46	29.7	14.9	.388	1.7	.179	5.3	.735	0.30	1.65	2.7	4.3	15.8	March	33	30.2	14.9	.384	1.8	.203	4.8	.667	0.33	1.36	2.5	4.3	15.0
vs. Div.	42	26.2	12.0	.397	1.4	.190	4.5	.670	0.36	1.21	2.0	4.2	12.8	Apr/May	30	28.0	12.8	.414	1.2	.162	4.8	.799	0.40	1.43	2.7	5.1	14.6
As Starter	38	38.8	20.3	.392	2.2	.250	7.1	.724	0.50	1.82	4.0	5.8	21.6	0 Days Rest	35	25.1	10.9	.420	1.0	.167	4.4	.752	0.29	1.49	2.0	3.6	12.7
Off Bench	94	19.5	8.4	.414	1.0	.172	2.8	.738	0.24	0.96	1.4	3.4	9.1	1 Days Rest	72	26.0	12.4	.389	1.4	.204	4.0	.727	0.33	1.14	2.3	4.1	13.0
In wins	61	21.5	10.1	.452	1.0	.297	3.1	.770	0.36	1.05	1.8	4.0	11.8	2 Days Rest	16	24.6	12.6	.433	1.7	.296	4.4	.700	0.44	1.00	2.3	3.7	14.4
In losses	71	28.2	13.3	.371	1.6	.159	4.8	.710	0.28	1.34	2.4	4.2	13.5	3+ Days Rest	9	18.9	9.1	.402	1.2	.182	1.8	.750	0.11	1.00	1.4	4.3	8.9

Lindsey Hunter

Detroit Pistons — Guard

1999-2000 Per Game Averages

	G	Min	FGA	FG%	3PA	3P%	FTA	FT%	Blk	Stl	Ast	Reb	Pts		G	Min	FGA	FG%	3PA	3P%	FTA	FT%	Blk	Stl	Ast	Reb	Pts
Total	82	35.6	10.9	.425	4.7	.432	1.9	.760	0.27	1.57	4.0	3.0	12.7	Pre All-Star	48	36.8	11.1	.429	4.8	.429	2.1	.758	0.27	1.65	4.4	3.1	13.2
Home	41	36.1	11.5	.434	5.0	.415	2.2	.791	0.39	1.51	4.2	3.3	13.8	Post All-Star	34	33.9	10.5	.419	4.6	.437	1.6	.764	0.26	1.47	3.5	3.0	12.1
Road	41	35.1	10.3	.415	4.4	.451	1.5	.714	0.15	1.63	3.8	2.8	11.6	November	15	37.6	11.9	.433	4.8	.417	1.8	.778	0.13	1.00	4.0	3.9	13.7
vs. Playoff	44	35.5	10.8	.426	4.8	.440	1.8	.628	0.23	1.52	3.6	3.1	12.4	December	14	36.9	10.1	.423	4.6	.406	2.4	.794	0.21	1.93	4.6	2.5	12.4
vs. Non-Playoff	38	35.7	10.9	.423	4.7	.422	2.0	.895	0.32	1.63	4.4	3.0	13.1	January	15	35.1	10.3	.406	4.8	.486	1.9	.643	0.40	1.73	4.2	2.6	11.9
vs. East	54	36.0	11.2	.427	4.6	.434	2.2	.761	0.31	1.70	4.1	3.3	13.2	February	12	39.6	14.6	.451	5.8	.429	2.3	.889	0.42	1.92	3.8	3.1	17.7
vs. West	28	34.8	10.3	.420	5.0	.429	1.3	.757	0.18	1.32	3.8	2.6	11.8	March	15	32.7	9.4	.411	4.8	.417	1.3	.789	0.27	1.47	3.7	2.7	10.7
vs. Div.	28	35.2	10.8	.429	4.5	.425	2.1	.724	0.25	1.86	4.3	3.2	12.7	April	11	33.5	9.2	.416	3.5	.436	1.7	.632	0.18	1.45	3.4	3.6	10.3
As Starter	82	35.6	10.9	.425	4.7	.432	1.9	.760	0.27	1.57	4.0	3.0	12.7	0 Days Rest	20	35.0	10.0	.417	4.6	.440	1.7	.848	0.15	1.35	3.8	3.1	11.7
Off Bench	0	—	—	—	—	—	—	—	—	—	—	—	—	1 Days Rest	45	35.9	11.1	.410	4.8	.394	1.9	.762	0.31	1.53	3.8	3.1	12.4
In wins	42	35.6	11.0	.455	4.9	.451	2.4	.822	0.36	1.88	4.2	3.2	14.2	2 Days Rest	8	35.1	9.4	.493	3.9	.484	2.1	.588	0.13	1.88	4.6	3.1	12.4
In losses	40	35.6	10.7	.393	4.6	.411	1.3	.642	0.18	1.25	3.7	2.9	11.2	3+ Days Rest	9	36.0	13.3	.458	5.7	.549	2.2	.750	0.44	2.00	4.8	2.7	17.0

Last Five Seasons

	G	Min	FGA	FG%	3PA	3P%	FTA	FT%	Blk	Stl	Ast	Reb	Pts		G	Min	FGA	FG%	3PA	3P%	FTA	FT%	Blk	Stl	Ast	Reb	Pts
Total	364	33.9	10.7	.405	4.3	.380	2.1	.749	0.23	1.51	3.0	3.0	11.9	Pre All-Star	175	35.8	11.6	.395	4.8	.383	2.3	.753	0.24	1.58	3.2	3.3	12.8
Home	181	33.9	10.8	.404	4.3	.356	2.1	.769	0.28	1.50	3.1	3.1	11.9	Post All-Star	140	30.8	9.7	.407	4.1	.376	1.9	.742	0.23	1.34	2.4	2.4	10.8
Road	183	33.9	10.7	.405	4.3	.405	2.1	.729	0.17	1.52	2.9	2.9	11.9	Oct/Nov	60	37.4	12.6	.411	4.9	.371	3.0	.775	0.20	1.53	3.1	3.8	14.5
vs. Playoff	198	34.1	10.9	.398	4.6	.391	1.9	.721	0.22	1.53	2.8	3.0	11.8	December	57	36.5	11.4	.386	4.7	.384	2.2	.756	0.23	1.39	3.3	3.2	12.2
vs. Non-Playoff	166	33.6	10.6	.413	4.0	.366	2.3	.777	0.23	1.50	3.2	3.0	12.0	January	45	33.8	10.6	.377	4.9	.400	1.8	.687	0.29	1.78	2.9	2.8	11.2
vs. East	251	33.9	10.7	.404	4.0	.372	2.2	.746	0.25	1.53	3.0	2.9	11.7	February	61	32.9	11.0	.416	4.4	.393	2.1	.792	0.20	1.59	2.6	3.0	12.6
vs. West	113	33.8	11.0	.405	5.0	.396	1.8	.758	0.18	1.48	3.0	3.3	12.2	March	79	30.5	9.0	.404	3.9	.369	1.8	.717	0.28	1.49	2.9	2.3	10.0
vs. Div.	127	33.6	10.4	.400	4.2	.371	1.8	.728	0.24	1.40	3.0	2.7	11.2	Apr/May	62	33.5	10.5	.426	3.3	.369	1.6	.737	0.16	1.37	3.1	3.1	11.4
As Starter	322	35.9	11.4	.405	4.6	.386	2.2	.752	0.24	1.61	3.2	3.2	12.6	0 Days Rest	89	34.0	10.8	.385	4.6	.370	2.2	.755	0.20	1.47	3.0	2.8	11.6
Off Bench	42	18.5	6.0	.394	2.3	.302	1.5	.721	0.10	0.74	1.4	1.2	6.5	1 Days Rest	196	34.0	10.7	.414	4.2	.380	2.0	.751	0.22	1.54	3.0	3.0	12.0
In wins	201	33.3	10.4	.436	4.0	.407	2.4	.771	0.24	1.60	3.2	3.1	12.5	2 Days Rest	49	34.1	10.0	.379	4.1	.374	1.9	.717	0.29	1.39	3.3	3.3	10.5
In losses	163	34.6	11.2	.369	4.6	.352	1.7	.713	0.20	1.40	2.8	2.8	11.1	3+ Days Rest	30	32.7	11.9	.436	4.6	.424	2.8	.762	0.23	1.70	2.8	3.2	14.5

Allen Iverson

1999-2000 Per Game Averages

	G	Min	FGA	FG%	3PA	3P%	FTA	FT%	Blk	Stl	Ast	Reb	Pts		G	Min	FGA	FG%	3PA	3P%	FTA	FT%	Blk	Stl	Ast	Reb	Pts
Total	70	40.8	24.8	.421	3.7	.341	8.9	.713	0.07	2.06	4.7	3.8	28.4	Pre All-Star	39	40.5	26.5	.423	4.3	.349	10.0	.733	0.10	1.97	4.6	3.8	31.3
Home	35	40.7	25.8	.420	4.2	.320	9.1	.710	0.06	2.23	5.6	4.3	29.4	Post All-Star	31	41.0	22.6	.417	3.0	.326	7.4	.678	0.03	2.16	4.8	3.8	24.8
Road	35	40.8	23.7	.421	3.3	.368	8.7	.716	0.09	1.89	3.7	3.3	27.4	November	12	40.8	25.8	.416	4.1	.531	10.0	.708	0.08	2.08	4.4	5.1	30.8
vs. Playoff	37	41.1	25.8	.403	4.2	.346	9.0	.705	0.08	1.86	4.8	4.4	28.5	December	10	39.5	24.8	.399	5.1	.275	10.2	.755	0.10	1.80	4.3	3.0	28.9
vs. Non-Playoff	33	40.4	23.6	.442	3.2	.333	8.7	.722	0.06	2.27	4.6	3.2	28.3	January	12	40.9	27.8	.419	3.9	.319	10.6	.724	0.00	2.25	5.2	3.0	32.3
vs. East	44	40.7	24.8	.422	3.9	.371	8.8	.679	0.07	2.05	4.5	3.8	28.4	February	12	40.4	25.3	.446	3.3	.256	7.9	.684	0.25	1.67	4.9	4.2	28.8
vs. West	26	40.9	24.7	.418	3.5	.286	8.9	.771	0.08	2.08	4.9	3.8	28.5	March	15	42.2	22.9	.410	3.5	.302	7.0	.724	0.00	2.20	4.5	3.9	24.9
vs. Div.	18	41.8	24.9	.396	4.2	.408	9.6	.711	0.00	2.50	4.9	3.9	28.3	April	9	40.0	21.6	.438	2.4	.364	7.9	.662	0.00	2.33	4.8	3.4	25.0
As Starter	70	40.8	24.8	.421	3.7	.341	8.9	.713	0.07	2.06	4.7	3.8	28.4	0 Days Rest	14	40.4	23.9	.412	3.6	.300	8.4	.729	0.07	1.93	3.5	3.4	26.9
Off Bench	0													1 Days Rest	38	41.1	24.0	.429	3.4	.349	8.7	.724	0.05	2.11	5.1	3.8	28.1
In wins	42	41.0	25.5	.445	3.8	.344	8.7	.734	0.07	2.24	5.0	4.0	30.4	2 Days Rest	9	41.7	26.8	.436	4.4	.350	9.3	.726	0.11	2.11	5.1	5.7	31.7
In losses	28	40.3	23.7	.382	3.6	.337	9.1	.682	0.07	1.79	4.3	3.6	25.5	3+ Days Rest	9	39.0	27.1	.385	4.7	.357	9.8	.636	0.11	2.00	4.6	2.6	28.8

Career (1996-97 thru 1999-2000)

	G	Min	FGA	FG%	3PA	3P%	FTA	FT%	Blk	Stl	Ast	Reb	Pts		G	Min	FGA	FG%	3PA	3P%	FTA	FT%	Blk	Stl	Ast	Reb	Pts
Total	274	40.3	20.8	.428	4.2	.323	7.9	.723	0.22	2.14	5.9	4.1	24.9	Pre All-Star	123	39.3	20.6	.421	4.6	.322	7.9	.714	0.28	2.23	6.2	3.8	24.5
Home	139	40.3	21.1	.427	4.3	.333	7.6	.725	0.21	2.25	6.6	4.4	25.0	Post All-Star	103	40.9	20.5	.444	3.7	.342	7.1	.715	0.18	1.97	6.1	3.9	24.5
Road	135	40.2	20.5	.429	4.0	.313	8.3	.720	0.24	2.03	5.2	3.7	24.8	Oct/Nov	36	38.8	20.4	.433	4.4	.411	7.7	.665	0.28	2.50	6.1	4.5	24.7
vs. Playoff	153	40.1	21.0	.422	4.6	.324	7.6	.727	0.26	2.03	5.8	4.3	24.8	December	35	39.1	20.0	.385	5.1	.274	8.1	.716	0.34	1.86	5.8	3.5	22.5
vs. Non-Playoff	121	40.5	20.5	.436	3.7	.322	8.3	.717	0.17	2.28	6.0	3.8	25.0	January	43	39.7	20.5	.424	4.5	.292	8.0	.745	0.26	2.37	6.4	3.5	24.7
vs. East	186	40.7	20.9	.426	4.2	.332	8.2	.714	0.24	2.16	5.5	4.2	25.1	February	50	39.4	20.7	.429	3.9	.309	7.5	.732	0.18	1.94	6.5	4.2	24.4
vs. West	88	39.6	20.6	.432	4.2	.306	7.3	.742	0.18	2.11	6.7	3.7	24.5	March	59	41.4	20.5	.437	3.6	.284	8.0	.726	0.17	2.00	5.4	4.1	24.7
vs. Div.	82	40.9	20.2	.404	4.5	.309	8.4	.714	0.24	2.35	5.6	4.4	23.7	Apr/May	51	42.3	22.4	.443	4.2	.380	8.3	.733	0.18	2.25	5.3	4.5	27.5
As Starter	272	40.4	20.9	.428	4.2	.323	7.9	.722	0.22	2.14	5.9	4.0	24.9	0 Days Rest	69	39.8	20.3	.431	4.2	.356	7.3	.738	0.20	1.94	5.2	3.8	24.4
Off Bench	2	27.5	13.5	.333	8.0	.375	6.5	.846	0.50	2.00	6.0	5.0	17.5	1 Days Rest	140	40.7	20.9	.432	4.1	.308	8.0	.740	0.23	2.19	6.1	4.1	25.2
In wins	121	41.1	21.7	.460	3.7	.333	8.6	.727	0.17	2.54	6.2	4.4	27.5	2 Days Rest	34	40.6	21.8	.427	4.4	.311	8.8	.686	0.29	2.35	5.9	4.9	26.1
In losses	153	39.7	20.1	.400	4.6	.317	7.4	.718	0.26	1.83	5.6	3.8	22.8	3+ Days Rest	31	39.3	20.6	.400	4.6	.317	7.4	.656	0.16	2.13	6.4	3.7	23.3

Jaren Jackson

1999-2000 Per Game Averages

	G	Min	FGA	FG%	3PA	3P%	FTA	FT%	Blk	Stl	Ast	Reb	Pts		G	Min	FGA	FG%	3PA	3P%	FTA	FT%	Blk	Stl	Ast	Reb	Pts
Total	81	20.9	6.0	.381	3.8	.353	0.6	.647	0.09	0.67	1.5	2.2	6.3	Pre All-Star	49	22.9	6.9	.355	4.1	.342	0.7	.528	0.12	0.80	1.8	2.7	6.7
Home	41	21.1	6.1	.402	3.8	.381	0.7	.759	0.07	0.66	1.6	2.0	6.9	Post All-Star	32	17.8	4.7	.440	3.3	.375	0.5	.933	0.03	0.47	0.9	1.6	5.8
Road	40	20.7	6.0	.360	3.8	.325	0.6	.500	0.10	0.68	1.3	2.5	5.8	November	16	23.1	7.1	.381	4.4	.400	0.6	.333	0.13	0.75	1.8	2.3	7.3
vs. Playoff	43	20.1	5.6	.326	3.3	.307	0.8	.576	0.07	0.70	1.2	2.1	5.1	December	15	23.9	7.6	.351	5.0	.293	0.7	.545	0.20	0.80	1.9	2.7	7.2
vs. Non-Playoff	38	21.7	6.6	.434	4.4	.392	0.5	.778	0.11	0.63	1.8	2.4	7.6	January	13	22.8	6.4	.325	2.9	.342	0.9	.667	0.08	0.77	2.0	3.2	5.8
vs. East	30	20.7	6.1	.390	4.0	.333	0.5	.600	0.10	0.80	1.2	2.1	6.4	February	12	17.3	4.8	.404	3.5	.333	0.7	.750	0.00	0.67	0.7	1.6	5.5
vs. West	51	21.0	6.0	.376	3.6	.366	0.7	.667	0.08	0.59	1.6	2.3	6.3	March	15	20.3	5.7	.459	3.9	.414	0.5	.875	0.07	0.40	1.3	1.5	7.3
vs. Div.	23	21.5	6.0	.428	4.1	.421	0.3	.833	0.04	0.35	1.5	2.0	7.1	April	10	15.6	3.6	.389	2.3	.304	0.3	1.000	0.00	0.60	0.8	1.9	3.8
As Starter	12	24.0	7.6	.330	4.2	.280	1.0	.667	0.17	0.83	2.2	3.3	6.8	0 Days Rest	18	18.6	5.0	.378	2.9	.283	0.6	.818	0.11	0.50	1.3	1.7	5.1
Off Bench	69	20.3	5.8	.393	3.7	.367	0.6	.641	0.07	0.64	1.3	2.0	6.2	1 Days Rest	41	21.8	6.7	.387	4.3	.358	0.7	.600	0.12	0.76	1.6	2.3	7.1
In wins	53	19.9	5.6	.400	3.5	.395	0.6	.750	0.09	0.62	1.5	2.3	6.4	2 Days Rest	18	20.7	5.4	.398	3.2	.431	0.5	.667	0.00	0.78	1.4	2.6	6.1
In losses	28	22.7	6.9	.352	4.3	.289	0.7	.474	0.07	0.75	1.4	2.2	6.4	3+ Days Rest	4	23.0	6.5	.269	4.8	.263	0.3	.000	0.00	0.00	1.0	3.0	4.8

Last Five Seasons

	G	Min	FGA	FG%	3PA	3P%	FTA	FT%	Blk	Stl	Ast	Reb	Pts		G	Min	FGA	FG%	3PA	3P%	FTA	FT%	Blk	Stl	Ast	Reb	Pts
Total	289	20.6	6.1	.389	3.2	.357	1.0	.767	0.14	0.70	1.3	2.2	6.6	Pre All-Star	140	22.0	6.8	.379	3.3	.354	1.1	.711	0.13	0.78	1.6	2.4	7.1
Home	144	20.5	6.2	.412	3.1	.366	1.1	.786	0.13	0.72	1.4	2.1	7.1	Post All-Star	102	19.6	5.2	.413	3.0	.360	1.0	.828	0.10	0.50	1.2	1.8	6.1
Road	145	20.6	6.0	.366	3.2	.348	0.9	.744	0.14	0.68	1.2	2.2	6.2	Oct/Nov	47	21.1	6.9	.404	3.2	.382	1.2	.737	0.09	0.68	1.5	2.1	7.7
vs. Playoff	150	20.3	5.9	.356	3.1	.327	1.0	.766	0.11	0.66	1.2	2.0	6.0	December	42	23.1	6.9	.392	3.8	.373	1.0	.625	0.19	0.90	1.7	2.4	7.4
vs. Non-Playoff	139	20.8	6.3	.422	3.2	.388	1.0	.767	0.17	0.77	1.5	2.1	7.3	January	41	22.1	6.6	.338	2.9	.303	1.0	.750	0.12	0.73	1.7	2.8	6.1
vs. East	118	19.3	5.5	.394	2.7	.346	1.0	.707	0.18	0.66	1.2	2.0	5.9	February	51	20.1	5.8	.362	3.1	.313	1.2	.669	0.18	0.78	1.2	2.2	6.1
vs. West	171	21.5	6.5	.386	3.4	.363	1.0	.807	0.11	0.72	1.5	2.3	7.1	March	63	18.8	5.3	.418	2.7	.401	0.8	.865	0.13	0.40	1.1	1.6	6.3
vs. Div.	90	20.2	6.4	.387	3.2	.356	1.0	.806	0.14	0.79	1.4	2.1	6.9	Apr/May	45	19.2	5.4	.416	3.4	.355	0.9	.872	0.13	0.80	1.0	2.1	6.5
As Starter	70	29.3	8.6	.385	4.4	.382	1.5	.792	0.19	0.64	2.1	3.1	9.5	0 Days Rest	67	19.5	5.4	.371	2.5	.267	1.0	.794	0.19	0.64	1.1	2.0	5.5
Off Bench	219	17.8	5.3	.391	2.8	.344	0.8	.751	0.12	0.64	1.1	1.9	5.7	1 Days Rest	144	21.5	6.5	.393	3.5	.364	1.1	.776	0.15	0.68	1.5	2.3	7.3
In wins	187	20.8	6.1	.407	3.0	.385	1.0	.780	0.16	0.72	1.4	2.3	6.9	2 Days Rest	52	21.3	6.3	.409	3.1	.413	0.8	.659	0.08	0.75	1.5	2.1	7.0
In losses	102	20.2	6.2	.357	3.4	.311	0.9	.740	0.10	0.65	1.2	1.9	6.2	3+ Days Rest	26	16.7	5.0	.357	3.0	.390	1.0	.808	0.08	0.81	0.9	2.3	5.5

Jim Jackson

Atlanta Hawks — Guard

1999-2000 Per Game Averages

	G	Min	FGA	FG%	3PA	3P%	FTA	FT%	Blk	Stl	Ast	Reb	Pts		G	Min	FGA	FG%	3PA	3P%	FTA	FT%	Blk	Stl	Ast	Reb	Pts
Total	79	35.0	15.6	.411	3.8	.386	2.7	.877	0.13	0.72	2.9	5.0	16.7	Pre All-Star	45	36.7	15.6	.434	3.9	.434	2.9	.871	0.11	0.53	2.9	5.6	17.8
Home	39	35.1	15.4	.433	3.9	.403	3.0	.873	0.18	0.62	2.9	4.9	17.6	Post All-Star	34	32.8	15.7	.379	3.8	.320	2.4	.888	0.15	0.97	2.9	4.2	15.2
Road	40	34.9	15.9	.390	3.7	.369	2.4	.883	0.08	0.83	3.0	5.1	15.8	November	15	35.3	14.0	.429	2.2	.364	2.4	.861	0.00	0.47	3.3	5.2	14.9
vs. Playoff	46	34.7	15.4	.411	4.0	.380	2.7	.864	0.17	0.72	2.9	4.6	16.5	December	12	39.1	16.5	.449	4.3	.549	3.6	.860	0.17	0.42	2.6	5.8	20.3
vs. Non-Playoff	33	35.5	16.0	.410	3.6	.395	2.6	.897	0.06	0.73	2.9	5.5	16.9	January	13	36.8	16.6	.426	5.8	.413	2.6	.882	0.23	0.69	2.8	5.6	18.8
vs. East	53	34.9	15.1	.414	4.0	.408	2.8	.872	0.13	0.66	3.1	4.9	16.6	February	12	36.8	16.8	.396	4.3	.385	2.5	.900	0.08	1.25	2.9	6.0	17.3
vs. West	26	35.3	16.8	.404	3.5	.333	2.5	.891	0.12	0.85	2.5	5.2	16.9	March	17	31.2	14.9	.379	3.4	.228	2.6	.864	0.24	0.76	2.4	3.9	14.3
vs. Div.	28	34.7	15.1	.450	4.5	.468	2.4	.868	0.07	0.68	3.5	4.8	17.8	April	10	31.9	15.6	.385	3.5	.371	2.5	.920	0.00	0.80	3.7	3.6	15.6
As Starter	76	35.1	15.7	.413	3.9	.386	2.7	.884	0.13	0.75	2.9	5.1	16.8	0 Days Rest	22	34.5	14.6	.391	4.0	.352	1.8	.821	0.00	0.77	3.1	5.0	14.3
Off Bench	3	33.0	15.0	.356	2.7	.375	1.7	.600	0.00	0.00	2.3	1.7	12.7	1 Days Rest	35	30.5	16.6	.418	3.8	.373	3.3	.904	0.26	0.66	3.1	5.1	18.3
In wins	27	36.4	15.4	.466	3.7	.455	2.9	.857	0.19	0.78	3.1	5.6	18.5	2 Days Rest	15	34.3	15.0	.387	3.0	.333	2.5	.838	0.07	0.73	2.3	4.8	14.7
In losses	52	34.3	15.8	.382	3.9	.351	2.6	.889	0.10	0.69	2.8	4.7	15.7	3+ Days Rest	7	38.4	15.3	.477	5.1	.583	3.1	.909	0.00	0.86	2.7	4.9	20.4

Last Five Seasons

	G	Min	FGA	FG%	3PA	3P%	FTA	FT%	Blk	Stl	Ast	Reb	Pts		G	Min	FGA	FG%	3PA	3P%	FTA	FT%	Blk	Stl	Ast	Reb	Pts
Total	366	34.5	13.8	.425	3.2	.352	3.6	.829	0.21	0.85	3.5	4.8	15.9	Pre All-Star	179	36.5	13.8	.444	3.1	.379	4.0	.817	0.21	0.82	3.5	5.2	16.7
Home	186	34.3	13.4	.433	3.0	.359	3.8	.821	0.20	0.82	3.7	4.8	15.8	Post All-Star	138	35.7	16.0	.407	3.8	.337	3.7	.844	0.25	0.88	3.9	4.9	17.4
Road	180	34.7	14.2	.418	3.3	.346	3.5	.838	0.23	0.89	3.4	4.9	16.0	Oct/Nov	55	35.6	12.9	.438	2.5	.350	3.8	.798	0.15	0.65	3.4	5.4	15.2
vs. Playoff	210	34.7	13.8	.419	3.3	.340	3.6	.817	0.22	0.80	3.5	4.7	15.7	December	54	37.0	13.7	.434	2.9	.422	3.8	.838	0.26	0.67	3.8	5.4	15.7
vs. Non-Playoff	156	34.3	13.7	.435	3.0	.370	3.6	.845	0.21	0.92	3.6	5.0	16.1	January	56	36.9	14.5	.459	3.6	.377	4.2	.814	0.21	1.09	3.5	4.9	18.1
vs. East	164	36.0	14.4	.430	3.4	.369	3.5	.822	0.24	0.77	3.7	5.0	16.5	February	58	33.0	13.4	.415	3.4	.337	3.3	.845	0.29	0.93	3.1	4.2	15.1
vs. West	202	33.3	13.3	.421	3.0	.337	3.7	.835	0.19	0.92	3.4	4.8	15.4	March	84	32.3	14.1	.398	3.1	.315	3.3	.839	0.14	0.85	3.1	4.7	14.9
vs. Div.	121	33.3	13.4	.429	3.3	.342	3.2	.849	0.20	0.81	3.4	4.8	15.4	Apr/May	59	33.7	14.0	.422	3.6	.338	3.5	.842	0.25	0.92	4.4	4.5	16.0
As Starter	322	36.1	14.7	.427	3.4	.357	3.8	.830	0.22	0.87	3.7	5.1	16.9	0 Days Rest	88	33.5	13.3	.420	3.2	.330	3.1	.804	0.15	0.80	3.2	5.0	14.8
Off Bench	44	23.1	7.5	.409	1.8	.282	2.2	.821	0.14	0.70	2.5	3.3	8.4	1 Days Rest	191	35.2	14.1	.434	3.2	.374	3.9	.834	0.26	0.80	3.8	4.8	16.7
In wins	137	34.0	13.2	.465	3.0	.412	4.0	.854	0.29	0.93	3.7	4.9	16.9	2 Days Rest	56	33.7	13.6	.385	2.8	.264	3.6	.824	0.18	1.00	3.0	5.0	14.1
In losses	229	34.8	14.1	.403	3.3	.319	3.4	.812	0.17	0.80	3.4	4.8	15.2	3+ Days Rest	31	35.1	13.4	.462	3.7	.414	3.1	.874	0.19	1.06	3.6	4.5	16.6

Mark Jackson

Indiana Pacers — Guard

1999-2000 Per Game Averages

	G	Min	FGA	FG%	3PA	3P%	FTA	FT%	Blk	Stl	Ast	Reb	Pts		G	Min	FGA	FG%	3PA	3P%	FTA	FT%	Blk	Stl	Ast	Reb	Pts
Total	81	27.0	7.0	.432	2.7	.403	1.2	.806	0.12	0.94	8.0	3.7	8.1	Pre All-Star	48	27.6	6.7	.428	2.9	.367	1.4	.815	0.15	1.02	8.3	3.9	7.9
Home	41	26.4	7.1	.450	2.8	.405	1.0	.738	0.20	0.93	8.1	3.5	8.3	Post All-Star	33	26.2	7.6	.436	2.5	.463	1.0	.788	0.09	0.82	7.6	3.4	8.5
Road	40	27.7	7.0	.412	2.6	.400	1.4	.857	0.05	0.95	8.0	3.9	8.0	November	15	26.5	6.3	.457	2.7	.439	1.0	.867	0.13	0.93	6.7	3.5	7.8
vs. Playoff	43	27.7	7.7	.415	3.0	.386	1.2	.827	0.14	1.02	8.1	3.8	8.5	December	14	28.7	6.1	.453	2.6	.432	1.1	.733	0.14	1.29	8.9	4.2	7.5
vs. Non-Playoff	38	26.3	6.3	.454	2.5	.426	1.2	.783	0.11	0.84	7.9	3.5	7.7	January	14	27.8	7.1	.364	3.5	.286	2.1	.800	0.07	0.93	9.6	3.6	7.9
vs. East	53	27.5	7.4	.449	2.8	.430	1.1	.845	0.17	0.96	8.4	3.6	8.8	February	13	28.2	8.3	.454	2.8	.444	0.7	.889	0.23	0.85	9.2	4.3	9.4
vs. West	28	26.2	6.3	.392	2.5	.343	1.4	.750	0.04	0.89	7.4	3.7	6.9	March	16	25.6	7.5	.442	2.2	.400	1.5	.750	0.13	0.88	6.8	2.6	8.6
vs. Div.	28	28.0	7.1	.467	2.8	.481	1.0	.793	0.14	0.89	9.4	4.0	8.8	April	9	25.0	7.0	.413	2.6	.478	0.6	1.000	0.00	0.67	7.0	4.0	7.0
As Starter	81	27.0	7.0	.432	2.7	.403	1.2	.806	0.12	0.94	8.0	3.7	8.1	0 Days Rest	20	28.4	7.0	.460	3.4	.493	1.0	.750	0.15	0.75	7.3	3.2	8.8
Off Bench	0	—	—	—	—	—	—	—	—	—	—	—	—	1 Days Rest	40	26.5	7.1	.415	2.6	.353	1.5	.810	0.13	0.85	7.9	3.9	8.0
In wins	55	27.1	7.0	.466	2.7	.438	1.0	.768	0.15	1.04	8.4	3.8	8.5	2 Days Rest	15	25.7	7.3	.409	2.7	.341	0.5	.857	0.07	1.07	8.7	3.9	7.3
In losses	26	26.9	7.1	.359	2.9	.333	1.6	.857	0.08	0.73	7.2	3.3	7.4	3+ Days Rest	6	29.7	6.2	.514	1.8	.545	2.2	.846	0.17	1.83	9.8	3.3	9.2

Last Five Seasons

	G	Min	FGA	FG%	3PA	3P%	FTA	FT%	Blk	Stl	Ast	Reb	Pts		G	Min	FGA	FG%	3PA	3P%	FTA	FT%	Blk	Stl	Ast	Reb	Pts
Total	375	31.2	7.5	.435	2.1	.373	2.0	.787	0.09	1.06	8.9	4.0	8.9	Pre All-Star	187	31.7	7.3	.437	2.1	.368	2.2	.793	0.11	1.13	9.4	4.3	9.3
Home	191	31.1	7.3	.437	2.0	.376	1.9	.768	0.09	1.01	8.9	4.0	8.6	Post All-Star	139	31.5	7.9	.436	2.2	.401	2.0	.768	0.06	1.05	8.5	3.7	9.3
Road	184	31.2	7.7	.433	2.2	.370	2.1	.805	0.08	1.13	8.8	4.1	9.2	Oct/Nov	55	29.3	5.8	.429	1.7	.418	2.2	.798	0.13	0.82	8.6	4.1	7.4
vs. Playoff	200	31.2	7.5	.428	2.2	.383	2.0	.805	0.07	0.98	8.5	3.9	8.9	December	58	32.7	7.6	.445	2.0	.397	2.4	.774	0.12	1.34	9.6	4.2	9.4
vs. Non-Playoff	175	31.1	7.4	.443	2.0	.360	2.1	.768	0.10	1.17	9.3	4.2	8.9	January	59	32.9	8.3	.429	2.5	.342	2.0	.792	0.07	1.25	9.8	4.6	9.6
vs. East	248	30.8	7.5	.429	2.1	.376	2.0	.809	0.10	1.04	8.7	3.8	8.8	February	65	31.1	7.9	.447	2.1	.367	2.0	.780	0.09	0.94	8.8	4.1	9.4
vs. West	127	31.8	7.4	.446	2.0	.367	2.1	.747	0.05	1.10	9.1	4.3	9.0	March	79	31.2	7.8	.434	2.1	.376	2.1	.761	0.08	1.08	8.6	3.8	9.1
vs. Div.	132	31.3	7.7	.440	2.2	.378	1.9	.798	0.08	1.06	9.1	4.1	9.1	Apr/May	59	29.5	7.2	.421	2.2	.359	1.6	.842	0.03	0.95	7.7	3.5	8.2
As Starter	375	31.2	7.5	.435	2.1	.373	2.0	.787	0.09	1.06	8.9	4.0	8.9	0 Days Rest	96	31.0	7.1	.435	2.2	.386	1.8	.800	0.07	0.99	8.8	3.7	8.5
Off Bench	0	—	—	—	—	—	—	—	—	—	—	—	—	1 Days Rest	194	31.3	7.6	.432	2.1	.360	2.1	.759	0.08	1.05	9.0	4.1	8.9
In wins	228	30.8	7.4	.457	2.0	.386	2.1	.781	0.09	1.19	9.3	4.2	9.2	2 Days Rest	54	30.5	7.9	.434	2.1	.381	1.9	.870	0.11	1.22	8.7	4.1	9.2
In losses	147	31.8	7.6	.401	2.2	.355	1.9	.799	0.07	0.87	8.2	3.7	8.4	3+ Days Rest	31	31.8	7.1	.457	1.8	.404	2.7	.798	0.10	1.13	8.6	4.2	9.4

Antawn Jamison

1999-2000 Per Game Averages

	G	Min	FGA	FG%	3PA	3P%	FTA	FT%	Blk	Stl	Ast	Reb	Pts		G	Min	FGA	FG%	3PA	3P%	FTA	FT%	Blk	Stl	Ast	Reb	Pts
Total	43	36.2	17.6	.471	0.2	.286	4.8	.611	0.35	0.70	2.1	8.3	19.6	Pre All-Star	43	36.2	17.6	.471	0.2	.286	4.8	.611	0.35	0.70	2.1	8.3	19.6
Home	21	38.3	18.1	.466	0.1	.333	4.8	.574	0.38	0.95	2.6	8.7	19.7	Post All-Star	0	—											
Road	22	34.1	17.1	.476	0.2	.250	4.9	.645	0.32	0.45	1.6	8.0	19.5	November	13	33.1	17.5	.419	0.4	.200	3.4	.568	0.08	0.46	1.7	7.6	16.6
vs. Playoff	22	35.6	16.6	.451	0.2	.400	4.3	.532	0.23	0.45	2.0	7.2	17.4	December	12	34.6	15.2	.478	0.1	1.000	4.8	.474	0.42	0.92	1.7	7.7	16.8
vs. Non-Playoff	21	36.8	18.6	.490	0.1	.000	5.4	.675	0.48	0.95	2.2	9.6	21.9	January	12	40.8	20.0	.492	0.1	.000	7.1	.694	0.67	1.00	2.5	10.5	24.6
vs. East	16	37.4	18.3	.498	0.3	.250	5.4	.756	0.44	0.75	2.1	8.4	22.4	February	6	36.8	17.8	.523	0.0	—	3.7	.727	0.17	0.17	3.0	7.0	21.3
vs. West	27	35.5	17.1	.454	0.1	.333	4.5	.508	0.30	0.67	2.1	8.3	17.9	March	0	—											
vs. Div.	10	34.1	17.2	.453	0.2	.500	3.3	.485	0.30	0.60	2.3	7.1	17.3	April	0	—											
As Starter	41	36.9	17.9	.475	0.2	.286	4.9	.619	0.37	0.71	2.1	8.5	20.1	0 Days Rest	11	36.0	18.7	.495	0.2	.500	3.0	.576	0.18	0.55	1.7	7.5	20.4
Off Bench	2	21.5	12.0	.333	0.0	—	3.0	.333	0.00	0.50	2.5	5.5	9.0	1 Days Rest	19	37.3	17.9	.479	0.1	.000	6.0	.588	0.47	0.84	2.1	8.7	20.7
In wins	10	35.2	17.7	.520	0.0	—	5.8	.655	0.40	0.90	2.6	9.2	22.2	2 Days Rest	7	33.0	15.0	.429	0.3	.500	4.1	.621	0.14	0.43	2.6	7.7	15.6
In losses	33	36.5	17.5	.456	0.2	.286	4.5	.593	0.33	0.64	1.9	8.1	18.8	3+ Days Rest	6	36.7	17.5	.438	0.3	.000	5.3	.719	0.50	0.83	2.3	9.7	19.2

Career (1998-99 thru 1999-2000)

	G	Min	FGA	FG%	3PA	3P%	FTA	FT%	Blk	Stl	Ast	Reb	Pts		G	Min	FGA	FG%	3PA	3P%	FTA	FT%	Blk	Stl	Ast	Reb	Pts
Total	90	29.0	12.8	.464	0.2	.294	4.0	.601	0.34	0.76	1.4	7.3	14.3	Pre All-Star	43	36.2	17.6	.471	0.2	.286	4.8	.611	0.35	0.70	2.1	8.3	19.6
Home	44	30.1	13.5	.465	0.2	.444	4.0	.597	0.34	0.80	1.7	8.2	15.0	Post All-Star	0	—											
Road	46	28.0	12.1	.464	0.2	.125	4.0	.605	0.35	0.72	1.1	6.5	13.7	Oct/Nov	13	33.1	17.5	.419	0.4	.200	3.4	.568	0.08	0.46	1.7	7.6	16.6
vs. Playoff	49	28.1	11.8	.447	0.2	.455	4.0	.541	0.29	0.55	1.2	7.0	12.8	December	12	34.6	15.2	.478	0.1	1.000	4.8	.474	0.42	0.92	1.7	7.7	16.8
vs. Non-Playoff	41	30.2	14.0	.482	0.1	.000	4.1	.671	0.41	1.00	1.6	7.7	16.2	January	12	40.8	20.0	.492	0.1	.000	7.1	.694	0.67	1.00	2.5	10.5	24.6
vs. East	22	32.7	15.2	.485	0.2	.200	4.9	.731	0.36	0.95	1.7	7.7	18.4	February	19	24.1	10.6	.468	0.2	.250	3.4	.554	0.32	0.42	1.4	6.8	11.8
vs. West	68	27.9	12.0	.458	0.3	.545	3.7	.545	0.34	0.69	1.3	7.2	13.0	March	15	21.9	8.0	.433	0.2	.000	3.9	.542	0.27	1.00	0.4	5.9	9.1
vs. Div.	28	26.6	11.1	.458	0.3	.429	3.6	.490	0.32	0.61	1.1	7.0	12.1	Apr/May	19	26.0	9.5	.489	0.2	.667	2.7	.745	0.37	0.84	1.1	6.6	11.4
As Starter	65	33.1	14.9	.481	0.2	.333	4.2	.644	0.37	0.78	1.7	7.9	17.2	0 Days Rest	27	28.1	12.7	.504	0.3	.286	3.6	.557	0.26	0.74	0.9	7.4	14.9
Off Bench	25	18.6	7.2	.374	0.2	.200	3.4	.465	0.28	0.68	0.6	5.8	7.0	1 Days Rest	41	30.2	13.1	.460	0.1	.333	4.4	.611	0.44	0.76	1.5	7.3	14.8
In wins	31	27.3	11.5	.480	0.1	.667	4.0	.629	0.35	0.77	1.5	7.5	13.7	2 Days Rest	13	26.7	11.0	.420	0.2	.500	3.2	.571	0.23	0.62	1.8	7.0	11.2
In losses	59	30.0	13.4	.457	0.2	.214	4.0	.586	0.34	0.75	1.3	7.3	14.7	3+ Days Rest	9	30.1	14.1	.425	0.2	.000	4.7	.690	0.33	1.00	1.6	8.0	15.2

Avery Johnson

1999-2000 Per Game Averages

	G	Min	FGA	FG%	3PA	3P%	FTA	FT%	Blk	Stl	Ast	Reb	Pts		G	Min	FGA	FG%	3PA	3P%	FTA	FT%	Blk	Stl	Ast	Reb	Pts
Total	82	31.4	10.4	.473	0.1	.111	1.9	.735	0.22	0.93	6.0	1.9	11.2	Pre All-Star	49	31.6	10.8	.467	0.2	.111	1.7	.683	0.22	0.96	6.0	1.8	11.2
Home	41	30.3	9.6	.528	0.1	.333	2.0	.738	0.22	0.85	6.0	1.7	11.6	Post All-Star	33	31.0	9.8	.483	0.0	—	2.2	.795	0.21	0.88	6.0	2.2	11.2
Road	41	32.4	11.2	.426	0.1	.000	1.8	.733	0.22	1.00	6.0	2.2	10.9	November	16	30.9	10.3	.430	0.1	.000	1.1	.706	0.19	1.00	6.3	1.8	9.6
vs. Playoff	44	32.3	11.0	.463	0.1	.200	2.0	.690	0.27	0.89	5.7	1.8	11.5	December	15	32.1	11.1	.431	0.3	.000	1.5	.478	0.33	0.53	5.7	1.7	10.3
vs. Non-Playoff	38	30.2	9.7	.486	0.1	.000	1.8	.794	0.16	0.97	6.3	2.1	10.9	January	13	31.5	10.4	.519	0.2	.333	2.2	.750	0.23	1.31	5.8	1.9	12.5
vs. East	30	31.1	10.3	.494	0.1	.000	1.5	.795	0.23	1.00	6.3	2.2	11.3	February	13	32.2	11.5	.497	0.0	—	2.3	.733	0.15	1.00	7.1	2.0	13.1
vs. West	52	31.5	10.4	.461	0.1	.143	2.1	.712	0.21	0.88	5.8	1.8	11.2	March	15	30.7	9.4	.511	0.0	—	2.8	.833	0.20	0.87	5.2	2.5	11.9
vs. Div.	24	32.4	11.3	.450	0.1	.000	2.3	.709	0.17	0.96	6.1	1.9	11.8	April	10	30.6	9.3	.462	0.0	—	1.5	.867	0.20	0.90	6.1	1.6	9.9
As Starter	82	31.4	10.4	.473	0.1	.111	1.9	.735	0.22	0.93	6.0	1.9	11.2	0 Days Rest	18	31.7	10.4	.439	0.1	1.000	1.6	.828	0.22	1.00	5.9	2.3	10.5
Off Bench	0	—												1 Days Rest	43	30.9	10.0	.480	0.1	.000	2.1	.697	0.23	0.70	5.8	1.8	11.1
In wins	53	30.9	10.4	.504	0.1	.000	1.5	.765	0.17	0.83	6.4	2.1	11.6	2 Days Rest	18	31.5	10.9	.503	0.1	.000	1.6	.724	0.17	1.06	6.2	1.8	12.2
In losses	29	32.1	10.3	.417	0.1	.333	2.6	.703	0.31	1.10	5.3	1.7	10.4	3+ Days Rest	3	34.7	11.7	.400	0.0	—	2.7	.875	0.33	3.00	7.7	2.3	11.7

Last Five Seasons

	G	Min	FGA	FG%	3PA	3P%	FTA	FT%	Blk	Stl	Ast	Reb	Pts		G	Min	FGA	FG%	3PA	3P%	FTA	FT%	Blk	Stl	Ast	Reb	Pts
Total	365	34.2	9.7	.480	0.2	.176	2.4	.702	0.23	1.17	7.5	2.1	11.1	Pre All-Star	187	35.5	10.2	.471	0.3	.176	2.6	.714	0.21	1.23	7.6	2.1	11.6
Home	184	33.1	9.2	.510	0.2	.179	2.4	.709	0.26	1.13	7.6	1.9	11.1	Post All-Star	128	32.5	9.2	.498	0.2	.214	2.4	.722	0.25	1.13	7.5	2.2	10.9
Road	181	35.3	10.3	.453	0.3	.175	2.4	.695	0.20	1.20	7.5	2.4	11.0	Oct/Nov	59	34.7	10.4	.466	0.3	.235	2.4	.647	0.27	1.34	7.3	2.1	11.3
vs. Playoff	199	34.8	10.3	.472	0.3	.173	2.4	.708	0.22	1.14	7.1	2.0	11.3	December	55	36.6	9.9	.462	0.2	.182	2.9	.720	0.22	1.20	8.1	2.1	11.3
vs. Non-Playoff	166	33.4	9.0	.491	0.2	.179	2.4	.695	0.24	1.22	8.1	2.2	10.6	January	59	35.1	10.4	.483	0.3	.176	2.7	.739	0.19	1.17	7.2	2.0	12.1
vs. East	119	34.9	10.0	.481	0.3	.030	2.4	.732	0.26	1.03	7.5	2.2	11.4	February	66	35.6	9.8	.471	0.2	.067	2.4	.703	0.26	1.14	7.8	2.3	10.9
vs. West	246	33.8	9.6	.480	0.2	.259	2.4	.687	0.21	1.23	7.6	2.1	10.9	March	67	33.3	9.3	.498	0.3	.167	2.4	.686	0.24	1.15	8.1	2.4	11.3
vs. Div.	115	33.5	10.1	.465	0.2	.261	2.6	.670	0.19	1.15	7.5	2.1	11.2	Apr/May	59	30.0	8.7	.502	0.2	.231	1.8	.717	0.19	1.02	6.7	1.9	10.1
As Starter	363	34.3	9.8	.480	0.3	.176	2.4	.702	0.23	1.17	7.6	2.1	11.1	0 Days Rest	82	34.4	9.5	.465	0.2	.176	2.5	.738	0.23	1.16	7.6	2.1	10.8
Off Bench	2	9.0	1.5	.667	0.0	—	0.0	—	0.00	0.00	1.0	0.0	2.0	1 Days Rest	199	34.4	9.7	.487	0.3	.186	2.4	.683	0.22	1.17	7.6	2.2	11.1
In wins	218	34.3	9.6	.503	0.2	.195	2.4	.711	0.22	1.19	8.2	2.3	11.4	2 Days Rest	58	34.5	10.1	.473	0.2	.000	2.1	.702	0.19	1.21	7.7	1.9	11.0
In losses	147	33.9	9.9	.447	0.3	.160	2.4	.689	0.23	1.13	6.6	1.9	10.6	3+ Days Rest	26	31.1	10.0	.490	0.2	.500	2.6	.731	0.38	1.08	7.1	1.8	11.7

Ervin Johnson
Milwaukee Bucks — Center

1999-2000 Per Game Averages

	G	Min	FGA	FG%	3PA	3P%	FTA	FT%	Blk	Stl	Ast	Reb	Pts		G	Min	FGA	FG%	3PA	3P%	FTA	FT%	Blk	Stl	Ast	Reb	Pts
Total	80	26.6	3.5	.516	0.0	.000	2.0	.605	1.59	1.01	0.6	8.1	4.8	Pre All-Star	49	26.5	3.3	.564	0.0	—	2.0	.606	1.55	1.04	0.6	7.7	5.0
Home	40	26.7	3.6	.517	0.0	.000	1.9	.608	1.43	1.00	0.5	8.4	4.9	Post All-Star	31	26.8	3.7	.448	0.0	.000	1.9	.603	1.65	0.97	0.5	8.7	4.5
Road	40	26.5	3.4	.515	0.0	—	2.1	.602	1.75	1.03	0.6	7.8	4.7	November	13	19.9	2.6	.588	0.0	—	2.2	.552	1.62	0.54	0.2	5.3	4.3
vs. Playoff	42	27.0	3.5	.510	0.0	—	1.7	.586	1.52	1.02	0.6	7.6	4.5	December	16	26.2	3.5	.518	0.0	—	2.3	.639	1.44	1.19	0.8	7.8	5.1
vs. Non-Playoff	38	26.2	3.5	.522	0.0	.000	2.3	.621	1.66	1.00	0.5	8.7	5.1	January	15	30.9	3.7	.600	0.0	—	2.1	.613	1.67	1.33	0.7	9.6	5.7
vs. East	52	26.1	3.4	.522	0.0	.000	1.7	.618	1.54	1.00	0.6	8.0	4.6	February	12	29.9	4.3	.462	0.0	—	1.2	.643	1.25	0.83	1.0	9.2	4.8
vs. West	28	27.6	3.6	.505	0.0	—	2.4	.588	1.68	1.04	0.4	8.3	5.1	March	13	25.5	3.0	.385	0.1	.000	1.5	.550	1.54	0.85	0.3	7.5	3.2
vs. Div.	27	25.6	3.2	.540	0.0	—	1.4	.622	1.19	1.04	0.7	7.5	4.3	April	11	27.1	3.9	.535	0.0	—	2.5	.630	2.09	1.27	0.4	9.4	5.7
As Starter	74	27.3	3.6	.506	0.0	.000	1.9	.622	1.61	1.04	0.6	8.4	4.8	0 Days Rest	19	28.2	3.3	.468	0.0	—	2.1	.641	2.16	1.05	0.5	7.9	4.4
Off Bench	6	18.3	2.3	.714	0.0	—	2.3	.429	1.33	0.67	0.2	5.0	4.3	1 Days Rest	45	26.2	3.4	.536	0.0	.000	1.6	.606	1.27	1.11	0.6	7.9	4.6
In wins	41	26.6	3.6	.544	0.0	.000	2.4	.629	1.73	1.15	0.5	8.8	5.4	2 Days Rest	5	25.8	4.4	.500	0.0	—	1.8	.889	1.40	0.80	0.6	7.4	6.0
In losses	39	26.6	3.4	.485	0.0	—	1.5	.567	1.44	0.87	0.6	7.3	4.2	3+ Days Rest	11	26.0	4.0	.523	0.0	—	3.5	.500	2.00	0.64	0.5	9.4	5.9

Last Five Seasons

	G	Min	FGA	FG%	3PA	3P%	FTA	FT%	Blk	Stl	Ast	Reb	Pts		G	Min	FGA	FG%	3PA	3P%	FTA	FT%	Blk	Stl	Ast	Reb	Pts
Total	374	25.5	4.7	.521	0.0	.167	2.1	.617	1.87	0.79	0.6	8.0	6.2	Pre All-Star	188	25.1	4.4	.521	0.0	.000	2.1	.607	1.79	0.86	0.7	7.6	5.9
Home	186	26.2	5.1	.538	0.0	.250	2.2	.627	1.96	0.76	0.8	8.6	6.9	Post All-Star	136	27.8	5.4	.525	0.0	.200	2.1	.633	2.24	0.76	0.7	9.2	7.0
Road	188	24.8	4.3	.501	0.0	.000	2.0	.606	1.77	0.81	0.5	7.5	5.5	Oct/Nov	58	23.2	4.3	.536	0.0	—	2.1	.605	1.59	0.79	0.6	6.7	5.9
vs. Playoff	205	25.4	4.5	.528	0.0	.000	1.8	.592	1.80	0.70	0.6	7.6	5.8	December	56	25.2	4.5	.526	0.0	—	2.3	.651	1.77	0.82	0.9	7.8	6.2
vs. Non-Playoff	169	25.6	5.0	.513	0.0	.200	2.4	.640	1.94	0.89	0.6	8.5	6.7	January	60	26.6	4.5	.513	0.0	.000	2.1	.561	1.93	0.90	0.5	8.4	5.8
vs. East	210	24.6	4.5	.522	0.0	.000	2.1	.612	1.64	0.76	0.7	7.5	6.0	February	60	25.4	4.7	.513	0.0	1.000	1.5	.630	2.00	0.62	0.7	7.6	5.8
vs. West	164	26.7	5.0	.520	0.0	.250	2.1	.624	2.15	0.82	0.6	8.7	6.5	March	77	26.5	4.8	.511	0.0	.000	2.2	.636	2.03	0.70	0.6	8.5	6.3
vs. Div.	126	25.7	4.9	.511	0.0	.000	2.1	.608	1.88	0.83	0.6	8.0	6.3	Apr/May	63	25.8	5.3	.531	0.0	.000	2.3	.614	1.83	0.90	0.6	8.9	7.1
As Starter	304	27.2	5.0	.516	0.0	.167	2.1	.619	2.04	0.83	0.7	8.6	6.5	0 Days Rest	98	24.5	4.4	.503	0.0	1.000	2.1	.688	1.80	0.74	0.6	7.6	5.9
Off Bench	70	18.3	3.2	.556	0.0	—	1.9	.604	1.10	0.59	0.4	5.5	4.7	1 Days Rest	188	26.1	4.7	.534	0.0	.000	2.0	.597	1.77	0.80	0.7	8.4	6.1
In wins	188	24.5	4.7	.539	0.0	.250	2.4	.626	1.93	0.77	0.7	8.0	6.6	2 Days Rest	56	24.0	4.9	.482	0.0	—	2.4	.575	2.09	0.68	0.6	7.0	6.1
In losses	186	26.5	4.7	.503	0.0	.000	1.8	.605	1.81	0.80	0.6	8.0	5.8	3+ Days Rest	32	27.4	5.5	.563	0.0	.000	2.4	.597	2.28	0.84	0.8	9.1	7.6

Larry Johnson
New York Knicks — Forward

1999-2000 Per Game Averages

	G	Min	FGA	FG%	3PA	3P%	FTA	FT%	Blk	Stl	Ast	Reb	Pts		G	Min	FGA	FG%	3PA	3P%	FTA	FT%	Blk	Stl	Ast	Reb	Pts
Total	70	32.6	9.3	.433	2.5	.333	2.4	.766	0.10	0.60	2.5	5.4	10.7	Pre All-Star	35	31.6	9.8	.447	2.6	.363	2.8	.765	0.11	0.60	2.5	5.4	11.8
Home	38	32.4	9.3	.437	2.7	.359	2.6	.765	0.13	0.63	2.4	4.9	11.1	Post All-Star	35	33.6	8.9	.416	2.4	.301	2.0	.768	0.09	0.60	2.5	5.4	9.6
Road	32	32.8	9.3	.428	2.2	.296	2.2	.768	0.06	0.56	2.6	6.1	10.3	November	8	31.0	10.4	.446	2.4	.263	2.6	.714	0.13	0.88	3.3	7.9	11.8
vs. Playoff	38	31.7	9.7	.427	2.9	.342	1.7	.723	0.13	0.68	2.4	5.2	10.5	December	12	31.7	10.0	.425	2.5	.333	3.9	.809	0.08	0.58	2.8	5.1	12.5
vs. Non-Playoff	32	33.7	8.9	.440	2.0	.317	3.2	.794	0.06	0.50	2.7	5.7	11.0	January	12	33.2	9.4	.478	2.7	.469	2.2	.731	0.00	0.50	2.3	5.0	11.8
vs. East	46	33.0	9.6	.457	2.4	.360	3.0	.766	0.11	0.48	2.5	5.5	11.9	February	11	33.3	9.8	.389	3.5	.308	2.0	.636	0.45	0.82	1.9	3.9	10.0
vs. West	24	31.9	8.8	.382	2.6	.286	1.3	.767	0.08	0.83	2.6	5.3	8.5	March	17	33.0	9.2	.401	2.2	.243	1.5	.880	0.00	0.47	2.9	5.5	9.2
vs. Div.	21	33.3	8.7	.475	2.1	.356	3.7	.795	0.10	0.38	2.1	5.8	12.0	April	10	32.8	7.1	.493	1.7	.412	2.6	.769	0.00	0.50	1.6	6.0	9.7
As Starter	68	32.9	9.3	.431	2.5	.335	2.4	.768	0.09	0.60	2.5	5.4	10.7	0 Days Rest	15	33.9	9.3	.400	2.3	.257	2.5	.892	0.00	0.33	2.5	6.1	10.3
Off Bench	2	23.5	9.0	.500	2.0	.250	1.5	.667	0.50	0.50	2.0	5.0	10.5	1 Days Rest	36	33.1	9.6	.403	2.7	.323	2.4	.761	0.11	0.69	2.6	5.0	10.5
In wins	43	33.8	9.7	.440	2.7	.350	2.4	.762	0.12	0.67	2.9	5.5	11.3	2 Days Rest	12	31.0	8.6	.524	2.5	.433	2.0	.708	0.17	0.67	2.3	5.6	11.5
In losses	27	30.6	8.7	.419	2.1	.298	2.3	.774	0.07	0.48	1.9	5.3	9.7	3+ Days Rest	7	29.7	8.9	.516	1.9	.385	2.6	.611	0.14	0.57	2.1	6.1	11.4

Last Five Seasons

	G	Min	FGA	FG%	3PA	3P%	FTA	FT%	Blk	Stl	Ast	Reb	Pts		G	Min	FGA	FG%	3PA	3P%	FTA	FT%	Blk	Stl	Ast	Reb	Pts
Total	346	35.3	11.4	.475	1.8	.335	4.2	.753	0.32	0.68	2.8	6.2	14.6	Pre All-Star	159	35.2	12.2	.474	1.9	.342	4.5	.721	0.35	0.64	2.9	6.2	15.3
Home	177	34.9	11.2	.493	1.8	.335	4.2	.757	0.33	0.64	3.0	6.3	14.8	Post All-Star	138	36.1	11.3	.482	1.6	.317	4.1	.774	0.31	0.72	2.8	6.4	14.6
Road	169	35.8	11.6	.457	1.8	.336	4.2	.748	0.30	0.72	2.6	6.1	14.4	Oct/Nov	50	33.9	12.1	.488	1.8	.272	5.0	.718	0.24	0.60	2.9	5.9	15.9
vs. Playoff	186	35.2	11.5	.449	1.9	.340	4.2	.753	0.33	0.73	2.8	6.2	14.1	December	47	35.2	12.3	.470	2.0	.411	4.3	.711	0.34	0.83	2.9	6.4	15.5
vs. Non-Playoff	160	35.4	11.4	.506	1.6	.329	4.2	.752	0.31	0.63	2.8	6.2	15.2	January	49	36.4	11.8	.445	1.9	.344	4.4	.698	0.45	0.57	3.1	6.2	14.2
vs. East	242	35.3	11.4	.482	1.8	.339	4.5	.756	0.30	0.65	2.7	6.1	15.0	February	61	35.8	11.4	.499	1.8	.333	4.1	.783	0.30	0.70	2.5	6.4	15.2
vs. West	104	35.4	11.5	.461	1.7	.326	3.4	.744	0.35	0.74	3.0	6.5	13.7	March	83	36.1	11.6	.490	1.7	.293	3.7	.779	0.31	0.63	3.1	6.1	14.7
vs. Div.	113	35.7	11.1	.493	1.7	.370	4.8	.763	0.27	0.69	2.9	6.3	15.2	Apr/May	56	34.0	9.6	.443	1.5	.384	4.1	.812	0.16	0.77	2.3	6.2	12.4
As Starter	343	35.4	11.4	.475	1.8	.336	4.2	.752	0.31	0.67	2.8	6.2	14.6	0 Days Rest	87	35.6	11.4	.460	1.8	.333	4.6	.786	0.24	0.64	2.6	6.1	14.7
Off Bench	3	25.7	9.3	.536	2.0	.333	2.0	.833	0.33	1.33	1.3	4.3	12.3	1 Days Rest	180	35.5	11.4	.476	1.8	.336	4.0	.742	0.33	0.66	2.9	6.2	14.5
In wins	200	35.3	11.2	.500	1.8	.363	4.2	.755	0.36	0.67	2.9	6.1	15.0	2 Days Rest	45	35.1	11.7	.477	1.6	.361	4.1	.763	0.38	0.82	2.8	6.2	14.9
In losses	146	35.4	11.7	.443	1.8	.300	4.2	.750	0.26	0.70	2.7	6.3	14.1	3+ Days Rest	34	33.9	11.1	.512	1.9	.308	4.3	.703	0.32	0.68	2.7	6.0	15.0

Eddie Jones
Charlotte Hornets — Guard-Forward

1999-2000 Per Game Averages

	G	Min	FGA	FG%	3PA	3P%	FTA	FT%	Blk	Stl	Ast	Reb	Pts
Total	72	39.0	15.5	.427	4.7	.375	5.8	.864	0.68	2.67	4.2	4.8	20.1
Home	38	38.9	15.2	.440	4.4	.387	6.3	.867	0.68	2.92	4.9	4.7	20.6
Road	34	39.1	15.9	.413	5.1	.364	5.3	.860	0.68	2.38	3.4	4.9	19.5
vs. Playoff	37	39.9	15.9	.428	5.1	.392	5.5	.847	0.62	2.68	4.1	4.8	20.2
vs. Non-Playoff	35	38.0	15.2	.427	4.3	.355	6.2	.880	0.74	2.66	4.4	4.7	20.0
vs. East	48	39.0	15.3	.453	4.9	.394	6.3	.868	0.60	2.71	3.7	4.4	21.3
vs. West	24	38.9	16.0	.378	4.4	.333	4.8	.852	0.83	2.58	5.3	5.4	17.6
vs. Div.	23	38.8	15.7	.458	5.4	.379	6.0	.849	0.52	3.04	3.6	4.7	21.5
As Starter	72	39.0	15.5	.427	4.7	.375	5.8	.864	0.68	2.67	4.2	4.8	20.1
Off Bench	0	—											
In wins	47	38.7	15.0	.454	4.8	.406	6.3	.872	0.77	3.06	4.7	4.7	21.1
In losses	25	39.4	16.5	.381	4.7	.316	4.8	.843	0.52	1.92	3.4	5.0	18.1
Pre All-Star	37	38.6	15.8	.434	4.5	.377	6.2	.843	0.65	3.00	4.5	4.8	20.6
Post All-Star	35	39.3	15.3	.419	5.0	.374	5.4	.889	0.71	2.31	3.9	4.7	19.5
November	14	38.6	15.3	.444	4.6	.385	6.1	.918	0.50	2.93	3.5	4.4	20.9
December	10	36.6	14.1	.404	3.9	.385	5.4	.815	0.90	2.70	6.0	5.4	17.3
January	8	39.1	16.8	.418	4.9	.308	7.6	.770	0.38	3.88	4.9	4.5	21.4
February	14	41.1	17.8	.422	5.0	.429	4.5	.873	0.79	2.43	4.1	5.1	21.1
March	15	39.4	15.4	.437	4.7	.386	6.3	.853	0.67	1.93	4.0	4.4	20.7
April	11	38.4	13.6	.427	5.3	.328	5.5	.934	0.82	2.73	3.5	4.8	18.5
0 Days Rest	18	38.6	15.0	.411	4.3	.321	5.5	.909	0.44	2.17	3.9	4.4	18.7
1 Days Rest	40	39.1	15.7	.435	5.0	.377	6.0	.840	0.63	2.95	4.0	4.9	20.5
2 Days Rest	6	42.0	17.3	.462	4.2	.480	6.0	.861	1.17	1.67	6.0	5.0	23.2
3+ Days Rest	8	37.0	14.8	.390	4.9	.410	5.8	.891	1.13	3.13	4.9	4.9	18.6

Last Five Seasons

	G	Min	FGA	FG%	3PA	3P%	FTA	FT%	Blk	Stl	Ast	Reb	Pts
Total	352	36.3	12.7	.454	4.2	.378	4.3	.804	0.73	2.26	3.6	4.0	16.6
Home	179	36.4	12.9	.455	4.1	.367	4.5	.814	0.76	2.35	4.1	4.0	16.6
Road	173	36.2	12.5	.452	4.2	.388	4.1	.793	0.69	2.17	3.0	3.9	16.3
vs. Playoff	191	37.2	12.8	.439	4.2	.371	4.2	.791	0.71	2.12	3.4	4.1	16.2
vs. Non-Playoff	161	35.3	12.6	.471	4.1	.386	4.4	.819	0.75	2.43	3.7	3.8	17.1
vs. East	166	37.1	13.1	.454	4.2	.358	4.9	.820	0.70	2.38	3.6	4.2	17.4
vs. West	186	35.6	12.4	.453	4.2	.395	3.8	.786	0.75	2.15	3.6	3.8	15.8
vs. Div.	110	35.9	12.4	.461	4.2	.354	4.8	.800	0.73	2.41	3.5	3.7	16.7
As Starter	348	36.5	12.8	.454	4.2	.377	4.3	.806	0.73	2.27	3.6	4.0	16.7
Off Bench	4	20.5	7.3	.414	1.8	.429	1.0	.250	0.50	1.50	2.8	1.8	7.0
In wins	241	36.0	12.7	.481	4.1	.407	4.5	.815	0.78	2.44	3.7	4.1	17.6
In losses	111	37.0	12.9	.395	4.2	.314	3.8	.777	0.61	1.87	3.2	3.8	14.5
Pre All-Star	165	36.1	13.1	.453	4.4	.382	4.3	.794	0.64	2.48	3.7	3.9	16.9
Post All-Star	137	36.1	12.6	.460	4.4	.382	4.0	.829	0.68	1.91	3.4	4.1	16.6
Oct/Nov	49	37.7	13.7	.489	5.0	.425	4.6	.806	0.57	2.55	3.4	4.0	19.3
December	55	34.0	11.5	.420	3.7	.345	3.5	.758	0.62	2.35	4.0	3.9	13.6
January	47	37.1	13.9	.443	4.6	.369	5.0	.809	0.70	2.77	3.8	3.7	18.0
February	63	36.4	13.3	.446	4.1	.387	3.7	.828	0.87	1.84	3.6	4.2	16.4
March	76	35.6	12.3	.457	3.9	.347	4.8	.788	0.68	1.75	2.9	3.9	16.4
Apr/May	62	37.4	12.1	.465	4.1	.391	4.3	.832	0.87	2.61	4.0	4.0	16.5
0 Days Rest	86	36.0	12.6	.449	4.0	.381	3.7	.844	0.63	2.13	3.5	4.0	15.9
1 Days Rest	194	36.9	12.8	.453	4.3	.374	4.6	.785	0.75	2.39	3.6	4.0	16.8
2 Days Rest	38	36.2	13.3	.485	3.8	.431	4.2	.807	0.71	2.03	3.7	3.8	17.9
3+ Days Rest	34	33.7	12.4	.433	4.2	.338	4.5	.829	0.88	2.09	3.4	3.6	15.9

Shawn Kemp
Cleveland Cavaliers — Forward

1999-2000 Per Game Averages

	G	Min	FGA	FG%	3PA	3P%	FTA	FT%	Blk	Stl	Ast	Reb	Pts
Total	82	30.4	14.1	.417	0.1	.333	7.7	.776	1.17	1.22	1.7	8.8	18.8
Home	41	30.4	13.9	.424	0.0	.500	8.3	.805	1.56	1.12	1.6	9.2	18.4
Road	41	30.3	14.4	.410	0.1	.250	7.2	.743	0.78	1.32	1.7	8.5	17.2
vs. Playoff	47	30.3	14.0	.384	0.1	.333	6.8	.781	1.02	1.17	1.7	8.4	16.1
vs. Non-Playoff	35	30.6	14.3	.460	0.1	.333	9.0	.772	1.37	1.29	1.6	9.4	20.2
vs. East	54	30.6	14.1	.413	0.1	.333	7.7	.788	1.11	1.19	1.8	9.1	17.8
vs. West	28	29.9	14.2	.425	0.0	—	7.9	.755	1.29	1.29	1.5	8.3	18.0
vs. Div.	28	30.1	13.9	.396	0.1	.333	6.8	.778	0.96	1.32	2.3	9.0	16.3
As Starter	82	30.4	14.1	.417	0.1	.333	7.7	.776	1.17	1.22	1.7	8.8	17.8
Off Bench	0	—											
In wins	32	30.4	13.7	.453	0.0	—	9.0	.836	1.53	1.53	1.6	9.7	19.9
In losses	50	30.4	14.4	.395	0.1	.333	7.0	.727	0.94	1.02	1.7	8.3	16.5
Pre All-Star	49	31.6	15.2	.406	0.1	.400	8.4	.759	1.12	1.12	1.7	9.2	18.8
Post All-Star	33	28.6	12.5	.438	0.0	.000	6.8	.809	1.24	1.36	1.6	8.3	16.5
November	13	33.2	16.2	.400	0.0	—	8.1	.829	1.00	1.00	1.9	10.7	19.6
December	16	31.1	15.7	.398	0.1	1.000	8.3	.773	0.88	1.13	1.8	8.3	19.0
January	15	31.1	13.9	.421	0.1	.000	7.9	.714	1.53	1.13	1.3	8.9	17.4
February	12	30.8	14.5	.385	0.1	.000	8.7	.769	1.25	1.25	1.7	9.0	17.8
March	15	28.6	12.8	.406	0.1	.000	6.7	.800	1.13	1.67	1.5	7.7	15.7
April	11	27.0	11.3	.540	—	—	6.8	.787	1.27	1.09	2.1	8.8	17.5
0 Days Rest	24	30.4	14.5	.441	0.0	—	7.8	.793	1.04	1.21	1.8	9.4	19.0
1 Days Rest	35	29.8	13.5	.366	0.1	.500	7.3	.765	1.09	1.17	1.7	8.5	15.5
2 Days Rest	16	31.6	14.1	.502	0.1	.000	8.4	.785	1.50	1.56	1.7	9.4	20.8
3+ Days Rest	7	30.7	16.4	.391	0.3	.500	8.1	.754	1.29	0.71	1.1	7.6	19.1

Last Five Seasons

	G	Min	FGA	FG%	3PA	3P%	FTA	FT%	Blk	Stl	Ast	Reb	Pts
Total	364	33.3	13.4	.479	0.2	.361	7.8	.753	1.21	1.30	2.1	9.8	18.8
Home	185	33.2	13.2	.499	0.2	.429	8.0	.766	1.32	1.26	2.1	9.8	19.3
Road	179	33.4	13.6	.458	0.2	.303	7.7	.739	1.09	1.35	2.1	9.8	18.2
vs. Playoff	199	33.5	13.3	.459	0.2	.333	7.4	.765	1.12	1.23	2.1	9.8	18.0
vs. Non-Playoff	165	33.1	13.4	.502	0.2	.387	8.3	.740	1.31	1.39	2.2	9.9	19.7
vs. East	202	33.5	13.8	.468	0.2	.452	7.7	.754	1.17	1.31	2.0	9.7	18.8
vs. West	162	33.0	12.8	.494	0.2	.267	8.0	.753	1.25	1.29	2.2	10.0	18.7
vs. Div.	120	33.1	13.2	.468	0.2	.263	7.7	.754	1.06	1.33	2.4	9.3	18.2
As Starter	355	33.5	13.5	.480	0.2	.367	7.9	.753	1.21	1.30	2.1	9.9	19.0
Off Bench	9	25.8	8.6	.429	0.1	.000	4.7	.738	1.00	1.33	1.9	6.6	10.8
In wins	218	33.4	12.9	.519	0.2	.394	8.1	.767	1.32	1.41	2.2	10.2	19.6
In losses	146	33.1	14.2	.425	0.2	.321	7.5	.730	1.03	1.14	1.9	9.1	17.5
Pre All-Star	188	34.1	14.1	.484	0.2	.405	8.1	.738	1.32	1.34	1.9	10.4	19.7
Post All-Star	134	31.6	12.3	.470	0.1	.235	7.0	.764	1.08	1.31	2.2	9.1	17.0
Oct/Nov	59	34.4	14.7	.506	0.2	.308	8.3	.747	1.32	1.34	2.0	11.1	21.1
December	57	34.0	13.9	.477	0.2	.400	8.2	.717	1.46	1.28	1.9	10.2	19.2
January	59	33.9	13.8	.471	0.3	.563	7.7	.748	1.31	1.31	1.9	10.1	18.9
February	58	33.7	13.1	.473	0.1	.125	8.0	.785	1.04	1.47	1.9	9.6	18.7
March	76	32.5	12.5	.455	0.1	.167	6.9	.770	0.96	1.14	2.6	8.7	16.8
Apr/May	55	31.4	12.4	.496	0.1	.375	8.2	.750	1.27	1.33	2.2	9.4	18.5
0 Days Rest	96	33.6	14.1	.487	0.1	.417	8.5	.750	1.22	1.23	2.0	10.1	20.2
1 Days Rest	171	33.7	13.1	.470	0.2	.300	7.8	.744	1.19	1.31	2.2	9.8	18.2
2 Days Rest	66	32.9	13.1	.518	0.2	.462	7.1	.784	1.29	1.44	2.1	9.8	19.2
3+ Days Rest	31	30.9	13.0	.419	0.2	.333	7.6	.755	1.06	1.19	1.7	8.7	16.7

Jerome Kersey
San Antonio Spurs — Forward

1999-2000 Per Game Averages

	G	Min	FGA	FG%	3PA	3P%	FTA	FT%	Blk	Stl	Ast	Reb	Pts		G	Min	FGA	FG%	3PA	3P%	FTA	FT%	Blk	Stl	Ast	Reb	Pts
Total	72	18.2	4.9	.412	0.1	.000	0.6	.707	0.65	0.93	1.0	3.1	4.5	Pre All-Star	40	16.2	4.6	.423	0.1	.000	0.7	.750	0.53	0.78	0.7	2.7	4.4
Home	36	18.5	5.0	.461	0.1	.000	0.8	.741	0.67	1.08	0.8	3.3	5.2	Post All-Star	32	20.7	5.4	.401	0.2	.000	0.4	.615	0.81	1.13	1.3	3.7	4.6
Road	36	17.9	4.8	.362	0.2	.000	0.4	.643	0.64	0.78	1.1	3.0	3.8	November	12	17.4	4.8	.448	0.0	—	0.4	.800	0.42	0.92	0.9	2.8	4.7
vs. Playoff	40	17.8	4.6	.411	0.1	.000	0.7	.759	0.53	0.88	0.8	3.2	4.4	December	10	15.2	4.6	.457	0.0	—	1.1	.545	0.40	0.60	0.8	2.2	4.8
vs. Non-Playoff	32	18.7	5.3	.414	0.2	.000	0.4	.583	0.81	1.00	1.1	3.0	4.6	January	13	16.5	4.2	.436	0.2	.000	0.8	1.000	0.46	0.69	0.5	3.0	4.5
vs. East	23	18.3	4.8	.445	0.1	.000	0.9	.650	0.48	0.78	0.7	2.8	4.8	February	12	17.5	5.2	.323	0.1	.000	0.8	.500	0.75	1.33	0.6	3.8	3.8
vs. West	49	18.2	5.0	.398	0.1	.000	0.4	.762	0.73	1.00	1.1	3.3	4.3	March	15	22.1	5.5	.427	0.3	.000	0.1	1.000	1.07	0.93	1.3	4.0	4.7
vs. Div.	21	16.4	4.3	.396	0.1	.000	0.6	.769	0.57	1.14	1.0	2.7	3.9	April	10	19.4	5.1	.392	0.1	.000	0.4	.750	0.70	1.10	1.7	2.8	4.3
As Starter	18	21.8	6.2	.393	0.3	.000	0.8	.667	0.89	1.28	0.9	4.3	5.4	0 Days Rest	16	18.1	5.0	.450	0.1	.000	0.8	.583	0.50	1.31	1.1	3.3	4.9
Off Bench	54	17.0	4.5	.421	0.1	.000	0.5	.731	0.57	0.81	1.0	2.7	4.1	1 Days Rest	35	19.0	5.2	.415	0.1	.000	0.6	.727	0.77	1.09	1.1	3.3	4.8
In wins	46	18.1	5.1	.410	0.1	.000	0.4	.737	0.65	1.00	1.0	3.3	4.5	2 Days Rest	16	17.8	4.4	.408	0.2	.000	0.2	1.000	0.56	0.44	0.6	3.1	3.8
In losses	26	18.3	4.6	.417	0.2	.000	0.8	.682	0.65	0.81	1.0	2.8	4.4	3+ Days Rest	5	14.2	4.0	.250	0.0	—	0.8	.750	0.60	0.20	0.8	1.2	2.6

Last Five Seasons

	G	Min	FGA	FG%	3PA	3P%	FTA	FT%	Blk	Stl	Ast	Reb	Pts		G	Min	FGA	FG%	3PA	3P%	FTA	FT%	Blk	Stl	Ast	Reb	Pts
Total	300	20.4	5.8	.409	0.4	.209	1.3	.629	0.56	1.22	1.2	4.1	5.6	Pre All-Star	136	19.7	5.5	.408	0.5	.258	1.5	.617	0.53	1.15	1.1	3.9	5.6
Home	155	20.5	5.9	.421	0.4	.254	1.5	.649	0.56	1.32	1.1	4.0	6.1	Post All-Star	119	22.9	6.6	.428	0.3	.114	1.4	.660	0.70	1.45	1.4	4.7	6.6
Road	145	20.2	5.6	.396	0.3	.146	1.1	.597	0.57	1.12	1.2	4.1	5.2	Oct/Nov	42	19.3	5.6	.413	0.2	.222	1.5	.600	0.40	1.29	1.0	3.8	5.6
vs. Playoff	165	19.6	5.6	.414	0.4	.169	1.3	.597	0.49	1.10	1.1	3.9	5.5	December	36	21.3	5.6	.448	0.5	.368	1.1	.610	0.50	1.28	1.2	4.1	5.9
vs. Non-Playoff	135	21.3	6.1	.403	0.4	.250	1.2	.671	0.65	1.36	1.3	4.2	5.8	January	46	18.7	5.3	.389	0.7	.242	1.9	.614	0.54	0.85	1.2	3.8	5.5
vs. East	91	21.1	5.9	.423	0.4	.200	1.5	.603	0.41	1.21	1.3	4.2	6.0	February	51	19.5	5.8	.375	0.3	.063	0.9	.604	0.57	1.18	1.1	4.0	4.9
vs. West	209	20.1	5.7	.403	0.4	.213	1.2	.643	0.63	1.22	1.1	4.0	5.4	March	68	21.5	5.8	.424	0.3	.130	1.0	.691	0.63	1.22	1.2	4.2	5.7
vs. Div.	92	19.6	5.4	.414	0.3	.129	1.4	.631	0.60	1.28	1.1	3.6	5.4	Apr/May	57	21.4	6.4	.409	0.3	.200	1.3	.640	0.65	1.47	1.4	4.3	6.1
As Starter	122	24.3	6.9	.412	0.5	.238	1.7	.637	0.70	1.42	1.3	5.0	6.9	0 Days Rest	66	19.8	5.5	.377	0.3	.095	1.2	.597	0.47	1.21	1.1	3.8	4.9
Off Bench	178	17.7	5.0	.406	0.3	.173	1.0	.619	0.47	1.08	1.1	3.4	4.7	1 Days Rest	154	21.2	6.1	.427	0.4	.242	1.5	.611	0.68	1.31	1.2	4.2	6.2
In wins	189	20.8	5.9	.423	0.4	.247	1.2	.629	0.59	1.34	1.3	4.3	5.8	2 Days Rest	46	19.3	5.5	.409	0.2	.182	0.9	.775	0.41	0.78	1.1	3.6	5.2
In losses	111	19.6	5.6	.384	0.3	.118	1.4	.627	0.52	1.01	1.0	3.7	5.2	3+ Days Rest	34	19.0	5.4	.379	0.5	.235	1.2	.643	0.44	1.41	1.3	4.2	5.0

Jason Kidd
Phoenix Suns — Guard

1999-2000 Per Game Averages

	G	Min	FGA	FG%	3PA	3P%	FTA	FT%	Blk	Stl	Ast	Reb	Pts		G	Min	FGA	FG%	3PA	3P%	FTA	FT%	Blk	Stl	Ast	Reb	Pts
Total	67	39.0	12.8	.409	2.5	.337	3.7	.829	0.42	2.00	10.1	7.2	14.3	Pre All-Star	48	39.7	14.3	.414	2.6	.360	3.6	.829	0.50	2.04	9.9	7.1	15.8
Home	35	37.4	12.1	.446	2.2	.308	3.7	.854	0.49	1.91	10.6	6.4	14.7	Post All-Star	19	37.5	9.0	.392	2.2	.268	3.7	.829	0.21	1.89	10.7	7.6	10.7
Road	32	40.8	13.5	.374	2.8	.364	3.6	.800	0.34	2.09	9.6	8.1	13.9	November	14	38.8	14.0	.464	2.2	.452	3.6	.804	0.50	1.86	8.3	5.8	14.6
vs. Playoff	36	39.9	13.1	.389	2.4	.314	3.4	.818	0.39	1.75	10.3	7.6	13.7	December	15	41.2	16.5	.433	2.7	.350	3.5	.887	0.67	2.33	10.6	8.2	18.3
vs. Non-Playoff	31	38.1	12.3	.435	2.6	.363	4.0	.839	0.45	2.29	9.9	6.8	15.0	January	14	40.4	13.1	.328	2.9	.300	3.7	.827	0.29	1.86	11.2	7.1	12.5
vs. East	27	38.7	11.2	.424	2.3	.295	3.8	.854	0.48	1.74	9.6	6.7	13.4	February	13	36.5	9.8	.383	2.3	.300	3.8	.755	0.31	2.08	8.6	7.1	11.1
vs. West	40	39.3	13.8	.401	2.6	.362	3.6	.810	0.38	2.18	10.5	7.5	14.9	March	11	37.6	9.2	.426	2.3	.280	3.6	.875	0.27	1.82	12.2	7.9	11.6
vs. Div.	17	38.7	13.9	.436	2.2	.500	3.8	.766	0.35	2.06	10.6	7.8	16.1	April	0	—	—	—	—	—	—	—	—	—	—	—	—
As Starter	67	39.0	12.8	.409	2.5	.337	3.7	.829	0.42	2.00	10.1	7.2	14.3	0 Days Rest	17	40.4	13.4	.346	2.8	.333	3.8	.877	0.35	2.12	9.9	8.4	13.6
Off Bench	0	—	—	—	—	—	—	—	—	—	—	—	—	1 Days Rest	31	38.2	11.9	.438	2.5	.372	3.9	.775	0.42	2.13	10.3	6.9	14.4
In wins	44	38.0	12.1	.442	2.3	.374	4.3	.843	0.50	2.20	10.3	7.1	15.2	2 Days Rest	14	39.8	13.9	.418	2.4	.212	3.3	.891	0.29	1.86	10.4	7.0	15.0
In losses	23	41.0	14.0	.356	2.9	.284	2.3	.778	0.26	1.61	9.8	7.4	12.7	3+ Days Rest	5	37.8	12.6	.444	1.4	.571	2.8	.857	1.00	1.20	9.2	5.6	14.4

Last Five Seasons

	G	Min	FGA	FG%	3PA	3P%	FTA	FT%	Blk	Stl	Ast	Reb	Pts		G	Min	FGA	FG%	3PA	3P%	FTA	FT%	Blk	Stl	Ast	Reb	Pts
Total	335	38.2	12.6	.407	3.2	.340	3.5	.750	0.36	2.12	9.7	6.4	14.0	Pre All-Star	162	38.2	12.4	.394	3.2	.333	3.6	.738	0.33	2.17	9.6	6.3	13.5
Home	170	37.7	12.0	.417	2.9	.319	3.5	.758	0.45	2.05	10.1	6.0	13.6	Post All-Star	123	36.9	12.4	.407	3.6	.340	3.0	.765	0.38	1.98	9.3	6.3	13.7
Road	165	38.7	13.3	.398	3.6	.358	3.6	.742	0.26	2.19	9.3	6.8	14.5	Oct/Nov	53	37.1	11.8	.415	3.0	.331	3.5	.707	0.36	2.21	8.7	6.0	13.3
vs. Playoff	182	38.7	13.1	.393	3.4	.331	3.4	.753	0.41	2.00	9.7	6.5	13.9	December	52	38.3	12.4	.394	2.8	.349	2.8	.734	0.35	2.37	9.5	6.1	12.8
vs. Non-Playoff	153	37.5	12.1	.425	3.1	.351	3.8	.747	0.29	2.25	9.6	6.3	14.2	January	44	39.6	12.8	.342	3.5	.276	4.6	.787	0.23	1.86	10.6	7.2	13.3
vs. East	111	37.2	11.5	.379	3.2	.306	3.2	.783	0.30	1.91	9.1	5.9	12.2	February	60	37.9	12.7	.433	3.3	.369	3.8	.765	0.45	2.02	9.8	6.5	15.1
vs. West	224	38.7	13.2	.419	3.2	.356	3.7	.736	0.38	2.22	10.0	6.6	15.0	March	78	36.9	12.5	.394	3.5	.321	3.0	.726	0.32	1.87	9.5	6.3	14.2
vs. Div.	103	38.8	13.1	.427	3.1	.379	3.6	.762	0.35	2.29	10.0	6.1	15.0	Apr/May	48	40.4	13.7	.456	3.3	.396	4.0	.777	0.42	2.50	10.2	6.3	16.9
As Starter	325	38.5	12.8	.407	3.2	.336	3.6	.750	0.35	2.12	9.8	6.5	14.2	0 Days Rest	76	39.1	12.4	.372	3.3	.307	3.1	.774	0.42	2.14	10.1	6.6	12.7
Off Bench	10	28.4	8.5	.412	2.8	.500	2.0	.750	0.40	1.90	6.8	3.4	9.9	1 Days Rest	179	38.0	13.0	.413	3.5	.352	3.6	.755	0.33	2.05	9.5	6.1	14.6
In wins	184	38.3	11.9	.440	2.8	.365	4.3	.771	0.35	2.29	10.2	6.6	14.8	2 Days Rest	56	38.4	12.3	.403	2.8	.312	3.9	.734	0.32	2.23	9.9	6.9	13.7
In losses	151	38.0	13.5	.371	3.8	.317	2.6	.710	0.36	1.91	9.0	6.1	13.1	3+ Days Rest	24	36.5	11.8	.486	2.1	.440	3.8	.692	0.42	2.25	9.2	6.7	15.0

Kerry Kittles

1999-2000 Per Game Averages

	G	Min	FGA	FG%	3PA	3P%	FTA	FT%	Blk	Stl	Ast	Reb	Pts		G	Min	FGA	FG%	3PA	3P%	FTA	FT%	Blk	Stl	Ast	Reb	Pts
Total	62	30.6	11.3	.437	3.9	.400	2.0	.795	0.31	1.27	2.3	3.6	13.0	Pre All-Star	36	31.8	11.9	.440	4.4	.409	2.3	.793	0.36	1.47	2.3	3.9	14.1
Home	33	30.7	12.2	.441	4.3	.390	1.9	.790	0.24	1.30	2.5	3.6	13.9	Post All-Star	26	28.9	10.3	.433	3.1	.383	1.7	.800	0.23	1.00	2.2	3.2	11.5
Road	29	30.4	10.2	.431	3.4	.414	2.2	.800	0.38	1.24	2.0	3.7	12.0	November	2	20.5	9.0	.278	1.5	.000	0.5	1.000	0.00	0.50	0.5	2.0	5.5
vs. Playoff	34	30.4	11.5	.418	4.0	.385	1.8	.790	0.24	1.35	2.3	3.5	12.6	December	15	31.3	11.8	.435	4.6	.435	2.7	.805	0.40	1.47	2.7	4.5	14.5
vs. Non-Playoff	28	30.9	10.9	.461	3.8	.419	2.3	.800	0.39	1.18	2.4	3.8	13.5	January	14	33.0	12.9	.453	5.1	.394	2.2	.806	0.43	1.43	1.9	4.1	15.5
vs. East	39	30.6	11.1	.419	3.6	.390	2.3	.822	0.28	1.23	2.7	3.5	12.6	February	12	34.0	12.2	.425	3.0	.333	1.9	.696	0.08	1.67	2.8	3.6	12.7
vs. West	23	30.5	11.5	.466	4.3	.414	1.6	.730	0.35	1.35	1.5	3.8	13.7	March	16	27.6	9.6	.481	3.2	.490	1.6	.800	0.38	0.88	2.1	2.8	12.1
vs. Div.	19	33.0	11.8	.433	3.8	.397	1.9	.861	0.21	1.26	2.5	4.0	13.4	April	3	24.3	7.3	.227	3.3	.100	2.0	1.000	0.00	0.67	2.3	3.0	5.7
As Starter	61	31.0	11.3	.440	3.9	.403	2.1	.794	0.31	1.30	2.3	3.7	13.2	0 Days Rest	13	31.0	10.3	.478	3.8	.420	1.2	.933	0.08	1.08	2.1	3.3	12.5
Off Bench	1	7.0	7.0	.143	2.0	.000	1.0	1.000	0.00	0.00	0.0	1.0	3.0	1 Days Rest	37	30.6	11.2	.439	3.9	.411	2.1	.785	0.46	1.24	2.1	3.9	13.1
In wins	29	29.9	11.3	.435	4.2	.415	1.9	.778	0.38	1.24	2.7	4.0	13.1	2 Days Rest	5	33.6	14.8	.432	5.0	.360	2.2	.636	0.00	1.80	4.0	4.0	16.0
In losses	33	31.2	11.2	.439	3.5	.385	2.2	.808	0.24	1.30	1.9	3.3	13.0	3+ Days Rest	7	27.6	10.7	.360	2.7	.316	3.1	.818	0.14	1.43	2.3	2.3	11.1

Career (1996-97 thru 1999-2000)

	G	Min	FGA	FG%	3PA	3P%	FTA	FT%	Blk	Stl	Ast	Reb	Pts		G	Min	FGA	FG%	3PA	3P%	FTA	FT%	Blk	Stl	Ast	Reb	Pts
Total	267	34.8	13.7	.423	4.0	.383	2.7	.788	0.44	1.67	2.6	4.1	15.3	Pre All-Star	125	36.2	13.6	.430	4.2	.395	2.8	.768	0.34	1.70	2.7	4.1	15.5
Home	134	34.6	13.8	.418	4.0	.361	2.7	.765	0.54	1.74	2.5	4.2	15.0	Post All-Star	96	33.4	14.0	.439	4.1	.394	2.6	.825	0.51	1.63	2.4	4.1	16.1
Road	133	35.0	13.6	.429	4.1	.405	2.7	.811	0.34	1.61	2.6	4.0	15.5	Oct/Nov	24	32.9	12.3	.391	3.1	.333	2.5	.820	0.25	1.50	2.8	3.3	12.7
vs. Playoff	145	34.8	13.7	.405	3.9	.360	2.4	.774	0.47	1.71	2.5	4.0	14.4	December	44	36.6	13.8	.450	4.3	.408	3.0	.750	0.41	1.77	2.7	4.3	16.4
vs. Non-Playoff	122	34.7	13.6	.445	4.3	.409	3.0	.802	0.40	1.63	2.6	4.2	16.3	January	45	37.4	14.2	.419	4.8	.386	2.8	.786	0.36	1.80	2.6	4.4	16.0
vs. East	183	35.5	13.9	.415	4.0	.357	2.7	.800	0.49	1.68	2.7	4.2	15.1	February	48	36.3	14.1	.419	3.8	.364	3.0	.726	0.52	1.77	3.0	4.2	15.4
vs. West	84	33.2	13.3	.443	4.2	.438	2.6	.760	0.33	1.65	2.2	3.9	15.6	March	62	32.7	13.0	.432	3.7	.411	2.2	.803	0.50	1.40	2.6	4.1	14.6
vs. Div.	85	36.1	14.0	.415	4.1	.364	2.7	.793	0.53	1.71	2.6	4.4	15.2	Apr/May	44	32.6	14.3	.412	4.2	.359	2.6	.879	0.48	1.82	1.9	4.0	15.6
As Starter	234	35.8	13.9	.424	4.1	.382	2.8	.788	0.42	1.70	2.6	4.3	15.7	0 Days Rest	71	36.1	14.0	.419	4.2	.359	2.3	.813	0.32	1.63	2.5	4.1	15.1
Off Bench	33	27.4	11.9	.416	3.7	.390	1.8	.787	0.58	1.48	1.9	3.0	12.8	1 Days Rest	138	34.5	13.5	.431	4.0	.390	2.8	.805	0.47	1.63	2.4	4.3	15.5
In wins	109	34.1	13.5	.441	4.1	.399	3.0	.790	0.44	1.72	2.6	4.6	15.9	2 Days Rest	33	34.9	14.7	.437	4.5	.416	3.0	.717	0.67	1.88	3.0	3.9	16.9
In losses	158	35.3	13.8	.411	4.0	.372	2.5	.787	0.44	1.64	2.6	3.8	14.8	3+ Days Rest	25	32.6	12.4	.369	3.4	.365	2.5	.730	0.28	1.76	2.9	3.5	12.2

Brevin Knight

1999-2000 Per Game Averages

	G	Min	FGA	FG%	3PA	3P%	FTA	FT%	Blk	Stl	Ast	Reb	Pts		G	Min	FGA	FG%	3PA	3P%	FTA	FT%	Blk	Stl	Ast	Reb	Pts
Total	65	27.0	8.6	.412	0.2	.200	2.8	.761	0.32	1.65	7.0	3.0	9.3	Pre All-Star	45	28.9	9.7	.416	0.2	.143	3.1	.763	0.27	1.84	7.3	3.3	10.4
Home	33	27.4	8.3	.398	0.1	.250	3.0	.765	0.52	2.00	7.9	3.2	8.9	Post All-Star	20	22.8	6.2	.398	0.2	.333	2.3	.756	0.45	1.20	6.6	2.2	6.7
Road	32	26.6	8.9	.426	0.2	.167	2.7	.756	0.13	1.28	6.2	2.8	9.6	November	13	29.8	10.2	.462	0.2	.500	3.4	.795	0.31	1.54	7.5	3.8	12.2
vs. Playoff	38	26.5	8.2	.433	0.2	.333	2.6	.765	0.32	1.26	6.5	3.1	9.1	December	15	28.5	9.0	.444	0.1	.000	3.7	.745	0.20	2.00	7.8	2.9	10.7
vs. Non-Playoff	27	27.7	9.1	.386	0.1	.000	3.2	.756	0.33	2.19	7.8	2.8	9.4	January	15	29.5	10.5	.361	0.3	.000	2.5	.789	0.27	1.93	6.9	3.5	9.6
vs. East	45	26.5	8.4	.417	0.2	.250	3.0	.769	0.31	1.69	6.9	2.9	9.4	February	3	22.7	5.3	.250	0.0	—	1.3	.250	0.67	1.67	5.0	2.0	3.0
vs. West	20	28.1	9.0	.402	0.1	.000	2.5	.740	0.35	1.55	7.4	3.2	9.1	March	10	22.9	7.2	.389	0.1	.000	2.8	.714	0.40	1.20	6.0	1.9	7.6
vs. Div.	23	23.7	7.4	.439	0.0	.000	3.0	.783	0.26	1.43	6.0	2.8	8.9	April	9	22.1	5.0	.444	0.2	.500	1.7	.867	0.44	1.22	7.1	2.4	6.0
As Starter	46	28.8	9.6	.413	0.2	.143	3.1	.759	0.28	1.83	7.3	3.3	10.3	0 Days Rest	18	25.9	7.9	.483	0.0	—	2.7	.792	0.17	1.06	7.1	2.8	9.8
Off Bench	19	22.5	6.2	.410	0.2	.333	2.3	.767	0.42	1.21	6.5	2.2	6.8	1 Days Rest	25	27.6	9.4	.369	0.2	.000	3.2	.750	0.36	1.96	6.6	3.2	9.4
In wins	27	28.3	8.9	.435	0.2	.200	3.5	.830	0.44	2.07	8.1	3.3	10.6	2 Days Rest	14	26.6	7.8	.413	0.2	.333	2.4	.727	0.50	2.29	8.2	2.7	8.2
In losses	38	26.0	8.4	.395	0.1	.200	2.4	.689	0.24	1.34	6.3	2.8	8.3	3+ Days Rest	8	28.3	8.8	.414	0.3	.500	2.9	.783	0.25	0.88	6.4	3.0	9.6

Career (1997-98 thru 1999-2000)

	G	Min	FGA	FG%	3PA	3P%	FTA	FT%	Blk	Stl	Ast	Reb	Pts		G	Min	FGA	FG%	3PA	3P%	FTA	FT%	Blk	Stl	Ast	Reb	Pts
Total	184	29.5	8.0	.427	0.1	.091	3.1	.774	0.25	2.03	7.7	3.1	9.2	Pre All-Star	90	30.2	8.5	.424	0.1	.100	3.0	.771	0.29	2.27	7.8	3.1	9.5
Home	92	30.0	7.8	.436	0.1	.091	3.3	.772	0.41	2.07	8.7	3.3	9.3	Post All-Star	55	27.7	7.0	.434	0.1	.143	3.0	.805	0.24	1.80	7.4	3.0	8.5
Road	92	29.0	8.1	.418	0.1	.091	3.0	.777	0.09	1.99	6.7	3.0	9.1	Oct/Nov	26	30.5	8.8	.443	0.1	.333	3.5	.767	0.27	2.27	7.9	3.5	10.5
vs. Playoff	104	28.5	7.7	.439	0.1	.182	2.9	.761	0.26	1.72	7.0	3.1	9.0	December	28	29.9	8.4	.445	0.0	.000	3.4	.768	0.25	2.43	7.9	2.9	10.1
vs. Non-Playoff	80	30.7	8.3	.411	0.1	.000	3.4	.790	0.24	2.43	8.6	3.2	9.5	January	31	30.8	8.5	.397	0.2	.000	2.4	.787	0.29	2.23	7.8	3.3	8.6
vs. East	130	29.2	7.9	.420	0.1	.105	3.1	.773	0.25	1.93	7.6	3.0	9.1	February	27	28.3	6.9	.368	0.1	.000	3.7	.768	0.33	1.81	6.9	2.6	7.9
vs. West	54	30.1	8.0	.442	0.1	.000	3.1	.776	0.26	2.26	8.0	3.4	9.6	March	38	28.5	8.1	.460	0.1	.000	2.9	.734	0.21	1.92	7.4	3.3	9.6
vs. Div.	65	28.7	8.2	.431	0.1	.000	3.1	.770	0.23	1.91	7.6	3.1	9.4	Apr/May	34	29.1	7.1	.428	0.2	.167	3.2	.824	0.18	1.62	8.2	3.3	8.8
As Starter	160	30.5	8.2	.427	0.1	.056	3.2	.775	0.22	2.10	7.9	3.2	9.5	0 Days Rest	49	29.6	7.7	.454	0.1	.000	2.9	.771	0.20	1.49	7.8	3.1	9.2
Off Bench	24	22.9	6.2	.423	0.2	.250	2.5	.767	0.46	1.54	6.3	2.5	7.2	1 Days Rest	83	30.0	8.5	.403	0.1	.000	3.6	.787	0.24	2.23	7.9	3.3	9.7
In wins	92	30.7	8.0	.458	0.1	.077	3.6	.794	0.28	2.43	8.8	3.5	10.3	2 Days Rest	34	28.9	7.1	.446	0.2	.250	2.2	.776	0.32	2.35	8.1	3.0	8.1
In losses	92	28.3	7.9	.395	0.1	.111	2.6	.747	0.22	1.62	6.6	2.8	8.2	3+ Days Rest	18	27.7	8.0	.438	0.1	.500	3.3	.712	0.28	1.94	5.9	2.7	9.4

Toni Kukoc
Philadelphia 76ers — Forward

1999-2000 Per Game Averages

	G	Min	FGA	FG%	3PA	3P%	FTA	FT%	Blk	Stl	Ast	Reb	Pts		G	Min	FGA	FG%	3PA	3P%	FTA	FT%	Blk	Stl	Ast	Reb	Pts
Total	56	31.9	13.0	.408	3.0	.262	4.7	.725	0.50	1.38	4.7	4.9	14.8	Pre All-Star	23	36.2	16.3	.385	3.3	.234	6.5	.752	0.83	1.91	5.3	5.5	18.2
Home	28	31.4	13.0	.412	3.0	.282	4.6	.711	0.68	1.54	4.6	4.9	14.8	Post All-Star	33	28.8	10.7	.432	2.8	.286	3.5	.690	0.27	1.00	4.3	4.4	12.5
Road	28	32.4	13.0	.404	3.0	.241	4.9	.737	0.32	1.21	4.8	4.9	14.8	November	4	30.5	14.0	.357	3.3	.231	6.5	.846	1.00	1.75	3.8	4.0	16.3
vs. Playoff	31	31.6	12.6	.383	2.8	.279	4.0	.718	0.39	1.58	4.0	4.3	13.3	December	0	—											
vs. Non-Playoff	25	32.2	13.4	.438	3.3	.244	5.6	.730	0.64	1.12	5.6	5.6	16.7	January	13	38.5	17.2	.362	3.5	.217	7.5	.714	0.92	2.31	6.5	6.2	18.6
vs. East	37	30.9	12.8	.381	3.2	.248	4.9	.710	0.51	1.38	5.3	4.8	14.5	February	13	30.6	12.2	.453	2.2	.310	3.5	.778	0.46	0.85	3.4	4.8	14.5
vs. West	19	33.6	13.5	.457	2.7	.294	4.3	.756	0.47	1.37	3.7	4.9	16.4	March	16	30.9	11.2	.419	3.4	.255	3.8	.639	0.31	1.19	4.3	4.6	12.7
vs. Div.	18	30.4	12.7	.376	3.6	.215	5.0	.644	0.50	1.28	4.9	5.1	13.6	April	10	27.0	11.0	.445	2.5	.320	3.5	.743	0.10	1.00	5.4	4.0	13.2
As Starter	31	36.4	15.4	.403	3.4	.250	6.2	.712	0.65	1.58	5.2	5.7	17.6	0 Days Rest	14	31.6	14.2	.437	3.1	.233	5.5	.701	0.43	1.29	4.8	5.1	17.0
Off Bench	25	26.2	10.0	.418	2.6	.281	3.0	.757	0.32	1.12	4.2	3.8	11.4	1 Days Rest	28	29.9	11.5	.427	3.1	.287	4.4	.699	0.36	1.25	4.6	4.2	13.8
In wins	30	31.8	12.6	.451	2.9	.318	5.3	.698	0.60	1.47	5.4	5.4	16.0	2 Days Rest	10	35.5	14.2	.387	2.4	.250	4.1	.732	0.80	1.90	5.4	6.2	14.6
In losses	26	32.0	13.5	.362	3.1	.200	4.1	.764	0.38	1.27	4.0	4.3	13.5	3+ Days Rest	4	37.0	16.5	.273	3.5	.214	6.0	.917	1.00	1.25	4.0	5.5	15.3

Last Five Seasons

	G	Min	FGA	FG%	3PA	3P%	FTA	FT%	Blk	Stl	Ast	Reb	Pts		G	Min	FGA	FG%	3PA	3P%	FTA	FT%	Blk	Stl	Ast	Reb	Pts
Total	312	30.1	11.9	.449	2.7	.335	3.7	.742	0.43	1.04	4.3	4.8	14.3	Pre All-Star	160	28.3	11.0	.443	2.4	.317	3.7	.739	0.44	1.11	4.2	4.3	13.2
Home	158	29.6	12.2	.474	2.8	.360	3.7	.749	0.37	1.15	4.4	4.9	15.3	Post All-Star	108	29.6	11.1	.476	3.1	.375	3.1	.749	0.47	0.93	4.2	4.5	14.1
Road	154	30.6	11.6	.422	2.6	.306	3.6	.735	0.49	0.94	4.3	4.7	13.2	Oct/Nov	50	26.8	10.5	.442	1.9	.323	3.7	.738	0.50	1.00	3.6	4.3	12.7
vs. Playoff	170	29.9	11.7	.439	2.8	.366	3.3	.746	0.38	1.08	4.0	4.4	13.8	December	40	28.3	10.7	.481	2.7	.383	3.4	.708	0.43	1.13	4.3	3.8	13.7
vs. Non-Playoff	142	30.3	12.1	.460	2.6	.295	4.1	.738	0.49	1.01	4.8	5.2	14.9	January	56	29.2	11.4	.426	2.5	.279	3.9	.753	0.38	1.25	4.5	4.9	13.3
vs. East	211	30.4	12.0	.448	2.8	.332	3.7	.738	0.43	1.09	4.4	4.7	14.4	February	62	30.4	12.4	.440	2.6	.315	3.3	.761	0.47	0.95	4.1	4.9	14.3
vs. West	101	29.5	11.7	.451	2.5	.340	3.5	.752	0.43	0.96	4.3	4.9	14.1	March	59	33.2	12.9	.450	3.3	.327	4.1	.736	0.53	1.10	4.7	5.5	15.7
vs. Div.	107	29.8	11.6	.443	2.8	.334	3.2	.699	0.42	1.07	4.2	4.5	13.4	Apr/May	45	32.0	13.1	.467	3.2	.393	3.4	.745	0.22	0.82	4.8	5.0	16.0
As Starter	162	35.6	14.3	.443	3.2	.334	4.2	.727	0.51	1.20	5.2	5.6	14.4	0 Days Rest	80	29.6	11.6	.454	2.6	.321	4.1	.727	0.39	0.89	4.4	5.1	14.4
Off Bench	150	24.1	9.3	.458	2.2	.335	3.0	.765	0.33	0.88	3.4	3.9	11.6	1 Days Rest	148	30.3	11.8	.449	2.9	.334	3.4	.731	0.45	1.01	4.4	4.5	14.0
In wins	221	29.1	11.1	.476	2.6	.373	3.6	.750	0.47	1.05	4.5	4.6	14.3	2 Days Rest	53	29.7	11.8	.423	2.4	.341	3.6	.771	0.32	1.30	4.2	5.1	13.6
In losses	91	32.4	13.7	.396	3.0	.256	3.7	.722	0.32	1.04	4.0	5.2	14.3	3+ Days Rest	31	30.9	13.1	.477	2.7	.361	3.9	.783	0.61	1.19	4.1	5.0	16.5

Christian Laettner
Detroit Pistons — Forward

1999-2000 Per Game Averages

	G	Min	FGA	FG%	3PA	3P%	FTA	FT%	Blk	Stl	Ast	Reb	Pts		G	Min	FGA	FG%	3PA	3P%	FTA	FT%	Blk	Stl	Ast	Reb	Pts
Total	82	29.8	9.8	.473	0.3	.292	3.6	.812	0.55	1.01	2.3	6.7	12.2	Pre All-Star	48	31.1	11.2	.460	0.4	.278	4.3	.795	0.60	0.96	2.3	6.9	13.8
Home	41	29.4	9.4	.463	0.2	.222	3.7	.796	0.59	0.93	2.2	7.2	11.7	Post All-Star	34	27.9	7.8	.500	0.2	.333	2.6	.851	0.47	1.09	2.3	6.5	10.0
Road	41	30.2	10.1	.483	0.4	.333	3.4	.829	0.51	1.10	2.3	6.3	12.7	November	15	29.0	11.1	.455	0.3	.500	4.0	.783	0.53	0.73	2.5	5.8	13.4
vs. Playoff	44	29.3	9.1	.464	0.2	.375	3.2	.837	0.52	0.93	2.3	6.8	11.2	December	14	31.8	10.7	.480	0.5	.286	4.4	.836	0.79	0.86	2.3	6.7	14.1
vs. Non-Playoff	38	30.3	10.6	.483	0.4	.250	4.0	.788	0.58	1.11	2.6	6.7	13.4	January	15	32.2	11.7	.466	0.4	.000	4.4	.773	0.53	1.20	1.9	7.9	14.3
vs. East	54	30.5	10.3	.470	0.3	.250	3.8	.797	0.54	0.98	2.1	7.2	12.8	February	12	30.3	8.6	.456	0.2	.500	3.8	.826	0.42	1.17	1.3	7.5	11.1
vs. West	28	28.5	8.8	.480	0.3	.375	3.4	.847	0.57	1.07	2.6	5.9	11.1	March	15	29.4	8.6	.527	0.3	.500	2.7	.875	0.40	1.13	3.1	7.1	11.5
vs. Div.	28	30.3	10.5	.471	0.3	.286	4.1	.817	0.43	0.93	2.1	7.0	13.4	April	11	25.1	6.9	.447	0.1	.000	1.7	.789	0.64	1.00	2.4	5.1	7.5
As Starter	82	29.8	9.8	.473	0.3	.292	3.6	.812	0.55	1.01	2.3	6.7	12.2	0 Days Rest	20	28.9	10.1	.537	0.3	.400	3.7	.822	0.75	0.90	2.7	5.1	13.9
Off Bench	0	—												1 Days Rest	45	29.5	9.5	.452	0.3	.200	3.3	.813	0.49	1.13	2.2	7.1	11.4
In wins	42	29.9	9.2	.456	0.2	.100	3.6	.808	0.50	1.14	2.5	7.4	11.3	2 Days Rest	8	31.3	11.0	.466	0.4	.667	3.0	.750	0.38	0.75	2.3	7.1	12.8
In losses	40	29.7	10.4	.489	0.4	.429	3.5	.816	0.60	0.88	2.0	6.1	13.2	3+ Days Rest	9	31.9	9.4	.435	0.1	.000	5.0	.822	0.56	0.89	1.9	8.3	12.3

Last Five Seasons

	G	Min	FGA	FG%	3PA	3P%	FTA	FT%	Blk	Stl	Ast	Reb	Pts		G	Min	FGA	FG%	3PA	3P%	FTA	FT%	Blk	Stl	Ast	Reb	Pts
Total	328	32.6	11.2	.480	0.6	.298	4.7	.825	0.81	1.04	2.5	7.2	14.8	Pre All-Star	181	35.0	12.6	.471	0.7	.323	5.2	.831	0.87	1.03	2.7	7.6	16.4
Home	158	32.3	11.0	.488	0.4	.214	4.6	.825	0.89	1.04	2.4	7.3	14.6	Post All-Star	131	30.7	9.9	.504	0.4	.235	4.1	.820	0.73	1.08	2.4	7.1	13.4
Road	170	32.9	11.4	.472	0.7	.351	4.8	.825	0.73	1.05	2.6	7.0	15.0	Oct/Nov	53	34.1	12.4	.476	0.8	.429	4.8	.821	0.92	0.85	2.7	7.2	16.1
vs. Playoff	172	32.9	11.0	.462	0.6	.295	4.5	.841	0.79	1.09	2.2	7.0	14.1	December	53	35.0	12.2	.494	0.6	.294	5.8	.843	0.74	1.02	2.7	7.7	17.1
vs. Non-Playoff	156	32.3	11.4	.498	0.6	.302	4.9	.809	0.83	0.99	2.9	7.3	15.5	January	61	35.9	12.7	.457	0.7	.267	5.4	.834	0.95	1.20	2.6	8.0	16.3
vs. East	208	32.6	11.1	.483	0.6	.292	4.8	.821	0.80	1.11	2.5	7.3	14.8	February	45	32.1	11.3	.478	0.3	.200	4.0	.800	0.73	0.96	2.1	6.9	14.0
vs. West	120	32.6	11.4	.474	0.5	.311	4.6	.834	0.82	0.93	2.5	7.0	14.8	March	69	30.3	9.9	.497	0.4	.161	4.4	.805	0.65	1.04	2.5	6.8	13.4
vs. Div.	112	32.2	11.2	.488	0.5	.271	4.9	.826	0.80	0.99	2.4	7.0	15.2	Apr/May	47	27.8	8.7	.479	0.3	.429	3.4	.846	0.87	1.17	2.3	6.3	11.3
As Starter	284	34.2	11.8	.482	0.6	.299	4.8	.828	0.82	1.09	2.6	7.6	15.5	0 Days Rest	83	32.6	11.0	.470	0.6	.333	4.9	.845	0.87	1.12	2.7	6.9	14.7
Off Bench	44	22.2	7.5	.458	0.3	.286	4.1	.802	0.75	0.73	1.6	4.7	10.3	1 Days Rest	170	32.3	11.1	.482	0.5	.232	4.5	.812	0.74	1.09	2.4	7.1	14.4
In wins	190	32.2	10.7	.493	0.4	.309	4.5	.808	0.82	1.07	2.7	7.4	14.3	2 Days Rest	38	35.0	12.8	.466	0.8	.345	4.6	.841	0.84	0.74	2.6	8.3	16.1
In losses	138	33.2	11.9	.463	0.7	.290	5.0	.847	0.79	1.01	2.3	6.8	15.4	3+ Days Rest	37	31.5	10.5	.505	0.5	.421	5.2	.824	0.97	0.95	2.6	7.1	15.1

Raef LaFrentz
Denver Nuggets — Forward-Center

1999-2000 Per Game Averages

	G	Min	FGA	FG%	3PA	3P%	FTA	FT%	Blk	Stl	Ast	Reb	Pts		G	Min	FGA	FG%	3PA	3P%	FTA	FT%	Blk	Stl	Ast	Reb	Pts
Total	81	30.1	10.9	.446	2.3	.328	2.9	.686	2.22	0.52	1.2	7.9	12.4	Pre All-Star	47	31.6	11.8	.448	2.7	.357	2.7	.659	2.23	0.47	1.2	7.8	13.3
Home	40	31.2	11.9	.454	2.6	.343	3.1	.696	3.15	0.45	1.2	8.7	13.8	Post All-Star	34	27.9	9.6	.442	1.7	.263	3.1	.720	2.21	0.59	1.2	8.1	11.2
Road	41	29.0	9.9	.437	2.0	.309	2.7	.676	1.32	0.59	1.2	7.2	11.1	November	13	33.0	11.5	.477	2.7	.457	3.2	.659	2.31	0.46	1.5	8.5	14.2
vs. Playoff	47	30.4	10.6	.422	2.5	.364	2.8	.634	2.13	0.57	1.2	7.8	11.6	December	14	33.4	12.6	.480	2.8	.385	3.1	.674	1.86	0.43	1.1	8.1	15.3
vs. Non-Playoff	34	29.6	11.2	.478	1.9	.262	3.1	.752	2.35	0.44	1.2	8.1	13.5	January	14	30.4	11.9	.404	2.9	.220	2.1	.690	3.14	0.50	1.4	7.2	11.6
vs. East	30	31.3	11.2	.458	2.2	.303	3.4	.670	2.33	0.47	1.4	8.7	13.2	February	13	25.8	9.3	.405	1.8	.348	2.3	.633	1.00	0.54	0.6	7.3	9.6
vs. West	51	29.3	10.6	.438	2.3	.342	2.6	.699	2.16	0.55	1.1	7.5	11.9	March	17	28.3	9.9	.414	1.9	.242	3.3	.679	2.12	0.41	1.3	8.6	10.9
vs. Div.	23	28.4	10.4	.444	2.1	.313	3.0	.721	1.91	0.65	1.0	8.0	12.0	April	10	29.7	9.7	.515	1.2	.333	3.7	.784	3.10	0.90	1.4	7.4	13.3
As Starter	80	30.1	10.8	.446	2.3	.326	2.9	.690	2.19	0.53	1.2	7.9	12.4	0 Days Rest	21	30.9	9.5	.420	2.1	.356	3.8	.663	1.81	0.43	1.1	7.1	11.3
Off Bench	1	24.0	13.0	.462	2.0	.500	4.0	.500	5.00	0.00	1.0	6.0	15.0	1 Days Rest	38	29.1	11.4	.450	2.3	.303	2.4	.648	2.18	0.45	1.2	8.0	12.5
In wins	34	32.8	11.6	.466	2.3	.338	3.7	.722	3.09	0.59	1.3	8.9	14.6	2 Days Rest	13	31.7	11.6	.503	2.4	.516	3.8	.816	2.77	0.77	1.5	9.0	16.0
In losses	47	28.1	10.3	.430	2.3	.321	2.3	.645	1.60	0.47	1.1	7.2	11.1	3+ Days Rest	9	30.0	10.6	.389	2.0	.056	1.8	.625	2.56	0.67	1.0	8.0	9.4

Career (1998-99 thru 1999-2000)

	G	Min	FGA	FG%	3PA	3P%	FTA	FT%	Blk	Stl	Ast	Reb	Pts		G	Min	FGA	FG%	3PA	3P%	FTA	FT%	Blk	Stl	Ast	Reb	Pts
Total	93	30.3	10.8	.447	2.3	.336	3.1	.697	2.12	0.55	1.1	7.9	12.6	Pre All-Star	47	31.6	11.8	.448	2.7	.357	2.7	.659	2.23	0.47	1.2	7.8	13.3
Home	46	31.6	11.8	.455	2.6	.347	3.3	.728	2.93	0.50	1.1	8.5	14.0	Post All-Star	34	27.9	9.6	.442	1.7	.263	3.1	.720	2.21	0.59	1.2	8.1	11.2
Road	47	29.1	9.9	.439	2.0	.323	2.8	.662	1.32	0.60	1.1	7.2	11.3	Oct/Nov	13	33.0	11.5	.477	2.7	.457	3.2	.659	2.31	0.46	1.5	8.5	14.2
vs. Playoff	56	30.9	10.8	.426	2.5	.366	3.0	.653	1.98	0.63	1.1	7.9	12.4	December	14	33.4	12.6	.480	2.8	.385	3.1	.674	1.86	0.43	1.1	8.1	15.3
vs. Non-Playoff	37	29.5	10.9	.479	1.9	.278	3.2	.761	2.32	0.43	1.1	7.9	13.4	January	14	30.4	11.9	.404	2.9	.220	2.1	.690	3.14	0.50	1.4	7.2	11.6
vs. East	30	31.3	11.2	.458	2.2	.303	3.4	.670	2.33	0.47	1.4	8.7	13.2	February	25	28.9	10.0	.432	2.2	.370	3.1	.705	1.20	0.64	0.6	7.4	11.6
vs. West	63	29.9	10.7	.442	2.3	.351	2.9	.713	2.02	0.59	1.0	7.5	12.3	March	17	28.3	9.9	.414	1.9	.242	3.3	.679	2.12	0.41	1.3	8.6	10.9
vs. Div.	29	28.7	10.1	.439	2.1	.311	3.2	.731	1.79	0.54	1.0	7.8	11.9	Apr/May	10	29.7	9.7	.515	1.2	.333	3.7	.784	3.10	0.90	1.4	7.4	13.3
As Starter	92	30.4	10.8	.447	2.3	.335	3.0	.700	2.09	0.55	1.1	7.9	12.6	0 Days Rest	25	30.4	9.4	.427	2.2	.382	3.5	.648	1.72	0.44	1.1	6.8	11.1
Off Bench	1	24.0	13.0	.462	2.0	.500	4.0	.500	5.00	0.00	1.0	6.0	15.0	1 Days Rest	44	29.9	11.6	.445	2.4	.302	2.8	.678	2.14	0.48	1.1	8.2	13.0
In wins	37	33.4	11.5	.468	2.3	.333	4.0	.745	3.03	0.59	1.2	8.9	14.6	2 Days Rest	13	31.7	11.6	.503	2.4	.516	3.8	.816	2.77	0.77	1.5	9.0	16.0
In losses	56	28.3	10.4	.432	2.3	.338	2.4	.644	1.52	0.52	1.1	7.2	11.3	3+ Days Rest	11	30.4	10.1	.423	2.0	.136	2.4	.731	2.18	0.82	0.9	7.8	10.5

Voshon Lenard
Miami Heat — Guard

1999-2000 Per Game Averages

	G	Min	FGA	FG%	3PA	3P%	FTA	FT%	Blk	Stl	Ast	Reb	Pts		G	Min	FGA	FG%	3PA	3P%	FTA	FT%	Blk	Stl	Ast	Reb	Pts
Total	53	27.1	10.6	.407	4.3	.390	2.0	.792	0.28	0.77	2.6	2.9	11.9	Pre All-Star	45	27.2	10.8	.413	4.3	.400	2.0	.793	0.31	0.73	2.6	2.8	12.3
Home	24	26.5	11.0	.399	4.7	.366	1.8	.786	0.33	0.75	2.5	2.5	11.8	Post All-Star	8	26.3	9.1	.370	4.1	.333	1.8	.786	0.13	1.00	2.6	3.3	9.5
Road	29	27.5	10.2	.414	4.0	.414	2.2	.797	0.24	0.79	2.6	3.2	11.9	November	14	22.2	9.1	.383	3.6	.373	2.1	.800	0.43	0.50	2.1	3.0	10.1
vs. Playoff	24	27.8	10.8	.368	3.9	.323	2.1	.840	0.33	0.79	2.2	3.3	10.9	December	14	28.5	11.4	.409	4.5	.397	1.9	.731	0.14	0.86	2.5	2.2	12.4
vs. Non-Playoff	29	26.5	10.4	.440	4.7	.437	1.9	.750	0.24	0.76	2.9	2.5	12.7	January	13	29.0	12.0	.462	5.2	.448	2.2	.828	0.23	0.77	3.0	2.8	15.2
vs. East	34	27.6	10.2	.412	4.2	.373	2.1	.789	0.26	0.76	2.7	3.1	11.6	February	12	28.9	9.8	.359	3.9	.319	1.8	.810	0.33	1.00	2.8	3.7	9.7
vs. West	19	26.1	11.2	.399	4.5	.419	1.8	.800	0.32	0.79	2.3	2.6	12.3	March	0	—											
vs. Div.	16	28.1	10.1	.441	3.8	.410	2.6	.805	0.31	0.69	2.9	2.8	12.5	April	0	—											
As Starter	13	33.6	11.5	.387	4.3	.385	1.5	.750	0.38	1.38	3.5	4.2	11.5	0 Days Rest	12	25.1	8.4	.396	3.7	.409	2.4	.724	0.25	0.92	2.3	2.7	9.9
Off Bench	40	24.9	10.3	.415	4.3	.412	2.2	.802	0.25	0.58	2.3	2.5	12.0	1 Days Rest	26	28.5	11.2	.390	4.9	.433	1.8	.854	0.31	0.69	2.5	3.3	12.5
In wins	34	26.1	10.4	.398	4.2	.378	2.3	.831	0.35	0.71	2.6	2.5	11.8	2 Days Rest	9	24.0	9.9	.416	3.0	.259	1.2	.818	0.22	0.56	2.6	1.7	10.0
In losses	19	28.7	10.8	.422	4.5	.412	1.5	.690	0.16	0.89	2.5	3.5	12.1	3+ Days Rest	6	29.5	13.0	.474	5.0	.300	3.0	.722	0.33	1.17	3.3	3.3	16.0

Career (1995-96 thru 1999-2000)

	G	Min	FGA	FG%	3PA	3P%	FTA	FT%	Blk	Stl	Ast	Reb	Pts		G	Min	FGA	FG%	3PA	3P%	FTA	FT%	Blk	Stl	Ast	Reb	Pts
Total	249	26.8	9.3	.427	4.8	.399	1.8	.795	0.20	0.63	2.1	2.9	11.3	Pre All-Star	142	26.4	9.2	.429	4.8	.399	1.7	.806	0.23	0.70	2.1	2.9	11.2
Home	122	27.0	9.6	.428	5.0	.415	1.6	.819	0.24	0.60	2.2	2.8	11.6	Post All-Star	95	28.9	9.8	.427	5.0	.405	2.0	.785	0.19	0.58	2.2	3.2	12.0
Road	127	26.6	9.1	.425	4.5	.383	1.9	.776	0.17	0.67	1.9	3.1	10.9	Oct/Nov	37	21.7	7.6	.381	3.4	.346	1.4	.824	0.22	0.49	1.6	2.6	8.1
vs. Playoff	127	27.5	9.4	.418	4.9	.380	1.7	.820	0.23	0.68	2.0	3.1	11.0	December	40	28.3	9.7	.439	5.0	.407	1.9	.816	0.23	0.93	2.1	2.7	12.1
vs. Non-Playoff	122	26.1	9.2	.436	4.6	.420	1.9	.773	0.18	0.59	2.1	2.7	11.5	January	49	27.9	10.1	.451	5.7	.425	1.7	.753	0.20	0.69	2.3	3.1	12.8
vs. East	165	27.2	9.2	.425	4.6	.389	1.7	.809	0.17	0.70	2.3	3.0	11.0	February	46	30.0	9.8	.428	4.9	.416	2.1	.800	0.28	0.65	2.5	3.8	12.1
vs. West	84	26.0	9.6	.430	5.0	.419	1.9	.769	0.27	0.51	1.7	2.8	11.8	March	39	26.9	9.3	.435	4.7	.393	2.0	.808	0.15	0.59	1.8	2.6	11.5
vs. Div.	71	28.6	9.5	.449	4.8	.399	2.0	.816	0.17	0.76	2.5	2.8	12.0	Apr/May	38	24.9	9.0	.404	4.4	.373	1.6	.780	0.13	0.42	2.0	2.5	10.1
As Starter	143	33.4	10.8	.435	5.4	.405	2.0	.794	0.24	0.80	2.5	3.6	13.2	0 Days Rest	53	27.3	9.1	.432	4.5	.418	1.8	.847	0.19	0.81	2.1	3.1	11.3
Off Bench	106	18.0	7.2	.410	3.9	.389	1.5	.798	0.16	0.42	1.5	2.1	8.7	1 Days Rest	118	29.2	10.4	.425	5.4	.422	1.9	.782	0.25	0.61	2.2	3.2	12.7
In wins	164	26.9	9.2	.443	4.6	.423	2.0	.807	0.23	0.63	2.2	2.9	11.8	2 Days Rest	42	27.6	8.6	.440	4.3	.346	1.7	.761	0.19	0.57	2.2	2.6	10.3
In losses	85	26.6	9.5	.396	5.0	.357	1.3	.759	0.15	0.65	1.8	3.0	10.3	3+ Days Rest	36	17.4	6.8	.407	3.7	.331	1.3	.804	0.11	0.53	1.4	2.3	7.8

Rashard Lewis

1999-2000 Per Game Averages

	G	Min	FGA	FG%	3PA	3P%	FTA	FT%	Blk	Stl	Ast	Reb	Pts
Total	82	19.2	6.9	.486	1.5	.333	1.5	.683	0.44	0.76	0.9	4.1	8.2
Home	41	19.5	6.7	.480	1.6	.369	1.8	.716	0.44	0.68	0.9	4.2	8.3
Road	41	18.9	7.1	.491	1.3	.291	1.2	.633	0.44	0.83	0.8	4.0	8.1
vs. Playoff	44	17.8	6.5	.470	1.6	.296	1.5	.631	0.41	0.57	1.0	3.7	7.5
vs. Non-Playoff	38	20.9	7.4	.502	1.3	.388	1.5	.741	0.47	0.97	0.7	4.6	9.1
vs. East	30	18.4	6.5	.469	1.5	.348	1.0	.621	0.27	0.77	0.7	3.4	7.3
vs. West	52	19.7	7.1	.495	1.4	.324	1.8	.702	0.54	0.75	0.9	4.5	8.8
vs. Div.	24	20.1	7.6	.519	1.7	.366	2.0	.646	0.75	0.75	1.0	4.6	9.8
As Starter	8	28.3	10.8	.465	2.8	.318	1.8	.929	0.50	1.63	2.0	5.9	12.5
Off Bench	74	18.2	6.5	.490	1.3	.337	1.5	.651	0.43	0.66	0.7	3.9	7.8
In wins	45	18.9	6.3	.502	1.2	.370	1.7	.697	0.44	0.91	0.7	4.2	7.9
In losses	37	19.5	7.6	.470	1.8	.303	1.3	.660	0.43	0.57	1.0	3.9	8.6

	G	Min	FGA	FG%	3PA	3P%	FTA	FT%	Blk	Stl	Ast	Reb	Pts
Pre All-Star	51	15.3	5.0	.496	0.8	.302	1.3	.672	0.47	0.55	0.5	3.4	6.1
Post All-Star	31	25.6	10.0	.477	2.5	.351	1.9	.695	0.39	1.10	1.4	5.3	11.7
November	15	11.8	3.5	.453	0.3	.200	0.9	.571	0.27	0.33	0.6	3.1	3.8
December	15	17.3	5.3	.513	0.9	.385	1.7	.731	0.40	0.40	0.8	3.7	7.1
January	15	16.5	5.3	.468	1.2	.278	0.8	.667	0.60	0.80	0.2	2.9	5.8
February	13	19.0	8.0	.481	1.5	.400	1.8	.696	0.46	0.92	0.8	4.5	9.5
March	14	25.4	9.0	.524	2.4	.324	2.1	.633	0.43	0.93	1.4	5.1	11.6
April	10	28.9	12.4	.460	3.0	.333	1.8	.778	0.50	1.40	1.6	6.0	13.8
0 Days Rest	21	18.0	7.0	.544	1.0	.318	1.0	.750	0.52	0.90	0.8	3.9	8.7
1 Days Rest	40	19.5	6.9	.478	1.6	.308	1.6	.641	0.35	0.68	0.9	4.3	8.1
2 Days Rest	17	20.5	7.0	.454	1.8	.400	1.9	.750	0.59	0.82	1.0	3.9	8.5
3+ Days Rest	4	17.0	6.5	.385	0.8	.333	1.8	.571	0.25	0.50	0.3	4.3	6.3

Career (1998-99 thru 1999-2000)

	G	Min	FGA	FG%	3PA	3P%	FTA	FT%	Blk	Stl	Ast	Reb	Pts
Total	102	16.9	6.1	.476	1.2	.325	1.3	.672	0.36	0.69	0.7	3.5	7.1
Home	51	17.4	6.1	.469	1.4	.362	1.5	.714	0.37	0.67	0.7	3.8	7.3
Road	51	16.4	6.1	.482	1.1	.281	1.2	.617	0.35	0.71	0.7	3.3	6.9
vs. Playoff	56	15.6	5.6	.452	1.3	.280	1.3	.630	0.32	0.54	0.8	3.2	6.2
vs. Non-Playoff	46	18.4	6.7	.500	1.1	.392	1.4	.719	0.41	0.87	0.6	4.0	8.1
vs. East	33	17.5	6.3	.452	1.5	.354	1.0	.636	0.27	0.76	0.6	3.2	6.8
vs. West	69	16.6	5.9	.488	1.1	.308	1.5	.683	0.41	0.65	0.8	3.7	7.2
vs. Div.	30	17.9	6.9	.507	1.4	.349	1.7	.640	0.60	0.73	0.9	4.0	8.6
As Starter	15	21.1	7.7	.452	1.7	.280	1.0	.867	0.27	1.13	1.3	4.3	8.3
Off Bench	87	16.1	5.8	.481	1.2	.337	1.4	.648	0.38	0.61	0.6	3.4	6.9
In wins	56	16.7	5.6	.491	1.0	.357	1.5	.679	0.36	0.84	0.6	3.7	6.9
In losses	46	17.1	6.6	.460	1.5	.300	1.2	.660	0.37	0.50	0.8	3.3	7.3

	G	Min	FGA	FG%	3PA	3P%	FTA	FT%	Blk	Stl	Ast	Reb	Pts
Pre All-Star	51	15.3	5.0	.496	0.8	.302	1.3	.672	0.47	0.55	0.5	3.4	6.1
Post All-Star	31	25.6	10.0	.477	2.5	.351	1.9	.695	0.39	1.10	1.4	5.3	11.7
Oct/Nov	15	11.8	3.5	.453	0.3	.200	0.9	.571	0.27	0.33	0.6	3.1	3.8
December	15	17.3	5.3	.513	0.9	.385	1.7	.731	0.40	0.40	0.8	3.7	7.1
January	15	16.5	5.3	.468	1.2	.278	0.8	.667	0.60	0.80	0.2	2.9	5.8
February	22	14.9	6.0	.462	1.0	.348	1.1	.680	0.27	0.77	0.5	3.5	6.7
March	20	19.2	7.0	.496	1.8	.306	2.0	.641	0.30	0.70	1.1	3.8	8.7
Apr/May	15	21.7	9.0	.459	2.1	.355	1.4	.714	0.40	1.07	1.1	4.3	10.0
0 Days Rest	26	15.8	6.0	.532	0.9	.304	0.9	.708	0.42	0.85	0.7	3.3	7.3
1 Days Rest	44	18.0	6.3	.478	1.5	.308	1.5	.632	0.32	0.64	0.8	3.4	7.4
2 Days Rest	20	19.1	6.4	.441	1.7	.364	1.6	.750	0.50	0.75	0.9	3.7	7.4
3+ Days Rest	12	11.2	4.9	.390	0.4	.400	1.1	.615	0.17	0.42	0.3	2.5	4.7

Luc Longley

1999-2000 Per Game Averages

	G	Min	FGA	FG%	3PA	3P%	FTA	FT%	Blk	Stl	Ast	Reb	Pts
Total	72	19.7	5.5	.466	0.0	—	1.3	.825	0.58	0.31	1.1	4.5	6.3
Home	35	20.1	5.8	.534	0.0	—	1.4	.854	0.63	0.23	1.0	4.7	7.4
Road	37	19.3	5.3	.395	0.0	—	1.3	.796	0.54	0.38	1.2	4.3	5.2
vs. Playoff	39	19.8	5.4	.460	0.0	—	1.7	.794	0.56	0.31	0.9	4.8	6.4
vs. Non-Playoff	33	19.5	5.7	.473	0.0	—	0.9	.897	0.61	0.30	1.3	4.1	6.2
vs. East	25	16.4	4.4	.455	0.0	—	1.1	.821	0.56	0.32	0.9	3.6	4.9
vs. West	47	21.4	6.1	.471	0.0	—	1.5	.826	0.60	0.30	1.1	5.0	7.0
vs. Div.	22	21.4	6.2	.431	0.0	—	1.4	.633	0.64	0.32	1.3	5.5	6.2
As Starter	68	19.9	5.6	.461	0.0	—	1.4	.828	0.60	0.31	1.1	4.6	6.3
Off Bench	4	16.3	4.8	.579	0.0	—	1.0	.750	0.25	0.25	1.0	3.0	6.3
In wins	45	19.1	5.4	.461	0.0	—	1.1	.843	0.62	0.22	1.1	4.5	5.9
In losses	27	20.6	5.9	.475	0.0	—	1.7	.804	0.52	0.44	1.0	4.5	6.8

	G	Min	FGA	FG%	3PA	3P%	FTA	FT%	Blk	Stl	Ast	Reb	Pts
Pre All-Star	41	21.4	5.9	.463	0.0	—	1.5	.790	0.59	0.32	1.1	5.0	6.7
Post All-Star	31	17.4	5.1	.471	0.0	—	1.1	.886	0.58	0.29	1.0	3.9	5.8
November	14	19.1	5.2	.425	0.0	—	1.5	.857	0.36	0.36	1.3	4.3	5.7
December	8	17.6	4.6	.486	0.0	—	1.5	.833	0.25	0.25	0.6	3.6	5.8
January	14	23.8	6.0	.452	0.0	—	1.5	.667	0.86	0.36	1.1	5.4	6.4
February	11	21.5	7.2	.506	0.0	—	1.5	.938	0.73	0.45	1.2	5.4	8.6
March	15	16.9	5.4	.420	0.0	—	1.1	.941	0.60	0.00	0.6	4.1	5.6
April	10	18.5	4.5	.556	0.0	—	1.0	.700	0.60	0.50	1.6	3.8	5.7
0 Days Rest	15	20.5	5.6	.488	0.0	—	1.5	.818	0.60	0.33	1.1	4.8	6.7
1 Days Rest	36	19.1	5.4	.469	0.0	—	0.9	.875	0.64	0.31	0.8	4.5	5.9
2 Days Rest	14	20.6	5.8	.457	0.0	—	2.1	.724	0.71	0.29	0.9	4.5	6.8
3+ Days Rest	7	18.9	5.4	.421	0.0	—	2.0	.929	0.00	0.29	2.4	3.7	6.4

Last Five Seasons

	G	Min	FGA	FG%	3PA	3P%	FTA	FT%	Blk	Stl	Ast	Reb	Pts
Total	290	24.7	7.9	.467	0.0	.000	1.9	.778	0.95	0.43	1.9	5.3	8.8
Home	145	25.1	8.2	.491	0.0	.000	1.9	.776	1.13	0.43	2.0	5.5	9.5
Road	145	24.3	7.6	.440	0.0	—	1.8	.779	0.77	0.43	1.8	5.1	8.1
vs. Playoff	159	24.8	7.9	.461	0.0	.000	1.9	.793	0.94	0.45	1.8	5.7	8.8
vs. Non-Playoff	131	24.6	7.9	.473	0.0	.000	1.8	.757	1.08	0.40	1.9	5.2	8.8
vs. East	148	24.5	8.2	.467	0.0	.000	1.9	.763	0.98	0.40	2.1	5.1	9.1
vs. West	142	24.9	7.5	.466	0.0	—	1.9	.793	0.92	0.46	1.6	5.5	8.5
vs. Div.	100	26.1	8.6	.482	0.0	.000	2.1	.745	0.96	0.47	2.2	5.7	9.8
As Starter	286	24.8	7.9	.466	0.0	.000	1.9	.778	0.96	0.43	1.9	5.3	8.8
Off Bench	4	16.3	4.8	.579	0.0	—	1.0	.750	0.25	0.25	1.0	3.0	6.3
In wins	211	25.0	7.8	.477	0.0	.000	2.0	.782	1.05	0.39	2.0	5.4	9.0
In losses	79	23.9	8.0	.440	0.0	—	1.7	.765	0.68	0.53	1.4	5.0	8.3

	G	Min	FGA	FG%	3PA	3P%	FTA	FT%	Blk	Stl	Ast	Reb	Pts
Pre All-Star	154	25.8	7.9	.458	0.0	.000	2.0	.770	0.97	0.41	2.0	5.4	8.8
Post All-Star	97	23.3	8.1	.473	0.0	.000	1.6	.794	1.07	0.39	1.9	5.1	8.9
Oct/Nov	55	25.0	7.7	.456	0.0	.000	2.2	.769	1.05	0.45	1.9	5.7	8.7
December	34	24.6	8.1	.460	0.0	—	2.2	.838	1.09	0.32	1.9	4.5	9.3
January	54	27.2	7.7	.451	0.0	—	1.8	.674	0.83	0.46	2.3	5.4	8.1
February	53	24.6	8.4	.490	0.0	—	2.0	.760	0.87	0.43	1.5	5.2	9.8
March	56	23.9	8.5	.470	0.0	.000	1.5	.849	1.02	0.38	1.7	5.6	9.3
Apr/May	38	22.2	6.4	.469	0.0	—	1.7	.813	0.84	0.50	1.9	4.9	7.4
0 Days Rest	75	25.1	8.0	.467	0.0	.000	1.9	.786	0.89	0.41	1.9	5.9	9.0
1 Days Rest	131	24.2	7.6	.458	0.0	—	1.6	.809	0.97	0.41	1.7	5.1	8.3
2 Days Rest	55	26.1	8.4	.484	0.0	—	2.1	.690	1.22	0.45	2.1	5.3	9.6
3+ Days Rest	29	23.3	7.8	.467	0.0	—	2.3	.809	0.48	0.48	2.3	4.5	9.1

George Lynch

1999-2000 Per Game Averages

	G	Min	FGA	FG%	3PA	3P%	FTA	FT%	Blk	Stl	Ast	Reb	Pts		G	Min	FGA	FG%	3PA	3P%	FTA	FT%	Blk	Stl	Ast	Reb	Pts
Total	75	32.2	8.6	.461	0.5	.417	2.4	.617	0.51	1.59	1.8	7.8	9.6	Pre All-Star	49	32.7	8.7	.460	0.4	.368	2.3	.658	0.53	1.69	2.1	8.1	9.7
Home	39	31.6	8.0	.457	0.4	.214	2.5	.653	0.46	1.74	1.9	7.8	9.1	Post All-Star	26	31.3	8.4	.463	0.7	.471	2.7	.551	0.46	1.38	1.2	7.0	9.5
Road	36	32.8	9.2	.465	0.6	.545	2.4	.576	0.56	1.42	1.7	7.8	10.3	November	16	34.1	9.6	.442	0.2	.667	3.3	.673	0.69	1.94	1.8	8.5	10.8
vs. Playoff	37	31.1	8.2	.484	0.5	.474	2.2	.627	0.46	1.59	1.8	7.4	9.6	December	16	33.6	8.1	.485	0.3	.200	2.1	.529	0.56	1.81	2.6	9.0	9.1
vs. Non-Playoff	38	33.3	8.9	.441	0.4	.353	2.6	.610	0.55	1.58	1.8	8.1	9.7	January	12	29.7	8.0	.469	0.7	.375	1.5	.833	0.33	1.08	1.9	7.1	9.0
vs. East	51	31.7	8.5	.463	0.5	.462	2.6	.579	0.43	1.43	1.4	7.1	9.6	February	12	32.3	8.1	.464	0.5	.500	1.7	.650	0.58	1.92	2.3	7.1	8.8
vs. West	24	33.4	8.8	.458	0.4	.300	2.1	.720	0.67	1.92	2.6	9.1	9.7	March	11	31.7	8.0	.466	0.7	.250	2.8	.548	0.45	1.00	0.9	7.0	9.2
vs. Div.	23	34.2	9.0	.418	0.6	.385	3.1	.542	0.48	1.39	1.2	7.8	9.5	April	8	30.1	9.9	.443	0.8	.667	3.5	.536	0.25	1.50	0.6	6.9	11.1
As Starter	75	32.2	8.6	.461	0.5	.417	2.4	.617	0.51	1.59	1.8	7.8	9.6	0 Days Rest	19	31.5	9.1	.497	0.5	.556	3.1	.621	0.42	1.42	1.7	7.2	11.2
Off Bench	0	—												1 Days Rest	39	33.0	8.3	.443	0.5	.300	2.3	.600	0.62	1.41	1.7	7.7	8.9
In wins	45	31.5	8.1	.449	0.3	.267	2.4	.633	0.53	1.69	1.9	7.5	8.9	2 Days Rest	8	32.8	8.5	.426	0.4	.333	2.3	.444	0.38	2.25	2.9	9.1	8.4
In losses	30	33.3	9.4	.477	0.7	.524	2.5	.595	0.47	1.43	1.7	8.1	10.8	3+ Days Rest	9	29.8	8.9	.488	0.4	.750	1.9	.882	0.33	2.11	1.6	7.8	10.7

Last Five Seasons

	G	Min	FGA	FG%	3PA	3P%	FTA	FT%	Blk	Stl	Ast	Reb	Pts		G	Min	FGA	FG%	3PA	3P%	FTA	FT%	Blk	Stl	Ast	Reb	Pts
Total	317	23.0	6.5	.457	0.4	.338	1.9	.648	0.40	1.20	1.5	5.3	7.3	Pre All-Star	182	22.8	6.6	.466	0.4	.321	2.1	.656	0.40	1.18	1.6	5.5	7.6
Home	163	23.4	6.5	.452	0.4	.250	2.0	.684	0.46	1.25	1.5	5.7	7.3	Post All-Star	92	19.9	5.8	.457	0.3	.344	1.6	.636	0.37	0.86	1.1	4.5	6.4
Road	154	22.6	6.6	.461	0.4	.420	1.8	.606	0.34	1.14	1.4	5.0	7.5	Oct/Nov	64	22.2	6.6	.444	0.5	.394	2.4	.632	0.38	1.25	1.5	5.5	7.5
vs. Playoff	171	22.2	6.3	.468	0.5	.373	1.9	.657	0.42	1.13	1.5	5.0	7.4	December	56	24.9	7.1	.494	0.4	.238	1.9	.625	0.46	1.30	1.8	5.8	8.2
vs. Non-Playoff	146	23.9	6.8	.444	0.3	.280	1.8	.637	0.39	1.27	1.4	5.7	7.3	January	50	21.6	5.9	.471	0.4	.316	2.0	.704	0.38	1.00	1.6	5.2	7.1
vs. East	160	24.9	6.9	.452	0.5	.411	1.9	.629	0.34	1.29	1.5	5.4	7.7	February	47	24.3	6.7	.473	0.4	.250	1.1	.611	0.47	1.45	1.6	5.1	7.1
vs. West	157	21.1	6.2	.462	0.4	.250	1.9	.668	0.46	1.10	1.4	5.2	7.0	March	56	22.8	6.5	.422	0.3	.316	1.8	.667	0.34	1.11	1.3	5.4	6.8
vs. Div.	94	23.5	6.4	.430	0.3	.313	2.3	.648	0.38	1.22	1.4	5.7	7.1	Apr/May	44	22.3	6.4	.434	0.5	.476	2.2	.642	0.41	1.05	0.9	4.8	7.2
As Starter	151	31.2	8.4	.452	0.6	.388	2.4	.635	0.48	1.70	1.8	7.3	9.3	0 Days Rest	82	22.3	6.7	.478	0.4	.382	1.8	.616	0.38	1.18	1.3	5.0	7.7
Off Bench	166	15.6	4.9	.463	0.3	.250	1.5	.667	0.33	0.73	1.1	3.6	5.6	1 Days Rest	162	23.7	6.5	.451	0.4	.319	2.0	.660	0.43	1.18	1.5	5.5	7.4
In wins	145	23.2	6.4	.445	0.3	.292	1.9	.649	0.39	1.32	1.4	5.4	7.0	2 Days Rest	38	23.1	6.5	.431	0.3	.385	1.8	.582	0.37	1.32	1.7	5.5	6.7
In losses	172	22.8	6.7	.466	0.5	.365	1.9	.647	0.41	1.09	1.5	5.3	7.6	3+ Days Rest	35	21.5	6.2	.458	0.4	.286	1.9	.721	0.37	1.17	1.3	5.2	7.2

Corey Maggette

1999-2000 Per Game Averages

	G	Min	FGA	FG%	3PA	3P%	FTA	FT%	Blk	Stl	Ast	Reb	Pts		G	Min	FGA	FG%	3PA	3P%	FTA	FT%	Blk	Stl	Ast	Reb	Pts
Total	77	17.8	6.1	.478	0.1	.182	3.4	.751	0.34	0.31	0.8	3.9	8.4	Pre All-Star	46	19.2	6.8	.489	0.2	.250	3.1	.722	0.30	0.33	0.7	4.1	8.9
Home	40	18.7	6.0	.465	0.2	.333	4.1	.741	0.35	0.38	1.0	4.4	8.7	Post All-Star	31	15.8	5.1	.456	0.1	.000	3.8	.786	0.39	0.29	0.9	3.7	7.6
Road	37	16.8	6.2	.491	0.1	.000	2.7	.768	0.32	0.24	0.5	3.5	8.1	November	13	15.5	5.8	.421	0.2	.000	2.1	.519	0.31	0.08	0.3	3.2	6.0
vs. Playoff	45	17.4	6.1	.482	0.2	.143	3.0	.707	0.36	0.31	0.6	3.7	8.0	December	12	21.6	7.7	.478	0.0	—	3.3	.795	0.50	0.42	0.8	4.8	9.9
vs. Non-Playoff	32	18.3	6.0	.472	0.1	.250	4.0	.797	0.31	0.31	1.1	4.2	8.9	January	17	19.8	6.7	.561	0.2	.500	3.7	.746	0.24	0.47	1.2	4.4	10.4
vs. East	52	17.6	5.8	.464	0.1	.167	3.6	.753	0.38	0.29	0.8	3.9	8.1	February	11	17.9	5.9	.431	0.3	.000	2.6	.828	0.09	0.09	0.8	3.5	7.3
vs. West	25	18.3	6.6	.503	0.2	.200	3.0	.747	0.24	0.36	0.8	4.0	8.9	March	15	17.9	6.3	.468	0.1	.000	4.4	.773	0.47	0.40	1.1	4.6	9.3
vs. Div.	23	16.3	5.5	.449	0.1	.333	3.6	.795	0.39	0.22	0.6	3.3	7.9	April	9	12.0	3.1	.429	0.0	—	4.1	.784	0.44	0.33	0.2	2.3	5.9
As Starter	5	21.2	9.2	.435	0.2	.000	2.2	.727	0.20	1.00	1.2	4.2	9.6	0 Days Rest	19	18.2	6.6	.460	0.2	.000	2.7	.712	0.47	0.37	0.7	4.2	8.1
Off Bench	72	17.6	5.9	.482	0.1	.200	3.5	.752	0.35	0.26	0.8	3.9	8.3	1 Days Rest	38	17.0	5.7	.465	0.1	.333	3.5	.758	0.24	0.29	0.8	3.8	8.0
In wins	37	18.1	6.1	.449	0.1	.200	4.0	.779	0.35	0.30	0.9	4.1	8.7	2 Days Rest	9	18.0	6.6	.525	0.2	.500	4.3	.769	0.56	0.33	0.2	3.2	10.3
In losses	40	17.5	6.1	.504	0.2	.167	2.8	.714	0.33	0.33	0.7	3.8	8.1	3+ Days Rest	11	19.6	6.1	.507	0.2	.000	3.5	.763	0.27	0.36	1.0	4.5	8.8

Dan Majerle

Miami Heat — Guard-Forward

1999-2000 Per Game Averages

	G	Min	FGA	FG%	3PA	3P%	FTA	FT%	Blk	Stl	Ast	Reb	Pts
Total	69	33.4	6.1	.403	4.4	.362	1.0	.812	0.25	1.29	3.0	4.8	7.3
Home	34	33.9	6.8	.407	4.8	.335	1.1	.892	0.21	1.18	3.1	5.4	8.1
Road	35	33.0	5.5	.398	4.0	.393	0.9	.719	0.29	1.40	2.9	4.3	6.6
vs. Playoff	37	33.1	6.1	.393	4.4	.362	1.0	.784	0.24	1.14	3.0	4.6	7.1
vs. Non-Playoff	32	33.8	6.2	.414	4.4	.362	1.0	.844	0.25	1.47	3.0	5.1	7.6
vs. East	43	32.2	6.2	.404	4.4	.353	0.9	.865	0.14	1.37	3.0	4.5	7.3
vs. West	26	35.5	6.0	.400	4.4	.377	1.2	.750	0.42	1.15	3.0	5.4	7.3
vs. Div.	18	34.9	6.8	.434	4.9	.375	0.8	.786	0.22	1.67	2.9	4.8	8.3
As Starter	69	33.4	6.1	.403	4.4	.362	1.0	.812	0.25	1.29	3.0	4.8	7.3
Off Bench	0	—	—	—	—	—	—	—	—	—	—	—	—
In wins	44	34.0	6.1	.438	4.2	.382	1.2	.808	0.23	1.32	3.1	5.3	7.9
In losses	25	32.4	6.2	.342	4.7	.331	0.7	.824	0.28	1.24	2.8	4.0	6.4

	G	Min	FGA	FG%	3PA	3P%	FTA	FT%	Blk	Stl	Ast	Reb	Pts
Pre All-Star	39	34.8	6.5	.435	4.8	.401	1.0	.800	0.38	1.33	3.1	5.1	8.4
Post All-Star	30	31.7	5.6	.353	3.9	.299	1.0	.828	0.07	1.23	2.9	4.5	5.9
November	14	32.6	6.2	.460	4.4	.393	1.3	.833	0.36	1.57	3.1	4.2	8.5
December	14	35.9	6.1	.388	4.6	.375	0.9	.615	0.43	1.29	3.1	5.5	7.0
January	11	36.2	7.5	.458	5.6	.435	0.8	.435	0.36	1.09	2.8	5.6	10.2
February	7	33.7	6.0	.357	4.6	.344	1.0	1.000	0.00	0.57	3.0	1.5	6.9
March	12	32.5	5.0	.300	3.3	.231	0.9	.545	0.00	1.67	2.2	5.3	4.3
April	11	29.5	5.9	.400	4.2	.326	1.0	1.000	0.18	1.18	3.6	3.2	7.1
0 Days Rest	16	33.4	6.2	.424	4.5	.375	1.1	.778	0.25	1.38	2.8	4.1	7.8
1 Days Rest	35	33.7	6.4	.391	4.4	.329	0.9	.806	0.23	1.23	3.0	5.1	7.2
2 Days Rest	11	34.1	5.5	.417	4.2	.457	1.1	.833	0.45	1.18	3.7	4.5	7.4
3+ Days Rest	7	31.1	5.4	.395	4.4	.355	1.1	.875	0.00	1.57	2.0	5.3	6.9

Last Five Seasons

	G	Min	FGA	FG%	3PA	3P%	FTA	FT%	Blk	Stl	Ast	Reb	Pts
Total	307	30.9	7.3	.406	4.6	.355	1.3	.734	0.28	1.07	2.7	4.2	8.5
Home	153	31.3	7.5	.406	4.8	.351	1.3	.755	0.33	1.10	2.8	4.5	8.7
Road	154	30.6	7.2	.406	4.5	.360	1.3	.711	0.23	1.05	2.7	3.8	8.4
vs. Playoff	162	31.5	7.3	.386	4.6	.336	1.4	.722	0.27	0.98	2.8	4.0	8.2
vs. Non-Playoff	145	30.2	7.4	.429	4.6	.377	1.2	.749	0.30	1.18	2.7	4.3	9.0
vs. East	212	30.0	7.1	.408	4.6	.353	1.1	.745	0.25	1.04	2.6	3.8	8.2
vs. West	95	33.1	8.0	.402	4.7	.359	1.6	.716	0.36	1.15	3.1	4.9	9.3
vs. Div.	96	30.9	7.3	.400	4.7	.336	1.1	.785	0.31	1.06	2.6	4.1	8.3
As Starter	180	35.4	7.9	.401	5.0	.350	1.2	.710	0.27	1.20	3.2	4.8	9.0
Off Bench	127	24.6	6.5	.415	4.0	.364	1.4	.763	0.31	0.90	2.1	3.3	8.0
In wins	199	30.9	7.2	.435	4.6	.384	1.2	.778	0.29	1.09	2.9	4.3	9.0
In losses	108	31.0	7.5	.356	4.7	.302	1.4	.658	0.27	1.06	2.5	4.0	7.7

	G	Min	FGA	FG%	3PA	3P%	FTA	FT%	Blk	Stl	Ast	Reb	Pts
Pre All-Star	151	29.8	7.3	.411	4.5	.353	1.3	.680	0.32	1.15	2.4	4.1	8.5
Post All-Star	108	31.2	8.0	.404	4.9	.365	1.3	.814	0.30	1.10	3.1	4.2	9.3
Oct/Nov	53	30.9	8.3	.422	4.9	.355	1.5	.636	0.28	1.23	2.8	3.9	9.7
December	49	30.9	6.9	.374	4.5	.336	1.2	.672	0.27	1.29	2.5	4.5	7.5
January	42	28.2	6.5	.423	3.9	.350	1.4	.733	0.38	1.00	1.9	4.0	7.9
February	47	29.7	6.7	.408	4.8	.385	1.2	.842	0.17	0.64	3.0	3.9	8.4
March	59	35.4	8.7	.401	4.9	.330	1.4	.716	0.34	1.27	3.4	5.1	9.6
Apr/May	57	29.3	6.6	.412	4.5	.376	1.0	.845	0.26	0.96	2.8	3.4	8.0
0 Days Rest	79	30.9	7.5	.405	4.9	.351	0.8	.701	0.22	0.92	2.6	3.9	8.4
1 Days Rest	148	31.2	7.5	.414	4.6	.361	1.4	.736	0.32	1.09	2.8	4.4	9.0
2 Days Rest	51	31.3	7.2	.375	4.5	.322	1.6	.788	0.31	1.20	3.1	4.1	8.1
3+ Days Rest	29	29.0	6.3	.429	4.2	.397	1.2	.657	0.21	1.21	2.2	4.0	7.8

Karl Malone

Utah Jazz — Forward

1999-2000 Per Game Averages

	G	Min	FGA	FG%	3PA	3P%	FTA	FT%	Blk	Stl	Ast	Reb	Pts
Total	82	35.9	18.0	.509	0.1	.250	9.0	.797	0.87	0.96	3.7	9.5	25.5
Home	41	36.0	17.2	.513	0.1	.333	9.8	.810	1.05	0.80	3.7	9.3	25.6
Road	41	35.9	18.8	.506	0.0	.000	8.3	.782	0.68	1.12	3.7	9.7	25.5
vs. Playoff	44	36.2	17.7	.496	0.1	.167	9.2	.793	0.61	0.86	3.8	9.9	24.9
vs. Non-Playoff	38	35.7	18.3	.524	0.1	.500	8.8	.802	1.16	1.08	3.6	9.1	26.3
vs. East	30	36.5	19.1	.530	0.0	—	9.9	.779	0.80	1.07	4.4	10.2	27.9
vs. West	52	35.6	17.4	.497	0.2	.250	8.5	.810	0.90	0.90	3.1	9.1	24.2
vs. Div.	24	36.2	18.4	.471	0.1	.333	8.5	.814	1.17	1.00	3.1	9.3	24.3
As Starter	82	35.9	18.0	.509	0.1	.250	9.0	.797	0.87	0.96	3.7	9.5	25.5
Off Bench	0	—	—	—	—	—	—	—	—	—	—	—	—
In wins	55	36.3	18.2	.534	0.1	.250	9.5	.810	1.05	1.00	3.8	9.6	27.1
In losses	27	35.1	17.6	.458	0.1	.250	8.1	.767	0.48	0.89	3.5	9.4	22.4

	G	Min	FGA	FG%	3PA	3P%	FTA	FT%	Blk	Stl	Ast	Reb	Pts
Pre All-Star	47	36.7	18.2	.508	0.1	.250	8.8	.793	0.96	1.02	3.7	9.5	25.5
Post All-Star	35	34.9	17.7	.511	0.1	.250	9.3	.802	0.74	0.89	3.7	9.5	25.6
November	14	37.0	17.9	.516	0.1	.000	8.8	.833	0.71	0.93	3.9	9.4	25.2
December	14	37.9	19.1	.500	0.0	—	9.9	.754	1.43	1.43	3.6	10.7	26.6
January	14	36.4	18.0	.512	0.2	.333	8.6	.775	0.86	0.86	3.4	8.9	25.1
February	13	37.2	18.9	.476	0.2	.000	10.0	.800	0.92	0.62	4.5	9.3	26.0
March	16	36.2	18.0	.538	0.0	—	8.9	.789	0.75	1.00	3.7	9.8	26.4
April	11	31.2	15.6	.512	0.2	.500	8.6	.853	0.45	0.91	3.1	8.7	23.5
0 Days Rest	19	35.9	18.1	.510	0.1	.500	8.9	.806	0.89	1.05	3.6	9.9	26.3
1 Days Rest	45	35.9	18.4	.512	0.1	.000	8.8	.797	0.82	0.91	3.5	9.6	25.8
2 Days Rest	12	35.4	16.9	.522	0.0	—	8.0	.802	0.92	1.08	4.7	9.4	24.1
3+ Days Rest	6	37.3	17.0	.461	0.3	.500	10.3	.790	1.00	0.83	3.3	7.8	24.0

Last Five Seasons

	G	Min	FGA	FG%	3PA	3P%	FTA	FT%	Blk	Stl	Ast	Reb	Pts
Total	376	37.0	18.2	.523	0.2	.294	9.2	.764	0.73	1.30	4.1	9.8	26.1
Home	187	36.1	17.4	.529	0.2	.318	9.4	.776	0.80	1.33	4.1	9.8	25.8
Road	189	38.0	19.0	.518	0.1	.250	8.9	.750	0.66	1.26	4.0	9.8	26.4
vs. Playoff	201	37.8	18.3	.511	0.2	.273	9.2	.765	0.63	1.24	4.0	9.9	25.8
vs. Non-Playoff	175	36.1	18.0	.538	0.2	.314	9.1	.761	0.84	1.36	4.2	9.7	26.4
vs. East	126	37.8	18.7	.519	0.1	.529	10.0	.745	0.68	1.42	4.2	10.5	27.0
vs. West	250	36.6	17.9	.525	0.2	.216	8.7	.774	0.75	1.24	4.0	9.5	25.6
vs. Div.	113	36.9	18.1	.509	0.2	.217	8.6	.759	0.88	1.22	3.9	9.7	25.0
As Starter	376	37.0	18.2	.523	0.2	.294	9.2	.764	0.73	1.30	4.1	9.8	26.1
Off Bench	0	—	—	—	—	—	—	—	—	—	—	—	—
In wins	271	36.5	17.9	.544	0.2	.357	9.4	.773	0.80	1.32	4.2	9.7	26.8
In losses	105	38.4	18.8	.473	0.2	.192	8.6	.737	0.52	1.24	3.9	10.2	24.2

	G	Min	FGA	FG%	3PA	3P%	FTA	FT%	Blk	Stl	Ast	Reb	Pts
Pre All-Star	188	37.5	18.6	.522	0.2	.278	8.9	.751	0.77	1.32	4.1	10.1	26.2
Post All-Star	139	36.3	18.2	.535	0.2	.323	9.3	.770	0.72	1.28	4.0	9.5	26.8
Oct/Nov	58	36.4	17.1	.534	0.2	.200	9.1	.772	0.81	1.31	4.1	10.0	25.3
December	58	38.3	19.6	.508	0.1	.375	8.3	.733	0.91	1.29	4.3	10.8	26.1
January	56	37.9	19.1	.520	0.2	.167	9.3	.743	0.68	1.41	3.8	9.7	26.8
February	61	37.2	18.8	.517	0.2	.429	9.1	.756	0.74	1.44	4.2	9.8	26.5
March	80	37.6	18.0	.521	0.1	.364	9.8	.756	0.63	1.21	4.3	10.0	26.5
Apr/May	63	34.8	16.7	.545	0.2	.231	9.1	.807	0.63	1.16	3.7	8.5	25.6
0 Days Rest	88	37.0	18.1	.528	0.2	.267	9.3	.760	0.74	1.30	3.8	9.4	26.2
1 Days Rest	208	36.7	18.1	.522	0.2	.324	9.1	.768	0.67	1.27	4.1	9.9	26.0
2 Days Rest	51	38.7	18.9	.519	0.2	.250	9.0	.753	0.84	1.41	4.3	10.1	26.5
3+ Days Rest	29	36.6	17.6	.528	0.3	.250	9.1	.758	0.90	1.31	4.4	9.8	25.6

Danny Manning
Milwaukee Bucks — Forward-Center

1999-2000 Per Game Averages

	G	Min	FGA	FG%	3PA	3P%	FTA	FT%	Blk	Stl	Ast	Reb	Pts		G	Min	FGA	FG%	3PA	3P%	FTA	FT%	Blk	Stl	Ast	Reb	Pts
Total	72	16.9	4.7	.440	0.1	.250	0.7	.654	0.40	0.86	1.0	2.9	4.6	Pre All-Star	49	18.2	5.2	.459	0.0	.000	1.0	.667	0.49	1.08	1.3	3.0	5.5
Home	33	17.7	5.0	.445	0.0	—	0.9	.677	0.18	0.97	1.1	3.0	5.1	Post All-Star	23	14.1	3.7	.381	0.1	.333	0.0	.000	0.22	0.39	0.5	2.7	2.8
Road	39	16.2	4.5	.434	0.1	.250	0.5	.619	0.59	0.77	0.9	2.8	4.3	November	14	20.6	5.9	.500	0.0	—	1.9	.731	0.43	1.57	1.3	3.3	7.2
vs. Playoff	40	17.2	4.6	.422	0.1	.000	0.9	.595	0.38	0.85	1.2	2.6	4.5	December	16	17.8	5.2	.373	0.1	.000	0.9	.643	0.75	0.69	1.6	3.8	4.4
vs. Non-Playoff	32	16.5	4.8	.461	0.0	1.000	0.5	.800	0.44	0.88	0.8	3.3	4.8	January	14	15.9	4.1	.466	0.0	—	0.5	.714	0.29	0.86	1.1	2.0	4.2
vs. East	46	17.5	5.1	.457	0.0	.000	0.8	.658	0.46	0.87	1.0	3.1	5.2	February	11	18.3	5.5	.475	0.1	1.000	0.5	.200	0.36	1.00	0.5	2.5	5.5
vs. West	26	15.8	4.0	.400	0.1	.333	0.5	.643	0.31	0.85	1.0	2.5	3.6	March	10	14.9	4.5	.422	0.2	.000	0.0	—	0.10	0.50	0.5	3.5	3.8
vs. Div.	25	18.2	5.5	.467	0.0	.000	0.8	.684	0.44	0.88	1.2	3.3	5.6	April	7	10.3	1.4	.200	0.0	—	0.0	—	0.29	0.14	0.6	1.6	0.6
As Starter	0	—	—	—	—	—	—	—	—	—	—	—	—	0 Days Rest	18	13.8	3.3	.383	0.1	.000	0.3	.833	0.17	0.67	0.6	2.6	2.8
Off Bench	72	16.9	4.7	.440	0.1	.250	0.7	.654	0.40	0.86	1.0	2.9	4.6	1 Days Rest	35	18.8	5.6	.497	0.0	.000	1.1	.649	0.37	1.17	1.3	2.9	6.3
In wins	36	18.3	5.1	.464	0.1	.500	0.6	.783	0.58	0.92	1.3	3.4	5.3	2 Days Rest	6	14.3	3.8	.391	0.0	—	0.3	1.000	1.00	0.67	1.2	2.0	3.3
In losses	36	15.6	4.3	.410	0.1	.000	0.8	.552	0.22	0.81	0.8	2.4	4.0	3+ Days Rest	13	17.2	4.5	.322	0.1	1.000	0.5	.429	0.54	0.38	0.8	3.7	3.2

Last Five Seasons

	G	Min	FGA	FG%	3PA	3P%	FTA	FT%	Blk	Stl	Ast	Reb	Pts		G	Min	FGA	FG%	3PA	3P%	FTA	FT%	Blk	Stl	Ast	Reb	Pts
Total	302	23.7	8.8	.499	0.2	.171	2.5	.723	0.70	0.95	1.9	4.7	10.6	Pre All-Star	139	24.0	9.1	.513	0.1	.091	2.4	.716	0.76	1.00	1.7	5.0	11.0
Home	150	23.8	9.0	.495	0.2	.152	2.8	.715	0.74	1.08	2.1	4.9	11.0	Post All-Star	113	23.2	9.0	.488	0.4	.200	2.7	.739	0.60	1.00	1.9	4.6	10.9
Road	152	23.6	8.6	.504	0.2	.189	2.2	.733	0.66	0.83	1.6	4.6	10.3	Oct/Nov	41	25.5	9.3	.512	0.0	.000	3.0	.744	0.73	1.22	1.6	5.8	11.8
vs. Playoff	169	24.2	9.0	.479	0.3	.149	2.8	.718	0.69	1.01	1.9	5.0	10.6	December	44	23.2	8.9	.522	0.1	.250	2.2	.688	0.61	0.80	1.8	5.2	10.8
vs. Non-Playoff	133	22.9	8.6	.526	0.2	.217	2.1	.730	0.71	0.89	1.8	4.5	10.7	January	39	23.5	8.7	.499	0.1	.000	2.1	.735	0.82	0.92	1.9	4.2	10.2
vs. East	120	23.5	8.6	.489	0.1	.176	2.3	.737	0.78	0.86	1.7	4.7	10.2	February	61	23.7	9.0	.477	0.3	.167	2.7	.704	0.69	0.89	1.8	4.6	10.5
vs. West	182	23.8	9.0	.506	0.3	.170	2.6	.714	0.64	1.02	2.0	4.8	11.0	March	72	24.1	9.1	.499	0.3	.125	2.7	.755	0.75	0.94	2.1	4.6	11.2
vs. Div.	100	23.7	9.1	.502	0.3	.185	2.7	.695	0.63	0.99	2.0	4.9	11.0	Apr/May	45	22.0	7.7	.496	0.4	.263	2.0	.682	0.58	1.00	1.9	4.2	9.0
As Starter	37	30.1	11.2	.498	0.3	.100	3.0	.736	0.97	1.11	2.4	6.0	13.4	0 Days Rest	72	22.1	8.1	.466	0.3	.263	2.0	.695	0.60	0.96	1.6	4.3	9.0
Off Bench	265	22.8	8.5	.500	0.2	.183	2.4	.720	0.66	0.93	1.8	4.6	10.3	1 Days Rest	163	24.3	9.2	.514	0.3	.119	2.6	.727	0.67	0.99	2.0	4.8	11.3
In wins	166	23.8	8.8	.517	0.2	.176	2.3	.735	0.72	0.99	2.1	4.8	10.9	2 Days Rest	35	24.8	9.3	.543	0.2	.167	3.3	.789	1.00	0.77	2.0	5.0	12.7
In losses	136	23.5	8.8	.478	0.3	.167	2.7	.710	0.67	0.90	1.6	4.6	10.4	3+ Days Rest	32	22.7	8.1	.436	0.1	.333	2.4	.654	0.75	0.94	1.7	5.2	8.7

Stephon Marbury
New Jersey Nets — Guard

1999-2000 Per Game Averages

	G	Min	FGA	FG%	3PA	3P%	FTA	FT%	Blk	Stl	Ast	Reb	Pts		G	Min	FGA	FG%	3PA	3P%	FTA	FT%	Blk	Stl	Ast	Reb	Pts
Total	74	38.9	17.8	.432	3.1	.283	7.2	.813	0.20	1.51	8.4	3.2	22.2	Pre All-Star	49	39.2	17.9	.432	3.3	.302	7.0	.820	0.18	1.55	8.5	3.2	22.2
Home	38	38.9	17.3	.418	2.5	.191	7.1	.804	0.26	1.76	9.6	3.4	20.7	Post All-Star	25	38.4	17.6	.433	2.8	.239	7.6	.801	0.24	1.44	8.2	3.3	22.0
Road	36	39.0	18.3	.446	3.9	.345	7.4	.823	0.14	1.25	7.2	3.1	23.7	November	15	40.4	20.8	.391	4.6	.319	8.2	.821	0.20	1.67	6.1	2.0	24.5
vs. Playoff	42	39.8	19.1	.433	3.4	.288	7.9	.823	0.19	1.62	8.4	3.1	24.0	December	15	36.7	16.3	.426	2.9	.233	5.5	.783	0.33	1.73	9.8	3.8	18.9
vs. Non-Playoff	32	37.8	16.1	.431	2.9	.277	6.3	.798	0.22	1.38	8.4	3.4	19.8	January	14	41.4	18.0	.476	2.7	.395	7.5	.838	0.07	0.93	9.1	3.9	24.5
vs. East	46	38.1	17.1	.420	3.2	.248	6.7	.803	0.15	1.46	8.4	3.0	20.6	February	12	39.3	17.2	.471	3.2	.316	8.7	.808	0.08	1.83	8.8	4.0	24.2
vs. West	28	40.3	18.9	.450	3.1	.341	8.1	.827	0.29	1.61	8.5	3.7	24.8	March	16	37.9	17.3	.424	2.6	.171	7.2	.809	0.31	1.50	8.6	2.8	20.9
vs. Div.	22	39.3	16.0	.394	2.8	.161	7.1	.827	0.18	1.64	8.6	3.1	19.0	April	2	33.0	13.5	.333	2.0	.000	3.0	.833	0.00	1.00	7.0	3.0	11.5
As Starter	74	38.9	17.8	.432	3.1	.283	7.2	.813	0.20	1.51	8.4	3.2	22.2	0 Days Rest	16	38.9	17.9	.411	4.1	.262	7.6	.820	0.25	1.19	8.3	3.3	22.1
Off Bench	0	—	—	—	—	—	—	—	—	—	—	—	—	1 Days Rest	43	38.7	17.4	.440	2.9	.270	7.3	.813	0.16	1.42	8.3	3.1	22.1
In wins	31	37.9	16.2	.446	2.5	.205	6.6	.800	0.29	1.48	9.6	3.6	20.3	2 Days Rest	9	39.8	17.0	.418	2.2	.250	7.3	.818	0.33	2.56	9.1	3.6	20.8
In losses	43	39.7	19.0	.423	3.6	.323	7.7	.822	0.14	1.53	7.5	3.0	23.5	3+ Days Rest	6	39.5	21.2	.449	3.7	.455	5.3	.781	0.17	1.50	8.2	3.7	24.8

Career (1996-97 thru 1999-2000)

	G	Min	FGA	FG%	3PA	3P%	FTA	FT%	Blk	Stl	Ast	Reb	Pts		G	Min	FGA	FG%	3PA	3P%	FTA	FT%	Blk	Stl	Ast	Reb	Pts
Total	272	37.5	15.8	.421	3.8	.322	5.9	.770	0.18	1.26	8.4	2.9	19.1	Pre All-Star	128	37.4	15.9	.426	3.8	.331	6.4	.756	0.17	1.38	8.1	2.9	19.7
Home	141	37.9	15.9	.417	3.4	.289	6.0	.773	0.26	1.35	8.9	2.9	19.0	Post All-Star	144	37.6	15.6	.417	3.6	.314	5.5	.783	0.20	1.15	8.6	3.0	18.6
Road	131	37.1	15.8	.426	4.2	.350	5.8	.765	0.09	1.16	7.8	2.9	19.3	Oct/Nov	38	36.5	16.6	.398	4.0	.327	7.0	.772	0.18	1.55	6.8	2.6	19.9
vs. Playoff	144	37.9	16.7	.412	4.1	.327	6.4	.778	0.17	1.31	8.2	3.0	20.1	December	44	36.8	15.5	.417	3.9	.295	5.5	.744	0.18	1.36	8.8	2.9	18.2
vs. Non-Playoff	128	37.2	14.8	.433	3.3	.315	5.3	.758	0.19	1.20	8.6	2.8	17.9	January	38	38.8	15.8	.465	3.4	.411	6.4	.749	0.18	1.13	8.3	3.2	20.9
vs. East	133	37.6	16.0	.414	3.9	.312	6.0	.777	0.17	1.19	8.4	2.8	19.2	February	46	37.3	16.2	.420	3.2	.252	5.9	.760	0.15	1.48	8.7	3.2	18.9
vs. West	139	37.5	15.7	.428	3.6	.333	5.7	.762	0.19	1.32	8.4	3.0	19.0	March	63	37.8	15.6	.399	3.6	.271	5.7	.773	0.16	1.08	8.4	2.9	17.8
vs. Div.	84	38.2	16.2	.422	3.4	.298	5.6	.786	0.19	1.37	8.4	3.0	19.1	Apr/May	43	38.0	15.5	.442	4.4	.398	5.0	.824	0.23	1.02	9.1	2.8	19.6
As Starter	268	37.7	15.9	.422	3.7	.320	5.9	.772	0.18	1.26	8.4	2.9	19.2	0 Days Rest	67	37.9	15.7	.409	4.2	.330	6.3	.780	0.16	1.07	8.6	3.0	19.1
Off Bench	4	25.3	11.5	.370	5.3	.429	3.0	.417	0.25	0.75	6.5	2.5	12.0	1 Days Rest	147	37.6	15.9	.432	3.6	.317	5.8	.773	0.17	1.26	8.4	3.0	19.4
In wins	133	37.3	14.6	.466	3.0	.362	5.6	.753	0.22	1.28	9.2	3.2	18.9	2 Days Rest	38	37.8	16.3	.417	3.6	.356	6.3	.741	0.29	1.55	8.6	2.8	19.5
In losses	139	37.8	17.1	.384	4.5	.297	6.2	.784	0.14	1.24	7.6	2.7	19.3	3+ Days Rest	20	35.5	15.3	.393	3.8	.267	4.3	.765	0.10	1.30	7.6	2.6	16.3

Shawn Marion

1999-2000 Per Game Averages

	G	Min	FGA	FG%	3PA	3P%	FTA	FT%	Blk	Stl	Ast	Reb	Pts
Total	51	24.7	9.2	.471	0.4	.182	1.7	.847	1.04	0.75	1.4	6.5	10.2
Home	26	25.1	9.3	.473	0.5	.083	1.8	.891	1.12	0.65	1.6	6.2	10.5
Road	25	24.3	9.1	.469	0.4	.300	1.6	.795	0.96	0.84	1.1	6.8	9.9
vs. Playoff	26	22.1	8.0	.481	0.3	.111	1.1	.862	0.96	0.69	1.2	5.5	8.7
vs. Non-Playoff	25	27.4	10.5	.464	0.5	.231	2.2	.839	1.12	0.80	1.6	7.6	11.8
vs. East	19	22.7	9.7	.467	0.3	.333	1.7	.879	1.26	0.74	1.0	5.7	10.7
vs. West	32	25.9	9.0	.474	0.5	.125	1.6	.827	0.91	0.75	1.6	7.0	9.9
vs. Div.	13	25.4	9.1	.492	0.2	.000	1.8	.750	0.69	0.62	1.8	8.2	10.3
As Starter	38	27.5	10.2	.459	0.4	.125	1.7	.844	1.11	0.82	1.6	7.3	10.8
Off Bench	13	16.6	6.4	.530	0.5	.333	1.6	.857	0.85	0.54	0.6	4.2	8.3
In wins	37	23.9	9.2	.479	0.3	.250	1.9	.843	0.95	0.81	1.4	6.7	10.5
In losses	14	26.8	9.4	.450	0.7	.100	1.1	.867	1.29	0.57	1.1	6.0	9.4

	G	Min	FGA	FG%	3PA	3P%	FTA	FT%	Blk	Stl	Ast	Reb	Pts
Pre All-Star	17	23.9	10.0	.424	0.5	.250	1.9	.906	1.53	0.53	1.4	5.9	10.3
Post All-Star	34	25.1	8.9	.498	0.4	.143	1.6	.811	0.79	0.85	1.3	6.8	10.1
November	14	24.9	10.4	.404	0.5	.286	1.7	.875	1.57	0.57	1.4	5.9	10.1
December	1	22.0	8.0	.500	1.0	.000	2.0	1.000	2.00	1.00	3.0	3.0	10.0
January	0	—	—	—	—	—	—	—	—	—	—	—	—
February	10	19.4	7.4	.514	0.3	.333	1.5	.933	1.10	0.50	0.5	5.4	9.1
March	16	25.7	9.4	.487	0.4	.143	1.9	.767	0.63	0.75	1.6	7.5	10.6
April	10	28.5	9.3	.516	0.4	.000	1.4	.857	0.80	1.20	1.7	7.3	10.8
0 Days Rest	11	25.9	9.1	.440	0.6	.286	2.1	.957	0.82	0.91	1.2	5.6	10.2
1 Days Rest	28	24.6	9.4	.477	0.4	.100	1.7	.792	1.14	0.82	1.4	6.7	10.3
2 Days Rest	8	22.4	7.3	.431	0.4	.000	1.3	.800	0.50	0.50	1.1	6.0	7.3
3+ Days Rest	4	26.5	12.8	.549	0.5	.500	1.0	1.000	2.00	0.25	2.3	8.5	15.3

Donyell Marshall

1999-2000 Per Game Averages

	G	Min	FGA	FG%	3PA	3P%	FTA	FT%	Blk	Stl	Ast	Reb	Pts
Total	64	32.4	13.1	.394	2.2	.355	4.0	.780	1.06	1.06	2.6	10.0	14.2
Home	33	32.5	12.6	.400	2.1	.343	4.8	.800	1.09	0.79	2.6	10.3	14.7
Road	31	32.2	13.7	.388	2.2	.368	3.1	.747	1.03	1.35	2.6	9.6	13.7
vs. Playoff	35	32.8	13.0	.412	2.5	.384	4.1	.769	0.86	1.17	2.5	9.5	14.8
vs. Non-Playoff	29	31.8	13.3	.373	1.8	.308	3.9	.795	1.31	0.93	2.7	10.5	13.6
vs. East	25	34.5	14.6	.407	2.5	.349	4.6	.784	1.16	0.96	3.1	11.3	16.7
vs. West	39	31.0	12.2	.384	1.9	.360	3.6	.777	1.00	1.13	2.3	9.1	12.8
vs. Div.	20	33.7	13.0	.442	2.4	.319	4.2	.795	1.00	1.40	2.5	9.2	15.6
As Starter	51	33.7	13.6	.394	2.1	.370	4.5	.772	1.12	1.14	2.9	10.2	14.9
Off Bench	13	27.2	11.3	.395	2.3	.300	2.1	.852	0.85	0.77	1.5	9.1	11.4
In wins	14	36.2	15.0	.402	2.1	.300	4.6	.738	1.64	1.64	3.5	11.7	17.6
In losses	50	31.3	12.6	.375	2.2	.370	3.8	.795	0.90	0.90	2.4	9.5	13.3

	G	Min	FGA	FG%	3PA	3P%	FTA	FT%	Blk	Stl	Ast	Reb	Pts
Pre All-Star	36	29.4	11.7	.382	1.9	.362	3.2	.733	0.86	1.00	2.1	9.6	12.0
Post All-Star	28	36.2	15.0	.406	2.5	.348	5.0	.820	1.32	1.14	3.3	10.5	17.1
November	10	27.1	11.7	.333	1.7	.294	3.6	.694	0.60	0.60	2.0	9.6	10.8
December	9	27.7	10.4	.394	1.7	.400	3.1	.643	0.44	1.33	1.1	7.6	10.9
January	11	32.4	12.7	.421	2.5	.370	3.1	.824	1.18	1.18	2.5	10.5	14.2
February	15	34.3	13.6	.422	2.5	.342	4.1	.836	1.47	1.20	3.2	11.9	15.7
March	16	36.9	15.9	.376	2.2	.286	5.0	.800	1.38	0.88	3.2	9.6	16.6
April	3	29.7	10.0	.467	2.0	.833	5.3	.813	0.33	1.67	3.7	8.7	15.3
0 Days Rest	14	32.4	13.4	.394	2.4	.424	3.6	.800	1.00	1.43	2.4	10.2	14.4
1 Days Rest	31	33.1	13.0	.399	2.0	.295	3.8	.805	1.29	0.68	2.7	9.4	14.0
2 Days Rest	9	32.6	13.3	.375	2.1	.368	5.6	.700	0.56	1.89	2.8	11.2	14.7
3+ Days Rest	10	29.9	12.8	.398	2.5	.400	3.7	.784	0.90	1.00	2.3	10.2	14.1

Last Five Seasons

	G	Min	FGA	FG%	3PA	3P%	FTA	FT%	Blk	Stl	Ast	Reb	Pts
Total	308	25.6	10.3	.408	2.0	.326	2.5	.737	0.83	0.83	1.6	6.8	10.9
Home	150	27.0	10.9	.427	2.2	.350	2.9	.727	0.79	0.88	1.8	7.5	12.2
Road	158	24.3	9.7	.387	1.8	.300	2.2	.751	0.87	0.79	1.4	6.2	9.7
vs. Playoff	183	25.0	9.9	.402	2.0	.311	2.4	.726	0.67	0.81	1.5	6.5	10.3
vs. Non-Playoff	125	26.6	10.8	.415	2.0	.348	2.7	.752	1.06	0.86	1.8	7.3	11.7
vs. East	102	26.7	11.0	.411	2.3	.346	2.7	.776	0.89	0.75	1.9	7.1	11.9
vs. West	206	25.1	9.9	.406	1.9	.314	2.4	.716	0.80	0.87	1.5	6.7	10.4
vs. Div.	94	26.0	10.2	.404	1.9	.266	2.6	.739	0.86	0.96	1.5	6.8	10.7
As Starter	170	33.2	13.5	.413	2.4	.336	3.2	.746	1.05	1.14	2.2	8.7	14.4
Off Bench	138	16.3	6.2	.393	1.6	.308	1.7	.716	0.56	0.46	0.8	4.5	6.6
In wins	92	26.1	10.4	.473	2.0	.393	2.6	.744	1.15	0.96	1.9	7.2	12.6
In losses	216	25.4	10.2	.380	2.0	.298	2.5	.735	0.69	0.78	1.5	6.6	10.2

	G	Min	FGA	FG%	3PA	3P%	FTA	FT%	Blk	Stl	Ast	Reb	Pts
Pre All-Star	142	24.2	9.6	.403	1.9	.327	2.3	.704	0.70	0.80	1.4	6.6	9.9
Post All-Star	118	27.2	11.1	.408	2.3	.316	2.8	.774	1.00	0.81	1.9	6.9	11.9
Oct/Nov	49	23.0	9.2	.397	1.9	.316	2.3	.675	0.59	0.59	1.3	7.0	9.5
December	39	23.2	8.6	.426	1.8	.352	2.3	.714	0.69	0.87	1.4	5.6	9.6
January	44	25.9	10.5	.405	2.1	.323	2.0	.711	0.80	0.98	1.3	6.6	10.7
February	52	25.9	10.8	.417	2.1	.300	3.0	.779	0.96	0.98	1.8	7.4	11.3
March	78	28.5	11.3	.391	2.1	.313	2.8	.769	1.04	0.79	2.0	7.2	11.6
Apr/May	46	25.1	10.1	.429	1.8	.381	2.3	.722	0.72	0.83	1.4	6.5	11.0
0 Days Rest	74	26.9	10.7	.398	2.0	.327	2.4	.725	0.88	0.89	1.6	7.2	10.9
1 Days Rest	142	26.5	10.7	.412	2.1	.327	2.6	.764	0.94	0.81	1.7	6.8	11.5
2 Days Rest	51	24.9	10.0	.414	2.0	.350	2.4	.689	0.67	0.96	1.7	7.0	10.6
3+ Days Rest	41	21.0	8.4	.403	1.8	.292	2.4	.720	0.56	0.66	1.2	6.0	9.0

Jamal Mashburn

1999-2000 Per Game Averages

	G	Min	FGA	FG%	3PA	3P%	FTA	FT%	Blk	Stl	Ast	Reb	Pts
Total	76	37.2	15.2	.445	3.7	.403	3.1	.778	0.18	1.04	3.9	5.0	17.5
Home	38	36.9	15.4	.459	3.9	.392	3.2	.833	0.24	1.08	3.6	4.9	18.3
Road	38	37.5	15.1	.430	3.4	.415	3.1	.723	0.13	1.00	4.3	5.1	16.6
vs. Playoff	39	37.6	15.2	.416	3.7	.396	3.0	.828	0.15	0.95	3.8	4.7	16.5
vs. Non-Playoff	37	36.8	15.3	.475	3.6	.410	3.3	.732	0.22	1.14	4.0	5.3	18.5
vs. East	52	37.3	15.0	.430	3.7	.387	3.3	.769	0.21	1.10	3.5	5.1	16.9
vs. West	24	37.1	15.8	.475	3.6	.437	2.8	.803	0.13	0.92	4.0	4.8	18.8
vs. Div.	23	37.8	14.4	.429	3.5	.363	3.5	.738	0.26	1.30	4.1	6.0	16.2
As Starter	76	37.2	15.2	.445	3.7	.403	3.1	.778	0.18	1.04	3.9	5.0	17.5
Off Bench	0	—	—	—	—	—	—	—	—	—	—	—	—
In wins	47	36.9	15.1	.480	3.6	.461	3.5	.795	0.23	0.98	3.9	5.1	19.0
In losses	29	37.7	15.4	.389	3.8	.315	2.5	.740	0.10	1.14	3.9	4.9	15.1

	G	Min	FGA	FG%	3PA	3P%	FTA	FT%	Blk	Stl	Ast	Reb	Pts
Pre All-Star	42	37.2	15.2	.456	3.5	.434	3.2	.728	0.24	1.21	4.5	5.3	17.8
Post All-Star	34	37.2	15.2	.431	3.9	.368	3.0	.845	0.12	0.82	3.2	4.7	17.1
November	14	38.4	16.0	.469	3.8	.491	3.9	.691	0.50	1.29	4.4	5.6	19.6
December	9	36.3	14.2	.445	3.1	.357	2.4	.682	0.00	1.00	4.6	4.6	15.4
January	15	36.3	15.0	.431	3.1	.413	2.5	.703	0.20	1.40	4.6	5.0	15.9
February	14	36.9	15.4	.435	3.9	.364	3.7	.827	0.00	0.64	3.1	6.1	17.9
March	13	40.2	16.5	.467	4.0	.327	2.6	.853	0.31	0.92	3.7	4.1	18.9
April	11	34.4	13.7	.411	4.0	.455	3.5	.897	0.00	0.91	4.1	4.3	16.3
0 Days Rest	17	35.9	15.4	.387	3.9	.333	3.0	.804	0.12	1.41	3.5	5.4	15.6
1 Days Rest	40	37.4	14.7	.454	3.5	.413	3.3	.782	0.18	0.98	3.8	4.8	17.4
2 Days Rest	13	38.7	16.2	.488	3.4	.523	2.2	.821	0.31	0.92	5.2	5.0	19.4
3+ Days Rest	6	36.7	16.3	.449	5.0	.333	4.5	.667	0.17	0.67	3.5	5.7	19.3

Last Five Seasons

	G	Min	FGA	FG%	3PA	3P%	FTA	FT%	Blk	Stl	Ast	Reb	Pts
Total	235	35.1	13.4	.421	3.4	.355	4.0	.751	0.20	1.00	3.2	4.9	15.5
Home	118	34.7	13.2	.425	3.3	.334	4.1	.774	0.19	1.05	3.2	4.7	15.5
Road	117	35.5	13.7	.418	3.6	.374	3.9	.726	0.20	0.94	3.3	5.1	15.6
vs. Playoff	121	35.9	13.5	.407	3.4	.365	4.0	.757	0.17	1.01	3.3	4.9	15.2
vs. Non-Playoff	114	34.2	13.4	.437	3.5	.345	4.0	.744	0.23	0.98	3.2	4.9	15.9
vs. East	152	36.2	13.6	.424	3.4	.351	4.0	.759	0.20	1.03	3.2	5.1	15.7
vs. West	83	33.1	13.2	.416	3.6	.361	4.0	.737	0.18	0.93	3.2	4.6	15.2
vs. Div.	74	36.1	13.1	.409	3.4	.339	4.0	.776	0.24	1.18	3.3	5.8	15.0
As Starter	216	36.1	13.8	.423	3.4	.357	4.2	.756	0.20	0.99	3.4	5.1	16.0
Off Bench	19	23.9	9.6	.404	3.8	.333	1.8	.629	0.11	1.05	1.8	3.0	10.2
In wins	131	35.3	13.3	.458	3.2	.401	4.1	.770	0.25	1.06	3.1	5.1	16.6
In losses	104	34.8	13.7	.377	3.7	.304	3.8	.725	0.13	0.91	3.4	4.6	14.2

	G	Min	FGA	FG%	3PA	3P%	FTA	FT%	Blk	Stl	Ast	Reb	Pts
Pre All-Star	139	34.2	13.7	.419	3.5	.358	4.2	.737	0.22	1.01	3.2	4.7	15.9
Post All-Star	72	36.6	13.2	.418	4.1	.341	3.4	.798	0.18	1.01	3.3	5.0	15.1
Oct/Nov	51	34.8	15.1	.424	4.0	.388	5.0	.744	0.33	0.84	2.9	4.6	18.1
December	35	32.5	12.8	.408	3.3	.313	3.7	.656	0.06	0.97	2.7	4.5	13.9
January	44	34.0	12.6	.405	2.9	.331	3.7	.762	0.23	1.23	3.9	4.5	14.0
February	33	35.7	14.0	.427	3.6	.350	4.1	.787	0.15	0.91	3.2	5.5	16.5
March	27	38.3	14.2	.435	4.4	.319	3.4	.772	0.22	1.04	3.5	5.0	16.4
Apr/May	45	36.0	12.0	.431	2.7	.402	3.6	.783	0.13	1.00	3.2	5.5	14.2
0 Days Rest	57	35.3	13.4	.435	3.3	.410	4.2	.739	0.21	1.12	3.0	4.9	16.1
1 Days Rest	114	35.6	13.4	.410	3.6	.333	3.6	.754	0.18	1.01	3.4	5.1	14.9
2 Days Rest	40	35.2	14.1	.421	3.4	.358	4.3	.769	0.20	0.80	3.4	4.9	16.4
3+ Days Rest	24	32.0	12.9	.445	3.2	.329	4.5	.734	0.25	0.96	2.5	4.3	15.9

Anthony Mason

1999-2000 Per Game Averages

	G	Min	FGA	FG%	3PA	3P%	FTA	FT%	Blk	Stl	Ast	Reb	Pts
Total	82	38.2	8.1	.480	0.0	.000	5.1	.746	0.35	0.90	4.5	8.5	11.6
Home	41	38.6	8.1	.489	0.0	.000	4.9	.785	0.37	0.98	5.0	8.4	11.8
Road	41	37.9	8.0	.470	0.0	—	5.4	.710	0.34	0.83	4.0	8.7	11.3
vs. Playoff	44	39.1	8.4	.480	0.0	—	5.2	.751	0.23	0.73	4.2	8.0	12.0
vs. Non-Playoff	38	37.2	7.6	.479	0.0	.000	5.1	.740	0.50	1.11	4.8	9.1	11.1
vs. East	54	39.0	8.3	.499	0.0	.000	5.5	.753	0.44	0.91	4.7	8.9	12.4
vs. West	28	36.8	7.6	.439	0.0	—	4.5	.730	0.18	0.89	4.0	7.8	9.9
vs. Div.	28	39.7	8.9	.504	0.0	.000	5.6	.756	0.46	0.93	5.0	8.9	13.2
As Starter	81	38.3	8.1	.481	0.0	.000	5.1	.742	0.36	0.91	4.5	8.6	11.6
Off Bench	1	28.0	2.0	.000	0.0	—	6.0	1.000	0.00	0.00	4.0	5.0	6.0
In wins	49	38.9	8.5	.514	0.0	.000	5.4	.760	0.43	0.94	5.3	8.9	12.9
In losses	33	37.2	7.4	.420	0.0	—	4.7	.721	0.24	0.85	3.2	8.0	9.6

	G	Min	FGA	FG%	3PA	3P%	FTA	FT%	Blk	Stl	Ast	Reb	Pts
Pre All-Star	47	36.6	7.4	.471	0.0	.000	5.4	.663	0.30	0.91	3.8	8.3	10.5
Post All-Star	35	40.4	9.0	.489	0.0	—	4.8	.870	0.43	0.89	5.3	8.9	13.0
November	14	37.3	8.4	.466	0.0	—	5.4	.613	0.29	0.93	3.4	10.0	11.1
December	15	36.6	7.6	.500	0.0	—	5.6	.655	0.20	1.00	4.7	8.5	11.3
January	13	36.2	6.5	.494	0.0	—	5.9	.688	0.38	0.92	3.0	6.8	10.5
February	14	36.9	7.1	.440	0.1	.000	4.0	.875	0.21	0.36	5.0	7.4	9.8
March	15	40.7	8.4	.484	0.0	—	4.4	.894	0.60	0.93	5.5	8.9	12.1
April	11	42.2	10.7	.492	0.0	—	5.7	.825	0.45	1.36	5.2	9.7	15.3
0 Days Rest	22	36.7	8.0	.418	0.0	—	4.3	.726	0.41	0.91	3.9	8.1	9.9
1 Days Rest	43	39.2	8.4	.461	0.0	.000	5.1	.747	0.42	0.93	5.0	8.5	11.6
2 Days Rest	8	36.1	8.1	.646	0.0	—	7.3	.724	0.13	1.13	4.1	9.8	15.8
3+ Days Rest	9	38.9	6.6	.593	0.0	—	5.2	.809	0.11	0.56	3.7	8.7	12.0

Last Five Seasons

	G	Min	FGA	FG%	3PA	3P%	FTA	FT%	Blk	Stl	Ast	Reb	Pts
Total	318	40.5	9.6	.521	0.0	.125	5.2	.716	0.36	0.90	4.7	9.8	13.7
Home	157	40.9	9.4	.535	0.0	.000	5.1	.730	0.33	0.90	4.9	9.7	13.9
Road	161	40.1	9.7	.507	0.0	.200	5.3	.703	0.39	0.91	4.4	9.9	13.6
vs. Playoff	171	40.7	9.6	.506	0.0	.200	5.2	.703	0.27	0.81	4.5	9.3	13.4
vs. Non-Playoff	147	40.3	9.5	.539	0.0	.000	5.3	.730	0.46	1.01	4.9	10.4	14.1
vs. East	209	40.8	9.6	.519	0.0	.167	5.4	.721	0.34	0.94	4.6	9.8	13.9
vs. West	109	39.9	9.5	.526	0.0	.000	5.0	.705	0.39	0.83	4.7	9.8	13.5
vs. Div.	103	40.5	9.9	.515	0.0	.200	5.5	.709	0.26	1.00	4.7	9.6	14.1
As Starter	316	40.6	9.6	.522	0.0	.125	5.2	.715	0.36	0.91	4.7	9.8	13.8
Off Bench	2	30.5	5.0	.300	0.0	—	5.0	.900	0.00	0.50	4.0	7.0	7.5
In wins	194	41.1	9.8	.549	0.0	.000	5.4	.728	0.40	0.98	5.2	10.2	14.7
In losses	124	39.7	9.3	.475	0.0	.200	4.9	.694	0.29	0.77	3.9	9.2	12.3

	G	Min	FGA	FG%	3PA	3P%	FTA	FT%	Blk	Stl	Ast	Reb	Pts
Pre All-Star	186	40.5	9.4	.505	0.0	.000	5.6	.690	0.30	0.89	4.4	9.5	13.3
Post All-Star	132	40.5	9.9	.543	0.0	.333	4.8	.759	0.44	0.92	5.1	10.2	14.3
Oct/Nov	56	39.9	9.0	.508	0.0	—	5.4	.650	0.18	0.79	4.5	9.3	12.6
December	59	40.7	9.9	.506	0.1	.000	5.5	.684	0.25	1.02	4.4	9.6	13.8
January	57	41.2	9.4	.511	0.0	—	6.1	.719	0.42	0.84	4.4	10.0	14.0
February	52	40.5	9.9	.532	0.1	.333	4.6	.789	0.37	1.04	5.0	9.6	14.2
March	54	39.9	8.7	.523	0.0	—	4.7	.718	0.50	0.83	5.1	10.7	12.5
Apr/May	40	40.5	10.9	.553	0.0	.000	5.1	.771	0.48	0.90	4.9	9.5	16.0
0 Days Rest	84	40.0	9.6	.502	0.0	.000	5.4	.716	0.37	0.83	4.5	9.3	13.5
1 Days Rest	154	40.6	9.6	.527	0.0	.000	5.0	.726	0.42	0.95	4.8	9.9	13.8
2 Days Rest	51	41.1	9.7	.523	0.1	.000	6.0	.694	0.25	0.92	4.9	10.6	14.3
3+ Days Rest	29	40.1	9.1	.540	0.0	1.000	4.9	.709	0.17	0.79	4.1	9.7	13.3

George McCloud

Denver Nuggets — Forward

1999-2000 Per Game Averages

	G	Min	FGA	FG%	3PA	3P%	FTA	FT%	Blk	Stl	Ast	Reb	Pts		G	Min	FGA	FG%	3PA	3P%	FTA	FT%	Blk	Stl	Ast	Reb	Pts
Total	78	27.2	8.2	.417	3.6	.378	2.3	.818	0.33	0.62	3.2	3.7	10.1	Pre All-Star	46	24.8	7.2	.402	3.2	.363	2.3	.792	0.30	0.70	2.7	3.8	8.8
Home	39	27.2	8.5	.425	3.9	.396	2.8	.802	0.46	0.56	3.5	3.8	11.1	Post All-Star	32	30.5	9.5	.433	4.3	.394	2.3	.853	0.38	0.50	3.9	3.5	11.9
Road	39	27.1	7.8	.408	3.3	.357	1.8	.843	0.21	0.67	2.8	3.5	9.1	November	13	22.8	7.5	.418	3.2	.381	2.1	.778	0.31	0.62	1.8	3.2	9.2
vs. Playoff	44	25.6	8.0	.396	3.4	.338	2.3	.767	0.32	0.77	2.8	3.6	9.3	December	13	25.1	6.5	.424	2.7	.429	2.2	.821	0.31	0.38	2.3	3.8	8.5
vs. Non-Playoff	34	29.1	8.4	.443	4.0	.422	2.3	.885	0.35	0.41	3.6	3.7	11.2	January	14	26.6	7.9	.400	3.7	.346	2.3	.781	0.21	1.14	3.7	3.7	9.4
vs. East	29	27.1	8.0	.418	4.1	.378	2.4	.775	0.34	0.34	3.1	3.8	10.1	February	12	21.6	5.4	.385	2.2	.308	2.2	.808	0.50	0.58	2.1	3.3	6.6
vs. West	49	27.2	8.3	.416	3.3	.378	2.2	.845	0.33	0.78	3.2	3.6	10.1	March	16	30.1	9.5	.408	4.6	.378	2.1	.824	0.31	0.25	4.1	3.3	11.3
vs. Div.	24	26.9	8.1	.415	2.9	.357	2.6	.841	0.46	0.63	2.4	3.0	10.0	April	10	38.2	12.8	.453	5.4	.407	3.4	.882	0.40	0.80	5.0	4.8	16.8
As Starter	11	37.2	11.4	.440	5.0	.400	2.3	.880	0.27	0.45	5.5	4.9	14.0	0 Days Rest	19	28.7	7.7	.370	3.4	.375	2.9	.855	0.32	0.68	3.5	4.0	9.4
Off Bench	67	25.5	7.7	.411	3.4	.373	2.3	.808	0.34	0.64	2.8	3.4	9.4	1 Days Rest	37	26.2	8.4	.427	3.8	.374	2.2	.838	0.32	0.46	3.1	3.6	10.4
In wins	33	27.6	7.9	.477	3.6	.471	2.0	.803	0.30	0.61	3.5	3.7	10.8	2 Days Rest	11	27.5	8.8	.412	4.1	.333	2.1	.739	0.09	0.73	3.1	2.6	10.2
In losses	45	26.8	8.4	.376	3.6	.311	2.6	.826	0.36	0.62	2.9	3.6	9.6	3+ Days Rest	11	27.4	7.8	.465	3.2	.457	2.1	.739	0.64	0.91	2.9	4.1	10.3

Last Five Seasons

	G	Min	FGA	FG%	3PA	3P%	FTA	FT%	Blk	Stl	Ast	Reb	Pts		G	Min	FGA	FG%	3PA	3P%	FTA	FT%	Blk	Stl	Ast	Reb	Pts
Total	332	26.9	9.8	.415	4.8	.379	1.9	.815	0.30	0.97	2.2	3.7	11.5	Pre All-Star	163	27.2	10.2	.415	4.7	.377	2.1	.805	0.32	0.99	2.2	3.9	12.0
Home	166	27.0	9.8	.408	4.9	.391	1.9	.807	0.39	0.90	2.3	3.7	11.5	Post All-Star	121	26.7	10.4	.410	5.4	.373	1.8	.812	0.27	0.94	2.4	3.5	12.0
Road	166	26.7	9.8	.423	4.6	.368	1.9	.823	0.21	1.04	2.1	3.7	11.6	Oct/Nov	45	22.8	8.7	.413	3.8	.393	2.2	.804	0.24	0.76	1.7	3.2	10.4
vs. Playoff	184	26.4	9.6	.400	4.5	.366	1.9	.802	0.24	0.96	1.9	3.6	10.8	December	52	30.3	11.4	.429	5.2	.394	1.9	.802	0.27	1.02	2.4	4.5	13.4
vs. Non-Playoff	148	27.4	10.0	.434	5.1	.394	2.0	.830	0.36	0.97	2.5	3.8	12.4	January	52	26.9	9.9	.397	4.8	.345	2.0	.810	0.38	1.17	2.2	3.6	11.2
vs. East	113	26.9	10.0	.406	5.0	.369	1.9	.768	0.28	0.91	2.2	3.9	11.4	February	55	27.5	9.7	.431	4.7	.415	2.0	.768	0.40	0.98	2.1	3.8	11.9
vs. West	219	26.8	9.7	.421	4.7	.385	2.0	.838	0.31	1.00	2.2	3.6	11.6	March	77	25.2	9.0	.386	5.0	.354	1.7	.846	0.19	0.92	2.1	3.3	10.1
vs. Div.	98	25.9	9.3	.424	4.3	.395	2.1	.831	0.38	0.99	2.1	3.3	11.3	Apr/May	51	28.7	10.2	.443	4.9	.391	1.9	.859	0.33	0.94	2.6	3.8	12.6
As Starter	131	36.1	14.6	.423	7.3	.382	2.5	.822	0.40	1.47	2.9	4.7	17.2	0 Days Rest	76	26.9	9.2	.400	4.4	.356	2.3	.855	0.24	1.12	2.1	3.5	10.9
Off Bench	201	20.8	6.7	.405	3.2	.376	1.6	.808	0.23	0.64	1.7	3.0	7.9	1 Days Rest	162	27.4	10.3	.418	5.3	.386	1.9	.818	0.33	0.93	2.3	3.7	12.1
In wins	149	25.5	8.6	.447	4.1	.417	1.8	.831	0.33	0.93	2.2	3.6	10.9	2 Days Rest	57	26.8	10.2	.413	4.7	.368	1.9	.771	0.21	0.96	2.0	3.7	11.6
In losses	183	27.9	10.8	.395	5.3	.355	2.1	.804	0.27	0.99	2.2	3.8	12.1	3+ Days Rest	37	24.2	8.3	.440	3.5	.420	1.6	.767	0.41	0.81	2.4	3.7	10.0

Antonio McDyess

Denver Nuggets — Forward

1999-2000 Per Game Averages

	G	Min	FGA	FG%	3PA	3P%	FTA	FT%	Blk	Stl	Ast	Reb	Pts		G	Min	FGA	FG%	3PA	3P%	FTA	FT%	Blk	Stl	Ast	Reb	Pts
Total	81	33.3	15.0	.507	0.0	.000	6.4	.626	1.72	0.85	2.0	8.5	19.1	Pre All-Star	47	33.2	14.3	.511	0.0	.000	6.8	.623	1.91	1.00	2.3	8.5	18.9
Home	40	33.3	14.7	.499	0.0	.000	6.4	.591	2.00	1.03	2.3	8.1	18.5	Post All-Star	34	33.5	15.9	.502	0.0	.000	5.7	.631	1.44	0.65	1.5	8.4	19.6
Road	41	33.3	15.2	.514	0.0	.000	6.3	.660	1.44	0.68	1.7	8.8	19.8	November	13	34.0	13.7	.483	0.0	—	5.9	.649	2.08	1.00	2.3	7.5	17.1
vs. Playoff	47	34.8	15.5	.490	0.0	.000	6.3	.617	1.85	0.85	2.2	8.5	19.1	December	14	32.9	13.1	.505	0.0	—	7.1	.570	2.00	1.21	2.4	9.6	17.4
vs. Non-Playoff	34	31.3	14.2	.533	0.0	.000	6.4	.638	1.53	0.85	1.6	8.4	19.1	January	14	31.9	14.6	.541	0.1	.000	7.4	.615	1.79	0.64	1.9	8.1	20.4
vs. East	30	33.3	15.2	.495	0.0	—	6.9	.609	1.60	0.67	2.1	8.3	19.2	February	13	34.0	17.3	.502	0.0	—	5.5	.653	1.92	1.00	2.1	7.8	21.0
vs. West	51	33.2	14.8	.515	0.0	.000	6.1	.638	1.78	0.96	1.9	8.5	19.1	March	17	31.8	16.2	.509	0.0	—	5.9	.640	0.94	0.47	1.4	8.1	20.2
vs. Div.	24	32.5	14.1	.527	0.0	—	5.6	.600	1.75	0.71	1.6	7.8	18.2	April	10	36.6	14.4	.493	0.1	.000	6.3	.651	1.80	0.90	1.8	10.2	18.3
As Starter	81	33.3	15.0	.507	0.0	.000	6.4	.626	1.72	0.85	2.0	8.5	19.1	0 Days Rest	21	34.6	15.7	.524	0.0	.000	7.1	.660	1.33	0.81	1.9	9.2	21.2
Off Bench	0	—	—	—	—	—	—	—	—	—	—	—	—	1 Days Rest	38	32.7	14.4	.497	0.0	.000	6.1	.604	1.76	0.95	2.2	7.7	18.0
In wins	34	32.3	13.9	.528	0.0	—	5.9	.604	1.79	1.03	2.1	8.1	18.2	2 Days Rest	13	32.1	14.0	.505	0.0	—	6.8	.607	2.38	0.77	1.1	9.5	18.1
In losses	47	34.0	15.7	.494	0.0	.000	6.7	.640	1.66	0.72	1.8	8.7	19.8	3+ Days Rest	9	34.7	16.7	.507	0.0	—	5.2	.660	1.44	0.67	2.6	8.4	20.3

Career (1995-96 thru 1999-2000)

	G	Min	FGA	FG%	3PA	3P%	FTA	FT%	Blk	Stl	Ast	Reb	Pts		G	Min	FGA	FG%	3PA	3P%	FTA	FT%	Blk	Stl	Ast	Reb	Pts
Total	362	32.9	14.0	.492	0.1	.135	5.0	.675	1.74	0.99	1.5	8.1	17.2	Pre All-Star	174	31.0	12.4	.494	0.1	.111	4.7	.641	1.66	0.95	1.5	7.6	15.3
Home	181	32.3	13.6	.502	0.1	.000	5.0	.674	2.04	0.99	1.5	7.8	17.1	Post All-Star	138	33.2	14.6	.500	0.2	.160	4.8	.714	1.63	0.86	1.3	7.9	18.0
Road	181	33.6	14.3	.482	0.2	.212	5.0	.676	1.44	0.98	1.5	8.5	17.2	Oct/Nov	54	31.0	12.1	.465	0.1	.000	4.3	.674	1.70	0.87	1.5	7.5	14.1
vs. Playoff	208	33.7	14.2	.477	0.1	.034	4.8	.662	1.71	1.06	1.5	8.1	16.8	December	53	30.6	12.4	.498	0.2	.250	4.7	.594	1.79	1.08	1.5	7.5	16.2
vs. Non-Playoff	154	31.9	13.6	.514	0.1	.261	5.2	.692	1.77	0.89	1.4	8.2	17.7	January	51	31.1	12.4	.519	0.0	.000	5.1	.638	1.57	0.86	1.6	7.7	16.1
vs. East	119	31.9	13.4	.510	0.1	.125	4.8	.671	1.57	0.77	1.4	7.8	16.9	February	65	33.1	14.2	.491	0.1	.000	4.6	.709	1.91	1.18	1.6	8.4	17.2
vs. West	243	33.5	14.3	.484	0.2	.136	5.1	.677	1.82	1.09	1.5	8.3	17.3	March	79	33.9	15.2	.509	0.2	.286	5.5	.715	1.61	0.76	1.3	8.3	19.5
vs. Div.	113	32.9	14.1	.488	0.2	.167	4.9	.665	1.84	1.05	1.3	8.4	17.0	Apr/May	60	36.8	16.6	.470	0.3	.067	5.6	.682	1.85	1.22	1.5	9.1	19.4
As Starter	360	33.0	14.0	.492	0.1	.135	5.0	.676	1.74	0.99	1.5	8.1	17.2	0 Days Rest	87	33.9	14.4	.499	0.2	.286	5.5	.711	1.67	0.82	1.5	8.5	18.0
Off Bench	2	20.0	6.5	.385	0.0	—	2.5	.400	0.50	1.00	0.0	6.5	6.0	1 Days Rest	185	32.9	14.2	.489	0.1	.048	5.0	.660	1.76	1.01	1.5	7.7	17.2
In wins	155	32.0	12.9	.526	0.0	.000	4.8	.687	2.04	1.08	1.6	8.1	16.9	2 Days Rest	59	32.7	13.1	.474	0.1	.000	4.4	.664	1.61	1.05	1.3	8.9	15.4
In losses	207	33.6	14.8	.470	0.2	.152	5.1	.667	1.51	0.92	1.4	8.1	17.3	3+ Days Rest	31	30.9	12.8	.526	0.1	.000	4.6	.671	2.03	1.26	1.5	7.6	16.6

Tracy McGrady
Toronto Raptors — Guard-Forward

1999-2000 Per Game Averages

	G	Min	FGA	FG%	3PA	3P%	FTA	FT%	Blk	Stl	Ast	Reb	Pts
Total	79	31.2	12.9	.451	0.8	.277	5.0	.707	1.91	1.14	3.3	6.3	15.4
Home	39	30.5	12.9	.455	0.7	.192	5.4	.717	2.67	1.31	3.4	6.4	15.8
Road	40	31.8	12.8	.446	1.0	.333	4.5	.694	1.18	0.98	3.3	6.3	14.9
vs. Playoff	41	30.7	12.4	.458	0.7	.286	5.3	.691	1.71	1.10	3.1	6.0	15.2
vs. Non-Playoff	38	31.7	13.4	.444	1.0	.270	4.6	.726	2.13	1.18	3.6	6.7	15.5
vs. East	51	31.0	13.0	.466	1.0	.308	4.5	.703	1.82	1.00	3.4	6.3	15.7
vs. West	28	31.5	12.6	.422	0.5	.154	5.7	.713	2.07	1.39	3.2	6.4	14.8
vs. Div.	26	30.9	13.1	.466	1.1	.321	3.9	.733	1.88	1.31	3.7	6.3	15.4
As Starter	34	37.1	14.8	.435	1.2	.275	5.4	.751	2.03	1.21	4.3	8.1	17.3
Off Bench	45	26.7	11.4	.466	0.6	.280	4.6	.667	1.82	1.09	2.6	5.0	13.9
In wins	44	31.5	12.7	.467	0.6	.346	5.1	.699	2.11	1.39	3.5	6.4	15.7
In losses	35	30.7	13.1	.431	1.1	.231	4.7	.717	1.66	0.83	3.1	6.3	14.9
Pre All-Star	44	27.0	11.5	.469	0.7	.200	4.6	.676	1.91	1.00	2.8	5.1	14.1
Post All-Star	35	36.5	14.6	.432	1.0	.343	5.4	.739	1.91	1.31	4.0	7.9	16.9
November	14	24.0	10.1	.426	0.5	.143	4.1	.741	2.14	1.00	2.3	4.3	11.7
December	13	29.5	12.7	.461	0.8	.091	4.5	.672	1.85	0.69	3.3	6.2	14.8
January	14	26.5	11.1	.542	0.8	.273	4.8	.612	1.79	1.07	3.1	4.8	15.1
February	11	31.8	13.5	.399	0.5	.400	6.5	.722	1.64	1.73	2.5	6.8	15.6
March	17	38.3	14.6	.418	0.7	.333	5.5	.745	2.12	1.35	4.2	8.5	16.6
April	10	37.0	16.0	.475	1.9	.368	4.3	.744	1.80	1.00	4.4	7.4	19.1
0 Days Rest	16	30.2	12.1	.466	1.2	.368	4.3	.721	1.50	0.88	3.6	6.3	14.8
1 Days Rest	46	31.8	13.2	.444	0.8	.211	5.5	.709	1.93	1.24	3.4	6.6	15.7
2 Days Rest	8	31.3	12.4	.475	0.3	.500	4.8	.684	2.13	0.63	3.5	6.3	15.1
3+ Days Rest	9	29.6	13.3	.442	0.7	.333	3.9	.686	2.33	1.56	2.3	5.4	14.7

Career (1997-98 thru 1999-2000)

	G	Min	FGA	FG%	3PA	3P%	FTA	FT%	Blk	Stl	Ast	Reb	Pts
Total	192	24.7	9.4	.448	0.7	.284	3.4	.712	1.45	0.99	2.5	5.5	11.1
Home	95	24.5	9.4	.455	0.6	.203	3.9	.734	1.89	1.11	2.7	5.7	11.6
Road	97	24.9	9.3	.440	0.8	.341	3.0	.684	1.01	0.89	2.3	5.2	10.5
vs. Playoff	105	24.3	9.1	.450	0.6	.303	3.2	.677	1.32	0.94	2.4	5.3	10.5
vs. Non-Playoff	87	25.2	9.8	.445	0.9	.267	3.7	.749	1.60	1.06	2.6	5.7	11.7
vs. East	139	25.0	9.5	.459	0.8	.288	3.2	.715	1.43	0.95	2.5	5.6	11.3
vs. West	53	24.1	9.0	.415	0.6	.267	4.0	.706	1.49	1.11	2.3	5.1	10.5
vs. Div.	72	24.8	9.5	.452	0.8	.339	3.0	.746	1.39	1.10	2.7	5.4	11.1
As Starter	53	34.0	12.6	.446	1.1	.322	4.0	.771	1.89	1.15	3.7	7.6	14.7
Off Bench	139	21.2	8.2	.448	0.6	.256	3.2	.684	1.28	0.94	2.0	4.6	9.7
In wins	80	26.5	10.0	.445	0.6	.265	4.0	.714	1.68	1.31	3.0	5.9	11.9
In losses	112	23.5	8.9	.449	0.8	.293	3.1	.711	1.29	0.77	2.1	5.2	10.4
Pre All-Star	75	21.0	8.6	.461	0.5	.237	3.3	.681	1.32	0.83	2.1	4.1	10.3
Post All-Star	68	30.3	11.4	.442	1.0	.338	3.8	.733	1.66	1.13	3.0	6.8	13.1
Oct/Nov	21	19.8	7.9	.430	0.4	.125	3.0	.734	1.62	0.81	1.8	3.9	9.0
December	23	23.1	9.3	.458	0.7	.133	3.3	.688	1.30	0.70	2.2	4.7	10.9
January	25	19.9	8.0	.525	0.5	.385	3.3	.610	1.12	0.84	2.2	3.8	10.6
February	33	24.0	9.8	.415	0.5	.294	4.3	.746	1.18	1.12	2.2	5.2	11.5
March	48	27.2	9.7	.406	1.0	.283	3.5	.710	1.67	1.15	2.8	6.4	10.6
Apr/May	42	28.6	10.3	.481	1.0	.333	3.0	.746	1.60	1.07	3.0	6.8	12.5
0 Days Rest	47	24.7	9.2	.463	1.0	.283	2.6	.760	1.38	0.87	2.7	5.2	10.8
1 Days Rest	103	25.9	9.7	.450	0.7	.247	4.0	.707	1.57	1.13	2.6	5.9	11.7
2 Days Rest	19	23.8	9.5	.433	0.5	.444	3.6	.667	1.21	0.58	2.1	5.7	10.8
3+ Days Rest	23	20.1	8.1	.414	0.6	.385	2.7	.705	1.22	1.00	1.5	3.8	8.8

Aaron McKie
Philadelphia 76ers — Guard

1999-2000 Per Game Averages

	G	Min	FGA	FG%	3PA	3P%	FTA	FT%	Blk	Stl	Ast	Reb	Pts
Total	82	23.8	7.2	.411	1.5	.364	1.8	.829	0.22	1.32	2.9	3.0	8.0
Home	41	23.8	7.2	.439	1.5	.468	2.1	.839	0.27	1.24	2.8	3.1	8.8
Road	41	23.8	7.3	.385	1.4	.254	1.4	.814	0.17	1.39	3.1	2.9	7.1
vs. Playoff	42	22.7	6.9	.421	1.3	.357	1.4	.850	0.17	1.12	2.8	2.8	7.5
vs. Non-Playoff	40	25.0	7.6	.403	1.6	.369	2.2	.814	0.28	1.53	3.0	3.2	8.5
vs. East	54	24.9	7.8	.424	1.6	.368	2.0	.822	0.24	1.37	2.9	3.2	8.8
vs. West	28	21.6	6.2	.382	1.2	.353	1.4	.846	0.18	1.21	3.0	2.5	6.3
vs. Div.	24	25.3	8.1	.400	1.6	.462	1.6	.795	0.29	1.50	2.4	3.0	8.5
As Starter	14	33.2	11.7	.390	1.9	.259	2.4	.824	0.14	1.36	4.0	4.6	11.6
Off Bench	68	21.9	6.4	.400	1.4	.394	1.6	.830	0.24	1.31	2.7	2.7	7.2
In wins	49	24.6	7.2	.435	1.5	.419	2.1	.843	0.27	1.37	3.3	3.1	8.7
In losses	33	22.6	7.2	.377	1.4	.277	1.3	.795	0.15	1.24	2.4	2.8	6.9
Pre All-Star	49	24.7	8.0	.417	1.3	.292	2.1	.842	0.22	1.22	2.9	3.2	8.8
Post All-Star	33	22.5	6.1	.401	1.7	.446	1.4	.800	0.21	1.45	3.0	2.6	6.8
November	16	22.1	8.5	.397	1.2	.316	1.8	.857	0.13	1.00	2.4	3.1	8.6
December	16	28.4	9.8	.439	1.4	.217	2.3	.838	0.31	1.50	3.5	4.0	10.9
January	12	23.6	6.0	.417	1.3	.438	2.7	.813	0.33	1.17	2.4	2.8	7.8
February	12	21.8	5.2	.355	1.3	.375	0.7	1.000	0.00	1.17	3.2	2.8	4.8
March	16	24.8	7.6	.426	2.1	.529	1.4	.783	0.44	1.75	3.3	2.4	8.8
April	10	20.3	4.4	.386	1.3	.154	1.8	.778	0.00	1.20	2.6	2.7	5.0
0 Days Rest	20	24.6	7.5	.436	1.4	.321	1.9	.763	0.30	1.00	3.7	3.0	8.4
1 Days Rest	45	23.7	7.4	.417	1.4	.369	1.8	.861	0.24	1.51	2.7	3.1	8.2
2 Days Rest	9	23.2	6.8	.311	1.9	.294	0.9	1.000	0.00	0.78	3.0	3.0	5.7
3+ Days Rest	8	23.1	6.3	.420	1.4	.545	2.6	.762	0.13	1.63	2.3	2.5	8.0

Last Five Seasons

	G	Min	FGA	FG%	3PA	3P%	FTA	FT%	Blk	Stl	Ast	Reb	Pts
Total	377	22.8	6.1	.420	1.2	.324	1.5	.788	0.20	1.17	2.3	3.0	6.7
Home	187	22.4	5.9	.418	1.3	.355	1.6	.798	0.22	1.29	2.2	3.0	6.6
Road	190	23.3	6.3	.422	1.3	.298	1.5	.779	0.19	1.05	2.5	3.1	6.8
vs. Playoff	207	22.1	5.8	.427	1.1	.322	1.5	.774	0.16	1.06	2.3	2.7	6.5
vs. Non-Playoff	170	23.8	6.4	.412	1.2	.327	1.6	.805	0.25	1.31	2.4	3.4	6.9
vs. East	219	23.4	6.2	.421	1.1	.327	1.5	.794	0.21	1.24	2.4	3.1	6.7
vs. West	158	22.0	6.0	.418	1.2	.321	1.6	.781	0.20	1.08	2.3	2.9	6.6
vs. Div.	115	23.4	6.3	.425	1.2	.304	1.3	.737	0.22	1.24	2.3	3.1	6.6
As Starter	134	29.7	8.5	.429	1.4	.306	2.1	.769	0.26	1.35	3.1	4.0	9.4
Off Bench	243	19.1	4.8	.411	1.0	.339	1.2	.808	0.17	1.07	1.9	2.5	5.2
In wins	203	23.0	6.3	.436	1.1	.369	1.8	.794	0.25	1.32	2.5	3.3	7.3
In losses	174	22.6	5.9	.400	1.2	.272	1.2	.779	0.15	0.99	2.2	2.7	6.0
Pre All-Star	190	22.6	6.3	.417	1.1	.297	1.7	.798	0.25	1.01	2.2	3.0	7.0
Post All-Star	137	24.5	6.2	.430	1.4	.374	1.3	.799	0.19	1.36	2.7	3.1	6.9
Oct/Nov	63	23.0	6.7	.444	1.1	.347	1.9	.786	0.27	1.05	2.1	3.1	7.8
December	58	23.6	7.1	.406	1.3	.256	1.7	.816	0.22	1.00	2.4	3.3	7.5
January	55	21.1	5.4	.399	0.9	.333	1.6	.770	0.29	1.02	1.9	2.8	5.8
February	63	21.3	5.2	.422	0.8	.415	1.4	.813	0.17	1.00	2.3	2.9	5.9
March	76	24.2	6.2	.419	1.3	.388	1.0	.810	0.21	1.53	2.8	3.0	6.5
Apr/May	62	23.3	6.0	.424	1.4	.233	1.6	.740	0.32	1.25	2.5	3.1	6.6
0 Days Rest	96	22.3	5.6	.428	1.3	.298	1.3	.800	0.19	1.01	2.7	3.0	6.3
1 Days Rest	201	23.0	6.3	.422	1.1	.325	1.6	.804	0.21	1.22	2.3	3.0	7.0
2 Days Rest	51	22.9	6.2	.413	1.0	.327	1.4	.732	0.20	1.00	2.1	3.2	6.5
3+ Days Rest	29	23.4	5.8	.393	1.2	.412	1.9	.741	0.21	1.66	2.3	3.0	6.4

1999-2000 Per Game Averages

	G	Min	FGA	FG%	3PA	3P%	FTA	FT%	Blk	Stl	Ast	Reb	Pts		G	Min	FGA	FG%	3PA	3P%	FTA	FT%	Blk	Stl	Ast	Reb	Pts
Total	68	35.0	15.9	.426	0.7	.313	4.0	.789	0.34	1.10	2.3	3.7	16.9	Pre All-Star	40	37.2	16.4	.443	1.0	.375	3.9	.788	0.40	0.98	2.8	4.1	18.0
Home	42	35.7	16.2	.433	0.7	.333	4.2	.826	0.50	1.12	2.6	4.0	17.7	Post All-Star	28	31.8	15.2	.400	0.3	.000	4.1	.789	0.25	1.29	1.7	3.1	15.4
Road	26	33.7	15.4	.414	0.7	.278	3.5	.717	0.08	1.08	1.9	3.2	15.5	November	13	39.2	17.5	.452	1.7	.500	3.9	.804	0.38	1.00	1.9	4.2	19.8
vs. Playoff	43	36.3	16.0	.418	0.5	.238	3.8	.794	0.26	1.16	2.5	3.9	16.5	December	10	36.5	15.7	.433	0.8	.125	5.1	.784	0.30	1.10	2.1	4.5	17.7
vs. Non-Playoff	25	32.7	15.7	.440	1.1	.370	4.2	.781	0.48	1.00	2.0	3.4	17.5	January	14	38.1	16.2	.445	0.6	.333	3.5	.776	0.50	0.64	4.1	3.8	17.4
vs. East	33	33.6	15.7	.404	0.6	.368	3.8	.825	0.24	1.42	2.1	3.2	16.0	February	10	29.6	14.9	.396	0.4	.000	3.1	.710	0.50	1.00	2.2	3.7	14.0
vs. West	35	36.3	16.1	.446	0.8	.276	4.1	.757	0.43	0.80	2.6	4.2	17.7	March	12	31.0	15.4	.422	0.0	—	4.3	.824	0.08	1.00	1.3	2.7	16.5
vs. Div.	25	34.5	16.5	.448	1.0	.269	4.0	.747	0.40	1.20	1.9	3.6	18.0	April	9	33.4	14.9	.381	0.6	.000	4.1	.811	0.22	2.22	1.9	3.2	14.7
As Starter	68	35.0	15.9	.426	0.7	.313	4.0	.789	0.34	1.10	2.3	3.7	16.9	0 Days Rest	11	35.5	15.5	.456	0.8	.667	4.7	.750	0.18	0.91	1.6	3.8	18.3
Off Bench	0	—	—	—	—	—	—	—	—	—	—	—	—	1 Days Rest	36	35.9	17.0	.440	0.6	.318	4.2	.822	0.31	1.22	2.6	3.6	18.7
In wins	34	35.3	16.9	.445	0.7	.320	4.4	.820	0.47	1.15	2.5	3.7	18.9	2 Days Rest	8	32.6	14.3	.430	1.1	.111	3.6	.793	0.75	1.25	1.6	3.1	15.3
In losses	34	34.6	14.9	.404	0.7	.304	3.5	.750	0.21	1.04	2.1	3.7	14.9	3+ Days Rest	13	33.2	14.0	.346	0.6	.125	2.8	.703	0.31	0.85	2.5	4.0	11.8

Career (1997-98 thru 1999-2000)

	G	Min	FGA	FG%	3PA	3P%	FTA	FT%	Blk	Stl	Ast	Reb	Pts		G	Min	FGA	FG%	3PA	3P%	FTA	FT%	Blk	Stl	Ast	Reb	Pts
Total	189	34.9	15.5	.437	0.6	.217	3.2	.808	0.28	1.41	2.3	3.6	16.2	Pre All-Star	85	33.6	14.5	.439	0.7	.274	3.4	.787	0.31	1.12	2.3	3.6	15.6
Home	104	35.6	15.8	.441	0.6	.194	3.4	.817	0.38	1.29	2.3	3.9	16.8	Post All-Star	63	34.7	15.7	.437	0.2	.071	3.2	.847	0.22	1.67	2.1	3.6	16.5
Road	85	34.0	15.2	.431	0.5	.256	2.9	.796	0.15	1.56	2.3	3.3	15.5	Oct/Nov	28	34.6	14.5	.462	1.1	.433	3.6	.765	0.36	1.04	1.9	3.9	16.7
vs. Playoff	109	35.6	15.7	.420	0.4	.184	3.2	.810	0.23	1.41	2.3	3.8	15.9	December	22	30.8	14.0	.440	0.6	.071	3.5	.756	0.18	1.23	1.7	3.7	15.0
vs. Non-Playoff	80	33.9	15.2	.460	0.7	.246	3.2	.806	0.34	1.41	2.3	3.4	16.7	January	30	35.7	15.2	.426	0.5	.214	3.5	.837	0.33	1.07	3.2	3.2	15.9
vs. East	120	34.9	15.4	.430	0.6	.214	3.0	.823	0.21	1.58	2.3	3.4	15.8	February	28	32.4	15.3	.436	0.3	.000	3.0	.795	0.39	1.39	2.2	4.0	15.7
vs. West	69	34.8	15.8	.448	0.5	.222	3.5	.787	0.39	1.12	2.3	4.0	17.0	March	45	35.1	16.3	.439	0.3	.143	3.2	.842	0.20	1.58	2.4	3.2	17.0
vs. Div.	62	35.1	15.7	.441	0.8	.234	3.3	.810	0.26	1.65	2.2	3.5	16.7	Apr/May	36	38.6	16.7	.424	0.8	.148	2.4	.826	0.22	1.92	2.1	4.0	16.3
As Starter	170	35.7	15.7	.435	0.6	.227	3.2	.805	0.28	1.38	2.4	3.6	16.4	0 Days Rest	38	35.4	15.1	.429	0.8	.367	3.3	.786	0.11	1.26	2.3	3.4	15.8
Off Bench	19	27.7	13.7	.450	0.5	.111	2.9	.839	0.21	1.68	1.4	3.4	14.8	1 Days Rest	104	35.6	16.2	.447	0.5	.189	3.2	.833	0.31	1.63	2.4	3.7	17.2
In wins	83	34.3	15.7	.455	0.6	.220	3.4	.809	0.33	1.40	2.3	3.7	17.1	2 Days Rest	23	33.7	14.9	.453	0.6	.077	3.1	.803	0.39	1.30	2.2	3.3	16.0
In losses	106	35.3	15.4	.422	0.5	.214	3.0	.808	0.24	1.42	2.4	3.6	15.5	3+ Days Rest	24	32.1	13.9	.381	0.4	.100	2.8	.731	0.29	0.79	2.2	3.8	12.7

Andre Miller
Cleveland Cavaliers — Guard

1999-2000 Per Game Averages

	G	Min	FGA	FG%	3PA	3P%	FTA	FT%	Blk	Stl	Ast	Reb	Pts		G	Min	FGA	FG%	3PA	3P%	FTA	FT%	Blk	Stl	Ast	Reb	Pts
Total	82	25.5	9.2	.449	0.6	.204	3.6	.774	0.21	1.02	5.8	3.4	11.1	Pre All-Star	49	22.2	8.6	.443	0.6	.233	3.3	.769	0.12	0.92	4.6	2.9	10.2
Home	41	25.7	9.0	.450	0.5	.250	3.4	.827	0.24	0.88	6.7	3.7	11.0	Post All-Star	33	30.4	10.2	.457	0.6	.158	4.0	.780	0.33	1.18	7.5	4.2	12.5
Road	41	25.4	9.4	.448	0.7	.172	3.7	.725	0.17	1.17	4.9	3.1	11.3	November	13	19.3	7.5	.510	0.5	.167	2.6	.735	0.00	0.85	4.4	2.8	9.7
vs. Playoff	47	25.8	9.1	.465	0.6	.231	3.6	.790	0.23	0.91	5.6	3.2	11.4	December	16	21.0	7.6	.380	0.6	.300	3.0	.813	0.13	0.88	5.0	2.9	8.4
vs. Non-Playoff	35	25.2	9.3	.428	0.7	.174	3.6	.752	0.17	1.17	6.1	3.7	10.7	January	15	20.9	8.2	.488	0.4	.167	3.5	.755	0.20	0.73	3.3	2.3	10.7
vs. East	54	24.8	8.7	.445	0.6	.158	3.3	.797	0.19	1.02	5.9	3.2	10.5	February	12	38.4	13.9	.413	1.2	.357	4.8	.741	0.25	1.83	9.4	5.2	15.5
vs. West	28	27.0	10.1	.456	0.4	.364	4.1	.739	0.25	1.04	5.6	3.9	12.4	March	15	30.7	10.1	.457	0.7	.000	4.1	.738	0.40	1.40	7.4	4.2	12.2
vs. Div.	28	26.9	9.9	.450	0.8	.174	3.4	.830	0.14	1.04	6.4	3.2	11.9	April	11	24.6	8.6	.474	0.2	.000	3.5	.895	0.27	0.45	6.0	3.5	11.3
As Starter	36	31.5	10.7	.442	0.7	.125	4.2	.787	0.31	1.25	7.8	4.4	12.8	0 Days Rest	24	25.3	9.5	.428	0.5	.231	3.1	.703	0.13	1.08	5.5	3.3	10.5
Off Bench	46	20.8	8.0	.457	0.5	.280	3.1	.761	0.13	0.85	4.2	2.7	9.8	1 Days Rest	35	26.3	9.2	.474	0.6	.150	3.9	.796	0.26	1.00	5.5	3.5	11.9
In wins	32	24.0	8.2	.460	0.5	.200	3.5	.788	0.22	1.25	6.1	3.5	10.4	2 Days Rest	16	25.8	8.9	.455	0.8	.231	3.2	.784	0.31	1.06	7.1	3.6	10.8
In losses	50	26.5	9.9	.443	0.7	.206	3.6	.765	0.20	0.88	5.6	3.3	11.6	3+ Days Rest	7	22.0	8.9	.387	0.4	.333	4.3	.833	0.00	0.86	5.3	3.1	10.6

Reggie Miller

1999-2000 Per Game Averages

	G	Min	FGA	FG%	3PA	3P%	FTA	FT%	Blk	Stl	Ast	Reb	Pts
Total	81	36.9	12.9	.448	5.0	.408	5.0	.919	0.31	1.05	2.3	3.0	18.1
Home	41	37.3	13.1	.467	5.1	.418	4.8	.929	0.41	1.15	2.4	2.8	18.8
Road	40	36.4	12.6	.427	4.9	.398	5.3	.910	0.20	0.95	2.2	3.1	17.5
vs. Playoff	43	37.8	13.9	.443	5.3	.424	5.3	.912	0.30	1.00	2.0	3.3	19.3
vs. Non-Playoff	38	35.8	11.7	.454	4.6	.389	4.7	.928	0.32	1.11	2.6	2.6	16.8
vs. East	53	36.4	12.5	.467	4.9	.417	5.2	.916	0.28	0.91	2.4	2.8	18.4
vs. West	28	37.7	13.5	.414	5.2	.393	4.8	.925	0.36	1.32	2.2	3.3	17.6
vs. Div.	28	36.4	12.2	.471	5.3	.416	4.3	.908	0.25	0.93	2.6	3.2	17.6
As Starter	81	36.9	12.9	.448	5.0	.408	5.0	.919	0.31	1.05	2.3	3.0	18.1
Off Bench	0	—											
In wins	55	37.3	12.8	.482	5.1	.447	5.4	.923	0.36	1.20	2.4	2.9	19.6
In losses	26	35.9	12.9	.376	4.7	.320	4.2	.908	0.19	0.73	2.0	3.1	15.0

	G	Min	FGA	FG%	3PA	3P%	FTA	FT%	Blk	Stl	Ast	Reb	Pts
Pre All-Star	48	37.3	13.4	.448	5.1	.430	5.4	.935	0.35	1.08	2.3	2.9	19.3
Post All-Star	33	36.2	12.1	.447	4.8	.375	4.4	.890	0.24	1.00	2.3	3.1	16.5
November	15	34.1	11.9	.363	3.9	.390	6.7	.910	0.13	1.40	2.3	2.5	16.3
December	14	37.6	13.9	.513	6.4	.489	4.9	.928	0.43	1.21	3.1	2.6	22.0
January	14	40.1	14.7	.471	5.4	.373	4.4	.967	0.50	0.79	1.9	3.6	20.1
February	13	37.0	12.0	.449	4.1	.415	5.7	.919	0.23	0.77	2.2	3.0	17.7
March	16	36.7	13.2	.427	5.4	.391	4.6	.878	0.31	1.13	2.1	3.2	17.4
April	9	35.6	10.4	.468	4.4	.350	3.1	.929	0.22	0.89	2.3	2.8	14.2
0 Days Rest	20	39.0	12.9	.447	5.4	.421	5.7	.912	0.35	1.20	2.3	2.9	19.0
1 Days Rest	40	35.8	12.7	.457	4.9	.403	4.6	.923	0.28	0.95	2.1	3.0	17.8
2 Days Rest	15	36.1	12.1	.423	4.4	.424	3.9	.949	0.33	1.13	2.8	3.0	15.9
3+ Days Rest	6	39.2	15.7	.447	5.8	.371	8.3	.880	0.33	1.00	3.0	2.8	23.5

Last Five Seasons

	G	Min	FGA	FG%	3PA	3P%	FTA	FT%	Blk	Stl	Ast	Reb	Pts
Total	369	35.7	13.8	.457	5.4	.415	5.6	.885	0.22	0.95	2.7	3.0	19.9
Home	185	35.3	13.5	.473	5.2	.403	5.5	.898	0.21	1.04	3.0	3.0	19.9
Road	184	36.0	14.1	.441	5.7	.425	5.7	.873	0.21	0.86	2.4	3.0	19.8
vs. Playoff	195	36.4	14.4	.443	5.7	.414	5.8	.883	0.24	0.92	2.7	3.0	20.3
vs. Non-Playoff	174	34.8	13.2	.474	5.2	.415	5.4	.887	0.21	0.99	2.7	3.0	19.4
vs. East	253	35.8	13.9	.455	5.5	.408	5.8	.891	0.22	0.90	2.7	2.9	20.1
vs. West	116	35.3	13.6	.462	5.2	.430	5.1	.872	0.23	1.07	2.7	3.1	19.2
vs. Div.	128	35.3	13.4	.465	5.7	.420	5.6	.891	0.27	0.85	2.7	2.9	19.3
As Starter	369	35.7	13.8	.457	5.4	.415	5.6	.885	0.22	0.95	2.7	3.0	19.9
Off Bench	0	—											
In wins	233	35.5	13.5	.488	5.2	.439	5.7	.893	0.24	0.97	2.8	3.1	20.6
In losses	136	36.0	14.3	.406	5.8	.376	5.5	.872	0.21	0.92	2.5	2.8	18.6

	G	Min	FGA	FG%	3PA	3P%	FTA	FT%	Blk	Stl	Ast	Reb	Pts
Pre All-Star	184	35.4	13.8	.470	5.2	.433	5.9	.888	0.24	1.01	2.7	3.0	20.5
Post All-Star	135	35.9	14.1	.446	5.7	.402	5.4	.871	0.22	0.96	2.9	3.1	19.5
Oct/Nov	53	34.6	13.8	.452	4.8	.412	7.0	.895	0.25	1.15	2.8	3.0	20.7
December	59	35.3	13.6	.473	5.2	.461	5.4	.897	0.17	0.78	3.1	2.8	20.1
January	57	36.1	14.0	.495	5.5	.424	5.6	.871	0.30	1.14	2.2	3.3	21.0
February	66	35.8	13.7	.440	5.2	.396	5.8	.888	0.23	0.91	2.4	3.0	19.3
March	78	36.3	14.2	.447	5.9	.416	5.5	.875	0.21	0.94	3.0	2.7	20.0
Apr/May	56	35.5	13.6	.440	5.7	.381	4.4	.890	0.21	0.84	2.6	3.3	18.0
0 Days Rest	99	35.4	13.8	.459	5.6	.431	5.4	.885	0.18	0.85	2.5	2.9	19.9
1 Days Rest	183	35.6	13.7	.452	5.2	.395	5.6	.886	0.20	1.02	2.7	3.0	19.3
2 Days Rest	53	35.9	14.0	.445	5.0	.397	5.7	.877	0.42	1.00	2.8	3.1	19.4
3+ Days Rest	34	36.0	14.5	.495	6.5	.477	6.1	.894	0.21	0.82	2.9	3.2	22.9

Terry Mills

1999-2000 Per Game Averages

	G	Min	FGA	FG%	3PA	3P%	FTA	FT%	Blk	Stl	Ast	Reb	Pts
Total	82	22.5	6.0	.439	3.0	.393	0.4	.735	0.29	0.46	1.0	4.8	6.7
Home	41	21.4	5.7	.451	2.7	.432	0.2	.667	0.32	0.32	0.9	4.5	6.4
Road	41	23.5	6.2	.427	3.2	.359	0.6	.760	0.27	0.61	1.2	5.0	6.9
vs. Playoff	44	23.9	6.8	.426	3.6	.377	0.3	.733	0.27	0.57	1.1	5.1	7.4
vs. Non-Playoff	38	20.8	5.0	.458	2.2	.422	0.5	.737	0.32	0.34	1.0	4.4	5.9
vs. East	54	23.2	6.2	.437	3.0	.400	0.6	.733	0.26	0.41	1.1	4.7	7.0
vs. West	28	21.1	5.5	.442	2.9	.378	0.1	.750	0.36	0.57	0.9	4.9	6.1
vs. Div.	28	24.8	6.2	.468	3.3	.407	0.6	.778	0.32	0.46	1.0	5.0	7.6
As Starter	78	22.9	6.0	.448	3.0	.405	0.4	.767	0.29	0.47	1.0	4.8	6.9
Off Bench	4	13.8	4.8	.211	2.5	.100	1.0	.500	0.25	0.25	1.0	3.3	2.8
In wins	42	21.9	5.3	.471	2.6	.464	0.3	.692	0.33	0.31	0.9	4.5	6.4
In losses	40	23.1	6.6	.411	3.3	.333	0.5	.762	0.25	0.63	1.2	5.0	6.9

	G	Min	FGA	FG%	3PA	3P%	FTA	FT%	Blk	Stl	Ast	Reb	Pts
Pre All-Star	48	24.1	6.5	.430	3.2	.399	0.6	.704	0.40	0.48	1.1	4.9	7.3
Post All-Star	34	20.1	5.1	.454	2.6	.382	0.2	.857	0.15	0.44	0.9	4.5	5.8
November	15	20.7	6.3	.337	3.5	.327	0.8	.667	0.33	0.60	0.7	4.4	5.9
December	14	24.8	6.5	.462	3.4	.362	0.3	1.000	0.50	0.50	1.6	4.4	7.5
January	15	26.1	6.5	.442	2.3	.486	0.5	.571	0.33	0.47	1.1	5.8	7.1
February	12	25.3	6.6	.519	4.2	.480	0.4	.800	0.33	0.25	0.9	5.0	9.2
March	15	18.9	5.1	.442	2.5	.324	0.0	—	0.00	0.53	1.1	4.5	5.3
April	11	18.7	4.5	.449	1.9	.381	0.5	.833	0.27	0.36	0.9	4.3	5.2
0 Days Rest	20	21.5	5.8	.414	2.7	.407	0.4	.857	0.30	0.70	1.5	4.3	6.2
1 Days Rest	45	23.2	6.1	.443	3.3	.399	0.4	.765	0.40	0.38	0.9	5.2	7.0
2 Days Rest	8	22.4	5.1	.463	2.4	.368	0.5	.750	0.00	0.63	1.1	3.1	6.0
3+ Days Rest	9	21.1	6.4	.448	2.3	.333	0.7	.500	0.00	0.22	0.8	4.8	6.9

Last Five Seasons

	G	Min	FGA	FG%	3PA	3P%	FTA	FT%	Blk	Stl	Ast	Reb	Pts
Total	294	21.4	7.1	.430	3.2	.399	1.0	.777	0.27	0.46	1.1	4.3	8.1
Home	148	20.4	6.7	.454	2.9	.418	0.9	.793	0.27	0.47	1.1	4.1	8.0
Road	146	22.5	7.5	.408	3.5	.384	1.1	.764	0.27	0.45	1.1	4.6	8.3
vs. Playoff	154	22.1	7.4	.415	3.5	.389	1.0	.782	0.24	0.47	1.1	4.5	8.3
vs. Non-Playoff	140	20.7	6.7	.447	2.9	.413	1.1	.772	0.31	0.45	1.1	4.2	8.0
vs. East	196	21.6	7.1	.433	3.2	.413	1.0	.766	0.23	0.44	1.1	4.3	8.2
vs. West	98	21.1	7.1	.423	3.3	.373	1.0	.800	0.36	0.49	1.1	4.3	8.0
vs. Div.	100	22.3	7.0	.441	3.4	.418	1.2	.774	0.25	0.40	1.1	4.2	8.5
As Starter	88	23.3	6.5	.458	3.1	.405	0.5	.800	0.28	0.45	1.0	4.9	7.6
Off Bench	206	20.7	7.3	.419	3.3	.397	1.2	.773	0.27	0.46	1.1	4.1	8.4
In wins	171	21.9	7.3	.465	3.4	.430	1.0	.814	0.31	0.42	1.2	4.4	9.0
In losses	123	20.8	6.8	.377	3.0	.351	1.0	.723	0.22	0.51	1.0	4.3	6.9

	G	Min	FGA	FG%	3PA	3P%	FTA	FT%	Blk	Stl	Ast	Reb	Pts
Pre All-Star	175	21.5	7.0	.432	3.0	.416	1.1	.773	0.25	0.47	1.1	4.3	8.1
Post All-Star	118	21.3	7.2	.427	3.5	.377	0.9	.789	0.31	0.43	1.2	4.4	8.2
Oct/Nov	58	20.5	6.9	.397	2.8	.383	1.2	.779	0.28	0.53	1.4	3.7	7.9
December	58	21.2	6.4	.472	2.9	.437	0.8	.783	0.28	0.53	1.4	3.7	7.9
January	48	22.9	7.6	.418	3.2	.419	1.2	.741	0.21	0.42	1.0	4.8	8.6
February	38	22.9	7.8	.477	4.0	.437	1.1	.791	0.42	0.42	1.0	4.8	10.1
March	52	21.4	7.0	.380	3.3	.301	0.8	.814	0.27	0.38	1.2	4.4	7.0
Apr/May	40	20.2	7.1	.450	3.5	.433	1.0	.763	0.28	0.48	1.1	4.2	8.6
0 Days Rest	76	21.4	7.0	.420	3.1	.390	1.2	.714	0.20	0.47	1.2	4.2	8.2
1 Days Rest	132	21.8	7.1	.425	3.4	.395	0.9	.815	0.35	0.42	1.4	4.7	8.1
2 Days Rest	48	21.8	7.3	.443	3.3	.419	1.0	.760	0.27	0.58	0.8	3.7	8.6
3+ Days Rest	38	19.7	6.3	.450	2.9	.404	0.8	.839	0.16	0.39	0.8	4.1	7.5

1999-2000 Per Game Averages

	G	Min	FGA	FG%	3PA	3P%	FTA	FT%	Blk	Stl	Ast	Reb	Pts		G	Min	FGA	FG%	3PA	3P%	FTA	FT%	Blk	Stl	Ast	Reb	Pts
Total	66	18.6	5.7	.447	0.3	.435	1.4	.880	0.21	0.41	1.7	2.1	6.5	Pre All-Star	45	20.1	6.1	.444	0.3	.357	1.7	.867	0.24	0.44	2.1	2.4	7.
Home	33	18.8	5.7	.418	0.3	.455	1.4	.872	0.18	0.45	1.8	2.3	6.2	Post All-Star	21	15.3	4.8	.455	0.4	.556	0.8	.941	0.14	0.33	0.9	1.5	5.
Road	33	18.4	5.7	.476	0.4	.417	1.4	.889	0.24	0.36	1.6	1.9	6.8	November	10	9.4	2.8	.321	0.2	.000	0.6	.833	0.20	0.20	0.7	1.1	2.
vs. Playoff	34	18.7	5.5	.425	0.4	.250	1.4	.898	0.26	0.53	1.6	2.1	6.0	December	15	17.4	5.5	.446	0.1	.500	1.7	.808	0.13	0.27	1.1	2.0	6.
vs. Non-Playoff	32	18.4	5.9	.468	0.3	.636	1.3	.860	0.16	0.28	1.7	2.0	6.9	January	15	28.1	8.4	.444	0.5	.429	2.6	.897	0.33	0.67	3.6	3.3	10.
vs. East	25	18.0	5.7	.458	0.3	.625	1.6	.878	0.16	0.32	1.6	1.8	6.8	February	8	25.6	7.8	.532	0.5	.250	1.1	1.000	0.38	0.50	2.4	2.4	9.
vs. West	41	19.0	5.7	.440	1.2	.333	1.2	.882	0.24	0.46	1.7	2.2	6.2	March	9	9.3	3.6	.483	0.4	.333	0.4	1.000	0.00	0.25	0.0	0.9	4.
vs. Div.	20	20.6	6.4	.433	0.4	.250	1.4	.821	0.25	0.45	1.9	2.0	6.8	April	10	17.1	4.8	.396	0.5	.800	0.9	.889	0.20	0.50	1.4	2.2	5.
As Starter	24	27.3	8.2	.477	0.5	.364	2.1	.920	0.33	0.63	3.2	3.0	9.9	0 Days Rest	15	18.2	5.9	.443	0.3	.000	1.3	.950	0.27	0.33	1.5	1.9	6.
Off Bench	42	13.6	4.3	.413	0.3	.500	1.0	.833	0.14	0.29	0.8	1.6	4.5	1 Days Rest	40	19.4	5.8	.450	0.4	.533	1.5	.852	0.20	0.43	1.9	2.3	6.
In wins	39	19.2	6.0	.459	0.3	.692	1.6	.885	0.18	0.38	1.9	2.3	7.1	2 Days Rest	3	11.7	3.7	.364	0.3	1.000	0.7	1.000	0.33	0.00	1.0	1.0	3.
In losses	27	17.8	5.3	.427	0.4	.100	1.1	.871	0.26	0.44	1.4	1.8	5.6	3+ Days Rest	8	18.0	5.8	.457	0.4	.333	1.1	.889	0.13	0.63	1.1	2.0	6.

Last Five Seasons

	G	Min	FGA	FG%	3PA	3P%	FTA	FT%	Blk	Stl	Ast	Reb	Pts		G	Min	FGA	FG%	3PA	3P%	FTA	FT%	Blk	Stl	Ast	Reb	Pts
Total	357	25.2	8.2	.454	0.4	.265	3.2	.803	0.27	0.63	1.3	3.8	10.1	Pre All-Star	184	24.7	7.3	.461	0.3	.212	3.3	.814	0.27	0.65	1.4	3.7	9.
Home	178	25.5	8.5	.457	0.5	.229	3.3	.821	0.30	0.64	1.6	4.0	10.6	Post All-Star	123	25.3	8.5	.467	0.5	.333	2.9	.802	0.26	0.59	1.0	4.1	10.
Road	179	24.9	7.8	.450	0.4	.313	3.1	.783	0.25	0.63	1.1	3.7	9.5	Oct/Nov	52	21.8	6.7	.450	0.2	.083	2.8	.784	0.29	0.54	1.1	3.2	8.
vs. Playoff	195	24.7	8.0	.451	0.5	.236	3.0	.798	0.28	0.61	1.4	3.7	9.7	December	59	24.3	7.2	.439	0.4	.286	3.4	.822	0.25	0.69	1.2	3.8	9.
vs. Non-Playoff	162	25.8	8.4	.457	0.4	.310	3.4	.808	0.27	0.67	1.2	4.1	10.5	January	58	27.3	8.0	.481	0.2	.214	3.7	.830	0.26	0.71	1.6	4.1	10.
vs. East	118	25.0	7.5	.458	0.4	.213	3.4	.812	0.22	0.56	1.3	3.6	9.7	February	59	24.6	8.0	.454	0.4	.208	3.1	.772	0.24	0.53	1.4	3.7	9
vs. West	239	25.3	8.5	.452	0.4	.290	3.1	.798	0.30	0.67	1.3	3.9	10.2	March	69	25.7	9.3	.432	0.5	.235	3.2	.789	0.28	0.61	1.0	4.1	10.
vs. Div.	111	25.6	8.7	.473	0.5	.288	3.1	.797	0.36	0.56	1.3	3.8	10.8	Apr/May	60	27.1	9.5	.468	0.7	.381	2.9	.813	0.33	0.72	1.6	4.1	11.
As Starter	124	31.7	10.4	.469	0.5	.350	3.7	.820	0.40	0.82	2.0	4.7	12.9	0 Days Rest	85	25.2	8.2	.453	0.4	.344	3.1	.785	0.24	0.59	1.2	3.6	10.
Off Bench	233	21.7	7.0	.442	0.4	.207	2.9	.791	0.21	0.53	1.0	3.4	8.6	1 Days Rest	196	25.5	8.4	.458	0.4	.235	3.2	.805	0.29	0.60	1.4	3.9	10.
In wins	172	25.0	8.5	.472	0.4	.296	3.4	.802	0.27	0.68	1.5	3.8	10.9	2 Days Rest	46	24.9	8.2	.451	0.4	.211	3.3	.831	0.30	0.78	1.3	4.2	10.
In losses	185	25.4	7.9	.435	0.4	.237	3.0	.803	0.28	0.59	1.2	3.9	9.3	3+ Days Rest	30	23.8	6.8	.429	0.4	.364	3.3	.788	0.27	0.77	0.9	3.5	8.

1999-2000 Per Game Averages

	G	Min	FGA	FG%	3PA	3P%	FTA	FT%	Blk	Stl	Ast	Reb	Pts		G	Min	FGA	FG%	3PA	3P%	FTA	FT%	Blk	Stl	Ast	Reb	Pt
Total	81	30.8	12.5	.430	3.6	.356	4.4	.847	0.40	1.07	2.6	3.6	15.8	Pre All-Star	50	30.9	11.9	.410	3.5	.333	4.2	.837	0.30	1.20	2.7	3.1	14.
Home	41	31.0	12.5	.447	3.8	.364	4.2	.832	0.44	0.95	2.7	3.7	16.1	Post All-Star	31	30.7	13.6	.459	3.7	.391	4.7	.862	0.55	0.87	2.4	4.3	18.
Road	40	30.6	12.6	.412	3.5	.348	4.5	.861	0.35	1.20	2.5	3.4	15.4	November	15	32.1	11.5	.382	3.7	.327	3.7	.857	0.33	1.27	2.9	2.9	13.
vs. Playoff	47	31.8	12.4	.405	4.0	.353	4.1	.870	0.43	1.00	2.5	3.3	15.0	December	15	32.1	12.7	.411	2.5	.368	5.4	.827	0.47	1.73	3.2	3.3	15.
vs. Non-Playoff	34	29.5	12.7	.464	3.1	.362	4.7	.820	0.35	1.18	2.7	3.9	16.8	January	14	29.3	11.4	.428	4.5	.349	3.3	.804	0.07	0.71	2.1	3.0	13
vs. East	30	31.2	13.0	.437	3.5	.385	4.3	.854	0.30	1.03	2.6	3.5	16.4	February	13	29.8	13.1	.441	4.1	.358	4.5	.897	0.46	0.92	2.0	3.3	17
vs. West	51	30.6	12.3	.426	3.7	.340	4.4	.843	0.45	1.10	2.5	3.6	15.4	March	14	29.5	12.8	.441	3.6	.340	4.1	.842	0.21	1.21	2.7	4.2	15.
vs. Div.	23	29.0	11.1	.426	3.0	.300	3.8	.807	0.48	0.91	1.6	3.0	13.5	April	10	32.2	14.5	.490	3.3	.424	5.5	.855	1.00	0.30	2.2	5.0	20.
As Starter	8	30.0	16.0	.375	4.4	.314	3.4	.889	0.38	1.38	3.6	4.9	16.4	0 Days Rest	17	29.5	12.0	.387	2.9	.280	4.0	.809	0.18	1.24	2.1	3.4	13
Off Bench	73	29.9	12.2	.438	3.5	.362	4.5	.844	0.40	1.04	2.5	3.4	15.7	1 Days Rest	43	29.7	12.0	.439	3.6	.357	4.6	.838	0.49	0.91	2.9	3.3	15
In wins	34	29.4	12.2	.455	3.4	.377	5.1	.833	0.50	1.06	2.9	3.6	16.6	2 Days Rest	17	34.3	14.5	.462	4.1	.435	4.4	.840	0.29	1.41	2.2	4.0	18
In losses	47	31.8	12.8	.413	3.8	.343	3.8	.860	0.32	1.09	2.3	3.6	15.1	3+ Days Rest	4	33.0	12.0	.354	4.8	.263	3.3	.923	0.75	0.75	2.3	4.0	12

Career (1998-99 thru 1999-2000)

	G	Min	FGA	FG%	3PA	3P%	FTA	FT%	Blk	Stl	Ast	Reb	Pts		G	Min	FGA	FG%	3PA	3P%	FTA	FT%	Blk	Stl	Ast	Reb	Pt
Total	130	30.4	10.9	.429	3.4	.357	3.6	.840	0.42	1.01	2.5	3.1	13.6	Pre All-Star	50	30.9	11.9	.410	3.5	.333	4.2	.837	0.30	1.20	2.7	3.1	14.
Home	66	30.9	11.1	.443	3.7	.359	3.5	.813	0.44	1.00	2.8	3.3	14.0	Post All-Star	31	30.7	13.6	.459	3.7	.391	4.7	.862	0.55	0.87	2.4	4.3	18
Road	64	29.9	10.8	.414	3.0	.354	3.6	.867	0.41	1.02	2.1	2.9	13.1	Oct/Nov	15	32.1	11.5	.382	3.7	.327	3.7	.857	0.33	1.27	2.9	2.9	13
vs. Playoff	71	30.5	10.7	.402	3.5	.347	3.3	.844	0.42	0.99	2.4	2.8	12.7	December	15	32.1	12.7	.411	2.5	.368	5.4	.827	0.47	1.73	3.2	3.3	15
vs. Non-Playoff	59	30.3	11.2	.459	3.3	.369	3.8	.836	0.42	1.03	2.7	3.4	14.7	January	14	29.3	11.4	.428	4.5	.349	3.3	.804	0.07	0.71	2.1	3.0	13
vs. East	36	30.6	12.3	.443	3.4	.411	3.9	.849	0.36	1.00	2.6	3.3	15.6	February	26	27.5	10.2	.424	3.0	.397	3.6	.894	0.38	0.73	1.8	2.5	13
vs. West	94	30.3	10.4	.422	3.4	.335	3.4	.836	0.45	1.01	2.5	3.0	12.8	March	31	30.5	10.1	.454	3.3	.350	3.2	.816	0.42	1.16	2.8	3.4	12
vs. Div.	44	30.0	9.8	.430	2.9	.302	3.2	.817	0.52	0.89	2.0	2.7	11.9	Apr/May	29	31.7	11.1	.444	3.6	.350	3.0	.830	0.66	0.72	2.6	3.2	13
As Starter	45	33.1	10.2	.417	3.6	.337	2.4	.830	0.49	0.98	3.0	2.9	11.7	0 Days Rest	33	29.5	10.2	.403	3.2	.346	3.1	.825	0.33	1.06	2.4	2.6	11
Off Bench	85	29.0	11.3	.434	3.3	.368	4.2	.843	0.39	1.02	2.3	3.1	14.6	1 Days Rest	69	29.9	10.7	.435	3.3	.342	3.8	.839	0.49	0.96	2.8	3.1	13
In wins	65	29.9	10.4	.455	3.3	.384	3.9	.831	0.46	1.02	2.8	3.1	14.0	2 Days Rest	22	33.2	13.1	.451	3.8	.410	3.8	.843	0.27	1.14	2.1	3.7	16
In losses	65	30.9	11.5	.405	3.4	.330	3.2	.851	0.38	1.00	2.2	3.0	13.2	3+ Days Rest	6	31.3	10.3	.387	3.7	.364	2.7	.938	0.67	0.83	1.8	3.0	11

Alonzo Mourning

1999-2000 Per Game Averages

	G	Min	FGA	FG%	3PA	3P%	FTA	FT%	Blk	Stl	Ast	Reb	Pts		G	Min	FGA	FG%	3PA	3P%	FTA	FT%	Blk	Stl	Ast	Reb	Pts
Total	79	34.8	15.0	.551	0.1	.000	7.4	.711	3.72	0.51	1.6	9.5	21.7	Pre All-Star	47	35.9	16.1	.543	0.1	.000	7.3	.710	4.04	0.40	1.6	9.6	22.7
Home	39	34.3	15.2	.553	0.1	.000	7.4	.717	3.97	0.56	1.5	9.9	22.2	Post All-Star	32	33.2	13.4	.564	0.0	.000	7.4	.713	3.25	0.66	1.6	9.4	20.4
Road	40	35.3	14.8	.548	0.1	.000	7.3	.705	3.48	0.45	1.6	9.2	21.4	November	14	36.4	16.5	.571	0.0	—	5.8	.654	3.29	0.36	1.4	9.9	22.6
vs. Playoff	40	36.2	15.4	.557	0.1	.000	7.3	.697	3.23	0.68	1.8	9.9	22.2	December	14	37.9	17.4	.533	0.2	.000	7.6	.698	5.29	0.57	1.8	10.5	23.9
vs. Non-Playoff	39	33.3	14.6	.544	0.0	.000	7.5	.726	4.23	0.33	1.4	9.1	21.3	January	15	33.9	15.3	.533	0.0	—	8.1	.711	4.00	0.20	1.6	8.9	22.0
vs. East	53	34.9	14.5	.560	0.1	.000	7.2	.704	3.62	0.51	1.6	9.5	21.4	February	12	35.4	14.0	.512	0.0	—	8.5	.814	3.83	0.42	1.3	9.2	21.3
vs. West	26	34.6	15.9	.533	0.0	—	7.7	.725	3.92	0.50	1.5	9.7	22.5	March	13	34.2	13.7	.562	0.0	—	8.8	.702	2.85	1.00	1.8	10.0	21.5
vs. Div.	23	36.2	15.0	.578	0.1	.000	8.2	.735	3.91	0.43	1.5	9.2	23.3	April	11	29.9	12.2	.612	0.1	.000	5.3	.655	2.82	0.55	1.4	8.5	18.4
As Starter	78	34.8	15.0	.548	0.1	.000	7.3	.712	3.74	0.50	1.5	9.6	21.7	0 Days Rest	17	35.5	14.9	.538	0.1	.000	6.4	.798	3.53	0.29	2.1	9.9	21.1
Off Bench	1	32.0	13.0	.769	0.0	—	12.0	.667	2.00	1.00	3.0	5.0	21.0	1 Days Rest	43	34.5	14.5	.558	0.0	.000	7.6	.689	3.74	0.65	1.4	9.4	21.3
In wins	50	34.3	15.1	.569	0.0	.000	7.2	.721	4.06	0.50	1.6	9.5	22.4	2 Days Rest	12	34.2	15.8	.582	0.0	—	7.1	.694	3.42	0.50	1.1	8.8	23.3
In losses	29	35.7	14.8	.519	0.1	.000	7.6	.695	3.14	0.52	1.4	9.7	20.7	3+ Days Rest	7	35.9	17.1	.492	0.1	.000	9.0	.698	4.57	0.14	2.0	10.3	23.1

Last Five Seasons

	G	Min	FGA	FG%	3PA	3P%	FTA	FT%	Blk	Stl	Ast	Reb	Pts		G	Min	FGA	FG%	3PA	3P%	FTA	FT%	Blk	Stl	Ast	Reb	Pts
Total	319	35.8	14.1	.535	0.1	.222	8.6	.673	3.08	0.75	1.6	10.0	21.0	Pre All-Star	154	35.5	14.7	.524	0.2	.237	8.4	.687	3.24	0.68	1.5	9.8	21.2
Home	157	35.8	14.5	.537	0.1	.190	8.6	.666	3.22	0.85	1.5	10.2	21.2	Post All-Star	119	35.4	13.5	.562	0.0	.200	8.7	.666	2.55	0.86	1.7	9.9	21.0
Road	162	35.9	13.8	.534	0.1	.250	8.7	.681	2.94	0.66	1.7	9.8	20.7	Oct/Nov	42	36.0	15.0	.541	0.3	.462	7.6	.692	3.05	0.62	1.5	9.8	21.7
vs. Playoff	167	35.9	13.9	.516	0.1	.350	8.4	.666	2.69	0.73	1.6	9.7	20.0	December	39	35.6	14.9	.511	0.2	.000	7.9	.669	3.67	0.67	1.8	10.6	20.5
vs. Non-Playoff	152	35.8	14.4	.556	0.2	.120	8.9	.681	3.51	0.78	1.6	10.4	22.1	January	58	34.9	14.6	.511	0.2	.214	9.0	.673	3.21	0.71	1.4	9.3	21.1
vs. East	223	36.4	14.1	.538	0.1	.240	8.6	.678	3.13	0.74	1.6	10.3	21.1	February	62	36.9	14.3	.524	0.1	.000	9.1	.702	3.23	0.79	1.4	10.2	21.4
vs. West	96	34.6	14.2	.530	0.2	.200	8.5	.662	2.95	0.79	1.5	9.5	20.8	March	61	35.8	13.7	.560	0.0	.000	9.1	.632	2.64	0.87	1.7	10.4	21.1
vs. Div.	98	37.2	15.0	.524	0.1	.200	9.0	.698	3.33	0.63	1.5	10.3	22.0	Apr/May	57	35.6	12.7	.563	0.1	.250	8.3	.679	2.88	0.79	1.9	10.0	20.0
As Starter	315	35.9	14.2	.534	0.1	.222	8.6	.675	3.09	0.75	1.6	10.1	21.2	0 Days Rest	73	35.7	13.4	.532	0.1	.333	8.2	.712	3.08	0.58	1.6	10.1	20.2
Off Bench	4	31.8	12.3	.633	0.0	—	10.0	.575	2.50	0.75	2.3	8.8	21.3	1 Days Rest	171	35.9	14.2	.537	0.1	.273	8.6	.663	3.01	0.86	1.7	10.2	21.0
In wins	209	35.7	14.0	.550	0.1	.167	8.5	.684	3.18	0.79	1.6	10.0	21.2	2 Days Rest	47	35.3	14.2	.541	0.1	.167	8.0	.676	2.89	0.81	1.3	9.4	20.7
In losses	110	36.2	14.5	.509	0.1	.333	8.9	.654	2.88	0.67	1.6	10.1	20.6	3+ Days Rest	28	36.9	15.5	.524	0.3	.000	10.8	.646	3.82	0.46	1.5	9.9	23.2

Lamond Murray

1999-2000 Per Game Averages

	G	Min	FGA	FG%	3PA	3P%	FTA	FT%	Blk	Stl	Ast	Reb	Pts		G	Min	FGA	FG%	3PA	3P%	FTA	FT%	Blk	Stl	Ast	Reb	Pts
Total	74	32.0	13.8	.451	1.9	.367	3.6	.761	0.49	1.42	1.8	5.7	15.9	Pre All-Star	41	31.0	13.0	.461	1.7	.333	3.4	.738	0.46	1.49	1.6	5.6	15.0
Home	36	33.0	14.0	.459	1.7	.419	3.9	.766	0.61	1.53	2.1	6.1	16.6	Post All-Star	33	33.1	14.8	.441	2.1	.400	3.8	.787	0.52	1.33	2.0	5.8	16.9
Road	38	31.0	13.5	.444	2.0	.325	3.3	.756	0.37	1.32	1.5	5.4	15.2	November	6	26.5	9.0	.519	1.0	.667	2.7	.813	0.67	1.17	2.0	5.7	12.2
vs. Playoff	43	32.1	14.0	.444	2.0	.357	3.3	.745	0.35	1.40	1.6	5.8	15.6	December	15	29.5	12.3	.405	1.3	.300	2.7	.756	0.47	1.60	1.6	5.1	12.5
vs. Non-Playoff	31	31.7	13.5	.462	1.8	.382	4.1	.780	0.68	1.45	2.1	5.6	16.3	January	15	33.5	14.1	.488	2.3	.265	5.2	.718	0.47	1.60	1.5	6.3	18.1
vs. East	47	31.0	13.6	.446	1.8	.400	3.2	.750	0.38	1.30	1.6	5.6	15.3	February	12	36.5	16.3	.474	2.3	.444	3.7	.864	0.42	1.50	2.2	6.7	19.7
vs. West	27	33.7	14.0	.460	2.0	.315	4.3	.776	0.67	1.63	2.1	5.9	16.9	March	15	32.7	13.9	.423	1.7	.346	4.4	.773	0.47	1.20	1.5	5.1	15.7
vs. Div.	26	30.8	14.6	.425	1.8	.362	3.2	.750	0.42	1.58	1.4	5.7	15.6	April	11	30.4	15.0	.442	2.4	.423	2.1	.652	0.55	1.27	2.3	5.5	15.6
As Starter	72	32.4	14.0	.451	1.9	.370	3.7	.761	0.49	1.44	1.8	5.8	16.2	0 Days Rest	21	30.6	12.7	.429	1.7	.444	3.7	.731	0.62	1.48	1.4	6.0	14.3
Off Bench	2	15.5	5.5	.455	0.5	.000	0.0	—	0.50	0.50	0.0	1.5	5.0	1 Days Rest	31	32.4	13.8	.452	2.0	.274	3.6	.786	0.45	1.35	1.9	5.5	15.9
In wins	27	32.6	14.2	.464	2.0	.455	5.0	.761	0.52	1.44	2.4	5.9	17.9	2 Days Rest	17	33.5	15.2	.471	1.9	.455	3.8	.703	0.41	1.41	2.1	5.4	17.9
In losses	47	31.6	13.5	.444	1.8	.310	2.9	.761	0.47	1.40	1.4	5.6	14.7	3+ Days Rest	5	29.6	13.0	.462	1.6	.375	2.8	1.000	0.40	1.60	1.6	6.8	15.4

Last Five Seasons

	G	Min	FGA	FG%	3PA	3P%	FTA	FT%	Blk	Stl	Ast	Reb	Pts		G	Min	FGA	FG%	3PA	3P%	FTA	FT%	Blk	Stl	Ast	Reb	Pts
Total	354	26.5	10.1	.445	1.7	.344	3.0	.758	0.46	1.12	1.3	4.5	11.9	Pre All-Star	174	27.6	10.0	.455	1.5	.327	2.8	.735	0.49	1.05	1.4	4.5	11.7
Home	177	26.4	9.8	.442	1.5	.332	2.8	.738	0.49	1.02	1.3	4.4	11.2	Post All-Star	130	25.0	9.8	.455	1.8	.369	3.2	.769	0.45	1.19	1.3	4.5	12.0
Road	177	26.6	10.5	.447	1.9	.353	3.2	.776	0.44	1.21	1.4	4.5	12.5	Oct/Nov	52	27.1	10.1	.484	1.4	.360	2.5	.750	0.56	1.00	1.6	4.8	12.2
vs. Playoff	203	26.6	10.1	.441	1.7	.342	2.9	.762	0.49	1.11	1.3	4.5	11.7	December	55	28.3	9.7	.431	1.5	.354	2.9	.730	0.47	1.16	1.5	4.2	11.0
vs. Non-Playoff	151	26.4	10.2	.449	1.7	.346	3.2	.753	0.43	1.12	1.4	4.4	12.1	January	53	28.6	10.5	.457	1.6	.264	3.5	.721	0.51	1.09	1.3	5.1	12.5
vs. East	137	27.4	10.5	.450	1.7	.348	2.8	.753	0.49	1.04	1.3	4.5	12.1	February	60	27.2	10.7	.431	1.8	.390	3.1	.766	0.45	1.03	1.3	4.8	12.3
vs. West	217	25.9	9.9	.441	1.7	.341	3.1	.761	0.45	1.16	1.4	4.4	11.7	March	76	24.0	9.5	.437	1.7	.356	3.1	.760	0.38	1.20	1.1	3.8	11.3
vs. Div.	112	27.0	11.1	.440	1.8	.356	3.2	.744	0.49	1.36	1.4	4.6	12.7	Apr/May	58	24.7	10.5	.435	2.1	.331	2.9	.819	0.45	1.17	1.3	4.4	12.2
As Starter	183	33.5	13.0	.456	2.0	.366	3.6	.753	0.55	1.47	1.8	5.7	15.3	0 Days Rest	94	24.9	10.0	.452	1.7	.372	3.1	.743	0.43	1.07	1.2	4.7	11.9
Off Bench	171	19.0	7.1	.423	1.4	.309	2.4	.766	0.37	0.74	0.9	3.2	8.2	1 Days Rest	166	27.8	10.3	.446	1.8	.341	3.1	.782	0.49	1.12	1.6	4.3	12.2
In wins	111	25.4	9.6	.469	1.6	.412	3.2	.761	0.38	1.02	1.5	4.2	12.1	2 Days Rest	56	28.4	11.5	.452	1.7	.330	3.2	.718	0.52	1.20	1.3	4.8	13.2
In losses	243	27.0	10.4	.434	1.7	.314	2.9	.757	0.50	1.16	1.3	4.6	11.8	3+ Days Rest	38	22.0	8.0	.398	1.2	.298	2.2	.750	0.37	1.08	0.8	4.1	8.4

Tracy Murray
Washington Wizards — Forward

1999-2000 Per Game Averages

	G	Min	FGA	FG%	3PA	3P%	FTA	FT%	Blk	Stl	Ast	Reb	Pts
Total	80	22.9	8.4	.433	3.3	.430	1.8	.851	0.30	0.56	0.9	3.4	10.2
Home	40	23.6	7.8	.410	3.0	.412	1.8	.918	0.35	0.58	0.9	3.5	9.3
Road	40	22.2	9.0	.453	3.6	.444	1.7	.779	0.25	0.55	0.9	3.3	11.0
vs. Playoff	45	23.7	8.5	.448	3.2	.396	1.8	.848	0.31	0.62	0.8	3.2	10.4
vs. Non-Playoff	35	21.8	8.2	.413	3.4	.471	1.8	.855	0.29	0.49	1.1	3.6	9.9
vs. East	52	22.8	8.2	.461	3.3	.480	1.9	.887	0.29	0.56	0.9	3.5	10.8
vs. West	28	23.1	8.7	.383	3.3	.337	1.6	.773	0.32	0.57	0.9	3.3	9.0
vs. Div.	22	21.9	7.9	.431	3.5	.487	2.1	.891	0.32	0.50	0.8	3.8	10.4
As Starter	8	34.8	9.4	.480	4.4	.371	2.3	.889	0.13	0.88	1.9	4.4	12.6
Off Bench	72	21.6	8.3	.427	3.2	.439	1.7	.846	0.32	0.53	0.8	3.3	9.9
In wins	28	21.6	7.9	.459	2.8	.429	1.5	.857	0.21	0.57	0.7	2.8	9.8
In losses	52	23.6	8.6	.420	3.6	.430	1.9	.848	0.35	0.56	1.0	3.7	10.6
Pre All-Star	49	21.4	8.2	.425	3.2	.397	1.7	.819	0.33	0.49	0.9	2.9	9.6
Post All-Star	31	25.2	8.6	.444	3.5	.477	1.9	.897	0.26	0.68	0.9	4.1	11.0
November	15	17.5	7.6	.386	2.7	.300	0.9	.857	0.20	0.33	0.5	3.1	7.5
December	15	18.1	7.5	.402	3.1	.413	2.1	.742	0.47	0.40	0.7	2.3	8.8
January	14	24.5	9.2	.457	3.4	.447	2.0	.857	0.36	0.79	1.2	3.1	11.6
February	12	31.7	10.3	.463	4.8	.474	1.7	.900	0.17	0.50	1.3	4.8	13.3
March	17	26.0	8.5	.428	3.4	.439	2.2	.892	0.35	0.82	1.1	3.9	10.7
April	7	18.9	6.7	.489	2.3	.563	1.6	.909	0.14	0.43	0.7	3.4	9.3
0 Days Rest	22	23.0	9.0	.487	3.5	.447	1.9	.769	0.32	0.77	0.9	3.2	11.7
1 Days Rest	37	23.6	8.2	.426	3.2	.453	1.9	.870	0.38	0.43	0.8	3.7	10.1
2 Days Rest	13	19.9	7.3	.347	3.0	.308	1.5	.950	0.15	0.54	1.0	2.5	7.5
3+ Days Rest	8	24.4	8.9	.423	3.9	.452	1.6	.846	0.13	0.63	1.3	4.1	10.6

Last Five Seasons

	G	Min	FGA	FG%	3PA	3P%	FTA	FT%	Blk	Stl	Ast	Reb	Pts
Total	362	24.8	10.2	.436	3.9	.393	2.1	.846	0.31	0.80	1.1	3.4	12.2
Home	182	25.0	10.2	.432	4.0	.405	2.1	.866	0.32	0.74	1.1	3.4	12.3
Road	180	24.7	10.1	.440	3.9	.381	2.1	.826	0.31	0.86	1.1	3.4	12.2
vs. Playoff	202	24.5	9.8	.433	3.7	.386	2.1	.835	0.27	0.77	1.0	3.3	11.7
vs. Non-Playoff	160	25.2	10.6	.439	4.3	.401	2.1	.860	0.38	0.83	1.2	3.5	12.9
vs. East	244	24.4	9.7	.433	3.8	.392	2.1	.857	0.30	0.75	1.1	3.4	11.7
vs. West	118	25.6	11.2	.441	4.2	.395	2.2	.823	0.36	0.91	1.1	3.5	13.3
vs. Div.	110	24.8	10.0	.434	4.0	.391	2.3	.883	0.29	0.79	1.0	3.6	12.3
As Starter	58	36.1	15.2	.463	5.3	.427	2.7	.866	0.38	1.26	1.6	5.1	18.6
Off Bench	304	22.7	9.2	.427	3.7	.384	2.0	.841	0.30	0.71	1.0	3.1	11.0
In wins	149	24.0	9.9	.463	3.9	.420	2.1	.844	0.26	0.79	1.1	3.2	12.6
In losses	213	25.4	10.3	.418	4.0	.375	2.2	.847	0.35	0.80	1.1	3.5	12.0
Pre All-Star	192	23.3	9.6	.432	3.7	.385	2.2	.828	0.33	0.72	1.1	3.1	11.6
Post All-Star	134	28.8	12.0	.453	4.6	.415	2.3	.876	0.33	0.97	1.2	4.2	14.7
Oct/Nov	61	22.1	9.3	.387	3.6	.341	2.0	.864	0.41	0.62	0.8	3.3	10.2
December	60	22.6	9.6	.447	3.9	.415	2.3	.763	0.37	0.65	1.2	3.1	11.6
January	56	23.4	9.5	.457	3.4	.402	2.3	.850	0.23	0.82	1.0	2.9	12.0
February	59	28.2	11.6	.428	4.4	.405	2.1	.833	0.34	1.00	1.3	3.5	13.5
March	80	26.1	10.1	.448	4.2	.398	1.8	.879	0.29	0.80	1.2	3.7	12.3
Apr/May	46	26.3	11.2	.449	4.0	.392	2.6	.890	0.24	0.93	1.0	4.1	13.9
0 Days Rest	97	24.7	10.1	.435	3.9	.359	2.1	.823	0.31	0.87	1.1	3.3	11.9
1 Days Rest	176	25.4	10.5	.431	4.0	.410	2.2	.854	0.33	0.78	1.1	3.5	12.3
2 Days Rest	58	23.9	9.5	.434	3.6	.392	2.2	.874	0.22	0.66	1.1	2.9	11.6
3+ Days Rest	31	23.4	9.9	.471	4.3	.403	1.9	.810	0.42	0.94	0.8	3.4	12.6

Dikembe Mutombo
Atlanta Hawks — Center

1999-2000 Per Game Averages

	G	Min	FGA	FG%	3PA	3P%	FTA	FT%	Blk	Stl	Ast	Reb	Pts
Total	82	36.4	7.0	.562	0.0	—	5.1	.708	3.28	0.33	1.3	14.1	11.5
Home	41	36.9	7.5	.627	0.0	—	5.5	.718	3.34	0.34	1.1	14.8	13.3
Road	41	36.0	6.5	.487	0.0	—	4.7	.696	3.22	0.32	1.5	13.4	9.6
vs. Playoff	47	36.4	7.1	.566	0.0	—	4.7	.701	2.60	0.38	1.4	13.6	11.3
vs. Non-Playoff	35	36.3	6.9	.556	0.0	—	5.7	.715	4.20	0.26	1.2	14.8	11.7
vs. East	54	35.4	7.0	.554	0.0	—	5.2	.710	3.02	0.37	1.5	14.0	11.5
vs. West	28	38.3	7.0	.577	0.0	—	4.9	.703	3.79	0.25	0.9	14.4	11.5
vs. Div.	28	35.2	6.4	.600	0.0	—	4.7	.750	2.75	0.21	1.6	13.3	11.3
As Starter	82	36.4	7.0	.562	0.0	—	5.1	.708	3.28	0.33	1.3	14.1	11.5
Off Bench	0	—	—	—	—	—	—	—	—	—	—	—	—
In wins	28	38.5	7.9	.613	0.0	—	5.1	.750	4.07	0.36	1.4	16.0	13.6
In losses	54	35.3	6.5	.530	0.0	—	5.1	.686	2.87	0.31	1.2	13.1	10.4
Pre All-Star	47	37.4	7.0	.556	0.0	—	6.2	.704	3.19	0.30	1.3	14.4	12.2
Post All-Star	35	35.0	6.9	.570	0.0	—	3.7	.715	3.40	0.37	1.2	13.7	10.5
November	15	38.1	8.1	.566	0.0	—	7.2	.620	3.60	0.33	1.3	14.6	13.7
December	14	37.1	6.1	.671	0.0	—	5.7	.725	3.64	0.07	1.4	14.1	12.3
January	13	36.7	6.4	.434	0.0	—	5.6	.753	2.54	0.62	1.1	14.9	9.8
February	12	39.3	8.3	.500	0.0	—	5.4	.769	4.50	0.25	1.5	15.4	12.5
March	17	32.8	6.3	.617	0.0	—	3.5	.750	2.65	0.24	0.9	12.4	10.4
April	11	35.2	6.9	.579	0.0	—	3.2	.657	2.91	0.55	1.7	13.6	10.1
0 Days Rest	24	34.7	7.1	.529	0.0	—	5.0	.692	3.96	0.29	1.5	14.3	11.0
1 Days Rest	37	35.9	6.8	.560	0.0	—	4.6	.669	2.76	0.43	1.1	13.2	10.7
2 Days Rest	14	39.1	7.1	.667	0.0	—	5.9	.793	3.36	0.14	1.1	17.1	14.1
3+ Days Rest	7	39.7	7.4	.481	0.0	—	7.1	.740	3.57	0.29	2.0	12.6	12.4

Last Five Seasons

	G	Min	FGA	FG%	3PA	3P%	FTA	FT%	Blk	Stl	Ast	Reb	Pts
Total	368	36.5	8.0	.529	0.0	.000	5.3	.693	3.50	0.45	1.3	12.2	12.1
Home	183	36.8	8.1	.556	0.0	—	6.0	.684	3.60	0.41	1.3	12.8	13.1
Road	185	36.1	7.9	.502	0.0	.000	4.5	.704	3.41	0.48	1.2	11.6	11.2
vs. Playoff	201	36.7	8.0	.516	0.0	.000	5.3	.696	3.18	0.48	1.2	12.0	11.9
vs. Non-Playoff	167	36.1	8.0	.546	0.0	—	5.3	.688	3.89	0.40	1.3	12.5	12.4
vs. East	233	36.5	8.0	.528	0.0	.000	5.6	.688	3.37	0.40	1.3	12.4	12.3
vs. West	135	36.4	8.0	.531	0.0	—	4.8	.702	3.73	0.53	1.1	11.9	11.8
vs. Div.	125	36.9	8.1	.550	0.0	—	5.4	.680	3.26	0.49	1.4	12.7	12.6
As Starter	368	36.5	8.0	.529	0.0	.000	5.3	.693	3.50	0.45	1.3	12.2	12.1
Off Bench	0	—	—	—	—	—	—	—	—	—	—	—	—
In wins	194	37.0	8.4	.545	0.0	—	5.4	.703	3.98	0.48	1.3	12.7	13.0
In losses	174	35.8	7.5	.510	0.0	.000	5.2	.681	2.97	0.41	1.2	11.7	11.2
Pre All-Star	188	37.2	8.2	.528	0.0	.000	5.5	.703	3.70	0.40	1.2	12.3	12.5
Post All-Star	130	35.3	8.1	.536	0.0	—	4.9	.679	3.43	0.56	1.3	12.1	12.0
Oct/Nov	60	37.9	9.6	.515	0.0	—	5.8	.656	3.62	0.35	1.1	12.6	13.7
December	53	37.6	7.8	.546	0.0	.000	5.4	.696	4.30	0.43	1.2	12.0	12.3
January	60	36.2	7.5	.529	0.0	—	5.1	.743	3.42	0.40	1.4	12.3	11.7
February	59	36.1	8.1	.523	0.0	—	4.7	.701	3.68	0.44	1.4	11.6	11.8
March	80	35.1	7.7	.545	0.0	—	5.3	.705	3.23	0.59	1.2	12.1	12.1
Apr/May	56	36.4	7.4	.517	0.0	—	5.5	.657	2.93	0.41	1.4	12.8	11.3
0 Days Rest	103	35.3	7.7	.530	0.0	—	5.2	.679	3.38	0.39	1.3	11.9	11.7
1 Days Rest	175	36.3	8.0	.516	0.0	.000	5.3	.679	3.30	0.53	1.2	12.0	11.9
2 Days Rest	55	39.0	7.9	.575	0.0	—	5.1	.743	3.93	0.38	1.4	13.6	12.9
3+ Days Rest	35	36.7	8.9	.524	0.0	—	5.7	.722	4.20	0.31	1.3	12.0	13.4

Steve Nash

1999-2000 Per Game Averages

	G	Min	FGA	FG%	3PA	3P%	FTA	FT%	Blk	Stl	Ast	Reb	Pts		G	Min	FGA	FG%	3PA	3P%	FTA	FT%	Blk	Stl	Ast	Reb	Pts
Total	56	27.4	6.5	.477	2.7	.403	1.5	.882	0.05	0.66	4.9	2.2	8.6	Pre All-Star	23	22.4	5.4	.460	2.3	.415	1.2	.821	0.04	0.78	3.7	1.9	6.9
Home	29	27.9	6.9	.490	2.9	.422	1.4	.905	0.03	0.52	4.8	2.1	9.3	Post All-Star	33	30.8	7.2	.485	2.9	.396	1.7	.912	0.06	0.58	5.7	2.3	9.8
Road	27	26.8	6.0	.460	2.4	.379	1.6	.860	0.07	0.81	5.0	2.2	7.9	November	13	23.5	5.9	.442	2.5	.406	0.8	.727	0.00	0.62	3.2	2.1	6.8
vs. Playoff	31	27.6	6.4	.482	2.6	.383	1.8	.893	0.06	0.71	4.8	2.0	8.7	December	0	—	—	—	—	—	—	—	—	—	—	—	—
vs. Non-Playoff	25	27.0	6.6	.470	2.7	.426	1.2	.862	0.04	0.60	4.9	2.4	8.4	January	5	17.2	2.2	.364	1.2	.333	1.6	1.000	0.00	1.20	2.6	1.6	3.6
vs. East	22	25.2	6.7	.439	2.8	.371	0.8	.833	0.05	0.64	4.2	1.7	7.6	February	13	23.6	6.7	.460	2.7	.400	1.4	.778	0.08	0.46	4.7	1.7	8.3
vs. West	34	28.7	6.3	.502	2.6	.425	2.0	.896	0.06	0.68	5.3	2.5	9.2	March	15	28.8	6.7	.446	3.1	.404	1.5	.955	0.07	0.53	5.0	1.9	8.7
vs. Div.	14	32.0	7.4	.534	2.7	.474	2.2	.935	0.07	0.71	6.2	2.8	11.2	April	10	40.1	8.7	.575	2.9	.414	2.6	.923	0.10	0.90	8.1	3.5	13.6
As Starter	27	34.7	7.9	.495	3.1	.381	1.7	.935	0.04	0.74	6.3	2.6	10.6	0 Days Rest	12	28.3	7.2	.465	3.0	.444	1.8	.905	0.00	0.75	4.9	2.8	9.6
Off Bench	29	20.6	5.1	.450	2.2	.431	1.3	.821	0.07	0.59	3.5	1.7	6.7	1 Days Rest	32	27.2	6.3	.500	2.4	.410	1.7	.868	0.03	0.72	4.9	2.0	8.7
In wins	31	31.6	7.0	.558	2.7	.512	2.1	.877	0.03	0.81	6.1	2.7	11.0	2 Days Rest	7	28.6	6.4	.378	3.1	.318	0.6	1.000	0.29	0.43	5.3	1.9	6.4
In losses	25	22.0	5.8	.356	2.6	.262	0.8	.900	0.08	0.48	3.4	1.5	5.6	3+ Days Rest	5	24.4	6.4	.500	2.6	.385	1.4	.857	0.00	0.40	4.0	1.8	8.6

Career (1996-97 thru 1999-2000)

	G	Min	FGA	FG%	3PA	3P%	FTA	FT%	Blk	Stl	Ast	Reb	Pts		G	Min	FGA	FG%	3PA	3P%	FTA	FT%	Blk	Stl	Ast	Reb	Pts
Total	237	21.7	6.1	.438	2.2	.402	1.1	.854	0.04	0.66	3.8	1.9	7.2	Pre All-Star	110	20.3	6.1	.458	2.0	.434	1.3	.847	0.04	0.75	3.5	1.8	7.6
Home	122	21.5	6.1	.437	2.2	.374	1.1	.864	0.02	0.65	3.6	1.9	7.1	Post All-Star	87	19.0	5.2	.461	2.0	.382	0.9	.885	0.03	0.43	3.4	1.6	6.3
Road	115	22.0	6.0	.439	2.2	.432	1.2	.846	0.05	0.68	3.9	1.9	7.2	Oct/Nov	40	20.7	6.2	.439	2.0	.405	1.3	.860	0.00	0.75	3.3	2.0	7.3
vs. Playoff	130	21.5	5.9	.429	2.1	.412	1.1	.891	0.04	0.64	3.6	1.8	6.9	December	22	21.1	7.5	.455	2.3	.420	1.8	.775	0.09	0.59	3.8	1.5	9.2
vs. Non-Playoff	107	22.0	6.3	.448	2.4	.391	1.2	.817	0.04	0.69	3.9	2.1	7.6	January	37	19.0	5.2	.482	1.7	.429	1.0	.889	0.03	0.81	3.3	1.9	6.6
vs. East	82	21.0	6.0	.443	2.0	.434	1.1	.879	0.02	0.67	3.6	1.7	7.2	February	49	21.1	6.0	.399	2.5	.421	1.0	.816	0.04	0.63	3.7	1.9	6.7
vs. West	155	22.1	6.1	.435	2.3	.387	1.1	.842	0.05	0.66	3.9	2.0	7.2	March	58	22.2	5.9	.396	2.5	.338	0.9	.909	0.05	0.50	3.7	1.8	6.4
vs. Div.	71	19.7	5.3	.441	1.8	.400	1.1	.852	0.04	0.52	3.5	1.7	6.4	Apr/May	31	26.8	6.4	.513	2.3	.458	1.2	.868	0.03	0.77	5.1	2.5	8.6
As Starter	78	32.3	8.0	.418	3.3	.364	1.3	.895	0.04	0.79	5.7	2.8	9.1	0 Days Rest	54	21.5	6.1	.444	2.5	.433	1.2	.864	0.04	0.69	3.6	2.0	7.5
Off Bench	159	16.5	5.1	.454	1.7	.439	1.0	.828	0.04	0.60	2.8	1.5	6.2	1 Days Rest	121	23.6	6.5	.433	2.3	.381	1.4	.855	0.04	0.64	4.1	2.0	7.6
In wins	125	22.2	6.1	.474	2.2	.444	1.3	.843	0.03	0.75	4.1	2.1	7.9	2 Days Rest	31	20.9	5.4	.440	2.0	.410	0.6	.947	0.06	0.65	3.5	2.0	6.2
In losses	112	21.2	6.0	.397	2.3	.356	1.0	.872	0.04	0.56	3.4	1.7	6.4	3+ Days Rest	31	15.7	5.1	.449	1.8	.421	0.6	.722	0.00	0.74	2.8	1.3	5.8

Tyrone Nesby

1999-2000 Per Game Averages

	G	Min	FGA	FG%	3PA	3P%	FTA	FT%	Blk	Stl	Ast	Reb	Pts		G	Min	FGA	FG%	3PA	3P%	FTA	FT%	Blk	Stl	Ast	Reb	Pts
Total	73	31.7	12.5	.398	3.8	.335	2.6	.791	0.42	1.03	1.7	3.8	13.3	Pre All-Star	43	30.1	11.3	.413	3.3	.333	2.4	.767	0.37	1.09	1.2	3.6	12.3
Home	40	30.2	12.0	.401	3.6	.317	3.1	.784	0.40	1.30	1.3	3.4	13.2	Post All-Star	30	34.1	14.3	.381	4.6	.336	2.9	.818	0.50	0.93	2.3	4.0	14.8
Road	33	33.6	13.2	.394	4.2	.353	2.0	.803	0.45	0.70	2.1	4.2	13.5	November	12	29.6	12.4	.336	3.3	.300	4.2	.680	0.50	1.08	1.1	4.5	12.2
vs. Playoff	44	31.3	12.3	.387	3.8	.331	3.0	.765	0.27	0.82	1.5	3.6	13.1	December	15	32.3	11.2	.435	3.5	.385	1.8	.852	0.67	1.27	1.3	4.1	12.6
vs. Non-Playoff	29	32.5	12.8	.414	4.0	.339	2.0	.847	0.66	1.34	1.9	4.0	13.7	January	12	27.4	10.3	.463	3.4	.317	1.3	.800	0.00	0.92	0.8	2.6	11.6
vs. East	25	31.2	12.4	.392	4.3	.333	2.0	.776	0.48	1.24	2.0	3.8	12.7	February	12	32.3	12.0	.368	3.3	.256	2.3	.889	0.42	1.33	2.6	3.3	11.7
vs. West	48	32.0	12.6	.401	3.6	.335	3.0	.796	0.40	0.92	1.5	3.8	13.6	March	13	31.5	13.8	.402	4.7	.311	2.6	.735	0.69	0.46	2.4	3.6	14.5
vs. Div.	22	33.2	13.3	.423	3.7	.383	3.4	.787	0.27	1.05	1.5	4.1	15.4	April	9	39.1	16.9	.388	5.3	.417	4.2	.868	0.11	1.11	1.8	4.6	19.0
As Starter	39	37.1	14.9	.406	4.8	.358	2.8	.798	0.62	1.04	2.2	4.5	16.1	0 Days Rest	16	34.3	13.2	.417	3.8	.328	3.0	.817	0.25	1.31	2.3	4.4	15.3
Off Bench	34	25.6	9.8	.383	2.8	.287	2.4	.780	0.21	1.03	1.1	2.9	10.2	1 Days Rest	35	31.6	12.3	.367	4.0	.331	2.0	.775	0.54	0.97	1.7	3.5	11.9
In wins	14	32.6	13.0	.489	4.1	.414	2.2	.839	0.64	1.57	2.0	4.6	16.3	2 Days Rest	13	31.3	12.4	.453	3.5	.391	2.8	.838	0.31	1.23	1.2	3.8	15.0
In losses	59	31.5	12.4	.375	3.8	.314	2.7	.781	0.37	0.90	1.6	3.6	12.6	3+ Days Rest	9	28.2	12.4	.402	3.9	.286	2.6	.696	0.44	0.44	1.1	3.6	12.9

Career (1998-99 thru 1999-2000)

	G	Min	FGA	FG%	3PA	3P%	FTA	FT%	Blk	Stl	Ast	Reb	Pts		G	Min	FGA	FG%	3PA	3P%	FTA	FT%	Blk	Stl	Ast	Reb	Pts
Total	123	29.3	10.7	.414	3.1	.342	2.6	.787	0.41	1.24	1.7	3.7	12.0	Pre All-Star	43	30.1	11.3	.413	3.3	.333	2.4	.767	0.37	1.09	1.2	3.6	12.3
Home	65	29.2	10.7	.426	2.8	.324	3.0	.783	0.42	1.45	1.4	3.5	12.4	Post All-Star	30	34.1	14.3	.381	4.6	.336	2.9	.818	0.50	0.93	2.3	4.0	14.8
Road	58	29.5	10.8	.400	3.3	.359	2.2	.794	0.41	1.00	2.0	3.9	11.5	Oct/Nov	12	29.6	12.4	.336	3.3	.300	4.2	.680	0.50	1.08	1.1	4.5	12.2
vs. Playoff	74	29.2	10.8	.396	3.0	.324	2.9	.765	0.31	1.11	1.6	3.8	11.8	December	15	32.3	11.2	.435	3.5	.385	1.8	.852	0.67	1.27	1.3	4.1	12.6
vs. Non-Playoff	49	29.4	10.7	.440	3.1	.368	2.2	.832	0.57	1.43	1.7	3.5	12.3	January	12	27.4	10.3	.463	3.4	.317	1.3	.800	0.00	0.92	0.8	2.6	11.6
vs. East	31	29.5	11.5	.398	3.9	.339	2.1	.815	0.45	1.13	2.0	3.5	12.2	February	24	22.7	8.3	.400	2.2	.302	1.7	.829	0.33	0.83	1.6	2.6	8.8
vs. West	92	29.2	10.5	.420	2.8	.344	2.8	.780	0.40	1.27	1.5	3.7	11.9	March	30	28.6	10.6	.429	3.1	.319	2.8	.821	0.60	1.03	1.9	3.2	12.4
vs. Div.	41	29.5	11.1	.430	2.8	.374	3.2	.789	0.41	1.37	1.4	4.0	13.2	Apr/May	30	34.4	12.0	.413	3.2	.392	3.6	.776	0.30	1.93	2.2	4.8	14.0
As Starter	75	33.7	12.2	.420	3.5	.356	3.0	.788	0.53	1.49	2.1	4.3	13.9	0 Days Rest	33	31.8	11.5	.453	3.2	.371	3.4	.811	0.33	1.85	2.2	4.4	14.3
Off Bench	48	22.5	8.4	.400	2.4	.310	2.1	.784	0.23	0.83	1.0	2.6	9.1	1 Days Rest	60	28.6	10.2	.379	3.0	.326	2.2	.791	0.45	1.03	1.7	3.3	10.5
In wins	23	33.1	11.3	.498	3.2	.405	3.2	.822	0.48	1.57	2.1	5.4	15.1	2 Days Rest	19	29.1	10.7	.451	2.8	.370	2.8	.796	0.42	1.26	1.1	3.7	13.0
In losses	100	28.4	10.6	.393	3.0	.327	2.5	.777	0.40	1.16	1.6	3.3	11.3	3+ Days Rest	11	26.0	11.1	.402	3.4	.297	2.3	.640	0.45	0.45	1.0	3.5	11.4

Radoslav Nesterovic

1999-2000 Per Game Averages

	G	Min	FGA	FG%	3PA	3P%	FTA	FT%	Blk	Stl	Ast	Reb	Pts		G	Min	FGA	FG%	3PA	3P%	FTA	FT%	Blk	Stl	Ast	Reb	Pts
Total	82	21.0	5.3	.476	0.0	.000	1.3	.573	1.04	0.26	1.1	4.6	5.7	Pre All-Star	47	24.5	6.5	.471	0.0	.000	1.7	.588	1.04	0.30	1.3	5.4	7.1
Home	41	20.2	5.3	.477	0.0	.000	1.1	.500	0.95	0.20	1.1	4.4	5.6	Post All-Star	35	16.3	3.6	.488	0.0	—	0.7	.522	1.03	0.20	0.9	3.5	3.9
Road	41	21.8	5.3	.475	0.0	—	1.4	.632	1.12	0.32	1.1	4.8	5.9	November	12	25.8	6.8	.463	0.1	.000	2.7	.500	1.50	0.42	1.0	5.5	7.7
vs. Playoff	44	21.1	5.2	.496	0.0	.000	1.2	.569	0.86	0.27	1.2	4.2	5.8	December	15	24.9	6.7	.465	0.0	—	1.7	.600	0.80	0.33	1.7	5.9	7.3
vs. Non-Playoff	38	20.9	5.4	.454	0.0	.000	1.4	.577	1.24	0.24	1.1	5.1	5.7	January	15	23.4	6.0	.489	0.1	.000	1.1	.765	0.80	0.20	1.3	5.4	6.7
vs. East	30	17.8	4.4	.458	0.0	—	1.3	.538	0.90	0.20	1.2	3.2	4.7	February	14	18.4	4.6	.554	0.0	—	0.7	.500	1.00	0.21	0.8	2.9	5.5
vs. West	52	22.9	5.8	.483	0.0	.000	1.2	.594	1.12	0.29	1.1	5.4	6.3	March	16	12.0	2.6	.488	0.0	—	0.9	.429	0.94	0.13	0.8	2.0	2.9
vs. Div.	24	22.8	5.3	.438	0.0	.000	1.3	.567	1.42	0.25	0.9	5.0	5.4	April	10	23.8	5.4	.389	0.0	—	0.5	.800	1.40	0.30	1.4	7.1	4.6
As Starter	55	23.4	6.1	.492	0.0	.000	1.1	.623	0.91	0.27	1.4	5.2	6.7	0 Days Rest	18	21.0	5.3	.442	0.0	—	1.2	.591	0.83	0.39	0.9	4.1	5.4
Off Bench	27	16.2	3.7	.420	0.0	.000	1.6	.500	1.30	0.22	0.7	3.4	3.9	1 Days Rest	51	21.4	5.4	.484	0.0	.000	1.3	.574	1.08	0.24	1.2	5.0	6.4
In wins	50	20.8	5.0	.488	0.0	.000	1.1	.607	1.16	0.18	1.2	4.7	5.6	2 Days Rest	5	23.6	5.0	.520	0.2	.000	1.4	.571	1.60	0.20	1.2	3.6	6.0
In losses	32	21.3	5.7	.459	0.0	—	1.5	.532	0.84	0.38	1.1	4.4	6.0	3+ Days Rest	8	17.1	4.8	.474	0.0	—	0.8	.500	0.88	0.13	1.0	4.3	4.9

Career (1998-99 thru 1999-2000)

	G	Min	FGA	FG%	3PA	3P%	FTA	FT%	Blk	Stl	Ast	Reb	Pts		G	Min	FGA	FG%	3PA	3P%	FTA	FT%	Blk	Stl	Ast	Reb	Pts
Total	84	20.9	5.3	.470	0.0	.000	1.3	.581	1.01	0.25	1.1	4.6	5.7	Pre All-Star	47	24.5	6.5	.471	0.0	.000	1.7	.588	1.04	0.30	1.3	5.4	7.1
Home	41	20.2	5.3	.477	0.0	.000	1.1	.500	0.95	0.20	1.1	4.4	5.6	Post All-Star	35	16.3	3.6	.488	0.0	—	0.7	.522	1.03	0.20	0.9	3.5	3.9
Road	43	21.5	5.3	.463	0.0	—	1.4	.644	1.07	0.30	1.1	4.8	5.8	Oct/Nov	12	25.8	6.8	.463	0.1	.000	2.7	.500	1.50	0.42	1.0	5.5	7.7
vs. Playoff	46	20.8	5.2	.483	0.0	.000	1.2	.585	0.83	0.26	1.1	4.2	5.7	December	15	24.9	6.7	.465	0.0	—	1.7	.600	0.80	0.33	1.7	5.9	7.3
vs. Non-Playoff	38	20.9	5.4	.454	0.0	.000	1.4	.577	1.24	0.24	1.1	5.1	5.7	January	15	23.4	6.0	.489	0.1	.000	1.1	.765	0.80	0.20	1.3	5.4	6.7
vs. East	30	17.8	4.4	.458	0.0	—	1.3	.538	0.90	0.20	1.2	3.2	4.7	February	14	18.4	4.6	.554	0.0	—	0.7	.500	1.00	0.21	0.8	2.9	5.5
vs. West	54	22.6	5.8	.475	0.0	.000	1.2	.606	1.07	0.28	1.1	5.4	6.3	March	16	12.0	2.6	.488	0.0	—	0.9	.429	0.94	0.13	0.8	2.0	2.9
vs. Div.	25	22.4	5.3	.432	0.0	.000	1.3	.594	1.36	0.24	0.8	4.9	5.3	Apr/May	12	22.3	5.5	.364	0.0	—	0.6	.857	1.17	0.25	1.3	6.6	4.5
As Starter	55	23.4	6.1	.492	0.0	.000	1.1	.623	0.91	0.27	1.4	5.2	6.7	0 Days Rest	19	20.8	5.4	.427	0.0	—	1.2	.591	0.79	0.37	0.9	4.2	5.3
Off Bench	29	16.1	3.9	.402	0.0	.000	1.5	.523	1.21	0.21	0.7	3.4	3.9	1 Days Rest	51	21.4	5.4	.484	0.0	.000	1.3	.574	1.08	0.24	1.2	5.0	6.0
In wins	50	20.8	5.0	.488	0.0	.000	1.1	.607	1.16	0.18	1.2	4.7	5.6	2 Days Rest	5	23.6	5.0	.520	0.2	.000	1.4	.571	1.60	0.20	1.2	3.6	6.0
In losses	34	20.9	5.7	.446	0.0	—	1.4	.551	0.79	0.35	1.0	4.4	5.9	3+ Days Rest	9	16.6	4.7	.452	0.0	—	0.9	.625	0.78	0.11	0.9	4.0	4.8

Johnny Newman

1999-2000 Per Game Averages

	G	Min	FGA	FG%	3PA	3P%	FTA	FT%	Blk	Stl	Ast	Reb	Pts		G	Min	FGA	FG%	3PA	3P%	FTA	FT%	Blk	Stl	Ast	Reb	Pts
Total	82	21.5	7.6	.446	2.3	.379	2.8	.838	0.13	0.65	0.8	1.9	10.0	Pre All-Star	49	20.8	7.2	.459	2.4	.398	2.6	.813	0.20	0.59	0.7	2.1	9.7
Home	41	20.0	7.2	.443	2.2	.356	3.2	.835	0.17	0.51	0.7	1.5	9.9	Post All-Star	33	22.5	8.2	.430	2.2	.347	3.1	.871	0.03	0.73	1.0	1.6	10.5
Road	41	23.0	8.0	.450	2.4	.400	2.3	.844	0.10	0.78	0.9	2.2	10.1	November	15	25.0	9.4	.426	3.2	.313	4.1	.836	0.47	0.67	0.9	2.8	12.
vs. Playoff	46	20.0	7.0	.474	2.0	.372	2.2	.788	0.15	0.72	0.7	1.7	9.1	December	15	18.1	6.4	.448	2.0	.400	2.1	.781	0.20	0.47	0.5	1.4	8.
vs. Non-Playoff	36	22.6	8.3	.417	2.7	.385	3.6	.877	0.11	0.56	0.9	2.1	11.1	January	14	19.7	6.1	.506	2.0	.500	1.1	.750	0.00	0.71	0.4	1.9	8.0
vs. East	54	21.5	7.5	.436	2.4	.378	3.0	.863	0.17	0.59	0.8	1.6	10.0	February	12	17.7	6.2	.405	1.9	.391	2.1	.800	0.00	0.58	1.0	1.6	7.4
vs. West	28	21.5	7.8	.465	2.3	.381	2.5	.783	0.07	0.75	0.8	2.4	10.0	March	16	20.7	6.4	.461	1.8	.345	2.4	.846	0.00	0.56	0.8	1.7	8.
vs. Div.	25	19.8	7.1	.399	2.5	.355	2.6	.924	0.16	0.36	0.8	1.7	9.0	April	10	29.8	12.5	.440	3.2	.375	5.6	.911	0.10	1.00	1.5	1.9	17.
As Starter	9	28.0	9.3	.452	2.4	.409	2.8	.920	0.44	0.89	0.8	2.3	12.0	0 Days Rest	20	22.8	7.9	.465	2.6	.423	2.7	.907	0.05	0.55	0.9	2.3	10.
Off Bench	73	20.7	7.4	.445	2.3	.375	2.8	.828	0.10	0.62	0.8	1.8	9.8	1 Days Rest	45	20.5	7.3	.465	2.3	.392	2.9	.820	0.11	0.64	0.8	1.7	9.8
In wins	31	19.6	7.0	.482	2.4	.452	2.7	.783	0.06	0.52	0.6	1.5	9.9	2 Days Rest	10	23.3	8.9	.382	2.4	.292	3.0	.700	0.40	0.80	0.6	2.4	9.
In losses	51	22.6	7.9	.427	2.3	.333	2.9	.870	0.18	0.73	0.9	2.1	10.0	3+ Days Rest	7	21.6	6.9	.375	1.7	.250	2.0	1.000	0.14	0.71	0.6	1.1	7.

Last Five Seasons

	G	Min	FGA	FG%	3PA	3P%	FTA	FT%	Blk	Stl	Ast	Reb	Pts		G	Min	FGA	FG%	3PA	3P%	FTA	FT%	Blk	Stl	Ast	Reb	Pts
Total	370	26.0	7.8	.451	1.7	.367	3.3	.808	0.21	0.87	1.4	2.0	10.3	Pre All-Star	181	26.3	7.6	.462	1.7	.362	3.2	.806	0.20	0.86	1.4	2.1	10.2
Home	186	26.3	7.9	.459	1.7	.358	3.6	.819	0.28	0.96	1.6	2.0	10.8	Post All-Star	139	28.2	8.9	.446	1.7	.370	4.1	.817	0.22	0.99	1.6	2.2	12.
Road	184	25.8	7.6	.443	1.7	.376	3.1	.797	0.14	0.77	1.2	2.1	9.9	Oct/Nov	56	27.7	8.3	.456	1.9	.317	3.6	.787	0.25	0.82	1.6	2.1	11.0
vs. Playoff	212	25.1	7.3	.438	1.5	.357	2.9	.802	0.20	0.93	1.2	1.9	9.3	December	58	25.7	7.2	.463	1.4	.333	3.2	.791	0.24	0.84	1.4	1.9	9.
vs. Non-Playoff	158	27.3	8.3	.467	1.8	.378	3.9	.815	0.23	0.78	1.7	2.3	11.7	January	53	25.1	7.0	.444	1.9	.414	2.3	.855	0.13	0.91	1.1	2.2	9.0
vs. East	232	25.5	7.4	.451	1.6	.383	2.8	.810	0.20	0.81	1.3	2.0	9.6	February	62	26.0	8.2	.449	1.7	.377	3.4	.783	0.26	0.92	1.6	2.3	10.
vs. West	138	25.6	7.8	.452	1.7	.342	4.2	.807	0.23	0.96	1.5	2.0	11.6	March	78	25.7	7.5	.455	1.6	.372	3.8	.821	0.21	0.78	1.4	2.0	10.
vs. Div.	125	25.6	7.6	.421	1.8	.382	2.9	.824	0.22	0.72	1.2	1.9	9.5	Apr/May	63	26.3	8.3	.442	1.6	.382	3.4	.824	0.19	0.95	1.3	1.9	10.
As Starter	112	32.3	8.6	.473	1.9	.363	3.1	.813	0.26	1.05	1.8	2.5	11.3	0 Days Rest	98	24.9	7.4	.436	1.7	.360	3.3	.815	0.14	0.94	1.4	2.2	9.
Off Bench	258	23.3	7.4	.440	1.6	.369	3.4	.807	0.19	0.79	1.2	1.9	9.9	1 Days Rest	184	26.3	7.8	.459	1.7	.377	3.5	.814	0.25	0.84	1.4	2.1	10.
In wins	122	25.1	7.3	.480	1.7	.435	3.6	.806	0.21	0.87	1.5	1.8	10.6	2 Days Rest	56	27.0	7.8	.439	1.7	.344	2.9	.778	0.25	0.73	1.2	1.9	9.
In losses	248	26.5	8.0	.438	1.6	.333	3.2	.810	0.21	0.87	1.4	2.1	10.1	3+ Days Rest	32	26.5	8.4	.470	1.6	.373	3.3	.798	0.16	1.06	1.5	1.6	11.

Dirk Nowitzki
Dallas Mavericks — Forward

1999-2000 Per Game Averages

	G	Min	FGA	FG%	3PA	3P%	FTA	FT%	Blk	Stl	Ast	Reb	Pts
Total	82	35.8	13.6	.461	3.7	.379	4.2	.830	0.83	0.77	2.5	6.5	17.5
Home	41	35.4	13.7	.449	3.3	.321	4.0	.798	0.88	0.73	2.1	6.4	16.5
Road	41	36.2	13.6	.472	4.1	.426	4.5	.859	0.78	0.80	2.8	6.6	18.5
vs. Playoff	48	36.2	13.7	.444	3.6	.372	3.9	.825	0.94	0.81	2.7	6.6	16.7
vs. Non-Playoff	34	35.3	13.6	.485	3.9	.388	4.7	.836	0.68	0.71	2.2	6.4	18.6
vs. East	30	36.4	13.6	.464	3.6	.439	4.8	.833	0.77	0.77	3.0	6.5	18.2
vs. West	52	35.5	13.7	.459	3.8	.347	3.9	.828	0.87	0.77	2.2	6.5	17.1
vs. Div.	24	35.8	13.8	.455	4.0	.333	3.5	.855	0.88	0.79	2.3	7.0	16.8
As Starter	81	35.9	13.7	.462	3.8	.380	4.3	.829	0.84	0.77	2.5	6.5	17.6
Off Bench	1	29.0	9.0	.333	1.0	.000	2.0	1.000	0.00	1.00	2.0	2.0	8.0
In wins	40	34.3	12.6	.480	4.0	.400	4.4	.842	0.83	0.70	2.5	6.3	17.4
In losses	42	37.3	14.6	.445	3.5	.356	4.1	.819	0.83	0.83	2.5	6.6	17.6

	G	Min	FGA	FG%	3PA	3P%	FTA	FT%	Blk	Stl	Ast	Reb	Pts
Pre All-Star	48	36.2	13.5	.461	2.9	.390	4.6	.834	0.90	0.77	2.5	6.2	17.5
Post All-Star	34	35.3	13.8	.460	4.9	.370	3.7	.824	0.74	0.76	2.5	6.9	17.5
November	16	34.0	12.4	.480	1.7	.407	5.0	.850	0.56	0.88	2.5	6.6	16.8
December	14	38.9	14.2	.492	3.6	.471	4.8	.821	0.86	1.07	3.0	6.6	19.6
January	13	37.0	14.2	.424	3.8	.300	4.3	.821	0.85	0.62	1.8	5.7	16.7
February	13	35.1	13.5	.434	3.4	.386	3.9	.824	1.23	0.77	2.8	6.0	16.2
March	16	36.5	14.5	.457	4.9	.392	3.8	.820	0.81	0.63	2.3	6.6	18.3
April	10	32.8	13.0	.477	5.5	.327	3.3	.848	0.70	0.60	2.4	7.8	17.0
0 Days Rest	18	36.0	13.7	.421	4.6	.373	4.4	.875	0.83	0.78	2.5	7.2	17.2
1 Days Rest	44	35.7	14.0	.468	3.6	.377	4.0	.795	0.73	0.73	2.3	6.4	17.6
2 Days Rest	16	36.6	13.1	.498	3.5	.429	4.7	.880	1.13	1.00	3.1	6.6	18.6
3+ Days Rest	4	33.3	11.5	.413	2.0	.125	4.3	.765	0.75	0.25	1.5	4.5	13.0

Career (1998-99 thru 1999-2000)

	G	Min	FGA	FG%	3PA	3P%	FTA	FT%	Blk	Stl	Ast	Reb	Pts
Total	129	30.2	11.3	.448	2.9	.348	3.7	.815	0.74	0.71	1.9	5.4	14.1
Home	63	29.6	11.3	.434	2.7	.304	3.6	.779	0.73	0.65	1.7	5.4	13.4
Road	66	30.8	11.3	.461	3.1	.383	3.8	.848	0.74	0.77	2.1	5.4	14.8
vs. Playoff	78	30.6	11.2	.440	2.8	.338	3.6	.800	0.86	0.76	2.0	5.5	13.7
vs. Non-Playoff	51	29.6	11.4	.459	3.0	.361	3.8	.837	0.55	0.65	1.9	5.2	14.7
vs. East	36	32.3	12.1	.460	3.1	.432	4.2	.828	0.75	0.72	2.6	5.7	16.0
vs. West	93	29.4	10.9	.442	2.8	.312	3.5	.809	0.73	0.71	1.7	5.3	13.4
vs. Div.	44	30.0	11.0	.440	2.8	.306	3.0	.835	0.80	0.75	1.6	5.8	13.1
As Starter	105	34.2	12.8	.452	3.3	.367	4.2	.813	0.82	0.79	2.2	6.2	16.2
Off Bench	24	12.6	4.6	.396	1.3	.129	1.6	.842	0.38	0.38	0.6	1.9	5.2
In wins	57	30.4	11.1	.471	3.2	.381	4.0	.819	0.68	0.65	2.2	5.7	14.9
In losses	72	30.1	11.4	.430	2.7	.316	3.5	.812	0.78	0.76	1.8	5.1	13.5

	G	Min	FGA	FG%	3PA	3P%	FTA	FT%	Blk	Stl	Ast	Reb	Pts
Pre All-Star	48	36.2	13.5	.461	2.9	.390	4.6	.834	0.90	0.77	2.5	6.2	17.5
Post All-Star	34	35.3	13.8	.460	4.9	.370	3.7	.824	0.74	0.76	2.5	6.9	17.5
Oct/Nov	16	34.0	12.4	.480	1.7	.407	5.0	.850	0.56	0.88	2.5	6.6	16.8
December	14	38.9	14.2	.492	3.6	.471	4.8	.821	0.86	1.07	3.0	6.6	19.6
January	13	37.0	14.2	.424	3.8	.300	4.3	.821	0.85	0.62	1.8	5.7	16.7
February	27	26.7	10.1	.392	2.3	.344	3.1	.810	0.96	0.52	1.8	4.8	11.2
March	32	24.6	9.7	.447	3.3	.337	2.8	.811	0.63	0.56	1.5	4.2	12.0
Apr/May	27	30.3	10.8	.464	3.0	.296	3.7	.788	0.63	0.85	1.8	5.9	13.8
0 Days Rest	33	30.9	10.9	.427	3.2	.346	3.7	.826	0.82	0.91	1.7	5.5	13.5
1 Days Rest	69	29.4	11.6	.453	2.8	.352	3.5	.795	0.65	0.62	1.8	5.2	14.2
2 Days Rest	19	34.8	12.4	.472	3.3	.387	4.8	.846	1.00	0.95	3.0	6.7	17.0
3+ Days Rest	8	23.0	7.6	.410	1.5	.083	3.1	.840	0.50	0.13	1.5	3.3	9.0

Charles Oakley
Toronto Raptors — Forward

1999-2000 Per Game Averages

	G	Min	FGA	FG%	3PA	3P%	FTA	FT%	Blk	Stl	Ast	Reb	Pts
Total	80	30.4	7.0	.418	0.5	.341	1.1	.776	0.56	1.28	3.2	6.8	6.9
Home	41	30.5	7.4	.434	0.5	.286	1.1	.756	0.68	1.24	3.6	7.0	7.4
Road	39	30.3	6.6	.399	0.5	.400	1.0	.800	0.44	1.31	2.7	6.5	6.3
vs. Playoff	41	30.1	6.4	.424	0.6	.440	1.1	.844	0.59	1.10	3.2	7.0	6.6
vs. Non-Playoff	39	30.6	7.6	.413	0.4	.188	1.0	.700	0.54	1.46	3.1	6.5	7.1
vs. East	52	30.2	7.0	.385	0.5	.357	1.1	.780	0.52	1.35	3.2	6.8	6.5
vs. West	28	30.8	6.9	.479	0.5	.308	0.9	.769	0.64	1.14	3.1	6.6	7.5
vs. Div.	27	30.2	7.4	.392	0.6	.353	1.1	.793	0.59	1.26	3.0	6.8	6.9
As Starter	80	30.4	7.0	.418	0.5	.341	1.1	.776	0.56	1.28	3.2	6.8	6.9
Off Bench	0	—	—	—	—	—	—	—	—	—	—	—	—
In wins	45	31.1	7.7	.438	0.5	.364	1.3	.776	0.73	1.44	3.7	6.7	7.9
In losses	35	29.4	6.1	.385	0.5	.316	0.8	.778	0.34	1.06	2.5	6.8	5.5

	G	Min	FGA	FG%	3PA	3P%	FTA	FT%	Blk	Stl	Ast	Reb	Pts
Pre All-Star	46	29.3	6.7	.429	0.2	.455	1.2	.759	0.54	1.35	3.5	7.3	6.7
Post All-Star	34	31.9	7.4	.405	0.9	.300	0.9	.806	0.59	1.18	2.7	6.0	7.0
November	15	26.7	5.1	.461	0.0	—	1.5	.696	0.60	1.13	3.3	6.1	5.7
December	14	29.9	6.7	.394	0.1	1.000	1.0	.857	0.29	1.36	3.2	9.6	6.2
January	13	31.8	8.6	.482	0.7	.444	1.3	.765	0.77	1.77	3.8	6.7	9.6
February	12	32.1	7.3	.443	0.7	.250	0.7	.875	0.75	1.33	3.8	5.0	7.3
March	17	31.8	6.9	.398	0.8	.538	1.0	.765	0.65	1.29	2.9	6.3	6.7
April	9	30.2	8.0	.306	1.1	.000	0.7	.833	0.22	0.50	1.8	6.8	5.4
0 Days Rest	17	29.1	6.4	.394	0.4	.429	1.2	.800	0.18	1.65	2.3	6.5	6.2
1 Days Rest	46	31.2	7.0	.435	0.5	.333	1.2	.774	0.76	1.11	3.4	7.0	7.2
2 Days Rest	9	30.6	7.7	.304	0.6	.400	1.0	.667	0.56	1.11	4.1	6.2	5.6
3+ Days Rest	8	28.4	7.5	.500	0.6	.200	0.4	1.000	0.25	1.63	2.5	6.4	8.0

Last Five Seasons

	G	Min	FGA	FG%	3PA	3P%	FTA	FT%	Blk	Stl	Ast	Reb	Pts
Total	342	33.5	8.0	.451	0.3	.278	2.1	.818	0.36	1.29	2.9	8.4	9.0
Home	175	34.0	8.1	.466	0.3	.296	2.1	.800	0.41	1.41	3.0	8.9	9.3
Road	167	33.0	7.9	.436	0.3	.256	2.0	.839	0.31	1.16	2.7	7.9	8.7
vs. Playoff	180	33.6	7.9	.457	0.3	.327	2.0	.824	0.32	1.19	2.7	8.7	9.0
vs. Non-Playoff	162	33.3	8.0	.445	0.3	.214	2.2	.813	0.41	1.39	3.1	8.1	9.0
vs. East	236	33.1	7.8	.442	0.3	.242	2.1	.816	0.35	1.25	2.9	8.4	8.6
vs. West	106	34.2	8.4	.471	0.3	.343	2.2	.823	0.39	1.37	2.8	8.6	9.8
vs. Div.	117	32.9	8.0	.433	0.3	.235	1.9	.821	0.44	1.21	2.8	8.3	8.5
As Starter	340	33.5	8.0	.451	0.3	.278	2.1	.818	0.36	1.29	2.9	8.4	9.0
Off Bench	2	23.0	7.5	.533	0.0	—	0.0	—	0.50	0.50	2.0	5.0	
In wins	198	33.9	8.1	.466	0.3	.288	2.5	.817	0.44	1.46	3.2	8.6	9.7
In losses	144	32.9	7.8	.431	0.3	.267	1.5	.822	0.24	1.05	2.5	8.2	8.1

	G	Min	FGA	FG%	3PA	3P%	FTA	FT%	Blk	Stl	Ast	Reb	Pts
Pre All-Star	179	33.0	8.0	.452	0.3	.286	2.4	.814	0.33	1.32	2.8	8.7	9.2
Post All-Star	113	34.6	8.6	.458	0.4	.279	1.8	.833	0.38	1.39	2.8	8.4	9.5
Oct/Nov	54	31.5	7.5	.491	0.4	.350	2.4	.836	0.26	1.19	2.7	7.6	9.5
December	56	32.8	7.7	.409	0.1	.125	2.5	.796	0.30	1.21	2.6	10.0	8.4
January	55	33.9	8.6	.487	0.3	.353	2.3	.819	0.40	1.56	3.0	8.2	10.4
February	53	35.6	8.5	.442	0.3	.267	2.2	.833	0.43	1.40	3.1	8.6	9.4
March	70	34.4	7.9	.441	0.3	.348	1.8	.806	0.39	1.39	3.0	8.6	8.5
Apr/May	54	32.5	7.6	.441	0.3	.071	1.5	.827	0.37	0.94	2.8	7.4	8.0
0 Days Rest	89	32.3	7.9	.442	0.2	.190	2.3	.817	0.19	1.11	2.8	8.2	8.9
1 Days Rest	170	34.0	7.8	.458	0.3	.318	1.8	.806	0.49	1.41	3.0	8.4	8.7
2 Days Rest	52	34.6	8.6	.438	0.4	.286	2.6	.851	0.27	1.13	2.5	8.5	9.8
3+ Days Rest	31	32.1	8.2	.469	0.4	.273	1.9	.817	0.29	1.35	2.8	8.8	9.4

Lamar Odom

1999-2000 Per Game Averages

	G	Min	FGA	FG%	3PA	3P%	FTA	FT%	Blk	Stl	Ast	Reb	Pts
Total	76	36.4	13.5	.438	2.2	.360	5.5	.719	1.25	1.20	4.2	7.8	16.6
Home	37	35.1	12.9	.426	2.2	.358	5.2	.701	1.35	1.32	4.1	8.0	15.4
Road	39	37.7	14.1	.449	2.1	.361	5.8	.735	1.15	1.08	4.3	7.7	17.6
vs. Playoff	44	37.4	13.5	.411	2.2	.327	5.9	.721	1.16	1.14	4.4	8.0	16.0
vs. Non-Playoff	32	35.1	13.4	.477	2.1	.409	5.1	.716	1.38	1.28	3.9	7.6	17.3
vs. East	26	37.5	13.4	.463	2.6	.373	4.7	.715	1.15	1.38	3.9	6.9	16.7
vs. West	50	35.8	13.5	.426	1.9	.351	5.9	.721	1.30	1.10	4.3	8.3	16.5
vs. Div.	23	36.7	14.6	.438	2.4	.418	6.6	.715	1.48	1.13	4.5	9.3	18.5
As Starter	70	37.3	13.8	.436	2.2	.346	5.6	.713	1.26	1.17	4.3	8.0	16.8
Off Bench	6	25.7	9.8	.475	1.8	.545	5.0	.800	1.17	1.50	2.7	5.5	14.3
In wins	15	39.1	15.1	.449	2.3	.371	6.6	.758	2.07	1.53	4.9	9.0	19.5
In losses	61	35.8	13.1	.435	2.1	.357	5.3	.707	1.05	1.11	4.0	7.5	15.9

	G	Min	FGA	FG%	3PA	3P%	FTA	FT%	Blk	Stl	Ast	Reb	Pts
Pre All-Star	48	37.2	13.9	.426	2.2	.324	5.5	.698	1.48	1.21	3.8	7.8	16.4
Post All-Star	28	35.0	12.7	.462	2.1	.424	5.5	.755	0.86	1.18	4.9	7.9	16.8
November	14	41.1	14.6	.417	2.7	.342	7.7	.713	1.21	1.36	3.6	7.8	18.6
December	15	35.0	13.8	.401	1.6	.250	4.9	.635	1.87	1.00	4.3	7.5	14.6
January	14	38.4	15.3	.467	2.7	.342	4.9	.783	1.43	1.36	3.6	9.1	19.1
February	13	33.1	11.1	.417	1.4	.500	4.5	.621	1.08	1.31	3.5	6.6	12.7
March	11	35.6	13.3	.500	2.6	.379	5.8	.750	0.45	0.73	5.6	7.8	18.6
April	9	34.0	12.1	.440	1.9	.412	5.2	.851	1.22	1.44	4.9	8.1	15.9
0 Days Rest	20	37.5	13.6	.449	1.9	.351	5.3	.755	1.35	1.10	4.1	7.5	16.9
1 Days Rest	35	36.4	13.4	.434	2.4	.373	5.6	.733	1.03	1.00	4.3	7.9	16.6
2 Days Rest	13	38.0	14.1	.410	2.2	.276	5.1	.727	1.69	1.54	4.6	8.6	15.8
3+ Days Rest	8	31.4	12.6	.485	1.9	.467	6.6	.585	1.25	1.75	3.1	7.1	17.0

Michael Olowokandi

1999-2000 Per Game Averages

	G	Min	FGA	FG%	3PA	3P%	FTA	FT%	Blk	Stl	Ast	Reb	Pts
Total	80	31.2	9.5	.437	0.0	—	2.4	.651	1.75	0.44	0.5	8.2	9.8
Home	40	30.3	8.5	.459	0.0	—	2.4	.604	1.53	0.50	0.4	7.8	9.3
Road	40	32.0	10.4	.418	0.0	—	2.3	.699	1.98	0.38	0.5	8.7	10.3
vs. Playoff	47	30.2	9.6	.437	0.0	—	2.4	.652	1.53	0.45	0.4	7.5	10.0
vs. Non-Playoff	33	32.5	9.2	.436	0.0	—	2.2	.649	2.06	0.42	0.6	9.2	9.5
vs. East	29	32.0	9.7	.436	0.0	—	2.7	.709	2.00	0.34	0.6	9.0	10.3
vs. West	51	30.7	9.3	.437	0.0	—	2.2	.609	1.61	0.49	0.4	7.7	9.5
vs. Div.	24	30.4	9.5	.395	0.0	—	2.3	.545	1.71	0.50	0.7	8.5	8.8
As Starter	77	31.5	9.6	.434	0.0	—	2.4	.647	1.75	0.42	0.5	8.4	9.9
Off Bench	3	23.7	6.0	.556	0.0	—	0.7	1.000	1.67	1.00	0.0	3.3	7.3
In wins	14	32.8	9.4	.443	0.0	—	3.4	.617	1.79	0.43	0.6	9.1	10.4
In losses	66	30.8	9.5	.435	0.0	—	2.2	.662	1.74	0.44	0.5	8.0	9.7

	G	Min	FGA	FG%	3PA	3P%	FTA	FT%	Blk	Stl	Ast	Reb	Pts
Pre All-Star	48	31.0	9.0	.449	0.0	—	2.5	.615	1.73	0.33	0.5	8.4	9.6
Post All-Star	32	31.4	10.1	.420	0.0	—	2.1	.716	1.78	0.59	0.5	7.8	10.0
November	14	29.6	7.6	.449	0.0	—	2.8	.615	1.71	0.43	0.4	7.1	8.6
December	14	31.5	9.5	.481	0.0	—	3.1	.605	1.43	0.36	0.6	8.3	11.0
January	14	32.4	9.9	.413	0.0	—	2.4	.576	2.00	0.29	0.6	10.0	9.5
February	14	30.1	9.2	.403	0.0	—	1.6	.864	2.07	0.29	0.2	8.1	8.8
March	15	29.9	10.5	.465	0.0	—	2.4	.694	1.47	0.47	0.3	7.7	11.4
April	9	34.9	10.2	.391	0.0	—	1.8	.625	1.89	1.00	1.0	7.9	9.1
0 Days Rest	21	32.6	10.9	.417	0.0	—	2.4	.627	1.86	0.48	0.6	8.4	10.6
1 Days Rest	37	30.2	8.9	.432	0.0	—	1.9	.681	1.70	0.49	0.4	7.6	8.9
2 Days Rest	15	32.0	8.7	.500	0.0	—	2.8	.643	1.27	0.40	0.6	8.2	10.5
3+ Days Rest	7	30.1	9.9	.406	0.0	—	3.9	.630	2.71	0.14	0.4	10.4	10.4

Career (1998-99 thru 1999-2000)

	G	Min	FGA	FG%	3PA	3P%	FTA	FT%	Blk	Stl	Ast	Reb	Pts
Total	125	30.2	9.2	.435	0.0	—	2.5	.586	1.56	0.50	0.5	8.1	9.5
Home	63	29.2	8.3	.458	0.0	—	2.4	.560	1.48	0.57	0.5	7.7	9.0
Road	62	31.2	10.2	.415	0.0	—	2.5	.611	1.65	0.42	0.5	8.5	10.0
vs. Playoff	73	29.1	9.2	.432	0.0	—	2.4	.588	1.29	0.49	0.5	7.5	9.4
vs. Non-Playoff	52	31.7	9.3	.438	0.0	—	2.5	.585	1.94	0.50	0.6	8.9	9.6
vs. East	34	31.3	9.7	.429	0.0	—	2.9	.680	2.03	0.38	0.5	8.6	10.2
vs. West	91	29.7	9.1	.437	0.0	—	2.3	.543	1.38	0.54	0.5	7.9	9.2
vs. Div.	42	28.8	8.6	.425	0.0	—	2.3	.505	1.43	0.40	0.7	7.9	8.8
As Starter	113	30.9	9.4	.430	0.0	—	2.4	.579	1.62	0.50	0.5	8.5	9.5
Off Bench	12	23.6	7.5	.489	0.0	—	3.0	.639	1.00	0.42	0.1	4.8	9.3
In wins	23	31.1	8.8	.446	0.0	—	2.6	.567	1.61	0.61	0.5	9.2	9.3
In losses	102	30.0	9.3	.432	0.0	—	2.4	.591	1.55	0.47	0.5	7.9	9.5

	G	Min	FGA	FG%	3PA	3P%	FTA	FT%	Blk	Stl	Ast	Reb	Pts
Pre All-Star	48	31.0	9.0	.449	0.0	—	2.5	.615	1.73	0.33	0.5	8.4	9.6
Post All-Star	32	31.4	10.1	.420	0.0	—	2.1	.716	1.78	0.59	0.5	7.8	10.0
Oct/Nov	14	29.6	7.6	.449	0.0	—	2.8	.615	1.71	0.43	0.4	7.1	8.6
December	14	31.5	9.5	.481	0.0	—	3.1	.605	1.43	0.36	0.6	8.3	11.0
January	14	32.4	9.9	.413	0.0	—	2.4	.576	2.00	0.29	0.6	10.0	9.5
February	25	29.5	9.1	.419	0.0	—	2.5	.635	1.76	0.32	0.3	8.0	9.2
March	28	28.3	9.5	.440	0.0	—	2.6	.658	1.36	0.54	0.3	7.6	10.1
Apr/May	30	31.1	9.5	.426	0.0	—	1.9	.411	1.37	0.80	0.9	8.3	8.8
0 Days Rest	36	30.2	9.7	.425	0.0	—	2.3	.583	1.56	0.56	0.6	8.0	9.6
1 Days Rest	60	29.8	9.2	.428	0.0	—	2.1	.563	1.52	0.55	0.5	8.0	9.1
2 Days Rest	19	31.9	8.5	.503	0.0	—	3.3	.613	1.42	0.37	0.5	8.2	10.5
3+ Days Rest	10	29.1	9.5	.389	0.0	—	3.5	.629	2.10	0.20	0.3	9.2	9.6

Shaquille O'Neal

Los Angeles Lakers — Center

1999-2000 Per Game Averages

	G	Min	FGA	FG%	3PA	3P%	FTA	FT%	Blk	Stl	Ast	Reb	Pts		G	Min	FGA	FG%	3PA	3P%	FTA	FT%	Blk	Stl	Ast	Reb	Pts
Total	79	40.0	21.1	.574	0.0	.000	10.4	.524	3.03	0.46	3.8	13.6	29.7	Pre All-Star	47	39.6	20.1	.574	0.0	.000	10.6	.476	3.43	0.53	3.5	14.2	28.0
Home	38	39.5	21.1	.578	0.0	.000	10.6	.521	3.55	0.53	4.2	15.1	29.9	Post All-Star	32	40.6	22.6	.575	0.0	—	10.3	.598	2.44	0.34	4.2	12.8	32.1
Road	41	40.5	21.0	.571	0.0	—	10.3	.527	2.54	0.39	3.4	12.3	29.4	November	14	37.4	19.6	.595	0.0	—	13.0	.418	3.36	0.43	3.0	13.4	28.7
vs. Playoff	42	41.5	21.6	.542	0.0	.000	10.0	.551	3.24	0.43	4.0	13.0	28.9	December	15	40.3	19.9	.544	0.1	.000	9.5	.469	3.20	0.67	3.4	15.5	26.1
vs. Non-Playoff	37	38.4	20.5	.613	0.0	—	10.9	.496	2.78	0.49	3.6	14.4	30.5	January	14	42.3	21.7	.559	0.0		8.1	.500	3.64	0.57	4.1	14.7	29.3
vs. East	30	40.9	21.2	.547	0.0	—	10.1	.543	3.47	0.43	3.9	14.4	28.7	February	13	39.9	18.6	.574	0.0	—	11.0	.608	3.38	0.38	4.6	12.8	28.1
vs. West	49	39.5	21.0	.591	0.0	.000	10.6	.513	2.76	0.47	3.7	13.2	30.3	March	16	39.4	23.5	.590	0.0	—	9.9	.608	2.13	0.38	4.0	12.3	33.8
vs. Div.	23	40.3	22.2	.586	0.0	.000	10.1	.543	2.43	0.39	3.0	14.0	31.5	April	7	42.0	24.4	.585	0.0	—	12.0	.583	2.14	0.14	3.4	12.7	35.6
As Starter	79	40.0	21.1	.574	0.0	.000	10.4	.524	3.03	0.46	3.8	13.6	29.7	0 Days Rest	22	38.7	19.6	.609	0.0	—	11.1	.549	2.82	0.45	3.5	14.6	30.0
Off Bench	0	—	—	—	—	—	—	—	—	—	—	—	—	1 Days Rest	38	41.1	22.0	.547	0.0	.000	9.9	.519	3.26	0.50	4.2	13.7	29.2
In wins	66	39.7	20.8	.576	0.0	.000	10.5	.540	3.05	0.48	3.9	13.9	29.7	2 Days Rest	11	40.1	20.3	.610	0.0	—	11.3	.468	2.73	0.36	4.3	11.8	30.0
In losses	13	42.0	22.2	.564	0.0	—	10.1	.443	2.92	0.31	3.3	12.3	29.5	3+ Days Rest	8	38.6	21.6	.572	0.0	—	10.0	.563	2.88	0.38	2.3	13.0	30.4

Last Five Seasons

	G	Min	FGA	FG%	3PA	3P%	FTA	FT%	Blk	Stl	Ast	Reb	Pts		G	Min	FGA	FG%	3PA	3P%	FTA	FT%	Blk	Stl	Ast	Reb	Pts
Total	293	37.3	19.5	.573	0.0	.125	10.2	.515	2.48	0.65	3.0	12.0	27.7	Pre All-Star	137	38.1	18.9	.580	0.0	.000	10.2	.474	3.05	0.68	3.1	13.0	26.8
Home	147	36.6	19.6	.579	0.0	.200	10.5	.512	2.82	0.69	3.1	12.5	28.0	Post All-Star	107	37.5	20.9	.565	0.0	.333	10.2	.556	2.12	0.58	3.1	11.4	29.3
Road	146	38.0	19.5	.568	0.0	—	10.0	.518	2.14	0.61	2.9	11.5	27.3	Oct/Nov	39	37.7	17.9	.600	0.1	.000	10.5	.444	2.85	0.64	2.7	12.9	26.2
vs. Playoff	163	38.3	19.5	.555	0.0	.000	10.3	.522	2.44	0.66	2.9	11.9	27.0	December	36	38.8	19.6	.548	0.1	.000	10.0	.517	3.17	0.75	3.3	13.5	26.6
vs. Non-Playoff	130	36.1	19.6	.596	0.0	.333	10.2	.505	2.54	0.65	3.0	12.2	28.5	January	50	38.6	20.0	.581	0.0	—	10.0	.454	3.18	0.72	3.3	13.3	27.8
vs. East	109	37.9	19.5	.569	0.0	.333	10.1	.508	2.78	0.72	3.2	12.5	27.3	February	55	36.0	18.8	.560	0.0	1.000	10.2	.529	2.42	0.73	3.0	11.0	26.4
vs. West	184	36.9	19.6	.576	0.0	.000	10.3	.519	2.30	0.61	2.8	11.7	27.9	March	65	37.2	20.2	.573	0.0	.000	10.0	.554	2.06	0.57	2.9	11.1	28.6
vs. Div.	94	37.2	20.7	.560	0.0	.000	10.4	.517	2.32	0.61	2.9	12.1	28.5	Apr/May	48	36.1	20.3	.580	0.0		10.7	.565	1.58	0.54	2.6	11.3	29.5
As Starter	288	37.4	19.6	.573	0.0	.125	10.2	.516	2.49	0.66	3.0	12.0	27.7	0 Days Rest	73	36.5	18.5	.584	0.0	.000	10.2	.532	2.36	0.68	2.7	11.8	27.1
Off Bench	5	29.0	17.4	.609	0.0	—	9.8	.449	1.80	0.20	2.6	11.0	25.6	1 Days Rest	151	38.2	19.9	.560	0.0	.000	10.2	.517	2.48	0.62	3.2	12.5	27.6
In wins	221	37.0	19.4	.577	0.0	.143	10.4	.524	2.57	0.64	3.1	12.2	27.9	2 Days Rest	36	37.5	19.7	.605	0.0	1.000	11.6	.489	2.81	0.53	2.9	10.9	29.6
In losses	72	38.1	19.8	.561	0.0	.000	9.7	.486	2.22	0.69	2.6	11.5	27.0	3+ Days Rest	33	34.8	19.9	.577	0.1	.000	8.7	.495	2.39	0.85	2.4	11.8	27.3

Greg Ostertag

Utah Jazz — Center

1999-2000 Per Game Averages

	G	Min	FGA	FG%	3PA	3P%	FTA	FT%	Blk	Stl	Ast	Reb	Pts		G	Min	FGA	FG%	3PA	3P%	FTA	FT%	Blk	Stl	Ast	Reb	Pts
Total	81	19.8	3.3	.464	0.0	.000	2.3	.636	2.12	0.25	0.2	6.0	4.5	Pre All-Star	46	19.3	3.3	.513	0.0	—	2.3	.594	1.80	0.26	0.2	5.7	4.7
Home	41	20.7	3.5	.472	0.0	—	2.3	.548	2.56	0.34	0.2	5.9	4.6	Post All-Star	35	20.5	3.3	.402	0.0	.000	2.3	.691	2.54	0.23	0.3	6.3	4.3
Road	40	19.0	3.1	.455	0.0	—	2.4	.723	1.68	0.15	0.2	6.1	4.5	November	14	23.4	3.6	.520	0.0	—	2.8	.564	1.71	0.36	0.1	6.7	5.3
vs. Playoff	44	19.5	3.3	.483	0.0	.000	2.5	.582	1.73	0.23	0.2	6.0	4.6	December	13	16.2	2.5	.606	0.0	—	1.9	.560	1.69	0.15	0.2	4.6	4.2
vs. Non-Playoff	37	20.2	3.4	.444	0.0	—	2.1	.714	2.59	0.27	0.2	5.9	4.5	January	14	17.4	3.1	.558	0.0	—	1.8	.520	1.86	0.14	0.2	5.8	4.4
vs. East	30	18.3	3.2	.448	0.0	—	2.4	.569	1.83	0.24	0.2	5.2	4.2	February	13	19.8	3.8	.400	0.0	—	2.5	.719	2.54	0.38	0.2	4.9	4.8
vs. West	51	20.7	3.4	.474	0.0	.000	2.3	.678	2.29	0.25	0.2	6.4	4.7	March	16	21.2	3.1	.440	0.0	—	2.3	.639	2.38	0.31	0.4	6.7	4.2
vs. Div.	24	21.4	3.1	.446	0.0	—	1.6	.579	2.42	0.25	0.2	6.4	3.7	April	11	20.8	3.7	.293	0.1	.000	2.7	.800	2.64	0.09	0.3	6.9	4.4
As Starter	3	17.7	3.3	.300	0.0	—	1.0	.667	0.67	1.00	0.0	4.3	2.7	0 Days Rest	18	18.5	2.7	.429	0.1	.000	3.2	.754	1.94	0.11	0.2	4.7	4.7
Off Bench	78	19.9	3.3	.471	0.0	.000	2.4	.636	2.18	0.22	0.2	6.0	4.6	1 Days Rest	44	20.1	3.5	.490	0.0	—	1.9	.600	2.05	0.27	0.3	6.1	4.6
In wins	54	20.4	3.4	.505	0.0	.000	2.3	.595	2.28	0.30	0.3	6.4	4.8	2 Days Rest	13	21.8	3.5	.444	0.0	—	2.4	.581	2.23	0.23	0.2	7.2	4.5
In losses	27	18.6	3.1	.373	0.0	—	2.3	.721	1.81	0.15	0.1	5.1	3.9	3+ Days Rest	6	17.8	3.3	.400	0.0	—	2.3	.500	3.00	0.50	0.2	6.0	3.8

Career (1995-96 thru 1999-2000)

	G	Min	FGA	FG%	3PA	3P%	FTA	FT%	Blk	Stl	Ast	Reb	Pts		G	Min	FGA	FG%	3PA	3P%	FTA	FT%	Blk	Stl	Ast	Reb	Pts
Total	326	20.6	4.0	.486	0.0	.000	2.2	.617	1.99	0.27	0.3	6.0	5.2	Pre All-Star	160	19.6	3.8	.508	0.0	.000	2.2	.586	1.73	0.28	0.3	5.6	5.2
Home	168	21.5	4.3	.486	0.0	.000	2.3	.591	2.45	0.32	0.4	6.5	5.5	Post All-Star	118	18.9	4.1	.463	0.0	.000	2.0	.661	2.06	0.28	0.3	6.0	5.1
Road	158	19.7	3.7	.486	0.0	—	2.1	.646	1.51	0.23	0.2	5.4	5.0	Oct/Nov	51	21.7	4.5	.463	0.0	.000	2.4	.533	1.98	0.35	0.2	6.2	5.4
vs. Playoff	173	20.5	3.8	.494	0.0	.000	2.2	.607	1.71	0.24	0.3	5.8	5.1	December	44	18.8	3.9	.567	0.0	.000	2.5	.577	1.48	0.23	0.2	5.3	5.9
vs. Non-Playoff	153	20.7	4.2	.478	0.0	.000	2.1	.628	2.32	0.31	0.4	6.1	5.4	January	49	18.8	3.0	.537	0.0	—	1.8	.581	1.76	0.20	0.3	5.4	4.2
vs. East	105	20.1	4.0	.512	0.0	.000	2.3	.588	1.94	0.24	0.2	5.7	5.4	February	50	19.5	3.9	.444	0.0	—	2.0	.700	2.18	0.30	0.3	5.5	4.9
vs. West	221	20.8	4.0	.474	0.0	.000	2.1	.632	2.02	0.29	0.3	6.1	5.1	March	67	21.4	4.0	.478	0.0	.000	2.2	.600	1.91	0.22	0.3	6.2	5.1
vs. Div.	98	21.5	3.9	.450	0.0	.000	2.1	.591	2.11	0.31	0.4	6.3	4.7	Apr/May	65	22.3	4.5	.468	0.0	.000	2.2	.699	2.48	0.32	0.4	6.7	5.8
As Starter	154	25.1	4.8	.491	0.0	.000	2.5	.635	2.34	0.32	0.4	7.0	6.3	0 Days Rest	76	20.2	3.3	.514	0.0	.000	2.4	.617	1.71	0.26	0.3	5.2	4.9
Off Bench	172	16.6	3.3	.480	0.0	.000	1.9	.595	1.69	0.23	0.2	5.0	4.3	1 Days Rest	172	21.5	4.3	.501	0.0	.000	2.1	.645	2.12	0.28	0.3	6.3	5.7
In wins	234	21.3	4.2	.509	0.0	.000	2.2	.613	2.19	0.31	0.4	6.4	5.6	2 Days Rest	44	18.4	3.4	.437	0.0	—	2.3	.588	1.84	0.23	0.3	5.7	4.4
In losses	92	18.8	3.5	.417	0.0	—	2.0	.627	1.49	0.18	0.1	4.9	4.2	3+ Days Rest	34	19.5	4.7	.419	0.0	—	2.0	.507	2.21	0.32	0.2	6.4	4.9

Bo Outlaw

Orlando Magic — Forward-Center

1999-2000 Per Game Averages

	G	Min	FGA	FG%	3PA	3P%	FTA	FT%	Blk	Stl	Ast	Reb	Pts
Total	82	28.4	4.1	.602	0.0	.000	2.0	.506	1.80	1.38	3.0	6.4	6.0
Home	41	28.4	4.3	.642	0.0	.000	2.0	.513	1.80	1.54	3.3	6.5	6.5
Road	41	28.3	4.0	.558	0.0	.000	2.0	.500	1.80	1.22	2.6	6.3	5.4
vs. Playoff	47	27.3	3.4	.609	0.1	.000	1.5	.549	1.70	1.19	2.5	6.1	5.0
vs. Non-Playoff	35	29.8	5.1	.596	0.0	—	2.6	.473	1.94	1.63	3.7	6.9	7.3
vs. East	54	28.6	4.2	.575	0.0	.000	2.0	.491	1.85	1.39	2.8	6.4	5.8
vs. West	28	27.9	4.0	.655	0.1	.000	1.9	.537	1.71	1.36	3.4	6.4	6.3
vs. Div.	25	29.8	4.5	.566	0.0	—	2.6	.500	2.08	1.32	3.3	7.2	6.4
As Starter	55	29.2	4.7	.602	0.0	.000	2.1	.487	1.62	1.35	3.4	6.6	6.6
Off Bench	27	26.7	3.1	.602	0.0	.000	1.7	.556	2.19	1.44	2.1	6.0	4.6
In wins	41	28.3	4.5	.630	0.0	—	2.2	.506	2.05	1.63	3.7	6.6	6.8
In losses	41	28.4	3.8	.568	0.1	.000	1.8	.507	1.56	1.12	2.3	6.2	5.2
Pre All-Star	50	28.1	3.8	.592	0.0	.000	1.8	.522	1.96	1.38	2.3	5.7	5.5
Post All-Star	32	28.7	4.6	.615	0.0	.000	2.2	.486	1.56	1.38	4.0	7.6	6.8
November	15	27.5	3.1	.435	0.0	—	1.5	.391	2.33	1.40	2.3	5.5	3.3
December	14	25.7	3.3	.674	0.1	.000	1.4	.500	1.79	1.50	2.2	5.6	5.1
January	17	30.8	4.8	.617	0.1	.000	2.4	.634	1.94	1.18	2.3	5.8	7.4
February	11	27.9	3.8	.643	0.1	.000	1.7	.421	1.45	0.91	4.4	6.4	5.6
March	16	28.3	4.6	.676	0.0	—	2.7	.535	1.31	1.69	4.1	8.1	7.7
April	9	30.1	5.6	.520	0.0	—	1.8	.375	2.00	1.56	3.0	7.2	6.4
0 Days Rest	22	28.2	4.2	.543	0.0	—	1.9	.500	1.68	0.91	2.4	6.6	5.5
1 Days Rest	42	27.9	4.1	.628	0.0	.000	1.9	.494	2.02	1.50	3.1	6.2	6.1
2 Days Rest	8	31.0	5.3	.595	0.1	.000	3.8	.533	1.13	1.88	3.8	7.6	8.3
3+ Days Rest	10	28.5	3.3	.636	0.1	.000	0.9	.556	1.70	1.50	3.1	5.9	4.7

Last Five Seasons

	G	Min	FGA	FG%	3PA	3P%	FTA	FT%	Blk	Stl	Ast	Reb	Pts
Total	357	26.1	4.6	.580	0.1	.048	2.7	.512	1.69	1.11	2.0	5.6	6.7
Home	178	26.9	4.9	.598	0.1	.083	3.1	.512	1.83	1.17	2.2	5.7	7.5
Road	179	25.3	4.3	.558	0.1	.000	2.3	.511	1.56	1.06	1.8	5.4	5.9
vs. Playoff	203	25.4	4.3	.559	0.1	.077	2.3	.495	1.59	1.03	1.8	5.3	5.9
vs. Non-Playoff	154	27.0	5.0	.603	0.1	.000	3.1	.508	1.84	1.22	2.3	5.9	7.7
vs. East	196	28.3	4.8	.569	0.0	.000	2.8	.517	1.81	1.16	2.2	6.0	6.8
vs. West	161	23.4	4.4	.593	0.1	.071	2.5	.505	1.56	1.06	1.8	5.0	6.5
vs. Div.	106	26.7	4.7	.586	0.1	.000	2.7	.510	1.81	0.96	2.2	5.9	6.9
As Starter	181	33.2	5.8	.571	0.0	.125	3.2	.519	1.99	1.33	2.9	7.2	8.3
Off Bench	176	18.7	3.4	.596	0.1	.000	2.2	.500	1.39	0.90	1.2	3.9	5.1
In wins	166	27.8	5.1	.601	0.0	.125	2.9	.524	1.90	1.29	2.5	6.0	7.7
In losses	191	24.6	4.1	.557	0.1	.000	2.4	.499	1.51	0.96	1.7	5.2	5.8
Pre All-Star	190	23.8	4.1	.591	0.0	.000	2.3	.517	1.54	1.05	1.5	5.0	6.1
Post All-Star	136	28.9	5.1	.574	0.1	.111	3.1	.521	1.99	1.16	2.9	6.4	7.5
Oct/Nov	62	22.2	4.1	.557	0.0	.000	2.3	.542	1.55	1.05	1.4	4.9	5.8
December	57	23.8	3.9	.595	0.0	.000	2.2	.488	1.33	1.18	1.3	4.6	5.7
January	58	25.5	4.4	.601	0.1	.000	2.5	.510	1.76	0.97	1.6	5.3	6.5
February	61	29.9	5.4	.558	0.1	.000	2.9	.531	1.87	1.21	2.7	6.6	7.6
March	68	28.1	5.0	.595	0.1	.250	3.2	.528	1.76	1.16	2.7	5.8	7.7
Apr/May	51	26.7	4.7	.576	0.1	.000	2.8	.455	1.90	1.12	2.5	6.0	6.7
0 Days Rest	92	27.0	4.6	.565	0.1	.000	2.5	.483	1.67	0.95	1.9	5.7	6.4
1 Days Rest	184	26.3	4.7	.589	0.1	.091	2.6	.538	1.83	1.17	2.1	5.6	7.0
2 Days Rest	42	24.9	4.6	.594	0.0	.000	3.4	.514	1.31	1.19	2.2	5.6	7.2
3+ Days Rest	39	24.0	4.2	.549	0.0	.000	2.2	.437	1.54	1.15	1.6	4.9	5.5

Billy Owens

Golden State Warriors — Forward

1999-2000 Per Game Averages

	G	Min	FGA	FG%	3PA	3P%	FTA	FT%	Blk	Stl	Ast	Reb	Pts
Total	62	21.0	5.8	.419	0.5	.324	1.7	.594	0.34	0.53	1.6	4.9	6.0
Home	30	20.1	5.0	.460	0.6	.421	1.6	.604	0.40	0.50	1.9	4.9	5.8
Road	32	21.9	6.5	.389	0.5	.200	1.8	.586	0.28	0.56	1.3	4.8	6.2
vs. Playoff	34	22.6	6.5	.371	0.7	.360	1.7	.534	0.29	0.59	1.4	5.1	6.0
vs. Non-Playoff	28	19.2	4.9	.496	0.3	.222	1.7	.667	0.39	0.46	1.3	4.6	6.1
vs. East	38	22.3	6.0	.410	0.5	.300	1.7	.578	0.37	0.68	1.8	5.1	6.1
vs. West	24	19.1	5.4	.434	0.6	.357	1.8	.619	0.29	0.29	1.2	4.4	6.0
vs. Div.	15	20.9	5.9	.382	0.4	.000	1.7	.615	0.47	0.47	1.6	4.9	5.6
As Starter	11	27.6	7.3	.400	0.8	.444	1.5	.625	0.36	1.36	1.9	5.1	7.1
Off Bench	51	19.6	5.5	.424	0.5	.280	1.8	.589	0.33	0.35	1.5	4.8	5.8
In wins	30	20.4	5.4	.497	0.5	.357	1.5	.568	0.47	0.77	1.6	4.7	6.4
In losses	32	21.6	6.1	.354	0.6	.300	1.9	.613	0.22	0.31	1.6	5.0	5.7
Pre All-Star	46	20.0	5.6	.434	0.6	.333	1.4	.594	0.35	0.57	1.3	4.2	5.9
Post All-Star	16	24.1	6.3	.380	0.4	.286	2.6	.595	0.31	0.44	2.4	6.8	6.4
November	15	25.4	7.4	.441	0.9	.357	1.9	.655	0.73	0.87	1.6	4.7	8.1
December	16	22.9	6.6	.453	0.6	.333	1.6	.600	0.13	0.50	1.4	5.4	7.1
January	11	12.0	2.5	.321	0.3	.333	0.6	.429	0.27	0.45	1.1	2.1	2.0
February	11	18.9	5.6	.419	0.3	.000	2.6	.483	0.18	0.36	1.7	5.9	6.0
March	9	24.2	5.7	.353	0.6	.400	1.8	.750	0.33	0.33	2.2	6.2	5.6
April	0	—											
0 Days Rest	18	22.2	6.4	.383	0.5	.111	1.4	.577	0.22	0.33	1.3	4.8	5.8
1 Days Rest	29	22.8	6.2	.456	0.4	.385	2.0	.621	0.41	0.59	1.6	5.3	7.1
2 Days Rest	6	13.2	4.0	.417	0.2	.000	1.7	.500	0.67	0.33	1.0	3.8	4.2
3+ Days Rest	9	18.4	4.3	.359	1.2	.455	1.3	.583	0.11	0.89	2.2	4.0	4.4

Last Five Seasons

	G	Min	FGA	FG%	3PA	3P%	FTA	FT%	Blk	Stl	Ast	Reb	Pts
Total	289	28.0	8.9	.458	0.7	.351	2.5	.637	0.44	0.86	2.6	6.1	10.0
Home	148	28.0	8.6	.473	0.7	.407	2.4	.589	0.48	0.95	2.8	6.3	10.3
Road	141	28.0	9.2	.444	0.7	.289	2.6	.683	0.39	0.77	2.3	5.9	10.1
vs. Playoff	167	28.2	9.0	.445	0.8	.359	2.3	.621	0.39	0.85	2.5	6.0	9.7
vs. Non-Playoff	122	27.6	8.8	.477	0.6	.338	2.8	.655	0.50	0.88	2.6	6.3	10.9
vs. East	129	28.2	8.9	.462	0.6	.361	2.7	.634	0.43	0.81	2.7	6.1	10.1
vs. West	160	27.4	8.9	.455	0.8	.344	2.4	.640	0.44	0.91	2.5	6.1	9.9
vs. Div.	91	28.2	9.0	.446	0.7	.281	2.4	.674	0.54	0.81	2.5	5.8	9.8
As Starter	215	30.4	9.8	.467	0.8	.361	2.7	.638	0.48	0.99	2.9	6.5	11.1
Off Bench	74	20.9	6.2	.420	0.5	.308	2.0	.633	0.31	0.50	1.7	4.9	6.6
In wins	123	27.9	9.0	.490	0.7	.346	2.6	.620	0.53	0.94	2.8	6.7	10.7
In losses	166	28.0	8.8	.434	0.7	.355	2.5	.650	0.37	0.80	2.4	5.7	9.5
Pre All-Star	163	29.0	9.1	.472	0.7	.339	2.5	.605	0.48	0.85	2.6	6.3	10.3
Post All-Star	105	27.7	8.8	.448	0.7	.355	2.7	.664	0.42	0.93	2.7	6.3	9.9
Oct/Nov	57	31.0	9.4	.484	0.8	.326	2.8	.635	0.65	0.75	2.7	6.4	11.1
December	49	30.3	9.5	.474	0.8	.325	2.7	.609	0.35	1.06	2.6	6.6	10.9
January	46	26.5	8.5	.435	0.5	.292	2.1	.561	0.50	0.78	2.5	5.8	8.7
February	49	28.8	9.5	.467	0.6	.333	3.3	.623	0.18	0.88	2.8	7.2	11.1
March	60	26.3	8.3	.442	0.8	.391	2.2	.705	0.38	0.78	2.5	5.5	9.2
Apr/May	28	22.4	7.7	.423	0.7	.474	1.6	.739	0.61	1.00	2.1	4.5	8.0
0 Days Rest	65	27.8	9.1	.449	0.7	.339	2.5	.679	0.42	0.71	2.4	5.8	10.1
1 Days Rest	152	28.7	9.0	.465	0.8	.362	2.6	.604	0.45	0.83	2.7	6.3	10.2
2 Days Rest	32	27.1	8.1	.458	0.8	.308	2.2	.671	0.47	1.03	2.3	5.5	9.2
3+ Days Rest	40	26.1	8.5	.450	0.7	.379	2.6	.673	0.38	1.10	2.5	4.9	9.6

Ruben Patterson

1999-2000 Per Game Averages

	G	Min	FGA	FG%	3PA	3P%	FTA	FT%	Blk	Stl	Ast	Reb	Pts
Total	81	25.9	8.2	.536	0.3	.444	4.0	.692	0.49	1.16	1.6	5.4	11.6
Home	40	27.3	8.6	.588	0.4	.438	4.0	.711	0.53	1.48	2.0	5.9	13.1
Road	41	24.5	7.8	.480	0.3	.455	4.0	.673	0.46	0.85	1.1	4.8	10.2
vs. Playoff	43	25.8	7.9	.512	0.5	.450	4.6	.663	0.47	1.12	1.5	4.9	11.3
vs. Non-Playoff	38	26.0	8.4	.561	0.2	.429	3.3	.736	0.53	1.21	1.6	5.8	12.0
vs. East	30	27.3	8.9	.526	0.6	.412	3.6	.685	0.57	1.27	1.5	5.6	12.1
vs. West	51	25.0	7.7	.542	0.2	.500	4.2	.695	0.45	1.10	1.6	5.2	11.4
vs. Div.	24	25.5	8.0	.534	0.2	.500	4.8	.711	0.50	1.00	1.2	5.2	12.0
As Starter	74	27.2	8.5	.537	0.4	.444	4.3	.686	0.54	1.19	1.6	5.6	12.2
Off Bench	7	12.4	4.7	.515	0.0	—	0.9	1.000	0.00	0.86	1.0	3.1	5.7
In wins	45	26.6	8.8	.569	0.3	.333	3.7	.702	0.53	1.33	1.9	5.7	13.1
In losses	36	25.1	7.4	.487	0.4	.533	4.3	.680	0.44	0.94	1.1	4.9	10.3

	G	Min	FGA	FG%	3PA	3P%	FTA	FT%	Blk	Stl	Ast	Reb	Pts
Pre All-Star	51	26.0	7.8	.549	0.2	.500	4.6	.697	0.55	1.08	1.5	5.5	11.9
Post All-Star	30	25.8	8.7	.515	0.6	.412	2.9	.678	0.40	1.30	1.6	5.2	11.2
November	15	29.2	9.6	.576	0.1	.500	5.7	.671	1.00	0.93	1.5	6.8	14.9
December	15	24.3	7.0	.457	0.1	.500	3.1	.739	0.47	1.40	1.8	5.6	8.7
January	15	25.7	7.4	.595	0.3	.750	5.2	.705	0.33	0.93	1.5	4.4	12.7
February	13	24.7	8.2	.538	0.2	.500	3.6	.702	0.23	1.15	1.2	4.9	11.5
March	13	28.8	9.9	.527	0.7	.444	3.0	.564	0.54	2.08	2.0	5.5	12.5
April	10	21.2	6.6	.485	0.2	.500	2.6	.808	0.30	0.30	1.1	4.7	8.6
0 Days Rest	21	22.7	6.6	.486	0.2	.000	2.8	.586	0.33	0.67	1.3	4.6	8.0
1 Days Rest	40	26.8	8.9	.551	0.4	.571	4.6	.696	0.60	1.28	1.6	5.4	13.2
2 Days Rest	15	28.7	8.3	.568	0.5	.375	4.3	.785	0.60	1.53	1.6	6.4	13.1
3+ Days Rest	5	24.0	8.4	.476	0.2	1.000	2.8	.643	0.00	1.20	2.0	5.2	10.0

Career (1998-99 thru 1999-2000)

	G	Min	FGA	FG%	3PA	3P%	FTA	FT%	Blk	Stl	Ast	Reb	Pts
Total	105	21.3	6.8	.527	0.3	.394	3.4	.693	0.41	0.94	1.2	4.4	9.6
Home	52	22.5	7.2	.573	0.4	.421	3.3	.724	0.42	1.15	1.6	4.9	10.8
Road	53	20.2	6.4	.475	0.3	.357	3.4	.665	0.40	0.74	0.9	4.0	8.4
vs. Playoff	58	20.1	6.2	.503	0.4	.417	3.7	.664	0.38	0.90	1.1	3.9	8.9
vs. Non-Playoff	47	22.9	7.4	.551	0.2	.333	2.9	.739	0.45	1.00	1.3	5.1	10.4
vs. East	33	25.4	8.3	.524	0.5	.412	3.3	.688	0.52	1.15	1.4	5.2	11.2
vs. West	72	19.5	6.1	.528	0.2	.375	3.4	.695	0.36	0.85	1.2	4.1	8.9
vs. Div.	34	20.4	6.4	.507	0.2	.429	3.9	.701	0.44	0.74	0.8	4.2	9.4
As Starter	76	26.8	8.4	.534	0.4	.429	4.2	.685	0.55	1.17	1.6	5.5	12.0
Off Bench	29	7.0	2.7	.468	0.2	.200	1.1	.774	0.03	0.34	0.3	1.6	3.3
In wins	59	21.9	7.3	.556	0.3	.333	3.2	.698	0.42	1.03	1.5	4.7	10.5
In losses	46	20.6	6.1	.482	0.4	.444	3.5	.687	0.39	0.83	0.8	4.0	8.5

	G	Min	FGA	FG%	3PA	3P%	FTA	FT%	Blk	Stl	Ast	Reb	Pts
Pre All-Star	51	26.0	7.8	.549	0.2	.500	4.6	.697	0.55	1.08	1.5	5.5	11.9
Post All-Star	30	25.8	8.7	.515	0.6	.412	2.9	.678	0.40	1.30	1.6	5.2	11.2
Oct/Nov	15	29.2	9.6	.576	0.1	.500	5.7	.671	1.00	0.93	1.5	6.8	14.9
December	15	24.3	7.0	.457	0.1	.500	3.1	.739	0.47	1.40	1.8	5.6	8.7
January	15	25.7	7.4	.595	0.3	.750	5.2	.705	0.33	0.93	1.5	4.4	12.7
February	19	17.9	5.8	.541	0.4	.250	2.6	.720	0.16	0.79	0.9	3.4	8.3
March	20	20.7	7.3	.517	0.5	.400	2.3	.565	0.40	1.35	1.3	4.0	9.0
Apr/May	21	14.1	4.6	.448	0.3	.286	2.2	.766	0.24	0.38	0.6	3.2	5.9
0 Days Rest	24	20.9	5.9	.479	0.2	.000	2.7	.594	0.29	0.58	1.2	4.1	7.3
1 Days Rest	49	22.9	7.6	.546	0.3	.500	4.0	.692	0.55	1.12	1.3	4.7	11.2
2 Days Rest	18	24.7	7.3	.557	0.5	.333	3.7	.791	0.50	1.33	1.3	5.5	11.2
3+ Days Rest	14	12.5	4.8	.463	0.2	.667	1.9	.692	0.00	0.43	0.7	2.7	5.9

Gary Payton

1999-2000 Per Game Averages

	G	Min	FGA	FG%	3PA	3P%	FTA	FT%	Blk	Stl	Ast	Reb	Pts
Total	82	41.8	20.3	.448	6.3	.340	5.2	.735	0.22	1.87	8.9	6.5	24.2
Home	41	41.1	20.4	.442	6.0	.339	4.9	.756	0.15	2.20	9.3	5.7	23.8
Road	41	42.4	20.2	.455	6.6	.342	5.4	.716	0.29	1.54	8.6	7.2	24.5
vs. Playoff	44	43.7	20.6	.445	7.0	.366	5.0	.723	0.25	1.75	8.6	6.8	24.5
vs. Non-Playoff	38	39.5	20.0	.452	5.6	.304	5.3	.749	0.18	2.00	9.3	6.1	23.8
vs. East	30	41.9	19.7	.444	6.7	.333	5.3	.719	0.10	1.73	8.5	6.6	23.6
vs. West	52	41.7	20.7	.451	6.1	.345	5.1	.745	0.29	1.94	9.2	6.4	24.5
vs. Div.	24	41.2	19.4	.433	6.1	.299	4.6	.685	0.17	2.00	9.4	5.8	21.8
As Starter	82	41.8	20.3	.448	6.3	.340	5.2	.735	0.22	1.87	8.9	6.5	24.2
Off Bench	0	—	—	—	—	—	—	—	—	—	—	—	—
In wins	45	41.3	20.6	.476	6.2	.362	5.6	.768	0.18	1.96	9.6	6.4	26.1
In losses	37	42.4	20.0	.414	6.5	.315	4.7	.688	0.27	1.76	8.1	6.5	21.8

	G	Min	FGA	FG%	3PA	3P%	FTA	FT%	Blk	Stl	Ast	Reb	Pts
Pre All-Star	51	41.7	19.2	.440	6.8	.366	4.8	.761	0.14	1.65	8.6	6.4	23.1
Post All-Star	31	41.9	22.1	.461	5.6	.289	5.7	.699	0.35	2.23	9.5	6.5	26.0
November	15	40.3	18.1	.426	5.7	.318	5.7	.709	0.13	2.27	9.6	6.6	21.3
December	15	42.2	19.1	.476	8.6	.426	4.8	.792	0.27	1.33	8.1	5.3	25.6
January	15	41.6	20.5	.430	6.3	.319	4.6	.783	0.07	1.27	8.1	6.7	23.2
February	13	42.8	20.0	.438	7.1	.391	4.3	.732	0.08	1.62	8.6	7.1	23.5
March	14	42.5	22.7	.465	5.0	.229	5.9	.711	0.29	2.57	10.7	5.6	26.5
April	10	41.1	22.3	.453	5.0	.260	5.7	.684	0.60	2.30	8.3	8.0	25.4
0 Days Rest	21	40.3	19.9	.440	5.9	.293	5.0	.769	0.29	1.24	8.0	5.9	23.0
1 Days Rest	40	41.9	19.9	.443	6.0	.335	5.2	.705	0.25	2.00	8.8	7.1	23.3
2 Days Rest	17	43.9	21.7	.455	7.5	.402	5.2	.784	0.12	2.29	10.2	6.1	26.8
3+ Days Rest	4	39.0	21.0	.512	7.8	.323	6.0	.667	0.00	2.00	9.8	5.0	28.0

Last Five Seasons

	G	Min	FGA	FG%	3PA	3P%	FTA	FT%	Blk	Stl	Ast	Reb	Pts
Total	377	39.7	17.6	.461	5.0	.326	4.6	.733	0.21	2.32	8.1	4.9	21.2
Home	188	38.7	17.7	.467	4.9	.316	4.7	.740	0.20	2.50	8.3	4.7	21.5
Road	189	40.6	17.5	.454	5.1	.335	4.5	.726	0.22	2.14	7.8	5.2	20.9
vs. Playoff	207	41.2	17.7	.459	5.3	.346	4.5	.724	0.23	2.26	8.1	5.0	21.4
vs. Non-Playoff	170	37.8	17.4	.462	4.6	.296	4.8	.744	0.19	2.39	8.1	4.9	21.0
vs. East	126	39.7	17.0	.452	5.0	.342	4.4	.730	0.24	2.30	7.7	4.8	20.3
vs. West	251	39.6	17.9	.465	5.0	.317	4.7	.734	0.20	2.33	8.2	5.0	21.6
vs. Div.	117	39.9	17.2	.468	4.9	.327	4.9	.743	0.11	2.36	8.6	4.8	21.3
As Starter	377	39.7	17.6	.461	5.0	.326	4.6	.733	0.21	2.32	8.1	4.9	21.2
Off Bench	0	—	—	—	—	—	—	—	—	—	—	—	—
In wins	251	38.8	17.4	.480	4.9	.340	4.7	.748	0.21	2.47	8.3	4.8	21.8
In losses	126	41.3	18.0	.422	5.2	.298	4.5	.702	0.21	2.03	7.6	5.3	19.9

	G	Min	FGA	FG%	3PA	3P%	FTA	FT%	Blk	Stl	Ast	Reb	Pts
Pre All-Star	191	39.5	17.2	.465	4.9	.345	4.5	.731	0.19	2.27	8.0	4.9	20.9
Post All-Star	136	39.7	17.8	.465	4.9	.311	4.4	.742	0.23	2.45	7.9	5.0	21.4
Oct/Nov	63	38.7	16.7	.454	4.2	.306	4.7	.724	0.17	2.57	8.8	4.8	19.9
December	57	39.6	17.0	.492	4.9	.355	5.0	.722	0.19	2.21	8.0	5.1	22.1
January	58	39.3	17.6	.450	5.2	.352	4.1	.757	0.19	2.07	7.1	4.7	20.8
February	59	40.8	17.7	.455	5.7	.334	4.7	.743	0.31	2.12	8.2	5.0	21.5
March	78	40.0	18.1	.456	5.1	.329	4.3	.748	0.24	2.56	8.2	5.1	21.4
Apr/May	62	39.5	18.1	.459	4.7	.272	4.9	.709	0.16	2.29	8.0	5.0	21.4
0 Days Rest	97	39.8	17.4	.443	4.8	.309	4.6	.756	0.26	1.93	7.9	4.7	20.4
1 Days Rest	188	39.3	17.4	.469	4.9	.333	4.7	.713	0.18	2.45	7.8	5.1	21.3
2 Days Rest	67	40.5	17.9	.462	5.3	.349	4.5	.769	0.24	2.55	9.1	5.0	21.9
3+ Days Rest	25	39.4	18.6	.458	5.1	.266	4.0	.697	0.20	2.28	8.2	4.9	21.2

Anthony Peeler

1999-2000 Per Game Averages

	G	Min	FGA	FG%	3PA	3P%	FTA	FT%	Blk	Stl	Ast	Reb	Pts		G	Min	FGA	FG%	3PA	3P%	FTA	FT%	Blk	Stl	Ast	Reb	Pts
Total	82	25.3	8.8	.436	3.1	.333	1.3	.798	0.12	0.76	2.4	2.8	9.8	Pre All-Star	47	25.6	8.7	.434	2.7	.317	1.4	.828	0.13	0.74	2.6	2.5	9.6
Home	41	26.1	9.0	.444	3.4	.348	1.3	.788	0.12	0.73	2.6	2.9	10.2	Post All-Star	35	24.8	9.0	.438	3.7	.349	1.3	.756	0.11	0.77	2.1	3.3	10.1
Road	41	24.4	8.7	.427	2.9	.316	1.4	.807	0.12	0.78	2.1	2.8	9.4	November	12	28.3	9.8	.410	3.8	.356	1.3	.875	0.00	0.75	3.2	3.3	10.5
vs. Playoff	44	25.0	8.7	.420	2.7	.319	1.3	.825	0.11	0.68	2.3	2.8	9.3	December	15	22.7	7.4	.414	2.1	.194	1.1	.875	0.13	0.73	2.6	1.4	7.5
vs. Non-Playoff	38	25.6	9.0	.453	3.6	.346	1.4	.769	0.13	0.84	2.5	2.9	10.4	January	15	26.1	8.7	.481	2.7	.350	1.5	.773	0.20	0.73	2.2	2.9	10.5
vs. East	30	24.0	8.3	.446	2.9	.307	1.2	.722	0.10	0.63	2.2	2.7	9.2	February	14	25.7	9.5	.414	3.4	.396	1.5	.762	0.21	0.79	2.1	2.9	10.4
vs. West	52	26.0	9.2	.431	3.2	.347	1.4	.836	0.13	0.83	2.5	2.9	10.2	March	16	24.8	9.1	.483	2.9	.340	1.0	.688	0.13	0.69	2.2	3.2	10.4
vs. Div.	24	27.4	9.0	.477	3.3	.425	1.5	.833	0.13	0.83	2.5	2.8	11.3	April	10	24.3	8.8	.386	4.4	.318	1.8	.833	0.00	0.90	2.1	3.6	9.7
As Starter	22	26.3	8.7	.424	2.9	.308	1.3	.893	0.09	0.82	3.0	2.3	9.5	0 Days Rest	18	23.9	8.3	.440	2.4	.372	1.7	.806	0.17	1.00	2.3	2.5	9.5
Off Bench	60	24.9	8.9	.440	3.2	.335	1.4	.765	0.13	0.73	2.1	3.0	9.9	1 Days Rest	51	25.6	9.0	.448	3.3	.343	1.3	.788	0.14	0.73	2.4	3.0	10.2
In wins	50	25.2	8.7	.447	3.1	.325	1.3	.781	0.16	0.78	2.6	3.0	9.8	2 Days Rest	5	22.8	7.6	.447	2.8	.214	2.0	.900	0.00	0.60	1.8	2.2	9.2
In losses	32	25.4	9.1	.419	3.1	.347	1.4	.822	0.06	0.72	2.1	2.6	9.8	3+ Days Rest	8	27.8	9.6	.351	3.6	.276	0.3	.500	0.00	0.50	3.0	2.8	7.9

Last Five Seasons

	G	Min	FGA	FG%	3PA	3P%	FTA	FT%	Blk	Stl	Ast	Reb	Pts		G	Min	FGA	FG%	3PA	3P%	FTA	FT%	Blk	Stl	Ast	Reb	Pts
Total	293	27.2	10.3	.423	3.7	.371	1.4	.776	0.17	1.10	2.7	2.8	11.2	Pre All-Star	142	27.2	10.7	.427	3.5	.359	1.4	.782	0.18	0.99	2.8	2.8	11.5
Home	143	27.9	10.3	.432	3.9	.368	1.4	.766	0.17	1.08	3.0	2.9	11.4	Post All-Star	123	26.9	10.1	.429	3.9	.401	1.4	.780	0.14	1.19	2.5	2.8	11.3
Road	150	26.6	10.4	.416	3.6	.374	1.4	.786	0.17	1.12	2.4	2.7	11.1	Oct/Nov	47	26.9	10.1	.418	3.6	.343	1.1	.750	0.15	0.74	2.7	2.9	10.5
vs. Playoff	160	27.1	10.2	.408	3.5	.377	1.5	.774	0.14	1.09	2.4	2.8	10.8	December	41	27.0	10.4	.464	3.3	.381	1.6	.769	0.20	1.10	3.0	2.2	12.1
vs. Non-Playoff	133	27.4	10.5	.442	4.0	.365	1.4	.780	0.20	1.11	3.0	2.8	11.8	January	42	27.9	11.4	.404	3.7	.350	1.5	.790	0.14	1.19	2.8	3.2	11.7
vs. East	97	26.2	9.9	.409	3.6	.348	1.2	.780	0.18	0.92	2.6	2.8	10.7	February	49	24.6	9.1	.402	3.3	.344	1.4	.761	0.24	1.00	2.4	2.6	9.5
vs. West	196	27.7	10.5	.430	3.8	.382	1.5	.775	0.16	1.19	2.7	2.8	11.7	March	69	28.3	10.8	.434	3.6	.375	1.6	.750	0.17	1.22	2.5	3.1	11.9
vs. Div.	90	27.1	10.1	.455	3.5	.422	1.4	.742	0.18	1.20	2.6	2.7	11.7	Apr/May	45	28.3	10.2	.416	4.9	.418	1.4	.855	0.09	1.31	2.7	2.8	11.7
As Starter	151	31.2	12.0	.416	4.2	.373	1.6	.790	0.21	1.39	3.3	3.2	12.9	0 Days Rest	71	27.1	10.5	.442	3.5	.411	1.3	.802	0.14	1.07	2.5	2.9	11.8
Off Bench	142	23.0	8.5	.434	3.2	.369	1.2	.756	0.13	0.79	2.0	2.4	9.5	1 Days Rest	157	28.1	10.7	.424	3.9	.378	1.5	.767	0.18	1.13	2.7	2.9	11.6
In wins	143	26.1	9.5	.467	3.5	.395	1.4	.763	0.19	1.01	2.7	2.7	11.3	2 Days Rest	31	25.9	9.0	.378	3.4	.231	1.7	.815	0.16	1.10	2.8	2.6	9.0
In losses	150	28.3	11.1	.388	4.0	.352	1.5	.788	0.15	1.19	2.6	2.9	11.2	3+ Days Rest	34	24.8	9.6	.418	3.8	.377	1.1	.718	0.18	1.00	2.9	2.1	10.3

Sam Perkins

1999-2000 Per Game Averages

	G	Min	FGA	FG%	3PA	3P%	FTA	FT%	Blk	Stl	Ast	Reb	Pts		G	Min	FGA	FG%	3PA	3P%	FTA	FT%	Blk	Stl	Ast	Reb	Pts
Total	81	20.0	5.4	.417	2.7	.408	1.2	.825	0.41	0.38	0.8	3.6	6.6	Pre All-Star	48	20.0	5.9	.431	3.0	.415	1.2	.825	0.23	0.33	0.8	3.5	7.3
Home	40	19.7	5.4	.419	3.0	.408	1.1	.841	0.50	0.43	1.1	3.5	6.7	Post All-Star	33	19.9	4.8	.394	2.3	.395	1.2	.825	0.67	0.45	0.9	3.7	5.7
Road	41	20.3	5.5	.416	2.4	.408	1.3	.811	0.32	0.34	0.6	3.7	6.6	November	15	20.8	5.3	.438	2.3	.412	1.2	.722	0.27	0.40	0.7	3.4	6.5
vs. Playoff	44	20.3	5.4	.426	2.8	.411	1.4	.823	0.43	0.32	0.8	3.3	6.9	December	14	17.3	5.3	.432	2.9	.425	0.8	.909	0.14	0.36	0.6	2.6	6.5
vs. Non-Playoff	37	19.7	5.5	.407	2.5	.404	0.9	.829	0.38	0.46	0.9	3.9	6.3	January	14	22.4	7.4	.442	4.1	.421	1.3	.778	0.29	0.36	0.7	4.4	9.3
vs. East	53	18.8	5.0	.440	2.3	.433	1.2	.841	0.40	0.30	0.8	3.5	6.4	February	13	19.1	4.8	.365	2.4	.411	1.5	.950	0.38	0.38	1.2	3.3	5.9
vs. West	28	22.2	6.3	.383	3.5	.378	1.2	.794	0.43	0.54	0.8	3.8	7.1	March	16	21.9	4.9	.380	2.4	.333	1.2	.792	0.75	0.50	0.8	4.4	5.8
vs. Div.	27	17.7	4.7	.425	2.2	.373	1.1	.833	0.37	0.26	0.8	3.3	5.7	April	9	17.0	4.6	.439	2.1	.474	0.7	.833	0.67	0.22	1.0	3.0	5.6
As Starter	0	—	—	—	—	—	—	—	—	—	—	—	—	0 Days Rest	21	19.8	5.5	.417	2.5	.358	1.3	.778	0.29	0.24	0.8	3.6	6.5
Off Bench	81	20.0	5.4	.417	2.7	.408	1.2	.825	0.41	0.38	0.8	3.6	6.6	1 Days Rest	40	20.3	5.4	.402	2.9	.430	1.0	.842	0.40	0.53	0.9	3.5	6.3
In wins	55	19.8	5.4	.426	3.0	.423	1.2	.800	0.45	0.38	0.9	3.7	7.1	2 Days Rest	14	19.1	5.6	.410	2.6	.361	1.7	.917	0.64	0.14	1.1	3.7	7.1
In losses	26	20.3	5.6	.400	2.1	.364	1.2	.875	0.31	0.38	0.6	3.4	6.3	3+ Days Rest	6	20.7	5.7	.529	2.5	.533	1.3	.625	0.33	0.50	0.2	4.0	8.2

Last Five Seasons

	G	Min	FGA	FG%	3PA	3P%	FTA	FT%	Blk	Stl	Ast	Reb	Pts		G	Min	FGA	FG%	3PA	3P%	FTA	FT%	Blk	Stl	Ast	Reb	Pts
Total	373	22.1	6.9	.418	3.2	.384	2.0	.797	0.46	0.70	1.2	3.6	8.6	Pre All-Star	187	23.2	7.2	.418	3.6	.381	2.1	.798	0.42	0.76	1.2	3.7	9.1
Home	187	21.0	6.5	.417	3.2	.391	2.1	.802	0.55	0.71	1.2	3.3	8.4	Post All-Star	138	22.4	7.4	.422	3.2	.388	2.2	.812	0.59	0.74	1.3	3.8	9.2
Road	186	23.1	7.2	.419	3.2	.377	1.9	.792	0.38	0.68	1.1	3.9	8.8	Oct/Nov	62	23.1	6.5	.435	3.0	.386	2.1	.771	0.40	0.95	1.2	3.4	8.4
vs. Playoff	198	22.9	6.9	.407	3.3	.388	2.2	.794	0.43	0.73	1.1	3.4	8.6	December	56	22.7	7.4	.428	3.9	.408	1.9	.787	0.46	0.80	1.2	3.8	9.4
vs. Non-Playoff	175	21.1	6.9	.431	3.1	.404	1.9	.801	0.50	0.66	1.2	3.9	8.7	January	57	24.0	7.9	.402	3.9	.360	2.1	.817	0.42	0.61	1.3	4.0	9.5
vs. East	185	20.7	6.1	.416	2.8	.387	1.7	.824	0.42	0.64	1.1	3.5	7.6	February	60	21.9	6.6	.431	3.2	.397	2.2	.792	0.38	0.70	1.2	3.2	8.7
vs. West	188	23.4	7.6	.420	3.6	.382	2.3	.778	0.51	0.76	1.2	3.8	9.6	March	80	21.0	6.8	.410	2.6	.398	2.3	.818	0.46	0.66	1.2	4.0	8.5
vs. Div.	119	21.1	6.7	.432	3.0	.409	2.1	.772	0.50	0.61	1.1	3.6	8.7	Apr/May	58	20.1	6.3	.407	2.9	.353	1.5	.788	0.66	0.45	0.9	3.2	7.3
As Starter	24	30.6	10.6	.388	5.0	.325	2.6	.746	0.58	0.96	2.1	5.9	11.8	0 Days Rest	94	21.9	6.9	.407	3.0	.389	2.3	.782	0.35	0.66	1.0	3.6	8.6
Off Bench	349	21.5	6.6	.422	3.1	.391	2.0	.802	0.46	0.68	1.1	3.4	8.3	1 Days Rest	189	21.6	6.6	.431	3.0	.389	1.7	.790	0.48	0.66	1.1	3.4	8.3
In wins	267	21.7	6.8	.436	3.3	.411	2.0	.803	0.51	0.75	1.2	3.7	8.9	2 Days Rest	61	23.4	7.6	.366	3.8	.322	2.3	.862	0.67	0.70	1.4	4.1	8.7
In losses	106	22.9	7.0	.376	3.0	.311	2.0	.783	0.34	0.57	1.0	3.5	7.8	3+ Days Rest	29	22.8	7.3	.493	3.9	.474	2.3	.750	0.31	1.03	1.0	3.8	10.8

Wesley Person
Cleveland Cavaliers — Guard

1999-2000 Per Game Averages

	G	Min	FGA	FG%	3PA	3P%	FTA	FT%	Blk	Stl	Ast	Reb	Pts
Total	79	26.0	8.3	.428	3.2	.424	1.0	.792	0.24	0.51	1.8	3.4	9.2
Home	39	27.8	9.0	.423	3.9	.424	1.1	.767	0.26	0.67	2.3	3.5	10.1
Road	40	24.3	7.6	.434	2.5	.424	0.9	.824	0.23	0.35	1.4	3.3	8.4
vs. Playoff	45	25.4	8.0	.414	3.1	.374	0.9	.800	0.22	0.56	1.5	3.2	8.5
vs. Non-Playoff	34	26.8	8.6	.446	3.3	.486	1.1	.784	0.26	0.44	2.3	3.6	10.1
vs. East	52	26.8	8.3	.448	3.0	.477	1.0	.784	0.27	0.56	1.7	3.3	9.6
vs. West	27	24.5	8.3	.390	3.5	.337	1.0	.808	0.19	0.41	2.1	3.6	8.4
vs. Div.	26	26.7	8.6	.424	2.7	.429	1.0	.846	0.19	0.50	1.8	3.5	9.3
As Starter	38	30.9	9.5	.446	3.5	.418	1.1	.762	0.21	0.63	2.3	4.1	10.8
Off Bench	41	21.5	7.1	.406	2.8	.431	0.9	.829	0.27	0.39	1.4	2.8	7.7
In wins	29	25.9	8.7	.448	3.2	.436	1.6	.778	0.21	0.55	2.2	3.7	10.4
In losses	50	26.1	8.0	.415	3.1	.417	0.6	.813	0.26	0.48	1.6	3.2	8.5
Pre All-Star	46	23.6	7.7	.408	3.0	.407	0.9	.814	0.26	0.43	1.7	3.0	8.3
Post All-Star	33	29.4	9.1	.452	3.3	.445	1.0	.765	0.21	0.61	2.0	3.9	10.5
November	12	23.9	7.2	.465	3.6	.419	1.0	.750	0.17	0.33	1.6	3.9	8.9
December	16	27.8	8.6	.445	3.4	.519	1.4	.773	0.38	0.63	1.8	3.0	10.4
January	13	13.2	5.7	.230	1.5	.105	0.5	1.000	0.23	0.31	1.2	1.4	3.2
February	12	38.5	11.6	.446	5.9	.408	1.3	.800	0.25	0.58	3.0	4.8	13.8
March	15	29.7	8.9	.459	3.2	.458	1.1	.750	0.27	0.53	1.9	4.4	10.4
April	11	22.5	7.7	.459	1.4	.467	0.5	.833	0.09	0.64	1.6	2.8	8.2
0 Days Rest	24	26.3	8.2	.408	3.6	.419	1.4	.818	0.25	0.50	2.1	3.1	9.3
1 Days Rest	31	26.5	8.6	.451	2.7	.447	0.8	.769	0.29	0.52	1.6	3.6	9.7
2 Days Rest	15	26.2	8.5	.422	3.5	.404	0.7	.800	0.20	0.53	2.1	3.9	9.1
3+ Days Rest	9	23.1	6.9	.403	3.0	.407	0.9	.750	0.11	0.44	1.3	2.4	7.4

Last Five Seasons

	G	Min	FGA	FG%	3PA	3P%	FTA	FT%	Blk	Stl	Ast	Reb	Pts
Total	368	31.3	10.4	.449	4.4	.407	1.6	.766	0.34	0.94	1.8	3.8	12.4
Home	184	31.4	10.5	.452	4.6	.418	1.7	.774	0.32	0.85	2.1	4.0	12.7
Road	184	31.2	10.3	.445	4.2	.395	1.6	.757	0.36	1.04	1.6	3.5	12.1
vs. Playoff	200	31.1	10.2	.443	4.3	.388	1.5	.755	0.30	0.84	1.7	3.8	11.8
vs. Non-Playoff	168	31.7	10.7	.455	4.5	.429	1.9	.776	0.39	1.07	2.0	3.7	13.1
vs. East	205	32.1	10.3	.462	4.4	.416	1.7	.744	0.38	0.98	1.9	3.8	12.6
vs. West	163	30.4	10.6	.433	4.4	.396	1.6	.793	0.29	0.90	1.8	3.8	12.2
vs. Div.	121	30.9	10.2	.443	4.2	.396	1.6	.745	0.38	0.88	1.7	3.8	12.1
As Starter	251	34.8	11.2	.450	4.7	.402	1.8	.751	0.38	1.12	2.1	4.2	13.3
Off Bench	117	23.9	8.7	.444	3.9	.421	1.3	.811	0.26	0.57	1.2	2.9	10.4
In wins	178	32.1	11.2	.481	4.7	.451	2.1	.775	0.38	1.07	2.0	4.2	14.6
In losses	190	30.6	9.6	.413	4.2	.361	1.2	.750	0.31	0.82	1.6	3.4	10.4
Pre All-Star	187	31.6	10.8	.437	4.2	.384	1.8	.793	0.28	1.01	2.0	3.8	12.4
Post All-Star	136	31.5	10.1	.464	4.7	.445	1.6	.764	0.43	0.90	1.6	3.9	12.7
Oct/Nov	55	31.3	11.1	.454	4.7	.342	2.2	.846	0.20	1.33	2.0	4.0	13.6
December	57	30.6	10.2	.439	4.2	.445	1.5	.735	0.30	0.89	2.1	3.3	11.8
January	60	31.4	10.9	.420	3.8	.369	1.6	.802	0.30	0.85	1.9	3.8	11.8
February	58	34.1	11.0	.457	5.1	.416	2.0	.733	0.33	1.02	1.8	4.0	13.6
March	77	29.1	9.5	.460	4.3	.421	1.5	.752	0.38	0.65	1.6	3.5	11.6
Apr/May	61	32.1	10.1	.460	4.6	.439	1.2	.693	0.52	1.03	1.7	4.1	12.1
0 Days Rest	93	31.2	10.2	.434	4.5	.370	1.8	.757	0.35	0.87	1.8	3.6	11.9
1 Days Rest	184	31.7	10.6	.460	4.5	.429	1.6	.769	0.36	0.85	1.9	3.8	12.9
2 Days Rest	61	30.8	10.2	.448	4.0	.428	1.4	.784	0.30	1.15	1.8	3.9	12.0
3+ Days Rest	30	30.6	10.2	.423	4.7	.355	1.5	.739	0.30	1.30	1.7	3.7	11.5

Eric Piatkowski
Los Angeles Clippers — Guard

1999-2000 Per Game Averages

	G	Min	FGA	FG%	3PA	3P%	FTA	FT%	Blk	Stl	Ast	Reb	Pts
Total	75	22.8	7.6	.415	3.2	.383	1.3	.850	0.17	0.59	1.1	3.0	8.7
Home	38	21.6	7.3	.414	2.9	.360	1.2	.867	0.16	0.58	1.0	3.2	8.1
Road	37	24.1	8.0	.417	3.6	.402	1.5	.836	0.19	0.59	1.2	2.8	9.3
vs. Playoff	42	22.6	7.5	.380	3.4	.362	1.2	.804	0.14	0.62	1.0	3.0	7.9
vs. Non-Playoff	33	23.1	7.9	.458	3.1	.412	1.5	.898	0.21	0.55	1.2	2.9	9.8
vs. East	28	21.4	6.8	.402	3.1	.345	1.5	.762	0.11	0.57	0.9	2.2	7.6
vs. West	47	23.7	8.2	.422	3.3	.404	1.2	.914	0.21	0.60	1.2	3.4	9.4
vs. Div.	23	25.0	8.5	.388	3.8	.345	0.8	.889	0.17	0.57	1.3	4.0	8.6
As Starter	23	33.0	11.2	.455	5.0	.466	2.7	.820	0.26	0.96	1.9	3.5	14.7
Off Bench	52	18.3	6.1	.383	2.4	.307	0.8	.897	0.13	0.42	0.7	2.7	6.1
In wins	13	26.8	9.0	.556	4.3	.518	2.2	.821	0.00	0.69	1.8	3.3	14.0
In losses	62	22.0	7.4	.379	3.0	.342	1.2	.861	0.21	0.56	0.9	2.9	7.6
Pre All-Star	42	21.0	6.9	.384	3.0	.362	0.9	.821	0.17	0.45	0.9	3.1	7.1
Post All-Star	33	25.2	8.6	.447	3.5	.405	1.8	.869	0.16	0.76	1.3	2.8	10.7
November	7	24.4	8.4	.356	4.4	.355	2.7	.789	0.14	0.71	0.9	4.0	9.7
December	15	23.9	8.3	.379	3.5	.358	0.5	.750	0.27	0.60	1.1	2.9	7.9
January	14	16.0	4.6	.369	2.3	.344	0.5	.857	0.14	0.29	0.6	3.1	4.6
February	15	20.5	6.5	.388	2.1	.344	0.9	.846	0.00	0.33	0.9	2.3	6.5
March	15	28.6	9.7	.455	3.9	.345	2.0	.900	0.40	0.93	1.5	3.9	11.9
April	9	24.8	9.1	.512	4.1	.568	2.6	.870	0.00	0.78	1.4	1.7	13.9
0 Days Rest	20	28.4	9.3	.405	3.7	.392	2.3	.867	0.20	0.85	1.2	3.9	10.9
1 Days Rest	35	20.1	6.8	.401	2.9	.356	0.9	.875	0.23	0.54	0.8	2.7	7.3
2 Days Rest	14	21.7	7.5	.467	3.5	.429	0.8	.818	0.00	0.50	1.6	2.6	9.1
3+ Days Rest	6	22.8	7.7	.413	3.2	.368	2.0	.750	0.17	0.17	1.3	2.7	9.0

Last Five Seasons

	G	Min	FGA	FG%	3PA	3P%	FTA	FT%	Blk	Stl	Ast	Reb	Pts
Total	321	19.4	6.5	.432	2.8	.392	1.7	.835	0.16	0.61	1.0	2.5	8.1
Home	164	19.5	6.6	.435	2.8	.387	1.7	.848	0.15	0.62	0.9	2.6	8.3
Road	157	19.3	6.5	.430	2.8	.397	1.6	.820	0.17	0.60	1.1	2.4	8.0
vs. Playoff	184	19.8	6.7	.427	3.0	.384	1.7	.795	0.15	0.64	1.0	2.5	8.3
vs. Non-Playoff	137	18.9	6.3	.441	2.6	.403	1.6	.891	0.18	0.58	1.0	2.5	8.0
vs. East	106	17.6	5.7	.405	2.6	.346	1.4	.799	0.13	0.60	0.9	2.2	6.6
vs. West	215	20.3	7.0	.443	2.9	.412	1.8	.848	0.17	0.61	1.0	2.7	8.9
vs. Div.	98	20.1	6.9	.434	3.1	.397	1.5	.816	0.13	0.55	1.1	2.9	8.4
As Starter	97	30.4	10.1	.455	4.4	.420	2.5	.850	0.21	1.00	1.5	3.5	13.2
Off Bench	224	14.6	5.0	.413	2.1	.367	1.3	.821	0.14	0.44	0.8	2.1	6.0
In wins	86	18.3	6.2	.474	2.8	.454	1.8	.839	0.15	0.60	1.1	2.3	8.7
In losses	235	19.8	6.6	.418	2.8	.370	1.6	.833	0.16	0.61	0.9	2.6	8.0
Pre All-Star	165	17.5	5.8	.414	2.6	.387	1.5	.805	0.16	0.55	0.9	2.5	7.0
Post All-Star	107	19.6	6.7	.457	2.9	.397	1.7	.859	0.17	0.58	1.1	2.3	8.8
Oct/Nov	48	16.7	5.5	.412	2.4	.357	2.2	.788	0.08	0.58	0.7	2.3	7.1
December	49	19.5	6.5	.404	2.9	.385	1.2	.702	0.18	0.65	1.1	2.6	7.2
January	53	16.1	5.3	.407	2.4	.409	1.4	.903	0.25	0.45	0.8	2.7	6.5
February	60	19.7	6.6	.428	2.9	.357	1.6	.851	0.05	0.50	1.0	2.2	8.0
March	69	20.5	6.8	.440	2.8	.381	1.8	.861	0.22	0.65	1.1	2.8	8.5
Apr/May	42	24.3	8.9	.484	3.6	.464	2.1	.865	0.17	0.88	1.3	2.4	12.1
0 Days Rest	81	21.2	7.3	.412	3.1	.382	1.9	.817	0.14	0.70	1.0	2.8	8.7
1 Days Rest	152	19.7	6.6	.427	2.8	.387	1.7	.836	0.19	0.65	1.0	2.6	8.1
2 Days Rest	48	19.0	6.3	.479	2.7	.431	1.5	.863	0.08	0.56	1.0	2.4	8.5
3+ Days Rest	40	14.9	5.3	.450	2.3	.387	1.4	.839	0.18	0.33	1.0	1.6	6.8

Paul Pierce
Boston Celtics — Forward

1999-2000 Per Game Averages

	G	Min	FGA	FG%	3PA	3P%	FTA	FT%	Blk	Stl	Ast	Reb	Pts		G	Min	FGA	FG%	3PA	3P%	FTA	FT%	Blk	Stl	Ast	Reb	Pts
Total	73	35.4	15.1	.442	3.8	.343	6.2	.798	0.85	2.08	3.0	5.4	19.5	Pre All-Star	40	35.4	15.6	.441	3.7	.383	6.0	.788	0.80	2.23	3.1	6.1	19.9
Home	38	35.4	15.6	.444	3.8	.384	6.0	.793	0.84	2.34	3.1	5.6	20.1	Post All-Star	33	35.4	14.4	.444	4.0	.298	6.4	.810	0.91	1.91	2.9	4.6	19.1
Road	35	35.4	14.4	.440	3.8	.299	6.4	.803	0.86	1.80	2.9	5.2	18.9	November	14	35.1	14.6	.466	3.6	.460	4.6	.734	0.86	1.57	2.9	6.6	18.6
vs. Playoff	41	36.7	16.2	.445	4.5	.370	6.0	.783	0.85	1.90	2.7	5.6	20.7	December	7	33.6	15.0	.400	4.0	.357	7.9	.800	0.71	3.29	4.3	5.6	19.7
vs. Non-Playoff	32	33.7	13.6	.438	3.0	.292	6.4	.816	0.84	2.31	3.4	5.3	18.1	January	13	35.2	16.9	.436	3.8	.300	6.4	.831	0.77	2.85	2.2	5.8	21.2
vs. East	49	36.2	14.9	.455	3.8	.344	6.1	.771	0.88	2.00	3.0	5.4	19.6	February	13	36.2	15.5	.433	3.9	.333	5.8	.842	0.85	1.85	3.8	5.7	19.6
vs. West	24	33.8	15.5	.418	3.9	.340	6.2	.852	0.79	2.25	3.1	5.5	19.5	March	16	36.6	15.8	.421	4.4	.286	7.1	.825	1.00	2.19	2.8	4.5	20.4
vs. Div.	21	36.6	15.6	.421	3.9	.272	7.0	.791	1.00	2.05	3.0	5.4	19.8	April	10	34.2	11.7	.513	3.1	.355	5.8	.707	0.80	1.10	2.9	4.4	17.2
As Starter	72	35.4	15.0	.444	3.8	.345	6.1	.795	0.86	2.08	3.0	5.4	19.5	0 Days Rest	19	35.4	14.5	.457	3.9	.413	5.8	.782	0.95	1.53	2.6	5.2	19.4
Off Bench	1	34.0	17.0	.353	5.0	.200	12.0	.917	0.00	2.00	7.0	6.0	24.0	1 Days Rest	36	35.9	15.2	.413	4.0	.297	6.6	.792	0.86	2.06	2.8	5.7	18.9
In wins	34	34.6	15.2	.461	3.9	.336	5.9	.796	0.88	2.82	3.2	5.9	20.1	2 Days Rest	8	31.0	13.5	.491	2.8	.318	3.9	.903	0.38	2.38	3.6	4.5	17.6
In losses	39	36.1	14.9	.425	3.8	.349	6.4	.799	0.82	1.44	2.8	5.1	19.1	3+ Days Rest	10	37.0	16.8	.482	3.8	.395	7.3	.795	1.00	3.00	4.2	5.6	23.5

Career (1998-99 thru 1999-2000)

	G	Min	FGA	FG%	3PA	3P%	FTA	FT%	Blk	Stl	Ast	Reb	Pts		G	Min	FGA	FG%	3PA	3P%	FTA	FT%	Blk	Stl	Ast	Reb	Pts
Total	121	34.8	14.4	.441	4.0	.372	5.3	.772	0.93	1.93	2.8	5.8	18.3	Pre All-Star	40	35.4	15.6	.441	3.7	.383	6.0	.788	0.80	2.23	3.1	6.1	19.9
Home	63	35.5	15.0	.438	4.4	.399	5.2	.759	0.90	2.02	2.9	6.2	18.8	Post All-Star	33	35.4	14.4	.444	4.0	.298	6.4	.810	0.91	1.91	2.9	4.6	19.1
Road	58	34.1	13.8	.445	3.6	.337	5.5	.785	0.95	1.84	2.7	5.4	17.8	Oct/Nov	14	35.1	14.6	.466	3.6	.460	4.6	.734	0.86	1.57	2.9	6.6	18.6
vs. Playoff	66	35.9	15.6	.445	4.6	.405	4.9	.782	0.92	1.77	2.5	6.0	19.6	December	7	33.6	15.0	.400	4.0	.357	7.9	.800	0.71	3.29	4.3	5.6	19.7
vs. Non-Playoff	55	33.6	13.1	.436	3.2	.315	5.8	.763	0.93	2.13	3.1	5.7	16.8	January	13	35.2	16.9	.436	3.8	.300	6.4	.831	0.77	2.85	2.2	5.8	21.2
vs. East	91	35.0	14.2	.448	4.1	.378	5.1	.748	0.98	1.78	2.8	5.9	18.1	February	24	36.0	15.5	.444	4.1	.378	5.9	.794	1.25	2.5	3.1	6.3	20.0
vs. West	30	34.3	15.2	.420	3.7	.351	6.0	.833	0.77	2.40	2.7	5.7	19.0	March	32	32.9	12.8	.407	3.8	.320	5.1	.784	0.88	1.63	2.3	4.9	15.6
vs. Div.	40	35.4	15.3	.433	4.3	.333	5.5	.771	1.05	2.00	2.8	6.3	18.8	Apr/May	31	35.9	14.1	.471	4.4	.412	4.5	.707	0.97	1.48	2.8	6.1	18.3
As Starter	119	35.0	14.5	.442	4.0	.374	5.3	.769	0.93	1.95	2.8	5.8	18.4	0 Days Rest	35	34.7	14.3	.445	3.9	.420	5.2	.746	0.94	1.51	2.5	5.9	18.3
Off Bench	2	23.5	9.5	.368	2.5	.200	6.0	.917	0.50	1.00	3.5	4.5	13.0	1 Days Rest	62	35.4	14.5	.422	4.3	.335	5.3	.774	0.89	1.85	2.7	6.0	17.8
In wins	53	34.5	14.7	.463	3.8	.353	5.5	.771	0.87	2.45	2.9	5.9	19.2	2 Days Rest	11	30.6	12.8	.482	3.0	.424	4.2	.848	0.64	2.64	2.9	4.6	17.2
In losses	68	35.1	14.2	.423	4.1	.386	5.2	.773	0.97	1.53	2.7	5.8	17.6	3+ Days Rest	13	36.2	15.8	.485	3.4	.409	6.9	.778	1.31	2.85	3.8	6.0	22.2

Scottie Pippen
Portland Trail Blazers — Forward

1999-2000 Per Game Averages

	G	Min	FGA	FG%	3PA	3P%	FTA	FT%	Blk	Stl	Ast	Reb	Pts		G	Min	FGA	FG%	3PA	3P%	FTA	FT%	Blk	Stl	Ast	Reb	Pts
Total	82	33.5	10.5	.451	3.2	.327	2.7	.717	0.50	1.43	5.0	6.3	12.5	Pre All-Star	49	34.8	10.2	.479	2.7	.343	2.7	.701	0.59	1.49	5.3	6.9	12.7
Home	41	33.3	11.1	.456	3.6	.318	3.0	.672	0.44	1.49	5.0	5.8	13.2	Post All-Star	33	31.6	10.9	.412	3.9	.310	2.7	.742	0.36	1.33	4.4	5.2	12.2
Road	41	33.8	9.9	.446	2.8	.339	2.5	.772	0.56	1.37	4.9	6.8	11.7	November	16	35.5	10.9	.477	2.6	.366	3.7	.695	0.75	1.31	5.1	7.1	13.9
vs. Playoff	44	34.8	10.6	.460	3.1	.326	2.9	.701	0.55	1.55	4.9	6.4	12.8	December	13	35.2	10.2	.466	3.0	.282	3.2	.619	0.46	1.46	5.2	6.6	12.4
vs. Non-Playoff	38	32.0	10.3	.440	3.3	.328	2.5	.740	0.45	1.29	5.1	6.1	12.1	January	14	34.3	9.6	.511	2.8	.359	1.3	.778	0.57	2.00	6.1	6.9	11.9
vs. East	30	31.1	9.4	.440	2.8	.310	2.6	.731	0.47	1.27	4.2	5.7	11.0	February	14	33.1	10.9	.434	4.4	.403	2.1	.767	0.29	1.29	4.6	5.9	12.9
vs. West	52	34.9	11.1	.457	3.4	.335	2.8	.710	0.52	1.52	5.4	6.6	13.3	March	14	33.8	11.6	.426	3.5	.245	3.4	.771	0.57	1.29	4.3	5.4	13.4
vs. Div.	24	35.7	11.4	.487	3.6	.384	2.8	.716	0.58	1.92	5.7	6.6	14.5	April	11	27.9	9.5	.375	3.0	.273	2.4	.731	0.27	1.18	4.2	5.4	9.6
As Starter	82	33.5	10.5	.451	3.2	.327	2.7	.717	0.50	1.43	5.0	6.3	12.5	0 Days Rest	22	32.3	10.3	.423	3.0	.323	3.2	.757	0.36	1.45	4.4	6.6	12.1
Off Bench	0	—	—	—	—	—	—	—	—	—	—	—	—	1 Days Rest	39	35.1	10.6	.472	3.2	.331	3.2	.702	0.51	1.74	5.1	6.2	13.3
In wins	59	33.5	10.1	.470	3.0	.349	2.6	.706	0.53	1.46	5.3	5.9	12.4	2 Days Rest	15	32.5	10.1	.430	3.5	.327	1.1	.706	0.73	0.60	5.5	6.5	10.6
In losses	23	33.5	11.4	.408	3.8	.284	3.0	.743	0.43	1.35	4.0	7.3	12.7	3+ Days Rest	6	30.2	11.2	.463	3.7	.318	2.0	.667	0.33	1.33	4.7	5.0	12.8

Last Five Seasons

	G	Min	FGA	FG%	3PA	3P%	FTA	FT%	Blk	Stl	Ast	Reb	Pts		G	Min	FGA	FG%	3PA	3P%	FTA	FT%	Blk	Stl	Ast	Reb	Pts
Total	335	36.8	14.2	.458	4.5	.352	3.6	.713	0.67	1.73	5.6	6.2	17.1	Pre All-Star	158	36.7	14.5	.472	4.3	.375	3.5	.685	0.73	1.69	5.7	6.5	17.7
Home	168	35.8	13.9	.464	4.7	.356	3.4	.707	0.59	1.72	5.7	6.0	16.9	Post All-Star	127	35.6	14.6	.449	4.7	.329	3.7	.744	0.55	1.70	5.3	5.9	17.4
Road	167	37.8	14.5	.452	4.2	.347	3.9	.719	0.74	1.75	5.4	6.5	17.4	Oct/Nov	46	36.5	13.7	.468	3.7	.369	4.0	.661	0.78	1.54	6.0	7.0	16.8
vs. Playoff	177	37.6	14.0	.454	4.6	.357	3.6	.698	0.69	1.71	5.6	6.5	16.9	December	42	37.6	15.9	.495	5.2	.413	3.8	.623	0.74	1.76	5.5	6.5	19.9
vs. Non-Playoff	158	36.0	14.4	.462	4.3	.345	3.6	.731	0.63	1.77	5.5	6.0	17.4	January	53	36.7	14.7	.467	4.4	.356	3.3	.743	0.64	1.85	6.0	6.1	17.7
vs. East	167	36.4	14.7	.452	4.6	.355	3.7	.721	0.61	1.65	5.6	5.9	17.6	February	67	37.4	14.7	.444	4.9	.350	3.8	.735	0.69	1.99	5.2	6.4	17.6
vs. West	168	37.3	13.7	.464	4.4	.349	3.6	.705	0.72	1.82	5.5	6.6	16.7	March	66	37.1	14.1	.442	4.1	.306	3.6	.788	0.67	1.56	5.6	6.2	16.5
vs. Div.	115	37.2	13.7	.457	4.4	.373	3.3	.710	0.60	1.65	5.7	6.1	16.5	Apr/May	61	35.6	12.5	.444	4.4	.336	3.6	.685	0.52	1.67	5.3	5.5	15.1
As Starter	335	36.8	14.2	.458	4.5	.352	3.6	.713	0.67	1.73	5.6	6.2	17.1	0 Days Rest	89	35.5	14.4	.467	4.4	.383	3.9	.717	0.76	1.60	5.4	5.7	17.9
Off Bench	0	—	—	—	—	—	—	—	—	—	—	—	—	1 Days Rest	161	38.0	14.2	.457	4.5	.337	3.6	.713	0.63	1.87	5.6	6.4	17.0
In wins	262	36.6	14.4	.473	4.4	.378	3.7	.713	0.72	1.78	5.7	6.2	17.9	2 Days Rest	57	36.1	13.9	.439	4.7	.353	3.4	.691	0.60	1.60	5.7	6.4	16.3
In losses	73	37.6	13.4	.399	4.7	.263	3.4	.716	0.47	1.56	5.0	6.5	14.3	3+ Days Rest	28	35.5	13.9	.472	4.0	.336	3.8	.743	0.71	1.68	5.6	6.6	17.3

Scot Pollard
Sacramento Kings — Forward-Center

1999-2000 Per Game Averages

	G	Min	FGA	FG%	3PA	3P%	FTA	FT%	Blk	Stl	Ast	Reb	Pts		G	Min	FGA	FG%	3PA	3P%	FTA	FT%	Blk	Stl	Ast	Reb	Pts
Total	76	17.6	3.7	.527	0.0	—	2.1	.717	0.78	0.72	0.6	5.3	5.4	Pre All-Star	48	15.8	3.1	.570	0.0	—	2.1	.727	0.73	0.63	0.5	4.8	5.1
Home	38	17.3	3.5	.553	0.0	—	2.2	.714	0.74	0.71	0.4	5.4	5.4	Post All-Star	28	20.6	4.7	.477	0.0	—	2.1	.700	0.86	0.89	0.8	6.3	6.0
Road	38	17.9	4.0	.503	0.0	—	2.0	.720	0.82	0.74	0.7	5.2	5.4	November	12	16.3	3.9	.511	0.0	—	1.9	.783	1.08	0.58	0.3	5.2	5.5
vs. Playoff	40	19.1	3.9	.484	0.0	—	2.3	.742	0.85	0.78	0.6	5.3	5.5	December	15	15.5	2.7	.659	0.0	—	2.2	.636	0.27	0.53	0.4	5.1	5.0
vs. Non-Playoff	36	15.9	3.5	.579	0.0	—	1.8	.682	0.69	0.67	0.6	5.3	5.3	January	16	15.8	3.3	.519	0.0	—	1.8	.759	0.88	0.69	0.8	4.2	4.8
vs. East	28	14.9	2.8	.532	0.0	—	1.9	.796	0.57	0.46	0.3	4.6	4.5	February	13	18.5	3.8	.520	0.0	—	2.5	.781	0.85	0.77	0.6	7.1	5.9
vs. West	48	19.1	4.3	.525	0.0	—	2.2	.676	0.90	0.88	0.7	5.8	5.9	March	9	20.7	3.8	.559	0.0	—	3.0	.630	0.78	1.33	0.6	5.6	6.1
vs. Div.	20	17.4	3.2	.531	0.0	—	2.4	.646	0.95	0.75	0.6	5.2	5.0	April	11	20.9	5.4	.441	0.0	—	1.4	.733	0.91	0.64	0.7	5.2	5.7
As Starter	5	24.4	7.0	.400	0.0	—	3.2	.750	0.40	0.60	0.6	5.6	8.0	0 Days Rest	17	21.3	5.1	.465	0.0	—	2.6	.705	1.00	0.76	0.9	6.2	6.5
Off Bench	71	17.1	3.5	.544	0.0	—	2.0	.713	0.80	0.73	0.6	5.3	5.2	1 Days Rest	46	16.9	3.5	.537	0.0	—	2.1	.705	0.67	0.72	0.4	5.2	5.2
In wins	40	16.7	3.2	.527	0.0	—	2.3	.700	0.70	0.68	0.6	5.1	5.0	2 Days Rest	7	17.9	4.0	.679	0.0	—	1.7	.750	0.86	0.57	1.0	5.4	6.7
In losses	36	18.6	4.3	.526	0.0	—	1.9	.739	0.86	0.56	0.6	5.6	5.9	3+ Days Rest	6	12.2	1.2	.429	0.0	—	1.3	.875	0.83	0.83	0.2	3.8	2.2

Career (1997-98 thru 1999-2000)

	G	Min	FGA	FG%	3PA	3P%	FTA	FT%	Blk	Stl	Ast	Reb	Pts		G	Min	FGA	FG%	3PA	3P%	FTA	FT%	Blk	Stl	Ast	Reb	Pts
Total	125	15.3	3.3	.524	0.0	—	1.6	.727	0.70	0.57	0.4	4.5	4.7	Pre All-Star	60	14.3	2.8	.562	0.0	—	1.8	.736	0.65	0.55	0.4	4.3	4.5
Home	63	15.4	3.5	.523	0.0	—	1.8	.705	0.71	0.59	0.4	4.8	4.9	Post All-Star	49	16.3	3.8	.484	0.0	—	1.5	.722	0.61	0.61	0.6	4.6	4.7
Road	62	15.2	3.2	.526	0.0	—	1.5	.753	0.68	0.55	0.5	4.2	4.5	Oct/Nov	19	14.4	3.2	.483	0.0	—	1.7	.813	0.84	0.47	0.2	4.4	4.4
vs. Playoff	66	16.3	3.3	.516	0.0	—	1.7	.743	0.76	0.61	0.4	4.6	4.6	December	18	13.6	2.3	.667	0.0	—	1.9	.629	0.28	0.44	0.3	4.3	4.3
vs. Non-Playoff	59	14.2	3.4	.533	0.0	—	1.6	.707	0.63	0.53	0.5	4.6	4.7	January	18	14.4	3.1	.536	0.0	—	1.6	.759	0.78	0.67	0.7	3.9	4.6
vs. East	48	12.8	2.6	.532	0.0	—	1.3	.774	0.50	0.42	0.3	3.6	3.8	February	19	16.2	3.3	.476	0.0	—	1.9	.806	0.63	0.53	0.5	5.8	4.7
vs. West	77	16.9	3.8	.521	0.0	—	1.9	.706	0.82	0.66	0.5	5.0	5.2	March	22	14.5	3.0	.561	0.0	—	1.6	.639	0.64	0.77	0.5	3.8	4.4
vs. Div.	38	14.9	3.1	.513	0.0	—	1.6	.672	0.79	0.53	0.5	4.4	4.2	Apr/May	29	17.5	4.4	.496	0.0	—	1.3	.730	0.90	0.52	0.4	4.7	5.3
As Starter	10	26.6	7.5	.507	0.0	—	2.9	.690	1.10	0.90	0.6	7.3	9.6	0 Days Rest	23	20.2	4.7	.509	0.0	—	2.4	.653	1.04	0.70	0.8	5.7	6.4
Off Bench	115	14.3	2.9	.528	0.0	—	1.5	.733	0.66	0.54	0.4	4.2	4.2	1 Days Rest	61	16.4	3.6	.527	0.0	—	1.8	.721	0.64	0.66	0.4	4.5	4.5
In wins	66	15.4	3.2	.524	0.0	—	1.9	.704	0.71	0.71	0.4	4.6	4.7	2 Days Rest	16	12.7	2.6	.619	0.0	—	0.9	.786	0.69	0.38	0.7	3.4	3.9
In losses	59	15.2	3.4	.525	0.0	—	1.4	.763	0.68	0.41	0.4	4.3	4.6	3+ Days Rest	25	9.9	1.7	.452	0.0	—	1.0	.840	0.52	0.36	0.0	3.2	2.4

Olden Polynice
Utah Jazz — Center

1999-2000 Per Game Averages

	G	Min	FGA	FG%	3PA	3P%	FTA	FT%	Blk	Stl	Ast	Reb	Pts		G	Min	FGA	FG%	3PA	3P%	FTA	FT%	Blk	Stl	Ast	Reb	Pts
Total	82	22.2	4.9	.510	0.0	.500	1.1	.311	1.02	0.37	0.5	5.5	5.3	Pre All-Star	47	22.7	4.7	.482	0.0	.000	0.7	.250	0.85	0.23	0.4	5.8	4.7
Home	41	21.1	4.5	.549	0.0	1.000	1.2	.333	1.10	0.41	0.5	5.5	5.4	Post All-Star	35	21.4	5.1	.545	0.0	1.000	1.7	.345	1.26	0.54	0.5	5.1	6.1
Road	41	23.3	5.2	.477	0.0	.000	1.0	.282	0.95	0.32	0.4	5.5	5.2	November	14	21.8	4.3	.400	0.0	—	0.6	.222	0.50	0.36	0.6	4.6	3.6
vs. Playoff	44	22.4	4.8	.469	0.0	.000	0.8	.382	1.02	0.30	0.4	5.4	4.8	December	14	25.9	4.9	.529	0.0	—	0.7	.200	1.57	0.14	0.5	7.1	5.3
vs. Non-Playoff	38	21.9	4.9	.557	0.0	1.000	1.5	.268	1.03	0.45	0.3	5.6	5.8	January	14	22.9	5.0	.514	0.1	.000	0.6	.333	0.71	0.29	0.4	6.5	5.4
vs. East	30	23.6	5.6	.569	0.0	—	0.8	.240	1.40	0.23	0.7	6.3	6.5	February	13	19.8	4.7	.475	0.0	—	1.0	.385	0.92	0.23	0.5	5.2	4.8
vs. West	52	21.4	4.4	.468	0.0	.500	1.3	.338	0.81	0.44	0.3	5.1	4.6	March	16	21.8	5.3	.583	0.1	1.000	1.6	.308	1.31	0.44	0.6	5.4	6.7
vs. Div.	24	20.3	4.0	.505	0.0	1.000	1.5	.194	0.58	0.42	0.3	5.3	4.4	April	11	20.5	5.0	.527	0.0	—	2.1	.348	1.09	0.82	0.1	4.1	6.0
As Starter	79	22.3	4.9	.505	0.0	.500	1.1	.307	1.03	0.35	0.4	5.6	5.3	0 Days Rest	19	22.9	4.9	.489	0.1	.000	1.4	.192	1.16	0.53	0.5	5.3	5.1
Off Bench	3	18.0	4.7	.643	0.0	—	0.7	.500	1.00	0.67	1.7	4.3	6.3	1 Days Rest	45	22.5	4.9	.511	0.0	1.000	1.0	.383	1.02	0.29	0.4	5.6	5.4
In wins	55	22.3	4.9	.546	0.0	—	1.2	.343	1.29	0.38	0.5	5.5	5.8	2 Days Rest	12	20.9	5.4	.508	0.0	—	1.1	.308	1.08	0.42	0.2	4.3	5.8
In losses	27	22.0	4.7	.433	0.1	.500	0.9	.217	0.48	0.33	0.4	5.6	4.3	3+ Days Rest	6	20.2	3.3	.600	0.0	—	0.7	.250	0.50	0.33	0.8	7.8	4.2

Last Five Seasons

	G	Min	FGA	FG%	3PA	3P%	FTA	FT%	Blk	Stl	Ast	Reb	Pts		G	Min	FGA	FG%	3PA	3P%	FTA	FT%	Blk	Stl	Ast	Reb	Pts
Total	363	27.8	8.5	.485	0.0	.231	2.1	.494	0.84	0.51	1.2	7.9	9.3	Pre All-Star	186	28.0	8.7	.481	0.0	.143	2.1	.512	0.84	0.47	1.2	7.9	9.5
Home	182	27.6	8.7	.492	0.0	.333	2.1	.523	0.86	0.53	1.2	8.1	9.6	Post All-Star	129	26.4	8.5	.494	0.0	.200	2.1	.534	0.92	0.60	1.3	7.5	9.5
Road	181	28.1	8.3	.477	0.0	.143	2.1	.466	0.82	0.49	1.2	7.7	8.9	Oct/Nov	60	27.9	7.9	.477	0.0	—	2.3	.532	0.68	0.48	1.2	6.9	8.8
vs. Playoff	205	27.7	8.5	.461	0.0	.125	1.8	.519	0.74	0.48	1.1	7.7	8.8	December	54	28.5	9.1	.484	0.1	.000	2.2	.513	0.94	0.44	1.1	8.4	9.9
vs. Non-Playoff	158	27.9	8.5	.515	0.0	.400	2.4	.470	0.97	0.55	1.3	8.0	9.9	January	55	28.2	9.5	.489	0.1	.333	2.0	.500	0.96	0.53	1.3	8.5	10.3
vs. East	123	28.0	8.4	.504	0.0	.250	2.1	.516	0.93	0.50	1.4	7.5	9.6	February	63	27.5	8.7	.488	0.0	.500	1.9	.521	0.92	0.37	1.3	8.5	9.5
vs. West	240	27.7	8.5	.475	0.0	.222	2.1	.483	0.79	0.51	1.1	8.0	9.1	March	72	27.6	7.5	.494	0.0	.500	2.2	.409	0.81	0.53	1.2	7.6	8.4
vs. Div.	111	27.5	8.3	.478	0.1	.333	2.4	.464	0.78	0.44	1.1	8.0	9.1	Apr/May	59	27.2	8.6	.473	0.0	—	1.8	.514	0.75	0.71	1.0	7.4	9.1
As Starter	313	29.5	8.8	.485	0.0	.231	2.2	.504	0.86	0.52	1.2	8.2	9.7	0 Days Rest	83	28.5	8.3	.480	0.0	.333	2.2	.457	0.90	0.54	1.1	7.8	9.0
Off Bench	50	17.3	6.4	.478	0.0	—	1.4	.397	0.70	0.46	1.2	5.5	6.7	1 Days Rest	196	28.0	8.8	.477	0.0	.333	2.0	.537	0.83	0.46	1.2	8.0	9.4
In wins	176	27.8	8.3	.512	0.0	.667	2.3	.467	0.99	0.51	1.1	8.1	9.5	2 Days Rest	53	27.6	8.6	.510	0.0	.000	2.2	.430	0.79	0.66	0.9	7.7	9.7
In losses	187	27.8	8.7	.460	0.1	.100	1.9	.524	0.70	0.51	1.2	7.6	9.0	3+ Days Rest	31	24.9	7.2	.507	0.1	.000	1.9	.448	0.84	0.48	1.7	7.5	8.1

Terry Porter

1999-2000 Per Game Averages

	G	Min	FGA	FG%	3PA	3P%	FTA	FT%	Blk	Stl	Ast	Reb	Pts
Total	68	23.7	6.8	.447	3.0	.435	2.5	.806	0.13	0.74	3.3	2.8	9.4
Home	33	23.9	6.9	.472	3.0	.500	2.3	.853	0.09	0.82	3.5	2.9	10.0
Road	35	23.5	6.7	.423	3.1	.374	2.7	.768	0.17	0.66	3.0	2.7	8.9
vs. Playoff	40	25.0	7.1	.423	3.1	.424	2.5	.792	0.10	0.70	3.3	3.1	9.3
vs. Non-Playoff	28	22.0	6.4	.486	2.9	.451	2.5	.826	0.18	0.79	3.2	2.5	9.6
vs. East	23	21.4	6.0	.486	3.0	.500	2.2	.820	0.13	0.61	2.6	3.3	9.1
vs. West	45	24.9	7.2	.431	3.1	.403	2.7	.800	0.13	0.80	3.6	2.5	9.6
vs. Div.	21	24.3	6.9	.444	2.6	.491	3.2	.851	0.14	0.57	3.0	2.4	10.1
As Starter	8	32.6	9.4	.533	3.1	.560	2.6	.905	0.25	0.63	3.4	4.0	14.1
Off Bench	60	22.5	6.5	.430	3.0	.418	2.5	.792	0.12	0.75	3.2	2.5	8.4
In wins	43	24.0	7.3	.481	3.0	.454	2.5	.806	0.16	0.77	3.1	3.0	10.4
In losses	25	23.2	6.0	.377	3.1	.403	2.5	.806	0.08	0.68	3.6	2.6	7.8

	G	Min	FGA	FG%	3PA	3P%	FTA	FT%	Blk	Stl	Ast	Reb	Pts
Pre All-Star	48	22.8	6.9	.428	3.2	.425	2.3	.800	0.13	0.69	2.8	2.8	9.1
Post All-Star	20	26.0	6.6	.496	2.7	.463	3.0	.817	0.15	0.85	4.4	2.8	10.2
November	16	21.9	7.6	.496	4.0	.531	1.9	.710	0.19	0.38	3.3	3.2	11.0
December	14	20.9	5.6	.342	3.1	.256	2.7	.921	0.00	0.79	2.2	1.8	7.1
January	13	23.9	7.2	.415	2.7	.457	2.3	.700	0.08	1.00	3.2	3.5	8.8
February	13	27.2	6.8	.489	2.5	.485	2.5	.906	0.23	0.77	3.5	3.1	10.1
March	2	35.0	8.0	.375	4.0	.250	3.5	.857	0.00	0.50	8.5	2.0	10.0
April	10	23.4	6.5	.492	2.4	.458	3.2	.750	0.20	0.90	3.4	2.5	9.9
0 Days Rest	15	25.0	7.5	.487	3.5	.547	2.7	.850	0.33	1.00	4.4	2.9	11.5
1 Days Rest	34	23.7	6.2	.412	2.9	.367	2.8	.792	0.09	0.65	3.1	2.6	8.4
2 Days Rest	14	25.4	7.9	.486	3.0	.429	1.8	.840	0.07	0.79	2.8	3.3	10.5
3+ Days Rest	5	15.0	5.6	.393	2.8	.500	1.8	.667	0.00	0.40	2.0	2.4	7.0

Last Five Seasons

	G	Min	FGA	FG%	3PA	3P%	FTA	FT%	Blk	Stl	Ast	Reb	Pts
Total	364	23.1	6.8	.443	2.8	.375	2.4	.809	0.17	0.84	3.8	2.4	9.0
Home	181	23.1	6.6	.441	2.9	.395	2.5	.813	0.20	0.89	4.0	2.5	9.0
Road	183	23.1	6.9	.445	2.7	.354	2.4	.804	0.14	0.78	3.6	2.4	9.0
vs. Playoff	202	23.0	6.7	.425	2.7	.369	2.4	.811	0.18	0.75	3.6	2.4	9.0
vs. Non-Playoff	162	23.2	6.8	.466	2.8	.383	2.5	.806	0.16	0.94	4.0	2.5	9.5
vs. East	158	23.2	6.8	.451	2.8	.390	2.3	.823	0.19	0.83	3.5	2.6	9.1
vs. West	206	23.0	6.8	.438	2.8	.364	2.5	.798	0.16	0.84	4.1	2.3	9.0
vs. Div.	113	24.3	7.0	.465	2.7	.417	2.9	.800	0.23	0.81	3.6	2.5	9.9
As Starter	77	29.2	8.0	.426	2.9	.323	3.0	.803	0.21	0.96	5.7	2.9	10.1
Off Bench	287	21.4	6.5	.449	2.7	.390	2.3	.811	0.16	0.80	3.3	2.3	8.7
In wins	187	23.4	6.7	.471	2.8	.409	2.7	.801	0.19	0.91	3.7	2.5	9.6
In losses	177	22.8	6.8	.415	2.8	.340	2.2	.819	0.15	0.75	3.9	2.4	8.4

	G	Min	FGA	FG%	3PA	3P%	FTA	FT%	Blk	Stl	Ast	Reb	Pts
Pre All-Star	187	22.3	6.5	.425	2.5	.353	2.3	.800	0.19	0.81	4.0	2.5	8.3
Post All-Star	127	22.7	7.0	.460	3.1	.389	2.4	.811	0.12	0.82	3.8	2.2	9.5
Oct/Nov	58	20.3	6.1	.424	2.6	.391	2.4	.789	0.19	0.64	3.8	2.3	8.1
December	58	21.9	6.4	.411	2.5	.310	2.2	.817	0.21	0.78	3.5	2.2	7.8
January	56	23.5	6.8	.413	2.5	.357	2.4	.761	0.13	1.00	4.9	3.0	8.3
February	64	24.8	7.1	.457	2.9	.410	2.8	.852	0.25	0.92	3.7	2.5	10.0
March	65	23.3	7.0	.466	2.9	.372	2.0	.792	0.14	0.85	3.5	2.2	9.2
Apr/May	63	24.4	7.3	.475	3.1	.396	2.9	.823	0.11	0.83	3.6	2.4	10.5
0 Days Rest	90	23.2	6.9	.462	2.7	.412	2.3	.804	0.26	0.92	3.8	2.4	9.3
1 Days Rest	190	23.4	6.7	.435	2.9	.355	2.7	.814	0.15	0.82	3.9	2.5	9.0
2 Days Rest	57	22.6	6.9	.457	2.5	.368	2.0	.807	0.14	0.65	3.5	2.5	8.8
3+ Days Rest	27	21.7	7.0	.413	2.7	.419	2.0	.782	0.11	1.04	3.8	2.2	8.5

James Posey

1999-2000 Per Game Averages

	G	Min	FGA	FG%	3PA	3P%	FTA	FT%	Blk	Stl	Ast	Reb	Pts
Total	81	25.3	6.6	.429	2.7	.373	1.9	.800	0.41	1.21	1.8	3.9	8.2
Home	40	23.9	6.6	.442	2.7	.383	2.0	.813	0.55	1.30	1.9	3.9	8.5
Road	41	26.7	6.6	.417	2.8	.363	1.7	.786	0.27	1.12	1.7	3.9	7.9
vs. Playoff	48	26.1	6.8	.432	2.6	.402	1.8	.786	0.46	1.31	2.0	4.1	8.3
vs. Non-Playoff	33	24.2	6.4	.425	2.8	.333	2.0	.818	0.33	1.06	1.5	3.7	8.0
vs. East	30	24.0	6.5	.434	2.6	.321	2.0	.754	0.50	1.03	1.3	3.9	8.0
vs. West	51	26.1	6.7	.426	2.8	.401	1.7	.831	0.35	1.31	2.1	3.9	8.3
vs. Div.	24	26.5	6.7	.429	2.8	.456	2.0	.830	0.54	1.17	1.9	4.0	8.7
As Starter	77	25.8	6.8	.426	2.8	.377	1.8	.806	0.42	1.26	1.8	4.0	8.3
Off Bench	4	15.5	3.3	.538	1.3	.200	2.8	.727	0.25	0.25	1.0	3.0	5.8
In wins	34	25.8	6.8	.474	3.0	.408	1.9	.818	0.41	1.26	2.1	4.2	9.3
In losses	47	25.0	6.5	.395	2.5	.342	1.8	.786	0.40	1.17	1.6	3.7	7.4

	G	Min	FGA	FG%	3PA	3P%	FTA	FT%	Blk	Stl	Ast	Reb	Pts
Pre All-Star	48	21.7	5.5	.425	2.1	.363	1.7	.790	0.46	1.17	1.3	3.9	6.8
Post All-Star	33	30.6	8.2	.433	3.6	.381	2.1	.812	0.33	1.27	2.6	3.9	10.2
November	13	24.5	5.4	.457	1.8	.348	2.8	.694	0.31	1.31	1.4	4.2	7.5
December	15	20.7	5.7	.388	2.3	.314	1.3	.789	0.40	1.20	1.0	3.5	6.1
January	14	17.9	4.6	.438	1.6	.364	1.3	.889	0.50	1.00	1.1	3.6	5.7
February	13	28.8	7.2	.394	3.0	.410	1.7	.955	0.54	1.31	2.6	5.1	8.5
March	16	29.2	8.2	.435	3.2	.333	2.6	.738	0.31	1.06	1.9	3.6	10.1
April	10	33.2	9.2	.467	5.0	.440	1.3	.923	0.40	1.50	3.3	3.6	12.0
0 Days Rest	21	25.7	6.6	.403	3.0	.391	1.8	.865	0.29	1.10	1.4	3.4	8.0
1 Days Rest	38	24.2	6.2	.464	2.6	.378	1.9	.764	0.50	1.18	1.3	3.7	8.2
2 Days Rest	13	30.1	8.2	.434	3.2	.429	2.4	.774	0.38	1.62	3.2	5.2	10.3
3+ Days Rest	9	22.2	6.0	.333	1.8	.125	1.1	.900	0.33	1.00	2.9	4.1	5.2

Vitaly Potapenko

1999-2000 Per Game Averages

	G	Min	FGA	FG%	3PA	3P%	FTA	FT%	Blk	Stl	Ast	Reb	Pts
Total	79	22.7	7.8	.499	0.0	.000	2.0	.681	0.37	0.52	1.0	6.3	9.2
Home	40	22.5	7.9	.513	0.0	.000	2.3	.678	0.25	0.63	1.1	6.3	9.6
Road	39	23.1	7.7	.485	0.0	—	1.8	.686	0.49	0.41	0.8	6.3	8.7
vs. Playoff	44	23.8	7.9	.473	0.0	.000	2.1	.624	0.39	0.52	1.1	6.0	8.8
vs. Non-Playoff	35	21.5	7.6	.534	0.0	—	1.9	.761	0.34	0.51	0.8	5.7	9.6
vs. East	53	23.2	7.5	.500	0.0	.000	2.1	.670	0.40	0.49	1.2	6.5	8.8
vs. West	26	21.8	8.4	.498	0.0	—	2.0	.706	0.31	0.58	0.6	6.0	9.8
vs. Div.	24	22.8	7.9	.481	0.0	—	2.4	.719	0.38	0.50	1.1	6.1	9.3
As Starter	72	22.8	7.9	.498	0.0	.000	2.1	.669	0.40	0.54	0.9	6.4	9.2
Off Bench	7	22.6	7.0	.510	0.0	—	1.7	.833	0.00	0.29	1.6	5.7	8.6
In wins	35	20.9	7.2	.474	0.0	.000	2.0	.700	0.34	0.60	1.1	6.3	8.3
In losses	44	24.3	8.2	.517	0.0	—	2.0	.667	0.39	0.45	0.9	6.3	9.9

	G	Min	FGA	FG%	3PA	3P%	FTA	FT%	Blk	Stl	Ast	Reb	Pts
Pre All-Star	46	24.2	8.0	.520	0.0	.000	2.2	.737	0.43	0.52	1.2	6.6	9.9
Post All-Star	33	20.7	7.5	.468	0.0	—	1.8	.590	0.27	0.52	0.7	5.9	8.1
November	14	23.9	6.5	.527	0.0	—	2.1	.724	0.50	0.36	1.6	6.6	8.4
December	11	22.5	7.6	.488	0.0	—	2.0	.818	0.36	0.55	1.0	4.6	9.1
January	15	25.4	9.3	.468	0.1	.000	2.9	.682	0.53	0.67	0.8	8.1	10.7
February	13	23.8	9.2	.592	0.0	—	1.3	.706	0.38	0.46	0.8	6.5	11.8
March	16	20.8	7.4	.454	0.0	—	1.8	.552	0.19	0.44	0.8	6.6	7.8
April	10	19.2	6.2	.452	0.0	—	1.9	.632	0.20	0.70	0.7	4.4	6.8
0 Days Rest	20	24.3	7.9	.494	0.0	—	2.3	.739	0.50	0.55	1.2	6.3	9.5
1 Days Rest	40	21.8	7.8	.474	0.0	.000	2.2	.670	0.35	0.48	1.1	6.2	8.8
2 Days Rest	9	23.7	8.8	.557	0.0	—	1.7	.600	0.22	0.56	0.3	6.6	10.8
3+ Days Rest	10	22.7	6.8	.559	0.0	—	1.1	.636	0.30	0.60	0.7	6.7	8.3

Career (1996-97 thru 1999-2000)

	G	Min	FGA	FG%	3PA	3P%	FTA	FT%	Blk	Stl	Ast	Reb	Pts
Total	289	20.2	6.7	.480	0.0	.200	2.0	.675	0.44	0.45	0.9	4.7	7.8
Home	149	20.3	6.7	.493	0.0	.000	2.0	.672	0.48	0.44	1.1	4.8	7.9
Road	140	20.1	6.8	.467	0.0	.333	2.0	.677	0.39	0.45	0.7	4.6	7.7
vs. Playoff	165	20.6	6.6	.473	0.0	.250	2.1	.664	0.37	0.41	0.9	4.8	7.6
vs. Non-Playoff	124	19.7	6.9	.490	0.0	.000	1.9	.691	0.53	0.49	0.8	4.6	8.1
vs. East	204	20.5	6.7	.477	0.0	.200	2.0	.667	0.45	0.46	1.0	4.9	7.8
vs. West	85	19.4	6.6	.489	0.0	—	2.1	.693	0.42	0.42	0.6	4.4	7.9
vs. Div.	97	19.6	6.6	.474	0.0	.250	1.8	.684	0.37	0.43	0.8	4.7	7.5
As Starter	119	25.2	8.2	.500	0.0	.000	2.5	.623	0.55	0.60	1.2	6.6	9.8
Off Bench	170	16.8	5.6	.460	0.0	.250	1.7	.729	0.36	0.34	0.6	3.4	6.4
In wins	142	19.1	6.5	.491	0.0	.000	2.1	.712	0.51	0.50	0.9	4.6	7.8
In losses	147	21.2	7.0	.471	0.0	.500	2.0	.637	0.37	0.39	0.9	4.9	7.8

	G	Min	FGA	FG%	3PA	3P%	FTA	FT%	Blk	Stl	Ast	Reb	Pts
Pre All-Star	138	18.2	6.2	.475	0.0	.000	1.9	.764	0.38	0.36	0.8	4.4	7.3
Post All-Star	101	19.2	6.6	.478	0.0	.333	1.7	.620	0.38	0.44	0.6	4.2	7.4
Oct/Nov	42	19.3	6.3	.468	0.0	—	2.2	.787	0.45	0.26	1.0	4.8	7.7
December	39	15.5	5.6	.479	0.0	—	1.7	.773	0.31	0.31	0.6	3.3	6.6
January	44	18.5	6.2	.465	0.0	.000	1.9	.718	0.45	0.50	0.7	4.8	7.1
February	49	20.6	7.0	.478	0.0	.000	1.4	.701	0.39	0.35	0.7	4.3	7.7
March	64	23.1	7.0	.488	0.0	.000	2.4	.616	0.50	0.55	0.8	5.4	8.3
Apr/May	51	22.1	7.7	.494	0.0	.500	2.4	.562	0.49	0.63	1.3	5.1	9.0
0 Days Rest	78	21.5	6.9	.469	0.0	—	2.3	.674	0.46	0.54	0.9	4.7	8.1
1 Days Rest	138	20.3	6.8	.475	0.0	.333	2.1	.664	0.42	0.41	1.0	4.9	7.9
2 Days Rest	47	18.2	6.1	.497	0.0	—	1.6	.675	0.53	0.38	0.7	4.1	7.1
3+ Days Rest	26	19.3	6.4	.521	0.0	.000	1.4	.757	0.31	0.46	0.6	4.8	7.8

Theo Ratliff

1999-2000 Per Game Averages

	G	Min	FGA	FG%	3PA	3P%	FTA	FT%	Blk	Stl	Ast	Reb	Pts
Total	57	31.5	8.6	.503	0.0	—	4.1	.771	3.00	0.56	0.6	7.6	11.9
Home	29	31.5	8.3	.481	0.0	—	4.0	.730	2.79	0.66	0.6	7.3	10.9
Road	28	31.5	8.9	.524	0.0	—	4.3	.810	3.21	0.46	0.7	8.0	12.9
vs. Playoff	29	31.4	9.3	.439	0.0	—	3.4	.786	2.52	0.55	0.6	6.8	10.9
vs. Non-Playoff	28	31.5	7.9	.582	0.0	—	4.9	.761	3.50	0.57	0.7	8.5	12.9
vs. East	40	31.8	8.0	.480	0.0	—	4.4	.787	3.03	0.56	0.6	7.4	11.1
vs. West	17	30.9	10.1	.547	0.0	—	3.6	.726	2.94	0.59	0.8	8.2	13.7
vs. Div.	18	34.2	7.7	.482	0.0	—	5.1	.815	3.33	0.44	0.6	8.2	11.6
As Starter	56	31.9	8.8	.504	0.0	—	4.2	.771	3.05	0.57	0.6	7.7	12.1
Off Bench	1	11.0	1.0	.000	0.0	—	0.0	—	0.00	0.00	1.0	2.0	2.0
In wins	34	31.8	8.1	.536	0.0	—	4.6	.783	3.15	0.62	0.5	8.0	12.3
In losses	23	31.0	9.3	.460	0.0	—	3.4	.747	2.78	0.48	0.9	7.1	11.2

	G	Min	FGA	FG%	3PA	3P%	FTA	FT%	Blk	Stl	Ast	Reb	Pts
Pre All-Star	24	30.7	8.3	.497	0.0	—	4.5	.752	2.71	0.54	0.7	7.9	11.7
Post All-Star	33	32.1	8.8	.507	0.0	—	3.8	.787	3.21	0.58	0.6	7.4	12.0
November	7	33.4	9.0	.381	0.0	—	4.9	.794	2.57	0.57	0.7	6.7	10.7
December	2	19.0	2.5	.400	0.0	—	4.0	.500	2.00	0.00	0.0	3.5	4.0
January	10	28.8	7.2	.500	0.0	—	4.6	.739	2.20	0.60	0.7	7.9	10.6
February	12	32.4	10.5	.603	0.0	—	4.4	.755	3.58	0.58	0.9	9.1	16.0
March	16	33.8	9.8	.494	0.0	—	3.6	.825	3.25	0.56	0.4	7.7	12.6
April	10	30.6	6.9	.464	0.0	—	3.8	.789	3.20	0.60	0.6	7.0	9.4
0 Days Rest	13	29.8	8.4	.468	0.0	—	2.8	.892	2.62	0.46	0.5	6.4	10.9
1 Days Rest	32	32.9	8.8	.504	0.0	—	4.7	.762	3.03	0.63	0.6	7.7	12.4
2 Days Rest	5	31.0	8.6	.581	0.0	—	4.6	.609	3.40	0.20	1.6	11.6	12.8
3+ Days Rest	7	28.4	8.4	.508	0.0	—	3.6	.800	3.29	0.71	0.3	6.6	11.4

Career (1995-96 thru 1999-2000)

	G	Min	FGA	FG%	3PA	3P%	FTA	FT%	Blk	Stl	Ast	Reb	Pts
Total	340	24.9	6.1	.510	0.0	.000	2.9	.724	2.37	0.51	0.4	5.7	8.3
Home	171	25.0	6.1	.505	0.0	—	3.0	.708	2.39	0.49	0.4	5.7	8.2
Road	169	24.8	6.1	.514	0.0	.000	2.8	.741	2.35	0.52	0.4	5.7	8.4
vs. Playoff	181	25.0	6.1	.487	0.0	—	2.7	.734	2.19	0.57	0.4	5.6	8.0
vs. Non-Playoff	159	24.8	6.1	.535	0.0	.000	3.1	.714	2.57	0.43	0.5	5.9	8.7
vs. East	234	25.2	6.1	.515	0.0	.000	3.1	.730	2.39	0.52	0.4	5.8	8.5
vs. West	106	24.3	6.0	.498	0.0	—	2.5	.708	2.32	0.48	0.4	5.5	7.8
vs. Div.	106	24.5	5.8	.526	0.0	.000	3.0	.730	2.33	0.48	0.4	5.5	8.3
As Starter	213	30.4	7.9	.502	0.0	—	3.7	.731	2.97	0.68	0.6	7.0	10.7
Off Bench	127	15.6	3.0	.543	0.0	.000	1.5	.694	1.35	0.21	0.1	3.5	4.5
In wins	189	24.4	6.0	.518	0.0	.000	2.9	.730	2.42	0.49	0.4	5.8	8.4
In losses	151	25.5	6.2	.499	0.0	—	2.9	.717	2.30	0.52	0.5	5.6	8.2

	G	Min	FGA	FG%	3PA	3P%	FTA	FT%	Blk	Stl	Ast	Reb	Pts
Pre All-Star	153	21.4	5.0	.520	0.0	.000	2.5	.711	2.05	0.40	0.4	5.0	6.9
Post All-Star	137	26.0	6.5	.520	0.0	—	2.7	.738	2.50	0.48	0.5	5.7	8.8
Oct/Nov	46	20.5	4.3	.457	0.0	—	2.2	.718	1.61	0.28	0.4	4.5	5.5
December	44	17.2	3.6	.529	0.0	—	2.0	.667	1.80	0.36	0.2	4.0	5.1
January	49	23.6	5.9	.530	0.0	.000	3.1	.713	2.55	0.49	0.4	5.5	8.4
February	64	28.5	7.6	.529	0.0	—	3.2	.709	2.84	0.61	0.5	7.0	10.3
March	75	27.5	7.1	.489	0.0	—	3.1	.742	2.50	0.63	0.6	6.2	9.3
Apr/May	62	27.8	6.7	.518	0.0	—	3.3	.752	2.50	0.63	0.6	6.2	9.4
0 Days Rest	85	24.7	6.3	.515	0.0	—	2.8	.708	1.96	0.51	0.4	5.6	8.4
1 Days Rest	175	26.5	6.5	.507	0.0	—	3.1	.725	2.65	0.50	0.5	6.0	8.9
2 Days Rest	43	21.9	5.0	.468	0.0	—	2.6	.727	2.28	0.53	0.4	5.4	6.6
3+ Days Rest	37	21.4	5.0	.562	0.0	.000	2.5	.758	2.08	0.49	0.3	5.0	7.5

Bryant Reeves

1999-2000 Per Game Averages

	G	Min	FGA	FG%	3PA	3P%	FTA	FT%	Blk	Stl	Ast	Reb	Pts
Total	69	25.7	8.1	.448	0.1	.000	2.4	.648	0.55	0.57	1.2	5.7	8.9
Home	36	26.4	8.5	.480	0.1	.000	2.6	.670	0.53	0.56	1.5	6.2	9.9
Road	33	25.0	7.8	.410	0.1	.000	2.2	.620	0.58	0.39	0.8	5.1	7.7
vs. Playoff	38	26.4	8.0	.475	0.1	.000	2.4	.587	0.66	0.66	1.2	6.2	9.0
vs. Non-Playoff	31	24.8	8.4	.417	0.0	.000	2.4	.726	0.42	0.26	1.2	5.0	8.7
vs. East	27	24.4	8.4	.436	0.0	.000	2.0	.727	0.33	0.30	1.3	5.6	8.8
vs. West	42	26.5	8.0	.457	0.1	.000	2.6	.609	0.69	0.60	1.1	5.7	8.9
vs. Div.	19	25.6	8.1	.425	0.1	.000	2.3	.744	0.89	0.74	1.1	6.1	8.5
As Starter	67	25.9	8.2	.453	0.1	.000	2.4	.650	0.54	0.49	1.2	5.7	9.0
Off Bench	2	17.5	5.0	.200	0.0	—	1.0	.500	1.00	0.00	0.5	3.5	2.5
In wins	20	25.4	8.0	.409	0.1	.000	2.4	.667	0.75	0.65	1.5	5.0	8.1
In losses	49	25.8	8.2	.464	0.1	.000	2.4	.641	0.47	0.41	1.1	5.9	9.2

	G	Min	FGA	FG%	3PA	3P%	FTA	FT%	Blk	Stl	Ast	Reb	Pts
Pre All-Star	41	27.4	9.1	.427	0.0	.000	2.4	.680	0.68	0.51	1.3	6.1	9.4
Post All-Star	28	23.3	6.8	.489	0.1	.000	2.3	.600	0.36	0.43	1.0	5.0	8.0
November	12	33.8	13.1	.452	0.0	—	3.5	.524	0.58	0.50	1.7	6.1	13.7
December	10	26.1	7.3	.411	0.0	—	2.3	.739	1.10	0.80	0.9	6.5	7.7
January	14	23.9	7.6	.425	0.1	.000	2.0	.821	0.50	0.36	1.3	6.0	8.1
February	11	22.6	6.7	.405	0.0	—	2.1	.696	0.45	0.36	0.8	5.2	6.9
March	12	25.9	7.6	.549	0.2	.000	2.8	.606	0.25	0.25	1.3	5.8	10.0
April	10	21.1	6.1	.426	0.0	—	1.6	.563	0.50	0.70	1.1	4.1	6.1
0 Days Rest	15	24.9	6.9	.452	0.0	—	2.4	.667	0.60	0.47	1.4	4.4	7.9
1 Days Rest	37	24.9	8.2	.421	0.1	.000	2.6	.646	0.59	0.38	1.0	5.9	8.6
2 Days Rest	6	30.7	10.0	.567	0.2	.000	2.3	.571	0.50	1.00	0.8	7.2	12.7
3+ Days Rest	11	26.7	8.5	.457	0.0	—	1.7	.684	0.36	0.55	1.6	5.8	9.0

Career (1995-96 thru 1999-2000)

	G	Min	FGA	FG%	3PA	3P%	FTA	FT%	Blk	Stl	Ast	Reb	Pts
Total	320	32.0	11.4	.477	0.1	.043	3.8	.692	0.78	0.49	1.7	7.2	13.5
Home	167	32.7	11.7	.480	0.1	.000	3.9	.704	0.84	0.51	1.8	7.5	13.9
Road	153	31.2	11.2	.474	0.1	.071	3.6	.677	0.70	0.47	1.5	6.8	13.1
vs. Playoff	186	32.4	11.3	.474	0.1	.067	3.3	.668	0.77	0.54	1.8	7.2	12.9
vs. Non-Playoff	134	31.5	11.6	.482	0.1	.000	4.4	.717	0.78	0.42	1.6	7.1	14.3
vs. East	113	32.5	11.9	.490	0.1	.000	4.2	.712	0.68	0.54	1.8	7.7	14.7
vs. West	207	31.7	11.2	.470	0.1	.077	3.5	.678	0.83	0.46	1.6	6.9	12.9
vs. Div.	99	31.9	11.5	.453	0.1	.000	3.6	.708	0.88	0.47	1.6	7.2	12.9
As Starter	293	33.1	11.8	.481	0.1	.048	3.8	.696	0.82	0.51	1.8	7.5	14.1
Off Bench	27	19.6	6.9	.409	0.1	.000	2.9	.623	0.33	0.30	0.7	3.7	7.4
In wins	68	32.2	11.4	.512	0.0	.000	4.5	.718	1.03	0.50	1.6	7.5	14.9
In losses	252	31.9	11.4	.468	0.1	.050	3.6	.683	0.71	0.49	1.7	7.1	13.1

	G	Min	FGA	FG%	3PA	3P%	FTA	FT%	Blk	Stl	Ast	Reb	Pts
Pre All-Star	180	31.7	10.6	.465	0.1	.083	3.2	.688	0.75	0.45	1.7	7.1	12.1
Post All-Star	115	33.3	13.0	.504	0.1	.000	4.4	.722	0.91	0.55	1.6	7.6	16.3
Oct/Nov	57	29.2	10.2	.454	0.1	.000	2.8	.631	0.67	0.51	1.5	5.8	11.0
December	48	33.3	11.1	.448	0.0	.000	3.3	.684	0.96	0.56	1.8	7.6	12.2
January	61	33.1	10.9	.491	0.1	.167	3.7	.726	0.74	0.36	1.8	7.9	13.4
February	55	31.7	11.2	.496	0.1	.000	4.4	.697	0.64	0.47	1.5	7.2	14.2
March	70	34.0	13.3	.487	0.1	.000	4.6	.694	0.77	0.53	1.8	7.8	16.2
Apr/May	29	28.8	11.4	.474	0.0	.000	3.3	.701	1.03	0.55	1.8	6.2	13.2
0 Days Rest	72	30.7	10.4	.448	0.0	.000	3.5	.737	0.61	0.53	1.8	6.4	11.9
1 Days Rest	178	32.4	11.9	.487	0.1	.000	4.1	.671	0.82	0.48	1.6	7.4	14.3
2 Days Rest	31	32.1	11.7	.481	0.1	.250	3.6	.726	0.68	0.45	1.5	6.6	13.9
3+ Days Rest	39	32.7	11.2	.476	0.1	.000	3.0	.690	0.95	0.49	1.9	7.7	12.7

Glen Rice

1999-2000 Per Game Averages

	G	Min	FGA	FG%	3PA	3P%	FTA	FT%	Blk	Stl	Ast	Reb	Pts
Total	80	31.6	12.3	.430	2.9	.367	5.0	.874	0.15	0.59	2.2	4.1	15.9
Home	40	30.5	11.8	.414	2.8	.310	5.3	.848	0.20	0.50	2.1	4.1	15.2
Road	40	32.8	12.7	.444	2.9	.422	4.6	.903	0.10	0.68	2.3	4.1	16.7
vs. Playoff	43	32.6	12.3	.438	3.3	.393	5.4	.876	0.09	0.65	2.2	4.4	16.8
vs. Non-Playoff	37	30.5	12.2	.419	2.4	.326	4.4	.871	0.22	0.51	2.3	3.7	14.9
vs. East	29	32.3	12.4	.457	3.1	.404	5.1	.879	0.17	0.90	2.1	4.3	17.1
vs. West	51	31.3	12.1	.414	2.7	.343	4.8	.870	0.14	0.41	2.3	4.0	15.2
vs. Div.	24	30.2	12.7	.387	2.8	.258	4.5	.889	0.08	0.54	1.9	4.0	14.3
As Starter	80	31.6	12.3	.430	2.9	.367	5.0	.874	0.15	0.59	2.2	4.1	15.9
Off Bench	0	—	—	—	—	—	—	—	—	—	—	—	—
In wins	65	31.0	12.0	.442	2.8	.374	5.3	.871	0.15	0.71	2.2	4.2	16.2
In losses	15	34.1	13.3	.382	3.3	.340	3.6	.889	0.13	0.07	2.3	3.8	14.5

	G	Min	FGA	FG%	3PA	3P%	FTA	FT%	Blk	Stl	Ast	Reb	Pts
Pre All-Star	47	32.3	12.4	.420	2.9	.366	5.8	.864	0.19	0.51	2.2	4.2	16.4
Post All-Star	33	30.6	12.1	.444	2.9	.368	3.8	.895	0.09	0.70	2.2	3.9	15.2
November	15	35.3	12.4	.457	2.6	.410	6.3	.883	0.07	0.53	2.7	4.4	17.9
December	14	30.8	13.1	.421	2.4	.235	5.4	.842	0.21	0.50	1.7	4.3	16.1
January	14	32.9	12.9	.398	3.6	.400	5.8	.864	0.29	0.57	2.6	4.1	16.7
February	13	29.8	11.0	.455	3.1	.450	4.2	.889	0.23	0.77	1.4	3.3	15.1
March	15	30.2	11.8	.418	2.7	.325	3.9	.862	0.07	0.60	2.4	4.3	14.1
April	9	30.0	12.2	.436	2.9	.346	3.7	.939	0.00	0.56	2.4	4.0	15.1
0 Days Rest	21	31.5	12.3	.461	2.9	.333	4.9	.882	0.10	0.57	2.3	4.0	16.6
1 Days Rest	39	32.3	12.3	.406	2.9	.348	4.8	.878	0.18	0.67	2.2	4.4	15.2
2 Days Rest	12	30.4	11.7	.400	2.3	.429	5.2	.859	0.17	0.17	1.7	3.5	14.7
3+ Days Rest	8	30.6	13.0	.500	3.6	.448	5.4	.884	0.13	0.88	2.6	3.5	19.4

Last Five Seasons

	G	Min	FGA	FG%	3PA	3P%	FTA	FT%	Blk	Stl	Ast	Reb	Pts
Total	347	38.4	16.1	.459	4.3	.428	5.5	.857	0.24	0.88	2.4	4.3	21.3
Home	174	38.3	16.0	.465	4.1	.413	6.0	.855	0.22	0.84	2.5	4.4	21.7
Road	173	38.4	16.1	.454	4.5	.441	5.0	.860	0.27	0.91	2.4	4.2	20.9
vs. Playoff	190	38.6	15.4	.455	4.4	.429	5.3	.858	0.21	0.88	2.4	4.3	20.4
vs. Non-Playoff	157	38.1	16.9	.464	4.3	.427	5.7	.857	0.29	0.87	2.4	4.2	22.4
vs. East	190	39.6	16.6	.465	4.3	.418	5.7	.861	0.29	0.99	2.4	4.3	22.3
vs. West	157	36.9	15.4	.452	4.2	.415	5.3	.852	0.18	0.74	2.3	4.2	20.2
vs. Div.	116	38.2	15.6	.444	4.3	.405	5.3	.849	0.24	0.77	2.3	4.1	20.1
As Starter	344	38.4	16.1	.460	4.3	.430	5.5	.858	0.25	0.88	2.4	4.3	21.4
Off Bench	3	29.7	15.0	.378	3.7	.182	2.7	.625	0.00	0.00	2.7	2.0	13.7
In wins	224	37.9	15.9	.475	4.1	.453	6.0	.860	0.23	0.84	2.5	4.3	22.2
In losses	123	39.2	16.3	.431	4.8	.390	4.5	.850	0.27	0.94	2.2	4.1	19.8

	G	Min	FGA	FG%	3PA	3P%	FTA	FT%	Blk	Stl	Ast	Reb	Pts
Pre All-Star	183	38.8	16.3	.456	4.3	.424	5.7	.849	0.25	0.93	2.3	4.5	21.5
Post All-Star	137	38.2	16.0	.469	4.3	.442	5.6	.869	0.25	0.85	2.3	4.1	21.8
Oct/Nov	54	37.5	14.9	.478	3.6	.431	5.4	.860	0.15	0.93	2.4	4.3	20.5
December	59	39.1	16.5	.454	4.4	.402	5.3	.826	0.24	0.97	2.3	4.3	21.1
January	57	40.5	17.9	.440	4.9	.433	6.5	.852	0.37	0.96	2.3	4.3	22.0
February	51	38.2	16.6	.465	4.5	.461	6.0	.891	0.18	1.12	2.4	4.2	22.8
March	69	37.2	15.2	.466	4.3	.438	5.1	.829	0.26	0.61	2.4	4.0	20.3
Apr/May	57	37.7	15.3	.457	4.3	.406	4.9	.892	0.26	0.75	2.4	3.9	20.1
0 Days Rest	90	38.4	16.0	.457	4.3	.385	5.3	.855	0.26	0.97	2.2	4.3	20.8
1 Days Rest	172	38.5	16.2	.457	4.3	.443	5.6	.861	0.26	0.79	2.4	4.4	21.5
2 Days Rest	50	38.8	16.0	.462	4.5	.458	5.5	.841	0.22	0.90	2.2	3.9	21.5
3+ Days Rest	35	37.1	15.8	.470	4.2	.422	5.2	.868	0.17	1.03	2.5	3.9	21.1

Mitch Richmond
Washington Wizards — Guard

1999-2000 Per Game Averages

	G	Min	FGA	FG%	3PA	3P%	FTA	FT%	Blk	Stl	Ast	Reb	Pts		G	Min	FGA	FG%	3PA	3P%	FTA	FT%	Blk	Stl	Ast	Reb	Pts
Total	74	32.4	14.2	.426	3.3	.386	4.6	.876	0.18	1.49	2.5	2.9	17.4	Pre All-Star	41	31.8	14.1	.440	3.1	.365	4.1	.840	0.29	1.39	2.5	2.6	17.0
Home	36	31.6	13.3	.411	3.1	.402	5.1	.874	0.22	1.44	2.7	2.6	16.6	Post All-Star	33	33.1	14.2	.409	3.5	.409	5.2	.912	0.03	1.61	2.5	3.2	17.8
Road	38	33.2	15.0	.439	3.4	.372	4.2	.880	0.13	1.53	2.3	3.2	18.1	November	14	25.1	10.8	.338	2.8	.231	3.8	.849	0.29	1.29	1.9	1.9	11.1
vs. Playoff	43	34.0	15.0	.430	3.3	.380	4.9	.885	0.16	1.51	2.4	3.2	18.5	December	15	35.6	16.2	.510	2.9	.386	5.5	.878	0.27	1.40	2.9	2.7	22.5
vs. Non-Playoff	31	30.1	13.0	.420	3.2	.394	4.2	.863	0.19	1.45	2.7	2.5	15.8	January	8	33.8	13.4	.407	3.3	.385	3.3	.731	0.50	1.25	2.6	3.6	16.1
vs. East	48	31.6	13.6	.414	3.2	.396	4.1	.862	0.17	1.48	2.6	2.7	16.1	February	11	34.3	13.2	.441	3.5	.462	3.5	.872	0.00	1.45	2.3	3.0	16.4
vs. West	26	33.9	15.2	.447	3.3	.368	5.5	.896	0.19	1.50	2.3	2.9	19.7	March	17	33.1	15.4	.441	3.6	.377	5.2	.909	0.06	1.94	2.4	3.6	19.6
vs. Div.	23	30.8	12.8	.427	3.2	.384	3.5	.850	0.13	1.65	2.9	2.5	15.1	April	9	33.4	14.0	.341	3.6	.500	5.8	.923	0.00	1.33	3.1	2.7	16.7
As Starter	69	32.9	14.4	.432	3.3	.398	4.5	.874	0.16	1.46	2.5	2.9	17.7	0 Days Rest	20	33.3	15.2	.442	3.2	.406	5.2	.885	0.20	1.55	2.2	3.3	19.3
Off Bench	5	24.8	11.2	.321	3.0	.200	6.0	.900	0.40	1.80	2.0	2.0	13.2	1 Days Rest	35	33.3	14.4	.436	3.2	.405	4.7	.890	0.06	1.54	2.8	2.9	18.0
In wins	27	31.9	14.1	.469	3.3	.438	4.9	.885	0.26	1.78	2.6	2.9	19.0	2 Days Rest	10	29.1	13.2	.371	3.2	.250	4.4	.841	0.70	1.30	2.3	2.9	14.3
In losses	47	32.7	14.2	.402	3.2	.355	4.4	.871	0.13	1.32	2.4	2.9	16.4	3+ Days Rest	9	30.6	12.1	.404	3.8	.412	3.2	.828	0.00	1.33	2.2	2.0	14.0

Last Five Seasons

	G	Min	FGA	FG%	3PA	3P%	FTA	FT%	Blk	Stl	Ast	Reb	Pts		G	Min	FGA	FG%	3PA	3P%	FTA	FT%	Blk	Stl	Ast	Reb	Pts
Total	356	36.4	16.9	.440	5.0	.404	6.0	.865	0.23	1.42	3.3	3.4	22.1	Pre All-Star	182	35.9	17.0	.456	4.5	.418	5.9	.866	0.26	1.43	3.5	3.4	22.6
Home	176	36.4	16.4	.441	4.9	.419	6.2	.859	0.21	1.42	3.5	3.5	21.8	Post All-Star	124	36.3	17.0	.427	6.0	.414	6.1	.866	0.19	1.45	3.4	3.4	22.3
Road	180	36.4	17.4	.439	5.2	.390	5.8	.870	0.24	1.42	3.2	3.3	22.3	Oct/Nov	61	34.1	15.4	.417	4.0	.359	5.4	.860	0.26	1.16	3.1	3.2	18.9
vs. Playoff	201	36.6	17.2	.430	5.0	.393	6.0	.864	0.22	1.44	3.2	3.3	22.0	December	56	36.7	17.2	.481	3.9	.432	6.4	.884	0.20	1.52	3.5	3.0	24.0
vs. Non-Playoff	155	36.1	16.5	.453	5.0	.417	5.9	.865	0.24	1.39	3.5	3.5	22.1	January	49	36.8	18.0	.464	5.1	.433	6.3	.839	0.35	1.69	3.9	4.0	24.3
vs. East	181	35.9	16.1	.436	4.7	.397	5.4	.867	0.20	1.33	3.2	3.2	20.6	February	62	37.7	18.1	.447	5.6	.401	6.0	.849	0.18	1.40	3.5	3.3	23.5
vs. West	175	36.9	17.7	.444	5.3	.410	6.6	.863	0.25	1.51	3.5	3.5	23.6	March	77	37.3	17.4	.433	5.9	.407	5.7	.889	0.19	1.49	3.1	3.4	22.6
vs. Div.	108	36.0	16.8	.444	5.3	.403	5.8	.853	0.23	1.49	3.2	3.2	22.0	Apr/May	51	35.4	15.0	.391	5.3	.393	6.1	.856	0.22	1.25	2.9	3.3	19.1
As Starter	351	36.5	17.0	.441	5.1	.406	6.0	.864	0.23	1.41	3.3	3.4	22.2	0 Days Rest	85	36.3	16.8	.446	4.8	.425	6.0	.868	0.22	1.44	2.7	3.0	22.2
Off Bench	5	24.8	11.2	.321	3.0	.200	6.0	.900	0.40	1.80	2.0	2.0	13.2	1 Days Rest	196	36.9	17.1	.432	5.1	.396	6.1	.867	0.22	1.38	3.5	3.5	22.1
In wins	144	36.6	16.5	.474	4.9	.457	6.4	.871	0.20	1.55	3.7	3.6	23.5	2 Days Rest	45	35.9	17.2	.452	5.0	.385	5.5	.871	0.29	1.51	3.4	3.7	22.4
In losses	212	36.2	17.2	.418	5.1	.369	5.7	.860	0.25	1.33	3.0	3.2	21.1	3+ Days Rest	30	34.9	15.6	.457	4.9	.426	5.6	.826	0.17	1.50	3.4	3.0	21.0

Isaiah Rider
Atlanta Hawks — Guard

1999-2000 Per Game Averages

	G	Min	FGA	FG%	3PA	3P%	FTA	FT%	Blk	Stl	Ast	Reb	Pts		G	Min	FGA	FG%	3PA	3P%	FTA	FT%	Blk	Stl	Ast	Reb	Pts
Total	60	34.7	17.9	.419	3.0	.311	4.3	.785	0.10	0.68	3.7	4.3	19.3	Pre All-Star	44	37.7	20.1	.419	3.6	.297	5.2	.789	0.11	0.73	4.0	4.7	22.0
Home	30	34.9	17.6	.445	3.0	.315	4.6	.791	0.13	0.80	3.7	4.6	20.3	Post All-Star	16	26.7	11.6	.419	1.4	.409	2.1	.758	0.06	0.56	2.8	3.3	11.9
Road	30	34.6	18.1	.393	3.0	.308	4.0	.777	0.07	0.57	3.6	4.0	18.3	November	13	33.2	18.5	.415	4.2	.338	4.7	.721	0.23	0.38	3.2	4.3	20.2
vs. Playoff	35	34.1	17.9	.404	3.3	.325	4.3	.812	0.14	0.74	3.7	4.0	19.0	December	13	41.4	22.0	.448	3.6	.234	6.4	.831	0.08	1.00	4.5	5.5	25.8
vs. Non-Playoff	25	35.6	17.8	.439	2.5	.286	4.4	.748	0.04	0.60	3.7	4.2	19.7	January	13	39.4	21.7	.390	3.8	.347	4.5	.831	0.08	0.85	3.9	3.9	22.0
vs. East	37	35.3	18.5	.406	3.2	.294	4.5	.792	0.16	0.70	3.7	3.9	19.6	February	12	36.0	17.3	.440	1.9	.391	3.5	.714	0.08	0.58	4.1	5.3	18.4
vs. West	23	33.8	16.9	.441	2.7	.344	4.0	.772	0.00	0.65	3.6	4.9	18.9	March	9	18.9	6.2	.357	0.8	.143	1.7	.800	0.00	0.56	1.6	1.9	5.9
vs. Div.	21	34.2	18.7	.413	3.4	.264	4.5	.779	0.19	0.67	4.1	3.8	19.9	April	0	—	—	—	—	—	—	—	—	—	—	—	—
As Starter	47	38.8	20.1	.428	3.3	.318	5.0	.784	0.13	0.74	4.0	4.9	22.2	0 Days Rest	18	35.2	17.8	.427	3.1	.357	4.8	.779	0.00	0.72	3.9	3.8	20.1
Off Bench	13	20.0	9.8	.354	1.8	.261	1.8	.792	0.00	0.46	2.2	2.2	8.8	1 Days Rest	23	34.3	17.6	.420	3.2	.219	4.2	.825	0.09	0.65	3.6	4.7	19.0
In wins	23	37.3	19.8	.461	2.9	.373	5.0	.784	0.26	0.65	4.1	5.1	23.3	2 Days Rest	11	33.5	16.4	.400	2.4	.385	4.4	.729	0.27	0.91	3.1	4.8	17.2
In losses	37	33.2	16.6	.388	3.1	.274	3.9	.785	0.00	0.70	3.4	3.8	16.8	3+ Days Rest	8	36.6	20.8	.422	3.1	.400	3.6	.759	0.13	0.38	3.9	3.6	21.5

Last Five Seasons

	G	Min	FGA	FG%	3PA	3P%	FTA	FT%	Blk	Stl	Ast	Reb	Pts		G	Min	FGA	FG%	3PA	3P%	FTA	FT%	Blk	Stl	Ast	Reb	Pts
Total	332	34.4	15.6	.438	3.7	.349	3.7	.809	0.23	0.64	2.9	4.3	18.0	Pre All-Star	173	36.0	16.4	.431	4.2	.338	4.2	.805	0.25	0.67	3.2	4.5	19.2
Home	167	34.7	15.9	.445	3.8	.342	3.9	.825	0.22	0.63	3.0	4.4	18.7	Post All-Star	112	34.0	14.9	.460	3.6	.361	3.3	.839	0.21	0.65	2.8	4.5	17.8
Road	165	34.0	15.2	.431	3.7	.357	3.5	.791	0.24	0.66	2.8	4.1	17.2	Oct/Nov	47	34.0	16.3	.408	5.1	.345	4.1	.791	0.23	0.51	3.1	4.6	18.2
vs. Playoff	187	34.5	15.5	.428	3.8	.361	3.8	.825	0.24	0.68	2.9	4.4	17.7	December	55	35.3	15.9	.448	4.2	.346	4.0	.786	0.25	0.85	3.5	4.4	18.9
vs. Non-Playoff	145	34.2	15.6	.452	3.7	.333	3.6	.788	0.21	0.59	2.9	4.1	18.2	January	57	38.2	17.7	.430	3.8	.322	4.3	.844	0.28	0.67	3.2	4.6	20.1
vs. East	125	35.6	15.3	.428	3.8	.328	4.0	.792	0.21	0.73	3.0	4.2	18.4	February	59	36.0	16.2	.454	3.2	.360	3.9	.803	0.17	0.59	2.7	4.4	19.0
vs. West	207	33.6	15.1	.445	3.7	.362	3.6	.821	0.24	0.59	2.7	4.4	17.7	March	67	31.8	13.7	.444	3.3	.339	3.1	.798	0.22	0.61	2.7	3.6	15.8
vs. Div.	106	33.9	15.6	.432	3.6	.350	4.1	.822	0.20	0.58	3.0	4.5	18.1	Apr/May	47	31.8	13.7	.442	3.2	.400	3.0	.835	0.15	0.62	2.3	4.2	15.9
As Starter	290	35.7	16.2	.438	3.8	.341	3.8	.811	0.24	0.66	3.0	4.4	18.6	0 Days Rest	89	33.9	15.5	.441	3.8	.362	3.7	.794	0.10	0.73	3.0	4.2	18.0
Off Bench	42	25.1	11.2	.445	3.1	.419	2.9	.793	0.14	0.52	2.5	3.5	13.6	1 Days Rest	155	34.7	15.6	.442	3.7	.326	3.8	.827	0.32	0.62	2.7	4.4	18.1
In wins	162	34.3	15.5	.478	3.6	.397	3.9	.822	0.27	0.64	3.0	4.5	19.4	2 Days Rest	45	35.3	15.9	.423	3.6	.401	3.8	.786	0.20	0.73	3.3	4.4	17.9
In losses	170	34.4	15.6	.401	3.9	.308	3.5	.796	0.19	0.65	2.8	4.1	16.5	3+ Days Rest	43	33.3	15.3	.435	3.9	.353	3.4	.796	0.21	0.47	2.9	3.8	17.4

Clifford Robinson
Phoenix Suns — Forward

1999-2000 Per Game Averages

	G	Min	FGA	FG%	3PA	3P%	FTA	FT%	Blk	Stl	Ast	Reb	Pts		G	Min	FGA	FG%	3PA	3P%	FTA	FT%	Blk	Stl	Ast	Reb	Pts
Total	80	35.5	14.3	.464	4.1	.370	4.8	.782	0.76	1.13	2.8	4.5	18.5	Pre All-Star	46	34.6	14.6	.473	4.1	.388	4.7	.784	0.72	0.87	2.9	4.3	19.1
Home	39	34.0	14.2	.474	4.0	.394	4.7	.781	0.69	1.00	3.3	4.4	18.7	Post All-Star	34	36.7	13.8	.452	4.0	.346	4.8	.779	0.82	1.47	2.6	4.8	17.6
Road	41	36.9	14.4	.455	4.1	.349	4.8	.783	0.83	1.24	2.4	4.6	18.3	November	12	27.6	10.4	.432	3.0	.250	3.9	.787	0.58	0.92	1.9	3.8	12.8
vs. Playoff	43	34.8	13.6	.430	4.0	.364	3.8	.750	0.72	1.00	2.7	4.4	16.0	December	15	37.8	16.9	.494	4.6	.478	4.7	.803	0.87	0.93	3.3	5.1	22.7
vs. Non-Playoff	37	36.3	15.1	.500	4.1	.377	5.9	.806	0.81	1.27	2.9	4.6	21.4	January	14	39.0	17.0	.496	5.0	.414	6.1	.729	0.86	0.71	3.2	4.1	23.4
vs. East	28	33.5	12.9	.457	3.6	.360	5.1	.764	1.00	0.96	2.7	3.9	17.0	February	13	31.7	12.0	.359	2.8	.250	3.2	.786	0.69	0.85	3.0	4.3	11.8
vs. West	52	36.6	15.0	.467	4.3	.375	4.6	.793	0.63	1.21	2.9	4.8	19.3	March	16	36.5	14.2	.489	4.4	.380	5.6	.844	0.69	1.94	2.6	4.6	20.3
vs. Div.	24	35.5	15.4	.462	4.3	.359	4.1	.758	0.58	1.04	2.7	4.6	18.9	April	10	39.9	14.3	.462	4.2	.310	4.6	.717	0.90	1.30	2.7	5.0	17.8
As Starter	67	37.1	14.9	.465	4.3	.377	4.9	.785	0.79	1.19	2.9	4.6	19.4	0 Days Rest	20	37.2	14.3	.441	4.5	.389	5.6	.820	0.80	0.80	2.7	4.7	18.9
Off Bench	13	26.9	10.8	.461	2.7	.314	3.9	.765	0.62	0.77	2.2	3.8	13.8	1 Days Rest	39	34.3	13.9	.465	3.9	.344	5.1	.747	0.74	1.21	2.6	4.2	18.1
In wins	51	35.1	14.2	.480	3.7	.365	4.7	.798	0.84	1.27	3.2	4.5	17.9	2 Days Rest	15	35.9	14.3	.481	3.8	.421	3.0	.844	0.87	1.40	3.3	4.5	17.9
In losses	29	36.2	14.4	.437	4.7	.378	4.8	.755	0.62	0.86	2.1	4.4	18.0	3+ Days Rest	6	36.3	16.3	.490	4.3	.346	4.5	.778	0.50	1.00	3.5	5.8	21.0

Last Five Seasons

	G	Min	FGA	FG%	3PA	3P%	FTA	FT%	Blk	Stl	Ast	Reb	Pts		G	Min	FGA	FG%	3PA	3P%	FTA	FT%	Blk	Stl	Ast	Reb	Pts
Total	369	35.2	13.6	.450	3.7	.368	4.9	.703	0.93	1.20	2.6	4.8	17.1	Pre All-Star	182	35.2	13.9	.451	4.0	.384	5.2	.675	0.86	1.05	2.7	4.6	17.6
Home	184	34.7	13.4	.457	3.5	.372	5.0	.694	0.89	1.11	2.8	4.8	17.0	Post All-Star	137	35.4	13.5	.439	3.6	.332	4.7	.747	0.94	1.28	2.6	5.1	16.6
Road	185	35.8	13.8	.443	3.9	.365	4.9	.713	0.97	1.29	2.5	4.7	17.1	Oct/Nov	55	34.4	13.1	.433	4.2	.355	5.2	.682	0.84	1.00	2.6	4.7	16.4
vs. Playoff	198	35.0	13.1	.434	3.8	.360	4.6	.696	0.95	1.15	2.5	4.7	15.9	December	59	35.6	14.1	.455	3.8	.410	5.4	.688	0.92	1.17	2.8	4.8	18.1
vs. Non-Playoff	171	35.4	14.1	.467	3.6	.379	5.4	.710	0.91	1.25	2.8	4.8	18.4	January	54	35.9	14.8	.469	4.2	.412	5.2	.644	0.83	0.93	2.6	4.3	18.9
vs. East	122	34.6	13.3	.447	3.8	.354	5.3	.691	0.98	1.02	2.6	4.5	16.9	February	64	33.2	12.4	.419	3.0	.309	4.4	.678	0.83	1.08	2.3	4.9	14.3
vs. West	247	35.5	13.7	.451	3.7	.376	4.8	.710	0.91	1.28	2.7	4.9	17.2	March	79	34.8	13.3	.465	3.4	.379	4.6	.752	1.10	1.38	2.6	4.8	17.1
vs. Div.	111	36.0	14.3	.448	3.7	.346	5.0	.718	0.93	1.12	2.8	4.9	17.6	Apr/May	58	37.7	14.2	.450	3.8	.333	5.1	.760	1.02	1.55	3.0	5.0	17.9
As Starter	321	36.1	14.1	.450	3.7	.371	5.1	.703	0.93	1.23	2.8	4.9	17.2	0 Days Rest	92	35.9	13.9	.444	4.1	.403	4.4	.723	0.92	1.25	2.9	4.6	17.2
Off Bench	48	25.5	10.1	.442	2.0	.330	3.9	.709	0.92	0.96	1.7	4.3	12.4	1 Days Rest	190	34.5	13.2	.454	3.5	.351	5.1	.691	0.92	1.19	2.4	4.6	16.7
In wins	223	34.9	13.5	.472	3.3	.389	5.0	.711	0.91	1.31	2.8	4.9	17.6	2 Days Rest	58	37.2	14.2	.451	3.9	.368	5.0	.712	1.05	1.33	3.0	5.1	17.8
In losses	146	35.7	13.7	.415	4.3	.344	4.8	.691	0.97	1.02	2.4	4.6	16.2	3+ Days Rest	29	34.0	14.3	.441	3.6	.356	5.2	.713	0.83	0.79	2.5	4.8	17.6

David Robinson
San Antonio Spurs — Center

1999-2000 Per Game Averages

	G	Min	FGA	FG%	3PA	3P%	FTA	FT%	Blk	Stl	Ast	Reb	Pts		G	Min	FGA	FG%	3PA	3P%	FTA	FT%	Blk	Stl	Ast	Reb	Pts
Total	80	32.0	12.9	.512	0.0	.000	6.4	.726	2.29	1.21	1.8	9.6	17.8	Pre All-Star	47	31.4	12.0	.492	0.0	.000	5.6	.701	2.34	1.00	1.8	9.8	15.7
Home	39	31.9	12.5	.506	0.0	.000	6.7	.738	2.77	1.08	1.7	9.4	17.6	Post All-Star	33	32.8	14.2	.536	0.0	.000	7.6	.752	2.21	1.52	1.8	9.4	20.9
Road	41	32.0	13.2	.517	0.0	.000	6.1	.713	1.83	1.34	1.8	9.9	18.1	November	15	28.7	9.7	.500	0.0	—	4.9	.699	3.00	0.93	2.1	8.6	13.1
vs. Playoff	43	33.4	13.4	.468	0.0	.000	6.7	.727	2.30	1.37	2.0	10.0	17.4	December	15	32.0	11.5	.451	0.0	—	5.9	.784	1.80	1.33	1.9	11.1	15.0
vs. Non-Playoff	37	30.3	12.3	.568	0.0	—	6.0	.725	2.27	1.03	1.6	9.2	18.4	January	13	32.7	13.8	.533	0.1	.000	5.8	.645	2.31	0.85	1.4	9.6	18.5
vs. East	29	32.0	12.1	.500	0.0	.000	6.0	.789	2.48	1.10	1.9	9.2	16.9	February	12	34.6	14.4	.503	0.1	.000	8.0	.719	2.42	1.67	1.5	9.8	20.3
vs. West	51	31.9	13.3	.518	0.0	.000	6.6	.693	2.18	1.27	1.7	9.8	18.4	March	15	32.6	14.3	.540	0.0	—	6.2	.742	1.93	1.13	1.8	9.5	20.1
vs. Div.	23	31.9	11.3	.517	0.0	.000	7.0	.744	2.13	1.30	1.5	8.9	16.9	April	10	31.7	14.4	.542	0.0	—	8.5	.753	2.30	1.50	1.8	8.8	22.0
As Starter	80	32.0	12.9	.512	0.0	.000	6.4	.726	2.29	1.21	1.8	9.6	17.8	0 Days Rest	17	32.1	12.1	.544	0.0	—	6.6	.735	2.35	1.06	1.6	9.5	18.1
Off Bench	0	—	—	—	—	—	—	—	—	—	—	—	—	1 Days Rest	42	32.3	13.4	.511	0.0	.000	6.3	.711	2.17	1.14	1.7	9.6	18.2
In wins	51	30.9	12.6	.522	0.0	.000	5.9	.730	2.47	1.20	1.8	9.5	17.5	2 Days Rest	16	31.3	13.1	.510	0.1	.000	6.6	.762	2.31	1.63	1.9	10.2	18.4
In losses	29	33.9	13.3	.496	0.0	.000	7.3	.720	1.97	1.24	1.8	9.8	18.5	3+ Days Rest	5	31.2	10.6	.415	0.0	—	5.4	.704	3.00	1.00	2.2	8.2	12.6

Last Five Seasons

	G	Min	FGA	FG%	3PA	3P%	FTA	FT%	Blk	Stl	Ast	Reb	Pts		G	Min	FGA	FG%	3PA	3P%	FTA	FT%	Blk	Stl	Ast	Reb	Pts
Total	290	33.6	14.0	.512	0.1	.250	8.3	.729	2.66	1.20	2.4	10.6	20.5	Pre All-Star	146	34.2	14.6	.517	0.1	.200	8.2	.732	2.69	1.06	2.5	11.0	21.1
Home	142	32.8	14.1	.514	0.1	.125	8.4	.730	3.09	1.20	2.4	10.8	20.6	Post All-Star	95	33.6	14.9	.507	0.1	.400	8.9	.754	2.73	1.29	2.4	10.4	21.9
Road	148	34.3	14.0	.511	0.1	.375	8.2	.727	2.24	1.20	2.4	10.5	20.4	Oct/Nov	43	32.5	13.7	.525	0.1	.167	7.8	.742	2.98	1.14	2.6	10.6	20.3
vs. Playoff	158	34.8	14.4	.480	0.1	.111	8.6	.713	2.70	1.26	2.6	10.8	19.9	December	49	34.2	14.6	.511	0.0	.000	8.8	.747	2.49	1.08	2.7	11.2	21.4
vs. Non-Playoff	132	32.1	13.7	.553	0.1	.429	7.9	.749	2.61	1.12	2.2	10.4	21.1	January	44	35.0	14.8	.516	0.0	.500	8.3	.716	2.70	0.95	2.3	11.0	21.2
vs. East	94	34.4	14.4	.518	0.1	.286	8.6	.737	2.81	1.27	2.5	10.6	21.3	February	45	34.4	13.9	.504	0.1	.250	8.7	.704	2.82	1.53	2.4	10.6	20.2
vs. West	196	33.2	13.9	.510	0.0	.222	8.1	.724	2.59	1.16	2.4	10.7	20.0	March	63	33.0	14.0	.510	0.0	.500	7.6	.745	2.62	1.22	2.2	10.0	20.1
vs. Div.	89	32.4	12.4	.532	0.0	.500	7.7	.735	2.53	1.17	2.3	10.4	18.9	Apr/May	46	32.4	13.3	.509	0.0	—	8.9	.713	2.39	1.26	2.3	10.6	19.9
As Starter	290	33.6	14.0	.512	0.1	.250	8.3	.729	2.66	1.20	2.4	10.6	20.5	0 Days Rest	63	34.4	13.7	.523	0.0	.333	8.2	.730	2.25	1.11	2.1	11.1	20.3
Off Bench	0	—	—	—	—	—	—	—	—	—	—	—	—	1 Days Rest	163	33.8	14.3	.504	0.0	.333	8.3	.732	2.82	1.18	2.4	10.6	20.5
In wins	199	32.9	13.8	.529	0.0	.429	8.2	.741	2.92	1.17	2.5	10.6	20.7	2 Days Rest	41	32.7	14.3	.542	0.1	.000	8.0	.752	2.49	1.41	2.4	10.4	21.5
In losses	91	35.1	14.5	.478	0.1	.111	8.6	.704	2.09	1.26	2.3	10.7	19.9	3+ Days Rest	23	31.3	12.6	.486	0.0	.000	9.3	.668	2.96	1.17	3.0	10.3	18.5

Glenn Robinson

1999-2000 Per Game Averages

	G	Min	FGA	FG%	3PA	3P%	FTA	FT%	Blk	Stl	Ast	Reb	Pts		G	Min	FGA	FG%	3PA	3P%	FTA	FT%	Blk	Stl	Ast	Reb	Pts
Total	81	35.9	18.0	.472	2.9	.363	3.5	.802	0.51	0.96	2.4	6.0	20.9	Pre All-Star	49	35.9	18.2	.496	3.1	.414	4.2	.807	0.65	0.96	2.2	5.9	22.7
Home	40	35.5	18.1	.486	2.9	.348	2.9	.826	0.45	1.05	2.2	5.7	21.0	Post All-Star	32	35.9	17.8	.436	2.7	.271	2.4	.789	0.28	0.97	2.7	6.2	18.1
Road	41	36.4	18.0	.459	3.0	.377	4.1	.786	0.56	0.88	2.6	6.3	20.8	November	14	34.7	16.7	.470	2.1	.483	4.8	.806	0.71	0.86	2.4	6.6	20.6
vs. Playoff	42	36.4	18.3	.476	3.1	.397	4.0	.849	0.45	0.93	2.4	5.9	22.0	December	15	35.2	18.3	.516	3.2	.396	3.5	.774	0.67	1.00	2.1	5.8	22.9
vs. Non-Playoff	39	35.4	17.7	.468	2.7	.321	3.0	.735	0.56	1.00	2.4	6.1	19.7	January	15	37.7	19.8	.475	3.7	.382	4.4	.833	0.80	1.20	2.1	5.9	23.9
vs. East	53	36.4	18.3	.468	2.9	.353	3.5	.804	0.47	0.96	2.3	5.7	20.9	February	12	36.3	18.8	.498	3.6	.419	3.2	.816	0.17	0.75	2.2	5.9	20.9
vs. West	28	35.1	17.6	.481	3.0	.381	3.5	.798	0.57	0.96	2.6	6.5	20.9	March	14	34.9	16.1	.420	2.3	.125	2.0	.857	0.21	1.00	3.1	5.4	15.6
vs. Div.	28	35.8	18.7	.493	2.9	.390	3.9	.817	0.50	0.96	2.3	5.4	22.8	April	11	36.8	18.5	.441	2.7	.333	2.8	.710	0.36	0.91	2.3	6.5	19.3
As Starter	81	35.9	18.0	.472	2.9	.363	3.5	.802	0.51	0.96	2.4	6.0	20.9	0 Days Rest	19	35.5	17.9	.476	3.0	.351	5.0	.747	0.37	0.89	2.4	6.6	21.8
Off Bench	0	—	—	—	—	—	—	—	—	—	—	—	—	1 Days Rest	48	36.4	18.1	.470	2.9	.319	3.0	.824	0.56	0.81	2.5	5.9	20.4
In wins	42	35.0	17.1	.477	2.7	.407	3.2	.809	0.67	1.12	2.4	5.9	20.0	2 Days Rest	5	35.0	20.0	.500	2.4	.667	4.6	.826	0.80	1.40	2.0	5.6	25.4
In losses	39	36.8	19.0	.468	3.2	.323	3.8	.796	0.33	0.79	2.4	6.1	21.8	3+ Days Rest	9	34.6	16.7	.460	3.0	.481	2.6	.870	0.33	1.67	2.2	5.2	19.0

Last Five Seasons

	G	Min	FGA	FG%	3PA	3P%	FTA	FT%	Blk	Stl	Ast	Reb	Pts		G	Min	FGA	FG%	3PA	3P%	FTA	FT%	Blk	Stl	Ast	Reb	Pts
Total	346	38.0	17.8	.464	2.4	.358	4.2	.811	0.65	1.13	2.9	6.0	20.9	Pre All-Star	184	38.9	18.4	.476	2.5	.375	4.7	.800	0.63	1.18	2.9	6.1	22.2
Home	175	37.8	17.6	.471	2.1	.370	4.3	.795	0.58	1.14	2.9	5.8	20.8	Post All-Star	115	38.3	17.7	.447	2.6	.323	3.8	.809	0.60	1.11	3.1	5.9	19.7
Road	171	38.1	18.1	.458	2.6	.348	4.2	.827	0.73	1.12	2.8	6.2	20.9	Oct/Nov	57	38.2	18.1	.467	2.2	.452	4.7	.801	0.74	1.25	2.8	6.1	21.7
vs. Playoff	188	38.3	17.6	.473	2.4	.353	4.3	.822	0.56	1.03	2.8	5.8	21.2	December	56	38.7	17.6	.492	2.5	.359	4.7	.798	0.64	1.20	3.2	6.0	22.0
vs. Non-Playoff	158	37.7	17.9	.455	2.4	.364	4.1	.797	0.76	1.25	3.0	6.2	20.4	January	57	40.1	19.7	.470	2.6	.313	4.9	.799	0.58	1.16	2.7	6.4	23.2
vs. East	238	38.2	17.6	.464	2.4	.365	4.3	.822	0.64	1.13	2.8	6.1	20.7	February	60	37.9	17.8	.459	2.2	.353	3.7	.809	0.67	0.93	2.5	5.7	20.1
vs. West	108	37.6	18.4	.465	2.4	.344	4.0	.784	0.69	1.14	2.9	5.9	21.1	March	66	36.8	17.0	.445	2.2	.313	3.8	.841	0.50	1.29	3.3	5.7	19.0
vs. Div.	122	38.2	17.3	.464	2.5	.373	4.2	.815	0.61	1.06	2.8	6.0	20.5	Apr/May	50	36.2	16.9	.454	2.6	.372	3.7	.821	0.84	0.92	2.6	6.1	19.3
As Starter	345	38.0	17.9	.465	2.4	.359	4.2	.811	0.65	1.13	2.9	6.0	20.9	0 Days Rest	89	37.7	17.9	.470	2.5	.383	5.0	.800	0.56	1.11	2.8	6.3	21.8
Off Bench	1	40.0	14.0	.357	2.0	.000	2.0	.500	1.00	2.00	7.0	2.0	11.0	1 Days Rest	176	38.1	17.6	.463	2.3	.332	4.0	.809	0.74	1.05	2.9	5.9	20.5
In wins	155	37.7	17.6	.486	2.0	.397	4.4	.817	0.77	1.15	3.0	6.1	21.5	2 Days Rest	48	37.5	18.2	.447	2.4	.381	3.8	.832	0.67	1.27	2.9	5.6	20.4
In losses	191	38.3	18.0	.448	2.7	.334	4.1	.805	0.55	1.12	2.8	5.9	20.3	3+ Days Rest	33	38.9	18.5	.479	2.5	.390	4.1	.830	0.42	1.39	2.7	5.8	22.1

Rodney Rogers

1999-2000 Per Game Averages

	G	Min	FGA	FG%	3PA	3P%	FTA	FT%	Blk	Stl	Ast	Reb	Pts		G	Min	FGA	FG%	3PA	3P%	FTA	FT%	Blk	Stl	Ast	Reb	Pts
Total	82	27.9	10.7	.486	3.2	.439	3.0	.639	0.57	1.15	2.1	5.5	13.8	Pre All-Star	48	26.4	9.2	.490	2.3	.413	2.6	.643	0.73	1.04	2.1	5.1	11.7
Home	41	27.2	10.2	.499	2.9	.445	3.1	.594	0.63	1.15	2.3	5.6	13.3	Post All-Star	34	30.0	12.9	.482	4.5	.458	3.6	.634	0.35	1.29	2.0	5.9	16.8
Road	41	28.6	11.3	.474	3.5	.434	3.0	.686	0.51	1.15	1.8	5.3	14.2	November	14	24.4	9.1	.480	2.5	.457	2.5	.600	0.86	0.79	1.8	4.9	11.4
vs. Playoff	44	28.7	10.9	.472	3.2	.423	2.9	.680	0.64	1.23	2.1	5.5	13.7	December	15	31.3	11.0	.479	3.0	.333	3.4	.627	0.80	1.53	2.5	6.2	13.7
vs. Non-Playoff	38	27.0	10.5	.503	3.2	.458	3.2	.595	0.50	1.05	2.1	5.4	13.9	January	14	22.6	7.3	.490	1.4	.450	2.1	.655	0.50	0.50	1.9	4.6	9.1
vs. East	30	26.4	9.9	.488	3.2	.421	3.5	.663	0.57	0.83	2.2	5.5	13.3	February	13	30.8	12.2	.579	3.5	.556	3.3	.721	0.77	2.00	1.7	5.3	18.5
vs. West	52	28.8	11.2	.485	3.2	.449	2.8	.621	0.58	1.33	2.0	5.4	14.1	March	16	28.8	13.4	.463	4.9	.462	3.2	.686	0.19	1.06	2.1	6.2	16.8
vs. Div.	24	30.0	11.8	.479	3.5	.440	2.9	.557	0.50	1.25	2.3	5.8	14.4	April	20	28.9	11.4	.412	3.9	.359	4.0	.525	0.30	1.00	2.6	5.3	12.9
As Starter	7	36.7	13.1	.467	3.1	.364	3.1	.591	0.57	1.57	2.7	7.3	15.3	0 Days Rest	20	27.5	9.6	.453	3.5	.435	2.2	.674	0.70	1.10	2.0	4.9	11.7
Off Bench	75	27.1	10.5	.488	3.2	.446	3.0	.643	0.57	1.11	2.0	5.3	13.6	1 Days Rest	42	28.5	11.0	.472	3.2	.407	3.6	.662	0.48	1.14	2.2	5.6	14.0
In wins	53	27.5	10.8	.517	3.1	.476	3.3	.624	0.64	1.26	2.3	5.9	14.6	2 Days Rest	15	26.2	11.1	.530	3.0	.467	2.8	.476	0.67	1.27	1.5	5.6	14.5
In losses	29	28.6	10.7	.429	3.4	.378	2.6	.671	0.45	0.93	1.7	4.6	12.2	3+ Days Rest	5	29.8	12.6	.571	2.6	.692	2.6	.769	0.60	1.00	3.2	5.8	18.2

Last Five Seasons

	G	Min	FGA	FG%	3PA	3P%	FTA	FT%	Blk	Stl	Ast	Reb	Pts		G	Min	FGA	FG%	3PA	3P%	FTA	FT%	Blk	Stl	Ast	Reb	Pts
Total	353	28.8	10.3	.467	2.5	.367	3.2	.660	0.58	1.12	2.4	4.9	12.7	Pre All-Star	219	29.5	10.3	.455	2.1	.352	3.5	.649	0.62	1.06	2.5	5.0	12.4
Home	179	28.4	9.7	.476	2.2	.364	3.5	.634	0.55	1.09	2.3	5.1	12.3	Post All-Star	134	30.9	11.7	.485	3.4	.390	3.4	.670	0.55	1.25	2.5	5.1	14.9
Road	174	29.3	10.9	.459	2.7	.369	3.0	.691	0.60	1.16	2.4	4.8	13.0	Oct/Nov	61	28.2	9.5	.466	1.9	.365	3.7	.655	0.48	1.00	2.2	4.5	12.0
vs. Playoff	199	28.9	10.3	.456	2.6	.373	3.1	.659	0.58	1.21	2.3	4.8	12.4	December	43	31.3	11.1	.470	2.2	.365	3.7	.658	0.86	1.21	2.9	5.5	13.7
vs. Non-Playoff	154	28.8	10.4	.481	2.3	.358	3.4	.661	0.56	1.01	2.5	5.2	13.0	January	54	29.0	10.6	.401	2.3	.293	3.2	.632	0.61	1.04	2.5	5.0	11.2
vs. East	109	28.2	10.0	.463	2.5	.342	3.6	.659	0.44	0.95	2.2	4.7	12.5	February	56	28.8	9.7	.533	2.4	.424	3.1	.665	0.59	1.13	2.1	5.0	13.4
vs. West	244	29.1	10.4	.469	2.5	.378	3.1	.651	0.64	1.20	2.5	5.0	12.8	March	80	29.3	11.1	.466	3.1	.394	3.3	.689	0.44	1.26	2.5	5.6	13.6
vs. Div.	113	29.5	10.6	.463	2.5	.356	3.5	.623	0.66	1.27	2.6	5.4	12.9	Apr/May	59	27.0	9.8	.470	2.6	.335	2.5	.642	0.61	1.08	2.2	4.1	11.7
As Starter	197	32.3	11.4	.467	2.6	.352	3.5	.660	0.62	1.18	2.7	5.2	13.8	0 Days Rest	92	29.0	10.2	.462	2.5	.349	3.5	.701	0.58	1.20	2.1	4.5	12.7
Off Bench	156	24.4	9.0	.467	2.3	.387	2.9	.659	0.51	1.06	1.9	4.6	11.2	1 Days Rest	177	28.8	10.1	.467	2.4	.368	3.2	.660	0.58	1.08	2.5	5.1	12.5
In wins	138	28.9	10.5	.510	2.4	.417	3.5	.640	0.65	1.09	2.8	5.7	14.0	2 Days Rest	53	29.3	11.0	.475	2.6	.399	3.0	.576	0.49	1.11	2.6	5.1	13.2
In losses	215	28.8	10.2	.438	2.5	.336	3.1	.674	0.53	1.14	2.1	4.5	11.8	3+ Days Rest	31	28.0	10.5	.466	2.5	.355	3.1	.660	0.68	1.16	2.2	4.9	12.7

Jalen Rose

1999-2000 Per Game Averages

	G	Min	FGA	FG%	3PA	3P%	FTA	FT%	Blk	Stl	Ast	Reb	Pts
Total	80	37.2	15.0	.471	2.5	.393	3.8	.827	0.61	1.05	4.0	4.8	18.2
Home	40	38.0	14.8	.489	2.0	.410	4.0	.851	0.73	1.13	4.0	5.5	18.7
Road	40	36.5	15.1	.453	3.0	.381	3.7	.801	0.50	0.98	4.0	4.2	17.7
vs. Playoff	43	38.0	15.0	.463	2.4	.423	3.5	.788	0.67	1.12	3.9	4.3	17.7
vs. Non-Playoff	37	36.4	14.9	.480	2.5	.359	4.2	.865	0.54	0.97	4.1	5.5	18.8
vs. East	53	37.4	14.9	.479	2.4	.375	4.2	.821	0.66	1.06	4.2	5.0	18.7
vs. West	27	36.9	15.0	.454	2.5	.426	3.1	.843	0.52	1.04	3.6	4.5	17.3
vs. Div.	27	37.3	15.3	.488	2.6	.391	4.5	.835	0.78	1.07	4.3	4.9	19.6
As Starter	80	37.2	15.0	.471	2.5	.393	3.8	.827	0.61	1.05	4.0	4.8	18.2
Off Bench	0	—	—	—	—	—	—	—	—	—	—	—	—
In wins	54	37.4	14.7	.486	2.3	.402	4.3	.820	0.59	1.09	4.1	4.8	18.8
In losses	26	37.0	15.4	.440	2.8	.378	2.8	.851	0.65	0.96	3.8	4.9	17.0

	G	Min	FGA	FG%	3PA	3P%	FTA	FT%	Blk	Stl	Ast	Reb	Pts
Pre All-Star	48	35.6	13.6	.467	2.6	.341	2.7	.847	0.52	1.02	4.0	4.6	15.9
Post All-Star	32	39.7	17.0	.475	2.2	.486	5.5	.813	0.75	1.09	4.0	5.3	21.7
November	15	33.5	12.5	.497	2.7	.488	2.1	.839	0.33	0.93	4.2	4.8	15.5
December	14	33.9	13.2	.454	2.9	.268	2.4	.824	0.79	1.00	3.7	3.9	14.8
January	14	38.2	13.9	.433	2.3	.281	3.0	.905	0.50	1.14	4.0	4.6	15.4
February	13	39.3	17.2	.516	2.2	.393	4.9	.859	0.85	1.15	3.5	4.8	22.8
March	14	40.4	17.8	.450	2.4	.545	5.8	.827	0.71	0.86	4.1	5.8	22.1
April	10	39.0	15.8	.475	2.1	.381	5.5	.727	0.50	1.30	4.7	5.2	19.8
0 Days Rest	20	38.0	15.1	.449	3.1	.393	3.8	.813	0.75	1.00	4.3	4.8	17.8
1 Days Rest	39	36.8	15.1	.458	2.4	.372	4.2	.835	0.49	1.03	3.8	4.7	18.2
3+ Days Rest	7	35.7	14.1	.455	1.6	.636	3.3	.870	0.29	1.29	2.3	4.4	16.7

Last Five Seasons

	G	Min	FGA	FG%	3PA	3P%	FTA	FT%	Blk	Stl	Ast	Reb	Pts
Total	357	25.9	9.2	.462	1.4	.335	3.2	.758	0.38	0.84	3.4	3.1	11.4
Home	179	26.0	9.0	.481	1.2	.343	3.3	.771	0.44	0.85	3.3	3.3	11.7
Road	178	25.8	9.4	.443	1.7	.329	3.0	.743	0.31	0.83	3.5	2.9	11.1
vs. Playoff	194	25.8	9.1	.457	1.5	.364	2.9	.743	0.38	0.85	3.3	3.0	11.0
vs. Non-Playoff	163	26.0	9.3	.468	1.3	.295	3.4	.773	0.38	0.83	3.6	3.3	11.8
vs. East	222	26.1	9.3	.461	1.4	.318	3.3	.774	0.38	0.83	3.1	3.1	11.6
vs. West	135	25.6	8.9	.464	1.6	.358	2.9	.728	0.38	0.85	3.9	3.1	11.0
vs. Div.	123	26.5	9.5	.486	1.4	.354	3.6	.778	0.45	0.82	3.4	3.2	12.5
As Starter	124	35.3	12.6	.475	2.0	.364	3.6	.783	0.63	0.97	5.1	4.4	15.5
Off Bench	233	20.9	7.4	.450	1.1	.307	2.9	.741	0.24	0.77	2.5	2.4	9.1
In wins	209	26.6	9.5	.480	1.4	.346	3.6	.770	0.41	0.83	3.4	3.3	12.3
In losses	148	24.9	8.7	.434	1.6	.320	2.6	.733	0.34	0.85	3.4	2.9	10.0

	G	Min	FGA	FG%	3PA	3P%	FTA	FT%	Blk	Stl	Ast	Reb	Pts
Pre All-Star	173	25.4	8.7	.461	1.6	.323	2.8	.753	0.35	0.74	3.6	3.1	10.7
Post All-Star	135	26.7	9.5	.486	1.2	.384	3.5	.752	0.44	0.90	3.7	3.1	12.3
Oct/Nov	53	24.1	8.1	.500	1.5	.427	2.5	.746	0.36	0.62	3.4	3.4	10.7
December	53	25.4	8.8	.414	2.1	.284	3.1	.750	0.42	0.70	3.7	3.4	10.2
January	54	26.2	8.6	.463	1.5	.291	2.8	.758	0.28	0.81	3.7	2.7	10.6
February	61	25.2	9.3	.483	1.1	.314	3.4	.756	0.51	1.15	3.2	2.8	11.9
March	76	25.0	9.1	.445	1.1	.345	3.1	.773	0.37	0.68	3.1	3.1	10.9
Apr/May	60	29.4	11.0	.470	1.5	.356	3.9	.754	0.33	1.07	3.6	3.4	13.8
0 Days Rest	93	26.2	8.9	.453	1.7	.327	3.2	.752	0.42	0.68	3.4	3.0	11.1
1 Days Rest	169	26.4	9.7	.470	1.4	.339	3.2	.771	0.38	0.91	3.3	3.3	12.1
2 Days Rest	59	26.1	9.3	.460	1.3	.329	3.0	.702	0.37	0.86	4.1	3.4	11.1
3+ Days Rest	36	22.3	7.3	.443	0.9	.353	2.8	.800	0.28	0.89	3.1	2.3	9.0

Malik Rose

1999-2000 Per Game Averages

	G	Min	FGA	FG%	3PA	3P%	FTA	FT%	Blk	Stl	Ast	Reb	Pts
Total	74	18.1	5.2	.457	0.0	.333	2.7	.722	0.70	0.47	0.6	4.5	6.7
Home	37	19.0	5.9	.447	0.1	.000	3.1	.772	0.68	0.38	0.6	5.1	7.6
Road	37	17.2	4.5	.470	0.0	1.000	2.3	.655	0.73	0.57	0.6	3.9	5.8
vs. Playoff	40	18.5	4.9	.442	0.0	1.000	2.2	.775	0.73	0.60	0.4	4.4	6.1
vs. Non-Playoff	34	17.7	5.5	.473	0.1	.000	3.2	.679	0.68	0.32	0.9	4.7	7.4
vs. East	26	17.3	5.1	.444	0.0	—	3.3	.709	0.85	0.46	0.6	4.4	6.9
vs. West	48	18.6	5.3	.464	0.1	.333	2.3	.732	0.63	0.48	0.6	4.6	6.6
vs. Div.	23	19.3	5.7	.454	0.1	.333	2.5	.702	0.78	0.43	0.8	4.6	6.9
As Starter	3	27.0	8.3	.520	0.3	1.000	3.3	.500	1.00	1.33	1.0	6.0	10.7
Off Bench	71	17.7	5.1	.453	0.0	.000	2.6	.734	0.69	0.44	0.6	4.5	6.5
In wins	48	17.9	5.4	.442	0.0	.000	2.5	.760	0.67	0.25	0.7	4.7	6.7
In losses	26	18.6	4.8	.488	0.1	.500	3.0	.662	0.77	0.88	0.5	4.2	6.7

	G	Min	FGA	FG%	3PA	3P%	FTA	FT%	Blk	Stl	Ast	Reb	Pts
Pre All-Star	49	17.6	4.9	.446	0.0	.000	2.6	.760	0.78	0.45	0.6	4.7	6.4
Post All-Star	25	19.1	5.8	.476	0.1	.500	2.8	.652	0.56	0.52	0.7	4.1	7.4
November	16	17.5	5.4	.517	0.1	.000	2.8	.795	1.31	0.06	0.9	5.1	7.8
December	15	16.9	4.1	.377	0.0	—	2.9	.727	0.67	0.80	0.6	4.8	5.2
January	13	17.8	4.8	.435	0.0	—	2.2	.759	0.46	0.54	0.3	3.8	5.8
February	13	21.7	6.9	.433	0.1	1.000	2.3	.733	0.77	0.69	0.7	4.8	7.8
March	8	11.6	3.9	.452	0.1	.000	1.8	.571	0.25	0.00	0.5	3.0	4.5
April	9	22.3	6.0	.519	0.0	—	4.1	.649	0.33	0.67	0.8	4.9	8.9
0 Days Rest	17	18.9	6.1	.485	0.1	.000	3.2	.673	0.65	0.35	0.4	4.7	8.1
1 Days Rest	35	18.9	5.2	.451	0.1	.500	3.1	.710	0.86	0.57	0.8	4.7	6.9
2 Days Rest	16	17.3	4.8	.421	0.0	—	1.5	.958	0.50	0.31	0.6	4.4	5.4
3+ Days Rest	6	13.7	4.0	.500	0.0	—	2.0	.583	0.50	0.67	0.5	3.2	5.2

Career (1996-97 thru 1999-2000)

	G	Min	FGA	FG%	3PA	3P%	FTA	FT%	Blk	Stl	Ast	Reb	Pts
Total	228	12.7	3.7	.458	0.0	.222	2.0	.681	0.43	0.54	0.6	3.4	4.5
Home	122	12.4	3.7	.445	0.1	.000	2.1	.702	0.46	0.52	0.6	3.3	4.7
Road	106	13.2	3.8	.471	0.0	1.000	2.0	.656	0.40	0.57	0.6	3.4	4.9
vs. Playoff	120	12.3	3.5	.432	0.0	.400	1.7	.663	0.42	0.61	0.4	3.3	4.1
vs. Non-Playoff	108	13.2	4.0	.483	0.0	.000	2.5	.694	0.44	0.47	0.7	3.5	5.6
vs. East	90	11.7	3.3	.481	0.0	—	1.7	.658	0.43	0.41	0.6	3.1	4.3
vs. West	138	13.4	4.0	.445	0.1	.222	2.3	.692	0.43	0.63	0.5	3.6	5.2
vs. Div.	83	13.2	4.0	.446	0.1	.400	2.0	.707	0.42	0.55	0.6	3.5	5.0
As Starter	4	23.3	7.0	.500	0.3	1.000	2.5	.500	1.00	1.00	1.0	5.0	8.5
Off Bench	224	12.5	3.7	.456	0.0	.125	2.0	.685	0.42	0.54	0.5	3.4	4.8
In wins	155	12.4	3.6	.473	0.0	.000	2.1	.685	0.43	0.50	0.6	3.4	4.8
In losses	73	13.4	4.0	.428	0.1	.333	2.0	.671	0.42	0.63	0.5	3.3	4.8

	G	Min	FGA	FG%	3PA	3P%	FTA	FT%	Blk	Stl	Ast	Reb	Pts
Pre All-Star	111	12.7	3.5	.446	0.0	.250	1.8	.722	0.45	0.51	0.5	3.5	4.5
Post All-Star	70	12.7	3.7	.471	0.1	.250	1.7	.621	0.37	0.39	0.6	2.8	4.6
Oct/Nov	40	11.8	3.5	.507	0.0	.000	2.0	.750	0.60	0.40	0.7	3.5	5.1
December	35	13.0	3.4	.378	0.0	1.000	1.8	.688	0.43	0.71	0.5	3.6	3.9
January	28	12.6	3.2	.456	0.0	.000	1.5	.714	0.36	0.50	0.4	3.0	4.0
February	36	14.4	4.7	.450	0.1	.333	1.9	.700	0.44	0.50	0.5	3.4	5.6
March	43	9.6	3.0	.408	0.0	.000	2.0	.671	0.30	0.35	0.4	2.6	3.8
Apr/May	46	15.0	4.4	.510	0.0	.000	2.7	.619	0.43	0.78	0.8	4.1	6.2
0 Days Rest	50	13.4	4.1	.483	0.0	.000	2.0	.647	0.38	0.54	0.4	3.4	5.3
1 Days Rest	104	13.5	3.8	.465	0.1	.167	2.3	.672	0.54	0.57	0.7	3.7	5.1
2 Days Rest	38	13.9	4.2	.413	0.0	.000	2.2	.759	0.32	0.63	0.7	3.9	5.1
3+ Days Rest	36	8.3	2.4	.447	0.0	1.000	1.1	.659	0.31	0.39	0.3	1.9	2.9

Bryon Russell
Utah Jazz — Forward

1999-2000 Per Game Averages

Split	G	Min	FGA	FG%	3PA	3P%	FTA	FT%	Blk	Stl	Ast	Reb	Pts
Total	82	35.4	11.1	.446	3.3	.396	3.9	.750	0.28	1.56	1.9	5.2	14.1
Home	41	35.3	11.4	.414	3.4	.381	3.4	.773	0.37	1.46	2.0	5.1	13.4
Road	41	35.4	10.9	.480	3.1	.411	4.3	.731	0.20	1.66	1.9	5.3	14.9
vs. Playoff	44	35.1	10.9	.418	3.3	.382	4.0	.764	0.39	1.52	1.8	5.0	13.4
vs. Non-Playoff	38	35.7	11.4	.478	3.3	.411	3.7	.732	0.16	1.61	2.0	5.5	15.0
vs. East	30	36.6	10.3	.423	2.9	.375	3.8	.752	0.27	1.53	2.3	5.3	12.7
vs. West	52	34.7	11.6	.459	3.5	.406	3.9	.749	0.29	1.58	1.7	5.2	15.0
vs. Div.	24	35.3	11.9	.472	3.4	.444	3.8	.733	0.17	1.00	1.5	4.8	15.5
As Starter	70	35.8	11.3	.443	3.4	.394	3.8	.747	0.29	1.60	2.1	5.3	14.2
Off Bench	12	32.8	10.1	.471	2.7	.406	3.9	.766	0.25	1.33	0.9	4.5	13.6
In wins	55	36.0	11.6	.469	3.8	.386	3.8	.774	0.25	1.64	2.1	5.3	15.1
In losses	27	34.1	10.3	.396	3.1	.417	4.0	.704	0.33	1.41	1.7	5.0	12.3
Pre All-Star	47	34.9	11.0	.441	2.8	.421	3.7	.750	0.30	1.47	1.8	5.0	13.7
Post All-Star	35	36.0	11.4	.454	3.9	.370	4.0	.750	0.26	1.69	2.1	5.5	14.8
November	14	32.9	10.1	.458	2.9	.375	3.8	.717	0.21	1.43	0.9	4.6	13.1
December	14	37.9	11.0	.429	2.5	.314	3.1	.744	0.29	1.71	2.2	5.4	12.5
January	14	35.9	12.9	.442	3.3	.500	4.3	.767	0.21	1.14	1.9	5.6	16.4
February	13	34.5	10.2	.439	3.9	.451	4.2	.836	0.38	2.08	2.4	4.3	14.2
March	16	36.7	11.1	.458	3.3	.358	4.5	.736	0.19	1.63	2.4	5.8	14.6
April	11	33.8	11.6	.453	3.9	.349	3.0	.667	0.45	1.36	1.7	5.5	13.9
0 Days Rest	19	35.4	11.5	.468	3.2	.361	3.8	.767	0.16	1.47	1.6	4.9	15.4
1 Days Rest	45	35.5	11.2	.429	3.5	.397	3.8	.734	0.33	1.42	2.0	5.0	13.8
2 Days Rest	12	34.9	10.8	.492	3.3	.462	3.6	.767	0.25	1.83	1.8	5.5	14.9
3+ Days Rest	6	34.8	10.5	.413	2.0	.333	2.3	.786	0.33	2.33	2.3	6.7	11.2

Last Five Seasons

Split	G	Min	FGA	FG%	3PA	3P%	FTA	FT%	Blk	Stl	Ast	Reb	Pts
Total	354	28.2	7.5	.451	2.6	.378	3.0	.748	0.29	1.28	1.4	4.1	10.1
Home	179	27.6	7.5	.461	2.6	.386	3.1	.746	0.33	1.23	1.4	3.8	10.2
Road	175	28.8	7.6	.441	2.7	.371	3.0	.750	0.26	1.33	1.3	4.3	10.0
vs. Playoff	186	29.1	7.6	.442	2.9	.388	3.0	.751	0.28	1.32	1.3	4.1	10.1
vs. Non-Playoff	168	27.3	7.5	.461	2.3	.365	2.9	.745	0.30	1.23	1.4	4.1	10.0
vs. East	118	27.9	7.1	.452	2.5	.392	3.0	.728	0.23	1.23	1.5	3.8	9.5
vs. West	236	28.4	7.8	.451	2.7	.372	3.1	.758	0.33	1.30	1.3	4.2	10.4
vs. Div.	107	28.7	8.0	.458	2.7	.384	3.1	.756	0.34	1.25	1.2	4.3	10.7
As Starter	217	33.1	9.0	.460	3.1	.387	3.3	.745	0.31	1.54	1.7	4.7	12.0
Off Bench	137	20.5	5.2	.425	1.9	.354	2.6	.754	0.27	0.86	0.9	3.1	7.0
In wins	261	27.8	7.5	.483	2.5	.413	3.1	.769	0.30	1.32	1.4	4.1	10.7
In losses	93	29.5	7.8	.365	2.9	.294	2.7	.681	0.27	1.16	1.4	4.1	8.4
Pre All-Star	176	26.7	7.1	.432	2.4	.381	2.9	.727	0.29	1.15	1.3	3.8	9.1
Post All-Star	128	27.5	7.4	.471	2.9	.385	3.1	.755	0.30	1.35	1.4	3.9	10.4
Oct/Nov	54	25.5	6.7	.440	2.2	.356	3.1	.738	0.33	1.11	1.0	3.6	9.0
December	55	29.4	7.4	.425	2.4	.351	3.1	.719	0.33	1.40	1.6	4.3	9.3
January	52	25.6	7.6	.428	2.6	.416	2.3	.702	0.13	0.87	1.3	3.6	9.3
February	58	28.5	7.3	.482	2.4	.362	3.3	.758	0.29	1.57	1.4	3.9	10.4
March	75	29.2	7.7	.453	2.9	.412	2.8	.767	0.29	1.27	1.4	4.4	10.3
Apr/May	60	30.3	8.4	.469	3.0	.357	3.5	.778	0.37	1.40	1.5	4.5	11.7
0 Days Rest	80	29.7	8.0	.448	2.7	.373	3.3	.745	0.29	1.24	1.3	4.2	10.6
1 Days Rest	183	29.6	7.9	.451	2.8	.388	3.3	.746	0.28	1.33	1.5	4.3	10.7
2 Days Rest	51	26.6	7.1	.471	2.7	.360	2.7	.750	0.35	1.27	1.2	4.0	9.7
3+ Days Rest	40	20.8	5.5	.427	1.8	.357	1.8	.775	0.28	1.13	1.0	3.0	6.7

Arvydas Sabonis
Portland Trail Blazers — Center

1999-2000 Per Game Averages

Split	G	Min	FGA	FG%	3PA	3P%	FTA	FT%	Blk	Stl	Ast	Reb	Pts
Total	66	25.6	9.1	.505	0.3	.368	3.0	.843	1.18	0.65	1.8	7.8	11.8
Home	29	25.6	9.1	.559	0.2	.429	3.1	.890	1.07	0.66	1.7	8.0	13.0
Road	37	25.6	9.1	.463	0.3	.333	2.9	.804	1.27	0.65	1.8	7.6	10.8
vs. Playoff	38	27.2	8.9	.507	0.3	.500	3.0	.860	0.95	0.63	2.0	8.1	11.8
vs. Non-Playoff	28	23.3	9.3	.502	0.3	.143	3.0	.821	1.50	0.68	1.5	7.4	11.8
vs. East	26	25.4	8.9	.530	0.3	.556	2.8	.824	1.35	0.54	1.8	7.9	12.0
vs. West	40	25.7	9.2	.489	0.3	.200	3.1	.855	1.08	0.73	1.8	7.7	11.7
vs. Div.	21	27.1	9.6	.510	0.3	.000	3.9	.864	1.43	0.90	2.2	8.9	13.1
As Starter	61	26.1	9.2	.506	0.3	.838	3.1	.838	1.25	0.66	1.9	8.0	11.8
Off Bench	5	18.8	7.8	.487	0.0	—	1.4	1.000	0.40	0.60	1.0	4.6	9.0
In wins	50	25.2	9.1	.521	0.3	.231	3.2	.829	1.20	0.62	1.8	8.0	12.2
In losses	16	26.9	8.8	.454	0.4	.667	2.5	.900	1.13	0.75	1.8	7.1	10.5
Pre All-Star	44	24.3	8.6	.470	0.3	.231	2.5	.817	1.39	0.64	1.6	7.1	10.2
Post All-Star	22	28.2	10.0	.566	0.3	.667	4.0	.876	0.77	0.68	2.1	9.1	15.0
November	16	25.1	8.7	.453	0.4	.333	2.3	.833	1.88	0.44	1.8	7.1	9.9
December	13	23.9	8.9	.440	0.3	.000	2.1	.778	1.54	0.62	1.8	6.9	9.5
January	10	25.3	8.4	.524	0.3	.333	3.0	.867	0.70	0.80	1.8	8.1	11.5
February	13	25.8	10.0	.531	0.0	—	4.5	.810	0.92	1.23	1.5	8.4	14.2
March	10	30.3	9.7	.598	0.6	.667	3.6	.889	0.80	0.40	2.4	9.3	15.2
April	4	21.0	8.0	.531	0.0	—	2.8	1.000	0.25	0.00	1.0	6.5	11.3
0 Days Rest	18	25.7	8.8	.503	0.5	.444	3.2	.845	1.78	0.61	1.7	8.1	11.8
1 Days Rest	25	26.4	9.4	.530	0.3	.286	2.7	.838	1.16	0.88	1.8	8.2	12.3
2 Days Rest	14	25.4	9.1	.469	0.1	.000	2.9	.878	0.64	0.43	1.7	6.9	11.1
3+ Days Rest	9	23.2	8.6	.494	0.2	.500	3.4	.806	0.89	0.44	2.1	7.2	11.3

Career (1995-96 thru 1999-2000)

Split	G	Min	FGA	FG%	3PA	3P%	FTA	FT%	Blk	Stl	Ast	Reb	Pts
Total	331	26.8	9.9	.507	1.2	.335	4.1	.788	1.16	0.81	2.2	8.4	13.7
Home	165	27.2	10.1	.518	1.2	.316	4.3	.802	1.10	0.93	2.4	8.7	14.3
Road	166	26.4	9.7	.495	1.2	.354	4.0	.773	1.21	0.70	2.0	8.0	13.1
vs. Playoff	179	27.5	9.7	.500	1.2	.354	4.0	.808	1.03	0.86	2.4	8.1	13.4
vs. Non-Playoff	152	25.9	10.2	.514	1.1	.310	4.3	.765	1.31	0.76	2.0	8.7	14.1
vs. East	110	26.7	9.9	.509	1.3	.378	4.0	.774	1.22	0.69	2.0	8.3	13.7
vs. West	221	26.8	9.9	.505	1.1	.311	4.2	.794	1.13	0.87	2.3	8.4	13.7
vs. Div.	109	26.8	10.1	.493	1.0	.307	4.0	.811	1.22	0.98	2.3	8.2	13.6
As Starter	271	27.8	10.2	.498	1.2	.320	4.3	.798	1.24	0.80	2.3	8.7	13.9
Off Bench	60	22.4	8.7	.554	1.2	.406	3.6	.732	0.80	0.87	1.8	6.8	12.7
In wins	209	26.5	9.9	.522	1.0	.355	4.1	.805	1.23	0.84	2.3	8.8	14.0
In losses	122	27.2	9.9	.480	1.5	.311	4.3	.759	1.02	0.77	2.1	7.6	13.2
Pre All-Star	169	26.5	9.7	.491	1.4	.335	4.2	.764	1.15	0.83	2.1	8.1	13.2
Post All-Star	112	27.2	10.4	.538	1.1	.344	4.3	.829	1.12	0.85	2.3	9.0	15.2
Oct/Nov	60	25.8	9.0	.513	1.5	.370	3.7	.745	1.30	0.73	2.3	8.2	12.5
December	50	26.1	9.7	.476	1.6	.333	4.0	.786	1.20	0.76	2.0	7.8	12.9
January	47	28.5	10.6	.485	1.4	.309	5.3	.769	0.96	1.02	2.2	8.6	14.7
February	57	26.6	9.6	.514	0.8	.319	4.1	.778	1.12	0.82	2.3	8.2	13.3
March	71	28.6	10.8	.535	1.1	.312	4.4	.816	1.25	0.89	2.3	9.3	15.4
Apr/May	46	24.5	9.7	.498	0.7	.375	3.5	.836	1.02	0.63	2.1	7.9	12.8
0 Days Rest	89	26.9	9.8	.507	1.0	.302	3.8	.802	1.33	0.80	1.9	8.2	13.2
1 Days Rest	150	26.7	10.0	.508	1.3	.352	4.4	.784	1.11	0.85	2.4	8.4	14.0
2 Days Rest	53	26.9	9.9	.512	1.3	.352	4.0	.792	0.94	0.75	2.1	8.7	13.8
3+ Days Rest	39	26.8	10.1	.491	1.1	.295	4.3	.765	1.26	0.77	2.3	8.3	13.5

Detlef Schrempf
Portland Trail Blazers — Forward

1999-2000 Per Game Averages

	G	Min	FGA	FG%	3PA	3P%	FTA	FT%	Blk	Stl	Ast	Reb	Pts		G	Min	FGA	FG%	3PA	3P%	FTA	FT%	Blk	Stl	Ast	Reb	Pts
Total	77	21.6	5.6	.432	0.7	.404	2.8	.833	0.22	0.48	2.6	4.3	7.5	Pre All-Star	47	21.7	5.9	.455	0.6	.481	2.7	.786	0.28	0.51	2.4	4.3	7.8
Home	40	21.9	5.9	.438	0.8	.355	2.7	.804	0.20	0.50	2.7	4.7	7.6	Post All-Star	30	21.4	5.1	.390	0.8	.320	3.0	.899	0.13	0.43	2.8	4.4	6.9
Road	37	21.2	5.4	.424	0.6	.476	2.9	.861	0.24	0.46	2.4	3.9	7.3	November	16	23.8	7.4	.471	0.5	.250	2.9	.809	0.19	0.31	1.9	4.5	9.5
vs. Playoff	40	21.9	5.6	.420	0.8	.419	2.7	.830	0.18	0.40	2.6	4.4	7.2	December	11	20.7	5.1	.393	0.5	.667	2.4	.692	0.45	0.45	2.9	4.3	6.0
vs. Non-Playoff	37	21.3	5.6	.445	0.6	.381	2.9	.835	0.27	0.57	2.6	4.2	7.7	January	14	20.2	5.4	.474	0.6	.625	2.0	.786	0.21	0.71	2.3	4.2	7.1
vs. East	30	22.8	5.9	.452	0.8	.360	3.0	.878	0.23	0.57	2.8	4.5	8.3	February	14	20.0	4.3	.417	0.7	.400	3.4	.854	0.14	0.71	3.0	4.0	6.8
vs. West	47	20.8	5.4	.418	0.6	.444	2.7	.800	0.21	0.43	2.4	4.2	6.9	March	14	22.3	5.3	.392	1.1	.333	2.4	.941	0.29	0.21	2.5	4.4	6.8
vs. Div.	23	20.3	5.0	.377	0.6	.462	3.2	.838	0.22	0.43	2.4	4.7	6.7	April	8	22.4	6.0	.396	0.6	.200	4.0	.875	0.00	0.50	3.1	4.9	8.4
As Starter	6	30.5	9.3	.482	1.2	.429	3.5	.667	0.50	0.67	2.3	5.2	11.8	0 Days Rest	21	21.3	5.8	.446	0.4	.375	3.0	.839	0.29	0.52	2.7	4.4	7.8
Off Bench	71	20.8	5.3	.424	0.6	.400	2.7	.851	0.20	0.46	2.6	4.2	7.1	1 Days Rest	35	21.2	5.6	.423	0.8	.444	2.9	.833	0.29	0.45	2.5	4.3	7.5
In wins	55	21.8	5.8	.437	0.7	.378	2.7	.826	0.20	0.49	2.7	4.6	7.5	2 Days Rest	14	23.8	5.8	.420	0.9	.417	3.1	.837	0.07	0.57	2.3	4.3	7.8
In losses	22	21.1	5.2	.417	0.7	.467	3.0	.848	0.27	0.45	2.2	3.6	7.2	3+ Days Rest	7	20.1	5.0	.457	0.7	.200	1.1	.750	0.00	0.43	2.9	4.4	5.6

Last Five Seasons

	G	Min	FGA	FG%	3PA	3P%	FTA	FT%	Blk	Stl	Ast	Reb	Pts		G	Min	FGA	FG%	3PA	3P%	FTA	FT%	Blk	Stl	Ast	Reb	Pts
Total	329	32.1	10.2	.478	1.9	.394	4.5	.813	0.26	0.78	3.8	6.0	14.2	Pre All-Star	167	31.7	10.2	.484	1.9	.397	4.5	.805	0.26	0.78	3.9	5.9	14.2
Home	167	31.2	9.9	.476	1.8	.370	4.5	.797	0.22	0.81	4.0	6.0	13.7	Post All-Star	112	31.3	9.8	.473	2.0	.387	4.5	.820	0.15	0.76	3.8	5.6	13.7
Road	162	33.0	10.4	.480	2.0	.416	4.6	.829	0.31	0.75	3.7	6.0	14.7	Oct/Nov	63	33.4	11.0	.499	2.1	.386	4.9	.799	0.30	0.70	3.7	5.9	15.7
vs. Playoff	180	33.1	10.5	.476	2.1	.399	4.6	.803	0.28	0.78	3.8	6.2	14.5	December	44	31.7	9.9	.455	2.0	.419	4.6	.798	0.27	0.84	4.4	6.2	13.5
vs. Non-Playoff	149	30.9	9.8	.481	1.7	.386	4.5	.826	0.23	0.79	3.9	5.8	13.7	January	47	29.9	9.5	.494	1.6	.425	3.7	.837	0.19	0.91	3.8	5.5	13.1
vs. East	107	31.9	10.0	.468	1.7	.380	4.7	.812	0.22	0.71	3.9	6.3	13.9	February	55	31.1	9.7	.449	1.6	.322	4.3	.787	0.20	0.96	3.5	5.5	12.6
vs. West	222	32.2	10.2	.483	2.0	.400	4.5	.813	0.28	0.82	3.8	5.9	14.3	March	63	32.4	9.8	.472	1.8	.384	4.9	.820	0.25	0.68	3.7	6.0	13.9
vs. Div.	106	32.5	10.1	.479	1.9	.372	4.8	.812	0.30	0.95	3.7	5.9	14.3	Apr/May	57	33.5	10.8	.490	2.4	.422	4.8	.838	0.33	0.65	4.1	6.6	15.6
As Starter	243	35.6	11.7	.486	2.3	.394	5.1	.803	0.27	0.89	4.3	6.5	16.3	0 Days Rest	86	32.3	10.4	.506	1.9	.429	4.4	.841	0.28	0.77	3.9	6.2	15.2
Off Bench	86	22.2	5.9	.435	0.8	.394	3.1	.857	0.23	0.48	2.6	4.7	8.1	1 Days Rest	157	32.1	9.9	.473	1.8	.399	4.6	.810	0.30	0.76	4.0	6.0	13.9
In wins	231	31.7	10.0	.483	1.9	.408	4.5	.808	0.21	0.87	4.1	6.0	14.1	2 Days Rest	60	33.1	10.8	.473	2.3	.378	4.6	.787	0.15	0.90	3.9	6.0	14.7
In losses	98	32.9	10.5	.467	2.0	.361	4.7	.823	0.38	0.56	3.2	6.1	14.4	3+ Days Rest	26	29.4	9.1	.419	1.7	.279	3.9	.794	0.23	0.69	2.7	5.7	11.2

Dennis Scott
Vancouver Grizzlies — Guard-Forward

1999-2000 Per Game Averages

	G	Min	FGA	FG%	3PA	3P%	FTA	FT%	Blk	Stl	Ast	Reb	Pts		G	Min	FGA	FG%	3PA	3P%	FTA	FT%	Blk	Stl	Ast	Reb	Pts
Total	66	19.1	5.0	.375	2.9	.376	0.9	.842	0.14	0.42	1.0	1.6	5.6	Pre All-Star	32	17.4	5.0	.365	2.6	.410	1.0	.871	0.06	0.22	0.8	1.8	5.5
Home	33	19.4	5.4	.369	3.3	.385	0.9	.759	0.18	0.64	1.2	1.7	5.9	Post All-Star	34	20.8	5.1	.385	3.1	.349	0.8	.808	0.21	0.62	1.3	1.4	5.6
Road	33	18.8	4.7	.383	2.4	.363	0.8	.929	0.09	0.21	0.8	1.5	5.2	November	0	—	—	—	—	—	—	—	—	—	—	—	—
vs. Playoff	39	18.8	4.9	.382	3.0	.419	0.6	.880	0.15	0.46	0.9	1.5	5.6	December	15	17.0	5.0	.347	2.6	.436	1.1	.882	0.00	0.00	0.5	1.8	5.6
vs. Non-Playoff	27	19.7	5.3	.366	2.7	.306	1.2	.813	0.11	0.37	1.3	1.7	5.6	January	12	17.3	5.3	.406	2.6	.387	0.8	.889	0.08	0.50	1.3	2.2	6.0
vs. East	24	16.5	5.0	.405	2.7	.422	1.0	.750	0.17	0.46	1.0	1.7	6.0	February	13	19.8	5.4	.400	3.2	.357	1.4	.722	0.15	0.38	1.0	1.5	6.5
vs. West	42	20.6	5.0	.358	3.0	.352	0.8	.909	0.12	0.40	1.0	1.6	5.4	March	15	18.2	5.0	.413	3.1	.413	0.5	1.000	0.20	0.60	1.3	1.3	5.9
vs. Div.	20	20.7	4.9	.327	2.8	.273	1.1	.938	0.10	0.40	1.1	1.3	4.7	April	11	24.5	4.5	.286	2.8	.258	0.5	.800	0.27	0.73	1.2	1.2	3.6
As Starter	0	—	—	—	—	—	—	—	—	—	—	—	—	0 Days Rest	15	18.9	5.5	.349	3.3	.384	1.1	.824	0.07	0.33	0.8	1.8	6.1
Off Bench	66	19.1	5.0	.375	2.9	.376	0.9	.842	0.14	0.42	1.0	1.6	5.6	1 Days Rest	38	19.6	4.7	.379	2.5	.347	1.0	.868	0.18	0.53	1.3	1.7	5.3
In wins	18	18.1	5.1	.391	2.8	.400	0.7	.750	0.11	0.28	1.3	1.9	5.6	2 Days Rest	5	18.8	5.2	.346	2.8	.357	0.0	—	0.00	0.20	0.4	1.0	4.6
In losses	48	19.5	5.0	.369	2.9	.367	0.9	.867	0.15	0.48	0.9	1.5	5.6	3+ Days Rest	8	17.6	5.9	.426	3.9	.452	0.3	.500	0.13	0.25	0.8	1.4	6.9

Last Five Seasons

	G	Min	FGA	FG%	3PA	3P%	FTA	FT%	Blk	Stl	Ast	Reb	Pts		G	Min	FGA	FG%	3PA	3P%	FTA	FT%	Blk	Stl	Ast	Reb	Pts
Total	331	28.7	9.8	.410	4.9	.397	1.6	.810	0.30	0.79	1.9	2.8	11.3	Pre All-Star	157	32.0	11.9	.404	5.4	.382	2.3	.817	0.41	0.81	2.2	3.4	13.6
Home	164	28.8	9.8	.415	5.2	.400	1.6	.805	0.37	0.81	2.0	2.6	11.5	Post All-Star	138	27.0	8.4	.421	5.0	.418	1.1	.805	0.23	0.86	1.9	2.4	10.0
Road	167	28.6	9.8	.406	4.7	.394	1.7	.814	0.23	0.76	1.9	3.0	11.1	Oct/Nov	32	33.7	14.6	.403	6.3	.383	2.7	.814	0.69	0.91	2.3	3.4	16.3
vs. Playoff	179	28.8	9.5	.410	4.8	.403	1.5	.795	0.20	0.84	1.8	2.8	11.0	December	54	33.1	12.3	.395	4.9	.405	2.7	.826	0.37	0.83	1.9	3.9	13.9
vs. Non-Playoff	152	28.6	10.1	.411	5.0	.391	1.8	.825	0.42	0.72	2.1	2.8	11.7	January	55	31.0	10.9	.419	5.5	.379	2.0	.824	0.35	0.85	2.4	3.3	12.9
vs. East	163	30.0	10.3	.412	5.3	.406	1.8	.823	0.28	0.85	2.2	2.9	12.2	February	66	25.9	8.6	.415	4.8	.386	1.1	.764	0.18	0.79	1.7	2.3	9.8
vs. West	168	27.5	9.2	.409	4.6	.388	1.4	.793	0.32	0.73	1.7	2.7	10.5	March	72	25.8	7.9	.419	4.8	.418	1.1	.789	0.19	0.72	1.6	2.3	9.5
vs. Div.	104	28.4	9.6	.414	4.9	.378	1.7	.790	0.28	0.72	2.0	2.8	11.2	Apr/May	52	26.2	7.1	.414	3.8	.410	1.1	.818	0.23	0.67	2.1	2.1	8.3
As Starter	198	35.5	12.7	.415	6.4	.406	2.2	.823	0.38	1.08	2.6	3.6	14.9	0 Days Rest	82	27.7	9.7	.403	4.4	.398	1.9	.849	0.13	0.79	2.1	2.6	11.2
Off Bench	133	18.5	5.5	.393	2.7	.368	0.8	.759	0.17	0.35	0.9	1.6	6.0	1 Days Rest	168	29.1	9.4	.410	4.9	.396	1.5	.796	0.33	0.88	1.9	2.8	10.9
In wins	163	29.2	10.2	.433	5.6	.412	1.7	.814	0.33	0.83	2.1	2.9	12.5	2 Days Rest	49	31.8	11.8	.438	6.0	.425	1.9	.821	0.51	0.67	2.1	3.3	14.4
In losses	168	28.2	9.4	.387	4.3	.379	1.6	.805	0.27	0.74	1.8	2.6	10.2	3+ Days Rest	32	24.3	8.8	.376	4.8	.346	1.1	.706	0.22	0.47	1.3	2.3	9.0

Malik Sealy

1999-2000 Per Game Averages

	G	Min	FGA	FG%	3PA	3P%	FTA	FT%	Blk	Stl	Ast	Reb	Pts		G	Min	FGA	FG%	3PA	3P%	FTA	FT%	Blk	Stl	Ast	Reb	Pts
Total	82	29.2	9.5	.476	0.4	.286	2.7	.812	0.23	0.93	2.4	4.3	11.3	Pre All-Star	47	27.7	9.6	.484	0.5	.364	2.7	.784	0.28	0.77	2.1	4.0	11.5
Home	41	29.4	9.9	.466	0.4	.333	2.5	.798	0.22	0.93	2.8	4.3	11.4	Post All-Star	35	31.2	9.4	.464	0.4	.154	2.7	.849	0.17	1.14	2.8	4.6	11.1
Road	41	28.9	9.1	.487	0.4	.235	2.8	.825	0.24	0.93	2.0	4.2	11.3	November	12	20.1	7.3	.494	0.2	.000	2.7	.688	0.17	0.33	1.2	3.1	9.0
vs. Playoff	44	30.1	9.7	.479	0.5	.318	2.4	.829	0.23	0.80	2.4	4.1	11.5	December	15	27.9	10.5	.490	0.3	.200	2.7	.850	0.27	0.73	1.8	4.1	12.6
vs. Non-Playoff	38	28.1	9.3	.472	0.3	.231	3.0	.796	0.24	1.08	2.4	4.5	11.2	January	15	34.0	11.3	.512	0.8	.500	2.7	.780	0.40	1.20	2.8	4.9	14.1
vs. East	30	31.4	10.2	.461	0.4	.273	2.9	.872	0.17	1.23	2.4	4.8	12.0	February	14	30.7	9.4	.450	0.4	.333	2.3	.844	0.21	1.00	2.9	4.1	10.5
vs. West	52	27.9	9.1	.485	0.5	.292	2.5	.773	0.27	0.75	2.4	4.0	10.9	March	16	32.6	9.1	.455	0.5	.125	2.9	.915	0.13	1.38	3.5	4.8	11.0
vs. Div.	24	27.3	8.9	.514	0.6	.286	3.1	.743	0.38	0.88	2.9	4.3	11.6	April	10	27.2	9.0	.433	0.2	.000	2.6	.731	0.20	0.70	1.7	4.7	9.7
As Starter	61	31.5	9.9	.474	0.5	.333	2.6	.832	0.23	1.11	2.8	4.6	11.7	0 Days Rest	18	29.7	9.9	.556	0.3	.333	3.1	.821	0.33	0.78	1.9	4.1	13.7
Off Bench	21	22.5	8.4	.483	0.2	.000	2.7	.754	0.24	0.38	1.4	3.4	10.1	1 Days Rest	51	29.3	9.5	.439	0.5	.261	2.4	.808	0.16	1.12	2.6	4.3	10.4
In wins	50	30.5	9.5	.488	0.4	.350	3.1	.805	0.32	1.04	2.8	4.6	11.9	2 Days Rest	5	31.2	10.0	.480	0.2	.000	3.6	.833	0.20	0.40	3.0	5.2	12.6
In losses	32	27.1	9.5	.456	0.5	.200	2.0	.828	0.09	0.75	1.8	3.8	10.4	3+ Days Rest	8	25.8	8.1	.523	0.6	.400	3.0	.792	0.50	0.38	1.4	4.0	11.1

Last Five Seasons

	G	Min	FGA	FG%	3PA	3P%	FTA	FT%	Blk	Stl	Ast	Reb	Pts		G	Min	FGA	FG%	3PA	3P%	FTA	FT%	Blk	Stl	Ast	Reb	Pts
Total	332	26.6	9.4	.426	1.3	.297	2.8	.837	0.35	1.14	1.8	3.4	10.7	Pre All-Star	173	28.5	10.0	.438	1.1	.289	3.3	.829	0.40	1.20	1.9	3.8	11.9
Home	161	26.5	9.4	.430	1.3	.317	2.9	.851	0.30	1.19	1.7	3.5	10.9	Post All-Star	128	24.7	9.0	.411	1.6	.308	2.3	.841	0.34	1.11	1.9	3.1	9.8
Road	171	26.7	9.4	.423	1.3	.278	2.7	.823	0.40	1.10	2.0	3.4	10.5	Oct/Nov	60	30.1	10.9	.423	1.2	.214	3.9	.791	0.40	1.27	1.8	3.9	12.5
vs. Playoff	182	26.5	9.1	.415	1.2	.273	2.7	.826	0.33	1.07	1.9	3.2	10.1	December	56	26.5	9.4	.447	1.0	.278	3.1	.857	0.36	1.09	1.8	3.4	11.4
vs. Non-Playoff	150	26.6	9.7	.439	1.3	.325	2.9	.851	0.38	1.23	1.8	3.7	11.4	January	48	29.5	10.0	.446	1.1	.340	3.0	.861	0.48	1.29	2.3	4.3	11.9
vs. East	139	25.6	8.8	.413	1.2	.265	2.6	.850	0.32	1.11	1.6	3.4	9.8	February	50	26.1	9.3	.443	1.5	.355	2.5	.821	0.30	1.22	1.7	3.2	10.8
vs. West	193	27.3	9.8	.435	1.3	.318	3.0	.829	0.38	1.17	2.0	3.5	11.4	March	69	24.3	8.2	.427	1.4	.326	2.3	.888	0.29	1.20	1.9	2.9	9.5
vs. Div.	103	24.7	8.7	.430	1.1	.293	2.7	.812	0.29	1.12	2.0	3.1	10.0	Apr/May	49	23.1	8.6	.364	1.5	.260	2.0	.816	0.31	0.73	1.6	3.0	8.3
As Starter	205	30.7	11.1	.425	1.7	.314	3.2	.845	0.43	1.39	2.3	3.8	12.6	0 Days Rest	78	26.9	9.3	.449	1.4	.264	3.1	.828	0.36	1.04	2.0	3.0	11.3
Off Bench	127	20.0	6.6	.429	0.6	.225	2.3	.820	0.22	0.74	1.1	2.9	7.1	1 Days Rest	183	27.0	9.5	.418	1.2	.311	2.9	.850	0.37	1.28	2.0	3.6	10.8
In wins	159	27.5	9.5	.452	1.1	.339	3.2	.846	0.39	1.25	2.0	3.9	11.7	2 Days Rest	39	26.2	9.5	.416	1.2	.311	2.4	.809	0.21	1.03	1.4	3.5	10.2
In losses	173	25.7	9.3	.402	1.4	.266	2.4	.827	0.32	1.04	1.7	3.0	9.8	3+ Days Rest	32	23.9	8.5	.434	1.3	.286	2.2	.817	0.38	0.75	1.3	3.4	9.6

Brian Shaw

1999-2000 Per Game Averages

	G	Min	FGA	FG%	3PA	3P%	FTA	FT%	Blk	Stl	Ast	Reb	Pts		G	Min	FGA	FG%	3PA	3P%	FTA	FT%	Blk	Stl	Ast	Reb	Pts
Total	74	16.9	4.4	.382	0.8	.310	0.7	.759	0.19	0.47	2.7	2.9	4.1	Pre All-Star	40	14.3	3.8	.360	0.4	.143	0.9	.730	0.18	0.48	2.2	2.4	3.4
Home	38	16.2	4.4	.373	0.8	.300	0.8	.742	0.16	0.55	2.6	2.8	4.1	Post All-Star	34	20.0	5.1	.401	1.3	.364	0.5	.824	0.21	0.47	3.4	3.6	4.9
Road	36	17.6	4.3	.391	0.8	.321	0.6	.783	0.22	0.39	2.8	3.1	4.1	November	15	19.3	5.7	.400	0.4	.167	1.5	.652	0.33	0.47	2.2	3.2	5.6
vs. Playoff	38	15.7	4.2	.316	1.0	.263	0.7	.778	0.18	0.45	2.3	2.9	4.1	December	9	9.4	2.3	.286	0.1	.000	0.7	.667	0.11	0.33	0.8	1.4	1.8
vs. Non-Playoff	36	18.1	4.6	.445	0.6	.400	0.8	.741	0.19	0.50	3.1	2.9	4.8	January	12	10.9	2.5	.367	0.5	.167	0.0	—	0.00	0.42	2.8	1.7	1.9
vs. East	27	15.7	3.7	.364	0.7	.211	0.9	.708	0.30	0.30	2.5	2.9	3.4	February	13	17.0	4.5	.356	0.5	.167	0.8	1.000	0.31	0.46	2.9	3.4	4.1
vs. West	47	17.5	4.7	.390	0.8	.359	0.6	.800	0.13	0.57	2.9	3.0	4.5	March	16	18.6	5.0	.450	1.6	.440	0.6	.778	0.19	0.38	2.9	3.2	5.6
vs. Div.	21	17.4	5.3	.375	1.0	.381	0.6	.909	0.10	0.62	2.9	3.0	4.9	April	9	24.9	5.2	.319	1.6	.286	0.7	.833	0.11	0.89	4.8	4.4	4.3
As Starter	2	33.0	7.5	.400	2.0	.250	0.0	—	0.00	0.00	8.0	8.5	6.5	0 Days Rest	18	19.3	5.2	.398	0.8	.429	1.2	.727	0.33	0.33	3.7	3.6	5.3
Off Bench	72	16.4	4.3	.381	0.8	.315	0.8	.759	0.19	0.49	2.6	2.8	4.1	1 Days Rest	33	17.0	4.5	.354	1.0	.333	0.5	.750	0.15	0.39	2.6	3.1	3.8
In wins	62	16.2	4.2	.400	0.7	.390	0.8	.766	0.19	0.45	2.6	2.9	4.2	2 Days Rest	12	16.7	4.0	.375	0.7	.000	0.9	.818	0.17	0.92	2.1	2.5	3.8
In losses	12	20.4	5.2	.306	1.4	.118	0.6	.714	0.17	0.58	3.2	3.3	3.8	3+ Days Rest	11	12.6	3.1	.471	0.3	.333	0.5	.800	0.09	0.45	2.0	1.8	3.4

Last Five Seasons

	G	Min	FGA	FG%	3PA	3P%	FTA	FT%	Blk	Stl	Ast	Reb	Pts		G	Min	FGA	FG%	3PA	3P%	FTA	FT%	Blk	Stl	Ast	Reb	Pts
Total	286	22.1	6.2	.366	1.7	.305	1.3	.775	0.24	0.73	3.9	3.0	6.0	Pre All-Star	171	23.0	6.6	.353	1.7	.301	1.4	.765	0.25	0.73	4.0	3.1	6.2
Home	144	21.9	5.7	.357	1.7	.298	1.1	.782	0.27	0.72	4.0	3.0	5.5	Post All-Star	114	21.0	5.6	.389	1.7	.312	1.1	.794	0.22	0.74	3.7	2.8	5.8
Road	142	22.4	6.7	.373	1.8	.312	1.4	.769	0.20	0.75	3.9	3.0	6.6	Oct/Nov	50	22.2	6.7	.324	1.2	.262	1.6	.709	0.24	0.64	3.3	3.2	5.8
vs. Playoff	149	21.4	6.2	.364	1.8	.305	1.1	.760	0.23	0.71	3.8	2.8	5.9	December	51	25.4	7.7	.361	2.2	.310	1.4	.753	0.22	0.92	4.5	3.1	7.3
vs. Non-Playoff	137	22.9	6.2	.367	1.6	.306	1.4	.788	0.24	0.75	4.1	3.1	6.1	January	56	22.6	6.0	.368	1.8	.310	1.0	.807	0.29	0.66	4.3	3.1	5.8
vs. East	153	22.6	5.9	.351	1.9	.297	1.5	.770	0.25	0.69	3.9	2.9	5.8	February	47	18.9	5.2	.374	1.4	.309	1.3	.803	0.32	0.62	3.6	2.7	5.4
vs. West	133	21.6	6.5	.382	1.5	.317	1.0	.783	0.23	0.78	3.9	3.1	6.2	March	56	21.4	5.9	.397	1.7	.289	1.0	.810	0.16	0.71	3.8	2.7	6.0
vs. Div.	89	22.1	6.2	.333	1.6	.336	1.2	.760	0.26	0.87	3.9	3.0	5.5	Apr/May	26	22.0	5.3	.387	2.0	.365	1.2	.813	0.19	0.92	3.8	2.7	5.8
As Starter	68	30.5	8.4	.354	2.3	.342	1.1	.730	0.31	0.93	5.3	3.8	7.6	0 Days Rest	70	23.3	6.9	.364	2.0	.271	1.2	.756	0.29	0.64	3.9	2.8	6.5
Off Bench	218	19.5	5.5	.372	1.5	.288	1.3	.787	0.22	0.67	3.5	2.7	5.6	1 Days Rest	137	22.5	6.3	.374	1.8	.333	1.3	.777	0.19	0.78	4.2	3.1	6.3
In wins	176	20.3	5.3	.385	1.4	.307	1.3	.800	0.26	0.71	3.7	2.9	5.6	2 Days Rest	45	22.5	5.7	.359	1.5	.265	1.2	.855	0.29	0.98	3.6	2.9	5.5
In losses	110	25.1	7.6	.345	2.3	.304	1.1	.728	0.20	0.76	4.3	3.1	6.8	3+ Days Rest	34	17.6	5.0	.343	1.1	.324	1.3	.705	0.26	0.38	2.9	2.9	4.7

Dickey Simpkins

1999-2000 Per Game Averages

	G	Min	FGA	FG%	3PA	3P%	FTA	FT%	Blk	Stl	Ast	Reb	Pts		G	Min	FGA	FG%	3PA	3P%	FTA	FT%	Blk	Stl	Ast	Reb	Pts
Total	69	23.9	4.0	.405	0.0	.000	1.7	.542	0.32	0.32	1.4	5.4	4.2	Pre All-Star	41	23.6	4.5	.410	0.0	.000	1.8	.542	0.22	0.34	1.5	4.8	4.6
Home	37	24.5	3.7	.423	0.0	.000	2.1	.532	0.35	0.35	1.5	5.8	4.2	Post All-Star	28	24.4	3.3	.396	0.0	—	1.7	.542	0.46	0.29	1.4	6.3	3.5
Road	32	23.3	4.3	.387	0.0	—	1.3	.558	0.28	0.28	1.4	4.9	4.1	November	8	22.3	5.4	.326	0.0	—	2.4	.579	0.25	0.00	1.5	5.0	4.9
vs. Playoff	39	22.7	3.9	.424	0.0	.000	1.6	.578	0.26	0.33	1.5	5.4	4.2	December	14	22.9	5.5	.455	0.1	.000	1.4	.579	0.29	0.50	1.9	4.2	5.8
vs. Non-Playoff	30	25.5	4.1	.382	0.0	—	1.9	.500	0.40	0.30	1.4	5.4	4.1	January	14	24.7	3.5	.367	0.0	—	2.1	.483	0.21	0.29	1.1	5.5	3.6
vs. East	46	24.0	4.0	.387	0.0	.000	1.9	.552	0.35	0.28	1.4	5.5	4.2	February	13	24.5	3.5	.500	0.0	—	2.1	.481	0.31	0.46	1.6	5.5	4.5
vs. West	23	23.8	3.8	.443	0.0	—	1.4	.515	0.26	0.39	1.5	5.2	4.1	March	16	25.1	3.1	.367	0.0	—	1.3	.667	0.50	0.19	1.4	6.3	3.1
vs. Div.	24	23.5	4.0	.371	0.0	.000	1.8	.523	0.33	0.33	1.4	5.8	4.0	April	4	21.3	2.5	.300	0.0	—	1.3	.400	0.25	0.50	1.0	6.0	2.0
As Starter	48	24.5	4.0	.407	0.0	—	1.9	.533	0.29	0.33	1.4	5.3	4.3	0 Days Rest	19	25.6	4.0	.382	0.0	—	1.4	.481	0.21	0.63	1.2	5.2	3.7
Off Bench	21	22.6	3.8	.400	0.0	.000	1.4	.567	0.38	0.29	1.6	5.6	3.9	1 Days Rest	29	24.5	3.6	.362	0.0	.000	2.0	.544	0.52	0.24	1.8	6.0	3.7
In wins	16	26.6	3.3	.404	0.0	—	2.4	.421	0.38	0.38	1.6	6.3	3.6	2 Days Rest	12	21.4	3.3	.425	0.0	—	1.3	.563	0.17	0.17	1.3	5.5	3.6
In losses	53	23.1	4.2	.405	0.0	.000	1.5	.598	0.30	0.30	1.4	5.1	4.3	3+ Days Rest	9	22.0	5.9	.509	0.0	—	2.2	.600	0.11	0.11	1.1	3.8	7.3

Last Five Seasons

	G	Min	FGA	FG%	3PA	3P%	FTA	FT%	Blk	Stl	Ast	Reb	Pts		G	Min	FGA	FG%	3PA	3P%	FTA	FT%	Blk	Stl	Ast	Reb	Pts
Total	267	17.3	3.5	.444	0.0	.222	2.1	.608	0.20	0.30	1.0	3.9	4.4	Pre All-Star	122	15.2	3.3	.423	0.0	.333	1.3	.538	0.16	0.22	1.0	3.3	3.5
Home	135	17.5	3.4	.447	0.0	.250	2.4	.577	0.21	0.30	1.0	4.1	4.4	Post All-Star	95	13.8	2.3	.452	0.1	.200	1.8	.623	0.22	0.19	0.9	3.1	3.2
Road	132	17.1	3.7	.440	0.0	.200	1.8	.650	0.18	0.30	1.0	3.7	4.4	Oct/Nov	32	16.6	4.1	.432	0.0	—	1.6	.462	0.19	0.09	1.1	3.9	4.3
vs. Playoff	144	16.8	3.3	.438	0.0	.000	2.0	.634	0.19	0.28	1.1	3.7	4.1	December	41	14.1	3.4	.447	0.0	.500	1.2	.580	0.15	0.24	1.0	3.0	3.8
vs. Non-Playoff	123	17.8	3.8	.449	0.0	.500	2.3	.581	0.20	0.33	0.9	4.0	4.8	January	37	14.9	2.7	.366	0.0	—	1.3	.553	0.16	0.22	0.8	3.4	2.7
vs. East	181	18.2	3.8	.444	0.0	.167	2.4	.619	0.22	0.33	1.0	4.1	4.9	February	46	16.9	2.7	.435	0.0	.000	2.4	.606	0.17	0.52	1.0	3.9	3.8
vs. West	86	15.3	3.0	.441	0.0	.333	1.5	.573	0.16	0.24	0.9	3.4	3.5	March	59	19.8	3.9	.450	0.1	.333	2.6	.706	0.24	0.36	1.0	4.4	5.4
vs. Div.	96	17.5	3.5	.469	0.0	.000	2.4	.661	0.19	0.35	0.9	3.9	4.9	Apr/May	52	19.4	4.1	.483	0.0	.000	3.0	.589	0.25	0.29	1.0	4.4	5.7
As Starter	95	26.7	5.4	.456	0.0	—	3.1	.593	0.28	0.41	1.4	6.0	6.7	0 Days Rest	65	20.8	4.4	.449	0.0	—	2.7	.586	0.20	0.43	1.0	4.3	5.5
Off Bench	172	12.0	2.5	.429	0.1	.222	1.6	.624	0.15	0.24	0.8	2.7	3.2	1 Days Rest	110	18.8	3.6	.414	0.1	.333	2.4	.627	0.26	0.35	1.1	4.4	4.5
In wins	142	14.1	2.9	.458	0.0	.333	2.0	.605	0.15	0.23	0.8	3.2	3.9	2 Days Rest	37	13.8	2.8	.394	0.0	—	1.1	.524	0.16	0.14	0.8	3.4	2.8
In losses	125	20.8	4.2	.433	0.0	.000	2.3	.611	0.26	0.38	1.3	4.6	5.1	3+ Days Rest	55	12.4	2.9	.541	0.1	.000	1.7	.634	0.09	0.16	0.8	2.8	4.2

Joe Smith

1999-2000 Per Game Averages

	G	Min	FGA	FG%	3PA	3P%	FTA	FT%	Blk	Stl	Ast	Reb	Pts		G	Min	FGA	FG%	3PA	3P%	FTA	FT%	Blk	Stl	Ast	Reb	Pts
Total	78	25.3	8.0	.464	0.0	1.000	3.3	.756	1.09	0.58	1.1	6.2	9.9	Pre All-Star	43	24.7	7.5	.463	0.0	—	3.2	.728	1.05	0.53	1.1	6.0	9.3
Home	40	25.1	8.4	.485	0.0	1.000	3.1	.726	1.10	0.55	1.3	6.5	10.4	Post All-Star	35	26.1	8.5	.465	0.0	1.000	3.5	.787	1.14	0.63	1.1	6.5	10.7
Road	38	25.6	7.6	.439	0.0	—	3.5	.784	1.08	0.61	1.0	5.9	9.4	November	12	22.6	7.6	.527	0.0	—	3.0	.694	1.00	0.58	1.0	5.8	9.3
vs. Playoff	42	24.5	7.3	.435	0.0	—	3.1	.738	0.88	0.67	1.1	5.9	8.6	December	11	31.5	8.9	.449	0.0	—	5.0	.818	0.91	0.27	1.5	7.7	12.1
vs. Non-Playoff	36	26.3	8.8	.492	0.0	1.000	3.6	.773	1.33	0.47	1.1	6.6	11.4	January	15	22.7	7.3	.445	0.0	—	2.5	.622	1.13	0.67	1.1	4.9	8.1
vs. East	28	27.6	8.1	.467	0.0	—	3.7	.779	0.93	0.54	1.3	6.7	10.5	February	14	22.6	7.4	.447	0.1	1.000	2.7	.789	1.21	0.57	1.1	5.2	8.8
vs. West	50	24.1	7.9	.462	0.0	1.000	3.1	.740	1.18	0.60	1.1	5.9	9.6	March	16	27.4	8.6	.438	0.0	—	3.4	.818	1.06	0.69	1.4	6.6	10.3
vs. Div.	23	24.0	8.3	.479	0.0	—	2.7	.683	1.61	0.48	0.9	6.0	9.8	April	10	26.2	8.4	.500	0.0	—	3.7	.730	1.20	0.60	0.7	7.7	11.1
As Starter	9	32.0	10.8	.485	0.0	—	3.8	.676	1.22	0.44	0.8	8.2	13.0	0 Days Rest	16	26.8	7.6	.459	0.0	—	4.0	.828	1.19	0.50	1.2	6.9	10.3
Off Bench	69	24.4	7.6	.460	0.0	1.000	3.2	.768	1.07	0.59	1.2	5.9	9.5	1 Days Rest	49	24.8	8.0	.459	0.0	1.000	3.1	.779	1.04	0.61	1.0	6.2	9.8
In wins	49	24.6	7.9	.499	0.0	1.000	3.5	.780	1.31	0.63	1.2	5.8	10.6	2 Days Rest	4	26.8	10.3	.610	0.0	—	4.0	.250	1.75	0.50	1.8	5.5	13.5
In losses	29	26.6	8.2	.408	0.0	—	2.9	.706	0.72	0.48	0.9	6.9	8.8	3+ Days Rest	9	25.0	7.6	.412	0.0	—	2.7	.750	0.89	0.56	1.2	5.4	8.2

Career (1995-96 thru 1999-2000)

	G	Min	FGA	FG%	3PA	3P%	FTA	FT%	Blk	Stl	Ast	Reb	Pts		G	Min	FGA	FG%	3PA	3P%	FTA	FT%	Blk	Stl	Ast	Reb	Pts
Total	362	32.2	12.5	.448	0.2	.267	4.2	.779	1.17	0.82	1.3	7.5	14.5	Pre All-Star	180	32.6	13.0	.458	0.3	.265	4.4	.780	1.19	0.89	1.3	7.4	15.5
Home	178	33.2	13.0	.467	0.2	.267	4.4	.792	1.17	0.87	1.4	7.9	15.7	Post All-Star	139	31.4	12.0	.442	0.2	.294	3.7	.785	1.01	0.76	1.1	7.3	13.6
Road	184	31.2	12.1	.429	0.2	.268	3.9	.764	1.16	0.78	1.1	7.0	13.4	Oct/Nov	55	31.5	12.6	.442	0.4	.200	3.7	.776	0.95	0.85	1.3	7.1	14.0
vs. Playoff	204	31.7	12.2	.427	0.3	.254	4.0	.764	1.10	0.84	1.2	7.3	13.5	December	53	33.3	13.3	.482	0.1	.333	4.8	.809	1.34	0.98	1.3	7.8	16.8
vs. Non-Playoff	158	32.8	12.9	.475	0.1	.304	4.4	.795	1.25	0.80	1.3	7.7	15.8	January	59	33.1	13.5	.446	0.4	.318	4.9	.761	1.31	0.88	1.3	7.3	15.9
vs. East	132	31.8	12.3	.480	0.3	.257	4.1	.780	1.02	0.76	1.3	7.3	15.1	February	64	31.4	12.6	.450	0.2	.286	3.9	.768	1.23	0.67	1.3	7.7	14.4
vs. West	230	32.4	12.7	.431	0.2	.275	4.2	.778	1.25	0.86	1.2	7.6	14.2	March	75	32.8	11.8	.431	0.2	.333	4.0	.786	1.21	0.83	1.3	7.7	13.4
vs. Div.	112	31.6	12.7	.424	0.2	.273	4.2	.785	1.37	0.87	1.2	7.6	14.1	Apr/May	56	30.7	11.5	.444	0.1	.000	3.8	.769	0.93	0.75	1.0	7.2	13.1
As Starter	268	35.1	14.2	.447	0.3	.265	4.5	.782	1.26	0.91	1.3	8.2	16.3	0 Days Rest	92	32.3	12.7	.436	0.2	.150	4.2	.792	1.22	0.79	1.2	7.3	14.4
Off Bench	94	23.7	7.8	.454	0.0	.333	3.1	.766	0.89	0.59	1.1	5.4	9.5	1 Days Rest	184	32.1	12.4	.444	0.3	.373	4.1	.790	1.17	0.82	1.2	7.7	14.4
In wins	156	31.6	11.8	.489	0.1	.222	4.5	.797	1.24	0.82	1.4	7.6	15.1	2 Days Rest	53	33.0	12.9	.482	0.2	.111	4.8	.723	1.26	0.75	1.7	7.3	15.9
In losses	206	32.6	13.1	.421	0.3	.279	3.9	.762	1.11	0.83	1.2	7.4	14.1	3+ Days Rest	33	30.8	12.1	.452	0.2	.000	3.5	.781	0.85	1.03	1.2	6.7	13.6

Steve Smith

1999-2000 Per Game Averages

	G	Min	FGA	FG%	3PA	3P%	FTA	FT%	Blk	Stl	Ast	Reb	Pts		G	Min	FGA	FG%	3PA	3P%	FTA	FT%	Blk	Stl	Ast	Reb	Pts
Total	82	32.8	11.0	.467	2.9	.398	4.1	.850	0.38	0.87	2.5	3.8	14.9	Pre All-Star	49	33.6	11.4	.478	3.1	.392	4.6	.831	0.49	0.84	2.5	4.2	15.9
Home	41	32.8	10.6	.460	2.7	.376	4.0	.865	0.37	0.76	2.8	4.0	14.1	Post All-Star	33	31.6	10.3	.449	2.7	.409	3.5	.887	0.21	0.91	2.6	3.3	13.5
Road	41	32.8	11.4	.473	3.2	.417	4.3	.836	0.39	0.98	2.3	3.7	15.7	November	16	34.6	11.0	.500	2.9	.370	4.6	.797	0.25	1.00	3.1	3.7	15.8
vs. Playoff	44	33.6	11.3	.417	3.2	.374	4.0	.834	0.30	0.98	2.6	3.8	14.0	December	13	34.5	11.9	.439	3.8	.388	3.6	.851	0.31	1.08	2.8	5.2	15.0
vs. Non-Playoff	38	31.8	10.6	.529	2.7	.431	4.3	.867	0.47	0.74	2.5	3.9	16.1	January	14	32.9	11.6	.457	2.8	.385	4.9	.824	0.68	0.57	2.0	4.1	15.6
vs. East	30	32.0	10.3	.461	2.8	.369	3.4	.892	0.50	0.80	2.5	3.9	13.5	February	14	30.4	10.4	.466	2.8	.462	4.5	.873	0.43	0.50	2.1	3.1	14.9
vs. West	52	33.3	11.4	.470	3.0	.414	4.6	.832	0.31	0.90	2.6	3.8	15.8	March	14	32.3	10.1	.430	2.6	.417	2.7	.868	0.21	1.14	2.1	3.9	12.1
vs. Div.	24	32.2	11.4	.429	3.2	.390	4.4	.849	0.25	1.13	2.6	4.2	14.8	April	11	31.7	10.8	.513	2.9	.375	4.5	.920	0.18	0.91	3.2	2.7	16.4
As Starter	81	32.8	11.0	.466	2.9	.392	4.1	.855	0.38	0.88	2.5	3.8	14.9	0 Days Rest	22	30.6	10.0	.509	2.4	.415	3.9	.837	0.23	0.77	2.4	3.7	14.5
Off Bench	1	29.0	12.0	.500	4.0	.750	10.0	.700	0.00	0.00	3.0	3.0	22.0	1 Days Rest	39	34.1	11.1	.439	3.2	.390	4.4	.855	0.33	1.00	3.0	3.8	14.7
In wins	59	32.3	10.6	.486	2.8	.435	4.3	.865	0.41	0.86	2.7	3.9	16.3	2 Days Rest	15	33.8	12.4	.446	3.1	.404	4.4	.894	0.60	0.67	2.1	4.0	16.3
In losses	23	34.1	11.9	.421	3.2	.315	3.9	.809	0.30	0.87	2.0	3.7	14.1	3+ Days Rest	6	29.8	10.2	.574	3.0	.389	2.7	.688	0.67	0.83	1.0	4.0	14.7

Last Five Seasons

	G	Min	FGA	FG%	3PA	3P%	FTA	FT%	Blk	Stl	Ast	Reb	Pts		G	Min	FGA	FG%	3PA	3P%	FTA	FT%	Blk	Stl	Ast	Reb	Pts
Total	343	36.5	14.1	.437	4.3	.348	5.2	.845	0.32	0.91	3.3	3.9	18.2	Pre All-Star	178	36.1	14.1	.437	4.3	.339	5.2	.838	0.34	0.81	3.2	4.1	18.1
Home	174	36.2	13.8	.438	4.1	.345	5.2	.846	0.34	0.85	3.4	3.9	18.0	Post All-Star	129	37.1	13.8	.449	4.3	.362	5.1	.854	0.30	1.02	3.5	3.6	18.3
Road	169	36.9	14.4	.436	4.4	.350	5.2	.844	0.30	0.97	3.3	3.9	18.5	Oct/Nov	49	34.9	13.5	.461	4.3	.402	4.7	.823	0.27	0.73	3.1	3.8	18.0
vs. Playoff	183	37.7	15.1	.421	4.7	.351	5.0	.837	0.30	0.94	3.3	3.8	18.6	December	51	35.0	14.0	.409	4.6	.331	4.5	.853	0.29	0.98	3.2	4.2	16.8
vs. Non-Playoff	160	35.2	12.9	.459	3.8	.343	5.5	.854	0.35	0.88	3.4	4.0	17.8	January	62	38.1	14.8	.438	4.2	.300	5.6	.824	0.45	0.79	3.4	4.0	18.8
vs. East	211	37.2	14.5	.426	4.3	.327	5.4	.850	0.34	0.93	3.4	4.1	18.3	February	58	36.5	14.0	.436	3.9	.354	6.2	.827	0.29	0.90	3.7	4.1	18.7
vs. West	132	35.6	13.5	.456	4.3	.381	5.0	.838	0.30	0.87	3.3	3.7	18.1	March	73	37.5	14.2	.441	4.5	.362	4.8	.865	0.27	0.95	3.3	3.7	18.3
vs. Div.	117	37.1	14.4	.418	4.5	.330	5.2	.846	0.29	0.98	3.4	3.6	17.9	Apr/May	50	36.4	13.9	.438	4.0	.343	5.6	.883	0.36	1.12	3.4	3.6	18.5
As Starter	342	36.6	14.1	.437	4.3	.347	5.2	.846	0.32	0.91	3.3	3.9	18.2	0 Days Rest	92	35.6	14.0	.439	4.4	.344	4.8	.850	0.29	0.84	3.1	3.7	17.9
Off Bench	1	29.0	12.0	.500	4.0	.750	10.0	.700	0.00	0.00	3.0	3.0	22.0	1 Days Rest	165	37.5	14.3	.441	4.1	.350	5.5	.854	0.34	0.96	3.5	3.9	18.7
In wins	224	36.2	13.5	.454	3.9	.374	5.6	.860	0.34	0.94	3.6	4.0	18.6	2 Days Rest	51	36.1	14.4	.418	4.9	.356	4.8	.841	0.29	0.80	3.4	4.2	17.8
In losses	119	37.2	15.1	.409	5.0	.309	4.6	.811	0.29	0.85	2.9	3.7	17.6	3+ Days Rest	35	35.2	13.0	.445	3.7	.331	5.8	.802	0.37	1.00	3.2	4.1	17.5

Rik Smits

1999-2000 Per Game Averages

	G	Min	FGA	FG%	3PA	3P%	FTA	FT%	Blk	Stl	Ast	Reb	Pts		G	Min	FGA	FG%	3PA	3P%	FTA	FT%	Blk	Stl	Ast	Reb	Pts
Total	79	23.4	11.3	.484	0.0	.000	2.7	.739	1.27	0.25	1.1	5.1	12.9	Pre All-Star	48	23.5	11.6	.488	0.0	—	2.5	.773	1.44	0.23	1.2	4.8	13.3
Home	40	25.0	12.2	.489	0.0	.000	3.2	.795	1.50	0.20	1.1	5.6	14.4	Post All-Star	31	23.3	10.7	.477	0.0	.000	3.0	.696	1.00	0.29	0.9	5.5	12.3
Road	39	21.9	10.3	.479	0.0	—	2.2	.655	1.03	0.31	1.0	4.5	11.3	November	15	24.9	11.7	.440	0.0	—	2.5	.676	1.33	0.27	1.2	4.9	11.9
vs. Playoff	42	22.9	10.5	.491	0.0	—	2.1	.744	1.10	0.26	1.0	5.0	11.9	December	14	24.1	11.0	.481	0.0	—	2.7	.737	1.64	0.14	1.1	5.5	12.6
vs. Non-Playoff	37	24.1	12.2	.478	0.0	.000	3.3	.736	1.46	0.24	1.2	5.1	14.0	January	14	21.6	12.0	.506	0.0	—	2.2	.935	1.36	0.36	1.3	3.9	14.2
vs. East	52	24.6	11.1	.515	0.0	.000	2.8	.740	1.06	0.17	1.3	5.1	13.5	February	10	23.2	11.6	.586	0.0	—	2.8	.750	1.40	0.20	1.0	5.6	15.7
vs. West	27	21.3	11.5	.428	0.0	—	2.4	.738	1.67	0.41	0.6	5.0	11.6	March	16	22.8	10.3	.448	0.0	—	3.8	.717	0.81	0.44	0.7	6.0	11.9
vs. Div.	27	24.5	11.0	.520	0.0	.000	2.7	.730	1.07	0.19	1.3	5.5	13.5	April	10	24.3	11.2	.473	0.1	.000	1.7	.588	1.10	0.00	1.3	4.4	11.6
As Starter	79	23.4	11.3	.484	0.0	.000	2.7	.739	1.27	0.25	1.1	5.1	12.9	0 Days Rest	20	22.4	11.9	.454	0.0	—	2.8	.661	0.95	0.35	1.4	5.8	12.7
Off Bench	0	—												1 Days Rest	38	22.8	10.1	.458	0.0	.000	2.1	.716	1.37	0.21	0.9	4.6	10.7
In wins	54	24.0	12.1	.491	0.0	.000	2.8	.730	1.46	0.30	1.2	5.5	13.9	2 Days Rest	14	26.1	13.4	.567	0.0	—	3.4	.830	1.79	0.14	1.1	5.4	17.9
In losses	25	22.2	9.5	.466	0.0	—	2.4	.763	0.84	0.16	0.8	4.1	10.7	3+ Days Rest	7	24.7	11.9	.506	0.0	—	3.9	.815	0.57	0.43	1.3	4.9	15.1

Last Five Seasons

	G	Min	FGA	FG%	3PA	3P%	FTA	FT%	Blk	Stl	Ast	Reb	Pts		G	Min	FGA	FG%	3PA	3P%	FTA	FT%	Blk	Stl	Ast	Reb	Pts
Total	316	27.3	13.3	.496	0.1	.158	3.5	.783	1.09	0.38	1.3	6.3	15.9	Pre All-Star	140	27.2	13.2	.498	0.1	.167	3.3	.800	1.19	0.37	1.5	6.1	15.8
Home	161	28.1	13.9	.494	0.0	.000	3.8	.795	1.12	0.40	1.3	6.5	16.7	Post All-Star	127	28.0	13.5	.496	0.1	.182	4.0	.759	0.99	0.40	1.3	6.7	16.4
Road	155	26.4	12.6	.498	0.1	.273	3.1	.768	1.06	0.36	1.3	6.0	15.0	Oct/Nov	29	27.7	13.1	.492	0.0	.000	2.7	.671	1.55	0.28	1.9	5.9	14.7
vs. Playoff	161	27.2	13.0	.479	0.1	.000	3.4	.765	0.99	0.38	1.3	6.2	15.1	December	42	27.7	13.0	.515	0.0	—	3.4	.840	1.17	0.36	1.3	6.1	16.3
vs. Non-Playoff	155	27.4	13.5	.513	0.1	.333	3.5	.802	1.19	0.39	1.3	6.3	16.7	January	54	26.2	12.9	.491	0.0	.000	3.4	.809	1.07	0.52	1.4	5.9	15.4
vs. East	223	27.7	13.0	.503	0.1	.154	3.5	.787	1.01	0.38	1.4	6.1	15.7	February	61	27.6	13.5	.504	0.1	.167	2.9	.764	1.00	0.33	1.4	6.9	15.9
vs. West	93	26.4	13.9	.480	0.1	.167	3.9	.774	1.28	0.40	1.1	6.5	16.3	March	77	27.7	13.7	.509	0.1	.333	4.0	.797	0.97	0.35	1.1	6.5	17.2
vs. Div.	114	27.9	13.2	.504	0.1	.111	3.4	.786	0.92	0.35	1.5	6.2	15.9	Apr/May	53	26.9	12.9	.458	0.1	.000	3.8	.759	1.06	0.43	1.2	5.9	14.8
As Starter	312	27.4	13.3	.497	0.1	.158	3.5	.785	1.10	0.39	1.3	6.3	15.9	0 Days Rest	80	27.0	13.8	.488	0.1	.000	3.1	.743	1.11	0.29	1.4	6.8	15.8
Off Bench	4	18.0	9.8	.385	0.0	—	3.5	.643	0.50	0.00	0.0	4.0	9.8	1 Days Rest	161	27.7	13.2	.496	0.1	.167	3.6	.795	1.04	0.40	1.3	6.1	15.9
In wins	205	27.4	13.5	.512	0.0	.375	3.5	.787	1.20	0.43	1.4	6.4	16.6	2 Days Rest	47	26.9	13.2	.502	0.0	.000	3.4	.796	1.43	0.47	1.1	5.9	16.0
In losses	111	27.1	12.7	.465	0.1	.000	3.5	.777	0.89	0.29	1.2	5.9	14.5	3+ Days Rest	28	26.6	12.3	.507	0.0	1.000	3.8	.794	0.71	0.43	1.4	6.0	15.6

Eric Snow

1999-2000 Per Game Averages

	G	Min	FGA	FG%	3PA	3P%	FTA	FT%	Blk	Stl	Ast	Reb	Pts		G	Min	FGA	FG%	3PA	3P%	FTA	FT%	Blk	Stl	Ast	Reb	Pts
Total	82	35.0	7.3	.430	0.5	.244	2.2	.712	0.10	1.71	7.6	3.2	7.9	Pre All-Star	49	33.3	7.4	.403	0.5	.154	2.3	.696	0.10	1.47	7.3	3.3	7.7
Home	41	34.3	7.7	.424	0.6	.250	2.0	.723	0.02	1.71	7.6	3.1	8.1	Post All-Star	33	37.3	7.0	.474	0.6	.368	1.9	.742	0.09	2.06	8.1	3.0	8.3
Road	41	35.6	6.9	.438	0.5	.238	2.3	.702	0.17	1.71	7.7	3.2	7.7	November	16	33.3	6.9	.378	0.4	.000	3.6	.649	0.13	1.38	5.9	3.6	7.6
vs. Playoff	42	35.0	7.4	.414	0.5	.304	2.0	.729	0.10	1.67	7.3	3.3	7.7	December	16	32.9	7.1	.354	0.5	.125	2.3	.703	0.00	1.00	6.4	2.8	6.7
vs. Non-Playoff	40	34.9	7.2	.448	0.6	.182	2.3	.696	0.10	1.75	7.9	3.1	8.2	January	12	32.4	7.7	.467	0.5	.167	1.4	.765	0.08	2.00	8.0	3.3	8.3
vs. East	54	36.1	7.4	.435	0.4	.167	2.5	.701	0.09	1.70	7.9	3.3	8.3	February	12	35.4	7.8	.457	0.9	.455	1.0	.917	0.25	1.83	9.7	3.7	8.5
vs. West	28	32.8	7.1	.422	0.8	.333	1.4	.750	0.11	1.71	7.1	3.0	7.3	March	16	40.1	8.1	.465	0.6	.300	1.9	.774	0.13	2.06	8.4	2.9	9.2
vs. Div.	24	36.9	7.6	.393	0.7	.118	2.9	.681	0.13	1.54	7.3	3.4	8.0	April	10	35.3	5.8	.500	0.3	.333	2.3	.652	0.20	2.30	8.1	2.9	7.4
As Starter	80	35.2	7.4	.428	0.6	.244	2.2	.707	0.09	1.74	7.6	3.2	8.0	0 Days Rest	20	34.0	7.1	.440	0.3	.200	2.1	.762	0.15	1.40	7.8	2.4	7.9
Off Bench	2	26.5	3.0	.667	0.0	—	1.5	1.000	0.50	0.50	6.5	2.5	5.5	1 Days Rest	45	35.7	7.5	.422	0.8	.286	2.0	.674	0.11	1.93	8.1	3.6	8.0
In wins	49	36.1	7.3	.461	0.5	.250	2.5	.710	0.04	1.90	8.4	3.2	8.7	2 Days Rest	9	34.9	6.4	.466	0.3	.000	3.3	.733	0.00	1.89	6.0	3.0	8.4
In losses	33	33.3	7.2	.385	0.6	.238	1.6	.717	0.18	1.42	6.4	3.2	6.9	3+ Days Rest	8	33.0	7.4	.424	0.3	.000	1.6	.769	0.00	1.00	6.5	2.9	7.5

Career (1995-96 thru 1999-2000)

	G	Min	FGA	FG%	3PA	3P%	FTA	FT%	Blk	Stl	Ast	Reb	Pts		G	Min	FGA	FG%	3PA	3P%	FTA	FT%	Blk	Stl	Ast	Reb	Pts
Total	304	21.9	4.6	.431	0.4	.222	1.7	.704	0.06	1.20	4.4	2.0	5.2	Pre All-Star	146	18.3	4.1	.411	0.3	.200	1.5	.685	0.05	0.88	3.8	1.8	4.4
Home	163	20.7	4.5	.430	0.4	.207	1.7	.722	0.02	1.29	4.2	1.9	5.1	Post All-Star	110	20.7	4.1	.460	0.4	.238	1.3	.701	0.07	1.25	4.3	1.8	4.8
Road	141	23.3	4.7	.433	0.4	.240	1.7	.683	0.10	1.09	4.6	2.2	5.3	Oct/Nov	46	18.5	3.9	.385	0.3	.154	1.6	.635	0.04	0.74	3.3	2.0	4.1
vs. Playoff	159	21.1	4.2	.416	0.4	.259	1.5	.726	0.04	1.19	4.0	1.9	4.7	December	46	19.4	4.2	.399	0.3	.250	1.7	.684	0.04	0.78	4.0	1.7	4.6
vs. Non-Playoff	145	22.9	5.0	.446	0.3	.180	1.9	.685	0.08	1.21	4.8	2.2	5.8	January	45	15.6	3.7	.446	0.3	.143	1.1	.700	0.04	0.98	3.4	1.4	4.1
vs. East	180	25.2	5.2	.434	0.4	.197	2.1	.704	0.06	1.38	4.9	2.3	6.0	February	52	22.3	4.5	.405	0.4	.318	1.7	.736	0.06	1.33	4.6	2.4	5.0
vs. West	124	17.2	3.7	.427	0.3	.262	1.1	.704	0.05	0.94	3.6	1.6	4.1	March	64	24.4	4.8	.458	0.2	.333	1.5	.713	0.05	1.48	4.6	2.0	5.6
vs. Div.	92	23.4	4.8	.410	0.5	.163	1.9	.682	0.05	1.23	4.4	2.2	5.3	Apr/May	51	29.4	6.1	.463	0.6	.156	2.5	.729	0.10	1.71	6.2	2.6	7.6
As Starter	129	35.4	7.3	.428	0.5	.242	2.5	.718	0.06	1.87	7.2	3.3	8.2	0 Days Rest	68	24.0	5.1	.442	0.3	.100	1.7	.748	0.06	1.19	5.0	2.0	5.8
Off Bench	175	12.0	2.6	.438	0.2	.190	1.1	.679	0.05	0.71	2.4	1.1	3.0	1 Days Rest	146	24.7	5.0	.431	0.5	.273	1.8	.706	0.08	1.42	4.9	2.4	5.8
In wins	193	21.2	4.4	.457	0.4	.210	1.8	.701	0.04	1.26	4.5	2.1	5.3	2 Days Rest	42	18.9	3.8	.415	0.3	.231	1.7	.704	0.02	1.00	3.5	1.5	4.4
In losses	111	23.2	4.9	.391	0.4	.239	1.5	.710	0.08	1.10	4.2	2.0	5.0	3+ Days Rest	48	13.3	3.2	.425	0.2	.111	1.2	.603	0.02	0.71	2.6	1.2	3.5

Latrell Sprewell

1999-2000 Per Game Averages

	G	Min	FGA	FG%	3PA	3P%	FTA	FT%	Blk	Stl	Ast	Reb	Pts		G	Min	FGA	FG%	3PA	3P%	FTA	FT%	Blk	Stl	Ast	Reb	Pts
Total	82	40.0	15.9	.435	1.5	.346	4.8	.866	0.27	1.33	4.0	4.3	18.6	Pre All-Star	47	40.6	16.6	.426	1.6	.403	4.9	.851	0.23	1.30	4.0	4.5	18.9
Home	41	39.9	15.6	.463	1.6	.424	5.0	.865	0.17	1.56	4.1	4.2	19.5	Post All-Star	35	39.0	15.0	.450	1.4	.260	4.8	.888	0.31	1.37	4.1	3.9	18.1
Road	41	40.0	16.2	.408	1.5	.262	4.6	.868	0.37	1.10	4.0	4.3	17.7	November	16	41.3	18.3	.386	1.1	.111	5.4	.895	0.19	1.19	4.5	5.2	19.1
vs. Playoff	44	40.3	16.0	.443	1.7	.351	4.8	.890	0.20	1.25	4.1	4.1	19.0	December	14	40.7	16.8	.451	2.0	.500	3.8	.792	0.29	1.21	4.2	4.4	19.0
vs. Non-Playoff	38	39.5	15.8	.426	1.4	.340	4.9	.840	0.34	1.42	4.0	4.4	18.1	January	12	39.8	15.3	.446	1.8	.429	5.8	.814	0.08	1.58	3.0	4.0	19.2
vs. East	54	40.2	15.9	.431	1.5	.341	4.6	.842	0.28	1.39	4.0	4.3	18.1	February	13	40.4	13.8	.433	1.5	.350	4.2	.927	0.38	1.31	4.6	4.6	16.5
vs. West	28	39.5	15.9	.444	1.6	.356	5.4	.907	0.25	1.21	4.1	4.3	19.6	March	17	39.4	16.4	.489	1.8	.387	5.6	.895	0.18	1.47	3.4	3.6	21.7
vs. Div.	24	40.6	15.7	.394	1.2	.276	4.1	.848	0.33	1.04	4.2	4.5	16.2	April	10	37.3	13.5	.393	0.9	.000	3.8	.842	0.60	1.20	4.8	3.1	13.8
As Starter	82	40.0	15.9	.435	1.5	.346	4.8	.866	0.27	1.33	4.0	4.3	18.6	0 Days Rest	20	40.8	16.1	.410	1.1	.273	4.9	.825	0.25	1.00	3.9	4.7	17.5
Off Bench	0	—	—	—	—	—	—	—	—	—	—	—	—	1 Days Rest	42	39.4	15.7	.439	1.6	.412	4.8	.871	0.24	1.48	4.1	4.3	18.6
In wins	50	39.9	15.8	.470	1.6	.427	5.4	.888	0.18	1.60	4.4	4.3	20.3	2 Days Rest	14	40.6	16.1	.478	1.7	.250	5.3	.905	0.43	1.14	4.4	3.6	20.6
In losses	32	40.1	16.2	.383	1.4	.200	4.0	.820	0.41	0.91	3.4	4.1	15.9	3+ Days Rest	6	39.5	16.3	.398	2.2	.308	4.2	.880	0.17	1.83	3.7	4.3	17.3

Last Five Seasons

	G	Min	FGA	FG%	3PA	3P%	FTA	FT%	Blk	Stl	Ast	Reb	Pts		G	Min	FGA	FG%	3PA	3P%	FTA	FT%	Blk	Stl	Ast	Reb	Pts
Total	291	39.4	16.3	.433	3.3	.329	5.9	.825	0.41	1.49	4.6	4.5	20.1	Pre All-Star	150	39.8	17.0	.428	3.6	.337	6.1	.832	0.47	1.44	4.7	4.7	20.8
Home	145	39.9	15.7	.451	3.2	.330	5.7	.831	0.39	1.55	4.9	4.4	20.0	Post All-Star	104	41.1	16.2	.447	3.2	.328	5.8	.820	0.45	1.64	5.0	4.3	20.3
Road	146	38.9	16.8	.417	3.4	.327	6.1	.820	0.42	1.42	4.2	4.5	20.2	Oct/Nov	56	39.7	17.8	.399	3.3	.286	6.3	.849	0.50	1.43	4.9	4.4	20.4
vs. Playoff	172	39.1	16.1	.422	3.4	.323	5.8	.833	0.34	1.42	4.5	4.2	19.5	December	42	38.8	16.0	.437	3.5	.356	5.7	.793	0.43	1.26	4.3	4.9	19.8
vs. Non-Playoff	119	39.9	16.6	.449	3.1	.339	6.0	.815	0.51	1.59	4.6	4.9	20.9	January	41	40.5	17.2	.449	4.1	.347	6.7	.840	0.44	1.63	5.0	5.1	22.5
vs. East	148	38.7	15.5	.423	2.7	.328	5.2	.820	0.37	1.37	4.2	4.3	18.3	February	39	40.8	16.1	.444	3.3	.352	5.1	.793	0.49	1.56	4.9	4.8	19.5
vs. West	143	40.1	17.2	.443	3.8	.329	6.6	.830	0.45	1.61	4.9	4.6	22.0	March	65	39.6	16.1	.446	3.1	.338	6.4	.840	0.32	1.58	4.6	4.0	19.8
vs. Div.	88	39.0	15.9	.408	3.0	.316	5.9	.824	0.38	1.49	4.4	4.5	18.8	Apr/May	48	37.3	14.6	.435	2.4	.293	4.9	.808	0.31	1.44	3.9	3.6	17.4
As Starter	256	40.3	16.6	.436	3.4	.334	6.0	.827	0.45	1.52	4.8	4.5	20.6	0 Days Rest	73	39.4	16.8	.413	3.1	.322	6.0	.816	0.40	1.56	4.1	4.6	19.8
Off Bench	35	33.2	14.1	.415	2.1	.270	5.1	.816	0.11	1.29	2.7	4.2	16.4	1 Days Rest	147	39.3	15.7	.434	3.2	.321	5.8	.831	0.39	1.45	4.6	4.3	19.6
In wins	132	40.0	16.5	.471	2.9	.387	6.4	.835	0.43	1.71	4.8	4.7	21.9	2 Days Rest	46	40.6	17.0	.464	3.3	.351	5.9	.837	0.54	1.48	5.3	4.1	21.9
In losses	159	39.0	16.2	.402	3.6	.290	5.5	.816	0.39	1.30	4.3	4.3	18.5	3+ Days Rest	25	37.9	17.0	.432	3.9	.347	5.8	.799	0.32	1.52	4.6	5.4	20.6

Jerry Stackhouse

1999-2000 Per Game Averages

	G	Min	FGA	FG%	3PA	3P%	FTA	FT%	Blk	Stl	Ast	Reb	Pts
Total	82	38.4	17.6	.428	3.5	.288	9.2	.815	0.44	1.26	4.5	3.8	23.6
Home	41	38.1	18.0	.440	3.3	.279	8.9	.821	0.49	1.32	4.4	3.8	24.0
Road	41	38.7	17.3	.415	3.7	.296	9.6	.810	0.39	1.20	4.5	3.9	23.2
vs. Playoff	44	38.4	17.6	.408	3.1	.287	9.3	.792	0.52	1.09	4.0	3.8	22.6
vs. Non-Playoff	38	38.4	17.7	.451	4.0	.289	9.2	.842	0.34	1.45	5.0	3.9	24.9
vs. East	54	38.7	17.6	.437	3.4	.268	9.4	.799	0.46	1.22	4.7	4.1	23.8
vs. West	28	37.8	17.8	.410	3.8	.324	9.0	.849	0.39	1.32	4.0	3.3	23.4
vs. Div.	28	38.6	17.8	.429	3.1	.244	8.9	.779	0.39	1.07	4.4	4.5	22.9
As Starter	82	38.4	17.6	.428	3.5	.288	9.2	.815	0.44	1.26	4.5	3.8	23.6
Off Bench	0	—	—	—	—	—	—	—	—	—	—	—	—
In wins	42	37.9	17.6	.464	3.8	.304	9.0	.834	0.50	1.19	4.7	3.8	25.0
In losses	40	39.0	17.7	.390	3.3	.269	9.5	.797	0.38	1.33	4.2	3.9	22.2

	G	Min	FGA	FG%	3PA	3P%	FTA	FT%	Blk	Stl	Ast	Reb	Pts
Pre All-Star	48	39.6	16.9	.427	3.1	.245	10.1	.790	0.35	1.27	4.7	4.5	23.2
Post All-Star	34	36.7	18.7	.428	4.1	.333	8.0	.860	0.56	1.24	4.1	2.9	24.3
November	15	38.1	15.7	.421	2.3	.294	9.2	.783	0.27	1.13	4.8	5.1	21.1
December	14	39.9	16.1	.440	3.1	.349	10.2	.839	0.36	0.64	4.1	4.3	23.8
January	15	40.5	18.3	.423	3.6	.130	11.6	.764	0.53	2.13	5.4	3.9	24.8
February	12	39.5	19.5	.419	3.4	.268	8.7	.837	0.75	1.33	4.4	4.1	24.5
March	15	37.4	18.3	.444	4.9	.342	8.3	.872	0.40	1.20	3.7	2.1	25.2
April	11	34.2	18.5	.417	3.9	.349	6.7	.824	0.36	1.00	4.1	3.5	22.4
0 Days Rest	20	37.4	17.0	.431	3.1	.262	7.4	.804	0.20	1.15	4.1	3.7	21.4
1 Days Rest	45	38.7	18.0	.421	3.6	.290	9.9	.812	0.58	1.42	4.7	3.9	24.3
2 Days Rest	8	37.8	16.4	.412	3.9	.323	9.0	.861	0.25	1.25	4.0	3.3	22.5
3+ Days Rest	9	39.4	18.6	.467	3.8	.294	10.1	.813	0.44	0.67	4.2	4.6	26.7

Career (1995-96 thru 1999-2000)

	G	Min	FGA	FG%	3PA	3P%	FTA	FT%	Blk	Stl	Ast	Reb	Pts
Total	356	35.8	14.9	.416	3.5	.290	7.4	.788	0.72	1.11	3.5	3.6	19.3
Home	180	36.3	15.5	.423	3.6	.291	7.3	.791	0.86	1.13	3.7	3.8	19.9
Road	176	35.4	14.4	.408	3.4	.288	7.5	.784	0.57	1.09	3.4	3.5	18.6
vs. Playoff	199	35.5	14.6	.410	3.3	.290	7.3	.779	0.66	1.06	3.2	3.4	18.6
vs. Non-Playoff	157	36.2	15.3	.424	3.7	.290	7.5	.799	0.80	1.17	3.9	3.9	20.1
vs. East	245	35.7	14.7	.418	3.4	.280	7.6	.781	0.71	1.09	3.4	3.5	19.2
vs. West	111	36.0	15.5	.412	3.7	.309	6.9	.804	0.73	1.15	3.7	3.9	19.5
vs. Div.	121	35.4	14.8	.424	3.1	.270	7.3	.776	0.66	1.06	3.4	3.5	18.4
As Starter	280	37.9	16.0	.416	3.8	.297	7.8	.786	0.76	1.17	3.7	3.9	20.6
Off Bench	76	27.9	11.0	.414	2.5	.246	5.9	.797	0.58	0.89	2.9	2.7	14.4
In wins	134	35.4	15.1	.454	3.5	.331	7.7	.811	0.69	1.13	3.9	3.7	21.1
In losses	222	36.1	14.8	.393	3.5	.264	7.2	.773	0.74	1.10	3.3	3.6	18.1

	G	Min	FGA	FG%	3PA	3P%	FTA	FT%	Blk	Stl	Ast	Reb	Pts
Pre All-Star	183	37.2	15.2	.416	3.5	.289	7.6	.770	0.78	1.16	3.7	4.1	19.5
Post All-Star	131	36.3	15.5	.428	3.7	.294	7.6	.797	0.72	1.13	3.6	3.3	20.4
Oct/Nov	55	36.1	15.1	.425	3.3	.322	7.1	.747	0.71	1.36	3.5	3.9	19.2
December	57	36.3	14.7	.402	3.4	.318	8.1	.834	0.88	0.75	3.6	4.1	19.7
January	60	39.1	15.8	.411	3.6	.229	7.6	.731	0.83	1.38	4.0	4.1	19.4
February	61	34.0	14.2	.415	3.2	.304	6.9	.781	0.61	1.07	3.0	3.1	18.1
March	76	35.5	14.9	.436	3.7	.288	7.6	.832	0.68	1.12	3.6	3.0	20.3
Apr/May	47	33.6	14.8	.398	3.7	.286	7.2	.780	0.60	0.94	3.5	3.8	18.4
0 Days Rest	90	36.7	15.2	.416	3.5	.295	7.3	.777	0.70	1.14	3.4	3.7	19.4
1 Days Rest	181	35.6	15.1	.416	3.4	.290	7.8	.798	0.77	1.12	3.7	3.7	19.7
2 Days Rest	43	35.0	14.0	.428	3.2	.309	6.7	.769	0.74	1.07	3.0	3.6	18.1
3+ Days Rest	42	35.4	14.6	.407	3.8	.261	6.9	.782	0.52	1.02	3.5	3.3	18.2

John Stockton

1999-2000 Per Game Averages

	G	Min	FGA	FG%	3PA	3P%	FTA	FT%	Blk	Stl	Ast	Reb	Pts
Total	82	29.7	8.8	.501	1.5	.355	3.1	.860	0.18	1.74	8.6	2.6	12.1
Home	41	29.5	9.0	.537	1.5	.371	2.9	.840	0.24	1.68	9.2	2.9	12.7
Road	41	29.9	8.7	.463	1.4	.339	3.4	.877	0.12	1.80	8.0	2.3	11.5
vs. Playoff	44	30.8	9.5	.528	1.6	.333	3.0	.865	0.18	1.77	8.2	2.7	13.2
vs. Non-Playoff	38	28.4	8.1	.464	1.3	.388	3.3	.855	0.18	1.71	9.0	2.5	10.8
vs. East	30	29.5	8.6	.494	1.4	.366	3.2	.885	0.13	1.87	8.4	2.6	11.9
vs. West	52	29.8	9.0	.504	1.6	.350	3.1	.845	0.21	1.67	8.7	2.6	12.2
vs. Div.	24	29.3	9.3	.498	1.5	.378	2.8	.909	0.25	1.67	9.2	2.2	12.3
As Starter	82	29.7	8.8	.501	1.5	.355	3.1	.860	0.18	1.74	8.6	2.6	12.1
Off Bench	0	—	—	—	—	—	—	—	—	—	—	—	—
In wins	55	29.8	8.3	.529	1.2	.379	3.3	.832	0.20	2.04	9.1	2.7	12.0
In losses	27	29.3	9.9	.451	2.0	.327	2.9	.923	0.15	1.15	7.4	2.4	12.2

	G	Min	FGA	FG%	3PA	3P%	FTA	FT%	Blk	Stl	Ast	Reb	Pts
Pre All-Star	47	28.6	8.9	.508	1.5	.329	2.9	.853	0.17	1.60	8.6	2.6	12.0
Post All-Star	35	31.1	8.8	.490	1.5	.392	3.5	.868	0.20	1.94	8.6	2.6	12.2
November	14	28.9	10.2	.531	1.6	.182	2.9	.927	0.21	1.71	8.7	2.4	13.9
December	14	26.9	7.9	.450	1.4	.368	3.3	.804	0.14	2.07	7.3	2.2	10.3
January	14	30.6	8.5	.529	1.6	.455	2.6	.833	0.14	1.29	10.2	3.1	11.9
February	13	28.5	9.5	.455	1.5	.368	3.0	.872	0.38	0.85	7.6	3.3	11.8
March	16	32.9	9.4	.527	1.6	.480	2.9	.848	0.06	2.69	9.5	2.1	13.1
April	11	29.6	7.2	.494	1.3	.214	4.5	.878	0.18	1.64	7.7	2.7	11.3
0 Days Rest	19	31.3	8.1	.468	1.6	.300	3.3	.889	0.26	1.74	8.4	2.4	11.0
1 Days Rest	45	29.2	9.0	.533	1.4	.369	2.9	.854	0.20	1.78	8.6	2.8	12.6
2 Days Rest	12	29.0	8.4	.455	1.2	.286	3.4	.878	0.08	1.92	8.3	2.7	11.0
3+ Days Rest	6	29.2	10.5	.444	2.0	.500	3.8	.783	0.00	1.17	9.3	2.2	13.3

Last Five Seasons

	G	Min	FGA	FG%	3PA	3P%	FTA	FT%	Blk	Stl	Ast	Reb	Pts
Total	360	32.0	9.0	.524	1.9	.403	3.5	.837	0.19	1.72	9.4	2.7	13.1
Home	179	31.3	8.7	.546	1.8	.441	3.1	.849	0.26	1.69	9.8	2.8	13.0
Road	181	32.7	9.2	.504	1.9	.367	3.9	.828	0.12	1.75	9.0	2.6	13.1
vs. Playoff	192	32.9	9.5	.531	2.0	.407	3.6	.836	0.18	1.77	9.3	2.8	13.9
vs. Non-Playoff	168	31.0	8.3	.514	1.7	.398	3.4	.839	0.20	1.66	9.5	2.6	12.1
vs. East	123	32.5	9.0	.519	1.8	.389	3.7	.848	0.15	1.65	9.6	2.6	13.4
vs. West	237	31.7	8.9	.527	1.9	.410	3.4	.831	0.21	1.76	9.3	2.8	13.0
vs. Div.	107	31.8	9.4	.522	1.9	.395	3.4	.859	0.27	1.84	9.4	2.5	13.4
As Starter	360	32.0	9.0	.524	1.9	.403	3.5	.837	0.19	1.72	9.4	2.7	13.1
Off Bench	0	—	—	—	—	—	—	—	—	—	—	—	—
In wins	262	31.5	8.4	.552	1.6	.449	3.7	.841	0.19	1.86	9.7	2.8	13.1
In losses	98	33.3	10.5	.463	2.6	.331	3.0	.826	0.17	1.35	8.8	2.4	13.1

	G	Min	FGA	FG%	3PA	3P%	FTA	FT%	Blk	Stl	Ast	Reb	Pts
Pre All-Star	170	32.7	9.5	.532	2.2	.416	3.2	.846	0.16	1.70	9.9	2.6	13.7
Post All-Star	140	32.5	8.6	.526	1.7	.401	4.0	.836	0.19	1.78	9.6	2.8	13.0
Oct/Nov	43	33.0	10.0	.558	2.5	.434	3.4	.864	0.21	1.67	10.0	2.6	15.1
December	55	31.0	8.7	.532	2.0	.429	3.4	.834	0.16	1.60	8.9	2.5	12.8
January	56	34.3	9.6	.521	2.1	.393	2.9	.821	0.16	1.82	10.7	2.9	13.2
February	61	31.4	9.1	.504	2.0	.433	3.9	.861	0.26	1.70	9.5	3.0	13.4
March	80	32.6	8.9	.530	1.5	.359	3.8	.831	0.16	1.89	9.2	2.7	13.1
Apr/May	65	29.9	7.9	.504	1.5	.368	3.7	.817	0.18	1.57	8.6	2.7	11.5
0 Days Rest	86	32.3	9.0	.513	1.9	.356	3.3	.845	0.17	1.87	9.5	2.6	12.9
1 Days Rest	200	31.7	8.9	.533	1.8	.431	3.3	.832	0.20	1.67	9.4	2.8	13.0
2 Days Rest	47	32.3	9.1	.505	1.8	.321	4.0	.832	0.17	1.60	8.9	3.0	13.2
3+ Days Rest	27	32.6	9.3	.530	2.1	.482	4.0	.853	0.19	1.81	10.4	2.2	14.3

Predrag Stojakovic
Sacramento Kings — Guard-Forward

1999-2000 Per Game Averages

	G	Min	FGA	FG%	3PA	3P%	FTA	FT%	Blk	Stl	Ast	Reb	Pts
Total	74	23.6	9.7	.448	3.6	.375	2.1	.882	0.09	0.70	1.4	3.7	11.9
Home	39	24.1	9.8	.438	4.0	.355	1.9	.880	0.08	0.62	1.4	3.7	11.7
Road	35	23.2	9.6	.458	3.2	.402	2.2	.885	0.11	0.80	1.5	3.8	12.1
vs. Playoff	37	24.4	10.0	.450	3.5	.406	2.4	.922	0.03	0.62	1.4	3.9	12.7
vs. Non-Playoff	37	22.9	9.4	.445	3.8	.345	1.7	.825	0.16	0.78	1.4	3.5	11.0
vs. East	25	21.6	8.9	.413	3.2	.370	1.6	.897	0.12	0.52	1.3	3.4	10.0
vs. West	49	24.7	10.1	.464	3.8	.376	2.3	.877	0.08	0.80	1.5	3.9	12.8
vs. Div.	22	26.3	11.4	.490	4.3	.400	2.7	.933	0.14	0.95	1.6	4.0	15.5
As Starter	11	35.5	15.9	.411	5.5	.279	3.1	.882	0.00	1.09	2.1	5.5	17.4
Off Bench	63	21.6	8.6	.459	3.3	.403	1.9	.882	0.11	0.63	1.3	3.4	10.9
In wins	41	22.5	8.9	.449	3.8	.377	2.0	.841	0.12	0.78	1.6	3.4	11.1
In losses	33	25.1	10.7	.446	3.4	.372	2.2	.930	0.06	0.61	1.2	4.1	12.8

	G	Min	FGA	FG%	3PA	3P%	FTA	FT%	Blk	Stl	Ast	Reb	Pts
Pre All-Star	43	21.0	8.0	.426	3.3	.352	1.9	.863	0.12	0.65	1.3	3.5	9.6
Post All-Star	31	27.3	12.0	.468	4.0	.400	2.4	.904	0.06	0.77	1.6	4.0	15.0
November	12	21.1	8.1	.454	3.8	.333	1.0	.917	0.17	0.75	1.7	3.7	9.5
December	15	21.4	8.7	.446	3.1	.340	2.7	.780	0.13	0.53	1.2	3.6	10.9
January	11	19.0	6.8	.347	2.9	.344	1.7	1.000	0.09	0.55	1.1	3.3	7.5
February	13	27.8	10.8	.496	3.9	.392	2.1	.889	0.00	0.85	1.3	3.5	14.2
March	12	25.9	11.3	.449	4.1	.408	2.1	.880	0.08	0.92	1.5	3.4	13.7
April	11	26.7	12.5	.449	3.9	.419	2.6	.931	0.09	0.64	1.9	5.0	15.4
0 Days Rest	15	25.8	10.9	.472	3.9	.390	2.9	.932	0.13	0.87	1.9	4.3	14.5
1 Days Rest	44	22.9	9.7	.424	3.5	.353	1.8	.914	0.07	0.55	1.3	3.7	11.1
2 Days Rest	8	25.0	9.0	.542	3.6	.483	1.4	.636	0.25	1.13	1.6	3.3	12.4
3+ Days Rest	7	22.3	8.1	.439	3.3	.348	2.4	.765	0.00	0.86	1.3	3.1	10.1

Career (1998-99 thru 1999-2000)

	G	Min	FGA	FG%	3PA	3P%	FTA	FT%	Blk	Stl	Ast	Reb	Pts
Total	122	22.7	8.9	.424	3.6	.353	1.9	.872	0.11	0.76	1.5	3.4	10.5
Home	63	23.4	9.4	.420	4.1	.342	1.7	.888	0.14	0.75	1.5	3.5	10.8
Road	59	22.0	8.5	.429	3.1	.368	2.0	.858	0.08	0.78	1.4	3.3	10.2
vs. Playoff	61	23.5	9.0	.421	3.5	.369	1.9	.923	0.05	0.80	1.6	3.6	10.7
vs. Non-Playoff	61	22.0	8.8	.427	3.8	.338	1.8	.818	0.18	0.72	1.3	3.3	10.3
vs. East	29	21.5	8.8	.408	3.3	.371	1.3	.897	0.10	0.45	1.2	3.6	9.6
vs. West	93	23.1	9.0	.429	3.7	.348	2.0	.867	0.12	0.86	1.5	3.4	10.8
vs. Div.	42	24.4	9.6	.449	4.2	.369	2.4	.900	0.12	1.05	1.6	3.6	12.3
As Starter	12	35.5	15.7	.399	5.6	.284	3.8	.848	0.00	1.00	2.0	5.5	17.3
Off Bench	110	21.3	8.2	.429	3.4	.365	1.6	.878	0.10	0.74	1.4	3.2	9.7
In wins	67	22.2	8.6	.434	3.8	.362	1.9	.847	0.16	0.85	1.6	3.4	10.4
In losses	55	23.4	9.3	.412	3.5	.340	1.9	.903	0.05	0.65	1.3	3.5	10.5

	G	Min	FGA	FG%	3PA	3P%	FTA	FT%	Blk	Stl	Ast	Reb	Pts
Pre All-Star	43	21.0	8.0	.426	3.3	.352	1.9	.863	0.12	0.65	1.3	3.5	9.6
Post All-Star	31	27.3	12.0	.468	4.0	.400	2.4	.904	0.06	0.77	1.6	4.0	15.0
Oct/Nov	12	21.1	8.1	.454	3.8	.333	1.0	.917	0.17	0.75	1.7	3.7	9.5
December	15	21.4	8.7	.446	3.1	.340	2.7	.780	0.13	0.53	1.2	3.6	10.9
January	11	19.0	6.8	.347	2.9	.344	1.7	1.000	0.09	0.55	1.1	3.3	7.5
February	25	25.2	9.7	.449	4.0	.354	1.2	.897	0.04	0.68	1.3	3.4	11.2
March	30	22.0	8.6	.438	3.6	.380	1.6	.872	0.07	0.87	1.5	2.8	10.3
Apr/May	29	24.1	9.9	.390	3.9	.342	2.7	.873	0.21	0.93	1.8	4.0	11.4
0 Days Rest	31	23.0	8.9	.425	3.7	.330	2.5	.873	0.13	0.84	2.0	3.5	11.0
1 Days Rest	67	22.4	9.1	.413	3.7	.355	1.7	.901	0.10	0.66	1.3	3.6	11.1
2 Days Rest	14	24.5	8.9	.484	3.6	.420	1.3	.778	0.21	1.14	1.6	3.5	11.1
3+ Days Rest	10	21.6	7.9	.405	3.2	.313	1.9	.789	0.00	0.70	1.0	2.4	8.9

Damon Stoudamire
Portland Trail Blazers — Guard

1999-2000 Per Game Averages

	G	Min	FGA	FG%	3PA	3P%	FTA	FT%	Blk	Stl	Ast	Reb	Pts
Total	78	30.4	11.5	.432	2.7	.377	1.9	.841	0.01	0.99	5.2	3.1	12.5
Home	37	30.2	11.5	.447	2.6	.365	1.5	.877	0.00	0.97	4.9	2.8	12.6
Road	41	30.6	11.4	.418	2.8	.388	2.1	.818	0.02	1.00	5.4	3.4	12.4
vs. Playoff	42	31.1	11.2	.418	2.5	.381	1.9	.873	0.02	0.88	5.3	3.0	12.7
vs. Non-Playoff	36	29.6	11.8	.447	3.0	.374	1.8	.803	0.00	1.11	5.0	3.3	13.1
vs. East	27	30.5	11.6	.462	3.0	.415	1.4	.949	0.00	1.07	5.5	2.7	13.4
vs. West	51	30.4	11.4	.416	2.5	.354	2.1	.802	0.02	0.94	5.0	3.3	12.0
vs. Div.	24	31.6	12.1	.448	2.7	.354	2.3	.873	0.04	0.79	5.2	3.6	13.8
As Starter	78	30.4	11.5	.432	2.7	.377	1.9	.841	0.01	0.99	5.2	3.1	12.5
Off Bench	0	—	—	—	—	—	—	—	—	—	—	—	—
In wins	57	30.0	11.2	.441	2.6	.342	1.9	.855	0.00	1.04	5.3	3.1	12.4
In losses	21	31.4	12.1	.408	3.1	.455	1.7	.800	0.05	0.86	4.8	3.2	12.7

	G	Min	FGA	FG%	3PA	3P%	FTA	FT%	Blk	Stl	Ast	Reb	Pts
Pre All-Star	47	30.0	11.3	.446	2.6	.361	1.9	.830	0.02	0.91	5.5	2.9	12.5
Post All-Star	31	31.0	11.8	.411	2.9	.400	1.8	.860	0.00	1.10	4.7	3.4	12.4
November	16	30.5	12.3	.437	3.0	.313	1.9	.800	0.00	1.06	6.4	3.6	13.2
December	12	28.2	9.7	.431	2.8	.471	1.6	.842	0.08	0.50	4.8	2.4	11.0
January	14	30.5	11.6	.466	1.8	.280	2.4	.824	0.00	1.29	4.9	2.9	13.4
February	13	32.2	11.8	.448	2.7	.400	2.2	.893	0.00	1.15	5.1	3.0	13.6
March	12	31.8	11.3	.382	2.6	.387	2.1	.840	0.00	0.75	5.5	3.6	11.4
April	11	28.9	11.6	.414	3.5	.410	0.8	.889	0.00	1.09	4.2	3.1	11.8
0 Days Rest	22	29.2	11.8	.458	3.1	.420	2.1	.872	0.00	0.68	5.2	2.6	14.0
1 Days Rest	35	30.9	11.1	.409	2.4	.349	1.7	.845	0.03	1.09	5.1	3.2	11.3
2 Days Rest	12	31.0	12.3	.473	3.5	.357	1.8	.727	0.00	1.17	5.2	4.1	14.3
3+ Days Rest	9	30.8	10.8	.392	2.0	.389	2.0	.889	0.00	1.11	5.6	2.6	11.0

Career (1995-96 thru 1999-2000)

	G	Min	FGA	FG%	3PA	3P%	FTA	FT%	Blk	Stl	Ast	Reb	Pts
Total	350	37.3	14.7	.413	4.3	.351	3.6	.811	0.13	1.31	7.6	3.8	16.6
Home	174	37.8	15.0	.422	4.2	.356	3.4	.801	0.14	1.30	8.2	3.8	16.9
Road	176	36.8	14.4	.404	4.4	.347	3.7	.821	0.11	1.32	7.0	3.7	16.2
vs. Playoff	195	37.7	14.8	.420	4.3	.347	3.2	.812	0.10	1.36	7.6	3.7	16.5
vs. Non-Playoff	155	36.9	14.7	.404	4.1	.358	4.0	.810	0.16	1.25	7.6	3.9	16.6
vs. East	166	39.3	16.0	.412	4.7	.340	4.0	.825	0.14	1.51	8.1	3.9	18.0
vs. West	184	35.5	13.6	.415	3.9	.364	3.2	.795	0.11	1.14	7.1	3.7	15.2
vs. Div.	126	37.8	14.8	.409	4.3	.338	3.6	.799	0.10	1.33	7.5	4.0	16.5
As Starter	350	37.3	14.7	.413	4.3	.351	3.6	.811	0.13	1.31	7.6	3.8	16.6
Off Bench	0	—	—	—	—	—	—	—	—	—	—	—	—
In wins	165	35.1	13.6	.435	3.7	.369	3.5	.810	0.13	1.27	7.3	3.7	16.1
In losses	185	39.3	15.7	.396	4.8	.339	3.6	.813	0.12	1.36	7.9	3.8	17.0

	G	Min	FGA	FG%	3PA	3P%	FTA	FT%	Blk	Stl	Ast	Reb	Pts
Pre All-Star	186	38.3	15.4	.417	4.3	.353	3.9	.820	0.15	1.37	7.8	3.9	17.6
Post All-Star	114	37.5	14.6	.413	4.8	.360	3.6	.820	0.11	1.37	7.8	3.8	16.7
Oct/Nov	60	38.1	14.9	.413	4.0	.321	3.8	.828	0.12	1.62	7.8	4.3	16.7
December	56	37.8	15.2	.406	4.2	.371	4.2	.798	0.14	1.02	7.5	3.9	17.2
January	55	38.9	16.4	.437	4.6	.385	3.7	.813	0.22	1.45	8.1	3.7	19.1
February	62	37.7	14.5	.398	4.3	.330	3.8	.831	0.08	1.53	7.5	3.5	16.2
March	65	37.0	13.9	.423	4.4	.382	3.1	.749	0.14	1.08	7.7	3.8	15.8
Apr/May	52	34.0	13.5	.397	4.1	.312	2.9	.859	0.06	1.17	6.9	3.4	14.4
0 Days Rest	88	36.0	14.0	.398	4.1	.337	3.4	.774	0.09	1.06	7.1	3.2	15.1
1 Days Rest	179	37.8	14.9	.418	4.3	.348	3.3	.817	0.14	1.42	7.9	3.9	16.6
2 Days Rest	54	37.8	15.3	.430	4.7	.364	4.2	.850	0.17	1.30	7.7	4.5	18.5
3+ Days Rest	29	37.4	14.5	.397	3.9	.393	4.7	.803	0.07	1.48	6.8	3.4	16.8

Erick Strickland
Dallas Mavericks — Guard

1999-2000 Per Game Averages

	G	Min	FGA	FG%	3PA	3P%	FTA	FT%	Blk	Stl	Ast	Reb	Pts
Total	68	29.8	10.7	.433	2.7	.392	2.9	.831	0.19	1.54	3.1	4.8	12.8
Home	35	30.5	11.6	.461	2.8	.388	2.8	.816	0.26	1.43	3.2	5.0	14.1
Road	33	29.0	9.8	.398	2.7	.398	2.9	.845	0.12	1.67	3.0	4.5	11.4
vs. Playoff	37	28.8	10.4	.465	3.0	.402	2.8	.838	0.19	1.57	2.9	4.5	13.2
vs. Non-Playoff	31	31.0	11.2	.398	2.4	.378	2.9	.822	0.19	1.52	3.4	5.0	12.2
vs. East	25	27.1	10.1	.411	2.7	.397	2.0	.800	0.24	1.48	3.3	4.2	11.0
vs. West	43	31.3	11.1	.444	2.7	.390	3.4	.841	0.16	1.58	3.0	5.1	13.8
vs. Div.	19	32.2	10.8	.413	2.3	.349	3.1	.879	0.21	1.32	2.6	4.7	12.4
As Starter	67	29.9	10.7	.432	2.7	.396	2.9	.828	0.19	1.57	3.1	4.8	12.7
Off Bench	1	20.0	12.0	.500	4.0	.250	3.0	1.000	0.00	0.00	2.0	2.0	16.0
In wins	36	30.8	11.3	.471	2.8	.410	3.8	.822	0.25	1.39	3.0	5.2	14.4
In losses	32	28.7	10.1	.385	2.7	.372	1.9	.850	0.13	1.72	3.2	4.3	10.3
Pre All-Star	34	28.5	9.6	.417	2.1	.366	2.5	.859	0.15	1.47	3.4	4.9	10.9
Post All-Star	34	31.1	11.9	.446	3.4	.409	3.2	.809	0.24	1.62	2.8	4.6	14.6
November	15	32.1	10.5	.376	2.3	.324	3.1	.915	0.27	1.60	3.3	5.5	11.5
December	1	13.0	3.0	.000	0.0	—	0.0	—	0.00	1.00	4.0	3.0	0.0
January	13	24.4	8.2	.421	1.5	.300	1.6	.810	0.08	1.38	3.9	4.2	8.7
February	13	27.6	10.5	.460	3.5	.455	3.5	.800	0.15	1.00	2.5	4.3	14.0
March	16	32.8	12.4	.447	3.8	.400	2.9	.787	0.19	2.13	2.9	4.1	14.9
April	10	33.0	12.7	.472	2.6	.462	3.5	.829	0.30	1.50	2.8	6.0	16.1
0 Days Rest	14	30.7	10.1	.401	2.9	.317	2.6	.806	0.21	1.93	3.7	4.9	11.1
1 Days Rest	38	30.6	11.4	.451	2.9	.402	3.3	.847	0.16	1.55	2.7	5.2	14.3
2 Days Rest	11	27.4	10.3	.451	2.1	.478	1.4	.800	0.27	1.00	3.5	3.2	11.4
3+ Days Rest	5	26.4	8.0	.300	2.0	.400	4.0	.800	0.20	1.60	3.8	4.2	8.8

Career (1996-97 thru 1999-2000)

	G	Min	FGA	FG%	3PA	3P%	FTA	FT%	Blk	Stl	Ast	Reb	Pts
Total	196	24.8	9.0	.400	2.6	.334	2.2	.814	0.14	1.16	2.6	3.4	9.8
Home	101	25.7	9.8	.423	2.8	.367	2.2	.849	0.19	1.18	2.8	3.5	11.2
Road	95	23.7	8.1	.371	2.3	.292	2.2	.777	0.09	1.15	2.4	3.2	8.4
vs. Playoff	118	25.0	9.0	.390	2.8	.319	2.1	.831	0.16	1.19	2.6	3.3	9.7
vs. Non-Playoff	78	24.5	9.0	.415	2.2	.363	2.3	.790	0.12	1.12	2.6	3.4	10.1
vs. East	59	25.6	9.2	.379	2.8	.321	1.9	.836	0.19	1.15	2.9	3.2	9.5
vs. West	137	24.4	8.9	.409	2.4	.340	2.3	.806	0.12	1.17	2.5	3.4	10.0
vs. Div.	66	24.4	8.9	.389	2.4	.312	2.3	.810	0.12	1.08	2.2	3.3	9.5
As Starter	103	31.2	10.9	.421	2.9	.357	2.8	.832	0.22	1.40	3.1	4.4	12.5
Off Bench	93	17.7	6.9	.364	2.2	.300	1.5	.777	0.05	0.90	2.0	2.2	6.8
In wins	71	27.8	10.1	.447	2.4	.374	3.1	.828	0.18	1.27	3.0	3.9	12.5
In losses	125	23.1	8.4	.368	2.6	.313	1.6	.798	0.12	1.10	2.4	3.0	8.3
Pre All-Star	70	24.5	8.7	.380	2.6	.339	1.9	.848	0.13	1.20	2.8	3.4	9.1
Post All-Star	93	27.7	10.0	.413	2.8	.337	2.4	.793	0.18	1.12	2.7	3.6	11.2
Oct/Nov	28	23.7	7.8	.381	2.3	.338	2.2	.852	0.18	1.25	2.7	3.5	8.6
December	8	21.4	8.8	.257	3.0	.292	0.9	1.000	0.25	0.63	2.5	2.5	6.3
January	26	24.9	8.7	.370	2.3	.305	1.4	.838	0.08	1.27	3.1	3.7	8.3
February	42	22.8	8.8	.418	2.8	.328	2.2	.830	0.10	0.90	2.0	2.9	10.1
March	53	27.6	9.8	.411	2.8	.333	2.5	.800	0.15	1.26	3.0	3.6	11.0
Apr/May	39	24.4	9.3	.423	2.1	.373	2.3	.767	0.18	1.28	2.4	3.4	10.5
0 Days Rest	42	25.3	8.8	.374	2.7	.259	2.1	.747	0.14	1.31	2.7	3.6	8.8
1 Days Rest	107	25.6	9.4	.415	2.6	.357	2.5	.846	0.14	1.16	2.6	3.5	10.9
2 Days Rest	26	25.9	9.6	.390	2.6	.382	1.3	.788	0.19	1.04	3.2	3.2	9.5
3+ Days Rest	21	18.2	6.6	.381	1.9	.300	1.8	.757	0.10	1.05	1.8	2.2	7.0

Rod Strickland
Washington Wizards — Guard

1999-2000 Per Game Averages

	G	Min	FGA	FG%	3PA	3P%	FTA	FT%	Blk	Stl	Ast	Reb	Pts
Total	69	31.7	11.0	.429	0.3	.048	4.4	.702	0.26	1.36	7.5	3.8	12.6
Home	35	32.8	11.6	.443	0.3	.000	4.9	.724	0.29	1.43	7.9	4.1	13.8
Road	34	30.6	10.5	.413	0.3	.100	4.0	.674	0.24	1.29	7.2	3.4	11.4
vs. Playoff	41	31.9	10.8	.437	0.3	.000	4.6	.700	0.37	1.32	7.6	3.7	12.7
vs. Non-Playoff	28	31.4	11.4	.418	0.3	.125	4.1	.704	0.11	1.43	7.4	3.9	12.4
vs. East	44	31.9	11.1	.457	0.3	.091	4.6	.682	0.25	1.32	7.9	4.2	13.3
vs. West	25	31.3	11.0	.380	0.4	.000	4.2	.740	0.28	1.44	6.9	2.9	11.4
vs. Div.	19	31.8	9.9	.429	0.4	.143	4.4	.667	0.26	1.21	7.3	3.8	11.5
As Starter	67	31.8	11.1	.429	0.3	.050	4.5	.703	0.27	1.37	7.6	3.8	12.7
Off Bench	2	28.5	10.0	.450	0.5	.000	1.0	.500	0.00	1.00	4.5	2.5	9.5
In wins	23	31.7	10.4	.452	0.3	.000	4.5	.777	0.39	1.43	8.0	4.0	12.9
In losses	46	31.7	11.4	.419	0.3	.067	4.4	.663	0.20	1.33	7.3	3.7	12.5
Pre All-Star	49	32.4	11.2	.438	0.3	.059	5.0	.705	0.18	1.35	7.5	4.3	13.4
Post All-Star	20	30.0	10.6	.406	0.2	.000	3.1	.689	0.45	1.40	7.5	2.5	10.7
November	15	30.1	9.9	.372	0.4	.167	4.1	.629	0.13	1.20	7.1	3.7	10.0
December	15	33.0	10.8	.463	0.4	.000	4.5	.662	0.33	1.39	6.9	3.3	13.0
January	14	34.2	12.9	.461	0.3	.000	5.8	.790	0.29	1.14	7.9	4.4	16.4
February	12	32.8	12.5	.420	0.4	.000	4.8	.741	0.33	1.25	7.3	4.3	14.1
March	13	28.5	9.4	.418	0.0	—	2.8	.639	0.46	1.38	7.8	2.4	9.6
April	0	—	—	—	—	—	—	—	—	—	—	—	—
0 Days Rest	20	31.9	11.4	.425	0.5	.111	4.6	.747	0.30	1.50	6.8	4.0	13.2
1 Days Rest	31	32.4	10.9	.404	0.3	.000	4.0	.688	0.32	1.48	7.8	3.3	11.6
2 Days Rest	12	29.8	11.0	.477	0.2	.000	6.1	.699	0.08	1.25	6.7	4.8	14.8
3+ Days Rest	6	31.3	10.5	.476	0.2	.000	2.7	.563	0.17	0.50	10.2	3.2	11.5

Last Five Seasons

	G	Min	FGA	FG%	3PA	3P%	FTA	FT%	Blk	Stl	Ast	Reb	Pts
Total	338	36.6	13.7	.444	0.9	.254	5.8	.712	0.23	1.59	9.2	4.5	16.5
Home	169	36.8	13.8	.452	0.8	.252	6.0	.720	0.22	1.60	9.3	4.7	17.0
Road	169	36.4	13.6	.436	0.9	.256	5.6	.703	0.24	1.57	9.2	4.3	16.0
vs. Playoff	181	36.9	13.8	.434	0.9	.223	5.6	.705	0.26	1.46	9.1	4.4	16.1
vs. Non-Playoff	157	36.2	13.6	.457	0.9	.289	6.0	.719	0.20	1.73	9.4	4.5	17.0
vs. East	207	36.4	13.5	.446	0.8	.222	5.7	.713	0.21	1.66	9.0	4.5	16.3
vs. West	131	36.8	14.0	.442	1.1	.291	5.9	.709	0.27	1.47	9.5	4.5	16.8
vs. Div.	101	36.6	13.0	.444	0.8	.207	5.9	.714	0.18	1.71	8.8	4.3	15.9
As Starter	330	36.8	13.7	.445	0.9	.256	5.8	.715	0.24	1.61	9.3	4.5	16.6
Off Bench	8	28.5	12.5	.430	0.8	.167	4.6	.541	0.00	0.75	5.4	4.0	13.4
In wins	158	36.4	13.4	.465	0.8	.299	6.4	.730	0.27	1.75	9.8	4.6	17.4
In losses	180	36.8	13.9	.427	1.0	.221	5.2	.692	0.20	1.44	8.8	4.3	15.7
Pre All-Star	190	36.7	13.7	.448	1.0	.264	5.6	.686	0.23	1.54	9.0	4.5	16.4
Post All-Star	104	36.1	13.7	.450	0.7	.213	6.2	.742	0.29	1.62	9.3	4.3	17.1
Oct/Nov	61	36.1	13.2	.434	1.0	.302	5.4	.659	0.25	1.59	8.7	4.3	15.3
December	59	37.0	13.4	.441	1.1	.262	5.6	.683	0.29	1.64	9.4	4.4	15.9
January	55	37.4	14.0	.453	0.8	.222	6.0	.715	0.15	1.42	8.9	4.7	17.2
February	56	36.8	14.9	.449	0.8	.279	6.0	.751	0.20	1.68	9.0	4.8	18.1
March	65	35.2	12.7	.432	0.5	.212	5.8	.724	0.29	1.52	9.6	3.9	15.3
Apr/May	42	37.4	14.1	.463	1.2	.220	6.0	.744	0.19	1.69	9.3	4.8	17.8
0 Days Rest	91	37.0	14.1	.448	0.9	.272	6.0	.712	0.23	1.60	8.9	4.3	17.2
1 Days Rest	158	36.3	13.5	.446	0.8	.221	5.6	.705	0.22	1.61	9.3	4.4	16.2
2 Days Rest	58	36.7	13.8	.443	0.9	.358	6.4	.728	0.31	1.69	8.9	4.8	17.2
3+ Days Rest	31	36.3	13.3	.425	1.1	.176	4.7	.712	0.16	1.19	10.2	4.7	14.8

Bob Sura

1999-2000 Per Game Averages

	G	Min	FGA	FG%	3PA	3P%	FTA	FT%	Blk	Stl	Ast	Reb	Pts		G	Min	FGA	FG%	3PA	3P%	FTA	FT%	Blk	Stl	Ast	Reb	Pts
Total	73	30.4	11.2	.437	4.5	.367	3.4	.697	0.26	1.25	3.9	3.9	13.8	Pre All-Star	45	32.4	11.9	.448	4.9	.419	4.0	.703	0.31	1.53	4.5	4.1	15.5
Home	37	29.7	11.5	.448	4.6	.388	3.6	.741	0.38	1.54	4.1	4.4	14.8	Post All-Star	28	27.0	10.0	.416	3.9	.264	2.5	.681	0.18	0.79	2.9	3.7	11.1
Road	36	31.0	10.8	.424	4.5	.346	3.2	.647	0.14	0.94	3.7	3.5	12.8	November	13	32.2	11.5	.443	4.2	.418	3.7	.771	0.31	1.77	4.5	2.9	14.8
vs. Playoff	41	30.7	11.7	.425	4.8	.376	3.3	.679	0.29	1.15	3.8	3.8	13.9	December	16	32.4	13.2	.474	5.3	.459	3.6	.632	0.38	1.13	3.7	4.8	17.2
vs. Non-Playoff	32	29.9	10.5	.454	4.2	.356	3.7	.718	0.22	1.38	4.0	4.1	13.7	January	15	32.9	10.9	.423	5.2	.385	4.9	.699	0.27	1.47	5.3	4.2	14.6
vs. East	49	30.3	11.7	.441	4.8	.376	3.8	.701	0.24	1.45	3.6	3.9	14.8	February	3	23.3	8.0	.333	3.7	.091	2.0	1.000	0.00	2.67	2.7	5.0	7.7
vs. West	24	30.5	10.0	.427	4.1	.347	2.7	.688	0.29	0.83	4.4	4.1	11.8	March	15	28.7	9.9	.423	3.5	.308	2.7	.600	0.33	0.73	3.7	4.4	11.1
vs. Div.	25	29.5	13.0	.431	4.9	.377	3.8	.723	0.24	1.20	3.0	3.6	15.8	April	11	26.0	10.8	.420	4.6	.255	2.5	.778	0.00	0.82	2.2	2.6	12.2
As Starter	45	32.4	11.9	.448	4.9	.419	4.0	.703	0.31	1.53	4.5	4.1	15.5	0 Days Rest	21	30.7	11.8	.460	4.7	.404	4.0	.714	0.33	1.05	4.2	4.2	15.6
Off Bench	28	27.0	10.0	.416	3.9	.264	2.5	.681	0.18	0.79	2.9	3.7	11.1	1 Days Rest	32	30.6	10.9	.451	4.5	.364	3.6	.632	0.25	0.81	3.7	3.9	13.8
In wins	30	30.7	10.7	.484	4.5	.407	3.7	.714	0.27	1.67	4.6	4.4	14.9	2 Days Rest	13	30.1	10.8	.383	4.7	.361	3.0	.846	0.15	2.31	4.4	3.8	12.5
In losses	43	30.1	11.5	.406	4.6	.340	3.2	.683	0.26	0.95	3.4	3.7	13.1	3+ Days Rest	7	28.9	10.9	.395	4.1	.276	2.0	.714	0.29	1.86	3.0	3.7	11.1

Career (1995-96 thru 1999-2000)

	G	Min	FGA	FG%	3PA	3P%	FTA	FT%	Blk	Stl	Ast	Reb	Pts		G	Min	FGA	FG%	3PA	3P%	FTA	FT%	Blk	Stl	Ast	Reb	Pts
Total	330	22.5	6.7	.415	2.1	.339	2.9	.644	0.28	0.99	3.7	2.8	8.1	Pre All-Star	148	22.7	7.4	.429	2.4	.387	2.9	.626	0.23	1.05	3.8	2.9	9.0
Home	165	22.1	6.8	.432	2.0	.372	3.0	.675	0.36	1.05	4.0	3.0	8.6	Post All-Star	132	24.4	6.8	.417	2.1	.300	3.2	.667	0.35	0.95	3.9	3.0	8.5
Road	165	22.9	6.6	.397	2.1	.306	2.7	.610	0.21	0.93	3.4	2.6	7.5	Oct/Nov	48	23.6	7.7	.427	2.2	.404	2.9	.624	0.21	1.17	4.0	2.7	9.3
vs. Playoff	184	23.1	6.7	.407	2.2	.346	2.7	.622	0.28	0.95	3.9	2.8	7.9	December	42	24.1	8.1	.460	2.8	.424	2.7	.634	0.24	0.88	3.6	3.5	10.3
vs. Non-Playoff	146	21.7	6.6	.424	1.9	.328	3.0	.670	0.29	1.05	3.5	2.8	8.3	January	47	21.5	6.8	.405	2.4	.369	2.9	.609	0.26	1.09	3.9	2.6	8.2
vs. East	235	22.6	6.6	.415	2.1	.344	3.0	.651	0.26	1.02	3.6	2.8	8.2	February	50	20.0	5.4	.433	1.4	.306	3.2	.621	0.24	1.06	3.5	2.6	7.7
vs. West	95	22.3	6.8	.415	2.1	.327	2.4	.623	0.35	0.92	4.0	2.8	7.8	March	80	23.0	6.7	.384	1.8	.280	2.9	.655	0.43	0.98	4.0	2.8	7.5
vs. Div.	124	22.2	6.9	.412	2.1	.328	3.0	.648	0.20	0.94	3.3	2.6	8.4	Apr/May	63	22.7	5.9	.402	2.1	.267	2.6	.708	0.25	0.83	3.4	2.9	7.1
As Starter	81	33.6	10.7	.437	3.8	.379	4.1	.696	0.42	1.48	5.0	4.2	13.7	0 Days Rest	90	23.7	6.9	.425	2.3	.337	3.2	.637	0.24	0.97	3.9	3.0	8.7
Off Bench	249	18.9	5.4	.401	1.5	.304	2.5	.617	0.24	0.83	3.2	2.3	6.3	1 Days Rest	156	21.9	6.5	.419	2.0	.350	2.8	.600	0.30	0.92	3.6	2.6	7.8
In wins	164	21.4	6.2	.452	1.8	.378	2.9	.661	0.36	0.98	3.9	3.0	8.2	2 Days Rest	56	22.3	6.9	.408	2.0	.357	2.9	.673	0.30	1.13	3.8	3.0	8.3
In losses	166	23.6	7.2	.384	2.3	.308	2.9	.628	0.21	1.01	3.6	2.7	8.0	3+ Days Rest	28	22.3	6.7	.372	2.0	.250	2.1	.707	0.29	1.21	3.8	2.8	7.3

Wally Szczerbiak

1999-2000 Per Game Averages

	G	Min	FGA	FG%	3PA	3P%	FTA	FT%	Blk	Stl	Ast	Reb	Pts		G	Min	FGA	FG%	3PA	3P%	FTA	FT%	Blk	Stl	Ast	Reb	Pts
Total	73	29.7	9.2	.511	1.1	.359	2.2	.826	0.32	0.79	2.8	3.7	11.6	Pre All-Star	38	25.6	8.1	.458	0.7	.240	1.9	.811	0.29	0.71	2.1	3.1	9.2
Home	35	29.7	9.2	.526	1.4	.354	2.2	.896	0.37	0.74	2.9	3.4	12.2	Post All-Star	35	34.3	10.3	.557	1.5	.415	2.5	.839	0.34	0.89	3.5	4.5	14.2
Road	38	29.7	9.1	.497	0.8	.367	2.2	.762	0.26	0.84	2.6	4.0	11.0	November	12	34.2	11.0	.492	1.3	.133	3.4	.854	0.42	1.25	3.0	4.1	13.9
vs. Playoff	39	28.3	8.8	.493	1.1	.341	1.9	.803	0.36	0.82	2.6	3.6	10.7	December	10	30.8	9.7	.433	0.4	.250	2.1	.667	0.30	0.70	2.3	4.4	9.9
vs. Non-Playoff	34	31.4	9.5	.531	1.0	.382	2.5	.847	0.26	0.76	2.9	3.8	12.6	January	11	13.2	4.2	.391	0.4	.250	0.3	1.000	0.18	0.27	0.9	1.0	3.6
vs. East	26	30.2	9.2	.521	1.1	.379	2.0	.830	0.31	0.73	2.6	3.8	11.7	February	14	27.4	8.5	.546	0.9	.538	2.0	.857	0.29	0.43	2.7	3.9	11.5
vs. West	47	29.5	9.1	.506	1.0	.347	2.3	.824	0.32	0.83	2.8	3.7	11.5	March	16	37.4	9.9	.544	1.6	.423	2.8	.864	0.38	1.06	4.0	4.8	13.8
vs. Div.	22	29.7	8.6	.484	0.8	.333	2.3	.882	0.32	0.77	3.0	3.2	10.7	April	10	32.6	11.7	.564	1.6	.375	2.4	.792	0.30	1.00	3.0	3.7	15.7
As Starter	53	34.7	10.6	.526	1.3	.343	2.6	.814	0.34	0.98	3.4	4.6	13.7	0 Days Rest	16	29.6	8.9	.479	0.9	.214	2.0	.875	0.25	0.63	2.8	3.5	10.4
Off Bench	20	16.5	5.4	.435	0.6	.455	1.1	.905	0.25	0.30	1.2	1.5	5.9	1 Days Rest	44	30.2	9.1	.535	1.0	.356	2.2	.813	0.39	0.91	2.8	3.5	11.9
In wins	45	30.3	9.0	.516	1.2	.327	2.4	.833	0.31	0.71	3.1	3.5	11.7	2 Days Rest	4	32.5	11.8	.511	2.5	.600	2.3	.889	0.00	1.00	5.0	4.0	15.5
In losses	28	28.9	9.4	.504	0.9	.423	1.9	.811	0.32	0.93	2.2	4.1	11.4	3+ Days Rest	9	26.3	8.9	.450	1.0	.333	2.7	.792	0.22	0.44	1.4	2.7	10.4

Maurice Taylor

1999-2000 Per Game Averages

	G	Min	FGA	FG%	3PA	3P%	FTA	FT%	Blk	Stl	Ast	Reb	Pts
Total	62	35.9	15.9	.464	0.1	.125	3.2	.711	0.77	0.82	1.6	6.5	17.1
Home	32	36.2	15.9	.464	0.2	.000	3.5	.732	0.75	0.84	1.5	7.0	17.3
Road	30	35.7	16.0	.463	0.1	.333	3.0	.685	0.80	0.80	1.7	5.9	16.9
vs. Playoff	34	35.8	16.1	.444	0.1	.000	2.8	.695	0.53	1.09	1.3	6.7	16.3
vs. Non-Playoff	28	36.1	15.7	.487	0.1	.250	3.8	.726	1.07	0.50	2.0	6.2	18.1
vs. East	23	37.4	16.0	.470	0.2	.200	3.1	.704	0.65	0.70	1.8	7.0	17.3
vs. West	39	35.0	15.9	.460	0.1	.000	3.3	.715	0.85	0.90	1.5	6.2	17.0
vs. Div.	18	34.8	15.8	.435	0.1	.000	2.6	.587	0.72	1.06	1.3	6.2	15.3
As Starter	60	36.1	15.9	.464	0.1	.125	3.2	.706	0.78	0.78	1.7	6.4	17.1
Off Bench	2	32.0	17.0	.441	0.0	—	3.5	.857	0.50	2.00	1.0	7.0	18.0
In wins	10	38.1	16.2	.481	0.1	.000	3.3	.697	1.20	0.40	2.0	6.8	17.9
In losses	52	35.5	15.9	.460	0.1	.143	3.2	.714	0.69	0.90	1.6	6.4	16.9
Pre All-Star	40	36.2	16.2	.466	0.2	.143	3.4	.716	0.90	0.75	1.6	6.6	17.5
Post All-Star	22	35.4	15.5	.459	0.0	.000	3.0	.701	0.55	0.95	1.8	6.3	16.4
November	7	30.3	14.0	.469	0.1	.000	3.6	.760	1.29	0.57	1.1	5.4	15.9
December	14	37.1	16.4	.489	0.2	.000	4.1	.690	0.71	0.86	1.6	6.4	18.9
January	14	39.1	16.7	.436	0.1	.500	3.1	.773	1.00	0.36	1.9	7.6	17.1
February	14	34.1	16.6	.448	0.1	.000	1.9	.692	0.36	1.36	1.1	5.1	16.1
March	9	36.9	15.1	.478	0.0	—	3.6	.594	1.00	0.89	2.7	7.2	16.6
April	4	35.0	14.8	.492	0.0	—	4.0	.813	0.25	0.75	1.0	7.8	17.8
0 Days Rest	13	36.3	15.8	.454	0.2	.500	2.4	.613	0.46	1.08	1.4	6.2	15.8
1 Days Rest	31	37.6	16.4	.464	0.2	.000	4.2	.754	0.97	0.74	1.9	6.9	18.4
2 Days Rest	9	36.6	17.1	.474	0.1	.000	2.4	.636	0.44	0.89	1.3	5.6	17.8
3+ Days Rest	9	29.0	13.3	.467	0.0	—	2.0	.667	0.89	0.67	1.4	6.1	13.8

Career (1997-98 thru 1999-2000)

	G	Min	FGA	FG%	3PA	3P%	FTA	FT%	Blk	Stl	Ast	Reb	Pts
Total	179	29.3	13.1	.466	0.1	.133	3.6	.716	0.65	0.56	1.2	5.2	14.8
Home	93	29.8	13.5	.475	0.1	.111	3.7	.712	0.72	0.66	1.4	4.7	14.1
Road	86	28.7	12.6	.456	0.1	.167	3.5	.720	0.58	0.47	1.4	4.7	14.1
vs. Playoff	102	28.7	13.0	.464	0.1	.000	3.5	.724	0.56	0.60	1.1	5.0	14.6
vs. Non-Playoff	77	30.1	13.1	.469	0.1	.250	3.8	.705	0.78	0.52	1.4	5.5	15.0
vs. East	51	31.0	13.4	.471	0.1	.200	3.5	.721	0.67	0.61	1.4	5.8	15.1
vs. West	128	28.6	12.9	.464	0.1	.100	3.7	.714	0.65	0.55	1.2	5.0	14.7
vs. Div.	57	27.4	12.4	.459	0.0	.000	3.2	.654	0.54	0.60	0.9	4.9	13.5
As Starter	108	34.5	15.4	.463	0.1	.143	3.8	.723	0.70	0.59	1.5	5.9	17.0
Off Bench	71	21.4	9.5	.473	0.0	.000	3.4	.704	0.58	0.52	0.8	4.2	11.4
In wins	35	29.3	13.1	.478	0.1	.500	4.0	.719	0.94	0.51	1.3	5.6	15.5
In losses	144	29.3	13.0	.463	0.1	.077	3.6	.715	0.58	0.58	1.2	5.2	14.6
Pre All-Star	84	27.8	12.4	.469	0.1	.125	3.3	.697	0.77	0.57	1.1	5.2	13.9
Post All-Star	49	28.6	12.7	.467	0.0	.000	3.5	.731	0.47	0.76	1.3	5.3	14.4
Oct/Nov	19	21.3	9.2	.514	0.1	.000	2.6	.740	0.95	0.26	0.6	4.1	11.4
December	28	28.1	12.1	.474	0.1	.000	3.3	.645	0.61	0.57	1.1	5.0	13.6
January	30	30.4	13.8	.451	0.1	.333	3.9	.720	0.90	0.60	1.4	6.0	15.3
February	34	30.4	13.9	.477	0.1	.000	2.9	.758	0.44	0.85	1.0	5.3	15.4
March	41	30.0	12.5	.463	0.0	.000	4.1	.749	0.59	0.46	1.8	4.9	14.6
Apr/May	27	32.5	15.7	.448	0.1	.250	4.6	.677	0.59	0.52	1.1	6.0	17.2
0 Days Rest	43	29.0	13.3	.474	0.1	.400	3.7	.684	0.63	0.72	1.1	4.7	15.2
1 Days Rest	88	30.7	13.3	.472	0.1	.000	3.9	.737	0.69	0.58	1.4	5.6	15.4
2 Days Rest	27	29.1	13.7	.453	0.1	.000	3.4	.707	0.44	0.41	1.0	4.9	14.8
3+ Days Rest	21	24.4	10.7	.438	0.0	.000	3.0	.694	0.81	0.38	1.0	5.0	11.4

Jason Terry

1999-2000 Per Game Averages

	G	Min	FGA	FG%	3PA	3P%	FTA	FT%	Blk	Stl	Ast	Reb	Pts
Total	81	23.3	7.4	.415	1.9	.293	1.7	.807	0.12	1.11	4.3	2.0	8.1
Home	41	25.8	8.1	.435	2.1	.337	1.9	.835	0.12	1.15	5.2	2.5	9.3
Road	40	20.7	6.7	.390	1.8	.239	1.5	.770	0.13	1.08	3.4	1.6	6.9
vs. Playoff	47	23.9	7.5	.432	2.0	.333	2.0	.813	0.11	1.26	4.5	2.0	8.8
vs. Non-Playoff	34	22.5	7.3	.391	1.8	.230	1.3	.795	0.15	0.91	4.0	2.1	7.1
vs. East	54	23.3	7.3	.416	2.0	.287	1.7	.828	0.11	1.22	4.1	2.0	8.0
vs. West	27	23.4	7.7	.413	1.8	.306	1.7	.766	0.15	0.89	4.5	2.2	8.3
vs. Div.	28	22.6	6.6	.400	2.0	.255	2.0	.807	0.11	1.21	4.5	1.9	7.4
As Starter	27	31.9	9.8	.442	2.0	.309	1.4	.846	0.07	1.33	7.0	2.2	10.5
Off Bench	54	19.0	6.2	.394	1.9	.284	1.9	.792	0.15	1.00	2.9	2.0	6.9
In wins	28	22.8	7.0	.441	1.4	.250	1.7	.792	0.07	1.07	4.3	2.5	7.9
In losses	53	23.6	7.6	.402	2.2	.308	1.7	.815	0.15	1.13	4.3	1.8	8.2
Pre All-Star	46	19.7	6.6	.405	2.1	.305	2.0	.817	0.15	1.09	3.0	2.0	7.6
Post All-Star	35	28.1	8.5	.426	1.8	.274	1.3	.787	0.09	1.14	5.9	2.1	8.7
November	15	20.3	7.0	.486	2.4	.444	2.1	.781	0.20	1.53	2.5	1.9	9.5
December	14	22.1	7.6	.355	2.4	.212	2.6	.838	0.14	1.00	3.4	2.9	8.1
January	12	17.9	5.9	.394	1.8	.286	1.5	.830	0.08	0.92	3.4	1.3	6.4
February	12	14.4	3.8	.333	0.8	.000	1.2	.643	0.08	0.33	2.2	1.5	3.3
March	17	32.1	9.5	.432	2.0	.206	1.5	.880	0.12	1.53	7.3	2.4	9.9
April	11	31.1	10.0	.427	2.2	.417	1.3	.786	0.09	1.09	6.4	2.1	10.5
0 Days Rest	23	22.6	7.5	.393	2.1	.208	1.3	.806	0.26	0.61	3.2	1.9	7.4
1 Days Rest	37	25.3	8.0	.420	2.1	.329	1.8	.846	0.05	1.43	5.5	2.3	8.9
2 Days Rest	14	24.0	7.1	.465	1.9	.333	2.3	.750	0.07	0.86	3.9	1.9	8.9
3+ Days Rest	7	13.9	4.7	.333	0.9	.333	1.7	.750	0.14	1.57	2.3	1.3	4.7

Kenny Thomas

Houston Rockets — Forward

1999-2000 Per Game Averages

	G	Min	FGA	FG%	3PA	3P%	FTA	FT%	Blk	Stl	Ast	Reb	Pts		G	Min	FGA	FG%	3PA	3P%	FTA	FT%	Blk	Stl	Ast	Reb	Pts
Total	72	25.0	7.4	.399	1.7	.262	2.9	.660	0.31	0.75	1.6	6.1	8.3	Pre All-Star	41	21.7	6.5	.421	1.2	.347	2.7	.652	0.27	0.61	1.1	5.4	7.7
Home	37	25.3	7.6	.399	1.7	.210	3.1	.664	0.30	0.70	1.9	6.6	8.4	Post All-Star	31	29.3	8.5	.377	2.4	.205	3.1	.670	0.35	0.94	2.1	7.0	9.0
Road	35	24.6	7.1	.400	1.7	.317	2.7	.656	0.31	0.80	1.3	5.5	8.1	November	6	5.8	1.7	.200	0.7	.250	0.3	.500	0.33	0.17	0.0	1.5	1.0
vs. Playoff	40	24.5	7.1	.408	1.8	.286	2.8	.649	0.23	0.60	1.3	5.5	8.1	December	15	19.9	6.3	.372	1.3	.300	2.6	.590	0.20	0.60	0.7	5.1	6.6
vs. Non-Playoff	32	25.5	7.8	.390	1.6	.231	3.1	.673	0.41	0.94	1.9	6.8	8.5	January	14	27.3	8.4	.453	0.6	.222	4.3	.683	0.21	0.64	1.6	6.8	10.6
vs. East	27	26.9	8.1	.418	1.9	.269	2.8	.592	0.37	1.00	2.3	6.7	9.0	February	13	30.5	9.2	.458	3.2	.390	2.6	.735	0.38	1.38	2.0	6.4	11.6
vs. West	45	23.8	6.9	.386	1.6	.257	3.0	.699	0.27	0.60	1.1	5.7	7.8	March	14	27.4	7.0	.357	2.1	.069	3.1	.545	0.43	0.93	2.4	6.4	6.9
vs. Div.	22	26.5	7.8	.378	1.6	.194	3.6	.696	0.41	0.68	1.4	6.5	8.7	April	10	30.0	9.2	.348	1.9	.263	3.0	.800	0.30	0.40	2.0	8.4	9.3
As Starter	29	29.0	8.5	.366	2.4	.200	3.0	.682	0.34	0.86	2.2	7.1	8.8	0 Days Rest	12	24.8	7.2	.453	1.8	.381	2.1	.720	0.25	0.83	1.3	6.1	8.7
Off Bench	43	22.2	6.6	.428	1.2	.346	2.8	.645	0.28	0.67	1.2	5.4	7.9	1 Days Rest	38	27.5	8.4	.401	1.8	.254	3.6	.667	0.34	0.84	2.0	7.0	9.6
In wins	33	26.3	8.3	.412	1.6	.333	2.8	.667	0.30	0.73	1.9	7.3	9.3	2 Days Rest	15	24.9	6.8	.343	1.9	.172	2.7	.634	0.27	0.67	1.3	5.2	6.7
In losses	39	23.8	6.6	.385	1.7	.206	3.0	.655	0.31	0.77	1.3	5.0	7.4	3+ Days Rest	7	11.6	3.4	.417	0.7	.400	1.1	.500	0.29	0.29	0.1	2.7	3.7

Kurt Thomas

New York Knicks — Forward

1999-2000 Per Game Averages

	G	Min	FGA	FG%	3PA	3P%	FTA	FT%	Blk	Stl	Ast	Reb	Pts		G	Min	FGA	FG%	3PA	3P%	FTA	FT%	Blk	Stl	Ast	Reb	Pts
Total	80	24.6	6.7	.505	0.0	.333	1.6	.781	0.53	0.64	1.0	6.3	8.0	Pre All-Star	45	24.5	6.9	.484	0.0	1.000	1.6	.740	0.49	0.67	1.0	6.2	7.9
Home	41	24.4	6.5	.521	0.0	1.000	1.6	.848	0.56	0.66	1.0	5.9	8.2	Post All-Star	35	24.8	6.4	.534	0.1	.000	1.6	.836	0.57	0.60	1.1	6.5	8.1
Road	39	24.9	6.9	.489	0.1	.000	1.6	.710	0.49	0.62	1.0	6.7	7.8	November	16	28.4	7.9	.488	0.1	1.000	1.8	.643	0.69	0.63	0.6	6.7	8.9
vs. Playoff	44	24.8	6.4	.472	0.1	.333	1.6	.786	0.45	0.66	1.0	7.0	7.3	December	12	24.1	7.1	.518	0.0	—	2.5	.800	0.58	0.58	1.0	7.3	9.3
vs. Non-Playoff	36	24.5	7.0	.542	0.0	—	1.6	.776	0.61	0.61	1.1	5.4	8.9	January	12	19.3	5.7	.500	0.0	—	0.8	.778	0.17	0.67	1.2	4.0	6.2
vs. East	52	24.7	6.6	.485	0.0	1.000	1.7	.756	0.56	0.65	1.1	6.3	7.7	February	13	29.0	6.7	.483	0.0	—	2.0	.923	0.77	1.00	1.4	7.5	8.3
vs. West	28	24.6	6.9	.539	0.1	.000	1.4	.842	0.46	0.61	0.8	6.3	8.6	March	17	23.2	5.4	.565	0.1	.000	1.0	.824	0.41	0.47	0.8	6.0	6.9
vs. Div.	22	25.0	7.3	.475	0.0	1.000	1.9	.714	0.73	0.68	1.5	6.6	8.3	April	10	22.5	7.6	.474	0.1	.000	1.8	.722	0.50	0.50	1.4	6.3	8.5
As Starter	21	31.2	7.9	.476	0.0	—	2.6	.745	0.71	0.81	1.2	8.7	9.5	0 Days Rest	20	25.2	7.0	.521	0.0	—	1.6	.645	0.70	0.80	1.1	6.8	8.3
Off Bench	59	22.3	6.3	.518	0.1	.333	1.2	.808	0.46	0.58	1.0	5.5	7.5	1 Days Rest	41	24.0	6.6	.493	0.1	.333	1.5	.871	0.44	0.54	0.9	6.5	7.9
In wins	49	24.9	6.8	.536	0.0	—	1.6	.833	0.51	0.53	1.1	6.2	8.6	2 Days Rest	13	25.8	6.8	.506	0.0	—	2.2	.679	0.54	0.77	1.2	5.7	8.4
In losses	31	24.3	6.5	.453	0.1	.333	1.6	.700	0.55	0.81	0.9	6.5	7.1	3+ Days Rest	6	24.7	5.7	.529	0.0	—	1.2	1.000	0.50	0.50	1.2	4.5	7.2

Career (1995-96 thru 1999-2000)

	G	Min	FGA	FG%	3PA	3P%	FTA	FT%	Blk	Stl	Ast	Reb	Pts		G	Min	FGA	FG%	3PA	3P%	FTA	FT%	Blk	Stl	Ast	Reb	Pts
Total	227	23.1	7.0	.481	0.0	.143	2.0	.695	0.46	0.69	0.9	6.0	8.2	Pre All-Star	108	21.7	6.6	.468	0.0	.250	2.0	.705	0.49	0.63	0.6	5.7	7.9
Home	114	22.7	6.7	.505	0.0	.500	2.0	.722	0.51	0.68	0.9	5.8	8.3	Post All-Star	69	25.1	7.0	.516	0.0	.000	2.0	.746	0.49	0.62	1.0	6.7	8.8
Road	113	23.6	7.4	.460	0.0	.000	2.1	.670	0.41	0.69	0.8	6.2	8.1	Oct/Nov	37	21.0	6.8	.433	0.1	.500	1.7	.688	0.49	0.54	0.5	5.6	7.1
vs. Playoff	124	23.0	6.8	.454	0.0	.200	2.1	.700	0.42	0.63	0.8	6.3	7.7	December	31	24.3	8.6	.494	0.1	.000	3.1	.740	0.68	0.74	0.6	6.8	10.8
vs. Non-Playoff	103	23.3	7.3	.511	0.0	.000	2.0	.689	0.50	0.76	1.0	5.7	8.9	January	31	20.0	5.7	.494	0.0	—	1.5	.652	0.32	0.58	0.6	4.4	6.6
vs. East	157	22.9	6.8	.466	0.0	.500	2.0	.670	0.46	0.64	0.9	5.9	7.7	February	39	23.8	6.6	.496	0.0	—	2.0	.679	0.33	0.79	1.1	6.1	7.9
vs. West	70	23.8	7.5	.511	0.1	.000	2.2	.747	0.44	0.79	0.7	6.4	9.2	March	49	24.3	6.9	.509	0.0	.000	2.0	.719	0.41	0.71	1.0	6.3	8.5
vs. Div.	67	23.3	7.3	.455	0.0	.500	2.1	.639	0.55	0.64	1.0	6.1	8.0	Apr/May	40	24.8	7.8	.460	0.1	.000	2.1	.663	0.55	0.73	1.2	6.5	8.5
As Starter	116	26.7	8.4	.475	0.0	.000	2.7	.690	0.56	0.84	1.0	7.0	9.8	0 Days Rest	55	24.3	7.9	.484	0.0	.000	2.2	.593	0.58	0.95	0.9	6.4	8.9
Off Bench	111	19.4	5.6	.491	0.0	.333	1.4	.706	0.35	0.52	0.7	5.0	6.5	1 Days Rest	122	23.4	7.0	.481	0.0	.200	2.0	.744	0.42	0.61	0.8	6.2	8.3
In wins	124	23.6	6.8	.510	0.0	.000	2.0	.731	0.51	0.66	1.0	6.0	8.4	2 Days Rest	28	23.0	7.3	.463	0.0	—	2.3	.698	0.46	0.75	0.9	5.4	8.4
In losses	103	22.6	7.3	.449	0.0	.200	2.1	.656	0.40	0.72	0.7	6.0	8.0	3+ Days Rest	22	18.8	4.8	.509	0.0	—	1.4	.710	0.36	0.41	0.9	4.6	5.9

Tim Thomas

1999-2000 Per Game Averages

	G	Min	FGA	FG%	3PA	3P%	FTA	FT%	Blk	Stl	Ast	Reb	Pts		G	Min	FGA	FG%	3PA	3P%	FTA	FT%	Blk	Stl	Ast	Reb	Pts
Total	80	26.2	9.4	.461	2.3	.346	3.0	.774	0.39	0.74	1.4	4.2	11.8	Pre All-Star	48	25.4	8.7	.473	2.0	.330	2.6	.752	0.44	0.73	1.4	3.9	10.9
Home	41	26.3	9.4	.468	2.3	.385	2.9	.767	0.39	0.71	1.5	4.3	11.9	Post All-Star	32	27.3	10.4	.446	2.8	.364	3.7	.797	0.31	0.75	1.4	4.5	13.3
Road	39	26.1	9.4	.454	2.2	.302	3.2	.780	0.38	0.77	1.3	4.0	11.7	November	12	22.6	6.9	.482	1.3	.313	2.5	.767	0.33	0.92	1.3	3.3	9.0
vs. Playoff	41	26.6	9.4	.452	2.5	.363	2.8	.784	0.44	0.80	1.4	4.0	11.6	December	16	25.1	8.9	.486	1.8	.179	2.5	.700	0.31	0.38	1.3	4.3	10.7
vs. Non-Playoff	39	25.7	9.4	.470	2.1	.325	3.3	.764	0.33	0.67	1.4	4.3	12.0	January	15	28.1	9.5	.497	2.5	.514	2.4	.778	0.40	1.13	1.5	4.1	12.6
vs. East	52	26.2	9.8	.471	2.5	.395	3.5	.781	0.48	0.77	1.4	4.5	12.9	February	12	25.3	9.4	.345	2.4	.138	3.4	.780	0.58	0.42	1.6	3.6	9.5
vs. West	28	26.1	8.8	.439	1.9	.226	2.1	.750	0.21	0.68	1.4	3.5	9.8	March	14	27.5	10.9	.487	3.2	.444	4.4	.803	0.43	0.71	1.2	4.5	15.5
vs. Div.	27	24.7	8.4	.502	2.2	.400	3.3	.798	0.48	0.81	1.6	4.7	12.0	April	11	28.3	10.9	.450	2.5	.370	3.2	.800	0.27	0.91	1.6	5.3	13.3
As Starter	1	35.0	14.0	.286	5.0	.400	6.0	.833	1.00	1.00	0.0	7.0	15.0	0 Days Rest	19	27.4	9.1	.445	1.8	.257	2.9	.625	0.58	0.42	1.5	3.9	10.4
Off Bench	79	26.1	9.4	.464	2.2	.345	3.0	.772	0.38	0.73	1.4	4.1	11.8	1 Days Rest	46	26.1	9.5	.471	2.4	.393	3.0	.800	0.39	0.78	1.5	4.4	12.3
In wins	42	25.1	9.1	.495	2.0	.376	2.7	.816	0.36	0.74	1.6	3.9	12.0	2 Days Rest	5	22.0	8.2	.415	1.8	.111	2.6	.923	0.00	0.40	2.0	3.6	9.4
In losses	38	27.3	9.8	.426	2.6	.320	3.4	.736	0.42	0.74	1.2	4.4	11.6	3+ Days Rest	10	26.0	10.2	.461	2.8	.346	3.4	.853	0.20	1.30	0.6	3.8	13.2

Career (1997-98 thru 1999-2000)

	G	Min	FGA	FG%	3PA	3P%	FTA	FT%	Blk	Stl	Ast	Reb	Pts		G	Min	FGA	FG%	3PA	3P%	FTA	FT%	Blk	Stl	Ast	Reb	Pts
Total	207	22.6	8.3	.457	2.0	.347	2.8	.737	0.29	0.67	1.2	3.6	10.4	Pre All-Star	90	23.5	8.6	.473	2.0	.350	2.7	.733	0.39	0.67	1.3	3.7	10.8
Home	108	22.4	8.2	.464	1.9	.362	2.8	.746	0.27	0.66	1.3	3.5	10.4	Post All-Star	67	26.2	9.9	.432	2.6	.358	3.5	.782	0.19	0.79	1.3	4.2	12.3
Road	99	22.9	8.4	.451	2.1	.332	2.9	.728	0.31	0.69	1.1	3.7	10.4	Oct/Nov	24	17.6	6.2	.483	1.0	.333	2.3	.704	0.33	0.67	1.0	2.7	7.9
vs. Playoff	112	22.5	8.1	.449	2.2	.360	2.7	.735	0.28	0.67	1.2	3.4	10.0	December	31	23.3	9.1	.484	1.8	.298	2.7	.711	0.35	0.55	1.1	4.2	11.2
vs. Non-Playoff	95	22.7	8.5	.467	1.8	.328	3.0	.739	0.31	0.67	1.3	3.8	10.8	January	28	28.5	9.8	.495	2.8	.449	2.8	.744	0.36	0.86	1.7	4.0	13.0
vs. East	150	22.3	8.3	.456	2.1	.360	3.0	.744	0.34	0.65	1.1	3.6	10.6	February	36	21.3	7.9	.385	2.1	.237	2.3	.810	0.28	0.69	1.3	3.4	8.4
vs. West	57	23.6	8.2	.461	1.8	.308	2.3	.712	0.16	0.74	1.4	3.6	9.8	March	47	21.7	8.1	.467	2.3	.409	3.5	.748	0.28	0.53	0.9	3.4	11.1
vs. Div.	73	22.0	8.1	.467	2.1	.368	3.3	.727	0.36	0.66	1.2	3.9	10.7	Apr/May	41	23.2	8.6	.444	1.9	.303	3.0	.702	0.20	0.78	1.4	3.9	10.3
As Starter	75	24.3	9.0	.447	2.3	.347	3.1	.718	0.23	0.76	1.1	3.8	11.1	0 Days Rest	55	22.4	8.3	.442	1.9	.327	2.9	.662	0.27	0.55	1.0	3.6	9.8
Off Bench	132	21.7	7.9	.464	1.9	.347	2.7	.750	0.33	0.62	1.3	3.5	10.1	1 Days Rest	114	23.3	8.4	.466	2.2	.347	3.0	.752	0.32	0.70	1.2	3.7	10.7
In wins	95	22.2	7.9	.480	1.8	.355	2.7	.762	0.26	0.71	1.4	3.6	10.2	2 Days Rest	18	19.4	7.2	.457	1.6	.429	2.5	.778	0.17	0.50	1.4	3.1	9.2
In losses	112	23.0	8.6	.440	2.2	.341	3.0	.719	0.31	0.64	1.0	3.6	10.5	3+ Days Rest	20	22.5	8.8	.451	2.1	.341	2.9	.828	0.30	1.00	1.2	3.3	11.0

Nick Van Exel

1999-2000 Per Game Averages

	G	Min	FGA	FG%	3PA	3P%	FTA	FT%	Blk	Stl	Ast	Reb	Pts		G	Min	FGA	FG%	3PA	3P%	FTA	FT%	Blk	Stl	Ast	Reb	Pts
Total	79	37.3	15.4	.390	5.1	.332	3.0	.817	0.14	0.86	9.0	3.9	16.1	Pre All-Star	45	36.4	14.9	.399	5.0	.338	2.9	.823	0.13	0.93	8.4	4.1	16.0
Home	39	38.5	14.7	.401	5.3	.369	3.1	.844	0.21	1.05	10.3	4.5	16.4	Post All-Star	34	38.6	15.9	.379	5.2	.324	3.2	.809	0.15	0.76	9.9	3.8	16.4
Road	40	36.2	16.0	.380	4.9	.292	3.0	.788	0.08	0.68	7.9	3.4	15.9	November	13	37.7	14.2	.411	5.7	.419	2.9	.789	0.08	0.77	8.4	4.2	16.4
vs. Playoff	45	37.1	15.5	.393	5.1	.357	3.0	.787	0.11	0.96	8.4	3.9	16.4	December	15	36.4	16.0	.379	4.7	.229	3.2	.854	0.00	1.07	8.9	4.5	15.9
vs. Non-Playoff	34	37.6	15.1	.386	5.0	.298	3.1	.856	0.18	0.74	9.9	4.0	15.8	January	13	36.5	14.5	.418	4.4	.298	3.2	.829	0.31	1.00	8.2	3.8	16.1
vs. East	29	37.1	15.1	.384	5.6	.337	2.9	.821	0.10	0.72	8.8	4.2	15.9	February	11	37.1	16.5	.376	5.8	.375	2.4	.846	0.09	0.91	9.3	3.2	16.5
vs. West	50	37.5	15.5	.394	4.8	.328	3.1	.814	0.16	0.94	9.2	3.8	16.3	March	17	36.5	13.1	.378	4.0	.338	2.4	.800	0.12	0.59	9.6	3.8	13.1
vs. Div.	23	37.7	15.4	.381	4.3	.260	3.4	.823	0.17	1.04	9.7	3.7	15.7	April	10	41.1	19.6	.383	6.8	.347	4.7	.787	0.30	0.90	10.0	4.0	20.9
As Starter	79	37.3	15.4	.390	5.1	.332	3.0	.817	0.14	0.86	9.0	3.9	16.1	0 Days Rest	19	34.4	14.3	.410	3.8	.329	2.8	.830	0.05	0.37	6.6	3.6	15.3
Off Bench	0	—	—	—	—	—	—	—	—	—	—	—	—	1 Days Rest	37	38.3	15.6	.384	5.5	.327	2.6	.837	0.16	0.97	10.1	4.0	16.0
In wins	35	39.6	17.2	.439	5.7	.398	4.4	.863	0.20	1.14	9.8	4.8	21.1	2 Days Rest	14	38.3	15.9	.350	5.7	.313	3.6	.800	0.07	1.07	10.0	3.5	15.8
In losses	44	35.5	13.9	.342	4.5	.265	2.0	.736	0.09	0.64	8.5	3.2	12.2	3+ Days Rest	9	38.1	15.7	.440	5.1	.391	4.3	.769	0.33	1.11	8.2	5.1	19.1

Last Five Seasons

	G	Min	FGA	FG%	3PA	3P%	FTA	FT%	Blk	Stl	Ast	Reb	Pts		G	Min	FGA	FG%	3PA	3P%	FTA	FT%	Blk	Stl	Ast	Reb	Pts
Total	346	35.4	13.7	.404	5.3	.356	2.9	.809	0.12	0.92	7.8	3.0	15.3	Pre All-Star	182	35.5	13.5	.409	5.2	.368	2.8	.813	0.10	0.90	8.0	3.1	15.3
Home	174	35.6	13.0	.411	5.1	.375	2.7	.814	0.13	0.92	8.7	3.0	14.8	Post All-Star	114	35.0	13.4	.399	5.6	.356	2.7	.803	0.17	0.99	7.7	3.0	14.8
Road	172	35.3	14.5	.397	5.5	.338	3.0	.805	0.10	0.91	7.0	2.9	15.8	Oct/Nov	59	35.4	13.0	.393	5.4	.359	3.0	.834	0.08	0.92	7.8	2.8	14.6
vs. Playoff	193	35.7	14.1	.395	5.3	.345	3.2	.800	0.10	0.94	7.7	3.0	15.5	December	61	35.1	13.7	.413	4.9	.377	3.0	.820	0.08	0.90	8.0	3.3	15.7
vs. Non-Playoff	153	35.1	13.3	.416	5.2	.371	2.4	.826	0.14	0.88	8.0	2.9	14.9	January	50	36.5	13.8	.418	5.3	.350	2.6	.771	0.12	0.94	8.2	3.4	15.4
vs. East	117	35.1	13.5	.401	5.4	.351	2.8	.777	0.09	0.91	7.6	3.3	14.9	February	53	35.5	14.2	.387	5.8	.367	2.7	.800	0.17	0.92	8.4	2.8	15.3
vs. West	229	35.3	13.8	.405	5.2	.359	2.9	.825	0.13	0.92	7.9	2.8	15.5	March	73	34.9	13.3	.404	5.1	.339	3.0	.820	0.15	0.89	7.2	2.8	14.9
vs. Div.	109	35.1	13.6	.396	5.1	.316	3.1	.804	0.14	1.02	7.9	2.8	14.9	Apr/May	50	35.5	14.7	.408	5.2	.347	2.8	.793	0.08	0.94	7.4	2.8	16.0
As Starter	328	35.9	14.0	.402	5.3	.357	2.9	.809	0.12	0.92	8.0	3.0	15.5	0 Days Rest	86	34.7	13.5	.421	5.0	.364	2.8	.806	0.06	0.72	7.4	2.7	15.5
Off Bench	18	26.9	8.8	.456	3.9	.338	2.2	.821	0.06	0.89	4.9	2.3	11.1	1 Days Rest	178	35.4	13.7	.395	5.3	.345	2.8	.825	0.13	0.94	7.8	3.0	14.9
In wins	196	35.1	13.5	.437	5.5	.407	3.0	.833	0.14	1.05	8.0	3.2	16.6	2 Days Rest	40	38.0	15.1	.384	5.8	.341	2.8	.784	0.13	1.00	8.9	2.8	15.7
In losses	150	35.9	14.0	.361	5.0	.284	2.7	.774	0.08	0.74	7.5	2.6	13.6	3+ Days Rest	42	34.3	13.2	.425	5.0	.406	3.5	.781	0.17	1.12	7.7	3.3	16.0

Keith Van Horn

New Jersey Nets — Forward

1999-2000 Per Game Averages

	G	Min	FGA	FG%	3PA	3P%	FTA	FT%	Blk	Stl	Ast	Reb	Pts
Total	80	34.8	15.7	.445	2.9	.368	4.9	.847	0.75	0.80	2.0	8.5	19.2
Home	40	34.8	16.1	.448	3.1	.387	5.5	.844	0.80	0.65	1.8	8.5	20.3
Road	40	34.8	15.3	.441	2.6	.346	4.4	.851	0.70	0.95	2.2	8.4	18.1
vs. Playoff	45	34.7	15.2	.433	2.8	.363	4.9	.859	0.60	0.96	1.9	7.9	18.4
vs. Non-Playoff	35	34.9	16.4	.458	3.0	.375	4.9	.832	0.94	0.60	2.1	9.1	20.3
vs. East	52	35.1	15.7	.464	3.0	.395	5.3	.864	0.83	0.83	2.1	8.5	20.3
vs. West	28	34.1	15.8	.410	2.5	.310	4.3	.808	0.61	0.75	1.7	8.4	17.2
vs. Div.	24	35.9	16.5	.428	3.5	.313	5.2	.839	1.00	0.83	2.0	9.6	19.5
As Starter	80	34.8	15.7	.445	2.9	.368	4.9	.847	0.75	0.80	2.0	8.5	19.2
Off Bench	0	—	—	—	—	—	—	—	—	—	—	—	—
In wins	30	32.4	15.2	.491	3.2	.433	4.9	.844	0.87	0.73	1.7	8.1	20.5
In losses	50	36.2	16.0	.418	2.6	.321	4.9	.850	0.68	0.84	2.1	8.7	18.4

	G	Min	FGA	FG%	3PA	3P%	FTA	FT%	Blk	Stl	Ast	Reb	Pts
Pre All-Star	48	34.3	15.6	.416	2.9	.372	4.8	.858	0.88	0.71	1.8	8.0	18.2
Post All-Star	32	35.6	15.9	.487	2.8	.363	5.0	.832	0.56	0.94	2.3	9.2	20.7
November	15	37.9	17.1	.358	1.3	.300	6.0	.900	0.67	1.00	1.9	10.0	18.1
December	14	31.8	15.6	.479	3.0	.452	3.7	.808	1.00	0.50	1.5	6.7	19.4
January	14	34.2	14.5	.419	4.1	.310	4.2	.814	1.00	0.64	1.8	6.7	16.9
February	11	32.6	14.3	.420	3.2	.429	5.6	.823	1.00	0.82	1.5	10.2	18.0
March	16	33.7	15.8	.500	2.9	.348	4.6	.863	0.50	1.00	2.3	8.6	20.7
April	10	39.1	16.9	.503	2.7	.370	5.7	.842	0.30	0.80	3.1	8.9	22.8
0 Days Rest	20	36.3	16.3	.446	2.9	.362	5.3	.857	0.60	1.00	2.3	7.5	20.1
1 Days Rest	43	33.7	15.0	.451	2.7	.365	4.7	.840	0.72	0.74	2.1	8.7	18.4
2 Days Rest	9	34.1	16.3	.435	2.9	.423	4.3	.795	1.11	0.78	1.6	8.8	18.9
3+ Days Rest	8	37.4	17.5	.421	3.6	.345	6.1	.898	0.88	0.63	1.0	9.3	21.5

Career (1997-98 thru 1999-2000)

	G	Min	FGA	FG%	3PA	3P%	FTA	FT%	Blk	Stl	Ast	Reb	Pts
Total	184	36.3	16.6	.434	2.7	.335	5.4	.850	0.75	0.93	1.8	7.8	19.9
Home	95	36.8	16.9	.443	2.9	.349	5.8	.861	0.81	0.81	1.7	7.8	21.0
Road	89	35.8	16.3	.425	2.6	.317	5.0	.837	0.69	1.06	1.9	7.9	18.8
vs. Playoff	99	36.4	16.5	.425	2.8	.347	5.2	.849	0.74	0.91	1.7	7.8	19.4
vs. Non-Playoff	85	36.3	16.8	.445	2.7	.320	5.7	.852	0.76	0.95	1.8	7.9	20.6
vs. East	132	36.8	16.8	.439	2.7	.346	5.7	.860	0.82	0.97	1.8	7.9	20.6
vs. West	52	35.2	16.2	.420	2.8	.306	4.6	.819	0.58	0.83	1.7	7.6	18.2
vs. Div.	59	36.8	17.2	.406	2.9	.305	5.6	.855	0.76	1.15	1.9	8.5	19.7
As Starter	184	36.3	16.6	.434	2.7	.335	5.4	.850	0.75	0.93	1.8	7.8	19.9
Off Bench	0	—	—	—	—	—	—	—	—	—	—	—	—
In wins	76	34.9	16.3	.468	2.9	.376	5.7	.872	0.75	0.96	1.8	7.4	21.3
In losses	108	37.4	16.8	.411	2.6	.303	5.2	.834	0.75	0.91	1.8	8.1	19.0

	G	Min	FGA	FG%	3PA	3P%	FTA	FT%	Blk	Stl	Ast	Reb	Pts
Pre All-Star	79	35.9	16.2	.413	3.5	.338	4.9	.852	0.70	0.87	1.6	7.2	18.7
Post All-Star	63	36.0	16.3	.464	2.8	.339	5.0	.840	0.48	0.94	2.2	8.2	20.3
Oct/Nov	15	37.9	17.1	.358	1.3	.300	6.0	.900	0.67	1.00	1.9	10.0	18.1
December	26	35.5	16.5	.448	3.9	.356	4.8	.810	0.69	0.88	1.1	6.7	20.1
January	30	36.0	15.6	.409	4.3	.313	4.3	.837	0.70	0.77	1.7	6.1	17.7
February	36	34.7	16.3	.406	2.5	.367	5.3	.833	0.89	0.86	1.6	8.4	18.6
March	42	35.9	16.7	.450	2.6	.324	5.0	.844	0.90	1.02	2.0	8.1	20.1
Apr/May	35	38.1	17.4	.485	1.7	.328	7.1	.879	0.54	1.03	2.3	8.3	23.7
0 Days Rest	50	36.7	16.7	.434	2.8	.312	5.7	.854	0.78	0.76	1.8	7.0	20.3
1 Days Rest	92	36.2	16.6	.427	2.7	.327	5.6	.862	0.75	1.04	1.9	8.2	19.8
2 Days Rest	24	35.3	16.6	.461	2.7	.391	4.3	.757	0.75	1.13	1.7	7.9	19.6
3+ Days Rest	18	37.2	16.7	.437	2.9	.365	5.1	.879	0.67	0.56	1.2	8.0	20.1

Antoine Walker

Boston Celtics — Forward

1999-2000 Per Game Averages

	G	Min	FGA	FG%	3PA	3P%	FTA	FT%	Blk	Stl	Ast	Reb	Pts
Total	82	36.6	18.4	.430	3.5	.256	5.4	.699	0.39	1.43	3.7	8.0	20.5
Home	41	36.3	17.5	.443	2.8	.267	5.5	.723	0.49	1.32	4.2	8.5	20.2
Road	41	37.0	19.3	.419	4.1	.249	5.4	.674	0.29	1.54	3.2	7.4	20.8
vs. Playoff	46	37.0	18.9	.417	3.6	.248	5.4	.685	0.33	1.46	3.5	8.2	20.4
vs. Non-Playoff	36	36.1	17.6	.449	3.3	.267	5.5	.716	0.47	1.39	4.0	7.6	20.6
vs. East	54	36.8	18.1	.428	3.5	.262	5.2	.719	0.35	1.54	3.9	8.0	20.2
vs. West	28	36.3	18.9	.434	3.4	.245	5.9	.665	0.46	1.21	3.3	7.9	21.1
vs. Div.	24	37.7	19.0	.429	3.8	.211	5.0	.708	0.46	1.50	3.8	8.6	20.6
As Starter	82	36.6	18.4	.430	3.5	.256	5.4	.699	0.39	1.43	3.7	8.0	20.5
Off Bench	0	—	—	—	—	—	—	—	—	—	—	—	—
In wins	35	35.9	17.2	.471	3.0	.298	5.3	.722	0.37	1.54	4.3	8.4	21.0
In losses	47	37.2	19.2	.403	3.9	.232	5.5	.682	0.40	1.34	3.3	7.6	20.1

	G	Min	FGA	FG%	3PA	3P%	FTA	FT%	Blk	Stl	Ast	Reb	Pts
Pre All-Star	49	36.5	18.7	.420	3.7	.263	5.4	.703	0.45	1.18	2.9	7.6	20.5
Post All-Star	33	36.8	17.8	.446	3.2	.245	5.5	.692	0.30	1.79	4.9	8.5	20.5
November	14	33.1	17.3	.420	3.6	.353	4.4	.677	0.21	1.14	2.2	6.6	18.9
December	14	36.4	17.9	.428	4.3	.233	6.1	.729	0.71	1.00	2.4	7.1	20.4
January	15	39.1	20.1	.429	3.4	.196	5.3	.722	0.47	1.27	4.1	8.3	21.7
February	13	38.1	20.5	.406	3.1	.225	5.7	.649	0.38	1.31	3.2	8.2	21.0
March	16	37.0	17.6	.468	3.3	.308	6.0	.729	0.19	1.88	4.8	9.6	21.9
April	10	35.7	16.5	.424	3.1	.194	4.9	.653	0.40	2.10	6.2	7.6	17.8
0 Days Rest	29	37.5	18.3	.414	4.4	.278	5.6	.699	0.32	1.41	3.2	6.9	20.3
1 Days Rest	42	35.7	18.1	.429	3.3	.264	4.9	.686	0.43	1.40	3.6	8.0	19.8
2 Days Rest	9	37.8	20.0	.483	2.1	.158	5.7	.667	0.11	1.89	6.1	9.8	23.4
3+ Days Rest	9	37.9	17.9	.416	3.2	.207	7.1	.766	0.67	1.11	3.0	8.2	21.0

Career (1996-97 thru 1999-2000)

	G	Min	FGA	FG%	3PA	3P%	FTA	FT%	Blk	Stl	Ast	Reb	Pts
Total	288	37.5	18.4	.424	3.2	.308	5.2	.646	0.60	1.48	3.4	9.0	19.1
Home	143	37.5	18.0	.426	3.1	.325	5.1	.650	0.68	1.49	3.7	9.2	19.7
Road	145	37.4	18.8	.423	3.3	.292	5.2	.642	0.52	1.48	3.1	8.7	20.2
vs. Playoff	161	37.5	18.7	.418	3.2	.301	5.1	.640	0.57	1.39	3.2	8.8	19.9
vs. Non-Playoff	127	37.4	18.0	.432	3.1	.317	5.3	.653	0.65	1.60	3.5	9.2	20.0
vs. East	198	37.4	18.1	.431	3.3	.312	4.9	.636	0.56	1.53	3.4	8.6	19.8
vs. West	90	37.5	19.1	.411	2.8	.298	5.7	.665	0.69	1.38	3.3	9.8	20.3
vs. Div.	89	37.3	18.4	.445	3.3	.312	4.8	.610	0.69	1.55	3.4	9.1	20.3
As Starter	273	38.0	18.7	.425	3.3	.307	5.2	.651	0.60	1.51	3.5	9.1	20.3
Off Bench	15	28.1	12.7	.408	1.1	.353	4.1	.532	0.60	0.93	1.8	7.6	13.0
In wins	102	37.5	18.0	.450	3.3	.334	5.0	.650	0.57	1.74	4.0	9.3	20.6
In losses	186	37.4	18.6	.411	3.1	.293	5.2	.644	0.62	1.34	3.0	8.8	19.6

	G	Min	FGA	FG%	3PA	3P%	FTA	FT%	Blk	Stl	Ast	Reb	Pts
Pre All-Star	142	36.3	17.9	.420	2.9	.272	5.1	.650	0.60	1.43	3.0	8.8	19.1
Post All-Star	104	39.2	19.5	.435	3.1	.321	5.3	.672	0.58	1.55	4.0	9.4	21.5
Oct/Nov	44	33.3	16.8	.419	3.2	.331	5.0	.626	0.43	1.55	2.8	7.9	18.3
December	39	35.4	16.8	.419	3.1	.217	5.0	.655	0.69	1.18	2.6	8.2	18.0
January	46	39.2	19.4	.429	2.7	.254	5.3	.659	0.72	1.50	3.2	9.6	20.8
February	51	38.6	19.7	.404	2.9	.289	6.0	.622	0.61	1.37	3.6	9.9	20.5
March	65	38.4	18.8	.433	3.2	.336	5.1	.666	0.54	1.52	3.4	9.4	20.7
Apr/May	43	38.9	18.3	.441	4.0	.374	4.4	.649	0.65	1.74	4.6	8.4	20.5
0 Days Rest	78	37.9	18.1	.417	3.6	.327	5.4	.622	0.47	1.49	2.9	8.2	19.6
1 Days Rest	147	37.4	18.5	.425	3.1	.296	5.1	.660	0.65	1.48	3.5	9.1	20.6
2 Days Rest	35	37.6	19.0	.450	2.7	.330	5.1	.606	0.57	1.69	3.9	10.1	21.1
3+ Days Rest	28	36.4	17.8	.410	3.0	.286	4.9	.699	0.75	1.21	3.2	8.9	18.8

Orlando Magic — Forward-Center

1999-2000 Per Game Averages

	G	Min	FGA	FG%	3PA	3P%	FTA	FT%	Blk	Stl	Ast	Reb	Pts		G	Min	FGA	FG%	3PA	3P%	FTA	FT%	Blk	Stl	Ast	Reb	Pts
Total	81	24.2	4.1	.503	0.0	—	1.4	.474	1.60	0.89	0.8	8.2	4.8	Pre All-Star	50	22.5	3.6	.475	0.0	—	1.3	.569	1.42	0.88	0.9	7.4	4.2
Home	40	24.6	4.6	.500	0.0	—	1.5	.450	1.53	0.83	0.7	8.1	5.2	Post All-Star	31	26.9	4.9	.536	0.0	—	1.6	.347	1.90	0.90	0.7	9.5	5.8
Road	41	23.8	3.7	.507	0.0	—	1.3	.500	1.68	0.95	0.9	8.3	4.4	November	15	19.7	3.2	.396	0.0	—	0.7	.636	1.20	0.53	0.8	7.1	3.0
vs. Playoff	46	23.4	3.9	.528	0.0	—	1.2	.439	1.28	0.89	1.0	7.9	4.7	December	14	21.5	3.8	.509	0.0	—	1.7	.542	1.57	0.93	1.1	7.0	4.8
vs. Non-Playoff	35	25.3	4.4	.474	0.0	—	1.6	.509	2.03	0.89	0.7	8.6	5.0	January	17	23.8	3.5	.492	0.0	—	1.1	.667	1.29	1.06	0.9	6.9	4.1
vs. East	53	24.3	4.2	.516	0.0	—	1.6	.440	1.53	0.91	0.8	8.6	5.1	February	11	25.9	4.1	.511	0.0	—	1.7	.368	1.55	0.91	0.7	9.1	4.8
vs. West	28	24.0	3.9	.477	0.0	—	1.1	.567	1.75	0.86	0.8	7.5	4.3	March	16	27.4	5.1	.573	0.0	—	1.9	.387	2.44	1.00	0.4	10.1	6.6
vs. Div.	25	26.6	4.7	.568	0.0	—	2.0	.388	1.76	0.80	0.8	10.2	6.1	April	8	29.4	5.9	.489	0.0	—	1.4	.273	1.50	0.88	1.1	10.0	6.1
As Starter	81	24.2	4.1	.503	0.0	—	1.4	.474	1.60	0.89	0.8	8.2	4.8	0 Days Rest	22	24.3	3.6	.513	0.0	—	1.7	.486	1.45	0.86	1.0	7.6	4.5
Off Bench	0													1 Days Rest	41	24.5	4.4	.503	0.0	—	1.3	.500	1.80	0.98	0.8	9.2	5.0
In wins	40	25.8	4.9	.495	0.0	—	2.0	.468	2.15	1.03	0.9	9.2	5.7	2 Days Rest	8	25.5	3.9	.613	0.0	—	1.5	.500	1.75	1.00	0.9	6.8	5.5
In losses	41	22.6	3.4	.514	0.0	—	0.9	.486	1.07	0.76	0.7	7.3	3.9	3+ Days Rest	10	21.7	4.4	.409	0.0	—	1.1	.273	1.00	0.50	0.7	6.5	3.9

Career (1996-97 thru 1999-2000)

	G	Min	FGA	FG%	3PA	3P%	FTA	FT%	Blk	Stl	Ast	Reb	Pts		G	Min	FGA	FG%	3PA	3P%	FTA	FT%	Blk	Stl	Ast	Reb	Pts
Total	228	19.8	3.3	.517	0.0	—	1.6	.390	1.33	0.84	0.5	6.3	4.0	Pre All-Star	106	15.3	2.5	.451	0.0	—	1.1	.464	0.98	0.68	0.5	5.0	2.7
Home	115	19.3	3.3	.520	0.0	—	1.7	.382	1.23	0.72	0.4	6.1	4.0	Post All-Star	76	21.9	3.7	.536	0.0	—	1.6	.358	1.43	0.91	0.5	6.8	4.5
Road	113	20.2	3.3	.514	0.0	—	1.5	.399	1.43	0.96	0.6	6.4	4.0	Oct/Nov	34	13.9	2.0	.391	0.0	—	0.7	.440	0.76	0.47	0.4	4.8	1.9
vs. Playoff	123	19.0	3.0	.537	0.0	—	1.6	.399	1.10	0.87	0.5	6.1	3.8	December	30	12.4	2.3	.457	0.0	—	1.2	.500	1.07	0.53	0.5	4.1	2.7
vs. Non-Playoff	105	20.7	3.6	.497	0.0	—	1.6	.380	1.60	0.80	0.4	6.4	4.2	January	33	16.5	2.5	.488	0.0	—	1.0	.455	0.91	0.70	0.5	5.0	2.9
vs. East	163	20.0	3.3	.518	0.0	—	1.7	.377	1.33	0.80	0.5	6.6	4.1	February	34	24.6	4.0	.489	0.0	—	1.6	.444	1.44	1.38	0.4	7.1	4.6
vs. West	65	19.1	3.0	.513	0.0	—	1.2	.438	1.34	0.94	0.5	5.6	3.6	March	56	21.0	3.4	.565	0.0	—	1.9	.358	1.52	0.93	0.3	7.1	4.6
vs. Div.	77	20.6	3.5	.515	0.0	—	1.9	.340	1.43	0.73	0.5	6.9	4.2	Apr/May	41	27.0	4.7	.568	0.0	—	2.6	.327	1.98	0.90	0.7	8.3	6.2
As Starter	113	26.6	4.4	.525	0.0	—	1.9	.419	1.75	1.05	0.8	8.6	5.4	0 Days Rest	54	22.6	3.4	.582	0.0	—	1.7	.380	1.31	0.91	0.6	6.6	4.6
Off Bench	115	13.1	2.1	.500	0.0	—	1.3	.349	0.91	0.63	0.1	4.0	2.6	1 Days Rest	104	21.5	3.7	.500	0.0	—	1.9	.379	1.61	0.89	0.5	7.5	4.4
In wins	112	19.7	3.4	.520	0.0	—	1.7	.412	1.54	0.94	0.5	6.4	4.3	2 Days Rest	31	19.5	2.9	.533	0.0	—	1.5	.440	1.16	0.90	0.5	5.2	3.8
In losses	116	19.9	3.1	.514	0.0	—	1.5	.365	1.13	0.74	0.5	6.1	3.7	3+ Days Rest	39	11.7	2.1	.434	0.0	—	0.8	.367	0.74	0.54	0.3	3.5	2.1

Rasheed Wallace

Portland Trail Blazers — Forward-Center

1999-2000 Per Game Averages

	G	Min	FGA	FG%	3PA	3P%	FTA	FT%	Blk	Stl	Ast	Reb	Pts		G	Min	FGA	FG%	3PA	3P%	FTA	FT%	Blk	Stl	Ast	Reb	Pts
Total	81	35.1	12.9	.519	0.6	.160	4.1	.704	1.32	1.07	1.8	7.0	16.4	Pre All-Star	48	34.8	12.7	.502	0.6	.172	4.0	.674	1.40	0.98	1.7	7.0	15.5
Home	40	34.9	12.3	.540	0.4	.059	3.9	.756	1.18	1.03	2.1	7.1	16.2	Post All-Star	33	35.6	13.2	.541	0.6	.143	4.3	.745	1.21	1.21	1.8	7.0	17.6
Road	41	35.4	13.5	.500	0.8	.212	4.3	.657	1.46	1.12	1.5	6.9	16.5	November	15	34.1	13.4	.443	0.8	.167	3.3	.673	1.60	1.00	1.7	7.2	14.2
vs. Playoff	43	36.1	13.1	.540	0.6	.280	5.0	.698	1.14	1.00	1.6	7.2	17.8	December	13	36.2	13.4	.552	0.8	.182	4.5	.695	2.00	0.85	1.5	7.8	18.1
vs. Non-Playoff	38	34.0	12.6	.494	0.7	.040	3.1	.716	1.53	1.16	1.9	6.7	14.7	January	14	33.6	11.9	.533	0.3	.250	4.3	.693	0.71	1.36	1.9	6.0	15.7
vs. East	30	36.9	13.1	.505	0.6	.158	4.9	.694	1.63	1.00	1.9	7.0	16.7	February	14	36.0	12.1	.459	0.4	.167	3.9	.648	1.36	1.36	1.6	7.2	13.7
vs. West	51	34.1	12.8	.527	0.6	.161	3.6	.712	1.14	1.12	1.6	7.0	16.2	March	14	38.2	14.1	.599	0.4	.167	4.9	.706	1.14	1.14	1.8	7.4	20.4
vs. Div.	23	34.2	13.0	.515	0.5	.182	3.7	.647	1.09	1.26	1.8	7.6	15.9	April	11	32.2	12.4	.529	1.0	.091	3.7	.854	1.09	0.64	2.2	6.1	16.4
As Starter	77	35.2	12.9	.520	0.6	.170	4.1	.703	1.30	1.08	1.8	7.0	16.4	0 Days Rest	21	34.1	12.0	.498	0.8	.063	3.5	.671	1.19	0.86	1.8	6.0	14.3
Off Bench	4	33.5	12.8	.490	0.8	.000	4.5	.722	1.75	1.00	1.5	6.8	15.8	1 Days Rest	39	35.9	12.6	.546	0.5	.278	5.1	.742	1.18	1.10	1.6	7.2	17.7
In wins	58	34.3	12.5	.519	0.6	.229	4.1	.695	1.34	1.21	1.9	7.1	15.9	2 Days Rest	14	35.9	15.3	.491	0.9	.083	2.8	.769	1.93	1.00	2.2	7.8	17.2
In losses	23	37.3	14.0	.519	0.7	.000	4.1	.726	1.26	0.74	1.5	6.8	17.5	3+ Days Rest	7	32.0	12.4	.494	0.6	.250	3.0	.333	1.29	1.71	1.6	7.4	13.4

Career (1995-96 thru 1999-2000)

	G	Min	FGA	FG%	3PA	3P%	FTA	FT%	Blk	Stl	Ast	Reb	Pts		G	Min	FGA	FG%	3PA	3P%	FTA	FT%	Blk	Stl	Ast	Reb	Pts
Total	334	32.4	10.9	.523	0.7	.277	3.5	.678	1.08	0.90	1.7	6.0	14.0	Pre All-Star	166	32.4	10.6	.522	0.7	.281	3.2	.657	1.14	0.80	1.6	6.0	13.3
Home	167	32.0	10.4	.526	0.6	.257	3.4	.696	0.99	0.83	1.7	6.0	13.5	Post All-Star	119	34.0	11.9	.529	0.8	.222	3.9	.681	0.99	1.00	1.9	6.4	15.4
Road	167	32.9	11.4	.520	0.8	.291	3.6	.661	1.18	0.97	1.7	6.0	14.5	Oct/Nov	56	32.1	10.5	.508	0.7	.154	3.2	.689	1.36	0.73	1.5	5.9	13.0
vs. Playoff	179	33.0	11.0	.532	0.8	.338	4.1	.679	0.97	0.92	1.5	6.0	14.7	December	53	30.2	10.0	.542	0.5	.321	3.0	.646	1.34	0.77	1.4	5.9	12.9
vs. Non-Playoff	155	31.8	10.8	.513	0.6	.188	2.9	.676	1.22	0.87	1.8	6.0	13.2	January	43	35.0	11.4	.528	0.9	.378	3.7	.642	0.77	0.88	1.8	6.2	14.8
vs. East	127	32.7	10.7	.516	0.7	.284	3.5	.664	1.06	0.78	1.6	6.0	13.6	February	63	32.3	11.0	.498	0.8	.313	3.5	.670	0.86	0.98	1.8	6.0	13.5
vs. West	207	32.3	11.0	.527	0.7	.271	3.5	.686	1.10	0.97	1.7	6.0	14.2	March	69	33.2	10.9	.530	0.8	.302	4.0	.672	1.04	1.01	1.8	6.1	14.5
vs. Div.	101	32.5	11.7	.515	0.8	.289	3.5	.680	1.15	0.94	1.8	6.1	14.7	Apr/May	50	32.2	11.8	.537	0.6	.167	3.7	.745	1.12	0.96	1.6	5.9	15.5
As Starter	279	34.0	11.4	.529	0.7	.281	3.6	.671	1.13	0.91	1.8	6.4	14.6	0 Days Rest	89	30.9	10.9	.519	0.7	.194	3.6	.694	0.98	0.80	1.7	5.9	13.9
Off Bench	55	24.3	8.6	.483	0.7	.250	3.0	.719	0.87	0.85	0.9	4.1	10.7	1 Days Rest	164	32.4	10.9	.535	0.7	.325	3.7	.689	1.05	0.88	1.6	6.0	14.5
In wins	202	32.1	10.8	.535	0.6	.316	3.5	.685	1.11	0.93	1.7	6.2	14.2	2 Days Rest	46	33.2	11.2	.499	0.7	.323	3.2	.638	1.28	1.07	1.7	6.2	13.5
In losses	132	33.0	11.1	.505	0.9	.237	3.5	.666	1.05	0.85	1.6	5.8	13.7	3+ Days Rest	35	30.4	10.4	.507	0.8	.214	3.0	.619	1.23	1.00	1.8	6.1	12.6

Charlie Ward

1999-2000 Per Game Averages

	G	Min	FGA	FG%	3PA	3P%	FTA	FT%	Blk	Stl	Ast	Reb	Pts		G	Min	FGA	FG%	3PA	3P%	FTA	FT%	Blk	Stl	Ast	Reb	Pts
Total	72	27.6	6.2	.423	3.7	.386	0.8	.828	0.22	1.32	4.2	3.2	7.3	Pre All-Star	46	28.5	6.7	.435	3.9	.399	0.9	.814	0.22	1.57	4.3	3.1	8.1
Home	34	27.9	5.9	.405	3.5	.356	1.2	.850	0.26	1.56	4.4	3.2	7.0	Post All-Star	26	25.9	5.3	.396	3.3	.360	0.6	.867	0.23	0.88	3.8	3.3	5.9
Road	38	27.3	6.5	.437	3.8	.411	0.5	.778	0.18	1.11	4.0	3.1	7.6	November	16	27.6	6.9	.432	4.0	.422	0.8	.750	0.19	1.25	4.9	3.0	8.3
vs. Playoff	37	26.9	6.1	.431	3.5	.400	0.8	.806	0.27	1.27	4.4	3.1	7.3	December	13	26.6	5.9	.390	3.4	.386	0.6	.625	0.23	1.23	2.8	2.9	6.3
vs. Non-Playoff	35	28.3	6.3	.414	3.8	.373	0.8	.852	0.17	1.37	3.9	3.3	7.3	January	12	28.8	6.7	.475	3.5	.381	1.4	.882	0.25	1.92	4.5	2.5	8.9
vs. East	47	27.8	6.4	.395	3.8	.343	0.8	.811	0.26	1.21	4.2	3.0	7.0	February	7	32.3	6.9	.417	4.7	.394	1.4	1.000	0.29	2.00	5.6	4.6	9.0
vs. West	25	27.2	5.8	.479	3.4	.477	0.8	.857	0.16	1.52	4.1	3.6	8.0	March	14	25.9	4.7	.470	2.5	.429	0.3	.500	0.14	0.79	4.1	3.5	5.6
vs. Div.	21	27.9	5.8	.377	3.7	.299	0.9	.833	0.29	1.29	3.2	3.3	6.2	April	10	26.3	6.5	.338	4.6	.304	0.7	1.000	0.30	1.10	3.4	3.1	6.5
As Starter	69	27.7	6.2	.430	3.7	.387	0.8	.839	0.22	1.36	4.2	3.2	7.4	0 Days Rest	18	26.4	6.3	.442	3.7	.448	0.8	.857	0.22	1.00	4.5	3.2	7.9
Off Bench	3	25.0	6.3	.263	3.7	.364	0.7	.500	0.33	0.33	3.3	2.0	5.0	1 Days Rest	35	28.3	6.4	.427	3.9	.390	0.8	.778	0.26	1.37	4.2	3.4	7.6
In wins	45	28.7	6.5	.440	3.9	.409	1.0	.818	0.22	1.62	4.5	3.0	8.1	2 Days Rest	11	25.1	5.6	.452	2.9	.344	0.5	.833	0.27	1.73	3.7	2.8	6.5
In losses	27	25.7	5.7	.390	3.3	.341	0.5	.857	0.22	0.81	3.6	3.4	6.0	3+ Days Rest	8	30.4	5.9	.319	3.6	.276	1.4	.909	0.00	1.25	3.9	2.8	6.0

Last Five Seasons

	G	Min	FGA	FG%	3PA	3P%	FTA	FT%	Blk	Stl	Ast	Reb	Pts		G	Min	FGA	FG%	3PA	3P%	FTA	FT%	Blk	Stl	Ast	Reb	Pts
Total	345	24.4	5.4	.421	2.6	.360	1.2	.762	0.24	1.39	4.3	2.9	6.4	Pre All-Star	168	23.2	5.3	.435	2.7	.367	1.1	.761	0.28	1.36	4.2	2.9	6.4
Home	171	24.5	5.3	.414	2.5	.350	1.5	.758	0.25	1.56	4.7	2.8	6.4	Post All-Star	127	23.3	4.9	.409	2.2	.351	1.3	.790	0.21	1.17	4.1	2.7	5.8
Road	174	24.2	5.4	.427	2.6	.369	1.0	.767	0.23	1.22	4.0	2.9	6.4	Oct/Nov	53	23.3	5.2	.487	2.5	.400	1.0	.692	0.36	1.15	4.8	2.9	6.7
vs. Playoff	179	24.0	5.5	.412	2.7	.356	1.1	.735	0.24	1.26	4.2	2.8	6.3	December	48	21.4	4.6	.408	2.2	.356	1.0	.870	0.31	1.23	3.4	2.6	5.4
vs. Non-Playoff	166	24.8	5.3	.430	2.4	.364	1.4	.785	0.23	1.52	4.5	3.0	6.5	January	54	24.0	5.9	.408	3.0	.363	1.3	.686	0.20	1.56	4.1	2.8	6.8
vs. East	239	24.8	5.5	.413	2.6	.356	1.2	.762	0.25	1.41	4.4	2.9	6.4	February	53	26.6	5.4	.437	2.4	.336	1.5	.778	0.17	1.70	4.6	2.8	6.7
vs. West	106	23.4	5.1	.440	2.4	.369	1.2	.762	0.21	1.35	4.1	2.8	6.3	March	78	26.2	5.5	.407	2.5	.354	1.6	.802	0.21	1.37	4.6	3.1	6.7
vs. Div.	108	24.3	5.4	.401	2.4	.323	1.2	.774	0.31	1.54	4.2	3.1	6.0	Apr/May	59	23.7	5.4	.389	2.7	.352	0.9	.717	0.20	1.32	4.3	2.9	5.8
As Starter	223	28.9	6.3	.437	3.0	.375	1.3	.774	0.30	1.65	5.2	3.4	7.7	0 Days Rest	87	25.1	5.2	.412	2.5	.359	1.4	.788	0.17	1.29	4.3	3.1	6.3
Off Bench	122	16.1	3.7	.368	1.7	.309	1.1	.735	0.12	0.90	2.8	2.0	4.0	1 Days Rest	168	25.3	5.7	.420	2.6	.359	1.2	.732	0.27	1.54	4.6	3.0	6.7
In wins	207	24.6	5.2	.450	2.4	.390	1.4	.759	0.26	1.51	4.5	2.9	6.7	2 Days Rest	52	22.0	5.0	.446	2.3	.392	1.2	.790	0.29	1.27	3.9	2.7	6.3
In losses	138	24.1	5.6	.379	2.8	.320	1.1	.767	0.21	1.20	4.1	2.8	5.9	3+ Days Rest	38	21.7	4.7	.412	2.6	.327	1.0	.795	0.16	1.13	3.9	2.4	5.5

Clarence Weatherspoon

1999-2000 Per Game Averages

	G	Min	FGA	FG%	3PA	3P%	FTA	FT%	Blk	Stl	Ast	Reb	Pts		G	Min	FGA	FG%	3PA	3P%	FTA	FT%	Blk	Stl	Ast	Reb	Pts
Total	78	20.7	5.4	.513	0.0	—	2.3	.738	0.63	0.65	1.2	5.8	7.2	Pre All-Star	44	18.6	4.8	.500	0.0	—	1.8	.738	0.70	0.77	1.3	5.3	6.1
Home	38	20.9	5.2	.566	0.0	—	2.3	.697	0.76	0.79	1.1	6.0	7.5	Post All-Star	34	23.4	6.1	.526	0.0	—	3.0	.738	0.53	0.50	1.1	6.4	8.7
Road	40	20.5	5.5	.466	0.0	—	2.4	.777	0.50	0.53	1.3	5.5	7.0	November	11	23.3	6.0	.485	0.0	—	1.9	.762	0.36	0.91	1.5	6.5	7.3
vs. Playoff	41	21.0	5.6	.478	0.0	—	2.6	.774	0.66	0.54	1.4	5.8	7.2	December	14	16.4	3.9	.418	0.0	—	1.9	.852	0.50	0.79	1.3	4.9	4.9
vs. Non-Playoff	37	20.4	5.2	.555	0.0	—	2.1	.688	0.59	0.78	1.4	5.8	7.2	January	15	16.4	4.6	.580	0.0	—	1.6	.625	0.93	0.60	0.8	4.9	6.3
vs. East	52	21.0	5.5	.516	0.0	—	2.6	.701	0.79	0.69	1.1	5.9	7.5	February	14	23.3	6.1	.535	0.0	—	2.7	.632	0.86	0.71	1.4	6.9	8.3
vs. West	26	20.2	5.2	.507	0.0	—	1.9	.837	0.31	0.58	1.3	5.5	6.8	March	13	25.1	6.9	.478	0.0	—	2.8	.861	0.69	0.69	1.2	5.7	9.0
vs. Div.	22	20.1	5.2	.548	0.0	—	2.4	.679	0.68	0.64	1.2	5.4	7.4	April	11	21.4	4.8	.585	0.0	—	3.4	.703	0.27	0.18	0.9	6.1	8.0
As Starter	2	37.5	10.0	.450	0.0	—	2.0	.750	0.50	0.50	1.5	10.5	10.5	0 Days Rest	17	21.5	5.5	.521	0.0	—	2.4	.775	0.53	0.59	1.5	5.5	7.6
Off Bench	76	20.1	5.3	.516	0.0	—	2.4	.737	0.63	0.66	1.2	5.6	7.2	1 Days Rest	43	20.8	5.3	.500	0.0	—	2.2	.663	0.63	0.70	1.3	5.8	6.8
In wins	49	21.5	5.3	.574	0.0	—	2.4	.720	0.65	0.71	1.2	6.2	7.8	2 Days Rest	11	20.0	5.3	.586	0.0	—	2.5	.821	0.82	0.45	1.0	5.0	8.3
In losses	29	19.4	5.6	.416	0.0	—	2.2	.769	0.59	0.55	1.1	5.0	6.3	3+ Days Rest	7	19.4	5.6	.462	0.0	—	2.9	.900	0.57	0.86	0.4	7.4	7.7

Last Five Seasons

	G	Min	FGA	FG%	3PA	3P%	FTA	FT%	Blk	Stl	Ast	Reb	Pts		G	Min	FGA	FG%	3PA	3P%	FTA	FT%	Blk	Stl	Ast	Reb	Pts
Total	366	30.1	8.5	.485	0.0	.125	3.6	.745	0.91	0.96	1.4	7.4	10.9	Pre All-Star	176	30.3	8.2	.485	0.0	.200	3.6	.724	0.88	0.95	1.4	7.6	10.6
Home	183	30.7	8.4	.495	0.0	.000	3.7	.738	0.93	1.03	1.4	7.8	11.0	Post All-Star	141	33.0	10.3	.476	0.0	.000	3.7	.754	1.15	1.09	1.6	8.1	12.3
Road	183	29.5	8.7	.476	0.0	.250	3.4	.752	0.89	0.89	1.4	7.0	10.8	Oct/Nov	47	30.9	8.2	.503	0.0	—	3.6	.713	0.60	1.06	1.4	8.3	10.7
vs. Playoff	205	29.9	8.2	.469	0.0	.000	3.4	.751	0.87	0.93	1.3	7.2	10.2	December	57	30.6	8.0	.446	0.0	.000	3.9	.741	0.86	0.93	1.4	7.0	10.0
vs. Non-Playoff	161	30.4	8.9	.505	0.0	.200	3.8	.737	0.97	0.99	1.5	7.8	11.8	January	61	29.5	8.3	.502	0.0	.333	3.7	.714	1.00	0.84	1.4	7.7	11.0
vs. East	242	29.7	8.3	.486	0.0	.000	3.7	.738	0.81	0.93	1.3	7.3	10.8	February	61	29.7	8.4	.501	0.0	.000	3.3	.767	1.28	1.02	1.5	7.5	11.0
vs. West	124	31.0	8.9	.485	0.0	.500	3.4	.758	1.12	1.02	1.6	7.8	11.2	March	76	31.6	9.5	.462	0.0	.000	3.9	.768	0.95	1.04	1.4	7.6	11.8
vs. Div.	111	30.0	8.2	.494	0.0	.000	3.5	.756	0.95	0.96	1.3	7.4	10.8	Apr/May	64	28.3	8.3	.508	0.0	—	3.1	.753	0.72	0.86	1.4	6.6	10.8
As Starter	211	36.8	10.7	.481	0.0	.125	4.3	.732	1.14	1.20	1.7	8.7	13.4	0 Days Rest	98	29.6	8.1	.483	0.0	.333	3.2	.758	0.61	0.83	1.4	7.0	10.3
Off Bench	155	21.1	5.5	.498	0.0	—	2.6	.773	0.61	0.62	1.0	5.7	7.5	1 Days Rest	189	30.4	8.9	.482	0.0	.000	3.6	.738	1.08	1.03	1.4	7.4	11.3
In wins	145	27.4	7.3	.529	0.0	.000	3.2	.756	1.05	0.96	1.4	7.1	10.1	2 Days Rest	42	30.3	8.0	.507	0.0	—	3.3	.734	0.74	0.83	1.5	7.6	10.6
In losses	221	31.9	9.3	.463	0.0	.143	3.8	.738	0.82	0.95	1.4	7.6	11.5	3+ Days Rest	37	29.9	8.1	.485	0.0	—	4.4	.755	1.03	1.08	1.3	8.2	11.2

Chris Webber
Sacramento Kings — Forward

1999-2000 Per Game Averages

	G	Min	FGA	FG%	3PA	3P%	FTA	FT%	Blk	Stl	Ast	Reb	Pts
Total	75	38.4	20.6	.483	1.3	.284	5.5	.751	1.71	1.60	4.6	10.5	24.5
Home	38	39.2	20.9	.485	0.9	.306	5.3	.735	1.97	1.61	5.3	11.2	24.4
Road	37	37.6	20.4	.481	1.6	.271	5.8	.766	1.43	1.59	3.8	9.8	24.5
vs. Playoff	40	38.8	21.5	.464	1.6	.258	5.1	.713	1.48	1.45	4.4	10.3	24.0
vs. Non-Playoff	35	37.9	19.7	.507	0.9	.333	6.1	.788	1.97	1.77	4.8	10.8	25.0
vs. East	28	38.3	20.3	.514	1.5	.366	5.5	.755	1.71	1.75	4.6	11.3	25.6
vs. West	47	38.5	20.9	.465	1.1	.222	5.5	.749	1.70	1.51	4.6	10.0	23.8
vs. Div.	23	38.4	20.8	.468	1.1	.200	5.5	.780	1.65	1.48	5.0	10.0	24.0
As Starter	75	38.4	20.6	.483	1.3	.284	5.5	.751	1.71	1.60	4.6	10.5	24.5
Off Bench	0	—											
in wins	41	37.8	19.3	.523	0.8	.382	5.4	.771	1.88	1.73	4.8	10.5	24.7
in losses	34	39.1	22.2	.442	1.8	.230	5.6	.728	1.50	1.44	4.5	10.1	24.1
Pre All-Star	45	36.7	20.3	.497	1.2	.377	5.7	.747	1.67	1.44	3.9	10.7	24.8
Post All-Star	30	41.0	21.2	.464	1.4	.167	5.2	.758	1.77	1.83	5.7	10.2	23.9
November	12	35.5	17.3	.522	0.4	.200	4.8	.632	1.75	1.58	3.9	10.8	21.1
December	13	36.2	20.6	.481	0.8	.600	6.1	.823	1.54	1.00	4.3	9.9	25.3
January	15	37.0	21.8	.495	1.9	.345	5.3	.772	1.80	1.67	3.3	11.1	26.3
February	13	40.5	23.4	.457	1.9	.280	6.5	.738	1.62	1.77	4.8	11.3	26.7
March	15	40.9	20.5	.477	1.6	.125	4.3	.813	1.73	1.67	5.6	9.9	23.3
April	7	41.0	19.1	.470	0.3	.000	7.3	.686	1.86	2.14	6.7	9.6	23.0
0 Days Rest	15	35.2	19.3	.484	1.4	.095	5.9	.739	1.87	1.60	3.3	9.4	23.1
1 Days Rest	43	39.7	20.9	.489	1.3	.345	5.7	.744	1.79	1.67	5.3	11.1	25.2
2 Days Rest	9	37.7	20.0	.494	0.9	.125	4.6	.854	1.22	1.67	4.6	9.6	23.8
3+ Days Rest	8	38.4	22.4	.441	1.4	.455	4.9	.718	1.50	1.13	3.3	10.1	23.9

Last Five Seasons

	G	Min	FGA	FG%	3PA	3P%	FTA	FT%	Blk	Stl	Ast	Reb	Pts
Total	275	39.2	18.6	.495	1.9	.329	4.7	.617	1.77	1.60	4.4	10.4	21.9
Home	139	39.8	18.8	.497	1.7	.326	4.7	.625	1.88	1.55	4.7	11.0	22.1
Road	136	38.5	18.4	.492	2.1	.332	4.8	.609	1.65	1.65	4.0	9.8	21.7
vs. Playoff	152	39.4	18.9	.469	2.1	.322	4.5	.618	1.70	1.53	4.2	10.0	21.1
vs. Non-Playoff	123	38.9	18.2	.527	1.6	.342	5.1	.616	1.85	1.69	4.6	10.9	22.9
vs. East	134	39.0	18.0	.496	2.3	.338	4.8	.607	1.63	1.51	4.3	10.1	21.6
vs. West	141	39.3	19.1	.493	1.5	.318	4.7	.627	1.91	1.68	4.4	10.7	22.3
vs. Div.	85	39.6	19.0	.475	1.9	.268	4.9	.616	1.76	1.64	4.5	10.4	21.6
As Starter	275	39.2	18.6	.495	1.9	.329	4.7	.617	1.77	1.60	4.4	10.4	21.9
Off Bench	0	—											
in wins	151	39.1	18.0	.527	1.6	.354	5.1	.630	1.76	1.87	4.8	10.7	22.7
in losses	124	39.3	19.3	.457	2.3	.308	4.3	.599	1.78	1.27	3.8	10.0	21.0
Pre All-Star	149	38.3	18.6	.500	2.0	.354	4.6	.638	1.74	1.57	4.2	9.7	22.3
Post All-Star	84	39.9	18.6	.488	2.3	.330	5.2	.649	1.65	1.74	4.8	10.3	22.3
Oct/Nov	41	37.4	17.5	.497	1.6	.313	4.4	.575	1.98	1.27	3.7	9.6	20.5
December	55	37.9	18.7	.513	1.6	.398	4.7	.640	1.42	1.73	4.3	9.5	22.8
January	45	39.9	19.4	.490	2.7	.352	4.5	.676	2.02	1.69	4.5	10.1	23.1
February	36	38.8	19.6	.483	1.7	.295	5.1	.641	2.06	1.44	4.3	11.7	22.7
March	57	39.9	18.5	.488	1.8	.324	5.0	.601	1.79	1.63	4.5	10.5	21.6
Apr/May	41	41.2	17.9	.492	1.9	.263	4.7	.565	1.49	1.76	4.9	11.4	20.8
0 Days Rest	70	38.2	17.4	.525	1.7	.322	4.7	.580	1.74	1.40	4.2	9.9	21.5
1 Days Rest	132	40.0	19.1	.483	1.9	.329	5.1	.633	1.85	1.73	4.7	11.0	22.3
2 Days Rest	40	39.2	18.0	.491	1.9	.270	4.2	.645	1.45	1.53	4.0	9.8	20.9
3+ Days Rest	33	38.1	19.5	.485	2.3	.400	4.2	.594	1.91	1.61	3.8	9.9	22.4

David Wesley
Charlotte Hornets — Guard

1999-2000 Per Game Averages

	G	Min	FGA	FG%	3PA	3P%	FTA	FT%	Blk	Stl	Ast	Reb	Pts
Total	82	33.7	11.6	.426	3.0	.355	3.4	.778	0.13	1.33	5.6	2.7	13.6
Home	41	33.1	11.4	.431	2.9	.370	3.2	.818	0.10	1.61	6.2	2.6	13.6
Road	41	34.2	11.9	.422	3.1	.341	3.5	.741	0.17	1.05	5.0	2.9	13.7
vs. Playoff	44	35.0	12.1	.395	3.2	.388	2.9	.798	0.16	1.25	5.7	2.9	13.1
vs. Non-Playoff	38	32.1	11.2	.465	2.9	.312	3.8	.760	0.11	1.42	5.6	2.6	14.2
vs. East	54	34.4	12.0	.437	3.1	.351	3.6	.760	0.11	1.48	5.8	2.8	14.3
vs. West	28	32.3	11.0	.404	2.9	.363	2.8	.823	0.18	1.04	5.4	2.7	12.2
vs. Div.	28	34.4	12.2	.436	3.0	.434	4.6	.813	0.11	1.43	5.4	2.4	15.6
As Starter	82	33.7	11.6	.426	3.0	.355	3.4	.778	0.13	1.33	5.6	2.7	13.6
Off Bench	0	—											
in wins	49	33.3	11.3	.446	2.5	.355	3.9	.795	0.10	1.29	5.9	2.8	14.0
in losses	33	34.2	12.2	.400	3.8	.355	2.6	.741	0.18	1.39	5.3	2.6	13.0
Pre All-Star	47	33.2	11.1	.410	3.9	.370	3.8	.817	0.11	1.36	6.3	2.7	13.6
Post All-Star	35	34.3	12.4	.446	1.8	.313	2.7	.705	0.17	1.29	4.8	2.8	13.6
November	14	33.9	10.1	.401	3.1	.326	4.5	.841	0.14	1.57	7.1	2.7	12.9
December	15	32.5	10.9	.442	3.3	.449	3.7	.800	0.07	1.27	6.8	2.2	14.0
January	13	32.2	11.6	.417	5.0	.415	2.5	.813	0.08	1.00	5.5	3.6	13.8
February	14	35.5	11.6	.352	3.6	.220	3.6	.843	0.14	1.50	5.4	3.1	12.0
March	15	34.9	13.3	.472	1.4	.333	2.7	.756	0.33	1.60	4.5	2.6	15.1
April	11	32.7	12.5	.464	1.8	.350	3.0	.515	0.00	0.91	4.3	2.2	13.8
0 Days Rest	22	32.8	11.0	.419	2.4	.415	3.0	.818	0.14	1.00	5.0	2.9	12.6
1 Days Rest	43	33.7	11.8	.459	3.3	.355	3.3	.790	0.14	1.35	5.8	2.8	14.6
2 Days Rest	8	31.1	10.6	.329	3.5	.250	4.1	.697	0.13	1.25	5.9	1.9	10.8
3+ Days Rest	9	37.8	13.4	.372	2.9	.346	3.7	.727	0.11	2.11	6.4	2.8	13.7

Last Five Seasons

	G	Min	FGA	FG%	3PA	3P%	FTA	FT%	Blk	Stl	Ast	Reb	Pts
Total	369	34.0	11.0	.448	3.1	.373	3.6	.785	0.20	1.66	6.1	3.1	13.9
Home	185	34.0	11.0	.435	3.1	.352	3.8	.790	0.22	1.73	6.5	2.9	13.7
Road	184	34.0	11.0	.462	3.1	.393	3.4	.779	0.18	1.58	5.6	3.2	14.1
vs. Playoff	206	34.2	11.2	.434	3.2	.377	3.5	.797	0.19	1.61	5.9	3.0	13.7
vs. Non-Playoff	163	33.7	10.9	.467	3.0	.367	3.8	.771	0.22	1.71	6.3	3.1	14.2
vs. East	256	34.6	11.4	.454	3.2	.382	3.6	.771	0.20	1.78	6.1	3.0	14.1
vs. West	113	32.6	11.0	.436	2.9	.350	3.5	.818	0.21	1.38	6.0	3.1	13.5
vs. Div.	124	34.5	11.1	.453	3.2	.388	3.7	.778	0.18	1.73	6.2	3.0	14.1
As Starter	339	35.4	11.5	.451	3.2	.378	3.7	.784	0.21	1.70	6.3	3.1	14.5
Off Bench	30	17.9	5.9	.384	2.4	.292	2.5	.797	0.10	1.20	3.4	2.5	7.2
in wins	171	34.1	10.8	.468	2.7	.400	4.1	.795	0.26	1.60	6.6	3.1	14.4
in losses	198	33.9	11.3	.432	3.5	.355	3.2	.773	0.15	1.70	5.6	3.0	13.4
Pre All-Star	178	31.6	10.2	.435	3.1	.363	3.4	.800	0.21	1.52	5.8	2.8	12.7
Post All-Star	141	36.0	12.2	.464	3.0	.390	3.8	.751	0.19	1.71	6.2	3.3	15.3
Oct/Nov	47	30.0	9.7	.424	3.0	.340	3.6	.766	0.21	1.32	5.9	2.5	12.0
December	57	30.2	9.1	.462	2.8	.426	3.3	.806	0.19	1.40	5.7	2.5	12.3
January	59	33.5	11.2	.427	3.2	.358	3.3	.840	0.24	1.58	5.9	3.2	13.5
February	64	35.9	11.5	.444	3.1	.300	3.8	.767	0.11	2.03	6.4	3.4	14.2
March	80	36.2	12.0	.451	3.1	.382	3.7	.795	0.25	1.71	6.2	3.3	15.0
Apr/May	62	36.1	11.9	.475	3.3	.396	4.0	.744	0.21	1.76	6.3	3.2	15.5
0 Days Rest	100	32.7	10.2	.451	3.0	.396	3.4	.779	0.17	1.59	5.6	3.0	13.1
1 Days Rest	188	34.5	11.5	.460	3.2	.378	3.7	.805	0.22	1.68	6.1	3.2	14.7
2 Days Rest	41	35.0	11.0	.424	3.5	.326	4.2	.750	0.34	1.61	6.8	2.8	13.7
3+ Days Rest	40	34.0	10.8	.411	2.5	.337	3.1	.740	0.05	1.75	6.1	2.9	12.0

1999-2000 Per Game Averages

	G	Min	FGA	FG%	3PA	3P%	FTA	FT%	Blk	Stl	Ast	Reb	Pts
Total	80	19.2	5.6	.507	0.0	—	2.6	.536	1.04	0.39	0.2	6.9	7.1
Home	39	19.3	5.6	.543	0.0	—	2.3	.511	0.90	0.21	0.2	6.8	7.3
Road	41	19.2	5.6	.472	0.0	—	3.0	.554	1.17	0.56	0.1	7.0	7.0
vs. Playoff	45	19.5	5.8	.502	0.0	—	2.6	.539	0.96	0.36	0.2	6.9	7.2
vs. Non-Playoff	35	18.8	5.5	.513	0.0	—	2.7	.531	1.14	0.43	0.1	6.9	7.1
vs. East	53	18.7	5.5	.497	0.0	—	2.6	.569	0.98	0.26	0.2	6.8	6.9
vs. West	27	20.1	5.9	.525	0.0	—	2.7	.473	1.15	0.63	0.1	7.2	7.4
vs. Div.	24	16.3	5.0	.445	0.0	—	2.0	.510	0.88	0.17	0.3	5.8	5.5
As Starter	59	22.1	6.3	.521	0.0	—	2.9	.558	1.15	0.42	0.2	7.6	8.2
Off Bench	21	11.1	3.6	.434	0.0	—	1.9	.436	0.71	0.29	0.2	5.0	4.0
In wins	28	19.5	6.0	.545	0.0	—	2.2	.597	1.14	0.32	0.3	6.6	7.8
In losses	52	19.0	5.4	.484	0.0	—	2.9	.510	0.98	0.42	0.1	7.1	6.7

	G	Min	FGA	FG%	3PA	3P%	FTA	FT%	Blk	Stl	Ast	Reb	Pts
Pre All-Star	47	18.0	5.3	.524	0.0	—	2.6	.537	0.94	0.26	0.2	7.0	7.0
Post All-Star	33	21.0	6.1	.485	0.0	—	2.7	.534	1.18	0.58	0.1	6.8	7.3
November	13	11.2	3.9	.392	0.0	—	1.8	.478	0.85	0.23	0.3	4.9	3.9
December	15	18.1	5.2	.590	0.0	—	3.1	.500	0.80	0.33	0.2	7.2	7.7
January	14	23.9	6.4	.567	0.0	—	3.2	.578	1.29	0.14	0.2	8.2	9.1
February	12	24.3	7.8	.505	0.0	—	3.2	.474	1.08	0.50	0.1	8.8	9.3
March	17	19.5	5.2	.420	0.0	—	1.8	.567	1.12	0.76	0.2	5.9	5.4
April	9	18.1	5.6	.540	0.0	—	3.2	.621	1.11	0.22	0.1	6.7	8.0
0 Days Rest	22	18.3	5.1	.434	0.0	—	2.0	.591	1.05	0.27	0.3	6.6	5.6
1 Days Rest	37	20.1	6.0	.525	0.0	—	2.9	.523	1.05	0.46	0.1	6.8	7.9
2 Days Rest	12	17.0	5.0	.550	0.0	—	2.8	.455	0.92	0.33	0.2	7.6	6.8
3+ Days Rest	9	20.9	6.0	.537	0.0	—	2.8	.600	1.11	0.44	0.3	7.2	8.1

Career (1998-99 thru 1999-2000)

	G	Min	FGA	FG%	3PA	3P%	FTA	FT%	Blk	Stl	Ast	Reb	Pts
Total	100	17.3	4.8	.508	0.0	—	2.5	.520	0.94	0.34	0.2	6.1	6.2
Home	49	17.1	4.8	.547	0.0	—	2.2	.486	0.84	0.18	0.2	5.9	6.3
Road	51	17.5	4.8	.472	0.0	—	2.7	.547	1.04	0.49	0.1	6.4	6.0
vs. Playoff	56	17.3	4.9	.513	0.0	—	2.4	.523	0.84	0.32	0.2	6.0	6.3
vs. Non-Playoff	44	17.2	4.7	.502	0.0	—	2.6	.518	1.07	0.36	0.1	6.2	6.1
vs. East	72	16.4	4.5	.500	0.0	—	2.4	.541	0.88	0.22	0.2	5.8	5.8
vs. West	28	19.5	5.6	.525	0.0	—	2.6	.473	1.11	0.64	0.1	7.0	7.2
vs. Div.	33	14.0	4.0	.443	0.0	—	1.7	.500	0.73	0.18	0.2	5.0	4.4
As Starter	59	22.1	6.3	.521	0.0	—	2.9	.558	1.15	0.42	0.2	7.6	8.2
Off Bench	41	10.4	2.6	.463	0.0	—	1.8	.432	0.63	0.22	0.1	4.0	3.2
In wins	34	17.5	5.2	.542	0.0	—	2.1	.571	1.06	0.26	0.2	6.0	6.8
In losses	66	17.2	4.6	.489	0.0	—	2.7	.500	0.88	0.38	0.1	6.2	5.8

	G	Min	FGA	FG%	3PA	3P%	FTA	FT%	Blk	Stl	Ast	Reb	Pts
Pre All-Star	47	18.0	5.3	.524	0.0	—	2.6	.537	0.94	0.26	0.2	7.0	7.0
Post All-Star	33	21.0	6.1	.485	0.0	—	2.7	.534	1.18	0.58	0.1	6.8	7.3
Oct/Nov	13	11.2	3.9	.392	0.0	—	1.8	.478	0.85	0.23	0.3	4.9	3.9
December	15	18.1	5.2	.590	0.0	—	3.1	.500	0.80	0.33	0.2	7.2	7.7
January	14	23.9	6.4	.567	0.0	—	3.2	.578	1.29	0.14	0.2	8.2	9.1
February	19	17.5	5.0	.516	0.0	—	2.2	.452	0.79	0.42	0.1	6.2	6.2
March	20	17.0	4.5	.422	0.0	—	1.7	.559	0.95	0.65	0.2	5.2	4.8
Apr/May	19	16.1	4.1	.526	0.0	—	2.9	.536	1.00	0.16	0.1	5.4	5.9
0 Days Rest	28	16.6	4.4	.439	0.0	—	2.1	.525	0.96	0.21	0.3	5.8	5.0
1 Days Rest	46	18.3	5.3	.523	0.0	—	2.7	.512	1.00	0.41	0.1	6.1	6.9
2 Days Rest	12	17.0	5.0	.550	0.0	—	2.8	.455	0.92	0.33	0.2	7.6	6.8
3+ Days Rest	14	15.5	4.0	.554	0.0	—	2.2	.613	0.71	0.36	0.3	5.4	5.8

1999-2000 Per Game Averages

	G	Min	FGA	FG%	3PA	3P%	FTA	FT%	Blk	Stl	Ast	Reb	Pts
Total	82	19.8	6.4	.417	3.1	.376	1.6	.848	0.06	0.67	3.8	1.6	7.8
Home	41	19.3	6.3	.453	3.2	.436	1.3	.873	0.05	0.68	4.1	1.4	8.3
Road	41	20.4	6.4	.380	3.0	.311	1.9	.831	0.07	0.66	3.5	1.8	7.4
vs. Playoff	46	18.0	5.7	.395	2.7	.376	1.3	.864	0.09	0.74	3.8	1.6	6.6
vs. Non-Playoff	36	22.2	7.2	.438	3.6	.377	2.0	.836	0.03	0.58	3.8	1.7	9.4
vs. East	54	19.8	6.0	.431	2.9	.429	1.7	.878	0.07	0.69	3.9	1.5	7.9
vs. West	28	20.0	7.0	.393	3.5	.293	1.5	.786	0.04	0.64	3.6	1.9	7.7
vs. Div.	24	19.7	5.8	.450	2.9	.429	1.8	.762	0.04	0.58	3.3	1.4	7.8
As Starter	15	35.7	11.2	.464	4.7	.400	2.7	.900	0.13	1.13	7.1	2.5	14.7
Off Bench	67	16.3	5.3	.394	2.8	.368	1.4	.826	0.04	0.57	3.1	1.4	6.3
In wins	29	20.9	5.9	.494	2.5	.486	1.7	.854	0.00	0.72	3.9	1.9	8.5
In losses	53	19.3	6.6	.378	3.5	.333	1.6	.845	0.09	0.64	3.8	1.5	7.5

	G	Min	FGA	FG%	3PA	3P%	FTA	FT%	Blk	Stl	Ast	Reb	Pts
Pre All-Star	49	15.3	5.1	.382	2.8	.350	1.3	.803	0.06	0.61	2.8	1.4	5.9
Post All-Star	33	26.6	8.2	.449	3.6	.407	2.0	.894	0.06	0.76	5.3	2.0	10.6
November	15	16.7	5.9	.348	3.3	.340	1.1	.647	0.00	0.73	3.3	1.3	6.0
December	15	13.9	4.2	.365	2.4	.306	1.1	.647	0.07	0.40	2.3	1.2	4.5
January	14	14.9	4.6	.431	2.1	.333	1.4	1.000	0.07	0.86	2.7	1.4	6.1
February	12	17.1	6.0	.431	3.5	.381	1.7	.900	0.08	0.50	3.2	1.5	8.0
March	17	25.1	8.2	.407	3.5	.367	1.9	.875	0.00	0.59	5.1	2.2	9.6
April	9	36.7	10.2	.511	4.1	.541	2.9	.923	0.22	1.11	7.4	2.4	15.3
0 Days Rest	22	18.5	6.3	.398	3.2	.394	1.5	.848	0.05	0.64	3.3	1.7	7.4
1 Days Rest	39	19.9	6.1	.437	2.9	.384	1.4	.855	0.10	0.62	4.1	1.5	7.6
2 Days Rest	13	20.2	6.2	.407	3.3	.349	2.0	.808	0.00	1.08	4.1	1.3	7.8
3+ Days Rest	8	22.5	8.6	.391	3.6	.345	2.3	.889	0.00	0.38	3.3	2.5	10.0

Last Five Seasons

	G	Min	FGA	FG%	3PA	3P%	FTA	FT%	Blk	Stl	Ast	Reb	Pts
Total	306	15.0	4.8	.405	2.4	.354	1.5	.873	0.06	0.57	2.7	1.4	6.0
Home	154	14.4	4.6	.408	2.3	.389	1.4	.888	0.05	0.53	2.6	1.4	5.9
Road	152	15.6	4.9	.402	2.4	.321	1.5	.860	0.07	0.61	2.7	1.4	6.1
vs. Playoff	170	14.5	4.7	.389	2.3	.338	1.4	.906	0.07	0.59	2.7	1.4	5.7
vs. Non-Playoff	136	15.7	4.9	.422	2.4	.372	1.6	.837	0.04	0.54	2.6	1.4	6.4
vs. East	213	15.3	4.6	.410	2.3	.367	1.5	.890	0.06	0.61	2.7	1.4	6.0
vs. West	93	14.4	5.1	.394	2.5	.326	1.3	.826	0.05	0.48	2.4	1.5	5.9
vs. Div.	97	15.5	4.8	.418	2.4	.362	1.8	.862	0.05	0.64	2.5	1.3	6.4
As Starter	23	34.5	10.6	.447	4.5	.369	2.5	.914	0.17	1.00	6.7	2.7	13.4
Off Bench	283	13.4	4.3	.396	2.2	.352	1.4	.867	0.05	0.53	2.3	1.3	5.4
In wins	141	14.8	4.3	.452	2.0	.428	1.7	.882	0.05	0.55	2.6	1.3	6.2
In losses	165	15.2	5.2	.371	2.7	.308	1.3	.863	0.07	0.58	2.7	1.5	5.8

	G	Min	FGA	FG%	3PA	3P%	FTA	FT%	Blk	Stl	Ast	Reb	Pts
Pre All-Star	145	13.9	4.4	.397	2.2	.361	1.4	.841	0.07	0.61	2.4	1.2	5.5
Post All-Star	122	17.5	5.5	.410	2.5	.352	1.7	.905	0.05	0.56	3.2	1.7	7.0
Oct/Nov	46	15.2	5.8	.383	3.0	.368	1.5	.836	0.07	0.70	2.4	1.3	6.7
December	45	13.1	3.4	.394	1.7	.316	1.2	.849	0.04	0.64	2.5	1.2	4.2
January	43	12.7	3.3	.434	1.6	.373	1.6	.841	0.09	0.58	2.1	1.0	4.8
February	47	13.7	4.7	.377	2.5	.347	1.2	.860	0.06	0.38	2.4	1.4	5.4
March	71	16.2	5.4	.413	2.6	.346	1.6	.913	0.03	0.52	2.8	1.5	6.8
Apr/May	54	17.9	5.5	.424	2.7	.368	1.6	.898	0.07	0.61	3.4	1.8	7.1
0 Days Rest	83	14.9	4.8	.411	2.5	.354	1.6	.873	0.08	0.58	2.6	1.4	6.0
1 Days Rest	143	15.1	4.7	.417	2.2	.382	1.3	.879	0.07	0.47	2.9	1.5	5.9
2 Days Rest	48	14.5	4.5	.359	2.4	.296	1.6	.867	0.02	0.79	2.5	1.2	5.3
3+ Days Rest	32	15.7	5.6	.400	2.6	.325	1.6	.860	0.00	0.66	2.0	1.5	6.7

Aaron Williams

Washington Wizards — Forward-Center

1999-2000 Per Game Averages

	G	Min	FGA	FG%	3PA	3P%	FTA	FT%	Blk	Stl	Ast	Reb	Pts		G	Min	FGA	FG%	3PA	3P%	FTA	FT%	Blk	Stl	Ast	Reb	Pts
Total	81	19.1	5.6	.522	0.0	.000	2.5	.726	1.14	0.51	0.7	5.0	7.6	Pre All-Star	49	19.8	5.5	.509	0.0	—	2.7	.748	1.22	0.59	0.6	5.1	7.6
Home	40	19.8	5.9	.561	0.1	.000	2.8	.727	1.25	0.58	0.7	5.2	8.7	Post All-Star	32	17.9	5.7	.541	0.1	.000	2.2	.686	1.00	0.38	0.9	4.9	7.6
Road	41	18.4	5.2	.479	0.0	.000	2.2	.725	1.02	0.44	0.7	5.0	6.6	November	15	20.9	5.9	.449	0.0	—	3.5	.712	1.20	0.67	0.5	5.5	7.8
vs. Playoff	46	18.5	5.4	.530	0.0	.000	2.5	.761	1.02	0.57	0.8	5.3	7.6	December	15	18.1	5.1	.481	0.0	—	1.7	.769	1.13	0.40	0.5	4.8	6.3
vs. Non-Playoff	35	19.9	5.8	.512	0.0	.000	2.4	.679	1.29	0.43	0.7	4.8	7.6	January	14	21.1	5.6	.570	0.0	—	3.1	.773	1.29	0.79	0.8	5.9	8.9
vs. East	54	18.3	5.3	.526	0.0	.000	2.4	.758	1.19	0.46	0.8	4.7	7.4	February	12	18.7	5.7	.529	0.1	.000	2.3	.704	1.08	0.58	1.3	5.3	7.6
vs. West	27	20.7	6.0	.515	0.0	.000	2.7	.671	1.04	0.59	0.6	5.8	8.0	March	16	20.5	6.3	.580	0.1	.000	2.9	.739	1.06	0.44	0.7	5.8	9.4
vs. Div.	24	19.1	5.1	.475	0.0	.000	2.6	.758	1.33	0.33	1.0	4.4	6.8	April	9	12.7	4.1	.514	0.1	.000	0.7	.333	1.00	0.00	0.8	1.8	4.4
As Starter	0	—	—	—	—	—	—	—	—	—	—	—	—	0 Days Rest	22	19.2	5.9	.500	0.0	—	2.6	.707	1.09	0.73	0.7	5.3	7.8
Off Bench	81	19.1	5.6	.522	0.0	.000	2.5	.726	1.14	0.51	0.7	5.0	7.6	1 Days Rest	38	17.4	5.1	.536	0.0	.000	2.3	.747	1.05	0.45	0.8	4.6	7.1
n wins	29	20.7	6.0	.595	0.0	—	2.6	.776	1.34	0.48	0.6	5.3	9.1	2 Days Rest	13	21.5	5.5	.535	0.0	—	2.3	.733	1.31	0.54	0.5	5.4	7.5
n losses	52	18.2	5.3	.477	0.1	.000	2.4	.696	1.02	0.52	0.8	4.9	6.8	3+ Days Rest	8	22.9	7.1	.509	0.1	.000	3.3	.692	1.38	0.13	0.9	5.9	9.5

Last Five Seasons

	G	Min	FGA	FG%	3PA	3P%	FTA	FT%	Blk	Stl	Ast	Reb	Pts		G	Min	FGA	FG%	3PA	3P%	FTA	FT%	Blk	Stl	Ast	Reb	Pts
Total	219	15.2	4.3	.518	0.0	.000	1.9	.731	0.84	0.41	0.5	3.8	5.8	Pre All-Star	92	16.2	4.4	.527	0.0	.000	2.1	.745	1.00	0.48	0.4	3.9	6.2
Home	106	16.0	4.6	.545	0.0	.000	2.1	.742	1.02	0.44	0.5	3.9	6.6	Post All-Star	87	15.8	4.7	.536	0.0	.000	1.6	.713	0.77	0.37	0.6	3.9	6.3
Road	113	14.4	4.0	.488	0.0	.000	1.6	.717	0.66	0.38	0.5	3.6	5.1	Oct/Nov	29	18.1	5.2	.507	0.0	—	2.6	.724	1.07	0.45	0.3	4.2	7.1
vs. Playoff	125	15.0	4.2	.521	0.0	.000	1.9	.737	0.77	0.46	0.5	3.9	5.8	December	29	13.9	3.7	.472	0.0	—	1.4	.775	0.83	0.52	0.3	3.7	4.5
vs. Non-Playoff	94	15.4	4.4	.513	0.0	.000	1.9	.723	0.93	0.35	0.5	3.6	5.9	January	26	17.0	4.7	.579	0.0	—	2.3	.763	1.12	0.54	0.5	4.1	7.1
vs. East	98	16.6	4.7	.524	0.0	.000	1.9	.751	1.00	0.38	0.6	4.2	6.4	February	42	14.5	4.1	.506	0.0	.000	2.0	.750	0.90	0.45	0.7	3.6	5.7
vs. West	121	14.0	4.0	.511	0.0	.000	1.8	.714	0.70	0.44	0.4	3.5	5.3	March	60	16.3	4.6	.527	0.1	.000	1.9	.717	0.70	0.35	0.6	4.3	6.2
vs. Div.	69	15.2	4.0	.487	0.0	.000	1.8	.705	0.80	0.43	0.7	3.5	5.1	Apr/May	33	11.0	3.5	.504	0.0	.000	1.1	.649	0.58	0.24	0.5	2.4	4.2
As Starter	12	18.6	4.8	.621	0.0	—	1.9	.696	1.25	0.30	0.3	3.3	7.3	0 Days Rest	47	15.9	4.8	.498	0.0	—	2.1	.727	0.79	0.49	0.6	4.1	6.3
Off Bench	207	15.0	4.3	.511	0.0	.000	1.9	.733	0.81	0.42	0.5	3.8	5.7	1 Days Rest	106	14.8	4.2	.518	0.0	.000	1.8	.755	0.79	0.39	0.6	3.6	5.7
n wins	101	14.6	4.1	.565	0.0	.000	1.9	.763	0.84	0.39	0.4	3.6	6.1	2 Days Rest	34	16.0	3.9	.508	0.0	.000	1.6	.679	0.88	0.35	0.3	4.1	5.1
n losses	118	15.7	4.5	.480	0.0	.000	1.9	.703	0.83	0.43	0.6	3.9	5.6	3+ Days Rest	32	14.7	4.4	.557	0.0	.000	1.9	.710	1.00	0.44	0.3	3.5	6.3

Eric Williams

Boston Celtics — Forward

1999-2000 Per Game Averages

	G	Min	FGA	FG%	3PA	3P%	FTA	FT%	Blk	Stl	Ast	Reb	Pts		G	Min	FGA	FG%	3PA	3P%	FTA	FT%	Blk	Stl	Ast	Reb	Pts
Total	68	20.3	5.7	.427	1.1	.347	2.5	.793	0.24	0.65	1.4	2.3	7.2	Pre All-Star	36	18.8	5.5	.416	0.6	.286	2.3	.756	0.14	0.69	1.3	2.5	6.4
Home	34	18.1	5.0	.474	0.8	.429	2.3	.844	0.21	0.71	1.2	2.4	7.0	Post All-Star	32	21.9	5.9	.439	1.6	.373	2.7	.828	0.34	0.59	1.5	2.1	8.0
Road	34	22.4	6.3	.391	1.3	.295	2.7	.750	0.26	0.59	1.5	2.2	7.4	November	13	13.9	4.5	.517	0.2	.000	2.6	.824	0.00	0.31	0.7	2.3	6.8
vs. Playoff	36	20.4	5.3	.417	0.9	.212	2.6	.789	0.17	0.58	1.1	2.3	6.7	December	14	26.1	7.1	.340	0.8	.455	2.3	.719	0.14	1.07	2.1	3.1	6.9
vs. Non-Playoff	32	20.1	6.1	.438	1.2	.462	2.3	.797	0.31	0.72	1.7	2.3	7.7	January	9	14.6	4.3	.462	0.8	.143	1.8	.688	0.33	0.67	0.8	1.8	5.3
vs. East	43	19.4	5.5	.447	1.2	.396	2.4	.816	0.21	0.56	1.3	2.3	7.4	February	7	19.1	3.7	.423	0.4	.000	2.6	.611	0.29	0.29	1.1	1.7	4.7
vs. West	25	21.8	6.0	.396	0.8	.211	2.6	.758	0.28	0.80	1.5	2.2	6.9	March	15	22.4	6.5	.439	1.6	.375	3.6	.889	0.40	0.40	1.3	1.9	9.5
vs. Div.	18	18.3	4.7	.482	0.8	.500	1.6	.893	0.33	0.44	1.2	2.5	6.3	April	10	23.0	6.6	.446	2.4	.417	1.5	.867	0.30	1.10	2.0	2.6	8.1
As Starter	17	25.6	6.7	.386	1.5	.385	2.0	.853	0.47	1.29	2.2	3.1	7.5	0 Days Rest	17	21.4	5.7	.433	1.4	.208	2.4	.725	0.35	0.82	1.4	2.8	6.9
Off Bench	51	18.5	5.3	.445	0.9	.326	2.6	.778	0.16	0.43	1.1	2.0	7.1	1 Days Rest	33	20.8	6.2	.419	1.2	.421	2.2	.795	0.21	0.64	1.3	2.2	7.4
n wins	30	16.8	4.8	.458	0.8	.500	2.2	.754	0.27	0.50	1.1	1.9	6.4	2 Days Rest	8	20.3	4.4	.514	0.6	.400	2.4	.842	0.13	0.50	1.9	1.5	6.8
n losses	38	23.0	6.4	.409	1.3	.271	2.7	.817	0.21	0.76	1.6	2.6	7.8	3+ Days Rest	10	16.4	5.1	.392	0.5	.400	3.7	.838	0.20	0.50	1.1	2.2	7.3

Career (1995-96 thru 1999-2000)

	G	Min	FGA	FG%	3PA	3P%	FTA	FT%	Blk	Stl	Ast	Reb	Pts		G	Min	FGA	FG%	3PA	3P%	FTA	FT%	Blk	Stl	Ast	Reb	Pts
Total	246	25.2	8.3	.435	0.5	.310	4.4	.740	0.20	0.83	1.4	3.3	10.6	Pre All-Star	120	25.2	8.4	.445	0.3	.300	4.3	.742	0.13	0.80	1.4	3.5	10.7
Home	127	24.0	7.8	.429	0.3	.341	4.4	.757	0.17	0.87	1.4	3.2	10.1	Post All-Star	88	27.3	9.2	.441	0.7	.350	4.9	.718	0.28	0.91	1.6	3.4	11.9
Road	119	26.5	8.8	.441	0.6	.293	4.5	.721	0.22	0.77	1.4	3.3	11.2	Oct/Nov	43	23.1	7.7	.474	0.1	.000	4.8	.732	0.09	0.56	1.2	3.4	10.8
vs. Playoff	139	25.3	8.3	.413	0.5	.227	4.4	.736	0.16	0.81	1.2	3.2	10.2	December	36	26.2	7.8	.429	0.4	.500	3.4	.736	0.14	0.78	1.6	3.6	9.4
vs. Non-Playoff	107	25.1	8.2	.464	0.5	.420	4.5	.744	0.24	0.85	1.6	3.3	11.2	January	33	25.4	8.6	.412	0.2	.125	4.2	.768	0.15	1.03	1.4	3.4	10.3
vs. East	143	25.7	8.7	.449	0.5	.361	4.7	.731	0.20	0.76	1.3	3.6	11.4	February	42	26.3	8.7	.439	0.2	.222	5.1	.704	0.24	0.93	1.5	3.0	11.3
vs. West	103	24.6	7.7	.413	0.4	.227	4.0	.754	0.18	0.92	1.5	2.8	9.5	March	61	27.5	9.0	.451	0.8	.348	5.3	.769	0.30	0.79	1.3	3.4	12.5
vs. Div.	79	25.5	8.9	.420	0.4	.379	4.8	.744	0.23	0.99	1.4	3.5	11.2	Apr/May	31	21.1	7.0	.366	1.1	.303	2.6	.695	0.19	0.97	1.5	2.7	7.3
As Starter	102	32.0	10.5	.433	0.4	.341	5.3	.757	0.24	1.10	1.9	4.2	13.2	0 Days Rest	67	25.7	8.2	.422	0.5	.194	4.2	.714	0.18	0.85	1.4	3.3	10.0
Off Bench	144	20.5	6.7	.437	0.5	.292	3.8	.722	0.17	0.63	1.0	2.6	8.7	1 Days Rest	113	25.4	8.1	.439	0.5	.403	4.3	.771	0.25	0.90	1.4	3.2	10.7
n wins	81	22.1	6.9	.499	0.3	.481	3.8	.715	0.23	0.78	1.3	2.9	9.8	2 Days Rest	28	27.4	9.3	.467	0.2	.333	5.5	.680	0.04	0.89	1.8	3.6	12.4
n losses	165	26.8	8.9	.411	0.5	.258	4.7	.749	0.18	0.85	1.4	3.5	11.0	3+ Days Rest	38	22.3	8.2	.420	0.3	.167	4.2	.745	0.18	0.50	1.1	3.2	10.1

Jason Williams
Sacramento Kings — Guard

1999-2000 Per Game Averages

	G	Min	FGA	FG%	3PA	3P%	FTA	FT%	Blk	Stl	Ast	Reb	Pts
Total	81	34.1	12.0	.373	6.2	.287	2.1	.753	0.10	1.44	7.3	2.8	12.3
Home	41	34.8	12.5	.390	6.4	.294	2.6	.726	0.10	1.29	6.9	2.8	13.5
Road	40	33.4	11.5	.354	6.1	.280	1.6	.797	0.10	1.60	7.7	2.9	11.1
vs. Playoff	43	35.2	12.0	.387	6.7	.313	2.4	.745	0.07	1.35	7.0	2.7	13.2
vs. Non-Playoff	38	32.8	12.0	.357	5.7	.253	1.8	.765	0.13	1.55	7.6	3.0	11.4
vs. East	30	35.4	12.5	.341	7.0	.280	2.2	.758	0.13	1.47	8.3	3.1	12.2
vs. West	51	33.3	11.7	.393	5.8	.293	2.0	.750	0.08	1.43	6.6	2.7	12.2
vs. Div.	23	33.5	11.5	.398	6.2	.296	1.7	.725	0.09	1.39	7.0	2.7	12.2
As Starter	81	34.1	12.0	.373	6.2	.287	2.1	.753	0.10	1.44	7.3	2.8	12.3
Off Bench	0	—	—	—	—	—	—	—	—	—	—	—	—
In wins	43	34.1	12.3	.382	6.3	.296	2.7	.784	0.14	1.51	7.2	2.8	13.4
In losses	38	34.1	11.6	.362	6.2	.277	1.4	.685	0.05	1.37	7.3	2.8	11.1

	G	Min	FGA	FG%	3PA	3P%	FTA	FT%	Blk	Stl	Ast	Reb	Pts
Pre All-Star	47	34.8	13.0	.361	6.7	.279	2.7	.752	0.15	1.57	8.3	3.0	13.3
Post All-Star	34	33.0	10.6	.394	5.6	.300	1.2	.756	0.03	1.26	5.9	2.6	10.9
November	12	30.9	13.9	.353	7.2	.244	3.6	.791	0.08	1.50	7.3	2.5	14.4
December	14	34.9	13.0	.374	6.1	.318	2.9	.707	0.14	1.07	8.1	3.2	13.7
January	16	36.8	12.2	.349	6.4	.265	2.3	.730	0.19	2.19	9.1	3.1	11.9
February	13	35.5	12.2	.358	6.7	.276	0.9	.917	0.08	1.31	7.4	3.3	11.5
March	15	31.6	10.1	.351	5.2	.256	1.4	.952	0.00	1.33	5.7	2.3	9.7
April	11	34.2	10.8	.487	6.1	.388	1.5	.438	0.09	1.09	5.5	2.5	13.5
0 Days Rest	17	31.9	11.9	.365	6.2	.286	1.5	.760	0.06	1.18	7.0	2.8	11.6
1 Days Rest	50	35.2	12.1	.375	6.3	.292	2.2	.722	0.08	1.48	7.3	3.0	12.4
2 Days Rest	9	31.8	11.1	.400	4.8	.279	1.9	.882	0.11	1.56	7.1	2.2	11.9
3+ Days Rest	5	34.2	13.4	.343	8.4	.262	4.0	.800	0.40	1.80	8.0	3.0	14.6

Career (1998-99 thru 1999-2000)

	G	Min	FGA	FG%	3PA	3P%	FTA	FT%	Blk	Stl	Ast	Reb	Pts
Total	131	34.8	12.1	.374	6.3	.296	2.1	.753	0.07	1.62	6.8	2.9	12.5
Home	66	35.1	12.6	.381	6.5	.295	2.6	.734	0.06	1.50	6.5	2.8	13.4
Road	65	34.6	11.7	.365	6.2	.297	1.6	.784	0.08	1.74	7.1	3.0	11.6
vs. Playoff	69	35.3	12.6	.378	6.7	.321	2.3	.763	0.06	1.61	6.3	2.6	13.4
vs. Non-Playoff	62	34.4	11.6	.368	5.9	.264	1.9	.739	0.08	1.63	7.3	3.3	11.5
vs. East	36	35.7	12.3	.352	6.9	.305	2.2	.725	0.11	1.69	7.9	3.1	12.4
vs. West	95	34.5	12.1	.382	6.1	.292	2.1	.764	0.05	1.59	6.4	2.9	12.6
vs. Div.	43	35.3	11.9	.389	6.4	.292	2.0	.773	0.05	1.53	6.5	3.0	12.7
As Starter	131	34.8	12.1	.374	6.3	.296	2.1	.753	0.07	1.62	6.8	2.9	12.5
Off Bench	0	—	—	—	—	—	—	—	—	—	—	—	—
In wins	70	34.8	12.2	.396	6.6	.320	2.6	.789	0.09	1.63	6.9	3.0	13.8
In losses	61	34.9	12.1	.348	6.0	.266	1.5	.678	0.05	1.61	6.6	2.9	11.0

	G	Min	FGA	FG%	3PA	3P%	FTA	FT%	Blk	Stl	Ast	Reb	Pts
Pre All-Star	47	34.8	13.0	.361	6.7	.279	2.7	.752	0.15	1.57	8.3	3.0	13.3
Post All-Star	34	33.0	10.6	.394	5.6	.300	1.2	.756	0.03	1.26	5.9	2.6	10.9
Oct/Nov	12	30.9	13.9	.353	7.2	.244	3.6	.791	0.08	1.50	7.3	2.5	14.4
December	14	34.9	13.0	.374	6.1	.318	2.9	.707	0.14	1.07	8.1	3.2	13.7
January	16	36.8	12.2	.349	6.4	.265	2.3	.730	0.19	2.19	9.1	3.1	11.9
February	26	36.3	13.0	.386	6.6	.327	1.2	.742	0.08	1.92	6.5	3.1	13.0
March	34	33.0	11.0	.348	5.3	.272	2.0	.794	0.00	1.38	5.5	2.4	10.7
Apr/May	29	36.2	11.6	.415	7.0	.319	1.9	.727	0.03	1.62	6.3	3.2	13.2
0 Days Rest	34	34.6	12.1	.353	6.1	.275	1.8	.721	0.03	1.53	6.4	2.9	11.5
1 Days Rest	76	35.1	12.0	.373	6.3	.295	2.1	.733	0.05	1.55	6.9	2.9	12.4
2 Days Rest	14	33.6	11.8	.430	5.9	.341	2.1	.867	0.07	1.71	6.8	3.1	14.0
3+ Days Rest	7	35.7	14.7	.369	8.3	.310	3.3	.826	0.43	2.57	7.1	3.0	16.1

Jerome Williams
Detroit Pistons — Forward

1999-2000 Per Game Averages

	G	Min	FGA	FG%	3PA	3P%	FTA	FT%	Blk	Stl	Ast	Reb	Pts
Total	82	25.6	5.6	.564	0.0	.000	3.5	.616	0.26	1.16	0.8	9.6	8.4
Home	41	26.4	5.8	.584	0.0	.000	3.5	.576	0.27	1.34	0.9	10.5	8.8
Road	41	24.9	5.3	.541	0.0	.000	3.4	.657	0.24	0.98	0.8	8.8	8.0
vs. Playoff	44	25.0	5.6	.538	0.1	.000	3.3	.601	0.23	0.95	0.7	9.6	8.0
vs. Non-Playoff	38	26.3	5.5	.593	0.0	—	3.7	.631	0.29	1.39	1.0	9.7	8.9
vs. East	54	25.9	5.5	.559	0.0	.000	3.6	.624	0.30	1.06	1.0	9.6	8.4
vs. West	28	25.2	5.7	.572	0.1	.000	3.1	.598	0.18	1.36	0.6	9.6	8.4
vs. Div.	28	25.0	5.9	.579	0.0	—	3.3	.615	0.32	1.07	1.1	9.2	8.8
As Starter	1	42.0	7.0	.429	0.0	—	6.0	.833	2.00	1.00	2.0	17.0	11.0
Off Bench	81	25.4	5.6	.566	0.0	.000	3.4	.612	0.23	1.16	0.8	9.5	8.4
In wins	42	26.8	5.7	.629	0.0	.000	3.9	.611	0.26	1.33	1.0	10.5	9.5
In losses	40	24.4	5.4	.491	0.1	.000	3.1	.623	0.25	0.98	0.6	8.7	7.2

	G	Min	FGA	FG%	3PA	3P%	FTA	FT%	Blk	Stl	Ast	Reb	Pts
Pre All-Star	48	26.6	5.5	.586	0.0	—	3.2	.623	0.25	1.33	0.8	9.9	8.4
Post All-Star	34	24.3	5.7	.534	0.1	.000	3.8	.608	0.26	0.91	0.9	9.2	8.4
November	15	28.3	6.7	.644	0.0	—	2.9	.682	0.27	1.60	0.7	10.6	10.7
December	14	26.9	5.0	.614	0.0	—	3.8	.585	0.21	1.14	1.1	9.9	8.4
January	15	25.0	4.9	.466	0.0	—	2.7	.575	0.27	1.13	0.7	9.4	8.9
February	12	25.8	5.2	.548	0.0	—	3.0	.694	0.33	1.25	0.8	9.2	7.8
March	15	22.9	5.3	.550	0.1	.000	3.2	.521	0.13	0.73	0.6	9.6	7.5
April	11	24.8	6.4	.529	0.1	.000	5.7	.651	0.36	1.09	1.3	8.3	10.5
0 Days Rest	20	25.3	5.2	.567	0.1	.000	3.2	.587	0.40	1.05	1.0	9.7	7.8
1 Days Rest	45	25.2	5.4	.541	0.0	.000	3.7	.627	0.20	1.13	0.8	9.3	8.2
2 Days Rest	8	25.3	7.0	.643	0.0	—	3.0	.667	0.13	1.38	1.1	9.1	11.8
3+ Days Rest	9	28.9	5.8	.577	0.0	—	3.4	.581	0.33	1.33	0.6	11.3	8.7

Career (1996-97 thru 1999-2000)

	G	Min	FGA	FG%	3PA	3P%	FTA	FT%	Blk	Stl	Ast	Reb	Pts
Total	242	19.6	4.3	.529	0.0	.000	2.6	.637	0.16	0.92	0.6	6.5	6.2
Home	123	19.5	4.4	.532	0.0	.000	2.6	.636	0.16	0.97	0.6	6.7	6.4
Road	119	19.7	4.2	.526	0.0	.000	2.6	.638	0.16	0.87	0.6	6.2	6.0
vs. Playoff	131	18.8	4.1	.494	0.0	.000	2.3	.628	0.12	0.73	0.5	6.2	5.4
vs. Non-Playoff	111	20.5	4.6	.566	0.0	—	3.0	.646	0.21	1.14	0.7	6.8	7.1
vs. East	168	20.5	4.4	.528	0.0	.000	2.8	.644	0.19	0.96	0.7	6.6	6.5
vs. West	74	17.6	4.0	.534	0.0	.000	2.1	.618	0.09	0.81	0.4	6.2	5.6
vs. Div.	85	19.6	4.6	.533	0.0	—	2.7	.655	0.24	1.05	0.8	6.3	6.6
As Starter	14	30.7	6.3	.636	0.0	—	3.6	.529	0.29	2.00	0.6	9.5	9.9
Off Bench	228	18.9	4.2	.519	0.0	.000	2.5	.647	0.15	0.85	0.6	6.3	6.0
In wins	125	20.3	4.6	.564	0.0	.000	2.8	.652	0.21	1.05	0.7	7.0	7.0
In losses	117	18.8	4.0	.486	0.0	.000	2.4	.618	0.11	0.78	0.5	5.9	5.4

	G	Min	FGA	FG%	3PA	3P%	FTA	FT%	Blk	Stl	Ast	Reb	Pts
Pre All-Star	103	18.9	4.2	.537	0.0	.000	2.3	.626	0.19	0.92	0.7	6.5	5.9
Post All-Star	89	18.4	4.1	.540	0.0	.000	2.6	.625	0.13	0.72	0.6	6.2	6.0
Oct/Nov	33	16.2	3.7	.603	0.0	—	1.6	.648	0.15	0.82	0.4	5.6	5.5
December	29	22.2	5.4	.526	0.0	—	3.2	.587	0.21	0.86	1.0	7.6	7.5
January	34	18.7	3.9	.489	0.0	.000	1.9	.636	0.21	1.03	0.6	6.8	5.1
February	42	19.0	4.1	.433	0.0	—	2.6	.685	0.21	0.79	0.4	6.3	5.3
March	57	19.0	3.8	.553	0.0	.000	2.7	.632	0.07	0.86	0.6	6.4	6.0
Apr/May	47	22.2	5.2	.564	0.0	.000	3.2	.636	0.17	1.13	0.7	6.5	7.5
0 Days Rest	53	21.1	4.5	.553	0.0	.000	3.1	.614	0.23	0.91	0.8	7.1	6.9
1 Days Rest	128	21.4	4.7	.517	0.0	.000	2.9	.655	0.14	0.98	0.6	7.0	6.7
2 Days Rest	26	16.7	4.3	.577	0.0	—	1.8	.681	0.15	1.08	0.6	5.1	6.2
3+ Days Rest	35	12.8	2.7	.495	0.0	—	1.4	.542	0.14	0.57	0.2	4.7	3.4

Monty Williams

1999-2000 Per Game Averages

	G	Min	FGA	FG%	3PA	3P%	FTA	FT%	Blk	Stl	Ast	Reb	Pts		G	Min	FGA	FG%	3PA	3P%	FTA	FT%	Blk	Stl	Ast	Reb	Pts
Total	75	20.0	7.2	.489	0.1	.400	2.2	.741	0.23	0.61	1.4	3.3	8.7	Pre All-Star	45	21.3	7.9	.468	0.1	.500	2.2	.770	0.24	0.67	1.6	3.2	9.1
Home	39	20.0	6.9	.519	0.1	.500	2.3	.756	0.21	0.62	1.4	3.1	8.9	Post All-Star	30	18.1	6.1	.530	0.0	.000	2.2	.697	0.20	0.53	1.1	3.5	8.0
Road	36	20.0	7.4	.459	0.1	.333	2.1	.724	0.25	0.61	1.4	3.6	8.4	November	15	24.5	8.8	.508	0.1	.000	1.9	.750	0.33	0.87	2.3	3.9	10.3
vs. Playoff	42	21.5	7.3	.484	0.1	.333	2.4	.723	0.21	0.74	1.4	3.2	8.8	December	14	22.2	8.8	.455	0.1	1.000	2.6	.811	0.29	0.57	1.4	3.7	10.2
vs. Non-Playoff	33	18.2	7.0	.496	0.1	.500	2.0	.769	0.24	0.45	1.5	3.5	8.5	January	12	16.4	6.1	.370	0.2	.500	1.3	.875	0.17	0.42	1.2	1.6	5.8
vs. East	49	20.1	7.3	.501	0.1	.333	2.5	.750	0.27	0.67	1.3	3.6	9.3	February	11	18.1	5.9	.538	0.0	—	2.7	.633	0.00	0.55	1.0	3.2	8.1
vs. West	26	19.8	6.9	.464	0.1	.500	1.6	.714	0.15	0.50	1.7	2.8	7.6	March	15	18.7	6.7	.525	0.0	—	2.1	.710	0.27	0.67	1.3	4.1	8.5
vs. Div.	24	19.0	7.0	.494	0.1	.000	2.5	.721	0.21	0.75	1.2	3.9	8.4	April	8	18.1	5.5	.568	0.1	.000	3.0	.708	0.25	0.50	0.9	2.9	8.4
As Starter	23	23.3	9.0	.449	0.1	.333	2.3	.808	0.22	0.70	1.8	3.7	10.0	0 Days Rest	20	20.2	7.7	.409	0.1	1.000	2.6	.731	0.30	0.65	1.1	3.1	8.3
Off Bench	52	18.6	6.4	.514	0.0	.500	2.2	.711	0.23	0.58	1.3	3.2	8.1	1 Days Rest	36	20.3	7.1	.553	0.1	.500	2.0	.718	0.28	0.61	1.3	3.4	9.3
In wins	39	20.1	7.5	.524	0.1	1.000	2.6	.733	0.33	0.59	1.4	3.5	9.8	2 Days Rest	8	18.8	6.8	.481	0.1	.000	2.4	.684	0.00	0.75	1.8	4.5	8.1
In losses	36	19.9	6.8	.447	0.1	.000	1.8	.754	0.11	0.64	1.4	3.1	7.5	3+ Days Rest	11	19.8	6.6	.438	0.1	.000	2.2	.875	0.09	0.45	2.1	2.6	7.7

Last Five Seasons

	G	Min	FGA	FG%	3PA	3P%	FTA	FT%	Blk	Stl	Ast	Reb	Pts		G	Min	FGA	FG%	3PA	3P%	FTA	FT%	Blk	Stl	Ast	Reb	Pts
Total	244	17.8	5.9	.480	0.0	.333	2.3	.683	0.39	0.58	1.2	2.8	7.2	Pre All-Star	145	17.1	5.4	.476	0.0	.333	2.0	.677	0.37	0.59	1.1	2.6	6.6
Home	129	16.9	5.5	.489	0.0	.250	2.2	.668	0.38	0.56	1.1	2.7	6.9	Post All-Star	98	19.0	6.6	.485	0.0	.333	2.6	.693	0.43	0.57	1.4	3.0	8.2
Road	115	18.8	6.3	.471	0.0	.400	2.4	.699	0.40	0.60	1.3	2.9	7.6	Oct/Nov	45	17.4	5.7	.490	0.0	.000	1.7	.636	0.42	0.51	1.3	2.8	6.6
vs. Playoff	133	18.4	6.0	.477	0.0	.400	2.2	.670	0.35	0.64	1.2	2.8	7.2	December	46	16.3	5.5	.464	0.0	.500	2.2	.723	0.28	0.59	1.0	2.8	6.7
vs. Non-Playoff	111	17.1	5.8	.483	0.0	.250	2.4	.698	0.43	0.50	1.2	2.8	7.2	January	45	17.4	5.0	.460	0.1	.333	1.9	.674	0.38	0.62	0.9	2.2	5.9
vs. East	115	18.7	6.2	.489	0.0	.250	2.5	.702	0.38	0.69	1.3	2.9	7.8	February	31	18.5	6.1	.489	0.1	.500	3.2	.673	0.42	0.45	1.2	3.1	8.2
vs. West	129	17.1	5.6	.470	0.0	.400	2.1	.663	0.40	0.48	1.1	2.6	6.7	March	49	18.1	6.4	.513	0.0	—	2.2	.710	0.41	0.69	1.4	2.9	8.1
vs. Div.	74	18.2	6.2	.484	0.1	.000	2.4	.682	0.42	0.61	1.1	3.1	7.6	Apr/May	28	20.4	7.2	.448	0.0	.000	3.1	.667	0.46	0.54	1.6	3.1	8.5
As Starter	65	25.8	9.3	.473	0.1	.250	3.3	.704	0.58	0.82	2.1	3.5	11.2	0 Days Rest	47	20.9	7.5	.444	0.0	1.000	2.7	.656	0.55	0.60	1.3	3.4	8.5
Off Bench	179	14.9	4.6	.485	0.0	.400	1.9	.671	0.32	0.49	0.9	2.5	5.8	1 Days Rest	117	18.4	5.8	.496	0.0	.250	2.2	.691	0.41	0.62	1.2	2.7	7.3
In wins	129	16.8	5.5	.508	0.0	.500	2.3	.689	0.37	0.53	1.2	2.7	7.2	2 Days Rest	34	14.9	4.9	.521	0.0	—	2.4	.646	0.26	0.53	0.9	2.8	6.6
In losses	115	19.0	6.3	.452	0.0	.200	2.2	.677	0.41	0.63	1.2	2.8	7.2	3+ Days Rest	46	15.3	5.3	.459	0.0	.000	1.9	.736	0.26	0.50	1.3	2.3	6.3

Scott Williams

1999-2000 Per Game Averages

	G	Min	FGA	FG%	3PA	3P%	FTA	FT%	Blk	Stl	Ast	Reb	Pts		G	Min	FGA	FG%	3PA	3P%	FTA	FT%	Blk	Stl	Ast	Reb	Pts
Total	68	21.9	6.3	.500	0.0	—	1.9	.729	0.97	0.59	0.4	6.6	7.6	Pre All-Star	36	24.7	7.0	.518	0.0	—	2.0	.736	1.06	0.64	0.4	8.1	8.8
Home	33	22.7	6.8	.511	0.0	—	1.7	.789	0.97	0.42	0.6	6.6	8.3	Post All-Star	32	18.7	5.4	.474	0.0	—	1.8	.719	0.88	0.53	0.4	4.9	6.4
Road	35	21.1	5.8	.488	0.0	—	2.1	.681	0.97	0.74	0.3	6.6	7.1	November	1	6.0	2.0	.500	0.0	—	2.0	1.000	0.00	0.00	0.0	4.0	4.0
vs. Playoff	35	23.2	6.4	.511	0.0	—	1.3	.702	0.91	0.60	0.5	7.2	7.5	December	15	25.3	7.0	.552	0.0	—	2.0	.600	1.07	0.87	0.3	7.5	8.9
vs. Non-Playoff	33	20.5	6.1	.488	0.0	—	2.5	.744	1.03	0.58	0.3	5.9	7.8	January	15	24.9	7.2	.509	0.0	—	2.5	.811	1.27	0.40	0.3	9.0	9.3
vs. East	45	21.7	6.2	.498	0.0	—	2.1	.720	0.96	0.51	0.4	6.6	7.7	February	12	25.8	7.3	.414	0.0	—	1.5	.889	0.92	0.50	0.7	7.0	7.3
vs. West	23	22.2	6.3	.503	0.0	—	1.6	.750	1.00	0.74	0.3	6.6	7.5	March	14	17.4	4.6	.508	0.0	—	1.9	.731	0.64	0.43	0.4	4.3	6.1
vs. Div.	23	22.0	6.0	.467	0.0	—	1.3	.806	0.91	0.65	0.5	6.4	6.7	April	11	15.8	5.4	.508	0.0	—	1.5	.563	1.00	0.82	0.4	5.2	6.3
As Starter	46	24.7	6.9	.497	0.0	—	2.0	.758	1.04	0.59	0.5	7.4	8.3	0 Days Rest	16	20.4	6.8	.623	0.0	—	2.1	.647	0.75	0.56	0.3	6.5	7.4
Off Bench	22	16.1	5.0	.509	0.0	—	1.7	.658	0.82	0.59	0.3	4.9	6.2	1 Days Rest	40	22.3	6.9	.484	0.0	—	1.7	.758	1.15	0.63	0.5	6.6	7.9
In wins	34	21.9	6.4	.532	0.0	—	1.8	.710	1.18	0.62	0.4	6.2	8.1	2 Days Rest	3	24.7	7.0	.333	0.0	—	1.7	.800	1.00	0.00	0.0	6.0	6.0
In losses	34	21.8	6.2	.467	0.0	—	2.0	.706	0.76	0.56	0.4	6.9	7.2	3+ Days Rest	9	22.0	5.9	.472	0.0	—	2.7	.750	0.56	0.67	0.3	7.1	7.6

Last Five Seasons

	G	Min	FGA	FG%	3PA	3P%	FTA	FT%	Blk	Stl	Ast	Reb	Pts		G	Min	FGA	FG%	3PA	3P%	FTA	FT%	Blk	Stl	Ast	Reb	Pts
Total	208	18.5	4.8	.487	0.0	.000	1.3	.741	0.66	0.53	0.5	5.4	5.6	Pre All-Star	116	19.3	4.8	.492	0.0	.000	1.2	.748	0.66	0.54	0.5	5.8	5.6
Home	108	18.9	5.1	.490	0.1	.000	1.3	.754	0.65	0.40	0.6	5.5	6.0	Post All-Star	85	18.4	5.1	.487	0.0	.000	1.4	.741	0.68	0.55	0.5	5.0	6.0
Road	100	18.0	4.5	.482	0.0	.000	1.3	.727	0.67	0.67	0.4	5.3	5.3	Oct/Nov	37	17.6	3.9	.466	0.1	.000	0.9	.818	0.59	0.65	0.6	4.9	4.4
vs. Playoff	118	19.3	4.8	.501	0.1	.000	1.2	.739	0.67	0.51	0.5	5.6	5.6	December	43	21.1	5.1	.511	0.0	—	1.3	.672	0.70	0.58	0.5	6.3	6.2
vs. Non-Playoff	90	17.5	4.9	.468	0.0	.000	1.4	.742	0.64	0.56	0.5	5.1	5.6	January	28	18.5	5.1	.507	0.0	—	1.8	.776	0.68	0.32	0.4	6.3	6.5
vs. East	138	18.1	4.9	.480	0.0	.000	1.4	.742	0.62	0.49	0.5	5.2	5.8	February	35	18.8	4.7	.427	0.0	.000	1.1	.872	0.71	0.46	0.4	5.2	5.0
vs. West	70	19.3	4.7	.500	0.1	.000	1.0	.735	0.73	0.60	0.5	5.7	5.4	March	38	19.5	5.5	.519	0.1	.000	1.6	.712	0.74	0.53	0.6	4.9	6.8
vs. Div.	68	18.3	5.1	.487	0.0	.000	1.1	.808	0.59	0.51	0.5	5.3	5.9	Apr/May	27	13.5	4.5	.467	0.0	—	1.0	.607	0.48	0.59	0.4	4.4	4.9
As Starter	106	23.4	6.1	.505	0.0	.000	1.8	.745	0.82	0.65	0.6	7.0	7.2	0 Days Rest	52	17.6	4.1	.549	0.0	—	1.1	.690	0.56	0.50	0.6	5.3	5.3
Off Bench	102	13.4	3.5	.452	0.1	.000	1.2	.736	0.49	0.40	0.4	3.7	4.0	1 Days Rest	95	20.3	5.5	.476	0.1	.000	1.4	.741	0.86	0.57	0.5	5.7	6.3
In wins	79	18.9	5.3	.522	0.0	.000	1.4	.754	0.86	0.56	0.4	5.5	6.6	2 Days Rest	19	21.5	5.6	.477	0.1	.000	1.4	.815	0.53	0.47	0.4	6.3	6.5
In losses	129	18.2	4.6	.462	0.0	.000	1.2	.730	0.53	0.51	0.5	5.3	5.1	3+ Days Rest	42	14.0	3.7	.442	0.0	.000	1.1	.761	0.38	0.50	0.4	4.4	4.1

Walt Williams

1999-2000 Per Game Averages

	G	Min	FGA	FG%	3PA	3P%	FTA	FT%	Blk	Stl	Ast	Reb	Pts		G	Min	FGA	FG%	3PA	3P%	FTA	FT%	Blk	Stl	Ast	Reb	Pts
Total	76	24.5	9.0	.458	3.4	.391	1.6	.821	0.58	0.64	2.1	4.0	10.9	Pre All-Star	48	23.2	8.1	.432	3.6	.363	1.3	.783	0.54	0.65	1.9	3.7	9.3
Home	37	24.7	9.2	.472	3.8	.390	1.5	.855	0.62	0.70	2.4	3.9	11.5	Post All-Star	28	26.7	10.4	.493	3.2	.444	2.3	.857	0.64	0.64	2.4	4.6	13.6
Road	39	24.3	8.7	.444	3.1	.392	1.7	.794	0.54	0.59	1.8	4.1	10.3	November	15	24.4	7.2	.407	4.2	.333	0.9	.929	0.53	0.67	2.1	2.9	8.1
vs. Playoff	43	24.7	8.4	.446	3.2	.390	1.7	.859	0.49	0.56	2.1	4.0	10.1	December	13	17.4	7.8	.392	3.5	.239	0.8	.727	0.54	0.46	1.3	3.2	7.6
vs. Non-Playoff	33	24.2	9.7	.472	3.8	.392	1.6	.769	0.70	0.76	2.0	4.1	11.8	January	14	26.7	8.9	.476	3.1	.465	2.3	.719	0.71	0.57	1.9	4.9	11.5
vs. East	28	22.8	8.8	.486	2.9	.383	1.9	.852	0.61	0.57	1.7	3.6	11.3	February	13	22.4	8.5	.409	2.8	.417	1.0	.846	0.31	0.69	1.8	3.5	8.9
vs. West	48	25.4	9.0	.442	3.8	.394	1.4	.797	0.56	0.69	2.3	4.3	10.6	March	12	26.7	11.9	.490	2.9	.314	2.8	.912	0.58	0.83	2.3	4.8	15.2
vs. Div.	22	26.4	9.5	.481	3.8	.405	1.7	.868	0.36	0.68	2.0	4.2	12.1	April	9	31.3	10.4	.574	4.2	.632	2.1	.789	0.89	0.67	3.4	5.6	16.3
As Starter	66	25.7	9.2	.456	3.6	.397	1.6	.825	0.58	0.57	2.3	4.1	11.1	0 Days Rest	15	25.7	10.1	.428	3.8	.386	0.9	.857	0.27	0.60	1.4	3.5	10.9
Off Bench	10	16.5	7.6	.474	2.2	.318	2.0	.800	0.60	0.10	0.7	3.6	9.5	1 Days Rest	40	27.1	9.4	.484	3.8	.413	2.1	.819	0.58	0.68	2.6	4.8	12.3
In wins	34	25.5	9.7	.486	4.1	.486	1.7	.789	0.82	0.82	2.6	4.2	12.7	2 Days Rest	14	20.5	8.2	.452	2.6	.351	1.3	.833	0.93	0.86	1.9	3.2	9.4
In losses	42	23.6	8.4	.432	2.9	.285	1.6	.848	0.38	0.50	1.6	3.9	9.4	3+ Days Rest	7	14.9	5.7	.350	2.4	.294	1.1	.750	0.57	0.14	0.9	2.4	5.6

Last Five Seasons

	G	Min	FGA	FG%	3PA	3P%	FTA	FT%	Blk	Stl	Ast	Reb	Pts		G	Min	FGA	FG%	3PA	3P%	FTA	FT%	Blk	Stl	Ast	Reb	Pts
Total	329	27.9	10.2	.430	4.1	.394	2.5	.780	0.69	0.99	2.4	4.1	12.4	Pre All-Star	158	30.2	11.2	.430	4.4	.381	2.7	.783	0.79	1.10	2.7	4.4	13.5
Home	161	28.5	10.6	.431	4.4	.393	2.7	.763	0.78	0.99	2.8	4.3	13.0	Post All-Star	123	27.4	10.1	.433	4.1	.400	2.4	.755	0.60	0.94	2.3	4.0	12.1
Road	168	27.4	9.8	.430	3.8	.396	2.3	.798	0.60	0.99	2.0	3.8	11.8	Oct/Nov	52	31.1	11.1	.413	4.4	.398	2.7	.816	0.79	1.40	2.7	4.4	13.2
vs. Playoff	176	27.7	10.0	.422	4.0	.389	2.4	.781	0.60	0.88	2.4	4.1	11.9	December	46	28.1	10.7	.433	4.3	.350	2.3	.766	0.61	0.91	2.3	4.1	12.6
vs. Non-Playoff	153	28.2	10.5	.439	4.2	.400	2.7	.778	0.80	1.12	2.4	4.1	13.0	January	43	31.0	11.6	.429	4.4	.356	3.3	.769	0.93	0.98	2.8	4.7	14.1
vs. East	148	29.6	10.8	.444	4.3	.403	2.8	.776	0.69	1.11	2.5	4.1	13.5	February	63	29.3	10.8	.448	4.5	.447	2.5	.780	0.78	0.94	2.6	3.9	13.6
vs. West	181	26.5	9.7	.418	3.9	.387	2.3	.783	0.69	0.90	2.3	4.0	11.5	March	71	25.3	9.4	.413	3.9	.348	2.3	.762	0.62	0.82	2.1	3.8	10.9
vs. Div.	107	27.1	9.5	.436	3.8	.394	2.1	.781	0.52	0.84	2.5	3.8	11.4	Apr/May	54	24.1	8.2	.450	3.2	.471	2.1	.784	0.46	0.98	1.9	3.6	10.6
As Starter	245	30.6	11.2	.434	4.5	.400	2.7	.762	0.77	1.11	2.7	4.5	13.6	0 Days Rest	74	27.7	9.9	.423	3.9	.401	2.1	.788	0.64	0.93	2.0	3.6	11.6
Off Bench	84	20.1	7.5	.414	2.9	.370	1.9	.855	0.46	0.65	1.5	2.9	8.9	1 Days Rest	167	28.6	10.2	.432	4.3	.395	2.9	.764	0.68	0.98	2.6	4.2	12.8
In wins	156	27.7	10.5	.454	4.4	.446	2.9	.774	0.78	1.06	2.7	4.2	13.7	2 Days Rest	52	26.8	10.6	.462	4.0	.399	1.7	.795	0.92	1.06	2.3	4.2	12.7
In losses	173	28.1	10.0	.408	3.8	.341	2.2	.786	0.61	0.94	2.1	3.9	11.2	3+ Days Rest	36	27.2	10.2	.391	4.0	.371	2.8	.824	0.50	1.08	2.6	3.8	11.8

Corliss Williamson

1999-2000 Per Game Averages

	G	Min	FGA	FG%	3PA	3P%	FTA	FT%	Blk	Stl	Ast	Reb	Pts		G	Min	FGA	FG%	3PA	3P%	FTA	FT%	Blk	Stl	Ast	Reb	Pts
Total	76	22.5	8.2	.500	0.0	—	2.8	.769	0.25	0.50	1.1	3.8	10.3	Pre All-Star	42	23.5	8.6	.496	0.0	—	2.9	.762	0.29	0.57	1.3	4.2	10.8
Home	39	22.1	8.2	.484	0.0	—	2.2	.793	0.26	0.44	1.2	3.8	9.7	Post All-Star	34	21.2	7.6	.506	0.0	—	2.6	.778	0.21	0.41	0.8	3.3	9.8
Road	37	22.8	8.2	.516	0.0	—	3.4	.752	0.24	0.57	0.9	3.8	11.0	November	12	20.9	8.0	.448	0.0	—	1.9	.565	0.25	0.33	1.4	3.3	8.3
vs. Playoff	40	23.1	8.0	.480	0.0	—	3.2	.837	0.33	0.50	1.1	3.8	10.4	December	15	25.5	10.3	.500	0.0	—	3.7	.768	0.33	1.00	1.3	5.4	13.1
vs. Non-Playoff	36	21.7	8.4	.521	0.0	—	2.3	.663	0.17	0.50	1.1	3.8	10.3	January	15	23.5	7.5	.531	0.0	—	2.9	.860	0.27	0.33	1.2	3.8	10.5
vs. East	26	22.5	8.2	.537	0.0	—	2.2	.732	0.42	0.35	1.2	3.8	10.4	February	8	19.9	7.5	.500	0.0	—	2.8	.727	0.00	0.38	0.4	2.5	9.5
vs. West	50	22.5	8.2	.480	0.0	—	3.1	.782	0.16	0.58	1.0	3.8	10.3	March	15	20.0	6.9	.529	0.0	—	1.9	.793	0.33	0.40	1.0	3.5	8.9
vs. Div.	24	23.0	8.7	.488	0.0	—	3.3	.788	0.21	0.71	1.0	3.8	11.1	April	11	23.9	8.6	.484	0.0	—	3.5	.795	0.18	0.45	0.9	3.6	11.2
As Starter	76	22.5	8.2	.500	0.0	—	2.8	.769	0.25	0.50	1.1	3.8	10.3	0 Days Rest	17	22.4	6.8	.461	0.0	—	3.0	.824	0.24	0.24	1.1	3.9	8.7
Off Bench	0	—	—	—	—	—	—	—	—	—	—	—	—	1 Days Rest	45	23.1	8.9	.512	0.0	—	3.2	.761	0.27	0.60	1.1	3.8	11.6
In wins	41	22.8	8.3	.538	0.0	—	2.9	.782	0.22	0.41	1.4	4.2	11.2	2 Days Rest	9	18.9	6.7	.550	0.0	—	0.8	.714	0.33	0.33	0.7	3.3	7.9
In losses	35	22.1	8.1	.454	0.0	—	2.7	.753	0.29	0.60	0.7	3.4	9.3	3+ Days Rest	5	23.6	9.0	.422	0.0	—	2.4	.667	0.00	0.80	1.4	4.4	9.2

Career (1995-96 thru 1999-2000)

	G	Min	FGA	FG%	3PA	3P%	FTA	FT%	Blk	Stl	Ast	Reb	Pts		G	Min	FGA	FG%	3PA	3P%	FTA	FT%	Blk	Stl	Ast	Reb	Pts
Total	337	25.2	9.9	.492	0.1	.050	3.5	.664	0.39	0.64	1.6	4.1	12.0	Pre All-Star	157	25.6	9.6	.481	0.1	.000	3.3	.683	0.44	0.71	1.8	4.3	11.5
Home	167	25.4	10.3	.488	0.1	.077	3.5	.679	0.46	0.68	1.7	4.4	12.4	Post All-Star	130	23.9	9.7	.510	0.1	.000	3.6	.653	0.43	0.57	1.4	3.9	12.2
Road	170	25.0	9.4	.497	0.0	.000	3.4	.649	0.33	0.60	1.4	3.8	11.6	Oct/Nov	44	26.5	9.6	.472	0.0	.000	3.1	.630	0.43	0.66	1.8	4.3	11.0
vs. Playoff	187	25.5	9.7	.483	0.0	.111	3.6	.684	0.40	0.59	1.5	3.9	11.9	December	49	26.8	10.5	.486	0.0	.000	3.9	.693	0.59	0.90	2.0	4.8	12.9
vs. Non-Playoff	150	24.9	10.0	.504	0.1	.000	3.3	.636	0.39	0.69	1.7	4.3	12.2	January	53	24.8	9.4	.480	0.1	.000	3.0	.725	0.25	0.58	1.6	4.3	11.2
vs. East	110	24.4	9.6	.492	0.1	.000	3.1	.693	0.35	0.65	1.7	3.9	11.6	February	58	24.8	9.7	.477	0.1	.000	3.4	.622	0.47	0.64	1.5	4.2	12.3
vs. West	227	25.6	10.0	.493	0.1	.077	3.7	.652	0.41	0.63	1.5	4.2	12.3	March	76	23.6	9.3	.516	0.0	.000	3.7	.650	0.33	0.50	1.2	3.8	12.0
vs. Div.	105	25.3	10.2	.513	0.0	.000	3.7	.645	0.39	0.63	1.5	4.2	12.9	Apr/May	57	25.9	10.8	.509	0.1	.167	3.8	.670	0.35	0.63	1.5	4.3	13.6
As Starter	235	28.9	11.2	.492	0.1	.077	4.0	.660	0.40	0.72	1.8	4.6	13.7	0 Days Rest	78	25.5	9.6	.490	0.0	.000	3.6	.681	0.28	0.54	1.5	3.9	11.8
Off Bench	102	16.8	6.9	.494	0.1	.000	2.3	.680	0.38	0.45	0.9	2.9	8.3	1 Days Rest	184	25.7	10.2	.491	0.1	.077	3.7	.670	0.42	0.66	1.7	4.1	12.5
In wins	147	24.9	9.7	.517	0.1	.000	3.4	.685	0.41	0.65	1.7	4.3	12.4	2 Days Rest	43	23.9	9.5	.511	0.0	.000	2.7	.649	0.51	0.65	1.4	4.3	11.4
In losses	190	25.5	10.0	.474	0.1	.083	3.5	.648	0.38	0.63	1.5	3.9	11.7	3+ Days Rest	32	23.7	9.0	.483	0.1	.000	3.3	.594	0.34	0.72	1.4	4.2	10.7

Kevin Willis
Toronto Raptors — Forward-Center

1999-2000 Per Game Averages

	G	Min	FGA	FG%	3PA	3P%	FTA	FT%	Blk	Stl	Ast	Reb	Pts		G	Min	FGA	FG%	3PA	3P%	FTA	FT%	Blk	Stl	Ast	Reb	Pts
Total	79	21.3	7.2	.415	0.0	.333	2.1	.799	0.61	0.46	0.6	6.1	7.6	Pre All-Star	47	20.6	7.2	.398	0.0	.000	2.2	.810	0.66	0.49	0.7	6.3	7.6
Home	41	21.5	7.2	.380	0.0	.000	2.1	.849	0.78	0.41	0.6	6.4	7.2	Post All-Star	32	22.2	7.2	.439	0.0	1.000	1.8	.780	0.53	0.41	0.6	5.9	7.8
Road	38	21.0	7.2	.453	0.1	.500	2.1	.744	0.42	0.50	0.6	5.8	8.1	November	15	20.5	7.2	.398	0.1	.000	2.4	.833	1.00	0.67	1.0	6.4	7.7
vs. Playoff	40	21.4	7.3	.390	0.1	.333	2.5	.780	0.58	0.45	0.6	6.3	7.6	December	14	20.6	7.1	.440	0.0	—	2.7	.842	0.79	0.14	0.6	6.6	8.6
vs. Non-Playoff	39	21.1	7.2	.441	0.0	—	1.6	.828	0.64	0.46	0.6	5.9	7.7	January	14	21.7	7.9	.400	0.1	.000	2.0	.714	0.29	0.64	0.4	6.3	7.7
vs. East	51	21.1	7.1	.404	0.0	.000	1.9	.811	0.57	0.47	0.6	5.5	7.3	February	12	17.8	5.8	.319	0.0	—	1.8	.810	0.58	0.58	0.3	4.6	5.1
vs. West	28	21.5	7.3	.434	0.1	.500	2.5	.783	0.68	0.43	0.7	7.1	8.3	March	17	23.2	7.7	.504	0.1	1.000	1.6	.704	0.41	0.24	0.5	6.8	8.9
vs. Div.	27	21.7	7.4	.385	0.0	.000	1.6	.814	0.48	0.41	0.6	5.7	7.0	April	7	24.3	7.3	.333	0.0	—	2.0	.929	0.57	0.57	0.4	5.0	6.7
As Starter	1	27.0	11.0	.091	0.0	—	4.0	.750	0.00	0.0	0.0	7.0	5.0	0 Days Rest	17	23.4	7.9	.459	0.1	1.000	2.5	.762	0.41	0.41	0.6	6.1	9.2
Off Bench	78	21.2	7.2	.421	0.0	.333	2.1	.800	0.62	0.46	0.6	6.1	7.7	1 Days Rest	45	20.2	6.6	.413	0.0	—	2.0	.784	0.62	0.38	0.5	5.9	7.0
in wins	45	21.3	6.9	.441	0.0	.500	1.6	.822	0.69	0.42	0.5	6.4	7.4	2 Days Rest	9	21.4	7.7	.406	0.0	—	1.3	.917	0.44	0.67	0.9	6.3	7.4
in losses	34	21.1	7.6	.384	0.0	.000	2.7	.780	0.50	0.50	0.6	5.7	7.9	3+ Days Rest	8	22.6	8.4	.343	0.3	.000	2.8	.864	1.13	0.75	0.8	6.8	8.1

Last Five Seasons

	G	Min	FGA	FG%	3PA	3P%	FTA	FT%	Blk	Stl	Ast	Reb	Pts		G	Min	FGA	FG%	3PA	3P%	FTA	FT%	Blk	Stl	Ast	Reb	Pts
Total	352	27.1	9.9	.466	0.1	.143	2.9	.765	0.53	0.55	0.9	7.7	11.5	Pre All-Star	181	26.9	9.8	.470	0.1	.150	2.9	.758	0.48	0.52	0.8	7.8	11.4
Home	187	27.8	10.3	.465	0.1	.118	2.9	.758	0.62	0.55	1.0	8.2	11.8	Post All-Star	129	26.7	9.9	.477	0.1	.154	2.7	.741	0.57	0.54	0.8	7.3	11.5
Road	165	26.2	9.6	.467	0.1	.167	2.9	.772	0.43	0.55	0.8	7.1	11.2	Oct/Nov	56	26.3	8.8	.469	0.1	.167	2.9	.753	0.45	0.52	1.2	7.5	10.5
vs. Playoff	196	26.8	9.8	.451	0.1	.190	2.9	.738	0.47	0.54	0.9	7.4	11.0	December	53	27.1	10.3	.498	0.0	.000	3.2	.786	0.53	0.47	0.7	7.9	12.8
vs. Non-Playoff	156	27.3	10.1	.484	0.1	.071	3.0	.797	0.60	0.56	0.9	8.0	12.2	January	58	26.7	10.0	.456	0.2	.222	2.7	.716	0.48	0.64	0.7	7.6	11.1
vs. East	184	26.9	9.6	.445	0.1	.143	2.8	.772	0.53	0.53	0.9	7.6	10.7	February	60	26.3	10.0	.445	0.1	.000	3.3	.759	0.52	0.47	0.9	8.1	11.4
vs. West	168	27.2	10.3	.487	0.1	.143	3.0	.757	0.53	0.57	0.9	7.8	12.4	March	72	28.2	10.8	.467	0.1	.333	2.6	.731	0.50	0.65	1.1	7.8	12.0
vs. Div.	117	27.1	10.1	.473	0.1	.111	2.8	.785	0.56	0.55	0.9	7.5	11.8	Apr/May	53	27.4	9.4	.462	0.1	.000	3.1	.846	0.74	0.51	0.9	7.1	11.2
As Starter	205	31.5	11.8	.471	0.1	.120	3.4	.779	0.53	0.64	1.1	9.0	13.8	0 Days Rest	70	27.1	9.9	.448	0.1	.200	3.5	.790	0.51	0.46	0.9	7.8	11.6
Off Bench	147	20.9	7.3	.454	0.1	.200	2.3	.736	0.53	0.42	0.6	5.9	8.3	1 Days Rest	198	26.9	9.8	.464	0.1	.167	2.8	.754	0.54	0.54	0.9	7.6	11.2
in wins	187	26.8	9.7	.477	0.1	.150	2.7	.773	0.59	0.56	1.0	7.8	11.3	2 Days Rest	50	26.6	10.6	.501	0.1	.200	2.6	.750	0.50	0.46	0.9	7.8	12.6
in losses	165	27.3	10.2	.454	0.1	.133	3.2	.757	0.46	0.53	0.8	7.6	11.7	3+ Days Rest	34	28.3	9.9	.458	0.2	.000	2.8	.781	0.59	0.91	1.1	8.0	11.3

Lorenzen Wright
Atlanta Hawks — Forward-Center

1999-2000 Per Game Averages

	G	Min	FGA	FG%	3PA	3P%	FTA	FT%	Blk	Stl	Ast	Reb	Pts		G	Min	FGA	FG%	3PA	3P%	FTA	FT%	Blk	Stl	Ast	Reb	Pts
Total	75	16.1	4.8	.499	0.0	.333	1.8	.644	0.53	0.39	0.3	4.1	6.0	Pre All-Star	44	15.1	4.0	.534	0.0	.000	1.9	.607	0.34	0.32	0.2	3.8	5.4
Home	39	16.9	5.0	.492	0.0	—	1.8	.676	0.56	0.38	0.3	4.6	6.2	Post All-Star	31	17.5	6.0	.465	0.1	.500	1.6	.706	0.81	0.48	0.4	4.4	6.8
Road	36	15.1	4.6	.506	0.1	.333	1.8	.609	0.50	0.39	0.3	3.5	5.8	November	15	16.8	4.3	.531	0.0	—	2.0	.500	0.47	0.27	0.0	4.1	5.5
vs. Playoff	42	16.5	5.4	.476	0.0	.500	1.8	.613	0.52	0.38	0.2	4.4	6.2	December	11	17.3	5.1	.536	0.1	.000	2.9	.625	0.45	0.55	0.3	5.0	7.3
vs. Non-Playoff	33	15.6	4.1	.537	0.0	.000	1.8	.683	0.55	0.39	0.3	3.7	5.7	January	13	13.5	3.2	.488	0.0	—	1.5	.700	0.23	0.31	0.3	2.8	4.2
vs. East	50	17.4	5.0	.490	0.1	.333	2.1	.673	0.60	0.40	0.3	4.0	6.4	February	11	8.6	2.5	.630	0.0	—	0.2	1.000	0.45	0.18	0.3	2.8	3.3
vs. West	25	13.5	4.4	.518	0.0	—	1.1	.536	0.40	0.36	0.2	4.2	5.2	March	17	18.0	6.5	.477	0.0	—	1.2	.700	0.71	0.53	0.4	4.6	7.1
vs. Div.	27	17.6	5.4	.538	0.1	.333	2.3	.661	0.44	0.41	0.4	4.3	7.3	April	8	23.3	7.8	.419	0.3	.500	3.9	.710	1.00	0.50	0.6	5.5	9.4
As Starter	0	—	—	—	—	—	—	—	—	—	—	—	—	0 Days Rest	20	16.7	4.8	.573	0.1	.500	2.8	.625	0.55	0.40	0.2	3.9	7.3
Off Bench	75	16.1	4.8	.499	0.0	.333	1.8	.644	0.53	0.39	0.3	4.1	6.0	1 Days Rest	33	17.2	5.2	.451	0.0	.000	2.0	.677	0.45	0.27	0.3	4.3	6.1
in wins	27	16.0	4.4	.567	0.0	—	1.7	.711	0.70	0.52	0.4	4.4	6.2	2 Days Rest	12	13.8	4.3	.471	0.0	—	0.8	.600	0.67	0.50	0.4	4.1	4.5
in losses	48	16.1	5.0	.465	0.1	.333	1.9	.611	0.44	0.31	0.2	3.9	5.8	3+ Days Rest	10	13.8	4.1	.561	0.0	—	0.4	.500	0.60	0.60	0.3	3.7	4.8

Career (1996-97 thru 1999-2000)

	G	Min	FGA	FG%	3PA	3P%	FTA	FT%	Blk	Stl	Ast	Reb	Pts		G	Min	FGA	FG%	3PA	3P%	FTA	FT%	Blk	Stl	Ast	Reb	Pts
Total	269	23.6	6.1	.469	0.0	.200	2.3	.644	0.83	0.59	0.6	6.5	7.3	Pre All-Star	125	21.8	6.0	.477	0.0	.200	2.4	.625	0.71	0.57	0.5	5.7	7.2
Home	140	24.0	6.4	.458	0.0	.000	2.3	.646	0.89	0.55	0.6	6.8	7.3	Post All-Star	96	25.8	6.8	.465	0.0	.250	2.1	.645	1.02	0.64	0.6	7.0	7.7
Road	129	23.1	5.9	.482	0.0	.333	2.3	.643	0.77	0.63	0.6	6.2	7.2	Oct/Nov	44	16.9	4.7	.481	0.0	.000	2.1	.634	0.77	0.52	0.2	3.9	5.9
vs. Playoff	154	24.1	6.6	.453	0.0	.286	2.3	.637	0.75	0.62	0.6	6.6	7.5	December	39	26.8	7.5	.466	0.0	.000	3.1	.667	0.77	0.69	0.9	7.2	9.1
vs. Non-Playoff	115	22.9	5.5	.495	0.0	.000	2.3	.654	0.94	0.54	0.5	6.3	7.0	January	33	22.8	5.9	.464	0.1	.333	2.1	.551	0.55	0.61	0.4	5.7	6.7
vs. East	110	23.1	6.1	.459	0.1	.167	2.5	.670	0.74	0.55	0.5	5.9	7.3	February	46	25.5	5.8	.474	0.0	—	2.1	.611	0.96	0.46	0.8	7.4	6.7
vs. West	159	23.9	6.2	.476	0.0	.250	2.1	.623	0.89	0.62	0.7	6.9	7.2	March	61	23.5	6.3	.484	0.0	.000	2.0	.681	0.72	0.67	0.6	6.8	7.4
vs. Div.	89	23.1	5.9	.482	0.0	.250	2.3	.608	0.72	0.60	0.7	6.2	7.1	Apr/May	46	26.1	6.6	.444	0.1	.333	2.7	.672	1.15	0.57	0.6	7.5	7.7
As Starter	104	32.2	8.1	.467	0.1	.167	2.8	.631	1.13	0.79	0.9	9.1	9.3	0 Days Rest	70	23.4	6.0	.466	0.1	.400	2.2	.656	0.80	0.51	0.6	6.5	7.1
Off Bench	165	18.2	4.9	.471	0.0	.250	2.0	.656	0.64	0.46	0.4	4.8	5.9	1 Days Rest	131	24.8	6.4	.462	0.0	.000	2.7	.634	0.83	0.55	0.7	6.9	7.6
in wins	84	22.7	5.7	.537	0.0	.000	2.2	.674	1.06	0.65	0.6	6.4	7.7	2 Days Rest	36	20.6	5.5	.457	0.0	—	1.7	.590	0.67	0.61	0.4	5.4	6.0
in losses	185	24.0	6.3	.441	0.0	.250	2.3	.632	0.72	0.56	0.6	6.5	7.1	3+ Days Rest	32	22.5	6.3	.520	0.0	.000	1.6	.745	1.06	0.88	0.4	6.0	7.8

Standings, Postseason Statistics & Team Statistics

Postseason and Team Statistics include all official stats for both the team in question and its opponents. In the Team Statistics, all league-leading totals appear in boldface. Because teams play different numbers of postseason games, only the percentage categories are eligible for bolding in the Postseason Statistics. There is an additional page dedicated to team records when certain criteria are met. For example, the Minnesota Timberwolves were 7-1 in overtime games and the Los Angeles Lakers were 57-2 when they had a higher field-goal percentage than their opponent.

Final 1999-2000

NBA Regular Season Standings

EASTERN CONFERENCE

ATLANTIC	W-L	Pct.	GB
Miami	52-30	.634	—
New York	50-32	.610	2
Philadelphia	49-33	.598	3
Orlando	41-41	.500	11
Boston	35-47	.427	17
New Jersey	31-51	.378	21
Washington	29-53	.354	23

CENTRAL	W-L	Pct.	GB
Indiana	56-26	.683	—
Charlotte	49-33	.598	7
Toronto	45-37	.549	11
Detroit	42-40	.512	14
Milwaukee	42-40	.512	14
Cleveland	32-50	.390	24
Atlanta	28-54	.341	28
Chicago	17-65	.207	39

WESTERN CONFERENCE

MIDWEST	W-L	Pct.	GB
Utah	55-27	.671	—
San Antonio	53-29	.646	2
Minnesota	50-32	.610	5
Dallas	40-42	.488	15
Denver	35-47	.427	20
Houston	34-48	.415	21
Vancouver	22-60	.268	33

PACIFIC	W-L	Pct.	GB
LA Lakers	67-15	.817	—
Portland	59-23	.720	8
Phoenix	53-29	.646	14
Seattle	45-37	.549	22
Sacramento	44-38	.537	23
Golden State	19-63	.232	48
LA Clippers	15-67	.183	52

2000 Postseason Results
(team in italics had home-court advantage)

East First Round
Indiana 3—Milwaukee 2
Miami 3—Detroit 0
New York 3—Toronto 0
Philadelphia 3—*Charlotte 1*

West First Round
LA Lakers 3—Sacramento 2
Utah 3—Seattle 2
Portland 3—Minnesota 1
Phoenix 3—*San Antonio 1*

East Semifinals
Indiana 4—Philadelphia 2
New York 4—*Miami 3*

West Semifinals
LA Lakers 4—Phoenix 1
Portland 4—Utah 1

Eastern Conference Finals
Indiana 4—New York 2

Western Conference Finals
LA Lakers 4—Portland 3

NBA Finals
LA Lakers 4—Indiana 2

1999-2000 NBA Postseason Team Totals

			Field Goals			3-Pt FGs			Free Throws			Misc			Fouls		Assists		Rebounds			Points	
Tm	G	Min	Made	Att	Pct	Md	Att	Pct	Made	Att	Pct	TO	Stl	Blk	PF	DQ	Ast	Avg	Off	Tot	Avg	Pts	Avg
LAL	23	5545	859	1849	**.465**	124	355	.349	453	727	.623	280	151	140	582	7	502	21.8	304	997	43.3	2295	**99.8**
Ind	23	5545	804	1814	.443	164	433	.379	484	585	**.827**	267	125	107	538	7	468	20.3	232	932	40.5	2256	98.1
Sac	5	1200	168	405	.415	33	87	.379	113	150	.753	60	34	18	110	2	84	16.8	59	206	41.2	482	96.4
Mil	5	1200	189	413	.458	18	58	.310	84	110	.764	59	33	28	125	1	103	20.6	57	214	42.8	480	96.0
Phi	10	2425	342	800	.428	39	123	.317	219	295	.742	127	65	45	226	2	191	19.1	135	424	42.4	942	94.2
Sea	5	1200	174	398	.437	35	82	**.427**	83	116	.716	73	41	17	109	2	99	19.8	62	205	41.0	466	93.2
Por	16	3840	519	1170	.444	87	234	.372	355	452	.785	203	118	61	404	5	308	19.3	156	611	38.2	1480	92.5
Cha	4	985	129	300	.430	18	60	.300	89	108	.824	62	33	23	88	1	91	22.8	54	176	44.0	365	91.3
Uta	10	2400	331	746	.444	46	123	.374	175	237	.738	149	69	54	250	1	236	23.6	103	403	40.3	883	88.3
Pho	9	2160	301	740	.407	42	151	.278	142	203	.700	138	73	56	247	2	189	21.0	125	404	44.9	786	87.3
Min	4	960	137	306	.448	12	39	.308	55	70	.786	47	24	16	95	1	94	23.5	41	140	35.0	341	85.3
NY	16	3865	499	1158	.431	72	183	.393	281	368	.764	188	104	65	367	5	234	14.6	129	615	38.4	1351	84.4
Tor	3	720	83	222	.374	13	47	.277	72	93	.774	43	27	13	78	0	57	19.0	39	128	42.7	251	83.7
Mia	10	2425	309	737	.419	47	149	.315	167	242	.690	140	72	51	261	5	191	19.1	105	434	43.4	832	83.2
SA	4	960	113	304	.372	12	44	.273	89	122	.730	65	35	30	83	0	60	15.0	49	185	**46.3**	327	81.8
Det	3	720	84	208	.404	13	35	.371	58	81	.716	51	18	5	74	1	44	14.7	18	103	34.3	239	79.7
Tot		36150	5041	11570	.436	775	2203	.352	2919	3959	.737	1952	1022	729	3637	42	2951	19.7	1668	6177	41.2	13776	91.8

1999-2000 NBA Postseason Opponent Totals

			Field Goals			3-Pt FGs			Free Throws			Misc			Fouls		Assists		Rebounds			Points	
Tm	G	Min	Made	Att	Pct	Md	Att	Pct	Made	Att	Pct	TO	Stl	Blk	PF	DQ	Ast	Avg	Off	Tot	Avg	Pts	Avg
Mia	10	2425	288	713	.404	39	114	.342	192	251	.765	128	67	33	233	3	139	13.9	78	381	38.1	807	**80.7**
SA	4	960	133	335	**.397**	16	59	**.271**	50	72	.694	62	37	39	101	0	83	20.8	56	192	48.0	332	83.0
NY	16	3865	487	1206	.404	92	278	.331	302	396	.763	198	101	68	368	3	299	18.7	177	682	42.6	1368	85.5
Min	4	960	125	287	.436	23	62	.371	76	91	.835	51	21	15	84	1	78	19.5	35	141	**35.3**	349	87.3
Tor	3	720	91	201	.453	16	34	.471	65	87	.747	48	24	15	72	1	36	**12.0**	23	111	37.0	263	87.7
Por	16	3840	519	1167	.445	77	230	.335	289	427	.677	210	89	86	426	6	362	22.6	152	599	37.4	1404	87.8
Det	3	720	103	215	.479	14	34	.412	50	73	.685	52	28	22	90	2	64	21.3	25	124	41.3	270	90.0
Pho	9	2160	287	696	.412	33	111	.297	212	309	.686	128	75	62	196	0	155	17.2	126	413	45.9	819	91.0
Uta	10	2400	336	758	.443	60	151	.397	200	273	.733	142	84	38	233	2	203	20.3	116	403	40.3	932	93.2
Cha	4	985	137	320	.428	24	60	.400	78	101	.772	51	28	24	97	1	85	21.3	52	162	40.5	376	94.0
Mil	5	1200	170	408	.417	24	81	.296	107	137	.781	58	21	17	109	0	92	18.4	66	209	41.8	471	94.2
Sea	5	1200	180	384	.469	30	65	.462	82	105	.781	79	41	29	111	0	126	25.2	56	210	42.0	472	94.4
Ind	23	5545	844	1857	.454	98	283	.346	409	594	.689	266	142	102	550	6	452	19.7	259	950	41.3	2195	95.4
Phi	10	2425	347	773	.449	63	180	.350	198	240	.825	133	74	61	239	3	231	23.1	110	408	40.8	955	95.5
LAL	23	5545	786	1804	.436	147	398	.369	522	667	.783	290	157	86	611	13	437	19.0	247	937	40.7	2241	97.4
Sac	5	1200	208	446	.466	19	63	.302	87	136	**.640**	56	33	32	117	1	109	21.8	90	255	51.0	522	104.4
Tot		36150	5041	11570	.436	775	2203	.352	2919	3959	.737	1952	1022	729	3637	42	2951	19.7	1668	6177	41.2	13776	91.8

1999-2000 NBA Regular Season Team Totals

Tm	G	Min	Field Goals Made	Att	Pct	3-Pt FGs Md	Att	Pct	Free Throws Made	Att	Pct	Misc TO	Stl	Blk	Fouls PF	DQ	Assists Ast	Avg	Rebounds Off	Tot	Avg	Points Pts	Avg
Sac	82	19805	**3276**	**7288**	.450	534	**1656**	.322	1521	2016	.754	1325	787	381	1729	15	1953	23.8	1056	3691	45.0	8607	105.0
Det	82	19830	3044	6635	.459	439	1223	.359	**1956**	**2506**	.781	1288	665	273	2011	27	1707	20.8	917	3375	41.2	8483	103.5
Dal	82	19730	3195	7047	.453	519	1326	.391	1407	1751	.804	1124	592	416	1770	22	1810	22.1	931	3375	41.2	8316	101.4
Ind	82	19730	3047	6640	.459	**583**	1487	**.392**	1629	2008	**.811**	1159	559	422	1786	**6**	1857	22.6	842	3454	42.1	8306	101.3
Mil	82	19855	3174	6827	.465	394	1069	.369	1558	1982	.786	1230	671	381	2020	21	1852	22.6	1016	3389	41.3	8300	101.2
LAL	82	19805	3137	6836	.459	344	1047	.329	1649	2368	.696	1143	613	534	1841	10	1921	23.4	1117	**3855**	**47.0**	8267	100.8
Orl	82	19755	3169	7014	.452	294	870	.338	1574	2142	.735	1443	743	467	1967	11	1709	20.8	1008	3594	43.8	8206	100.1
Hou	82	19830	3001	6664	.450	581	1625	.358	1573	2145	.733	1425	613	438	**1663**	7	1774	21.6	1108	3528	43.0	8156	99.5
Bos	82	19730	3054	6880	.444	417	1260	.331	1621	2175	.745	1152	**795**	286	1776	11	1878	22.9	1042	3525	43.0	8146	99.3
Sea	82	19830	3108	6946	.447	546	1611	.339	1363	1960	.695	1363	657	345	1962	25	1911	23.3	1073	3663	44.7	8125	99.1
Den	82	19855	3057	6911	.442	470	1397	.336	1531	2116	.724	1281	554	**618**	1962	25	1911	23.3	1073	3580	43.7	8115	99.0
Pho	82	19805	3093	6771	.457	458	1246	.368	1467	1934	.759	1369	744	433	1973	17	1913	23.3	1016	3487	42.5	8111	98.9
Min	82	**19905**	3226	6910	.467	248	716	.346	1379	1769	.780	1379	622	444	1913	25	**2205**	26.9	884	3519	42.9	8079	98.5
Cha	82	19780	2935	6533	.449	339	1001	.339	1863	2458	.758	1206	732	480	1670	16	2023	24.7	1040	3355	40.9	8072	98.4
NJ	82	19830	2979	6881	.433	477	1374	.347	1601	2041	.784	**1119**	720	393	1913	19	1688	20.6	966	3526	43.0	8036	98.0
Por	82	19780	3021	6430	**.470**	407	1128	.361	1542	2029	.760	1243	633	396	1865	11	1925	23.5	966	3526	43.0	7991	97.5
Tor	82	19755	2980	6882	.433	425	1171	.363	1583	2068	.765	1137	666	544	1989	22	1947	23.7	1098	3547	43.3	7968	97.2
Cle	82	19855	2977	6734	.442	343	919	.373	1653	2205	.750	1427	715	363	2219	34	1941	23.7	1010	3509	42.8	7950	97.0
Was	82	19805	3010	6681	.451	335	890	.376	1566	2107	.743	1320	593	383	2149	20	1771	21.6	1064	3502	42.7	7921	96.6
Uta	82	19755	2962	6380	.464	329	854	.385	1661	2150	.773	1220	629	446	2013	11	2041	24.9	936	3362	41.0	7914	96.5
SA	82	19855	2952	6393	.462	330	882	.374	1652	2214	.746	1233	614	551	1716	**6**	1819	22.2	927	3593	43.8	7886	96.2
GS	82	19755	2996	7140	.420	345	1069	.323	1497	2147	.697	1302	731	356	2043	27	1851	22.6	**1300**	3738	45.6	7834	95.5
Phi	82	19830	2993	6776	.442	208	643	.323	1577	2226	.708	1284	791	386	1939	17	1817	22.2	1147	3615	44.1	7771	94.8
Mia	82	19830	2974	6462	.460	446	1202	.371	1345	1827	.736	1231	582	524	1947	23	1931	23.5	921	3540	43.2	7739	94.4
Atl	82	19830	3000	6807	.441	258	814	.317	1477	1987	.743	1266	500	461	1718	16	1548	18.9	1146	3716	45.3	7735	94.3
Van	82	19855	2892	6441	.449	324	898	.361	1594	2060	.774	1381	608	346	1881	19	1700	20.7	1005	3323	40.6	7702	93.9
NY	82	19830	2897	6374	.455	351	937	.375	1410	1805	.781	1201	515	349	1983	23	1588	19.4	802	3323	40.5	7555	92.1
LAC	82	19705	2877	6757	.426	429	1267	.339	1363	1826	.746	1325	578	494	1821	37	1479	18.0	955	3332	40.6	7546	92.0
Chi	82	19805	2565	6180	.415	340	1032	.329	1482	2089	.709	1557	646	383	1908	18	1645	20.1	1032	3355	40.9	6952	84.8
Tot		574270	87591	195220	.449	11513	32614	.353	45094	60111	.750	36789	18868	12293	55408	557	53130	22.3	29526	102062	42.9	231789	97.5
Avg	82	19802	3020	6732	.449	397	1125	.353	1555	2073	.750	1269	651	424	1911	19	1832	22.3	1018	3519	42.9	7993	97.5

1999-2000 NBA Regular Season Opponent Totals

Tm	G	Min	Field Goals Made	Att	Pct	3-Pt FGs Md	Att	Pct	Free Throws Made	Att	Pct	Misc TO	Stl	Blk	Fouls PF	DQ	Assists Ast	Avg	Rebounds Off	Tot	Avg	Points Pts	Avg
SA	82	19855	2884	6781	.425	355	1036	.343	**1276**	**1726**	.739	1181	645	429	1893	25	1667	20.3	986	3396	41.4	7399	90.2
NY	82	19830	**2711**	6398	.424	404	1197	.338	1609	2153	.747	1161	603	354	1799	17	1609	19.6	927	3368	41.1	7435	90.7
Por	82	19780	2825	6557	.431	394	1195	.330	1422	1985	**.716**	1186	652	350	1872	22	1705	20.8	974	3315	40.4	7466	91.0
Mia	82	19830	2782	6595	.422	408	1130	.361	1512	2022	.748	1150	621	364	1795	12	1620	19.8	887	**3123**	**38.1**	7484	91.3
Uta	82	19755	2781	**6240**	.446	388	1097	.354	1598	2141	.746	1270	588	411	2023	**42**	1597	19.5	1007	3538	43.1	7548	92.0
LAL	82	19805	2838	6824	**.416**	372	1142	.326	1518	2045	.742	1196	627	345	1977	29	1828	22.3	1065	3566	43.5	7566	92.3
Phi	82	19830	2867	6595	.435	417	1172	.356	1510	2001	.755	1444	631	531	1794	11	1700	20.7	1071	3566	43.7	7661	93.4
Pho	82	19805	2825	6665	.424	403	1146	.352	1630	2205	.739	1422	733	427	1966	18	1902	23.2	1000	3416	41.7	7683	93.7
Chi	82	19805	2916	6396	.456	358	1049	.341	1533	2070	.741	1244	853	461	2076	21	1903	23.2	966	3516	42.9	7723	94.2
Cha	82	19780	3048	6811	.448	380	1066	.356	1644	2185	.752	1232	591	344	1685	19	1737	21.2	916	3356	40.9	7853	95.8
Min	82	19905	2924	6576	.445	380	1066	.356	1374	1821	.755	1126	610	323	1910	18	1735	21.2	1040	3585	43.7	7872	96.0
Ind	82	19730	3113	6982	.446	**329**	1006	.327	1631	2136	.764	1250	557	434	1874	15	1790	21.8	961	3513	42.8	7929	96.7
Tor	82	19755	3002	6615	.454	346	1021	.339	1343	1795	.748	1258	590	433	1839	13	1939	23.6	1084	3695	45.1	7981	97.3
Sea	82	19780	3132	6941	.451	440	1293	.340	1503	2012	.747	1366	568	469	1869	14	1866	22.8	1129	3786	46.2	8047	98.1
NJ	82	19830	3125	6741	.464	368	1013	.363	1567	2104	.745	**1488**	724	475	2008	16	1991	24.3	1094	3567	43.5	8121	99.0
Orl	82	19755	3076	6919	.445	431	1277	.338	1530	1989	.769	1234	725	519	1912	28	1932	23.6	970	3306	40.3	8150	99.4
Van	82	19855	3136	6613	.474	361	1083	.333	1381	1796	.769	1001	655	404	1830	13	1886	23.0	1052	3526	43.0	8163	99.5
Atl	82	19830	3211	7060	.455	373	1015	.367	1790	2405	.744	1225	686	404	1967	17	1793	21.9	962	3380	41.2	8176	99.7
Was	82	19805	3005	6547	.459	390	1052	.371	1929	2563	.753	1395	638	473	1928	21	1798	21.9	**857**	3391	41.4	8190	99.9
Bos	82	19730	2960	6304	.470	359	995	.361	1599	2136	.753	1126	735	433	1833	17	1863	22.7	1027	3478	42.4	8208	100.1
Hou	82	19830	3226	7074	.456	350	**990**	.354	1425	1829	.779	1389	659	500	2058	26	1942	23.7	1013	3599	43.9	8227	100.3
Cle	82	19855	2983	6736	.443	420	1229	.342	1851	2385	.776	1303	637	340	1870	14	1987	24.2	1037	3405	41.5	8237	100.5
Mil	82	19855	3033	6644	.457	531	1357	.391	1685	2241	.752	1179	616	462	2003	22	2003	24.4	1027	3633	44.3	8282	101.0
Den	82	19855	3129	6953	.450	391	1126	.347	1632	2174	.751	1318	604	416	1937	22	1901	23.2	1251	3970	48.4	8289	101.1
Dal	82	19730	3225	7053	.457	429	1244	.345	1484	2005	.740	1400	652	396	1814	12	1893	23.1	973	3477	42.4	8363	102.0
Det	82	19830	3119	6706	.465	458	1234	.371	1669	2237	.746	1437	753	396	1943	19	1950	23.8	1143	3904	47.6	8365	102.0
Sac	82	19730	3269	7239	.452	369	1123	.353	1434	1910	.751	1172	621	469	1887	18	1975	24.1	1038	3737	45.6	8368	102.0
LAC	82	**19705**	3281	6879	.477	417	1077	.387	1512	2041	.741	1339	690	377	1731	8	2036	24.8	1091	3782	46.1	8491	103.5
GS	82	19755	3165	6776	.467	427	1163	.367	1755	2328	.754	1339	690	469	1887	18	1887	23.0	1091	3782	46.1	8512	103.8
Tot		574270	87591	195220	.449	11513	32614	.353	45094	60111	.750	36789	18868	12293	55408	557	53130	22.3	29526	102062	42.9	231789	97.5
Avg	82	19802	3020	6732	.449	397	1125	.353	1555	2073	.750	1269	651	424	1911	19	1832	22.3	1018	3519	42.9	7993	97.5

1999-2000 NBA Regular Season Team Records

		Location		All-Star		Monthly						Versus				Game Situation		
Tm	Total	Home	Road	Pre	Post	Nov	Dec	Jan	Feb	Mar	Apr	Div	East	West	Playoff	OT	3 Pts or Less	10+ Pts
LAL	67-15	36-5	31-10	37-11	30-4	11-4	14-1	9-5	12-1	15-1	6-3	20-4	27-3	40-12	34-10	2-2	8-1	34-7
Por	59-23	30-11	29-12	38-11	21-12	13-3	9-4	11-3	12-2	7-7	7-4	21-3	21-9	38-14	30-14	3-1	4-7	32-7
Ind	56-26	36-5	20-21	32-16	24-10	8-7	12-2	8-6	11-2	9-7	8-2	20-8	36-18	20-8	26-18	1-1	8-5	28-13
Uta	55-27	31-10	24-17	29-18	26-9	8-6	10-4	9-5	8-5	14-2	6-5	14-10	22-8	33-19	24-20	1-1	7-8	31-9
Pho	53-29	32-9	21-20	29-19	24-10	10-4	8-7	7-7	10-3	12-4	6-4	15-9	23-7	30-22	22-22	2-2	7-9	27-10
SA	53-29	31-10	22-19	32-17	21-12	13-3	8-7	7-6	9-4	10-5	6-4	16-8	20-10	33-19	21-23	6-1	8-7	31-11
Mia	52-30	33-8	19-22	30-17	22-13	11-3	8-6	8-7	9-5	9-5	7-4	18-6	34-20	18-10	24-19	4-1	9-2	26-15
Min	50-32	26-15	24-17	27-20	23-12	7-5	6-9	12-3	7-7	12-4	6-4	18-6	18-12	32-20	23-21	7-1	11-4	23-15
NY	50-32	33-8	17-24	29-18	21-14	8-8	10-4	8-4	8-5	11-6	5-5	14-10	32-22	18-10	25-19	3-3	9-5	20-13
Cha	49-33	30-11	19-22	27-20	22-13	8-6	10-5	6-7	7-7	9-6	9-2	20-8	36-18	13-15	20-24	2-2	7-5	24-16
Phi	49-33	29-12	20-21	27-22	22-11	8-8	9-7	7-5	7-5	11-5	7-3	13-11	36-18	13-15	18-24	5-0	17-8	18-14
Sea	45-37	24-17	21-20	31-20	14-17	11-4	7-8	10-5	7-6	6-8	4-6	12-12	14-16	31-21	15-29	2-2	8-7	22-17
Tor	45-37	26-15	19-22	26-21	19-16	9-6	8-6	7-7	6-6	10-7	5-5	16-12	29-25	16-12	23-19	0-3	13-4	20-20
Sac	44-38	30-11	14-27	30-18	14-20	10-2	7-8	10-6	5-8	9-6	3-8	9-15	19-11	25-27	17-27	1-4	3-6	28-16
Det	42-40	27-14	15-26	25-23	17-17	7-8	8-6	7-8	6-6	8-7	6-5	16-12	30-24	12-16	17-27	2-3	6-6	21-16
Mil	42-40	23-18	19-22	26-24	16-16	8-6	9-7	8-7	3-9	6-8	8-3	16-12	28-26	14-14	14-29	2-4	11-7	18-17
Orl	41-41	26-15	15-26	24-26	17-15	7-8	8-6	5-12	6-5	11-5	4-5	12-13	27-27	14-14	15-32	1-2	6-7	20-16
Dal	40-42	22-19	18-23	20-28	20-14	5-11	4-10	8-5	7-6	7-9	9-1	12-12	12-18	28-24	18-30	2-0	6-7	18-19
Bos	35-47	26-15	9-32	21-28	14-19	7-7	5-9	8-7	3-10	7-9	5-5	12-12	24-30	11-17	13-33	0-1	4-13	18-19
Den	35-47	25-16	10-31	21-27	14-20	6-7	9-6	5-9	5-8	4-13	6-4	10-14	13-17	22-30	21-27	5-2	10-8	12-27
Hou	34-48	22-19	12-29	20-30	14-18	4-11	6-9	7-7	5-8	5-10	7-3	8-16	11-19	23-29	13-35	2-3	6-7	16-22
Cle	32-50	22-19	10-31	19-30	13-20	7-6	5-11	6-9	4-8	6-9	4-7	8-20	20-34	12-16	9-38	3-4	7-11	12-21
NJ	31-51	22-19	9-32	19-30	12-21	2-13	10-5	5-9	5-7	9-7	0-10	9-19	21-33	10-18	15-31	1-4	6-14	15-15
Was	29-53	17-24	12-29	15-34	14-19	5-10	5-10	4-10	2-10	10-7	3-6	7-17	19-35	10-18	13-33	1-3	6-10	15-22
Atl	28-54	21-20	7-34	19-28	9-26	6-9	5-9	5-8	6-6	4-13	2-9	11-17	20-34	8-20	13-34	2-3	4-7	11-32
Van	22-60	12-29	10-31	14-34	8-26	3-11	3-12	6-8	6-7	1-14	3-8	6-18	10-20	12-40	6-42	1-5	5-10	10-33
GS	19-63	12-29	7-34	12-35	7-28	2-11	4-12	3-9	7-8	1-16	2-7	2-22	10-20	9-43	4-44	1-1	2-4	10-39
Chi	17-65	12-29	5-36	10-37	7-28	1-12	1-13	6-8	4-10	2-14	3-8	5-23	13-41	4-24	6-41	1-3	6-9	3-38
LAC	15-67	10-31	5-36	11-38	4-29	4-10	5-10	2-12	1-14	2-13	1-8	5-19	7-23	8-44	6-42	0-1	3-5	3-47
Avg	41-41	25-16	16-25	24-24	17-17	7-7	7-7	7-7	6-6	8-8	5-5	13-13	22-21	19-20	17-28	2-2	7-7	20-20

1999-2000 NBA Regular Season Team Records

	After 1 Qtr		At Half		After 3 Qtr		100 Pts		FG %		3-Pt Att		Rebounds		Turnovers		2nd
Tm	Lead	Trail	Lead	Trail	Lead	Trail	Score 100+	Allow <100	Higher than opp	Lower than opp	More than opp	Less than opp	More than opp	Less than opp	More than opp	Less than opp	Bk2Bk
LAL	43-5	18-8	50-5	15-10	59-4	7-11	42-5	55-7	57-7	10-12	23-7	40-7	50-4	16-10	25-4	37-10	20-2
Por	40-14	16-8	43-10	14-12	49-5	8-17	26-6	55-15	55-6	4-17	24-11	33-10	43-15	14-8	30-15	27-5	16-6
Ind	37-7	18-19	44-5	9-21	46-7	9-19	39-7	39-7	43-6	13-20	43-26	8-0	26-9	28-15	19-21	32-5	14-7
Uta	38-6	16-17	38-6	12-19	43-3	11-23	28-3	50-13	47-4	8-23	17-10	35-15	41-12	12-14	14-19	35-4	14-5
Pho	35-10	16-17	41-8	11-19	45-8	4-21	32-6	40-13	47-3	6-26	28-20	22-5	37-10	14-19	21-13	28-12	12-8
SA	29-10	22-18	40-12	11-17	41-4	12-22	28-3	51-20	48-8	5-21	20-13	29-14	38-10	13-18	24-15	23-12	12-6
Mia	34-8	18-13	38-12	12-18	41-3	8-27	23-2	43-21	45-12	6-18	34-15	17-13	38-11	12-17	25-20	24-8	9-9
Min	37-13	12-17	32-8	17-21	39-4	10-26	36-6	35-11	39-6	11-26	8-5	37-27	36-12	13-19	18-16	30-15	11-7
NY	29-13	17-18	31-10	17-18	40-5	8-27	17-2	45-23	45-11	5-20	13-10	32-21	25-9	23-22	27-15	21-13	7-13
Cha	33-13	15-20	39-7	9-23	44-7	5-24	35-3	35-14	37-8	11-24	19-16	25-16	24-8	21-23	19-13	27-17	10-12
Phi	23-8	23-24	30-9	17-22	33-8	14-24	27-4	40-22	38-5	11-28	5-8	41-28	29-12	19-20	13-10	30-22	11-9
Sea	34-9	9-23	33-12	11-23	41-6	4-29	31-10	34-12	36-6	9-31	27-28	15-8	24-9	18-28	12-16	30-17	10-11
Tor	33-8	11-26	32-8	11-28	32-3	12-33	25-6	35-10	28-5	17-32	22-24	19-10	20-16	21-18	13-13	30-21	8-10
Sac	29-15	18-19	33-14	10-31	34-6	8-29	40-17	25-7	34-3	10-35	34-29	10-7	17-11	21-26	14-18	28-19	8-10
Det	25-14	16-21	30-9	11-29	32-11	8-27	35-17	28-8	28-6	14-34	20-20	21-18	26-10	15-30	15-18	24-17	9-11
Mil	27-15	11-24	28-14	14-25	32-12	8-28	31-17	30-10	31-8	11-32	10-10	32-23	16-15	20-21	9-24	28-12	9-10
Orl	27-16	11-23	28-9	11-31	36-10	3-29	33-14	30-12	34-13	7-28	7-12	33-26	24-20	14-19	11-26	28-12	11-11
Dal	32-14	14-30	29-7	10-34	30-6	8-36	31-13	24-8	32-6	8-36	18-23	19-19	7-6	32-35	9-13	30-27	7-11
Bos	23-17	11-29	23-16	11-30	27-13	7-33	23-20	29-12	24-7	11-40	21-33	11-14	25-16	9-25	9-23	23-22	3-19
Den	16-10	16-34	14-12	19-30	25-8	10-37	24-13	24-12	26-9	8-38	25-28	9-12	23-13	11-26	21-28	11-15	8-13
Hou	25-9	7-38	28-9	4-37	30-8	4-39	25-12	24-13	27-12	6-35	25-42	7-5	24-23	9-23	20-40	9-7	5-12
Cle	20-21	8-27	24-21	6-28	23-13	9-36	24-11	20-17	27-14	5-36	8-13	24-29	19-15	10-33	13-29	15-17	10-14
NJ	21-15	9-33	23-15	8-35	28-11	2-39	20-14	23-18	20-8	11-43	23-39	6-12	11-9	18-40	3-14	25-35	6-14
Was	18-13	10-35	18-14	11-39	20-11	8-41	19-16	22-18	24-14	4-39	10-20	18-31	17-27	10-22	11-35	16-15	5-17
Atl	13-20	10-31	13-17	13-33	23-9	4-42	18-10	21-21	26-13	2-41	4-22	22-30	23-31	4-23	17-38	10-12	5-19
Van	11-22	9-36	13-17	6-40	17-8	5-47	14-8	18-18	14-11	8-49	5-22	17-32	17-23	5-31	8-38	12-16	6-13
GS	9-14	9-48	9-9	8-53	14-3	5-60	15-14	12-19	17-3	2-59	8-27	9-35	12-21	5-38	4-33	14-24	3-17
Chi	8-8	8-10	7-38	8-52	8-5	8-59	3-2	16-35	11-15	6-50	7-34	9-28	12-21	5-39	11-48	6-14	4-20
LAC	11-19	2-44	10-13	3-51	11-9	4-56	8-14	11-21	10-10	5-57	9-42	5-22	9-14	5-51	6-45	7-16	4-18
Avg	26-13	13-26	28-11	11-28	32-7	7-32	26-9	32-15	33-8	8-33	18-21	21-18	25-14	14-25	15-23	23-15	9-12

Team Profiles

Team Profiles list per-game averages for a number of situational breakdowns.

Also listed for each team are its opponents' per-game averages. When reviewing the opponents' per-game averages for the Atlanta Hawks, for example, the home and road splits on the left side of the table refer to Atlanta's home and road games. The "In wins" and "In losses" splits also refer to the Hawks' decisions. On the other hand, the starters and bench splits on the left side of the table refer to players who make up Atlanta's opponents.

For comparison's sake, a profile for the entire NBA appears following the Washington Wizards' profile.

Atlanta Hawks

1999-2000 Per Game Averages

	W	L	FGA	FG%	3PA	3P%	FTA	FT%	Blk	Stl	Ast	Reb	Pts		W	L	FGA	FG%	3PA	3P%	FTA	FT%	Blk	Stl	Ast	Reb	Pts
Total	28	54	83.0	.441	9.9	.317	24.2	.743	5.62	6.10	18.9	45.3	94.3	Pre All-Star	19	28	83.6	.449	10.6	.333	27.3	.747	5.38	5.72	18.7	46.3	98.9
Home	21	20	82.2	.457	9.9	.325	25.4	.755	5.54	5.88	19.2	46.5	97.5	Post All-Star	9	26	82.3	.430	9.0	.292	20.1	.736	5.94	6.60	19.2	44.0	88.2
Road	7	34	83.8	.425	10.0	.309	23.0	.730	5.71	6.32	18.6	44.1	91.1	November	6	9	83.5	.466	9.8	.340	27.0	.686	5.40	5.60	18.1	46.7	99.7
vs. Playoff	13	34	83.1	.437	10.6	.322	23.0	.744	4.91	6.21	18.9	44.2	93.1	December	5	9	82.8	.448	11.1	.323	29.4	.757	6.07	5.00	18.4	47.1	100.0
vs. Non-Playoff	15	20	82.9	.446	9.1	.309	25.9	.743	6.57	5.94	18.9	46.9	96.0	January	5	8	84.0	.429	12.4	.366	25.7	.784	4.92	6.92	19.2	44.1	96.8
vs. East	20	34	82.0	.446	10.2	.322	25.7	.756	5.63	6.17	19.1	44.3	95.9	February	6	6	84.5	.438	8.1	.320	20.8	.764	7.00	6.08	19.3	49.2	92.5
vs. West	8	20	85.0	.430	9.4	.305	21.4	.715	5.61	5.96	18.5	47.3	91.3	March	4	13	80.5	.428	8.4	.211	20.0	.738	5.18	6.18	18.6	42.8	85.5
vs. Div.	11	17	82.9	.460	11.1	.332	25.1	.754	5.04	5.86	20.6	43.4	98.9	April	2	9	83.6	.433	10.2	.339	22.4	.744	5.36	7.09	20.1	42.3	92.5
Starters	—	—	58.0	.449	7.0	.337	16.6	.746	4.46	3.66	13.0	32.8	66.8	0 Days Rest	5	19	83.7	.436	10.7	.307	25.7	.734	6.50	5.83	18.8	47.2	95.1
Bench	—	—	25.1	.422	2.9	.270	7.6	.737	1.16	2.44	5.8	12.5	27.6	1 Days Rest	12	25	83.0	.433	10.1	.300	23.8	.755	4.97	6.32	19.1	43.7	92.8
In wins	28	0	84.3	.478	8.6	.361	24.5	.765	6.82	6.39	20.9	48.4	102.4	2 Days Rest	7	7	83.3	.453	8.7	.320	22.9	.720	5.64	5.29	17.6	47.9	94.7
In losses	0	54	82.4	.421	10.6	.298	24.1	.732	5.00	5.94	17.9	43.7	90.1	3+ Days Rest	4	3	80.0	.479	8.3	.466	24.1	.763	6.00	7.43	20.9	42.4	98.9

Opponents' 1999-2000 Per Game Averages

	W	L	FGA	FG%	3PA	3P%	FTA	FT%	Blk	Stl	Ast	Reb	Pts		W	L	FGA	FG%	3PA	3P%	FTA	FT%	Blk	Stl	Ast	Reb	Pts
Total	54	28	86.1	.455	12.4	.367	21.9	.769	4.93	7.99	23.0	43.0	99.7	November	9	6	87.3	.449	13.5	.320	24.1	.771	6.67	7.80	22.7	42.3	101.3
Home	20	21	86.5	.450	12.4	.375	21.8	.775	4.05	8.54	20.9	40.6	99.5	December	9	5	89.0	.452	13.4	.378	21.8	.777	4.21	9.07	25.1	42.1	102.4
Road	34	7	85.7	.459	12.3	.360	22.0	.763	5.80	7.44	25.1	45.4	100.0	January	8	5	83.7	.460	11.2	.352	25.5	.774	4.38	6.77	21.2	43.7	100.6
vs. Div.	17	11	85.3	.460	13.7	.367	24.8	.813	4.36	7.68	24.3	41.5	103.6	February	6	6	87.1	.411	13.8	.373	19.1	.755	4.58	6.75	21.8	44.3	91.3
Starters	—	—	59.8	.457	8.4	.374	15.0	.777	3.24	5.45	16.9	28.0	69.4	March	13	4	84.4	.468	11.6	.394	17.9	.774	3.82	8.88	22.1	41.9	97.4
Bench	—	—	26.3	.450	4.0	.354	7.0	.753	1.68	2.54	6.1	15.0	30.3	April	9	2	85.1	.490	10.5	.400	23.9	.757	6.18	8.27	25.5	44.6	105.7
In wins	0	28	86.7	.416	14.6	.320	21.1	.780	3.79	7.43	19.0	40.6	93.2	0 Days Rest	19	5	85.3	.448	11.7	.375	24.9	.752	5.38	7.92	21.9	43.5	99.6
In losses	54	0	85.8	.475	11.2	.400	22.3	.763	5.52	8.28	25.1	44.2	103.1	1 Days Rest	25	12	86.2	.465	11.8	.363	21.5	.782	4.89	8.24	23.1	43.6	101.2
Pre All-Star	28	19	86.6	.451	13.2	.349	23.6	.778	5.06	7.72	23.1	42.3	101.1	2 Days Rest	7	7	87.4	.454	13.4	.404	18.8	.749	4.86	7.64	24.5	41.1	98.8
Post All-Star	26	9	85.4	.460	11.3	.396	19.6	.755	4.74	8.34	22.9	43.9	97.9	3+ Days Rest	3	4	85.7	.425	15.6	.303	20.3	.803	3.71	7.57	23.6	41.9	93.9

Boston Celtics

1999-2000 Per Game Averages

	W	L	FGA	FG%	3PA	3P%	FTA	FT%	Blk	Stl	Ast	Reb	Pts		W	L	FGA	FG%	3PA	3P%	FTA	FT%	Blk	Stl	Ast	Reb	Pts
Total	35	47	83.9	.444	15.4	.331	26.5	.745	3.49	9.70	21.2	43.0	99.3	Pre All-Star	21	28	82.7	.444	14.9	.334	25.3	.746	3.61	9.37	21.1	42.2	97.3
Home	26	15	84.4	.449	15.0	.364	26.3	.753	3.98	10.49	23.2	45.0	101.0	Post All-Star	14	19	85.6	.444	16.1	.326	28.4	.744	3.30	10.18	21.5	44.3	102.4
Road	9	32	83.4	.439	15.7	.300	26.8	.738	3.00	8.90	19.3	41.0	97.7	November	7	7	81.6	.454	15.4	.407	25.8	.745	4.07	9.64	20.9	42.1	99.5
vs. Playoff	13	33	84.3	.437	15.6	.343	25.8	.733	3.26	9.28	20.0	43.2	97.9	December	5	9	82.8	.444	14.6	.293	24.1	.727	3.71	10.00	21.3	41.3	95.4
vs. Non-Playoff	22	14	83.4	.453	15.1	.315	27.4	.760	3.78	10.22	22.8	42.8	101.2	January	8	7	83.1	.431	15.1	.283	26.1	.747	3.20	9.27	20.8	43.4	95.3
vs. East	24	30	83.7	.444	16.4	.339	26.1	.748	3.50	9.69	21.4	42.9	99.4	February	3	10	84.2	.440	13.5	.314	27.5	.760	3.23	8.77	20.4	42.6	99.3
vs. West	11	17	84.3	.444	13.4	.311	27.3	.741	3.46	9.71	20.9	43.3	99.2	March	7	9	87.5	.436	15.6	.317	29.1	.766	3.63	9.94	21.4	46.3	103.6
vs. Div.	12	12	84.7	.436	16.3	.307	25.8	.752	4.25	9.42	21.3	44.3	99.1	April	5	5	83.7	.467	18.9	.376	26.2	.710	2.90	10.80	23.1	45.1	103.9
Starters	—	—	58.4	.442	11.0	.321	18.2	.743	2.06	7.11	15.2	27.2	68.7	0 Days Rest	3	19	81.7	.439	16.4	.313	26.3	.728	3.36	9.36	19.3	38.9	96.0
Bench	—	—	25.5	.448	4.4	.356	8.3	.750	1.43	2.59	6.1	15.9	30.6	1 Days Rest	22	20	85.9	.438	16.0	.331	26.4	.740	3.57	9.90	22.1	44.7	100.1
In wins	35	0	83.7	.462	15.4	.363	26.6	.747	4.14	11.20	23.1	46.1	102.9	2 Days Rest	4	5	84.3	.457	11.9	.355	25.6	.770	2.44	9.44	22.3	44.0	101.0
In losses	0	47	84.0	.430	15.3	.307	26.5	.744	3.00	8.57	19.8	40.7	96.7	3+ Days Rest	6	3	79.7	.471	13.6	.361	28.7	.783	4.44	9.78	20.8	44.1	102.4

Opponents' 1999-2000 Per Game Averages

	W	L	FGA	FG%	3PA	3P%	FTA	FT%	Blk	Stl	Ast	Reb	Pts		W	L	FGA	FG%	3PA	3P%	FTA	FT%	Blk	Stl	Ast	Reb	Pts
Total	47	35	76.9	.470	12.1	.361	31.3	.753	5.77	7.78	21.9	41.4	100.1	November	7	7	78.0	.471	14.1	.359	28.9	.757	5.07	7.43	21.8	40.8	100.4
Home	15	26	78.1	.453	11.9	.358	28.6	.743	4.78	8.12	20.1	41.3	96.3	December	9	5	73.8	.469	12.1	.324	33.0	.710	6.50	7.79	22.3	42.6	96.5
Road	32	9	75.7	.486	12.4	.363	33.9	.760	6.76	7.44	23.8	41.4	103.9	January	7	8	76.7	.470	12.5	.367	28.7	.770	5.80	7.93	22.1	41.6	98.9
vs. Div.	12	12	76.9	.467	11.3	.380	30.2	.738	5.29	7.67	20.4	40.5	98.4	February	10	3	78.0	.486	11.7	.355	31.3	.779	5.92	8.08	24.4	41.1	104.4
Starters	—	—	52.3	.474	7.9	.371	20.8	.766	3.95	5.01	15.4	27.2	68.5	March	9	7	79.6	.462	12.0	.385	31.8	.750	6.06	7.69	20.9	41.7	101.9
Bench	—	—	24.6	.460	4.2	.342	10.4	.726	1.82	2.77	6.5	14.2	31.6	April	5	5	74.1	.459	9.5	.379	35.1	.755	5.00	7.80	19.9	39.9	98.1
In wins	0	35	77.7	.428	12.3	.310	28.6	.720	5.11	7.37	19.0	40.7	93.2	0 Days Rest	19	3	74.2	.496	11.8	.385	32.2	.748	5.86	7.18	23.4	41.0	102.3
In losses	47	0	76.2	.501	12.0	.400	33.2	.773	6.26	8.09	24.1	41.9	106.9	1 Days Rest	20	22	77.6	.457	11.9	.348	31.4	.760	5.64	7.90	20.7	42.0	99.0
Pre All-Star	28	21	76.3	.473	12.9	.357	30.2	.755	5.76	7.71	22.1	41.4	99.6	2 Days Rest	5	4	78.6	.487	12.9	.405	28.7	.740	6.89	8.11	23.8	40.4	102.9
Post All-Star	19	14	77.7	.464	11.0	.367	32.9	.749	5.79	7.88	21.6	41.2	100.8	3+ Days Rest	3	6	78.4	.448	13.2	.319	30.9	.741	5.00	8.33	22.1	40.1	97.3

Charlotte Hornets

1999-2000 Per Game Averages

	W	L	FGA	FG%	3PA	3P%	FTA	FT%	Blk	Stl	Ast	Reb	Pts		W	L	FGA	FG%	3PA	3P%	FTA	FT%	Blk	Stl	Ast	Reb	Pts
Total	49	33	79.7	.449	12.2	.339	30.0	.758	5.85	8.93	24.7	42.9	98.4	Pre All-Star	27	20	80.4	.444	12.9	.335	32.5	.748	6.30	10.00	25.1	42.6	100.0
Home	30	11	78.4	.464	12.2	.351	30.5	.769	6.44	9.41	27.3	42.8	100.6	Post All-Star	22	13	78.7	.456	11.3	.344	26.6	.774	5.26	7.49	24.1	43.3	96.3
Road	19	22	80.9	.435	12.2	.326	29.4	.746	5.27	8.44	22.0	43.0	96.3	November	8	6	81.9	.430	14.3	.325	32.2	.743	5.71	10.71	24.9	42.4	99.0
vs. Playoff	20	24	79.0	.440	12.1	.353	28.7	.753	5.18	8.70	23.6	42.1	95.4	December	10	5	81.6	.475	10.3	.351	31.3	.740	6.00	10.67	27.7	41.9	104.4
vs. Non-Playoff	29	9	80.5	.460	12.3	.322	31.4	.763	6.63	9.18	25.9	43.9	102.0	January	6	7	77.8	.433	13.1	.353	33.5	.750	6.38	9.31	23.4	43.5	97.2
vs. East	36	18	78.9	.456	12.5	.345	31.4	.761	5.59	9.17	25.2	41.8	100.1	February	7	7	79.7	.425	14.1	.330	25.5	.804	5.93	6.71	23.9	45.6	92.9
vs. West	13	15	81.3	.437	11.6	.326	27.3	.751	6.36	8.46	23.7	45.1	95.3	March	9	6	78.8	.472	10.6	.327	27.1	.769	5.67	7.60	24.0	41.5	98.7
vs. Div.	20	8	78.4	.454	12.4	.352	31.8	.769	5.39	9.25	25.3	41.6	100.0	April	9	2	77.5	.457	11.0	.355	30.6	.751	5.36	8.45	23.7	42.8	97.8
Starters	—	—	58.2	.445	9.5	.362	22.7	.774	4.43	6.05	18.1	31.4	72.8	0 Days Rest	10	12	79.8	.432	10.7	.319	29.8	.757	5.91	7.95	22.5	43.1	94.9
Bench	—	—	21.4	.461	2.7	.256	7.3	.710	1.43	2.88	6.6	11.6	25.6	1 Days Rest	30	13	79.9	.463	13.1	.350	29.3	.773	5.58	9.09	26.0	43.1	101.2
In wins	49	0	79.0	.476	11.7	.359	31.8	.769	6.35	9.14	27.3	43.9	103.2	2 Days Rest	3	5	82.1	.461	12.3	.337	31.0	.746	7.25	10.00	26.6	39.9	103.0
In losses	0	33	80.7	.411	13.0	.312	27.3	.739	5.12	8.61	20.7	41.5	90.5	3+ Days Rest	6	3	76.2	.414	11.7	.324	32.9	.706	5.78	9.56	22.0	44.2	90.1

Opponents' 1999-2000 Per Game Averages

	W	L	FGA	FG%	3PA	3P%	FTA	FT%	Blk	Stl	Ast	Reb	Pts		W	L	FGA	FG%	3PA	3P%	FTA	FT%	Blk	Stl	Ast	Reb	Pts
Total	33	49	83.1	.448	13.2	.378	22.0	.745	5.13	7.37	23.2	42.9	95.8	November	6	8	82.1	.454	11.6	.309	23.9	.743	5.07	8.00	23.9	44.0	95.9
Home	11	30	83.0	.441	13.3	.368	20.9	.749	4.17	7.02	22.9	41.2	93.8	December	5	10	85.6	.445	14.9	.372	23.1	.746	5.80	7.00	23.3	43.9	99.0
Road	22	19	83.1	.454	13.2	.387	23.2	.742	6.10	7.71	23.5	44.5	97.8	January	7	6	82.8	.463	14.9	.454	20.7	.740	5.77	9.38	24.5	41.5	98.7
vs. Div.	8	20	83.4	.445	14.0	.402	22.1	.786	3.86	7.57	23.9	43.0	97.2	February	7	7	81.6	.444	12.6	.381	20.9	.706	5.00	7.07	23.3	42.2	92.0
Starters	—	—	56.0	.450	8.7	.395	14.9	.771	3.50	5.26	16.4	28.1	65.2	March	6	9	83.9	.445	12.1	.365	22.5	.777	4.67	5.87	20.9	43.7	96.5
Bench	—	—	27.1	.443	4.6	.344	7.2	.692	1.63	2.11	6.8	14.8	30.5	April	2	9	81.7	.433	13.6	.373	20.6	.758	4.36	7.09	23.9	41.4	91.5
In wins	0	49	83.7	.433	13.2	.322	21.3	.734	4.39	6.98	22.2	41.2	92.4	0 Days Rest	12	10	83.0	.452	11.3	.353	22.7	.766	6.18	7.00	24.1	42.0	96.5
In losses	33	0	82.1	.470	13.3	.459	23.1	.761	6.24	7.94	24.6	45.3	100.8	1 Days Rest	13	30	83.0	.443	14.5	.376	21.7	.740	4.79	7.21	23.1	42.3	95.0
Pre All-Star	20	27	83.5	.454	13.7	.382	22.5	.744	5.51	7.94	23.7	43.4	97.8	2 Days Rest	5	3	84.9	.482	13.9	.477	25.0	.755	5.00	8.50	24.3	45.0	107.3
Post All-Star	13	22	82.5	.438	12.6	.371	21.4	.747	4.63	6.60	22.5	42.2	93.0	3+ Days Rest	3	6	81.8	.425	11.6	.337	19.7	.706	4.33	8.00	20.8	46.0	87.3

Chicago Bulls

1999-2000 Per Game Averages

	W	L	FGA	FG%	3PA	3P%	FTA	FT%	Blk	Stl	Ast	Reb	Pts		W	L	FGA	FG%	3PA	3P%	FTA	FT%	Blk	Stl	Ast	Reb	Pts
Total	17	65	75.4	.415	12.6	.329	25.5	.709	4.67	7.88	20.1	40.9	84.8	Pre All-Star	10	37	76.9	.416	12.6	.319	25.4	.692	4.55	8.53	19.6	40.4	85.6
Home	12	29	76.2	.407	13.4	.339	26.6	.696	5.41	8.02	22.4	43.4	85.1	Post All-Star	7	28	73.3	.413	12.5	.344	25.6	.732	4.83	7.00	20.6	41.5	83.7
Road	5	36	74.5	.424	11.8	.318	24.3	.724	3.93	7.73	17.7	38.5	84.5	November	1	12	78.2	.401	11.1	.333	27.6	.694	4.54	8.54	19.1	39.1	85.6
vs. Playoff	6	41	74.3	.415	12.7	.344	25.0	.705	4.51	8.57	20.2	39.3	83.6	December	1	13	78.4	.406	12.1	.300	22.8	.705	4.64	7.64	19.4	42.6	83.3
vs. Non-Playoff	11	24	76.8	.415	12.5	.310	26.1	.715	4.89	6.94	19.9	43.1	86.3	January	6	9	76.3	.431	13.9	.325	27.0	.664	5.07	9.64	21.2	42.0	88.1
vs. East	13	41	74.6	.424	13.1	.346	25.4	.722	5.00	7.61	20.3	41.3	86.1	February	4	10	74.1	.417	13.1	.372	22.8	.702	4.07	6.43	20.0	38.8	82.6
vs. West	4	24	76.9	.399	11.5	.294	25.6	.686	4.04	8.39	19.7	40.3	82.3	March	2	14	74.6	.398	11.7	.305	25.2	.759	4.81	8.06	20.3	42.3	82.1
vs. Div.	5	23	76.9	.426	13.5	.333	24.4	.719	4.54	7.39	20.7	41.8	87.5	April	3	8	69.7	.450	14.0	.344	28.3	.730	4.91	6.73	20.4	40.4	88.2
Starters	—	—	48.6	.425	6.5	.335	16.8	.709	3.17	5.20	12.7	25.9	55.4	0 Days Rest	4	20	73.7	.426	12.5	.329	26.4	.719	4.50	7.33	19.0	39.3	86.0
Bench	—	—	26.8	.397	6.1	.324	8.6	.710	1.50	2.68	7.3	15.0	29.4	1 Days Rest	10	27	75.4	.411	12.8	.323	24.9	.720	5.00	7.89	20.6	41.6	84.0
In wins	17	0	75.8	.425	13.5	.389	29.4	.679	5.24	7.24	20.9	44.8	88.0	2 Days Rest	3	10	76.4	.416	13.6	.356	26.5	.666	4.62	9.46	21.2	42.4	86.0
In losses	0	65	75.8	.412	12.4	.313	24.5	.719	4.52	8.05	19.8	39.9	83.9	3+ Days Rest	0	8	78.5	.401	10.0	.313	23.8	.705	3.75	6.88	18.8	40.0	82.9

Opponents' 1999-2000 Per Game Averages

	W	L	FGA	FG%	3PA	3P%	FTA	FT%	Blk	Stl	Ast	Reb	Pts		W	L	FGA	FG%	3PA	3P%	FTA	FT%	Blk	Stl	Ast	Reb	Pts
Total	65	17	78.0	.456	12.8	.341	25.2	.741	5.62	10.40	23.2	41.7	94.2	November	12	1	74.6	.485	10.2	.361	30.9	.746	8.62	10.23	22.8	42.2	99.1
Home	29	12	78.8	.437	12.7	.337	24.7	.705	5.17	10.10	24.1	42.6	90.5	December	13	1	78.1	.457	11.1	.368	25.4	.770	5.07	8.93	23.2	41.0	94.9
Road	36	5	77.2	.475	12.9	.345	25.8	.774	6.07	10.71	22.3	40.7	97.8	January	8	6	77.7	.448	13.9	.313	23.9	.710	5.07	10.79	24.2	40.9	90.9
vs. Div.	23	5	78.6	.452	12.5	.353	25.3	.755	5.25	10.00	23.0	40.6	94.6	February	10	4	78.5	.458	15.8	.317	20.4	.741	6.79	10.36	23.2	42.2	92.0
Starters	—	—	51.4	.468	7.9	.350	17.7	.741	3.89	6.94	15.5	26.9	64.0	March	14	2	79.9	.436	12.7	.330	27.3	.739	5.19	11.81	24.1	44.6	94.1
Bench	—	—	26.6	.432	4.9	.328	7.6	.741	1.73	3.46	7.7	14.8	30.2	April	8	3	78.8	.460	12.9	.387	23.2	.733	2.64	10.00	21.1	37.9	94.5
In wins	0	17	78.8	.407	14.5	.251	20.6	.681	5.24	8.29	20.7	40.9	81.8	0 Days Rest	20	4	76.7	.483	11.5	.354	25.7	.754	4.42	10.46	23.5	39.6	97.6
In losses	65	0	77.8	.469	12.3	.369	26.4	.753	5.72	10.95	23.8	41.9	97.4	1 Days Rest	27	10	78.7	.443	13.5	.343	24.2	.726	5.97	9.89	22.9	42.5	92.0
Pre All-Star	37	10	77.2	.467	12.5	.334	25.6	.747	6.11	10.04	23.7	41.0	95.4	2 Days Rest	10	3	77.8	.442	11.7	.316	27.6	.719	5.92	12.00	23.2	42.7	92.3
Post All-Star	28	7	79.1	.441	13.2	.350	24.8	.732	4.97	10.89	22.5	42.5	92.5	3+ Days Rest	8	0	79.0	.456	14.9	.336	24.6	.807	7.13	10.00	23.4	42.0	96.9

Cleveland Cavaliers

1999-2000 Per Game Averages

	W	L	FGA	FG%	3PA	3P%	FTA	FT%	Blk	Stl	Ast	Reb	Pts		W	L	FGA	FG%	3PA	3P%	FTA	FT%	Blk	Stl	Ast	Reb	Pts
Total	32	50	82.1	.442	11.2	.373	26.9	.750	4.43	8.72	23.7	42.8	97.0	Pre All-Star	19	30	82.4	.437	11.0	.379	28.4	.742	4.49	9.43	23.6	43.2	97.4
Home	22	19	83.0	.446	11.8	.413	28.6	.768	5.51	9.12	26.4	44.7	100.8	Post All-Star	13	20	81.6	.449	11.5	.365	24.6	.763	4.33	7.67	23.8	42.2	96.3
Road	10	31	81.3	.438	10.7	.330	25.2	.729	3.34	8.32	20.9	40.9	93.1	November	7	6	81.4	.451	11.2	.397	28.4	.770	4.92	9.08	25.0	43.8	99.7
vs. Playoff	9	38	82.0	.432	11.3	.366	25.5	.740	4.02	8.34	22.7	42.3	93.9	December	5	11	83.6	.432	11.1	.449	28.5	.730	3.81	9.13	23.5	42.2	98.1
vs. Non-Playoff	23	12	82.3	.455	11.0	.383	28.8	.761	4.97	9.23	25.0	43.5	101.0	January	6	9	81.7	.432	10.5	.291	29.5	.731	4.80	10.47	22.7	43.2	95.1
vs. East	20	34	82.2	.439	11.4	.387	27.5	.748	4.30	8.78	23.8	42.3	97.2	February	4	8	82.4	.437	12.4	.389	24.1	.782	4.42	7.92	23.0	43.3	95.7
vs. West	12	16	81.9	.447	10.9	.345	25.7	.753	4.68	8.61	23.4	43.8	96.4	March	6	9	80.7	.445	11.1	.347	25.5	.749	4.60	8.13	23.2	41.8	94.8
vs. Div.	8	20	84.4	.435	11.1	.374	26.5	.748	3.93	8.79	23.6	42.4	97.5	April	4	7	83.1	.462	11.0	.355	24.3	.753	4.00	7.00	25.0	42.7	98.9
Starters	—	—	53.6	.438	6.5	.384	19.2	.754	2.83	5.94	15.4	27.6	63.9	0 Days Rest	10	14	81.0	.452	10.8	.396	27.2	.743	4.04	8.08	24.0	42.9	97.7
Bench	—	—	28.5	.450	4.7	.358	7.7	.738	1.60	2.78	8.3	15.2	33.0	1 Days Rest	12	23	82.3	.431	11.1	.356	27.1	.741	4.31	8.83	22.3	42.7	95.0
In wins	32	0	81.9	.466	11.1	.410	31.4	.776	5.31	10.16	27.1	45.1	105.2	2 Days Rest	9	7	83.0	.459	11.8	.381	25.8	.774	5.06	9.50	26.7	43.2	100.7
In losses	0	50	82.3	.427	11.3	.350	24.0	.728	3.86	7.80	21.5	41.3	91.7	3+ Days Rest	1	6	82.9	.426	11.7	.366	27.4	.766	4.86	8.57	22.6	42.1	95.9

Opponents' 1999-2000 Per Game Averages

	W	L	FGA	FG%	3PA	3P%	FTA	FT%	Blk	Stl	Ast	Reb	Pts		W	L	FGA	FG%	3PA	3P%	FTA	FT%	Blk	Stl	Ast	Reb	Pts
Total	50	32	82.1	.443	15.0	.342	29.1	.776	6.10	8.04	23.7	43.9	100.5	November	6	7	85.0	.418	15.6	.330	30.8	.800	5.77	8.38	22.1	44.9	100.8
Home	19	22	83.0	.428	15.7	.354	28.9	.772	5.88	7.73	24.0	43.0	98.9	December	11	5	81.8	.452	13.4	.335	31.4	.777	6.38	7.88	24.1	44.3	102.9
Road	31	10	81.3	.458	14.3	.329	29.3	.780	6.32	8.34	23.4	44.8	102.0	January	9	6	81.9	.437	15.7	.357	27.7	.778	5.87	8.07	22.4	43.4	98.7
vs. Div.	20	8	80.8	.448	15.5	.335	31.1	.781	6.71	7.36	23.5	45.0	101.9	February	8	4	82.5	.449	16.1	.337	26.6	.787	7.08	8.50	25.2	43.0	100.5
Starters	—	—	56.0	.447	9.5	.338	19.7	.793	4.22	5.30	16.9	29.2	68.9	March	9	6	80.4	.454	14.7	.330	27.1	.762	5.53	7.53	25.3	43.6	98.6
Bench	—	—	26.1	.435	5.5	.350	9.3	.740	1.88	2.73	6.8	14.6	31.5	April	7	4	80.2	.452	14.6	.366	31.1	.751	6.09	8.00	22.9	44.1	101.3
In wins	0	32	83.8	.414	15.7	.318	28.7	.777	5.75	7.59	21.9	42.0	96.7	0 Days Rest	14	10	82.6	.430	14.8	.327	31.3	.767	5.96	7.54	22.8	43.9	99.9
In losses	50	0	81.1	.462	14.5	.359	29.3	.776	6.32	8.32	24.8	45.1	102.9	1 Days Rest	23	12	82.4	.457	13.7	.339	27.4	.782	6.23	8.46	24.4	43.8	101.3
Pre All-Star	30	19	82.7	.439	15.1	.341	29.7	.784	6.06	8.16	22.9	44.2	101.0	2 Days Rest	7	9	80.9	.437	17.8	.352	29.0	.776	5.56	7.81	23.3	43.3	99.5
Post All-Star	20	13	81.3	.449	14.8	.343	28.2	.763	6.15	7.85	24.8	43.5	99.7	3+ Days Rest	6	1	82.3	.431	15.9	.378	30.0	.781	7.14	8.14	23.9	45.6	100.3

Dallas Mavericks

1999-2000 Per Game Averages

	W	L	FGA	FG%	3PA	3P%	FTA	FT%	Blk	Stl	Ast	Reb	Pts		W	L	FGA	FG%	3PA	3P%	FTA	FT%	Blk	Stl	Ast	Reb	Pts
Total	40	42	85.9	.453	16.2	.391	21.4	.804	5.07	7.22	22.1	41.2	101.4	Pre All-Star	20	28	87.0	.452	14.7	.393	22.1	.797	5.48	7.33	22.6	41.2	102.0
Home	22	19	86.4	.457	15.6	.387	21.1	.805	6.22	7.00	21.6	42.1	102.0	Post All-Star	20	14	84.5	.456	18.2	.389	20.2	.814	4.50	7.06	21.4	41.1	100.6
Road	18	23	85.5	.449	16.8	.396	21.6	.802	3.93	7.44	22.6	40.2	100.8	November	5	11	89.0	.442	13.4	.360	22.1	.811	5.00	8.13	22.6	40.6	101.5
vs. Playoff	18	30	85.8	.451	16.1	.397	20.2	.788	5.00	7.21	21.4	40.8	99.6	December	4	10	87.1	.448	15.4	.423	21.1	.756	6.00	6.43	21.6	40.1	100.4
vs. Non-Playoff	22	12	86.1	.457	16.2	.384	23.0	.822	5.18	7.24	23.1	41.7	103.9	January	8	5	84.8	.463	15.1	.383	22.4	.804	5.23	6.92	23.5	42.6	102.4
vs. East	12	18	86.3	.441	16.5	.404	20.5	.787	5.37	6.73	22.5	40.7	98.9	February	7	6	85.5	.451	16.4	.399	21.2	.801	5.15	6.62	22.4	41.5	100.8
vs. West	28	24	85.8	.461	16.0	.384	21.8	.813	4.90	7.50	21.8	41.4	102.9	March	7	9	84.1	.447	18.3	.384	20.1	.816	3.81	7.31	20.2	41.2	98.5
vs. Div.	12	12	85.4	.455	15.0	.362	21.1	.822	4.79	7.04	20.8	40.5	100.5	April	9	1	84.3	.480	19.6	.403	21.4	.841	5.60	7.90	22.7	41.0	106.9
Starters	—	—	61.8	.461	11.5	.394	15.8	.821	3.38	5.17	16.5	28.9	74.4	0 Days Rest	7	11	86.2	.433	18.1	.387	20.9	.809	3.50	8.06	22.4	41.9	98.6
Bench	—	—	24.2	.435	4.7	.384	5.6	.755	1.70	2.05	5.6	12.3	27.0	1 Days Rest	23	21	85.5	.455	15.9	.385	22.7	.794	5.02	7.16	20.8	40.7	102.0
In wins	40	0	84.0	.480	16.0	.432	23.9	.820	5.88	7.55	23.4	41.9	104.9	2 Days Rest	8	8	86.9	.468	15.3	.430	17.4	.824	6.69	6.94	24.9	41.4	102.3
In losses	0	42	87.8	.430	16.3	.353	18.9	.784	4.31	6.90	20.8	40.4	96.0	3+ Days Rest	2	2	85.8	.464	14.3	.333	24.0	.823	6.25	5.25	23.3	41.8	104.0

Opponents' 1999-2000 Per Game Averages

	W	L	FGA	FG%	3PA	3P%	FTA	FT%	Blk	Stl	Ast	Reb	Pts		W	L	FGA	FG%	3PA	3P%	FTA	FT%	Blk	Stl	Ast	Reb	Pts
Total	42	40	86.0	.457	15.2	.345	24.5	.740	5.07	7.37	23.2	48.4	102.0	November	11	5	90.0	.460	17.4	.342	24.6	.731	6.00	7.63	25.1	53.1	106.7
Home	19	22	85.7	.451	15.0	.330	25.3	.752	5.24	7.00	20.8	49.1	101.2	December	10	4	85.8	.467	12.7	.337	24.0	.774	5.07	7.57	24.0	47.6	103.0
Road	23	18	86.3	.464	15.4	.360	23.6	.728	4.90	7.73	25.5	47.7	102.7	January	5	8	85.1	.429	15.8	.307	28.3	.745	5.15	7.62	21.4	48.2	99.0
vs. Div.	12	12	85.1	.458	15.1	.333	24.6	.745	5.92	6.67	23.5	47.3	101.4	February	6	7	85.9	.459	13.8	.335	23.2	.748	5.69	7.69	24.3	45.5	100.4
Starters	—	—	57.4	.465	9.1	.357	16.2	.742	3.13	4.98	16.1	31.3	68.7	March	9	7	82.2	.470	15.1	.390	23.6	.730	4.56	6.88	21.9	46.1	100.4
Bench	—	—	28.6	.441	6.1	.327	8.2	.736	1.94	2.39	7.1	17.1	33.2	April	1	9	87.4	.453	16.3	.350	22.7	.705	3.50	6.70	21.9	48.5	100.9
In wins	0	40	86.4	.425	15.6	.307	26.5	.731	4.88	6.95	20.7	48.1	97.6	0 Days Rest	11	7	86.6	.458	13.6	.331	23.4	.735	5.11	8.89	24.3	48.8	101.1
In losses	42	0	85.6	.488	14.8	.383	22.5	.751	5.26	7.76	25.5	48.8	106.2	1 Days Rest	21	23	85.4	.459	15.4	.356	25.0	.745	5.02	6.64	22.8	48.7	102.5
Pre All-Star	28	20	87.3	.453	15.2	.323	25.8	.743	5.40	7.71	23.6	49.8	103.2	2 Days Rest	8	8	87.4	.455	15.1	.306	23.6	.729	5.25	8.50	23.4	47.6	101.3
Post All-Star	14	20	84.2	.463	15.1	.375	22.6	.736	4.62	6.88	22.6	46.4	100.2	3+ Days Rest	2	2	85.0	.441	19.5	.410	26.5	.745	4.75	4.00	22.0	46.8	102.8

Denver Nuggets

1999-2000 Per Game Averages

	W	L	FGA	FG%	3PA	3P%	FTA	FT%	Blk	Stl	Ast	Reb	Pts		W	L	FGA	FG%	3PA	3P%	FTA	FT%	Blk	Stl	Ast	Reb	Pts
Total	35	47	84.3	.442	17.0	.336	25.8	.724	7.54	6.76	23.3	44.7	99.0	Pre All-Star	21	27	83.8	.442	16.6	.334	26.0	.717	8.04	6.92	22.6	44.0	98.2
Home	25	16	85.6	.445	17.5	.367	27.0	.723	9.98	6.93	25.5	46.3	102.0	Post All-Star	14	20	85.0	.443	17.7	.339	25.6	.733	6.82	6.53	24.3	45.6	100.1
Road	10	31	83.0	.440	16.6	.304	24.7	.724	5.10	6.59	21.1	43.0	95.9	November	6	7	82.3	.442	16.8	.394	26.4	.717	8.31	7.46	20.7	42.5	98.3
vs. Playoff	21	27	84.4	.436	16.8	.342	24.7	.703	7.46	7.08	22.5	44.3	96.7	December	9	6	83.2	.438	15.9	.277	28.5	.722	7.60	7.00	20.8	46.0	97.9
vs. Non-Playoff	14	20	84.1	.452	17.3	.329	27.4	.750	7.65	6.29	24.5	45.3	102.2	January	5	9	84.6	.444	16.1	.316	23.6	.697	8.57	6.36	25.1	41.8	96.6
vs. East	13	17	82.5	.434	17.6	.319	27.6	.717	7.27	6.03	22.6	44.8	96.9	February	5	8	87.2	.438	17.3	.347	24.4	.741	6.77	7.23	23.8	46.7	100.5
vs. West	22	30	85.3	.447	16.7	.347	24.8	.728	7.69	7.17	23.7	44.6	100.1	March	4	13	83.7	.441	15.6	.320	26.2	.730	6.29	5.71	23.9	46.1	98.0
vs. Div.	10	14	84.5	.446	15.8	.311	26.2	.717	7.33	6.67	22.7	43.7	99.1	April	6	4	85.2	.453	22.5	.373	25.3	.735	8.10	7.20	26.3	44.5	104.2
Starters	—	—	60.2	.444	11.5	.340	17.4	.719	5.07	4.16	16.7	29.3	69.9	0 Days Rest	8	13	79.2	.443	16.2	.341	27.3	.729	5.86	6.00	20.5	44.3	95.5
Bench	—	—	24.0	.439	5.5	.330	8.4	.732	2.46	2.60	6.6	15.4	29.0	1 Days Rest	16	24	86.1	.445	17.4	.330	25.1	.722	7.70	6.83	24.2	44.6	100.4
In wins	35	0	85.2	.466	17.4	.387	26.2	.739	9.43	7.03	25.1	47.0	105.4	2 Days Rest	7	6	83.5	.440	18.2	.360	27.6	.738	8.62	8.00	24.2	44.8	100.3
In losses	0	47	83.6	.425	16.8	.298	25.5	.711	6.13	6.55	22.0	43.0	94.2	3+ Days Rest	4	4	89.9	.435	15.5	.315	22.8	.687	9.38	6.38	24.5	45.9	98.8

Opponents' 1999-2000 Per Game Averages

	W	L	FGA	FG%	3PA	3P%	FTA	FT%	Blk	Stl	Ast	Reb	Pts		W	L	FGA	FG%	3PA	3P%	FTA	FT%	Blk	Stl	Ast	Reb	Pts
Total	47	35	84.8	.450	13.7	.354	26.5	.751	5.63	7.51	24.4	44.3	101.1	November	7	6	84.2	.475	11.8	.351	22.9	.688	5.00	7.08	24.4	43.0	99.9
Home	16	25	85.0	.435	13.9	.344	26.2	.748	6.20	6.93	23.7	44.2	98.3	December	6	9	83.7	.441	12.3	.319	26.3	.734	5.60	7.47	23.6	43.6	97.1
Road	31	10	84.6	.466	13.6	.365	26.8	.753	5.07	8.10	25.2	44.4	103.9	January	9	5	85.1	.460	14.6	.420	24.1	.774	6.00	7.00	25.9	45.5	103.1
vs. Div.	14	10	84.2	.456	12.2	.365	26.5	.756	5.33	7.42	23.7	43.1	101.9	February	8	5	86.4	.451	14.8	.342	27.0	.746	6.23	8.38	25.1	44.8	103.1
Starters	—	—	57.7	.447	8.5	.343	17.8	.770	3.49	4.83	17.3	29.4	68.1	March	13	4	84.0	.433	14.5	.340	29.5	.778	5.94	7.82	23.8	43.7	100.6
Bench	—	—	27.1	.457	5.2	.372	8.7	.711	2.15	2.68	7.1	15.0	32.9	April	4	6	86.1	.445	14.2	.352	29.3	.768	4.70	7.20	24.0	44.4	104.1
In wins	0	35	86.9	.419	13.7	.316	24.4	.746	5.71	6.69	23.0	43.1	95.4	0 Days Rest	13	8	83.4	.439	13.3	.355	29.5	.766	4.33	8.29	22.5	43.2	100.5
In losses	47	0	83.3	.474	13.7	.383	28.1	.754	5.57	8.13	25.5	45.2	105.3	1 Days Rest	24	16	84.0	.461	13.7	.353	26.9	.736	6.00	7.38	24.7	44.3	102.1
Pre All-Star	27	21	84.5	.456	13.3	.357	25.5	.733	5.75	7.46	24.6	44.4	100.5	2 Days Rest	6	7	86.7	.442	12.9	.339	24.3	.747	6.23	7.08	25.5	44.3	99.2
Post All-Star	20	14	85.2	.441	14.4	.350	28.0	.774	5.47	7.59	24.2	44.2	101.9	3+ Days Rest	4	4	89.3	.440	16.5	.379	20.1	.795	6.25	6.88	26.5	47.1	100.8

Detroit Pistons

1999-2000 Per Game Averages

	W	L	FGA	FG%	3PA	3P%	FTA	FT%	Blk	Stl	Ast	Reb	Pts		W	L	FGA	FG%	3PA	3P%	FTA	FT%	Blk	Stl	Ast	Reb	Pts
Total	42	40	80.9	.459	14.9	.359	30.6	.781	3.33	8.11	20.8	41.2	103.5	Pre All-Star	25	23	81.6	.453	14.8	.345	31.9	.780	3.15	8.13	21.0	41.3	104.0
Home	27	14	80.8	.460	14.7	.353	31.3	.778	3.34	8.05	20.3	42.6	103.9	Post All-Star	17	17	79.9	.467	15.1	.378	28.6	.782	3.59	8.09	20.6	40.9	102.7
Road	15	26	81.0	.457	15.1	.365	29.9	.783	3.32	8.17	21.3	39.7	103.0	November	7	8	84.1	.441	14.1	.308	30.4	.781	2.73	7.27	21.1	43.4	102.3
vs. Playoff	17	27	80.7	.447	15.2	.360	29.8	.774	3.09	7.61	19.4	41.5	100.8	December	8	6	78.9	.460	13.9	.361	33.5	.804	3.14	7.71	21.5	39.7	104.5
vs. Non-Playoff	25	13	81.1	.472	14.6	.358	31.4	.787	3.61	8.68	22.5	40.8	106.6	January	7	8	80.5	.454	15.4	.364	32.9	.755	3.67	9.53	20.7	39.9	103.5
vs. East	30	24	81.2	.457	14.8	.357	31.1	.777	3.24	8.07	21.0	41.4	103.6	February	6	6	83.6	.464	16.6	.387	26.2	.806	4.33	8.08	19.7	41.5	105.0
vs. West	12	16	80.4	.463	15.1	.363	29.4	.788	3.50	8.18	20.5	40.6	103.1	March	8	7	80.4	.473	15.2	.342	29.3	.782	2.40	7.93	20.8	40.9	104.3
vs. Div.	16	12	82.3	.455	14.8	.362	30.3	.776	2.96	8.18	21.2	41.5	103.8	April	6	5	77.4	.464	14.5	.406	30.3	.760	4.09	8.09	20.9	41.6	100.7
Starters	—	—	62.1	.454	12.8	.372	22.6	.802	2.18	5.68	16.5	24.9	79.3	0 Days Rest	9	11	79.6	.468	14.4	.366	30.6	.747	3.65	7.10	20.8	39.0	102.6
Bench	—	—	18.8	.474	2.1	.278	7.9	.719	1.15	2.43	4.3	16.3	24.1	1 Days Rest	23	22	80.7	.452	15.3	.345	30.4	.789	3.56	8.67	20.2	41.8	102.2
In wins	42	0	80.0	.485	14.8	.385	31.5	.791	3.31	8.83	21.9	42.5	108.1	2 Days Rest	4	4	80.9	.465	14.5	.371	27.6	.801	1.63	8.00	23.6	40.0	102.8
In losses	0	40	81.9	.432	15.1	.332	29.6	.769	3.35	7.35	19.7	39.7	98.6	3+ Days Rest	6	3	84.9	.467	14.4	.408	33.7	.795	3.00	7.67	21.4	43.7	112.0

Opponents' 1999-2000 Per Game Averages

	W	L	FGA	FG%	3PA	3P%	FTA	FT%	Blk	Stl	Ast	Reb	Pts		W	L	FGA	FG%	3PA	3P%	FTA	FT%	Blk	Stl	Ast	Reb	Pts
Total	40	42	81.8	.465	15.0	.371	27.3	.746	4.83	7.95	23.1	42.4	102.0	November	8	7	83.1	.468	15.1	.388	27.1	.736	5.67	7.93	22.9	43.4	103.5
Home	14	27	80.5	.461	14.7	.358	27.4	.743	4.29	8.24	22.0	40.8	99.9	December	6	8	85.6	.450	12.8	.313	25.6	.735	6.64	8.36	21.9	44.6	99.9
Road	26	15	83.1	.469	15.4	.384	27.1	.749	5.37	7.66	24.2	44.0	104.2	January	8	7	80.8	.500	12.3	.429	26.3	.736	3.87	8.13	23.9	42.1	105.4
vs. Div.	12	16	81.0	.464	14.4	.395	27.9	.762	5.18	7.86	23.8	42.5	102.1	February	6	6	83.8	.446	18.6	.395	25.8	.803	4.25	7.42	21.8	43.8	102.9
Starters	—	—	56.4	.477	10.2	.383	18.2	.756	3.09	5.15	16.0	27.8	71.5	March	7	8	78.7	.476	16.1	.344	29.1	.752	4.33	8.00	23.7	38.9	102.3
Bench	—	—	25.4	.439	4.9	.347	9.0	.726	1.74	2.80	7.1	14.6	30.5	April	5	6	78.5	.440	16.4	.356	30.2	.720	4.00	7.73	24.3	41.8	96.6
In wins	0	42	81.1	.445	15.1	.356	26.4	.725	4.10	8.07	21.0	40.1	96.7	0 Days Rest	11	9	81.9	.476	14.9	.396	27.2	.766	5.35	7.80	23.0	42.9	104.7
In losses	40	0	82.5	.486	15.0	.387	28.2	.767	5.60	7.83	25.3	44.9	107.6	1 Days Rest	22	23	81.5	.460	15.6	.369	27.0	.738	4.71	8.27	23.1	41.9	100.7
Pre All-Star	23	25	83.3	.471	13.7	.366	26.5	.743	5.21	8.21	22.8	43.3	103.2	2 Days Rest	4	4	82.1	.454	11.8	.330	26.9	.763	5.13	7.38	22.4	43.6	98.9
Post All-Star	17	17	79.7	.456	16.9	.377	28.3	.750	4.29	7.59	23.6	41.2	100.3	3+ Days Rest	3	6	82.6	.476	15.8	.359	29.1	.729	4.00	7.22	24.1	42.8	105.6

Golden State Warriors

1999-2000 Per Game Averages

	W	L	FGA	FG%	3PA	3P%	FTA	FT%	Blk	Stl	Ast	Reb	Pts
Total	19	63	87.1	.420	13.0	.323	26.2	.697	4.34	8.91	22.6	45.6	95.5
Home	12	29	86.7	.429	13.2	.309	27.4	.688	4.22	8.73	24.7	47.2	97.3
Road	7	34	87.5	.410	12.8	.337	25.0	.708	4.46	9.10	20.5	44.0	93.8
vs. Playoff	4	44	86.5	.409	13.2	.316	25.9	.687	3.90	8.71	21.7	44.9	92.9
vs. Non-Playoff	15	19	87.8	.434	12.9	.332	26.6	.711	4.97	9.21	23.8	46.6	99.3
vs. East	10	20	88.0	.417	14.5	.307	27.1	.694	4.37	8.60	23.5	48.1	96.6
vs. West	9	43	86.5	.421	12.2	.333	25.7	.699	4.33	9.10	22.1	44.2	94.9
vs. Div.	2	22	87.6	.423	12.7	.311	24.2	.675	4.13	9.92	22.7	44.4	94.5
Starters	—	—	61.5	.417	9.2	.328	16.5	.677	3.29	5.80	16.1	31.5	65.5
Bench	—	—	25.6	.425	3.9	.310	9.6	.732	1.05	3.11	6.4	14.0	30.0
In wins	19	0	86.4	.477	12.0	.355	27.6	.681	4.47	9.89	27.3	47.5	105.6
In losses	0	63	87.3	.402	13.3	.314	25.8	.702	4.30	8.62	21.2	45.0	92.5
Pre All-Star	12	35	88.4	.425	14.0	.346	23.6	.690	3.87	8.19	23.1	45.9	96.2
Post All-Star	7	28	85.3	.413	11.8	.286	29.6	.705	4.97	9.89	21.8	45.2	94.6
November	2	11	89.1	.406	12.7	.358	23.0	.716	4.77	7.00	21.9	47.8	93.3
December	4	12	89.5	.426	13.9	.320	23.4	.644	3.19	8.56	23.6	45.8	95.8
January	3	9	88.3	.424	15.3	.350	25.3	.707	3.83	9.17	23.3	45.7	98.1
February	7	8	85.9	.435	14.5	.341	25.1	.702	4.13	9.20	23.3	47.9	97.3
March	1	16	84.1	.399	11.0	.251	29.4	.696	6.24	9.29	19.8	42.8	90.4
April	2	7	85.7	.435	10.6	.316	32.7	.731	3.22	10.78	24.9	43.6	101.7
0 Days Rest	3	17	88.2	.415	12.8	.355	24.6	.711	3.95	8.60	21.4	46.0	95.2
1 Days Rest	10	34	86.8	.421	12.4	.320	27.0	.701	4.77	8.77	22.7	45.2	96.0
2 Days Rest	4	7	87.4	.418	13.8	.283	27.8	.660	3.00	9.55	23.7	46.4	95.4
3+ Days Rest	2	5	85.4	.428	16.7	.316	22.7	.698	4.86	9.71	23.1	45.7	94.3

Opponents' 1999-2000 Per Game Averages

	W	L	FGA	FG%	3PA	3P%	FTA	FT%	Blk	Stl	Ast	Reb	Pts
Total	63	19	82.6	.467	14.2	.367	28.4	.754	6.04	8.41	24.8	46.1	103.8
Home	29	12	83.2	.457	14.2	.395	27.5	.751	4.98	8.29	23.9	46.7	102.3
Road	34	7	82.0	.477	14.2	.339	29.2	.756	7.10	8.54	25.8	45.5	105.3
vs. Div.	22	2	82.3	.471	15.9	.365	28.3	.742	5.71	8.58	25.3	46.5	104.3
Starters	—	—	55.3	.466	8.6	.352	20.1	.754	4.22	5.29	17.0	30.5	69.7
Bench	—	—	27.3	.470	5.6	.390	8.3	.753	1.82	3.12	7.8	15.7	34.1
In wins	0	19	84.8	.419	13.6	.322	25.9	.712	3.89	6.95	20.7	44.7	93.9
In losses	63	0	82.0	.482	14.4	.380	29.1	.765	6.68	8.86	26.1	46.6	106.8
Pre All-Star	35	12	83.8	.466	14.0	.341	26.9	.754	5.72	8.40	24.6	45.7	103.1
Post All-Star	28	7	81.1	.469	14.5	.401	30.4	.754	6.46	8.43	25.1	46.7	104.7
November	11	2	84.0	.470	14.4	.406	25.9	.763	4.92	8.08	25.8	46.5	104.5
December	12	4	82.3	.467	13.1	.306	27.3	.722	6.13	7.75	24.4	44.6	100.6
January	9	3	84.9	.462	14.3	.308	29.0	.767	6.17	9.50	24.3	47.5	105.2
February	8	7	83.5	.446	14.1	.393	27.9	.761	5.93	8.53	22.7	45.5	101.3
March	16	1	81.6	.473	14.5	.382	30.7	.745	7.71	8.18	26.4	47.8	105.6
April	7	2	78.6	.496	15.3	.413	29.7	.783	4.33	8.89	25.7	44.3	107.6
0 Days Rest	17	3	82.4	.468	14.4	.373	28.8	.763	6.45	9.00	24.9	46.6	104.3
1 Days Rest	34	10	81.9	.475	14.6	.365	29.7	.764	6.18	8.59	25.1	45.8	105.8
2 Days Rest	7	4	84.2	.456	12.5	.380	24.4	.690	4.73	7.45	24.9	48.6	98.3
3+ Days Rest	5	2	85.7	.438	13.6	.347	25.4	.747	6.00	7.14	22.9	48.3	98.9

Houston Rockets

1999-2000 Per Game Averages

	W	L	FGA	FG%	3PA	3P%	FTA	FT%	Blk	Stl	Ast	Reb	Pts
Total	34	48	81.3	.450	19.8	.358	26.2	.733	5.34	7.48	21.6	43.8	99.5
Home	22	19	82.2	.458	20.3	.360	25.3	.726	5.54	7.29	23.4	44.8	101.1
Road	12	29	80.3	.442	19.4	.355	27.0	.740	5.15	7.66	19.9	42.8	97.8
vs. Playoff	13	35	79.0	.442	20.1	.354	25.5	.748	4.77	7.21	20.5	42.1	96.1
vs. Non-Playoff	21	13	84.5	.461	19.4	.362	27.0	.714	6.15	7.85	23.3	46.2	104.2
vs. East	11	19	80.0	.449	19.1	.359	25.7	.732	5.80	7.30	21.5	42.7	98.9
vs. West	23	29	82.0	.451	20.2	.357	26.4	.734	5.08	7.58	21.7	44.5	100.6
vs. Div.	8	16	80.1	.442	19.1	.334	28.0	.721	5.25	6.58	20.1	42.9	97.4
Starters	—	—	50.1	.454	12.7	.350	15.1	.736	3.13	4.68	14.7	27.0	61.0
Bench	—	—	31.2	.445	7.1	.371	11.1	.730	2.21	2.79	7.0	16.8	38.4
In wins	34	0	82.5	.478	20.6	.417	26.4	.735	5.88	7.71	24.4	45.4	106.9
In losses	0	48	80.4	.430	19.3	.313	26.0	.732	4.96	7.31	19.7	42.7	94.2
Pre All-Star	20	30	82.4	.441	19.6	.348	26.3	.714	5.42	7.74	21.2	44.7	98.4
Post All-Star	14	18	79.5	.465	20.1	.372	25.9	.765	5.22	7.06	22.3	42.5	101.2
November	4	11	83.7	.439	20.2	.323	25.1	.721	5.87	8.47	20.7	47.1	98.3
December	6	9	81.0	.451	18.0	.367	26.5	.680	5.87	7.40	21.6	43.3	97.7
January	7	7	81.7	.438	20.4	.358	27.9	.736	4.57	6.64	21.6	45.3	99.4
February	5	8	84.2	.432	21.8	.345	23.8	.742	4.54	9.00	21.6	42.5	98.0
March	5	10	78.0	.458	19.1	.341	27.3	.748	5.20	7.67	22.5	41.4	98.4
April	7	3	78.5	.498	19.6	.439	26.2	.794	6.10	5.00	22.0	43.2	107.6
0 Days Rest	5	12	82.1	.431	18.3	.360	25.4	.729	5.18	7.88	19.5	42.6	95.9
1 Days Rest	23	22	81.4	.459	20.2	.359	26.9	.740	5.31	7.11	22.7	44.0	101.9
2 Days Rest	5	12	80.5	.447	19.7	.349	24.9	.723	5.71	8.24	20.6	44.1	96.8
3+ Days Rest	2	1	79.7	.448	23.3	.371	26.3	.709	4.67	6.33	23.0	45.3	98.7

Opponents' 1999-2000 Per Game Averages

	W	L	FGA	FG%	3PA	3P%	FTA	FT%	Blk	Stl	Ast	Reb	Pts
Total	48	34	86.3	.456	12.1	.354	22.3	.779	5.28	8.96	22.7	42.4	100.3
Home	19	22	86.8	.442	12.3	.337	22.1	.768	4.46	8.49	21.5	41.9	97.9
Road	29	12	85.7	.470	11.9	.370	22.5	.790	6.10	9.44	23.9	42.9	102.7
vs. Div.	16	8	84.8	.476	11.3	.367	22.0	.809	5.67	8.58	25.0	40.9	102.8
Starters	—	—	59.0	.466	7.4	.340	16.4	.780	3.35	5.88	15.9	27.5	70.3
Bench	—	—	27.3	.434	4.5	.376	5.9	.778	1.93	3.09	6.9	14.9	30.0
In wins	0	34	87.3	.426	13.4	.294	22.1	.755	5.26	7.79	20.6	42.0	95.1
In losses	48	0	85.6	.477	11.1	.404	22.4	.796	5.29	9.79	24.2	42.7	104.1
Pre All-Star	30	20	85.6	.457	11.5	.354	23.0	.763	5.36	8.82	22.1	42.7	99.9
Post All-Star	18	14	87.3	.454	12.9	.353	21.2	.806	5.16	9.19	23.7	41.9	101.0
November	11	4	87.5	.441	12.5	.374	24.7	.776	4.73	10.07	22.1	43.5	101.1
December	9	6	82.7	.460	10.3	.316	24.0	.764	6.00	9.33	20.5	40.7	97.7
January	7	7	87.1	.455	13.1	.377	22.3	.753	5.14	8.29	23.5	43.0	101.0
February	8	5	85.1	.476	10.6	.384	20.9	.768	6.08	7.92	23.8	44.7	101.2
March	10	5	85.5	.466	10.7	.394	19.8	.808	4.33	9.13	23.9	41.5	98.0
April	3	7	91.3	.434	16.7	.275	21.7	.820	5.60	8.80	22.8	41.0	101.6
0 Days Rest	12	5	86.2	.462	10.8	.386	20.6	.809	6.12	7.94	22.9	45.0	100.5
1 Days Rest	22	23	86.4	.452	12.1	.339	22.7	.777	5.11	8.56	22.6	41.4	99.9
2 Days Rest	12	5	86.3	.458	13.1	.369	22.4	.774	5.47	11.12	22.8	42.9	101.2
3+ Days Rest	2	1	84.0	.472	13.0	.308	25.7	.688	2.00	8.67	22.3	39.7	101.0

Indiana Pacers

1999-2000 Per Game Averages

	W	L	FGA	FG%	3PA	3P%	FTA	FT%	Blk	Stl	Ast	Reb	Pts		W	L	FGA	FG%	3PA	3P%	FTA	FT%	Blk	Stl	Ast	Reb	Pts
Total	56	26	81.0	.459	18.1	.392	24.5	.811	5.15	6.82	22.6	42.1	101.3	Pre All-Star	32	16	82.0	.460	19.0	.379	24.3	.816	5.42	6.88	23.4	42.1	102.4
Home	36	5	80.5	.472	17.6	.405	25.5	.818	5.63	7.00	23.0	42.4	104.0	Post All-Star	24	10	79.5	.458	16.9	.413	24.8	.805	4.76	6.74	21.6	42.2	99.7
Road	20	21	81.5	.446	18.6	.380	23.5	.804	4.66	6.63	22.2	41.8	98.6	November	8	7	83.6	.445	17.6	.383	24.7	.784	5.73	7.00	21.7	41.9	100.5
vs. Playoff	26	18	80.4	.449	18.6	.397	23.1	.818	4.82	6.50	22.1	42.0	98.5	December	12	2	80.9	.469	20.1	.397	24.0	.815	5.36	7.57	24.3	41.9	103.4
vs. Non-Playoff	30	8	81.6	.470	17.6	.386	26.1	.804	5.53	7.18	23.3	42.3	104.5	January	8	6	82.4	.455	20.7	.366	23.5	.845	4.79	6.43	24.1	41.2	102.4
vs. East	36	18	79.6	.472	17.7	.397	24.5	.808	5.15	6.17	23.3	41.2	102.0	February	11	2	77.9	.479	15.6	.399	26.2	.826	5.54	6.77	23.2	42.5	102.5
vs. West	20	8	83.5	.434	19.0	.383	24.5	.818	5.14	8.07	21.4	43.9	99.9	March	9	7	80.7	.448	17.8	.407	27.2	.807	4.56	6.94	20.2	42.9	101.4
vs. Div.	20	8	79.3	.478	18.3	.393	23.4	.813	5.25	6.32	24.8	41.9	102.1	April	8	2	79.5	.465	16.3	.411	19.8	.783	4.90	5.90	22.9	42.3	96.2
Starters	—	—	54.3	.467	10.5	.401	15.5	.822	3.48	3.99	16.1	26.5	67.7	0 Days Rest	14	7	80.1	.454	19.0	.401	24.0	.786	5.14	6.62	21.8	42.0	99.3
Bench	—	—	26.7	.442	7.6	.379	9.0	.794	1.67	2.83	6.5	15.6	33.6	1 Days Rest	27	14	81.1	.452	18.4	.384	24.0	.828	4.80	6.78	22.5	42.1	100.2
In wins	56	0	80.3	.478	17.8	.420	25.5	.805	5.39	7.39	23.6	42.1	104.9	2 Days Rest	9	5	82.9	.486	17.0	.399	23.2	.822	6.93	6.93	25.0	42.9	106.4
In losses	0	26	82.5	.418	18.8	.335	22.2	.827	4.62	5.58	20.1	42.1	95.7	3+ Days Rest		0	78.7	.460	16.2	.402	32.0	.776	3.33	7.50	21.0	41.3	103.7

Opponents' 1999-2000 Per Game Averages

	W	L	FGA	FG%	3PA	3P%	FTA	FT%	Blk	Stl	Ast	Reb	Pts		W	L	FGA	FG%	3PA	3P%	FTA	FT%	Blk	Stl	Ast	Reb	Pts
Total	26	56	85.1	.446	12.3	.327	22.2	.755	3.94	7.44	21.2	43.7	96.7	November	7	8	84.9	.446	11.5	.349	24.3	.769	3.87	8.27	20.6	45.8	98.4
Home	5	36	86.0	.436	12.7	.313	20.9	.750	3.73	7.24	19.2	43.6	94.7	December	2	12	83.2	.433	12.1	.329	21.5	.678	3.93	6.29	19.9	44.1	90.7
Road	21	20	84.3	.455	11.9	.342	23.6	.759	4.15	7.63	23.1	43.8	98.7	January	6	8	85.7	.455	12.3	.285	23.1	.735	3.79	7.71	21.9	43.4	98.5
vs. Div.	8	20	85.1	.438	12.4	.323	22.8	.746	3.68	7.71	21.4	42.5	95.7	February	2	11	86.2	.443	14.2	.324	18.8	.775	3.54	7.15	21.0	41.3	95.6
Starters	—	—	60.6	.451	8.0	.350	15.3	.759	2.70	4.80	15.4	30.0	69.0	March	7	9	88.1	.458	11.8	.383	22.5	.792	4.56	7.94	22.4	45.1	102.9
Bench	—	—	24.5	.434	4.2	.284	6.9	.746	1.24	2.63	5.8	13.8	27.6	April	2	8	81.3	.433	11.9	.269	22.8	.781	3.80	7.00	21.0	41.5	91.4
In wins	0	56	85.0	.433	12.8	.309	21.0	.751	3.77	7.20	19.9	43.1	93.4	0 Days Rest	7	14	82.9	.447	11.0	.365	23.3	.753	3.48	7.52	20.5	42.2	95.6
In losses	26	0	85.5	.472	11.1	.372	24.8	.761	4.31	7.96	24.0	45.0	103.8	1 Days Rest	14	27	85.2	.445	12.6	.322	21.3	.757	4.27	7.46	22.3	43.8	96.1
Pre All-Star	16	32	84.9	.444	12.2	.329	22.8	.729	3.88	7.46	20.8	44.0	96.0	2 Days Rest	5	9	90.0	.442	12.5	.314	22.0	.769	3.50	7.07	19.9	46.3	100.4
Post All-Star	10	24	85.6	.448	12.3	.325	21.4	.794	4.03	7.41	21.7	43.3	97.6	3+ Days Rest	0	6	81.2	.456	13.8	.277	25.2	.715	4.33	7.83	18.8	42.2	95.8

Los Angeles Clippers

1999-2000 Per Game Averages

	W	L	FGA	FG%	3PA	3P%	FTA	FT%	Blk	Stl	Ast	Reb	Pts		W	L	FGA	FG%	3PA	3P%	FTA	FT%	Blk	Stl	Ast	Reb	Pts
Total	15	67	82.4	.426	15.5	.339	22.3	.746	6.02	7.05	18.0	40.6	92.0	Pre All-Star	11	38	81.8	.429	15.3	.326	22.6	.734	6.37	6.94	17.5	40.9	91.8
Home	10	31	82.0	.432	15.0	.321	23.6	.752	5.83	7.78	17.3	40.5	93.4	Post All-Star	4	29	83.3	.421	15.6	.357	21.8	.766	5.52	7.21	18.8	40.3	92.3
Road	5	36	82.8	.420	15.9	.355	20.9	.740	6.22	6.32	18.7	40.7	90.6	November	4	10	77.8	.409	15.2	.324	30.1	.732	7.00	7.14	14.7	41.8	90.5
vs. Playoff	6	42	81.8	.417	15.3	.337	22.7	.739	5.46	6.90	17.2	39.9	90.1	December	5	10	83.5	.434	15.4	.333	21.1	.699	6.87	7.07	20.3	41.5	92.3
vs. Non-Playoff	9	25	83.3	.439	15.6	.341	21.6	.758	6.82	7.26	19.2	41.9	94.8	January	2	12	83.9	.447	14.6	.327	18.9	.762	6.00	6.00	17.4	41.9	94.2
vs. East	7	23	81.7	.431	16.1	.345	21.8	.744	6.07	7.30	18.1	40.1	92.2	February	1	14	82.8	.398	15.3	.343	18.3	.749	5.53	7.87	17.1	38.3	84.9
vs. West	8	44	82.8	.423	15.1	.335	22.6	.748	6.00	6.90	18.0	41.0	91.9	March	2	13	83.4	.438	16.3	.307	22.1	.771	5.20	6.87	19.9	40.1	95.1
vs. Div.	5	19	84.3	.411	16.0	.328	23.2	.722	5.46	7.33	17.6	42.1	91.3	April	1	8	83.1	.430	16.0	.431	24.1	.783	5.33	7.44	18.8	40.1	97.3
Starters	—	—	61.1	.436	9.7	.355	16.8	.746	4.10	4.73	13.2	29.7	69.3	0 Days Rest	4	18	82.5	.420	15.8	.340	22.1	.739	5.77	7.91	17.5	41.0	90.9
Bench	—	—	21.3	.396	5.8	.311	5.4	.749	1.93	2.32	4.8	11.0	22.7	1 Days Rest	6	33	82.1	.425	14.8	.349	21.9	.762	6.51	6.23	18.7	40.8	91.5
In wins	15	0	81.7	.457	16.2	.412	24.4	.749	7.13	7.80	21.0	42.5	99.6	2 Days Rest	5	10	82.5	.438	17.5	.324	22.7	.730	4.60	7.87	18.1	39.3	94.5
In losses	0	67	82.6	.419	15.3	.321	21.8	.746	5.78	6.88	17.4	40.2	90.3	3+ Days Rest	0	6	84.3	.425	13.3	.300	24.3	.719	7.33	7.17	15.7	41.3	93.2

Opponents' 1999-2000 Per Game Averages

	W	L	FGA	FG%	3PA	3P%	FTA	FT%	Blk	Stl	Ast	Reb	Pts		W	L	FGA	FG%	3PA	3P%	FTA	FT%	Blk	Stl	Ast	Reb	Pts
Total	67	15	83.9	.477	13.1	.387	24.9	.741	4.60	7.59	24.1	45.6	103.5	November	10	4	83.4	.452	11.3	.361	24.6	.733	5.29	8.07	22.9	44.4	97.4
Home	31	10	82.8	.475	13.2	.384	25.3	.734	3.98	7.39	21.3	44.1	102.3	December	10	5	84.3	.466	13.0	.385	25.2	.720	4.87	6.93	22.2	45.8	101.7
Road	36	5	85.0	.478	13.1	.390	24.5	.748	5.22	7.78	26.8	47.0	104.8	January	12	2	88.1	.461	11.2	.363	25.5	.739	4.07	7.86	23.1	47.1	104.2
vs. Div.	19	5	85.7	.482	13.7	.337	24.4	.716	4.17	7.92	25.3	46.6	104.7	February	14	1	82.9	.488	14.2	.413	21.2	.792	5.20	7.93	26.4	47.4	103.6
Starters	—	—	57.0	.486	8.0	.396	17.1	.744	3.13	4.85	16.6	29.7	71.3	March	13	2	82.5	.506	14.3	.377	26.7	.738	3.87	7.27	24.8	44.3	108.7
Bench	—	—	26.9	.458	5.2	.373	7.8	.734	1.46	2.73	7.5	15.8	32.3	April	8	1	81.4	.494	15.6	.421	27.0	.724	4.11	7.44	25.7	43.8	106.6
In wins	0	15	84.9	.431	13.5	.297	22.9	.706	4.47	6.33	18.9	42.7	93.3	0 Days Rest	18	4	85.7	.477	14.1	.339	24.0	.729	4.95	7.86	25.2	45.9	104.0
In losses	67	0	83.7	.487	13.1	.408	25.3	.748	4.63	7.87	25.2	46.2	105.8	1 Days Rest	33	6	83.7	.476	12.3	.432	24.8	.739	5.05	7.64	24.0	45.9	103.4
Pre All-Star	38	11	84.5	.468	12.0	.373	24.9	.745	4.67	7.65	23.0	45.3	102.2	2 Days Rest	10	5	81.5	.476	13.7	.359	24.2	.766	2.73	6.93	22.6	42.5	101.1
Post All-Star	29	4	83.0	.490	14.9	.403	24.9	.735	4.48	7.48	25.7	46.0	105.6	3+ Days Rest	6	0	84.7	.480	13.5	.370	30.8	.735	5.00	7.83	24.0	49.7	109.0

Los Angeles Lakers

1999-2000 Per Game Averages

	W	L	FGA	FG%	3PA	3P%	FTA	FT%	Blk	Stl	Ast	Reb	Pts		W	L	FGA	FG%	3PA	3P%	FTA	FT%	Blk	Stl	Ast	Reb	Pts
Total	67	15	83.4	.459	12.8	.329	28.9	.696	6.51	7.48	23.4	47.0	100.8	Pre All-Star	37	11	83.0	.453	12.4	.322	30.3	.672	7.06	7.92	22.1	47.5	99.6
Home	36	5	84.1	.458	13.0	.304	30.6	.697	7.37	8.10	24.1	49.4	102.3	Post All-Star	30	4	83.8	.468	13.3	.337	26.8	.735	5.74	6.85	25.2	46.4	102.6
Road	31	10	82.6	.460	12.5	.354	27.1	.695	5.66	6.85	22.7	44.6	99.3	November	11	4	79.5	.460	11.5	.343	30.6	.614	6.00	7.67	21.6	45.2	95.9
vs. Playoff	34	10	82.8	.446	13.6	.297	28.2	.710	6.75	7.34	22.5	46.7	98.0	December	14	1	83.0	.443	10.7	.281	31.9	.695	7.00	8.07	20.5	49.4	98.8
vs. Non-Playoff	33	5	84.0	.473	11.8	.371	29.6	.681	6.24	7.63	24.5	47.4	104.0	January	9	5	88.5	.448	15.7	.332	26.6	.700	7.86	8.14	23.6	48.1	103.1
vs. East	27	3	81.4	.460	12.0	.341	30.1	.708	7.43	7.23	23.6	46.1	100.3	February	12	1	79.5	.472	11.8	.357	28.6	.726	7.85	7.31	26.3	44.3	100.1
vs. West	40	12	84.5	.458	13.2	.322	28.2	.689	5.98	7.62	23.3	47.6	101.1	March	15	1	83.8	.480	13.0	.361	28.1	.733	5.50	6.63	24.8	46.6	105.8
vs. Div.	20	4	85.0	.458	13.2	.306	28.2	.706	5.75	7.46	22.0	48.7	101.8	April	6	3	87.1	.445	14.8	.278	26.2	.737	4.33	6.89	24.4	49.0	101.0
Starters	—	—	60.0	.483	6.8	.339	23.2	.681	4.51	4.34	15.2	33.1	76.1	0 Days Rest	20	2	84.0	.466	13.7	.326	29.6	.699	5.55	6.68	24.2	47.5	103.4
Bench	—	—	23.4	.397	6.0	.316	5.6	.760	2.00	3.13	8.2	13.9	24.7	1 Days Rest	33	8	83.4	.451	12.4	.326	28.8	.700	6.85	7.56	22.8	47.7	99.4
In wins	67	0	82.7	.469	12.4	.349	30.0	.707	6.69	7.66	23.9	48.0	103.1	2 Days Rest	7	5	81.0	.459	12.3	.331	29.8	.664	6.50	7.67	23.2	44.2	98.2
In losses	0	15	86.3	.417	14.6	.251	23.7	.637	5.73	6.67	21.3	42.7	90.6	3+ Days Rest	7	0	85.1	.483	12.7	.348	25.9	.729	7.57	9.14	25.0	46.6	105.6

Opponents' 1999-2000 Per Game Averages

	W	L	FGA	FG%	3PA	3P%	FTA	FT%	Blk	Stl	Ast	Reb	Pts		W	L	FGA	FG%	3PA	3P%	FTA	FT%	Blk	Stl	Ast	Reb	Pts
Total	15	67	83.2	.416	13.9	.326	24.9	.742	4.21	7.65	19.5	43.1	92.3	November	4	11	78.9	.414	13.2	.348	27.9	.742	5.07	7.93	17.5	43.0	90.7
Home	5	36	83.6	.401	14.3	.341	25.7	.732	4.00	8.37	18.3	43.0	90.8	December	1	14	83.7	.394	13.7	.335	24.9	.733	4.27	8.00	19.0	44.1	88.9
Road	10	31	82.8	.431	13.5	.310	24.2	.753	4.41	6.93	20.6	43.3	93.7	January	5	9	83.1	.420	15.9	.302	25.4	.772	4.64	7.00	19.1	44.4	94.2
vs. Div.	4	20	85.9	.415	16.0	.300	23.3	.708	4.00	7.96	19.2	44.2	92.6	February	1	12	84.3	.408	13.5	.301	21.0	.744	3.85	7.85	20.8	42.3	88.5
Starters	—	—	58.2	.425	9.1	.339	16.6	.753	2.78	4.99	14.2	28.5	65.1	March	1	15	82.9	.431	13.4	.341	25.3	.723	3.38	6.94	19.5	40.3	94.4
Bench	—	—	25.0	.394	4.8	.300	8.3	.721	1.43	2.66	5.2	14.6	27.1	April	3	6	88.9	.431	14.0	.325	24.3	.744	4.00	8.56	22.2	46.1	99.3
In wins	0	67	84.1	.405	13.8	.315	24.5	.731	4.03	7.63	19.3	42.6	90.4	0 Days Rest	2	20	83.5	.414	14.1	.312	26.9	.736	4.09	7.41	19.7	42.7	93.4
In losses	15	0	79.2	.468	14.4	.370	26.9	.787	5.00	7.73	20.3	45.5	100.7	1 Days Rest	8	33	83.8	.410	14.4	.337	24.2	.740	3.98	8.10	18.9	43.9	91.5
Pre All-Star	11	37	82.2	.408	14.1	.325	25.7	.747	4.69	7.58	18.6	43.8	90.9	2 Days Rest	5	7	79.9	.449	12.2	.342	24.1	.754	5.00	6.92	21.4	41.5	94.2
Post All-Star	4	30	84.7	.427	13.6	.326	23.9	.735	3.53	7.74	20.7	42.3	94.2	3+ Days Rest	0	7	84.4	.403	13.6	.274	24.4	.754	4.57	7.00	18.7	42.9	90.1

Miami Heat

1999-2000 Per Game Averages

	W	L	FGA	FG%	3PA	3P%	FTA	FT%	Blk	Stl	Ast	Reb	Pts		W	L	FGA	FG%	3PA	3P%	FTA	FT%	Blk	Stl	Ast	Reb	Pts
Total	52	30	78.8	.460	14.7	.371	22.3	.736	6.39	7.10	23.5	43.2	94.4	Pre All-Star	30	17	80.5	.469	14.5	.391	22.2	.740	6.98	7.04	24.4	43.9	97.5
Home	33	8	80.5	.473	15.4	.358	22.1	.746	6.85	7.41	24.0	44.7	98.1	Post All-Star	22	13	76.6	.448	14.9	.345	22.4	.731	5.60	7.17	22.5	42.1	90.1
Road	19	22	77.1	.447	13.9	.386	22.5	.726	5.93	6.78	23.0	41.6	90.7	November	11	3	82.9	.470	17.1	.402	24.8	.749	6.43	8.00	25.0	45.0	103.4
vs. Playoff	24	19	77.7	.451	14.4	.368	21.6	.746	5.91	6.56	23.0	42.6	91.4	December	8	6	76.4	.469	12.6	.352	21.4	.736	7.79	5.93	23.9	43.1	91.7
vs. Non-Playoff	28	11	80.0	.471	14.9	.375	23.1	.726	6.92	7.69	24.2	43.8	97.6	January	8	7	81.9	.471	13.9	.413	20.0	.703	6.93	6.80	25.1	43.5	96.9
vs. East	34	20	79.2	.456	15.3	.360	22.9	.727	6.44	7.54	23.4	42.7	94.4	February	9	5	79.2	.430	15.5	.355	22.2	.788	6.43	7.07	21.6	45.4	94.1
vs. West	18	10	78.1	.469	13.5	.394	21.0	.755	6.29	6.25	23.8	44.0	94.4	March	9	5	75.9	.461	13.9	.340	23.8	.721	5.21	7.71	22.6	39.6	91.9
vs. Div.	18	6	77.7	.463	15.2	.373	23.8	.726	6.50	7.54	22.8	42.8	94.9	April	7	4	75.7	.459	15.3	.351	21.5	.713	5.27	7.09	22.8	42.1	90.2
Starters	—	—	55.6	.465	11.2	.373	15.6	.750	4.89	4.66	17.1	29.4	67.6	0 Days Rest	9	9	76.7	.441	14.7	.345	22.8	.768	6.22	6.61	22.3	43.2	90.1
Bench	—	—	23.2	.448	3.5	.364	6.7	.704	1.50	2.44	6.4	13.8	26.8	1 Days Rest	29	16	78.2	.459	14.8	.382	21.3	.721	6.16	7.04	23.3	43.0	92.8
In wins	52	0	79.1	.481	14.6	.399	23.5	.748	6.94	7.19	24.8	44.8	99.2	2 Days Rest	9	4	79.5	.499	12.7	.418	20.8	.737	6.62	7.15	25.9	40.3	100.0
In losses	0	30	78.4	.423	14.8	.323	20.2	.713	5.43	6.93	21.5	40.4	85.5	3+ Days Rest	5	1	78.8	.444	18.0	.296	31.3	.745	8.17	8.83	24.2	50.5	106.7

Opponents' 1999-2000 Per Game Averages

	W	L	FGA	FG%	3PA	3P%	FTA	FT%	Blk	Stl	Ast	Reb	Pts		W	L	FGA	FG%	3PA	3P%	FTA	FT%	Blk	Stl	Ast	Reb	Pts
Total	30	52	80.4	.422	13.8	.361	24.7	.748	4.44	7.57	19.3	40.4	91.3	November	3	11	84.6	.429	13.9	.395	25.6	.741	4.71	7.21	18.9	42.1	97.1
Home	8	33	80.7	.415	13.6	.326	24.8	.740	3.85	7.56	16.8	39.8	89.6	December	6	8	84.6	.417	13.5	.323	21.9	.743	4.00	8.50	20.6	41.8	91.2
Road	22	19	80.2	.429	14.0	.395	24.6	.756	5.02	7.59	21.8	41.0	92.9	January	7	8	80.3	.418	14.0	.357	27.4	.764	5.73	8.00	20.0	40.3	93.1
vs. Div.	6	18	82.1	.415	12.8	.366	24.1	.750	4.17	8.17	18.6	41.5	89.1	February	5	9	80.4	.412	13.9	.436	22.5	.742	4.43	6.64	17.9	40.8	93.1
Starters	—	—	56.3	.426	8.7	.367	16.9	.760	2.87	5.07	14.1	27.1	64.0	March	5	9	76.9	.435	14.1	.315	24.5	.741	4.00	7.07	20.1	39.1	89.4
Bench	—	—	24.2	.412	5.0	.351	7.7	.722	1.57	2.50	5.2	13.4	27.2	April	4	7	74.3	.421	13.1	.333	26.1	.742	3.45	8.09	17.8	37.9	86.3
In wins	0	52	81.8	.407	13.5	.340	23.8	.743	3.79	7.19	18.5	39.8	88.8	0 Days Rest	9	9	79.9	.420	13.3	.346	25.4	.749	4.33	8.06	21.2	40.2	90.8
In losses	30	0	78.0	.449	14.3	.396	26.1	.755	5.57	8.23	20.7	41.5	95.5	1 Days Rest	16	29	78.7	.419	14.0	.378	24.0	.748	4.40	7.69	18.1	39.7	89.3
Pre All-Star	17	30	83.1	.423	13.6	.367	25.0	.754	4.70	7.89	20.0	41.3	94.1	2 Days Rest	4	9	82.2	.441	14.0	.341	24.2	.743	4.85	7.00	21.2	39.8	95.2
Post All-Star	13	22	76.9	.420	14.0	.354	24.2	.739	4.09	7.14	18.4	39.3	87.5	3+ Days Rest	1	5	91.0	.405	13.0	.321	28.3	.753	4.17	6.50	18.2	47.8	99.2

Milwaukee Bucks

1999-2000 Per Game Averages

	W	L	FGA	FG%	3PA	3P%	FTA	FT%	Blk	Stl	Ast	Reb	Pts		W	L	FGA	FG%	3PA	3P%	FTA	FT%	Blk	Stl	Ast	Reb	Pts
Total	42	40	83.3	.465	13.0	.369	24.2	.786	4.65	8.18	22.6	41.3	101.2	Pre All-Star	26	24	83.6	.469	13.6	.372	24.6	.804	4.66	8.44	22.9	40.8	103.3
Home	23	18	82.9	.472	12.9	.361	23.3	.798	4.02	8.20	23.7	41.5	101.5	Post All-Star	16	16	82.7	.458	12.1	.362	23.6	.757	4.63	7.78	22.1	42.2	98.0
Road	19	22	83.6	.458	13.2	.376	25.0	.775	5.27	8.17	21.5	41.1	101.0	November	8	6	82.1	.469	13.2	.384	27.3	.809	4.50	9.21	21.9	38.8	104.1
vs. Playoff	14	29	82.7	.458	14.1	.378	23.0	.804	4.16	7.72	22.2	39.9	99.7	December	9	7	82.9	.467	11.7	.353	22.7	.769	4.63	8.19	23.1	42.1	98.9
vs. Non-Playoff	28	11	83.8	.472	11.9	.356	25.4	.768	5.18	8.69	23.1	42.9	102.9	January	8	7	85.5	.469	15.6	.393	24.6	.832	4.87	7.93	24.1	41.9	106.7
vs. East	28	26	83.5	.467	13.2	.383	24.3	.789	4.87	8.26	22.9	41.8	102.3	February	3	9	85.6	.453	13.3	.346	21.5	.822	4.08	6.67	20.8	40.5	99.8
vs. West	14	14	82.7	.461	12.7	.340	23.9	.780	4.21	8.04	22.0	40.4	99.1	March	6	8	81.1	.468	12.7	.354	21.4	.746	4.07	8.21	22.9	40.6	96.4
vs. Div.	16	12	83.6	.479	13.1	.403	23.7	.819	4.36	8.75	24.1	41.0	104.8	April	8	3	82.5	.461	11.5	.373	28.3	.733	5.91	8.82	22.2	44.5	101.0
Starters	—	—	58.8	.470	9.1	.386	17.8	.812	3.39	5.37	16.5	28.6	73.2	0 Days Rest	9	10	80.7	.464	13.5	.359	25.5	.764	5.16	8.00	21.6	41.4	99.2
Bench	—	—	24.5	.454	3.9	.328	6.4	.715	1.26	2.82	6.1	12.7	28.1	1 Days Rest	24	25	83.8	.468	12.8	.367	23.3	.786	4.47	8.33	22.7	40.9	101.5
In wins	42	0	82.8	.487	12.0	.410	25.6	.798	5.29	9.17	24.3	42.7	106.1	2 Days Rest	3	2	85.4	.452	12.0	.383	21.2	.877	4.80	7.60	24.8	40.2	100.4
In losses	0	40	83.7	.441	14.1	.332	22.7	.772	3.98	7.15	20.8	39.9	96.1	3+ Days Rest	6	3	84.6	.457	13.8	.387	27.8	.788	4.44	8.11	22.8	44.0	104.6

Opponents' 1999-2000 Per Game Averages

	W	L	FGA	FG%	3PA	3P%	FTA	FT%	Blk	Stl	Ast	Reb	Pts		W	L	FGA	FG%	3PA	3P%	FTA	FT%	Blk	Stl	Ast	Reb	Pts
Total	40	42	81.0	.457	16.5	.391	27.3	.752	4.15	7.77	24.2	41.5	101.0	November	6	8	82.0	.463	15.0	.376	29.7	.728	4.14	6.14	23.8	43.0	103.1
Home	18	23	80.1	.449	15.6	.395	25.9	.743	3.39	7.51	22.7	40.6	97.3	December	7	9	80.8	.437	18.3	.380	27.3	.752	4.44	7.50	22.1	40.9	97.9
Road	22	19	82.0	.464	17.5	.388	28.8	.760	4.90	8.02	25.8	42.5	104.7	January	7	8	84.4	.457	18.7	.367	28.9	.758	4.60	8.73	25.5	43.4	105.8
vs. Div.	12	16	78.7	.455	15.5	.389	28.0	.759	4.14	7.61	23.0	39.8	98.9	February	9	3	79.3	.493	14.5	.477	27.2	.755	4.42	7.75	27.0	41.1	105.6
Starters	—	—	55.3	.465	11.1	.413	18.8	.763	2.59	5.12	17.1	26.5	70.3	March	8	6	77.2	.463	16.0	.362	22.5	.781	3.00	8.64	23.3	38.8	94.8
Bench	—	—	25.7	.439	5.5	.347	8.6	.726	1.56	2.65	7.2	15.0	30.7	April	3	8	82.4	.432	16.0	.420	28.6	.743	4.27	7.82	24.3	41.9	99.1
In wins	0	42	81.5	.429	17.2	.366	26.3	.737	3.98	6.71	21.8	41.1	95.6	0 Days Rest	10	9	83.6	.451	17.5	.411	27.1	.740	3.53	8.42	24.9	43.1	102.6
In losses	40	0	80.5	.486	15.9	.420	28.4	.767	4.33	8.88	26.8	41.9	106.7	1 Days Rest	25	24	80.3	.459	16.3	.390	27.3	.764	4.27	7.86	24.2	41.0	100.9
Pre All-Star	24	26	82.2	.457	17.3	.389	28.2	.749	4.40	7.58	24.1	42.2	103.1	2 Days Rest	2	3	78.8	.485	12.2	.393	28.2	.723	6.00	7.20	24.4	41.0	101.6
Post All-Star	16	16	79.1	.455	15.4	.396	26.0	.757	3.75	8.06	24.5	40.4	97.8	3+ Days Rest	3	6	81.0	.442	18.2	.354	27.3	.728	3.78	6.22	22.7	41.4	97.9

Minnesota Timberwolves

1999-2000 Per Game Averages

	W	L	FGA	FG%	3PA	3P%	FTA	FT%	Blk	Stl	Ast	Reb	Pts		W	L	FGA	FG%	3PA	3P%	FTA	FT%	Blk	Stl	Ast	Reb	Pts
Total	50	32	84.3	.467	8.7	.346	21.6	.780	5.41	7.59	26.9	42.5	98.5	Pre All-Star	27	20	84.1	.460	7.7	.320	22.3	.767	5.70	7.38	26.2	42.2	96.9
Home	26	15	84.8	.470	9.2	.345	20.9	.775	5.85	7.20	28.6	43.2	99.1	Post All-Star	23	12	84.5	.476	10.1	.374	20.6	.797	5.03	7.86	27.8	42.9	100.7
Road	24	17	83.7	.464	8.3	.348	22.2	.784	4.98	7.98	25.2	41.9	97.9	November	7	5	86.0	.461	8.8	.295	23.5	.745	6.50	8.17	26.1	44.3	99.4
vs. Playoff	23	21	83.6	.461	8.5	.335	21.3	.770	5.16	7.39	26.2	41.5	96.2	December	6	9	84.1	.444	7.2	.250	23.1	.772	5.00	7.00	25.9	42.4	94.3
vs. Non-Playoff	27	11	85.1	.474	9.0	.359	21.9	.790	5.71	7.82	27.7	43.8	101.2	January	12	3	82.6	.484	6.9	.404	20.3	.784	5.53	6.93	27.9	40.6	98.7
vs. East	18	12	83.7	.465	8.4	.351	22.9	.798	5.10	7.40	27.1	42.0	99.0	February	7	7	82.7	.472	9.9	.345	21.1	.790	5.79	6.86	26.9	41.3	98.2
vs. West	32	20	84.6	.468	8.9	.344	20.8	.768	5.60	7.69	26.8	42.7	98.2	March	12	4	83.8	.492	8.9	.385	20.9	.803	4.94	8.81	27.9	41.4	102.8
vs. Div.	18	6	84.0	.483	8.7	.370	20.7	.781	6.54	7.63	26.5	41.6	100.5	April	6	4	87.8	.436	11.7	.385	20.5	.780	4.80	7.80	26.2	47.0	97.1
Starters	—	—	57.7	.484	4.9	.356	13.8	.807	3.40	5.44	20.3	28.1	68.7	0 Days Rest	11	7	83.4	.468	8.5	.373	23.3	.810	5.11	7.11	25.2	42.4	100.2
Bench	—	—	26.6	.431	3.8	.334	7.8	.730	2.01	2.15	6.6	14.4	29.8	1 Days Rest	33	18	84.2	.471	8.5	.337	20.8	.776	5.35	7.76	27.3	42.9	98.3
In wins	50	0	83.3	.497	8.3	.383	22.5	.791	5.80	7.74	29.0	43.3	103.6	2 Days Rest	3	2	85.0	.485	9.2	.413	22.6	.735	5.20	8.20	28.2	38.8	102.8
In losses	0	32	85.8	.422	9.5	.297	20.2	.760	4.81	7.34	23.5	41.4	90.5	3+ Days Rest	3	5	86.4	.430	10.1	.309	21.6	.757	6.63	7.13	27.5	42.5	93.8

Opponents' 1999-2000 Per Game Averages

	W	L	FGA	FG%	3PA	3P%	FTA	FT%	Blk	Stl	Ast	Reb	Pts		W	L	FGA	FG%	3PA	3P%	FTA	FT%	Blk	Stl	Ast	Reb	Pts
Total	32	50	80.2	.445	13.0	.356	26.6	.752	4.20	7.21	21.2	40.9	96.0	November	5	7	81.4	.427	12.2	.370	26.2	.768	3.75	6.92	21.4	41.4	94.1
Home	15	26	80.0	.440	13.1	.349	25.6	.765	4.24	7.05	21.9	39.3	94.5	December	9	6	82.3	.458	13.0	.349	25.1	.724	4.67	7.47	20.9	42.5	98.1
Road	17	24	80.4	.449	12.9	.364	27.7	.740	4.15	7.37	20.5	42.5	97.5	January	3	12	81.3	.439	13.1	.383	25.3	.729	3.87	6.33	20.9	40.9	94.9
vs. Div.	6	18	80.0	.438	12.2	.342	26.3	.739	4.42	5.92	19.5	40.4	94.0	February	7	7	76.9	.445	12.4	.345	29.8	.765	5.21	7.57	20.9	40.1	95.5
Starters	—	—	56.4	.451	8.2	.358	19.1	.762	2.85	4.70	15.0	27.8	68.4	March	4	12	79.3	.453	12.6	.347	27.3	.766	3.50	7.25	20.7	39.5	97.0
Bench	—	—	23.8	.429	4.8	.355	7.5	.729	1.34	2.51	6.2	13.1	27.6	April	4	6	80.0	.441	15.3	.346	26.1	.766	4.20	7.90	23.0	41.4	95.9
In wins	0	50	80.0	.430	12.8	.342	26.5	.738	3.66	6.66	19.5	38.6	92.7	0 Days Rest	7	11	80.2	.467	12.3	.385	26.2	.715	4.44	7.06	22.6	40.6	98.3
In losses	32	0	80.5	.467	13.4	.379	26.9	.774	5.03	8.06	23.8	44.5	101.1	1 Days Rest	18	33	79.3	.441	12.9	.355	26.3	.758	3.98	7.33	20.7	40.0	94.4
Pre All-Star	20	27	81.6	.442	12.7	.365	26.4	.741	4.36	6.94	21.1	42.3	96.3	2 Days Rest	2	3	78.2	.414	11.8	.322	35.8	.799	4.80	6.60	19.2	44.8	97.2
Post All-Star	12	23	78.3	.449	13.5	.346	27.0	.768	3.97	7.57	21.3	39.1	95.7	3+ Days Rest	5	3	87.0	.440	16.3	.331	24.4	.759	4.63	7.13	22.1	45.4	100.4

New Jersey Nets

1999-2000 Per Game Averages

	W	L	FGA	FG%	3PA	3P%	FTA	FT%	Blk	Stl	Ast	Reb	Pts		W	L	FGA	FG%	3PA	3P%	FTA	FT%	Blk	Stl	Ast	Reb	Pts
Total	31	51	83.9	.433	16.8	.347	24.9	.784	4.79	8.78	20.6	40.9	98.0	Pre All-Star	19	30	83.4	.428	17.6	.358	24.7	.789	4.98	8.96	19.8	41.1	97.2
Home	22	19	84.9	.435	16.7	.334	27.2	.790	5.10	8.68	21.9	42.6	101.0	Post All-Star	12	21	84.7	.440	15.5	.328	25.2	.778	4.52	8.52	21.7	40.7	99.2
Road	9	32	82.9	.431	16.8	.360	22.6	.778	4.49	8.88	19.3	39.2	95.0	November	2	13	83.7	.398	14.0	.314	29.0	.791	4.33	8.87	16.8	42.7	94.0
vs. Playoff	15	31	83.2	.430	16.5	.336	25.1	.786	4.67	9.11	19.9	39.8	96.9	December	10	5	85.4	.432	18.8	.362	21.1	.778	6.07	8.80	21.5	42.3	97.1
vs. Non-Playoff	16	20	84.9	.436	17.0	.361	24.6	.782	4.94	8.36	21.5	42.4	99.4	January	5	9	82.5	.441	19.6	.378	23.8	.778	4.43	8.79	19.9	39.1	98.6
vs. East	21	33	83.6	.435	16.7	.350	25.1	.783	4.89	9.00	21.0	40.5	98.2	February	5	7	81.8	.434	17.7	.344	25.3	.782	5.92	9.08	20.6	39.9	96.8
vs. West	10	18	84.6	.429	16.9	.342	24.4	.788	4.61	8.36	19.8	41.6	97.6	March	9	7	85.4	.459	16.9	.351	25.3	.790	4.81	8.81	23.2	40.8	104.3
vs. Div.	9	16	83.5	.422	17.5	.341	25.3	.780	4.96	9.04	20.2	41.3	96.1	April	0	10	84.3	.431	12.4	.298	25.0	.784	2.70	8.20	21.7	39.9	95.9
Starters	—	—	59.0	.432	10.5	.348	17.9	.792	3.23	5.79	15.7	24.6	68.8	0 Days Rest	6	14	81.8	.448	17.2	.363	23.3	.785	3.95	8.15	19.8	38.3	97.9
Bench	—	—	24.9	.435	6.3	.346	7.0	.766	1.56	2.99	4.9	16.3	29.2	1 Days Rest	19	26	84.0	.431	16.9	.352	25.4	.787	5.13	8.58	21.2	41.6	98.4
In wins	31	0	84.8	.459	18.0	.370	25.0	.786	5.68	9.52	23.4	43.7	104.2	2 Days Rest	4	6	86.1	.415	14.5	.269	24.7	.769	5.50	10.10	20.6	42.2	94.3
In losses	0	51	83.4	.417	16.0	.332	24.8	.783	4.25	8.33	18.9	39.2	94.2	3+ Days Rest	2	5	86.7	.427	18.0	.365	26.4	.789	4.00	10.00	19.0	42.6	101.4

Opponents' 1999-2000 Per Game Averages

	W	L	FGA	FG%	3PA	3P%	FTA	FT%	Blk	Stl	Ast	Reb	Pts		W	L	FGA	FG%	3PA	3P%	FTA	FT%	Blk	Stl	Ast	Reb	Pts
Total	51	31	82.2	.464	12.4	.363	24.5	.747	5.72	6.93	22.8	46.2	99.0	November	13	2	81.4	.484	12.3	.319	27.3	.727	5.87	9.07	22.9	45.6	102.6
Home	19	22	81.3	.456	12.1	.347	26.1	.768	4.90	6.80	20.7	45.4	98.5	December	5	10	78.7	.436	11.1	.365	25.6	.727	4.80	5.93	17.3	45.9	91.3
Road	32	9	83.1	.471	12.6	.379	23.0	.723	6.54	7.05	24.8	47.0	99.6	January	9	5	80.6	.483	11.8	.436	22.6	.789	4.64	7.00	22.4	42.7	100.9
vs. Div.	16	9	80.7	.455	11.4	.333	25.8	.726	5.60	7.04	20.5	47.0	95.9	February	7	5	82.9	.441	11.8	.326	26.1	.764	6.25	7.08	23.2	47.7	96.9
Starters	—	—	57.1	.470	8.1	.365	17.4	.755	3.84	4.65	16.6	30.8	69.8	March	7	9	86.3	.450	14.3	.341	22.1	.780	6.63	6.06	25.8	47.9	104.1
Bench	—	—	25.1	.449	4.3	.360	7.1	.726	1.88	2.28	6.2	15.4	29.3	April	10	0	83.5	.496	12.6	.413	23.4	.688	6.30	6.30	25.9	48.4	104.1
In wins	0	31	83.6	.425	13.4	.337	23.0	.757	4.52	6.03	19.8	45.4	92.9	0 Days Rest	14	6	81.5	.490	11.9	.367	23.8	.746	5.45	7.15	24.6	45.0	102.0
In losses	51	0	81.4	.488	11.7	.381	25.5	.742	6.45	7.47	24.5	46.7	102.8	1 Days Rest	26	19	83.5	.448	12.6	.353	24.2	.756	5.96	6.56	22.2	46.8	97.6
Pre All-Star	30	19	80.7	.464	11.7	.367	25.5	.752	5.06	7.45	21.0	45.1	98.2	2 Days Rest	6	4	77.4	.466	13.8	.377	24.7	.725	5.10	7.90	21.9	46.5	95.3
Post All-Star	21	12	84.5	.464	13.4	.358	23.2	.738	6.70	6.15	25.3	47.8	100.2	3+ Days Rest	5	2	82.6	.486	9.9	.406	28.7	.731	5.86	7.29	22.0	45.0	105.3

New York Knicks

1999-2000 Per Game Averages

	W	L	FGA	FG%	3PA	3P%	FTA	FT%	Blk	Stl	Ast	Reb	Pts		W	L	FGA	FG%	3PA	3P%	FTA	FT%	Blk	Stl	Ast	Reb	Pts
Total	50	32	77.7	.455	11.4	.375	22.0	.781	4.26	6.28	19.4	40.5	92.1	Pre All-Star	29	18	78.5	.453	12.1	.395	22.5	.769	4.77	6.70	19.5	40.8	93.2
Home	33	8	76.6	.461	11.1	.383	23.4	.803	4.41	6.71	20.3	40.3	93.7	Post All-Star	21	14	76.7	.456	10.6	.343	21.4	.798	3.57	5.71	19.2	40.2	90.7
Road	17	24	78.8	.448	11.8	.366	20.6	.756	4.10	5.85	18.4	40.8	90.6	November	8	8	77.9	.443	11.6	.384	23.1	.786	4.44	6.06	20.7	41.6	91.6
vs. Playoff	25	19	78.9	.452	12.1	.391	21.1	.778	3.82	5.86	20.1	40.9	92.5	December	10	4	78.6	.438	11.8	.364	24.5	.735	6.21	6.36	17.3	42.1	91.1
vs. Non-Playoff	25	13	76.4	.457	10.6	.352	23.1	.784	4.76	6.76	18.5	40.1	91.7	January	8	4	80.1	.482	12.3	.439	19.3	.801	4.00	8.00	19.3	39.3	98.0
vs. East	32	22	77.1	.452	11.5	.378	22.4	.770	4.61	6.19	19.3	40.6	91.3	February	8	5	75.0	.446	11.2	.345	21.5	.778	4.00	6.15	20.4	38.4	87.5
vs. West	18	10	78.9	.459	11.3	.368	21.3	.804	3.57	6.46	19.4	40.3	93.7	March	11	6	76.9	.477	10.6	.378	20.4	.827	2.53	5.71	19.1	39.8	94.2
vs. Div.	14	10	76.3	.436	10.7	.346	25.0	.754	4.83	6.29	17.2	40.6	89.2	April	5	5	78.5	.434	11.4	.325	23.7	.759	4.80	5.60	19.4	42.1	89.9
Starters	—	—	57.7	.455	9.7	.384	16.3	.804	2.35	4.63	13.6	26.2	69.4	0 Days Rest	7	13	77.9	.439	11.1	.333	20.2	.772	3.95	6.05	18.8	40.4	87.7
Bench	—	—	20.0	.452	1.7	.321	5.7	.714	1.90	1.65	5.7	14.3	22.7	1 Days Rest	30	12	78.6	.455	11.6	.381	22.4	.789	4.33	6.29	19.9	40.8	93.6
In wins	50	0	76.9	.476	11.8	.405	22.6	.805	4.60	6.76	21.0	41.5	96.2	2 Days Rest	9	5	76.5	.473	11.4	.394	21.9	.772	4.14	6.43	19.3	39.6	93.9
In losses	0	32	79.0	.422	10.8	.322	21.1	.742	3.72	5.56	16.8	39.0	85.8	3+ Days Rest	4	2	74.3	.455	11.5	.420	25.5	.778	5.00	6.67	17.5	41.0	92.3

Opponents' 1999-2000 Per Game Averages

	W	L	FGA	FG%	3PA	3P%	FTA	FT%	Blk	Stl	Ast	Reb	Pts		W	L	FGA	FG%	3PA	3P%	FTA	FT%	Blk	Stl	Ast	Reb	Pts
Total	32	50	78.0	.424	14.6	.338	26.3	.747	4.32	7.35	19.6	41.1	90.7	November	8	8	77.1	.406	14.3	.342	31.0	.728	4.94	6.50	19.5	41.2	89.9
Home	8	33	77.9	.416	14.4	.319	26.1	.731	2.88	7.22	18.6	40.6	88.5	December	4	10	80.2	.400	15.2	.319	27.7	.740	4.07	7.00	17.2	45.0	89.5
Road	24	17	78.1	.432	14.8	.356	26.4	.763	5.76	7.49	20.6	41.5	92.9	January	4	8	79.5	.423	15.5	.366	29.6	.738	3.83	8.25	17.8	43.4	94.8
vs. Div.	10	14	79.7	.423	13.9	.338	24.5	.727	4.67	8.54	18.7	42.9	89.9	February	5	8	77.2	.433	14.7	.361	20.3	.784	3.31	6.77	21.2	40.6	88.0
Starters	—	—	55.7	.428	9.3	.383	18.2	.762	2.93	5.07	14.6	28.1	64.7	March	6	11	75.1	.446	13.0	.290	25.1	.738	4.24	7.59	20.1	36.9	89.2
Bench	—	—	22.3	.412	4.8	.367	8.1	.715	1.39	2.28	5.0	13.0	26.0	April	5	5	80.8	.439	15.8	.361	22.3	.794	5.70	8.50	22.5	40.2	94.4
In wins	0	50	79.1	.408	14.9	.316	25.6	.725	3.62	7.34	18.3	39.9	87.7	0 Days Rest	13	7	76.0	.430	14.8	.338	27.0	.750	4.70	8.20	20.2	41.2	90.5
In losses	32	0	76.4	.450	14.2	.373	27.3	.780	5.41	7.38	21.7	42.9	95.3	1 Days Rest	12	30	78.5	.430	14.5	.347	25.2	.742	4.33	6.38	19.8	40.5	91.2
Pre All-Star	18	29	78.9	.413	15.1	.350	28.3	.737	4.23	7.15	18.7	42.8	91.4	2 Days Rest	5	9	77.4	.406	14.9	.303	28.9	.743	3.79	8.29	18.4	42.4	88.9
Post All-Star	14	21	76.9	.438	13.9	.319	23.5	.764	4.43	7.63	20.9	38.7	89.7	3+ Days Rest	2	4	83.0	.402	14.2	.353	25.2	.788	4.17	9.17	19.5	41.8	91.5

Orlando Magic

1999-2000 Per Game Averages

	W	L	FGA	FG%	3PA	3P%	FTA	FT%	Blk	Stl	Ast	Reb	Pts		W	L	FGA	FG%	3PA	3P%	FTA	FT%	Blk	Stl	Ast	Reb	Pts
Total	41	41	85.5	.452	10.6	.338	26.1	.735	5.70	9.06	20.8	44.9	100.1	Pre All-Star	24	26	86.5	.452	9.8	.324	27.6	.741	5.76	9.22	21.1	45.5	101.8
Home	26	15	86.3	.464	11.0	.351	26.8	.732	5.39	9.27	21.7	45.5	103.6	Post All-Star	17	15	84.1	.451	11.8	.356	23.9	.724	5.59	8.81	20.4	44.1	97.3
Road	15	26	84.7	.439	10.2	.324	25.4	.737	6.00	8.85	20.0	44.4	96.5	November	7	8	88.9	.447	10.8	.284	25.9	.728	5.40	9.27	21.7	47.7	101.4
vs. Playoff	15	32	85.3	.443	11.3	.317	25.7	.728	5.13	8.85	19.6	44.2	97.9	December	8	6	87.2	.448	10.7	.327	28.9	.745	5.93	9.57	20.6	45.4	103.1
vs. Non-Playoff	26	9	85.8	.464	9.7	.371	26.6	.744	6.46	9.34	22.5	45.9	102.9	January	5	12	84.6	.448	8.4	.364	27.2	.767	6.12	8.65	19.8	43.9	99.7
vs. East	27	27	84.4	.445	10.5	.332	26.8	.734	5.87	8.67	20.6	45.7	98.2	February	6	5	85.6	.481	12.2	.358	23.4	.681	4.82	8.18	23.7	42.5	102.6
vs. West	14	14	87.8	.465	10.9	.349	24.9	.737	5.36	9.82	21.3	43.5	103.8	March	11	5	82.8	.464	10.1	.398	24.7	.729	6.00	9.13	20.2	45.3	98.9
vs. Div.	12	13	84.5	.447	10.8	.326	25.6	.727	6.48	8.28	20.6	46.1	97.7	April	4	5	83.7	.417	13.3	.292	26.0	.735	5.56	9.67	19.3	43.9	92.8
Starters	—	—	45.5	.447	5.5	.313	12.8	.743	3.70	5.83	12.5	24.8	51.9	0 Days Rest	11	11	84.5	.439	9.4	.343	26.0	.717	5.77	8.64	20.1	44.5	96.1
Bench	—	—	40.0	.457	5.1	.364	13.3	.727	2.00	3.23	8.3	20.1	48.2	1 Days Rest	22	20	86.5	.456	10.8	.341	25.3	.749	6.12	9.29	21.4	45.4	101.5
In wins	41	0	85.4	.473	9.8	.368	28.1	.731	6.71	9.76	23.0	45.9	104.9	2 Days Rest	3	5	82.5	.459	10.6	.259	30.8	.724	5.50	8.63	19.0	44.5	100.8
In losses	0	41	85.7	.431	11.5	.313	24.1	.739	4.68	8.37	18.7	44.0	95.3	3+ Days Rest	5	5	86.0	.457	12.4	.371	26.2	.729	3.90	9.40	21.6	44.4	102.3

Opponents' 1999-2000 Per Game Averages

	W	L	FGA	FG%	3PA	3P%	FTA	FT%	Blk	Stl	Ast	Reb	Pts		W	L	FGA	FG%	3PA	3P%	FTA	FT%	Blk	Stl	Ast	Reb	Pts
Total	41	41	84.4	.445	15.6	.338	25.7	.745	5.79	8.83	24.3	43.5	99.4	November	8	7	85.5	.460	16.7	.375	24.8	.718	5.80	9.20	24.9	43.6	102.7
Home	15	26	83.4	.443	16.0	.315	24.9	.726	5.49	7.59	23.2	41.7	96.9	December	6	8	88.1	.436	14.5	.345	25.1	.773	6.86	8.36	26.8	45.6	101.3
Road	26	15	85.4	.446	15.2	.362	26.5	.762	6.10	10.07	25.4	45.3	101.9	January	12	5	84.9	.450	16.0	.338	27.1	.761	5.82	9.18	24.4	43.6	102.5
vs. Div.	13	12	84.4	.437	15.4	.345	22.6	.740	5.48	8.08	23.9	41.7	95.7	February	5	6	83.5	.453	15.4	.361	25.6	.762	5.55	7.45	23.8	44.4	100.7
Starters	—	—	55.9	.437	9.5	.333	17.2	.744	3.96	5.94	16.6	28.8	64.7	March	5	11	81.8	.430	15.2	.276	26.4	.733	5.44	9.31	22.1	40.5	93.8
Bench	—	—	28.5	.460	6.1	.344	8.5	.747	1.83	2.89	7.7	14.7	34.7	April	5	4	81.4	.437	15.4	.338	23.9	.712	5.00	9.11	23.8	44.0	93.3
In wins	0	41	83.4	.419	15.8	.287	25.3	.735	5.41	7.32	22.4	43.0	92.9	0 Days Rest	11	11	85.4	.443	15.5	.315	25.8	.761	6.64	9.27	25.8	46.4	100.2
In losses	41	0	85.4	.470	15.3	.390	26.0	.754	6.17	10.34	26.1	44.0	105.9	1 Days Rest	20	22	83.9	.442	14.8	.343	26.0	.728	5.57	8.88	23.5	42.4	98.2
Pre All-Star	26	24	85.6	.448	15.6	.348	25.8	.750	6.02	8.68	25.0	44.1	101.5	2 Days Rest	5	3	84.4	.439	18.8	.340	25.0	.820	4.38	7.50	22.9	41.0	100.9
Post All-Star	15	17	82.5	.439	15.5	.321	25.4	.736	5.44	9.06	23.1	42.6	96.1	3+ Days Rest	5	5	84.1	.463	16.6	.361	24.3	.720	6.00	8.70	25.6	44.0	101.3

Philadelphia 76ers

1999-2000 Per Game Averages

	W	L	FGA	FG%	3PA	3P%	FTA	FT%	Blk	Stl	Ast	Reb	Pts		W	L	FGA	FG%	3PA	3P%	FTA	FT%	Blk	Stl	Ast	Reb	Pts
Total	49	33	82.6	.442	7.8	.323	27.1	.708	4.71	9.65	22.2	44.1	94.8	Pre All-Star	27	22	84.2	.432	7.4	.304	27.4	.714	4.63	9.55	21.2	45.0	94.5
Home	29	12	83.3	.449	8.3	.334	27.6	.718	4.63	10.17	23.1	45.4	97.4	Post All-Star	22	11	80.4	.457	8.4	.349	26.8	.700	4.82	9.79	23.6	42.7	95.2
Road	20	21	82.0	.434	7.4	.311	26.7	.699	4.78	9.12	21.2	42.8	92.2	November	8	8	82.9	.420	7.1	.398	28.3	.684	5.94	9.94	19.3	44.6	91.8
vs. Playoff	18	24	84.6	.432	8.6	.334	25.4	.697	4.29	9.29	21.7	43.3	93.7	December	9	7	83.7	.422	7.5	.233	24.8	.712	3.50	9.25	21.3	43.9	90.0
vs. Non-Playoff	31	9	80.6	.452	7.0	.310	29.0	.719	5.15	10.03	22.7	44.9	95.9	January	7	5	84.8	.447	7.5	.322	31.9	.728	3.58	9.75	22.0	45.9	101.5
vs. East	36	18	81.6	.443	7.8	.333	28.2	.706	4.67	9.30	21.4	44.6	94.9	February	7	5	82.8	.466	7.3	.330	24.6	.722	6.00	9.83	24.8	47.0	97.3
vs. West	13	15	84.6	.439	7.9	.305	25.1	.714	4.79	10.32	22.7	44.4	94.7	March	11	5	82.4	.444	10.1	.333	25.6	.712	4.94	9.19	22.8	41.4	94.8
vs. Div.	13	11	79.1	.421	8.6	.340	29.5	.707	5.21	9.00	20.0	43.5	90.4	April	7	3	78.0	.472	7.0	.329	28.9	.696	4.10	10.20	24.2	42.2	96.0
Starters	—	—	58.2	.446	5.1	.325	19.8	.703	3.37	6.79	16.0	30.3	67.5	0 Days Rest	11	9	82.5	.441	7.0	.307	24.6	.701	4.75	8.40	21.6	41.6	92.1
Bench	—	—	24.4	.431	2.8	.322	7.4	.723	1.34	2.85	6.2	13.7	27.3	1 Days Rest	27	18	81.6	.442	8.0	.321	27.6	.716	4.73	9.91	22.4	44.4	94.4
In wins	49	0	81.9	.467	7.8	.345	28.0	.726	4.45	10.43	24.0	44.9	99.5	2 Days Rest	7	2	83.9	.453	8.2	.284	29.4	.694	4.78	9.89	23.2	50.7	98.8
In losses	0	33	83.7	.406	8.0	.293	25.8	.680	5.09	8.48	19.5	42.9	87.8	3+ Days Rest	4	4	87.5	.431	8.9	.408	28.8	.700	4.38	11.00	21.1	41.5	99.3

Opponents' 1999-2000 Per Game Averages

	W	L	FGA	FG%	3PA	3P%	FTA	FT%	Blk	Stl	Ast	Reb	Pts		W	L	FGA	FG%	3PA	3P%	FTA	FT%	Blk	Stl	Ast	Reb	Pts
Total	33	49	80.4	.435	14.3	.356	24.4	.755	6.48	7.68	22.3	43.5	93.4	November	8	8	77.1	.414	12.5	.330	30.1	.730	8.19	7.31	20.1	45.1	89.9
Home	12	29	80.4	.431	14.4	.341	24.4	.743	5.20	7.76	22.1	42.9	92.4	December	7	9	79.8	.437	15.3	.302	25.6	.741	5.69	8.13	21.1	44.8	93.3
Road	21	20	80.5	.438	14.2	.370	24.4	.766	7.76	7.61	22.5	44.1	94.5	January	5	7	81.8	.440	16.6	.347	27.1	.791	7.25	6.33	23.8	41.3	99.2
vs. Div.	11	13	81.6	.417	13.9	.311	24.0	.763	6.00	8.25	20.2	45.4	90.6	February	5	7	81.8	.428	15.8	.407	20.8	.775	6.25	8.25	22.8	47.0	92.5
Starters	—	—	55.8	.440	9.2	.352	17.3	.760	4.22	5.20	16.3	28.3	65.5	March	5	11	81.8	.444	11.9	.403	21.9	.766	6.44	8.00	23.3	44.6	94.2
Bench	—	—	24.6	.423	5.1	.362	7.1	.743	2.26	2.49	6.0	15.2	28.0	April	3	7	81.5	.449	14.8	.365	18.6	.737	4.40	8.00	23.6	43.1	92.3
In wins	0	49	80.7	.421	14.8	.341	23.9	.753	5.45	7.92	21.1	41.8	91.0	0 Days Rest	9	11	78.0	.454	14.0	.351	25.5	.772	7.60	7.80	22.9	43.5	95.5
In losses	33	0	80.1	.455	13.5	.380	25.1	.757	8.00	7.33	24.1	46.0	97.1	1 Days Rest	18	27	81.3	.431	14.3	.362	23.1	.747	6.33	8.22	22.3	42.9	92.5
Pre All-Star	22	27	79.7	.433	15.5	.343	27.1	.752	7.16	7.59	21.9	43.7	94.6	2 Days Rest	2	7	81.2	.391	17.7	.296	26.2	.725	4.56	7.22	18.3	42.9	87.8
Post All-Star	11	22	81.5	.438	12.5	.380	20.4	.760	5.45	7.82	22.8	43.2	91.6	3+ Days Rest	4	4	80.8	.458	11.3	.433	27.1	.783	6.63	4.88	25.1	47.4	100.1

309

Phoenix Suns

1999-2000 Per Game Averages

	W	L	FGA	FG%	3PA	3P%	FTA	FT%	Blk	Stl	Ast	Reb	Pts
Total	53	29	82.6	.457	15.2	.368	23.6	.759	5.28	9.07	25.6	43.7	98.9
Home	32	9	82.2	.471	14.8	.365	23.8	.768	5.93	9.12	27.3	43.7	101.1
Road	21	20	82.9	.443	15.6	.370	23.3	.749	4.63	9.02	23.9	43.7	96.7
vs. Playoff	22	22	81.5	.441	15.7	.358	22.5	.756	4.84	8.45	24.1	42.5	94.6
vs. Non-Playoff	31	7	83.8	.474	14.6	.379	24.8	.762	5.79	9.79	27.3	45.0	103.9
vs. East	23	7	80.4	.464	14.8	.366	24.6	.769	6.33	9.60	25.6	42.5	99.0
vs. West	30	22	83.8	.453	15.4	.369	23.0	.752	4.67	8.77	25.6	44.3	98.9
vs. Div.	15	9	83.4	.461	15.1	.388	22.5	.708	4.38	8.08	26.0	45.9	98.7
Starters	—	—	55.7	.456	8.6	.345	15.6	.795	3.18	5.90	19.1	29.0	66.1
Bench	—	—	26.9	.459	6.6	.398	8.0	.688	2.10	3.17	6.5	14.7	32.8
In wins	53	0	82.5	.477	14.0	.385	24.8	.771	5.96	10.09	27.7	45.2	103.2
In losses	0	29	82.7	.421	17.4	.341	21.4	.732	4.03	7.21	24.8	40.9	91.1
Pre All-Star	29	19	83.4	.455	15.4	.366	23.0	.752	5.69	8.73	25.4	43.7	98.8
Post All-Star	24	10	81.5	.460	14.9	.370	24.4	.767	4.71	9.56	25.9	43.6	99.1
November	10	4	83.0	.454	12.2	.351	23.9	.737	6.79	9.50	25.1	46.3	97.2
December	8	7	86.1	.464	18.7	.389	23.5	.751	5.67	9.07	25.5	42.3	104.9
January	7	7	81.9	.428	16.9	.360	22.8	.746	4.93	6.86	24.8	41.9	93.2
February	10	3	80.5	.467	11.6	.391	21.8	.784	4.92	10.77	26.2	44.2	96.8
March	12	4	82.9	.466	15.8	.365	25.3	.790	4.75	9.81	26.9	43.8	102.9
April	6	4	79.7	.462	15.6	.340	24.0	.733	4.40	8.20	24.5	43.4	96.5
0 Days Rest	12	8	83.0	.442	17.4	.378	24.0	.798	5.25	8.85	24.7	43.0	99.1
1 Days Rest	27	15	81.1	.465	14.4	.362	24.4	.744	5.38	9.29	25.6	43.3	98.8
2 Days Rest	10	5	83.9	.447	14.5	.350	22.4	.729	5.13	9.07	24.9	43.1	96.3
3+ Days Rest	4	1	89.2	.478	15.4	.416	18.8	.819	5.00	8.20	31.0	50.8	107.0

Opponents' 1999-2000 Per Game Averages

	W	L	FGA	FG%	3PA	3P%	FTA	FT%	Blk	Stl	Ast	Reb	Pts
Total	29	53	81.3	.424	14.0	.352	26.9	.739	5.21	8.94	20.7	43.1	93.7
Home	9	32	81.3	.415	13.5	.350	26.9	.736	4.76	9.29	19.7	42.4	92.0
Road	20	21	81.2	.433	14.5	.354	26.9	.743	5.66	8.59	21.8	43.9	95.4
vs. Div.	9	15	81.6	.416	15.5	.330	28.0	.696	5.00	8.96	19.9	43.0	92.5
Starters	—	—	56.7	.428	9.2	.353	18.2	.744	3.65	6.07	14.9	28.9	65.4
Bench	—	—	24.5	.414	4.8	.349	8.7	.728	1.56	2.87	5.8	14.3	28.3
In wins	0	53	82.5	.404	14.3	.333	25.9	.740	4.98	9.02	19.4	42.2	90.5
In losses	29	0	79.0	.463	13.3	.389	28.7	.738	5.62	8.79	23.2	44.8	99.4
Pre All-Star	19	29	81.6	.430	13.9	.347	27.1	.723	5.42	9.15	21.3	43.0	94.6
Post All-Star	10	24	80.8	.415	14.1	.358	26.6	.762	4.91	8.65	19.9	43.3	92.5
November	4	10	80.6	.409	12.1	.282	28.1	.711	5.64	9.36	19.7	42.7	89.3
December	7	8	83.7	.466	15.3	.376	26.1	.689	5.87	9.07	23.9	43.7	101.7
January	7	7	80.1	.432	13.6	.366	29.6	.746	5.43	9.21	21.5	44.0	96.2
February	3	10	80.9	.389	14.4	.332	23.3	.779	4.69	8.38	17.9	41.5	85.8
March	4	12	79.6	.426	14.2	.344	26.3	.772	4.69	8.56	19.6	42.4	93.1
April	4	6	83.5	.411	14.2	.415	28.1	.747	4.80	9.10	21.8	44.8	95.5
0 Days Rest	8	12	82.5	.424	13.2	.319	29.4	.744	5.25	9.15	20.7	45.3	96.3
1 Days Rest	15	27	80.8	.423	13.4	.361	26.0	.739	4.81	9.12	20.5	42.2	92.4
2 Days Rest	5	10	80.1	.434	14.7	.350	25.2	.720	5.33	8.33	21.5	43.4	92.9
3+ Days Rest	1	4	84.2	.404	20.0	.390	27.2	.772	8.00	8.40	20.2	41.6	96.8

Portland Trail Blazers

1999-2000 Per Game Averages

	W	L	FGA	FG%	3PA	3P%	FTA	FT%	Blk	Stl	Ast	Reb	Pts
Total	59	23	78.4	.470	13.8	.361	24.7	.760	4.83	7.72	23.5	43.0	97.5
Home	30	11	77.5	.480	13.6	.339	24.7	.764	4.20	7.41	24.1	43.0	97.9
Road	29	12	79.3	.460	13.9	.382	24.8	.756	5.46	8.02	22.8	43.0	97.0
vs. Playoff	30	14	77.5	.467	13.4	.368	25.0	.756	3.98	7.45	22.9	42.6	96.3
vs. Non-Playoff	29	9	79.4	.473	14.2	.353	24.5	.765	5.82	8.03	24.1	43.4	98.8
vs. East	21	9	78.5	.477	14.2	.362	25.7	.764	5.70	7.70	23.9	43.1	99.0
vs. West	38	14	78.4	.466	13.5	.360	24.2	.758	4.37	7.73	23.2	42.9	96.2
vs. Div.	21	3	79.5	.470	13.5	.375	25.2	.775	4.33	8.58	24.0	44.7	99.3
Starters	—	—	54.0	.475	9.8	.355	15.9	.775	3.30	5.01	16.0	27.6	67.1
Bench	—	—	24.4	.459	4.0	.375	8.9	.733	1.52	2.71	7.5	15.4	30.4
In wins	59	0	77.3	.486	13.0	.374	25.4	.759	4.93	8.08	24.5	43.3	99.3
In losses	0	23	81.3	.430	15.7	.333	23.0	.762	4.57	6.78	20.9	42.3	92.6
Pre All-Star	38	11	78.3	.473	13.2	.357	24.7	.746	5.24	7.57	24.0	43.4	97.1
Post All-Star	21	12	78.5	.466	14.6	.366	24.8	.780	4.21	7.94	22.7	42.3	97.9
November	13	3	80.3	.467	12.9	.325	24.8	.758	5.81	7.50	24.8	44.3	97.9
December	9	4	79.2	.458	15.4	.365	23.2	.721	5.85	7.38	24.0	44.0	94.8
January	11	3	75.9	.494	11.3	.373	24.7	.731	4.14	8.64	23.9	42.3	97.3
February	12	2	78.9	.457	14.2	.402	27.4	.799	4.50	8.64	22.0	43.9	99.0
March	7	4	77.3	.474	13.9	.371	24.6	.762	4.43	6.79	22.3	41.7	97.1
April	7	4	78.9	.470	15.5	.327	23.5	.787	4.00	7.27	23.7	41.3	97.7
0 Days Rest	16	6	79.6	.472	14.1	.371	26.0	.781	5.09	7.36	23.2	43.6	100.7
1 Days Rest	29	10	76.2	.472	13.2	.366	26.0	.750	4.41	7.92	23.2	41.7	96.2
2 Days Rest	9	6	80.7	.457	14.7	.335	21.7	.791	5.13	6.60	23.1	44.9	96.0
3+ Days Rest	1	2	82.8	.479	14.0	.357	19.5	.650	5.83	10.50	27.0	44.7	97.0

Opponents' 1999-2000 Per Game Averages

	W	L	FGA	FG%	3PA	3P%	FTA	FT%	Blk	Stl	Ast	Reb	Pts
Total	23	59	80.0	.431	14.6	.330	24.2	.716	4.27	7.95	20.8	39.0	91.0
Home	11	30	79.4	.437	14.6	.339	22.9	.709	3.51	8.10	20.9	36.9	90.5
Road	12	29	80.5	.425	14.5	.320	25.5	.723	5.02	7.80	20.7	41.1	91.6
vs. Div.	3	21	83.1	.423	16.8	.313	23.0	.675	4.00	8.67	20.9	39.6	93.3
Starters	—	—	56.1	.434	10.0	.340	16.8	.717	2.77	5.05	15.4	26.3	64.1
Bench	—	—	23.9	.423	4.6	.307	7.5	.715	1.50	2.90	5.4	12.7	26.9
In wins	0	59	80.8	.416	14.2	.305	23.3	.697	3.69	8.14	20.1	38.6	87.7
In losses	23	0	77.9	.471	15.6	.388	26.5	.761	5.74	7.48	22.6	40.1	99.6
Pre All-Star	11	38	81.2	.418	14.1	.325	23.8	.707	4.31	7.96	20.4	39.8	89.3
Post All-Star	12	21	78.2	.450	15.3	.337	24.8	.729	4.21	7.94	21.4	37.8	93.6
November	3	13	82.1	.396	12.9	.316	26.6	.721	4.88	7.75	18.9	43.0	88.3
December	4	9	82.2	.430	16.0	.332	21.3	.690	3.77	7.92	22.8	40.2	90.6
January	3	11	78.5	.421	12.9	.309	24.0	.685	4.50	7.71	20.2	37.0	86.6
February	2	12	82.1	.433	15.8	.321	22.9	.745	3.79	9.14	20.3	39.6	93.3
March	7	7	78.4	.458	15.9	.345	26.1	.756	3.50	8.07	21.9	36.9	97.1
April	4	7	75.4	.461	14.2	.359	23.6	.688	5.27	6.91	21.2	36.4	90.8
0 Days Rest	6	16	83.0	.425	14.9	.336	24.5	.720	4.82	7.77	20.2	41.9	93.1
1 Days Rest	10	29	78.7	.433	14.2	.308	24.6	.716	3.97	7.92	20.8	37.6	90.0
2 Days Rest	6	9	79.4	.445	14.4	.375	23.1	.746	4.87	7.87	21.9	36.5	93.3
3+ Days Rest	1	5	78.8	.408	16.7	.330	23.2	.626	2.67	9.00	20.3	43.8	84.3

Sacramento Kings

1999-2000 Per Game Averages

	W	L	FGA	FG%	3PA	3P%	FTA	FT%	Blk	Stl	Ast	Reb	Pts
Total	44	38	88.9	.450	20.2	.322	24.6	.754	4.65	9.60	23.8	45.0	105.0
Home	30	11	89.3	.458	21.0	.331	24.1	.749	5.00	9.00	24.1	46.7	106.8
Road	14	27	88.4	.441	19.4	.313	25.0	.759	4.29	10.20	23.5	43.3	103.1
vs. Playoff	17	27	88.0	.440	20.0	.334	24.9	.751	4.30	8.93	22.6	43.6	102.0
vs. Non-Playoff	27	11	89.9	.460	20.4	.309	24.3	.758	5.05	10.37	25.3	46.6	107.4
vs. East	19	11	87.7	.459	21.7	.324	23.5	.757	4.83	9.20	24.5	45.2	105.3
vs. West	25	27	89.6	.444	19.3	.321	25.2	.753	4.54	9.83	23.4	44.9	104.8
vs. Div.	9	15	88.3	.447	19.3	.313	26.3	.749	4.58	9.50	23.6	44.0	104.7
Starters	—	—	60.7	.448	13.5	.304	15.5	.725	3.37	6.04	17.5	29.6	69.7
Bench	—	—	28.2	.453	6.7	.359	9.1	.804	1.28	3.56	6.4	15.4	35.3
In wins	44	0	87.5	.474	20.8	.338	26.1	.769	5.00	10.14	25.2	45.7	110.1
In losses	0	38	90.4	.422	19.6	.303	22.9	.735	4.24	8.97	22.3	44.2	99.0

	W	L	FGA	FG%	3PA	3P%	FTA	FT%	Blk	Stl	Ast	Reb	Pts
Pre All-Star	30	18	89.4	.446	21.5	.317	25.3	.755	4.94	9.85	24.1	45.9	105.5
Post All-Star	14	20	88.2	.455	18.4	.332	23.6	.753	4.24	9.24	23.4	43.7	104.2
November	10	2	91.7	.448	23.6	.304	23.7	.739	5.25	9.33	25.0	48.2	106.8
December	7	8	88.7	.439	17.5	.304	28.5	.745	4.33	9.13	23.5	45.7	104.4
January	10	6	88.8	.449	21.7	.331	24.1	.766	4.85	10.00	23.8	44.8	105.4
February	5	8	90.3	.448	23.4	.329	22.2	.792	4.85	10.00	23.8	44.8	106.2
March	9	6	86.4	.461	17.7	.317	23.7	.753	4.13	9.00	23.5	42.6	103.2
April	8	7	87.9	.452	17.6	.356	25.1	.732	4.09	9.45	23.1	44.6	104.1
0 Days Rest	8	10	88.6	.437	20.2	.321	25.6	.783	4.94	9.39	23.4	44.2	104.0
1 Days Rest	26	24	89.4	.451	20.2	.315	24.2	.745	4.56	9.56	23.4	45.8	105.0
2 Days Rest	6	3	86.2	.485	18.6	.347	21.1	.747	4.44	9.78	26.3	41.8	105.8
3+ Days Rest	4	1	89.0	.422	23.4	.350	30.8	.753	4.80	10.40	24.4	45.4	106.6

Opponents' 1999-2000 Per Game Averages

	W	L	FGA	FG%	3PA	3P%	FTA	FT%	Blk	Stl	Ast	Reb	Pts
Total	38	44	88.3	.452	13.7	.353	23.3	.751	4.93	9.18	23.4	47.6	102.0
Home	11	30	88.4	.433	12.9	.343	23.8	.735	4.76	9.00	21.5	46.3	97.9
Road	27	14	88.1	.470	14.5	.352	23.8	.766	5.10	9.37	26.1	48.9	106.2
vs. Div.	15	9	89.5	.448	14.3	.334	23.9	.749	4.71	9.42	24.3	49.4	102.9
Starters	—	—	62.6	.458	9.1	.369	16.3	.754	3.37	6.43	17.6	32.1	73.1
Bench	—	—	25.7	.435	4.6	.320	7.0	.743	1.56	2.76	6.2	15.5	29.0
In wins	0	44	87.9	.431	14.2	.323	22.8	.738	4.27	8.73	20.8	45.8	97.3
In losses	38	0	88.8	.475	13.1	.390	23.8	.765	5.68	9.71	27.2	49.7	107.6
Pre All-Star	18	30	89.2	.449	14.0	.341	23.3	.756	4.48	9.27	23.4	48.4	102.5
Post All-Star	20	14	87.0	.455	13.3	.369	23.3	.743	5.56	9.06	24.3	46.4	101.4

	W	L	FGA	FG%	3PA	3P%	FTA	FT%	Blk	Stl	Ast	Reb	Pts
November	2	10	92.8	.436	13.3	.346	18.4	.747	3.92	8.92	22.4	50.4	99.2
December	8	7	88.5	.458	14.7	.348	25.7	.751	4.93	8.33	23.7	47.6	105.5
January	6	10	87.9	.457	13.2	.355	24.0	.758	4.75	10.38	24.4	47.3	103.1
February	8	5	86.8	.452	14.8	.391	24.2	.771	5.23	9.69	25.1	47.5	102.9
March	6	9	86.9	.443	15.0	.302	22.7	.726	4.40	8.40	22.1	48.1	98.1
April	8	3	87.2	.465	10.5	.400	24.1	.751	6.64	9.36	25.3	44.5	103.4
0 Days Rest	10	8	89.5	.455	14.2	.329	22.6	.764	5.56	9.72	24.7	48.9	103.3
1 Days Rest	24	26	88.0	.450	13.7	.361	24.1	.748	4.88	9.04	23.0	47.2	102.1
2 Days Rest	3	6	87.3	.455	13.4	.314	20.1	.718	4.56	9.22	24.2	45.9	98.2
3+ Days Rest	1	4	88.6	.447	12.4	.435	23.8	.790	3.80	8.60	27.8	49.6	103.4

San Antonio Spurs

1999-2000 Per Game Averages

	W	L	FGA	FG%	3PA	3P%	FTA	FT%	Blk	Stl	Ast	Reb	Pts
Total	53	29	78.0	.462	10.8	.374	27.0	.746	6.72	7.49	22.2	43.8	96.2
Home	31	10	77.9	.469	10.9	.402	27.7	.752	7.54	7.39	22.4	44.9	98.3
Road	22	19	78.0	.454	10.7	.346	26.3	.740	5.90	7.59	22.0	42.8	94.0
vs. Playoff	21	23	77.6	.440	10.3	.347	26.6	.740	6.52	7.64	20.6	43.7	91.5
vs. Non-Playoff	32	6	78.4	.487	11.3	.403	27.4	.753	6.95	7.32	24.0	44.0	101.5
vs. East	20	10	76.6	.465	11.1	.377	26.3	.747	7.53	7.07	22.0	43.0	95.1
vs. West	33	19	78.7	.460	10.5	.372	27.4	.746	6.25	7.73	22.3	44.3	96.8
vs. Div.	16	8	76.8	.468	10.5	.427	28.4	.778	6.78	8.00	22.6	42.8	96.3
Starters	—	—	52.0	.475	4.0	.356	19.1	.754	5.07	4.57	14.8	29.7	65.2
Bench	—	—	26.0	.436	6.7	.385	7.9	.726	1.65	2.91	7.4	14.1	31.0
In wins	53	0	79.6	.477	10.5	.408	26.7	.752	7.21	7.62	23.1	46.1	100.3
In losses	0	29	74.9	.433	11.2	.317	27.5	.736	5.83	7.24	20.5	39.6	88.6

	W	L	FGA	FG%	3PA	3P%	FTA	FT%	Blk	Stl	Ast	Reb	Pts
Pre All-Star	32	17	78.7	.456	11.1	.363	27.1	.741	6.92	7.35	21.9	45.2	96.0
Post All-Star	21	12	76.8	.470	10.3	.391	26.8	.753	6.42	7.70	22.7	41.7	96.5
November	13	3	80.6	.471	11.8	.466	23.7	.710	8.50	6.00	23.8	46.6	98.2
December	8	7	77.1	.435	12.0	.289	29.5	.756	6.33	7.27	20.2	44.1	92.8
January	7	6	77.3	.463	9.6	.336	28.4	.748	6.23	8.62	21.5	43.3	96.0
February	9	4	78.5	.457	10.0	.408	26.6	.746	6.23	9.08	22.2	40.8	95.8
March	10	5	77.5	.475	10.9	.348	25.7	.782	6.27	6.40	22.0	44.3	97.5
April	6	4	75.8	.472	9.4	.404	29.3	.730	6.40	8.30	23.6	40.1	96.8
0 Days Rest	12	6	77.4	.464	10.3	.360	26.7	.777	6.78	8.00	22.6	42.8	96.3
1 Days Rest	26	17	78.3	.458	11.4	.376	27.5	.729	6.56	7.49	22.0	43.9	96.8
2 Days Rest	14	4	77.8	.478	9.7	.379	26.4	.758	6.56	7.22	21.9	44.9	98.1
3+ Days Rest	1	2	77.3	.405	10.7	.406	25.3	.750	9.67	6.00	24.0	42.3	86.0

Opponents' 1999-2000 Per Game Averages

	W	L	FGA	FG%	3PA	3P%	FTA	FT%	Blk	Stl	Ast	Reb	Pts
Total	29	53	82.7	.452	12.6	.343	21.0	.739	5.23	7.87	20.3	41.4	90.2
Home	10	31	82.8	.424	11.7	.337	20.3	.744	5.39	7.73	20.2	40.0	89.2
Road	19	22	82.6	.427	13.5	.348	21.8	.735	5.07	8.00	20.4	42.8	91.2
vs. Div.	8	16	80.8	.441	12.0	.358	21.6	.769	6.04	7.42	21.0	39.5	92.2
Starters	—	—	58.0	.437	7.9	.366	15.1	.744	3.49	5.11	15.0	27.7	64.7
Bench	—	—	24.7	.399	4.7	.303	6.0	.727	1.74	2.76	5.4	13.7	25.5
In wins	0	53	83.8	.406	12.5	.312	20.2	.734	5.26	7.66	19.3	40.7	86.8
In losses	29	0	80.6	.462	12.8	.398	22.7	.747	5.17	8.24	22.2	42.7	96.5
Pre All-Star	17	32	83.4	.418	12.2	.347	21.4	.716	5.39	7.90	19.7	42.1	89.3
Post All-Star	12	21	81.6	.436	13.2	.336	20.5	.776	5.00	7.82	21.2	40.3	91.6

	W	L	FGA	FG%	3PA	3P%	FTA	FT%	Blk	Stl	Ast	Reb	Pts
November	3	13	84.8	.398	11.4	.335	21.5	.721	5.19	8.19	17.3	43.4	86.8
December	7	8	83.1	.425	11.8	.362	23.2	.716	4.47	8.07	20.7	42.2	91.4
January	6	7	83.3	.435	12.8	.367	18.7	.700	5.85	7.69	21.2	41.2	90.2
February	4	9	81.2	.413	13.8	.322	22.8	.758	6.46	7.38	21.3	42.9	88.8
March	5	10	82.2	.444	12.0	.350	18.2	.780	5.00	7.80	20.9	37.3	91.3
April	4	6	80.7	.447	15.1	.318	22.1	.774	4.40	8.00	21.4	41.6	94.1
0 Days Rest	6	12	81.8	.430	14.6	.342	22.4	.708	5.33	8.28	19.9	41.3	91.2
1 Days Rest	17	26	82.9	.431	12.0	.355	21.2	.751	5.02	7.67	20.7	41.8	91.6
2 Days Rest	4	14	83.1	.409	13.3	.310	19.4	.745	5.28	7.61	19.4	40.6	86.6
3+ Days Rest	2	1	82.7	.411	6.3	.421	21.0	.746	7.33	9.67	22.7	41.0	86.3

Seattle SuperSonics

1999-2000 Per Game Averages

	W	L	FGA	FG%	3PA	3P%	FTA	FT%	Blk	Stl	Ast	Reb	Pts
Total	45	37	84.7	.447	19.6	.339	23.9	.695	4.21	8.01	22.9	43.0	99.1
Home	24	17	84.2	.454	19.5	.341	23.7	.706	4.10	8.68	24.3	43.0	99.8
Road	21	20	85.2	.441	19.8	.337	24.1	.685	4.32	7.34	21.5	43.0	98.3
vs. Playoff	15	29	83.9	.426	21.2	.333	23.5	.681	4.14	7.25	21.1	41.8	94.6
vs. Non-Playoff	30	8	85.7	.471	17.8	.347	24.3	.711	4.29	8.89	25.0	44.4	104.3
vs. East	14	16	82.9	.438	20.4	.315	24.6	.682	4.23	7.17	21.7	42.7	95.9
vs. West	31	21	85.7	.453	19.2	.354	23.5	.704	4.19	8.50	23.6	43.2	100.9
vs. Div.	12	12	85.1	.440	19.2	.343	24.0	.686	4.17	8.46	22.7	44.1	98.0
Starters	—	—	59.5	.460	12.0	.360	17.7	.713	2.74	5.60	18.5	31.7	71.6
Bench	—	—	25.2	.419	7.6	.305	6.2	.645	1.46	2.41	4.4	11.3	27.4
In wins	45	0	84.7	.473	18.8	.358	24.8	.717	4.09	8.82	25.1	44.3	104.6
In losses	0	37	84.7	.417	20.7	.318	22.8	.666	4.35	7.03	20.2	41.4	92.4

	W	L	FGA	FG%	3PA	3P%	FTA	FT%	Blk	Stl	Ast	Reb	Pts
Pre All-Star	31	20	83.1	.444	19.9	.345	24.4	.706	4.22	7.59	22.3	43.2	97.9
Post All-Star	14	17	87.4	.452	19.3	.329	23.0	.676	4.19	8.71	23.9	42.6	101.0
November	11	4	86.0	.452	18.9	.300	26.2	.679	4.13	8.20	24.1	44.2	101.2
December	7	8	83.0	.431	21.5	.376	24.7	.732	4.07	6.93	21.7	42.9	97.6
January	10	5	80.5	.449	19.2	.340	24.7	.709	4.33	7.47	21.8	43.4	96.3
February	7	6	83.0	.449	20.9	.382	20.9	.658	4.15	7.85	22.1	43.4	96.2
March	6	8	84.8	.458	17.9	.296	22.9	.694	3.79	9.71	23.6	39.5	98.9
April	4	6	93.7	.447	19.6	.327	23.4	.688	5.00	8.00	24.6	45.1	106.3
0 Days Rest	10	11	85.2	.453	19.2	.337	22.5	.685	4.48	7.24	22.8	41.9	99.0
1 Days Rest	23	17	84.8	.447	18.7	.327	24.2	.703	4.25	7.88	22.7	43.3	98.9
2 Days Rest	8	9	83.6	.438	21.8	.364	24.1	.710	4.29	8.76	23.1	43.1	98.4
3+ Days Rest	4	0	86.3	.464	22.5	.344	27.5	.618	2.00	10.25	25.3	45.5	104.8

Opponents' 1999-2000 Per Game Averages

	W	L	FGA	FG%	3PA	3P%	FTA	FT%	Blk	Stl	Ast	Reb	Pts
Total	37	45	84.6	.451	15.8	.340	21.9	.748	5.28	7.20	23.6	45.1	98.1
Home	17	24	82.6	.447	15.5	.331	22.7	.751	4.61	7.02	23.3	43.2	96.0
Road	20	21	86.7	.455	16.1	.349	21.1	.745	5.95	7.37	24.0	46.9	100.2
vs. Div.	12	12	85.1	.452	16.9	.383	22.8	.734	5.21	7.83	23.8	44.5	100.2
Starters	—	—	59.1	.458	10.5	.329	15.6	.753	3.74	4.90	17.3	30.2	69.4
Bench	—	—	25.5	.435	5.2	.364	6.3	.737	1.54	2.29	6.3	14.9	28.7
In wins	0	45	84.6	.433	16.2	.322	21.3	.719	4.80	6.89	22.4	43.2	93.8
In losses	37	0	84.7	.474	15.3	.364	22.6	.781	5.86	7.57	25.2	47.3	103.5
Pre All-Star	20	31	84.3	.451	15.1	.340	22.1	.734	5.37	7.29	23.6	44.7	97.3
Post All-Star	17	14	85.3	.452	16.9	.341	21.5	.772	5.13	7.03	23.7	45.7	99.5

	W	L	FGA	FG%	3PA	3P%	FTA	FT%	Blk	Stl	Ast	Reb	Pts
November	4	11	87.6	.454	14.5	.355	21.5	.724	5.13	6.87	23.6	46.1	100.2
December	8	7	82.7	.451	13.5	.371	24.9	.730	5.93	8.40	24.1	44.3	97.9
January	5	10	83.5	.445	17.5	.308	21.5	.730	5.47	7.00	23.0	44.3	95.3
February	6	7	85.2	.435	16.6	.315	19.2	.771	4.77	7.69	22.2	44.7	94.2
March	8	6	81.4	.479	13.4	.305	20.1	.772	4.64	6.71	24.9	43.5	97.6
April	6	4	88.7	.441	20.8	.394	24.6	.780	5.80	6.20	24.2	48.4	105.6
0 Days Rest	11	10	84.8	.463	16.3	.371	21.9	.767	5.71	6.90	25.0	45.3	101.4
1 Days Rest	17	23	85.3	.450	15.1	.339	21.6	.743	5.30	7.13	23.4	45.7	97.3
2 Days Rest	9	8	84.1	.447	16.1	.307	21.7	.748	4.94	8.18	24.0	43.5	96.4
3+ Days Rest	0	4	80.0	.419	18.8	.333	25.8	.709	4.25	5.25	17.3	44.5	91.5

Toronto Raptors

1999-2000 Per Game Averages

	W	L	FGA	FG%	3PA	3P%	FTA	FT%	Blk	Stl	Ast	Reb	Pts
Total	45	37	83.9	.433	14.3	.363	25.2	.765	6.63	8.12	23.7	43.3	97.2
Home	26	15	83.9	.434	14.4	.361	24.2	.779	8.93	8.24	24.9	42.6	96.9
Road	19	22	84.0	.432	14.2	.365	26.2	.753	4.34	8.00	22.6	44.0	97.5
vs. Playoff	19	23	84.4	.420	14.5	.359	25.9	.762	6.36	7.57	22.7	44.1	95.2
vs. Non-Playoff	26	14	83.5	.447	14.1	.367	24.6	.769	6.93	8.70	24.9	42.4	98.7
vs. East	29	25	84.1	.432	14.9	.361	25.1	.769	6.65	8.30	24.1	43.0	97.4
vs. West	16	12	83.5	.435	13.1	.367	25.4	.758	6.61	7.79	23.0	43.8	96.6
vs. Div.	16	12	84.2	.437	16.1	.376	23.1	.790	6.61	8.00	24.8	42.5	98.0
Starters	—	—	56.9	.438	9.3	.377	17.9	.781	4.49	5.49	16.2	29.5	67.3
Bench	—	—	27.0	.423	5.0	.337	7.3	.727	2.15	2.63	7.5	13.8	29.9
In wins	45	0	82.8	.460	14.0	.415	25.0	.793	7.60	9.02	25.5	43.1	101.9
In losses	0	37	85.3	.401	14.6	.303	25.4	.732	5.46	7.03	21.6	43.5	91.4

	W	L	FGA	FG%	3PA	3P%	FTA	FT%	Blk	Stl	Ast	Reb	Pts
Pre All-Star	26	21	85.1	.437	13.0	.369	26.1	.770	6.79	8.28	24.2	44.1	99.2
Post All-Star	19	16	82.3	.428	16.0	.357	24.1	.759	6.43	7.91	23.2	42.1	94.4
November	9	6	82.1	.446	13.9	.413	25.5	.775	7.00	8.33	23.4	43.7	98.7
December	8	6	86.3	.425	13.2	.330	26.1	.764	6.64	7.57	24.4	47.6	97.7
January	7	7	85.4	.448	11.4	.356	26.4	.756	7.07	8.86	25.1	41.1	100.4
February	6	6	84.3	.429	14.8	.337	25.3	.773	6.58	8.67	23.8	41.7	96.9
March	10	7	83.3	.427	15.2	.391	25.9	.768	6.24	7.94	23.3	42.9	97.0
April	5	5	82.0	.418	18.2	.330	20.8	.750	6.20	7.20	22.2	42.0	90.2
0 Days Rest	8	10	84.8	.441	14.1	.394	26.3	.755	4.17	9.33	23.4	44.1	100.2
1 Days Rest	27	21	83.9	.427	14.3	.351	25.0	.761	7.29	7.73	23.5	43.6	95.7
2 Days Rest	6	3	83.4	.445	15.2	.380	24.3	.785	7.11	7.89	25.9	39.8	99.1
3+ Days Rest	4	3	82.6	.441	13.4	.340	24.9	.799	7.86	8.00	23.7	43.4	97.3

Opponents' 1999-2000 Per Game Averages

	W	L	FGA	FG%	3PA	3P%	FTA	FT%	Blk	Stl	Ast	Reb	Pts
Total	37	45	80.7	.454	12.5	.339	26.0	.764	5.29	6.79	21.8	42.8	97.3
Home	15	26	79.0	.462	11.7	.366	24.4	.751	6.29	6.46	20.9	41.0	95.7
Road	22	19	82.3	.446	13.2	.315	27.7	.774	4.29	7.12	22.8	44.7	99.0
vs. Div.	12	16	79.1	.464	12.3	.372	26.4	.780	4.89	6.75	22.2	41.2	98.6
Starters	—	—	55.7	.454	8.3	.345	18.7	.768	3.57	4.56	15.1	28.8	67.9
Bench	—	—	24.9	.452	4.1	.287	7.4	.751	1.72	2.23	6.7	14.0	29.4
In wins	0	45	81.1	.436	12.6	.297	24.0	.744	5.29	6.33	20.9	41.4	92.3
In losses	37	0	80.1	.476	12.3	.390	28.5	.784	5.30	7.35	22.9	44.6	103.5
Pre All-Star	21	26	81.9	.450	12.2	.351	27.5	.764	5.38	7.00	21.3	43.2	99.0
Post All-Star	16	19	79.1	.459	12.8	.324	24.1	.763	5.17	6.51	22.5	42.3	95.1

	W	L	FGA	FG%	3PA	3P%	FTA	FT%	Blk	Stl	Ast	Reb	Pts
November	6	9	84.4	.433	13.2	.369	25.3	.723	5.73	7.13	21.0	44.2	96.2
December	6	8	83.4	.437	12.1	.365	26.8	.755	6.00	7.71	22.6	42.0	97.5
January	7	7	77.3	.484	11.1	.353	29.5	.804	5.43	6.50	21.4	41.6	102.5
February	6	6	78.2	.464	12.7	.355	26.0	.760	4.00	5.67	20.5	42.4	96.8
March	7	10	81.7	.459	13.8	.281	24.8	.779	4.94	7.24	23.9	43.6	98.1
April	5	5	77.3	.450	11.0	.327	23.6	.750	5.60	6.00	20.5	42.9	90.9
0 Days Rest	10	8	81.6	.458	13.3	.364	26.0	.776	4.89	7.17	22.1	43.5	99.8
1 Days Rest	21	27	80.8	.450	12.8	.309	26.4	.767	5.73	6.83	21.9	43.0	96.9
2 Days Rest	3	6	78.9	.475	9.7	.345	23.4	.720	4.78	5.33	21.8	42.1	95.1
3+ Days Rest	3	4	79.7	.441	11.4	.488	27.4	.760	4.00	7.43	20.9	41.3	96.7

Utah Jazz

1999-2000 Per Game Averages

	W	L	FGA	FG%	3PA	3P%	FTA	FT%	Blk	Stl	Ast	Reb	Pts		W	L	FGA	FG%	3PA	3P%	FTA	FT%	Blk	Stl	Ast	Reb	Pts
Total	55	27	77.8	.464	10.4	.385	26.2	.773	5.44	7.67	24.9	41.0	96.5	Pre All-Star	29	18	77.6	.465	9.7	.368	25.4	.773	5.11	7.64	24.7	40.4	95.5
Home	31	10	77.7	.480	11.2	.394	26.3	.775	6.39	7.34	26.5	41.0	99.4	Post All-Star	26	9	78.1	.463	11.4	.405	27.3	.773	5.89	7.71	25.2	41.7	97.9
Road	24	17	77.9	.448	9.6	.375	26.2	.770	4.49	8.00	23.2	41.0	93.6	November	8	6	76.9	.465	10.3	.347	25.0	.800	4.50	7.14	23.2	39.9	95.0
vs. Playoff	24	20	77.7	.448	10.7	.353	25.8	.768	4.77	7.14	23.6	41.4	93.2	December	10	4	75.9	.466	8.9	.328	25.8	.756	5.86	8.79	24.2	39.5	93.1
vs. Non-Playoff	31	7	77.9	.483	10.1	.424	26.7	.778	6.21	8.29	26.4	40.6	100.3	January	9	5	79.8	.471	9.6	.418	26.1	.759	5.07	7.29	25.9	42.4	98.9
vs. East	22	8	77.9	.471	10.2	.387	26.0	.764	5.40	7.67	25.6	41.1	97.2	February	8	5	80.1	.445	12.1	.433	25.8	.789	6.15	6.54	25.1	40.8	96.8
vs. West	33	19	77.7	.460	10.6	.384	26.3	.777	5.46	7.67	24.5	40.9	96.1	March	14	2	76.4	.483	10.4	.440	26.3	.762	5.50	8.44	26.3	41.1	98.4
vs. Div.	14	10	77.8	.465	9.9	.408	24.5	.767	5.88	7.29	24.3	40.0	95.2	April	6	5	78.2	.450	11.6	.320	28.9	.774	5.64	7.64	24.3	42.8	96.5
Starters	—	—	51.3	.489	6.4	.402	18.9	.788	2.55	5.41	17.3	25.1	67.7	0 Days Rest	14	5	75.5	.452	10.3	.347	29.5	.771	5.21	7.89	23.5	40.4	94.5
Bench	—	—	26.5	.417	4.0	.359	7.3	.733	2.89	2.26	7.6	15.9	28.9	1 Days Rest	30	15	78.5	.475	10.3	.405	24.8	.773	5.49	7.38	25.3	41.0	97.8
In wins	55	0	77.5	.486	10.0	.397	26.9	.776	6.00	8.36	26.3	41.7	100.3	2 Days Rest	9	3	79.2	.457	11.1	.398	26.7	.778	5.50	8.58	25.8	42.3	97.5
In losses	0	27	78.3	.420	11.2	.364	24.8	.764	4.30	6.26	22.1	39.6	88.8	3+ Days Rest	2	4	77.3	.440	10.5	.333	24.3	.761	5.67	7.33	24.3	40.3	91.2

Opponents' 1999-2000 Per Game Averages

	W	L	FGA	FG%	3PA	3P%	FTA	FT%	Blk	Stl	Ast	Reb	Pts		W	L	FGA	FG%	3PA	3P%	FTA	FT%	Blk	Stl	Ast	Reb	Pts
Total	27	55	76.1	.446	13.4	.354	26.1	.746	5.01	7.17	19.8	38.1	92.0	November	6	8	74.4	.457	12.6	.339	27.8	.712	4.79	7.64	19.7	37.0	92.1
Home	10	31	75.7	.450	13.3	.373	25.7	.748	5.12	6.83	18.7	36.1	92.3	December	4	10	76.2	.429	13.7	.297	26.1	.726	5.43	6.29	18.8	39.2	88.4
Road	17	24	76.5	.441	13.4	.335	26.5	.744	4.90	7.51	20.8	40.1	91.8	January	5	9	79.9	.442	11.9	.337	24.1	.734	5.29	7.71	19.7	39.6	92.4
vs. Div.	10	14	77.0	.447	13.5	.340	25.1	.762	5.04	7.29	20.4	38.0	92.5	February	5	8	75.5	.457	13.7	.410	28.8	.771	5.62	6.77	18.8	38.2	96.9
Starters	—	—	53.2	.451	8.7	.352	18.2	.753	3.34	4.68	14.4	25.7	64.8	March	2	14	74.4	.444	12.9	.369	24.4	.769	3.56	6.88	20.6	37.4	89.5
Bench	—	—	22.9	.433	4.7	.357	7.9	.732	1.67	2.49	5.4	12.4	27.3	April	5	6	76.4	.446	16.2	.371	25.8	.771	5.82	7.91	20.9	37.0	94.1
In wins	0	55	75.9	.432	13.1	.327	25.5	.740	4.69	6.69	18.5	36.9	88.7	0 Days Rest	5	14	77.3	.441	13.2	.339	25.5	.748	4.32	7.37	21.1	40.0	91.7
In losses	27	0	76.4	.473	14.0	.404	27.4	.758	5.67	8.15	22.3	40.6	98.8	1 Days Rest	15	30	76.2	.441	13.2	.342	26.6	.756	5.07	6.98	18.5	37.3	91.9
Pre All-Star	18	29	76.4	.445	12.9	.339	26.6	.729	5.38	7.34	19.7	38.3	91.8	2 Days Rest	3	9	74.2	.455	14.2	.406	25.8	.735	6.08	7.50	21.3	37.1	92.2
Post All-Star	9	26	75.6	.446	14.0	.371	25.5	.771	4.51	6.94	19.9	37.7	92.3	3+ Days Rest	4	2	75.2	.477	13.3	.375	24.8	.691	4.67	7.33	21.7	39.7	93.8

Vancouver Grizzlies

1999-2000 Per Game Averages

	W	L	FGA	FG%	3PA	3P%	FTA	FT%	Blk	Stl	Ast	Reb	Pts		W	L	FGA	FG%	3PA	3P%	FTA	FT%	Blk	Stl	Ast	Reb	Pts
Total	22	60	78.5	.449	11.0	.361	25.1	.774	4.22	7.41	20.7	40.6	93.9	Pre All-Star	14	34	79.8	.443	9.8	.355	25.5	.774	4.33	7.35	19.7	41.5	93.9
Home	12	29	79.5	.450	11.5	.364	23.0	.774	4.93	7.73	21.7	42.5	93.6	Post All-Star	8	26	76.8	.458	12.6	.367	24.6	.774	4.06	7.50	22.2	39.3	94.0
Road	10	31	77.6	.448	10.4	.357	27.2	.774	3.51	7.10	19.8	38.7	94.3	November	3	11	80.1	.447	8.0	.313	25.1	.724	4.21	7.36	19.9	42.5	92.2
vs. Playoff	6	42	76.4	.448	11.2	.379	25.2	.768	4.02	6.92	20.7	39.3	92.0	December	3	12	79.7	.443	10.3	.364	24.1	.767	4.53	6.27	18.9	39.8	92.7
vs. Non-Playoff	16	18	81.5	.451	10.6	.334	25.0	.782	4.50	8.12	20.7	42.4	96.6	January	6	8	78.0	.441	10.7	.387	28.2	.810	4.14	8.36	20.4	41.9	95.9
vs. East	10	20	76.8	.446	10.4	.383	25.7	.784	4.33	8.10	21.0	40.3	92.6	February	6	7	79.5	.451	11.7	.368	24.4	.782	4.23	8.62	22.6	41.5	95.1
vs. West	12	40	79.6	.451	11.3	.349	24.8	.768	4.15	7.02	20.6	40.8	94.7	March	1	14	74.2	.465	13.2	.348	24.2	.755	4.07	6.73	21.8	38.4	91.9
vs. Div.	6	18	82.0	.443	10.9	.317	23.4	.797	4.04	7.25	20.4	40.2	94.9	April	3	8	80.5	.447	12.0	.379	24.8	.810	4.09	7.36	21.1	39.5	96.6
Starters	—	—	61.3	.461	7.4	.372	19.5	.789	3.12	5.07	16.3	29.5	74.6	0 Days Rest	6	13	76.6	.446	11.9	.389	27.1	.778	3.79	7.74	20.8	38.5	94.0
Bench	—	—	17.2	.408	3.6	.338	5.6	.722	1.10	2.34	4.4	11.0	19.3	1 Days Rest	11	36	78.9	.451	11.0	.359	25.0	.783	4.55	7.38	20.6	41.1	94.6
In wins	22	0	78.9	.473	10.6	.446	27.2	.800	4.82	9.05	22.8	43.5	101.1	2 Days Rest	1	6	78.4	.470	8.6	.317	24.4	.696	3.29	7.14	21.3	37.9	93.4
In losses	0	60	78.4	.440	11.1	.331	24.4	.763	4.00	6.82	20.0	39.5	91.3	3+ Days Rest	4	5	80.9	.431	10.8	.330	22.1	.774	4.11	7.11	21.0	44.4	90.4

Opponents' 1999-2000 Per Game Averages

	W	L	FGA	FG%	3PA	3P%	FTA	FT%	Blk	Stl	Ast	Reb	Pts		W	L	FGA	FG%	3PA	3P%	FTA	FT%	Blk	Stl	Ast	Reb	Pts
Total	60	22	80.6	.474	13.2	.333	24.3	.769	6.33	8.84	23.6	40.3	99.5	November	11	3	82.5	.466	13.6	.316	25.9	.735	6.43	10.00	22.5	41.6	100.1
Home	29	12	81.4	.462	13.0	.326	23.8	.758	5.78	9.12	22.0	41.0	97.4	December	12	3	78.2	.479	12.9	.326	28.0	.786	7.13	7.93	23.7	40.5	101.1
Road	31	10	79.9	.487	13.4	.341	24.8	.780	6.88	8.56	25.3	39.7	101.7	January	8	6	80.3	.464	12.6	.345	23.6	.752	7.43	8.50	24.6	39.7	96.5
vs. Div.	18	6	78.8	.485	13.7	.384	25.7	.771	7.42	7.29	23.9	41.2	101.5	February	7	6	80.8	.468	12.8	.353	20.5	.764	4.77	9.15	23.1	40.0	95.9
Starters	—	—	56.9	.486	8.8	.338	16.8	.773	4.39	5.85	17.2	27.1	71.3	March	14	1	81.1	.484	12.0	.311	24.3	.772	5.67	10.53	22.7	39.1	100.9
Bench	—	—	23.7	.445	4.4	.324	7.5	.760	1.94	2.99	6.4	13.2	28.3	April	8	3	81.3	.487	16.0	.352	22.4	.817	6.45	6.36	25.2	41.3	103.0
In wins	0	22	80.1	.443	14.0	.330	21.9	.739	6.50	7.36	20.0	38.5	91.7	0 Days Rest	13	6	79.8	.482	11.5	.344	26.5	.758	6.32	8.37	24.7	40.5	101.0
In losses	60	0	80.9	.486	12.9	.335	25.1	.779	6.27	9.38	24.9	41.0	102.4	1 Days Rest	36	11	81.1	.468	14.2	.325	23.3	.786	6.15	8.87	23.1	40.1	98.9
Pre All-Star	34	14	80.0	.468	13.0	.337	25.2	.765	6.85	8.67	23.4	40.4	98.6	2 Days Rest	6	1	80.1	.504	15.9	.387	25.7	.789	7.57	9.43	25.9	40.4	107.3
Post All-Star	26	8	81.5	.482	13.5	.328	22.9	.775	5.59	9.09	23.9	40.2	100.9	3+ Days Rest	5	4	80.7	.466	9.6	.302	23.1	.692	6.33	9.22	21.7	40.9	94.0

Washington Wizards

1999-2000 Per Game Averages

	W	L	FGA	FG%	3PA	3P%	FTA	FT%	Blk	Stl	Ast	Reb	Pts
Total	29	53	81.5	.451	10.9	.376	25.7	.743	4.67	7.23	21.6	42.7	96.6
Home	17	24	80.7	.463	10.5	.391	26.4	.758	4.85	7.37	22.0	41.9	98.7
Road	12	29	82.3	.439	11.2	.363	25.0	.728	4.49	7.10	21.2	43.5	94.5
vs. Playoff	13	33	81.5	.451	10.5	.356	25.8	.751	4.24	7.33	21.8	42.7	96.6
vs. Non-Playoff	16	20	81.5	.450	11.4	.401	25.6	.734	5.22	7.11	21.4	42.8	96.6
vs. East	19	35	81.1	.461	10.7	.407	25.8	.754	4.69	7.19	22.5	42.4	98.5
vs. West	10	18	82.2	.432	11.2	.319	25.5	.721	4.64	7.32	19.9	43.4	92.9
vs. Div.	7	17	78.4	.447	11.4	.407	25.1	.749	4.92	7.17	21.3	40.9	93.6
Starters	—	—	51.1	.455	4.7	.358	16.5	.746	2.15	4.55	14.8	25.9	60.5
Bench	—	—	30.4	.442	6.2	.390	9.1	.737	2.52	2.68	6.8	16.8	36.0
In wins	29	0	80.1	.489	9.5	.425	25.6	.794	4.97	8.03	22.7	42.2	102.6
In losses	0	53	82.2	.430	11.6	.354	25.8	.716	4.51	6.79	21.0	43.0	93.3
Pre All-Star	15	34	80.6	.453	10.1	.345	26.8	.733	4.78	7.00	21.1	43.9	96.1
Post All-Star	14	19	82.7	.448	12.0	.415	24.1	.761	4.52	7.58	22.3	40.9	97.3
November	5	10	82.7	.415	10.9	.287	25.8	.729	4.40	7.80	20.5	45.7	90.6
December	5	10	77.8	.464	9.1	.346	27.5	.697	4.80	7.07	20.9	43.5	94.5
January	4	10	81.2	.478	9.1	.344	28.2	.765	5.36	6.57	21.6	42.6	102.3
February	2	10	82.4	.440	12.8	.429	25.4	.728	4.08	6.33	21.1	44.2	96.5
March	10	7	82.8	.454	11.5	.379	22.6	.784	4.53	8.18	22.4	40.7	97.2
April	3	6	82.1	.456	12.6	.504	24.8	.767	4.89	7.00	23.6	38.6	100.2
0 Days Rest	5	17	82.8	.443	11.3	.387	27.3	.737	4.59	7.55	20.5	44.1	97.8
1 Days Rest	14	25	81.6	.454	10.4	.394	24.6	.747	4.74	7.15	22.1	41.7	96.5
2 Days Rest	6	7	79.6	.447	10.7	.309	27.2	.737	5.00	7.92	21.2	44.4	94.5
3+ Days Rest	4	4	80.5	.461	12.4	.374	24.0	.755	4.00	5.63	22.8	40.8	97.0

Opponents' 1999-2000 Per Game Averages

	W	L	FGA	FG%	3PA	3P%	FTA	FT%	Blk	Stl	Ast	Reb	Pts
Total	53	29	79.8	.459	12.8	.371	29.3	.744	6.13	8.37	21.9	41.2	99.9
Home	24	17	79.1	.464	13.0	.381	29.0	.747	5.61	7.95	21.0	39.6	100.1
Road	29	12	80.6	.454	12.7	.360	29.7	.742	6.66	8.78	22.7	42.8	99.7
vs. Div.	17	7	79.0	.460	11.8	.363	29.1	.749	5.96	9.08	21.0	40.4	98.8
Starters	—	54	54.8	.464	8.4	.355	20.7	.763	4.13	5.54	15.1	27.3	69.7
Bench	—		25.0	.447	4.4	.401	8.7	.699	2.00	2.83	6.8	14.0	30.2
In wins	0	29	79.3	.430	12.3	.321	26.7	.762	5.24	6.48	18.9	39.1	92.6
In losses	53	0	80.1	.474	13.1	.396	30.8	.736	6.62	9.40	23.5	42.4	103.9
Pre All-Star	34	15	80.7	.457	12.9	.374	29.7	.740	6.71	9.12	23.4	40.2	100.6
Post All-Star	19	14	78.5	.462	12.8	.366	28.8	.751	5.27	7.24	19.6	42.8	98.8
November	10	5	81.1	.448	13.2	.389	27.7	.742	6.67	8.87	23.5	42.6	98.3
December	10	5	78.5	.452	12.2	.372	30.0	.711	6.93	8.40	21.7	37.9	96.9
January	10	4	82.6	.468	13.9	.374	29.9	.768	5.93	10.07	25.5	39.7	105.6
February	10	2	82.0	.455	13.8	.364	29.9	.744	6.42	8.67	21.9	42.4	101.9
March	7	10	76.9	.452	12.6	.377	27.7	.760	5.35	6.59	18.7	42.2	95.4
April	6	3	78.2	.491	10.7	.323	32.4	.740	5.33	7.78	19.7	43.3	104.3
0 Days Rest	17	5	80.9	.469	12.2	.347	31.2	.751	6.45	8.50	22.6	41.3	103.9
1 Days Rest	25	14	78.6	.457	13.3	.390	28.8	.761	6.18	8.00	21.3	41.2	98.9
2 Days Rest	7	6	81.8	.444	12.4	.354	28.5	.701	6.31	9.15	22.2	40.8	97.0
3+ Days Rest	4	4	79.6	.466	13.1	.362	28.1	.711	4.75	8.50	22.0	41.9	99.0

National Basketball Association

1999-2000 Per Game Averages

	G	FGA	FG%	3PA	3P%	FTA	FT%	Blk	Stl	Ast	Reb	Pts
Total	2378	82.1	.449	13.7	.353	25.3	.750	5.17	7.93	22.3	42.9	97.5
Home	1189	82.2	.456	13.8	.356	25.7	.755	5.62	8.06	23.4	43.8	99.2
Road	1189	82.0	.442	13.6	.349	24.9	.746	4.71	7.81	21.3	42.0	95.7
vs. Playoff	1312	81.7	.440	13.9	.351	24.7	.747	4.81	7.69	21.5	42.3	95.2
vs. Non-Playoff	1066	82.6	.459	13.4	.355	26.0	.754	5.62	8.23	23.3	43.7	100.2
vs. East	1230	81.3	.449	13.7	.357	25.8	.752	5.24	7.88	22.4	42.6	97.4
vs. West	1148	82.9	.448	13.7	.349	24.7	.748	5.09	7.99	22.3	43.3	97.6
vs. Div.	730	82.0	.449	13.8	.353	25.4	.751	5.08	7.90	22.2	42.7	97.5
Starters	—	56.7	.454	8.9	.357	17.5	.758	3.46	5.26	15.9	28.5	67.9
Bench	—	25.4	.437	4.9	.346	7.8	.732	1.71	2.67	6.4	14.5	29.6
In wins	1189	81.6	.475	13.4	.387	26.4	.762	5.75	8.52	24.4	44.3	102.9
In losses	1189	82.6	.422	14.0	.321	24.2	.737	4.59	7.35	20.3	41.5	92.0

	G	FGA	FG%	3PA	3G%	FTA	FT%	Blk	Stl	Ast	Reb	Pts
Pre All-Star	1400	82.5	.447	13.6	.350	25.7	.746	5.33	8.00	22.2	43.2	97.8
Post All-Star	978	81.5	.450	13.8	.357	24.7	.756	4.94	7.85	22.5	42.5	97.0
November	418	82.8	.444	13.3	.351	26.2	.739	5.45	8.06	21.8	43.8	97.5
December	426	82.4	.445	13.4	.343	25.7	.738	5.37	7.84	22.1	43.2	96.9
January	408	82.4	.451	13.9	.356	25.6	.753	5.22	8.11	22.6	42.8	98.6
February	376	82.1	.446	14.1	.363	23.9	.763	5.21	7.87	22.5	42.9	96.6
March	454	81.2	.454	13.5	.346	24.8	.759	4.82	7.88	22.4	42.1	97.3
April	296	81.5	.453	14.2	.363	25.4	.751	4.90	7.82	22.8	42.5	98.0
0 Days Rest	591	81.4	.445	13.7	.354	25.6	.750	4.91	7.69	21.5	42.4	96.5
1 Days Rest	1245	82.3	.449	13.7	.351	25.2	.753	5.23	7.96	22.5	43.0	97.6
2 Days Rest	345	82.1	.455	13.8	.356	24.7	.743	5.35	8.10	23.0	43.0	98.0
3+ Days Rest	197	83.1	.446	13.5	.357	26.2	.748	5.29	8.22	22.5	43.7	98.5

Team Game Logs

Any superscript number following the score in a game denotes the number of overtimes played in that game. For most columns in the regular season section, we've bolded the *best* single-game performance by team, along with the top single-game points, rebounds and assists performances by individual players.

Atlanta Hawks 1999-2000 Game Log (28-54)

Date	Opp	Score	W/L	Rec	Atl FG Att–Pct.	Opp FG Att–Pct.	Atl FT Att–Pct.	Opp FT Att–Pct.	Atl Reb	Opp Reb	Points	Rebounds	Assists
11/02	@Was	87-94	L	0-1	78–.397	88–.443	30–.767	16–.813	50	42	McLeod 22, Jackson 17	2 with 12	Coles 5
11/04	Mil	109-119	L	0-2	83–.494	90–.456	30–.700	36–.917	46	38	Jackson 19, Rider 19	Mutombo 16	Coles 6
11/06	Chi	113-97	W	1-2	81–.543	80–.438	34–.647	35–.686	42	39	Rider 18, Mutombo 16	Mutombo 13	Terry 5
11/08	@Den	100-115	L	1-3	82–.476	96–.469	30–.733	24–.792	39	49	Rider 28, Jackson 16	Mutombo 13	Coles 8
11/10	@Van	97-102[1]	L	1-4	92–.424	92–.478	24–.750	16–.813	41	49	Coles 20, Crawford 18	2 with 8	Coles 8
11/13	@Por	95-131	L	1-5	90–.422	81–.654	22–.636	32–.656	36	47	Henderson 22, Terry 17	Henderson 8	Johnson 6
11/14	@LAL	88-93	L	1-6	81–.395	84–.429	33–.576	33–.515	56	47	Rider 24, Henderson 14	Mutombo 16	Rider 5
11/16	Cha	103-98	W	2-6	86–.465	84–.452	29–.690	22–.818	49	39	Terry 22, Jackson 20	Mutombo 17	2 with 5
11/19	@Ind	105-99	W	3-6	96–.448	83–.434	22–.773	25–.880	46	43	Jackson 19, 3 with 16	Mutombo 16	2 with 3
11/20	Orl	103-107	L	3-7	90–.478	100–.460	22–.591	15–.800	53	46	Mutombo 22, Jackson 19	Mutombo 21	Coles 7
11/23	Mia	113-106	W	4-7	81–.556	90–.467	28–.714	16–.813	46	33	Rider 32, 2 with 21	Mutombo 16	3 with 3
11/24	@Mia	91-93	L	4-8	80–.450	85–.412	21–.714	22–.773	47	43	Rider 28, Mutombo 20	Mutombo 18	2 with 4
11/26	@Det	91-93	L	4-9	85–.424	84–.381	22–.591	29–.897	51	47	Jackson 18, 3 with 16	Mutombo 20	Jackson 4
11/27	Bos	94-84	W	5-9	69–.493	78–.385	32–.781	25–.800	47	30	Rider 30, Mutombo 17	Mutombo 17	Coles 6
11/30	@Tor	107-89	W	6-9	79–.544	95–.379	26–.615	16–.688	51	42	Rider 23, Jackson 15	Mutombo 11	Rider 6
12/02	Sac	110-100	W	7-9	87–.517	101–.406	22–.727	13–.846	51	53	Rider 32, Jackson 26	Mutombo 18	Coles 7
12/04	Det	112-110	W	8-9	76–.513	87–.483	34–.882	20–1.000	40	34	Jackson 33, Rider 30	2 with 9	Coles 8
12/08	LAC	99-81	W	9-9	87–.506	87–.368	14–.643	17–.765	50	43	Rider 38, Mutombo 16	Mutombo 14	Rider 7
12/10	GS	99-107	L	9-10	82–.427	99–.475	33–.697	17–.647	43	46	Rider 34, Terry 16	Mutombo 14	Terry 6
12/11	@Cle	116-127	L	9-11	79–.418	92–.500	55–.782	39–.744	42	41	Rider 27, Henderson 21	Mutombo 13	2 with 5
12/14	Min	105-94	W	10-11	87–.471	96–.417	26–.731	15–.733	60	39	Mutombo 27, Jackson 23	Mutombo 29	2 with 6
12/16	LAL	88-95	L	10-12	78–.385	87–.402	36–.722	36–.694	46	51	Rider 33, Henderson 13	Mutombo 11	Rider 5
12/18	Uta	96-106	L	10-13	75–.427	87–.494	40–.775	17–.941	41	36	Rider 24, Jackson 22	Mutombo 11	Rider 4
12/19	@NJ	88-96	L	10-14	77–.442	89–.472	21–.762	9–.444	49	41	Rider 20, Jackson 15	Mutombo 13	3 with 3
12/22	@Bos	81-98	L	10-15	79–.405	83–.482	25–.640	11–.818	45	41	Coles 13, Ellis 13	Mutombo 13	Terry 4
12/23	Cle	108-90	W	11-15	92–.446	89–.371	29–.828	24–.792	56	40	Rider 30, Jackson 19	Mutombo 21	Rider 5
12/27	@Cha	104-108	L	11-16	76–.474	71–.493	31–.839	45–.800	31	42	Rider 25, Jackson 20	Mutombo 10	Rider 5
12/29	Ind	89-116	L	11-17	85–.412	91–.516	22–.682	16–.875	46	43	Jackson 19, Rider 16	2 with 9	Terry 7
12/30	@Det	105-106[1]	L	11-18	99–.424	87–.460	24–.750	26–.731	60	39	Jackson 26, Ellis 16	Mutombo 13	2 with 8
1/04	@Mil	113-116	L	11-19	81–.568	88–.557	18–.833	15–.867	35	34	Jackson 30, Coles 25	Mutombo 10	Coles 7
1/05	Det	108-120	L	11-20	75–.560	81–.556	24–.792	33–.818	29	38	Rider 27, Mutombo 15	Mutombo 8	2 with 6
1/07	Tor	105-97	W	12-20	81–.506	79–.430	19–.895	31–.806	42	36	Jackson 31, Rider 27	Mutombo 11	Coles 5
1/08	@Dal	85-95	L	12-21	98–.347	77–.416	16–.625	27–.889	55	50	Rider 24, Jackson 18	Mutombo 19	Rider 5
1/14	@Chi	89-83	W	13-21	79–.443	88–.386	19–.737	14–.857	37	46	Rider 24, Jackson 18	Mutombo 13	Johnson 8
1/15	Phi	98-101	L	13-22	77–.455	83–.494	24–.792	24–.750	40	37	Rider 35, Jackson 16	Mutombo 16	Terry 6
1/17	Mil	101-107	L	13-23	83–.482	89–.449	23–.826	20–.850	43	40	Henderson 20, Jackson 17	Ellis 13	Terry 8
1/19	@Phi	89-107	L	13-24	85–.341	83–.494	38–.763	32–.781	41	53	Henderson 22, Rider 17	Mutombo 12	2 with 5
1/21	@Mia	79-101	L	13-25	92–.304	83–.506	30–.733	26–.577	48	50	Jackson 18, Henderson 14	Mutombo 20	Coles 4
1/22	Was	111-93	W	14-25	84–.464	92–.402	37–.757	21–.762	53	49	Rider 28, Jackson 20	Mutombo 19	Coles 9
1/25	Chi	96-89	W	15-25	84–.452	81–.395	23–.783	29–.724	52	42	Rider 28, Jackson 21	Mutombo 23	Rider 5
1/28	NY	98-96[1]	W	16-25	93–.355	84–.429	27–.926	24–.708	56	43	Rider 22, Mutombo 18	Mutombo 24	Terry 4
1/29	@Orl	87-103	L	16-26	80–.363	80–.463	36–.750	36–.750	42	50	Jackson 15, 2 with 12	Mutombo 12	Jackson 5
2/02	@NJ	97-89	W	17-26	79–.456	83–.422	30–.767	14–.786	45	40	Rider 25, Henderson 22	Mutombo 16	4 with 4
2/04	Por	90-97	L	17-27	91–.363	83–.446	27–.815	24–.708	52	44	Jackson 25, Henderson 18	Mutombo 13	Jackson 4
2/05	@Cle	102-94	W	18-27	89–.438	83–.386	25–.920	30–.867	50	42	Rider 23, 2 with 16	Mutombo 17	Rider 9
2/08	@Tor	88-109	L	18-28	75–.427	94–.479	29–.793	13–1.000	43	40	Mutombo 22, Rider 12	Mutombo 15	Terry 3
2/09	Hou	116-100	W	19-28	89–.562	83–.422	20–.750	31–.774	52	32	Jackson 23, Coles 16	Coles 8	2 with 5
2/15	NJ	103-86	W	20-28	80–.500	95–.326	27–.704	21–.762	49	46	Henderson 21, Mutombo 21	Mutombo 13	Coles 7
2/18	@Pho	73-85	L	20-29	75–.360	90–.411	30–.600	15–.600	60	45	Mutombo 12, Henderson 10	Mutombo 25	2 with 3
2/21	@Uta	94-96	L	20-30	79–.519	83–.470	13–.692	16–.688	40	37	Rider 22, Jackson 15	Mutombo 16	Terry 5
2/23	@Sac	100-94	W	21-30	104–.433	92–.413	10–.800	16–.938	50	52	Rider 33, Jackson 17	Jackson 12	Rider 7
2/25	@Sea	95-87	W	22-30	85–.447	85–.424	17–.706	16–.625	45	51	Rider 24, Jackson 23	Mutombo 13	Coles 10
2/26	@LAC	77-78	L	22-31	84–.405	85–.376	5–1.000	13–.692	52	44	Coles 16, Rider 16	Mutombo 17	Rider 7
2/28	@GS	75-80	L	22-32	84–.345	89–.371	17–.824	20–.600	52	58	Rider 24, Jackson 21	Mutombo 22	Coles 5

Date	Opp	Score	W/L	Rec	Atl FG Att–Pct.	Opp FG Att–Pct.	Atl FT Att–Pct.	Opp FT Att–Pct.	Atl Reb	Opp Reb	Points	Rebounds	Assists
3/01	Was	83-102	L	22-33	75–.427	76–.526	22–.773	23–.739	41	37	Jackson 22, Mutombo 16	Mutombo 17	Terry 5
3/03	NY	83-**70**	W	23-33	75–.453	82–.366	14–.929	11–.727	50	**30**	Terry 17, Ellis 16	Mutombo 20	Terry 5
3/04	Sea	81-93	L	23-34	82–.415	84–.464	19–.526	18–.611	49	40	3 with 11	Mutombo 12	Terry 7
3/06	@Mil	78-111	L	23-35	75–.467	86–.558	8–.625	11–.636	21	51	Wright 18, 2 with 12	2 with 5	Terry 11
3/07	@Chi	82-89	L	23-36	85–.435	90–.356	9–.778	23–.870	52	44	Henderson 15, 2 with 12	Mutombo 21	Terry 9
3/09	SA	79-105	L	23-37	76–.434	84–.512	13–.846	19–.737	35	41	McLeod 15, Terry 13	Mutombo 11	Terry 10
3/11	Van	91-86	W	24-37	73–.534	76–.487	18–.722	17–.647	37	**30**	Jackson 22, Henderson 20	Mutombo 10	**Terry 12**
3/14	@SA	79-94	L	24-38	85–.424	79–.506	8–.750	13–.923	42	39	Jackson 22, Mutombo 14	Mutombo 12	Terry 9
3/15	Ind	107-113	L	24-39	80–.475	79–.519	37–.757	31–.774	45	38	Henderson 21, Jackson 17	Mutombo 9	Jackson 6
3/17	Bos	90-114	L	24-40	72–.431	99–.495	34–.765	11–.818	35	45	Jackson 26, Mutombo 19	2 with 6	Terry 5
3/19	Dal	85-89	L	24-41	88–.352	85–.400	30–.667	17–.824	**64**	45	Henderson 24, Jackson 20	Mutombo 18	Terry 7
3/21	Mia	82-77	W	25-41	87–.379	81–.383	18–.833	12–1.000	45	45	Henderson 15, Jackson 15	Mutombo 14	Terry 11
3/22	@Orl	90-103	L	25-42	86–.419	88–.455	30–.567	28–.750	40	57	3 with 18	Jackson 6	Glover 5
3/24	@NY	83-95	L	25-43	82–.427	79–.494	14–.786	17–.882	39	38	Terry 17, Jackson 12	2 with 6	Terry 8
3/25	Cha	70-86	L	25-44	87–.333	84–.429	16–.688	15–.733	46	51	Henderson 17, Mutombo 11	Mutombo 20	Terry 6
3/28	Den	**116**-111	W	26-44	82–.549	89–.483	31–.806	26–.692	47	33	Henderson 24, Mutombo 24	Mutombo 10	Terry 6
3/30	Pho	74-118	L	26-45	79–.354	94–.521	19–.842	13–.923	40	49	Jackson 11, Terry 11	Mutombo 10	Terry 9
4/01	@Hou	93-115	L	26-46	103–.369	89–.506	15–.800	27–.778	44	58	Jackson 21, Henderson 20	Mutombo 15	Terry 10
4/04	@Min	76-86[1]	L	26-47	81–.420	95–.379	11–.455	12–.750	46	52	Jackson 13, Terry 11	Mutombo 16	Coles 5
4/05	@Phi	86-107	L	26-48	76–.447	84–.548	25–.680	23–.652	38	45	Glover 18, Coles 13	Mutombo 16	2 with 5
4/07	Tor	84-104	L	26-49	81–.407	77–.532	18–.722	18–.833	42	39	Henderson 24, 2 with 14	Mutombo 15	Terry 7
4/08	@Was	98-108	L	26-50	78–.462	81–.506	28–.857	29–.724	39	42	Henderson 22, 2 with 15	Mutombo 9	Coles 6
4/10	@Bos	94-99	L	26-51	68–.485	79–.481	31–.774	20–.800	38	31	Jackson 27, Henderson 14	Mutombo 15	2 with 4
4/12	@Cha	87-119	L	26-52	82–.439	81–.543	18–.778	31–.806	31	42	Glover 14, 2 with 13	2 with 7	Terry 8
4/14	Phi	92-104	L	26-53	84–.429	75–.547	16–.938	31–.710	39	38	Terry 20, Mutombo 16	Mutombo 12	Terry 9
4/16	Cle	104-101	W	27-53	74–.527	84–.476	31–.645	25–.760	47	34	Henderson 19, Jackson 17	Mutombo 18	Terry 11
4/18	NJ	111-109[2]	W	28-53	101–.446	101–.426	24–.792	25–.720	60	52	Ellis 16, Terry 16	Mutombo 22	Terry 9
4/19	@Ind	92-111	L	28-54	92–.370	90–.489	29–.690	22–.818	41	58	Wright 23, Jackson 16	Ellis 10	Terry 6

Boston Celtics 1999-2000 Game Log (35-47)

Date	Opp	Score	W/L	Rec	Bos FG Att–Pct.	Opp FG Att–Pct.	Bos FT Att–Pct.	Opp FT Att–Pct.	Bos Reb	Opp Reb	Points	Rebounds	Assists
11/02	@Tor	103-90	W	1-0	73–.521	75–.440	22–.773	30–.700	39	36	Pierce 30, Walker 22	2 with 8	Griffin 7
11/03	Was	112-101	W	2-0	88–.511	79–.456	23–.739	33–.727	43	43	Potapenko 20, 2 with 19	2 with 8	Anderson 10
11/05	Cha	103-100	W	3-0	87–.448	75–.480	29–.724	34–.735	46	41	Anderson 24, Battie 18	Griffin 10	Potapenko 7
11/06	@Ind	108-115	L	3-1	80–.525	75–.480	23–.783	40–.825	38	39	Walker 21, Anderson 20	Potapenko 11	2 with 5
11/10	Det	92-110	L	3-2	75–.413	84–.464	28–.821	29–.897	40	46	Pierce 26, Walker 18	Walker 10	Barros 6
11/12	NY	80-**74**	W	4-2	72–.389	68–.397	27–.556	25–.640	49	36	Walker 22, Pierce 19	Griffin 15	2 with 4
11/13	@Chi	91-92	L	4-3	82–.378	71–.479	35–.743	28–.679	43	44	Walker 24, Anderson 20	Potapenko 11	Anderson 7
11/17	Cle	114-103	W	5-3	81–.432	80–.475	45–.844	34–.735	47	38	Pierce 30, Griffin 23	2 with 11	2 with 4
11/19	NJ	109-96	W	6-3	86–.500	88–.420	23–.739	24–.708	49	39	Walker 25, Pierce 17	Griffin 11	3 with 5
11/20	@Mia	92-110	L	6-4	80–.450	78–.513	21–.667	28–.750	37	37	Walker 18, Pierce 15	Walker 8	Walker 4
11/22	Ind	95-85	W	7-4	82–.451	89–.382	21–.571	15–.733	51	41	Pierce 17, Barros 15	Pierce 12	3 with 4
11/24	SA	98-121	L	7-5	89–.449	81–.580	19–.789	21–.905	36	43	Williams 16, Walker 15	2 with 6	Anderson 5
11/26	Mil	112-114	L	7-6	89–.483	80–.538	20–.800	31–.774	42	41	Walker 27, 2 with 22	Potapenko 11	Overton 5
11/27	@Atl	84-94	L	7-7	78–.385	69–.493	25–.800	32–.781	30	47	Anderson 17, Walker 16	Ellison 8	2 with 3
12/03	Mia	96-84	W	8-7	77–.455	74–.446	31–.710	24–**.500**	47	40	Pierce 26, Anderson 22	Battie 12	Griffin 5
12/04	@Phi	74-77	L	8-8	76–.421	69–.464	15–.533	17–.706	37	37	Pierce 22, Battie 16	Battie 15	Anderson 4
12/08	Den	115-90	W	9-8	91–.516	71–.408	20–.850	44–.682	48	40	Walker 20, 2 with 15	Battie 12	Pierce 8
12/10	Hou	100-96	W	10-8	83–.470	79–.494	25–.760	21–.619	40	45	Anderson 20, Pierce 19	Griffin 10	Griffin 7
12/12	@NY	97-99	L	10-9	89–.393	68–.515	23–.826	34–.765	50	**32**	Walker 24, Potapenko 21	3 with 9	Griffin 5
12/14	@Cle	88-115	L	10-10	80–.413	81–.531	21–.810	24–.958	32	42	Battie 16, Griffin 16	Battie 7	3 with 4
12/15	Uta	86-96	L	10-11	77–.403	68–.500	29–.724	38–.684	41	42	Walker 36, Anderson 14	Walker 12	Walker 4
12/17	@SA	94-103	L	10-12	90–.411	63–.460	22–.636	54–.778	35	46	Barros 18, Battie 16	2 with 6	2 with 5
12/18	@Hou	94-100	L	10-13	80–.488	76–.447	24–.625	40–.700	38	48	Walker 24, Anderson 23	Griffin 9	Anderson 5
12/20	LAL	90-99	L	10-14	89–.404	65–.523	18–.833	41–.683	43	45	Walker 24, Anderson 21	Griffin 9	Anderson 10
12/22	Atl	98-81	W	11-14	83–.482	79–.405	11–.818	25–.640	41	45	Walker 24, Barros 15	Griffin 10	Anderson 10
12/26	@LAC	100-103	L	11-15	77–.494	88–.466	29–.759	21–.619	44	36	Walker 28, Pierce 24	Griffin 9	Pierce 7
12/28	@Sac	101-114	L	11-16	89–.449	75–.520	24–.667	32–.875	39	44	Walker 23, Anderson 17	Griffin 10	Anderson 9
12/30	@Den	102-94	W	12-16	78–.423	77–.390	45–.689	47–.660	43	53	Walker 26, Pierce 21	2 with 8	2 with 6
1/03	Cle	105-98	W	13-16	78–.462	80–.438	37–.811	33–.788	48	38	Walker 32, Pierce 17	Walker 13	2 with 6
1/04	@NY	88-96	L	13-17	81–.395	**60**–.550	31–.710	30–.833	36	36	Pierce 23, Anderson 22	Fortson 8	Anderson 4
1/07	Sac	101-93	W	14-17	86–.477	92–.424	19–.737	**10**–.900	51	45	Pierce 19, Walker 17	3 with 10	Walker 9
1/08	@Chi	79-96	L	14-18	68–.426	67–.493	27–.704	32–.719	37	38	Pierce 20, Walker 16	3 with 6	Anderson 5
1/10	Van	103-112	L	14-19	88–.455	74–.486	22–.773	42–.762	42	43	Pierce 23, Anderson 22	Walker 11	Anderson 8
1/12	LAC	95-88	W	15-19	93–.376	80–.463	26–.731	11–.727	46	47	Pierce 22, Walker 19	Potapenko 11	Anderson 5
1/13	@Min	85-103	L	15-20	83–.373	81–.519	26–.731	19–.789	44	44	Pierce 17, Walker 14	Walker 10	Cheaney 4
1/15	@NJ	99-96	W	16-20	85–.482	76–.382	21–.714	45–.778	42	49	**Walker 39**, Pierce 15	2 with 11	3 with 5
1/17	@Was	105-101	W	17-20	80–.450	69–.507	34–.912	36–.833	37	34	Pierce 34, Walker 31	Walker 11	Anderson 4
1/19	Tor	94-90	W	18-20	84–.393	81–.432	32–.625	19–.789	54	42	Pierce 30, Walker 19	2 with 12	Walker 8
1/21	Sea	111-86	W	19-20	91–.484	93–.376	22–.727	23–.696	60	42	Pierce 21, Walker 21	Fortson 13	2 with 5
1/22	@Cha	96-110	L	19-21	92–.457	75–.520	13–.769	37–.757	41	40	Potapenko 18, Fortson 16	Potapenko 11	Anderson 8
1/25	@Mia	89-115	L	19-22	85–.400	78–.551	25–.760	29–.690	36	47	Walker 28, Barros 18	Potapenko 8	Overton 5
1/26	@Orl	89-111	L	19-23	75–.413	65–.600	24–.833	43–.721	34	34	Walker 26, Potapenko 11	McCarty 13	Anderson 7
1/28	Pho	91-88	W	20-23	78–.410	80–.388	32–.656	22–.864	43	45	Pierce 31, Walker 24	Potapenko 12	Griffin 5
2/01	@Ind	96-99	L	20-24	88–.477	74–.486	12–.583	30–.800	45	42	Walker 27, 2 with 16	Potapenko 12	Anderson 7
2/02	Mia	103-105	L	20-25	87–.414	75–.480	31–.742	31–.903	40	44	Walker 35, Pierce 27	Pierce 10	Anderson 6
2/04	NJ	100-95	W	21-25	78–.474	80–.438	28–.750	24–.792	49	36	Pierce 19, Potapenko 16	Walker 9	Anderson 8
2/06	Por	94-100	L	21-26	77–.455	75–.440	27–.741	39–.769	37	42	Potapenko 19, Pierce 16	Walker 10	Anderson 10
2/08	@NJ	113-131	L	21-27	89–.438	81–.580	34–**.971**	35–.857	46	36	Walker 27, Pierce 17	Pierce 11	Pierce 9
2/09	Ind	104-113	L	21-28	87–.471	78–.564	17–.824	22–.864	31	38	Pierce 27, Potapenko 21	2 with 10	Pierce 7
2/15	@Uta	101-99	W	22-28	77–.468	80–.400	34–.765	33–.879	39	44	Anderson 33, Pierce 20	Walker 9	Anderson 6
2/18	@GS	100-122	L	22-29	78–.385	84–.512	**53**–.679	45–.733	50	51	Fortson 18, Barros 16	Walker 11	Pierce 7
2/19	@Sea	91-94	L	22-30	86–.384	82–.500	26–.808	16–.625	42	44	Pierce 23, Walker 21	3 with 10	Walker 5
2/21	@Por	92-105	L	22-31	86–.372	73–.493	28–.857	40–.775	44	39	Walker 24, 2 with 14	Fortson 14	Anderson 7
2/24	@Van	101-77	W	23-31	81–**.568**	74–.419	13–.538	19–.684	44	**32**	Pierce 25, Walker 24	Fortson 8	Anderson 6

Date	Opp	Score	W/L	Rec	Bos FG Att–Pct.	Opp FG Att–Pct.	Bos FT Att–Pct.	Opp FT Att–Pct.	Bos Reb	Opp Reb	Game Leaders Points	Rebounds	Assists
2/25	@LAL	96-109	L	23-32	89–.416	77–.532	30–.667	38–.658	38	47	Walker 25, Pierce 19	Battie 8	Anderson 10
2/28	Dal	100-108	L	23-33	92–.413	81–.469	25–.800	35–.771	49	38	Walker 23, Pierce 21	Battie 11	2 with 7
3/01	Tor	94-96	L	23-34	86–.430	85–.400	31–.581	27–.815	51	45	Walker 27, Pierce 22	Potapenko 11	Anderson 6
3/03	@Tor	104-114	L	23-35	85–.447	79–.494	28–.857	33–.848	42	38	Williams 22, Anderson 17	Fortson 11	Overton 5
3/05	Orl	97-91	W	24-35	92–.391	82–.463	24–.750	13–.692	46	48	Pierce 19, Walker 18	Griffin 11	Pierce 7
3/08	Mil	112-101	W	25-35	97–.412	83–.470	30–.867	25–.600	**65**	38	Walker 30, Pierce 20	**Walker 19**	Walker 10
3/10	Chi	104-**74**	W	26-35	84–.452	65–.385	32–.750	33–.727	50	39	Anderson 16, Pierce 15	Battie 11	Anderson 7
3/12	Phi	93-77	W	27-35	93–.387	73–.411	25–.800	29–.517	50	44	Pierce 29, Walker 25	Walker 13	Anderson 7
3/13	@Det	115-124	L	27-36	81–.444	71–.563	45–.756	49–.755	40	39	Pierce 38, Walker 30	Potapenko 14	Walker 7
3/15	GS	**121**-104	W	28-36	82–.488	68–.441	44–.818	58–.707	41	39	Walker 25, Pierce 19	Fortson 13	Anderson 7
3/17	@Atl	114-90	W	29-36	99–.495	72–.431	11–.818	34–.765	45	35	Walker 30, 2 with 16	Fortson 9	Anderson 9
3/18	@Dal	104-99	W	30-36	81–.494	87–.437	21–.762	21–.762	47	40	Walker 29, Williams 18	2 with 10	Walker 6
3/20	@Pho	106-110	L	30-37	93–.387	82–.451	34–.882	36–.889	54	42	Pierce 27, Walker 22	Fortson 15	Anderson 5
3/22	Min	106-109	L	30-38	76–.539	81–.481	28–.714	31–.903	33	42	Pierce 25, Walker 22	Potapenko 7	**Anderson 12**
3/24	@Phi	115-117²	L	30-39	**106**–.396	97–.402	32–.719	46–.739	**65**	57	Pierce 31, Walker 24	Potapenko 18	Walker 9
3/26	@Mil	84-99	L	30-40	74–.405	81–.506	28–.714	21–.667	36	34	Walker 22, Williams 14	Fortson 17	Walker 3
3/28	@Orl	87-122	L	30-41	92–.370	85–.553	27–.556	33–.697	33	52	Barros 19, Griffin 11	Potapenko 10	Walker 5
3/31	Was	102-104	L	30-42	79–.481	82–.500	26–.923	19–.895	42	35	Walker 21, Pierce 18	Walker 14	Anderson 5
4/01	@Cle	103-109	L	30-43	89–.404	80–.500	33–.667	30–.833	41	47	Pierce 22, Potapenko 19	Potapenko 9	Anderson 7
4/04	@Cha	105-112	L	30-44	82–.512	65–.569	19–.789	45–.756	28	40	Anderson 23, Walker 22	Walker 7	Walker 10
4/05	@Det	106-111	L	30-45	80–.475	66–.470	33–.606	56–.768	37	38	Anderson 24, Pierce 20	Walker 9	Pierce 6
4/07	Phi	97-102	L	30-46	92–.413	77–.468	17–.882	38–.763	51	40	Anderson 28, Pierce 18	Battie 11	2 with 6
4/10	Atl	99-94	W	31-46	79–.481	68–.485	20–.800	31–.774	31	38	Walker 34, Anderson 24	Fortson 9	Pierce 7
4/12	Orl	95-91	W	32-46	88–.409	82–.402	25–.680	27–.815	50	46	Anderson 23, Walker 22	Fortson 14	Walker 8
4/14	Chi	106-91	W	33-46	82–.488	63–.444	26–.769	38–.789	39	35	Fortson 21, Pierce 20	Fortson 10	Walker 7
4/16	Cha	102-105	L	33-47	83–.446	81–.506	36–.639	25–.760	44	44	Walker 21, Williams 20	Walker 8	Walker 10
4/18	@Was	114-81	W	34-47	84–.536	76–**.368**	27–.593	32–.688	53	34	Fortson 17, Pierce 16	Fortson 12	Walker 4
4/19	NY	112-85	W	35-47	78–.526	83–.398	26–.846	29–.586	41	37	Pierce 19, Anderson 18	Fortson 13	Anderson 6

Charlotte Hornets 1999-2000 Game Log (49-33)

Date	Opp	Score	W/L	Rec	Cha FG Att–Pct.	Opp FG Att–Pct.	Cha FT Att–Pct.	Opp FT Att–Pct.	Cha Reb	Opp Reb	Points	Rebounds	Assists
11/02	Orl	100-86	W	1-0	82–.415	80–.425	37–.595	27–.667	47	48	Jones 24, Phills 20	Campbell 9	Wesley 9
11/04	Ind	98-89	W	2-0	87–.437	71–.479	29–.621	20–.800	38	47	Jones 22, Wesley 17	Mason 10	Wesley 7
11/05	@Bos	100-103	L	2-1	75–.480	87–.448	34–.735	29–.724	41	46	Wesley 17, Phills 15	Mason 8	Wesley 7
11/07	@Tor	99-109	L	2-2	68–.441	88–.545	40–.775	9–.778	38	35	Jones 26, Wesley 23	2 with 10	Wesley 5
11/10	Mil	117-111	W	3-2	79–.519	77–.494	36–.806	29–.862	32	38	Jones 33, Wesley 20	Mason 8	Wesley 10
11/12	NJ	96-92	W	4-2	77–.429	72–.486	34–.794	24–.750	34	39	Jones 24, 2 with 17	Campbell 11	Wesley 11
11/13	@SA	79-95	L	4-3	87–.356	83–.470	20–.750	14–.857	43	48	Coleman 13, Phills 13	2 with 10	Wesley 8
11/16	@Atl	98-103	L	4-4	84–.452	86–.465	22–.818	29–.690	39	49	Jones 20, Mason 20	Mason 16	Wesley 6
11/17	Dal	104-99	W	5-4	82–.402	89–.416	41–.829	26–.808	60	35	Jones 24, Coleman 21	Coleman 18	Jones 9
11/19	@Orl	103-92	W	6-4	86–.477	84–.440	21–.524	24–.625	46	47	Jones 30, Phills 27	Mason 15	Mason 8
11/20	Por	96-100[1]	L	6-5	89–.382	90–.433	36–.694	22–.864	52	41	Campbell 24, Jones 22	Campbell 11	Wesley 9
11/24	Van	89-73	W	7-5	71–.423	78–.385	39–.718	23–.565	41	45	Jones 14, 3 with 12	Mason 10	Wesley 8
11/26	Was	118-85	W	8-5	89–.494	85–.424	33–.788	21–.619	43	42	Campbell 19, R Davis 15	Miller 10	Wesley 10
11/27	@Cle	89-106	L	8-6	90–.333	80–.450	29–.897	38–.816	40	56	Jones 22, Phills 15	Mason 13	B Davis 4
12/01	@Por	90-94	L	8-7	84–.417	72–.514	24–.708	24–.583	38	41	Campbell 19, Coleman 17	Campbell 11	Wesley 11
12/03	@Van	113-94	W	9-7	83–.554	71–.507	22–.773	28–.679	33	35	Wesley 28, Coleman 22	Mason 6	Jones 12
12/05	@Sea	103-81	W	10-7	87–.483	87–.345	22–.773	22–.636	54	42	Coleman 26, Robinson 18	Coleman 11	Wesley 9
12/08	GS	113-106	W	11-7	84–.524	103–.427	28–.750	19–.579	45	55	Jones 30, Coleman 17	Mason 15	Jones 10
12/10	Den	106-99	W	12-7	80–.488	98–.429	29–.828	11–.727	47	43	Mason 21, Miller 17	Mason 12	2 with 8
12/11	@Phi	106-84	W	13-7	94–.457	89–.371	25–.720	27–.667	50	51	Miller 19, R Davis 16	Miller 12	**Wesley 13**
12/15	Min	103-98	W	14-7	75–.520	86–.453	35–.629	21–.857	33	44	Coleman 20, Jones 19	Mason 13	2 with 8
12/17	Cle	99-86	W	15-7	80–.425	92–.380	35–.800	13–.846	51	43	Phills 19, Jones 17	Mason 13	5 with 5
12/18	@Mia	106-89	W	16-7	85–.447	82–.451	32–.750	19–.632	50	36	Jones 24, Coleman 19	Coleman 10	B Davis 8
12/20	@NY	109-112[1]	L	16-8	82–.463	95–.411	35–.743	32–.813	38	57	Jones 23, Wesley 19	Mason 13	Wesley 7
12/23	Orl	106-110	L	16-9	96–.417	86–.465	33–.788	30–.767	43	51	Coleman 20, Robinson 19	3 with 9	B Davis 9
12/26	@Det	96-114	L	16-10	76–.447	73–.562	38–.658	36–.806	31	48	Mason 28, Coleman 17	3 with 6	Wesley 9
12/27	Atl	108-104	W	17-10	71–.493	76–.474	45–.800	31–.839	42	31	Coleman 25, Wesley 23	Coleman 16	Wesley 12
12/29	Mil	109-105	W	18-10	69–.536	89–.483	40–.775	13–.846	36	37	Coleman 27, Campbell 17	Campbell 13	Mason 7
12/30	@Ind	99-109	L	18-11	78–.487	85–.471	27–.593	20–.900	37	42	Wesley 17, Campbell 15	3 with 6	B Davis 9
1/04	@Pho	80-86	L	18-12	81–.321	80–.425	32–.688	13–.692	47	56	Campbell 18, Wesley 18	Coleman 19	Wesley 5
1/05	@Uta	96-118	L	18-13	78–.410	81–.617	37–.730	16–.813	32	42	Wesley 19, 2 with 14	2 with 6	Wesley 5
1/07	@LAL	83-87	L	18-14	73–.411	80–.338	32–.656	34–.735	46	52	3 with 17	Campbell 13	B Davis 5
1/08	@Den	92-97	L	18-15	83–.398	83–.398	29–.724	28–.750	51	38	Coleman 21, Miller 20	Coleman 14	B Davis 6
1/10	@Mil	87-137	L	18-16	82–.402	86–.640	18–.889	15–.933	30	43	Wesley 23, Campbell 12	Miller 8	Campbell 5
1/15	@NY	79-91	L	18-17	69–.333	79–.456	39–.744	12–.833	44	43	Jones 23, Coleman 17	Coleman 13	Wesley 9
1/17	Tor	115-94	W	19-17	68–.515	90–.433	55–.745	24–.625	42	42	Jones 25, Coleman 24	Coleman 11	Wesley 9
1/19	@Chi	96-86	W	20-17	77–.429	83–.398	38–.763	24–.583	54	36	Jones 26, Coleman 20	Coleman 13	Wesley 11
1/20	Phi	109-100	W	21-17	72–.458	87–.448	46–.826	29–.690	42	40	Coleman 23, Jones 23	Mason 9	Jones 8
1/22	Bos	110-96	W	22-17	75–.520	92–.457	37–.757	13–.769	40	41	Coleman 24, Jones 18	2 with 11	2 with 8
1/25	Sac	99-110	L	22-18	86–.430	83–.530	25–.720	17–.765	42	42	Coleman 24, 2 with 16	Campbell 11	Jones 9
1/27	Det	117-102	W	23-18	88–.523	74–.473	24–.708	29–.828	44	34	Jones 25, 2 with 24	Miller 9	Coleman 8
1/29	Pho	100-79	W	24-18	80–.475	78–.397	24–.833	15–.733	51	31	Jones 20, Coleman 19	Miller 12	2 with 6
2/01	@Hou	104-19	L	24-19	87–.368	89–.427	21–.667	21–.714	47	49	Jones 20, 2 with 14	Coleman 11	B Davis 5
2/03	@Dal	96-106	L	24-20	81–.370	75–.533	43–.767	29–.793	46	43	Jones 21, Coleman 19	Campbell 10	2 with 5
2/05	@Was	110-102	W	25-20	72–.458	83–.458	55–.764	25–.800	41	45	Campbell 27, 3 with 20	Coleman 10	2 with 5
2/07	NY	95-85	W	26-20	79–.430	77–.468	18–.944	13–.769	42	39	**Jones 34**, Coleman 29	Coleman 13	Wesley 8
2/09	Cle	103-95	W	27-20	76–.474	89–.427	34–.794	21–.667	39	50	Jones 32, Wesley 30	Campbell 10	2 with 5
2/15	@Phi	95-93	W	28-20	85–.412	88–.455	27–.778	16–.625	57	41	Jones 27, Campbell 19	2 with 12	Wesley 7
2/16	LAL	85-92	L	28-21	77–.416	88–.386	22–.864	28–.821	42	46	Coleman 19, 2 with 18	Campbell 13	Wesley 8
2/18	LAC	115-87	W	29-21	88–.545	85–.400	14–.786	21–.714	52	32	Coleman 17, Jones 16	Campbell 12	B Davis 7
2/20	Mia	80-85	L	29-22	69–.406	72–.389	20–.850	26–.654	41	42	Jones 18, Coleman 16	Coleman 12	Mason 7
2/22	Hou	102-97	W	30-22	83–.494	83–.494	17–.941	11–.636	47	37	Coleman 32, Wesley 21	Coleman 12	Mason 11
2/24	SA	70-72	L	30-23	78–.359	75–.387	13–.692	15–.800	50	42	Coleman 19, Jones 17	**Coleman 20**	Mason 6
2/26	@NJ	93-104	L	30-24	82–.402	83–.482	27–.815	27–.778	45	44	Coleman 24, Jones 23	Coleman 10	Wesley 7

Date	Opp	Score	W/L	Rec	Cha FG Att–Pct.	Opp FG Att–Pct.	Cha FT Att–Pct.	Opp FT Att–Pct.	Cha Reb	Opp Reb	Points	Rebounds	Assists
											Game Leaders		
2/28	Sea	81-84	L	30-25	87–.368	76–.421	15–.867	26–**.462**	51	41	Jones 23, 2 with 14	Mason 13	Wesley 9
2/29	@Min	92-87	W	31-25	72–.444	80–.488	31–.839	14–.571	38	40	Campbell 22, Jones 17	2 with 8	Jones 5
3/02	@Orl	96-104	L	31-26	84–.464	78–.500	18–.778	27–.778	36	45	Campbell 22, 2 with 17	Mason 13	2 with 5
3/03	Uta	87-89	L	31-27	77–.455	82–.451	14–.714	16–.750	39	43	Jones 31, B Davis 13	Campbell 11	Jones 7
3/05	Chi	100-94	W	32-27	75–.427	75–.480	40–.775	22–.727	33	45	Coleman 26, Jones 23	2 with 7	Wesley 11
3/07	@GS	102-99	W	33-27	78–.436	82–.415	42–.762	40–.750	49	49	**Coleman 34**, Jones 19	Coleman 17	Mason 8
3/08	@Sac	92-105	L	33-28	78–.474	92–.511	21–.762	13–.692	42	43	Wesley 21, Coleman 17	Campbell 13	Wesley 6
3/10	@LAC	118-101	W	34-28	86–.523	85–.471	35–.714	18–.778	45	42	Coleman 31, Jones 21	2 with 12	B Davis 7
3/15	Chi	77-74	W	35-28	68–.397	82–.341	27–.778	17–.882	47	48	Jones 18, Wesley 18	**Campbell 20**	Jones 8
3/17	NY	99-118	L	35-29	81–.494	76–.553	24–.750	31–.903	33	39	Wesley 24, Campbell 20	Campbell 10	B Davis 7
3/18	@Ind	99-113	L	35-30	85–.424	79–.532	29–.793	29–.828	36	45	Coleman 28, Campbell 21	2 with 10	Jones 4
3/20	Phi	96-102	L	35-31	75–.507	91–.462	27–.630	23–.609	41	46	Jones 28, Wesley 17	Mason 11	Wesley 10
3/22	NJ	**119**-103	W	36-31	82–.561	86–.465	27–.778	23–.783	39	38	Jones 26, 2 with 22	3 with 7	3 with 7
3/24	@Tor	102-84	W	37-31	79–.494	84–.357	22–.864	17–.941	48	36	Jones 25, Mason 20	Coleman 12	Mason 6
3/25	@Atl	86-**70**	W	38-31	84–.429	87–**.333**	15–.733	16–.688	51	46	Jones 24, Mason 12	2 with 15	Mason 11
3/29	@Det	98-91	W	39-31	71–.493	91–.385	36–.750	24–.750	44	46	Mason 22, Wesley 18	Campbell 13	Mason 8
3/31	Tor	110-101[1]	W	40-31	79–.494	89–.438	30–.933	21–.762	40	45	Jones 32, Mason 31	Mason 14	Mason 11
4/01	@Chi	90-87	W	41-31	76–.421	72–.486	30–.733	23–.652	38	38	Campbell 25, Jones 23	2 with 9	Mason 7
4/04	Bos	112-105	W	42-31	65–**.569**	82–.512	45–.756	19–.789	40	**28**	Mason 27, 2 with 25	Coleman 14	Wesley 9
4/06	@Mia	70-76	L	42-32	81–.309	74–.419	25–.720	11–.636	41	50	Mason 14, 2 with 12	Mason 15	2 with 3
4/07	Det	82-97	L	42-33	79–.380	82–.427	32–.594	21–.762	48	48	B Davis 14, 2 with 10	2 with 10	Coleman 5
4/09	Ind	96-80	W	43-33	74–.419	84–.369	38–.789	14–.857	51	44	3 with 19	Campbell 13	2 with 5
4/10	@Was	107-105	W	44-33	81–.506	80–.513	37–.649	26–.769	42	34	Jones 26, Wesley 21	Coleman 16	Mason 9
4/12	Atl	**119**-87	W	45-33	81–.543	82–.439	31–.806	18–.778	42	31	Wesley 29, Miller 15	Miller 8	Mason 10
4/14	@Mil	109-106[1]	W	46-33	89–.449	88–.420	26–.808	28–.857	46	45	Jones 29, Wesley 24	Coleman 12	2 with 6
4/16	@Bos	105-102	W	47-33	81–.506	83–.446	25–.760	36–.639	44	44	Jones 25, Robinson 16	Mason 12	B Davis 5
4/18	@Cle	103-88	W	48-33	83–.458	100–.350	25–.800	17–.824	47	57	Wesley 23, Coleman 21	2 with 11	4 with 5
4/19	Mia	83-73	W	49-33	63–.492	72–.403	23–.913	14–.857	32	36	Jones 14, Mason 14	Campbell 8	B Davis 7

Postseason

Date	Opp	Score	W/L	Rec	Cha FG Att–Pct.	Opp FG Att–Pct.	Cha FT Att–Pct.	Opp FT Att–Pct.	Cha Reb	Opp Reb	Points	Rebounds	Assists
4/22	Phi	82-92	L	0-1	65–.369	78–.423	39–.769	31–.710	51	36	Coleman 23, 3 with 14	Coleman 16	Wesley 4
4/24	Phi	108-98[1]	W	1-1	83–.530	86–.430	16–.875	19–.842	41	42	Coleman 29, Campbell 20	Campbell 14	Jones 8
4/28	@Phi	76-81	L	1-2	71–.352	78–.346	25–.880	28–.786	40	48	Jones 18, 2 with 14	Coleman 17	Mason 7
5/01	@Phi	99-105	L	1-3	81–.444	78–.513	28–.821	23–.783	44	36	Campbell 21, Mason 21	2 with 11	Jones 8

Chicago Bulls 1999-2000 Game Log (17-65)

Date	Opp	Score	W/L	Rec	Chi FG Att–Pct.	Opp FG Att–Pct.	Chi FT Att–Pct.	Opp FT Att–Pct.	Chi Reb	Opp Reb	Game Leaders Points	Rebounds	Assists
11/03	NY	74-84	L	0-1	69–.304	76–.474	**40**–.725	**9**–.889	32	48	Simpkins 17, 2 with 14	Brand 8	2 with 3
11/05	Mia	87-105	L	0-2	78–.385	71–.507	27–.741	30–.800	38	41	Kukoc 25, Hoiberg 11	Brand 6	Hoiberg 7
11/06	@Atl	97-113	L	0-3	80–.438	81–.543	35–.686	34–.647	39	42	Brand 21, Kukoc 21	Brand 12	Kukoc 5
11/09	Pho	80-103	L	0-4	74–.365	72–.556	38–.632	32–.656	36	43	Brand 11, 2 with 10	Perdue 7	Hoiberg 4
11/12	@Phi	86-92	L	0-5	79–.430	69–.493	14–**.929**	33–.697	33	40	Hawkins 30, Hoiberg 14	Simpkins 7	Hawkins 7
11/13	Bos	92-91	W	1-5	71–.479	82–.378	28–.679	35–.743	44	43	Hoiberg 19, Brown 18	2 with 7	2 with 4
11/16	@GS	79-99	L	1-6	**92**–.348	87–.437	21–.524	30–.700	52	59	Brand 17, 2 with 14	2 with 9	Artest 6
11/17	@Pho	81-105	L	1-7	64–.422	76–.553	35–.686	22–.818	30	35	Brand 19, Artest 14	Brand 6	4 with 2
11/19	@LAL	95-103	L	1-8	86–.360	**63**–.460	38–.684	64–.672	41	46	Brand 29, Artest 20	Brand 17	2 with 4
11/20	@Den	86-95	L	1-9	87–.414	86–.430	20–.700	34–.765	41	37	Anstey 18, David 17	Brand 9	Brown 6
11/24	@Mil	95-102	L	1-10	76–.487	77–.442	19–.737	34–.912	36	36	Brand 16, Hawkins 15	Perdue 10	Brown 6
11/26	@SA	78-101	L	1-11	79–.354	74–.514	32–.656	27–.741	43	44	Brand 24, Hawkins 15	David 8	Brown 6
11/27	@Dal	83-95	L	1-12	82–.439	75–.493	12–.833	18–.944	43	34	Brand 18, 2 with 12	2 with 9	Brown 6
12/02	Dal	95-101	L	1-13	88–.386	84–.476	36–.694	24–.708	55	37	Artest 20, Brand 14	Anstey 15	Willoughby 5
12/04	Mil	91-92	L	1-14	79–.380	70–.543	33–.758	20–.800	44	34	Artest 21, Brand 19	Brand 17	2 with 6
12/08	@Cle	93-107	L	1-15	82–.451	77–.494	24–.667	35–.686	35	40	Benjamin 15, Perdue 13	2 with 7	Brown 4
12/10	NJ	71-69	W	2-15	75–.360	72–.375	24–.583	17–.588	54	38	Brand 16, Artest 14	Brand 14	Artest 7
12/11	@Orl	87-108	L	2-16	75–.427	82–.488	21–.762	27–.889	37	40	Artest 20, Brand 16	Brand 10	Willoughby 5
12/15	@Ind	91-102	L	2-17	82–.488	79–.430	12–.667	28–.893	37	40	Willoughby 21, 2 with 16	Perdue 10	Willoughby 8
12/17	@Phi	74-77	L	2-18	73–.411	73–.425	13–.923	22–.682	38	32	Benjamin 16, Artest 15	Brand 11	Armstrong 7
12/18	Orl	74-83	L	2-19	83–.337	86–.384	16–.875	23–.652	51	51	Brand 19, Benjamin 13	Brand 10	Benjamin 5
12/20	Sea	84-93	L	2-20	80–.425	74–.459	18–.667	24–.750	42	43	Benjamin 19, 3 with 14	Brand 9	Artest 7
12/22	Min	86-106	L	2-21	81–.407	80–.525	28–.679	28–.750	39	42	Brand 17, 2 with 14	Brand 8	LaRue 5
12/26	@NJ	76-103	L	2-22	77–.364	85–.435	27–.741	28–.821	45	47	Brand 22, Benjamin 15	Brand 11	Artest 5
12/27	Ind	91-103	L	2-23	81–.432	80–.500	22–.636	21–.810	49	36	Artest 22, Brand 22	Brand 13	2 with 7
12/29	Det	77-91	L	2-24	71–.408	80–.363	22–.636	36–.806	40	44	Armstrong 22, Brand 17	Brand 10	Artest 7
12/30	@Min	76-94	L	2-25	70–.400	71–.507	23–.696	23–.870	30	39	Benjamin 21, 2 with 9	Ruffin 8	Reeves 8
1/03	Por	63-88	L	2-26	77–.338	72–.500	17–.529	19–.737	43	39	Brand 23, Benjamin 19	Brand 10	Armstrong 7
1/05	Was	77-**66**	W	3-26	75–.360	84–**.286**	29–.655	20–.700	56	46	Kukoc 18, 2 with 16	Brand 16	2 with 5
1/07	@Was	**110**-103	W	4-26	69–**.594**	75–.533	27–.778	27–.630	34	26	Kukoc 33, Artest 19	Brand 13	**Kukoc 10**
1/08	Bos	96-79	W	5-26	67–.493	68–.426	32–.719	27–.704	38	37	Brand 26, Kukoc 23	Brand 14	Kukoc 8
1/11	@NY	88-95	L	5-27	70–.443	70–.471	37–.541	27–.926	36	37	Artest 24, Brand 22	2 with 7	Kukoc 8
1/14	Atl	83-89	L	5-28	88–.386	79–.443	14–.857	19–.737	46	37	Anstey 19, Kukoc 19	Brand 14	Kukoc 9
1/15	Hou	90-93	L	5-29	76–.434	76–.500	27–.741	21–**.476**	38	41	Kukoc 29, Brand 15	Brand 11	Kukoc 7
1/18	@Mia	92-85[1]	W	6-29	80–.438	75–.413	31–.613	26–.692	43	42	Brand 24, Kukoc 23	Brand 13	Kukoc 4
1/19	Cha	86-96	L	6-30	83–.398	77–.429	24–.583	38–.763	36	54	Brand 24, Artest 19	Brand 11	Kukoc 5
1/22	Det	98-92	W	7-30	67–.463	87–.391	**40**–.700	31–.613	53	39	Kukoc 22, Brand 20	2 with 14	Kukoc 5
1/24	Ind	83-82	W	8-30	75–.440	85–.400	30–.533	12–.833	40	49	Brand 28, Artest 17	Brand 8	Artest 7
1/25	@Atl	89-96	L	8-31	81–.395	84–.452	29–.724	23–.783	42	52	Brand 22, Artest 17	Simpkins 11	Kukoc 5
1/28	Sac	90-102	L	8-32	81–.432	86–.477	24–.667	19–.632	45	41	Brand 30, Carr 16	**Brand 18**	Brown 6
1/29	Tor	89-106	L	8-33	79–.456	70–.586	17–.765	25–.720	38	32	Artest 18, Brand 16	Brand 9	Brand 6
2/01	@Por	81-92	L	8-34	80–.388	78–.474	17–.765	20–.850	34	51	Brand 22, Kukoc 12	Brand 8	Kukoc 4
2/02	@Sea	88-81	W	9-34	77–.442	73–.466	24–.750	12–.583	39	34	Kukoc 31, Artest 24	Simpkins 10	Brown 6
2/04	@Van	76-101	L	9-35	70–.400	81–.481	23–.783	22–.818	34	46	Kukoc 27, Brand 22	Perdue 8	3 with 2
2/06	@LAC	100-90	W	10-35	70–.543	75–.493	24–.792	18–.778	36	**24**	Brand 21, Kukoc 20	Brand 8	**Kukoc 10**
2/08	@Sac	80-119	L	10-36	72–.431	94–.511	19–.632	11–1.000	41	41	Brand 25, Kukoc 12	Brand 10	Brown 6
2/09	@Uta	86-113	L	10-37	63–.476	77–.584	29–.690	26–.731	25	37	Brand 13, Brown 12	Hawkins 5	Brown 6
2/15	LAL	76-88	L	10-38	77–.377	82–.402	15–.867	20–.850	37	49	Artest 16, Kukoc 14	Brand 8	Maloney 5
2/17	Mia	83-76	W	11-38	75–.360	79–.405	27–.815	11–.545	47	40	Brand 26, Hawkins 20	Brand 10	Brand 5
2/19	LAC	74-72	W	12-38	77–.286	78–.385	**40**–.575	13–.538	46	55	Carr 19, Hawkins 14	**Brand 18**	2 with 4
2/22	Van	81-85	L	12-39	77–.443	70–.414	28–.571	32–.800	40	48	Brand 25, Starks 17	Brand 9	3 with 4
2/24	@Ind	83-100	L	12-40	81–.444	75–.493	8–.875	22–.818	34	42	Brand 38, Starks 11	2 with 7	Simpkins 4
2/25	SA	78-91	L	12-41	76–.382	76–.461	27–.630	26–.654	48	39	Hoiberg 18, 3 with 10	Brand 12	Brown 4
2/27	@Det	90-93	L	12-42	75–.427	76–.421	23–.783	36–.750	44	37	Brand 28, 2 with 14	Brand 12	2 with 4

Date	Opp	Score	W/L	Rec	Chi FG Att–Pct.	Opp FG Att–Pct.	Chi FT Att–Pct.	Opp FT Att–Pct.	Chi Reb	Opp Reb	Game Leaders Points	Rebounds	Assists
2/29	@Tor	80-87	L	12-43	74–.459	85–.412	15–.533	17–.706	38	48	Brand 26, Carr 13	2 with 8	Artest 5
3/02	Cle	**110**-114[1]	L	12-44	80–.488	91–.462	36–.833	30–.800	45	42	Brand 30, Artest 15	Brand 11	Brown 6
3/04	Phi	84-95	L	12-45	70–.414	86–.430	26–.692	25–.680	33	49	Artest 18, Maloney 17	Brand 8	Maloney 6
3/05	@Cha	94-100	L	12-46	75–.480	75–.427	22–.727	40–.775	45	33	Brand 24, Hoiberg 20	Brand 11	Brown 7
3/07	Atl	89-82	W	13-46	90–.356	85–.435	23–.870	**9**–.778	44	52	Brand 31, Hoiberg 14	Simpkins 9	Brown 7
3/08	@Orl	67-103	L	13-47	69–.333	81–.506	24–.708	21–.857	40	46	Carr 13, Brand 11	Brand 11	3 with 2
3/10	@Bos	74-104	L	13-48	65–.385	84–.452	33–.727	32–.750	39	50	Brand 16, Brown 15	Brand 9	Maloney 4
3/13	Uta	79-87	L	13-49	64–.391	80–.350	33–.818	35–.743	45	43	Brand 26, Carr 14	Brand 12	Brown 5
3/15	@Cha	74-77	L	13-50	82–.341	68–.397	17–.882	27–.778	48	47	Carr 18, Brand 12	Brand 12	Hoiberg 6
3/17	GS	92-95[2]	L	13-51	81–.420	78–.423	30–.667	38–.632	45	43	Brand 26, Hoiberg 18	Simpkins 12	Brown 7
3/18	@Was	88-101	L	13-52	65–.462	88–.443	33–.788	21–.905	38	48	Brand 24, Artest 14	Simpkins 10	Armstrong 4
3/20	Orl	86-88[1]	L	13-53	85–.400	83–.373	20–.650	35–.686	**65**	39	Brand 18, 2 with 12	Brand 17	Hawkins 7
3/22	@NY	67-78	L	13-54	69–.362	73–.452	17–.824	11–.909	36	42	Brand 22, 2 with 14	Brand 13	Maloney 7
3/24	Den	70-68	W	14-54	79–.304	75–.333	28–.679	29–.552	46	55	Brand 26, Artest 15	Brand 15	Brown 9
3/26	@Hou	78-123	L	14-55	81–.407	85–.529	11–.909	23–.783	33	47	Brand 24, Artest 22	Artest 8	Brand 4
3/29	Cle	81-86	L	14-56	81–.383	76–.421	18–.722	27–.667	43	39	Brand 27, Hawkins 20	Anstey 11	Hawkins 6
3/30	@Mia	80-105	L	14-57	58–.466	71–.535	32–.750	34–.765	31	39	Brand 17, Hoiberg 15	2 with 5	Brown 4
4/01	Cha	87-90	L	14-58	72–.486	76–.421	23–.652	30–.733	38	38	Brand 24, Artest 20	Brand 8	2 with 5
4/02	@Cle	83-74	W	15-58	71–.408	74–.392	32–.656	15–.800	52	32	Brand 23, Artest 18	Brand 14	Brown 5
4/04	@Mil	73-92	L	15-59	67–.358	83–.446	31–.742	20–.750	45	40	Brand 18, Artest 16	Simpkins 9	Hawkins 5
4/06	Mil	90-88	W	16-59	70–.443	90–.400	31–.677	21–.714	45	47	Brand 20, Hawkins 20	Brand 13	Hawkins 6
4/08	Tor	79-98	L	16-60	66–.394	75–.520	28–.786	16–.500	38	38	Artest 17, Brand 16	Brand 11	Armstrong 5
4/11	NJ	100-93	W	17-60	67–.537	82–.427	29–.586	28–.786	45	36	Brand 22, Maloney 19	Brand 15	Brand 7
4/13	Was	103-109	L	17-61	77–.519	82–.476	23–.826	26–.808	34	38	**Brand 44**, Carr 14	Brand 12	Maloney 7
4/14	@Bos	91-106	L	17-62	63–.444	82–.488	38–.789	26–.769	35	39	Brand 18, Ruffin 14	Ruffin 10	2 with 4
4/16	@Tor	84-85	L	17-63	72–.444	78–.410	23–.783	18–.889	41	36	Brand 24, Carr 15	Ruffin 10	Carr 4
4/18	Phi	89-93	L	17-64	70–.486	76–.474	21–.762	30–.633	37	42	Brand 26, Anstey 17	Brand 10	Maloney 7
4/19	@Det	91-112	L	17-65	72–.417	69–.638	32–.781	25–.680	34	31	Brand 32, Hoiberg 15	Brand 11	2 with 4

Cleveland Cavaliers 1999-2000 Game Log (32-50)

Date	Opp	Score	W/L	Rec	Cle FG Att–Pct.	Opp FG Att–Pct.	Cle FT Att–Pct.	Opp FT Att–Pct.	Cle Reb	Opp Reb	Game Leaders Points	Rebounds	Assists
11/02	@NY	84-92	L	0-1	77–.390	74–.432	23–.739	27–.815	38	44	Kemp 17, Person 16	DeClercq 7	Sura 8
11/03	NJ	97-90	W	1-1	81–.469	82–.341	20–.850	35–.857	48	40	Kemp 27, Knight 16	Kemp 15	2 with 7
11/05	@Orl	104-99	W	2-1	90–.489	95–.389	14–.786	27–.815	41	51	Knight 18, Miller 18	Kemp 10	2 with 7
11/06	NY	102-93	W	3-1	72–.444	82–.439	44–.795	19–.842	44	40	Kemp 25, Knight 18	Kemp 9	Knight 7
11/11	Sea	103-109	L	3-2	103–.408	94–.447	17–.706	27–.630	54	53	Kemp 22, DeClercq 19	Kemp 14	Knight 7
11/13	Mil	117-112	W	4-2	81–.469	84–.452	49–.735	39–.795	41	42	Sura 23, Knight 18	Kemp 12	Knight 12
11/17	@Bos	103-114	L	4-3	80–.475	81–.432	34–.735	45–.844	38	47	Kemp 27, Sura 14	Kemp 8	Knight 6
11/19	@Det	90-101	L	4-4	84–.393	74–.432	27–.704	45–.800	35	53	Miller 23, Sura 18	Kemp 13	4 with 3
11/20	Ind	98-107	L	4-5	77–.519	91–.495	16–.813	14–.571	43	34	Kemp 29, Sura 21	Kemp 15	2 with 7
11/23	Por	103-100	W	5-5	76–.500	88–.398	27–.852	28–.893	34	51	Kemp 28, Murray 20	Kemp 10	Knight 12
11/26	@Phi	83-106	L	5-6	71–.423	82–.439	28–.679	41–.732	42	49	Murray 15, Sura 15	2 with 8	Knight 11
11/27	Cha	106-89	W	6-6	80–.450	90–.333	38–.816	29–.897	56	40	DeClercq 16, Murray 16	**Murray 16**	2 with 6
11/30	Dal	106-99	W	7-6	86–.442	88–.409	32–.813	24–.792	55	40	Kemp 25, DeClercq 17	DeClercq 15	Knight 10
12/01	@Was	111-108	W	8-6	76–.434	82–.463	53–.755	41–.659	43	43	Kemp 27, Sura 18	Kemp 14	Knight 6
12/03	Phi	100-102[1]	L	8-7	81–.444	91–.451	33–.667	23–.826	44	49	Murray 22, Sura 20	Kemp 11	Knight 12
12/07	@Tor	98-101	L	8-8	80–.438	89–.427	35–.714	20–.800	41	47	Knight 20, Kemp 16	DeClercq 10	Knight 11
12/08	Chi	107-93	W	9-8	77–.494	82–.451	35–.686	24–.667	40	35	Sura 29, Kemp 21	DeClercq 12	2 with 6
12/10	@Ind	88-136	L	9-9	101–.337	79–.620	27–.667	37–.757	49	51	Person 13, DeClercq 12	2 with 7	2 with 6
12/11	Atl	127-116	W	10-9	92–.500	79–.418	39–.744	55–.782	41	42	Kemp 29, Sura 24	Kemp 11	**Knight 15**
12/14	Bos	115-88	W	11-9	81–.531	80–.413	24–**.958**	21–.810	43	**32**	Sura 22, Murray 20	2 with 8	Sura 10
12/15	@NJ	101-111	L	11-10	73–**.562**	82–.463	22–.591	31–.903	30	38	Kemp 36, Person 22	2 with 5	Miller 9
12/17	@Cha	86-99	L	11-11	92–.380	80–.425	13–.846	35–.800	43	51	Kemp 15, Murray 15	Kemp 10	Miller 7
12/18	NJ	74-98	L	11-12	77–.364	77–.455	24–.667	23–.913	43	42	Kemp 14, Sura 12	Knight 7	Knight 11
12/20	Min	94-100	L	11-13	76–.447	77–.416	31–.742	44–.818	40	46	Sura 20, 2 with 16	DeClercq 14	Sura 7
12/22	Orl	97-103	L	11-14	90–.378	86–.477	27–.741	29–.586	51	44	Sura 28, Kemp 18	Kemp 11	Miller 7
12/23	@Atl	90-108	L	11-15	89–.371	92–.446	24–.792	29–.828	40	56	Kemp 17, Sura 17	Kemp 8	Knight 9
12/26	Tor	95-98	L	11-16	88–.364	77–.455	31–.806	25–.960	44	44	Murray 20, Sura 20	Kemp 13	Knight 9
12/29	Was	96-94	W	12-16	84–.464	82–.439	24–.625	28–.643	41	40	Kemp 35, Murray 15	DeClercq 11	Knight 9
12/30	@Mil	90-91	L	12-17	81–.457	74–.419	14–.714	37–.757	42	41	Sura 19, Murray 11	Sura 12	Knight 6
1/03	@Bos	98-105	L	12-18	80–.438	78–.462	33–.788	37–.811	38	48	Kemp 23, Murray 22	2 with 9	Knight 10
1/04	Sac	107-111	L	12-19	83–.518	83–.434	24–.667	41–.707	42	42	Sura 26, Kemp 21	Kemp 11	Knight 12
1/06	GS	90-**75**	W	13-19	89–.427	98–**.306**	21–.571	14–.786	53	53	Murray 20, Miller 13	Murray 8	Miller 7
1/08	@NY	89-86	W	14-19	73–.411	75–.453	28–.821	20–.700	39	33	Sura 25, Murray 15	Bryant 8	2 with 5
1/10	LAC	111-106	W	15-19	82–.476	80–.425	39–.744	31–.903	45	**32**	Murray 20, Sura 20	Kemp 7	Knight 14
1/12	@Por	75-95	L	15-20	73–.384	79–.532	24–.667	12–.750	36	40	Kemp 16, Murray 17	DeClercq 8	Knight 4
1/14	@Van	82-80	W	16-20	82–.415	77–.403	18–.778	19–.842	44	39	Kemp 24, Knight 16	2 with 10	Sura 11
1/16	@Sac	102-113	L	16-21	92–.424	86–.488	31–.774	29–.690	56	39	Kemp 20, 2 with 18	2 with 11	2 with 5
1/18	@Sea	80-99	L	16-22	83–.373	74–.514	19–.789	23–.783	38	41	Murray 20, Kemp 13	DeClercq 8	2 with 4
1/19	@LAL	86-95	L	16-23	84–.381	81–.346	32–.656	50–.700	50	59	Miller 20, Knight 15	2 with 8	Knight 6
1/21	@GS	103-115	L	16-24	84–.440	87–.471	36–.694	29–.828	44	49	**Murray 38**, Kemp 18	Kemp 14	Kemp 5
1/22	@Pho	88-101	L	16-25	71–.479	76–.447	25–.640	29–.897	30	38	Kemp 20, Sura 12	Kemp 9	2 with 10
1/25	Det	116-107[1]	W	17-25	88–.455	85–.424	41–.756	39–.718	46	50	Sura 31, Murray 19	2 with 10	Sura 9
1/27	Orl	102-90	W	18-25	77–.442	87–.402	43–.744	17–.824	48	45	Murray 24, Kemp 20	Kemp 14	2 with 7
1/29	@Was	98-103	L	18-26	84–.417	82–.488	28–.821	25–.840	39	40	Sura 23, Kemp 14	Kemp 10	Knight 10
2/01	Was	112-108	W	19-26	83–.434	80–.488	47–.702	30–.700	44	45	Kemp 28, Ferry 18	Kemp 12	Miller 7
2/04	@Det	96-105	L	19-27	82–.500	80–.425	16–.750	34–.824	36	46	Kemp 22, Murray 19	Kemp 7	Person 5
2/05	Atl	94-102	L	19-28	83–.386	89–.438	30–.867	25–.920	42	50	Miller 28, Person 18	Miller 10	Miller 12
2/08	@Hou	83-91	L	19-29	82–.439	85–.447	13–.692	15–.600	51	40	Kemp 23, Miller 21	Kemp 10	Miller 7
2/09	@Cha	95-103	L	19-30	89–.427	76–.474	21–.667	34–.794	50	39	Murray 31, Kemp 16	Person 12	Miller 13
2/15	SA	92-81	W	20-30	81–.420	75–.387	24–.833	23–.783	43	35	Murray 27, Miller 20	Murray 12	2 with 7
2/17	Den	119-101	W	21-30	87–.529	85–.424	24–.875	32–.824	47	40	Murray 24, Person 24	2 with 9	Miller 13
2/18	@Phi	75-104	L	21-31	83–.349	78–.487	18–.778	37–.676	43	50	Kemp 17, Person 15	Kemp 13	Miller 10
2/21	Van	109-108[1]	W	22-31	83–.458	88–.477	30–.833	23–.913	42	42	Kemp 26, Murray 25	Kemp 11	Miller 14
2/23	LAL	98-116	L	22-32	79–.468	89–.517	23–.783	16–.813	41	36	Kemp 23, Miller 23	3 with 8	Miller 9

Date	Opp	Score	W/L	Rec	Cle FG Att–Pct.	Opp FG Att–Pct.	Cle FT Att–Pct.	Opp FT Att–Pct.	Cle Reb	Opp Reb	Points	Rebounds	Assists
2/25	@Mia	82-87	L	22-33	78–.410	80–.400	17–.706	19–.895	38	48	Murray 28, Miller 12	Kemp 10	Miller 7
2/29	Pho	93-100	L	22-34	79–.418	85–.424	26–.846	31–.742	43	45	Murray 18, Miller 16	Murray 9	Miller 12
3/02	@Chi	114-110[1]	W	23-34	91–.462	80–.488	30–.800	36–.833	42	45	Kemp 25, Miller 24	Kemp 10	Miller 12
3/04	@LAC	109-99	W	24-34	67–.478	78–.436	54–.778	34–.794	45	37	Kemp 22, 2 with 18	Murray 9	Miller 7
3/05	@Den	100-92	W	25-34	82–.439	93–.376	30–.767	23–.696	49	51	Murray 20, Miller 15	2 with 9	Miller 9
3/07	@Uta	95-113	L	25-35	74–.500	80–.600	21–.714	20–.750	34	36	Miller 15, 2 with 14	2 with 6	Miller 8
3/10	Ind	92-95	L	25-36	94–.426	68–.471	9–.667	30–.733	41	45	Murray 25, Miller 17	Murray 11	Miller 14
3/12	@Mil	72-103	L	25-37	68–.397	85–.459	28–.643	24–.875	33	49	Murray 16, Miller 15	Kemp 7	2 with 3
3/14	Phi	97-98[1]	L	25-38	87–.425	82–.427	22–.818	34–.735	45	42	Murray 16, Ferry 15	4 with 7	Miller 8
3/16	Uta	86-107	L	25-39	79–.418	78–.474	23–.739	35–.829	39	43	Ferry 15, Kemp 13	Ferry 9	Sura 5
3/18	Mia	90-92[1]	L	25-40	76–.355	89–.371	41–.756	30–.600	49	48	Kemp 22, Murray 14	Kemp 12	2 with 6
3/20	Hou	98-85	W	26-40	83–.470	75–.467	19–.842	23–.522	44	39	Kemp 17, Murray 17	Kemp 10	Knight 10
3/21	@Min	107-111[1]	L	26-41	91–.495	89–.483	17–.706	28–.857	45	44	Murray 16, 2 with 15	Murray 9	Knight 8
3/23	@Dal	104-98	W	27-41	84–.488	92–.391	22–.864	26–.808	52	44	Kemp 22, Henderson 15	Kemp 12	Knight 11
3/25	@SA	76-96	L	27-42	78–.410	77–.481	18–.611	22–.773	31	51	Miller 15, Murray 14	2 with 6	Miller 8
3/28	Tor	96-99	L	27-43	80–.488	74–.459	21–.762	24–.833	39	37	Murray 30, Kemp 20	Kemp 9	Miller 14
3/29	@Chi	86-81	W	28-43	76–.421	81–.383	27–.667	18–.722	39	43	Sura 20, Murray 16	Kemp 11	Knight 6
4/01	Bos	109-103	W	29-43	80–.500	89–.404	30–.833	33–.667	47	41	Kemp 22, Henderson 20	Kemp 14	Knight 12
4/02	Chi	74-83	L	29-44	74–.392	71–.408	15–.800	32–.656	32	52	Murray 16, Bryant 12	Bryant 8	Miller 4
4/04	@Mia	85-111	L	29-45	71–.479	82–.537	25–.560	21–.810	30	42	Person 14, Boykins 12	Ketner 5	Miller 5
4/07	@Ind	94-95	L	29-46	83–.470	78–.449	21–.762	29–.759	44	43	Kemp 23, Murray 20	Kemp 13	Miller 7
4/08	Det	117-98	W	30-46	83–.482	89–.360	38–.816	38–.737	57	46	Kemp 25, 2 with 21	Kemp 13	Miller 7
4/10	@Tor	103-112	L	30-47	84–.512	76–.526	20–.750	34–.765	36	40	Kemp 22, Sura 19	Murray 7	Knight 7
4/12	Mil	100-101	L	30-48	82–.427	81–.457	36–.667	30–.800	44	46	Person 21, 2 with 15	DeClercq 8	Knight 8
4/15	NY	106-96	W	31-48	87–.471	70–.414	18–.833	40–.850	42	39	Miller 18, Murray 16	Bryant 8	2 with 9
4/16	@Atl	101-104	L	31-49	84–.476	74–.527	25–.760	31–.645	34	47	Kemp 20, Sura 18	Murray 10	Miller 5
4/18	Cha	88-103	L	31-50	100–.350	83–.458	17–.824	25–.800	57	47	Sura 20, Miller 16	Kemp 14	Miller 10
4/19	@NJ	111-108	W	32-50	86–.535	89–.449	22–.727	29–.793	47	42	Murray 27, Kemp 23	Kemp 13	Knight 12

Dallas Mavericks 1999-2000 Game Log (40-42)

Date	Opp	Score	W/L	Rec	Dal FG Att–Pct.	Opp FG Att–Pct.	Dal FT Att–Pct.	Opp FT Att–Pct.	Dal Reb	Opp Reb	Points	Rebounds	Assists
											Game Leaders		
11/02	GS	108-96	W	1-0	85–.459	82–.415	34–.824	27–.778	41	51	Ceballos 27, Finley 26	2 with 7	Strickland 5
11/04	@Sea	96-106	L	1-1	89–.472	100–.420	15–.667	20–.850	41	58	Ceballos 34, Nowitzki 15	Bradley 8	Pack 11
11/06	@GS	120-97	W	2-1	89–.506	106–.358	26–.885	23–.739	44	59	Finley 23, Ceballos 22	Ceballos 13	Pack 8
11/07	@LAL	97-105	L	2-2	82–.427	86–.465	30–.800	37–.541	42	51	Finley 29, Nowitzki 20	Nowitzki 9	Nash 7
11/09	LAL	101-123	L	2-3	91–.418	85–.624	22–.818	28–.429	35	53	Finley 19, Strickland 19	2 with 7	Strickland 4
11/11	@Mia	105-128	L	2-4	97–.412	88–.557	20–.850	22–.864	33	54	Nowitzki 23, Strickland 15	Nowitzki 9	3 with 5
11/13	Orl	**125**-117	W	3-4	87–.506	85–.529	39–.744	26–.731	39	45	Finley 28, 3 with 21	Ceballos 12	Pack 10
11/16	Hou	114-95	W	4-4	88–.523	92–.370	24–.833	35–.629	44	57	Finley 28, Ceballos 19	Finley 13	Pack 10
11/17	@Cha	99-104	L	4-5	89–.416	82–.402	26–.808	41–.829	35	60	Pack 27, 2 with 16	Ceballos 14	**Pack 14**
11/19	Sac	94-103	L	4-6	101–.396	91–.396	12–.917	32–.875	58	58	Finley 24, Pack 20	Finley 12	Finley 8
11/20	@SA	90-106	L	4-7	92–.402	102–.461	16–.813	**5**–.400	48	58	Finley 19, 2 with 16	Nowitzki 12	Davis 7
11/23	@Hou	99-119	L	4-8	91–.462	90–.533	15–.800	20–.700	37	48	Nowitzki 31, Finley 29	Finley 8	2 with 6
11/24	@Orl	100-112	L	4-9	92–.446	93–.462	14–.786	25–.760	41	47	Finley 35, Nowitzki 20	2 with 9	Strickland 11
11/27	Chi	95-83	W	5-9	75–.493	82–.439	18–.944	12–.833	34	43	Finley 24, 2 with 17	Ceballos 7	2 with 7
11/29	@NY	82-107	L	5-10	88–.352	90–.511	19–.737	9–.889	38	52	Finley 20, Bradley 15	Finley 8	Nowitzki 6
11/30	@Cle	99-106	L	5-11	88–.409	86–.442	24–.792	32–.813	40	55	Davis 27, Nowitzki 20	Finley 12	Finley 11
12/02	@Chi	101-95	W	6-11	84–.476	88–.386	24–.708	36–.694	37	55	Finley 30, Nowitzki 18	Finley 9	Davis 6
12/04	@Min	103-84	W	7-11	83–.458	94–.330	29–.793	24–.875	44	50	Finley 32, Ceballos 25	Ceballos 12	Finley 5
12/05	@Mil	97-103	L	7-12	81–.407	85–.494	26–.769	19–.895	37	43	Finley 29, 2 with 18	Nowitzki 10	Nowitzki 8
12/07	Van	95-104	L	7-13	85–.447	88–.432	22–.682	27–.815	38	51	Nowitzki 31, Ceballos 23	Ceballos 12	Pack 12
12/08	@Uta	79-85	L	7-14	87–.356	80–.450	15–.800	15–.733	36	49	Ceballos 19, Nowitzki 15	Finley 10	Finley 8
12/11	Pho	120-115	W	8-14	87–.529	93–.441	26–.692	38–.763	45	48	Finley 33, Pack 24	Finley 14	Pack 11
12/14	SA	93-111	L	8-15	88–.409	89–.506	18–.833	22–.773	38	51	Ceballos 27, Finley 15	Ceballos 10	Pack 8
12/16	NY	93-100	L	8-16	89–.416	81–.494	20–.800	19–.842	39	47	Nowitzki 24, Finley 20	Bradley 10	2 with 7
12/18	Min	104-108	L	8-17	91–.462	80–.538	19–.789	25–.800	42	41	Finley 26, Davis 25	2 with 10	Finley 7
12/20	Mia	89-92	L	8-18	77–.429	73–.466	23–.696	21–.762	37	49	Trent 22, Finley 13	Bradley 10	2 with 4
12/23	@Pho	111-110	W	9-18	85–.518	86–.500	20–.750	19–.632	48	34	Finley 33, Nowitzki 24	Finley 13	Finley 13
12/26	@Sac	111-118	L	9-19	101–.455	84–.560	15–.867	26–.654	41	40	Finley 23, Trent 20	Finley 8	Finley 8
12/27	@LAL	106-108	L	9-20	93–.441	90–.489	21–.667	22–.773	46	55	Nowitzki 30, Finley 24	Trent 13	Finley 8
12/30	Tor	104-109	L	9-21	89–.461	90–.478	17–.824	23–.870	34	54	Nowitzki 32, Ceballos 26	Finley 7	Jones 9
1/04	@Den	96-98	L	9-22	84–.452	88–.455	18–.889	19–.579	39	48	Finley 28, Trent 20	Finley 8	Finley 10
1/06	Uta	92-105	L	9-23	85–.435	83–.446	20–.700	39–.795	43	49	Finley 30, Nowitzki 24	Ceballos 14	Finley 8
1/08	Atl	95-85	W	10-23	77–.416	98–.347	27–.889	16–.625	50	55	Finley 28, Nowitzki 18	Ceballos 14	Finley 9
1/10	@Por	94-107	L	10-24	77–.481	79–.532	22–.591	22–.727	33	47	Nowitzki 19, Ceballos 18	Ceballos 11	Finley 5
1/11	@GS	109-102	W	11-24	78–.487	86–.442	33–.848	29–.724	42	46	Ceballos 29, Finley 21	Ceballos 12	Finley 10
1/15	Por	113-105	W	12-24	90–.467	78–.436	22–.864	40–.775	45	42	Finley 32, Davis 21	Ceballos 11	Finley 8
1/17	Hou	111-121	L	12-25	94–.436	82–.500	28–.893	39–.795	47	48	**Ceballos 39**, Finley 31	Ceballos 9	Strickland 7
1/19	@Was	104-86	W	13-25	93–.462	80–.375	15–.800	30–.733	42	51	Finley 23, Nowitzki 22	Nowitzki 9	Finley 9
1/22	@NJ	95-98	L	13-26	87–.471	83–.446	8–.750	27–.778	44	42	Ceballos 36, Davis 13	Bradley 11	Finley 9
1/23	@Det	99-91	W	14-26	81–.469	89–.393	28–.679	23–.652	45	46	Ceballos 22, Finley 18	2 with 10	2 with 6
1/25	GS	117-103	W	15-26	86–.488	93–.409	31–.871	33–.788	41	56	Finley 30, Nowitzki 23	Bradley 12	Finley 10
1/27	LAC	99-90	W	16-26	87–.471	77–.403	14–.857	27–.926	39	45	Nowitzki 24, Finley 20	Bradley 10	Finley 10
1/29	Den	107-96	W	17-26	84–.488	90–.422	25–.760	24–.583	44	51	Ceballos 31, Strickland 15	Ceballos 10	Strickland 6
2/01	Phi	100-101	L	17-27	92–.413	83–.506	21–.810	21–.810	39	54	Ceballos 26, Finley 21	Ceballos 12	Nash 8
2/03	Cha	106-96	W	18-27	75–.533	81–.370	29–.793	43–.767	43	46	Finley 32, Strickland 23	Finley 9	Nash 6
2/05	@LAC	119-106	W	19-27	81–.494	91–.462	33–.879	29–.586	40	50	Strickland 24, Nowitzki 20	Finley 10	Finley 9
2/06	@Van	103-99[1]	W	20-27	89–.393	89–.416	29–.828	31–.710	44	53	Finley 34, Nash 24	Strickland 9	Nash 7
2/09	Sea	106-117	L	20-28	90–.500	100–.510	11–.909	15–.533	44	46	Ceballos 26, Finley 26	Rodman 13	2 with 5
2/15	Mil	99-112	L	20-29	84–.476	92–.457	22–.727	20–.800	42	46	Bradley 20, Finley 19	Rodman 16	Finley 6
2/17	Det	106-97	W	21-29	91–.462	82–.415	14–.714	25–.840	44	43	Nowitzki 22, 2 with 21	Nowitzki 12	Strickland 7
2/20	@Tor	100-96	W	22-29	80–.463	84–.488	26–.692	17–.706	38	41	Ceballos 23, Finley 23	Rodman 16	Nash 4
2/21	@Ind	93-94	L	22-30	90–.433	77–.468	9–.778	19–.947	44	38	Nowitzki 23, Finley 22	Rodman 18	2 with 4
2/24	Uta	85-92	L	22-31	87–.402	86–.419	13–.769	18–.833	44	47	Ceballos 26, Strickland 16	Rodman 12	Finley 6
2/26	Den	98-96	W	23-31	87–.460	87–.437	19–.842	21–.714	44	49	Ceballos 22, Pack 22	Rodman 14	Pack 12

Date	Opp	Score	W/L	Rec	Dal FG Att–Pct.	Opp FG Att–Pct.	Dal FT Att–Pct.	Opp FT Att–Pct.	Dal Reb	Opp Reb	Points	Rebounds	Assists
2/28	@Bos	108-100	W	24-31	81–.469	92–.413	35–.771	25–.800	38	49	Nowitzki 26, Strickland 19	Rodman 16	2 with 8
2/29	@Phi	87-106	L	24-32	85–.388	73–.630	15–.933	18–.667	34	43	Finley 15, 2 with 12	Rooks 11	Pack 4
3/02	NJ	102-103	L	24-33	98–.439	91–.484	6–1.000	14–.429	53	49	Strickland 31, 2 with 21	**Rodman 21**	Pack 9
3/04	@Pho	96-110	L	24-34	85–.435	93–.462	22–.727	19–.789	47	46	Ceballos 33, Finley 22	Rodman 19	Pack 9
3/06	@Sac	109-130	L	24-35	88–.466	93–.538	23–.783	27–.593	40	50	Ceballos 27, Nowitzki 25	Rodman 8	Finley 5
3/07	@Sea	86-101	L	24-36	84–.393	82–.500	19–.789	20–.600	40	52	Finley 31, Nowitzki 22	Rodman 15	3 with 5
3/09	Min	79-100	L	24-37	73–.438	83–.518	20–.650	12–.750	34	43	Bradley 26, Nowitzki 15	Bradley 9	Finley 5
3/11	Pho	104-99	W	25-37	79–.418	81–.444	43–.744	35–.657	48	47	Strickland 36, Finley 22	Bradley 12	Pack 8
3/14	Ind	111-90	W	26-37	95–.484	94–**.330**	10–1.000	25–.920	50	52	Nowitzki 28, Nash 21	Buckner 11	Finley 11
3/16	@SA	110-88	W	27-37	79–.519	68–.441	17–.941	34–.706	34	41	Strickland 26, Finley 22	Rooks 11	Nash 11
3/18	Bos	99-104	L	27-38	87–.437	81–.494	21–.762	21–.762	40	47	Finley 28, Buckner 25	Nowitzki 11	2 with 6
3/19	@Atl	89-85	W	28-38	85–.400	88–.352	17–.824	30–.667	45	64	Finley 31, Nowitzki 16	2 with 7	2 with 5
3/21	SA	97-96	W	29-38	89–.449	64–.516	14–.929	34–.824	31	41	Finley 24, Strickland 14	Bradley 8	Nash 4
3/23	Cle	98-104	L	29-39	92–.391	84–.488	26–.808	22–.864	44	52	Finley 29, Nowitzki 17	Finley 10	Nash 6
3/25	Was	86-93	L	29-40	79–.418	79–.456	16–.813	20–.900	41	47	Nowitzki 18, Finley 15	Bradley 14	Nash 7
3/27	@Uta	113-105	W	30-40	69–**.580**	79–.481	29–.897	31–.710	38	**34**	Finley 31, 2 with 16	Nowitzki 17	Nash 11
3/28	@LAC	112-102	W	31-40	85–.482	83–.506	18–.944	15–.867	41	37	Finley 20, Nowitzki 20	Finley 12	Finley 10
3/30	@Por	85-96	L	31-41	78–.423	72–.542	20–.800	19–.632	33	36	Finley 30, Nowitzki 16	Finley 7	Nash 7
4/02	@Van	100-86	W	32-41	79–.468	81–.407	18–**1.000**	26–.731	45	45	Nowitzki 22, Finley 18	Bradley 10	Nash 10
4/04	Sac	105-102	W	33-41	79–.544	97–.474	8–.750	12–.667	32	47	Finley 38, Strickland 21	Bradley 7	Nash 10
4/06	@Den	116-115[1]	W	34-41	90–.489	85–.506	28–.786	25–.760	38	44	Nowitzki 32, Finley 23	Nowitzki 9	Nash 10
4/08	LAC	98-96	W	35-41	83–.410	84–.440	29–.724	16–.813	40	57	Finley 19, Strickland 19	Finley 8	2 with 7
4/11	Por	92-**81**	W	36-41	76–.447	81–.346	18–.889	33–.576	37	59	Finley 24, Nowitzki 21	Nowitzki 14	Nash 6
4/13	@Hou	102-111	L	36-42	88–.420	79–.532	26–.808	25–.760	37	44	Finley 35, Nowitzki 15	2 with 9	Finley 9
4/14	Sea	117-103	W	37-42	93–.527	92–.424	14–.857	30–.733	57	41	Strickland 21, Ceballos 19	Nowitzki 10	Nash 8
4/16	Van	114-106	W	38-42	91–.484	88–.443	22–.818	29–.793	45	51	Finley 25, Strickland 19	Strickland 11	Nash 9
4/18	LAL	112-102	W	39-42	87–.483	92–.467	28–.893	20–.450	41	56	Finley 25, Nash 23	Strickland 10	Nash 8
4/19	@Min	113-107	W	40-42	77–.532	95–.484	23–.913	11–.818	38	41	Nash 22, Finley 18	Nash 8	Nash 10

Denver Nuggets 1999-2000 Game Log (35-47)

					Den FG	Opp FG	Den FT	Opp FT	Den	Opp	Game Leaders		
Date	Opp	Score	W/L	Rec	Att–Pct.	Att–Pct.	Att–Pct.	Att–Pct.	Reb	Reb	Points	Rebounds	Assists
11/02	Pho	107-102[1]	W	1-0	89–.449	111–.387	26–.731	14–.500	55	58	Van Exel 34, McDyess 18	2 with 9	Van Exel 9
11/05	@Por	83-95	L	1-1	74–.432	78–.474	19–.737	28–.607	37	43	LaFrentz 17, Van Exel 16	McDyess 8	Van Exel 9
11/06	@Van	94-109	L	1-2	70–.457	81–.556	28–.857	20–.850	31	41	Mercer 31, LaFrentz 19	McDyess 8	Van Exel 7
11/08	Atl	115-100	W	2-2	96–.469	82–.476	24–.792	30–.733	49	39	LaFrentz 24, Van Exel 23	2 with 11	**Van Exel 20**
11/12	Por	78-93	L	2-3	82–.366	89–.416	19–.684	13–.846	48	46	McDyess 17, Van Exel 15	McDyess 12	Posey 5
11/14	@Sac	116-126	L	2-4	90–.500	95–.547	17–.765	25–.680	40	46	Van Exel 26, LaFrentz 23	LaFrentz 13	Van Exel 7
11/16	NY	95-102	L	2-5	71–.451	71–.563	38–.658	26–.731	34	33	Mercer 30, McDyess 26	Mercer 7	Van Exel 7
11/18	LAL	93-82	W	3-5	76–.434	75–.453	31–.645	22–**.364**	45	35	Mercer 24, Van Exel 23	McDyess 13	Van Exel 8
11/20	Chi	95-86	W	4-5	67–.463	87–.414	34–.765	20–.700	37	41	McDyess 21, Mercer 19	Clark 9	Van Exel 8
11/24	Tor	109-84	W	5-5	105–.419	73–.425	17–.824	19–.895	53	44	Van Exel 19, 3 with 13	LaFrentz 18	2 with 6
11/26	Min	114-105	W	6-5	89–.472	87–.460	32–.719	33–.697	46	43	Mercer 27, 2 with 21	LaFrentz 20	Van Exel 10
11/27	@SA	87-106	L	6-6	81–.444	81–.519	20–.500	21–.667	32	53	Mercer 26, McDyess 20	LaFrentz 6	Van Exel 7
11/30	@Min	92-109	L	6-7	80–.388	85–.518	38–.684	27–.704	46	37	McDyess 16, Mercer 16	2 with 9	Van Exel 7
12/01	Det	100-96	W	7-7	74–.486	71–.451	30–.767	37–.757	47	28	McDyess 24, Mercer 23	McDyess 11	Billups 6
12/03	Orl	100-112	L	7-8	99–.384	82–.512	24–.750	33–.788	51	47	McDyess 25, Billups 20	2 with 12	Van Exel 11
12/05	@NY	80-78	W	8-8	78–.372	80–.375	28–.643	19–.737	48	47	Van Exel 20, McDyess 16	LaFrentz 12	Van Exel 5
12/06	@Phi	94-77	W	9-8	72–.472	83–.373	28–.786	25–.600	43	43	Van Exel 34, 2 with 17	McDyess 10	Van Exel 7
12/08	@Bos	90-115	L	9-9	71–.408	91–.516	44–.682	20–.850	40	48	McDyess 20, Billups 19	LaFrentz 12	Billups 4
12/10	@Cha	99-106	L	9-10	98–.429	80–.488	11–.727	29–.828	43	47	LaFrentz 20, Van Exel 20	McDyess 13	Van Exel 5
12/11	@Mil	101-99	W	10-10	86–.419	88–.443	27–.667	24–.667	42	49	Van Exel 27, McCloud 21	McDyess 14	Van Exel 8
12/14	@Sea	84-109	L	10-11	84–.345	87–.506	30–.767	28–.536	44	49	LaFrentz 15, 2 with 14	McDyess 13	Van Exel 9
12/16	Sac	116-106	W	11-11	104–.452	89–.438	25–.800	30–.800	58	40	Van Exel 38, Mercer 25	Clark 16	Van Exel 10
12/18	SA	86-84	W	12-11	82–.415	74–.392	27–.630	29–.724	53	37	Mercer 25, Clark 18	Clark 16	Van Exel 9
12/20	Por	97-88	W	13-11	82–.488	85–.400	20–.750	17–.765	37	47	Mercer 22, McDyess 20	2 with 7	Van Exel 13
12/23	@Van	91-93	L	13-12	77–.481	87–.425	21–.667	21–.857	39	46	LaFrentz 29, Mercer 18	LaFrentz 10	Van Exel 10
12/26	Van	109-86	W	14-12	78–.513	89–.393	30–.800	19–.737	47	39	McDyess 22, Van Exel 22	McDyess 10	Van Exel 13
12/28	LAC	128-105	W	15-12	86–.535	91–.473	36–.778	18–.722	45	44	McDyess 22, 2 with 20	LaFrentz 11	Van Exel 13
12/30	Bos	94-102	L	15-13	77–.390	78–.423	47–.660	45–.689	53	43	Mercer 20, Clark 18	McDyess 11	Van Exel 14
1/03	@Uta	89-109	L	15-14	72–.458	87–.506	38–.553	20–.800	38	39	McDyess 24, 2 with 16	2 with 6	Van Exel 10
1/04	Dal	98-96	W	16-14	88–.455	84–.452	19–.579	18–.889	48	39	McDyess 27, McCloud 19	McDyess 13	Van Exel 13
1/06	Ind	87-102	L	16-15	83–.422	79–.481	23–.565	15–.933	43	42	McDyess 21, LaFrentz 15	2 with 9	Van Exel 11
1/08	Cha	97-92	W	17-15	83–.398	83–.398	28–.750	29–.724	38	51	Van Exel 32, Mercer 24	LaFrentz 10	Van Exel 8
1/10	@LAL	95-130	L	17-16	85–.435	107–.486	24–.750	26–.692	38	59	McDyess 23, Mercer 18	McDyess 9	2 with 4
1/12	Sea	93-103	L	17-17	84–.476	70–**.500**	13–.615	23–.957	36	41	McDyess 26, Mercer 25	LaFrentz 8	Van Exel 8
1/14	Mia	87-92	L	17-18	79–.418	82–.451	25–.680	20–.600	41	45	McDyess 26, 2 with 12	McDyess 15	Herren 6
1/16	@Pho	100-113	L	17-19	89–.438	79–.532	22–.864	28–.786	42	45	Mercer 25, LaFrentz 16	LaFrentz 11	Van Exel 6
1/20	@Hou	115-122	L	17-20	97–.495	95–.474	20–.900	28–.786	40	48	McDyess 40, Van Exel 31	McDyess 12	Van Exel 11
1/21	Pho	99-101	L	17-21	78–.436	85–.447	26–.846	22–.955	38	44	McDyess 26, LaFrentz 22	McDyess 11	Van Exel 7
1/24	Van	110-98	W	18-21	90–.456	82–.451	28–.821	31–.742	48	40	Mercer 24, Van Exel 18	LaFrentz 10	Van Exel 9
1/28	Hou	104-98	W	19-21	85–.471	88–.420	24–.750	25–.720	37	52	Mercer 24, Van Exel 21	2 with 7	Van Exel 8
1/29	@Dal	96-107	L	19-22	90–.422	84–.488	24–.583	25–.760	51	44	Stith 27, Posey 15	LaFrentz 11	Herren 6
1/31	Phi	83-80	W	20-22	81–.432	86–.360	16–.438	27–.630	47	48	Mercer 15, Van Exel 14	2 with 9	Mercer 8
2/02	Mil	135-112	W	21-22	84–**.631**	96–.458	21–.810	28–.750	38	40	Van Exel 28, McDyess 26	2 with 10	Van Exel 11
2/04	@GS	101-103	L	21-23	89–.438	80–.513	20–.750	25–.600	39	49	McDyess 30, 2 with 12	McDyess 11	Van Exel 8
2/05	Min	97-105[1]	L	21-24	84–.357	88–.364	46–.674	49–.755	64	48	Posey 23, McDyess 20	LaFrentz 13	Alexander 7
2/07	@LAL	98-106	L	21-25	93–.419	83–.506	14–.786	28–.571	48	47	McDyess 24, Van Exel 18	McDyess 12	Van Exel 6
2/09	SA	97-106	L	21-26	85–.447	85–.435	21–.762	38–.789	45	45	Gatling 19, Posey 15	Clark 11	Van Exel 6
2/10	@Sac	84-96	L	21-27	85–.365	84–.393	24–.792	26–.846	51	51	McDyess 21, Clark 19	2 with 9	Alexander 7
2/15	@Min	107-104[1]	W	22-27	96–.490	83–.470	15–.533	22–1.000	46	34	Van Exel 25, McDyess 23	Posey 9	2 with 9
2/17	@Cle	101-119	L	22-28	85–.424	87–.529	32–.813	24–.875	40	47	Clark 19, McDyess 16	LaFrentz 12	Van Exel 15
2/18	@Tor	95-91	W	23-28	74–.432	91–.407	33–.848	22–.545	49	41	McDyess 24, LaFrentz 18	LaFrentz 14	Van Exel 6
2/21	Sac	123-117[1]	W	24-28	99–.475	100–.440	27–.630	28–.714	51	55	McDyess 29, Van Exel 27	McDyess 13	Van Exel 15
2/22	@Pho	67-86	L	24-29	82–.317	74–.432	18–.611	24–.667	42	53	Posey 14, McDyess 12	Jones 8	2 with 3
2/24	@Hou	106-97	W	25-29	91–.451	85–.459	25–.840	18–.778	45	42	Van Exel 23, McCloud 17	Clark 11	Van Exel 11

Date	Opp	Score	W/L	Rec	Den FG Att–Pct.	Opp FG Att–Pct.	Den FT Att–Pct.	Opp FT Att–Pct.	Den Reb	Opp Reb	Game Leaders Points	Rebounds	Assists
2/26	@Dal	96-98	L	25-30	87–.437	87–.460	21–.714	19–.842	49	44	McDyess 22, Clark 20	Clark 13	Van Exel 12
3/01	NJ	81-94	L	25-31	93–.333	88–.432	23–.609	20–.750	50	56	McCloud 22, McDyess 22	McDyess 11	Van Exel 11
3/03	GS	122-88	W	26-31	96–.542	97–.361	21–.714	25–.600	63	42	Clark 29, 2 with 18	Clark 16	Van Exel 16
3/05	Cle	92-100	L	26-32	93–.376	82–.439	23–.696	30–.767	51	49	Van Exel 20, 2 with 16	2 with 10	Van Exel 13
3/07	@Ind	89-90	L	26-33	98–.398	78–.385	8–.750	32–.719	60	43	McDyess 23, LaFrentz 17	**Clark 22**	Van Exel 8
3/08	@Det	116-130	L	26-34	81–.556	85–.518	31–.710	38–.868	43	32	McDyess 29, Van Exel 19	LaFrentz 10	Van Exel 8
3/10	@Mia	88-96	L	26-35	82–.427	78–.462	29–.586	30–.733	41	39	Clark 28, McDyess 19	3 with 9	Van Exel 13
3/11	@Orl	107-110	L	26-36	67–.507	82–.451	40–.875	47–.723	36	40	McDyess 35, McCloud 25	McDyess 8	Herren 8
3/13	LAL	108-118	L	26-37	88–.443	80–.513	27–.852	37–.811	36	47	Gatling 25, Clark 18	Gatling 10	Van Exel 15
3/14	@LAC	106-110	L	26-38	77–.571	76–.526	18–.778	25–.840	37	**25**	McDyess 31, Gatling 19	Gatling 8	McCloud 6
3/17	LAC	114-87	W	27-38	87–.471	104–.356	30–.800	**11–.909**	56	51	McDyess 23, LaFrentz 21	McDyess 15	Van Exel 8
3/18	@SA	82-102	L	27-39	81–.370	79–.392	26–.769	40–.875	39	53	Gatling 23, McDyess 16	McDyess 8	2 with 6
3/21	@Uta	83-96	L	27-40	82–.390	75–.493	24–.667	22–.682	43	37	McDyess 25, Clark 19	McDyess 12	Van Exel 13
3/23	Was	86-100	L	27-41	80–.338	85–.435	40–.625	28–.750	44	55	McCloud 18, Van Exel 18	LaFrentz 12	Van Exel 8
3/24	@Chi	68-**70**	L	27-42	75–.333	79–**.304**	29–.552	28–.679	55	46	Clark 18, Van Exel 12	LaFrentz 15	Van Exel 4
3/26	@NJ	112-110	W	28-42	88–.500	87–.425	14–**1.000**	33–.848	51	40	Van Exel 28, LaFrentz 22	LaFrentz 18	Van Exel 12
3/28	@Atl	111-116	L	28-43	89–.483	82–.549	26–.692	31–.806	33	47	McDyess 28, Van Exel 24	McDyess 11	Van Exel 11
3/29	@Was	101-93	W	29-43	66–.485	91–.363	36–.833	24–.875	45	41	Van Exel 26, Posey 25	McDyess 12	2 with 8
4/01	Uta	112-92	W	30-43	79–.506	76–.434	26–.808	26–.808	41	34	McDyess 33, Van Exel 27	LaFrentz 11	Van Exel 14
4/04	@Sea	93-106	L	30-44	87–.414	88–.466	19–.632	21–.857	41	48	McCloud 28, McDyess 17	McDyess 15	Van Exel 10
4/06	Dal	115-116[1]	L	30-45	85–.506	90–.489	25–.760	28–.786	44	38	McCloud 23, 2 with 18	McDyess 13	Van Exel 12
4/08	Sea	105-97	W	31-45	92–.413	86–.442	29–.655	21–.714	55	39	McCloud 20, Posey 19	McDyess 9	Van Exel 12
4/09	@GS	103-117	L	31-46	82–.451	85–.506	27–.778	48–.625	46	46	McDyess 25, Herren 17	McDyess 12	Van Exel 7
4/11	Hou	93-103	L	31-47	89–.416	80–.450	17–.941	38–.632	37	52	Van Exel 27, LaFrentz 16	Gatling 7	Van Exel 11
4/14	GS	105-97	W	32-47	79–.430	88–.364	34–.794	34–.824	49	47	LaFrentz 23, Van Exel 22	LaFrentz 12	Van Exel 7
4/15	@LAC	115-114[1]	W	33-47	89–.483	94–.426	27–.704	36–.833	53	45	**Van Exel 44**, McDyess 30	McDyess 21	Van Exel 8
4/18	Uta	105-104[1]	W	34-47	89–.416	88–.455	33–.727	20–.900	40	50	LaFrentz 32, Gatling 19	LaFrentz 17	Van Exel 10
4/19	@Por	96-95	W	35-47	81–.506	86–.419	16–.500	21–.905	39	45	McDyess 22, Van Exel 22	McDyess 8	Van Exel 9

Detroit Pistons 1999-2000 Game Log (42-40)

Date	Opp	Score	W/L	Rec	Det FG Att–Pct.	Opp FG Att–Pct.	Det FT Att–Pct.	Opp FT Att–Pct.	Det Reb	Opp Reb	Points	Rebounds	Assists
11/02	@Mia	122-128[2]	L	0-1	99–.434	106–.387	43–.721	48–.750	**54**	66	Hill 41, Stckhse 26	2 with 11	Hill 5
11/03	@Orl	94-103	L	0-2	80–.438	93–.462	25–.760	24–.625	34	58	Hill 30, Laettner 18	Williams 12	Hill 7
11/05	NY	91-103	L	0-3	83–.386	72–.542	32–.750	23–.783	37	42	Stckhse 30, Hill 23	Williams 12	Hill 6
11/06	@Mil	111-121	L	0-4	83–.506	89–.506	26–.692	25–.880	39	37	Stckhse 20, 2 with 18	Hill 8	2 with 7
11/10	@Bos	110-92	W	1-4	84–.464	75–.413	29–.897	28–.821	46	40	Stckhse 30, Williams 20	Williams 16	Hunter 9
11/11	Tor	106-123	L	1-5	90–.389	84–.536	40–.775	31–.871	37	51	Hill 25, Stckhse 21	Williams 10	Stckhse 7
11/13	Sea	107-99	W	2-5	85–.459	89–.416	29–.828	29–.621	48	44	Hill 34, Stckhse 24	2 with 11	Stckhse 8
11/16	@Tor	85-89	L	2-6	92–.391	70–.443	12–.833	33–.727	38	45	Stckhse 26, Williams 26	Williams 10	Hill 10
11/17	NJ	109-107	W	3-6	84–.536	76–.474	24–.667	31–.806	40	37	Hill 32, Laettner 20	Williams 14	Laettner 6
11/19	Cle	101-90	W	4-6	74–.432	84–.393	45–.800	27–.704	53	35	Hill 28, Stckhse 26	2 with 10	Hunter 7
11/21	Mil	113-94	W	5-6	77–.532	79–.494	35–.743	18–.611	43	28	Hill 31, Hunter 21	2 with 12	Hill 7
11/25	@Ind	107-99	W	6-6	80–.450	83–.494	36–.806	16–.625	46	34	Stckhse 26, Hill 22	2 with 9	Stckhse 6
11/26	Atl	93-91	W	7-6	84–.381	85–.424	29–.897	22–.591	47	51	Hill 30, Hunter 20	Williams 13	2 with 4
11/28	Orl	99-108	L	7-7	87–.414	85–.482	29–.793	35–.743	49	45	Hill 24, Stckhse 21	Williams 13	Stckhse 10
11/30	@SA	87-106	L	7-8	80–.425	76–.592	22–.773	16–.750	40	38	Hill 30, 2 with 9	Reid 7	2 with 5
12/01	@Den	96-100	L	7-9	71–.451	74–.486	37–.757	30–.767	28	47	Hill 39, Laettner 19	Hill 7	Stckhse 4
12/03	SA	102-80	W	8-9	82–.451	**65**–.369	33–.758	35–.829	45	37	Hill 28, Stckhse 21	Mills 9	Hill 6
12/04	@Atl	110-112	L	8-10	87–.483	76–.513	20–**1.000**	34–.882	34	40	Hill 33, Hunter 22	Hill 10	Hill 6
12/07	@Mil	116-112	W	9-10	74–.527	95–.516	34–.853	15–.733	23	48	Hill 31, Stckhse 26	Williams 10	**Hill 12**
12/10	LAC	107-83	W	10-10	84–.488	82–.415	22–.864	17–.588	52	37	Hill 27, Stckhse 23	2 with 12	Hunter 8
12/12	@LAL	93-101	L	10-11	78–.385	100–.420	36–.750	25–.600	40	63	Hill 25, Stckhse 24	Hill 12	Hill 7
12/14	@Pho	104-114	L	10-12	81–.444	86–.512	28–.893	24–.833	35	38	Stckhse 35, Laettner 26	Williams 10	Stckhse 7
12/16	@GS	116-108	W	11-12	75–.507	92–.413	43–.860	35–.714	42	51	Hill 25, Stckhse 23	2 with 8	Stckhse 11
12/18	Phi	104-91	W	12-12	79–.443	91–.418	38–.763	21–.667	48	42	Stckhse 26, Hill 20	Williams 16	Hill 7
12/20	@Phi	121-122[1]	L	12-13	79–.519	101–.495	41–.805	22–.682	39	41	Hill 32, Stckhse 23	Mills 8	2 with 6
12/21	Was	83-97	L	12-14	75–.360	91–.440	39–.718	17–.882	39	50	Hill 25, Stckhse 20	Williams 11	Mills 4
12/26	Cha	114-96	W	13-14	73–.562	76–.447	36–.806	38–.658	48	31	Hill 30, Stckhse 22	**Williams 21**	Hunter 7
12/29	@Chi	91-77	W	14-14	80–.363	71–.408	36–.806	22–.636	44	40	Stckhse 23, Hill 20	Williams 12	Hill 5
12/30	Atl	106-105[1]	W	15-14	87–.460	99–.424	26–.731	24–.750	39	60	Stckhse 33, Hill 25	3 with 9	**Hill 12**
1/03	@Orl	118-106	W	16-14	**99**–.455	79–.506	28–.714	31–.677	48	46	**Hill 42**, Hunter 25	Laettner 14	Hill 8
1/05	@Atl	120-108	W	17-14	81–.556	75–.560	33–.818	24–.792	38	29	**Hill 42**, Stckhse 28	Laettner 12	Stckhse 7
1/06	Mil	101-95	W	18-14	78–.474	80–.413	31–.677	22–.864	49	37	Hill 31, Laettner 20	Williams 17	2 with 7
1/08	Min	105-110	L	18-15	78–.449	78–.500	43–.651	39–.769	38	42	Hill 40, Stckhse 16	Williams 12	Hill 9
1/12	NY	114-108	W	19-15	72–.500	90–.533	39–.872	**9**–.889	37	35	3 with 29	Laettner 9	Hill 7
1/14	Was	105-98	W	20-15	78–.487	76–.539	32–.750	20–.650	34	42	Stckhse 32, Hill 30	Williams 13	Hunter 6
1/15	@Was	112-107	W	21-15	80–.500	74–.527	37–.784	35–.771	32	41	Hill 39, Stckhse 27	Williams 14	2 with 5
1/17	@NY	94-105	L	21-16	81–.432	90–.489	27–.704	18–.667	38	48	Laettner 23, Stckhse 19	Williams 12	Stckhse 9
1/20	@NJ	120-122	L	21-17	72–.542	90–.511	42–.905	24–.875	34	38	Laettner 28, Stckhse 28	Laettner 8	Stckhse 9
1/22	@Chi	92-98	L	21-18	87–.391	67–.463	31–.613	40–.700	39	53	Mills 20, Laettner 19	Mills 9	Stckhse 6
1/23	Dal	91-99	L	21-19	89–.393	81–.469	23–.652	28–.679	46	45	Stckhse 36, Buechler 12	Williams 10	Hunter 7
1/25	@Cle	107-116[1]	L	21-20	85–.424	88–.455	39–.718	41–.756	50	46	Stckhse 38, Hunter 17	Mills 12	Stckhse 7
1/27	@Cha	102-117	L	21-21	74–.473	88–.523	29–.828	24–.708	34	44	Stckhse 34, Hill 28	Williams 7	Stckhse 6
1/29	Phi	90-88	W	22-21	79–.380	75–.453	29–.828	30–.600	44	47	Stckhse 26, Laettner 15	Laettner 16	Stckhse 5
1/31	@Mia	82-104	L	22-22	75–.373	81–.556	31–.742	**9**–.778	37	39	Stckhse 17, Laettner 15	Williams 9	Stckhse 5
2/02	Sac	110-113	L	22-23	90–.456	83–.518	26–.769	23–.826	46	42	Stckhse 35, Mills 24	Williams 16	Stckhse 5
2/04	Cle	105-96	W/L	23-23	80–.425	82–.500	34–.824	16–.750	46	36	Hunter 26, Stckhse 22	Laettner 10	Hunter 10
2/06	Hou	109-105	W	24-23	83–.530	83–.458	23–.826	30–.767	35	41	Hill 36, Stckhse 23	Williams 9	Stckhse 7
2/09	Tor	115-108[1]	W	25-23	89–.483	92–.359	31–.710	46–.870	52	49	Hill 30, Hunter 28	Hill 13	2 with 4
2/15	@Hou	102-107	L	25-24	81–.469	82–.476	30–.700	25–.760	36	46	Stckhse 29, Hill 23	Hill 11	Hill 6
2/17	@Dal	97-106	L	25-25	82–.415	91–.462	25–.840	14–.714	43	46	Stckhse 22, Hill 20	Williams 17	Hill 6
2/19	@Uta	87-91	L	25-26	75–.413	77–.364	21–.905	33–.879	37	48	Hunter 24, Stckhse 21	Hill 9	Hill 8
2/21	Mia	95-87	W	26-26	82–.439	80–.413	17–.765	16–.875	44	38	Hill 26, 2 with 22	3 with 9	Stckhse 9
2/23	Ind	111-118	L	26-27	89–.506	74–.527	17–.941	36–.861	31	39	Hill 24, Hunter 20	Mills 7	Hill 6
2/25	GS	**131**-99	W	27-27	84–.571	102–.392	27–.889	20–**.500**	46	50	Hill 30, Stckhse 29	Williams 12	Stckhse 7

Date	Opp	Score	W/L	Rec	Det FG Att–Pct.	Opp FG Att–Pct.	Det FT Att–Pct.	Opp FT Att–Pct.	Det Reb	Opp Reb	Game Leaders Points	Rebounds	Assists
2/27	Chi	93-90	W	28-27	76–.421	75–.427	36–.750	23–.783	37	44	Stckhse 27, Laettner 17	Williams 14	Stckhse 5
2/29	@Ind	105-115	L	28-28	92–.424	85–.482	27–.852	28–.857	45	47	Hill 37, Stckhse 32	Laettner 12	2 with 5
3/01	Uta	94-107	L	28-29	70–.457	82–.537	40–.675	24–.667	37	42	Hill 26, Stckhse 17	Williams 11	4 with 3
3/04	@Was	94-100	L	28-30	75–.467	78–.487	24–.750	28–.786	38	42	Stckhse 26, Hill 24	Laettner 9	Hill 6
3/08	Den	130-116	W	29-30	85–.518	81–.556	38–.868	31–.710	32	43	Stckhse 40, Hill 27	2 with 8	Hill 10
3/10	Van	111-97	W	30-30	83–.518	67–.448	28–.821	38–.842	38	37	Hill 27, Stckhse 27	Williams 12	Hill 6
3/11	Por	94-99	L	30-31	71–.479	73–.479	26–.769	28–.786	36	41	Hill 30, Stckhse 22	Laettner 8	3 with 4
3/13	Bos	124-115	W	31-31	71–.563	81–.444	49–.755	45–.756	39	40	Stckhse 36, Hunter 25	Laettner 10	Hunter 8
3/15	Orl	113-91	W	32-31	88–.477	68–.441	29–.897	36–.750	50	26	Stckhse 32, Hill 24	Laettner 17	Stckhse 6
3/17	LAL	82-110	L	32-32	85–.353	92–.489	29–.690	22–.727	45	49	Stckhse 18, 3 with 12	Williams 13	Hunter 5
3/19	@Van	101-99	W	33-32	76–.487	74–.514	23–.913	17–.882	27	38	Hill 31, Stckhse 23	Williams 11	Laettner 5
3/21	@Sea	100-90	W	34-32	82–.463	90–.389	25–.800	23–.696	47	41	Hill 33, Stckhse 21	Williams 14	Hill 8
3/22	@Por	104-95	W	35-32	75–.520	85–.447	28–.714	21–.714	39	38	Hill 24, Stckhse 23	Williams 13	Hill 6
3/24	@Sac	103-113	L	35-33	91–.429	75–.480	27–.741	44–.705	41	46	Hill 35, Stckhse 24	Hill 9	2 with 5
3/25	@LAC	126-107	W	36-33	79–.633	84–.476	23–.696	23–.783	48	**22**	Stckhse 31, Hunter 20	Williams 11	Stckhse 7
3/29	Cha	91-98	L	36-34	91–.385	71–.493	24–.750	36–.750	46	44	Hill 26, Stckhse 19	Williams 11	Stckhse 6
3/31	Pho	97-98	L	36-35	84–.393	79–.468	27–.926	20–.750	51	34	Hill 28, Stckhse 19	Williams 12	2 with 4
4/02	@NJ	113-92	W	37-35	93–.505	84–.405	18–.722	29–.655	51	44	Stckhse 34, Hill 32	Hill 12	Hill 8
4/04	@Tor	104-88	W	38-35	75–.493	89–.371	39–.692	17–.824	39	50	Hill 32, Stckhse 28	Hill 9	Stckhse 3
4/05	Bos	111-106	W	39-35	66–.470	80–.475	**56**–.768	33–.606	38	37	Hill 27, Stckhse 22	Hill 9	2 with 3
4/07	@Cha	97-82	W	40-35	82–.427	79–.380	21–.762	32–.594	48	48	Stckhse 23, Crotty 14	Williams 11	Stckhse 7
4/08	@Cle	98-117	L	40-36	89–.360	83–.482	38–.737	38–.816	46	57	Williams 19, Stckhse 14	Williams 11	Hill 5
4/10	@Min	100-102	L	40-37	71–.423	82–.427	42–.833	37–.757	39	42	Hill 36, Laettner 12	Laettner 10	Laettner 5
4/12	Mia	90-**73**	W	41-37	73–.397	69–**.333**	27–.815	33–.667	53	35	Stckhse 29, Hunter 17	Williams 15	2 with 3
4/15	@Phi	94-100	L	41-38	81–.481	79–.481	20–.600	30–.733	39	50	Stckhse 15, Williams 12	Williams 12	Hunter 7
4/16	Ind	101-112	L	41-39	85–.482	76–.566	19–.842	21–.762	40	32	Stckhse 26, Curry 23	3 with 6	Hunter 6
4/18	@NY	88-100	L	41-40	67–.448	70–.514	28–.857	30–.767	34	31	Stckhse 24, Moore 14	3 with 6	Crotty 5
4/19	Chi	112-91	W	42-40	69–**.638**	72–.417	25–.680	32–.781	31	34	Stckhse 21, Buechler 14	Williams 8	2 with 7

Postseason

Date	Opp	Score	W/L	Rec	Det FG Att–Pct.	Opp FG Att–Pct.	Det FT Att–Pct.	Opp FT Att–Pct.	Det Reb	Opp Reb	Game Leaders Points	Rebounds	Assists
4/22	@Mia	85-95	L	0-1	67–.433	73–.466	32–.656	24–.833	37	35	Stckhse 23, Hill 13	2 with 9	Hill 5
4/25	@Mia	82-84	L	0-2	68–.471	71–.451	18–.778	24–.667	32	42	Stckhse 26, Mills 11	2 with 7	Hill 4
4/29	Mia	72-91	L	0-3	73–.315	71–.521	31–.742	25–.560	34	47	Stckhse 25, Curry 14	Laettner 7	Stckhse 3

Golden State Warriors 1999-2000 Game Log (19-63)

Date	Opp	Score	W/L	Rec	GS FG Att–Pct.	Opp FG Att–Pct.	GS FT Att–Pct.	Opp FT Att–Pct.	GS Reb	Opp Reb	Game Leaders Points	Rebounds	Assists
11/02	@Dal	96-108	L	0-1	82–.415	85–.459	27–.778	34–.824	51	41	Starks 20, Mills 18	Marshall 9	2 with 4
11/04	@SA	81-104	L	0-2	88–.341	81–.494	25–.720	31–.613	51	45	Jamison 18, Farmer 11	Jamison 11	Blaylock 6
11/06	Dal	97-120	L	0-3	106–.358	89–.506	23–.739	26–.885	59	44	Jamison 21, Mills 21	Marshall 11	Blaylock 8
11/09	SA	89-118	L	0-4	95–.347	88–.534	27–.815	26–.654	48	52	Farmer 19, Mills 11	Marshall 8	Starks 5
11/12	@Van	103-93	W	1-4	86–.465	85–.447	21–.810	21–.714	39	47	Starks 22, Mills 20	Foyle 8	Mills 8
11/13	Hou	95-103	L	1-5	95–.400	85–.400	19–.842	32–.813	57	49	Jamison 27, Mills 19	Marshall 15	Jones 10
11/16	Chi	99-79	W	2-5	87–.437	92–.348	30–.700	21–.524	59	52	Jamison 20, Mills 14	Marshall 18	Blaylock 7
11/17	@Sea	108-111	L	2-6	88–.523	85–.529	19–.579	22–.773	40	**33**	Jamison 27, 3 with 16	T Cummings 10	Blaylock 12
11/20	NY	79-86	L	2-7	86–.326	77–.403	27–.630	23–.783	45	54	Marshall 19, Mills 17	Marshall 11	Starks 5
11/24	NJ	84-92	L	2-8	88–.364	75–.427	23–.739	28–.750	43	54	Farmer 19, Jamison 12	Foyle 12	2 with 8
11/26	@Sac	95-124	L	2-9	97–.412	90–.533	18–.667	24–.792	50	49	Starks 16, Jamison 15	Jamison 11	Blaylock 7
11/27	Tor	88-106	L	2-10	89–.404	87–.460	17–.706	22–.864	54	43	Jamison 25, Farmer 16	Foyle 15	V Cummings 7
11/29	@Uta	99-115	L	2-11	71–.521	73–.575	23–.565	27–.889	25	41	Jones 17, 2 with 15	Jamison 6	Blaylock 10
12/01	@LAL	75-93	L	2-12	84–.333	93–.376	22–.727	29–.759	52	57	Blaylock 13, Carr 13	Farmer 15	Blaylock 6
12/02	Sea	108-117	L	2-13	96–.417	85–.494	30–.667	34–.735	47	52	V Cummings 19, Jamison 18	2 with 8	Blaylock 5
12/04	Uta	82-94	L	2-14	80–.400	70–.457	29–.552	32–.844	48	35	Mills 24, Jamison 17	Mills 10	Blaylock 8
12/07	@NY	83-89	L	2-15	90–.333	84–.440	31–.710	21–.619	54	45	Jamison 25, T Cummings 15	Jamison 17	Blaylock 6
12/08	@Cha	106-113	L	2-16	103–.427	84–.524	19–.579	28–.750	55	45	Starks 28, Jamison 26	Caffey 13	Starks 9
12/10	@Atl	107-99	W	3-16	99–.475	82–.427	17–.647	33–.697	46	43	Mills 20, Jamison 19	Jamison 10	**Blaylock 19**
12/11	@Min	104-76	W	4-16	85–.482	80–.413	23–.739	**14**–.714	41	41	Starks 27, Mills 23	Farmer 8	Blaylock 11
12/14	Mia	102-97	W	5-16	89–.461	79–.494	25–.640	23–.652	43	39	Mills 23, Starks 21	Caffey 12	Starks 10
12/16	Det	108-116	L	5-17	92–.413	75–.507	35–.714	43–.860	51	42	Starks 22, Caffey 21	Caffey 11	V Cummings 7
12/17	@LAC	91-92	L	5-18	94–.394	78–.436	17–.706	33–.606	46	47	Farmer 19, Starks 18	2 with 10	Starks 7
12/20	Sac	111-99	W	6-18	86–.523	101–.396	32–.625	24–.667	47	57	Caffey 26, 2 with 20	Caffey 14	Starks 12
12/22	LAC	99-103	L	6-19	96–.438	85–.471	14–.571	16–.875	44	45	Starks 22, Caffey 16	Jamison 9	V Cummings 13
12/23	@Por	91-111	L	6-20	89–.416	77–.481	16–.875	40–.775	35	40	Marshall 18, Starks 18	Caffey 9	2 with 5
12/26	@Pho	88-108	L	6-21	80–.438	76–.579	27–.519	24–.583	34	41	Jamison 17, Caffey 16	Caffey 10	Starks 7
12/27	SA	83-105	L	6-22	85–.424	88–.523	15–.467	19–**.474**	41	47	Starks 27, Jamison 14	Jamison 10	V Cummings 11
12/29	Phi	94-97	L	6-23	84–.440	80–.488	22–.545	23–.783	48	38	V Cummings 23, Jamison 21	Marshall 13	2 with 5
1/03	@Was	87-99	L	6-24	77–.455	84–.476	20–.650	18–.778	35	42	Jamison 21, Starks 16	Marshall 9	Blaylock 8
1/05	@Phi	92-113	L	6-25	87–.402	81–.531	21–.762	34–.735	37	54	Jamison 26, Marshall 17	Marshall 10	Blaylock 7
1/06	@Cle	75-90	L	6-26	98–.306	89–.427	14–.786	21–.571	53	53	Jamison 22, Blaylock 16	Foyle 13	Blaylock 8
1/09	Sea	95-100[1]	L	6-27	88–.398	82–.451	31–.581	30–.733	48	54	Blaylock 20, Jamison 20	Marshall 11	Blaylock 10
1/11	Dal	102-109	L	6-28	86–.442	78–.487	29–.724	33–.848	46	42	Jamison 28, Marshall 21	Marshall 16	Blaylock 6
1/13	Hou	100-108	L	6-29	81–.457	101–.426	29–.690	22–.727	47	51	Blaylock 25, Caffey 24	Caffey 10	Blaylock 11
1/15	Sac	99-114	L	6-30	98–.418	75–.493	15–.733	43–.837	46	49	Jamison 23, 2 with 16	Marshall 10	Blaylock 6
1/17	Orl	113-100	W	7-30	92–.511	86–.453	25–.600	20–.800	45	41	Jamison 32, 2 with 20	Marshall 13	Blaylock 8
1/21	Cle	115-103	W	8-30	87–.471	84–.440	29–.828	36–.694	49	44	Jamison 37, Marshall 25	Jamison 18	Blaylock 11
1/23	Min	81-99	L	8-31	87–.356	82–.476	22–.682	24–.792	44	50	Blaylock 14, Caffey 13	2 with 7	Blaylock 4
1/25	@Dal	103-117	L	8-32	93–.409	86–.488	33–.788	31–.871	56	41	Jamison 33, Jacobson 15	Jamison 21	Blaylock 7
1/27	@Hou	115-110	W	9-32	86–.477	91–.418	36–.694	36–.750	42	49	Jamison 25, V Cummings 23	Marshall 12	Blaylock 11
2/01	@LAC	107-76	W	10-32	90–**.533**	81–.346	7–.714	18–.833	46	36	Jamison 24, Starks 20	Marshall 13	2 with 6
2/02	Van	101-95	W	11-32	73–.521	89–.427	23–.783	20–.750	37	45	Blaylock 25, Jamison 21	Foyle 8	Blaylock 10
2/04	Den	103-101	W	12-32	80–.513	89–.438	25–.600	20–.750	49	39	Jamison 19, Caffey 17	Marshall 12	V Cummings 7
2/06	@NJ	90-110	L	12-33	93–.376	81–.457	20–.700	36–.833	46	49	Jamison 25, Blaylock 18	Marshall 13	Blaylock 9
2/07	@Orl	100-120	L	12-34	92–.424	80–.575	29–.655	31–.806	41	44	Jamison 22, V Cummings 19	Marshall 8	2 with 4
2/09	@Mia	100-115	L	12-35	78–.449	90–.533	29–.862	18–.778	35	48	Blaylock 17, Jamison 17	Marshall 12	Starks 6
2/15	Por	83-92	L	12-36	77–.403	95–.368	28–.571	23–.652	54	58	Marshall 23, Starks 15	Marshall 17	3 with 5
2/16	@Por	95-99	L	12-37	79–.456	71–.465	16–**.938**	29–.862	38	39	Blaylock 22, Marshall 18	Dampier 16	V Cummings 8
2/18	Bos	**122**-100	W	13-37	84–.512	78–.385	45–.711	53–.679	51	50	Hughes 21, Blaylock 18	Dampier 10	V Cummings 7
2/20	Was	112-103	W	14-37	96–.490	90–.411	21–.667	40–.600	58	48	Caffey 25, Marshall 19	Caffey 16	Hughes 7
2/22	@Min	89-112	L	14-38	80–.350	75–.560	36–.833	34–.735	35	48	Hughes 14, 3 with 11	Hughes 7	Blaylock 5
2/23	@Mil	91-86	W	15-38	88–.386	81–.407	30–.633	20–.800	**62**	40	Marshall 37, Dampier 12	Marshall 21	Blaylock 14
2/25	@Det	99-131	L	15-39	102–.392	84–.571	20–.500	27–.889	50	46	Hughes 24, Caffey 18	Owens 13	Blaylock 4

Date	Opp	Score	W/L	Rec	GS FG Att–Pct.	Opp FG Att–Pct.	GS FT Att–Pct.	Opp FT Att–Pct.	GS Reb	Opp Reb	Points	Rebounds	Assists
2/26	@Ind	88-104	L	15-40	88–.375	85–.424	27–.741	32–.781	58	40	Hughes 24, Marshall 16	**Marshall 23**	Marshall 5
2/28	Atl	80-**75**	W	16-40	89–.371	84–**.345**	20–.600	17–.824	58	52	Hughes 23, Marshall 23	Marshall 21	Blaylock 8
3/03	@Den	88-122	L	16-41	97–.361	96–.542	25–.600	21–.714	42	63	V Cummings 21, Farmer 17	Marshall 14	V Cummings 5
3/05	Ind	95-114	L	16-42	80–.425	94–.436	30–.767	27–.741	46	50	Marshall 27, Caffey 18	Caffey 10	Blaylock 12
3/07	Cha	99-102	L	16-43	82–.415	78–.436	40–.750	42–.762	49	49	Hughes 21, Marshall 19	Owens 9	Blaylock 7
3/09	LAL	92-109	L	16-44	82–.427	83–.482	37–.595	27–.852	46	49	Hughes 41, Marshall 16	Marshall 12	Blaylock 6
3/10	@Sea	85-99	L	16-45	84–.417	86–.430	17–.588	26–.769	44	44	Marshall 27, Hughes 26	Marshall 12	Blaylock 10
3/12	LAC	103-112	L	16-46	86–.442	89–.528	28–.857	22–.591	43	46	Hughes 30, Marshall 22	Hughes 10	Blaylock 10
3/14	@Tor	78-85	L	16-47	90–.378	72–.403	13–.462	28–.750	47	44	Hughes 25, Marshall 12	2 with 10	Marshall 7
3/15	@Bos	104-121	L	16-48	68–.441	82–.488	58–.707	44–.818	39	41	Hughes 32, V Cummings 23	Marshall 10	2 with 4
3/17	@Chi	95-92[2]	W	17-48	78–.423	81–.420	38–.632	30–.667	43	45	Blaylock 23, Marshall 21	2 with 8	Blaylock 8
3/19	Pho	82-99	L	17-49	88–.352	83–.446	30–.633	20–.700	47	55	Hughes 25, Caffey 20	2 with 9	Blaylock 8
3/21	@Van	82-98	L	17-50	76–.342	81–.457	32–.813	37–.595	43	50	Marshall 16, Farmer 14	Marshall 9	V Cummings 5
3/22	@LAL	96-119	L	17-51	90–.400	84–.500	34–.647	38–.763	40	53	Hughes 26, Caffey 17	Caffey 14	2 with 4
3/24	Por	83-96	L	17-52	74–.419	**68**–.500	24–.792	31–.645	37	**33**	Farmer 18, V Cummings 17	Marshall 10	Blaylock 6
3/26	@Pho	82-90	L	17-53	83–.386	73–.452	25–.640	32–.750	41	45	Marshall 28, Hughes 16	Marshall 11	Blaylock 5
3/28	@Hou	86-121	L	17-54	96–.396	88–.500	15–.533	32–.813	38	55	Hughes 22, Blaylock 14	2 with 7	Hughes 6
3/30	@SA	90-102	L	17-55	85–.424	78–.474	19–.842	29–.793	38	44	Blaylock 19, Hughes 17	Foyle 9	Blaylock 6
3/31	@Uta	97-114	L	17-56	91–.363	72–.528	35–.771	36–.861	44	47	Hughes 27, Marshall 18	Marshall 16	Marshall 4
4/02	Mil	113-117	L	17-57	85–.435	79–.519	38–.842	39–.769	42	42	Hughes 32, Blaylock 24	Caffey 11	Blaylock 7
4/05	LAL	104-111	L	17-58	96–.417	79–.506	26–.692	30–.767	58	40	Marshall 32, Caffey 21	Marshall 18	Hughes 9
4/07	Uta	84-105	L	17-59	80–.400	73–.521	22–.818	28–.821	40	39	Hughes 14, V Cummings 13	Caffey 9	Hughes 9
4/09	Den	117-103	W	18-59	85–.506	82–.451	48–.625	27–.778	46	46	**Hughes 44**, Foyle 18	Foyle 13	Blaylock 11
4/11	Van	109-97	W	19-59	82–.524	76–.513	29–.759	20–.850	41	35	Hughes 28, 2 with 25	Davis 12	Blaylock 10
4/13	@Sac	107-130	L	19-60	93–.419	80–.575	35–.800	46–.717	45	43	Hughes 35, Jacobson 19	Hughes 12	V Cummings 5
4/14	@Den	97-105	L	19-61	88–.364	79–.430	34–.824	34–.794	47	49	Blaylock 21, Farmer 18	Foyle 11	Blaylock 6
4/17	Min	96-101	L	19-62	78–.474	83–.446	29–.586	25–.840	35	54	Hughes 33, Davis 13	Foyle 8	Blaylock 8
4/19	Pho	88-99	L	19-63	84–.381	76–.513	33–.667	18–.778	38	51	Hughes 20, Blaylock 14	2 with 8	Davis 7

333

Houston Rockets 1999-2000 Game Log (34-48)

Date	Opp	Score	W/L	Rec	Hou FG Att–Pct.	Opp FG Att–Pct.	Hou FT Att–Pct.	Opp FT Att–Pct.	Hou Reb	Opp Reb	Points	Rebounds	Assists
11/02	Mil	93-98	L	0-1	75–.453	79–.481	29–.655	28–.679	42	35	Francis 14, 2 with 13	2 with 11	Olajuwon 7
11/04	@Uta	82-98	L	0-2	68–.441	77–.532	18–.833	19–.737	28	37	Mobley 17, Olajuwon 12	Mssenbrg 6	Barkley 6
11/05	SA	85-95	L	0-3	83–.398	77–.455	23–.652	23–.826	45	42	Williams 19, Barkley 18	Barkley 13	Francis 3
11/08	Orl	97-102	L	0-4	79–.430	99–.374	37–.730	36–.750	48	56	Mobley 25, Barkley 18	Barkley 17	Francis 6
11/10	LAL	88-89	L	0-5	74–.405	81–.395	33–.667	24–.833	44	42	Francis 26, Olajuwon 15	2 with 10	3 with 5
11/12	@LAL	97-81	W	1-5	71–.493	83–.337	23–.913	25–.880	44	39	Francis 22, Rogers 16	Olajuwon 11	Francis 7
11/13	@GS	103-95	W	2-5	85–.400	95–.400	32–.813	19–.842	49	57	Francis 27, Williams 16	Barkley 16	Francis 8
11/15	Ind	87-96	L	2-6	86–.430	83–.398	14–.714	27–.926	50	40	3 with 18	**Barkley 24**	Francis 12
11/16	@Dal	95-114	L	2-7	92–.370	88–.523	35–.629	24–.833	57	44	Drew 15, Anderson 14	Barkley 11	Francis 6
11/18	Sac	110-128	L	2-8	97–.474	99–.455	19–.737	31–.774	51	43	Olajuwon 31, 2 with 16	Barkley 16	Francis 11
11/20	@Sea	107-110	L	2-9	91–.451	87–.483	19–.632	31–.710	52	41	Francis 27, Mobley 19	Barkley 11	2 with 5
11/21	@Sac	105-110	L	2-10	95–.453	99–.485	13–.923	9–.778	47	50	Francis 21, Olajuwon 20	Olajuwon 15	Barkley 5
11/23	Dal	119-99	W	3-10	90–.533	91–.462	20–.700	15–.800	48	37	Barkley 26, Francis 17	Barkley 15	Francis 7
11/26	@Por	88-91[1]	L	3-11	83–.337	88–.398	32–.781	26–.654	55	47	Mobley 25, 2 with 13	Cato 12	Barkley 6
11/29	@Van	118-110[1]	W	4-11	87–.517	86–.453	30–.600	34–.706	46	42	Francis 24, Barkley 22	Cato 10	Francis 10
12/01	@Pho	122-128[2]	L	4-12	94–.489	103–.427	33–.636	39–.846	51	44	Francis 24, Cato 23	Barkley 13	Francis 10
12/02	@LAC	109-96	W	5-12	80–.475	76–.474	35–.686	29–.793	40	39	Anderson 27, 2 with 15	Barkley 10	Barkley 7
12/04	Pho	105-95	W	6-12	85–.482	80–.450	16–.750	29–.690	35	44	Anderson 26, Barkley 21	Cato 8	Drew 10
12/06	Van	102-99	W	7-12	81–.469	79–.481	28–.643	31–.677	40	40	Barkley 25, Rogers 18	Barkley 11	2 with 7
12/08	@Phi	73-83	L	7-13	71–.366	84–.417	21–.714	15–.800	41	45	Francis 18, Mobley 14	Rogers 7	Francis 7
12/10	@Bos	96-100	L	7-14	79–.494	83–.470	21–.619	25–.760	45	40	Mobley 23, 2 with 15	Rogers 13	Drew 7
12/11	@NJ	94-106	L	7-15	79–.430	88–.500	25–.760	16–.813	45	41	Drew 18, Mobley 18	Hamilton 11	Hamilton 4
12/14	NY	90-101	L	7-16	74–.459	74–.527	18–.722	17–.941	32	34	Francis 20, Mobley 14	Rogers 8	Francis 5
12/15	@SA	77-83	L	7-17	75–.400	74–.405	26–.538	28–.750	44	39	Francis 24, Anderson 13	Bullard 8	Francis 4
12/18	Bos	100-94	W	8-17	76–.447	80–.488	40–.700	24–.625	48	38	Cato 27, Mobley 21	Cato 12	Anderson 6
12/21	Por	79-89	L	8-18	71–.437	90–.444	17–.706	6–.833	46	42	Mobley 20, Francis 14	Rogers 8	Francis 7
12/23	Was	105-89	W	9-18	80–.438	77–.468	37–.730	26–.577	41	40	Cato 20, Mobley 20	Cato 12	Francis 11
12/26	@Was	92-103	L	9-19	89–.393	77–.506	28–.571	25–.880	45	41	Francis 21, Williams 20	Hamilton 13	Francis 7
12/28	Tor	99-100	L	9-20	87–.425	91–.418	29–.759	27–.815	49	46	Mobley 21, Rogers 19	Rogers 8	Francis 12
12/30	LAC	122-100	W	10-20	94–.532	85–.447	23–.696	23–.783	47	38	Cato 21, Francis 19	Cato 11	2 with 11
1/04	Sea	96-103	L	10-21	82–.415	92–.467	25–.720	19–.684	48	48	Francis 27, Bullard 20	Rogers 14	Francis 7
1/06	@Mia	99-111	L	10-22	74–.419	86–.535	34–.882	20–.750	35	41	Francis 22, 2 with 17	2 with 7	Francis 6
1/08	Uta	87-103	L	10-23	68–.397	85–.435	42–.738	26–.846	42	45	Rogers 28, Anderson 16	Miller 11	2 with 4
1/11	@Sac	93-110	L	10-24	86–.407	88–.477	26–.731	22–.864	53	41	Francis 16, Mobley 14	Miller 12	Francis 4
1/13	@GS	108-100	W	11-24	101–.426	81–.457	22–.727	29–.690	51	47	Mobley 23, Francis 19	Miller 13	Francis 10
1/15	@Chi	93-90	W	12-24	76–.500	76–.434	21–.476	27–.741	41	38	Francis 27, Williams 17	Williams 9	Francis 11
1/17	@Dal	121-111	W	13-24	82–.500	94–.436	39–.795	28–.893	48	47	Francis 31, Thomas 20	Thomas 12	Francis 11
1/18	Por	90-89	W	14-24	79–.456	86–.430	23–.565	16–.688	40	46	Francis 26, Thomas 22	Thomas 14	Francis 12
1/20	Den	122-115	W	15-24	95–.474	97–.495	28–.786	20–.900	48	40	Anderson 26, Francis 22	Anderson 13	Francis 7
1/23	Mia	101-88	W	16-24	81–.469	93–.398	10–1.000	8–.625	43	47	Bullard 24, Mobley 18	Anderson 12	Francis 9
1/25	Min	84-92	L	16-25	73–.397	85–.494	28–.679	8–.750	37	42	Francis 24, Mobley 18	Thomas 8	Anderson 6
1/27	GS	110-115	L	16-26	91–.418	86–.477	36–.750	36–.694	49	42	Francis 25, Miller 19	Francis 17	**Francis 14**
1/28	@Den	98-104	L	16-27	88–.420	85–.471	25–.720	24–.750	52	37	Francis 27, Bullard 18	Cato 10	Francis 10
1/30	LAL	89-83	W	17-27	68–.426	86–.360	31–.742	29–.621	47	41	Francis 17, Mobley 15	Olajuwon 10	Mobley 4
2/01	Cha	99-83	W	18-27	89–.427	87–.368	21–.714	21–.667	49	47	Mobley 23, Francis 22	2 with 8	Francis 8
2/03	Phi	109-106	W	19-27	82–.451	85–.518	32–.719	22–.727	48	39	Anderson 32, Olajuwon 14	Thomas 12	Francis 7
2/04	@Min	85-102	L	19-28	84–.381	80–.563	23–.696	10–.800	36	47	Drew 20, 2 with 15	Cato 9	Drew 10
2/06	@Det	105-109	L	19-29	83–.458	83–.530	30–.767	23–.826	41	35	Cato 23, Drew 20	Cato 12	Drew 6
2/08	Cle	91-83	W	20-29	85–.447	82–.439	15–.600	13–.692	40	51	Anderson 23, Williams 17	Anderson 10	2 with 5
2/09	@Atl	100-116	L	20-30	83–.422	89–.562	31–.774	20–.750	32	52	Mobley 30, Francis 13	2 with 5	Drew 3
2/15	Det	107-102	W	21-30	82–.476	81–.469	25–.760	30–.700	46	36	Anderson 25, Mobley 21	Cato 13	Francis 7
2/18	@SA	92-116	L	21-31	78–.423	86–.523	31–.742	24–.792	42	40	Francis 18, Anderson 14	Francis 8	Mobley 4
2/20	SA	111-113[1]	L	21-32	89–.449	85–.518	28–.786	21–.810	44	38	Olajuwon 21, Mobley 20	2 with 9	Francis 12
2/22	@Cha	97-102	L	21-33	83–.494	83–.494	11–.636	17–.941	37	47	Francis 24, Thomas 20	Thomas 8	Francis 8

334

Date	Opp	Score	W/L	Rec	Hou FG Att–Pct.	Opp FG Att–Pct.	Hou FT Att–Pct.	Opp FT Att–Pct.	Hou Reb	Opp Reb	Points	Rebounds	Assists
2/24	Den	97-106	L	21-34	85–.459	91–.451	18–.778	25–.840	42	45	Mobley 24, Anderson 14	Rogers 8	2 with 4
2/27	@LAL	85-101	L	21-35	81–.358	77–.532	25–.800	23–.565	39	49	Mobley 29, Thomas 14	Miller 8	2 with 4
2/28	@LAC	96-**77**	W	22-35	90–.378	97–**.268**	20–.750	23–.913	56	55	Mobley 21, Bullard 14	2 with 8	Norris 7
3/02	Sac	102-99	W	23-35	83–.434	95–.411	26–.808	19–.789	48	51	Mobley 22, Anderson 19	Thomas 9	Francis 9
3/04	NJ	99-92[1]	W	24-35	88–.455	91–.385	20–.700	22–.864	53	37	Francis 15, Mobley 14	2 with 8	Thomas 5
3/07	Pho	101-108	L	24-36	86–.488	82–.476	13–.692	26–.923	42	42	Francis 32, Anderson 20	Olajuwon 8	Francis 8
3/09	@Uta	82-101	L	24-37	65–.477	72–.569	22–.682	15–.733	30	36	Anderson 16, Norris 16	Rogers 8	Francis 6
3/11	Min	86-100	L	24-38	78–.372	87–.483	35–.657	14–.929	47	44	Francis 19, Rogers 12	2 with 7	Norris 5
3/14	@NY	85-91	L	24-39	68–.441	**70**–.486	30–.667	25–.880	29	36	Francis 32, Anderson 17	Olajuwon 6	Francis 4
3/16	@Mil	96-106	L	24-40	72–.417	74–.554	32–.875	30–.700	36	40	Francis 22, Mobley 20	Cato 7	Francis 6
3/17	@Ind	102-111	L	24-41	80–.475	86–.488	23–.870	25–.840	38	40	Francis 25, Anderson 22	Cato 8	Anderson 6
3/19	@Tor	98-100	L	24-42	74–.459	91–.440	30–.733	20–.850	39	47	Anderson 25, Williams 19	2 with 8	Francis 7
3/20	@Cle	85-98	L	24-43	75–.467	83–.470	23–.522	19–.842	39	44	Francis 17, Williams 17	2 with 7	4 with 4
3/23	LAC	110-95	W	25-43	83–.566	85–.447	19–.526	21–.762	40	39	Francis 34, Mobley 30	Francis 9	**Francis 14**
3/24	@Orl	96-112	L	25-44	75–.387	102–.441	34–.882	19–.789	43	54	**Anderson 35**, Mobley 19	2 with 9	2 with 6
3/26	Chi	**123**-78	W	26-44	85–.529	81–.407	23–.783	11–.909	47	**33**	Williams 24, Francis 19	Thomas 10	Anderson 8
3/28	GS	121-86	W	27-44	88–.500	96–.396	32–.813	15–**.533**	55	38	Anderson 20, Williams 20	Williams 11	2 with 6
3/30	@Min	90-122	L	27-45	70–.371	87–.598	**47**–.809	16–.750	35	41	Williams 18, 2 with 16	2 with 7	Francis 4
4/01	Atl	115-93	W	28-45	89–.506	103–.369	27–.778	15–.800	**58**	44	Mobley 24, Cato 21	Thomas 22	Thomas 6
4/04	@Van	100-102	L	28-46	82–.476	92–.424	16–.938	24–.833	51	40	Francis 30, Mobley 18	Cato 13	Francis 5
4/05	@Por	118-105	W	29-46	71–**.620**	87–.471	24–.875	18–.778	34	35	Anderson 30, Mobley 22	Anderson 10	Francis 7
4/07	@Sea	119-116	W	30-46	82–.537	101–.465	24–.917	21–.762	36	46	Francis 31, Anderson 28	Cato 9	2 with 7
4/09	Uta	99-90	W	31-46	69–.435	87–.379	32–.813	27–.852	40	42	Francis 26, Williams 21	Thomas 12	Francis 7
4/11	@Den	103-93	W	32-46	80–.450	89–.416	38–.632	17–.941	52	37	Williams 23, 2 with 15	Williams 12	Francis 11
4/13	Dal	111-102	W	33-46	79–.532	88–.420	25–.760	26–.808	44	37	Williams 21, Mobley 20	2 with 11	Francis 7
4/16	Sea	112-121	L	33-47	81–.506	105–.476	25–.800	21–.762	43	45	**Mobley 35**, Francis 20	3 with 9	Norris 10
4/18	@Pho	107-98	W	34-47	70–.486	87–.448	35–.771	19–.737	42	41	**Anderson 35**, Francis 27	Cato 9	Francis 8
4/19	Van	92-96	L	34-48	82–.439	74–.473	16–.813	29–.897	32	43	Williams 20, Thomas 13	Thomas 8	Francis 7

Indiana Pacers 1999-2000 Game Log (56-26)

Date	Opp	Score	W/L	Rec	Ind FG Att–Pct.	Opp FG Att–Pct.	Ind FT Att–Pct.	Opp FT Att–Pct.	Ind Reb	Opp Reb	Points	Rebounds	Assists
11/02	@NJ	119-112	W	1-0	78–.474	81–.444	53–.736	46–.761	43	45	Miller 27, Davis 23	Davis 13	Jackson 5
11/04	@Cha	89-98	L	1-1	71–.479	87–.437	20–.800	29–.621	47	38	Miller 20, Harrington 15	2 with 7	Jackson 7
11/06	Bos	115-108	W	2-1	75–.480	80–.525	40–.825	23–.783	39	38	Miller 29, Jackson 15	Davis 11	Jackson 8
11/09	@Mia	101-113	L	2-2	95–.411	93–.516	19–.789	20–.700	47	52	Rose 17, Harrington 15	Davis 10	Jackson 4
11/11	Orl	116-101	W	3-2	74–.568	89–.472	31–.742	15–.733	36	42	Miller 21, Harrington 19	Rose 8	Rose 7
11/13	Was	105-83	W	4-2	83–.458	92–.370	29–.793	18–.833	45	55	Rose 16, 2 with 15	Davis 8	2 with 6
11/15	@Hou	96-87	W	5-2	83–.398	86–.430	27–.926	14–.714	40	50	Harrington 18, Miller 17	Davis 11	Jackson 7
11/16	@SA	87-90[1]	L	5-3	94–.394	83–.386	6–.833	30–.767	51	48	Rose 28, Perkins 16	Davis 10	3 with 4
11/19	Atl	99-105	L	5-4	83–.434	96–.448	25–.880	22–.773	43	46	Miller 21, Smits 21	Harrington 8	Jackson 12
11/20	@Cle	107-98	W	6-4	91–.495	77–.519	14–.571	16–.813	34	43	Rose 22, Smits 18	Croshere 8	2 with 9
11/22	@Bos	85-95	L	6-5	89–.382	82–.451	15–.733	21–.571	41	51	Davis 19, Miller 18	Davis 12	Jackson 8
11/25	Det	99-107	L	6-6	83–.494	80–.450	16–.625	36–.806	34	46	Smits 23, Davis 21	Davis 8	Jackson 10
11/26	Van	105-86	W	7-6	79–.532	78–.410	17–.882	25–.840	34	39	Smits 17, Rose 15	2 with 5	Best 6
11/28	@Sea	91-102	L	7-7	91–.352	87–.437	27–.815	25–.920	49	48	Davis 19, Mullin 12	Davis 15	Best 5
11/29	@Por	93-91	W	8-7	85–.376	83–.398	31–.742	24–.875	45	46	Rose 22, 2 with 15	Davis 12	Jackson 9
12/01	@Van	96-89	W	9-7	77–.442	80–.438	28–.786	18–.833	38	45	Miller 26, Davis 17	Croshere 9	Jackson 10
12/03	@Uta	100-75	W	10-7	80–.513	79–.380	14–.714	21–.667	43	42	Miller 31, Rose 17	Davis 13	Jackson 9
12/07	SA	83-77	W	11-7	80–.363	81–.407	27–.704	15–.600	49	47	Miller 23, Smits 18	Davis 16	Jackson 9
12/10	Cle	136-88	W	12-7	79–.620	101–.337	37–.757	27–.667	51	49	Smits 25, Rose 23	Davis 20	Miller 8
12/11	LAC	108-90	W	13-7	86–.442	84–.440	29–.828	21–.619	47	42	Miller 26, Smits 16	Davis 18	Jackson 9
12/14	@Tor	97-105	L	13-8	79–.468	94–.436	22–.909	22–.818	35	50	Rose 21, Croshere 18	Davis 10	Best 7
12/15	Chi	102-91	W	14-8	79–.430	82–.488	28–.893	12–.667	40	37	Croshere 21, Smits 19	Smits 8	Jackson 5
12/17	Uta	89-74	W	15-8	78–.385	80–.363	26–.808	23–.609	44	49	Miller 19, Perkins 15	Croshere 11	Jackson 6
12/18	@Mil	95-109	L	15-9	76–.461	84–.500	18–.833	26–.692	40	40	Miller 21, Rose 19	Davis 15	Jackson 10
12/21	Sea	113-103	W	16-9	87–.529	85–.459	10–.900	20–.850	37	45	Miller 31, 2 with 19	Davis 9	2 with 11
12/25	NY	101-90	W	17-9	76–.408	71–.521	40–.800	25–.600	41	40	Miller 26, 2 with 14	Croshere 10	Jackson 7
12/27	@Chi	103-91	W	18-9	80–.500	81–.432	21–.810	22–.636	36	49	Davis 21, Rose 20	Davis 8	Jackson 13
12/29	@Atl	116-89	W	19-9	91–.516	85–.412	16–.875	22–.682	43	46	Miller 25, Davis 19	Davis 12	Jackson 14
12/30	Cha	109-99	W	20-9	85–.471	78–.487	20–.900	27–.593	42	37	Miller 30, Jackson 18	Davis 11	Jackson 11
1/04	NJ	116-111	W	21-9	80–.563	81–.519	26–.808	25–.800	41	30	Miller 24, Smits 22	Smits 9	Jackson 15
1/06	@Den	102-87	W	22-9	79–.481	83–.422	15–.933	23–.565	42	43	Miller 20, Smits 17	3 with 7	Jackson 10
1/08	@LAC	94-107	L	22-10	74–.446	87–.483	31–.774	26–.654	37	41	Best 20, Rose 17	3 with 6	Jackson 6
1/09	@Sac	113-116	L	22-11	99–.414	81–.543	24–.833	29–.724	44	41	Croshere 22, Best 20	Davis 12	Best 8
1/12	Was	117-102	W	23-11	87–.494	91–.440	28–.786	27–.704	38	55	Rose 25, Smits 19	Davis 13	Jackson 13
1/14	LAL	111-102	W	24-11	84–.476	94–.457	23–.957	16–.750	48	42	Miller 22, Rose 19	Croshere 12	Jackson 8
1/15	@Orl	96-89	W	25-11	82–.451	91–.407	19–.684	21–.667	45	50	Croshere 14, 2 with 13	Davis 11	Rose 6
1/17	@Min	100-101	L	25-12	79–.443	93–.462	27–.926	18–.778	40	44	Smits 20, Miller 17	Croshere 13	Jackson 11
1/19	Mil	106-84	W	26-12	80–.463	89–.382	27–.889	14–.786	47	42	Miller 29, 4 with 12	Davis 13	Jackson 12
1/21	@Was	113-123	L	26-13	87–.460	85–.600	27–.889	24–.875	35	35	Miller 21, Rose 21	Davis 9	Jackson 13
1/22	@Phi	97-103	L	26-14	81–.444	82–.439	21–.857	32–.938	33	48	Miller 28, Perkins 16	Davis 15	Jackson 9
1/24	@Chi	82-83	L	26-15	85–.400	75–.440	12–.833	30–.533	49	40	Rose 18, 2 with 13	Davis 11	Jackson 12
1/25	Pho	93-87	W	27-15	79–.430	83–.398	22–.818	20–.750	43	44	Miller 21, Rose 15	2 with 9	Jackson 8
1/29	Mia	94-84	W	28-15	78–.410	85–.388	27–.852	19–.789	35	52	Miller 30, Smits 22	2 with 6	Jackson 8
2/01	Bos	99-96	W	29-15	74–.486	88–.477	30–.800	12–.583	43	45	Smits 26, Rose 20	Davis 14	Jackson 7
2/04	Sac	104-94	W	30-15	88–.432	87–.391	27–.889	24–.792	55	43	Rose 22, Smits 18	Davis 13	Jackson 15
2/05	@Orl	102-107	L	30-16	77–.455	80–.463	38–.789	43–.651	49	43	Rose 25, Smits 14	Davis 14	3 with 4
2/07	Phi	109-84	W	31-16	80–.538	92–.402	12–.917	9–.778	43	39	Miller 32, Rose 20	Rose 7	2 with 6
2/09	@Bos	113-104	W	32-16	78–.564	87–.471	22–.864	17–.824	38	31	Rose 23, 3 with 16	Davis 11	Jackson 9
2/16	Tor	109-101	W	33-16	80–.538	88–.466	19–.789	21–.667	39	39	Rose 32, Croshere 15	Davis 13	Jackson 15
2/17	@Mil	92-90	W	34-16	61–.492	85–.412	34–.765	20–.900	38	42	Miller 23, Rose 20	3 with 9	Jackson 9
2/19	@NY	73-87	L	34-17	79–.342	74–.514	21–.762	10–.900	42	43	Miller 16, Rose 12	Davis 16	Jackson 6
2/21	Dal	94-93	W	35-17	77–.468	90–.433	19–.947	9–.778	38	44	Rose 28, Davis 16	2 with 8	Jackson 6
2/23	@Det	118-111	W	36-17	74–.527	89–.506	36–.861	17–.941	39	31	Smits 29, 2 with 23	Smits 9	Jackson 14
2/24	Chi	100-83	W	37-17	75–.493	81–.444	22–.818	8–.875	42	34	Rose 22, Croshere 17	McKey 10	Jackson 7

Date	Opp	Score	W/L	Rec	Ind FG Att–Pct.	Opp FG Att–Pct.	Ind FT Att–Pct.	Opp FT Att–Pct.	Ind Reb	Opp Reb	Game Leaders Points	Rebounds	Assists
2/26	GS	104-88	W	38-17	85–.424	88–.375	32–.781	27–.741	40	58	Rose 29, Miller 15	Perkins 7	Jackson 9
2/29	Det	115-105	W	39-17	85–.482	92–.424	28–.857	27–.852	47	45	Miller 24, Rose 20	Smits 12	Jackson 13
3/02	@Pho	87-118	L	39-18	79–.392	93–.505	18–.889	21–.857	43	49	Best 20, Rose 19	2 with 9	Jackson 8
3/03	@LAL	92-107	L	39-19	76–.395	89–.461	36–.722	26–.808	39	50	Miller 22, Croshere 15	Davis 13	Jackson 6
3/05	@GS	114-95	W	40-19	94–.436	80–.425	27–.741	30–.767	50	46	Croshere 18, 3 with 15	Davis 8	Jackson 8
3/07	Den	90-89	W	41-19	78–.385	98–.398	32–.719	8–.750	43	60	Rose 19, Best 13	Davis 11	Rose 9
3/09	Por	127-119[1]	W	42-19	86–.477	85–.482	46–.783	40–.800	48	41	Jackson 23, Smits 22	Davis 13	Jackson 9
3/10	@Cle	95-92	W	43-19	68–.471	94–.426	30–.733	9–.667	45	41	Miller 28, Smits 17	2 with 8	Jackson 9
3/12	Mia	96-105	L	43-20	75–.493	78–.500	16–.875	28–.750	32	38	Miller 26, Rose 21	Davis 8	Jackson 7
3/14	@Dal	90-111	L	43-21	94–.330	95–.484	25–.920	10–1.000	52	50	Best 26, Rose 18	2 with 13	Best 5
3/15	@Atl	113-107	W	44-21	79–.519	80–.475	31–.774	37–.757	38	45	Rose 32, Miller 28	Croshere 11	Jackson 10
3/17	Hou	111-102	W	45-21	86–.488	80–.475	25–.840	23–.870	40	38	**Rose 35**, Croshere 22	Croshere 13	Jackson 8
3/18	Cha	113-99	W	46-21	79–.532	85–.424	29–.828	29–.793	45	36	Rose 22, Miller 20	Smits 12	Jackson 9
3/21	NY	95-91	W	47-21	74–.459	87–.460	28–.857	10–.800	38	43	Rose 28, Smits 20	Croshere 8	Jackson 7
3/23	Mil	84-105	L	47-22	72–.375	85–.506	29–.793	19–.895	36	47	Rose 22, Miller 16	Croshere 7	Jackson 5
3/26	Phi	101-111	L	47-23	83–.434	94–.500	24–.917	23–.696	40	51	Rose 19, Best 17	Smits 7	2 with 5
3/28	@NJ	106-111	L	47-24	86–.453	94–.436	23–.913	30–.800	48	40	Rose 27, Croshere 15	Croshere 10	Jackson 11
3/31	Min	109-85	W	48-24	82–.537	92–.380	16–.750	17–.706	50	46	Best 27, Miller 26	2 with 9	Best 7
4/02	@Tor	104-83	W	49-24	81–.481	81–.383	18–.889	20–.950	43	43	Rose 23, Perkins 22	2 with 7	Jackson 10
4/05	NJ	105-101	W	50-24	82–.537	80–.488	15–.733	21–.952	42	32	Smits 25, Rose 17	Davis 11	Jackson 8
4/07	Cle	95-94	W	51-24	78–.449	83–.470	29–.759	21–.762	43	44	Rose 26, Best 16	Rose 13	Jackson 6
4/09	@Cha	80-96	L	51-25	84–.369	74–.419	14–.857	38–.789	44	51	Rose 18, Davis 12	Davis 14	Jackson 8
4/10	@NY	81-83	L	51-26	73–.384	78–.462	24–.750	**7**–.857	44	39	Jackson 13, Smits 12	Davis 12	Jackson 5
4/12	Tor	77-**73**	W	52-26	76–.382	81–**.333**	18–.833	20–.650	43	47	Rose 24, Croshere 15	Davis 14	2 with 4
4/14	@Mia	105-101	W	53-26	76–.513	77–.519	25–.800	25–.760	31	36	Miller 26, Rose 22	Davis 7	Jackson 5
4/16	@Det	112-101	W	54-26	76–.566	85–.482	21–.762	19–.842	32	40	Miller 21, Rose 20	Davis 15	Jackson 9
4/17	@Phi	92-90	W	55-26	79–.481	82–.415	12–.583	28–.679	43	42	Mullin 21, Rose 20	Smits 10	Rose 9
4/19	Atl	111-92	W	56-26	90–.489	92–.370	22–.818	29–.690	**58**	41	Rose 19, Best 14	Foster 13	Jackson 8

Postseason

Date	Opp	Score	W/L	Rec	Ind FG Att–Pct.	Opp FG Att–Pct.	Ind FT Att–Pct.	Opp FT Att–Pct.	Ind Reb	Opp Reb	Game Leaders Points	Rebounds	Assists
4/23	Mil	88-85	W	1-0	86–.372	83–.361	26–.731	26–.808	47	43	Rose 26, Miller 21	Davis 17	Jackson 11
4/27	Mil	91-104	L	1-1	80–.388	77–.532	35–.714	25–.720	44	42	Croshere 16, Best 14	Davis 12	Jackson 5
4/29	@Mil	109-96	W	2-1	84–.488	86–.465	19–.947	19–.684	35	42	Miller 34, Rose 27	Croshere 11	2 with 5
5/01	Mil	87-100	L	2-2	75–.400	85–.494	32–.844	15–.733	39	44	Rose 17, Miller 15	Davis 10	Jackson 6
5/04	Mil	96-95	W	3-2	83–.434	82–.439	25–.720	25–.840	44	43	Miller 41, Rose 14	Davis 12	Jackson 8
5/06	Phi	108-91	W	1-0	79–.494	82–.439	21–.905	22–.727	37	42	Miller 40, Rose 40	Croshere 11	Jackson 10
5/08	Phi	103-97	W	2-0	76–.487	78–.436	25–.840	37–.703	38	39	Rose 30, Croshere 20	Rose 7	Jackson 14
5/10	@Phi	97-89	W	3-0	78–.487	77–.416	15–.800	32–.750	40	42	Miller 29, Best 19	Davis 17	Jackson 8
5/13	@Phi	90-92	L	3-1	80–.388	78–.385	25–.840	43–.674	37	53	Smits 20, 2 with 16	Davis 11	Jackson 7
5/15	Phi	86-107	L	3-2	84–.405	78–.500	20–.750	32–.813	34	45	Smits 15, 2 with 13	Davis 8	2 with 6
5/19	@Phi	106-90	W	4-2	76–.513	87–.391	26–.808	28–.714	46	41	Miller 25, Rose 21	Davis 11	Jackson 11
5/23	NY	102-88	W	1-0	83–.482	80–.438	12–1.000	17–.706	43	35	Croshere 22, Miller 19	Davis 16	Jackson 13
5/25	NY	88-84	W	2-0	77–.364	78–.436	38–.737	18–.778	49	45	Rose 24, Miller 19	Davis 16	Jackson 5
5/27	@NY	95-98	L	2-1	70–.514	74–.527	18–.889	24–.750	33	28	Rose 26, Smits 25	Davis 16	2 with 6
5/29	@NY	89-91	L	2-2	79–.456	71–.493	10–.900	16–.688	32	41	Miller 24, Rose 18	Davis 11	Jackson 7
5/31	NY	88-79	W	3-2	79–.367	75–.400	25–.800	17–.765	45	43	Best 24, Rose 18	McKey 9	Jackson 7
6/02	@NY	93-80	W	4-2	74–.392	74–.419	31–.903	19–.737	42	34	Miller 34, Rose 11	Davis 16	2 with 4
6/07	@LAL	87-104	L	0-1	76–.421	88–.511	23–.783	19–.579	36	48	Jackson 18, Croshere 16	Davis 8	Jackson 7
6/09	@LAL	104-111	L	0-2	88–.375	75–.480	39–.846	57–.561	46	47	Rose 30, Croshere 24	Davis 10	Jackson 8
6/11	LAL	100-91	W	1-2	78–.462	76–.500	24–.875	19–.421	39	33	Miller 33, Rose 21	Davis 12	Jackson 6
6/14	LAL	118-120[1]	L	1-3	84–.500	93–.516	28–.857	30–.667	39	42	Miller 35, Smits 24	Davis 8	Jackson 7
6/16	LAL	120-87	W	2-3	68–.574	90–.400	36–.889	21–.524	46	34	Rose 32, Miller 25	Croshere 9	Jackson 7
6/19	@LAL	111-116	L	2-4	77–.468	90–.478	32–.844	33–.606	41	44	Rose 29, Miller 25	Davis 14	Jackson 11

Los Angeles Clippers 1999-2000 Game Log (15-67)

Date	Opp	Score	W/L	Rec	LAC FG Att–Pct.	Opp FG Att–Pct.	LAC FT Att–Pct.	Opp FT Att–Pct.	LAC Reb	Opp Reb	Points	Rebounds	Assists
11/02	Sea	92-104	L	0-1	78–.449	93–.398	27–.593	32–.719	45	53	Odom 30, Anderson 19	Olwkandi 16	2 with 3
11/03	@Por	98-121	L	0-2	80–.450	74–.608	30–.833	33–.818	29	41	Odom 23, Taylor 22	Odom 7	Anderson 4
11/05	Phi	91-81	W	1-2	69–.435	86–.337	31–.871	34–.647	52	44	Anderson 21, Odom 18	Skinner 11	Anderson 6
11/08	Uta	79-94	L	1-3	73–.342	76–.487	35–.771	23–.783	36	44	Taylor 23, 2 with 11	2 with 8	Odom 4
11/10	SA	94-99	L	1-4	71–.451	85–.424	33–.758	28–.786	40	45	Anderson 28, Taylor 18	2 with 9	Hudson 6
11/14	@Van	89-109	L	1-5	81–.407	79–.570	29–.690	15–.800	41	37	Odom 16, Olwkandi 14	Odom 12	Anderson 5
11/16	@Mil	93-101	L	1-6	95–.389	78–.500	26–.615	24–.833	54	43	Anderson 27, Odom 22	Skinner 17	2 with 5
11/17	@Min	89-85	W	2-6	90–.389	82–.476	32–.719	20–.650	43	48	Odom 22, Nesby 20	Olwkandi 12	Murdock 7
11/19	@Tor	100-106	L	2-7	83–.434	80–.475	30–.667	28–.821	43	40	Hudson 20, Piatkowski 19	Skinner 16	2 with 4
11/20	@Was	98-89	W	3-7	72–.444	93–.398	31–.774	16–.750	37	50	Piatkowski 25, Hudson 22	Skinner 13	Murdock 6
11/23	NY	100-95	W	4-7	77–.403	81–.432	32–.875	31–.774	41	39	Odom 24, Anderson 23	Skinner 10	Odom 5
11/26	@Sea	93-98	L	4-8	78–.449	79–.494	21–.810	25–.520	35	40	Anderson 29, Nesby 18	2 with 8	Odom 6
11/27	Por	71-88	L	4-9	79–.329	87–.425	25–.520	9–.889	45	47	Nesby 16, Odom 15	Piatkowski 10	Odom 6
11/30	Pho	80-94	L	4-10	76–.342	86–.442	**39**–.692	27–.593	44	51	Anderson 25, Taylor 15	Skinner 10	2 with 4
12/02	Hou	96-109	L	4-11	76–.474	80–.475	29–.793	35–.686	39	40	Anderson 23, Odom 22	Odom 8	Anderson 4
12/04	Sea	89-102	L	4-12	87–.368	72–.514	29–.759	29–.793	40	40	Anderson 19, Taylor 19	Odom 8	Murdock 6
12/06	Mia	91-99	L	4-13	91–.429	82–.512	12–.833	15–.800	47	41	Odom 20, Taylor 17	Anderson 10	**Anderson 12**
12/08	@Atl	81-99	L	4-14	87–.368	87–.506	17–.765	14–.643	43	50	Taylor 22, Olwkandi 17	**Olwkandi 20**	Anderson 8
12/10	@Det	83-107	L	4-15	82–.415	84–.488	17–.588	22–.864	37	52	Olwkandi 16, Anderson 14	Taylor 7	Anderson 5
12/11	@Ind	90-108	L	4-16	84–.440	86–.442	21–.619	29–.828	42	47	Olwkandi 21, Taylor 16	Olwkandi 13	Odom 7
12/13	Van	102-90	W	5-16	83–.506	75–.413	17–.706	33–.727	39	39	Taylor 26, Hudson 18	Olwkandi 10	Hudson 11
12/14	@LAL	68-95	L	5-17	80–.325	91–.429	17–.529	25–.640	42	59	Nesby 18, Olwkandi 13	Olwkandi 10	Hudson 8
12/17	GS	92-91	W	6-17	78–.436	94–.394	33–.606	17–.706	47	46	Odom 23, Hudson 20	Odom 13	Odom 7
12/19	@Van	84-85	L	6-18	69–.464	75–.400	22–.591	24–.792	35	46	Taylor 20, Odom 20	Olwkandi 11	Hudson 9
12/22	@GS	103-99	W	7-18	85–.471	96–.438	16–.875	14–.571	45	44	Nesby 28, 2 with 22	Odom 11	Hudson 9
12/23	Sac	97-91	W	8-18	86–.430	86–.419	24–.750	33–**.485**	49	47	Hudson 16, Taylor 14	Taylor 10	Hudson 10
12/26	Bos	103-100	W	9-18	88–.466	77–.494	21–.619	29–.759	36	44	Taylor 26, Nesby 22	Odom 11	Hudson 9
12/28	@Den	105-128	L	9-19	91–.473	86–.535	18–.722	36–.778	44	45	Taylor 30, Nesby 16	Odom 10	Hudson 8
12/30	@Hou	100-122	L	9-20	85–.447	94–.532	23–.783	23–.696	38	47	Taylor 31, Piatkowski 24	Odom 13	Odom 10
1/04	LAL	98-122	L	9-21	101–.406	104–.481	17–.706	27–.704	52	59	Nesby 22, Odom 22	Odom 12	Hudson 10
1/05	@LAL	101-118	L	9-22	86–.453	100–.500	23–.783	23–.652	42	60	Odom 26, Nesby 23	Odom 12	Hudson 7
1/08	Ind	107-94	W	10-22	87–.483	74–.446	26–.654	31–.774	41	37	Olwkandi 24, 2 with 23	Olwkandi 17	Hudson 5
1/10	@Cle	106-111	L	10-23	80–.425	82–.476	31–.903	39–.744	32	45	Anderson 29, Odom 28	Odom 7	Anderson 5
1/12	@Bos	88-95	L	10-24	80–.463	93–.376	11–.727	26–.731	47	46	Odom 26, Taylor 22	Olwkandi 15	Hudson 4
1/13	@NJ	105-110	L	10-25	82–**.537**	87–.483	15–.667	28–.821	29	48	Odom 26, Anderson 23	Olwkandi 10	4 with 4
1/15	@Uta	75-112	L	10-26	81–.383	91–.505	13–.769	19–.789	36	56	Anderson 18, Olwkandi 18	Odom 8	Anderson 8
1/17	SA	93-99	L	10-27	85–.447	76–.553	16–.688	26–.500	39	44	Taylor 22, Anderson 17	Taylor 12	2 with 5
1/18	@Sac	98-104	L	10-28	90–.422	95–.432	25–.720	20–.850	54	48	Taylor 22, Odom 19	Olwkandi 15	Hudson 4
1/21	Min	89-95	L	10-29	82–.476	86–.430	13–.615	22–.864	44	39	Odom 18, 2 with 14	Odom 14	Odom 5
1/23	Orl	89-102	L	10-30	80–.450	89–.438	19–.737	30–.700	45	48	Anderson 20, Taylor 19	Olwkandi 13	Hudson 4
1/25	@SA	82-105	L	10-31	85–.412	81–.469	10–.800	37–.703	36	54	Anderson 22, Odom 16	Olwkandi 13	Murdock 7
1/27	@Dal	90-99	L	10-32	77–.403	87–.471	27–.926	14–.857	45	39	**Anderson 35**, Odom 21	Olwkandi 14	Odom 6
1/29	NJ	98-93	W	11-32	79–.506	88–.409	19–.789	15–.800	44	36	Taylor 23, Odom 21	Olwkandi 13	Murdock 10
2/01	GS	76-107	L	11-33	81–.346	90–.533	18–.833	7–.714	36	46	Nesby 20, Taylor 16	Olwkandi 10	4 with 2
2/02	@Pho	68-114	L	11-34	78–.295	85–.576	19–.842	17–.824	34	50	Nesby 17, Piatkowski 10	2 with 9	3 with 4
2/05	Dal	106-119	L	11-35	91–.462	81–.494	29–.586	33–.879	50	40	Taylor 17, Odom 14	Olwkandi 11	Hudson 6
2/06	Chi	90-100	L	11-36	75–.493	70–.543	18–.778	24–.792	24	36	Taylor 23, Hudson 19	Olwkandi 8	Hudson 8
2/09	@Por	100-107	L	11-37	85–.494	68–.529	8–.875	36–.889	29	39	Taylor 23, Hudson 22	Odom 7	Odom 6
2/10	Van	90-112	L	11-38	83–.434	82–.512	14–.929	22–.909	35	40	Anderson 29, Olwkandi 14	Odom 7	Odom 7
2/15	@Mia	88-107	L	11-39	86–.384	89–.461	26–.692	24–.750	37	63	Murdock 15, Piatkowski 15	Olwkandi 9	Murdock 5
2/16	@Orl	96-129	L	11-40	97–.402	92–.554	19–.684	21–.857	47	49	Taylor 19, 2 with 13	Olwkandi 15	Hudson 4
2/18	@Cha	87-115	L	11-41	85–.400	88–.545	21–.714	14–.786	32	52	Taylor 22, Odom 16	Odom 10	Odom 6
2/19	@Chi	72-**74**	L	11-42	78–.385	77–**.286**	13–.538	40–.575	55	46	Hudson 22, Odom 19	Skinner 12	Hudson 8
2/21	@NY	76-87	L	11-43	70–.400	74–.446	18–.667	21–.905	36	39	Odom 14, Taylor 14	Olwkandi 8	Odom 7

Date	Opp	Score	W/L	Rec	LAC FG Att–Pct.	Opp FG Att–Pct.	LAC FT Att–Pct.	Opp FT Att–Pct.	LAC Reb	Opp Reb	Game Leaders Points	Rebounds	Assists
2/23	@Phi	78-94	L	11-44	78–.397	84–.464	16–.750	21–.667	34	58	Odom 20, Anderson 19	Odom 9	Hudson 4
2/24	@Min	91-116	L	11-45	73–.452	90–.556	20–.850	13–.769	27	45	Taylor 22, Nesby 19	Avent 7	Jones 6
2/26	Atl	78-77	W	12-45	85–.376	84–.405	13–.692	5–1.000	44	52	Anderson 21, Nesby 14	Odom 12	Odom 7
2/28	Hou	77-96	L	12-46	97–.268	90–.378	23–.913	20–.750	55	56	Odom 20, 3 with 12	Anderson 12	Jones 3
3/04	Cle	99-109	L	12-47	78–.436	67–.478	34–.794	54–.778	37	45	Odom 17, Nesby 14	Olwkandi 12	2 with 3
3/06	LAL	103-123	L	12-48	93–.409	82–.610	31–.742	34–.588	40	50	Taylor 25, Anderson 21	Odom 11	Odom 4
3/08	Tor	94-95	L	12-49	74–.446	78–.462	25–.960	25–.640	38	36	Anderson 21, Nesby 21	Olwkandi 14	Odom 8
3/10	Cha	101-118	L	12-50	85–.471	86–.523	18–.778	35–.714	42	45	Anderson 24, Nesby 20	Odom 10	Odom 11
3/12	@GS	112-103	W	13-50	89–.528	86–.442	22–.591	28–.857	46	43	Odom 29, Piatkowski 20	Odom 14	Odom 7
3/14	Den	110-106	W	14-50	76–.526	77–.571	25–.840	18–.778	25	37	Piatkowski 31, Odom 25	2 with 5	Odom 9
3/15	@Sac	78-98	L	14-51	88–.352	84–.452	17–.765	23–.826	52	47	Odom 21, Olwkandi 16	Olwkandi 14	Odom 10
3/17	@Den	87-114	L	14-52	104–.356	87–.471	11–.909	30–.800	51	56	Taylor 21, Anderson 11	Olwkandi 9	McInnis 7
3/18	Sac	83-104	L	14-53	77–.442	84–.464	19–.632	27–.778	48	34	Anderson 25, Odom 18	Piatkowski 13	Anderson 5
3/20	Was	93-105	L	14-54	79–.405	89–.461	30–.733	22–.773	46	46	Nesby 20, Anderson 18	Taylor 11	2 with 4
3/22	@SA	78-103	L	14-55	76–.395	84–.500	21–.714	25–.640	41	48	Anderson 17, Olwkandi 16	Chilcutt 9	Anderson 6
3/23	@Hou	95-110	L	14-56	85–.447	83–.566	21–.762	19–.526	39	40	Odom 28, Anderson 20	Closs 11	McInnis 7
3/25	Det	107-126	L	14-57	84–.476	79–.633	23–.783	23–.696	22	48	Nesby 22, Anderson 19	2 with 4	McInnis 8
3/28	Dal	102-112	L	14-58	83–.506	85–.482	15–.867	18–.944	37	41	Piatkowski 28, Olwkandi 27	Olwkandi 8	McInnis 9
3/30	Mil	85-104	L	14-59	80–.400	87–.494	20–.750	19–.737	38	48	McInnis 20, Nesby 17	Olwkandi 10	McInnis 7
4/04	Uta	93-103	L	14-60	82–.476	76–.513	13–.923	33–.667	36	41	Anderson 20, 2 with 16	Taylor 9	McInnis 6
4/06	Min	90-112	L	14-61	65–.462	91–.505	32–.750	16–.813	31	45	Taylor 23, Piatkowski 13	Closs 8	McInnis 4
4/08	@Dal	96-98	L	14-62	84–.440	83–.410	16–.813	29–.724	57	40	Nesby 29, Taylor 24	Taylor 15	McInnis 7
4/11	Pho	88-95	L	14-63	82–.415	74–.446	17–.824	32–.750	40	47	Odom 26, Anderson 25	Odom 15	Odom 6
4/12	@Uta	93-102	L	14-64	76–.434	73–.479	23–.739	39–.769	35	40	Piatkowski 35, Nesby 23	Odom 7	Odom 8
4/14	@Pho	88-112	L	14-65	80–.338	85–.471	38–.737	30–.733	40	53	Nesby 21, Olwkandi 15	Olwkandi 12	Odom 4
4/15	Den	114-115[1]	L	14-66	94–.426	89–.483	36–.833	27–.704	45	53	Anderson 31, Nesby 25	Odom 13	Odom 5
4/18	Por	100-116	L	14-67	91–.451	75–.640	18–.667	18–.833	28	40	Anderson 20, Nesby 20	Olwkandi 14	2 with 4
4/19	@Sea	114-106	W	15-67	94–.436	87–.506	24–.833	19–.526	49	35	Odom 33, Piatkowski 27	Odom 14	2 with 7

Los Angeles Lakers 1999-2000 Game Log (67-15)

Date	Opp	Score	W/L	Rec	LAL FG Att–Pct.	Opp FG Att–Pct.	LAL FT Att–Pct.	Opp FT Att–Pct.	LAL Reb	Opp Reb	Points	Rebounds	Assists
11/02	@Uta	91-84	W	1-0	76–.434	**67**–.433	26–.654	28–.821	45	38	Rice 28, O'Neal 23	O'Neal 13	Fisher 7
11/03	Van	103-88	W	2-0	91–.505	73–.411	17–.588	40–.700	47	40	O'Neal 28, Rice 17	O'Neal 10	Fisher 8
11/06	@Por	82-97	L	2-1	78–.397	69–.551	34–.500	21–.952	39	40	O'Neal 21, Rice 14	2 with 10	Harper 9
11/07	Dal	105-97	W	3-1	86–.465	82–.427	37–.541	30–.800	51	42	O'Neal 30, Rice 20	O'Neal 20	Fisher 8
11/09	@Dal	123-101	W	4-1	85–**.624**	91–.418	28–.429	22–.818	53	35	O'Neal 27, Rice 21	O'Neal 10	Shaw 5
11/10	@Hou	89-88	W	5-1	81–.395	74–.405	24–.833	33–.667	42	44	Rice 24, 2 with 14	Green 12	Harper 6
11/12	Hou	81-97	L	5-2	83–.337	71–.493	25–**.880**	23–.913	39	44	Rice 11, 3 with 10	Green 9	Green 4
11/14	Atl	93-88	W	6-2	84–.429	81–.395	33–.515	33–.576	47	56	O'Neal 23, Fisher 20	O'Neal 11	Harper 5
11/15	@Pho	91-82	W	7-2	76–.382	87–.368	46–.674	19–.737	52	44	O'Neal 34, Rice 23	O'Neal 18	2 with 4
11/18	@Den	82-93	L	7-3	75–.453	76–.434	22–.364	31–.645	35	45	O'Neal 36, Fisher 15	Green 9	Fisher 9
11/19	Chi	103-95	W	8-3	63–.460	86–.360	**64**–.672	34–.684	46	41	O'Neal 41, Rice 17	O'Neal 17	Harper 4
11/21	Tor	102-111	L	8-4	91–.462	86–.442	27–.519	33–.758	50	52	O'Neal 37, Rice 29	O'Neal 19	2 with 5
11/24	Uta	90-82	W	9-4	64–.484	80–.375	41–.634	23–.783	44	40	O'Neal 39, Rice 21	O'Neal 18	2 with 4
11/26	NJ	103-80	W	10-4	83–.542	81–.346	14–.643	21–.905	44	42	O'Neal 30, Harper 17	O'Neal 16	O'Neal 7
11/30	@Sea	101-77	W	11-4	77–.519	79–.392	21–.762	24–.583	44	42	O'Neal 27, Rice 19	O'Neal 10	Fisher 8
12/01	GS	93-75	W	12-4	93–.376	84–.333	29–.759	22–.727	57	52	O'Neal 28, Bryant 19	O'Neal 23	Fisher 4
12/03	Por	93-80	W	13-4	86–.360	76–.342	41–.659	25–.840	57	42	Bryant 23, O'Neal 21	O'Neal 16	O'Neal 6
12/05	Orl	117-100	W	14-4	82–.488	78–.397	37–.703	38–.868	44	36	O'Neal 27, Rice 24	O'Neal 10	O'Neal 7
12/07	Was	91-80	W	15-4	72–.444	89–.360	38–.658	20–.650	45	50	O'Neal 30, Bryant 21	O'Neal 16	Harper 7
12/08	@Sac	91-103	L	15-5	83–.422	82–.451	23–.783	35–.714	37	45	Bryant 27, O'Neal 27	O'Neal 9	Bryant 5
12/11	@Van	106-94	W	16-5	81–.481	81–.469	34–.794	15–.867	42	37	O'Neal 30, Rice 22	O'Neal 10	Bryant 7
12/12	Det	101-93	W	17-5	100–.420	78–.385	25–.600	36–.750	**63**	40	Bryant 26, O'Neal 22	**O'Neal 24**	Bryant 6
12/14	LAC	95-68	W	18-5	91–.429	80–.325	25–.640	17–**.529**	59	42	O'Neal 21, Bryant 18	O'Neal 19	3 with 4
12/16	@Atl	95-88	W	19-5	87–.402	78–.385	36–.694	36–.722	51	46	Bryant 30, Rice 11	O'Neal 13	2 with 4
12/17	@Min	97-88	W	20-5	78–.449	83–.470	33–.697	17–.588	46	37	Bryant 28, O'Neal 24	O'Neal 13	**Bryant 12**
12/19	@Tor	94-88	W	21-5	75–.427	89–.393	40–.700	23–.652	44	50	Bryant 26, O'Neal 24	O'Neal 15	Rice 4
12/20	@Bos	99-90	W	22-5	65–.523	89–.404	41–.683	18–.833	45	43	O'Neal 34, Bryant 27	O'Neal 20	2 with 4
12/25	SA	99-93	W	23-5	83–.458	85–.376	32–.688	33–.758	43	53	O'Neal 32, Rice 25	O'Neal 11	3 with 5
12/27	Dal	108-106	W	24-5	90–.489	93–.441	22–.773	21–.667	55	46	O'Neal 35, Bryant 25	O'Neal 14	Horry 8
12/29	Pho	103-87	W	25-5	79–.519	90–.378	23–.609	18–.667	53	42	O'Neal 27, Bryant 18	O'Neal 19	O'Neal 7
1/04	@LAC	122-98	W	26-5	104–.481	101–.406	27–.704	17–.706	59	52	O'Neal 38, Bryant 29	O'Neal 15	Shaw 7
1/05	LAC	118-101	W	27-5	100–.500	86–.453	23–.652	23–.783	60	42	O'Neal 40, Bryant 26	O'Neal 19	Shaw 8
1/07	Cha	87-83	W	28-5	80–.338	73–.411	34–.735	32–.656	52	46	O'Neal 23, Rice 17	O'Neal 16	2 with 4
1/08	@Sea	110-100	W	29-5	76–.526	86–.419	28–.750	29–.724	41	48	Bryant 31, Rice 24	O'Neal 9	O'Neal 6
1/10	Den	130-95	W	30-5	107–.486	85–.435	26–.692	24–.750	59	38	O'Neal 31, Bryant 30	O'Neal 19	O'Neal 9
1/12	@Mil	103-94	W	31-5	81–.481	78–.397	25–.760	28–1.000	42	37	O'Neal 27, Bryant 22	O'Neal 10	Fisher 6
1/14	@Ind	102-111	L	31-6	94–.457	84–.476	16–.750	23–.957	42	48	Rice 23, O'Neal 22	O'Neal 14	Harper 7
1/15	@Min	104-91	W	32-6	82–.488	85–.388	24–.542	26–.731	52	38	O'Neal 26, Bryant 22	O'Neal 19	2 with 7
1/17	Sea	81-82	L	32-7	83–.398	74–.405	20–.600	20–.700	42	40	O'Neal 30, Bryant 15	Bryant 14	2 with 6
1/19	Cle	95-86	W	33-7	81–.346	84–.381	50–.700	32–.656	59	50	O'Neal 27, Bryant 25	O'Neal 23	Bryant 4
1/22	Por	91-95	L	33-8	82–.451	87–.460	20–.700	17–.706	37	45	Bryant 28, O'Neal 17	O'Neal 16	O'Neal 7
1/24	@Uta	101-105[2]	L	33-9	98–.408	83–.446	23–.783	32–.875	44	51	O'Neal 36, Bryant 26	O'Neal 9	Harper 8
1/28	Mil	117-89	W	34-9	85–.529	89–.382	28–.786	21–.810	43	40	O'Neal 30, Bryant 23	O'Neal 8	Harper 10
1/30	@Hou	83-89	L	34-10	86–.360	68–.426	29–.621	31–.742	41	47	O'Neal 27, Bryant 17	O'Neal 19	Bryant 5
2/01	@SA	81-105	L	34-11	78–.436	82–.524	20–.600	19–.737	33	46	O'Neal 31, Bryant 19	2 with 7	Bryant 8
2/04	Uta	113-**67**	W	35-11	69–.493	81–**.296**	55–.727	26–.731	53	39	O'Neal 25, Rice 20	Green 10	Bryant 9
2/07	Den	106-98	W	36-11	83–.506	93–.419	28–.571	14–.786	47	48	O'Neal 35, Bryant 29	O'Neal 13	Bryant 11
2/09	Min	114-81	W	37-11	79–.481	88–.341	42–.833	27–.704	54	39	O'Neal 37, Bryant 24	O'Neal 16	Shaw 7
2/15	@Chi	88-76	W	38-11	82–.402	77–.377	20–.850	15–.867	49	37	O'Neal 29, Bryant 21	O'Neal 20	Fisher 6
2/16	@Cha	92-85	W	39-11	88–.386	77–.416	28–.821	22–.864	46	42	Bryant 26, Rice 21	O'Neal 14	Bryant 9
2/18	@Orl	107-99[1]	W	40-11	81–.494	97–.454	27–.852	11–.636	38	44	O'Neal 39, Rice 20	O'Neal 16	Fisher 8
2/20	@Phi	87-84	W	41-11	80–.450	85–.388	19–.579	21–.619	39	51	O'Neal 22, 2 with 18	O'Neal 16	O'Neal 9
2/22	@NJ	97-89	W	42-11	82–.463	78–.436	29–.690	26–.731	42	42	O'Neal 35, Bryant 21	O'Neal 13	4 with 4
2/23	@Cle	116-98	W	43-11	89–.517	79–.468	16–.813	23–.783	36	41	Bryant 21, Horry 20	O'Neal 8	O'Neal 7

Date	Opp	Score	W/L	Rec	LAL FG Att–Pct.	Opp FG Att–Pct.	LAL FT Att–Pct.	Opp FT Att–Pct.	LAL Reb	Opp Reb	Points	Rebounds	Assists
2/25	Bos	109-96	W	44-11	77–.532	89–.416	38–.658	30–.667	47	38	O'Neal 28, Rice 20	O'Neal 15	Harper 7
2/27	Hou	101-85	W	45-11	77–.532	81–.358	23–.565	25–.800	49	39	Bryant 31, O'Neal 24	O'Neal 13	O'Neal 8
2/29	@Por	90-87	W	46-11	69–.449	89–.404	27–.815	14–.786	43	44	O'Neal 23, Bryant 22	O'Neal 10	Horry 5
3/01	Van	103-91	W	47-11	87–.448	76–.447	27–.704	19–.789	42	39	Bryant 27, O'Neal 25	O'Neal 17	2 with 5
3/03	Ind	107-92	W	48-11	89–.461	76–.395	26–.808	36–.722	50	39	O'Neal 31, Bryant 22	O'Neal 15	Bryant 7
3/05	Mia	93-80	W	49-11	76–.395	72–.417	36–.750	24–.667	48	42	Rice 23, O'Neal 17	O'Neal 11	O'Neal 7
3/06	@LAC	123-103	W	50-11	82–.610	93–.409	34–.588	31–.742	50	40	**O'Neal 61**, Bryant 22	O'Neal 23	3 with 5
3/09	@GS	109-92	W	51-11	83–.482	82–.427	27–.852	37–.595	49	46	Bryant 30, O'Neal 29	O'Neal 13	2 with 4
3/12	Sac	109-106	W	52-11	98–.469	85–.482	21–.667	19–.789	59	33	Bryant 40, O'Neal 39	O'Neal 20	Bryant 8
3/13	@Den	118-108	W	53-11	80–.513	88–.443	37–.811	27–.852	47	36	O'Neal 40, Bryant 22	2 with 9	O'Neal 7
3/16	@Was	102-109	L	53-12	74–.500	76–.500	32–.719	35–.800	38	37	O'Neal 40, Rice 22	O'Neal 12	Bryant 7
3/17	@Det	110-82	W	54-12	92–.489	85–.353	22–.727	29–.690	49	45	O'Neal 35, Bryant 25	O'Neal 11	Bryant 6
3/19	@NY	92-85	W	55-12	80–.425	81–.407	32–.594	20–.700	46	48	O'Neal 43, Bryant 24	O'Neal 10	Bryant 7
3/20	@Mia	100-89	W	56-12	75–.507	81–.420	23–.870	24–.792	37	**32**	O'Neal 28, Rice 28	O'Neal 12	Bryant 4
3/22	GS	119-96	W	57-12	84–.500	90–.400	38–.763	34–.647	53	40	O'Neal 22, Bryant 18	Knight 10	Harper 7
3/24	Pho	109-101	W	58-12	83–.482	85–.471	33–.750	18–.722	38	48	O'Neal 40, Bryant 28	O'Neal 14	Bryant 7
3/26	@Sac	90-89	W	59-12	89–.382	87–.437	25–.720	13–.692	53	44	O'Neal 34, Bryant 24	Bryant 14	Bryant 4
3/29	@Van	108-99	W	60-12	90–.500	74–.541	19–.632	19–.737	37	38	Bryant 28, O'Neal 19	Horry 7	O'Neal 8
3/31	Phi	100-88	W	61-12	79–.532	96–.375	18–.778	20–.700	50	38	O'Neal 37, Harper 16	O'Neal 14	3 with 5
4/02	NY	106-82	W	62-12	76–.513	91–.374	29–.828	**8**–1.000	50	37	O'Neal 34, Bryant 17	O'Neal 12	Bryant 8
4/04	@Pho	84-83	W	63-12	82–.402	84–.393	25–.680	19–.737	48	45	O'Neal 32, Horry 11	Horry 11	Harper 8
4/05	@GS	111-104	W	64-12	79–.506	96–.417	30–.767	26–.692	40	58	O'Neal 49, Bryant 16	O'Neal 13	Bryant 11
4/08	SA	80-98	L	64-13	95–.316	75–.467	24–.708	32–.813	50	50	Bryant 26, Rice 17	Green 9	Bryant 5
4/10	Sea	106-103[1]	W	65-13	95–.400	96–.406	30–.867	28–.571	56	49	Bryant 33, Rice 28	Bryant 10	2 with 6
4/14	Sac	121-114	W	66-13	89–.551	93–.452	27–.704	33–.758	43	38	O'Neal 41, Bryant 31	O'Neal 16	Harper 10
4/16	Min	101-95	W	67-13	74–.486	90–.433	31–.871	21–.762	40	46	O'Neal 33, Bryant 25	O'Neal 14	Bryant 10
4/18	@Dal	102-112	L	67-14	92–.467	87–.483	20–.450	28–.893	56	41	O'Neal 38, Bryant 16	O'Neal 20	Shaw 9
4/19	@SA	98-103[1]	L	67-15	102–.402	88–.466	20–.600	24–.625	58	51	Bryant 23, O'Neal 22	Shaw 10	Shaw 7

Postseason

Date	Opp	Score	W/L	Rec	LAL FG Att–Pct.	Opp FG Att–Pct.	LAL FT Att–Pct.	Opp FT Att–Pct.	LAL Reb	Opp Reb	Points	Rebounds	Assists
4/23	Sac	117-107	W	1-0	99–.525	85–.435	14–.714	35–.743	54	37	O'Neal 46, Bryant 23	O'Neal 17	2 with 5
4/27	Sac	113-89	W	2-0	84–.488	80–.425	35–.714	20–.800	48	40	Bryant 32, O'Neal 23	O'Neal 19	O'Neal 6
4/30	@Sac	91-99	L	2-1	86–.407	81–.432	32–.500	34–.706	48	46	Bryant 35, O'Neal 21	O'Neal 17	Harper 4
5/02	@Sac	88-101	L	2-2	87–.379	82–.439	29–.655	27–.741	51	48	Bryant 32, O'Neal 25	O'Neal 16	2 with 4
5/05	Sac	113-86	W	3-2	90–.522	77–.338	26–.654	34–.794	54	35	O'Neal 32, Bryant 17	O'Neal 18	2 with 6
5/07	Pho	105-77	W	1-0	92–.435	77–.364	26–.808	27–.667	52	42	O'Neal 37, Bryant 25	O'Neal 14	Shaw 4
5/10	Pho	97-96	W	2-0	73–.534	85–.435	28–.571	22–.773	37	43	O'Neal 38, Bryant 15	O'Neal 20	Bryant 6
5/12	@Pho	105-99	W	3-0	70–.457	77–.455	51–.686	34–.735	40	40	O'Neal 37, Bryant 25	O'Neal 17	2 with 4
5/14	@Pho	98-117	L	3-1	77–.442	86–.523	45–.622	27–.630	40	44	O'Neal 24, Bryant 23	2 with 9	Bryant 5
5/16	Pho	87-65	W	4-1	80–.363	80–.288	37–.622	21–.714	59	43	Bryant 17, O'Neal 15	O'Neal 21	Shaw 4
5/20	Por	109-94	W	1-0	71–.535	78–.423	43–.558	24–.875	36	39	O'Neal 41, Rice 15	O'Neal 11	O'Neal 7
5/22	Por	77-106	L	1-1	69–.391	74–.446	32–.531	45–.778	34	49	O'Neal 23, Bryant 12	O'Neal 12	3 with 4
5/26	@Por	93-91	W	2-1	71–.535	69–.507	22–.636	17–.824	35	28	O'Neal 26, Bryant 25	O'Neal 12	Bryant 7
5/28	@Por	103-91	W	3-1	71–.465	77–.390	34–.912	34–.765	42	37	O'Neal 25, Rice 21	O'Neal 11	Bryant 7
5/30	Por	88-96	L	3-2	79–.380	74–.432	30–.733	34–.765	44	43	O'Neal 31, Bryant 17	O'Neal 21	Horry 5
6/02	@Por	93-103	L	3-3	75–.453	74–.500	27–.481	34–.824	34	43	Bryant 33, O'Neal 17	O'Neal 11	Horry 7
6/04	Por	89-84	W	4-3	63–.492	77–.416	37–.541	16–.750	41	33	O'Neal 25, Bryant 18	Bryant 11	Bryant 7
6/07	Ind	104-87	W	1-0	88–.511	76–.421	19–.579	23–.783	48	36	O'Neal 43, Bryant 14	O'Neal 19	2 with 5
6/09	Ind	111-104	W	2-0	75–.480	88–.375	57–.561	39–.846	47	46	O'Neal 40, 2 with 21	O'Neal 24	Shaw 7
6/11	@Ind	91-100	L	2-1	76–.500	78–.462	19–.421	24–.875	33	39	O'Neal 33, Harper 14	O'Neal 13	Fisher 10
6/14	@Ind	120-118[1]	W	3-1	93–.516	84–.500	30–.667	28–.857	42	39	O'Neal 36, Bryant 28	O'Neal 21	Bryant 5
6/16	@Ind	87-120	L	3-2	90–.400	68–.574	21–.524	36–.889	34	46	O'Neal 35, Rice 11	O'Neal 11	Harper 5
6/19	Ind	116-111	W	4-2	90–.478	77–.468	33–.606	32–.844	44	41	O'Neal 41, Bryant 26	O'Neal 12	Harper 9

Miami Heat 1999-2000 Game Log (52-30)

Date	Opp	Score	W/L	Rec	Mia FG Att–Pct.	Opp FG Att–Pct.	Mia FT Att–Pct.	Opp FT Att–Pct.	Mia Reb	Opp Reb	Points	Rebounds	Assists
11/02	Det	**128**-122[2]	W	1-0	**106**–.387	99–.434	**48**–.750	43–.721	**66**	54	Hardaway 32, Mashburn 21	Wthrspn 15	2 with 5
11/04	@Tor	86-97	L	1-1	83–.434	86–.430	15–.667	18–.722	46	40	Mourning 18, 2 with 17	Brown 13	Mashburn 6
11/05	@Chi	105-87	W	2-1	71–.507	78–.385	30–.800	27–.741	41	38	Lenard 22, Mashburn 21	Mourning 8	Hardaway 6
11/09	Ind	113-101	W	3-1	93–.516	95–.411	20–.700	19–.789	52	47	Mourning 33, Hardaway 19	Mourning 16	**Hardaway 14**
11/11	Dal	**128**-105	W	4-1	88–.557	97–.412	22–.864	20–.850	54	33	Mashburn 34, Mourning 18	Brown 11	Carter 10
11/12	@Was	104-95	W	5-1	77–.494	88–.398	29–.724	26–.769	40	49	Mourning 25, Mashburn 22	Mourning 9	Hardaway 11
11/14	@NY	94-88	W	6-1	70–.486	82–.390	32–.688	24–.792	34	40	Mourning 25, Brown 21	3 with 7	Hardaway 9
11/16	Por	96-101	L	6-2	83–.446	72–.514	16–.750	29–.759	54	42	Mourning 23, Mashburn 21	Mourning 9	Hardaway 10
11/17	@Phi	98-93	W	7-2	82–.439	88–.386	30–.667	34–.706	54	44	Mourning 27, Mashburn 19	Mourning 14	Hardaway 7
11/20	Bos	110-92	W	8-2	78–.513	80–.450	28–.750	21–.667	37	37	Mashburn 23, Mourning 22	Majerle 7	2 with 6
11/23	@Atl	106-113	L	8-3	90–.467	81–.556	16–.813	28–.714	33	46	Mourning 26, Mashburn 22	Mourning 11	Mashburn 7
11/24	Atl	93-91	W	9-3	85–.412	80–.450	22–.773	21–.714	43	47	Mourning 25, Majerle 18	Mourning 13	Carter 8
11/27	Was	89-86	W	10-3	75–.467	72–.431	19–.737	28–.750	41	34	Mourning 30, Mashburn 16	Brown 11	Mashburn 10
11/29	Sac	98-88	W	11-3	80–.488	87–.379	20–.850	21–.714	53	38	Mashburn 22, Brown 18	Mourning 11	Walters 5
12/01	Phi	90-83	W	12-3	73–.452	78–.423	23–.870	24–.667	44	36	Mourning 28, Brown 14	Mourning 15	Carter 8
12/03	@Bos	84-96	L	12-4	74–.446	77–.455	24–.500	31–.710	40	47	Lenard 23, Mourning 21	Mashburn 10	Mashburn 6
12/06	@LAC	99-91	W	13-4	82–.512	91–.429	15–.800	12–.833	41	47	Mourning 25, 2 with 20	Mourning 9	Carter 5
12/07	@Por	86-76	W	14-4	69–.478	80–.388	21–.667	14–.714	43	40	Mourning 17, Mashburn 16	Brown 9	Mashburn 8
12/10	@Sac	107-97	W	15-4	76–.539	106–.358	29–.759	19–.684	44	45	Mourning 37, Mashburn 18	2 with 11	2 with 9
12/11	@Sea	88-92	L	15-5	68–.441	81–.395	26–.846	27–.778	47	29	Mourning 23, Mashburn 21	Mourning 10	Carter 5
12/14	@GS	97-102	L	15-6	79–.494	89–.461	23–.652	25–.640	39	43	Mourning 26, Lenard 18	Brown 11	Carter 9
12/16	Mil	95-96	L	15-7	88–.398	81–.457	20–.800	20–.950	44	44	Lenard 29, Mourning 21	**Mourning 18**	Walters 8
12/18	Cha	89-106	L	15-8	82–.451	85–.447	19–.632	32–.750	36	50	Mourning 18, Mashburn 12	Mourning 11	Carter 10
12/20	@Dal	92-89	W	16-8	73–.466	77–.429	21–.762	23–.696	49	37	Brown 25, Mourning 18	Brown 13	Carter 7
12/22	Uta	74-72	W	17-8	76–.434	68–.456	6–.833	15–**.467**	38	37	Mourning 17, Carter 16	Mourning 10	Carter 5
12/26	@Mil	85-93	L	17-9	68–.441	87–.414	34–.676	19–.895	38	45	Mourning 25, Carter 15	Wthrspn 9	Carter 9
12/28	Min	89-78	W	18-9	82–.439	89–.348	16–.813	15–.867	60	40	Mourning 30, Thorpe 12	Mourning 13	Carter 8
12/29	@Orl	109-106	W	19-9	79–.570	96–.406	22–.818	31–.774	41	45	Mourning 28, Carter 21	Mourning 11	Carter 9
1/02	Orl	111-103[1]	W	20-9	93–.409	97–.361	32–.844	34–.882	45	63	Lenard 24, Mashburn 22	Brown 15	Carter 10
1/04	Van	87-91	L	20-10	80–.463	74–.392	15–.600	37–.757	39	48	Mashburn 21, Brown 14	Brown 10	Carter 10
1/06	Hou	111-99	W	21-10	86–.535	74–.419	20–.750	34–.882	41	35	Mourning 28, Mashburn 19	Brown 9	Carter 6
1/08	NJ	89-90	L	21-11	79–.481	74–.432	14–.500	23–.696	46	32	Mourning 23, Majerle 20	**Mourning 18**	Mashburn 8
1/11	@Min	116-106	W	22-11	81–.556	81–.531	16–.938	16–.875	36	25	Majerle 33, Lenard 18	2 with 7	Carter 13
1/13	@Uta	83-93	L	22-12	80–.400	74–.432	28–.750	38–.711	40	42	Mourning 27, Lenard 25	Mourning 9	Carter 7
1/14	@Den	92-67	W	23-12	82–.451	79–.418	20–.600	25–.680	45	41	Mourning 28, Lenard 24	Mourning 13	Mashburn 6
1/16	@Van	94-83	W	24-12	77–.494	78–.436	22–.636	20–.650	48	32	Mourning 27, Brown 19	2 with 10	Carter 8
1/18	Chi	85-92[1]	L	24-13	75–.413	80–.438	26–.692	31–.613	42	43	Carter 20, Mourning 20	Mashburn 9	Mashburn 8
1/21	Atl	101-79	W	25-13	83–.506	92–**.304**	26–.577	30–.733	50	48	Mashburn 28, Mourning 20	2 with 10	Hardaway 11
1/23	@Hou	88-101	L	25-14	93–.398	81–.469	8–.625	**10**–1.000	47	43	Mourning 23, Lenard 20	Mourning 11	2 with 6
1/25	Bos	115-89	W	26-14	78–.551	85–.400	29–.690	25–.760	47	36	Lenard 21, Mourning 20	Wthrspn 9	2 with 8
1/28	@Tor	93-108	L	26-15	85–.471	83–.482	16–.688	30–.767	36	45	Mourning 26, 2 with 10	Mourning 8	Mashburn 6
1/29	@Ind	84-94	L	26-16	85–.388	78–.410	19–.789	27–.852	52	35	Mourning 24, Mashburn 15	**Mourning 18**	Hardaway 8
1/31	Det	104-82	W	27-16	81–.556	75–.373	9–.778	31–.742	39	37	Mashburn 23, Mourning 20	Mashburn 8	3 with 6
2/02	@Bos	105-103	W	28-16	75–.480	87–.414	31–.903	31–.742	44	40	Mashburn 23, Mourning 23	Mourning 8	Lenard 5
2/04	Was	99-92	W	29-16	76–.421	91–.429	35–.857	**10**–.900	45	46	Mourning 32, Mashburn 24	Brown 10	Hardaway 7
2/06	@NY	80-94	L	29-17	83–.386	74–.473	13–.692	27–.741	41	39	Hardaway 23, Mashburn 21	Brown 9	Hardaway 6
2/09	GS	115-100	W	30-17	90–.533	78–.449	18–.778	29–.862	48	35	Mashburn 26, 2 with 17	Brown 13	Hardaway 8
2/15	LAC	107-88	W	31-17	89–.461	86–.384	24–.750	26–.692	63	37	Mashburn 26, Mourning 20	Mourning 13	Carter 8
2/17	@Chi	76-83	L	31-18	79–.405	75–.360	11–.545	27–.815	40	47	Mourning 15, Hardaway 14	Mourning 11	Hardaway 9
2/18	@NJ	84-91	L	31-19	74–.473	79–.392	17–.647	34–.676	51	35	Hardaway 18, 2 with 15	2 with 11	Hardaway 6
2/20	@Cha	85-80	W	32-19	72–.389	69–.406	26–.654	20–.850	42	41	Hardaway 23, Mourning 21	3 with 8	Hardaway 12
2/21	@Det	87-95	L	32-20	80–.413	82–.439	16–.875	17–.765	38	44	Mourning 20, Mashburn 14	Mourning 8	Hardaway 8
2/23	NJ	99-85	W	33-20	80–.463	94–.372	35–.657	14–.786	56	45	**Mourning 43**, Wthrspn 14	Mourning 16	Hardaway 7
2/25	Cle	87-82	W	34-20	80–.400	78–.410	19–.895	17–.706	48	38	Mashburn 18, Wthrspn 13	Wthrspn 16	Hardaway 7

Date	Opp	Score	W/L	Rec	Mia FG Att–Pct.	Opp FG Att–Pct.	Mia FT Att–Pct.	Opp FT Att–Pct.	Mia Reb	Opp Reb	Points	Rebounds	Assists
2/26	@Was	98-88	W	35-20	74–.459	82–.390	28–.857	19–.895	31	44	Mourning 28, Hardaway 23	2 with 6	Hardaway 9
2/28	NY	85-76	W	36-20	76–.434	80–.388	14–**1.000**	13–.692	45	40	Mashburn 24, Wthrspn 14	Wthrspn 12	Hardaway 6
2/29	@SA	69-93	L	36-21	81–.296	71–.479	24–.833	31–.581	44	41	Brown 16, Causwell 13	Wthrspn 12	Majerle 4
3/02	Sea	101-83	W	37-21	70–**.586**	84–.369	17–.824	20–.800	42	36	Mashburn 29, Hardaway 18	Wthrspn 12	Hardaway 8
3/05	@LAL	80-93	L	37-22	72–.417	76–.395	24–.667	36–.750	42	48	Mourning 21, Mashburn 17	Mourning 9	Hardaway 7
3/06	@Pho	92-100	L	37-23	71–.437	77–.532	28–.857	27–.630	36	37	Mourning 25, Brown 22	Brown 11	Hardaway 11
3/10	Den	96-88	W	38-23	78–.462	82–.427	30–.733	29–.586	39	41	Mourning 28, Mashburn 23	Mourning 10	Hardaway 7
3/12	@Ind	105-96	W	39-23	78–.500	75–.493	28–.750	16–.875	38	32	Mourning 35, Hardaway 22	Brown 12	Hardaway 12
3/14	Mil	108-104	W	40-23	78–.526	80–.488	31–.645	27–.778	36	36	Mashburn 28, Mourning 22	Mourning 17	Hardaway 8
3/16	Phi	92-77	W	41-23	83–.470	77–.442	8–.625	11–.636	40	37	Mourning 21, Hardaway 18	Hardaway 9	**Hardaway 14**
3/18	@Cle	92-90[1]	W	42-23	89–.371	76–.355	30–.600	41–.756	48	49	Mashburn 29, Hardaway 21	2 with 8	Hardaway 7
3/20	LAL	89-100	L	42-24	81–.420	75–.507	24–.792	23–.870	32	37	Mourning 33, Hardaway 15	Mourning 13	Hardaway 7
3/21	@Atl	77-82	L	42-25	81–.383	87–.379	12–**1.000**	18–.833	45	45	Mashburn 20, Mourning 18	Mourning 11	Hardaway 7
3/24	@Mil	99-87	W	43-25	74–.554	74–.486	14–.857	**10**–.800	37	32	Mourning 24, Mashburn 22	Mourning 11	Hardaway 8
3/26	@Orl	69-94	L	43-26	76–.368	78–.449	24–.458	22–.727	34	48	Mourning 14, 2 with 12	Mourning 13	Hardaway 5
3/28	Pho	81-78	W	44-26	60–.467	78–.321	29–.690	31–.677	46	38	Hardaway 20, Mourning 20	2 with 12	2 with 7
3/30	Chi	105-80	W	45-26	71–.535	58–.466	34–.765	32–.750	39	31	Hardaway 16, Mourning 15	Wthrspn 7	Carter 9
4/02	SA	88-84	W	46-26	69–.449	65–.446	26–.731	31–.677	40	32	Mourning 26, Mourning 15	Brown 13	2 with 4
4/04	Cle	111-85	W	47-26	82–.537	71–.479	21–.810	25–.560	42	30	Mashburn 17, Mourning 15	Mourning 11	Hardaway 10
4/06	Cha	76-**70**	W	48-26	74–.419	81–.309	11–.636	25–.720	50	41	Mourning 26, Majerle 12	Mourning 17	Hardaway 6
4/07	@NJ	103-85	W	49-26	76–.500	77–.364	30–.633	35–.771	50	43	Mashburn 21, 2 with 15	Mourning 11	Hardaway 8
4/09	NY	95-94[1]	W	50-26	87–.437	87–.437	16–.625	15–.733	43	47	Mourning 33, Hardaway 16	Mourning 11	Hardaway 10
4/10	@Phi	80-96	L	50-27	73–.411	72–.500	22–.727	22–.818	41	35	Mashburn 16, Mourning 13	2 with 8	Hardaway 7
4/12	@Det	73-90	L	50-28	69–.333	73–.397	33–.667	27–.815	35	53	Mashburn 22, Mourning 16	Mourning 10	Carter 6
4/14	Ind	101-105	L	50-29	77–.519	76–.513	25–.760	25–.800	36	31	Mourning 28, Mashburn 19	Brown 7	Majerle 7
4/16	Orl	95-84	W	51-29	73–.521	76–.408	17–.765	25–.720	38	35	Mourning 18, Mourning 16	Mourning 8	Mashburn 7
4/18	Tor	97-73	W	52-29	81–.494	76–.316	22–.682	34–.676	52	38	Carter 17, Mashburn 16	Wthrspn 9	Carter 6
4/19	@Cha	73-83	L	52-30	72–.403	63–.492	14–.857	23–.913	36	32	Carter 16, Mashburn 15	Brown 10	Carter 4

Postseason

Date	Opp	Score	W/L	Rec	Mia FG Att–Pct.	Opp FG Att–Pct.	Mia FT Att–Pct.	Opp FT Att–Pct.	Mia Reb	Opp Reb	Points	Rebounds	Assists
4/22	Det	95-85	W	1-0	73–.466	67–.433	24–.833	32–.656	35	37	Mashburn 29, Mourning 20	Majerle 10	Carter 7
4/25	Det	84-82	W	2-0	71–.451	68–.471	24–.667	18–.778	42	32	Mashburn 24, Mourning 22	Mourning 8	Carter 13
4/29	@Det	91-72	W	3-0	71–.521	73–.315	25–.560	31–.742	47	34	Wthrspn 18, Mourning 12	2 with 10	Carter 9
5/07	NY	87-83	W	1-0	71–.465	78–.423	23–.783	20–.750	41	40	Mourning 26, Mashburn 21	Brown 16	Hardaway 7
5/09	NY	76-82	L	1-1	74–.338	68–.353	33–.576	42–.738	50	43	Mashburn 25, Mourning 17	Mourning 17	3 with 3
5/12	@NY	77-76[1]	W	2-1	85–.365	64–.406	14–.786	24–.833	45	34	Mourning 23, Mashburn 16	Brown 12	Carter 8
5/14	@NY	83-91	L	2-2	72–.431	78–.423	22–.773	22–.773	48	37	Mourning 27, 2 with 13	Mourning 14	Carter 7
5/17	NY	87-81	W	3-2	74–.419	74–.473	27–.741	12–.667	42	32	Mashburn 21, Mourning 18	Brown 12	Carter 5
5/19	@NY	70-72	L	3-3	66–.333	71–.380	29–.724	19–.789	41	46	Mourning 22, Carter 15	2 with 10	Majerle 7
5/21	NY	82-83	L	3-4	80–.413	72–.361	21–.524	31–.903	43	46	Mourning 29, Hardaway 15	Mourning 13	Hardaway 7

Milwaukee Bucks 1999-2000 Game Log (42-40)

Date	Opp	Score	W/L	Rec	Mil FG Att–Pct.	Opp FG Att–Pct.	Mil FT Att–Pct.	Opp FT Att–Pct.	Mil Reb	Opp Reb	Points	Rebounds	Assists
11/02	@Hou	98-93	W	1-0	79–.481	75–.453	28–.679	29–.655	35	42	Cassell 35, Allen 19	Johnson 7	Cassell 11
11/04	@Atl	119-109	W	2-0	90–.456	83–.494	36–.917	30–.700	38	46	Allen 31, Cassell 24	Thomas 8	Cassell 8
11/06	Det	121-111	W	3-0	89–.506	83–.506	25–.880	26–.692	37	39	Cassell 28, Allen 26	Reid 8	Cassell 8
11/08	@NY	101-111[1]	L	3-1	91–.396	87–.414	31–.774	37–.892	48	47	Robinson 23, Allen 18	Robinson 9	Cassell 10
11/10	@Cha	111-117	L	3-2	77–.494	79–.519	29–.862	36–.806	38	32	Allen 24, Robinson 24	Robinson 9	Cassell 9
11/12	Pho	107-92	W	4-2	77–.532	86–.384	25–.800	28–.714	37	48	Robinson 27, Allen 20	Robinson 12	Cassell 14
11/13	@Cle	112-117	L	4-3	84–.452	81–.469	39–.795	49–.735	42	41	Robinson 32, 2 with 22	Traylor 10	Cassell 7
11/16	LAC	101-93	W	5-3	78–.500	95–.389	24–.833	26–.615	43	54	Robinson 24, Cassell 20	Robinson 10	Cassell 9
11/18	SA	99-88	W	6-3	85–.447	69–.435	17–.824	36–.694	40	44	Allen 26, Robinson 22	2 with 8	Robinson 4
11/20	Uta	100-111	L	6-4	78–.487	80–.550	28–.750	23–.783	34	39	Allen 23, Robinson 18	Robinson 8	Cassell 8
11/21	@Det	94-113	L	6-5	79–.494	77–.532	18–.611	35–.743	28	43	Allen 33, Robinson 20	Traylor 8	Allen 10
11/24	Chi	102-95	W	7-5	77–.442	76–.487	34–.912	19–.737	36	36	Robinson 22, Allen 18	Traylor 9	Cassell 6
11/26	@Bos	114-112	W	8-5	80–.538	89–.483	31–.774	20–.800	41	42	Cassell 28, Robinson 21	3 with 6	Cassell 12
11/27	Phi	79-82	L	8-6	85–.365	88–.386	17–.824	22–**.545**	46	49	Allen 23, Cassell 16	Reid 9	Cassell 7
12/02	NY	80-84	L	8-7	70–.329	85–.400	36–.806	13–.692	41	43	Allen 25, Cassell 16	Johnson 9	Cassell 4
12/04	@Chi	92-91	W	9-7	70–.543	79–.380	20–.800	33–.758	34	44	Cassell 23, 2 with 19	3 with 6	Cassell 15
12/05	Dal	103-97	W	10-7	85–.494	81–.407	19–.895	26–.769	43	37	Allen 20, Robinson 17	3 with 6	Cassell 18
12/07	Det	112-116	L	10-8	95–.516	74–.527	15–.733	34–.853	48	23	Robinson 30, Allen 21	Johnson 10	Cassell 12
12/08	@NJ	90-107	L	10-9	78–.449	79–.481	28–.571	31–.742	47	37	Robinson 25, Allen 14	Williams 10	Cassell 5
12/10	@Tor	107-91	W	11-9	84–.524	87–.391	18–.778	19–.737	37	42	Cassell 22, Robinson 22	Robinson 6	Cassell 10
12/11	Den	99-101	L	11-10	88–.443	86–.419	24–.667	27–.667	49	42	Allen 25, Robinson 24	Johnson 13	Cassell 12
12/15	@Orl	116-99	W	12-10	93–.505	82–.390	19–.947	40–.825	49	44	Allen 29, Robinson 25	Williams 15	Allen 7
12/16	@Mia	96-95	W	13-10	81–.457	88–.398	20–.950	20–.800	44	44	Allen 28, Cassell 20	Johnson 10	Cassell 7
12/18	Ind	109-95	W	14-10	84–.500	76–.461	26–.692	18–.833	40	40	Robinson 24, Manning 19	Robinson 10	Cassell 6
12/20	@Pho	101-108	L	14-11	83–.494	92–.457	17–.765	24–.750	38	47	Allen 31, 2 with 19	Allen 7	Cassell 10
12/21	@Sac	95-108	L	14-12	84–.452	85–.447	23–.565	34–.735	37	52	Cassell 20, Robinson 19	2 with 6	Cassell 6
12/23	@SA	94-91	W	15-12	81–.420	80–.425	29–.793	29–.655	43	44	Cassell 27, Robinson 25	Johnson 14	Cassell 8
12/26	Mia	93-85	W	16-12	87–.414	68–.441	19–.895	34–.676	45	38	Robinson 30, Allen 22	Williams 11	Cassell 11
12/29	@Cha	105-109	L	16-13	89–.483	69–.536	13–.846	40–.775	37	36	Robinson 36, Allen 28	Johnson 9	**Cassell 19**
12/30	Cle	91-90	W	17-13	74–.419	81–.457	37–.757	14–.714	41	42	Cassell 20, Robinson 17	Johnson 9	Allen 7
1/03	@Phi	120-124[1]	L	17-14	96–.448	88–.523	31–.839	41–.683	46	39	Allen 25, Robinson 25	Johnson 15	Cassell 11
1/04	Atl	116-113	W	18-14	88–.557	81–.568	15–.867	18–.833	34	35	Robinson 36, Allen 25	Johnson 8	Cassell 18
1/06	@Det	95-101	L	18-15	80–.413	78–.474	22–.864	31–.677	37	49	Robinson 31, Thomas 16	Williams 10	Workman 5
1/08	Was	130-129[2]	W	19-15	**97**–.495	93–.473	38–.737	42–.762	48	48	Robinson 34, Allen 28	**Johnson 18**	Cassell 10
1/10	Cha	**137**-87	W	20-15	86–**.640**	82–.402	15–.933	18–.889	43	30	Allen 26, Thomas 21	Johnson 13	Cassell 12
1/12	LAL	94-103	L	20-16	78–.397	81–.481	28–**1.000**	25–.760	37	42	Allen 25, Cassell 24	Johnson 8	Cassell 13
1/14	@Tor	110-115	L	20-17	83–.530	84–.464	21–.810	32–.906	36	38	Robinson 37, Allen 25	Williams 8	Cassell 10
1/15	Tor	118-97	W	21-17	66–.561	99–**.333**	**44**–.818	33–.727	40	53	Allen 33, Cassell 24	2 with 7	Cassell 9
1/17	@Atl	107-101	W	22-17	89–.449	83–.482	20–.850	23–.826	40	43	Cassell 31, Allen 23	Williams 14	Cassell 11
1/19	@Ind	84-106	L	22-18	89–.382	80–.463	14–.786	27–.889	42	47	Robinson 25, Allen 16	Williams 13	Cassell 9
1/20	Sea	96-104	L	22-19	86–.465	81–.469	18–.722	27–.815	44	41	Robinson 21, Cassell 19	Williams 11	Allen 13
1/26	Sac	112-104	W	23-19	90–.444	97–.392	36–.750	19–.586	52	57	Allen 22, Cassell 21	Johnson 15	Cassell 13
1/28	@LAL	89-117	L	23-20	89–.382	85–.529	21–.810	28–.786	40	43	Cassell 18, Del Negro 15	Williams 9	2 with 4
1/29	@Sea	101-99	W	24-20	84–.452	75–.400	25–.840	37–.703	50	40	Robinson 24, 2 with 18	Williams 10	Cassell 9
1/31	@Van	92-87	W	25-20	81–.432	79–.418	21–.952	22–.636	39	46	Robinson 25, Cassell 21	Johnson 10	Cassell 7
2/02	@Den	112-135	L	25-21	96–.458	84–.631	28–.750	21–.810	40	38	Allen 22, Cassell 21	Williams 8	Cassell 8
2/03	@Uta	102-99	W	26-21	79–.468	84–.452	22–.864	21–.810	36	46	Allen 36, Robinson 30	Johnson 11	Cassell 10
2/05	Tor	95-98	L	26-22	86–.407	88–.420	29–.828	26–.692	54	47	Robinson 29, Cassell 25	Johnson 13	Cassell 5
2/07	Por	111-115	L	26-23	84–.560	75–.533	15–.800	34–.765	34	34	Robinson 27, Allen 26	2 with 7	Cassell 13
2/09	NY	103-109	L	26-24	80–.500	75–.533	20–.800	23–.826	30	39	Allen 24, Robinson 19	Williams 10	2 with 7
2/15	@Dal	112-99	W	27-24	92–.457	84–.476	20–.800	22–.727	46	42	Robinson 29, Cassell 28	Johnson 12	Cassell 13
2/17	Ind	90-92	L	27-25	85–.412	**61**–.492	20–.900	34–.765	42	38	Cassell 23, Robinson 22	Williams 11	Cassell 9
2/19	Van	100-111	L	27-26	81–.481	70–.514	26–.808	39–.795	39	31	Allen 32, Robinson 21	Robinson 9	Cassell 10
2/22	@Was	101-126	L	27-27	96–.427	86–.581	16–.875	22–.818	40	41	Allen 17, Robinson 15	Johnson 12	Cassell 6

344

Date	Opp	Score	W/L	Rec	Mil FG Att–Pct.	Opp FG Att–Pct.	Mil FT Att–Pct.	Opp FT Att–Pct.	Mil Reb	Opp Reb	Points	Rebounds	Assists
2/23	GS	86-91	L	27-28	81–.407	88–.386	20–.800	30–.633	40	62	Allen 24, Robinson 24	Johnson 11	Cassell 6
2/25	Phi	83-97	L	27-29	85–.424	70–.471	11–.818	39–.718	35	38	Robinson 24, Allen 15	Johnson 9	Cassell 11
2/27	Orl	102-95	W	28-29	82–.439	86–.442	31–.839	15–.733	50	37	Allen 26, Cassell 22	Johnson 12	Allen 4
3/02	@NY	94-109	L	28-30	69–.420	66–.591	42–.738	23–.826	32	32	Thomas 26, Allen 25	Williams 6	Cassell 8
3/04	Min	84-91	L	28-31	83–.410	74–.459	17–.824	20–1.000	35	44	Allen 28, Robinson 21	Robinson 10	Cassell 9
3/06	Atl	111-78	W	29-31	86–.558	75–.467	11–.636	**8**–.625	51	**21**	Cassell 21, Robinson 17	Ham 13	Cassell 12
3/08	@Bos	101-112	L	29-32	83–.470	97–.412	25–.600	30–.867	38	65	Allen 28, 2 with 14	Robinson 10	2 with 7
3/10	NJ	80-108	L	29-33	84–.405	85–.518	11–.636	15–.800	44	43	Thomas 19, Allen 16	Allen 9	2 with 7
3/12	Cle	103-**72**	W	30-33	85–.459	68–.397	24–.875	28–.643	49	33	Thomas 22, 2 with 18	Ham 11	Cassell 8
3/14	@Mia	104-108	L	30-34	80–.488	78–.526	27–.778	31–.645	36	36	Allen 26, Cassell 22	Robinson 8	Cassell 7
3/16	Hou	106-96	W	31-34	74–.554	72–.417	30–.700	32–.875	40	36	Allen 28, Cassell 22	Johnson 13	2 with 7
3/18	@NJ	90-92[1]	L	31-35	87–.425	84–.405	19–.684	23–.783	47	47	Thomas 23, Cassell 20	Williams 8	Cassell 7
3/19	@Min	82-109	L	31-36	78–.372	82–.561	24–.833	14–.714	36	39	Robinson 20, Cassell 17	Thomas 7	Cassell 6
3/23	@Ind	105-84	W	32-36	85–.506	72–.375	19–.895	29–.793	47	36	Cassell 30, Allen 26	Ham 10	Cassell 9
3/24	Mia	87-99	L	32-37	74–.486	74–.554	10–.800	14–.857	32	37	Allen 36, Robinson 19	Williams 6	Cassell 10
3/26	Bos	99-84	W	33-37	81–.506	74–.405	21–.667	28–.714	34	36	Allen 27, Cassell 22	Johnson 11	Cassell 11
3/30	@LAC	104-85	W	34-37	87–.494	80–.400	19–.737	20–.750	48	38	Allen 35, Robinson 17	2 with 9	Cassell 16
4/01	@Por	79-113	L	34-38	76–.408	84–.512	25–.600	25–.720	35	45	Cassell 22, Allen 13	Johnson 6	Cassell 6
4/02	@GS	117-113	W	35-38	79–.519	85–.435	39–.769	38–.842	42	42	Cassell 31, Allen 27	Johnson 14	Robinson 7
4/04	Chi	92-73	W	36-38	83–.446	67–.358	20–.750	31–.742	40	45	Cassell 19, Allen 18	3 with 6	Cassell 12
4/06	@Chi	88-90	L	36-39	90–.400	70–.443	21–.714	31–.677	47	45	Robinson 24, Allen 19	2 with 12	Cassell 9
4/08	NJ	109-101	W	37-39	91–.505	78–.513	17–.706	20–.700	47	30	Allen 21, 3 with 20	Johnson 7	Cassell 11
4/10	Orl	104-87	W	38-39	83–.470	83–.349	24–.750	40–.700	42	42	Allen 33, Cassell 18	Ham 8	Cassell 8
4/12	@Cle	101-100	W	39-39	81–.457	82–.427	30–.800	36–.667	46	44	Cassell 29, Allen 27	2 with 9	Cassell 6
4/14	Cha	106-109[1]	L	39-40	88–.420	89–.449	28–.857	26–.808	45	46	**Robinson 38**, Allen 26	Johnson 11	Cassell 8
4/15	@Was	120-116[1]	W	40-40	80–.513	93–.462	42–.690	25–.720	**55**	37	Cassell 34, Robinson 31	Johnson 15	Allen 7
4/17	@Orl	85-83	W	41-40	76–.408	86–.349	33–.667	21–.810	50	41	Thomas 21, Cassell 19	Johnson 13	Cassell 10
4/19	Was	110-105	W	42-40	80–.525	89–.438	32–.750	22–.818	41	44	Williams 19, Del Negro 16	Manning 7	Cassell 7

Postseason

Date	Opp	Score	W/L	Rec	Mil FG Att–Pct.	Opp FG Att–Pct.	Mil FT Att–Pct.	Opp FT Att–Pct.	Mil Reb	Opp Reb	Points	Rebounds	Assists
4/23	@Ind	85-88	L	0-1	83–.361	86–.372	26–.808	26–.731	43	47	Allen 26, Cassell 18	2 with 8	Cassell 6
4/27	@Ind	104-91	W	1-1	77–.532	80–.388	25–.720	35–.714	42	44	Allen 20, Cassell 20	Johnson 12	Cassell 8
4/29	Ind	96-109	L	1-2	86–.465	84–.488	19–.684	19–.947	42	35	Allen 26, Robinson 26	Johnson 13	Cassell 12
5/01	Ind	100-87	W	2-2	85–.494	75–.400	15–.733	32–.844	44	39	Allen 20, Williams 20	Johnson 9	Cassell 13
5/04	@Ind	95-96	L	2-3	82–.439	83–.434	25–.840	25–.720	43	44	Cassell 22, 2 with 18	Thomas 9	Cassell 6

Minnesota Timberwolves 1999-2000 Game Log (50-32)

Date	Opp	Score	W/L	Rec	Min FG Att–Pct.	Opp FG Att–Pct.	Min FT Att–Pct.	Opp FT Att–Pct.	Min Reb	Opp Reb	Points	Rebounds	Assists
11/05	@Sac	95-100	L	0-1	**99**–.394	95–.358	14–.786	27–.852	54	55	Garnett 34, Brandon 18	Garnett 17	Brandon 12
11/06	Sac	114-101	W	1-1	91–.516	84–.488	19–.842	24–.583	50	37	Garnett 31, Peeler 19	Garnett 12	Brandon 13
11/11	NY	93-90	W	2-1	78–.423	84–.429	31–.806	16–.813	40	42	Garnett 35, Szczerbiak 23	Garnett 14	Brandon 10
11/13	Pho	111-100	W	3-1	92–.533	87–.425	15–.733	22–.955	47	38	Nesterovic 23, Brandon 21	Garnett 12	Brandon 9
11/17	LAC	85-89	L	3-2	90–.389	77–.403	20–.650	32–.719	48	43	Garnett 23, Sealy 17	Garnett 20	Brandon 12
11/19	Uta	89-84	W	4-2	78–.436	75–.373	28–.714	31–.871	40	38	Garnett 11, Peeler 13	Garnett 11	Brandon 6
11/21	@Van	105-81	W	5-2	80–.550	73–.384	23–.652	29–.759	47	37	Szczerbiak 19, Brandon 18	Garnett 14	Brandon 8
11/22	@Uta	93-108	L	5-3	73–.479	78–.577	27–.815	19–.684	32	30	Brandon 21, Garnett 20	Garnett 7	Brandon 7
11/24	Por	81-88	L	5-4	97–.340	76–.382	18–.722	28–.857	52	54	Szczerbiak 26, Brandon 22	Garnett 19	Garnett 7
11/26	@Den	105-114	L	5-5	87–.460	89–.472	33–.697	32–.719	43	46	Smith 18, Brandon 17	2 with 9	Brandon 7
11/27	Van	113-82	W	6-5	82–.524	79–.443	27–.815	16–.750	41	31	Garnett 20, Peeler 17	Jackson 7	Brandon 6
11/30	Den	109-92	W	7-5	85–.518	80–.388	27–.704	38–.684	37	46	Smith 26, 2 with 18	Smith 9	2 with 6
12/02	Orl	93-103	L	7-6	89–.382	93–.452	29–.759	24–.708	**55**	45	Smith 18, Garnett 17	Smith 13	Brandon 8
12/04	Dal	84-103	L	7-7	94–.330	83–.458	24–.875	29–.793	50	44	Garnett 20, Peeler 14	Smith 17	Garnett 5
12/08	@Sea	94-110	L	7-8	81–.469	94–.436	21–.714	21–.810	36	50	Garnett 22, Szczerbiak 16	Garnett 12	Brandon 10
12/09	@Por	86-90	L	7-9	72–.458	66–.485	26–.692	32–.781	26	37	Garnett 26, Brandon 20	Garnett 7	Brandon 11
12/11	GS	76-104	L	7-10	80–.413	85–.482	14–.714	23–.739	41	41	Nesterovic 23, Garnett 12	Nesterovic 13	2 with 6
12/14	@Atl	94-105	L	7-11	96–.417	87–.471	15–.733	26–.731	39	60	Garnett 22, Brandon 16	Garnett 15	Garnett 10
12/15	@Cha	98-103	L	7-12	86–.453	75–.520	21–.857	35–.629	46	33	Sealy 27, Garnett 17	Garnett 20	Brandon 7
12/17	LAL	88-97	L	7-13	83–.470	78–.449	17–.588	33–.697	37	46	Garnett 28, Brandon 22	Garnett 21	Brandon 9
12/18	@Dal	108-104	W	8-13	80–.538	91–.462	25–.800	19–.789	41	42	Garnett 27, Brandon 20	Garnett 14	Brandon 6
12/20	@Cle	100-94	W	9-13	77–.416	76–.447	44–.818	31–.742	46	40	Garnett 24, Brandon 17	Garnett 18	Brandon 11
12/22	@Chi	106-86	W	10-13	80–.525	81–.407	28–.750	28–.679	42	39	Garnett 27, Sealy 19	Garnett 13	Brandon 11
12/23	Sea	109-102	W	11-13	96–.458	87–.437	25–.760	19–.684	54	40	Brandon 30, Garnett 23	Garnett 14	Brandon 9
12/27	@Orl	107-105	W	12-13	88–.511	86–.523	20–.700	18–.611	44	31	Garnett 26, 2 with 18	**Garnett 23**	Brandon 15
12/28	@Mia	78-89	L	12-14	89–.348	82–.439	15–.867	16–.813	40	60	Garnett 16, 2 with 14	Garnett 9	Brandon 6
12/30	Chi	94-**76**	W	13-14	71–.507	70–.400	23–.870	23–.696	39	30	Garnett 22, 4 with 12	Garnett 11	Brandon 7
1/04	SA	91-88	W	14-14	84–.452	85–.400	18–.667	24–.750	45	42	Sealy 22, Garnett 21	Garnett 11	Brandon 13
1/06	Por	98-96	W	15-14	74–.500	**65**–.538	29–.759	34–.676	37	29	Garnett 27, Sealy 27	Brandon 8	Brandon 14
1/08	@Det	110-105	W	16-14	78–.500	78–.449	39–.769	43–.651	42	38	Brandon 28, Garnett 22	Garnett 14	2 with 8
1/09	@Phi	**123**-112	W	17-14	81–**.642**	89–.449	16–.938	35–.743	36	40	Garnett 27, Sealy 23	Brandon 10	Brandon 14
1/11	Mia	106-116	L	17-15	81–.531	81–.556	16–.875	16–.938	25	36	Garnett 35, Peeler 16	Garnett 9	Brandon 11
1/13	Bos	103-85	W	18-15	81–.519	83–.373	19–.789	26–.731	44	44	Brandon 20, Garnett 19	Garnett 10	Brandon 11
1/15	LAL	91-104	L	18-16	85–.388	82–.488	26–.731	24–.542	38	52	Garnett 22, Brandon 21	Garnett 10	Brandon 8
1/17	Ind	101-100	W	19-16	93–.462	79–.443	18–.778	27–.926	44	40	Garnett 37, 2 with 16	Garnett 13	Garnett 7
1/19	@Uta	91-88	W	20-16	81–.457	74–.486	22–.727	21–.619	37	44	Garnett 31, Sealy 19	Garnett 10	Jackson 8
1/21	@LAC	95-89	W	21-16	86–.430	82–.476	22–.864	13–.615	39	44	Mitchell 20, Garnett 18	Sealy 8	Jackson 7
1/23	@GS	99-81	W	22-16	82–.476	87–.356	24–.792	22–.682	50	44	Garnett 22, 2 with 15	Garnett 15	Brandon 9
1/25	@Hou	92-84	W	23-16	85–.494	73–.397	8–.750	28–.679	42	37	Garnett 27, Brandon 26	Garnett 12	Brandon 8
1/27	@SA	80-92	L	23-17	84–.405	84–.429	12–.917	22–.773	40	49	Garnett 26, Jackson 12	Garnett 8	2 with 4
1/29	Uta	96-94	W	24-17	85–.447	83–.434	22–.727	25–.800	43	38	Garnett 29, 2 with 15	Garnett 13	2 with 7
1/31	Sac	105-90	W	25-17	79–.582	95–.358	14–.786	20–.900	47	36	Garnett 31, Peeler 18	Garnett 12	Jackson 12
2/02	@Was	93-103	L	25-18	75–.520	78–.487	14–.857	29–.759	30	40	Garnett 22, Jackson 21	Garnett 11	2 with 3
2/04	Hou	102-85	W	26-18	80–.563	84–.381	10–.800	23–.696	47	36	Garnett 23, Mitchell 17	Garnett 18	Garnett 9
2/05	@Den	105-97[1]	W	27-18	88–.364	84–.357	**49**–.755	46–.674	48	64	Garnett 30, Jackson 20	Garnett 14	Jackson 5
2/09	@LAL	81-114	L	27-19	88–.341	79–.481	27–.704	42–.833	39	54	Garnett 29, Hammonds 12	Garnett 6	Jackson 6
2/10	@Pho	85-101	L	27-20	89–.393	78–.487	15–.800	30–.800	44	47	Mitchell 16, Garnett 12	Garnett 13	2 with 5
2/15	Den	104-107[1]	L	27-21	83–.470	96–.490	22–**1.000**	15–.533	34	46	Garnett 24, Mitchell 16	Garnett 11	Brandon 12
2/16	@NY	89-93	L	27-22	76–.461	71–.465	24–.750	29–.828	39	35	Garnett 23, Mitchell 13	Garnett 13	Brandon 10
2/18	Van	103-91	W	28-22	78–.513	75–.467	21–.905	20–.800	33	37	Brandon 21, Sealy 18	Garnett 10	2 with 9
2/20	NJ	89-91	L	28-23	94–.372	70–.443	19–.737	32–.750	51	38	Garnett 27, Sealy 16	Garnett 18	Jackson 7
2/22	GS	112-89	W	29-23	75–.560	80–**.350**	34–.735	36–.833	48	35	Brandon 21, Szczerbiak 21	Garnett 14	Szczerbiak 10
2/24	LAC	116-91	W	30-23	90–.556	73–.452	13–.769	20–.850	45	**27**	Smith 18, 2 with 16	3 with 8	Brandon 8
2/25	@Tor	107-85	W	31-23	81–.531	68–.441	17–.882	27–.704	40	33	Garnett 28, 2 with 18	Garnett 12	2 with 8

346

Date	Opp	Score	W/L	Rec	Min FG Att–Pct.	Opp FG Att–Pct.	Min FT Att–Pct.	Opp FT Att–Pct.	Min Reb	Opp Reb	Points	Rebounds	Assists
2/27	SA	102-98	W	32-23	81–.531	69–.493	16–.875	37–.730	40	32	Garnett 29, Brandon 20	Garnett 16	Brandon 7
2/29	Cha	87-92	L	32-24	80–.488	72–.444	14–.571	31–.839	40	38	Garnett 21, Szczerbiak 17	Garnett 9	Brandon 8
3/02	@SA	108-102	W	33-24	83–.530	69–.507	19–.737	31–.806	40	33	Garnett 23, Sealy 20	Garnett 13	Sealy 8
3/04	@Mil	91-84	W	34-24	74–.459	83–.410	20–1.000	17–.824	44	35	Brandon 22, Garnett 21	Smith 13	Sealy 7
3/05	Sea	105-100[1]	W	35-24	80–.538	86–.477	19–.842	19–.684	40	33	Garnett 21, Brandon 20	Garnett 13	Brandon 11
3/07	Was	86-90	L	35-25	84–.405	75–.480	21–.714	19–.684	41	40	Garnett 26, Szczerbiak 26	Garnett 13	Brandon 11
3/09	@Dal	100-79	W	36-25	83–.518	73–.438	12–.750	20–.650	43	34	Garnett 22, Brandon 17	Garnett 13	2 with 6
3/11	@Hou	100-86	W	37-25	87–.483	78–.372	14–.929	35–.657	44	47	Brandon 24, Szczerbiak 19	Garnett 15	Brandon 9
3/14	@Pho	100-107	L	37-26	80–.513	75–.413	20–.750	49–.878	37	43	Garnett 18, Garnett 17	Garnett 11	Brandon 9
3/16	@Por	96-92	W	38-26	80–.500	74–.514	19–.737	19–.632	29	41	Brandon 25, Garnett 17	Garnett 12	Garnett 8
3/19	Mil	109-82	W	39-26	82–.561	78–.372	14–.714	24–.833	39	36	Brandon 28, Szczerbiak 27	Garnett 8	Brandon 13
3/21	Cle	111-107[1]	W	40-26	89–.483	91–.495	28–.857	17–.706	44	45	Garnett 29, Brandon 24	Garnett 14	**Brandon 16**
3/22	@Bos	109-106	W	41-26	81–.481	76–.539	31–.903	28–.714	42	33	**Garnett 40**, Sealy 24	2 with 8	Brandon 9
3/24	@NJ	116-115[1]	W	42-26	89–.506	93–.419	30–.833	35–.829	43	47	Garnett 38, 2 with 17	3 with 8	Brandon 9
3/26	Tor	106-101[1]	W	43-26	85–.471	89–.416	32–.781	30–.767	52	37	Garnett 34, Brandon 23	Garnett 10	Brandon 11
3/28	Phi	100-102	L	43-27	85–.459	76–.487	23–.739	30–.800	38	43	Garnett 31, Brandon 14	Smith 12	Brandon 12
3/30	Hou	122-90	W	44-27	87–.598	70–.371	16–.750	47–.809	41	35	Garnett 25, Brandon 21	Smith 10	Brandon 13
3/31	@Ind	85-109	L	44-28	92–.380	82–.537	16–.706	16–.750	46	50	Brandon 24, Garnett 14	Garnett 12	Brandon 5
4/02	Pho	86-87	L	44-29	85–.388	77–.455	17–.941	19–.789	48	39	Sealy 19, Szczerbiak 18	Garnett 13	Brandon 11
4/04	Atl	86-**76**[1]	W	45-29	95–.379	81–.420	12–.750	**11**–.455	52	46	Garnett 18, Smith 18	Garnett 14	Avery 7
4/06	@LAC	112-90	W	46-29	91–.505	**65**–.462	16–.813	32–.750	45	31	Garnett 28, Szczerbiak 23	Nesterovic 13	Brandon 13
4/07	@Sac	95-92	W	47-29	81–.457	90–.356	22–.818	32–.750	45	50	Brandon 30, Garnett 21	Garnett 14	Brandon 9
4/10	Det	102-100	W	48-29	82–.427	71–.423	37–.757	42–.833	42	39	Garnett 25, Brandon 16	Garnett 9	Brandon 9
4/12	@Sea	83-110	L	48-30	84–.345	90–.433	33–.667	28–.786	48	52	Garnett 18, Szczerbiak 14	Smith 10	2 with 5
4/14	@Van	104-94[2]	W	49-30	92–.489	97–.402	11–.727	14–.714	49	44	3 with 20	2 with 12	Brandon 10
4/16	@LAL	95-101	L	49-31	90–.433	74–.486	21–.762	31–.871	46	40	Brandon 18, Szczerbiak 16	Garnett 15	Brandon 8
4/17	@GS	101-96	W	50-31	83–.446	78–.474	25–.840	29–.586	54	35	Brandon 21, Smith 14	2 with 11	Brandon 8
4/19	Dal	107-113	L	50-32	95–.484	77–.532	11–.818	23–.913	41	38	Peeler 22, Jackson 21	2 with 8	Jackson 9

Postseason

Date	Opp	Score	W/L	Rec	Min FG Att–Pct.	Opp FG Att–Pct.	Min FT Att–Pct.	Opp FT Att–Pct.	Min Reb	Opp Reb	Points	Rebounds	Assists
4/23	@Por	88-91	L	0-1	82–.476	75–.413	14–.643	23–.913	34	37	Sealy 23, Brandon 17	Garnett 10	Brandon 12
4/26	@Por	82-86	L	0-2	71–.437	70–.443	22–.818	23–.783	34	36	Garnett 23, Brandon 20	Garnett 10	Brandon 6
4/30	Por	94-87	W	1-2	71–.535	76–.421	16–.750	18–.944	33	28	Brandon 28, Garnett 23	Garnett 13	Brandon 12
5/02	Por	77-85	L	1-3	82–.354	66–.470	18–.889	27–.741	39	40	Garnett 17, Brandon 13	Garnett 10	Garnett 9

New Jersey Nets 1999-2000 Game Log (31-51)

Date	Opp	Score	W/L	Rec	NJ FG Att–Pct.	Opp FG Att–Pct.	NJ FT Att–Pct.	Opp FT Att–Pct.	NJ Reb	Opp Reb	Points	Rebounds	Assists
11/02	Ind	112-119	L	0-1	81–.444	78–.474	46–.761	53–.736	45	43	Marbury 39, Van Horn 16	Feick 17	Marbury 7
11/03	@Cle	90-97	L	0-2	82–.341	81–.469	35–.857	20–.850	40	48	Marbury 27, Van Horn 20	Feick 13	Van Horn 4
11/05	Tor	92-112	L	0-3	89–.382	87–.506	28–.786	29–.724	38	52	Marbury 25, Harris 19	Feick 9	Marbury 3
11/07	Was	112-87	W	1-3	89–.427	86–.407	34–.794	22–.636	50	46	Newman 25, Van Horn 23	Van Horn 18	Marbury 8
11/10	Pho	89-104	L	1-4	84–.381	85–.471	28–.821	26–.808	41	53	Marbury 27, Newman 26	Feick 13	Marbury 5
11/12	@Cha	92-96	L	1-5	72–.486	77–.429	24–.750	34–.794	39	34	Marbury 31, Van Horn 18	Feick 8	Marbury 8
11/15	Sea	92-100	L	1-6	101–.356	72–.486	24–.792	38–.737	47	49	Marbury 24, 2 with 15	2 with 12	Marbury 5
11/17	@Det	107-109	L	1-7	76–.474	84–.536	31–.806	24–.667	37	40	Marbury 35, Van Horn 30	Feick 11	Marbury 7
11/19	@Bos	96-109	L	1-8	88–.420	86–.500	24–.708	23–.739	39	49	Marbury 26, Van Horn 16	Van Horn 13	Gill 6
11/20	Phi	96-100	L	1-9	71–.408	74–.486	46–.783	35–.714	42	36	Marbury 22, Van Horn 20	Van Horn 13	Marbury 4
11/23	@Sac	92-105	L	1-10	100–.390	85–.518	17–.647	18–.556	46	57	Marbury 31, Douglas 13	Van Horn 17	Marbury 8
11/24	@GS	92-84	W	2-10	75–.427	88–.364	28–.750	23–.739	54	49	Newman 22, Van Horn 22	Van Horn 11	Marbury 8
11/26	@LAL	80-103	L	2-11	81–.346	83–.542	21–.905	14–.643	42	44	Newman 24, Van Horn 20	Feick 14	Marbury 5
11/27	@Pho	90-129	L	2-12	86–.337	83–.639	32–.875	22–.818	35	50	Marbury 25, Newman 13	2 with 10	Marbury 7
11/30	Was	78-85	L	2-13	80–.388	72–.431	17–.765	29–.655	46	40	Van Horn 24, Feick 15	Feick 16	Marbury 12
12/02	SA	94-96	L	2-14	89–.416	71–.493	20–.600	25–.880	38	43	Marbury 20, Van Horn 20	Feick 13	Marbury 13
12/04	NY	82-92	L	2-15	90–.311	77–.416	28–.821	29–.793	50	48	Marbury 19, Van Horn 16	Feick 23	Marbury 8
12/06	Sac	109-95	W	3-15	91–.473	82–.415	16–.875	27–.889	47	41	Van Horn 27, Marbury 26	Feick 16	Marbury 14
12/08	Mil	107-90	W	4-15	79–.481	78–.449	31–.742	28–.571	37	47	Marbury 25, Van Horn 20	Feick 10	Marbury 14
12/10	@Chi	69-71	L	4-16	72–.375	75–.360	17–.588	24–.583	38	54	Van Horn 19, Marbury 18	Van Horn 11	Marbury 9
12/11	Hou	106-94	W	5-16	88–.500	79–.430	16–.813	25–.760	41	45	Van Horn 21, Gill 17	Feick 14	Marbury 7
12/15	Cle	111-101	W	6-16	82–.463	73–.562	31–.903	22–.591	38	30	Van Horn 27, Marbury 23	2 with 8	Marbury 7
12/16	@Was	104-108	L	6-17	73–.507	79–.595	28–.679	20–.500	28	41	Van Horn 23, Marbury 20	Feick 9	Marbury 11
12/18	@Cle	98-74	W	7-17	77–.455	77–.364	23–.913	24–.667	42	43	Kittles 18, Marbury 18	Feick 13	5 with 3
12/19	Atl	96-88	W	8-17	89–.472	77–.442	9–.444	21–.762	41	49	Van Horn 20, Feick 16	Feick 13	Marbury 11
12/21	@Tor	87-116	L	8-18	85–.400	90–.500	18–.778	27–.741	35	51	Newman 22, Marbury 18	Feick 12	Marbury 6
12/23	Phi	99-94	W	9-18	91–.429	77–.351	19–.789	43–.860	49	46	Van Horn 25, 2 with 21	Van Horn 12	Marbury 7
12/26	Chi	103-76	W	10-18	85–.435	77–.364	28–.821	27–.741	47	45	Van Horn 17, Gill 14	Feick 14	Marbury 11
12/28	NY	89-83	W	11-18	80–.413	79–.380	20–.850	25–.720	47	48	Gill 23, Kittles 21	Feick 17	Marbury 13
12/30	Orl	102-92	W	12-18	110–.382	90–.422	12–.833	17–.647	57	57	Marbury 21, Van Horn 20	Feick 15	Marbury 13
1/04	@Ind	111-116	L	12-19	81–.519	80–.563	25–.800	26–.808	30	41	Kittles 33, Marbury 26	2 with 8	Marbury 10
1/07	Van	91-101	L	12-20	80–.425	78–.449	16–.750	21–1.000	32	51	Kittles 21, 2 with 19	Kittles 6	Marbury 11
1/08	@Mia	90-89	W	13-20	74–.432	79–.481	23–.696	14–.500	32	46	Marbury 20, 2 with 16	3 with 5	Marbury 11
1/10	@Orl	100-94	W	14-20	93–.398	85–.412	20–.750	28–.750	53	41	Marbury 22, Van Horn 20	Feick 13	Marbury 9
1/13	LAC	110-105	W	15-20	87–.483	82–.537	28–.821	15–.647	48	29	Kittles 22, Marbury 21	Feick 14	Marbury 9
1/15	Bos	96-99	L	15-21	76–.382	85–.482	45–.778	21–.714	49	42	Kittles 20, Van Horn 20	2 with 11	Marbury 7
1/17	@Phi	96-101	L	15-22	83–.434	83–.398	24–.708	37–.838	36	51	Marbury 31, Van Horn 20	Van Horn 14	Marbury 9
1/19	@NY	89-90	L	15-23	82–.390	76–.487	18–.889	14–.714	42	44	Marbury 23, Van Horn 16	Van Horn 9	Marbury 10
1/20	Det	122-120	W	16-23	90–.511	72–.542	24–.875	42–.905	38	34	Marbury 34, Van Horn 28	Feick 25	Marbury 15
1/22	Dal	98-95	W	17-23	83–.446	87–.471	27–.778	8–.750	42	44	Gill 23, Marbury 20	Feick 12	Marbury 8
1/24	@Por	87-101	L	17-24	77–.442	77–.519	16–.750	20–.800	31	44	Marbury 21, Van Horn 17	Feick 6	2 with 4
1/26	@Sea	92-95	L	17-25	90–.400	86–.430	20–.700	24–.667	41	55	Marbury 24, Gill 18	Van Horn 9	Marbury 7
1/27	@Van	106-108	L	17-26	71–.507	80–.500	32–.781	28–.821	38	32	Marbury 42, Van Horn 19	Feick 8	Marbury 9
1/29	@LAC	93-98	L	17-27	88–.409	79–.506	18–.800	19–.789	36	44	Kittles 24, Marbury 23	Feick 7	Marbury 7
2/02	Atl	89-97	L	17-28	83–.422	79–.456	14–.786	30–.767	40	45	Van Horn 28, Marbury 15	Feick 16	Marbury 10
2/04	@Bos	95-100	L	17-29	80–.438	78–.474	24–.792	28–.750	36	49	Marbury 20, Newman 15	Van Horn 11	Marbury 11
2/06	GS	110-90	W	18-29	81–.457	93–.376	36–.833	20–.700	49	46	Gill 25, Newman 23	McIlvaine 16	Marbury 11
2/08	Bos	131-113	W	19-29	81–.580	89–.438	35–.857	34–.971	36	46	Marbury 30, Van Horn 30	Van Horn 9	Marbury 10
2/09	@Phi	90-92	L	19-30	70–.471	82–.415	15–.933	25–.840	28	52	Gill 21, Marbury 17	Newman 7	Marbury 9
2/15	@Atl	86-103	L	19-31	95–.326	80–.500	21–.762	27–.704	46	49	Marbury 27, Harris 15	Eschmeyer 7	2 with 4
2/18	Mia	91-84	W	20-31	79–.392	74–.473	34–.676	17–.647	35	51	Van Horn 19, 2 with 18	Van Horn 11	Kittles 7
2/20	@Min	91-89	W	21-31	70–.443	94–.372	32–.750	19–.737	38	51	Marbury 39, Harris 14	Kittles 8	Marbury 5
2/22	LAL	89-97	L	21-32	78–.436	82–.463	26–.731	29–.690	42	42	Marbury 33, Gill 18	Van Horn 16	Marbury 6
2/23	@Mia	85-99	L	21-33	94–.372	80–.463	14–.786	35–.657	45	56	Kittles 24, Marbury 21	Van Horn 11	Marbury 7

348

Date	Opp	Score	W/L	Rec	NJ FG Att–Pct.	Opp FG Att–Pct.	NJ FT Att–Pct.	Opp FT Att–Pct.	NJ Reb	Opp Reb	Points	Rebounds	Assists
											Game Leaders		
2/26	Cha	104-93	W	22-33	83–.482	82–.402	27–.778	27–.815	44	45	Van Horn 29, Gill 23	Van Horn 11	**Marbury 15**
2/28	@Uta	101-106	L	22-34	87–.425	82–.488	25–.760	22–.818	40	40	Marbury 34, Kittles 22	Van Horn 13	Marbury 11
3/01	@Den	94-81	W	23-34	88–.432	93–**.333**	20–.750	23–.609	56	50	Van Horn 25, Marbury 20	2 with 11	Marbury 8
3/02	@Dal	103-102	W	24-34	91–.484	98–.439	14–.429	**6**–1.000	49	53	Marbury 25, 2 with 23	Van Horn 11	Marbury 11
3/04	@Hou	92-99[1]	L	24-35	91–.385	88–.455	22–.864	20–.700	37	53	Marbury 35, Van Horn 24	Van Horn 12	Marbury 6
3/06	@SA	104-106	L	24-36	77–.494	85–.471	28–.857	27–.778	31	52	Marbury 34, Van Horn 23	Feick 11	Marbury 6
3/08	Por	115-103	W	25-36	82–.451	80–.463	41–.805	31–.742	43	45	Marbury 24, Feick 16	Burrell 9	Marbury 13
3/10	@Mil	108-80	W	26-36	85–.518	84–.405	15–.800	11–.636	43	44	Burrell 19, Kittles 16	Feick 11	2 with 8
3/12	Orl	129-91	W	27-36	87–.563	86–.453	30–.767	14–.857	35	44	Newman 26, Burrell 16	Feick 10	Marbury 10
3/18	Mil	92-90[1]	W	28-36	84–.405	87–.425	23–.783	19–.684	47	47	Van Horn 27, Marbury 19	Van Horn 12	Marbury 11
3/19	Uta	88-92	L	28-37	73–.466	72–.458	16–.875	26–.885	35	39	Marbury 23, 2 with 14	Feick 11	Marbury 12
3/21	@Tor	100-93	W	29-37	83–.506	86–.372	18–.611	27–.852	37	55	Gill 24, Marbury 18	Van Horn 9	Marbury 7
3/22	@Cha	103-119	L	29-38	86–.465	82–.561	23–.783	27–.778	38	39	Marbury 23, 2 with 17	2 with 5	Perry 5
3/24	Min	115-116[1]	L	29-39	93–.419	89–.506	35–.829	30–.833	47	43	Kittles 27, Marbury 27	Van Horn 15	Marbury 10
3/26	Den	110-112	L	29-40	87–.425	88–.500	33–.848	14–1.000	40	51	Newman 20, Van Horn 20	Van Horn 10	Marbury 11
3/28	Ind	111-106	W	30-40	94–.436	86–.453	30–.800	23–.913	40	48	Van Horn 30, Marbury 28	Van Horn 10	Marbury 10
3/30	Tor	107-103	W	31-40	78–.474	91–.418	32–.875	30–.767	40	47	Van Horn 32, Marbury 17	Feick 9	2 with 5
3/31	@Orl	97-103	L	31-41	87–.437	85–.506	24–.708	26–.615	35	50	Gill 21, Van Horn 20	Feick 10	Marbury 5
4/02	Det	92-113	L	31-42	84–.405	93–.505	29–.655	18–.722	44	51	Newman 22, Van Horn 11	2 with 7	Marbury 10
4/04	@Was	93-102	L	31-43	80–.413	76–.526	29–.862	23–.696	42	36	Van Horn 24, Marbury 13	Eschmeyer 8	2 with 4
4/05	@Ind	101-105	L	31-44	80–.488	82–.537	21–.952	15–.733	32	42	Van Horn 26, Newman 20	Van Horn 9	Burrell 4
4/07	Mia	85-103	L	31-45	77–.364	76–.500	35–.771	30–.633	43	50	Gill 18, Perry 18	Feick 15	Gill 7
4/08	@Mil	101-109	L	31-46	78–.513	91–.505	20–.700	17–.706	30	47	Newman 21, Van Horn 19	Feick 7	2 with 6
4/11	@Chi	93-100	L	31-47	82–.427	**67**–.537	28–.786	29–.586	36	45	Van Horn 25, Gill 19	Feick 12	Perry 5
4/12	@NY	89-91[1]	L	31-48	88–.398	80–.450	17–.941	27–.593	42	50	Van Horn 32, Newman 16	Feick 10	2 with 5
4/14	Orl	88-96	L	31-49	84–.429	83–.434	17–.706	29–.759	36	56	Newman 27, Van Horn 25	Van Horn 17	Gill 6
4/18	@Atl	109-111[2]	L	31-50	101–.426	101–.446	25–.720	24–.792	52	60	Van Horn 24, Harris 22	Van Horn 14	Gill 9
4/19	Cle	108-111	L	31-51	89–.449	86–.535	29–.793	22–.727	42	47	Newman 29, Van Horn 29	Feick 12	Perry 7

349

New York Knicks 1999-2000 Game Log (50-32)

Date	Opp	Score	W/L	Rec	NY FG Att–Pct.	Opp FG Att–Pct.	NY FT Att–Pct.	Opp FT Att–Pct.	NY Reb	Opp Reb	Points	Rebounds	Assists
11/02	Cle	92-84	W	1-0	74–.432	77–.390	27–.815	23–.739	44	38	L Johnson 24, Houston 18	Camby 17	Houston 5
11/03	@Chi	84-74	W	2-0	76–.474	69–.304	9–.889	40–.725	48	32	Houston 23, Sprewell 19	L Johnson 9	Ward 9
11/05	@Det	103-91	W	3-0	72–.542	83–.386	23–.783	32–.750	42	37	Houston 29, Camby 19	Camby 13	Childs 8
11/06	@Cle	93-102	L	3-1	82–.439	72–.444	19–.842	44–.795	40	44	Houston 22, Sprewell 22	Sprewell 11	**Ward 10**
11/08	Mil	111-101[1]	W	4-1	87–.414	91–.396	37–.892	31–.774	47	48	Houston 30, Camby 23	Camby 13	Childs 7
11/11	@Min	90-93	L	4-2	84–.429	78–.423	16–.813	31–.806	42	40	Houston 29, Sprewell 20	Camby 11	Ward 7
11/12	@Bos	74-80	L	4-3	68–.397	72–.389	25–.640	27–.556	36	49	Houston 16, L Johnson 16	L Johnson 12	L Johnson 4
11/14	Mia	88-94	L	4-4	82–.390	70–.486	24–.792	32–.688	40	34	Camby 22, Houston 20	Thomas 9	2 with 5
11/16	@Den	102-95	W	5-4	71–.563	71–.451	26–.731	38–.658	33	34	Sprewell 26, Houston 23	L Johnson 7	2 with 6
11/17	@Uta	90-98	L	5-5	82–.463	74–.473	19–.632	33–.788	33	46	Sprewell 24, Camby 18	L Johnson 10	Childs 6
11/19	@Pho	81-96	L	5-6	66–.409	69–.464	35–.714	30–.833	36	41	Houston 17, Wallace 16	Dudley 11	Brunson 5
11/20	@GS	86-79	W	6-6	77–.403	86–.326	23–.783	27–.630	54	45	Houston 24, 2 with 14	Lang 10	2 with 5
11/23	@LAC	95-100	L	6-7	81–.432	77–.403	31–.774	32–.875	39	41	Sprewell 32, Thomas 18	2 with 9	Sprewell 5
11/27	Orl	99-96	W	7-7	84–.476	81–.444	14–.929	29–.724	35	44	Houston 30, Sprewell 30	3 with 6	2 with 6
11/29	Dal	107-82	W	8-7	90–.511	88–.352	9–.889	19–.737	52	38	Ward 25, Thomas 20	Lang 9	Sprewell 8
11/30	@Phi	70-74	L	8-8	70–.300	75–.387	32–.813	28–.500	44	48	Houston 20, Sprewell 18	Thomas 16	2 with 3
12/02	@Mil	84-80	W	9-8	85–.400	70–.329	13–.692	36–.806	43	41	Houston 25, Sprewell 23	2 with 11	Ward 7
12/04	@NJ	92-82	W	10-8	77–.416	90–.311	29–.793	28–.821	48	50	Houston 24, Sprewell 20	Thomas 11	Houston 6
12/05	Den	78-80	L	10-9	80–.375	78–.372	19–.737	28–.643	47	48	Houston 15, Sprewell 14	Thomas 13	Childs 7
12/07	GS	89-83	W	11-9	84–.440	90–.333	21–.619	31–.710	45	54	Sprewell 21, 2 with 15	Camby 9	Childs 8
12/10	Phi	85-78	W	12-9	80–.413	85–.365	26–.692	25–.600	46	55	Sprewell 31, 2 with 12	Ewing 10	4 with 3
12/12	Bos	99-97	W	13-9	68–.515	89–.393	34–.765	23–.826	32	50	Houston 26, L Johnson 23	2 with 7	3 with 5
12/14	@Hou	101-90	W	14-9	74–.527	74–.459	17–.941	18–.722	34	32	Sprewell 22, 2 with 20	2 with 5	L Johnson 7
12/16	@Dal	100-93	W	15-9	81–.494	89–.416	19–.842	20–.800	47	39	Houston 31, Camby 17	Camby 12	2 with 5
12/18	Was	83-95	L	15-10	76–.382	67–.493	28–.857	29–.828	31	38	Houston 20, Ewing 18	2 with 8	Childs 5
12/20	Cha	112-109[1]	W	16-10	95–.411	82–.463	32–.813	35–.743	57	38	Houston 31, Sprewell 30	Ewing 18	Ward 6
12/22	Tor	91-90	W	17-10	79–.456	86–.407	22–.591	30–.633	42	50	Sprewell 25, Houston 18	Thomas 10	Houston 5
12/25	@Ind	90-101	L	17-11	71–.521	76–.408	25–.600	40–.800	40	41	Sprewell 23, 2 with 16	Camby 15	Sprewell 6
12/28	@NJ	83-89	L	17-12	79–.380	80–.413	25–.720	20–.850	48	47	Wallace 20, Houston 19	Ewing 16	Sprewell 3
12/30	@Was	89-86	W	18-12	71–.437	67–.478	33–.636	25–.560	30	47	L Johnson 24, Houston 19	Ewing 9	Sprewell 5
1/04	Bos	96-88	W	19-12	60–.550	81–.395	30–.833	31–.710	36	36	**Houston 37**, Sprewell 16	Ewing 12	2 with 5
1/07	@Orl	94-86	W	20-12	79–.506	99–.354	16–.625	21–.619	39	58	Houston 23, Sprewell 19	L Johnson 10	Sprewell 5
1/08	Cle	86-89	L	20-13	75–.453	73–.411	20–.700	28–.821	33	39	Houston 23, Camby 13	Camby 8	Ward 8
1/11	Chi	95-88	W	21-13	70–.471	70–.443	27–.926	37–.541	37	36	L Johnson 19, Houston 15	Ewing 14	Childs 6
1/12	@Det	108-114	L	21-14	90–.533	72–.500	9–.889	39–.872	35	37	Sprewell 23, Houston 22	Ewing 9	Ward 6
1/15	Cha	91-79	W	22-14	79–.456	69–.333	12–.833	39–.744	43	44	Sprewell 20, L Johnson 17	Camby 10	Childs 9
1/17	Det	105-94	W	23-14	90–.489	81–.432	18–.667	27–.704	48	38	Sprewell 23, Camby 22	Camby 15	Houston 6
1/19	NJ	90-89	W	24-14	76–.487	82–.390	14–.714	18–.889	44	42	Ward 19, 2 with 17	Ewing 14	Ward 7
1/22	@SA	83-96	L	24-15	82–.420	71–.479	8–.625	32–.750	37	50	Houston 17, Childs 16	2 with 8	Houston 4
1/24	Sea	112-106	W	25-15	88–.466	76–.526	29–.862	34–.559	37	45	Houston 27, Sprewell 24	Houston 9	2 with 4
1/28	@Atl	96-98[1]	L	25-16	84–.429	93–.355	24–.708	27–.926	43	56	Houston 22, Sprewell 21	Ewing 15	Ward 6
1/30	Sac	**120**-111	W	26-16	82–.537	87–.494	24–**1.000**	22–.818	39	40	Sprewell 32, Houston 28	Ewing 12	2 with 8
2/01	Orl	77-98	L	26-17	77–.403	73–.521	15–.800	28–.679	36	44	Camby 23, L Johnson 17	Ward 7	Childs 7
2/03	Por	98-88	W	27-17	79–.418	83–.422	35–.686	13–.769	38	46	Houston 22, Ewing 20	2 with 9	Ward 9
2/06	Mia	94-80	W	28-17	74–.473	83–.386	27–.741	13–.692	39	41	Ewing 25, Houston 25	Ewing 14	3 with 5
2/07	@Cha	85-95	L	28-18	77–.468	79–.430	13–.769	18–.944	39	42	Houston 26, Ewing 15	Thomas 13	Ward 8
2/09	@Mil	109-103	W	29-18	75–.533	80–.500	23–.826	20–.800	39	30	Sprewell 27, Houston 22	Ewing 16	Sprewell 7
2/15	@Tor	70-91	L	29-19	74–.392	82–.427	19–.421	18–.778	42	45	Houston 17, Thomas 14	Ewing 9	Childs 7
2/16	Min	93-89	W	30-19	71–.465	76–.461	29–.828	24–.750	35	39	Sprewell 19, Houston 18	Ewing 8	Childs 6
2/19	Ind	87-73	W	31-19	74–.514	79–.342	10–.900	21–.762	43	42	Houston 19, Sprewell 17	Thomas 11	Childs 9
2/21	LAC	87-76	W	32-19	74–.446	70–.400	21–.905	18–.667	39	36	Houston 24, 2 with 16	Ewing 12	Sprewell 9
2/23	Tor	88-99	L	32-20	70–.443	72–.486	26–.885	30–.833	34	34	Ewing 24, Sprewell 19	Ewing 10	3 with 4
2/25	Pho	84-79	W	33-20	79–.430	75–.413	18–.833	14–.929	36	42	Ewing 25, Sprewell 21	Sprewell 11	Childs 5
2/27	Phi	89-88	W	34-20	71–.437	75–.413	30–.833	33–.727	39	42	Ewing 18, 2 with 15	2 with 10	Sprewell 6

Date	Opp	Score	W/L	Rec	NY FG Att–Pct.	Opp FG Att–Pct.	NY FT Att–Pct.	Opp FT Att–Pct.	NY Reb	Opp Reb	Points	Rebounds	Assists
2/28	@Mia	76-85	L	34-21	80–.388	76–.434	13–.692	14–1.000	40	45	L Johnson 20, Houston 15	Thomas 11	2 with 5
3/02	Mil	109-94	W	35-21	66–.591	69–.420	23–.826	42–.738	32	32	Sprewell 32, Houston 24	Ewing 8	**Childs 10**
3/03	@Atl	70-83	L	35-22	82–.366	75–.453	11–.727	14–.929	30	50	Sprewell 17, Houston 16	Ewing 7	2 with 4
3/05	Uta	79-88	L	35-23	71–.394	69–.449	30–.733	31–.710	31	46	Sprewell 22, Houston 20	Ewing 9	Sprewell 5
3/07	Van	111-86	W	36-23	66–**.621**	74–.392	30–.867	31–.742	39	**28**	Houston 22, Sprewell 22	2 with 7	Ward 6
3/08	@Was	113-118[1]	L	36-24	79–.544	75–.613	33–.758	30–.833	33	31	Sprewell 33, 2 with 23	Ewing 16	L Johnson 4
3/10	@Phi	82-77	W	37-24	79–.405	75–.373	20–.750	25–.680	52	34	Ewing 19, 2 with 14	Ewing 15	2 with 4
3/12	SA	93-80	W	38-24	70–.486	83–.386	24–.833	18–.722	46	37	Sprewell 24, Ewing 21	Ewing 15	Sprewell 7
3/14	Hou	91-85	W	39-24	70–.486	68–.441	25–.880	30–.667	36	29	Sprewell 27, Wallace 17	3 with 7	Childs 5
3/17	@Cha	118-99	W	40-24	76–.553	81–.494	31–.903	24–.750	39	33	Houston 27, Sprewell 23	L Johnson 10	3 with 6
3/19	LAL	85-92	L	40-25	81–.407	80–.425	20–.700	32–.594	48	46	Houston 20, 2 with 13	Ewing 16	Houston 4
3/21	@Ind	91-95	L	40-26	87–.460	74–.459	10–.800	28–.857	43	38	Ewing 23, 2 with 17	Camby 10	L Johnson 5
3/22	Chi	78-**67**	W	41-26	73–.452	69–.362	11–.909	17–.824	42	36	Sprewell 21, L Johnson 14	2 with 9	2 with 4
3/24	Atl	95-83	W	42-26	79–.494	82–.427	17–.882	14–.786	38	39	Sprewell 30, Houston 27	Camby 12	Ward 8
3/26	@Por	93-89	W	43-26	78–.487	76–.474	11–.909	17–.706	35	37	3 with 19	Ewing 9	Sprewell 9
3/28	@Sac	95-103	L	43-27	86–.442	77–.506	14–1.000	28–.750	40	38	Houston 33, Sprewell 18	Thomas 10	2 with 3
3/29	@Sea	110-95	W	44-27	82–.524	81–.420	20–.850	32–.625	57	30	Houston 19, 2 with 18	Camby 19	Ward 7
3/31	@Van	89-83	W	45-27	82–.451	69–.478	16–.813	14–.857	36	44	Houston 24, Sprewell 23	Ewing 11	Ward 5
4/02	@LAL	82-106	L	45-28	91–.374	76–.513	8–1.000	29–.828	37	50	Ewing 14, L Johnson 13	2 with 8	Houston 5
4/06	Was	101-92	W	46-28	70–.471	84–.405	39–.872	23–.870	46	32	Ewing 30, Camby 21	Camby 15	Sprewell 5
4/07	@Orl	96-89	W	47-28	82–.439	80–.425	23–.870	28–.607	46	36	Ewing 28, Thomas 14	Ewing 18	Sprewell 5
4/09	@Mia	94-95[1]	L	47-29	87–.437	87–.437	15–.733	16–.625	47	43	Houston 20, Sprewell 19	Ewing 10	Childs 5
4/10	Ind	83-81	W	48-29	78–.462	73–.384	7–.857	24–.750	39	44	Houston 20, Sprewell 20	Ewing 10	Childs 8
4/12	NJ	91-89[1]	W	49-29	80–.450	88–.398	27–.593	17–.941	50	42	Sprewell 21, Ewing 18	L Johnson 11	2 with 6
4/14	@Tor	71-86	L	49-30	74–.405	88–.398	19–.579	14–.786	49	38	Ewing 16, 2 with 11	Camby 12	Houston 5
4/15	@Cle	96-106	L	49-31	70–.414	87–.471	**40**–.850	18–.833	39	42	Houston 21, 2 with 15	Thomas 8	**Sprewell 10**
4/18	Det	100-88	W	50-31	70–.514	**67**–.448	30–.767	28–.857	31	34	Houston 29, Sprewell 16	Ewing 9	Ward 9
4/19	@Bos	85-112	L	50-32	83–.398	78–.526	29–.586	26–.846	37	41	Wallace 17, Ewing 15	Thomas 7	Sprewell 5

Postseason

Date	Opp	Score	W/L	Rec	NY FG Att–Pct.	Opp FG Att–Pct.	NY FT Att–Pct.	Opp FT Att–Pct.	NY Reb	Opp Reb	Points	Rebounds	Assists
4/23	Tor	92-88	W	1-0	72–.486	81–.370	21–.810	28–.714	34	47	Houston 21, Sprewell 21	Ewing 9	Ward 5
4/26	Tor	84-83	W	2-0	67–.403	58–.414	38–.737	41–.805	37	35	Sprewell 25, Ewing 19	Camby 13	Houston 4
4/30	@Tor	87-80	W	3-0	62–.468	83–.349	28–.714	24–.792	40	46	Houston 23, L Johnson 14	Ewing 11	Sprewell 6
5/07	@Mia	83-87	L	0-1	78–.423	71–.465	20–.750	23–.783	40	41	Houston 21, Ewing 17	Camby 13	Childs 6
5/09	@Mia	82-76	W	1-1	68–.353	74–.338	42–.738	33–.576	43	50	Ewing 13, Ward 13	2 with 8	Sprewell 4
5/12	Mia	76-77[1]	L	1-2	64–.406	85–.365	24–.833	14–.786	34	45	Houston 24, Sprewell 23	Ewing 9	Ward 4
5/14	Mia	91-83	W	2-2	78–.423	72–.431	22–.773	22–.773	37	48	Ward 20, Houston 17	Ewing 11	Sprewell 6
5/17	@Mia	81-87	L	2-3	74–.473	74–.419	12–.667	27–.741	32	42	Sprewell 24, Ewing 16	Ewing 11	Sprewell 6
5/19	Mia	72-70	W	3-3	71–.380	66–.333	19–.789	29–.724	46	41	Houston 21, 2 with 15	Ewing 18	Ward 4
5/21	@Mia	83-82	W	4-3	72–.361	80–.413	31–.903	21–.524	46	43	Sprewell 24, Ewing 20	Camby 12	Sprewell 5
5/23	@Ind	88-102	L	0-1	80–.438	83–.482	17–.706	12–1.000	35	43	Sprewell 22, Ewing 21	2 with 8	Houston 4
5/25	@Ind	84-88	L	0-2	78–.436	77–.364	18–.778	38–.737	45	49	L Johnson 25, Houston 15	Camby 11	Sprewell 6
5/27	Ind	98-95	W	1-2	74–.527	70–.514	24–.750	18–.889	28	33	Sprewell 32, Houston 28	Sprewell 8	Ward 9
5/29	Ind	91-89	W	2-2	71–.493	79–.456	16–.688	10–.900	41	32	L Johnson 25, Houston 17	Camby 8	Ward 7
5/31	@Ind	79-88	L	2-3	75–.400	79–.367	17–.765	25–.800	43	45	Houston 25, Ewing 13	4 with 7	Ward 7
6/02	Ind	80-93	L	2-4	74–.419	74–.392	19–.737	31–.903	34	42	Sprewell 32, Ewing 18	Ewing 12	Ward 6

Orlando Magic 1999-2000 Game Log (41-41)

Date	Opp	Score	W/L	Rec	Orl FG Att–Pct.	Opp FG Att–Pct.	Orl FT Att–Pct.	Opp FT Att–Pct.	Orl Reb	Opp Reb	Points	Rebounds	Assists
11/02	@Cha	86-100	L	0-1	80–.425	82–.415	27–.667	37–.595	48	47	Gatling 15, Armstrong 12	2 with 7	Atkins 4
11/03	Det	103-94	W	1-1	93–.462	80–.438	24–.625	25–.760	58	34	Garrity 20, Armstrong 17	Ab-Wahad 11	Armstrong 7
11/05	Cle	99-104	L	1-2	95–.389	90–.489	27–.815	14–.786	51	41	Gatling 21, 2 with 20	Wallace 9	3 with 3
11/06	@Was	107-104	W	2-2	81–.469	87–.425	38–.737	29–.793	37	51	Armstrong 20, Harpring 16	Ab-Wahad 8	Armstrong 11
11/08	@Hou	102-97	W	3-2	99–.374	79–.430	36–.750	37–.730	56	48	Gatling 22, Amaechi 18	Gatling 16	5 with 3
11/10	Phi	110-105	W	4-2	86–.512	91–.473	25–.760	21–.667	40	47	Garrity 25, Armstrong 20	Wallace 9	Armstrong 10
11/11	@Ind	101-110	L	4-3	89–.472	74–.568	15–.733	31–.742	42	36	Armstrong 22, Doleac 14	Gatling 8	Armstrong 6
11/13	@Dal	117-125	L	4-4	85–.529	87–.506	26–.731	39–.744	45	39	Gatling 31, Armstrong 29	Gatling 10	Williams 5
11/17	Por	79-81	L	4-5	91–.341	83–.410	19–.789	19–.579	60	43	Gatling 21, Armstrong 13	2 with 10	Armstrong 6
11/19	Cha	92-103	L	4-6	84–.440	86–.477	24–.625	21–.524	47	46	Armstrong 18, Williams 14	Outlaw 7	Armstrong 10
11/20	@Atl	107-103	W	5-6	100–.460	90–.478	15–.800	22–.591	46	53	Gatling 28, Armstrong 21	Gatling 11	Armstrong 8
11/24	Dal	112-100	W	6-6	93–.462	92–.446	25–.760	14–.786	47	41	**Armstrong 33**, Gatling 19	Gatling 12	**Armstrong 14**
11/27	@NY	96-99	L	6-7	81–.444	84–.476	29–.724	14–.929	44	35	Gatling 17, Armstrong 16	Ab-Wahad 8	Armstrong 8
11/28	@Det	108-99	W	7-7	85–.482	87–.414	35–.743	29–.793	45	49	Doleac 20, Williams 18	Wallace 12	Armstrong 8
11/30	Sac	102-111	L	7-8	92–.457	91–.462	24–.667	20–.850	49	44	Armstrong 29, Gatling 17	Outlaw 9	Armstrong 12
12/02	@Min	103-93	W	8-8	93–.452	89–.382	24–.708	29–.759	45	55	Gatling 22, Atkins 18	Amaechi 10	Armstrong 7
12/03	@Den	112-100	W	9-8	82–.512	99–.384	33–.788	24–.750	47	51	Armstrong 20, Amaechi 16	2 with 8	Atkins 8
12/05	@LAL	100-117	L	9-9	78–.397	82–.488	38–.868	37–.703	36	44	Armstrong 20, Garrity 16	Wallace 8	Armstrong 9
12/07	@Pho	107-110	L	9-10	100–.460	84–.476	19–.737	30–.767	54	32	Armstrong 16, 2 with 14	Wallace 9	Armstrong 7
12/11	Chi	108-87	W	10-10	82–.488	75–.427	27–.889	21–.762	40	37	5 with 16	2 with 8	Armstrong 8
12/15	Mil	99-116	L	10-11	82–.390	93–.505	40–.825	19–.947	44	49	Ab-Wahad 15, Atkins 15	Gatling 11	Atkins 5
12/17	Tor	112-98	W	11-11	89–.427	91–.396	40–.750	30–.767	52	45	Atkins 16, Maggette 16	Wallace 14	Armstrong 8
12/18	@Chi	83-74	W	12-11	86–.384	83–.337	23–.652	16–.875	51	51	Amaechi 13, Gatling 10	Ab-Wahad 9	Armstrong 7
12/20	Uta	104-102	W	13-11	85–.471	74–.500	35–.657	32–.750	39	39	Armstrong 22, 2 with 14	2 with 8	Armstrong 8
12/22	@Cle	103-97	W	14-11	86–.477	90–.378	29–.586	27–.741	44	51	Atkins 22, Williams 14	Williams 8	2 with 6
12/23	@Cha	110-106	W	15-11	86–.465	96–.417	30–.767	33–.788	51	43	Armstrong 28, Williams 15	Wallace 15	Armstrong 10
12/27	Min	105-107	L	15-12	86–.523	88–.511	18–.611	20–.700	31	44	Ab-Wahad 16, Armstrong 16	Ab-Wahad 8	2 with 3
12/29	Mia	106-109	L	15-13	96–.406	79–.570	31–.774	22–.818	45	41	Ab-Wahad 21, Gatling 21	Gatling 9	Armstrong 10
12/30	@NJ	92-102	L	15-14	90–.422	110–.382	17–.647	**12**–.833	57	57	Ab-Wahad 18, Armstrong 18	Ab-Wahad 17	2 with 4
1/02	@Mia	103-111[1]	L	15-15	97–.361	93–.409	34–.882	32–.844	**63**	45	Ab-Wahad 22, Armstrong 16	2 with 10	Outlaw 5
1/03	Det	106-118	L	15-16	79–.506	99–.455	31–.677	28–.714	46	48	Gatling 26, Maggette 20	Gatling 11	Atkins 5
1/05	Van	116-96	W	16-16	80–.538	79–.418	25–.875	32–.844	38	32	Gatling 23, Ab-Wahad 17	2 with 6	Atkins 8
1/07	NY	86-94	L	16-17	99–.354	79–.506	21–.619	16–.625	58	39	Armstrong 16, Maggette 14	2 with 10	Armstrong 6
1/08	@SA	92-127	L	16-18	84–.452	84–.583	17–.824	31–.806	30	48	Maggette 17, 2 with 13	2 with 6	Atkins 5
1/10	NJ	94-100	L	16-19	85–.412	93–.398	28–.750	20–.750	41	53	Armstrong 29, Outlaw 16	Wallace 14	Armstrong 8
1/12	@Tor	102-108	L	16-20	72–.486	86–.465	34–**.912**	32–.813	38	37	Ab-Wahad 23, Doleac 20	Wallace 10	Atkins 7
1/14	@Phi	100-102	L	16-21	82–.427	90–.422	33–.848	27–.815	48	41	Doleac 18, Gatling 18	Doleac 13	2 with 5
1/15	Ind	89-96	L	16-22	91–.407	82–.451	21–.667	19–.684	50	45	Ab-Wahad 18, Armstrong 17	2 with 8	Armstrong 4
1/17	@GS	100-113	L	16-23	86–.453	92–.511	20–.800	25–.600	41	45	Ab-Wahad 19, Armstrong 18	Wallace 7	Armstrong 6
1/20	@Sac	103-111	L	16-24	88–.466	95–.453	26–.769	19–.737	41	51	Maggette 18, Armstrong 16	Outlaw 8	Armstrong 6
1/22	@Van	85-82	W	17-24	80–.438	81–.383	18–.667	18–.889	39	49	Ab-Wahad 16, Atkins 16	Wallace 11	Armstrong 7
1/23	@LAC	102-89	W	18-24	89–.438	80–.450	30–.700	19–.737	48	45	Armstrong 17, Ab-Wahad 16	2 with 9	Armstrong 6
1/26	Bos	111-89	W	19-24	65–**.600**	75–.413	43–.721	24–.833	34	34	Ab-Wahad 19, Amaechi 16	2 with 7	Armstrong 8
1/27	@Cle	90-102	L	19-25	87–.402	77–.442	17–.824	43–.744	45	48	Armstrong 21, Ab-Wahad 17	Outlaw 9	Armstrong 7
1/29	Atl	103-87	W	20-25	80–.463	80–.363	36–.750	36–.750	50	42	Gatling 19, Maggette 18	Gatling 12	2 with 4
1/31	Pho	113-117	L	20-26	95–.484	78–.538	22–.636	39–.692	37	40	Armstrong 26, Ab-Wahad 19	Maggette 10	Armstrong 11
2/01	@NY	98-77	W	21-26	73–.521	77–.403	28–.679	15–.800	44	36	Atkins 22, 2 with 14	Outlaw 11	2 with 7
2/05	Ind	107-102	W	22-26	80–.463	77–.455	43–.651	38–.789	43	49	Amaechi 19, Garrity 18	Wallace 11	Atkins 7
2/07	GS	120-100	W	23-26	80–.575	92–.424	31–.806	29–.655	44	41	Amaechi 25, Doleac 23	Wallace 9	Atkins 13
2/09	Was	107-96	W	24-26	97–.495	74–.473	20–.500	24–.750	44	42	Maggette 15, 2 with 14	Wallace 16	Atkins 9
2/16	LAC	**129**-96	W	25-26	92–.554	97–.402	21–.857	19–.684	49	47	Armstrong 26, Amaechi 23	Maggette 8	Armstrong 9
2/18	LAL	99-107[1]	L	25-27	97–.454	81–.494	11–.636	27–.852	44	38	Armstrong 24, Doleac 16	Outlaw 9	Outlaw 9
2/22	@Sea	91-127	L	25-28	93–.387	85–.529	25–.520	28–.786	42	54	Atkins 21, Maggette 13	Wallace 7	Atkins 4
2/24	@Por	92-111	L	25-29	91–.440	79–.557	15–.667	19–.842	39	40	Armstrong 16, Atkins 16	Wallace 12	Atkins 7

Date	Opp	Score	W/L	Rec	Orl FG Att–Pct.	Opp FG Att–Pct.	Orl FT Att–Pct.	Opp FT Att–Pct.	Orl Reb	Opp Reb	Game Leaders Points	Rebounds	Assists
2/25	@Uta	88-96	L	25-30	67–.463	82–.415	36–.667	33–.788	38	45	Amaechi 24, Mercer 19	Wallace 13	Outlaw 4
2/27	@Mil	95-102	L	25-31	86–.442	82–.439	15–.733	31–.839	37	50	Garrity 32, 2 with 13	Outlaw 9	2 with 6
2/29	Sea	103-94	W	26-31	86–.512	93–.409	12–.833	19–.526	44	46	Mercer 27, Armstrong 18	Wallace 9	Armstrong 9
3/02	Cha	104-96	W	27-31	78–.500	84–.464	27–.778	18–.778	45	36	Mercer 19, Atkins 14	Outlaw 10	Atkins 5
3/05	@Bos	91-97	L	27-32	82–.463	92–.391	13–.692	24–.750	48	46	Armstrong 19, Atkins 17	2 with 8	Armstrong 6
3/06	@Was	87-85	W	28-32	92–.402	73–.425	16–.500	23–.826	51	38	Atkins 15, Maggette 14	Wallace 16	2 with 5
3/08	Chi	103-**67**	W	29-32	81–.506	69–.333	21–.857	24–.708	46	40	Armstrong 17, Amaechi 16	Outlaw 7	Maggette 5
3/11	Den	110-107	W	30-32	82–.451	**67**–.507	**47**–.723	40–.875	40	36	Amaechi 31, Armstrong 23	Outlaw 13	Armstrong 5
3/12	@NJ	91-129	L	30-33	86–.453	87–.563	14–.857	30–.767	44	35	Armstrong 15, Amaechi 14	Outlaw 11	Atkins 5
3/14	Was	107-98	W	31-33	72–.528	86–.465	32–.813	18–.667	31	37	Williams 19, Mercer 18	Wallace 12	Armstrong 6
3/15	@Det	91-113	L	31-34	68–.441	88–.477	36–.750	29–.897	26	50	Amaechi 27, Mercer 19	Outlaw 6	3 with 4
3/17	@Tor	91-95	L	31-35	82–.488	83–.398	13–.538	32–.813	46	41	Atkins 14, Wallace 14	Doleac 10	Armstrong 6
3/19	@Phi	85-89	L	31-36	81–.432	78–.462	13–.846	26–.654	47	39	Mercer 26, Armstrong 16	Wallace **21**	Armstrong 8
3/20	@Chi	88-86[1]	W	32-36	83–.373	85–.400	35–.686	20–.650	39	65	Armstrong 20, Mercer 19	2 with 9	2 with 6
3/22	Atl	103-90	W	33-36	88–.455	86–.419	28–.750	30–.567	57	40	Armstrong 27, Amaechi 16	Wallace 16	Armstrong 10
3/24	Hou	112-96	W	34-36	**102**–.441	75–.387	19–.789	34–.882	54	43	Armstrong 21, 2 with 14	Wallace 14	Armstrong 9
3/26	Mia	94-69	W	35-36	78–.449	76–.368	22–.727	24–.**458**	48	34	Atkins 20, Armstrong 16	Wallace 11	Atkins 5
3/28	Bos	122-87	W	36-36	85–.553	92–.370	33–.697	27–.556	52	33	Mercer 23, Atkins 21	Outlaw 14	Outlaw 10
3/31	NJ	103-97	W	37-36	85–.506	87–.437	26–.615	24–.708	50	35	Mercer 22, Amaechi 17	Wallace 14	Armstrong 9
4/04	SA	107-97	W	38-36	81–.543	69–.536	17–.706	28–.643	40	29	Amaechi 24, Armstrong 23	Outlaw 11	Atkins 6
4/07	NY	89-96	L	38-37	80–.425	82–.439	28–.607	23–.870	36	46	Armstrong 15, Atkins 14	Outlaw 9	Atkins 5
4/09	Phi	92-80	W	39-37	99–.384	79–.**329**	16–.688	31–.710	53	54	Mercer 17, Armstrong 14	Wallace 12	Armstrong 9
4/10	@Mil	87-104	L	39-38	83–.349	83–.470	40–.700	24–.750	42	42	Mercer 14, Armstrong 13	Wallace 13	Armstrong 6
4/12	@Bos	91-95	L	39-39	82–.402	88–.409	27–.815	25–.680	46	50	Amaechi 22, Mercer 14	Amaechi 9	Armstrong 5
4/14	@NJ	96-88	W	40-39	83–.434	84–.429	29–.759	17–.706	56	36	Armstrong 23, Mercer 22	Wallace 20	Armstrong 6
4/16	@Mia	84-95	L	40-40	76–.408	73–.521	25–.720	17–.765	35	38	Armstrong 16, Maggette 15	Wallace 10	Armstrong 3
4/17	Mil	83-85	L	40-41	86–.349	76–.408	21–.810	33–.667	41	50	Atkins 18, Garrity 15	Mercer 9	2 with 6
4/19	Tor	106-100	W	41-41	83–.470	99–.414	31–.806	17–.647	46	51	Mercer 27, Armstrong 22	Strong 8	Atkins 7

353

Philadelphia 76ers 1999-2000 Game Log (49-33)

Date	Opp	Score	W/L	Rec	Phi FG Att–Pct.	Opp FG Att–Pct.	Phi FT Att–Pct.	Opp FT Att–Pct.	Phi Reb	Opp Reb	Points	Rebounds	Assists
11/02	@SA	76-89	L	0-1	83–.361	72–.431	21–.714	29–.724	35	50	Iverson 28, Hughes 10	Lynch 10	McKie 4
11/04	@Pho	80-84	L	0-2	80–.363	73–.397	26–.808	31–.774	40	49	Hill 14, Iverson 11	Lynch 15	Snow 5
11/05	@LAC	81-91	L	0-3	86–.337	**69**–.435	34–.647	31–.871	44	52	Iverson 21, Lynch 15	Lynch 8	2 with 2
11/08	Sea	117-98	W	1-3	**102**–.480	83–.446	17–.765	31–.548	56	40	Iverson 37, Hughes 27	2 with 10	2 with 6
11/10	@Orl	105-110	L	1-4	91–.473	86–.512	21–.667	25–.760	47	40	Iverson 46, Lynch 15	MacCulloch 12	Snow 10
11/12	Chi	92-86	W	2-4	69–.493	79–.430	33–.697	14–.929	40	33	Iverson 35, Lynch 15	2 with 7	Snow 10
11/14	@Tor	93-90	W	3-4	84–.440	78–.372	22–.636	33–.818	42	43	Iverson 30, Ratliff 17	Ratliff 8	Iverson 6
11/16	@Was	95-73	W	4-4	70–.471	79–.342	37–.649	31–.516	45	52	Iverson 39, Owens 18	2 with 9	Snow 11
11/17	Mia	93-98	L	4-5	88–.386	82–.439	34–.706	30–.667	44	54	Lynch 26, Iverson 24	Lynch 12	Snow 9
11/19	Por	91-97	L	4-6	85–.412	71–.507	26–.692	35–.600	45	42	Iverson 26, Owens 14	Lynch 10	2 with 5
11/20	@NJ	100-96	W	5-6	74–.486	71–.408	35–.714	46–.783	36	42	Iverson 37, Hughes 16	2 with 7	Iverson 8
11/22	SA	91-94	L	5-7	92–.370	84–.405	26–.731	29–.690	49	53	Iverson 35, 2 with 15	Lynch 12	Snow 10
11/24	Was	93-101	L	5-8	78–.449	81–.407	30–.733	39–.795	44	39	McKie 17, 2 with 15	Hill 10	Snow 7
11/26	Cle	106-83	W	6-8	82–.439	71–.423	41–.732	28–.679	49	42	McKie 23, Hill 22	Hill 8	Snow 10
11/27	@Mil	82-79	W	7-8	88–.386	85–.365	22–.545	17–.824	49	46	Snow 18, MacCulloch 16	Hill 14	Snow 7
11/30	NY	74-**70**	W	8-8	75–.387	70–**.300**	28–.500	32–.813	48	44	Hughes 25, Snow 11	MacCulloch 13	2 with 4
12/01	@Mia	83-90	L	8-9	78–.423	73–.452	24–.667	23–.870	36	44	Hill 20, McKie 20	Hill 8	Snow 4
12/03	@Cle	102-100[1]	W	9-9	91–.451	81–.444	23–.826	33–.667	49	44	McKie 25, 2 with 22	Hill 16	McKie 9
12/04	Bos	77-74	W	10-9	69–.464	76–.421	17–.706	15–.533	37	37	Hill 14, Lynch 13	3 with 9	Snow 11
12/06	Den	77-94	L	10-10	83–.373	72–.472	25–.600	28–.786	43	43	Hill 16, McKie 12	Lynch 13	Snow 8
12/08	Hou	83-73	W	11-10	84–.417	71–.366	15–.800	21–.714	45	41	McKie 16, Snow 16	Hill 11	Snow 5
12/10	@NY	78-85	L	11-11	85–.365	80–.413	25–.600	26–.692	55	46	Hill 16, Hughes 13	Owens 12	Snow 6
12/11	Cha	84-106	L	11-12	89–.371	94–.457	27–.667	25–.720	51	50	McKie 16, Owens 12	Lynch 9	McKie 4
12/15	Tor	93-91	W	12-12	92–.391	84–.405	24–.667	27–.704	48	56	Iverson 37, Hughes 12	Geiger 9	Snow 7
12/17	Chi	77-74	W	13-12	73–.425	73–.411	22–.682	13–.923	43	38	Iverson 19, 2 with 16	2 with 9	Iverson 7
12/18	@Det	91-104	L	13-13	91–.418	79–.443	21–.667	38–.763	42	48	Iverson 19, Geiger 17	Geiger 11	Iverson 6
12/20	Det	122-121[1]	W	14-13	101–.495	79–.519	22–.682	41–.805	41	39	Iverson 32, Hill 22	Hill 7	McKie 6
12/23	@NJ	94-99	L	14-14	77–.351	91–.429	43–.860	19–.789	46	49	Iverson 42, Hill 14	Hill 13	Snow 12
12/26	@Sea	92-86	W	15-14	81–.420	81–.333	33–.667	33–.727	49	45	Iverson 34, Hughes 12	Lynch 14	Snow 3
12/27	@Van	100-93	W	16-14	82–.463	83–.482	29–.793	15–.800	44	42	Iverson 29, Geiger 20	Lynch 14	Iverson 6
12/29	@GS	97-94	W	17-14	80–.488	84–.440	23–.783	22–.545	38	48	Iverson 34, 2 with 15	Hill 15	Snow 9
12/30	@Por	90-108	L	17-15	83–.434	75–.493	23–.652	31–.806	35	48	Iverson 32, Geiger 12	Lynch 9	Snow 11
1/03	Mil	**124**-120[1]	W	18-15	88–.523	96–.448	41–.683	31–.839	39	46	Iverson 45, Hill 22	Hill 9	Snow 7
1/05	GS	113-92	W	19-15	81–.531	87–.402	34–.735	21–.762	54	37	Iverson 34, Geiger 26	Hill 11	**Snow 15**
1/09	Min	112-123	L	19-16	89–.449	81–.642	35–.743	16–.938	40	36	Iverson 37, McKie 17	Geiger 13	Snow 11
1/14	Orl	102-100	W	20-16	90–.422	82–.427	27–.815	33–.848	41	48	Iverson 35, Ratliff 18	Ratliff 14	2 with 4
1/15	@Atl	101-98	W	21-16	83–.494	77–.455	24–.750	24–.792	37	40	Iverson 31, Geiger 22	Hill 13	Snow 11
1/17	NJ	101-96	W	22-16	83–.398	83–.434	27–.667	24–.708	51	36	Iverson 34, McKie 14	Lynch 11	Snow 12
1/19	Atl	107-89	W	23-16	83–.494	85–.341	32–.781	38–.763	53	41	Iverson 25, Hughes 18	Hill 13	Iverson 5
1/20	@Cha	100-109	L	23-17	87–.448	72–.458	29–.690	46–.826	40	42	Iverson 35, Hill 17	Hill 7	Snow 9
1/22	Ind	103-97	W	24-17	82–.439	81–.444	32–**.938**	21–.857	48	33	Iverson 37, Hill 16	Geiger 11	Snow 8
1/26	Pho	87-93	L	24-18	90–.367	77–.429	35–.543	26–.769	53	46	Iverson 18, Ratliff 14	Ratliff 14	Iverson 7
1/29	@Det	88-90	L	24-19	75–.453	79–.380	30–.600	29–.828	47	44	Iverson 27, Lynch 13	2 with 11	Iverson 6
1/31	@Den	80-83	L	24-20	86–.360	81–.432	27–.630	16–**.438**	48	47	Iverson 29, 2 with 11	Lynch 14	2 with 4
2/01	@Dal	101-100	W	25-20	83–.506	92–.413	21–.810	21–.810	54	39	Iverson 29, Ratliff 25	Ratliff 13	Snow 11
2/03	@Hou	106-109	L	25-21	85–.518	82–.451	22–.727	32–.719	39	48	Iverson 40, Ratliff 25	Hill 12	Snow 10
2/06	Sac	119-108	W	26-21	99–.465	90–.422	33–.788	33–.667	57	49	Iverson 40, Ratliff 15	Hill 14	Snow 13
2/07	@Ind	84-109	L	26-22	92–.402	80–.538	9–.778	12–.917	39	43	**Iverson 50**, Ratliff 15	Ratliff 13	**Snow 15**
2/09	NJ	92-90	W	27-22	82–.415	70–.471	25–.840	15–.933	52	**28**	Iverson 41, Snow 12	Lynch 12	Snow 14
2/15	Cha	93-95	L	27-23	88–.455	85–.412	16–.625	27–.778	41	57	Iverson 28, 2 with 13	Hill 14	Snow 7
2/18	Cle	104-75	W	28-23	78–.487	83–.349	37–.676	18–.778	50	43	Iverson 19, Ratliff 16	Ratliff 11	2 with 6
2/20	LAL	84-87	L	28-24	85–.388	80–.450	21–.619	19–.579	51	39	Ratliff 20, Iverson 16	Hill 12	Iverson 8
2/23	LAC	94-78	W	29-24	84–.464	78–.397	21–.667	16–.750	**58**	34	Iverson 22, Kukoc 18	Kukoc 14	Snow 11
2/25	@Mil	97-83	W	30-24	70–.471	85–.424	39–.718	11–.818	38	35	Iverson 25, Hill 17	2 with 7	Snow 9

Date	Opp	Score	W/L	Rec	Phi FG Att–Pct.	Opp FG Att–Pct.	Phi FT Att–Pct.	Opp FT Att–Pct.	Phi Reb	Opp Reb	Points	Rebounds	Assists
2/27	@NY	88-89	L	30-25	75–.413	71–.437	33–.727	30–.833	42	39	Iverson 26, Hill 19	**Hill 20**	3 with 5
2/29	Dal	106-87	W	31-25	73–**.630**	85–.388	18–.667	15–.933	43	34	Iverson 35, Ratliff 19	Lynch 8	Snow 11
3/02	@Was	87-84	W	32-25	81–.383	79–.405	28–.679	17–.882	42	43	Kukoc 19, Ratliff 17	2 with 11	Kukoc 7
3/04	@Chi	95-84	W	33-25	86–.430	70–.414	25–.680	26–.692	49	33	Iverson 29, Ratliff 21	Ratliff 13	Snow 14
3/08	Van	107-90	W	34-25	80–.488	69–**.478**	31–.806	28–.714	35	40	Iverson 20, Kukoc 20	Lynch 10	Kukoc 8
3/10	NY	77-82	L	34-26	75–.373	79–.405	25–.680	20–.750	34	52	Iverson 30, McKie 14	Lynch 10	Iverson 7
3/12	@Bos	77-93	L	34-27	73–.411	93–.387	29–.517	25–.800	44	50	Iverson 21, Snow 18	Geiger 13	Iverson 5
3/14	@Cle	98-97[1]	W	35-27	82–.427	87–.425	34–.735	22–.818	42	45	Iverson 28, McKie 20	Hill 12	2 with 7
3/16	@Mia	77-92	L	35-28	77–.442	83–.470	11–.636	**8**–.625	37	40	Ratliff 20, McKie 14	Hill 10	Snow 10
3/17	Uta	99-97	W	36-28	82–.500	75–.453	12–.917	28–.750	36	43	Iverson 24, Kukoc 14	Hill 10	2 with 9
3/19	Orl	89-85	W	37-28	78–.462	81–.432	26–.654	13–.846	39	47	Iverson 18, Hill 15	Lynch 11	Iverson 10
3/20	@Cha	102-96	W	38-28	91–.462	75–.507	23–.609	27–.630	46	41	Iverson 25, Hill 16	Hill 14	Snow 10
3/22	Tor	106-93	W	39-28	74–.554	86–.442	22–.909	22–.682	36	43	Iverson 44, Hill 20	Hill 12	Snow 14
3/24	Bos	117-115[2]	W	40-28	97–.402	106–.396	**46**–.739	32–.719	57	65	Iverson 21, Snow 21	Ratliff 14	Snow 8
3/26	@Ind	111-101	W	41-28	94–.500	83–.434	23–.696	24–.917	51	40	Iverson 33, 2 with 19	2 with 10	Kukoc 10
3/28	@Min	102-100	W	42-28	76–.487	85–.459	30–.800	23–.739	43	38	Iverson 43, Hill 18	Hill 14	Snow 12
3/29	Uta	84-98	L	42-29	77–.416	78–.500	25–.680	17–1.000	34	44	Iverson 18, Kukoc 18	Hill 8	Snow 8
3/31	@LAL	88-100	L	42-30	96–.375	79–.532	20–.700	18–.778	38	50	Geiger 20, Kukoc 19	Ratliff 13	Snow 8
4/02	@Sac	95-117	L	42-31	82–.488	83–.566	21–.667	20–.650	38	40	Iverson 23, 2 with 15	Hill 8	Snow 9
4/05	Atl	107-86	W	43-31	84–.548	76–.447	23–.652	25–.680	45	38	Iverson 30, Hill 21	2 with 10	Kukoc 9
4/07	@Bos	102-97	W	44-31	77–.468	92–.413	38–.763	17–.882	40	51	Geiger 20, Iverson 16	Lynch 9	2 with 6
4/09	@Orl	80-92	L	44-32	79–.329	99–.384	31–.710	16–.688	54	53	Hill 22, Iverson 18	Hill 14	Snow 9
4/10	Mia	96-80	W	45-32	72–.500	73–.411	22–.818	22–.727	35	41	Iverson 33, 2 with 12	2 with 6	Snow 10
4/12	Was	93-84	W	46-32	74–.473	78–.410	35–.600	17–.882	38	50	Iverson 24, Kukoc 23	Ratliff 10	Snow 10
4/14	@Atl	104-92	W	47-32	75–.547	84–.429	31–.710	16–.938	38	39	Iverson 27, Hill 20	Ratliff 13	Snow 9
4/15	Det	100-94	W	48-32	79–.481	81–.481	30–.733	20–.600	50	39	Iverson 30, Lynch 17	Lynch 15	Iverson 7
4/17	Ind	90-92	L	48-33	82–.415	79–.481	28–.679	12–.583	42	43	Iverson 24, Lynch 16	Hill 14	Snow 12
4/18	@Chi	93-89	W	49-33	76–.474	70–.486	30–.633	21–.762	42	37	Snow 20, Kukoc 18	Geiger 9	McKie 8

Postseason

Date	Opp	Score	W/L	Rec	Phi FG Att–Pct.	Opp FG Att–Pct.	Phi FT Att–Pct.	Opp FT Att–Pct.	Phi Reb	Opp Reb	Points	Rebounds	Assists
4/22	@Cha	92-82	W	1-0	78–.423	65–.369	31–.710	39–.769	36	51	Iverson 40, 3 with 10	Ratliff 8	Snow 9
4/24	@Cha	98-108[1]	L	1-1	86–.430	83–.530	19–.842	16–.875	42	41	Kukoc 20, Snow 19	Hill 13	Snow 13
4/28	Cha	81-76	W	2-1	78–.346	71–.352	28–.786	25–.880	48	40	Iverson 24, 2 with 12	Ratliff 11	McKie 5
5/01	Cha	105-99	W	3-1	78–.513	81–.444	23–.783	28–.821	36	44	Iverson 26, McKie 25	Geiger 10	McKie 11
5/06	@Ind	91-108	L	0-1	82–.439	79–.494	22–.727	21–.905	42	37	Iverson 28, Hill 20	Lynch 14	Snow 7
5/08	@Ind	97-103	L	0-2	78–.436	76–.487	37–.703	25–.840	39	38	Iverson 28, 2 with 15	Hill 8	Iverson 10
5/10	Ind	89-97	L	0-3	77–.416	78–.487	32–.750	15–.800	42	40	Iverson 29, McKie 20	Hill 14	Kukoc 4
5/13	Ind	92-90	W	1-3	78–.385	80–.388	43–.674	25–.840	53	37	Iverson 19, Hill 18	Hill 15	Iverson 5
5/15	@Ind	107-86	W	2-3	78–.500	84–.405	32–.813	20–.750	45	34	Iverson 37, Ratliff 26	2 with 10	McKie 9
5/19	Ind	90-106	L	2-4	87–.391	76–.513	28–.714	26–.808	41	46	McKie 19, Iverson 18	2 with 9	McKie 4

Phoenix Suns 1999-2000 Game Log (53-29)

Date	Opp	Score	W/L	Rec	Pho FG Att–Pct.	Opp FG Att–Pct.	Pho FT Att–Pct.	Opp FT Att–Pct.	Pho Reb	Opp Reb	Points	Rebounds	Assists
11/02	@Den	102-107[1]	L	0-1	111–.387	89–.449	14–.500	26–.731	**58**	55	Gugliotta 22, Rogers 21	**Gugliotta 19**	Kidd 8
11/04	Phi	84-80	W	1-1	73–.397	80–.363	31–.774	26–.808	49	40	Kidd 22, Hardaway 18	Gugliotta 10	3 with 3
11/07	SA	77-74	W	2-1	83–.398	84–.381	14–.571	16–.**375**	47	52	Kidd 23, Rogers 18	Hardaway 10	Kidd 7
11/09	@Chi	103-80	W	3-1	72–.556	74–.365	32–.656	38–.632	43	36	3 with 19	Gugliotta 12	Kidd 9
11/10	@NJ	104-89	W	4-1	85–.471	84–.381	26–.808	28–.821	53	41	Hardaway 25, Gugliotta 18	Miller 10	Hardaway 5
11/12	@Mil	92-107	L	4-2	86–.384	77–.532	28–.714	25–.800	48	37	Hardaway 19, Kidd 17	Gugliotta 10	2 with 4
11/13	@Min	100-111	L	4-3	87–.425	92–.533	22–.955	15–.733	38	47	Hardaway 21, Marion 13	Miller 8	Kidd 7
11/15	LAL	82-91	L	4-4	87–.368	76–.382	19–.737	46–.674	44	52	Kidd 20, 2 with 12	Longley 10	Kidd 10
11/17	Chi	105-81	W	5-4	76–.553	64–.422	22–.818	35–.686	35	**30**	Gugliotta 18, Hardaway 18	Gugliotta 7	Kidd 11
11/19	NY	96-81	W	6-4	69–.464	66–.409	30–.833	35–.714	41	36	Day 20, Kidd 16	Gugliotta 9	Kidd 10
11/21	Sea	99-86	W	7-4	88–.443	91–.385	24–.625	19–.526	49	53	Kidd 25, Gugliotta 16	Robinson 8	Kidd 14
11/23	Tor	94-93	W	8-4	76–.474	89–.427	24–.792	14–.786	42	40	Hardaway 17, 2 with 16	2 with 7	Kidd 15
11/27	NJ	**129**-90	W	9-4	83–.**639**	86–.337	22–.818	32–.875	50	35	Marion 27, 2 with 21	2 with 8	2 with 7
11/30	@LAC	94-80	W	10-4	86–.442	76–.342	27–.593	39–.692	51	44	Kidd 20, Robinson 19	Gugliotta 11	Kidd 10
12/01	Hou	128-122[2]	W	11-4	103–.427	94–.489	39–.846	33–.636	44	51	Robinson 25, Hardaway 21	3 with 8	Kidd 11
12/04	@Hou	95-105	L	11-5	80–.450	85–.482	29–.690	16–.750	44	35	Hardaway 21, Robinson 21	Hardaway 9	2 with 5
12/05	Por	90-92	L	11-6	82–.439	68–.485	13–.692	36–.722	32	41	Gugliotta 19, Robinson 19	Longley 9	Kidd 10
12/07	Orl	110-107	W	12-6	84–.476	100–.460	30–.767	19–.737	32	54	Kidd 29, Day 19	Miller 8	Kidd 11
12/09	Was	99-85	W	13-6	79–.519	78–.423	13–.846	31–.581	44	36	Robinson 31, Gugliotta 27	Gugliotta 8	Kidd 9
12/11	@Dal	115-120	L	13-7	93–.441	87–.529	38–.763	26–.692	48	45	Robinson 28, Kidd 19	Kidd 13	Kidd 9
12/14	Det	114-104	W	14-7	86–.512	81–.444	24–.833	28–.893	38	35	Chapman 22, Kidd 18	Kidd 9	Kidd 11
12/17	@Por	110-102	W	15-7	90–.489	84–.488	19–.684	17–.647	43	44	Kidd 32, Robinson 23	Gugliotta 14	Kidd 10
12/18	Sac	119-103	W	16-7	94–.447	87–.414	31–.806	35–.657	**58**	52	Robinson 33, Kidd 27	Kidd 14	Kidd 14
12/20	Mil	108-101	W	17-7	92–.457	83–.494	24–.750	27–.765	47	38	Rogers 24, Robinson 19	Rogers 13	Kidd 11
12/21	@SA	90-91[1]	L	17-8	92–.370	87–.379	17–.765	32–.719	52	55	Robinson 26, Chapman 19	Miller 12	Kidd 10
12/23	Dal	110-111	L	17-9	86–.500	85–.518	19–.632	20–.750	34	48	Robinson 30, Kidd 25	Robinson 9	Kidd 15
12/26	GS	108-88	W	18-9	76–.579	80–.438	24–.583	27–.519	41	34	Robinson 25, Kidd 19	Robinson 8	Kidd 7
12/27	@Uta	91-92	L	18-10	65–.538	77–.429	15–.867	32–.719	36	35	Chapman 29, Kidd 16	Kidd 12	Kidd 15
12/29	@LAL	87-103	L	18-11	90–.378	79–.519	18–.667	23–.609	42	53	Robinson 24, Chapman 18	Robinson 8	Kidd 11
1/04	Cha	86-80	W	19-11	80–.425	81–.321	13–.692	32–.688	56	47	Robinson 30, Day 13	Gugliotta 10	Kidd 10
1/07	SA	83-102	L	19-12	89–.371	88–.420	15–.733	32–.781	46	56	Robinson 22, Gugliotta 14	Longley 10	Kidd 13
1/08	@Por	91-96	L	19-13	88–.409	71–.479	21–.571	37–.676	36	47	Chapman 20, Day 15	Gugliotta 9	Kidd 14
1/11	@Sea	88-101	L	19-14	87–.425	77–.481	12–.583	24–.792	38	43	Robinson 17, Chapman 13	Gugliotta 9	Kidd 15
1/12	@Van	95-92	W	20-14	90–.389	70–.357	27–.741	45–.889	41	50	Kidd 20, Longley 15	Kidd 10	Kidd 10
1/14	Por	83-105	L	20-15	76–.421	74–.473	30–.600	36–.806	37	36	Robinson 23, Kidd 17	Rogers 10	Kidd 8
1/16	Den	113-100	W	21-15	79–.532	89–.438	28–.786	22–.864	45	42	**Robinson 50**, Day 15	2 with 8	Kidd 13
1/21	@Den	101-99	W	22-15	85–.447	78–.436	22–.955	26–.846	44	38	Kidd 24, Robinson 24	Gugliotta 15	Kidd 12
1/22	Cle	101-88	W	23-15	76–.447	71–.479	29–.897	25–.640	38	**30**	Kidd 16, Rogers 16	Gugliotta 9	Kidd 12
1/25	@Ind	87-93	L	23-16	83–.398	79–.430	20–.750	22–.818	44	43	Robinson 24, Kidd 22	Gugliotta 10	Kidd 8
1/26	@Phi	93-87	W	24-16	77–.429	90–.367	26–.769	35–.543	46	53	Hardaway 27, Robinson 19	Kidd 13	Kidd 8
1/28	@Bos	88-91	L	24-17	80–.388	78–.410	22–.864	32–.656	45	43	Robinson 37, Hardaway 18	Kidd 12	Kidd 14
1/29	@Cha	79-100	L	24-18	78–.397	80–.475	15–.733	24–.833	31	51	Hardaway 24, Robinson 16	Gugliotta 11	Kidd 6
1/31	@Orl	117-113	W	25-18	78–.538	95–.484	39–.692	22–.636	40	37	Robinson 28, Hardaway 21	2 with 8	Kidd 14
2/02	LAC	114-68	W	26-18	85–.576	78–.**295**	17–.824	19–.842	50	34	Robinson 21, Gugliotta 14	Longley 9	Kidd 8
2/04	@Sea	86-94	L	26-19	80–.413	79–.468	18–.889	20–.650	44	45	Rogers 26, Hardaway 17	Kidd 12	Kidd 6
2/06	Sea	105-93	W	27-19	83–.494	85–.376	22–.773	25–.800	46	41	Kidd 22, Rogers 22	Gugliotta 9	Kidd 12
2/08	Van	94-76	W	28-19	75–.547	82–.329	9–**1.000**	21–.952	42	31	Longley 20, Hardaway 13	Hardaway 8	Kidd 9
2/10	Min	101-85	W	29-19	78–.487	89–.393	30–.800	15–.800	47	44	Kidd 16, Robinson 16	Longley 12	Kidd 7
2/15	@Sac	117-108	W	30-19	87–.517	87–.471	23–.957	20–.700	46	33	Rogers 36, Gugliotta 18	Kidd 10	Kidd 11
2/18	Atl	85-73	W	31-19	90–.411	75–.360	15–.600	30–.600	45	60	Rogers 24, Longley 15	2 with 9	Kidd 9
2/21	@SA	98-89	W	32-19	88–.409	78–.410	21–.810	29–.793	44	44	Rogers 22, Gugliotta 21	Gugliotta 11	Kidd 11
2/22	Den	86-**67**	W	33-19	74–.432	82–.317	24–.667	18–.611	53	42	Rogers 17, 2 with 12	Hardaway 10	Kidd 7
2/24	@Was	92-83	W	34-19	74–.459	84–.381	28–.679	19–.737	40	45	Gugliotta 20, Rogers 16	Gugliotta 8	Kidd 9
2/25	@NY	79-84	L	34-20	75–.413	79–.430	14–.929	18–.833	42	36	Gugliotta 16, Hardaway 14	Kidd 10	Kidd 13

Date	Opp	Score	W/L	Rec	Pho FG Att–Pct.	Opp FG Att–Pct.	Pho FT Att–Pct.	Opp FT Att–Pct.	Pho Reb	Opp Reb	Points	Rebounds	Assists
2/27	@Tor	102-103	L	34-21	73–.493	75–.400	31–.742	43–.884	31	42	Hardaway 28, Rogers 28	Gugliotta 7	Hardaway 5
2/29	@Cle	100-93	W	35-21	85–.424	79–.418	31–.742	26–.846	45	43	Hardaway 22, Kidd 21	Kidd 9	2 with 6
3/02	Ind	118-87	W	36-21	93–.505	79–.392	21–.857	18–.889	49	43	Robinson 22, Gugliotta 19	Kidd 9	Kidd 15
3/04	Dal	110-96	W	37-21	93–.462	85–.435	19–.789	22–.727	46	47	Rogers 29, Robinson 27	Gugliotta 14	Kidd 14
3/06	Mia	100-92	W	38-21	77–.532	71–.437	27–.630	28–.857	37	36	Hardaway 28, Gugliotta 15	Kidd 9	**Kidd 17**
3/07	@Hou	108-101	W	39-21	82–.476	86–.488	26–.923	**13**–.692	42	42	Hardaway 24, Gugliotta 23	Kidd 12	Hardaway 10
3/10	Uta	96-99	L	39-22	71–.479	72–.528	23–.957	24–.792	30	34	Hardaway 28, Longley 17	Longley 7	Kidd 12
3/11	@Dal	99-104	L	39-23	81–.444	79–.418	35–.657	43–.744	47	48	Robinson 29, Kidd 19	Rogers 11	Kidd 9
3/14	Min	107-100	W	40-23	75–.413	80–.513	**49**–.878	20–.750	43	37	Hardaway 26, Robinson 24	Marion 12	Kidd 12
3/17	@Van	101-86	W	41-23	96–.448	65–.431	12–.917	31–.774	44	38	Robinson 27, Rogers 26	Marion 11	Kidd 15
3/19	@GS	99-82	W	42-23	83–.446	88–.352	20–.700	30–.633	55	47	Robinson 25, Rogers 21	Marion 13	Kidd 14
3/20	Bos	110-106	W	43-23	82–.451	93–.387	36–.889	34–.882	42	54	Robinson 22, Marion 18	2 with 9	Kidd 11
3/22	Sac	114-93	W	44-23	85–.541	87–.391	22–.682	26–.769	52	36	Robinson 26, Rogers 18	Marion 9	Kidd 7
3/24	@LAL	101-109	L	44-24	85–.471	83–.482	18–.722	32–.750	48	38	Hardaway 25, Robinson 22	Marion 14	Hardaway 7
3/26	GS	90-82	W	45-24	73–.452	83–.386	32–.750	25–.640	45	41	Hardaway 33, Marion 15	Marion 14	Livingston 7
3/28	@Mia	78-81	L	45-25	78–.321	**60**–.467	31–.677	29–.690	38	46	Rogers 22, Robinson 20	Hardaway 9	Hardaway 5
3/30	@Atl	118-74	W	46-25	94–.521	79–.354	13–.923	19–.842	49	40	Rogers 21, Marion 16	Rogers 8	Hardaway 11
3/31	@Det	98-97	W	47-25	79–.468	84–.393	20–.750	27–.926	34	51	Robinson 20, Rogers 17	2 with 8	Hardaway 12
4/02	@Min	87-86	W	48-25	77–.455	85–.388	19–.789	17–.941	39	48	Rogers 23, Hardaway 22	Marion 9	Hardaway 9
4/04	LAL	83-84	L	48-26	84–.393	82–.402	19–.737	25–.680	45	48	Hardaway 23, Robinson 20	Hardaway 10	2 with 6
4/06	@Uta	85-105	L	48-27	71–.451	87–.460	26–.808	30–.667	35	50	Hardaway 13, Johnson 12	Hardaway 8	Johnson 5
4/09	@Sac	102-97	W	49-27	78–.500	98–.378	32–.594	23–.696	48	52	Hardaway 25, Robinson 20	Hardaway 12	Johnson 9
4/11	@LAC	95-88	W	50-27	74–.446	82–.415	32–.750	17–.824	47	40	Robinson 22, Day 18	Marion 12	Hardaway 8
4/12	Van	122-116[1]	W	51-27	93–.495	91–.407	26–.846	34–.882	44	41	Robinson 36, Livingston 23	Robinson 10	Livingston 7
4/14	LAC	112-88	W	52-27	85–.471	80–.338	30–.733	38–.737	53	40	Rogers 22, Marion 20	2 with 11	Hardaway 8
4/16	Uta	82-96	L	52-28	72–.444	76–.474	19–.579	29–.690	31	49	Hardaway 16, Marion 15	Miller 8	Livingston 7
4/18	Hou	98-107	L	52-29	87–.448	70–.486	19–.737	35–.771	41	42	Hardaway 20, Robinson 20	Hardaway 10	Hardaway 12
4/19	@GS	99-88	W	53-29	76–.513	84–.381	18–.778	33–.667	51	38	Robinson 23, Hardaway 17	2 with 8	2 with 5

Postseason

Date	Opp	Score	W/L	Rec	Pho FG Att–Pct.	Opp FG Att–Pct.	Pho FT Att–Pct.	Opp FT Att–Pct.	Pho Reb	Opp Reb	Points	Rebounds	Assists
4/22	@SA	72-70	W	1-0	82–.366	73–.370	10–.900	21–.571	47	50	Hardaway 17, Robinson 17	Marion 9	Johnson 6
4/25	@SA	70-85	L	1-1	86–.326	81–.358	19–.579	26–.923	46	49	Hardaway 19, Rogers 18	Blount 11	2 with 3
4/29	SA	101-94	W	2-1	87–.437	77–.390	24–.750	36–.806	50	43	Hardaway 17, 2 with 16	Marion 14	Hardaway 13
5/02	SA	89-78	W	3-1	80–.463	73–.370	19–.632	39–.615	49	43	Hardaway 23, Rogers 23	2 with 10	Kidd 10
5/07	@LAL	77-105	L	0-1	77–.364	92–.435	27–.667	26–.808	42	52	Hardaway 25, Robinson 13	2 with 7	Kidd 7
5/10	@LAL	96-97	L	0-2	85–.435	73–.534	22–.773	28–.571	43	37	Robinson 30, Hardaway 27	2 with 9	Hardaway 8
5/12	LAL	99-105	L	0-3	77–.455	70–.457	34–.735	51–.686	40	40	Hardaway 31, Robinson 23	Robinson 9	Kidd 12
5/14	LAL	117-98	W	1-3	86–.523	77–.442	27–.630	45–.622	44	40	Robinson 32, Kidd 22	Kidd 10	Kidd 16
5/16	@LAL	65-87	L	1-4	80–.288	80–.363	21–.714	37–.622	43	59	Day 10, Rogers 9	Rogers 8	Robinson 4

Portland Trail Blazers 1999-2000 Game Log (59-23)

Date	Opp	Score	W/L	Rec	Por FG Att–Pct.	Opp FG Att–Pct.	Por FT Att–Pct.	Opp FT Att–Pct.	Por Reb	Opp Reb	Points	Rebounds	Assists
11/02	@Van	106-86	W	1-0	82–.549	75–.400	18–.722	34–.706	39	41	Smith 22, Pippen 14	Wallace 7	2 with 8
11/03	LAC	121-98	W	2-0	74–.608	80–.450	33–.818	30–.833	41	29	Stdamre 23, 2 with 22	Sabonis 13	Stdamre 9
11/05	Den	95-83	W	3-0	78–.474	74–.432	28–.607	19–.737	43	37	Smith 22, Pippen 18	Schrempf 8	Stdamre 7
11/06	LAL	97-82	W	4-0	69–.551	78–.397	21–.952	34–**.500**	40	39	Pippen 19, 2 with 17	Pippen 8	2 with 5
11/09	@Uta	87-92	L	4-1	73–.411	67–.433	31–.742	38–.868	40	34	Smith 26, Stdamre 19	Sabonis 9	Pippen 5
11/12	@Den	93-78	W	5-1	89–.416	82–.366	13–.846	19–.684	46	48	Wallace 19, Schrempf 15	Wallace 11	Pippen 8
11/13	Atl	**131**-95	W	6-1	81–**.654**	90–.422	32–.656	22–.636	47	36	Stdamre 20, O'Neal 17	O'Neal 10	Stdamre 7
11/16	@Mia	101-96	W	7-1	72–.514	83–.446	29–.759	16–.750	42	36	Wallace 22, Pippen 20	Pippen 13	2 with 5
11/17	@Orl	81-79	W	8-1	83–.410	91–.341	19–.579	19–.789	43	45	Wallace 13, 3 with 11	Wallace 11	Stdamre 8
11/19	@Phi	97-91	W	9-1	71–.507	85–.412	35–.600	26–.692	42	45	Wallace 21, Smith 19	Sabonis 10	Pippen 9
11/20	@Cha	100-96[1]	W	10-1	90–.433	89–.382	22–.864	36–.694	41	52	Anthony 24, Wallace 17	Sabonis 8	Stdamre 8
11/23	@Cle	100-103	L	10-2	88–.398	76–.500	28–.893	27–.852	51	34	Schrempf 22, Smith 18	Pippen 11	Stdamre 10
11/24	@Min	88-81	W	11-2	76–.382	97–.340	28–.857	18–.722	54	52	Smith 18, Stdamre 18	2 with 10	Stdamre 9
11/26	Hou	91-88[1]	W	12-2	88–.398	83–.337	26–.654	32–.781	47	55	Pippen 19, 2 with 15	Wallace 10	Pippen 7
11/27	@LAC	88-71	W	13-2	87–.425	79–.329	9–.889	25–.520	47	45	Stdamre 24, Smith 13	Wallace 12	Pippen 10
11/29	Ind	91-93	L	13-3	83–.988	85–.376	24–.875	31–.742	40	45	Pippen 20, Wallace 20	Wallace 11	Stdamre 6
12/01	Cha	94-90	W	14-3	72–.514	84–.417	24–.583	24–.708	41	38	Schrempf 18, Sabonis 16	3 with 9	Anthony 7
12/03	@LAL	80-93	L	14-4	76–.342	86–.360	25–.840	41–.659	42	57	Stdamre 23, Smith 18	Pippen 10	Stdamre 6
12/05	@Pho	92-90	W	15-4	68–.485	82–.439	36–.722	13–.692	41	32	Wallace 21, Sabonis 18	Sabonis 10	Pippen 8
12/07	Mia	76-86	L	15-5	80–.388	69–.478	14–.714	21–.667	40	43	Anthony 19, Wallace 14	Wallace 8	Anthony 7
12/09	Min	90-86	W	16-5	66–.485	72–.458	32–.781	26–.692	37	**26**	Wallace 23, Smith 18	B Grant 10	Smith 6
12/11	@Sac	101-96	W	17-5	93–.419	91–.396	23–.739	25–.760	58	44	Pippen 24, Wallace 24	2 with 11	**Stdamre 11**
12/16	@Sea	107-81	W	18-5	85–.529	84–.393	15–.467	10–.600	45	42	Stdamre 20, Anthony 17	2 with 9	Schrempf 7
12/17	Pho	102-110	L	18-6	84–.488	90–.489	17–.647	19–.684	44	43	Stdamre 22, Pippen 19	Pippen 10	Pippen 6
12/20	@Den	88-97	L	18-7	85–.400	82–.488	17–.765	20–.750	47	37	Stdamre 19, Wallace 14	Wallace 10	Stdamre 5
12/21	@Hou	89-79	W	19-7	90–.444	71–.437	6–.833	17–.706	42	46	Smith 22, Sabonis 15	2 with 8	Pippen 8
12/23	GS	111-91	W	20-7	77–.481	89–.416	**40**–.775	16–.875	40	35	Wallace 20, Smith 19	Sabonis 7	2 with 7
12/28	Sea	94-89	W	21-7	78–.500	85–.400	21–.571	22–.545	49	44	Wallace 24, Pippen 19	2 with 8	2 with 6
12/30	Phi	108-90	W	22-7	75–.493	83–.434	31–.806	23–.652	46	35	Wallace 23, Smith 20	Wallace 11	Anthony 7
1/03	@Chi	88-**63**	W	23-7	72–.500	77–.338	19–.737	17–.529	39	43	Stdamre 16, Wells 15	Sabonis 8	2 with 6
1/04	@Tor	114-90	W	24-7	77–.545	85–.412	28–.786	24–.708	44	34	Stdamre 22, Smith 19	Sabonis 10	Schrempf 8
1/06	@Min	96-98	L	24-8	65–.538	74–.500	34–.676	29–.759	29	37	Wallace 24, Smith 20	B Grant 7	Pippen 7
1/08	Pho	96-91	W	25-8	71–.479	88–.409	37–.676	21–.571	47	36	Wells 23, B Grant 21	B Grant 11	Pippen 9
1/10	Dal	107-94	W	26-8	79–.532	77–.481	22–.727	22–.591	47	33	3 with 17	2 with 8	3 with 6
1/12	Cle	95-75	W	27-8	79–.532	73–.384	12–.750	24–.667	40	36	Wallace 25, Smith 18	2 with 9	Pippen 8
1/14	@Pho	105-83	W	28-8	74–.473	76–.421	36–.806	30–.600	36	37	Sabonis 23, Smith 22	Sabonis 10	2 with 7
1/15	@Dal	105-113	L	28-9	78–.436	90–.467	**40**–.775	22–.864	42	45	Pippen 22, Smith 19	Pippen 9	2 with 4
1/18	@Hou	89-90	L	28-10	86–.430	79–.456	16–.688	23–.565	46	40	Smith 21, Wallace 17	Pippen 9	Pippen 8
1/19	@SA	105-95	W	29-10	75–.560	67–.463	27–.667	38–.816	40	35	Wallace 22, Sabonis 17	2 with 7	2 with 7
1/22	@LAL	95-91	W	30-10	80–.425	82–.451	17–.706	20–.700	45	37	Smith 27, Stdamre 22	Wallace 12	Pippen 7
1/24	NJ	101-87	W	31-10	77–.519	77–.442	20–.800	16–.750	44	31	Sabonis 21, Wallace 17	Sabonis 13	Pippen 10
1/27	Uta	85-75	W	32-10	77–.468	79–**.316**	14–.643	28–.750	48	35	O'Neal 14, Stdamre 13	B Grant 12	Stdamre 7
1/29	SA	81-67	W	33-10	66–.455	75–.360	24–.750	22–.591	45	39	Smith 15, Pippen 14	Sabonis 8	2 with 4
2/01	Chi	92-81	W	34-10	78–.474	80–.388	20–.850	17–.765	51	34	B Grant 19, Wallace 14	Wallace 9	Pippen 7
2/03	@NY	88-98	L	34-11	83–.422	79–.418	13–.769	35–.686	46	38	Smith 18, Wells 18	2 with 9	Stdamre 5
2/04	@Atl	97-90	W	35-11	83–.446	91–.363	24–.708	27–.815	44	52	Smith 21, Sabonis 17	Sabonis 12	Stdamre 6
2/06	@Bos	100-94	W	36-11	75–.440	77–.455	39–.769	27–.741	42	37	Smith 23, Pippen 19	2 with 8	Stdamre 7
2/07	@Mil	115-111	W	37-11	75–.533	84–.560	34–.765	15–.800	34	34	Smith 24, Wallace 17	B Grant 7	2 with 6
2/09	LAC	107-100	W	38-11	68–.529	85–.494	36–.889	**8**–.875	39	29	Sabonis 23, Smith 19	Wallace 13	Pippen 9
2/15	@GS	92-83	W	39-11	**95**–.368	77–.403	23–.652	28–.571	58	54	Sabonis 21, Pippen 17	**Sabonis 16**	Stdamre 5
2/16	GS	99-95	W	40-11	71–.465	79–.456	29–.862	16–.938	39	38	Sabonis 20, Stdamre 19	Sabonis 11	3 with 4
2/18	Was	93-85	W	41-11	81–.370	74–.419	34–.824	31–.677	51	36	Sabonis 17, Stdamre 15	2 with 11	2 with 4
2/20	@Sac	108-103[1]	W	42-11	86–.453	98–.418	26–.846	24–.750	47	47	Wallace 24, Pippen 21	Sabonis 14	Pippen 6
2/21	Bos	105-92	W	43-11	73–.493	86–.372	**40**–.775	28–.857	39	44	Sabonis 19, Wallace 16	Sabonis 8	Pippen 8

Date	Opp	Score	W/L	Rec	Por FG Att–Pct.	Opp FG Att–Pct.	Por FT Att–Pct.	Opp FT Att–Pct.	Por Reb	Opp Reb	Game Leaders Points	Rebounds	Assists
2/24	Orl	111-92	W	44-11	79–.557	91–.440	19–.842	15–.667	40	39	Stdamre 30, Wells 15	Sabonis 8	3 with 5
2/27	Uta	101-92	W	45-11	68–.485	79–.443	33–.818	23–.652	41	29	Sabonis 17, Wallace 17	Wallace 9	Stdamre 9
2/29	LAL	87-90	L	45-12	89–.404	69–.449	14–.786	27–.815	44	43	Pippen 19, Sabonis 16	Sabonis 11	Pippen 4
3/03	Van	101-91	W	46-12	77–.506	71–.465	26–.769	27–.741	47	29	Smith 19, 2 with 16	Wallace 9	Pippen 7
3/06	Tor	90-109	L	46-13	77–.442	81–.469	24–.792	27–.741	45	40	Wallace 27, Sabonis 16	Sabonis 11	Anthony 4
3/08	@NJ	103-115	L	46-14	80–.463	82–.451	31–.742	41–.805	45	43	Wallace 19, Sabonis 16	O'Neal 9	2 with 5
3/09	@Ind	119-127[1]	L	46-15	85–.482	86–.477	40–.800	46–.783	41	48	Wells 29, Wallace 24	2 with 11	Stdamre 4
3/11	@Det	99-94	W	47-15	73–.479	71–.479	28–.786	26–.769	41	36	Wallace 24, Pippen 18	2 with 7	3 with 4
3/12	@Was	102-86	W	48-15	68–.515	89–.382	24–.917	21–.571	48	33	Stdamre 16, 2 with 15	Sabonis 13	Stdamre 6
3/14	Sac	96-91	W	49-15	87–.414	83–.410	25–.800	28–.714	59	37	Sabonis 20, Wallace 19	Sabonis 16	3 with 4
3/16	Min	92-96	L	49-16	74–.514	80–.500	19–.632	19–.737	41	29	Pippen 21, 2 with 19	2 with 9	2 with 4
3/18	@Sea	97-96	W	50-16	78–.487	81–.469	21–.905	23–.609	41	34	Wallace 24, Wells 23	Sabonis 11	2 with 6
3/22	Det	95-104	L	50-17	85–.447	75–.520	21–.714	28–.714	38	39	Smith 20, Wallace 20	Wallace 9	Stdamre 7
3/24	@GS	96-83	W	51-17	68–.500	74–.419	31–.645	24–.792	33	37	Stdamre 26, Smith 21	O'Neal 10	Stdamre 8
3/26	NY	89-93	L	51-18	76–.474	78–.487	17–.706	11–.909	37	35	3 with 20	Wallace 10	Stdamre 8
3/28	SA	85-89	L	51-19	82–.402	69–.478	18–.778	24–.917	32	43	Pippen 25, Wallace 17	2 with 6	2 with 5
3/30	Dal	96-85	W	52-19	72–.542	78–.423	19–.632	20–.800	36	33	Wallace 34, Smith 22	Wallace 9	Pippen 8
4/01	Mil	113-79	W	53-19	84–.512	76–.408	25–.720	25–.600	45	35	Stdamre 31, Wells 18	Schrempf 8	Stdamre 6
4/02	Sea	95-82	W	54-19	80–.413	80–.400	30–.800	26–.538	47	42	Smith 21, Pippen 18	Schrempf 8	Stdamre 6
4/05	Hou	105-118	L	54-20	87–.471	71–.620	18–.778	24–.875	35	34	Smith 24, Wallace 21	B Grant 12	Pippen 5
4/06	@Van	87-89	L	54-21	86–.395	66–.500	15–1.000	23–.696	38	39	Wallace 28, Smith 14	Pippen 9	Stdamre 6
4/08	Van	98-85	W	55-21	63–.556	70–.486	32–.781	23–.609	31	30	Smith 27, Wallace 21	Wallace 8	Pippen 6
4/10	@Uta	90-86	W	56-21	69–.449	60–.417	30–.800	41–.756	30	38	B Grant 16, Smith 16	2 with 7	2 with 4
4/11	@Dal	81-92	L	56-22	81–.346	76–.447	33–.576	18–.889	59	37	Wallace 13, Augmon 12	B Grant 12	6 with 2
4/13	@SA	93-77	W	57-22	69–.565	70–.429	15–.733	23–.696	34	36	Wallace 27, 2 with 13	Wallace 8	Pippen 7
4/16	Sac	102-95	W	58-22	88–.455	88–.420	21–.905	23–.696	50	42	Wallace 18, 2 with 15	Wallace 9	Pippen 9
4/18	@LAC	116-100	W	59-22	75–.640	91–.451	18–.833	18–.667	40	28	Smith 24, Pippen 18	2 with 8	3 with 5
4/19	Den	95-96	L	59-23	86–.419	81–.506	21–.905	16–.500	45	39	Wells 18, Smith 15	O'Neal 11	Anthony 5

Postseason

Date	Opp	Score	W/L	Rec	Por FG Att–Pct.	Opp FG Att–Pct.	Por FT Att–Pct.	Opp FT Att–Pct.	Por Reb	Opp Reb	Game Leaders Points	Rebounds	Assists
4/23	Min	91-88	W	1-0	75–.413	82–.476	23–.913	14–.643	37	34	Pippen 28, Stdamre 18	Pippen 9	Stdamre 4
4/26	Min	86-82	W	2-0	70–.443	71–.437	23–.783	22–.818	36	34	Pippen 21, Sabonis 19	2 with 7	Stdamre 6
4/30	@Min	87-94	L	2-1	76–.421	71–.535	18–.944	16–.750	28	33	Smith 22, Sabonis 17	B Grant 7	2 with 6
5/02	@Min	85-77	W	3-1	66–.470	82–.354	27–.741	18–.889	40	39	Sabonis 15, Wallace 15	Sabonis 11	Pippen 6
5/07	Uta	94-75	W	1-0	73–.384	76–.368	41–.829	23–.696	41	42	Pippen 20, Stdamre 14	Sabonis 14	Sabonis 4
5/09	Uta	103-85	W	2-0	64–.563	73–.452	35–.714	21–.762	35	33	Smith 19, Wells 17	2 with 8	3 with 4
5/11	@Uta	103-84	W	3-0	78–.513	70–.400	24–.792	31–.742	38	39	Sabonis 22, Smith 21	Sabonis 8	Pippen 7
5/14	@Uta	85-88	L	3-1	72–.375	68–.456	34–.706	34–.676	40	41	B Grant 20, Smith 19	B Grant 13	2 with 4
5/16	Uta	81-79	W	4-1	73–.425	75–.413	23–.652	23–.652	44	38	Pippen 23, Sabonis 16	2 with 9	Pippen 8
5/20	@LAL	94-109	L	0-1	78–.423	71–.535	24–.875	43–.558	39	36	Pippen 19, Wells 17	Pippen 11	Pippen 5
5/22	@LAL	106-77	W	1-1	74–.446	69–.391	45–.778	32–.531	49	34	Wallace 29, Smith 24	Wallace 12	Anthony 4
5/26	LAL	91-93	L	1-2	69–.507	71–.535	17–.824	22–.636	28	35	Stdamre 19, Wallace 19	Pippen 9	Pippen 6
5/28	LAL	91-103	L	1-3	77–.390	71–.465	34–.765	34–.912	37	42	Wallace 34, Smith 20	Wallace 13	Stdamre 5
5/30	@LAL	96-88	W	2-3	74–.432	79–.380	34–.765	30–.733	43	44	Pippen 22, Wallace 22	Wallace 10	Schrempf 6
6/02	LAL	103-93	W	3-3	74–.500	75–.453	34–.824	27–.481	43	34	Smith 26, Wells 20	Sabonis 11	Sabonis 6
6/04	@LAL	84-89	L	3-4	77–.416	63–.492	16–.750	37–.541	33	41	Wallace 30, Smith 18	Pippen 10	3 with 3

Sacramento Kings 1999-2000 Game Log (44-38)

Date	Opp	Score	W/L	Rec	Sac FG Att–Pct.	Opp FG Att–Pct.	Sac FT Att–Pct.	Opp FT Att–Pct.	Sac Reb	Opp Reb	Points	Rebounds	Assists
11/05	Min	100-95	W	1-0	95–.358	99–.394	27–.852	14–.786	55	54	Anderson 17, 2 with 15	Webber 15	Williams 6
11/06	@Min	101-114	L	1-1	84–.488	91–.516	24–.583	19–.842	37	50	Webber 22, Divac 19	Webber 10	Williams 8
11/12	Uta	105-92	W	2-1	88–.443	88–.386	29–.690	23–.826	48	51	Webber 20, Williams 18	Webber 9	Williams 4
11/14	Den	126-116	W	3-1	95–.547	90–.500	25–.680	17–.765	46	40	Webber 32, 2 with 16	2 with 12	Williams 6
11/16	Van	81-77	W	4-1	96–.323	83–.373	24–.667	25–.520	53	56	Webber 19, Divac 11	Corbin 10	2 with 4
11/18	@Hou	128-110	W	5-1	99–.455	97–.474	31–.774	19–.737	43	51	Williams 23, Stojakovic 20	Pollard 9	Williams 10
11/19	@Dal	103-94	W	6-1	91–.396	101–.396	32–.875	12–.917	58	58	Webber 24, 2 with 15	Pollard 12	Martin 5
11/21	Hou	110-105	W	7-1	99–.485	95–.453	9–.778	13–.923	50	47	Webber 28, Williams 25	Webber 11	Williams 12
11/23	NJ	105-92	W	8-1	85–.518	100–.390	18–.556	17–.647	57	46	Webber 26, Funderburke 18	Webber 22	Webber 10
11/26	GS	124-95	W	9-1	90–.533	97–.412	24–.792	14–.667	49	50	Webber 20, 2 with 14	Webber 9	Williams 12
11/29	@Mia	88-98	L	9-2	87–.379	80–.488	21–.714	20–.850	38	53	Webber 18, Williams 17	Webber 10	Williams 8
11/30	@Orl	111-102	W	10-2	91–.462	92–.457	20–.850	24–.667	44	49	Webber 22, Anderson 18	2 with 11	2 with 5
12/02	@Atl	100-110	L	10-3	101–.406	87–.517	13–.846	22–.727	53	51	Webber 26, Williams 18	Divac 11	Williams 12
12/04	@Was	114-104	W	11-3	94–.511	78–.449	22–.727	43–.744	37	50	Webber 25, Williamson 21	Webber 11	Webber 10
12/06	@NJ	95-109	L	11-4	82–.415	91–.473	27–.889	16–.875	41	47	Webber 25, Divac 21	Webber 14	Williams 7
12/08	LAL	103-91	W	12-4	82–.451	83–.422	35–.714	23–.783	45	37	Webber 20, 2 with 19	Webber 12	Williams 5
12/10	Mia	97-107	L	12-5	106–.358	76–.539	19–.684	29–.759	45	44	Webber 26, Anderson 16	Webber 10	Williams 12
12/11	Por	96-101	L	12-6	91–.396	93–.419	25–.760	23–.739	44	58	Webber 36, Williams 16	Webber 12	Williams 12
12/15	@Van	109-106	W	13-6	92–.413	86–.430	37–.811	35–.743	49	55	Webber 21, Stojakovic 17	Webber 13	Divac 6
12/16	@Den	106-116	L	13-7	89–.438	104–.452	30–.800	25–.800	40	58	Webber 26, Stojakovic 19	Divac 7	Williams 7
12/18	@Pho	103-119	L	13-8	87–.414	94–.447	35–.657	31–.806	52	58	Williams 22, Divac 21	Divac 11	Williams 8
12/20	@GS	99-111	L	13-9	101–.396	86–.523	24–.667	32–.625	57	47	Williamson 24, Stojakovic 19	Delk 11	Williams 11
12/21	Mil	108-95	W	14-9	85–.447	84–.452	34–.735	23–.565	52	37	Williams 28, Stojakovic 19	Divac 12	Williams 6
12/23	@LAC	91-97	L	14-10	86–.419	86–.430	33–.485	24–.750	47	49	Webber 33, Williamson 17	Williamson 11	Divac 8
12/26	Dal	118-111	W	15-10	84–.560	101–.455	26–.654	15–.867	40	41	Webber 31, Williams 23	Divac 13	Williams 8
12/28	Bos	114-101	W	16-10	75–.520	89–.449	32–.875	24–.667	44	39	Webber 23, Stojakovic 19	Webber 11	Williams 7
12/29	@Sea	113-104	W	17-10	75–.493	90–.422	35–.886	20–.950	39	43	Webber 31, Martin 21	Webber 10	Martin 7
1/04	@Cle	111-107	W	18-10	83–.434	83–.518	41–.707	24–.667	42	42	Webber 37, Williams 18	Webber 10	Williams 18
1/06	@Tor	89-101	L	18-11	89–.404	106–.425	16–.938	9–.667	49	52	Webber 27, Barry 14	Webber 19	Williams 4
1/07	@Bos	93-101	L	18-12	92–.424	86–.477	10–.900	19–.737	45	51	Anderson 24, Webber 21	Webber 11	Williams 7
1/09	Ind	116-113	W	19-12	81–.543	99–.414	29–.724	24–.833	41	44	Webber 31, Anderson 25	Williamson 9	Williams 15
1/11	Hou	110-93	W	20-12	88–.477	86–.407	22–.864	26–.731	41	53	Webber 26, Martin 17	Webber 12	Williams 5
1/13	SA	107-103	W	21-12	101–.386	79–.430	30–.733	41–.780	59	48	Webber 34, Williams 22	Webber 19	3 with 3
1/15	@GS	114-99	W	22-12	75–.493	98–.418	43–.837	15–.733	49	46	Webber 37, Williamson 23	Webber 16	Williams 10
1/16	Cle	113-102	W	23-12	86–.488	92–.424	29–.690	31–.774	39	56	Webber 25, Williams 20	Webber 11	Williams 12
1/18	LAC	104-98	W	24-12	95–.432	90–.422	20–.850	25–.720	48	54	Webber 30, Anderson 19	Divac 11	Williams 12
1/20	Orl	111-103	W	25-12	95–.453	88–.466	19–.737	26–.769	51	41	Divac 17, Stojakovic 17	Divac 12	Williams 8
1/22	Uta	101-104	L	25-13	88–.443	81–.519	19–.789	21–.714	36	44	Williams 22, Webber 21	Divac 10	Williams 6
1/25	@Cha	110-99	W	26-13	83–.530	86–.430	17–.765	25–.720	42	42	Webber 30, Anderson 29	Divac 12	Williams 9
1/26	@Mil	104-112	L	26-14	97–.392	90–.444	29–.586	36–.750	57	52	Anderson 24, Corbin 14	Divac 12	Williams 11
1/28	@Chi	102-90	W	27-14	86–.477	81–.432	19–.632	24–.667	41	45	Webber 24, 2 with 19	Webber 12	Williams 9
1/30	@NY	111-120	L	27-15	87–.494	82–.537	22–.818	24–1.000	40	39	Webber 26, Divac 17	2 with 6	Williams 12
1/31	@Min	90-105	L	27-16	95–.358	79–.582	20–.900	14–.786	36	47	Webber 14, 3 with 13	Webber 7	Williams 7
2/02	@Det	113-110	W	28-16	83–.518	90–.456	23–.826	26–.769	42	46	Webber 39, Williams 23	Webber 10	Williams 11
2/04	@Ind	94-104	L	28-17	87–.391	88–.432	24–.792	27–.889	43	55	Webber 26, Divac 17	Divac 14	Williams 8
2/06	@Phi	108-119	L	28-18	90–.422	99–.465	33–.667	33–.788	49	57	Webber 32, Stojakovic 20	Webber 15	2 with 7
2/08	Chi	119-80	W	29-18	94–.511	72–.431	11–1.000	19–.632	41	41	Webber 22, Anderson 19	2 with 10	Williams 8
2/10	Den	96-84	W	30-18	84–.393	85–.365	26–.846	24–.792	51	51	Webber 22, Anderson 20	Webber 14	Williams 8
2/15	Pho	108-117	L	30-19	87–.471	87–.517	20–.700	23–.957	33	46	Webber 27, 2 with 15	Webber 9	Williams 8
2/17	@Uta	108-119	L	30-20	77–.442	80–.525	43–.814	38–.737	37	43	Webber 22, Williamson 18	Pollard 9	Williams 9
2/18	Sea	118-85	W	31-20	99–.465	84–.357	15–1.000	21–.810	50	41	Stojakovic 21, Williamson 15	Pollard 14	Williams 7
2/20	Por	103-108[1]	L	31-21	98–.418	86–.453	24–.750	26–.846	47	47	Webber 33, Stojakovic 25	Webber 15	Webber 7
2/21	@Den	117-123[1]	L	31-22	100–.440	99–.475	28–.714	27–.630	55	51	Stojakovic 30, Webber 25	Webber 15	Williams 8
2/23	Atl	94-100	L	31-23	92–.413	104–.433	16–.938	10–.800	52	50	Webber 28, Divac 18	Webber 20	Williams 7

Date	Opp	Score	W/L	Rec	Sac FG Att–Pct.	Opp FG Att–Pct.	Sac FT Att–Pct.	Opp FT Att–Pct.	Sac Reb	Opp Reb	Points	Rebounds	Assists
2/26	@Van	90-102	L	31-24	94–.436	81–.481	7–.571	21–.810	41	49	Webber 36, Anderson 18	2 with 10	Divac 7
2/29	Van	112-87	W	32-24	89–.506	74–.486	18–.778	20–.550	41	41	Webber 23, 3 with 13	Pollard 10	Williams 8
3/02	@Hou	99-102	L	32-25	95–.411	83–.434	19–.789	26–.808	51	48	Webber 29, Barry 19	Webber 11	Barry 8
3/04	@SA	108-103[1]	W	33-25	95–.474	82–.476	15–.733	28–.714	40	49	Webber 31, Williams 15	Pollard 9	Webber 5
3/06	Dal	**130**-109	W	34-25	93–.538	88–.466	27–.593	23–.783	50	40	Webber 22, Divac 19	2 with 10	Webber 11
3/08	Cha	105-92	W	35-25	92–.511	78–.474	13–.692	21–.762	43	42	Divac 27, Webber 22	Divac 11	Williams 6
3/10	Tor	103-88	W	36-25	94–.415	82–.415	24–.917	29–.552	49	50	Webber 25, Williamson 24	Webber 12	Williamson 6
3/12	@LAL	106-109	L	36-26	85–.482	98–.469	19–.789	21–.667	33	59	Webber 24, Stojakovic 22	Divac 13	Williams 8
3/14	@Por	91-96	L	36-27	83–.410	87–.414	28–.714	25–.800	37	59	Stojakovic 22, Webber 21	Webber 11	2 with 5
3/15	LAC	98-78	W	37-27	84–.452	88–**.352**	23–.826	17–.765	47	52	Webber 25, Stojakovic 17	Divac 15	3 with 4
3/18	@LAC	104-83	W	38-27	84–.464	77–.442	27–.778	19–.632	34	48	Divac 20, Stojakovic 20	Webber 9	Webber 5
3/21	Was	98-86	W	39-27	79–.443	99–.384	32–.781	13–.615	54	42	Divac 24, Webber 22	Divac 12	2 with 3
3/22	@Pho	93-114	L	39-28	87–.391	85–.541	26–.769	22–.682	36	52	Webber 16, 2 with 14	Webber 6	Williams 7
3/24	Det	113-103	W	40-28	75–.480	91–.429	44–.705	27–.741	46	41	Webber 29, Anderson 28	Webber 14	Williams 10
3/26	LAL	89-90	L	40-29	87–.437	89–.382	13–.692	25–.720	44	53	Webber 28, Williams 21	Webber 15	Webber 8
3/28	NY	103-95	W	41-29	77–.506	86–.442	28–.750	14–1.000	38	40	Webber 21, Stojakovic 20	Webber 10	Webber 11
3/31	@Sea	108-123	L	41-30	86–.512	91–.538	18–.778	30–.733	37	47	Stojakovic 23, Webber 22	Webber 12	Williams 10
4/02	Phi	117-95	W	42-30	83–.566	82–.488	20–.650	21–.667	40	38	Webber 26, Williams 18	Divac 11	Divac 11
4/04	@Dal	102-105	L	42-31	97–.474	79–.544	12–.667	**8**–.750	47	32	Williamson 20, Divac 16	2 with 10	Williams 10
4/05	@SA	108-98	W	43-31	77–.506	80–.463	26–.923	22–.955	41	33	Williamson 28, Divac 20	Williamson 11	Williams 8
4/07	Min	92-95	L	43-32	90–.356	81–.457	32–.750	22–.818	50	45	Divac 20, Stojakovic 19	Divac 12	Divac 9
4/09	Pho	97-102	L	43-33	98–.378	78–.500	23–.696	32–.594	52	48	Williams 24, Webber 17	Webber 13	Webber 5
4/11	SA	92-98[1]	L	43-34	83–.446	93–.387	21–.571	34–.676	48	51	Divac 17, Williams 17	Webber 12	Williams 9
4/13	GS	**130**-107	W	44-34	80–**.575**	93–.419	**46**–.717	35–.800	43	45	Webber 22, Divac 15	Divac 11	3 with 5
4/14	@LAL	114-121	L	44-35	93–.452	89–.551	33–.758	27–.704	38	43	Webber 36, Anderson 22	Webber 10	Williams 9
4/16	@Por	95-102	L	44-36	88–.420	88–.455	23–.696	21–.905	42	50	Webber 21, Stojakovic 18	Divac 14	Webber 8
4/18	Sea	112-119[1]	L	44-37	99–.424	112–.446	18–.833	19–.632	52	54	Webber 23, Williams 23	Pollard 11	Webber 13
4/19	@Uta	86-95	L	44-38	79–.405	84–.429	22–.727	24–.833	38	50	Martin 16, Funderburke 14	2 with 10	Martin 4

Postseason

Date	Opp	Score	W/L	Rec	Sac FG Att–Pct.	Opp FG Att–Pct.	Sac FT Att–Pct.	Opp FT Att–Pct.	Sac Reb	Opp Reb	Points	Rebounds	Assists
4/23	@LAL	107-117	L	0-1	85–.435	99–.525	35–.743	14–.714	37	54	Webber 28, Williams 20	Funderburke 6	Divac 8
4/27	@LAL	89-113	L	0-2	80–.425	84–.488	20–.800	35–.714	40	48	Webber 22, Divac 14	Webber 12	Webber 6
4/30	LAL	99-91	W	1-2	81–.432	86–.407	34–.706	32–.500	46	48	Webber 29, Stojakovic 19	Webber 14	Webber 8
5/02	LAL	101-88	W	2-2	82–.439	87–.379	27–.741	29–.655	48	51	Webber 23, Barry 17	Webber 13	Webber 8
5/05	@LAL	86-113	L	2-3	77–.338	90–.522	34–.794	26–.654	35	54	Webber 20, Barry 9	Delk 6	2 with 4

361

San Antonio Spurs 1999-2000 Game Log (53-29)

Date	Opp	Score	W/L	Rec	SA FG Att–Pct.	Opp FG Att–Pct.	SA FT Att–Pct.	Opp FT Att–Pct.	SA Reb	Opp Reb	Points	Rebounds	Assists
11/02	Phi	89-76	W	1-0	72–.431	83–.361	29–.724	21–.714	50	35	Duncan 20, Porter 15	Duncan 16	Johnson 8
11/04	GS	104-81	W	2-0	81–.494	88–.341	31–.613	25–.720	45	51	Robinson 19, Walker 16	Duncan 14	Porter 6
11/05	@Hou	95-85	W	3-0	77–.455	83–.398	23–.826	23–.652	42	45	Porter 18, Elie 15	Robinson 11	Johnson 9
11/07	@Pho	74-77	L	3-1	84–.381	83–.398	16–.375	14–.571	52	47	Duncan 15, 2 with 12	Duncan 17	Johnson 6
11/09	@GS	118-89	W	4-1	88–.534	95–.347	26–.654	27–.815	52	48	Rose 21, Duncan 19	Duncan 11	2 with 5
11/10	@LAC	99-94	W	5-1	85–.424	71–.451	28–.786	33–.758	45	40	Duncan 22, Johnson 14	Duncan 17	Johnson 6
11/13	Cha	95-79	W	6-1	83–.470	87–.356	14–.857	20–.750	48	43	Duncan 22, Robinson 16	Duncan 12	Johnson 12
11/15	@Uta	85-91	L	6-2	70–.457	74–.459	27–.667	23–.696	31	46	Duncan 32, 2 with 12	Robinson 10	2 with 3
11/16	Ind	90-87[1]	W	7-2	83–.386	94–.394	30–.767	6–.833	48	51	Duncan 22, Robinson 22	Duncan 15	Porter 5
11/18	@Mil	88-99	L	7-3	69–.435	85–.447	36–.694	17–.824	44	40	Duncan 29, Robinson 21	Duncan 14	Johnson 6
11/20	Dal	106-90	W	8-3	102–.461	92–.402	5–.400	16–.813	58	48	Jackson 23, Brown 16	Duncan 17	Johnson 8
11/22	@Phi	94-91	W	9-3	84–.405	92–.370	29–.690	26–.731	53	49	Duncan 26, Robinson 19	Duncan 17	Johnson 8
11/24	@Bos	121-98	W	10-3	81–.580	89–.449	21–.905	19–.789	43	36	Duncan 31, Elie 25	Duncan 15	Johnson 9
11/26	Chi	101-78	W	11-3	74–.514	79–.354	27–.741	32–.656	44	43	Duncan 23, Rose 13	Duncan 10	Johnson 5
11/27	Den	106-87	W	12-3	81–.519	81–.444	21–.667	20–.500	53	32	Rose 21, Porter 19	Duncan 17	Johnson 8
11/30	Det	106-87	W	13-3	76–.592	80–.425	16–.750	22–.773	38	40	Duncan 28, Johnson 22	Duncan 10	Elie 7
12/02	@NJ	96-94	W	14-3	71–.493	89–.416	25–.880	20–.600	43	38	Robinson 27, Duncan 26	Robinson 13	Johnson 7
12/03	@Det	80-102	L	14-4	65–.369	82–.451	35–.829	33–.758	37	45	Robinson 15, Duncan 14	Duncan 12	Johnson 6
12/05	@Tor	92-98	L	14-5	86–.419	81–.457	21–.667	24–.875	40	45	Duncan 27, Johnson 20	Duncan 13	Elie 6
12/07	@Ind	77-83	L	14-6	81–.407	80–.363	15–.600	27–.704	47	49	Duncan 30, Johnson 15	Robinson 17	2 with 4
12/09	Van	99-91	W	15-6	65–.508	77–.468	37–.838	20–.850	39	25	Duncan 42, Robinson 19	Duncan 14	Johnson 6
12/11	Was	89-99	L	15-7	75–.413	82–.476	30–.767	22–.773	37	47	Duncan 23, Robinson 16	Duncan 13	Johnson 4
12/14	@Dal	111-93	W	16-7	89–.506	88–.409	22–.773	18–.833	51	38	Duncan 29, Johnson 16	Duncan 12	Jackson 7
12/15	Hou	83-77	W	17-7	74–.405	75–.400	28–.750	26–.538	39	44	Duncan 20, Robinson 14	Duncan 10	Porter 5
12/17	Bos	103-94	W	18-7	63–.460	82–.411	54–.778	22–.636	46	35	Duncan 30, Brown 13	Duncan 17	Johnson 6
12/18	@Den	84-86	L	18-8	74–.392	82–.415	29–.724	27–.630	37	53	Duncan 33, Porter 12	Robinson 12	Johnson 5
12/21	Pho	91-90[1]	W	19-8	87–.379	92–.370	32–.719	17–.765	55	52	Duncan 25, Robinson 21	Duncan 16	Johnson 7
12/23	Mil	91-94	L	19-9	80–.425	81–.420	29–.655	29–.793	44	43	Duncan 18, Johnson 16	Duncan 15	Johnson 10
12/25	@LAL	93-99	L	19-10	85–.376	83–.458	33–.758	32–.688	53	43	Duncan 28, Johnson 15	Robinson 19	Johnson 6
12/27	@GS	105-83	W	20-10	88–.523	85–.424	19–.474	15–.467	47	41	Robinson 28, Duncan 16	Robinson 14	Johnson 9
12/30	@Van	98-88	W	21-10	73–.452	79–.443	33–.879	16–.813	46	35	Duncan 32, Robinson 19	Duncan 15	Duncan 4
1/04	@Min	88-91	L	21-11	85–.400	84–.452	24–.750	18–.667	42	45	Duncan 27, Johnson 17	Duncan 19	2 with 5
1/05	Sea	96-99	L	21-12	79–.481	88–.477	16–.750	17–.412	44	41	Duncan 24, Robinson 20	Duncan 12	Johnson 9
1/07	@Pho	102-83	W	22-12	82–.488	89–.371	32–.781	15–.733	56	46	Robinson 24, Duncan 19	Duncan 15	2 with 5
1/08	Orl	127-92	W	23-12	84–.583	84–.452	31–.806	17–.824	48	30	Duncan 22, Rose 19	Robinson 13	Porter 6
1/10	Uta	93-86	W	24-12	68–.471	74–.419	26–.885	23–.783	35	39	Duncan 46, Porter 16	Duncan 14	Johnson 6
1/13	@Sac	103-107	L	24-13	79–.430	101–.386	41–.780	30–.733	48	59	Duncan 33, Robinson 17	Duncan 20	Johnson 6
1/14	@Sea	85-91	L	24-14	68–.485	80–.425	22–.773	26–.577	45	38	Duncan 32, Robinson 20	Duncan 16	Johnson 7
1/17	@LAC	99-93	W	25-14	76–.553	85–.447	26–.500	16–.688	44	39	Robinson 38, Duncan 23	Duncan 13	Johnson 9
1/19	Por	95-105	L	25-15	67–.463	75–.560	38–.816	27–.667	35	40	Robinson 29, Johnson 18	Robinson 12	Porter 7
1/22	NY	96-83	W	26-15	71–.479	88–.420	32–.750	8–.625	50	37	Duncan 33, Porter 18	Duncan 15	Johnson 6
1/25	LAC	105-82	W	27-15	81–.469	85–.412	37–.703	10–.800	54	36	Duncan 24, Robinson 22	2 with 13	2 with 5
1/27	Min	92-80	W	28-15	84–.429	84–.405	22–.773	12–.917	49	40	Duncan 20, Robinson 19	Duncan 14	Johnson 8
1/29	@Por	67-81	L	28-16	75–.360	66–.455	22–.591	24–.750	39	45	Johnson 15, 2 with 12	Robinson 10	Johnson 5
2/01	LAL	105-81	W	29-16	82–.524	78–.436	19–.737	20–.600	46	33	Duncan 29, Johnson 22	Duncan 18	Johnson 9
2/03	Tor	112-95	W	30-16	82–.488	92–.380	37–.811	24–.750	49	41	Duncan 32, Johnson 19	Duncan 17	2 with 7
2/06	@Uta	90-93	L	30-17	78–.423	69–.464	26–.808	33–.788	32	39	Duncan 32, Robinson 11	Duncan 10	Johnson 6
2/08	Sea	79-77	W	31-17	79–.405	80–.375	20–.600	15–.733	48	45	Duncan 22, Robinson 19	Robinson 11	Johnson 5
2/09	@Den	106-97	W	32-17	85–.435	85–.447	38–.789	21–.762	45	45	Robinson 30, Duncan 24	Duncan 13	Johnson 8
2/15	@Cle	81-92	L	32-18	75–.387	81–.420	23–.783	24–.833	35	43	Duncan 21, Robinson 20	Robinson 11	Johnson 10
2/18	Hou	116-92	W	33-18	86–.523	78–.423	24–.792	31–.742	40	42	Duncan 19, Porter 17	Duncan 8	Johnson 8
2/20	@Hou	113-111[1]	W	34-18	85–.518	89–.449	21–.810	28–.786	38	44	Duncan 25, Elie 19	Duncan 11	Johnson 13
2/21	Pho	89-98	L	34-19	78–.410	88–.409	29–.793	21–.810	44	44	Robinson 31, Rose 17	Robinson 18	Porter 7
2/24	@Cha	72-70	W	35-19	75–.387	78–.359	15–.800	13–.692	42	50	Robinson 16, Duncan 15	Duncan 12	Johnson 7

Date	Opp	Score	W/L	Rec	SA FG Att–Pct.	Opp FG Att–Pct.	SA FT Att–Pct.	Opp FT Att–Pct.	SA Reb	Opp Reb	Points	Rebounds	Assists
											Game Leaders		
2/25	@Chi	91-78	W	36-19	76–.461	76–.382	26–.654	27–.630	39	48	Robinson 23, Rose 17	Rose 11	Johnson 5
2/27	@Min	98-102	L	36-20	69–.493	81–.531	37–.730	16–.875	32	40	Robinson 29, Johnson 17	Robinson 9	Porter 7
2/29	Mia	93-**69**	W	37-20	71–.479	81–**.296**	31–.581	24–.833	41	44	Robinson 19, Porter 15	Walker 11	Johnson 5
3/02	Min	102-108	L	37-21	69–.507	83–.530	31–.806	19–.737	33	40	Robinson 24, 2 with 18	Walker 12	Porter 10
3/04	Sac	103-108[1]	L	37-22	82–.476	95–.474	28–.714	15–.733	49	40	Robinson 23, Duncan 22	Duncan 15	Johnson 8
3/06	NJ	106-104	W	38-22	85–.471	77–.494	27–.778	28–.857	52	31	Robinson 25, Duncan 17	2 with 13	Johnson 11
3/09	@Atl	105-79	W	39-22	84–.512	76–.434	19–.737	13–.846	41	35	Daniels 18, Johnson 18	Robinson 9	Daniels 6
3/10	@Was	106-99[1]	W	40-22	80–.525	88–.443	26–.769	23–.739	44	40	Duncan 23, Robinson 21	Robinson 11	2 with 5
3/12	@NY	80-93	L	40-23	83–.386	70–.486	18–.722	24–.833	37	46	Robinson 22, Duncan 15	Duncan 13	Johnson 4
3/14	Atl	94-79	W	41-23	79–.506	85–.424	13–.923	8–.750	39	42	Robinson 26, Johnson 22	Duncan 13	Johnson 10
3/16	Dal	88-110	L	41-24	68–.441	79–.519	34–.706	17–.941	41	34	Robinson 20, Rose 14	2 with 7	4 with 3
3/18	Den	102-82	W	42-24	79–.392	81–.370	40–.875	26–.769	53	39	Walker 18, 2 with 13	Robinson 12	Johnson 8
3/21	@Dal	96-97	L	42-25	64–.516	89–.449	34–.824	14–.929	41	31	Robinson 30, Duncan 26	Robinson 17	Duncan 5
3/22	LAC	103-78	W	43-25	84–.500	76–.395	25–.640	21–.714	48	41	Duncan 30, Walker 18	Walker 12	Daniels 6
3/25	Cle	96-76	W	44-25	77–.481	78–.410	22–.773	18–.611	51	31	Duncan 17, Jackson 16	Duncan 17	Duncan 11
3/27	@Sea	90-82	W	45-25	82–.463	89–.404	15–.733	10–.500	49	40	Duncan 30, Robinson 23	Duncan 18	2 with 5
3/28	@Por	89-85	W	46-25	69–.478	82–.402	24–.917	18–.778	43	32	Duncan 36, Robinson 15	Duncan 15	Duncan 6
3/30	GS	102-90	W	47-25	78–.474	85–.424	29–.793	19–.842	44	38	Robinson 27, Duncan 19	Duncan 17	Jackson 5
4/02	@Mia	84-88	L	47-26	65–.446	69–.449	31–.677	26–.731	32	40	Robinson 28, Duncan 19	Duncan 11	Johnson 6
4/04	@Orl	97-107	L	47-27	69–.536	81–.543	28–.643	17–.706	29	40	Robinson 30, Daniels 14	Duncan 9	2 with 6
4/05	Sac	98-108	L	47-28	80–.463	77–.506	22–**.955**	26–.923	33	41	Duncan 28, Robinson 23	Robinson 8	Porter 7
4/08	@LAL	98-80	W	48-28	75–.467	95–.316	32–.813	24–.708	50	50	Duncan 26, Robinson 15	Duncan 16	Porter 6
4/09	@Van	107-99	W	49-28	71–.577	81–.444	27–.778	19–1.000	37	34	Duncan 31, Porter 22	Duncan 11	Johnson 10
4/11	@Sac	98-92[1]	W	50-28	93–.387	83–.446	34–.676	21–.571	51	48	Robinson 26, Duncan 18	Robinson 14	Johnson 6
4/13	Por	77-93	L	50-29	70–.429	69–.565	23–.696	15–.733	36	34	Robinson 16, Walker 13	Walker 10	Johnson 4
4/15	Uta	106-83	W	51-29	74–.500	80–.400	38–.763	21–.857	41	38	Robinson 19, 2 with 15	Robinson 12	Johnson 8
4/17	Van	100-93	W	52-29	73–.479	70–.457	34–.706	32–.844	41	33	Robinson 27, Johnson 24	Robinson 10	Johnson 7
4/19	LAL	103-98[1]	W	53-29	88–.466	102–.402	24–.625	20–.600	51	58	Robinson 17, Rose 14	2 with 9	Daniels 10
							Postseason						
4/22	Pho	70-72	L	0-1	73–.370	82–.366	21–.571	10–.900	50	47	Elliott 15, Johnson 14	Walker 16	2 with 4
4/25	Pho	85-70	W	1-1	81–.358	86–.326	26–.923	19–.579	49	46	Robinson 25, Johnson 21	Robinson 15	Johnson 6
4/29	@Pho	94-101	L	1-2	77–.390	87–.437	36–.806	24–.750	43	50	Robinson 37, Elie 12	Robinson 13	Johnson 6
5/02	@Pho	78-89	L	1-3	73–.370	80–.463	39–.615	19–.632	43	49	Robinson 21, Elie 12	Robinson 16	Johnson 5

363

Seattle SuperSonics 1999-2000 Game Log (45-37)

Date	Opp	Score	W/L	Rec	Sea FG Att–Pct.	Opp FG Att–Pct.	Sea FT Att–Pct.	Opp FT Att–Pct.	Sea Reb	Opp Reb	Points	Rebounds	Assists
11/02	@LAC	104-92	W	1-0	93–.398	78–.449	32–.719	27–.593	53	45	Maxwell 29, Payton 22	Grant 13	Payton 13
11/04	Dal	106-96	W	2-0	100–.420	89–.472	20–.850	15–.667	**58**	41	Baker 22, Maxwell 22	Baker 13	Payton 13
11/06	Uta	99-94	W	3-0	79–.519	79–.468	20–.600	18–.944	36	38	Payton 22, Patterson 21	Grant 8	Barry 8
11/08	@Phi	98-117	L	3-1	83–.446	102–.480	31–.548	17–.765	40	56	Payton 28, Patterson 22	2 with 9	Grant 5
11/10	@Was	109-95	W	4-1	87–.517	90–.478	15–.667	12–.583	37	39	Maxwell 24, Payton 20	Grant 8	**Payton 17**
11/11	@Cle	109-103	W	5-1	94–.447	103–.408	27–.630	17–.706	53	54	Payton 27, Baker 24	Baker 13	Payton 9
11/13	@Det	99-107	L	5-2	89–.416	85–.459	29–.621	29–.828	44	48	Payton 30, Patterson 16	Baker 10	Payton 8
11/15	@NJ	100-92	W	6-2	72–.486	101–.356	**38**–.737	24–.792	49	47	Baker 21, Maxwell 21	2 with 11	Payton 9
11/17	GS	111-108	W	7-2	85–.529	88–.523	22–.773	19–.579	33	40	Baker 23, Payton 21	Patterson 9	Payton 11
11/18	@Van	110-108	W	8-2	85–.435	74–.541	35–.743	33–.697	36	55	Maxwell 27, Payton 24	2 with 9	Payton 10
11/20	Hou	110-107	W	9-2	87–.483	91–.451	31–.710	19–.632	41	52	Payton 26, Maxwell 24	2 with 9	Payton 10
11/21	@Pho	86-99	L	9-3	91–.385	88–.443	19–.526	24–.625	53	49	Maxwell 20, 2 with 13	Baker 14	Payton 9
11/26	LAC	98-93	W	10-3	79–.494	78–.449	25–.520	21–.810	40	35	Baker 24, Payton 20	Grant 8	Payton 11
11/28	Ind	102-91	W	11-3	87–.437	91–.352	25–.920	27–.815	48	49	Payton 31, Grant 23	Grant 11	Payton 8
11/30	LAL	77-101	L	11-4	79–.392	77–.519	24–.583	21–.762	42	44	Patterson 19, 2 with 12	Baker 10	Payton 5
12/02	@GS	117-108	W	12-4	85–.494	96–.417	34–.735	30–.667	52	47	Payton 27, Baker 25	Baker 13	Payton 8
12/04	@LAC	102-89	W	13-4	72–.514	87–.368	29–.793	29–.759	40	40	Payton 19, Baker 16	Lewis 8	Grant 6
12/05	Cha	81-103	L	13-5	87–.345	87–.483	22–.636	22–.773	42	54	Payton 17, 3 with 12	Patterson 8	Payton 8
12/08	Min	110-94	W	14-5	94–.436	81–.469	21–.810	21–.714	50	36	Payton 36, Baker 22	Baker 13	Payton 10
12/10	@Uta	83-101	L	14-6	76–.395	86–.453	26–.615	25–.800	34	49	Payton 22, Barry 10	Baker 10	Payton 10
12/11	Mia	92-88	W	15-6	81–.395	**68**–.441	27–.778	26–.846	29	47	Payton 26, Baker 25	Baker 9	Payton 6
12/14	Den	109-84	W	16-6	87–.506	84–.345	28–.536	30–.767	49	44	Payton 25, Patterson 16	Baker 9	Payton 7
12/16	Por	81-107	L	16-7	84–.393	85–.529	10–.600	15–.467	42	45	Payton 22, Barry 13	**Grant 19**	2 with 5
12/18	Van	112-89	W	17-7	77–.481	70–.443	35–.886	34–.647	45	**32**	Payton 26, Baker 15	Patterson 11	2 with 8
12/20	@Chi	93-84	W	18-7	74–.459	80–.425	24–.750	18–.667	43	42	Baker 25, Payton 22	Grant 10	Payton 13
12/21	@Ind	103-113	L	18-8	85–.459	87–.529	20–.850	**10**–.900	45	37	Payton 28, Baker 24	Barry 13	Payton 12
12/23	@Min	102-109	L	18-9	87–.437	96–.458	19–.684	25–.760	40	54	Payton 33, Maxwell 15	Grant 11	Payton 8
12/26	Phi	86-92	L	18-10	81–.333	81–.420	33–.727	33–.667	45	49	Payton 32, Barry 12	Grant 12	Payton 9
12/28	@Por	89-94	L	18-11	85–.400	78–.500	22–.545	21–.571	44	49	Payton 24, Baker 16	Lewis 8	Payton 13
12/29	Sac	104-113	L	18-12	90–.422	75–.493	20–.950	35–.886	43	39	Payton 25, Barry 24	Grant 10	Barry 5
1/04	@Hou	103-96	W	19-12	92–.467	82–.415	19–.684	25–.720	48	48	Payton 29, Baker 19	Baker 18	Payton 10
1/05	@SA	99-96	W	20-12	88–.477	79–.481	17–.412	16–.750	41	44	Payton 24, Grant 16	2 with 8	Payton 10
1/08	LAL	100-110	L	20-13	86–.419	76–.526	29–.724	28–.750	48	41	Baker 31, Payton 23	3 with 10	Payton 9
1/09	@GS	100-95[1]	W	21-13	82–.451	88–.398	30–.733	31–.581	54	48	Baker 30, Lewis 19	Baker 18	Payton 12
1/11	Pho	101-88	W	22-13	77–.481	87–.425	24–.792	12–.583	43	38	Payton 23, Barry 21	Grant 11	Payton 13
1/12	@Den	103-93	W	23-13	70–.500	84–.476	23–**.957**	13–.615	41	36	Payton 35, Barry 21	Payton 10	Barry 8
1/14	SA	91-85	W	24-13	80–.425	**68**–.485	26–.577	22–.773	38	45	Payton 25, Baker 23	2 with 9	Payton 8
1/17	@LAL	82-81	W	25-13	74–.405	83–.398	20–.700	20–.600	40	42	Payton 36, Barry 17	Baker 13	Payton 7
1/18	Cle	99-80	W	26-13	74–.514	83–.373	23–.783	19–.789	41	38	Baker 28, Payton 25	Baker 8	Payton 8
1/20	@Mil	104-96	W	27-13	81–.469	86–.465	27–.815	18–.722	41	44	Baker 31, Payton 22	Payton 10	Payton 7
1/21	@Bos	86-111	L	27-14	93–.376	91–.484	23–.696	22–.727	42	60	Baker 19, Lewis 14	Payton 9	Payton 5
1/23	@Tor	77-94	L	27-15	74–.405	83–.446	15–.867	22–.818	34	53	Payton 29, Baker 11	Payton 9	Payton 6
1/24	@NY	106-112	L	27-16	76–.526	88–.466	34–.559	29–.862	45	37	Williams 22, 2 with 21	Baker 12	Williams 5
1/26	NJ	95-92	W	28-16	86–.430	90–.400	24–.667	20–.700	55	41	Baker 23, Williams 18	Baker 13	Payton 9
1/29	Mil	99-101	L	28-17	75–.400	84–.452	37–.703	25–.840	40	50	Payton 29, Patterson 22	Patterson 9	Payton 12
2/01	@Uta	104-96	W	29-17	76–.487	81–.469	25–.800	14–.929	35	36	Payton 35, Baker 33	Barry 8	Payton 7
2/02	Chi	81-88	L	29-18	73–.466	77–.442	12–.583	24–.750	34	39	Baker 19, Barry 13	2 with 7	Payton 10
2/04	Pho	94-86	W	30-18	79–.468	80–.413	20–.650	18–.889	45	44	Payton 23, Baker 22	Payton 13	Payton 7
2/06	@Pho	93-105	L	30-19	85–.376	83–.494	25–.800	22–.773	41	46	Lewis 21, Barry 14	Lewis 8	Payton 7
2/08	@SA	77-**79**	L	30-20	80–.375	79–.405	15–.733	20–.600	45	48	Baker 18, Payton 17	Payton 16	2 with 5
2/09	@Dal	117-106	W	31-20	100–.510	90–.500	15–.533	11–.909	46	44	Lewis 30, Payton 25	Lewis 12	Payton 14
2/15	Was	114-85	W	32-20	81–.506	82–.366	34–.559	30–.733	41	50	Payton 41, Patterson 14	McCoy 9	Payton 5
2/18	@Sac	85-118	L	32-21	84–.357	99–.465	21–.810	15–1.000	41	50	Barry 21, Baker 19	Baker 8	Payton 12
2/19	Bos	94-91	W	33-21	82–.500	86–.384	16–.625	26–.808	44	42	Payton 27, Baker 17	2 with 8	Payton 9

Date	Opp	Score	W/L	Rec	Sea FG Att–Pct.	Opp FG Att–Pct.	Sea FT Att–Pct.	Opp FT Att–Pct.	Sea Reb	Opp Reb	Points	Rebounds	Assists
2/22	Orl	**127**-91	W	34-21	85–.529	93–.387	28–.786	25–.520	54	42	Lewis 21, 3 with 17	Patterson 9	Payton 7
2/25	Atl	87-95	L	34-22	85–.424	85–.447	16–.625	17–.706	51	45	3 with 21	Grant 10	Payton 16
2/28	@Cha	84-81	W	35-22	76–.421	87–.368	26–.462	15–.867	41	51	Payton 32, Barry 13	Grant 13	Payton 8
2/29	@Orl	94-103	L	35-23	93–.409	86–.512	19–.526	12–.833	46	44	Payton 29, Baker 19	Grant 10	Davis 6
3/02	@Mia	83-101	L	35-24	84–.369	70–.586	20–.800	17–.824	36	42	Patterson 24, Baker 23	2 with 9	Payton 7
3/04	@Atl	93-81	W	36-24	84–.464	82–.415	18–.611	19–.526	40	49	Payton 28, Baker 16	2 with 8	Payton 5
3/05	@Min	100-105[1]	L	36-25	86–.477	80–.538	19–.684	19–.842	33	40	Payton 34, Baker 20	Baker 9	Payton 12
3/07	Dal	101-86	W	37-25	82–.500	84–.393	20–.600	19–.789	52	40	Patterson 32, Payton 19	3 with 8	Payton 9
3/10	GS	99-85	W	38-25	86–.430	84–.417	26–.769	17–.588	44	44	Payton 27, 2 with 13	2 with 10	Payton 16
3/12	Tor	97-99	L	38-26	95–.421	82–.427	21–.667	29–.793	50	46	Lewis 28, Payton 22	Grant 12	Payton 10
3/13	@Van	113-103	W	39-26	86–.500	81–.519	32–.719	17–.882	38	40	Payton 40, Patterson 15	Grant 11	Payton 11
3/16	Van	117-103	W	40-26	86–**.547**	83–.542	18–.889	18–.667	32	35	Payton 30, 2 with 21	Baker 7	Payton 16
3/18	Por	96-97	L	40-27	81–.469	78–.487	23–.609	21–.905	34	41	Payton 24, Patterson 15	Patterson 11	Payton 11
3/21	Det	90-100	L	40-28	90–.389	82–.463	23–.696	25–.800	41	47	Payton 22, 2 with 18	Grant 10	Payton 12
3/24	Uta	95-98	L	40-29	66–.500	83–.446	28–.714	27–.778	36	42	Payton 28, Baker 25	Barry 10	Payton 9
3/27	SA	82-90	L	40-30	89–.404	82–.463	10–.500	15–.733	40	49	Baker 21, Payton 21	Baker 10	Payton 7
3/29	NY	95-110	L	40-31	81–.420	82–.524	32–.625	20–.850	30	57	Payton 21, Lewis 18	Lewis 5	Payton 10
3/31	Sac	123-108	W	41-31	91–.538	86–.512	30–.733	18–.778	47	37	Payton 35, Lewis 20	Baker 14	Payton 15
4/02	@Por	82-95	L	41-32	80–.400	80–.413	26–.538	30–.800	42	47	Payton 21, Lewis 18	2 with 8	Payton 11
4/04	Den	106-93	W	42-32	88–.466	87–.414	21–.857	19–.632	48	41	Grant 26, Payton 21	Grant 12	Payton 13
4/07	Hou	116-119	L	42-33	101–.465	82–.537	21–.762	24–.917	46	36	Payton 29, Lewis 22	2 with 10	Payton 9
4/08	@Den	97-105	L	42-34	86–.442	92–.413	21–.714	29–.655	39	55	Payton 30, Barry 20	Payton 10	Grant 8
4/10	@LAL	103-106[1]	L	42-35	96–.406	95–.400	28–.571	30–.867	49	56	Williams 28, Payton 22	Payton 12	Payton 8
4/12	Min	110-83	W	43-35	90–.433	84–**.345**	28–.786	33–.667	52	48	Payton 29, Maxwell 20	Grant 12	Payton 9
4/14	@Dal	103-117	L	43-36	92–.424	93–.527	30–.733	14–.857	41	57	Baker 25, Borrell 15	2 with 7	Williams 4
4/16	@Hou	121-112	W	44-36	105–.476	81–.506	21–.762	25–.800	45	43	**Payton 43**, Baker 16	2 with 11	2 with 7
4/18	@Sac	119-112[1]	W	45-36	**112**–.446	99–.424	19–.632	18–.833	54	52	Payton 33, Baker 23	Lewis 13	Payton 14
4/19	LAC	106-114	L	45-37	87–.506	94–.436	19–.526	24–.833	35	49	Williams 17, McCoy 15	McCoy 8	Williams 10

Postseason

Date	Opp	Score	W/L	Rec	Sea FG Att–Pct.	Opp FG Att–Pct.	Sea FT Att–Pct.	Opp FT Att–Pct.	Sea Reb	Opp Reb	Points	Rebounds	Assists
4/22	@Uta	93-104	L	0-1	89–.427	80–.463	16–.563	26–.885	45	50	Payton 24, Williams 23	Payton 11	Payton 6
4/24	@Uta	87-101	L	0-2	69–.464	72–.556	24–.708	20–.650	37	38	Payton 20, Lewis 19	Baker 7	Williams 10
4/29	Uta	89-78	W	1-2	70–.414	74–.405	36–.694	18–.778	46	38	Payton 23, Baker 15	Baker 11	Payton 10
5/03	Uta	104-93	W	2-2	88–.443	77–.416	23–.783	26–.885	42	43	Payton 35, Lewis 20	Payton 10	Payton 11
5/05	@Uta	93-96	L	2-3	82–.439	81–.506	17–.824	15–.600	35	41	Payton 27, Lewis 20	3 with 7	Payton 9

Toronto Raptors 1999-2000 Game Log (45-37)

Date	Opp	Score	W/L	Rec	Tor FG Att–Pct.	Opp FG Att–Pct.	Tor FT Att–Pct.	Opp FT Att–Pct.	Tor Reb	Opp Reb	Points	Rebounds	Assists
11/02	Bos	90-103	L	0-1	75–.440	73–.521	30–.700	22–.773	36	39	Christie 20, Williams 13	2 with 7	Bogues 5
11/04	Mia	97-86	W	1-1	86–.430	83–.434	18–.722	15–.667	40	46	Christie 28, Carter 24	Davis 13	Oakley 7
11/05	@NJ	112-92	W	2-1	87–.506	89–.382	29–.724	28–.786	52	38	Carter 26, Willis 20	3 with 9	McGrady 4
11/07	Cha	109-99	W	3-1	88–.545	68–.441	9–.778	40–.775	35	38	Carter 25, 2 with 14	Davis 12	Bogues 11
11/11	@Det	**123**-106	W	4-1	84–.536	90–.389	31–.871	40–.775	51	37	Christie 24, Carter 22	Willis 13	Bogues 7
11/14	Phi	90-93	L	4-2	78–.372	84–.440	33–.818	22–.636	43	42	Carter 27, Christie 19	Carter 11	Carter 5
11/16	Det	89-85	W	5-2	70–.443	92–.391	33–.727	**12**–.833	45	38	Davis 24, Carter 21	Davis 15	Bogues 6
11/18	@Was	81-92	L	5-3	85–.329	76–.395	30–.633	37–.811	46	56	Carter 23, Brown 11	Carter 11	Oakley 6
11/19	LAC	106-100	W	6-3	80–.475	83–.434	28–.821	30–.667	40	43	Davis 20, Carter 19	Oakley 8	2 with 5
11/21	@LAL	111-102	W	7-3	86–.442	91–.462	33–.758	27–.519	52	50	Carter 34, 2 with 15	Carter 13	2 with 4
11/23	@Pho	93-94	L	7-4	89–.427	76–.474	14–.786	24–.792	40	42	Carter 19, Willis 16	3 with 7	2 with 5
11/24	@Den	84-109	L	7-5	73–.425	105–.419	19–.895	17–.824	44	53	Carter 16, 2 with 13	2 with 8	Christie 5
11/26	@Uta	100-87	W	8-5	69–.478	88–.398	37–.838	22–.636	46	36	Carter 18, McGrady 17	2 with 9	Carter 4
11/27	@GS	106-88	W	9-5	87–.460	89–.404	22–.864	17–.706	43	54	Davis 28, Carter 22	McGrady 7	3 with 4
11/30	Atl	89-107	L	9-6	95–.379	79–.544	16–.688	26–.615	42	51	Davis 16, Carter 14	Davis 12	Brown 5
12/03	Was	95-93	W	10-6	82–.439	82–.451	24–.750	25–.720	40	48	Carter 23, McGrady 21	Oakley 9	Oakley 7
12/05	SA	98-92	W	11-6	81–.457	86–.419	24–.875	21–.667	45	40	Carter 39, McGrady 16	Oakley 11	Christie 9
12/07	Cle	101-98	W	12-6	89–.427	80–.438	20–.800	35–.714	47	41	Carter 32, Brown 17	Oakley 9	Bogues 8
12/10	Mil	91-107	L	12-7	87–.391	84–.524	19–.737	18–.778	42	37	Carter 25, Christie 14	Willis 10	Christie 6
12/12	Uta	88-103	L	12-8	77–.351	72–.486	44–.682	33–.909	46	39	Carter 16, Willis 16	2 with 10	3 with 3
12/14	Ind	105-97	W	13-8	94–.436	79–.468	22–.818	22–.909	50	35	Carter 24, McGrady 21	Davis 14	3 with 6
12/15	@Phi	91-93	L	13-9	84–.405	92–.391	27–.704	24–.667	**56**	48	Carter 19, McGrady 18	**Davis 18**	2 with 6
12/17	@Orl	98-112	L	13-10	91–.396	89–.427	30–.767	40–.750	45	52	Carter 23, McGrady 20	Davis 13	McGrady 6
12/19	LAL	88-94	L	13-11	89–.393	75–.427	23–.652	40–.700	50	44	Carter 29, Davis 19	Davis 16	Brown 5
12/21	NJ	116-87	W	14-11	90–.500	85–.400	27–.741	18–.778	51	35	Carter 24, Christie 20	Willis 10	Williams 12
12/22	@NY	90-91	L	14-12	86–.407	79–.456	30–.633	22–.591	50	42	Carter 36, Davis 12	Davis 17	2 with 4
12/26	@Cle	98-95	W	15-12	77–.455	88–**.364**	25–.960	31–.806	44	44	Carter 36, Christie 20	2 with 10	Carter 8
12/28	@Hou	100-99	W	16-12	91–.418	87–.425	27–.815	29–.759	46	49	Carter 35, Williams 17	Carter 12	2 with 5
12/30	@Dal	109-104	W	17-12	90–.478	89–.461	23–.870	17–.824	54	34	McGrady 24, Carter 22	Davis 15	Carter 8
1/04	Por	90-114	L	17-13	85–.412	77–.545	24–.708	28–.786	34	44	McGrady 18, 2 with 17	Willis 8	2 with 4
1/06	Sac	101-89	W	18-13	**106**–.425	89–.404	9–.667	16–.938	52	49	Oakley 20, Christie 16	Oakley 16	Williams 10
1/07	@Atl	97-105	L	18-14	79–.430	81–.506	31–.806	19–.895	36	42	Carter 34, Oakley 14	3 with 7	Christie 5
1/09	Van	97-107	L	18-15	83–.482	72–.458	22–.727	46–.870	39	45	Carter 20, Davis 20	Carter 10	2 with 6
1/11	@Was	89-117	L	18-16	83–.386	79–.532	32–.750	36–.889	36	40	Carter 19, McGrady 16	Davis 15	Bogues 6
1/12	Orl	108-102	W	19-16	86–.465	72–.486	32–.813	34–.912	37	38	Carter 30, Bogues 22	Davis 9	Carter 9
1/14	Mil	115-110	W	20-16	84–.464	83–.530	32–.906	21–.810	38	36	Carter 47, Christie 20	Oakley 12	Christie 8
1/15	@Mil	97-118	L	20-17	99–.333	**66**–.561	33–.727	44–.818	53	40	Christie 31, Carter 24	Willis 12	2 with 5
1/17	@Cha	94-115	L	20-18	90–.433	68–.515	24–.625	55–.745	42	42	Carter 24, Christie 14	Stewart 8	Carter 6
1/19	@Bos	90-94	L	20-19	81–.432	84–.393	19–.789	32–.625	42	54	Carter 20, 2 with 14	Oakley 10	2 with 5
1/23	Sea	94-77	W	21-19	83–.446	74–.405	22–.818	15–.867	53	34	Davis 17, McGrady 17	Willis 12	Christie 6
1/26	Was	120-105	W	22-19	83–.542	73–.548	34–.676	34–.706	37	36	Carter 26, Christie 21	Willis 9	Oakley 8
1/28	Mia	108-93	W	23-19	83–.482	85–.471	30–.767	16–.688	45	36	Carter 23, McGrady 20	Davis 12	Oakley 7
1/29	@Chi	106-89	W	24-19	70–**.586**	79–.456	25–.720	17–.765	32	38	Carter 22, Willis 21	3 with 6	Christie 9
2/03	@SA	95-112	L	24-20	92–.380	82–.488	24–.750	37–.811	41	49	McGrady 21, Carter 19	Davis 8	2 with 5
2/05	@Mil	98-95	W	25-20	88–.420	86–.407	26–.692	29–.828	47	54	Carter 30, Curry 16	Carter 11	Oakley 7
2/08	Atl	109-88	W/L	26-20	94–.479	75–.427	13–**1.000**	29–.793	40	43	Carter 36, Christie 16	2 with 9	Bogues 12
2/09	@Det	108-115[1]	L	26-21	92–.359	89–.483	**46**–.870	31–.710	49	52	Carter 34, McGrady 20	Carter 13	2 with 4
2/15	NY	91-**70**	W	27-21	82–.427	74–.392	18–.778	19–**.421**	45	42	Carter 29, McGrady 18	Davis 14	**Christie 13**
2/16	@Ind	101-109	L	27-22	88–.466	80–.538	21–.667	19–.789	39	39	Carter 21, McGrady 20	Davis 13	Christie 6
2/18	Den	91-95	L	27-23	91–.407	74–.432	22–.545	33–.848	41	49	Carter 31, Davis 14	2 with 8	Bogues 5
2/20	Dal	96-100	L	27-24	84–.488	80–.463	17–.706	26–.692	41	38	Carter 24, Davis 20	Davis 8	2 with 7
2/23	@NY	99-88	W	28-24	72–.486	70–.443	30–.833	26–.885	34	34	Carter 33, Christie 22	Carter 9	Carter 9
2/25	Min	85-107	L	28-25	68–.441	81–.531	27–.704	17–.882	33	40	Carter 23, McGrady 20	McGrady 9	2 with 4
2/27	Pho	103-102	W	29-25	75–.400	73–.493	43–.884	31–.742	42	**31**	**Carter 51**, McGrady 15	Davis 11	Christie 7

Date	Opp	Score	W/L	Rec	Tor FG Att–Pct.	Opp FG Att–Pct.	Tor FT Att–Pct.	Opp FT Att–Pct.	Tor Reb	Opp Reb	Game Leaders Points	Rebounds	Assists
2/29	Chi	87-80	W	30-25	85–.412	74–.459	17–.706	15–.533	48	38	Carter 26, Oakley 14	McGrady 15	Christie 7
3/01	@Bos	96-94	W	31-25	85–.400	86–.430	27–.815	31–.581	45	51	Carter 28, Christie 21	McGrady 11	McGrady 6
3/03	Bos	114-104	W	32-25	79–.494	85–.447	33–.848	28–.857	38	42	Carter 30, 2 with 24	Carter 7	Carter 7
3/05	@Van	94-92	W	33-25	84–.464	74–.419	19–.684	35–.714	43	43	Carter 28, Curry 16	McGrady 10	Bogues 7
3/06	@Por	109-90	W	34-25	81–.469	77–.442	27–.741	24–.792	40	45	Carter 35, Christie 26	Willis 8	2 with 5
3/08	@LAC	95-94	W	35-25	78–.462	74–.446	25–.640	25–.960	36	38	Carter 23, Christie 18	Davis 11	Carter 5
3/10	@Sac	88-103	L	35-26	82–.415	94–.415	29–.552	24–.917	50	49	Carter 25, Willis 13	Davis 15	Christie 4
3/12	@Sea	99-97	W	36-26	82–.427	95–.421	29–.793	21–.667	46	50	Carter 34, McGrady 19	Willis 13	McGrady 6
3/14	GS	85-78	W	37-26	72–.403	90–.378	28–.750	13–.462	44	47	Carter 23, McGrady 20	Willis 15	Bogues 7
3/17	Orl	95-91	W	38-26	83–.398	82–.488	32–.813	13–.538	41	46	Carter 30, Christie 22	McGrady 13	Christie 7
3/19	Hou	100-98	W	39-26	91–.440	74–.459	20–.850	30–.733	47	39	Carter 37, Willis 19	Willis 13	Christie 5
3/21	NJ	93-100	L	39-27	86–.372	83–.506	27–.852	18–.611	55	37	Carter 23, McGrady 22	2 with 12	Christie 7
3/22	@Phi	93-106	L	39-28	86–.442	74–.554	22–.682	22–.909	43	36	Carter 26, McGrady 20	Davis 9	Christie 8
3/24	Cha	84-102	L	39-29	84–.357	79–.494	17–.941	22–.864	36	48	Carter 18, McGrady 16	Christie 11	2 with 4
3/26	@Min	101-106[1]	L	39-30	89–.416	85–.471	30–.767	32–.781	37	52	Carter 38, McGrady 21	2 with 7	McGrady 8
3/28	@Cle	99-96	W	40-30	74–.459	80–.488	24–.833	21–.762	37	39	Carter 34, McGrady 18	3 with 8	Carter 6
3/30	@NJ	103-107	L	40-31	91–.418	78–.474	30–.767	32–.875	47	40	Carter 39, Davis 15	Davis 13	Carter 7
3/31	@Cha	101-110[1]	L	40-32	89–.438	79–.494	21–.762	30–.933	45	40	Carter 31, McGrady 16	McGrady 13	Bogues 7
4/02	Ind	83-104	L	40-33	81–.383	81–.481	20–.950	18–.889	43	43	McGrady 24, Carter 17	Davis 11	2 with 5
4/04	Det	88-104	L	40-34	89–.371	75–.493	17–.824	39–.692	50	39	McGrady 28, Carter 24	Davis 12	3 with 5
4/07	@Atl	104-84	W	41-34	77–.532	81–.407	18–.833	18–.722	39	42	Carter 23, McGrady 21	Davis 11	Carter 9
4/08	@Chi	98-79	W	42-34	75–.520	66–.394	16–.500	28–.786	38	38	Brown 19, McGrady 19	Oakley 7	Bogues 8
4/10	Cle	112-103	W	43-34	76–.526	84–.512	34–.765	20–.750	40	36	Carter 31, McGrady 27	Carter 11	Carter 10
4/12	@Ind	73-77	L	43-35	81–.333	76–.382	20–.650	18–.833	47	43	Carter 28, McGrady 19	McGrady 14	McGrady 8
4/14	NY	86-71	W	44-35	88–.398	74–.405	14–.786	19–.579	38	49	Carter 34, Davis 17	McGrady 9	2 with 6
4/16	Chi	85-84	W	45-35	78–.410	72–.444	18–.889	23–.783	36	41	Carter 25, Davis 17	Davis 9	McGrady 5
4/18	@Mia	73-97	L	45-36	76–.316	81–.494	34–.676	22–.682	38	52	Carter 17, McGrady 15	Oakley 9	Christie 4
4/19	@Orl	100-106	L	45-37	99–.414	83–.470	17–.647	31–.806	51	46	Davis 14, McGrady 14	Stewart 11	Christie 5

Postseason

Date	Opp	Score	W/L	Rec	Tor FG Att–Pct.	Opp FG Att–Pct.	Tor FT Att–Pct.	Opp FT Att–Pct.	Tor Reb	Opp Reb	Points	Rebounds	Assists
4/23	@NY	88-92	L	0-1	81–.370	72–.486	28–.714	21–.810	47	34	McGrady 25, Carter 16	Willis 11	2 with 6
4/26	@NY	83-84	L	0-2	58–.414	67–.403	41–.805	38–.737	35	37	Carter 27, Willis 16	Willis 10	Carter 5
4/30	NY	80-87	L	0-3	83–.349	62–.468	24–.792	28–.714	46	40	Davis 18, Carter 15	Oakley 14	Carter 8

Utah Jazz 1999-2000 Game Log (55-27)

Date	Opp	Score	W/L	Rec	Uta FG Att–Pct.	Opp FG Att–Pct.	Uta FT Att–Pct.	Opp FT Att–Pct.	Uta Reb	Opp Reb	Points	Rebounds	Assists
11/02	LAL	84-91	L	0-1	67–.433	76–.434	28–.821	26–.654	38	45	Hornacek 23, Stockton 15	Ostertag 7	Stockton 8
11/04	Hou	98-82	W	1-1	77–.532	68–.441	19–.737	18–.833	37	28	Malone 21, Stockton 18	Ostertag 10	Stockton 7
11/06	@Sea	94-99	L	1-2	79–.468	79–.519	18–.944	20–.600	38	36	Malone 31, Russell 20	Malone 13	Malone 7
11/08	@LAC	94-79	W	2-2	76–.487	73–.342	23–.783	35–.771	44	36	Malone 24, Hornacek 16	2 with 9	Stockton 10
11/09	Por	92-87	W	3-2	67–.433	73–.411	38–.868	31–.742	34	40	Malone 24, Russell 19	Russell 9	Stockton 9
11/12	@Sac	92-105	L	3-3	88–.386	88–.443	23–.826	29–.690	51	48	Malone 20, Hornacek 14	Ostertag 13	Stockton 9
11/15	SA	91-85	W	4-3	74–.459	70–.457	23–.696	27–.667	46	31	Malone 20, Stockton 20	2 with 11	Eisley 6
11/17	NY	98-90	W	5-3	74–.473	82–.463	33–.788	19–.632	46	33	Malone 33, Stockton 17	Malone 11	Stockton 11
11/19	@Min	84-89	L	5-4	75–.373	78–.436	31–.871	28–.714	38	40	Malone 19, Stockton 18	Ostertag 10	Stockton 8
11/20	@Mil	111-100	W	6-4	80–.550	78–.487	23–.783	28–.750	39	34	**Malone 40**, Russell 19	Malone 8	Stockton 12
11/22	Min	108-93	W	7-4	78–.577	73–.479	19–.684	27–.815	30	32	Malone 34, Russell 14	Malone 11	Stockton 15
11/24	@LAL	82-90	L	7-5	80–.375	64–.484	23–.783	41–.634	40	44	Malone 22, Hornacek 14	Malone 12	Stockton 9
11/26	Tor	87-100	L	7-6	88–.398	69–.478	22–.636	37–.838	36	46	Malone 24, Stockton 16	Malone 13	Stockton 8
11/29	GS	115-99	W	8-6	73–.575	71–.521	27–.889	23–.565	41	**25**	Malone 27, 2 with 16	Malone 8	Malone 10
12/03	Ind	75-100	L	8-7	79–.380	80–.513	21–.667	14–.714	42	43	Malone 16, Hornacek 10	Malone 10	Stockton 6
12/04	@GS	94-82	W	9-7	70–.457	80–.400	32–.844	29–.552	35	48	Malone 29, Russell 17	Malone 14	Stockton 7
12/06	Was	102-96	W	10-7	73–.507	69–.493	34–.706	32–.781	34	34	Malone 32, Eisley 18	Malone 11	Stockton 10
12/08	Dal	85-79	W	11-7	80–.450	87–.356	15–.733	15–.800	49	36	Malone 29, Russell 13	Malone 11	2 with 7
12/10	Sea	101-83	W	12-7	86–.453	76–.395	25–.800	26–.615	49	34	Malone 21, Hornacek 19	Malone 11	Stockton 10
12/12	@Tor	103-88	W	13-7	72–.486	77–.351	33–.909	44–.682	39	46	Malone 28, Russell 17	Malone 14	Eisley 6
12/14	@Was	101-80	W	14-7	79–.532	67–.448	19–.684	29–.690	34	39	Malone 34, Hornacek 21	Malone 12	Stockton 7
12/15	@Bos	96-86	W	15-7	68–.500	77–.403	38–.684	29–.724	42	41	Malone 27, 2 with 15	Ostertag 11	Stockton 7
12/17	@Ind	74-89	L	15-8	80–.363	78–.385	23–.609	26–.808	49	44	Malone 16, Hornacek 15	Malone 13	Malone 5
12/18	@Atl	106-96	W	16-8	87–.494	75–.427	17–.941	40–.775	36	41	Malone 33, Russell 19	Polynice 11	Stockton 11
12/20	@Orl	102-104	L	16-9	74–.500	85–.471	32–.750	35–.657	39	39	Malone 29, Stockton 15	Malone 13	Malone 8
12/22	@Mia	72-**74**	L	16-10	68–.456	76–.434	15–.467	**6**–.833	37	38	Malone 21, 2 with 12	Polynice 11	Stockton 8
12/27	Pho	92-91	W	17-10	77–.429	65–.538	32–.719	15–.867	35	36	Malone 26, Russell 14	Polynice 9	Eisley 6
12/29	Van	101-90	W	18-10	70–.529	75–.427	25–.960	25–.880	33	30	Malone 29, Hornacek 22	Malone 11	Stockton 13
1/03	Den	109-89	W	19-10	87–.506	72–.458	20–.800	38–.553	39	38	Malone 33, Russell 17	2 with 8	**Stockton 18**
1/05	Cha	118-96	W	20-10	81–**.617**	78–.410	16–.813	37–.730	42	32	Malone 30, 2 with 16	Polynice 10	2 with 7
1/06	@Dal	105-92	W	21-10	83–.446	85–.435	39–.795	20–.700	49	43	Malone 24, Russell 20	Polynice 12	Stockton 10
1/08	@Hou	103-87	W	22-10	85–.435	68–.397	26–.846	42–.738	45	42	Malone 32, Russell 25	Russell 10	2 with 6
1/10	@SA	86-93	L	22-11	74–.419	68–.471	23–.783	26–.885	39	35	Malone 23, Eisley 16	Malone 8	Stockton 11
1/13	Mia	93-83	W	23-11	74–.432	70–.400	38–.711	28–.750	42	40	Russell 19, Malone 18	Malone 9	Stockton 13
1/15	LAC	112-75	W	24-11	**91**–.505	81–.383	19–.789	13–.769	**56**	36	Malone 24, 2 with 17	Gilliam 12	2 with 6
1/19	Min	88-91	L	24-12	74–.486	81–.457	21–.619	22–.727	44	37	Stockton 23, Malone 21	Ostertag 12	Stockton 12
1/20	@Van	94-89	W	25-12	65–.538	89–.449	31–.710	8–.875	38	41	Malone 32, Russell 25	Malone 12	Stockton 12
1/22	@Sac	104-101	W	26-12	81–.519	88–.443	21–.714	19–.789	44	36	Malone 24, Russell 24	Malone 9	Stockton 13
1/24	LAL	105-101[2]	W	27-12	83–.446	98–.408	32–.875	23–.783	51	44	Malone 31, Stockton 18	Ostertag 14	Stockton 15
1/26	Van	99-116	L	27-13	77–.494	79–.570	26–.615	26–.769	31	39	Russell 16, Malone 13	Polynice 6	Stockton 11
1/27	@Por	75-85	L	27-14	79–.316	77–.468	28–.750	14–.643	35	48	Gilliam 15, 2 with 12	2 with 7	Eisley 5
1/29	@Min	94-96	L	27-15	83–.434	85–.447	25–.800	22–.727	38	43	Malone 35, Hornacek 13	Malone 13	Stockton 7
2/01	Sea	96-104	L	27-16	81–.469	76–.487	14–.929	25–.800	36	35	Malone 26, Russell 19	Malone 11	2 with 8
2/03	Mil	99-102	L	27-17	84–.452	79–.468	21–.810	22–.864	46	36	Malone 28, Stockton 18	Malone 10	Stockton 7
2/04	@LAL	67-113	L	27-18	81–.296	69–.493	26–.731	55–.727	39	53	Malone 14, Ostertag 10	2 with 6	Stockton 4
2/06	SA	93-90	W/L	28-18	69–.464	78–.423	33–.788	26–.808	39	32	Malone 25, Hornacek 17	2 with 7	Stockton 9
2/09	Chi	113-86	W	29-18	77–.584	**63**–.476	26–.731	29–.690	37	**25**	Malone 30, Hornacek 15	Malone 10	Stockton 8
2/15	Bos	99-101	L	29-19	80–.400	77–.468	33–.879	34–.765	44	39	Malone 32, Eisley 19	Malone 9	Stockton 9
2/17	Sac	**119**-108	W	30-19	80–.525	77–.442	38–.737	43–.814	43	37	Malone 30, 2 with 22	Malone 13	Stockton 10
2/19	Det	91-87	W	31-19	77–.364	75–.413	33–.879	21–.905	48	37	Malone 33, Russell 14	Malone 13	Hornacek 4
2/21	Atl	96-94	W	32-19	83–.470	79–.519	16–.688	13–.692	37	40	Malone 25, Hornacek 21	Polynice 11	Stockton 10
2/24	@Dal	92-85	W	33-19	86–.419	87–.402	18–.833	13–.769	47	44	Russell 25, Malone 18	2 with 10	Stockton 10
2/25	Orl	96-88	W	34-19	82–.415	67–.463	33–.788	36–.667	45	38	Malone 19, Russell 15	Malone 10	Stockton 8
2/27	@Por	92-101	L	34-20	79–.443	68–.485	23–.652	33–.818	29	41	Malone 23, Russell 23	2 with 6	Eisley 7

Date	Opp	Score	W/L	Rec	Uta FG Att–Pct.	Opp FG Att–Pct.	Uta FT Att–Pct.	Opp FT Att–Pct.	Uta Reb	Opp Reb	Points	Rebounds	Assists
2/28	NJ	106-101	W	35-20	82–.488	87–.425	22–.818	25–.760	40	40	Malone 35, Hornacek 27	Malone 12	Malone 9
3/01	@Det	107-94	W	36-20	82–.537	70–.457	24–.667	40–.675	42	37	Malone 31, Gilliam 19	Malone 13	Eisley 9
3/03	@Cha	89-87	W	37-20	82–.451	77–.455	16–.750	14–.714	43	39	Stockton 22, Malone 19	Malone 13	Stockton 7
3/05	@NY	88-79	W	38-20	69–.449	71–.394	31–.710	30–.733	46	31	Malone 30, Russell 19	2 with 8	Stockton 12
3/07	Cle	113-95	W	39-20	80–.600	74–.500	20–.750	21–.714	36	34	Malone 30, Hornacek 18	Russell 10	**Stockton 18**
3/09	Hou	101-82	W	40-20	72–.569	65–.477	15–.733	22–.682	36	30	Eisley 17, Stockton 17	Polynice 10	Eisley 7
3/10	@Pho	99-96	W	41-20	72–.528	71–.479	24–.792	23–.957	34	30	Malone 29, Russell 22	Ostertag 9	Stockton 12
3/13	@Chi	87-79	W	42-20	80–.350	64–.391	35–.743	33–.818	43	45	Malone 31, Stockton 19	Malone 13	Stockton 9
3/16	@Cle	107-86	W	43-20	78–.474	79–.418	35–.829	23–.739	43	39	Eisley 23, Malone 21	**Russell 15**	Stockton 8
3/17	@Phi	97-99	L	43-21	75–.453	82–.500	28–.750	12–.917	43	36	Malone 31, Hornacek 16	Malone 13	2 with 7
3/19	@NJ	92-88	W	44-21	72–.458	73–.466	26–.885	16–.875	39	35	Malone 32, 2 with 15	Malone 10	Stockton 10
3/21	Den	96-83	W	45-21	75–.493	82–.390	22–.682	24–.667	37	43	Malone 28, Russell 16	Malone 10	Stockton 11
3/24	@Sea	98-95	W	46-21	83–.446	66–.500	27–.778	28–.714	42	36	Malone 21, Russell 18	2 with 12	Stockton 10
3/25	@Van	84-75	W	47-21	74–.419	79–.354	33–.606	15–.933	48	47	Malone 25, Russell 14	Malone 14	2 with 5
3/27	Dal	105-113	L	47-22	79–.481	69–.580	31–.710	29–.897	34	38	Malone 26, Russell 20	Malone 10	Stockton 14
3/29	Phi	98-84	W	48-22	78–.500	77–.416	17–**1.000**	25–.680	44	34	Malone 30, Stockton 20	Ostertag 13	Stockton 8
3/31	GS	114-97	W	49-22	72–.528	91–.363	36–.861	35–.771	47	44	Malone 22, Hornacek 16	Gilliam 9	Stockton 9
4/01	@Den	92-112	L	49-23	76–.434	79–.506	26–.808	26–.808	34	41	Malone 27, Russell 17	Malone 13	Stockton 7
4/04	@LAC	103-93	W	50-23	76–.513	82–.476	33–.667	13–.923	41	36	Malone 34, Russell 18	Ostertag 11	2 with 8
4/06	Pho	105-85	W	51-23	87–.460	71–.451	30–.667	26–.808	50	35	Malone 19, Gilliam 14	Polynice 14	Eisley 13
4/07	@GS	105-84	W	52-23	73–.521	80–.400	28–.821	22–.818	39	40	Malone 19, Russell 17	Ostertag 9	Stockton 10
4/09	@Hou	90-99	L	52-24	87–.379	69–.435	27–.852	32–.813	42	40	Stockton 23, Malone 20	Russell 10	Stockton 7
4/10	Por	86-90	L	52-25	60–.417	69–.449	41–.756	30–.800	38	30	Malone 29, 2 with 18	Malone 14	Stockton 9
4/12	LAC	102-93	W	53-25	73–.479	76–.434	39–.769	23–.739	40	35	Malone 27, Russell 16	2 with 7	Stockton 7
4/15	@SA	83-106	L	53-26	80–.400	74–.500	21–.857	38–.763	38	41	Malone 23, Hornacek 13	Malone 11	Stockton 5
4/16	@Pho	96-82	W	54-26	76–.474	72–.444	29–.690	19–.579	49	31	Malone 32, Russell 16	**Malone 15**	Stockton 9
4/18	@Den	104-105[1]	L	54-27	88–.455	89–.416	20–.900	33–.727	50	40	Padgett 13, 2 with 12	Ostertag 13	Vaughn 9
4/19	Sac	95-86	W	55-27	84–.429	79–.405	24–.833	22–.727	50	38	Hornacek 18, Malone 18	3 with 8	Stockton 9

Postseason

Date	Opp	Score	W/L	Rec	Uta FG Att–Pct.	Opp FG Att–Pct.	Uta FT Att–Pct.	Opp FT Att–Pct.	Uta Reb	Opp Reb	Points	Rebounds	Assists
4/22	Sea	104-93	W	1-0	80–.463	89–.427	26–.885	16–.563	50	45	Malone 50, Hornacek 13	Malone 12	Hornacek 11
4/24	Sea	101-87	W	2-0	72–.556	69–.464	20–.650	24–.708	38	37	Malone 23, Stockton 21	Ostertag 12	Stockton 11
4/29	@Sea	78-89	L	2-1	74–.405	70–.414	18–.778	36–.694	38	46	Malone 30, Hornacek 15	3 with 6	Stockton 13
5/03	@Sea	93-104	L	2-2	77–.416	88–.443	26–.885	23–.783	43	42	Russell 26, Malone 23	Malone 14	Stockton 14
5/05	Sea	96-93	W	3-2	81–.506	82–.439	15–.600	17–.824	41	35	Malone 27, Stockton 17	Malone 8	Stockton 15
5/07	@Por	75-94	L	0-1	76–.368	73–.384	23–.696	41–.829	42	41	Malone 22, Vaughn 11	2 with 8	Stockton 6
5/09	@Por	85-103	L	0-2	73–.452	64–.563	21–.762	35–.714	33	35	Malone 15, Russell 12	Polynice 6	Stockton 6
5/11	Por	84-103	L	0-3	70–.400	78–.513	31–.742	24–.792	39	38	Malone 28, Hornacek 24	Malone 11	Stockton 12
5/14	Por	88-85	W	1-3	68–.456	72–.375	34–.676	34–.706	41	40	Malone 27, Stockton 18	Polynice 11	Stockton 9
5/16	@Por	79-81	L	1-4	75–.413	73–.425	23–.652	23–.652	38	44	Malone 27, Russell 18	Malone 11	Stockton 9

Vancouver Grizzlies 1999-2000 Game Log (22-60)

Date	Opp	Score	W/L	Rec	Van FG Att–Pct.	Opp FG Att–Pct.	Van FT Att–Pct.	Opp FT Att–Pct.	Van Reb	Opp Reb	Points	Rebounds	Assists
11/02	Por	86-106	L	0-1	75–.400	82–.549	34–.706	18–.722	41	39	Abdr-Rhm 19, Reeves 15	Parks 11	Bibby 8
11/03	@LAL	88-103	L	0-2	73–.411	91–.505	40–.700	17–.588	40	47	Abdr-Rhm 19, Dickerson 19	Abdr-Rhm 11	2 with 4
11/06	Den	109-94	W	1-2	81–.556	70–.457	20–.850	28–.857	41	31	Abdr-Rhm 27, Reeves 22	Abdr-Rhm 10	**Bibby 16**
11/10	Atl	102-97[1]	W	2-2	92–.478	92–.424	16–.813	24–.750	49	41	Abdr-Rhm 22, Harrington 21	2 with 12	Abdr-Rhm 9
11/12	GS	93-103	L	2-3	85–.447	86–.465	21–.714	21–.810	47	39	Abdr-Rhm 21, 2 with 20	Abdr-Rhm 15	2 with 7
11/14	LAC	109-89	W	3-3	79–**.570**	81–.407	15–.800	29–.690	37	41	Dickerson 23, Harrington 20	Harrington 9	Abdr-Rhm 10
11/16	@Sac	77-81	L	3-4	83–.373	96–**.323**	25–.520	24–.667	**56**	53	Abdr-Rhm 24, Harrington 22	Abdr-Rhm 18	Bibby 5
11/18	Sea	108-110	L	3-5	74–.541	85–.435	33–.697	35–.743	55	36	Abdr-Rhm 31, Harrington 25	Abdr-Rhm 14	2 with 5
11/21	Min	81-105	L	3-6	73–.384	80–.550	29–.759	23–.652	37	47	Harrington 18, Abdr-Rhm 15	Abdr-Rhm 11	Dickerson 4
11/23	@Was	87-89	L	3-7	85–.400	73–.425	20–.850	30–.800	35	47	Reeves 25, Abdr-Rhm 23	2 with 8	4 with 3
11/24	@Cha	73-89	L	3-8	78–.385	71–.423	23–.565	39–.718	45	41	Dickerson 16, Abdr-Rhm 15	Abdr-Rhm 21	Bibby 6
11/26	@Ind	86-105	L	3-9	78–.410	79–.532	25–.840	17–.882	39	34	Abdr-Rhm 22, Harrington 16	3 with 6	Bibby 7
11/27	@Min	82-113	L	3-10	79–.443	82–.524	16–.750	27–.815	31	41	Harrington 18, Lopez 11	Abdr-Rhm 9	3 with 5
11/29	Hou	110-118[1]	L	3-11	86–.453	87–.517	34–.706	30–.600	42	46	Bibby 25, Abdr-Rhm 23	Harrington 11	2 with 5
12/01	Ind	89-96	L	3-12	80–.438	77–.442	18–.833	28–.786	45	38	Abdr-Rhm 24, Harrington 15	Abdr-Rhm 10	Bibby 7
12/03	Cha	94-113	L	3-13	71–.507	83–.554	28–.679	22–.773	35	33	Dickerson 29, Abdr-Rhm 15	Parks 8	Bibby 9
12/06	@Hou	99-102	L	3-14	79–.481	81–.469	31–.677	28–.643	40	40	Abdr-Rhm 24, Harrington 18	Parks 8	Parks 5
12/07	@Dal	104-95	W	4-14	88–.432	85–.447	27–.815	22–.682	51	38	Abdr-Rhm 26, Dickerson 21	Abdr-Rhm 15	Bibby 7
12/09	@SA	91-99	L	4-15	77–.468	65–.508	20–.850	37–.838	25	39	Abdr-Rhm 30, Harrington 18	Parks 7	Bibby 7
12/11	LAL	94-106	L	4-16	81–.469	81–.481	15–.867	34–.794	37	42	Bibby 23, Abdr-Rhm 19	Abdr-Rhm 9	Bibby 8
12/13	@LAC	90-102	L	4-17	75–.413	83–.506	33–.727	17–.706	39	39	Abdr-Rhm 24, Dickerson 21	Abdr-Rhm 16	Bibby 3
12/15	Sac	106-109	L	4-18	86–.430	82–.413	35–.743	37–.811	55	49	Bibby 26, Dickerson 22	Abdr-Rhm 15	Bibby 11
12/18	@Sea	89-112	L	4-19	70–.443	77–.481	34–.647	35–.886	32	45	Abdr-Rhm 25, Dickerson 14	2 with 8	Bibby 8
12/19	LAC	85-84	W	5-19	75–.400	69–.464	24–.792	22–.591	46	35	Dickerson 26, Abdr-Rhm 20	Harrington 12	Bibby 6
12/23	Den	93-91	W	6-19	87–.425	77–.481	21–.857	21–.667	46	39	Abdr-Rhm 29, Dickerson 22	Abdr-Rhm 13	Bibby 11
12/26	@Den	86-109	L	6-20	89–.393	78–.513	19–.737	30–.800	39	47	Abdr-Rhm 20, 3 with 14	Abdr-Rhm 10	Bibby 10
12/27	Phi	93-100	L	6-21	83–.482	82–.463	15–.800	29–.793	42	44	Abdr-Rhm 24, 2 with 18	Abdr-Rhm 12	Bibby 13
12/29	@Uta	90-101	L	6-22	75–.427	70–.529	25–.880	25–.960	30	33	Dickerson 25, Abdr-Rhm 18	Reeves 10	Bibby 8
12/30	SA	88-98	L	6-23	79–.443	73–.452	16–.813	33–.879	35	46	Abdr-Rhm 24, Bibby 21	2 with 7	Bibby 11
1/04	@Mia	91-87	W	7-23	74–.392	80–.463	37–.757	15–.600	48	39	Bibby 22, Abdr-Rhm 20	Harrington 13	Bibby 4
1/05	@Orl	96-116	L	7-24	79–.418	80–.538	32–.844	32–.875	32	38	Abdr-Rhm 17, Dickerson 16	Long 10	Bibby 9
1/07	@NJ	101-91	W	8-24	78–.449	80–.425	21–**1.000**	16–.750	51	32	Dickerson 28, Bibby 20	Harrington 12	Bibby 9
1/09	@Tor	107-97	W	9-24	72–.458	83–.482	46–**.870**	22–.727	45	39	Abdr-Rhm 29, Dickerson 21	2 with 7	Bibby 6
1/10	@Bos	112-103	W	10-24	74–.486	88–.455	42–.762	22–.773	43	42	Bibby 33, Harrington 27	2 with 12	Dickerson 6
1/12	Pho	92-95	L	10-25	70–.357	90–.389	45–.889	27–.741	50	41	Harrington 19, 2 with 17	2 with 10	Bibby 6
1/14	Cle	80-82	L	10-26	77–.403	82–.415	19–.842	18–.778	39	44	Dickerson 23, Long 13	Harrington 10	Bibby 4
1/16	Mia	83-94	L	10-27	78–.436	77–.494	20–.650	22–.636	32	48	Dickerson 23, Abdr-Rhm 20	Long 7	Bibby 9
1/20	Uta	89-94	L	10-28	89–.449	65–.538	8–.875	31–.710	41	38	Bibby 22, Harrington 22	Abdr-Rhm 12	Bibby 9
1/22	Orl	82-85	L	10-29	81–.383	80–.438	18–.889	18–.667	49	39	3 with 16	2 with 10	Bibby 8
1/24	@Den	98-110	L	10-30	82–.451	90–.456	31–.742	28–.821	40	48	Abdr-Rhm 24, Bibby 18	Abdr-Rhm 13	Bibby 9
1/26	@Uta	116-99	W	11-30	79–**.570**	77–.494	26–.769	26–.615	39	31	Abdr-Rhm 30, Bibby 28	2 with 9	Bibby 11
1/27	NJ	108-106	W	12-30	80–.500	71–.507	28–.821	32–.781	32	38	Dickerson 29, Abdr-Rhm 23	Abdr-Rhm 7	Bibby 11
1/31	Mil	87-92	L	12-31	79–.418	81–.432	22–.636	21–.952	46	39	Reeves 22, 3 with 16	Reeves 15	Bibby 12
2/02	@GS	95-101	L	12-32	89–.427	73–.521	20–.750	23–.783	45	37	Abdr-Rhm 25, Dickerson 19	Abdr-Rhm 10	Bibby 5
2/04	Chi	101-**76**	W	13-32	81–.481	70–.400	22–.818	23–.783	46	34	Dickerson 20, Bibby 16	Reeves 9	Bibby 7
2/06	Dal	99-103[1]	L	13-33	89–.416	89–.393	31–.710	29–.828	53	44	Abdr-Rhm 36, Dickerson 14	**Abdr-Rhm 22**	Bibby 8
2/08	@Pho	76-94	L	13-34	82–.329	75–.547	21–.952	9–1.000	31	42	Dickerson 19, Abdr-Rhm 13	Abdr-Rhm 10	Bibby 4
2/10	@LAC	112-90	W	14-34	82–.537	83–.434	22–.909	14–.929	40	35	**Dickerson 40**, Abdr-Rhm 22	Abdr-Rhm 8	Bibby 8
2/16	Was	92-87	W	15-34	79–.418	85–.400	27–.815	26–.615	44	48	Bibby 21, 2 with 19	Abdr-Rhm 14	Bibby 7
2/18	@Min	91-103	L	15-35	75–.467	78–.513	20–.800	21–.905	37	33	Dickerson 27, Bibby 18	Abdr-Rhm 9	Bibby 8
2/19	@Mil	111-100	W	16-35	70–.514	81–.481	39–.795	26–.808	31	39	Dickerson 26, Abdr-Rhm 24	Harrington 6	Bibby 10
2/21	@Cle	108-109[1]	L	16-36	88–.477	83–.458	23–.913	30–.833	42	42	Bibby 27, Dickerson 27	Abdr-Rhm 9	Bibby 11
2/22	@Chi	85-81	W	17-36	70–.414	70–.443	32–.688	28–.571	48	40	Dickerson 25, Reeves 15	Abdr-Rhm 14	Bibby 10
2/24	Bos	77-101	L	17-37	74–.419	81–.568	19–.684	13–**.538**	32	44	Abdr-Rhm 20, Dickerson 18	2 with 7	2 with 6

Date	Opp	Score	W/L	Rec	Van FG Att–Pct.	Opp FG Att–Pct.	Van FT Att–Pct.	Opp FT Att–Pct.	Van Reb	Opp Reb	Points	Rebounds	Assists
2/26	Sac	102-90	W	18-37	81–.481	94–.436	21–.810	**7**–.571	49	41	Abdr-Rhm 22, Harrington 20	Abdr-Rhm 11	Bibby 15
2/29	@Sac	87-112	L	18-38	74–.486	89–.506	20–.550	18–.778	41	41	Harrington 20, Abdr-Rhm 19	Long 10	Bibby 12
3/01	@LAL	91-103	L	18-39	76–.447	87–.448	19–.789	27–.704	39	42	Abdr-Rhm 18, Dickerson 18	Abdr-Rhm 11	Bibby 8
3/03	@Por	91-101	L	18-40	71–.465	77–.506	27–.741	26–.769	29	47	Bibby 25, Abdr-Rhm 21	Abdr-Rhm 9	Bibby 14
3/05	Tor	92-94	L	18-41	74–.419	84–.464	35–.714	19–.684	43	43	Abdr-Rhm 22, Harrington 22	Abdr-Rhm 14	Bibby 8
3/07	@NY	86-111	L	18-42	74–.392	66–.621	31–.742	30–.867	28	39	Abdr-Rhm 18, Bibby 15	Abdr-Rhm 8	2 with 4
3/08	@Phi	90-107	L	18-43	69–.478	80–.488	28–.714	31–.806	40	35	Harrington 20, Abdr-Rhm 17	Harrington 8	Bibby 10
3/10	@Det	97-111	L	18-44	67–.448	83–.518	38–.842	28–.821	37	38	Harrington 25, Abdr-Rhm 16	2 with 8	Bibby 9
3/11	@Atl	86-91	L	18-45	76–.487	73–.534	17–.647	18–.722	30	37	Bibby 20, Abdr-Rhm 14	Abdr-Rhm 10	Bibby 6
3/13	Sea	103-113	L	18-46	81–.519	86–.500	17–.882	32–.719	40	38	Reeves 31, Abdr-Rhm 17	Reeves 12	Bibby 9
3/16	@Sea	103-117	L	18-47	83–.542	86–.547	18–.667	18–.889	35	32	Dickerson 24, Bibby 23	Abdr-Rhm 9	Bibby 13
3/17	Pho	86-101	L	18-48	65–.431	96–.448	31–.774	12–.917	38	44	Abdr-Rhm 14, Dickerson 14	2 with 8	Lopez 4
3/19	Det	99-101	L	18-49	74–.514	76–.487	17–.882	23–.913	38	**27**	Dickerson 24, Abdr-Rhm 22	Harrington 9	Bibby 9
3/21	GS	98-82	W	19-49	81–.457	76–.342	37–.595	32–.813	50	43	Dickerson 25, Lopez 14	Abdr-Rhm 13	2 with 8
3/25	Uta	75-84	L	19-50	79–.354	74–.419	15–.933	33–.606	47	48	Scott 16, Abdr-Rhm 15	Reeves 9	Bibby 9
3/29	LAL	99-108	L	19-51	74–.541	90–.500	19–.737	19–.632	38	37	Dickerson 32, Abdr-Rhm 30	Abdr-Rhm 13	Bibby 14
3/31	NY	83-89	L	19-52	69–.478	82–.451	14–.857	16–.813	44	36	Dickerson 28, Abdr-Rhm 21	Harrington 16	Bibby 10
4/02	Dal	86-100	L	19-53	81–.407	79–.468	26–.731	18–1.000	45	45	Abdr-Rhm 23, 2 with 14	Bibby 11	Bibby 11
4/04	Hou	102-100	W	20-53	92–.424	82–.476	24–.833	16–.938	40	51	Bibby 27, Abdr-Rhm 21	Abdr-Rhm 14	Bibby 10
4/06	Por	89-87	W	21-53	66–.500	86–.395	23–.696	15–1.000	39	38	Dickerson 27, Abdr-Rhm 18	2 with 9	Bibby 9
4/08	@Por	85-98	L	21-54	70–.486	**63**–.556	23–.609	32–.781	30	31	Dickerson 20, Abdr-Rhm 17	Abdr-Rhm 9	Bibby 10
4/09	SA	99-107	L	21-55	81–.444	71–.577	19–1.000	27–.778	34	37	Bibby 24, Abdr-Rhm 23	Abdr-Rhm 11	Bibby 8
4/11	@GS	97-109	L	21-56	76–.513	82–.524	20–.850	29–.759	35	45	Dickerson 24, Abdr-Rhm 23	Abdr-Rhm 13	Bibby 9
4/12	@Pho	**116**-122[1]	L	21-57	91–.407	93–.495	34–.882	26–.846	41	44	Dickerson 35, Harrington 20	Harrington 12	Bibby 11
4/14	Min	94-104[2]	L	21-58	**97**–.402	92–.489	14–.714	11–.727	44	49	Abdr-Rhm 27, Dickerson 22	Abdr-Rhm 17	Bibby 12
4/16	@Dal	106-114	L	21-59	88–.443	91–.484	29–.793	22–.818	51	45	Harrington 27, Abdr-Rhm 19	Abdr-Rhm 13	Bibby 8
4/17	@SA	93-100	L	21-60	70–.457	73–.479	32–.844	34–.706	33	41	Dickerson 29, Abdr-Rhm 27	Abdr-Rhm 10	Bibby 7
4/19	@Hou	96-92	W	22-60	74–.473	82–.439	29–.897	16–.813	43	32	Dickerson 20, Harrington 18	Abdr-Rhm 11	Bibby 8

Washington Wizards 1999-2000 Game Log (29-53)

Date	Opp	Score	W/L	Rec	Was FG Att–Pct.	Opp FG Att–Pct.	Was FT Att–Pct.	Opp FT Att–Pct.	Was Reb	Opp Reb	Points	Rebounds	Assists
11/02	Atl	94-87	W	1-0	88–.443	78–.397	16–.813	30–.767	42	50	Howard 21, Strickland 12	Austin 11	Strickland 10
11/03	@Bos	101-112	L	1-1	79–.456	88–.511	33–.727	23–.739	43	43	Richmond 20, Whitney 15	Austin 10	Richmond 6
11/06	Orl	104-107	L	1-2	87–.425	81–.469	29–.793	38–.737	51	37	Howard 22, Strickland 18	Smith 12	Strickland 13
11/07	@NJ	87-112	L	1-3	86–.407	89–.427	22–.636	34–.794	46	50	Hamilton 14, 2 with 10	Smith 9	3 with 3
11/10	Sea	95-109	L	1-4	90–.478	87–.517	12–.583	15–.667	39	37	Howard 16, Hamilton 15	White 6	Whitney 11
11/12	Mia	95-104	L	1-5	88–.398	77–.494	26–.769	29–.724	49	40	Murray 15, 2 with 13	King 9	Strickland 15
11/13	@Ind	83-105	L	1-6	92–.370	83–.458	18–.833	29–.793	55	45	King 20, Murray 12	**King 16**	Strickland 8
11/16	Phi	73-95	L	1-7	79–.342	70–.471	31–.516	37–.649	52	45	Hamilton 17, Howard 13	2 with 11	Strickland 4
11/18	Tor	92-81	W	2-7	76–.395	85–**.329**	37–.811	30–.633	**56**	46	Austin 20, 2 with 12	Austin 13	Strickland 5
11/20	LAC	89-98	L	2-8	93–.398	72–.444	16–.750	31–.774	50	37	Howard 19, A Williams 15	Austin 12	Strickland 5
11/23	Van	89-87	W	3-8	73–.425	85–.400	30–.800	20–.850	47	35	Richmond 19, Austin 16	A Williams 9	Strickland 6
11/24	@Phi	101-93	W	4-8	81–.407	78–.449	39–.795	30–.733	39	44	Murray 19, Austin 15	Austin 9	Strickland 10
11/26	@Cha	85-118	L	4-9	85–.424	89–.494	21–.619	33–.788	42	43	Hamilton 16, Strickland 11	White 9	Strickland 10
11/27	@Mia	86-89	L	4-10	72–.431	75–.467	28–.750	19–.737	34	41	Richmond 20, Howard 13	3 with 6	2 with 4
11/30	@NJ	85-78	W	5-10	72–.431	80–.388	29–.655	17–.765	40	46	Howard 23, Hamilton 14	Smith 13	2 with 4
12/01	Cle	108-111	L	5-11	82–.463	76–.434	41–.659	53–.755	43	43	Richmond 30, 2 with 15	Smith 11	Strickland 7
12/03	@Tor	93-95	L	5-12	82–.451	82–.439	25–.720	24–.750	48	40	Richmond 18, Strickland 16	Smith 11	Strickland 12
12/04	Sac	104-114	L	5-13	78–.449	94–.511	**43**–.744	22–.727	50	37	Richmond 23, A Williams 16	Smith 9	Strickland 10
12/06	@Uta	96-102	L	5-14	69–.493	73–.507	32–.781	34–.706	34	34	Richmond 25, Strickland 16	Smith 9	Howard 5
12/07	@LAL	80-91	L	5-15	89–.360	72–.444	20–.650	38–.658	50	45	Richmond 23, Strickland 15	Howard 9	Strickland 10
12/09	@Pho	85-99	L	5-16	78–.423	79–.519	31–.581	**13**–.846	36	44	Howard 15, Richmond 14	3 with 5	2 with 6
12/11	@SA	99-89	W	6-16	82–.476	75–.413	22–.773	30–.767	47	37	Richmond 31, Murray 15	Smith 15	Strickland 7
12/14	Uta	80-101	L	6-17	67–.448	79–.532	29–.690	19–.684	39	34	Strickland 18, Richmond 17	Smith 9	2 with 5
12/16	NJ	108-104	W	7-17	79–.595	73–.507	20–.500	28–.679	41	**28**	Howard 28, Richmond 22	Smith 10	Strickland 14
12/18	@NY	95-83	W	8-17	67–.493	76–.382	29–.828	28–.857	38	31	Richmond 19, White 15	White 10	Strickland 8
12/21	@Det	97-83	W	9-17	91–.440	75–.360	17–.882	39–.718	50	39	Richmond 33, Howard 16	Smith 13	Whitney 8
12/23	@Hou	89-105	L	9-18	77–.468	80–.438	26–.577	37–.730	40	41	Richmond 18, Howard 16	Smith 12	Strickland 7
12/26	Hou	103-92	W	10-18	77–.506	89–.393	25–.880	28–.571	41	45	Richmond 27, 2 with 15	White 9	Richmond 7
12/29	@Cle	94-96	L	10-19	82–.439	84–.464	28–.643	24–.625	48	41	Strickland 20, White 16	Smith 14	Howard 9
12/30	NY	86-89	L	10-20	67–.478	71–.437	25–.560	33–.636	47	30	Richmond 24, Murray 15	White 13	Strickland 6
1/03	GS	99-87	W	11-20	84–.476	77–.455	18–.778	20–.650	42	35	Richmond 19, Strickland 15	Howard 8	Strickland 10
1/05	@Chi	66-**77**	L	11-21	84–.286	75–.360	20–.700	29–.655	46	56	Murray 18, Howard 12	Howard 10	Strickland 6
1/07	Chi	103-110	L	11-22	75–.533	69–.594	27–.630	27–.778	26	34	Howard 19, Richmond 17	Smith 12	Strickland 12
1/08	@Mil	**129**-130[2]	L	11-23	93–.473	97–.495	42–.762	38–.737	48	48	Murray 27, Richmond 25	A Williams 13	Strickland 12
1/11	Tor	117-89	W	12-23	79–.532	83–.386	36–.889	32–.750	48	36	A Williams 17, Strickland 15	A Williams 10	Strickland 7
1/12	@Ind	102-117	L	12-24	91–.440	87–.494	27–.704	28–.786	55	38	Howard 23, Richmond 17	2 with 11	Howard 7
1/14	@Det	98-105	L	12-25	76–.539	78–.487	20–.650	32–.750	42	34	Richmond 29, Howard 20	Austin 9	Strickland 8
1/15	Det	107-112	L	12-26	74–.527	80–.500	35–.771	37–.784	41	32	Strickland 27, Murray 17	A Williams 8	2 with 5
1/17	Bos	101-105	L	12-27	69–.507	80–.450	36–.833	34–.912	34	37	Howard 31, Strickland 24	Smith 9	Strickland 6
1/19	Dal	86-104	L	12-28	80–.375	93–.462	30–.733	15–.800	51	42	Murray 17, White 16	White 15	Strickland 3
1/21	Ind	123-113	W	13-28	85–.600	87–.460	24–.875	27–.889	35	35	**Howard 36**, Strickland 27	Howard 10	Strickland 7
1/22	@Atl	93-111	L	13-29	92–.402	84–.464	21–.762	37–.757	49	53	Hamilton 19, Strickland 19	A Williams 11	Strickland 6
1/26	@Tor	105-120	L	13-30	73–.548	83–.542	34–.706	34–.676	36	37	Howard 22, 2 with 17	White 10	Strickland 13
1/29	Cle	103-98	W	14-30	82–.488	84–.417	25–.840	28–.821	43	39	Strickland 26, Hamilton 21	White 12	Strickland 11
2/01	@Cle	108-112	L	14-31	80–.488	83–.434	30–.700	47–.702	45	44	Murray 23, Hamilton 22	Howard 11	Strickland 9
2/02	Min	103-93	W/L	15-31	78–.487	75–.520	29–.759	14–.857	40	30	Richmond 19, Strickland 15	Howard 13	Howard 7
2/04	@Mia	92-99	L	15-32	91–.429	76–.421	10–.900	35–.857	46	45	Richmond 21, Strickland 20	Austin 10	Strickland 8
2/05	Cha	102-110	L	15-33	83–.458	72–.458	25–.800	55–.764	45	41	Richmond 22, Strickland 20	2 with 10	Strickland 8
2/09	@Orl	96-107	L	15-34	74–.473	97–.495	24–.750	20–**.500**	42	44	Howard 20, Richmond 14	**White 16**	Strickland 10
2/15	@Sea	85-114	L	15-35	82–.366	81–.506	30–.733	34–.559	50	41	Murray 16, 2 with 12	Austin 11	Strickland 7
2/16	@Van	87-92	L	15-36	85–.400	79–.418	26–.615	27–.815	48	44	Richmond 18, Strickland 16	A Williams 8	Strickland 6
2/18	@Por	85-93	L	15-37	74–.419	81–.370	31–.677	34–.824	36	51	Strickland 18, Howard 15	Howard 8	Strickland 8
2/20	@GS	103-112	L	15-38	90–.411	96–.490	40–.600	21–.667	48	58	White 23, Strickland 14	White 14	Strickland 11
2/22	Mil	126-101	W	16-38	86–.581	96–.427	22–.818	16–.875	41	40	Richmond 26, 2 with 18	White 11	Whitney 8

Date	Opp	Score	W/L	Rec	Was FG Att–Pct.	Opp FG Att–Pct.	Was FT Att–Pct.	Opp FT Att–Pct.	Was Reb	Opp Reb	Points	Rebounds	Assists
2/24	Pho	83-92	L	16-39	84–.381	74–.459	19–.737	28–.679	45	40	Richmond 19, Whitney 13	White 10	Whitney 4
2/26	Mia	88-98	L	16-40	82–.390	74–.459	19–.895	28–.857	44	31	Murray 20, Howard 17	Howard 11	Strickland 6
3/01	@Atl	102-83	W	17-40	76–.526	75–.427	23–.739	22–.773	37	41	Richmond 18, King 17	King 8	Strickland 11
3/02	Phi	84-87	L	17-41	79–.405	81–.383	17–.882	28–.679	43	42	Richmond 16, Murray 13	2 with 7	2 with 5
3/04	Det	100-94	W	18-41	78–.487	75–.467	28–.786	24–.750	42	38	A Williams 27, Strickland 14	2 with 8	Strickland 8
3/06	Orl	85-87	L	18-42	73–.425	92–.402	23–.826	16–.500	38	51	Hamilton 25, Murray 14	King 12	Strickland 7
3/07	@Min	90-86	W	19-42	75–.480	84–.405	19–.684	21–.714	40	41	Murray 17, Richmond 14	White 9	Strickland 7
3/08	NY	118-113[1]	W	20-42	75–**.613**	79–.544	30–.833	33–.758	31	33	Richmond 32, Howard 29	King 9	Strickland 10
3/10	SA	99-106[1]	L	20-43	88–.443	80–.525	23–.739	26–.769	40	44	Howard 29, Richmond 22	Howard 12	Strickland 13
3/12	Por	86-102	L	20-44	89–.382	68–.515	21–.571	24–.917	33	48	Richmond 18, Murray 17	A Williams 10	Strickland 8
3/14	@Orl	98-107	L	20-45	86–.465	72–.528	18–.667	32–.813	37	31	Murray 26, Richmond 16	2 with 8	3 with 5
3/16	LAL	109-102	W	21-45	76–.500	74–.500	35–.800	32–.719	37	38	Richmond 32, Howard 14	White 8	**Strickland 16**
3/18	Chi	101-88	W	22-45	88–.443	65–**.462**	21–**.905**	33–.788	48	38	Strickland 13, 3 with 12	King 10	Strickland 9
3/20	@LAC	105-93	W	23-45	89–.461	79–.405	22–.773	30–.733	46	46	Richmond 21, Howard 20	2 with 8	Whitney 9
3/21	@Sac	86-98	L	23-46	**99**–.384	79–.443	13–.615	32–.781	42	54	Richmond 26, Howard 21	White 10	Whitney 6
3/23	@Den	100-86	W	24-46	85–.435	80–.338	28–.750	40–.625	55	44	Howard 22, Richmond 22	Howard 11	Whitney 7
3/25	@Dal	93-86	W	25-46	79–.456	79–.418	20–.900	16–.813	47	41	Whitney 29, Richmond 20	White 10	Howard 4
3/29	Den	93-101	L	25-47	91–.363	66–.485	24–.875	36–.833	41	45	Richmond 22, Howard 17	Murray 10	Whitney 8
3/31	@Bos	104-102	W	26-47	82–.500	79–.481	19–.895	26–.923	35	42	Richmond 30, Hamilton 20	A Williams 14	Whitney 6
4/04	NJ	102-93	W	27-47	76–.526	80–.413	23–.696	29–.862	36	42	Whitney 18, Howard 16	3 with 6	Howard 8
4/06	@NY	92-101	L	27-48	84–.405	70–.471	23–.870	39–.872	32	46	Richmond 23, Howard 20	2 with 8	2 with 5
4/08	Atl	108-98	W	28-48	81–.506	78–.462	29–.724	28–.857	42	39	Whitney 19, Hamilton 16	White 14	Whitney 7
4/10	Cha	105-107	L	28-49	80–.513	81–.506	26–.769	37–.649	34	42	Richmond 21, Hamilton 19	White 6	Whitney 10
4/12	@Phi	84-93	L	28-50	78–.410	74–.473	17–.882	35–.600	50	38	Hamilton 19, Howard 13	Howard 10	Howard 5
4/13	@Chi	109-103	W	29-50	82–.476	77–.519	26–.808	23–.826	38	34	Hamilton 26, Whitney 17	King 9	Whitney 8
4/15	Mil	116-120[1]	L	29-51	93–.462	80–.513	25–.720	42–.690	37	55	Howard 21, Richmond 21	King 6	Whitney 14
4/18	Bos	81-114	L	29-52	76–.368	84–.536	32–.688	27–.593	34	53	Whitney 25, 2 with 12	2 with 6	Whitney 9
4/19	@Mil	105-110	L	29-53	89–.438	80–.525	22–.818	32–.750	44	41	Richmond 27, Whitney 22	King 9	2 with 7

Team Player-By-Player Statistics

Included for each team is a page that lists all individual player stats for the 1999-2000 regular season and postseason. Team leaders are bolded in the regular-season section based on the NBA minimums to qualify for leadership in a category for a season. Therefore, Jim Jackson is bolded as the Hawks' team leader in points per game because he met the NBA requirement of having played in 70 games or having scored 1,400 points. Postseason leaders are bolded based on the NBA regular-season minimums divided by the number of postseason games played by a team. We've also included an interesting "Did You Know?" fact on these pages, specific to each team.

Atlanta Hawks 1999-2000 Regular Season Totals (28-54)

Player	G	GS	Min	Field Goals			3-Pt FGs			Free Throws			Misc			Fouls		Assists		Rebounds			Points	
				Md	Att	Pct	Md	Att	Pct	Md	Att	Pct	TO	Stl	Blk	PF	DQ	Ast	Avg	Off	Tot	Avg	Pts	Avg
Isaiah Rider	60	47	2084	449	1072	.419	56	180	.311	204	260	.785	168	41	6	132	3	219	3.7	63	258	4.3	1158	19.3
Jim Jackson	79	76	2767	507	1235	.411	117	303	.386	186	212	.877	185	57	10	167	0	230	2.9	101	394	5.0	1317	16.7
Alan Henderson	82	82	2775	429	930	.461	1	10	.100	224	334	.671	139	81	54	233	3	77	0.9	265	571	7.0	1083	13.2
D. Mutombo	82	82	2984	322	573	.562	0	0	—	298	421	.708	174	27	269	248	3	105	1.3	304	1157	14.1	942	11.5
LaPhonso Ellis	58	8	1309	209	464	.450	3	21	.143	66	95	.695	52	32	25	133	1	59	1.0	98	290	5.0	487	8.4
Jason Terry*	81	27	1888	249	600	.415	46	157	.293	113	140	.807	156	90	10	133	0	346	4.3	24	166	2.0	657	8.1
Bimbo Coles	80	54	1924	276	607	.455	8	39	.205	85	104	.817	103	58	11	178	1	290	3.6	30	172	2.2	645	8.1
Roshown McLeod	44	20	860	131	332	.395	2	13	.154	54	70	.771	59	16	5	84	0	52	1.2	41	138	3.1	318	7.2
Dion Glover*	30	1	446	66	171	.386	12	45	.267	51	70	.729	28	15	4	28	0	27	0.9	15	38	1.3	195	6.5
Lorenzen Wright	75	0	1205	180	361	.499	1	3	.333	87	135	.644	66	29	40	203	3	21	0.3	117	305	4.1	448	6.0
Chris Crawford	55	11	668	91	229	.397	7	27	.259	63	81	.778	37	17	16	83	1	33	0.6	51	99	1.8	252	4.6
Cal Bowdler*	46	0	423	49	115	.426	0	1	.000	24	38	.632	21	14	9	46	1	14	0.3	22	85	1.8	122	2.7
Anthony Johnson†	38	2	423	36	103	.350	1	6	.167	19	24	.792	24	23	2	41	0	59	1.6	15	39	1.0	92	2.4
Drew Barry†	8	0	74	6	15	.400	4	9	.444	3	3	1.000	7	0	0	9	0	16	2.0	0	4	0.5	19	2.4
Total	82	410	19830	3000	6807	.441	258	814	.317	1477	1987	.743	1266	500	461	1718	16	1548	18.9	1146	3716	45.3	7735	94.3
Opponent	82	410	19830	3211	7060	.455	373	1015	.367	1381	1796	.769	1001	655	404	1830	13	1886	23.0	1052	3526	43.0	8176	99.7

* indicates rookie; † indicates player played with another team in 1999-2000; bold indicates team leader

Did You Know?

The Hawks forced only 12.2 turnovers per game last season, fewest by any team in the 27 seasons in which turnovers have been recorded.

Boston Celtics 1999-2000 Regular Season Totals (35-47)

Player	G	GS	Min	Field Goals			3-Pt FGs			Free Throws			Misc			Fouls		Assists		Rebounds			Points	
				Md	Att	Pct	Md	Att	Pct	Md	Att	Pct	TO	Stl	Blk	PF	DQ	Ast	Avg	Off	Tot	Avg	Pts	Avg
Antoine Walker	82	82	3003	648	1506	.430	73	285	.256	311	445	.699	259	117	32	263	4	305	3.7	199	652	8.0	1680	20.5
Paul Pierce	73	72	2583	486	1099	.442	96	280	.343	359	450	.798	178	152	62	237	5	221	3.0	83	396	5.4	1427	19.5
Kenny Anderson	82	82	2593	434	986	.440	85	220	.386	196	253	.775	130	139	8	230	4	420	5.1	55	225	2.7	1149	14.0
Vitaly Potapenko	79	72	1797	307	615	.499	0	1	.000	109	160	.681	145	41	29	239	4	77	1.0	182	499	6.3	723	9.2
Danny Fortson	55	5	856	140	265	.528	0	0	—	139	189	.735	67	20	5	180	4	29	0.5	141	366	6.7	419	7.6
Eric Williams	68	17	1378	165	386	.427	25	72	.347	134	169	.793	66	44	16	165	3	93	1.4	55	156	2.3	489	7.2
Dana Barros	72	0	1139	196	435	.451	59	144	.410	66	76	.868	66	31	4	80	0	133	1.8	13	99	1.4	517	7.2
Adrian Griffin*	72	47	1927	175	413	.424	16	57	.281	119	158	.753	93	116	15	222	3	177	2.5	128	372	5.2	485	6.7
Tony Battie	82	4	1505	219	459	.477	1	8	.125	102	151	.675	67	47	70	249	4	63	0.8	152	410	5.0	541	6.6
Calbert Cheaney	67	19	1309	120	273	.440	18	54	.333	9	21	.429	46	44	14	158	3	80	1.2	23	138	2.1	267	4.0
Walter McCarty	61	5	879	78	230	.339	34	110	.309	39	54	.722	67	24	23	83	1	70	1.1	33	110	1.8	229	3.8
Jamel Thomas*†	3	0	19	5	10	.500	0	1	.000	1	1	1.000	1	0	0	0	0	2	0.7	0	2	0.7	11	3.7
Doug Overton	48	0	432	61	154	.396	10	28	.357	20	21	.952	20	10	0	46	0	53	1.1	14	33	0.7	152	3.2
Pervis Ellison	30	5	269	19	43	.442	0	0	—	15	21	.714	13	10	8	67	1	13	0.4	29	67	2.2	53	1.8
Wayne Turner*	3	0	41	1	6	.167	0	0	—	2	6	.333	3	0	0	4	0	5	1.7	1	3	1.0	4	1.3
Total	82	410	19730	3054	6880	.444	417	1260	.331	1621	2175	.745	1259	795	286	2223	36	1741	21.2	1108	3528	43.0	8146	99.3
Opponent	82	410	19730	2960	6304	.470	359	995	.361	1929	2563	.753	1395	638	473	1928	21	1798	21.9	857	3391	41.4	8208	100.1

* indicates rookie; † indicates player played with another team in 1999-2000; bold indicates team leader

Did You Know?

Last season the Celtics posted 17 more home wins (26) than road wins (nine). The differential was the largest for any NBA team since the 1994-95 Orlando Magic won 21 more home games than road games.

Charlotte Hornets 1999-2000 Regular Season Totals (49-33)

Player	G	GS	Min	Field Goals Md	Att	Pct	3-Pt FGs Md	Att	Pct	Free Throws Md	Att	Pct	Misc TO	Stl	Blk	Fouls PF	DQ	Assists Ast	Avg	Rebounds Off	Tot	Avg	Points Pts	Avg
Eddie Jones	72	72	2807	**478**	1119	.427	**128**	341	**.375**	**362**	419	**.864**	160	**192**	49	176	1	305	4.2	81	343	4.8	**1446**	**20.1**
Derrick Coleman	74	64	2347	446	979	.456	51	141	.362	296	377	.785	**173**	34	130	195	2	175	2.4	124	632	**8.5**	1239	16.7
David Wesley	**82**	**82**	2760	407	955	.426	88	248	.355	214	275	.778	159	109	11	186	2	**463**	**5.6**	39	225	2.7	1116	13.6
Bobby Phills	28	9	825	152	335	.454	30	91	.330	47	65	.723	48	41	8	72	2	79	2.8	17	71	2.5	381	13.6
Elden Campbell	78	77	2538	370	829	.446	0	6	.000	247	358	.690	127	56	**150**	**269**	6	129	1.7	**168**	590	7.6	987	12.7
Anthony Mason	**82**	81	**3133**	317	661	**.480**	0	1	.000	314	**421**	.746	160	74	29	220	0	367	4.5	145	**699**	8.5	948	11.6
Brad Miller	55	4	961	135	293	.461	0	2	.000	153	195	.785	48	23	35	111	1	45	0.8	113	293	5.3	423	7.7
Eddie Robinson*	67	8	1112	212	386	.549	0	4	.000	47	64	.734	39	48	25	67	0	32	0.5	54	184	2.7	471	7.0
Baron Davis*	**82**	0	1523	182	433	.420	25	111	.225	97	153	.634	140	97	19	201	1	309	3.8	48	165	2.0	486	5.9
Ricky Davis	48	4	570	94	187	.503	0	4	.000	39	51	.765	46	30	8	39	0	62	1.3	29	83	1.7	227	4.7
Chucky Brown†	33	2	494	66	152	.434	1	7	.143	11	21	.524	17	12	8	61	1	25	0.8	24	90	2.7	144	4.4
Todd Fuller	41	2	399	51	122	.418	0	0	—	32	53	.604	27	9	8	46	0	5	0.1	36	110	2.7	134	3.3
Dale Ellis†	24	5	240	19	58	.328	14	35	.400	3	4	.750	13	7	0	22	0	8	0.3	6	22	0.9	55	2.3
Eldridge Recasner	7	0	28	3	7	.429	1	4	.250	0	0	—	0	0	0	1	0	5	0.7	0	4	0.6	7	1.0
Michael Hawkins	12	0	36	3	13	.231	1	5	.200	1	2	.500	3	0	0	2	0	13	1.1	0	7	0.6	8	0.7
Derek Hood*	2	0	4	0	3	.000	0	0	—	0	0	—	0	0	0	0	0	0	0.0	0	1	0.5	0	0.0
Jason Miskiri*	1	0	3	0	1	.000	0	0	—	0	1	.000	0	0	0	2	0	1	1.0	0	0	0.0	0	0.0
Total	82	410	19780	2935	6533	.449	339	1001	.339	1863	2458	.758	1206	732	480	1670	16	2023	24.7	884	3519	42.9	8072	98.4
Opponent	82	410	19780	3048	6811	.448	410	1086	.378	1347	1807	.745	1297	604	421	2076	21	1903	23.2	966	3516	42.9	7853	95.8

* indicates rookie; † indicates player played with another team in 1999-2000; bold indicates team leader

Charlotte Hornets 1999-2000 Postseason Totals (1-3)

Player	G	GS	Min	Field Goals Md	Att	Pct	3-Pt FGs Md	Att	Pct	Free Throws Md	Att	Pct	Misc TO	Stl	Blk	Fouls PF	DQ	Assists Ast	Avg	Rebounds Off	Tot	Avg	Points Pts	Avg
Derrick Coleman	4	4	169	27	57	**.474**	5	16	.313	**22**	28	.786	13	3	12	11	1	14	3.5	10	**50**	**12.5**	81	20.3
Eddie Jones	4	4	171	22	**58**	.379	9	26	.346	15	16	.938	5	**10**	3	12	0	19	4.8	4	20	5.0	68	17.0
Elden Campbell	4	4	150	22	47	.468	0	1	.000	13	14	.929	8	2	4	16	0	4	1.0	9	33	8.3	57	14.3
Anthony Mason	4	4	**179**	18	38	**.474**	0	1	.000	14	20	.700	**13**	4	0	13	0	**22**	**5.5**	**16**	39	9.8	50	12.5
David Wesley	4	4	152	16	48	.333	3	10	.300	9	9	**1.000**	6	8	0	**17**	0	19	4.8	3	12	3.0	44	11.0
Brad Miller	4	0	62	9	17	.529	0	0	—	12	15	.800	9	0	3	11	0	3	0.8	8	13	3.3	30	7.5
Baron Davis	4	0	57	10	23	.435	1	6	.167	2	4	.500	3	4	0	6	0	6	1.5	3	6	1.5	23	5.8
Eddie Robinson	4	0	45	5	12	.417	0	0	—	2	2	1.000	1	2	1	2	0	4	1.0	1	3	0.8	12	3.0
Total	4	20	985	129	300	.430	18	60	.300	89	108	.824	62	33	23	88	1	91	22.8	54	176	44.0	365	91.3
Opponent	4	20	985	137	320	.428	24	60	.400	78	101	.772	51	28	24	97	1	85	21.3	52	162	40.5	376	94.0

Did You Know?

The Hornets recorded assists on 68.9 percent of their field goals in 1999-2000, the best ratio of any NBA team. It was the first time since 1992-93 that a team other than the Utah Jazz led the league in this category.

Chicago Bulls 1999-2000 Regular Season Totals (17-65)

Player	G	GS	Min	Field Goals Md	Att	Pct	3-Pt FGs Md	Att	Pct	Free Throws Md	Att	Pct	Misc TO	Stl	Blk	Fouls PF	DQ	Assists Ast	Avg	Rebounds Off	Tot	Avg	Points Pts	Avg
Elton Brand*	81	80	2999	630	1306	.482	0	2	.000	367	536	.685	228	66	132	259	3	155	1.9	348	810	10.0	1627	20.1
Toni Kukoc†	24	23	868	148	388	.381	18	78	.231	118	155	.761	75	44	19	51	0	124	5.2	37	130	5.4	432	18.0
Ron Artest*	72	63	2238	309	759	.407	60	191	.314	188	279	.674	166	119	39	159	0	202	2.8	62	308	4.3	866	12.0
Chris Carr†	50	2	1092	185	463	.400	31	93	.333	91	106	.858	112	30	14	101	0	81	1.6	36	160	3.2	492	9.8
Rusty LaRue	4	1	129	15	43	.349	2	14	.143	5	7	.714	7	7	0	9	0	11	2.8	1	10	2.5	37	9.3
Fred Hoiberg	31	11	845	89	230	.387	32	94	.340	69	76	.908	43	40	2	66	0	85	2.7	7	110	3.5	279	9.0
Hersey Hawkins	61	49	1622	159	375	.424	55	141	.390	107	119	.899	100	74	15	146	1	134	2.2	31	175	2.9	480	7.9
Corey Benjamin	48	10	862	145	350	.414	31	89	.348	49	82	.598	74	31	22	122	2	54	1.1	21	88	1.8	370	7.7
D. Willoughby*	25	1	508	61	179	.341	29	98	.296	39	51	.765	37	23	2	32	0	66	2.6	11	51	2.0	190	7.6
John Starks†	4	0	82	11	34	.324	3	10	.300	5	5	1.000	3	5	1	9	0	11	2.8	0	10	2.5	30	7.5
B.J. Armstrong	27	18	583	83	186	.446	13	29	.448	22	25	.880	40	7	1	34	0	78	2.9	2	47	1.7	201	7.4
Kornel David†	26	5	443	63	148	.426	0	3	.000	42	52	.808	31	13	2	49	0	16	0.6	22	73	2.8	168	6.5
Randy Brown	59	55	1625	157	435	.361	3	6	.500	62	84	.738	105	61	15	120	1	202	3.4	23	144	2.4	379	6.4
Matt Maloney	51	12	1175	114	318	.358	62	174	.356	37	45	.822	63	32	3	42	0	138	2.7	10	64	1.3	327	6.4
Chris Anstey	73	11	1007	161	364	.442	1	6	.167	116	147	.789	80	29	25	180	4	65	0.9	90	280	3.8	439	6.0
Dickey Simpkins	69	48	1651	111	274	.405	0	1	.000	65	120	.542	128	22	22	217	4	100	1.4	124	372	5.4	287	4.2
Khalid Reeves	3	0	48	3	12	.250	0	3	.000	5	5	1.000	6	2	0	8	0	13	4.3	2	4	1.3	11	3.7
Will Perdue	67	15	1012	59	168	.351	0	0	—	50	105	.476	78	14	42	126	1	65	1.0	88	262	3.9	168	2.5
Michael Ruffin*	71	6	975	58	138	.420	0	0	—	43	88	.489	59	26	26	170	1	44	0.6	117	250	3.5	159	2.2
Lari Ketner*†	6	0	41	4	10	.400	0	0	—	2	2	1.000	3	1	1	8	1	1	0.2	0	7	1.2	10	1.7
Total	82	410	19805	2565	6180	.415	340	1032	.329	1482	2089	.709	1557	646	383	1908	18	1645	20.1	1032	3355	40.9	6952	84.8
Opponent	82	410	19805	2916	6396	.456	358	1049	.341	1533	2070	.741	1244	853	461	1966	18	1902	23.2	1000	3416	41.7	7723	94.2

* indicates rookie; † indicates player played with another team in 1999-2000; bold indicates team leader

---

Did You Know?

The Bulls produced two of the NBA's eight worst shooting performances last season, a 28.6-percent effort vs. the Clippers, and a 30.4-percent showing vs. the Nuggets. On both occasions, Chicago won the game.

Cleveland Cavaliers 1999-2000 Regular Season Totals (32-50)

Player	G	GS	Min	Md	Att	Pct	Md	Att	Pct	Md	Att	Pct	TO	Stl	Blk	PF	DQ	Ast	Avg	Off	Tot	Avg	Pts	Avg
				Field Goals			**3-Pt FGs**			**Free Throws**			**Misc**			**Fouls**		**Assists**		**Rebounds**			**Points**	
Shawn Kemp	82	82	2492	484	1160	.417	2	6	.333	493	635	.776	291	100	96	371	13	138	1.7	231	725	8.8	1463	17.8
Lamond Murray	74	72	2365	460	1019	**.451**	51	139	.367	204	268	.761	184	105	36	208	2	132	1.8	127	423	5.7	1175	15.9
Bob Sura	73	45	2216	356	815	.437	122	332	.367	175	251	.697	148	91	19	201	0	284	3.9	50	288	3.9	1009	13.8
Andre Miller*	82	36	2093	339	755	.449	10	49	.204	226	292	.774	166	84	17	194	1	**476**	5.8	85	280	3.4	914	11.1
Brevin Knight	65	46	1754	230	558	.412	2	10	.200	140	184	.761	157	**107**	21	185	2	458	**7.0**	38	193	3.0	602	9.3
Wesley Person	79	38	2056	280	654	.428	106	250	**.424**	61	77	.792	60	40	19	119	1	146	1.8	44	267	3.4	727	9.2
Danny Ferry	63	3	1326	189	380	.497	33	75	.440	52	57	.912	55	22	24	181	1	67	1.1	55	238	3.8	463	7.3
Andrew DeClercq	82	31	1831	225	443	.508	0	0	—	94	160	.588	108	63	66	275	6	58	0.7	156	439	5.4	544	6.6
Mark Bryant	75	50	1712	174	346	.503	0	0	—	76	94	.809	87	31	31	250	5	61	0.8	126	352	4.7	424	5.7
Cedric Henderson	61	7	1107	129	326	.396	1	15	.067	69	104	.663	68	39	17	99	0	55	0.9	34	140	2.3	328	5.4
Earl Boykins†	25	0	253	53	112	.473	8	20	.400	18	23	.783	17	12	1	23	0	45	1.8	11	25	1.0	132	5.3
Trajan Langdon*	10	0	145	15	40	.375	8	19	.421	11	11	1.000	6	5	0	16	0	11	1.1	4	15	1.5	49	4.9
Ryan Stack	25	0	198	17	51	.333	0	1	.000	18	27	.667	17	4	11	47	3	5	0.2	15	45	1.8	52	2.1
Kornel David†	6	0	31	4	9	.444	0	0	—	3	4	.750	2	4	1	7	0	1	0.2	4	8	1.3	11	1.8
Donny Marshall	6	0	39	3	11	.273	0	3	.000	5	6	.833	3	2	0	7	0	0	0.0	0	1	0.2	11	1.8
Lari Ketner*†	16	0	91	9	22	.409	0	0	—	6	10	.600	7	3	2	12	0	0	0.0	12	27	1.7	24	1.5
M. Hendrickson†	10	0	47	5	7	.714	0	0	—	2	2	1.000	3	2	1	7	0	3	0.3	2	11	1.1	12	1.2
A.J. Bramlett*	8	0	61	4	21	.190	0	0	—	0	0	—	3	1	0	13	0	0	0.0	12	22	2.8	8	1.0
Benoit Benjamin	3	0	8	1	3	.333	0	0	—	0	0	—	0	0	1	1	0	0	0.0	0	1	0.3	2	0.7
Pete Chilcutt†	6	0	30	0	2	.000	0	0	—	0	0	—	0	0	0	3	0	1	0.2	4	9	1.5	0	0.0
Total	82	410	19855	2977	6734	.442	343	919	.373	1653	2205	.750	1427	715	363	2219	34	1941	23.7	1010	3509	42.8	7950	97.0
Opponent	82	410	19855	2983	6736	.443	420	1229	.342	1851	2385	.776	1389	659	500	2058	26	1942	23.7	1013	3599	43.9	8237	100.5

* indicates rookie; † indicates player played with another team in 1999-2000; bold indicates team leader

---

Did You Know?

Shawn Kemp's 371 personal fouls in 1999-2000 were the fourth-most in a single season in NBA history, and the most since 1983-84, when Darryl Dawkins committed an NBA-record 386 fouls.

Dallas Mavericks 1999-2000 Regular Season Totals (40-42)

Player	G	GS	Min	Field Goals			3-Pt FGs			Free Throws			Misc			Fouls		Assists		Rebounds			Points	
				Md	Att	Pct	Md	Att	Pct	Md	Att	Pct	TO	Stl	Blk	PF	DQ	Ast	Avg	Off	Tot	Avg	Pts	Avg
Michael Finley	82	82	3464	748	1636	.457	99	247	.401	260	317	.820	196	109	32	171	1	438	5.3	122	518	6.3	1855	22.6
Dirk Nowitzki	82	81	2938	515	1118	.461	116	306	.379	289	348	.830	141	63	68	256	4	203	2.5	102	532	6.5	1435	17.5
Cedric Ceballos	69	25	2064	447	1002	.446	44	134	.328	209	248	.843	125	56	24	165	3	90	1.3	172	462	6.7	1147	16.6
Gary Trent	11	11	301	70	142	.493	0	2	.000	11	21	.524	25	8	3	28	0	22	2.0	20	52	4.7	151	13.7
Erick Strickland	68	67	2025	316	730	.433	73	186	.392	162	195	.831	102	105	13	190	3	211	3.1	69	323	4.8	867	12.8
Robert Pack	29	22	665	96	230	.417	4	11	.364	63	78	.808	76	31	3	44	0	168	5.8	7	42	1.4	259	8.9
Steve Nash	56	27	1532	173	363	.477	60	149	.403	75	85	.882	102	37	3	122	1	272	4.9	34	121	2.2	481	8.6
Shawn Bradley	77	54	1901	266	555	.479	1	5	.200	114	149	.765	74	71	190	260	7	60	0.8	160	497	6.5	647	8.4
Hubert Davis	79	15	1817	217	464	.468	82	167	.491	67	77	.870	70	24	3	109	0	141	1.8	17	134	1.7	583	7.4
Greg Buckner*	48	1	923	111	233	.476	10	26	.385	43	63	.683	36	38	20	148	1	55	1.1	56	174	3.6	275	5.7
Sean Rooks	71	13	1001	122	283	.431	0	0	—	65	89	.730	70	29	52	169	0	68	1.0	82	248	3.5	309	4.4
Damon Jones†	42	0	416	55	154	.357	30	91	.330	25	39	.641	25	12	1	21	0	57	1.4	12	39	0.9	165	3.9
Rick Hughes*	21	0	224	35	72	.486	0	1	.000	12	26	.462	14	3	1	30	0	9	0.4	24	49	2.3	82	3.9
Dennis Rodman	12	12	389	12	31	.387	0	1	.000	10	14	.714	19	2	1	41	2	14	1.2	48	171	14.3	34	2.8
Bruno Sundov	14	0	61	12	31	.387	0	0	—	2	2	1.000	4	2	2	16	0	2	0.1	5	12	0.9	26	1.9
Randell Jackson	1	0	1	0	0	—	0	0	—	0	0	—	0	0	0	0	0	0	0.0	0	0	0.0	0	0.0
Rodrick Rhodes	1	0	8	0	3	.000	0	0	—	0	0	—	2	2	0	0	0	0	0.0	1	1	1.0	0	0.0
Total	82	410	19730	3195	7047	.453	519	1326	.391	1407	1751	.804	1124	592	416	1770	22	1810	22.1	931	3375	41.2	8316	101.4
Opponent	82	410	19730	3225	7053	.457	429	1244	.345	1484	2005	.740	1318	604	416	1814	12	1901	23.2	1251	3970	48.4	8363	102.0

* indicates rookie; † indicates player played with another team in 1999-2000; bold indicates team leader

Did You Know?

Michael Finley's 7,109 career points are the most among active players who have never played in a playoff game.

Denver Nuggets 1999-2000 Regular Season Totals (35-47)

Player	G	GS	Min	Field Goals			3-Pt FGs			Free Throws			Misc			Fouls		Assists		Rebounds			Points	
				Md	Att	Pct	Md	Att	Pct	Md	Att	Pct	TO	Stl	Blk	PF	DQ	Ast	Avg	Off	Tot	Avg	Pts	Avg
Antonio McDyess	81	81	2698	**614**	1211	**.507**	0	2	.000	**323**	**516**	.626	**230**	69	139	**316**	**12**	159	2.0	234	**685**	8.5	**1551**	**19.1**
Ron Mercer†	37	37	1408	272	612	.444	15	39	.385	119	151	.788	87	33	15	75	0	104	2.8	29	152	4.1	678	18.3
Nick Van Exel	79	79	**2950**	473	**1213**	.390	**133**	**401**	.332	196	240	.817	221	68	11	148	0	**714**	**9.0**	34	311	3.9	1275	16.1
Raef LaFrentz	81	80	2435	392	879	.446	60	183	.328	162	236	.686	96	42	**180**	292	6	97	1.2	170	641	7.9	1006	12.4
Chris Gatling†	40	0	770	155	340	.456	11	47	.234	95	128	.742	64	34	13	104	2	31	0.8	63	205	5.1	416	10.4
George McCloud	78	11	2118	266	638	.417	107	283	**.378**	148	181	**.818**	134	48	26	180	2	246	3.2	72	285	3.7	787	10.1
T. Abdul-Wahad†	15	10	373	51	131	.389	1	2	.500	31	42	.738	19	6	12	31	0	26	1.7	24	52	3.5	134	8.9
Chauncey Billups	13	5	305	34	101	.337	7	41	.171	37	44	.841	24	10	2	27	0	39	3.0	8	34	2.6	112	8.6
Keon Clark	81	20	1850	286	528	.542	1	8	.125	121	176	.688	125	45	114	231	1	71	0.9	162	505	6.2	694	8.6
James Posey*	81	77	2052	230	536	.429	82	220	.373	120	150	.800	95	**98**	33	207	1	146	1.8	85	317	3.9	662	8.2
Bryant Stith	45	6	691	86	189	.455	17	56	.304	64	77	.831	33	18	12	56	0	61	1.4	23	84	1.9	253	5.6
Chris Herren*	45	1	597	45	124	.363	24	67	.358	27	40	.675	42	15	2	74	0	111	2.5	12	52	1.2	141	3.1
Cory Alexander	29	2	329	28	98	.286	9	35	.257	17	22	.773	28	24	2	39	0	58	2.0	8	42	1.4	82	2.8
Popeye Jones	40	1	330	44	104	.423	2	3	.667	14	19	.737	13	3	6	50	1	19	0.5	41	103	2.6	104	2.6
Ryan Bowen*	52	0	589	46	117	.393	1	9	.111	38	53	.717	14	39	13	95	0	20	0.4	75	114	2.2	131	2.5
Roy Rogers	40	0	355	35	88	.398	0	1	.000	19	41	.463	10	2	38	36	0	9	0.2	33	80	2.0	89	2.2
Johnny Taylor†	1	0	5	0	2	.000	0	0	—	0	0	—	0	0	0	1	0	0	0.0	0	1	1.0	0	0.0
Total	82	410	19855	3057	6911	.442	470	1397	.336	1531	2116	.724	1281	554	618	1962	25	1911	23.3	1073	3663	44.7	8115	99.0
Opponent	82	410	19855	3129	6953	.450	399	1126	.354	1632	2174	.751	1179	616	462	1937	22	2003	24.4	1027	3633	44.3	8289	101.1

* indicates rookie; † indicates player played with another team in 1999-2000; bold indicates team leader

Did You Know?

Last season the Nuggets became the first team since the 1983-84 Philadelphia 76ers to lead the NBA in blocked shots despite not using a single player 7'0" or taller.

Detroit Pistons 1999-2000 Regular Season Totals (42-40)

Player	G	GS	Min	Field Goals			3-Pt FGs			Free Throws			Misc			Fouls		Assists		Rebounds			Points	
				Md	Att	Pct	Md	Att	Pct	Md	Att	Pct	TO	Stl	Blk	PF	DQ	Ast	Avg	Off	Tot	Avg	Pts	Avg
Grant Hill	74	74	2776	**696**	1422	**.489**	34	98	.347	480	604	.795	240	103	43	190	0	**385**	**5.2**	97	490	6.6	1906	**25.8**
Jerry Stackhouse	82	82	3148	619	**1447**	.428	83	288	.288	618	758	.815	**311**	103	36	188	1	365	4.5	118	315	3.8	**1939**	23.6
Lindsey Hunter	82	82	2919	379	892	.425	**168**	389	**.432**	117	154	.760	145	**129**	22	216	2	327	4.0	35	250	3.0	1043	12.7
Christian Laettner	82	82	2443	379	801	.473	7	24	.292	237	292	.812	186	83	**45**	**326**	**10**	186	2.3	175	553	6.7	1002	12.2
Jerome Williams	82	1	2102	257	456	.564	0	3	.000	175	284	.616	105	95	21	196	0	68	0.8	**277**	**789**	**9.6**	689	8.4
Mikki Moore	29	0	488	87	140	.621	0	0	—	54	68	.794	23	9	31	104	5	17	0.6	44	112	3.9	228	7.9
Terry Mills	82	78	1842	214	488	.439	95	242	.393	25	34	.735	46	38	24	242	4	85	1.0	50	390	4.8	548	6.7
Michael Curry	82	3	1611	182	379	.480	1	5	.200	141	168	**.839**	73	33	5	209	3	87	1.1	21	104	1.3	506	6.2
John Crotty	69	0	937	106	251	.422	33	80	.413	80	93	.860	54	27	5	104	0	128	1.9	17	75	1.1	325	4.7
Jud Buechler	58	5	657	55	156	.353	18	83	.217	2	7	.286	13	25	16	50	1	33	0.6	30	91	1.6	130	2.2
Loy Vaught	43	0	292	32	89	.360	0	3	.000	11	16	.688	11	6	4	45	0	11	0.3	26	91	2.1	75	1.7
Don Reid†	21	3	165	16	34	.471	0	0	—	3	6	.500	11	5	12	45	1	1	0.0	5	25	1.2	35	1.7
Marcus Brown	6	0	45	4	14	.286	0	7	.000	2	2	1.000	3	0	0	8	0	3	0.5	3	7	1.2	10	1.7
J. Jackson*	7	0	73	1	11	.091	0	1	.000	5	8	.625	7	3	0	7	0	4	0.6	1	11	1.6	7	1.0
Eric Montross	51	0	332	17	55	.309	0	0	—	6	12	.500	22	6	9	81	0	7	0.1	18	72	1.4	40	0.8
Total	82	410	19830	3044	6635	.459	439	1223	.359	1956	2506	.781	1288	665	273	2011	27	1707	20.8	917	3375	41.2	8483	103.5
Opponent	82	410	19830	3119	6706	.465	458	1234	.371	1669	2237	.746	1400	652	396	2219	33	1893	23.1	973	3477	42.4	8365	102.0

* indicates rookie; † indicates player played with another team in 1999-2000; bold indicates team leader

Detroit Pistons 1999-2000 Postseason Totals (0-3)

Player	G	GS	Min	Field Goals			3-Pt FGs			Free Throws			Misc			Fouls		Assists		Rebounds			Points	
				Md	Att	Pct	Md	Att	Pct	Md	Att	Pct	TO	Stl	Blk	PF	DQ	Ast	Avg	Off	Tot	Avg	Pts	Avg
Jerry Stackhouse	3	3	120	24	59	.407	3	7	.429	23	31	.742	14	2	0	4	0	10	3.3	1	12	4.0	74	24.7
Grant Hill	2	2	55	6	16	.375	1	2	.500	9	10	.900	10	1	0	7	0	9	4.5	0	11	5.5	22	11.0
Michael Curry	3	1	79	12	23	**.522**	0	0	—	4	6	.667	2	1	0	5	0	3	1.0	0	3	1.0	28	9.3
Lindsey Hunter	3	3	93	10	32	.313	1	9	.111	4	6	.667	5	5	1	4	0	5	1.7	0	7	2.3	25	8.3
Terry Mills	3	3	77	9	15	.600	6	9	.667	1	2	.500	2	2	0	12	1	1	0.3	0	6	2.0	25	8.3
Christian Laettner	3	3	75	7	17	.412	0	0	—	6	8	.750	3	0	1	14	0	6	2.0	2	15	5.0	20	6.7
Mikki Moore	3	0	42	5	12	.417	0	0	—	8	8	**1.000**	4	1	0	9	0	3	1.0	7	12	4.0	18	6.0
Jerome Williams	3	0	73	7	14	.500	0	0	—	1	8	.125	3	3	0	8	0	2	0.7	7	**21**	**7.0**	15	5.0
Jud Buechler	3	0	34	2	7	.286	2	5	.400	0	0	—	0	0	1	4	0	1	0.3	0	4	1.3	6	2.0
John Crotty	3	0	51	2	10	.200	0	3	.000	2	2	1.000	4	1	1	4	0	4	1.3	0	4	1.3	6	2.0
Eric Montross	2	0	5	0	0	—	0	0	—	0	0	—	0	0	0	2	0	0	0.0	0	2	1.0	0	0.0
Loy Vaught	2	0	16	0	3	.000	0	0	—	0	0	—	1	2	0	1	0	0	0.0	1	6	3.0	0	0.0
Total	3	15	720	84	208	.404	13	35	.371	58	81	.716	51	18	5	74	1	44	14.7	18	103	34.3	239	79.7
Opponent	3	15	720	103	215	.479	14	34	.412	50	73	.685	52	28	22	90	2	64	21.3	25	124	41.3	270	90.0

Did You Know?

The Pistons increased their scoring average by an NBA-high 13.1 points per game from 1998-99 to 1999-2000. Detroit scored 90.4 points per game two seasons ago, 103.5 last year.

Golden State Warriors 1999-2000 Regular Season Totals (19-63)

Player	G	GS	Min	Field Goals Md	Att	Pct	3-Pt FGs Md	Att	Pct	Free Throws Md	Att	Pct	Misc TO	Stl	Blk	Fouls PF	DQ	Assists Ast	Avg	Rebounds Off	Tot	Avg	Points Pts	Avg
Larry Hughes†	32	32	1306	267	686	.389	18	74	.243	173	235	.736	100	61	16	97	2	130	4.1	61	190	5.9	725	22.7
Antawn Jamison	43	41	1556	**356**	756	.471	2	7	.286	127	208	.611	113	30	15	115	0	90	2.1	172	359	8.3	841	19.6
Chris Mills	20	11	649	123	292	.421	8	30	.267	68	84	.810	25	18	4	60	0	47	2.4	46	123	6.2	322	16.1
John Starks†	33	30	1108	192	508	.378	56	161	**.348**	45	54	.833	64	37	3	93	1	170	5.2	10	91	2.8	485	14.7
Donyell Marshall	64	51	2071	331	**840**	.394	49	138	.355	199	255	**.780**	123	68	68	180	1	167	2.6	**189**	**637**	10.0	**910**	14.2
Jason Caffey	71	56	2159	323	675	**.479**	0	2	.000	**206**	**345**	.597	**170**	62	20	**269**	11	119	1.7	**189**	482	6.8	852	**12.0**
Mookie Blaylock	73	**72**	**2459**	327	837	.391	**101**	**301**	.336	67	95	.705	143	**146**	22	122	0	**489**	**6.7**	55	270	3.7	822	11.3
V. Cummings*	75	11	1793	265	655	.405	49	151	.325	127	169	.751	132	91	13	174	4	247	3.3	57	184	2.5	706	9.4
Terry Cummings	22	0	398	76	177	.429	0	0	—	32	39	.821	27	13	8	74	0	21	1.0	45	107	4.9	184	8.4
Erick Dampier	21	12	495	70	173	.405	0	0	—	27	51	.529	29	8	15	75	1	19	0.9	48	134	6.4	167	8.0
Billy Owens†	16	4	386	38	100	.380	2	7	.286	25	42	.595	24	7	5	47	0	38	2.4	36	109	6.8	103	6.4
Tony Farmer	74	9	1199	127	312	.407	8	44	.182	203	265	.766	82	66	16	167	1	74	1.0	118	295	4.0	465	6.3
Mark Davis	23	7	464	56	137	.409	0	2	.000	31	47	.660	40	25	4	52	0	38	1.7	31	84	3.7	143	6.2
Chris Carr†	7	0	74	11	33	.333	1	8	.125	16	19	.842	5	0	1	12	0	3	0.4	5	13	1.9	39	5.6
Adonal Foyle	**76**	59	1654	193	380	.508	0	0	—	34	90	.378	71	26	**136**	218	2	42	0.6	174	424	5.6	420	5.5
Damon Jones†	13	1	196	25	54	.463	11	23	.478	7	9	.778	15	6	0	13	0	39	3.0	0	16	1.2	68	5.2
Sam Jacobson†	49	5	663	103	203	.507	9	24	.375	30	39	.769	31	29	3	112	3	30	0.6	25	70	1.4	245	5.0
Sam Mack	23	5	333	37	122	.303	21	64	.328	19	20	.950	19	18	1	45	0	24	1.0	7	39	1.7	114	5.0
Tim Legler	23	4	284	28	78	.359	7	21	.333	14	18	.778	6	4	1	33	0	24	1.0	4	23	1.0	77	3.3
Drew Barry†	8	0	85	9	18	.500	3	9	.333	1	2	.500	6	2	0	14	0	17	2.1	0	8	1.0	22	2.8
Bill Curley†	24	0	259	23	57	.404	0	1	.000	18	25	.720	17	11	4	51	1	14	0.6	14	42	1.8	64	2.7
Tim Young*	25	0	137	13	39	.333	0	0	—	28	36	.778	9	2	1	18	0	5	0.2	13	35	1.4	54	2.2
Jamel Thomas*†	4	0	27	3	8	.375	0	2	.000	0	0	—	4	1	0	2	0	4	1.0	1	3	0.8	6	1.5
Total	82	410	19755	2996	7140	.420	345	1069	.323	1497	2147	.697	1302	731	356	2043	27	1851	22.6	1300	3738	45.6	7834	95.5
Opponent	82	410	19755	3165	6776	.467	427	1163	.367	1755	2328	.754	1339	690	495	1887	18	2036	24.8	1091	3782	46.1	8512	103.8

* indicates rookie; † indicates player played with another team in 1999-2000; bold indicates team leader

---

Did You Know?

The Warriors' Donyell Marshall shot .402 on two-point field goals last season, the lowest percentage in the league (minimum 500 two-point attempts). Teammate Mookie Blaylock had the league's third-lowest overall field goal percentage among qualifiers, .391.

Houston Rockets 1999-2000 Regular Season Totals (34-48)

Player	G	GS	Min	Field Goals			3-Pt FGs			Free Throws			Misc			Fouls		Assists		Rebounds			Points	
				Md	Att	Pct	Md	Att	Pct	Md	Att	Pct	TO	Stl	Blk	PF	DQ	Ast	Avg	Off	Tot	Avg	Pts	Avg
Steve Francis*	77	77	**2776**	497	1117	.445	**107**	310	.345	287	365	.786	**306**	**118**	29	231	2	**507**	**6.6**	**152**	409	5.3	**1388**	**18.0**
Cuttino Mobley	81	8	2496	437	1016	.430	104	292	.356	**299**	353	**.847**	186	87	32	171	0	208	2.6	59	288	3.6	1277	15.8
Charles Barkley	20	18	620	106	222	.477	6	26	.231	71	110	.645	44	14	4	48	0	63	3.2	71	209	10.5	289	14.5
S. Anderson	**82**	**82**	2700	368	778	**.473**	79	225	.351	194	253	.767	194	96	32	182	0	239	2.9	91	384	4.7	1009	12.3
Walt Williams	76	66	1859	312	681	.458	102	261	.391	101	123	.821	73	49	44	190	2	157	2.1	69	306	4.0	827	10.9
Hakeem Olajuwon	44	28	1049	193	421	.458	0	2	.000	69	112	.616	71	33	**124**	88	1	26	0.6	65	274	6.2	455	10.3
Kelvin Cato	65	32	1581	216	402	.537	0	4	.000	135	208	.649	112	54	22	175	0	61	0.9	102	389	6.0	567	8.7
Kenny Thomas*	72	29	1797	212	531	.399	32	122	.262	138	209	.660	63	14	34	167	0	113	1.6	147	**437**	**6.1**	594	8.3
Carlos Rogers	53	15	1101	170	324	.525	1	14	.071	81	137	.591	81	14	34	77	0	42	0.8	98	275	5.2	422	8.0
Moochie Norris	30	0	502	69	159	.434	12	29	.414	57	73	.781	30	23	1	32	0	94	3.1	16	68	2.3	207	6.9
Matt Bullard	56	27	1024	139	340	.409	79	177	**.446**	25	30	.833	36	19	13	85	0	63	1.1	13	138	2.5	382	6.8
Bryce Drew	72	5	1293	158	413	.383	59	163	.362	45	53	.849	66	41	1	79	0	162	2.3	23	103	1.4	420	5.8
Tony Massenburg	10	0	109	16	36	.444	0	0	—	14	16	.875	9	2	5	13	0	3	0.3	7	27	2.7	46	4.6
Thomas Hamilton	22	7	273	35	79	.443	0	0	—	12	23	.522	28	11	14	25	0	15	0.7	31	90	4.1	82	3.7
Anthony Miller	35	14	476	52	97	.536	0	0	—	26	51	.510	19	2	10	68	1	16	0.5	49	164	4.7	130	3.7
Bill Curley†	4	0	50	6	11	.545	0	0	—	0	0	—	4	5	0	10	1	0	0.0	4	8	2.0	12	3.0
Devin Gray	21	2	124	15	37	.405	0	0	—	19	29	.655	19	5	3	22	0	5	0.2	11	25	1.2	49	2.3
Total	82	410	19830	3001	6664	.450	581	1625	.358	1573	2145	.733	1425	613	438	1663	7	1774	21.6	1008	3594	43.8	8156	99.5
Opponent	82	410	19830	3226	7074	.456	350	990	.354	1425	1829	.779	1126	735	433	1833	17	1863	22.7	1027	3478	42.4	8227	100.3

* indicates rookie; † indicates player played with another team in 1999-2000; bold indicates team leader

---

Did You Know?

Last season the Rockets scored an NBA-high 21.4 percent of their points on three-point field goals.

Indiana Pacers 1999-2000 Regular Season Totals (56-26)

Player	G	GS	Min	Field Goals Md	Att	Pct	3-Pt FGs Md	Att	Pct	Free Throws Md	Att	Pct	Misc TO	Stl	Blk	Fouls PF	DQ	Assists Ast	Avg	Rebounds Off	Tot	Avg	Points Pts	Avg
Jalen Rose	80	80	2978	563	1196	.471	77	196	.393	254	307	.827	188	84	49	234	1	320	4.0	42	387	4.8	1457	18.2
Reggie Miller	81	81	2987	466	1041	.448	165	404	.408	373	406	.919	129	85	25	126	0	187	2.3	50	239	3.0	1470	18.1
Rik Smits	79	79	1852	431	890	.484	0	1	.000	156	211	.739	108	20	100	249	1	85	1.1	94	401	5.1	1018	12.9
Austin Croshere	81	14	1885	288	653	.441	63	174	.362	196	231	.848	121	44	60	203	2	89	1.1	135	516	6.4	835	10.3
Dale Davis	74	72	2127	302	602	.502	0	0	—	139	203	.685	91	52	94	203	1	64	0.9	256	729	9.9	743	10.0
Travis Best	82	0	1691	271	561	.483	35	93	.376	156	190	.821	107	76	5	204	1	272	3.3	16	142	1.7	733	8.9
Mark Jackson	81	81	2190	246	570	.432	89	221	.403	79	98	.806	174	76	10	111	0	650	8.0	63	296	3.7	660	8.1
Sam Perkins	81	0	1620	184	441	.417	89	218	.408	80	97	.825	63	31	33	136	0	68	0.8	64	289	3.6	537	6.6
Al Harrington	50	0	854	121	264	.458	8	34	.235	78	111	.703	65	25	9	130	0	38	0.8	47	159	3.2	328	6.6
Chris Mullin	47	2	582	80	187	.428	45	110	.409	37	41	.902	28	28	9	60	0	37	0.8	14	76	1.6	242	5.1
Derrick McKey	32	0	634	43	108	.398	10	23	.435	43	56	.768	19	29	13	81	0	35	1.1	29	135	4.2	139	4.3
Jonathan Bender*	24	1	130	23	70	.329	2	12	.167	16	24	.667	7	1	5	18	0	3	0.1	4	21	0.9	64	2.7
Jeff Foster*	19	0	86	13	23	.565	0	1	.000	17	25	.680	2	5	1	18	0	5	0.3	12	32	1.7	43	2.3
Zan Tabak	18	0	114	16	34	.471	0	0	—	5	8	.625	11	3	9	13	0	4	0.2	16	32	1.8	37	2.1
Total	82	410	19730	3047	6640	.459	583	1487	.392	1629	2008	.811	1159	559	422	1786	6	1857	22.6	842	3454	42.1	8306	101.3
Opponent	82	410	19730	3113	6982	.446	329	1006	.327	1374	1821	.755	1126	610	323	1910	18	1735	21.2	1040	3585	43.7	7929	96.7

* indicates rookie; † indicates player played with another team in 1999-2000; bold indicates team leader

Indiana Pacers 1999-2000 Postseason Totals (13-10)

Player	G	GS	Min	Field Goals Md	Att	Pct	3-Pt FGs Md	Att	Pct	Free Throws Md	Att	Pct	Misc TO	Stl	Blk	Fouls PF	DQ	Assists Ast	Avg	Rebounds Off	Tot	Avg	Points Pts	Avg
Reggie Miller	22	22	892	174	385	.452	58	147	.395	121	129	.938	28	23	10	37	0	60	2.7	9	53	2.4	527	24.0
Jalen Rose	23	23	964	171	391	.437	30	70	.429	107	133	.805	50	16	11	71	0	78	3.4	10	101	4.4	479	20.8
Rik Smits	22	21	461	103	207	.498	0	1	.000	35	40	.875	27	10	20	84	1	21	1.0	24	78	3.5	241	11.0
Austin Croshere	23	2	490	64	153	.418	15	37	.405	73	87	.839	25	9	16	51	1	19	0.8	31	109	4.7	216	11.0
Travis Best	23	0	463	77	179	.430	13	30	.433	37	44	.841	25	19	4	61	1	66	2.9	15	57	2.5	204	8.9
Dale Davis	23	23	714	79	151	.523	0	0	—	32	59	.542	18	11	31	83	4	17	0.7	83	263	11.4	190	8.3
Mark Jackson	23	23	634	69	176	.392	21	67	.313	28	31	.903	43	19	2	42	0	178	7.7	12	86	3.7	187	8.1
Sam Perkins	23	0	417	34	105	.324	23	66	.348	19	21	.905	8	4	6	45	1	10	0.4	17	73	3.2	110	4.8
Chris Mullin	9	1	90	10	21	.476	2	8	.250	9	11	.818	4	6	1	7	0	5	0.6	2	14	1.6	31	3.4
Derrick McKey	23	0	352	15	32	.469	1	6	.167	16	20	.800	19	7	4	45	0	14	0.6	25	79	3.4	47	2.0
Jonathan Bender	9	0	21	4	6	.667	1	1	1.000	3	6	.500	0	1	0	2	0	0	0.0	0	3	0.3	12	1.3
Zan Tabak	10	0	47	4	8	.500	0	0	—	4	4	1.000	1	0	2	10	0	0	0.0	4	16	1.6	12	1.2
Total	23	115	5545	804	1814	.443	164	433	.379	484	585	.827	267	125	107	538	7	468	20.3	232	932	40.5	2256	98.1
Opponent	23	115	5545	844	1857	.454	98	283	.346	409	594	.689	266	142	102	550	6	452	19.7	259	950	41.3	2195	95.4

Did You Know?

Over the last four seasons Mark Jackson has recorded 2,684 assists and 2,523 points. He is the only player who has played at least 20 games over that span to have more assists than points.

Los Angeles Clippers 1999-2000 Regular Season Totals (15-67)

Player	G	GS	Min	Field Goals			3-Pt FGs			Free Throws			Misc			Fouls		Assists		Rebounds			Points	
				Md	Att	Pct	Md	Att	Pct	Md	Att	Pct	TO	Stl	Blk	PF	DQ	Ast	Avg	Off	Tot	Avg	Pts	Avg
Maurice Taylor	62	60	2227	458	988	.464	1	8	.125	143	201	.711	169	51	48	217	4	101	1.6	96	400	6.5	1060	17.1
Derek Anderson	64	58	2201	377	860	.438	55	178	.309	271	309	.877	167	90	11	149	2	220	3.4	80	258	4.0	1080	16.9
Lamar Odom*	76	70	2767	449	1024	.438	59	164	.360	302	420	.719	258	91	95	291	13	317	4.2	159	595	7.8	1259	16.6
Tyrone Nesby	73	39	2317	364	915	.398	94	281	.335	151	191	.791	102	75	31	205	5	121	1.7	82	275	3.8	973	13.3
M. Olowokandi	80	77	2493	330	756	.437	0	0	—	123	189	.651	177	35	140	304	10	38	0.5	194	656	8.2	783	9.8
Troy Hudson	62	38	1592	204	541	.377	60	193	.311	77	95	.811	108	43	0	65	0	242	3.9	28	148	2.4	545	8.8
Eric Piatkowski	75	23	1712	238	573	.415	93	243	.383	85	100	.850	57	44	13	140	0	81	1.1	74	222	3.0	654	8.7
Jeff McInnis	25	10	597	80	186	.430	7	21	.333	13	17	.765	27	15	2	55	0	89	3.6	18	72	2.9	180	7.2
Eric Murdock	40	15	693	79	205	.385	16	42	.381	51	80	.638	58	47	5	67	0	108	2.7	15	77	1.9	225	5.6
Brian Skinner	33	9	775	68	134	.507	0	0	—	43	65	.662	37	16	44	75	0	11	0.3	63	201	6.1	179	5.4
Keith Closs	57	6	820	96	197	.487	0	3	.000	46	78	.590	34	13	73	80	0	25	0.4	65	179	3.1	238	4.2
Charles Jones	56	0	662	66	201	.328	39	118	.331	17	23	.739	28	30	5	46	0	94	1.7	17	62	1.1	188	3.4
Pete Chilcutt†	24	2	347	31	63	.492	5	16	.313	6	6	1.000	11	10	6	39	2	16	0.7	27	79	3.3	73	3.0
E. Bohannon†	11	0	113	7	13	.538	0	0	—	12	20	.600	8	2	6	24	0	5	0.5	12	30	2.7	26	2.4
Anthony Avent	49	3	377	29	96	.302	0	0	—	23	32	.719	24	16	15	62	1	11	0.2	23	74	1.5	81	1.7
Marty Conlon	3	0	9	1	2	.500	0	0	—	0	0	—	0	0	0	1	0	0	0.0	1	2	0.7	2	0.7
Mario Bennett	1	0	3	0	3	.000	0	0	—	0	0	—	0	0	0	1	0	0	0.0	1	2	2.0	0	0.0
Total	82	410	19705	2877	6757	.426	429	1267	.339	1363	1826	.746	1325	578	494	1821	37	1479	18.0	955	3332	40.6	7546	92.0
Opponent	82	410	19705	3281	6879	.477	417	1077	.387	1512	2041	.741	1172	621	377	1731	8	1975	24.1	1038	3737	45.6	8491	103.5

* indicates rookie; † indicates player played with another team in 1999-2000; bold indicates team leader

Did You Know?

Of the 20 players drafted either first or second overall in the 1990s, Michael Olowokandi is the only one with a career scoring average under 10 points per game. Olowokandi is averaging 9.5 points per game.

Los Angeles Lakers 1999-2000 Regular Season Totals (67-15)

Player	G	GS	Min	Field Goals			3-Pt FGs			Free Throws			Misc			Fouls		Assists		Rebounds			Points	
				Md	Att	Pct	Md	Att	Pct	Md	Att	Pct	TO	Stl	Blk	PF	DQ	Ast	Avg	Off	Tot	Avg	Pts	Avg
Shaquille O'Neal	79	79	3163	956	1665	.574	0	1	.000	432	824	.524	223	36	239	255	2	299	3.8	336	1078	13.6	2344	29.7
Kobe Bryant	66	62	2524	554	1183	.468	46	144	.319	331	403	.821	182	106	62	220	4	323	4.9	108	416	6.3	1485	22.5
Glen Rice	80	80	2530	421	980	.430	84	229	.367	346	396	.874	114	47	12	179	0	176	2.2	56	327	4.1	1272	15.9
Ron Harper	80	78	2042	212	531	.399	33	106	.311	100	147	.680	132	85	39	164	0	270	3.4	96	337	4.2	557	7.0
Rick Fox	82	1	1473	206	498	.414	59	181	.326	63	78	.808	87	52	26	203	1	138	1.7	63	198	2.4	534	6.5
Derek Fisher	78	22	1803	167	483	.346	52	166	.313	105	145	.724	75	80	3	150	1	216	2.8	22	143	1.8	491	6.3
Tyronn Lue	8	0	146	19	39	.487	4	8	.500	6	8	.750	9	3	0	17	0	17	2.1	2	12	1.5	48	6.0
Robert Horry	76	0	1685	159	363	.438	29	94	.309	89	113	.788	73	84	80	189	0	118	1.6	133	361	4.8	436	5.7
A.C. Green	82	82	1929	173	387	.447	1	4	.250	66	95	.695	53	53	18	127	0	80	1.0	160	486	5.9	413	5.0
Brian Shaw	74	2	1249	123	322	.382	18	58	.310	41	54	.759	75	35	14	105	0	201	2.7	45	216	2.9	305	4.1
Sam Jacobson†	3	0	18	5	9	.556	0	0	—	0	2	.000	2	1	0	1	0	2	0.7	0	1	0.3	10	3.3
Devean George*	49	1	345	56	144	.389	16	47	.340	27	41	.659	21	10	4	54	0	12	0.2	29	75	1.5	155	3.2
John Celestand*	16	0	185	15	45	.333	2	9	.222	5	6	.833	16	7	0	22	0	20	1.3	1	11	0.7	37	2.3
Travis Knight	63	0	410	46	118	.390	0	0	—	17	28	.607	26	6	23	88	1	23	0.4	46	129	2.0	109	1.7
John Salley	45	3	303	25	69	.362	0	0	—	21	28	.750	18	8	14	67	1	26	0.6	20	65	1.4	71	1.6
Total	82	410	19805	3137	6836	.459	344	1047	.329	1649	2368	.696	1143	613	534	1841	10	1921	23.4	1117	3855	47.0	8267	100.8
Opponent	82	410	19805	2838	6824	.416	372	1142	.326	1518	2045	.742	1196	627	345	2099	42	1597	19.5	1007	3538	43.1	7566	92.3

* indicates rookie; † indicates player played with another team in 1999-2000; bold indicates team leader

Los Angeles Lakers 1999-2000 Postseason Totals (15-8)

Player	G	GS	Min	Field Goals			3-Pt FGs			Free Throws			Misc			Fouls		Assists		Rebounds			Points	
				Md	Att	Pct	Md	Att	Pct	Md	Att	Pct	TO	Stl	Blk	PF	DQ	Ast	Avg	Off	Tot	Avg	Pts	Avg
Shaquille O'Neal	23	23	1000	286	505	.566	0	0	—	135	296	.456	56	13	55	67	1	71	3.1	119	355	15.4	707	30.7
Kobe Bryant	22	22	857	174	394	.442	22	64	.344	95	126	.754	55	32	32	89	1	97	4.4	26	98	4.5	465	21.1
Glen Rice	23	23	766	93	228	.408	28	67	.418	71	89	.798	36	15	4	50	0	48	2.1	10	92	4.0	285	12.4
Ron Harper	23	23	643	78	181	.431	9	39	.231	33	47	.702	28	23	13	63	0	73	3.2	30	85	3.7	198	8.6
Robert Horry	23	0	618	59	145	.407	17	59	.288	40	57	.702	30	20	19	88	3	58	2.5	38	123	5.3	175	7.6
Brian Shaw	22	1	408	45	107	.421	16	48	.333	13	16	.813	17	11	4	46	1	67	3.0	7	51	2.3	119	5.4
Derek Fisher	21	0	322	34	79	.430	12	29	.414	19	25	.760	9	11	1	30	0	41	2.0	4	22	1.0	99	4.7
Rick Fox	23	0	331	33	73	.452	18	39	.462	16	21	.762	16	9	0	68	1	28	1.2	11	38	1.7	100	4.3
A.C. Green	23	23	429	37	90	.411	0	0	—	16	23	.696	9	14	3	44	0	13	0.6	43	96	4.2	90	3.9
Devean George	9	0	45	7	19	.368	2	10	.200	6	11	.545	3	1	0	5	0	2	0.2	4	10	1.1	22	2.4
Travis Knight	14	0	48	8	15	.533	0	0	—	2	6	.333	6	1	3	16	0	0	0.0	3	5	0.4	18	1.3
John Salley	18	0	78	5	13	.385	0	0	—	7	10	.700	4	1	6	16	0	4	0.2	9	22	1.2	17	0.9
Total	23	115	5545	859	1849	.465	124	355	.349	453	727	.623	280	151	140	582	7	502	21.8	304	997	43.3	2295	99.8
Opponent	23	115	5545	786	1804	.436	147	398	.369	522	667	.783	290	157	86	611	13	437	19.0	247	937	40.7	2241	97.4

Did You Know?

Shaquille O'Neal's 61 points against the Clippers on March 6, 2000 were the most ever by an NBA player on his birthday.

Miami Heat 1999-2000 Regular Season Totals (52-30)

Player	G	GS	Min	Field Goals Md	Att	Pct	3-Pt FGs Md	Att	Pct	Free Throws Md	Att	Pct	Misc TO	Stl	Blk	Fouls PF	DQ	Assists Ast	Avg	Rebounds Off	Tot	Avg	Points Pts	Avg
Alonzo Mourning	79	78	2748	652	1184	.551	0	4	.000	414	582	.711	217	40	294	308	8	123	1.6	215	753	9.5	1718	21.7
Jamal Mashburn	76	76	2828	515	1158	.445	112	278	.403	186	239	.778	180	79	14	215	3	298	3.9	64	381	5.0	1328	17.5
Tim Hardaway	52	52	1672	246	638	.386	94	256	.367	110	133	.827	119	49	4	112	0	385	7.4	25	150	2.9	696	13.4
Voshon Lenard	53	13	1434	228	560	.407	89	228	.390	84	106	.792	80	41	15	127	2	136	2.6	37	153	2.9	629	11.9
P.J. Brown	80	80	2302	322	671	.480	0	1	.000	120	159	.755	100	65	61	264	4	145	1.8	216	600	7.5	764	9.6
Dan Majerle	69	69	2308	170	422	.403	110	304	.362	56	69	.812	62	89	17	156	1	206	3.0	27	333	4.8	506	7.3
C. Weatherspoon	78	2	1615	215	419	.513	0	0	—	135	183	.738	100	51	49	165	1	93	1.2	128	449	5.8	565	7.2
Anthony Carter*	79	30	1859	201	509	.395	3	23	.130	93	124	.750	173	93	5	167	0	378	4.8	48	199	2.5	498	6.3
Otis Thorpe	51	1	777	125	243	.514	0	3	.000	29	48	.604	59	26	9	136	4	33	0.6	56	166	3.3	279	5.5
Bruce Bowen†	27	2	567	46	121	.380	26	56	.464	19	31	.613	14	14	10	81	0	18	0.7	13	60	2.2	137	5.1
Mark Strickland	58	5	663	122	224	.545	0	0	—	40	56	.714	24	15	18	68	0	22	0.4	44	140	2.4	284	4.9
Rodney Buford*	34	0	386	62	151	.411	7	29	.241	16	22	.727	9	10	8	44	0	21	0.6	10	48	1.4	147	4.3
Rex Walters	33	0	389	38	91	.418	5	20	.250	12	16	.750	29	6	0	44	0	65	2.0	8	36	1.1	93	2.8
Tim James*	4	0	23	5	14	.357	0	0	—	1	3	.333	2	0	3	1	0	2	0.5	3	4	1.0	11	2.8
Duane Causwell	25	2	185	20	37	.541	0	0	—	26	38	.684	10	2	16	42	0	2	0.1	11	47	1.9	66	2.6
Harold Jamison*	12	0	74	7	20	.350	0	0	—	4	18	.222	4	2	1	17	0	4	0.3	16	21	1.8	18	1.5
Total	82	410	19830	2974	6462	.460	446	1202	.371	1345	1827	.736	1231	582	524	1947	23	1931	23.5	921	3540	43.2	7739	94.4
Opponent	82	410	19830	2782	6595	.422	408	1130	.361	1512	2022	.748	1150	621	364	1795	12	1582	19.3	974	3315	40.4	7484	91.3

* indicates rookie; † indicates team played with another team in 1999-2000; bold indicates team leader

Miami Heat 1999-2000 Postseason Totals (6-4)

Player	G	GS	Min	Field Goals Md	Att	Pct	3-Pt FGs Md	Att	Pct	Free Throws Md	Att	Pct	Misc TO	Stl	Blk	Fouls PF	DQ	Assists Ast	Avg	Rebounds Off	Tot	Avg	Points Pts	Avg
Alonzo Mourning	10	10	376	76	157	.484	0	1	.000	64	96	.667	24	2	33	40	1	14	1.4	31	100	10.0	216	21.6
Jamal Mashburn	10	10	423	63	157	.401	13	33	.394	36	42	.857	24	11	2	30	0	32	3.2	9	46	4.6	175	17.5
Rodney Buford	1	0	16	4	8	.500	1	2	.500	2	2	1.000	0	0	0	3	0	1	1.0	0	1	1.0	11	11.0
Dan Majerle	10	10	372	30	71	.423	20	50	.400	10	14	.714	11	21	1	34	0	32	3.2	5	70	7.0	90	9.0
Tim Hardaway	7	7	182	20	68	.294	7	34	.206	7	10	.700	11	5	0	10	0	33	4.7	1	15	2.1	54	7.7
Anthony Carter	10	3	275	32	77	.416	1	6	.167	12	16	.750	24	12	2	23	0	56	5.6	8	40	4.0	77	7.7
P.J. Brown	10	10	308	35	82	.427	0	0	—	5	6	.833	11	8	4	42	3	11	1.1	26	82	8.2	75	7.5
C. Weatherspoon	10	0	170	25	60	.417	0	0	—	14	24	.583	8	4	3	23	0	1	0.1	18	41	4.1	64	6.4
Bruce Bowen	10	0	157	10	27	.370	5	22	.227	10	16	.625	6	7	4	27	1	8	0.8	1	10	1.0	35	3.5
Otis Thorpe	10	0	136	13	27	.481	0	1	.000	7	14	.500	11	0	2	29	0	3	0.3	6	29	2.9	33	3.3
Mark Strickland	1	0	10	1	3	.333	0	0	—	0	2	.000	1	2	0	0	0	0	0.0	0	0	0.0	2	2.0
Total	10	50	2425	309	737	.419	47	149	.315	167	242	.690	140	72	51	261	5	191	19.1	105	434	43.4	832	83.2
Opponent	10	50	2425	288	713	.404	39	114	.342	192	251	.765	128	67	33	233	3	139	13.9	78	381	38.1	807	80.7

Did You Know?

Twice in the last 14 seasons, NBA playoff series have ended with a one-point decision in Game 7. On both occasions, Dan Majerle was a member of the losing team—with Miami last season vs. New York, and with Phoenix in 1995 vs. Houston.

Milwaukee Bucks 1999-2000 Regular Season Totals (42-40)

Player	G	GS	Min	Field Goals			3-Pt FGs			Free Throws			Misc			Fouls		Assists		Rebounds			Points	
				Md	Att	Pct	Md	Att	Pct	Md	Att	Pct	TO	Stl	Blk	PF	DQ	Ast	Avg	Off	Tot	Avg	Pts	Avg
Ray Allen	**82**	**82**	**3070**	642	1411	.455	**172**	**407**	**.423**	353	398	**.887**	183	**110**	19	187	1	308	3.8	83	359	4.4	**1809**	**22.1**
Glenn Robinson	81	81	2909	**690**	**1461**	**.472**	86	237	.363	227	283	.802	223	78	41	212	3	193	2.4	107	485	6.0	1693	20.9
Sam Cassell	81	81	2899	545	1170	.466	26	90	.289	**390**	445	.876	**267**	102	8	255	5	**729**	**9.0**	69	301	3.7	1506	18.6
Tim Thomas	80	1	2093	347	753	.461	63	182	.346	188	243	.774	129	59	31	227	3	113	1.4	100	332	4.2	945	11.8
Scott Williams	68	46	1488	213	426	.500	0	0	—	94	129	.729	65	40	66	230	3	28	0.4	177	448	6.6	520	7.6
Dale Ellis†	18	0	324	47	101	.465	23	65	.354	6	9	.667	7	6	0	23	0	7	0.3	7	34	1.9	123	6.8
Vinny Del Negro	67	0	1211	153	325	.471	8	24	.333	35	39	.897	48	36	0	81	0	160	2.4	9	107	1.6	349	5.2
Darvin Ham	35	21	792	71	128	.555	0	1	.000	35	78	.449	29	29	29	102	1	42	1.2	85	172	4.9	177	5.1
Ervin Johnson	80	74	2129	144	279	.516	0	1	.000	95	157	.605	80	81	**127**	298	6	44	0.6	**233**	**648**	**8.1**	383	4.8
Danny Manning	72	0	1217	149	339	.440	1	4	.250	34	52	.654	55	62	29	183	2	73	1.0	50	208	2.9	333	4.6
J.R. Reid	34	7	602	53	127	.417	1	7	.143	43	56	.768	20	19	5	81	2	18	0.5	29	117	3.4	150	4.4
Robert Traylor	44	16	447	58	122	.475	0	4	.000	41	68	.603	27	25	25	79	0	20	0.5	50	115	2.6	157	3.6
Mirsad Turkcan*†	10	0	65	12	28	.429	0	4	.000	5	8	.625	7	1	1	10	0	4	0.4	11	23	2.3	29	2.9
H. Workman†	23	1	248	23	62	.371	11	29	.379	9	13	.692	14	11	0	23	0	44	1.9	1	17	0.7	66	2.9
Rafer Alston*	27	0	361	27	95	.284	3	14	.214	3	4	.750	29	12	0	29	0	70	2.6	5	23	0.9	60	2.2
Total	82	410	19855	3174	6827	.465	394	1069	.369	1558	1982	.786	1230	671	381	2020	26	1852	22.6	1016	3389	41.3	8300	101.2
Opponent	82	410	19855	3033	6644	.457	531	1357	.391	1685	2241	.752	1303	637	340	1870	14	1987	24.2	1037	3405	41.5	8282	101.0

* indicates rookie; † indicates player played with another team in 1999-2000; bold indicates team leader

Milwaukee Bucks 1999-2000 Postseason Totals (2-3)

Player	G	GS	Min	Field Goals			3-Pt FGs			Free Throws			Misc			Fouls		Assists		Rebounds			Points	
				Md	Att	Pct	Md	Att	Pct	Md	Att	Pct	TO	Stl	Blk	PF	DQ	Ast	Avg	Off	Tot	Avg	Pts	Avg
Ray Allen	**5**	**5**	186	40	90	.444	10	26	.385	20	22	.909	9	8	0	10	0	13	2.6	10	33	6.6	**110**	**22.0**
Sam Cassell	5	5	178	30	72	.417	1	5	.200	18	21	.857	9	4	0	19	1	**45**	**9.0**	0	17	3.4	79	15.8
Glenn Robinson	5	5	174	32	79	.405	2	7	.286	11	13	.846	15	8	4	18	0	13	2.6	0	21	4.2	77	15.4
Tim Thomas	5	0	142	29	59	.492	5	15	.333	14	17	.824	1	1	4	14	0	10	2.0	6	24	4.8	77	15.4
Scott Williams	5	0	93	23	36	**.639**	0	0	—	5	6	.833	4	2	5	16	0	2	0.4	9	28	5.6	51	10.2
Ervin Johnson	5	5	155	10	20	.500	0	0	—	11	18	.611	3	6	6	19	0	2	0.4	14	**49**	**9.8**	31	6.2
Vinny Del Negro	5	0	93	13	30	.433	0	2	.000	0	0	—	3	3	0	4	0	9	1.8	0	8	1.6	26	5.2
Darvin Ham	5	5	144	11	17	.647	0	1	.000	3	9	.333	7	1	**8**	**22**	0	7	1.4	**17**	29	5.8	25	5.0
Mirsad Turkcan	2	0	10	1	5	.200	0	1	.000	2	2	1.000	3	0	0	1	0	0	0.0	0	2	1.0	4	2.0
Rafer Alston	4	0	16	0	3	.000	0	1	.000	0	2	.000	1	0	0	0	0	1	0.3	0	0	0.0	0	0.0
Danny Manning	1	0	5	0	1	.000	0	0	—	0	0	—	0	0	0	0	0	0	0.0	0	1	1.0	0	0.0
Robert Traylor	1	0	4	0	1	.000	0	0	—	0	0	—	0	0	1	2	0	1	1.0	1	2	2.0	0	0.0
Total	5	25	1200	189	413	.458	18	58	.310	84	110	.764	59	33	28	125	1	103	20.6	57	214	42.8	480	96.0
Opponent	5	25	1200	170	408	.417	24	81	.296	107	137	.781	58	21	17	109	0	92	18.4	66	209	41.8	471	94.2

Did You Know?

On November 26, 1999, the Bucks overcame an 18-point halftime deficit to win in Boston, 114-112. It was the largest halftime deficit from which any NBA team came back to win during the 1999-2000 campaign.

Minnesota Timberwolves 1999-2000 Regular Season Totals (50-32)

Player	G	GS	Min	Field Goals Md	Att	Pct	3-Pt FGs Md	Att	Pct	Free Throws Md	Att	Pct	Misc TO	Stl	Blk	Fouls PF	DQ	Assists Ast	Avg	Rebounds Off	Tot	Avg	Points Pts	Avg
Kevin Garnett	81	81	3243	759	1526	.497	30	81	.370	309	404	.765	268	120	126	205	1	401	5.0	223	956	11.8	1857	22.9
Terrell Brandon	71	71	2587	486	1042	.466	53	132	.402	187	208	.899	184	134	30	158	1	629	8.9	44	238	3.4	1212	17.1
Wally Szczerbiak*	73	53	2171	342	669	.511	28	78	.359	133	161	.826	83	58	23	175	3	201	2.8	89	272	3.7	845	11.6
Malik Sealy	82	61	2392	371	780	.476	10	35	.286	177	218	.812	110	76	19	197	1	197	2.4	119	352	4.3	929	11.3
Joe Smith	78	9	1975	289	623	.464	1	1	1.000	195	258	.756	119	45	85	302	8	88	1.1	186	484	6.2	774	9.9
Anthony Peeler	82	22	2073	316	725	.436	85	255	.333	87	109	.798	85	62	10	171	1	195	2.4	58	232	2.8	804	9.8
Sam Mitchell	66	24	1227	168	376	.447	10	23	.435	81	92	.880	44	27	14	116	0	111	1.7	28	138	2.1	427	6.5
R. Nesterovic	82	55	1723	206	433	.476	0	2	.000	59	103	.573	71	21	85	262	9	93	1.1	135	379	4.6	471	5.7
Bobby Jackson	73	10	1034	140	346	.405	13	46	.283	76	98	.776	58	48	7	114	0	172	2.4	50	153	2.1	369	5.1
William Avery*	59	1	484	56	181	.309	18	63	.286	24	36	.667	42	14	2	60	0	88	1.5	8	40	0.7	154	2.6
Tom Hammonds	56	0	372	42	97	.433	0	0	—	33	56	.589	21	8	3	55	1	10	0.2	34	101	1.8	117	2.1
Dean Garrett	56	23	604	48	108	.444	0	0	—	18	26	.692	21	8	40	94	1	19	0.3	41	140	2.5	114	2.0
Andrae Patterson	5	0	20	3	4	.750	0	0	—	0	0	—	1	1	0	4	0	1	0.2	1	2	0.4	6	1.2
Total	82	410	19905	3226	6910	.467	248	716	.346	1379	1769	.780	1139	622	444	1913	25	2205	26.9	1016	3487	42.5	8079	98.5
Opponent	82	410	19905	2924	6576	.445	380	1066	.356	1644	2185	.752	1232	591	344	1685	19	1737	21.2	916	3356	40.9	7872	96.0

* indicates rookie; † indicates player played with another team in 1999-2000; bold indicates team leader

Minnesota Timberwolves 1999-2000 Postseason Totals (1-3)

Player	G	GS	Min	Field Goals Md	Att	Pct	3-Pt FGs Md	Att	Pct	Free Throws Md	Att	Pct	Misc TO	Stl	Blk	Fouls PF	DQ	Assists Ast	Avg	Rebounds Off	Tot	Avg	Points Pts	Avg
Terrell Brandon	4	4	162	32	63	.508	4	11	.364	10	11	.909	8	3	0	11	0	34	8.5	4	23	5.8	78	19.5
Kevin Garnett	4	4	171	30	78	.385	2	3	.667	13	16	.813	11	5	3	12	0	35	8.8	13	43	10.8	75	18.8
Malik Sealy	4	4	122	19	41	.463	1	3	.333	11	16	.688	8	2	0	10	0	5	1.3	5	18	4.5	50	12.5
Anthony Peeler	4	0	90	11	24	.458	2	10	.200	6	8	.750	1	3	1	9	0	5	1.3	2	9	2.3	30	7.5
R. Nesterovic	4	4	126	11	25	.440	0	0	—	3	6	.500	4	3	7	20	1	6	1.5	5	13	3.3	25	6.3
Wally Szczerbiak	4	4	94	12	30	.400	0	3	.000	0	0	—	1	3	1	7	0	2	0.5	2	8	2.0	24	6.0
Sam Mitchell	4	0	68	9	18	.500	2	5	.400	3	3	1.000	4	0	1	5	0	2	0.5	2	7	1.8	23	5.8
Bobby Jackson	3	0	30	4	8	.500	1	3	.333	6	6	1.000	2	2	1	4	0	4	1.3	0	5	1.7	15	5.0
Joe Smith	4	0	79	8	17	.471	0	1	.000	2	2	1.000	4	3	1	15	0	1	0.3	7	12	3.0	18	4.5
Dean Garrett	3	0	16	1	2	.500	0	0	—	1	2	.500	0	0	1	2	0	0	0.0	1	2	0.7	3	1.0
Tom Hammonds	1	0	2	0	0	—	0	0	—	0	0	—	0	0	0	0	0	0	0.0	0	0	0.0	0	0.0
Total	4	20	960	137	306	.448	12	39	.308	55	70	.786	47	24	16	95	1	94	23.5	41	140	35.0	341	85.3
Opponent	4	20	960	125	287	.436	23	62	.371	76	91	.835	51	21	15	84	1	78	19.5	35	141	35.3	349	87.3

Did You Know?

The Timberwolves have 12 overtime wins over the last three seasons, most of any team.

New Jersey Nets 1999-2000 Regular Season Totals (31-51)

Player	G	GS	Min	Field Goals Md	Att	Pct	3-Pt FGs Md	Att	Pct	Free Throws Md	Att	Pct	Misc TO	Stl	Blk	Fouls PF	DQ	Assists Ast	Avg	Rebounds Off	Tot	Avg	Points Pts	Avg
Stephon Marbury	74	74	2881	569	1317	.432	66	233	.283	436	536	.813	270	112	15	195	4	622	8.4	61	240	3.2	1640	22.2
Keith Van Horn	80	80	2782	559	1257	.445	84	228	.368	333	393	.847	245	64	60	258	5	158	2.0	200	676	8.5	1535	19.2
Kendall Gill	76	75	2355	396	956	.414	20	78	.256	181	255	.710	89	139	41	211	3	210	2.8	82	283	3.7	993	13.1
Kerry Kittles	62	61	1896	305	698	.437	96	240	.400	101	127	.795	56	79	19	120	0	142	2.3	46	225	3.6	807	13.0
Johnny Newman	82	9	1763	278	623	.446	72	190	.379	192	229	.838	89	53	11	207	0	65	0.8	39	154	1.9	820	10.0
Lucious Harris	77	11	1510	198	463	.428	38	115	.330	79	99	.798	42	65	6	98	0	100	1.3	53	187	2.4	513	6.7
Scott Burrell	74	9	1336	165	419	.394	82	232	.353	39	50	.780	38	67	44	173	1	72	1.0	65	256	3.5	451	6.1
Sherman Douglas	20	2	309	45	90	.500	5	16	.313	25	28	.893	24	17	0	26	0	34	1.7	13	29	1.5	120	6.0
Jamie Feick	81	17	2241	181	423	.428	3	3	1.000	94	133	.707	59	43	38	206	2	68	0.8	264	755	9.3	459	5.7
Elliot Perry	60	5	803	128	294	.435	11	39	.282	50	62	.806	60	39	1	47	0	139	2.3	13	61	1.0	317	5.3
G. Muresan	30	2	267	41	90	.456	0	0	—	23	38	.605	16	0	12	52	0	9	0.3	24	68	2.3	105	3.5
Evan Eschmeyer*	31	5	373	38	72	.528	0	0	—	15	30	.500	21	8	21	84	2	21	0.7	40	108	3.5	91	2.9
Jim McIlvaine	66	53	1048	64	154	.416	0	0	—	29	56	.518	38	26	117	205	2	36	0.5	106	230	3.5	157	2.4
Michael Cage	20	7	242	12	24	.500	0	0	—	3	3	1.000	4	8	8	30	0	9	0.5	33	81	4.1	27	1.4
M. Hendrickson†	5	0	24	0	1	.000	0	0	—	1	2	.500	0	0	0	1	0	3	0.6	1	2	0.4	1	0.2
Total	82	410	19830	2979	6881	.433	477	1374	.347	1601	2041	.784	1119	720	393	1913	19	1688	20.6	1040	3355	40.9	8036	98.0
Opponent	82	410	19830	3125	6741	.464	368	1013	.363	1503	2012	.747	1366	568	469	1869	14	1866	22.8	1129	3786	46.2	8121	99.0

* indicates rookie; † indicates player played with another team in 1999-2000; bold indicates team leader

Did You Know?

The Nets' 46-point first quarter against the Celtics on February 8 was the highest-scoring quarter by any NBA team during the 1999-2000 campaign. For the season, New Jersey averaged only 24.4 points per quarter.

New York Knicks 1999-2000 Regular Season Totals (50-32)

Player	G	GS	Min	Field Goals			3-Pt FGs			Free Throws			Misc			Fouls		Assists		Rebounds			Points	
				Md	Att	Pct	Md	Att	Pct	Md	Att	Pct	TO	Stl	Blk	PF	DQ	Ast	Avg	Off	Tot	Avg	Pts	Avg
Allan Houston	82	82	3169	614	1271	.483	106	243	.436	280	334	.838	186	65	14	219	1	224	2.7	38	271	3.3	1614	19.7
Latrell Sprewell	82	82	3276	568	1305	.435	44	127	.346	344	397	.866	226	109	22	184	0	332	4.0	49	349	4.3	1524	18.6
Patrick Ewing	62	62	2035	361	775	.466	0	2	.000	207	283	.731	142	36	84	196	1	58	0.9	140	604	9.7	929	15.0
Larry Johnson	70	68	2281	282	652	.433	58	174	.333	128	167	.766	94	42	7	205	1	175	2.5	87	380	5.4	750	10.7
Marcus Camby	59	11	1548	226	471	.480	1	2	.500	148	221	.670	72	43	116	204	5	49	0.8	174	461	7.8	601	10.2
Kurt Thomas	80	21	1971	270	535	.505	1	3	.333	100	128	.781	105	51	42	278	6	82	1.0	144	505	6.3	641	8.0
Charlie Ward	72	69	1986	189	447	.423	102	264	.386	48	58	.828	102	95	16	176	3	300	4.2	22	228	3.2	528	7.3
John Wallace	60	0	798	155	332	.467	0	3	.000	82	102	.804	63	10	14	103	0	22	0.4	42	135	2.3	392	6.5
Chris Childs	71	2	1675	146	357	.409	37	104	.356	47	59	.797	105	36	4	240	4	285	4.0	17	147	2.1	376	5.3
Andrew Lang	19	10	244	28	64	.438	0	0	—	3	7	.429	5	8	6	31	0	3	0.2	16	60	3.2	59	3.1
Rick Brunson	37	0	289	29	70	.414	2	13	.154	11	18	.611	31	9	1	35	0	49	1.3	3	27	0.7	71	1.9
E. Bohannon†	2	0	5	0	4	—	0	0	—	3	4	.750	2	0	0	1	0	0	0.0	1	1	0.5	3	1.5
D. Johnson*	5	0	37	3	9	.333	0	0	—	0	0	—	3	1	0	5	0	0	0.0	3	7	1.4	6	1.2
Chris Dudley	47	3	459	23	67	.343	0	0	—	9	27	.333	18	7	21	95	2	5	0.1	63	136	2.9	55	1.2
Mirsad Turkcan*†	7	0	25	2	10	.200	0	2	.000	0	0	—	1	2	0	4	0	1	0.1	2	10	1.4	4	0.6
David Wingate	7	0	32	1	9	.111	0	0	—	0	0	—	0	0	0	7	0	3	0.4	1	2	0.3	2	0.3
Total	82	410	19830	2897	6374	.455	351	937	.375	1410	1805	.781	1201	515	349	1983	23	1588	19.4	802	3323	40.5	7555	92.1
Opponent	82	410	19830	2711	6398	.424	404	1197	.338	1609	2153	.747	1161	603	354	1799	17	1609	19.6	927	3368	41.1	7435	90.7

* indicates rookie; † indicates player played with another team in 1999-2000; bold indicates team leader

New York Knicks 1999-2000 Postseason Totals (9-7)

Player	G	GS	Min	Field Goals			3-Pt FGs			Free Throws			Misc			Fouls		Assists		Rebounds			Points	
				Md	Att	Pct	Md	Att	Pct	Md	Att	Pct	TO	Stl	Blk	PF	DQ	Ast	Avg	Off	Tot	Avg	Pts	Avg
Latrell Sprewell	16	16	700	110	266	.414	10	30	.333	69	88	.784	37	18	5	28	0	58	3.6	12	70	4.4	299	18.7
Allan Houston	16	16	654	103	235	.438	19	38	.500	56	65	.862	36	19	3	42	0	26	1.6	3	52	3.3	281	17.6
Patrick Ewing	14	14	461	71	170	.418	0	0	—	62	89	.697	27	16	20	48	0	6	0.4	29	133	9.5	204	14.6
Larry Johnson	16	16	589	70	152	.461	13	33	.394	27	34	.794	23	8	2	47	1	26	1.6	15	80	5.0	180	11.3
Charlie Ward	16	16	439	57	113	.504	21	53	.396	15	21	.714	20	22	5	40	1	65	4.1	11	68	4.3	150	9.4
Chris Childs	16	0	334	27	70	.386	9	28	.321	24	28	.857	14	7	0	53	1	39	2.4	1	37	2.3	87	5.4
Marcus Camby	16	0	386	29	86	.337	0	1	.000	19	31	.613	12	8	23	51	1	6	0.4	34	111	6.9	77	4.8
Kurt Thomas	16	0	251	31	61	.508	0	0	—	7	10	.700	14	3	6	44	1	5	0.3	19	51	3.2	69	4.3
Chris Dudley	5	2	43	1	2	.500	0	0	—	2	2	1.000	1	1	1	11	0	2	0.4	5	12	2.4	4	0.8
Rick Brunson	3	0	4	0	1	.000	0	0	—	0	0	—	0	1	0	2	0	1	0.3	0	0	0.0	0	0.0
John Wallace	1	0	4	0	2	.000	0	0	—	0	0	—	1	1	0	1	0	0	0.0	0	1	1.0	0	0.0
Total	16	80	3865	499	1158	.431	72	183	.393	281	368	.764	188	104	65	367	5	234	14.6	129	615	38.4	1351	84.4
Opponent	16	80	3865	487	1206	.404	92	278	.331	302	396	.763	198	101	68	368	3	299	18.7	177	682	42.6	1368	85.5

Did You Know?

The Knicks' combined total of steals and blocked shots last season was 864, lowest in the NBA. But New York allowed only 90.7 points per game, second-fewest in the league.

Orlando Magic 1999-2000 Regular Season Totals (41-41)

Player	G	GS	Min	Md	Att	Pct	Md	Att	Pct	Md	Att	Pct	TO	Stl	Blk	PF	DQ	Ast	Avg	Off	Tot	Avg	Pts	Avg
				Field Goals			**3-Pt FGs**			**Free Throws**			**Misc**			**Fouls**		**Assists**		**Rebounds**			**Points**	
Darrell Armstrong	82	82	2590	484	1119	.433	137	403	.340	225	247	.911	248	169	9	137	0	501	6.1	65	270	3.3	1330	16.2
Ron Mercer†	31	31	969	188	468	.402	0	9	.000	94	119	.790	64	42	8	76	2	54	1.7	35	98	3.2	470	15.2
Chris Gatling†	45	0	1041	210	462	.455	7	23	.304	171	245	.698	105	48	10	142	0	40	0.9	91	297	6.6	598	13.3
T. Abdul-Wahad†	46	46	1205	223	515	.433	2	21	.095	115	151	.762	87	53	16	116	1	72	1.6	77	239	5.2	563	12.2
John Amaechi	80	53	1684	306	700	**.437**	1	6	.167	223	**291**	.766	139	35	37	161	1	95	1.2	62	266	3.3	836	10.5
Chucky Atkins*	82	0	1626	314	741	.424	57	163	.350	97	133	.729	142	52	3	137	1	306	3.7	20	126	1.5	782	9.5
Monty Williams	75	23	1501	263	538	.489	2	5	.400	123	166	.741	109	46	17	187	1	106	1.4	96	250	3.3	651	8.7
Corey Maggette*	77	5	1370	224	469	.478	2	11	.182	196	261	.751	138	24	26	169	1	61	0.8	123	303	3.9	646	8.4
Pat Garrity	82	1	1479	258	585	.441	79	197	**.401**	80	111	.721	85	31	19	197	1	58	0.7	44	210	2.6	675	8.2
Michael Doleac	81	29	1335	242	535	.452	1	2	.500	80	95	.842	65	29	34	**224**	3	63	0.8	89	334	4.1	565	7.0
Earl Boykins†	1	0	8	3	4	.750	0	0	—	0	0	—	0	0	0	0	0	3	3.0	1	1	1.0	6	6.0
Bo Outlaw	82	55	2326	204	339	.602	0	3	.000	82	162	.506	133	113	**148**	203	0	245	3.0	202	525	6.4	490	6.0
Ben Wallace	81	81	1959	168	334	.503	0	0	—	54	114	.474	67	72	130	162	0	67	0.8	211	665	**8.2**	390	4.8
Matt Harpring	4	0	63	4	17	.235	2	2	1.000	6	7	.857	1	5	1	7	0	8	2.0	5	12	3.0	16	4.0
Anthony Parker	16	0	185	24	57	.421	1	14	.071	8	11	.727	11	8	4	13	0	10	0.6	5	27	1.7	57	3.6
Anthony Johnson†	18	4	214	26	61	.426	1	5	.200	9	15	.600	8	10	2	17	0	13	0.7	6	12	0.7	62	3.4
Derek Strong	20	0	148	21	48	.438	1	4	.250	11	14	.786	12	5	2	15	0	4	0.2	11	44	2.2	54	2.7
Johnny Taylor†	5	0	29	5	12	.417	1	1	1.000	0	0	—	2	1	1	4	0	1	0.2	2	5	1.0	11	2.2
Kiwane Garris	3	0	23	2	10	.200	0	1	.000	0	0	—	1	0	0	0	0	2	0.7	0	1	0.3	4	1.3
Total	82	410	19755	3169	7014	.452	294	870	.338	1574	2142	.735	1443	743	467	1967	11	1709	20.8	1145	3685	44.9	8206	100.1
Opponent	82	410	19755	3076	6919	.445	431	1277	.338	1567	2104	.745	1488	724	475	2008	17	1991	24.3	1094	3567	43.5	8150	99.4

* indicates rookie; † indicates player played with another team in 1999-2000; bold indicates team leader

Did You Know?

The Magic got an NBA-high 48.2 points per game from their bench last season. No other bench averaged as much as 39 points per game.

Philadelphia 76ers 1999-2000 Regular Season Totals (49-33)

Player	G	GS	Min	Field Goals			3-Pt FGs			Free Throws			Misc			Fouls		Assists		Rebounds			Points	
				Md	Att	Pct	Md	Att	Pct	Md	Att	Pct	TO	Stl	Blk	PF	DQ	Ast	Avg	Off	Tot	Avg	Pts	Avg
Allen Iverson	70	70	2853	**729**	**1733**	.421	**89**	**261**	.341	**442**	**620**	.713	230	**144**	5	162	1	328	4.7	71	267	3.8	**1989**	**28.4**
Toni Kukoc†	32	8	916	149	340	.438	26	90	.289	74	110	.673	71	33	9	61	0	141	4.4	38	143	4.5	398	12.4
Tyrone Hill	68	65	2155	318	656	.485	0	1	.000	179	259	.691	124	64	27	**243**	3	52	0.8	**220**	**625**	9.2	815	12.0
Theo Ratliff	57	56	1795	247	491	.503	0	0	—	182	236	**.771**	108	32	**171**	185	4	36	0.6	140	435	7.6	676	11.9
Larry Hughes†	50	5	1018	192	461	.416	11	51	.216	106	142	.746	95	54	12	94	0	75	1.5	52	159	3.2	501	10.0
Matt Geiger	65	20	1406	260	589	.441	0	4	.000	109	140	.779	91	29	22	194	1	39	0.6	154	387	6.0	629	9.7
George Lynch	75	75	2416	297	644	.461	15	36	.417	113	183	.617	120	119	38	231	2	136	1.8	216	582	**7.8**	722	9.6
Aaron McKie	82	14	1952	244	593	.411	44	121	.364	121	146	.829	113	108	18	194	3	240	2.9	47	246	3.0	653	8.0
Eric Snow	82	80	2866	257	597	.430	11	45	.244	126	177	.712	162	140	8	243	2	**624**	7.6	42	261	3.2	651	7.9
Billy Owens†	46	7	919	112	258	.434	9	27	.333	38	64	.594	61	26	16	119	1	59	1.3	63	192	4.2	271	5.9
Todd MacCulloch*	56	6	528	89	161	.553	0	0	—	28	54	.519	26	11	37	94	0	13	0.2	48	146	2.6	206	3.7
Stanley Roberts	5	1	51	5	16	.313	0	1	.000	0	3	.000	2	1	1	15	0	3	0.6	6	15	3.0	10	2.0
Nazr Mohammed	28	3	190	21	54	.389	0	0	—	12	22	.545	18	4	12	29	0	2	0.1	16	50	1.8	54	1.9
Kevin Ollie	40	0	290	22	49	.449	0	0	—	28	37	.757	10	10	0	27	0	46	1.2	4	31	0.8	72	1.8
Jumaine Jones*	33	0	138	22	58	.379	2	4	.500	11	18	.611	14	6	5	10	0	5	0.2	16	38	1.2	57	1.7
Bruce Bowen†	42	0	311	26	73	.356	1	2	.500	6	12	.500	5	9	5	37	0	16	0.4	14	36	0.9	59	1.4
Antonio Lang†	3	0	6	1	1	1.000	0	0	—	1	1	1.000	0	0	0	1	0	1	0.3	0	0	0.0	3	1.0
Ira Bowman*	11	0	20	2	2	1.000	0	0	—	1	2	.500	1	1	0	0	0	1	0.1	0	2	0.2	5	0.5
Total	82	410	19830	2993	6776	.442	208	643	.323	1577	2226	.708	1284	791	386	1939	17	1817	22.2	1147	3615	44.1	7771	94.8
Opponent	82	410	19830	2867	6595	.435	417	1172	.356	1510	2001	.755	1444	631	531	1977	29	1828	22.3	1065	3566	43.5	7661	93.4

* indicates rookie; † indicates player played with another team in 1999-2000; bold indicates team leader

Philadelphia 76ers 1999-2000 Postseason Totals (5-5)

Player	G	GS	Min	Field Goals			3-Pt FGs			Free Throws			Misc			Fouls		Assists		Rebounds			Points	
				Md	Att	Pct	Md	Att	Pct	Md	Att	Pct	TO	Stl	Blk	PF	DQ	Ast	Avg	Off	Tot	Avg	Pts	Avg
Allen Iverson	10	10	**444**	91	237	.384	12	39	.308	68	92	.739	32	12	1	24	0	45	4.5	14	40	4.0	**262**	**26.2**
Aaron McKie	10	6	331	50	103	.485	12	35	**.343**	26	31	**.839**	16	4	2	26	0	**46**	**4.6**	4	36	3.6	138	13.8
Theo Ratliff	10	10	374	48	101	.475	0	0	—	34	47	.723	17	10	30	35	1	9	0.9	28	79	7.9	130	13.0
Tyrone Hill	10	10	352	46	100	.460	0	1	.000	31	44	.705	12	9	1	**38**	0	9	0.9	36	**97**	**9.7**	123	12.3
Toni Kukoc	10	0	257	36	93	.387	11	34	.324	10	17	.588	15	10	3	26	0	17	1.7	7	37	3.7	93	9.3
Matt Geiger	8	0	128	25	50	.500	0	0	—	20	25	.800	5	5	2	23	0	2	0.3	17	40	5.0	70	8.8
Eric Snow	5	4	138	15	31	.484	3	4	.750	4	4	1.000	7	4	1	14	0	35	7.0	0	10	2.0	37	7.4
George Lynch	10	10	293	22	65	.338	1	7	.143	14	18	.778	8	9	5	33	1	14	1.4	26	71	7.1	59	5.9
Kevin Ollie	10	0	65	6	12	.500	0	0	—	8	9	.889	3	2	0	5	0	12	1.2	0	5	0.5	20	2.0
Todd MacCulloch	5	0	24	2	3	.667	0	0	—	4	6	.667	0	0	0	2	0	0	0.0	3	9	1.8	8	1.6
Jumaine Jones	4	0	8	1	3	.333	0	2	.000	0	0	—	0	0	0	0	0	0	0.0	0	0	0.0	2	0.5
Ira Bowman	7	0	11	0	2	.000	0	1	.000	0	2	.000	0	0	0	0	0	2	0.3	0	0	0.0	0	0.0
Total	10	50	2425	342	800	.428	39	123	.317	219	295	.742	127	65	45	226	2	191	19.1	135	424	42.4	942	94.2
Opponent	10	50	2425	347	773	.449	63	180	.350	198	240	.825	133	74	61	239	3	231	23.1	110	408	40.8	955	95.5

Did You Know?

On December 23 of last season, Allen Iverson scored 42 points without collecting a single assist in Philadelphia's loss to New Jersey. He became the first guard to score 40 points without an assist since Chicago's Michael Jordan had a 41-point, no-assist game on December 29, 1997.

Phoenix Suns 1999-2000 Regular Season Totals (53-29)

Player	G	GS	Min	Field Goals			3-Pt FGs			Free Throws			Misc			Fouls		Assists		Rebounds			Points	
				Md	Att	Pct	Md	Att	Pct	Md	Att	Pct	TO	Stl	Blk	PF	DQ	Ast	Avg	Off	Tot	Avg	Pts	Avg
Clifford Robinson	80	67	2839	530	1142	.464	120	324	.370	298	381	.782	166	90	61	239	3	224	2.8	105	359	4.5	1478	18.5
A. Hardaway	60	60	2253	378	798	.474	33	102	.324	226	286	.790	153	94	38	164	1	315	5.3	91	347	5.8	1015	16.9
Jason Kidd	67	67	2616	350	855	.409	56	166	.337	203	245	.829	226	134	28	148	2	678	10.1	96	483	7.2	959	14.3
Rodney Rogers	82	7	2286	428	881	.486	115	262	.439	159	249	.639	163	94	47	290	5	170	2.1	138	447	5.5	1130	13.8
Tom Gugliotta	54	54	1767	310	645	.481	1	8	.125	117	151	.775	106	80	31	152	2	124	2.3	141	425	7.9	738	13.7
Shawn Marion*	51	38	1260	222	471	.471	4	22	.182	72	85	.847	51	38	53	113	0	69	1.4	105	332	6.5	520	10.2
Todd Day	58	1	941	130	330	.394	64	165	.388	72	108	.667	50	44	22	127	1	65	1.1	31	129	2.2	396	6.8
Kevin Johnson	6	0	113	16	28	.571	1	1	1.000	7	7	1.000	7	2	0	6	0	24	4.0	0	16	2.7	40	6.7
Rex Chapman	53	19	957	124	320	.388	41	123	.333	59	78	.756	38	22	1	70	0	62	1.2	10	80	1.5	348	6.6
Oliver Miller	51	9	1088	137	233	.588	0	0	—	49	73	.671	74	42	80	132	1	68	1.3	87	261	5.1	323	6.3
Luc Longley	72	68	1417	186	399	.466	0	0	—	80	97	.825	136	22	42	221	1	77	1.1	100	323	4.5	452	6.3
Randy Livingston	79	15	1081	155	373	.416	19	55	.345	52	62	.839	92	49	13	129	1	170	2.2	25	130	1.6	381	4.8
Toby Bailey	46	2	449	58	140	.414	2	10	.200	45	65	.692	24	13	4	55	0	30	0.7	26	72	1.6	163	3.5
Corie Blount	38	1	446	44	89	.494	0	2	.000	19	33	.576	28	15	7	78	0	10	0.3	52	113	3.0	107	2.8
Don MacLean	16	0	143	18	49	.367	2	6	.333	4	6	.667	8	2	1	24	0	8	0.5	6	23	1.4	42	2.6
Ben Davis	5	0	22	2	6	.333	0	0	—	0	0	—	3	1	1	2	0	2	0.4	3	9	1.8	4	0.8
Mark West	22	2	127	5	12	.417	0	0	—	5	8	.625	6	2	4	23	0	2	0.1	6	31	1.4	15	0.7
Total	82	410	19805	3093	6771	.457	458	1246	.368	1467	1934	.759	1369	744	433	1973	17	2098	25.6	1022	3580	43.7	8111	98.9
Opponent	82	410	19805	2825	6665	.424	403	1146	.352	1630	2205	.739	1422	733	427	1794	11	1700	20.7	1071	3536	43.1	7683	93.7

* indicates rookie; † indicates player played with another team in 1999-2000; bold indicates team leader

Phoenix Suns 1999-2000 Postseason Totals (4-5)

Player	G	GS	Min	Field Goals			3-Pt FGs			Free Throws			Misc			Fouls		Assists		Rebounds			Points	
				Md	Att	Pct	Md	Att	Pct	Md	Att	Pct	TO	Stl	Blk	PF	DQ	Ast	Avg	Off	Tot	Avg	Pts	Avg
A. Hardaway	9	9	386	67	145	.462	5	19	.263	44	62	.710	25	14	9	29	0	51	5.7	14	44	4.9	183	20.3
Clifford Robinson	9	9	333	56	145	.386	13	40	.325	33	45	.733	18	11	7	35	0	19	2.1	18	54	6.0	158	17.6
Rodney Rogers	9	0	263	48	115	.417	8	36	.222	23	31	.742	15	10	10	31	1	14	1.6	16	61	6.8	127	14.1
Jason Kidd	6	6	229	22	55	.400	8	22	.364	7	9	.778	23	11	1	14	0	53	8.8	8	40	6.7	59	9.8
Shawn Marion	9	9	281	36	86	.419	1	6	.167	9	11	.818	7	6	14	17	0	7	0.8	21	79	8.8	82	9.1
Corie Blount	9	0	162	17	31	.548	0	0	—	10	18	.556	13	6	6	36	0	3	0.3	25	56	6.2	44	4.9
Todd Day	9	0	100	16	35	.457	5	16	.313	5	10	.500	4	4	1	24	0	4	0.4	6	10	1.1	42	4.7
Luc Longley	9	9	162	18	51	.353	0	0	—	2	3	.667	10	4	4	36	1	8	0.9	12	30	3.3	38	4.2
Kevin Johnson	9	0	129	12	37	.324	0	3	.000	5	6	.833	13	3	1	10	0	23	2.6	0	13	1.4	29	3.2
Randy Livingston	7	3	63	6	27	.222	2	6	.333	0	0	—	4	4	1	6	0	4	0.6	2	7	1.0	14	2.0
Oliver Miller	7	0	37	2	9	.222	0	3	.000	2	4	.500	2	0	2	8	0	1	0.1	2	8	1.1	6	0.9
Toby Bailey	5	0	15	1	4	.250	0	0	—	2	4	.500	0	0	0	1	0	2	0.4	1	2	0.4	4	0.8
Total	9	45	2160	301	740	.407	42	151	.278	142	203	.700	138	73	56	247	2	189	21.0	125	404	44.9	786	87.3
Opponent	9	45	2160	287	696	.412	33	111	.297	212	309	.686	128	75	62	196	0	155	17.2	126	413	45.9	819	91.0

Did You Know?

The Suns had six players score at least 10.0 points per game last season, tying Sacramento for the most on any team (minimum 50 games played with the team).

Portland Trail Blazers 1999-2000 Regular Season Totals (59-23)

Player	G	GS	Min	Field Goals			3-Pt FGs			Free Throws			Misc			Fouls		Assists		Rebounds			Points	
				Md	Att	Pct	Md	Att	Pct	Md	Att	Pct	TO	Stl	Blk	PF	DQ	Ast	Avg	Off	Tot	Avg	Pts	Avg
Rasheed Wallace	81	77	2845	542	1045	.519	8	50	.160	233	331	.704	157	87	107	216	2	142	1.8	129	566	7.0	1325	16.4
Steve Smith	82	81	2689	420	900	.467	96	241	.398	289	340	.850	117	71	31	214	0	209	2.5	123	313	3.8	1225	14.9
D. Stoudamire	78	78	2372	386	894	.432	80	212	.377	122	145	.841	149	77	1	173	0	405	5.2	61	243	3.1	974	12.5
Scottie Pippen	82	82	2749	388	860	.451	86	263	.327	160	223	.717	208	117	41	208	0	406	5.0	114	513	6.3	1022	12.5
Arvydas Sabonis	66	61	1688	302	598	.505	7	19	.368	167	198	.843	97	43	78	184	3	118	1.8	97	513	7.8	778	11.8
Bonzi Wells	66	0	1162	236	480	.492	20	53	.377	88	129	.682	97	69	12	153	3	97	1.5	78	182	2.8	580	8.8
Detlef Schrempf	77	6	1662	187	433	.432	21	52	.404	179	215	.833	100	37	17	182	0	197	2.6	79	332	4.3	574	7.5
Brian Grant	63	14	1322	173	352	.491	1	2	.500	112	166	.675	84	32	28	166	2	64	1.0	121	344	5.5	459	7.3
Greg Anthony	82	3	1548	169	416	.406	88	233	.378	88	114	.772	85	59	9	143	0	208	2.5	17	133	1.6	514	6.3
Gary Grant	3	0	24	6	14	.429	0	0	—	0	0	—	2	1	0	3	0	1	0.3	0	3	1.0	12	4.0
Jermaine O'Neal	70	8	859	108	222	.486	0	1	.000	57	98	.582	47	11	55	127	1	18	0.3	97	229	3.3	273	3.9
Stacey Augmon	59	0	692	83	175	.474	0	2	.000	37	55	.673	38	27	11	69	0	53	0.9	42	116	2.0	203	3.4
Antonio Harvey	19	0	137	17	30	.567	0	0	—	7	12	.583	12	1	6	20	0	5	0.3	8	33	1.7	41	2.2
Joe Kleine	7	0	31	4	11	.364	0	0	—	3	3	1.000	2	1	0	7	0	2	0.3	0	6	0.9	11	1.6
Total	82	410	19780	3021	6430	.470	407	1128	.361	1542	2029	.760	1243	633	396	1865	11	1925	23.5	966	3526	43.0	7991	97.5
Opponent	82	410	19780	2825	6557	.431	394	1195	.330	1422	1985	.716	1186	652	350	1872	22	1705	20.8	978	3198	39.0	7466	91.0

* indicates rookie; † indicates player played with another team in 1999-2000; bold indicates team leader

Portland Trail Blazers 1999-2000 Postseason Totals (10-6)

Player	G	GS	Min	Field Goals			3-Pt FGs			Free Throws			Misc			Fouls		Assists		Rebounds			Points	
				Md	Att	Pct	Md	Att	Pct	Md	Att	Pct	TO	Stl	Blk	PF	DQ	Ast	Avg	Off	Tot	Avg	Pts	Avg
Rasheed Wallace	16	16	605	110	225	.489	8	13	.615	58	75	.773	23	15	20	52	0	28	1.8	31	103	6.4	286	17.9
Steve Smith	16	16	604	88	181	.486	29	53	.547	69	78	.885	27	19	4	44	0	44	2.8	13	40	2.5	274	17.1
Scottie Pippen	16	16	614	88	198	.419	21	70	.300	52	70	.743	37	32	7	49	1	69	4.3	22	114	7.1	239	14.9
Arvydas Sabonis	16	16	493	68	150	.453	6	21	.286	39	49	.796	26	14	13	59	2	31	1.9	19	107	6.7	181	11.3
D. Stoudamire	16	16	447	56	135	.415	10	30	.333	20	24	.833	19	8	4	43	1	58	3.6	8	42	2.6	142	8.9
Bonzi Wells	14	0	188	37	83	.446	2	10	.200	29	41	.707	16	7	0	33	0	13	0.9	12	35	2.5	105	7.5
Detlef Schrempf	15	0	276	22	56	.393	1	6	.167	39	47	.830	15	4	0	29	0	30	2.0	10	53	3.5	84	5.6
Brian Grant	16	0	320	29	65	.446	0	0	—	29	39	.744	17	6	6	53	1	8	0.5	37	92	5.8	87	5.4
Greg Anthony	15	0	213	19	52	.365	10	31	.323	12	16	.750	12	13	4	27	0	25	1.7	2	16	1.1	60	4.0
Jermaine O'Neal	8	0	38	3	11	.273	0	0	—	6	9	.667	0	0	3	9	0	1	0.1	2	7	0.9	12	1.5
Stacey Augmon	7	0	34	4	12	.333	0	0	—	1	2	.500	0	0	0	6	0	0	0.0	0	2	0.3	9	1.3
Gary Grant	2	0	8	0	2	.000	0	0	—	1	2	.500	0	0	0	0	0	1	0.5	0	0	0.0	1	0.5
Total	16	80	3840	519	1170	.444	87	234	.372	355	452	.785	203	118	61	404	5	308	19.3	156	611	38.2	1480	92.5
Opponent	16	80	3840	519	1167	.445	77	230	.335	289	427	.677	210	89	86	426	6	362	22.6	152	599	37.4	1404	87.8

Did You Know?

The Blazers outrebounded their opponents by 4.0 boards per game last season, the best differential of any team.

Sacramento Kings 1999-2000 Regular Season Totals (44-38)

Player	G	GS	Min	Field Goals			3-Pt FGs			Free Throws			Misc			Fouls		Assists		Rebounds			Points	
				Md	Att	Pct	Md	Att	Pct	Md	Att	Pct	TO	Stl	Blk	PF	DQ	Ast	Avg	Off	Tot	Avg	Pts	Avg
Chris Webber	75	75	**2880**	**748**	1548	.483	27	95	.284	**311**	414	.751	218	120	128	264	7	345	4.6	189	787	10.5	1834	24.5
Jason Williams	81	81	2760	363	973	.373	145	505	.287	128	170	.753	296	117	8	140	0	589	7.3	22	230	2.8	999	12.3
Vlade Divac	**82**	81	2374	384	764	**.503**	7	26	.269	230	333	.691	190	103	103	251	2	244	3.0	174	656	8.0	1005	12.3
P. Stojakovic	74	11	1749	321	717	.448	100	267	.375	135	153	**.882**	88	52	7	97	0	106	1.4	74	276	3.7	877	11.9
Nick Anderson	72	72	2094	306	782	.391	132	397	.332	37	76	.487	95	94	16	118	0	123	1.7	83	339	4.7	781	10.8
Corliss Williamson	76	76	1707	311	622	.500	0	0	—	163	212	.769	110	38	19	192	0	82	1.1	122	290	3.8	785	10.3
Jon Barry	62	1	1281	161	346	.465	66	154	**.429**	107	116	.922	85	75	7	104	1	150	2.4	38	159	2.6	495	8.0
L. Funderburke	75	1	1026	184	352	.523	0	2	.000	115	163	.706	40	32	20	91	0	33	0.4	98	234	3.1	483	6.4
Tony Delk	46	1	682	120	279	.430	9	40	.225	47	59	.797	32	35	5	58	0	55	1.2	36	88	1.9	296	6.4
Darrick Martin	71	1	893	133	350	.380	38	124	.306	98	119	.824	62	28	2	89	0	122	1.7	7	44	0.6	402	5.7
Scot Pollard	76	5	1336	149	283	.527	0	0	—	114	159	.717	50	55	59	213	3	43	0.6	168	404	5.3	412	5.4
Ryan Robertson*	1	0	25	2	6	.333	0	2	.000	1	1	1.000	0	0	0	0	0	0	0.0	0	0	0.0	5	5.0
Tyrone Corbin	54	5	941	88	247	.356	10	44	.227	33	39	.846	29	36	5	99	2	60	1.1	40	165	3.1	219	4.1
Bill Wennington	7	0	57	6	19	.316	0	0	—	2	2	1.000	1	2	2	13	0	1	0.1	5	19	2.7	14	2.0
Total	82	410	19805	3276	7288	.450	534	1656	.322	1521	2016	.754	1325	787	381	1729	15	1953	23.8	1056	3691	45.0	8607	105.0
Opponent	82	410	19805	3269	7239	.452	396	1123	.353	1434	1910	.751	1437	753	404	1943	19	1950	23.8	1143	3904	47.6	8368	102.0

* indicates rookie; † indicates player played with another team in 1999-2000; bold indicates team leader

Sacramento Kings 1999-2000 Postseason Totals (2-3)

Player	G	GS	Min	Field Goals			3-Pt FGs			Free Throws			Misc			Fouls		Assists		Rebounds			Points	
				Md	Att	Pct	Md	Att	Pct	Md	Att	Pct	TO	Stl	Blk	PF	DQ	Ast	Avg	Off	Tot	Avg	Pts	Avg
Chris Webber	5	5	196	47	110	.427	1	5	.200	27	34	.794	8	8	10	14	1	27	5.4	14	48	9.6	122	24.4
Tony Delk	5	0	101	18	41	**.439**	3	5	**.600**	17	23	.739	8	3	0	11	0	7	1.4	11	18	3.6	56	11.2
Vlade Divac	5	5	160	20	56	.357	0	2	.000	16	23	.696	9	7	4	22	0	14	2.8	9	36	7.2	56	11.2
Jason Williams	5	5	145	18	48	.375	8	25	.320	8	10	.800	8	3	0	8	0	12	2.4	1	8	1.6	52	10.4
P. Stojakovic	5	0	129	16	40	.400	6	13	.462	6	9	.667	5	4	0	7	0	3	0.6	2	17	3.4	44	8.8
Jon Barry	5	0	102	9	21	.429	7	12	.583	14	16	.875	4	3	0	7	0	12	2.4	2	12	2.4	39	7.8
Nick Anderson	5	5	132	11	34	.324	7	20	.350	7	8	.875	4	1	3	9	0	2	0.4	4	17	3.4	36	7.2
Corliss Williamson	5	5	87	11	16	.688	0	0	—	11	12	**.917**	5	1	0	8	0	1	0.2	4	15	3.0	33	6.6
Darrick Martin	2	0	21	3	9	.333	1	3	.333	3	4	.750	3	1	0	4	0	2	1.0	1	3	1.5	10	5.0
Scot Pollard	5	0	70	9	16	.563	0	0	—	2	6	.333	3	2	1	18	1	1	0.2	6	16	3.2	20	4.0
L. Funderburke	4	0	34	4	9	.444	0	0	—	2	4	.500	0	1	0	0	0	0	0.0	4	11	2.8	10	2.5
Tyrone Corbin	3	0	23	2	5	.400	0	2	.000	0	1	.000	0	0	0	2	0	3	1.0	1	5	1.7	4	1.3
Total	5	25	1200	168	405	.415	33	87	.379	113	150	.753	60	34	18	110	2	84	16.8	59	206	41.2	482	96.4
Opponent	5	25	1200	208	446	.466	19	63	.302	87	136	.640	56	33	32	117	1	109	21.8	90	255	51.0	522	104.4

Did You Know?

Jason Williams has missed 583 three-point field goal attempts over the last two seasons (while making 245), the most of any player over that span.

San Antonio Spurs 1999-2000 Regular Season Totals (53-29)

Player	G	GS	Min	Field Goals Md	Att	Pct	3-Pt FGs Md	Att	Pct	Free Throws Md	Att	Pct	Misc TO	Stl	Blk	Fouls PF	DQ	Assists Ast	Avg	Rebounds Off	Tot	Avg	Points Pts	Avg
Tim Duncan	74	74	2875	**628**	**1281**	.490	1	11	.091	**459**	**603**	.761	**242**	66	165	210	1	234	3.2	**262**	**918**	**12.4**	**1716**	**23.2**
David Robinson	80	80	2557	528	1031	.512	0	2	.000	371	511	.726	164	**97**	**183**	247	1	142	1.8	193	770	9.6	1427	17.8
Avery Johnson	**82**	**82**	2571	402	850	.473	1	9	.111	114	155	.735	140	76	18	150	0	**491**	**6.0**	33	158	1.9	919	11.2
Terry Porter	68	8	1613	207	463	.447	90	207	**.435**	137	170	.806	100	50	9	79	0	221	3.3	24	191	2.8	641	9.4
Mario Elie	79	79	2217	195	457	.427	74	186	.398	126	149	**.846**	130	73	9	156	0	193	2.4	48	249	3.2	590	7.5
Malik Rose	74	3	1341	176	385	.457	1	3	.333	143	198	.722	99	35	52	232	**2**	47	0.6	133	335	4.5	496	6.7
Jaren Jackson	81	12	1691	186	488	.381	**108**	**306**	.353	33	51	.647	66	54	7	157	1	118	1.5	34	181	2.2	513	6.3
Chucky Brown†	30	27	602	82	176	.466	1	3	.333	25	31	.806	28	8	10	53	0	41	1.4	11	77	2.6	190	6.3
Antonio Daniels	68	1	1195	163	344	.474	22	66	.333	72	101	.713	58	55	5	73	0	177	2.6	16	86	1.3	420	6.2
Sean Elliott	19	19	391	38	106	.358	13	37	.351	25	32	.781	19	12	2	34	0	28	1.5	6	47	2.5	114	6.0
Samaki Walker	71	7	980	137	305	.449	0	0	—	86	126	.683	64	10	35	108	1	38	0.5	77	272	3.8	360	5.1
Derrick Dial*	8	0	95	17	46	.370	3	12	.250	3	5	.600	6	1	1	10	0	5	0.6	14	26	3.3	40	5.0
Jerome Kersey	72	18	1310	146	354	.412	0	9	.000	29	41	.707	51	67	47	161	0	69	1.0	58	225	3.1	321	4.5
Steve Kerr	32	0	268	32	74	.432	16	31	.516	9	11	.818	7	4	0	14	0	12	0.4	3	19	0.6	89	2.8
Felton Spencer	26	0	149	15	33	.455	0	0	—	20	30	.667	9	6	8	32	0	3	0.1	15	39	1.5	50	1.9
Total	82	410	19855	2952	6393	.462	330	882	.374	1652	2214	.746	1233	614	551	1716	6	1819	22.2	927	3593	43.8	7886	96.2
Opponent	82	410	19855	2884	6781	.425	355	1036	.343	1276	1726	.739	1181	645	429	1893	25	1667	20.3	986	3396	41.4	7399	90.2

* indicates rookie; † indicates player played with another team in 1999-2000; bold indicates team leader

San Antonio Spurs 1999-2000 Postseason Totals (1-3)

Player	G	GS	Min	Field Goals Md	Att	Pct	3-Pt FGs Md	Att	Pct	Free Throws Md	Att	Pct	Misc TO	Stl	Blk	Fouls PF	DQ	Assists Ast	Avg	Rebounds Off	Tot	Avg	Points Pts	Avg
David Robinson	4	4	155	31	83	.373	0	1	.000	32	42	.762	8	7	12	15	0	10	2.5	17	55	13.8	94	23.5
Avery Johnson	4	4	144	19	42	.452	0	0	—	10	14	.714	10	4	0	10	0	21	5.3	2	9	2.3	48	12.0
Sean Elliott	4	4	119	15	40	.375	5	13	.385	5	8	.625	4	0	2	13	0	5	1.3	1	22	5.5	40	10.0
Samaki Walker	4	4	121	14	31	.452	0	0	—	8	12	.667	8	1	12	13	0	2	0.5	13	45	11.3	36	9.0
Mario Elie	4	4	115	6	22	.273	1	7	.143	17	18	**.944**	12	5	0	4	0	7	1.8	5	17	4.3	30	7.5
Antonio Daniels	4	0	82	9	23	.391	2	8	.250	9	13	.692	6	7	0	5	0	6	1.5	2	10	2.5	29	7.3
Malik Rose	4	0	83	8	18	.444	0	0	—	5	9	.556	7	2	3	12	0	1	0.3	5	19	4.8	21	5.3
Terry Porter	4	0	89	8	31	.258	4	14	.286	0	0	—	7	6	0	4	0	5	1.3	0	1	0.3	20	5.0
Derrick Dial	2	0	8	2	4	.500	0	0	—	1	2	.500	0	0	0	1	0	0	0.0	2	2	1.0	5	2.5
Jaren Jackson	2	0	19	0	3	.000	0	1	.000	2	4	.500	1	0	1	1	0	2	1.0	0	1	0.5	2	1.0
Jerome Kersey	2	0	25	1	7	.143	0	0	—	0	0	—	1	2	1	5	0	1	0.5	2	4	2.0	2	1.0
Total	4	20	960	113	304	.372	12	44	.273	89	122	.730	65	35	30	83	0	60	15.0	49	185	46.3	327	81.8
Opponent	4	20	960	133	335	.397	16	59	.271	50	72	.694	62	37	39	101	0	83	20.8	56	192	48.0	332	83.0

Did You Know?

The Spurs went 8-10 (.444) against the six teams that averaged more than 100 points per game in 1999-2000. Against the rest of the NBA, San Antonio went 45-19 (.703).

Seattle SuperSonics 1999-2000 Regular Season Totals (45-37)

Player	G	GS	Min	Field Goals			3-Pt FGs			Free Throws			Misc			Fouls		Assists		Rebounds			Points	
				Md	Att	Pct	Md	Att	Pct	Md	Att	Pct	TO	Stl	Blk	PF	DQ	Ast	Avg	Off	Tot	Avg	Pts	Avg
Gary Payton	82	82	3425	747	1666	.448	177	520	.340	311	423	.735	224	153	18	178	0	732	8.9	100	529	6.5	1982	24.2
Vin Baker	79	75	2849	514	1129	.455	2	8	.250	281	412	.682	213	47	66	288	6	148	1.9	227	605	7.7	1311	16.6
Brent Barry	80	74	2726	327	707	.463	164	399	.411	127	157	.809	142	103	31	228	4	291	3.6	50	372	4.7	945	11.8
Ruben Patterson	81	74	2097	354	661	.536	12	27	.444	222	321	.692	144	94	40	190	0	126	1.6	218	434	5.4	942	11.6
Vernon Maxwell	47	0	989	169	490	.345	67	223	.300	108	148	.730	53	38	9	83	0	75	1.6	15	79	1.7	513	10.9
Rashard Lewis	82	8	1575	275	566	.486	40	120	.333	84	123	.683	78	62	36	163	0	70	0.9	127	336	4.1	674	8.2
Horace Grant	76	76	2688	266	599	.444	0	4	.000	80	111	.721	61	55	60	192	0	188	2.5	167	591	7.8	612	8.1
S. Williams	43	5	517	84	225	.373	24	81	.296	33	51	.647	40	18	0	39	0	78	1.8	12	52	1.2	225	5.2
Jelani McCoy	58	2	746	102	177	.576	0	0	—	45	91	.495	45	15	46	127	0	24	0.4	54	159	3.1	249	4.3
Emanual Davis	54	2	701	80	220	.364	31	103	.301	26	38	.684	44	38	5	72	0	70	1.3	15	100	1.9	217	4.0
Lazaro Borrell*	17	6	167	28	63	.444	0	3	.000	6	11	.545	6	6	3	9	0	10	0.6	14	40	2.4	62	3.6
Greg Foster	60	5	718	91	224	.406	3	15	.200	18	28	.643	28	10	18	105	0	41	0.7	16	107	1.8	203	3.4
Chuck Person	37	0	340	37	123	.301	24	95	.253	4	8	.500	12	5	2	56	1	22	0.6	6	53	1.4	102	2.8
Vladimir Stepania	30	1	202	29	79	.367	0	6	.000	17	36	.472	22	10	11	44	0	3	0.1	21	47	1.6	75	2.5
Fred Vinson	8	0	40	5	17	.294	2	7	.286	1	2	.500	4	3	0	2	0	0	0.0	0	1	0.1	13	1.6
Total	82	410	19780	3108	6946	.447	546	1611	.339	1363	1960	.695	1152	657	345	1776	11	1878	22.9	1042	3525	43.0	8125	99.1
Opponent	82	410	19780	3132	6941	.451	440	1293	.340	1343	1795	.748	1258	590	433	1839	13	1939	23.6	1084	3695	45.1	8047	98.1

* indicates rookie; † indicates player played with another team in 1999-2000; bold indicates team leader

Seattle SuperSonics 1999-2000 Postseason Totals (2-3)

Player	G	GS	Min	Field Goals			3-Pt FGs			Free Throws			Misc			Fouls		Assists		Rebounds			Points	
				Md	Att	Pct	Md	Att	Pct	Md	Att	Pct	TO	Stl	Blk	PF	DQ	Ast	Avg	Off	Tot	Avg	Pts	Avg
Gary Payton	5	5	221	50	113	.442	9	23	.391	20	26	.769	18	9	1	16	0	37	7.4	8	38	7.6	129	25.8
Rashard Lewis	5	5	157	26	59	.441	9	19	.474	16	20	.800	10	5	3	11	0	3	0.6	12	31	6.2	77	15.4
Vin Baker	5	4	177	30	75	.400	0	1	.000	10	17	.588	16	5	2	19	0	10	2.0	16	38	7.6	70	14.0
S. Williams	5	2	99	18	33	.545	7	11	.636	8	11	.727	6	8	0	3	0	18	3.6	2	11	2.2	51	10.2
Brent Barry	5	3	155	12	33	.364	8	20	.400	10	14	.714	7	3	3	20	2	15	3.0	3	13	2.6	42	8.4
Ruben Patterson	5	0	84	14	26	.538	0	2	.000	13	15	.867	8	3	2	6	0	2	0.4	9	15	3.0	41	8.2
Lazaro Borrell	2	1	26	4	7	.571	0	0	—	2	4	.500	1	0	0	2	0	1	0.5	3	11	5.5	10	5.0
Horace Grant	5	5	185	11	27	.407	0	0	—	2	4	.500	1	8	5	12	0	10	2.0	8	31	6.2	24	4.8
Greg Foster	5	0	68	7	19	.368	2	5	.400	2	2	1.000	3	0	1	14	0	1	0.2	1	11	2.2	18	3.6
Jelani McCoy	3	0	26	2	5	.400	0	0	—	0	3	.000	2	0	0	6	0	2	0.7	0	6	2.0	4	1.3
Chuck Person	2	0	2	0	1	.000	0	1	.000	0	0	—	0	0	0	0	0	0	0.0	0	0	0.0	0	0.0
Total	5	25	1200	174	398	.437	35	82	.427	83	116	.716	73	41	17	109	2	99	19.8	62	205	41.0	466	93.2
Opponent	5	25	1200	180	384	.469	30	65	.462	82	105	.781	79	41	29	111	0	126	25.2	56	210	42.0	472	94.4

Did You Know?

Gary Payton scored or assisted on 47.6 percent of the Sonics' field goals in 1999-2000, the highest percentage in the NBA. Payton was involved in 1,479 Seattle field goals; no other player's total of field goals plus assists was as high as 1,300.

Toronto Raptors 1999-2000 Regular Season Totals (45-37)

Player	G	GS	Min	Field Goals			3-Pt FGs			Free Throws			Misc			Fouls		Assists		Rebounds			Points	
				Md	Att	Pct	Md	Att	Pct	Md	Att	Pct	TO	Stl	Blk	PF	DQ	Ast	Avg	Off	Tot	Avg	Pts	Avg
Vince Carter	82	82	3126	788	1696	.465	95	236	.403	436	551	.791	178	110	92	263	2	322	3.9	150	476	5.8	2107	25.7
Tracy McGrady	79	34	2462	459	1018	.451	18	65	.277	277	392	.707	160	90	151	201	2	263	3.3	188	501	6.3	1213	15.4
Doug Christie	73	73	2264	311	764	.407	99	275	.360	182	216	.843	144	102	43	167	1	321	4.4	63	285	3.9	903	12.4
Antonio Davis	79	78	2479	313	712	.440	0	0	—	284	371	.765	121	38	100	267	2	105	1.3	235	696	8.8	910	11.5
Kevin Willis	79	1	1679	236	569	.415	1	3	.333	131	164	.799	98	36	48	256	3	49	0.6	201	482	6.1	604	7.6
Dell Curry	67	9	1095	194	454	.427	95	242	.393	24	32	.750	40	32	9	66	0	89	1.3	11	100	1.5	507	7.6
Dee Brown	38	12	673	93	258	.360	67	187	.358	11	16	.688	39	24	5	62	1	86	2.3	9	54	1.4	264	6.9
Charles Oakley	80	80	2431	234	560	.418	14	41	.341	66	85	.776	154	102	45	294	6	253	3.2	117	540	6.8	548	6.9
Alvin Williams	55	28	779	114	287	.397	16	55	.291	48	65	.738	47	34	11	78	0	126	2.3	27	85	1.5	292	5.3
Muggsy Bogues	80	5	1731	157	358	.439	17	51	.333	79	87	.908	59	65	4	119	0	299	3.7	25	135	1.7	410	5.1
A. Radojevic*	3	0	24	2	7	.286	0	0	—	3	6	.500	5	2	1	5	0	1	0.3	2	8	2.7	7	2.3
John Thomas	55	6	477	49	107	.458	0	1	.000	16	41	.390	14	12	14	106	1	9	0.2	37	75	1.4	114	2.1
Sean Marks	5	0	12	2	6	.333	0	1	.000	4	4	1.000	3	1	1	3	0	2	0.4	0	2	0.4	8	1.6
H. Workman†	13	1	102	8	28	.286	3	14	.214	1	2	.500	4	9	0	14	1	17	1.3	0	9	0.7	20	1.5
Michael Stewart	42	1	389	20	53	.377	0	0	—	18	32	.563	17	5	19	81	3	6	0.1	33	94	2.2	58	1.4
Antonio Lang†	7	0	32	0	5	.000	0	0	—	3	4	.750	2	4	1	7	0	1	0.1	0	5	0.7	3	0.4
Total	82	410	19755	2980	6882	.433	425	1171	.363	1583	2068	.765	1137	666	544	1989	22	1947	23.7	1098	3547	43.3	7968	97.2
Opponent	82	410	19755	3002	6615	.454	346	1021	.339	1631	2136	.764	1250	557	434	1874	15	1790	21.8	961	3513	42.8	7981	97.3

* indicates rookie; † indicates player played with another team in 1999-2000; bold indicates team leader

Toronto Raptors 1999-2000 Postseason Totals (0-3)

Player	G	GS	Min	Field Goals			3-Pt FGs			Free Throws			Misc			Fouls		Assists		Rebounds			Points	
				Md	Att	Pct	Md	Att	Pct	Md	Att	Pct	TO	Stl	Blk	PF	DQ	Ast	Avg	Off	Tot	Avg	Pts	Avg
Vince Carter	3	3	119	15	50	.300	1	10	.100	27	31	.871	8	3	4	12	0	19	6.3	9	18	6.0	58	19.3
Tracy McGrady	3	3	111	17	44	.386	2	7	.286	14	16	.875	10	3	3	10	0	9	3.0	10	21	7.0	50	16.7
Antonio Davis	3	3	105	14	24	.583	0	0	—	11	14	.786	4	1	4	9	0	3	1.0	7	25	8.3	39	13.0
Kevin Willis	3	0	76	12	33	.364	0	0	—	15	20	.750	2	2	0	11	0	1	0.3	6	26	8.7	39	13.0
Charles Oakley	3	3	110	14	29	.483	2	7	.286	0	1	.000	5	6	1	14	0	11	3.7	2	23	7.7	30	10.0
Muggsy Bogues	3	2	87	6	21	.286	3	9	.333	1	3	.333	4	4	0	4	0	5	1.7	3	6	2.0	16	5.3
Doug Christie	3	1	61	3	13	.231	3	8	.375	3	6	.500	4	4	1	10	0	6	2.0	1	5	1.7	12	4.0
Dell Curry	3	0	30	2	4	.500	2	3	.667	1	2	.500	2	2	0	4	0	1	0.3	1	2	0.7	7	2.3
Dee Brown	3	0	19	0	4	.000	0	3	.000	0	0	—	1	2	0	4	0	2	0.7	0	2	0.7	0	0.0
John Thomas	1	0	1	0	0	—	0	0	—	0	0	—	0	0	0	0	0	0	0.0	0	0	0.0	0	0.0
Alvin Williams	1	0	1	0	0	—	0	0	—	0	0	—	0	0	0	0	0	0	0.0	0	0	0.0	0	0.0
Total	3	15	720	83	222	.374	13	47	.277	72	93	.774	43	27	13	78	0	57	19.0	39	128	42.7	251	83.7
Opponent	3	15	720	91	201	.453	16	34	.471	65	87	.747	48	24	15	72	1	36	12.0	23	111	37.0	263	87.7

Did You Know?

Dee Brown attempted 422 field goals last year, of which 72.0 percent (304) were three-point attempts. This was the highest such percentage ever by a player with at least 300 field goal attempts in a season.

Utah Jazz 1999-2000 Regular Season Totals (55-27)

Player	G	GS	Min	Field Goals Md	Att	Pct	3-Pt FGs Md	Att	Pct	Free Throws Md	Att	Pct	Misc TO	Stl	Blk	Fouls PF	DQ	Assists Ast	Avg	Rebounds Off	Tot	Avg	Points Pts	Avg
Karl Malone	82	82	2947	752	1476	.509	2	8	.250	589	739	.797	231	79	71	229	1	304	3.7	169	779	9.5	2095	25.5
Bryon Russell	82	70	2900	408	914	.446	106	268	.396	237	316	.750	101	128	23	255	3	158	1.9	99	427	5.2	1159	14.1
Jeff Hornacek	77	77	2133	358	728	.492	66	138	.478	171	180	.950	113	66	16	149	1	202	2.6	49	182	2.4	953	12.4
John Stockton	82	82	2432	363	725	.501	43	121	.355	221	257	.860	179	143	15	192	0	703	8.6	45	215	2.6	990	12.1
Howard Eisley	82	5	2096	282	675	.418	60	163	.368	84	102	.824	132	59	9	223	2	347	4.2	23	170	2.1	708	8.6
Armen Gilliam	50	0	782	133	305	.436	0	1	.000	67	86	.779	55	12	16	83	0	42	0.8	72	209	4.2	333	6.7
Olden Polynice	82	79	1819	203	398	.510	1	2	.500	28	90	.311	70	30	84	260	1	37	0.5	166	453	5.5	435	5.3
Greg Ostertag	81	3	1606	124	267	.464	0	1	.000	119	187	.636	79	20	172	196	2	18	0.2	172	482	6.0	367	4.5
Quincy Lewis*	74	0	896	111	298	.372	23	63	.365	38	52	.731	46	24	15	158	0	40	0.5	46	113	1.5	283	3.8
Jacque Vaughn	78	0	884	109	262	.416	14	34	.412	57	76	.750	77	32	0	92	0	121	1.6	11	65	0.8	289	3.7
Scott Padgett*	47	9	432	44	140	.314	13	44	.295	19	27	.704	22	14	8	55	1	25	0.5	24	88	1.9	120	2.6
Adam Keefe	62	3	604	53	130	.408	0	1	.000	29	36	.806	46	17	13	90	0	34	0.5	45	136	2.2	135	2.2
Pete Chilcutt†	26	0	224	22	62	.355	1	10	.100	2	2	1.000	9	5	4	31	0	10	0.4	15	43	1.7	47	1.8
Total	82	410	19755	2962	6380	.464	329	854	.385	1661	2150	.773	1220	629	446	2013	11	2041	24.9	936	3362	41.0	7914	96.5
Opponent	82	410	19755	2781	6240	.446	388	1097	.354	1598	2141	.746	1270	588	411	2023	16	1620	19.8	887	3123	38.1	7548	92.0

* indicates rookie; † indicates player played with another team in 1999-2000; bold indicates team leader

Utah Jazz 1999-2000 Postseason Totals (4-6)

Player	G	GS	Min	Field Goals Md	Att	Pct	3-Pt FGs Md	Att	Pct	Free Throws Md	Att	Pct	Misc TO	Stl	Blk	Fouls PF	DQ	Assists Ast	Avg	Rebounds Off	Tot	Avg	Points Pts	Avg
Karl Malone	10	10	386	103	198	.520	2	2	1.000	64	79	.810	27	7	7	31	0	31	3.1	19	89	8.9	272	27.2
Bryon Russell	10	10	371	48	114	.421	13	45	.289	31	41	.756	15	16	5	27	0	21	2.1	9	52	5.2	140	14.0
Jeff Hornacek	10	10	297	43	102	.422	9	22	.409	20	24	.833	15	10	0	28	0	33	3.3	9	30	3.0	115	11.5
John Stockton	10	10	350	41	89	.461	7	18	.389	23	30	.767	26	13	2	30	0	103	10.3	7	30	3.0	112	11.2
Olden Polynice	10	10	260	28	52	.538	0	0	—	3	6	.500	13	3	8	36	1	5	0.5	24	66	6.6	59	5.9
Howard Eisley	10	0	200	17	55	.309	9	19	.474	8	9	.889	13	6	1	24	0	19	1.9	1	18	1.8	51	5.1
Jacque Vaughn	7	0	67	10	28	.357	1	2	.500	7	8	.875	9	4	1	5	0	11	1.6	4	12	1.7	28	4.0
Greg Ostertag	8	0	172	10	19	.526	0	0	—	10	22	.455	8	2	17	20	0	2	0.3	19	45	5.6	30	3.8
Armen Gilliam	10	0	132	15	46	.326	0	0	—	5	13	.385	11	4	4	15	0	4	0.4	6	29	2.9	35	3.5
Quincy Lewis	8	0	106	10	27	.370	2	6	.333	4	5	.800	3	3	7	24	0	2	0.3	2	15	1.9	26	3.3
Scott Padgett	8	0	59	6	16	.375	3	9	.333	0	0	—	4	1	2	10	0	5	0.6	3	17	2.1	15	1.9
Total	10	50	2400	331	746	.444	46	123	.374	175	237	.738	149	69	54	250	1	236	23.6	103	403	40.3	883	88.3
Opponent	10	50	2400	336	758	.443	60	151	.397	200	273	.733	142	84	38	233	2	203	20.3	116	403	40.3	932	93.2

Did You Know?

Jerry Sloan's 637 wins as Jazz head coach are the second-most by any coach with a single team in NBA history. Only Red Auerbach, who won 795 games with Boston, has more victories with one team.

Vancouver Grizzlies 1999-2000 Regular Season Totals (22-60)

Player	G	GS	Min	Field Goals			3-Pt FGs			Free Throws			Misc			Fouls		Assists		Rebounds			Points	
				Md	Att	Pct	Md	Att	Pct	Md	Att	Pct	TO	Stl	Blk	PF	DQ	Ast	Avg	Off	Tot	Avg	Pts	Avg
S. Abdur-Rahim	82	82	3223	594	1277	.465	29	96	.302	446	551	.809	249	89	87	244	3	271	3.3	218	825	10.1	1663	20.3
Michael Dickerson	82	82	3103	554	1270	.436	119	291	.409	269	324	.830	165	116	45	226	0	208	2.5	78	279	3.4	1496	18.2
Mike Bibby	82	82	3155	459	1031	.445	77	212	.363	195	250	.780	247	132	15	171	1	665	8.1	73	306	3.7	1190	14.5
Othella Harrington	82	82	2677	420	830	.506	0	2	.000	236	298	.792	217	36	58	287	3	97	1.2	196	563	6.9	1076	13.1
Bryant Reeves	69	67	1773	252	562	.448	0	4	.000	107	165	.648	119	33	38	245	8	82	1.2	126	390	5.7	611	8.9
Dennis Scott	66	0	1263	125	333	.375	71	189	.376	48	57	.842	30	28	9	104	0	69	1.0	16	106	1.6	369	5.6
Grant Long	42	1	920	74	167	.443	0	4	.000	55	71	.775	49	45	10	108	1	43	1.0	86	234	5.6	203	4.8
Felipe Lopez	65	0	781	111	261	.425	3	18	.167	67	109	.615	53	32	17	94	0	44	0.7	59	124	1.9	292	4.5
Doug West	38	0	581	59	145	.407	0	3	.000	34	40	.850	19	12	8	80	1	43	1.1	18	71	1.9	152	4.0
Brent Price	41	0	424	41	119	.345	25	68	.368	34	39	.872	47	17	1	63	0	69	1.7	8	37	0.9	141	3.4
Obinna Ekezie*	39	0	351	41	88	.466	0	0	—	43	64	.672	26	9	4	61	0	8	0.2	34	92	2.4	125	3.2
Antoine Carr	21	0	221	28	64	.438	0	0	—	11	14	.786	9	3	6	42	0	7	0.3	8	32	1.5	67	3.2
Joe Stephens	13	0	181	19	51	.373	0	8	.000	3	4	.750	6	7	3	9	0	11	0.8	13	36	2.8	41	3.2
Cherokee Parks	56	14	808	72	145	.497	0	1	.000	24	37	.649	28	29	45	115	2	35	0.6	55	183	3.3	168	3.0
Milt Palacio*	53	0	394	43	98	.439	0	2	.000	22	37	.595	44	20	0	32	0	48	0.9	17	51	1.0	108	2.0
Total	82	410	19855	2892	6441	.449	324	898	.361	1594	2060	.774	1381	608	346	1881	19	1700	20.7	1005	3329	40.6	7702	93.9
Opponent	82	410	19855	3136	6613	.474	361	1083	.333	1530	1989	.769	1234	725	519	1912	28	1932	23.6	970	3306	40.3	8163	99.5

* indicates rookie; † indicates player played with another team in 1999-2000; bold indicates team leader

Did You Know?

The Grizzlies had four players—Shareef Abdur-Rahim, Mike Bibby, Michael Dickerson and Othella Harrington—start all 82 games in 1999-2000. In the 19 seasons during which the NBA has officially recorded games started, only one other team, the 1991-92 New York Knicks, has had four players start all 82 of its games.

Washington Wizards 1999-2000 Regular Season Totals (29-53)

Player	G	GS	Min	Field Goals Md	Att	Pct	3-Pt FGs Md	Att	Pct	Free Throws Md	Att	Pct	Misc TO	Stl	Blk	Fouls PF	DQ	Assists Ast	Avg	Rebounds Off	Tot	Avg	Points Pts	Avg
Mitch Richmond	74	69	2397	447	1049	.426	93	241	.386	298	340	.876	154	110	13	191	2	185	2.5	37	213	2.9	1285	17.4
Juwan Howard	82	82	2909	509	1108	.459	0	7	.000	202	275	.735	225	67	21	299	2	247	3.0	132	470	5.7	1220	14.9
Rod Strickland	69	67	2188	327	762	.429	1	21	.048	214	305	.702	187	94	18	147	1	519	7.5	73	259	3.8	869	12.6
Tracy Murray	80	8	1831	290	670	.433	113	263	.430	120	141	.851	84	45	24	185	2	72	0.9	63	271	3.4	813	10.2
Richard Hamilton*	71	12	1373	254	605	.420	28	77	.364	103	133	.774	84	28	6	142	2	108	1.5	38	129	1.8	639	9.0
Chris Whitney	82	15	1627	217	521	.417	96	255	.376	112	132	.848	107	55	5	166	1	313	3.8	20	134	1.6	642	7.8
Aaron Williams	81	0	1545	235	450	.522	0	3	.000	146	201	.726	80	41	92	234	3	58	0.7	159	409	5.0	616	7.6
Jahidi White	80	59	1537	228	450	.507	0	0	—	113	211	.536	94	31	83	234	2	15	0.2	202	553	6.9	569	7.1
Isaac Austin	59	23	1173	151	352	.429	1	4	.250	94	137	.686	107	17	38	128	0	74	1.3	64	282	4.8	397	6.7
Don Reid†	17	0	333	44	78	.564	0	0	—	21	28	.750	12	19	19	73	4	10	0.6	26	77	4.5	109	6.4
Michael Smith	46	46	1145	108	192	.563	0	1	.000	73	101	.723	45	27	23	127	0	56	1.2	121	331	7.2	289	6.3
Gerard King	62	28	1060	139	277	.502	0	0	—	49	66	.742	41	34	15	132	1	49	0.8	84	250	4.0	327	5.3
Calvin Booth*	11	0	143	16	46	.348	0	0	—	10	14	.714	6	3	14	23	0	7	0.6	15	32	2.9	42	3.8
Lorenzo Williams	8	0	76	7	9	.778	0	0	—	0	0	—	3	3	6	13	0	1	0.1	12	25	3.1	14	1.8
Laron Profit*	33	1	225	21	59	.356	3	17	.176	4	10	.400	19	7	4	26	0	25	0.8	2	26	0.8	49	1.5
Reggie Jordan	36	0	243	17	53	.321	0	1	.000	7	13	.538	19	12	2	29	0	32	0.9	16	41	1.1	41	1.1
Total	82	410	19805	3010	6681	.451	335	890	.376	1566	2107	.743	1320	593	383	2149	20	1771	21.6	1064	3502	42.7	7921	96.6
Opponent	82	410	19805	3005	6547	.459	390	1052	.371	1790	2405	.744	1225	686	503	1967	17	1793	21.9	962	3380	41.2	8190	99.9

* indicates rookie; † indicates player played with another team in 1999-2000; bold indicates team leader

Did You Know?

In 2000-01, Leonard Hamilton will become Washington's seventh head coach in a span of five seasons. Only two other franchises, the Blackhawks/Hawks (1949-54) and Cavaliers (1978-83 and 1981-86), have had as many as seven head coaches in a span of five years.

2000 NBA Draft

Each player chosen in the 2000 NBA Draft is shown with the team that drafted him, along with his complete college statistics (unless otherwise noted).

A dagger following a player's name indicates the player has changed teams since the draft. All footnoted materials have an explanation following a player's stat box.

2000 NBA Rookie Draft

First Round

Kenyon Martin—New Jersey (1)

College: Cincinnati **Ht:** 6'9" **Wt:** 230 **Born:** 12/30/76 **Age:** 24

Year	G	GS	Min	FGM	FGA	Pct	3PM	3PA	Pct	FTM	FTA	Pct	TO	Stl	Blk	PF	DQ	Ast	Avg	OReb	TReb	Avg	Pts	Avg
96-97	22	3	233	26	40	.650	0	0	—	10	32	.313	16	14	24	51	2	10	0.5	28	74	3.4	62	2.8
97-98	30	30	858	124	198	.626	0	1	.000	50	105	.476	52	30	83	109	3	41	1.4	106	267	8.9	298	9.9
98-99	33	33	900	142	248	.573	0	1	.000	50	89	.562	67	37	78	109	6	49	1.5	84	228	6.9	334	10.1
99-00	31	31	908	221	389	.568	2	7	.286	141	206	.684	57	43	105	71	1	42	1.4	77	300	9.7	585	18.9
Total	116	97	2899	513	875	.586	2	9	.222	251	432	.581	192	124	290	340	12	142	1.2	295	869	7.5	1279	11.0

Stromile Swift—Vancouver (2)

College: Louisiana State **Ht:** 6'9" **Wt:** 225 **Born:** 11/21/79 **Age:** 21

Year	G	GS	Min	FGM	FGA	Pct	3PM	3PA	Pct	FTM	FTA	Pct	TO	Stl	Blk	PF	DQ	Ast	Avg	OReb	TReb	Avg	Pts	Avg
98-99	16	7	319	45	110	.409	1	8	.125	30	50	.600	46	15	35	43	2	5	0.3	33	69	4.3	121	7.6
99-00	34	33	1013	208	342	.608	7	25	.280	127	206	.617	80	50	95	88	3	32	0.9	103	279	8.2	550	16.2
Total	50	40	1332	253	452	.560	8	33	.242	157	256	.613	126	65	130	131	5	37	0.7	136	348	7.0	671	13.4

Darius Miles—LA Clippers (3)

College: None# **Ht:** 6'9" **Wt:** 217 **Born:** 10/9/81 **Age:** 19

Year	G	GS	Min	FGM	FGA	Pct	3PM	3PA	Pct	FTM	FTA	Pct	TO	Stl	Blk	PF	DQ	Ast	Avg	OReb	TReb	Avg	Pts	Avg
99-00	—	—	—	—	—	—	—	—	—	—	2.4	7.2	—	—	3.4	—	—	12.4	—	—	22.1			

Attended East St. Louis High School 1999-2000.

Marcus Fizer—Chicago (4)

College: Iowa State **Ht:** 6'8" **Wt:** 250 **Born:** 8/10/78 **Age:** 22

Year	G	GS	Min	FGM	FGA	Pct	3PM	3PA	Pct	FTM	FTA	Pct	TO	Stl	Blk	PF	DQ	Ast	Avg	OReb	TReb	Avg	Pts	Avg
97-98	30	25	816	173	365	.474	0	2	.000	101	164	.616	80	32	27	76	3	19	0.6	74	202	6.7	447	14.9
98-99	30	29	961	190	422	.450	6	28	.214	153	208	.736	68	29	23	78	1	34	1.1	66	229	7.6	539	18.0
99-00	37	37	1243	327	562	.582	15	42	.357	175	239	.732	77	29	39	103	0	41	1.1	100	285	7.7	844	22.8
Total	97	91	3020	690	1349	.511	21	72	.292	429	611	.702	225	90	89	257	4	94	1.0	240	716	7.4	1830	18.9

Mike Miller—Orlando* (5)

College: Florida **Ht:** 6'8" **Wt:** 218 **Born:** 2/19/80 **Age:** 20

Year	G	GS	Min	FGM	FGA	Pct	3PM	3PA	Pct	FTM	FTA	Pct	TO	Stl	Blk	PF	DQ	Ast	Avg	OReb	TReb	Avg	Pts	Avg
98-99	28	19	677	115	233	.494	31	87	.356	80	114	.702	69	35	7	52	1	58	2.1	48	146	5.2	341	12.2
99-00	37	37	1058	175	368	.476	47	139	.338	124	170	.729	71	46	15	70	0	91	2.5	80	243	6.6	521	14.1
Total	65	56	1735	290	601	.483	78	226	.345	204	284	.718	140	81	22	122	1	149	2.3	128	389	6.0	862	13.3

* From Golden State.

DerMarr Johnson—Atlanta (6)

College: Cincinnati **Ht:** 6'9" **Wt:** 200 **Born:** 5/5/80 **Age:** 20

Year	G	GS	Min	FGM	FGA	Pct	3PM	3PA	Pct	FTM	FTA	Pct	TO	Stl	Blk	PF	DQ	Ast	Avg	OReb	TReb	Avg	Pts	Avg
99-00	32	32	879	140	293	.478	52	140	.371	70	95	.737	46	31	30	64	0	45	1.4	36	123	3.8	402	12.6

Chris Mihm†—Chicago* (7)

College: Texas **Ht:** 7'0" **Wt:** 262 **Born:** 7/16/79 **Age:** 21

Year	G	GS	Min	FGM	FGA	Pct	3PM	3PA	Pct	FTM	FTA	Pct	TO	Stl	Blk	PF	DQ	Ast	Avg	OReb	TReb	Avg	Pts	Avg
97-98	31	28	769	148	288	.514	2	11	.182	86	133	.647	63	12	90	107	4	14	0.5	79	248	8.0	384	12.4
98-99	32	32	1027	144	321	.449	0	4	.000	149	218	.683	78	13	84	90	2	19	0.6	130	351	11.0	437	13.7
99-00	33	33	1014	206	394	.523	7	15	.467	164	232	.707	81	11	87	90	2	22	0.7	115	346	10.5	583	17.7
Total	96	93	2810	498	1003	.497	9	30	.300	399	583	.684	222	36	261	287	8	55	0.6	324	945	9.8	1404	14.6

† Rights traded to Cleveland for the rights to Jamal Crawford plus cash. * From Washington.

Jamal Crawford†—Cleveland (8)

College: Michigan **Ht:** 6'6" **Wt:** 190 **Born:** 3/20/80 **Age:** 20

Year	G	GS	Min	FGM	FGA	Pct	3PM	3PA	Pct	FTM	FTA	Pct	TO	Stl	Blk	PF	DQ	Ast	Avg	OReb	TReb	Avg	Pts	Avg
99-00	17	16	577	105	255	.412	33	101	.327	40	51	.784	53	19	16	19	0	76	4.5	7	47	2.8	283	16.6

† Rights traded to Chicago plus cash for the rights to Chris Mihm.

Joel Przybilla†—Houston (9)

College: Minnesota **Ht:** 7'1" **Wt:** 260 **Born:** 10/10/79 **Age:** 21

Year	G	GS	Min	FGM	FGA	Pct	3PM	3PA	Pct	FTM	FTA	Pct	TO	Stl	Blk	PF	DQ	Ast	Avg	OReb	TReb	Avg	Pts	Avg
98-99	28	26	714	79	141	.560	0	0	—	30	52	.577	64	16	83	89	4	41	1.5	53	163	5.8	188	6.7
99-00	21	19	638	122	199	.613	0	0	—	55	111	.495	77	17	81	61	2	50	2.4	54	174	8.3	299	14.2
Total	49	45	1352	201	340	.591	0	0	—	85	163	.521	141	33	164	150	6	91	1.9	107	337	6.9	487	9.9

† Rights traded to Milwaukee for the rights to Jason Collier and a future first-round draft pick.

Keyon Dooling† —Orlando* (10)

College: Missouri Ht: 6'3" Wt: 184 Born: 5/8/80 Age: 20

Year	G	GS	Min	FGM	FGA	Pct	3PM	3PA	Pct	FTM	FTA	Pct	TO	Stl	Blk	PF	DQ	Ast	Avg	OReb	TReb	Avg	Pts	Avg
98-99	28	10	676	78	170	.459	8	28	.286	79	110	.718	55	32	12	47	1	85	3.0	15	58	2.1	243	8.7
99-00	31	30	987	145	373	.389	59	170	.347	124	167	.743	79	44	17	56	1	113	3.6	17	84	2.7	473	15.3
Total	59	40	1663	223	543	.411	67	198	.338	203	277	.733	134	76	29	103	2	198	3.4	32	142	2.4	716	12.1

† Rights traded to LA Clippers along with Corey Maggette, Derek Strong plus cash for a future first-round draft pick. * From Denver.

Jerome Moiso—Boston (11)

College: UCLA Ht: 6'10" Wt: 235 Born: 6/15/78 Age: 22

Year	G	GS	Min	FGM	FGA	Pct	3PM	3PA	Pct	FTM	FTA	Pct	TO	Stl	Blk	PF	DQ	Ast	Avg	OReb	TReb	Avg	Pts	Avg
98-99	29	22	689	131	269	.487	4	18	.222	48	78	.615	52	24	26	83	4	26	0.9	67	169	5.8	314	10.8
99-00	33	30	973	170	339	.501	1	6	.167	87	142	.613	88	37	55	93	4	40	1.2	84	252	7.6	428	13.0
Total	62	52	1662	301	608	.495	5	24	.208	135	220	.614	140	61	81	176	8	66	1.1	151	421	6.8	742	12.0

Etan Thomas—Dallas (12)

College: Syracuse Ht: 6'9" Wt: 256 Born: 4/1/78 Age: 22

Year	G	GS	Min	FGM	FGA	Pct	3PM	3PA	Pct	FTM	FTA	Pct	TO	Stl	Blk	PF	DQ	Ast	Avg	OReb	TReb	Avg	Pts	Avg
96-97	25	11	408	55	103	.534	0	0	—	33	71	.465	33	9	48	58	1	3	0.1	52	105	4.2	143	5.7
97-98	35	35	1009	144	236	.610	0	0	—	109	178	.612	58	27	138	99	3	15	0.4	87	230	6.6	397	11.3
98-99	33	33	913	148	240	.617	0	0	—	109	190	.574	56	27	131	92	1	17	0.5	95	243	7.4	405	12.3
99-00	29	29	940	148	246	.602	0	0	—	99	146	.678	59	22	107	92	1	16	0.6	100	269	9.3	395	13.6
Total	122	108	3270	495	825	.600	0	0	—	350	585	.598	206	85	424	341	6	51	0.4	334	847	6.9	1340	11.0

Courtney Alexander† —Orlando (13)

College: Fresno State# Ht: 6'5" Wt: 210 Born: 4/27/77 Age: 23

Year	G	GS	Min	FGM	FGA	Pct	3PM	3PA	Pct	FTM	FTA	Pct	TO	Stl	Blk	PF	DQ	Ast	Avg	OReb	TReb	Avg	Pts	Avg
95-96	27	22	727	147	302	.487	18	35	.514	63	82	.768	46	20	9	57	1	36	1.3	26	122	4.5	375	13.9
96-97	26	20	732	142	338	.420	40	90	.444	60	79	.759	31	20	1	50	0	37	1.4	6	70	2.7	384	14.8
98-99	32	32	980	264	563	.469	50	158	.316	106	140	.757	76	50	7	82	2	82	2.6	28	121	3.8	684	21.4
99-00	27	27	980	252	564	.447	58	175	.331	107	137	.781	67	36	4	62	0	92	3.4	29	128	4.7	669	24.8
Total	112	101	3462	805	1767	.456	166	458	.362	336	438	.767	220	126	21	251	3	247	2.2	89	441	3.9	2112	18.9

† Rights traded to Dallas for a future first-round draft pick plus cash. # Attended Fresno State 1998-99 thru 1999-2000, attended Virginia 1995-96 thru 1996-97.

Mateen Cleaves—Detroit (14)

College: Michigan State Ht: 6'2" Wt: 205 Born: 9/7/77 Age: 23

Year	G	GS	Min	FGM	FGA	Pct	3PM	3PA	Pct	FTM	FTA	Pct	TO	Stl	Blk	PF	DQ	Ast	Avg	OReb	TReb	Avg	Pts	Avg
96-97	29	24	750	111	277	.401	18	76	.237	57	79	.722	117	17	4	61	2	146	5.0	23	73	2.5	297	10.2
97-98	30	29	1005	161	403	.400	51	152	.336	111	158	.703	117	73	6	80	1	217	7.2	14	75	2.5	484	16.1
98-99	38	38	1185	159	392	.406	42	144	.292	85	108	.787	141	69	2	77	0	274	7.2	12	62	1.6	445	11.7
99-00	26	24	820	109	259	.421	32	85	.376	65	86	.756	95	36	4	57	0	179	6.9	5	46	1.8	315	12.1
Total	123	115	3760	540	1331	.406	143	457	.313	318	431	.738	470	195	16	275	3	816	6.6	54	256	2.1	1541	12.5

Jason Collier† —Milwaukee (15)

College: Georgia Tech# Ht: 7'0" Wt: 260 Born: 9/8/77 Age: 23

Year	G	GS	Min	FGM	FGA	Pct	3PM	3PA	Pct	FTM	FTA	Pct	TO	Stl	Blk	PF	DQ	Ast	Avg	OReb	TReb	Avg	Pts	Avg
96-97	33	27	778	112	258	.434	6	13	.462	80	117	.684	72	16	32	76	1	24	0.7	48	188	5.7	310	9.4
97-98	9	8	226	36	64	.563	0	0	—	24	36	.667	19	6	9	18	0	9	1.0	14	47	5.2	96	10.7
98-99	25	25	849	153	347	.441	32	90	.356	92	128	.719	88	15	34	87	3	36	1.4	48	182	7.3	430	17.2
99-00	30	30	975	178	376	.473	31	84	.369	122	166	.735	96	23	33	80	2	49	1.6	81	276	9.2	509	17.0
Total	97	90	2828	479	1045	.458	69	187	.369	318	447	.711	275	60	108	261	6	118	1.2	191	693	7.1	1345	13.9

† Rights traded to Houston plus a future first-round draft pick for the rights to Joel Pryzbilla. # Attended Indiana 1996-97 thru 1997-98, attended Georgia Tech 1998-99 thru 1999-2000.

Hidayet Turkoglu—Sacramento (16)

College: None# Ht: 6'8" Wt: 202 Born: 3/19/79 Age: 21

Year	G	GS	Min	FGM	FGA	Pct	3PM	3PA	Pct	FTM	FTA	Pct	TO	Stl	Blk	PF	DQ	Ast	Avg	OReb	TReb	Avg	Pts	Avg
96-97	2	—	—	0	0	—	0	0	—	0	0	—	—	—	—	—	—	0	0.0	—	0	0.0	0	0.0
97-98	9	—	—	8	16	.500	2	6	.333	3	6	.500	—	—	—	—	—	3	0.3	—	12	1.3	25	2.8
98-99	17	—	—	24	50	.480	11	42	.262	15	24	.625	—	—	—	—	—	23	1.4	—	60	3.5	96	5.6
99-00	22	—	—	82	131	.626	27	81	.333	54	86	.628	—	—	—	—	—	59	2.7	—	101	4.6	299	13.6
Total	50	—	—	114	197	.579	40	129	.310	72	116	.621	—	—	—	—	—	85	1.7	—	173	3.5	420	8.4

Played in EuroLeague 1996-97 thru 1999-2000.

Desmond Mason—Seattle (17)

College: Oklahoma State Ht: 6'5" Wt: 215 Born: 10/11/77 Age: 23

Year	G	GS	Min	FGM	FGA	Pct	3PM	3PA	Pct	FTM	FTA	Pct	TO	Stl	Blk	PF	DQ	Ast	Avg	OReb	TReb	Avg	Pts	Avg
96-97	32	12	543	52	138	.377	17	52	.327	23	37	.622	42	13	10	45	1	22	0.7	45	80	2.5	144	4.5
97-98	29	29	947	157	299	.525	22	69	.319	86	126	.683	47	51	19	75	3	45	1.6	76	223	7.7	422	14.6
98-99	34	34	1180	196	408	.480	27	79	.342	106	142	.746	73	53	30	82	1	28	0.8	89	267	7.9	525	15.4
99-00	34	34	1202	211	423	.499	64	149	.430	125	163	.767	60	41	33	69	1	52	1.5	56	225	6.6	611	18.0
Total	129	109	3872	616	1268	.486	130	349	.372	340	468	.726	222	158	92	271	6	147	1.1	266	795	6.2	1702	13.2

Quentin Richardson—LA Clippers* (18)

College: DePaul **Ht:** 6'6" **Wt:** 225 **Born:** 4/13/80 **Age:** 20

Year	G	GS	Min	FGM	FGA	Pct	3PM	3PA	Pct	FTM	FTA	Pct	TO	Stl	Blk	PF	DQ	Ast	Avg	OReb	TReb	Avg	Pts	Avg
98-99	31	29	1039	203	425	.478	44	127	.346	136	183	.743	61	24	8	69	2	32	1.0	174	327	10.5	586	18.9
99-00	33	33	1151	202	468	.432	73	194	.376	84	119	.706	77	35	9	75	0	72	2.2	118	325	9.8	561	17.0
Total	64	62	2190	405	893	.454	117	321	.364	220	302	.728	138	59	17	144	2	104	1.6	292	652	10.2	1147	17.9

* From Toronto via Atlanta, Philadelphia and New York.

Jamaal Magloire—Charlotte (19)

College: Kentucky **Ht:** 6'10" **Wt:** 260 **Born:** 5/21/78 **Age:** 22

Year	G	GS	Min	FGM	FGA	Pct	3PM	3PA	Pct	FTM	FTA	Pct	TO	Stl	Blk	PF	DQ	Ast	Avg	OReb	TReb	Avg	Pts	Avg
96-97	40	23	625	75	153	.490	0	0	—	45	82	.549	64	25	77	120	6	15	0.4	82	177	4.4	195	4.9
97-98	38	12	567	77	158	.487	0	0	—	43	64	.672	46	10	66	99	0	11	0.3	52	161	4.2	197	5.2
98-99	34	6	668	94	177	.531	0	0	—	49	85	.576	42	16	66	79	1	18	0.5	48	151	4.4	237	7.0
99-00	33	33	978	148	296	.500	0	0	—	139	203	.685	95	17	57	91	0	17	0.5	116	300	9.1	435	13.2
Total	145	74	2838	394	784	.503	0	0	—	276	434	.636	247	68	266	389	7	61	0.4	298	789	5.4	1064	7.3

Speedy Claxton—Philadelphia (20)

College: Hofstra **Ht:** 5'11" **Wt:** 180 **Born:** 5/8/78 **Age:** 22

Year	G	GS	Min	FGM	FGA	Pct	3PM	3PA	Pct	FTM	FTA	Pct	TO	Stl	Blk	PF	DQ	Ast	Avg	OReb	TReb	Avg	Pts	Avg
96-97	27	27	914	134	310	.432	6	38	.158	132	187	.706	77	50	4	85	5	91	3.4	34	123	4.6	406	15.0
97-98	31	31	1081	182	375	.485	2	11	.182	138	189	.730	104	67	8	87	3	224	7.2	42	144	4.6	504	16.3
98-99	30	28	970	136	282	.482	6	19	.316	121	151	.801	86	69	16	74	1	159	5.3	42	131	4.4	399	13.3
99-00	31	31	1089	253	538	.470	51	134	.381	149	195	.764	101	102	5	71	0	186	6.0	47	168	5.4	706	22.8
Total	119	117	4054	705	1505	.468	65	202	.322	540	722	.748	368	288	33	317	9	660	5.5	165	566	4.8	2015	16.9

Morris Peterson—Toronto* (21)

College: Michigan State **Ht:** 6'7" **Wt:** 215 **Born:** 8/26/77 **Age:** 23

Year	G	GS	Min	FGM	FGA	Pct	3PM	3PA	Pct	FTM	FTA	Pct	TO	Stl	Blk	PF	DQ	Ast	Avg	OReb	TReb	Avg	Pts	Avg
95-96	4	0	12	1	1	1.000	0	0	—	0	1	.000	1	0	0	2	0	0	0.0	0	3	0.8	2	0.5
96-97	29	18	518	72	166	.434	16	59	.271	36	51	.706	23	19	6	60	1	18	0.6	42	97	3.3	196	6.8
97-98	27	0	503	81	182	.445	23	69	.333	32	58	.552	32	21	3	61	2	24	0.9	42	94	3.5	217	8.0
98-99	38	6	907	190	343	.554	22	59	.373	114	140	.814	62	33	22	97	4	36	0.9	92	216	5.7	516	13.6
99-00	39	38	1136	218	469	.465	85	200	.425	136	176	.773	84	46	11	79	0	49	1.3	79	235	6.0	657	16.8
Total	137	62	3076	562	1161	.484	146	387	.377	318	426	.746	202	119	42	299	7	127	0.9	255	645	4.7	1588	11.6

* From Minnesota.

Donnell Harvey†—New York (22)

College: Florida **Ht:** 6'8" **Wt:** 216 **Born:** 8/26/80 **Age:** 20

Year	G	GS	Min	FGM	FGA	Pct	3PM	3PA	Pct	FTM	FTA	Pct	TO	Stl	Blk	PF	DQ	Ast	Avg	OReb	TReb	Avg	Pts	Avg
99-00	37	9	746	144	284	.507	0	1	.000	86	141	.610	60	27	31	101	3	37	1.0	99	258	7.0	374	10.1

† Rights traded to Dallas along with John Wallace for Erick Strickland and the rights to Pete Mickeal.

DeShawn Stevenson—Utah* (23)

College: None# **Ht:** 6'5" **Wt:** 210 **Born:** 4/3/81 **Age:** 19

Year	G	GS	Min	FGM	FGA	Pct	3PM	3PA	Pct	FTM	FTA	Pct	TO	Stl	Blk	PF	DQ	Ast	Avg	OReb	TReb	Avg	Pts	Avg
99-00	—	—	—	—	—	—	—	—	—	—	—	—	—	—	—	—	—	—	6.2	—	—	9.7	—	30.4

* From Miami. # Attended Washington Union High School 1999-2000.

Dalibor Bagaric—Chicago* (24)

College: None# **Ht:** 7'1" **Wt:** 255 **Born:** 2/7/80 **Age:** 20

Year	G	GS	Min	FGM	FGA	Pct	3PM	3PA	Pct	FTM	FTA	Pct	TO	Stl	Blk	PF	DQ	Ast	Avg	OReb	TReb	Avg	Pts	Avg
97-98	25	—	—	57	99	.576	0	—	—	35	40	.875	—	—	—	—	—	9	0.4	—	72	2.9	149	6.0
98-99	11	—	—	27	39	.692	0	—	—	21	26	.808	—	—	—	—	—	4	0.4	—	54	4.9	75	6.8
99-00	22	—	—	147	249	.590	0	—	—	109	167	.653	—	—	—	—	—	15	0.7	—	228	10.4	403	18.3
Total	58	—	—	231	387	.597	0	3	.000	165	233	.708	—	—	—	—	—	28	0.5	—	354	6.1	627	10.8

* From San Antonio. # Played for Benston Zagreb (Croatia) 1997-98 thru 1999-2000.

Iakovos Tsakalidis—Phoenix (25)

College: None# **Ht:** 7'2" **Wt:** 282 **Born:** 6/10/79 **Age:** 21

Year	G	GS	Min	FGM	FGA	Pct	3PM	3PA	Pct	FTM	FTA	Pct	TO	Stl	Blk	PF	DQ	Ast	Avg	OReb	TReb	Avg	Pts	Avg
96-97	1	—	—	1	2	.500	0	0	—	2	2	1.000	—	—	—	—	—	0	0.0	—	4	4.0	4	4.0
97-98	18	—	—	35	63	.571	0	0	—	24	43	.558	—	—	—	—	—	4	0.2	—	101	5.6	94	5.2
98-99	25	—	—	63	121	.521	0	0	—	35	55	.636	—	—	—	—	—	5	0.2	—	149	6.0	161	6.4
99-00	22	—	—	73	123	.593	0	0	—	57	103	.553	—	—	—	—	—	14	0.6	—	153	7.0	203	9.2
Total	66	—	—	172	309	.557	0	0	—	118	203	.581	—	—	—	—	—	23	0.3	—	407	6.2	462	7.0

Played for AEK (Greece) 1996-97 thru 1999-2000.

Mamadou N'diaye—Denver* (26)

College: Auburn **Ht:** 7'0" **Wt:** 245 **Born:** 6/16/75 **Age:** 25

Year	G	GS	Min	FGM	FGA	Pct	3PM	3PA	Pct	FTM	FTA	Pct	TO	Stl	Blk	PF	DQ	Ast	Avg	OReb	TReb	Avg	Pts	Avg
96-97	31	13	350	42	86	.488	0	1	.000	10	19	.526	30	13	25	72	2	7	0.2	33	76	2.5	94	3.0
97-98	30	30	747	89	177	.503	0	0	—	61	99	.616	83	16	73	106	9	22	0.7	83	208	6.9	239	8.0
98-99	33	33	785	88	180	.489	0	0	—	63	97	.649	63	33	77	100	4	29	0.9	106	247	7.5	239	7.2
99-00	34	33	903	100	188	.532	0	1	.000	103	155	.665	73	26	66	105	6	18	0.5	95	267	7.9	303	8.9
Total	128	109	2785	319	631	.506	0	2	.000	237	370	.641	249	88	241	383	21	76	0.6	317	798	6.2	875	6.8

* From Utah.

Primoz Brezec—Indiana (27)

College: None# **Ht:** 7'0" **Wt:** 240 **Born:** 10/2/79 **Age:** 21

Year	G	GS	Min	FGM	FGA	Pct	3PM	3PA	Pct	FTM	FTA	Pct	TO	Stl	Blk	PF	DQ	Ast	Avg	OReb	TReb	Avg	Pts	Avg
97-98	30	—	—	164	283	.580	16	52	.308	201	258	.779	—	—	—	—	—	12	0.4	—	207	6.9	577	19.2
98-99	12	—	—	36	47	.766	0	0	—	28	41	.683	—	—	—	—	—	4	0.3	—	38	3.2	100	8.3
99-00	23	—	—	40	52	.769	0	0	—	31	45	.689	—	—	—	—	—	4	0.2	—	40	1.7	111	4.8
Total	65	—	—	240	382	.628	16	52	.308	260	344	.756	—	—	—	—	—	20	0.3	—	285	4.4	788	12.1

Played for Olimpija Ljubljana (Slovenia) 1997-98 thru 1999-2000.

Erick Barkley—Portland (28)

College: St. John's **Ht:** 6'1" **Wt:** 185 **Born:** 2/21/78 **Age:** 22

Year	G	GS	Min	FGM	FGA	Pct	3PM	3PA	Pct	FTM	FTA	Pct	TO	Stl	Blk	PF	DQ	Ast	Avg	OReb	TReb	Avg	Pts	Avg
98-99	37	37	1228	157	397	.395	57	166	.343	129	167	.772	77	83	10	93	2	175	4.7	34	118	3.2	500	13.5
99-00	28	27	1033	159	400	.398	50	160	.313	81	122	.664	68	84	8	64	2	127	4.5	20	84	3.0	449	16.0
Total	65	64	2261	316	797	.396	107	326	.328	210	289	.727	145	167	18	157	4	302	4.6	54	202	3.1	949	14.6

Mark Madsen—LA Lakers (29)

College: Stanford **Ht:** 6'9" **Wt:** 240 **Born:** 1/28/76 **Age:** 25

Year	G	GS	Min	FGM	FGA	Pct	3PM	3PA	Pct	FTM	FTA	Pct	TO	Stl	Blk	PF	DQ	Ast	Avg	OReb	TReb	Avg	Pts	Avg
96-97	25	0	410	51	95	.537	0	0	—	45	74	.608	22	6	11	73	4	5	0.2	59	126	5.0	147	5.9
97-98	27	24	706	116	197	.589	0	1	.000	83	132	.629	35	11	11	70	3	20	0.7	92	220	8.1	315	11.7
98-99	33	33	969	153	253	.605	0	1	.000	127	218	.583	51	17	21	75	3	16	0.5	109	297	9.0	433	13.1
99-00	23	20	628	108	184	.587	0	0	—	65	113	.575	34	13	21	52	0	25	1.1	84	214	9.3	281	12.2
Total	108	77	2713	428	729	.587	0	2	.000	320	537	.596	142	47	64	270	10	66	0.6	344	857	7.9	1176	10.9

Second Round

Marko Jaric—LA Clippers (30)

College: None# **Ht:** 6'7" **Wt:** 198 **Born:** 12/10/78 **Age:** 22

Year	G	GS	Min	FGM	FGA	Pct	3PM	3PA	Pct	FTM	FTA	Pct	TO	Stl	Blk	PF	DQ	Ast	Avg	OReb	TReb	Avg	Pts	Avg
96-97	30	—	—	27	52	.519	0	3	.000	22	33	.667	—	—	—	—	—	15	0.5	—	36	1.2	76	2.5
97-98	29	—	—	50	98	.510	9	24	.375	38	49	.775	—	—	—	—	—	35	1.2	—	73	2.5	165	5.7
98-99	25	—	—	42	73	.575	23	59	.390	43	49	.878	—	—	—	—	—	34	1.4	—	73	2.9	196	7.8
99-00	26	—	—	72	126	.571	19	58	.328	57	77	.740	—	—	—	—	—	36	1.4	—	74	2.8	258	9.9
Total	110	—	—	191	349	.547	51	144	.354	160	208	.769	—	—	—	—	—	120	1.1	—	256	2.3	695	6.3

Played for Peristeri (Greece) 1996-97 thru 1997-98, played for Fortitudo Bologna (Italy) 1998-99 thru 1999-2000.

Dan Langhi†—Dallas* (31)

College: Vanderbilt **Ht:** 6'11" **Wt:** 220 **Born:** 11/28/77 **Age:** 23

Year	G	GS	Min	FGM	FGA	Pct	3PM	3PA	Pct	FTM	FTA	Pct	TO	Stl	Blk	PF	DQ	Ast	Avg	OReb	TReb	Avg	Pts	Avg
96-97	31	2	477	33	76	.434	9	27	.333	55	74	.743	27	11	4	32	0	9	0.3	24	76	2.5	130	4.2
97-98	31	2	496	68	162	.420	24	67	.358	36	47	.766	41	11	6	47	0	14	0.5	38	91	2.9	196	6.3
98-99	29	28	954	162	388	.418	47	122	.385	141	167	.844	70	23	7	52	1	36	1.2	65	211	7.3	512	17.7
99-00	30	29	1033	222	465	.477	58	144	.403	162	186	.871	53	13	9	56	0	24	0.8	47	181	6.0	664	22.1
Total	121	61	2960	485	1091	.445	138	360	.383	394	474	.831	191	58	26	187	1	83	0.7	174	559	4.6	1502	12.4

† Rights traded to Houston for the rights to Eduardo Najera and a future second-round draft pick. * From Chicago.

A.J. Guyton—Chicago* (32)

College: Indiana **Ht:** 6'1" **Wt:** 185 **Born:** 2/13/78 **Age:** 22

Year	G	GS	Min	FGM	FGA	Pct	3PM	3PA	Pct	FTM	FTA	Pct	TO	Stl	Blk	PF	DQ	Ast	Avg	OReb	TReb	Avg	Pts	Avg
96-97	33	29	1107	157	361	.435	56	145	.386	80	94	.851	71	40	17	42	0	129	3.9	22	110	3.3	450	13.6
97-98	32	30	1089	188	402	.468	79	180	.439	82	107	.766	79	36	8	60	0	118	3.7	15	112	3.5	537	16.8
98-99	34	34	1158	198	435	.455	76	187	.406	71	94	.755	78	22	14	42	0	88	2.6	23	117	3.4	543	16.0
99-00	29	29	995	204	444	.459	72	172	.419	90	114	.789	69	29	13	27	0	68	2.3	17	80	2.8	570	19.7
Total	128	122	4349	747	1642	.455	283	684	.414	323	409	.790	297	127	52	171	0	403	3.1	77	419	3.3	2100	16.4

* From Golden State.

Jake Voskuhl—Chicago* (33)

College: Connecticut **Ht:** 6'11" **Wt:** 245 **Born:** 11/1/77 **Age:** 23

Year	G	GS	Min	FGM	FGA	Pct	3PM	3PA	Pct	FTM	FTA	Pct	TO	Stl	Blk	PF	DQ	Ast	Avg	OReb	TReb	Avg	Pts	Avg
96-97	33	30	678	48	99	.485	0	0	—	36	57	.632	37	23	46	110	9	20	0.6	66	181	5.5	132	4.0
97-98	37	37	877	100	177	.565	0	0	—	56	83	.675	66	25	49	128	6	27	0.7	88	262	7.1	256	6.9
98-99	34	34	728	66	129	.512	0	0	—	54	87	.621	61	20	51	106	2	38	1.1	63	218	6.4	186	5.5
99-00	34	34	778	109	191	.571	0	0	—	71	104	.683	62	18	47	93	1	39	1.1	73	219	6.4	289	8.5
Total	138	135	3061	323	596	.542	0	0	—	217	331	.656	226	86	193	437	18	124	0.9	290	880	6.4	863	6.3

* From Vancouver via Houston.

Khalid El-Amin—Chicago* (34)

College: Connecticut **Ht:** 5'10" **Wt:** 203 **Born:** 4/25/79 **Age:** 21

Year	G	GS	Min	FGM	FGA	Pct	3PM	3PA	Pct	FTM	FTA	Pct	TO	Stl	Blk	PF	DQ	Ast	Avg	OReb	TReb	Avg	Pts	Avg
97-98	37	36	1105	211	498	.424	81	222	.365	90	113	.796	100	68	5	68	0	156	4.2	25	108	2.9	593	16.0
98-99	36	35	1031	174	422	.412	51	151	.338	98	126	.778	95	59	1	82	0	140	3.9	33	101	2.8	497	13.8
99-00	35	35	1118	195	475	.411	63	177	.356	107	120	.892	93	59	4	73	0	183	5.2	22	110	3.1	560	16.0
Total	108	106	3254	580	1395	.416	195	550	.355	295	359	.822	288	186	10	223	0	479	4.4	80	319	3.0	1650	15.3

* From Atlanta.

Mike Smith—Washington (35)

College: Louisiana-Monroe **Ht:** 6'8" **Wt:** 195 **Born:** 4/15/76 **Age:** 24

Year	G	GS	Min	FGM	FGA	Pct	3PM	3PA	Pct	FTM	FTA	Pct	TO	Stl	Blk	PF	DQ	Ast	Avg	OReb	TReb	Avg	Pts	Avg
98-99	27	25	927	166	383	.433	55	187	.294	113	153	.739	120	48	17	54	1	51	1.9	54	185	6.9	500	18.5
99-00	28	27	1011	187	441	.424	75	222	.338	113	141	.801	121	42	25	56	0	96	3.4	71	264	9.4	562	20.1
Total	55	52	1938	353	824	.428	130	409	.318	226	294	.769	241	90	42	110	1	147	2.7	125	449	8.2	1062	19.3

Soumaila Samake—New Jersey (36)

College: None# **Ht:** 7'2" **Wt:** 230 **Born:** 3/18/78 **Age:** 22

Year	G	GS	Min	FGM	FGA	Pct	3PM	3PA	Pct	FTM	FTA	Pct	TO	Stl	Blk	PF	DQ	Ast	Avg	OReb	TReb	Avg	Pts	Avg
98-99	30	—	—	81	123	.659	0	1	.000	49	86	.570	—	—	—	—	—	4	0.1	—	147	4.9	211	7.0
99-00	60	—	—	235	413	.569	0	2	.000	114	165	.691	—	—	—	—	—	39	0.7	—	458	7.6	584	9.7
Total	90	—	—	316	536	.590	0	3	.000	163	251	.649	—	—	—	—	—	43	0.5	—	605	6.7	795	8.8

Played for Slovan (Slovenia) 1998-99, played for Cincinnati Stuff (IBL) 1999-2000.

Eddie House—Miami* (37)

College: Arizona State **Ht:** 6'1" **Wt:** 180 **Born:** 5/14/78 **Age:** 22

Year	G	GS	Min	FGM	FGA	Pct	3PM	3PA	Pct	FTM	FTA	Pct	TO	Stl	Blk	PF	DQ	Ast	Avg	OReb	TReb	Avg	Pts	Avg
96-97	30	22	885	151	363	.416	57	179	.318	18	28	.643	39	59	8	66	1	108	3.6	19	84	2.8	377	12.6
97-98	32	31	983	143	331	.432	55	137	.401	22	29	.759	43	64	6	80	1	93	2.9	16	96	3.0	363	11.3
98-99	30	30	1106	206	477	.432	66	167	.389	91	115	.791	84	61	3	87	2	93	3.1	36	147	4.9	568	18.9
99-00	32	31	1189	263	623	.422	73	200	.365	137	164	.835	72	74	2	66	1	111	3.5	51	175	5.5	736	23.0
Total	124	114	4163	763	1794	.425	250	683	.366	268	336	.798	238	258	19	299	5	405	3.3	122	502	4.0	2044	16.5

* From Denver via Cleveland.

Eduardo Najera†—Houston (38)

College: Oklahoma **Ht:** 6'8" **Wt:** 240 **Born:** 7/11/76 **Age:** 24

Year	G	GS	Min	FGM	FGA	Pct	3PM	3PA	Pct	FTM	FTA	Pct	TO	Stl	Blk	PF	DQ	Ast	Avg	OReb	TReb	Avg	Pts	Avg
96-97	30	16	739	72	178	.404	3	15	.200	64	92	.696	36	38	17	87	6	32	1.1	79	167	5.6	211	7.0
97-98	30	20	857	119	280	.425	13	49	.265	64	101	.634	56	37	20	93	3	42	1.4	66	163	5.4	315	10.5
98-99	32	32	1100	187	451	.415	51	149	.342	70	109	.642	83	59	27	87	3	69	2.2	101	266	8.3	495	15.5
99-00	34	34	1162	234	514	.455	18	82	.220	139	202	.688	82	59	25	97	4	72	2.1	92	314	9.2	625	18.4
Total	126	102	3858	612	1423	.430	85	295	.288	337	504	.669	257	193	89	364	16	215	1.7	338	910	7.2	1646	13.1

† Rights traded to Dallas plus a future second-round draft pick for the rights to Dan Langhi.

Lavor Postell—New York* (39)

College: St. John's **Ht:** 6'6" **Wt:** 212 **Born:** 2/26/78 **Age:** 22

Year	G	GS	Min	FGM	FGA	Pct	3PM	3PA	Pct	FTM	FTA	Pct	TO	Stl	Blk	PF	DQ	Ast	Avg	OReb	TReb	Avg	Pts	Avg
96-97	27	27	689	51	140	.364	9	47	.191	41	62	.661	71	34	14	83	1	60	2.2	44	89	3.3	152	5.6
97-98	32	32	931	100	221	.452	17	51	.333	100	121	.826	54	33	11	69	2	50	1.6	83	162	5.1	317	9.9
98-99	37	12	1001	172	387	.444	41	99	.414	100	126	.794	52	32	12	68	1	35	0.9	108	236	6.4	485	13.1
99-00	33	33	1155	171	400	.428	25	85	.294	106	131	.809	49	30	21	79	0	60	1.8	94	229	6.9	473	14.3
Total	129	104	3776	494	1148	.430	92	282	.326	347	440	.789	226	129	58	299	4	205	1.6	329	716	5.6	1427	11.1

* From Boston.

Hanno Möttölä—Atlanta* (40)

College: Utah **Ht:** 6'10" **Wt:** 245 **Born:** 9/9/76 **Age:** 24

Year	G	GS	Min	FGM	FGA	Pct	3PM	3PA	Pct	FTM	FTA	Pct	TO	Stl	Blk	PF	DQ	Ast	Avg	OReb	TReb	Avg	Pts	Avg
96-97	32	1	579	78	133	.586	0	2	.000	48	77	.623	38	8	9	95	6	29	0.9	27	91	2.8	204	6.4
97-98	34	34	958	158	323	.489	16	55	.291	92	122	.754	78	12	16	76	1	27	0.8	65	181	5.3	424	12.5
98-99	33	33	1023	186	386	.482	34	96	.354	100	120	.833	58	13	13	96	4	47	1.4	53	178	5.4	506	15.3
99-00	21	19	574	116	233	.498	21	60	.350	105	127	.827	63	4	12	68	1	36	1.7	27	101	4.8	358	17.0
Total	120	87	3134	538	1075	.500	71	213	.333	345	446	.774	237	37	50	335	12	139	1.2	172	551	4.6	1492	12.4

* From Denver.

Chris Carrawell—San Antonio* (41)

College: Duke **Ht:** 6'6" **Wt:** 215 **Born:** 11/25/77 **Age:** 23

Year	G	GS	Min	FGM	FGA	Pct	3PM	3PA	Pct	FTM	FTA	Pct	TO	Stl	Blk	PF	DQ	Ast	Avg	OReb	TReb	Avg	Pts	Avg
96-97	31	11	503	72	125	.576	0	2	.000	27	47	.574	29	22	21	39	0	34	1.1	47	97	3.1	171	5.5
97-98	32	10	710	121	251	.482	14	38	.368	66	103	.641	49	19	23	38	0	35	1.1	53	117	3.7	322	10.1
98-99	39	38	1116	144	317	.454	19	55	.345	79	137	.577	84	30	34	71	1	130	3.3	59	188	4.8	386	9.9
99-00	34	34	1212	205	422	.486	29	77	.377	137	176	.778	69	34	36	58	0	110	3.2	52	206	6.1	576	16.9
Total	136	93	3541	542	1115	.486	62	172	.360	309	463	.667	231	105	114	206	1	309	2.3	211	608	4.5	1455	10.7

* From Dallas.

Olumide Oyedeji—Seattle* (42)

College: None# **Ht:** 6'10" **Wt:** 240 **Born:** 5/11/81 **Age:** 19

Year	G	GS	Min	FGM	FGA	Pct	3PM	3PA	Pct	FTM	FTA	Pct	TO	Stl	Blk	PF	DQ	Ast	Avg	OReb	TReb	Avg	Pts	Avg
98-99	23	—	—	73	126	.579	2	5	.400	32	51	.627	—	—	—	—	—	12	0.5	—	176	7.7	184	8.0
99-00	24	—	—	114	203	.562	0	1	.000	70	138	.507	—	—	—	—	—	15	0.6	—	370	15.4	298	12.4
Total	47	—	—	187	329	.568	2	6	.333	102	189	.540	—	—	—	—	—	27	0.6	—	546	11.6	482	10.3

* From Orlando. # Played for DJK Wurzburg (Germany) 1998-99 thru 1999-2000.

Michael Redd—Milwaukee (43)

College: Ohio State **Ht:** 6'6" **Wt:** 215 **Born:** 8/24/79 **Age:** 21

Year	G	GS	Min	FGM	FGA	Pct	3PM	3PA	Pct	FTM	FTA	Pct	TO	Stl	Blk	PF	DQ	Ast	Avg	OReb	TReb	Avg	Pts	Avg
97-98	30	30	1137	241	550	.438	46	152	.303	130	211	.616	104	61	8	67	2	91	3.0	74	194	6.5	658	21.9
98-99	36	36	1183	261	560	.466	46	135	.341	135	220	.614	89	51	2	61	1	85	2.4	77	203	5.6	703	19.5
99-00	30	30	1002	197	452	.436	34	108	.315	90	116	.776	62	37	6	56	1	64	2.1	56	196	6.5	518	17.3
Total	96	96	3322	699	1562	.448	126	395	.319	355	547	.649	255	149	11	184	4	240	2.5	207	593	6.2	1879	19.6

Brian Cardinal—Detroit (44)

College: Purdue **Ht:** 6'8" **Wt:** 245 **Born:** 5/2/77 **Age:** 23

Year	G	GS	Min	FGM	FGA	Pct	3PM	3PA	Pct	FTM	FTA	Pct	TO	Stl	Blk	PF	DQ	Ast	Avg	OReb	TReb	Avg	Pts	Avg
96-97	30	30	860	100	220	.455	21	63	.333	98	139	.705	63	51	8	105	6	58	1.9	65	182	6.1	319	10.6
97-98	36	32	925	140	275	.509	30	70	.429	122	155	.787	50	65	12	119	6	66	1.8	69	178	4.9	432	12.0
98-99	34	34	960	118	246	.480	37	99	.374	114	147	.776	66	78	14	99	3	82	2.4	75	186	5.5	387	11.4
99-00	32	29	943	137	333	.411	42	124	.339	130	169	.769	74	65	10	86	4	71	2.2	61	203	6.3	446	13.9
Total	132	125	3688	495	1074	.461	130	356	.365	464	610	.761	253	259	44	409	19	277	2.1	270	749	5.7	1584	12.0

Jabari Smith—Sacramento (45)

College: Louisiana State **Ht:** 6'11" **Wt:** 250 **Born:** 2/12/77 **Age:** 23

Year	G	GS	Min	FGM	FGA	Pct	3PM	3PA	Pct	FTM	FTA	Pct	TO	Stl	Blk	PF	DQ	Ast	Avg	OReb	TReb	Avg	Pts	Avg
98-99	27	24	808	115	227	.507	12	49	.245	100	145	.690	95	32	32	73	1	51	1.9	92	262	9.7	342	12.7
99-00	34	34	969	156	282	.553	13	35	.371	100	168	.595	88	24	33	84	1	75	2.2	83	239	7.0	425	12.5
Total	61	58	1777	271	509	.532	25	84	.298	200	313	.639	183	56	65	157	2	126	2.1	175	501	8.2	767	12.6

DeeAndre Hulett—Toronto (46)

College: None# **Ht:** 6'8" **Wt:** 205 **Born:** 12/29/80 **Age:** 20

Year	G	GS	Min	FGM	FGA	Pct	3PM	3PA	Pct	FTM	FTA	Pct	TO	Stl	Blk	PF	DQ	Ast	Avg	OReb	TReb	Avg	Pts	Avg
98-99	37	—		434	829	.524	79	220	.359	115	178	.646	—	—	—	—	—	57	1.5	—	310	8.4	1062	28.7
99-00	56	—		186	371	.501	4	37	.108	93	142	.655	—	—	—	—	—	32	0.6	—	145	2.6	469	8.4
Total	93	—		620	1200	.517	83	257	.323	208	320	.650	—	—	—	—	—	89	1.0	—	455	4.9	1531	16.5

Attended College of The Sequoias 1998-99, played for Las Vegas Silver Bandits (IBL) 1999-2000.

Josip Sesar[†]—Seattle (47)

College: None# **Ht:** 6'6" **Wt:** — **Born:** —/—/78 **Age:** —

Year	G	GS	Min	FGM	FGA	Pct	3PM	3PA	Pct	FTM	FTA	Pct	TO	Stl	Blk	PF	DQ	Ast	Avg	OReb	TReb	Avg	Pts	Avg
96-97	18	—		78	147	.531	41	95	.432	108	137	.788	—	—	—	—	—	43	2.4	—	32	1.8	387	21.5
97-98	22	—		118	198	.596	44	100	.440	119	152	.783	—	—	—	—	—	43	2.0	—	32	1.5	487	22.1
98-99	11	—		62	106	.585	21	57	.368	65	85	.765	—	—	—	—	—	17	1.5	—	24	2.2	252	22.9
99-00	20	—		70	108	.648	42	102	.412	54	69	.783	—	—	—	—	—	60	3.0	—	20	1.0	320	16.0
Total	71	—		328	559	.587	148	354	.418	346	443	.781	—	—	—	—	—	163	2.3	—	108	1.5	1446	20.4

† Rights traded to Boston for two future second-round draft picks. # Played for Cibona Zagreb (Croatia) 1996-97 thru 1999-2000.

Mark Karcher—Philadelphia (48)

College: Temple **Ht:** 6'5" **Wt:** 215 **Born:** 11/22/78 **Age:** 22

Year	G	GS	Min	FGM	FGA	Pct	3PM	3PA	Pct	FTM	FTA	Pct	TO	Stl	Blk	PF	DQ	Ast	Avg	OReb	TReb	Avg	Pts	Avg
98-99	35	31	1042	158	431	.367	67	228	.294	85	131	.649	63	51	4	97	3	78	2.2	69	203	5.8	468	13.4
99-00	32	32	1022	180	476	.378	82	235	.349	62	109	.569	65	59	5	64	0	70	2.2	53	146	4.6	504	15.8
Total	67	63	2064	338	907	.373	149	463	.322	147	240	.613	128	110	9	161	3	148	2.2	122	349	5.2	972	14.5

Jason Hart—Milwaukee* (49)

College: Syracuse **Ht:** 6'3" **Wt:** 181 **Born:** 4/29/78 **Age:** 22

Year	G	GS	Min	FGM	FGA	Pct	3PM	3PA	Pct	FTM	FTA	Pct	TO	Stl	Blk	PF	DQ	Ast	Avg	OReb	TReb	Avg	Pts	Avg
96-97	32	32	1144	113	298	.379	23	70	.329	58	84	.690	99	88	2	85	2	184	5.8	30	113	3.5	307	9.6
97-98	35	35	1198	120	328	.366	25	96	.260	91	133	.684	123	79	3	98	2	174	5.0	38	126	3.6	356	10.2
98-99	33	32	1068	167	407	.410	53	145	.366	71	96	.740	103	101	6	100	2	143	4.3	22	98	3.0	458	13.9
99-00	32	32	1083	125	304	.411	38	115	.330	94	128	.734	111	59	3	78	0	208	6.5	16	96	3.0	382	11.9
Total	132	131	4493	525	1337	.393	139	426	.326	314	441	.712	436	327	14	361	7	709	5.4	106	433	3.3	1503	11.4

* From Charlotte.

Kaniel Dickens—Utah* (50)

College: Idaho **Ht:** 6'8" **Wt:** 235 **Born:** 7/21/78 **Age:** 22

Year	G	GS	Min	FGM	FGA	Pct	3PM	3PA	Pct	FTM	FTA	Pct	TO	Stl	Blk	PF	DQ	Ast	Avg	OReb	TReb	Avg	Pts	Avg
98-99	26	1	426	66	138	.478	0	3	.000	31	51	.608	47	21	14	54	2	7	0.3	43	124	4.8	163	6.3
99-00	29	23	795	119	243	.490	13	34	.382	102	160	.638	65	26	25	96	4	27	0.9	30	192	6.6	353	12.2
Total	55	24	1221	185	381	.486	13	37	.351	133	211	.630	112	47	39	150	6	34	0.6	73	316	5.7	516	9.4

* From New York.

Igor Rakocevic—Minnesota (51)

College: None# **Ht:** 6'2" **Wt:** 175 **Born:** 3/29/78 **Age:** 22

Year	G	GS	Min	FGM	FGA	Pct	3PM	3PA	Pct	FTM	FTA	Pct	TO	Stl	Blk	PF	DQ	Ast	Avg	OReb	TReb	Avg	Pts	Avg
96-97	12	—		10	24	.417	5	20	.250	16	21	.762	—	—	—	—	—	8	0.7	—	2	0.2	51	4.3
97-98	26	—		88	155	.568	35	77	.455	55	73	.753	—	—	—	—	—	33	1.3	—	35	1.3	336	12.9
98-99	16	—		70	132	.530	27	73	.370	82	99	.828	—	—	—	—	—	35	2.2	—	30	1.9	303	18.9
99-00	17	—		73	121	.603	23	54	.426	53	74	.716	—	—	—	—	—	31	1.8	—	35	2.1	268	15.8
Total	71	—		241	432	.558	90	224	.402	206	267	.771	—	—	—	—	—	107	1.5	—	102	1.4	958	13.5

Played for Red Star Belgrade (Yugoslavia) 1996-97 thru 1999-2000.

Ernest Brown—Miami (52)

College: Indian Hills CC# **Ht:** 7'0" **Wt:** 255 **Born:** 5/17/79 **Age:** 21

Year	G	GS	Min	FGM	FGA	Pct	3PM	3PA	Pct	FTM	FTA	Pct	TO	Stl	Blk	PF	DQ	Ast	Avg	OReb	TReb	Avg	Pts	Avg
98-99	29	—	—	283	361	.784	0	0	—	92	152	.605	—	—	—	—	—	20	0.7	—	444	15.3	658	22.7
99-00	33	—	—	168	276	.609	0	0	—	59	113	.522	—	—	—	—	—	21	0.6	—	227	6.9	395	12.0
Total	62	—	—	451	637	.708	0	0	—	151	265	.570	—	—	—	—	—	41	0.7	—	671	10.8	1053	17.0

Attended Mesa Community College 1998-99, attended Indian Hills Community College 1999-2000.

Dan McClintock—Denver* (53)

College: Northern Arizona **Ht:** 7'0" **Wt:** 260 **Born:** 4/19/77 **Age:** 23

Year	G	GS	Min	FGM	FGA	Pct	3PM	3PA	Pct	FTM	FTA	Pct	TO	Stl	Blk	PF	DQ	Ast	Avg	OReb	TReb	Avg	Pts	Avg
96-97	28	1	509	117	178	.657	0	0	—	58	95	.611	49	6	43	61	3	13	0.5	26	90	3.2	292	10.4
97-98	29	0	463	110	175	.629	0	1	.000	59	94	.628	49	15	41	78	2	17	0.6	25	90	3.1	279	9.6
98-99	27	0	452	125	187	.668	0	0	—	59	88	.670	49	8	42	72	1	13	0.5	35	104	3.9	309	11.4
99-00	31	31	754	190	318	.597	0	0	—	103	151	.682	57	11	70	88	1	36	1.2	50	202	6.5	483	15.6
Total	115	32	2178	542	858	.632	0	1	.000	279	428	.652	204	40	196	299	7	79	0.7	136	486	4.2	1363	11.9

* From Phoenix.

Cory Hightower[†]—San Antonio (54)

College: Indian Hills CC **Ht:** 6'8" **Wt:** 200 **Born:** 7/30/79 **Age:** 21

Year	G	GS	Min	FGM	FGA	Pct	3PM	3PA	Pct	FTM	FTA	Pct	TO	Stl	Blk	PF	DQ	Ast	Avg	OReb	TReb	Avg	Pts	Avg
98-99	33	—	—	174	354	.492	40	121	.331	51	61	.836	—	—	—	—	5	93	2.8	—	97	2.9	439	13.3
99-00	33	—	—	254	528	.481	87	207	.420	150	200	.750	—	—	—	—	5	145	4.4	—	193	5.8	745	22.6
Total	66	—	—	428	882	.485	127	328	.387	201	261	.770	—	—	—	—	5	238	3.6	—	290	4.4	1184	17.9

† Rights traded to LA Lakers for two future second-round draft picks.

Chris Porter—Golden State* (55)

College: Auburn **Ht:** 6'7" **Wt:** 218 **Born:** 5/9/78 **Age:** 22

Year	G	GS	Min	FGM	FGA	Pct	3PM	3PA	Pct	FTM	FTA	Pct	TO	Stl	Blk	PF	DQ	Ast	Avg	OReb	TReb	Avg	Pts	Avg
98-99	30	28	862	179	381	.470	8	22	.364	113	179	.631	71	64	13	76	1	34	1.1	107	259	8.6	479	16.0
99-00	26	26	755	141	304	.464	4	17	.235	94	139	.676	54	52	9	70	3	30	1.2	94	191	7.3	380	14.6
Total	56	54	1617	320	685	.467	12	39	.308	207	318	.651	125	116	22	146	4	64	1.1	201	450	8.0	859	15.3

* From Utah.

Jaquay Walls—Indiana (56)

College: Colorado **Ht:** 6'3" **Wt:** 170 **Born:** 4/3/78 **Age:** 22

Year	G	GS	Min	FGM	FGA	Pct	3PM	3PA	Pct	FTM	FTA	Pct	TO	Stl	Blk	PF	DQ	Ast	Avg	OReb	TReb	Avg	Pts	Avg
98-99	33	28	801	114	291	.392	28	92	.304	129	175	.737	105	46	7	96	5	129	3.9	14	104	3.2	385	11.7
99-00	32	32	985	167	379	.441	57	147	.388	153	203	.754	82	49	7	87	2	143	4.5	23	101	3.2	544	17.0
Total	65	60	1786	281	670	.419	85	239	.356	282	378	.746	187	95	14	183	7	272	4.2	37	205	3.2	929	14.3

Scoonie Penn—Atlanta* (57)

College: Ohio State# **Ht:** 5'10" **Wt:** 185 **Born:** 1/9/77 **Age:** 24

Year	G	GS	Min	FGM	FGA	Pct	3PM	3PA	Pct	FTM	FTA	Pct	TO	Stl	Blk	PF	DQ	Ast	Avg	OReb	TReb	Avg	Pts	Avg
95-96	30	30	1036	134	306	.438	55	175	.314	74	98	.755	69	35	4	59	2	106	3.5	17	103	3.4	397	13.2
96-97	26	26	886	109	271	.402	49	148	.331	73	94	.777	62	53	1	49	2	81	3.1	15	82	3.2	340	13.1
98-99	36	36	1247	202	450	.449	88	229	.384	117	158	.741	96	70	4	79	0	154	4.3	17	140	3.9	609	16.9
99-00	30	30	1045	147	381	.386	65	208	.313	108	143	.755	78	66	2	60	0	130	4.3	13	131	4.4	467	15.6
Total	122	122	4214	592	1408	.420	257	760	.338	372	493	.755	305	224	11	247	4	471	3.9	62	456	3.7	1813	14.9

* From Portland via Detroit. # Attended Ohio State 1998-99 thru 1999-2000, attended Boston College 1995-96 thru 1996-97.

Pete Mickeal[†]—Dallas* (58)

College: Cincinnati **Ht:** 6'5" **Wt:** 230 **Born:** 2/22/78 **Age:** 22

Year	G	GS	Min	FGM	FGA	Pct	3PM	3PA	Pct	FTM	FTA	Pct	TO	Stl	Blk	PF	DQ	Ast	Avg	OReb	TReb	Avg	Pts	Avg
98-99	33	33	1117	182	312	.583	5	16	.313	124	177	.701	66	51	9	77	1	57	1.7	87	236	7.2	493	14.9
99-00	32	31	1002	143	284	.504	21	60	.350	125	173	.723	69	46	16	88	2	58	1.8	65	203	6.3	432	13.5
Total	65	64	2119	325	596	.545	26	76	.342	249	350	.711	135	97	25	165	3	115	1.8	152	439	6.8	925	14.2

† Rights traded to New York along with Erick Strickland for John Wallace and the rights to Donnell Harvey. * From LA Lakers.

Leader Boards

In the following section you'll find the NBA leaders in various statistical categories for the 1999-2000 season, as well as all-time league leaders and leaders among active players.

For all the percentage categories in any of the leader boards, we've included the minimum number of points, minutes played, etc., needed to qualify in that particular category.

In the all-time leader boards, we've highlighted any active players (those who logged at least one minute of action in 1999-2000) in bold.

There are leader boards for all-time players in per-game averages in six categories: points, rebounds, assists, steals, turnovers and blocked shots.

In addition, there are also postseason leader boards, which are similar to the regular-season all-time lists.

1999-2000 NBA Leader Boards

Points Per Game
(minimum 70 G or 1400 Pts)

Player, Team	Pts	G	Avg
S. O'Neal, LAL	**2344**	**79**	**29.7**
A. Iverson, Phi	1989	70	28.4
G. Hill, Det	1906	74	25.8
V. Carter, Tor	2107	82	25.7
K. Malone, Uta	2095	82	25.5
C. Webber, Sac	1834	75	24.5
G. Payton, Sea	1982	82	24.2
J. Stackhouse, Det	1939	82	23.6
T. Duncan, SA	1716	74	23.2
K. Garnett, Min	1857	81	22.9

Rebounds Per Game
(minimum 70 G or 800 Reb)

Player, Team	Reb	G	Avg
D. Mutombo, Atl	**1157**	**82**	**14.1**
S. O'Neal, LAL	1078	79	13.6
T. Duncan, SA	918	74	12.4
K. Garnett, Min	956	81	11.8
C. Webber, Sac	787	75	10.5
S. Abdur-Rahim, Van	825	82	10.1
E. Brand, Chi	810	81	10.0
D. Davis, Ind	729	74	9.9
D. Robinson, SA	770	80	9.6
Je. Williams, Det	789	82	9.6

Assists Per Game
(minimum 70 G or 400 Ast)

Player, Team	Ast	G	Avg
J. Kidd, Pho	**678**	**67**	**10.1**
N. Van Exel, Den	714	79	9.0
S. Cassell, Mil	729	81	9.0
G. Payton, Sea	732	82	8.9
T. Brandon, Min	629	71	8.9
J. Stockton, Uta	703	82	8.6
S. Marbury, NJ	622	74	8.4
M. Bibby, Van	665	82	8.1
M. Jackson, Ind	650	81	8.0
E. Snow, Phi	624	82	7.6

Points

Player, Team	Points
S. O'Neal, LAL	**2344**
V. Carter, Tor	2107
K. Malone, Uta	2095
A. Iverson, Phi	1989
G. Payton, Sea	1982
J. Stackhouse, Det	1939
G. Hill, Det	1906
K. Garnett, Min	1857
M. Finley, Dal	1855
C. Webber, Sac	1834

Rebounds

Player, Team	Reb
D. Mutombo, Atl	**1157**
S. O'Neal, LAL	1078
K. Garnett, Min	956
T. Duncan, SA	918
S. Abdur-Rahim, Van	825
E. Brand, Chi	810
Je. Williams, Det	789
C. Webber, Sac	787
K. Malone, Uta	779
D. Robinson, SA	770

Assists

Player, Team	Ast
G. Payton, Sea	**732**
S. Cassell, Mil	729
N. Van Exel, Den	714
J. Stockton, Uta	703
J. Kidd, Pho	678
M. Bibby, Van	665
M. Jackson, Ind	650
T. Brandon, Min	629
E. Snow, Phi	624
S. Marbury, NJ	622

Points Per 48 Minutes
(minimum 500 Min or 1400 Pts)

Player, Team	Pts	Min	Avg
S. O'Neal, LAL	**2344**	**3163**	**35.6**
K. Malone, Uta	2095	2947	34.1
A. Iverson, Phi	1989	2853	33.5
G. Hill, Det	1906	2776	33.0
V. Carter, Tor	2107	3126	32.4
C. Webber, Sac	1834	2880	30.6
A. Mourning, Mia	1718	2748	30.0
J. Stackhouse, Det	1939	3148	29.6
T. Duncan, SA	1716	2875	28.6
R. Allen, Mil	1809	3070	28.3

Rebounds Per 48 Minutes
(minimum 500 Min or 800 Reb)

Player, Team	Reb	Min	Avg
D. Fortson, Bos	**366**	**856**	**20.5**
D. Mutombo, Atl	1157	2984	18.6
Je. Williams, Det	789	2102	18.0
J. White, Was	553	1537	17.3
D. Davis, Ind	729	2127	16.5
S. O'Neal, LAL	1078	3163	16.4
B. Wallace, Orl	665	1959	16.3
C. Barkley, Hou	209	620	16.2
J. Feick, NJ	755	2241	16.2
T. Duncan, SA	918	2875	15.3

Assists Per 48 Minutes
(minimum 500 Min or 400 Ast)

Player, Team	Ast	Min	Avg
M. Jackson, Ind	**650**	**2190**	**14.2**
J. Stockton, Uta	703	2432	13.9
B. Knight, Cle	458	1754	12.5
J. Kidd, Pho	678	2616	12.4
R. Pack, Dal	168	665	12.1
S. Cassell, Mil	729	2899	12.1
T. Brandon, Min	629	2587	11.7
N. Van Exel, Den	714	2950	11.6
R. Strickland, Was	519	2188	11.4
T. Hardaway, Mia	385	1672	11.1

Points in a Game

Player, Team	Date	Opp	Pts
S. O'Neal, LAL	**03/06**	**@LAC**	**61**
V. Carter, Tor	02/27	Pho	51
C. Robinson, Pho	01/16	Den	50
A. Iverson, Phi	02/06	Sac	50
S. O'Neal, LAL	04/05	@GS	49
V. Carter, Tor	01/14	Mil	47
A. Iverson, Phi	11/10	@Orl	46
T. Duncan, SA	01/10	Uta	46
A. Iverson, Phi	01/03	Mil	45
4 tied with			44

Rebounds in a Game

Player, Team	Date	Opp	Reb
D. Mutombo, Atl	**12/14**	**Min**	**29**
J. Feick, NJ	01/20	Det	25
D. Mutombo, Atl	02/18	@Pho	25
C. Barkley, Hou	11/15	Ind	24
S. O'Neal, LAL	12/12	Det	24
D. Mutombo, Atl	01/28	NY	24
7 tied with			23

Assists in a Game

Player, Team	Date	Opp	Ast
N. Van Exel, Den	**11/08**	**Atl**	**20**
M. Blaylock, GS	12/10	@Atl	19
S. Cassell, Mil	12/29	@Cha	19
S. Cassell, Mil	12/05	Dal	18
J. Stockton, Uta	01/03	Den	18
S. Cassell, Mil	01/04	Atl	18
Ja. Williams, Sac	01/04	@Cle	18
J. Stockton, Uta	03/07	Cle	18
G. Payton, Sea	11/10	@Was	17
J. Kidd, Pho	03/06	Mia	17

1999-2000 NBA Leader Boards

Steals Per Game
(minimum 70 G or 125 Stl)

Player, Team	Stl	G	Avg
E. Jones, Cha	**192**	**72**	**2.67**
P. Pierce, Bos	152	73	2.08
D. Armstrong, Orl	169	82	2.06
A. Iverson, Phi	144	70	2.06
M. Blaylock, GS	146	73	2.00
J. Kidd, Pho	134	67	2.00
T. Brandon, Min	134	71	1.89
G. Payton, Sea	153	82	1.87
K. Gill, NJ	139	76	1.83
J. Stockton, Uta	143	82	1.74

Blocked Shots Per Game
(minimum 70 G or 100 Blk)

Player, Team	Blk	G	Avg
A. Mourning, Mia	**294**	**79**	**3.72**
D. Mutombo, Atl	269	82	3.28
S. O'Neal, LAL	239	79	3.03
T. Ratliff, Phi	171	57	3.00
S. Bradley, Dal	190	77	2.47
D. Robinson, SA	183	80	2.29
T. Duncan, SA	165	74	2.23
R. LaFrentz, Den	180	81	2.22
G. Ostertag, Uta	172	81	2.12
M. Camby, NY	116	59	1.97

Turnovers Per Game
(minimum 70 G or 200 TO)

Player, Team	TO	G	Avg
S. Francis, Hou	**306**	**77**	**3.97**
J. Stackhouse, Det	311	82	3.79
Ja. Williams, Sac	296	81	3.65
S. Marbury, NJ	270	74	3.65
S. Kemp, Cle	291	82	3.55
L. Odom, LAC	258	76	3.39
J. Kidd, Pho	226	67	3.37
K. Garnett, Min	268	81	3.31
S. Cassell, Mil	267	81	3.30
A. Iverson, Phi	230	70	3.29

Steals

Player, Team	Stl
E. Jones, Cha	**192**
D. Armstrong, Orl	169
G. Payton, Sea	153
P. Pierce, Bos	152
M. Blaylock, GS	146
A. Iverson, Phi	144
J. Stockton, Uta	143
E. Snow, Phi	140
K. Anderson, Bos	139
K. Gill, NJ	139

Blocked Shots

Player, Team	Blk
A. Mourning, Mia	**294**
D. Mutombo, Atl	269
S. O'Neal, LAL	239
S. Bradley, Dal	190
D. Robinson, SA	183
R. LaFrentz, Den	180
G. Ostertag, Uta	172
T. Ratliff, Phi	171
T. Duncan, SA	165
T. McGrady, Tor	151

Turnovers

Player, Team	TO
J. Stackhouse, Det	**311**
S. Francis, Hou	306
Ja. Williams, Sac	296
S. Kemp, Cle	291
S. Marbury, NJ	270
K. Garnett, Min	268
S. Cassell, Mil	267
A. Walker, Bos	259
L. Odom, LAC	258
S. Abdur-Rahim, Van	249

Steals Per 48 Minutes
(minimum 500 Min or 125 Stl)

Player, Team	Stl	Min	Avg
E. Jones, Cha	**192**	**2807**	**3.3**
E. Murdock, LAC	47	693	3.3
R. Bowen, Den	39	589	3.2
D. Armstrong, Orl	169	2590	3.1
Ba. Davis, Cha	97	1523	3.1
B. Knight, Cle	107	1754	2.9
A. Griffin, Bos	116	1927	2.9
B. Wells, Por	69	1162	2.8
M. Blaylock, GS	146	2459	2.8
K. Gill, NJ	139	2355	2.8

Blocked Shots Per 48 Mins
(minimum 500 Min or 100 Blk)

Player, Team	Blk	Min	Avg
J. McIlvaine, NJ	**117**	**1048**	**5.4**
G. Ostertag, Uta	172	1606	5.1
A. Mourning, Mia	294	2748	5.1
S. Bradley, Dal	190	1901	4.8
T. Ratliff, Phi	171	1795	4.6
D. Mutombo, Atl	269	2984	4.3
K. Closs, LAC	73	820	4.3
A. Foyle, GS	136	1654	3.9
K. Cato, Hou	124	1581	3.8
S. O'Neal, LAL	239	3163	3.6

Turnovers Per 48 Minutes
(minimum 500 Min or 200 TO)

Player, Team	TO	Min	Avg
S. Kemp, Cle	**291**	**2492**	**5.6**
R. Pack, Dal	76	665	5.5
S. Francis, Hou	306	2776	5.3
Ja. Williams, Sac	296	2760	5.1
C. Maggette, Orl	138	1370	4.8
C. Carr, GS-Chi	117	1166	4.8
J. Stackhouse, Det	311	3148	4.7
L. Longley, Pho	136	1417	4.6
D. Armstrong, Orl	248	2590	4.6
S. Marbury, NJ	270	2881	4.5

Steals in a Game

Player, Team	Date	Opp	Stl
E. Jones, Cha	**11/04**	**Ind**	**9**
P. Pierce, Bos	12/03	Mia	9
A. Iverson, Phi	**03/19**	**Orl**	**9**
T. Duncan, SA	02/09	@Den	8
T. Brandon, Min	03/24	@NJ	8
14 tied with			7

Blocked Shots in a Game

Player, Team	Date	Opp	Blk
D. Mutombo, Atl	**02/15**	**NJ**	**11**
A. Mourning, Mia	12/18	Cha	9
D. Mutombo, Atl	12/23	Cle	9
A. Mourning, Mia	01/06	Hou	9
R. LaFrentz, Den	01/08	Cha	9
14 tied with			8

Turnovers in a Game

Player, Team	Date	Opp	TO
T. Kukoc, Chi	**01/14**	**Atl**	**10**
D. Anderson, LAC	11/05	Phi	9
J. Kidd, Pho	11/09	@Chi	9
J. Kidd, Pho	12/27	@Uta	9
K. Garnett, Min	01/08	@Det	9
J. Stackhouse, Det	02/02	Sac	9
E. Brand, Chi	02/29	@Tor	9
S. Francis, Hou	04/16	Sea	9
44 tied with			8

1999-2000 NBA Leader Boards

Field Goal Percentage
(minimum 300 FG made)

Player, Team	FGM	FGA	Pct
S. O'Neal, LAL	**956**	**1665**	**.574**
D. Mutombo, Atl	322	573	.562
A. Mourning, Mia	652	1184	.551
R. Patterson, Sea	354	661	.536
R. Wallace, Por	542	1045	.519
D. Robinson, SA	528	1031	.512
W. Szczerbiak, Min	342	669	.511
K. Malone, Uta	752	1476	.509
A. McDyess, Den	614	1211	.507
O. Harrington, Van	420	830	.506

Free Throw Percentage
(minimum 125 FTM)

Player, Team	FTM	FTA	Pct
J. Hornacek, Uta	**171**	**180**	**.950**
R. Miller, Ind	373	406	.919
D. Armstrong, Orl	225	247	.911
T. Brandon, Min	187	208	.899
R. Allen, Mil	353	398	.887
P. Stojakovic, Sac	135	153	.882
Ji. Jackson, Atl	186	212	.877
D. Anderson, LAC	271	309	.877
M. Richmond, Was	298	340	.876
S. Cassell, Mil	390	445	.876

3-Point FG Percentage
(minimum 50 3PM)

Player, Team	3PM	3PA	Pct
H. Davis, Dal	**82**	**167**	**.491**
J. Hornacek, Uta	66	138	.478
M. Bullard, Hou	79	177	.446
Rod. Rogers, Pho	115	262	.439
A. Houston, NY	106	243	.436
T. Porter, SA	90	207	.435
L. Hunter, Det	168	389	.432
T. Murray, Was	113	263	.430
J. Barry, Sac	66	154	.429
W. Person, Cle	106	250	.424

Field Goals Made

Player, Team	FGM
S. O'Neal, LAL	**956**
V. Carter, Tor	788
K. Garnett, Min	759
K. Malone, Uta	752
M. Finley, Dal	748
C. Webber, Sac	748
G. Payton, Sea	747
A. Iverson, Phi	729
G. Hill, Det	696
G. Robinson, Mil	690

Free Throws Made

Player, Team	FTM
J. Stackhouse, Det	**618**
K. Malone, Uta	589
S. Kemp, Cle	493
G. Hill, Det	480
T. Duncan, SA	459
S. Abdur-Rahim, Van	446
A. Iverson, Phi	442
V. Carter, Tor	436
S. Marbury, NJ	436
S. O'Neal, LAL	432

3-Point Field Goals Made

Player, Team	3PM
G. Payton, Sea	**177**
R. Allen, Mil	172
L. Hunter, Det	168
R. Miller, Ind	165
B. Barry, Sea	164
Ja. Williams, Sac	145
D. Armstrong, Orl	137
N. Van Exel, Den	133
N. Anderson, Sac	132
E. Jones, Cha	128

Field Goals Attempted

Player, Team	FGA
A. Iverson, Phi	**1733**
V. Carter, Tor	1696
G. Payton, Sea	1666
S. O'Neal, LAL	1665
M. Finley, Dal	1636
C. Webber, Sac	1548
K. Garnett, Min	1526
A. Walker, Bos	1506
K. Malone, Uta	1476
G. Robinson, Mil	1461

Free Throws Attempted

Player, Team	FTA
S. O'Neal, LAL	**824**
J. Stackhouse, Det	758
K. Malone, Uta	739
S. Kemp, Cle	635
A. Iverson, Phi	620
G. Hill, Det	604
T. Duncan, SA	603
A. Mourning, Mia	582
S. Abdur-Rahim, Van	551
V. Carter, Tor	551

3-Point FGs Attempted

Player, Team	3PA
G. Payton, Sea	**520**
Ja. Williams, Sac	505
R. Allen, Mil	407
R. Miller, Ind	404
D. Armstrong, Orl	403
N. Van Exel, Den	401
B. Barry, Sea	399
N. Anderson, Sac	397
L. Hunter, Det	389
E. Jones, Cha	341

FGs Attempted Per Game
(minimum 70 G or 300 FGM)

Player, Team	FGA	G	Avg
A. Iverson, Phi	**1733**	**70**	**24.8**
S. O'Neal, LAL	1665	79	21.1
V. Carter, Tor	1696	82	20.7
C. Webber, Sac	1548	75	20.6
G. Payton, Sea	1666	82	20.3
M. Finley, Dal	1636	82	20.0
G. Hill, Det	1422	74	19.2
K. Garnett, Min	1526	81	18.8
A. Walker, Bos	1506	82	18.4
G. Robinson, Mil	1461	81	18.0

FTs Attempted Per Game
(minimum 70 G or 125 FTM)

Player, Team	FTA	G	Avg
S. O'Neal, LAL	**824**	**79**	**10.4**
J. Stackhouse, Det	758	82	9.2
K. Malone, Uta	739	82	9.0
A. Iverson, Phi	620	70	8.9
G. Hill, Det	604	74	8.2
T. Duncan, SA	603	74	8.1
S. Kemp, Cle	635	82	7.7
A. Mourning, Mia	582	79	7.4
S. Marbury, NJ	536	74	7.2
S. Abdur-Rahim, Van	551	82	6.7

3-Point FGs Att Per Game
(minimum 70 G or 50 3PM)

Player, Team	3PA	G	Avg
G. Payton, Sea	**520**	**82**	**6.3**
Ja. Williams, Sac	505	81	6.2
N. Anderson, Sac	397	72	5.5
N. Van Exel, Den	401	79	5.1
R. Miller, Ind	404	81	5.0
B. Barry, Sea	399	80	5.0
R. Allen, Mil	407	82	5.0
T. Hardaway, Mia	256	52	4.9
D. Brown, Tor	187	38	4.9
D. Armstrong, Orl	403	82	4.9

1999-2000 NBA Leader Boards

Minutes

Player, Team	Min
M. Finley, Dal	3464
G. Payton, Sea	3425
L. Sprewell, NY	3276
K. Garnett, Min	3243
S. Abdur-Rahim, Van	3223
A. Houston, NY	3169
S. O'Neal, LAL	3163
M. Bibby, Van	3155
J. Stackhouse, Det	3148
A. Mason, Cha	3133

Points Per FG Attempt
(minimum 300 FGM)

Player, Team	Pts	FGA	Avg
B. Barry, Sea	818	707	1.16
S. O'Neal, LAL	1912	1665	1.15
D. Mutombo, Atl	644	573	1.12
Rod. Rogers, Pho	971	881	1.10
A. Mourning, Mia	1304	1184	1.10
R. Patterson, Sea	720	661	1.09
J. Hornacek, Uta	782	728	1.07
W. Williams, Hou	726	681	1.07
W. Szczerbiak, Min	712	669	1.06
J. Stockton, Uta	769	725	1.06

Double Doubles

Player, Team	DD
S. O'Neal, LAL	63
T. Duncan, SA	60
K. Garnett, Min	57
C. Webber, Sac	49
D. Mutombo, Atl	46
K. Malone, Uta	43
S. Abdur-Rahim, Van	42
E. Brand, Chi	42
G. Payton, Sea	41
A. Mourning, Mia	38

Minutes Per Game
(minimum 70 G or 2000 Min)

Player, Team	Min	G	Avg
M. Finley, Dal	3464	82	42.2
G. Payton, Sea	3425	82	41.8
A. Iverson, Phi	2853	70	40.8
S. O'Neal, LAL	3163	79	40.0
K. Garnett, Min	3243	81	40.0
L. Sprewell, NY	3276	82	40.0
S. Abdur-Rahim, Van	3223	82	39.3
J. Kidd, Pho	2616	67	39.0
E. Jones, Cha	2807	72	39.0
S. Marbury, NJ	2881	74	38.9

Assist/Turnover Ratio
(minimum 400 Ast or 200 TO)

Player, Team	Ast	TO	Ratio
J. Stockton, Uta	703	179	3.93
E. Snow, Phi	624	162	3.85
M. Jackson, Ind	650	174	3.74
Av. Johnson, SA	491	140	3.51
M. Blaylock, GS	489	143	3.42
T. Brandon, Min	629	184	3.42
G. Payton, Sea	732	224	3.27
N. Van Exel, Den	714	221	3.23
K. Anderson, Bos	420	130	3.23
J. Kidd, Pho	678	226	3.00

Triple Doubles

Player, Team	TD
J. Kidd, Pho	5
C. Webber, Sac	5
M. Finley, Dal	4
A. Mason, Cha	3
L. Odom, LAC	3
G. Payton, Sea	2
16 tied with	1

Offensive Reb Per Game
(minimum 70 G or 260 OReb)

Player, Team	OReb	G	Avg
E. Brand, Chi	348	81	4.3
S. O'Neal, LAL	336	79	4.3
D. Mutombo, Atl	304	82	3.7
T. Duncan, SA	262	74	3.5
D. Davis, Ind	256	74	3.5
Je. Williams, Det	277	82	3.4
J. Feick, NJ	264	81	3.3
A. Henderson, Atl	265	82	3.2
A. Davis, Tor	235	79	3.0
E. Johnson, Mil	233	80	2.9

Steal/Turnover Ratio
(minimum 125 Stl or 200 TO)

Player, Team	Stl	TO	Ratio
K. Gill, NJ	139	89	1.56
B. Russell, Uta	128	101	1.27
E. Jones, Cha	192	160	1.20
K. Anderson, Bos	139	130	1.07
M. Blaylock, GS	146	143	1.02
L. Hunter, Det	129	145	0.89
E. Snow, Phi	140	162	0.86
P. Pierce, Bos	152	178	0.85
J. Stockton, Uta	143	179	0.80
T. Brandon, Min	134	184	0.73

Personal Fouls

Player, Team	PF
S. Kemp, Cle	371
C. Laettner, Det	326
A. McDyess, Den	316
A. Mourning, Mia	308
M. Olowokandi, LAC	304
J. Smith, Min	302
J. Howard, Was	299
E. Johnson, Mil	298
C. Oakley, Tor	294
R. LaFrentz, Den	292

Defensive Reb Per Game
(minimum 70 G or 540 DReb)

Player, Team	DReb	G	Avg
D. Mutombo, Atl	853	82	10.4
S. O'Neal, LAL	742	79	9.4
K. Garnett, Min	733	81	9.0
T. Duncan, SA	656	74	8.9
C. Webber, Sac	598	75	8.0
K. Malone, Uta	610	82	7.4
S. Abdur-Rahim, Van	607	82	7.4
D. Robinson, SA	577	80	7.2
D. Coleman, Cha	508	74	6.9
A. Mourning, Mia	538	79	6.8

Two-Point FG Percentage
(minimum 250 2PM)

Player, Team	2PM	2PA	Pct
S. O'Neal, LAL	956	1664	.575
Je. Williams, Det	257	453	.567
D. Mutombo, Atl	322	573	.562
A. Mourning, Mia	652	1180	.553
K. Clark, Den	285	520	.548
R. Patterson, Sea	342	634	.539
R. Wallace, Por	534	995	.537
W. Szczerbiak, Min	314	591	.531
J. Stockton, Uta	320	604	.530
S. Anderson, Hou	289	553	.523

Disqualifications

Player, Team	DQ
S. Kemp, Cle	13
L. Odom, LAC	13
A. McDyess, Den	12
J. Caffey, GS	11
C. Laettner, Det	10
M. Olowokandi, LAC	10
R. Nesterovic, Min	9
A. Mourning, Mia	8
B. Reeves, Van	8
J. Smith, Min	8

Career NBA Leader Boards—1999-2000 Active Players

Points

Player	Points
K. Malone	**31041**
H. Olajuwon	25822
C. Barkley	23757
P. Ewing	23665
R. Miller	19792
M. Richmond	19639
T. Cummings	19460
D. Ellis	19004
D. Robinson	18142
C. Mullin	17796
O. Thorpe	17462
J. Stockton	16781
S. Pippen	16735
G. Rice	16643
J. Hornacek	15659

Rebounds

Player	Reb
H. Olajuwon	**12950**
K. Malone	12618
C. Barkley	12546
D. Rodman	11954
C. Oakley	11009
P. Ewing	10759
K. Willis	10662
O. Thorpe	10225
A. Green	9160
D. Robinson	8651
M. Cage	8646
T. Cummings	8630
D. Mutombo	8439
H. Grant	8176
S. Kemp	7836

Assists

Player	Ast
J. Stockton	**13790**
M. Jackson	8574
R. Strickland	6723
M. Bogues	6721
K. Johnson	6711
T. Porter	6704
T. Hardaway	6310
G. Payton	5548
M. Blaylock	5396
J. Hornacek	5281
Av. Johnson	5148
S. Pippen	5143
S. Douglas	4392
K. Anderson	4233
C. Barkley	4215

Points Per Game
(minimum 250 G or 5000 Pts)

Player	Pts	G	Avg
S. O'Neal	**14687**	**534**	**27.5**
K. Malone	31041	1192	26.0
A. Iverson	6818	274	24.9
D. Robinson	18142	765	23.7
H. Olajuwon	25822	1119	23.1
P. Ewing	23665	1039	22.8
M. Richmond	19639	875	22.4
C. Barkley	23757	1073	22.1
G. Hill	9393	435	21.6
A. Mourning	11259	534	21.1
G. Robinson	8970	426	21.1
S. Abdur-Rahim	6138	294	20.9
C. Webber	8447	405	20.9
G. Rice	16643	825	20.2
A. Walker	5739	288	19.9

Rebounds Per Game
(minimum 250 G or 3000 Reb)

Player	Reb	G	Avg
D. Rodman	**11954**	**911**	**13.1**
S. O'Neal	6615	534	12.4
D. Mutombo	8439	685	12.3
C. Barkley	12546	1073	11.7
H. Olajuwon	12950	1119	11.6
D. Robinson	8651	765	11.3
K. Malone	12618	1192	10.6
P. Ewing	10759	1039	10.4
A. Mourning	5377	534	10.1
C. Webber	4075	405	10.1
D. Coleman	5882	586	10.0
C. Oakley	11009	1098	10.0
S. Kemp	7836	829	9.5
K. Willis	10662	1141	9.3
K. Garnett	3350	367	9.1

Assists Per Game
(minimum 250 G or 2000 Ast)

Player	Ast	G	Avg
J. Stockton	**13790**	**1258**	**11.0**
J. Kidd	3848	414	9.3
K. Johnson	6711	735	9.1
T. Hardaway	6310	712	8.9
M. Jackson	8574	1007	8.5
S. Marbury	2285	272	8.4
R. Strickland	6723	840	8.0
D. Stoudamire	2659	350	7.6
M. Bogues	6721	886	7.6
N. Van Exel	3831	507	7.6
G. Payton	5548	786	7.1
K. Anderson	4233	601	7.0
M. Blaylock	5396	785	6.9
G. Hill	2720	435	6.3
S. Douglas	4392	706	6.2

Points Per 48 Minutes
(minimum 5000 Min or 5000 Pts)

Player	Pts	Min	Avg
S. O'Neal	**14687**	**20148**	**35.0**
K. Malone	31041	44608	33.4
D. Robinson	18142	27921	31.2
P. Ewing	23665	37586	30.2
H. Olajuwon	25822	41299	30.0
A. Iverson	6818	11038	29.6
M. Richmond	19639	32384	29.1
C. Barkley	23757	39330	29.0
C. Ceballos	8432	14153	28.6
A. Mourning	11259	19034	28.4
T. Cummings	19460	33898	27.6
R. Miller	19792	35073	27.1
T. Duncan	4531	8042	27.0
C. Mullin	17796	31789	26.9
K. Bryant	4240	7579	26.9

Rebounds Per 48 Minutes
(minimum 5000 Min or 3000 Reb)

Player	Reb	Min	Avg
D. Rodman	**11954**	**28839**	**19.9**
C. Dudley	5192	15370	16.2
D. Mutombo	8439	25114	16.1
S. O'Neal	6615	20148	15.8
P. Jones	3123	9789	15.3
C. Barkley	12546	39330	15.3
E. Johnson	3406	10722	15.2
W. Perdue	3900	12302	15.2
H. Olajuwon	12950	41299	15.1
K. Willis	10662	34067	15.0
A. Sabonis	2770	8867	15.0
D. Robinson	8651	27921	14.9
C. Oakley	11009	35591	14.8
S. Kemp	7836	25345	14.8
T. Hill	5494	17826	14.8

Assists Per 48 Minutes
(minimum 5000 Min or 2000 Ast)

Player	Ast	Min	Avg
J. Stockton	**13790**	**40526**	**16.3**
K. Johnson	6711	25061	12.9
M. Jackson	8574	32122	12.8
M. Bogues	6721	25395	12.7
B. Knight	1416	5423	12.5
J. Kidd	3848	15460	11.9
R. Strickland	6723	27620	11.7
T. Hardaway	6310	26285	11.5
G. Grant	3012	12585	11.5
R. Pack	2106	9290	10.9
Av. Johnson	5148	22906	10.8
S. Marbury	2285	10212	10.7
S. Douglas	4392	20054	10.5
N. Van Exel	3831	17899	10.3
K. Anderson	4233	19806	10.3

Career NBA Leader Boards—1999-2000 Active Players

Steals

Player	Stl
J. Stockton	**2844**
H. Olajuwon	2018
S. Pippen	1986
M. Blaylock	1888
G. Payton	1756
R. Harper	1677
K. Malone	1654
C. Barkley	1648
H. Hawkins	1589
J. Hornacek	1536
C. Mullin	1514
T. Porter	1486
J. Kersey	1425
R. Strickland	1397
M. Jackson	1385

Blocked Shots

Player	Blk
H. Olajuwon	**3652**
P. Ewing	2758
D. Robinson	2506
D. Mutombo	2443
A. Mourning	1666
B. Benjamin	1581
S. Bradley	1520
S. O'Neal	1436
M. West	1403
V. Divac	1261
E. Campbell	1229
S. Kemp	1190
R. Smits	1111
And. Lang	1099
H. Grant	1005

Turnovers

Player	TO
K. Malone	**3704**
J. Stockton	3651
H. Olajuwon	3488
C. Barkley	3376
P. Ewing	3321
O. Thorpe	2742
S. Pippen	2739
M. Jackson	2625
C. Oakley	2537
S. Kemp	2484
T. Porter	2477
M. Richmond	2455
R. Strickland	2419
C. Mullin	2296
K. Willis	2283

Steals Per Game
(minimum 250 G or 500 Stl)

Player	Stl	G	Avg
M. Blaylock	**1888**	**785**	**2.41**
J. Stockton	2844	1258	2.26
G. Payton	1756	786	2.23
E. Jones	926	416	2.23
A. Iverson	587	274	2.14
J. Kidd	860	414	2.08
S. Pippen	1986	965	2.06
A. Hardaway	812	429	1.89
D. Christie	789	437	1.81
H. Olajuwon	2018	1119	1.80
T. Hardaway	1272	712	1.79
K. Gill	1271	718	1.77
R. Harper	1677	962	1.74
H. Hawkins	1589	924	1.72
T. Gugliotta	907	533	1.70

Blocked Shots Per Game
(minimum 250 G or 500 Blk)

Player	Blk	G	Avg
D. Mutombo	**2443**	**685**	**3.57**
D. Robinson	2506	765	3.28
H. Olajuwon	3652	1119	3.26
S. Bradley	1520	473	3.21
A. Mourning	1666	534	3.12
S. O'Neal	1436	534	2.69
P. Ewing	2758	1039	2.65
M. Camby	550	231	2.38
T. Ratliff	805	340	2.37
G. Ostertag	650	326	1.99
B. Benjamin	1581	807	1.96
C. Webber	736	405	1.82
K. Garnett	653	367	1.78
J. McIlvaine	676	383	1.77
A. McDyess	629	362	1.74

Turnovers Per Game
(minimum 250 G or 500 TO)

Player	TO	G	Avg
A. Iverson	**978**	**274**	**3.57**
J. Stackhouse	1224	356	3.44
S. Marbury	900	272	3.31
G. Hill	1433	435	3.29
J. Kidd	1357	414	3.28
G. Robinson	1393	426	3.27
T. Duncan	667	206	3.24
P. Ewing	3321	1039	3.20
A. Mourning	1699	534	3.18
C. Barkley	3376	1073	3.15
A. Walker	900	288	3.13
S. Abdur-Rahim	917	294	3.12
H. Olajuwon	3488	1119	3.12
K. Malone	3704	1192	3.11
K. Johnson	2258	735	3.07

Steals Per 48 Minutes
(minimum 5000 Min or 500 Stl)

Player	Stl	Min	Avg
J. Stockton	**2844**	**40526**	**3.37**
E. Murdock	830	11882	3.35
B. Knight	373	5423	3.30
M. Blaylock	1888	28075	3.23
G. Grant	821	12585	3.13
R. Brown	643	10027	3.08
D. Armstrong	403	6387	3.03
J. Barry	407	6464	3.02
E. Jones	926	14761	3.01
G. Payton	1756	28190	2.99
E. Perry	549	8954	2.94
D. Christie	789	13060	2.90
S. Pippen	1986	34617	2.75
G. Anthony	770	13480	2.74
C. Ward	481	8453	2.73

Blocked Shots Per 48 Mins
(minimum 5000 Min or 500 Blk)

Player	Blk	Min	Avg
J. McIlvaine	**676**	**5734**	**5.66**
S. Bradley	1520	13384	5.45
D. Mutombo	2443	25114	4.67
G. Ostertag	650	6713	4.65
T. Ratliff	805	8446	4.56
D. Robinson	2506	27921	4.31
H. Olajuwon	3652	41299	4.24
A. Mourning	1666	19034	4.20
M. Camby	550	6392	4.13
D. Causwell	749	9025	3.98
E. Johnson	787	10722	3.52
P. Ewing	2758	37586	3.52
B. Benjamin	1581	21911	3.46
And. Lang	1099	15344	3.44
S. O'Neal	1436	20148	3.42

Turnovers Per 48 Minutes
(minimum 5000 Min or 500 TO)

Player	TO	Min	Avg
R. Pack	**1109**	**9290**	**5.73**
G. Grant	1268	12585	4.84
S. Kemp	2484	25345	4.70
D. Armstrong	624	6387	4.69
J. Stackhouse	1224	12748	4.61
S. Cassell	1142	12104	4.53
K. Johnson	2258	25061	4.32
J. Stockton	3651	40526	4.32
A. Mourning	1699	19034	4.28
B. Price	612	6888	4.26
A. Iverson	978	11038	4.25
I. Austin	636	7198	4.24
P. Ewing	3321	37586	4.24
S. Marbury	900	10212	4.23
J. Kidd	1357	15460	4.21

Career NBA Leader Boards—1999-2000 Active Players

Field Goal Percentage
(minimum 1000 FGM)

Player	FGM	FGA	Pct
M. West	2528	4356	.580
S. O'Neal	5896	10210	.577
G. Muresan	1265	2206	.573
B. Outlaw	1218	2131	.572
O. Thorpe	6813	12462	.547
D. Davis	2530	4661	.543
C. Barkley	8435	15605	.541
O. Miller	1483	2774	.535
D. Mutombo	3098	5864	.528
C. Gatling	2344	4443	.528

Free Throw Percentage
(minimum 500 FTM)

Player	FTM	FTA	Pct
D. Armstrong	589	660	.892
R. Miller	5015	5690	.881
J. Hornacek	2973	3390	.877
R. Allen	1076	1233	.873
H. Hawkins	3410	3920	.870
T. Brandon	1506	1735	.868
D. Anderson	684	789	.867
C. Mullin	3592	4150	.866
D. Barros	1158	1347	.860
M. Elie	1390	1623	.856

3-Point FG Percentage
(minimum 250 3PM)

Player	3PM	3PA	Pct
S. Kerr	618	1332	.464
H. Davis	581	1317	.441
T. Legler	260	603	.431
B. Armstrong	436	1026	.425
D. Barros	1022	2476	.413
W. Person	777	1890	.411
A. Houston	777	1917	.405
G. Rice	1353	3339	.405
R. Miller	1867	4629	.403
D. Curry	1138	2822	.403

Field Goals Made

Player	FGM
K. Malone	11435
H. Olajuwon	10272
P. Ewing	9260
C. Barkley	8435
T. Cummings	8045
D. Ellis	7323
M. Richmond	7000
O. Thorpe	6813
C. Mullin	6704
S. Pippen	6587

Free Throws Made

Player	FTM
K. Malone	8100
C. Barkley	6349
D. Robinson	5263
H. Olajuwon	5253
P. Ewing	5126
R. Miller	5015
D. Schrempf	4463
M. Richmond	4376
J. Stockton	4049
S. Kemp	3984

3-Point Field Goals Made

Player	3PM
R. Miller	1867
D. Ellis	1719
G. Rice	1353
M. Richmond	1263
D. Majerle	1224
V. Maxwell	1222
C. Person	1220
T. Hardaway	1219
D. Scott	1214
H. Hawkins	1209

Field Goals Attempted

Player	FGA
K. Malone	21777
H. Olajuwon	20005
P. Ewing	18224
T. Cummings	16628
C. Barkley	15605
M. Richmond	15287
D. Ellis	15275
S. Pippen	13768
R. Miller	13460
G. Rice	13415

Free Throws Attempted

Player	FTA
K. Malone	11027
C. Barkley	8643
H. Olajuwon	7339
D. Robinson	7122
P. Ewing	6904
R. Miller	5690
O. Thorpe	5588
D. Schrempf	5558
S. O'Neal	5418
S. Kemp	5388

3-Point FGs Attempted

Player	3PA
R. Miller	4629
D. Ellis	4266
V. Maxwell	3820
M. Blaylock	3549
T. Hardaway	3443
D. Majerle	3382
C. Person	3370
G. Rice	3339
J. Starks	3314
M. Richmond	3222

FGs Attempted Per Game
(minimum 250 G or 1000 FGM)

Player	FGA	G	Avg
A. Iverson	5700	274	20.8
S. O'Neal	10210	534	19.1
V. Carter	2462	132	18.7
A. Walker	5300	288	18.4
K. Malone	21777	1192	18.3
H. Olajuwon	20005	1119	17.9
G. Robinson	7583	426	17.8
P. Ewing	18224	1039	17.5
C. Webber	7085	405	17.5
M. Richmond	15287	875	17.5

FTs Attempted Per Game
(minimum 250 G or 500 FTM)

Player	FTA	G	Avg
S. O'Neal	5418	534	10.1
D. Robinson	7122	765	9.3
K. Malone	11027	1192	9.3
A. Mourning	4593	534	8.6
C. Barkley	8643	1073	8.1
A. Iverson	2173	274	7.9
G. Hill	3420	435	7.9
J. Stackhouse	2640	356	7.4
S. Abdur-Rahim	2149	294	7.3
T. Duncan	1443	206	7.0

3-Point FGs Att Per Game
(minimum 250 G or 250 3PM)

Player	3PA	G	Avg
N. Van Exel	2697	507	5.3
D. Scott	3060	629	4.9
T. Hardaway	3443	712	4.8
V. Lenard	1184	249	4.8
V. Maxwell	3820	812	4.7
J. Starks	3314	725	4.6
R. Miller	4629	1013	4.6
M. Blaylock	3549	785	4.5
R. Allen	1281	296	4.3
D. Stoudamire	1491	350	4.3

Career NBA Leader Boards—1999-2000 Active Players

Minutes

Player		Min
K. Malone		**44608**
H. Olajuwon		41299
J. Stockton		40526
C. Barkley		39330
O. Thorpe		39175
P. Ewing		37586
S. Perkins		35599
C. Oakley		35591
A. Green		35141
R. Miller		35073

Points Per FG Attempt
(minimum 1000 FGM)

Player	Pts	FGA	Avg
M. West	**5056**	**4356**	**1.16**
S. O'Neal	11793	10210	1.16
G. Muresan	2530	2206	1.15
B. Outlaw	2437	2131	1.14
S. Kerr	4144	3631	1.14
C. Barkley	17408	15605	1.12
J. Stockton	12732	11592	1.10
R. Miller	14777	13460	1.10
O. Thorpe	13629	12462	1.09
D. Davis	5060	4661	1.09

Double Doubles
(since 1991-92)

Player	DD
K. Malone	**417**
S. O'Neal	402
D. Mutombo	389
J. Stockton	372
D. Robinson	367
S. Kemp	365
H. Olajuwon	362
P. Ewing	357
C. Barkley	356
K. Willis	311

Minutes Per Game
(minimum 250 G or 5000 Min)

Player	Min	G	Avg
A. Iverson	**11038**	**274**	**40.3**
L. Sprewell	20518	519	39.5
M. Finley	14911	379	39.3
G. Hill	17007	435	39.1
T. Duncan	8042	206	39.0
J. Howard	15864	410	38.7
G. Robinson	16103	426	37.8
S. O'Neal	20148	534	37.7
C. Webber	15277	405	37.7
S. Marbury	10212	272	37.5

Assist/Turnover Ratio
(minimum 2000 Ast or 500 TO)

Player	Ast	TO	Ratio
M. Bogues	**6721**	**1429**	**4.70**
J. Stockton	13790	3651	3.78
Av. Johnson	5148	1532	3.36
M. Jackson	8574	2625	3.27
N. Van Exel	3831	1179	3.25
V. Del Negro	2356	786	3.00
K. Anderson	4233	1424	2.97
K. Johnson	6711	2258	2.97
T. Brandon	3560	1221	2.92
T. Hardaway	6310	2170	2.91

Triple Doubles
(since 1991-92)

Player	TD
J. Kidd	**31**
G. Hill	29
S. Pippen	13
C. Webber	13
M. Jackson	11
C. Barkley	10
D. Mutombo	9
G. Payton	9
D. Robinson	8
2 tied with	7

Offensive Reb Per Game
(minimum 250 G or 1000 OReb)

Player	OReb	G	Avg
D. Rodman	**4329**	**911**	**4.8**
S. O'Neal	2162	534	4.0
C. Barkley	4260	1073	4.0
D. Mutombo	2554	685	3.7
H. Olajuwon	3812	1119	3.4
D. Davis	2185	646	3.4
P. Jones	1277	380	3.4
C. Oakley	3673	1098	3.3
D. Robinson	2521	765	3.3
S. Kemp	2726	829	3.3

Steal/Turnover Ratio
(minimum 500 Stl or 500 TO)

Player	Stl	TO	Ratio
E. Jones	**926**	**742**	**1.25**
B. Russell	568	485	1.17
D. Majerle	1093	1046	1.04
M. Blaylock	1888	1902	0.99
R. Brown	643	652	0.99
M. Bogues	1367	1429	0.96
G. Lynch	532	567	0.94
T. Corbin	1226	1307	0.94
A. McKie	477	510	0.94
L. Hunter	723	786	0.92

Personal Fouls

Player	PF
H. Olajuwon	**4095**
O. Thorpe	4038
C. Oakley	3890
T. Cummings	3836
K. Malone	3813
P. Ewing	3676
K. Willis	3613
J. Kersey	3419
J. Stockton	3355
D. Schrempf	3317

Defensive Reb Per Game
(minimum 250 G or 2000 DReb)

Player	DReb	G	Avg
D. Mutombo	**5885**	**685**	**8.6**
D. Rodman	7625	911	8.4
S. O'Neal	4453	534	8.3
H. Olajuwon	9138	1119	8.2
D. Robinson	6130	765	8.0
K. Malone	9486	1192	8.0
P. Ewing	8191	1039	7.9
C. Barkley	8286	1073	7.7
D. Coleman	4215	586	7.2
A. Mourning	3756	534	7.0

Two-Point FG Percentage
(minimum 750 2PM)

Player	2PM	2PA	Pct
C. Barkley	**7897**	**13585**	**.581**
M. West	2528	4352	.581
B. Outlaw	1217	2103	.579
S. O'Neal	5895	10193	.578
G. Muresan	1265	2205	.574
O. Thorpe	6810	12398	.549
M. Smith	843	1543	.546
C. Rogers	758	1388	.546
J. Stockton	5271	9679	.545
D. Davis	2530	4658	.543

Disqualifications

Player	DQ
S. Kemp	**109**
O. Thorpe	85
H. Olajuwon	80
R. Smits	73
C. Oakley	61
G. Long	58
A. Carr	56
T. Cummings	56
T. Hill	54
M. West	52

Career NBA Leader Boards—All Time

Points

	Player	Points
1	Kareem Abdul-Jabbar	38387
2	Wilt Chamberlain	31419
3	**Karl Malone**	31041
4	Michael Jordan	29277
5	Moses Malone	27409
6	Elvin Hayes	27313
7	Oscar Robertson	26710
8	Dominique Wilkins	26668
9	John Havlicek	26395
10	**Hakeem Olajuwon**	25822
11	Alex English	25613
12	Jerry West	25192
13	**Charles Barkley**	23757
14	**Patrick Ewing**	23665
15	Robert Parish	23334
16	Adrian Dantley	23177
17	Elgin Baylor	23149
18	Clyde Drexler	22195
19	Larry Bird	21791
20	Hal Greer	21586
21	Walt Bellamy	20941
22	Bob Pettit	20880
23	George Gervin	20708
24	Tom Chambers	20049
25	**Reggie Miller**	19792
26	Bernard King	19655
27	**Mitch Richmond**	19639
28	Walter Davis	19521
29	**Terry Cummings**	19460
30	Bob Lanier	19248
31	Eddie A. Johnson	19202
32	Gail Goodrich	19181
33	Reggie Theus	19015
34	**Dale Ellis**	19004
35	Chet Walker	18831
36	Isiah Thomas	18822
37	Bob McAdoo	18787
38	Mark Aguirre	18458
39	Dolph Schayes	18438
40	Rick Barry	18395
41	Julius Erving	18364
42	Dave Bing	18327
43	**David Robinson**	18142
44	World B. Free	17955
45	Calvin Murphy	17949
46	Lou Hudson	17940
47	**Chris Mullin**	17796
48	Lenny Wilkens	17772
49	Bailey Howell	17770
50	Magic Johnson	17707

Rebounds
(since 1950-51)

	Player	Reb
1	Wilt Chamberlain	23924
2	Bill Russell	21620
3	Kareem Abdul-Jabbar	17440
4	Elvin Hayes	16279
5	Moses Malone	16212
6	Robert Parish	14715
7	Nate Thurmond	14464
8	Walt Bellamy	14241
9	Wes Unseld	13769
10	Buck Williams	13017
11	**Hakeem Olajuwon**	12950
12	Jerry Lucas	12942
13	Bob Pettit	12849
14	**Karl Malone**	12618
15	**Charles Barkley**	12546
16	Paul Silas	12357
17	**Dennis Rodman**	11954
18	Elgin Baylor	11463
19	Dolph Schayes	11256
20	Bill Bridges	11054
21	**Charles Oakley**	11009
22	Jack Sikma	10816
23	**Patrick Ewing**	10759
24	**Kevin Willis**	10662
25	Dave Cowens	10444
26	Bill Laimbeer	10400
27	**Otis Thorpe**	10225
28	Red Kerr	10092
29	Bob Lanier	9698
30	Sam Lacey	9687
31	Dave DeBusschere	9618
32	Bailey Howell	9383
33	Artis Gilmore	9161
34	**A.C. Green**	9160
35	Johnny Green	9083
36	Larry Bird	8974
37	Leroy Ellis	8709
38	**David Robinson**	8651
39	**Michael Cage**	8646
40	**Terry Cummings**	8630
41	**Dikembe Mutombo**	8439
42	Willis Reed	8414
43	**Horace Grant**	8176
44	Larry Smith	8125
45	Bob McAdoo	8048
46	Larry Foust	8041
47	Happy Hairston	8019
48	John Havlicek	8007
49	**Shawn Kemp**	7836
50	Oscar Robertson	7804

Assists

	Player	Ast
1	**John Stockton**	13790
2	Magic Johnson	10141
3	Oscar Robertson	9887
4	Isiah Thomas	9061
5	**Mark Jackson**	8574
6	Maurice Cheeks	7392
7	Lenny Wilkens	7211
8	Bob Cousy	6955
9	Guy Rodgers	6917
10	**Rod Strickland**	6723
11	**Muggsy Bogues**	6721
12	**Kevin Johnson**	6711
13	**Terry Porter**	6704
14	Derek Harper	6577
15	Tiny Archibald	6476
16	John Lucas	6454
17	Reggie Theus	6453
18	Norm Nixon	6386
19	**Tim Hardaway**	6310
20	Jerry West	6238
21	Clyde Drexler	6125
22	John Havlicek	6114
23	Larry Bird	5695
24	Kareem Abdul-Jabbar	5660
25	**Gary Payton**	5548
26	Dennis Johnson	5499
27	Dave Bing	5397
28	**Mookie Blaylock**	5396
29	Kevin Porter	5314
30	**Jeff Hornacek**	5281
31	Rickey Green	5221
32	Norm Van Lier	5217
33	Sleepy Floyd	5175
34	**Avery Johnson**	5148
35	**Scottie Pippen**	5143
36	Walt Frazier	5040
37	Michael Jordan	5012
38	Nate McMillan	4893
39	Doc Rivers	4889
40	Mark Price	4863
41	Gail Goodrich	4805
42	Brad Davis	4709
43	Fat Lever	4696
44	Wilt Chamberlain	4643
45	Joe Dumars	4612
46	Gus Williams	4597
47	Hal Greer	4540
48	Randy Smith	4487
49	Calvin Murphy	4402
50	**Sherman Douglas**	4392

Career NBA Leader Boards—All Time

Games		Minutes (since 1951-52)		Personal Fouls	
Player	**G**	**Player**	**Min**	**Player**	**PF**
1 Robert Parish	1611	1 Kareem Abdul-Jabbar	57446	1 Kareem Abdul-Jabbar	4657
2 Kareem Abdul-Jabbar	1560	2 Elvin Hayes	50000	2 Robert Parish	4443
3 Moses Malone	1329	3 Wilt Chamberlain	47859	3 Buck Williams	4267
4 Buck Williams	1307	4 John Havlicek	46471	4 Elvin Hayes	4193
5 Elvin Hayes	1303	5 Robert Parish	45704	5 **Hakeem Olajuwon**	4095
6 John Havlicek	1270	6 Moses Malone	45071	6 James Edwards	4042
7 **John Stockton**	1258	7 **Karl Malone**	44608	7 **Otis Thorpe**	4038
8 Paul Silas	1254	8 Oscar Robertson	43886	8 **Charles Oakley**	3890
9 **Sam Perkins**	1222	9 Buck Williams	42464	9 Jack Sikma	3879
10 **Dale Ellis**	1209	10 **Hakeem Olajuwon**	41299	10 Hal Greer	3855
11 **Otis Thorpe**	1208	11 Bill Russell	40726	11 **Terry Cummings**	3836
12 Derek Harper	1199	12 **John Stockton**	40526	12 **Karl Malone**	3813
Eddie A. Johnson	1199	13 Hal Greer	39788	13 Tom Chambers	3742
14 **A.C. Green**	1196	14 **Charles Barkley**	39330	14 **Patrick Ewing**	3676
15 Alex English	1193	15 **Otis Thorpe**	39175	15 Bill Laimbeer	3633
16 **Karl Malone**	1192	16 Walt Bellamy	38940	16 **Kevin Willis**	3613
17 **Terry Cummings**	1183	17 Dominique Wilkins	38113	17 Walt Bellamy	3536
18 James Edwards	1168	18 Lenny Wilkens	38064	18 Caldwell Jones	3527
19 Tree Rollins	1156	19 Alex English	38063	19 Rick Mahorn	3499
20 **Kevin Willis**	1141	20 Derek Harper	37786	20 Bailey Howell	3498
21 **Michael Cage**	1140	21 **Patrick Ewing**	37586	21 Danny Schayes	3494
22 Danny Schayes	1138	22 Clyde Drexler	37537	22 Sam Lacey	3473
23 **Jerome Kersey**	1131	23 Jack Sikma	36943	23 Dolph Schayes	3432
24 Hal Greer	1122	24 Jerry West	36571	24 **Jerome Kersey**	3419
Terry Porter	1122	25 Dennis Johnson	35954	25 Tree Rollins	3377
26 **Hakeem Olajuwon**	1119	26 Michael Jordan	35887	26 Bill Bridges	3375
27 Rick Mahorn	1117	27 Nate Thurmond	35875	27 **John Stockton**	3355
28 **Detlef Schrempf**	1110	28 Wes Unseld	35832	28 **Detlef Schrempf**	3317
29 Tom Chambers	1107	29 **Sam Perkins**	35599	29 **Charles Barkley**	3287
Jack Sikma	1107	30 **Charles Oakley**	35591	30 Clyde Drexler	3285
31 Herb Williams	1102	31 Isiah Thomas	35516	Lenny Wilkens	3285
32 Maurice Cheeks	1101	32 **A.C. Green**	35141	32 John Havlicek	3281
33 Dennis Johnson	1100	33 Joe Dumars	35139	33 Calvin Murphy	3250
34 **Charles Oakley**	1098	34 **Reggie Miller**	35073	34 **Shawn Kemp**	3219
35 **Mark West**	1090	35 Paul Silas	34989	35 Alvan Adams	3214
36 Clyde Drexler	1086	36 Maurice Cheeks	34845	36 Alton Lister	3179
37 **Jeff Hornacek**	1077	37 **Dale Ellis**	34778	37 Wayne Cooper	3144
Lenny Wilkens	1077	38 **Scottie Pippen**	34617	38 LaSalle Thompson	3143
39 Dominique Wilkins	1074	39 Reggie Theus	34603	39 **Mark West**	3136
40 **Charles Barkley**	1073	40 Larry Bird	34443	40 **Sam Perkins**	3116
Byron Scott	1073	41 Adrian Dantley	34151	41 Paul Silas	3105
42 Caldwell Jones	1068	42 **Kevin Willis**	34067	42 Mickey Johnson	3101
Bill Laimbeer	1068	43 **Jeff Hornacek**	33964	43 Dennis Johnson	3087
44 Johnny Green	1057	44 Bill Laimbeer	33956	44 Moses Malone	3076
45 Don Nelson	1053	45 Tom Chambers	33922	45 **Antoine Carr**	3063
46 **Tyrone Corbin**	1050	46 **Terry Cummings**	33898	46 Bob Lanier	3048
47 Leroy Ellis	1048	47 Elgin Baylor	33863	47 Tom Sanders	3044
48 Wilt Chamberlain	1045	48 Gail Goodrich	33527	48 Alex English	3027
49 Walt Bellamy	1043	49 Chet Walker	33433	49 **Rik Smits**	3011
50 Danny Ainge	1042	50 Magic Johnson	33245	50 Reggie Theus	3008

Career NBA Leader Boards—All Time

Steals (since 1973-74)			Blocked Shots (since 1973-74)			Turnovers (since 1977-78)		
	Player	Stl		Player	Blk		Player	TO
1	John Stockton	2844	1	Hakeem Olajuwon	3652	1	Moses Malone	3804
2	Maurice Cheeks	2310	2	Kareem Abdul-Jabbar	3189	2	Karl Malone	3704
3	Michael Jordan	2306	3	Mark Eaton	3064	3	Isiah Thomas	3682
4	Clyde Drexler	2207	4	Patrick Ewing	2758	4	John Stockton	3651
5	Alvin Robertson	2112	5	Tree Rollins	2542	5	Magic Johnson	3506
6	Hakeem Olajuwon	2018	6	David Robinson	2506	6	Reggie Theus	3493
7	Scottie Pippen	1986	7	Dikembe Mutombo	2443	7	Hakeem Olajuwon	3488
8	Derek Harper	1957	8	Robert Parish	2361	8	Charles Barkley	3376
9	Mookie Blaylock	1888	9	Manute Bol	2086	9	Patrick Ewing	3321
10	Isiah Thomas	1861	10	George T. Johnson	2082	10	Robert Parish	3183
11	Gary Payton	1756	11	Larry Nance	2027	11	Clyde Drexler	2977
12	Magic Johnson	1724	12	Elvin Hayes	1771	12	Alex English	2821
13	Ron Harper	1677	13	Artis Gilmore	1748	13	Larry Bird	2816
14	Fat Lever	1666	14	Moses Malone	1733	14	Bernard King	2791
15	Karl Malone	1654	15	Kevin McHale	1690	15	Buck Williams	2784
16	Charles Barkley	1648	16	Alonzo Mourning	1666	16	Otis Thorpe	2742
17	Gus Williams	1638	17	Herb Williams	1605	17	Scottie Pippen	2739
18	Hersey Hawkins	1589	18	Benoit Benjamin	1581	18	Dominique Wilkins	2669
19	Doc Rivers	1563	19	Wayne Cooper	1535	19	Mark Jackson	2625
20	Larry Bird	1556	20	Shawn Bradley	1520	20	Michael Jordan	2589
21	Nate McMillan	1544	21	Caldwell Jones	1517	21	Jack Sikma	2586
22	Jeff Hornacek	1536	22	Alton Lister	1473	22	Tom Chambers	2549
23	Chris Mullin	1514	23	Hot Rod Williams	1456	23	Walter Davis	2541
24	Julius Erving	1508	24	Shaquille O'Neal	1436	24	Charles Oakley	2537
25	Terry Porter	1486	25	Mark West	1403	25	Kareem Abdul-Jabbar	2527
26	Dennis Johnson	1477	26	Terry Tyler	1342	26	Adrian Dantley	2503
27	Micheal Ray Richardson	1463	27	Julius Erving	1293	27	Shawn Kemp	2484
28	Jerome Kersey	1425	28	James Donaldson	1267	28	Terry Porter	2477
29	Randy Smith	1403	29	Vlade Divac	1261	29	Mitch Richmond	2455
30	Rod Strickland	1397	30	Elden Campbell	1229	30	Dennis Johnson	2448
31	Mark Jackson	1385	31	Harvey Catchings	1227	31	Rod Strickland	2419
32	Dominique Wilkins	1378	32	Shawn Kemp	1190	32	Norm Nixon	2368
33	Muggsy Bogues	1367	33	Elmore Smith	1183	33	Artis Gilmore	2347
34	Rickey Green	1348	34	Sam Lacey	1160	34	Derek Harper	2334
35	Quinn Buckner	1337	35	Bob McAdoo	1147	35	Julius Erving	2323
36	T.R. Dunn	1316	36	Charles Jones	1134	36	Mark Aguirre	2306
37	Alvan Adams	1289	37	Joe Barry Carroll	1121	37	Chris Mullin	2296
38	Walter Davis	1280	38	Dan Roundfield	1117	38	Kevin Willis	2283
39	John Lucas	1273	39	Rik Smits	1111	39	Maurice Cheeks	2268
40	Tim Hardaway	1272	40	Bob Lanier	1100	40	Kevin Johnson	2258
41	Kendall Gill	1271		Buck Williams	1100	41	Sleepy Floyd	2251
42	Terry Cummings	1255	42	Andrew Lang	1099	42	Detlef Schrempf	2240
43	Tyrone Corbin	1226	43	Thurl Bailey	1086	43	Terry Cummings	2200
44	Byron Scott	1224	44	Mychal Thompson	1073	44	Alvan Adams	2194
45	Robert Parish	1219	45	Jack Sikma	1048	45	Ron Harper	2189
46	Charles Oakley	1213	46	Bill Walton	1034	46	Tim Hardaway	2170
47	Reggie Theus	1206	47	Darryl Dawkins	1023	47	George Gervin	2137
48	Ray Williams	1198	48	Rick Mahorn	1007	48	Alvin Robertson	2116
49	Norm Nixon	1187	49	Horace Grant	1005	49	David Robinson	2108
50	David Robinson	1170	50	Mike Gminski	989	50	Mychal Thompson	2104

Career NBA Leader Boards—All Time

Field Goal Percentage
(minimum 2000 FGM)

	Player	FGM	FGA	Pct
1	Artis Gilmore	5732	9570	.599
2	**Mark West**	2528	4356	.580
3	**S. O'Neal**	5896	10210	.577
4	Steve Johnson	2841	4965	.572
5	Darryl Dawkins	3477	6079	.572
6	James Donaldson	3105	5442	.571
7	Jeff Ruland	2105	3734	.564
8	K. Abdul-Jabbar	15837	28307	.559
9	Kevin McHale	6830	12334	.554
10	Bobby Jones	3412	6199	.550
11	Buck Williams	6404	11661	.549
12	**Otis Thorpe**	6813	12462	.547
13	Larry Nance	6370	11664	.546
14	Cedric Maxwell	3433	6293	.546
15	**Dale Davis**	2530	4661	.543
16	**Charles Barkley**	8435	15605	.541
17	Adrian Dantley	8169	15121	.540
18	Wilt Chamberlain	12681	23497	.540
19	Gene Banks	2134	3961	.539
20	Swen Nater	2432	4528	.537
21	Robert Parish	9614	17914	.537
22	Brad Daugherty	3823	7189	.532
23	Larry Smith	2519	4743	.531
24	**D. Mutombo**	3098	5864	.528
25	Calvin Natt	4003	7580	.528
26	**Chris Gatling**	2344	4443	.528
27	**A. Mourning**	3985	7576	.526
28	**Karl Malone**	11435	21777	.525
29	Bill Cartwright	4656	8868	.525
30	K. Vandeweghe	6139	11699	.525
31	Clifford Ray	2333	4450	.524
32	Lewis Lloyd	2172	4144	.524
33	Maurice Cheeks	4906	9374	.523
34	Mitch Kupchak	2003	3832	.523
35	**David Robinson**	6427	12306	.522
36	Tree Rollins	2592	4963	.522
37	**Dennis Rodman**	2766	5310	.521
38	James Worthy	6878	13204	.521
39	Bill Walton	2552	4900	.521
40	Magic Johnson	6211	11951	.520
41	Frank Brickowski	2873	5538	.519
42	Bernard King	7830	15109	.518
43	Marques Johnson	5733	11065	.518
44	**John Stockton**	6001	11592	.518
45	**Anthony Mason**	2616	5060	.517
46	Walt Bellamy	7914	15340	.516
47	Cliff Levingston	2333	4524	.516
48	**Tyrone Hill**	2353	4563	.516
49	**Michael Cage**	3317	6445	.515
50	Bob Lanier	7761	15092	.514

Free Throw Percentage
(minimum 1000 FTM)

	Player	FTM	FTA	Pct
1	M. Abdul-Rauf	1029	1132	.909
2	Mark Price	2135	2362	.904
3	Rick Barry	3818	4243	.900
4	Calvin Murphy	3445	3864	.892
5	Scott Skiles	1548	1741	.889
6	Larry Bird	3960	4471	.886
7	Bill Sharman	3143	3559	.883
8	**Reggie Miller**	5015	5690	.881
9	**Jeff Hornacek**	2973	3390	.877
10	Ricky Pierce	3389	3871	.875
11	**Ray Allen**	1076	1233	.873
12	Kiki Vandeweghe	3484	3997	.872
13	Jeff Malone	2947	3383	.871
14	**Hersey Hawkins**	3410	3920	.870
15	Mike Newlin	3005	3456	.869
16	**Terrell Brandon**	1506	1735	.868
17	Micheal Williams	1545	1780	.868
18	**Chris Mullin**	3592	4150	.866
19	John Long	1814	2104	.862
20	**Dana Barros**	1158	1347	.860
21	Fred Brown	1896	2211	.858
22	Johnny Dawkins	1082	1262	.857
23	**Mario Elie**	1390	1623	.856
24	**B.J. Armstrong**	1184	1383	.856
25	**Sam Cassell**	1624	1899	.855
26	Larry Siegfried	1662	1945	.854
27	James Silas	1440	1690	.852
28	Walter Davis	3128	3676	.851
29	Jack Sikma	4292	5053	.849
30	Dolph Schayes	6712	7904	.849
31	Flynn Robinson	1597	1881	.849
32	Kelly Tripucka	3106	3660	.849
33	Michael Adams	2158	2543	.849
34	**Mitch Richmond**	4376	5161	.848
35	Magic Johnson	4960	5850	.848
36	Spud Webb	1946	2296	.848
37	**Glen Rice**	2966	3501	.847
38	Danny Ainge	1676	1980	.846
39	Junior Bridgeman	1875	2216	.846
40	Jon McGlocklin	1167	1381	.845
41	George Gervin	4541	5383	.844
42	Joe Dumars	3423	4059	.843
43	Jack Marin	2405	2852	.843
44	Mike Gminski	2531	3002	.843
45	Ricky Sobers	2272	2695	.843
46	Brian Winters	1443	1713	.842
47	**Dell Curry**	1169	1388	.842
48	Larry Costello	2432	2891	.841
49	**Kevin Johnson**	3943	4691	.841
50	**Bryant Stith**	1379	1641	.840

3-Point FG Percentage
(minimum 500 3PM)

	Player	3PM	3PA	Pct
1	**Steve Kerr**	618	1332	.464
2	**Hubert Davis**	581	1317	.441
3	**Dana Barros**	1022	2476	.413
4	**Wesley Person**	777	1890	.411
5	Trent Tucker	575	1410	.408
6	**Allan Houston**	777	1917	.405
7	**Glen Rice**	1353	3339	.405
8	**Reggie Miller**	1867	4629	.403
9	**Dell Curry**	1138	2822	.403
10	Dale Ellis	1719	4266	.403
11	**Jeff Hornacek**	828	2055	.403
12	Mark Price	976	2428	.402
13	Craig Hodges	563	1408	.400
14	Kenny Smith	664	1665	.399
15	**Dennis Scott**	1214	3060	.397
16	**Hersey Hawkins**	1209	3062	.395
17	**Tracy Murray**	667	1692	.394
18	**Mitch Richmond**	1263	3222	.392
19	**Terry Mills**	530	1370	.387
20	**Danny Ferry**	543	1409	.385
21	**Chris Mullin**	796	2068	.385
22	**Terry Porter**	1151	3013	.382
23	Joe Dumars	990	2592	.382
24	**John Stockton**	730	1913	.382
25	Scott Skiles	524	1381	.379
26	Danny Ainge	1002	2651	.378
27	**Eddie Jones**	645	1713	.377
28	Larry Bird	649	1727	.376
29	**Walt Williams**	736	1973	.373
30	**Lindsey Hunter**	700	1879	.373
31	Byron Scott	775	2093	.370
32	**Sean Elliott**	534	1443	.370
33	**George McCloud**	783	2117	.370
34	**Anthony Peeler**	549	1488	.369
35	Craig Ehlo	621	1684	.369
36	**Mario Elie**	538	1472	.365
37	**Sam Perkins**	811	2238	.362
38	**Chuck Person**	1220	3370	.362
39	**Dan Majerle**	1224	3382	.362
40	**Nick Anderson**	1032	2877	.359
41	**Dee Brown**	592	1653	.358
42	**Clifford Robinson**	697	1955	.357
43	**Nick Van Exel**	955	2697	.354
44	**Tim Hardaway**	1219	3443	.354
45	Derek Harper	1070	3026	.354
46	**D. Stoudamire**	524	1491	.351
47	**Isaiah Rider**	627	1789	.350
48	Rex Chapman	805	2301	.350
49	**Kenny Anderson**	519	1490	.348
50	**Steve Smith**	831	2402	.346

Career NBA Leader Boards—All Time

Points Per Game
(minimum 250 G or 5000 Pts)

	Player	Pts	G	Avg
1	Michael Jordan	29277	930	31.5
2	Wilt Chamberlain	31419	1045	30.1
3	**Shaquille O'Neal**	14687	534	27.5
4	Elgin Baylor	23149	846	27.4
5	Jerry West	25192	932	27.0
6	Bob Pettit	20880	792	26.4
7	George Gervin	20708	791	26.2
8	**Karl Malone**	31041	1192	26.0
9	Oscar Robertson	26710	1040	25.7
10	**Allen Iverson**	6818	274	24.9
11	D. Wilkins	26668	1074	24.8
12	K. Abdul-Jabbar	38387	1560	24.6
13	Larry Bird	21791	897	24.3
14	Adrian Dantley	23177	955	24.3
15	Pete Maravich	15948	658	24.2
16	**David Robinson**	18142	765	23.7
17	Rick Barry	18395	794	23.2
18	George Mikan	10156	439	23.1
19	**H. Olajuwon**	25822	1119	23.1
20	Paul Arizin	16266	713	22.8
21	**Patrick Ewing**	23665	1039	22.8
22	Bernard King	19655	874	22.5
23	**Mitch Richmond**	19639	875	22.4
24	**Charles Barkley**	23757	1073	22.1
25	David Thompson	11264	509	22.1
26	Bob McAdoo	18787	852	22.1
27	Julius Erving	18364	836	22.0
28	Geoff Petrie	9732	446	21.8
29	**Grant Hill**	9393	435	21.6
30	Alex English	25613	1193	21.5
31	**Alonzo Mourning**	11259	534	21.1
32	**Glenn Robinson**	8970	426	21.1
33	Elvin Hayes	27313	1303	21.0
34	**S. Abdur-Rahim**	6138	294	20.9
35	**Chris Webber**	8447	405	20.9
36	Billy Cunningham	13626	654	20.8
37	John Havlicek	26395	1270	20.8
38	John Drew	15291	739	20.7
39	Moses Malone	27409	1329	20.6
40	Clyde Drexler	22195	1086	20.4
41	Dan Issel	14659	718	20.4
42	Dave Bing	18327	901	20.3
43	World B. Free	17955	886	20.3
44	**Glen Rice**	16643	825	20.2
45	Lou Hudson	17940	890	20.2
46	John Williamson	5802	288	20.1
47	Marques Johnson	13892	691	20.1
48	Walt Bellamy	20941	1043	20.1
49	Bob Lanier	19248	959	20.1
50	Mark Aguirre	18458	923	20.0

Rebounds Per Game
(minimum 250 G or 3000 Reb)

	Player	Reb	G	Avg
1	Wilt Chamberlain	23924	1045	22.9
2	Bill Russell	21620	963	22.5
3	Maurice Stokes	3492	202	17.3
4	Bob Pettit	12849	792	16.2
5	Jerry Lucas	12942	829	15.6
6	Nate Thurmond	14464	964	15.0
7	Wes Unseld	13769	984	14.0
8	Walt Bellamy	14241	1043	13.7
9	Dave Cowens	10444	766	13.6
10	Elgin Baylor	11463	846	13.5
11	George Mikan	4167	311	13.4
12	**Dennis Rodman**	11954	911	13.1
13	Willis Reed	8414	650	12.9
14	Gus Johnson	7379	582	12.7
15	Elvin Hayes	16279	1303	12.5
16	**Shaquille O'Neal**	6615	534	12.4
17	**D. Mutombo**	8439	685	12.3
18	Moses Malone	16212	1329	12.2
19	Dolph Schayes	11256	932	12.1
20	Bill Bridges	11054	926	11.9
21	Harry Gallatin	6684	562	11.9
22	**Charles Barkley**	12546	1073	11.7
23	**H. Olajuwon**	12950	1119	11.6
24	Neil Johnston	5856	516	11.3
25	**David Robinson**	8651	765	11.3
26	Walter Dukes	6223	553	11.3
27	K. Abdul-Jabbar	17440	1560	11.2
28	Red Kerr	10092	905	11.2
29	Dave DeBusschere	9618	875	11.0
30	Swen Nater	5297	489	10.8
31	Elmore Smith	5962	562	10.6
32	**Karl Malone**	12618	1192	10.6
33	Bill Walton	4923	468	10.5
34	Ray Scott	7154	684	10.5
35	Zelmo Beaty	5949	570	10.4
36	**Patrick Ewing**	10759	1039	10.4
37	Happy Hairston	8019	776	10.3
38	Clyde Lee	7626	742	10.3
39	Jeff Ruland	3378	332	10.2
40	Billy Cunningham	6638	654	10.1
41	Bob Lanier	9698	959	10.1
42	Artis Gilmore	9161	909	10.1
43	**Alonzo Mourning**	5377	534	10.1
44	**Chris Webber**	4075	405	10.1
45	**Derrick Coleman**	5882	586	10.0
46	**Charles Oakley**	11009	1098	10.0
47	Roy Tarpley	2803	280	10.0
48	Larry Bird	8974	897	10.0
49	Buck Williams	13017	1307	10.0
50	Bailey Howell	9383	951	9.9

Assists Per Game
(minimum 250 G or 2000 Ast)

	Player	Ast	G	Avg
1	Magic Johnson	10141	906	11.2
2	**John Stockton**	13790	1258	11.0
3	Oscar Robertson	9887	1040	9.5
4	**Jason Kidd**	3848	414	9.3
5	Isiah Thomas	9061	979	9.3
6	**Kevin Johnson**	6711	735	9.1
7	**Tim Hardaway**	6310	712	8.9
8	**Mark Jackson**	8574	1007	8.5
9	**S. Marbury**	2285	272	8.4
10	Norm Nixon	6386	768	8.3
11	Kevin Porter	5314	659	8.1
12	**Rod Strickland**	6723	840	8.0
13	Guy Rodgers	6917	892	7.8
14	**D. Stoudamire**	2659	350	7.6
15	**Muggsy Bogues**	6721	886	7.6
16	**Nick Van Exel**	3831	507	7.6
17	Bob Cousy	6955	924	7.5
18	Johnny Moore	3866	520	7.4
19	Tiny Archibald	6476	876	7.4
20	**Gary Payton**	5548	786	7.1
21	**Kenny Anderson**	4233	601	7.0
22	M. Ray Richardson	3899	556	7.0
23	Norm Van Lier	5217	746	7.0
24	John Lucas	6454	928	7.0
25	**Mookie Blaylock**	5396	785	6.9
26	Mark Price	4863	722	6.7
27	Maurice Cheeks	7392	1101	6.7
28	Lenny Wilkens	7211	1077	6.7
29	Jerry West	6238	932	6.7
30	Pooh Richardson	4180	639	6.5
31	Scott Skiles	3881	600	6.5
32	Michael Adams	4209	653	6.4
33	Phil Ford	3083	482	6.4
34	Larry Bird	5695	897	6.3
35	Reggie Theus	6453	1026	6.3
36	**Grant Hill**	2720	435	6.3
37	Fat Lever	4696	752	6.2
38	**Sherman Douglas**	4392	706	6.2
39	**A. Hardaway**	2658	429	6.2
40	**Avery Johnson**	5148	837	6.2
41	Nate McMillan	4893	796	6.1
42	Slick Watts	2678	437	6.1
43	Walt Frazier	5040	825	6.1
44	Dave Bing	5397	901	6.0
45	John Bagley	3980	665	6.0
46	**Terry Porter**	6704	1122	6.0
47	**Allen Iverson**	1612	274	5.9
48	**Sam Cassell**	2548	434	5.9
49	**Terrell Brandon**	3560	614	5.8
50	Micheal Williams	2385	413	5.8

Career NBA Leader Boards—All Time

Steals Per Game
(minimum 250 G or 500 Stl)

	Player	Stl	G	Avg
1	Alvin Robertson	2112	779	2.71
2	M. Ray Richardson	1463	556	2.63
3	Michael Jordan	2306	930	2.48
4	**Mookie Blaylock**	1888	785	2.41
5	**John Stockton**	2844	1258	2.26
6	**Gary Payton**	1756	786	2.23
7	**Eddie Jones**	926	416	2.23
8	Fat Lever	1666	752	2.22
9	Slick Watts	961	437	2.20
10	**Allen Iverson**	587	274	2.14
11	Maurice Cheeks	2310	1101	2.10
12	**Jason Kidd**	860	414	2.08
13	**Scottie Pippen**	1986	965	2.06
14	Clyde Drexler	2207	1086	2.03
15	Rick Barry	1104	554	1.99
16	Gus Williams	1638	825	1.99
17	Johnny Moore	1017	520	1.96
18	Ron Lee	869	448	1.94
19	Nate McMillan	1544	796	1.94
20	Magic Johnson	1724	906	1.90
21	Isiah Thomas	1861	979	1.90
22	Walt Frazier	681	359	1.90
23	**A. Hardaway**	812	429	1.89
24	Quinn Buckner	1337	719	1.86
25	Mike Gale	840	453	1.85
26	Brian Taylor	606	330	1.84
27	Ray Williams	1198	655	1.83
28	Eddie Jordan	766	420	1.82
29	Doc Rivers	1563	864	1.81
30	Norm Van Lier	767	424	1.81
31	**Doug Christie**	789	437	1.81
32	Julius Erving	1508	836	1.80
33	**H. Olajuwon**	2018	1119	1.80
34	Larry Steele	846	472	1.79
35	Don Buse	1160	648	1.79
36	**Tim Hardaway**	1272	712	1.79
37	**Kendall Gill**	1271	718	1.77
38	George McGinnis	923	528	1.75
39	**Ron Harper**	1677	962	1.74
40	Micheal Williams	717	413	1.74
41	Larry Bird	1556	897	1.73
42	Wilbur Holland	475	276	1.72
43	**Hersey Hawkins**	1589	924	1.72
44	Randy Smith	1403	818	1.72
45	Darwin Cook	1044	612	1.71
46	**Tom Gugliotta**	907	533	1.70
47	**Kerry Kittles**	447	267	1.67
48	**Rod Strickland**	1397	840	1.66
49	Michael Adams	1081	653	1.66
50	**Latrell Sprewell**	851	519	1.64

Blocked Shots Per Game
(minimum 250 G or 500 Blk)

	Player	Blk	G	Avg
1	**D. Mutombo**	2443	685	3.57
2	Mark Eaton	3064	875	3.50
3	Manute Bol	2086	624	3.34
4	**David Robinson**	2506	765	3.28
5	**H. Olajuwon**	3652	1119	3.26
6	**Shawn Bradley**	1520	473	3.21
7	**Alonzo Mourning**	1666	534	3.12
8	Elmore Smith	1183	408	2.90
9	**Shaquille O'Neal**	1436	534	2.69
10	**Patrick Ewing**	2758	1039	2.65
11	K. Abdul-Jabbar	3189	1239	2.57
12	George T. Johnson	2082	848	2.46
13	**Marcus Camby**	550	231	2.38
14	**Theo Ratliff**	805	340	2.37
15	Bill Walton	1034	468	2.21
16	Larry Nance	2027	920	2.20
17	Tree Rollins	2542	1156	2.20
18	Nate Thurmond	553	269	2.06
19	**Greg Ostertag**	650	326	1.99
20	Elvin Hayes	1771	894	1.98
21	**Benoit Benjamin**	1581	807	1.96
22	Artis Gilmore	1748	909	1.92
23	**Chris Webber**	736	405	1.82
24	**Kevin Garnett**	653	367	1.78
25	Sam Bowie	909	511	1.78
26	**Jim McIlvaine**	676	383	1.77
27	Kevin McHale	1690	971	1.74
28	Roy Hinson	882	507	1.74
29	**Antonio McDyess**	629	362	1.74
30	Harvey Catchings	1227	725	1.69
31	**Elden Campbell**	1229	728	1.69
32	**Bo Outlaw**	793	475	1.67
33	Jawann Oldham	546	329	1.66
34	Ralph Sampson	752	456	1.65
35	**Oliver Miller**	732	445	1.64
36	Hot Rod Williams	1456	887	1.64
37	**Ervin Johnson**	787	483	1.63
38	**Pervis Ellison**	750	465	1.61
39	Joe Barry Carroll	1121	705	1.59
40	**Vlade Divac**	1261	797	1.58
41	Charles Jones	1134	726	1.56
42	Wayne Cooper	1535	984	1.56
43	Julius Erving	1293	836	1.55
44	Alton Lister	1473	953	1.55
45	Terry Tyler	1342	871	1.54
46	Bob Lanier	1100	716	1.54
47	Sam Lacey	1160	761	1.52
48	**Derrick Coleman**	884	586	1.51
49	Dan Roundfield	1117	746	1.50
50	**Andrew Lang**	1099	737	1.49

Turnovers Per Game
(minimum 250 G or 500 TO)

	Player	TO	G	Avg
1	Magic Johnson	3506	906	3.87
2	Isiah Thomas	3682	979	3.76
3	Pete Maravich	530	142	3.73
4	Jeff Ruland	1212	332	3.65
5	**Allen Iverson**	978	274	3.57
6	Kevin Porter	1133	326	3.48
7	George McGinnis	1291	372	3.47
8	Eric Money	712	207	3.44
9	**Jerry Stackhouse**	1224	356	3.44
10	Reggie Theus	3493	1026	3.40
11	M. Ray Richardson	1854	556	3.33
12	**Stephon Marbury**	900	272	3.31
13	**Grant Hill**	1433	435	3.29
14	**Jason Kidd**	1357	414	3.28
15	**Glenn Robinson**	1393	426	3.27
16	**Tim Duncan**	667	206	3.24
17	Ray Williams	2099	655	3.20
18	**Patrick Ewing**	3321	1039	3.20
19	Bernard King	2791	874	3.19
20	**Alonzo Mourning**	1699	534	3.18
21	**Charles Barkley**	3376	1073	3.15
22	Larry Bird	2816	897	3.14
23	**Antoine Walker**	900	288	3.13
24	**S. Abdur-Rahim**	917	294	3.12
25	**H. Olajuwon**	3488	1119	3.12
26	**Karl Malone**	3704	1192	3.11
27	Norm Nixon	2368	768	3.08
28	Julius Erving	2323	754	3.08
29	**Kevin Johnson**	2258	735	3.07
30	Moses Malone	3804	1247	3.05
31	**Tim Hardaway**	2170	712	3.05
32	George Gervin	2137	709	3.01
33	Shawn Kemp	2484	829	3.00
34	**Latrell Sprewell**	1552	519	2.99
35	Ralph Sampson	1363	456	2.99
36	Andrew Toney	1394	468	2.98
37	**Juwan Howard**	1220	410	2.98
38	Ricky Sobers	1973	664	2.97
39	**Chris Webber**	1203	405	2.97
40	**A. Hardaway**	1273	429	2.97
41	Truck Robinson	1592	537	2.96
42	**D. Stoudamire**	1037	350	2.96
43	Campy Russell	1025	346	2.96
44	**Keith Van Horn**	542	184	2.95
45	**Derrick Coleman**	1720	586	2.94
46	**Jim Jackson**	1538	527	2.92
47	Mickey Johnson	2050	704	2.91
48	**Shaquille O'Neal**	1554	534	2.91
49	**John Stockton**	3651	1258	2.90
50	Charlie Scott	656	227	2.89

Career Postseason NBA Leader Boards—All Time

	Points			Offensive Rebounds (since 1973-74)			Rebounds (since 1950-51)	
	Player	Points		Player	OReb		Player	Reb
1	Michael Jordan	5987	1	Dennis Rodman	626	1	Bill Russell	4104
2	Kareem Abdul-Jabbar	5762	2	Robert Parish	571	2	Wilt Chamberlain	3913
3	Jerry West	4457	3	Charles Barkley	510	3	Kareem Abdul-Jabbar	2481
4	Karl Malone	4203		Moses Malone	510	4	Wes Unseld	1777
5	Larry Bird	3897	5	Kareem Abdul-Jabbar	505	5	Karl Malone	1769
6	John Havlicek	3776	6	Horace Grant	501	6	Robert Parish	1765
7	Hakeem Olajuwon	3727	7	Charles Oakley	499	7	Elgin Baylor	1724
8	Magic Johnson	3701	8	Hakeem Olajuwon	462	8	Larry Bird	1683
9	Elgin Baylor	3623	9	Kevin McHale	456	9	Dennis Rodman	1676
10	Wilt Chamberlain	3607	10	Scottie Pippen	454	10	Hakeem Olajuwon	1602
11	Scottie Pippen	3529	11	Karl Malone	446	11	Charles Barkley	1582
12	Kevin McHale	3182	12	Shaquille O'Neal	410	12	Scottie Pippen	1527
13	Dennis Johnson	3116	13	A.C. Green	389		Paul Silas	1527
14	Julius Erving	3088	14	Larry Bird	360	14	Magic Johnson	1465
15	James Worthy	3022		Julius Erving	360	15	Patrick Ewing	1413
16	Clyde Drexler	2963	16	Clyde Drexler	359	16	Charles Oakley	1369
17	Sam Jones	2909	17	Buck Williams	351	17	Horace Grant	1330
18	Charles Barkley	2833	18	Magic Johnson	349	18	Bill Bridges	1305
19	Robert Parish	2820	19	Paul Silas	339	19	Bob Pettit	1304
20	Patrick Ewing	2787	20	Elvin Hayes	336	20	Moses Malone	1295
21	Bill Russell	2673	21	Patrick Ewing	332	21	Dave Cowens	1285
22	Shaquille O'Neal	2469	22	Dale Davis	317	22	Kevin McHale	1253
23	Byron Scott	2451	23	Shawn Kemp	311	23	Elvin Hayes	1244
24	Reggie Miller	2320	24	Wes Unseld	306	24	John Havlicek	1186
25	John Stockton	2281	25	Michael Jordan	305	25	Dave DeBusschere	1155
26	Isiah Thomas	2261	26	Jerome Kersey	283	26	Michael Jordan	1152
27	Bob Pettit	2240	27	David Robinson	277	27	Nate Thurmond	1101
28	Elvin Hayes	2194	28	Caldwell Jones	267	28	Bill Laimbeer	1097
29	Jeff Hornacek	2092	29	Dennis Johnson	262	29	Shaquille O'Neal	1085
30	Moses Malone	2077	30	Bill Laimbeer	257	30	A.C. Green	1080
31	Tom Heinsohn	2058		James Worthy	257	31	Dolph Schayes	1051
32	Kevin Johnson	2026	32	Sam Perkins	254	32	Clyde Drexler	1002
33	Bob Cousy	2018	33	Terry Cummings	252	33	Caldwell Jones	999
34	Bob Dandridge	1967	34	Jamaal Wilkes	251	34	Julius Erving	994
35	Gus Williams	1929	35	John Salley	244	35	David Robinson	973
36	Walt Frazier	1927	36	Dave Cowens	243	36	Tom Heinsohn	954
37	Chet Walker	1916	37	Kurt Rambis	236	37	Jack Sikma	945
38	Maurice Cheeks	1910	38	Cedric Maxwell	233	38	Buck Williams	941
	Oscar Robertson	1910	39	Jack Sikma	226	39	Sam Perkins	932
40	Danny Ainge	1902	40	Mychal Thompson	224	40	Dale Davis	917
41	Dolph Schayes	1887	41	Derrick McKey	222	41	Jerry West	855
42	Hal Greer	1876	42	Bobby Jones	219	42	Shawn Kemp	830
43	Sam Perkins	1856	43	Anthony Mason	217	43	Red Kerr	827
44	Cliff Hagan	1834	44	Kevin Willis	215	44	Willis Reed	801
45	Rick Barry	1833	45	Bill Cartwright	207	45	Dennis Johnson	781
46	Jamaal Wilkes	1820	46	Robert Horry	203	46	Rudy LaRusso	779
47	David Robinson	1807	47	Clifford Ray	196	47	Kurt Rambis	764
48	Horace Grant	1793	48	Vlade Divac	189	48	Tom Sanders	763
49	Joe Dumars	1752		Sidney Moncrief	189	49	Bob Dandridge	754
50	Mark Aguirre	1747	50	Larry Nance	184	50	James Worthy	747

Career Postseason NBA Leader Boards—All Time

	Assists			Games			Minutes	
							(since 1951-52)	
	Player	Ast		Player	G		Player	Min
1	Magic Johnson	2346	1	Kareem Abdul-Jabbar	237	1	Kareem Abdul-Jabbar	8851
2	John Stockton	1716	2	Scottie Pippen	198	2	Scottie Pippen	7814
3	Larry Bird	1062	3	Danny Ainge	193	3	Wilt Chamberlain	7559
4	Michael Jordan	1022	4	Magic Johnson	190	4	Magic Johnson	7538
5	Scottie Pippen	1011	5	Robert Parish	184	5	Bill Russell	7497
6	Dennis Johnson	1006	6	Byron Scott	183	6	Michael Jordan	7474
7	Isiah Thomas	987	7	Dennis Johnson	180	7	Dennis Johnson	6994
8	Jerry West	970	8	Michael Jordan	179	8	Larry Bird	6886
9	Bob Cousy	937	9	John Havlicek	172	9	John Havlicek	6860
10	Kevin Johnson	935	10	Kevin McHale	169	10	Karl Malone	6556
11	Maurice Cheeks	922		Dennis Rodman	169	11	Jerry West	6321
12	Clyde Drexler	891	12	Michael Cooper	168	12	Robert Parish	6177
13	Mark Jackson	857		John Stockton	168	13	John Stockton	5922
14	John Havlicek	825	14	Bill Russell	165	14	Kevin McHale	5716
15	Bill Russell	770	15	Larry Bird	164	15	Hakeem Olajuwon	5663
16	Oscar Robertson	769		Sam Perkins	164	16	Horace Grant	5622
17	Kareem Abdul-Jabbar	767	17	Paul Silas	163	17	Clyde Drexler	5572
18	Michael Cooper	703	18	Wilt Chamberlain	160	18	Elgin Baylor	5510
19	Wilt Chamberlain	673	19	Karl Malone	158	19	Byron Scott	5365
20	Danny Ainge	656	20	Sam Jones	154	20	James Worthy	5297
21	Walt Frazier	599	21	Jerry West	153	21	Julius Erving	5288
22	Julius Erving	594	22	Horace Grant	150	22	Patrick Ewing	5140
23	Terry Porter	572		A.C. Green	150	23	Danny Ainge	5038
24	Gary Payton	543		Don Nelson	150	24	Wes Unseld	4889
25	Elgin Baylor	541	25	Clyde Drexler	145	25	Charles Barkley	4849
26	Jeff Hornacek	525	26	James Worthy	143	26	Maurice Cheeks	4848
27	Avery Johnson	521	27	Julius Erving	141	27	Dennis Rodman	4789
28	Derek Harper	513	28	Jeff Hornacek	140	28	Jeff Hornacek	4766
29	Joe Dumars	512		Hakeem Olajuwon	140		Sam Perkins	4766
30	Nate McMillan	505	30	Kurt Rambis	139	30	Michael Cooper	4744
31	Karl Malone	483	31	Patrick Ewing	135	31	Charles Oakley	4717
32	Charles Barkley	482	32	Elgin Baylor	134	32	Sam Jones	4654
33	Doc Rivers	479		Derrick McKey	134	33	Paul Silas	4619
34	Gus Williams	469		John Salley	134	34	Isiah Thomas	4216
35	Norm Nixon	464	35	Maurice Cheeks	133	35	Dan Majerle	4168
36	James Worthy	463	36	Charles Oakley	132	36	Elvin Hayes	4160
37	Hakeem Olajuwon	456	37	Tom Sanders	130	37	Bob Cousy	4120
38	Wes Unseld	453	38	Jerome Kersey	126	38	A.C. Green	4098
39	Jo Jo White	452	39	Bobby Jones	125	39	Joe Dumars	4097
40	Tom Henderson	431	40	Bill Cartwright	124	40	Walt Frazier	3953
41	Paul Pressey	420	41	Charles Barkley	123	41	Bob Dandridge	3882
42	K.C. Jones	396	42	Dan Majerle	120	42	Kevin Johnson	3879
43	Hal Greer	393	43	Caldwell Jones	119	43	Reggie Miller	3872
44	John Starks	391		John Paxson	119	44	Jamaal Wilkes	3799
45	Byron Scott	390		Wes Unseld	119	45	Robert Horry	3797
46	Lenny Wilkens	372	46	Robert Horry	118	46	Moses Malone	3796
47	Rod Strickland	371	47	Mark Jackson	116	47	Dave Cowens	3768
48	Bob Dandridge	365		Vinnie Johnson	116	48	Bill Laimbeer	3735
49	Tim Hardaway	364	49	3 tied with	113	49	Derrick McKey	3711
50	Sam Jones	358				50	Buck Williams	3710

Career Postseason NBA Leader Boards—All Time

	Personal Fouls			Steals (since 1973-74)			Blocked Shots (since 1973-74)	
	Player	PF		Player	Stl		Player	Blk
1	Kareem Abdul-Jabbar	797	1	**Scottie Pippen**	383	1	Kareem Abdul-Jabbar	476
2	**Scottie Pippen**	650	2	Michael Jordan	376	2	**Hakeem Olajuwon**	468
3	**Dennis Rodman**	630	3	Magic Johnson	358	3	Robert Parish	309
4	Robert Parish	617	4	**John Stockton**	309	4	**Patrick Ewing**	299
5	Dennis Johnson	575	5	Larry Bird	296	5	Kevin McHale	281
6	Kevin McHale	571	6	Maurice Cheeks	295	6	**David Robinson**	247
7	**Karl Malone**	558	7	Clyde Drexler	278	7	Julius Erving	239
8	**Hakeem Olajuwon**	553	8	Dennis Johnson	247	8	Caldwell Jones	223
9	Bill Russell	546	9	**Hakeem Olajuwon**	238	9	Elvin Hayes	222
10	Michael Jordan	541	10	Julius Erving	235	10	Mark Eaton	210
11	Danny Ainge	533	11	Isiah Thomas	234	11	**Shaquille O'Neal**	193
12	John Havlicek	527	12	Byron Scott	226	12	**Scottie Pippen**	181
13	Magic Johnson	524	13	**Karl Malone**	216	13	Darryl Dawkins	165
14	**Patrick Ewing**	510	14	Michael Cooper	203	14	**Horace Grant**	159
15	Tom Sanders	508	15	**Charles Barkley**	193		**John Salley**	159
16	**John Stockton**	491	16	Kareem Abdul-Jabbar	189	16	Michael Jordan	158
17	Clyde Drexler	486	17	James Worthy	177	17	Bobby Jones	156
18	Michael Cooper	474	18	Gus Williams	174	18	Moses Malone	151
	Charles Oakley	474	19	Danny Ainge	172		Bob McAdoo	151
20	Paul Silas	469	20	**Jeff Hornacek**	170	20	**Alonzo Mourning**	150
21	Larry Bird	466	21	**Jerome Kersey**	168	21	**Greg Ostertag**	146
22	**Horace Grant**	465	22	**Charles Oakley**	166	22	Larry Bird	145
23	Jerry West	451	23	**Dan Majerle**	161	23	Larry Nance	144
24	Byron Scott	445	24	**Robert Horry**	156	24	Alton Lister	142
25	Darryl Dawkins	438	25	**Horace Grant**	153	25	**Shawn Kemp**	137
	Sam Perkins	438		**Gary Payton**	153	26	**Dikembe Mutombo**	134
27	Elgin Baylor	435	27	Derek Harper	148		Tree Rollins	134
28	Jack Sikma	432	28	Robert Parish	145	28	**Sam Perkins**	126
29	**Jerome Kersey**	427	29	**Ron Harper**	137	29	**Karl Malone**	124
30	Caldwell Jones	426		Jamaal Wilkes	137	30	**Robert Horry**	121
31	**Derrick McKey**	424	31	**Kevin Johnson**	132	31	Mark West	119
32	**John Salley**	420		Bobby Jones	132	32	**Vlade Divac**	117
33	**Rik Smits**	419	33	Nate McMillan	131	33	**Dale Davis**	113
34	Tom Heinsohn	417	34	Doc Rivers	125		Dennis Johnson	113
35	Bill Cartwright	412	35	**Terry Porter**	122	35	**Charles Barkley**	108
	Wilt Chamberlain	412	36	**Patrick Ewing**	121		Clyde Drexler	108
37	**Charles Barkley**	408	37	**John Starks**	119	37	Mychal Thompson	106
	Bill Bridges	408	38	**Mark Jackson**	118	38	George T. Johnson	101
	Bill Laimbeer	408		**Sam Perkins**	118	39	Bob Lanier	99
40	Julius Erving	403	40	**Mookie Blaylock**	116	40	Gar Heard	98
41	Bobby Jones	400		**Hersey Hawkins**	116		**Dennis Rodman**	98
42	Don Nelson	399		Paul Pressey	116	42	Michael Cooper	96
43	Dave Cowens	398	43	Lionel Hollins	114		Wayne Cooper	96
44	Vern Mikkelsen	397	44	**David Robinson**	113		James Worthy	96
45	Sam Jones	391	45	**Derrick McKey**	109	45	**Elden Campbell**	94
46	Buck Williams	386	46	Rick Barry	106		**Clifford Robinson**	94
47	**Robert Horry**	385		**Reggie Miller**	106		Marvin Webster	94
48	**Jeff Hornacek**	384		Sidney Moncrief	106	48	**Antoine Carr**	92
49	**Antoine Carr**	383		Robert Reid	106	49	**Rik Smits**	90
50	Elvin Hayes	378		**Dennis Rodman**	106	50	**Derrick McKey**	86

Career Postseason NBA Leader Boards—All Time

Field Goal Percentage
(minimum 300 FGM)

	Player	FGM	FGA	Pct
1	**Otis Thorpe**	319	555	.575
2	**Shaquille O'Neal**	961	1690	.569
3	Kevin McHale	1204	2145	.561
4	**Dale Davis**	320	578	.554
5	Darryl Dawkins	542	992	.546
6	Cedric Maxwell	375	688	.545
7	James Worthy	1267	2329	.544
8	**Horace Grant**	741	1365	.543
9	Larry Nance	440	813	.541
10	Bobby Jones	553	1034	.535
11	K. Abdul-Jabbar	2356	4422	.533
12	Bob Lanier	508	955	.532
13	**Anthony Mason**	321	606	.530
14	**H. Olajuwon**	1492	2825	.528
15	Adrian Dantley	531	1012	.525
16	Wilt Chamberlain	1425	2728	.522
17	Buck Williams	436	839	.520
18	**Antoine Carr**	301	586	.514
19	**Charles Barkley**	1009	1965	.513
20	Maurice Cheeks	772	1509	.512
21	Walt Frazier	767	1500	.511
22	Kiki Vandeweghe	419	822	.510
23	George Gervin	622	1225	.508
24	**Rik Smits**	623	1230	.507
25	Magic Johnson	1291	2552	.506
26	Robert Parish	1132	2239	.506
27	Calvin Natt	320	636	.503
28	Alex English	668	1328	.503
29	**Shawn Kemp**	504	1004	.502
30	**Terry Cummings**	678	1351	.502
31	Mychal Thompson	449	897	.501
32	**Avery Johnson**	364	731	.498
33	Don Nelson	585	1175	.498
34	Dan Issel	402	810	.496
35	Walter Davis	591	1192	.496
36	**Chris Mullin**	366	740	.495
37	John Paxson	306	620	.494
38	Wes Unseld	513	1040	.493
39	**Vlade Divac**	361	735	.491
40	Bob McAdoo	698	1423	.491
41	**Dennis Rodman**	442	902	.490
42	Marques Johnson	471	964	.489
43	**Alonzo Mourning**	362	744	.487
44	Michael Jordan	2188	4497	.487
45	Julius Erving	1187	2441	.486
46	Mark Aguirre	696	1435	.485
47	Caldwell Jones	322	665	.484
48	Maurice Lucas	472	975	.484
49	Rolando Blackman	434	897	.484
50	**Larry Johnson**	351	727	.483

Free Throw Percentage
(minimum 125 FTM)

	Player	FTM	FTA	Pct
1	Mark Price	202	214	.944
2	Calvin Murphy	165	177	.932
3	Bill Sharman	370	406	.911
4	**Hersey Hawkins**	287	315	.911
5	Kiki Vandeweghe	235	259	.907
6	Larry Bird	901	1012	.890
7	**Reggie Miller**	605	683	.886
8	**Jeff Hornacek**	488	551	.886
9	Bobby Wanzer	212	241	.880
10	**Allan Houston**	246	281	.875
11	Rick Barry	392	448	.875
12	Cazzie Russell	134	154	.870
13	Rolando Blackman	233	268	.869
14	Ricky Pierce	350	404	.866
15	Steve Mix	153	177	.864
16	Eddie A. Johnson	197	228	.864
17	Alex English	325	377	.862
	Jay Vincent	150	174	.862
19	**Chris Mullin**	183	213	.859
20	Joe Dumars	407	476	.855
21	Oscar Robertson	560	655	.855
22	Larry Costello	196	230	.852
23	Jeff Malone	190	223	.852
24	Kenny Smith	127	150	.847
25	Phil Chenier	212	251	.845
26	**Sam Cassell**	190	225	.844
27	**Glen Rice**	162	192	.844
28	**Steve Smith**	264	313	.843
29	Gene Shue	155	184	.842
30	**Mario Elie**	239	285	.839
31	Magic Johnson	1068	1274	.838
32	John Havlicek	874	1046	.836
33	Dave Gambee	131	157	.834
34	Thurl Bailey	201	241	.834
35	Larry Siegfried	256	307	.834
36	**Kevin Johnson**	594	713	.833
37	**B.J. Armstrong**	149	179	.832
38	**Terry Porter**	418	503	.831
39	Jack Sikma	338	407	.830
40	Walter Davis	263	317	.830
41	Paul Arizin	364	439	.829
42	Danny Ainge	296	357	.829
43	Dan Issel	223	269	.829
44	**Rik Smits**	290	350	.829
45	Jo Jo White	256	309	.828
46	Michael Jordan	1463	1766	.828
47	Tom Chambers	421	509	.827
48	Tiny Archibald	195	236	.826
49	Frank Ramsey	393	476	.826
50	Michael Cooper	293	355	.825

3-Point FG Percentage
(minimum 50 3PM)

	Player	3PM	3PA	Pct
1	**B.J. Armstrong**	51	113	.451
2	Kenny Smith	117	261	.448
3	**Jeff Hornacek**	122	282	.433
4	**Steve Smith**	114	273	.418
5	**Eddie Jones**	60	144	.417
	Trent Tucker	50	120	.417
7	**Voshon Lenard**	54	131	.412
8	**Allan Houston**	70	170	.412
9	**Chris Mullin**	67	164	.409
10	**Reggie Miller**	243	599	.406
11	**Hersey Hawkins**	98	246	.398
12	Danny Ainge	172	433	.397
13	Byron Scott	134	339	.395
14	Michael Cooper	124	316	.392
15	**Chuck Person**	77	197	.391
16	**A. Hardaway**	87	227	.383
17	**Terry Porter**	133	350	.380
18	**Mario Elie**	88	232	.379
19	**Robert Horry**	148	398	.372
20	**John Starks**	175	471	.372
21	**Detlef Schrempf**	55	150	.367
22	Derek Harper	96	263	.365
23	**Dennis Scott**	95	261	.364
24	**Sam Perkins**	151	415	.364
25	**Steve Kerr**	72	198	.364
26	Craig Hodges	90	248	.363
27	**Gary Payton**	100	276	.362
28	**Bryon Russell**	110	305	.361
29	Joe Dumars	53	148	.358
30	**Glen Rice**	65	182	.357
	Sam Cassell	50	140	.357
32	**Sean Elliott**	65	183	.355
33	**Dan Majerle**	177	499	.355
34	**Dale Ellis**	71	202	.351
35	**Mookie Blaylock**	125	357	.350
36	Isiah Thomas	81	234	.346
37	**Mark Jackson**	90	261	.345
38	**Charlie Ward**	52	151	.344
39	Craig Ehlo	57	166	.343
40	Doc Rivers	50	148	.338
41	Mark Price	56	166	.337
42	**Brian Shaw**	52	155	.335
43	**John Stockton**	109	325	.335
44	**Nick Anderson**	89	267	.333
45	Michael Jordan	148	446	.332
46	**Toni Kukoc**	88	267	.330
47	Larry Bird	80	249	.321
48	**Tim Hardaway**	106	331	.320
49	Eddie A. Johnson	67	216	.310
50	**Vernon Maxwell**	84	274	.307

Career Postseason NBA Leader Boards—All Time

<table>
<tr><td colspan="4">

Points Per Game
(minimum 25 G or 625 Pts)
</td><td colspan="4">

Offensive Reb Per Game
(minimum 25 G or 50 OReb)
</td><td colspan="4">

Rebounds Per Game
(minimum 25 G or 200 Reb)
</td></tr>
<tr>
<td></td><td>Player</td><td>Pts</td><td>G</td><td>Avg</td>
<td>Player</td><td>OReb</td><td>G</td><td>Avg</td>
<td>Player</td><td>Reb</td><td>G</td><td>Avg</td>
</tr>
<tr><td>1</td><td>Michael Jordan</td><td>5987</td><td>179</td><td>33.4</td><td>Moses Malone</td><td>510</td><td>94</td><td>5.4</td><td>Bill Russell</td><td>4104</td><td>165</td><td>24.9</td></tr>
<tr><td>2</td><td>Jerry West</td><td>4457</td><td>153</td><td>29.1</td><td>Roy Tarpley</td><td>115</td><td>24</td><td>4.8</td><td>Wilt Chamberlain</td><td>3913</td><td>160</td><td>24.5</td></tr>
<tr><td>3</td><td>Shaquille O'Neal</td><td>2469</td><td>89</td><td>27.7</td><td>Shaquille O'Neal</td><td>410</td><td>89</td><td>4.6</td><td>Wes Unseld</td><td>1777</td><td>119</td><td>14.9</td></tr>
<tr><td>4</td><td>Elgin Baylor</td><td>3623</td><td>134</td><td>27.0</td><td>Charles Barkley</td><td>510</td><td>123</td><td>4.1</td><td>Bob Pettit</td><td>1304</td><td>88</td><td>14.8</td></tr>
<tr><td>5</td><td>George Gervin</td><td>1592</td><td>59</td><td>27.0</td><td>Shawn Kemp</td><td>311</td><td>78</td><td>4.0</td><td>Walt Bellamy</td><td>680</td><td>46</td><td>14.8</td></tr>
<tr><td>6</td><td>H. Olajuwon</td><td>3727</td><td>140</td><td>26.6</td><td>Elvin Hayes</td><td>336</td><td>85</td><td>4.0</td><td>Dave Cowens</td><td>1285</td><td>89</td><td>14.4</td></tr>
<tr><td>7</td><td>Karl Malone</td><td>4203</td><td>158</td><td>26.6</td><td>Wes Unseld</td><td>306</td><td>79</td><td>3.9</td><td>George Mikan</td><td>665</td><td>48</td><td>13.9</td></tr>
<tr><td>8</td><td>Bob Pettit</td><td>2240</td><td>88</td><td>25.5</td><td>Clifford Ray</td><td>196</td><td>51</td><td>3.8</td><td>Moses Malone</td><td>1295</td><td>94</td><td>13.8</td></tr>
<tr><td>9</td><td>D. Wilkins</td><td>1423</td><td>56</td><td>25.4</td><td>Vin Baker</td><td>57</td><td>15</td><td>3.8</td><td>Nate Thurmond</td><td>1101</td><td>81</td><td>13.6</td></tr>
<tr><td>10</td><td>Rick Barry</td><td>1833</td><td>74</td><td>24.8</td><td>Charles Oakley</td><td>499</td><td>132</td><td>3.8</td><td>Elvin Hayes</td><td>1244</td><td>96</td><td>13.0</td></tr>
<tr><td>11</td><td>Bernard King</td><td>687</td><td>28</td><td>24.5</td><td>Kevin Garnett</td><td>60</td><td>16</td><td>3.8</td><td>Derrick Coleman</td><td>219</td><td>17</td><td>12.9</td></tr>
<tr><td>12</td><td>Alex English</td><td>1661</td><td>68</td><td>24.4</td><td>Dave Cowens</td><td>243</td><td>65</td><td>3.7</td><td>Elgin Baylor</td><td>1724</td><td>134</td><td>12.9</td></tr>
<tr><td>13</td><td>K. Abdul-Jabbar</td><td>5762</td><td>237</td><td>24.3</td><td>Dennis Rodman</td><td>626</td><td>169</td><td>3.7</td><td>Charles Barkley</td><td>1582</td><td>123</td><td>12.9</td></tr>
<tr><td>14</td><td>Paul Arizin</td><td>1186</td><td>49</td><td>24.2</td><td>Jeff Ruland</td><td>62</td><td>17</td><td>3.6</td><td>Roy Tarpley</td><td>307</td><td>24</td><td>12.8</td></tr>
<tr><td>15</td><td>George Mikan</td><td>1680</td><td>70</td><td>24.0</td><td>D. Mutombo</td><td>130</td><td>38</td><td>3.4</td><td>Walter Dukes</td><td>432</td><td>35</td><td>12.3</td></tr>
<tr><td>16</td><td>Larry Bird</td><td>3897</td><td>164</td><td>23.8</td><td>Horace Grant</td><td>501</td><td>150</td><td>3.3</td><td>Dolph Schayes</td><td>1051</td><td>86</td><td>12.2</td></tr>
<tr><td>17</td><td>Reggie Miller</td><td>2320</td><td>100</td><td>23.2</td><td>David Robinson</td><td>277</td><td>83</td><td>3.3</td><td>Shaquille O'Neal</td><td>1085</td><td>89</td><td>12.2</td></tr>
<tr><td>18</td><td>Charles Barkley</td><td>2833</td><td>123</td><td>23.0</td><td>Dan Roundfield</td><td>126</td><td>38</td><td>3.3</td><td>D. Mutombo</td><td>462</td><td>38</td><td>12.2</td></tr>
<tr><td>19</td><td>David Thompson</td><td>619</td><td>27</td><td>22.9</td><td>H. Olajuwon</td><td>462</td><td>140</td><td>3.3</td><td>Dave DeBusschere</td><td>1155</td><td>96</td><td>12.0</td></tr>
<tr><td>20</td><td>Bob Love</td><td>1076</td><td>47</td><td>22.9</td><td>Dale Davis</td><td>317</td><td>97</td><td>3.3</td><td>David Robinson</td><td>973</td><td>83</td><td>11.7</td></tr>
<tr><td>21</td><td>Elvin Hayes</td><td>2194</td><td>96</td><td>22.9</td><td>Ralph Sampson</td><td>124</td><td>38</td><td>3.3</td><td>Bill Bridges</td><td>1305</td><td>113</td><td>11.5</td></tr>
<tr><td>22</td><td>Wilt Chamberlain</td><td>3607</td><td>160</td><td>22.5</td><td>Buck Williams</td><td>351</td><td>108</td><td>3.3</td><td>H. Olajuwon</td><td>1602</td><td>140</td><td>11.4</td></tr>
<tr><td>23</td><td>Tim Duncan</td><td>581</td><td>26</td><td>22.3</td><td>Derrick Coleman</td><td>55</td><td>17</td><td>3.2</td><td>Karl Malone</td><td>1769</td><td>158</td><td>11.2</td></tr>
<tr><td>24</td><td>Oscar Robertson</td><td>1910</td><td>86</td><td>22.2</td><td>Tom Boerwinkle</td><td>58</td><td>18</td><td>3.2</td><td>Neil Johnston</td><td>257</td><td>23</td><td>11.2</td></tr>
<tr><td>25</td><td>Moses Malone</td><td>2077</td><td>94</td><td>22.1</td><td>Marques Johnson</td><td>173</td><td>54</td><td>3.2</td><td>Harry Gallatin</td><td>592</td><td>53</td><td>11.2</td></tr>
<tr><td>26</td><td>John Havlicek</td><td>3776</td><td>172</td><td>22.0</td><td>Larry Kenon</td><td>99</td><td>31</td><td>3.2</td><td>Zelmo Beaty</td><td>696</td><td>63</td><td>11.0</td></tr>
<tr><td></td><td></td><td></td><td></td><td></td><td>Larry Smith</td><td>99</td><td>31</td><td>3.2</td><td>Red Kerr</td><td>827</td><td>76</td><td>10.9</td></tr>
<tr><td>27</td><td>Julius Erving</td><td>3088</td><td>141</td><td>21.9</td><td></td><td></td><td></td><td></td><td></td><td></td><td></td><td></td></tr>
<tr><td>28</td><td>David Robinson</td><td>1807</td><td>83</td><td>21.8</td><td>Paul Silas</td><td>339</td><td>107</td><td>3.2</td><td>Shawn Kemp</td><td>830</td><td>78</td><td>10.6</td></tr>
<tr><td>29</td><td>Marques Johnson</td><td>1163</td><td>54</td><td>21.5</td><td>Marvin Webster</td><td>150</td><td>48</td><td>3.1</td><td>Tim Duncan</td><td>276</td><td>26</td><td>10.6</td></tr>
<tr><td></td><td></td><td></td><td></td><td></td><td>Anthony Roberts</td><td>50</td><td>16</td><td>3.1</td><td>Ralph Sampson</td><td>400</td><td>38</td><td>10.5</td></tr>
<tr><td>30</td><td>A. Hardaway</td><td>1162</td><td>54</td><td>21.5</td><td></td><td></td><td></td><td></td><td></td><td></td><td></td><td></td></tr>
<tr><td>31</td><td>Jo Jo White</td><td>1720</td><td>80</td><td>21.5</td><td>Robert Parish</td><td>571</td><td>184</td><td>3.1</td><td>K. Abdul-Jabbar</td><td>2481</td><td>237</td><td>10.5</td></tr>
<tr><td>32</td><td>Doug Collins</td><td>687</td><td>32</td><td>21.5</td><td>Lonnie Shelton</td><td>157</td><td>52</td><td>3.0</td><td>Patrick Ewing</td><td>1413</td><td>135</td><td>10.5</td></tr>
<tr><td>33</td><td>Adrian Dantley</td><td>1558</td><td>73</td><td>21.3</td><td>Reggie King</td><td>69</td><td>23</td><td>3.0</td><td>Charles Oakley</td><td>1369</td><td>132</td><td>10.4</td></tr>
<tr><td>34</td><td>Lou Hudson</td><td>1300</td><td>61</td><td>21.3</td><td>Kevin Willis</td><td>215</td><td>73</td><td>2.9</td><td>Willis Reed</td><td>801</td><td>78</td><td>10.3</td></tr>
<tr><td>35</td><td>James Worthy</td><td>3022</td><td>143</td><td>21.1</td><td>Tim Duncan</td><td>75</td><td>26</td><td>2.9</td><td>Larry Bird</td><td>1683</td><td>164</td><td>10.3</td></tr>
<tr><td>36</td><td>Walt Frazier</td><td>1927</td><td>93</td><td>20.7</td><td>George McGinnis</td><td>97</td><td>34</td><td>2.9</td><td>Brad Daugherty</td><td>419</td><td>41</td><td>10.2</td></tr>
<tr><td>37</td><td>Patrick Ewing</td><td>2787</td><td>135</td><td>20.6</td><td>Xavier McDaniel</td><td>145</td><td>51</td><td>2.8</td><td>Arnie Risen</td><td>561</td><td>55</td><td>10.2</td></tr>
<tr><td>38</td><td>Clyde Drexler</td><td>2963</td><td>145</td><td>20.4</td><td>Karl Malone</td><td>446</td><td>158</td><td>2.8</td><td>Jack Coleman</td><td>621</td><td>61</td><td>10.2</td></tr>
<tr><td>39</td><td>Hal Greer</td><td>1876</td><td>92</td><td>20.4</td><td>D. Wilkins</td><td>158</td><td>56</td><td>2.8</td><td>Clyde Lee</td><td>519</td><td>51</td><td>10.2</td></tr>
<tr><td>40</td><td>Alonzo Mourning</td><td>1060</td><td>52</td><td>20.4</td><td>Curtis Rowe</td><td>78</td><td>28</td><td>2.8</td><td>Clifford Ray</td><td>608</td><td>60</td><td>10.1</td></tr>
<tr><td>41</td><td>Cliff Hagan</td><td>1834</td><td>90</td><td>20.4</td><td>Curtis Perry</td><td>97</td><td>35</td><td>2.8</td><td>Gene Wiley</td><td>272</td><td>27</td><td>10.1</td></tr>
<tr><td>42</td><td>Isiah Thomas</td><td>2261</td><td>111</td><td>20.4</td><td>P.J. Brown</td><td>107</td><td>39</td><td>2.7</td><td>Tom Gola</td><td>391</td><td>39</td><td>10.0</td></tr>
<tr><td>43</td><td>George Yardley</td><td>933</td><td>46</td><td>20.3</td><td>George T. Johnson</td><td>136</td><td>50</td><td>2.7</td><td>Jerry Lucas</td><td>717</td><td>72</td><td>10.0</td></tr>
<tr><td>44</td><td>Bob Dandridge</td><td>1967</td><td>98</td><td>20.1</td><td>Larry Nance</td><td>184</td><td>68</td><td>2.7</td><td>Dan Roundfield</td><td>378</td><td>38</td><td>9.9</td></tr>
<tr><td></td><td></td><td></td><td></td><td></td><td>Grant Long</td><td>92</td><td>34</td><td>2.7</td><td>George Yardley</td><td>457</td><td>46</td><td>9.9</td></tr>
<tr><td>45</td><td>Latrell Sprewell</td><td>774</td><td>39</td><td>19.8</td><td></td><td></td><td></td><td></td><td></td><td></td><td></td><td></td></tr>
<tr><td>46</td><td>Tom Heinsohn</td><td>2058</td><td>104</td><td>19.8</td><td>Kevin McHale</td><td>456</td><td>169</td><td>2.7</td><td>Dennis Rodman</td><td>1676</td><td>169</td><td>9.9</td></tr>
<tr><td>47</td><td>Gus Williams</td><td>1929</td><td>99</td><td>19.5</td><td>Bob Lanier</td><td>179</td><td>67</td><td>2.7</td><td>Sam Lacey</td><td>287</td><td>29</td><td>9.9</td></tr>
<tr><td>48</td><td>Magic Johnson</td><td>3701</td><td>190</td><td>19.5</td><td>Kevin Kunnert</td><td>61</td><td>23</td><td>2.7</td><td>Ray Scott</td><td>246</td><td>25</td><td>9.8</td></tr>
<tr><td>49</td><td>Dolph Schayes</td><td>1887</td><td>97</td><td>19.5</td><td>Alonzo Mourning</td><td>137</td><td>52</td><td>2.6</td><td>Alonzo Mourning</td><td>508</td><td>52</td><td>9.8</td></tr>
<tr><td>50</td><td>Dan Issel</td><td>1029</td><td>53</td><td>19.4</td><td>Mike Green</td><td>52</td><td>20</td><td>2.6</td><td>Bill Laimbeer</td><td>1097</td><td>113</td><td>9.7</td></tr>
</table>

Career Postseason NBA Leader Boards—All Time

	Assists Per Game				Steals Per Game				Blocked Shots Per Game		
	(minimum 25 G or 100 Ast)				(minimum 25 G or 25 Stl)				(minimum 25 G or 25 Blk)		
	Player	Ast	G	Avg	Player	Stl	G	Avg	Player	Blk	G	Avg
1	Magic Johnson	2346	190	12.3	M. Ray Richardson	50	18	2.78	D. Mutombo	134	38	3.53
2	John Stockton	1716	168	10.2	Alvin Robertson	36	13	2.77	H. Olajuwon	468	140	3.34
3	Jason Kidd	164	18	9.1	Slick Watts	43	17	2.53	David Robinson	247	83	2.98
4	Oscar Robertson	769	86	8.9	Jason Kidd	43	18	2.39	Alonzo Mourning	150	52	2.88
5	Kevin Johnson	935	105	8.9	Maurice Cheeks	295	133	2.22	Mark Eaton	210	74	2.84
6	Isiah Thomas	987	111	8.9	Rick Barry	106	48	2.21	Manute Bol	77	29	2.66
7	Bob Cousy	937	109	8.6	Mookie Blaylock	116	54	2.15	Tim Duncan	68	26	2.62
8	Rod Strickland	371	44	8.4	Walt Frazier	32	15	2.13	Elvin Hayes	222	85	2.61
9	Johnny Moore	344	41	8.4	Isiah Thomas	234	111	2.11	Mike Green	52	20	2.60
10	Norm Nixon	464	58	8.0	Michael Jordan	376	179	2.10	Theo Ratliff	52	21	2.48
11	John Bagley	142	19	7.5	Scottie Pippen	383	198	1.93	K. Abdul-Jabbar	476	196	2.43
12	Mark Jackson	857	116	7.4	Sam Lacey	56	29	1.93	Patrick Ewing	299	135	2.21
13	Tim Hardaway	364	50	7.3	Clyde Drexler	278	145	1.92	Shaquille O'Neal	193	89	2.17
14	M. Ray Richardson	129	18	7.2	Magic Johnson	358	190	1.88	Larry Nance	144	68	2.12
15	Slick Watts	120	17	7.1	Fat Lever	89	48	1.85	George T. Johnson	101	50	2.02
16	Mark Price	327	47	7.0	A. Hardaway	100	54	1.85	Greg Ostertag	146	73	2.00
17	Maurice Cheeks	922	133	6.9	John Stockton	309	168	1.84	Derrick Coleman	34	17	2.00
18	Darnell Valentine	177	26	6.8	Larry Bird	296	164	1.80	Marvin Webster	94	48	1.96
19	Avery Johnson	521	77	6.8	Randy Smith	43	24	1.79	Chris Webber	31	16	1.94
20	Mookie Blaylock	357	54	6.6	Allen Iverson	32	18	1.78	Elmore Smith	25	13	1.92
21	Randy Smith	157	24	6.5	Gus Williams	174	99	1.76	Nate Thurmond	51	27	1.89
22	Tiny Archibald	306	47	6.5	Norm Van Lier	47	27	1.74	Benoit Benjamin	34	18	1.89
23	Larry Bird	1062	164	6.5	Tim Hardaway	87	50	1.74	Caldwell Jones	223	119	1.87
24	Walt Frazier	599	93	6.4	Muggsy Bogues	33	19	1.74	Roy Tarpley	43	24	1.79
25	A. Hardaway	345	54	6.4	Gary Payton	153	89	1.72	Oliver Miller	73	41	1.78
26	Jerry West	970	153	6.3	Johnny Moore	70	41	1.71	Shawn Kemp	137	78	1.76
27	Sherman Douglas	106	17	6.2	Hersey Hawkins	116	68	1.71	Tom Burleson	26	15	1.73
28	Guy Rodgers	286	46	6.2	H. Olajuwon	238	140	1.70	Gar Heard	98	57	1.72
29	Fat Lever	297	48	6.2	Micheal Williams	27	16	1.69	Julius Erving	239	141	1.70
30	Norm Van Lier	234	38	6.2	Julius Erving	235	141	1.67	Marcus Camby	61	36	1.69
31	Clyde Drexler	891	145	6.1	Kendall Gill	35	21	1.67	Bill Walton	83	49	1.69
32	Gary Payton	543	89	6.1	Don Chaney	66	40	1.65	Artis Gilmore	71	42	1.69
33	Sleepy Floyd	219	36	6.1	Charlie Ward	101	62	1.63	Joe Barry Carroll	32	19	1.68
34	Doc Rivers	479	81	5.9	Otis Birdsong	56	35	1.60	Robert Parish	309	184	1.68
35	Nick Van Exel	212	36	5.9	Michael Adams	32	20	1.60	Kevin McHale	281	169	1.66
36	Lenny Wilkens	372	64	5.8	Charles Barkley	193	123	1.57	Alton Lister	142	87	1.63
37	Kevin Porter	191	33	5.8	Calvin Murphy	79	51	1.55	Mike Gminski	57	35	1.63
38	Michael Jordan	1022	179	5.7	Paul Pressey	116	75	1.55	Kevin Garnett	26	16	1.63
39	Terry Porter	572	101	5.7	Doc Rivers	125	81	1.54	Moses Malone	151	94	1.61
40	Jo Jo White	452	80	5.7	Darnell Valentine	40	26	1.54	Bob McAdoo	151	94	1.61
41	Muggsy Bogues	107	19	5.6	Norm Nixon	89	58	1.53	Vlade Divac	117	73	1.60
42	Paul Pressey	420	75	5.6	Derek Harper	148	97	1.53	Sam Lacey	44	29	1.52
43	Dennis Johnson	1006	180	5.6	Eddie Jones	61	40	1.52	Darryl Dawkins	165	109	1.51
44	Dick McGuire	350	63	5.6	Lionel Hollins	114	77	1.48	Ralph Sampson	57	38	1.50
45	Tom Henderson	431	80	5.4	Butch Beard	34	23	1.48	Elden Campbell	94	63	1.49
46	Rory Sparrow	161	30	5.4	Nick Anderson	72	49	1.47	Bob Lanier	99	67	1.48
47	Rickey Green	294	55	5.3	Winston Garland	29	20	1.45	Dan Roundfield	56	38	1.47
48	Derek Harper	513	97	5.3	Jimmy Jones	26	18	1.44	Tree Rollins	134	93	1.44
49	Nate McMillan	505	98	5.2	Jerry Sloan	27	19	1.42	Sam Bowie	41	29	1.41
50	Michael Adams	103	20	5.2	Gar Heard	80	57	1.40	Clifford Ray	70	51	1.37

Abbreviations

Assists	Ast	Minutes Played	Min
Attempts	Att	Offensive Rebounds	Off, OReb
Average	Avg	Opponent	Opp
Blocks	Blk	Percentage	Pct
Double Doubles	DD	Personal Fouls	PF
Division	Div	Points	Pts
Disqualifications	DQ	Rebounds	Reb
Defensive Rebounds	DReb	Steals	Stl
Field Goal Attempts	FGA	Two-Point Attempts	2PA
Field Goals Made	FGM	Two-Pointers Made	2PM
Field Goal Percentage	FG%	Three-Point Attempts	3PA
Free Throw Attempts	FTA	Three-Pointers Made	3PM
Free Throws Made	FTM	Three-Point Percentage	3P%
Free Throw Percentage	FT%	Triple Doubles	TD
Games Played	G	Total Rebounds	Tot, TReb
Games Started	GS	Turnovers	TO
Made	Md		

Team Abbreviations

Atlanta Hawks	Atl	Minnesota Timberwolves	Min
Boston Celtics	Bos	New Jersey Nets	NJ
Charlotte Hornets	Cha	New York Knicks	NY
Chicago Bulls	Chi	Orlando Magic	Orl
Cleveland Cavaliers	Cle	Philadelphia 76ers	Phi
Dallas Mavericks	Dal	Phoenix Suns	Pho
Denver Nuggets	Den	Portland Trail Blazers	Por
Detroit Pistons	Det	Sacramento Kings	Sac
Golden State Warriors	GS	San Antonio Spurs	SA
Houston Rockets	Hou	San Diego Clippers	SDC
Indiana Pacers	Ind	Seattle SuperSonics	Sea
Kansas City Kings	KC	Toronto Raptors	Tor
Los Angeles Clippers	LAC	Utah Jazz	Uta
Los Angeles Lakers	LAL	Vancouver Grizzlies	Van
Miami Heat	Mia	Washington Bullets/Wizards	Was
Milwaukee Bucks	Mil		

College Abbreviations

Alabama	Ala	Indiana	Ind	Purdue	Pur
American International	AmInt	Iowa State	IaSt	Rhode Island	RI
Arizona	Ari	Jackson State	JkSt	Richmond	Rich
Arizona State	AriSt	Jacksonville	Jac	Rutgers	Rut
Arkansas	Ark	Kansas	Kan	Saint Louis	StL
Arkansas-Little Rock	Ak-LR	Kansas State	KanSt	San Diego State	SDSU
Auburn	Aub	Kentucky	Kty	San Jose State	SJSU
Auburn-Montgomery	Ab-Mn	La Salle	LaSal	Santa Clara	SanCl
Augsburg	Aug	Long Beach State	LgBch	Seton Hall	SetHl
Ball State	BlSt	Long Island	LIU	South Alabama	SoAl
Baylor	Bay	Longwood	Lngwd	South Carolina	SCar
Boise State	Boi	Louisiana State	LSU	South Florida	SoFl
Boston College	BC	Louisiana Tech	LaTch	Southeastern Oklahoma St.	SEOk
Bowling Green	BlGr	Louisville	Lou	Southern California	USC
Bradley	Brad	Marquette	Marq	Southern Illinois	SIU
Brigham Young	BYU	Marshall	Mrsh	Southern Mississippi	SoMs
Cal State Bakersfield	CS-Bk	Maryland	Myld	Southern University	Sou
Cal State Fullerton	CSF	Massachusetts	Mass	Southwest Texas State	SWTx
California	Cal	Memphis	Mem	St. John's (NY)	StJn
Cameron	Cam	Mercer	Mer	St. Mary's (CA)	StMry
Central Arkansas	CnAk	Miami (FL)	Mia-Fl	Stanford	Stan
Central Connecticut State	CenCt	Miami (OH)	Mia-O	Stetson	Stet
Central Michigan	CenMi	Michigan	Mich	Syracuse	Syr
Central Oklahoma	CnOk	Michigan State	MchSt	Temple	Tem
Charleston	Char	Minnesota	Minn	Tennessee	Tenn
Chattanooga	Chat	Mississippi State	MisSt	Tennessee State	TnSt
Cincinnati	Cin	Missouri	Misou	Texas Christian	TCU
Clemson	Clem	Murray State	Mur	Texas Tech	TxTch
Colgate	Colg	Nebraska	Neb	Thomas More	ThMr
Colorado	Colo	New Mexico	NM	Tulsa	Tuls
Colorado State	ColSt	New Mexico State	NMSt	UC-Santa Barbara	UCSB
Connecticut	Conn	New Orleans	UNO	UCLA	UCLA
Creighton	Cre	Nicholls State	Nich	UNLV	UNLV
Davidson	Dav	North Carolina	UNC	Utah	Utah
Delaware State	DeSt	North Carolina Charlotte	NC-Ch	UTEP	UTEP
DePaul	DeP	North Carolina State	NCSt	Valparaiso	Val
Detroit	Det	Northwestern	NW	Vanderbilt	Van
Drexel	Drex	Notre Dame	ND	Villanova	Vill
Eastern Michigan	EstMi	Ohio State	OhSt	Virginia	UVa
Fayetteville State	Fay	Oklahoma	Okla	Virginia Tech	VTch
Florida	Fla	Oklahoma State	OkSt	Virginia Union	VaUn
Florida State	FlaSt	Old Dominion	ODU	Wake Forest	Wake
Fresno State	Fres	Oral Roberts	OrRob	Washington	Wash
George Mason	GMas	Oregon	Ore	Washington State	WshSt
Georgetown	GTwn	Oregon State	OreSt	West Florida	WstFl
Georgia	UGa	Pacific (CA)	Pac	Wichita State	Wich
Georgia Southern	GaSo	Penn State	PSU	Winston-Salem	W-Sal
Georgia Tech	GTch	Pennsylvania	Penn	Wisconsin	Wisc
Gonzaga	Gonz	Pepperdine	Pep	Wisconsin-Green Bay	Wis-GB
Hartford	Hart	Pfeiffer	Pfe	Wisconsin-Stevens Point	Wis-SP
Hawaii	Haw	Pittsburgh	Pitt	Wright State	Wri
Houston	Hou	Portland	Por	Wyoming	Wyo
Illinois	Ill	Providence	Prov	Xavier	Xav

About STATS, Inc.

STATS, Inc. is the nation's leading sports information and statistical analysis company, providing detailed sports services for a wide array of commercial clients. In January 2000, STATS was purchased by News Digital Media, the digital division of News Corporation. News Digital Media engages in three primary activities: operating FOXNews.com, FOXSports.com, FOXMarketwire.com and FOX.com; developing related interactive services; and directing investment activities and strategy for News Corporation, as they relate to digital media.

As one of the fastest growing companies in sports, STATS provides the most up-to-the-minute sports information to professional teams, print and broadcast media, software developers and interactive service providers around the country. STATS recently was recognized as "one of Chicago's 100 most influential technology players" by *Crain's Chicago Business* and has been one of 16 finalists for KPMG/Peat Marwick's Illinois High Tech Award for three consecutive years. Some of our major clients are Fox Sports, the Associated Press, America Online, *The Sporting News*, ESPN, Electronic Arts, MSNBC, SONY and Topps. Much of the information we provide is available to the public via STATS On-Line. With a computer and a modem, you can follow action in the four major professional sports, as well as NCAA football and basketball and other professional and college sports. . . as it happens!

STATS Publishing, a division of STATS, Inc., produces 13 annual books, including the *Major League Handbook*, *The Scouting Notebook*, the *Pro Football Handbook*, the *Pro Basketball Handbook* and the *Hockey Handbook*. In 1998, we introduced two baseball encyclopedias, the *All-Time Major League Handbook* and the *All-Time Baseball Sourcebook*. Together they combine for more than 5,000 pages of baseball history. Also available is *From Abba Dabba to Zorro: The World of Baseball Nicknames*, a wacky look at monikers and their origins. A new football title was launched in 1999, the *Pro Football Scoreboard*, and we added the *Pro Football Sourcebook* in 2000. These publications deliver STATS' expertise to fans, scouts, general managers and media around the country.

In addition, STATS offers the most innovative—and fun—fantasy sports games around, from Bill James Fantasy Baseball and Bill James Classic Baseball to STATS Fantasy Football and our newest game, Diamond Legends Internet Baseball. Check out our immensely popular Fantasy Portfolios and our great new web-based product, STATS Fantasy Advantage.

Information technology has grown by leaps and bounds in the last decade, and STATS will continue to be at the forefront as both a vendor and supplier of the most up-to-date, in-depth sports information available. For those of you on the information superhighway, you always can catch STATS in our area on America Online or at our Internet site.

For more information on our products or on joining our reporter network, contact us via:

America Online — Keyword: STATS

Internet — www.stats.com

Toll-Free in the USA at 1-800-63-STATS (1-800-637-8287)

Outside the USA at 1-847-470-8798

Or write to:

STATS, Inc.
8130 Lehigh Ave.
Morton Grove, IL 60053

Notes

Notes

Notes

More Than Meets the Ice!

STATS Hockey Handbook 2000-01

- Career stats for every NHL player who made an appearance in 1999-2000
- In-depth player profiles identifying strengths and weaknesses
- Leader boards for forwards, defensemen and goaltenders
- Team game logs

"STATS scores again with the *Hockey Handbook*."
— Bill Clement, ESPN Hockey Analyst

Item #HH01, $19.95, Available Now

*Here is an example of the great coverage you'll find in the *STATS Hockey Handbook*:

Joe Sakic
(statistical profile on page 382)

Pos: C   Shoots: L   Ht: 5'11"   Wt: 185   Born: 7/7/69—Burnaby, British Columbia   Age: 31

Year	Tm	GP	G	A	Pts	+/-	GW	GT	S	SPct	G	A	Pts	G	A	Pts	Num	PIM	Maj	Mnr	Fgt	Rgh	HHT	Hat	P/G
				Over	all						Power	Play		Short	hand				Pena	lty				Mi	sc
88-89	Que	70	23	39	62	-36	2	1	148	15.5	10	–	–	0	–	–	–	24	–	–	–	–	–	2	.89
89-90	Que*	80	39	63	102	-40	2	1	234	16.7	8	–	–	1	–	–	–	27	–	–	–	–	–	1	1.28
90-91	Que*	80	48	61	109	-26	7	1	245	19.6	12	21	33	3	1	4	12	24	0	12	0	0	7	1	1.36
91-92	Que*	69	29	65	94	5	1	1	217	13.4	6	25	31	3	4	7	10	20	0	10	0	1	9	1	1.36
92-93	Que*	78	48	57	105	-3	4	1	264	18.2	20	27	47	2	1	3	20	40	0	20	0	2	7	0	1.35
93-94	Que*	84	28	64	92	-8	9	1	279	10.0	10	23	33	1	1	2	9	18	0	9	0	0	7	0	1.10
94-95	Que	47	19	43	62	7	5	0	157	12.1	3	19	22	2	1	3	11	30	0	10	0	1	5	0	1.32
95-96	Col*	82	51	69	120	14	7	1	339	15.0	17	33	50	6	2	8	22	44	0	22	0	5	10	0	1.46
96-97	Col*	65	22	52	74	-10	5	0	261	8.4	10	26	36	2	1	3	17	34	0	17	0	0	6	1	1.14
97-98	Col*	64	27	36	63	0	2	1	254	10.6	12	16	28	1	0	1	25	50	0	25	0	0	17	0	.98
98-99	Col	73	41	55	96	23	6	1	255	16.1	12	22	34	5	1	6	13	29	1	12	1	0	10	1	1.32
99-00	Col	60	28	53	81	30	5	0	242	11.6	5	17	22	1	0	1	14	28	0	14	0	0	3	2	1.35
12 Years		852	403	657	1060	-44	55	9	2895	13.9	125	–	–	27	–	–	–	368	–	–	–	–	–	9	1.24

Postseason

Year	Tm	GP	G	A	Pts	+/-	GW	OT	S	SPct	G	A	Pts	G	A	Pts	Num	PIM	Maj	Mnr	Fgt	Rgh	HHT	Hat	P/G
92-93	Que	6	3	3	6	-3	0	0	24	12.5	1	1	2	0	0	0	1	2	0	1	0	0	0	0	1.00
94-95	Que	6	4	1	5	-4	1	0	15	26.7	1	1	2	1	0	1	0	0	0	0	0	0	0	1	.83
95-96	Col	22	18	16	34	10	6	2	98	18.4	6	10	16	0	0	0	7	14	0	7	0	1	4	1	1.55
96-97	Col	17	8	17	25	5		0	50	16.0	3	9	12	0	0	0	7	14	0	7	0	0	4	0	1.47
97-98	Col	6	2	3	5				24	8.3		2	2		0	1	3	6	0	3	0	0	2	0	.83
98-9										10.7	1	5	6				4	8	0	4	0	0	3	0	1.00

Order From STATS Today!

1-800-63-STATS   847-470-8798   www.stats.com

Free First-Class Shipping for Books Over $10
Order form in back of this book

STATS Power Hitters

Bill James Presents:

STATS Major League Handbook 2001

- Career stats for every 2000 major leaguer
- Bill James' & STATS' exclusive player projections for 2001
- Complete fielding stats for every player at every position
- Expanded and exclusive leader boards
- Managerial performances and tendencies

"STATS consistently provides a thorough and innovative analysis of the game of baseball."
  —Ron Schueler, GM, Chicago White Sox

Item #HB01, $19.95, Available November
Comb-bound #HC01, $24.95, Available November
2000 Edition Currently Available-50% OFF!

The Scouting Notebook 2001

- Extensive scouting reports on over 650 major league players
- Evaluations of more than 400 minor league prospects
- Expert analysis from nationally known writers
- Manager profiles evaluate skipper styles and strategies

"A phenomenal resource!"
  —Jayson Stark, ESPN

Item #SN01, $19.95, Available January 2001
Comb-bound #SC01, $24.95, Available January 2001
2000 Edition Currently Available -50% OFF!

Order From STATS Today!
1-800-63-STATS   847-470-8798   www.stats.com

Free First-Class Shipping for Books Over $10
Order form in back of this book

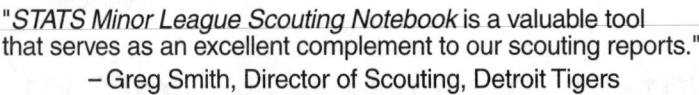

Player Portfolio   Real-time Game Coverage   Comprehensive Statistics

www.stats.com

Player & Team News & Notes   Injury Updates   STAT Search

Books (Free first-class shipping for books over $10)

Qty	Product Name	Item Number	Price	Total
	STATS Major League Handbook 2001	HB01	$ 19.95	
	STATS Major League Handbook 2001 (Comb-bound)	HC01	$ 24.95	
	The Scouting Notebook 2001	SN01	$ 19.95	
	The Scouting Notebook 2001 (Comb-bound)	SC01	$ 24.95	
	STATS Minor League Handbook 2001	MH01	$ 19.95	
	STATS Minor League Handbook 2001 (Comb-bound)	MC01	$ 24.95	
	STATS Player Profiles 2001	PP01	$ 19.95	
	STATS Player Profiles 2001 (Comb-bound)	PC01	$ 24.95	
	STATS Minor League Scouting Notebook 2001	MN01	$ 19.95	
	STATS Batter Vs. Pitcher Match-Ups! 2001	BP01	$ 24.95	
	STATS Ballpark Sourcebook: Diamond Diagrams	BSDD	$ 24.95	
	STATS Baseball Scoreboard 2001	SB01	$ 19.95	
	STATS Diamond Chronicles 2001	CH01	$ 19.95	
	STATS Pro Football Handbook 2000	FH00	$ 19.95	
	STATS Pro Football Handbook 2000 (Comb-bound)	FC00	$ 24.95	
	STATS Pro Football Scoreboard 2000	SF00	$ 19.95	
	STATS Pro Football Sourcebook 2000	PF00	$ 19.95	
	STATS Hockey Handbook 2000-01	HH01	$ 19.95	
	STATS Pro Basketball Handbook 2000-01	BH01	$ 19.95	
	STATS All-Time Major League Handbook, 2nd Edition	ATHB	$ 79.95	
			Total	

Books Under $10 (Please include $2.00 S&H for each book/magazine)

	From Abba Dabba to Zorro: The World of Baseball Nicknames	ABBA	$ 9.95	
	STATS Baseball's Terrific 20	KID1	$ 9.95	
	STATS Player Projections Update 2001	PJUP	$ 9.95	
			Total	

Previous Editions (Please Circle appropriate years and include $2.00 S&H for each book)

	STATS Major League Handbook	'91 '92 '93 '94 '95 '96 '97 '98 '99 '00	$ 9.95	
	The Scouting Notebook/Report	'94 '95 '96 '97 '98 '99 '00	$ 9.95	
	STATS Player Profiles	'93 '94 '95 '96 '97 '98 '99 '00	$ 9.95	
	STATS Minor League Handbook	'92 '93 '94 '95 '96 '97 '98 '99 '00	$ 9.95	
	STATS Minor League Scouting Notebook	'95 '96 '97 '98 '99 '00	$ 9.95	
	STATS Batter Vs. Pitcher Match-Ups!	'94 '95 '96 '97 '98 '99 '00	$ 9.95	
	STATS Diamond Chronicles	'97 '98 '99 '00	$ 9.95	
	STATS Baseball Scoreboard	'92 '93 '94 '95 '96 '97 '98 '99 '00	$ 9.95	
	Pro Football Revealed: The 100-Yard War	'94 '95 '96 '97 '98	$ 9.95	
	STATS Pro Football Handbook	'95 '96 '97 '98 '99	$ 9.95	
	STATS Pro Football Scoreboard	'99	$ 9.95	
	STATS Hockey Handbook	'96-97 '97-98 '98-99 '99-00	$ 9.95	
	STATS Pro Basketball Handbook	'93-94 '94-95 '95-96 '96-97 '97-98 '98-99 '99-00	$ 9.95	
	All-Time Major League Handbook (Slightly dinged)	First Edition	$ 45.00	
	All-Time Major League Sourcebook (Slightly dinged)	First Edition	$ 45.00	
			Total	

	Bill James Classic Baseball	BJCB	$ 129.95	
	Bill James Fantasy Baseball	BJFB	$ 89.95	
	STATS Fantasy Football	SFF	$ 49.95	
			Total	

TOTAL

1st Fantasy Team Name (ex. Colt 45's):_____
Which Fantasy Game is the team for?_____

2nd Fantasy Team Name (ex. Colt 45's):_____
Which Fantasy Game is the team for?_____

Note: $1.00/player is charged for all roster moves and transactions.

SPORTS TEAM ANALYSIS & TRACKING SYSTEMS

Mail:
STATS, Inc.
8130 Lehigh Avenue
Morton Grove, IL 60053

Phone:
1-800-63-STATS
(847) 677-3322

Fax:
(847) 470-9140

Bill To:
Company_____
Name_____
Address_____
City_____State_____Zip_____
Phone (   )_____Ext.____Fax (   )_____
E-mail Address_____

Ship To: *(Fill in this section if shipping address differs from billing address)*
Company_____
Name_____
Address_____
City_____State_____Zip_____
Phone (   )_____Ext.____Fax (   )_____
E-mail Address_____

Method of payment:
All prices stated
in U.S. Dollars

❑ Charge to my *(circle one)*
  Visa
  MasterCard
  American Express
  Discover

❑ Check or Money Order
  (U.S. funds only)

Please include credit card number
and expiration date with charge orders!

Exp. Date [/   ]
Month   Year

X_____
Signature *(as shown on credit card)*

Totals for STATS Products:	
Books	
Books Under $10 *	
Prior Book Editions *	
order 2 or more books/subtract: $1.00/book *(Does not include prior editions)*	
Illinois residents add 8.5% sales tax	
Sub Total	

Shipping Costs		
Canada	Add $4.00/book	
* All books under $10	Add $2.00/book	
Fantasy Games		
Grand Total		
(No other discounts apply)		

(Orders subject to availability)

Free First-Class Shipping for Books Over $10